To inspire ambition, to stimulate the imagination, to provide the inquiring mind with accurate information told in an interesting style, and thus lead into broader fields of knowledge—such is the purpose of this work

The New
BOOK OF KNOWLEDGE
Volume Eight

Other Famous Works
of
Popular Instruction
by
the Same Editor

❖ ❖ ❖

PRACTICAL KNOWLEDGE FOR ALL
Six Vols.

NEW UNIVERSAL ENCYCLOPEDIA
Ten Vols.

UNIVERSAL HISTORY OF THE WORLD
Eight Vols.

THE SECOND GREAT WAR
Nine Vols.

PEOPLES OF ALL NATIONS
Two Vols.

COUNTRIES OF THE WORLD
Two Vols

WONDERS OF THE PAST
Two Vols.

MANNERS AND CUSTOMS OF
MANKIND
Three Vols

OUR WONDERFUL WORLD
Four Vols.

WORLD'S GREAT BOOKS IN OUTLINE
Seven Vols.

MASTERPIECE LIBRARY OF SHORT
STORIES
Twenty Vols.

MADE AND PRINTED IN GREAT BRITAIN BY THE AMALGAMATED PRESS, LTD.

SOME BRITISH COMMONWEALTH FLAGS AND ARMS

WHITE ENSIGN (R.N.)   BLUE ENSIGN (R.N.R.)   RED ENSIGN (M.N.)   WORN BY BRITISH GOVERNMENT — OWNED VESSELS OF THE COLONIES AND PROTECTORATES. DISK SHOWS POSITION OF THE HERALDIC BEARINGS

STANDARD OF SCOTLAND

TRINITY HOUSE JACK

UNION FLAG

PORT OF LONDON AUTHORITY

CEYLON

ROYAL STANDARD

TRINIDAD   BRIT HONDURAS

St HELENA

BRIT. GUIANA

GAMBIA   N.W. TERRITORIES

GOLD COAST   NIGERIA

ALBERTA

BRIT. COLUMBIA

GIBRALTAR   MALTA

N BORNEO   SINGAPORE

YUKON   SARAWAK

PAPUA

PR. EDWARD I

QUEBEC

PAPUA   FIJI

BAHAMAS   TURKS & CAICOS IS   BERMUDAS   SASKATCHEWAN

MANITOBA   NEW BRUNSWICK   ONTARIO

NOVA SCOTIA   SOLOMON IS   MAURITIUS   SEYCHELLES

CANADA

NEW S WALES   QUEENSLAND   S. AUSTRALIA

AUSTRALIA

TASMANIA   W AUSTRALIA   VICTORIA

BARBADOS   St LUCIA

SOMALILAND   ZANZIBAR

GRENADA   St VINCENT

NEW ZEALAND   SOUTH AFRICA

KENYA   UGANDA

WINDWARD IS   JAMAICA

INDIA   PAKISTAN

N. RHODESIA   S. RHODESIA

The NEW BOOK OF KNOWLEDGE

A Pictorial Treasury of Reading & Reference for Young and Old

Edited by

SIR JOHN HAMMERTON

COMPLETE IN EIGHT VOLUMES
Alphabetically Arranged

OVER SIX THOUSAND ILLUSTRATIONS
OVER 600 IN COLOUR AND GRAVURE

VOLUME EIGHT
Through the Year : Study Outlines
EASY REFERENCE FACT-INDEX

THE WAVERLEY BOOK COMPANY LTD.
Farringdon Street, London, E.C.4

THROUGH THE YEAR

with the New Book of Knowledge

A DAY-TO-DAY CALENDAR OF HOME STUDIES

JANUARY

THIS Calendar has been devised to vivify home study by relating historic events and personalities to their particular days. Under date January 28, for example, we find that Henry VII was born on that day in 1457. The page numbered in heavy type **1612** contains the main article about him, but there are other articles that ought to be consulted : Bosworth, page 530 ; Tudor, page 3253 ; Wars of the Roses, page 2828. You can thus learn quite a lot about Henry VII on his birthday, and this applies to a very large number of other famous personages and historic events. A page numbered in italic thus, *675, 2073,* signifies that it has a portrait or other picture illustrating the subject. Remember, too, that the Fact-Index contains a large number of additional entries as well as a vast amount of supplementary information ; where that information will be specially useful, the letters *f-i* occur as a reference to the Fact-Index. At the end of each day are a few helps to Nature Study.

1 NEW YEAR'S DAY, **2350** ; Calendar, 661.
1347 Edward III captured Calais, **1091.** Calais, 655 ; France : History, 1365 ; Hundred Years' War, 1652.
1785 *The Times* founded, *f-i.* Newspapers, 2344.
1901 Commonwealth of Australia inaugurated, **307.** British Commonwealth, 580 ; Government, 1488 ; Parliament, 2521.
1943 Siege of Leningrad raised, **1923.** Germany : History, 1447 ; Russia, 2852 ; World Wars, 3421.
1946 Hirohito, Emperor of Japan, publicly denied his " divine origin," **1629.** Japan, 1795.
1947 Ownership of U.K. coal mines passed to the State. Coal, 855 ; Mines, 2181 ; Socialism, 2996.
1948 Control of U.K. railways passed to the State. Railways, 2734 ; Socialism, 2996.

Big flocks of fieldfares are conspicuous, 2171.
The first spikes of crocus leaves appear, 932.

2 **1492** GRANADA, last stronghold of the Moors, captured by Spaniards, **1498.** Spain : History, 3036.
1905 Port Arthur surrendered to the Japanese. Japan, 1795 ; Russia, 2848.
1947 Cupro-nickel coins issued in U.K. to replace silver, *f-i.* Alloys, 122 ; Money, 2200.

Hibernating butterflies are found indoors, 1622.
Migrant waders are seen on the seashore, 3331.

3 **106** B.C. CICERO, Roman orator, born, **827.** Latin Literature, 1894.
A.D. **1823** Robert Whitehead, inventor of torpedo, born. Artillery, 257 ; Torpedoes, 3224.
1883 Clement Richard Attlee, British statesman, born, **300.** Labour movement, 1875 ; Socialism, 2996 ; United Kingdom, 3282.

Small birds come to the garden food-table, 437.
You may uncover a hibernating hedgehog in a leaf-filled ditch, 1622.

4 **1642** CHARLES I attempted arrest of Five Members, **755.** Cromwell, Oliver, 933 ; English History, 1196 ; Parliament, 2521.

1749 Charles James Fox, British statesman, born, *f-i.*
1878 Edwin Augustus John, British artist, born, *f-i.* English Art, *1192.*
1948 Burma became an independent republic, **623.**

Perch are well fed and easy to catch, 2549.
Dandelions are already flowering, 967.

5 **1477** BATTLE OF NANCY and death of Charles the Bold, Duke of Burgundy, **759.** France : History, 1365.
1896 Phenomena of X-rays made public by Professor Röntgen. Medicine, 2132 ; X-rays, 3430.
1922 Sir Ernest Shackleton, Antarctic explorer, died in the Antarctic, **2931.** Antarctica, 173 ; Polar Exploration, 2644.

An early skylark sings, 1893.
Female winter moths crawl up the apple trees, 3388.

6 FEAST OF THE EPIPHANY. Twelfth Night. Christianity, 817 ; Christmas, 819.
1367 Richard II, King of England, born, **2777.** Edward III, 1091 ; Henry IV, 1611 ; English History, 1193, *1197* ; Tyler, Wat, 3269.

From an engraving by Hollar
Jan. 4, 1642. Charles I attempting to arrest the Five Members for intriguing with the Scots, to find them flown.

1833 Gustave Doré, French artist, born, *f-i.* France : Art, 1377.

Sea-gulls come inland for food, **1555.**
Stray red campion flowers are found, **674.**

7 1327 EDWARD II of England deposed, **1089.** Edward I, 1089 ; English History, 1193.
1610 Galileo discovers Jupiter's satellites, **1414.** Astronomy, 276, *280* ; Planets, 2617 ; Telescope, 3178.
1785 First Channel crossing by air (Blanchard and Jeffries). Balloon, 347, *349.*

An occasional hive bee is seen, **390.**
Chickweed flowers in sheltered hedges, f-i.

8 1679 LA SALLE, French explorer, reached Niagara Falls, **1894.** America : Discovery, 139 ; Mississippi, 2191 ; Niagara, 2361.
1823 Alfred Russel Wallace, British scientist, born, *f-i.* Darwin, 975 ; Pacific, 2469 ; Asia, 263 ; East Indies, *map, 1074–75.*
1836 Sir Lawrence Alma-Tadema, British artist, born, *f-i.* English Art, 1177.
1868 Sir Frank Watson Dyson, Astronomer Royal from 1910 to 1932, born, *f-i.* Astronomy, 275 ; Stars, 3077 ; Telescope, 3178.
1886 Severn Tunnel (4 miles, 624 yards) opened. Railways, 2734 ; Tunnels, 3258.

Carp are hidden deep in the mud, **704.**
Female chaffinches are still in small flocks, **1272.**

9 1735 JOHN JERVIS, Earl St. Vincent, British sailor, born. Navy, 2293.
1816 Davy's safety lamp first used in coal-mine, **979.** Lamps, *1889* ; Mines, 2181.
1819 William Powell Frith, British painter, born, *f-i.* English Art, 1177 ; Highwaymen, *1625.*
1863 Metropolitan Railway opened. London, 2009 ; Railways, 2734.

Widgeon appear on inland waters, 1051.

10 1769 MICHEL NEY, French marshal, born at Saarlouis, **2360.** Napoleon I, 2275 ; France : History, 1365.
1776 George Birkbeck, English educational reformer, born, **457.**
1840 Penny Postage introduced. Hill, Sir R., *f-i.* ; Post Office, 2661 ; Stamps, 3074.
1920 League of Nations established, **1908.** Geneva, 1428 ; Peace Movements, 2531 ; United Nations, 3283 ; World Wars, 3414.
1946 First General Assembly of the United Nations

Jan. 12, 1856. John Singer Sargent, painter of "Carnation, Lily, Lily, Rose" (above), was born.

opened in London, **3283.** League of Nations, 1908 ; World Wars, 3424.

Crossbills are seen in the pine woods, 1272.
A landslide displays new soil, full of fossils. **1353.**

11 1753 SIR HANS SLOANE, British physician and collector, died. British Museum, 584 ; Museums, 2259.
1859 Marquess Curzon of Kedleston, English statesman, born, *f-i.* India : History, 1714.
1866 Royal Aeronautical Society founded. Aeroplane, 41 ; Airship, 92 ; Balloon, 347.
1883 Royal Courts of Justice opened, **921.** Law, *1902* ; London, 2009.

Queen wasps are awakening indoors, **3345.**
Notice how weather affects the actions of birds, **437.**

12 1628 CHARLES PERRAULT, French author, born, *f-i.* Folklore, 1333 ; Literature for Children, 1964.
1729 Edmund Burke, Irish statesman and orator, born, **621.** French Revolution, 1393.
1856 John Singer Sargent, American artist, born, **2874.** English Art, 1177 ; Prophets, *2691.*
1876 Jack London, U.S. author, born, *f-i.* Novel, 2401 ; Socialism, 2996.
1879 Zulu War began. South Africa, 3019 ; Zulus, 3488.

Squirrels are energetic as ever, **3071.**
The wren's lusty song is heard, **3425.**

13 1399 DELHI captured and plundered by Tamerlane, **987.** India, *1713* ; Lutyens, Sir E. L., 2041 ; Mongols, 2205.
1879 William Reid Dick, Scottish sculptor, born, *f-i.* Sculpture, 2903.
1935 Saar plebiscite taken. Germany : History, 1447.

Snowdrop spikes peep through the snow, 2992.
Burying beetles are busy on dead creatures, 400.

14 ST. HILARY'S DAY, traditionally the coldest day of the year in England ; 10 weeks' frost began in 1205. Climate, 840 ; Frost, 1400.
1797 Napoleon defeats Austrians at Battle of Rivoli. France : History, 1365 ; Napoleon I, 2275.
1836 Théodore Fantin-Latour, French painter, born, *f-i.* France : Art, 1377 ; Painting, 2475.
1907 Kingston, Jamaica, destroyed by earthquake. Earthquake, 1069 ; Jamaica, 1792 ; West Indies, 3368.
1943 Casablanca Conference of war opened, *f-i.* Churchill, 824 ; Roosevelt, 2823 ; World Wars, 3420.

Nuthatches may visit the bird-table, **2407.**
Salmon return to the sea, **2865.**

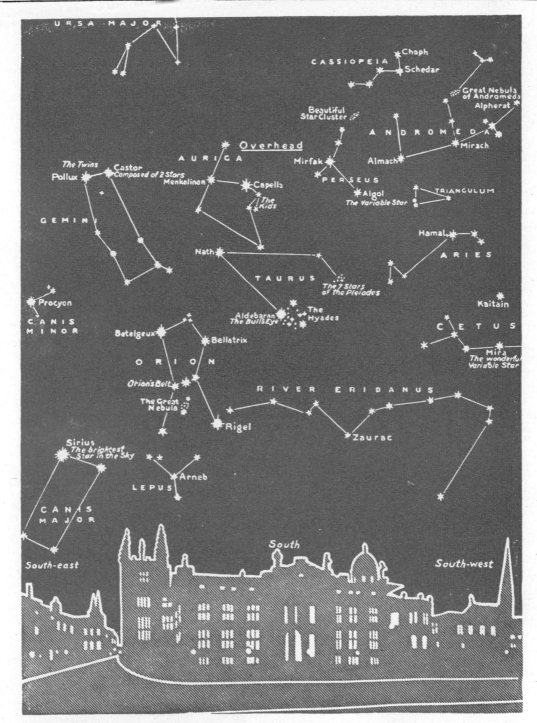

THE STARS IN JANUARY. Here we give the first of a series of charts showing how to read the stars month by month. They are shown as they appear at about 9 p.m. (Greenwich Time) in the middle of the month and about four minutes earlier each succeeding evening. With this map we can study the stars from the middle of January to the middle of February. We are looking southward in Oxford towards Hertford College and the Bodleian Library, but the stars are seen in practically the same position, looking south, from all parts of Britain.

JANUARY

15 1622 MOLIERE, French dramatist, baptized, **2198.** France : Literature, *1381*.

1759 Brit**i**sh Museum opened, **584.** Elgin Marbles, 1143 ; Greek Art, *1536*, *1537* ; Library, 1930 ; London, 2009 ; Museums, 2259.

1778 Captain Cook discovered the Sandwich Islands, **898.** Pacific Ocean, 2469.

The hedge-sparrow is in song, 3052.

16 1780 RODNEY defeated the Spanish fleet off Cape St. Vincent, *f-i*. United Kingdom, 3276 ; Navy, 2293.

1809 Battle of Corunna. Moore, Sir John, 2227 ; Napoleon I, 2275.

1874 Robert William Service, Canadian poet, born. Canadian Literature, 684.

1941 Siege of Malta began, **2072.** World Wars, 3418.

Tortoiseshell butterflies emerge from hibernation, 1322

17 1600 PEDRO CALDERON DE LA BARCA, Spanish dramatist, born, *f-i*. Spanish Literature, 3051.

1706 Benjamin Franklin, American scientist, born, **1386.** Electricity, 1127 ; Lightning, 1945.

1860 Anton Tchekhov, Russian dramatist, born, **3159.** Drama, 1037 ; Russian Literature, 2855.

1863 David Lloyd George, Welsh politician, born, **1976.** Liberals, 1929 ; World Wars, 3409.

1871 Earl Beatty, British sailor, born, **386.** World Wars, 3411 ; Jellicoe, 1816 ; Navy, 2293.

1912 Captain Scott reached the South Pole, **2895.** Antarctica, 173 ; Polar Exploration, 2644.

1945 Warsaw captured by the Red Army, **3341.** Germany : History, 1447 ; Poland, 2640 ; World Wars, 3424.

Gorse is already in flower, f-i.

18 1486 HENRY VII married Elizabeth of York, so uniting the rival houses of York and Lancaster, **1612.** Wars of the Roses, 2828.

1871 William I, King of Prussia, proclaimed German Emperor, 3317. Germany : History, 1447 ; Franco-Prussian War, 1384 ; France : History, 1365.

1882 A. A. Milne, British author and dramatist, born, *f-i*. Literature for Children, 1964.

Warm weather tempts out an early frog or two, **1398.**

19 1736 JAMES WATT, British engineer, born, **3356.** Industrial Revolution, 1721 ; Steam-engine, 3085.

1807 Robert E. Lee, American soldier, born, **1917.** American Civil War, *f-i*. ; United States : History, 3291.

1809 Edgar Allan Poe, American writer, born, **2633.** United States : Literature, 3293.

1812 Battle of Ciudad Rodrigo, Napoleon I, 2275 ; Wellington, Duke of, 3363.

1813 Sir Henry Bessemer, English inventor, born, **420.** Iron and Steel, 1752.

1839 Paul Cézanne, French artist, born, **749.** France : Art, *1375* ; Painting, 2475.

Rooks are back at the rookery once more, 2823.
Spring usher moths are on the wing, f-i.
Notice the purple catkins of the alder, 104.

20 1265 FIRST ENGLISH PARLIAMENT met in Westminster Hall. English History, 1193 ; Government, 1488 ; Parliament, 2521.

21 1649 Trial of Charles I began, **755,** *756.* Cromwell, Oliver, 933 ; English History, 1196, *1199*, *1206*.

1841 Hong Kong ceded to Britain by China, **1639.** British Commonwealth, 580 ; China, 807.

1936 Death of George V and accession of Edward VIII, **1442, 1092.** George VI, 1442 ; United Kingdom, 3282.

The house-sparrow gets his breeding dress, 3052.

21 1780 RODNEY relieved Gibraltar. Gibraltar, 1462 ; United Kingdom, 3277.

1793 Louis XVI of France guillotined, **2030.** French Revolution, 1393 ; Marie Antoinette, 2102.

1824 " Stonewall " Jackson, Confederate general, born, **1789.** Lincoln, Abraham, 1951.

1846 First issue of the *Daily News* published. Dickens, Charles, 1012 ; Newspapers, 2344.

1926 Sennar Dam, on the Nile, opened. Dam, 958 ; Egypt, 1095 ; Nile, 2370.

Plover are still in enormous flocks, 2629.
Crayfish are active in muddy streams, 926.

22 1561 FRANCIS BACON, Viscount St. Albans, English philosopher and essayist, born, **333.** English Literature, 1210 ; Essay, 1224 ; Physics, 2591.

1788 George Gordon Byron, Lord Byron, born, **634.** English Literature, 1210 ; Poetry, 2634.

1849 August Strindberg, Swedish dramatist, born, *f-i*. Drama, 1037 ; Sweden, 3131.

1858 Frederick Dealtry Lugard, British colonial administrator, born, *f-i*. Africa, 65 ; Niger, 2367.

1901 Death of Queen Victoria and accession of Edward VII, **3320, 1092.** Albert, Prince Consort, 101 ; United Kingdom, 3279.

1944 Allied landing at Anzio, *f-i*. Italy, 1774 ; World Wars, 3422.

Shepherd's purse flowers, **2944.**

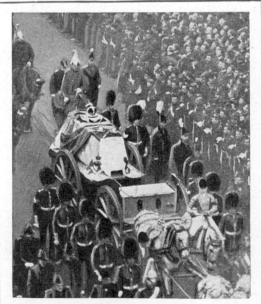

Jan. 22, 1901. Death of Queen Victoria at Osborne. Above, the funeral procession on its way to Windsor.

3512

23

1570 ROYAL EXCHANGE opened in London by Queen Elizabeth. Elizabeth, 1146; London, 2009.

1894 Lobengula, King of the Matabele, killed. Boer War, 486; Rhodes, Cecil, 2771; S. Africa, 3019.

1896 Grand Duchess Charlotte of Luxemburg born, 2041; anniversary kept as national holiday.

1900 Battle of Spion Kop in South African War. Boer War, 486; South Africa, 3019.

1943 Eighth Army captured Tripoli. Montgomery, 2221; Rommel, *f-i.*; World Wars, 3420.

Earthworms burrow deeply in the frost, 1070.
Shoveller ducks appear on the ponds, 1051.

24

1712 FREDERICK II (the Great), King of Prussia, born, **1389.** Germany: History, 1447; Germany: Literature, 1456; Prussia, 2696.

1749 Charles James Fox, British politician, born, *f-i.* Pitt, 2614; United Kingdom, 3277.

1891 First train crossed the Forth Bridge. Bridge, 564; Caisson, 654; Railways, 2734.

1946 U.S. Army signal corps contacted the moon by radar, 2726.

Dead teasels still stand in the hedges, 3163.

25

FEAST OF THE CONVERSION OF ST. PAUL, **2529.** Christianity, 817.

1759 Robert Burns, Scottish poet, born, **625.** English Literature, 1210; Poetry, 2634.

1806 Daniel Maclise, British painter, born, *f-i.* Ainsworth, H., *87*; Cobbett, W., *858*; Coleridge, S. T., *869*; Hamlet, *1570.*

1906 Simplon Tunnel through the Alps opened. Alps, 126; Railways, 2734; Tunnels, 3257.

Magpies are forming small flocks, 2065.
The mistle-thrush is in fine song, 3205.

26

1763 CHARLES XIV of Sweden (Bernadotte), born, *f-i.* French Revolution, 1393; Napoleon I, 2275; Sweden, 3131.

1788 Sydney founded, **3144;** anniversary kept as Australia Day. Australia, 307; New S. Wales, 2343.

1885 Khartum captured by Mahdi, and Gordon killed. Egypt, 1095; Gordon, 1486; Khartum, 1855; Kitchener, Earl, 1862.

Many moth chrysalises may be found in the soil, in nooks and crannies and beneath the bark of trees, 628.

27

1756 WOLFGANG AMADEUS MOZART, Austrian composer, born, **2249.** Music, 2261; Opera, 2435.

1832 Lewis Carroll (Rev. Charles L. Dodgson), British author and mathematician, born, **707.** Literature for Children, 1964.

1859 William II, German Emperor, born, **3378.**

Germany: History, 1447; Edward VII, 1092; World Wars, 3409.

1943 Siege of Stalingrad raised, **3073.** Germany: History, 1447; Russia, 2852; World Wars, 3421.

Tracks of rabbits and other non-hibernating mammals are visible in the snow, 2721.

28

1457 HENRY VII, King of England, born, **1612;** his tomb, *2765.* Bosworth, 530; Tudor, 3253; Richard III, 2777; Wars of the Roses, 2828.

1833 Charles George Gordon, British soldier, born, **1486.** China, 807; Egypt, 1095; Khartum, 1855.

1867 Luigi Pirandello, Italian dramatist, born, *f-i.* Drama, 1037; Italy: Literature, 1786.

1871 Paris surrendered to Germans. Franco-Prussian War, 1384; Paris, 2514.

1884 Auguste Piccard, Swiss scientist, born, *f-i.* Air, 88, *89*; Balloons, 347.

The Dartford warbler is found about this time in heathy districts, 3341.

29

1688 EMANUEL SWEDENBORG, Swedish mystic, born, **3131.**

1737 Thomas Paine, English writer, born, **2474.** French Revolution, 1393.

1833 Reform Parliament of England opened. United Kingdom, 3278; Parliament, 2521.

1863 Frederick Delius, British composer, born, **988.** Music, 2261.

Mallard drakes are in breeding plumage, 1051.
Birch tree catkins begin to lengthen, 436.

30

1649 CHARLES I executed, **755.** Charles II, 756; Cromwell, Oliver, **933;** English History. 1196, **1199.**

1775 Walter Savage Landor, English poet, born, **1890.** English Literature, 1210.

1882 Franklin Delano Roosevelt, American President, born, **2823.** United States: History, 3292; World Wars, 3419.

1948 Mahatma Gandhi assassinated, **1416;** India: History, 1714.

The robin's spring song is heard, 2790.

31

1606 GUY FAWKES, conspirator, executed, **1264.** Beefeater, *plate f. 397*; James I. 1793.

1797 Franz Peter Schubert, Austrian composer, born, **2887.** Music, 2261.

1846 Corn Laws abolished. Bright, John, 569; Ireland, 1744; Peel, Sir Robert, 2535; United Kingdom, 3278.

1858 Great Eastern steamship launched. Cable, *642*; Brunel, I. K., 593; Industrial Revolution, 1721; Ships, 2945.

Pintail ducks are often seen now. 1052

Jan. 25, 1759. Robert Burns, Scotland's great lyric poet, was born. Above, his birthplace at Alloway, near Ayr.

1 1757 John Philip Kemble, Shakespearian actor, born, *f-i.* Drama, 1037.
1811 Inchcape Rock Lighthouse first lit, *f-i.* Lighthouses, 1943; Navigation, 2290; Southey, Robert, ballad, 3028.
1873 Dame Clara Butt, famous singer, born, *f-i.*
1908 Charles I, king of Portugal, and the Crown Prince assassinated. Portugal, 2658.

The raven, the earliest nesting bird, is building, 2747.

2 Presentation of Jesus in the Temple (Candlemas). Jesus Christ, 1821; Christianity, 817.
1461 Battle of Mortimer's Cross between Yorkists and Lancastrians. English History, 1193; Roses, Wars of the, 2828.
1535 Buenos Aires founded by Pedro de Mendoza, **601.** Argentina, 228; South America, 3022.
1801 First Parliament of Great Britain and Ireland. Ireland, 1746; Parliament, 2521; United Kingdom, 3276.

In the woods, the first hazel catkins are opening, 1590. The yellow-hammer is beginning to sing, 616.

3 1660 General Monk entered London with his army. Charles II, 756; English History, 1198, *1199, 1207.*
1807 British captured Montevideo, Uruguay, **2220.** South America, 3022; Uruguay, 3298.
1809 Felix Mendelssohn-Bartholdy, German composer, born, **2141.** Music, 2261.
1830 Robert Cecil, 3rd Marquess of Salisbury, British statesman, born, *f-i.* Boer War, 486; Conservatives, 892; Disraeli, 1018; Victoria, Queen, 3319.

Over flooded meadows the roach search for worms, 2781. Snowdrops are now in flower in the south, 2992.

4 1805 William Harrison Ainsworth, English novelist, born, **87.** English Literature, 1210; Novel, 2401.
1902 Charles Augustus Lindbergh, American aviator, born, **1953.** Aeroplane, 41; Atlantic Ocean, 290.
1945 Yalta (Crimea) Conference of war opened, *f-i.* Churchill, 824; Roosevelt, 2823; Stalin, 3073; World Wars, 3424.
1948 Ceylon Independence Act came into force, **748.** British Commonwealth, 580.

Wood-pigeons are cooing loudly in the woods, 2605. The first toad pushes his way out from the soil, 3219.

5 1788 Sir Robert Peel, English statesman, born, 2535. Police, 2647; Victoria, Queen, 3319.
1814 Thames Ice Fair, bank to bank at London Bridge. Frost, 1400; Thames, 3193.

1837 Dwight L. Moody, American evangelist, born, *f-i.* Hymns, 1678.
1856 Victoria Cross instituted. Orders and Decorations, 2448; Victoria, Queen, 3319; Roberts, Earl, 2789.
1866 Sir Arthur Keith, English scientist, born, *f-i.* Man, 2078.

6 1665 Anne, Queen of England, born, **163.** English History, 1200; English Literature, 1212; James II, 1794; Marlborough, 1st Duke of, 2105.
1838 Sir Henry Irving, English actor, born, **1759.** Drama, 1037; Shakespeare, 2932.
1840 Treaty of Waitangi signed, ceding New Zealand to British Crown. British Commonwealth, 580; New Zealand, 2357.
1941 British Army of the Nile captured Benghazi, *f-i.* Italy, 1774; Libya, 1932; World Wars, 3418.
1946 Sarawak ceded to Britain, **2873.** Brooke, Sir James, *f-i.*; East Indies, *map, 1074–75*; Pacific, 2473.

Blue tits are making the woods ring with their strange, squeaky little song, 3218.

7 1478 Sir Thomas More, English statesman and writer, born, **2228.** English Literature, 1210; Henry VIII, 1612; Renaissance, 2764.
1812 Charles Dickens born, **1012.** English Literature, 1215; "Christmas Carol," 820; Novel, 2402.
1865 First issue of *Pall Mall Gazette.* Newspapers, 2344; Printing, 2684.
1885 Sinclair Lewis, American novelist, born. Novel, 2403; United States Literature, *3295.*

Flocks of linnets are still seen in the fields, 1955. Red dead-nettle is in flower, 2335.

8 1577 Robert Burton, author of "The Anatomy of Melancholy," born, 1211.
1587 Mary Queen of Scots beheaded, **2115.** Elizabeth, *1148*; James I, 1793; Knox, John, 1871; Scotland, 2892.
1819 John Ruskin, English writer, born, **2843.**

Feb. 4, 1945. War conference of Mr. Churchill, President Roosevelt, and Marshal Stalin opened at Yalta, in the Crimea. Behind the three leaders are Mr. Anthony Eden, Mr. Stettinius, and Mr. Molotov.

English Literature, 1215 ; Economics, 1080.

1828 Jules Verne, French writer, born, **3316**. Literature for Children, 1964 ; Submarines, 3104.

Snails are coming out of hibernation, to fall a prey to the song-thrushes, 161.

9 **1473** NICOLAS COPERNICUS, Polish astronomer, born, **905**. Astronomy, 276 ; Galileo, 1415 ; Planets, 2617.

1824 John Quincy Adams elected U.S. President, 23. United States : History, 3291.

1853 Sir Leander Starr Jameson, British administrator, born, *f-i.* Boer War, 486 ; Rhodes, Cecil, 2771 ; South Africa, 3019.

1897 Sir Charles Kingsford-Smith, Australian airman, born, 1858. Aeroplane, 41.

Signs of life are seen on the outside of the ant-hill, 168. The elms are purple with swelling flower-buds, 1152.

10 **1567** LORD DARNLEY, husband of Mary Queen of Scots, killed. Mary Stuart, 2115 ; Scotland, 2892.

1763 Canada annexed to England by Treaty of Paris, **682**. British Commonwealth, 580.

1775 Charles Lamb, English essayist, born, **1886**. English Literature, 1214 : Essay, 1224.

1824 Samuel Plimsoll, English politician, born, *f-i.* Merchant Navy, 2143 ; Ships, 2951.

1840 Marriage of Queen Victoria to Prince Albert. Albert, Prince Consort, 101 ; Edward VII, 1092 ; Victoria, Queen, 3319.

1904 Tsar Nicholas II declared war on Japan. Russia, 2848 ; Japan, 1800.

The green woodpecker's loud " yaffle " is heard, 3403. Wheat fields are green with young blades, 3374

11 **1573** SIR FRANCIS DRAKE first sighted the Pacific, **1036**. Balboa, 341 ; Pacific Ocean, 2469.

1836 London University chartered, **2021**. Education, 1088 ; Universities, 3296.

1847 Thomas Alva Edison, American inventor, born, **1087**. Cinema, 828 ; Gramophone, 1495.

1920 King Farouk of Egypt born, *f-i.*; Egypt, 1095.

Bluebell leaves are showing in the woods, 479 The woodlark is now in song, 1893.

12 **1541** SANTIAGO, Chile, founded by Valdivia, **2872**. Chile, 802 ; South America, 3022.

1554 Lady Jane Grey beheaded, **1544**. Henry VIII, 1612 ; Mary I, 2113 ; Reformation, 2758.

1809 Charles Robert Darwin, English biologist, born, **975**. Biology, 430 ; Ecology, 1079 ; Evolution, 1244 ; Huxley, T. H., 1661.

1809 Abraham Lincoln, American President, born, **1951**. Slavery, 2981 ; United States: History, 3291.

These purplish-brown elm flowers are very conspicuous in February.

1828 George Meredith, British author, born, **2146**. English Literature, 1215 ; Novel, 2402.

1851 Gold discovered in New South Wales. Australia, 307 ; Gold, 1479 ; New South Wales, 2343.

1912 Pu Yi, Emperor of China, abdicated. China, 813.

Rats may migrate now, driven on by floods and food-scarcity, 2746.

13 **1542** CATHERINE HOWARD, fifth wife of Henry VIII of England, executed on Tower Hill. Henry VIII, 1612.

1692 Massacre of Glencoe, *f-i.* James II, 1794 ; William III, 3380.

1728 John Hunter, British physiologist and anatomist, born, *f-i.* Anatomy, 151 ; Medicine, 2134.

1743 Sir Joseph Banks, British naturalist, born, **359**. Kew Gardens, 1854 ; Fingal's Cave, 3071.

1754 Charles Maurice de Talleyrand-Périgord, French statesman, born, **3149**. French Revolution, 1393 ; Napoleon I, 2275.

1788 Trial of Warren Hastings began in Westminster Hall, **1581**. Calcutta, 661 ; India: History, 1714.

1885 Mersey railway tunnel opened. Liverpool, 1968 ; Railways, 2734 ; Tunnels, 3255.

Black-headed gulls are getting their black heads again 1556.

14 ST. VALENTINE'S DAY, **2862**, feast day of St. Valentinus, an Italian saint.

1779 Captain James Cook killed at Hawaii, **898**. Australia, 308 310 ; New South Wales, 2343 ; New Zealand, 2360 ; Pacific Ocean, 2472.

1946 Bill to nationalize the Bank of England received Royal Assent, **356**. Banks, *357* ; Money, 2200 ; Socialism, 2996.

Spring salmon run up the rivers, 2865 White butterflies are on the wing, plate f. 632.

The Autocar

Feb 13, 1692. The Pass of Glencoe, above, was the scene of the massacre of the Macdonalds.

FEBRUARY

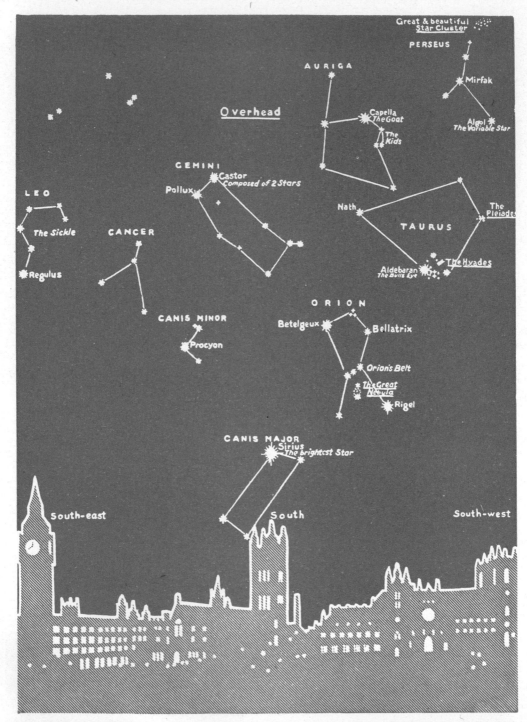

THE STARS IN FEBRUARY. With the aid of this picture any boy or girl in Britain can study the stars between the middle of February and the middle of March. We are supposed to be standing in Parliament Square, facing due south, with the Houses of Parliament and Westminster Abbey in front of us. The thin lines join up the stars of each constellation. The objects underlined, such as the Great Nebula in Orion, should be looked at through a telescope, or, if that is not available, through field- or opera-glasses.

15

1564 GALILEO GALILEI, Italian mathematician and astronomer, born, **1415**. Astronomy, 276; Gravitation, 1513; Mechanics, 2127; Microscope, 2163.

1763 Seven Years' War ended by Peace of Hubertsburg, **2924**. Frederick the Great, 1389; Quebec, 2715; Wolfe, James, 3401.

1874 Sir Ernest Shackleton. British explorer, born, **2931**. Antarctica, 173; Polar Exploration, 2645; Scott, Robert Falcon, 2895.

1900 Relief of Kimberley. Boer War, 486; Rhodes, Cecil, 2771; South Africa, 3019.

1942 Singapore surrendered to the Japanese, **2974**. Japan, 1800; Pacific, 2473; World Wars, 3420.

16

1804 HOBART, Tasmania, founded. British Commonwealth, 580; Tasmania, 3156.

1822 Sir Francis Galton, English anthropologist, born, *f-i*. Eugenics, 1230; Genetics, 1427; Heredity, 1617.

1876 George Macaulay Trevelyan, English historian, born, *f-i*. History, 1630.

1906 British battleship Dreadnought launched at Portsmouth. Navy, 2293; Ships, 2945.

17

1600 GIORDANO BRUNO, Italian philosopher, burnt at the stake in Rome, *f-i*.

1766 Thomas Robert Malthus, British economist, born, *f-i*. Economics, 1080; Philosophy, 2571; Population, 2656.

1862 Sir Edward German, British composer, born, **1444**. Gilbert and Sullivan, 1464; Music, 2261; Opera, 2435.

Mistle-thrushes are collecting nesting material, 3205. Musk-rats may already have their first litter, 2268.

18

1516 MARY I, Queen of England, born, **2113**. Elizabeth, 1146; Henry VIII, 1612; Philip II (Spain), 2567.

1609 Edward Hyde, Earl of Clarendon, English historian and politician, born, *f-i*. Charles II, 756; English History, 1193; History, 1630.

1745 Alessandro Volta, inventor of voltaic cell, born, *f-i*. Battery, 376.

1775 Thomas Girtin, English painter, born, *f-i*. English Art, 1177; Painting, 2475.

1784 Nicolo Paganini, Italian violinist, born, *f-i*. Musical Instruments, 2266; Violin, 3324.

1861 First Italian Parliament met. Garibaldi, 1418; Italy, 1769.

1948 John Aloysius Costello became prime minister of Eire, *f-i*. De Valera, 998; Irish Free State, 1750.

The yellow bill and metallic spring plumage of the cock starling are now conspicuous, 3083.

19

1717 DAVID GARRICK, British actor, born, *f-i*. Drama, 1037; Johnson, Dr., 1836.

1719 George Brydges Rodney, Lord Rodney, English admiral, born, *f-i*. Navy, 2293.

1792 Sir Roderick Murchison. British geologist, born. Geology, 1432.

1865 Sven Hedin, Swedish explorer, born, *f-i*. Deserts, 996.

1945 U.S. marines landed on Iwo Jima, *f-i*. Japan, 1800; Pacific Ocean, 2473; World Wars, 3424.

Newts are making their way to the ponds for spawning, f-i.

20

1803 KANDY, Ceylon, captured by British. British Commonwealth, 580; Ceylon, 749.

1809 Battle of Saragossa. Napoleon I, 2275; Wellington, Duke of, 3363.

1810 Andreas Hofer, Tirolese patriot, shot, *f-i*. Austria-Hungary, 319; Tirol, 3215.

1864 Henry Seymour Rawlinson, 1st Baron, British soldier, born, *f-i*. Haig, Earl, 1564; World Wars, 3409.

The great tit's curious song is heard in the woods, 3218. Signs of straw and grass round the " earth " show that the badger has awakened from his winter sleep, 337.

21

1788 SIR FRANCIS RONALDS, English scientist, born, *f-i*. Telegraphy, 3164.

1801 Cardinal John Henry Newman born, **2342**. Hymns, 1678.

1815 Jean Louis Meissonier, French painter, born, *f-i*. France: Art, 1377; Painting, 2475.

1859 George Lansbury, British politician, born, *f-i*. Labour Movement, 1875; London, 2015.

1901 Cuba became a republic, **940**.

1916 Battle of Verdun opened. France: History, 1366; World Wars, 3410.

1918 Jericho captured by Lord Allenby, **121**. Palestine, 2481; World Wars, 3414.

22

1732 GEORGE WASHINGTON, American soldier and president, born, **3342**. American Independence, 144; United States: History, 3291.

1810 Frédéric François Chopin, Polish musician, born, **816**. Music, 2261; Piano, 2604.

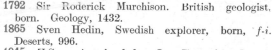

Feb. 16, 1906. H.M.S. Dreadnought, first of the modern all-big-gun battleships, launched.

February   The male of the common or smooth newt has a fine crest in the breeding season.

FEBRUARY

1819 James Russell Lowell, American poet, born, *f-i.* Poetry, 2634 ; United States : Literature, 3294.

1857 Lord Baden-Powell, British soldier and founder of Boy Scouts, born, **337.** Boer War, 486 ; Boy Scouts, 538.

1946 Discovery of streptomycin announced, **3103.** Antiseptics, 179 ; Medicine, 2132.

Herons are starting to repair their nests, 3099.
Flocks of finches begin to break up into pairs, 1272.

23 **1633** SAMUEL PEPYS, English diarist, born, **2547.** Charles II, 756 ; English Literature, 1212 ; Navy, 2293.

1685 George Frederick Handel, Anglo-German composer, born, **1572.** Music, 2264 ; Musical Instruments, *2266* ; Opera, 2435.

Feb. 23, 1685. Handel born At Whitchurch, in Edgware (above), he used to play the organ.

1817 George Frederic Watts, English painter, born, *f-i.* English Art, 1182 ; Orpheus, *2454* ; Mill, John Stuart, *2175.*

Cock pheasants fight for mates in the woods, 2565.
Bracken " handles " appear amid dead leaves, 543.

24 FEAST OF ST. MATTHIAS.
1525 Battle of Pavia ; Francis I taken prisoner, **1383.** France : History, 1365.

1619 Charles Le Brun, French painter, born in Paris, *f-i.* France : Art, 1377.

1877 Avonmouth Dock, Bristol, opened. Bristol, 571 ; Docks, 1022.

The goldcrest sings in the tall conifers, 443.
First rooks' eggs may now be found. 451.

25 **1634** ALBRECHT VON WALLENSTEIN, German general assassinated, *f-i.* Germany : History, 1447 ; Thirty Years' War, 3202.

1778 José de San Martin, S. American patriot, born, *f-i.* Andes, 152 ; Argentina, 229 ; South America, 3022.

1841 Pierre Firmin Auguste Renoir. French Impressionist painter, born, *f-i.* France : Art, *1376, 1378* ; Impressionism, 1689.

1852 Wreck of the Birkenhead with loss of 485 lives. **457.** Ships, 2945.

1873 Enrico Caruso, Italian tenor, born, *f-i.* Opera, 2435.

Daisies are flowering in garden and meadow, 956.
An occasional bat may now be seen, 370.

26 **1802** VICTOR HUGO, French poet, novelist and dramatist, born, **1650.** Drama, 1037 ; France : Literature, 1381.

1815 Napoleon escaped from Elba before the " Hundred Days," **2275.** France : History, 1366 ; Wellington, Duke of, 3363.

1842 Camille Flammarion, French astronomer, born, *f-i.* Astronomy, 275.

1845 Buffalo Bill (W. F. Cody), American pioneer and showman, born, **603.**

Feb. 26, 1842. Flammarion, French astronomer, born.

The cock chaffinch has his fine spring plumage, 1272.
Look out for the first brimstone butterfly, plate f. 632

27 **1807** HENRY WADSWORTH LONGFELLOW, American poet, born, **2022.** Poetry, 2634. United States : Literature, 3294.

1823 Joseph Ernest Renan, French writer, born, *f-i.* France : Literature, 1381 ; Philosophy, 2571.

1847 Ellen Terry, British actress, born, *f-i.* Drama, 1037 ; Irving, Sir H., 1759 ; Sargent, J. S., 2874.

1848 Sir Hubert Parry, British composer, born, *f-i.* Music, 2266 ; Orchestra, 2445.

Strange little butcher's broom is in flower, f-i.

28 **1533** MICHEL DE MONTAIGNE, French essayist, born, **2218.** Essay, 1224 ; France : Literature, 1380.

1820 Sir John Tenniel, British artist, born, *f-i.* Carroll, Lewis, *709* ; Nicknames, *2366.*

1865 Sir Wilfred Grenfell, British doctor and missionary, born, **1543.** Eskimos, 1222 ; Labrador, 1875.

1881 Battle of Majuba Hill. Boer War, 486 ; South Africa, 3019.

1900 Relief of Ladysmith. Boer War, 486 ; South Africa, 3019.

1948 The last British troops left India, 1716. Gandhi, 1416 ; Pakistan, 2479.

Many migrant birds are slowly making their way northwards by this date, 2171.

29 **1712** MARQUIS DE MONTCALM. French soldier, born, **2218.** Canada, 681 ; Quebec, 2716 ; Wolfe, James, 3401.

1792 Gioachino Antonio Rossini, Italian composer, born, *f-i.* Music, 2261 : Opera, 2438.

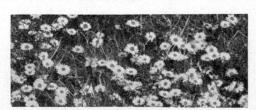

Towards the end of February the fields are often white with daisy heads, heralds of the spring.

1 ST. DAVID'S DAY. David or Dewi, patron saint of Wales.

1711 First number of *The Spectator*, Addison and Steele's periodical. Addison, 23 ; Essay, 1224 ; English Literature, 1213.

1880 Lytton Strachey, British author, born, *f-i.* Biography, 430 ; English Literature, 1217.

1896 Abyssinians defeated Italian army of invasion at Adowa, Abyssinia, 14.

1900 Relief of Ladysmith. Boer War, 486 ; South Africa, 3019.

The red deer loses his fine antlers, 984.
Barren strawberry may be found in flower, 3103.

2 1545 THOMAS BODLEY, founder of Bodleian Library, born. Library, 1930 ; Oxford, 2465.

1825 Work started on Thames Tunnel. Brunel, I. K., 593 ; Tunnels, 3257 ; Thames, 3194.

1922 First woman member admitted to House of Lords (Viscountess Rhondda). Parliament, 2521 ; Peerage, 2536.

Lapwing flocks break up as the birds go to their breeding grounds, 2629.

3 1652 THOMAS OTWAY, English dramatist, born, *f-i.* Drama, 1037 ; English Literature, 1210.

1793 William Charles Macready, English actor, born, *f-i.* Drama, 1037 ; Shakespeare, 2932.

1847 Alexander Graham Bell, inventor of the telephone, born, **408.** Sound, 3011 ; Telephone, 3173.

1853 Vincent Van Gogh, Dutch painter, born, **3305.** Impressionism, *1687* ; Netherlands : Art, 2335 ; Painting, 2477.

1861 Serfdom abolished in Russia. Russia, 2848 ; Slavery, 2982.

1869 Sir Henry Joseph Wood, British conductor, born, *f-i.* Music, 2261 ; Orchestra, 2445.

1918 Treaty of Brest-Litovsk between Germany and Russia. Russia, 2849 ; World Wars, 3412.

There are eggs, if not young, in the raven's nest, 2747.

4 1394 PRINCE HENRY THE NAVIGATOR born at Oporto, **1613.** Africa, 69 ; Portugal, 2659.

1756 Sir Henry Raeburn, Scottish painter, born. English Art, 1180 ; Painting, 2475.

1805 Foundation stone of East India Docks, London, laid. Docks, 1022 ; London, 2010 ; Thames, 3193.

1824 Royal National Lifeboat Institution founded. Lifeboat, 1935.

1890 Forth Bridge opened. Bridge, *567* ; Railways, 2734.

1941 British raid on the Lofoten Islands, *f-i.* Army, 244 ; Norway, 2398 ; World Wars, 3418.

1947 Anglo-French treaty of alliance signed at Dunkirk, 1055. Bevin, E., 422 ; Bidault, G., *f-i.*

Song-thrushes are building in sheltered gardens, 3205.
Daffodils are coming into bloom, 955.

5 1133 HENRY II of England born, **1609.** Becket, Thomas, 389 ; John, King, 1833 ; Newcastle, 2337 ; Richard I, 2776.

1512 Gerard Mercator, Flemish geographer, born, *f-i.* Maps, 2094.

1817 Sir Austen Layard, British orientalist, born. Archaeology, 206 ; Babylonia, 329 ; Nineveh, 2371.

1850 Menai (Britannia tubular) Bridge opened. Anglesey, *155* ; Bridge, 565.

1943 U.S. victory in the Bismarck Sea, *f-i.* Japan, 1800 ; Pacific, 2474 ; World Wars, 3421.

Migrant buntings and finches are beginning to leave for their northern nesting places, 2171.
Ground beetles are active in the garden, 399.

6 1475 MICHELANGELO, Italian artist and sculptor, born, **2160.** Adonis, *28* ; Italy : Art, *1783*, 1785 ; Renaissance, *2765*, 2766.

1806 Elizabeth Barrett Browning, English poetess, born, **589.** Browning, Robert, 590 ; English Literature, 1215 ; Poetry, 2634.

1834 George Du Maurier, English artist and writer, born, *f-i.* English Literature, 1210 ; Novel, 2401.

The chaffinch's cheery song is heard, 1272.
Green tips show through the lilac buds, 1947.

7 1802 SIR EDWIN LANDSEER, English painter, born, **1890.** English Art, 1177 ; London, 2019.

1804 British and Foreign Bible Society founded. Bible, 423 ; Borrow, George, 527 ; Christianity, 817.

1849 Luther Burbank, American horticulturist, born, **621.** Plant Life, 2620.

1850 Thomas Masaryk, first President of Czechoslovakia, born, **2117.** Czechoslovakia, 953.

1866 Albert Medal instituted. Albert, Prince Consort, 101 ; Orders and Decorations, 2448.

1945 U.S. troops crossed the Rhine at Remagen, *f-i.* Germany, 1453 ; Rhine, 2769 ; World Wars, 3422.

Many house sparrows' nests now contain eggs, 3052.

Courtesy of the High Commissioner for South Africa
March 4, 1394. Prince Henry the Navigator (after a painting by J. A. Amshewitz), born.

MARCH

8 1726 RICHARD, Earl Howe, British admiral, born, *f-i.* Navy, 2293.
1858 Ruggiero Leoncavallo, Italian composer, born, *f-i.* Opera, 2438 ; " I Pagliacci," 2439.

The first blackbird is heard, 463.
Larch trees are green with needles and purple with their first young cones, 1892.

9 1566 DAVID RIZZIO, secretary to Mary Queen of Scots, murdered at Holyrood. Mary Stuart, *2115* ; Scotland, 2892.
1749 Mirabeau, French statesman and orator, born, **2189.** French Revolution, 1393, *1394.*
1762 William Cobbett, British writer and reformer, born, **858.** English Literature, 1210.
1799 Royal Institution of Great Britain founded, *f-i.* Davy, Sir H., 980 ; Faraday, 1260 ; Tyndall, 3270.
1847 Mary Anning, girl discoverer of the first ichthyosaurus, died, **164.** Prehistoric Animals, *2681.*
1850 Sir William Hamo Thornycroft, British sculptor, born, *f-i.* Sculpture, 2906.
1851 Owens College, Manchester, opened. Manchester, 2084 ; Universities, 3296.

" Mad " March hares are now fighting for their mates, 1578.

10 1628 MARCELLO MALPIGHI, Italian anatomist, born, *f-i.* Blood, 477 ; Microscope, 2163.
1801 First Census taken in England. Census, 742 ; Population, 2656.
1863 Marriage of Edward VII and Alexandra, **108, 1092.** George V, 1442.
1873 Guildhall Library opened. Library, 1930 ; London, *frontis., vol. 5,* 2010.
1948 Jan Masaryk, Czech politician, committed suicide, 2117. Czechoslovakia, 953.

Bramblings prepare to leave for farther north, 2171.

11 1544 TASSO, Italian poet, born, **3157.** Italy : Literature, 1786 ; Poetry, 2634.
1682 Chelsea Hospital founded. Army, 244 ; Charles II, 756.
1885 Sir Malcolm Campbell born, **674.**
1941 U.S. Lease-Lend bill became law, *f-i.* Roosevelt, 2824 ; United States : History, 3292 ; World Wars, 3418.

Partridges chase each other in the open fields, 2526.
The roe-buck now has his new antlers, 984.

12 1507 CESARE BORGIA, Italian tyrant, killed, **525.** Italy, 1764.
1609 Bermudas become an English colony, **418.** British Commonwealth, *581.*
1838 Sir W. H. Perkin, founder of aniline dye industry, born. Coal-tar, 857 ; Dyes, 1059.
1864 Gabriele d'Annunzio, Italian poet and patriot, born, *f-i.* Italy, 1770.
1917 Outbreak of Russian Revolution. Bolshevism, 495 ; Lenin, 1922 ; Nicholas II, 2365 ; Russia, 2849.
1939 Coronation of Cardinal Eugênio Pacelli as Pope Pius XII. Pius, 2616 ; Papacy, 2495.

Green plovers call as they select their nesting sites. 2629.
Hairy bitter-cress is now in flower, 3354.

13 1733 JOSEPH PRIESTLEY, English physicist, born, **2683.** Oxygen, 2466.
1855 Percival Lowell, American astronomer, born. Astronomy, 275 ; Planets, 2618 ; Pluto, 2631.
1881 Assassination of Tsar Alexander II. Russia, 2848 ; Slavery, 2982.
1938 Annexation (*Anschluss*) of Austria to Germany, **316.** Hitler, 1631 ; National-Socialist Party, 2281.

Trout, after spawning, are feeding hungrily 3251.

14 1757 ADMIRAL BYNG shot in Portsmouth Harbour " to encourage the others," *f-i.* Balearic Islands, 342.
1864 Albert Nyanza discovered and named by Sir Samuel Baker, **340.** Africa, 72.
1879 Albert Einstein, German physicist, born, **1122.** Gravitation, 1514 ; Relativity, 2760.
1885 First production of Gilbert and Sullivan's " Mikado " at the Savoy, **1463.** Opera, 2438.

Watch the " display " of the male hedge sparrow, 3052.
Queen wasps are seeking sites for their nests, 3345

15 44 B.C. JULIUS CAESAR murdered, **651.** Britain, 573 ; Cleopatra, *838* ; Latin Literature, 1895 ; Rome : History, 2811.
A.D. 1767 Andrew Jackson, President of United States, born. United States : History, 3291.
1779 Lord Melbourne, British statesman, born, *f-i.* United Kingdom, 3278 ; Peel, Sir R., 2535 ; Victoria, Queen, 3319.
1939 German occupation of Czechoslovakia, **953.** Germany, 1451 ; Hitler, 1631.

Wagtails and pipits move northwards, 3332, 2611.

March 11, 1682. Foundation of the Royal Hospital for Invalid Soldiers, Chelsea. The engraving, by T. Bowles, reproduced above, shows the hospital as it appeared from the river in 1751.

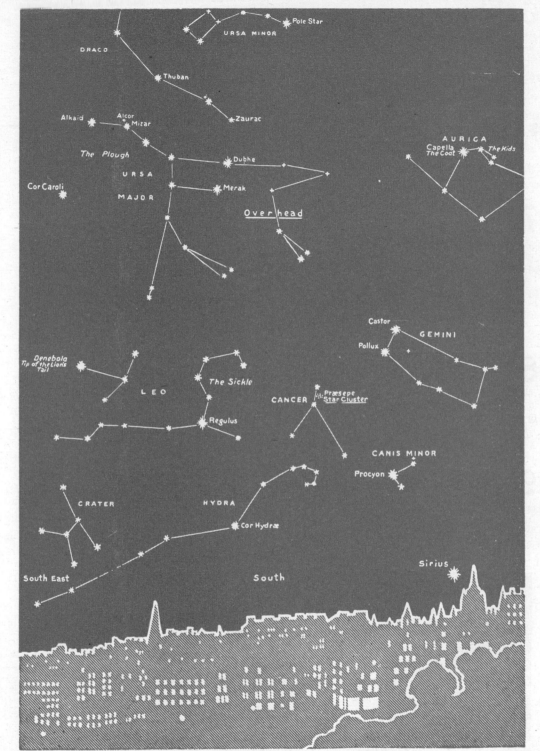

THE STARS IN MARCH. With this map we can study the stars from the middle of March to the middle of April. We are looking south in Edinburgh. Many of the stars in last month's diagram will be seen in the west and south-west. Throw the head well back to see the stars above the point marked Overhead.

16

1774 MATTHEW FLINDERS, British sailor and explorer, born. South Australia, 3028; New South Wales, 2343.

March 16, 1774. Matthew Flinders born.

1878 Émile Cammaerts, Belgian poet, born, *f-i.* Poetry, 2634.

1922 Sultan Ahmed Fuad proclaimed king of independent Egypt, 1102; British Commonwealth, 580.

Pike are leaving the deep water to spawn in the shallows, **2606.**

Lunar dung beetle burrows are visible in sandy soil, **400.**

17

St. PATRICK'S DAY, **2528.** Ireland, 1744.

1787 Edmund Kean, English actor, born, *f-i.* Drama, 1037; Shakespeare, 2932.

1839 John Pettie, British painter, born, *f-i.* Jacobites, *1791.*

1846 Kate Greenaway, British artist, born, *f-i.* Literature, Children's, 1964.

1948 50-year treaty of alliance signed at Brussels by Britain, France and the Benelux countries. European History, 1242; World Wars, 3424.

Early house flies appear, having passed the winter as larvae in the soil, **1329.**

18

978 EDWARD THE MARTYR assassinated, **1089.** English History, 1193.

1869 Arthur Neville Chamberlain, British statesman, born, **750.** Baldwin, Earl, 341; Munich, 2256; United Kingdom, 3282; World Wars, 3416.

1913 King George I of Greece assassinated, 1525. Balkan Peninsula, 343.

Pale green catkins make the hornbeam trees conspicuous, f-i.

19

1821 SIR RICHARD FRANCIS BURTON, British traveller, born, **626.** Mahomet, 2066; Mecca, 2125.

1834 Gottlieb Daimler, German engineer, born, *f-i.* Internal Combustion Engine, 1737; Motor Vehicles, 2241.

1858 Relief of Lucknow, **2035.** India: History, 1714

1872 Sergei Pavlovich Diaghileff, Russian impresario, born, *f-i.* Ballet, 345; Dancing, 965.

1932 Sydney Bridge opened, **3144.** Bridge, *567, 569.*

The robin begins to build, **2790.**

20

43 B.C. OVID, Roman poet, born. Latin Literature, *1897;* Poetry, 2634.

A.D. 1828 Henrik Ibsen, Norwegian dramatist, born, **1679.** Drama, 1040; Norway, 2392.

1836 Sir Edward Poynter, British painter, born, *f-i.* English Art, 1182; Atalanta, *283.*

1945 Mandalay recaptured from the Japanese by the British, *f-i.* Burma, 625; Japan, 1800; Slim, Sir Wm., *f-i.* World Wars, 3424.

Cock greenfinches are getting their handsome breeding plumage— brilliant yellow and rich green, **1272**

Greenfinch, a common British hedgerow bird.

21

FIRST DAY OF SPRING. Month, 2223; Seasons, 2914.

1556 Thomas Cranmer, Archbishop of Canterbury, burned at stake, **925.** Mary I, 2113; Reformation, 2758.

1685 Johann Sebastian Bach, German composer, born, **333.** Music, 2264.

1763 Jean Paul Richter, German poet, born, *f-i.* Germany, Prose and Poetry, 1456.

1801 Abercromby's victory over the French at Aboukir, *f-i.* France: History, 1365; Napoleon I, 2275; Nelson, 2313.

1918 Great German offensive opened against British Fifth Army. World Wars, 3412.

Now wheatears are seen, the first of our summer migrants, though even these are travelling on, **2171.**

22

1599 SIR ANTHONY VAN DYCK, Dutch painter, born. Netherlands: Art, 2333.

1644 Newark capitulated to Prince Rupert. English History, 1196.

1822 Rosa Bonheur, French painter, born, **499.** France: Art, 1377.

1939 Annexation of Memel to Germany, *f-i.* Hitler, 1631; National-Socialist Party, 2281.

The gannet lays its solitary egg, **1418.**

23

1801 PAUL I, Tsar of Russia murdered. Russia: History, 2846.

1854 Lord Milner, British statesman, born, *f-i.* Boer War, 486; Egypt, 1102.

1876 Muirhead Bone. English etcher, born, Engraving, 1219.

Lombardy poplar catkins open, **2655.**

March 17, 1948. At the signing of the Brussels Treaty of Western Union: left to right, M. Spaak (Belgium), M. Bidault (France), M. Bech (Luxemburg), Baron van Boetzelaer van Oosterhout (Netherlands), and Mr. Bevin (United Kingdom)

24

1607 MICHAEL ADRIANSZOON DE RUYTER, Dutch sailor, born, *f-i.* Blake, Robert, 101 ; Charles II. 756 ; Navy, 1809.

1834 William Morris, English poet and artist, born, 2232. Furniture, 1412 ; English Art, 1182 ; Bookbinding, 518 ; Pre-Raphaelites, 2682.

March 24, 1944. Gen. Orde Wingate (above) died.

1944 Orde Wingate, British general, killed in air crash, *f-i.* Burma, 623 ; Chindits, 815.

1945 Allied armies crossed the Rhine in force, 2769. Germany : History, 1453 ; Montgomery, 2222 ; World Wars, 3422.

The chiff-chaff has arrived and sings in southern woodlands, 3341. Perch are now spawning, 2549.

25

FEAST OF THE ANNUNCIATION. Lady Day. Madonna, 2052.

1807 Slave Trade abolished by British Parliament. Africa, 72 ; Cameroons, 672 ; Hawkins, Sir John, 1588 ; Henry the Navigator, 1613.

1821 Greece revolted against the Ottoman Empire ; anniversary kept as Greek Independence Day, **1525.** European History, 1237 ; Turkey, 3265.

1881 Mary Webb, English novelist, born, *f-i.* English Literature, 1210 ; Novel, 2401.

Curlew have left the lowlands and returned to the moors, where they will breed, 2169.

26

1838 WILLIAM EDWARD HARTPOLE LECKY, British historian, born, *f-i.* History, 1630.

1859 A. E. Housman, British poet, born, *f-i.* English Literature, 1216 ; Poetry, 2634.

1868 Maxim Gorki, Russian author, born, *f-i.* Novel, 2401 ; Russian Literature, *2856.*

1884 Wilhelm Backhaus, German pianist, born, *f-i.* Music, 2261 ; Piano, 2601.

Slow-worms now bask in the warm sun, 1973. Look for the first primroses, 2684.

27

1797 ALFRED DE VIGNY, French poet, born, *f-i.* France : Literature, 1379 ; Poetry, 2634.

1809 Georges Eugène, Baron Haussmann, French administrator, born. Paris, 2518.

1835 Sir William Orchardson, British painter, born, *f-i.* English Art, 1177 ; Painting, 2475.

1845 Wilhelm Konrad Röntgen, discoverer of X-rays, born, *f-i.* Atom, 294 ; X-rays, 3430.

1942 British Commando raid on St. Nazaire, *f-i.* Army, 245 ; World Wars, 3420.

1945 Last rocket bomb of the Second World War fell in England, **2791.**

See the long red and yellow catkins of the black Italian poplar, 2655.

28

1483 RAPHAEL born (or April 6), **2745.** Italy: Art, *1777,* 1785 ; Madonna, 2052, *2053* ; Paul, St., *2530.*

1660 George I, King of England, born, **1440.** Anne, 163 ; United Kingdom, 3276 ; Jacobites, 1790.

1749 Pierre Simon Laplace, French astronomer, born, *f-i.* Planets, 2618 ; Nebulae, 2310.

1862 Aristide Briand, French statesman, born, **560.** France : History, 1367.

1941 British naval victory over Italians at Matapan, *f-i.* Italy, 1774 ; Mediterranean, 2135 ; Navy, 2293.

Lady's smock is flowering in the meadows, 3354. The first sand-martins are here, 3125.

Cuckoo-flower, or Lady's Smock.

29

1869 SIR EDWIN LUTYENS, British architect, born, **2590.** Architecture, 212 ; Liverpool, 1968.

1871 Albert Hall opened. Albert, Prince Consort, 101 ; Organ, *2450.*

1918 Marshal Foch appointed generalissimo in France, **1332.** Haig, Earl, 1564 ; World Wars, 3412.

1939 End of the Civil War in Spain, **3040.** Franco, 1384 ; Madrid, 2055.

1945 Last flying bomb of the Second World War fell in England, **1330.** Jet Propulsion, 1826.

Willow warblers are singing in the woods, 3340.

March 29, 1871. The huge Albert Hall, London, opened as a memorial to the Prince Consort.

30

1282 " SICILIAN VESPERS " (massacre of French in Sicily). Sicily, 2968.

1844 Paul Verlaine, French poet, born, *f-i.* Poetry, 2634.

1856 Peace of Paris signed, ending Crimean War, 931. Russia, 2848.

*Jackdaws are starting to build, **1789.** On the ponds, duckweed plants begin to reappear, 3355.*

31

1596 RENÉ DESCARTES, French philosopher, born, **995.** Philosophy, 2572.

1621 Andrew Marvell, English poet, born. Charles I, 755 ; Milton, *2177.*

1732 Joseph Haydn, Austrian composer, born, **1589.** Music, 2264.

1811 Robert Wilhelm Bunsen, German chemist, born. Bunsen Burner, 615 ; Blowlamp, 477.

1900 Henry, Duke of Gloucester, brother of George VI, born, *f-i.* George V, 1442 ; George VI, 1442 ; Mary, Queen Mother, 2114.

*Moles, fighting for their mates, appear on the surface of the soil, oblivious to their normal enemies, **2196.***

1 APRIL FOOLS' DAY, **191.**

1578 William Harvey, discoverer of the circulation of the blood, born, **1581.** Anatomy, 151 ; Blood, 477.

1815 Otto von Bismarck, German statesman, born, *f-i.* Franco-Prussian War, 1384 ; Germany : History, 1449.

1918 Royal Air Force formed, **2832.** Aeroplane, *34-39, 46* ; Air Force, 91.

1945 U.S. forces landed on Okinawa, *f-i.* Japan, 1800 ; Pacific Ocean, 2474.

1947 Nationalization of electricity supply in U.K. came into force. Grid, 1545 ; Power Station, 2673.

1949 Newfoundland became the tenth province of Canada, **2337.**

Stitchwort's white flowers line the wayside, 3092.
Queen bumble-bees are on the move, 392.

2 742 CHARLEMAGNE, King of the Franks, born, **753.** Aachen, 9 ; France : History, 1365 ; Holy Roman Empire, 1636.

1801 Nelson's victory at Copenhagen. Copenhagen, 905 ; Navy, 2293 ; Nelson, Lord, 2313.

1805 Hans Christian Andersen, Danish author, born, **152.** Folklore, 1333 ; Literature for Children, 1965.

1827 Holman Hunt, English painter, born. English Art, 1182 ; Jesus Christ, *1825* ; Pre-Raphaelites, 2681 ; Painting, 2476.

1840 Émile Zola, French novelist, born, **3444.** Dreyfus, *f-i* ; France : Literature, 1381 ; Novel, 2404.

Yellow catkins are opening on the crack willows, 3382.
The blue tit is nesting in an old tree, 3218.

3 1593 GEORGE HERBERT, English divine and poet, born, *f-i.* Poetry, 2634.

1783 Washington Irving, American essayist and historian, born, **1759.** Novel, 2401 ; United States : Literature, 3293.

1933 First flight over Mt. Everest, **1243.** Aeroplane, 41 ; Asia, 263 ; Himalayas, 1626, *1627.*

The house martins are here again, 3124.
Hedge sparrows are beginning to build, 442.

4 1581 SIR FRANCIS DRAKE knighted by Queen Elizabeth aboard the Golden Hind, **1036.** Armada, 236 ; Elizabeth, Queen, 1146.

1648 Grinling Gibbons, English sculptor and woodcarver, born, **1462.**

1758 John Hoppner, English portrait painter, born, *f-i.* Burke, Edmund, *622* ; English Art, 1180.

1933 U.S. dirigible Akron lost. Airships, *94.*

1949 Signing of the North Atlantic Treaty by twelve nations, *f-i.* Bevin, E., 422 ; Truman, H. S., 3252.

The last redwings and other winter visitors are now leaving us, 2171.

5 1784 LOUIS SPOHR, German composer and violinist, born. Music, 2261 ; Opera, 2435.

1795 Sir Henry Havelock, English general, born, *f-i.* India : History, 1714 ; Lucknow, 2035.

1827 Joseph, Baron Lister, British surgeon, born, **1963.** Antiseptics, 178 ; Medicine, 2135 ; Pasteur, Louis, 2528.

1837 Algernon Charles Swinburne, British poet, born, **3137.** English Literature, 1215 ; Poetry, 2634.

Blackcaps arrive and settle down in the bushy places, 3340
Fox cubs are born now, 1355.

6 1767 HENRY BELL, builder of steamship Comet, born, *f-i.* Industrial Revolution, 1721 ; Ships, 2945 ; Steam Engine, 3085.

1773 James Mill, Scottish philosopher and economist, born, *f-i.* Economics, 1080 ; Philosophy, 2571.

1821 Greek War of Independence began. Greece, 1525 ; Byron, 634.

1872 Gold Coast becomes a British Colony. Africa, 68 ; British Commonwealth, 580.

1917 U.S.A. declared war on Germany. United States : History, 3291 ; World Wars, 3412.

1941 Germany invaded Yugoslavia and Greece, **1452.** Balkan Peninsula, 345 ; Greece, 1526 ; World Wars, 3418 ; Yugoslavia, 3440.

April 6, 1767. Birthday of Henry Bell, whose Clyde steamer Comet is seen above. It was built in 1811.

Big shoals of roach go to the shallows to breed, 2781.
Wood anemones flower, 154.

7 1506 ST. FRANCIS XAVIER, Spanish Jesuit missionary, born, **3429.** Christianity, 817 ; India : History, 1799 ; Japan, 1799 ; Loyola, Ignatius de, 2032.

1770 William Wordsworth, English poet, born, **3408.** Coleridge, S. T., 869 ; English Literature, *1214* ; Poetry, 2634.

1781 Sir Francis Legatt Chantrey, English sculptor, born, *f-i.* English Art, 1177 ; National Gallery, 2280 ; Sculpture, 2903.

1891 David Low, Australian cartoonist, born, *f-i.* Drawing, 1044.

1921 Dr. Sun Yat Sen elected president of Chinese Republic, *f-i.* China, *813* ; Nanking, *2273.*

1939 Italy invaded Albania, **100.** Italy, 1773 ; Mussolini, 2269.

Swallows return to their favourite nesting sites, 3124.
White dead-nettle flowers in the hedges, 2335.

April 4, 1933. U.S. dirigible Akron was lost in a storm. Above, we see the remains of the airship being salvaged.

APRIL

8 46 B.C. JULIUS CAESAR defeats Scipio's republican army at Thapsus in Africa, 881. Rome : History, 2811.

A.D. 1875 Albert I, King of the Belgians, born, **102**. Belgium, 407 ; Leopold III, 1928 ; World Wars, 3409.

1898 Battle of Atbara. Kitchener, Earl, 1862 : Sudan, 3110.

1943 Eighth Army and U.S. forces met in Tunisia, 3254. Army, 249 ; Italy, 1774 ; Libya, 1932 ; Montgomery, 2222 ; World Wars, 3420.

Whitethroats may now be heard in song, 3340.
The long aspen catkins are very conspicuous, 2655.
Ladybird beetles are seen in the garden, 1883.

9 1649 JAMES, Duke of Monmouth, born, *f-i.* Charles II, 756 ; James II, 1794.

1806 Isambard Kingdom Brunel, British engineer, born, **593**. Bridge, 568 ; Railways, 2734 ; Ships, *2957.*

Grayling, a member of the salmon family which spawns in spring.

1835 Leopold II, King of the Belgians, born, **1928**. Africa, 72 ; Albert I, 102 ; Belgium, 407 ; Congo States, 887.

1838 National Gallery, London, opened, **2280**. Italy : Art, *1778, 1779, 1782* ; London, *2012,* 2015, *2019.*

1865 Erich von Ludendorff, German soldier, born, *f-i.* World Wars, 3409.

1898 Paul Robeson, famous Negro singer, born, *f-i.*

1940 Germany invaded Denmark and Norway, **1452**. Denmark, 992 ; Norway, 2398 ; World Wars, 3416.

Stoats bring forth their young, 1222.
Grayling are spawning now, f-i.

10 1739 DICK TURPIN hanged at York. Highwaymen, 1625.

1778 William Hazlitt, English critic and essayist, born, *f-i.* English Literature, 1210 ; Essay, 1224 ; Lamb, Charles, 1886.

1829 General William Booth, founder of Salvation Army, born, **520**. Salvation Army, 2868.

1829 Catholic Emancipation Bill passed by Parliament. O'Connell, D., 2419 ; United Kingdom, 3278 ; Vote, 3330.

1870 Lenin (Vladimir Ilyich Ulianov) born, **1922**. Bolshevism, 495 ; Moscow, 2233 ; Russia, 2850.

Young fledgelings of such birds as thrushes and blackbirds are already in evidence ; the rookery is loud with the squawks of the young birds, 446–455.

11 1713 TREATY OF UTRECHT, 3300 ; Gibraltar ceded to Britain, 1463.

1770 George Canning, British statesman, born, *f-i.* United Kingdom, 3277.

1829 Alexander Buchan, Scottish meteorologist, born. *f-i.* Meteorology, 2149.

1861 Civil War opened in America. American Civil War, *f-i.* Lee, R. E., 1917 ; Lincoln, Abraham, 1951.

The nightingale reaches our shores, 2367.
Cowslips bloom in the meadows, 924.

12 1782 BATTLE OF THE SAINTS. Rodney defeated the French off the West Indies. Navy, 2293 ; United Kingdom, 3277.

1799 Church Missionary Society founded. Christianity, 817 ; Church of England, 825.

1945 Death of Franklin Delano Roosevelt, U.S. President, **2823**. United States : History, 3292 : World Wars, 3422.

Female crayfish may be found, laden with their berry-like eggs, 926.
Bilberries flower on the moors, 428.

13 1593 THOMAS WENTWORTH, Earl of Strafford, English statesman, born, *f-i.* Charles I, 755 ; Laud, Archbishop, *1899.*

1598 Edict of Nantes promulgated, giving religious freedom. Henry IV (France), 1613 ; Huguenots, 1656.

1743 Thomas Jefferson, U.S. president, born, **1816.**

1771 Richard Trevithick, builder of first moving steam carriage, born, **3247**. Locomotives, 1981.

1912 Royal Flying Corps constituted by royal warrant. Air Force, 91 ; Royal Air Force, 2832.

Tawny owls are now sitting on their large white eggs, plate f. 2460.
Lichens of various sorts begin to grow again, 1932.

14 1471 BATTLE OF BARNET. Edward IV, 1091 ; English History, 1193 ; Roses, Wars of the, 2828.

1629 Christian Huygens, Dutch astronomer, born, *f-i.* Astronomy, 275 ; Clocks and Watches, 844 ; Light, 1941 ; Pendulum, 2543.

1865 Abraham Lincoln, U.S. President, shot in theatre by John Wilkes Booth, **1951**. United States : History, 3290.

1865 President F. Solano Lopez of Paraguay began the disastrous war with Argentina, Brazil and Uruguay. Paraguay, 2512 ; Argentina, 229.

1931 Spain became a republic, **3037**. Alfonso XIII, *f-i.*

Now at last you may hear the cuckoo in southern England. 941.
The curved fronds of bracken are unfolding, 542.

April 14, 1471 Battle of Barnet commemorative stone at Hadley.

THE STARS IN APRIL. With this map we can study the stars from the middle of April to the middle of May. We are looking south in Chamberlain Square, Birmingham. The Great Bear, Ursa Major, is prominent overhead.

15 1755 Dr. Samuel Johnson published his Dictionary, 1896. Dictionary, 1015 ; English Literature, *1213*.

1800 Sir James Clark Ross, British admiral and explorer, born, *f-i*. Antarctica, 173 ; Polar Exploration, 2645.

1814 John Lothrop Motley, American historian, born, *f-i*. Netherlands : History, 2321 ; United States : Literature, 3294.

Apr. 15, 1912. The Titanic struck an iceberg on her maiden voyage and sank. The news reaches London.

1847 Opening of the new House of Lords, London, *2013* ; Parliament, *2520* ; Peerage, *2536*.

1912 Titanic sunk. Icebergs, 1682 ; Ships, 2945.

1923 Insulin discovered by Sir F. G. Banting. Digestion, 1016 ; Gland, 1471 ; Medicine, *2133*.

Bluebells begin to flower in the woods. **479**.
The little holly blue is in evidence again, plate f. **633**.

16 1746 Battle of Culloden. Jacobites, 1790 ; Macdonald, Flora, *2047* ; Pretender, 2682.

1786 Sir John Franklin, British sailor and explorer, born, **1387**. Arctic Regions, 223 ; Polar Exploration, 2644.

1821 Ford Madox Brown, English painter, born, *f-i*. English Art, 1182 ; Pre-Raphaelites, *2682*.

1844 Anatole France, French novelist, born, *f-i*. France : Literature, 1381, *1382* ; Novel, 2404.

1867 Wilbur Wright, pioneer airman, born, **3427**. Aeroplane, 45.

1889 "Charlie" Chaplin, born, *f-i*. Cinema, *828*.

1942 Malta awarded the George Cross, *2073*. Orders and Decorations, 2449.

Wood warblers sing in the woods once more, 3340.
The wild cherries make a fine show of bloom, **778**.

17 1492 Ferdinand and Isabella sign their grant to Columbus, **1760**. America : Discovery, 139 ; Columbus, Christopher, 878.

1876 Ian Hay, British author and dramatist, born, *f-i*. English Literature, 1210 ; Novel, 2401.

The corncrake reaches Britain, 2734.
Toothwort flowers in the hazel coppice, 2621.

18 1856 Aldershot Camp publicly inaugurated by Queen Victoria. Army, 244 ; Victoria, Queen, 3319.

1874 David Livingstone, British missionary and explorer buried in Westminster Abbey, **1970**. Africa, 72 ; Congo, 887.

1881 Natural History Museum, South Kensington, opened. London, 2015 ; Museums, *2259, 2260*.

1946 International Court of Justice opened. The Hague, 1563. International Law, 1905 ; United Nations, 3283.

The plane tree seed-balls burst and scatter their seeds, each armed with a parachute of fine hairs, **2616**.
Newts are spawning in the ponds, f-i.

19 1775 Battle of Lexington, opening of American War of Independence, 144. United States : History, 3291.

1839 Belgium became an independent kingdom, **407**. European History, 1240.

1881 Benjamin Disraeli, Earl of Beaconsfield, died, **1018** ; the anniversary celebrated as Primrose Day. Conservatives, 892 ; Peel, Sir Robert, 2535.

1915 British captured Hill 60. World Wars, 3409.

By the riverside, sedge-warblers vie with each other in noisy, chattering song, **3340**.

20 1657 Admiral Blake defeated the Spanish fleet off the Canary Islands, **465**.

1689 Opening of the siege of Londonderry, **2021**. Ireland, 1744 ; James I, 1793 ; William III, 3380.

1808 Napoleon III, Emperor of the French, born, **2278**. France : History, 1366 ; Franco-Prussian War, 1384.

1889 Adolf Hitler, German President and Chancellor, born, **1631**. Germany : History, 1450.

1947 Christian X, King of Denmark, died, **816**. Denmark, 991 ; Frederick IX, *f-i*.

Swifts begin to arrive in southern England, **3124**.
Hunting spiders and other species are on the look-out for their insect prey, **3062**.

21 1782 Friedrich Wilhelm August Froebel, German educationist, born, **1398**. Education, 1088 ; School, 2883.

1816 Charlotte Brontë, English novelist, born, **586**. English Literature, 1210 ; Novel, 2402.

1926 Princess Elizabeth born, **1150**. Elizabeth, Queen Consort, 1149 ; George VI, 1442.

The early purple orchid flowers, **2448**.
Oak trees are beginning to burst their buds, their catkins gradually expanding, **2409**.

22 1707 Henry Fielding, English novelist, born, 1269. English Literature, 1213 ; Novel, 2402.

1724 Immanuel Kant, German philosopher, born, **1846**. Germany : Prose and Poetry, 1457 ; Philosophy, 2572.

1857 Opening of first Parliament in South Australia. South Australia, 3028 ; Australia, 307 ; Parliament, 2521.

1918 Attack on Zeebrugge launched. Navy, 2293 ; World Wars, 3412.

Bugle, a plant of the sage family.

Meadow pipits and skylarks are nesting on the moors and in the fields, 2611, **1893**.
Bugle flowers in the woods, **3207**.

23

St. George's Day, 1440.

1616 William Shakespeare died, **2932**. Drama. *1039*, 1040, *1041*; English Literature, 1211, *1212*; Poetry, 2634.

1662 Connecticut chartered as a British colony, **891**. America: Discovery, 139; United States: History, 3290.

1858 Dame Ethel Mary Smyth, composer and conductor, born, *f-i*.

1861 Lord Allenby, British general, born, **121**. Palestine, 2480; World Wars, 3409.

1915 Rupert Brooke, British poet, died at Lemnos, 587. English Literature, 1216; Poetry, 2634.

Garden warblers reach us now, 3340.
Notice the green fruits on the wych elms, 1152.
Primroses are at their best in the north, 2684.

24

1500 Brazil discovered by Pedro Alvarez Cabral, **550**. South America, 3022.

1743 Edmund Cartwright, inventor of power-loom, born, **712**. Weaving, 3361.

1815 Anthony Trollope, English novelist, born, **3250**. English Literature, 1215; Novel, 2402.

1916 Outbreak of Easter Rebellion in Dublin. Dublin, 1051; Ireland, 1744.

Adders sun themselves in the dry bracken, 3325.
The grey wagtail is nesting, 3332.

25

Feast of St. Mark. Bible, 423; Christianity, 817.

1284 Edward II, King of England, born, **1089**. English History, 1193; Battle of Bannockburn, 359.

1792 John Keble, English poet and divine, born, *f-i*. Hymns, 1678; Oxford, 2462.

1862 Lord Grey of Fallodon, English statesman, born, **1544**. United Kingdom, 3276; World Wars, 3409.

1874 Guglielmo Marconi, Italian inventor, born, **2098**. Wireless, 3391.

1915 Landing of Australian and New Zealand Army Corps at Gallipoli (Anzac Day). World Wars, 3410.

1945 San Francisco Conference of the Allied nations opened, **2872**. United Nations, 3283.

Moorhens build their big platform of reeds, 2734.
Perch spawn, gathering along the river banks in well-regulated shoals, 2549.

April 26, 1948. King George VI and Queen Elizabeth driving to a thanksgiving service at St. Paul's on their Silver Wedding day.

26

121 Marcus Aurelius Antoninus, Roman Emperor, born, **2099**. Latin Literature, 1897; Rome: History, 2812.

1711 David Hume, Scottish philosopher, born, *f-i*. Philosophy, 2572.

1769 First exhibition of the Royal Academy opened. Academy, 17; English Art, 1179; Painting, *2477*.

1923 Marriage of George VI (then Duke of York) to Lady Elizabeth Bowes-Lyon. Elizabeth, Queen Consort, 1149; George VI, 1442.

Tiger-beetles may be seen in warm weather, 399.
Lilac flowers in the south, 1947.

27

1737 Edward Gibbon, English historian, born, **1461**. History, 1630; Roman History, 2811.

1791 Samuel Finley Breese Morse, inventor of electric telegraph, born, **2232**. Cable, 641; Telegraphy, 3164.

1818 Order of St. Michael and St. George founded. Knighthood, 1863; Orders, 2449.

1820 Herbert Spencer, English philosopher, born, *f-i*. Philosophy, 2572.

Snipe breed on the damp, marshy moors, 2991.
Apple-blossom is at its best, 190, plate f. 1400

28

1220 Foundation Stones of Salisbury Cathedral laid, **2864**. Architecture, *219*; Cathedral, *721*; Church of England, 825.

1442 Edward IV, King of England, born, **1091**. English History, 1193; Roses, Wars of the, 2828.

1789 Mutiny of the Bounty. Pacific, *2472, 2473*.

1801 Anthony Ashley-Cooper, 7th Earl of Shaftesbury, English reformer, born, **2031**.

1945 Benito Mussolini, Italian dictator, executed by partisans, **2268**. Fascism, 1261; Italy, 1770; World Wars, 3424.

Young rabbits now provide an easy prey for cats, stoats, and weasels, 2721.
Trout fatten on newly emerged flies, 3251.

29

1429 Joan of Arc relieves Orleans, **1831**. France: History, 1365; Hundred Years' War, 1652.

1783 David Cox, English landscape painter, born, *f-i*. English Art, 1181; Painting, 2475.

1879 Sir Thomas Beecham, British musical conductor, born, **395**. Opera, 2438; Orchestra, 2447.

1884 Statute passed at Oxford University admitting women to examinations. Oxford, 2464.

Jackdaws' eggs are laid, 1789.
Great activity is visible round the entrance to the bee hive, plate f. 393.

30

1789 George Washington inaugurated as first President of U.S.A., **3342**. American Independence, 144; U.S.A.: History, 3291.

1827 Foundation stone of London University laid 2021. Universities, 3296.

1834 Sir John Lubbock (Lord Avebury), British writer and entomologist, born, **323**. Holidays, 1635.

1945 Death of Adolf Hitler, German dictator, **1631**. Germany, 1451; National-Socialist Party, 2281; World Wars, 3424.

Buttercups begin to flower in the fields, 628.
The bullfinch nests in thick hedges, 1272.

MAY

1 FEAST OF ST. PHILIP AND ST. JAMES. May Day Month ????

1672 Joseph Addison, English poet and essayist, born, **23.** English Literature, 1213; Essay, 1224.

1707 Act of Union between Scotland and England. Anne, Queen, 163; English History, 1200, *1208*; Parliament, 2524.

1851 Great Exhibition opened in Hyde Park. Albert, Prince Consort, 101; Victoria, Queen, 3319.

1931 Prof. Auguste Piccard, Swiss scientist, made the first balloon ascent into the stratosphere, *f-i.* Air, *89*; Balloon, 349.

1949 Gas industry in U.K. passed into State ownership, **1423.** Socialism, 2996.

Young animals of all sorts are now common in the woods and fields.
Tawny owls begin hunting in early evening, 2460.

2 1611 AUTHORIZED VERSION of the Bible published, **426.** James I, 1793.

1670 Hudson's Bay Company chartered, **1650.** Canada, 682; Furs, 1412; Labrador, 1875.

1729 Catherine II (the Great), Empress of Russia, born. Odessa, 2420; Russia: History, 2847.

1859 Jerome K. Jerome, British novelist and dramatist, born, *f-i.* Drama, 1037; Novel, 2401.

1945 Berlin captured by the Red Army, **416.** Germany, 1453; Hitler, 1631; World Wars, 3424.

Sand lizards are active if the weather is sunny, 1972.
Young blue tits call from the nest. 3218.

3 1469 NICCOLO MACHIAVELLI, Italian diplomat and writer, born, **2049.** Medici Family, 2131. Italy: Literature, 1786.

1791 Poland's first liberal constitution accepted by the Diet; anniversary kept as Poland's National Day, **2642.** Kosciusko, 1873.

1844 Richard D'Oyly Carte, producer of Gilbert and Sullivan operas, born, *f-i.* Gilbert and Sullivan, 1463; Opera, 2438.

1926 General Strike began. Trade Union, 3233.

Lesser stitchwort flowers plentifully along the roadside, 3092.
Common blue butterflies are on the wing, plate f. 632.

4 1471 BATTLE OF TEWKESBURY. English History, 1193; Henry VI, 1611; Roses, Wars of. 2828. 1769 Sir Thomas Lawrence, English painter, born. English Art, 1180; Moore, Sir John, *2227*; Painting, 2475.

1825 Thomas H. Huxley, English biologist, born, **1661.** Darwin, 978; Evolution, 1244.

1896 First issue of the *Daily Mail*, founded by Alfred Harmsworth (Lord Northcliffe), **2385.**

Now the nightingale's song may be heard, 2367.
Wasps and bumble-bees are making their new colonies. 3345, 392

5 1818 KARL MARX born at Trèves, **2113.** Communism, 881; Philosophy, 2571; Socialism, 2996. 1826 Empress Eugénie, wife of Napoleon III, born. France: History, 1365; Napoleon III, 2278.

1882 Sir Douglas Mawson, British explorer, born. Antarctica, 173; Polar Exploration, *2645.*

Hawthorn is beginning to flower, 1588.
The curious spider orchis may now be found. 2448.

After the painting by H. Selous

May 1, 1851. Queen Victoria opened the Great Exhibition in Hyde Park. The building was afterwards re-erected at Sydenham and called the Crystal Palace.

6 1856 SIGMUND FREUD, Austrian scientist, born, **1396** Mind, 2180; Psychology, 2697; Psychoanalysis, 2697.

1856 Robert E. Peary, discoverer of North Pole, born, **2534.** Arctic, *223*; Polar Exploration, 2645.

1882 Phoenix Park murders in Dublin, Ireland, 1744; Parnell, C. S., 2525.

1910 Death of Edward VII and accession of George V, **1092, 1442.** United Kingdom, 3280.

Swifts scream round their old haunts again, 3124.
Newt tadpoles may be found in the ponds. f-i.

7 1765 NELSON's flagship, H.M.S. Victory, launched. Navy, 2293; Nelson, 2313; Trafalgar, 3234. 1812 Robert Browning, English poet, born, **590.** English Literature, 1215; Poetry, 2634.

1833 Johannes Brahms, German composer and pianist, born, **544.** Music, 2264; Orchestra, 2445.

1840 Piotr Ilyitch Tchaikovsky, Russian composer, born, **3158.** Music, 2266; Orchestra, 2445.

1915 Lusitania torpedoed. United States: History, 3290; World Wars, 3412.

1945 Unconditional surrender of all German forces. Germany, 1453; World Wars, 3424.

One of our latest migrants, the red-backed shrike, has settled down again, 2962.
The bee hawk moth may be seen in warm localities, f-i

8 1837 ALPHONSE LEGROS, French painter, born *f-i.* Browning, Robert, *590*; France: Art, 1377. 1902 Eruption of Mont Pelée, Martinique, **2112.** West Indies, 3368; Volcanoes, 3328.

1942 Allied victory over Japan in the battle of the Coral Sea, *f-i.* Japan, 1800; Pacific, 2473.

1945 VE-Day; public holiday to celebrate surrender of Germany in the Second World War, 3424.

The strange flowers of the ash appear, 262.
There are eggs in the buzzard's nest, 633.

9 1671 ATTEMPT by Thomas Blood to steal the Crown Jewels, **477.** Charles II, 756; Crown Jewels, 935, *Vol. 2 frontis.*

1800 John Brown, American hero, born, **588.** Slavery, 2981; United States: History, 3291.

1860 Sir James Matthew Barrie, Scottish author and dramatist, born, **364.** Drama, 1037; English Literature, 1210; Novel, 2401.

1946 Victor Emmanuel III, King of Italy, abdicated, 3319. Italy, 1775; Mussolini, 2269.

Woods ring with the fascinating song of the wood-warbler, 3340.
Rowan trees are now in flower, 3376.

10 1727 ANNE ROBERT JACQUES TURGOT, French statesman, born. France: History, 1365; French Revolution, 1393.

May 10, 1857. Outbreak of the Indian Mutiny. Above, ghat at Cawnpore where Europeans were massacred.

1760 Claude-Joseph Rouget de Lisle, author of the Marseillaise, born, 19 3. France: History, 1365; French Revolution, 1393; National Songs, 2883.

1857 Outbreak of the Indian Mutiny. British Commonwealth, 580; India, 1714; Lucknow, 2035.

1940 Germany, 1452, invaded the Netherlands, Belgium, and Luxembourg, **403, 2041, 2318.** Winston Churchill became Prime Minister, **824.**

Swallows are rebuilding old nests or constructing new ones, 3124.
Roe deer fawns are born now, 984.

11 1740 MARIA THERESA crowned at Prague, **2101.** Austria-Hungary, 320; Germany: History, 1447.

1824 Léon Gérôme, French artist, born. Cleopatra, *838*; Caesar, Julius, *652*; France: Art, 1377.

1868 Public executions in U.K. abolished. Prison, 2686.

Sheldrakes are nesting in the sand dunes, 1051, 456
White butterflies' eggs are laid, 630.

12 1812 EDWARD LEAR, English writer, born, **1910.** English Literature, 1210; Limericks, 1950; Literature for Children, 1965.

1820 Florence Nightingale, English nurse, born, **2368.** Crimea, 931; Hospitals, 1648; Nursing, 2406.

1828 Dante Gabriel Rossetti, English poet and painter, born, *f-i.* English Art, 1182, *1190*; Poetry, 2634; Pre-Raphaelites, 2681.

1937 Coronation of George VI, **1442.** Coronation, *912*; Crown Jewels, 935, *Vol. 2 frontis.*

1943 German surrender in Tunisia complete, **3254.** Eisenhower, 1123; Rommel, *f-i.*

Flycatchers arrive from abroad again, 1330.
Holly is in flower, 1636.

13 1792 PIUS IX, Pope, born, **2615.** Garibaldi, 1418; Italy: History, 1769.

1840 Alphonse Daudet, French novelist, born, **979.** France: Literature, 1379.

1842 Sir Arthur Seymour Sullivan, English composer, born. Gilbert and Sullivan, *1463*; Opera, 2438.

1857 Sir Ronald Ross, British physician, born. Medicine, 2133; Mosquito, 2236; Panama Canal, 2488.

Young blackbirds have already flown from their nests, 447, 463.
White evening campion is in flower, 674.

14 1264 BATTLE OF LEWES. Edward I, 1089; Henry III, 1611; Montfort, Simon de, 2221.

1686 Gabriel Daniel Fahrenheit, German scientist, born, *f-i.* Heat, 1593; Thermometer, 3200.

1727 Thomas Gainsborough, English painter, baptized, **1413.** English Art, 1179, *1187*; Pitt, *2614.*

1847 Sir Frederick William Borden, Canadian statesman, born, *f-i.* British Commonwealth, 580; Canada, 676.

1948 State of Israel proclaimed, *f-i.* Jews, 1831; Palestine, 2483.

The whitethroat is nesting now, f-i.
Young red squirrels are born, 3071.

15 1567 MARRIAGE of Mary Queen of Scots to the Earl of Bothwell, **2115.** Elizabeth, 1146; Scotland: History, 2892.

1679 Ashmolean Museum, Oxford, founded. Museums, 2259; Oxford, 2465.

1773 Prince Metternich, Austrian statesman, born, *f-i.* European History, 1240; Napoleon I, 2275.

1847 Sir Edwin Ray Lankester, English scientist, born, *f-i.* Anatomy, 150; Biology, 430.

1859 Pierre Curie, co-discoverer of radium, born, 944. Radium, 2731.

1942 British evacuated Burma, **625.** Japan, 1800; World Wars, 3420.

Cliff birds, such as the guillemot and razorbill, are laying their eggs on bare, rocky ledges, f-i, 304.
Carp spawn now in ponds, 704.

Guillemot (right) and razorbill, sea-birds that breed in May on the steep cliffs of Britain.

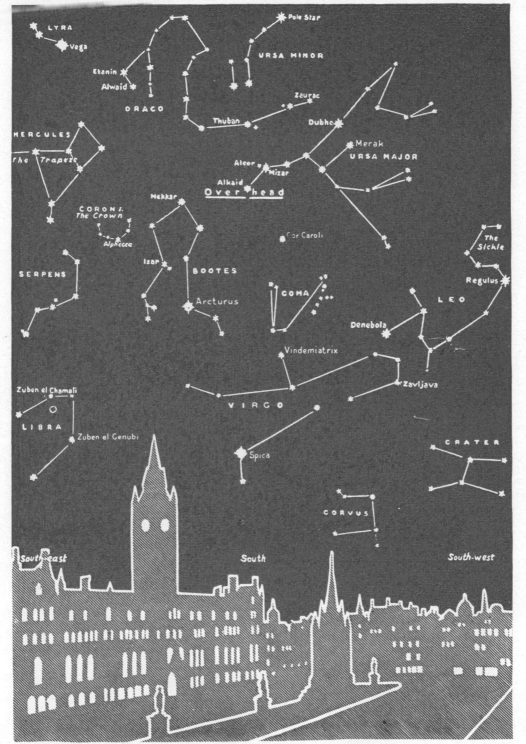

THE STARS IN MAY. With this map we can study the stars from the middle of May to the middle of June. We are looking south in Albert Square, Manchester, with the Town Hall on the left of us. The constellation Draco, " the dragon," lies high above our heads.

16 1782 JOHN SELL COTMAN, British painter, born, **917**. English Art, *1189* ; Norwich. 2398 ; Painting, 2475.

1811 French defeated by Allies at Albuera. Napoleon I, 2275 ; Wellington, Duke of, 3364.

May 16, 1811. British, Portuguese, and Spaniards, under Beresford defeated the French at Albuera.

1911 Victoria Memorial, London, unveiled. Buckingham Palace, *599* ; Victoria, Queen, 3319.

Starlings are busy feeding their young, 3083, 446.
Various species of vetch are in flower by the wayside. f-i.

17 1673 JACQUES MARQUETTE set out to explore the Mississippi, **2107**. America : Discovery, 143 ; Mississippi, 2192.

1749 Edward Jenner, discoverer of vaccination, born, **1818**. Medicine, 2132.

1814 Norway's constitution adopted at Eidsvold, **2392**; anniversary kept as Norway's National Day.

1877 Edward Iliffe, 1st Baron, British newspaper proprietor, born, **1686**. Newspapers, 2344.

1886 Alfonso XIII, King of Spain, born, **110**. Spain, 3037.

1900 Mafeking relieved. Boer War, 486 ; South Africa, 3019.

Grasshopper warblers sing on the moors, 3340.
Bats are numerous now, 370.

18 1857 BRITISH MUSEUM Reading Room opened, *585*. Library, 1930.

1868 Nicholas II, Tsar of Russia, born, **2365**. Russia : History, 2848.

1872 Bertrand Russell, British philosopher, born, *f-i.* Mathematics, 2120 ; Philosophy, 2572.

1882 New Eddystone Lighthouse opened, **1084**. Lighthouses, *plate f. 1944*.

Young ducklings are common on the ponds, 1051
House martins lay their eggs now, 3124.

19 1588 SPANISH ARMADA sailed from the Tagus, **236**, *plate facing 236*. Drake, Sir F., 1036 ; English History, 1195 ; Navy, 2293.

1692 French fleet defeated off Cape La Hogue. Louis XIV, 2029 ; Navy, 2293.

1859 Dame Nellie Melba, Australian singer, born, *f-i.* Opera, 2435.

20 1501 ASCENSION ISLAND discovered. Atlantic Ocean, 290.

1780 Elizabeth Fry, English Quakeress and reformer, born, **1403**. Prisons, 2686.

1799 Honoré de Balzac, French novelist, born, **352**. France : Literature, 1381 ; Novel, 2404.

21 1806 John Stuart Mill, British philosopher and economist, born, **2175**. Carlyle, Thomas, 702 ; Economics, 1081 ; Philosophy, 2572.

Pine woods are yellow with falling pollen, 2609.
Cockchafers begin to appear on warm evenings, 399.
The coot's nest is full of brown-spotted eggs, 2734.

21 1471 ALBRECHT DÜRER, German artist, born, **1058**. Engraving, *1217* ; Germany : Art, 1454.

1618 Opening of Thirty Years' War, 3202. Europe, 1239 ; Germany : History, 1449 ; Gustavus Adolphus, 1558.

1894 Manchester Ship Canal opened by Queen Victoria. Canal, 686, *688* ; Manchester, 2084.

1916 Summer Time Act first came into force. Daylight Saving, 980.

1927 Lindbergh arrived at Le Bourget on his Transatlantic flight, **1953**. Aeroplane, 41 ; Atlantic, 291.

May-flies begin to appear on southern streams, 2122.
Sticklebacks make their nests, to be ferociously
defended by the males, 3091.

22 1455 FIRST BATTLE OF ST. ALBANS. Roses, Wars of the, 2828 ; St. Albans, 2861.

1813 Wilhelm Richard Wagner, German composer, born, **3331**. Music, 2264 ; Nibelungs, 2263 ; Opera, 2437 ; Stories, 2439, 2440.

1856 Opening of the first Parliament of New South Wales, **2343**. Australia, 307 ; British Commonwealth, 580 ; Parliament, 2521.

1859 Sir Arthur Conan Doyle born, **1032**. English Literature, 1210 ; Novel, 2401.

1915 Railway disaster at Gretna Green—157 killed and 200 injured. Railways, 2734.

1931 Whipsnade Zoo Park opened to the public. Zoological Gardens, 3445.

The kestrel's eggs are laid by now, 1587, 453.
Water-crowfoot is in bloom on the pond, 3355.

23 1706 MARLBOROUGH defeats the French at Ramillies, **2105**. Anne, Queen, 163.

1707 Carl Linné or Linnaeus, Swedish botanist, born, **1954**. Biology, 435 ; Botany, 531.

1734 Franz Anton Mesmer, German physician, born, *f-i.* Medicine, 2132 ; Psycho-analysis, 2697.

Partridges brood their eggs closely beneath the hedgerows, 2526.
The furniture beetle appears on the wing, f-i.
Horse chestnuts come into flower, 1647.

The furniture beetle, shown much magnified.

24 1819 QUEEN VICTORIA born, **3319**. Empire Day (founded 1904). British Commonwealth, 580.

1862 Westminster Bridge opened. Bridge, 564 ; Caisson, 654 ; London, 2014 ; Thames, 3193.

1870 F.-M. Jan Christiaan Smuts, South African statesman, born, **2987**. Boer War, 456 ; South Africa, 3019.

1930 Amy Johnson finished her solo flight from England to Australia at Port Darwin, **1834.** Aeroplane, 41.

There are now young in the chiff-chaff's nest, 3340.
Tree-pipits are in song in the woods, 2612.

25 1659 RICHARD CROMWELL resigned the Protectorate, *f-i.* Cromwell, Oliver, 933; English History. 1198.

1803 Ralph Waldo Emerson, American poet and essayist, born, **1156.** Essay, 1224; United States: Literature, 3294.

1803 Lord Lytton, English novelist and dramatist, born, **2044.** Drama, 1037; English Literature, 1210; Pompeii, 2654.

1810 The people of Buenos Aires deposed the Spanish viceroy; anniversary kept as Argentina's Independence Day, **228.**

1871 Bank Holidays Act passed. Avebury, Lord, 323; Holidays, 1635.

1946 Transjordan became an independent state, **3238.** Arabia, 195, *map, 197*; Palestine, 2483.

Red deer are now getting their new set of antlers, 984.
In the reed beds, reed warblers are beginning to build, 3340.

26 735 THE VENERABLE BEDE, English historian and translator of the Scriptures, died, *f-i.* Bible, *423.*

1867 Queen Mary, Consort of George V, born, **2114.** Edward VIII, 1092; George V, 1442; George VI, 1442.

The nightjar's strange " churring " is heard at night, 2369.
White willows glisten silvery in full leaf, 3382.

27 1679 HABEAS CORPUS ACT passed. Charles II, 756; Law, 1902; Prisons, 2686.

1703 St. Petersburg founded by Peter the Great. Leningrad, 1923; Peter the Great, 2562; Russia, 2847.

1819 Julia Ward Howe, American poetess, born, *f-i.* National Songs, 2282; United States: Literature, 3293.

1867 Enoch Arnold Bennett, British novelist, born, **414.** English Literature, 1215; Novel, 2403.

The spindle tree with its pink berries.

Goldfinches are rearing their first brood, 1272.
The spindle tree is in flower, f-i.

28 1759 WILLIAM PITT THE YOUNGER, English statesman, born, **2614.** United Kingdom, 3277; Napoleon I, 2275.

1779 Thomas Moore, Irish poet, born. Irish Literature, 1751; Poetry, 2634.

1807 Louis Agassiz, Swiss-American naturalist, born, **75.** Botany, 531.

Rock pipits are nesting along the foreshore, 2611, and the sea birds swarm on the cliffs.

May 24, 1862. Westminster Bridge (above) was opened. It is 1,160 ft. long and 85 ft. wide.

29 1453 TURKS captured Constantinople. Istanbul, **1761**; Renaissance, 2764; Turkey, 3264.

1630 Charles II, King of England, born, **756.** Charles I, 755; English History, 1198, *1207.*

1660 Entry of Charles II into London at the Restoration; Oak Apple Day, **756.** English History, 1198.

1860 Opening of Queensland's first Parliament, **2716.** British Commonwealth, 580; Australia, 307; Parliament, 2521.

1874 Gilbert Keith Chesterton, English writer, born, **781.** English Literature, 1216.

1940 Evacuation of British and Allied forces at Dunkirk began, **1056.** Army, 244; World Wars, 3417.

Terneries are loud with the cries of the nesting birds, 1555.
Small copper butterflies are on the wing, plate f. 632.

30 1431 JOAN OF ARC burned at stake, **1831.** Charles VII, 757; Hundred Years' War, 1653; France: History, 1365.

1672 Peter the Great, Tsar of Russia born, **2562.** Russia, 2847.

1746 Toussaint l'Ouverture, Negro leader, born. Haiti, 1565; West Indies, 3368.

1935 Earthquake at Quetta — approximately 40,000 deaths. Baluchistan, 352; Earthquake, 1069; India, 1691; Pakistan, 2479.

May 30, 1746. Toussaint l'Ouverture, Negro leader, born.

*The water-rail is sitting now on its well-hidden nest, 2286, **2733.***
Stag-beetles are seen on warm evenings, 398.

31 1819 WALT WHITMAN, American poet, born, **3376.** Poetry, 2637; U.S.: Literature, 3294.

1902 Peace of Vereeniging, ending Boer War, **486.** South Africa, 3019.

1910 Union of South Africa established; anniversary celebrated as Union Day. South Africa, 3019.

1916 Battle of Jutland. Jellicoe, Lord, 1816; World Wars, 3411.

Merlins nest on northern moorlands, 1588.
Beech trees, now in full leaf, are flowering also, 395.

JUNE

1 **1794** LORD HOWE's victory over the French in the Atlantic Ocean : the "Glorious First of June." French Revolution, 1393 ; Navy, 2293.
1875 John Masefield, poet laureate, born, **2117.** English Literature, 1216 ; Poet Laureate, 2634.

June 1, 1794. Lord Howe (seen above on his flagship, the Queen Charlotte) defeated the French.

1927 The new Regent Street, London, opened by George V. Architecture 212 ; London, 2015, *2017.*
1941 British forces evacuated Crete, **927.** Greece, 1526 ; Mediterranean, 2135 ; World Wars, 3418.
Robins are making their second-brood nests, 2790.
Young field voles are to be seen now, f-i.

2 **1793** OPENING OF REIGN OF TERROR. France : History, 1366 ; French Revolution, 1396.
1840 Thomas Hardy, British novelist and poet, born, **1577.** Dorset, 1030 ; English Literature, *1215* ; Novel 2402.
1857 Sir Edward Elgar, British composer, born, **1143.** Music, 2266 ; Orchestra, 2445.
1858 G. B. Donati, Italian astronomer, discovered comet now known by his name, *f-i.* Astronomy, 275 ; Comet, 880 ; *back of plate f. 881.*

The grasshopper warbler nests now, 3340.
Large skipper butterflies are common, plate f. 633.
Whitebeam flowers on the chalk downs, 3376.

3 **1771** SYDNEY SMITH, British divine and wit, born, *f-i.* English Literature, 1210.
1804 Richard Cobden, British politician, born, **858.** Bright, John, *569* ; Peel, Sir Robert, 2535.
1853 Sir Flinders Petrie, British Egyptologist, born, *f-i.* Archaeology, 206 ; Egypt : Ancient, 1113.
1865 George V, King of England, born, **1442.** Edward VII, 1092 ; Edward VIII, 1092 ; Mary, Queen Mother, 2114 ; United Kingdom, 3280.

Reed buntings are building now by the waterside, 616.
Flowers of the yellow archangel are common in the woods.

4 **1738** GEORGE III, King of England (reign 1760–1820), born, **1441.** Eton, 1229 ; United Kingdom, 3278.
1823 Garnet Joseph, Viscount Wolseley, British soldier, born, *f-i.* Egypt : Modern, 1101 ; Gordon, General, 1486.

1944 Rome liberated by the Allies, **2804.** Italy, 1774 ; World Wars, 3422.
Dragon-flies fly to and fro over the water, 1034.
The ringed plover lays its eggs now, 443, plate f. 440.

5 **755** ST. BONIFACE, Apostle of Germany, murdered, 500. Christianity, 817 ; Germany, 1449.
1723 Adam Smith, British economist, born, 2896. Economics, 1081.
1819 John Couch Adams, English astronomer, born, *f-i.* Astronomy, 275.
1849 Denmark's liberal constitution came into force ; anniversary kept as Constitution Day, **991.**
1916 Lord Kitchener drowned, **1862.** World Wars, 3411.
1947 George G. Marshall, U.S. Secretary of State, outlined at Harvard the "Marshall Plan" to assist Europe, **2111.** European Recovery Programme, *f-i.* European History, 1242.

Swans with their cygnet family are now a common sight, 449, 3126.
In shallow, gentle streams minnows are spawning, 704.

6 **1599** DIEGO RODRIGUEZ DA SILVA Y VELAZQUEZ, Spanish painter, baptized, **3307.** Murillo, 2257 ; Painting, 2475 ; Spanish Art, 3049.
1606 Pierre Corneille, French dramatist, born, **910.** Drama, 1040 ; France : Literature, 1380.
1799 Alexander Pushkin, Russian poet, born, *f-i.* Russian Literature, 2855.
1921 Southwark Bridge opened. Bridge, 564 ; London, 2009 ; Thames, 3193.
1942 U.S. victory in the Battle of Midway Island, *f-i.* Japan, 1800 ; Pacific, 2474 ; World Wars, 3421.
1944 D-Day. Allied invasion of Normandy, **2377.** France, 1368 ; Germany, 1453 ; World Wars, 3422.

Young lizards may be found already, 1973.
The orange-tip butterfly is about, plate f. 632.

7 **1566** FOUNDATION STONE of London's first Royal Exchange (destroyed in the Great Fire) laid by Sir Thomas Gresham. London, 2009.

1773 Guatemala City. Guatemala, wiped out by earthquake. Central America, 743 ; Earthquake, 1069 ; Guatemala, 1552.
1811 Sir James Young Simpson, Scottish physician, born, *f-i.* Anaesthesia, 148 ; Medicine, *2133* ; Victoria, Queen, 3319.
1832 Reform Bill received the Royal Assent. Parliament, 2522 ; Vote, 3330.
1848 Paul Gauguin, French artist, born in Paris. France : Art, 1379 ; Impressionism, *1689* ; Painting, 2477.

Yellow archangel, or dead-nettle, common in June in woods.

Herring gulls are nesting on the cliffs. 1557.
The swifts lay their long, white eggs in roofs or old buildings, 3124.

8 **1652** WILLIAM DAMPIER, English navigator, baptized, **964**. Australia, 310.

1810 Robert Schumann, German composer, born, **2887**. Music, 2265.

1814 Charles Reade, British novelist, born, *f-i*. English Literature, 1210 ; Novel, 2402.

1821 Sir Samuel White Baker, English explorer, born, **340**. Africa, 65 ; Nile, 2370.

1829 Sir John Everett Millais, British painter, born. English Art, 1182 ; Carlyle, *703* ; Huguenots, *1651* ; Martyrs, *2112* ; Moses, *2235* ; Pre-Raphaelites, 2681.

The whinchat's nest, deeply hidden in grass, now contains eggs, 3375.
The lesser water plantain is in flower, 3356.

9 **1781** GEORGE STEPHENSON born, **3087**. Locomotives, 1 9 8 1 ; Steam Engine, 3085.

1859 Sir F. C. Doveton Sturdee, British sailor, born, *f-i*. World Wars, 3409.

1873 Alexandra Palace destroyed by fire, *f-i*. Fire-Fighting, 1285 ; London, 2009.

The common seal's young are born now, 2912.
Puss-moth eggs may be found on willow or poplar leaves, which the caterpillars will eat later on, 720.

10 **1688** JAMES FRANCIS EDWARD, the " Old Pretender," born. Jacobites, 1790 ; Pretender, 2682.

1921 H.R.H. Prince Philip, Duke of Edinburgh, born, *f-i*. Elizabeth, Princess, *1151*.

1940 Italy declared war on Britain and France, **1773**. Mussolini, 2269 ; World Wars, 3417.

1942 The Czech village of Lidice destroyed by the Germans, *f-i*. National-Socialist Party, 2281.

Turtle doves have hatched their young now. 2606.
Giant puff-balls appear in the fields, plate f 1408.

11 FEAST OF ST. BARNABAS.

1685 James, Duke of Monmouth, landed at Lyme Regis to seize the throne, *f-i*. Charles II, 756 ; James II, 1794.

1776 John Constable, British painter, born, **893**. English Art, 1181, *1188* ; National Gallery, 2280 ; Painting, 2476.

1864 Richard Strauss, German composer, born, **3103**. Opera, 2438, 2440, *2441*.

Late nests of green plover may yet contain eggs, 2629.
Thistles are beginning to come into bloom, 3203.

12 **1802** HARRIET MARTINEAU, English writer for young people, born, *f-i*.

1819 Charles Kingsley, English divine and author, born, **1858**. English Literature, 1210 ; Literature for Children, 1966.

Effigy in Canterbury Cathedral
June 15, 1330. Edward, the " Black Prince," born.

1837 First electric telegraph patented by Cooke and Wheatstone, **3164**. Cable, 640 ; Edison, 1087 ; Morse, 2232 ; Post Office, 2661.

1851 Sir Oliver Joseph Lodge, English scientist, born, **1988**. Physics, 2594 ; Wireless, 3391.

1897 Robert Anthony Eden, British politician, born, **1085**. Conservatives, 892 ; League of Nations, 1908 ; United Kingdom : History, 3282 ; World Wars, 3415.

1943 Trans-Canada Highway opened to coast-to-coast traffic. Canada, 676 ; Roads, 2783.

Pheasants sit close on their large clutch of eggs, 2565.
On the buckthorn feed the green caterpillars of the lovely brimstone butterfly, plate f. 632.

13 **1752** FRANCES (FANNY) BURNEY, Madame d'Arblay, English novelist, born, *f-i*. Johnson, Samuel, 1835.

1795 Dr. Thomas Arnold, British educationist, born, *f-i*. Rugby, *f-i*. ; School, 2883.

1841 First Canadian Parliament opened at Ottawa. Canada, 684 ; British Commonwealth, 580 ; Ottawa, *2458* ; Parliament, 2521.

1865 William Butler Yeats, Irish poet and dramatist, born. Irish Literature, *1751*.

The Arctic tern lays its eggs on the shore, 1557.
Numerous young birds and small mammals provide food for stoats and weasels and their families. 1222.

14 **1645** BATTLE OF NASEBY. Charles I, 755 ; Cromwell, Oliver, 933 ; English History, 1196.

1811 Harriet Beecher Stowe, author of " Uncle Tom's Cabin," born, *f-i*. Slavery, 2982 ; United States : Literature, 3294.

1919 First Atlantic flight started (Alcock and Whitten Brown). Aeroplane, 47 ; Atlantic Ocean, 290.

The long-eared bat produces its single young one, 372.
Goat's-beard is in flower, f-i.

15 **1215** MAGNA CARTA sealed by King John at Runnymede, **2059**. Government, 1489 ; English History, 1194 ; John, King, 1834.

1330 Edward the Black Prince born at Woodstock. Edward III, 1091 ; Hundred Years' War, 1652 ; Richard II, 2777.

The redshank's cleverly hidden eggs are ready to hatch, 3331.
The marsh orchis is in flower, f-i.

Marsh orchis, a purple-flowered species.

JUNE

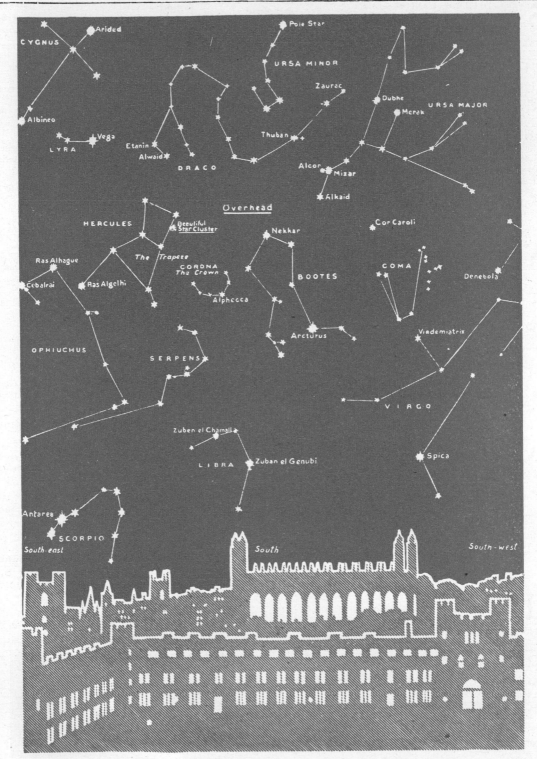

THE STARS IN JUNE. Here we can study the stars from the middle of June to the middle of July. We are looking south in Cambridge, towards King's College Chapel. Antares in Scorpio is a beautiful red star.

16

1722 JOHN CHURCHILL, Duke of Marlborough, died, **2105.** Anne, Queen, 163 ; Blenheim, Battle of, 470.

1824 Royal Society for the Prevention of Cruelty to Animals founded by Richard Martin, M.P., *f-i.* Animals' Behaviour, 159.

The sea-bird's cliff haunts are loud with the sounds of the nesting season, now in full swing.
Stinkhorn fungi betray themselves by their horrible smell, f-i.

17

ST. ALBAN'S DAY, **100.**

1239 Edward I, King of England, born, **1089.** English History, 1193 ; Montfort, Simon de, 2221 ; Parliament, *2522.*

1682 Charles XII of Sweden born, **758.** Peter the Great, 2563 ; Sweden, 3131.

1703 John Wesley, founder of Methodism, born, **3365.** Christianity, 817 ; Free Churches, 1390.

1818 Charles François Gounod, French composer, born, *f-i.* Opera, 2437, 2438, *2441.*

1832 Sir William Crookes, British scientist, born. Radium, 2732 ; X-rays, 3430.

1841 First issue of *Punch* published. Newspapers, 2344.

Nightingales have nearly all stopped singing by now, **2367.**
Whirligig beetles gyrate on the smooth surface of pond and ditch, 400.

18

1643 JOHN HAMPDEN, English statesman and patriot, mortally wounded at Chalgrove Field, **1571.** Buckinghamshire, 599 ; Cromwell, Oliver, 933.

1815 Battle of Waterloo, **3354.** France: History, 1365 ; Napoleon I, 2275 ; United Kingdom, 3278 ; Wellington, Duke of, 3364.

1817 Old Waterloo Bridge opened. Bridge, 564 ; London, 2009 ; Thames, 3193.

Young moles are large enough now to fend for themselves, 2196.
The glow-worm's dull light may now be seen, 1288.

19

1566 JAMES I, King of England, born, **1793.** Fawkes, Guy, 1264 ; Mary Stuart, 2115.

1623 Blaise Pascal, French philosopher and scientist, born, *f-i.* Calculating Machines, 656 ; France : Literature, 1380 ; Hydraulics, 1666.

1861 Earl Haig, British general, born, **1564.** World Wars, 3409.

1867 Maximilian, Emperor of Mexico, shot. Mexico, 2159.

1895 Kiel Canal opened, **1856.** Canal, 689 ; Germany, 1445.

Lime trees are now coming into bloom, a resort for bees and for birds which feed on them, **1949.**
House flies begin to become more numerous, **1329.**

20

1756 BLACK HOLE OF CALCUTTA, **660,** *661.* Clive, Lord, 842 ; India: History, 1714.

1837 Death of William IV and accession of Victoria. William IV, 3381 ; Victoria, Queen, 3319.

1867 Alaska sold to U.S.A. by Russia, **97.** Russia, 2844 ; United States, 3291.

1897 Queen Victoria's Diamond Jubilee. Victoria, Queen, 3319.

Reed warblers' nests may now be found, often several quite close together, **3340**
Buttercups are now at their best in the meadows, **628.**

21

LONGEST DAY OF THE YEAR.

1675 Foundation stone of new St. Paul's Cathedral laid, **2862,** *2863.* Architecture, *219* ; Cathedral, 729 ; London, 2010, *2020* ; Wren, 3425.

1813 William Aytoun, Scottish poet, born, *f-i.* Flodden Field, 1315 ; Scotland: Literature, 2894.

1917 Order of the British Empire instituted. Orders and Decorations, 2449.

1942 Surrender of Tobruk to the Germans, *f-i.* Libya, 1932 ; World Wars, 3420.

Young sandpipers may be seen by river or lake, f-i.
Hover-flies are about, their larvae feeding on aphids, 1731.

22

FESTIVAL OF ST. ALBAN, **100.** St. Albans, 2861.

1805 Giuseppe Mazzini, Italian patriot, born, 2124. Garibaldi, G., 1418 ; Italy, 1769.

1904 Cape to Cairo Railway opened. Africa, 65 ; Railways, 2734 ; Rhodes, Cecil, 2771.

1911 Coronation of George V and Queen Mary, **1442, 2114.** Coronation, 912.

1940 Franco-German armistice signed at Compiègne, *f-i.* France : History, 1368 ; Germany : History, 1452 ; World Wars, 3417.

1941 Invasion of Russia by Germany, **1452.** Russia, 2852, *2853* ; World Wars, 3418.

The golden eagle has young in its eyrie, 1064.
Young fallow deer are born now ; stags of this species have shed their horns, 984.

June 19, 1867. Ferdinand Maximilian, Emperor of Mexico, shot. This painting by Jean Paul Laurens depicts his last moments.

2 c 8

23 1757 BATTLE OF PLASSEY. Calcutta, 660; Clive, Lord, 842; India: History, 1714.
1879 William Ewert Berry, 1st Viscount Camrose, born, 675. Newspapers, 2344.
1894 Edward VIII, King of England, later Duke of Windsor, born, *1091*, 1092. George V, 1442; George VI, 1442; Mary, Queen Mother, 2114.

Trout are now at their best from the angler's point of view, 3251.
Bee orchids are in flower on the chalk hills, 2448.

24 ST. JOHN THE BAPTIST'S DAY: Midsummer Day. Month, 2223; Seasons, 2914.
1314 Battle of Bannockburn, 359. Bruce, Robert, *591*; Scotland, 2892.
1340 Battle of Sluys. Edward III, 1091; Hundred Years' War, 1652.
1859 French defeated Austrians at Solferino. Napoleon III, 2278; Red Cross, 2752.

Yellow-hammers have their second brood, 616.
Look for the water-spider in clear ponds, 2287.

25 1807 NAPOLEON and the Tsar Alexander I held interview at Tilsit. Napoleon I, 2275; Russia, 2848.
1900 Earl Mountbatten of Burma born, 2248. Army, 244; Burma, 625; India: History, 1716; Royal Family, table, *f-i*.

Young cuckoos clamour for food from their over-worked foster-parents, 942.

26 1553 CHRIST'S HOSPITAL granted its charter. Edward VI, 1091; Lamb, Charles, 1886; Coleridge, S. T., 869; School, 2883.
1763 George Morland, English artist, born. English Art, 1182; Painting, 2475.
1824 Lord Kelvin, British physicist, born, *1849*. Cable, 642; Joule, 1840.
1945 United Nations Charter signed by 50 nations at San Francisco, 2872. United Nations, 3283.

Various fritillaries are now on the wing, especially in open woodlands and along the hedges, plate f. 632, 633.
The flowering rush blooms in muddy ditches, 3356.

27 1550 CHARLES IX, King of France, born, 758. France · History, 1365; Henry IV (France), 1613; Huguenots, 1650.
1867 Luigi Pirandello, Italian playwright, born, *f-i*. Drama, 1042; Italy: Literature, 1787.
1880 Helen Adams Keller, American blind deaf-mute, born. Blind, Education of, 471; Deaf, 981.

Young barn owls are nearly ready to fly, 2460.
Shrews breed now in their nests of leaves and grass, f-i.

28 1491 HENRY VIII, King of England, born, 1612. English History, 1193; Germany: Painting, *1455*; More, Sir Thomas, 2228; Reformation, 2759; Wolsey, 3402.

June 26, 1553. Christ's Hospital (the Blue Coat School), boys from which are seen above, was granted its charter.

1712 Jean Jacques Rousseau, French philosopher, born, 2831. Biography, 430; France: Literature, 1380; French Revolution, 1393.
1914 Assassination of Archduke Francis Ferdinand at Sarajevo. Serbia, 2922; World Wars, 3409.
1919 Treaty of Versailles ending the First World War signed. Versailles, 3317; World Wars, 3414.

Young starlings are forming into vast flocks, 3083.
The dragonet spawns now, and the male is at his best with brilliant colours, 1034.

29 ST. PETER'S DAY, 2562.
1577 Peter Paul Rubens, Flemish artist, born, 2838. Cadmus, *649*; Loyola, *2034*; Netherlands · Art, *2327*, *2333*; Painting, 2475.
1855 First issue of the *Daily Telegraph* published. Camrose, 675; Newspapers, 2344.
1895 Foundation stone of Westminster Cathedral laid. Architecture, 212; Cathedrals, 729.

Mallard drakes lose their breeding dress and enter their "eclipse" plumage, 1051.
In beech woods look for the lovely butterfly orchis, 2448.

30 1837 USE OF PILLORY abolished by Parliament. Defoe, 985; Prisons, 2686.
1894 Tower Bridge opened. Bridge, *567*, *568*; London, 2009, *2017*; Thames, 3193.
1934 Nazi coup ("blood purge") in Germany. Germany: History, 1451; Hitler, Adolf, 1632.
1940 German forces occupied the Channel Islands, 752.

Water-rails' nests still contain eggs, 2286, 2733.
The privet hawk moth may now be seen, plate f. 633.
Toads are now common in the field and garden, 3219.

June 29, 1895. Foundation stone of Westminster Cathedral (above) laid.

1 1690 (Old Style). BATTLE OF THE BOYNE, 607, anniversary celebrated as Orange Day in N. Ireland on July 12. Ireland, 1745 ; William III, 3380.

1867 Dominion of Canada founded, **680,** 683 ; anniversary kept as Dominion Day. British Commonwealth, 580.

1916 First Battle of the Somme began. World Wars, 3410.

1946 Experimental atomic bomb exploded at Bikini Atoll (a second was exploded July 24), *f.-i.* Atom, 299.

Families of stoats may be seen, hunting together, one behind the other in a line, 1222.
Tortoiseshell butterfly caterpillars swarm on the nettles, plate f. 632, 720.

2 1489 THOMAS CRANMER, Archbishop of Canterbury, born, **925.** Church of England, 825 ; Reformation, 2758.

1644 Battle of Marston Moor. Charles I, 756 ; Cromwell, Oliver, 933 ; English History, 1196.

1857 Siege of Lucknow began, **2035.** India : History, 1714.

1862 Sir William Bragg, British scientist, born, *f.-i.* Crystal, 940 ; Ions, 1739 ; X-rays, 3431.

Young partridges have left the nest and run to and fro in the cornfields, 2526.

3 1737 JOHN SINGLETON COPLEY, Anglo-American painter, born, *f.-i.* English Art, 1177 ; Painting, 2475.

1866 Austrians defeated by the Prussians at Sadowa (Königgratz). Germany : History, 1449; William I of Germany, 3378.

1900 Count Zeppelin, German aeronaut, made the first flight in a rigid airship, **3442.** Airship, 93 ; World Wars, 3409.

The cuckoo's call is now irregular, 941.
Great water plantain flowers in the muddy ditch, 3356.

4 1776 DECLARATION OF AMERICAN INDEPENDENCE, **144.** United States : History, 3291 ; Washington, George, 3342.

1804 Nathaniel Hawthorne, American writer, born, **1589.** Literature for Children, 1966 ; Novel, 2401 ; United States : Literature, 3294.

July 8, 1921. King George V opened the London dock (seen above) named after him.

1807 Giuseppe Garibaldi, Italian patriot, born, **1418.** Cavour, 737 ; Italy, 1769.

1946 Philippine Islands became an independent republic, **2569.** Pacific, 2473 ; United States : History, 3293.

The robin is one of the few birds whose song can still be heard, for after breeding most species are moulting and are silent, 2790.

5 1781 SIR STAMFORD RAFFLES, founder of Singapore, born ; he died on the same day in 1826. British Commonwealth, 580 ; Singapore, 2974.

1803 George Borrow, English writer, born, **527.** Bible, 423.

1804 George Sand, French novelist, born. Chopin, Frédéric, 816 ; France : Literature, 1381.

1853 Cecil Rhodes, British statesman and Empire pioneer, born, **2771.** British Commonwealth, 580 ; South Africa, 3019.

National Portrait Gallery
July 5, 1781. Sir Stamford Raffles born.

1948 National Health Service came into operation in the U.K. Health, Ministry of, 1590 ; Insurance, 1735 ; Social Insurance, 2994.

Harvest mice are nesting now in the corn, plate f. 2248.
Grasshoppers sing their lustiest now, 1510.

6 1415 JOHN HUSS, Bohemian reformer and champion of Czech nationalism, burned at the stake, **1660.** Reformation, 2758.

1685 Battle of Sedgemoor, last battle fought on English soil ; the Duke of Monmouth (*f.-i.*) defeated by the troops of James II. James II, 1794.

1755 John Flaxman, English sculptor, born at York, *f.-i.* Pottery, 2665 ; Sculpture, 2906.

The goldfinch is hatching its second brood now, 1272.
Now is the time to collect many species of grasses, flowering by the wayside, in the woods and on the hills, 1509, frontis. Vol. 4.

7 1752 JOSEPH MARIE JACQUARD, French inventor, born. Automatic Control, 321 ; Industrial Revolution, 1721 ; Jacquard Loom, 1790 ; Lace, 1877 ; Weaving, 3361.

1929 Vatican constituted a sovereign state. Vatican City and State, **3306.**

1937 China-Japan conflict began ; anniversary kept in China as Double-Seventh Day, **814.** Japan, 1800 : Manchuria, 2087.

Female bats, caught in their daytime hiding places, have their single young one clinging to their own bodies, 370.
Small pike hunt now in the streams and ditches, 2606.

8 1621 JEAN DE LA FONTAINE, French poet and fabulist, born, **1884.** France : Literature, 1379.

1836 Joseph Chamberlain, English statesman, born, **749.** Conservatives, 892.

July 12, 1870. Opening of Victoria Embankment. The above photograph was taken just after its completion.

1921 George V opened London dock named after him. Docks, 1022 ; George V, 1442.

Nests of the greater whitethroat may still have eggs, and the cock bird sings occasionally even now, 3340.

9 **1777** HENRY HALLAM, English historian, born, *f-i.* History, 1630.
1819 Elias Howe, inventor of sewing-machine. born. Clothes, 851 ; Sewing-machine, 2929.

In the hot, clear sunny weather, trout and other fish are unwilling to feed, and lie basking in the shallows.

10 **1509** JOHN CALVIN, French reformer, born, **664.** Christianity, 817 ; Geneva, 1428 ; Reformation, 2758.
1584 William the Silent assassinated, **3381** ; Netherlands : History, 2321.
1792 Captain Frederick Marryat, English sailor and novelist, born, 2109. English Literature, 1210.
1834 James McNeill Whistler, American artist, born, *f-i.* English Art, 1182 ; Painting, 2477.
1943 Allied invasion of Sicily, **2969.** Italy, 1774 ; World Wars, 3421.

*One of the coolest places is the beech wood, where the shade even now is intense, **395.***
Late swarms of hive bees may occur, 391.

11 **1274** ROBERT BRUCE born, **590.** Bannockburn, 359 ; Scotland, 2892.
1708 Battle of Oudenarde. Marlborough, Duke of, 2105.
1882 Bombardment of Alexandria, **110.** Egypt : Modern, 1101.

Woodcock may now be seen carrying their young as they fly to the feeding grounds. 3403.

12 **1174** HENRY II did penance at Canterbury for murder of Becket. Becket, Thomas, 389 ; Canterbury, 692 ; Henry II, 1609.

1691 (Old Style). Battle of Aughrim, 537. Ireland, 1745 ; William III, 3380. Anniversary kept as Orange Day (*see* July 1).
1817 Henry David Thoreau, American author and naturalist, born, **3204.** U.S. Literature, 3294.
1854 George Eastman, American inventor, born. Photography, 2580.
1870 Victoria Embankment opened by Prince of Wales (Edward VII). London, 2012 ; Thames, 3193.

*The swallows are rearing their second brood, **3124.***
White admiral butterflies are on the wing, plate f. 632.

13 **1525** CHRIST CHURCH COLLEGE, Oxford, founded as Cardinal College by Cardinal Wolsey. Oxford, 2464.
1607 Wenceslaus Hollar, Bohemian engraver, born, *f-i.* Engraving, 1217.
1793 Assassination of Jean Paul Marat by Charlotte Corday, **2096.** France : History, 1365 ; French Revolution, *1394,* 1396.

*Wasps' nests may be discovered, excavated and robbed by badgers, **3345.***
Harebells are in flower, 479.

14 **1602** JULES MAZARIN, French cardinal and statesman, born, *f-i.* France : History, 1365 ; Louis XIV, 2029 ; Opera, 2435.
1789 Bastille taken by Paris mob ; commemorated as National Fête. France : History, 1365 ; French Revolution, 1394, *1395* ; Paris, 2514.
1865 First ascent of the Matterhorn by Edward Whymper. Alps, 128, *131* ; Mountaineering, 2247.
1940 Annexation of Estonia, Latvia amd Lithuania to the Soviet Union, **1226, 1899, 1967.** Russia, 2852 ; World Wars, 3418.

*Linnets' nests may still be found in the hedges and gorse thickets, **1955.***
*Adders are born now, **3325.***

15 ST. SWITHIN'S DAY, **2862.**
1573 Inigo Jones, English architect, born, **1836.** Architecture, 220.
1606 Rembrandt van Rijn, Dutch painter, born,

July 10, 1834. James McNeill Whistler born. Above is a typical etching by him, dated 1859, of the Pool of London.

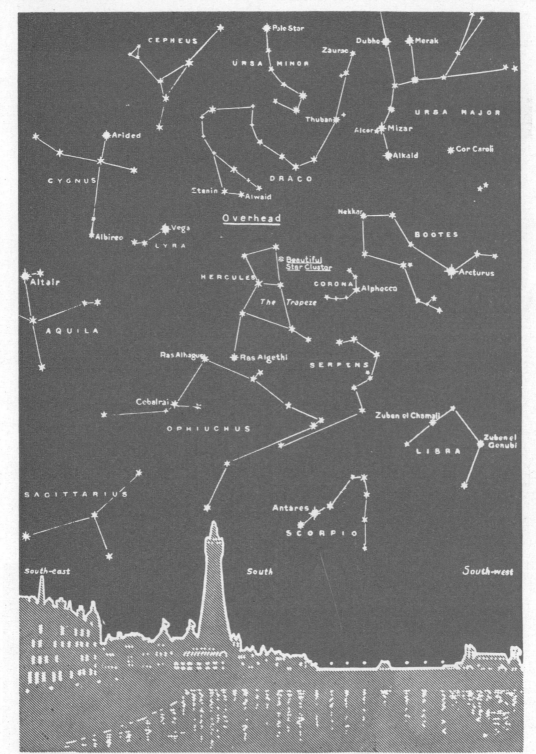

THE STARS IN JULY. With this map we can study the stars from the middle of July to the middle of August. We are looking southward in Blackpool, but the holiday-maker will find the same splendid spectacle wherever he may go in Britain.

JULY

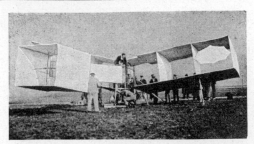

July 20, 1873. Santos-Dumont, seen above in his box-kite form of aeroplane, was born.

2762. Engraving, *1219* : Netherlands ; Art, *2328*, 2333. Painting, 2476.

1865 Alfred Harmsworth, Viscount Northcliffe, born, **2385 ;** Newspapers, 2344 ; World Wars, 3409.

> *The strange and interesting fruits of many mosses may be found in the shady woods, 2238.*

16 1486 ANDREA DEL SARTO, Italian painter, born. Herod, *1620* ; Italy : Art, 1775. 1723 Sir Joshua Reynolds, English painter, born, **2768.** English Art, 1179, *1186* ; Gainsborough, Thomas, 1413 ; Painting, 2476.

1821 Mary Baker Eddy, founder of Christian Science, born, *f-i.* Free Churches, 1390.

> *Look out for the nests of the potter wasps on twigs and small branches, 1732.*
> *Strange little green hydra is common in pond water,* **1664.**

17 1674 DR. ISAAC WATTS, English divine and hymn-writer, born, *f-i.* Hymns, 1678. 1796 Camille Jean Baptiste Corot, French painter, born, **913,** *914.* Fine Arts, *1274,* 1275 ; France : Art, 1378.

1797 Paul Delaroche, French painter, born, *f-i.* France : Art, 1377 ; Laud, Archbishop, *1899.*

1936 Civil War began in Spain, 3039. European History, 1242 ; Franco, 1384.

1945 Potsdam Conference opened, *f-i.* Attlee, 300 ; Churchill, 824 ; Germany, 1453 ; Stalin, 3073 ; Truman, 3252 ; World Wars, 3424.

> *Young house sparrows chirp almost incessantly in the eaves,* **3052.**
> *The green oak tortrix is on the wing, f-i.*

18 1720 GILBERT WHITE, clergyman and naturalist, born, **3376.** English Literature, 1210 ; Nature Study, 2283.

1811 William Makepeace Thackeray born, **3193.** English Literature, 1215 ; Novel, 2402, *2403.*

1848 Dr. W. G. Grace born, *f-i.* Cricket, 928.

1870 Doctrine of Papal Infallibility promulgated. Christianity, 817 ; Papacy, 2495.

1934 Mersey Tunnel opened by King George V. Birkenhead, *457* ; Lancashire, 1890 ; Liverpool, 1968 ; Tunnels, 3255.

> *In thundery weather, swarms of winged ants are in flight, and so are minute " rove " beetles, called " thunderbugs " by the country people.*

19 1924 LIVERPOOL CATHEDRAL consecrated, **1968.** Architecture, *219* ; Cathedrals, 729. 1932 Lambeth Bridge opened by King George V. Bridge, 564 ; London, 2009 ; Thames, 3193.

> *Water-plants are especially conspicuous, and among them the wild iris is one of the most beautiful,* **1748.**

20 1304 PETRARCH, Italian poet, born. Italian Literature, *1786* ; Poetry, 2636. 1873 Alberto Santos-Dumont, Brazilian aeronaut, born, *f-i.* Aeroplane, 45 ; Airships, 93.

1944 Attempted assassination of Adolf Hitler, **1631.**

> *The reed bunting still chatters by the riverside, 617. Green, cone-like fruits are ripening on the alders,* **104.**

21 1403 BATTLE OF SHREWSBURY and death of Hotspur. Henry IV, 1611 ; Henry V, 1611. 1817 Sir John Gilbert, British artist, born. Agincourt, *76* ; Charles I, *756* ; Merchant of Venice, *2145.*

1831 Belgium became a separate kingdom under Leopold I, *403 ;* anniversary kept as Independence Day. Leopold, 1928 ; Netherlands, 2323.

1897 Tate Gallery (London) opened. English Art, 1177 ; National Gallery, 2280.

> *Young swifts may be discovered, having fallen to the ground in trying to fly,* **3124.**
> *Summer broods of many butterflies are now seen, plate f. 632.*

22 ST. MARY MAGDALENE'S DAY. 1298 Battle of Falkirk. Edward I, 1089 ; English History, 1193 ; Scotland, 2892 ; Wallace, Sir Wm., 3337.

1822 Gregor Mendel, Austrian scientist, born, **2139.** Genetics, 1427 ; Heredity, 1617.

> *Young barn owls are losing their white down for a suit of real feathers,* **2460.**
> *Yellow-horned poppy is in flower on sea cliffs, 2655.*

23 1423 LOUIS XI of France born, **2028.** Charles the Bold, 759 ; France : History, 1365.

1823 Coventry Patmore, British poet, born, *f-i.* English Literature, 1210.

July 18, 1934. The Mersey Tunnel, the Liverpool entrance to which is seen above, was opened.

1840 Vaccination Act passed by Parliament. Anti-toxin, 180 ; Jenner, Edward, 1819 ; Medicine, 2132.

1883 F.-M. Lord Alanbrooke, British soldier, born, **96**. Army, 244 ; Montgomery, 2222.

The downy thistle seeds blow from field to garden, settling down to provide next year's weeds, 3203.
Rowan berries are beginning to change colour, 3376.

24 1704 CAPTURE OF GIBRALTAR, **1462**.
1802 Alexandre Dumas the Elder, French novelist, born, **1053**. France : Literature, 1381 ; Novel, 2404.

1898 Amelia Earhart, American airwoman, born, *f-i.* Aeroplane, 41.

1927 Menin Gate at Ypres unveiled by Lord Plumer. Belgium, *407* ; World Wars, 3409.

Various weevils are common now, devouring leaves, seeds and twigs of trees, 3362.
Wild raspberries are ripening, 2745.

25 FEAST OF ST. JAMES (the Greater).
1554 Marriage of Mary I to Philip of Spain, **2113, 2567**.

1848 Arthur James, 1st Earl Balfour, British states-man, born, **343**. Chamberlain, Joseph, 749 ; Pale-stine, 2482.

1909 Louis Blériot, French aviator, made the first cross-Channel aeroplane flight, **470**. Aeroplane, 45.

1934 Engelbert Dollfuss, Austrian statesman, assas-sinated. Austria, 318.

Deadly hemlock flowers in the hedges ; you know it by the purple blotches on its stems, 1608.

26 1847 LIBERIA, the Negro Republic, declared independent, **1929**. Africa, 70 ; Slavery, 2981.

1856 George Bernard Shaw, Irish writer, born, **2939**. Drama, 1040, *1042* ; English Literature, 1215, *1216*.

1875 Carl Jung, Swiss scientist, born, **1840**. Psychology, 2697 ; Psycho-analysis, 2697.

1894 Aldous Leonard Huxley, English author, born, **1662**. English Litera-ture, 1216.

Sand-martins begin to collect in huge flocks, 3124.
Hedgehogs may be found wandering in the garden after dark, 1604.

27 1809 BATTLE OF TALAVERA. Wellington, Duke of, 3364.
1836 Adelaide, S. Australia, founded, **26**. Australia, 307 : South Australia, 3028.

1870 Hilaire Belloc, British author, born, **409**. Chesterton, G. K., 781.

Great thickets of bracken cover the waste places, 542
The lovely chalk-hill blue butterfly is on the wing, plate f. 633.

28 1726 JEDEDIAH STRUTT, English inventor, born. Arkwright, R., 235 ; Knitting Machines, 1865.

1794 Maximilien Robespierre, French revolution-

July 24, 1927. Menin Gate at Ypres, seen in this photograph, unveiled by Lord Plumer.

ary, guillotined, **2789**. French Revolution, 1396 : Marat, 2096.

" Codlins-and-cream "—the great hairy willow-herb—is in flower, 3382.
Strange little burnet moths may be seen on the downs, plate f. 633.

29 1900 KING HUMBERT of Italy assassinated, *f-i.* Italy, 1770.
1948 Opening of XIV Olympiad at Wembley, *2433.* Olympic Games Results, *f-i.*

Cuckoos are useful now, for alone of birds they eat the destructive, hairy cater-pillars, 941.
Great black slugs are on the dewy grass, 2989.

30 1818 EMILY JANE BRONTË born, **586**. English Litera-ture, 1210 ; Novel, 2402.

1856 Richard Burdon Haldane, 1st Viscount, born. Army, 244.

1863 Henry Ford, American manu-facturer, born, **1346**. Conveyors, *897*; Internal Combustion Engine, 1735 ; Motor Vehicles, 2241.

As late as this, an occasional yellow-hammer's nest is found containing eggs, 616.
Water-lilies flower on the ponds, 3354.

July 29, 1948. Opening of XIV Olympiad. Above, Mrs. F. Blankers-Koen winning the 100 metres.

31 1835 PAUL BELLONI DU CHAILLU, French explorer, born, *f-i.* Africa, 72 ; Pygmies, 2707.

1908 Boy Scout movement instituted by Sir Robert Baden-Powell, **538**. Baden-Powell, Lord, 337 ; Girl Guides, 1465.

1917 Third Battle of Ypres. World Wars, 3411 ; Ypres, 3436.

Heather flowers now, and the bees produce from it their finest honey, 1596.
Look for the great water beetles in small ponds, 401.

1 1759 BATTLE OF MINDEN; French defeated by English and Hanoverians. Seven Years' War, 2924.

1798 Battle of the Nile, at which Nelson destroyed French fleet. Napoleon I, 2275; Nelson, Lord, 2313.

1831 London Bridge opened. Bridge, 564; London, 2012; Thames, 3193.

1834 Emancipation of slaves in the British dominions. Slavery, 2982.

Aug. 1, 1798. Nelson's victory at the Nile. Above we see the French flagship blowing up.

1874 Discovery of D.D.T. first announced, *f-i*. Antiseptics, 179.

1883 Parcel post introduced. Post Office, 2661.

By the seaside, notice the points of difference between our common species of gulls and other sea-birds, **1555, 2931.**

2 216 B.C. HANNIBAL'S VICTORY over Rome at Cannae, **1573.** Carthage, 711; Rome: History, 2808.

A.D. 1100 William Rufus shot in the New Forest, **3380.** English History, 1193.

1802 Cardinal Wiseman, English scholar and prelate, born. Newman, John Henry, 2342.

1858 Sir William Watson, English poet, born, *f-i*. English Literature, 1210; Poetry, 2634.

Brambles are in full bloom, their flowers being extremely popular with insects of all sorts, 463.

3 1492 COLUMBUS SAILED in the Santa Maria, **878.** America: Discovery, *139*; Isabella of Castile, 1760; Navigation, 2290; Ships, 2946.

1805 First recorded Eton v. Harrow match. Cricket, 928; Eton, 1229; School, *2885.*

1867 Earl Baldwin, English premier, born. **341.** Chamberlain, A. N., 750; Conservatives, 893; MacDonald, J. Ramsay, 2048; United Kingdom, 3282; World Wars, 3414.

The breeding season among birds is virtually over, and young of many species are common in field and garden.

4 1265 SIMON DE MONTFORT defeated at Evesham, **2221.** Edward I, 1089; Henry III, 1611.

1347 Calais surrendered to the English, **655.** Edward III, 1091; Hundred Years' War, *1653.*

1792 Percy Bysshe Shelley, English poet, born, **2942.** English Literature, *1214*; Poetry, 2636.

1839 Walter Pater, English essayist, born, *f-i*. English Literature, 1215; Renaissance, 2764.

1900 Elizabeth, consort of George VI, born, **1149.** Elizabeth, Princess, 1150; George VI, 1442; Margaret, Princess, 2100.

1914 Great Britain declared war on Germany. Germany: History, 1450; Grey of Fallodon, 1544; United Kingdom, 3280; William II (Germany), 3378; World Wars, 3409.

Watch the worker wasps as they strip thin slivers of wood from convenient boards and palings; these are chewed up to make the "paper" for the nest, **3345.**

5 1583 SIR HUMPHREY GILBERT took possession of Newfoundland, 2338. America: Discovery, 142; British Commonwealth, 580.

1850 Guy de Maupassant, French novelist, born, *f-i*. French Literature, 1382; Novel, 2401.

1858 First telegraph message sent from England to America, 3164; Cable, 642; Morse, Samuel, 2232.

Flocks of young lapwings are now in evidence on the moors and marshlands, 2629.

On moist heaths in the south you may find the lovely marsh gentian, 1429.

6 1809 ALFRED, Lord Tennyson, English poet, born, **3186.** English Literature, 1214; Poetry, 2637.

1820 Lord Strathcona born, **3102.** British Commonwealth, 580; Canadian History, 681.

1891 F.-M. Sir W. J. Slim, British soldier, born, *f-i*. Burma, 625; World Wars, 3424.

1915 Anzacs landed at Suvla Bay. Australia, 312; New Zealand, 2357; World Wars, 3410.

1926 Gertrude Ederle swam the Channel—the first woman to do so, *f-i*. Swimming, 3135.

1945 Atomic bomb dropped on Hiroshima, **1629.** Atom, 299; Japan, 1800; Pacific, 2474; World Wars, 3424.

The male stickleback has on his brilliant mating suit, and is ready to defend his nest with great ferocity, even against his own mate, **3091.**

7 1858 OTTAWA proclaimed capital of Canada, **2458.** Canada, *683*; Ontario, 2434.

1904 British entered Lhasa, forbidden city of Tibet. Tibet, 3208.

1942 U.S. troops landed on Guadalcanal, *f-i*. Japan, 1800; Pacific, 2474; Solomon Islands, 3421.

Corn buntings continue to make their curious noise, hardly worth the name of song, 617.

Vapourer moths are common even in the towns, the males flying in search of the wingless females, 3388.

8 1646 SIR GODFREY KNELLER, English painter, born, *f-i*. Addison, Joseph, *24*; Dryden, John, *1050*; English Art, 1177; Marlborough, Duke of, *2106.*

1786 Summit of Mt. Blanc first reached—by Paccard and Balmat, 127. Alps, *127*; Mountaineering, 2247.

1940 Battle of Britain began, **575.** Germany, 1452 ; Royal Air Force, 2832 ; World Wars, 3417.

Young of slow-worms are born now ; these are lizards, not snakes, although they superficially resemble the latter, 2985, 1973.
Look for the neat little nests of the potter wasps, often built on heather stems, 1732.

9 **1387** HENRY V, King of England, born, **1611.** Agincourt, 76 ; Hundred Years' War, 1652.
1593 Izaak Walton, author of "The Compleat Angler," born, **3339.** English Literature, 1210.
1631 John Dryden, English poet, born, **1050.** English Literature, 1212 ; Poet Laureate, 2634.
1757 Thomas Telford, Scottish engineer, born, **3184.** Canal, 686 ; Roads, 2783.
1870 Elementary Education Act passed. Education, 1088 ; School, 2884.
1896 Otto Lilienthal, German flying pioneer, killed while gliding. Aeroplane, *44* ; Glider, 1474.
1945 Atomic bomb dropped on Nagasaki, *299.* Japan, 1800 ; Pacific, 2474 ; World Wars, 3424.

Hedge sparrows and one or two other birds sing again now after their silence during July, 454.
Bladderwort flowers in watery marshes, its yellow blooms projecting just above the surface of the water, plate f. 2621.

10 **1675** ROYAL OBSERVATORY, GREENWICH, founded. Astronomy, *281* ; Latitude and Longitude, *1898* ; Observatory, *2411.*
1810 Cavour, Count, Italian patriot, born, **737.** Garibaldi, G., 1418 ; Italy : History, 1769.
1895 First Promenade Concert given in Queen's Hall, London. Music, 2266 ; Orchestra, 2445.

High over the hills of the West Country you may see a big brown bird soaring—a buzzard, 633.
Wood-boring larvae, especially those of " long-horn " beetles, may be found in dead or dying branches, 401.

11 **1576** SIR MARTIN FROBISHER entered the Strait now called after him, **1398.** America : Discovery, 142 ; Polar Exploration, 2644.
1942 German offensive against Stalingrad opened, **3073.** Germany, 1452 ; Russia, 2852 ; World Wars, 3421.

The stoat goes through its curious " dance," a series of strange antics designed to fascinate rabbits and other prey within striking distance, 1222.
Marigolds flower in the cornfields, 2102.

12 GROUSE SHOOTING begins, **1550.**
1753 Thomas Bewick, English wood engraver, born. Engraving, 1217.
1762 George IV, King of England, born, **1441.** Brighton, 570 ; United Kingdom, 3278.
1774 Robert Southey, English poet and writer, born, **3028.** Coleridge, S. T., 869 ; Landor, Walter Savage, 1890 ; Wordsworth, W., 3408.
1854 Sir Alfred Gilbert, English sculptor and metal-worker, born. English Art, 1177 ; London, *2017* ; Sculpture, 2906, *2907.*

Little owls are often seen out in the daylight, either resting on fences, or hunting, towards dusk, 2460.
The nettle-leaved bell-flower, a wild " Canterbury bell," is conspicuous in southern woodlands.

13 **1704** MARLBOROUGH'S VICTORY AT BLENHEIM, **470.** Marlborough, Duke of, 2105.
1814 Cape Colony ceded to Britain by the Dutch, **695.** British Commonwealth, 580.
1889 C. R. W. Nevinson, English painter, born, *f-i.* English Art, *1183*, 1184.

The quail is preparing to leave us, 2711.
Purple hairstreak butterflies are seen in the oak woods, plate f. 632.
Strange little sundew flowers on wet heaths, 3120.

14 **1836** SIR WALTER BESANT, English novelist, born, *f-i.* English Literature, 1210 ; Novel, 2401.
1867 John Galsworthy, British novelist and playwright, born, **1415.** Drama, 1037 ; English Literature, 1215 ; Novel, 2403.
1880 Cologne Cathedral completed, having been building since 1248, **872.** Architecture, 218 ; Cathedrals, 729.
1945 Japan capitulated to the Allies (surrender terms signed Sept. 2), **1800.** World Wars, 3424.

On rugged cliffs in the West you may see the peregrine falcon, our finest member of its tribe, 1258.
Cornfields on poor soil are red with poppies, 2655.

15 **1057** MACBETH, King of Scotland, slain, **2047.** Scotland : History, 2892.
1769 Napoleon I, Emperor of the French, born, **2275.** Bonaparte, 497 ; European History, 1240 ; France : History, 1366, 1396 ; Josephine, Empress, 1838 ; Wellington, Duke of, 3363.
1771 Sir Walter Scott, novelist and poet, born, **2898.** Abbotsford, *10* ; Kenilworth, 1851 ; English Literature, 1214 ; Novel, 2402.
1785 Thomas de Quincey, English writer, born, **994.** English Literature, 1214 ; Essay, 1224.
1875 Samuel Coleridge-Taylor, composer, born, *f-i.* Hiawatha, 2022 ; Music, 2261.
1914 Panama Canal opened to commerce, **2486.** Canal, 689 ; Mosquito, 2236.
1945 VJ-Day ; public holiday to celebrate surrender of Japan in the Second World War, 1800. World Wars, 3424.
1947 Dominions of India and Pakistan inaugurated, **1691, 2479.**

Notice the rock pipit, a nervous little brown bird that flits ahead of you on a seaside walk, 2611.

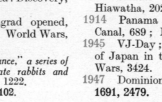

The rock pipit is often seen on the shore in August.

16 **1536** ST. LAWRENCE RIVER named by Cartier, **2861.** America : Discovery, 143 ; Cartier, Jacques, 712 ; North America, 2380.
1807 First London street (Golden Lane) lighted by gas. Gas Manufacture, *1422*, 1423 ; Murdock, William, 2256 ; Roads, 2783.

Fine, pure white flowers of the great field convolvulus are conspicuous on the hedges, 898

AUGUST

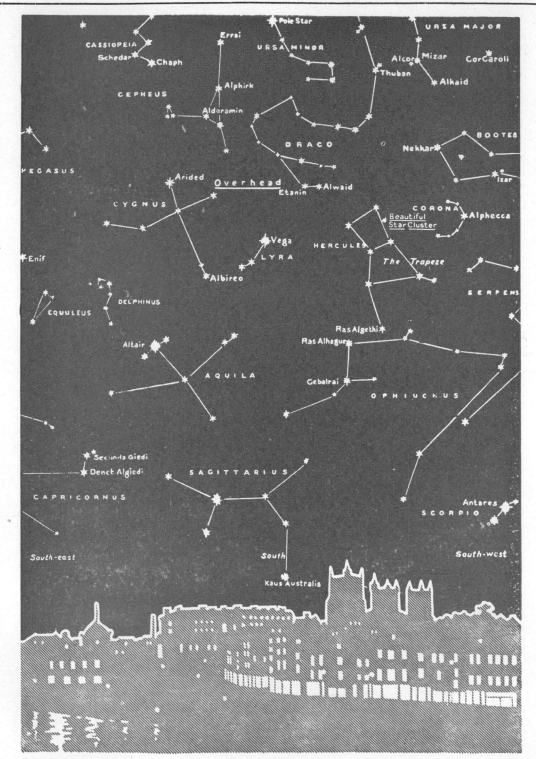

THE STARS IN AUGUST. With this map those of us who live in the British Isles can study the stars from the middle of August to the middle of September. We are looking south in Bristol, and on the right hand are the towers of the cathedral.

AUGUST

17 1648 CROMWELL'S VICTORY AT PRESTON, **933.** Charles I, 755 ; English History, 1196.

1859 Charles Blondin, French acrobat, first crossed Niagara on a tightrope, **473.**

1943 Quebec Conference of war opened. Churchill, 824 ; Pacific, 2473 ; Roosevelt, 2824.

*A seaside visit gives an opportunity to study the strange ways of the hermit crabs, as well as more normal types of these creatures, **924.***

18 1792 EARL (LORD JOHN) RUSSELL, British statesman, born. United Kingdom, 3278 ; Peel, Sir R., 2535.

1830 Francis Joseph I, emperor of Austria-Hungary, born, **1383.** Austria-Hungary, 319.

*Roebucks are bad-tempered now, for this is their pairing season, **984.***
Marbled white butterflies are seen on the chalk downs plate f. 632.

Aug. 18, 1792. Earl (Lord John) Russell, born.

19 1646 JOHN FLAMSTEAD, first Astronomer Royal, born, *f-i.* Astronomy, 275 ; Observatory, 2411 ; Stars, 3077.

1745 Charles Edward Stuart, the Young Pretender, raised his standard at Glenfinnan, in Scotland. Jacobites, 1790 ; Pretender, 2682.

1808 James Nasmyth, Scottish engineer and inventor, born. Iron and Steel, 1758.

1871 Orville Wright, American airman, born, **3427.** Aeroplane, 45.

1942 Canadian and British Commandos raided Dieppe, *f-i.* Army, 244 ; World Wars, 3420.

Swifts take their leave ; they are often the earliest birds to make the autumn migration to warmer climes, 3124.
*The lovely blue cornflower is now in bloom, **910.***

20 1860 RAYMOND POINCARÉ, French President, born, *f-i.* France : History, 1367 ; World Wars, 3409.

1897 Sir Ronald Ross discovered malaria parasites in the mosquito, **2236** ; anniversary kept as Mosquito Day. Medicine, 2133 ; Panama Canal, 2488.

1940 Leon Trotsky, Russian revolutionary, assassinated, **3251**; Russia, 2850 ; Stalin, 3072.

Notice the varied life of rock-pools left by the receding tide ; sea-anemones, shrimps, and many marine creatures are easily observed there, 2103.

21 1765 WILLIAM IV, King of England, born, **3380.** Victoria, Queen, 3319.

1808 Wellington defeats the French at Vimiera. France : History, 1366 ; Wellington, 3364.

1930 Princess Margaret born, **2100.** Elizabeth, Queen Consort, 1149 ; George VI, 1442.

*Among the first birds to leave us are the shrikes, now on their way southward, **2962.***

22 1138 SCOTS DEFEATED at battle of the Standard. Scotland . History, 2892.

1642 Charles I raised his standard at Nottingham, **755.** Cromwell, O., 933 ; English History, 1196.

1906 First aeroplane flight in Europe made by Santos-Dumont. Aeroplane, 45 ; Airship, 93.

Goldfinches are often seen now feeding on thistle seeds, a welcome sight to the farmer, 1272.
The speckled wood butterfly is on the wing, plate f. 632.

23 1305 SIR WILLIAM WALLACE, Scottish patriot, executed, **3338.** Scotland : History, 2892.

1628 George Villiers, Duke of Buckingham, murdered at Portsmouth, **598.** Charles I, 755 ; English History, 1196.

1754 Louis XVI, King of France, born, 2030. French Revolution, 1393 ; Marie Antoinette, 2102.

1852 Arnold Toynbee, economist and social worker, born, *f-i.*

1914 Opening of battle of Mons. World Wars, 3409 ; Ypres, Earl of, 3436.

1939 Russo-German non-aggression pact signed, 1242. Hitler, 1632 : Molotov, 2199 ; Russia, 2852 ; World Wars, 3416.

On oak and birch trees, many of the leaves are partly cut across, then neatly rolled up ; this is the work of leaf-rolling weevils, 3362.

24 79 HERCULANEUM AND POMPEII DESTROYED by Vesuvius, **2653.** Vesuvius, 3319 ; Volcanoes, 3328.

1572 St. Bartholomew's Day. Massacre of the Huguenots in Paris, **1650.** Charles IX, 758 ; Coligny, Admiral, 870 ; France : History, 1366 ; Henry IV, 1613.

1686 Calcutta founded by Job Charnock, **660.** Bengal, 413 ; Jute, 1844.

1759 William Wilberforce, British philanthropist, born, *f-i.* Slavery, 2982.

In the cornfields, wheat is ready for harvest, and sparrows amongst many other birds feed off the ripe ears, 3052.
Among the butterflies, fritillaries are also especially fond of cornfields, plates f. 632, 633.

Aug. 24, A.D. 79. On this day Pompeii (some of whose excavated ruins are seen here) was destroyed.

25

1770 THOMAS CHATTERTON, English poet, committed suicide, **760**. English Literature, 1210 ; Poetry, 2634.

1825 Uruguay proclaimed independent, **3299**; anniversary kept as Uruguay's Independence Day.

1839 Francis Bret Harte, American writer, born, **1579**. United States : Literature, 3294.

1931 National Government formed in Britain. Government, 1488 ; United Kingdom, 3282. MacDonald, J. R., 2048.

1944 Liberation of Paris, **2521**. France, 1368 ; Normandy Invasion, 2377 ; World Wars, 3422.

Carline thistles are found on the chalk and limestone hills, their curious flowers having a yellow, dried-up appearance, 2917.
Now is the time to " sugar " for night-flying moths, 632

26

1346 EDWARD III defeated the French at Crécy, **1091**. Hundred Years' War, 1052.

1676 Sir Robert Walpole, first British Prime Minister, born, **3338**. Cabinet, 640 ; Government, 1488.

1819 Albert, Prince Consort, born, **101**. Victoria, Queen, 3319.

1875 John Buchan (Lord Tweedsmuir), British author and administrator, born, **597**. Novel, 2401.

Many wild species of grass are still in bloom, such as the wild oat, which grows in cornfields, 1509.
On the hawthorn hedge are many species of " stick " or " looper " caterpillars, 720.

27

1816 ALGIERS, stronghold of the Barbary pirates, bombarded by Lord Exmouth, 118. Pirates, 2612.

1871 Theodore Dreiser, American novelist, born, *f-i.* Novel, 2401; United States : Literature, 3295.

1886 Eric Coates, English composer, born, *f-i.* Music, 2261.

1908 Sir Donald George Bradman, Australian cricketer, born, **543**. Cricket, 928.

Conspicuous at the seaside is the cormorant, 2931.

Aug. 27, 1908. Sir Don Bradman, Australian cricketer, born.

28

1749 JOHANN WOLFGANG VON GOETHE, German poet, born, **1478**. Faust, 1264; Germany : Literature, 1456 ; Novel, *2404.*

1833 Sir Edward Burne-Jones, English painter, born, *f-i.* English Art, 1182. Morris, William, 2232 ; Pre-Raphaelites, 2681.

1850 First submarine telegraph (Cape Gris Nez to Dover) opened. Cable, *641* ; Morse, Samuel, 2232 ; Telegraph, 3164.

On northern moorlands the golden plover is a common bird now, 2629 ; the merlin, too, is the characteristic bird of prey of these districts, 1588.

Aug. 29, 1935. Queen Astrid of the Belgians accidentally killed in Switzerland. Above is the memorial chapel at Kuessnacht.

29

410 ALARIC, King of Visigoths, sacks Rome, **96**. Rome : History, 2812.

1632 John Locke, English philosopher, born, *f-i.* English Literature, 1210 ; Philosophy, 2572.

1817 John Leech, English caricaturist, born, *f-i.* Christmas, *821* ; Drawing, 1044.

1835 City of Melbourne founded, **2136**. Australia, 307 ; Victoria (Australia), 3321.

1862 Maurice Maeterlinck, Belgian poet and dramatist, born, **2055**. Bees, 390.

1935 Astrid, Queen of the Belgians, killed in motor accident. Albert I, 102 ; Leopold III, 1928.

Bittersweet or woody nightshade is now in flower, 462.

30

30 B.C. CLEOPATRA poisoned herself, **838**. Mark Antony, 2105.

A.D. **1797** Mary Wollstonecraft Shelley born, *f-i.* Shelley, P. B., 2942. English Literature, 1210.

1871 Lord Rutherford, English physicist, born, **2858**. Atom, 296, 298 ; Quantum Theory, 2711 ; Radium, 2731.

1905 Alberta constituted a Canadian province, **102**. Calgary, 663 ; Canada, *679* ; Fuel, *1406.*

Fungi are now coming into evidence, especially the dangerous rusts and smuts, 2857.

31

12 CALIGULA, Roman Emperor, born, **664**. Rome : History, 2811.

1290 Jews exiled from England, **1829**. English History, 1193.

1591 Sir Richard Grenville in the Revenge engaged the whole Spanish Fleet, **1543**. English History, 1193.

1870 Maria Montessori, Italian educationist, born, **2220**. Children, 801 ; School, 2883.

1880 Queen Wilhelmina of the Netherlands born, *f-i.* Netherlands, 2323.

Tunny fish are now seen off Scarborough and other East Coast resorts, 3258 ; at many places, too, you may see schools of porpoises close inshore, 2657.

1 **1804** ASTEROID JUNO discovered by Professor Harding. Astronomy, 275; Planets, 2617, *2618*.
1870 Battle of Sedan. Franco-Prussian War, 1384; Napoleon III, 2278.
1923 Tokyo and Yokohama devastated by earthquake. Earthquake, 1069; Japan, 1796; Tokyo, 3221.
1939 Germany invaded Poland. Germany, 1451; Poland, 2643; World Wars, 3416.

Throughout this month, our migrant summer visitors are departing for the south, plate f. 2171.
Late broods of many butterflies hatch out and new flowers still come into bloom.

2 **31 B.C.** BATTLE OF ACTIUM. Augustus (Octavian) defeats Antony. Augustus, 303; Mark Antony, 2165; Rome: History, 2811.
A.D. 1666 Great Fire of London began. Fire, 1278; Fire-fighting, 1285; London, 2010.
1898 Battle of Omdurman. Kitchener, Earl, 1862; Sudan, 3110.

Among birds leaving now is the sand martin, 3124.
Filmy strands of gossamer float in the warm air, each with its passenger, a tiny spider, 3062.

3 OLIVER CROMWELL'S "lucky day." On this date were fought the battles of Dunbar (1650) and Worcester (1651), and on this date he died (1658). Cromwell, Oliver, 933.
1939 Great Britain and France declared war on Germany. Chamberlain, N., 750; World Wars, 3416.
1943 Allied landings on the Italian mainland, and surrender of Italy, **1774**. World Wars, 3421.
1944 Liberation of Brussels, **595**. Belgium, 407; Germany, 1453.
1948 Death of Dr. Edward Benes, Czech statesman, **412**. Czechoslovakia, 954; Masaryk, Jan, 2117.

Some young swallows are still unfledged, 3124.
Many salmon now enter the rivers and swim strongly upstream to their spawning grounds, 2865.

4 **1768** FRANÇOIS RENÉ DE CHÂTEAUBRIAND, French author, born, *f-i*. France: Literature, 1379.
1850 Count Luigi Cadorna, Italian soldier, born, *f-i*. World Wars, 3411; Italy, 1770.

Natterjack toads are now in their mature dress, 3219.
Devil's-bit scabious is at its best, f-i.

In September devil's-bit scabious makes a blue haze.

5 **1585** CARDINAL RICHELIEU, French ecclesiastic and statesman, born, **2778**. France: History, 1365, *1369*; Louis XIII, 2028.
1638 Louis XIV of France born, **2029**. France: History, 1366; France: Literature, 1380, *1381*.
1905 Treaty of Portsmouth (New Hampshire, U.S.A.), including Russo-Japanese War. Japan, 1800; Russia, 2848.

The chiff-chaff repeats its monotonous song for a few weeks before leaving us, 3340.
Among fine autumn butterflies the red admiral is conspicuous, plate f. 632.

6 **1620** THE PILGRIM FATHERS sailed from Plymouth in the Mayflower, **2606**. Massachusetts, 2118; Mayflower, 2121, *2123*.
1766 John Dalton, British chemist, born, **957**. Atom, 294; Chemistry, 766.

Sept. 2, 1666. The Great Fire of London (commemorated by the Monument above) began.

1869 Sir Walford Davies, British composer and conductor, born, *f-i*. Music, 2261.
1914 First Battle of the Marne opened. World Wars, 3409; Joffre, Marshal, 1832.
1948 Juliana invested as Queen of the Netherlands, 2323.

Partridges are now plentiful in the root fields, 2526.
The wasp population is at its greatest, and these busy workers take great toll of ripe fruit, 3345.

7 **1533** QUEEN ELIZABETH born, **1146**. Armada, 236; Henry VIII, 1612; Mary Stuart, 2116.
1707 Georges Louis Leclerc, Comte de Buffon, French naturalist, born, **603**. Nature Study, 2283.
1880 Wild Birds' Protection Act passed. Birds, 437.
1940 London "blitz" opened with air raid on the docks, **2016**. Britain, Battle of, 575.

Some of the finest dragon-flies are only now reaching the adult stage, amongst them the great "horse-stingers" of the genus Aeschna, 1034.

SEPTEMBER

8 1157 RICHARD I, King of England, born, 2776. Crusades, 936.
1565 Great siege of Malta ended in decisive victory over the Turks, **2072**; anniversary kept as Malta's National Day.
1841 Antonin Dvorak, Bohemian composer, born, *f-i.* Music, 2261.
1886 Johannesburg founded, **1833.** Gold, 1479; South Africa, 3019.
1944 First rocket bomb of the Second World War fell on London, **2791.** London, 2016; World Wars, 3422.

Fallow deer bucks fight now to add to their following of hinds, 984.
Lovely blue meadow crane's-bill, our largest wild geranium, is a conspicuous flower, 1444.

9 1513 BATTLE OF FLODDEN FIELD, 1315. Scotland, 2892.
1737 Luigi Galvani, Italian scientist, born, **1416.** Electricity, 1127.
1828 Count Leo Tolstoy, Russian novelist and reformer, born, **3222.** Novel, 2404; Russian Literature, 2856.

Dace, though relatives of the bottom-feeding roach, now greedily feed on flies at the surface, 2781.

10 1753 SIR JOHN SOANE, British architect, born, *f-i.* Architecture, 220; Museums, 2260.
1847 Gold discovered in California, **663.** Gold, 1479.
1872 K. S. Ranjitsinhji, Indian prince and cricketer, born, *f-i.* Cricket, 928.

Lavender, flowering in the garden, attracts large numbers of moths at night, 1901.
Many types of dung beetles, English " scarabs," may be found now, 399.

11 1524 PIERRE DE RONSARD, French poet, born, *f-i.* France: Literature, 1380.
1709 Battle of Malplaquet. Anne, Queen, 163; Marlborough, Duke of, 2106.
1877 Sir James Hopwood Jeans, British scientist, born, **1815.** Astronomy, 275; Planets, 2620.
1885 David Herbert Lawrence, British novelist and poet, born, *f-i.* English Literature, 1216; Novel, 2401.
1948 Mahomed Ali Jinnah, first Governor-General of Pakistan, died, **1831.** India, 1716; Pakistan, 2479.

Flycatchers, typical summer visitors, are going, 1330.
On the figwort (f-i.) you find many sorts of weevil.

12 1440 ETON COLLEGE received its first charter, 1229 Henry VI, 1611.
1494 Francis I, King of France, born, **1383.**

Sept. 12, 1905. On this day this fine bridge over the Zambezi River was opened.

1649 Capture and sack of Drogheda by Cromwell, **933.** Ireland, 1745.
1846 Marriage of Robert Browning and Elizabeth Moulton Barrett, **589, 590.**
1852 Herbert Henry Asquith, Earl of Oxford and Asquith, British statesman, born, **2465.** Liberals, 1929; World Wars, 3409.
1905 Bridge over Zambezi R., near Victoria Falls, opened. Africa, 65; Bridge, 564.

Blackberries are ripening now. On the fruits (463) you can find many beetles, flies, and other insects; birds love blackberries, too.

13 1759 WOLFE stormed the Heights of Abraham and was mortally wounded, 3401. British Commonwealth, 580; Canada, 681; Montcalm, 2218; Quebec, *2716.*
1860 John Pershing, American soldier, born, *f-i.* World Wars, 3409.
1865 Lord Birdwood, British soldier, born, *f-i.* World Wars, 3409.
1882 Battle of Tel-el-Kebir. Egypt, 1102.

Nightjars leave us now, 2369.
Damp weather leads to great growth of fungi, and mushrooms are at their best, 2260

Sept. 10, 1753. Sir John Soane born. His house in Lincoln's Inn Fields, London (above), is a museum.

14 1618 SIR PETER LELY, Anglo-Dutch painter, born, *f-i.* English Art, *1178.*
1735 Robert Raikes, British philanthropist, founder of Sunday Schools, born. School, 2883.
1769 Alexander von Humboldt, German explorer and naturalist, born. Ape, 182; Monkey, *2209.*

Red squirrels have lost their long ear-tufts now, and the hair of their tails is often almost white, 3071.

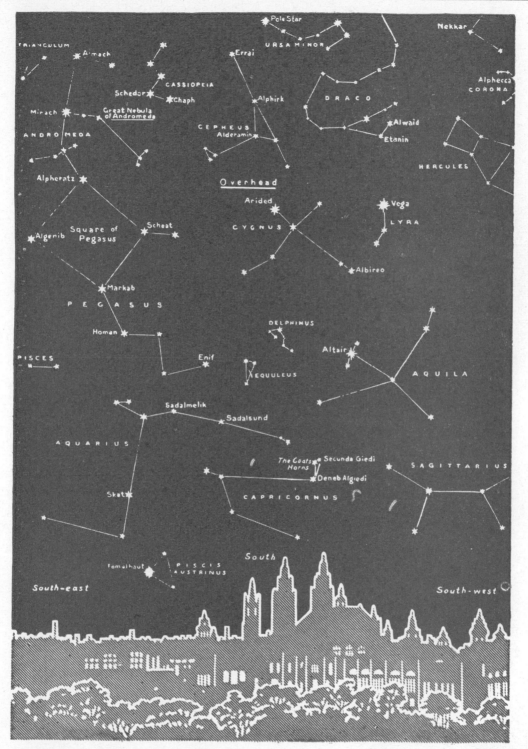

THE STARS IN SEPTEMBER. With this map we can study the stars from the middle of September to the middle of October. We are looking south in Glasgow, and on the right hand can be seen the Art Gallery. The stars are seen practically in this position from all parts of Britain at about nine o'clock in the middle of September.

SEPTEMBER

15 1789 JAMES FENIMORE COOPER, American novelist, born, **902**. Novel, 2401 ; United States : Literature, 3293.

1830 Opening of Liverpool and Manchester Rly. ; William Huskisson killed. Industrial Revolution, *1723* ; Railways *2735, 2736*.

1916 First appearance of tanks in the First World War. Armour, 242 ; Army, 244 ; Tanks, 3151 ; World Wars, 3409.

Sept. 18, A.D. 53. The Roman emperor Trajan was born near Seville. His martial deeds in Dacia are celebrated on this column at Rome.

1917 Russia proclaimed a republic, **2849**. World Wars, 3411.

Water-voles are often so tame that, if you sit still, they will run over your feet as you rest on the river's bank. They swim and dive at speed, f-i.

16 1518 TINTORETTO, Italian painter, born, *f-i*. Italian Art, 1776.

1795 British take Cape Town, **697**. British Commonwealth, 580 ; South Africa, 3019.

1812 Great Fire of Moscow, **2235**. Napoleon I, 2275.

1947 John Cobb established new land-speed record of 394·196 m.p.h., *f-i*. Records, *f-i*.

The robin's autumn song is now heard everywhere ; though it means the end of summer, it is one of the sweetest of all bird sounds, 2790.

17 1631 BATTLE OF BREITENFELD. Gustavus Adolphus defeats Tilly. Gustavus Adolphus, 1558 ; Thirty Years' War, 3202.

1939 Russia invaded Poland, **2643**. Russia, 2852 ; World Wars, 3416.

1944 Allied air-borne landings at Arnhem, Nijmegen and Eindhoven, *f-i*. Netherlands, 2230 ; Rhine, 2769 ; World Wars, 3422.

1948 Count Folke Bernadotte, Swedish humanitarian, assassinated in Jerusalem, *f-i*. Palestine 2483 ; United Nations, 3283.

Family flocks of long-tailed tits are common now, 3218 The grass-snake's eggs, laid in refuse heaps or other hot places, are now hatching, 1512.

18 53 TRAJAN, Roman emperor, born. Rome : History, 2812.

1709 Samuel Johnson, English author and lexicographer, born, **1835**. Boswell, James, 529 ; English Literature, *1213*.

1900 Commonwealth of Australia proclaimed, **307**. British Commonwealth, 580.

All but a very few of our nightingales have left for Africa. 2367.

Autumnal lady's tresses is in flower, f-i.

19 1356 BATTLE OF POITIERS, Edward III, 1091 ; Hundred Years' War, 1652.

1551 Henry III of France born, **1613**. France : History, 1365.

1802 Louis Kossuth, Hungarian patriot, born, **1874**. Hungary, 1656.

Willow warblers sing a soft departing song, 3340.
Great bunches of fruits, called " keys " by countryfolk, hang from the ash tree's boughs, 262.

20 1771 MUNGO PARK, Scottish explorer, born, **2521**. Africa, 72 ; Niger, 2367.

1792 Battle of Valmy ; French Republicans defeated Prussian-Austrian invaders. French Revolution, 1396.

1854 Battle of the Alma. Crimea, 931.

1909 South African Union Bill received Royal Assent. British Commonwealth, 580 ; Parliament, 2521 ; South Africa, 3019.

Wagtails and pipits are assembling into small flocks, and many are travelling southwards, 3332, 2611.

21 ST. MATTHEW'S DAY.

1452 Girolamo Savonarola, Florentine reformer, born, **2876**. Florence, 1319 ; Reformation, 2758.

1745 Battle of Prestonpans—victory for the Young Pretender. Jacobites, 1790 ; Pretender, 2682 ; George II, 1440.

1756 John Loudon McAdam, road-maker, born at Ayr, **2045**. Roads, 2783.

1866 Herbert George Wells, British novelist and " popular educator," born, **3364**. English Literature, 1215 ; Novel, 2403.

In the orchard many birds attack ripe fruit, but as often for the insects thereon as for the apples or pears themselves. This excuse does not hold for such birds as jays, blackbirds, and thrushes, 1401.

22 1586 BATTLE OF ZUTPHEN. Sir Philip Sidney mortally wounded, *f-i*.

1694 Philip Stanhope, Earl of Chesterfield, born. English Literature, 1210.

1791 Michael Faraday, British physicist, born, **1260**. Dynamo, 1060 ; Electricity, 1127, 1132 ; Magnetism, 2060.

At this time daddy-long-legs flies often hatch out in enormous numbers ; you frequently find their pupal cases sticking out from the grass of the lawn, 1732.

23

480 B.C. EURIPIDES, Greek dramatist, born, **1231.** Drama, 1038; Greek Language and Literature, 1540.

A.D. 1831 Formation of the British Association for the Advancement of Science, *f-i.*

1846 The planet Neptune discovered, **2315.** Astronomy, 279; Uranus, 3298.

1940 George Cross and Medal instituted by King George VI, *f-i.* Malta, **2073**; Orders and Decorations, 2449.

Flocks of house sparrows are common in the farmyard, 3052.
Teasels flower by the wayside in dry places, 3163.

24

1625 JAN DE WITT, Dutch statesman, born, *f-i.* Netherlands, 2318.

1717 Horace Walpole, 4th Earl of Orford, English writer, born, **3338.** English Literature, 1210; Novel, 2401.

Burdock is now a common wayside flower, its prickly bracts catching in all sorts of passing objects, 2917.
The horse-fly, a terrible biter, is common now; it is a member of the same group as the house-fly, 1330.

25

1066 KING HAROLD II of England defeated the Norwegians under Harold Hardrada at Stamford Bridge. Harold, King, **1579.**

1513 Vasco Nuñez de Balboa discovers Pacific Ocean, **341.** America, 140; Pacific Ocean, 2472.

1857 Lucknow relieved by Havelock, **2035.** India: History, 1714.

Great reed-mace, or "cat's tail," the so-called bulrush, is now producing its conspicuous, poker-like fruits, 615.
Stock-doves' eggs may still be found in hollow trees or masonry, 2606.

26

1750 CUTHBERT, Baron Collingwood, British admiral, born, **870.** Nelson, Lord, 2313; Trafalgar, 3234.

1907 New Zealand granted Dominion status; anniversary kept as New Zealand Dominion Day, **2357.**

1934 Cunard liner s.s. Queen Mary launched by Queen Mary. Docks, *1023*; Ships, *2949, 2950, 2960.*

Trout are very plump now, for they are nearly ready to spawn, 3251.
Corncrakes, migrating southwards, often fall to the sportsman's gun, 2734.

27

1404 WILLIAM OF WYKEHAM, founder of Winchester School, died, *f-i.* School, *2885.*

1627 Jacques Bénigne Bossuet, French preacher, born, *f-i.* France: Literature, 1380.

1792 George Cruikshank, British illustrator and caricaturist, born, *f-i.* Drawing, 1044.

The wheatear reappears in the south of England, now on its way to its winter home, 3514.
Brimstone butterflies are seen in the woods; these are insects of the summer brood, plate f. 632.

28

490 B.C. BATTLE OF MARATHON, Persians defeated by Greeks. Persian Wars, 2555; Greece, 1522.

A.D. 1824 Francis Turner Palgrave, compiler of "Golden Treasury," born, *f-i.* English Literature, 1210; Poetry, 2634.

1841 Georges Clemenceau, French statesman, born, **837.** France: History, 1366; World Wars, 3409.

1852 The Earl of Ypres (Sir John French), born, **3437.** Boer War, 486; World Wars, 3409.

Rowan berries, among the earliest to ripen, are quickly stripped by blackbirds and thrushes, 3376.
Clustered bell-flower is in evidence—flowers on the chalk downs.

29

FEAST OF ST. MICHAEL AND ALL ANGELS (Michaelmas).

1725 Robert, Lord Clive, British soldier and statesman, born, **842.** Calcutta, 660; Hastings, Warren, 1581; India: History, 1714.

1758 Horatio, Viscount Nelson, British admiral, born, **2313.** United Kingdom, 3277; Trafalgar, 3234.

Sept. 29, 1938. Signing of the Munich Agreement. Above, Mr. Neville Chamberlain signs.

1829 Peel's police force commenced duty, **2647.** Peel, Sir Robert, 2535, *2536.*

1938 Munich Agreement signed, 2256. Chamberlain, N., 750; Czechoslovakia, 954; Hitler, A., 1632; World Wars, 3416.

Amongst birds now leaving us are the terns; some of these fly as far as the Southern Hemisphere every autumn, 1556, 2171.

30

1832 EARL ROBERTS of Kandahar born, **2789.** Afghanistan, 56; Boer War, 486.

1852 Sir Charles Villiers Stanford, Irish composer, born, *f-i.* Music, 2261.

1856 William Willett, promoter of daylight-saving, born. Daylight Saving, 980.

1928 Discovery of penicillin first announced, **2544.** Antiseptics, 180; Fleming, Sir Alexander, 1314.

Spruce cones are now conspicuous as long, green objects hanging from the smaller branches, 3070; compare them with those of the silver firs, which stand erect on the shoots, 1278.

1

1207 HENRY III, King of England, born, **1611.** Edward I, 1089, Montfort, Simon de, 2221.

1754 Paul I, Tsar of Russia, born. Russia, 2848.

1847 Paul von Hindenburg, German soldier and president, born, *f-i.* World Wars, 3409; Germany: History, 1451; Hitler, 1632.

Oct. 1, 1754. Paul I, Tsar of Russia, born

The last wrynecks leave us now, migrating southwards, 2171.

Ivy flowers now, its greenish blooms being most attractive to flies, 1788.

2

1452 RICHARD III of England born, **2777.** Bosworth Field, 530; Henry VII, 1612; Roses, Wars of the, 2828.

1351 Ferdinand Foch, French soldier, born, **1332.** Haig, Earl, 1564; World Wars, 3409,

1852 Sir William Ramsay, British chemist, born, **2744.** Air, 88; Neon, 2315.

Redwings reach us now from the north, among the earliest of our autumn immigrants, 3205.

Rowan berries are now ripening; their colour is a particularly brilliant scarlet, 3376.

3

1614 CHARTERHOUSE SCHOOL opened in London. School, 2883.

1844 Sir Patrick Manson, British physician, born, *f-i.* Medicine, 2133; Mosquito, 2236; Panama Canal, 2488.

Beneath the birch trees you may find several interesting species of fungi; the fly agaric, Amanita muscaria, red with yellow spots, is one of these, a very poisonous species, plate f. 1408.

4

1472 LUCAS CRANACH THE ELDER, German painter, born, *f-i.* Germany: Art, 1454.

1787 François Guizot, French statesman and historian, born, *f-i.* France: History, 1365; France: Literature, 1379.

1872 Admiral Lord Keyes, British sailor, born, *f-i.* Navy, 2293; World Wars, 3409.

House martins are departing southwards for the winter, 3124.

A few butterflies are still about, among them the comma, plate f. 632.

5

1925 OPENING OF LOCARNO CONFERENCE. European History, 1241; Chamberlain, Sir Austen, 750; Peace Movement, 2531.

1930 R 101 wrecked near Beauvais. Airships, 94, *95.*

Whinchats are now leaving this country; their close relatives, the stonechats, stay behind, however, and are true residents, 3374.

6

1510 JOHN CAIUS, founder of Caius College, Cambridge, born, *f-i.* Cambridge, 666.

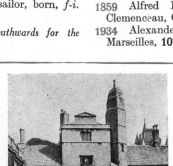

Oct. 6, 1510. The founder of Caius College, Cambridge (above), was born.

1732 Nevil Maskelyne, English astronomer, born, *f-i.* Astronomy, 275; Stars, 3077; Tides, 3209.

1820 Jenny Lind, Swedish soprano, born, *f-i.* Opera, 2435.

1846 George Westinghouse, American inventor, born, *f-i.* Brakes, 549; Railways, 2734.

Two brilliant flowers of the heaths and commons are the dwarf gorse and the autumnal gorse, which closely resembles the common species; gorse, f-i.

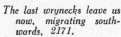

Dwarf gorse is brilliant in October.

7

1571 BATTLE OF LEPANTO. Navy, *2294;* Turkey: History, 3264.

1573 William Laud, Archbishop of Canterbury, born, **1899.** Charles I, 755; English History, 1196.

1854 Christian Rudolf De Wet, Boer soldier, born. Boer War, 486; South Africa, 3019.

1885 Niels Henrik David Bohr, Danish physicist, born, **487.** Atom, 294; Physics, *2594;* Quantum Theory, 2711.

Male wasps are now seen, recognizable by their long, narrow bodies and long antennae; they are unable to sting, 3345.

8

451 FOURTH GENERAL COUNCIL of the Church at Chalcedon. Christianity, 817.

1831 Opening of King's College, London. London University, 2021.

1885 Bechuanaland proclaimed British territory. Boer War, 486; South Africa, 3019.

The vast wood-ants' nest assumes a quieter appearance as the inhabitants prepare for winter by transferring their activities to the underground galleries, 168.

9

1547 MIGUEL DE CERVANTES SAAVEDRA, Spanish author, baptized, **745.** Spanish Literature, 3050.

1859 Alfred Dreyfus, French soldier, born, *f-i.* Clemenceau, Georges, 837; Zola, Émile, 3445.

1934 Alexander I of Yugoslavia assassinated at Marseilles, **107.** Yugoslavia, 3439.

Red deer stags are dangerous now, for this is their "rutting" season; angrily they bellow at each other, and fierce fights occur for the possession of each harem of the more timid hinds, 984.

10

732 SARACENS defeated by Franks at battle of Tours. Charles Martel, 759; France: History, 1365; Mahomet, 2067.

1684 Jean Antoine Watteau, French painter, born, *f-i.* France: Art, 1377; Painting, 2475.

1731 Henry Cavendish, English scientist, born, **736.** Chemistry, 766; Gravitation, 1512.

1738 Benjamin West, American painter, born, *f-i.* Cromwell, Oliver, *934*; Nelson, Lord, *2314*; Penn, William, *2545*.

1813 Giuseppe Verdi, Italian composer, born, **3315.** Opera, 2438, 2439, 2440.

1861 Dr. Fridtjof Nansen, Norwegian explorer, born, **2273.** Arctic Regions, *223*; Polar Exploration, 2644.

1877 William Richard Morris, Viscount Nuffield, British manufacturer and philanthropist, born, **2404.** Conveyors, *896*; Motor Vehicles, 2241; Oxford, 2465.

1911 Opening of republican revolution in China, **813**; anniversary kept as China's Double Tenth Day.

The ring ouzel, a blackbird with a white " collar," leaves us now ; it breeds in the north of Britain and is seen in the south only when on migration, 2171.

J. Dixon-Scott

Oct. 14, 1644. William Penn, whose grave lies outside this Quaker meeting-house at Jordans, Bucks, was born.

11 **1399** ORDER OF THE BATH formally constituted. Orders and Decorations, 2449.

1521 Title " Defender of the Faith " conferred on Henry VIII by Pope Leo X. Church of England, 825 ; Henry VIII, 1612 ; Papacy, 2495.

1811 Steam-ferry (first in world) established between New York and Hoboken. New York, 2351 ; Ships, 2945 ; Steam Engine, 3085.

1899 Boer War opened, **486.** South Africa, 3019.

Many birds assemble into flocks at this season, those of the starlings being the most conspicuous, 3083.

12 **1492** COLUMBUS discovered the Bahamas, **878**; anniversary kept in U.S.A. as Columbus Day. America: Discovery, 139 ; Bahamas, 339.

1537 Edward VI, King of England, born, *1090*, **1091.** Church of England, 825 ; English History, 1193 ; Henry VIII, 1612 ; School, 2883.

1866 J. Ramsay MacDonald, British statesman, born, **2048.** Baldwin, Earl, 341 ; Labour Movement, 1875.

1915 Nurse Cavell shot, *f-i.* World Wars, 3409.

Red admiral butterflies are seen now, typical of autumn. They delight to feed on rotting apples and other fruits, plate f. 632.

13 **1630** SOPHIA, Electress of Hanover, born. George I, 1440 ; United Kingdom, 3276.

1821 Rudolf Virchow, German pathologist. born, *f-i.* Medicine, 2132.

1944 Liberation of Athens, **287.** Greece, 1526 ; World Wars, 3422.

It is not too late to study ferns still, and the polypody is a conspicuous species, easy to identify by its simple fronds, which are not quite pinnate but are termed pinnatifid ; polypody, f-i.

14 **1066** BATTLE OF HASTINGS, **1581.** Harold, King, 1579 ; William I, 3379.

1633 James II, King of England, born, **1794.** English History, 1200 ; Jacobites, 1790 ; Pretender. 2682.

1644 William Penn, Quaker and founder of Pennsylvania, born,

Oct. 12, 1915. Nurse Cavell was shot. This is her statue in London.

2544. Pennsylvania, 2546 ; Philadelphia, *2566*.

1882 Eamon de Valera, Irish statesman, born, **998.** Irish Free State, 1749.

You may still see a straggling warbler, such as a blackcap, if the weather is warm, 3340.
Look for the curious fruits of the medlar tree, found wild in some of the southern counties, 2718.

15 **1586** MARY QUEEN OF SCOTS tried for conspiracy against Queen Elizabeth, **2115.** Elizabeth, Queen, 1146 ; James I, 1793.

1608 Evangelista Torricelli, Italian physicist, inventor of barometer, born, *f-i.* Air, 88 ; Barometer, 363.

1686 Allan Ramsay, Scottish poet, born, *f-i.* Scotland : Literature, 2894.

1856 Oscar Wilde, author and dramatist, born, *f-i.* Drama, 1042 ; English Literature, 1210.

1945 Pierre Laval, French politician, executed, *f-i.* Abyssinia, 13 ; France : History, 1365 ; Germany, 1451.

1946 Hermann Goering, German politician and war leader, committed suicide, *f-i.* National-Socialist Party, 2281.

Fewer bees are out now, for the cool weather keeps them at home, and stragglers in late afternoon are overtaken by the cold evenings and die before they can reach the hive, 390.

16 **1555** NICHOLAS RIDLEY and HUGH LATIMER, bishops, burned at the stake, *f-i.* Church of England, 825 ; Mary I, 2113.

1758 Noah Webster, American lexicographer, born, *f-i.* Dictionary, 1015.

1793 Marie Antoinette, Queen of France, guillotined in Paris, **2102.** French Revolution, 1393 ; Louis XVI, 2030.

1863 Sir Austen Chamberlain, British statesman, born, **750.** European History, 1241 ; Peace Movement, 2531.

1869 Girton College for women founded in a Hitchin (Herts)

OCTOBER

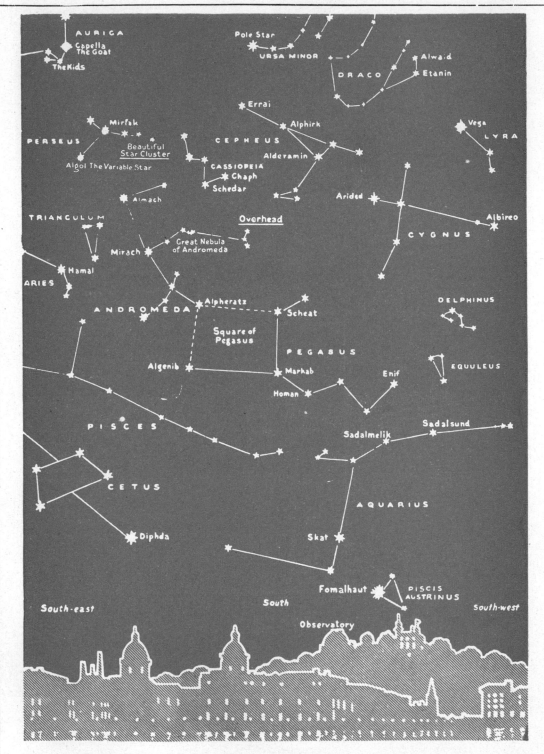

THE STARS IN OCTOBER. With this map we can study the stars from the middle of October to the middle of November. We are looking south in Greenwich, and we are on the meridian line that is marked 0 on our maps. The building containing the telescope that marks the meridian is next to the dome.

house. Cambridge, 666, 669 ; Universities, 3296.

1946 Execution of the ten major German war criminals at Nuremberg, **2406**. Germany: History, 1453 ; National-Socialist Party, 2282.

Many caterpillars are now found wandering in search of winter quarters, among them those of the fox moth, typical examples of the " woolly bear," for they are covered with a thick coat of long, brown hairs, 720.

17 **1777** BATTLE OF SARATOGA ; British defeated by Americans. American Independence, 144 ; British Commonwealth, 580.

1854 Siege of Sevastopol opened. Crimea, 931 ; Balaclava, 341.

Among autumn flowers are the autumn crocus and saffron crocus, two mauve-flowered species now in bloom ; they have narrow leaves and must not be confused with the lovely meadow saffron, which resembles them but whose broad leaves appeared in spring and then died away again, 932, f-i.

18 St. LUKE'S DAY.
1469 Isabella of Castile married Ferdinand of Aragon, **1760**. Columbus, Christopher, 878.

1663 Prince Eugene of Savoy, Austrian soldier, born, *f-i.* European History, 1237 ; Marlborough, 1st Duke of, 2106.

1697 Antonio Canaletto, Venetian painter, born, *f-i.* Italy : Art, 1776.

Swallows assemble in great numbers on the telegraph wires. Some have been " ringed " by ornithologists, who can discover where they go and whether they return next year, 3124.

19 **1605** SIR THOMAS BROWNE, English physician and writer, born (and died in 1682), *f-i.* English Literature, 1212.

1784 Leigh Hunt, British poet and essayist, born, *f-i.* English Literature, 1210 ; Essay, 1224.

1833 Adam Lindsay Gordon, Australian poet, born, *f-i.* Australian Literature, 315.

1943 Moscow Conference of war opened, **2233**. Churchill, 824 ; Stalin, 3073.

Now is the time to study the way in which plants distribute their seeds : thistles and dandelions use the wind, burdocks make use of passing animals, other plants expel seeds violently for a few feet on every side, 2917.

20 **1632** SIR CHRISTOPHER WREN, English architect, born, **3425**. Architecture, 220 ; London, 2010 ; St. Paul's, 2862, *2863.*

1822 Thomas Hughes, British author, born, *f-i.* English Literature, 1210 ; School, 2887.

1944 U.S. forces landed in Leyte, Philippine Islands, **2569**. Japan, 1800 ; Pacific, 2474.

Gnats and small midges are still common in damp places ; the larger forms provide food for such surface-feeding fish as chub, dace and grayling.

21 **1772** SAMUEL TAYLOR COLERIDGE, English poet, born, **869**. Albatross, 101 ; English Literature, 1214 ; Lamb, Charles, 1886.

1790 Alphonse de Lamartine, French poet, born, *f-i.* France : Literature, 1377.

1805 Battle of Trafalgar and death of Nelson, **3234**, **2313**. Collingwood, Lord, 870 ; Napoleon I, 2275.

1833 Alfred Nobel, Swedish scientist, born, 2375. Dynamite, 1060 ; Explosives, 1250.

Eels migrate now towards the sea, often making cross-country journeys at night. Only those which are going to breed this season do that, the others remaining in streams and ponds, perhaps for years, 1092.

22 **741** CHARLES MARTEL, king of the Franks, died, **759**.

1685 Edict of Nantes revoked. Louis XIV, 2029 ; Huguenots, 1650 ; France : History, 1366.

1811 Franz Liszt, Hungarian composer and pianist, born, **1964**. Music, 2261 ; Piano, 2601.

1845 Sarah Bernhardt, French actress, born, **419**. Drama, 1037.

Sandpipers have nearly all left us now, but their places are taken by many species of waders reaching us from farther north, 3331.

Wallace Collection
Oct. 18, 1697. Canaletto, Venetian painter, was born. This picture of the Grand Canal at Venice is typical of his work.

23 **1844** ROBERT BRIDGES, poet laureate, born, *f-i.* English Literature, 1216 ; Poet Laureate, 2634.

1917 Battle of Caporetto opened. Italy, 1770 ; World Wars, 3411.

1942 Battle of El Alamein opened, *f-i.* Army, 249 ; Montgomery, 2222 ; World Wars, 3420.

Turtle-doves, unlike our other pigeons, are migratory and have now left us until the following spring, 2606. Beech trees are at their best in their glorious copper autumnal foliage, 395.

24 **1648** THIRTY YEARS' WAR ended by Peace of Westphalia, **3202**. European History, 1239 ; Germany : History, 1449 ; Gustavus Adolphus, 1558.

OCTOBER

1881 Pablo Picasso, Spanish painter, born, **2604**. France. Art, 1379 ; Painting, 2477.

1888 Richard Evelyn Byrd, American admiral and explorer, born, *f-i.* Antarctica, 174 ; Arctic Regions, 223 ; Polar Exploration, 2646.

1945 Charter of the United Nations came into force, **3283**. Peace Movement, 2531 ; San Francisco, 2872.

Grey phalaropes (f-i.) are now spreading southwards ; they are among the first birds to reach us from the north.
The red-necked phalarope, strangely enough, is one of the waders that visit us in summer, to breed in Scotland.

1636 Harvard University founded. Boston (Mass.), 529 ; Universities, 3296.

1918 Czechoslovakia proclaimed a republic, **953** ; anniversary kept as Czechoslovakia's Independence Day. Bohemia, 487 ; Masaryk, T. G., 2117.

1940 Greece invaded by Italian forces, **1526**. World Wars, 3418.

Now is the time to collect acorns, if you wish to grow your own oak-trees—a fascinating way of studying the development of our finest tree. Choose the big acorns from the finest trees if you want the best results. 2283

25 1415 BATTLE OF AGINCOURT, **76**. Henry V, 1611 ; Hundred Years' War, 1652.

1800 Lord Macaulay, British historian and politician, born, **2046**. English Literature, 1215 ; Essay 1224 ; History, 1630.

1825 Johann Strauss, Austrian composer, born. **3102**. Dancing, 967 ; Music, 2261.

1854 Battle of Balaclava ; Charge of the Light Brigade, **341**. Crimea, 931.

The autumn colouring of trees makes a fascinating study at this time of the year. Amongst the most brilliant are introduced species of oaks, such as the red oak, and maples, which reached us from America, 2409.

Privet berries are noticeable now in the hedgerows

26 1664 ROYAL MARINES formed. Navy, 2306, 2308.

1759 Georges Jacques Danton, French revolutionist, born, **971**. French Revolution, 1396 ; Marat, Jean Paul, 2096 ; Robespierre, 2790.

1800 Helmuth Karl, Count von Moltke, Prussian soldier, born. Franco-Prussian War, 1385.

Spiders are still very active, and the dewy mornings show up their webs better than at any other season of the year. Often the whole countryside seems covered with sheets of gossamer, while every web is pearly with dewdrops, 3062.

27 1728 CAPTAIN JAMES COOK, British sailor and explorer, born, **898**. Australia, *308*, 310 ; New Zealand, 2360 ; Pacific Ocean, 2472.

1858 Theodore Roosevelt, American president, born, **2824**. Panama, 2486 ; United States, 3291.

1870 Capitulation of Metz, 2155. Alsace-Lorraine, 133 ; Franco-Prussian War, 1385.

Young thrushes may sometimes be heard trying out their voices. 3205.

28 FEAST OF ST. SIMON AND ST. JUDE.

c. 1466 Desiderius Erasmus, Dutch scholar, born, **1221**. Holbein, 1635 ; More, Sir Thomas, 2228 ; Renaissance, 2764.

29 1618 SIR WALTER RALEIGH, English soldier and writer, beheaded, **2743**. America, 142 ; Carolina, 704 ; Guiana, 1552 ; Orinoco, 2452.

1656 Edmund Halley, English astronomer, born, *f-i.* Astronomy, 280 ; Comets, 880, *plate f. 881* ; Newton, Sir Isaac, 2349.

1740 James Boswell, Scottish author, born, **529**. Johnson, Samuel, 1836.

1795 John Keats, British poet, born, **1849**. English Literature, 1214.

1889 British South Africa Company received its charter. Rhodes, Cecil, 2771 ; South Africa, 3019.

1923 Turkey became a republic, **3265** ; anniversary kept as her National Day. Kemal Atatürk, 1850.

Among hedgerow fruits are those of the privet—round, shining purple-black berries of which the birds are especially fond. To Man, however, they are poisonous ; privet, f-i.

30 1485 THE YEOMEN OF THE GUARD (Beefeaters) instituted by Henry VII, **396**.

1751 Richard Brinsley Sheridan, British dramatist, born, **2944**. Drama, 1040.

1822 Caledonian Canal opened. Canal, 686 ; Inverness-shire, 1737.

Swan families are often seen on quiet waters, the young cygnets conspicuous in their brownish plumage, 3125.
Elderberries may be gathered now to be made into an excellent wine. 1124.

31 HALLOWE'EN, **1566**.

1620 John Evelyn, English diarist, born, **1243**. Gibbons, Grinling, 1462.

1632 Jan Vermeer, Dutch painter, born, **3315**. Netherlands : Art, *2325*, 2334.

1940 The Battle of Britain ended, **575**. Royal Air Force, 2832 ; World Wars, 3417.

Apples are ripening now, though those of many of the wild " crabs " are too tart to be edible. Yet birds like them, and the trees are often stripped long before the fruits have a chance to fall, 190, plate f. 1400.

Oct. 30, 1822. The Caledonian Canal was opened. Above are the locks at Fort Augustus.

NOVEMBER

1
ALL SAINTS' DAY.
1500 Benvenuto Cellini, Florentine sculptor and goldsmith, born. Italy: Art, *1784*, 1785; Renaissance, 2766.
1517 Luther nailed his 95 Theses to the church door at Wittenberg, **2040.** Reformation, 2758.
1755 Earthquake in Lisbon destroyed the city. Earthquake, 1070; Lisbon, 1962.
1757 Antonio Canova, Italian sculptor, born. Italy: Art, 1775; Sculpture, 2906.
1914 Battle of Coronel. World Wars, 3411.
1944 The Home Guard, British citizen army of the Second World War, stood down, **1637.** Army, 244; World Wars, 3417.

Bird visitors still reach our shores from the colder lands to the north and east, and on the east coast in particular these migrants may be seen, often in a state of exhaustion after a long battle with autumn gales, 2171.

2
ALL SOULS' DAY.
1877 Victor Trumper, Australian cricketer, born, *f-i.* Cricket, 928.
1903 The *Daily Mirror* first issued in London. Newspapers, 2344; Northcliffe, Lord, 2386.
1917 The Balfour Declaration on Zionism. Balfour, Lord, 343; Jews, 1831; Palestine, 2482.

A few bats are still seen if the weather is fairly mild, but a great many have already retired to their hibernating places, 370.

3
1534 ACT OF SUPREMACY, making the King the head of the English Church. Church of England, 825; Henry VIII, 1612; Reformation, 2759.
1879 Vilhjalmur Stefansson, Arctic explorer, born, *f-i.* Arctic Regions, 223; Polar Exploration, 2644.
1901 Leopold III, King of the Belgians, born, **1928.** Albert I, 102; Belgium, 407.

The refuse of dead leaves, sticks, and other vegetable material floating in flood water is an excellent place for finding many strange insects, especially beetles, swept away from their usual haunts.

4
1575 GUIDO RENI, Italian painter, born, *f-i.* Aurora, *304*; Italy: Art, 1775.
1590 Gerard van Honthorst, Dutch painter, born. Buckingham, Duke of, *598*; Netherlands: Art, 2333.
1650 William III born, **3380.** English History, 1200; James II, 1794; Mary II, 2114.

The last of the autumn colours on trees can still be studied; notice the yellow of the English elms long after the other species have lost their foliage, 1152

5
1605 GUNPOWDER PLOT. Fawkes, Guy, 1264; James I, 1793; Parliament, 2521.
1688 William of Orange (later King William III of England) landed at Torbay, **3380.** English History, 1200.
1854 Battle of Inkerman. Crimea, 931.
1914 Cyprus annexed by Britain. Cyprus, 952.

Finches and their relatives haunt the beech woods, for the nuts or mast form an important article of their winter food, 1272

Nov. 1, 1517. Martin Luther nailed his theses to the door of Wittenberg church.

6
1671 COLLEY CIBBER, English poet laureate, born, *f-i.* Drama, 1037; English Literature, 1210; Poet Laureate, 2634.
1848 Richard Jefferies, British naturalist and writer, born, **1816.** English Literature, 1210; Nature Study, 2283.
1869 New Blackfriars Bridge, London, opened. London, 2012.

The bareness of the trees now enables us to see more of many of our own birds and arboreal creatures; among these the red squirrel is conspicuous, and it is possible now to watch his acrobatics in the tree-tops, 3071.

7
1867 MME. CURIE, co-discoverer of radium, born, **944.** Atom, 296; Radium, 2731.
1885 Completion of Canadian Pacific Rly.; Lord Strathcona drove in last spike. Canada, 678; Railways, 2734; Strathcona, Lord, 3102.
1917 (Oct. 25 Old Style) Lenin and the Bolsheviks seized power in Russia (the " October revolution "). Bolshevism, 495; Lenin, 1923; Russia, 2849.

Groundsel is among the flowers still out, for, like other common weeds, it is open practically the whole year round, f-i. Badgers have retired for their winter sleep, 337.

In November groundsel is still out.

8
1866 HERBERT AUSTIN, 1st Baron Austin, motor-manufacturer, born, **306.** Motor Vehicles, 2241.
1942 Allied landings in N.W. Africa. Algeria, 118; Tunisia, 3254; World Wars, 3420.

Nov. 9. The Lord Mayor's coach makes a glittering spectacle as it arrives at the Mansion House, in London.

Now queen wasps enter the house or garden shed to find safe winter quarters, **3345.**
The "old man's beard," a mass of silky white seeds, makes the wild clematis conspicuous, 836.

9 LORD MAYOR'S SHOW DAY. The show is held on Nov. 8 or 10 if Nov. 9 falls on Sunday.
1841 Edward VII, King of England, born, *1091*, **1092.** Albert, Prince Consort, 101 ; Alexandra, 108 ; George V, 1442 ; Victoria, 3319.
1880 Sir Giles Gilbert Scott, British architect, born, *f-i.* Architecture, 212 ; Liverpool, 1968.
1918 William II, German Emperor, abdicated, **3378.** Germany : History, 1450 ; World Wars, 3414.
1918 Polish independence proclaimed. Poland, 2642.

Fieldfare flocks are conspicuous now ; you can distinguish this big thrush by its pale rump and generally richer plumage than that of the mistle-thrush, 3206.

10 1483 MARTIN LUTHER, German reformer, born, **2040.** Charles V, Emperor, 754 ; Reformation, 2758.
1697 William Hogarth, British artist, born, **1634.** English Art, 1178, *1185.*
1728 Oliver Goldsmith, Irish novelist and dramatist, born, **1482.** English Literature, *1213* ; Johnson, S., 1836 ; Novel, 2402.
1759 Friedrich Schiller, German poet and dramatist, born, **2882.** Germany : Literature, 1456 ; Goethe, J. W. von, 1479.
1880 Jacob Epstein, British sculptor, born, **1221.** Hudson, W. H., *1649* ; Sculpture, 2911.

Mice are now hibernating, and the nests of some species may be discovered in masses of leaves or thick evergreen foliage, each with its curled-up inhabitant, **1029, 2248.**

11 1822 FEODOR MIKHAILOVITCH DOSTOIEVSKI, Russian novelist, born, **1030.** Novel, 2404 ; Russian Literature, 2856.
1869 Victor Emmanuel II, King of Italy, born, **3319.** Italy, 1769.
1918 First World War ended by Armistice, which took effect at 11 a.m., **239.** World Wars, 3414.

Big bunches of fruits hang from the hornbeam boughs, giving these trees a strangely leafy appearance, considering the time of year, f-i.

12 1684 EDWARD VERNON, British sailor, born, *f-i.* Navy, 2293.
1842 Lord Rayleigh, British physicist, born, *f-i.* Air, 88 ; Neon, 2315.
1847 Sir James Young Simpson first used chloroform in surgery. Anaesthetics, 149 ; Medicine, *2133.*
1940 British victory over Italians at Taranto, *f-i.* Italy, 1774 ; Mediterranean, 2135 ; Navy 2293.

The larch, a deciduous conifer, looks strangely bare now, **1892.**
The mottled umber moth is one of the few now seen on the wing, 3388.

13 1312 EDWARD III, King of England, born, *1090*, 1091. Calais, 655 ; Hundred Years' War, 1652, *1653* ; Orders, *2448.*
1850 Robert Louis Stevenson, Scottish author, born, **3089.** English Literature, 1215 ; Novel, 2402 ; Samoa, 2869.

Resident wildfowl have had their numbers enormously increased by visitors from the north, even in the case of ducks, such as mallard and teal, 1051.

14 1840 CLAUDE MONET, French painter, born, *f-i.* France : Art, *1375*, 1378 ; Impressionism, 1687.
1840 Auguste Rodin, French sculptor, born, **2795**, *2796.* Sculpture, 2906.
1922 British Broadcasting Company sent out its first daily programme, from 2LO. Marconi, G., 2098 ; Wireless, 3398.
1940 Coventry severely bombed by German aircraft, **923.** World Wars, 3417.
1948 Prince Charles, son of Princess Elizabeth and the Duke of Edinburgh, born, *f-i.* Elizabeth, Princess, 1150.

Red deer come down from the hilltops to the shelter and food of the deeply-wooded valleys, 984.
Medlars are "bletted" now and more or less fit to eat, 2718.

15 1708 WILLIAM PITT, Earl of Chatham, British statesman, born, **759.** American Independence, 144 ; Pitt, William, 2614 ; United Kingdom, 3276.
1731 William Cowper, English poet, born, **923.** English Literature, 1213.
1738 Sir William Herschel, English astronomer, born, *f-i.* Astronomy, 275 ; Planets, 2618.
1889 Revolution in Brazil overthrew monarchy and

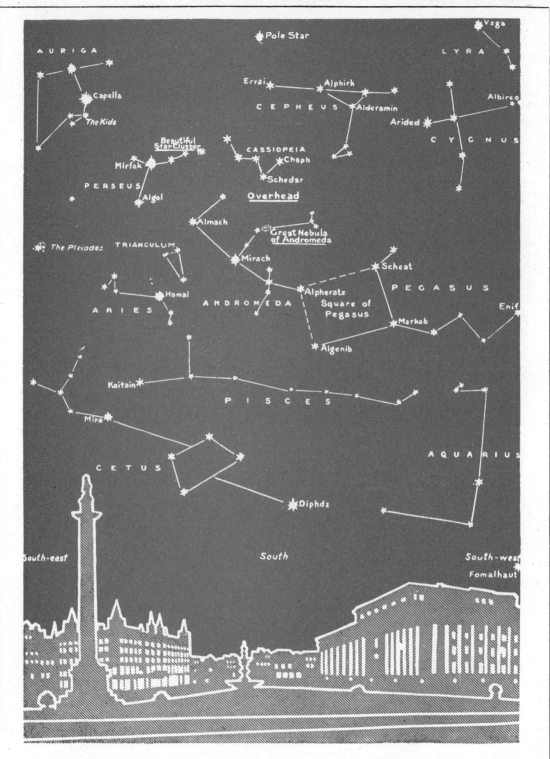

THE STARS IN NOVEMBER.   With this map we can study the stars from the middle of November to the middle of December.   We are looking south in Lime Street, Liverpool, and on the right hand is St. George's Hall.   Many stars in last month's diagram will be seen in the west and south-west.

established republic ; anniversary kept as Brazil's National Day, **554.**

> *London's winter birds, the black-headed gulls, are now in residence, their numbers swelled by a few lesser black-backed gulls, some of which are immigrants from Scandinavia,* **1555.**

16 **1632** BATTLE OF LÜTZEN and death of Gustavus Adolphus, **1558.** Thirty Years' War, 3202.

1811 John Bright, British statesman, born, **569.** Cobden, Richard, 858 ; Liberals, 1929 ; Peel, Sir Robert, 2535.

Nov. 19, 1946. Opening of first U.N.E.S.C.O. conference. Above, M. Bidault welcomes the delegates to Paris.

1918 Hungary proclaimed a republic, **1656.** World Wars, 3414.

> *In the south ivy is still in flower, its blooms often covered with sleepy, half-drunken flies,* **1788.**
> *On honeysuckle you may find the hibernaculum of the white admiral butterfly's little caterpillar, 1622, plate f. 632.*

17 **1755** LOUIS XVIII, King of France, born, **2030.** France : History, 1365.

1869 Suez Canal opened, **3110.** Canal, 689 ; Egypt, 1101, *1103.*

1887 F.-M. Lord Montgomery, British soldier, born, **2221.** Army, 244 ; Libya, 1932 ; Normandy Invasion, 2377 ; World Wars, 3420.

> *Plump trout may be found in tiny streams, usually in pairs, for they are there for spawning,* **3251.**
> *Red "haws," the fruits of the hawthorn, cover the bare hedges with masses of bright colour,* **1588.**

18 **1626** CONSECRATION OF ST. PETER'S, ROME. Rome, *2802* ; Vatican, 3306.

1785 Sir David Wilkie, Scottish painter, born, *f-i.* English Art, 1182 ; Knox, John, *1871.*

1789 Louis Jacques Daguerre, pioneer of photography, born, *f-i.* Photography, 2580.

1836 Sir William Schwenck Gilbert, English dramatist, born. Gilbert and Sullivan, 1463 ; Opera, 2438.

1887 Frank Dobson, English sculptor, born, *f-i.* Sculpture, 2911.

> *Along our coasts, especially those of East Anglia, the wild geese have begun to assemble,* **1484.**

19 **1600** CHARLES I, King of England, born, **755,** *756.* Charles II, 756 ; Cromwell, Oliver, 933 ; English History, 1196, *1206.*

1770 Bertel Thorvaldsen, Danish sculptor, born, *f-i.* Sculpture, 2906.

1805 Ferdinand, Vicomte de Lesseps, engineer of Suez Canal, born, *f-i.* Canal, 686 ; Panama Canal, 2487 ; Suez Canal, 3110.

1849 Sir Ambrose Fleming, British scientist, born, *f-i.* Electronic Devices, 1138 ; Thermionic Valve, 3198.

1946 First general conference of U.N.E.S.C.O. opened in Paris, *f-i.* United Nations, 3283.

> *House flies are hibernating now—a few as adults, more as maggots, hidden deep in garden refuse heaps or the farmyard dunghill,* **1329.**

20 **1759** BATTLE OF QUIBERON BAY. Seven Years' War, *2925.*

1841 Sir Wilfred Laurier, Canadian statesman, born, *f-i.* Canadian History, 681.

1847 Rev. H. F. Lyte, English divine, died, *f-i.* Hymns, 1678.

1947 Marriage of Princess Elizabeth and Prince Philip, Duke of Edinburgh, *1151.*

> *Flocks of golden plover are seen on arable land, river-estuaries and marshes, 2630*

21 **1694** VOLTAIRE (François Marie Arouet), French writer, born, **3329.** France : Literature, 1380 ; French Revolution, 1393.

1918 Surrender of the German fleet. Beatty, Earl, 386 ; World Wars, 3414.

> *Notice how the flocks of chaffinches comprise either females only or males only ; often the male birds go about singly, whence the alternative name, " bachelor finch,"* **1272.**

22 **1428** RICHARD NEVILLE, Earl of Warwick (the " Kingmaker "), born, *f-i.* English History, 1193 ; Roses, Wars of the, 2828.

1643 René Robert Cavelier, Sieur de La Salle, French explorer, born, **1894.** America : Discovery, 143 ; Mississippi, 2192.

1819 George Eliot (Marian Evans), English novelist, born, **1145.** English Literature, 1215 . Novel, 2402.

1943 Cairo Conference of war opened, **654.** Chiang Kai-shek, 783 ; Churchill, 824.

> *The second-year cones of the Scots pines are now turning greyish and hard, for the seeds within are almost ripe. 2610.*
> *Salmon are running far up the rivers to spawn, 2865.*

23 **1862** SIR GILBERT PARKER, Canadian novelist, born, *f-i.* Canadian Literature, 685.

1890 Queen Wilhelmina (*f-i.*) became Queen of the Netherlands. Netherlands, 2323.

> *In the pine woods the cole tit flits from tree to tree seeking insects,* **3218.**

24 1642 ABEL TASMAN Dutch navigator, discovered Van Diemans Land (Tasmania), **3156**. Australia, 310 ; New Zealand, 2358 ; Pacific Ocean, 2472.

1718 Laurence Sterne, British author, born, *f-i.* English Literature, 1210 ; Novel, 2402.

1859 Darwin's " Origin of Species " published, **975**. Evolution, 1244.

> *Now is the time to put out the bird-table and to arrange coconuts and other suitable food in a place where you can watch the birds feeding,* **437**.
> *In the woods a fine crop of hazel nuts is ready for the gathering,* 1590.

25 1562 LOPE DE VEGA, Spanish poet and dramatist, born. Spanish Literature, 3051. 1835 Andrew Carnegie, Scottish manufacturer and philanthropist, born, **703**. Library, 1930.

1877 Harley Granville-Barker, English dramatist and producer, born, *f-i.* Theatre, 3194.

> *Coots collect in vast flocks on freshwater lakes, as well as in shallow harbours and estuaries,* 2734.
> *Snails have retired among the ivy, behind refuse or beneath the garden shed, each with the entrance to his shell sealed by a lid,* **2989**.

26 1379 NEW COLLEGE, OXFORD, founded by William of Wykeham. Oxford, 2464 ; Winchester, 3383.

1862 Sir Mark Aurel Stein, British archaeologist, born, *f-i.* Baluchistan, 352 ; Turkistan, 3266.

1948 First movable bridge of aluminium alloy opened at Sunderland. Alloys, 122 ; Aluminium, 134 ; Bridge, 564.

> *Harvest mice do not go into a hibernatory sleep, and may be disturbed in a lively condition in farmyard stacks or corn ricks, plate f.* 2248.

27 1635 MME. DE MAINTENON, second wife of Louis XIV, born. France : History, 1365 ; Louis XIV, *2029*.

1701 Anders Celsius, Swedish astronomer, born, *f-i* Astronomy, 275 ; Thermometer, 3200.

1853 Sir Frank Dicksee, English artist, born, *f-i.* English Art, 1177.

1878 Sir William Orpen, British artist, born, *f-i.* English Art, *1183*, 1184.

1941 Surrender of Gondar (*f-i.*) and end of the Abyssinian campaign. Abyssinia, 15 ; E. Africa, *map*, *1072* ; Italy, 1774 ; World Wars, 3419.

> *Thick white hoar-frost now covers the trees and fields ; it enables us to see the characteristic form of each species of tree,* **3245**.

28 1757 WILLIAM BLAKE, British artist and poet, born, **466**. English Art, 1182 ; English Literature, 1213 ; Literature for Children, 1965.

1836 London University granted charter, **2021**. Universities, 3296.

1912 Albania declared independent of Turkey, **100**. Turkey, 3265.

1943 Teheran Conference of war opened. Churchill, 824 ; Iran, 1742 ; Roosevelt, 2824 ; Stalin, 3073.

> *Now nuthatches can be tempted indoors by a line of hazel nuts. In near-by oak trees we find the broken shells, wedged in cracks of the bark, and hammered open by the bird's sharp bill,* 2407.

Turkey oak acorns may be seen now.

29 1797 GAETANO DONIZETTI, Italian composer, born, *f-i.* Opera, 2439.

1832 Louisa May Alcott, American authoress, born, *f-i.* Literature for Children, 1965 ; United States : Literature, 3294.

> *Rare waders may often be discovered mingling with the flocks of commoner species on the shore and the mud-flats,* 3331.

30 ST. ANDREW'S DAY.

1667 Jonathan Swift, British satirist, born, **3132**. English Literature, 1213 ; Literature for Children, 1965.

1835 Mark Twain, American humorist, born, **3269**. Literature for Children, 1966 ; United States : Literature, 3295.

1874 Rt. Hon. Winston Churchill, British statesman, born, 824. Marlborough, 1st Duke, 2105 ; Northcliffe, Lord, *2386* ; World Wars, 3409, 3417.

1936 Crystal Palace destroyed by fire. Fireworks, 1289.

1939 Finland invaded by the Red Army, **1278**. Russia, 2852 ; World Wars, 3416.

> *The stonechat is a conspicuous bird on the downs and bare hills and moors ; unlike its relative, the whinchat it is not a migrant,* 3374.

Nov. 30, 1936. For miles around, London's millions gathered to watch the flaming end of the Crystal Palace.

1 1768 ROYAL ACADEMY OF ART founded, **17.** English Art, 1179 ; Painting, *2477.*

1844 Queen Alexandra, consort of Edward VII, born, **108.** Edward VII, 1092 ; George V, 1442.

1919 Lady Astor, first woman M.P. to do so, took her seat in the House of Commons, *f-i.* Parliament, 2521 ; Vote, 3330.

> *Study the lovely forms of frost and snow crystals, each a perfectly symmetrical design, however complex ; a strong lens or small microscope comes in useful for this,* **1400,** *2992.*

2 1697 CHOIR OF THE REBUILT ST. PAUL'S CATHEDRAL, London, opened. St. Paul's Cathedral, 2862. Architecture, *219* ; Cathedral, 729 ; London, 2010, *2020* ; Wren, Sir C., 3425.

1805 Battle of Austerlitz. Napoleon I, 2275 ; Pitt, William, 2614.

> *Many coarse fish, such as tench and some carp, have buried themselves in the muddy bottom of the lakes, keeping away from the cold,* **704.**

3 1753 SAMUEL CROMPTON, British inventor, born, **933.** Industrial Revolution, 1721.

1795 Sir Rowland Hill, British reformer, born, *f-i.* Post Office, 2661.

1830 Frederick, Baron Leighton, President of the Royal Academy, born, **1919,** *1921.* English Art, 1182 ; Hero, *1619.*

> *In cold weather, many birds that live normally in the woods or open fields now become tamer and enter the garden, even coming near the house in their search for food.*

4 1795 THOMAS CARLYLE, British essayist and historian, born, **702.** English Literature, 1215 ; Essay, 1224.

1833 George Henry Boughton, British painter, born, *f-i.* Milton, John, *2177.*

> *Look for the cocoons of moths in nooks and crannies of old walls, garden fences and outhouses ; on the trunk of willow or poplar you may find the iron-hard cocoon of the fine puss-moth,* **628,** *f-i.*

Dec. 2, 1805. The battle of Austerlitz. Napoleon's great victory over the Austrians and Russians in Moravia was the most decisive in his career.

5 1830 CHRISTINA ROSSETTI, English poetess, born, *f-i.* English Literature, 1210 ; Poetry, 2634.

1859 Lord Jellicoe, British sailor, born, **1816.** Beatty, Earl, 386 ; World Wars, 3411.

1901 Walter Disney, American cartoonist, born, *f-i.* Cinema, 829.

> *The brambling is one of our winter visitors of the finch tribe ; you will find it in small flocks feeding on beech " mast " or on the hornbeam seeds,* 1272.

The brambling is a December visitant.

6 1421 HENRY VI, King of England, born, **1611.** English History, 1193 ; Roses, Wars of the, 2828.

1732 Warren Hastings, British statesman, born, **1581.** Calcutta, 660 ; India : History, 1714.

1857 Joseph Conrad, British novelist, born, **891.** English Literature, 1215 ; Novel, 2403.

1917 Finland declared her independence, **1278.**

> *In Devon or Cornwall occasional blackcaps or garden warblers or even swallows may be seen ; these normally migrate overseas, but have stayed in Britain for a change,* **3340.**

7 1598 GIOVANNI LORENZO BERNINI, Italian sculptor, born. Sculpture, 2903.

1839 Sir Redvers Buller, English soldier, born, *f-i.* Boer War, 486.

1941 Pearl Harbour attacked by Japanese aircraft, **2533.** Hawaii, 1587 ; Japan, 1800 ; Pacific, 2473 ; United States : History, 3292 ; World Wars, 3419.

> *Among the few flowers still regularly found in bloom is herb robert, our commonest wild member of the geranium tribe,* 1444.
> *Little auks are occasionally found far inland, driven down and exhausted by the wind,* 304.

8 1832 BJÖRNSTJERNE BJÖRNSON, Norwegian novelist and dramatist, born, **462.** Scandinavia, 2880.

1848 Joel Chandler Harris, American author of " Uncle Remus," born, *f-i.*

1865 Jean Sibelius, Finnish composer, born, **2965.** Music, 2266.

1914 Battle of the Falkland Isles, **1259.** World Wars, 3411.

1934 England - Australia air mail instituted. Aeroplane, 51 ; Post Office, 2662.

> *Over flooded meadows, where the river bank is no longer visible, migrant ducks of many species swim to and fro, often stalked by the wildfowler in his punt,* **1051.**

9 1594 GUSTAVUS ADOLPHUS, King of Sweden, born, **1558.** Army, 251 ; Sweden, 3131 ; Thirty Years' War, 3202.

1608 John Milton, British poet, born, **2176.** English Literature, 1211, *1212.*

Big birds of prey such as the white-tailed or sea eagle are sometimes seen in southern England, where they have taken up their winter quarters. These are usually young male birds, 1063.

10 1891 F.-M. LORD ALEXANDER, British soldier, born, **107.** Burma, 625 ; Dunkirk, 1057 ; Montgomery, 2221.

1902 Assuan Dam opened. Dam, *959* ; Egypt, *1102* ; Nile, 2370.

1936 Abdication of Edward VIII, **1092.** George V, 1442 ; George VI, 1442.

1941 British battleships *Prince of Wales* and *Repulse* sunk by Japanese aircraft. Japan, 1800 ; Pacific, 2473 ; World Wars, 3420.

Roe deer lose their antlers now, 984.
Hibernating butterflies such as small tortoise-shells and peacocks are often found indoors, 1622.

11 1803 HECTOR BERLIOZ, French composer, born, *f-i.* Music, 2261 ; Orchestra, 2446.

1843 Robert Koch, German bacteriologist, born. Germs, 1458 ; Medicine, *2133.*

1941 Germany and Italy declared war on the U.S.A., **1452, 1774.** World Wars, 3420.

1945 Formal opening of the new Waterloo Bridge, *566* ; London, *2011.*

In pine and larch logs you may discover the fat, whitish larvae of the wood wasps such as Sirex, f-i. ; also those of many wood-boring beetles, 398.
House crickets chirp now behind the kitchen stove or in other warm, dark places, 927.

12 1724 SAMUEL, Viscount Hood, British sailor, born, *f-i.* Navy, 2293 ; United Kingdom, 3276.

1821 Gustave Flaubert, French novelist, born, *f-i.* France : Literature, 1381 ; Novel, 2404.

1901 Marconi received his first transatlantic wireless message, **2098.** Wireless, 3391.

Vast flocks of crossbills now often appear on our eastern seaboard, sometimes spreading southwards. These birds have come from Scandinavia or N. Germany, and have nothing to do with the native Scottish crossbills, 1272.

13 1553 HENRY IV (Henry of Navarre), born, **1613.** France : History, 1366 ; Huguenots, 1650 ; Nantes, 2274.

1797 Heinrich Heine, German poet, born, **1604.** Germany : Literature, 1457.

1816 Ernst Werner von Siemens, German engineer, born. Iron and Steel, 1756.

1939 Battle of the River Plate, *f-i.* Navy, 2293 ; World Wars, 3417.

Snow gives an opportunity to study the footprints and other signs of animals.

Dec. 11, 1945. At the formal opening of the new Waterloo Bridge, London, Mr. Morrison cut the tape.

14 1546 TYCHO BRAHE, Danish astronomer, born, **622.** Astronomy, 275 ; Kepler, Johann, 1852.

1824 Pierre Puvis de Chavannes, French painter, born, *f-i.* France : Art, 1378 ; Painting, 2475.

1895 George VI, King of England, born, **1442.** Elizabeth, Queen Consort, 1149 ; Elizabeth, Princess, 1150 ; Margaret, Princess, 2100.

1897 Kurt Schuschnigg, Austrian politician, born, *f-i.* Austria, 318 ; Hitler, Adolf, 1632.

Redpolls are seen now in birch woods in southern England; they are small relatives of the linnet, 1955.

15 37 NERO, Roman Emperor, born, **2315.** Christianity, 817 ; Rome : History, 2811.

1610 David Teniers (younger), Flemish painter, baptized. Netherlands : Art, *2330*, 2333.

1734 George Romney, British painter, born, *f-i.* English Art, 1180.

1832 Alexandre Eiffel, French engineer, born. Paris, 2517, 2518.

Among flowers seen at this season are colt's-foot and lesser celandine, f-i.
Look out for the white wagtail, a migrant easily mistaken for the pied species, 3332.

16 1714 GEORGE WHITE-FIELD, English preacher, born, *f-i.* Free Churches, 1390 ; Wesley, John, 3365.

1770 Ludwig van Beethoven, German composer, born, **397,**

After John Hoppner

Dec. 12, 1724. Admiral Lord Hood, commander of Britain's fleet in the American War, was born.

DECEMBER

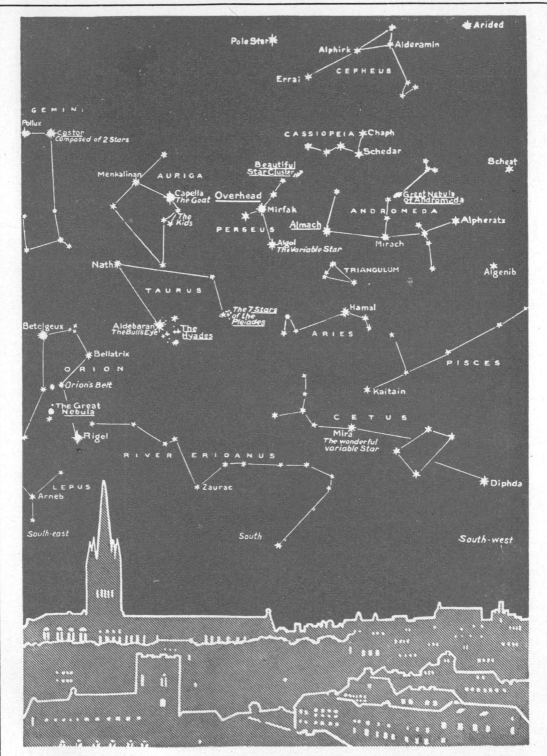

THE STARS IN DECEMBER. With this map we can study the stars from the middle of December to the middle of January. We are looking southward in Norwich and can see the cathedral on the left of the picture. All the stars that are underlined in the map should be viewed with a telescope or with field- or opera-glasses.

Dec. 16, 1773. Resenting the British government's attempt to enforce the tax of 3d. per lb. on tea, a party disguised as Red Indians boarded the tea ships in Boston, Massachusetts, harbour, and threw the tea overboard. This drawing of the town was made by a British lieutenant in 1775.

Music, 2264; Orchestra, 2445; Piano, 2602, 2603.

1773 "Boston Tea Party," opening the War of American Independence, 144. United States: History, 3290.

1775 Jane Austen, English novelist, born, **306.** English Literature, 1214; Novel, 2402.

1838 Defeat of Dingaan, Zulu chief, by the Boers; anniversary kept in S. Africa as Dingaan's Day. Natal, 2279; S. Africa, 3019.

1899 Noel Coward, actor, composer and dramatist, born, f-i. Drama, 1037.

Now is the time to see the lesser spotted woodpecker, for this species, preferring the tops of the trees, is hard to discover when they are in leaf, 3404.

17 **1619** PRINCE RUPERT OF BAVARIA born, f-i. Charles I, 755; Hudson's Bay Co., 1650. **1778** Sir Humphry Davy, British inventor, born, **979.** Faraday, Michael, 1260; Lamp, *1889.*

1807 John Greenleaf Whittier, American poet, born, f-i. United States: Literature, 3294.

1903 Wright brothers made the first flight in a heavier-than-air machine, **3427.** Aeroplane, 45.

The great grey shrike is one of the winter visitors sometimes seen in East Anglia, 2962.
Green spikes showing through the soil are signs of bulbs such as snowdrops, crocuses or daffodils, 2992.

18 **1707** CHARLES WESLEY, English divine and hymn-writer, born, 3365. Free Churches, 1390; Hymns, 1678.

1786 Carl Maria von Weber, German composer, born, f-i. Music, 2261; Opera, 2436.

1859 Francis Thompson, English poet, born, f-i. English Literature, 1210; Poetry, 2634.

1865 Slavery abolished in U.S.A., **2982.** United States: History, 3291.

Puffins, guillemots and other marine divers are all far out at sea, for most of these strange birds spend the winter on the waves, 304.

19 **1790** SIR WILLIAM PARRY, British Arctic explorer, born, f-i. Arctic Regions, 223; Polar Exploration, 2644.

1915 British troops withdrawn from Gallipoli. World Wars, 3410.

Winter enables us to study the bare twigs of trees, and to learn how to identify each species by them; those of the walnut, for example, are distinguishable by their buds, by the small, conical male catkins and by their chambered pith, 3338.

20 **1192** RICHARD COEUR DE LION captured by Leopold of Austria, **2776.** Crusades, 936. **1769** Sir Martin Archer Shee, British artist, born, f-i. English Art, 1177.

Acorns and hazel nuts, punctured by neat little round holes, and with ruined contents, have been the home of species of weevil, 3362.

21 ST. THOMAS'S DAY. **1118** Thomas Becket, English prelate, born, **389.** Canterbury, 692; Henry II, 1609.

1571 Johann Kepler, German astronomer, born, **1852.** Astronomy, 275; Planets, 2617.

1849 John Seymour Lucas, British painter, born, f-i. Armada, *236*; Drake, Sir F., 1036.

1879 Josef Vissarionovitch Stalin, Russian dictator, born, **3072.** Bolshevism, 495; Russia: History, 2850; Trotsky, 3251; World Wars, 3418.

The strangely shaped, greenish-grey pupa of the large white butterfly is often found on garden outhouses, walls, or palings, 631.
Now is the time to find the "pixie cup" lichens, 1933.

22 **1639** JEAN RACINE, French poet and dramatist, baptized, **2725.** Drama, 1040; France: Literature, 1380.

1768 John Crome ("Old Crome"), British painter, born, f-i. English Art, *1180*, 1181; Norwich, 2398.

1896 Sir Henry O. D. Segrave, British racing motorist, born, **2919.** Motor Vehicles, 2241.

Many species of marine diving ducks may be seen off our coasts; almost all are winter visitors, 1051.

23 **1732** SIR RICHARD ARKWRIGHT, English inventor, born, **235.** Cotton, 917; Industrial Revolution, 1721.

1777 Alexander I, Emperor of Russia, born. Napoleon I, 2275; Russia, 2848.

1805 Joseph Smith, Mormon leader, born. Mormons, 2230.

1832 Britain annexes the Falkland Isles, **1259.** British Commonwealth, 580.

1948 Execution of Gen. Tojo (*f-i.*) and other major Japanese war criminals. Japan, 1800; World Wars, 3424.

Mistletoe hangs in great bunches on the trees, especially apples, lime, and poplars. The berries are ripe now, popular food with birds, 2194.

24

1167 JOHN, King of England, born, **1833.** English History, 1194, *1196*; Government, 1489; Magna Carta, 2059.

1491 Ignatius de Loyola, founder of the Jesuits, born, **2032.** Reformation, 2760.

1818 James Prescott Joule, British physicist, born, **1839.** Heat, 1593.

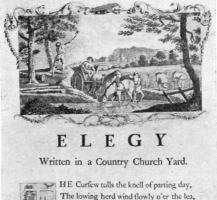

Christmas rose, Helleborus niger

1822 Matthew Arnold, British poet, essayist and critic, born, *f-i.* English Literature, 1215.

1838 John, Viscount Morley, British statesman and writer, born, *f-i.* Gladstone, W. E., 1469; History, 1630.

Christmas roses flower now in the garden, f-i.
The red berries of butcher's broom make this strange little plant conspicuous, f-i.

25

CHRISTMAS DAY, **819.** Christianity, 817; Jesus Christ, 1821.

1648 Sir Isaac Newton, English mathematician and scientist, born, **2348.** Astronomy, 276; Gravitation, 1512; Mechanics, 2127; Physics, 2593; Rockets, 2793.

1941 Hong Kong surrendered to the Japanese, **1640.** Japan, 1800; Pacific, 2473; World Wars, 3420.

This is the traditional time for holly berries, although often they are ripe a month earlier and sometimes they are still red when spring is with us, 1636.

26

ST. STEPHEN'S DAY. Martyrs, *2112.*

1716 Thomas Gray, English poet, born, **1514.** English Literature, 1213; Poetry, 2634.

Many strange fungi are at their best now; look out for the curious velvety, purple-brown "Jew's ear" on dead or dying elder boughs, f-i.

27

ST. JOHN THE EVANGELIST'S DAY.

1822 Louis Pasteur, French chemist, born, **2527.** Antiseptics, 178; Germs, 1458; Lister, Lord, 1963; Medicine, 2135.

1939 Earthquakes at Erzingan, Turkey, killed 23,000. Earthquake, 1069; Turkey, 3262.

Many mosses fruit now, 2238.

28

HOLY INNOCENTS DAY.

1065 Westminster Abbey consecrated, **3369.** Edward the Confessor, 1089; London, 2014; Poetry, *2635.*

1856 Woodrow Wilson, President of U.S.A., born, **3383.** League of Nations, 1908; Peace Movement, 2531; World Wars, 3412.

1882 Sir Arthur Stanley Eddington, British astronomer, born, **1083.** Astronomy, 275.

The "Glastonbury thorn," a variety of the hawthorn, flowers now; legend says that it grew originally from the staff of St. Joseph of Arimathea, f-i.

29

1809 WILLIAM EWART GLADSTONE, British statesman, born, **1469.** Ireland, 1746; Liberals, 1929; Victoria, Queen, 3320.

1940 Great fire-bomb air raid on the City of London, **2016.** Germany, 1452; World Wars, *3418.*

A sweep with a small-meshed net in any pond or ditch will show that life under the water is almost as active as during the summer months: grubs of may-flies, 2122, caddis flies, f-i., and water beetles, 400, are discovered in large numbers.

30

1460 RICHARD, Duke of York, slain at battle of Wakefield. Roses, Wars of, 2828.

1858 André Messager, French composer, born, *f-i.* Music, 2261; Opera, 2435.

1865 Rudyard Kipling, British poet and writer, born, **1859.** English Literature, 1215.

1869 Stephen Leacock, Canadian humorist and educationist, born, *f-i.* Canadian Literature, 685.

1947 King Michael of Rumania abdicated, *f-i.* Rumania, 2841.

Among waders visiting us in vast flocks are dunlins, knots, and various rare sandpipers, 3331.

31

1384 JOHN WYCLIFFE, English reformer and translator of the Bible, died, **3427.** Bible, *425.*

1491 Jacques Cartier, French explorer, born, **712.** America: Discovery, 143; Canadian History, 681; Montreal, 2224; Quebec, 2715.

1600 Honourable East India Company (*f-i.*) chartered by Queen Elizabeth. Hastings, Warren, 1582; India: History, 1714.

1617 Bartolomé Esteban Murillo, Spanish painter, born, 2257. Spanish Art, 3049.

1720 Charles Edward Stuart, the Young Pretender, born, **2682.** Jacobites, 1790.

An occasional mistle-thrush or hedge sparrow adds his voice to the song of the robin which has been heard almost the whole year. A few daisies, dandelions, and other common weeds can also be found.

E L E G Y

Written in a Country Church Yard.

THE Curfew tolls the knell of parting day,
The lowing herd wind slowly o'er the lea,
The plowman homeward plods his weary way,
And leaves the world to darkness and to me.

British Museum

Dec. 26, 1716. The poet, Thomas Gray, was born. The above is from the 1753 edition of his famous "Elegy."

STUDY OUTLINES

For Student, Teacher and Every Reader

A Note about
Our Study Outlines

While the Fact-Index, which begins in page 3695, brings out details of subjects and tells you exactly where to find them, our Study Outlines do exactly the opposite. They gather up all the information in The New Book of Knowledge into great groups—the groups which form the main divisions of human knowledge—and present it arranged progressively for systematic study. The Geography Outline, for instance, brings together into a single consecutive chain all the material of Geography contained in Volumes 1 to 7, fitting each part into the other, link by link, until the whole of Geography has been surveyed.

These Study Outlines, however, are much more than mere "guides to reading," much more than mere titles of articles or of portions of articles arranged in tabular form. A glance through them will show you that their subdivisions consist for the most part of sentences or phrases, of brief notes and explanations, which serve to bring out the significance of each step and its relations to what precedes and what follows. In other words, they are skilled teachers in print. It would be profitable, indeed, merely to read through many of these Outlines, even if you did not look up a single page reference, for this would give you a rapid and quite intelligible survey of the subject in question. On the other hand, they are so arranged that those interested in only a single section of a wide field of study may use that section independently. Attached to the Outlines will be found lists of books (obtainable from any good public library) for supplementary reading. Numerous carefully-framed Interest Questions, which serve as pointers to attractive subjects in the text of our work, are also provided.

As in the other sections in this volume, a page reference in heavy black type indicates the main article or source of information on the subject; the references in ordinary type are to other articles containing supplementary or related information; figures given in italic type indicate the pages on which illustrations appear.

Special Index of Study Outlines

NATURE STUDY
Preliminary Readings for Young Children

FOR children not yet old enough to begin Nature Study in a systematic way, the story method is the best introduction to the subject. Interested at first in the adventures of their animal heroes, they soon develop a desire to find out more about the animals themselves and the natural surroundings in which the animals live. The following stories, selected from the " Tales for the Story Hour " to be found in these volumes, will prove admirably suited to this purpose. While retaining the full imaginative flavour that appeals so directly to the young reader, they serve at the same time to bring out the principal characteristics and habits of the animals in question.

TALES OF THE ANIMAL WORLD

General Outline for Older Students

THE following references provide a foundation for practical Nature Study, such as can be carried out in Britain. While such exotic creatures as some popular pets have been included, in general it is confined to those manifestations of plant or animal life that can be found in the British Isles, and it is so arranged as to give a broad basis on which to work. The Study Outlines on Biology (3614), Zoology (3622) and Botany (3616) should also be studied in order to grasp the scientific basis on which all modern Nature Study is founded. It is especially useful to have read the main articles, to many of which references are given below, and to have come to appreciate the main inter-relationships between animals and plants, before you start field trips. It should be borne in mind that, no matter how small an area the student is forced to work in, there will be enough material for a prolonged study. If it is desired to go outside the boundaries of Nature Study as set out in this Outline, a detailed study of Weather, 2149, Soils, 2998, and Geology, 1432, will be necessary.

I. NATURE STUDY, 2283.

II. PLANT LIFE, 2620.

    A. **Lower Plants** : Bacteria, 335 ; Algae, Seaweeds, 111, 2914 ; Fungi, Mushrooms, 1407, 2260 ; Lichens, 1932 ; Moss, 2238 ; Liverworts, 1969 ; Ferns, 1266.

    B. **Flowering Plants** : Flowers, 1321 ; Grass, 1509 ; Cacti, 648 ; Water Plants, 3355 ; Trees, 3245.

III. ANIMAL KINGDOM, 156.

    A. Some of the commoner animal types.

        a. **Lower Types** : Amoeba, 2695 ; Protozoa, 2695 ; Worms, 3425.

        b. **Arthropods** : Crabs, 924 ; Lobsters, 1977 ; Insects, 1726 ; Ant, 165 ; Bee, 390 ; Beetle, 398 ; Butterflies and Moths, 628 ; Caterpillars, 720 ; Fly, 1329 ; Grasshopper, 1510 ; Wasps, 3345 ; Centipedes, Millepedes, Woodlouse, 742, 3403 ; Spiders, 3062.

        c. **Molluscs**, 2199 : Cockles and Mussels, 860 ; Snails and Slugs, 2989 ; Cuttlefish, Squids, 945.

        d. **Fishes**, 1296 : Carp, 704 ; Eel, 1092 ; Salmon, 2865 ; Roach, 2781.

        e. **Amphibians** : Frog, 1398 ; Toad, 3219 ; Newt, *f-i.*

        f. **Reptiles**, 2767 : Lizards, 1972 ; Snakes, 2990 ; Tortoises, 3229.

        g. **Birds**, 437.

        h. **Mammals**, 2074 :

            1. Cattle, 730 ; Horses, and other hoofed creatures, 1645.

            2. Rodents, 2795 ; Rabbits, 2721 ; Squirrels, 3071.

            3. Cats, 718, and Dogs, 1025.

            4. Mole, 2196 ; Hedgehog, 1604.

            5. Bats, 370.

NATURE STUDY ALL THE YEAR ROUND

THERE are no fixed rules for Nature Study. You may begin anywhere, at any time. You may start with the whale and work down to the tiny bacteria, or you may begin at the other end. You may start with animals or you may start with plants, but no matter where you begin, if you ask questions about the common everyday things of life you will find yourself very quickly following the fascinating paths through Nature's great garden-menagerie. There are two important rules to follow in finding your way through these paths. First, begin with the animals and plants that are near you, those that you can *see for yourself*; secondly, from those that are around you, choose at the outset the animals and plants that you like the best, for love of Nature and sympathy with Nature are essential.

Do not try to do too much. Among the experiments suggested, pick out a few and *carry them out to the end*. If you try to keep four or five different kinds of pets, take care of a flower garden, cultivate vegetables, and make several different collections, all at the same time, you will not do any one thing well and so you will become dissatisfied. Pick out not more than one or two for each season, and leave the others until next year.

While you are at work, always bear these main principles in mind :

A. **All Nature is unified.** Every part is connected with every other part. Plants depend on soil and climate ; animals depend upon plants or upon other animals. No living thing can ever be entirely independent. Nature Study is the study of the marvellous adjustment of those fascinating relations.

B. **Everything in Nature has a reason.** The shape of every leaf, every flower, every seed, the form and colour of all animals, the arrangement of their feet, their teeth, their fur, their feathers, the way every bird builds its nest, the way every creature looks after its young, every detail of structure and habit, large or small—all these things have a reason. Nature Study is the study of those reasons.

Note : Reference to the Nature notes for each day in the Through the Year Calendar in this volume will be of considerable help in suggesting what creatures or plants to look out for at any particular time. Remember that in general the North of England is a fortnight or so later in Spring and Summer than the South, while its summer birds leave earlier, and our winter visitors appear there first.

SPRING

Spring is the season of birth and awakening after the Winter months of rest. In this section of this Outline, the basis of work for the rest of the year is also given.

PLANTS—

I. STUDY OF BUDS.

A. **Order of Opening.** Examine the trees of your neighbourhood. See which buds open first. Note the effect of a day of brilliant sunshine, a day of rain, a night of frost.

B. **How the Buds Develop.** Gather twigs of Beech (**395**), Elm (**1152**), Horse Chestnut (**1647**), or other trees. Put them in water at home, using a fruit jar or wide-mouthed bottle. Place them where they will get plenty of sun every day, and watch carefully the development of the buds. See how the tiny leaves were curled in the bud. Note the difference between the young leaves and the young flowers, and if possible make drawings at regular intervals.

Note : All good Naturalists keep notebooks. But a very good plan is to have one small, pocket-size notebook for " Field Notes," and another larger, loose-leaf one for " Experiments." The first will cover what you *see* on your trips outdoors ; the second what you *do* at home ; and rough notes from the first can later be neatly written up and filed in a loose-leaf system for reference. Before starting a field trip, try to have some definite plan in mind about what you intend to find and study, and make your notes accordingly. Always put down the date of the trip, where you went, and what the weather was like. Do not try to write too much—just the most striking things. In your notes of experiments you should go into greater detail. If you have to make or build anything, describe how you did it. Whenever you get a chance, *make a drawing of what you see or do*. Drawing is far better than writing, for once you have drawn a thing you will never forget how it looks. Never mind if your first drawings seem crude ; you will be surprised how rapidly you improve with practice. And remember that your notebooks are intended for your own benefit and pleasure, not for someone else. Never think of what others will say about them.

II. STUDY OF FLOWERING PLANTS.

A. **Flowers.** Watch for the appearance of the first Spring flowers and note them, year by year. Notice that trees usually bud in the Spring before the smaller flowering plants spring up from the ground. Which gets warm first, the air or the ground ?

B. **Collecting Flowers.** When Spring is well under way, you may start to collect wild flowers.

    a. When you get home with your flowers, how do they look ? How does the stem look ? Notice that those you carry home in your hand suffer more than those you take in a tin collecting box.

    b. Now put them in water and watch carefully what happens.

    c. Put a few of the flowers into water stained with red ink or some bright water colour. The next day cut through the stem, half-way up ; examine the cut ends. What do they tell you about how flowers drink ?

   d. See how many of the flowers you can name, using a good book such as those in the Biblio-
      graphy, page 3580. Make sketches of one or two in your field notes.

Note. One way of learning about wild plants is to make a collection of dried specimens. This is
very easy to do. Whenever you find a new kind, take it home, lay it out between two sheets of blotting
or other coarse-grained paper, put the sheets between two boards, and place heavy weights, such as four
or five big books, on the top board. Change the paper after 12 hours and again after 24 hours, so that
the plants will dry quickly and not lose their natural colours. The plant should be so arranged as to
show the root-leaves (those at the base of the stem) as well as those on the stem ; flower buds, flowers—
neatly spread open—and fruits, should all be included, if possible on the same sheet. Notes as to date
and locality MUST be added. Pressed flowers without notes are worthless. When thoroughly dry,
mount them on special sheets by pasting narrow loops of paper across the stems at suitable places. The
special mounting paper should be fairly heavy and about 8 by 10 inches in size. Your mounted collection
should be kept in stiff card folders, which may be bought cheaply ; one family or genus will go in each
folder. In a large herbarium—as such a collection is called—each species has one or more folders to
itself.

III. THE PARTS OF A FLOWER, 1321.

   A. The important parts of a flower are the **peduncle** (stalk), the **sepals** and **petals** (combining to form
      the **perianth**), the **stamens** (each consisting of the **filament** and the **anther** which bears the **pollen**),
      the **pistil** (which consists of the **ovary** containing the **ovules**, the **style**, and the **stigma**).
      a. Take a flower and examine it, pulling it to pieces if necessary, and learn to recognize the
         parts mentioned above. If you are to learn the purposes of things in Nature, it is important
         to know their technical names, for this will make it much easier for you to think and observe
         correctly, and to describe things to others clearly.
      b. Remember that the primary purpose of every flower is to develop seed. A fruit is that
         part of the flower which contains the seed ; some flowers, however, are sterile and are
         used to attract insects to the less showy, fertile ones, as in Guelder Rose (*f-i*).

IV. SEEDS, 2916.

   A. **Seed Structure.** Get a handful of dry Broad Beans (*381*). Examine one of them carefully.
      Notice the small knob on the inner edge. That is part of the **young plant** or **embryo**. Peel off
      the tough outer hull, called the **seed-coat** or **testa**. Notice how the inside of the bean is divided
      into two halves, which are united only at the young plant. These halves are called the **cotyledons.**
   B. **The Seed Comes to Life.** Fill a small wooden box with rich moist soil. Plant a number of the
      beans a quarter of an inch deep, covering them quite firmly and marking with a match where
      each is planted. Keep the soil moist, but not soaking.
      a. After two days, dig one of them up, and note what has happened to the embryo and the
         seed-coat. Dig another up very carefully every other day and observe the development
         of the rootlet (called the radicle), of the first small leaves (called plumules), of the stem.
         What has become of the cotyledons ?
      b. Note how long after planting the first stem appears above the ground. You will see that
         it is arched ; the root end is the anchor, and the other side of the arch is pulling upwards
         just as hard as it can to free the first leaves.
         1. The cotyledons are simply storage houses for the embryo's food. When we eat
            cooked beans we are nourished by the food which was really intended to give the
            sprouting bean plant its first start in life.
         2. Here is a simple way of testing this. The food stored in the cotyledons is mostly
            starch. Iodine turns blue when it touches starch ; the more starch there is, the
            deeper and darker the blue. Keeping that in mind, put a drop of weak solution of
            iodine on one of the cotyledons, when a bean first starts to sprout. Note the colour.
            Now put a drop of iodine on a cotyledon after a young bean plant has straightened
            up above the ground. What change do you notice, and what does it indicate ?
         3. An even simpler test is to remove the cotyledons from one of the young plants a day
            after it appears above the ground, and then compare its rate of growth with the others.
   C. **Differences in Seeds.** Study the seeds of other plants. Plant seeds of onion, lilies, radish,
      nasturtium, pansy, hollyhock, sunflower, cabbage, pine or fir tree, or any other available variety,
      selecting a half-dozen as varied as possible in size and shape. Note how each behaves in sprout-
      ing. (Be sure to label each group of seeds so that you can identify the sprouts.)
      Note. Some seeds have only one cotyledon. This is an important point in the scientific
         classification of plants, all the most highly developed plants and trees being grouped as
         either Monocotyledons (with one cotyledon) or Dicotyledons (with two or more cotyledons).
         The pine, belonging to a lower group (*see* Outline on Botany), has a number of cotyledons.

V. MAKING A GARDEN.

   A. Remember that you, as a Nature student, are interested in the lives of your garden vegetables.
      Learn to know them all, how they sprout, what their flowers are like, and other similar details.
   B. While you are taking care of the garden, learn the *reason* for everything you do. Why must the
      soil be dug and made fine before seeding time ? What harm do weeds do ? What are the chief
      enemies of your garden, besides weeds ?

ANIMALS—

Plants and animals are intimately connected in Nature. Where there are no plants, there can be no permanent animal life, for plants are the original manufacturers of all food, and animals live upon this food, directly or indirectly. If some are able to exist as flesh-eaters, it is because they live upon others which eat vegetable food. I follows, therefore, that the structure and habits of all animals are closely associated with the character of their plant neighbours.

I. FAMILIAR PETS.

Note. Begin your study of animals with those nearest to you. Such studies are intended to bring out some of the most striking points in the bodily structure of these familiar animals, points which you might perhaps overlook, but which illustrate the great fundamental law of *natural fitness*. By the use of intelligence, men train themselves to be fit for special tasks. But the fitness of animals for the many different lives they lead has been trained and developed through untold ages by Nature. While most domestic animals have been greatly changed in appearance by the long breeding carried on by men for their own purposes, these animals retain most of the forms, instincts, and habits that were so useful to their wild ancestors. A study of these forms and habits, therefore, will be most useful in helping you to work out problems of wild life.

A. Dogs and Cats.

Examine a Dog and a Cat. Observe the extraordinary length of their eye-teeth or " canine " teeth, characteristic of the carnivorous or flesh-eating animals. Does a cat behave in the same way when you give it a saucer of milk as it does when you give it a piece of meat ? In the same way, note the differences in their general build, their claws, eyes, fur, etc., in relation to their different modes of life.

B. Other Pets.

Examine the front teeth of a Rodent (2797), such as a Rabbit, Guinea-pig, or Mouse. How do they differ from the teeth of the cat and dog ?

C. Bird Pets and Poultry, 2671.

Gather as many interesting notes as you can about the habits of bird pets, such as canaries, parrots, and pigeons and farmyard poultry. How do birds get along without teeth ? How do their beaks differ in relation to their food ? Notice the arrangement of their claws. Notice particularly how bright and active little chicks are as soon as they break out of the egg. Compare them with young pigeons. Remember that chickens are descended from birds which nested and spent most of their lives on the ground, where the young, if they were not quite alert from birth, would be at the mercy of every chance foe. Pigeons, on the other hand, are descended from birds that built their nests in high, inaccessible places, where the young were comparatively safe.

II. FARM ANIMALS : Horse, 1647 ; Cattle, 730 ; Sheep, 2940 ; Pig, 2605 ; Goat, 1478.

a. Watch these animals when they are feeding. See how they gather up the grass. Do they stop to chew very much ? Watch them when they are lying down after feeding. What are their jaws doing ? This is one of the most remarkable habits in the whole animal kingdom. Read about it in the article on Cattle, **730.** Do horses or pigs " chew the cud " in this fashion ?

b. Notice the feet of these beasts (*1342*). How many toes have they ? Look again and see if you can see two more. Nearly all Mammals, except elephants, bears, monkey ; Man, and a few other groups, *walk on their toes*. Some walk on one toe, like the horses, some on two toes, like the cow ; some on four toes like the cat and dog. In each case, traces of the remaining toe or toes are to be found higher up on the leg. The " hock " on the hind leg of a cow or horse is really the heel, while the " stifle " is the knee. What we call the " knee " on the front leg is really the wrist.

c. Examine the teeth of cattle, sheep, pigs, and goats. Remember that the organs for eating and moving are usually the best indications of the habits of animals. If an animal is to survive, 437, these, above all others, must be suited to their task.

III. WILD BIRDS, 437.

A. Bird Diary.

Right at the beginning of the year you can start a bird diary, for our own resident birds are moving, singing, and building their nests long before summer visitors begin to arrive. Notice, too, the movements of the big flocks of starlings, finches, and other birds, as well as those of our winter visitors. In later spring, you will be kept busy with notes on the arrival and departure of various migrants. Observe when various species start to sing, when they get their breeding plumage, when and where they first begin to build. A bird diary, even if your activities are confined to one small garden, may have several entries for every day of the year.

B. Nest Boxes.

Build small bird-boxes such as those shown in page *445*. Place them fairly high up on big trees, but not too close to the house. Keep a good watch on them and note which birds use them or inspect them, when they begin to build, etc. Be careful not to disturb them by going close too often, and resist the temptation to look inside and see what is going on !

C. Field Notes on Birds.

a. Watch for birds' nests on your field trips. Note the position of each with small sketch maps in your notebook, so that you can return from time to time to watch the progress of the feathered families. Notice the size, shape, and colour of the eggs. Do not yield, however, to the temptation to collect birds' eggs. A blown egg in a box at home soon becomes most uninteresting, while that same egg left in the nest will quickly turn into a fascinating youngster. Do not, moreover, visit any nest more than once a week or the birds may desert it. When the young have gone you can examine the nest and note the materials of which it is made.

b. Try your hand at sketching some of your favourite birds. Make sketches *from your personal observations*. There is little profit in copying someone else's drawings. Try filling in the outlines of the sketches with water colours.

c. Learn to identify birds by their song and their manner of flying as well as by their shape and colour. Use a good book for this. It is no use having an inaccurate or incomplete book for any serious Nature Study.

IV. THE LIFE OF STREAM AND POND.

A. The home Aquarium, 192.

One of the most delightful ways of studying Nature is to keep an aquarium at home. You might begin modestly with a small fruit jar, or you may buy a larger glass tank, or even build yourself an aquarium of the large oblong kind, with plate-glass sides cemented into a wooden or metal frame.

a. Plants for the Aquarium. Cover the bottom of your aquarium one inch deep at least with clean, fresh sand. Go to the nearest pool or stream and gather small water-plants, taking a little of the mud or stones on which they are growing. Read the article on Water-plants (**3355**), and try to identify all the plants you collect. Arrange them in your aquarium, and leave them alone for a few days.

b. Animals for the Aquarium. Gather in a net or in glass jars any of the water creatures you find in the same place as you found the plants. For this purpose, a shallow net of strong netting, stretched on a cross-stick frame, will do very well. Just comb it through the water-plants or along the muddy bottom.

1. Try to get some water-snails (**2989**), some of the smaller water-beetles (**400**) and other insects. These will be enough to start with. If you find strange insect-like creatures in your net which you cannot identify, place them with a few plants in separate jars. They will probably turn out to be insect larvae, such as the larvae of dragon flies (*1305*), which are very fierce and would kill your other captives if placed in the same aquarium. Later you may add small fish or crayfish to the collection.

2. If the water in your aquarium tends to become cloudy, change it and try putting in or taking out a few more plants, and watch the result. Experiment in this way until the water remains clear without changing. Such an aquarium is said to be " balanced," the plants providing the oxygen that the animals need, and the animals the gas (carbon dioxide) that the plants need. Water-snails are especially useful for keeping the water clear and clean. (Read the article on Respiration, **2768**).

3. Cover the aquarium with cloth netting or a wire screen to prevent such insects as water-boatmen and water-beetles from flying away. Always keep the water cold. Do not let direct rays of the sun shine on the aquarium for long.

c. Raising Frogs and Toads. Go to a pond where there are frogs (**1398**) or toads (**3219**), and collect their jelly-like spawn. Place these in the aquarium, and watch them develop. Note carefully the stages through which each one passes.

SUMMER

In summer you continue your general Nature observations and notes, always bearing in mind that now all animal and plant life is growing, developing to maturity, preparing for the fruitful tasks of the Autumn.

I. PLANTS AT WORK. Review in detail the Plant Life article (**2620**).

A. Leaves, 1914. Read this article carefully.

a. Start a Collection of Leaves. Follow the detailed directions given for the flower collection, page 3572. Be sure to identify each leaf, noting the principal points which distinguish it from other leaves.

Note : Remember, in looking up the names of plants and animals, that they often have different popular names in different parts of the country. If you cannot find a certain name in your books on flowers, consult a good dictionary, and you will possibly find that the plant or animal in question is more widely known under some other name, which will be the one used in those volumes.

b. Leaves and Water. Suspend a drinking glass mouth downwards over a well-watered growing plant, so that some of the leaves are imprisoned inside the glass. Cover the soil with oiled silk. Leave it overnight. What do you find on the inside of the glass in the morning ? Where did it come from ?

c. Leaves and Light. Place a house plant, like the so-called geranium (**1443**), in a room that has only one window. Examine it a week later. Which way are all the leaves facing ? What must you do with a potted plant to make it keep its shape in such a room ?

d. Leaves and Their Work. If the leaves are stripped from a plant it will stop growing, and if the stripping continues for long, the plant will die. Why is this ? Notice that when there is a bad attack of defoliating caterpillars such as winter moths (**3388**), trees may be so weakened that they are attacked by other pests ; if it happens several years running they may even die.

1. Crush a leaf in your fingers. Can you see the green colouring matter (chlorophyll) separating itself from the pulp ?
2. What kinds of plants can you find that are not green ? Read the articles on Fungi (**1407**), Mushrooms (**2260**) and *see* page *2621*. Do you know now why mushrooms can be grown in dark cellars, where green plants would die ?

B. Flowers, 1321.
    a. Select a Few Common Flowers for Study. Identify the different parts of each flower, as you did when working on spring blossoms.
        1. Touch the anther at the tip of the stamen in one of your flowers with your moistened finger. Note the fine yellowish dust that comes off. That is the pollen.
        2. Read the section on the development of a flower, **1322**. Now cut your flower open carefully and see if you can find the parts there described.
    b. Go out in the evening and notice how flowers go to sleep at night, *957*, *2624*. (*See also* below.)

Note : An evening or night walk is full of interest at all times. Watch for flowers that are open, for birds such as the nightjar (**2369**), for bats (**370**), glow-worms (*1288*) and all the many moths. If you are quiet you will hear all sorts of animals moving.

II. POLLINATION OF FLOWERS (*1323–1328*).

The fertilizing pollen is carried from the male anthers to the female stigmas in various ways. While it would be possible for many flowers to fertilize themselves, this is in general avoided, for it is one of the rules of Nature that cross-fertilization should be achieved whenever possible : indeed, it is essential if the race is to continue strong and vigorous. Many flowers are therefore of one sex only, bearing either stamens or pistils, but not both. In some trees this is most noticeable : thus you often see a holly tree that never bears berries, although it flowers frequently. Make a note of such a tree and examine its flowers in spring : they are all males. Cross-pollination is brought about in various ways. If the anthers ripen first, the plant is said to be protandrous ; if the stigmas ripen first, it is proterogynous.

    A. Insect pollination. You can see this by examining almost any flower that attracts insects. Notice that when a bee enters the flower, it brushes against the anthers, collecting some of the yellow pollen (often it has gone to the flower expressly to collect pollen to make " bee-bread " to feed its grubs on, *391*). The pollen on the bee's legs or back rubs against the sticky stigmas of the next similar flower visited by the bee, and fertilization is ensured. Some orchids are fertilized by moths which take away the whole pollen-sac, called a " pollinium," and if you examine the tongues of these moths you find these sacs sticking to them, *2447*. Many flowers are pollinated by one species of insect only.

    B. Wind pollination. Notice the masses of yellow dust in the pine woods. This is pollen, blown from the curious catkin-like male flowers, and floating about until it comes to rest on a young female cone (*2610*). Most conifers and other big trees are pollinated in this fashion ; so are early flowering trees, such as cherries, which bloom before insects are about. But they also bloom before there are any leaves, and their petals open exceptionally wide, giving the pollen every chance of finding the stigmas.

    C. Other Types. A few plants are water-pollinated, the pollen being floated on the surface of pond or stream ; these are, of course, water-plants whose blooms are close to, or on, the surface. Many tropical species rely on small birds such as humming birds ; they usually have red flowers. Self-pollination occurs in early flowers such as crocus (**932**), narcissus, etc., and may occur in others if they have not been visited by insects, the anthers bending inwards to the stigmas in the later blooms.

III. SEED PRODUCTION : The transformation of the flower into fruit (1402) and seed (2916).

    a. Watch a flower as it fades and note what happens to the various parts. Remember that from the point of view of the plant, the purpose of the flower is simply to produce the seed.
    b. Make notes of the seed development on the trees and other plants of your neighbourhood.
    c. Find how flowerless plants, like Ferns (**1266**), Mosses (**2238**) or Liverworts (**1969**), reproduce themselves.

IV. WHAT PLANTS NEED FOR LIFE.

A. Light.
Plant half a dozen French beans in a box or flower-pot and put it in a dark place. Give them all the water they need. Note how they differ from some planted in the light.

B. Water.
Plant three separate colonies of French beans. Keep one colony soaked with water ; keep the second colony moderately damp ; and give the third colony no water at all. Compare the results.

C. Air.
Plant some French beans inside a fruit jar and keep the top screwed on tightly. You will not have to water them, since no water evaporates. Watch what happens.

D. Minerals.
Besides the article on Plant Life, **2620**, read also that on Soil, **2916**.

V. INSECTS AT WORK.

A. What is an Insect (**1726**) ? Be sure you know one when you see it. Is a Spider an insect (**3062**)?

B. **Social Insects :** Ant, **165** ; Bee, **390** ; Wasps, **3345**.

    a. **Studying Ants at Home.** Get a large fruit jar and fill it two-thirds full of moderately damp earth—a soil containing a fair amount of sand is best. Find a nest of ants, any one of the smaller varieties that build in the ground, and capture its inhabitants. A good way to do this is to scoop up the whole nest with a garden trowel and put it, ants and all, straight into the empty jar. Be careful not to injure the ants, or the larvae and pupae. The former are tiny white grubs, the latter like little grains of rice. Also search carefully for the queen, whom you will recognize by her greater size.

        1. Transfer all your captives to the jar you have prepared, and fasten over the top a fine screen or a paper punched full of pin-holes. Now make a cylinder of heavy black or dark brown paper which will fit snugly round the outside of the jar, yet be free to slide up and down. Put a little sugar, some bits of raw apple, or some tiny pieces of meat in the jar, and place it for a few days in a corner, where there is not too much sun.

        2. After some days, slide the paper cylinder down, and you will find the ants have made galleries down the sides, just inside the glass. They have taken advantage of the fact that the glass offers them support for one side of their tunnels. You may watch the structure of the tunnels for a few minutes, but do not leave them exposed to the light too long, or the ants will abandon those tunnels and dig out of sight.

        3. Make notes on the way the ants work, how they eat, how they look after their young, etc. New larvae and pupae of the same species will be welcomed, cared for, and brought up most cheerfully. If at any time the earth seems to be drying up, scatter a few drops of water inside the jar. Feed the ants from time to time on fruit or meat.

    b. **Field Work on Ants.** Although bees and wasps are difficult to study in the field, since they sting, ants may be examined with comparative impunity. Even the stings of the large wood ants are only irritating and you can do a good deal of work without getting stung at all. Dig carefully into and examine the nests of different sorts of ants, capturing specimens of the inhabitants and identifying them.

        The big wood ants' nest (**168**) are the easiest of all to study. Some way from the nest you will find a trail leading inwards and outwards, along it moving a stream of workers. In the nest itself, if you can pluck up courage to sit down and really examine the inside, you may find some of the rare beetles and other insects which are the " guests " of the ants, secreting " honey-dew " for their benefit and being fed in return. Some of them are also scavengers in the nests. Then there are other ants beneath the bark of trees, under stones or in old masonry. Look, too, for the ants which " milk " the aphides or green-fly (**185**) on garden plants—especially the roses—and notice how carefully they look after these strange " cattle." Finally, when the hot, sultry, thundery weather comes in mid-summer, watch the mating flight of the male and female ants, and the way in which the winged forms break off their wings when this flight is over. Notice that this flight always occurs under certain weather conditions.

C. **Insect Transformation,** 1728.

    a. **Caddis Flies.** To study these you will require an aquarium as described on page 3575. Go out to the nearest pond or stream and examine the shallow water near the edges. If you look long enough you will probably see some small bundles of criss-crossed sticks, which move about in a mysterious way. Scoop a few up and carry them home in a jar full of water, and put them in your aquarium. They are the larvae of Caddis Flies (*f-i*). In time they will turn into pupae and then, a little later, they will emerge from the water as adult, four-winged flies.

    b. **Caterpillars,** **720.** Find caterpillars of various types. Take them home and keep them in a well-aired tin, or a box one of whose sides is covered with zinc-gauze or muslin. Keep them on sprigs of the tree or plant on which you found them and renew this *daily*. See that they get plenty of light, but no direct sunlight. Clean the box each day, removing all the food but that on to which they are actually holding. They will crawl of their own accord on to the fresh food. Never touch the caterpillars if you can help it. When they are full grown after changing their skin several times, see that there is an inch or two of earth in the bottom of the cage or box, also bits of bark. If you can identify them, you can find out where they will pupate. Some go underground, others make a silk cocoon in a corner of the box, others weave leaves together. Some will emerge as adults this year, others may wait until the spring. If you have a male and female adult of the same sort they may mate and you will then be able to breed more from their eggs.

VI. **BIRD LIFE.**

    A. **Summer Activities.** Continue your spring time notes, with especial reference to the young of the birds you have seen arriving. Notice their plumage, its differences from that of their parents ; observe how the latter stop singing and begin to moult after the breeding season. Ducks, for example, go into an " eclipse " plumage (**1051**).

    B. **Feathers,** **1264.**

        a. Examine all the feathers you can find. Cut up a feather, examine the quill. Pull apart the " barbs," which make up the flat part or " vane " of the feather. If you have a magnifying glass, examine the structure of these barbs.

AUTUMN

Autumn is the season of fruitfulness. Plants, which have reached maturity or gained new vitality in the summer months, now put forth their seeds and fruit. New generations of animals are growing up. All Nature is busy preparing for Winter.

I. SEEDS AND SPORES, 2916.

A. **Seeds and Fruits** : Make a collection of seeds, or observe and draw those of all the plants you can find in your neighbourhood. Note how the seed-containers are fastened to the plant, and see how each is adapted to distribution by some means.

    a. **Distribution by Wind** : Observe fruits of the ash (**262**), sycamore (**3143**), and pines (**2609**).

    b. **By Animals** : Notice the burrs of burdock (*2917*).

    c. **By Birds**, as in mistletoe (**2194**) or yew (**3434**).

    d. **By Water** : Alder seeds (**104**) are dropped over streams, then floated down.

    e. "**Mechanical**" distribution : Seeds of hairy bittercress (**3354**) and many other plants are expelled violently from their pods for a foot or more. Remember that what we commonly call " fruit " consists simply of seeds enclosed in a pulp which is intended to induce animals to swallow the seeds and drop them again far away from the parent plant (**1402**).

B. **Spores** :

    a. **Ferns as Examples of Spore-bearing Plants, 1266.** Examine the under side of Fern fronds until you find one covered with little brown dots. These are the " spore cases." What is the difference between seeds and spores ? Do ferns have flowers ?

    b. **Mosses and Liverworts (2238, 1969).** Note the differences between them and the ferns.

    c. **Fungi and Mushrooms (1407, 2260).** This is the great season for these parasites and saprophytes. Notice the different types of fungi, the way they grow and how they spread. Examine fairy rings (*1258*). Make a collection of the special insects found in connexion with these fungi.

II. HOW PLANTS GROW.

A. **Trees as Examples of Growth, 3245.**

    a. **Examine a Fresh Tree Stump.** Note the rings in the wood. You can tell the age of the tree by counting those rings. Which is harder and tougher—the heart-wood near the centre or the sap-wood near the bark ? Peel off the bark and try to identify the cambium.

    b. **How Sap Circulates.** In summer, even in spring if possible, select on a growing tree a small branch which may be destroyed without harm. With a sharp knife cut off a narrow ring of bark, so as to leave a bare strip completely encircling the branch. Be sure you cut through the cambium to the woody fibre. Now watch that branch daily. Before long it will die from the ring to the tip, for the circulation of the life-giving sap is stopped.

    c. **Autumn Foliage.** Notice when the leaves in your neighbourhood begin to change colour and observe the order in which they change. Some very similar trees, such as certain elms and poplars, can be distinguished by the time of leaf-fall. Gather leaves from the different trees of your neighbourhood after they have changed colour, and put them with the Summer leaves in your collection.

        1. What happens to the chlorophyll when the leaves change colour (**1915**) ? In the winter, when the leaves are gone, the trees stop growing.

        2. What happens when a leaf falls (**1917**) ?

B. **Roots and Their Work, 2825,** *2622.* Dig out any small plant, taking up plenty of soil with it. Now wash off the soil so as not to injure the roots. Examine the fine root hairs.

    a. Read about the remarkable process of root pressure in pages 2621 and 2622, and if possible perform the interesting experiment shown in the lower picture in page 2621.

    b. Study the text on page **2621**, then read the article on Soil, page **2998**.

    c. What are the underground parts of plants besides roots ? Read the article headed Bulb, page 612, and plant examples of the various plant storage organs in pots indoors, setting them aside until the winter or spring—crocus corms, narcissus bulbs, tubers of potato, Solomon's seal rhizomes.

III. ANIMAL STUDIES.

A. **Spiders and Their Webs, 3062.**

    a. Notice the different types of webs and their owners. Agitate a big " orb " web by moving a blade of grass against it. Watch the behaviour of the spider. Make a drawing of the web pattern. Now poke a hole in the web with a stick. Come back the next day, and you will probably find the web mended. Notice by comparison with your drawing how the patch was put in.

    b. Notice the difference between the spiral threads and the coarser cross-threads of the web. Why are some elastic and others rigid ?

    c. Study the remarkable structure of a large spider beneath a lens and note especially ways in which it differs from insects.

B. **Snakes, 2990 ; Lizards, 1972** : Remember that there is in Great Britain only one species of poisonous snake—the adder or viper. The other snakes are not only harmless but, like the adder, they do a great deal of good to the farmer by devouring vermin.

    a. You may examine a grass-snake (**1512**) without fear. Note the absence of eyelids. See how the scales on the under side are arranged for catching in the ground and pulling the snake along. You can feel them pulling if you let the snake crawl over your hand.

b. Try to catch a slow-worm or a lizard. These make interesting pets and are not hard to keep in captivity. Compare your slow-worm with a snake and see that really they are quite different.

IV. ANIMAL PREPARATIONS FOR THE WINTER.
A. Storing Away Food :
a. **Outside Storage.** Watch a squirrel during the autumn months. Throw nuts where it can find them and try to see what it does with them.

b. **Inside Storage.** If you can catch a hedgehog (*1604*) or dormouse (*1029*) in the autumn, notice how very fat it is. It is storing its winter's food inside its body in the form of fat.

c. **What other animals do you know that hibernate (1622) ?**
B. Migration, 2169.
a. **Birds.** Watch during the autumn months for the southward migration of birds. What kinds leave your neighbourhood ? Note when you last see them. Notice, too, that some sing a little before leaving, while others are silent. Discover what kinds pass through your neighbourhood from the north—these are " passage migrants."

b. **Other Types of Migration.** Eel, 1092 ; Salmon, 2865.

WINTER

This is the season of rest. Most of Nature lies dormant awaiting the call of Spring to burst forth into new life. But for those animals which neither migrate nor sleep through this season Winter is often a period of hard struggle and hunger.

I. PLANT LIFE IN WINTER.
A. Evergreens, 1243.
a. **Conifers, 890.** Make a list in your notes of all the cone-bearing trees you can find and identify in your neighbourhood : notice and draw the arrangement of the needles, the form of the cones and the shape of the tree as a whole. Notice that some cone-bearing trees shed their needles in the winter : Larch, 1892.

b. **Other Evergreens.** Laurel, 1900 ; Holly, 1636 ; Holm Oak, 2409.
B. Trees which Lose Their Leaves (deciduous).
a. **Bark Formation.** Winter gives you an opportunity to learn to know trees by their bark. Study the trees of your neighbourhood until you can recognize them in this way. In your leaf collection make sketches of the bark of the tree to which each leaf belongs.

b. **Arrangement of Branches.** Note that the shape and arrangement of branches differ in nearly all species of trees. An interesting experiment for winter field trips consists in guessing the names of trees from a distance, judging merely from the appearance of the branches against the sky, then verifying them by closer inspection of the bark or twigs.

c. **Twigs.** The examination of the twigs is the surest way of all for identifying trees in winter. Even those of such difficult groups as the elms, willows, and poplars may in the end be distinguished thus, though it is often only after long practice. Notice that some twigs bear now the young, tightly-closed catkins of next year's flowers, as in the case of the walnut (**3338**), birch (**436**) and hazel (**1590**) while others still bear bunches of fruits (hornbeam, *f-i*).
C. Winter Sleep of Plants.
Learn to distinguish annuals, biennials, and perennials (2624). Note that nearly all plants whose *seeds* are used for food are *annuals*, such as corn, oats, beans, peas. Nearly all plants whose *roots* or *leaves* are used for food are *biennials*, such as carrots, turnips, beets, and cabbages. In the first case the parent throws all of its strength into the seed and dies ; in the second the first year's strength is thrown into root, stem, or leaf.

II. ANIMAL LIFE IN WINTER.
Although many animals are asleep or hibernating, there is ample opportunity to observe those that are still about.
A. Deer (984) and other Mammals.
Red deer, which are common in parks all over Britain, have their antlers at their best. In autumn they " rutted," fighting fiercely for the collection of hinds which now follow them meekly about. Roe deer, on the other hand, have mated already, and the bucks have lost their little pointed horns. If there is snow, you can find tracks of many animals ; foxes, cats, dogs, rats, weasels all leave their characteristic footmarks, which you can learn to recognize with a little practice. Make drawings of each type of track and, if possible, add the measurements between the foot-marks in every direction so that you know its real size.
B. Birds.
a. **Winter Visitors :** Birds also leave tracks in the snow, and this gives you a chance to see the different ways in which they progress on the ground. Thus, rooks (**2823**) walk, members of the thrush tribe (**3205**) hop, and wagtails (**3332**) run. Sea-birds such as gulls (**1555**) come inland and leave strange markings with their webbed feet, and the curiously leaf-like toes of the moorhen (*2734*) also make a very distinct track.

Then there are the winter visitors : go to your nearest large pond and see how many kinds of duck (**1051**) you can find. Notice that they are as easy to distinguish in flight as on the water. Rare birds from northern parts may be seen here, too ; and on the mud-flats on big marshes, all sorts of unusual wading birds (**3331**) are seen.

b. **Flocking and Small Migrations.** Notice how many common birds gather into vast flocks in winter. Finches (**1274**), starlings (**3083**), and green plovers (**2629**) are the most conspicuous, unless you live near the sea, when enormous flocks of waders are conspicuous on the shore. Coots (*2734*), too, form big congregations at this time of year. There are all sorts of interesting small migrations to be watched even among the common birds of the garden. Thus, robins, thrushes, and other birds are much more bold when hunger drives them, and many tits and other species you never normally see in the garden will put in an appearance at the bird-table. Put out a good supply of food of all sorts, but see that cats cannot reach it or get at the birds.

C. **Insects.** Many insects are resting now, often in one or other of their immature stages. On the apple trees, for example, you may find the eggs of the lackey moth (*f-i*) laid in neat bands round the twigs ; on other trees, other eggs are found, while every nook and cranny of the garden shed may shelter a chrysalis or cocoon, from which in the spring you can rear the moths. Digging in the deep mossy floor beneath big trees, such as oaks, will also yield more pupae. Beetles, wood-lice, and many garden pests are ever active, while even among the butterflies a few come out on warm sunny days. After the New Year, start looking out already for their first appearances for your new Nature Diary. Remember that Nature's year has little to do with that of the calendar, and your new diary can be as full of entries now, in its first two months, as it will be in Spring and Summer.

Some Books for the Nature Student

General

Outline of Nature in the British Isles, edited by Sir John Hammerton. The best all-round book on Natural History in the British Isles.

Handbooks in Series

The " **Shown** " **Series.** This series is suitable for small children, and includes volumes on Birds, Flowers, Butterflies and Moths, Bees, the Seashore, etc. Another excellent series is the **Wayside and Woodland** series, which comprises what are in many ways the best available books on their respective subjects : Birds (3 vols.), Animals, Butterflies and Moths (3 vols.), Spiders, Bees, Wasps, and allied Insects, Fishes, Ferns, Trees, Flowers (3 vols.) and " Life of the Wayside and Woodland." The last is especially useful as it is arranged month by month.

Individual Works

The Country Book. E. Golding.
A Bird Book for the Pocket. E. Sandars.
How to Find and Name Wild Flowers. F. Fox.
Catkin-bearing Trees. H. Gilbert Carter.
Nature by Day. Nature by Night. Arthur R. Thompson.
Natural History of Selborne. Gilbert White.
The Charm of Birds. Lord Grey of Fallodon.
British Insect Life. E. Step.
British Beetles. Pond Life. Rev. C. A. Hall.
Common Objects of the Microscope. Common Objects of the Seashore. Rev. J. G. Wood.
Shell Life. E. Step.
Edible Fungi. Poisonous Fungi. John Ramsbottom. (King Penguins).

These are all books to be bought and kept. There are innumerable others in your nearest Public Library.

Interest-Questions in Natural History

" It has a beak like a duck, hair like a cat, and a tail like a beaver. It has four legs and web feet. It lives both on land and in the water, lays eggs and hatches them like a bird, but feeds its young with milk." What is it ? 1053.
What fish are hatched in a pouch in the male parent's body ? 2911.
Why have certain plants developed the power of eating insects ? 2624
Why have some plants developed poisonous properties ? 2637.
What animal spends nearly its whole life upside down ? 2985.
How are certain animals able to live all winter without food ? 1622.
How do water spiders get air into their nests at the bottom of ponds ? 2287, 3064.
Does the flying squirrel really fly ? 3071.
How can you tell butterflies from moths ? 628.
What bird takes her little ones riding on her back ? 1516. What animal does the same ? 2442.
What happens to insects in the winter time ? 1729.
Why do plants grown in the dark remain white ? 2623.
Which animals walk on their toes ? 1342.
Why do leaves change colour in the autumn ? 1917.
What reptile runs on its hind feet like a man ? Plate f. p. 1972.
Why are most plants green ? 2620.
Where do earthworms spend the winter ? *1071.*
What is caviare ? 3104.
Why are birds' eggs variously coloured ? 442.
Why do many water plants have long slender leaves ? 3355.
What animal of the United States carries its young in a pouch, as the kangaroo does ? 2442.
What use has the camel's hump ? 670.
Does a plant get most of its food from the soil or from the air ? 2622.
How long can a camel go without water ? 670.
What does a bird's foot tell you about its habits ? 448.
Are whales fish ? 3371.
What insects sometimes travel in such clouds that they darken the sky ? 1511.
How is it that tulips and crocuses are able to get such a start over most other plants in the spring ? 612.
Can cats see in total darkness ? 718.
For what does an elephant use its trunk ? 1141.
Do male birds ever hatch eggs ? 444.
How far can a lion travel at one bound ? 1960.
How do flowering plants breathe ? 1322.
Is a king-crab really a crab ? Plate f. p. 925.
What birds have a " third eyelid " ? 438.
What fish sleep through the dry season inside balls of mud ? 2038.

Which insect looks after its family after they have hatched ? 1071.
How tall do bamboos grow ? 353.
How fast can an ostrich run ? 2456.
How can you tell the age of a colt by its teeth ? 1646.
What common coniferous tree sheds its leaves in winter ? 1892.
Are sponges plants or animals ? 3067.
What is the only class of animals that grows hair ? 2074.
What insect fights with " poison gas " ? 399.
What is the largest land animal that ever lived ? 1140. The largest sea animal ? 3371.
What is the largest creature that has ever flown ? 2680.
How do insects breathe ? 1732.
What gives butterfly wings their beautiful colouring ? 628.
Was there ever a bird with teeth ? *437.*
What are the ants' " cows " ? 166.
Why are a bird's bones hollow ? 437.
Why should an aquarium contain plants as well as fish ? 192.
Can fishes hear ? 1296.
Why does the ant-lion dig holes in the sand ? 181.
Which fish travels on land and climbs trees ? 1297.
What purpose is served by the colour and fragrance of flowers ? 1321.
What makes it possible for a fly to walk on the ceiling ? 1239.
Why do beavers build dams ? 387
What birds lay their eggs in other birds' nests ? 941.
What insect lives 17 years underground ? 826.
Why do whales " blow " ? 3371.
What animal absorbs its tail as it grows ? *1399.*
How does a grasshopper " sing " ? 1511. A cricket ? 927.
What group of plants lives entirely on food manufactured by other plants and animals ? 1407.
Do both male and female mosquitoes bite ? 2238.
Why does the giraffe have such long legs and neck ? 1464.
Which is the largest of all bird families ? 1272.
What is the use of the glow-worm's light ? *1288.*
Was there ever such a creature as a flying reptile ? 2767.
Why are coconut palms found in so many parts of the world ? 862.
What plants " go into partnership " ? 1932
What is the " sensitive plant " ? 2623.
What tree has roots springing from its branches ? 359.
What lizards look like snakes ? *1973.*
What are " ant-guests " ? 168.
Are the flat-fish's eyes on top of its head ? 1298.
What is a true albino ? 447.
Where do hermit crabs live ? *924.*

GEOGRAPHY

IF you could make from memory an accurate map of every country in the world, placing every mountain, every river, every gulf, every island, every boundary, every city in its exact and proper place, you might still know very little about Geography. You must learn to see a map as you see the frame of a picture, which your imagination fills with visions of bold scenery, flowing rivers, cloud-capped mountains, fertile plains, great green forests, wind-swept deserts, and, above all, people at work and play.

Geography, as we treat it here, is the study of the Earth *as the home of Man*. Thus, it deals with such things as the races of mankind, their character, and their customs ; the influence of climate upon crops and industries ; the kinds of plants and animals that thrive in various regions ; the ties of trade that bind nations and peoples together ; the causes of wealth and poverty in different parts of the world—in fact, with the whole *present* structure of civilization. In so far as the past physical history of the world helps us to understand the present, Geography enters the special field of Geology. And in so far as the past customs of peoples have influenced their present manners, it enters the field of History proper. Political Science, Economics, and every other branch of the " social sciences " are of prime importance to a complete understanding of geographical problems.

PHYSICAL GEOGRAPHY

The Earth as a Whole and Its Relation to the Sun

I. THE EARTH, 1067.

A. Its Form and Size, 1067.
  a. Gravitation, 1512.
  b. Magnetism, 881, 2060.

B. Motions of the Earth.
  a. Rotation on its axis, 1067.
  b. Revolution round the Sun, 276.

C. Results of Earth's Motions.
  a. Rotation on axis causes day and night, 980.
  b. Revolution round Sun, coupled with inclined axis, causes changing seasons, 2914.

II. ZONES OF THE EARTH.

A. The Tropical or Torrid Zone : the region of greatest heat—that portion of the earth where, at some time during the year, the sun is *directly overhead at noon*, so that the rays strike down perpendicularly, 840, 1221.
  a. Extent. Since the earth's axis is 23½ degrees from the perpendicular, the Tropical Zone occupies a belt of 23½ degrees wide on each side of the Equator. This makes the whole tropical belt 47 degrees wide, which amounts on the earth's surface to about 3,030 miles.
  b. Boundary Lines. North of Equator is Tropic of Cancer. South of Equator is Tropic of Capricorn.

B. Frigid Zones : regions of greatest cold—those portions of the earth surrounding the Poles, where, *at least once* in every year, the sun does not rise above the horizon at noon, and where, *at least once* in every year, the sun does not sink below the horizon at midnight. At the Poles the sun remains continuously above the horizon for six months, and then remains below the horizon for six months.
  a. Extent. 23½ degrees on each side of the two Poles, or 47 degrees in all. Because the earth is slightly flattened at the Poles (an oblate spheroid), 47 degrees there amount to nearly 3,300 miles.
  b. Boundary Lines. North Frigid Zone bounded by the Arctic Circle. South Frigid Zone bounded by the Antarctic Circle.

C. Temperate Zones : regions of moderate heat and cold—those portions of the earth lying between the Tropical Zone and the Frigid Zones, where the sun is never directly overhead and yet where it never fails to appear in the course of 24 hours.
  Extent. Since there are 90 degrees between the Equator and the Poles, 23½ of which are in the Tropical Zone and 23½ in the Frigid Zones, it follows that the two Temperate Zones are each 43 degrees in width, or about 2,960 miles. They are called respectively North Temperate Zone and South Temperate Zone.

The Story of the Earth's Materials

III. GEOLOGY, 1432 ; PHYSIOGRAPHY, 2595.

Note : Geology deals with the history of the earth's crust and of the materials which compose it. Physiography deals with the characteristic relief features of the earth's surfaces and with the causes which produced them.

IV. ATMOSPHERE OR AIR.

A. Nature and Functions of the Atmosphere, 88.

B. Atmosphere and Climate, 840.

  a. Temperature: How the earth gets heat from the sun, 1595 ; Temperature and weather maps—the meaning and usefulness of " isotherms," 841.

  b. Moisture, 840 : Moisture in the atmosphere, 88 ; How moisture is measured with the hygrometer, 1677 ; How moisture gets into the atmosphere by evaporation, 1243 ; How

Chief Features of the Earth's Surface and Their Origin

RACES OF MANKIND

FOR the student of geography it is not so important to know the relationships and origin of peoples as it is to have a convenient method for grouping them according to their present-day customs, their degree of civilization, and their geographical distribution. The grouping followed in this Outline brings out some of the more generally accepted racial affinities, but in the main its purpose is to emphasize the geographical and cultural side of this great and important subject.

I. MAN'S PLACE IN NATURE, 2078.

II. RACES OF MANKIND.

A. The Many Methods of Classification, 2723.
  a. Differences in hair, 1565.
  b. Differences in language, 1891.
  c. Geographical distribution, 2723.

B. The Races Based on Colour and Geographical Distribution.
  a. The Caucasian, European, or White Race.
  b. The Ethiopian, African, or Black Race.
  c. The Mongolian, Asiatic, or Yellow Race.
  d. The Amerind, American, or Red Race.
  e. The Malay and Polynesian, or Brown Race.

III. THE WHITE RACE.

Note : Certain peoples, once important in history but now no longer existing as separate groups, have been included in this list ; these are indicated by italic type.

A. South Mediterranean.
  a. Hamitic—Present-day types found chiefly in North Africa : Berbers, 2231, 2860 ; *Ancient Aegeans*, 29 ; *Etruscans* or *Tyrrhenians*, 1229 ; Tuaregs, 2860 ; Copts, 1098 ; Fellahin, 1095, 1104 ; Kabyles, Masai, Gallas, Somalis, 70.

  Note : The people known today as "Moors" are largely of Berber origin, but Arab and Negro blood is distinctly traceable among them. Historically the term is applied to the Mahomedan invaders of Spain.

  b. Semitic—Present-day types found chiefly in the Arabian Peninsula, Asia Minor, and North Africa : Arabs, 195 ; Armen'an·, 238, 239 ; *Assyrians*, 330 ; *Carthaginians*, 711 ; *Hittites*, 1633 ; Israelites (Jews), 1829 ; *Phoenicians*, 2573 ; *Canaanites*, 1829 ; Syrians, 3145 ; *Philistines*, 2570.

B. North Mediterranean.
Note : The Europeans of today are the chief representatives of this great division, and therefore it is called the " North Mediterranean " branch of the white race. It includes, however, several Asiatic groups. The term " Aryan," which is often used to describe those members of the white race which are believed to have originated in western Asia, is synonymous with " Indo-European " and can properly be used only when people are being classified according to languages, 261.
  a. Primitive European Types : Basques, *1361*, 3032 ; Iberians (Spain) ; Ligurians (Genoa), 1763.
  b. Celts, 740 ; Bretons, 585, *1361* ; *Britons*, 574 ; *Gauls*, 1365 ; Irish, 740, 1744 ; *Picts* and *Scots*, 2892 ; Welsh, 3333.
  c. Latin Type, 1763, 2804 ; French, 1358 ; Italians, 1763, 2000 ; Portuguese, 2658 ; Rumanians (Rumans or Vlachs), 1527, 2840 ; *Sabines*, 2804 ; Spanish, 3032.

  d. Illyric Peoples : Albanians, 100 ; *Illyrians*, 100.
  e. Hellenic Peoples : Greeks, 1517 ; *Macedonians*, 2049.
  f. Lettic Peoples : Letts, 1899 ; Lithuanians, 1967.
  g. Teutons, 1237, 3190 ; East Teutons— Danes, 991, 1194 ; *Goths*, 1447, 1487 ; *Northmen* or *Normans*, 1358, 2376 ; Scandinavians, 2880 ; *Vandals*, 1237, 3304 ; *Burgundians*, 1237 ; West Teutons—Angles, 1194 ; Dutch, 2318, *2322* ; English, 1195 ; *Franks*, 1365, 1447 ; Germans, 1447 ; *Saxons*, 1237, 1447, 1449 ; *Alemannians*, 1237 ; *Lombards* or *Langobards*, 1237.
  h. Slavs, 1237, 2982, 3438 ; Bulgarians, *613* ; Croatians, 3438 ; Czechs or Bohemians, 487, 953; Montenegrins, 2219; Poles, 2640; Russians, 2844 ; Serbs, 2922 ; Ruthenians or Ukrainians, 3273 ; Dalmatians, Moravians, Slovaks, 2985 ; Wends, etc.
  i. Indo-Iranians : Armenians, 237, 732 ; Baluchis (inhabitants of Baluchistan), *352* ; Kurds, 239 ; *Medes*, 2554 ; Persians, 2554 ; Hindus, 1703 ; Ceylonese or Sinhalese, 749.
  j. Caucasic Type : Circassians, Georgians, 732.

IV. THE BLACK RACE.

A. Negrito Type, 2312.
  a. Equatorial Pigmies, *67*.
  b. South African Branches : Bushmen, Hottentots, 70, 2312.
  c. East Indian Groups : Negritos of Philippines, 2568 ; Andaman Islanders, 1692 ; Semangs and Sakais, 2069.
  d. Australian Groups : Blackfellows, 307 ; Tasmanians.

Note : The list of peoples named above presents unusual difficulties to the ethnologists. The student is specially cautioned against regarding this arrangement as an implication of true racial affinity. They are grouped together because of their general resemblance to the Negro type and because they present on the whole the lowest forms of civilization found in the world today.

B. True Negro Type, 2312.
  a. Sudanese Negroes, 70.
  b. Guinea Coast Negroes : Ashantis, 68.

C. Negroid or Bantu Type, 70, 2312 : Basutos (Natives of Basutoland) ; Bechuanas (Natives of Bechuanaland) ; Kaffirs, 3013 ; Swahilis ; Zulus, 70.

V. THE YELLOW RACE.

A. Eastern Mongolian Type.
  a. Southern Chinese, 807.
  b. Indo-Chinese, 1718 : Annamese, 1718 ; Burmese, 623 ; Siamese, 2964 ; Tonkinese, 1718 ; Shans, Chins, Kachins, 623.

c. Tibetan Group, 1703 : Bhutanese ; Nepalese, 2315 ; Tibetans, 3208.

B. Western Mongolian Type. This type is sometimes called " Ural Altaic."
  a. Manchu Group.
  b. Mongol-Tartar Group, 2205 : Kalmuks, 2207 ; Cossacks, 916 ; Tartars, 3155 ; *Huns,* 1657 ; Kirghiz, 271 ; True Mongols, 2205 ; Turkomans, 3266 ; Turks, 3262.
  c. Finnish Group : Estonians or Ests, 1226 ; Finns, 1277 ; Lapps, 1891 ; Magyars, 2065.
  d. Japanese-Korean Group.

VI. THE BROWN RACE.

A. Dravidian Group : Gonds, Bhils, Tamils, 1703 ; Veddahs, 749.

B. Malayan Type, 2069.
  a. East-Indian Group : Dyaks, 525 ; Javanese, 1813 ; Malays, 2069 ; Sumatrese, 3118 ; Igorots and Moros, 2568.
  b. Madagascar Group : Hovas and Malagasies, 2051.

C. Oceanic Type.
  a. Papuan or Melanesian Group, 2470 : New Guineans, 2338 ; New Hebrideans, New Caledonians, Solomon Islanders ; Fijians (in part), 1271.
  b. Micronesian Group : Inhabitants of the Ladrones, Pelew, Caroline, Marshall, and Gilbert Islands, 2470.
  c. Polynesian Group, 2471 ; Hawaiians, 1585 ; Maoris, 2358 ; Samoans, 2869 ; Fijians (in part), 1271 ; Tahitians, Tongans, Marquesans, 2471 ; and other inhabitants of the more eastern Pacific islands.

Note : Some ethnologists regard the Polynesians as descendants of an ancient Aryan or white stock which came across south-eastern Asia and over the waters of the Pacific centuries ago, settling in one after the other of the islands they now inhabit.

VII. THE RED RACE, 2753.

A. Arctic Type : Eskimos and Aleutian Islanders or Aleuts, 99, 1222.

B. North American Types (Alaska, Canada, and United States) : Athabascan, Algonquian, Iroquoian, Muskhogean, Siouan, Shoshonean, and other groups, 2753.

Note : The so-called " Pueblo " Indians did not belong to any single tribe or group, but consisted of several independent stocks in various parts of the South-west who were distinguished by their settled and semi-civilized life in tribal villages.

C. Mexican and Central American Types.
  a. Nahuan Group : Aztecs, 325.
  b. Mayan Group : Mayas, in northern regions of Central America.

D. South American Types. The chief groups are : Chibcan (Colombia) ; Quechuan (Peru ; Incas, 1689) ; Aymaran (southern Peru, Bolivia, and northern Chile) ; Calchaquan (northern Argentina) ; Araucanian (Chile and western Argentina, 802); Cariban (Venezuela, Guiana, and Amazon delta) ; Tupi-Guarani (Brazil) ; Arawakan (formerly inhabiting Haiti, Porto Rico, Cuba, the Bahamas, etc., as well as their present home in the Amazon Valley) ; Patagonian (Southern Argentina, 226) ; Fuegian (Tierra del Fuego) and extending a short distance north of the Strait of Magellan.

EUROPE

JUDGED by its size alone, Europe is a minor division of the Earth's surface. Indeed, it is little more than a broken and irregular peninsula projecting westward from the vast land mass of Asia, and it is treated as a separate continent only because of its racial and historical individuality. Yet, in the history of modern civilization and in the broadest geographical sense, Europe has played by far the most important part of all the continents. It has given its " point of view " to the world.

Why has Europe prevailed over so much of the world ? An adequate answer to that question would involve countless subtle forces and influences which it is perhaps impossible to analyze fully, but it is certain that Geography would play an important part in the solution of the problem.

I. POSITION AND AREA, 1232.

A. Europe is situated in the centre of the land masses of the globe, giving it an enormous commercial and political advantage. This advantage of position will be made apparent by a glance at a map of the world.

B. The area of Europe (about 3,724,000 square miles) is about half that of South America ; about two-fifths of North America ; about one-third of Africa ; and slightly more than one-fifth of Asia. The overcrowding of this comparatively small area forced Europe to seek food supplies in other lands, and an outlet for its surplus population.

II. PHYSIOGRAPHY, 1233.

A. Geological Influences :
  a. The Glaciers of the Ice Age, 1468, 1680 (*picture*).
  b. The Sinking of the Land. To this is due

the exceedingly irregular outline of Europe, with its countless peninsulas and bays, its land-locked seas, and its numerous islands (1234).

B. Mountains and Highlands. The mountains of Europe are, as a whole, comparatively low and scattered, and nowhere do they cut off large interior areas from the moist sea winds.
  a. Central and Southern Mountain Groups : Alps, 126 ; Apennines, 184 ; Dinaric Alps, 1233 ; Transylvanian Alps, 2839 ; Carpathian Mountains, 704 ; Balkan Mountains and Pindus Mountains, 343.
  b. Central Highlands : French Highlands, 1359-60 ; Jura Mountains, 1842 ; Vosges Mountains, 3330 ; Black Forest, 464 ; Bavarian Highlands, 377 ; Thuringian Hills and Harz Mountains, 1445 ; and Bohemian Mountains, 487.

c. South-Western Mountains and Highlands. Pyrenees, **2709** : Sierra Nevada and other ranges and plateaux forming part of the Iberian or Spanish Peninsula, 3030.

d. **North-West Highlands** : Brittany Highlands, 1360 ; Highlands of England and Wales, Ireland and Scotland, 1161, 1744, 2889, 3333 ; Kiolen Mountains of Scandinavia, 3126 ; Mountains of Finland, 1277.

e. Mountains of the extreme East and South-East : Ural Mts., 2844 ; Caucasus Mts., 732.

C. Lowlands.

a. **Great Central Lowland** : English Plain, 1161 ; Paris Basin, 1360 ; Lowlands of Belgium and Holland, 403, 2318 ; North German Plain, 1444 ; Plains of Denmark and S. Sweden, 991, 3126 ; and Great Plains of Russia, 2844.

b. Smaller European Lowlands : Hungarian Plain, 2137 ; Lombardy Plain or Basin of the Po River, 1233 ; Garonne Basin, 1360.

D. Seas and Chief Rivers flowing into them :

a. **Mediterranean**, 2135 : Rhône, **2772** ; chief divisions of the Mediterranean, Adriatic Sea, 29, into which empties the Po, **2663** ; and Aegean Sea, **29**.

b. **Atlantic Ocean**, *290, 291* : Rivers of the Iberian Peninsula : Guadalquivir, Guadiana, Tagus, and Douro. French rivers : Garonne and Loire, **2000**.

c. **North Sea**, **2390**, and **English Channel** : Seine, **2919** ; Thames, **3193** ; Meuse, **2156** ; Rhine, **2769** ; Elbe, 1124.

d. **Baltic Sea**, 351 : Oder, 1445 ; Vistula, **3326**.

e. **White Sea**, *2845*, with the Dvina ; and Arctic Ocean, *223*, with the Pechora river.

f. **Black Sea**, **464** : Danube, **972** ; Dnieper, Don, Dniester.

g. **Caspian Sea**, **712** : Volga, **3329**.

E. Chief Islands belonging to Europe : Iceland, **1684** ; British Isles, **582** ; Danish Islands, 991 ; Balearic Isles, **342** ; Corsica, **914** : Sardinia, **2873** ; Sicily, **2968** ; Crete, **927** ; Malta, **2072** ; Aegean Is., *1518*.

III. CLIMATE.

A. Climate of Europe is chiefly Oceanic, 840.

a. Russia has continental climate, 2844.

b. Gulf Stream warms Western Europe, **1554**.

c. Effect of warm west winds, 1232.

B. Rainfall, 1237.

The British Isles

CUT off by water from the rest of Europe, the British Isles (**582**) have been compelled to develop their commerce by sea. As the population of these small islands increased, the products of the home farms no longer sufficed to feed the inhabitants, and Britain was obliged to buy foreign food. To pay for this food, manufacturing industries had to be developed. The presence of coal and minerals on the islands favoured this development. To maintain the manufacturing industries, raw materials had to be imported. To establish sure sources of raw materials and to control markets for manufactured products, Britain struggled for and obtained colonies in all quarters of the globe. To protect this colonial empire, Britain built a powerful navy. These (and the discovery of America, which put Britain on the world's main sea routes), are the chief factors in the evolution of these small islands into a world-power.

I. PHYSIOGRAPHY, 582.

A. Islands with Irregular Coastline produced by sinking of Land, *582*.

B. General characteristics.

a. Description of English country, 1161.

b. Wales, a country of hills and low mountains, **3333**.

c. Scotland and its highlands, **2889**.

d. Ireland, an inland plain surrounded by low mountains, **1744**.

C. Soil. Fertile in England, 1161 ; good in Scottish lowlands, poor in highlands, 2889 ; thin in Ireland, 1744.

D. Lesser Islands : Hebrides, **1601** ; Shetland Islands, **2945** ; Isle of Man, **2084** ; Isle of Wight, **3377**; Orkney Islands, **2453**; Channel Islands, *751.*

II. CLIMATE AND NATURAL RESOURCES.

A. Climate Tempered by Westerlies and Gulf Stream drift, 1554.

B. Fairly Heavy Rainfall.

C. Natural Resources.

a. Many good harbours.

b. Coal, iron, tin, copper, zinc, and lead, 1162, 2889, 3333.

c. Rich fishing ground in the North Sea, *1304*.

III. CHIEF INDUSTRIES.

A. Manufacturing : Cotton goods, *919*, 1165 ; woollens ; linen ; silk ; porcelain and pottery,

1165 ; iron and steel products, 1168 ; shipbuilding, 1168.

B. Mining.

C. Fisheries, *1304-08*.

D. Agriculture, 78, *81–84*, 1745, 1747.

E. Stock Raising and Dairying, *1162*, 1745, 1747.

IV. COMMERCE AND TRANSPORT.

A. Importance of Colonial Trade, 70, 308, 2358.

B. Transport.

a. British Shipping ; importance of sea power, 1195, 2144, 2293, 3277.

b. Rivers and Canals, *686*, 1165.

c. Arterial Roads, 2784.

d. Railways, 2734.

e. Air Transport, 47.

V. IMPORTANT CITIES.

A. In England : London, **2009** ; Birmingham, **457** ; Liverpool, **1968** ; Manchester, **2084** ; Sheffield, **2941** ; Leeds, **1918** ; Bristol, **571** ; Newcastle-upon-Tyne, **2336** ; Plymouth, **2631** ; Southampton, **3027** ; Dover, **1030**, etc.

B. In Scotland : Glasgow, **1471** ; Edinburgh, **1086** ; Aberdeen, **11**, etc.

C. In Ireland : Dublin, **1050** ; Belfast, **402** ; Cork, **910**, etc.

Note : *See also* separate articles on all the counties of the British Isles.

The British Commonwealth of Nations

(Flags, col. frontispiece Vol. 8. *See also* historical introduction, page 580.)

I. SELF-GOVERNING DOMINIONS.

Australia, **307** ; Canada, **676** ; Ceylon, **748** ; New Zealand, **2357** ; Pakistan, *1702*, **2479** ; Union of South Africa, **3013**.

II. ASSOCIATED INDEPENDENT STATES.

A. Republic of India, *1702*, **1714** ; an independent republic within the Commonwealth, recognizing the British Sovereign as First Citizen.

B. Republic of Ireland ; also called Eire or Irish Free State, **1749** ; an independent republic outside the Commonwealth but not recognized as a foreign country.

III. COLONIES, PROTECTORATES, AND DEPENDENCIES.

A. In Europe: Gibraltar, **1462** ; Malta, **2072**.

B. In Africa:

   a. British Somaliland, *map facing page* 68, and *map, 1072*.

   b. British East Africa, **1072**. This includes Kenya Colony and Protectorate (former East Africa Protectorate), Uganda Protectorate, Tanganyika Territory (former German East Africa), Zanzibar Protectorate and Pemba.

   c. Nyasaland Protectorate, **2772**, *map, 1073*.

   d. South Africa. British possessions not part of Union of South Africa: Rhodesia, **2771** ; Bechuanaland, **3016** ; Swaziland, **3016** ; and Basutoland, **3015**.

   e. South-west Africa Protectorate (former German colony now administered by Union of South Africa), **3029**.

   f. West Africa Colonies, **3366**. These include Nigeria, Gold Coast, Sierra Leone, Gambia, and portions of the former German colonies of Cameroon, **672**, and Togoland.

   g. Islands. Mauritius, **2121**, St. Helena and Ascension Island, *map facing page* 68 ; Tristan da Cunha, **290**, *f-i*.

Note. The Anglo-Egyptian Sudan, **3110**, is a Condominium, ruled jointly by Britain and Egypt.

C. In Asia : Cyprus, **952** ; Aden, **26** ; Bahrein Islands, **2557** ; Seychelles Islands, *f-i.* ; Andaman and Nicobar and Maldive Islands, *f-i.* ; Singapore Colony, **2069**, **2974** ; Federation of Malaya, **2069** ; Hong Kong, **1639**.

D. In North and South America : Bermudas, **418** ; Bahamas, **339** ; Barbados, **460** ; British Honduras, **1638** ; Jamaica, **1792** ; other West Indian Islands, **3368** ; Trinidad and Tobago, **3248** ; British Guiana, **1552** ; Falkland Islands and Dependencies, **1259**.

E. Islands of the Pacific : British North Borneo (including Brunei and Sarawak), **525** ; British New Guinea (including Papua and the former German section of the island), **2338** ; New Britain Islands (formerly the Bismarck Archipelago), **2470** ; New Hebrides (ruled jointly with France), **2470** ; Fiji Islands, **1271** ; British Samoa, British Solomon Islands, Gilbert and Ellice Islands, Tokelau Islands, Tonga Islands, Pitcairn Island, Cook Islands, **2470–73**.

Note: After the First World War former German territories in New Guinea, New Britain and the Solomons were mandated to Australia, German Samoa to New Zealand. These territories and British mandated former German colonies in Africa were placed under U.N. trusteeship in 1947.

France

STRETCHING from the North Sea to the Mediterranean, and facing the Atlantic Ocean on the west, France (**1358**) has broad open gateways to all avenues of world commerce. Her position gives her a variety of climate, ranging from semi-tropical to temperate, so that the soil will produce, with the aid of the abundant rains, almost any kind of crops. Able to satisfy with home products virtually all their frugal requirements, the French have had in the past little incentive to strive for foreign commerce. France's position as a world power, therefore, was based mainly on the bonds of French nationalism. She had a large colonial empire, which after the vicissitudes of the Second World War was reconstituted as French Overseas Departments and Territories.

I. PHYSIOGRAPHY.

A. Mountains and Highlands, **1358**.

   a. Chief Ranges : Alps, **126** ; Pyrenees, **2709** ; Jura Mts., **1842** ; Vosges Mts., **3330**.

   b. Lesser Ranges and Highlands : Ardennes Hills, **1359** ; Auvergne Mts., Cevennes Chain, Highlands of Brittany and Normandy, **1360**.

B. Plains, **1565** ; Paris Basin, **1360**.

C. Chief Rivers, **1360** : Seine, **2919** ; Loire, **2000** ; Garonne, **1360** ; Rhône, **2772**.

D. Island of Corsica, **914**.

II. CLIMATE.

The winds from the Atlantic bring abundant moisture, keep the temperature mild, **840**, **1358**.

III. NATURAL RESOURCES.

A. Fertile soil, **1360**.

B. Minerals : coal, iron, and building stone, **1361**.

C. Forest lands, **1361**.

D. Rivers form valuable links, **1360**.

IV. CHIEF INDUSTRIES AND PRODUCTS.

A. Agriculture is the most important industry, **1360**.

   a. Principal Crops : Wheat, oats, rye, barley, potatoes, and sugar-beet.

   b. France leads in Grape Growing, **1360**.

   c. Livestock : Cattle, horses, sheep, goats, pigs, and poultry.

B. Fisheries : Cod, oysters, sardines, **1361**.

C. Mining and Quarrying, **1361**.

D. Manufacturing, **1361** : Textiles and leather, wine, gloves, perfumes, soap, porcelains, iron and steel products, sugar.

E. Transport :

   a. Rivers and Canals, **686**, **1360**, **2156**, **2774**.

   b. Wonderful System of Roads, **1362**.

   c. Railways owned by Government, **1362**.

V. CHIEF CITIES.

Paris (capital), **2514** ; Marseilles, **2110** ; Lyons, **2043** ; Bordeaux, **524** ; Lille, **1947** ; Nantes, **2274** ; Toulouse ; St. Étienne, **1361** ; Nice, **2364** ; Havre, **1585** ; Rouen, **2829** ; Reims, **2760** ; Amiens, *1362* ; Brest, **560** ; Calais, **655** ; Orléans, **2454** ; Metz, **2155** ; Versailles, **3317** ; Dunkirk, **1055**.

FRENCH OVERSEAS DEPTS. and TERRITORIES

forming, with France itself, the French Union.

I. IN AFRICA.

A. On the Mediterranean : Algeria (Northern Algeria is part of metropolitan France ; Southern Algeria is a separate colony), **117** ; Tunisia, **3254** ; Morocco, **2230**.

B. French West Africa, **3367** : Senegal, French Guinea, Ivory Coast, Dahomey, French Sudan and the Niger, Mauritania, Togo (part of the former German Togoland), and most of the Sahara Desert.

C. French Equatorial Africa : Gabun, Middle Congo, Ubanghi Shari, Chad and a part of the former German Cameroon, **672**, *map*, *888*.

D. Other Depts. and Territories : Madagascar and its dependencies, **2051** ; French Somaliland, *map*, *1072*, **3000** ; Réunion and its dependencies, **1362**, *f-i*.

Note : The former German colonies of Togoland and the Cameroon, mandated to France after the First World War, were placed under United Nations trusteeship in 1947.

II. IN ASIA.

India Establishments, **1692** ; Indo-China, comprising Viet-Nam (Annam and Tonking), Cochin-China, Laos and Cambodia, **1718**.

III. IN AMERICA.

St. Pierre and Miquelon, *f-i.* ; Guadeloupe, **1551** ; Martinique, **2112** ; French Guiana, **1553**.

IV. IN PACIFIC OCEAN.

These possessions, **2470**, include New Hebrides (jointly with Britain), Loyalty Islands, New Caledonia, Marquesas Islands, Tuamotu Group, Society Islands (including Tahiti), Tubuai Islands, and Wallis Islands.

Belgium and Luxemburg

BELGIUM (**403**) is primarily a manufacturing nation. Most of the population is crowded into industrial centres, while the countryside is covered with small farms which are made to yield enormous crops by intensive cultivation on scientific lines.

I. PHYSIOGRAPHY, 403.

A. General character of the country : Sand-dunes along the sea, hills (Ardennes) in the south, fertile plains in between.

B. Chief Rivers : Scheldt, *404* (*map*) ; Meuse, **2156**.

II. CLIMATE.

Like that of northern France and southern England, with mild winters, cool summers, and an abundance of rain.

III. NATURAL RESOURCES.

A. Chief minerals : Coal, iron, sand for making glass, **404**.

B. Good farm land, **403**.

IV. CHIEF INDUSTRIES.

A. Agriculture : Principal crops are wheat, rye, flax, and sugar-beet.

B. Mining and fisheries, **404**.

C. Manufacturing : Chief products are iron and steel, artificial silk, motor-cars, glass, lace, linen, wool, gloves, and sugar.

D. River and canal navigation, **404**, **686**.

V. CHIEF CITIES.

Brussels (capital), **594** ; Antwerp, **181** ; Liége, **1934** ; Ghent, **1460** ; Bruges, **592** ; Ostend, **404**, *f-i.* ; Louvain, **2032**.

VI. BELGIAN COLONIAL TERRITORY.

Belgian Congo, **887**.

GRAND DUCHY OF LUXEMBURG.

This small territory (**2041**) lies between France, Belgium, and Germany. Its industries and other characteristics are similar to those of Belgium.

Switzerland

SWITZERLAND (**3138**) is a land normally devoted to agriculture, manufacturing and commerce—all on a small scale. Among the principal assets of the country are the scenery and climate, which, in normal times, attracts thousands of tourists annually.

I. PHYSIOGRAPHY, 3138.

A. Mountains : Alps, **126**, *129–132* ; Jura Mountains, **1842**.

B. Narrow Plateau between the two ranges.

C. Rivers rising in Switzerland : Rhine, Rhône, Aar, Ticino, Inn, **3138**, **3140**.

D. Other Physical Features : Many lakes ; majestic glaciers.

II. CLIMATE.

Much cooler than that of the surrounding lowlands. There are heavy rains in summer and great snowfalls in winter.

III. NATURAL RESOURCES.

The chief resources are the scenery, the pasture land, and the plentiful supply of water-power.

IV. CHIEF INDUSTRIES.

A. Tourist industry.

B. Dairying and agriculture : Goats and cattle supply the very important dairying industry ; crops are wheat, rye, oats, and potatoes.

C. Manufacturing : Chief products are watches and clocks, silk and cotton goods, cheese and condensed milk, chocolate, machinery, clothing, and salt.

V. CHIEF CITIES.

Berne (capital), **418** ; Zürich, **3448** ; Geneva, **1428** ; Basle, **370**.

The Netherlands

HOLLAND or the Netherlands (2318) is primarily a commercial nation, whose prosperity rests upon thrift and the Dutch merchant's world-wide reputation for rigid honesty. The early merchants sailed East and West in search of new lands and markets, and founded colonies which, in the East, developed into independent States.

I. PHYSIOGRAPHY, 2318.

A. Alluvial soil brought by three rivers.
B. Nearly half the land is below sea level, 2318. How the sea is kept out, *2319*. How the marshes are reclaimed, 2318–19.
C. Land is not naturally fertile.
D. Rivers : Rhine, **2769** ; Meuse or Maas River, 2156 ; Scheldt, 1232.

II. CLIMATE.

Damp and cool ; severe cold in winter, 2319.

III. NATURAL RESOURCES.

A favourable situation for ocean commerce, a considerable area of pasture land, some coal and deposits of pottery clay.

IV. CHIEF INDUSTRIES.

A. Dairying and dairy products, 2321.
B. Agriculture : Chief crops are rye, oats, potatoes, sugar-beet, wheat and flax ; tulip-raising, 2320.
C. Manufacturing : Textiles, ropes, dyes, chemicals, sugar refineries, aircraft factories, etc., 147 ; diamond-cutting, 147, 2321, and pottery.

D. Shipbuilding, 147.

V. COMMERCE AND TRANSPORT.

A. Large amount of shipping.
B. Canals, rivers, railways, 688–89, 1233, 2320–21.
C. Colonial trade, 2321.

VI. CHIEF CITIES.

Amsterdam, **147** ; Rotterdam, **2829** ; The Hague (capital), **1563** ; Utrecht, **3300**.

DUTCH WEST INDIES

Dutch Guiana or Surinam, 1555 ; Curaçao Island Group or Netherlands Antilles, *map, 3309*.

FORMER DUTCH EAST INDIES

(Now known as **Indonesia** or the **United States of Indonesia**), **1720**, *map, 1075*.

Principal Islands : Java, **1813** ; Sumatra, **3117** ; Borneo (northern part belongs to Great Britain), **525** ; Celebes, **738** ; Molucca Islands, 1076 ; Timor, *1074–75, map* (eastern half belongs to Portugal). Western half of New Guinea remains in Dutch hands, eastern half belongs to Great Britain.

Germany

NEITHER her soil nor climate, nor the temper of her people, has inclined Germany (**1444**) to remain an agricultural nation. After the unification of the German state in 1871 Germany rapidly developed into a powerful manufacturing and commercial country. There were few outlets for her industry, however, for most of the world was already divided by, or under the control of, the great powers. Germany then sought a re-division of the world's markets and colonies in her favour. After her unsuccessful attempt in 1914–18, she was re-organized as an aggressor nation by the Nazis, only to suffer complete defeat and economic eclipse in 1939–45.

I. PHYSIOGRAPHY.

A. Highlands in the South :
   a. Bavarian Highlands, **377** ; Black Forest, **464**.
   b. Thuringian Hills and Harz Mountains, **1581**.
   c. Erzgebirge or " Ore Mountains " of Saxony, 2878.
B. Northern Germany is part of great European plain, 1445 ; Alps of Austrian Tirol, 319.
C. Chief Rivers : Rhine, **2769** ; Ems, *f-i.* ; Weser, *f-i.* ; Elbe, **1124** ; Oder, 1445 ; Vistula, 1445, **3326** ; Danube, **972**.

II. CLIMATE.

Drier and marked by greater extremes of temperature than in the lands to the west. The winds from the Atlantic have lost much of their moisture and equable temperature by the time they reach central Germany.

III. NATURAL RESOURCES.

A. Minerals : Coal, iron, zinc, copper, tin, nickel, lead, potash, sulphur, silver, gold, and building stone.
B. Forests, 464, 1351, 1445.

C. Water-power, from the many rivers of the mountains.

IV. INDUSTRIES.

A. Manufacturing : Iron and steel products, 1753, motor-cars, textiles, chemicals and dyes, pottery and porcelain ; beer, wine, jewelry, and toys ; wood products.
B. Agriculture : Principal crops are wheat, rye, barley, oats, sugar-beet, hops, potatoes, flax, tobacco, 1445, and grapes.
C. Livestock.
D. Shipbuilding and fisheries, 1568.

V. TRANSPORT.

A. Railways, rivers and canals, 688, 689, 972, 1124, 1568, 2769.
B. Roads.

VI. MAIN DIVISIONS OF GERMANY.

A. Before the Second World War : Prussia, **2696** ; Bavaria, **377**, **1447** ; Württemberg, *f-i.* ; Baden, 1445 ; Saxony, **2878** ; Thuringia, 1445 ; Hesse, 1445 ; Hamburg, **1568** ; Lübeck, *f-i.* ; Bremen, **559**.

B. **After the Second World War** : In 1945 part of E. Prussia was incorporated in Russia ; rest of Germany east of the Oder administered by Poland. The other occupation zones were :

a. British (N.W.) Schleswig-Holstein, N. Rhine-Westphalia, Hamburg, Lower Saxony.

b. French (W.) Rhineland-Palatinate, Baden, Wurttemberg-Hohenzollern, Saar.

c. U.S. (S.W.) Bavaria, Wurttemberg-Baden, Bremen, Hesse.

d. Russian (E.) Brandenburg, Saxony, Saxony-Anhalt, Mecklenburg.

In May 1949 the W. German Federal Republic was set up, with Bonn as capital. In October 1949 the Russians proclaimed the E. German Republic, capital E. Berlin.

VII. CHIEF CITIES.

Berlin, **416** ; Bonn, **500** ; Hamburg, **1568** ; Munich, **2256** ; Leipzig, **1920** ; Dresden, **1048** ; Cologne, **871** ; Frankfort-on-Main, **1385** ; Hanover, **1574**.

Austria

PART of the Dual Monarchy of Austria-Hungary before the First World War, Austria (**316**) was, after her defeat, reduced to a small republic in which the urban population far outweighed the rural, resulting in economic unbalance. Annexed by Germany in 1938, she was restored as a separate country but occupied by the Allies in 1945.

I. PHYSIOGRAPHY.

A. **Mountains :** Alps (**316**) in the Western, Central and Southern regions ; Moravian Hills in the North.

B. **Lowlands :** The valley of the Danube (**972**) lies between the highlands ; and there is a small strip of the Hungarian plain in the East.

C. **Rivers, etc. :** The Inn (**1725**) is the most important tributary of the Danube (**317, 972**) ; there are many fine lakes.

II. CLIMATE.

Austria has a varied inland continental climate (**316–17**), with heavy rainfall and snows in the mountains.

III. NATURAL RESOURCES.

In the lowlands and foothills farmland and pasture ; timber in the highlands (35 per cent of total area is forested) ; deposits (**318**) of iron, copper, zinc, lead, coal and lignite ; hydro-electric power.

IV. INDUSTRIES.

A. **Agriculture :** Principal crops (**317**) are wheat, rye, barley, oats, potatoes and turnips. Grapes for wine. Horses, cattle and sheep.

B. **Manufactures** (**318**) : Textiles, pianos, iron and steel goods, perfumes and fashion goods.

V. CHIEF CITIES.

Vienna (capital), **3322** ; Graz, *f-i.* ; Salzburg, 318 ; Innsbruck, **1725**.

VI. MAIN DIVISIONS.

Provinces of Upper Austria (divided between U.S. and Russian zones of occupation) ; Lower Austria (Russian zone) ; Burgenland (Russian zone) ; Salzburg (U.S. zone) ; Tirol and Vorarlberg (French zone) ; Carinthia, East Tirol, Styria (British zone).

Denmark

DENMARK (**991**) consists of the peninsula of Jutland and several islands lying at the entrance of the Baltic Sea. Although their land borders on Germany, the Danes are more closely connected by race, customs, and traditions with Sweden and Norway (**3126, 2392**). Denmark's prosperity was the outgrowth of the thrift and enterprise of the people, their marvellous co-operative industries, and the high degree of public education.

I. PHYSIOGRAPHY.

A. **Peninsula of Jutland :** stormy barren west coast and protected smiling east coast.

B. **Islands** large part of total area : Fünen, Zealand, Laaland, Falster, Moen, and Bornholm.

C. **Character of the surface :** low plains, woodlands, and swamps.

D. **Coastline** faces North Sea and Baltic.

II. CLIMATE.

Denmark is exposed to cold and damp winds, which bring an abundance of moisture.

III. NATURAL RESOURCES.

Farmland, pasture land, pottery clay, and fishing waters are the only natural sources of wealth ; forestry is very scientifically worked.

IV. INDUSTRIES.

A. **Agriculture** (**991**) is the chief industry.
a. **Chief crops :** oats, rye, barley, potatoes, sugar-beet, hay.

b. **Importance of dairying.**
c. **Effective work of co-operative societies.**

B. **Fisheries :** Cod, salmon, shrimp, lobster, haddock, herring, and flounder, **991**.

C. **Manufacture of porcelain, 991.**

V. CHIEF CITIES.

Copenhagen (capital), **904** ; Aarhus, Aalborg, and Odense, **991**.

VI. POSSESSIONS OF DENMARK.

A. **Faroe Islands, 991.** These islands, lying about midway between Scotland and Iceland, are considered part of Denmark, having representatives in the Danish Legislature, but retain a measure of self-government. Chief industries : fishing and sheep raising.

B. **Greenland, 1541.** This, the largest island in the world, is the only true colony of Denmark. Population mostly Eskimos. Chief industries : fishing, seal hunting, trapping, cryolite mining.

Iceland

THE twentieth century has seen the progressive loosening of the ties between Iceland (1684) and Denmark, of which it was for centuries a part. In 1904 the Iceland parliament became more or less independent for internal matters, in 1918 the two countries were declared free and equal states under one king, and in 1944 Iceland voted for a completely independent republican constitution.

I. PHYSIOGRAPHY

A. Mountainous Plateau : Volcanic rocks, with glaciers and snowfields, comprising most of the island. Chief volcano is Hekla.

B. Lowlands : Amounting to only one-fifteenth of total area, in S. and S.W. Unproductive and sandy.

C. Coasts : Rugged high cliffs, with deep fiords affording harbours.

II. CLIMATE.

Iceland has an Arctic climate, cold and stormy, but modified by prevailing S.W. winds and warm Atlantic drift.

III. NATURAL RESOURCES.

Fish in great quantities ; hot water geysers (1685) and many swift mountain streams providing water-power ; small deposits of lignite and sulphur, and Iceland spar.

IV. INDUSTRIES.

A. Fisheries. Cod the chief fish ; salmon and trout in inland waters.

B. Agriculture : Ponies, sheep and cattle ; dairying.

V. CHIEF CITIES.

The only town of any size is Reykjavik, the capital, 1685.

Sweden and Norway

THE Scandinavian Peninsula (map, 2395), occupied by Sweden and Norway, is virtually an island in the commercial and economic sense. The front door of Sweden and Norway is the sea. Norway, exposed to the tempering winds of the North Sea, has on the whole a warmer, moister climate than Sweden, despite the fact that Sweden is farther to the south. The Baltic Sea harbours of Sweden are usually ice-locked throughout the winter, whilst most of the Norwegian seaports, snug in their deep fiords, are free all the year round. While this makes Norway a more important seafaring nation than Sweden, the excessive rains, combined with the poor soil, keep its agricultural development far behind that of Sweden.

I. SWEDEN.

A. Physiography, 3126.
  a. Separated from Norway by Kiolen Mts.
  b. Divided into three natural regions : Götaland, a fertile region in the extreme south ; Svealand, a middle region of lakes and hills ; Norrland, a northern region of vast forest-covered mountains ; includes part of Lapland.
  c. Coastline irregular, rocky in places, sandy in others ; part of southern coast faces the Kattegat branch of the North Sea.

B. Climate. Summers in Sweden are short, winters are long. The extremes of temperature are greater than in Norway. The mountains also cut off much of the moisture carried by winds from the sea.

C. Natural Resources.
  a. Fertile soil in the south.
  b. Fish plentiful in Baltic and inland waters.
  c. Forests and mineral deposits.
  d. Navigable rivers and water power.

D. Industries.
  a. Agriculture is the most important industry. Chief crops are oats, rye, barley, potatoes, and sugar-beet.
  b. Lumbering and mining (iron, copper, silver, and zinc).
  c. Fisheries.
  d. Manufacturing : Chief products are matches, furniture, wood pulp, paper, porcelain, glass, textiles, iron and steel products, and sugar.
  e. Transport : Railways, rivers, canals, and shipping.

E. Chief Cities : Stockholm (capital), 3092 ; Göteborg, Malmö, Norrköping and Helsingborg.

II. NORWAY.

A. Physiography, 2392.
  a. Separated from Sweden by the Kiolen Mts.
  b. Nearly all Norway covered with rugged mountains and plateaux.
  c. Coastline broken by countless fiords and bordered with small islands.
  d. The North Sea (2930) and the Skagerrak.
  e. Spitsbergen Islands (Svalbard), 3067.

B. Climate. The temperate ocean winds and the effect of the Gulf Stream (1554) help to make the climate of Norway milder than that of Sweden and the lands farther east. The winters, however, are long and the summers short. The northern third of Norway lies inside the Arctic Circle.

C. Natural Resources.
  a. Great forests of pine and fir.
  b. Fish plentiful in coastal waters.
  c. Some minerals (iron, copper, nickel, silver) ; immense coal deposits on Spitsbergen Islands.
  d. Agricultural land confined to small valleys.
  e. Water power ; countless natural harbours.

D. Industries.
  a. Fisheries : Cod, herring, mackerel, salmon, whale.
  b. Lumbering and lumber products.
  c. Agriculture : oats, rye, barley, potatoes.
  d. Stock raising and dairying ; reindeer are raised in the extreme north.
  e. Manufacturing : Chemicals, machinery, and woodenware.
  f. Transport. Norway is one of the important shipping countries of the world.

E. Chief Cities. Oslo (Christiania) (capital), 2455 ; Bergen, Trondhjem, Stavanger, Narvik, Hammerfest.

Finland

FROM the 13th to the 18th century a possession of Sweden, and from 1809 to 1917 a grand duchy of tsarist Russia, Finland (**1277**) is among the most progressive and independent of the new countries created after the First World War. During the Second she suffered two defeats at the hands of the Soviet Union, losing some territory in the peace settlements of 1940 and 1944.

I. PHYSIOGRAPHY.

A. **Plateau**, rising in the North, covers most of the country ; surface is marshy and pitted with thousands of lakes.

B. **Coastline** : indented, low, and island-fringed, with narrow coastal plain.

II. CLIMATE.

Long, cold winters and short, hot summers.

III. RESOURCES AND PRODUCTS.

A. **Forests** : over half the land area ; timber, wood-pulp and paper ; shipbuilding.

B. **Grazing land** : cattle, sheep, goats, pigs, horses and reindeer ; chief crops are oats, barley, rye and potatoes.

C. **Fisheries** : herring, seal, salmon, trout.

D. **Water-power**, from many short rivers.

IV. CHIEF CITIES.

Helsinki (capital), **1607** ; Turku, Oulu, Tampere.

Poland

LYING in the middle of the Great European Plain at the crossroads of commerce, Poland (**2640**) has always been a storm centre of international politics. Her position at the meeting point of diverse racial groups—Germanic, Scandinavian, Slavic, and Mongolian peoples—has been a further cause of unrest. By the partitions of 1772, 1793, and 1795 Poland was divided between Germany, Austria, and Russia, and was not independent again until 1918. Occupied by Germany and Russia in 1939, in 1945 she became independent once more, but with new frontiers. Territory east of the " Curzon Line " was ceded to U.S.S.R., and Poland was compensated with German areas up to the R. Oder (*see maps, 2641, 2642*).

I. PHYSIOGRAPHY.

A. Part of great central lowland of Europe, 1234.
B. Much of the land is marshy and dotted with lakes.
C. Carpathian Mountains on southern boundary, 704.
D. Vistula river and its tributaries drain most of Poland, 3326.
E. Coastline on the Baltic Sea.

II. CLIMATE.

Winters are long ; springs are rainy ; summers are dry and often extremely hot.

III. RESOURCES AND PRODUCTS.

A. **Agriculture** : rye, oats, wheat, barley, sugar-beet, potatoes, hemp, and hops.

B. **Minerals and mining** : coal, iron, zinc, tin, copper, and sulphur.

C. **Manufacturing** : textiles, leather and leather-goods, lumber and wood products, metal products, beet-sugar.

IV. CHIEF CITIES.

Warsaw (capital), **3341**, Lodz ; Cracow, **925** ; Danzig (Gdansk), **793**.

Czechoslovakia, Hungary, and Rumania

THESE three countries have been called for convenience the Central European States. The first two came into separate existence as a result of the First World War, having formerly been a part of the empire of Austria-Hungary. All three countries lie, in whole or in part, in the great Danube Basin. Controlling the Central Mountains and Highlands which surround the Hungarian Plain, they thus control many of the most important avenues of commerce between northern and southern Europe. Liberated by the Red Army in 1945, they all fell under Russian influence.

I. CZECHOSLOVAKIA.

Made up of the former Austrian provinces of Bohemia (**487**), Moravia and Slovakia.

A. Physiography, 953.

a. Mountains and highlands : Moravian Hills, Bohemian Forest (Böhmer Wald), Ore Mountains (Erzgebirge), and Giant Mountains (Riesengebirge of Sudetic Chain), Carpathian Mountains.

b. Rivers : Head waters of Elbe, **1124** ; Danube on southern boundary and tributaries of Danube in the East, **972**.

B. Climate.
Abundant rainfall ; cold winters and hot summers.

C. Resources and Products.
a. Timber and Timber Products.
b. Agriculture : Wheat, rye, barley, oats, potatoes, beets, hops.
c. Minerals and Mining : Coal, iron, graphite, gold, silver, copper, lead, radio-active ores.
d. Manufacturing : Textiles, glass, furniture machinery, paper, chemicals, beet-sugar, ar beer.

D. Capital and chief city : Prague, **2677**,

II. HUNGARY.

A. **Physiography, 1654.**
    a. **Slopes of Carpathians** form Northern boundary.
    b. **Great Hungarian Plain (Alföld).** Covers remainder of Hungary and extends eastward into Rumania and southward into Yugoslavia.
    c. **Chief Rivers :** Danube flowing across central Hungary, Theiss (or Tisza) in the east, Drava on the southern boundary.

B. **Climate.** Hungarian Plain has less moisture than surrounding highlands, but rainfall is most abundant in the late spring, which favours the early growth of crops, while the late summer is hot and dry, which helps the crops to ripen ; the winters are extremely cold.

C. **Resources and Products.**
    a. **Agriculture :** The Hungarian Plain is the richest agricultural region in Europe. Chief crops : Wheat, rye, barley, oats, corn, sugar-beet, hops, grapes, tobacco, flax.
    b. **Stock Growing and Dairying.**
    c. **Minerals and Mining :** Coal, iron, and bauxite.

D. **Chief City :** Budapest (capital), **600.**

III. RUMANIA.

A. **Physiography, 2839.**
    a. **Mountains :** Southern spurs of Carpathian Mountains including Transylvanian Alps.

    b. **Uplands of Transylvania** west of mountains.
    c. **Strip of Hungarian plain** on western border.
    d. **Lowland plain in east and south** comprising lower Danube basin and stretching to Black Sea. This is the south-western tip of the Russian plain, which forms a part of the Great Central Lowland of Europe.
    e. **Rivers :** Danube and its tributaries the Pruth (north-eastern boundary) and Sereth.

B. **Climate.** Mountains and western slopes have typical Central European climate ; eastern plains suffer from extremes of heat and cold.

C. **Resources and Products.**
    a. **Agriculture :** wheat, rye, barley, oats, maize, beans, potatoes, sugar-beet, tobacco, grapes, and fruit.
    b. **Timber and timber products.**
    c. **Minerals and mining :** coal, salt, silver, iron, lead, copper, and marble.
    d. **Important oil fields, 2426.**

D. **Chief Cities :** Bucharest (capital), **597 ;** Jassy, Constanza.

LIECHTENSTEIN.

This principality (**1934**) lying between Austria and Switzerland and formerly dependent upon Austria-Hungary, was given its independence in 1918. Chief products of the principality are :—grain, wine, fruit, timber, livestock, cotton goods, leather, and pottery.

Spain and Portugal

THE Iberian Peninsula, upon which Spain and Portugal are situated, is almost as isolated from the rest of Europe as if it were an island. The formidable wall of the Pyrenees bars the only approach by land. The coastline (*see map* in page 3030) has very few natural harbours large enough to accommodate modern ships, and most of the rivers are rushing mountain streams unfit for navigation. The interior of the country consists chiefly of a high rough plateau, criss-crossed by ridges which interfere with transport from one part of the peninsula to the other. Furthermore, the climate and soil of this interior plateau are not favourable to agriculture on a large scale. The future prosperity of the peninsula must depend to a great extent upon the development of the immense mineral resources of the mountains and upon the establishment of industries to make use of the raw materials so obtained. Portugal has the more favourable climate and soil.

I. SPAIN.

A. **Physiography, 3030.**
    a. **Mountains :** Pyrenees, **2709 ;** Cantabrian Mountains, Sierra Nevada, Sierra Morena.
    b. **Central Tableland or Plateau.**
    c. **Lowland Plains.** These include the valley of the Ebro, a narrow strip on the Gulf of Valencia, and the valley of the Guadalquivir broadening out on the Gulf of Cadiz.
    d. **Guadalquivir and Ebro** are the only navigable streams.
    e. **Smooth Coastline** with few natural harbours.
    f. **Balearic Islands** off the East Coast, **342.**

B. **Climate.** The rainfall on the Atlantic coast is extremely heavy ; it is lighter on the Mediterranean coast ; and in many parts of the mountain-ringed interior semi-desert conditions prevail. Extremes of heat and cold exist in the interior, but on the coast the temperature is usually milder.

C. **Resources and Products.**
    a. **Agriculture :** Wheat barley, oats, rye, maize, beans, peas, sugar-beet, grapes (3032),

olives, oranges, lemons, flax, and hemp. Importance of irrigation, 3032.
    b. **Stock Raising :** Sheep (3030), goats, pigs, poultry, cattle, horses, mules, and asses.
    c. **Minerals and Mining, 3032 :** Coal, iron, lead, copper, mercury, zinc, sulphur, silver, potash, salt.
    d. **Fisheries :** Sardines, tunny.
    e. **Manufacturing :** Cotton goods, woollens silk, wine, leather, paper, glass, cork, lumber
    f. **Supply of Water-Power** is large but little developed.

D. **Chief Cities :** Madrid (capital), **2054 ;** Barcelona, **360 ;** Valencia, **3302 ;** Seville, **2925.**

E. **Spanish Possessions :** Canary Islands, **690 ;** Rio de Oro and Rio Muni, on West Coast of Africa

II. PORTUGAL.

A. **Physiography, 2658.** Portugal is made up o a continuation of the great Iberian plateau, with several small lowland areas on the coast. Its principal rivers are the Douro and the Tagus both navigable.

B. **Climate.** Being more exposed to the tempering winds of the Atlantic, Portugal has on the whole a milder and moister climate than Spain.

C. **Resources and Products.**
 a. **Agriculture :** Wheat, maize, oats, rye, barley, grapes, olives, figs, tomatoes, oranges, onions, nuts, and potatoes.
 b. **Stock Raising :** Sheep, goats, cattle, pigs.
 c. **Forests :** Lumber and cork (909) are among the chief sources of wealth.
 d. **Minerals :** Tungsten, iron, copper, manganese, lead, tin, kaolin, sulphur, and gold.
 e. **Fisheries :** Sardines, tunny, cod.
 f. **Manufacturing :** Wine, chemicals, leather, olive oil, woollens, cotton goods, lace, tiles.

D. **Chief Cities :** Lisbon (capital), 1962, Oporto.

E. **Portuguese Possessions.**
 a. **Atlantic Islands :** Azores, 324 ; Madeira, 2051 ; Cape Verde Islands, 698 ; St. Thomas and Principe.
 b. **African Colonies :** Portuguese Guinea, Angola, and Mozambique.
 c. **Asiatic and East Indian Colonies :** Portuguese India (including Goa, Damao, and Diu) ; Macao, part of Timor Island.

ANDORRA.

This tiny semi-independent republic lies in the Pyrenees between Spain and France. Area 191 square miles ; population, 5,231 (2709).

Italy

ITALY (1763), with its commanding position in the Mediterranean Sea, dominated the world in the days when the Mediterranean was the centre of civilization, and its position along the highways of trade between Europe, Africa, and Asia still gives it great importance. Italy was stripped of its colonial empire as a result of the Second World War.

I. PHYSIOGRAPHY.

A. **Mountains, 1763.**
 a. **Alps along the Northern boundary, 126.**
 b. **Apennines form backbone of Peninsula, 184.**
 1. Highlands of Sicily (2968) are part of same land formation as the Apennines.
 2. Volcanoes : Vesuvius, 3318 ; Etna, 1228.

B. **Lowlands.** These include the plains of Lombardy and the valley of the Po, the plains of Tuscany, the Roman Campagna, and other coastal plains along the Mediterranean Sea (2135) and the Adriatic Sea (29).

C. **Chief Rivers:** Po, 2633 ; Tiber, Adige, and Arno.

D. **Principal Lakes :** Maggiore, Como.

E. **Islands :** Sicily, 2968 ; Sardinia, 2873.

II. CLIMATE.

The Alps cut off the cold winds from the north. The summers are hot throughout the peninsula ; except in the higher mountain regions the winters become increasingly mild towards the south. Rainfall is usually plentiful.

III. NATURAL RESOURCES.

A. **Rich Soil and Forests.**

B. **Minerals.** With the exception of marble (2097), the mainland of Italy contains little mineral wealth. However, Sardinia provides many metals, principally iron, zinc, and lead ; and Sicily yields sulphur.

C. **Water-power.**

IV. INDUSTRIES.

A. **Agriculture :** Wheat, maize, potatoes, sugar-beet, grapes, olives, oats, beans, rice, barley, rye, lemons, oranges and tomatoes.

B. **Stock Raising:** Sheep, cattle, goats, pigs, horses, mules, and asses.

C. **Mining and Quarrying :** Sulphur, marble, iron, zinc, lead, mercury, and manganese.

D. **Fisheries :** Tunny, sardines, coral.

E. **Manufacturing :** Silk, cotton goods, wines, olive oil, hemp, hats, rubber goods, leather, motor-cars, iron and steel products, pottery, glass, paper, chemicals, sugar, macaroni, soap.

V. CHIEF CITIES.

Naples, 2274 ; Milan, 2170 ; Rome (capital), 2799 ; Turin, 3260 ; Palermo, 2968 ; Genoa, 1429 ; Florence, 1318 ; Bologna, 494 ; Venice, 3310 ; Ravenna, 2747 ; Pisa, 2612.

VI. FORMER ITALIAN POSSESSIONS.

Libya, 1931 ; Eritrea and Italian Somaliland, 1072 (*map*), 1073 ; the Island of Rhodes, 2770 ; Abyssinia (occupied 1936 to 1941), 13. Trieste and the area around it was taken from Italy after the Second World War and placed under Allied military occupation pending its establishment as a free territory under U.N. control.

SAN MARINO.

This is a small independent republic completely surrounded by Italian territory, 2872.

Yugoslavia, Bulgaria, Albania, and Greece

OCCUPYING as they do the Balkan Peninsula (343) and adjacent territory, these four countries are known as the Balkan States. Their history has been one of strife and confusion, much of which can be explained in geographical terms. Their growing commercial importance, and their positions in relation to the Near East and the Soviet Union involved them in intense political intrigues. After the Second World War, with the exception of Greece, they underwent drastic social changes and came within the aegis of the U.S.S.R. Greece was influenced by Britain and U.S.A.

I. YUGOSLAVIA.

This state, newly created after the 1914–18 War, consists of what formerly was Serbia (2922), Montenegro (2219), Bosnia and Herzegovina (528), and other lands on the Adriatic, previously belonging to Austria-Hungary, including **Croatia** and **Slavonia** and most of **Dalmatia** (957). The northern boundary extends into the **Hungarian Plain** (1654).

A. **Physiography, 3438.**
    a. Mountains. All of Yugoslavia, except the northern strip of the Hungarian Plain, is covered with rugged forested highlands and mountains, including the **Dinaric Alps**, which form a link between the Alps proper in the west and the Balkan ranges in the east.
    b. Lowlands. The strip of **Hungarian Plain** includes the valleys of the **Save** and the **Drava** and a rich part of the **Danube valley** (1233).

B. **Climate.** The climate, particularly on the southern mountain slopes, is mild. Extremes of cold are found only in the highest interior ranges. Rainfall is plentiful along the coast and in the foothills to the north, but scanty in some of the enclosed tablelands.

C. **Resources and Products :**
    a. Agriculture : Wheat, barley, oats, maize, potatoes, grapes, rye, sugar-beet, hops, tobacco, fruit (particularly plums), and hay.
    b. Stock Raising : Sheep, goats, and cattle.
    c. Minerals and Mining : Coal, iron, copper, lead, zinc, antimony, manganese, mercury, gold, silver.
    d. Manufacturing : Flour, beer, silk, wines, leather, textiles, carpets, meat-packing, pottery, iron products, cement, and lumber.

D. **Chief Cities :** Belgrade (capital), 408 ; Agram or Zagreb ; Split or Spalato.

II. BULGARIA.

A. **Physiography, 612.** The Balkan Mountains lie across the middle of Bulgaria from west to east. To the north is a lowland plain extending to the boundary, which is mostly formed by the **Danube** (972). South of the Balkan Mountains are highlands surrounding a strip of plain which extends to the **Black Sea** (464).

B. **Climate.** Generally mild with cold winters in the mountains of the interior.

C. **Resources and Products :**
    a. Agriculture : Wheat, maize, barley, rye, tobacco, grapes, fruit, sugar-beet, and rice.
    b. Stock Raising : Sheep, cattle, and goats.
    c. Minerals and Mining : Coal, iron, gold, silver, lead, zinc, manganese, and copper.
    d. Manufacturing : Foodstuffs, leather, perfumes.

D. **Chief Cities :** Sofia (capital), 2997 ; Philippopolis (Plovdiv).

III. ALBANIA.

A. **Physiography, 100.** Rugged mountains encircle a narrow strip of coastal plain on the Adriatic.

B. **Climate.** Extremely mild, except in the highest mountain regions, where the winters are severe.

C. **Resources and Products :**
    a. Agriculture: Wheat, maize, tobacco, olives.
    b. Stock Raising : Sheep, goats, and cattle.
    c. Minerals : Coal, copper, silver, gold, and lead.
    d. Manufacturing : Olive oil and cloth for home use.

D. **Chief Cities :** Tirana (capital) ; Shkodra ; Durazzo.

IV. GREECE.

A. **Physiography, 1517.**
    a. Mountains and Plains. All of Greece is criss-crossed by ranges of low mountains and hills, with small valleys and plains between. The **Pindus Range** (343), extending down from the north-west border, is the most important of the mountain systems.
    b. Coastline. Marked by countless gulfs and peninsulas, among which the most important are the **Gulf of Corinth** and the **Peninsula of Morea.**
    c. Surrounding Islands : Crete, 927 ; Aegean Islands (Sporades and Cyclades), 30 (*map*) ; Ionian Islands, *1518* (*map*).

B. **Climate.** Temperate, with moist winters and dry summers.

C. **Resources and Products :**
    a. Agriculture : Wheat, maize, barley, grapes, currants, olives, oats, tobacco, cotton, oranges, lemons, rice, figs, and nuts.
    b. Stock Raising and Dairy Products : Sheep, cattle, cheese.
    c. Minerals and Mining. Greece is poor in minerals, particularly coal ; the most important are iron and zinc.
    d. Manufacturing : Olive oil, wines, textiles, leather, soap, glass, and paper.

D. **Chief Cities :** Athens (capital), 284, *285* ; Thessaloniki, 3202 ; Piraeus (port of Athens), 284.

TURKEY IN EUROPE. Of its former possessions in Europe, Turkey retains control only of Istanbul and Adrianople (29), with Chatalja and Eastern Thrace, totalling about 9,000 square miles.

Russia

R USSIA (2844), last of the European states to come under the influence of western civilization, belongs as much to Asia as it does to Europe. This Outline deals only with European Russia, the boundaries of which, as a result of the Second World War, were extended westwards to include the former Baltic republics of Estonia, Latvia and Lithuania, Poland east of the "Curzon Line," Petsamo and the Karelian territory of Finland, Bessarabia and the Northern Bukovina (ceded by Rumania), Ruthenia (ceded by Czechoslovakia), and the larger part of East Prussia, *map, 2850*. The regions of Asiatic Russia are treated in the Outline on Asia, 3599.

I. PHYSIOGRAPHY.

A. **Most of Russia is a great Lowland Plain,** 2844, 1233.
    a. The fertile " Black Belt."
    b. Steppes and barren tundras.

B. **Mountains :**
    a. Low chain of Ural Mountains on eastern boundary of Europe, 2844.
    b. Rugged Caucasus Mountains on southern boundary, 732.

C. Rivers, Lakes, and Inland Seas, 464, 712, 1232, 2844.
   a. Volga, the largest river in Europe, 1232.
   b. Lake Ladoga, the largest lake in Europe.
   c. Black Sea, 464 ; Caspian Sea, 712.

II. CLIMATE.

The great interior plains of Russia have a wide variation in temperature between winter and summer, dry winds, and uncertain rainfall. The Russian plains extend from the frozen Arctic Zone to the temperate regions of the south.

III. RESOURCES AND PRODUCTS.

A. Agriculture and Stock Raising, 931, 2844-45.
   a. Great areas of extremely fertile soil.
   b. Chief Crops : Wheat, rye, oats, barley, cotton, potatoes, flax, hemp, sugar-beet, to-bacco, and rice.
   c. Livestock: Sheep, cattle, horses, pigs, goats.

B. Forests and Timber Products. Lumber, wood-pulp, tar, turpentine, and resin.

C. Fish and Fisheries. Chief products of Fisheries are Salmon and Sturgeon (3104), the latter yielding Caviare and Isinglass, 1760.

D. Minerals and Mining. Coal, platinum, petroleum, iron, manganese, cobalt, sulphur, mercury or quicksilver, copper, zinc, gold, silver, iridium, lead, asphalt, peat, and precious stones.

E. Manufacturing. Among the principal manufactures in normal times are iron and steel products, machinery, cement, textiles, furs, hides, chemicals, paper, sugar, and shoes.

IV. TRADE AND TRANSPORT.

A. River and Canal Transportation, 2844.

B. Importance of Black Sea and Caspian, 464, 717.

C. Railways. There are over 30,000 miles of railway in operation in European Russia.

V. MAIN DIVISIONS.

The U.S.S.R. (Union of Soviet Socialist Republics) consists of 16 Union Republics, of which seven are entirely within Europe, one (the R.S.F.S.R.) is divided between Europe and Asia, three are on the borderland between the continents, and five are entirely within Asia, map, 2850.

A. The R.S.F.S.R. (Russian Socialist Federal Soviet Republic), the largest of the Republics, includes the Eastern half of European Russia.
   a. Products : in the North, reindeer, furs, fish, timber ; in the Centre, cereals, cattle ; in the South, wine, tobacco, cotton. Coal, oil, iron, copper, precious metals and stones, salt, etc. are found throughout the Republic, especially in the Urals.
   b. Chief Cities : Moscow (capital), 2233 ; Gorki, Rostov, Stalingrad, 3073 ; Grozny, Taganrog, Magnetogorsk.

B. Ukraine, 3273, in the South-west of European Russia, was increased by the Polish Ukraine, Northern Bukovina and Ruthenia after the Second World War. The area was devastated during the war.
   a. Products : coal (Donetz basin), iron (Krivoi Rog), chemicals in the South ; sugar beet in the central steppes ; cereals and cattle.
   b. Chief Cities : Kiev (capital), 1856 ; Kharkov, 1854 ; Odessa, 2420 ; Dnepropetrovsk, Stalino, Lwow.

C. White Russia (Byelorussia), in the western half of European Russia.
   a. Products : where the marshes are drained agriculture is pursued ; wood and engineering products.
   b. Chief Cities : Minsk (capital), Vitebsk, Gomel.

D. Moldavia, in the S.W., adjoins Rumania, which ceded Bessarabia to it in 1940.
   a. Products : wine, fruit, vegetables.
   b. Capital : Kishinev.

E. Estonia, 1226.
   a. Products : rye, wheat, barley, potatoes, sugar-beet ; livestock ; wood products, boats, textiles.
   b. Capital : Tallinn.

F. Latvia, 1899.
   a. Products : agricultural, similar to Estonia's ; ships, timber products, chemicals, textiles.
   b. Capital : Riga, 2779.

G. Lithuania, 1967.
   a. Products : agricultural, similar to Estonia's ; dairying; timber and wooden goods.
   b. Chief Cities : Vilnius (Vilna, capital) ; Kaunas (Kovno).

H. Karelo-Finnish S.S.R., in the N.W., bordering Finland.
   a. Products : timber, wood-pulp ; granite.
   b. Capital : Petrozavodsk.

I. Borderland Republics. For the republics of Azerbaijan, Georgia and Armenia, see Asiatic Russia, in the Outline on Asia, p. 3600.

AFRICA

AFRICA (65) is the second in size of the continents, ranking next to Asia. It has been known to civilized people ever since the days of the ancient Egyptians, yet it is today the most backward in civilization. By far the greater part of the continent lies in the tropics, and, in addition to the oppressive heat, a host of tropical diseases besets the white man. The Negro population of the interior lives in a state of primitive savagery. Territorial rivalries between the European nations themselves have complicated the problem of civilization, so that the task of developing the natural wealth of the Dark Continent has made no more than a beginning.

I. POSITION AND AREA.

Africa extends an equal distance north and south of the Equator. With its area of 11,500,000 square miles it is about three times as large as Europe and contains one-fifth of the globe's land surface.

II. PHYSIOGRAPHY.

(See Colour Plate facing page 69).

A. The great mass of Africa consists of a High Tableland surrounded by narrow Coastal Plains.

B. Former land connexion with Europe, 3030.

C. **Mountains and Highlands.** Most of the higher mountain ranges are on or near the sea coast.

   a. **Atlas Mountains** in the North-west, 2231.

   b. **Highlands of the East.** These include the Tableland of Nubia, the Abyssinian Mountains (*14*), and the East African Ranges (*1073*, *map*). The latter, mostly of volcanic origin, contain Kilimanjaro, the highest peak on the continent, the " Great Rift Valley," and Ruwenzori.

   c. **South African Highlands** (*map*), 3015.

D. **Lowlands.** Congo Lowland, 887; narrow Coastal Lowlands.

E. **Forests, Grasslands, and Deserts :**

   a. Great forests of Central Africa, 888.

   b. Savanna region of the Sudan north of the great forests, 69, 3109.

   c. Veldt region to the South, 3013.

   d. Sahara Desert, the largest arid waste in the world, **2859**. The Libyan Desert, 1931, the Nubian Desert, and the Arabian Desert are eastern continuations of the Sahara.

   e. Kalahari Desert in South Africa, 69, *map*, 3015.

F. **Chief Rivers and Lakes :**

   a. Nile, the only large African river flowing into the Mediterranean, 1095, **2370**.

   b. Congo and its vast basin, **887**.

   c. Niger, **2367** ; Zambezi and Victoria Falls, 3441.

   d. Lake Chad, Victoria Nyanza, 1072 ; Lake Tanganyika, 1072 ; Albert Nyanza, Albert Edward Nyanza, and Lake Nyasa, 1072.

G. **Coastline is Unbroken—Few Natural Harbours.** Mediterranean Coast (*map*), *2136* ; Red Sea Coast, 2758; Indian Ocean, 1718; Atlantic Ocean, **290** ; Cape of Good Hope, 695.

H. **Islands off the Coast of Africa :**

   a. Madagascar, the only large island, 2051.

   b. Small Islands in the Atlantic : Madeira Islands, **2051** ; Canary Islands, 690; Cape Verde Islands, **698** ; Ascension, 290.

c. Small Islands in the Indian Ocean : Zanzibar and Pemba, **3441** ; Mauritius, **2121** ; Comoro Islands, Réunion, and Seychelles.

III. CLIMATE.

A. **Hot Equatorial Climate** modified in places by altitude, 840.

B. **Climate of the Mediterranean Coast,** 117, 2231.

C. **Desert Climate,** 840.

D. **Bracing Climate of South Africa,** 3013.

E. **Rainfall,** 2741. *See* Colour Plate facing page 69. Reasons for lack of rain in the Sahara, **2859**.

IV. MINERAL RESOURCES OF AFRICA.

A. **In North Africa :** petroleum, copper, antimony, iron, lead, zinc, sulphur, silver, gold, manganese, phosphates, mercury.

B. **In East Africa :** coal, iron, lead, copper.

C. **In South Africa :** gold, diamonds, copper, coal, iron, tin, lead, silver.

V. VEGETABLE AND ANIMAL LIFE.
(*See* Colour Plates between pages 72–73).

A. **Typical Vegetation of Africa :** Monkey-bread Tree or Baobab, 69 ; Mangrove, **2088** ; Ebony, **1076** ; Cypress, **952** ; Lotus, 2027 ; Papyrus Plant, **2500** ; Elephant Grass, Date Palm, **978**; Oil Palm, 2485 ; Bamboo Palm, **353** ; Groundnut, **1549** ; Banana, 354.

B. **Typical Animals of Africa :** Aardvark, **9** ; Leopard, **1927** ; Lion, **1959** ; Elephant, **1140** ; Hippopotamus, **1628** ; Rhinoceros, **2770** ; Monkey, **2207** ; Baboon and Mandrill ; Chimpanzee, **805** ; Gorilla, **1487** ; Buffalo, **602** ; Camel, **669** ; Giraffe, **1464** ; Wild Ass, **273** ; Zebra, **3442** ; Eland, Springbok, Gnu, and other Antelopes, 71, **176** ; Hartebeest ; Wart Hog, **3341** ; Crocodile, **931** ; Cobra, **859** ; Horned Viper, 3325 ; Ostrich, **2456**; Guinea Fowl, **1554** ; Tsetse Fly, 68, **3252** ; White Ants or Termites, 3188.

Divisions of Africa

I. NORTHERN AFRICA.

A. **Egypt, 1095** (Independent sovereign state).

   a. **Chief Products :** cotton, wheat, barley, maize, millet, rice, sugar, clover, petroleum, cotton and silk goods, morocco leather, pottery.

   b. **Chief Cities :** Cairo, **653** ; Alexandria, **109** ; Port Said, Tanta, Assiut, Suez, 3110; Damietta.

B. **Anglo-Egyptian Sudan, 3110** (British Condominium).

   a. **Chief Products :** gum arabic, ivory, cotton, ostrich feathers, palm nuts, dates, sesame, hides, skins, and gold.

   b. **Chief Cities :** Khartum, **1855**, and Omdurman.

C. **Libya, 1931** (formerly Italian ; status undecided).

   a. **Chief Products :** Dates, olives, lemons, figs, grapes, cereals, saffron, almonds, bananas, barley, cattle, sponges.

   b. **Chief Cities :** Tripoli and Benghazi.

D. **Tunisia, 3254** (French Associated State).

   a. **Chief Products :** olives, wheat, barley, oats, grapes, dates, almonds, oranges, lemons, pistachios, alfa-grass, henna, cork, sheep, goats, cattle, sardines, tunny, lead, zinc, iron and manganese.

   b. **Chief Cities :** Tunis; Sfax ; Susa ; Kairwan.

E. **Algeria, 117** (French Government-General).

   a. **Chief Products :** wheat, barley, oats, maize, potatoes, artichokes, beans, peas, tomatoes, flax, silk, tobacco, wine, tropical fruits, olive oil, cotton, cork, sheep, goats, cattle, sardines, tunny, iron, lead, zinc, and coal.

   b. **Chief Cities :** Algiers, *118*; Oran ; Constantine.

F. **Morocco, 2230** (French, Spanish, and Neutral).

   a. **Chief Products :** barley, wheat, beans, oats, maize, linseed, olives, oranges, lemons, dates, almonds, figs, sardines, tunny, sheep, goats, cattle, horses, iron, and silver.

b. **Chief Cities:** Morocco or Marrakesh ; Fez, 2231 ; Tangier, **3151.**

G. **Rio de Oro and Adrar** (Spanish), 3366.
  a. **Products :** This colony is virtually desert land, without important products.
  b. **Capital :** Villa Cisneros.

II. EAST AFRICA.

A. **Eritrea,** 1072, **1222** (formerly Italian). Chief products : livestock, meat, hides, butter, pearls and mother of pearl, vegetable ivory, salt, gold. Chief cities : Asmara ; Massowah.

B. **Somaliland,** 1073.
  a. **Somalia** (formerly It. Somaliland). Chief industries : cattle, agriculture. Chief city : Mogadisho.
  b. **British Somaliland.** Chief products : skins, hides, gum, resin, cattle, sheep. Chief city : Berbera.
  c. **French Somaliland,** 1073. Chief products : coffee, ivory, hides, skins, salt. Chief city : Djibouti.

C. **Abyssinia,** 13, 1073 (or Ethiopia).
  a. **Resources and Products :** hides, skins, coffee, wax, ivory, civet, barley, millet, wheat, tobacco, iron, gold, coal, silver, sulphur, timber, and rubber.
  b. **Chief City :** Addis Ababa.

D. **British East Africa, 1072.**
  a. **Kenya Colony,** 1072. Resources and products : rice, coconuts, cotton, ground-nuts, casava, sugar-cane, bananas, wheat, barley, maize, flax, coffee, sisal-hemp, livestock, timber. Chief cities : Mombasa ; Nairobi. (capital).
  b. **Uganda** (protectorate), 1072. Resources and products : cotton, coffee, para rubber, cocoa, oil-seeds, timber, bananas, ivory. Chief cities : Entebbe (British capital), Buganda (native capital).
  c. **Tanganyika Territory,** 1072, 3939 (under U.N. trusteeship). Resources and products : coco-palms, coffee, rubber, sugar, cotton, tea, ground-nuts, cardamom, sisal-hemp, livestock, and timber. Chief city : Dar-es-Salaam (capital).
  d. **Islands of Zanzibar and Pemba,** *map, 1073,* **3441.** Products : cloves, coconuts (copra), hides, pottery, coir-fibre, rope, soap, oil, jewelry, mats. Chief city : Zanzibar.

E. **Nyasaland** (British protectorate), 2772. Resources and products : cotton, tobacco, coffee, tea, livestock. Chief trade centre : Port Herald.

F. **Mozambique or Portuguese East Africa,** 1073.
  a. **Chief Products :** sugar, coconuts, rubber, beeswax, ivory, gold, coal.
  b. **Chief Cities :** Mozambique ; Lourenço Marquez.

III. WEST AFRICA.

Products typical of Western Africa **(3366)** are mahogany, ebony, ivory, rubber, ground-nuts, manioc, yams, gum, palm-oil and kernels, dyewoods, hides, skins and feathers.

A. **French West Africa and the Sahara,** 3367.
  a. **Senegal.** Chief cities : St. Louis (capital) ; Dakar.

b. **French Guinea.** Chief city : Konakry.
c. **Ivory Coast.** Chief cities : Adidjan (capital) ; Grand Bassam.
d. **Dahomey.** Chief city : Porto Novo.
e. **French Sudan,** 3879. Chief cities : Bamako (capital) ; Timbuktu.
f. **Togo** (under U.N. trusteeship). Chief cities : Lome ; Anecho.
g. **Mauritania and Colony of the Niger :** desert land.

B. **British West Africa,** 3366.
  a. **Nigeria** (colony and protectorate). Chief city : Lagos.
  b. **Cameroon** (under U.N. trusteeship). Chief city : Victoria.
  c. **Gambia.** Chief city : Bathurst.
  d. **Sierra Leone** (colony and protectorate). Chief city : Freetown.
  e. **Gold Coast** (includes part of former German Togoland under U.N. trusteeship). Chief city : Accra.

C. **Spanish West Africa,** 3368 : Rio Muni and Fernando Po.

D. **Portuguese Guinea,** 3368. Chief city : Bolama.

E. **Liberia,** 3366 (independent Negro Republic under protection of United States). Chief city : Monrovia.

F. **Angola,** 3368 (Portuguese).
  a. **Resources and Products :** coffee, rubber, wax, coconuts, ivory, fish, tobacco, petroleum, asphalt, copper, iron, salt, gold.
  b. **Chief Cities:** Loanda (capital) ; Benguela.

IV. MIDDLE AFRICA.

A. **French Equatorial Africa,** 888.
  a. **Products and Resources :** rubber, palm-oil, ivory, coffee, livestock, copper, zinc, lead, and wild forest products similar to those listed under West Africa.
  b. **Chief Ports :** Port Gentil ; Libreville.

B. **Cameroon** (French, under U.N. trusteeship), 672. Chief products : coffee, tobacco, palm-oil, ivory.

C. **Congo State** (Belgian), 887.
  a. **Products and Resources :** rubber, palm-nuts, palm-oil, cocoa, ivory, coffee, rice, cotton, tobacco, cattle, uranium, gold, diamonds, copper, coal, iron, tin and manganese.
  b. **Chief Cities:** Boma (capital) ; Leopoldville.

V. SOUTH AFRICA (British).

A. **Basutoland,** 3015. Products and resources : wool, wheat, maize, kaffir-corn, livestock, iron, copper, coal. Chief city : Maseru (capital).

B. **Bechuanaland** (protectorate), 3016. Chief products : cattle, sheep, goats, maize, kaffir-corn, gold, silver. Chief cities : Francistown ; Mafeking.

C. **Rhodesia, 2771.**
  a. **Products and Resources :** cattle, sheep, goats, dairy-products, hides and skins, gold, silver, copper, zinc, lead, coal, diamonds, maize, cotton, wheat, fruits, rubber, timber.
  b. **Chief Cities:** Salisbury (capital of Southern Rhodesia), 2865 ; Bulawayo, Livingstone (capital of Northern Rhodesia).

D. **Swaziland** (protectorate), 3016. Products and resources : tin, gold, cattle, sheep, goats, pigs, horses, tobacco. Capital and chief town, Mbabane.

E. **South-West Africa** (administered by the Union of S. Africa), **3029.**
  a. **Products and Resources :** diamonds, copper, tin, marble, cattle, sheep, goats, maize, wheat.
  b. **Capital and Chief City :** Windhuk.

F. **Union of South Africa, 3013.** This includes the provinces of Cape of Good Hope, 697 ; Natal, 2279 ; Zululand, 3448 ; Transvaal, **3239** ; Orange Free State, **2444.**
  a. **Chief Products and Resources :**
    1. Agricultural products : wheat, barley, oats, kaffir-corn, potatoes, tobacco, cotton, sugar.
    2. Livestock and dairy products : butter, cheese, sheep, goats, cattle, pigs, horses, mules, asses, ostriches, wool, mohair, hides, skins, ostrich feathers.

3. **Minerals :** gold, diamonds, coal, copper.
4. **Manufactures :** leather, tobacco, dynamite, soap, rope, wine, furniture, vehicles.
  b. **Chief Cities :** Cape Town (capital of Cape Province), 697 ; Kimberley, Port Elizabeth, Pietersmaritzburg (capital of Natal), Pretoria (capital of Transvaal), 2682 ; Johannesburg, 1833 : Bloemfontein (capital of Orange Free State).

VI. MADAGASCAR (French).
A. **Resources and Products, 2051.**
  a. **Agriculture :** rice, sugar, coffee, manioc, cotton, vanilla, tobacco, cloves, rubber.
  b. **Mineral Resources :** gold, iron, copper, lead, silver, zinc, nickel, sulphur, graphite, and coal.
  c. **Manufacturing :** silk, cotton goods, straw hats, metal and food products.

C. **Chief Cities :** Antananarivo (capital), *2051*, Tamatave.

ASIA

A SIA (263), the giant of the continents, presents many extreme contrasts. It contains Mt. Everest, the highest peak in the world, and the Dead Sea basin, the lowest valley —more than 1,000 feet below ocean level. It has the most extensive tablelands and the greatest area of lowland plains ; the bleakest and most barren desert and the most fertile and densely populated farm lands ; regions of the severest cold and of the greatest heat. Asia is the home of more than half the human race, and out of Asia have come so many great contributions to human progress that it is often called " the Mother of Civilization." The great variety of climate, the almost impassable desert, and the mountain barriers account in great measure for the sharp racial distinctions which exist upon the continent. White, yellow, and brown peoples dwell there today, and some scientists believe that the black and red races of the world likewise originated there.

I. POSITION AND AREA.
The northern tip of Siberia lies nearly 600 miles inside the Arctic Circle, while the southern tip of the Malay Peninsula almost touches the Equator. Connected by land in the west to Europe and Africa, the continent reaches in the extreme northeast to within 50 miles of America. One-third of the land surface of the globe is included in Asia.

II. PHYSIOGRAPHY.
A. **Mountains and Interior Plateaux.**
  a. Plateau of Asia Minor or Anatolia, and Taurus Mountains, **271.**
  b. Elburz Mountains and Hindu Kush, marking northern boundary of the Iranian Plateau.
  c. Great Pamir, the meeting-place of the Hindu Kush, Karakoram and Tien Shan Ranges, 263.
  d. Himalaya Mountains, forming a vast wall between the Central Highlands and the plains of India, **1626.** Mount Everest, the highest mountain in the world, **1243.**
  e. Plateau of Tibet between Himalayas and Kuenlun Mountains, 806, 3208.
  f. Plateau of Eastern or Chinese Turkistan between Tien Shan and Kuenlun Mountains, 3267.
  g. Gobi Desert and Plateau of Mongolia between Altai, Yablonoi, and Khingan Mountains, 807, 2204.

B. **Detached Ranges :**
  a. Caucasus and Ural Mountains on boundary of Europe, 732, 3297.

  b. Volcanic Ranges on Pacific side extending through Kamchatka, Sakhalin Island, the Kurile Islands, the islands of Japan, the Korean Peninsula, and Formosa.

C. **Lowland Plains and worn-down Tablelands :**
  a. Arabian Plateau and Plains of Iraq, 195, 1743.
  b. Plains of India and the Deccan, 1691.
  c. Highlands and Plains of Indo-China and Siam, 1718, 2963.
  d. Lowlands of Eastern China and Manchuria, 807, 2085.
  e. Great Siberian Plains and Siberian Highlands, 2966.
  f. Lowlands of Western or Russian Turkistan, 3267.

D. **Chief Rivers and Lakes.**
  a. Rivers flowing into the Arctic Ocean : Ob, Yenisei, and Lena.
  b. Into the Pacific : Amur, Hwang, and Yangtze.
  c. Into the Bay of Bengal and Indian Ocean : Brahmaputra, Ganges, and Irrawaddy.
  d. Into the Arabian Sea and Persian Gulf : Indus, Tigris, and Euphrates.
  e. Lakes and Inland Seas : Black Sea, **464** ; Caspian Sea, **712** ; Sea of Aral with its two tributaries, Syr-Daria and Amu, 203 ; Lake Balkash, and Lake Baikal.

III. CLIMATE.
A. Great variety of Asiatic climate. (*See plate facing* 265.)

B. High mountain ranges and interior plateaux suffer from extremes of heat and cold and from lack of well-distributed rain. The great " Desert Belt " stretching over from Africa.

C. Siberia has dry steppes, frozen tundras, and rain-soaked eastern coast.

D. Tropical climate with heavy rains in the south and south-east.

E. Tremendous importance of monsoon winds to southern Asia.

IV. MINERAL RESOURCES.

Almost every known mineral is found in Asia, but there has been comparatively little development of these resources. *See* under the separate countries of Asia.

V. VEGETATION AND ANIMAL LIFE.

A. Typical Plants of Asia.
> a. Siberia. Falls into three zones : (1) the Arctic tundras, where little grows except moss and berries ; (2) the forest lands, where there is enough rain to support growths of pine, fir, larch, birch, willow, and poplar ; and (3) the dry steppes, where grasses are the prevailing vegetation.
> b. Central Highlands and Deserts. Except in rare sheltered valleys, desert oases, or the southern slopes of a few ranges, little vegetation of importance is found here.
> c. Temperate Slopes of the Himalayas. The southern sides of the great mountain barrier support a dense vegetation of trees and undergrowth. Typical forms are the rhododendron magnolia, deodar, bamboo, and cane.
> d. Plains of India. Typical forms here are the babul, mango, banyan, plantain, and betel palm.
> e. Tropical South. Typical forms are teak, sandalwood, satinwood, ironwood, ebony, rosewood, bamboo, orchids, catechu plant, and innumerable spice plants.
> f. Eastern Coast. Coastal plains of China are so densely inhabited and so closely cultivated that there is virtually no wild vegetation.

B. Typical Animals of Asia.
> a. Northern Zone : reindeer, 2760 ; polar bear and brown bear, 385 ; seal, 2912 ; wolf, 3400 ; fox, 1355 ; badger, 337 ; ermine, 1222 ; mink, 2186 ; sable-marten, 2111 ; otter, 2459 ; grey squirrel, 3071 ; hare, 1578.
> b. Central and Southern Zone : monkeys, 2207 ; elephant, 1140 ; rhinoceros, 2770 ; tiger, 3211 ; lion, 1959 ; leopard, 1927 ; Himalayan bear and sun bear, 385 ; hyena, 1675 ; jackal, 1785 ; wild dog, 1027 ; wild ass, 273 ; camel, 669 ; yak, 3433 ; buffalo, 602 ; ibex and other wild goats, 1478, 1679 ; many species of wild sheep, 2940 ; antelopes, 176 ; and deer, 984 ; wild boar, 480 ; mongoose, 2207 ; squirrel, 3071 ; bats, 370 ; hornbill, 1643 ; pheasant, 2565 ; peacock, 2532 ; weaver-bird, 3360 ; crocodile, 931 ; cobra, 859 ; python, 2710 ; adjutant, 27.

Asiatic Russia

THE Asiatic portion of the U.S.S.R. comprises the Eastern half of the R.S.F.S.R. from the Urals to Vladivostok on the Pacific Ocean, five Union Republics, three Republics on the Europe-Asia borders and lands taken from Japan after the Second World War. Every type of climate and product is found, and much development of mineral resources was proceeding during and after the Second World War when so much of European Russia was occupied or devasted by battle.

I. PHYSIOGRAPHY.

A. Siberian Plains—divided into Arctic tundras, central timber lands, and southern steppes, 2966.

B. Plains and Deserts of Western Turkistan.

C. Mountains and Highlands :
> a. Ural Mountains on the boundary between European and Asiatic Russia, 3297.
> b. Eastern Highlands ; Stanovoi Mountains.
> c. Tien Shan, Pamir, Hindu Kush, and Elburz on Southern Border.

D. Rivers : Ob, Yenisei, Lena, and Amur.

E. Lakes and Inland Seas : Caspian Sea, 717 ; Sea of Aral, 203 ; Lake Baikal ; Lake Balkash.

II. RESOURCES AND PRODUCTS.

A. Agriculture : wheat, rye, oats, barley, vegetables.

B. Stock Raising and Dairying : cattle, sheep, camels, eggs, butter.

C. Timber and Timber Products.

D. Minerals and Mining : coal, iron, petroleum, copper, lead, silver, gold, platinum, nickel, graphite, tin, zinc, salt, mica, precious stones, and radio-active ores.

E. Fur Industry : seal, fox, ermine, mink, sable-marten, otter, grey squirrel.

F. Manufacturing : rugs, textiles, leather.

III. THE R.S.F.S.R.

A. Western Siberian Region.
> a. Products : coal, grain, livestock, timber.
> b. Chief Towns : Novosibirsk (capital), Tomsk, Barnaul, Biisk.

B. Eastern Siberian Region.
> a. Products : coal, mica, non-ferrous metals ; timber, furs, gold.
> b. Capital : Irkutsk.

C. Far Eastern Region.
> a. Products : wheat, soya beans, cattle ; gold, silver, iron ; fish, firs, timber.
> b. Chief Towns : Khabarovsk, Vladivostok.

D. Yakutsk A.S.S.R.
> a. Products : furs, gold, silver, lead, coal, salt ; livestock.
> b. Capital : Yakutsk.

E. Buriat-Mongol A.S.S.R.
> a. Products : cattle, leather, poultry, honey, furs, glass.
> b. Chief Town : Udinsk.

F. Tuva A.P. Formerly the nominally independent republic of Tannu-Tuva, this became an autonomous province of the R.S.F.S.R. in 1944.
> a. Products : cattle, gold, asbestos.
> b. Capital : Kysylchoto (Russ. Krasny), formerly called Khem-Belder.

IV. BORDERLAND REPUBLICS.

A. Azerbaijan.
- a. Products : grain, cotton, wine, tobacco, silk, cattle, oil.
- b. Chief Town : Baku, 341.

B. Georgia, 1443.
- a. Products : wine, tobacco, tea, timber ; manganese, coal, oil.
- b. Chief Towns : Tbilisi (Tiflis), Signakh, Telav.

C. Armenia, 237.
- a. Products : cereals, wine, cotton, soap, canned food, carpets, chemicals.
- b. Chief Town : Erevan.

V. REPUBLICS IN CENTRAL ASIA.

A. Turkmenistan, 3257.
- a. Products : cotton, wool, silk, Astrakhan fur, carpets ; horses, sheep ; oil, salt, sulphur ; soda.
- b. Chief Towns : Ashkhabad (capital), Merv, Leninsk, Kerki.

B. Uzbekistan, 3267.
- a. Products : cotton, lucerne, rice, grapes, apricots ; coal, oil, gold.
- b. Chief Towns : Tashkend (capital), Bokhara, Khiva, Namanghan, Samarkand.

C. Tajikstan, 3267.
- a. Products : cereals, cotton, fruit, grapes ; cattle and sheep ; coal, lead, zinc, oil, radium, mica, sulphur.
- b. Chief Town : Stalinabad.

D. Kirghiz, 3267.
- a. Products : sugar, hemp, cotton ; sheep, cattle ; coal, oil, gold, silver.
- b. Capital : Frunze.

E. Kazakhstan. This republic includes the remaining districts of Turkistan, and stretches from the Volga to China.
- a. Products : copper and other metals, coal, oil.
- b. Chief Towns : Alma-Ata (capital) ; Karaganda.

VI. OTHER RUSSIAN LANDS IN ASIA.

A. Sakhalin : an island to the North of Japan ; the northern half was a Russian possession from 1857, the southern part (Karafuto) was at first Japanese, then Russian from 1875 to 1905, then Japanese until taken by Russia in 1945.
- a. Products : fish ; coal, oil ; timber.
- b. Chief Town : Alexandrovsk.

B. The Kurile Islands (Chishima), between Japan and Kamchatka. Acquired by Russia in 1945.
Products : fish—cod, herring ; seal.

Japan

LESS than a century ago Japan (**1795**) was an isolated state, having apparently no interest in the outside world. Its people pursued agricultural and primitive crafts, unmindful of the march of western civilization. Then, as if by magic, all this was transformed. Within the span of one man's lifetime, Japan became a power in world politics and in world commerce. The Japanese built up manufacturing industries, developed foreign commerce, emigrated in large numbers to foreign lands. Japan built a powerful navy and organized a large and efficient standing army. A victorious war with Russia, an alliance with Great Britain, and a strategic position during the First World War extended her empire. The annexation of Manchuria and the invasion of China followed, and in 1940 Japan challenged U.S.A. and the Allies for the hegemony of Asia. Her subsequent downfall in the Second World War saw the dissolution of her empire and her reduction to impotence in world affairs.

I. PHYSIOGRAPHY.

A. Volcanic Mountains.
- a. Most prominent peak Mount Fujiyama, 1795.
- b. Earthquakes, 1069.

B. Important Lowlands, 1797.

C. Broken Coastlines provide many good Harbours, 1796.

II. NATURAL RESOURCES AND PRODUCTS.

A. Agriculture : Rice, tea, wheat, barley, rye, tobacco, vegetables, bamboo.

B. Mining and Minerals : copper, iron, petroleum, sulphur, gold, silver, kaolin clay, coal (abundant but of low quality).

C. Forests and Forest Products.

D. Fresh and Salt Water Fisheries : sturgeon, mackerel, salmon, flounder, halibut, shad, herring, oysters.

E. Manufacturing : cotton goods, silk, woollens, iron and steel products, matches, toys, pottery, glassware, lacquer-ware, paper, camphor, art objects, ink, machinery, and chemicals.

III. CHIEF CITIES.

Tokyo (capital), **3221** ; Osaka, **2454** ; Kobe, Kyoto, **1874** ; Nagoya, **2271** ; Yokohama, **3435**.

IV. FORMER POSSESSIONS.

A. Korea (northern half occupied by Russia from 1945 ; southern occupied by Americans but independent as republic from 1948, with American aid), **1872**. Products : rice, wheat, beans, tobacco, cotton, livestock, gold, copper, iron, coal. Chief city, Seoul.

B. Formosa. Restored to China. See Outline on China.

C. South Sakhalin. Restored to Russia. See Outline on Asiatic Russia.

D. Other Former Possessions : Kurile Islands taken by Russia in 1945 (see Outline on Asiatic Russia) and Nansei (Ryukyu) Islands ; Marianas, Pelew, Caroline, Marshall Islands (in American occupation) ; Kwangtung (territory in Manchuria), restored to China.

China

CHINA (807) has an area larger than that of the United States, Mexico, and Central America put together ; and its population is almost as great as the combined population of North America, South America, and Africa. Yet the power latent in this vast land and its countless people is for the most part lost through lack of organization. For long there were signs of national feeling in China, aroused largely by fourteen years of struggle against Japan ; but the successful conclusion of that conflict saw China again plunged into disorder by civil war. (*Map*, 808.)

I. DIVISIONS OF GREATER CHINA.

China proper occupies the south-eastern corner of the country. The other main divisions are Mongolia (2204) in the north, Sinkiang including Chinese Turkistan (3267) in the west, and Tibet (3208) in the south-west. Manchuria (2085), in the north-east, was the Japanese puppet state of Manchukuo from 1932 to 1945 and afterwards fell under Russian influence.

II. PHYSIOGRAPHY.

A. Plains of China and Manchuria. Rich " loess " soil.

B. Mountains and Plateaux.
 a. Khingan Mountains of Manchuria and Mongolia, 2204 (*map*).
 b. Altai Mountains and the Plateau of Mongolia, including the Gobi Desert, 2204 (*map*).
 c. Tien Shan and Kuenlun Mountains enclosing the Plateau of Chinese Turkistan.
 d. Plateau of Tibet bordered on the South by the Himalayas.

C. Rivers : Yantze, Hwang, Amur, Si-kiang.

D. Island of Hainan, 808 (*map*).

III. RESOURCES AND PRODUCTS.

A. Agriculture : Rice, wheat, barley, maize, millet, sugar, indigo, tobacco, soya beans, tea, ginseng, bamboo, cotton.

B. Livestock : Pigs, cattle, buffaloes, sheep.

C. Fisheries.

D. Minerals and Mining : Coal, iron, petroleum, copper, tin, antimony, gold, silver, lead, bismuth.

E. Silk Industry and pearl fishing.

F. Manufacturing : Textiles, pottery, and porcelain ; rugs, lacquer-ware, paper, pig bristles.

G. Transport : There are few railways in China, but the network of rivers and canals, including the Grand Canal, is very important to commerce.

IV. CHIEF CITIES.

A. China Proper, 807. Peking (Peiping), 2536 ; Shanghai, 2937 ; Canton, 693 ; Tientsin, 3211 ; Nanking, 2273 ; Foochow, 1335 ; Hankow, 1573 ; Hangchow, 1573.

B. Kwantung. Dairen, Port Arthur.

C. Manchuria, 2085. Changchun (later Hsinkiang, former capital), Mukden, Harbin.

D. Mongolia, 2204. Urga.

E. Sinkiang, including Chinese Turkistan, 3267. Urumchi (capital), Yarkand, Khotan, Kashgar.

F. Tibet, 3208. Lhasa.

V. POSSESSIONS OF FOREIGN COUNTRIES ON CHINESE COAST.

A. Hong Kong, 1639 (British). Chief city, Victoria (commonly called Hong Kong).

B. Macao (Portuguese).

Note: The former French leased territory of Kwangchow was restored to China in 1945.

VI. FORMOSA (TAIWAN).

This island off the Chinese coast was restored to China in 1945, after being a Japanese possession since 1895.

A. Products : Rice, tea, sugar, sweet potatoes ; camphor, coal ; fish, livestock.

B. Capital. Taipei.

Indo-China and Malay Peninsula

THE peninsula of Indo-China (1718) is divided into the Federation of Indo-China, comprising the Viet-Nam Republic and other Indo-Chinese states within the French Union, in the east ; Kingdom of Siam (2963) in the centre, extending down to Malay Peninsula (2069) and a narrow strip of Burma in the west.

I. PHYSIOGRAPHY.

Northern highlands spread like a fork down the east and west coasts, enclosing central lowlands and narrow coastal plains.

II. PRODUCTS AND RESOURCES.

A. Agriculture : Rice, rubber, maize, tobacco, tropical fruits, sago, sugar-cane, tapioca, spices, tea, coffee, cotton.

B. Forests : Ebony, rosewood, teakwood, ironwood, rattan.

C. Minerals and Mining : Tin, coal, tungsten, gold, lead, iron, copper, zinc, precious stones.

III. POLITICAL DIVISIONS.

A. The Federation of Indo-China, within French Union, 1718 : Viet-Nam Republic, consisting of Tonking, Annam and Cochin-China, 3323 ; Cambodia, 664 ; and Laos. Chief Cities : Hanoi, Saigon, Cholon, Pnom Penh, and Binh-Dinh.

B. Siam, 2963 (Independent). Capital and chief city : Bangkok (355).

C. Malayan Federation, 2069. Capital : Kuala Lumpur.

D. Singapore Colony, 2069 (British). Chief city : Singapore, 2974.

India and Pakistan

THE sub-continent of India (1691) is the home of a population almost as great as China's, and of a civilization more ancient than that of Europe. It consists of four distinct geographical areas; the Himalayan mountain and hill regions in the north; the river plains of the Indus, Ganges and Lower Brahmaputra; the Deccan plateau; and the southern hills known as the Eastern and Western Ghats. In 1947 British India was partitioned into India, 1691, and Pakistan, 2479.

I. PHYSIOGRAPHY.
A. Mountains and Plateaux :
  a. Himalaya Mountains and Hindu Kush on northern border, 1626.
  b. Baluchistan Highlands in the extreme west, 352.
  c. Deccan Tableland in the south, surrounded by the Vindhya Mountains and the Eastern and Western Ghats.
B. Plains of Hindustan between northern mountains and Deccan.
C. Rivers : Indus, 1721 ; Ganges, 1417 ; Brahmaputra.

II. CLIMATE.
A. Tropical in southern half.
B. Dry, with cold winters, in north.
C. Moist and cold in Himalayan region.
D. Immense importance of monsoon rains (S.W. in June, N.E. in Madras area in autumn), 1692.

III. RESOURCES AND PRODUCTS.
A. Agriculture : millet, rice, wheat, cotton, flax, jute, sugar-cane, tea, indigo, mustard, tobacco.
B. Live-stock : cattle, buffaloes, sheep, goats.
C. Forests and Timber : teak and sandalwood.
D. Minerals and Mining : coal, gold, oil, manganese, salt, lead, tungsten, mica, precious stones.
E. Manufacturing : cotton, silk, jute, sugar, shawls, rugs, lacquer-ware, leather, opium, hemp.

IV. MAIN DIVISIONS AND CHIEF CITIES
A. India (independent republic within the British Commonwealth) is a Union of 27 States.
  a. State of Assam. Chief city, Shillong.
  b. State of Bihar. Chief city, Patna.
  c. State of Bombay. Chief city, Bombay, 495 ; others Ahmedabad ; Poona.
  d. Central Provinces and Berar (Madhya Pradesh). Chief city, Nagpur.
  e. State of Madras (chief city, Madras, 2054), includes the Laccadive Islands ; other cities, Madura and Trichinopoly.
  f. State of Orissa. Chief city, Cuttack.
  g. State of Punjab (East Punjab). Chief cities : Simla, Amritsar.
  h. United Provinces (Uttar Pradesh). Chief cities, Allahabad ; Lucknow, 2035 ; Benares ; Cawnpore.
  i. State of West Bengal. Chief city, Calcutta.
  j. State of Hyderabad. Chief city, Hyderabad.
  k. Madhya Bharat. Chief city, Gwalior.
  l. State of Mysore. Chief city, Mysore.
  m. Patiala and East Punjab States Union. Chief city, Patiala.
  n. Rajasthan. Chief city, Jaipur.
  o. Saurashtra. Chief cities, Jamnagar ; Rajkot.
  p. Travancore-Cochin. Chief city, Trivandrum.
  q. Ten centrally administered areas, being Ajmer ; Bhopal ; Bilaspur ; Coorg ; Delhi ; Himalchal Pradesh ; Kutch ; Manipur ; Tripura ; Vindhya Pradesh.
  r. Andaman and Nicobar Islands. Chief city, Port Blair.
  s. State of Jammu and Kashmir (*Disputed with Pakistan*). Chief city, Srinagar.
B. Pakistan (British Dominion).
  a. Province of West Punjab. Chief cities : Lahore, Rawalpindi, Multan.
  b. Province of Sind. Chief city, Karachi (capital of Pakistan).
  c. North-West Frontier Province. Chief city, Peshawar.
  d. Province of East Bengal. Chief cities, Dacca ; Chittagong.
  e. Baluchistan. Chief city, Quetta.

Note : Pakistan is divided into two regions, one in the N.E. of the sub-continent (E. Bengal), the other to the N.W. (all other provinces).

V. NEIGHBOURING STATES AND FOREIGN POSSESSIONS.
A. Nepal, 2315, between the republic of India and the Himalayas. Chief city, Khatmandu.
B. Bhutan on the S.E. of the Himalayas. Chief city, Punakha.
C. French India, 1692. Four small territories : Pondicherry, Karikal, Yanaon, Mahé.
D. Portuguese India. Goa, Damao, and Diu.

Burma

THE Independent Union of Burma (623) came into being on Jan. 4, 1948 ; it comprises Burma proper, the Chin Hill and Kachin Hill tracts, the Shan States, and the Karenni States, and lies between Tibet and China to the north, India and Pakistan to the north-west, Bay of Bengal on the west, and China, Indo-China and Siam on the east and north-east. It was part of British India until 1937, was overrun by the Japanese 1941–45, and became a free and independent republic after the Second World War.

I. PHYSIOGRAPHY.
A. Mountains : Parallel ranges running generally north and south form the Western Hills, Central Belt, and Shan Plateau.
B. Rivers : Irrawaddy, Sittang and Salween.

II. RESOURCES AND PRODUCTS.
A. Agriculture in the fertile valleys : chief crop, rice ; also sesame, ground-nuts, cotton, maize.
B. Forests on the mountains yield teak.
C. Minerals : silver, lead, wolfram ; oil ; rubies, sapphires, jade.

III. CHIEF CITIES.
Rangoon (capital), 2744 ; Bassein, Pegu, Prome, Bhamo, Moulmein.

Ceylon

THE island of Ceylon (**748**), off the southern tip of the Indian sub-continent, was possessed in turn by the Portuguese, Dutch and British. A British Crown colony from 1802, it became a dominion on February 4, 1948, after two years of self-government. The Maldive Islands are closely associated with Ceylon.

I. PHYSIOGRAPHY.

A. Plateau and mountains : in south central portion (Adam's Peak).

B. Plain : in north and north central area.

C. Rivers : short, unnavigable, some drying up in summer.

II. RESOURCES AND PRODUCTS.

A. Agriculture : chief crops : tea, rubber, rice, copra, oils, cacao, cinnamon.

B. Minerals : plumbago, vanadium, gem-stones.

C. Pearl fishing.

III. CHIEF CITIES.

Colombo (capital) ; Kandy, Trincomalee.

Persia (Iran) and Afghanistan

THESE two countries occupy the rugged mountains and arid tablelands which divide what we call the Near East from Central Asia and the Far East. They are among the least progressive of the Asiatic states, having few railways or native industries.

I. PERSIA (IRAN).

A. Physiography, 1740. The Elburz Mountains in the north, and the vast stretches of the Iranian Plateau in the centre and south are the chief physical features. The Caspian Sea (**712**) forms part of the northern boundary, while, in the south, Persia extends along the Persian Gulf and the Gulf of Oman.

B. Resources and Products.

1. Agriculture and Live-stock : wheat, barley, rice, fruits, sheep, camels, cattle, goats.

b. Minerals : most important, petroleum ; also iron, coal, copper, lead, manganese, borax, nickel.

c. Manufacturing : silk, woollens, carpets, opium, gums, leather.

C. Chief Cities : Teheran (capital), Tabriz, Ispahan.

II. AFGHANISTAN.

A. Physiography, 55. The north-eastern half of Afghanistan is covered by the ridges and spurs of the Hindu Kush Mountains ; the south-western half is a continuation of the Iranian Plateau, extending over from Persia.

B. Resources and Products.

a. Agriculture and Live-stock : wheat, barley, rice, millet, maize, fruits, tobacco, sheep, goats, camels, cattle.

b. Minerals : copper, lead, iron, gold, precious stones.

c. Manufacturing : silks, felt, carpets, leather, food products.

C. Capital and Chief City : Kabul.

Countries of South-western Asia

BEFORE the First World War this area formed part of the Turkish Empire ; it is better for geographical purposes to divide this part of Asia into four large natural regions rather than to attempt to study separately each of the many states, principalities, emirates, mandates, or other political units into which it is now divided.

I. ASIATIC TURKEY OR ANATOLIA.

A. Physiography, 3262. The plateau of Asia Minor (**271**) is surrounded on all sides by mountains extending to the shores of the Black Sea and the Mediterranean, the most important being the Taurus Mountains in the south and south-east.

B. Resources and Products.

a. Agriculture and Live-stock : wheat, oats, barley, tobacco, cotton, opium, grapes, olives, figs ; sheep, cattle, goats, asses, horses.

b. Minerals : Chrome ore, copper, coal, zinc, lead, antimony, manganese, borax, salt, gold, silver, corundum.

c. Forests and Forest Products : timber, gums, wild fruit.

d. Manufacturing : cotton goods, woollens, silk, rugs, leather, opium, olive oil.

C. Chief Cities : Ankara, 162 ; Smyrna (Izmir), 2988 ; Bursa ; Trabzon (Trebizond).

II. SYRIA, LEBANON, PALESTINE AND THE KINGDOM OF THE JORDAN

A. Physiography, 3144, 2480, 3238. Low mountains rise from the Mediterranean coast, except in the extreme south, where there is a strip of coastal plain. Beyond these mountains lie narrow river valleys parallel to the coast. Beyond these again lie the great Arabian Desert.

B. Resources and Products.

a. Agriculture and Live-stock : wheat, barley, millet, fruits, tobacco, cotton, hemp, olives ; sheep, goats, cattle, camels, asses, horses.

b. Manufacturing : silk, olive oil, wine.

C. Chief Cities :

a. Syria : Damascus, 961 ; Aleppo, Homs.

b. Lebanon : Beirut (capital) ; Tyre, Sidon.

c. Palestine : Jerusalem, 1819; Tel Aviv, Jaffa.

d. Jordan : Amman (capital), Irbid.

III. IRAQ.

A. Physiography, 1743. Iraq consists of a lowland plain which forms the valleys of the Tigris (**3212**) and the Euphrates (**1231**). It is for the most part treeless, and, except along the rivers, is an unproductive desert. However, with irrigation, the soil becomes exceedingly fertile.

B. Resources and Products : wheat, barley, cotton, dates, petroleum.

C. Chief Cities : Baghdad, 339 ; Basra, Mosul.

IV. ARABIA.

The land of Arabia (195) is divided into a group of independent and semi-independent native states, the most important, the Kingdom of Saudi Arabia, which includes Nejd, Hejaz, and Asir; Yemen along the Red Sea coast; Kuwait at the head of the Persian Gulf; and Muscat and Oman, extending round the eastern tip of the Arabian peninsula from the Persian Gulf to the Indian Ocean. The British Colony of Aden (26) occupies the other tip of the peninsula at the mouth of the Red Sea.

The Bahrein Islands form a separate entity, and there are seven small sheikhdoms.

A. **Physiography**: Arabia is mostly a great desert tableland bordered by narrow coastal plains and, in the south, by low mountain ranges.

B. **Resources and Products**: dates, livestock, hides, wool, coffee (from Mocha in Yemen), petroleum.

C. **Chief Cities**: Mecca, 2125; Jeddah, Medina, Riyadh, Muscat, Hodeida, Aden, 26.

East Indies (Indonesia)

THIS is the large group of islands lying between the south-east coast of Asia and the continent of Australia. The island of Sumatra marks the western extremity of the group, the Philippines the northern extremity, and the island of New Guinea the eastern extremity, the islands outside these limits being considered as belonging to Asia, to Australia, or to some of the Pacific Ocean archipelagoes. The islands forming the former Netherlands East Indies were renamed the United States of Indonesia after the Second World War, but geographically the name Indonesia (1720) is also applied to the whole area of the East Indies; Malay Archipelago is another geographical term.

I. PHYSIOGRAPHY AND CLIMATE.

A. **Islands of Volcanic Origin, containing many Active and Extinct Cones** (1075; *map, 1074-75*).

B. **Typical Formation**: Most of the islands have mountainous interiors, cut up by river valleys and surrounded by coastal plains.

C. **Hot Equatorial Climate.**

II. RESOURCES AND PRODUCTS.

A. **Agriculture and Forest Products**: rice, maize, tea, soya beans, spices, pepper, coffee, canesugar, cacao, coconuts, bananas, tobacco, manila hemp, indigo, quinine, rubber, gutta-percha, ebony, teak, sandalwood.

B. **Minerals and Mining**: copper, iron, gold, tin, petroleum, coal, mercury, precious stones.

III. MAIN DIVISIONS.

A. **Philippine Islands** (independent republic), 2568. Capital and chief city, Manila, 2088.

B. **Portuguese possession**: part of Timor. Chief city, Deli.

C. **British possessions.**
  a. Borneo, 525:
    1. British North Borneo. Chief city, Sandakan.
    2. Brunei. Chief city, Brunei.

  3. Sarawak, 2873. Chief cities, Kuching (capital); Sibu.
  b. New Guinea, 2338:
    1. Papua (Australian). Chief city, Port Moresby.
    2. Former German possessions, mandated to Australia in 1920 and from 1947 administered by Australia under U.N. trusteeship. These areas comprise North-Eastern New Guinea and adjacent islands (chief cities, Lae, Wewak); the Bismarck Archipelago; the Admiralty Islands; Bougainville and Buka, in the Solomon Islands.

D. **United States of Indonesia** (an independent republic within the Netherlands-Indonesian Union), 1075.
    a. Sumatra, 3117. Chief cities, Padang, Palembang.
    b. Java, 1813. Chief cities, Djakarta (Batavia), Bandoeng.
    c. Madura.
    d. Part of Borneo. Chief cities, Pontianak, Banjermasin.
    e. Flores.
    f. Part of Timor. Chief city, Kupang.
    g. Celebes. Chief city and capital, Macassar.
    h. Molucca Islands. Chief city, Amboyna.
    i. Federation of Bangka, Billiton and Riouw.

AUSTRALASIA

AUSTRALIA (307) is the smallest of the continents. It was the last of the inhabitable portions of the globe to be explored and settled by white men. In size Australia, including Tasmania, is nearly 60 times larger than England. Occupying the same latitude as South Africa, it resembles South Africa in many important geographical features, chief of which is the division of the country into an arid western zone and a rainy eastern zone. South-east of Australia lies New Zealand, the largest group of islands in the Pacific outside the East Indies. The remainder of the Pacific Islands lie scattered over the vast watery stretches which separate Asia and Australia from the two Americas.

I. AUSTRALIA.

A. **Physiography, 307.**
  a. Western Australian Plateau, including the Desert Region.
  b. Great Central Plains.
  c. East Australian Highlands, including the

Great Dividing Range.
  d. Murray and Darling Rivers form only important river system of Australia.
  e. Coastline smooth, very slightly indented. Great Barrier Reef.
  f. Tasmania, 3156.

B. Climate.

a. Typical tropical climate in the north.

b. Seasonal change in the south; high temperature of the interior.

c. Rainfall: Uncertain and insufficient in the interior and on the west coast; heavy on eastern coast.

d. Temperate climate of Tasmania.

C. Vegetation and Animal Life.

a. Typical Vegetation: eucalyptus, *314*; acacia, **16**; tree ferns, gigantic tulips and lilies, tall tropical grasses.

b. Typical Animals, *313*: rabbit, dingo (wild dog); kangaroo, **1845**; wombat, bandicoot; grey opossum, Tasmanian devil, Tasmanian wolf; duckbill, *1053*; spiny ant-eater, 176; frilled lizard, 1973; laughing jackass; emu, **1157**; cassowary, black swan, lyre bird, brush turkey and mallee-bird; bower birds, **534**.

D. Natural Resources and Industries, *311*.

a. Sheep and Cattle Raising the Most Important Industry, *312*.

b. Agriculture: wheat, oats, barley, maize, hay, potatoes, sugar-cane, grapes, fruit.

c. Minerals and Mining: coal, gold, silver, lead, copper, tin, zinc, iron, tungsten.

d. Manufacturing: wool, leather, chemicals, metal products, lumber.

F. Divisions of Australia.

a. New South Wales, 2343. Capital and chief city, Sydney, 3144.

b. Victoria, 3321. Capital and chief city, Melbourne, 2136.

c. Queensland, 2716. Capital and chief city, Brisbane, 571.

d. South Australia, 3028. Capital and chief city, Adelaide, 26.

e. Western Australia, 3368. Capital and chief city, Perth, 2557.

f. Tasmania, 3156. Capital and chief city, Hobart, 1633.

g. Territories.

1. Federal Capital Territory, Canberra, 690.
2. Northern Territory. Chief city, Port Darwin.

h. Possessions administered by the Australian Commonwealth: Territory of Papua; U.N. Trusteeship Territory of New Guinea (former German New Guinea), with that part of the Solomon Islands formerly owned by Germany.

II. NEW ZEALAND.

The Dominion of New Zealand (**2357**) consists of two large islands (North Island and South Island), and a smaller island (Stewart Island) lying near the southern tip of South Island. The group is situated about 1,300 miles south-east of Australia. Attached to the Dominion of New Zealand are several small islands and island groups, of which the most important are the Auckland Islands, Chatham Islands, Cook Islands, and Kermadec Islands.

A. Physiography and Climate.

a. North Island consists of Plains and Plateaux marked by Volcanic Cones and Hot Springs.

b. Rugged Cloud-capped Peaks of " Southern Alps " on South Island flanked by the Canterbury Plains.

c. Climate: Semi-tropical conditions prevail in the north, while the south is temperate. Rainfall is abundant everywhere.

C. Resources and Products.

a. Agriculture and Livestock: wheat, oats, barley, hay; sheep, cattle, pigs, horses.

b. Forests and Forest Products: lumber and kauri gum.

c. Fisheries: whaling is an important industry.

d. Minerals and Mining: coal, gold, silver, tungsten, copper, iron, lead, zinc, antimony.

e. Manufacturing: wool, leather, meat-packing, dairy products, clothing, shoes, metalware.

D. Chief Cities: Wellington (capital); Auckland, 301; Christchurch, Dunedin.

III. PACIFIC ISLANDS.

A. Resources and Products (2469).

a. Wild and Cultivated Products: coconuts and copra, breadfruit, sugar, pineapples, bananas, taro, yams, sago, coffee, rubber, tea, rare woods.

b. Sea Products: pearl shell, turtle-shell, trepang or bêche-de-mer.

c. Minerals: phosphate, nickel.

B. Principal Islands of the Pacific.

a. Melanesia, 2470: Bismarck or New Britain Archipelago, Solomon Islands, and Santa Cruz (British); New Hebrides (British and French); New Caledonia and Loyalty Islands (French).

b. Micronesia, 2470: Marianas or Ladrones (formerly Japanese, except Guam); Pelew Islands, Caroline Islands and Marshall Islands (formerly Japanese); Gilbert Islands (British).

c. Polynesia, 2471: Hawaiian Islands (United States); Fiji Islands (British); Samoan Islands (United States and British); Ellice Islands, Tokelau Islands, Tonga or Friendly Islands, and Cook Islands (British); Society Islands, Tubuai or Austral Islands, Marquesas, and Tuamotu or Low Archipelago (French).

POLAR REGIONS

SURROUNDING each of the poles of the Earth is a region of extreme cold, where permanent settlement is difficult if not impossible. The North Polar or Arctic Region (223) consists for the most part of a great ocean into which are thrust the northern ends of Europe, Asia, and North America. The South Polar or Antarctic Region (173), on the other hand, consists chiefly of a vast and lofty land mass isolated by hundreds of miles of open water.

I. ARCTIC REGIONS.

A. Physiography and Climate.

a. Arctic Ocean; Bering Strait, 415; Baffin Bay.

b. Chief Islands in Arctic Circle. Greenland (1541), Spitsbergen, Fridtjof Nansen Land, Nova Zembla, New Siberia, Lenin Land, Baffin Land, Banks Land, Victoria Land, Grant Land, Wrangel Island.

c. Arctic Plains or Tundras : In North America ; in Europe ; in Asia.

d. North Magnetic Pole, *map, 223*, 2390, 2644.

e. Climate. Extreme cold, sunless winters ; midnight sun.

B. Animals and Vegetation, 156.

a. Sea Life : whale, 3371 ; dolphin, 1027 ; seal, 2912 ; walrus, 3339.

b. Land Mammals : arctic fox, 1355 ; polar hare ; white wolf ; polar bear, *383* ; ermine, 1222 ; musk ox.

c. Reindeer, the domestic animal of the North, 2760.

d. Birds : auk, 303 ; eider duck, 1052 ; puffin, ptarmigan, sandpiper ; snowy owl, *2461* ; tern ; teal, 1051.

e. Vegetation : lichens and mosses, 1932, 2238.

C. Natives of the Arctic Region : Eskimos, 1222 ; Lapps, 1891.

D. Natural Resources and Industries : fur-bearing animals ; fishing ; whaling ; sealing ; walrus hunting ; coal.

E. North Polar Explorations, 225, 2644.

II. ANTARCTIC REGIONS.

A. Physiography and Climate, 173.

a. High Plateaux and Lofty Mountains. Average elevation as compared with other continents.

b. South Magnetic Pole.

c. Severe Antarctic Climate because of altitude and land mass.

B. Animals, 156.

a. Only few Birds can bear the rigorous climate : penguin, *170, 172*, 2544 ; petrel, 2563 ; albatross, 101.

b. Sea Mammals : seal, sea-lion, sea-elephant, 175, 2912 ; whales, 3371 ; dolphin, 1027.

c. Vegetation : mosses and lichens, 1932, 2238.

C. South Polar Explorations, 175, 2645.

NORTH AMERICA

THE Arctic Circle cuts across the American continent far to the north, and the Tropic of Cancer crosses Central Mexico. This means that the great bulk of North America (2379) lies in the *temperate* zone, with a climate suited to the greatest variety of human enterprises. South America, on the other hand, has its largest area in the *tropical* zone. In contrasting the progress of North and South America it is also important to note that South America was chiefly colonized by Spaniards and Portuguese, who did not regard the New World as a land to be settled and developed, but as a treasure-house to be exploited for the benefit of the governments at home ; whereas the English, Dutch, and French settlers of North America sought the New World as a permanent home.

I. GEOLOGICAL HISTORY.

A. Growth of the Continent, 2384.

B. Formation of Mountain Ranges and Plateaux.

a. The Laurentian Plateau—extending from northern Labrador to western tip of Lake Superior, and north to Hudson Bay plain.

b. The Appalachian Mountains—extending from Gulf of St. Lawrence parallel with Atlantic Coast almost to the Gulf of Mexico, **190**.

C. Plains.

a. The Great Central Plain, 2384.

b. Northern Plain—between the Laurentian Plateau and Hudson Bay.

c. Coastal Plains : The Atlantic coastal plain ; the Gulf coastal plain.

II. RIVERS AND LAKES EAST OF THE CONTINENTAL DIVIDE.

A. The St. Lawrence System and the Great Lakes.

B. The Rivers of the Atlantic Coastal Plain.

a. Chief rivers rising in the northern division of the Appalachians : St. John, Penobscot and Kennebec, Merrimac, Connecticut.

b. The Hudson.

c. Chief Rivers rising in the southern division of the Appalachians : Delaware, Susquehanna, Potomac, Neuse, Cape Fear, Peedee and Santee, Savannah, Altamaha.

C. Rivers of the Gulf Coastal Plain (excluding the Mississippi and Rio Grande Systems).

D. The Mississippi-Missouri System.

E. The Rio Grande System.

III. RIVERS WEST OF THE CONTINENTAL DIVIDE.

A. The Colorado System.

B. Columbia System.

C. The Yukon System.

IV. RIVERS FLOWING INTO THE ARCTIC OCEAN AND HUDSON BAY.

A. The Mackenzie-Athabaska System.

B. The Nelson-Saskatchewan System.

United States

THE study of the natural resources of the country and of the multitude of uses to which they have been put are the most interesting and important points in the geography of the United States. From this point of view, the territory may be divided into several natural regions, each of which is particularly adapted to certain classes of industries and occupations. A comprehensive account of the natural resources and industries, as well as of the principal cities, will be found in the article on the United States, **3285**. Each State in the Union is also the subject of a separate article.

NOTE : For exact boundaries of natural divisions of the U.S.A., consult map, *3286*.

I. NORTHERN DIVISION OF THE APPALACHIAN HIGHLANDS.

This region, which includes all New England, is essentially a manufacturing district. The surface of the land is generally broken and rocky ; the only portions suitable for farming on an important scale are the narrow river valleys and lake bottoms. The extensive forests in the north contribute chiefly the wood-pulp used in the paper mills. While poor in metals, the rock-ribbed hills of the interior yield building stone of great value. An inexhaustible source of power is found in the swift streams.

The principal centres of manufacturing and trade include Boston, **529** ; Providence, Worcester, New Haven, Bridgeport, and Hartford.

II. THE ATLANTIC COASTAL PLAIN.

The southern ridges and plateaux of the Appalachian Highlands are separated from the sea by a strip of lowland called the Atlantic Coastal Plain, composed of layers of soil washed down from the ancient mountains. A natural boundary called the " Fall Line " separates this region from that part of the Appalachian Highlands known as the " Piedmont Plateau " ; here the rivers, emerging from the western hills, plunge in falls or rapids to the plains below, at the same time putting an end to upstream navigation from the sea and providing a rich source of water-power. The Atlantic Coastal Plain is at once a manufacturing and an agricultural region. Its chief manufacturing and trade centres are grouped round the great natural harbours to the north ; its agricultural districts become increasingly important towards the south.

Important cities include New York, **2351** ; Philadelphia, **2566** ; Baltimore, **352** ; and Jersey City.

III. SOUTHERN DIVISION OF THE APPALACHIAN HIGHLANDS.

This is one of the busiest mining and industrial regions in the world. From the ancient seams of the mountains there pours forth a vast volume of coal which lights the furnaces of thousands of factories. Drawing raw materials—iron ore chiefly—from the western districts, and provided with a convenient outlet for manufactured products to the east, this busy territory sets the pace for all other American industrial life.

Pennsylvania mines one half of the United States supply of coal, and the mining of iron, copper, petroleum, and natural gas are extensive industries. The agricultural products of this region are almost as important as the minerals.

The region has many cities, chiefly mining and manufacturing centres, such as Pittsburgh, **2614**, and Rochester.

IV. GULF COASTAL PLAIN.

This portion of the Coastal Plain, for the most part low and flat, is formed by the accumulated sediment of ages. It is an extremely fertile region, including as it does the lower reaches of the vast Mississippi Valley. Most of the population is devoted to agriculture and there are comparatively few large cities.

Cotton is the chief product of the region, Texas being the leading cotton state, followed by Mississippi and Alabama. Lumber is the most important manufacturing product.

V. CENTRAL PLAINS AND INTERIOR HIGHLANDS.

This is the great farming region. The vast stretch of cultivable land which forms the upper Mississippi Valley, the lower Ohio Valley, and the Great Lakes Plain has a gently sloping surface composed chiefly of exceedingly fertile alluvial and glacial soils. Abundant rains and a warm summer climate favour successful agriculture. The region possesses extensive waterways, water-power, coal, oil, natural gas, and other great mineral resources, which have helped to turn many of its sections into great industrial districts—among the richest and busiest in the nation.

Of the agricultural crops maize leads, followed by wheat. The Mesaba range, *1752*, is the world's greatest iron-mining centre. Niagara Falls lie in this region. Michigan leads the world in the production of motor cars, and Chicago, **783**, is the greatest meat-packing centre. The largest flour mills in the U.S.A. are at Minneapolis.

VI. GREAT PLAINS.

Between the Central Plains and the Rocky Mountains and stretching from Canada to Mexico lies a broad belt of almost treeless grassland called the Great Plains, for the most part flat or very gently undulating. Most of this semi-arid land is given over to stock raising. But the wilderness is gradually being brought under cultivation, either with the aid of irrigation or through the special methods of " dry-farming." Coal in great quantities has been found, and oil fields have been discovered. There are few large cities, owing to the fact that there are not many great manufacturing industries to bring large numbers of people together.

VII. ROCKY MOUNTAINS.

Rising abruptly from the Great Plains, the Rocky Mountains form a great barrier which comes down from Canada and reaches seven-eighths of the way across the United States towards Mexico. These mountains constitute the most important watershed in North America, giving rise to four of the largest river systems in the United States—the Missouri-Mississippi, the Columbia, the Colorado, and the Rio Grande systems. Vast stores of mineral wealth have been brought to light in these rugged ranges. In the sheltered valleys agriculture and stock-raising flourish, while the swift mountain streams provide a boundless source of water-power.

Beautiful scenery is preserved in the many National Parks. Cities include Denver, Cheyenne, and Laramie.

VIII. WESTERN PLATEAUX.

Between the Rocky Mountains and the Pacific Coast Ranges lies a long stretch of broken land, the greater part of which has less than 10 inches of rain a year. There are many real deserts in this region ; the soil, however, is extraordinarily fertile, and in those districts where irrigation is possible or where the rainfall is somewhat above the average, tremendous crops can be grown. While consisting for the most part of high plateaux, this section contains also deep basins, in one case—Death Valley—actually reaching below sea level.

The chief natural resources are minerals. Though the amount of agricultural land is relatively small, the yields per acre are enormous.

IX. PACIFIC RANGES AND LOWLANDS.

Nowhere in the world are the effect of mountains on climate and the effect of climate upon life better demonstrated than in crossing the great ranges which separate the Western Plateaux and the Great Basin from the Pacific slopes of the United States. On the one side is an arid parched region subject to violent changes of temperature, on the other a paradise with ample rainfall, equable temperature, luxuriant vegetation, flourishing fields, great cities, and thriving industries. The secret of this tremendous contrast lies in the fact that when the warm moisture-laden winds from the Pacific strike the mountain ranges, they are cooled and release their moisture in the form of rain or mountain snows. The vast Pacific Ocean does not vary much in temperature the year round, so that it remains warmer than the atmosphere in the winter and cooler than the atmosphere in the summer.

This is the leading fruit producing region of the U.S.A., oranges, lemons, grapes, apples, and other fruits being grown in profusion. Food products and iron and steel products are among the principal manufactures. Near Los Angeles is the famous film city, Hollywood, 2026 ; Yosemite National Park contains magnificently wild scenery.

X. POSSESSIONS OF THE UNITED STATES.

United States has few colonies or outlying possessions. This is due to the fact that it is the youngest among the great nations of the world, having never suffered from that overcrowding and fierce trade competition which led the nations of Europe to seek foreign territory and the control of distant markets.

A. Alaska, 97.

B. Island Possessions.
    a. In the Atlantic : Puerto Rico, 2698 ; U.S. Leeward Is.
    b. In the Pacific : Hawaiian Islands, 1585 ; Eastern Samoan Islands ; Guam. (the Philippines, 2568, became independent in 1945 ; U.S.A. also administers former Jap. islands).

C. Panama Canal Zone, 2486.

Canada

THE British Dominion of Canada (676), with an area larger than the United States including Alaska, is a much younger country from the point of view of development. The commercial centres on the Atlantic and Pacific coasts, and along the great interior waterways of Canada, present a picture of thriving industry, but in the interior of the Dominion and in the north are vast stretches of wilderness still beckoning to the pioneer and settler. Except where the Arctic climate makes agriculture impossible, however, land is rapidly being brought under the plough, and with tremendous natural resources in fertile soil, waterways, water power, forests, minerals, and fisheries, Canada is every year taking a more and more important place in the commerce of the world.

I. POLITICAL DIVISIONS.
(See Map facing page 680).

a. Maritime Provinces: Nova Scotia, 2400 ; Prince Edward Island, 2684 ; New Brunswick, 2336 ; Newfoundland, 2337.

b. Eastern Provinces : Quebec, 2714 ; Ontario, 2434.

c. Prairie Provinces : Manitoba, 2088 ; Saskatchewan, 2874 ; Alberta, 102.

d. Western Province : British Columbia, 578.

e. Territories : Yukon Territory, 3440 ; North-west Territories, 2392.

II. PHYSIOGRAPHY.

A. Mountains and Plateaux.

    a. Appalachian Highlands. Extending northward from U.S.A. into Maritime Provinces of Canada, 190.

    b. Laurentian Plateau. Oldest land formation in North America, 676. Covers more than half of Canada.

    c. Ranges of the Cordillera System in the West, 2384. The Canadian Rocky Mountains (676) and the Coast Ranges enclose a great valley and plateau, which run parallel with the Pacific coast from the United States boundary to Alaska.

B. Plains.

    a. Central Plains. Extending from U.S.A. to tongue of land between Lakes Huron, Erie, and Ontario.

    b. Great Plains. Between Laurentian Plateau and Rocky Mountains (676), the Great Plains include south-western Manitoba, central and southern Saskatchewan, all of Alberta except a south-western strip, a western strip through the Provisional District of Mackenzie.

C. Rivers and Lakes.

    a. St. Lawrence River, 2861.

    b. Nelson-Saskatchewan System, 676 ; Red River of the north.

    c. Mackenzie-Athabaska System, 676, 2050. Peace River.

    d. Yukon, 3440.

    e. Fraser, 676.

    f. Great Lakes, 1515.

    g. Other Large Lakes : Lake Winnipeg, 676 ; Great Slave Lake and Great Bear Lake, 676.

D. Coastline.

    a. Deep Fiords and Bays on Coasts of Labrador and British Columbia, 1875.

    b. Hudson Bay and Northern Island Groups.

E. Important Islands : Cape Breton Island, 695 ; Vancouver Island, 3303 ; Newfoundland, 2337.

III. CLIMATE.

a. Prevailing climate is of "Continental" type, with great variations in temperature.

b. Influence of Great Lakes.

c. The Atlantic maritime provinces have comparatively mild climate; the harbours are free from winter ice, but fog prevails in Newfoundland.

d. On the Pacific coast warm winds from the ocean keep the winters mild.

e. Hudson Bay district is ice-bound most of the year, but the long summer days help to make up for the shortness of the warm season.

f. Rainfall.

IV. NATURAL RESOURCES.

A. **Fertile Soil.** Vast districts still uncultivated; good grazing land.

B. **Vast Forests of Valuable Timber.** Forests, composed chiefly of evergreen trees, cover almost all of the uncultivated surface of Canada, except the Great Plains and the Arctic Regions.

C. **Minerals.**

a. Gold and silver.

b. Sudbury district of Ontario produces most of the world's nickel.

c. Most of the world's asbestos comes from Quebec.

d. Coal and petroleum.

e. Other minerals: Copper, iron, zinc and lead; cobalt, mica, molybdenite, uranium, and graphite.

D. **Fish.**

E. **Fur-Bearing Animals.**

F. **Waterways and Water-Power.** The Great Lakes and the St. Lawrence River form one of the most important systems of water transport in the world.

G. **National Parks.** These include the famous Banff, Buffalo, and Rocky Mountain Parks, etc.

V. INDUSTRIES.

A. **Agriculture the most important industry.** Wheat is the largest crop; oats, barley, rye, flax, hay, potatoes, fruit, irrigation and dry farming.

B. **Stock Raising, Dairying, and Dairy Products.**

C. **Mining.** Only a small part of Canada's vast mineral resources have been developed.

D. **Lumber and Lumber Products.** Wood pulp for making paper is an important product.

E. **Fisheries.** The fish caught include cod, hake, haddock, alewife, halibut, pollack, mackerel, herring, smelt, shad, sardine, flounder, trout, pike, whitefish, pickerel, and sturgeon. Oysters are found in the Gulf of St. Lawrence. Salmon canning in British Columbia. Importance of Newfoundland Banks, 2338.

F. **Fur Industry.**

G. **Manufacturing.** The most important manufacturing region in Canada is southern Ontario. 2434.

VI. COMMUNICATIONS.

A. **Water Transport.** In addition to the natural waterways, numerous canals facilitate commerce in the Dominion. Chief among these are the Welland Canal, **3363**, the Trent Canal, the Rideau-Ottawa Canal system, the Rideau Canal.

B. **Railways.** The chief railways are the Canadian National and the Canadian Pacific.

VII. CHIEF CITIES.

A. **Seaports:** Halifax, **1566**; Saint John, **2861**; St. John's, *2338*; Vancouver, **3303**; Victoria, **3321.**

B. **River Ports:** Montreal, **2226**; Quebec, **2714**; Ottawa (capital), **2458.**

C. **Lake Ports:** Toronto, **3223**; Kingston, Hamilton, Fort William.

D. **Interior Cities:** Winnipeg, **3388**; Regina, London, Edmonton, Calgary.

CENTRAL AMERICA AND WEST INDIES

THE continents of North and South America may be said to be connected by two sets of mountain chains. One of these forms the great isthmus which we call Central America (**743**). The other is partially submerged, leaving only its loftiest peaks and plateaux exposed. These form the great chain of islands known as the West Indies or Antilles, the Yucatan Peninsula and the Florida Peninsula. All of Central America and all of the West Indies, except a few small islands to the north, lie in the Tropical Zone.

Central America

I. BOUNDARIES AND AREA, 743.

A. Geographically, Central America is usually considered a part of North America, although its climate, its plant and animal life, and its people have more in common with tropical South America.

B. The total area of Central America is about four times that of England.

II. PHYSIOGRAPHY AND CLIMATE.

A. **Backbone of Mountains** belonging to Cordillera Chain, 2384, Chain broken by Nicaragua basin.

B. **Atlantic or Caribbean Coastal Region.** Generally low and swampy, hot, and unhealthy, **701.**

III. PRODUCTS.

A. **Hot Lowland Region.** Bananas, mahogany, logwood, chicle, guayule rubber, coconuts.

B. **Upland Region.** Coffee, tobacco, cacao, maize, rice, beans, sugar, henequen, gold, silver, copper, iron, and coal.

IV. POLITICAL DIVISIONS.

A. **Guatemala, 1551.** Chief cities : Guatemala City (capital) ; Atlantic coast port, Puerto Barrios ; Pacific coast port, San José ; Quirigua.

B. **Honduras, 1638.** Chief cities : Tegucigalpa (capital) ; Atlantic coast port, Puerto Cortes ; Pacific coast port, Amapala.

C. **Salvador, 2868.** Chief cities : San Salvador (capital) ; Santa Ana ; no Atlantic coastline ; Pacific coast ports, Acajutla and La Union.

D. **Nicaragua, 2363.** Chief cities : Managua (capital), Leon, Granada ; Atlantic coast port, Bluefields ; Pacific coast ports, Corinto, San Juan del Sur.

E. **Costa Rica, 916.** Chief cities : San José (capital), Cartago ; Atlantic coast port, Limon ; Pacific coast port, Puntarenas.

F. **Panama, 2486.** Chief cities: Panama (capital and Pacific coast port); Atlantic coast port, Colon.

G. **Foreign Territory.**
   a. British Honduras, 1638. Capital, Belize.
   b. Panama Canal Zone (United States), 2486.

West Indies

I. POSITION AND AREA.

The West Indies (**3368**) stretch from the entrance to the Gulf of Mexico eastward and southward to the coast of South America, forming the northern and eastern boundary of the Caribbean Sea. With the exception of a part of the Bahamas, they lie entirely within the tropical zone. The Bahamas reach within 60 miles of the coast of Florida.

II. PHYSIOGRAPHY AND CLIMATE.

A. Bahamas consist of coral formations resting on submerged mountains, **339**.

B. Remainder of West Indies chiefly of volcanic formation, **2112**. Most of the islands have important mountains, sometimes snow-capped. Mont Pelée is an active volcano.

C. Rolling plains on some islands and low swampy coast lands, **940**.

D. Usually hot and damp with abundant rainfall, **1565, 2112**.

E. Hurricanes are frequent.

III. PRODUCTS.

A. Cane-sugar, tobacco, fruits, cotton, and coffee.

B. **Rare Woods** : mahogany, lignum vitae, ebony, rosewood, logwood, and satinwood.

C. Livestock.

IV. DIVISIONS OF WEST INDIES.

(1) The **Bahamas** ; (2) the **Greater Antilles**, including Cuba, Jamaica, Haiti, and Porto Rico ; and (3) the **Lesser Antilles**, including the Leeward Islands, the Windward Islands, Barbados, Trinidad and Tobago, and the chain of small islands off the north coast of South America, the most important of which form the Curaçao group.

A. **Bahamas, 339** (British). Comprise more than 3,000 islands and islets. Capital and chief city, Nassau. The Turks and Caicos Islands belong geographically to the Bahamas, but are under the government of Jamaica.

B. **Cuba, 940** (Independent). Chief cities : Havana (capital), Camaguey, Cienfuegos, Santiago de Cuba, Guantanamo, Santa Clara, Matanzas, and Manzanillo.

C. **Jamaica, 1792** (British). Capital and chief city, Kingston.

D. **Haiti, 1565.** This island is divided politically into two parts :
   a. Republic of Haiti. Capital and chief city, Port-au-Prince.
   b. Dominican Republic. Capital and chief city, Ciudad Trujillo. (Formerly both republic and capital were called Santo Domingo).

E. **Puerto Rico, 2698** (United States). Capital and chief city, San Juan.

F. **British Leeward Islands.** Principal islands : British Virgin Islands, comprising Tortola, Virgin Gorda, Anegada, Jost Van Dykes, and about 30 smaller islands ; St. Kitts, Nevis and Anguilla ; Antigua, Barbuda, and Redonda ; Montserrat ; and Dominica. Chief city, St. John, on Antigua Island.

G. **French Leeward Islands.** Principal islands : Guadeloupe and Marie Galante. Chief cities, Basse-Terre (capital) and Pointe-à-Pitre. Under the Guadeloupe government is included one-half the island of St. Martin, the other half, with St. Eustache (or Eustatius), belonging to the Dutch colony of Curaçao (*see* below).

H. **Leeward Islands** (United States). Consisting of part of Virgin Islands. Principal islands : St. Croix, St. Thomas, and St. John. Chief city, St. Thomas (formerly Charlotte Amalie).

I. **Windward Islands** :
   a. Martinique, 2112 (French). Capital and chief city, Fort de France.
   b. British Windward Islands. Principal islands: St. Lucia, St. Vincent, Grenada, and the Grenadines. Chief cities : St. George, Castries, and Kingstown.

J. **Barbados, 360** (British). Capital and chief city, Bridgetown.

K. **Trinidad and Tobago, 3248** (British). Chief cities : Port of Spain (capital) and Scarborough.

L. **Curaçao Group** (Dutch). Principal islands : Curaçao, Bonaire, and Aruba. Capital and chief city, Willemstad. The government of Curaçao extends to the Dutch possessions in the Leeward Islands—St. Eustache and one-half of St. Martin.

SOUTH AMERICA

SOUTH AMERICA (3022) is endowed with unlimited natural resources, every variety of climate and land formation, rich mineral deposits, great rivers, vast forests, and fertile plains. Many South American cities rank as the most progressive centres in the world, not only in engineering, sanitation, schools, and transport, but also in fostering the higher arts and general education. Politically, however, the South American republics are unstable and prone to revolution and despotism.

I. PHYSIOGRAPHY.

A. Mountains and Highlands.

    a. Andes, extending along the west coast from Isthmus of Panama to Cape Horn, 152.

    b. Brazilian Highlands or Tableland in the east, 551.

    c. Guiana Highlands and Plateau in the north, 1552.

B. Plains.

    a. Amazon Lowland, 136, 550. Covered with a dense tropical forest.

    b. Guiana Lowlands and Coastal Plain, 1552.

    c. Temperate Zone Forests cover portions of South Central Plains such as the Gran Chaco, 226, 2511.

    d. Treeless Grasslands : Llanos of Colombia and Venezuela, 873, 3308. Grasslands of Southern Brazil, Paraguay, and Uruguay. Pampas of Argentina, 226. Savannas of Guiana, 1552.

C. Rivers and Lakes of South America. All the important rivers of South America empty into the Atlantic Ocean.

    a. Magdalena in the extreme north, 873.

    b. Orinoco, 2452.

    c. Amazon with more than 200 tributaries, 136.

    d. Tocantins and São Francisco rivers, 552.

    e. Plata river formed by the junction of the Uruguay and Paraná.

    f. Rio Negro forming the northern boundary of Patagonia.

    g. Lake Titicaca, largest lake in South America, 491, *492*.

D. Chief Islands Near South America :

    a. Tierra del Fuego Group, 802.

    b. Trinidad, 3248.

    c. Falkland Islands, 1259.

    d. Juan Fernandez Island, 804, 937.

    e. Galapagos Islands, 1083.

II. CLIMATE.

Intensely hot and damp in tropical lowlands and coastal plains ; temperate in south.

A. Rainfall.

    a. Tropical Lowlands east of Andes have heavy rainfall, 226, 552.

    b. Prevailing easterly winds in tropical north deposit their moisture on eastern slopes of Andes, leaving most of west coast arid, 152.

    c. Prevailing westerly winds in temperate south deposit moisture on Pacific side of Andes, leaving interior mountain slopes and plains arid, 152, 226.

    d. Tremendous rainfall in the extreme south, 802.

III. MINERAL RESOURCES.

A. In Northern Andes. Amethysts and emeralds, platinum, gold, silver, mercury, copper, lead, zinc, magnesium, antimony, iron, coal, petroleum, and asphalt.

B. In Central Andes. Gold, silver, tin, nickel, copper, tungsten, lead, iron, manganese, antimony, bismuth, sulphur, coal, gypsum, borax, and nitrates.

C. In Southern Andes. Coal.

D. In Guiana Highlands. Gold, aluminium, copper, iron, coal, petroleum, and asphalt.

E. In Brazilian Highlands. Diamonds, iron, and gold are most important ; others are platinum, thorium, silver, copper, lead, mercury, manganese, coal, and graphite.

IV. VEGETATION AND ANIMAL LIFE.

A. Typical South American Plants :

    a. Native Plants : quebracho, 2511 ; brazilwood ; rubber trees, 2833 ; ivory palm, 632 ; araucarian pine ; cinchona, 2559 ; sarsaparilla ; indigo, 1718 ; tolu balsam, 2550 ; fustic or dye wood, 1060 ; bamboo, 353 ; cacao, 648 ; coca, 2559 ; maté ; orchids, 2447 ; giant water-lilies ; cotton, 920 ; potato, 2664 ; tomato, 3223 ; tobacco, 3219 ; pineapple, 2611.

    b. Introduced Plants : coffee, 864 ; sugarcane ; oranges, 2442 ; bananas, 354.

B. Typical South American Animals : Monkeys, 2207 ; jaguar, 1791 ; puma, 2702 ; tapir, 3154 ; llama, 1975 ; alpaca and vicuña, 124 ; pudu or dwarf deer, pampas deer, and guemal, 984 ; peccary ; chinchilla, 815 ; sloth, 2985 ; armadillo, 237 ; ant-eater, 176 ; vampire bat, 372 ; manatee or sea cow ; opossum, 2442 ; rhea ; condor, 885 ; toucan, 3230 ; hoatzin ; parrots and macaws, 2525 ; white ibis, flamingo, 1312 ; alligator, 121 ; matamata turtle, 3230 ; iguana and teguexin, 1686 ; boa constrictor and anaconda.

Countries of South America

A. Colombia, 872. Chief Products : coffee, petroleum, sugar, cocoa, bananas, cotton, hides, platinum, gold, and emeralds. Chief cities : Bogotá (capital), Barranquilla, and Cartagena.

B. **Venezuela, 3308.** Chief products : petroleum, cotton, coffee, cocoa, rubber, sugar, hides, and gold. Chief cities : Caracas (capital), Valencia, and Maracaibo.

C. **Brazil, 550.** Chief products : Brazil produces two-thirds of the world's coffee. Other products : rubber, sugar, hides and leather, grain, rice, cotton, meat, cocoa, tobacco, beans, yerba maté, timber, diamonds, platinum, gold, and manganese. Chief cities : Rio de Janeiro (capital), **2779** ; São Paulo, Bahia, Pernambuco, Para (or Belem), Porto Alegre, and Manaos.

D. **Ecuador, 1081.** Chief products : cocoa, coffee, rubber, vegetable ivory, tobacco, gold, and panama hats. Chief cities : Guayaquil and Quito (capital).

E. **Peru, 2558.** Chief products : sugar, cotton, rice, cocoa, coffee, wool, hides, quinine, cocaine, rubber, copper, coal, iron, lead, quicksilver, sulphur, zinc, vanadium, petroleum, and silver. Chief cities : Lima (capital), **1948**, and Callao.

F. **Bolivia, 491.** Chief products : tin, silver, rubber, copper, lead, zinc, cocoa, and coffee. Chief cities : La Paz (the actual seat of government), Cochabamba, Sucre (the nominal capital).

G. **Chile, 802.** Chief products : nitrates, copper, coal, manganese, silver, wheat, grapes, beans, hides and leather, meat, and wool. Chief cities :

Santiago (capital), **2872**, Valparaiso, **3302**, Concepción, Antofagasta.

H. **Paraguay, 2511.** Chief products : livestock, meat and hides, yerba maté, tobacco, oranges, and sugar. Chief cities : Asunción (capital) and Villa Rica.

I. **Argentina, 226.** Chief products : meat, hides, wool, wheat, maize, flax, oats, cotton, sugar, grapes, tobacco, clothing and petroleum. Chief cities : Buenos Aires (capital), **601**, Rosario, Cordoba, La Plata, Avellanida, Tucuman, Santa Fé, and Bahia Blanca.

J. **Uruguay, 3298.** Chief products : cattle, wool, hides, wheat, flax, oats, grapes, tobacco, olives, gold. Chief cities : Montevideo (capital), **2220**, and Salto.

K. **Guiana, 1552.**

   a. **British Guiana.** Chief products : sugar, coffee, rubber, rum, timber, coconuts, rice, bauxite, diamonds, and gold. Capital and chief city : Georgetown.

   b. **Dutch Guiana or Surinam.** Chief products : sugar, cocoa, bananas, coffee, rice, maize, molasses, rubber, and gold. Capital and chief city : Paramaribo.

   c. **French Guiana.** Chief products : gold, silver, iron, phosphates, rice, maize, sugar, and tobacco. Capital and chief city : Cayenne.

MEXICO

M EXICO (2156) is a land of enormous natural wealth, but its resources lie for the most part undeveloped. For its Spanish conquerors Mexico was simply a great mine of gold and silver, a storehouse of rare woods and spices, to be exploited for the benefit of the royal government and its favoured representatives. To carry out this plan the natives were virtually enslaved. When the land finally won its independence, it thus had a population untrained in government or individual industry, and sharply divided into a small educated class and a large ignorant class. The result was political chaos. Today, however, a new national spirit animates the country and education and modernization are bearing fruit.

I. PHYSIOGRAPHY.

A. **Mountains, 2156.** These form part of the great Cordillera system, and are divided into two principal ranges : Sierra Madre Oriental or Eastern Sierra Madre, and Sierra Madre Occidental or Western Sierra Madre. The central Mexican plateau or tableland lies between the two ranges.

B. **Coastal Plains.** The eastern coastal plain, an extension of the Gulf Coastal Plain of the United States, broadens out in the south to cover most of the Yucatan Peninsula. The coast is low and has no good natural harbours. The western coastal plain is narrow, 2157 (map), but has many fine harbours.

C. **Rivers.** With the exception of the Rio Grande, the rivers of Mexico are of no great size.

II. CLIMATE.

Coastal plains exceedingly hot ; Central Plateau mild ; mountains cold. Yucatan and lower California generally hot and dry. Heavy rains in the south, but mountains cut off moisture from interior.

III. NATURAL RESOURCES AND INDUSTRIES.

A. **Rich Soil and extensive Grazing Lands.**
   a. **Chief Food Crops :** maize, wheat, beans, sugar-cane, coffee, cacao, fruits, and spices.
   b. **Fibre Crops :** cotton, agave or sisal plant.
   c. **Other Crops :** tobacco, guayule rubber.
   d. **Stock Raising on the Northern Plateaux.**

B. **Minerals.**
   a. **Anthracite Coal in Sonora ; Graphite.**
   b. **Metals.** Silver, gold, copper, lead, iron, antimony, quicksilver, zinc, manganese.
   c. **Vast Supplies of Oil, 3044.**

C. **Great Forests of Valuable Timber.**

D. **Manufacturing.** Meat-packing, cotton-milling, rope and twine, soap, cigars and cigarettes, sugar, rubber.

V. CHIEF CITIES.

Mexico City, 2159 ; Guadalajara, 2156 ; Vera Cruz, 3313.

Interest-Questions in Geography

What does the name of the Himalaya Mountains mean ?   1626.

How did a volcano preserve an ancient civilization for us ?   2653.

What regulates the rainfall ?   2741.

How do we measure rainfall ?   2742.

What is the most important agent in shaping land surfaces ?   3349.

Why is the Sahara a Desert ?   2860.

What makes sand ?   2870.

How are wandering sand dunes kept at home ?   2870.

Where can you dip fresh water from the Atlantic Ocean ?   136.

What great continent lies uninhabited by Man ?   173.

How can boats float upstairs ?   688.

In what city are there many floating homes ?   694.

Where is the oldest existing canal ?   686.

Why is the Hwang Ho called " China's Sorrow " ?   1662.

How does a mountain reveal its age ?   2595.

How does it happen that many people living on the Equator suffer from cold ?   840.

Where is ivory mined ?   2966.

Where are the Pillars of Hercules ?   1463.

How did the Latin Quarter of Paris get its name ?   2516.

Where is there a great wall of ice 500 miles long ?   173.

What island of the East Indies is the third largest in the world ?   2338.

What makes a geyser spout ?   1459.

What made Niagara Falls ?   2362.

Why is a rain storm feared in Lima, Peru ?   1948.

What queer lake helps us to surface our roads ?   3248.

What is the name of the northernmost town in the world ?   2394.

Where does most of the world's nickel come from ?   3366.

What country is the holy land of three religions ?   2480.

Why does the Dead Sea deserve its name ?   2480.

In what country do we get most of our platinum ?   2627.

Where do birds catch fish for their masters ?   814.

What tiny island was called the Gibraltar of the North Sea ?   1607.

Where does there still live a race of pygmies ?   2707.

How does infertile Chile make the world fertile ?   803.

Why did Africa remain a dark continent so long ?   65.

Why is it possible to grow strawberries in Alaska ?   841.

What region leads the world in volcanoes ?   744.

How does manufacturing help to make fogs ?   1333.

Why is the Red Sea red ?   2758.

In what continent did the human race probably originate ?   2170.

What causes earthquakes ?   1070.

What single river basin is almost as large as the United States ?   137.

Which is the longest mountain system ?   152.

What country is supported by gambling ?   2219.

What Canadian seaport is nearly 1,000 miles from the sea ?   2224.

What country has more canals than railways ?   2321.

What French port was benefited most by the opening of the Suez Canal ?   2111.

What kingdom is political ruler of Mecca ?   2127.

What sea was the first to be navigated by white men ?   2135.

Why is Iraq, once a garden spot, all but desert now ?   1743.

What important French river flows through a natural tunnel for three miles ?   2156.

Which is the smallest county in England ?   2858.

What wild animals are still at large in Europe ?   1237.

How large is the British Empire ?   580.

Which is Britain's highest mountain ?   414.

Which port is the " Gibraltar of the East " ?   2974.

What places have the greatest and smallest variations in temperature ?   840.

Where are there famous hot springs ?   1459.

In what country is Bohemia ?   487.

Where is Devil's Island ?   1553.

Which is Canada's chief winter port ?   2861.

Where is the world's largest cave ?   734.

How did Florida get its name ?   1319.

Which is the world's deepest canyon ?   1916.

In what part of the British Isles is French the official language ?   752.

What is the largest city in South America ?   602.

Where are the most dangerous volcanoes in America ?   2863.

Why is London warmer than Labrador ?   1554.

Which French mountains are extinct volcanoes ?   1360.

Where are the world's chief gold-fields ?   1479.

Which is Great Britain's longest river ?   1164.

Which is the largest city in India ?   660.

How did Carolina get its name ?   704.

Which is Europe's " oldest state " ?   2872.

Where is the heaviest rainfall ?   841, 1701.

What is another name for Shropshire ?   2963.

Which is the deepest ocean ?   2469.

Where is Whipsnade Zoo ?   1622.

Where is the Atlantic west of the Pacific ?   2487.

What is the Pearl of the Orient ?   748.

What is the Garden of the Gulf ?   2684.

Which is the City of Steel or Iron City of U.S.A. ?   2614.

What is a hacienda ?   744.

What did Khufu build ?   2707.

Where is the Gran Chaco ?   491.

Is Buda or Pest the older part of Budapest ?   600.

What was the Polish Corridor ?   2642.

Where is one of the world's longest breakwaters ?   558.

Where and what is the Wallace Line ?   1074–75 (map).

Why are the monsoons so important to India ?   1701.

Where and what is the heating apparatus of N.W. Europe ?   1554.

Who live on the top of a " mesa " ?   2698.

What and where is the Plain of Armageddon ?   2481.

How long is the Khyber Pass ?   1691.

Can you tell a Persian from a Turkish carpet ?   705.

What is the Heidelberg tun ?   1604.

Where is the " Valley of Death " ?   2482.

Where is the ruined " city of palms " ?   2485.

Where are the Fortunate Isles believed to be ?   690.

What are Rum, Eigg and Muck ?   1737.

Where is " la ville lumière " ?   2514.

Is there a Sydney in Canada ?   695.

What is Hull's full name ?   1651.

Where is the Icarian Sea and who was it named after ?   1680.

Where is the " city of peace " ?   1819.

Which is the Keystone State of the U.S.A. ?   2546.

What is " Peruvian bark " used for ?   2559.

Books for the Student of Geography

Countries of the World.   Ed. Sir J. Hammerton.

Peoples of All Nations.   Ed. Sir J. Hammerton.

Human Geographies.   J. Fairgrieve and E. Young.

The Home of Mankind.   H. Van Loon.

Commercial Geography.   G. G. Chisholm.

Britain and the British Seas.   Sir H. J. Mackinder.

Geography and World Power.   J. Fairgrieve.

An Atlas of Current Affairs.   J. F. Horrabin.

A Brief Survey of the British Empire.   Mrs. H. A. L. Fisher.

A Geography of the World.   O. J. R. Howarth and W. A. Bridewell.

A Geography of Everyday Things.   Visct. Sandon and F. E. West.

Commercial Geography of the World.   O. J. R. Howarth.

The World and Its Discovery.   H. B. Wetherell.

Descriptive Geography of the World.   F. D. and A. J. Herbertson.

The Antiquity of Man.   Sir A. Keith.

The Races of Europe.   W. Z. Ripley.

Textbook of Geology.   Sir A. Geikie.

Geology for Beginners.   W. W. Watts.

Man and his Conquest of Nature.   M. Newbigin.

The British Empire.   Sir C. Lucas.

Physical Geography.   Philip Lake.

Mirror of the Sea.   Joseph Conrad.

Famous Explorers.   R. J. Finch.

The Study of Man.   A. C. Haddon.

A Study of the Oceans.   J. Johnstone.

Earthquakes and Mountains.   H. Jeffries.

BIOLOGY

THE most wonderful thing in the world is Life. Since the earliest days of civilized thought philosophers have wondered at its manifold problems and have sought in vain to penetrate its mysteries. What is life ? What is that magic thing, possessed alike by the tiniest plant and the great genius among men, which serves to set them apart from the " dead " rock of the hillside ? We are perhaps very little nearer to a final definition of life than were the old Greek sages. Yet of the facts *about* life we know vastly more. It is with these facts that Biology (430) deals. It was not until the beginning of the 19th century that Biology was organized definitely as a separate science. About that time the knowledge of botany and zoology, anatomy and physiology, had developed far enough to suggest to scientists that certain great principles must run through all forms of Life, a study which became known as the science of biology. In the Outline on Nature Study (3571) we examine many of the most interesting and significant facts about plants and animals—without, however, emphasizing any general biological laws. Here we shall survey briefly the scope of biology as a science and examine simply some of the more important characteristics common to all forms of life.

I. THE SCOPE OF BIOLOGICAL SCIENCE.

A. Biology is the Science of All Life.

a. Botany (531)—Biology applied to Plant Life (2620) ; Zoology (3446)—Biology applied to the Animal Kingdom (156).

b. Relations of Biology to Other Sciences.

1. Chemistry (766) supplies data and methods for studying substances involved in life (food, tissues, fluids, such as blood and the sap of plants). An example is the chemistry of digestion (1016). This aspect of chemistry is often called Organic Chemistry (774), and it is, in fact, the chemistry of carbon compounds. A more definite term—Biochemistry (429)—however, is used to describe the specific chemistry of life's processes.

2. Physics (2591) supplies data and methods for studying the effects upon life of physical states and forces, such as light, heat, electricity, etc. For instance, physics helps to tell why sap rises (*2621*).

3. Geology (1432) supplies data concerning how the " life environment "—that is, the earth's crust, the air, the waters of the earth—came to have its present form. It helps to trace the history of life by studying the age of fossils, and this study is often given a separate name—Palaeontology 434, 1353.

B. Chief Subdivisions of Biology.

a. Cytology deals with the composition and structure of cells (738), the basic units from which all living things are built ; Histology deals with the manner in which these cells are organized into living tissues ; Anatomy (150) investigates the arrangement of tissues into organs, and the arrangement of organs in the living organism.

b. Embryology 433, 1154, studies the development of individual organisms from the first single cell ; Morphology (531) applies the principles of the foregoing branches to a study of the causes governing the structure and forms of all living organisms ; Physiology (434, 533) investigates and describes the functions of the parts of the organisms.

c. Ecology (1079, 434, 531) deals with the relations of plants and animals to one another, to environment, effects of climate, etc.

d. Genetics (433, 621, 1427) includes the study of the laws governing heredity in plants and animals. Eugenics (1230) is a branch or outgrowth of Genetics, applied to animals. Plant breeding (533, 621) is an important modern development.

e. Taxonomy (434, 531) is the classification and naming of living things, closely linked with, and almost the same as, Systematy.

II. BIOLOGY'S TEACHINGS—THE LIFE PROCESS.

A. Things Necessary to Life.

a. Chemical Elements, 775. Of all those of which the earth is composed, 10 elements only, besides a number of so-called " trace-elements," are required by vegetable organisms. These are carbon, oxygen, hydrogen, nitrogen, iron, sulphur, phosphorus, potassium, magnesium, calcium; trace-elements include cobalt, copper, iodine, etc. (*See* articles on these elements).

b. Water essential to Life, 3347.

c. Heat and Light essential to Life, 1915.

d. The Nitrogen Cycle, 2373.

B. Combination of Matter into Life Forms.

a. The Cell (738) is the Combining Unit. The cell is the unit of all tissue (432). Many primitive plants and animals consist of single cells—Amoeba (2695), Yeast (3433). Higher forms start as single cells in the reproductive process and grow by cell-division (433, *739*).

b. Chemical Nature of Cells. Protoplasm (2695) is the universal material. Plant structures are stiffened primarily with cellulose (739), animal structures usually with compounds of calcium and silicon.

c. Basic Chemical and Physical Processes.

1. Life materials are obtained from lifeless air, earth, and water by the process of " Photosynthesis " (2589). This is the scientific name of the process by which plants with the aid of sunlight use their green colouring matter (chlorophyll) to extract carbon from the carbon dioxide of the air, and then combine that carbon with the minerals and water from the earth to manufacture the materials from which plant cells are built.

2. Plants alone possess the chlorophyll necessary for Photosynthesis (2589). Animals live directly or indirectly on the food manufactured by plants.

3. Many life processes are carried out through the action of Enzymes (1220).

d. Food Absorption and Conversion.

1. Single-celled animals and plants obtain their food by absorbing it through the cell walls (*432*). Many-celled types usually have some kind of container into which food is drawn and held while being absorbed.

2. Chemical nature of food conversion— partly by chlorophyll in plants (2621) ; by digestive ferments in animals (1266, 1470).

e. Distribution of Food.

1. Circulation of sap in higher plants, 2621.

2. Circulation of blood in animals, **474**, *475*, 1591.

f. Respiration necessary to all Forms of Life, **2768**, 2621.

g. Indirect Ways of obtaining Life Substances.

1. Parasitism (2512), living upon body material of another living organism (*434*, **1407**, *2621*). Typical parasites among plants : rusts and smuts, **2857**. Usually accompanied by degeneration of the parasite (2513).

2. Saprophytism, living upon material of dead organisms, *1408*, 2621. Mushrooms (**2260**) are typical plant saprophytes.

3. Symbiosis (2514), strictly a combination of two forms of life into a partnership, each carrying on a separate share of the life process, as in Lichens (**1932**). In many cases, only one organism may attain apparent benefit (924).

h. Disposing of used and waste Materials.

1. By Excretion, 1017, 1470, 1855.

2. By Respiration, 2768.

3. By Bacterial Action, 335.

C. Organization of Life Processes.

a. Life Processes are carried out only through Individual Organisms.
It is characteristic of all the phenomena of life that they are invariably found associated with individuals *functioning as units*. The parts of each unit are so co-ordinated that they act together toward a common end.

b. Co-ordinating Mechanism of Plants.
Little is known of the forces which control this feature of plant life. The manner in which the various parts of a great tree, for instance, " communicate " with one another so that each performs its proper part in relation to the whole tree is still a mystery. Evidence of delicate co-ordination in Plants is well shown in the mechanism for fertilization by insects, *531*, 2447 ; also in the Sensitive Plant, *2625*.

c. Co-ordinating Mechanism in Animals.
The very low types of animals, such as Sponges, present the same mystery in this respect as do plants. But, beginning with the Jelly-fish, there appears a distinct equipment definitely suited for the co-ordinating process—that is, a nervous system.

1. Nerves and their work, 2316.

2. Nervous systems of higher animals culminate in Man's brain (545, *546*), the highest development of the co-ordinating mechanism. *See also* articles on Animals, Behaviour of, 159 ; Migration, 2169.

Note : Both Animals and Plants react to light, heat, chemicals, etc., by a series of *tropisms*, which some authorities think control all life. *See* Leaves, **1914** ; Migration, **2169** ; Plant Life, 2622.

D. Reproduction of Life.

a. Asexual Reproduction.
This consists of the production of one or more new organisms from a single organism. It may take place in one of the following ways :

1. By Fission, or the division into two approximately equal parts, as in Amoeba (2695) and Bacteria (**335**).

2. By Budding, or the outgrowth of one or more new organisms which, sooner or later, may be separated from the parent organism —Hydra (**1664**), Sponges (**3067**), Yeast (**3433**) and some plants such as Frogbit (**3356**).

3. By Spore Formation, 2918—that is, by the production of minute bodies, usually consisting of a single cell which is liberated and can grow into a new organism. Ferns (**1266**) and Fungi (**1407**) all produce spores.

b. Sexual Reproduction, *431*, 432.
This type consists of the union of two reproducing cells or Gametes (1617). Often the two types of cells are found upon the same individual, as in the case of most flowers (**1322**).

1. The male cell is called a sperm.

2. The female cell is called an ovum or egg cell. In some cases " Parthenogenesis " takes place, an unfertilized female being capable of producing young, usually themselves infertile females, as in certain aphides (**185**) and in many sawflies.

Note: Many organisms reproduce by a process which combines the asexual and the sexual method, and this is known as alternation of generations. The process in plants consists of (1) the asexual production of a spore ; (2) the growth of the spore into a " gametophyte " or sexual plant ; (3) the sexual production by the gametophyte of a " sporophyte " or non-sexual plant, which in turn produces spores again by the asexual process. Examples of this process are seen in Moss (*2238*) and Ferns (**1266**). In some insects, such as Aphides (**185**), there is a different alternation of generations. This occurs also in many parasites (2512).

E. Development of Life.

a. Embryology, 1154.

b. Egg, **1093**, 442 ; Seeds and Spores, 2916.

III. HISTORY OF LIFE.

A. Evolution, **1244**, *158*.

a. Various Theories : Buffon's Doctrine, 603 ; Darwin, **975** ; Modern Theories, 1246.

b. What Geology Tells Us of Evolution, **1432** ; the story of Fossils, **1353**.

c. Some Examples of Evolution : Horse, 1645; Elephant, *1140* ; Flatfish, *1298*. Survival of primitive types : Marsupials, **2111** ; Opossum, **2442**.

B. Heredity and What It Means, **1617**.

Books for the Biology Student

Note : The list of books which accompanies the Outline on Nature Study deals with the habits of plants and animals from the point of view of common experience and observation. The books listed here emphasize mainly the fundamental laws of life, the structure and physiology of living creatures, and the history of life and its evolution. They were chosen for their importance, their clearness, and their interest, and while they may present a few technical difficulties to the newcomer in Biology, they will soon prove as fascinating as any story of travel or adventure. Further lists will be found under Zoology and Botany.

Elements of Plant Biology. A. G. Tansley.
Life ; Hunting Under the Microscope. Sir A. E. Shipley.
Common Objects of the Microscope. Rev. J. G. Wood.
A History of Science. H. S. and E. H. Williams.
The Science of Life. Sir J. Arthur Thomson.
Essays of a Biologist ; Rare Animals, and the Disappearance of Wild Life. J. Huxley.
Life in Ponds and Streams. W. S. Furneaux.
Life—Outlines of General Biology. Sir J. A. Thomson and Sir P. Geddes.
Origin and Problem of Life. A. E. Baines.

The Cell in Development and Inheritance. Edmund B. Wilson.
Living Machinery. A. V. Hill.
The Origin of Species. Charles Darwin.
Mendel's Principles of Heredity. William Bateson.
Species and Varieties, Their Origin by Mutation. Hugo de Vries.
The Evolution Theory. August Weismann.
Man's Place in Nature. Thomas H. Huxley.
What is Eugenics ? Leonard Darwin.
Origin and Evolution of Life. Henry Fairfield Osborn.
The Phenomena of Life. George Crile.
The Nature of Living Matter. L. Hogben.
The Science of Life (3 vols.). H. G. Wells, J. S. Huxley and G. P. Wells.
Biology for Everyman, edited by Sir J. Arthur Thomson.
Animal Ecology. C. E. Elton.
Biology in Everyday Life. J. R. Baker and G. B. S. Haldane.
World Natural History. E. G. Boulenger.
Animal Biology. Grove and Newall.
Adaptive Coloration in Animals. H. B. Cott.
Microbe Hunters. P. de Kruif.
The Virus, Life's Enemy. K. M. Smith.

BOTANY
Classification of Plants

COUNTLESS difficulties confront botanists in the classification of plants, and the various writers differ widely in their arrangements. But such differences are not important to the general student. The classification below does not pretend to be complete, but includes only those groups which are either of scientific importance or can be simply studied. Students should begin this Outline by reading the general articles on **Botany (531)**, **Flowers (1321)**, **Leaves (1914)**, **Roots (2825)**, **Plant Life (2620)**, **Seeds (2916)**, **Trees (3245)**. The divisions in the classification of plants, as in that of animals (435), are Phylum, Sub-phylum, Class, Order, Family, Genus. In each case the phylum is indicated by a Roman numeral (I, II, III, etc.), the sub-phylum by " sub-ph.," and the others by the following abbreviations : " Cl., Ord., Fam., Gen." An explanation of the meaning of these group names is given in page 435. **Note :** A simple classification is given in page 2620.

I. THALLOPHYTA.

Simplest plants, usually distinguished by having a " thallus," that is, a body which has no differentiated organs, such as flowers, wood fibres, leaves, roots, etc. Forms range from microscopic size to enormous growths as the giant kelp. Most types reproduce by simple division or by spore formation, but higher types have primitive sexual characteristics. The simpler Thallophytes are frequently grouped together as Protophyta, equivalent to the Protozoa (2695) of the Animal Kingdom. Among the classes of the Protophyta are many of those included among the Algae and placed there in the table below. Others, however, show features more akin to those of animals than plants, being for example motile ; these are sometimes called Flagellata. Among these simplest forms were the ancestors of all the higher plants.

Sub-ph. **ALGAE, 111, 2914.** Includes those Thallophyta which contain chlorophyll.

Cl. **Chlorophyceae :** " Green Algae," simple one-celled forms and multicellular forms, with no colouring matter other than chlorophyll. Reproduction either sexual or asexual.

Ord. **Volvocales :** Single-celled plants capable of moving about with the aid of " cilia " or vibrating hair-like organs ; often classed as animals in the group Flagellata. Typical genera, *Volvox* (432), *Chlamydomonas.*

Ord. **Protococcales :** One- or many-celled motile or non-motile forms. Typical genera, *Pleurococcus,* Green Slime, often found in colonies on damp stones, tree trunks ; *Hydrodictyon,* Water Net, forming net-like colonies sometimes a foot long.

Ord. **Ulotrichales :** Simple unbranched filaments of many cells. *Ulothrix* is a common fresh-water genus.

Ord. **Oedogoniales :** Fresh-water filamentous forms. Typical genus, *Oedogonium.*

Ord. **Ulvales :** Thallus flat or tubular. Best-known genus, *Ulva,* Sea Lettuce.

Ord. **Siphonales :** Lack of cross-walls in body gives continuous cavity. Typical genus, *Vaucheria* (pond-scum, " green felt ").

Ord. **Conjugales :** Forms a complex mass of fused tubes. Typical genus, *Spirogyra* (112), which consists of delicate filaments, found in pond-scum.

Cl. **Characeae :**

Ord. **Charales :** " Stoneworts " ; grow on bottom of ponds. Thallus has definite points from which branches and reproducing cells originate.

Cl. **Rhodophyceae :** " Red Algae " (111, 2914) Some have simple, others have very complicated structure. Sexual reproduction is highly developed.

Cl. **Phaeophyceae :** " Brown Algae," the big seaweeds (2914), chiefly marine (111). Includes Ord. **Laminariales,** the Kelps ; Ord. **Fucales** the Bladder Wracks to which *Sargassum,* the gulf-weed, belongs.

Cl. **Cyanophyceae :** " Blue-green Algae " formerly placed in the Sub-phylum Schizomycetes. Now regarded as the most primitive class of Algae, and thus included in the Protophyta.

Sub-ph. **FUNGI, 1407.** Parasitic and saprophytic forms, lacking chlorophyll. Consist of a mycelium of thread-like filaments (hyphae) which penetrate the food supply and also give rise to the spore-producing parts. Believed by some authorities to be degenerate forms of algae.

Cl. **Phycomycetes** : Hyphae have continuous cavity, cross-walls only being formed in connexion with reproduction. Includes false " mildews " and Black Moulds (1408, **2173**).

Cl. **Ascomycetes** : Hyphae divided by cross-walls ; spores contained in sacs (asci). Includes Morels (1408), Truffles (1408), Ergot (2858), and true Mildews and Moulds (**2173**) ; also the Yeasts, **3433**.

Cl. **Basidiomycetes** : Spores borne on outgrowth from a cell, or row of cells, called a " basidium " ; these are most of the common fungi, the mushrooms and toadstools. Typical examples, Rusts and Smuts (**2857**), Mushrooms (**2260**), Toadstools (*1258, 1408, 2288*).

Note : The sub-phylum **Myxomycetes** or Slime Fungi were once included with the Fungi because they possess spore cases. They do not, however, have the mycelium. The young swarm cells gather into amoeba-like groups, which leads some biologists to class them as animals under the Mycetozoa (*see* Zoology Outline under Protozoa (3622).

Sub-ph. **SCHIZOMYCETES** : Bacteria (335, 2373, *2374*). Usually classed with the Fungi. Reproduction by fission and by spores. Read also Germs in Disease (**1458**).

Note : The **Lichens, 1932**, are partnership plants, consisting of a Fungus which imprisons algae, forming a combination that is mutually helpful. Lichens can be made artificially by placing the proper plants together. They are usually classified by means of the Fungus which enters into the combination. For instance, the genera *Parmelia* and *Physia* are **Ascolichenes**, because the Fungus is an Ascomycete.

II. BRYOPHYTA.

Probably evolved from Green Algae and adapted to land life. Characterized by well developed " alternation of generations " in which the gametophyte (plant of the sexual generation) is the commonly visible form.

Cl. **Hepaticae** : Liverworts (**1969**), probably evolved from Algae and ancestors of Mosses ; spore case opens by splitting or decay of walls

Cl. **Musci** : Mosses (**2238**) ; spore case opens by means of a lid or by slits ; plant differentiated into primitive stems and leaves.

III. PTERIDOPHYTA.

This group is characterized by the appearance of a **Vascular Structure**, that is, a system of specialized cells for conducting sap through the plant body. A striking alternation of generations occurs, the familiar form being the sporophyte (the asexual generation). The gametophyte is a small, simple, green object. The best-known classes are :

Cl. **Equisetales** : The " Horsetails." The only living genus is *Equisetum*, stems jointed, leaves grow in whorls, being united in each whorl into a sheath.

Cl. **Lycopodiales** : Divided into various orders, the Lycopodiaceae or " Club mosses " being the typical one. Stems slender, branched, closely covered with small leaves, moss-like in appearance.

Cl. **Filicales** : Ferns (*434*, **1266**, *1432*) ; leaves bear spores in " sori " or groups on their under surface. Two sub-classes : **Filicineae**, the true Ferns, such as *Pteris*, Bracken (**542**), and **Hydropteridineae**, the Water Ferns.

Note : In prehistoric times members of this and other primitive groups formed huge trees, the forests of their day (*855*).

IV. SPERMATOPHYTA.

Plants in which fertilization results in the production of a seed, a resting embryo embedded in the food store (2918). (In the preceding groups the fusion of the gametes does not result in a resting embryo.) There are two main sub-phyla : (1) Gymnosperms ; (2) Angiosperms.

Note : Many of the less important families are omitted in the classification below.

Sub-ph. **GYMNOSPERMS** : " Naked-seeded " plants in which the seed is exposed to the air. This is a very ancient group, going far back in geological time, and showing evident descent from the ferns ; yet at the same time, its higher members point the way to the Angiosperms. The extant classes are :

Cl. **Cycadales** : Primitive, fern-like or palm-like forms, confined to the tropics. The single stem bears a few large leaves. Typical genera, *Cycas* (Asiatic) and *Zamia* (American).

Cl. **Ginkgoales** : Sole surviving example, the Ginkgo or maidenhair tree (**1464**).

Cl. **Coniferales** : Chief group, the conifers (**890**), found in temperate zones ; tall, erect trees, usually evergreen with needle-like leaves.

Fam. **Araucariaceae** : Male and female cones similar, with numerous pointed scales. Typical genera *Araucaria*, Monkey Puzzle or Chili Pine (*f-i.*) ; *Agathis*, Kauri Gum (2611).

Fam. **Podocarpaceae** : Small trees and shrubs ; cones small. An unimportant group.

Fam. **Pinaceae** : Trees and shrubs. Male cones superficially catkin-like ; females consisting of overlapping scales, usually hard (*890, 2610*). Important genera : *Pinus*, Pines (**2609**) ; *Abies*, Fir (**1278**) ; *Picea*, Spruce (**3070**) ; *Tsuga*, Hemlock (**1608**) ; *Pseudotsuga*, Douglas Fir (*890*) ; *Larix*, Larch (**1892**) ; *Cedrus*, Cedar (**737**).

Fam. **Cupressaceae** : Scales fewer than in Pinaceae, leaves often of two types. Typical genera, *Cupressus*, Cypress (**952**) ; *Taxodium*, Deciduous or Swamp Cypress (952, 3355) ; *Juniperus*, Juniper (**1840**), in which cone-scales are amalgamated to form a berry-like fruit ; *Sequoia*, Redwoods (**2921**, *3241*).

Fam. **Taxaceae** : Seeds often in fleshy capsules, or with naked ovules. Typical genus, *Taxus*, Yew (*2639*, **3434**).

Sub-ph. **GNETALES** (*f-i.*). Plants intermediate between the later Coniferous orders and the Angiosperms, possibly the true ancestors of the latter. Examples, *Ephedra*, *Gnetum*.

Sub-ph. **ANGIOSPERMS**. The highest plants. Members of this group have true flowers ; seeds are enclosed in seed case. Angiosperms fall into two great classes : (1) **Monocotyledons** and (2) **Dicotyledons**.

Note : The classification of Angiosperms depends chiefly upon the development of and variation in their flowers (1321) and, to a slight extent, their leaves. If the flowers, for example, have their parts arranged in a spiral, they are termed " spiral " ; but in the higher groups they are often in a series of definite, separate whorls, in which case they are " cyclic." The number of families is very large and only important ones are given below.

Cl. Monocotyledons : Seeds have only one cotyledon ; flowers with parts usually arranged in threes ; vascular tissue (3245) usually scattered through the stems, which have no secondary thickening ; leaves are mostly parallel-veined, the main veins being connected by finer veins, while in the leaves of the Dicotyledons there is usually one main vein sending branches to the margin.

Ord. Pandanales : Spiral flowers without perianth ; all forms water-loving. Typical example : Fam. Typhaceae, Gen. Typha, Reed Mace (615).

Ord. Heliobieae : Water plants ; usually cyclic flowers, often enclosed in a spathe.

Fam. Alismaceae, 3356 ; Alisma, Water Plantain ; Sagittaria, Arrowhead, 3356 ; Butomus, Flowering Rush.

Ord. Glumales : Individual flowers protected by bracts or hairs.

Fam. Gramineae : Grass family (1509) ; includes most cereal grains. Typical genera : Avena, Oats (2410) ; Triticum, Wheat (1337, 3372) ; Secale, Rye (2858) ; Oryza, Rice (2774) ; Hordeum, Barley (361) ; Zea, Maize (2068) ; Phragmites, Reed, (Frontis. Vol. 4) ; Sorghum ; Panicum, Millet (2175) ; Bambusa, Bamboo (353) ; Saccharum, Sugar-cane (3112).

Fam. Cyperaceae : Sedges (f-i.) Distinguished from grasses by solid leaf-sheath enclosing stem. Typical genera : Cyperus, Papyrus Reed ; Carex, Common Sedge.

Ord. Palmales : Consists of one family, Palmaceae, the Palms (2483) ; rudimentary perianth present ; flower cluster sheltered by great bract. Typical genera : Phoenix, Date Palm (978) ; Areca, Betel (2408) ; Cocos, Coconut (862) ; Metroxylon, Sago Palm (2859) ; Phytelephas, Ivory Palm (632, 2485).

Ord. Arales : Flowers with highly specialized type of bract ; broad, net-veined leaves.

Fam. Araceae : Arums. Typical genera : Arum, Arum (3332), Richardia, Arum Lily (1948).

Fam. Lemnaceae : Duckweeds (3355) ; leafless, whole plant resembling simple frond ; form scum on ponds.

Ord. Farinales : Flowers primitive, but often with differentiated calyx and corolla.

Fam. Commelinaceae : Spiderworts. Typical genus : Tradescantia, Spiderwort.

Fam. Bromeliaceae : Bromelia family ; most types epiphytic ; leaves often scaly. Typical genera : Tillandsia ; Ananas, Pineapple (2611).

Ord. Lileales : Perianth varies from primitive to petal-like type ; root system often a bulb, rhizome or corm (612).

Fam. Liliaceae : Floral elements set below ovaries (hypogynous) ; regarded as primitive family. Typical genera : Lilium, Lilies (1947) ; Allium, Onion (2434), Garlic, Leek ; Asparagus, Asparagus (271) ; Convallaria, Lily of the Valley ; Tulipa, Tulip (3253) ; Yucca, Yucca ; Hyacinthus, Hyacinth (1663) ; Ruscus, Butcher's Broom, f-i. ; Scilla, Bluebell (479).

Fam. Juncaceae : Rushes, f-i. Flowers resemble lilies but are clustered ; suited to wind pollination ; leaves grasslike.

Fam. Dioscoreaceae : Tuber roots, climbing stems. Typical genus : Dioscorea, Yam (f-i.) ; Tamus, Black Bryony (f-i.).

Fam. Amaryllidaceae : Floral elements rise from top of ovary (epigynous). Typical genera : Narcissus, Narcissus (2278) ; Daffodil (955) ; Galanthus, Snowdrop (2992) ; Agave, Agave (75) ; Sisal (2975).

Fam. Iridaceae : Iris family ; most highly specialized family ; flowers epigynous. Typical examples : Iris, Iris (1748) ; Gladiolus (f-i.) ; Crocus (130, 932) ; Freesia, (f-i.).

Ord. Scitaminales : Flowers have petal-like stamens ; leaf sheaths build up false stem.

Fam. Musaceae : Banana family. Typical genus : Musa, Banana (354, 690).

Fam. Cannaceae or Scitaminaceae : Canna family. Typical example, Canna.

Fam. Zingiberaceae : Ginger family. Typical genera : Zingiber, Ginger (1464, 3061) ; Maranta, Arrowroot.

Ord. Orchidales : Most highly specialized of all Monocotyledons.

Fam. Orchidaceae : Orchids (2447), including " air plants " (epiphytes) and normal forms, the latter frequently saprophytic or parasitic. Most flowers have a well-developed labellum, or "lip." Typical genera : Orchis, including many of the best known species ; Ophrys, insect-mimicking types, such as the bee and spider orchids ; Laelio-cattleya (2447) ; Cypripedium, Lady's Slipper (1883) ; Vanilla, Vanilla (3305, 1337, 3061) ; Spiranthes, Lady's Tresses (2448).

Cl. Dicotyledons : Plants whose seeds contain two cotyledons (381). Vascular tissue (3245) forms tube or cylinder including central pith ; stems show secondary thickening ; leaf veins usually end at edge of leaf ; flowers have parts in fours or fives.

Note : The Dicotyledons fall into two sub-classes : (1) the Archichlamydeae, in which the flowers are either devoid of corolla (apetalous) or else have one or several separate petals (polypetalous), and (2) the Sympetalae, in which the petals are usually fused into a cup or tube at the base (sympetalous). The classification begins with the Archichlamydeae ; only important families are mentioned.

Ord. Piperales : Primitive form ; naked flowers. Typified by family Piperaceae, genus Piper, Pepper (2547, 3061).

Ord. Salicales : The Willow order with one family ; flowers grow on aments or " catkins," comprising numerous simple flowers, each concealed by a horny sheath or bract.

Fam. Salicaceae : Typical genera : Salix, Willows (3382) ; Populus, Poplars (2655)

Ord. **Juglandales** : The Walnut order, with one family. Flowers in catkins similar to willows, but show beginnings of petal and sepal structure ; compound leaves.

Fam. **Juglandaceae** : Flowers monoecious (1321). Typical genera : *Juglans*, Walnut (3338) ; *Carya*, Hickory ; Pecan.
Ord. **Fagales** : Flowers in catkins similar to those of the Walnut order, but leaves simple.

Fam. **Fagaceae** : Typical genera : *Fagus*, Beech (395) ; *Quercus*, Oak (2409, 909) ; *Castanea*, Spanish Chestnut (782).

Fam. **Betulaceae** : Typical genera : *Betula*, Birch (436) ; *Corylus*, Hazel (1590) ; *Alnus*, Alder (104).
Ord. **Urticales** : Perianth distinct but bracteate instead of having true petals and sepals ; flowers cyclic.

Fam. **Urticaceae** : Nettle family ; alternate leaves. Typical genus ; *Urtica*, Nettle (2335). Fam. **Ulmaceae** : Elm family ; alternate, simple leaves. Examples : *Ulmus*, Elm (1152) ; *Celtis*, Lotus or Nettle tree (2027). Fam. **Moraceae** : Mulberry family. Typical genera : *Morus*, Mulberry (2250) ; *Cannabis*, Hemp (1608) ; *Ficus*, Fig (1270) ; Rubber Plant ; Banyan (359) ; *Artocarpus*, Breadfruit (557) ; *Humulus*, Hop (*1337*, 1641).

Note: All the catkin-bearing plants are now often grouped together as **Amentiferae**.

Ord. **Santalales** : Flowers cyclic as in above order, but calyx and corolla are differentiated.

Fam. **Santalaceae** : Typical genus : *Santalum*, Sandalwood.

Fam. **Loranthaceae** : Most members tropical and parasitic. Typical example : *Viscum*, Mistletoe (2194).
Ord. **Polygonales** : Flowers cyclic ; perianth segments in threes.

Fam. **Polygonaceae** : The Dock family. Typical genera : *Polygonum*, Knotgrass ; *Rumex*, Dock ; *Rheum*, Rhubarb (2774).
Ord. **Centrospermales** : Transitional forms ranging from bracteate flowers of **Chenopodiaceae** to well-differentiated perianth of **Caryophyllaceae**.

Fam. **Chenopodiaceae:** Goosefoot family ; leaves adapted to avoid evaporation of water. Typical genera : *Chenopodium*, Goosefoot ; *Beta*, Beet (396).

Fam. **Caryophyllaceae** : Pinks ; flowers well developed with calyx tending to fuse into tube in some types. Typical genera ; *Silene*, *Lychnis*, Campions (674) ; *Dianthus*, Pink (2611), Carnation (703), Sweet William ; *Stellaria*, Stitchwort (3092), Chickweed (*f-i.*).
Ord. **Ranales** : Ranges from primitive types with spiral flowers to well-developed cyclic flowers having true perianth.

Fam. **Ranunculaceae** : Crowfoot family. Typical genera : *Ranunculus*, Buttercup (628) ; Crowfoot (*3355*) ; *Delphinium*, Larkspur (1893) ; *Paeonia*, Peony (2546) ; *Clematis*, Traveller's Joy (836) ; *Helleborus*, Hellebore, Christmas Rose (*f-i.*) ;

Aquilegia, Columbine (878) ; *Hepatica*, Hepatica ; *Caltha*, Marsh Marigold ; *Aconitum*, Monkshood (2639) ; *Anemone* (154).
Fam. **Berberidaceae** : Typical genus : *Berberis*, Barberry.

Fam. **Nymphaeaceae** : Typical genera ; *Nuphar*, Yellow Water Lily (532, 3354) ; *Nymphaea*, White Water Lily (2288, 3354) ; Sacred Lotus (*2027*).

Fam. **Magnoliaceae** : Magnolia family. Typical genera : *Magnolia*, Magnolia (2064) ; *Liriodendron*, Tulip Tree (*f-i.*).

Fam. **Myristicaceae** : Nutmeg family ; tropical trees and shrubs. Typical genus : *Myristica*, Nutmeg (2407, *3061*).

Fam. **Lauraceae** : Laurel family. Typical genera : *Laurus*, Bay Laurel (1900) ; *Cinnamomum*, Cinnamon (*3061*), Camphor (674).
Ord. **Rhoedales** : An advance on the Ranales.

Fam. **Papaveraceae** : The Poppy family, from which the other families may have evolved. Typical genus : *Papaver*, Poppy (2655), Opium (2442).

Fam. **Resedaceae** : Typical genus : *Reseda*, Mignonette (2169).

Fam. **Cruciferae** : The Cabbage family (639). Typical genus : *Brassica*, Cabbage, Turnip, Mustard (2270) ; *Raphanus*, Radish (640) ; *Nasturtium*, Watercress (3353) ; *Capsella*, Shepherd's Purse ; *Iberis*, Candytuft (640) ; *Cardamine*, Lady's Smock, Bittercress (3353) ; *Cheiranthus*, Wallflower (640).
Ord. **Sarraceniales** : In this order are included many insect-catching plants.

Fam. **Sarraceniaceae** : American forms. Typical genus : *Sarracenia*, Pitcher Plants (2613).

Fam. **Nepenthaceae** : Asiatic forms ; pitchers at tip of tendrils. Typical genus : *Nepenthes*, Pitcher Plants (2613, *f. 2621*).

Fam. **Droseraceae** : Leaves exude sticky fluid. Typical genera : *Drosera*, Sundew (3120) ; *Dionoea*, Venus's Fly-Trap (3313).
Ord. **Rosales** : This is the dominant order in the sub-class **Archichlamydeae**, with over 14,000 species. The fruits are highly specialized in a large variety of forms. Types supposed to have evolved from Buttercup family, Ranunculaceae.

Fam. **Saxifragaceae** : Most primitive types ; regarded as ancestors of other families in the order. Typical genera : *Saxifraga*, Saxifrage (2877) ; *Hydrangea* (1665) ; *Ribes*, Gooseberry (1486), Currant (944).

Fam. **Rosaceae** : The Rose family. Typical genera : *Spiraea*, Spiraea, Meadow Sweet ; *Alchemilla*, Lady's mantle ; *Rosa*, Rose (2827) ; *Fragaria*, Strawberry (3103) ; *Potentilla*, Barren Strawberry (3103) ; *Rubus*, Raspberry (2745), Blackberry (463), Loganberry (*f-i.*) ; *Prunus*, Apricot (191), Sloe, Plum (2630), Peach (2531), Cherry (778), Cherry Laurel (1900, *2639*) ; *Crataegus*, Hawthorn (1588) ; *Pyrus*, Pear (2532), Apple

(190); genus *Pyrus* is now usually subdivided into *Pyrus* (Pear), *Malus* (Apple), *Sorbus* (Rowan, Service), Whitebeam (3376); *Mespilus*, Medlar; *Amygdalus*, Almond (124); *Cydonia*, Quince (2718).

Fam. Leguminosae : Pod-bearing plants ; roots often harbour nitrifying bacteria (337); genus *Mimosa* is typical of the stock from which other types of Leguminosae evolved. This family is divided into three sub-families according to flower structure.

Sub-fam. Mimosoideae : Tropical and semi-tropical forms ; corolla regular. Typical genera : *Mimosa*, Mimosa, Sensitive Plant (*2625*); *Acacia*, Acacia (16).

Sub-fam. Caesalpinioidae : Flower partially " papilionaceous," that is butterfly-shaped. Typical genera : *Gleditschia*, Honey Locust ; *Tamarindus*, Tamarind (1401); *Cercis*, Judas Tree.

Sub-fam. Papilionoidae : Flower completely papilionaceous. Typical genera: *Phaseolus*, Bean (380); *Glycine*, Soya Bean (3029); *Pisum*, Pea (2530); *Lathyrus*, Sweet Pea (2530); *Lens*, Lentil (1925); *Arachis*, Groundnut (1549); *Trifolium*, Clover (852), Shamrock (2936); *Melilotus*, Sweet Clover (854); *Medicago*, Alfalfa (110); *Astragalus*, Milk Vetch, Tragacanth (1558); *Glycyrrhiza*, Liquorice (1962); *Lotus*, Bird's-foot Trefoil (2027); *Robinia*, Locust, False Acacia ; *Indigofera*, Indigo (1718); *Haematoxylon*, Logwood (*f-i.*).

Fam. Platanaceae : Typical genus : *Platanus*, Plane Tree (2616).

Fam. Hamamelidaceae : Typical genus : *Hamamelis*, Witch-hazel (*f-i.*).

Ord. Geraniales : Flowers completely cyclic ; carpels tend to fuse into " compound pistils " in higher families.

Fam. Geraniaceae : Geranium family, 1444. Typical genera : *Pelargonium*, so-called "Geranium"; *Geranium*, true Geranium.

Fam. Tropaeolaceae : Typical genus : *Tropaeolum*, Nasturtium (2279).

Fam. Linaceae : Type: *Linum*, Flax (1313).

Fam. Meliaceae : Typical genus : *Swietenia*, Mahogany (2065).

Fam. Euphorbiaceae : Spurge family. Typical genera : *Euphorbia*, Spurge (*f-i.*); *Ricinus*, Castor Bean (1263); *Hevea*, Para Rubber (2833); *Manihot*, Cassava (3153).

Fam. Oxalidaceae : Typical genus : *Oxalis*, Oxalis, Wood Sorrel (2936).

Fam. Rutaceae : Typical genus : *Citrus*, Orange (2442), Lemon (1920), Lime (1949), Grapefruit (1499).

Ord. Sapindales : Flower forms similar to Geraniales ; distinguished by structure of ovules.

Fam. Hippocastanaceae : Typical genus : *Æsculus*, Horse Chestnut (1647, *2284*): by some this family is retained within fam. Sapindaceae.

Fam. Anacardiaceae : Typical genera : *Rhus*, Sumach (2638), Lacquer (1881); *Mangifera*, Mango (2087).

Fam. Aceraceae : Maple family. Typical genus : *Acer*, Maple (2092); Sycamore (3143).

Fam. Buxaceae: Type: *Buxus*, Box (*f-i.*).

Fam. Aquifoliaceae : Typical genus : *Ilex*, Holly (1636).

Ord. Rhamnales : Flowers tetra-cyclic, that is, the parts of the perianth arise from four distinct circles or whorls. Otherwise order resembles Sapindales.

Fam. Rhamnaceae : Buckthorn family. Typical genus : *Rhamnus*, Buckthorn.

Fam. Vitaceae : Shrubs, climbing vines. Typical genera : *Vitis*, Grape Vine (944, 1499); *Ampelopsis*, Virginia Creeper.

Ord. Malvales : Most types have carpels fused into compound pistil (syncarpous).

Fam. Malvaceae : Mallow family ; stamens fused into tube around pistil. Typical genera : *Malva*, Mallow (2071); *Gossypium*, Cotton (917, 986); *Althaea*, Hollyhock (1636); *Eriodendron*, Kapok tree (1847).

Fam. Tiliaceae : Lime family ; carpels fused ; stamen form variable. Typical genera : *Tilia*, Lime Tree (1948); *Corchorus*, Jute (1844).

Fam. Bombacaceae : Silk cottons ; seeds covered with silky hairs. Typical genus : *Adansonia*, Baobab.

Fam. Sterculiaceae : Cola nut family ; flowers often have stamens fused. Typical genera : *Sterculia*, Bottle tree (533); *Theobroma*, Cacao (648, *861, 1337*).

Ord. Parietales : Complex group showing marked relation to Ranales.

Fam. Passifloraceae : Typical genus : *Passiflora*, Passion Flower (*f-i.*).

Fam. Begoniaceae : Typical genus : *Begonia*, Begonia (402).

Fam. Theaceae : the Tea family. Typical genera : *Thea*, Tea (3159, *1337*); *Camellia*, Camellia (671).

Fam. Violaceae : Violet family. Typical genus : *Viola*, Violet (3324), Pansy (2494).

Ord. Opuntiales : The Cactus order (648, *2288*). Contains one family, Cactaceae. Typical genera ; *Cereus*, *Opuntia*, *Echinocactus*.

Ord. Myrtales : Stamens always cyclic ; some perigynous, some epigynous.

Fam. Myrtaceae : Myrtle family. Typical genera : *Myrtus*, Myrtle (*f-i.*); *Eucalyptus*, Eucalyptus (1230); *Eugenia*, Allspice (*3061*) and Clove (854, *3061*).

Fam. Onagraceae : Typical genus : *Epilobium*, Willow-herbs (3382); *Fuchsia*, Fuchsia (1404).

Fam. Punicaceae : Typical genus : *Punica*, Pomegranate (2652).

Fam. Rhizophoraceae : Typical genus : *Rhizophora*, Mangrove (2088).

Ord. Umbellales : Most highly developed forms in the sub-class, Archichlamydeae. Stamens always cyclic. Flowers epigynous.

Fam. Araliaceae : Typical genus : *Hedera*, Ivy (1788).

Fam. Cornaceae : Typical genus : *Cornus*, Dogwood (*f-i.*).

Fam. **Umbelliferae** : The Parsley family ; flowers usually very small and numerous, in umbrella-shaped clusters (umbels). Typical genera : *Apium*, Celery (**738**) ; *Peucedanum*, Parsnip (**2526**) ; *Daucus*, Carrot ; *Conium*, Hemlock (**1608**).

Note : This point marks the end of the sub-class **Archichlamydeae** and the beginning of the sub-class **Sympetalae**, in which the petals are fused into a more or less tubular corolla.

Ord. **Ericales**: Most primitive of Sympetalae.
Fam. **Ericaceae** : Heath family. Typical genera : *Erica*, Heaths (**1597**), *Calluna*, Heather (**1596**) ; *Vaccinium*, Cranberry, Bilberry (**428**) ; Azalea (**324**) ; *Arbutus*, Strawberry Tree (**204**) ; Rhododendron (**2772**).

Ord. **Primulales** : Single cycle of stamens, opposite petals ; seed-supporting structure " free " inside ovary.
Fam. **Primulaceae** : Primrose family. Typical genera : *Primula*, Primrose (**2684**), Cowslip (**924**) ; *Lysimachia*, Yellow Loosestrife, Pimpernel (*f-i.*) ; *Cyclamen*, Shepherd's Weather Glass.

Ord. **Ebenales**: Members show both primitive polypetalous forms and advanced epigynous characteristics.
Fam. **Ebenaceae** : Ebony family. Typical genus : *Diospyros*, Ebony (**1076**), Persimmon.
Fam. **Sapotaceae** : Sapodilla family. Typical genera : *Chrysophyllum*, Star Apple (**1401**) ; *Sapota*, Sapodilla ; *Palaquium*, Gutta percha Tree (**1559**).

Ord. **Gentianales** : Flowers stable in type, usually with five petals and stamens, and two carpels ; corolla twisted in bud.
Fam. **Gentianaceae** : Gentian family. Typical genus : *Gentiana*, Gentian (**1429**).
Fam. **Oleaceae**: Olive family ; leaves often leathery ; many types grow flowers in clusters. Typical genera : *Olea*, Olive (**2431**); *Ligustrum*, Privet (*f-i.*) ; *Syringa*, Lilac (**1947**) ; *Jasminum*, Jasmine (**1812**), *Fraxinus*, Ash (**262**).
Fam. **Loganiaceae** : Typical genera : *Strychnos*, *S. nux-vomica* (*f-i.*) ; *Gelsemium*, Yellow or Carolina Jasmine.
Fam. **Apocynaceae** : Dogbane or Periwinkle family. Highly evolved, except that carpels are distinct. Typical genera : *Nerium*, Oleander ; *Vinca*, Periwinkle.

Ord. **Polemoniales** : Flowers symmetrical with several planes of symmetry.
Fam. **Polemoniaceae** : Typical genus : Phlox (**2572**).
Fam. **Convolvulaceae** : Twining, climbing plants. Typical genera : *Ipomaea*, Morning Glory ; Convolvulus (**898**) ; *Cuscuta*, Dodder (*2514*).

Ord. **Boraginales** : Types tend to evolve lobed ovary, resulting in four-part form.
Fam. **Boraginaceae** : Borage family ; members usually have hairy stems. Typical genera : *Myosotis*, Forget-me-not (**1351**) ; *Heliotropium*, Heliotrope (*f-i.*).

Ord. **Labiatales** : Flower forms tend to develop about only one axis of symmetry.

Fam. **Lentibulariaceae** : Insectivorous, marsh-loving plants. Typical genera : *Utricularia*, Bladderwort (**2624**, *plate f.* 2621*) ; *Pinguicula*, Butterwort (*2624*).
Fam. **Verbenaceae** : The more primitive forms. Typical genera : Verbena ; *Tectona*, Teak (**3162**).
Fam. **Labiatae** : Most of the garden herbs belong to this family (**3206**). Typical genera : *Mentha*, Mint (**2187**) ; *Nepeta*, Ground Ivy (*f-i.*) ; *Lamium*, Dead Nettle (**2335**) ; *Thymus*, Thyme (**3206**) ; *Lavandula*, Lavender (**1901**).

Ord. **Personales** : Flowers highly zygomorphic (developed about one axis of symmetry).
Fam. **Solanaceae** : Nightshade family ; members frequently poisonous (**2637**). Typical genera : *Solanum*, Nightshade (**2369**, *2639*), Potato (**2664**) ; Bittersweet (**462**) ; *Nicotiana*, Tobacco (**3219**) ; *Capsicum*, Cayenne Pepper (**2547**) ; *Atropa*, Belladonna, Deadly Nightshade, *2369*, *2639* ; *Petunia*, Petunia ; *Lycopersicon*, Tomato (**3223**).
Fam. **Bignoniaceae** : Trees and woody climbers ; flowers often irregular. Typical genera : *Catalpa*, Catalpa, Indian Bean.
Fam. **Scrophulariaceae** : Figwort family ; fruit two-celled, many-seeded capsule. Contains more than 2,000 species. Typical examples : Toadflax, *Linaria* (*f-i.*) ; *Digitalis*, Foxglove ; Calceolaria ; *Scrophularia*, Figwort (*f-i.*) ; *Verbascum*, Mullein (*f-i.*).
Fam. **Orobanchaceae** : Brown or whitish, leafless, parasitic plants, flowers lipped. *Orobanche*, Broom-rape ; *Lathraea*, Toothwort (*2621*).

Ord. **Rubiales** : Anthers usually distinct ; flowers epigynous.
Fam. **Rubiaceae** : Madder family ; opposite or whorled leaves with interposed stipules. Typical genera : *Cinchona*, Quinine (**2718**) ; *Coffea*, Coffee (**864**, *1337*) ; *Gardenia*, Gardenia.
Fam. **Caprifoliaceae** : Honeysuckle family ; flat-topped flower clusters. Typical genera : *Sambucus*, Elder (**1124**) ; *Lonicera*, Honeysuckle (**1639**).
Fam. **Dipsaceae** : Typical genus : *Dipsacus*, Teasel (**3163**); *Scabiosa*, Scabious (*f-i.*).

Ord. **Campanulales** : Contains highest forms of Angiosperms. Anthers often converge or fuse ; more than 14,500 species in order.
Fam. **Campanulaceae** : Primitive stock of this last order. Typical genus : *Campanula*, Harebell (**479**), Canterbury Bells, Bellflower (*f-i.*).
Fam. **Cucurbitaceae** : The Gourd and Melon family. Typical genera : *Cucurbita*, Marrow (**2109**) ; Squash, Pumpkin (**2702**); *Cucumis*, Musk Melon, Cantelupe (**2137**), Cucumber (**2109**) ; *Citrullus*, Water Melon (**2137**) ; *Lagenaria*, Gourds ; *Bryonia*, Bryony (*f-i.*).

Note : This family is sometimes placed in a separate order, Cucurbitales.
Fam. **Compositae** : The Compositae are the dominant and most highly evolved family of plants, containing over 12,500 species.

Characterized by "compound" inflorescences (1321) ; seeds usually wind-borne on "parachute" (*968, 2917*). Regarded as the highest type known. Typical genera : Aster (**274**) ; Chrysanthemum (**823**) ; *Helianthus*, Jerusalem Artichoke (**256**), Sunflower (**3120**) ; *Taraxacum*, Dandelion (**937**) ; *Lactuca*, Lettuce ; *Cichorium*, Chicory and Endive ; *Dahlia*, Dahlia (**955**) ; *Carduus* and *Cnicus*, Thistles (**3203**); *Tussilago*, Colt's-foot (*f-i.*); *Bellis*,

Daisy (**956**) ; *Anthemis*, Camomile (**673**); *Calendula*, Marigold (**2102**) ; *Centaurea*, Cornflower (**910**), Knapweed ; *Cynara*, Globe Artichoke (**256**). The Compositae are often divided into **Tubuliflorae**, which have a composite floral head made up of small tubular flowers usually surrounded by large "ray" flowers, with conspicuous perianth, and **Liguliflorae**, whose floral head is composed entirely of ray flowers.

Books for the Botany Student

A number of good books on our wild flowers are mentioned in the Bibliography on Nature Study, and some of general interest are included in that on Biology. The following are further useful books on various aspects of Botany.
Practical Plant Ecology. A. G. Tansley.
British Trees and Shrubs. H. Gilbert-Carter.
Trees of Britain. Barbara Briggs.
Wild Flowers Month by Month. Edward Step.

Hayward's Botanist's Pocket Book.
Student's Flora of the British Isles Sir Joseph Hooker.
Flowers of the Field. Forest Trees of Britain. Rev. C. A. Johns.
A Flower Book for the Pocket. Macgregor Skene.
British Grasses. Margaret Plues.
British Ferns, British Fungi, British Mosses. Pub. Epworth Press.
The Advance of the Fungi. E. C. Large.
The Romance of the Fungus World. R. T. and F. W. Rolfe.

ZOOLOGY
Classification of Animals

THE members of the animal kingdom (156) present a far greater variety of structure and function than those of the plant kingdom, for the conditions of animal life are far less fixed and stable than those of plant life. Most plants obtain their food directly from the air and soil ; animals are for the most part compelled to move about in search of food and to adjust themselves to a far greater variety of diet. The struggle between animals for survival is more violent and active than between plants, so that the means of attack and escape are much more highly developed and versatile. Because of the greater variety of forms, animals are even more difficult to classify than plants. Countless differences of opinion exist among authorities, and the systems of classification are subject to change from year to year. The tendency, however, is always to arrive at a classification which will bring out the *natural* relationships between animals from the evolutionary point of view (1244). The method followed here is based upon the best established modern systems, with the omission of many of the less important subdivisions ; other systems are given in pages 156, *158*. Consult the Botany Outline for key to abbreviations (3616) ; read also the main article on **Zoology, 3446** ; **Evolution, 1244** ; **Marine Life, 2103.**

Phylum I. PROTOZOA.
This is a largely unnatural classification consisting principally of microscopic, unicellular, aquatic organisms of primitive and simple form (2695). It is equivalent to the Protophyta among the plants (3616), and like that group contains a number of forms claimed by animals and plants alike. The following classification, based largely on organs of locomotion, is an artificial one ; the more important groups only are indicated.

Cl. **Mastigophora (Flagellata)** : Move by means of a whip-like "flagellum." Numerous orders, including :

Ord. **Euglenoidina** : one or two flagella; type, *Euglena*, common in stagnant fresh water to which they give green colour.

Ord. **Dinoflagellata** : two flagella, often cellulose armour; many parasitic types. *Noctiluca* is a phosphorescent form found at sea.

Ord. **Phytoflagellata** : higher forms multicellular ; often claimed as plants (3616). Types, *Chlamydomonas, Volvox (432).*

Ord. **Protomonadina** : parasitic forms : *Trypanosoma*, sleeping sickness parasite (3252).

Cl. **Rhizopoda** : move by means of "pseudopodia," outgrowths of the cell substance.

Ord. **Amoebina** : *Amoeba* (*f-i.*), a typical example.

Ord. **Foraminifera** (749, *2103*, 2695) : larger forms with complex calcareous shell. Examples, *Polystomella, Globigerina*, found in plankton, *Nummulites* (a common fossil "giant" form).

Ord. **Radiolaria** : large forms with radiating, siliceous skeleton, living in marine plankton (*433*).

Ord. **Mycetozoa** : Slime fungi, forming gigantic amoeba-like masses such as "flowers of tan," *Fuligo varians*.

Cl. **Sporozoa**: parasitic forms. Sub-cl. **Telosporidia** typified by Ord. **Haemosporidia**, including malaria parasite, *Plasmodium* (*2237*).

Sub-cl. **Neosporidia (Sporozoa)** : genus *Nosema* cause important diseases of bees and silkworms.

Cl. **Ciliophora** : Move by means of "cilia," numerous minute hairs. Ord. **Ciliata (Infusoria)** contains numerous forms common in pond water, *Paramoecium* (2695), *Vorticella*, or Bell animalcule, etc.

Note: The animals from this point on are known collectively as **Metazoa**, meaning "advanced" forms, as distinguished from **Protozoa**, meaning "primitive" forms. While the **Protozoa** are mainly single-celled, the structure of the Metazoa consists of groups of cells.

Phylum II. PORIFERA.

The Sponges (**3067**). Sac-like body of connective tissue with single opening ; feed through pores in body wall. Have "skeletons," or stiffening matter, arranged in innumerable " spicules " (*3067*). Typical classes : **Hexactinellida**, skeleton of silica rods (Venus's Flower Basket, Glass-Rope Sponges) ; **Calcarea**, skeleton of carbonate of lime ; **Demospongiae**, mixed types, skeleton of silica or spongin or both (Cup Sponges, Horny or Bath Sponges, Boring Sponges).
Note: Some authorities give the Sponges rank as a separate sub-kingdom, **Parazoa**, divided into Phylum I (**Nuda**), to which belong the **Hexactinellida**, and Phylum II (**Gelatinosa**) containing all other sponges.

Phylum III. COELENTERATA.

Sac-like body ; food swept into single orifice or " mouth " by fringe of tentacles ; rudimentary sense organs, nerve cells, either scattered throughout body or forming connected system.

Cl. **Hydrozoa** : Primitive types, tubular or umbrella-shaped. Typical orders : **Hydroida**, least developed forms (genus *Hydra*, 1664, *1665*) ; **Hydrocorallinae**, gather into coral-like colonies with limy skeletons (Millepore Coral, 908, *plate f. 2104*) ; **Siphonophora**, attached to floating bladders or air-sacs (genus *Physalia*, Portuguese Man-of-War, *1817*).

Cl. **Scyphozoa** : Body umbrella-shaped ; specialized reproductive and sense organs. Jelly-fish (**1817**). Typical order : **Discomedusae** ; genus *Aurelia*, common Jelly-fish (**1817**, *1818*).

Cl. **Anthozoa** (**Actinozoa**) : Individual forms (Sea Anemones, *2105*, **2911**), and colonial forms (Corals, 908, *plate f. 2104*, 2105). Have oesophagus and primitive muscular tissue in tentacles ; colonial types have stiffening matter of carbonate of lime or horny matter.

Sub-cl. **Alcyonaria** : Eight tentacles. Typical families : **Pennatulidae**, Sea-Pens, with feather-shaped upper end ; **Gorgoniidae**, Sea-Fans (*plate f. 908*), Sea-Whips, and Precious Coral of Mediterranean, 908.

Sub-cl. **Zoantharia** : Forms with variable structure. Includes order **Actiniidae**, divisible into sub-orders **Actinaria**, Sea Anemones (**2911**, *924, 2103, 2105*), and **Madreporaria**, Madrepore Corals.

Phylum IV. CTENOPHORA.

Transparent, delicate jelly-fish, but not related closely to Coelenterates.

Phylum V. PLATYHELMINTHES.

Flatworms (**3425**) ; mainly parasitic. Alimentary canal and nervous system well developed ; rudimentary blood vessels and muscles.

Cl. **Turbellaria**, aquatic, ciliated types ; Cl. **Trematoda**, parasitic upon animals (genus *Distomum*, the Liver Fluke) ; Cl. **Cestoda**, Tapeworms.

Phylum VI. NEMERTINA.

Small group of unsegmented marine " worms."

Phylum VII. ROTIFERA.

Wheel Animalcules. Microscopic ; have " wheel " of cilia about free end ; have points of similarity to flat worms, primitive ringed-worms, and molluscs.

Phylum VIII. CHAETOGNATHA.

Bristles about mouth, fins on tail (genus *Sagitta*, a sea-worm).

Phylum IX. ACANTHOCEPHALA.

Cylindrical parasitic forms possibly related to next phylum.

Phylum X. NEMATHELMINTHES.

Round-worms (**3425**) ; muscular, sucking oesophagus, thick skin, parasitic in plants and animals.

Cl. **Nematoda** : Thread-shaped, from microscopic length to 1 yard long ; frequently parasitic, disease-causing forms. Typical genera : *Ascaris*, Round-worm ; *Oxyuris*, Pinworm ; *Ankylostoma*, Hookworm ; *Trichina*, cause of trichinosis ; *Filaria*, cause of elephantiasis.

Ord. **Gordiacea** : Hairy worms ; typified by Horse-hair Worm.

Phylum XI. ANNELIDA (Chaetopoda).

Ringed worms (**3425**) ; cylindrical ; body segmented or " ringed " ; usually locomotion by bristles. Classes : **Polychaeta**, marine types (*3425*) ; **Oligochaeta**, fresh-water and soil types (Earthworm, **1070**). **Hirudinei** : Have suckers instead of bristles for locomotion ; the Leeches (**3425**).

Phylum XII. ARTHROPODA.

Resemble Annelid Worms in segmentation of body, but appendages are jointed to segments ; heavily armoured with chitin ; nervous structure resembles spinal cord ; organs highly developed. The Arthropods are divided into five main living classes : (1) **Crustacea**, Lobsters, Crabs, Shrimps, and Barnacles ; (2) **Arachnida**, Scorpions, Spiders, and Mites ; (3) **Diplopoda**, Millepedes ; (4) **Chilopoda**, Centipedes ; (5) **Hexapoda**, Insects. In addition, there is the small class **Onycophora**, consisting of the strange caterpillar-like *Peripatus*, and considered to be in many ways ancestral ; and the small group of spider-like marine creatures, the class **Pycnogonida**.
Note: Because of the vast size and many subdivisions of the phylum Arthropoda, considerable space has had to be devoted to each of its divisions.
1. Class **CRUSTACEA**, Crustaceans.
Chitinous shell strengthened with lime ; gills (modified for air-breathing in land types) ; appendages develop several branches in swimming types ; have horny carapace or " shell " over combined head and thorax (cephalothorax).

Sub-cl. **Branchiopoda** : Primitive, aquatic forms ; typical order, **Cladocera**, including Water-Fleas. The sub-classes **Ostracoda** and **Copepoda** contain a large variety of usually small marine forms. These, with the **Branchiopoda** and **Cirripedia** were formerly grouped as one heterogeneous sub-class, **Entomostraca**.

Sub-cl. **Cirripedia** : Degenerate, parasitic types. Barnacles (**361**) ; *Sacculina* (**2513**).

Sub-cl. **Malacostraca** : Have 20 or 21 body segments ; most types have eyes on stalks. Principal order : **Decapoda** (" ten-footed "). Five segments of thorax have walking legs ; have strong pincer-like grasping claws (chelae).

Sub-o. **Macrura** : Abdomen large, long. Typical families : Homaridae, Lobsters (**1917**) ; Crangonidae, Shrimps (**2962**) ; Palaemonidae, Prawns (**2962**) ; Astacidae, Crayfish (**926**) ; Paguridae, Hermit Crabs (*924, 925*).

Sub.-o. **Brachyura** : True Crabs (**924**) ; abdomen short or rudimentary ; includes Common Crabs, Spider Crabs, and Land Crabs (*plate f. 924*).

2. Class **ARACHNIDA**, Scorpions, Spiders, Mites. Cephalothorax (fused head and thorax) bears six pairs of appendages, the first two used for grasping, last four pairs as legs. Land forms have either lungs, or **tracheae** (tubes passing air through the body), or both. Among extinct members of this class are grouped the Trilobites and Eurypterids, while the King-Crabs, **Xiphosura** (*plate f. 925*) are grouped here rather than in the Crustacea. Apart from these, there are now considered to be two sub-classes :

Sub.-cl. **Pectinifera** : possessing a pair of pectinei or combs formed from abdominal appendages ; tail-end of body elongated.
Ord. **Scorpiones**, Scorpions, **2888**.

Sub.-cl. **Epectinata** : no pectinei, rear end not elongated.

Super-ord. **Caulogastra** : abdomen constricted from cephalothorax by narrow waist or " pedicle."
Ord. **Pedipalpi** : Whip-scorpions.
Ord. **Araneae** : Spiders (**3062**) ; have silk glands (spinnerets). Typical families ; **Theraphosidae** or **Mygalidae**, including " Bird-Eating " Spiders (*plate f. 3064*), and Trap-Door Spiders (*3064*) ; **Lycosidae**, Wolf Spiders, Tarantula (**3154**); **Argyronetidae**, Water Spider (*2287*), **Attidae**, Leaping Spiders ; **Argiopidae** or **Epeiridae**, including common Garden Spiders (*3062–64*) ; **Agelenidae**, Labyrinth Spiders.
Super-ord. **Pseudoscorpiones** : No " waist," silk glands open on to mandibles. " Book-scorpions."
Super-ord. **Phalangiomorphae** : Includes **Phalangidae**, " Harvest-men," with pill-like body, long slender legs.
Super-ord. **Rhyncostomi** : Order **Acari** : Mites. Abdomen fused with cephalothorax ; mouth formed into sucking beak. Includes Red Mites, Water Mites, Ticks, "Itch" Parasites, Cheese Mites, Follicle Mites ; Fam. **Eriophyidae** are the gall-mites of plants.

3. Class **DIPLOPODA**, Millepedes. Body cylindrical, divided into numerous segments ; each two segments covered by single plate, making it appear as if two pairs of legs spring from each segment (hence " Diplopoda," meaning double-footed) ; internal anatomy differs markedly from that of Centipedes.

4. Class **CHILOPODA**, Centipedes. Centipedes (**742**) resemble insects except for numerous segments of body and many legs.

Note : Some authorities retain a class **Myriapoda**, which includes Millepedes in sub-class Diplopoda and Centipedes in sub-class **Chilopoda**.

5. Class **INSECTA**, Insects. The Insects (**1726**) are distinguished from other Arthropoda by having 3 pairs of legs. Head, body, and abdomen are separate ; they breathe by tracheae (air tubes). The manner in which the young develop (1893) leads to a division of

Insects into two sub-classes :
(1) Apterygota ; (2) Pterygota.
Sub-cl. **Apterygota** : New-born young closely resemble parents. Orders : **Thysanura**, primitive, wingless forms, including *Machilis*, the " Silver-fish " ; **Collembola**, the Spring Tails.
Sub-cl. **Pterygota**, with two divisions :
Division I. **Exopterygota** : Young (nymphs) superficially resemble parents, but with wings undeveloped ; some orders show partial metamorphosis (*1035*).

Ord. **Orthoptera** : " Straight-winged," the front pair stiffened into covers ; mouth adapted for biting and chewing. Includes three sub-orders (1) **Cursoria** or " Runners " such as Cockroaches (**861**, *1732*) ; (2) **Gressoria** or "Walkers " such as Mantis (**2090**), Stick Insects (*1728*), and Leaf Insects (*1728*) ; (3) **Saltatoria** or " Jumpers" such as Grasshoppers and Locusts (**1510**, *plate f. 1512*), and Crickets (**927**) ; also the Mole Cricket (*1727*).
Ord. **Dermaptera** : Front wings hardened into covers but wings sometimes absent ; tip of abdomen bears pincers. Typical family ; **Forficulidae**, Earwigs (**1071**).
Ord. **Plecoptera** : Stone Flies ; nymphs aquatic, with gills.
Ord. **Ephemeroptera** : Consists of a single family **Ephemeridae**, May-flies (**2122**).
Ord. **Odonata** : Dragon-flies (**1034**, *1035*) ; strong biting jaws ; nymphs aquatic.
Ord. **Isoptera** : Social habits similar to ants, but otherwise different. White Ants or Termites (**3188**, *1733*).
Ord. **Embioptera**. Small, gregarious or semi-social insects.
Ord. **Psocoptera** (**Corrodentia**) : Very small forms, biting mouth parts. Single family **Psocidae**, Book Lice.
Ord. **Anoplura** : Very small, flattened, wingless forms ; parasitic.
Sub-ord. **Siphunculata**, sucking mouth parts, Lice.
Sub-ord. **Mallophaga**, biting mouth parts, Bird-lice (**2513**).
Ord. **Thysanoptera** : Thrips ; small forms with hairy wings ; sucking mouth.
Ord. **Hemiptera** : True Bugs ; mouth parts developed for piercing and sucking. Divided into sub-orders : (1) **Heteroptera**, fore and hind wings of different types, as in the Water Bugs, Bed Bugs ; (2) **Homoptera**, all four wings similar, as in Cicadas (**826**), Aphids (**185**), Scale Insects (**1881**, **2878**), Frog-hoppers (*1732*), and Cochineal (**859**).
Division 2. **Endopterygota** : Young (larvae) undergo complete metamorphosis with resting (pupal) stage ; illustrated in mosquito (**2236**) ; butterfly (*630, 631*).
Ord. **Neuroptera** : Membraneous, net-veined wings ; usually carnivorous on other insects. Examples, Ant-lions (**181**), lace-wing flies (*f-i.*), lantern flies.
Ord. **Coleoptera** : Beetles (**398**, *399*) ; fore wings hardened as "elytra," wing-covers; biting mouth-parts (*1729*). Sub-ord. **Adephaga**

includes ground, tiger (*399*) and water beetles (400, *401*) ; all predaceous forms Sub-ord. Polyphaga includes rest of beetles, in six super-families : (1) **Staphylinoidea**, rove beetles, devil's coach horse (*f-i.*) ; (2) **Diversicornia** ; burying beetles (*400*) ; lady-birds (**1883**, *1731*) ; glow-worm (**1288**) ; click beetles (399) ; " death-watch " (399) ; (3) **Heteromera**, oil beetles, " Spanish fly " (400, *401*) ; (4) **Phytophaga**, leaf-eating beetles, long-horns (*401*), wood-borers (*1731*) ; (5) **Rhyncophora**, weevils (3362) ; (6) **Lamellicornia**, cockchafers ; scarabs, dor beetles (*400*) ; stag beetles (*398*). Many individuals are figured on *401*.

Ord. **Strepsiptera** : Minute forms, females parasitic on other insects ; example, *Stylops*, the bee louse (400).

Ord. **Mecoptera** : Scorpion flies ; family **Panorpidae** ; pupa free-living ; transparent, net-veined wings.

Ord. **Trichoptera** : Caddis flies ; larvae aquatic, live in tubes of sand, stones or sticks.

Ord. **Lepidoptera** : Butterflies and Moths, **628**. Scales on wings ; larvae usually " caterpillars " (**720**).

Sub-ord. **Homoneura** : Primitive forms, including Swift moths (*Hepialus*).

Sub-ord. **Heteroneura** : Venation of fore and hind wings different, not same as in Homoneura.

Super-fam. **Cossoidea** : Goat moth, larva bores in trees.

Super-fam. **Tineoidea** : Clothes moths ; boll-worm of cotton, *Pectinophora*, etc.

Super-fam. **Pyraloidea** : Small forms, including *Ephestia*, flour moths.

Super-fam. **Psychoidea** : Genus *Zygaena*, burnet moths (*plate f. 633*).

Super-fam. **Lasiocampoidea** : Eggar moths ; vapourer ; lackey (*f-i.*).

Super-fam. **Noctuoidea** : Principally night-flying moths, including " cut-worms " and " army-worms " ; fam. **Arctiidae** " woolly-bears," tiger-moths (*plate f. 633, 720*).

Super-fam. **Notodontoidea** : Puss-moth ; hawk moths, fam. **Sphingidae** (*plate f. 633*) ; group **Geometrina** have " looper " larvae ; winter moths (3388).

Super-fam. **Bombycoidea** : Silk-worms (*2970*), Atlas moths (*plate f. 633*).

Super-fam. **Papilionoidea** : All the butterflies (*plate f. 632*). Fam. **Papilionidae**, swallow-tails (720) ; **Nymphalidae**, peacocks, tortoise-shells, etc. ; **Pieridae**, whites, etc. (*630*) ; **Lycaenidae**, blues ; **Argynnidae**, fritillaries (*plate f. 628* and *f-i.*).

Note : The old grouping of the Lepidoptera into Rhopalocera, Butterflies, and Heterocera, moths, was not founded on scientific evidence ; nor is that adopted by collectors of dividing the order into Micro- (small) and Macro- (large) lepidoptera.

Ord. **Diptera** : true flies, **1329**, distinguished by having only one pair of wings, the rear pair being represented by " halteres," balancers. Two sub-orders : (1) **Nematocera**, forms with long antennae, larva has

obvious head, includes fam. **Tipulidae**, Daddy-long-legs (*1732, f-i.*) ; fam. **Culicidae**, gnats (**2238**), mosquitoes (1732, **2236**) ; and various families of midges. (2) **Brachycera**, antennae short, larva has no evident head ; two groups, (1) **Orthorrhapha**, pupa free ; horse flies, robber flies, bee-flies, (2) **Cyclorrhapha**, pupa enclosed in puparium ; hover flies (*1731*), house flies (**1329**) and bluebottles ; sheep ked or tick (**2513**) belongs to super-fam. **Pupipara**, in which larvae are borne ready to pupate from body of female. The tsetse fly, *Glossina*, also reproduces in this manner (3252).

Ord. **Siphonaptera** (**Aphaniptera**) ; Fleas (**1313**, **2512**) ; wingless ; larvae free-living, adults semi-parasitic, sucking mouth-parts.

Ord. **Hymenoptera** : Four membranous wings ; higher forms most highly developed of all insects. Has two sub-orders :

Sub-o. **Symphyla** : Sawflies, primitive types with no waist constriction (**2877**).

Sub-o. **Apocrita** : With constricted waists; divided into seven super-families, first three of which are termed **Parasitica**, rest **Aculeata**, being armed with stings.

1. **Cynipoidea** : Gall flies. Lay eggs in plant tissue, producing " gall " (*1730*).

2. **Chalcidoidea** : Usually bright metallic colours ; include fig wasps (*1270*), but chiefly parasitic on other insects.

3. **Ichneumonoidea** : Ichneumon flies (**1685**) ; long, curved ovipositors, for laying eggs in larvae of other insects.

4. **Vespoidea** : Wasps (**3345**). Typical families : **Vespidae**, social wasps, including hornets (**1643**) ; **Eumemidae**, solitary potter wasps (*1732*) ; **Ammophila**, sand wasps (*3346*) ; **Odynerus**, mud wasp ; **Mutillidae**, solitary, females wingless, ant-like, parasitic.

5. **Sphecoidea** : Mud-dauber wasps ; solitary types, usually preying on other insects.

6. **Apoidea** : Bees (**390**) ; honey feeders. Typical families : **Apidae**, hive bees (**390**), tongue short, social life highly organized ; **Bombidae**, bumble bees (**394**), tongue long, make " honey-pots " instead of combs ; **Megachilidae**, solitary mason, leaf-cutter (*1729*), and potter bees ; **Xylocopidae**, carpenter bees (*394*) ; **Andrenidae**, burrowing bees.

7. **Formicoidea** : Ants (**165**) ; females differentiated into queens and workers ; social life highly organized. Social ants form a single great family, **Formicidae**.

Phylum XIII. MOLLUSCA.

Molluscs (**2199**, *2943*) ; specialized mouth, eyes, gills, or primitive lungs, digestive tract, heart and blood vessels, nervous system. Most forms have " mantle " or fold of skin secreting shell on its outer surface (2942).

Cl. **Amphineura** : Primitive types, especially the wormlike forms without shells. Shelled type, with eight plates, enabling animal to roll into ball, include Chitons (2199).

Cl. **Gastropoda** : Usually snail-like types (2199) ; conical or spiral shell ; foot usually a creeping sole ; primitive eyes ; gills in water types, lungs in land types ; heart, nerves, and muscles; rasp-like palate. The following is one of several modern classifications of this group.

Ord. **Prosobranchia (Streptoneura)** : Gills. Typical families : **Patellidae**, Limpets (2199), ring-like gills ; **Haliotidae**, Abalones, two comb-like gills ; **Muricidae**, secrete valuable purplish dye ; **Buccinidae**, Whelks, carnivorous ; **Cypraeidae**, Cowries, carnivorous ; **Ampullaridae**, Ampulla or " Watering Pot " Shell ; **Littorinidae**, Periwinkles ; **Tritoniidae**, Tritons, turret-like, siphonated shells ; **Strombidae**, foot narrow, soleless, Conches, Wing Shells.

Ord. **Pulmonata** : Lungs, consisting of cavity with network of blood vessels. Typical families : **Helicidae**, Snails (2989) ; **Limacidae**, Slugs, shell reduced (2989) ; **Limnaeidae**, Pond Snails (2943).

Cl. **Scaphopoda** : Tooth-Shells ; mantle secretes tusk-shaped shell ; a small group.

Cl. **Lamellibranchiata (Pelecypoda)**. Bivalves (2199); mantle divided along back, hinged shells.

Ord. **Filibranchia** : Gill juncture non-vascular, ciliated. Typical genera : *Mytilus*, Mussels (860); *Pecten*, free-swimming, eyes on edge of mantle, Scallops (2879).

Ord. **Eulamellibranchia** : Gill juncture vascular. Typical genera : *Ostrea*, Oysters (2446, 2533) ; *Cardium*, Cockle, (860); *Veneris*, *Mya*, Clams (860); *Teredo* (f-i.), boring types, Shipworm ; *Unio*, *Anodon*, Fresh-water Mussels (860).

Cl. **Cephalopoda** (2199) : Foot bent under and joined to head ; tentacles surrounding mouth ; shell rudimentary (" cuttlebone ") or absent. Bodily structure highly organized ; well-developed eyes.

Sub-Cl. **Tetrabranchia** : Primitive forms, organs grouped in fours ; genus *Nautilus* only living type (2943) ; Ord. **Ammonoidea**, Ammonites (146), common fossils.

Sub-Cl. **Dibranchia** : Organs grouped in twos. Ord. **Decapoda** : Ten tentacles. Examples, *Loligo*, common Squid (946) ; *Sepia*, Cuttlefish (945) ; *Architeuthis*, Giant Squid (945). Ord. **Octopoda** : Eight-armed. Typical families : **Octopodidae**, Octopus (945) ; **Argonautidae**, Argonaut or " Paper Nautilus," female has boat-like shell (230).

Phylum XIV. POLYZOA (BRYOZOA).
Live in colonies resembling some Hydrozoans ; sometimes called " Sea Moss " ; entirely aquatic.

Phyla XV, PHORONIDEA and XVI, GEPHYRAEA.
Two small phyla of marine creatures, more highly evolved than molluscs.

Phylum XVII. BRACHIOPODA.
Have mollusc-like shells (2943) ; *Lingula*, lamp shell, has not changed since Cambrian times, and is one of the oldest living creatures.

Phylum XVIII. ECHINODERMA.
Literally, " spiny-skinned " animals : starfish and sea-urchins (3082) ; internal structure, like 5-rayed star, with alimentary canal as axis ; skin has limy plates ; body has " arms " for locomotion. Circulatory system, muscles, nerves, and sense organs

present. Typical classes : **Crinoidea**, Sea Lilies (1244), mouth turned upward, arms branched and fringed, lower surface attached to bottom by stalk ; **Asteroidea**, five arms, mouth on lower surface (genus *Asterias*, common Starfish, 3082) ; **Ophiuroidea**, Brittle-Stars (3083) ; **Echinoidea**, Sea Urchins (3083), globular ; **Holothuroidea**, Sea Cucumbers (2911), limy plates embedded, leaving surface leathery; axis horizontal instead of vertical.

Phylum XIX. CHORDATA (VERTEBRATA).
Body-wall cylindrical, usually with appendages (fins, wings, limbs, etc.). Body stiffened in primitive forms by gristly rod called a *notochord*, lying along spinal cord (158) ; in higher forms notochord develops vertebrae of bone, many of them supporting ribs (3318).

Sub-ph. **HEMICHORDA** : Worm-like body ; short spinal column, connected by nerve collar to another system along abdomen. Typical genus, *Balanoglossus*.

Sub-ph. **UROCHORDA** : Sea-Squirts : usually have mollusc-like mantle or tunic containing cellulose ; rudimentary heart.

Sub-ph. **CEPHALOCHORDA** : Body pointed at both ends ; only appendage, tail fin ; internal structure extremely primitive ; very small fish-like creatures, swimming or lying buried in sand. Typical of this group is the genus *Amphioxus*, the Lancelet.

Sub-ph. **VERTEBRATA (Craniata)** : Vertebrates. Notochord in embryo of all true Vertebrates, and remains as cartilaginous skeleton among the lower fishes : higher types develop true bony skeleton (2977). The Vertebrates are divided into six classes : (1) **Cyclostomata**, Lampreys, etc.; (2) **Pisces**, Fishes; (3) **Amphibia** or **Batrachia**, Amphibians ; (4) **Reptilia**, Reptiles ; (5) **Aves**, Birds ; (6) **Mammalia**, Mammals.

Note: The sub-phylum **Craniata** includes all the remaining members of the Animal Kingdom. Scientists believe that the first Vertebrates were primitive Fishes ; that certain of these Fishes gave rise to the Amphibians ; that certain of the Amphibians gave rise to the primitive Reptiles ; and that from these in turn were evolved the Reptiles, Birds, and Mammals.

Class CYCLOSTOMATA, Lampreys, etc.
Sucker mouth instead of jaws ; primitive cartilaginous skull, spine consists of chord and notochord rod. Lampreys and Hagfishes (1886).

Class PISCES, Fishes.
All Fishes (1296) are water dwellers, and are especially adapted to this life ; breathe with gills ; skeleton structure varies from primitive notochord forms to highly organized bony forms. Of many classifications, that below is one of the simplest.

Sub-cl. **Elasmobranchii (Chondrichthyes)** : Snout overhangs mouth ; true jaws ; skeleton cartilaginous ; skin smooth with limy dots. Typical orders : **Selachii**, Sharks (2938), Dogfishes (2939) ; **Batoidei**, Skates and Rays (2976), Torpedo-Fish (3228), Sawfish (2877).

Sub-cl. **Teleostomi (Osteichthyes)** : Fishes with well-developed jaws and skulls ; body skeleton varies from partly cartilaginous to well-developed bony type.

Ord. **Crossopterygii** : Fins have bony axis

fringed with spines or rays. Numerous fossil types; two living African genera. These primitive fish, the "Fringe-Finned Ganoids," are important because they are believed to belong to the ancestral stock of all the higher Vertebrates.

Ord. **Dipneusti** (Dipnoi) : Lung-fishes (**2038**) ; gristly skeleton ; swim bladder has unusually rich lining of blood-vessels and serves as primitive lung when fish are out of water. Numerous in Palaeozoic times ; few living types.

Ord. **Ganoidei** : The Ganoids (**1298**). Skeletons vary between primitive (cartilaginous) and advanced (bony) types ; skin covered with bony plates, almost scale-like in some types. Typical sub-orders : **Chondrostei**, including Sturgeons (**3104**) ; **Holostei**, including Garpike and Bowfins.

Ord. **Teleostei** : Bony fishes ; well-developed skeleton and scales ; divided conveniently into following sub-orders :

1. **Malacopterygii** (**Physostomi**) : fin-rays soft. Following principal families : **Salmonidae**, salmon (**2865**), trout (**3251**), char, smelt, grayling ; **Scombresidae**, flying fish (**1332**) ; **Clupeidae**, herring (**1620**), sprat (*1621*), sardine, etc.

2. **Apodes** : Eels (**1092**), pelican fish.

3. **Haplomi** : Genus *Esox*, pike (**2606**).

4. **Ostariophysi** : A very large and various group ; families include **Cyprinidae**, carp (**704**), roach (**2781**), dace (*2781*), bream (**558**), goldfish (**1481**), minnow, etc. ; **Blennidae**, blennies, catfish (**729**) ; electric eel ; suckers.

5. **Thoracostei** : Includes sticklebacks (**3091**) : sea-horses (**2911**).

6. **Anacanthini** : Soft-finned types ; fam. **Gadidae**, cod (**864**), haddock (**1563**), pollack, etc. Fam. **Pleuronectidae**, includes most of the flatfish, plaice (*1298*), sole, halibut (**1566**), turbot, flounder, etc.

7. **Acanthopterygii** : Bony spines in fins. A very large group comprising many different forms. **Percidae**, perch (**2549**), bass (**370**, *1296, 1302*) ; sea bream ; gurnards ; dragonet (**1034**) ; angler fish (*2418*); angel fish (*1303*); **Scombridae**, mackerel (**2050**), tunny (**3258**) ; swordfish (**3143**) ; mullets ; lumpsucker (*1303*).

8. **Plectognathi** : Highly specialized forms ; sunfish (**3120**).

Note : There is very little agreement between authorities on the classification of fishes. Some, for example, rank these sub-orders as orders; others place the flatfish in an order of their own ; others, again, place the catfish group in the Acanthopterygii, and confine the Ostariophysi to the carp group ; the position of many small groups is a matter of complete uncertainty. This classification, however, follows generalized lines and is intended to give an idea of the main relationships.

Class **AMPHIBIA** (**BATRACHIA**), Amphibians.

The Amphibians mark an intermediate stage between Fishes and Reptiles. As their name indicates (*amphi*, on both sides, *bios*, life), they are fitted for life in water and on land. The typical Amphibians undergo metamorphosis ; that is, they hatch from the eggs (*1155*) as gill-breathing larvae (tadpoles, for example, *1399*) which then develop into lung-breathing adults. There are, however, exceptions to this rule. The fins of the Fishes are in the Amphibians replaced by legs ; the skin is soft and glandular ; heart is three-chambered. In former geologic periods Amphibians were abundant, but today there are comparatively few species, mostly divided into the following two orders :

Ord. **Caudata** or **Urodela** : Tailed forms ; types able to regenerate lost parts. Includes Salamanders (**2864**) and Newts (*f-i.*),

Ord. **Ecaudata** or **Anura** : Tail-less forms, Typical sub-orders : **Aglossa**, tongue degenerate, such as Pipa Toad ; **Phaneroglossa**, tongue developed, including Toads (**3219**) and Frogs (**1398**).

Class **REPTILIA**, Reptiles.

The Reptiles (**2767**) have no larval stage ; skeleton specialized for land life ; four-chambered heart ; aquatic forms breathe at surface ; skin covered with scales or bony plates. The most primitive Reptile stock (**1433**) is supposed to have evolved two great branches. The first, springing from Theromorphodont stock (*see* sub-class Theromorpha below) gave rise to the first Mammals and various specialized Reptiles of which the Turtles are highest. The second branch came from stock of which the Tuatera or *Sphenodon* is a living example, and gave rise to the first Birds and specialized Reptiles, of which the Crocodiles, Snakes, and Lizards are the living forms. These two great groups are marked " Evolutionary Group A " and " Evolutionary Group B."

Evolutionary Group A.

Sub-cl. **Theromorpha** : Varied extinct forms, with many skeletal details and teeth transitional between Amphibia and Mammals.

Sub-cl. **Plesiosauria** : Plesiosaurs (**2678**). Extinct forms ; long necks, paddle limbs ; comparatively slow-moving, aquatic types.

Sub-cl. **Ichthyosauria** : Ichthyosaurs (**2680**). Extinct forms, short necks, toothed beaks, swift-moving, whale-like forms, exclusively aquatic ; bore living young.

Sub-cl. **Chelonia** :

Ord. **Chelonia** : Tortoises and Turtles (**3229**, *plate f. 3228*). Toothless, horny beak ; body protected by bony case ; limbs developed for walking or swimming. Divided into two sub-orders : (1) **Athecae**, shell leathery, including Leathery Turtles ; (2) **Thecophora**, shell hard, including Land Tortoises and all the remaining Turtles.

Note: The Order **Chelonia** of this classification is divided by some authorities into 2 Orders of which **Testudinata** contains tortoises and **Chelonida** turtles.

Evolutionary Group B.

Sub-cl. **Prosauria** : Typical sub-order is **Rhynchocephalia**, of which the Tuatera or *Sphenodon* (**1975**) is the only living representative. First birds may have developed from Prosaurian stock.

Sub-cl. **Pterosauria** : Extinct flying reptiles, in wing development like bats. Typical order : **Pterodactyli**, the Pterodactyls (**2860**), *Pteranodon* (**2680**).

Sub-cl. **Dinosauria** : Extinct : represented by

many prehistoric monsters (2678, *1354*). Some had many bird-like features (hollow bones, etc.), but birds already existed when these forms flourished.

Sub-cl. **Crocodilia** :

Ord. **Crocodilia** : Differ from other reptiles chiefly in skull structure. Crocodiles (931, *2767*) and Alligators (121).

Sub-cl. **Sauria** : Lizards and Snakes. Differ from other reptiles chiefly in structure of skeleton.

Ord. **Ophidia** : Snakes (2990). Lack limbs ; halves of lower jaw connected by elastic tissue. Anaconda (*550*), Boa Constrictor (*3025*), Python (2710), Cobra (859), Vipers (3325), Rattlesnake (2746), Grass-snake.

Ord. **Lacertilia** : Lizards (1972) ; limbs usually developed and functional ; halves of lower jaw fused solidly together. Divided into three sub-orders : (1) **Lacertae**, most typical Lizards, including Common Lizards (*1973*), Iguanas (1686), Komodo Dragons (*plate f.* 1973), Horned Toad (1974), Gila Monster (*1974*), Flying Lizard (*plate f.* 1972), Slow Worm (2985, *1973*), Glass Snakes ; (2) **Geckones**, the Geckos ; (3) **Chamaleontes**, Chameleons (750, *plate f.* 752, 753).

· Note : Some authorities place snakes and lizards in Order **Squamata**, divided into Sub-order **Ophidia** : Snakes (2990), Sub-order **Lacertilia** : Lizards.

Class **AVES**, Birds (437, 2170, *2171*)

The skeleton of a bird resembles the reptile type, save in modifications for flying (*438, 1572*) ; the skin produces feathers (1264) ; there is a four-chambered heart ; teeth absent in living forms ; all organs show adaptations for flying, evolved from reptile stock, after unsuccessful experiments such as *Pteranodon* (2680).

Sub-cl. **Archaeornithes** : Extinct forms, possessed teeth ; *Archaeopteryx* (437, 2681). Sub-cl. **Neornithes**. Three super-orders : (1) **Odontognathae**, fossil forms such as *Hesperornis*. (2) **Palaeognathae** (Ratites), a heterogeneous group that have lost the " keel " to the breast bone and are flightless. Various orders, represented by *Struthio*, Ostrich (2456), two-toed, Old World ; *Rhea* (*3029*) three-toed, New World ; *Casuariiformes*, Cassowary, Emus (*313*, 1157), Australian ; *Dinornis*, Moa, New Zealand ; *Apteryx*, Kiwi (191), New Zealand ; Tinamous, S. America. (3) **Neognathae** (Carinatae) ; all the normal birds ; breastbone has a keel for attachment of flying muscles.

Ord. **Sphenisciformes** ; Penguins (2544).

Ord. **Gaviiformes** ; Loon, divers.

Ord. **Colymbiformes** ; Grebes (1516).

Ord. **Tubinares** or **Procellariiformes** ; Albatross (101), Shearwaters, Petrels (2563).

Ord. **Pelecaniformes** ; Pelican (2538), Gannet (1418), Shag, Cormorant (2931, *446*), Frigate-birds (1397).

Ord. **Ciconiiformes** : Sub-ord. **Ardeae**, Heron (*3101*, 3098), Bittern (461), Egret (*3098*). Sub-ord. **Balaenicipites**, Shoe-bill (*3098*). Sub-ord. **Ciconiae**, Stork, 3097, Ibis (*3099*), *plate f.* 3100), Spoonbill (*3100*). Sub-ord. **Phoenicopteri**, Flamingo (1312).

Ord. **Anseriformes** : Ducks (1051, *456*), Geese (1484), Swan (3125, *449*).

Ord. **Falconiformes** ; Condor (885), Vultures (3330), Adjutant (27), Hawks and falcons (1587, *452*), Turkey Buzzard (634), Eagle (1063, *1064, 438*), Secretary Bird (2916), Buzzard (633), Kite (1863).

Ord. **Galliformes** ; Game birds and poultry (2671), Grouse (1550), Partridge (2526), Peacock (2532), Pheasants (2565), Guinea-fowl (1554), Turkey (3261, *441*), Quail (2711).

Ord. **Gruiformes** ; Crane (*3101*), Rail (2733, *2286*), Moorhen, Coot, and Corncrake (2734).

Ord. **Charadriiformes** ; Waders (3331) and Plovers (2629) ; Oyster-catcher (*456*), Plover (*443*, 2629), Snipe (2991), Woodcock (3403), Avocet (3331), Phalarope (520). Sub-ord. **Lari** includes Gulls (1555), Terns (*1557*), Skua ; Sub-ord. **Alci**, Auk (303), Guillemot, Razorbill (*3530*, 304), Puffin (*f-i.*).

Ord. **Columbiformes** ; Dodo (1025), Pigeons and Doves (2605).

Ord. **Cuculiformes** ; Cuckoo (941).

Ord. **Psittaciformes** ; Parrots (2525), Macaws (2047, *2049*), Cockatoos (859) ; Budgerigars (*2526*).

Ord. **Strigiformes** ; Owls (2460, *439*).

Ord. **Caprimulgiformes** ; Night-jars (2369).

Ord. **Cypseliformes** or **Micropodiformes** ; Swift (3125), Humming-birds (1651).

Ord. **Coraciiformes** ; Kingfisher (1857), Hornbill (1643).

Ord. **Piciformes** ; Toucan (3231, 3025), Woodpeckers (*plate f.* 3405, 3403), Wryneck.

Ord. **Passeriformes** ; the highest birds, including all the song birds. In general, adapted for perching ; named from *passer*, Latin for sparrow. Important families :

Menuridae ; Lyre-bird (2043).
Alaudidae ; Larks (1893).
Hirundinidae ; Swallow, Martins (3124).
Corvidae ; Crow (935), Rook (2823), Raven (2747), Jay (1815, *455*), Magpie (2065), Jackdaw (1789).
Ptilinorrhyncidae ; Bower-bird (534).
Paradiseidae ; Birds of Paradise (2511).
Paridae ; Tits (3218, *443*).
Sittidae ; Nuthatch (2407).
Certhiidae ; Tree-creeper (2407).
Cinclidae ; Dipper (*f-i.*).
Troglodytidae ; Wren (3425, *439*).
Turdidae ; Thrushes (3205, *161*), Blackbird (463), Robin (2790), Nightingale (2367, *450*), Wheatear (3374), Stone- and Whinchats (3374), Orioles (2452), Hedge Sparrow (*454*).
Sylviidae ; Warblers (3340, *443*).
Regulidae ; Gold-crest (*443*).
Muscicapidae ; Flycatchers (1330, *2289*).
Motacillidae ; Wagtails (3332), Pipits (2611).
Laniidae, Shrike (2962).
Sturnidae ; Starling (3083, *446*).
Ploceiidae ; Weaver-birds (3360).
Thraupidae ; Tanager (3150).
Fringillidae ; Finches (614, 1272), Cardinal Bird, Bunting (616), Cross-bill Canary (689), Linnet (1955), Sparrow (3052, *444*), Chaffinch (1272).

Class MAMMALIA, Mammals.

The Mammals (2074) include all vertebrates which have true hair (1564) and the young of which are nourished with their mother's milk. The class is here subdivided into three sub-classes according to the degree of development of the young at the time of birth. It is generally believed by scientists that mammals evolved from reptile or amphibian stock, although the course of evolution thereafter is uncertain. The earliest known Mammals lived at about the same geological period as the giant Reptiles and the first Birds.

Sub-cl. **Prototheria** : Primitive types ; lay eggs and hatch young ; one living order, **Monotremata**. Includes Duckbill (*313*, **1052**) and Spiny Ant-Eaters (*313*, 1053).

Sub-cl. **Metatheria** : Young born alive but not perfectly formed ; development completed in a skin-pouch on mother's body. One living order, **Marsupialia**, divided into two sub-orders : (1) **Diprotodonta**, teeth adapted to vegetable food : includes Wombats (2111), Phalangers, Kangaroo (*313*, **1845**), Koala (*313*, **1872**) ; (2) **Polyprotodonta**, teeth adapted to animal food ; includes Opossums (2442), Tasmanian Devil—and Tasmanian Wolf, Bandicoots.

Sub-cl. **Eutheria** (Placentalia) : Young completely developed when born ; includes all other Mammals.

Group Unguiculata.

Ord. **Insectivora** : The most primitive of the higher Mammals ; teeth suited for eating insects ; feet plantigrade (sole-walking) ; most types nocturnal. Includes Tree Shrews (placed by some authorities in the Primates), Elephant or Jumping Shrews, Moles (2196), Shrews (*f-i.*), Hedgehogs (1604, 1622).

Ord. **Dermoptera** : Flying Lemurs ; curious Malayan forms, with affinities to Insectivora, Bats, and Lemurs. Only two species are known.

Ord. **Chiroptera** : Bats (370) ; fore-limbs winged (*1572*, *2585*) ; internal structure modified for true flight. Typical sub-orders : (1) **Megachiroptera**, teeth adapted to fruit-eating, Flying Foxes (372) ; (2) **Microchiroptera**, adapted to eating insects or sucking blood ; includes Vampires (372), and all the British Bats (370).

ote : Many older authorities place the order Primates in a group separated from the other orders ; they are here included with orders showing some affinities, following the grouping of G. G. Simpson (*f-i.*).

Ord. **Primates** : Five-fingered hands and five-toed feet, with nails ; eyes directed forward.

Sub-o. **Prosimii** or **Lemuroidea** : Lemurs (1922). Face long and fox-like ; tails not suited for grasping.

Sub-o. **Anthropoidea** : Face rounded, cranium comparatively high ; internal organs more highly developed than in Lemurs. Divisible into : (1) **Platyrrhina**, New World types, nostrils far apart, tail often prehensile, three pairs of premolar teeth in each jaw ; (2) **Catarrhina**, Old World types, nostrils close together, tail never prehensile, two pairs of premolar teeth in each jaw. First two families are New World types, remainder Old World.

Fam. **Cebidae** : New World Monkeys (2207) with opposable thumbs, more or less naked ears, and flat or curved nails.

Fam. **Hapalidae** : Marmosets (2208). Thumbs not opposable, nails clawlike.

Fam. **Hylobatidae** : Gibbons (1462, *183*), long-armed, tailless ; thumb short, backbone without S-shaped curve.

Fam. **Cercopithecidae** : Old World Monkeys (2207), including Baboons, Mandrill (*2210*). Wedge-shaped chest ; arms shorter than legs ; tail usually present.

Fam. **Simiidae** or **Pongidae** : Higher Apes (182, *183*). Broad chest ; arms longer than legs, but shorter than in Gibbons ; S-shaped curve of backbone partially developed ; prominent canine teeth ; jaws not curved at sides as in Man ; cerebrum smaller than in Man. Includes Orang-utan (2445, *183*), Chimpanzee (805, *183*), Gorilla, 1487, *183*.

Fam. **Hominidae** : The human type. Single living genus, with one living species—*Homo sapiens*, Man (2078).

Ord. **Edentata**: Toothless or with rudimentary teeth in rear of jaw ; exceedingly varied types. Two sub-orders : (1) **Pilosa**, hairy types, including Sloths (2985, *550*, *2077*), Ant-Eaters (176) ; (2) **Dasypoda**, armoured types, including Armadilloes (237).

Ord. **Pholidota** : True Scaly Ant-Eaters or Pangolins. Covered with horny, overlapping scales.

Group Glires.

Ord. **Rodentia** : Rodents (2795, *2075*) ; teeth and jaws adapted to gnawing. Single pair of incisors in upper jaw ; families differ in skull structure and dentition. Includes Squirrels (3071), Chipmunk (815), Prairie Dogs, Marmots, Beavers (387), Kangaroo Rats, Dormice (1029), Jerboas (*71*, **1819**), Hamsters, Vole (*f-i.*), Lemmings, Musk-rats (2268), Rats (2746) and Mice (2248), Porcupine (2656), Guinea-Pig (1554, *1555*), Capybara, Chinchilla (815).

Ord. **Lagomorpha** (by many authorities retained as Sub-order **Duplicidentata** of Order **Rodentia**). Two pairs of incisors in upper jaw. Includes Hares (1578) and Rabbits (2721), Agouti (77).

Group Mutica or Cetacea.

Order **Cetacea** (Mammals with Flippers), (2074, *2076*).

Sub-ord. **Odontoceti** : Toothed Whales (3371) ; includes Sperm-Whales, Dolphins (1027), Porpoises (2657), Grampuses, and Narwhals (*f-i.*).

Sub-ord. **Mystacoceti** : Whalebone Whales (3371). *Also* Right Whales, Rorquals, Humpbacks.

Group Ferungulata.

Ord. Carnivora : Flesh-eaters, though some forms are omnivorous and one or two entirely vegetarian. Teeth and skeletal structure adapted to seizing and killing prey. Divided into sub-orders according to internal structure.

Sub-ord. **Fissipeda :**

Fam. **Canidae :** Dogs (**1025**, *plate f. 1024*), Dingo (*313*), Wolves (**3400**) and Coyotes (**3400**), Jackal (**1789**), Fox (**1355**). In all these there are special adaptations to running down prey ; feet digitigrade.

Fam. **Ursidae :** Bears (**382**) ; teeth adapted to partly vegetarian diet ; feet plantigrade.

Fam. **Procyonidae :** Raccoons (**2722**) ; feet plantigrade, but usually arboreal creatures. The Pandas (**2494**) come between the raccoons and the bears. They are vegetarian and have plantigrade feet.

Fam. **Mustelidae :** Weasel family, a highly successful group of mainly small, very active, carnivorous forms ; feet partly digitigrade, body long and slender. Marten (**2111**), Stoat or Ermine (**1222**), Weasel (**3359**), Polecat and Ferret (**1268**), Mink (**2186**), Wolverine, Skunk (**2980**), Badger (**337**), Otter (**2459**).

Super-Fam. **Feloidea :**

Fam. **Viverridae :** Civets, etc., with the Sub-fam. **Herpestinae :** Mongooses (**2207**).

Fam. **Hyaenidae :** Hyaenas (**1675**).

Fam. **Felidae :** Cats (**718**). Very highly specialized for predaceous habit. Domestic Cats (*719*), Jaguar (**1791**), Leopard or Panther (**1927**), Lion (**1959**, *1961*), Ocelot (**1928**), Puma (**2702**), Tiger (**3211**), Lynx (**2043**), Cheetah (*1928*).

Sub-order **Pinnipedia :**

The Pinnipede series contains three families : **Otariidae**, in which are the Sea-lions and Fur-seals (**2912**) ; **Odobaenidae**, containing the Walrus (**3339**) ; and **Phocidae**, the true Seals (**2912**), Sea-elephants (**2913**).

Ord. Tubulidentata : Aardvarks (**9**). Tubular snout, large number of lumbar vertebrae.

Note : The following Orders have by many authorities been grouped together broadly as **Ungulata.**

Ord. Proboscidea : Nose and upper lip extended to form trunk. Elephants (**1140, 60**, **1788**), Mammoths (*735*, **2077**), Mastodons (*1140*).

Ord. Hyracoidea : some unique skull features ; cheek teeth like those of rhinoceros ; in size and habits like hares. Hyrax or Rock-Rabbit (*2074*).

Ord. Sirenia : Aquatic mammals with flippers ; eat vegetable food, in contrast with Cetaceans (*see* Group Mutica or Cetacea) and the Seals (*see* Ord. Carnivora) ; internal structure indicates descent from ancestor of Proboscideans. Includes Sea-cows, Manatees (*f-i.*) and Dugongs.

Ord. Perissodactyla : Hoofed animals, usually odd-toed ; where toes are even in number, they are not symmetrical about the vertical plane of the hoof.

Fam. **Equidae :** Foot structure highly evolved (**1342**), teeth unusually long. Includes Horse (**1645**), Ass (**273**), Zebra (*back of plate f. 73*).

Fam. **Tapiridae :** Tapirs (**3154**, *550*) ; have proboscis, small tusks and simple teeth ; front foot has four toes.

Fam. **Rhinocerotidae :** Rhinoceroses (**735**, *59 back of plate f. 73*, **2770**).

Ord. Artiodactyla : Hoofed animals, usually even-toed ; odd-toed types have digits symmetrical about the vertical plane of the hoof.

Sub-o. **Suina :** Lower leg not fused into cannon bone ; upper incisor teeth always present, often tusked. Stomach varies from simple to ruminant type.

Fam. **Suidae :** Pigs (**2605**) ; Wild Boar (**480**) ; Wart-hog (**3341**, *plate f. 3340*). Snout has fleshy button, tusks of male curve upwards ; stomach simple ; four toes on each foot, outside two off ground.

Fam. **Tayassuidae :** Peccaries (*3025*). Tusks small, point downward ; front feet have four toes (two not touching ground) and rear feet only three.

Fam. **Hippopotamidae :** Hippopotamus (**1628**). Muzzle broad, rounded ; stomach complex ; all four toes touch ground.

Sub-o. **Tylopoda :** Feet have large, cushioned pads ; stomach complex but not completely ruminant. Typical family : **Camelidae**, Camel (**669**), Alpaca (**124**), Llama (**1975**).

Sub-o. **Pecora :** True ruminants ("cud chewers ").

Fam. **Giraffidae :** Giraffes (**1464**). Adapted to browsing ; solid-horned. Also the Okapi (*71*, *f-i.*).

Fam. **Cervidae :** Deer (**984**). Antlers solid horned, shed annually, 984. Caribou (**702**), Moose (**2228**), Musk Deer (**2268**), Reindeer (**2760**), Wapiti (**2382**).

Fam. **Antilocapridae :** American Antelope or Pronghorns (*f-i.*). Hollow horns growing from bony cores and shed annually. Fam. **Bovidae :** Permanent hollow horns from bony horn-core, **1641**. Includes Cattle (**730**), True Buffalo (*71*), Yak (**3433**), Sheep (**2940**), Goats (**1478**), Ibex (**1679**), Bison (**459**, *1234*), Aurochs (*460*), Musk Ox (**2268**). True Antelopes (*71*, **176**), Chamois (**750**), Rocky Mountain Goat (**176**), Gazelle (*back of plate f. 72*). Permanent hollow horns growing from bony horn-core.

Books for the Zoology Student

Wonders of Animal Life. Ed. Sir John Hammerton. Amalgamated Press, Ltd.

Habits and Characters of British Wild Animals. H. Mortimer Batten.

Life in the Animal World. F. H. Shoosmith.

How Birds Live. E. M. Nicholson.

At the Zoo. Julian Huxley.

Nonsuch, Land of Water. William Beebe.

World Nature History. E. G. Boulenger. *See also* under Biology, page 3616.

The Invertebrata. Borradaile and Potts.

HISTORY

HISTORY (1630) occupies a more important place in the field of knowledge today than it has ever occupied before, for if we are to form sound opinions upon world affairs we must know the historical background of world politics. Moreover, we shall understand the social and economic questions of our own times far better if we are able to trace their origin and their development down the ages. History, as it is taught and written today, is no longer a narrative of isolated incidents, of wars and intrigue, of marriages and deaths of kings and queens, or of the detached deeds of famous men and women. Rather it is an account of the origin and development of human institutions and ideas. It deals with the conditions under which ordinary men lived in various ages and countries ; it deals with their customs, arts, and ideals, with the growth of law and government, and with the influence of leaders upon the fate of peoples. At all times it seeks material on which to base general principles of human conduct, so that we in the present may profit by the mistakes and successes of the past.

Books for further study are listed at the end of each section, but for a proper grasp of the historical process the student should read some general survey of world history, such as H. G. Wells's " Outline of History " or his " Short History of the World." Throughout reference may be made to " The Universal History of the World," edited by Sir John Hammerton.

ANCIENT HISTORY
The Dawn of Civilization

I. PREHISTORIC PERIOD.

For thousands of years before the oldest kind of writing was invented, men and women and children had been working and playing in many parts of the world. By carefully studying the things they have left us—stone tools, pieces of pottery, and pictures on cave walls—we have learned a great deal about the way these people lived and can trace the almost unbelievably slow steps by which they learned the arts of civilization. But, because they lived before there was any *written* history, we call them prehistoric men.

A. Stone Age Man, 3094.
  a. Eolithic Age, 2080.
  b. Old Stone Age (Palaeolithic Age), 2080.
    1. Cave Dwellers, **734** ; col. plate facing 737.
    2. Remarkable artistic ability, 2475 ; drawings, colour plate facing 736.
  c. Mesolithic Age, 2080.
  d. New Stone Age (Neolithic Age), 2080.
    1. Beginnings of settled life and division of labour.
    2. Interesting remains. Lake Dwellers, 1237.

B. Dawn of History with Bronze Age.
  a. Discovery of Metals quickens march of progress. Relics, *587*.
  b. Invention of Writing ends Prehistoric Age, 1630.

II. DEVELOPMENT OF CIVILIZATION ALONG THE NILE.

A. Favourable Situation of Northern Egypt, 1095. The fertile strip of the Nile Valley, sheltered on all sides by deserts and the sea, was an ideal situation for the beginnings of civilization. The rich soil brought down by the Nile supported a dense population ; the river itself was a great highway ; the quarries of the neighbouring deserts furnished unlimited building materials.

B. Great Epochs of Egyptian History. The History Chart in the Fact-Index should be consulted.

a. Long period of Early Development culminating in the union of Upper and Lower Egypt.
b. Pyramid Age. The building of monumental Pyramid tombs to gratify the vanity of the Pharaohs became the dominant interest, exhausted the wealth, and took a terrific toll of the slave labour, 2707, *2708*, 212, 1114.
c. Feudal Period—when nobles ruled vast estates. During a long struggle between rival rulers and sections Egypt became so weak that it fell before foreign conquerors, the Hyksos or Semitic " Shepherd Kings."
d. Defeat of Shepherd Kings and Rise of the Empire.
  1. Egyptian nobles revolted against the Hyksos and drove them out (c. 1600 B.C.).
  2. Great Temple of Karnak crowned revival of art, *216*.
e. Fall of the Empire. Pursuing the Shepherd Kings into Asia, the Egyptians began a period of foreign conquest, which for many centuries added to Egypt's glory, but which finally led to the invasion and subjugation of Egypt, first by the Assyrians (670 B.C.) and later by the Persians (525 B.C.). With these invasions ended the period of distinctive Egyptian culture.

Note : The Egyptian rulers are often grouped into dynasties beginning with Menes (3400 B.C.). The IVth Dynasty marked the height of the Pyramid Age ; the XVIIIth began and the XXXIst ended the Imperial Period.

C. How the Ancient Egyptians Lived.
  a. Religion.
    1. Belief in a life after death shown by careful preservation of bodies (mummies) and building of suitable tombs, 2255.
    2. Important gods, 1760, 2455.
    3. Sacred animals, 399, *400*, 719, 931, 1427, 2207, 3097.
    4. Priesthood.
  b. Industrial Life. Agriculture, *1115* ; Boats and ships, 2945 ; Bread, *555* ; Brick making, 561 ; Enamelling, 1158 ; Fisheries, 1298.

Furniture, *1410* ; Harps, *1579* ; Beasts of burden, *1109, 1115* ; Ink, 1725 ; Papyrus, 2500 ; Spinning and weaving, 920, 1113 ; Water-clock, 843 ; Mining, 1479 ; Canals and Irrigation, 686, 1118.

c. Art and Science. Architecture, 212, 2707 ; Astronomy, 275 ; Books, 509 ; Language and Writing, 2496, *125* ; beginnings of Mathematics, 112, 1434 ; Painting, 2475 ; Sculpture, 2904, 3058, *3059*.

III. EARLY CIVILIZATIONS OF WESTERN ASIA.

That part of Asia which we call today the Near East, consisting of Asia Minor, Syria, and the Arabian Peninsula, was the ancient home of civilizations which were of immense importance, because of their profound influence upon subsequent culture and history. These civilizations grew up in what has been called the Fertile Crescent, consisting of that borderland between the mountains in the north and the Arabian desert where crops could be grown and cities built.

A. Mesopotamia or Iraq—the Eastern part of the Fertile Crescent, 1743.

   a. Sumerian Culture. The Sumerians (a non-Semitic people), in their group of city states along the Rivers Tigris and Euphrates, originated the characteristic culture of Mesopotamia which was to endure through centuries of conquest (329). Cuneiform Writing, oldest known Library, 2371.

   b. Babylonian Empire, 329. Established by Semitic tribes who conquered Sumerian cities. The conquerors absorbed and modified the Sumerian culture, developing a highly organized social and political system. Architecture, 212 ; Brick, 561 ; Street Paving, 2783 ; Education, 331 ; Writing, 331, 1623 ; Engraved Seals, 1427 ; Origin of Seven-day Week, 3361 ; Invention of Sundial, 843.

   c. Assyria absorbs Babylonia in Great Assyrian Empire.

     1. Improvements in art of warfare make possible the conquest of a vast military empire, 329 ; introduction of iron weapons increases fighting efficiency.

     2. Conquest of Hittites and Israelite Tribes, 1633 ; 1829.

     3. Nineveh, the capital built by Sennacherib, 330 ; 2371.

     4. Artistic advance especially marked by sculptures depicting the conquests, 330 ; use of stone in building, 212 ; Painting, 2475 ; Engraving, 1427 ; Library at Nineveh, 331, 333, 2371.

Note: It is important to keep in mind that slavery was an essential part of all ancient civilizations ; the conquered people formed the slave class and without them the great construction projects would have been impossible.

   d. Chaldean Empire—east Semitic empire, 331.

     1. Babylon rebuilt, *330*, 331 ; famous Hanging Gardens, 331, 2923, colour plate facing 329 ; Nebuchadrezzar's canal, 686, 1231.

     2. Babylonian captivity of the Jews, which did much to advance Hebrew culture, 1830.

B. Syria—The Western end of the Fertile Crescent.

   a. Phoenicians—the early traders who carried the alphabet to all civilized lands. Although they had built their cities on the " battleground of empires," these peaceful merchants suffered little from the successive conquests, for they were content to pay tribute to any conqueror as long as they were allowed to continue their trading enterprises.

   b. Hebrews—a people who retained an intense racial and religious unity despite conquests and oppression, 1829.

     1. Nomadic wanderings begun by Abraham, 13 ; terminated by Moses, 2235.

     2. Kingdom established under David and his son Solomon, 979, 2999 ; capital is Jerusalem, 1819.

   c. Philistines. These cousins of the Cretans are the enemies of the Israelites of whom we read so much in the Bible.

C. Asia Minor.

   a. Hittites, 1633. Through their wars with the Hittites the Assyrians and Egyptians learned the use of iron for tools and weapons and the value of the horse.

   b. Lydians. These people of Asia Minor rose to such prosperity that the name of their king Croesus, is still the symbol for fabulous wealth, 932 ; earliest known use of coins, 2201.

D. Indo-European supremacy supplants Semitic power. The Indo-European races moving southward from the mountains north of the Fertile Crescent belonged to the same race as the peoples of modern Europe.

   a. The Medes, 2131, 2554.

   b. The short-lived Persian Empire, 2554.

     1. Religion of Zoroaster, the first universal religion, 3447.

     2. Rising power of Greece stays westward tide of Persian conquest, 2554.

     3. Alexander's conquest ends great Asiatic Empires, 105.

The Greeks

I. THE RISE OF EUROPEAN CIVILIZATION.

Aegean Civilization, 29, 927. This civilization developed in Crete and spread over the Aegean World.

   a. Effect on European civilization, 1517, 30 (*map*). The islands of the Aegean were the stepping-stones that brought civilization to Europe.

   b. Discoveries of archaeologists. Excavations of Schliemann, 32.

II. GREEK INVASION OF THE AEGEAN WORLD

A. Nomad tribes from the North, 1517, 32. The Greeks came down from the unknown North and conquered the Aegeans ; adopted much of the Aegean culture. The Greeks were a northern branch (Indo-European) of the same stock as the Medes and Persians (Indo-Iranians) who had invaded the Semitic world of western Asia.

B. Homeric Age marks the high tide of the migration, 1518.

a. Trojan War, 3248.

b. Culture of the Achaeans. An account of the culture of those early Greeks is preserved for us in the Iliad and Odyssey of Homer, 1518, 1637.

III. DEVELOPMENT OF GREEK CITY STATES.

A. Lack of unity among the Greeks. This is the keynote of Greek political history, and was largely due to geographical influences, 1518.

B. Evolution of Democracy, 1519.

a. Athens, the intellectual leader of Greece, 284, 1522. Reforms of Solon make government more democratic, 2999.

b. Sparta, the military state, 3052. Lycurgus, the great law-giver, 2042.

Note : It must be remembered in discussing Greek democracy that it was limited to an aristocratic class, the citizens of the states. In the Greek cities the greater part of the menial and skilled labour was done by slaves and free men who were not citizens, 1523, 3053.

IV. PERSIAN WARS.

A. Greece checks Persian invasion and saves Europe from Asiatic domination, 2554, 1522.

a. Famous battles : Marathon, 2097 ; Salamis, 230 ; Thermopylae, 3201.

b. Leaders : Themistocles, 1522 ; Aristides, 230.

B. Results of the Wars. They led to the foundation of the Delian Confederacy, which became the Athenian Empire, 231, 1522.

V. AGE OF PERICLES, OR THE " GOLDEN AGE " OF GREECE.

A. " Plain living and high thinking " in ancient Athens, 286, 1523, 2551.

B. Far-reaching effects of this period. It served to crystallize all the previous culture of Greece ; it stimulated new and immortal achievements ; and it established such high and firm standards in art, literature, and philosophy that Greece continued to be the intellectual leader of the world long after the political power of the Greek states was broken.

VI. CULTURE OF THE GREEKS.

A. Literature, 1539.

a. Poetry : Homeric epics, 1637 ; Lyric poetry, 1539.

b. Drama : evolved from dialogues and choruses of religious festivals, 1037, 1540.

1. Aeschylus, 53 ; Sophocles, 3000 ; Euripides, 1231 ; and Aristophanes, 231, 1540.

2. Greek Theatres, 3194.

c. Prose : developed by historians and orators, 1540, 2769.

1. Herodotus, the " father of history," 1620.

2. Demosthenes, greatest of orators, 990.

B. Art and Architecture, 1528, 213.

a. Pheidias, the master sculptor and builder, 2566.

b. Glories of the Acropolis, 21, *286*, *1521*.

C. Music Among the Greeks, 2261.

D. Influence of religion. A survey of the Greek gods and goddesses will be found in the Mythology Outline, 3648–51. Olympic Games, 2432 ; Oracles, 188, 988.

E. The work of the Philosophers, 1540, 2572—Socrates, 2996 ; Plato, 2628 ; Aristotle, 231.

VII. CIVIL WARS AND DECLINE OF THE POWER OF THE CITY STATES.

A. Peloponnesian Wars establish Spartan supremacy, 3053, 286.

B. Leadership Passes to Thebes, 3197.

VIII. GREECE UNDER MACEDONIAN RULE.

A. Philip of Macedon builds up a great military power, 1524.

B. Alexander, Philip's son, becomes a world conqueror, 105.

a. Subjugation of Persian Empire, including Egypt, 105, 2554.

b. Alexander carries Greek culture to most of known world, 1524.

C. Sunset glory of Greece—the Hellenistic Age, 1524.

a. In Egypt, 2697, 837. Alexandria becomes literary and scientific capital of world, 109, 1930.

b. Art and Literature of Hellenistic Age, 1528, 1539.

c. Development of Science, 1434, 1431, 2697.

IX. GRECIAN WORLD ABSORBED BY ROMAN EMPIRE, 1524.

Rise and Fall of the Roman Empire

I. BEGINNINGS OF ROME.

A. Sunny Italy : the generous mistress of the Mediterranean. Italy was more hospitable to the enterprises of men than Greece. The ridge of the Apennines near the Adriatic coast was a high garden wall which kept curious easterners from trespassing ; the sunny hillsides sloping to the western Mediterranean could support a large population ; communication was not difficult. If the lack of good harbours tended to keep the early Romans at home, it also kept invaders away.

B. Inhabitants of ancient Italy.

a. The Etruscans, 1229. These were perhaps related to the Cretans.

b. The Latins, 1763, 2805. Entered Italy from north, belonged to same stock (Indo-European) as invaders of Greece.

C. Founding of Rome. Nothing definite is known of the founding of Rome, as there is little historical evidence to support the legends of Aeneas or of Romulus and Remus, 1763, 2804.

D. Progress and prosperity of Rome under Etruscan rule, 2805.

E. Etruscan Kings expelled, 1230, 2804. Story of Horatius, 2804.

II. THE REPUBLIC.

A. Long fight waged by common people (Plebs) against the ruling aristocracy (Patricians) for political power, 2805.

B. Military conquest and territorial expansion.

a. All Italy comes under Roman rule, 2807.

1. Defeat of Pyrrhus at Beneventum leads to capture of Greek colonies, 2709.

2. Wise political organization of conquered territories aids governmental stability, 2807.

3. Story of Cincinnatus, 828.

b. Triumph in Punic Wars gives Rome naval supremacy, 2808.

1. Carthage—its rise and fall, 711.

2. Hannibal—a genius in victory and defeat, 1573.

c. Other Conquests. With Carthage defeated, the way was now clear for the conquest of a Mediterranean empire ; victory followed victory ; and sooner or later most of the known world fell before the Roman legions : Syracuse, 210 ; Spain, 3033 ; Greece, 1524 ; Pompey in the East, 2654 ; Gaul, 1365.

C. Collapse of the Republic.

a. Causes, 2803. Here again crops out that fundamental weakness of the ancient civilizations, the slave systems. The rich grew richer and the poor grew poorer, until they were worse off than the actual slaves in the rich man's home. The flooding of the slave-market with military captives made the employment of free labour unprofitable. There were no stabilizing " middle class," no newspapers, no effective civil service, and no national school system to enlighten the public.

b. Civil War, a period of personal rivalries and class struggle, 2808 ; Spartacus slave revolt, 3053. During this period many famous characters appeared : Cicero, 827 ; Pompey, 2654 ; Antony, 2105, and Cleopatra, 837.

c. Julius Caesar masters the Roman world and becomes " Imperator," 652, 2811.

III. THE EMPIRE.

A. First Century of Imperial glory, 3517.

a. Augustus encourages era of intellectual and Imperial development, 303.

b. The infamous Nero, the last of the Augustan line, ends the century, 2315.

B. Second Century of Imperial glory—empire reaches greatest extent, 2808 (map).

a. Conquest of Britain, 1193.

b. Rule of Blood and Iron. Destruction of Jerusalem, 1821 ; Annihilation of Palmyra, 2485.

c. Marcus Aurelius, the Emperor-philosopher, 2099.

C. Life in Imperial Rome.

a. Luxury the keynote of Roman life. Every-day affairs in Pompeii, 2653 ; performances of gladiators, 1469.

b. Practical Progress.

1. " Modern " improvements two thousand years ago : public baths (2804, 2654) ; drainage systems, 2804 ; aqueducts and water supply, 194, 2818 ; utensils, 2809.

2. Greatest system of communication in the ancient world ; roads, 2783, 574 ; postal service, 2661 ; lighthouses, 1943.

c. Artistic Achievements.

1. Roman architects modify Greek style and develop engineering technique, 212.

2. In sculpture and painting, also, the Romans followed Greek models, 2812.

d. Literature, 1894.

1. Golden Age of Latin literature : 1895 ; Cicero the great prose stylist, 827 ; Horace and Virgil poets, 1641, 3325.

2. Silver Age, 1897. " Meditations " of Marcus Aurelius, a classic of all ages, 2099.

e. Religion. In religion, too, the Romans borrowed from the Greeks. For a survey of Roman gods and goddesses consult the Mythology Outline, 3648-51.

IV. DECLINE AND FALL OF THE EMPIRE.

A. Internal Decay.

a. Emperors under control of army, 3519.

b. Constantine ends the political power of Rome by removing capital to Constantinople, 893.

1. This paved the way for the formal division of the Empire, 1237.

2. Justinian I preserves Roman Law in famous code, 1844.

c. The Byzantine Empire at Constantinople, 635. This empire is chiefly interesting in connexion with Roman history because it preserved for posterity the classic culture that was destroyed in Rome.

B. The Coming of the Barbarians : Beyond the last Roman outposts restless peoples were ever eager to push into the southern lands of sunshine and plenty. Centuries before, the Gauls had ravaged Italy and even sacked Rome, 1365. With the weakening of the Roman military power these tribes began to pour into the Empire, 1237, 1487.

C. Fall of Rome.

a. Visigoth victory at Adrianople foreshadows doom of Rome, 1487.

b. Rome is captured by Alaric, 96.

c. Pope Leo I saves city from ravages of Huns under Attila, 1654, 1926.

d. Theodoric, the Ostrogoth, establishes short-lived rule in Italy, 1763.

e. Vandals plunder by land and sea, 3304.

f. Lombards found kingdom in Northern Italy, 2000.

D. The Christian Church takes up the burden dropped by the dying Empire.

Some Books on Ancient History

Men of the Old Stone Age. H. F. Osborn
Ancient Hunters. W. J. Sollas.
Everyday Life in the Old Stone Age, also New Stone, Bronze, and Early Iron Ages. M. and C. H. B. Quennell.
The Antiquity of Man. Sir Arthur Keith.
Dawn of European Civilization. V. Gordon Childe.
Digging up the Past. Sir C. L. Woolley.
Progress of Early Man. Stuart Piggott.
Our Forerunners. M. C. Burkitt.
History of the Ancient Egyptians. J. H. Breasted.
The Dawn of History. J. L. Myres.

Babylonian Life and History. Sir E. Wallis Budge.
The Greek View of Life. G. Lowes Dickinson.
History of Greece. J. B. Bury.
Decline and Fall of the Roman Empire. E. Gibbon.
The Greek Commonwealth. Sir A. E. Zimmern.
Everyday Things in Homeric Greece, Everyday Things in Classical Greece. M. and C. H. B. Quennell.
Roman Society from Nero to M. Aurelius. S. Dill.
Plutarch's Lives.
Herodotus' History.
Cambridge Ancient History.

MEDIEVAL HISTORY

I. CHARLEMAGNE'S EMPIRE.

A. Foundation of the Frankish Empire.

    a. Clovis unites all Franks and conquers modern France, 854, 1365. The conversion of Clovis to Orthodox Christianity led to Frankish support of the Pope.

    b. Charles Martel saves Europe from Mahomedan conquest at Tours, 759.

B. Charlemagne, the empire builder of the Middle Ages, 753.

C. Disruption of Charlemagne's empire, the starting point of modern Germany and France, 1365, 1449. Charlemagne's son, Louis the Pious, was unable to maintain order in the vast domain left him, and upon his death his three sons divided the lands between them—the Partition of Verdun. Louis the German received the portion beyond the Rhine ; Charles the Bold, that west of the Rhône and Schelde ; Lothair, the middle strip including Italy.

II. THE MEDIEVAL CHURCH.

A. Bishop of Rome, as Pope, becomes the most powerful ruler of the Middle Ages, 2495.

B. Work of the monks and monasteries, 510, 2212.

    a. Missionary enterprises, 302, 500.

    b. The Friars, 2212 ; Franciscans, 1363.

III. FEUDALISM.

A. Result of the collapse of Roman government, 1268.

    a. General causes of Feudalism. This system was not peculiar to Europe ; it has often grown up in countries where the central government has been weak ; Japan, 1795.

    b. The castle, the stronghold of Feudalism, 717.

    c. Rule of " might makes right." In England, 1161 ; in France, 2027 ; in Germany, 1447.

B. Life under the Feudal System.

    a. Knighthood and chivalry, 1863.

    1. Armour, 240, 241 ; heraldry, 1614.

    2. Life in the castle, 717 ; the importance of the minstrels, 2262 ; courtly sport of falconry, 1258.

    b. Country life. System of land holding, 1268 ; dependent position of serfs ; agricultural methods, 78.

    c. Town life, 461, 1751. Fairs and markets, 1256 ; Flemish trade, 403 ; Hanseatic League, 1575 ; trade with the East, 1158, 3174 ; guilds, the medieval forerunner of the trade unions, 1555.

C. Decline of Feudalism, 1269. Black Death breaks down agricultural system, 85 ; effects of Crusades, 937, 2766 ; Peasants' revolt, 3269 ; invention of gunpowder, 1558 ; rise of infantry and professional armies, 76 ; inventions which changed the tide of power, 1721, 1881, 2684.

IV. CULTURAL DEVELOPMENT OF THE MIDDLE AGES.

A. Literature embodied in Minstrels' Songs, 2798, 2262, 2401.

    a. Modern survivals. Tales of King Arthur, 255 ; Robin Hood, 2790, 3469 ; Song of Roland, 2797.

    b. Froissart the Chronicler, 1399.

    c. Books and Libraries, 510, 1930.

B. Beginnings of the Modern Drama. Pageants, Miracle and Mystery Plays, 1039, 2189.

C. Architecture and Art.

    a. Gothic architecture, 216 ; Cathedrals, 729 ; stained glass, 218 ; sculpture, 2904.

    b. Other arts. Painting, 2476 ; tapestries, 3152 ; ivory carving, 1788 ; illumination of books, 512.

D. Living Conditions. Meagre house furnishings, 1409 ; floor coverings, 706 ; inadequate water supply, 3347 ; table utensils, 1867 ; limited diet, 3060 ; bad roads, 2783.

E. Education carried on by the Church.

    a. Medieval universities, 2462, 494, 2275.

    b. Importance of Abélard, 11 ; Roger Bacon, 334.

V. THE CRUSADES.

A. The East at the time of the Crusades.

    a. Byzantine Empire, the stronghold of culture in Europe, 635.

    b. Rising tide of Mahomedanism, 2066, 1872. Movement into Europe through Spain, 2227 ; checked at Tours, 759.

B. The Crusades, 936.

    a. Causes. Seljuk Turks capture Jerusalem, threaten Constantinople, and stop pilgrimages to Palestine, 936.

    b. General character.

    1. Famous leaders : Richard the Lionhearted, 2776 ; Saladin, 2864 ; Louis IX of France, 2028 ; Frederick Barbarossa, 1388 ; Philip Augustus, 2567.

    2. Corruption into economic crusades, 638, 927, 953.

    3. Part played by Crusading Orders, 1865, 2072.

C. Effects, 937. Agriculture improved by introduction of new plants ; use of Arabic notation,
2405 ; influence on architecture, 218.

VI. GROWTH OF MONARCHY IN FRANCE.

A. Capetian Kings begin Unification of France,
1238, 1365. When Hugh Capet came to the
throne, the kingly power was disputed by great
barons, of whom the Duke of Normandy was the
most powerful ; Henry I fails to subdue vassals ;
how the Northmen conquered Normandy, 2376.

   a. Louis the Fat brings order to France by
   defeating feudal barons, 2027.

   b. Philip Augustus conquers Normandy from
   John of England, 2567. Normandy became
   an English possession when the Duke of
   Normandy became king of England, 2376-77.

   c. Louis the Saint's administrative reforms,
   2028.

   d. Philip the Fair, 2567. Calls the first States-
   General.

B. Hundred Years' War, 1652.

   a. Causes. 1652. English claims to France.

   b. How the war was fought.
   1. Royal leaders, 757, 758, 1091, 1611.
   2. Important battles : Crécy, 926 ; 1652 ;
   Poitiers, 1652 ; Agincourt, 76, 1653 ; first
   use of cannon, 260.
   3. How Joan of Arc saved France, 1831,
   757.

   c. Results, 1265, 1611.

C. Growth of Absolute Monarchy under Louis XI,
2028. Defeat of Charles the Bold, Duke of Burgundy, 759.

Note: For the history of England in the Middle
Ages, *see* page 3643.

VII. THE EMPIRE AND THE PAPACY.

A. The Beginnings of the Holy Roman Empire,
1636.

   a. Coronation of Charlemagne, the " central
   fact of the Middle Ages," 753, *1366*.

b. Conflict between Popes and Emperors, 1636.
Since both Pope and Emperor claimed that
their power was derived from God, a difference
in interests was bound to lead to a conflict.

c. Revived under Otto I, 2459. For the next
few centuries the history of Germany and Italy
became that of the Empire and the Papacy.

B. Great Investiture Conflict.

   a. Begun by Henry IV and Pope Gregory VII
   (Hildebrand), 1609, 1542. Settled by Concordat of Worms.

   b. Conflict in England, 3380.

C. Quarrels of the Hohenstaufens and the Popes.

   a. Fundamental causes. The office of Emperor
   was theoretically elective, and the Guelfs
   disputed the claims of the Hohenstaufens
   (Ghibellines). Since the coronation of the
   Emperor by the Pope was necessary to the
   imperial power, the Pope was forced to take
   sides in the disputes. The Hohenstaufens
   were the most formidable rivals of the papacy,
   1637, 1449.

   b. Frederick Barbarossa, one of the greatest
   of the emperors, 1388.

   c. Innocent III strengthens the papal position,
   2215 ; humbles John of England, 1725.

   d. Frederick II restores Hohenstaufen House ;
   cultural development of this period in Naples
   and Sicily, 1389.

D. Golden Bull establishes a " Constitution " for
the Empire, 1637 ; hinders growth of centralized government in Germany, 1449.

VIII. FALL OF THE EASTERN (BYZANTINE) EMPIRE.

A. Rise of the Ottoman Turks, 3262.

B. Fall of Constantinople, 1761, 638. This put
an end to the Byzantine Empire and gave the
Turks undisputed control of the eastern Mediterranean and of a large corner of Europe ; it
stimulated the era of exploration and discovery
by forcing western Europe to seek new ways of
reaching the Far East.

Books on Medieval History

The Holy Roman Empire. James Bryce.
The Crusades. T. A. Archer and C. L. Kingsford.
Medieval Europe. H. W. C. Davis.
Stories from Froissart. Ed. by Sir Henry Newbolt.

Cambridge Medieval History. Ed. by H. M. Gwatkin.
Life in Medieval France. Joan Evans.
Medieval People. Eileen Power.
Universal History of the World, Vol. 5. Ed. by Sir John Hammerton.

MODERN HISTORY
The Renaissance

1. FORERUNNERS AND CONTRIBUTING CAUSES.

A. Crusades—Contact with Eastern culture stimulated thought of Crusaders, 936.

B. Invention of Printing and more general use of
paper promoted interchange of ideas, 2684.

C. Growth of Creative Impulse as shown in medieval
Architecture, 212.

II. LITERARY RENAISSANCE.

Study of classical learning and beginnings of
national literatures, 2764.

A. In Italy, 2764, 1786.

   a. Dante, the forerunner of the Renaissance,
   969.

   b. Revival of Greek and Latin hampers distinctly national literature, 1539, 1894.

B. North of the Alps, 2764.
    a. France, 1379 ; Froissart the Chronicler, 1399.
    b. England, 1210, 1612 ; early influence of Chaucer, 761, and Wycliffe, 3428, on English language ; Sir Thomas More and the Oxford Reformers, 2228.

III. ARTISTIC RENAISSANCE.

A. In Italy, 2764, 2476, 2904.
    a. Florence the centre of the movement ; Patronage of the Medici, 2131.
    b. Italian Masters : Giotto, 1464 ; Ghiberti, 1460 ; Leonardo da Vinci, 1926 ; Michelangelo, 2160´; Raphael, 2745 ; Titian, 3217.
    c. The Church a patron of art : The Borgias, 525 ; Leo X, 1926.
B. Northern Artists, 2766 ; Dürer, 1058 ; Holbein, 1635.
C. Architecture : Return to the classic styles, 220.

IV. BEGINNINGS OF SCIENCE.

A. Roger Bacon, who foreshadowed experimental science, 334.
B. Advance in Astronomy :
    a. Copernicus, the founder of modern astronomy, 905.
    b. Galileo continues work of Copernicus, 1414, 1513.
C. Important Inventions : Compass, 881 ; gunpowder, 1558.

V. EXPLORATIONS AND DISCOVERIES.

A. Prince Henry the Navigator and the Portuguese in the East, 1613.
    a. Bartholomew Diaz discovers the Cape of Good Hope, 695.
    b. Vasco da Gama reaches India, 3306.
B. Columbus discovers America, 878.
C. Magellan circumnavigates the world, 2056.

The Reformation and Religious Wars

I. CAUSES OF THE REFORMATION.
A. Effect of the Renaissance, 2766. Social and political unrest in Germany, 2758 ; printing and translation of Bible into national languages, 425.
B. Forerunners of the Reformation, 2758 : Wycliffe and the Lollards, 3428 ; John Huss attacks corruption of the Church in Bohemia, 1660 ; influence of Erasmus, 1221, 2764.

II. POLITICAL AND SOCIAL CONDITIONS OF EUROPE.
A. Consolidation of Spain, 3036.
    a. Marriage of Ferdinand and Isabella, 3036.
    b. Moorish power broken, 2227.
    c. Charles V rules the Holy Roman Empire and all Hapsburg possessions, 754, 2759, 1239.
B. French Designs on Italy, 758.
    a. Battle of Ravenna, 2748.
    b. Savonarola preaches moral and religious revival, 2876.
    c. Invasions of Italy distract attention from religious revolt, 1764.

III. REFORMATION BEGINS IN GERMANY.
A. Why Germany was ready for the Reformation, 2758.

B. Luther and his teachings, 2040, 2758.
C. Peace of Augsburg ends civil wars, 2759. Since this peace left to each ruler the right to establish either Lutheranism or Catholicism, the people who disagreed with their rulers were forced to emigrate.

IV. CALVINISM.
A. In Switzerland.
    a. Zwingli preaches radical reform, 3448. In the disagreement between Zwingli and Luther lay the germ of much future Protestant dissension.
    b. Calvin and his teachings, 664.
B. Huguenots in France, 1650.
    a. Persecutions and St. Bartholomew Massacre, 1366, 1650, 2274.
    b. Henry IV and Edict of Nantes, 2274.
    c. Richelieu destroys political power of Huguenots, 2778.
C. In Scotland, 2892. John Knox founds Scottish Presbyterianism, 1871.

Note : For the Reformation in England, see page 3643.

Period of Civil Strife

I. SPAIN AND REVOLT OF THE PROTESTANT NETHERLANDS.
A. Catholic Policy of Philip II, 2568.
B. Dutch Fight for independence, 2321. William the Silent ; Treaty of Westphalia, 2323, 3381, 3202.

II. COUNTER-REFORMATION.
A. Earlier Churchmen's attempts to end abuses. Savonarola, 2876 ; Ximenes, 427.
B. Reform within the Catholic Church, 2760. Loyola and the Jesuits, 2032 ; Francis Xavier, 3429.
C. The Inquisition, 1726.

III. THE THIRTY YEARS' WAR.
A. Last Great Religious War spreads from German Empire into all Europe, 3202.
    a. Gustavus Adolphus, the Protestant champion, 1558, 3202. Originates modern army.
    b. Richelieu aids Protestant cause, 2778. By this time the religious significance of the war had been lost sight of.
B. Results of War.
    a. Religious question settled in Germany, 3203.
    b. Political adjustments, 1239.
    c. Terrific devastation of invaded countries.
Note : For the Civil War, Commonwealth, and Restoration in England, see page 3643.

Struggle for Power and Possessions

I. THE AGE OF LOUIS XIV IN FRANCE.

A. Louis XIV, the *Grand Monarque*, 2029.

a. Inherits strong monarchy, built by Richelieu and Mazarin, 2778, 2124. Absolutism illustrated by incident of the " Man in the Iron Mask," 1758.

b. Internal administration under Colbert, 868. Persecution of the Huguenots, 1650.

c. Foreign policy—wars to extend French power, 2029. Louis systematically paid foreign court officials and even rulers to support his cause, as in the case of James II, King of England, 1794.

B. French Society during Reign of Louis XIV.

a. Court at Versailles.
Spectacular extravagance, 2029 : Art under royal patronage, 1377.

b. Golden age of French literature, 1380. Corneille, 910 ; Molière, 2198 ; Racine, 2725 ; Voltaire, 3329.

II. STRUGGLE FOR BALANCE OF POWER.

A. What " Balance of Power " means. In the 17th century there appeared in European politics a new factor, the " Balance of Power," the maintenance of a balance of equality between the great nations of Europe. At this period it was Louis XIV who threatened the balance of power.

B. War of the Spanish Succession, 2029.

a. Marlborough, the great English general, 2105.

b. By the Treaty of Utrecht (1713), Britain obtained Gibraltar, Newfoundland, Nova Scotia, etc.

C. War of the Austrian Succession, 2101, 2924.

D. Seven Years' War, 2924.

a. Preceded by diplomatic revolution. France and Austria against Prussia and Great Britain, 2101 ; importance of Chatham, 759 ; weak rule of Louis XV, 2030.

b. Overseas contest. In America, 2924 ; in India, 1715, 660, 842, 413.

c. Results of the war, 2920. Extension of British Empire, 581 ; losses of France, 1366 ; gains of Prussia, 1752.

III. RACE FOR COLONIAL EMPIRES.

A. Results of Discoveries. It was the inevitable result of the discoveries in the western hemisphere that each European country should hasten to seize as much as possible of the New World. Claims to the new territories were based upon priority of discovery and settlement.

B. Spanish America.

a. Columbus establishes Spanish claim to New World, 880. Explorations continued by Balboa, 341 ; Ponce de Leon, 1319 ; Vespucius, 3318 ; De Soto, 2192.

b. Spain's empire. South America, 3025 ; West Indies, 3368 ; Central America, 743 ; Mexico, 2158.

1. Conquest of native peoples. Cortes in Mexico, 914 ; Pizarro in Peru, 2616.

2. Las Casas, Dominican monk, protector of the Indians, *f-i.*

c. Spanish colonial policy was one of ruthless exploitation.

C. Portugal obtains great colony of Brazil, 550.

D. French in North America, 681.
Cartier, 712 ; Champlain, 751 ; Marquette and Joliet, 2107 ; La Salle, 1894.

E. Other Settlements in North America.
Dutch Colonies in New World, 986.

Note: For British exploration and settlement, and colonial results of the Seven Years' War, *see* page 3645.

Rise of Prussia and Russia

I. THE BEGINNINGS OF PRUSSIAN POWER.

A. Early Duchy under the Hohenzollerns, 2696. Prussia had been converted to Christianity by Teutonic Knights, 1238.

B. Frederick the Great raises Prussia to state of first rank, 1390, 2696.

a. Seizure of Silesia and Seven Years' War, 1389, 2924.

b. Partition of Poland, 2640.

II. FORMATION OF THE RUSSIAN EMPIRE.

A. Russia before Peter the Great, 2846.

a. Early leadership of Kiev, 1856.

b. Mongol invasion shuts off contact with Western Europe, 2205.

c. Grand Dukes of Muscovy reorganize Russia, 1787.

B. Peter the Great, 2562. How one man lashed a medieval empire into a modern state, 2846.

a. Defeat of Charles XII of Sweden, 758.

b. Baltic provinces annexed, 1899.

C. Catherine II continues Peter's policies, 2847.

a. Seven Years' War, 2924.

b. Shares in partition of Poland, 2640 ; Kosciusko, saviour of Poland, 1873.

c. Ambitions along the Black Sea, 2420.

III. LESSER EUROPEAN STATES IN EIGHTEENTH CENTURY.

A. Decline of Spanish Power, 3036.

B. Italy without political unity, 1763. Bourbons succeed Hapsburgs in Naples and Sicily, 2275, 2968.

C. Weakness of Austria. After the death of the Emperor Charles V, Austria was ruled by the Austrian branch of the Hapsburgs, 320.

a. Lack of racial unity.

b. Reign of Maria Theresa, 2101, 320 ; Loss of Silesia, 1389 ; Seven Years' War, 2924 ; partition of Poland, 2640.

The French Revolution and Napoleon

1. REVOLUTION IN FRANCE, 1755.

A. Sources of the Revolutionary Movement.

    a. **Influence of Liberal thinkers.** Voltaire, **3329** ; Rousseau, **2381** ; the Encyclopedists.

    b. Abuses of the old regime, 1366, 1393.

    c. Failure of reforms under Louis XVI, 1393, 2030. Influence of Marie Antoinette, 1393, 2030, 2102.

B. Overthrow of the Old Regime.

    a. **Meeting of the States-General,** 1393 ; Bastille stormed and social revolution, 1395 ; serfdom ended, 1394 ; royal family escorted to Paris, 2030.

    b. **Constitution drawn up,** 1395. Declaration of the Rights of Man, 1394.

    c. **Leaders :** Mirabeau, **2189** ; Lafayette, **1884,** 1394 ; Talleyrand, **3149.**

    d. **Flight of king** leads to abolition of monarchy, 2030. Execution of Louis XVI, 2030.

C. Reign of Terror, Government by the Convention, 1393.

    a. **Dominated by Jacobins,** 1790, 1396. Robespierre, **2789** ; Danton, **971.**

    b. **Control by terrorism.** Execution of Lavoisier, **1901** ; Madame Roland, **2797** ; Marie Antoinette, **2102** ; Jean Paul Marat, 1394, **2096.**

D. Directory Established, 1367.

    a. **Wars with foreign powers :** The hostility of France's neighbours to the revolutionary spirit had brought on a whole series of wars, 1366, 2275.

    b. **Napoleon Bonaparte,** the " man of the hour," 2275. Early life and education, 2275 ; marriage to Josephine Beauharnais, **1838** ; campaigns under the Directory, 2275 ; Egyptian campaign, 2275, 2313.

II. NAPOLEONIC ERA.

A. Bonaparte overthrows the Directory and establishes the Consulate, 2275.

    a. Wars against second coalition, 2275.

    b. **Battle of the Baltic,** 905, 2313 ; peace of Amiens, 2276.

B. Napoleonic Empire.

    a. **Imperial conquests** extended over most of Europe, 2276–77. Naval power crushed at Trafalgar, 2276, **3234.**

    b. **Napoleon as statesman,** 2276.

    c. **Effects of Continental System :** In Europe, 2277 ; in United States they led to war with Britain, 3291.

C. Napoleon's downfall through national risings and military reverses, 2277.

    a. **Peninsular War,** 2660 ; retreat from Moscow, 2277, 2235.

    b. **Hundred Days and Waterloo,** 2278.

    c. **Exile to St. Helena,** *2277,* 2278.

III. CONGRESS OF VIENNA AND PERIOD OF REACTION.

A. Partition of Napoleonic Empire among European powers, 1240. Talleyrand's work for France, **3149.**

B. Formation of Grand and Holy Alliances ; The Quadruple (Grand) Alliance was formed by Austria, Russia, Prussia, and Great Britain ; the last subsequently withdrew, and France was included.

Note : In reconstructing Europe the Congress of Vienna was guided by dynastic rather than national claims. The representatives of the old aristocracy in seeking to restore the " balance of power " sowed the seeds of later conflicts.

C. **Age of Metternich.** For thirty years after the Congress of Vienna, the moving spirit of European politics was Prince Metternich (*f-i.*), the famous Austrian statesman. He was the consistent foe of democracy and set his face against any suggestions of change.

D. Decline of Reactionary Power.

    a. Great Britain joins United States in Monroe doctrine, 3291.

    b. Russia supports Greece in war of independence, 1525.

    c. Revolution of 1830 in France overthrows Charles X, **758.**

The Industrial Revolution

I. OLD INDUSTRIAL CONDITIONS.

The Renaissance had had little effect on the everyday life of the people. Nearly all the work of the world was done by hand labour with a few inefficient tools, 1721 ; communication was slow and hazardous, the masses of the people continued to live in the Middle Ages. Then, in about a generation, the adoption of a few practical inventions radically changed living conditions.

II. HOW THE CHANGE CAME ABOUT.

A. Inventions in spinning and weaving, 3066, 3361.

    a. **Hargreaves'** spinning jenny, 1578. Improvements by Arkwright and Crompton, **235, 933.**

    b. **Cartwright's** power loom, **712.**

    c. **Whitney's** cotton gin adds impetus to textile industry, 918.

B. Invention of Steam-engine fills great industrial need ; Watt, father of the steam-engine, **3356.**

C. Rise of the Factory System, 802, 1722.

D. Improvement in Communications.

    a. Building of Roads and Canals, 2783, 686.

    b. Application of steam-engine to problems of transport, **3085.** Fulton's work with the steamboat, **1407** ; locomotives and railways, **1981, 2734** ; Stephenson's locomotive, **3086.**

    c. Use of Electricity. Morse invents telegraph, **2232** ; submarine cables unite continents, **641.**

E. Improvement of Agricultural Methods, 79, 80.
Better ploughs, reaping machines, etc.

III. SOME RESULTS OF THE INDUSTRIAL REVOLUTION.

A. Economic, 1721.

Factory System and its problems, 1721. Medieval apprenticeship system, 1553 ; child labour a social menace, 802 ; growth of trade union movement, **3233**.

B. Influence upon Literature, 1040, 1088, 2402.

Europe in the Nineteenth Century

I. DEMOCRACY AND REACTION IN FRANCE.

A. **Bourbon Restoration** under Louis XVIII, **2030**. Reactionary policies of Charles X and the Revolution of 1830, 1366, **758**.

B. **Louis Philippe**, the Citizen King, **2031**.

C. **Revolution of 1848** and Second Republic, 1366, 2031.

D. **Napoleon III** and the Second Empire, 1366, **2278**.
a. Foreign policy : Participates in Crimean War, 931 ; aids Italy against Austria, 737, 1769 ; interferes in Mexico, 2159.
b. Domestic administration marked by prosperity and public improvements ; Paris rebuilt, 2518.

E. **Franco-Prussian War** and the Third Republic.
a. Germany crushes France in Franco-Prussian War, **1384**. Siege of Metz, **2155** ; disaster at Sedan, 2278.
b. Third Republic, 1366. Commune of Paris suppressed, 1385.

II. FOUNDING OF THE GERMAN EMPIRE.

A. **Revolution of 1848** seeks democratic and united government, 1449.

B. **Bismarck** builds up Prussia's power, 1384, 2696, 1449, 3378. Schleswig-Holstein seized, 992 ; Seven Weeks' War with Austria and formation of North German Confederation, 1449.

C. **Franco-Prussian War** and Empire proclaimed.
a. Germany defeats France in short campaign, 1366.
b. Germany united as a Hohenzollern empire, 1449.

III. FORMATION OF AUSTRIA-HUNGARY.

A. **Revolution of 1848** in Hapsburg lands, 319, 1656.
a. Kossuth and Hungarian Republic, 1656, 1874.

b. Insurrection in Italy led by Sardinia-Piedmont, 1769.
c. Revolt in Bohemia, 487.

B. **Francis Joseph** begins long reign, **1383**.
a. Loss of Italian provinces, 1769, 737, 1418.
b. Defeated by Prussia in Seven Weeks' War, 2696.

C. **Dual Monarchy Formed**, 1656, 319.

IV. UNIFICATION OF ITALY, 1769.

A. **Mazzini** and the Republic of Rome, 1769.

B. **Sardinian leadership** under Victor Emmanuel and his great minister, Cavour, **737**.
a. Garibaldi and his " thousand red-shirts," 1418.
b. Why the Pope opposed the new kingdom, 2615.

Note : For Great Britain in the 19th century, *see* page 3644.

V. OTHER EUROPEAN COUNTRIES.

A. **Scandinavian Countries.**
a. **Denmark.** Loses Norway after Napoleonic Wars, 992, 2398 ; Prussia and Austria seize Schleswig-Holstein, 816, 992.
b. **Sweden.** Loss of Finland, 1277 ; loss of Norway, **3131**, 2398.
c. **Norway** becomes an independent kingdom, 2398.

B. **Iberian Peninsula.**
a. **Spain** loses most of colonial empire. Insurrections in Cuba and war with United States, 3036, 941.
b. **Portugal**, 2658. Revolution of 1910, 2660.

C. **Belgium and Holland.**
a. **Belgium** revolts from Netherlands, 2323, 407.
b. **Kingdom of Belgium**, **407**. Leopold II secures Congo region, **887**, **1928**.

Awakening of the Far East

I. EUROPEANS IN CHINA.

A. **China opened to Foreigners** through treaty ports, 810. Great Britain obtains Hong Kong through Opium War, 1639, 2442.

B. **Exploitation by Foreign Powers**, 810.
a. Defeat by Japan leads to foreign intervention, 1800.
b. German holdings in Shantung, **2938**.
c. Manchuria falls under Russian and later under Japanese influence, **2087**.
d. " Open door " agreement saves national integrity.

C. **Revolution** establishes republican government, 813 ; failure of " Boxer " rising, 812.

II. RUSSIA TURNS TO THE EAST.

A. **Reaction** after the Crimean War, 2848.
a. Alexander, the " Tsar liberator," frees the serfs, 2848.
b. Return of tyrannical policies, 2365. Influences of Nihilist movement, 2856 ; Tolstoy, the voice of Russia, 3222.

B. **Advance in Asia.**
a. March to the Pacific.
Trans-Siberian Railway links Leningrad with the Pacific, 2967 ; Port Arthur taken, 1800 ; influence extended through Manchuria, 2087.

b. **Central Asia.**
Conquest of Transcaucasia and Turkistan, 732 ; pressure on Indian border buffer state of Afghanistan, 55.

III. TRANSFORMATION OF JAPAN.

A. Country opened to Foreigners, 1799.
    a. Matthew Perry's expedition, 1795 ; Marco Polo's visit, 1799.
    b. Earlier Contact with Westerners, 1799.

B. **War with China,** 1800. Chinese attitude towards Japan, 814
C. Russo-Japanese War makes Japan a world-power, 1800.
    a. Annexation of Korea, **1873,** 1800.
    b. Japanese influence in Manchuria, 1800, **2085.**
    c. Independent state of Manchukuo (Manchuria) set up ; conflict with China, 1800, 814, **2085.**
D. " Unofficial " War, 1800.

Europe before the First World War

I. ARMED PEACE IN EUROPE.

A. **Triple Alliance** between Germany, Austria, and Italy, 1240. A serious weakness of this alliance lay in the fact that Italy was linked with her ancient enemy Austria, who still held Italian territories (*Italia Irredenta*, "Unredeemed Italy"); Italy had joined the alliance from pique at France for seizing Tunis and fear of her interference on behalf of the Pope.

B. **Triple Entente** of France, Russia, and Great Britain, 1240. Originally a Dual Alliance of Russia and France, it was enlarged to include Great Britain during Edward VII's reign, **1092.**
Note : France and Russia were balanced against Germany and Austria. Italy joined the latter because of the North African quarrel, while Great Britain, fearing the growing sea-power of Germany, threw its weight on the side of France and Russia.

C. **Germany's Industrial Growth** and need for new markets.
    a. William II backs economic ambitions with militarism, 3378.
    b. Effect of struggle for colonial possessions, 1450.

D. Hague Peace Conference, an attempt to combat militarism, 2365.

II. THE NEAR EAST AND THE DISMEMBERMENT OF TURKEY.

A. Russia looks to the Mediterranean.

    a. Crimean War, **931.**
    b. Russo-Turkish War, 344, 1019.
Note : The Western Powers rushed to the aid of Turkey in order to prevent Russia from securing any considerable influence in Constantinople and the Dardanelles. The Triple Entente came much later.

B. **Balkan Wars** deprive Turkey of most of its European territory, 344. Territorial gains of Greece, **1525** ; Serbia, **2922** ; Montenegro, 2219 ; Rumania, **2841.**

C. **Central Powers** look towards the Near East.
    a. Germany's Balkan policy and the Baghdad railway, 339, 343, 1743.
    b. Austria, 343, 2922. Annexation of Bosnia-Herzegovina, 320, 2922.

III. SCRAMBLE FOR AFRICA.

A. **Modern Explorations** disclose vast resources, 72. Livingstone and Stanley, **1970, 3076** ; Leopold II of Belgium starts the race for Africa, 1928.

B. **Partition of Africa** at Congress of Berlin, 72.

C. For the British Empire in Africa, *see* page 3646.

D. **Extension of French Influence.**
    a. The French in Algeria and Tunis before Congress of Berlin, 118.
    b. Germany challenges French rights in Morocco, 2230.

E. **Italy obtains Libya** in war with Turkey, 1770.

The First World War and its Consequences

I. CAUSES.

A. **The Spirit of Aggression.** The fundamental cause of the catastrophe was the aggressive nationalism which had been steadily growing in the great European states. International relations were regarded as essentially competitive and it was only in rare instances, as the International Postal Union (2662), that true cooperation had obtained. In the half century of diplomacy before 1914 national ambitions found an outlet in imperialistic colonial enterprises and a military rivalry that turned Europe into an armed camp.

B. **The Spark** that started the blaze. The immediate cause was the crisis raised by the assassination of the heir to the Austrian throne, 345, **3409,** 2922.
For the military and naval operations and the general course of the War reference should be made to the article on the First World War, 2409, and those on the various countries concerned, and

to the Chronologies and list of battles in the Fact-Index, World Wars.

II. PEACE CONFERENCE AT PARIS, 1241.

A. **Representatives** from all Allied and associated powers attend, 2531, *1241.*
    a. **Dominated by " big four."** Lloyd George, **1976** ; Clemenceau, **837** ; Woodrow Wilson, **3383** ; Orlando.
    b. **Other influential delegates.** Borden, **524** ; Smuts, **2987** ; Venizelos, 1525.

B. **Treaty of Versailles** with Germany, 2531, 3414, *1241.* Subsidiary Treaties with Austria 3415 ; Hungary, 3414 ; Bulgaria, 3415 ; Turkey (Sèvres), 3415 ; (Lausanne), 3415.

C. **League of Nations** established, **1908.**

III. RUSSIAN REVOLUTION.

    a. How the Revolution was accomplished, 2848–49.
    b. Abdication of Nicholas II, 2365, 2848.

Between the Wars

After the First World War sweeping alterations were made in the grouping of the European states, changes based mainly on the principle of nationalism. Monarchism was at a discount, Republicanism in the ascendant, Parliamentary government tended to break down, and government by dictators became increasingly common, 1241–42, 3414–16. *See also* on the financial crisis, 1242, 1482.

A. Russia, 2844.
   a. The Bolshevists and their leaders. Lenin, 1922, Trotsky, 3251, and Stalin, 3072.
   b. Disruption of the Empire, 1241, 2849. Loss of Finland, 1277 ; Estonia, 1226 ; Latvia, 1299 ; Lithuania, 1967 ; Russian Poland, 2641 ; Bessarabia, 2841 ; Siberia, 2966 ; Ukraine, 3273.

B. Germany, 1450, 1241.
   a. The Weimar Republic and Stresemann, 1450.

b. Hitler, 1631 ; the Nazi State, 1242, 1451, 2281, 3415.

C. Italy, 2284.
   a. Mussolini, 1242, 2268, 1770, 3415.
   b. The Fascist State, 1261, 1770, 3415.
   c. Conquest of Abyssinia, 13, 3415.

D. Turkey, 3262. Kemal Atatürk, 1850.

E. Dissolution of Austria-Hungary and the formation of new states, 3415.
   a. Czechoslovakia obtains independence, 953, 1241.
   b. Slavs of Austria-Hungary join Serbia and Montenegro to form Yugoslavia, 1241, 3438.
   c. Austria stripped of former possessions 3414, becomes part of German Reich, 3416, 318
   d. Hungary given independence, 1656, 1241

F. Spain. Civil War, *3414*, 1242, 1384.

The Second World War and Its Consequences

I. CAUSES.

A. **Nationalist Aggression.** Under their dictators Germany and Italy found the peace-loving democracies unwilling to resist their demands by force, while the League of Nations could not combine to inflict any but economic sanctions upon aggressors. Mussolini's grandiose ideas led him to attempt to erect a greater Italian empire in Africa, 1773. Hitler's plan to refute Versailles Treaty met with unopposed success :
   a. Re-militarization of the Rhineland, 1451, 1632, 3415.
   b. " Anschluss " with Austria, 318, 1242, 1632, 3416.
   c. The Munich Crisis and Agreement, 1451, 2256, 3416.
   d. Occupation of Czechoslovakia, 1242, 1451, 1632, 3416.
   e. Memel and Danzig, 1242, 1451, 3414, 3416.

B. **Isolationism in U.S.A. and Russia,** 2852, 3292.

C. **Non-Aggression Pact between Germany and Russia,** by securing Germany's rear, gives Hitler the signal for aggression, 1242, 2852.

D. **Japan's successes against China,** and her " mission " to create a New Order in East Asia led her to challenge Britain and U.S.A., 3415.

II. COURSE OF THE WAR.

For the general course of the War reference should be made to World Wars (3416) and the various countries, operations, battles and commanders ; the Fact-Index contains Chronologies and a list of battles, under World Wars.

III. CONSEQUENCES.

A. In Europe.
   a. Germany devastated, defeated and occupied, 1452–53.

b. **Italy,** having surrendered, becomes republic, 1775 ; loses colonies, 1222, 3000.
   c. **Russia** acquires territory lost in the disruption of the Tsarist empire ; e.g. in Poland and Finland, Latvia, Lithuania and Estonia 1226, 1278, 1899, 1967–68, 2643.
   d. **Tension** between the Western Democracies and Communism leads to the erection of " Iron Curtain " between Communist-controlled and democratic countries.
   e. **Treaty of Brussels** between Britain, France and Benelux countries, the beginning of Western Union, *f-i.*
   f. **North Atlantic Treaty** signed by U.S.A. Brussels Treaty Powers, Canada, Norway Italy, Portugal and Iceland, 3282, 3293.
   g. " **Marshall Aid** " from U.S.A. helps Wester Europe's economic recovery, 1242, 2111, 329:
   h. **Palestinian Jews,** reinforced by Europea refugees, set up state of Israel, *f-i.*, 2483.

B. In Asia.
   a. **Japan,** devastated and defeated in ever field, surrenders and is occupied, 1242, 1800 loses her overseas possessions, *f-i.*
   b. **Russia** acquires S. Sakhalin, the Kuri Islands, etc., from defeated Japan, *f-i.*
   c. Japan's nationalist influence, together wit Communist movements, in liberated countrie leads to independence demands in Indonesi 1720, and Indo-China, 1718.
   d. **Self-government** granted by Britain t India, 1717, 3283, Pakistan, 1717, 2479, 328 Burma, and Ceylon, 3283.
   e. Civil War in China, 814.

C. **United Nations Organization** replaces tl League of Nations, 1242, 3283.

Some Books on Modern History

History of Europe. H. A. L. Fisher.
A Short History of the Renaissance in Italy. J. Addington Symonds.
Garibaldi and the Making of Italy. G. M. Trevelyan.
The Rise of the Dutch Republic. J. L. Motley.
The Conquest of Peru ; The Conquest of Mexico. W. H. Prescott.
The French Revolution from the Age of Louis XIV to the Coming of Napoleon ; The Story of Napoleon. H. F. B. Wheeler.
Short History of France. A. M. F. Duclaux.
France. J. E. C. Bodley.
Life of Napoleon. J. Holland Rose.
The Destiny of France. Alexander Werth.
A Short History of Germany. E. F. Henderson.
History of European Nations . . .to the Beginning of the 20th Cent. A. S. Rappoport.

Bismarck and Foundation of the German Empire. Headlam.
A History of Russia to Modern Times. R. Beazley, N. Forbes, a G. A. Birkett.
China, Japan and Korea. J. O. P. Bland.
The Influence of Sea Power upon History. A. T. Mahan.
Modern Italy, Modern Germanies, Modern France, etc. Cice Hamilton.
Modern Democracies. James Bryce.
A History of the World War, 1914-1918. B. H. Liddell Hart.
World War, A Pictured History. Ed. by Sir John Hammerton.
The Economic Consequences of the Peace. J. M. Keynes.
A Survey of Modern Europe. G. D. H. Cole.
The Second Great War, 1939-45. Ed. Sir John Hammerton.
The Gathering Storm. Winston S. Churchill.

The History of England

I. ENGLAND IN THE MIDDLE AGES.

A. Early History.

a. Roman Britain, **1193**.

b. Anglo-Saxon Period. Teutonic invasion, 3190, 1194, 740 ; Christianity returns, 302 ; Alfred, the first great English king, **110** ; Danish Invasions, 1194, 110, 1089 ; Canute rules all England, 694 ; Edward the Confessor restores Saxon line, 1089.

B. Norman Conquest.

a. Normans under **William the Conqueror** defeat Harold at Hastings, **1581**. Death of Harold, last Saxon king, **1579**.

b. Norman rule established, 1194. Feudalism reaches height under Stephen, 1609.

c. Results of conquest. While the Norman Conquest brought continental influences to England, in the end the Normans (2378) became English.

C. Growth of Constitutional Government, 1194.

a. Beginning of systematic government under Henry II, 1609.

   1. Attempt to regulate the clergy fails, 389 ; jury trials extended, 1842.

   2. Administrative methods continued by Richard I, **2776**.

b. Magna Carta, the Great Charter that made the king amenable to the law, **2059**. Extorted from John by rebellious barons, 1833.

c. Growth of parliamentary power. How Simon de Montfort called the First Parliament, 2221, **2521** ; result of Barons' war against Henry III, 1611 ; Model Parliament, 2521 ; Edward I encourages idea of law and order, 1089 ; Parliament divided into two houses, **2521**; Parliament, under Edward II, begins to restrict the power of the king, 1091 ; quarrels with Richard II, **2777**.

D. England reaches out for more territory.

a. Edward I attempts to unite Scotland and England, 2892, 1089. Resisted by Wallace (**3337**) and Bruce, Scottish heroes, 590.

b. Conquest of Wales, 1089.

c. Loss of Normandy under John left Aquitaine chief English possession in France, 1089, 2376.

E. Struggle for Social Justice—Beginning of conflict between Capital and Labour. Black Death causes decline of serfdom, 85 ; Peasants' Revolt, 3269.

F. Birth of a National Spirit.

a. Effect of the Hundred Years' War. This struggle was largely carried on by the English people united by a common interest, not by a body of personal retainers to further the design of some feudal lord.

b. Beginnings of a national literature, 1210. Chaucer, **761** ; Wycliffe's English Bible, **3427** ; John Gower ; Langland, *f-i*.

G. Wars of the Roses, 2828, 2777, 1612. Resulted in establishing powerful Tudor monarchy, **3253** ; Court of Star Chamber, 1612.

Note: For England's part in the Renaissance, *see* page 3637.

II. REFORMATION IN ENGLAND.

A. Henry VIII's divorce leads to break with Rome, 1612.

a. Opposition of Sir Thomas More, **2228**.

b. Underlying issues : The changes under Henry VIII had to do with Papal control rather than religious reform, 1612 ; Protestant doctrines had little influence before Edward VI, 1091.

B. Catholic Reaction under Queen Mary, **2113**, 1146. Tragedy of Lady Jane Grey, **1544**.

C. Elizabeth secures England's position as Protestant kingdom, **1146**.

a. Mary Queen of Scots centre of Catholic movement, **2113**.

b. Defeat of Spanish Armada, **236**. This marked the beginning of British sea-power, 2305.

c. Elizabethan age in literature, 1210, 2401. Shakespeare, **2932** ; Bacon, **333** ; Jonson, **1837**.

III. QUARRELS BETWEEN STUART KINGS AND PARLIAMENT.

A. James I attempts to rule by " Divine Right," **1793**.

B. Charles I continues the policy, **755**. John Hampden leads resistance to ship money, **1571**. Long Parliament begins, 2524.

C. Failure to settle Religious Question.

a. Gunpowder Plot to blow up Parliament, 1264.

b. Persecution of Puritans and " great migration," 2707, 2121.

c. Bishops' wars in Scotland, 2802.

IV. CIVIL WAR, COMMONWEALTH, AND PROTECTORATE.

A. Parliament leads War against King, 755, 756, 2892. Scotland aids Parliament, 2892.

B. Cromwell in Power, **933**. King Charles is put to death, 756.

a. Irish rebellion crushed, 1745 ; the " levellers," **933**.

b. Growth of sea-power in war with Netherlands, 465, 2323.

V. THE RESTORATION.

A. Charles II seeks absolute power, 755. Habeas Corpus Act passed, **1563**.

B. James II's attempt to secure Catholic restoration brings revolution, 1794. Stuart claims upheld by " Pretenders," **2682**.

C. Age of Puritan and Cavalier in literature, 1211.

a. Influence of King James's Bible, 426.

b. Great Puritan writers ; Milton, **2176** ; Bunyan, 617.

VI. CONSTITUTIONAL MONARCHY ESTABLISHED.

A. After the Revolution against James II.

a. William and Mary re-establish Protestant rule. Bill of Rights fixes supremacy of Parliament, **429** ; Toleration Act begins peaceful adjustment of religious rights.

b. Union of Scotland and England, 2893.

c. Age of Queen Anne. Marlborough and the War of the Spanish Succession, **2105**; period of intellectual activity, 1213; rise of newspapers and periodicals, 1224 ; Dryden, **1050** ; Pope, **2654** ; Swift, **3132** ; Sir Isaac Newton, **2348**.

B. Limitation of King's power under early Hanoverians.

a. Growth of Cabinet government, 1440, 1490. Work of Lord Chatham, **759**.

b. Whigs strengthen position of House of Commons.

C. Reaction under George III, 1441.

a. Dismissal of Chatham and close of Seven Years' War, 759, 2924.

b. Failure of Tory colonial policy, 3277. Burke, the champion of Whig policies towards America, 621.

c. Wars with Revolutionary France and Napoleon, 1395, 2276. Work of William Pitt, **2614** ; Nelson secures British supremacy of the seas, 2313 ; War of 1812 with United States, 3291 ; Wellington and the battle of Waterloo, **3354, 3363**.

VII. GREAT BRITAIN IN THE NINETEENTH CENTURY.

A. Beginnings of Political and Social Reforms.

a. Industrial Revolution brings demand for more democratic government and remedy of social abuses, 1721, 3278.

b. Catholic Emancipation Act, 2420, 2535. The laws prohibiting " Dissenters " from holding office had already been repealed ; in 1858 political privileges were extended to the Jews.

c. Reform Act of **1832** transfers political power to middle classes, 2522.

d. Factory Laws, 802.

e. Repeal of Corn Laws and establishing of Free Trade, 2535.

B. Victorian Age.

a. Influence of Queen Victoria, **3319**.

b. Reflected in literature, 1214.

C. Victorian Foreign Policies.

a. Crimean War and the integrity of Turkey, 931.

b. Neutrality in American Civil War. Arbitration of Alabama claims, 203.

D. Continuation of Reform Movement.

a. Political reforms. Suffrage extended, **2522**; women's suffrage, adoption of secret method of voting, 351, 2522 ; veto power of the House of Lords restricted, 2522, 1976, 3282.

b. Social reforms. Employers' Liability Act : old age pensions, 1976 ; trade unions given legal status ; Lloyd George's land reform and social legislation, 1976 ; National Insurance Act, 2546.

c. Religious reform. Disestablishment of the Irish Church, 1470, 1746 ; religious qualifications removed from Universities, 1470 ; Welsh Church disestablished, 3280, 3334.

d. The Irish question, 3280, 1746. Gladstone's attempt to solve it, **1470** ; work of Parnell, 2525.

VIII. GREAT BRITAIN IN THE TWENTIETH CENTURY.

A. Edward VII. Edward the Peacemaker's exceptional knowledge of the men and movements of his time was of the greatest use in British foreign policy ; Entente with France, 1092.

B. George V.

a. First World War, **3409**.

b. Name of Royal House changed to Windsor 1442.

c. Ties between Crown and dominions strengthened, 580.

d. Statute of Westminster gives self-governing dominions equality with mother country, 580

e. Britain goes off the gold standard, **1482**.

C. Edward VIII. Abdication, 1092.

D. George VI.

a. New Constitution in Eire, 1746 ; Eire sever last link with U.K. in the Republic o Ireland Act, 3283.

b. Second World War, **3416**, *f-i*.

c. India (**1691**, **1717**), Pakistan (**2479**) an Ceylon (**748**) granted dominion status, Indi later becoming a republic. Burma become independent (625).

d. Further Social Reforms. Beveridge report *f-i*.; National Health Scheme, **1590**, 1735 Labour govt. introduces nationalization c coal, transport, electricity and gas, civ aviation, iron and steel, 3282.

Note : For Outline on the British Commonwealth *see* next page.

Some Books on English History

Outline of English History. S. R. Gardiner.
A Short History of the English People. J. R. Green.
History of England. Lord Macaulay.
English Social History. G. M. Trevelyan.
Oxford Manuals of English History. Ed. by Sir C. W. C. Oman.
Celtic Britain. Sir John Rhys.
Roman Britain. R. W. Collingwood.
England before the Norman Conquest. Sir C. W. C. Oman.
Anglo-Saxon England. F. M. Stenton.
The Life and Times of Alfred the Great. C. Plummer.
English Wayfaring Life in the Middle Ages. J. A. Jusserand.
England under the Normans and Angevins, 1066-1272. H. W. C. Davis.
Medieval England. Ed. by H. W. C. Davis.
History of England, 1485-1547. H. A. L. Fisher.
England under the Tudors. A. D. Innes.
Life of Sir Walter Raleigh. E. Edwards.
Queen Elizabeth. Mandell Creighton.
Henry VIII, Thomas Cranmer, Wolsey, History of England, 1547-1603. A. F. Pollard.
Thomas More. R. W. Chambers.
Oliver Cromwell. Lord Morley.
Charles II. A. Bryant.
Social Life in Stuart England. M. Coate.
The Early Stuarts, 1603-1660. G. Davies.
History of England, 1660-1702. R. Lodge.

England under Queen Anne. G. M. Trevelyan.
Marlborough, his Life and Times. Winston S. Churchill.
History of England in the Eighteenth Century. W. E. A. Leck.
History of the English People. E. Halévy.
Walpole. Lord Morley.
The Life of Nelson. Robert Southey.
Life of Wellington. Sir H. Maxwell.
Peel. J. R. Thursfield.
Clive. C. Wilson.
Life of William Pitt, Earl of Chatham. B. Williams.
A History of the Four Georges and of William IV ; A History Our Own Times. Justin McCarthy.
England, 1870-1914. R. C. K. Ensor.
Queen Victoria. L. Strachey.
England since Waterloo. J. A. N. Marriott.
Disraeli. André Maurois.
Life of Gladstone. Lord Morley.
British History in the Nineteenth Century. G. M. Trevelyan.
Victorian England. G. M. Young.
The Life of Joseph Chamberlain. J. L. Garvin.
Edwardian England. F. J. C. Hearnshaw.
Our Own Times, 1913-1934. S. King-Hall.
Short History of Our Times. J. A. Spender.
The Reign of King George V. D. C. Somervell.
War Memoirs. D. Lloyd George.
The Gathering Storm ; Their Finest Hour. Winston S. Church

The British Commonwealth

It was the discovery of the New World that started the race for colonial empires. The British Commonwealth was built up not only by fighting and conquest, but also, as in the case of Australia, by discovery, exploration, and peaceful settlement. A separate article is devoted to the British Commonwealth as a whole, **580**, and also to the story of the British rule and after in India, 1714.

A. British Exploration and Settlement, 681.

a. **Early voyages** the basis of English claims. The Cabots, **647** ; Drake, **1036** ; Hudson's explorations, 1649.

b. **Early colonizing enterprises.** Raleigh's lost colony, 2744 ; Founding of the Thirteen Colonies, 144 ; Hudson's Bay Company, 1650.

B. Colonial Results of the Seven Years' War between England and France, **2924**.

a. **In America.** French loss of Canada, 2925, 2400.

b. **In the East.** General situation in the East Indies, **1075** ; Ceylon, **748** ; French and British in India, 1714 ; Clive establishes British rule, **842**, 2924, 660, 413 ; Warren Hastings continues Clive's work, **1581**.

C. British Empire in Africa.

a. **Occupation of Egypt,** 1101. Control of Suez Canal, 1019 ; conquest of Anglo-Egyptian Sudan, 1102 ; " Chinese " Gordon and Kitchener, 1486, 1862.

b. **Control of South Africa.** Boer War, **486** ; Cecil Rhodes, **2771**.

D. Growth of the Empire.

a. **Disraeli** lays foundation of modern British imperialism, 1018. Control of Suez Canal, 3111.

b. **Britain " discovers " India** in Indian Mutiny, 1715. Victoria crowned Empress of India, 1019.

E. Mandated Territories.

a. Former German colonies in Africa and the Pacific mandated by League of Nations to Britain, Australia and New Zealand after First World War.

b. Former Turkish territory mandated to Britain (Palestine).

I. CANADA.

A. **Exploration and Early Settlement** under the French, 681.

a. **First Explorers.** The Northmen, 139, 2388 ; John Cabot, **647**, 2338 ; Cartier, **712** ; Henry Hudson, **1648**.

b. **Beginnings of settlement.** First French settlement at Nova Scotia, 2400 ; Champlain founds Quebec, **751** ; founding of Montreal, 2224.

c. **Extension into interior.** Marquette and Joliet, 2107 ; La Salle, **1894** ; Hennepin, 2192.

B. Conflict of French and British.

a. **British claims to Canada.** Nova Scotia

and Newfoundland, 17, 2337. Hudson Bay Region, 1649.

b. **Hudson's Bay Company,** a rival to French fur-trading interests, **1649**, 1412.

c. **Wars over colonial territory.** King William's war : British capture Acadia and attack Quebec, but restore conquests in treaty of peace. Queen Anne's war : cession of Hudson Bay Region, Newfoundland, and Acadia to British ; French fishing rights secured, 2338. King George's war : Conquests restored at peace. Seven Years' War ends French rule in Canada, 2924, 2401. Deportation of Acadians, 17 ; Wolfe and Montcalm at Quebec, 2218, 2715.

C. A Century of British Rule.

a. **Development of Self-Government,** 683. Rebellion of 1837. Papineau leads French in Lower Canada, 2715 ; Mackenzie in Upper Canada ; Union of Upper and Lower Canada with a responsible government : The Act of Union was passed by the British Parliament upon the recommendations of Lord Durham, whose famous report upon British North America became the basis of Britain's system of imperial government ; establishing a Dominion government, 2048.

b. **Westward Expansion.** Mackenzie's explorations, 2050 ; Hudson's Bay Company and the fur trade, 1649 ; Early colonization of Manitoba, 683, 2089.

D. Under Dominion Government.

a. **Territorial Expansion,** 681. Purchase of territory of Hudson's Bay Company, 2392, 6150 ; Organization of Manitoba precipitates Red River Rebellion, 2089 ; British Columbia joins federation, 580 ; Canadian Pacific Railway opens western prairies to settlement, 580 ; Yukon organized, **3440**.

b. **Imperial Relations,** 580. Participation in the Boer War ; Canada's part in the First World War, 525 ; in Second, 684, 3422.

II. AUSTRALIA.

A. Early Visitors.

a. Luis de Torres and Tasman, 310.

b. Dampier, **964**, 310.

B. **Captain Cook.** Cook the " real discoverer " of Australia, 310, 581, **898**.

C. **Exploration of Interior.** E. J. Eyre, **1254**.

D. Early Settlement.

a. New South Wales founded, **2344**.

b. Discovery of gold, 1479.

c. Penal settlements, 2344, 2718, 3156.

E. Federation.

a. Federal Constitution adopted, 312.

b. New South Wales, **2344**.

c. Victoria, **3321**.

d. South Australia, **3028**.

e. Queensland, **2718**.

Books on the History of the British Commonwealth

Cambridge History of the British Empire.
The British Empire. D. C. Somervell.
Peoples and Problems of India. Sir T. Holderness.
New Zealand : A Short History. J. C. Beaglehole.
Australia. W. K Hancock.
Short History of Australia. E. Scott.
History of Canada. C. G. D. Roberts.
Life of Lord Strathcona. Beckles Willson.
Cambridge Shorter History of India.

Constitutional History of India. A. Berreidale Keith.
History of South Africa. E. A. Walker.
South Africa from the Great Trek to the Union. F. R. Can
The Opening Up of Africa. Sir Harry Johnston.
The British in Tropical Africa. I. L. Evans.
Political Geography of the British Empire. C. B. Fawcett.
The Third British Empire. Sir A. Zimmern.
Evolution of the British Empire and Commonwealth. J. Marriot
Story of the British Colonial Empire. D. Woodruff.

The United States of America

B. Beginning of Pacific Island Interests.

    a. United States share in division of the Samoan Islands, 2869.

    b. Annexation of Hawaii, 1587.

C. Development of the Monroe Doctrine.

    a. France forced to withdraw from Mexico, 2158.

    b. Arbitration of British-Venezuelan boundary dispute, 203.

    c. Hostility of South America softened by Pan-American Movement ; Monroe Doctrine recognized by League of Nations.

D. Spanish-American War, 3291, 3037.

E. Panama Canal, 2486.

F. American Contributions to International Peace.

    a. Policy of International Arbitration, 203.

    b. Relation to the League of Nations, 1908, 3292.

    c. Relation to U.N. and post-war world, 3293.

G. U.S.A. and the World Wars, 3291, 3292, 3412, 3419.

III. INTERNAL AFFAIRS IN THE TWENTIETH CENTURY.

A. Theodore Roosevelt inaugurates an era of reform ; combats trusts and the sinister alliance of politics and industry, 3291, 2824.

B. Democracy under Woodrow Wilson, 3291, 3383 ; Prohibition, 3292.

Note : For events connected with World Wars, *see* Fact-Index and under World Wars.

C. Roosevelt and the " New Deal," 2823, 3292.

D. Truman and the post-war world, 3293, 3252.

The States of Latin America

A. SOUTH AMERICA.

South America was discovered by Columbus (878, 1025) and for 300 years was, with the exception of Brazil, ruled by Spain. In 1500 Brazil came into the possession of Portugal. Latin America now comprises ten republics and the three colonies of British, French and Dutch Guiana.

The history of each State is given in the respective articles : Argentina, 226 ; Bolivia, 491 ; Brazil, 650, 2658 ; Chile, 802 ; Colombia, 872 ; Ecuador, 1081 ; Paraguay, 2511 ; Peru, 2558 ; (Pizarro, 2616 ; Incas, 1689) ; Uruguay, 3298 ; Venezuela, 3308 ; Guiana, 1552.

B. CENTRAL AMERICA.

Discovered by Columbus (878, 744) and originally belonging to Spain (3036 ; Cortes, 914), Central America now consists of six republics, together with British Honduras. For particulars of their history *see* Guatemala, 1551 ; Salvador, 2868 ; Nicaragua, 2363 ; Honduras, 1638 ; Costa Rica, 916 ; Panama, 2156 ; British Honduras, 1638. For the early (pre-conquest) history of South and Central America *see* the articles on Aztecs (Mexico), 325, Incas (Peru), 1689 ; Yucatan (Maya), 3437.

C. MEXICO, 2156.

Some Books on American History

U.S.A.
Cambridge Modern History. Vol. 7.
Short History of the American People. R. G. Caldwell.
Recent History of the U.S.A. F. L. Paxson.
The American Revolution. John Fiske.
Political and Social History of the U.S.A. Hockett and Schlesinger.
History of American Life. Fox and Schlesinger.
Our Times. Mark Sullivan.
Rise of American Civilization. C. A. and M. R. Beard.
America : the Story of a Free People. A. Nevins and H. S. Commager.

SOUTH AMERICA.
A History of South America. C. E. Akers.
The South American Republics. T. C. Dawson.
The River Plate Republics. W. E. Browning.
Green Hell : Adventures in the Mysterious Jungles of E. Bolivia. J. Duguid.

CENTRAL AMERICA.
Central American Archaeology. T. A. Joyce.
Maya and Mexican Art. T. A. Joyce.
Mexico. S. Hale.

Interest-Questions in History

What king sat on his throne for more than 300 years ? 9.

Where is there a painting 20,000 years old ? *459.*

How do we know that 10,000 years ago European lakes were inhabited by men ? 2083.

How did a pick and shovel make a myth come true ? 3252.

Why was India not conquered by Alexander the Great ? 106.

How did Alfred the Great defeat the Danes ? 111.

What Belgian king studied shipping by being a reporter ? 102.

Who discovered America 500 years before Columbus ? 139.

How did science keep the Romans out of Syracuse three years ? 211.

Between what two countries does a colossal bronze figure stand as a symbol of peace ? *228.*

How did Aristides help to banish himself ? 230.

What great philosopher through one pupil sent the culture of his country throughout the civilized world ? 232.

How did Sir Francis Drake " singe the Spanish king's beard " ? 236.

What great king was overthrown by Cortes when he conquered the New World ? 325.

What European king owned an African state independent of his kingdom ? 887.

What great English essayist, philosopher, and statesman was convicted of receiving bribes ? 334.

What famous king followed a spider's example and led his army to victory ? 590.

Why did the Portuguese give Bombay to England ? 496.

What explorer received ten pounds for discoveries in the New World ? 648.

Why was Cairo built on the east bank of the Nile ? 654.

What famous English explorer advertised Newfoundland Fisheries ? 681.

What gave Canada an English-speaking population ? 682.

Why did a king of England order the sea to flow back ? 695.

How did victory for the little colony of Quebec in 1610 lead to defeat in 1759 ? 751.

What early Frank put down anarchy ? 753.

Why did the old Venetians throw a wedding ring in the sea every year ? 29.

What king owed his throne to a girl general. 1831.

What early government always had two kings at the same time ? 3053.

How can stones tell the progress of Man ? 3095.

How did a thistle save the Scots from Norse invaders ? 3203.

At what period in the history of the world were the poor paid to enjoy music and drama ? 2551.

How did being blind in one eye help a famous English naval officer to victory ? 2313.

How many hundreds of years after the Crusades did the Christians as conquerors enter the Holy Land ? 2480.

What great explorer was killed by the natives of Hawaii ? 899.

What famous early explorer was cast adrift by his men to perish in the Arctic ? 1648.

How was Greek influence brought to India ? 1714.

How did a king and queen give to Europe a new nation and to the world a new continent ? 1760.

How was a baby responsible for a revolution in England ? 1794.

Who were the first merchants to come to England for tin ? 1193.

What statesman escaped from his beleaguered capital by balloon ? 1385.

How did a single monk stop the gladiatorial contests of ancient Rome ? 1469.

How did ancient Greece educate its conqueror ? 1525.

What English queen reigned only nine days and died on the scaffold ? 1544.

What famous king was killed just as his troops won a great battle ? 1558.

What French king, too stingy to buy himself a new hat, helped to unify France ? 2028.

What king returned from war with only two companions ? 758.

What silver-tongued orator of Rome lost his life because of his famous " Philippics " ? 990.

What beautiful queen conquered two great warriors with her charms but failed with the third ? 837.

What foreign minister of France was able to keep his position through the Directory, the Napoleonic empire, and the restored Bourbon monarchy ? 3149.

Who was the earliest European to describe the city of Hangchow, China ? 1573.

How did the phrase " Fabian policy " originate ? 1574.

How did the Northmen finally conquer the English from the south instead of the north ? 1579.

Why did the response of Europe to the Byzantine Emperor's call for help lead to the downfall of the Empire ? 638.

Why were castles built during the Middle Ages ? 717.

How did throwing a king's representative out of a window involve Europe in 30 years of war ? 3203.

What country recently had for its leader a musician ? 2474.

What Tsar worked in a shipyard ? 2563.

What Spaniard accepted a ransom of gold and silver to the value of £3,000,000 for a great Indian chief, and then killed him ? 2616.

What early European served the Grand Khan Kublai ? 2652.

Why did a European monarch live in South America for many years ? 2660.

What great Mahomedan leader is remembered because of his courtesy and kindness of heart ? 2864.

When was Florence a city of Puritans ? 2876.

Why was the scallop the pilgrim's badge in the Middle Ages ? 2879.

What Scottish queen was forced to abdicate in favour of her infant son ? 2116.

How did a tiny club grow into a revolution ? 1790.

What French nobleman took part in three revolutions on the popular side ? 1884.

Who were the first Europeans to visit Japan ? 1799.

What were the trade unions of the Middle Ages called ? 1553.

What are Russia's Five-Year Plans ? 2850-54.

When did the " tanks " first go into action ? 3151.

Which was the first Christian nation to abolish the slave trade 2982.

When was Britain's first Labour Government ? 1875.

Who was first President of Turkey ? 1850.

When was Austria incorporated in Germany ? 3323.

Who were the first Bolsheviks ? 495.

Which British king fought a great naval battle ? 1443.

Which English writer took part in two great revolutions ? 2474.

When was the Zulu power broken ? 3448.

When did " bobbies " wear top-hats ? 2536.

What was the Maginot Line ? 1367.

When was the Nazi " blood purge " ? 1451.

When was the Vatican State constituted ? 3307.

MYTHOLOGY

THE fascinating stories of mythology represent the first efforts of primitive people to explain the origin of the world and to solve the mysteries of life which surrounded them. Woven out of the fresh imaginations of ancient generations and carried down through ages of popular approval, they need no justification on the score of interest. A study of these stories helps us to understand the early history and customs of the people who originated them. In this connexion, a comparison of the myths of different early peoples often indicates that they had the same origin and thus sheds light upon prehistoric connexions of race and culture. And, besides, a ready understanding and appreciation of many of the finest passages in our literature is impossible unless the reader is familiar with the classical myths to which allusions are so frequently made.

I. BABYLONIAN MYTHS OF LIFE AND DEATH, 329—Etana, the shepherd who attempted to fly ; Adapa, a fisherman who refused immortality ; Babylonian story of the Flood.

II. ANCIENT EGYPTIAN MYTHOLOGY.

A. Osiris. Legendary king of Egypt and chi of the gods, 2455.

B. Isis : The Moon Goddess, wife of Osiris, 176

Greek and Roman Mythology

THE mythology of the ancient Romans, a practical people, is based very largely on that of their imaginative and poetical Greek neighbours. For this reason we shall consider Greek and Roman mythology together, giving the Roman names in brackets after the Greek names.

I. ANCIENT GREEK THEORY OF THE CREATION.

A. The Origin of Heaven and Earth. How Uranus (Heaven) and Gaea (Earth) came into being (3298) ; their children—the Cyclopes, Hundred-Handers, and Titans (949) ; temporary power of Kronos and Rhea, and how their son, Zeus, finally became the ruler of the universe (3443).

B. The Origin of Man. The Greeks held several theories regarding the creation of Man. One story relates that Prometheus, son of the Titan

Iapetus, fashioned Man at the request of t gods. By his devotion to mankind, howeve Prometheus so enraged Zeus that Zeus caus a woman, Pandora, to be made to bring troub to Man (2494), and ordered Prometheus to chained to a rock (2690). When, later, men h fallen into evil ways, Zeus destroyed them by flood, saving only Deucalion (f-i.), son Prometheus, and his wife, Pyrrha.

II. HEAVEN AND THE DEITIES WHO DWE THERE.

The Heaven of the Greek gods was a high mou tain, Olympus, with a gate of clouds, opened by t Hours or Seasons. Each god had a separa dwelling, but at the command of Zeus all repair to his palace, where they feasted on ambro and nectar poured by Hebe and listened to t music of Apollo and the Muses.

A. The Greater Gods who dwelt on Mount Olympus.

a. Zeus (Jupiter), Son of the Titans, Kronos and Rhea. Supreme ruler of the universe, **3443**, *plate f. 1524*, **1841**.

b. Hera (Juno), his sister and wife. Queen goddess and guardian of women, **1614, 1841**.

c. Apollo, son of Zeus and Leto (Latona). God of light and manly beauty and of prophecy, and in later times the Sun-God, **186**.

d. Artemis (Diana), Apollo's twin sister. Virgin goddess, huntress, as well as guardian, of wild beasts, and later, the Moon-Goddess, **251**.

e. Ares (Mars), son of Zeus and Hera. God of war, **2110**.

f. Hephaestus (Vulcan), son of Zeus and Hera. God of fire and the blacksmith of the gods, **1613**.

g. Aphrodite (Venus). Goddess of love, who sprang full-grown from the sea-foam, **186**, *1538*.

h. Hermes (Mercury), son of Zeus. Cunning and swift-footed messenger of Heaven, *1536*, **1619**.

i. Athena (Minerva), who sprang fully armed from the head of Zeus. Goddess of storms, of war and of wisdom, of spinning and weaving, and of agriculture, and protectress of cities, **283**.

j. Hestia (Vesta), sister of Zeus and eldest daughter of Kronos and Rhea. Goddess of the hearth and divinity of the home, **3318**.

B. Most Noteworthy of the Lesser Deities of Heaven.

a. Eros (Cupid). Small god of love, son of Aphrodite, **943**.

b. Hebe, daughter of Zeus and Hera. Cupbearer of the gods, **1600**.

c. Ganymede : a Trojan boy who succeeded Hebe as cup-bearer.

d. The Graces, daughters of Zeus. Goddesses who presided over social matters.

e. The Muses, daughters of Zeus. Presided over the arts and sciences, **2259**.

f. Themis, a Titan, daughter of Uranus. Goddess of justice who sat beside Zeus on his throne.

g. The Fates. Controlled human destiny, **1262**.

h. Nemesis, daughter of Night. Represented righteous anger and the vengeance of the gods, **2314**.

i. Aesculapius, son of Apollo. His function was the art of healing, **53**.

j. Boreas, Zephyrus, Notus, and Eurus. The winds.

k. Helios, Selene, and Eos (Aurora), children of the Titan Hyperion. Helios, charioteer of the Sun, was the more ancient Greek Sun-god, frequently identified with his successor Apollo. Selene was the early Moon-goddess, whose attributes and adventures were later merged in those of Artemis. Eos was the rosy-fingered goddess of Dawn, mother of the stars and of the morning and evening breezes, **304**.

l. Orion, son of Neptune. Mighty hunter, **2453**.

m. Iris. Goddess of the rainbow, **1748**.

n. Nike (Victoria). Goddess of victory.

III. THE EARTH AND THE GODS WHO MADE IT THEIR ABODE.

The Greeks believed that the earth was a flat circle in the centre of which was either Mount Olympus or Delphi, famous for the oracle of Apollo. It was crossed from east to west by the Sea (the Mediterranean and Euxine or Black Sea), while around it flowed in a steady current the Ocean Stream (personified as the Titan Oceanus), from which the sea and all rivers received their waters. Beyond the mountains of the North Wind, in a region inaccessible by land or sea, dwelt the Hyperboreans, in bliss and everlasting spring. In the south, close to the Ocean, dwelt the Ethiopians, a people greatly favoured by the gods. On the western margin lay the **Elysian Plain**, the abode of the blessed. The dawn, the sun, the moon, and most of the stars rose out of the Ocean to give their light to Man.

A. The Chief Gods of Earth.

a. Demeter (Ceres), sister of Zeus. Goddess of agriculture and of civilized life, **989**.

b. Gaea, or Ge, the Mother Earth, wife of Uranus. One of the older order of gods.

c. Rhea, wife of Kronos and mother of Zeus. Another goddess of earth.

d. Dionysus (Bacchus), son of Zeus and Semele. God of wine and of animal life and vegetation, **1018**.

B. The Lesser Divinities of Earth.

a. Pan, son of Hermes. God of the flocks and pastures, of fields and forests, **2485**.

b. The Nymphs, including the **Dryads** or tree nymphs ; the **Oreads**, nymphs of the mountains and grottoes ; and the **Napaeads**, shy valley nymphs, **2408**.

c. The Satyrs (Fauns). Goatlike deities of woods and fields.

IV. THE UNDERWORLD AND ITS DIVINITIES.

" Beneath the secret places of the Earth " lay a realm of darkness bounded by awful rivers—the sacred **Styx** and **Acheron**, river of woe—where Hades, whose name is given to the region, in a dark and gloomy palace haunted by strange apparitions, ruled the spirits of the dead.

A. Principal Deities of Hades.

a. Hades (Pluto), brother of Zeus, ruler of the underworld, **989**.

b. Persephone (Proserpina), daughter of Demeter and wife of Hades. Goddess of death and also spring.

B. Lesser Divinities.

a. Aeacus, Rhadamanthus, and Minos, sons of Zeus and judges of the dead. Minos during his life had been king of Crete, **927**.

b. Eumenides or Erinyes (Furies), born of the

blood of wounded Uranus. Deities who punished those who had escaped from or defied justice.

c. **Hecate.** Goddess of sorcery and witch-craft.

d. **Hypnos (Somnus) or Sleep, and Thanatos or Death,** sons of Night.

V. THE GODS OF THE WATERS.

A. The Older Dynasty. The Sea had two sets of rulers, the earlier of which flourished during the reign of Kronos. The Titan **Oceanus** and his sister and queen **Tethys,** from whom sprang thousands of rivers and numerous ocean-nymphs, ruled the waters from their beautiful palace beyond the boundaries of Earth. There was also **Pontus** (the deep sea), who was the father of **Nereus,** a genial old man famous for his prophetic gifts and his love of truth and justice. Nereus' wife was **Doris,** and their children were the fifty fair **Nereids.** Of these beautiful daughters the most famous were **Panope, Galatea, Thetis** (19), and **Amphitrite.**

B. The Younger Dynasty.

a. **Poseidon (Neptune),** brother of Zeus. Ruler of the waters, **2660.**

b. **Amphitrite,** daughter of Oceanus and wife of Poseidon.

c. **Triton,** son of Poseidon. A lesser divinity, trumpeter of Ocean.

d. **Proteus.** Little old man of the sea. He had prophetic powers and could change his shape at will, **2694.**

e. **The Harpies,** children of Thaumas, a son of Pontus and Gaea.

f. **The Graeae.** Three hoary witches, grey-haired from birth.

g. **The Gorgons.** Three horrible sisters, whose glance was death, 2552.

h. **The Sirens.** Sea muses who, by their singing, lured mariners to destruction, 2421.

i. **Scylla.** Six-headed monster destructive to mariners, 2422.

j. **Atlas.** A Titan, who supported the universe on his shoulders, 1615. Three groups of nymphs—the **Pleiades (2629), Hyades** and **Hesperides (1615)**—were daughters of Atlas.

k. **The Water-Nymphs**—the **Oceanides, Nereids,** and the **Naiads.** The last of these daughters of Zeus were of most importance.

VI. ITALIAN GODS.

Besides the Roman gods already mentioned, there were certain other deities always peculiar to Roman Mythology. Among them the most important were : **Saturn,** the introducer of agriculture (whom some have attempted to identify with Kronos), and **Ops,** his wife, goddess of sowing and harvest (later confounded with Rhea) ; **Janus,** god of doors or of beginnings, the most important native Italian deity, **2223 ; Quirinus,** a war god, the deified Romulus ; **Bellona,** a war goddess ; **Lucina,** a goddess of light and of childbirth (a name applied to both Juno and Diana) ; **Faunus,** grandson of Saturn, god of fields, of shepherds, and

of prophecy (his name in the plural refers to a group of woodland deities like the Greek Satyrs, 2485) ; **Sylvanus,** god of the forest glades ; **Flora,** goddess of flowers, 2223 ; **Pomona,** goddess of fruit trees ; the **Lares** and **Penates,** household gods, the former being considered as the deified spirits of ancestors who watched over their descendants. **Sol** (the Sun), **Luna** (the Moon), **Juventas** (Youth), **Fides** (Honesty), **Fortuna** (Fortune), 1352, and other personifications were also worshipped by the Romans.

VII. LEGENDARY HEROES.

Besides these divine beings, the Greeks and Romans held in veneration a large number of demigods and heroes, some of whom were offspring of the gods.

A. Older Heroes :

a. **Perseus :** hero of Argos, son of Zeus and Danaë, who was the daughter of King Acrisius of Argos, 2552.

b. **Heracles (Hercules) :** national hero of the Greeks, son of Zeus and Alcmene, the grand-daughter of Perseus, 1615.

c. **Cadmus :** founder of Thebes, a descendant of Zeus, 649.

d. **Orpheus :** famous musician, son of Apollo and the muse Calliope, 2454.

e. **Minos :** King of Crete, son of Zeus and Europa, 927.

f. **Oedipus :** King of Thebes, descendant of Cadmus.

g. **Theseus :** son of King Aegeus of Athens, a " second Hercules," slayer of the Minotaur, 3201.

h. **Jason :** heir to the throne of Iolcus in Thessaly, leader of the Argonauts, 229.

i. **Peleus :** grandson of Zeus, husband of the sea nymph Thetis, and father of Achilles.

j. **Pelops :** son of Tantalus.

k. **Castor and Pollux :** twin sons of Zeus, 718.

B. The Younger Heroes : These were sons and grandsons of the Older Heroes and chieftains in the Theban and Trojan Wars and in numerous other military expeditions. Among them were **Achilles, Nestor, Agamemnon, Hector, Aeneas.**

VIII. MYTHS OF THE GODS.

A. Stories of the Greater Gods.

a. Myths of Zeus : his love for Io, *plate f. 2532 ;* Zeus and Callisto, a maid of Arcadia, 894 ; abduction of Europa, 650 ; the punishment of Tantalus, 3152.

b. Myths of Athena, **283 ;** her birth ; helping the Greeks at Troy ; the naming of Athens ; weaving contest with Arachne, 283.

c. Myths of Apollo and Artemis : Apollo and the deadly python, 186 ; Hyacinthus and Apollo, 1663 ; the punishment of Niobe, Apollo's revenge on King Midas, 2372 ; the musical contest of Apollo and Marsyas, 187 ; Apollo's love for the nymph Daphne, 1900 ; the fate of Actaeon at the hands of Artemis, 251 ; Orion and Artemis, 2453.

d. Myths of Aphrodite : Birth, 186 ; Aphrodite and Adonis, 28 ; wedding of Aphrodite and Hephaestus, 186 ; Atalanta's race, 282 ; Hero and Leander, 1619.

e. Early adventures of Hermes, 1619.

f. Dionysus and the pirates, 1018.

g. Abduction of Persephone by Hades, 989, 1921.

h. Poseidon and the building of Troy, 2660.

B. Myths of the Lesser Divinities.

a. Myth of Phaethon, son of Helios, and the nymph Clymene, 2564.

b. Aesculapius and Cheiron, 54.

c. Myth of the Pleiades, nymphs of Artemis' train, 2629.

d. Cupid and Psyche, 943.

e. Aurora and Tithonus, 304.

f. Pan and Syrinx, 2485.

g. Echo (an Oread) and Narcissus, 2278.

IX. MYTHS OF THE DEMIGODS AND HEROES.
A. Stories of the Older Heroes.

a. Myths of Perseus, 2552 ; the doom of King Acrisius ; Perseus and Medusa ; Perseus and Atlas ; Perseus and Andromeda.

b. Myths of Heracles, 1615 ; his youth ; his labours ; further exploits ; death.

c. The Argonauts' quest of the Golden Fleece, 229.

d. Myths of King Minos of Crete : the Minotaur, 3201 ; Daedalus and Icarus, 955, 1681.

e. Myths of Theseus : Theseus and Ariadne ; Theseus and Pirithoüs and the battle with the Centaurs, 3201.

f. Orpheus and Eurydice, 2454.

g. Founding of Thebes by Cadmus, 650.

B. Myths of the Younger Heroes.

a. The Trojan War.

1. Its Origin : The story of Paris, son of King Priam of Troy, 2514 ; Marriage feast of Peleus and Thetis, 3248 ; Paris abducts Helen, wife of King Menelaus, 3249.

2. Greek Heroes who took part : Achilles, son of Peleus and Thetis, the bravest of the warriors, 19 ; Odysseus, King of Ithaca, 2421 ; Ajax the Great, second only to Achilles in strength and bravery, 95 ; Agamemnon, King of Mycenae, commander-in-chief of the Greek forces, 74 ; gallant Diomedes, aged Nestor, King of Pylos, and others.

3. Chief Trojan Leaders : Hector, son of King Priam, one of the noblest figures of antiquity, 1603 ; Aeneas, son of Anchises and Aphrodite, 30. Among the Trojans' allies was Memnon, King of Ethiopia, 2138.

4. Story of the War : The wrath of Achilles, 19 ; the shield of Achilles, 19 ; the Amazons, 137 ; the death of Hector, 1603 ; story of the Wooden Horse and the fall of Troy, 3249 ; the return of Menelaus to Greece, 2694.

b. The Wanderings of Odysseus : The lotus-eaters, 2421 ; the Cyclops, 949 ; Odysseus and Circe, 2421 ; the Sirens, Scylla and Charybdis, the island of Calypso, the Princess Nausicaa, Penelope and the suitors, return of Odysseus, 2422.

c. Adventures of Aeneas, 30.

Norse and Teutonic Mythology

THE mythology of the Northmen, who inhabited the countries now known as Sweden, Denmark, Norway, and Iceland, has come down to us chiefly through the Eddas and Sagas (2880). Cradled in the frozen North, the Scandinavian myths image the spirit of the hardy Viking race, and while their gods lack the graceful fancy of the Greek deities, they have a rugged personality well calculated to inspire the warlike Northmen to deeds of prowess.

1. THE GODS AND THEIR MYTHS.

A. The Creation : Scandinavian myths, like those of the Greeks, tell of the development of the world from darkness and chaos. Originally there existed a world of mist, a bottomless deep, and a world of light. From the mist-world issued twelve rivers whose frozen waters gradually filled up the bottomless deep. Then from the world of light issued warm winds which melted the ice, producing vapours which rose and formed clouds. From these clouds sprang Ymir, the rime-cold giant, and his progeny, and a cow, Audhumbla, whose milk furnished nourishment to the giant, and who in turn was nourished by licking the hoar frost and salt from the ice. Finally there appeared first the hair, then the head, and at length the whole form of a god of

great beauty and power. This was Bori, from whom and his wife, a daughter of the giants, sprang Odin, Vili, and Ve. These three slew Ymir and from his body and blood formed heaven and earth. Of his eyebrows they built a fence around Midgard, the destined abode of man. Having created the world, they fashioned man from an ashen spar and woman from a piece of elm. To these first human beings Odin gave life and soul, Vili, reason and motion, and Ve, the senses, features, and speech. The universe was supported by Ygdrasil, a mighty ash tree (2421).

B. Asgard, abode of the Gods, and its Chief Deities, 2421.

a. Odin or Woden : ruler of Heaven, Earth, and the Underworld, who lived in a golden palace called Valhalla, 2420.

b. Frigga : Odin's wife, who knows all things.

c. The Valkyries : warlike virgins mounted on horse and armed with helmet, shield, and spear, who conveyed fallen warriors from the battlefields to Valhalla.

d. Thor : The Thunderer, eldest son of Odin, 3204.

e. Bragi : son of Odin, and god of poetry.

f. **Iduna** : Bragi's wife ; custodian of the casket of magic apples, which produce immortal youth, 2881.

g. **Balder** : son of Odin ; beautiful god of sunlight, spring, and gladness, 341, 1750.

h. **Hoder** : son of Odin, blind god of winter, 341.

i. **Frey** : god of Fruitfulness; Freyja; his sister, goddess of love.

j. **Tyr** : A wrestler, "god of battles."

k. **Loki** : The mischief-maker, who, though of the demon race, forced himself into the company of the gods. One of his children was the Midgard Serpent, who encircled the Earth.

C. **Jotunheim and the Frost Giants,** enemies of the gods, 2421.

D. **Some Myths of the Gods :**

a. Odin at the fountain of knowledge, **2421.**

b. The apples of Iduna, **2881.**

c. Thor's visit to Jotunheim, 3204.

d. The death of Balder, **341.**

II. **MYTHS OF NORSE AND OLD GERMAN HEROES.**

In the Norse Saga of the Volsungs are gathered many ancient legends, with Sigurd, a great hero never equalled in comeliness, valour, and greatheartedness, as the central figure. The great epic, Nibelungenlied, is the German version of these hero-tales, with certain variations of name, character, and incident. Here Sigurd appears as Siegfried.

A. The Story of Siegfried, 2969.

B. The Songs of the Nibelungs, 2363.

Some Books to Read on Mythology

Myth, Ritual, and Religion. Andrew Lang.
Primitive Culture. E. B. Tylor.
Man, Past and Present. A. H. Keane.
The Golden Bough. Sir J. G. Frazer.
The Legend of Perseus. E. S. Hartland.
Religion of Babylonia and Assyria. Morris Jastrow.
The Heroic Age. H. M. Chadwick.
Stories from Ancient Greece. A. J. Church.
The Heroes, or Greek Fairy Tales. Charles Kingsley.
Heroes and Kings. Stories from the Greek. A. J. Church.
The Children's Iliad. A. J. Church.

Tales of Troy and Greece. Andrew Lang.
The Children's Æneid. A. J. Church.
Stories from Ancient Rome. A. J. Church.
Popular Tales from the Norse. Sir G. W. Dasent.
The Heroes of Asgard. A. & E. Keary.
The Fall of the Niebelungs. Margaret Armour.
Harrap's Myths Series. Various Authors.
Harrap's " Told Through the Ages " Series.
Boys and Girls and Gods. N. Mitchison.
The Odyssey (prose trans.), T. E. Lawrence; another by E. V. Rieu.

Interest-Questions in Mythology

What goddess sprang from the sea-foam ? 186.

How did the ancient Greeks explain the change of seasons ? 989.

Why is the laurel associated with poets ? 2634.

How did it happen that the most beautiful of the Greek goddesses became the wife of the most awkward of the gods ? 186.

How did the ancient Greeks explain the origin of fire ? 2690.

How did three golden apples help a hero to win a race and a wife ? 282.

What great Greek city is named after a goddess ? 283.

What woman, according to the Greeks, was responsible for all the ills of mankind ? 2494.

What happened when a man was given immortal life without immortal youth ? 304.

How, according to the Babylonians, was the gift of immortality lost to mankind ? 332.

What girl was turned into a spider ? 283.

What did the sowing of a dragon's teeth have to do with the founding of a great city ? 649.

What god had wings on his sandals ? 1619.

What god was most often represented in Greek art ? 186.

What is meant when a horseman is said to " ride like a Centaur " ? 742.

What sorceress changed men into beasts ? 834.

What woman brought disaster on herself through her curiosity concerning her husband ? 943.

What connexion is there between " cereal " and a Roman goddess ? 989.

Who, according to the ancient Greeks, was the first man to fly ? 955.

What Babylonian hero attempted to soar to heaven on an eagle's back ? 332.

What flower sprang from the blood of a beautiful youth ? 1663.

How, according to the Greeks, did the peacock get the " eyes " in its tail ? plate f. 2533.

Why should sudden unreasonable fear be called a " panic " ? 2485.

How did the Romans get the name of their chief god ? 1841.

What youth gazed at his own image until he was transformed into a beautiful flower ? 2278.

How did the ancient Greeks think their poets and artists were inspired ? 2259.

How did the Northmen explain the coming of winter ? 2881

How did a polished shield help Perseus to slay a monster ? 2552.

What hero removed his war helmet because his little son was afraid of it ? 1603.

How was a northern hero enabled to understand the language of birds and beasts ? 2969.

How did Odysseus and his men get past the giant Polyphemus without being caught ? 949.

What river in Africa was made to overflow by the tears of a goddess ? 1760.

How did the god of the vine keep a ship from moving ? 1018.

Who was the mischievous god that escaped from his cradle and began his adventures when only a few hours old ? 1619.

Which of the Greek heroes was called " the crafty " ? 2421.

What common metal was named after a god, and why ? 2145.

How did a goddess punish a mortal who saw her unattired ? 251.

What goddess sprang from the head of Zeus ? 283.

Who was the god of music ? 186.

What planet is named after the Roman war god, and why ? 2110.

What strait was called " Oxford " in Greek, and why ? 528.

How was the lyre invented ? 1619.

What flower is named after the goddess of the rainbow ? 1748.

Who was the first person to be " tantalized " ? 3152.

In what mythical country did woman have all the rights ? 137.

What hero in disguise was recognized by his dog though no one else knew him ? 2424.

What Norse god gave an eye for wisdom ? 2421.

After what god is the fourth day of the week named ? 2421.

What wife of a Greek hero was noted for her fidelity ? 2423.

How did a maiden in trying to protect her lover bring about his death ? 2969.

How did a wooden horse bring victory when brave warriors failed ? 3249.

What teacher who was half a horse instructed many famous heroes ? 742.

What old man of the sea tried to avoid prophesying by changing form ? 2694.

How did a woman's beauty lead to a great war ? 3248.

From what Greek hero is the tendon of the heel named, and why ? 19.

What flower sprang from the tears of a goddess ? 154.

What power moved the god of the underworld to allow one of the dead to return to life ? 2454.

SOCIAL SCIENCES

UNDER the name of "Social Sciences" are included those branches of knowledge which deal with the problems of men in their relations with one another. Just as Biology is concerned with the natural laws which govern the physical structure and function of individual organisms, so the Social Sciences seek to discover the laws which govern the structure and function of social organisms. The Social Sciences deal with human conduct and with the influences which shape human conduct. For practical purposes they are usually divided into **Sociology, Economics (1080)**, and political science or **Government (1488)**.

The name Sociology is often applied broadly to the whole group of Social Sciences, but in its more restricted sense it deals with those phases of human conduct which are governed by usage and custom rather than those which are the outgrowth of political or economic necessity ; it seeks to investigate the "social habits" of the human race and their effects upon human welfare. Economics deals with the activities of men in producing, distributing, and consuming the valuable things of the earth. Political science deals with the organization and life of the State. The name of "civics" is often given to that department of political science which deals with the practical machinery of our own government and our duties as citizens. The science of **Education (1088)**, which deals with political as well as purely sociological problems, has come to be so important that it is often made a fourth great division of the Social Sciences. The articles on Geography (**1430**) and History (**1630**) will provide a valuable background.

SOCIOLOGY

I. ANTHROPOLOGY.
The study of Man's physical development, his place in Nature, and the origin of culture, with particular reference to primitive life and the survival of primitive modes of living and methods of thought (2723). Read also the article on **Man, 2078**, and that on **Anthropometry, 2724**, the science dealing with the physical measurements of the races of mankind.

II. ETHNOLOGY.
The study of the various races and their customs, with a view to finding out their origin and relationships, **1227**.
A. Races of Mankind, **2723** ; Aryans, **261** ; Teutons, **3190**.
B. Cave-dwellers, **734**.
C. Stone Age, **3094**.
D. Superstitions and Magic Practices of Primitive Peoples, **2056**.
E. Mythology, **2270**.
F. Legends, **1918**.

III. PHILOLOGY.
The science which deals with the formation of languages (2570). By the study of words used by early peoples, scientists have been able to ascertain many important things about the people who made the words and their mode of life. Alphabet, **125**.

IV. CUSTOMS AND INSTITUTIONS.
A. Family, **1259**. Its origin and importance as a social unit. Clan, **835** ; Marriage, **2107**.
B. Origin of names, **2272** ; Nicknames, **2366**.
C. Magic and Witchcraft, **2056**.
D. Folklore, **1333**. The tales and songs and dances which furnished amusement for the peoples of long ago and the modern revival of folk dancing.
E. Architecture, and What it Tells us of Human Progress, **212**.
F. Costume and Adornment.
 a. Tattooing, **3158**.
 b. Armour, **240**.
 c. Uniforms. Army badges, **245** ; Navy, *facing p. 2292*.

d. Boots and shoes of different periods and lands, **521**.
e. The history of hats and caps, **1582**.
f. How buttons came into use, **632**.
g. Lace and its history, **1876**.
h. Orders and decorations, **2448**.
i. Crowns and coronets, **936**.
j. Heraldry, **1614**.
G. Etiquette, **1227**. The essentials of good manners as established by custom.
H. Holidays and Festivals, **1635** ; Calendar, **661**.
 a. Christmas and how it is celebrated in different countries, **819**.
 b. Easter—its significance and some customs connected with it, **1073**.
 c. Hallowe'en and its superstitions, **1566**.
 d. New Year's Day in various parts of the World, **2350**.
 e. Armistice Day or Remembrance Sunday, **239**.
 f. Eisteddfod, **1123**.
 g. The Passover, **2527**.
 h. The Sabbath, **2859**.
 i. Harvest Home, **1580**.
 j. Royal Coronation, **912**.
 k. St. Valentine's Day, **2862**.

V. AMUSEMENTS, GAMES AND SPORTS.
A. Olympic Games, Ancient and Modern, **2433**.
B. Gladiatorial Combats of the Romans, **1469**.
C. Medieval Tournaments, **2900**.
D. Modern Sports and Games.
 a. Outdoor Games : Badminton, **338** ; Baseball, **367** ; Basket Ball, **369** ; Bowls, **534** ; Cricket, **928** ; Curling, **944** ; Fives, **1312** ; Football, **1344** ; Golf, **1483** ; Hockey, **1633** ; Hurling, **1660** ; Lacrosse, **1882** ; Lawn Tennis, **1905** ; Netball, **2317** ; Quoits, **2720**, etc.
 b. Sports : Bathing, **374** ; Boxing, **535** ; Cycling, **947** ; Hunting, **1657** ; Riding, **2779** ; Skating, **2976** ; Swimming and Diving, **3135**, etc.
 c. Indoor Pastimes : Billiards, **428** ; Chess,

779; Dancing, 965; Darts, 975; Dominoes, 1029; Draughts, 1044; Stamp Collecting, 3074, etc.

d. Athletics, 287.

E. Theatre and the Drama, 1037, 3194.

a. Miracle and morality plays of the Middle Ages, 2189.

b. Ballet, 345.

c. Pantomime, 2495 ; Punch and Judy, 2705 ; Puppets, 2706.

d. Cinema, 828.

e. Television, 3182.

VI. SOCIAL ORGANIZATIONS.

In the complicated social life of today one great branch of Man's activities centres about the clubs and societies which have been formed for the pursuit of a common interest.

A. Religious or Semi-Religious Organizations.

a. Crusading Orders, 1865.

b. Monasticism, 2212, 412.

c. Salvation Army, 2868.

B. Fraternal Organizations. Freemasonry, 1390.

C. Boys' and Girls' Societies. Boy Scouts, 538 ; Girl Guides, 1465.

VII. PROBLEMS OF SOCIOLOGY.

One of the greatest problems of Sociology is the care of those who are incapable of self-support, of whom there are many in every community or nation.

A. Protection of the Weak and Unfortunate.

a. Child Welfare : Children, 801 ; Compulsory Education, 1088.

b. Care of the Poor, Old and Disabled : Insurance, 1733 ; Pensions, 2546 ; Education of the Blind, 470 ; Deaf and Dumb, 981.

c. Care of Defectives and Delinquents : Prisons and Punishment, 2686.

B. Organizations and Institutions for the Preservation of Health and the Relief of Suffering.

a. Hospitals, 1648.

b. National Health Service, 1590. Factory and Food inspection, etc.

c. Red Cross Societies, 2752.

d. Nursing, 2406.

C. Social Insurance, 2994.

D. Private Philanthropy. Besides the public channels through which social work is carried on, individuals often contribute their personal efforts or their fortunes to the relief of suffering, the advance of education, and to various other causes which are of benefit to humanity.

a. Well-known Philanthropies : Gifts of John D. Rockefeller, 2791 ; Andrew Carnegie's gifts, 703 ; Rhodes Scholarships, 2771 ; Nobel Prizes, 2375 ; Lord Nuffield's gifts, 2404.

b. Some Prominent Philanthropists : Florence Nightingale, the greatest of war nurses, 2368 ; George Peabody and his " Buildings," 2530 ; Jane Addams, American social worker, 23 ; Thomas John Barnardo, friend of " Street Arabs," 362 ; Jeremy Bentham, law reformer, 414 ; General Booth of the Salvation Army, 520 ; Lord Shaftesbury, 2931.

E. The Future Race. Eugenics, 1230.

Books for the Student of Sociology

A library catalogue will provide students with titles of many books on the myriad minor subjects included under the main heading Sociology ; the following list is restricted to a few reliable works on the subject in general.

Primitive Culture. E. B. Tylor.
Principles of Sociology. L. T. Hobhouse.
The Social Contract. Rousseau.
Ancient Law, Its Connection with the Early History of Society and Its Relation to Modern Ideas. Sir Henry Maine.
Plato's Republic.
The Social Structure of England & Wales. Carr-Saunders & Jones.
Sociology ; The Psychology of Society. M. Ginsberg.

An Introduction to Social Psychology. W. McDougall.
Human Nature in Politics. The Great Society. G. Wallas.
Social Psychology. K. Young.
A Study of History. A. I. Toynbee.
Poverty and Progress. B. S. Rowntree.
England Speaks. Sir Philip Gibbs.
English Journey. J. B. Priestley.
Modern England. Cicely Hamilton.

ECONOMICS

Economics (1080), or Political Economy as it was called, is the " bread-and-butter " science, dealing with the production, distribution and exchange of all forms of wealth.

I. LAND.

Land is considered the basis of all wealth, because it is the source of all the raw materials of production. The share which Land receives from the production of wealth may be measured in terms of Rent. The development of Agriculture and its economic effect, 78.

II. LABOUR AND CAPITAL.

The second great factor in the production of wealth

is Labour, and Labour's share of wealth is measured in Wages. The third element is Capital, or accumulated wealth from which its owner expects to derive an income ; its share of wealth is measured in Interest.

A. Division of Labour, 1080.

B. Enforced Labour—Slavery and Serfdom, 2981.

C. Industrial Revolution and the Factory System, 1721.

D. Organization of Labour. Medieval Guilds, 1553 ; forerunners of modern Trade Unions, 3223.

E. Arbitration in Labour Questions, 203.

F. Socialism, 2996.

G. Labour Movement, 1875.

H. Communism, 881.

III. MANAGEMENT AND THE ENTREPRENEUR.

The last agency in the production of wealth is the man of enterprise, or manager, through whose efforts Land, Labour, and Capital are brought together and put to productive use. Generally nowadays the " manager " is an official of a limited liability company.

IV. FINANCE.

The work of obtaining and using money and credit for the support of public and private enterprises.

A. Money, 2200.

B. Credit and Banking, 356, 926.

    a. Postal Savings Bank and Postal Money Orders, 357.

    b. Banknotes, 2202.

    c. Cheques, 357.

    d. Interest.

    e. Bankruptcy, 356.

    f. Foreign Exchange, 1347.

C. Public Finance.

    a. Taxation, 3158.

      1. Customs and Tariffs, 944.

      2. Stamp duties, 3158.

      3. Income Tax and Estate or Death Duties, 3158.

      4. Licences and excises, 3158.

    b. National Debt.

    c. Gold Standard, 1479.

    d. Social Credit, f-i.

    e. Managed Currency, 2203.

D. Stocks and Shares, 3093.

V. PRODUCTION AND DISTRIBUTION.

A. Organizations for Production and Their Regulation.

    a. Companies, 3093.

    b. Trusts.

    c. Co-operative Societies, 903.

    d. Municipal Undertakings.

    e. Nationalization and Government Ownership, 3282, 2996.

    f. Building Societies.

B. Commerce and Transport.

    a. Railways, 2734.

    b. Post Office, 2661.

    c. Telephones, 3173.

    d. Ships, 2945.

    e. Roads and Streets, 2783.

    f. Fairs and Markets, 1256.

    g. Hire Purchase.

C. Board of Trade, 3233.

VI. INSURANCE, 1733.

Books for the Student of Economics

Work, Wealth and Happiness of Mankind. H. G. Wells.
Intelligent Man's Guide through World Chaos. G. D. H. Cole.
Economics and the General Reader. Henry Clay.
The Intelligent Woman's Guide to Socialism, Capitalism, and Fascism. G. Bernard Shaw.
Wealth. Edwin Cannan.
The Meaning of Money. Hartley Withers.
Essays in Persuasion. J. M. Keynes.
What Everybody Wants to Know about Money. Ed. G. D. H. Cole.
Fabian Essays in Socialism. G. B. Shaw and Others.
The Economics of Everyday Life. Sir Henry Benson.
Economics of Industry. J. H. Marshall.
The Douglas Manual (Social Credit). P. Mairet.
Plan or No Plan. Barbara Wootton.
An Outline of Money. G. Crowther.
Full Employment in a Free Society. W. H. Beveridge.

Classics
The Wealth of Nations. Adam Smith.
Principles of Political Economy and Taxation. D. Ricardo.
Principles of Political Economy. J. S. Mill.
Lombard Street. W. Bagehot.
Capital. Karl Marx.

History
Economic Organization of England. W. J. Ashley.
English Economic History. W. J. Ashley.
Industrial and Commercial Revolutions in Great Britain. Economic Development of the British Overseas Empire. Economic Development in the 19th century. L. C. A. Knowles.
The Town Labourer, The Village Labourer, The Skilled Labourer, The Age of the Chartists, J. L. and B. Hammond.
History of Trade Unionism. S. J. and B. Webb.
English Economic Documents.
Economic History of Europe. A. Birnie.
English Farming, Past and Present. Lord Ernle.

POLITICAL SCIENCE (CIVICS)

I. ORIGIN OF GOVERNMENT.

If Man were a solitary creature who did not come in contact with his fellows he might do as he pleased without any restraint, except by the law of Nature. But Man early learned that it was to his advantage to live and work with his fellow-men, and found himself better able to survive and make progress in society than out of it. And so his liberty became limited by such rules as were necessary for the public good. An early social unit was the Family (1259) but it is not yet known whether this originated before or after the development of tribal or patriarchal government. By gradual evolution this early system gave place to the complex organization now known as the State, a term used primarily to designate any community having an independent existence and possessing a sovereign government. Government (1488), then, is the machinery by which a State makes or enforces the rules of action which are necessary to enable men to live together in peace and security. It is the subject matter of Politics (2651).

II. FORMS OF GOVERNMENT.

A. Monarchy. A government in which the sovereign authority is vested in one person, called a sovereign, monarch, king, emperor, etc., while those under his rule are called his subjects ; it is usually hereditary, but may be elective. Monarchies are divided into two classes :

    a. Absolute Monarchy. One in which the monarch's power is unlimited by any principles of government ; it is sometimes called an autocracy, and if the rule is cruel or severe, a despotism or tyranny.

    b. Limited Monarchy. One in which the ruler is limited in the exercise of his power by a constitution ; it is also called a constitutional monarchy. Great Britain is an example, as are also Denmark, Norway, Sweden, etc.

c. **Feudal System, 1268.** Under this system the king was the nominal owner of all the land. It was distributed, however, as " fiefs " among his vassals, who owed him in return homage and military aid in time of need. These royal vassals in turn distributed their land in smaller fiefs to lesser vassals, and so on down.

B. **Aristocracy.** A State ruled by a few nobles ; literally the name means " rule of the best," and the ideal aristocracy (as in Plato's " Republic," 2629) was controlled by a few men of superior wisdom. When those who held the power did so, not by virtue of character but by virtue of birth or wealth, and allowed their own selfish interests to predominate, the aristocracy became an **Oligarchy** (1519). In modern states the aristocracy plays an inconsiderable part in government as the Peerage, **2536.**

C. **Democracy, 989.** A government in which all the members of the State possess an equal share of the sovereignty.

> a. **Pure Democracy.** One in which the government is carried on directly by all the people of a community, as ancient Athens (1519). This form is now found only among savage tribes and as a form of local government in small towns.

> b. **Representative Democracy, Republic, or Commonwealth.** One in which the government is delegated to a body of men, elected by the members of the State or **Citizens.** The vote is usually by **Ballot (351).**

D. **Dictatorship.** Dictators are no new thing in history, but the modern dictator exercises a far greater influence than the dictators who, in critical moments in the State's history, were called to supreme power in ancient Greece and Rome. The modern dictator exercises his power over countries which are " totalitarian," i.e., all the citizens and resources of the State are at his disposal as the personal representative and embodiment of the State. The outstanding modern Totalitarian States have been Germany (**1444**) under Adolf Hitler (**1631**), Italy (**1763**) under Benito Mussolini (**2268**), and Spain under Francisco Franco (**1384**).

E. **Communism (881).** Under the name of **Socialism (2996)** or **Communism (881)** are included those plans of government in which the State owns and controls for the benefit of every citizen all essential industries and means of distribution. The Bolshevist or Soviet government of Russia is the only full-scale test of Socialism that has been made (**2996** ; Stalin, **3072**).

F. **Anarchism.** This demands the complete abolition of the State as it exists today, substituting instead some form of industrial co-operation. Only in Spain and Italy was Anarchism of any real importance as a political force.

Note : A government may be single or **Unitary**; that is, it may consist of a single State in which there is single sovereignty ; or it may be **Federal,** consisting of a union of States which have surrendered their right to act independently in matters pertaining to the common interest, while in other respects they have retained complete independence. France has a unitary government. The United States, Australia, and the Soviet Union have federal governments.

III. CONSTITUTIONS.

With the wane of absolute monarchies and the growing tendency towards democracy the authority of rulers came to be limited or defined by Constitutions. The first such in England took the form of a charter, the famous Magna Carta, granted to the English barons in 1215 by King John (**1833**). Other historic documents of the kind are the Bill of Rights (**429**), several provisions of which are found almost word for word in amendments to the United States Constitution ; and the constitution prepared by the French Assembly at the time of the Revolution, which contained the immortal " Declaration of the Rights of Man " (**834**). A constitution may be either written or unwritten.

IV. FUNCTIONS OF GOVERNMENT.

A government, no matter what its form may be, has three functions, known as Legislative, Judicial, and Executive.

V. LEGISLATIVE BRANCH.

The function of the legislative department of a government is to make the laws. In countries like Britain, which have the parliamentary form of government, the line between the legislative and executive branches is not very clearly drawn, but in the United States, for instance, the legislative branch is sharply separated from the executive branch of the government.

A. **Law, 1902** ; Justinian and the Roman Civil Law, 1854 ; the Code Napoléon, 2276.

B. **British Parliament, 2521.** The law-making body for the British Isles and the Crown Colonies, and one of the oldest legislative assembles in existence ; **Cabinet, 640.**

VI. EXECUTIVE BRANCH, OR CIVIL SERVICE.

That branch of government which administers and enforces the laws, **835.** For the main departments *see* Home Office, **1637** ; Ministry of Health, **1590** ; Ministry of Transport, **3238**, etc.

VII. JUDICIAL BRANCH, OR JUDICIARY.

The branch which applies and interprets the laws (Statute or Common), 1902.

A. **Courts of Justice, 921.** Their criminal and civil functions ; different classes of courts.

> a. **Habeas Corpus, 1563.**

> b. **Jury, 1842.**

> c. **Prisons and Punishments, 2686.**

B. **Police, 2647.**

VIII. TAXATION.

How a government obtains money to conduct its affairs ; how a tax is levied ; different kinds of taxes, **3158.**

IX. POLITICAL PARTIES.

In parliamentary constitutions a large part in the working of the political machine is played by parties, i.e., organizations of men and women who are joined together to promote the political aims they have in common. In Britain the principal parties are Conservative (**892**), Labour or Socialist (**1875, 2996**) and the Liberal (**1929**).

X. INTERNATIONAL LAW.

A. Treaties, **3240.**

B. Arbitration of Disputes, **203.**

C. Some Rules of War.

   a. Blockade, **473.**

   b. Armistice and Truce.

   c. Red Cross, **2752.**

E. League of Nations, **1903.**

F. United Nations, **3283.**

Books for the Student of Politics

Guide to Modern Politics. G. D. H. Cole.
Modern Political Theory. C. E. M. Joad.
English Political Theory. Ivor Brown.
Short History of Democracy. A. F. Hattersley.
Political Thought in England. (Vols. in Home University Library.)
Parliament. Sir H. Ilbert.
Conservatism Lord Hugh Cecil.

Political Parties and Policies. E. Royston Pike.
Everybody's Political What's What. G. Bernard Shaw.
Soviet Communism. S. and B. Webb.
The Republic. Plato.
Utopia. Sir T. More.
Reflections on the French Revolution. E. Burke.
On Liberty. Representative Government. J. S. Mill.

EDUCATION

This outline is intended only as a very brief survey of the principal articles on educational subjects. For fuller information of the modern educational movements and theories the reader is referred to the short bibliography below.

I. PSYCHOLOGY IN EDUCATION.

A. The Mind, **2180, 2697.**

B. Heredity, **1617.**

C. Memory, **2138.**

D. Habits, **2697.**

II. EDUCATIONAL THEORIES AND METHODS.

A. Training Young Children.

   a. Froebel and the Kindergarten, **1398, 2886.**

   b. Montessori Method, **2220.**

B. Educating the Blind, and Deaf and Dumb, **470, 981.**

C. Athletics, **287.**

D. Eurhythmics, **1231.**

E. Methods of Study.

   a. The study of Grammar as a basis for correct thinking, **1493.**

   b. Mind-training through reading, **2750.**

F. School Subjects.

   a. Arithmetic, **233** ; Fun with Figures, **3457.**

   b. Mathematics, **2120** ; Algebra, **112** ; Geometry, **1434.**

   c. Botany, **531** ; Biology, **430.**

   d. Geography, **1430.**

   e. History, **1630.**

   f. Chemistry, **766.**

   g. Physics, **2591** ; Heat, **1593** ; Light, **1939** ; Sound, **3009** ; Electricity, **1127** ; Magnetism, **2060** ; Mechanics, **2127** ; Hydraulics, **1665.**

   h. Book-keeping, **518.**

G. Examinations, **1246.**

III. BRITAIN'S EDUCATIONAL SYSTEM.

A. Schools and their History, **2883.**

B. Colleges and Universities, **3296** ; Cambridge, **666** ; London, **2021** ; Oxford, **2462.**

C. Auxiliary Institutions and Organizations.

   a. Libraries and how to use them, **1930** ; Children's Literature, **1964.**

   b. Boy Scouts, **538**, Girl Guides, **1465.**

Some Books on Education

Education : Its Data and First Principles. Sir Percy Nunn.
History of Elementary School Education. Charles Birchenough.
Secondary School Education in the 19th century. R. L. Archer.
Hadow Report of Re-organization.
Ministry of Education Reports on the Teaching of Various Subjects.
British Universities. Ernest Barker.
School Hygiene. James Kerr.
Emile. Rousseau.
Teacher's Handbook of Psychology J. Sully.
The Education of Man. Froebel.
The Montessori Method. M. Montessori.

Physical Education : A Guide for Teachers. H. P. Haley.
The Young Delinquent. Cyril Burt.
The School and the Child: The School and Society J. Dewey.
The Education of the Whole Man. L. P. Jacks.
On Education. Bertrand Russell.
Education in Transition. H. C. Dent.
Educational Experiments in England. A. Woods.
Education Through Art. Herbert Read.
The Fleming Report.
The Norwood Report.

HOUSEHOLD SCIENCE

THE study of Household Science, which deals with the natural, economic, and social foundations of home life, has come to have an important place in general education. The four main topics of which it treats are shelter, food, clothing, and home management. In this Outline there are gathered together the chief articles and portions of articles which will be of assistance to anyone interested in the art of home-making. The most complete guide to the running of a home is the "Concise Household Encyclopedia."

I. THE HOME AND ITS EQUIPMENT.

A. Heating and Ventilation, 1597. Importance of keeping the house at the proper temperature; different heating systems; how to keep the air fresh; fan, 1259; coal, 855.

B. Lamps and Lighting, 1887.
   a. Electric lighting, 1134.
   b. Gas lighting, 1423, 615.
   c. Gas and electric meters, 2152, *2153*.
   d. Matches, 2119.

C. Plumbing and Sewerage, 611.

D. Locks and Keys, 1978.

E. Furnishings and Decoration.
   a. Wall coverings: Wallpaper, 2496; Tapestry, 3152.
   b. Floor coverings : Carpets and rugs, 705 ; Linoleum, 1956.
   c. Furniture, 1409.
   d. Baskets and pottery, 368 and 2665.
   e. Paints, 2477 ; Varnish, 3305.

F. Electrical Labour-saving Devices : Vacuum-cleaner, 3301 ; electric clock, 1125 ; time switches, 3214.

II. SANITATION, VENTILATION AND HYGIENE.

A. Keeping the Home in Sanitary Condition : House-cleaning ; care of food ; keeping the drinking water pure. Heating and Ventilation, 1597. Laundry and dry cleaning, 1900.
   a. Insect pests : flies, 1329.
   b. Mice and rats, 2248, 2746.
   c. Mildews and moulds, 2173.

B. Personal Hygiene.
   a. The science of healthy living, 1675.
   b. First Aid, 1291.

C. Fire Prevention, 1289.

III. FOOD.

A. Food Materials, 1336.
   a. Carbohydrates, 1338, *1339;* Starch, 3082 ; Sugars and their food value, 3112.
   b. Fats, 1262, 1339.
   c. Proteins, 2693, *1339*.
   d. Mineral Salts : how they are absorbed by plants and passed on to Man, 2181.
   e. Vitamins, 3326.

B. Some Important Foods, 1336.
   a. Meat, 2124.
   b. Food Fishes, 1298 : Cod, 864 ; Haddock, 1563 ; Herring, 1620 ; Skate, 2976, etc.
   c. Eggs—their food value : Varieties of Eggs used as Food, 1093.
   d. Milk and its Products, 2173 ; Dairying, 955 ; Cheese, 765 ; Butter, 627 ; Margarine, 2100.

e. Grain Foods : Breakfast Cereals, 745 ; Flour, 1320 ; Wheat, 3372 ; Barley, 361 ; Rice, 2774.

f. Legumes or " Pod " Foods : Beans, 380 ; Peas, 2530 ; Lentils, 1925.

g. Root, Bulb and Tuber Foods : Radishes, Turnips, Beets, 396, 612 ; Carrots, 2825 ; Onions, 2434 ; Potatoes, 2664.

h. Leaf and Stalk Foods : Cabbages and Cauliflower, 639 ; Artichoke, 256 ; Asparagus, 271 ; Celery, 738 ; Lettuce, Spinach, Rhubarb, 2774.

i. Other Vegetables : Tomatoes, 3223 ; Cucumbers, 943 ; Marrows, 2109 ; Parsnips, 2526.

j. Fruits, 1401 ; Orange, 2442 ; Pears, 2532 ; Prunes, 2695 ; Raspberry, 2745 ; Strawberry, 3103 ; Nuts, 2407 ; Apples, 190 ; Bananas, 354 ; Grapes, 1499 ; Gooseberry, 1486.

k. Foods Used for their Taste or Flavour : Sugar, 3112 ; Spices and Condiments, 3060 ; Pepper, 2547 ; Salt, 2865.

l. Confectionery : Chocolate, 861.

C. Cookery, 900 : Bread, 554, 901 ; Cakes, 902 ; Jam, 1792.

D. Preservation of Foods, 1340.
   a. Freezing, Cold Storage and Refrigeration, 1391.
   b. Canning, 692.

E. Drinks.
   a. Beer, 103.
   b. Cocoa and Chocolate, 861.
   c. Coffee, 864.
   d. Spirits, 103, 3066.

F. Some Pointers about Table Manners, 122; History of the Use of Knives and Forks, 1867.

IV. CLOTHING.

A. The History of Dress, 851.

B. Textiles.
   a. Kinds of Cloth, 850 ; Cotton, 917 ; Linen, 1953 ; Silk, 2970 ; Wool, 3404 ; Rayon and Nylon, 2748.
   b. Spinning and Weaving, 3065.
   c. Bleaching and Dyeing : Dyes, 469, 1059.

C. How Clothing is Manufactured, 850.
   a. Hats and Caps, 1582.
   b. Boots and Shoes, 521.
   c. Socks and Stockings, *1866, 1867*.
   d. Gloves, 1477.
   e. Buttons, 632.

D. Sewing and Mending, 2927.
   a. Sewing machines, 2929.
   b. Needles, 2311 ; Thread, 3205.
   c. Embroidery, 1152.

V. DOMESTIC ANIMALS.

Dog, 1025 ; Cat, 718 ; Poultry, 2671.

PHYSIOLOGY, HYGIENE & MEDICINE

A SOUND knowledge of the structure of the human body and the normal function of its various parts is an essential of modern life. This Outline is intended merely as a brief survey of the chief parts of the body and their work, the simple laws of hygiene, and a few of the outstanding features of medical history and practice. For information fuller and wider than that given in this work, see " The New People's Physician " (Waverley Book Co., Ltd.) and " The Concise Home Doctor " (Amalgamated Press, Ltd.).

I. THE HUMAN BODY.

Anatomy, 150 ; Physiology, 2598.
A. Framework of the Body.
    a. Skeleton, 2977, *151*.
    b. Composition of Bone, 498.
    c. Hands, 1572 ; Feet, 1342.
B. Muscles—How the Body is moved, 2258.
C. Digestion—the Process by which the Food is changed so that it can be absorbed by the Body, 1016.
    a. The Teeth—Preparing the food for digestion, 3163.
    b. The Tongue, 3223.
    c. The Stomach and how it works, 3094.
    d. The Liver—the largest gland organ in the body, 1968.
    e. Other glands that aid digestion, 1470.
    f. Enzymes—Chemical substances that aid digestion, 1220, 2547.
D. Circulation, *2600*.
    a. The Blood and its journey through the body, 474, 1458.
    b. The Heart—the centre of the Circulatory System, 1591.
    c. Function of the Lungs in circulation, 2039.
    d. The Pulse, 2701.
E. Respiration, 2768.
    a. The Lungs, 2039.
    b. The Diaphragm—the principal muscle of respiration, 2039.
    c. The Voice and its organs, 3327.
F. Removal of Body Wastes.
    a. Function of the Intestines, 1017.
    b. The Kidneys—the filtering plant for the blood, 1855.
    c. The Sweat Glands, 2979.
G. Special Glands, 1470.
H. How the Body is Governed.
    a. The Brain—the executive offices of the body, 545.
    b. The Nerves—the body's telephone system, 2316.
    c. The Special Senses and their organs. Eye, 1252 ; Ear, 1065 ; Tongue and organs of taste, 3223, 3157 ; Sense of Smell, 2986 ; Touch, 3231.
The Skin—the Covering of the Body, 2979.
    a. Hair, 1564.
    b. Nails, 1643.
Note: Students should also read the main article on Biochemistry, 429.

II. THE CARE OF THE BODY.

Hygiene, 1675.
A. Exercise.
    a. Physical Training, 2589.
    b. Athletics, 287.
    c. Sports and Games ; Archery, 209 ; Badminton, 338 ; Baseball, 367 ; Basketball, 369 ; Boxing, 535 ; Cricket, 928 ; Curling, 944 ; Cycling, 947 ; Dancing, 965 ; Fencing, 1266 ; Fives, 1312 ; Football, 1344 ; Golf, 1483 ; Hockey, 1633 ; Ice Hockey, 1682 ; Lacrosse, 1882 ; Lawn Tennis, 1905 ; Netball, 2317 ; Riding, 2779 ; Rowing, 483 ; Skating, 2976 ; Ski-ing, 2978 ; Squash, 3070 ; Swimming, 3135 ; Table Tennis, 3147 ; Water-polo, 3356 ; Wrestling, 3426.
    d. Eurhythmics, 1231.
B. Food—What to Eat to Build Healthy Bodies, 1336.
    a. Proteins and the foods which contain them. 2693.
    b. Vitamins—substances essential to proper growth and preservation of the body, 3326.
C. The Value of Sleep, 2983.
D. Sanitation and Ventilation.
    a. Personal Cleanliness, 1675.
    b. Heating and Ventilation, 1597 ; at school, *1591*.
    c. Uses of Antiseptics, 177.
E. Public Health.
    a. Plumbing and Sewerage, 611.
    b. Waterworks, 3347.
Note: Additional information on Hygiene is contained in many of the articles on the different parts and organs of the body listed in Section I, and in the following section on Medicine and Surgery.

III. HUMAN ILLNESS.

Medicine and Surgery, 2132.
A. Germs in Disease, 1458.
    a. Bacteria, 335.
    b. Protozoa, 2695 ; Malaria parasite, *2237*.
B. Disease Carriers.
    a. Mosquito—the carrier of Malaria and Yellow Fever, 2236.
    b. Flea—the Bubonic Plague carrier, 1313.
    c. Tsetse Fly—the insect which produces the dreaded Sleeping Sickness, 3252.
    d. House Fly—carrier of Typhoid Fever, Cholera, and many other diseases, 1329.
C. Prevention and Treatment of Disease.
    a. Antitoxins and Serums, 180.
        1. Vaccination, 3301.
        2. Pasteur's work, 2527.
    b. Surgery, 2132.
        1. Anaesthetics, 148.
        2. Use of Antiseptics, 177.
        3. Use of the X-Rays and Radium, 3430, 2731.
    c. Drugs, 1048 ; Penicillin, 2544 ; Sulpha drugs, 3116 ; Streptomycin, 3103.
    Note: Many of the common drugs improperly used are poisons. For some of the principal poisons and their antidotes read the articles on Poisons and First Aid, 2638, 1291.
    d. Dentistry, 3163.
D. Auxiliary Medical Agencies.
    a. Hospitals, 1648.
    b. Nursing and First Aid, 2406, 1291 ; Red Cross, 2752.

LANGUAGE AND LITERATURE

Language is the tool of thought. To think clearly and to grasp firmly the expressed thoughts of others requires a sure knowledge of words and of the manner in which words are put together into phrases and sentences. But language is a gradual growth, rooted in custom and tradition, improved by centuries of development, and enriched by the skilful use of generations of great minds. The study of grammar alone will not, therefore, give us the mastery of language essential to clear thought and understanding. We must get a certain intuitive " feel " for our own tongue, and this can be obtained only by steeping ourselves in the great literature of the past and the present.

I. THE THEORY OF LANGUAGE.

A. Philology : the science of the growth and relationship of languages, **2570**.
  a. Etymology, the History of Words, 2570.
    1. Etymology of English words, 1209.
    2. How personal names originated, 2272.
  b. Language Types, **2570**.
B. Grammar, the Science of the Correct Use of Language, **1493**.
  a. Sentence, **2920**, 1493. Phrases and clauses ; sentences classified according to structure.
  b. Parts of Speech, 1494. Nouns, **2399** ; Verbs, **3313** ; Pronouns, **2690** ; Adjectives, 27 ; Adverbs, 29 ; Conjunctions, **891** ; Prepositions, **2681** ; Interjections, 1494.
  c. Punctuation, 2705.
C. Rhetoric, the Art of effective and pleasing use of Language, **2769** ; Figures of Speech, 1270.

II. THE LANGUAGES OF VARIOUS PEOPLES.

A. National Characteristics, 1891.
B. African Languages, 70, **73**.
C. Asiatic Languages.
  a. Chinese, 808.
  b. Indian, 1691, 1703.
  c. Hebrew, 1600.
D. European Languages.
  a. Aryan, 261.
    1. Teutonic, 3190, **2570**. English, 1209 ; German, 1456 ; Scandinavian, 2880.
    2. Celtic, 740, **1750**. Erse, Manx, Gaelic, Welsh and Breton.
    3. Romance, 2798. French, 1379 ; Italian, 1786 ; Spanish, 3050.
    4. Slavonic, 2983. Russian, Polish, Serbian, etc.
  b. Non-Aryan. Magyar, 1655 ; Finnish, 1277.
E. Languages of Indigenous American Peoples :
  a. Indian, 2753.
  b. Eskimo (also in Asia), 1222.
F. Universal Languages. Esperanto, 1223 ; Volapuk ; Basic English, 1210.
G. Ancient Languages : Greek, **1539** ; Latin, **1894** ; Sanskrit, 2570.

III. WRITTEN LANGUAGE.

A. Writing.
  a. Picture-writing and Hieroglyphic Writing, 125, 1623. See also in Fact-Index panels describing history of each letter of the Alphabet.
  b. Cuneiform Writing, 2573, 329, 331.
  c. Alphabetic Writing, 125.
  d. Methods and materials : Handwriting, 510 ; Shorthand, **2961** ; Typewriter, **3271** ; Pen, **2539** ; Paper, **2496** ; Ink, **1724** ; Pencil, 2541.
B. Printing, 2684.
  a. Type and Type-making, 3270.
    1. Linotype, 1956.

2. Monotype, 2215.
3. Electrotyping and Stereotyping, **1140**, 3088.
  b. Products of the Press : Books, 509 ; Newspapers, **2344** ; Journalism, 2344 ; Magazines, 1213 ; Bibliography, **427**.

IV. FORMS OF LITERATURE.

A. Poetry and its Forms, **2634**.
  a. Lyric, 2637.
  b. Dramatic, 2637, **1037**. Shakespeare's plays furnish an excellent example of dramatic poetry.
  c. Epic, 2637. Milton's " Paradise Lost," 2176 ; Spenser's " Faerie Queene."
B. Prose Forms : Romance, 2798 ; Novel, 2401 ; Essay, 1224 ; Biography, 430 ; Diary, 2547.
C. Drama, 1037 ; Miracle Plays, 2189.

V. NATIONAL LITERATURES.

A. Hebrew Literature, **1600**. Read the article on the Bible, **423**, and those on the Books of Job, **1832** ; Esther, **1225** ; and Ruth, 2857.
B. Other Asiatic Literatures :
  a. Arabian. See Arabian Nights, 202, and story of Aladdin's Lamp, 3450.
  b. Chinese, 808.
  c. Hindu, 1626.
C. Greek and Latin Literature, 1539, 1894.
  a. Great Greek Authors : Homer, **1637** (stories from the Iliad, 19, 1603 ; stories from the Odyssey, 2421, 949); Aesop and his Fables, 54 ; Herodotus, 1621 ; Socrates, 2996 ; Plato, 2628 ; Aristotle, 231 ; Xenophon, 3429 ; Demosthenes, 990 ; Plutarch, 2630.
  b. Some Great Roman Authors : Cicero, 827 ; Caesar, 651 ; Virgil, 3325 (the story of the Wooden Horse from the Aeneid, 3249) ; Horace, 1641 ; Livy, 1972.
  c. Greek Drama, 1037 : Aeschylus, 53 ; Sophocles, 3000 ; Euripides, 1231 ; Aristophanes, 231.
  d. Mythology : See the Study Outline, 3648.
D. English Literature : 1210.
  a. Early Literature : " Beowulf," the great Anglo-Saxon epic, 415; Arthurian Legends, 255, 2830, 1413 ; Legends of Robin Hood, 3469.
  b. Chief Poets and their Works : Caedmon, 650 ; Geoffrey Chaucer, 761 (tales told by the Canterbury Pilgrims, 762) ; Edmund Spenser, 3058 ; Christopher Marlowe, 2107 ; Sir Walter Raleigh, 2743 ; Ben Jonson, 1837 ; William Shakespeare, 2932 (" As You Like It," 282 ; " Hamlet," 1570 ; " King Lear," 1858 ; " Macbeth," 2047 ; " Merchant of Venice," 2144 ; "Midsummer Night's Dream," 2169 ; "Othello," 2457; "Romeo and Juliet, 2821 ; " The Tempest," 3185 ; " Winter"

Tale," **3389**); John Milton, **2176** (the story of "Paradise Lost," **2178**); John Dryden, **1050**; Alexander Pope, **2654**; William Cowper, **923**; William Blake, **465**; Robert Burns, **625**; Sir Walter Scott, **2895**; Samuel Taylor Coleridge, **869**; William Wordsworth, **3408**; Lord Byron, **634**; Percy Bysshe Shelley, **2942**; John Keats, **1849**; Elizabeth Barrett Browning, **589**; Robert Browning, **590**; Lord Tennyson, **3186**; Rudyard Kipling, **1859**; John Masefield, **2117**; T. S. Eliot, 1216.

c. Chief Prose Writers and their Works : Sir Thomas Malory's " Morte d'Arthur," 255 ; Francis Bacon, **333** ; John Bunyan, **617** (story of " Pilgrim's Progress," 618) ; Daniel Defoe, **985** ; Jonathan Swift, **3132** (story of " Gulliver's Visit to Lilliput and Other Lands," 3133) ; Joseph Addison, **23** ; Samuel Johnson, **1835** ; James Boswell, **529** ; Oliver Goldsmith, **1482** ; Edmund Burke, **621** ; Charles Lamb, **1886** ; Sir Walter Scott, **2898** ; Jane Austen, **306** ; George Borrow, **527** ; The Brontës, **586** ; Lord Macaulay, **2046** ; Thomas Carlyle, **702** ; John Ruskin, **2843** ; William Makepeace Thackeray, **3193** ; Charles Dickens, **1012** (story of " Pickwick Papers," 1013 ; story of " A Christmas Carol," 820) ; George Eliot, **1145** ; Charles Kingsley, **1858** ; Lewis Carroll, **707** (story of " Alice in Wonderland," 708) ; Thomas Hardy, **1577** ; Robert Louis Stevenson, **3089** (story of "Treasure Island," 3090) ; Rudyard Kipling, **1859** (story of " Mowgli," 1860) ; Sir James Matthew Barrie, **364** (story of " Peter Pan,") ; Hilaire Belloc, **409** ; Arnold Bennett, **414** ; G. K. Chesterton, **781** ; John Galsworthy, **1415** ; H. G. Wells, **3364** ; James Joyce, **2403** ; J. B. Priestley, **2683**.

d. Drama and Chief Dramatists, **1210**, **1037**, **2189**.

E. Irish Literature, **1750**.

F. American Literature :

a. Chief Poets : William Cullen Bryant, **597** ; Edgar Allan Poe, **2633** ; Ralph Waldo Emerson, **1156** ; Henry David Thoreau, **3204** ; Henry Wadsworth Longfellow, **2022** (story of " The Song of Hiawatha," 2022) ; Oliver Wendell Holmes, **1636** ; Walt Whitman, **3376**.

b. Chief Prose Writers : Benjamin Franklin, **1386** ; Washington Irving, **1759** ; James Fenimore Cooper, **902** ; Edgar Allan Poe, **2633** ; Nathaniel Hawthorne, **1589** ; Oliver Wendell Holmes, **1636**; Henry David Thoreau, **3204**; Bret Harte, **1579** ; Henry James, **2403** ;

Upton Sinclair, 3295 ; Sinclair Lewis, 3295 ; Ernest Hemingway, 2403.

G. Canadian Literature, **684**.

H. Australian Literature, **315**.

I. South African Literature, **3020**.

J. French Literature, **1379**.

a. Early Romance, **2798**. Story of Roland, 2797.

b. Chief Poets and Prose Writers : Jean Froissart, **1399** ; François Rabelais, **2722** ; Michel de Montaigne, **2218** ; Pierre Corneille, **910** ; Madame de Sévigné, **1380** ; Jean Baptiste Racine, **2725** ; Molière, **2198** ; Voltaire, **3329** ; Jean Jacques Rousseau, **2831** ; Honoré de Balzac, **352** ; Victor Hugo, **1650** ; Alexandre Dumas, **1053** ; Émile Zola, **3444** ; Alphonse Daudet, **979** ; Guy de Maupassant, **1382** ; Anatole France, **1382** ; M. Proust, **1382**.

c. Drama and Chief Dramatists, **1040**.

K. German Literature, **1456**.

a. Early Literature, **1456** : Nibelungs, **2363**.

b. Some Important Figures : Martin Luther, **2040** ; Johann Wolfgang Goethe, **1478** ; Johann Christoph Friedrich Schiller, **2882** ; Heinrich Heine, **1604** ; Richard Wagner, **3331** ; Heinrich and Thomas Mann, **2404** ; Franz Kafka, **2404**.

L. Russian Literature, **2855**. Feodor Dostoievski, **1030** ; Ivan Turgeniev, **3260** ; Leo Tolstoy, **3222** ; Alexander Pushkin, **2855** ; Tchekhov, **3159**.

M. Italian Literature, **1786**. Dante Alighieri, **969** (story of Dante's " Divine Comedy," **970**) ; Torquato Tasso, **3157** ; Francesco Petrarch, **910** ; Giovanni Boccaccio, **1786** ; Gabriele d'Annunzio, 1787.

N. Spanish Literature, **3050**. Miguel de Cervantes Saavedra, **745** (story of " Don Quixote," 746).

O. South American Literature, **3027**.

P. Scandinavian Literature, **2880**.

a. Early Literature. See the Outline on Mythology under the heading Norse and Teutonic Mythology, 3651.

b. Some Scandinavian Writers. Selma Lagerlöf, **1885** ; Björnstjerne Björnson, **462** ; Henrik Ibsen, **1679** ; Hans Christian Andersen, **152** ; Johan Bojer, Knut Hamsun, 2881.

Q. Other European Literatures :

a. Belgian : Maurice Maeterlinck, **2055** (story of " The Blue Bird," 3465).

b. Dutch : Erasmus, **1221**.

VI. READING, 2750.

A. Literature for Children, **1964**.

B. Libraries and How to Use Them, **1930**.

Books for the Literature Student

The Making of English. Henry Bradley.
The Study of Words. R. C. Trench.
The Waverley Children's Dictionary. Edited by Harold Wheeler.
The Cambridge History of English Literature. Edited by A. W. Ward and A. R. Waller.
English Literature : Medieval. W. P. Ker.
The Facts of Fiction. Norman Collins.
Short History of French Literature. George Saintsbury.
Literature of Germany. J. G. Robertson.
Story of Italian Literature. Richard Garnett.
Story of Spanish Literature. J. Fitzmaurice-Kelly.
An Outline of Russian Literature. M. Baring.
Story of Ancient Greek Literature. Gilbert Murray.
Latin Literature J. W. Mackail.
Familiar Studies of Men and Books. R. L. Stevenson.
Essays in Criticism. Matthew Arnold.

Studies in Literature. Edward Dowden.
The Choice of Books. Frederic Harrison.
The Author's Craft. Arnold Bennett.
The Making of English Literature. W. H. Crawshaw.
A Short History of the English Drama. B. Brawley.
An Introduction to the Study of Literature. W H. Hudson.
Contemporary American Literature. J. M. Manly and E. Rickert.
Short History of English Literature. B. Ifor Evans (Penguin).
The Tyranny of Words. S. Chase.
The Oxford Book of English Verse.

The reader is recommended, for general reading, to make selections from the series of classics published by Dent (" Everyman's Library "), Oxford University Press (" World's Classics "), and Collins. The " English Men of Letters " series contains biographies of all our greatest writers.

FINE ARTS

A RT is as old as the human race. Long before men learned to write, they were striving to express in concrete form their faith and their fears, their ideals and their hopes. Crude monuments to the dead, figures carved in bone, horn, and ivory, drawings upon cave walls are among the most valuable records we possess of the civilization which existed before the dawn of history. Ancient traditions and legends were embodied in songs which were passed on from generation to generation before alphabets were invented. And, as civilization grew, men placed more and more emphasis upon the expression of their emotions and their sense of beauty through the arts. Artists were honoured above all other workers, and took their station by the side of kings and nobles. Today we build veritable palaces in which to house great paintings and statues ; we exalt those who can play or sing with special skill the masterpieces of music ; we travel half-way round the world to view the outlines of some famous building. But apart from the pleasure it gives us, a study of art has an educational importance often overlooked. The history of art is also the history of the manners and customs of people in all periods and countries. It contains a vivid narrative of the development of ideas and ideals, and gives us a key to the story of mankind often more valuable than any written record.

I. THE MAJOR FINE ARTS.

What are usually regarded as the Major Fine Arts are three in number : Architecture (212), Sculpture (2903), and Painting (2475). To these are often added Music and Poetry.

The following pages include Study Outlines on the first four of these subjects, and a shorter outline on the Minor Fine Arts. Poetry will be found in the Outline on Language and Literature.

II. THE MINOR FINE ARTS.

Among the many minor Fine Arts may be mentioned Drama, **1037** ; Dancing, **965** ; Engraving and Drawing, **1044** ; Mosaic Working, **2233** ; Tapestry Weaving, **3360**; Cabinet-making, **1409**; Embroidery, **1152**; Glass Making, **1472**; Ceramics, **1665**; the Arts of making Medals, Cameos, **671**, Jewelry, **1427**, Enamels, **1157**, etc. Drama is dealt with under the heading Language and Literature; see Outline, **3660**.

ARCHITECTURE

I. EGYPTIAN ARCHITECTURE.

A. **Characteristics**, 212, **1095** : Vast tombs of kings and solemn temples of the gods built by an enslaved population, massive stone buildings of the " column and lintel " type, with walls often sloping instead of perpendicular on the outside ; use of column foreshadowing Greek architecture, *216* ; profuse ornamentation, both carved and painted, *1116*.

B. **Some Notable Examples** : Pyramids, *2707*, *212* ; Temples, *212*, *1112*, *1121*; columns, *1111*; pylon, *1110* ; Sphinxes, *3058*, *3060* ; obelisks, *839*.

II. BABYLONIAN AND ASSYRIAN ARCHITECTURE.

A. **Characteristics**, 212, 329. Gorgeous temples and palaces set on broad terraces, approached by imposing stairways and built of baked or sun-dried brick and enamelled tile ; stone used in later period ; arch and turret forms often employed.

B. **Typical Examples**: Hanging Gardens of Babylon, *plate f.* 329 ; palace of an Assyrian King, *332*, *330* ; Sumerian Shrine, *3297* ; House at Ur, *13*.

III. GREEK ARCHITECTURE.

A. **Characteristics**, **1528**, 213, *285*, *1521* : The Aegean civilizations of Crete, **29**, 213, and Mycenae, *1519*, laid the foundations of Western Architecture from which the Greeks evolved their own ; characteristics of Greek architecture are : noble temples, theatres, gymnasia, etc. ; " column and lintel " type of structure, built of marble or of coarser stone covered with stucco, sometimes without a roof, sometimes roofed with tiles or slabs supported on wooden beams ; three styles or " orders "—Doric, Ionic, and Corinthian, *215*.

B. The Three Great Styles :
a. **Doric**. Parthenon, *plates f.* 21, *212* ; temple at Bassae, *1530*; of Poseidon, Paestum, *plate f.* 212; of Zeus, Olympia, *plates f.* 1520 1524.

b. **Ionic**. Temple of the Wingless Victory 1530 ; Mausoleum at Halicarnassus, and Temple of Diana, *plate f.* 2924 ; Erechtheum *back of plate f.* 1524 ; temple in Rome, 215

c. **Corinthian** : Monument of Lysicrates, *1529*

IV. ROMAN ARCHITECTURE.

A. **Characteristics**, 213, *216*. Stately, showy temples, monuments, basilicas, forums, amphitheatres, and circuses, and highly practical aqueducts and baths ; richly ornamented structures built of brick, stone, and cement and concrete, and faced with brick, marble, or mosaic structural forms included. The arch, the vault the dome, and columns of the three Greek order are all found frequently.

B. **Some Notable Examples** : Pantheon, 214, *2802* Colosseum, *2803* ; Forum, *2801*, *2803* ; Baths of Caracalla, *plate f.* *2805* ; Castle of Sant' Angelo or Mausoleum of Hadrian, *2805* ; Arch of Severus, *2801*, of Titus, *2803*, of Constantine *2819*, Hadrian's Wall, *2391* ; aqueducts, *19 227*, *2818* ; residences at Pompeii, *2653*, *2820*.

V. BYZANTINE ARCHITECTURE.

A. **Characteristics**, 214, *636* : Huge squat churches with magnificent interiors ; domes placed over rectangular compartments by means of pendentives ; buildings constructed of brick and stone faced with precious marbles and gorgeous mosaics ; much of this style is seen in Russian and Mahomedan architecture.

B. **Some Notable Examples** : Santa Sophia Constantinople, *213* ; St. Mark's Cathedral Venice, *3311* ; Church, Leningrad, *2854*.

VI. MAHOMEDAN ARCHITECTURE

A. **Characteristics :** The art of the Mahomedans—called also Moorish, Saracenic and Arab architecture—has many common features, throughout the range of their religion. These include graceful gay-hued mosques with bulbous domes, round, lancet, and horseshoe arches, slender minarets, and fretted screens in geometric patterns or arabesques ; built of all structural materials, including marble, and decorated with exquisite mosaics and inlays of silver, gold, enamels, and semi-precious stones.

B. **Typical Examples :**

   a. **India :** Delhi, *987, plates f. 988, 989* ; Taj Mahal, *3147, 3148.*

   b. **Persia and Near East :** Gateway at Kum, *1741* ; Cairo, *plates f. 652, 653.*

   c. **North Africa and Spain :** Moroccan gateway, *2231* ; Alhambra, **119**, *plate f. 120* ; Cordoba, 3043 ; Seville, *2926.*

VII. ROMANESQUE ARCHITECTURE.

Called "Lombard" and "Tuscan" in Italy, "Romane" in France, "Rheinish" in Germany, and including the "Saxon" and "Norman" of Britain, *219.* Probably originated about A.D. 600 in Lombardy and thence spread about A.D. 1000 westward and northward as well as south (to Sicily). To this period belong the great castles of Britain, **717.**

A. **Characteristics, 216 :** Dignified churches and palaces and massive castles ; round arches framing doors and windows and springing from round columns or piers, thick stone walls pierced with small windows ; roofs at first flat and timbered, later vaulted in stone by means of the plain barrel or groined vault ; decoration varies locally from crude and spare to rich and exuberant.

B. **Some Notable Examples :**

   a. **Southern Romanesque :** Pisa, *2613* ; the domed central chapel at Aachen shows very early Southern influence, 9.

   b. **Northern Romanesque :** Durham, *723, 729* ; Norwich, *2398* ; Tower of London, **3231**, *2017* ; *plate f.* 3232 ; Carnarvon Castle, *716.*

VIII. GOTHIC ARCHITECTURE.

Divided into periods in different countries—"Lancet," "Rayonnant," and "Flamboyant" in France ; and "Early English," "Decorated," and "Perpendicular" in England. This is the great period of cathedral building, **729.**

A. **Characteristics, 217, 216–220.** Wonderfully varied forms, emphasizing the vertical line, and reaching to new heights, with great lofty window spaces filled with stained glass ; pointed arch completely supersedes rounded types, and ogival vaulting with flying buttresses permits stone walls to be far thinner than in Romanesque buildings and to be largely replaced by windows ; decoration varied, often consisting, in ecclesiastical buildings, of finely-sculptured figures.

Notable Examples :

   a. **Continental Northern Gothic :** Notre Dame, Paris, *2519, plate f. 2516* ; Amiens, *1362* ; Rouen, *2376* ; Cologne, *872* ; Danzig, *973* ; Antwerp, *406* ; Mons, *405* ; Bruges, *592* ; Ypres, *407* ; **Southern Gothic :** Milan, *1236* ; Florence, *1319.*

   b. **English Gothic :** (i) Early English, transitional from Norman. York, *725* ; Lincoln,

722 ; Salisbury, *219, 721* ; Wells, *219, 728.* (ii) Decorated, typified by florid ornament, "rose" windows ; Lichfield, *726* ; Glasgow, *1471.* (iii) Perpendicular ; tall, narrow, rectangular windows, fan vaulting ; nave at Canterbury, *724* ; Gloucester, *1476* ; Magdalen Tower, Oxford, *2463* ; Henry VII chapel, Westminster, *3369.*

   c. **Domestic architecture :** Houses in Brussels, *594* ; Strasbourg, 134, typical of Continental practice in this period ; "Tudor" timbered houses in Britain, *218* ; to the same period belong the "rows" of Chester, *781* ; typical English "Gothic" castle, *218* ; Hampton Court, *3402.*

IX. RENAISSANCE ARCHITECTURE.

A. **Characteristics, 217,** 220 ; Sumptuous palaces, châteaux, and churches, expressing not the spirit of whole peoples but the whims and moods of luxurious intellectual aristocracies ; formal and classical by intention, and in detail consisting largely of borrowings from Roman antiquity ; degenerating finally into a frenzy of over-ornamentation in the Baroque and Rococo ; no new structural features.

B. **Some Notable Examples :**

   a. **Continental :** St. Peter's, Rome, *2802* ; Palace, Rome, *2803* ; Palazzo Vecchio, Florence, 1771, an early example ; Louvre, Paris, *2033* ; Opera House, *2516.*

   b. **In England :** This was the great period of English architecture, with which are associated the names of Wren, **3425**, Inigo Jones, **1836**, Vanbrugh, Nash, and, later still, the brothers Adam, **22.** St. Paul's Cathedral, *219, 2020, 2863* ; St. Bride's, typical Wren church, *2010.* The later architects, working at first in the classical "Palladian" style, evolved gradually the fine English "Georgian" houses, *220*, from which modern English domestic architecture is descended ; Buckingham Palace, *599*, a modernized example.

X. MODERN ARCHITECTURE.

A. **Characteristics, 220 ;** After the Renaissance the broad national movements in Architecture virtually ceased and the new designs were the products of individual architects (*see* above), who originated a wide variety of schools more or less independent of one another. It was only with the advent of steel and concrete that great new structural principles were evolved, but even so, in many ways old traditions lingered, and as noted the traditional big English house is directly descended from "Georgian" structures. From C. R. Mackintosh (*f-i.*) through Le Corbusier (*f-i.*) and Mallet Stevens, "functionalism" (222) spread everywhere ; in this style materials and buildings were primarily suited to their express purposes, and an effort was made, for example, to provide ideal conditions for the *use* of a building. Thus, a factory, where workers work better with plenty of light, is all windows : similarly, a school, 1591 ; a theatre is expressly built as a theatre, *3101* ; a private house, while still retaining an English dignity, is simple, light and airy, 611 ; a power house expresses the purpose of its building, *221* ; an exhibition hall, again, calls forth new problems, 608. Read also **Building Construction, 604.**

B. Further Examples :

a. America : In America, steel and concrete bred the peculiarly local "skyscraper," an effort to house more people in the same ground-area and to provide light and air for all, *222.* New York, *2354–55* ; Chicago, *783* ; Pittsburgh, *2615.*

b. Continental and elsewhere : Berlin, shop, *417* ; Russia, *2851, 2854* ; Oslo, *2455* ; Stockholm, *3127* ; Tel-Aviv, *2482.*

c. English :

1. Besides such examples as those referred to above, functional simplicity extends to public works, as in *885* ; London University, *607, 2021* ; Masonic Temple, *1391* ; Battersea Power Station, *221.*

2. Where necessary, old or traditional styles are followed : Bank of England, *357* ; County Hall, London, *2013* ; Stormont Park, Belfast, *1747.*

3. Much revived " Gothic " was built in Britain in the 19th century ; Law Courts, *1902* ; Houses of Parliament, 2013 ; Balmoral, *351.*

XI. OTHER ANCIENT ARCHITECTURE.

This includes isolated types of architecture which have played no part in the great chain of development dealt with above.

A. Chinese and Japanese Architecture.

a. Characteristics : Gay, bright, comparatively fragile pagodas and memorial gateways built of wood, brick, glazed tile, and, less often, of stone ; feature is the tent-like curved roof.

b. Examples : Temple of Heaven, *2537* ; the Great Wall, *806* ; Japan, 1801.

B. Hindu and Buddhist Architecture (including Javanese and Cambodian).

a. Characteristics : Strange tombs, shrines, and temples, often scooped from the living rock of caves and hills, or built of stone with high pyramidal towers, fantastically ornamented.

b. Examples : Buddhist temple, *270, 1814* ; Rock Temple, *1664* ; Karli, *1710* ; Jaipur, *1711* ; Siam, *2963* ; Angkor Vat, *665, 666.*

C. American Indian Architecture.

a. Inca Architecture : Structures composed of stones, often huge boulders, without mortar, but cut and fitted with extreme accuracy, *1688.*

b. Maya Architecture. Earliest great period in Central America and Mexico. Stone, faced with stucco. Narrow rooms, wide roofs necessitated by the false arch.

c. Toltec and Aztec Architecture. Houses of sun-dried brick and great pueblos, usually of stone ; pyramid-temples and palaces of brick or stone elaborately decorated with carvings and gilding, *327.*

d. North American Indian Architecture : Log dwellings of most advanced hunting tribes ; stone dwellings of the Cliff Dwellers, *234* ; sun-dried brick dwellings of the Pueblo Indians, *2698, 2699.*

SCULPTURE

I. SCULPTURAL PRACTICE.

A. Incised Design : This simple method of drawing with a sharp point was practised by cavemen in prehistoric times, *736, plates f. 736, 2084.* Though not what we would today call sculpture, it may very well have been its direct ancestor.

B. Sculpture in Relief, *2903.*

a. Bas-Relief or Low Relief, *283, 1649, 2906, 3443.* In these sculptures the figures project only a little from the background.

b. High Relief, *1537, 2815.* Here the composition as a whole is part of the slab, but limbs and heads of individual figures here and there are almost free.

c. Sunk Relief. In this method the artist cuts into a flat surface so as to leave the figures standing in relief on a sunken ground.

C. Intaglio, *2903.* In this method—the opposite of relief—the design is hollowed out below the surface. It is used mainly in the carving of precious stones and in making seals, etc.

D. Sculpture " in the Round," *2903.* This is the most " complete " form of sculpture, the figures being, in part at least, completely " free," so that they may be viewed from all sides.

II. PRIMITIVE SCULPTURE.

The beginnings of sculpture arise wherever men have the impulse to adorn articles of use with decorative shapes, or to give outward form to their imaginings concerning the gods or spirits they worship, as did some of the Stone Age races, *2082, 2083,* and the Alaskan tribesmen who carved totem-poles (*97*) ; or to erect memorials bearing the features of the dead, as possibly did the mysterious unknown race that carved the " stone man " of Easter Island, *1074, 1075.*

III. EARLY DEVELOPMENT.

A. Egyptian Sculpture.

a. Characteristics and Materials, 2904.

b. Typical Examples : The Sphinx, *3059* ; statues, etc., *1111, 1114, 3138, plates f. 1120* etc. ; Reliefs, *1110, 1115, 1119, 1121.*

B. Babylonian and Assyrian Sculpture.

a. Characteristics, 2904.

b. Typical Examples : Assyrian animal sculpture, *331* ; warriors, *329* ; winged bulls, which are as typical of Assyrian sculpture as the Sphinx is of Egyptian, *plate f. 585* ; Hittite sculpture, 1633.

C. Aegean Sculpture, 29, *1519*

IV. GREEK AND ROMAN SCULPTURE.

A. Archaic (Attic) Greek, 1528, *1531.*

B. The Great Age of Greek Sculpture, 1528.

**a. The work of Myron and Polycleitus, and of Pheidias, greatest of Greek sculptors, 1537 ; " Discus Thrower " of Myron, *1532* ; Pheidias' statue of Zeus, *plate f. 1524* ; Parthenon frieze, *1143, 1144, 1537* ; the Venus de Milo, *1535* ; Erechtheum Caryatids, *back of plate f. 1521*

**b. The work of Praxiteles, Scopas, and Lysippus, 1537. The " Hermes " of Praxiteles, 1533 ; other works, *106, 1535* ; to this period, too, belongs the Alexander sarcophagus, *106*

C. Later Greek and Roman Sculpture, 1538.
Despite a gradual loss of directness and simplicity and an increasing tendency towards realism, affectation, and ostentation, many beautiful works were produced in Greece in the 4th century B.C., and the Romans created fine portrait statues before art was extinguished in the West about the 4th century A.D. ; Etruscan work also influenced them.

    a. Late Greek Sculpture : "Dying Gaul," *1538* ; Bronze horses, *1773*.

    b. Roman Sculpture, influenced by that of the Greeks, *2813–16, 651, 1573, 730*.

V. MEDIEVAL AND RENAISSANCE SCULPTURE.

A. Medieval, 2904.

    a. Byzantine. Largely confined to carving and small work, often of great beauty, 638.

    b. Early Gothic. Sculpture in the early Christian centuries, hampered by literal interpretation of the commandment against making "any graven image," was confined chiefly to sarcophagi (*1610*), crucifixes, and objects for the adornment and use of the Church. With the rise of Romanesque and Gothic cathedrals and churches, sculpture was more and more freely used as an adjunct to architecture. Early Gothic artists worked "for the glory of God" and not for fame, and their names are lost. Many religious sculptures, i.e., the Irish Romanesque crosses, show the various stages of artistic development.

    c. Late Gothic in Italy. Many of the Italian sculptors of this period were painters and architects as well. Such were Niccolo Pisano, whose work shows a study of the antique and thus foreshadows the Renaissance ; Giovanni Pisano, son of Niccolo ; and Andrea Pisano, pupil of Giovanni.

B. Renaissance, 2764.

    a. Italian Renaissance. Among the great sculptors of the Renaissance were Ghiberti, **1460**; Donatello, *f.-i.*; the Della Robbias, *2765*; Verrocchio, *1776, 1784* ; Leonardo da Vinci, *1926* ; Michelangelo, *2160, 1783, 2765, 28* ; Benvenuto Cellini, *1784* ; Torrigiano, *2765* ; Giovanni da Bologna, *1619*.

    b. French Renaissance. The Renaissance dawned late in France. Jean Goujon and Germain Pilon were its most important sculptors, and their work, though graceful and often vigorous, is not free from the florid affectation of a declining age.

VI. 'BAROQUE' AND THE LATE CLASSICAL REVIVAL.

A. "Baroque," 2906. In Post-Renaissance sculpture (17th-century) statuesque dignity gave way to violent fluttering movement and florid excesses. The chief sculptor and architect of this period was the Italian J. L. Bernini, 2631, a man of great talent and versatility, who filled Rome with "an almost incredible quantity of sculpture of the most varying degrees of merit and hideousness." From Italy this movement spread all over Europe.

B. Classicist Revival, 2906. A period of cold formal classicism followed the extravagances of the "Baroque" style. The leading figures in this

movement were Canova, an Italian sculptor, and Thorwaldsen, a Dane, 830J. John Flaxman was a notable follower of this manner in Britain.

VII. NINETEENTH-CENTURY AND MODERN SCULPTURE.

A. The Nineteenth Century, 2906.

    a. In France especially there was great revival of a new, more living sculpture as a revolt against the classical manner. This was led by such men as Rude, Chapu and Barye, and, in Britain, by our greatest native sculptor, Alfred Stevens, 2906. Gradually, too, the influence of even greater freedom began to be felt.

    b. The outcome of the reaction from pure "naturalism" was the work of Auguste Rodin, **2795**, which, beginning in 19th-century Impressionism, continued into the next period.

B. Modern Sculpture.

    a. On the Continent. From Rodin onwards, sculpture developed rapidly, and each successive school in painting was reflected in its sister art. The work of Ivan Mestrovic, *2906*, is typical of much fine modern work.

    b. In Britain. Although a majority of fine sculptors continued to develop in the academic tradition, as exemplified by the work of Sir Alfred Gilbert, *2907*, Sir George Frampton, *2908*, Charles Wheeler, *2910*, and W. Hardiman, *2910*, others turned to more original styles. C. S. Jagger and Eric Gill, *2910*, show two types of development, the latter being especially moved by religious feeling and interest in the classicism of Rome.

    c. Epstein and the Later Movements. Jacob Epstein, **1221**, *1649*, had tremendous influence in the 20th century, both in his large architectural works, and in his smaller, but far finer modelled portrait busts. Among still more modern sculptors, Frank Dobson, Barbara Hepworth, and Henry Moore, *2909*, showed abstract, at times Surrealist (**3122**) influence, while Maurice Lambert was one of those who combined naturalism with up-to-date ideas.

VIII. ORIENTAL SCULPTURE.

A. Indian Sculpture, 1708. In India, sculpture went back to thousands of years B.C., being at one time influenced by the art of Greek invaders, *1708*. In general, it is a naturalistic style tending toward the monstrous and exuberant, *1707, 1709, 1712*.

B. Chinese and Japanese Sculpture, 1809.

    a. Japanese Sculpture. The Japanese, refined and delicate artists though they are, seem to care little for the beauty of the human figure. Yet the "Nara school" of sculpture (6th to 12th century A.D.) takes rank with the Florentine school of European sculpture. As elsewhere in the Orient, religion had the greatest influence on sculpture, *600*.

    b. Chinese Sculpture. The Chinese have practised sculpture in stone from early times, and with the rise of Buddhism a school of sculptors sprang up, but their art was largely dominated by Indian models, *695, 812*. The real beauty of Chinese sculpture lies in the exquisite bronzes and ivory carvings of the Golden Age, which have cast their influence over the art of many lands.

PAINTING AND THE GRAPHIC ARTS

WITH painting (2475), the graphic arts of drawing and pastel work, together with engraving (1217) and illumination (2090), are indissolubly linked ; when a school of one branch died out, its place was often taken by men working in another medium. *See also* Engraving. Originally, painting was essentially a religious art, interpreting Scriptures for the people. When the development of the printed book made this unnecessary, painting was freed from religion and it is now largely a decorative art ; at the same time, the modern painter works more and more in conjunction with advertising industry, and with other arts such as Drama, in his capacity of designer.

I. PRIMITIVE PAINTING.

Stone Age, 2475, **734**, 2078. Spirited paintings done in three colours on the walls of caves, often with incised outlines, give evidence of the adroitness of hand and keenness of observation of the men of the Old Stone Age, *459, plates f.* 736, 2080, 2084. From these, the arts of Painting and Sculpture may both have sprung.

II. DEVELOPMENT OF PAINTING IN THE WEST.

A. Egyptian, *1115, 1119*, 2475. Paintings intended not only to decorate walls, but to furnish historical records ; conventionalized and symbolic figures often done in brilliant colours which were decorative but not realistic.

B. Babylonian and Assyrian, 2475. Human figures less conventionalized, but also less spirited, animals more truly portrayed than by Egyptians.

C. Aegean Painting, 2475, *31*. Aegean art showed extraordinary power and vigour, less knowledge and accuracy than that of the Egyptian, but greater artistry ; animals and plants delightfully rendered.

D. Greek and Roman Painting, 2475, 2812.

   a. Greek. An art which we can judge only from the descriptions of ancient writers who tell of the fine work of Polygnotus, the reputed founder of Greek painting, of Zeuxis, Parrhasius, Apelles, and others ; vase-paintings, *1528, 1536,* show us Greek skill in one branch.

   b. Roman. The great masterpieces of Roman painting, too, are lost to use, and only mural paintings preserved at Pompeii (*2817*) and elsewhere remain. They show that the art of the Augustan Age gave local colour, natural flesh tints, and rounded modelling to figures. Although the Greek art was their model, it is believed that the Romans developed considerable originality in painting. Mosaic work reached a high standard, especially in formal design, and this influenced later work, 206.

III. EARLY CHRISTIAN PAINTING AND ILLUMINATION.

A. Roman Christian, 2476. From crude religious decorations painted by persecuted Christians on the walls of the catacombs, *817*, and later on walls of churches, a really distinct style in mural painting evolved, 1775.

B. Byzantine, 638. Stiff and inexpressive but richly coloured paintings and illuminated religious books overlaid with gorgeous conventional ornament. Byzantine art had some influence on illumination, especially on that of E. Europe.

C. Medieval and Gothic. A period when the painter, as a rule, was an artisan employing his highest skill in following the instructions of the clergy who ordered religious paintings and dictated costume, pose, and composition. In France, 1377, a good deal of fine painting was done, and doubtless there were artists at work all over Western Europe.

D. Illumination, 2090. This art had tremendous influence on European painting and must be considered with it. The Byzantine and Irish Romanesque schools first reached high standards ; later those of France, 1377, *2167*, Flanders and England, 1177, reached great heights. Through miniatures they influenced portrait painting in the one direction, book illustration and engraving in another. *See also* Outline, page 3669.

IV. THE SCHOOLS OF ITALIAN PAINTING.

A. Florentine School. These artists were the first to paint from Nature ; they acquired also the mastery of perspective (2557) and developed technique in painting.

   a. Early Renaissance (14th Century). Cimabue, a half-legendary figure, 1775, and his great pupil Giotto, *1384*, **1464**, 1775, who is looked upon as the founder of the Florentine School, stand at the dawn of this period. Among the greatest of the " Giottesques " was Andrea di Cione, who called himself Orcagna ; these early painters all worked in tempera or fresco (2476).

   b. Later Renaissance (15th and 16th Centuries), 2764. Fra Angelico, Masaccio, Botticelli, *186, 1779* ; Andrea del Castagno, *1786* ; Fra Filippo Lippi, Uccello, *1778* ; Verrocchio, Ghirlandajo, Fra Bartolommeo, and Andrea del Sarto, 1775–76. These are some of the great Florentine names before the school reaches its climax in the high Renaissance with the work of Leonardo da Vinci, **1926**, *189, 2033*, and Michelangelo, 2160.

B. Sienese School. This school, taking a good deal from Byzantine art, started as early as that of Florence, which it perhaps surpassed in poetry and tenderness. Early in the 15th century it had begun to decline.

C. Venetian School, 1776. Neither the exquisite Florentine line, nor the intellectual mysticism of Florence, but sumptuous, vibrant colour that reflected the gay and brilliant life of the Venetians marked the painting of this school.

   a. The Great Period : Carpaccio, Gentile, and Giovanni Bellini, *1782*, Giogione, Titian, *1780*, Paolo Veronese, *1781*, and Tintoretto.

   b. Later Masters. The Venetian was the longest lived of all Italian schools, for after its great period came a revival under Tiepolo, the greatest baroque decorator, Canaletto, *3557* and Francesco Guardi, *1781*, who worked til almost the end of the 18th century.

D. Umbrian School, 1776. The heir of the Sienese School produced an art full of freshness and poetry, yet limited and childish. Its masters were Piero della Francesca, Perugino and Pinturicchio.

E. Raphael and the Roman School, 2745. The work of Perugino's great pupil, Raphael, 2900, 2749, 2765, was divided into three periods, Umbrian, Florentine, and Roman. At Rome he became head of a school where his successor Giulio Romano or "Jules Romain," *187, 894,* was an able and prolific imitator whose work marks the beginning of Italian decadence.

F. Other Italian Schools and Masters. In the late 15th century Padua produced a mighty genius, Mantegna, whose work had a marked influence on Venetian art, *1776* ; the glory of Parma was Correggio, *1785* ; and many other towns produced lesser masters. The Bolognese or Eclectic School was one of incipient decadence ; its masters were the Caracci, Domenichino, Guido Reni, and Guercino, *1785.* The Naturalist School was led by Caravaggio, with interest in chiaroscuro and foreshortening, and Neapolitan landscape painter, Salvator Rosa.

V. THE NETHERLANDS AND GERMANY.

Northern artists pursued no visions of ideal beauty ; they painted the world around them, and their art is influenced in manner by religion and in technique by the sister arts of illumination and miniature, 2476.

A. Flanders, 2324. Minute detail, rich colour, and homely dignity characterize this art.

    a. **Early Workers :** These evolved on their own a school which rapidly became the equal of contemporary Italian work ; the Van Eycks, *2324, 2326,* who discovered oil painting ; Memling, *2333,* painter of religious masterpieces ; Patinir, first landscape artist ; Rogier Van der Weyden ; Quentin Matsys ; *genre* painters like the Brueghels, *592* ; and Mabuse, through whom Italian influence came in.

    b. **Later Masters :** Still keeping their native originality, these men profited by study in Italy ; Rubens, **2838,** *2327,* the "Titian of the North" ; his pupil, Van Dyck, **3304,** who with Kneller and other portraitists vastly influenced English painting, 1178 ; Teniers, *2330,* who linked the Flemish with the Dutch schools.

B. Holland, 2333 : A homely, essentially *genre* art, which depicted the scenes of its country, fine portraits, superb still life, and religious subjects ; the Dutch school of marine-painters is the greatest of its type there has ever been.

    a. **Portrait Painters :** Rembrandt, **2762,** *2328,* a genius who excelled in whatever he touched ; Frans Hals, **1568,** *2329* ; Ter Borch.

    b. **Genre and Interior Painters :** The Van Ostades ; Gerard Dou ; Metsu ; Pieter de Hooch, *2334* ; Jan Vermeer, **3315,** *2325,* greatest of "little masters" ; Jan Steen ; Beerstraaten, *2331.*

    c. **Landscape and Animal Painters :** Van Goyen ; Cuyp ; Ruisdael ; Hobbema, *2330* ; Paul Potter ; Wouwerman.

    d. **Marine Painters :** The Van de Veldes, *2331* ; Van de Cappelle ; Backhuysen.

    e. **Still-life Painters :** Van Huysum, *2332* ; De Heem ; Hondecoeter.

    f. **Modern Dutch :** In the 19th century a Dutch landscape school arose which achieved enormous popularity ; its exponents were Josef Israels ; J. Maris ; Anton Mauve ; Jongkind, an impressionist, was of the same date.

C. Germany, 1454. Harsh realism, combined in early works with a certain religious mysticism, characterizes this art.

    a. **Dürer, 1058, and Holbein, 1635 :** These great masters of the 16th century stand far above all others in Germany ; both excelled in portraiture and religious art, both were fine engravers of wood.

    b. **Other painters :** Cologne school, the Cranachs, *1454* ; Hans Holbein the elder.

VI. SPANISH, FRENCH, AND BRITISH PAINTING DOWN TO 1800.

A. Spain, 3040. The natural tendency of Spanish artists has always been towards an ascetic style and only by its greater artists is Spanish painting released from the grip of Spanish mysticism.

    Noted Painters : José di Ribera (Lo Spagnoletto), a follower of the Neapolitan Naturalist School (1785) ; Zurbaran, *3049,* first great Spanish master : Velazquez, **3307,** *3045, 3050,* one of world's greatest artists ; Murillo, another of world's great masters, **2257,** *3049* ; the bold and versatile Goya, **1492,** *3047, 3363* ; El Greco, mystic hailed by the moderns, *3044.*

B. France, 1377. For centuries painting in France was connected with the Church, then with the court, and it has been one of the country's industries since the time of Louis XIV. Nowhere does the artist receive such official encouragement or find such freedom, and nowhere does art reflect so well the country's history. The classical landscape was a French development in the reign of Louis XIV. Then the keynote changed to frivolous gaiety and elegance, though the "back-to-nature" work of Greuze and Chardin found ready appreciation.

    Noted Painters : Jehan Fouquet, greatest early French artist ; the brothers Le Nain, *1371,* portrayers of peasant life ; Nicolas Poussin, a really great painter ; Charles Le Brun, court painter to Louis XIV, *2102* ; Claude Lorrain, the "discoverer of sunlight," who developed the classical landscape, *1370* ; Antoine Watteau, one of France's greatest masters, in whose work French elegance and vivacious charm find their first expression ; Nattier, painter of the great ladies of Louis XV's court ; Boucher, *1372,* and Fragonard, in whose work beauty tends toward mere prettiness ; sentimental Greuze and unaffected Chardin, *1373,* painters of humble people, Philip de Champaigne, *1369,* typical portraitist.

C. Britain, 1177. Influenced at first by illumination, and later by Holbein and the miniature painters, British art then came under further influence of the Flemish portraitists. In the 18th century it came into its own, chiefly as a school of portraiture. In landscape, in watercolour and sporting painting England established a position of great importance.

    a. **Miniature painters :** Nicholas Hilliard, influenced by illumination ; the Hoskins ; Samuel Cooper ; Richard Cosway.

    b. **Portraiture :** Lely, *1178,* and Kneller, *2106* ; Hogarth, also a great genre painter, **1634,** *1185* ; Reynolds, **2768,** *1186* ; Gainsborough, **1413,** *1187* ; Romney ; Raeburn ; Hoppner ; Lawrence, *1177.*

c. **Landscape** : Richard Wilson, *1191*, Samuel Scott ; J. M. W. Turner, **3267**, *1189*, *1275* ; John Constable, **893**, *1188* ; " Old " Crome, *1180* ; J. S. Cotman, *917*, *1189*.

d. **Genre and Sporting Painters.** The Devis family and Zoffany, founder of the " conversation piece " ; Morland ; Wheatley ; Stubbs, *1179*.

e. **Water-colour School, 3352.** Pre-eminent in this branch of painting is the English school, whose development is traced from Paul Sandby and Girtin, *3352*, through the Cozens family to de Wint, David Cox, **3353**, and Birket Foster. Great oil-painters who also did fine work in this medium are Turner, Constable, Cotman, *917*, and R. P. Bonington, *3353*. Here, too, comes William Blake, **466**.

VII. MODERN PAINTING.

In the 19th century France assumed the position of teacher in the graphic fine arts that had been held earlier by Italy. Most of the modern movements in painting have radiated from Paris, though England claims a notable school of landscape painting headed by Constable and Turner, and the Pre-Raphaelite movement (**2681**) was born and died in this country. In France, **1377**, revolutionary classicism was followed by Romanticism and that by the Barbizon School, after which a number of movements were on foot at the same time (**2476**).

A. In France.

a. **Classicism**, which coincided largely with Napoleon : David, *1372*, and Ingres were its great exponents.

b. **Romanticism**, a reaction led by Gericault and Delacroix, *1377*.

c. **The Barbizon School**, led by Corot, **913**, *1274*, and J. F. Millet, **2176**, *1374* ; Rousseau ; a minor group was that following Courbet.

d. **Impressionism, 1687.** This almost world-wide movement began with the work of Claude Monet, *1375* ; the group also included Édouard Manet, *1687* ; Degas, *346* ; Renoir, *1376* ; Pissarro, in France ; in Germany, Liebermann, Slevogt and Corinth ; in Spain, Sorolla and to a certain extent, Zuloaga, *3048*.

e. **The Post-Impressionists, 2477.** Having comparatively little in common, these painters continued to revolt against academic art and laid the foundations of the most modern groups. Gauguin, *1689* ; Van Gogh, **3305**, *1687* ; and Cezanne, *1375*, were its prime movers.

f. **Later Groups, 2477.** From Matisse, Braque, Rouault, and Picasso, **2604**, greatest of modern masters, most later schools have evolved. The first of these was concerned with new scales of colour and pattern, and founded the "Fauvist " school ; the second with a strange type of picture derived from still-life ; the fourth, great above all as a draughtsman, remains a ceaseless experimenter. To him, with Cezanne's influence, was due Cubism, **2604** ; German Expressionism, *f-i.*, was a revolt against Impressionism. Futurism, an Italian manner, was short-lived ; and Vorticism was founded by Wyndham Lewis, an Englishman. In Surrealism, **3122**, a number of artists combined to remove painting further than ever from public appreciation.

B. Modern Painting in England.

a. **Portraiture.** A continued tradition of fine portraiture can be traced from the days of Lawrence to modern times. Alfred Stevens, *1181*, and G. F. Watts, **2454**, were outstanding in the mid-19th century ; more recent are the American Sargent, **2874** ; Orpen, *1183* ; Augustus John, *1192* ; McEvoy, etc.

b. **Pre-Raphaelites, 2681.** In an attempt to get away from academism, these painters, Rossetti, Holman Hunt, and Millais, with their followers and with such artists as Burne-Jones, Ford Madox Brown, *2682*, Lord Leighton, **1919**, *1921*, etc., formed the backbone of later Victorian art, but they left few successors and had little lasting influence.

c. **Impressionism, Vorticism, and Surrealism.** After the dull, purely representational 19th century came an anglicized Impressionism, whose chief exponents were Whistler, *1189*, Sickert, Wilson Steer, *1191*, Tonks and members of the Camden Town and London Groups, such as Harold Gilman and Charles Ginner, Henry Lamb, headed later by Duncan Grant ; also Percy Wyndham Lewis, inventor of Vorticism, the English equivalent of Cubism.

d. **Other Figures.** William Etty was a fine painter of the nude, J. Crawhall and Landseer of animals, and Frith of *genre* subjects. Among the more modern artists are Augustus John, excelling as portraitist, 1184, *1192* ; Nevinson, *1183*, Ben Nicholson, Christopher Wood, Henry Moore, and the brothers John and Paul Nash, while others are Stanley Spencer, *1184*, Wadsworth, and William Roberts.

MINOR FINE ARTS

UNDER this heading are grouped a number of the lesser Fine Arts referred to in page 3662. Most of them are definitely related to the major Arts and have been, as a rule, practised by exponents of the latter.

I. ENGRAVING.

This heading, **1217**, includes a large number of very different modes of working, although the principal is the same in every case : the production of a block or plate, from which can be printed numerous copies of the artist's original drawing.

A. Wood-engraving. For centuries a great art in China and Japan, 1811. Used for the earliest illustration of printed books, 511, and continued for its own sake, as well as for this purpose, ever since. In recent years there has been a great revival in this art. Closely allied to it, though usually used for rougher work, is the new art of lino-cut, in which a linoleum block replaces the wood.

a. **Continental Work** : Dürer, greatest of wood-engravers, 1058, *1217*; Holbein, another great engraver, 1635.

b. **Modern English Engravers** : Clare Leighton, *f-i.* ; Gertrude Hermes, most original of modern engravers ; Eric Gill, 1178 ; Robert Gibbings, *f-i.*

c. **Japanese Masters :** Hosoda Eishi, *1806* ; Hokusai, *1807* ; Hiroshige, *f-i.*

B. **Engraving on Metal Plates :** This includes line-engraving, in which the design is cut in a steel or copper plate ; **dry-point**, in which the plate, often of zinc, in engraved directly with a sharp instrument ; **etching**, in which the plate is covered with a layer of wax, in which the design is cut, the metal then being eaten away with acid. Many masters of all the great schools of painting have practised etching. **Aquatint** is often used to assist etching, as well as on its own. The plate is covered with sand or powdered resin, and bitten through this with acid, producing a finely reticulated surface.

a. **Early Workers :** Dürer, greatest of early engravers and still unrivalled as a line-engraver, *1217* ; Rembrandt, greatest etcher of all time, *1219*, **2762** ; Van Dyck, **3304** ; Van Ostade, a great Dutch engraver, *2334*; Leonardo da Vinci, and many others of the great Italian masters were fine engravers. Line-engravers : Canot, *2954* ; J. Payne, *2955* ; B. Picart, *1616, 2694.*

b. **Modern Masters.** In the 19th century, etching especially underwent a tremendous revival. The Frenchmen, Meryon, *f-i.*, and Legros were leaders in this art ; in Britain, Seymour Hayden and Whistler, *f-i.*, **3540**, were followed by Brangwyn, *f-i.*, Muirhead Bone, *f-i.*, etc. ; America's great etcher is J. Pennell ; from Scandinavia came Anders Zorn, another modern master. Sir Frank Short is an outstanding modern aquatinter.

C. **Engraving for Reproduction.** Several types of engraving are used, chiefly for the reproduction of paintings by great masters. Among these is **mezzo-tinting**. " Stipple engraving " is a somewhat similar art, *1218*. Finally, there is **lithography**, **1967**, *2946*, which is at present very popular for original work, and in which a stone block is used instead of a metal plate (1218). This is really a method of surface-printing, not strictly engraving. **Process-engraving**, *2688*, the modern method of illustrating many books and magazines, cannot be ranked as a fine art. " Scraper-board," a specially prepared board or thin card covered with a uniform layer of kaolin brushed over with ink, on which a design is scraped out, is much used in modern reproduction where speed is essential.

Great English Mezzotinters. The English mezzotinters reached their greatest perfection during the 18th century. They included Valentine Green ; Bartolozzi ; John Raphael Smith and many others.

II. OTHER GRAPHIC ARTS.

A. **Crayon and pencil drawing and pastel.** Though closely allied to painting, and practised by all artists and designers, drawing is also an art of its own, and much fine work has been done with pencil, crayon, or pastel. The latter especially can be used to produce fine effects.

a. **Early Draughtsmen :** Jehan (Jean) Fouquet, 1377, whose drawings are of tremendous value ; François Clouet, *870*. Cartoon by Leonardo da Vinci, *1927* ; drawing by him, *1046*.

b. **Modern Examples :** Degas, an outstanding artist in pastel, *f-i.* ; George Cruikshank ;

Harry Furniss, typical English 19th-century illustrator in pen-and-ink, *1014*.

B. **Illumination, Miniature Painting and Printing,** *2090, 1177.*

From illuminated manuscripts came the first books, in which the illustrations were drawn separately in each copy. From the miniature portraits thus introduced came the art of miniature painting, reaching its highest standard in England in 16th, 17th and 18th centuries. Together with these arts has survived that of **calligraphy**, or fine writing, still practised in heraldry and in drawing up agreements and deeds.

a. **Manuscripts and Book Illustration :** French, *2090, 2167, 2652* ; Irish Romanesque, *510* ; English, Winchester School, *1177* ; Luttrell Psalter, *2091* ; *plate f. 1864.*

b. **Fine Printing, Book Production :** William Morris, *2232*; Bible, *427*; Grolier Binding, *517.*

III. CERAMICS.

The art of making pottery is a world-wide one, having been discovered independently by many primitive peoples, 2082. Porcelain, on the other hand, is an oriental discovery, copied in Western Europe within comparatively recent times. Read **Pottery and Porcelain, 2665.**

a. **Early European Pottery :** Cretan, *31* ; Greek, *1523, 1524, 1528, 1536, 1537* ; Roman, *2809* ; Portland Vase, *facing p. 585.*

b. **Oriental Pottery and Porcelain :** *2668* ; Chinese, *810, 811* ; Japanese, *1809.*

c. **European,** *2669* ; Della Robbia, *2670.*

d. **American :** Inca Ware, *1690.*

IV. METAL WORK, JEWELRY, ETC.

A. **Metal Work.** One of the most practical of arts, metal work has been practised since pre-history, for even in the earliest times ornamental as well as useful metal-work was produced. Examples : Celtic shield, *740* ; Spanish, *2926* ; Japanese sword-guard, *1809* ; Italian, *1784* ; Indian bronze, *1713.*

B. **Jewelry, 1427, and Allied Crafts.** Closely allied to ornamental metal-work, the art of making jewelry is also an extremely ancient one.

a. **Egyptian and other Ancient Work :** *1116* ; *backs of plates f. 1120, 1121* ; Chaldean, *2147* ; Aztec work, *326.*

b. **Cameos, 671.**

c. **Carving.** Though closely allied to Sculpture carving often entails more detailed work. Wood carving has been practised for centuries. Great carvers, Grinling Gibbons, **1462** ; Montanes, *3045.* Ivory carving, *1812.*

C. **Enamelling,** *1157.* This difficult art combines skilled metal-work with jewelry, *110.*

V. CABINET-MAKING AND INTERIOR DECORATION.

A. **Furniture.** Allied with Architecture, cabinet-making, *1409*, has often been practised by the same men. From early times, the rich devoted great attention to interior decoration and furnishing of their homes or even their tombs.

a. **Early Furnishings :** Egypt, *1404, 1410, 1120* ; Roman, **1410.**

b. **European Furniture :** From early, crude works of local woods (e.g., oak in the case of England, *1410*), furniture gradually became artistic. The Renaissance did much to aid its appreciation. In England, the line can be traced from simply designed, often well ornamented Elizabethan and Tudor work, *1410*, through the more delicate Jacobean, to the walnut furniture of William and Mary, and thence to Chippendale, *1411*, *f-i.*, Hepplewhite, *1411*, Sheraton, *1411*, and Adam, *22*, when mahogany and rosewood replaced local woods. French influence was then paramount for fifty years. In the late 19th century William Morris's group of workers such as Ernest Gimson, *f-i.*, revived fine furniture. In modern times, the family of Heal, Gordon Russell and many others have renewed interest in English woods and created a modern " period " style.

B. **Tapestry.** Allied with interior decoration was the art of **Tapestry-weaving, 3152**, now more or less dead. From the Middle Ages to the 18th century, tapestry was a usual wall covering, the most famous being that made at the Gobelins factory, 1378. Famous artists such as Raphael designed tapestries for their great patrons, *2530*. Examples : Bayeux Tapestry, **378** ; French, 15th century, *3153*.

C. **Weaving, Embroidery, etc.** These domestic arts, which are all of great age, have now largely disappeared in the age of machines, though many examples exist in museums and private collections.

    a. Spinning and Weaving, 3065, 3360.

    b. Embroidery, 1152, and lace-making, 1876 ; Japanese embroidery, *1810*.

MUSIC

I. NATURE OF MUSIC.

A. **Music and its Physical Basis, 2261.** *See also* Sound in the Physics Outline, 3676.

B. **Three Elements of Music, 2263.**

    a. **Rhythm :** Regular recurrence of tone groups in which individual notes are symmetrically arranged according to accent and time value.

    b. **Melody :** A succession of simple tones constituting a musical phrase.

    c. **Harmony:** Simultaneous blending of sounds called " chords " and with the interweaving of " parts " or voices.

C. **Written Music, 2262.**

    a. **Staff and Notes,** *2262*.

    b. **Time in Music, 3214.**

II. SOME IMPORTANT FORMS OF MUSICAL EXPRESSION.

A. **Suite, 2264.** A composition consisting of several varied movements, originally intended for one instrument, now often written for an orchestra.

B. **Sonata :** An instrumental composition in three or four movements, for piano or for solo instrument with piano accompaniment.

C. **Concerto :** A composition in sonata form for a solo instrument and the orchestra.

D. **Symphony :** A large scale sonata for an orchestra. A few " choral " symphonies also exist.

E. **Oratorio :** A semi-dramatic sacred choral work of large scope with vocal solos and orchestra.

F. **Opera, 2435 :** Musical form of drama with solos, choruses, orchestra, scenery, and acting.

G. **Cantata :** A composition either sacred or secular for solo voices and chorus ; shorter than an Oratorio or Opera.

H. **Anthem :** A composition in common use in church services ; sometimes for full choir throughout or for two choirs, and sometimes with solo parts introduced ; organ accompaniment is usual.

I. **Hymn :** A form of composition used in religious services ; it varies considerably in measure owing to the variety of metres used in the words.

J. **Canon :** A composition in which one part follows another over the same notes, separated perhaps by an octave, but exactly imitating its movement.

K. **Rondo :** A bright movement in which the principal subject keeps recurring, in the same key.

L. **Fugue :** A movement beginning with a subject in single notes, which is given out by one part and answered by other parts in turn, the subject and counter-subjects forming an harmonious whole.

III. MUSICAL INSTRUMENTS.

A. **Stringed Instruments :** **2266**, *2267* : Piano, **2601** ; Harp, **1579** ; Violin (Viola, Violoncello, and Double Bass), **3324** ; Guitar, *f-i.* ; Mandolin, *f-i.* ; Banjo, **356**.

B. **Wind Instruments,** *2267*.

    a. **Woodwind Instruments :** Flute, Piccolo, Fife, Oboe, English Horn, Bassoon, and Clarinet.

    b. **Brasses :** French Horn, Trumpet, Cornet, Trombone, Tuba, and Saxophone.

    c. **Other Wind Instruments :** Accordion (bellows-mechanism) ; Bagpipe, **339** ; organ, **2449**.

C. **Percussion Instruments,** *2267*.

    a. **Drums, 1049 :** Kettledrum, Tympani, Bass Drum, and Side or Snare Drum.

    b. **Bells, 409 :** Triangle, Glockenspiel, Xylophone, Cymbals, etc.

D. **Orchestra, 2445 :** Group use of instruments.

IV. HISTORY OF MUSIC.

A. **Hebrew Music, 2261.**

B. **Greek Music, 2261.**

C. **Development from the 4th to the 17th century A.D., 2261.**

    a. **Guido of Arezzo and the Invention of the Musical Staff, 2261.**

    b. **Rise of Secular Music, 2262.**

    c. **Development of Counterpoint, 2263.**

    d. **Palestrina and the Perfection of the Mass, 2263.**

D. **Great Modern Composers and their Contribution to the Development of Music.**

    a. **Henry Purcell, 2706.** England's first great composer.

    b. **Johann Sebastian Bach, 333.** The world's most profound and original musical thinker and the link between medieval polyphonic and modern harmonic styles.

c. **George Frederick Handel, 1572.** Great Master of the Oratorio.

d. **Christoph Willibald Gluck, *f-i.*** Reformer of the Opera and greatest writer of dramatic music before Mozart.

e. **Franz Joseph Haydn, 1589.** The earliest great master of the symphony and the orchestra.

f. **Wolfgang Amadeus Mozart, 2249.** Universal genius in music, who raised all musical forms, except the Oratorio and the Fugue, to a point never reached before, and Comic Opera to a height " never since approached within classical limits."

g. **Ludwig van Beethoven, 397.** Greatest orchestral composer of the 19th century, and profoundest symphonist of all time.

h. **Carl von Weber, *f-i.*** Founder of the Romantic School of German Opera.

i. **Franz Schubert, 2887.** The first and perhaps the greatest classical song writer.

j. **Felix Mendelssohn, 2141.** Modern classical master, one of the earliest of moderns to appreciate and be influenced by Bach.

k. **Frédéric François Chopin, 816.** Created a new style of composition for the piano and added a new national element to music.

l. **Hector Berlioz, *f-i.*** Master of Impressionist orchestration.

m. **Robert Schumann, 2887.** Romanticist

composer whose songs rank with those of Schubert and his " piano lyrics " with those of Chopin.

n. **Franz Liszt, 1964.** Pioneer of the symphonic poem.

o. **Giuseppe Verdi, 3315.** Greatest Italian composer of the 19th century ; a master of opera.

p. **Richard Wagner, 3331.** Creator of a new form of music drama.

q. **Johannes Brahms, 544.** A prolific and versatile master of orchestration ; adapted romantic material to classical forms.

r. **Peter Ilyitch Tchaikovsky, 3158.** Greatest of Russian composers.

s. **Antonin Dvorak, *f-i.*** Made extensive use of folk-melodies, especially of Slavonic origin.

t. **Jan Sibelius, 2965.** Has recently been recognized as the greatest symphonist of the 20th century ; Finland's first great national composer.

u. **Richard Strauss, 3103.** Perfecter of the dramatic " symphonic poem," brilliant and inventive orchestrator, lyric and operatic master.

v. **Other composers, 2266.** Britten, 2266, *2437* ; Debussy ; Delius, 988 ; Elgar, 1143 ; German, 1444 ; Grieg ; Holst, 2266 ; Mahler ; Parry ; Ravel ; Rawsthorne ; Shostakovitch, 2266 ; W. Johann Strauss, 3102 ; Stravinsky, 2266 ; Sullivan, 1463 ; Vaughan Williams ; Walton.

Careers in the Fine Arts

FOR artists of all sorts, as well as teachers of the arts, and for musicians, there will always be a demand. Music and drawing can be studied from a very early age. Later, after leaving school, most students go to a local teacher and then enter one of the bigger Art Schools. In London there is the Royal College of Art, under the Ministry of Education, for training artists in commerce and as teachers ; also the Slade School, the Royal Academy Schools, and many others. There is a famous School of Art at Glasgow. Most of the provincial cities have Conservatoires of Music, and in London there are the Royal College and the Royal Academy of Music.

Some Books on the Fine Arts

Art Through the Ages. Helen Gardner.
Arts and Crafts in Ancient Egypt. Sir Flinders Petrie.
The Legacy of Greece. E. R. W. Livingstone.
Legacy of Rome. Cyril Bailey.
Medieval Art. W. R. Lethaby.
Art. Clive Bell.
Vision and Design. Roger Fry.
Art in My Time. Frank Rutter.
The Meaning of Art. Herbert Read.
The Musical Companion. A. L. Bacharach.

The Meaning of Modern Sculpture. R. H. Wilenski.
The Modern Movement in Painting. T. W. Earp.
Modern Painting in England. Mary Chamot.
Groves' Dictionary of Music and Musicians.
Bryan's Dictionary of Painters and Engravers.
Chats on Old China, etc. : A series on objets d'art of all sorts.
The House : A Machine to Live in. Anthony Bertram.
The New Architecture. A. Roth.
On the European Schools there are innumerable excellent books in most libraries ; this applies also to Architecture.

Interest-Questions in Arts and Literature

What keeps an arch from falling ? 205.
How can a dome be put over a square room ? 214.
What is the entablature of a building ? 215.
What are flying buttresses ? 218.
What is " baroque " art ? 220.
How did the geography of Greece influence Greek art ? 1528.
What is " relief " in sculpture and what is its opposite ? 2903.
Were Greek statues all white ? 1528.
Who were the great animal painters 20,000 years ago ? 2475.
Where were the first Christian paintings made ? 2476.
What is a " fresco " ? 2476.
What is " tempera " in painting ? 2476.
What is " impressionism " ? " Post-impressionism " ? 1687, 1689.
What composer became deaf at the height of his success ? 397.
What musician began to compose at the age of five ? 2249.
When was the first piano made ? 2601.
What people were the first to leave written music ? 2261.

What is a " sonata " ? 2264.
Who was the " father of English poetry " ? 761.
What great literary work was burned by a servant-maid ? 703.
Who was the poet who said of himself " I awoke one morning to find myself famous " ? 635.
What English poet died while fighting for the freedom of Greece ? 635.
What great religious allegory was written in prison ? 617.
Who was the " real Robinson Crusoe " ? 937.
What book written as a cutting satire on human nature has become a children's classic ? 3132.
What Scottish writer developed his gift of humour through trying to make his mother laugh ? 364.
How many actors were there in the Greek drama ? 1037.
What great Spanish novelist was sold into slavery ? 746.
What world language did not have to be invented ? 1894.
What Russian writer gave up his wealth to live as a peasant ? 3222.

PHYSICAL SCIENCES

THE principal physical sciences are **Physics (2591)**, **Chemistry (766)**, and **Astronomy (275)**, but there is no sharp line dividing one from the other ; and indeed there is in practice no sharp line dividing the physical sciences from the biological sciences, for we have such departments as biological chemistry or biochemistry, **429**, and biophysics. Because of the countless technical principles involved in the physical sciences, it is possible to present here only a brief survey of the primary points in each field.

PHYSICS

I. DEFINITION.

Physics attempts to discover the nature of the physical universe and the character of the laws that rule it. Physics, therefore, has for a goal the explanation, with mathematical exactness and in conformity with these laws, of all phenomena of the inanimate universe. It has had greater success in this field than in defining the " matter " of which the universe is composed, although modern research into the physics of the atom has reduced to fact what was for centuries pure hypothesis. Fresh fields of study are constantly opening before the physicist, whose discoveries have as yet perhaps only touched the fringe of the mystery of the universe.

II. SOME BASIC LAWS OF PHYSICS.

A. **The Law of Causation.** Physics assumes that everything which takes place in the physical universe is the result of causes, exactly proportional to the effect produced.

B. **Newton's Three Laws of Mechanical Action, 2130.**

C. The " Conservation of Energy " Law, 1160, 2592.

D. The " Conservation of Mass " Law, 1161, 2592.

Today the Law of the Conservation of Mass, and the Law of the Conservation of Energy are re-stated by combining these two laws : matter *can* be annihilated, in certain circumstances ; an equivalent amount of energy is then liberated (2592). Albert Einstein promulgated his Law of the Equivalence of Mass and Energy (297) : by losing mass a substance could liberate energy (1161).

States and Properties of Matter

I. BASIC PROPERTIES OF MATTER.

A. **Extension or Volume.** Every material thing in the world takes up some room in it.

B. **Mass.** The quantity of matter in a body. This is indicated by the amount of force necessary to produce a given amount of motion in the body in a given time. The symbol used in physical formulae to indicate Mass is m.

C. **Weight.** The downward pressure which a body exerts in response to **Gravity (1512)**. Weight depends both upon the *force of gravity* at the place of measurement, and the *mass* of the article weighed. If a body of given mass be placed at different distances from the centre of the earth, its weight will vary (1513, *1513*) while its mass remains constant.

D. **Density.** The mass of a substance per unit of volume. When we say that lead is " heavier " than cork, we mean that it has a greater density. When expressed as the *ratio* of the density of a given substance to the density of water (taken as unity), we use the term *specific gravity* (3054). The s.g. of gases is expressed in relation to the density of air.

E. **Inertia.** The tendency to " stay put," either motionless or in straight-line motion at uniform speed. Newton's first law of motion (2130) is sometimes called the Law of Inertia.

F. **Other Properties.** Elasticity, plasticity, cohesiveness, adhesiveness, malleability, ductility, hardness.

II. STATES OF MATTER.

A. **Solid.** A solid possesses a definite mass, a definite size or volume, and a definite shape.

B. **Liquid.** A liquid possesses a definite mass and a definite size or volume, but has no definite shape.

C. **Gas.** A gas has definite mass only. A gas not only changes shape, but it does not remain within any definite volume (1419). A quantity of water poured into a container will more or less fill the container ; a quantity of gas introduced into a container will spread out until it entirely fills the receptacle.

III. TRANSFORMING MATTER.

Such transformations, as from solid to liquid, or solid to gas or liquid to gas, are produced by heat, temperature and pressure changes, chemical action, or radio-activity.

IV. MECHANICS—THE EFFECTS OF FORCE, 2127.

A. **Force.** Force is " pull, push, pressure, tension, attraction, or repulsion." Therefore, to exert force, a body must meet resistance. Force is exerted by a moving object *only in the quantity necessary to overcome resistance*. This is the meaning of Newton's Third Law of Motion (2130).

   a. **Units of Force.** The unit of force in physics is the **dyne**. A dyne is a force sufficient to impart, in one second, an acceleration of one centimetre a second to a body weighing one gramme. The dyne, therefore, is a unit in the metric or " centimetre-gramme-second " (C.G.S.) system of units. The amount of force which, acting on a pound, will produce, at the end of a second, motion of one foot a second, is called a **poundal**. It is equivalent to 13,825 dynes. The symbol of force in physical formulae is F, and is expressed in dynes.

   b. **The Force of Gravity.** Since in one second gravity imparts an acceleration of 981 centimetres a second to a gramme of matter, the force of gravity is taken as 981 dynes.

B. Measurement of Force. Since force is called forth by reaction, the amount exerted may be measured by the reaction or " effect " produced. This is done by multiplying the mass of the body affected, by the **acceleration** produced. In symbols, it is expressed as **F = ma**, in which **m** is the symbol for mass, and **a** acceleration. This relation is expressed in Newton's Second Law of Motion (2130).

C. Composition of Forces. When two or more forces act on a body at a given point and at the same time, the result is the same as if a single force, called the resultant, were applied.

Note : The Parallelogram of Forces. If a parallelogram be constructed in which the sides are drawn to scale, so as to represent the true proportions between two component forces, and if the angle between the sides be made equal to the angle between the component forces, then the diagonal which intersects that angle will represent on the same scale, the resultant of the two forces (*2127, 2128*).

D. Resolution of Forces. Division of a known force into the component forces causing it is called " resolution of forces." It is performed by constructing the parallelogram of forces in the reverse manner.

E. Kinds of Motion :

    a. Translation. The change of position of the whole body in some direction. Example : an arrow in flight.

    b. Rotation. The turning of a body about a stationary axis. Example : a fly-wheel.

    c. Vibration or Undulation. To-and-fro motion of parts without changing the position of the whole. Example: a plucked banjo string.

F. Qualities of Motion :

    a. Speed. Speed in physics means the rate of a moving body, *at any particular instant*. In order to define speed simply, assume an object travelling at a uniform speed. Measure the distance travelled in a given time, and divide this distance by the time. The answer is the speed.

In symbols, $S = \dfrac{d}{t}$. (S is the customary symbol for speed, and t for time ; d is used for distance travelled.)

    b. Velocity. Velocity is speed *in a certain direction*. The symbol for velocity is **v**. Velocities may be " compounded " and " resolved " by the parallelogram method.

    c. Acceleration. When a train starts, its velocity, or speed in a given direction, changes constantly. If its speed increases, the rate of this *change* is called **Acceleration.** We determine acceleration by measuring the velocity at any given instant and again a few instants later. The difference is the acceleration over the period of time. The answer may be obtained by using the following formula :

$a = \dfrac{v_2 - v_1}{t_2 - t_1}$ (v_1 and t_1 are the velocity at the first observation and the time of taking it, while v_2 and t_2 are for the second observation). The acceleration produced by gravity at the surface of the earth is approximately 32 feet or 981 centimetres per second per second (1513).

G. Properties of a Body in Motion—Kinetics.

    a. Momentum : The amount of force required to set a body of a given mass in motion at a particular speed, or, what is the same thing, the amount of resistance required to stop the body when once it is moving at that speed. Both the mass of the body and its velocity determine its momentum. In symbols, momentum = **mv** (mass *times* velocity).

    b. Kinetic Energy : The *striking power* of a moving object, as opposed to its momentum, is $\frac{1}{2}mv^2$.

    c. Centrifugal and Centripetal Force : As stated in Newton's first law, a moving body will continue to move in the same straight line unless forced to do otherwise. In order, then, to swing a stone at the end of a string, we must apply force to keep the stone in a curved path. This force is supplied through the string. The force tending to make the stone fly outwards is called **centrifugal force (745)**, and the restraining force of the string is called **centripetal force.** The formula for centrifugal force is

$$F = \frac{mv^2}{r}$$

where **m** is the mass of the object exerting the force ; **v** is its velocity ; and **r** is the radius of the curve of its motion.

H. Determination of Work, Power, and Energy :

    a. Work : In physics, the Work done upon a body is defined as the amount of motion, or the strain, compression, or distortion produced in it ; but work is not done if the point of application does not move. The amount of work is the product of the force exerted by the distance traversed. In symbols, work is equal to **Fd** where **F** is the force and **d** is the distance. The engineering unit of work is the foot-pound, the amount of work required to raise one avoirdupois pound through one foot against gravity. The C.G.S. unit is the work required to move a gramme one centimetre against a resistance of one dyne. This unit is called an **erg.** Since it is so small, a **joule,** or 10^7 ergs, is used in practice.

    b. Power : Under the definition of work given above, the work is the same if an object be moved a foot in a second or an hour. In ordinary life, however, the time element is important ; and **Power** is force which does the work *in a certain time.* In physics the unit of power is **an erg a second**—that is, the force which will move one gramme one centimetre in one second against a resistance of one dyne. The larger unit of a joule a second is called a **watt** (10^7 ergs per second). The engineering unit is the **horse-power,** equivalent to 746 watts ; 1 **kilowatt** (1,000 watts) is equivalent to 1·34 horse-power.

    c. Kinds of Energy (1160, 2593) : Energy is defined as the *capacity for doing work.* A hanging weight has the capacity for doing work when it is let fall. This " stored energy " is called **Potential Energy.** When falling, the weight has the capacity for doing work upon any object in its path. This energy is called **Kinetic Energy.**

    d. Measurement of Energy : The amount of

potential energy stored by raising an object against gravity = mgh (mass of the object, times **force of gravity** in dynes, times **height** to which the object is raised).

I. Properties of a Body at Rest—Statics, 2127.

a. Balanced Forces : Every motionless body is subject to two forces—the force of gravity and the equal resistance of the foundation on which the body stands. The opposing forces are " balanced." The science of balanced forces is called **Statics**.

b. Centre of Gravity : So long as a body remains structurally rigid, all its weight may be considered as concentrated at one point, called the **Centre of Gravity** (41, 1513, *1514*). The centre of gravity always tends to get as low as possible. If, therefore, a body be suspended by an edge or corner, the centre of gravity will be vertically below the point of suspension.

c. Equilibrium : The condition called Equilibrium—that is, balance of forces—exists in a body when the sum of all forces acting upon it in one direction equals the sum of those acting upon it in the opposite direction.

J. Machines.

a. Purpose of Machines : A machine is (1) a device, such as a petrol motor (1736), for transforming energy of one kind into another ; (2) a device, such as the connecting-rod of a locomotive (*f. p. 1980*) for transferring energy from one place or direction to another ; (3) a device, such as a block and tackle (2701) for changing the relative speed and strength of action of a force.

b. The Law of Machines and the Principle of Mechanical Advantage : We can get out from a machine only the energy we put into it, and some of this energy will be wasted in the form of heat, caused by friction. But we can make the energy applied move a small weight over a large distance, or a large weight over a small distance. Ignoring losses caused by friction (**1396**) within the machine, these two quantities must equal each other. This equality is the **law of machines**, which may be stated in symbols thus : $F l = md$. (F is the force put in, l the distance over which it operates ; m is the mass of the object moved, and d the distance over which it moves.) The amount by which the power of a machine is multiplied, at a corresponding loss in distance lifted, is called its **mechanical advantage** (2700).

c. Six Types of Machines in Physics : The six simple machines known in mechanics are the **lever** (*2130*), **wheel and axle** (2700, 3375), **pulley** (2698), **inclined plane** (2128, *2902*), **wedge** (2129, *2902*) and **screw** (**2901**). All machines, in so far as they involve the transformation of mechanical energy, are combinations of these simple types.

V. MECHANICS OF LIQUIDS—HYDRAULICS.

A. Definition and Subject Matter of Hydraulics.
Hydraulics is the science of Liquids. "Fluids" include both liquids and gases ; and since gases at low velocities have many of the properties of liquids, those principles of Hydraulics which describe the effects of pressure are also applicable to gases, at ordinary temperatures. Hydraulics is divided into two branches : (1) **Hydrostatics**, or the science of liquids at rest ; (2) **Hydrodynamics**, or the science of liquids in motion. Since hydrodynamics involves such problems as the design of water turbines, the theory of vortices in flowing streams, and so on, needing the use of higher mathematics in their solution, the discussion in this Study Outline will be confined to Hydrostatics (**1665**).

B. Pressure and Flow : Apart from gravity, the great force causing phenomena within liquids is **Pressure**. Pressure arises from : (1) Atmospheric pressure upon the surface of the liquid ; (2) the weight of overlying liquid ; and (3) cohesion, or the tendency of molecules to cling together, within the liquid. The symbol of pressure is **P**. In this connexion it is well to remember that all liquids are virtually " incompressible." A number of machines such as the pump (*2703*), hydraulic ram (*2704*), hydraulic press (*1666*) and the hydraulic lift (1937) make use of this important fact.

a. Qualities of Pressure.

1. Pressure due to Atmosphere : This is computed by multiplying the total area of the surface by the atmospheric pressure. This pressure is the same throughout the liquid.

2. Pressure due to Gravity : Since weight is merely downward pressure caused by gravity, the gravitational pressure at any level is the weight of the vertical column of liquid above that level. Since liquids tend to move sideways as well as downwards, this pressure acts equally both downwards and sideways at any given level against the walls of the container. Pressure against a side is always exerted at right angles to the side, no matter what the slope of the side may be.

3. Uniformity of Pressure throughout a Liquid : If the pressure upon a confined liquid be increased by a certain amount at any point, the liquid will transmit that same increase of pressure equally throughout its whole extent. It is this principle which makes possible the hydraulic press (*1666*). " Hydrostatic paradox " is the term applied to the fact that a mass of 100 lbs. on a piston of 1 square inch in area can support a mass of 90,000 lbs. on a piston of 900 square inches in area if they are connected hydraulically.

4. " Water Finds its own Level " : The uniformity of pressure within liquids explains why a liquid reaches the same level in open vessels that are connected no matter what their sizes or shapes (*252*).

5. Principle of the Siphon (2975) : atmospheric pressure and the difference in weight between the water in the short limb and the long limb of the siphon causes the water flow

b. Phenomena of Immersion.

1. Principle of Archimedes : This principle (211) states that a body immersed in a fluid is buoyed up by a force equal to the weight of the volume of fluid it displaces.

2. Why some Bodies Sink and Others Float .
A liquid buoys the body up ; the body's weight forces it down. If its weight is greater than the weight of the water it displaces, the downward force will be the greater and it will sink. But if the body's weight is, for instance, only half that of an equal volume of water, it ceases to sink when half of its volume is immersed, the upward thrust of the displaced water then being equal to the downward thrust of its weight. This principle is utilized in the Hydrometer (**1674**) to measure specific gravity, *3053*.

c. Surface Tension and Capillarity : The molecules of a liquid " stick together " with appreciable force. This " clinging tendency " is called **Cohesion**, and creates a force called **Surface Tension (3121)** on liquid surfaces. Surface tension causes the phenomena of **Capillary Attraction (698)**.

VI. MECHANICS OF GASES—PNEUMATICS.

A. Nature of Gases, 1419. Unlike both liquids and solids, gases are practically indefinitely elastic. At ordinary temperatures many are soluble in liquids or solids without appreciably increasing their volumes. They become liquids or even solids when cooled to a low temperature under compression.

B. Relation of Pneumatics to Hydraulics. Hydraulic principles relating to fluid pressure apply also to gases not in motion. But since gases are compressible, principles involving the incompressibility of liquids, such as the hydrostatic paradox, are not applicable.

C. Relations of Temperature, Pressure, and Volume. As may be understood from considering the molecular nature of gases (**1419**) and the molecular nature of heat (**1593**), the temperature, pressure, and volume of a gas are intimately dependent upon each other, as follows :

a. Boyle's Law (537, 1419). This law states that, at a given temperature, the volume of a gas decreases proportionately as the pressure increases. This law may be stated as a proportion: $\dfrac{P_1}{P_2} = \dfrac{V_2}{V_1}$, in which P_1 is the initial pressure and P_2 is the increased pressure ; V_1 is the initial volume and V_2 is the volume due to the increased pressure.

b. Charles's Law. This law asserts that, at constant pressure, the volume of a gas increases regularly with increased temperature. The amount of increase is called the coefficient of expansion, and is, for all gases, nearly the same: almost exactly $\frac{1}{273}$, or 0·003663 of the volume for each degree C. rise in temp.

c. Avogadro's Law. Avogadro's Law states that equal volumes of gases at equal temperatures and pressures contain an equal number of molecules, whatever the gases may be. The law is of immense importance in chemistry in determining atomic weights.

D. Atmospheric Pressure and the Barometer. *See* Air (**88**), Barometer (**362**), and Steam (**3084**).

Heat and its Principles

I. NATURE OF HEAT.

According to modern theory, heat is due to *motion* of the molecules within a substance (**1593**), and the amount of heat present is determined by the total amount of motion present. When there is no motion, there is no heat—that is, the body is at **absolute zero** (−273° Centigrade) in temperature (**1391, 1594**). The theory that heat is a consequence of molecular motion is called the **kinetic theory of heat**.

II. BASIC LAWS OF HEAT.

A. Law of the Conservation of Energy, 1160.

B. Law of the Dissipation of Useful Energy. If we want to heat a body, we cannot do so by transferring a portion of their heat from colder bodies and so " build up " heat (**1599**). We must do so by abstracting heat from a still hotter body ; or by using chemical energy such as we have in unburned coal (**1595**) ; or by using potential mechanical energy such as we have in a raised hammer.

III. ATTRIBUTES OF HEAT.

Since heat is due to molecular motion, the amount present in a body depends upon two factors : (1) the average *speed* of the moving molecules, and (2) the *number* of moving molecules.

A. Temperature. Temperature is the " relative hotness " of any body, as compared with any convenient standard. The most convenient standard is the comparison of the expansion produced in some substance (e.g. mercury in a narrow tube) by the temperature in question, with the known expansion produced by some standard temperature (e.g. that of melting ice or boiling water). Instruments for doing this are Thermometers (**3199**) and Pyrometers (**2709**). The " absolute scale " of temperatures with zero at the " absolute zero " or complete lack of molecular motion, is often used in science (**1391, 1594**).

B. Specific Heat. It takes more energy to raise the average speed of the molecules—that is, to raise the temperature—in substances where they are bound tightly by physical or chemical forces, than it does in others. The amount required to raise the temperature of a given substance one degree, as compared with the amount required for the same mass of water, is called the **Specific Heat** (**1596**) of the substance.

C. Latent Heat. A parallel to specific heat is **Latent Heat**, or the heat absorbed in changing the physical state of a substance (**1391, 3084**), as in changing ice to water or water to steam. While a body is absorbing heat, in the course of fusion or evaporation, its temperature remains unaltered. When the change is reversed, as in changing water to ice, or condensing steam to water, the latent heat is *given out* by the changing substance.

D. Measurement of Heat. Since the quantity of heat, or amount of molecular motion in a substance, depends upon (1) its temperature,

(2) its mass, and (3) its specific heat, the unit of heat must contain these quantities. The commonest units are the **calorie** (1596), and the **British Thermal Unit** (1596) which is equivalent to 778 foot-pounds of work.

Note : Calorie, the unit of heat, must not be confused with " caloric," the name given to the imaginary substance (1593) which, in the 18th century, was supposed to be the actual source and medium of heat.

IV. EFFECTS OF HEAT ON MATTER.

A. Expansion. Since heating a body makes its molecules move more rapidly, they push each other farther apart, and the substance expands. The amount of expansion of a bar of unit length when its temperature is raised one degree is called its **coefficient of thermal expansion.**

a. In Solids. Practically all solids expand at an approximately uniform rate as heat is applied, up to the point where they become liquid. The alloy invar (2543) is valuable because of its remarkably low coefficient of expansion. It is used for pendulum rods of clocks.

b. In Liquids. Most liquids (water being a notable exception) expand proportionately to temperature increase. Water, however, when near the freezing point, actually expands with a further *drop* in temperature (1680). Water reaches its greatest density at a temperature of 39·2° Fahrenheit (3351).

c. In Gases. All gases at normal temperature, irrespective of their chemical nature, have nearly the same coefficient of expansion, as explained under Pneumatics—Charles's Law, *see above.*

B. Change of Physical State. When sufficient heat is applied, matter changes state. That is,

because their particles are speeded up, solids become liquids and liquids become gases. Lowering of temperature reverses the process. The change is also affected by pressure alterations. *See above* under Pneumatics. *See* Freezing (1391) ; Evaporation (1243).

a. Change from Solid to Liquid. Melting points are the temperatures at which the change from solid to liquid takes place. Melting points are also the " freezing points " at which cooling liquids become solids.

b. Change from Liquid to Gas. This change is accomplished by : (1) Evaporation, (2) Boiling or Ebullition, and (3) Explosion. In **Evaporation** (1243), molecules shoot off from the surface of the liquid into surrounding space, thus transforming the liquid gradually into vapour. **Boiling** is violent evaporation that takes place not only on the surface but within the liquid, giving rise to bubbles of vapour (*see* Distillation, **1019** ; Steam, **3084**). **Explosion** is a change so violent that the liquid " bursts," so to speak, into gas all at once. The reverse process, by which gas is transformed into liquid, is called **Condensation,** discussed under Dew (**1000**) and Steam (**3084**).

c. Change from Solid to Gas. This process, with the intermediate liquid stage omitted, is called sublimation, and is comparatively rare (e.g. Camphor, **674**). The reverse process is an extremely rapid condensation.

C. Transmission of Heat. Heat is transferred by Conduction, Convection, and Radiation, as explained on page 1595.

D. Machines for Transforming Heat into Work. The chief devices for doing this are Steam Engines (**3085**), centred upon the Boiler (**488**) ; and Internal Combustion Engines (**1735**). The heat pump (**1600**) is a specialized form.

Sound and Its Principles

I. NATURE OF SOUND.

Sound (3009) is produced by a vibrating object ; and is carried by longitudinal or " compression and rarefaction " waves in elastic matter (e.g. air). Sound vibrations set up in a solid substance travel through that substance and generate air waves which are receivable by the ear and are interpreted by the brain as noise, or musical sounds, or speech (3010).

II. VELOCITY OF SOUND.

A. General Law of Velocity. In any medium the velocity varies directly as the square root of the elasticity and inversely as the square root of the density of the medium.

B. Some Figures for Sound Velocity. The velocity in air is about 350 metres per second. Liquids, though denser than gases, are still more elastic, and therefore convey sound more rapidly (about 1,500 metres per second is the rate in water). Elastic solids are best of all and about 5,000 metres a second is the velocity in iron. Temperature affects the velocity ; and at 0° Centigrade the velocity through air is 331 metres. For every degree C. by which the temperature rises, the velocity increases by 60 centimetres per second (3010).

III. REFLECTION OF SOUND.

Sound waves impinging upon a cloud mass, or upon a body of air of greater density than that of the air near by, cause reflections which magnify the sharp " crack " of a lightning flash into the familiar rumble of thunder. When a brass band is marching along a street at right angles to the street in which we are standing, although we cannot see the players, the sound they make reaches us by reflection from the walls of the houses at the angle of the streets. Gunfire is reflected from walls, cliff faces and similar solid surfaces. According to the distance between the originating sound-source and the obstacle which reflects the noise, we hear echoes (1077), more or less sharply defined, and at a longer or shorter time-interval. The relation between the wavelength of the sound on the one hand, and the distance on the other, governs the nature of the echo.

IV. REFRACTION OF SOUND.

Sound is bent or refracted whenever it passes obliquely from one medium into another, in which its velocity is different. Varying air currents in the atmosphere, and the varying density of air masses due to pressure differences, refract sound sometimes we hear the noise made by an aircraft clearly, while at other times the noise may be hardly perceptible.

V. DISTINCTION BETWEEN "MUSICAL" NOTES AND NOISES.

If the pulses of a sound wave are regular, they produce an effect upon the ear which we call a " note." If the pulses of the wave are irregular, a noise results. **Loudness, pitch,** and **quality** of sounds (3010). The range of sound frequencies audible to Man (3011). Singing is the production by the vocal organs of " musical " notes—i.e. notes of which the vibrations are in a definite mathematical relation to one another (3328).

VI. PROPERTIES OF NOTES.

A. **Pitch.** By Pitch is meant the relative " highness " or " lowness " of a sound. The pitch of a note depends upon the **frequency** rate of vibration.

B. **Intensity.** The intensity, or " energy of motion " of the waves governs the loudness of a sound ; also the extent to which the waves are checked, broken up or absorbed in passing through intervening mediums (3010). Intensity depends upon : (1) The power of the original pulse, (2) the distance from the source of sound, and (3) the density of the transmitting medium. A pistol shot produces a feeble sound in the rarefied air of a high mountain top.

C. **Quality.** That quality which distinguishes, for example, a note played on a violin from the same note played on a flute depends upon intensity and frequency ; and upon the **overtones** and **harmonics** and their relation to the **fundamental** frequency.

D. **Effect of Motion on Pitch.** When the source of sound is approaching rapidly, the pitch rises ; when the source recedes, the pitch falls. This is known as the **Doppler Effect.**

VII. PRODUCTION OF NOTES.

A. **In Strings.**
   a. **Effect of Length.** Tension and diameter being constant, the frequency (which determines pitch) varies inversely as the length ("the shorter the string, the higher the note ").
   b. **Effect of Tension.** Length and diameter being constant, the frequency varies inversely as the square root of the tension (" the tauter the string, the higher the note ").
   c. **Effect of Mass.** Length and tension being constant, the frequency varies inversely as the square root of the mass of a unit length (" the thinner the string, the higher the note "). Mass is determined by the material and the diameter of the string.
   d. **Tuning.** Since in a stringed instrument such as a pianoforte the length, material, and size of each string are fixed, tuning is accomplished by varying the tension. But in the violin family, although the strings are tuned to an " open " string note, the performer varies the note by " stopping " the open string at longer or shorter lengths (*see* **a**, *above*).

B. **In Enclosed Columns of Air.** In wind instruments (1643, **3009**, *3010*) the pipe or tube acts as a resonator for vibrations produced in the air blown into them.
   a. **Effect of Length.** Frequency, and therefore pitch, varies inversely as the length of the vibrating air column. Thus, doubling the length gives a tone an octave lower. "Stops " enable the player to vary the length of the vibrating column, and therefore the pitch of the note.
   b. **Open and Closed Pipes.** An open pipe gives a tone an octave higher than a closed pipe of the same length. Stated in another way, to produce any given fundamental pitch, the closed pipe need be only half as long as the open pipe.
   c. **Voice.** The human vocal organs are a type of reed instrument in which the vocal cords of the larynx (3327) are the reeds.

VIII. COMBINED NOTES.

A. **Forced Vibrations.** When a strongly vibrating body is pressed against another, the second is forced to vibrate, too, regardless of what its natural frequency might be. Such a vibration is a **forced vibration.** Stringed instruments use forced vibrations of sounding bodies to amplify the sound produced by the strings themselves. The sounding board of the piano and the wooden shells of the guitar, violin, and mandolin are examples.

B. **Sympathetic Vibrations.** Forced vibrations are produced by strong external force. A slight force, however, is quite enough to set in vibration an agent which is naturally capable of vibrating with the same frequency. Even slight air pulses, carrying a tone of the proper frequency, or even a strong overtone, are enough. These are termed **sympathetic vibrations.**

C. **Resonance.** When one vibrating body sets another in sympathetic motion, the second emits pulses which in turn help the first. Such a " building up " is called **resonance.**

D. **Interference.** Two waves with the same characteristics " cancel " each other if they are " out of step," i.e., when the crest of one wave coincides with the trough of the other. Such a " cancellation " is called interference. " Soundless zones " are produced accidentally where reflected sound from a fog signal interferes with the direct sound from the signal. (Study of the similar phenomena of the interference of light— *see* page 1941—is helpful here.)

E. **Beats.** If two instruments are sounding nearly but not quite the same note, we get alternate resonance and interference. At first the waves reinforce each other, and we have resonance ; then the vibrations of the lower-pitched instrument lag until they are half a vibration behind, whereupon the vibrations oppose each other and we have interference. When the " lag " amounts to a full vibration we have resonance again— and so on. This alternate resonance and interference produces a vibration—known as one with the " beat frequency "—having a frequency equal to the *difference* between those of the two originating notes. This is explained in page 3394, where the application of the principle to heterodyne wireless transmission and reception is described.

F. Musical Intervals and Scales (2262). Notes whose frequencies bear simple ratios to each other are pleasing to us when played in various combinations.

a. Musical Intervals. The simpler musical combinations of notes are called Octaves, Thirds, Fifths, etc. When a note has twice the frequency of another, it is said to be an octave above the other. When they are in the ratio of two to three, the interval is a fifth (C to the next higher G). A ratio of 3 to 4 gives a fourth (G to C above) ; one of 4 to 5, a major third (C to E) ; one of 5 to 6, a minor third (E to G) ; and one of 24 : 25, a chromatic semitone. When one note is sounded after another, they form an interval ; when sounded together, a chord. A combination of three notes with frequency ratios of 4, 5, and 6 is termed a major chord and sounds very pleasing to the ear. There are three major chords, C, E, G ; F, A, C ; G, B, D ; a fact which probably played an important part in fixing the scale.

b. The Diatonic Scale. If between the two notes of an octave we insert a selection of notes with simple intermediate rates of vibration, we have a pleasing succession of tones known as a scale. In the major diatonic scale, the notes, beginning with C for the lower end of the octave, are as follows, the vibration ratio of each note to the one next above it being given in parentheses : C (vibration ratio with D, 8 to 9) ; D (ratio with E, 9 to 10) ; E (ratio with F, 15 to 16) ; F (ratio with G, 8 to 9) ; G (ratio with A, 9 to 10) ; A (ratio with B, 8 to 9) ; B (ratio with upper C, 15 to 16). Each of these intervals has one of three values : 8 to 9, called a major tone ; 9 to 10, a minor tone ; 15 to 16, a major semitone. The C upon which the scale begins is called the fundamental of the scale, and the other notes are the second, third, etc., up to the next C, which is the eighth, or octave. A sharp is a chromatic semitone above the note, and a flat is a tone lowered by a chromatic semitone. Chromatic semitones may be inserted between all tones of the scale except the two " major semitone " intervals (E to F and B to C).

c. The Tempered Scale. If the diatonic scale were to be used on pianos and other musical instruments it would be possible to play music only in one key. Hence instruments are not tuned to this scale, but to an equally tempered scale which is only a compromise. The frequencies of the notes in the tempered scale are in the ratios :

C	D	E	F	G	A	B	C
1	$2^{\frac{2}{12}}$	$2^{\frac{4}{12}}$	$2^{\frac{5}{12}}$	$2^{\frac{7}{12}}$	$2^{\frac{9}{12}}$	$2^{\frac{11}{12}}$	2

IX. SOUND RECORDING AND REPRODUCTION, 3011.

Light and Its Principles

I. NATURE AND PROPAGATION OF LIGHT.

A. Theories of Light Propagation. Newton's corpuscular theory (1941). Huyghens and a wave theory (1941). 20th century wave theory, of propagation through a " luminiferous ether." Measurement of light velocity (1939). Attempts to demonstrate existence of the ether (1227).

a. Wave theory fails to explain some observed phenomena of light propagation. The quantum theory (2711) and " wave mechanics." Effect of Einstein's relativity theory upon our ideas of the nature of light (2730, 2762).

b. Recent theory proposes that light may be regarded as a stream of particles (harking back somewhat to Newton's corpuscular theory), but that such particle streams may have associated with them certain wave-like properties (2711).

c. Photo-electric effects (1943, 2574). Photo-chemical effects (2574). Phosphorescence and luminescence (2573).

d. Light waves are electro-magnetic waves, occupying only a small portion of the complete electro-magnetic spectrum (1942, 2729, f.p. 3056, 3057).

B. Luminous and Non-Luminous Bodies. Luminous bodies are those like the sun, which have sufficient energy in their natural state to emit light. Other bodies are naturally non-luminous and are distinguished, with reference to their behaviour toward light, by one of the following three properties :

a. Transparency. Substances like air, water, and glass let the light pass through so freely that we can see through them objects placed on the other side of them. Such bodies are transparent.

b. Translucency. Substances like horn, ground glass, fine porcelain, and paper, transmit light, but not clearly enough to permit objects on the other side of them to be seen distinctly. Such bodies are translucent.

c. Opacity. Substances like wood, stone, and cold metal block the passage of light. Such bodies are opaque.

C. Velocity. The velocity of light and its measurements are described on page 1939.

D. The Path of Light. In all ordinary light phenomena, such as casting shadows, behaviour in lenses, etc., light seems to travel outward from its source in straight lines. It was this fact that led Newton to accept the corpuscular theory (1945), which was displaced by the wave theory later. As explained under " Theories of Light Propagation " above, scientists today envisage light as being propagated by particles in streams which have certain wave-like characteristics but the pure wave theory serves to explain many light phenomena. When we use the term " ray " we mean a line perpendicular to the wave front at the point considered—that is, a radius prolonged. When we say that a " ray " is bent, we really mean that the geometric centre of the wave-front has shifted. (See diagrams in page 1940).

E. Intensity of Light. The intensity of light depends upon the energy of the disturbance creating it. This disturbance spreads out in al directions, so at any given distance the energy may be regarded as distributed round the surface of a sphere whose radius is the distance. In order to compare intensity at different distances, we must therefore compare these surfaces. Since the surfaces of spheres are to each other as the squares of their radii, we get the rule : **The intensity of illumination from a given source varies as the square of the distance from the source.**

F. **Standard Unit of Illumination or Candlepower.** The illuminating power of a candle made of spermaceti weighing one-sixth of a pound and burning at the rate of 120 grains an hour was the standard source of light used in computing illumination (691). A " foot-candle " was the intensity of illumination given on a cardboard screen at one foot distance from a standard candle. The **international standard candle** is the present unit (renamed the " **new candle** " in 1948), measured with reference to special electric filament lamps. The science of measuring the intensity of illumination is called **Photometry.** Units of illumination are the *lumen,* the *lux* and the *phot* (*f-i.*).

II. REFLECTION OF LIGHT.

A. Laws of Reflection, *1940*, 2191. The manner in which light is reflected is described by the following laws :
  a. The angles of Incidence and Reflection are equal.
  b. The Incident and the Reflected Rays lie in one plane perpendicular to the reflecting surface.
  c. The Incident and Reflected Rays lie on opposite sides of the normal through their point of intersection.
B. Mirrors, 1940, **2190** : Behaviour of plane and curved mirrors (2191). The mirror as an optical device (2191).

III. REFRACTION OF LIGHT.

A. **Cause of Refraction, and Refractive Index.** In water, glass, and other " optically dense " substances, light moves at a velocity less than in air. Therefore a light wave entering water or glass obliquely from air is slowed down at the side which first enters the denser medium, and this " drag " changes the direction of the wave. The **Law of Refraction** is discussed in page 1940. The amount of refraction produced at the boundary surface of two media is called the **refractive index** for the media in question.
B. **Refraction, Partial Reflection, and Total Reflection.** In any case of refraction, only part of the light passes from one medium into another and is refracted ; the rest is reflected from the boundary surface. The portion reflected increases as the angle becomes more oblique, and at a certain value, called the **critical angle,** the

refracted ray lies along the boundary surface. At more oblique angles, all the light is reflected. We thus get **total internal reflection** (*1940*).
C. Lenses (**1924**) and Prisms, 1940, 2163, 2553.
D. **Spherical Aberration** and **Chromatic Aberration,** 2163.
E. The Lens of the Eye, 1252.

IV. DIFFRACTION AND INTERFERENCE.

Light waves, in passing through narrow openings or across the sharp edges of objects, are radiated out from the points of contact in paths which intersect the waves which have not been so disturbed. This is known as **diffraction** (1941). The diffracted waves alternately reinforce and counteract the undisturbed waves in such a way as to produce bands or zones of light and dark (*see* diagram, page 1941). This phenomenon is called **interference,** *1941.* The diffraction grating, a series of closely spaced lines on glass, is used in some types of spectrometer (*plate f. p.* 3057). The first such grating was made by Joseph Fraunhöfer. The interferometer (1941) (used to measure the wavelength of light waves) utilizes the phenomenon of interference.

V. PHENOMENA OF COLOUR.

The general nature of colour and its perception in objects are given in page **874.**
A. **Refraction of Coloured Light.** The amount of refraction (*see* " Refraction " *above*) caused in light depends upon its wavelength. Since difference in colour is due to difference in wavelength, it follows that in refraction **light of different colour will be refracted by a different amount.** This behaviour is the cause of **Rainbows (2741),** and is made use of in such instruments as the Spectroscope (3056, *f. p.* 3057). Longer waves are refracted less than shorter. Since red light has the longest wave, it is the least refracted.
B. **Chromatic Aberration,** 2163. Since light of different colours is refracted differently, it follows that a convex lens focuses light of each colour at a different point, the violet rays being focused nearest the lens, and the red farthest away. This behaviour is known as **chromatic aberration,** or colour aberration (1925), and is corrected by using compound or " achromatic " lenses, made of different types of glass with differing refractive indexes (1925, 2163).

VI. POLARIZED LIGHT.

The behaviour of Polarized Light, and some of its uses, are explained in page 1942.

VII. OTHER TYPES OF RADIATION.

X-rays, Gamma rays, Cosmic rays, Ultra-violet light, Infra-red rays, Radar and Wireless waves differ from light in their wavelengths (2729, *f. p.* 3057). The apparatus used and the peculiarities of each phenomenon are described in the articles on X-rays (**3430**), Radar (2726), Infra-red rays (**1722**), and Wireless (**3391**). The article on Radiation (**2728**) deals with them all.

Nuclear Physics

I. DEFINITION.

Nuclear physics is a general term describing the study of the structure, composition and behaviour of the nucleus of the atom, the invisible core of the physical universe. As explained in the article

on the Atom (294), an atom consists of a central nucleus surrounded by a number of **electrons (1137)** arranged in " shells " or orbits. The electrons are electrically *negative,* and the nucleus contains an equal and opposite *positive* charge. The number of electrons surrounding the nucleus gives us the **atomic number** (297, 1137) ; the latter may also be regarded as the number of units of positive charge on the nucleus.

II. STRUCTURE OF THE NUCLEUS.

A. **Protons, 296.** These are the positive electric charges in the nucleus. The number of protons defines an element's chemical properties, and gives its atomic number (297) ; it varies in different elements but is equal to the number of electrons.

B. **Neutrons, 297.** These are " neutral " particles, having no electric charge, and, with the protons, they make up the nucleus. The number of neutrons in a nucleus varies in different elements ; added to the number of protons it gives the **atomic weight** (769) of an element.

C. **Protons plus Neutrons.** Added together, these constituents of a nucleus have fractionally *more* mass than the mass of the nucleus ; the additional mass is believed to be the force that holds the atom (and the universe) together. Though *mass* and *weight* are not the same thing, we may say in simple language that the nucleus weighs a tiny amount *less* than do the neutrons and protons added together.

D. **Isotopes, 1760.** The element may have several forms that are chemically the same, since they have the same number of protons in their nuclei ; but these forms have different atomic weights because the number of neutrons are different. These forms of the same element are called isotopes (296, 769, **1760**).

E. **Positrons.** In 1933 Carl D. Anderson (U.S.A.) discovered evidence of a new kind of particle while investigating cloud-chamber photographs of cosmic rays. This particle, which Anderson named a **positron** (297), appeared to be an electron having a *positive* charge instead of a negative charge. Other experiments showed that positrons could be made artificially in the disintegration of elements. The life of the positron is probably very brief.

F. **Theories of Nuclear Energy.**
    a. Equivalence of Mass and Energy : a theory framed by Einstein, 297, **1122.**
    b. The Quantum Theory, **2711.**

III. NUCLEAR FISSION.

A. **Radio-activity, 2731.** In naturally occurring radio-active elements, e.g. Radium (**2731**), the nucleus breaks up of its own accord and the atom changes its chemical nature, becoming in course of time another element (*2732*). In doing so it gives off alpha, beta and gamma rays (2731).

B. **Transmutation, 296, 2733.** It is possible to change one element into another by bombarding its nuclei with atomic particles ; it is similarly possible to render radio-active a non-radio-active element.

C. **" Splitting the Atom."** This process is today carried out by such machines as the Cyclotron (**950**) and Betatron (**422**), which enable an atom to be bombarded with atomic particles having enormous velocity ; these " bullets " knock particles out of the bombarded atom, and such particles in turn may split a neighbouring atom, the process continuing in a " chain reaction " that can produce a tremendous explosion of energy (297).

D. **The Atomic Bomb, 299.** An " explosion " resulting from the chain reaction in pieces of radio-active elements (e.g. Plutonium, 778 ; Uranium, 3297), which have been made more than normally unstable by " bombardment." (The " new " elements neptunium and plutonium were produced by bombarding uranium).

E. **The " Pile."** This is a carefully shielded structure in which experiments in nuclear fission are carried out. To prevent unwanted " explosions," the bombarding particles can be slowed down by passing them through heavy water (998), or some of them can be captured in rods of graphite, boron, etc. In the pile, new " artificial " elements are created ; also common elements can be made radio-active for use as "tracers " in medical and biochemical study (1761, 2733).

F. **Instruments.** For the detection and counting of atomic particles and radio-active emanations two interesting instruments have been invented —the **Geiger-Müller counter** and the **Wilson cloud chamber,** both based on the phenomenon of the ionization of gases by atomic particle (1739).

Electricity and Magnetism

I. NATURE OF ELECTRICITY.

The electric current is a flow of **electrons** (1137) from a negatively charged source to a positive body. Owing to the earlier use of the convention of the " one-fluid " theory (1128), practical electrical science is based on the rule that an electric current flows from positive to negative. This apparent contradiction is retained for reasons of practical convenience. Electricity, we say, flows from a point of **high potential** towards a point of **low potential** (1129)—that is, from positive to negative (+ to −)—in accordance with this convention.

II. PROPERTIES OF ELECTRIC CHARGES.

A. **Static Electricity, or Electricity at Rest.** Strictly speaking, electricity is not " produced " or " generated," but is the result of converting some other kind of energy (e.g. heat, chemical energy, energy of moving water) into electrical energy. " Static " charges can be produced by friction (e.g. by rubbing a stick of sealing wax with a piece of dry flannel) ; a *negative* charge then appears on the sealing wax (1127) but, as we cannot produce a charge of one " sign " without also creating a charge of opposite sign, an equal *positive* charge appears on the flannel, though this is soon dissipated. Rubbing a glass rod with a piece of silk usually endows the rod with a positive charge. Free electrons travel readily in certain classes of substances, particularly the metals ; these substances are called conductors. It is difficult to create charges by rubbing two conductors together, because the charges leak away. Frictional charges are best created upon non-conducting substances, known as insulators. These terms are relative ; it is best to regard an insulator as a substance having very poor conducting powers.

B. **Attraction, Repulsion, and Polarity.** The mutual behaviour of electric charges is summed up in the simple rule, " like attracts unlike, and repels like " (1131). The sign of a charge (+ or -) is its **polarity**.

C. **Induction across Space.** A charged body upsets the balance between positive and negative charges in neighbouring bodies. A positively charged body placed close to the end of an insulated rod will attract electrons to the nearer end of the rod, leaving a negative charge at the other end (*1131*). When the inducing positively charged body is removed, these effects disappear.

D. **Potential.** The **potential** (really potential energy) of an electric charge is the pressure, or attractive power, tending to pull separated charges of opposite signs together. When two charged bodies each having a potential of the same sign are connected, the body of greater potential will drive part of its charge to the other, until the two are equalized. The " driving pressure " or **electromotive force (E.M.F.)** moving the charge is the **potential difference (P.D.)** between the areas. If the potentials are of opposite sign, the E.M.F. is the sum of the potentials. The strength of a static charge may be measured by an electroscope (*1133*).

E. **Electrostatic Capacity.** A considerable number of free electrons may be accommodated between the molecules of some substances, without any great upset in the potential of the substance. In other substances, the addition of a few electrons produces a marked change in potential. This relation between the amount of charge— that is, the quantity of electrons absorbed—and the resulting change in potential is called the capacity of the substance (1132).

F. **Condensers.** If an insulated body, such as a metal plate, be charged and another plate which is connected to the earth be brought near it, the capacity of the first plate for holding electricity is increased. Such a device, which may consist of many plates separated by insulators, is called a condenser (1132), and is used in many practical ways, where it is desired to accumulate electric charges.

a. **Effect of Intervening Insulator or Dielectric.** Experiments show that the potential caused by the presence of the charges occurs in the surfaces of the intervening insulator or **dielectric**. When the strain becomes more than the dielectric can bear, a spark passes, and the charges unite. The capacity of a condenser, therefore, depends upon the ability of the dielectric to withstand electric stress.

b. **Leyden Jars.** The oldest known form of condenser is the Leyden jar (1929). Such jars were used in the early days of wireless transmission (3392).

II. MOVING CHARGES—ELECTRIC CURRENTS.

A. **Nature.** An electric current is a flow of electrons through a conductor. Such a flow is set up by discharging a condenser, but is over almost instantly. In order to have a steady current,

we must have some means for creating a charge, or potential difference, as rapidly as the flowing electrons carry the charge away. Such a current can be produced by **electro-chemical** means ; the dissolving of a metal electrode by an electrolyte in a battery (**375**) ; or by an **electro-thermal** process, in which heat energy is transformed (e.g. a thermocouple ; the junction of two dissimilar metals is heated, 1132) ; or by **electro-magnetic induction**—most important practical means, as in the dynamo (**1060**). The dynamo may be driven by a prime mover such as a steam engine or an internal combustion engine ; or even by a machine which is rotated by pedals operated as in the bicycle (emergency generating appliance, as used in military operations when no other source of mechanical power is available). Water power may be used to drive water turbines (**hydro-electric installations, 1669**), and so to rotate dynamos or alternators.

B. **Creation of Currents by Chemical Means.** The first and simplest means of creating a galvanic current is by the chemical energy of a so-called **voltaic cell** (**376**).

a. **Voltaic Cells.** A familiar example is the Leclanché cell (**375**). The electrodes here are a zinc rod or cylinder, and a carbon rod ; the electrolyte is a solution of ammonium chloride. The Leclanché is the common " wet cell." In the common " dry cell " a moist packing is substituted for the watery solution. In other types of cell the electrodes may be two metal rods or plates (e.g. **Daniell cell**, zinc and copper), with sulphuric acid as the electrolyte.

b. **Storage Cells, or " Accumulators."** These depend upon the alteration in chemical composition of the metallic " plates " when the cell is slowly charged from a source of electric current ; after charging, and upon connexion to an external circuit, the chemical process reverses, and chemical energy is then transformed into electric energy. In the **lead-acid accumulator** (**377**) the plates are grids of lead, filled with a paste of red lead (positive plate) or litharge (negative plate) ; the electrolyte is sulphuric acid diluted with water. In another type (**nickel-iron cell**), the active materials are nickel oxide and iron oxide, with potassium hydroxide as the electrolyte.

c. **Polarization.** In the simple voltaic cell, the chemical action gradually accumulates hydrogen upon the carbon plate. When a certain amount has accumulated, it blocks further action, and current output ceases. This blocking is known as polarization, and is avoided by using chemicals, such as manganese dioxide, to remove the hydrogen (*376*).

C. **Creation of Currents by Irradiation.** The thermocouple (*see* **A**, *above*) may be heated by the radiation from a hot body, and the electric current so produced can be measured with a delicate instrument in order to determine the amount of radiation. Another method (2575) of producing electricity is to allow light to fall upon a photosensitive substance (e.g. iron coated with a selenium compound, in contact with a thin film of silver). Only a tiny current is thus produced. The main types of photo-electric cells are those in which the shining of a light upon the sensitive surface lessens electrical resistance (e.g. selenium), or acts as a " valve " in causing an electron flow from the sensitive surface in proportion to the amount of illumination (e.g. photocell sensitized with caesium and silver).

D. **Creation of Currents by Mechanical Means.** Usually when traced back these devices depend upon heat engines. But the hydro-electric generator and pedal-operated machines mentioned under A, above, are purely mechanical devices.

E. **Creation of Currents by Contraction and Expansion of Crystals.** This phenomenon is known as Piezo-electricity (**2604**).

IV. LAWS OF ' DIRECT ' CURRENTS.

A. **Direct and Alternating Currents (1130).** A current may flow steadily in one direction, as it does from a voltaic cell, or as it is delivered from the commutator of a dynamo (*1061*). Or it may reverse direction periodically—many times per second, as in the case of current delivered by an alternator ; a given point will then be negative at one instant, and negative at another instant (1130). The first type is a dire**c**t current (D.C.) and the second is an alternating current (A.C.). Since alternating currents are created by electro-magnetic induction, we shall discuss direct currents only at this point.

B. **Attributes of a Direct Current.** The characteristics of a direct current are determined by the following elements : the **quantity** of current (symbol I), measured in **amperes** ; the **pressure** which drives the current (symbol E), measured in **volts** ; and the **resistance** which the current encounters (symbol R), measured in **ohms**. The **pressure** is the " potential difference " between the terminals of the generating unit supplying the current. It is usually called the **electromotive force (E.M.F.).** The **power** of the current depends upon both the quantity of current and the pressure under which it flows, and the product of the voltage and the current. **Power** is measured in **watts** (1128).

C. **Ohm's Law.** The relation between potential, current, and resistance is expressed by Ohm's Law (1128), which states that the current in a circuit is equal to the voltage (V) divided by the resistance (R). Thus $I = \dfrac{V}{R}$.

D. **Divided Currents.** When a current passes through one element after another in a circuit—as when it passes through a number of lamps (*1129*)—the elements are said to be connected **in series.** When branches divide the circuit and send a part of the current through each element, the elements are said to be connected **in parallel** (*1129*).

E. **Measurement of Current (1133).** Electric currents are measured by means of instruments of various kinds and types. Resistance is measured by **Ohmeters.** Those which measure amperes are called **Ammeters**, and those which measure volts are called **Voltmeters.**

V. MAGNETISM : NATURAL MAGNETS.

The theory of magnetic " domains " explains **the** properties of magnets as being due to the symmetric arrangement of " molecular " magnets within the body.

A. **Polarity.** The " north-and-south-pole " phenomenon in magnets is explained in page 2060 and in the article on the Compass (**881**). The magnetized needle of a compass, placed at any point in the earth's magnetic field, aligns itself with that field to point towards the magnetic pole (*2061*). The article on the Compass also explains what is meant by **magnetic deviation**, and by **variation.**

B. **Magnetic Dip.** A Magnetic needle so mounted as to be able to move freely in all directions will be found, if observed anywhere but on the magnetic equator or " aclinic " line, to dip at one end. The angle which it makes with the horizontal is called the **inclination** or **magnetic dip.**

C. **Magnetic Substances and Magnetic Penetration.** Substances which can be magnetized either temporarily or permanently are said to be magnetic. The important ones besides iron and steel are other ferrous metals, such as nickel and cobalt and certain alloys. Magnetic force acts freely through all non-magnetic substances (*2062*), but is " screened " by sheets of magnetic substances. Substances only weakly magnetic are said to be **para-magnetic** ; substances which are anti-magnetic and which cause the lines of force to diverge are said to be **dia-magnetic** (*2062*).

D. **Lines and Fields of Magnetic Force.** Magnetic flux seems to act along lines called **lines of force** (*2060*), flowing out from the north pole and into the south pole. These lines can be demonstrated by placing a glass plate or a stiff paper over a magnet and dusting iron filings upon it. The filings arrange themselves along the " lines." A **magnetic field** is the complete group or pattern of lines depicting magnetic conditions.

E. **Natural and Artificial Magnets.** Pieces of magnetic iron ore, or of natural magnetic iron known as **lodestones** (2060, 2062) were known to the ancients as having the power of attracting iron. Later, lodestones were used for compasses. By stroking a piece of ferrous metal with one pole of a bar magnet, the piece of metal is magnetized in turn, and acquires N. and S. polarity. Permanent magnets are made today, however, by placing a piece of suitable metal in the field of an electro-magnet (*see* following Section, VI).

VI. ELECTRO-MAGNETIC INDUCTION.

The fact that electricity and magnetism are related phenomena was discovered when Oersted found that an electric current had magnetic effects (*1132, 2063*), and Faraday (**1260**) found that a magnetic field generated electric current (1060).

A. **Magnetic Field of a Current.** When direct electric current passes through a wire, a magnetic field is created. In any plane cutting squarely across a straight wire, the lines of force are formed as concentric circles with the wire as centre (*2063*). If a wire carrying a current is bent into a loop, all the lines of force enter the loop at one face and come out at the other face.

If several loops are put together to form a coil, practically all the lines of force will pass around the outside and through the centre of the coil, as if it were a single wire (*2063*). If an iron core be placed within the loops of the coil, the power is greatly increased, and the device is known as an electro-magnet (2063). The strength of an electro-magnet depends upon the ampere-turns, i.e. the strength of the current and the number of loops or turns of wire which form the coil.

B. Induction of Current by a Magnetic Field. Faraday found that when lines of magnetic force move across a conductor, or when a conductor moves across lines of magnetic force, a current is set up or " induced " in the conductor. It is this discovery which makes it possible to turn mechanical energy into electrical energy by the dynamo (1060).

C. Character of Induced Currents. Current is induced as described above only when the conductor is moving in the magnetic field ; and the strength of the induced E.M.F. varies directly as the speed of the moving conductor. If it is the magnetic field which moves and the conductor which remains stationary, the effect is the same. Any induced current has such a direction that the magnetic action it sets up after it starts tends to resist or oppose the motion which produces it.

D. Currents Induced by Other Currents. A change may be produced in the field of an electro-magnet by altering the intensity of the current which flows through it and produces the field. Thus if the coil of the magnet be fed with direct current rapidly interrupted, we get such a flow of current rapidly varying in intensity at each " make " and " break " of the circuit (1720), though not reversing in direction. If the current be rapidly turned on and off in this manner it will set up an induced current in any conductor which lies across the lines of force. It is upon this principle that the induction coil (1720) operates.

Books for the Student of Physics

Everyday Physics. H. E. Hadley.
Class Book of Physics. Sir Richard Gregory and H. E. Hadley.
Text-Book of Physics. J. Duncan and S. G. Starling.
Practical Physics. R. A. Millikan and H. G. Gale.
Matter, Energy and Radiation. J. R. Dunning and H. C. Paxton.

CHEMISTRY

I. CHEMICAL VIEW OF MATTER.

Chemistry is the study of the composition of matter ; and of the behaviour of different substances when mixed. By analysis, natural substances are taken apart to learn of what these substances are composed. By synthesis, chemists recombine the parts into other substances, or into purer forms of the original substances (760). Chemistry is thus concerned with the kinds of matter, and with changes in the composition of matter.

A. Pure Substances. All specimens of pure iron show the same set of general properties—grey colour, hardness, etc. Pure zinc, again, shows a characteristic set of qualities. We can also buy " commercial " zinc, which answers for some experiments, and does quite well ; but being of insufficient purity for fine and accurate experiments, we must sometimes use the pure substance instead. Metallic iron and zinc are " elementary substances," or chemical elements. (*See* the Periodic Table, in page 768).

a. Physical State. A substance may be either solid, liquid, or gaseous, according to its temperature.

b. Crystalline Substances and Amorphous Substances, 1190 ; If the particles of a solid substance have a definite geometrical form, the substance is crystalline. If the particles show no definite form, the substance is amorphous (meaning " without form "). A picture in page 770 shows lampblack, an amorphous form of carbon, alongside diamond and graphite, crystalline forms of the same element, carbon. All three are allotropes of the same substance.

B. Mixtures, 767. It is possible to mix substances and produce mixtures of fairly definite properties. The component substances do not lose their identity and may be recovered by mechanical means from the mixture. A mixture of iron with sulphur is an example. The ingredients of a mixture are called components because they are simply placed together without change, and can be separated without change. Elements and compounds occur naturally as mixtures (e.g. air, soil, mineral ores, water, body fluids). Examples of artificial mixtures are beverages, paints, inks, and most of the pharmacist's prescriptions (767).

C. Solutions. Many substances, such as iron in the form of filings, can be shaken up in liquid substances, such as water, without undergoing immediate change. Other substances, such as salt, when mixed with water, promptly disappear or dissolve. They are recoverable, however, apparently unchanged, by physical means, such as evaporation. When a solid disappears in a liquid, but without apparent change of its inherent properties, it is said to be in solution. The substance so dissolved is called the solute, and the liquid is called the solvent. The two together are known as the solution. If particles of a finely divided substance be shaken up in a liquid, but gradually settle down, the mixture is not a solution but a mere suspension. In a solution, the dissolved substance remains invisible and in solution. The " magnetic " theory of varying solubility is described in page 773. Water dipoles and polar compounds. Oils and similar liquids which are non-polar. Colloids, natural and artificial (773, 871).

D. Chemical Change. While iron filings will disappear in time when placed in aerated water, they do not dissolve, as salt does. They change to iron-rust (2586), a substance entirely different from iron. The change is not a mere mixture; it is not a solution; it is a **genuine transformation of substance.**

Formation of Compounds. Suppose we examine this rusting more closely by moistening the interior of a glass tube closed at one end, sprinkling some powdered iron upon the interior surface, and setting the tube mouth downwards in a dish of water. As the moist iron slowly rusts, the water pushes farther up into the tube. Evidently part of the air has been absorbed and the water has been forced up to take its place. Apparently, then, this lost air or some part of it has **combined** with the iron to make rust. Portions of two substances have **reacted**, and in their places **we have a new substance.** Such a union, in which the constituent substances have lost their identity, is called a **compound.** This is an example of **oxidation** (2586). Oxygen from the atmosphere, in the presence of water, combines with the iron to form the compound we call rust, an oxide of iron.

E. The Field of Chemistry. The examination of such transformations in substance and the conditions under which they occur, constitutes a large part of the field of chemistry. Formerly a sharp distinction used to be made on the one hand between the chemistry of **inorganic** substances, such as salt, soda and sulphuric acid, derived from mineral substances, and on the other hand the **organic** substances such as sugars, fats and proteins, produced by plants and animals. At that time it was thought that all organic substances resulted from some power of chemical synthesis possessed only by living beings. Later it was proved that no such fundamental distinction between inorganic and organic substances existed. Many thousands of organic substances are synthesized in the chemical laboratory or manufactured by industrial chemists.

Since all organic substances (whether natural or artificial) contain carbon as an essential part of their structure, the division "organic chemistry" has survived as a name for the chemistry of the **carbon compounds** (699, 774).

Other departments of chemistry are **biochemistry (429)**; **agricultural chemistry,** with subdivisions such as soil chemistry; **pharmaceutical chemistry,** concerned with drugs and medicines; **metallurgical chemistry**; and **physical chemistry,** where chemists and physicists work in close association on research and practice. **Industrial chemistry** includes the work of chemists in all our important industries, from building to the making of plastics.

II. ELEMENTS.

Countless experiments in the past and present have broken up many substances into constituent substances, and combined many substances to form others. In all purely chemical experiments, however, certain substances, such as Iron, Copper, and Sulphur, stand out as unbreakable. They can be combined with other substances, but they can never be broken up chemically, into other substances. Any substance which appears to be chemically irreducible is called an **element** (768, 775).

Note: Transmutation of one element into another does occur, however, in nature in radioactive substances, and can be made to occur in other substances by physical means. *See* Outline on Nuclear Physics, 3679.

III. COMBINATION OF ELEMENTS TO FORM COMPOUNDS.

A. Law of Constant Proportions (or constant combining weights). When iron rusts, there is the same percentage of iron and oxygen in the rust, no matter where the metal rusted. Wherever common salt is mined, it contains the same percentage of sodium and chlorine. The law at the beginning of this paragraph runs thus: The composition of a pure compound never varies; its elements are present in a **definite proportion by weight** (767). This law has had to be modified by the discovery of **isotopes**: for many elements there exist atoms of different weight (296, 767, 769, **1760**). Though identical in chemical properties, isotopes of the same element have differing atomic weights.

B. Law of Multiple Proportions. Experiments with the various compounds of an element show that while an element may have different combining weights in different compounds, the **higher combining weights are always multiples of the lowest one obtained.** This is the *Law of multiple proportions*, enunciated by Dalton. It may be stated simply thus: Combinations between atoms take place in simple ratios of whole numbers.

C. The Atomic Theory. From these various phenomena, chemists began to build up the atomic theory. This theory says that any given element is composed of minute particles, which are called **atoms** (294). If, then, we suppose that compounds are formed by union between the atoms of the elements concerned, the laws of "constant proportions" and of "multiple proportions" become clear. If, for example, two elements combine atom for atom, it does not matter what quantities of the two elements be used; the total mass of each element entering into the compound will be in the same ratio as the masses of the two kinds of particles. If the combining mass of an element in one compound is twice as in another compound, we need only say that two atoms of the element have entered into one compound while only one atom entered into the other.

a. **Molecules** (769). When atoms of two or more different elements unite to form a compound, the smallest possible particle of this compound is called a **molecule.**

b. **Atom Structure.** As explained in the articles on the Atom (294) and the Electron (1137), the atoms of elements are not indivisible as formerly supposed, but consist of a nucleus containing **protons** and **neutrons,** surrounded by **electrons** and other particles. The atomic structure theories of Niels Bohr and of Lewis and Langmuir are illustrated diagrammatically in page **295**.

D. Atomic Weights. If we assign an arbitrary number to express the weight of one atom of an element, we can express the comparative weight of an atom of any other element in terms of the element chosen as a standard. Such a method gives us the so-called **atomic weights** of the elements. Formerly chemists used the lightest element, the gas **Hydrogen**, with a value of **1**, as the standard. But an atom of **oxygen** was found to weigh 15·88 times as much as a hydrogen atom. However, the hydrogen-oxygen ratio is taken as 1 to 16 in general discussions. On this basis, with the oxygen atom taken as the unit, the atomic weight of hydrogen is 1·008 (295). The atomic weights of the known elements are given on page 768, and in the Fact-Index under each element. A list and brief description of the elements is printed in pages 775–78.

E. Molecular Weights. Taking the atomic weight of oxygen as 16, its molecular weight is 32, owing to the fact that two atoms of oxygen combine to form one molecule. Three atoms of oxygen can be made to combine forming a compound known as Ozone, with a molecular weight of 48. In other words, **the molecular weight of a compound is the sum of the atomic weights of the constituent elements.**

F. Chemical Symbols for Elements and Compounds. In order to express chemical changes simply, chemists have devised an international " shorthand " system :

a. For Elements. Every element is assigned an initial, as **H** for hydrogen, **C** for carbon, etc. When two or more elements would have the same initial letters under this system, another letter is added to the initial to distinguish them, as **Ca** for calcium, **Cl** for chlorine. The symbol is frequently based on the Latin name, as **Fe** for iron (*ferrum*), and **Pb** for lead (*plumbum*), or on the name in some language of northern Europe (767). The symbols are chosen by international agreement and the same symbols are used throughout the world by chemists.

b. Formulae and Simple Equations. The composition of simple compounds can be stated by setting down the necessary symbols for the elements, and the result is a **formula**. For example, **Ferrous Sulphide** may be indicated by the symbols **FeS** (**Fe** for iron, and **S** for sulphur). Other rules for naming compounds are given in page 767. A mere mixture of iron and sulphur is shown by the plus sign, thus : **Fe+S**. When the mixture is fused into ferrous sulphide by heat, we indicate the direction of the change by an arrow, thus **Fe+S$\longrightarrow$FeS**. Such an array of symbols, showing a **reaction**, is called a **chemical equation**. When only a single atom of an element enters the reaction, the symbol for that element is given without qualification as (**Fe** or **S** in this case). But when more than one atom of an element is present in a compound, it is indicated by a small number placed at the lower right-hand corner of the symbol, as **H$_2$O**, meaning that **two** atoms of hydrogen have combined with **one** atom of oxygen. When more than one molecule is concerned in a reaction the number is put in front of the symbols describing the molecule. Thus two molecules of water are written **2H$_2$O**.

G. Valence. The atoms of different elements possess in varying degrees the power of combining with atoms of other elements. Thus an atom of hydrogen or an atom of chlorine can never combine with more than **one** atom of any other element. One atom of oxygen, however, can combine with **two** atoms of another element, while one atom of carbon can combine with **four** atoms of another element, and so on. This " capacity for combination " in an element is known as its **Valence** (770). The valence of an element is defined by comparing it with hydrogen or with chlorine, both of which have the same combining power. Thus the valence of any element is determined by the number of chlorine or hydrogen atoms which one atom of the element in question will hold (770). Greek prefixes are used to distinguish valences : elements with a valence of 1 are **monovalent** ; those with a valence of 2 are **divalent** ; with a valence of 3, **trivalent** ; and with a valence of 4, **tetravalent**, and so on. The lowest valence is zero ; the highest is 8. *See* diagram in page 770.

H. Radicals, 767. The formula for sulphuric acid is **H$_2$SO$_4$**. When it combines with potassium, it forms potassium sulphate, **K$_2$SO$_4$**. With copper it gives copper sulphate, **CuSO$_4$**, and so on— the **SO$_4$** always being present. Such a group persisting throughout a number of reactions is called a **radical**. In this case **SO$_4$** is the radical of sulphuric acid ; and this acid forms **salts** by combining its radical with other elements in proportion to their valencies. Another radical is the hydroxyl (**OH**) which unites with an atom of hydrogen to form water (3351), an atom of sodium (120) to form hydroxide (**NaOH**) or caustic soda (20), and so on. Ethyl alcohol is a combination of two radicals—the " ethyl " radical, or **C$_2$H$_5$**, and a hydroxyl (**OH**). If instead of the " ethyl " radical we have methyl (**CH$_3$**), the result is methyl alcohol or " wood spirit."

Inorganic Chemistry

(General Properties of the Elements)

I. FAMILIES OF ELEMENTS.
The elements could be classified broadly as metals and non-metals (770), but many show such similar properties that they have been placed together in groups. The most conspicuous examples are the **halogens, 1567,** fluorine, chlorine, bromine, iodine, and the **inert gases** (769, 1420), helium (**1607**), neon (**2314**), argon, krypton and xenon (**3429**).

II. PERIODIC LAW.

The existence of families among the elements long ago convinced chemists that there must be some simple way of arranging the elements so that related groups with a similarity of properties would fall into order. The most obvious plan was to arrange them in the order of their atomic weights, and in 1869 Mendeléev (**2140**), by leaving hydrogen out of account, succeeded in producing the **periodic system** of elements. The table in page 768 shows the up-to-date form of this system. Mendeléev's original table had many gaps, left in order to bring the elements into their proper positions in the groups ; as elements were discovered since his time, they were invariably found to fit the gaps in his scheme. Mendeléev's Periodic Law may be stated thus : The properties of elements are periodic functions of their atomic weights.

III. COMPOUNDS.

In writing the formula of a compound we give the name of the metal first. If only two elements are in the compound, the name of the metal ends in -ic or -ous, followed by the non-metal with the ending -ide. If the elements can combine in different proportions, the -ic ending is used for the compound containing the smaller proportion of the metallic element. Examples : ferric sulphide (Fe_2S_3) and ferrous sulphide (FeS). If oxygen forms a third element in a compound, a smaller amount is indicated by the ending -ite, and a larger amount by -ate. Examples are sodium sulphite Na_2SO_3 ; sodium sulphate, Na_2SO_4.

IV. ACIDS.

A. **Definition.** An **acid (20)** is a hydrogen compound in which the hydrogen can be replaced by a metal. The other part of the compound is called the **acid radical** (767). The strongest acids are the mineral ones : sulphuric, nitric, hydrochloric acids.

B. **Solubility.** Acids are generally soluble and **dissociate** in solution. *See* Outline on Physical Chemistry III, B).

C. **Ionization Theory,** 1738, 771–72, 20. Compounds are classed according to their **Ionization.**

V. BASES AND ALKALIS.

A. **Definition.** A base is a substance which combines with an acid to form a salt and water and nothing else. This includes the oxides and hydroxides of metals and basic radicals such as the ammonium group (NH_4). Bases which are soluble in water are known as **alkalis (20)**, e.g., caustic soda (sodium hydroxide), **NaOH**. The **hydroxyl radical,** an oxygen-hydrogen unit which acts in many chemical exchanges as if it were a single element (20).

B. **Solubility.** All alkalis are, of course, soluble in water, but many of the bases of heavy metals are insoluble.

C. **Types of Acids and Bases.** Acids containing one, two or three replaceable hydrogen atoms are known as mono-, di-, and tri-basic acids. Similarly bases containing one, two, and three hydroxyl radicals are termed mono-, di-, and tri-acid bases.

VI. SALTS.

A. **Definition.** A salt is a compound formed from a metal and an acid radical. A **normal salt (20)** is one in which *all* the hydrogen in an acid is replaced by a metal. An **acid salt** is one in which only *part* of the hydrogen is so replaced. A **basic salt** is a salt formed when *all* the hydrogen of the acid had been replaced by the metal, but some surplus metal has carried over hydroxyl into the new combination.

B. **Properties of Normal Salts.** Salts that are soluble in water dissociate, but their solutions do not turn red litmus blue or blue litmus red (unless they are " complex salts," such as potassium ferrocyanide).

C. **Methods of Formation of Salts.**

    a. By Reaction of Acids and Bases. When an acid is neutralized by a base the hydrogen of the acid unites with the hydroxyl of the base to form water, while the basic and acid radicals unite to form a perfectly neutral salt : e.g.,

$$NaOH + HCl \longrightarrow NaCl + H_2O.$$

    b. By Action of an Acid on Metal. Many metals dissolve in acids with the evolution of hydrogen and the formation of a salt : e.g.,

$$Zn + H_2SO_4 \longrightarrow ZnSO_4 + H_2.$$

    c. By Double Decomposition of a Salt and Acid. When two compounds change their radicals during a reaction they are said to undergo double decomposition. If the substances are an acid and a salt, a new salt and acid will be formed : e.g.,

$$2NaCl + H_2SO_4 \longrightarrow Na_2SO_4 + 2HCl.$$ *See page* 1667.

    d. By Double Decomposition of Two Salts Two new salts are formed when double decomposition takes place between two salts e.g.,

$$(NH_4)_2CO_3 + 2NaCl \longrightarrow 2NH_4Cl + Na_2CO_3.$$

    e. By Direct Union of the Elements. Some salts such as ferric chloride are prepared from the elements, in this case by passing chlorine gas over heated iron : $2Fe + 3Cl_2 \longrightarrow 2FeCl_3.$

Organic Chemistry

(The Chemistry of Carbon Compounds)

FIELD COVERED. This branch of chemistry is called **Organic Chemistry** (1774), because until 1828 it was supposed that only living organisms could produce the substances studied. *See* Outline on Chemistry, I, E. Very many organic compounds can be synthesized in the laboratory.

A. **Nature of Organic Compounds.** Organic compounds consist of various radicals, arranged in different combinations, but all containing carbon (774). A molecule of the natural substance urea contains the same atoms as a molecule of ammonium cyanate, but differently arranged ; thi difference is responsible for sharply different properties in the two substances—a phenomenon named **isomerism** (774).

B. Classes of Organic Compounds.

a. Hydrocarbons. Compounds containing carbon and hydrogen only.

1. Aliphatic, open chain, or Paraffin Series. In these compounds, carbon atoms are united in a line or " open chain," thus :—Ċ-Ċ—..., with hydrogen grouped about the edge. Important members : methane (CH_4), ethane (C_2H_6), propane (C_3H_8), butane (C_4H_{10}), pentane (C_5H_{12}). This group is often called the paraffin series because many of its members are found in paraffin. The type of formula of this group is C_nH_{2n+2}, which means that the number of hydrogen atoms is equal to twice the number of carbon atoms plus two. The names of the radicals end in -**ane**. When a hydrogen atom is removed, in order to permit entering into combination, the ending changes to -**yl**. Examples : methane, CH_4, methyl CH_3.
These are also called **saturated** hydrocarbons, since the chemical valences of their carbon atoms are believed to be fully utilized by attached hydrogen atoms, or by the attachment between successive carbon atoms.

2. Ethylene Series. These radicals have certain carbon valences unsatisfied, and are, therefore, more reactive. They are of the type : C_nH_{2n}. Example : ethylene (C_2H_4), a constituent of illuminating gas.

3. Acetylene Series. Type formula : C_nH_{2n-2}. Example : acetylene, C_2H_2. The types represented by **2** and **3** are known as **unsaturated** hydrocarbons.

4. Aromatic or Benzene Series. This is an exceedingly important series in which the carbon chain is a **closed chain**, having as its fundamental unit the " benzene ring." The chain is bent round until it links up, forming a six-sided ring, as in benzene, C_6H_6 :
The general formula of this series is C_nH_{2n-6}.

```
          H
          |
          C
        /   \
   H—C       C—H
     |        |
   H—C       C—H
        \   /
          C
          |
          H
```

b. Carbohydrates are compounds containing carbon and the elements of water, i.e., hydrogen and oxygen in the proportion of 2 to 1—i.e. the proportion of the water molecule, H_2O. The **sugars** (3114) belong to this class. On treatment with dilute acid they are hydrolyzed to mono-saccharides. The chief types of carbohydrates are :

1. Mono-saccharides (3114). These are compounds of the type $C_6H_{12}O_6$, differing chiefly in optical and complex chemical properties. Examples : glucose (1447) or grape sugar ; fructose (3114) or fruit sugar. Glucose and fructose are also called **dextrose** and **laevulose**, respectively, because of their optical action (3114).

2. Di-saccharides. These consist of two mono-saccharide molecules, less the equivalent of a water molecule, in combination. Typical formula : $C_{12}H_{22}O_{11}$. Examples : sucrose or cane sugar (3112), maltose (3116), lactose.

3. Poly-saccharides. Contain more than two mono-saccharide molecules, less the equivalent of some water in combination. Typical formula : $(C_6H_{10}O_5)$. Examples : starch (**3082**) and cellulose (**739**).

C. Substitution Compounds.

a. In Aliphatic Radicals.

1. If hydrogen atoms are replaced by halogens (1567) (e.g., chlorine, **816**), **alkyl halides** such as chloroform $CHCl_3$ and ethyl chloride C_2H_5Cl are formed.

2. Substitution of an hydroxyl radical for a hydrogen atom gives an **alcohol** (**103**, 774). This can be brought about by the fermentation (**1266**) of sugar or the *hydrolysis* (3114) of an alkyl halide by an alkali, such as potassium hydroxide :
$$CH_3I + KOH \longrightarrow CH_3OH + KI.$$

3. Substitution of a **carboxyl radical** (COOH) gives an organic acid (774). This is achieved by oxidizing an alcohol. Partial oxidation of methyl alcohol produces formaldehyde (775), a simple **aldehyde** containing a (COH) radical, while complete oxidation gives formic acid :
$$CH_3OH \longrightarrow HCOH \longrightarrow HCOOH.$$

b. In Aromatic Radicals.

1. Substitution of one, two, or three nitro groups (NO_2), in a benzene ring give mono-, di-, and tri-**nitrobenzenes**, e.g., $C_6H_5NO_2$.

2. Substitution of an amino group (NH_2) gives an **amine**. This is done by replacing the oxygen atoms in a nitro group by hydrogen atoms. In this way nitrobenzene gives the amine commonly known as aniline (857, 1059) :
$$C_6H_5NO_2 + 3H_2 \longrightarrow C_6H_5NH_2 + 2H_2O.$$

3. Replacement of a hydrogen atom by two nitrogen atoms gives us a **diazo** compound. This is done by the action of *nitrous acid* on an amine. Diazo compounds are of immense importance in the manufacture of dyes.

4. Phenols such as carbolic acid C_6H_5OH (**699**, 857) are prepared from diazo compounds by boiling with water :
$$C_6H_5N_2 + H_2O \longrightarrow C_6H_5OH + H.$$

5. Phenols contain a hydroxyl radical and are therefore alcohols, although they are acids, too. **Aromatic aldehydes** and **acids** can be prepared from the phenols in much the same way as the alipathic aldehydes and acids are produced.

D. **Electrovalent Compounds, or Polar Compounds,** 772. These names are given to *compounds that ionize*—i.e. those formed by the **transfer of electrons** between the elements which compose such compounds.

Contrasted with the electrovalent compounds are the **covalent or non-polar compounds,** in which the elements unite by **sharing electrons** (772). The effect of the presence of ions in their crystals upon the boiling point of salts (773). Solubility in polar liquids (773). Why non-polar liquids (such as petrol or fats) do not mix completely with water (773).

E. **Polymerisation, 775.** Much of modern synthetic chemistry is concerned with the bringing about of changes in compounds so that their molecules can be made to join together to form larger and larger molecules (called **polymers**). " Plastics " are synthesized by this means; polymerisation also plays an important part in the drying of paints and varnishes containing linseed oil and other " drying oils," and in the formation of synthetic rubber and of natural rubber.

Physical Chemistry

I. STRUCTURE OF THE ATOM.

The generally accepted theory that the atom has a " planetary " structure is set out in the Physics Outlines. There also are brief notes on the electrical nature of the atom; the theories of natural and artificial radio-activity; nuclear disintegration; atomic energy and the atomic bomb.

II. THE STATES OF MATTER.

Matter can exist in three " states " according to its temperature. These are the solid, liquid, and gaseous states. (*See, further,* Physics Outlines.)

III. EFFECT OF SOLUTION UPON CHEMICAL AFFINITY.

A. **Physical Properties of Solutions.** A dissolved substance " disappears " in a solution because its particles break up into their constituent molecules, and the molecules diffuse, or become dispersed, among the molecules of the liquid. The degree to which a substance will disappear in this way is called its **solubility** (773). Modern theories to account for the wide difference in solubility of various substances: The **Debye-Huckel theory** of ion-scattering by dilution of a strong solution (773). The " magnetic " theory of solution; how mixing is controlled (*773*). Polar and non-polar liquids; " water dipoles " and mixing (773). How crystals dissolve by the water dipoles dragging ions from the crystal surface of a salt (*773*).

a. **Concentration.** The proportion of dissolved molecules (**solute**) to the molecules of the liquid (**solvent**) is called the **concentration** of the solution. A dilute solution is one with small concentration of solute.

b. **Saturated Solutions.** When once dissolved, the molecules of the solute wander about and from time to time encounter each other. When this happens they tend to resume their solid form. The more molecules dissolved, the greater will be this tendency; and at a certain point the tendency to solidify again equals the dissolving tendency of the liquid. Then no more solid can pass into solution, and the liquid is said to be **saturated.**

c. **Diffusion.** All dissolved substances tend to diffuse within the solution until the concentration of the latter is the same at all points. This tendency gives rise to " osmotic pressure " in solutions.

B. **Dissociation.** When compound substances are dissolved in water, the bonds uniting the constituent elements or radicals are weakened, and the compound tends to fall apart into electrically charged portions called **ions** (1738). This " falling apart " is called **dissociation.**

IV. ELECTRO-CHEMISTRY

The theory of the electrical structure of the atom (296) and the phenomena of ionization (1738, 772) suggest that the various types of chemical affinity are due to an electrical cause. The difference between liquids which are capable of conducting electricity (**electrolytes**) and those that are not thus capable (**non-electrolytes**) exists before any electric current is applied to the liquids. In electrolytes a certain proportion of the molecules is always broken up (dissociated) into **negative** and **positive ions,** the electrical charges upon which balance each other at any given moment. The connexion between ionization and the electrical theory of valence (772).

V. THE BASIC PHENOMENA OF CHEMICAL REACTIONS.

A. **Combination.** When elements or radicals unite we have a case of chemical combination.

B. **Decomposition.** When a compound breaks up into its constituent elements or radicals we have chemical decomposition.

C. **Substitution.** When two compounds exchange their constituent parts, we have a case of substitution or double decomposition.

D. **Catalysis.** Many elements and radicals which will not combine of themselves do so readily in the presence of certain substances, which only enter into the reaction temporarily and are left unchanged at the end. The presence of spongy platinum, for example, unites oxygen and hydrogen. Substances such as these are called catalysts, **720.**

VI. PHOTO-CHEMISTRY.

Some reactions are caused by the effect of light on the activity of the molecules. If a mixture of hydrogen and chlorine is kept in the dark no reaction takes place. When placed in the sunlight, however, they immediately combine with a loud explosion. Such reactions are termed photo-chemical, 2574. The photosynthesis of carbo-hydrates by plants through the medium of chlorophyll is another well-known example of a photo-chemical process (2589).

VII. COLLOIDS AND THE COLLOIDAL STATE.

In the first part of the Outline we divided solid matter into crystalline and amorphous forms. With the exceptions now to be noted, when solids are placed in a solvent, they either fall to the bottom or dissolve. The exceptions concern the substances known as Colloids (773, 871). Colloids are mixtures in which one substance is evenly distributed throughout another substance in the form of extremely small particles without being dissolved or broken up into separate molecules or into ions. Milk, asphalt and rubber latex are examples. In a suspension the particles of insoluble substance remain unchanged in form. In a solution, the particles break up into individual molecules, and these, being practically as light as the molecules of the solvent, remain suspended indefinitely. In the state known as a colloidal suspension, taken by various kinds of substances, the particles are kept evenly distributed throughout the solution.

Books for the Student of Chemistry

Everyday Chemistry. J. R. Partington.
Modern Practical Chemistry. A. E. Bell.
Reference Book of Inorganic Chemistry. W. M. Latimer and J. M. Hildebrand.

Outlines of Organic Chemistry. E. J. Holmyard.
Textbook of Organic Chemistry. A. H. Holleman.
Industrial Chemistry of Colloids and Amorphous Materials. W. K. Lewis, L. Squires and G. Broughton.

ASTRONOMY

ASTRONOMY has been called the " Mother of the Sciences." Long before any of the other great sciences had been organized, men were busy investigating the mysteries of the heavens, and out of the speculations and observations of these early " star-gazers " came some of the most profound scientific truths. The great names associated with Astronomy are those of Galileo, Kepler, Newton—all leaders in the science of their day. We must not think that a knowledge of the sun, and the moon, the planets and the stars is far removed from the practical affairs of our daily life. Not only is Astronomy fascinating and full of inspiration in itself, but an understanding of its chief principles is absolutely essential for a proper grasp of most of the other branches of knowledge whose fields lie much nearer home. Some of its uses are outlined in page 277.

Books for the Student of Astronomy

Stars Shown to the Children. Ellison Hawks.
A Voyage in Space. H. H. Turner.
The Stars in Their Courses. Sir James Jeans.
General Astronomy. H. S. Jones.
The Mysterious Universe. Sir James Jeans.

Story of the Heavens. Sir Robert Ball.
The Expanding Universe. Sir Arthur Eddington.
The Universe Around Us. Sir James Jeans.
An Outline of the Universe. J. G. Crowther.
Relativity. James Rice.

Interest-Questions in Astronomy

What did astronomy have to do with the discovery of America ?   281.

When does the comet's tail precede and when does it follow the comet ?   880.

How do we know that " nothing ever happens " on the moon ?   2224.

Why was there no such day as " October 5th " in the year 1582 ?   662.

How can you sail in a ship " from today to yesterday " ?   3214.

Light travels with speed enough to flash round the earth more than seven times in a second. How many years does it take the light from the nearest star to reach us ?   3078.

What makes a star twinkle ?   3079.

What leads some scientists to think there may be inhabitants on the planet Mars ?   2617.

What planet wears three rings ?   2618.

If you could travel at the speed of light, how long would it take you to reach the nearest fixed star ?   280.

How is time measured by the sun ?   661–62.

How many days did Russia lose when she accepted the new style calendar ?   662.

What is the difference between a sun day and a star day ?   980.

Who established the theory that the earth revolved about the sun ?   905.

Why cannot the solar year be divided evenly into months and days ?   662.

By what method are the solar year and the calendar year kept together ?   662.

What keeps the planets in their paths ?   1512.

Why were many large constellations not known to the Greeks ?   896.

When can the stars be seen in the daytime ?   1079.

What are " shooting stars " ?   2151.

How was the planet Pluto discovered ?   2618.

AGRICULTURE

IT was a great day in the history of the human race when some ancient nomad first decided to settle down and begin scratching the soil with a sharp stick so that it would grow crops for him. Gradually men added one food plant after another to their stock ; they learned to domesticate animals ; they grew flax and clipped the wool of their sheep that wives and daughters might spin and weave clothes for the household. Meanwhile, the sharpened stick had given way to the ploughshare, and the forward march of human culture was measured by the improvements in agriculture. To this day agriculture remains the foundation of civilization. Read first the article on **Agriculture** (**78**), then follow the Outline.

I. SOIL AND ITS COMPOSITION, 2998.

A. Water essential to fertile soil, 2741.

B. Artificial treatment of the soil :

a. How moisture is supplied ; Irrigation and drainage, 958, 253.

b. How chemical elements are supplied : fertilizers, 2664 ; guano, *f-i.* ; nitrogen and soil-enriching crops, 2372 ; lucerne, 2034 ; clover, 852 ; mustard, 2270 ; soya bean, 3029.

Note : For soil formation and kinds of soil, *see* Physiography, 2595.

II. DOMESTIC PLANTS.

A. Breeding and Propagation, 621. Seeds and seed selection, 2625, 2139 ; bulbs, tubers, rootstocks, 612 ; grafting, *1402* ; harvesting, 1580 ; cereals, 1580.

B. Cereals, 745, 1320 : Wheat, 3372 ; oats, 2410 ; rye, 2858 ; barley, 361 ; rice, 2774, *79, 2568* ; millet, 2175 ; maize, 2068.

C. Pasture and Hay Crops. Grasses, 1509 ; clover, 852 ; lucerne, 2034 ; legumes, *2374* ; soya bean, 3029.

D. Vegetables.

a. Legumes : Beans, 380 ; peas, 2530 ; lentils, 1925.

b. Bulbs, Tubers, Roots, etc., 612 ; Beet, 396 ; parsnips, 2526 ; onions, 2434 ; potatoes, 2664 ; radishes, *639* ; turnips, *639* ; artichokes, 256 ; tapioca, 3153.

c. Other Vegetables : Asparagus, 271 ; cabbage, 639 ; brussels sprouts, kale, cauliflower, *639* ; watercress, 3353 ; celery, 738 ; cucumber, 943 ; lettuce, *f-i.* ; rhubarb, 2774 ; spinach, *f-i.* ; tomato, 3223.

E. Spices and Condiments, 3060 : Ginger, 1464 ; mint, 2187 ; mustard, 2270 ; nutmeg and mace, 2407 ; pepper, 2547 ; vanilla, 3305.

F. Sugar, 3112 ; cacao, 648 ; coffee, 864 ; tea, 3159 ; tobacco, 3219 ; hops, 1641.

G. Fibre Crops : Cotton, 917, *2383* ; flax, *1313,* 1313 ; hemp, 1608 ; jute, 1844 ; sisal, 2975.

H. Fruits and Fruit-Growing, 1401.

a. Orchard Fruits : Apple, 190 ; apricot, 191 ; cherry, 778 ; mulberry, 2250 ; peach, 2531 ; pear, 2532 ; plum, 2630 ; prunes, 2695 ; quince, medlar, 2718.

b. Bush Fruits : Currants, 944 ; gooseberry, 1486 ; grape, 1499 ; loganberry, *f-i.* ; raspberry, 2745 ; strawberry, 3103.

c. Tropical and Semi-Tropical Fruits : Banana, 354 ; breadfruit, 557 ; date, 978 ; fig, 1270 ; grapefruit, 1499 ; lemon, 1920 ; lime, 1949 ; mango, 2087 ; melon, 2137 ; olive, 2431 ; orange, 2442 ; pineapple, *1586,* 2611 ; pomegranate, 2652.

I. Nuts, 2407.

a. Temperate Zone Nuts : Chestnuts, 782 ; pistachio, *2408* ; hazel, cobnut, etc., 1590 ; walnut, 3338.

b. Tropical Nuts : Almond, 124 ; brazil nut, *2408* ; coconut, 862.

J. Vegetable Oil Crops.
Fats and oils, 1262 ; ground-nuts, 1549 ; coconut palm (copra), 862 ; cotton, 917 ; olive, 2431 ; sunflower, 3121 ; soya bean, 3029.

K. Medicinal and Miscellaneous Crops : Opium, 2442 ; quinine, 2718 ; camphor, 674 ; rubber, 2833 ; maple sugar, 2092 ; cork, 909.

III. LIVESTOCK AND LIVESTOCK PRODUCTS.

A. Stock Raising and the Effects of Careful Breeding, 79, 730, 2671.

B. Common Domestic Animals and their Products :

a. Draught Animals : Horse, 1645 ; mule, 2253 ; ass, 273, *1115.*

b. Cattle and Pigs, 730, *731,* 2605 ; meat, 2124 ; leather, 1910.

c. Sheep and Wool, 2940.

d. Goats, 1478.

e. Poultry, 2671. Turkey, 3261 ; duck, 1051 ; goose, 1484 ; guinea-fowl, 1554 ; pigeons and doves, 2605.

f. Insect Products : Bees and honey, 390 ; silkworms, 2970 ; shellac, 1881 ; cochineal, 859.

g. Dairying and Dairy Products, 955. Milk, 2173 ; butter, 627 ; cheese, 765, *336.*

h. Other animal products : Leather, 1910 ; feathers, 1264 ; 2456.

C. Domestic Animals peculiar to certain regions : Alpaca, 124 ; buffalo, 602 ; camel, 669 ; llama, 1975 ; reindeer, 2760 ; yak, 3433 ; ostrich, 2456, *3018.*

IV. ENEMIES AND FRIENDS OF THE FARMER.

A. **Animal Pests** : Mice, **2248** ; rats, **2746** ; insects, **1726**, *2513* ; aphids, **185** ; beetles, **398** ; caterpillars, **720**, *1728* ; grasshoppers and locusts, **1510**, *plate f. 1512* ; scale insects, **2878** ; weevils, **3362**.

B. **Harmful Plants** : Poisonous plants, **2637** ; thistles, **3203** ; rusts and smuts, **2857**.

C. **Farmers' Helpers** : Bats, **370** ; birds, **437** ; dogs, *1026* ; frogs, **1398** ; toads, **3219** ; moles, **2196** ; ladybirds, **1883** ; hover-flies, *1731* ; bacteria, **335** ; centipedes, **742**.

V. FARMING MACHINERY, ETC.

Windmill, **3386** ; ploughs, *80*, **2629**, *671*, *2089* ; reapers, etc., *679*, *78*, *1509–10*.

Books for the Student of Agriculture

The Principles of Agriculture. J. R. Ainsworth Davis.
Farming and Mechanized Agriculture. R. G. Stapledon (ed.).
The Evolution of the English Farm. M. E. Seebohm.
Growth of English Industry and Commerce during the Early and Middle Ages. W. Cunningham.
Agricultural Writers from Sir Walter of Henley to Arthur Young, 1200–1800. D. McDonald.
The Soil. Sir A. D. Hall.
The Feeding of Crops and Stock. Sir A. D. Hall.

The Farmer's Year. Claire Leighton.
The Small Farm and its Management. J. Long.
Dairy Farming. R. H. Leitch.
English Farming, Past and Present. R. E. Prothero (Lord Ernle).
Bee Keeping for All. E. Tickner Edwardes.
Notebook of Agricultural Facts and Figures. Primrose MacConnell.
Farmer's Glory, and other books. A. G. Street.
Corduroy, and similar works. Adrian Bell.
Pests of Fruit and Hops. A. M. Massee.
Text Book of Plant Virus Diseases. K. M. Smith.

Interest-Questions in Agriculture

Is the potato a root ? 2664.
Why do cows swallow their food first and chew it afterwards ? 732.
Why would the earth become sterile without the earthworm ? 1070.
How long does a hen's egg take to hatch ? A duck's egg ? 444.
How large a load can a camel carry and how far can it travel in a day ? 669.
What orchard tree does not come into full bearing until it is 30 years old ? 2431.
What bird lays a 3-lb. egg ? 2456.
How does the palm tree get its name ? 2483.
Why does the horse have only one toe on each foot ? 1645.
How did one coffee tree supply three-quarters of the world ? 864.
Why must coffee be grown 1,200 to 2,000 feet above sea-level ? 864.
To what is the flavour of a spice due ? 3061.
How does the fruit grower keep Jack Frost out of his garden ? 1401.
What plant is harvested from July to November ? 918.

What does a farmer mean by " heavy " soil ? 2998
How is soil enriched by certain plants ? 2372.
Why are the tea plants kept pruned ? 3159.
What fruit is picked green and packed away to ripen ? 2472.
What accounts for the small size of the Shetland pony ? 1647.
How do bees collect pollen ? 391.
What fruit cannot be grown without the aid of an insect ? 1270.
What familiar fruit comes from the same genus of trees as the india-rubber tree ? 1270.
What familiar fruits are closely related to the rose ? 463.
Why do cows pull grass instead of cutting it off with their teeth ? 732.
How is it possible to develop new varieties of fruits and vegetables ? 621.
Why can cattle eat coarse foods that horses cannot ? 732.

INDUSTRIES AND APPLIED SCIENCES

INDUSTRIES and applied sciences form the very backbone of modern civilization. A complete study of their field would encompass the whole fabric of our practical daily lives and would branch out into such subjects as geography, botany, zoology, the physical sciences, the social sciences, and many other departments of knowledge. This Outline is intended merely as a general survey of the chief materials of industry and of the principal ways in which they are obtained and used, together with a summary of the important sources of power and methods of transport and communication.

I. RAW MATERIALS AND HOW THEY ARE OBTAINED.

A. Minerals, 2180.

a. Mining, 2181.

1. Coal, **855** ; oil, **2426**, **2564** ; natural gas, **1607**, **2428**.

2. Metals, **2148** : iron, **1752** ; copper, **906** ; lead, **1908** ; aluminium, **134** ; mercury, **2145** ; nickel, **2365** ; tungsten, **3253**.

3. Precious Metals : gold, **1479** ; silver, **2973** ; platinum, **2627** ; radium, **2731**.

4. Gems, **1427** ; diamonds, **1009**.

5. Other Common Minerals : salt, **2865** ; sulphur, **3116** ; potash, **2662**.

b. Quarrying, 2712.

1. Building Stones : granite, **1498** ; marble, **2097** ; slate, **2981**.

2. Other Minerals : clay, **836** ; sand, **2870** ; chalk, **749** ; asbestos, **261** ; mica, **2159**.

B. Plant Materials.

a. Food Crops : grains, **745** ; fruit, **1401** ; vegetables ; spices, **3060** ; nuts, **2407** ; groundnuts, 1549.

b. Timber, **3247**, **1349**, **2035**.

1. Woods : *see* articles on the various trees and conifers, **896**.

2. Forestry Protection, 1351.

c. Some Other Plant Materials : tobacco, **3219** ; camphor, **674** ; cellulose, **739** ; cork, **909** ; coconut palm, **862** ; lacquer, **1881** ; rubber, **2883** ; cotton, **917** ; kapok, **1847**.

C. Animal Materials. Domestic animals are treated in the Outline on Agriculture, 3691.

a. Hunting.

1. Furs, 1412.

2. Ivory, **1788** ; Bone, **498**.

3. Perfume, 2549.

4. Feathers, 1264.

b. Fishing.

1. Fish and Fisheries, 1296 ; *see* articles on the various fishes.

2. Sea Mammals : Whale, 3371 ; Porpoise, 2657 ; Seal, 2912 ; Walrus, 3339.

3. Reptiles, 2767 ; Turtle, 3229.

4. Shellfish : Oyster, 2466 ; Crab, 924 ; Lobster, 1977 ; Shrimp, 2962.

5. Other Sea Products, 1020 ; Coral, 908 ; Pearls, 2533 ; Sponges, 3067.

c. Raw Materials used for Cloth Making : Silk, 2970 ; Wool, 3404.

d. Other Animal Materials : Honey, 390 ; Lac, 1881.

II. POWER AND HOW IT IS APPLIED.

A. Fuels. Steam Engine, 3085 ; Boilers, 488 ; Diesel engine, 1015 ; Gas engine, 1420 ; Gas turbine, 1424 ; Bunsen burner, 615 ; Petrol engine, 1735 ; Motors, 2239.

B. Water. Dams and Barrages, 958 ; Hydro-electric installations, 1669 ; Hydraulic Machinery, 1665 ; Water Turbine, 3259.

C. Air. Windmill, 3258, 3386 ; Pneumatic Appliances, 549, 2632.

D. Electricity. Dynamos, 1060, and Batteries, 375 ; Power stations, 2673 ; Electronic devices, 1138 ; Photo-electric devices, 2574 ; Electric motor, 2239 ; Thermionic valve, 3198.

E. Animals. Agricultural machinery, Carriages, Wagons, 78.

III. TRANSPORT AND COMMUNICATION.

A. Land Transport.

a. Roads and Streets, 2783 ; bridges, 564 ; tunnels, 3255 ; railways, 2734.

b. Vehicles : cycles, 947 ; motor-cars, 2241 ; tramcar, trolleybus, and omnibus, 2246, 3235.

B. Water Transport.

a. Waterways : canal, 686 ; lakes, 1885 ; ocean routes, *290*.

b. Craft : boats and yachts, 481 ; ships, 2945.

C. Air Transport : airships, 92 ; aeroplanes, 41 ; autogiros (320) and helicopters (1604).

D. Communication : telephone, 3173 ; radar, 2726 ; teleprinter, 3164 ; telegraph, 3164 ; wireless, 3391 ; cable, 640 ; television, 3182.

IV. MANUFACTURING.

A. Metal-Working.

a. Industries Concerned with the Extraction of Metals : metallurgy, 2148 ; smelting and refining, 1754.

b. Industries Concerned with Shaping and Finishing Metals : blast-furnace, 467 ; welding, 3362 ; electroplating, 1139.

c. Metal Products.

1. Chief Metals and their uses : (*see* under Minerals, in this Outline).

2. Machinery : *See* list of machines under the entry " Machinery " in the Fact-Index.

3. Other devices made of metal : armour-plate, 240 ; cables, 640 ; tin cans, 692 ; firearms, 1281 ; artillery, 257 ; clocks and watches, 843 ; nails, 2271 ; pins, 2609 ; plough, 2629 ; steamship, 2946 ; stoves, 1597 ; wire, 3389.

B. Building Materials, 604 : iron and steel, 1752 ; granite, 1498 ; marble, 2097 ; slate, 2981 ; cement, 740 ; concrete, 883 ; bricks and tiles, 561.

C. Wood Products and Associated Industries.

a. Furniture Making, 1409.

b. Other Products : Aeroplane parts, 48 ; Baskets, 368 ; Cricket Bats, 3382 ; Beams, 379 ; Bows, 3434 ; Paper Pulp, 2496 ; Pencils, 1500, 2541 ; Roof, 2821.

D. Ceramic Industries : China clay, 814 ; porcelain and pottery, 2665 ; enamel, 1157 ; glass, 1472.

E. Cloth and Clothing.

a. Processes in Cloth Making : loom, 2024 ; spinning, 3065 ; weaving, 3360, 850 ; knitting, 1865 ; bleaching, 469 ; dyeing, 1059, 1718.

b. Products.

1. Cloth, 850 ; cotton, 917 ; felt, 1265 ; linen, 1953 ; rayon, 2748 ; silk, 2970 ; wool, 3404.

2. Other products : thread, 3205 ; lace, 1876 ; carpets and rugs, 705.

c. Clothes, 851.

1. Sewing, 2927 ; embroidery, 1152 ; Clothing Industry, 850.

2. Garments : hats and caps, 1582 ; gloves, 1477 ; boots and shoes, 521.

F. Rubber and Products, 2833. Tires, *2835*, 2836 ; Synthetic Rubber, 2838.

G. Leather.

a. Leather Making, 1910 ; chamois, 750 ; pigskin, 2605 ; shagreen, 2938 ; crocodile, 931.

b. Chief Products. Gloves, 1477 ; boots and shoes, 521.

H. Food Manufactures.

a. Flour Milling, 1320 ; Bread, 554 ; Cereals, 745.

b. Sugar and Sugar Products, 3112 ; maple, 2092.

c. Cocoa and Chocolate, 861 ; Coffee, 864 ; Tea, 3159 ; Salt, 2865. Butter, 627 ; Cheese, 765 ; Margarine, 2100 ; Biscuits, 557.

d. Preserving of Food : canning industry, 692 ; refrigeration, 1391.

I. Paper Making, 2496.

J. Printing, 2684.

a. Printing Processes : electrotyping, 1140 ; engraving, 1217 ; stereotyping, 3088 ; process engraving, 2688 ; Linotype, 1956 ; Monotype, 2215.

b. Books, 509 ; Newspaper, 2344.

K. Photographic Industry, 2577.

L. Amusement Industries : Cinema, 828 ; Circus, *f.p. 820* ; Television, 3182 ; Wireless, 3391 ; Theatre, 3194.

M. Miscellaneous Manufactures : drugs, 1048 ; opium, 2442 ; explosives, 1250 ; detergents, 998, and soap, 2993 ; candle, 691 ; celluloid, 739 ; plastics, 2625 ; turpentine, 3268 ; musical instruments, 2266 ; coal-tar, 857.

V. ENGINEERING AND ENGINEERING CONSTRUCTION.

A. Building Construction, 604, 212.

B. Ship Building, 2945.

C. Heating, 1278, 1597 ; Lighting, 1134.

D. Sanitation : waterworks, 3347 ; aqueducts, 194 ; reservoirs, 958.

E. Highway and Waterway Construction : roads, 2783 ; railways, 2734 ; tunnels, 3255 ; bridge, 564 ; harbours and ports, 1576 ; canal, 686 ; dredgers, 1046, and excavators, 1247.

F. Mine Construction, 2181.

Books for the Student of Applied Sciences

Markets of London. Cuthbert Maughan.
Commodities of Commerce. J. A. Slater.
Shipping. Arnold Hall.
History and Development of Road Transport. James Paterson.
The Clothing Industry. B. W. Poole.

Silk : Its Production and Manufacture. L. Hooper.
Introduction to Textiles. A. E. Lewis.
Timber : From the Forest to its Use in Commerce. W. Bullock.
Coal-Tar and Some of Its Products. A. R. Warnes.
The Story of Steel. J. B. Walker.

THE HOW AND WHY OF THINGS
Interest-Questions on Many Subjects

What is the peculiar property of type metal that distinguishes it from most other substances ? 124.
Why are coins not made of pure gold and silver ? 122.
What is the difference between grain alcohol and wood or methyl alcohol ? 103.
Why is the upper wing of a biplane set farther forward than the lower wing ? 41.
What instrument is used to determine the height of mountains ? 362.
What mineral is woven into cloth ? 261.
What supports an aeroplane in the air ? 41.
Why is the sky blue ? 88.
Why is coffee roasted ? 866.
How does a barometer help to forecast the weather ? 363.
What makes a balloon rise ? 347.
Who was the first man to go up in a balloon ? 348.
What makes the water spurt up in an artesian well ? 252.
How does chloride of lime bleach cloth ? 469.
Why is the hour divided into 60 minutes ? 329.
What part of your weight is blood ? 474.
How high does the atmosphere extend ? 88.
Which falls faster in a vacuum—a feather or a ball of lead ? 88.
Why did the Ancient Egyptians put straw in their bricks, though we do not ? 561.
Does a compass needle point exactly north ? 881.
What is colour blindness ? 1254.
How does smoke cause fogs ? 2986.
Why are the roofs of tunnels rounded ? 205.
Why do the stones in the middle of an arch not fall through ? 205.
Where is most of the world's amber obtained ? 138.
Why is the outer rail of a railway track raised higher than the inner rail at a curve ? 744.
How does a lampwick raise oil to the burner ? 698.
Why are buttons put on men's coat sleeves ? 632.
What is the difference between a musket and a rifle ? 1281.
How can you have fire without flame ? 1280.
How does a wasp help to make figs ? 1270.
How do feathers grow ? 1264.
Why, though an inverted image is formed on the retina, do we not see things upside-down ? 1252.
Where does rain fall from the clouds without reaching the ground ? 1243.
What is emery ? 1156.
Why do " perpetual motion " machines always fail ? 1160.
What is the difference between wealth and riches ? 1080.
How does the earthworm help the farmer ? 1070.
What part of the ear has nothing to do with hearing ? 1065.
Where does eiderdown come from ? 1052.
Why does a dog turn round before lying down ? 1025.
Why does a dog howl at night ? 1025.
Why must a deep-sea diver come up slowly ? 1019.
Why does dew not form on cloudy nights ? 1000.
How can a wire screen prevent explosions ? 980.
How much cream does it take to make a pound of butter ? 956.
How does a cream separator work ? 955.
How are railway sleepers kept from rotting ? 927.
Why does cork float ? 909.
What was the first metal worked by Man ? 906.
What element is a black useful drudge and a brilliant jewel ? 699.
Why is aluminium kitchen-ware only a few decades old ? 134.
What metal is used to protect iron from rust ? 3443.

What metal was named after a mischievous goblin ? 857.
Why does phosphorus shine in the dark ? 2573.
What gas was discovered on the sun before it was found on the earth ? 1607.
Why does a hat have a little bow on the inside ? 1584.
How are felt hats made of fur ? 1584.
Why does a stick look bent in water ? 1939.
What plant rivals the elephant for ivory ? 1788.
How did " pig iron " get its name ? 1753.
What kind of compass is independent of the earth's magnetism ? 1559.
What fish can climb trees ? 1297.
What gives fireworks their colours ? 1289.
What people used baskets for carrying water ? 369.
Why does a piece of iron get hot when it is hammered ? 1593.
Why is fire hot ? 1595.
What mineral can be made as thin as tissue paper ? 2159.
Why must safety matches be struck on the box ? 2119.
What are " paste " gems ? 1427.
Why, if mercury is a liquid, will it not wet paper ? 2145.
How was cooking done in a basket ? 369.
Why is basket-making called the parent of cloth-making ? 368.
How can a flame manufacture water ? 1673.
What animals make paper ? 2496.
Why do so many people have the name " Smith " ? 2272.
What plants eat animals ? Plate f. p. 2621.
How can you tell how far away a thunderstorm is ? 3010.
Why did the fruit-growers of California import Australian lady-birds ? 2878.
If you plant a seed upside down, will the root grow upward instead of downward ? 2622.
What fruit gets its name from Corinth, Greece ? 944.
How many earthworms are there in an average acre of soil ? 1071.
What plant gives us gum arabic ? 16.
What animals have four stomachs ? 732.
What sort of birds' nests are used as food ? 3125.
How can a clay statue be made into a marble one ? 2904.
How does a potter " throw " a vase ? 2665.
What animal has a hide over an inch thick ? 1628.
From what fish do we get caviare and isinglass ? 3104.
How fast can a homing pigeon fly ? 2606.
How far can a rattlesnake reach when it strikes ? 2746.
What snake can throw its poison from a distance ? 859.
What bird builds nests six feet across ? 1063.
Where do crabs climb trees ? Plate f. p. 924.
Why is spider's silk not used for making cloth ? 3065.
How does a chameleon change its colour ? 750.
What animal has been known to tunnel more than 75 yards in one night ? 2196.
Why has the penguin lost its power of flight ? 2544.
How did the camellia get its name ? 671.
What causes the phosphorescence of the ocean ? 2573.
Why cannot a snake close its eyes ? 2990.
If a tiger should attack a buffalo, which would probably win the fight ? 602.
Can any animal remain standing up continuously for years ? 1141.
Why does a white cat with pink eyes make a poor mouser ? 718.
Where do ferns and lilies and tulips grow as large as trees ? 309.
Why is spruce the best wood for aeroplane construction ? 3070.
What animal can eat its own weight in food every day ? 446.

EASY REFERENCE
FACT-INDEX

*A Guide to the Contents of
Volumes 1—7 with Thousands
of Additional Entries*

Editor's Note

As the Editor has pointed out at the beginning of each volume, whenever the immediate object is to secure some particular piece of information, the reader should first refer to the FACT-INDEX. If the information is anywhere recorded in the NEW BOOK OF KNOWLEDGE, the FACT-INDEX will tell you where, or may even directly yield the information.

The FACT-INDEX itself presents the essential facts about a very large proportion of the entries which it contains. When the main source of the information desired is to be found in the preceding volumes, the page numbers in **black-face** type show the reader where to turn for the chief article that deals with the particular subject. The titles and page numbers of other articles in the preceding volumes which contain still further information relating in any way to the subject inquired about are also given.

PICTURES have not been separately indexed where they appear on the same pages with text references, except occasionally for special emphasis or to prevent confusion. But pages containing pictures related to the subject indexed are shown in *italic* type (*201*). In many cases the pages numbered in **black-face** type also contain illustrations relating to the subject indexed.

The latest census populations of cities, towns, etc., are given, usually in round numbers correct to the previous thousand, *e.g.* 171,760 would be stated as 171,000. Distances between points are map distances, not distances by railway.

Key to Pronunciation

Most of the subject-headings in THE NEW BOOK OF KNOWLEDGE require no special indication in the way in which they should be pronounced. There are also many for whose proper pronunciation it is only necessary to know which syllable is stressed ; in these cases the stress is shown *after* the syllable, thus, A′jax. The pronunciations given are those preferred by the most recent authorities. For foreign names the native pronunciation is given except where the English pronunciation is well established. Where further guidance is necessary, the following signs are employed :

ah = a as in father
aw = a as in ball
ê = vowel sound in fern, word, girl, curl
ow = vowel sound in now, bout
oi = vowel sound in noise, boy
Unmarked vowels have their **short sound,** as a in hat, e in bet, i in bit, o in not, u in but, oo in book
Marked vowels have their **long sound,** as in hāte, bē, bīte, nōte, tūne, boŏn

Vowels in italics have a slurred or obscure sound as in abet (*a*-bet′), recent (rē′-s*e*nt), conform (k*o*n-form′), nation (nā′-sh*u*n), tailor (tā′-l*o*r

th = first sound in thing, thank
th = first sound in the, that
zh = s in measure, leisure
g = hard g, as in good, girl
j = soft g, as in gem, ginger
kh = guttural in loch

Abbreviations Used in the Fact-Index

The abbreviations most commonly used in this work are noted below ; a much longer list of abbreviations often met with in reading or conversation is given under **Abbreviations** in the Fact-Index:

a., area
agric., agriculture
Amer., America, American
anc., ancient
bor., borough
Brit., Britain, British
cap., capital
cath., cathedral
Cath., Catholic
cent., central, century
ch., church
Co., county
co-ed., co-educational
comm., commercial
Cong., Congregational
dept., department
dist., district, distributed
Eg., Egypt, Egyptian
Eng., England, English
esp., especially
est., estimated
f., facing (of plates)
Fr., France, French
frontis., frontispiece

Ger., Germany, German
Gk., Greek
govt., government
Gt., Great
hist., history
h.q., headquarters
inc., incl., including, included
inst., instrument
Ire., Ireland
isl., island
It., Italy, Italian
L., Lake
lit., literally
marit., maritime
Mex., Mexico, Mexican
mfg., manufacturing
mfr(s)., manufacture(s)
mil., military
mkt., market
Mt., mount, mountain
mus., music, musical
myth., mythology
nr., near
N.Y., New York
NZ., New Zealand.

occupn., occupation
Parl., Parliament, Parliamentary
Pk., park
pl., plate
Port., Portugal, Portuguese
Pres., President
Prot., Protestant
prov., province
rev., revolution
r., riv., river
rly., railway
Rom., Roman
Rus., Russia, Russian
Scot., Scotland, Scottish
sec., secretary
Sp., Spain, Spanish
spt., seaport
stn., station
tn., town
univ., university
U.S.S.R., Union of Socialist Soviet Republics
vil., village
Vol., volume
yrs., years

MANY of our letters derive from picture-writings of animals, birds, and parts of the body. The birds, indeed, gave us a large number of letters. The owl, for example, with his horns and his beak, gave us our M. The letter Z was originally a duck of ancient Egypt, while the eagle grew into our A. In Egyptian picture-writing the eagle first had its proper shape like this: Then as it came to be made by the Egyptian scribe in writing a running hand, it was simplified to this: When the letter in this second form passed over into the Phoenician alphabet and was used in stone inscriptions, it was found easier to carve by using straight strokes of the chisel, and it was made like this: After the Greeks had got it from the Phoenicians and put it into their alphabet, they gradually straightened it up to a horizontal position, thus: A making the letter as we have it today.

A1. Shipping term, denoting that a vessel is in good condition, 9.

Aachen (ah′-khen) or **Aix-la-Chapelle** (āks-lah-sha-pel′), Germany ; almost destroyed in 2nd World War ; 9, 754.

Aaland Is. *See* Aland Is.

Aalborg (awl′borg) (" Eel-town "), Denmark, port of Jutland ; pop. 55,652 ; exports fish, grain ; important commercially from medieval times ; 991, 992.

Aar (ahr). Largest r. (180 m.) entirely within Switzerland ; rises in Aar Glazier and flows N.W., falling into Rhine opposite Waldshut ; 3140 ; at Berne, 418.

Aardvark (ahr′vark), giant ant-eater, 9, 10, 176.

Aard′wolf (" earth wolf "), a hyena-like mammal of Africa ; food chiefly termites and carrion, 69.

Aarhus (awr′-hoos), 2nd largest city of Denmark ; pop. 100,000 ; large trade in grain, cattle ; shipyards, iron foundries ; seat of bishop since 10th cent. ; fine 13th cent. cath. ; 991, 992.

Aaron (ãr′-on). First high priest of Israelites, brother of Moses ; spokesman for Moses before Pharaoh ; with Moses led Israelite exodus from Egypt ; made idol Golden Calf while Moses was on Mt. Sinai.

Aaron's Rod. Various tall flowering plants (golden-rod, mullein, etc.) named after budding and flowering of Aaron's rod (Num. xvii) ; in architecture, ornamental rod with leaves or entwined serpent.

Aba (ab′-a), a sleeveless outer garment, usually of camel's or goat's hair, frequently of striped pattern, worn by Arabs.

Abaca (ab′-a-ka), a plant (*Musa textilis*), source of Manila hemp, 2569.

Abacus (ab′a′kus), framework with movable beads for counting, 233 ; in architecture, the slab which forms the top of a capital, 215.

Abadan′, Persia. Island in the delta of Shatt-el-Arab ; pop. 40,000 ; large refineries of Anglo-Iranian Oil Co. are here, and port is important for loading oil. Occupied during 2nd World War by Brit. and Indian troops.

Abalone (ab-a-lō′-ne), a shell-fish.

Ab′ana or **Amanah** (now **Barada**) and **Pharpar** (now **Awaj**). Two famous " rivers of Damascus " mentioned in Bible (2 Kings v. 12).

Abattoir (ab′-at-war′), a public slaughter-house.

Abbas I, " the Great " (c. 1557–c. 1628), ruler of Persia, 2555.

Abbas II, Hilmi (1874–1944). Third and last Khedive of Egypt ; ruled under Brit. supervision until deposed (1914) for plotting with Turks.

Abbasides (a-bas′-idz). Second great dynasty of Mahomedan caliphs ; ruled at Baghdad 750–1258 ; based claim on descent from Abbas, uncle of Mahomet ; most famous sovereign Harun-al-Raschid.

Abbé, Ernst (1840–1905). Ger. scientist, from 1888 owner of Zeiss optical works ; invented Abbé refracto-meter ; improvement to microscope, 2163.

Abbess, head of a convent, 2214.

Abbeville (ab-vēl), France. Picturesque town on Somme, 12 m. from the English Channel, known from 9th cent. ; pop. 20,373 ; mfrs. cloth, carpets, hemp goods, sugar ; has shipbuilding yards ; trades in grain. In 1st World War base for B.E.F. In 2nd World War captured by Germans 1940, and cathedral of S. Vulfran gutted ; liberated by Canadians and Poles 1944.

Abbey, a monastery or nunnery, 2212.

Abbey Craig, Wallace Memorial at, 2894.

Abbey Theatre, Dublin, 1050, 1751.

Abbot, George (1562–1633). Archbishop of Canterbury ; helped to translate the Bible.

Abbot, head of a monastery, 2214.

Abbotsbury, fishing vil., Dorset ; swannery, 3125.

Ab′botsford, home of Sir W. Scott, 10, 2832, 2898.

Abbott, Lyman (1835–1922). Amer. Cong. preacher and author.

Abbreviations, 10. The most commonly used abbreviations and their meanings are given in the list in pages 3698–3703. For abbreviations used in this Index *see* page 3696.

Abd-el-Kader (abd-el-kah′-dār). (c. 1807–83). Arab chief ; struggled for 15 yrs. against Fr. conquest of Algeria ; surrendered in 1847.

Abd el Krim, Mohammed ben (born 1883 ?). Riffian chief, 2231.

Abdication, renunciation of an office, usually by a ruler. In Britain a king cannot abdicate without the consent of Parliament : in absolute monarchies he may abdicate when he pleases. Among rulers who have abdicated are Diocletian, Roman Emperor (305), Romulus Augustulus, Roman Emperor (476), Richard II of England (1399), Charles V, Holy Roman Emperor (1556). Mary Stuart of Scotland (1567), James II of England (1688), Napoleon I of France (1814 and 1815), Pedro II of Brazil (1889), Manoel II of Portugal (1910), Pu-Yi (Hsuan Tung) of China (1911), Nicholas II of Russia (1917), Ferdinand I of Bulgaria (1918), William II of Germany (1918), Charles I of Austria-Hungary (1918), Mohammed VI of Turkey (1922), Edward VIII of England (1936), Carol of Rumania (1940), Victor Emmanuel III of Italy and his son Humbert (1946), and Michael of Rumania (1947).

Abdomen (ab-dō′-men *or* ab′dō-men), in the human body, the lower cavity containing liver, pancreas, spleen, kidneys, stomach, intestines, etc., 150 ; of insects, 1726, 1733.

Abdul-Aziz (ab′-dul-ah-zēz) (1830–76). Sultan of Turkey from 1861 until deposed in 1876.

Abdul-Hamid (hah-mēd′) **II** (1842–1918). Sultan of Turkey ; succeeded in 1876 ; encouraged massacres of Christian subjects ; ruled by terror and spy system ; deposed in 1909 ; 3265.

Abdul′lah Ibn Hussein′ (b. 1882), second son of Hussein Ibn Ali, recognized as Amir of Transjordan in 1921 ; assumed title of king, 1946, 3238.

Abdul-Mejid, Turkish statesman ; proclaimed Caliph by the Turkish Parliament at Angora in 1922, and was ruling Caliph of Islam until the Caliphate was abolished in 1924.

Abdul-Mejid (1823–61). Sultan of Turkey ; succeeded in 1839 ; kindly but weak would-be reformer ; France and England fought Crimean War on his behalf.

A Becket. *See* Becket.

A′bel. Younger son of Adam and Eve ; killed by Cain, his brother (Gen. iv).

Abel, Sir Frederick Augustus (1827–1902). Eng. chemist ; noted authority on explosives, part inventor of cordite ; gave name to Abel Test of petroleum.

Abel, John Jacob (1857–1938), American chemist ; professor of pharmacology, Johns Hopkins University after 1893 ; discovered method of forming crystalline insulin.

Ab′élard (ab′-ā-lar), **Pierre** (1079–1142). Fr. scholar and philosopher, 2572.

Abercorn, James Edward Hamilton, 3rd Duke of, (b. 1869). First Governor of Northern Ireland (from 1922).

Abercrombie (ab′er-krom-bi), **Sir (Leslie) Patrick** (b. 1879). Brit. architect ; prof. of Town Planning, London Univ., 1935–46 ; planned reconstruction of London, Edinburgh, Plymouth, etc.

Abercromby, Sir Ralph (1734–1801). Brit. soldier, fatally wounded at his great victory at Alexandria over Napoleon's army in Egypt.

Aberdare (ab-er-dār′), Wales. Coal-mining and market town in Glamorgan ; brickworks, breweries ; pop. 48,750.

Aberdeen, George Hamilton Gordon, 4th Earl of (1784–1860). Brit. statesman ; Prime Minister, 1852–55.

Aberdeen and Temair, John Campbell Gordon, 1st Marquess of (1847–1934). Gov.-gen. of Canada, (1893–8), Lord-lieut. of Ireland (1886, 1905–15) ; Lord Rector of St. Andrews University (1913).

Aberdeen, 3rd largest city in Scotland : pop. over 181,000 ; 11, 12.

Aberdeen, Angus, breed of beef-cattle, 732.

Aberdeen′shire, Co. of Scot. ; 1,970 sq. m. ; pop. over 300,000 ; 12, 1499.

Aberneth′y, John, (1764–1831), English surgeon, famous for his lectures at Bart's, for his eccentric rudeness to private patients, and for his book " The Constitutional Origin and Treatment of Local Diseases."

Aberra′tion, in lenses, 2163–64 ; chromatic, 1925, 2163 ; in telescopes, 3178.

Aberystwyth (ab-er-ist′-with), Wales. Seaport tn. of Cardiganshire ; pop. 9,474 ; National Library of Wales ; university college ; seaside resort ; 701.

" Abide With Me," hymn, 1678.

Abies (ab′-i′-ēz), the fir genus, 1278.

Abietic Acid, main constituent of rosin, 2768.

Abigail (ab′-i-gāl). Wife of Nabal ; ministered to the fleeing David, who married her on Nabal's death (1 Sam. xxv, 14–42) ; name used to mean a waiting-maid.

Abimelech (a-bim′-e-lek). A judge of Israel who set himself up as king and reigned for three years in Shechem. During an uprising against him he was struck on the head by a piece of millstone thrown by a woman, whereupon at his own order he was slain by his armour-bearer (Judges viii, ix).

Ab'lett, Thomas Robert (1849–1945). Brit. art teacher; founded Royal Drawing Soc., 1885. His system encouraged memory drawing.

Abney, Sir William de Wiveleslie (1844–1920). English chemist and physicist; made valuable photographic and colour printing researches.

Abo. *See* **Turku.**

Aborigines (ab-*o*-rij'-i-nĕz). Name given by Romans to a people of cent. Italy, traditionally said to have descended from their mountain home near Reate upon Latium, where they settled down as Latini. Term now applied to original, or earliest known, inhabitants of any country; of Australia; 307, *309*, 310.

Abou-ben-Adhem. In Leigh Hunt's poem, sees in a vision an angel writing "the names of those who love the Lord "; asks to be counted as one who loves his fellow-men, and learns that the love of Man is the love of God.

Aboukir (ab-ōō-kēr') or **Abukir Bay.** On N. coast of Egypt, w. of Rosetta mouth of Nile; Casablanca at the battle of (1798); 2313.

About (ah-bōō'), **Edmond François Valentin** (1828–85). Fr. novelist and dramatist; works include "Contemporary Greece," "Tolla, a Tale of Modern Rome."

A'braham. Founder of Hebrew nation, 13, 1829, 2480.

Abraham, Plains of. Battlefield near Quebec, where Wolfe defeated Montcalm (1759), 2715, *2716*.

A'brahams, Harold Maurice (b. 1899). Brit. athlete; represented Gt. Brit. in Olympic Games 1920 and 1924; won the 100 metres sprint in 1924: captained Brit. team in 1928.

Ab'rial, Jean Marie Charles (b. 1888). Fr. naval commander; under Pétain, resident-gen. Algiers, 1940; sec. of state for Navy, 1942–43; sentenced to 10 years' hard labour as collaborator 1946; released 1947.

Abruzzi (ah-brood'-zi), **Luigi, Duke of the** (1873–1933). It. royal prince, explorer, and scientist; first to ascend Mt. St. Elias, Alaska (1897); commanded It. fleet in 1st World War.

Abruzzi and Malise. Dept. in cent. It.; about 5,900 sq. m.; pop. 1,677,146; includes highest point of Apennines. Gran Sasso d'Italia (" great rock of Italy "), culminating in Mt. Corno. Scene of heavy fighting in 2nd World War, *184*, 1763, *1768*.

Ab'salom. Rebellious son of David; caught by his long hair in tree and slain (2 Sam. xiv-xviii); 979.

" Absalom and Achit'ophel." Allegorical satire by Dryden, in which Duke of Monmouth figures as Absalom, and Shaftesbury as Achitophel, 1050.

Ab'scess. A collection of pus in a body tissue.

LIST OF ABBREVIATIONS

A

A—argon.
A1—at Lloyd's, first-class ship on the register; first-class in physique, etc.
A.A.—Automobile Association; Associate in Arts; Antiaircraft.
A.A.A.—Amateur Athletic Association.
A.A.F.—Auxiliary Air Force.
A.A.G.—Assistant Adjutant-General.
A.A.I.—Associate of the Auctioneers' Institute.
A. and M.—Ancient and Modern (hymn-book).
A.A.Q.M.G.—Acting Assistant Quartermaster-General.
A.B.—able-bodied seaman; Bachelor of Arts, usually B.A.
A.B.A.—Amateur Boxing Association.
A B C—the alphabet; alphabetical railway guide.
ab init.—L *ab initio*, from the beginning.
A.C.—Appeal Court; Alpine Club; Athletic Club; Alternating Current.
Ac—actinium.
A.C.A.—Associate of the Institute of Char*ered Accountants.
a/c—account.
A.C.G.I.—Associate of the City and Guilds of London Institute.
A.C.I.S.—Associate of the Chartered Institute of Secretaries.
A.D.—L. *Anno Domini*, in the year of our Lord.
ad.—advertisement.
A.D.C.—aide-de-camp; Amateur Dramatic Club.
ad eund.-L. *ad eundem* (*gradum*) admitted to the same degree (at another university).
ad fin.—L. *ad finem*, at, to the end.
ad lib.—L. *ad libitum*, at pleasure.
Adm.—Admiral, Admiralty; Administrator.
admor.—administrator.
A.D.O.S.—Assistant Director of Ordnance Services.
ad val.—L. *ad valorem*, according to the value.
advt.—advertisement.
Æ—third-class ship at Lloyd's.
aegrot.—L. *aegrotat*, he is ill, in English universities, certificate that student is too ill to take exam.
aet., aetat.—L. *aetatis*, aged (so many years).
A.E.U.—Amalgamated Engineering Union.
A.F.A.—Amateur Football Association.

A.F.C.—Air Force Cross.
A.F.M.—Air Force Medal.
A.F.R.Ae.S.—Associate Fellow of the Royal Aeronautical Society.
A.G.—Adjutant-General; Attorney-General; Accountant-General; Agent-General.
Ag.—L. *argentum*, silver.
A.G.S.M.—Associate of the Guildhall School of Music.
A.I.A.—Associate of the Institute of Actuaries.
A.I.C E.—Associate of the Institution of Civil Engineers.
A.I.D.—Aeronautical Inspection Directorate.
A.I.Mech.E.—Associate of the Institution of Mechanical Engineers.
A.R.I.C.—Associate of the Royal Institute of Chemistry.
A.I.S.A.—Associate of the Incorporated Secretaries' Association.
Al—aluminium.
Ala.—Alabama.
Alban.—St. Albans, in signature of Bishop.
A.L.C.M.—Associate of the London College of Music.
A.L.S.—Associate of the Linnean Society.
a.m.—L. *ante meridiem*, before noon.
Am.—Americium.
A.M.D.G.—L. *ad majorem Dei gloriam*, to the greater glory of God—motto of the Jesuits.
A.M.I.C.E.—Associate Member of the Institution of Civil Engineers.
A.M.I.E.E.—Associate Member of the Institution of Electrical Engineers.
A.M.I.Mech.E.— Associate Member of the Institution of Mechanical Engineers.
amp.—ampere.
anon.—anonymous.
anr.—another.
A.N.Z.A.C. (Anzac)—Australian and New Zeland Army Corps.
A.O.D.—Ancient Order of Druids.
A.O.F.—Ancient Order of Foresters.
A.O H —Ancient Order of Hibernians.
A.P.M.—Assistant Provost-Marshal.
appro.—approval.
approx.—approximately.
A.Q.M.G.—Assistant Quartermaster-General.
A.R.A.—Associate of the Royal Academy.
A.R.A.M.—Associate of the Royal Academy of Music.
A.R.B.A.—Associate of the Royal Society of British Artists.

A.R.C.—Automobile Racing Club.
A.R.C.A.—Associate of the Royal College of Art; Associate of the Royal Cambrian Academy.
A.R.C.I.—Associate of the Royal Colonial Institute.
A.R.C.M.—Associate of the Royal College of Music.
A.R.C.O.—Associate of the Royal College of Organists.
A.R.C.S.—Associate of the Royal College of Science.
A.R.E.—Associate of the Royal Society of Painter-Etchers and Engravers.
A.R.H.A.—Associate of the Royal Hibernian Academy.
A.R.I.B.A.—Associate of the Royal Institute of British Architects.
Ariz.—Arizona.
Ark.—Arkansas.
A.R.M.S.—Associate of the Royal Society of Miniature Painters.
A.R.P.—Air Raid Precautions.
A.R.P.S.—Associate of the Royal Photographic Society.
A.R.S.A.—Associate of the Royal Scottish Academy.
A.R.S.M.—Associate of the Royal School of Mines (now Royal College of Science).
A.R.S.W.—Associate of the Royal Scottish Society of Painters in Water Colours.
A.R.W.S.—Associate of the Royal Society of Painters in Water Colours.
A.-S.—Anglo-Saxon.
As—arsenic.
A.S.A.A.—Associate of the Society of Incorporated Accountants and Auditors.
Asaph.—St. Asaph, in signature of Bishop.
A.S.E.—Amalgamated Society of Engineers.
A.S.L E. and F.—Associated Society of Locomotive Engineers and Firemen.
A.S.R.S. — Amalgamated Society of Railway Servants.
Assn.—association.
Asst.—assistant.
A.T.C.L.—Associate of Trinity College (of Music), London.
A.T.S.—Auxiliary Territorial Service (Women)
A.U.—Angström unit.
Au—L. *aurum*, gold.
A.U.C.—L. *ab urbe condita*, or *anno urbis conditae*, in the year of, or from the foundation of, the city (Rome).
A.V.—Authorized Version (Bible).
A.V.C.—Automatic volume control.

B

B—boron; black (of pencil lead).
b.—born; (cricket) bowled, bye
B.A.—Bachelor of Arts; British Academy; British Association.
Ba—Barium.
B. Agr(ic).—Bachelor of Agriculture.
B. & W.—Bath and Wells, in signature of Bishop.
Bart.—Baronet.
Bart's.—St. Bartholomew's Hospital.
Bath. & Well.—Bath and Wells, in signature of Bishop.
BB—double black (of pencil lead).
B.B.B.—treble black (of pencil lead).
B.B.C.—British Broadcasting Corporation.
B.C.—before Christ; British Columbia.
B.Ch.—L. *Baccalaureus Chirurgiae*, Bachelor of Surgery.
B.Ch.D.—Bachelor of Dental Surgery.
B.C.L.—Bachelor of Civil Law
B.Com.—Bachelor of Commerce.
B.D.—Bachelor of Divinity.
B.D.S.—Bachelor of Dental Surgery.
B.E.—Bachelor of Engineering
Be—beryllium.
B.E.A.—British European Airways.
Beds—Bedfordshire.
B.E.F.—British Expeditionary Force.
B.Eng.—Bachelor of Engineering.
Berks—Berkshire.
B. ès L.—Fr. *Bachelier ès Lettres*, Bachelor of Letters.
B. ès S.—Fr. *Bachelier ès Sciences*, Bachelor of Science
b.h.p.—brake-horse-power.
Bi—bismuth.
B.I.F.—British Industries Fair
B.L.—Bachelor of Law.
b.l.—bill of lading.
B.Litt.—Bachelor of Letters.
B LL.—Bachelor of Laws, more commonly LL.B.
B.M.—Bachelor of Medicine more commonly M.B.
B.M.A.—British Medical Association.
B.M.E.—Bachelor of Mining Engineering.
B.Mus.—Bachelor of Music more commonly Mus.Bac.
B.N.C.—Brasenose College, Oxford.
B.O.A.C.—British Overseas Airways Corporation.
B.O.T.—Board of Trade.
Br—bromine.

Ab'solute, Sir Anthony. In Sheridan's comedy " The Rivals," blustering kind-hearted old gentleman ; his son Captain Absolute makes way by humorous strategy.

Absolute alcohol, the purest form, containing 95·5 per cent alcohol, 103.

Absolute zero, −459·4° F., 1391, 1594.

Absorp'tion, of heat, 1595 ; of light, 875 ; in plants, 2621 ; spectrum, *plate f.* 3057.

Abt (ahpt), **Franz** (1819–85). Ger. song composer (" When the Swallows Homeward Fly ").

Abu Bekr (ah'-bōō-bek'r). First Mahomedan caliph, father-in-law of Mahomet.

Abydos (a-bī'-dos), Asia Minor. Anc. city at narrowest point of Hellespont, where Xerxes built bridge of boats ; home of Leander, 1619.

Abydos, Egypt. Anc. city on Nile, once second only to Thebes ; held sacred as burial-place of Osiris.

Abyssinia (ab-i-sin'-i-*a*). Country in N.E. Africa (anc. Ethiopia) ; about 350,000 sq. m. ; pop. est. 8,000,000 ; 13, 1072, 1227 ; *maps, 13, 1072* ; Italian invasion and conquest, 14, 1073, 1773, 3415 ; reconquered 1941, 15, 3418.

Acacia (*a*-kā'-sha). Widely distributed genus of shrubs and trees, **16** ; source of gum arabic, 1558.

Acad'emy, 16 ; of anc. Athens, *17*, 2628 ; British, 17 ; French, 17, 1380, 2779 ; Royal, 17, *2477*.

Acadia (*a*-kā'-di-*a*). Former Fr. colony in N. Amer., 17, 682, 2400.

Acanthus (*a*-kan'-thus), a plant, found chiefly in the tropics and S. Europe ; leaves inspired Corinthian capital in architecture, 213, *215*.

Acapulco (ah-k*a*-pool'-kō). Mex. spt. on Pacific, 230 m. s.w. of Mexico City ; pop. 21,000 ; exports copper, fruit, hides ; 2156.

Acari (ak'-*a*-rī). An order of arachnids including mites.

Accelera'tion, in mechanics, 1513, 2130.

Accel'erator, motor-car, *2242*, 2243.

Accident, social insurance against, 2994.

Accipitres (ak-sip'-i-trēz). Order of diurnal birds of prey.

Accolade (ak-*o*-lād), in ceremony of knighthood, 1864.

Accountant. A person who has charge of the accounts of a business or other concern ; as career, 519.

Accounting machine, 17.

Accra (ak-rah'). Cap. of Brit. Gold Coast Colony, w. Africa ; rly. and air terminus ; site of Achimota College, *f-i.* ; pop. 73,000 ; 3366.

Accrington. Tn. in Lancashire, 23 m. n.w. of Manchester ; cotton industry, dyeing, chemicals, engineering ; pop. about 40,000 ; 1890.

Accu'mulator, an electrical storage battery, *376*.

Acer (ā-sēr). The maple genus of trees, 2092.

Acetaldehyde, a colourless inflammable

LIST OF ABBREVIATIONS (*continued*)

B.R.—British Railways.
Brecon—Brecknockshire.
Brit.—Britain, Britannia, British.
Britt. — L. *Brit(t)an(n)iarum*, of (all) the Britains, on coins.
Bros.—Brothers (commercial).
B.S.—Bachelor of Surgery ; Bachelor of Science (U.S.A.).
B S A —British South Africa ; Birmingham Small Arms Co.
B.S.A.A.—British South American Airways.
B.Sc.—Bachelor of Science.
B.S.T.—British Summer Time.
Bt.—Baronet.
B.Th.—Bachelor of Theology.
B.Th.U.—British thermal unit.
B.T.U.—(elect.) Board of Trade unit.
Bucks—Buckinghamshire.
B.V.M.—L. *Beata Virgo Maria*, the blessed Virgin Mary.
B.W.G. — Birmingham wire gauge.
B.W.I.—British West Indies.

C

C—L. *centum*, 100 ; carbon.
C.—Centigrade.
c.—L. *circa, circum, circiter*, about ; (cricket) caught.
C3—lowest in physique, state of health, etc.
C.A.—Chartered Accountant.
Ca—calcium.
Cal.—California.
Cambs—Cambridgeshire.
c. & b.—caught and bowled (cricket).
Cantab. — L. *Cantabrigiensis*, member of Cambridge University.
Cantuar.—L. *Cantuariensis*, of Canterbury, in signature of Archbishop.
cap.—L. *capitulum*, chapter ; capital letter ; number of statute in year of reign.
Capt.—Captain.
Carliol.—Carlisle, in signature of Bishop.
C.B.—Companion of the Bath ; confined to barracks, as punishment in army.
Cb—columbium.
C.B.E.—Commander of the British Empire.
c.c.—cubic centimetre.
Cd—cadmium.
C.D.—Civil Defence.
c.d.v.—Fr.*carte-de-visite*(photograph size).
C.E.—Civil Engineer ; Chief Engineer ; Church of England.
Ce—cerium.
cent.—L. *centum*, 100 ; centigrade.
Cestr.—Chester, in signature of Bishop.

cf.—L. *confer*, compare.
c.f.i.—cost, freight, insurance.
C.G.S.—centimetre - gramme - second system of scientific measurement.
C.H.—Companion of Honour.
Ch.—Church.
Chas.—Charles.
Ch.B.—L. *Chirurgiae Baccalaureus*, Bachelor of Surgery.
Ch.M.—L. *Chirurgiae Magister*, Master of Surgery.
C.I.—(Imperial Order of the) Crown of India (for ladies).
Cicestr.—Chichester, in signature of Bishop.
C.I.D.—Criminal Investigation Department, New Scotland Yard.
C.I.E. — Companion of the Order of the Indian Empire.
C.I.G.S.—Chief of the Imperial General Staff.
C.I.Mech.E.—Companion of the Institution of Mechanical Engineers.
C.I.V.—City Imperial Volunteers.
Cl—chlorine.
Cm.—Curium.
C.M.—L. *Chirurgiae Magister*, Master of Surgery.
cm.—centimetre.
C.M.G. — Companion of St. Michael and St. George.
C.M.S.—Church Missionary Society.
C.N.R.—Canadian National Railways ; Civil Nursing Reserve.
C.O. — Commanding Officer ; Colonial Office ; Conscientious Objector.
Co—cobalt.
Co.—company ; county.
c/o—care of.
C.O.D.—cash on delivery.
Col.—Colonel.
Colo.—Colorado.
Com. — Commander, Commissioner, Commodore.
Con—L. *Contra*, against.
Conn.—Connecticut.
Consols—Consolidated Stock.
Co-op.—Co-operative (Stores).
Cor. Fel.—Corresponding Fellow (of society or academy).
Cor. Mem. — Corresponding Member (of society or academy).
Cor. Sec.—Corresponding Secretary (of society or academy).
cos.—cosine (trigonometry).
C.P.R.—Canadian Pacific Railway.
Cr—chromium.
Cr.—credit(or).
cresc.—Ital. *crescendo*, with increasing loudness.
Cs—caesium.
C.S.I.—Companion of the Star of India.

C.T.C.—Cyclists' Touring Club.
Cu—L. *cuprum*, copper ; cubic.
C.V.O.—Commander of the Royal Victorian Order.
C.W.S.—Co-operative Wholesale Society.
cwt.—hundredweight.

D

D.—500 (Roman numeral) ; deuterium.
d.—L. *denarius*, a penny ; died.
Dak.—Dakota.
D.B.E.—Dame Commander of the British Empire.
D.C.—direct current ; District of Columbia (U.S.A.).
d.c.—Ital. *da capo*, repeat from the beginning (music).
D.C.L.—Doctor of Civil Law.
D.D.—Doctor of Divinity.
D.D.S.—Doctor of Dental Surgery.
D.D.T. — dichlor-diphenyl-trichlorethene.
Del.—Delaware ; delete.
del(t).—L. *delineavit*, he (she) drew (it).
D.Eng.—Doctor of Engineering.
D.F.—Defender of the Faith (more often *Fid Def* or F.D.).
D.F.C.—Distinguished Flying Cross.
D.F.M.—Distinguished Flying Medal.
D.G.—L. *Dei gratia*, by the Grace of God.
D.I.C.—Diploma of the Imperial College.
dim.—Ital. *diminuendo*, getting gradually softer.
div.—dividend.
D.Lit.—Doctor of Literature.
D.Litt.—(at Aberdeen) Doctor of Letters.
dm.—decimetre.
D.M.R.E.—Diploma in Medical Radiology and Electrology.
d.—*ditto*, the same.
D.O.M.—L. *Deo optimo maximo*. to God the best and greatest.
D.O.M.S.—Diploma in Ophthalmic Medicine and Surgery.
D.O.R.A.—Defence of the Realm Act(s).
D.P.H.—Diploma in, Department of, Public Health.
Dr.—Doctor ; debtor.
dr.—drachm.
D.S.C.—Distinguished Service Cross.
D.Sc.—Doctor of Science.
D.S.M.—Distinguished Service Medal.
D.S.O.—Distinguished Service Order.
D.T.M.—Diploma in Tropical Medicine.
Dunelm.—Durham, in signature of Bishop.
D.V.—L. *Deo volente*, God willing.

D.V.M.—Doctor of Veterinary Medicine.
D.V.S.—Doctor of Veterinary Science or Surgery.
dwt.—pennyweight.
Dy.—dysprosium.
D.Z.—Doctor of Zoology.

E

E.—east ; second-class ship at Lloyd's ; Egyptian in £E.
E. & O.E.—errors and omissions excepted.
Ebor.—L. *Eboracensis*, of *Eboracum*, York, in signature of Archbishop.
E.C.—East Central (London postal district).
Edin.—Edinburgh.
e.g.—L. *exempli gratia*, for example.
E.G.M.—Empire Gallantry Medal.
elect.—electricity.
Em.—emanation.
E.M.D.P.—electromotive difference of potential.
E.M.F.—electromotive force.
E.M.S.—Emergency Medical Service.
E.M.U.—electromagnetic units.
Eng.—England.
E.N.S.A.—Entertainment National Service Association.
E.P.D.—Excess Profits Duty.
E.P.N.S. — Electro-plated nickel silver.
Er—erbium.
E.R. (et I.)—L. *Eduardus Rex (et Imperator)*, Edward King (and Emperor).
Esq —Esquire.
E.S.U.—Electrostatic units.
et. al.—L. *et alibi*, and elsewhere ; *et alii*, and other people ; *et alia*, and other things.
etc.—L. *et cetera*, and (the other things, and so forth).
et seq.—L. *et sequens, et sequentia*, and the following.
E.T.U.—Electrical Trades Union.
Eu—europium.
Exon.—Exeter, in signature of Bishop.

F

F—fluorine (chemistry) ; firm (of pencil-lead).
F.—Fahrenheit.
f—acceleration (mechanics) ; force ; foot or feet.
f—Ital. *forte*, loud ; lens aperture.
F.A.—Football Association.
Fahr.—Fahrenheit.
F.A.I.—Fellow of the Auctioneers' Institute.
F.A.N.Y.—First Aid Nursing Yeomanry.

solvent liquid, made from alcohol and acetylene, 18.

Acetan'ilide. A drug used in headache powders and as a febrifuge ; obtained from coal-tar.

Acetate (as'-i-tāt). A salt of acetic acid ; lead (" sugar of lead "), 1724 ; rayon, 2748, 2749.

Acetic (a-sē'-tik) **acid**, composition of, 699 ; vinegar from, 3324.

Ace'tone. An organic compound used as a solvent, and absorbent in cylinders of acetylene, 18 ; from petroleum, 2430 ; in rayon mfr., 2749.

Acetylene (a-set'-i-lēn). An illuminating and heating gas, 18, 1420 ; in lighthouse lamps, 1945 ; specific gravity, 3054.

Achaea (a-kē'-a). District of Greece on N. coast of Peloponnesus ; Achaean League, a confederation of its anc. towns, crushed by Rome, 146 B.C.

Achaeans. One of the main divisions of the anc. Greeks, 1517, 1518.

Achates (a-kā'-tēz). In Virgil's " Aeneid," Trojan hero noted for loyalty to Aeneas ; hence phrase *fidus Achates*, " faithful Achates."

Acheron (ak'-ē-ron). In Gk. myth., river of underworld ; also the underworld in general.

Acheson (atch'-es-on), **Dean G.** (b. 1893). Amer. statesman ; successively asst.-sec., 1941–45, undersec., 1945–47, and Secretary of State from Jan. 7, 1949 ; U.S. signatory of the North Atlantic Treaty, April 4, 1949.

Achill (ak'-il). Largest isl. of Ireland, part of co. Mayo, Eire ; 15 m. by 12 m. ; pop. 4,800 ; tillage and turf-cutting ; knitting industry at Dooagh.

Achill Head. Westernmost point of the mountainous isl. of Achill.

Achilles (a-kil'-ēz). Gk. hero of Trojan War, 19 ; and Amazons, 137 ;

and Chiron, 742 ; slays Hector, 1603 ; statue, *19* ; story of his shield, 19.

Achilles (ak-ill'-eez), **H.M.S.** Brit. cruiser, N.Z. div. ; took part in battle of riv. Plate ; 3417 ; *See* Plata River, battle of.

Achilles tendon, *1342* ; origin of name, 19 ; and shoes, 1677.

Achimota College, for Africans ; estab. 1927, near Accra, Gold Coast ; comprising Secondary School and Teacher Training Coll., and in 1949 temporarily housing Gold Coast University Coll. ; 73.

Achinese (ach-i-nēz). Natives of Achin or Atcheen, a former native kingdom, Atjeh, at N. end of Sumatra ; of shorter stature and darker colour than other Sumatrans.

Achro'matism, of reflecting telescope, 3178.

Acids and Alkalis, in chemistry, 20 ; acetic, 699 ; benzoic, 857 ; carbolic, 699, 857 ; carbonic, 699 ; in

---

LIST OF ABBREVIATIONS (*continued*)

F.A.O.—Food and Agricultural Organization.
F.B.A.—Fellow of the British Academy.
F.B.H.—fire brigade hydrant.
F.B.I.—Federation of British Industries.
F.C.A.—Fellow of the Institute of Chartered Accountants.
F.C.G.I.—Fellow of the City and Guilds of London Institute.
F.C.I.I.—Fellow of the Chartered Insurance Institute.
F.C.I.S.—Fellow of the Chartered Institute of Secretaries.
rep.—foolscap.
F.C.S.—Fellow of the Chemical Society.
F.D.—L. *Fidei Defensor*, defender of the faith.
Fe—L. *ferrum*, iron.
fec.—L. *fecit*, he (she) did, made (it).
ff.—Ital. *fortissimo*, very loud.
F.F.A.—Fellow of the Faculty of Actuaries.
F.G.S.—Fellow of the Geological Society.
F.H.—fire hydrant.
F.I.A.—Fellow of the Institute of Actuaries.
F.I.A.A.—Fellow (Architect Member) of the Incorporated Association of Architects and Surveyors.
F.I.A.S.—Fellow (Surveyor Member) of the Incorporated Association of Architects and Surveyors.
F.I.A.T.—Ital. *Fabrica Italiana Automobile Torino*, make of motor-car.
F.I.C.A.—Fellow of the Institute of Chartered Accountants.
Fid. Def.—L. *Fidei Defensor*, defender of the faith.
fig.—figure (illustration).
F.I.I.A.—Fellow of the Institute of Industrial Administration.
F.I.Inst.—Fellow of the Imperial Institute.
F.Inst.P.—Fellow of the Institute of Physics.
F.I.O.—Fellow of the Institute of Ophthalmic Opticians.
F.I.S.A.—Fellow of the Incorporated Secretaries' Association.
F.J.I.—Fellow of the Institute of Journalists.
Fl.—florin.
Fla.—Florida.
F.L.A.A.—Fellow of London Association of Accountants.
F.L.A.S.—Fellow of the Land Agents' Society.
F.L.S.—Fellow of the Linnean Society.
F.M.—Field-Marshal.
F.O.—Foreign Office, Field Officer.
f.o.b.—free on board.

f.p.a.—free of particular average.
F.Phys.S. — Fellow of the Physical Society.
Fr.—French.
F.R.A.I.—Fellow of the Royal Anthropological Institute.
F.R.A.M.—Fellow of the Royal Academy of Music.
F.R.A.S.—Fellow of the Royal Astronomical Society, of the Royal Asiatic Society.
F.R.Ae.S.—Fellow of the Royal Aeronautical Society.
F.R.B.S.—Fellow of the Royal Botanic Society.
F.R.C.I.—Fellow of the Royal Colonial Institute.
F.R.C.M.—Fellow of the Royal College of Music.
F.R.C.O.—Fellow of the Royal College of Organists.
F.R.C.P.—Fellow of the Royal College of Physicians.
F.R.C.S.—Fellow of the Royal College of Surgeons.
F.R.C.V.S. — Fellow of the Royal College of Veterinary Surgeons.
F.R.Econ.Soc.—Fellow of the Royal Economic Society.
F.R.G.S.—Fellow of the Royal Geographical Society.
F.R.Hist.S.—Fellow of the Royal Historical Society.
F.R.Hort.S.—Fellow of the Royal Horticultural Society.
F.R.I.B.A.—Fellow of the Royal Institute of British Architects.
F.R.I.C.—Fellow of the Royal Institute of Chemistry.
F.R.Met.S.—Fellow of the Royal Meteorological Society.
F.R.M.S.—Fellow of the Royal Microscopical Society.
F.R.N.S.A.—Fellow of the Royal Naval School of Architects.
F.R.P.S.—Fellow of the Royal Photographic Society.
F.R.S.—Fellow of the Royal Society.
F.R.S.A.—Fellow of the Royal Society of Arts.
F.R.S.E.—Fellow of the Royal Society of Edinburgh.
F.R.S.L.—Fellow of the Royal Society of Literature.
fs.—foot-second.
F.S.A.—Fellow of the Society of Antiquaries.
F.S.A.A.—Fellow of the Society of Incorporated Accountants and Auditors.
F.S.I.—Fellow of the Surveyors' Institute.
ft.—foot, feet.
F.W.B—four wheel brake.
F.W.D.—four wheel drive.
F.Z.S.—Fellow of the Zoological Society of London.

G

g.—gramme ; gravity.
Ga—gallium.
Ga.—Georgia.
gal.—gallon.
G.B.—Great Britain.
G.B.E.—Knight (or Dame) Grand Cross of British Empire.
G.C.—George Cross.
G.C.B.—Knight Grand Cross of the Bath.
G.C.F.—greatest common factor.
G.C.H.—Knight Grand Cross of Hanover.
G.C.I.E.—Knight Grand Commander of the Indian Empire.
G.C.L.H.—Knight Grand Cross of the Legion of Honour.
G.C.M.—greatest common measure.
G.C.M.G.—Knight Grand Cross of St. Michael and St. George.
G.C.S.I.—Knight Grand Commander of the Star of India.
G.C.V.O.—Knight Grand Cross of the Royal Victorian Order.
Gd—gadolinium.
Ge—germanium.
Gen.—General.
Ger.—German.
G.H.Q.—General Headquarters.
Gib.—Gibraltar.
Gk.—Greek.
Gl—glucinum (beryllium).
Glam—Glamorganshire.
Glos—Gloucestershire.
G.M.—Grand Master (nighthood and freemasonry) ; Gold Medallist (Bisley) ; George Medal.
gm.—gramme ; grain.
G.M.C.—General Medical Council.
G.M.I.E.—Grand Master of the Indian Empire.
G.M.M.G.—Grand Master of St. Michael and St. George.
G.M.S.I.—Grand Master of the Star of India.
G.M.T.—Greenwich Mean Time.
G.O.C.—General Officer Commanding.
G.P.O.—General Post Office.
G.R.—L. *Georgius Rex*, George King.
Gr.—Greek.
gr.—gramme.
grm.—gramme.
gym.—gymnasium, gymnastics.

H

H—hydrogen ; hard (of pencil-lead).
H.—Hydrant.
H.A.C.—Honourable Artillery Company.
h. & c.—hot and cold running water.
Hants—Hampshire.

HB—hard black (of pencil-lead).
H.B.M.—His (Her) Britannic Majesty.
H.C.F.—highest common factor.
H.E.—His Eminence ; His Excellency ; high explosive.
He—helium.
Herts.—Hertfordshire.
Hf—hafnium.
H.F.—high frequency.
Hg—L. *hydrargyrum*, mercury.
H.H.—His (Her) Highness ; His Holiness (the Pope).
hhd.—hogshead.
HH—double hard (of pencil-lead).
HHH—trebly hard (of pencil-lead).
H.I.H.—His (Her) Imperial Highness.
H.I.M.—His (Her) Imperial Majesty.
H.M.—His (Her) Majesty.
H.M.S.—His (Her) Majesty's Ship (Service).
Ho—holmium.
Hon.—Honourable, honorary.
H.P.—half-pay ; horse-power ; high pressure ; hire-purchase.
H.Q.—headquarters.
H.R.H.—His (Her) Royal Highness.
H.S.H.—His (Her) Serene Highness.
H.T.—high tension.
Hunts—Huntingdonshire.
Hy.—Henry.
hydro—hydropathic establishment.

I

I—(Roman numeral) one ; iodine ; amperes (electricity)
Ia.—Iowa.
ib., ibid.—L. *ibidem*, in the same place.
I.B.U.—International Boxing Union.
i.c.—internal combustion.
I.C.I.—Imperial Chemical Industries.
I.C.S.—Indian Civil Service.
id.—L. *idem*, the same.
Ida.—Idaho.
I.D.B.—Illicit diamond buying, buyer (South Africa).
i.e.—L. *id est*, that is.
I.G.—Inspector-General.
i.h.p.—indicated horse-power.
I.H.S.—L. *Jesus Hominum Salvator*, Jesus, Saviour of Mankind.
Il—illinium.
Ill.—Illinois.
I.L.O.—International Labour Office.
I.L.P.—Independent Labour Party.
In—indium.
in.—inch, inches.
inc.—incorporated, inclusive.

digestion, 1016; formic, 165; hydrochloric, 1016, 1667; hydrocyanic (prussic), 947; lactic, 2174; nitric, 1250; picric, 857, 1250; salicylic, 857; sulphuric, 3117; tartaric, 3155.

Aclin'ic Line, or Magnetic Equator. An imaginary irregular line round the earth, near geographical equator, marking perfect balance between attraction of North and South Magnetic Poles; at any point on this line the compass needle does not dip.

Acoma Indians. Pueblo people, *2699*.

Aconcagua (ah-kon-kah'-gwa). Highest peak of Andes and S. Amer. (23,080 ft.); gives its name to river and prov. in Chile; 153, *3024*.

Aconi'tum. A genus of about 70 species of poisonous plants of the buttercup family, including some medicinal species; also called monk's-hood, from large showy flowers with hooded sepals : 2637, *2639*; roots, 2825.

Acon'itine, poison, 2638.

Acorn. Fruit of oak tree, *2410*.

Acorn barnacle, 362.

Acoustic mine, 2186.

Acoustics (*a*-kŏŏ'-stiks *or a*-kow'-stiks). Science of sound, 3009.

Acre (ah'-kêr *or* ă-kêr). Spt. of Palestine; pop. 9,800; taken by Richard the Lion-Hearted in 3rd Crusade (1191), 937; siege, *937*; taken by Brit. in 1918, 3414.

Acre. Unit of land measure (4,840 sq. yd.). *See* **Weights and Measures,** *f-i.*

Acres (ă'-kêrz), **Bob.** In Sheridan's comedy " The Rivals," a swaggering coward.

Acridiidae (ak-ri-dī'-i-dē). The locust family, 1511.

Acrisius (*a*-kris'-i-*u*s), in Gk. myth., king of Argos, grandfather of Perseus, 2552.

Acromegaly (ak-rō-meg'-*a*-li), produces a form of giantism, 1461.

Acropolis (*a*-krop'-*o*-lis), of Athens, **21**, *plate f. 212*, 284, *285*, 286; statue of Athena, *283*.

Acropolis, of Thebes, anc. Gk. city, 3197.

Acros'tic. A puzzle, competition, or verse form in which the initial, and sometimes final letters of the lines form words.

Acteon or Actaeon (ak-tē'-on), in Gk. myth., hunter who spied on Diana bathing, 251, *252*.

Acting, hints on, 1044; as career, 1044. *See in Index* Drama.

Ac'tinism. Property of light by which chemical changes are produced; makes photography possible, 2577.

Actin'ium (Ac). A radio-active element of the aluminium group; of unknown atomic weight; disintegration product of the element proto-actinium, occurring in pitch-blende; radio-active properties, 778, *2732*.

Actinomyco'sis. A disease of cattle and Man, characterized by tumours

---

LIST OF ABBREVIATIONS (*continued*)

incl.—including, inclusive.
incog.—incognito.
Ind.—Indiana.
inf.—L. *infra*, below.
infra dig.—L. *infra dignitatem*, beneath one's dignity.
I.N.R.I.—L. *Jesus Nazarenus Rex Judaeorum*, Jesus of Nazareth, King of the Jews.
inst.—instant (the present month).
int.—interest.
I.O.G.T.—Independent Order of Good Templars.
I.O.M.—Isle of Man.
I.O.O.F.—International Order of Oddfellows.
I.O.U.—I owe you.
I.O.W.—Isle of Wight.
ipecac.—ipecacuanha.
Ir—iridium.
I.R.A.—Irish Republican Army.
Is.—Island.
I.S.C.—Indian Staff Corps.
Isl.—Island.
I.S.O.—Imperial Service Order.
I.T.—Indian Territory (U.S.A.)
Ital.—Italian. Italics.
I.W.—Isle of Wight.
I.W.W.—Industrial Workers of the World.

J

Jap.—Japanese.
Jas.—James.
Jno.—John.
jnr.—junior.
J.P.—Justice of the Peace.
jr.—junior.
junr.—junior.

K

K—L, *kalium*, potassium.
Kan.—Kansas.
K.B.—Knight Bachelor.
K.B.E.—Knight Commander of British Empire.
K.C.—King's Counsel.
kc.—kilocycle.
K.C.B.—Knight Commander of the Bath.
K.C.H.—Knight Commander of Hanover.
K.C.I.E.—Knight Commander of the Indian Empire.
K.C.M.G.—Knight Commander of St. Michael and St. George.
K.C.S.I.—Knight Commander of the Star of India.
K.C.V.O.—Knight Commander of the Victorian Order.
K.G.—Knight of the Garter.
kg.—kilogramme.
kilo(g).—kilogramme.
kilo(l).—kilolitre.
kilo(m).—kilometre.
kl.—kilolitre.
K.L.H.—Knight of the Legion of Honour.
K.M.—Knight of Malta.
km.—kilometre (km².—square kilometre).

K.P.—Knight of St. Patrick.
Kr—krypton.
K.T.—Knight Templar; Knight of the Thistle.
Kt.—Knight.
kv.—kilovolt.
kw.—kilowatt.
kw.-hr.—kilowatt-hours.
Ky.—Kentucky.

L

L—(Roman numeral) fifty.
L.—Lake; Liberal; left; Latin.
l.—left; litre; lira.
La—lanthanum.
La.—Louisiana.
Lancs—Lancashire.
Lat.—Latin. Latitude.
lb.—pound(s) (weight).
l.b.—(cricket) leg-bye.
l.b.w.—leg before wicket.
l.c.—lower case (type).
L.C.C.—London County Council(lor).
L.C.J.—Lord Chief Justice.
L.C.M.—least common multiple.
L.Cpl.—lance-corporal.
L.D.S.—Licentiate of Dental Surgery.
L.F.—low frequency.
L.F.B.—London Fire Brigade.
l.h.—left hand.
Li—lithium.
Lieut.—Lieutenant.
Lincs—Lincolnshire.
Lit. Hum.—L. *Literae Humaniores*, Final Classical Honour School, Oxford.
Litt.B.—Bachelor of Literature.
Litt.D.—Doctor of Literature.
L.J.—Lord Justice.
L.L.A.—Lady Literate in Arts.
LL.B.—Bachelor of Laws.
LL.D.—Doctor of Laws.
LL.M.—Master of Laws.
L.M.T.—Length, mass, time (physics).
loc. cit.—L. *loco citato*, in the place cited.
log—logarithm.
Londin., also London.—London, in signature of Bishop.
long.—longitude.
log.—L. *loquitur*, (he) speaks.
L.P.O.—London Philharmonic Orchestra.
L.R.A.M.—Licentiate of the Royal Academy of Music.
L.R.B.—London Rifle Brigade.
L.R.C.P.—Licentiate of the Royal College of Physicians.
L.R.C.S.—Licentiate of the Royal College of Surgeons.
L.S.D.—L. *librae, solidi, denarii*, pounds, shillings, pence.
L.S.O.—London Symphony Orchestra.
Lt.—Lieutenant.

L.T.—low tension; London Transport.
L.T.A.—Lawn Tennis Association.
Ltd.—Limited.
L.T.E.—London Transport Executive.
Lu—lutecium.
L.-U.—Liberal-Unionist.

M

M—(Roman numeral) 1000.
M.—Monsieur; maiden (over, cricket).
m.—miles; mass (physics).
Ma—masurium.
M.A.—Master of Arts.
Maj.—Major.
Mancun. — L. *Mancunium*, Manchester, in signature of Bishop.
M. and B.—May and Baker (firm of mfr. chemists).
Mass.—Massachusetts.
maths.—mathematics.
matric.—matriculation.
M.B.—Bachelor of Medicine.
M.B.E.—Member of the Order of the British Empire.
M.C.—Master of Ceremonies; Military Cross.
M.C.C. — Marylebone Cricket Club.
M.Com.—Master of Commerce (Birmingham).
M.Comm.—Master of Commerce and Administration (Manchester).
M.D.—Doctor of Medicine.
Md.—Maryland.
Mddx.—Middlesex.
M.D.S. — Master of Dental Surgery.
Me.—Maine.
mem.—L. *memento*, remember; memorandum.
memo.—L. *memorandum*, to be remembered.
Messrs.—Messieurs, Gentlemen; also as plural of Mr.
Met.—Metropolitan (Railway).
mf—Ital. *mezzo forte*, moderately loud.
mfd.—microfarad.
M.F.H.—Master of Foxhounds.
mfrs.—manufacturers.
Mg—magnesium.
mg.—milligramme.
Mgr.—Monsignor.
mho—unit of conductivity, reciprocal of ohm.
M.I.C.E.—Member of the Institution of Civil Engineers.
Mich.—Michigan; Michaelmas.
Middx.—Middlesex.
M.I.E.E.—Member of the Institution of Electrical Engineers.
M.I.J.—Member of the Institute of Journalists.
M.I.Mech.E.—Member of the Institution of Mechanical Engineers.

Minn.—Minnesota.
M.Inst.C.E.—Member of the Institution of Civil Engineers.
M.Inst.Mech.E.—Member of the Institution of Mechanical Engineers.
M.Inst.Min.E.—Member of the Institution of Mining Engineers.
Miss.—Mississippi.
ml.—millilitre.
Mlle.—Mademoiselle.
MM.—Messieurs.
mm.—millimetre (mm², square millimetre; mm³, cubic millimetre).
M.M.—Military Medal.
Mme.—Madame.
Mn—manganese.
M.N.—Merchant Navy.
M.O.—Money Order; Medical Officer.
Mo—molybdenum.
Mo.—Missouri.
Mods.—Moderations (Oxford).
M.O.H.—Medical Officer of Health; Master of Otter Hounds; Ministry of Health.
Mon.—Monmouthshire.
Mont.—Montana.
M.O.O.—Money order office.
M.P.—Member of Parliament; Military Police.
mp—Ital. *mezzo piano*, moderately soft.
m.p.h.—miles per hour.
M.P.S.—Member of the Pharmaceutical Society. Philological Society.
Mr.—Mister.
M.R.A.S.—Member of the Royal Asiatic Society; Member of the Royal Academy of Science.
M.R.C.P. — Member of the Royal College of Physicians.
M.R.C.S. — Member of the Royal College of Surgeons.
M.R.C.V.S.—Member of the Royal College of Veterinary Surgeons.
M.R.I.—Member of the Royal Institution.
Mrs.—Mistress.
M.R.S.L.—Member of the Royal Society of Literature.
MS.—manuscript.
M.S.—Master in Surgery; motor ship.
M.Sc.—Master of Science.
M.S.H.—Master of Stag Hounds.
MSS—manuscripts.
Mt.—mount(ain).
Muc. Bac.—Bachelor of Music.
Mus. Doc.—Doctor of Music.
M.V.—motor vessel.
M.V.O.—Member of the Victorian Order.
M.W.B.—Metropolitan Water Board.
Mx.—Middlesex.

of the mouth and jaws, and caused by a fungus.

Actinozo'a. A class of coelenterates.

Actium (ak'-ti-um) (now Akri). Promontory of N.W. Greece; battle of (31 B.C.) 303, 2305.

Act of Parliament, 1489, 1490.

Act of Union (of 1707), unites Scot. to Eng., 1515; (of 1800), Ire., 1515, 1746.

Ac'ton, John Emerich, first Baron (1834–1902). Eng. historian and editor; led liberal Cath. movement in Eng.

Ac'ton. Borough of Middlesex, 7 m. w. of City of London; pop. 70,500; engineering works, printing, food products, laundries; 2168.

Acts of the Apostles. 5th book of New Testament, giving history of Church from Ascension of Christ to imprisonment of St. Paul in Rome; authorship, 189.

Adagio (ad-ah'-jō), in music, 2264.

Ada'lia. Spt. of Turkey in S. Asia Minor; important trade centre; pop. 28,000.

Adam. First created man; Babylonion version, 332; in "Back to Methuselah," 1042; in Milton's "Paradise Lost," 2178; creation of, by Michelangelo, 2161; statue by Rodin, 2796.

Adam, Robert (1728–92). Brit. architect and furniture-maker, most celebrated of four brothers, 22, 1409, 1412; designs by, 22, 23.

Adamawa (ad-ah-mah'-wah). Former native kingdom of W.-Cent. Africa, divided between Nigeria and Cameroon; largely mountainous, with thick forests. Palm and banana grown extensively; trade in ivory and rubber.

"Adam Bede." Novel by George Eliot, 1146.

Adams, Abraham (" Parson "). In Fielding's " Joseph Andrews," eccentric good-hearted country

curate, unsuspecting and ignorant of the world.

Adams, Charles Francis (1807–86). Amer. diplomatist, son of John Quincy Adams; he was minister to Gt. Brit. 1861–68, 23.

Adams, John (1735–1826), 2nd Pres. of U.S.A., 23.

Adams, John (c.1760–1829). Assumed name of Alexander Smith, one of the mutineers of the Bounty, 2473.

Adams, John Couch (1819–92). Eng. astronomer, one of the discoverers of Neptune, 2315, 2618.

Adams, John Quincy (1767–1848), 6th Pres. of U.S.A., 23.

Adams, Samuel (1722–1803). Amer. patriot and statesman who was largely responsible for bringing about the independence of the U.S.A.

Adam's apple. Origin of name, 191.

Adam's Bridge. Reefs and sand banks between India and Ceylon.

LIST OF ABBREVIATIONS (*continued*)

N

N—nitrogen.
N.—north.
Na—L. *natrium*, sodium.
N.A.—Nursing Auxiliary.
N.A.A.F.I.—Navy, Army, and Air Force Institutes.
N.B.—L. *nota bene*, note well; North Britain; New Brunswick.
n.b.—(cricket) no ball.
Nb—niobium.
N.C.—North Carolina.
N.C.O. — non-commissioned officer.
Nd—neodymium.
N.D.C.—National Defence Contribution.
Ne—neon.
Neb.—Nebraska.
nem. con.—L. *nemine contradicente*, "no one contradicting," unanimously.
Nev.—Nevada.
N.H.—New Hampshire.
n.h.p.—nominal horse-power.
N.H.S.—National Health Service.
Ni—nickel.
N.J.—New Jersey.
No(s).—Ital.*numero*,number(s).
non seq.—L. *non sequitur*, it does not follow.
Northants—Northamptonshire.
Norvic.—Norwich, in signature of Bishop.
Notts—Nottinghamshire.
Np—Neptunium.
N.P.—Notary Public.
N.R.—National Register.
N.R.A.—National Rifle Association; National Recovery Administration (U.S.A.).
N S.—New Style, of Gregorian Calendar; Nova Scotia; L. *non satis*, not sufficient (funds), on cheque.
N.S.D.A.P.—(Ger.) National Socialist (Nazi) Party.
N.S.P.C.C.—National Society for the Prevention of Cruelty to Children.
N.S.W.—New South Wales.
N.T.—New Testament; Northern Territory (Australia).
Nt—niton.
N.U.R.—National Union of Railwaymen.
N.W.T.—North-Western Territories (Canada).
N.Y.—New York (state).
N.Y.C.—New York City.
N.Z.—New Zealand.

O

O—oxygen.
O.—Ohio.
o/a—on account.
ob.—*obiit*, died.
O.B.E.—Officer of Brit. Empire.
O.C.—Officer Commanding.

O.E. — Old English; Old Etonian.
O.H.M.S.—On His (Her) Majesty's Service.
Okla.—Oklahoma.
O.M.—Order of Merit.
Ont.—Ontario.
O.P.—opposite prompt (theatre); out of print.
o.p.—over proof (spirits).
op.—L. *opus*, a work.
op. cit.—L. *opere citato*, in the work cited.
Oreg.—Oregon.
O.S.—Old Style (calendar).
O.S.B.—Order of St. Benedict.
Os—osmium.
O.T.—Old Testament.
O.T.C.—Officers' Training Corps.
O.U.D.S.—Oxford University Dramatic Society.
Oxon.—Oxfordshire; Oxford University; Oxford, in signature of Bishop.
Oz.—ounce(s).

P

P—phosphorus.
p.—page.
p—Ital. *piano*, soft.
Pa.—Pennsylvania.
P. & O. — Peninsular and Oriental (steamship line).
par.—paragraph.
P.A.Y.E.—pay as you earn (Income Tax).
Pb—L. *plumbum*, lead.
P.C.—Privy Council; Privy Councillor; Police Constable.
p.c.—L. *per centum*, by the hundred; post card.
Pd—palladium.
P.E.P.—Political Economic Planning.
per cent—L. *per centum*, per hundred.
per pro.—*per procurationem*, by proxy, as agent.
Petriburg.—Peterborough, in signature of Bishop.
pf—Ital. *piano-forte*, soft, then loud.
Ph.B.—Bachelor of Philosophy.
Ph.D.—Doctor of Philosophy.
Phila.—Philadelphia.
P.L.A. — Port of London Authority.
p.m.—L. *post meridiem*, after noon.
P.M.G.—Postmaster-General.
P.O.—Post Office; postal order; petty officer (naval).
Po—polonium.
P.O.O.—Post Office Order.
pop.—population, popular.
p.p.—L. *per pro*. (*q.v.*).
pp.—pages.
pp—Ital. *pianissimo*, very soft.
ppp—Ital. *pianissimo*,as soft as possible.

P.P.S.—additional postscript; Parliamentary and Private Secretary.
Pr—praseodymium.
P.R.—Proportional Representation.
P.R.A.—President of the Royal Academy.
pref.—preference; preferred (stock or shares).
prep.—preparation, preparatory (school, etc.).
pro.—professional (golf, etc.).
P.R.O.—Public Relations Officer.
Proc.—Proceedings (of learned society).
Prof.—Professor.
pro tem.—L. *pro tempore*, for the time being.
prox.—L.*proximo* (*mense*), next month.
P.R.S.—President of the Royal Society.
P.R.S.A.—President of the Royal Scottish Academy.
P.S.—L. *post scriptum*, postscript; prompt side (theatre).
p.s.—(military) passed School (of Instruction).
p.s.a.—graduate of the Royal Air Force Staff College.
p.s.c.—graduate of the Military (or Naval) Staff College.
P.T.—physical training.
Pt.—Point; Port.
Pt—platinum.
P.T.O—please turn over.
p.v.c—polyomyl chloride.
Pu—plutonium.
P.W.D.—Public Works Department.

Q

Q.—Coulomb.
Q.C.—Queen's Counsel.
Q.E.D.—L. *quod erat demonstrandum*, which was to be proved (theorem).
Q.E.F.—L. *quod erat faciendum*, which was to be done (problem).
Q.M.G.—Quartermaster-General.
qq.v.—L. *quae vide*, which (things) see.
qt.—quart.
quad.—quadrangle, quadrant.
q.v.—L. *quod vide*, which see.

R

R.—L. *rex*, king; L. *regina*, queen; right; river; ohm; Réaumur (thermometer).
r.—right; run (cricket).
R.A.—Royal Academy; Royal Academician; Royal Artillery; Rear-Admiral; Road Association.
Ra—radium.

R.A.C.—Royal Automobile Club; Royal Armoured Corps.
R.A.D.A.—Royal Academy of Dramatic Art.
R.A.F.—Royal Air Force.
R.A.F.V.R.—Royal Air Force Volunteer Reserve.
R.A.M.—Royal Academy of Music.
R.A.M.C.—Royal Army Medical Corps.
R.A.O.B.—Royal Antediluvian Order of Buffaloes.
R.A.O.C.—Royal Army Ordnance Corps.
R.A.P.C.—Royal Army Pay Corps.
R.A.R.O.—Regular Army Reserve of Officers.
R.A.S.— Royal Asiatic Society; Royal Astronomical Society.
R.A.S.C.—Royal Army Service Corps.
R.A.V.C.—Royal Army Veterinary Corps.
R.B.—Rifle Brigade.
Rb—rubidium.
R.B.A.—Royal Society of British Artists.
R.B.S.—Royal Society of British Sculptors.
R.C.—Roman Catholic; right centre (stage).
R.C.M.—Royal College of Music.
R.C.P.—Royal College of Physicians.
R.C.S.—Royal College of Surgeons.
R.D.—refer to drawer (on cheques).
Rd.—Road.
R.D.I.—Royal Designer for Industry.
Re—rhenium.
R.E.—Royal Engineers.
recd.—received.
R. et I.—L. *Rex* (*Regina*) *et Imperator* (*Imperatrix*), King (Queen) and Emperor (Empress).
Reg.—L. *regina*, Queen.
Reg. Prof.—Regius Professor.
R.E.M.E.—Royal Electrical and Mechanical Engineers.
Rev.—Reverend.
rev.—revolution (mechanics).
R.F.C.—Royal Flying Corps.
R.F.U.—Rugby Football Union
Rh—rhodium.
r.h.—right hand.
R.H.S.—Royal Horticultural Society; Royal Historical Society.
R.I.—Rhode Island; Royal Institute (of Painters in Water Colours); Royal Institution.
R.I.B.A.—Royal Institute of British Architects.
R.I.P.—L. *requiescat in pace* may he (she) rest in peace.

Adam's Peak. Mt. in Ceylon, 7,319 ft.; pilgrim resort, 748.

Adana (ah-dah′-na) or **Seyhan.** City and vilayet of Turkey in S.E. Asia Minor; pop. city, 100,300, vilayet, 387,000; strategic position near passes of Taurus Mts.

Adapa (ah′dah-pah), in Babylonian myth, 332.

Adapta′tion, in biology, 156, 1079, 1080, *plate f. 1080,* 1246; alpaca, 125; birds, 437; fishes, 1298; giraffe, 1464; plants, 948.

Adder, or common viper, 2991, 3325; confused with slow-worm, 2986.

Adding machine. *See* **Calculating Machine.**

Addis Ababa (ad′is ab-ā′ba). Cap. of Abyssinia; pop. 150,000; *15*; Italian occupation, 1936–41; liberated, 3418.

Addison, Christopher, 1st Baron Addison of Stallingborough (b. 1869). Brit. politician and doctor of medicine; Minister of Munitions (1916–

17); Reconstruction (1917); first Min. of Health (1919–21); Agric. and Fisheries (1930–31); peer 1937. Dominions Sec., Leader of House of Lords, 1945; K.G. 1946; 1st Sec. for Commonwealth Relations, July–Oct. 1947; Lord Privy Seal, Nov. 1947.

Addison, Joseph (1672–1719). Eng. poet and essayist, **23**, *24*; essays, 1213.

Addition, 24; law in algebra, 114, 115; fractions, 1356; decimals, 982.

Address, forms of. Forms to be used in addressing persons of high rank or official position are :

Ambassador : "His Excellency the —— Ambassador." Begin letter : "Your Excellency."

Archbishop : "The Most Reverend His Grace the Lord Archbishop of ——." Begin letter : "My Lord Archbishop"; "Your Grace."

Bishop : "The Right Reverend the

Lord Bishop of ——" (Ch. of Eng. and Rom. Cath.). Begin letter : "Right Reverend Sir," or "Dear Sir."

Governor of Colony : "His Excellency the Governor of ——." Begin letter: "Sir," or "Dear Sir."

King : "The King's Most Excellent Majesty. King ——." Begin letter : "Sir," or "May it please your Majesty."

Lord Mayor : "The Right Honorable the Lord Mayor of ——." Begin letter : "My Lord."

Pope : "His Holiness the Pope." Begin letter : "Most Holy Father."

Queen : "The Queen's Most Excellent Majesty." Begin letter : "Madam," or "May it please your Majesty."

Adelaide, Queen (1792–1849). Consort of William IV of England.

Adelaide. Cap. and trade centre of S. Australia. 3rd largest city of Commonwealth; pop. with suburbs 390,000, **26,** 3028.

LIST OF ABBREVIATIONS (*continued*)

rit(ard).—Ital. *ritardando,* gradually slower.
R.L.O.—Returned Letter Office.
R.L.S.—Robert Louis Stevenson.
Rly.—Railway.
R.M.—Resident Magistrate (Ireland) ; Royal Marine.
R.M.A.—Royal Military Academy ; Royal Marine Artillery.
R.M.S.—Royal Mail Steamer.
R.N.—Royal Navy.
Rn—radon.
R.N.C.—Royal Naval College.
R.N.L.I.—Royal National Lifeboat Institution.
R.N.R.—Royal Naval Reserve.
R.N.S.R.—Royal Naval Special Reserve.
R.N.V.R.—Royal Naval Volunteer Reserve.
Robt.—Robert.
R.O.F.—Royal Ordnance Factory.
Roffen.—Rochester, in signature of Bishop.
r.p.m.—revolutions per minute.
Rs.—rupees.
R.S.F.S.R.—Russian Socialist Federal Soviet Republic.
R.S.P.C.A.—Royal Society for the Prevention of Cruelty to Animals.
R.S.V.P.—Fr. *Répondez s'il vous plaît,* please reply.
R.T.C.—Royal Tank Corps.
R.T.S.—Religious Tract Society.
Rt. Hon.—Right Honourable.
Rt. Rev.—Right Reverend.
Ru—ruthenium.
R.V.—Revised Version (of the Bible).
R.W.S.—Royal Society of Painters in Water Colours.
Ry.—Railway.
R.Y.S.—Royal Yacht Squadron.

S

S.—sulphur; distance (physics).
S.—south ; Saint.
s.—L. *solidus,* shilling.
Sa—samarium.
S.A.—South Africa ; (Ger.) Sturm Abteilung (Storm Division).
Salop.—Shropshire.
S. and M.—Sodor and Man, in signature of B's lop.
Sarum.—Salisbury, in signature of Bishop.
Sb—L. *stibium,* antimony.
S.C.—South Carolina.
s.c.—small capital letters.
Sc—scandium.
S.C.A.P.A. (Scapa)—Society for Checking the Abuses of Public Advertising.
s.caps.—small capital letters.

sculps.—L. *sculpsit,* he (she) engraved (it).
sd.—said.
S.Dak.—South Dakota.
S.D.F.—Social Democratic Federation.
S.D.P.—Social Democratic Party.
Se—selenium.
Sec.—secretary.
senr.—senior.
seq., seqq. — L. *sequens, sequentia,* the following.
sf—ital. *sforzando,* with sudden emphas **s**.
S.G.—specific gravity.
s.h.p.—shaft horse-power.
Si—silicon.
S.I.C.—specific inductive capacity.
sin—sine (trigonometry).
S.J.—Society of Jesus (Jesuits).
Sm—samarium.
Sn—L. *stannum,* tin.
S.O.—Sub-office (postal).
Soc.—Socialist.
S O S—wireless distress signal.
S.P.C.K.—Society for the Promotion of Christian Knowledge.
S.P.G.—Society for the Propagation of the Gospel.
sp.gr.—Specific gravity.
S.P.Q.R.—L. *Senatus Populusque Romanus,* the Roman Senate and People ; small profits and quick returns.
sq.—square.
Sr—strontium.
Sr.—Senior.
S.R.N.—State Registered Nurse.
S.S.—steamship ; (Ger.) Schutz Staffeln.
SS.—Saints.
St.—Saint ; Strait ; Street.
st.—stone (weight) ; stumped (cricket).
Staffs—Staffordshire.
Supt.—Superintendent.
s.v.—L. *sub voce,* under the word, heading.
S.W.G.—standard wire gauge.

T

t—time (physics).
T.A.—Territorial Army.
Ta—tantalum.
tan—tangent.
Tb—terbium.
T.B.—tuberculosis.
T.C.D.—Trinity College, Dublin.
Te—tellurium.
t.e.g—top edges gilt (of books).
temp.—L. *tempore,* in the time of.
Tenn.—Tennessee.
Tex.—Texas.
Th—thorium.
Ti—titanium.

Tl—thallium.
Tm—thulium.
T.M.O.—Telegraph Money Order.
T.N.T.—trinitrotoluene.
T.O.—Turn over ; telegraph office.
Toc H.—Talbot House.
T.R.H.—Their Royal Highnesses.
Trs.—trustees.
trs.—transpose.
Truron.—Truro, in signature of Bishop.
T.S.F.—Fr. *télégraphie, téléphonie sans fil,* wireless.
T.T.—Tourist Trophy ; torpedo tubes ; teetotaller ; tuberculin tested.
T.U.C.—Trades Union Congress ; Trades Union Council.
Tv.—television.

U

U—uranium.
U.—Unionist.
u—initial velocity (mechanics).
U.A.B.—Unemployment Assistance Board.
u.c.—upper case (printing).
U.D.C—Union of Democratic Control ; Urban District Council.
U.K.—United Kingdom.
ult.—L. *ultimo (mense),* last month.
U.N.—United Nations.
U.N.A.—United Nations Association.
U.N.E.S.C.O.—United Nations Educational, Scientific and Cultural Organization.
U.N.R.R.A.—United Nations Relief and Rehabilitation Organization.
u.p.—under proof (spirits).
U.S.—United Services ; United States.
U.S.A.—United States of America.
U.S.S.R.—Union of Soviet Socialist Republics.
Ut.—Utah.

V

V—five (Roman numeral) ; vanadium ; volt.
Va.—Virginia.
V.A.D.—Voluntary Aid Detachment.
V.C.—Victoria Cross.
V.D.H.—valvular disease of the heart.
Ven.—Venerable.
verb. (sat.) sap.—L. *verbum satis sapienti,* a word is enough to the wise.
Vet.—Veterinary surgeon.
V.G.—Vicar-General.

viz.—L. *videlicet,* namely.
vol.—volume.
Vt.—Vermont.

W

W—(wolfram) tungsten.
W.—west.
W.A.A.C. — Women's Army Auxiliary Corps (1914–8 war).
W.A.—Western Australia.
W.A.A.F.—Women's Auxiliary Air Force.
W.C.—west central (London postal district).
W.D.—War Department.
w.f.—wrong fount (printing).
W.H.O.—World Health Organization.
W.I.—West Indies.
Wigorn.—Worcester, in signature of Bishop.
Wilts—Wiltshire.
Winton—Winchester, in signature of Bishop.
Wis.—Wisconsin.
W.L.—Wave-length.
W.O.—War Office ; warrant officer.
W.P.B.—waste-paper basket.
W.R.—War Reserve (Police).
W.R.A.C.—Women's Royal Army Corps.
W.R.A.F.—Women's Royal Air Force.
W.R.N.S.—Women's Royal Naval Service.
W.S.—Writer to the Signet.
wt.—weight.
W. Va.—West Virginia.
W.V.S.—Women's Voluntary Services.
Wyo.—Wyoming.

X

X—ten (Roman numeral).
x-cp.—(excluding) coupon.
xd., x-div.—(excluding) dividend.
Xe—xenon.
Xmas—Christmas.
Xt(ian)—Christ(ian).
XX, XXX, double X, triple-X denoting strength of ales.

Y

Yb—ytterbium.
Y.H.A.—Youth Hostel Association.
Y.M.C.A.—Young Men's Christian Association.
Yt—yttrium.
Y.W.C.A.—Young Women's Christian Association.

Z

Zn—zinc.
Zr—zirconium.

Adélie Land (ad-ā-lē´). A portion of the Antarctic Continent, discovered by Dumont d'Urville, a Frenchman, in 1840 ; sheer cliffs of ice ; has whaling possibilities.

Adelphi (a-del´-fi). London terrace near Charing Cross built by the brothers Adam, 23 ; demolished 1936.

"**Adelphi**" ("The Brothers"). Latin comedy by Terence based partly on one in Greek by Menander ; treats question of whether it is better to bring up children indulgently or sternly.

A'den. Brit. tn. and Colony on s.w. coast of Arabia, Crown Colony since 1937 ; a. 75 sq. m. (inc. Protectorate about 112,000 sq. m.) ; pop., about 46,000 ; **26**, *27*, 196 ; *map, 197* ; water supply, 26.

Adenauer (ad´enower), **Konrad** (b. 1876). Elected Chancellor of the W. German Federal Republic in Sept. 1949 ; 1453.

Ad'enoids. Excessive growth of tissue in the nasal pharynx, 1676.

Adige (ah´-dē-jä). R. of N. Italy rises in Tirolese Alps and empties into Gulf of Venice ; length about 240 m., 1763, 3310.

Adirondack (ad-i-ron´-dak) **Mts.** in N.E. New York, U.S.A., highest summit, Mt. Marcy, 5,385 ft., 3288.

Ad'jective, 27, 1494 ; phrase or clause as, 2920.

Ad'jutant. A large East Indian stork, **27**, 3097, *3099*.

Adjutant, in army, 27.

Ad'ler, Alfred (1870-1937). Austrian psychologist and psychiatrist, associated with Freud but broke away from psycho-analytic school and founded Society for Individual Psychology ; explained maladjustment as due to "inferiority complex," 2697.

Ad'mirable Crichton (krī´-ton). *See* Crichton.

Ad'miral, in Brit. Navy, **28** ; rank sleeve stripes, and flags, *28*.

Admiral of the Fleet, in Brit. Navy, 28.

Ad'miralty. Dept. of Brit. govt. having, under Parliament, supreme charge of naval affairs, 28.

Admiralty Arch, in London, *2018*.

Admiralty Islands. Group of small isls. in Bismarck Archipelago ; native pop. 13,400 ; coconuts, pearls ; in Australian trust territory of New Guinea ; *map f. 2472*.

Admiralty Law. Legal system governing criminal and civil cases arising on the high seas ; originally administered in Eng. by Lord High Admiral.

Adobe (ad-ō´-bi), sun-dried brick, or the clay of which bricks are made, 561.

"**Adonais.**" Elegy by Shelley on death of Keats, 2944.

Ado'nis. In Gk. myth., a youth beloved of Aphrodite, **28**.

Adowa (ad´-o-wa). Tn. in Abyssinia ; pop. 5,000 ; Italians defeated in 1896, 14 ; held by Italians 1935-41.

Adre'nalin. Astringent drug from adrenal gland of cattle, 1471 ; in anaesthetics, 149 ; and emotion, 1157.

A'dria. City of Italy ; pop. 14,000, 29.

A'drian. Popes. *See* Pope.

Adrian IV (1100 ?-59). Nicholas Breakspear, only Eng. Pope ; elected 1154 ; quarrelled with the Emperor Frederick Barbarossa, initiating long contest between Papacy and house of Hohenstaufen.

Adrianople (ā-dri-a-nō-´pl) ("Hadrian's City") (in Turkish *Edirne*). City of European Turkey ; pop. about 46,000, **29**; battle of, 2166.

Adrianople, Peace of (1829), between Russia and Turkey, secured Gk. independence, 1525.

Adriatic (ā-dri-at´-ik) **Sea.** An arm of the Mediterranean, E. of Italy, **29**, 1233; Albania, 100 ; Venice, 3310 ; Yugoslavia, 3438.

Adsorption. Taking up of a gas upon, but not within, a body ; in charcoal, 753 ; colloids, 871.

Adul'lam, Cave of, 979.

Adúr. River of Sussex, Eng. ; old bridge at Shoreham, *566*.

Ad'verb, 29, 1494 ; conjunctive, 891.

Advocates' Library. Library of the Faculty of Advocates, in Edinburgh, Scot. ; founded in 1682.

Æ. Pen name of George William Russell (1867-1935), Irish lyric poet, essayist, painter, and nationalist leader ("The Earth-Breath and other Poems" : "Deirdre"), 1751.

Aegean (ē-jē´-an) **Civilization** (flourished 3000-1200 B.C.), in Crete and neighbouring isls. and mainland, **29**, 927 ; architecture, 213 ; art, *31* ; in Homer's poems, 1638 ; influence on Gk. civilization, 1517 ; paintings, *31*, 2475.

Aegean Sea. Arm of Mediterranean between mainland of Greece and Asia Minor, 29, 1517 ; *map, 30, 1518* ; origin of name, 3201 ; islands in 2nd World War, 32.

Aegeus (ē´-jūs). Mythical king of Athens, 3201.

Aegina (ē-jī´-na). Gk. isl. in Saronic Gulf ; 40 sq. m. ; important anc. state ; conquered by Athens c. 456 B.C. ; 1527.

Aegisthus (ē-jis´-thus). In Gk. myth., son of Thyestes and adopted son of Atreus, whom he slew ; aided Clytemnestra in slaying Agememnon, his cousin, 74, 75.

Aegospotami (ē-gos-pot´-a-mī). Anc. name of small stream on Peninsula of Gallipoli, emptying into Hellespont ; Athenian fleet captured (405 B.C.), 1524.

Ælfric (c. 955-1022). Celebrated English scholar ; called Grammaticus from his "Latin Grammar" ; wrote a life of Æthelwold, whose pupil he was ; chiefly famous for his "Homilies" and "Colloquium."

Aemilian (ē-mil´-i-an) **Way.** Road in anc. Italy over 180 m. long, Rimini to Milan ; built 187 B.C.

Aeneas (ē-nē´-as). Fabled ancestor of Romulus and Remus, hero of Virgil's epic Aeneid, **32** ; and Dido, 711.

Aene'id, epic poem by Virgil, 32, *1895*, 1896, 3325 ; "Story of the Wooden Horse," 3249-50.

Aeolian (ē-ō´-li-an) **Islands.** *See* Lipari Islands.

Aeolians. One of the four great divisions of the Gk. race, 1517.

Aeol'ic dialect, 1541.

Ae'olus. In Gk. myth., ruler of the winds ; he was the son of Poseidon (Neptune) ; gave his name to Aeolian harp, a stringed mus. instr. played by winds.

Aerials (ār´-i-alz), or antennae, in wireless, 3392, 3293 ; directional, 3397 ; television, 3183.

Aerodrome (ār´-o-drōm). Name formerly applied to flying machine, now given to flying grounds and stations.

Aerolite (ār´-ō-līt) or meteorite, 2151, *2152*.

Aeronau'tics. *See* **Aeroplane** ; **Airship**; **Balloons**; list of terms, 3705.

Aeroplane. Strictly speaking, a power-driven, heavier-than-air flying machine, **41**; aero-engines, 50, 1737 ; aircraft-carriers, 2296, *2300* ; air freighters, 51, 52 ; air mail, 2662 ; airport, *48* ; airscrew, 2903 ; Atlantic flights, 47, 1950 ; autogiro, 320 ; Jean Batten, *375* ; Blériot, *45*, 46, *470* ; camouflage, 674 ; controls, 42 ; compass, *882* ; dive-bombers, 1056; flight, theory of, 41, 2127, *2128* ; flying boat, 51 ; gas turbine, 1424; glider, 1474 ; Grahame-White, *46* ; helicopter, 1605, *1606* ; highest flight, 3102 ; instruments, *43* ; jet-propelled, *49*, *1826* ; Amy Johnson, 1834 ; Kingsford-Smith, 1858 ; map-making from, 2095 ; models, *2196* ; Moore-Brabazon, 46 ; navigation, 2292, 2293 ; Pacific route, *2473* ; parachute, 2509 ; pilotless, 1330 ; radar, 2726 ; Royal Air Force, 2832 ; seaplanes, *51* ; speeds, 48 ; "Spitfire," chasing flying bomb, *1332* ; to relay television, 3184 ; torpedo-carrying, *3227* ; Tudor, *40* ; used in traffic control, 2787 ; Vickers Viking, *47*, *1826* ; Wright brothers

45, 3427. *See also* types by name, and **Records**.

Aeschines (ēs´-ki-nēz) (389-314 B.C.). Athenian orator and statesman.

Aeschylus (ēs´-kil´us) (525-456 B.C.). First great tragic dramatist of Greece, **53**, 1038, 1540, 2690 ; and Agamemnon, 75.

Aesculapius (ēs-kū-lā´-pi-us) or **Asclepios.** In Gk. and Rom. myth., god of medicine, son of Apollo ; his staff with a serpent coiled round it is often used as medical insignia, **53**, 742 ; serpents, 2991.

Aesop (ē´-sop) (c. 620-560 B.C.). Gk. writer of fables, **54**.

Aesthetics (ēs-thet´-iks). Branch of philosophy, defined, 2572.

Aestivation. Summer sleep, 1623.

Aetius (ā-ē´-shi-us) (d. 454). Rom. general, saviour of Europe by his victory (451) over Attila at Châlons ; murdered by Valentinian III.

Aetolia (ē-tō´-li-a). District of Greece N. of Gulf of Corinth ; Aetolian League became chief rival of Achaean League in the 4th and 3rd cents. B.C.

Af'ferent nerves, 2317.

Afforestation. The conversion of waste land into forest ; over 430,000 acres had been planted in Great Britain by 1939, 1351.

Afghanistan. Mountainous inland country of Asia between Pakistan and Iran ; a. 255,000 sq. m. ; pop. 10,000,000 ; **55**, *maps*, *55*, *plate f. 264*; Khyber Pass, **56**, 1691 ; stamp, 3075.

Afghan Wars, 56.

Africa. Second largest continent ; a. 11,500,000 sq. m. ; pop. 155,000,000; **65** ; *map f. 68, f. 69, f. 72*; animals, 69, *71, plates f. 72, 73* ; climate, *plate f. 69* ; deserts, 68, 997, 2859 ; East Africa, 1072, 1550 ; elevation, *plate f. 69* ; flags of, *frontis.*, *Vol. 8*; modern exploration and partition, 72 ; former land connexion with other continents, 2051 ; Kenya, 1072 ; languages, 70 ; Mahomedanism, 2066 ; natives, *65, 66, 67, 69, 70* ; population, *68, plate f. 69* ; resources and products, 73 ; Sahara, 997, 2859 ; Somaliland, 2999 ; South Africa, 3013 ; Sudan, 3109 ; transport, 72 ; vegetation, *plate f. 69* ; West Africa, 3366 ; 1st World War, 3411 ; 2nd World War, 3418, 3419, 3420, *3421* ; Zambezi country, *3441* ; Zulus, 3448. *See also* under chief rivers, countries and cities.

Africa Star. Brit. award of Second World War, instit. Aug. 1943, for service in N. Africa between June 10, 1940, and May 1943 ; with clasp for 8th and 1st army for service between Oct. 23, 1942, and May 12, 1943.

Afrika Korps, 1452.

Afrikaans (af-ri-kahnz´). S. African Dutch, 73 ; literature in, 74, 3020.

Afrikan'der, 74.

Agadir (ah-gah-dēr´). Spt. in French Protectorate of Morocco ; said to have been important trading centre in Roman era ; was closed to commerce for 165 years ; reopened 1930 ; the Agadir "incident," 2230.

Aga Khan III (ah´-ga´kahn´) (Aga Sultan Sir Mohammed Shah) (b. 1877). Mahomedan leader of vast influence which he exerted to raise Indian standards and to encourage co-operation with British ; a famous racehorse owner.

Agamemnon (ag-a-mem´-non). In Gk. myth., king of Mycenae, 19, **74** 3249 ; and Iphigenia, *1740*.

"**Agamemnon.**" Drama by Aeschylus, 53, 75.

Agar agar. Red algae used in mfr. of foodstuffs, and in bacteriological cultures, 112.

Agassiz (ag´-a-sē), **Louis Jean Rodolphe** (1807-73). Swiss-Amer. naturalist and geologist, 75.

Agate, James Evershed (1877-1947) English essayist and dramatic critic notably in "Sunday Times."

Ag'ate. A semi-precious stone of whitish-brown or grey, 2713.

Ag'atha, St. Patron saint of Malta ; noble Sicilian woman who was martyred about A.D. 251.

Agave (*a-gā̆ -vī*). A genus of Amer. plants of amaryllis family, **75**, 2157.

Age of animals, variation, 156.

"Age of Innocence." Painting by Sir Joshua Reynolds, *1186*.

"Age of Reason, The," by Thos. Paine, 2475.

Agglu'tinative languages, 2571.

Agheila (a-gā'-lah), **El.** Village of Cyrenaica, 100 m. s. of Benghazi; changed hands three times during 1941–42; limit of Wavell's advance from Egypt, 3418; taken by Montgomery Dec. 1942, 3420, *3421*.

Agincourt (ah-zhan-k'ŏōr). Vil. in N. France; decisive battle of Hundred Years' War (1415), **76**, 1611. 1653.

Aglaia (a-glā'-ya). In Gr. myth., one of the three Graces.

Agnes, St. Virgin martyr (d. 306), patron of girls; symbol, a lamb.

Agora (ag'o-ra). Market-place; of anc. Athens, *1521*, 1523.

Agouti (a-goo'-ti). S. Amer. rodent, 76, *77*.

Agra and Oudh. United Province of N.W. India. Agra, 77, 3284; Benares, 411; Lucknow, 2035; Taj Mahal, 3147, *3148*.

Agram. See **Zagreb.**

Agricola (a-grik'-o-la) **Gnaeus Julius** (A.D. 37–93). Rom. general and gov. of Britain; **78**, 574, 1897.

Agricola, Georgius (1490–1555), Ger. mineralogist ("De re metallica," first scientific text-book on mining and metallurgy); 3443.

Agriculture, the science and art of cultivating the soil, **78**, *81–84*; in ancient Egypt, *1115*; breeding of plants and animals, 79, 621; cereals, 745 (see also names of different crops); climate, 840; co-operative societies, 904; crop rotation, 85, 2374; dairying, 955; fertilizers, 2373, 2574; harvest, *84*, 1580; haymaking, *1509*, *1510*; insect pests, 438, 1511, *1730*, *1731*, 1732; irrigation and reclamation, 1100, 1721; livestock, 730, 1645, 2125; modern methods introduced, 85; nitrifying bacteria and legumes, 336, 852, *2034*, 2373, *2374*; orchard crops, 1401; pasture lands, 1509; ploughing, 2629; poultry, 2671; primitive methods, *87*, 809, 1797; rusts and smuts, 2857; soil, 2998.

Agriculture and Fisheries, Ministry of, Govt. Department of G. Britain, 86.

Agrippina (ag-ri-pī'na) (A.D. *c*. 15–59). Rom. empress, wife of Claudius and mother of Nero, 2315.

Aguecheek (ă'-gŭ-chēk), **Sir Andrew.** In Shakespeare's "Twelfth Night," comic country squire in love with Olivia.

Agulhas (ah-gŏōl'yahs), **Cape,** southernmost point of Africa.

Ahab. King of Israel, 875–853 B.C.; married Jezebel; rebuked by Elijah for permitting idolatry (1 Kings xvi-xxii).

Ahasuerus (ă-haz-ū-ēr-*us*), anc. king of Persia identified with Xerxes the Great, 1225.

Ahasuerus, the legendary Wandering Jew, 3340.

Ahmedabad (ah-med-ah-bahd'), India. City in Bombay Province; founded in 1412; pop. 591,000; magnificent temples; silk and cotton mfg., 496.

Ahmed Mirza (ah'-med mêr-zah) (1898–1930). Shah of Persia; succeeded his father, who abdicated in 1909; deposed in 1925.

Ahriman (ah'-ri-mahn), in Zoroastrianism, 3448.

Ahura (ah-hŏōr'-*a*) **Mazda** (Ormuzd), in Zoroastrianism, 3448.

"Aida" (ah-ē'-da), opera by Verdi; scene laid in anc. Egypt; story, 2438; 3315.

Aidan, St. (d. 651). From 635 first bishop of Lindisfarne. he converted Northumbria.

Ailanthus (ā-lan'-thus), a genus of trees including the tree of heaven, commonly seen in suburban gardens; leaves resemble those of ash, but are much larger; valuable for feeding silkworms.

Aileron (ā'-le-ron). Aeroplane control surface, *42*, *43*.

Ailsa Craig (ăl'-sa), Scot. Island rock of basalt in Firth of Clyde.

Ain (an), river of E. France; rises in Jura Mts., flows s.w. 119 m. to Rhône.

Ainley, Henry (1879–1945). British actor: famous in Shakespearian roles.

Aino (I-nō) or **Ainu** ("man"), an aboriginal race found in northern isls. of Japan, more European than Mongolian in type.

Ainsworth, William Harrison (1805–82). Eng. novelist, **87**, 2862.

Ainu (I'-nŏō). Same as **Aino.**

Air, 88, *89*, 1067, 1243; composition of, 88, 700, 1598; compressed, 90, 1016, 1020, 1425, 2246, 2478, 2632, *2633*; circulation, 1598; conditioning, 1597; convection, *1594*, 1598; extent of atmosphere, 88. 89; fixed

TERMS COMMONLY USED IN AERONAUTICS

Aerobatics. Manoeuvres performed voluntarily other than those used in normal flight (i.e. "stunts").

Aerodynamics. Science dealing with the motion of air and other gaseous fluids, and with the forces acting on solids in motion relative to such fluids.

Aerofoil. A sustaining surface of an aeroplane (i.e. a wing).

Aileron. Hinged portion on the rear edge of the wing-tip of an aeroplane to provide lateral control.

Airframe. An aeroplane complete, less engine.

Air-pocket. A pouch or vacuum in space.

Airport. A commercial Customs aerodrome.

Airscrew. A propeller.

Air speed. Velocity relative to the air.

Altimeter. Instrument showing approximate height of machine while in flight.

Amphibian. Flying-machine able to alight on land or water.

Autogiro. Aircraft having overhead rotor instead of wings, able almost to hover.

Banking. Tilting an aeroplane inwards at an angle when turning.

Biplane. Aeroplane with two superimposed mainplanes.

Camber. Curvature of an aerofoil.

Captive balloon. One attached to the ground by cable.

Ceiling. Maximum height attainable.

Chock. A block placed in front of an aeroplane's wheels to prevent it from moving when the engine is started.

Chord. Distance from leading to trailing edge (of a wing, etc.).

Cockpit. Opening in fuselage to accommodate pilot or passenger.

Cruising speed The normal, economic speed of an aircraft.

Dihedral. Angle of inclination of wings to transverse axis of aircraft.

Dope. Varnish applied to aeroplane fabric.

Drag. Head-resistance.

Elevator. Hinged flap on tailpiece governing longitudinal control.

Endurance. The time for which an aeroplane can remain aloft.

Fairing. Any structure added to reduce drag.

Fin. Fixed stabilizing surface.

Flaps. Hinged surface of an aerofoil, especially to slow machine when landing.

Float. Watertight alighting gear of a seaplane.

Flying-boat. Seaplane with a boat-like hull.

Fuselage. The body of an aeroplane.

Hangar. Shed for housing aircraft.

Helicopter. Heavier-than-air flying-machine with overhead horizontal airscrews, able to rise and descend almost vertically.

Interference. The spoiling of a wing's lift owing to the proximity of another surface.

Jet. Aircraft with jet-propulsion unit; a **jet-prop** has both jet propulsion and airscrews.

Joystick. Control lever of an aircraft.

Landplane. Aeroplane with a wheeled undercarriage.

Leading edge. Front edge of an aerofoil.

Lift. Force component tending to make an aircraft rise.

Longeron. Main structural member of the fuselage.

Monoplane. Aeroplane with a single mainplane.

Pitch. The angle of airscrew blades to the airflow; the **variable-pitch airscrew** is a modern device to aid efficiency.

Power dive. Diving an aeroplane steeply and at full throttle.

Pusher. Engine driving airscrew at rear.

Radial. An engine with cylinders arranged in a circle around the crankshaft.

Reduction gear. Gearing between engine and airscrew so that latter runs more slowly than the engine.

Rib. Lateral member of the wing structure.

Roll. Manoeuvre entailing a complete revolution around the longitudinal axis.

Seaplane. Aeroplane capable of alighting on, or taking-off from, the water.

Slipstream. Body of air thrown back by the airscrew.

Slots. Safety device on the leading edge of the wing to delay the stall and maintain lateral control beyond the stall.

Span. Length of a wing or other aerofoil.

Spar. Principal longitudinal member of wing structure.

Spin. Downward corkscrew manoeuvre that usually follows the stall.

Spinner. Streamlined fairing, sometimes fitted to the front of, and revolving with, the airscrew.

Squadron. An R.A.F. unit, usually consisting of nine aircraft with three in reserve.

Stagger. An arrangement on a biplane whereby one wing is placed in front of or behind the other.

Stalling. Allowing an aeroplane to lose its forward impetus, so as to deprive the aerofoils of sustaining power.

Step Step-like projection on the bottom of a float or flying-boat hull.

Streamline. Shape given to cause the minimum of resistance.

Strut. A structural member holding other parts in place and taking loads.

Take-off. To ascend from the ground or water.

Tarmac. Concrete area on an aerodrome.

Three-pointer. Landing in which both wheels and tail-skid or wheel touch at the same moment.

Thrust. Forward force provided by airscrew.

Tractor. An aeroplane in which the airscrew is in front and had a tractive motion.

Undercarriage. Wheeled landing-gear; many types are retractable in flight to lessen resistance, while others are of the tricycle type.

Wind sock or sleeve. A conical streamer to indicate wind direction.

Wind tunnel Apparatus producing uniform windflow for research purposes.

nitrogen from, 2372; importance of "fresh air," 1676; a gas, 1419; humidity, 1000, 1243, 1677; liquid air, 1391; meteorology, 2149; neon in, 2315; nitrogen in, 2373, oxygen in, 2466; pneumatic appliances, 2632; pressure maintained by barometer, 90, *362, 363*; purified by plants, 88, 2621; resistance, 41, 90; respiration, 2039; roof supported by, 2823; sound waves in, 1495, *3009*, 3010; specific gravity, 3054; of stratosphere, 3102; sunlight reflected and refracted by, 88; ventilation, 1598, 1676; wind, 3384–86; xenon in, 3429.

Airborne Troops. *See* **Army Air Corps.**

Air Council, of the R.A.F., 2832.

Aircraft. *See* **Aeroplane; Airship; Balloons.**

Aircraft-carrier, 2296, *2300*.

Air currents, in dew formation, 1000; in fog formation, 1333.

Aird, Sir John, Bart. (1833–1911). Brit. engineering contractor; built the Assuan Dam on R. Nile.

Airdrie (ār'-drē). Scot. Mfg. tn. in Lanarkshire, engineering; cottons, silks; iron and brass works; pop. 25,900, 1890.

Aire, river, Eng., trib. of Ouse, 1918.

Airedale terrier, *plate f. 1024*.

Air Force. A state's war aircraft, **91.** *See* **Royal Air Force.**

Air Force Cross (A.F.C.). Decoration instituted 1918 for officers in R.A.F., for acts of courage or devotion to duty when flying, but not against enemy.

Air Force Medal, (A.F.M.). Similar decoration (1918) for warrant and N.C.O.s and men of R.A.F.

Air Gun. Gun fired by compressed air.

"Air Horse." Type of helicopter, *1606*.

Air Liner. Tudor, *40*; Vickers Viking, *47, 1826*.

Air-log. Device controlling duration of flying bomb's flight, 1332.

Air mail, 48, 51, 2662; stamps, 3076.

Air Ministry. Govt. dept. controlling aviation, formed 1918; weather forecasts, 2149.

Air plants, or epiphytes; vanilla, 3305; orchids, 2447.

Airport. A commercial customs aerodrome; London, *48*, 52.

Air pump, principle, 90, 2702; used in diving, 1019.

Air Rangers. Branch of the Girl Guides, *1467*.

Airscrew, correct term for aeroplane propeller, 41, 2903; of helicopter, 1605.

Airship, 92; buoyancy of hydrogen, 93, 1674; use of helium, 95, 1607; Akron, *94*; R34 and R101, *95*; Zeppelins, *92*, 93, 3442.

Air Training Corps (A.T.C.). Brit. voluntary organization estab. Feb. 1941 to provide training for prospective candidates in the R.A.F. or Naval Aviation. In 1946 reorganized under Reserve Command in six Regional Groups; 2833.

Airy, Sir George Biddell, (1801–92). Brit. astronomer; originator of photographic record of sun spots; his transit instrument, *3214*.

Aisle, in architecture, 216.

Aisne (ān), r. in N. France (175 m.); famous battleground in War of 1914–18, 3409. 3412: 2nd World War, 3917.

Aiton, William (1731–93), laid out Kew Gardens, 1854.

Aix (-en-Provence), France. Historic tn., former cap. of Provence; pop. 38,300; founded 123 B.C.; hot springs; univ. (established 1409).

Aix-la-Chapelle (āks-lah-sha-pel'). Fr. name of Aachen. 9, 754; treaties of, 9, 2101, 3276.

Ajaccio (ah-yah'-chō), cap. of Corsica; pop. about 25,000; birthplace of Napoleon, 914, 2275.

Ajanta, India, village of Hyderabad. noted for cave dwellings dating back to 200 B.C.; temple frescoes, *1663*, *1712*.

Ajax (ā'-jaks), "the Great," in Gk. myth., a hero of Trojan War, 95.

Ajax, "the lesser," the son of Oïleus, whose death by drowning was caused by Poseidon, 96.

Ajax, H.M.S. Brit. cruiser, flagship of Commodore Harwood; took part in battle of riv. Plate, 3417; listed for scrapping, April 1949. *See* **Plata River,** battle of.

Ajmer-Merwara, small state of India; a. 2,400 sq. m.; pop. 583,600.

Ajusco (ah-hês'-kō) Mts., of Mexico, volcanic chain forming part of s. wall of cent. plateau; greatest height, 13,628 ft.; 2159.

Akaba (ak-ah'-bah). Tn. of Trans-jordan on E. side of Gulf of Akaba, an arm of Red Sea; near boundaries of Israel and Egypt.

Ak'bar (1542–1605), greatest of Mogul emperors of India, 77, *1712*, 1714, 2206.

A'kenside, Mark (1721–70). Brit. physician and poet; wrote "Pleasures of Imagination."

Akershus (ah'kêrs-hūs). Norwegian fortress, 2455.

Akhnaton (Spirit of the Sun). Name assumed by son of Amenophis (Amenhotep) III, Egyptian king of the XVIIIth dynasty, when he tried to introduce worship of the sun, *1118*.

Ak'ron, U.S. airship, *94*.

Ak'ron, tn. Ohio, U.S.A., 35 m. S.E. of Cleveland; known as "rubber capital" of world; pop. 244,700, 2426.

Akyab'. Island and spt. of Arakan, Burma; the spt. is on E. side of the island; rice mills; exports rice, oil, timber; pop. 36,569. On May 8, 1942, taken by Japs; chief Jap. base for air raids on Calcutta, 1942–43; evacuated by Japs. during 1944; re-occupied by Allies Jan. 1945.

Alaba'ma, a Gulf state of U.S.A.; a. 51,600 sq. m.; pop. 2,800,000, **96.**

"Alabama" Claims, 203.

Alabamine (Ab). Chemical element of radio-active series, atomic number 85; atomic weight 221; discovery, since disputed, claimed by Allison in 1931; 768, 778.

Al'abaster, 1559.

"Aladdin," story, 3450.

Alagoas (al-*a*-gō'-as), state of Brazil.

Alame'da, California, U.S.A. City 6 m. across bay from San Francisco; pop. 35,000; ships, motors; petroleum and borax-refining plants.

Alamein, El. Battle of, 249, 1452; Alexander and, 3420; Montgomery and, 2222, 3420, *3421*.

Alanbrooke, Alan Francis Brooke, 1st Viscount (b. 1883). Chief of Imperial General Staff, 1941–46. C.-in-C. Home Forces 1940–41; **96.**

A'land Islands. Archipelago at entrance to Gulf of Bothnia, 6,854 islands; strategic importance. Ceded to Russia by Sweden (1809), awarded by League of Nations to Finland (1921). Fortification, forbidden by Convention of 1921, allowed in 1939.

Alarcón (ah-lahr-kōn'), **Pedro Antonio de** (1833–91), Sp. novelist, 3051.

Alarcón y Mendoza (ah-lahr-kōn' ē mān-dō'-thah), **Juan Ruiz de** (*c.* 1581–1639). Sp. dramatist ("Truth Suspected," adapted by Corneille as "Le Menteur"; "The Weaver of Segovia"); 3051.

Alard (al'ard), **Gervase,** first commissioned admiral, 28.

Al'aric (376–410), king of Visigoths, 96 1488; sacks Rome (A.D. 410), 2802 2812.

Alaska, a territory of the U.S.A.; a. 586,400 sq. m.; pop., 90,000; **97** *map*, 99; caribou, *702*; dogs, 1026; forests, 2384; glaciers, 2384; Ice Age, 2384; Mt. McKinley, *2380*; Northwest Highway, 99; resources. 2384; reindeer, 2760; Yukon, 2379.

Alaska Highway, constructed 1942. to carry war materials from U.S.A. to Alaska, via Edmonton, Ft. Nelson, Whitehorse, to Fairbanks (Alaska); total length, 1,671 m., of which Canadian portion 1,257 m.

Alas'tor. In Gk. myth., the spirit of revenge personified; or a man driven by such a spirit. Title of a poem by Shelley.

Alba. *See* **Alva.**

Albacore (al'b*a*-kawr), a fish of the tunny family, 3258.

Al'ba Lon'ga. It. city of anc. Latium, founded, according to tradition, by Ascanius, son of Aeneas; birthplace of Romulus and Remus; 2821.

Alban (awl'ban), **St.,** Britain's first martyr, 100.

Albani (ahl-bah-nē), **Dame Emma Marie** (1852–1930), Canadian soprano vocalist; oratorio and opera.

Alba'nia. Country in w. Balkans, a. 10,629 sq. m.; pop. 1,003,000; **100,** 343, 345; *map, 344*; people, 100, 1527; King Zog I, 100; invaded by Italy, April 1939, when King Zog fled, 1773, 3416; liberated 1945; proclaimed republic 1946.

Albany, New York, U.S.A. Cap. and 2nd oldest city of State; pop. 127,000; 2353.

Albany, spt. tn. of w. Australia, on arm of King George Sound; pop. 5,000.

Al'batross, largest of sea birds, 101, 441.

Albemarle, George Monk, Duke of. *See* **Monk, George.**

Albert (1819–61), prince of Saxe-Coburg-Gotha, consort of Queen Victoria of Eng., 101, 102, 500, 3320.

Albert I (1875–1934), king of the Belgians, 102, 407.

Albert (ahl-bār'), France, tn. in extreme N.; in First World War, 3413.

Alberta. Province in w. Canada; a. 255,200 sq. m.; pop. 796,000; **102**; Calgary, 663; Hudson's Bay Company, 683; natural gas, *1406*; oil, 102; parks, *103*, 680; prairies, 102, 676; wheat harvest, *679*.

Albert Canal, in Belgium, *689*.

Albert Hall, Royal. Concert and meeting hall in Kensington, London, in memory of the Prince Consort, *2265*; has one of the largest organs in the world, *2450*; can seat 8,000 people; opened in 1871.

Albert Medal. Decoration instituted by Queen Victoria in 1866. It is open to all and is awarded for acts of gallantry in saving life at sea or on land.

Albert Memorial. Monument in Kensington Gardens, London, in memory of the Prince Consort; designed by Sir Gilbert Scott.

Albert Nyan'za (Lake Albert). Lake in E. Cent. Africa, one of chief sources of Nile, 69; discovery, 340.

Albigenses (al-bi-jen'-sēz), heretical sect prominent in early 13th cent., named from Albi, France, their cap.

Albi'no. A person or animal whose skin, hair, and eyes lack colouring matter; birds, 447, cats, 718; ferrets, 1268; peacock, *facing p. 2533*.

Albion. Anc. name of Britain; lit. "white land" (from Latin *albus*), referring to chalk cliffs of s. coast.

Albula Rly., in Engadine valley, *133*.

Al bumen, a protein, found in eggs and meat, 2694.

Albumin. Any protein resembling albumen in properties.

Albuquerque (ahl-bōō-kar'-kā), **Alfonso d'** (1453–1515), "the Great." Conqueror of Goa, and founder of Port. power in E. Indies, 2342.

Alcalá de Henares (ahl-kah-lah' dä en-ah'-res), old town in Spain near Madrid; pop. 11,700; birthplace of Cervantes.

Alcantara (ahl-kahn'-tah-rah), Spain. Anc. tn. on Tagus; owes name (Arabic "bridge") to Rom. bridge built by Trajan; about 1215 became stronghold of knightly Order of Alcantara, organized for defence against Moors, *2818*.

Alcazar (al-kah'-zahr), Span. or Moorish palace, originally a fort; at Seville, 2926. *3033*; at Toledo (besieged in 1936), 3030, 3039.

Alcestis (al-ses'-tis), in Gk. myth., wife of King Admetus, whom she saves by dying in his stead; rescued from Hades, 1615.

Alcibiades (al-si-bī-*a*-dēz) (*c.* 450–404 B.C.) handsome, brilliant, unscrupulous Athenian statesman and general; nephew of Pericles; pupil of Socrates, 2997; precipitates 3rd Peloponnesian War, 1524.

Alcinoüs (al-sin'-ō-*us*), in Odyssey king of Phaeacia, 2422.

Alcmaeonidae (alk-mē-ōn'-i-dē), a wealthy and powerful family of anc. Athens, claiming descent from Alcmaeon, great-grandson of Nestor, 2551.

Alcmene (alk-mē'-nē), the mother of Hercules, 1615.

Alcock, Sir John (1892–1919), first non-stop transatlantic aeroplane flight, 47.

Alcohol, 103, 774 ; fermentation, 103, 1266, 3434 ; as fuel, 1406, 2564, 2792 ; from petroleum, 2430 ; from potatoes, 2665 ; and soap-making, 2594 ; specific gravity, 3054 ; spirits, 3066 ; synthetic rubber from, 2838.

Alcoholic beverages, 3066, 3388.

Alcott, Louisa May (1832–88). Amer. author, born at Concord, Mass. ; began to write at 8, sold first story at 16 ; "Little Women" (1868), "Good Wives," "Little Men," "Jo's Boys," "Eight Cousins," "An Old-Fashioned Girl" were her best-known books.

Alcuin (735–804), Eng. scholar and churchman, head of Charlemagne's palace school, 754.

Alcyone (al'-si-*o*-nē, al-sī'-*o*-nē) or **Halcyone**, in Gk. myth., daughter of Aeolus ; name gave origin to phrase halcyon days.

Aldabra (ahl-dah'-brah). Group of small isls. in Indian Ocean, part of Brit. colony of Seychelles.

Aldebaran (al-deb'-*a*-r*an*), a prominent fixed star, 3079, *3080* ; in the eye of Taurus, the Bull, *895*.

Aldeburgh (awld'-brĕ), coast tn. in Suffolk ; birthplace of Crabbe ; pop. 2,480 ; 3112.

Alden, John (1599–1687), Mayflower Pilgrim ; immortalized in Long-fellow's poem, "The Courtship of Miles Standish."

Alder, Common Brit. tree, 104, *105* ; classified, 3247.

Alder fly. Species of large, net-veined insect peculiar to Amer. ; larvae (dobsons) used as bait for still-fishing ; eggs, *1094*.

Alderney (awl'd*er*-ni), one of Channel Isls. ; pop. 1,250 ; a. 3 sq. m., 751, 752. From July 1948 social services admin. by Guernsey.

Alderney, H.M.S., Brit. submarine, *3107*.

Aldershot (awl'-d*er*-shot), tn. and Army camp in Hampshire, pop. 34,000 ; 1571.

Aldhelm, St. (*c.* 640–709), Abbot of Malmesbury and first Bishop of Sherborne.

Aldington, Richard (b. 1892). Brit. author ; leader of "imagist" school ("Images Old and New" ; "Death of a Hero").

Aldus Manutius (al'd*us* m*a*-nū'-shi-*us*) (1450–1515), famous Venetian printer, 2705.

Aldwych (awld'wich). Curved London thoroughfare, opened in 1905, entering Strand at western end of Gaiety Theatre and at eastern end near St. Clement Danes. Island between Aldwych and Strand occupied by Australia House and Bush House. Damaged by "flying bomb," 1944.

Alekhine, Alexander (1892–1946). Russian chess player. Chess champion of the world, 1927–35 ; championship regained 1937–46.

Alemán, Mateo (1547–*c.* 1609), Spanish novelist, 3051.

Alemán, Miguel (b. 1902). President of Mexico ; elected Dec. 1946.

Alemanni (al-*e*-man'-i) or **Alamanni** ("all-men"), confederacy of Ger. tribes, 1237 ; conquered in 495 by Clovis ; name Allemagne applied by French to modern Germany.

Alembert (al-ahm-bèr') **Jean le Rond d'** (1717–83). Fr. mathematician and philosopher, associated with Diderot on the "Encyclopédie," 1160.

Alemtejo (ah-lahn-tā-zhō), province of S. Portugal, famous for cork industry ; 9,200 sq. m. ; pop. 669,700 ; 2658.

Alençon (al-ahn-sawn). Tn. of France ; pop. 16,600 ; linen and woollen goods ; lace manufactures ("point d'Alençon"), 1880.

Aleppo (Arabic *Haleb*), metropolis of N. Syria ; pop. 320,100 ; for centuries centre of caravan trade between Baghdad and Damascus, *3145*.

Alessandria (ah-les-san'-dri-ah). It. fortified city in Piedmont ; pop. 79,300 ; rly. centre ; textiles, clothing.

Aletschhorn (ah'lech-horn), a peak (13,723 ft.) in the Swiss Alps, 3138 ; the Aletsch glacier, 16 m. long, is the largest in the Alps.

Aleutian (a-lū'-sh*an*) **Islands**, chain of small isls. extending 1,200 m. w. from Alaska, 98, *99*, 2469 ; bound Bering Sea, 415 ; route of prehistoric migration, 2379 ; in 2nd World War, 3421.

Aleuts, natives of Aleutian Isls. and N. side of Alaskan peninsula, 99 ; allied to Eskimos, 1222.

Al'evin. A young salmon, 2865.

Alewife, or gaspereau, a shad-like fish found in N. America.

Alexander the Great (356–323 B.C.). King of Macedon, and one of history's greatest conquerors, 105 ; anecdote, 1018 ; Aristotle instructs, 232 ; cameo of, 671 ; captures Tyre, 2573 ; conquers Egypt, 106 ; Persia, 105 ; and family of Darius III, 1781 ; founder of Alexandria, 109 ; Hellenizes the East, 1524 ; influence on India, 1714.

Alexander, Popes. See **Pope**.

Alexander. Name of three tsars of Russia. **Alexander I** (1777–1825), at first allied with Britain, Austria and Prussia against Napoleon, made peace with him at Tilsit ; rejoined alliance before retreat from Moscow, 1812 ; founder of the Holy Alliance. **Alexander II** (1818–81), nephew of Alexander I, succeeded in 1855. The Tsar Liberator, he fed serfs 1861, but was assassinated by Nihilists. **Alexander III** (1845–94), his second son, succeeded him ; married sister of Queen Alexandra.

Alexander I (Obrenovitch) (1876–1903), King of Serbia ; succeeded in 1889 ; assassinated, 2922.

Alexander (1893–1920), King of the Hellenes, succeeded in 1917 ; 1525.

Alexander I (1888–1934), King of Yugoslavia, 107, 3439.

Alexander, Albert V., 1st Viscount Alexander of Hillsborough (b. 1885). Parl. Sec. to Board of Trade (1924) ; First Ld. of Admiralty (1929–31, 1940–45, and 1945–46). Min. of Defence (1946). C.H. (1941). Chancellor of Duchy of Lancaster in 1950.

Alexander, F.-M. Viscount Harold (b. 1891), British soldier. Organized evacuation at Dunkirk, 1940, and of Burma, 1942 ; c.-in-c. Middle East, 1942–43 ; gov.-gen. of Canada, 1946, 107 ; at Dunkirk, 1057.

Alexander, Sir George (1858–1918). Eng. comedy actor. From 1891 was manager of St. James's Theatre.

Alexander, Severus (205–235). Rom. emperor ; succeeded Heliogabalus in 222 ; murdered in insurrection.

Alexan'dra (1844–1925), queen of Edward VII, 108, 816, 1092.

Alexandra Day, popularly known as Rose Day, started by Queen Alexandra in 1912 ; 108.

Alexandra Feodorovna (1872–1918). Tsarina of Russia ; was Princess Alix of Hesse, granddaughter of Queen Victoria ; shot with her husband and family by the Ural regional Soviet at Ekaterinburg, 2849.

Alexandra Palace, public place of amusement at Muswell Hill, London, named after Q. Alexandra ; present structure completed 1875 ; during the 1914–18 War German prisoners were interned here ; television stn. opened 1936 ; *3183*, 3184, 3399.

Alexandretta (now Iskanderun). Turkish seaport on the Mediterranean, 70 m. from Aleppo ; capital of the sanjak of Alexandretta, now Hatay, made by the League of Nations in 1937 a separate entity, with full independence ; pop. 13,900 ; ceded to Turkey June 1939.

Alexandria, chief spt. of Egypt ; pop. 686,000 ; centre of late Gr. culture, 109 ; 1098, 1100, 1101 ; centre for Christian study, 425 ; library, 109, 1930 ; Pharos, one of the Seven Wonders of the Ancient World, 1943, 2924 ; skyscraper at, *1104* ; in 2nd World War, 1102. *map, 3421*.

Alexandr a, Battle of. Fought in 1801, between British and French, and paved way for British occupation of Alexandria a few months later ; Sir Ralph Abercromby was fatally wounded and Sir John Moore wounded.

Alexius (*a*-lek'-si-*us*) **I, Comrenus** (1048–1118). Byzantine emperor, succeeded in 1081 ; brilliant soldier, efficient administrator.

Alfal'fa. Feeding stuff. See **Lucerne**.

Alfieri (al-fē-ār'ē), **Count Vittorio** (1749–1803). It. tragic poet, 1787.

Alföld (ahl'-feld), large, fertile plain of cent. Hungary, 972, 1654.

Alfon'so I (1094–1185). Founder of Port. kingdom ; proclaimed king after victory of Ourique (1139) over Moors.

Alfonso XII (1857–85). King of Spain, 110.

Alfonso XIII (1886–1941). King of Spain, 110.

Alfred the Great. King of Eng. (848–901), 110, 1194 ; in the Danish camp, *1202* ; grand jury, *1843* ; literary work, 111 ; as minstrel, 2262 ; rebuilds London, 2009, 2016 ; and Oxford University, 2462 ; son, 1089 ; statue, *111*.

Alfred's Jewel, in the Ashmolean Museum, Oxford, 110.

Algae (al'-gē), a low type of plants, including seaweeds, 111, 2620 ; combine with fungi to form lichens, 1932, 2514 ; in geysers, 1459 ; sea-weed forms, *111* ; alginate rayon from seaweed, 2750.

Algarroba (al-gah-rō'-ba), a species of locust tree.

Algebra. A branch of mathematics, 112, 2120, 2068 ; equation, *113*.

Algeciras (ahl-je-sēr'-*as*). Spt. of S. Spain ; pop. 20,500 ; 3030 ; conference, 2230.

Alger'ia. Fr. possession in N. Africa ; became Government-General in 1946, recd. measure of self-govt. 1947 ; 847,000 sq. m. ; pop. 6,300,000 ; 117 ; *maps f. 68*, *117* ; date palm, *2484* ; desert, *2800* ; oasis, *119* ; children of, *791* ; Allied landings, 1942, 118, 3420.

Algiers (al-jērz'). A fortified spt., cap. of Algeria ; pop. 252,000 ; coaling station ; extensive trade, 117, *118* ; occupied by Allies, 1942, 118 ; temp. cap. of France, 119.

Algol. A variable star in Perseus, *895*, 3079.

Algonquian or **Algonkian stock**, group of N. Amer. Indians ranging from Labrador to Rocky Mts., 2753.

Alham'bra. Beautiful palace and fortress in Granada, 119 ; *plates f. 120, 121* ; 1498, 3032.

Ali (ah'-lē) (600 ?–661). Fourth Mahomedan caliph ; married Mahomet's daughter, founding Fatimite line, 2067.

Ali Baba. Hero of an "Arabian Nights" tale ; obtains wealth of the "Forty Thieves" by learning magic password "Open sesame."

Alibi (al'-i-bī) (Latin, "elsewhere"). A form of defence in criminal cases by which the accused undertakes to show that he was elsewhere when the crime was committed.

Alicante (ah-lē-kahn'tā). Seaport of w. Sp. ; pop. 78,000 ; exports wine, fruit, oil.

"Alice's Adventures in Wonderland," story, by Lewis Carroll, 708, 709, 711.

Aligarh (ah-li-gahr'), India. Cap. of Aligarh dist., United Provinces ; pop. 112,600 ; has celebrated Mahomedan University.

Alimen'tary canal, the system of connected internal organs by which higher animals assimilate food ; conducts digestion, 1016, *2599*, *2600* ; in earthworms, 1071.

Al'ington, Cyril (b. 1872). Brit. divine, schoolmaster, and writer; headmaster of Shrewsbury, then Eton; Dean of Durham in 1933; wrote detective stories.

Aliwal (ah-li-wahl'), India. Vil. in the E. Punjab, on r. Sutlej; here the Brit. beat the Sikhs in 1846.

Aliz'arin, dye-base of "lake" colours, obtained from coal-tar, 857.

Al'kali, a base that is soluble in water; and acids, 20; caustic potash, 2664; caustic soda, 2997; cellulose, 2749; in soap-making, 2993.

Alkali Metals, univalent metals of the first group in the periodic system, combining with water forming alkalis, **120**; potassium, 2662; sodium, 2997.

Al'kaline earth metals, bivalent metallic elements of the second group forming compounds resembling alkali metals, 120.

Alkaline soils, 2999, 1559.

Al'kaloids, poisonous vegetable compounds with alkaline properties; 21, 2638; tea, 3160.

Alkmaar (ahlk'-mahr), Netherlands, town on N. Holland Canal; pop. 31,700; unsuccessfully besieged by Spaniards in 1573; cheese trade, 2320.

Alkyd Resins, 2768.

Allah. Arabic name used by Mahomedans for God, 2066, 1872.

Allahabad (ah-lah-hah-bahd'), India ("City of God"), at junction of Ganges and Jumna, in United Provinces; airport; university; pop. 284,000; pilgrimage centre for Hindus, 1417; trade in cotton, grain, sugar, 3284.

Al'lah ak'bar (" Allah is great "). War cry of the Mahomedans.

Allan, Sir William (1782–1850). Scottish painter of historical subjects; portrait of Burns writing, 626; portrait of Scott, 2899.

" All Blacks," N.Z. Rugby football team.

Allbutt, Sir Clifford (1836–1925). Eng. physician; invented the short clinical thermometer.

Allegheny (al'-e-gen-i) or **Alleghany Mts.**, part of Appalachian system, 190.

Allegheny, r., rises in N. cent. Pennsylvania, U.S.A.; drains N.W. quarter of Pa. and south N.Y.; 2426, 2614, 2615.

Al'legory, a presentation of abstract thoughts or principles by means of stories, either in words or in pictures; parables and fables are forms of allegory; examples: Cupid and Psyche, 943; Dante's " Divine Comedy," 970; " Pilgrim's Progress," 618.

Alle'gri, Antonio, known as **Correggio.**

Alleluia. Same as **Hallelujah.**

Allen, Sir Hugh (1869–1946). Director of Royal College of Music from 1918 to 1937, then Prof. Music, Oxford Un.

Allen of Hurtwood, Reginald Clifford, 1st Baron (1889–1939). English Labour politician.

Allen, Ralph (1694–1774), Eng. philanthropist, " the Man of Bath," 374; postal reforms, 2661.

Allen, William (1532–94). Eng. cardinal; established (1568) college at Douai, France, for Eng. Rom. Cath. exiles; Bible translation, 427.

Al'lenby, Edmund, 1st Viscount (1861–1936). Brit. field-marshal, commander of Palestine expedition in First World War, **121**; enters Jerusalem, 121, 2480, 3411. High Commissioner for Egypt and the Sudan (1919–1925).

Allenstein (ahl'-en-shtīn), town formerly in E. Prussia, pop. 38,000; chief city of Masurian Lakes region, scene of Hindenburg's operations in 1914–15; captured by Russ. and incorp. in Poland, 1945, and under Polish name Olsztyn made cap. of Masuria prov.

Allergy. Abnormal sensitivity to certain substances, e.g. pollen, which causes hay fever; white of egg, which causes urticaria, eczema, or asthma:

these complaints being known as allergic diseases; and the liver, 1968, in " protein shock therapy," 2694.

Alleyn (al-ān'), **Edward** (1566–1626). Eng. actor; contemporary of Shakespeare; founded Dulwich College in 1619; **121.**

All Fools' Day. See **April Fools' Day.**

Al'lia. Small r. in anc. Italy; joins Tiber 12 m. above Rome; here Gauls defeated Romans, 390 B.C.

Allies, in First World War, 3409, 3410. In Second, 3416, 3420.

Al'ligator, an American reptile, **121**, 2767; distinguished from crocodile, 932; protective coloration, 2692; the armoured amphibious craft, 247.

Alligator Pear, fruit of a West Indian tree, also called avocado.

Allitera'tion, 1271.

Al'lium, the onion genus, 2434.

Allosaurus, prehistoric animal.

Allot'ropy, a change in physical properties without accompanying chemical change; three forms of carbon, 770; oxygen, 2466; phosphorus, 2574; sulphur, 3116.

Alloys, mixtures or combinations of metals, **122**; aluminium, 135; brass, 122, 3443; bronze, 122, 906, 2148; chromium, 123; coins, 1481; ferrous, 123; invar, 2365; manganese, 123; permanent magnets, 2062; pewter, 3215; tantalum, 3152; titanium, 3217; tungsten, 123, 3253; type metal, 124, 3270; vanadium steel, 3303; of zinc, 3444; zirconium steel, 3444. See also under names of the various metals and alloys.

All Saints' Day, formerly called All Hallows Day in Great Britain; Christian Church festival held Nov. 1.

All Souls' College, Oxford, 2462, 2464.

All Souls' Day. Nov. 2, day set aside in Rom. Cath. Church for prayer and almsgiving on behalf of the faithful departed.

Allspice or **pimento**, 3062, 1792; belongs to myrtle family, 2547.

" All's Well that Ends Well," a comedy by Shakespeare (about 1595); plot based on story in Boccaccio's " Decameron."

Allu'vial soil, 2999, 2598; deposits by Ganges, 1418, Hwang Ho, 1662, Mississippi, 2191, Nile, 1095, 2371.

Allyl, in onions, 2434.

Al'ma, small r. of the Crimea; near its mouth in Black Sea, British, French, and Turks defeated Russians (1854).

Almaden (ahl-mah-then'), Spain, town 65 m. N. of Cordova; pop. 10,000; mercury mines, 2145.

" Almagest " (al'-ma-jest), book on astronomy by Ptolemy, 2697.

Al'manac, a book or pamphlet containing a calendar and astronomical data, usually also lists of holidays, important recent events, and a variety of other miscellaneous information; " Poor Richard's," 1386.

Almansa (ahl'-mahn-sah), Span. city; scene of Brit. defeat by France and Spain in 1707.

Alma-Tadema (al'ma-tad'-e-ma). **Sir Laurence** (1836–1912). Eng. painter. b. in Netherlands; portrayed Gk. and Rom. life.

Almeida (ahl-mā'-i-dah), **Antonio José de** (1866–1929). President of Portugal (1919–23).

Almeria (ahl-mā-rē'-ah), Spain. Seaport 60 m. S.E. of Granada, cap. of province of same name; pop. 84,900; founded by Phoenicians, became flourishing port and pirate headquarters under Moors; exports fruit; bombarded by Ger. battleship Deutschland in 1937.

Almond, a tree of the rose family, **124**, 2408; essential oil from, 1263.

Almonry, a place where alms are given, 2214.

Alnwick (an'-ik), co. tn. of Northumberland; corn trade, brewing; pop. 7,200, 2391.

Aloe (al'-ō), or century plant, a species of agave, 75.

Alost (ah'-lŏst). Historic tn. in Belgium, midway between Brussels and

Ghent; pop. 41,000; anc. cap. of Flanders; contained one of first printing presses in Europe; captured by Germans in 1914 and in 1940.

Alpac'a, a S. Amer. animal of the camel family, **124**, 492; cloth, 125, 850, 3405.

Alp-Arslan (ahlp-ahr-slahn') (1029–72) Seljuk sultan (1063–72); conquered large part of Asia.

Alpenhorn, a long, curved wooden Swiss bugle, 1644.

Alpenstock, a long spiked pole used by mountaineers.

Al'pha, α, A. (Rom. a, A). First letter of Gk. alphabet; much used in scientific nomenclature; in astronomy, the chief star of the constellation.

Alphabet, 125; Braille, for the blind, 471; Burmese, 126; Cadmus myth, 650; Cyrillic, 423, 2855; deaf and dumb, 981; Gothic, 423, 1456; Hebrew, 1601; invented by Phoenicians, 2573; Japanese, 1809; Morse, 3166; origin, 125. See also individual letters in Fact-Index.

Alpha Centau'ri, nearest fixed star, 280, 3078.

Alpha Crucis, star, 3079.

Alpha Particles. Positively charged helium nuclei expelled by radio-active substances, 298, 2732.

Alpha rays, 297; of radium, 2731, 2733.

Alpheus (al-fe'-us), r. of Peloponnesus; in myth, 1615.

Alphonso. See **Alfonso.**

Alpine Club, 2247.

Alpine plants, 130.

Alpine race, 2725.

Alps, the greatest mountain system of Europe, **126**, 129–132, 1233, 1235, 1447, 3138, 3139; Austrian, 129, 133, 316; chamois, 751; French, 1360. 2248; glaciers, 1468; Hannibal crosses, 1573; in Italy, 1763, 1764; mountaineering, 2247; roads, 128; St. Bernard dogs, 128, plate f. 1024, 1025; ski-ing, 2978; in Switzerland, 127, 130, 131, 132, 1235, 3139; tunnels, 3138, 3257; Tirol, 1725, 3215–16.

Alsace-Lorraine (al-sas-lo-rän), region in N.E. France taken by Germany (1871), restored to France (1919) after 1st World War; 5,605 sq. m.; pop. 1,700,000; **133**; capital Strasbourg, 134; map, 1359; iron, 1361, 1753; people, 134, plate f. 1360.— History; Charles the Bold invades, 759; Alsace won by France (1648), 3203; in Franco-Prussian War, 1385; ceded to Germany, 1449; restored to France, 133, 1367; occupied by Germany (1940), 133; liberated (1945), 133.

Alsatian. Large breed of intelligent dog favoured as a guard.

Alster, r. of Germany, 1568.

Altai (ahl'-tī) **Mts.**, in Mongolia and S. Siberia; highest point Byelukha (14,800 ft.); rich minerals.

Altair, star, 3078, 3079.

Altamira (al-ta-mēr'-a), **Cave of**, Spain; prehistoric paintings, 2475, plate f. 2084.

Alt'dorf, Switzerland, cap. of canton of Uri, on L. Lucerne; scene of story of William Tell, 3185.

Altenburg (ahl'-ten-bŏŏrg), Germany. Mfg. tn. in Thuringia; pop. 42,500; grain and cattle trade.

Alternating current (A.C.), electric, 1130; from dynamo, 1061; in grid, 1545; from induction coil, 1720; in electric motor, 2240; rectifier, 2757 3198; rectified by transformer, 3237 in wireless, 3394.

Alterna'tion of generations, 3615; in moss, 2238.

Alternator, A.C. dynamo, 1062, 2674 high frequency, 1623; in hydro electric installations, 1670.

Althing, the legislative body of Ice land; founded 930, has functioned almost continuously for more than 1,000 years; but present form from 1874; formerly under the Danish crown, it became independent in 1944; composed of 42 elected members who form an upper and a lower house, 2521.

Al'timeter. Height-finding instrument, 2093.

Al'titude, affects climate and plant life, 840, 1081, 2156, 3022 ; heights attained by aeroplanes, 48, 89, 3102 ; by balloons, 89, 349 ; shown by barometer, 363 ; and temperature. 3084.

Alt'mark. Ger. prison ship ; captured Feb. 1940 by the Cossack (Capt. Vian) in Joessing Fjd., Norway ; 299 survivors of Brit. ships, imprisoned in holds, were set free.

Altmühl, river of central Bavaria, 972.

Alto. The highest male voice in a choir.

Al'tona, Germany, seaport now forming part of city of Hamburg : pop. 241,000, 1568.

Alto-relievo (al'-tō-rā-lyä'-vō), or "high relief," in sculpture, 2903.

Altrincham (al'-tring-am). Bor. of Cheshire ; iron working and other industries ; pop. 21,400.

Al'truists (from Latin alter, "other"). in philosophy, 2571.

Al'um, potassium aluminium sulphate, used as astringent in medicine, as mordant in dyeing, in tanning, fire-proofing and shower-proofing ; coal-gas by-product ; 3117.

Alu'mina, aluminium oxide, 135 ; found in clay, 836 ; as corundum, 1157.

Alumin'ium (Al), a light metallic element of the boron group ; atomic weight, 26·96 ; melts at 1210° F. ; 134 ; alloys, 123, 124, 135 ; "anodising " of, 1140 ; diving suit, 1020 ; in electric supply lines, 1547 ; confuses radar signals, 2728 ; oxide, 1157 ; paint, 2478 ; properties, 776 ; refined by electrolysis, 135, 1137. 1567 ; rods and tubes of, 1667 ; silicates, 1265, 2160 ; specific gravity, 3054.

Aluminium bronze, 587.

Alun'dum. Artificial abrasive made from aluminium oxide, 136.

Al'va or **Alba, Duke of** (1508–83), Span. general ; set up " Council of Blood " in Netherlands, 2321, 3381.

Alvarado (ahl-vär-ah'-thō), **Pedro de** (c. 1495–1541). Span. cavalier, companion of Cortes in conquest of Mexico ; names Salvador. 2868.

Alveo'li, of the lungs, 2039.

Alwar. Cap. of native State of Alwar. in Rajputana ; pop. 44,700 ; mausoleum of Bakhtawar Singh, 1700.

Amadeus I (am-a-dē'-oos) (1845–90). King of Spain, son of Victor Emmanuel II of Italy ; accepted crown from revolutionists (1870) ; abdicated in 1873.

Am'adis of Gaul. Hero of famous medieval prose romance, 746.

Amager (am'-ah-jêr) **Island**, Denmark. pop. 26,000 ; 904.

Amalekites (a-mal'e-kīts). An anc. tribe of Edomites, foes of the Israelites : crushed by Saul and David.

Amal'fi. Seaport of Italy ; pop. 7,400; 13th-cent. cathedral and old Capuchin monastery ; in Middle Ages it was a republic and rivalled Genoa and Pisa. Bitter fighting following Salerno landings, Sept. 1943. Soap. paper, macaroni made.

Amal'gam. A mixture of mercury with another metal, 2145 ; with gold, 1480.

Amalgamated Press. Lord Camrose and, 675 ; composing room. 3271 ; process dept., plate 1. 2689.

Amanul'lah (b. 1892). Amir or King of Afghanistan (1926–29), 56.

Ama'ra, Iraq. Tn. on the Tigris, about 150 m. N. of Persian Gulf : taken by British (1915).

Am'aranth. Flowering plant of the genus Amaranthus, such as love-lies-bleeding and Joseph's coat.

Amaryl'lis family of plants allied to the lily and iris families, and including amaryllis, narcissus, and agave.

Amateur Athletic Association (A.A.A.) Governing body for amateur athletics in Gt. Brit. ; founded in 1880 at Oxford, 288.

Amati (a-mah -tē). Ital. family of violin-makers at Cremona, of whom the most famous was Nicolo (1596–1684), 3324.

Am'azon. R. of S. Amer.. world's largest r. in point of drainage area (3,350 m. long), 136, 550, 3022 ; maps, 136, 551 ; Indians, 1430 ; rubber, 2833 ; tributaries, 136, 550. 873 ; giant water-lily, 3354.

Amazons. In Gk. myth., a nation of female warriors, 137 ; Hippolyte. 1615.

Am'ba Alagi (al-ah'-gē). Abyssinian mountain fortress, 9,000 ft. alt., near Magdala ; Duke of Aosta's surrender here in May 1941 to Imperial forces was virtual end of It. resistance in Abyssinia.

Ambala (um-bah'-lah), or **Umballa.** Cap. of E. Punjab, 3 m. E. of R. Ghaggar ; pop. 76,300.

Ambas'sador. Representative of one Power in the chief city of another, 138 ; 3290 ; of the Pope, 2496.

Amber. A fossilized resin, 138, 2768 : plastics, substitute, 138.

Am'bergris. Secretion of sperm whale : used in perfumery, 138.

Amboy'na or **Amboina.** Chief city and comm. centre of Molucca Isls., Indonesia, on Amboyna Isl. in N. of Banda Sea ; pop. of isl., about 278.000.

Ambrose, St. (c. 340–397), bishop of Milan ; among first hymn writers ; won earliest great victory of Church over temporal power ; 138, 2172.

Ambro'sia. In anc. myth., the food or drink of the gods, giving immortality ; name later applied only to food, and drink of the gods was called nectar.

Ambush, H.M.S., Brit. submarine, 3105.

Amen. Hebrew word, also used by Christians to conclude prayers and hymns, where it has the sense " So be it," 138.

Amenho'tep III, King of Egypt from 1411 to 1375 B.C. ; great warrior and builder ; temple of Luxor, 1112 ; statue, 2138.

Ameno'phis or **Amenhotep II**, Eg. king of 18th dynasty, reigned 26 yrs. in 15th cent. B.C. ; grandfather of Amenhotep III.

America, discovery of, 139, 141 ; flags of, 326, frontis. vol. 8 ; Indians, 140, 143, 1689, 2753 ; origin of name, 139. 3318. See also **Canada ; Central America ; North America ; South America ; United States of America.** etc.

American Civil War (1861–65). Struggle between the existing Federal government in the north and the new confederation in the south, which gave to the opposing forces their names of Federals and Confederates. The main cause of the war was the desire of the latter to secede from the union. After the bombardment of Fort Sumter by the Confederates, April 12, 1861, no fewer than 2,260 battles, sieges and skirmishes took place before the last of the Confederate armies surrendered on May 26, 1865. The main battles were Bull Run, July 21, 1861 ; Shiloh, April 6, 1862 ; Fair Oaks, May 31, 1862 ; Antietam, September 17, 1862 ; Fredericksburg, December 13, 1862 ; Chancellorsville, May 1, 1863 ; Siege of Vicksburg, June-July, 1863 ; Gettysburg, July 1-3, 1863 ; Cold Harbor, June 3, 1864 ; naval battle of Mobile Bay, August 1864 ; Nashville, December 1864. The long struggle came to an end when the Southern general. Robert E. Lee, was forced to abandon his lines at Petersburg, where, for nine months, he had resisted all Gen. Grant's attempts to break through. His retreat was blocked at Appomattox Court House, where he surrendered, April 9, 1865 ; 3291 ; leaders and chief events, 1789, 1790, 1917, 1918, 1951, 1952 ; and slavery. 2982.

American Independence, 144 ; colonization. 144 ; Declaration of. 145.

3291 ; War of, 144, 3276, 3291. See also **United States : History.**

American literature. Drama, 1042 ; national beginnings, 597, 902, 1759. See also **United States, literature of,** and under names of chief writers.

American marten, 2112.

American, Amerind, or **Red, race, 2723,** 2753 ; civilization, 143.

America Cup. Trophy offered in 1851 for a race between British and American yachts ; first secured by the schooner America. Recent results are—1930, Enterprise (U.S.A.) bt. Shamrock V ; 1934, Rainbow (U.S.A.) bt. Endeavour ; 1937, Ranger (U.S.A.) bt. Endeavour II.

Americ'ium (Am), new element, atomic number 95, named by Glenn T. Seaborg in 1946 ; produced by artificial radio-activity.

Americus Vespu'cius, 139, 3318.

Amery, Leopold Charles Maurice Stennett (b. 1873). Brit. journalist and politician ; " The Times " war correspondent in Boer War ; First Lord of Admiralty (1922–24) ; Sec. for Colonies from 1924, and also for Dominion Affairs from 1925 to 1929 ; Sec. for India, May 1940–45.

Amethyst. A precious stone, found in Germany, Hungary, Brazil, and Ceylon, 1427, 2181, 2713.

Amharic. Modern Ethiopian language. 16.

Am'herst, Jeffrey Amherst, Baron (1717–97). Brit. soldier, succeeded Abercromby as commander in conquest of Canada from French ; gov.-gen. of Brit. N. Amer. (1759–63) ; commander-in-chief Brit. army (1772–82, 1783–95).

Amherst, William Pitt, Earl (1773–1857). Brit. diplomatist ; acted as envoy to China (1816) ; governor-general of India (1823–8) ; raised to peerage (1826).

Amicis (ah-mē'-chēs), **Edmondo de** (1846–1908). It. novelist and writer of books of travel ; " Cuore " (" The Heart of a Boy ").

Amiens. Mfg. city in France, 81 m. from Paris, pop. 93,700 ; silk, woollen, cotton mfrs. : cathedral, 1362 ; in Second World War, captured by Germans, May 21, 1940. 3417 ; liberated, Aug. 31, 1944.

Amiens, Treaty of (1802). 2276, 3248.

Amino acids, in proteins. 20, 2693.

Amman. Capital of Jordan ; the Rabbath-Ammon of the Bible and the Gk. Philadelphia ; capt. by Brit. troops from Turks in Sept. 1918 : 3238.

Amman, Jost. Swiss engraver (1539–91) ; woodcuts, 511.

Ammersee. Lake 10 m. long in S. Bavaria.

Am'meter. A galvanometer used to measure electric current, 1124 ; for high amperages, 3238.

Ammon, or Ammon-Re. Chief god in Eg. myth., originally local god of Thebes ; represented with ram's horns ; temple at Karnak, 1116, 1117.

Ammo'nia. A compound of nitrogen with three parts of hydrogen, 146 ; in batteries, 146 ; in gas manufacture, 1805 ; dissolves in water, 1420 ; from hydrogen, 1674 ; made from " fixed " atmospheric nitrogen, 2374 ; evaporation of, 1243 ; in refrigeration, 146, 1392 ; preserves rubber latex, 2834.

Am'monite. Fossil mollusc, 146, 1353.

Ammonites. Semitic tribe living E. of the Jordan, 1829 ; finally subdued by Judas Maccabaeus.

Ammo'nium salts, 146, 375, 2373, 2748, 2997, 3303.

Ammunition, for artillery, 258, 260 ; for small arms, 1281 ; gunpowder, 1558.

Amne'sia. Medical term for loss of memory.

Amoeba (a-mē-ba). The simplest known animal, consisting of one cell and multiplying by division ; 156, 738 ; breathing, 2768 ; classified among protozoa, 2695.

Amor. Cupid, 943.

Amor'phous substances, 940.

Amos. Hebrew prophet (8th cent. B.C.), earliest of " writing prophets " (Book of Amos), 2691.

Amoy, China. Treaty port on isl. opposite Formosa ; pop. 234,000 ; exports tea, porcelain, paper. Name from Chinese *Hiamun.* Chinese sovereignty restored 1945.

Amp re, André Marie (1775–1836). Fr. physicist ; a pioneer of electro-dynamics.

Ampere (amp.). A unit of electric current, 1128 ; ampere-turns, 2063.

Amphibia. A class of vertebrate animals including the frogs and toads, 156 ; eggs, 1094 ; frogs, 1155, 1398 ; place in the evolution of animals, 156, 1298, 2767 ; salamanders, 2864 ; toads, 3219. The term " amphibian " is also applied to any machine (e.g., aeroplane and tank) that can travel on land or water, 247, 3422.

Amphineur'a. A class of molluscs, in-cluding chitons, 2199.

Amphiox'us, also called lancelet. Genus of aquatic sand-burrowing animals resembling primitive verte-brates.

Amphisbaena. A legless lizard, 1973, 1974.

Amphitheatres. Buildings in which the spectators' seats surround the place used by the performers, 3194 ; outside Athens, 287 ; Colosseum at Rome, 2803 ; Rom. arena at Nimes, 1363 ; theatre of Epidaurus, 1540.

Amphitrite (am-fi-trī-ti). In Gk. myth., sea-queen, daughter of Nereus and wife of Poseidon.

Am plifier, of sound, 3012; in tele-graphy, 644 ; in telephony, 3174; triode as, 3199 ; in wireless, 3393.

Am plitude, of wave, 3358 ; modula-tion, 3393.

Amritsar, India. Cap. of dist. of same name in E. Punjab ; pop. 391,000 ; centre of Sikh faith ; silks, shawls, carpets ; scene of riot in 1919.

Amsterdam. Capital of Netherlands on R. Amstel ; pop. 814,000 ; **147** ; diamond-cutting. 1012 ; inaugura-tion of Queen Juliana, 2323.

Amu, or **Amu Darya** (anc. Oxus). Great r. of cent. Asia, rising on Pamir Plateau and flowing about 1,500 m. N.W. to Aral Sea.

Am'ulet, 2058.

Amundsen, Roald (1872–1928). Nor-wegian navigator and explorer, 147, 148, 2645, 2646 ; voyage through North-West Passage, 148, 682 ; map, 223 ; and Scott, 2895, 2896.

Amur. Great navigable r. of E. Asia (2,920 m.) ; gives name to province in Siberia N. of river, 265 ; map, 2086, 2966.

Amylop'sin. Starch-digesting ferment secreted by pancreas, 1017.

Anabap'tists. A 16th-cent. religious sect.

" Anab'asis." Xenophon's account of the expedition sent by Cyrus the Younger against Artaxerxes ; 3429.

Anab'olism. The chemical pro ess by which living matter builds up com-plex proteins.

Anaconda. A snake, 2991.

Anacos'tia. Tributary of the Potomac.

Anac'reon (563–478 B.C.). Gk. lyric poet ; famous for songs of love.

Anadir, r. of Far Eastern Region. U.S.S.R., about 500 m. long. 415.

Anaesthesia. Temporary or perman-ent loss of power to feel sensation, 148.

Anaesthet'ics. Drugs administered in surgery to render the body or part of the body free from pain, 148, 1048; carbon dioxide, 2039 ; and enzymes, 1220 ; ether, 1227 ; opiates, 2442.

An'agram. A puzzle.

An'alects of Confucius, 886.

Anal'ysis, in grammar, 1494 ; types of chemical analysis, 773 ; in psycho-logy, 2697.

Ananda, Mahidol (1926–46). King of Siam, 2965. Reigned from 1935 to his death.

Ananias (an-*a*-n'-*as*). An early Chris-tian who, with his wife Sapphira, was struck dead for lying (Acts v, 1–10).

An'apaest, in poetry, 2635, 2636.

An'archism. Theory that all govern-ment is an evil.

Anatolia. Modern Gk. name for Asia Minor, 271, 3262.

Anatol'ic languages, 2571.

Anat'omy. Name given to the study of the bodily structure of animals, 150, 151 ; comparative, 1245 ; Leon-ardo's work, 1927 ; microscopic (histology), 3447 ; of plants, 531 ; related to physiology, 2601 ; skele-ton, 2977. See also **Physiology.**

Anatomy, comparative, 1245 ; supports evolution theory, 1245.

" Anatomy of Melancholy." One of the most famous books in Eng. literature ; written by Robert Burton (1577–1640), published 1621 ; a vast accumulation of learning on a variety of subjects.

Anaxagoras (an-aks-ag'-o-ras). Gk. philosopher of 5th cent. B.C., teacher of Pericles ; introduced philosophy into Athens, 2551.

Ancestor worship, Africa, 2270 ; Japan (Shintoism), 1798.

Anchises (an-kī-sēz), in Rom. myth.. Trojan hero, father of Aeneas, 32.

Ancho'vies. Small herring-like fish, abundant in Mediterranean, 1621.

" Ancient Mariner." Poem by Cole-ridge, 101, 869.

Ancient Society of College Youths, bell-ringers, 410.

Anco na. It. spt. off N.E. coast ; pop. 89,000 ; triumphal arch of Trajan, A.D. 115 ; sugar refining, shipbuild-ing, silk, paper, 29.

Ancona. A breed of fowls, 2671.

Ancus Marcius. Legendary king of Rome, reigned 640–616 B.C., 2804.

Andalu'sia. Beautiful fertile dist. (formerly province) in S. Spain ; chief city, Seville ; fruit, olives, grain ; 3032 ; map, 3030.

Andalusian. Breed of fowls, 2671.

An'daman Islands, in Bay of Bengal ; together with Nicobars form prov. of India. Penal settlement, 1692.

Andan'te, in music, 2264.

Andersen, Hans Christian (1805–75), Danish fairy-tale author, 152, 1965, 2880 ; birthplace, 991.

Anderson, Carl David (b. 1905). Amer. physicist ; during research on gamma and cosmic rays, discovered the positron, 297 ; Nobel prize (physics) in 1936.

Anderson, Elizabeth Garrett (1836–1917). First Eng. woman physician ; first Eng. woman mayor ; a London hospital was named after her.

Anderson, Sir John (b. 1882). Brit. politician and civil servant. Gov. of Bengal (1932–37), app. Lord Privy Seal (Oct. 1938) with special powers as Minister of Civil Defence. Sec. of State for Home Defence and Minister of Home Security, Sept. 1939–Oct. 1940 ; gave name to Anderson shelter ; Lord President of the Council, Oct. 1940 ; chancellor of the Exchequer, 1943–45 ; chair-man of atomic energy commission, 1945–48.

Anderson, Lt.-Col. Sir Kenneth A. N. (b. 1891). Brit. soldier ; G.O.C.-in-C. Eastern Command, April 1942 ; Nov. 1942 Commander of Brit. 1st Army in Tunisian campaign, and to end of African campaign 1943 ; G.O.C.-in-C. E. Africa, 1945–46.

An'derson, Maxwell (b. 1888). Amer. author, playwright ; plays " Satur-day's Children," " Winterset " (blank verse).

Andes (an'-dēz), mts. in western S. Amer. ; length 4,500 m. ; highest peak. 23,097 ft. ; 152. 3022 ; Mt. Aconcagua, 153, 3024 ; animals. 815, 885, 1975 ; in Argentina, 226, map, 227 ; in Bolivia, 491, 492 ; in Chile, 802, 805 ; effect on climate. 226, 2559 ; in Colombia, 872, 873 ; in Ecuador, 1081 ; minerals, 228. 492, 802, 803, 2559, 3024 ; in Peru, 2558, 2559 ; railways, 153, 804, 3024 ; statue of Christ. 228, 805 ; in Vene-zuela, 3308.

Andijan, Tn. in Uzbekistan, U.S.S.R. ; pop. 83,000 ; terminus Trans-Caspian Rly. ; centre of vast cotton dist.

Andor'ra. Republic in Pyrenees under joint suzerainty of Fr. Pres. and Sp. Bishop of Urgel ; area 191 sq. m. ; pop. 5,230 ; sheep-raising, farming, 2709.

Andras y, Count Julius (1823–90). Hungarian statesman, chief architect of Hungarian state after formation of Dual Monarchy, and its first Premier (1867).

Andrée, Salomon August (1854–97). Swedish scientist and aeronaut, 154, 349, 2645.

Andrew, Saint (d. c. 70). One of the Twelve Apostles ; patron saint of Scot. and Rus., 188, 2562 ; cross used in Union flag, 580, 1312.

Andreyev (an'-drä'-yef), **Leonid** (1870–1919). Rus. writer, mystic and fatalist, 2856.

Andrianzoon, Jacob. Telescope made by, 276.

" Androcles (an'-drō-klēz) **and the Lion,"** story, 1605.

Andromache (an-drom'-*a*-kē). In Gk. myth., wife of Hector, 1603.

Andromeda (an-drom'-e-d*a*). In Gk. myth., dau. of Cassiopeia, 2554.

Andromeda, nebula, 2310.

Androni'cus Livi us (3rd cent. B.C.), first Rom. poet, 1895.

An'dros, Greece. Fertile mountainous isl. in Aegean Sea ; one of the Cyclades.

Ane'mograph, inst. for recording wind pressure and direction, 3384.

Anemom'eter, 3385–86.

Anemone (*a*-nem'-*o*-ni), or " wind flower," 154 ; in myth., 154.

Anemone, sea. A coelenterate animal related to the corals, 924, 2103, 2105.

An'eroid barometer. A portable form of barometer, 363 ; as altimeter, 2293 ; controls altitude of flying bomb, 1332.

Angara, in Siberia, important affluent of the Yenisei, length about 1,300 miles.

Angel-fish, sometimes called angel-shark, a fish with wing-like fins, belonging to the chaetodon family, found chiefly in tropics, plate f. 192, 193, 1303.

Angelico, Fra (frah an-jel'-i-kō) (1387–1455), the painter friar Fra Giovanni da Fiesole, painted only sacred subjects, 1775.

" Angel Inn," Grantham, 1499.

Angell, Sir Norman (b. 1874). English publicist (" The Great Illusion ").

Angels. According to apocalyptic liter-ature, the chief archangels are Michael, the prince ; Gabriel, the angel interpreter ; and Raphael, who, with Uriel, Chamuel, Jophiel, and Zadkiel, stands before God.

An'gelus. A bell rung in Cath. countries morning, noon, and night, inviting faithful to prayer ; painting by J. F. Millet, 1374.

Angers (ahn'-zhā), France. Mfg. city on r. Mayenne ; pop. 87,000 ; cap. former duchy of Anjou ; slate quarries.

Angina pectoris. A disease of the heart due to over-exertion.

Angiosperms (an'-ji-ō-spêrmz). The greatest division of seed-bearing plants (spermatophytes), including the true " flowering " types, 2620 ; divided into dicotyledons and mono-cotyledons, 2918 ; include most trees, 3247.

Angkor', Indo-China. Ruined city and former cap. of Cambodia, 10 m. N. of Tonle Sap (Great Lake) ; 666 ; Angkor Vat, 270, 665, 666.

Angle, in geometry, 1435 ; of refraction. 1925.

Angler fish, tropical species, 1297.

Angles. Ger. tribe which settled in Britain in 5th cent., 574, 1194, 1237 See also **Anglo-Saxons.**

Anglesey, Wales. isl. county in Irish Sea connected by bridge with main land ; 275 sq. m. ; pop. 49,000 155. map f. 1164 ; Llanfair Pg. (ful name has 52 letters), 155.

Anglicans. Members of Church of England, 985.

Angling. Fishing as a sport, 1309, *1311*; tackle, *1309*.

Anglo-Egyptian Sudan. *See* Sudan.

Anglo-Irish Treaty (1921), 1746, 1748.

" Anglo-Saxon Chronicle " 111, 1210 ; quoted, 3379.

Anglo-Saxons, 1237, 2388 ; conquer Brit., 992, 1194, 2878 ; Christianity introduced, 1194 ; jury system, 1843 ; language, 1209 ; laws, 1843 ; literature, 415, 650, 1210 ; witenagemot, 1488 ; 2521. *See also* Britain.

Ango'la or Portuguese West Africa, colony on s.w. coast ; 481,350 sq. m. ; pop. 3,738,000 ; cap. Loanda ; *map, plate f. 68* ; natives of, *62* ; occupied by Portugal, 72, 3368.

Angor'a. *See* Ankara.

Angora cat, or Persian, 720.

Angora goat, a long-haired species, 850, 1478.

Angoulême (ahn-gōō-lām). Fr. city on r. Charente ; pop. 36,700 ; paper, wine, linen ; cathedral begun in 1101.

Angström unit. One ten-millionth of a millimetre ; used in the measurement of minute distances, such as the wavelength of light, *plate f. 3056* ; named after Anders Jonas Angström (1814–74), Swedish physicist, who measured wavelength of light.

Angular measure. *See* **Weights and Measure**, *f-i*.

Angus. Scot. county, formerly called Forfarshire, area 873 sq. m. ; population 273,000, 155.

Anhalt. State in cent. Ger., former duchy ; 890 sq. m. ; pop. 436,200 ; cap. Dessau ; agriculture ; coal and other minerals.

Anhwei. Inland province of China in E. ; 87,900 sq. m. ; pop. 22,705,000 ; cap. Hwaining.

Aniline dyes, 857, 1059, 1724.

Animal'cule. An animal of microscopic size, as rotifers or " wheel animalcules."

Animal Kingdom, 156.

Animals, 156, *2075*, 3446–47 ; adaptations, 156, 1080 ; behaviour, 159 ; breeding of livestock, 730 ; cells, 738, 1155 ; classification, 156 ; cries, **162** ; development (embryology), 1155 ; distinguished from plants, 156 ; distribution (ecology), 841, 1080 ; domestication a step in civilization, 273, 1025 ; evolution, 156, 160, 1214 ; hibernation, 1622 ; instinct and intelligence, 159, *160, 161*; length of life, 156 ; lowest forms, 335, 2695 ; mammals, 2074 ; migration, 2169 ; Nature Study, 2283 ; parasites, 2512 ; prehistoric, *1245, 1246, 2678–81; protective coloration, 673, 2692, *2693*. *See also* **Biology** ; **Cell** ; **Ecology** ; **Embryology** ; **Evolution** ; **Heredity** ; **Reproduction,** etc. ; and the individual animals and animal groups such as **Birds** ; **Fish** ; **Insects.**

Animal worship, 2270 ; in anc. Egypt, 719, 931, 2256 ; in India, 601, 859, *1703*, 2211.

An'imism. The attribution of a living soul to inanimate objects and natural phenomena.

An'ion. Ion flowing to anode, or positive pole, in electrolysis, 1136, 1738 ; chloric ions, *1739*.

Anis. A tropical communistic bird, 441.

Anise. A plant of the parsley family, native of N. Africa, widely cultivated in Ger., S. Europe, India ; aniseed, 3061 ; essential oil from, 1263.

Anjou (ahn-zhōō). Fief of medieval Fr. on both sides of Loire ; cap. Angers ; held by Eng. (1154–1204) ; 1238, 1609.

Ank'ara (Angora). Modern capital of Turkey ; pop. 227,000 ; **162**, *163*, *3263*, 3266.

Ankle. Part of foot, 1342.

Anna. Indian coin ; 16 to the rupee.

" Anna Karenina " (an'a kä-rā'-nin-a). Novel by Tolstoy, and its heroine ; intense psychological study ; 3222.

Annam, Indo-China ; part of Viet-Nam ; pop. 6,211,200 ; sugar, rice, cotton, 1718.

Annamese race. Habits and characteristics, *1719*.

Annan. Scot. spt. tn., Dumfriesshire ; oat products ; boiler-making, and leather, rope, cotton industries ; pop. 4,300.

Annapolis. Cap. of Maryland, U.S.A. ; has U.S. naval academy ; oyster canning industry ; pop. 13,000 : 2116.

Annap'olis Royal, Nova Scotia. Tn. on arm of Bay of Fundy, 95 m. w. of Halifax ; pop. about 800 ; founded as Port Royal, 2401.

Anne. Queen of Eng. (1665–1714), **163**, *164, 1200;* accession, 1200 ; architecture under, *163;* deserts James II, 1794 ; favours Marlborough, 2106 ; literature under, 1212 ; and Act of Union, *1208*.

Anne Boleyn (1507–36). 2nd Queen of Henry VIII of Eng., *490*, 1612.

Anne of Austria (1601–66). Daughter of Philip III of Spain ; Queen of Louis XIII of Fr. ; regent during minority of her son Louis XIV ; her chief minister Mazarin.

Anne of Cleves (1515–57), 4th Queen of Henry VIII of Eng., 1612.

Annealing. Process of heating substance and cooling slowly to make it less brittle, 1472 ; iron, 1756.

An'nelids. Animal group containing the segmented worms, 3425.

" Annie Laurie." Famous 18th-cent. Scots song by William Douglass ; a real person, daughter of Sir Robert Laurie, first baronet of Maxwelton.

Anning, Mary (1799–1847). Eng. geologist, discovered the Ichthyosaurus, etc., **164**.

Annual parallax of stars, 3078.

Annual plants, for the flower garden, 2624.

Annunzio (ah-noont'-sē-ō), **Gabriele D'.** *See* D'Annunzio.

Anode (an'-ōd), *1739;* of Crookes tube, 3430 ; of therm*i*onic valve, 1138, 3198, *3199*.

Anodynes (an'-ō-dīnz). Pain-soothing drugs, 1048.

Anopheles (an-of'-el-ēz) mosquitoes, 2236.

Anschluss. German, " a joining." Denotes a union between two countries, either politically or under a customs agreement. Applied particularly to the proposal to join Austria to the German Reich, which was effected in March 1938, and ended May 1945 ; 3416.

Anrep, Boris. Russian artist, 2855.

Anselm, St. (1033–1109). Archbishop of Canterbury (1093–1109) ; and William Rufus, 3380.

Anson, George, Lord (1697–1762). Brit. admiral ; commanded victorious expedition against Spaniards (1740) ; defeated Fr. navy off Finisterre (1747), for which he was raised to peerage. First Lord of the Admiralty, 1751–56.

Anson, H.M.S. Brit. battleship, displacing 35,000 tons ; covered munitions convoys to N. Russia ; flagship of Rear Adm. Harcourt at Jap. surrender, Aug. 30, 1945.

" Answers." Lord Northcliffe's paper, 2385.

Ant. R. of Norfolk, Eng., *1168*.

Ant, 165, 1726, 1733 ; fossil, 138 ; research by Lord Avebury, 323 ; Forel's researches, 1349 ; instinct, 159 ; mandibles, *1729;* nests and community life, 165 ; use aphides and caterpillars as " cows," 166 ; at war, *165, 167;* white, *see* Termites.

Antaeus (an-tē-us). Giant slain by Hercules, 1615.

Antananarivo (an-tan-an-a-rē'-vō) or **Tananarivo,** Madagascar. Cap. and largest city ; pop. 126,500 ; *2051*. Captured by British 1942.

Antarctica (Antarctic Continent), *169–172;* **173** ; *map, 173;* exploration, 175, 899, 2544, 2896, 2931 ; ice-cap, 1468 ; ownership, 175 ; penguins, *170;* position of S. Pole, 2390.

Antarctic Circle, *173*, 1899 ; first crossed by Capt. Cook, 899.

Antarctic Ocean. Waters surrounding Antarctic Continent ; some modern geographers consider these waters

as southern ends of Atlantic, Pacific, and Indian oceans, 173.

Ant-eater. A mammal, **173** ; related to armadillo, 237 ; " spiny," 176, *313*, 1053.

Antelope, 176, 2075, 2842.

Antenna. *See* Aerials.

Anten'nae, of animals, 1730 ; ant, 165 ; bee, *plate f. 392:* bee drone, *391* ; beetle, *401;* crab, *pl. f. 924, 925* ; different in moths and butterflies, *628, 629;* lobster, 1977.

Anten'nule, a small feeler in front of the true antennae of crustaceans.

Anther, in plants, *532, 1321, 1323, 1324, 1325.*

Antherid'ia. Structures in moss, 2238, 2919.

Anthony, St. (*c.* 251–356), b. in Egypt, lived in solitude for years, resisted many temptations which are favourite subjects in literature and art ; founded Christian monasticism, 2212.

Anthony of Padua, St. (1195–1231), most celebrated of followers of St. Francis of Assisi ; wonderful preacher ; legends tell of tissues leaping from the water to hear him ; fine scholar.

Anthozo'a. Class of coelenterate animals ; corals, 908.

Anthracene oil. Obtained from coaltar, 857.

Anthracite or **hard coal,** 855, 2986 ; slates, 2981.

Anthrax. An infectious disease ; bacillus discovered, *1458*; Pasteur discovers vaccine, 2528.

Anthropoid. Name given to a group of apes, *183*.

Anthropol'ogy. The science of Man, his physical structure, customs and languages, arts and religions, distribution and civilization ; classification of Man, by language, 2570 ; by skin colour, 2723 ; by skull measurements, 2723 ; origin of Man, 156, 1245, 2078 ; prehistoric Man, 734, 2078 ; races of mankind, 2723.

Anthropom'etry. Science of the physical measurement of Man, his height, weight, and skull shape ; a branch of Anthropology.

Anthropomor'phism. Representation of God, or of the gods, in human form.

Anti-aircraft gun, 260 ; rocket-gun, 258, 2794; Home Guard, 1637.

Antibody. Substance created in the body to combat disease germs; also artificially prepared, 429.

Antibiot'ic. Substance produced by a living organism which inhibits the growth of certain germs or kills them, 179 ; such are penicillin, from the mould *Penicillium notatum*, 179 ; streptomycin, from the soil fungus *Streptomyces griseus*, 3103.

An'ticline. A rock fold with the convex side upward, *2427.*

Anti-Com'intern Pact. Signed between Ger. and Jap., Nov. 25, 1936, aimed against Communism ; on Nov. 6, 1937, Italy joined ; Manchukuo, Jan. 1939 ; Hungary, Feb. 1939 ; Spain, April 1939. Pact fell into abeyance on signing of Ger.-Russ. non-aggression pact, Aug. 1939 ; was revived June 1941, when Ger. attacked the U.S.S.R.

Anti-Corn Law League. (Cobden), 858.

Anticy'clone. Area of high meteorological pressure, 2150.

An'tidotes for poisons, 2638.

Antigone (an-tig'-o-nē). In Gk. myth., dau. of Oedipus ; follows father into exile ; buries brother in defiance of king's order ; tragedy of Sophocles, 3000.

Antigua (an-tig'-wa). Isl. of Brit. W. Indies, incl. in Leeward Is. group. of which St. John is cap. A. 108 sq. m. ; pop. 36,500 ; 3368.

" Anti-knock," desirable in petrol, 2564 ; tellurium in, 3185.

Antilles (an-til-ēz). All W. Indies isls. except Bahamas, 3368.

An'timony (Sb). A metallic element of the nitrogen group ; atomic weight, 121·7 ; melts at 1166° F. ; **176**, 2148; properties, 777 ; sulphide, 2119 ; in tartar emetic, 3155 ; used in alloys, 122, 123, 124, 3270.

Antinous (an-tin'-ō-us). Favourite page of Hadrian ; portrait, *2816.*

Antioch (an'-ti-ok), Turkey. Anc. centre of Gk. culture; transferred from Syria to Turkey, 1939; modern tn. Antakiveh; pop. 28,000; **177, 936.**

Antiochus (an-ti'-o-kus) **I, Soter.** King of Seleucid dynasty in Syria; ruled *c.* 280–271 B.C.; conquered Palestine.

Antiochus III, the Great, of Syria; ruled 223–187 B.C.; sheltered Hannibal and warred with Rome.

Antiochus IV, Epiphanes (e-pif'-*a*-nēz), of Syria; ruled 176–164 B.C.; oppresses Jews, 1830.

Antipater (an-tip'-*a*-ter) **the Idumean** (d. 43 B.C.), 1830.

Antipodes (an-tip'-ŏdēz) ("with the feet opposite"). A region on the opposite side of the earth; New Zealand is regarded as the Antipodes of England; also small uninhabited isl. S.E. of New Zealand.

Antipope. A usurping pontiff or one elected in opposition to the pope canonically chosen; Clement VII, 3298; Benedict XIII, 1543.

Antirrhinum. Favourite perennial garden plant, the snapdragon. Dwarf or tall varieties are obtainable in many colours. A Brit. species is found in cornfields.

Anti-rust alloy, 2365.

Anti-Semitism. Repressive measures against Jews (Semites) formed part of the policy of several countries before the 2nd World War, notably the German Reich, Italy, Poland, and Rumania.

Antiseptics. Germ-killing substances such as carbolic acid, iodine, and coal-tar preparations, used for medicinal and other purposes, **177,** 1048; alcohol, 104; bichloride of mercury, 2146; carbolic acid, 699; creosote, 857, 927; cyanides, 947; D.D.T., 179; hydrogen peroxide, 179; insecticides, 179; iodine, 179, 1738; Lister, 1963; M. & B., 179; Pasteur, 2528; penicillin, *178,* 179, 180, 2544; streptomycin, 179, 3103; sulphur, 3116; ultra-sonic waves, 3011; ultra-violet, 178, 1942.

Anti-slavery movement, 2982.

Antitoxin. A serum used in the treatment of cases of poisoning by bacteria, such as diphtheria and tetanus, **180,** 1818.

Antlers. Deer, *984, 985;* moose, *2228;* reindeer, 2760.

Anti-lion. Larva of an insect, **181.**

Antofagasta (an-tō-fa-gas'-ta). Spt. in N. Chile, cap. of prov. of same name; pop. 53,000; ships much nitrate; silver smelters.

Antonine Period. Roman Art, *2813.*

Antoninus Pius (A.D. 86–161). Rom. emperor; succeeded A.D. 139, adopted as son and successor by Hadrian; 2812.

Antonio (an-tō'-ni-ō). The merchant, friend of Bassanio, in Shakespeare's "Merchant of Venice," 2144.

An'tony, Mark. *See* **Mark Antony.**

Antrim. Co. and co. tn. of Northern Ire.; 1,176 sq. m.; pop. without Belfast, 197,000; **181,** 1747, *1954;* tn. of Antrim, pop. 2,000.

Antry'cide. Synthetic drug which gives cattle immunity for about six months from cattle disease caused by the tsetse fly.

Antwerp. City of Belgium; pop. (1938) 786,161; (1949) 254,000; **181,** *182,* 406; *map, 182;* architecture, *182;* guild halls, 1554; "city of Rubens," 2838; dialect, 404; in 1914–18 War, 3409. Connected with the r. Meuse by the Albert Canal. Germans occupied, May 18, 1940, 3417; liberated Sept. 4, 1944, 3422; flying bombs and rockets, 182.

Anu'bis. Anc. Eg. deity. Conducted souls of dead to lower world and assisted Osiris at final judgement.

An'zacs. Members of the Australian-New Zealand Army Corps in 1st World War; served in Gallipoli campaign, later in Fr.; the word is made by taking the initial letters.

An'zio Beaches, Battle of. Landings made to N. of Anzio by Anglo-U.S. forces on Jan. 22, 1944; ground held under constant bombardment and 270 attacks by Luftwaffe, until link-

up by patrols of 5th army from S.E. on May 25; 3421.

Aorta (ā-or'-ta), an artery, 1592.

Aosta (ah-os'-tah), **Aimone, Duke of** (b. 1900). It. nobleman; younger brother of Amadeo Umberto; in May 1941 made King Tomislav of Croatia, at Mussolini's instigation, after whose fall he renounced crown, having never visited his kingdom.

Aosta, Amadeo Umberto, Duke of (1898 –1942). It. soldier; second cousin of King Victor Emmanuel III; succeeded Graziani as Viceroy of Abyssinia in 1937; became c.-in-c. It. E. Africa; at Amba Alagi his surrender to Brit. forces virtually ended Abyssinian campaign; died in captivity.

Apaches (a-pach'-ēz). Tribe of roving predatory Indians of S.W. U.S.A.; in Arizona, 235. The name (pron. a-pash') is applied to violent street hooligans, esp. in Paris.

Apatite (ap'-a-tīt). A glassy phosphate of calcium containing chlorine or fluorine; yields phosphorus, 2574.

Ape, 182, *183, 184;* chimpanzee, *183;* gorilla, *183,* 1487; not a monkey, 2207; orang-utan, *183.*

Apeldoorn. Netherlands city; pop. 71,100; summer palace of Queen; the chief industry is paper making.

Apelles (a-pel'-ēz) (4th cent. B.C.), most celebrated Gk. painter; court painter of Philip of Macedon and Alexander the Great, 1528.

Ape-man. *Pithecanthropus erectus,* 182, 2079.

Apennines (ap'-e-nīnz). Mts. in It.; 800 m. long; highest peak, 9,585 ft., **184,** 1233, 1763; *map, 1764.*

Apet'alous plants, examples among trees, 3247.

Aphis (af'-is). Greenfly or plant louse, **185,** 1729; "domesticated" by ants, 166; and ladybird, 1883.

Aphrodite (af-rō-dī-tē), in Gk. myth., goddess of love and beauty, **186;** Adonis, 28, 154; Atalanta, 282; judgement of Paris, 3249; statue ("Venus de Milo"), *1535,* 1537, 2033.

Apia (ah'-pi-a). Trade centre of Samoa; rainfall, 2741; R. L. Stevenson died here, 2869.

A'piary. A place where bees are kept.

Apis (ā'-pis). In Eg. myth., sacred bull worshipped at Memphis; represented an incarnation of the god Osiris, 2455.

Apis. The genus of honey-bees, 395.

Apocalypse (a-pok'-a-lips) ("Revelation"), last book of New Testament.

Apocrita (a-pok'-ri-ta). Sub-order of insect ord. *Hymenoptera;* contains all members of order except sawflies, 3625.

Apocrypha (a-pok'-ri-fa). Writings of doubtful authenticity; of O.T., 424.

Apoidea. The bee family, 395.

Apollo (a-pol'-ō). In Gk. myth., god of light, **186,** *187, 974;* aids Trojans, 1603; causes d. of Achilles, 19; Daphne, *974;* Hermes, 1619; Hyacinthus, 1663; and Midas, 2166; oracle at Delphi, 988.

Apollo Bel'vedere. Famous Gk. statue, *187,* 1538.

Apollonius Rhodius (222–181 B.C.). Gk. poet, 1541.

Apoll'yon, "the destroyer"; "the angel of the bottomless pit" (Rev. ix. 11); in Bunyan's "Pilgrim's Progress," 619.

Apostle (a-pos'-l), **188,** *189.* The Twelve were Peter, Andrew, James the Elder, John, Philip, Bartholomew, Matthew, Thomas, James the Younger, Simon, Jude and Judas Iscariot; emblems, *188.* Name was applied in later days to others than the Twelve; Apostle of the Eng., St. Augustine; of the Fr., St. Denis; of Ger., St. Boniface; of the Highlanders, St. Columba; to the Indians, John Eliot; of the Indies, Bartolomé de Las Casas; of Ire., St. Patrick; to the Scots, St. Andrew, John Knox.

Apostle spoon. Spoon bearing image of one of the Apostles; a set numbers 13, including one with figure of Jesus. Apostle jugs had relief figures of Apostles in 12 panels round them.

Apos'trophe, use of, 2705.

Apothecaries' Weight. *See* **Weights and Measures,** *f-i.*

Appalachians (ap-a-lach'-i-anz). Mts. in E. N. Amer.; highest peak, 6,711 ft., *190;* effect on climate, 2385; effect on early settlement, 190, 3285, 3287; and exploration, 2380; geological history, 190, 2385; minerals, 3289; routes of travel, 3287.

Appeal, Courts of, 922.

Appendix, vermiform. Worm-like tube attached to lower right-hand end of large intestine; rudimentary character, 1245. Inflammation of appendix is called appendicitis.

Appenzell (a-pent-sel'). Canton of Switzerland traversed by Alps; textile industry, 3142.

Appia, Adolphe. Italian-Swiss theatrical designer. Stage production, 1043.

Ap'pian. Rom. historian, flourished during the reigns of Trajan and Hadrian, 1541.

Appian Way. Oldest and most famous of Rom. roads, Rome to Brundisium, 360 m.; begun 312 B.C.; *2799;* Spartacans crucified, 3053. It was "Route 6" of the Allied advance on Rome, May-June 1944.

Apple, 190, *plates f. 1400, 1401,* 1402; grafting, *1402;* in laboratory, *1403;* mistletoe on, 2194; ripening, 1220.

Appleby. Co. tn. of Westmorland; grammar school; pop. 1,600; 3371.

"Apples of Iduna, The," 2881.

Appleton, Sir Edward, G.B.E., K.C.B., F.R.S. (b. 1892). Sec. Dept. of Scientific and Industrial Research from 1939; researched in radar. G.B.E., Jan. 1946.

Appleton Layer. Ionized layer of upper atmosphere, 150 m. above earth; reflects short-wave electro-magnetic radiations used in broadcasting; named after Sir E. Appleton; 89.

Appomattox (ap-ō-mat'-oks) **Court House,** Virginia, U.S.A. Lee's surrender, *1918.*

Appren'tice, in medieval guilds, 1553.

Approved School, 2688.

Apricot (ā'-pri-kot), **191,** 937; *plate f. 1400.*

April, 4th month in calendar, 2223.

April Fools' Day, 191.

Apse, in architecture, 216.

Apsheron. Promontory of Transcaucasia, extending for 40 m. on W. coast of Caspian Sea; forms E. extremity of Caucasus Mts.

Apsley House, at Hyde Pk. Corner, London; formerly Duke of Wellington's residence. Given to nation 1947.

Apterygota. Sub-class of wingless insects, 1733.

Apteryx (ap'-te-riks) or kiwi, a wingless New Zealand bird, **191,** *192;* foot, *448.*

Apu'lia. Dept. of S.E. It.; 7,400 sq. m.; pop. 2,610,000; 1763.

Aqua Fortis. Original name for nitric acid, 2372.

Aquae Sextiae. Anc. name of Aix; here Marius defeated Teutones (102 B.C.).

Aqua re'gia. Mixture of concentrated nitric and hydrochloric acids, 1481.

Aquarium (a-kwär'-i-um), **192;** *plate f. 192;* at Naples, 2275; how to make your own, 193.

Aquar'ius. Sign of Zodiac, 3444.

Aquatint (ak'-wa-tint). A kind of etching on copper.

Aqueduct (ak'-wē-dukt), **194,** 3347; at Carthage, *2818;* modern type *195;* of anc. Roms., 194, 2818, 3347; at Segovia, 194, *3038;* Brindley's aqueduct, *571.*

Aqueous humour, of the eye, *1252.*

Aquileja (ak-wi-lā'-ya). It. Tn. with pop. about 2,600; once one of chief cities of Rom. Empire with 400,000 pop.; destroyed by Attila A.D. 452.

Aquinas (a-kwī'-nas), **Saint Thomas** (1227–74), theologian and scholastic philosopher, called the "Angelic Doctor"; next to St. Augustine in influence on Catholic doctrine ("Summa Theologiae," a summary of general knowledge as well as theology); 2572.

Aquincum. Roman Buda, 600.

TERMS USED IN ARCHITECTURE AND BUILDING

Alcove. A recess of considerable size in a room, and frequently separated from it by an arch or a beam.

Apse. A semicircular space opposite the entrance of a basilica.

Arabesque. A form of ornamentation highly developed during the Roman and Renaissance periods, of a fanciful character. The name means Arabian, but true Arabian ornamentation is called Moresque.

Arcade. A series of open arches supporting a roof or an upper storey; also a long gallery that is arched and has shops on either side; sometimes a narrow street that is covered over.

Architrave. The lowest part of the entablature, resting on the capital of the column. Also the moulding round a door or window.

Archivolt. Band of mouldings, etc., carried around a curved opening.

Arris. Corner where two planes meet.

Ashlar. Squared or "dressed" blocks of stone.

Basilica. Originally a hall of justice among the Greeks and Romans. In the early days of Christianity churches were given the same general plan, which was that of an oblong building with a nave, aisles, apse, narthex, and sometimes a transept.

Batten. A narrow strip of wood.

Batter. Slope of a wall face as it diminishes in thickness with increase in height.

Bay. An offset in a wall, as one of the compartments between pilasters or pillars; also part of a room forming a recess; a window opening with its framing.

Beam. A horizontal supporting member of timber, steel, or concrete, resting on two or more supports.

Bevel. Finished surface at an angle other than a right angle. When a sharp corner is cut off it leaves a flat surface called the bevel. When a corner is bevelled off equally by removing the arris, it produces a chamfer.

Bond. In a wall of stone, brick, or similar units, the arrangement of the units to "break joint" and afford strength; also the pattern produced on the face of the wall by this arrangement.

Bracket. A projecting member supporting an overhanging weight; often an ornamental member to carry a statue or similar object.

Bridging. Cross-pieces between joists or studs to act as stiffeners.

Bungalow. A small house of one storey. If there are upper rooms they are contained within the roof and lighted by dormers.

Butt joint. The joint formed by placing two members end to end.

Buttress. A brickwork or masonry mass which projects beyond a wall to take its thrust. When detached from the wall at the foot and arched over, it is termed a flying buttress.

Caisson. A watertight enclosure or casing sunk into the ground to allow work on the foundations of a building.

Capital. The ornamental head to a column. It identifies the order to which the column belongs.

Casement. A window which opens on hinges or pivots.

Clerestory. A part of a building that rises above and clear of other parts of the roof; it contains windows for lighting the interior. Originally that part of a church above the roofing of the aisles by means of which the upper part of the nave was lighted.

Conduit. A channel or pipe to carry water. The pipe or casing through which electric wires are run.

Coping. The cap run continuously around the top of a wall.

Corbel. A support projecting from a wall; courses set beyond the lower ones in brickwork or masonry form corbel courses.

Cove. A surface that is continuously concave. A quarter-circular hollow moulding.

Dormer. A vertical-framed window in a sloping roof; a structure projecting from a roof, having a window in it.

Dowel. A pin of wood or metal let into two parts or members to hold them together.

Drip. The grooved underside of a sill or moulding or other part that projects. The groove causes rain to drip instead of running back to the wall. Also the step in a lead gutter or lead flat where sheets overlap.

Façade. The front of a building, especially its principal front, when architecturally treated.

Fan-light. Originally a fan-shaped window in the head of a door or window. Now applied to rectangular lights in that position; often hinged or pivoted to open for ventilation.

Finial. The decorative piece, frequently in the form of a knot or bunch of foliage, which finishes off a pinnacle or gable.

Firring. Strips of wood on the inside of a brick, stone, or concrete wall to give a level surface for boarding, etc.

Flashing. Metal placed at joints between walls and roof to prevent water entering.

Flat. Suite of rooms on a single floor in a building of two or more storeys.

Flue. A passage to carry off air, smoke, or gas.

Fluting. Channels which are cut on the shafts of columns. Each channel is a flute.

Footings. Courses of brickwork or masonry resting on the foundations, made wider than the walls in order to give greater bearing.

Foundations. Lowest part of a structure, that transmits the weight of a building to the ground on which it is built. Usually of concrete, made wide so as to spread the load over a greater area. (See **Grillage**.)

Frame. A structural member built up of ties and struts in a series of triangles. (See **Truss**.)

Framing. The timber or steelwork skeleton of a building.

Fresco. A decoration in water colour on fresh plaster.

Frieze. An entablature has three divisions, and the frieze is the middle one. It is sometimes ornamented. Top part of a wall, above the picture rail.

Girder. Any main horizontal member which supports the floor beams or a partition. Similar principal member of a bridge.

Grillage. A mattress of steel or iron beams bolted together, usually in two layers with the beams of each at right angles to the other, used as a foundation in bad ground.

Grille. A screen of wood or metal, especially of wrought iron in an ornamental design, used in arches, fences, etc.

Half-timber Work. Method of house construction in which the walls are of timber frames having the openings filled in with brickwork.

Head. The upper horizontal member of a door or window opening.

Header. The end or short face of a brick, as it shows in the face of a wall. The long face is termed the "stretcher."

Inglenook. An alcove-like space near a fireplace, fitted with seats.

Jamb. Vertical sides of a door or window opening, etc.

Joist. A horizontal timber or steel beam to carry a floor or ceiling.

Lath. Strips of wood on which to put plaster work; metal lath is a mesh used for the same purpose.

Lintel. Horizontal member of timber, stone, etc., spanning an opening.

Metope. In the Doric frieze the spaces between the triglyphs are called metopes. In the Parthenon they were sculptured.

Mitre. A joint in which the members are cut at an angle and butted together.

Mortise. An opening or pocket cut in a member to take the tenon of a mortise-and-tenon joint.

Mullion. The upright posts or divisions in window openings.

Muntin. Vertical members between panels of a door. The outside vertical members are "stiles"; the horizontal ones, "rails."

Nave. The central part of a church or cathedral from the entrance to the altar. The nave is usually lighted from above by the windows in the clerestory.

Newel-post. Central post in a winding staircase, supporting inner ends of the steps; post carrying the handrail.

Nosing. A rounded edge which projects, as on a stair-tread.

Pier. A post or pillar used to sustain a beam; may be detached (or separate), or may be attached (built into a wall). (See **Pilaster**.)

Pilaster. A pier of rectangular shape usually set in the wall of a building with a projection of about one-third its width. Frequently treated to give the appearance of a column.

Plate. A horizontal timber used as a bearing, as a wall plate.

Rail. A member placed horizontally as in a door, a fence, panelling, etc.

Rebate. A recess cut or formed in the edge of a member to take a frame, etc.

Return. A structural member that turns and ends against a surface.

Reveal. The sides of a door or window opening at right angles to the face of a wall.

Ridge. The member which extends along the top of a roof, and to which the top ends of the rafters are fastened.

Riser. The upright piece in a stair step.

Rose window. Any circular window that is decorated, as with tracery. Also called wheel window.

Sash. The frame holding the glass in a window.

Sill. A principal member placed horizontally under a structure for a bearing, at the bottom of a frame; also the horizontal piece at the bottom of a door or window opening.

Sleeper. A horizontal timber for the support of floor joists or other timbers. A sleeper wall is a low wall to take ground-floor joists.

Stile. A member placed vertically in panelling, as a stile on a door. The inner verticals are termed "muntins."

Stop. The small strip that holds a window or door in place.

Stretcher. The longest face of a brick.

Strut. A member used in compression in a building; that is, one that sustains a pressure. It is usually a diagonal member. (See **Frame**).

Stud. One of the vertical members of a frame (e.g. in a timber partition).

Tie. A building unit which holds other members in tension, being the opposite to a strut. (See **Frame**).

Transept. The lateral parts of a church, between the nave and the choir, which extend beyond the walls of the structure, giving it the form of a cross.

Tread. The horizontal member on which the foot rests in a stair step.

Trim. The woodwork or metalwork used for the interior finish of a room.

Trimmer. A timber at the side of a framed (or "trimmed") opening that butts into and is supported by a trimming joist. The trimmer carries the ends of trimmed or "tail" joists, as at a fireplace opening.

Truss. A framework of timbers or steel, braced to resist the strains of pressure and pull, as a roof-truss. In its simplest form the rafters, king-post and tie-beam of a house roof. (See **Frame**.)

Aquitaine (ak-wi-tān') or **Aquitania**. Old Fr. province and duchy, 1238, 1834, 2028.

Arabesque (a-ra-besk'). Term applied to any intricate and fantastic design or composition; originally meant only patterns used by Arabs and Moors on their buildings.

Arabi, Ahmed. Same as **Arabi Pasha.**

Arabia (a-rā'-bi-a). Vast peninsula of S.W. Asia, including geographically Palestine, Syria, Iraq, and Transjordan, and politically Saudi Arabia, Yemen, Aden, Hadhramaut, Oman and Kuwait; 1,000,000 sq. m.; pop. est. 10,000,000; *195*; *maps, 197, facing 264*; coffee, 864; exploration, 195; history, 268; 1907; Mahomet, 2066; Mecca, 2125; primitive skyscraper cities, *196, 199*; spices, 3060.

Arabian camel, 199, 201, *670, 671.*

Arabian horse, *1646.*

"Arabian Nights," 202, 339. Story of Aladdin, 3450.

Arabian Sea. Portion of Indian Ocean between Arabia and India, 264.

Ar'abic numerals, 233, 2068, 2405.

Arabi Pasha (c. 1839–1911). Egyptian rebel; defeated by Wolseley (1882) at Tel-el-Kebir, 110.

Arab League, 200. Formed March 22, 1945, between Egypt, Iraq, Lebanon, Transjordan, Syria, Yemen, Saudi Arabia. *See* under names of these countries, and under Palestine.

Arabs, 195, *57, 790*; bring sugar plant to Europe, 3112; commerce, 2067; culture, 268, 2067; horses, *1646, 1647*; invade N. Africa, 2227, 3254; Semitic race, 2920; Spain, 2227; Syria, 3145; language, 1601; and Jews in Palestine, 2438, *pl. f. 2480*; religion, 2066; in Sahara, *997*; textiles, 3191.

Araceae (a-rā'-si-ē). The Arum family of plants, 3618.

Arachne (a-rak'-nē). In Gk. myth., maiden who was turned into a spider, 283–4, 3063.

Arach'nids. A class of arthropod animals, 3065; origin of name, 3063; scorpions, 2888; spiders, 3062.

Arad, Rumania. Tn. on r. Maros; pop. 77,000; formerly strong fortress; one of world's largest distilleries.

Arafat, Mt. Holy mt. near Mecca, 2125, 2127. In Mahomedan legend it was scene of reunion between Adam and Eve after their fall from Paradise.

Ar'ago, Dominique (1786–1853). Fr. astronomer and physicist; founder of electro-dynamics.

Aragon (a'-ra-gon). Former kingdom of N.E. Sp., 1238, *map 3030*, 3030; united with Castile and Leon, 1760.

Aragon, Louis (b. 1895). Fr. poet, novelist, etc.; a founder of surrealism; poems "Le Crève-Coeur," "Les Yeux d'Elsa."

Araguaya (a-ra-gwī'-ya). R. of Brazil, 1,300 m. long; joins Tocantins; *map, 551.*

Arakan'. W. coast area of Burma, from S. of Chittagong (just inside E. Bengal border) to Ramree Is.; cap. Akyab; overrun by the Japs April 1942; in Maungdaw-Buthidaung areas Brit. and Indian forces prevented Jap. breakthrough to India.

Ar'al Sea. 2nd largest body of water in Asia, 203, 717.

Aram, Eugene (1704–59). Eng. schoolmaster hanged for murder; subject of novel by Bulwer-Lytton and poem by Hood.

Aramae'ans. An anc. branch of Semites centred in N. Syria and Iraq; alphabet, 125.

Aramaic (a-ra-mā'-ik) **language.** Used by Jews, 425, 1601.

Aramis (a-ra-mis). One of the "Three Musketeers" in Dumas' novel; mild and gracious; finally enters the Church; 1054.

Aran, Isles of. Off Galway, Ireland. Three islands with a total area of 18 sq. m. Pop. about 2,680. Archaeological remains.

Araneida (a-rā'-ni-ida). The spider order of arachnids, 3065.

Aranyakas. Hindu sacred books, 1713.

Ararat (a'-ra-rat). Double volcanic mt. peak in E. Armenia, 238, 265; legendary resting-place of Noah's Ark.

Arauca'nian Indians. Aboriginal inhabitants of S. Chile, *804.*

Arbela. Modern Erbil or Arbil, tn. in Iraq S.E. of Mosul; battle of (331 B.C.), 106.

Arbitra'tion. Settlement of disputes between nations and individuals, and in industry, 203; national tribunal, 3234; Alaskan boundary, 99, treaties of, 3240.

Arblay, Frances d'. *See* Burney, Fanny.

Arbor Day. Day set apart in U.S.A. for planting trees; it is an official holiday; it is also observed in some places in Eng. and in other countries.

Arbutus (ar-bū'-tus). The strawberry tree, 204.

Arc, in geometry, 1436.

Arc, electric, in lighting, 1134, 1136; temperature attained, 1594; used in electric furnace, 1409; in switches, 1133; in welding, 3362.

Arcadia (ar-kā'-di-a). Dist. in Greece, 204, *1518.*

Arcadian stag. In Gk. myth., slain by Hercules, 1615

Arc de Triomphe (ark dē trē-onf), Paris. Largest triumphal arch in the world, *2515, 2516.*

Arch, in building, 204; in Babylonian architecture, 212; in bridge-building, 564–569; Gothic, 218; Roman, 214, *216*; Romanesque, *214*, 216, 218; Arch of Constantine, Rome, *2819*; Arch of Septimius Severus, Rome, *2799*; Arch of Titus, Rome, *2803*; steel, *568*; in Tientsin street, 3211.

Arch, of foot, 1342.

Archaean (ar-kē'-an) **period,** in geology, 1432.

Archaeology (ar-ki-ol'-o-ji). The science which studies the relics of Man's handiwork, such as buildings and utensils, 206; Babylonia, 329; Crete, 208, 927; Egypt, *206*, 208, 1113; in Britain, *206, 207, 209, 323*; Pompeii, 2653; in Rome, *2800, 2801, 2802, 2803, p. f. 2805*; H. Schliemann, 2883; Ur, 207.

Archaeopteryx (ar-ki-op'-te-riks), a primitive bird, known through fossil remains, *437*, 2681.

Archangel. Rus. spt. on R. Dvina near White Sea; pop. 281,000; ice-bound, 2844, 2849; 2nd World War convoys to, 3419.

Archangel tar, 3154.

Archbishop, Anglican costume, *825*, *826*; of Canterbury, 692; in Parliament, 2522.

Archegonium, male organ of spore-bearing plants, 2238, 2919.

Archer, Frederick James (1857–86). Eng. jockey. Rode in 8,084 races and won 2,748. Won five Derbys, six St. Legers, four Oaks, and five Two Thousand Guineas.

Archer, William (1856–1924). Brit. dramatic critic and author; mainly responsible for bringing before Brit. public dramas of Ibsen, whose works he edited; dramas, "War is War" and "The Green Goddess."

Archer (Sagittarius). A sign of the Zodiac, *3444.*

Archery, 209, *210.*

Archilochus (7th cent. B.C.). Greek lyric poet.

Archimedes (ar-ki-mē'-dēz) (c. 287–212 B.C.). Gk. mathematician and inventor, 210; lever, 2128; as a physicist, 2593.

Arch medes' law, in hydrostatics, 211.

Archimedes' Screw, 210, 211.

Architecture, 212; Adam brothers, *22, 23*; Aegean, 32, 213; Amer., *222*; Asiatic, 270, *666, 1814*; Babylonian and Assyrian, 212, *plate f. 329, 330, 332*; Byzantine, *213*, 214, *636, 637*; Egyptian, 212, *216, 1110, 1111, 1112, 1116, 1121*, 2708; Gothic, 216, *595, 1236, 1362, 3370*; Gk., *plate f. 212, 213, 213, 215, 216, 285, 286, 2800*; India, *plates f. 987, 988, 1700, 1706, 1710, 1711, 1713*, 3147; Japanese, *1801*; Inigo Jones, 1836; Lutyens, 2041; Mahomedan, *plate f. 119, 120*;

models, 2195; modern, *221, 222, 607, 608, 611, 783, 885, 987, 1104, 1793, 2354, 2355, plate f. 2352, back of plates f. 2352–53, 2854, 3101, 3127*; naval, 2951; Renaissance, *219*, 220, 2765; Rom. (anc.), *213, 214, 216, 2800, 2803*; Romanesque, 214, 2612; Russ., 2854; S. Amer. (anc.), *327, 1688, 1690*; styles, *219*; Wren, 3425. *See also* Building Construction; Castle; Cathedral; and list of architectural terms, 3713.

Architrave, in architecture, *215.*

Archons. Elected officials of anc. Athens.

Arc lamp, principle, 1134.

Arco. It. city nr. L. Garda, *1765.*

Arcot, siege of, 842, 1714.

Arctic Circle, *223*, 1899, 2390.

Arctic Ocean. Waters surrounding North Pole; a. 5,400,000 sq. m.; *223*; *map, 223*; size, 2413; sea life and fisheries, 225, 2844.

Arctic Regions, 223; *map, 223*; Asia, 2966; Eskimos, 224, *1223*; Europe, 2394, 2844; explorations, *148, 224, 1387, 2273, 2534, 2644, 2852, 2967*; Greenland, *1223, 1541*; N. Amer., 2385; Norway, 2392, 2393; plant life, 225, *226, 2620*; reindeer, 2760; Spitsbergen, 3067; "midnight sun," *plate f. 2168, 2169. See also* Polar Exploration.

Arctic tern, 1556, *1557.*

Arctur'us. The brightest star N. of the celestial equator, *3078.*

Ardèche. R. in S. Fr., 2774.

Arden, former forest in Warwickshire, 282, 3341.

Arden, Enoch. Hero of Tennyson's poem, "Enoch Arden"; shipwrecked sailor who, returning years later, finds his wife married again; leaves her untroubled and conceals his identity until death.

Ardennes (ahr-den'). Hilly wooded dist. in W. Europe, 226; Fr., 1359; Belgium, 407; Luxemburg, 2041; German counter-offensive, 1944, 226, 3422.

Ardennes, Fr. Dept. bordering Belg. and Luxemburg; a. 2,026 sq. m., pop. 293,000; cap, Mézières; **226.**

"Ardil," an artificial fibre made from ground-nuts, 2749.

Ardnacrusha, Co. Clare, Eire. Power station, 1950.

Ardnamurchan Point. Westernmost point of the mainland of Gt. Brit., in Argyllshire, Scot. It has a lighthouse.

Ardrossan. Scot. spt., Ayrshire; fishing, engineering works; pop. 8,500.

Area, in geometry, 1437.

Areca. Genus of tropical palms; produces betel-nut.

Area of Nîmes. One of the finest Rom. ruins in existence; 437 ft. long by 332 ft. wide.

"Areopagitica" (a-rē-op-a-git'-i-ka). Milton's pamphlet on freedom of press, 1211, 2177.

Areopagus (a-rē-op'-a-gus), of Athens, 286, 2111.

Arequipa (ar-ā-kē'-pa). City, trade centre in S. Peru, 100 m. N.E. of port Mollendo; pop. 46,000; mfrs., 2560.

Ares (ār'-ēz). In Gk. myth., god of war, 2111.

Arezzo (a-ret'-sō). It. city; pop. 60,200; 13th cent. cath.; art treasures; birthplace of Guido, Petrarch; anc. Arretium, one of 12 great cities of Etruria. Heavily damaged during 2nd World War.

Argali. Wild sheep of Altai Mts. and Tibet, 2940.

Argand, Aimé (1755–1803). Swiss chemist, mathematician; improved oil lamps, 1945; invented Argand smokeless gas burner, 1888.

Argent, in heraldry, 1614.

Argentina (ar-jen-tē'-na). Republic in S.E. of S. Amer.; 1,153,119 sq. m.; pop. about 16,000,000, 226; *map, 227*; cap., Buenos Aires, 601, *602*; and Chile boundary, *805*; climate, 2741, 3022; cowboys (gauchos), *228*; foreign commerce, 602, 3289; rlys., 602; war with Uruguay, 3299.

Argo. Ship of the Argonauts, 229.

Ar'gol. A tartrate in wine lees, 1500, 3155.

Ar'golis. Anc. Gk. dist. in N.E. Peloponnesus, *map, 1518* ; conquered by Argos, 1518.

Ar'gon (A) A colourless element of the inert gas group ; atomic weight, 39·94 ; occurs in the air, 88, 1420 ; has been liquefied at −302° F. ; 2744 ; properties, 776 ; in electric lamps, 1135, 1136.

Argonaut (ar'-gō-nawt). Paper nautilus, 230.

Argonauts, in Gk. myth., **229**, *230* ; Orpheus, 2454 ; Theseus, 3201.

Argonne (ar-gon') **Forest.** Wooded region in N.E. Fr. ; in First World War, 3413.

Argos, Greece. Anc. city 20 m. s. of Corinth, *map, 30* ; conquers Argolis, 1518.

Argosy. Originally, merchant ship of Ragusa (Argouse) ; now, poetically, any richly laden vessel.

Argus. In Gk. myth., hundred-eyed giant ; markings of peacock, 2532 ; pheasant, *2565*.

Argus. Odysseus' dog, 2423.

Argyll, John Douglas Sutherland Campbell, 9th Duke of (1845–1914). Gov.-gen. of Canada (1878–83) ; long known as Marquess of Lorne ; married Princess Louise, daughter of Queen Victoria.

Argyllshire, Scot. Second largest co., situated in the w. ; a. 3,100 sq. m. ; pop. 63,000 ; Co. tn., Lochgilphead ; 230.

Aria (ah'-ri-*a*). An elaborate solo in opera.

Ariadne (a-ri-ad'-ni). In Gk. myth., daughter of Minos, king of Crete ; aids Theseus, 3201. Deserted by him on Naxos, she was found and married by Dionysus.

Ar'ianism. The doctrine, repudiated by early Christian Church as heresy, that the Son is finite and created by the Father ; founded by Arius, 109 ; Nicene Council, 893.

Arica (a-rē'-ka). Spt. in N. Chile ; pop. 13,100 ; large trade with Bolivia.

Ariel (ār'-i-el). Fairy spirit in Shakespeare's "Tempest," 3185.

Aries (a'-ri-ēz) or **Ram.** Sign of the Zodiac, 3444.

Arion (a-rī-on), in Gk. myth., poet-musician, who saved his life, when forced to jump into the sea, by charming the dolphins with song.

Ariosto (a-ri-os'-tō), **Ludovico** (1474–1533). Ital. epic poet ; "Orlando Furioso," 1786.

Aristi'des (a-ris-ti'-dēz), "the Just" (c. 550–467 B.C.). Athenian general, **230**, *231*.

Aristip'pus (c. 430–360 B.C.). Gk. philosopher, pupil of Socrates.

Aristoc'racy (govt.), in anc. Athens. 1519 ; anc. Rome, 2805.

Aristogeiton (a-ris-tō-gī'-ton), 1522.

Aristophanes (a-ris-tof'-*a*-nēz) (c. 445–c. 385 B.C.). Athenian comic dramatist, **231** ; 1038, 1540.

Aristotle (a'-ris-totl) (384–322 B.C.). Gk. philosopher, **231**. *232*, 1541 ; and Alexander the Great, 105, 107 ; classification of plants, 531 ; falling bodies, 1513 ; pupil of Plato, 2628 ; on rhetoric, 2769 ; as a zoologist, 3446, 1092, 1244.

Arita (ar-ē'-ta). Tn. in isl. of Kiushu, Japan ; porcelain, 1809.

Arithmetic, 233 ; accounting machine, 17 ; addition, 24 ; calculating machines, 656 ; compared with algebra, 112, 113 ; decimals, 982 ; division, 1021 ; factors, 1255 ; fractions, 1355 ; Fun with Figures, 3457 ; logarithms, 1998 ; multiplication, 2253 ; percentage and interest, 2548 ; Rom. and Arabic numerals, 2405 ; slide rule, 2985 ; subtraction, 3107.

Arius (256–336). Alexandrian theologian, founder of Arianism, 109.

Arizona. State in s.w. U.S.A. ; 113,900 sq. m. ; pop. 500,000 ; **234**, 3291 ; animal life, *1974* ; Grand Canyon, *pl. f. 1496*, 1498 ; plant life, *648*.

Arizonite, an ore of titanium, 3217.

Ark, Noah's. *See* **Noah.**

Ark of the Covenant, Chest containing the laws given to Moses on Mount Sinai.

Arkansas (ah'-kan-saw). State in s. cent. U.S.A. ; 53,000 sq. m. ; pop. 1,950,000 ; 235.

Arkansas River. Largest Mississippi affluent except Missouri ; rises in Rocky Mts., flows s.E. 2,000 m.

Ark Royal, H.M.S., Lord Howard's flagship, *1198*. The 2nd Ark Royal (1914) was a seaplane carrier. The 3rd was an aircraft carrier (completed 1938, torpedoed 1941). The 4th, also an aircraft carrier, was launched at Birkenhead, Cheshire, by H.M. Queen Elizabeth in 1950.

Ark'wright, Sir Richard (1732–92). Inventor of the spinning frame, 235, 712, 3361.

Arlandes, Marquis d'. Fr. balloonist, *348*.

Arlen, Michael (b. 1895). Author of "The Green Hat," etc.

Arles (arl) (anc. Arelate), Fr. Important tn. in Rom. times ; remains of huge Rom. amphitheatre ; pop. 32,400 ; on Rhône, 2774.

Arlington, Virginia, U.S.A. Vil. on Potomac r. ; national cemetery and burial place of America's unknown soldier who fell in the 1st World War, and of F.-M. Sir John Dill ; *3343*.

Arliss, George (1868–1946). English-American actor ; film successes in "Disraeli," "The House of Rothschild," "The Green Goddess."

Arm, muscles, 2258, how to bandage, *1292*.

Armada, Spanish (1588), **236**, *237*, *plates f. 236, 237,* 1146 ; British Navy and, 2305 ; Drake, **236**, *1036*; Elizabeth and, 1146 ; Hawkins and, 1588 ; Philip II and, 2568 ; Raleigh and, 2744 ; monument, Plymouth, *2631* ; results, 142, 1146, 1195 ; type of ships in, 2946.

Armadil'lo. Armour-clad animal, 237.

Armageddon (ah-ma-ged'-on). Battlefield mentioned in Rev. xvi, 16, where final struggle between good and evil is to occur on Judgement Day ; hence any great battle ; supposed site in Palestine, 2482.

Armagh (ah-mah'). Co. of Northern Ire. ; 419 sq. m. ; pop. 109,000 ; **237.**

Armagh. City of N. Ire. ; co. tn. of Co. Armagh, and seat of Archbishops; pop. 7,000 ; 237.

Ar'mature, in electric motors, 2239 ; part of dynamo, *1061, 1062.*

Armenia. A country in w. Asia, of uncertain area, **237**, *238* ; language, 261 ; massacres, 239 ; people, 732.

Armenia. Republic of Soviet Russia, in Transcaucasia ; a. 12,000 sq. m. ; pop. 1,300,000 ; **237**, *238*.

Armenian Church. 238.

Armenti res (ahr-mahn-ti-ār'). Fr. mfg. and border tn. on r. Lys ; pop. 24,000 ; in 1914–18 War was Allied anchor to s. flank of Ypres salient until captured by Germans in April 1918.

Armin'ianism. A doctrine of modified predestination, making salvation depend on acts of individuals ; formulated by Jacob Arminius (Dutch, Harmensen) (1560–1609), anti-Calvinist theologian.

Armin'ius (17 B.C.–A.D. 21). Ger. chieftain, 1447.

Ar'mistice Day (Nov. 11), commemorating end of 1914–18 War, **239.**

Armitage, Edward (1817–96). English painter.

Armor'ican tribes, 586.

Armour, 240 ; heraldic devices, 1614 ; medieval knights, 1864, *plate f. 1864*; in modern war, 242 ; tanks, *242, 243*, *2794*, 3151.

Armoured car, *243.*

Armoured division, composition, 242.

Armoured fighting vehicles, in army, 242, *243* ; flail tank, 2185.

Armour-piercing shell, 260.

Armour-plate, of warships, 240, 2295 ; and meteorite metal, 2151 ; armour-piercing shell, 260 ; zirconium steel, 3444.

Arms (heraldry), 1614.

Arms (weapons). *See* **Artillery ; Firearms ; Machine-gun.**

Arms, Royal College of, Queen Victoria St., London ; dates from 1484 ; present building designed by Wren on the site of former building burnt in Great Fire ; also called Heralds' College ; constitution and function, 1615.

Armstrong, Anthony (b. 1897). Brit. humorist and playwright ("Warriors at Ease," "Full House," "Ten Minute Alibi ").

Armstrong, William George, 1st Baron (1810–1900). Brit. solicitor and engineer ; invented the hydraulic crane and other mechanical appliances ; also the Armstrong gun ; founder of important ordnance and shipbuilding works at Elswick, Northumberland.

Army, the land fighting forces, **244** ; airborne units, 244 ; artillery, 245, 257 ; badges, *245* ; branches, 244 ; catering, *246* ; commandos, 245 ; conscription, 246, 248 ; decorations, 2448 ; engineers, 246, 248 ; gas warfare, 3409 ; Gurkhas, 249 ; Home Guard, 1637 ; machine-guns, 2049 ; medals, 2448 ; ordnance, 248 ; physical training, 2589 ; Pioneers, 248 ; police, 249 ; ranks, *245*, 699 ; rocket weapons, *2794* ; Service corps, 246 ; small arms, 1281 ; tanks, *242, 243, 2794*, 3151 ; Territorials, 250 ; vehicles, *247*. *See also* **Territorial Army.**

Army Air Corps (Brit.). Formed Feb. 1942 ; comprising the Glider Pilot Regt., the Parachute Regt., and Airborne Infantry Units, *251, 1475* ; at Arnhem, 2320, 3422 ; in Normandy Invasion, 2378 ; training of parachute troops, 2509 ; in Rhine fighting, 2769, 2770.

Army Cadet Force (Brit.). Pre-service Army training organization for boys of 14 to 18 yrs. ; c.-in-c. King George VI.

Army Catering Corps, 248.

Army Corps. Division of an army, first introduced by Napoleon ; its composition varies, but usually it consists of about 40,000 officers and men.

Army Council. Controlling body of Brit. Army.

Arne, Thomas Augustine (1710–78). Brit. musical composer ; works include oratorios, operas, operettas ; best known for his "Rule, Britannia " in " The Masque of Alfred."

Arnhem. Netherlands mfg. tn. on Rhine ; pop. 78,000. Famous allied airborne attack, Sept. 17–26, 1944, 2320, 2769, 3422.

Ar'ni Al'to, a kind of marble, *2097.*

Ar'nica. A genus of flowering plants of family *Compositae*, found in N. Europe and w. part of U.S.A. ; tincture a household remedy for sprains and bruises.

Arno. R. of It., rises in Apennines, flows 150 m. to Mediterranean, through Florence and Pisa, 2612. Fierce fighting during German retreat of 1944.

Arnold, Matthew (1822–88). Eng. man of letters ; grave austere poet (" Sohrab and Rustum "), brilliant essayist and critic (" Culture and Anarchy ") ; swept away old pompous, acridly personal school of literary criticism, 1215, 1224.

Arnold, Thomas (1795–1842). Father of Matthew Arnold ; headmaster of Rugby, portrayed in Thomas Hughes' " Tom Brown's School Days."

Arnold of Brescia (bresh'a) (c. 1100–55). It. priest and reformer ; preached against vices and riches of clergy ; led revolt against papal rule in Rome ; executed at instigation of Adrian IV.

Arosa. Noted health resort in canton Grisons, Switzerland ; nearly 6,000 ft. high ; pop. 1,800.

Arquebus (ah'-kwi-bus). Early handgun, 1281, *1282.*

Ar'ran. Isl. of Buteshire, Scot., noted for igneous rocks and beautiful scenery ; largest isl. in Firth of Clyde (165 sq. m.) ; pop. 4,500.

Arras (ar'-ah). City in N. France ; pop. 26,000 ; strategic point in War of 1914–18, when ancient town hall and cath. were destroyed ; in Second World War, Brit. H.Q. of 1939–40 ; heavy rly. damage, 1940–44 ; liberated, 3422 ; tapestry, 3153.

Arrhenius (ar-ā´-ni-us), **Svante** (1859–1927). Swedish chemist and physicist ; originator of the ionic theory of electrolytes, 1739 ; Nobel prizewinner (1903) ; advocate of theory that the energy of the world is self-renewing.

Arrol, Sir William (1839–1913). Brit. engineer, contractor and politician ; head of firm which built the Tay, Forth and Tower Bridges and Manchester Ship Canal.

Arromanches, Fr. vil. in dept. of Calvados, Normandy, 7 m. N.E. of Bayeux ; Brit. landing-craft beached here on D-day, 2377 ; site of Mulberry Harbour, 2252.

Arrowhead, water-plant, 3356.

Arrowroot. Starchy powder obtained from roots of W. Indies and trop. Amer. plants ; an invalid food ; name comes from S. Amer. Indian use for wounds made by poisoned arrows.

Arsenal. Place for manufacture or storage of armaments ; Chorley (Lancs) supplements Woolwich as principal Royal Arsenal.

Arsenal. Famous Association football club with h.q. at Highbury, London ; First Division champions in 1931, 1933–35, 1938, and 1948.

Arsenic (As). A highly poisonous element of the nitrogen group ; atomic weight, 74·91 ; occurs chiefly as sulphides ; does not melt but volatilizes at 212° F. ; used in mfr. of lead shot, rat poisons, insecticides, etc. ; properties, 777.

Art. *See* Fine arts.

Artaxerxes (ah-tak-zêrk´-sēz) **I.** King of Persia, son of Xerxes I, ruled 464–424 B.C.

Artaxerxes II. King of Persia 404–358 B.C., succeeding his father Darius II ; life told by Plutarch.

Artaxerxes III. King of Persia 358–338 B.C. ; weak and despotic ruler.

Artemis (ar´-tem-is). In Gk. myth., goddess of the chase, 251, *252* ; statue, *2033* ; temple at Ephesus, 2923.

Artemisia (ar-te-mis´ya), queen of Halicarnassus ; Mausoleum, *2924.*

Artemisium. Region on N. coast of Euboea, isl. in Aegean Sea ; naval victory of Gks. over Persians. 480 B.C., 2556.

Arter'ial blood, 477, 1591, 1592.

Arterial road. A main first-class highway, 2754.

Ar'teries. Blood-vessels which carry blood from heart to body tissues, 477, 1591 ; aorta, *1592* ; bleeding, how to stop, 1295 ; hepatic, 1968 ; pulmonary, 1592 ; pulse, 1593, 2701.

Arte'sian wells, 252, 3069 ; in Australia, 308.

Artevelde (ar-te-vel´-dê), **Jacob Van** (c. 1290–1345). Flemish leader in revolt of Ghent (1337) against Count of Flanders. His son Philip (1340–82) was killed in similar revolt.

Ar'thropods. The phylum of animals with jointed legs, 156, 1730, 3065.

Arthur. King of Brit., in 6th cent. ; hero of many legends ; founder of the Order of the Round Table ; 255.

Arthur (1187–1203). Duke of Brittany, 254 ; and King John, 1833.

Arthurian legends, 255, 2830 ; Galahad, 1413 ; popularized by Geoffrey of Monmouth, 1210, by Malory, 1210, by Tennyson, 1214, 3187 ; Stories : "How Arthur Won His Crown," 256 ; "The Ninth Diamond," 2830 ; "The Kitchen Boy Who Became a Knight," 2831.

Arthur's Seat. Hill overlooking Edinburgh from S. (822 ft.).

Ar'tichoke. A vegetable, **256** ; yields fructose, 3114.

Artif'icer, in the Royal Navy, 2308.

Artificial respiration. Methods, *1294.*

Artificial silk, 739, 2748, *2749, 2750,* 2973.

Artificial substances. *See* Synthetic products.

Artillery, "the guns," **257,** 245 ; anti-aircraft, 257, *260* ; fuses, 258 ; howitzer, 257 ; naval, 2305, 2306 ; predictor, 257 ; radar, 257, *260* ; rockets, *258, 2794* ; Rumford's experiments, 2842 ; self-propelled, *257. See also* **Firearms, Machine-gun.**

Artois (ahr-twah). Former province in N. France, cap. Arras ; now department of Pas-de-Calais ; desperate fighting in First World War (Cambrai, Loos, Neuve Chapelle) ; gives name to artesian well.

Arts Council of Great Britain, formed early in 2nd World War to encourage knowledge and practice of the arts : C.E.M.A. (Committee for Encouragement of Music and the Arts) provided plays, concerts and art exhibitions for forces, war workers, and general public ; given permanent form June 1945 ; govt.-controlled.

Arts, Royal Society of. Institution whose functions are indicated by its full title, Royal Society for the Encouragement of Arts, Manufactures and Commerce. Founded in 1754.

Aru or **Arru Islands.** Group in Indonesia, S.W. of New Guinea ; pop. 18,000 ; *map, 1075* ; pearls, 2534.

Arum, wild, or wake-robin, 3332.

Arum lily. Not a lily, 1948.

Arun. R. ; rises in St. Leonard's Forest and flows through Sussex into the Eng. Channel at Littlehampton. Arundel Castle overlooks it.

Arundel. Anc. tn. of Sussex on r. Arun ; pop. 2,480 ; the 10th cent. castle, destroyed during Civil War and rebuilt towards end of 18th cent., is the seat of Duke of Norfolk.

Arundel Marbles. Collection of antiquities bequeathed in 1667 by 6th Duke of Norfolk to Oxford University, 2465.

Aruwimi (a-rōō-wē´-mē). Tributary of r. Congo ; rises W. of Lake Albert, flows W. 800 m. through jungles of equatorial Africa ; partly explored by Stanley (1887) ; *map, 888.*

Aryan (är´-i-an), 261, 1714, 2570.

Asa. Third kind of Judah, zealous uprooter of idolatry (1 Kings xv. ; 2 Chron. xiv-xvi).

Asafoetida (as-a-fē´-ti-da). A resin, with smell of garlic.

Asaph (ā´-saf). Leader of David's temple choir. The hereditary choirs of the temple were called "sons of Asaph" (1 Chron. xxv).

Asbestos. A fibrous mineral used in fireproof fabrics, 261, 1286 ; in Quebec, 2714 ; a silicate, 2181.

Ascalon (as´-ka-lon) or **Askelon.** Anc. Philistine city on the Mediterranean ; centre of Hellenistic culture ; birthplace of Herod the Great ; scene of battles in Crusades, 2570.

Ascension. Isolated Brit. isl. near middle of S. Atlantic Ocean ; 34 sq. m. ; govt. sanatorium ; noted for large turtles ; *map, 290.*

Ascham (as´-kam), **Roger** (1515–68). Eng. classical scholar and writer ; tutor of Queen Elizabeth ; noted for defence of gentle methods of teaching ("The Schoolmaster").

Asche, Oscar (1872–1936). Brit. actor-manager ; b. in Australia ; first appeared in London 1893 ; presented "Chu Chin Chow."

Asclepios. *See* Aesculapius.

Ascomycetes (as-kō-mī-sēts). A class of fungi bearing spores inside special cells, 1408 ; yeast, 3434.

Ascor'bic acid, med. name for Vitamin C, 3327.

Ascot. Vil. of Berkshire ; fashionable horse-racing meeting, 1648.

As'culum, battle of, 2710.

As'dic (Anti- or Admiralty Submarine Detection Investigation Committee). R.N. method of detection of submarines by means of sound waves (or echoes) thrown back by the submarine's hull.

Asep'sis and Antiseptics, 177.

Asgard. In Norse myth., home of gods, 341, 2421, 2881.

Ash. A hardwood tree, 262, *3244.*

Ash, or mineral salts ; in food, 1338, *2174* ; potash, 2664 ; seaweed, 2914 ; volcanic, 3328.

Ashanti (ash-an´-ti). Inland territory in Gold Coast Colony, Brit. W. Africa ; cap. Kumasi ; 3366.

Ash'burton. Goldfield in W. Australia.

Ashburton shield. Challenge shield shot for annually at Bisley, for the best eight from public school J.T.Cs. Seven shots at 200 and 500 yds. are fired.

Ashby-de-la-Zouch (zōōsh). Mkt. tn. of Leicestershire. Remains of castle in which Mary Queen of Scots was imprisoned ; pop. 5,000.

Ash'dod. Anc. Philistine city, 2570.

Ashdown Forest. In Sussex ; the only remaining part of the immense forest known to the Saxons as the Andredsweald.

Asher (Hebrew "blessed"). Son of Jacob ; ancestor of tribe of Asher.

"Ashes." Origin of name in cricket, 930.

Ashfield, Albert H. S., 1st Baron (1874–1948). Brit. business man and politician ; chairman London Transport ; one of first four members of British Transport Commn.

Ashkhabad. Cap. of Russ. republic of Turkmenistan, formerly Polterask ; pop. 127,000 ; a commercial centre, 3267.

Ashmole, Elias (1617–92). Eng. astrologer and antiquary ; founder of Ashmolean Museum, Oxford, 2465.

Ashridge. Name of park and house in Herts, former seat of Lord Brownlow ; mansion now a Conservative college founded as a memorial to Bonar Law.

Ashton, Frederick, W. M., C.B.E. (b. 1906). Brit. choreographer and dancer ; created "Facade," "Les Patineurs."

Ashton, Lucy. Heroine of Scott's "Bride of Lammermoor" ; betrothed to Ravenswood but forced to marry another ; stabs her husband on wedding night, and goes mad ; story used by Donizetti in opera "Lucia di Lammermoor."

Ashton-under-Lyne. Mfg. tn., Lancashire ; pop. 51,500 ; silk, cotton, bleaching, dyeing, hat, iron-founding industries ; coal mines near by.

Ash'toreth. Same as Astarte.

Ashurbanipal, or **Assur-bani-pal.** Last great Assyrian emperor (7th cent. B.C.); called Sardanapalus by Greeks; his library, *331,* 1930 ; palace at Nineveh, 2371.

Ash Wednesday. First day of Lent, 1074.

Ashwell, Lena (b. 1872). Brit. actress-manager ; took part of Mrs. Dane in "Mrs. Dane's Defence" ; played title-role in "Leah Kleschna."

Asia. Largest of the continents, 17,000,000 sq. m. ; 263 ; *map plate f. 264* ; pop. 1,155,000,000 ; climate, *plate f. 265, 841* ; deserts, 264, 996, *997* ; elevation, 263, *plate f. 265* ; flags of, *frontis. vol. 8* ; history, 265 ; mountains and plateaus, 264 ; oil-fields, 2426 ; political history, 271 ; pop., *plate f. 265, 267* ; railways, 2736 ; religions, 268, 269 ; rivers, 265 ; Soviet Central Asia, 264 ; steppes, 265 ; tundras, 263 ; vegetation, *plate f. 265. See also* under names of chief physical features, political divisions, and cities.

Asia Minor or Anatolia. Peninsula of Asia between Black Sea and Mediterranean, now largely in modern Turkey, 271, 3262; importance of Smyrna, 2988.—History: Aegean civilization, 29–31 ; Hittites, 1633 ; Lydian empire, 932 ; Gk. colonies, 105, 1519, 255 ; Rome conquers, 2808 ; Mongols, 2206, 3264 ; St. Paul, 2530 ; Greeks expelled by Turks, 1525.

Asia'go. It. tn., centre of small plateau dist. S.E. of former Austrian Trentino ; scene of Austrian offensive in 1916.

Asiat'ic elephant, 1141.

Askari. Native African soldier trained and officered by Europeans, particularly Italian in E. Africa.

Asmara. Cap. of Eritrea ; pop. 85,000 ; 1073, 1222.

Asoka (as-ō'-ka). Emperor of India 264–c. 228 B.C. ; great conqueror, most powerful sovereign of his time, who devoted himself to spreading Buddhist religion. He conducted a remarkable missionary campaign and built pillars with inscriptions setting forth Buddhist doctrines.

Asp, or African cobra, 859.

Asparagus. A plant, 271 ; belong to lily family, 1947 ; blanching, 2623.

Aspasia (as-pā'-zi-a) (5th cent. B.C.). Beautiful Gk. woman. b. Miletus ; she greatly influenced Pericles.

As'pen, or trembling poplar, 2655.

Aspern, Austria. Vil. on Danube opposite Vienna ; here French were defeated by Austrians in 1809.

Asphalt (as'-falt). A mineral, 272 ; artificial, 2429 ; as fossil bed, 1354 ; Trinidad, 272, 3248 ; Venezuela, 3024, 3309 ; used in paving, 272.

Asphodel (as'-fō-del). Plant genus of lily family ; in Gk. legend, most famous of all plants associated with underworld.

Asquith, H. H. See Oxford and Asquith, Earl of.

Ass, 273.

Assam (as-sam'). Prov. in N.E. India, bordering China and Burma ; 55,000 sq. m. ; pop. 8,500,000, 273 ; highest rainfall, 265, 1701 ; in Second World War, 274.

Assam Highway, from Chungking to Sadiya, rail-head of Bengal-Assam rly. ; 2,200 m. long ; rises to 9,000 ft. ; begun 1940.

Assas'sins. Mahomedan sect, 274.

Assay'ing. Process of finding how much of a given metal is in an ore or alloy.

Assiniboine (as-in-i-boin') River. In S. Saskatchewan and Manitoba, Canada ; flows 450 m. S.E. ; 2088.

Assisi (as-sē'-si). Tn. in cent. It. ; pop. 20,000 ; birthplace of St. Francis, 1383.

Assiut (as-i-ūt'), Egypt. City near w. bank of Nile ; pop. 60,000 ; once starting point of caravan route into Libyan desert and Sudan ; site of a Nile barrage.

Assizes. In Eng., 922.

Association football, 1344, 1345. See also Cup Final ; Football.

Association of ideas, and memory, 2138.

Assuan, or Aswan. Anc. Syene, tn. and resort in Upper Egypt on Nile ; pop. 22,200 ; near fine ruins ; great Nile dam, 959, 1102, 2371.

Assur. Original name of Assyria and earliest cap. on Tigris ; destroyed by Medes and Chaldeans 606 B.C. ; 330.

Assur-bani-pal (as-ēr-bah'-ni-pal). See Ashurbanipal.

Assyrian Empire, 274, 330 ; architecture, 212 ; art, 584, 585 ; enamelling, 1158 ; language, 1601 ; library of Ashurbanipal, 331, 1930 ; Nineveh, cap., 2371 ; paintings, 2475 ; sculpture, 331, 2904.—History : Israel conquered, 1829 ; Hittite empire conquered, 1633 ; Medes overthrow, 2131. See also Babylonia and Assyria.

Astarte (as-tar'-ti) or Ash'toreth. Phoenician goddess ; corresponds to Gk. Aphrodite.

Astatine, chem. element, 778. See Alabamine.

Aster. Perennial and annual flowering plants, 274.

Asteroidea. Starfish class of echinoderms.

As'teroids. Small planets, 2617, 3119.

Astig'matism. A defect of vision, 1254 ; corrected by lenses, 1925 ; in microscope, 2163.

Aston, Francis William (1877–1945). Brit. scientist and inventor of mass spectrograph ; work on isotopes, 1760.

Aston Villa. Famous Association football club (Birmingham) ; winners of F.A. Cup six times ; in 1896–7 won Cup and League competitions.

Astor, John Jacob (b. 1886). Brit. newspaper proprietor ; became chief proprietor of " The Times " in 1922.

Astor, Nancy Witcher, Viscountess (b. 1879) ; b. Virginia, U.S.A. ; first woman actually to take seat in Brit. Parliament (1919).

Astragal (as'tra-gal). A small moulding or bead semicircular in form ; called also a roundel ; the circular moulding close to the mouth of a gun.

Astrakhan (as-tra-kan'). Town of R.S.F.S.R. ; pop. 254,000 ; chief port on Caspian Sea, 275, 717, 3329.

Astrakhan. A breed of sheep, 2940 ; fur, 275.

Astrid, Queen of the Belgians (1905– 35) ; death, 1928.

As'trolabe. Steering by, 2290.

Astrol'ogy. The forerunner of astronomy ; fortune-telling by the stars, 281, 3444.

Astronom'ical telescope. One showing an inverted image, 3180.

Astronomy, 275 ; aurora borealis, 304, plate f. 304, 305, 305 ; comets, 880, plates f. 880–81 ; constellations, 894, 895 ; earth, 1067 ; eclipses, plates f. 1076, 1077, 1078, 1079 ; equinoxes and solstices, 1221 ; ether and space, 1226 ; gravitation, 1512 ; how gravity deflects light, 1079 ; meteors and meteorites, 2151, 2152 ; moon, 2224, plates f. 2224, 2225 ; nebulae, 280, 2310 ; observatory, 281, 2411 ; planets, plates f. 280, 281, 2617 (see also under names of the planets) ; relativity, 2760 ; spectroscope, 3055 ; stars, 3077 ; sun and solar system, 3119 ; telescopes, 3178 ; in time determinations, 3212 ; zodiac, 3444. — History : Tycho Brahe, 544 ; Chaldeans, 332 ; Copernicus, 905 ; Eddington, 1083 ; Galileo, 1414 ; Jeans, 1815 ; Kepler, 1852, 1853 ; Newton's theory of gravitation, 1512 ; Ptolemy, 2697 ; Pythagoreans, 2710. See also, in Index and Astronomy Study Outline, chief topics named above.

Astur'ias. Anc. prov. of N.W. Sp., corresponding roughly to modern Oviedo, map 3030, 3036.

Astyages (as'-ti-a-jēz). Median king ; reigned 584–550 B.C.

Astyanax (as'-ti-a-naks). In Gk. myth. son of Hector ; 1603.

Asunción (as-un-si-ōn'). Paraguay, cap., on Paraguay r. ; pop. 130,000 ; trade in Paraguay tea, tobacco, fruits, etc., 2512.

Asyn'chronous Motor, a type of A.C. motor, 2014.

" As You Like It," comedy by Shakespeare, 282.

Atacama (ah-ta-kah'-ma), Desert of. Large elevated tract in N. Chile, barren, but rich in minerals ; nitrates, 803.

Atahualpa (ah-ta-hwal'-pa) (c. 1495– 1533), last Inca of Peru, captured by Pizarro, 2616.

Atalanta. In Gk. myth., a maiden famous for beauty and fleetness, 282, 283.

" Atalanta's Race," by Sir Edward Poynter, 283.

Atatürk. See Kemal Atatürk.

At'avism. " Throw-back " to racial or family ancestor, 1427.

Atbara (at-bah'-ra), r., rises in N. Abyssinia and flows N.W. 500 m. to Nile, 2371 ; battle in 1898 saw victory

of British under Kitchener over the Mahdi.

Atchana-Alakakh. Ancient Hittite cap. of Hatay, Turkey, excavated in 1947 ; 208.

At'ebrin. Synthetic substitute for quinine ; also called Mepacrine.

Athabaska or Athabasca. Lake in N. Alberta and Saskatchewan, Canada ; 2,842 sq. m. ; 2050.

Athabaska River, in Alberta, Canada ; flows 776 m. N.E. to Athabaska L. ; becomes Mackenzie r., 2050 ; oil-soaked sands, 102.

Athaliah (ath-a-lī'-a). Daughter of Ahab and wife of Jehoram ; slaughtered grandsons except one, and seized power ; was put to death six years later on coronation of Joash, the heir who had been kept in hiding (2 Kings xi.) ; subject of Racine's tragedy " Athalie."

Athana'sius, Saint (297–373). Bishop of Alexandria, chief defender of orthodox doctrine of Trinity against Arianism, 109 ; Nicene council, 893.

Ath'elstan or Æthelstan (c. 895–940). Saxon king, succeeded 924 ; grandson of Alfred the Great ; first Saxon king to be called king of all Brit. ; defeated Celts and Danes at Brunanburgh in 937.

Athena (a-thē-na). In Gk. myth., goddess of wisdom, 283 ; Achilles, 1603 ; Gorgon's head, 2552 ; Odysseus, 2422 ; Paris, judgement of, 3249 ; statues by Pheidias, 22.

Athenaeum (ath-e-nē-um) Club. Famous institution in Pall Mall, London, founded in 1824. Members are men of considerable eminence in the literary, scientific, or artistic world.

Athe'nia, S.S. Brit. trans-Atlantic liner of Donaldson line, first U-boat victim of Second World War ; sunk Sept. 3, 1939, 250 m. N.W. of Ireland with loss of 128 persons.

Athens. Cap. of Greece ; pop. 400,000 ; with Piraeus and suburbs over 1,000,000, 284, 285 ; plate f. 212 ; plate f. 1524, 1525 ; 1529, 1530, back of plate f. 1524 ; Acropolis, 21, 1521 ; Elgin Marbles, 1143, 1144, 1537 ; Erechtheum, back of plate f. 1524 ; stages of government, 1519 ; Parthenon, 22, 1144, plate f. 212 ; theatre of Dionysus, 3194.—History : 286 ; legend of Theseus, 3201 ; rise of democracy, 1519 ; in Persian wars, 230, 1522, 2550 ; under Themistocles, 1522 ; origin of name, 286 ; in age of Pericles, 1923, 1924, 2551 ; Peloponnesian wars, 1923, 3053 ; Pheidias and, 2566 ; Macedonian conquest, 990, 1524, 3198 ; Sparta and, 3052 ; temple of Wingless Victory, 1530 ; occupied by Germany, 1941–44 ; rebel fighting in, 1944–45 ; 287. See also Greece ; Greek Art.

Athletics, 287, 289 ; in Gk. art, 1532 ; Olympic Games, 2432 ; physical training, 2589 ; running, 2843. See also Records ; Sports and Games.

Athlone, Eire. Tn. on Shannon ; pop. 7,500 ; high-power wireless station.

Athlone, Earl of. English title held by Alexander Augustus Cambridge (b. 1874), 3rd son of Duke of Teck and Princess Mary Adelaide and brother of Queen Mary. Married Princess Alice of Albany in 1904. Governor-general of the Union of S. Africa (1923–31) ; Governor-general of Canada, 1940–46. (Earldom created in 1917.)

Athor (ah'thor) or Hathor. Egyptian goddess, sometimes identified with Isis and Gk. Aphrodite ; usually represented with cow's head or horns.

Athos. One of the Three Musketeers in Dumas' novel ; 1054.

Athos. Peninsula N.E. Greece ; Mt. Athos (6,350 ft.), 2212.

Atlant'a. Cap. of Georgia, U.S.A. ; pop. 302,300 ; mfrs. cotton goods, engines, machinery, 1443.

Atlantic. Class of locomotive, 1988.

Atlantic, Battle of, 291, 3417.

Atlantic Charter. Eight-point declaration issued by Roosevelt and

Churchill, and announced by Attlee, Aug. 14, 1941, formulating Brit. and U.S. war and peace aims ; signed by 26 nations, Jan. 1, 1942 ; 3283.

Atlantic City. City and seaside resort of New Jersey, U.S.A., 56 m. S.E. of Philadelphia ; pop. 64,100.

Atlantic flights, 47, 291 ; by Lindbergh, 1953 ; R34, 94 ; base at Foynes, 1950 ; fastest crossing, 291.

Atlantic Ocean. 2nd largest of the oceans, 290, map, 290 ; battle of. 291 ; currents, 291, 1554, 2414, 2419 ; first use by ships, 2945, 2946 ; fastest crossing, 291, 2949 ; fisheries, 1299 ; icebergs, 1682 ; Sargasso Sea, 2914 ; submarine cables, 642, 643.

Atlantic Pact or Treaty. See **North Atlantic Treaty.**

Atlantic Star. Brit. Empire medal for service in Battle of Atlantic, 2nd World War, amounting to six months afloat in R.N. or M.N. in Atlantic or home waters.

Atlan'tis, fabled isl., 294.

Atlantosaur'us, prehistoric reptile, 2678.

At'las. In Gk. myth., rebellious Titan, brother of Prometheus ; condemned to bear the heavens on his shoulders, 1615 ; a series of maps.

Atlas Mts., range in N.W. Africa, 65 ; in Algeria, 117 ; Morocco, 2231.

Atmosphere. Unit of pressure (=14·7 lb. per sq. in. approx.). See **Air ; Meteorology.**

Atoll, coral islet, 908, 2597.

Atom. Smallest or " unit " particle of a chemical element, 294, 767, 769–775, 1137, 1138 ; atomic theory of John Dalton, 294, 958 ; of chlorine, 771, 1739 ; composition of, 296, 2733 ; cyclotron in experiments, 951 ; of deuterium, 998 ; in dyes, 1060 ; electrons in, 1137 ; energy release, 298, 2733 ; fission, 298 ; in ionization, 1738 ; isotopes, 296, 1760 ; artificially large ones, 2733 ; of mica, 2160 ; neptunium, 2315 ; quantum theory, 2711 ; radio-activity, 2731 ; Rutherford and, 2858 ; of sodium, 771, 1739 ; sun's energy from, 1161 ; split, 298 ; uranium, 3297.

Atomic Bomb, 299 ; damage to Hiroshima, 609 ; isotype of uranium in, 1760 ; effect in Pacific War, 2474, 3293, 3424.

Atomic Energy Commission, set up by U.N. to discuss the international control of atomic energy ; suspended activities 1948 for lack of agreement between Russia and other members.

Atomic Number, position in Periodic Table, 295, 768, 769, 1137.

Atomic Pile, in " atom-splitting " experiments, 1595 ; heat from, 1595 ; neptunium and other elements produced, 2315.

Atomic weight, relative weight of an atom to that of hydrogen, 295, 769.

Atonement, Day of. Fast day of the Jews ; Yom Kippur, observed on 10th day of 7th month of sacred year.

Atox'yl, a remedy for sleeping sickness.

Atrato (ah-trah'-tō) **River,** in W. Colombia, 873.

Atreus (ā'-trūs). In Gk. myth., father of the Atridae, Agamemnon and Menelaus ; slew children of his brother Thyestes and served them to him as food, thus drawing down curse on his race ; reconstruction of treasury, 1519.

Atrophy. Wasting away of the body or its organs through disease or want of nourishment.

A'tropine, a poisonous aklaloid derived from deadly nightshade, 21, 2370, 2638.

Atropos (a'-tro-pos). In Gk. myth., the eldest Fate, who cuts the thread of life, 1262.

Attar of roses, 2551, 2827 ; Bulgaria, 612, 613 ; Iran, 1740 ; Kashmir, 1848.

Atterbury, Francis (1662–1732). Eng. scholar, politician and divine ; became Bishop of Rochester in 1713 ; committed to Tower of London for plotting against George I and later banished from Eng.

Attica (at'ik-a). Anc. division of E. cent. Greece on Aegean Sea, map, 1518 ; Athens, ruling city, 1518 ; inhabitants today, 1527 ; mts., 284 ; Peloponnesian War, 1524 ; pottery, 1536 ; silver mines, 1523, 2973. See also **Athens.**

At'tila (d. 453). king of the Huns, known as " the scourge of God," 1657 ; in Ger. myth, 1456.

Attlee, Clement Richard (b. 1883). British Labour politician ; Prime Minister, July 1945, 300, 3284.

At'tock. Fort in Punjab, India, on r. Indus.

Attorney-General. Principal law officer of govt. of certain countries.

Attraction, electrical, 1128.

Attraction (gravitation), 1512.

Attwell, Mabel Lucie (b. 1879). Brit. artist ; creator of a popular type of chubby child.

Aube, r. of N.E. Fr., 150 m. long, 2919.

Auber, Daniel (1782–1871). Fr. musical composer, regarded as founder of Fr. grand opera (" Fra Diavolo").

Aubrey, John (1626–97), Eng. antiquary, student of Avebury, Stonehenge, etc. ; his " Miscellanies " contain a host of anecdotes and curiosities ; the Aubrey holes at Stonehenge, 3096.

Aubusson (ō-bew-sawn). Tn. of cent. France, dept. of Creuse ; famous for mfr. of carpets for 400 yrs.

Auchinleck, Field-Marshal Sir Claude (b. 1884). G.O.C. Middle East, 1941–1942 ; c.-in-c. India, 1943–47 ; 300.

Auckland. Largest city of New Zealand, pop. (1945) 263,000, 301, 2357.

Auckland Islands, uninhabited group, 200 m. s. of New Zealand, 2360.

Auction. A public sale in which each bidder offers a higher price than the preceding.

Auction Bridge. A card game, a development of the game of bridge. For two, three or four players.

Auden, Wystan Hugh (b. 1907). English poet and dramatist. " Poems " (1930) ; " The Orators " (1932) ; " The Dance of Death " (1933) ; in collaboration with Christopher Isherwood, " The Dog Beneath the Skin " (1935) and " The Ascent of F.6 " (1936), 1042, 1216.

Audio-frequency, the low frequencies perceptible by the human ear ; in telegraphy, 3167 ; wireless, 3384.

Auditor. One appointed to audit, i.e. examine, accounts.

Auditory nerve, 1065.

Audubon (aw'-doo-bon), **John James** (c. 1780–1851). Amer. naturalist and artist, 301.

Augean (aw-jē'-an) **stables,** in Gk. myth., cleaned by Hercules, 1615.

Aughrim (aw'-grim), **Battle of.** Fought at Aughrim, Galway, Ire., between Eng. and combined forces of Ir. and Fr., July 12, 1691 ; ended in victory for the Eng., 537.

Augite (aw'-g t), crystal, 939.

Augsburg (owgs'-bōōrkh), Ger. mfg. city on r. Leck ; pop. 185,700 ; textiles ; founded 14 B.C. ; 1447.

Augsburg Confession, standard of Lutheran faith, 2759.

Augsburg, Peace of (1555), 2759.

Augurs. In anc. Rome, members of a religious college whose duty it was to interpret the signs (auspices) of approval or disapproval sent by the gods in reference to any proposed undertaking ; these signs were found in the sky (as thunder and lightning), in flight and feeding of birds, condition of entrails of animals sacrificed, etc.

August, the 8th month, originally called Sextilis and renamed in honour of the Roman Emperor Augustus, 2223.

Augusta. Capital of Maine, U.S.A., on r. Kennebec, 40 m. from sea ; pop. 20,000 ; mfg. city, 2068.

Augus'tan Age, in Latin literature, 303, 1896. Term also sometimes applied to reign of Queen Anne, as epoch of great literary achievement.

Augustine, St. (354–430), bishop of Hippo, greatest of Church Fathers, 302, 430.

Augustine, St. (d. 604), apostle to Eng., 302, 1194.

Augustin'ian friars, 2214 ; Luther joins, 2040.

Augus'tus (63 B.C.–A.D. 14), emperor of Rome, 303, 2811, 2814, 2816.

Auk, a sea bird, 303, 304.

Auld Lang Syne (Scot., " old long since "). A Scot. popular song ; words written by Robert Burns ; probably set to music by George Thomson (1799).

Aulus Plautius, conquers Britain, 574.

Au'ricle, of heart, 1592.

Auriga (aw-rī'-ga) or **Charioteer.** A constellation, 895, 896.

Aurignac (ō-rēn-yak). A town in N. France where valuable palaeolithic remains were found ; type of man to which they belonged is known as Aurignacian.

Auriol (ō-rĕ-ol), **Vincent** (b. 1884). Fr. statesman ; pres. constituent assembly 1946 ; first pres. fourth republic, 1947.

Aurochs (aw'-roks). European bison, 460, 461.

Auror'a, in Rom. myth., goddess of dawn, 304.

Aurora Australis, streamers of light seen in the southern sky, 306.

Aurora Borealis (baw-rē-ā'-lis). Streamers of light seen in the northern sky, 304 ; plates f. 304, 305 ; 305 ; caused by gaseous ionization, 1739 ; in stratosphere, 3102.

" Aurora Leigh." Poem by Elizabeth Barrett Browning, 589.

Aurungzebe (aw-rung-zĕb) or **Aurungzeb** (1618–1707), last powerful Mogul emperor of India, 1714, 2206.

Auschwitz (owsh'-vitz). Pol. Oswiecim (os-wĕ-ett-sim). Tn. of Polish Silesia, 33 m. w. of Cracow ; site of Ger. concentration camp taken by Russians Jan. 1945 ; " extermination camp " with gas chambers ; barbarous medical experiments ; Rudolf Hoess, commander, exec. April 1947.

Aussig (ows'-sikh) or **Usti,** Czechoslovakia. City in Bohemia on Elbe ; pop. 43,800 ; coal traffic ; chemicals ; 1124.

Austen, Jane (1775–1817). Eng. novelist, 306, 1214, 1571, 2402.

Aus'terlitz, Czechoslovakia. Vil. 12 m. S.E. of Brno ; battle of (1805), 2276, 3277.

Austin, Alfred (1835–1913). Eng. poet laureate (1896–1913), edited " The National Review " from 1883 to 1893 ; much of his work was only mediocre, but expressed a great love of Nature.

Austin, Herbert, Baron (1866–1941). English motor manufacturer, 306.

Austin, Herbert Wilfred (b. 1906). Eng. lawn tennis player ; finalist at Wimbledon in 1932 and 1938, and for many years a " star " of Britain's Davis Cup team.

Australasia (os-tra-lā'-sha). All the isls. of the s. Pacific, including Australia, New Zealand, Tasmania, New Guinea, Polynesia and Melanesia ; maps, plate f. 308, 309, 581 ; Wallace's line, 1074.

Australia. Island-continent in s. Hemisphere ; a Dominion (Commonwealth) of the Brit. Empire ; pop. over 8 m. ; area (with Tasmania) 2,974,581 sq. m. ; 307, maps, plates f. 308, 309, 310 ; agriculture, 80, 1510 ; animal life, 309, 313, 1053, 1845, 1872, 2043, 2111, 2721 ; boomerang, 520 ; broadcasting, 3399 ; chief cities, 26, 312, 571, 690, 2136, 3144, 3368 ; commerce and industries, 308, 311, 3144, 3368, 3407 ; emblem, 16 ; exploration and settlement, 310, 581, 898, 1254, 3368 ; government, 312 ; Great Barrier Reef, 908 ; history, 310 ; irrigation, 308 ; natives (aborigines), 309, 310, 1280, 2108 ; Parliament House, 691 ;

physical features, 307, 308, *plate f. 309*, 3368 ; plant life, 308, 3368 ; pop., *plate f. 309* ; rabbits in, 2721 ; sheep-farming, 2941 ; sponge fisheries, 3069 ; states, 2343, 2716, 3028, 3156, 3321, 3368 ; uranium, 3297 ; vegetation, *plate f. 309* ; in 1st World War, 312, 3411 ; in 2nd World War, 312, 2473, 3416, 3418, 3420, 3421.

Australia House. London H.Q. of the Australian Commonwealth at corner of Strand and Aldwych.

Australian Alps. Range in s.E. Australia nearly parallel with coast : includes Mt. Kosciusko (7,328 ft.), highest point on continent.

Australian literature, 315.

Austria. Part of the Austro-Hungarian Empire up to the 1st World War, and afterwards an independent republic ; 316 ; area, 32,369 sq. m. ; pop. (1934) 6,760,233 ; *map, 316, plate f. 1232* ; Tirol, 3215, Vienna, cap., 3322.—*History :* 318, 319 ; Hapsburgs, 320 ; under Charles V, 754 ; Thirty Years' War (1618–48), 3202 ; Bohemia acquired, 487 ; under Marie Theresa, 320, 2101 ; Seven Years' War, 2924 ; in Napoleonic Wars, 2275, 2276 ; Holy Roman Empire dissolved (1806), 1449, 2276 ; Congress of Vienna, *1240*, 1449, 3323 ; Francis Joseph I, 319, *1383* ; Dual Monarchy formed (1867), 319, 1656 ; in Triple Alliance, 1240 ; Balkan policy, 345, 2922, 3409 ; after 1918 War, 316, 318, 319 ; part of Germany, 318, 3416 ; in 2nd World War, 318.

Austria-Hungary. Former dual monarchy in Cent. Europe, 319, 1656 ; *map, 320*, 3409, 3414.

Austrian Netherlands. Name given to Span. Netherlands after their cession to Austria (1713) : consisted chiefly of provinces now composing Belgium.

Austrian Succession, War of (1740–48), 2101, 3276 ; in America, 144.

Authorized Version (A.V.) of the Bible. Translation, authorized by James I. of England, 426, *427*.

Autobahnen (ow-tō-bah-nen). German high-speed motor-roads.

Autobiography, and biography, **430.**

" Autocar, The." Motoring journal founded by Lord Iliffe, 1686.

Autoclave, type of boiler, 488.

Autocracy (aw-tok'-ra-si). A form of government in which a single person has absolute power (from Greek words for " self " and " power ").

" Autocrat of the Breakfast Table The." By O. W. Holmes, 1636.

Auto-da-fé (aw'-tō-dah-fā). In Inquisition, 1726.

Autogiro, 320, *321* ; not a helicopter, 1605.

Autolycus (aw-tol'-i-kus). Pedlar in Shakespeare's " The Winter's Tale," 3389.

Automatic Control, 321 ; coin-slot machines, 866 ; operated by electronic devices, 1139 ; of lifts, 1937 ; of lightships, 1944 ; of navigation (aircraft), *42*, 2293 ; by punched cards, 1791 ; by photo-electricity, 2574 ; on railways, 2739 ; of road traffic, 2784 ; of rocket bombs, 2793 ; telephone, 3172 ; time switches, 3214.

Automatic firearms, 1283.

Automatic Pilot. Instrument which by means of a gyroscope keeps an aeroplane on a pre-set course, 1562.

Automatic telephone, *3172.*

Automobile Association (A.A.). Founded in 1905. Headquarters : Fanum House, New Coventry Street, London, W.1. Among its activities are legal aid to members summoned for motoring offences, a comprehensive system of road signs, and an extensive system of road patrols.

Autonomy (aw-ton'-o-mi), self-govt. Used not only in absolute sense, but especially of countries which, while subject in some matters to another power, are in other respects self-governing.

Aut'oplasty. Surgical operation to mend or replace an injured or diseased part from a sound part of a patient's body.

Autostrade (ow-tō-strah-dā). Name of It. high-speed motor-roads.

Auto-suggestion. The hypnotic power of the mind to influence the self, in mind or body ; exploited by Émile Coué. *See* Coué.

Auto-transformer (elec.), 3238.

Autumn. Third season in the year ; the Amer. " fall " ; 2914 ; begins about Sept. 21 ; leaves in, *1917* ; Nature study in, 2289.

Autumnal equinox, 1221.

Auvergne (ō-vār'-nyê), France. Former province of s.-central France ; has highest mountain of interior.

Auvergne Mts. Branch of Cévennes in s.-cent. France ; picturesque scenery ; 1360 ; crater lakes, 3328.

Auxiliary Air Force (A.A.F.). Equivalent of Territorial Army.

Auxiliary Territorial Service (A.T.S.). *See* **Women's Royal Army Corps** (W.R.A.C.).

Auxins (awk'-zinz). Substances produced by plants which control rate of growth ; synthetic auxins (e.g. colchicine) used to produce abnormally large plants, flowers, or fruits.

Auxiliary verbs, 3314.

Av'alanche, *322* ; 2992.

Av'alon. In Arthurian legends, 255, *256.*

A'vars. A people of Ural-Altaic stock allied to the Huns ; settled Dacia about 555 ; 1238.

Avatcha. Bering Island, 415.

Avebury. Vil. in Wiltshire, with interesting prehistoric ruins, 323, 3383.

Avebury, Sir John Lubbock, 1st Baron (1834–1912), Eng. archaeologist, anthropologist and entomologist, 323 ; experiment with bees, 394.

Avena (a-vē'-na). The oat genus, 2411.

Aventine Hill. Southernmost of the seven hills of Rome.

Aver'nus. Small L. near Naples, It., in crater of extinct volcano ; ancients thought it entrance to infernal regions.

Averroes (a-ver'-ō-ēz) (1126–98). Arabian philosopher ; commentaries on Aristotle.

Avertin. Type of anaesthetic, 149.

Avery, Captain John. Famous pirate of the 17th cent., 2612.

Aves (ā'-vēz). The bird class of animals, 448.

A'viary. Large cage for keeping birds.

Aviation. *See* **Aeroplane ; Airships ; Balloons.**

Avicenna (av-i-sen'-a) (980–1037). Arabian philosopher and physician ; European medicine in Middle Ages guided by his works, based on Galen, Hippocrates, and Aristotle.

Avignon (av-ē'-nyawn), Fr., pop' 59,100 ; medieval walls ; silk mills, extensive trade ; on Rhône, *1364*, 2774 ; seat of the Popes, 500.

Avila (ah'-vē-lah). Sp. fortified city ; pop. 15,200 ; *3034.*

Avlo'na, Vlone or **Valona.** Chief port of Albania ; pop. 6,500.

Avocet (av'-ō-set). Rare Brit. bird, related to the snipe ; nested again in the U.K. (E. Anglia) in 1947 and 1948 after an interval of perhaps a century.

Avogadro (av-ō-gah'-drō), **Amadeo** (1776–1856). It. physicist ; formulator of Avogadro's law.

Avogadro's law. That under the same temperature and pressure equal volumes of all gases contain the same number of molecules.

Avoirdupois (av-ê-dū-poiz') **weight.** *See* **Weights and Measures,** *f-i.*

Avon. Several rivs. in Gt. Brit. ; among them are the Avon or Lower Avon, flowing 75 m. through Gloucestershire, Wiltshire and Somerset, to the Bristol Channel at Avonmouth, 572 ; the Avon or Upper Avon, rising in Northamptonshire, and extending for 96 m. to the Severn at

Tewkesbury ; the Little or Middle Avon, another tributary of the Severn ; and the East Avon, 48 m. long, emptying into the Eng. Channel. Upper and Lower Avon canal.

Avory, Sir Horace Edmund (1851–1935), Brit. judge ; a great prosecuting counsel, Mr. Justice Avory became a judge of the King's Bench Division in 1910.

Awe, Loch. Longest L. in Scot., in Argyllshire (22 m.) ; has many isls., on one of which is the ruined castle of Kilchurn.

Awn, or beard, of barley, *361* ; of oats, 2410 ; of " animated " oat, 2411 ; of rye, *2858.*

Axis. Term used to describe Italo-German collaboration 1936–43 ; 3416. In 1940 it became the Berlin-Rome-Tokyo Axis, when Japan joined. *See* **Anti-Comintern Pact.**

Axis deer. Native to India, 984.

Axminster. Market tn. of Devonshire, on r. Axe ; pop. 2,327 ; ancient church ; celebrated for rugs made there : factory at, *707.*

Axminster carpet, *707.*

Ax'olotl. A kind of salamander found in Mexico.

Ayala, Ramón Pérez de (b. 1880). Spanish poet, critic, and novelist ; called greatest of modern Spanish poets ; ambassador to Gt. Brit. in 1931 ; (" Tiger Juan "), *3051.*

Aycliffe or **Newton Aycliffe.** Proposed satellite town for Darlington.

Aye-aye. A Madagascar lemur, 1922.

Ayesha (c. 611–c. 678). Wife of Mahomet.

Aylesbury. Co. tn. of Buckinghamshire, 600 ; pop. about 20,000 ; noted for ducks and dairy produce ; book-binding, engineering, felt processing, butter-blending.

Aymara Indians. S. Amer. tribe, living around L. Titicaca ; high culture before conquest by Incas ; *3026.*

Ayolas, Juan de, founded Asunción, Paraguay.

Ayr, Scot. Spt. on Firth of Clyde ; co. tn. of Ayrshire ; pop. 41,600 ; woollens, carpets, engineering, ship-building, 324.

Ayrshire, Scot. Co. bordered by Firth of Clyde ; a. 1,130 sq. m.; pop. 299,000 ; 324 ; Burns' birthplace, 625.

Ayrshire cattle, *731*, 732.

Aytoun, William Edmondstoune (1813–65). Scot. poet ; wrote " Lays of the Scottish Cavaliers " ; 2895.

Aza'lea. Plant, 324.

Azaña, Manuel (1880–1940). Spanish statesman, barrister, and lecturer at Madrid University. Arrested 1930 for revolutionary activities ; president of Spanish republic 1931–33, and elected again in 1936. Resigned, Feb. 1939.

Azerbaijan (az-êr-bī'-jan). A republic of Soviet Rus. on w. coast of Caspian Sea ; 32,000 sq. m. ; pop. 3,209,000 ; oil fields ; cap. Baku ; 341, 733. 2844. 2849.

Azerbaijan. Prov. of N.W. Persia on Caspian Sea ; 33,640 sq. m. ; pop. 2,096,000 ; iron, lead, copper, marble ; cap. Tabriz, 214,000 ; 1741.

Azores. Group of Portuguese isls. in Atlantic, about midway between Europe and Amer. ; Allied air bases, 1942–45 ; 324 ; geology, 290.

Azorin (Jose Martinez Ruiz) (b. 1874). Leading Sp. literary critic, 3051.

Azov. Russ. tn. on s. arm of Don. 20 m. from mouth ; pop. 17,000 ; captured by Peter the Great, 325.

Azov, Sea of. Northern arm of Black Sea, formed by the Crimea peninsula; 14,500 sq. m. ; 325, 465, 717 ; *map, 465* ; 2nd World War, 3419.

Azrael (az'-rā-el) (Hebrew, " help of God "). Mahomedan angel of death.

Aztecs, 325, *327* ; build Mexitli (Mex. City), 2159 ; Cortes conquers, 915 ; use of vanilla, 3305.

Azulejo (ah-thōōl-ā'-hō). A roofing tile, made in Spain, 3302.

Azure. In heraldry, 1614.

OUR letter B seems to have started its career in the shape of a crane (bird), in Egyptian picture-writing. Presently the Egyptian scribes gave it a simpler form, which resembled the outline of a tent. So when the Phoenicians and Hebrews took the symbol into their alphabets, they named it *Beth*, which means " house." The Phoenician form of the letter resembled a tent supported by its pole, but some of these early B's or Beths, it seems, were more aristocratic than the tent Beths, for Dr. Isaac Taylor in his story of the alphabet says : " Other forms suggest . . . a two-chambered eastern house (notice that our big B has two rooms) with the men's apartment on one side and the women's on the other." In sound B is closely related to *p, f, v* and *m.* Martial said of the Spaniards, who pronounce *b* as *v* and *v* as *b*, that *vivere* (to live) is *bibere* (to drink) ; the ancient Spaniards not only mixed their *b's* and *v's*, but were heavy drinkers.

Baal (bä'-*al*). Semitic name for a lord, master, or god ; especially sun-god of Canaanites and Phoenicians.

Baalbek (bahl'-bek), Syria. Vil. famous for splendid Rom. ruins ; called Heliopolis by Greeks.

Ba'ba, Cape. Asia Minor, 264.

Babar the Tiger (c. 1483–1530). Mahomedan conqueror and founder of Mogul dynasty, 1714, 2206 ; conquest of Agra, 77.

Bab'assu, type of nut, 2408.

Bab'bage, Charles (1792–1871). Eng. mathematician ; invented calculating machine, 656 ; wrote " Logarithms."

Babbitt. Chief character in Sinclair Lewis's novel of that name ; typifies the self-satisfied " small-town " Amer. business man.

Babbitt metal. A soft alloy, 124 ; in bearings, 385.

Babel, Isaac (b. 1894), Rus. writer, 2856.

Babel (bä'-bel), **Tower of.** Built by Noah's descendants to guard against future floods ; during construction occurred the " confusion of tongues " (Gen. xi.) ; 329.

Bab el Man'deb (" Gate of Tears "). Strait, 26, 264, 2758.

Bab'ington, Anthony (1561–86). Page to Mary Queen of Scots ; executed for conspiracy to murder Elizabeth, 2116.

Babirussa (bab-i-rōō-s*a*). A species of wild hog, native of the East Indies.

Baboons', or dog-headed monkeys, 2210, 2211.

Babrius (1st cent. A.D.). Collector of Aesop's fables, 55.

Babylon (bab'-i-lon). Cap. of anc. Babylonia, on Euphrates, 70 m. s. of modern Baghdad, 328, 329 ; Hanging gardens, plates f. 328, 329 ; 2923 ; plate f. 2924.

Babylonia and Assyria. An empire of Tigris-Euphrates valley, 329 ; map, 1113 ; agriculture, 80 ; architecture, 212 ; Babylon, 328 ; canals, 686 ; engraving, 1427 ; excavations at Babylon, 328 ; at Nineveh, 2371 ; irrigation, 1231 ; libraries, 1930, 2371 ; myths, 332 ; Nineveh, 2371 ; painting, 2475 ; sculpture, 2904 ; sun-dial invented, 843 ; Tigris, 3212 ; writing, 331.

Babylonian captivity, of Jews, 1830.

Bacchanalia (bak-*a*-nā'-lia). Rom. festival, 1018.

Bacchantes (bak-an'-tēz). Attendants of Bacchus, 1018.

Bac'chus. Rom. name for Dionysus, god of wine, 1018.

Bach (bahkh), **Johann Christian** (1735–82). Ger. musician, son of J. S. Bach, 333.

Bach, Johann Sebastian (1685–1750). Ger. composer of immense influence, 333, 2264.

Bach, Karl Philipp Emanuel (1714–88). Ger. musician and composer, third son of J. S. Bach, 333.

Bach'elor. Word applied to an unmarried man and to students granted the lowest degree (B.A., M.B., B.Sc., etc.).

Bacillus (b*a*-sil'-*us*). Rod-shaped bacterium, 335, 336, 1458, 1459.

Back, in football, 1344, 1345.

Backbone. See Spine.

Backhaus, Wilhelm (b. 1884). Ger. pianist, formerly professor at Manchester College of Music.

Backhuysen, Ludolf (1631–1708). Dutch painter, 2335.

Back lighting, in photography, 2581.

Backs, The. Part of the river Cam at Cambridge, 666, 667.

" Back to Methuselah." Play by G. B. Shaw, 1042, 2940.

Bacon, Francis, Baron Verulam and Viscount St. Albans (1561–1626), Eng. philosopher, statesman and writer, 333, 334, 1211, 1224 ; author of " New Atlantis," 334 ; and physics, 2593.

Bacon, Sir Nicholas (1509–79). Father of Francis Bacon ; lord keeper of the great seal during Elizabeth's reign.

Bacon, Roger (c. 1214–94). Eng. monk, alchemist, and author, 334 ; invented gunpowder, 1558 ; telescope, 334, 3178.

Bacteria (bak-tēr'-i-*a*). A group of microscopic plants, 335 ; in cheese, 765 ; cause disease, 1458 ; destroyed or checked by heat, 692 ; in milk, 956, 2528 ; nitrogen-fixing types, 2373, 2374, 2624 ; as parasites, 2513 ; soil-making, 2998 ; reproduced by spores, 2919 ; attacked by virus, 335, 1459 ; vaccination, 3301 ; in water purification, 3348, 3349 ; resemble yeasts, 3433. For animal germs, see **Microbes ; Protozoa.**

Bacteriology, 335, 533 ; antitoxin, 180 ; germ theory of disease, 1458 ; Koch, 1458, 2528 ; Lister, 1963 ; microscope, 2163 ; Pasteur, 2135, 2528 ; vaccination, 3301.

Bacter'iophage, a virus that destroys bacteria, 335, 1459.

Bac'tria. Anc. country (modern Balkh) N. of Hindu Kush Mts., famous for horses and camels ; conquered by Cyrus the Great and Alexander.

Bactrian camel, 670.

Badajoz (bad'-*a*-hōth), Sp. City on Guadiana ; pop. 43,000 ; taken by French (1811) and recaptured and sacked by British (1812).

" Bad Child's Book of Beasts," by Hilaire Belloc, 409.

Baddeleyite, oxide of zirconium, 3444.

Baden (bah'-d*e*n). State of s.w. Ger., former grand duchy ; 5,800 sq. m. ; pop. 2,518,000 ; mountainous and wooded, partly in Black Forest ; mfrs. toys, textiles, cigars, chemicals, pottery, jewelry (pforzheim) ; grows cereals, sugar-beet, hops, grapes ; cap. Karlsruhe ; Mannheim largest city ; 1445.

Ba'den or **Ba'den-Ba'den.** Ger. health resort in Baden at edge of Black Forest ; pop. 25,000.

Baden-Powell (bä'-d*e*n pō'-*e*l), **Robert Stephenson Smyth Baden-Powell, 1st Baron** (1857–1941). British gen., founder of Boy Scouts, 337, 538, 1465.

Bader, Douglas R. S. (b. 1910). Brit. R.A.F. pilot who lost both legs in crash in 1933 ; squadron leader in Battle of Britain ; prisoner-of-war, 1941–45 ; led post-war Battle of Britain fly-past, Sept. 1945.

Badger. Animal of weasel family, 337 ; fur, 1412.

Badges, of Boy Scouts, plate f. 542 ; in the British Army, 245 ; of the British Commonwealth, vol. 8, frontispiece ; of Girl Guides, plate f.

1468 ; of Naval Officers, plate f. 2292 ; of Naval ratings, 2293.

Badminton. Indoor sport, 338.

Badoglio (ba-dō'-lyō), **Pietro** (b. 1871). It. soldier ; governor of Tripoli (1928) ; commander in Abyssinia (1936) ; resigned from C. of Staff, 1940 ; prime minister and Foreign min., 1943–44 ; signed armistice, 3421.

Baedeker, Karl (1801–59). German publisher and writer of guide books, which have been translated into many languages.

Baekeland, Leo Hendrik (1863–1944). Amer. chemist, b. in Belgium ; invented bakelite, 2625.

Baer, K. E. von (1792–1876). Father of embryology, 1155, 3447.

Baeyer (bī'-y*ẽr*), **Adolph von** (1835–1917). Ger. chemist ; won Nobel prize in chemistry (1905) ; synthetic indigo, 1718.

Baf'fin, William (1584–1622). Eng. Arctic explorer, discovered Baffin Bay in 1615 ; 2644.

Baffin Bay. Large gulf of N.E. N. Amer. ; 800 m. by 280 m.

Baffin Island. Barren isl. belonging to Canada ; w. of Greenland ; about 237,000 sq. m.

Bagan'da. African tribe, 1072.

Bagasse', sugar cane pulp, 3112.

Bagehot (baj'-*ot*), **Walter** (1826–77), Eng. political philosopher, economist, and literary critic, 338.

Baggat'away. Indian name for game of lacrosse, 1882.

Baghdad or **Bagdad,** Chief city of Iraq ; pop. 270,000 ; 350 m. N. of Persian Gulf on Tigris, 339, 1744 ; in 1st World War, 3411.

Baghdad Railway, 339, 3262.

Bagnold, Enid. 20th-cent. Eng. author ; novels " National Velvet," " The Squire " ; play " Lottie Dundass."

Bagpipe. A wind instrument, 339, plate f. 2893.

Bahamas (b*a*-hah'-m*a*z). Group of isls., Brit. W. Indies ; 4,400 sq. m. ; pop. 69,000 ; 339, 3368, 3369 ; Duke of Windsor governor, 1940–47.

Bahia (b*a*-hē'-*a*) or **Sao Salvador.** 3rd city of Brazil and former cap. ; pop. 363,700 ; 554.

Bahi'a Blan'ca, Argentina. Seaport and rly. centre ; pop. 119,100, exports wheat, wool ; govt. naval station.

Bahrein or **Bahrain Islands.** Nr. Arabian shore of Persian Gulf ; pop 120,000 ; ruled by a native sheikh under Brit. protection ; cap. Manama (28,000) ; petroleum, pearl fisheries, 197.

Baikal, Lake. In s. of E. Siberia ; the largest fresh-water lake in Asia (13,350 sq. m. in a., and depth about 5,000 ft.) ; Trans-Siberian Rly. skirts the s. shore, 2966 ; region home of Mongols, 2205.

Bail (cricket), 928.

Bailey, Henry Christopher (b. 1878) Eng. author of historical and detective fiction, etc. (" Mr. Fortune Please.")

Bailey, Philip James (1816–1902). Eng poet ; son of a Nottingham newspaper owner, he is chiefly remembered for his " Festus," a long poem published anonymously, which enjoyed much popularity.

Bailey bridge. To cross rivers, etc., up to 240 ft. wide without pontoons or supports; erected in about 24 hrs. from prefabricated panels; 10-ft. sections constructed on shore; *250*; invented by Sir D. Bailey.

Bailey wall, of medieval castle, *717*.

Baillie, Joanna (1762–1851). Scot. poet and dramatist; best known for her " Plays on the Passions "·(1798–1812); friend of Sir Walter Scott.

Baily, Edward Hodges (1788–1867). Eng. sculptor of the Nelson statue in Trafalgar Square.

Baily, Francis (1774–1844). Eng. astronomer; assisted in founding Astronomical Society (1820); Baily's beads, phenomena occurring during eclipses of sun, named after him, *plate f. 1077.*

Bain, Alexander (1818–1903). Scot. philosopher, taught at Aberdeen and Glasgow (" Logic ").

Baird, John Logie (1888–1946). Scot. pioneer of television, 3184.

Baireuth. *See* Bayreuth.

Bairns'father, Bruce (b. 1887). Brit. humorous artist and soldier; creator of " Old Bill " and author of " The Better 'Ole " (1917).

Bait, for fishing, 1309.

Baja (ba-hah') **California,** Mexico. A territory including peninsula of Lower Cal.; 55,000 sq. m.; pop. 95,000; cap. and chief port, La Paz.

Bajazet (baj-*a*-zet') or **Bayazid I** (1347–1403). First Ottoman sultan, victor over allied Christian armies at Nicopolis (1396); defeated by Mongols; 3264.

Ba'kelite. An artificial plastic material, 857, *2626.*

Baker, Sir Benjamin (1840–1907). Eng. engineer, associated with the building of the Forth Bridge and Assuan Dam.

Baker, Sir Herbert (1862–1946). Eng. architect; in S. Africa designed Groote Schuur, Govt. House (Pretoria) and Rhodes Memorial; also architect for Bank of England, New Delhi, etc.; *2683.*

Baker, Sir Samuel White (1821–93). Eng. explorer, discoverer of Albert Nyanza, 340.

Bakeries, employing automatic machinery, 555, *556*; mobile army, *246.*

Bakerloo Tube, 3275.

Bakewell, Robert (1725–95). Farmer of Dishley, Leics, who established scientific stock-breeding, 85.

Bakhtawar Singh. Mausoleum at Alwar, *1700.*

Baking, cookery process, 901. *See also* Bread and Biscuit.

Baking powder. Chemically prepared substance with a similar action to yeast, 3155.

Bakst, Leon Nikolaievitch (1886–1924). Rus. designer of stage settings and costumes, 347, 2855.

Baku, oil centre. Cap. of Republic of Azerbaijan, on w. coast of Caspian; fifth city of U.S.S.R.; pop. 809,300, 341, 717, 733, 1420.

Bakunin, Mikhail (1814–76). Rus. anarchist and political agitator.

Bala. Largest lake in Wales, in Merionethshire.

Balaam. Prophet disobedient to divine command until miraculously rebuked by his ass; compelled against his will (Num. xx-xxiv) to bless Israel.

Balaclava (bal-*a*-klah'-v*a*) or **Balaklava.** Small port of the Crimea, 6 m. from Sevastopol; scene of famous " Charge of the Light Brigade " in battle of Oct. 25, 1854, during Crimean War, 341, 931.

Balance (Libra). A sign of the zodiac.

Balance, sense of, in ear, *1065*, 1066.

Balance of Nature, 1080.

Balance of Power. Diplomatic term for the principle of maintaining an equilibrium between states or groups of states by means of alliances so that no one state can become predominantly powerful; 1240.

Balance wheel, of watch, 846.

Balaton. Lake in Hungary; area 250 sq. m.; discharges into the Danube; home of many rare birds.

Balbo, Italo (1896–1940). It. statesman and airman; led formation flights over Atlantic in 1931 and 1933; in 1933 he was appointed Governor of Libya. On June 28, 1940, he was killed in an aeroplane accident in mysterious circumstances.

Balboa. Pacific port of Panama Canal Zone, 2490.

Balboa, Vasco Nuñez de (1475–1517). Span. explorer, discoverer of Pacific, 341, 140, 2472.

Balbrig'gan. Cotton goods, hosiery, etc., made of fine unbleached fibre; named after Irish town where first made.

Balcon, Sir Michael (b. 1896). Brit. film producer and director; " Rome Express," " Yank at Oxford," " The Overlanders," " Scott of the Antarctic."

Balder. In Norse myth., god of light, 341, 2881.

Bald-headed eagle, 1063, *1065.*

Baldwin I (1058–1118). Adventurer prince of First Crusade, first king of Jerusalem; crowned 1100; brother of Godfrey of Bouillon.

Baldwin, Oliver, 2nd Earl (b. 1899). Brit. administrator; Governor and C.-in-C. of Leeward Is., Feb. 1948.

Baldwin, Robert (1804–58). Canadian statesman; the champion of responsible govt.

Baldwin of Bewdley, Stanley, 1st Earl (1867–1947). Brit. statesman (Conservative), 341; premierships, 3281.

Balearic (bal-ē-ar'-ik) **Islands.** Span. province off Mediterranean coast of Spain, including Majorca and Minorca; a. 1,935 sq. m.; pop. 410,000; 342, *maps, 2136, 3030,* 3032.

Baleen' whales, 3371, *3372.*

Balfe, Michael William (1808–70). Irish composer; wrote " Bohemian Girl " and other light operas; song music, " Killarney," " The Arrow and the Song," etc.

Balfour, Arthur James, 1st Earl of (1848–1930). Brit. Unionist statesman, 343.

Balfour Declaration on Palestine, 2482.

Bali (bah'-li). Isl. of Indonesia, E. of Java; 2,160 sq. m.; exports rice, cocoa, coffee; 1076; temple dances, *967*; Battle of Bali Straits, Feb. 19, 1942; in Jap. occupn., 3420.

Balik' Papan'. Oil pt. on S.E. coast of State of E. Borneo (former Dutch Borneo); its oil wells were fired by the Dutch in 1942; occupied by Japanese (1942–45).

Balilla. It. Fascist organization of boys from 6 to 12 years of age, started in 1926, disbanded 1943.

Baliol (bāl'-yol), **John de** (1249–1315). King of Scot., son of the founder of Balliol College, Oxford; claimed Scot. throne on death of Margaret (1290) and became king (1292); invading Eng., he was forced to surrender to Edward I.

Balkan (bawl'-k*a*n) **Entente.** A pact of regional political understanding signed in Feb. 1934 between Greece, Rumania, Turkey, and Yugoslavia.

Balkan Mts., in the Balkan Peninsula, an extension of the Carpathians; beginning at Iron Gates of Danube, extend S. through Serbia, then turn sharply E. to Black Sea, 343, 1233.

Balkan Peninsula, S.E. peninsula of Europe, 343; *map, 344*; Austrian policy, 1383, 2922, 3409; Macedonia, 2049; mountains, 1233; people, *345*, 3439; Russo-Turkish War, 1019, 2922, 3265; First World War, 3409, 3410, 3414; Second World War, 3418, 3424.

Balkan Wars (1912–13), 344, 1240; Adrianople taken, 29; Bulgaria, 613; Greece, 1525; Macedonia, 2049; Montenegro, 2219; Serbia, 2922; Treaty of Bucharest, 598; Turkey, 3265.

Balkash. Salt lake in Kazakstan, near Chinese border; 330 m. long; no outlet; 4th largest lake in Eurasia.

Balkh. Dist. of Afghanistan between Hindu Kush Mts. and Amu-Darya r.; anc. Bactria.

Ball, cricket, 318; football, *1344.*

Ball, Albert (1896–1917). Brit. flying officer of the 1st World War; victor of over 40 combats; killed in France, May 7, 1917; awarded V.C. after death.

Ball, John (d. 1381). A leader in Wat Tyler's Rebellion, 3269.

Ballads, defined, 2637; folk songs, 1333; Robin Hood, 2790.

Ballantyne, Robert Michael (1825–94). Scot. author of more than 80 books for boys, including " Coral Island "; was in service in Hudson's Bay Co., 1841–47.

Ballarat, Australia, 3rd city of Victoria; pop. 40.181; 3321.

Ballet. The art of telling a story by gestures and dancing, 345, 965; music for, 2264; Russian, 2855.

Bal'lin, Albert (1857–1918). " One of the makers of modern (pre-1914) Germany "; general director of Hamburg-Amer. steamship line, which he developed from insignificance to predominance.

Ballistics. The science of projectiles, 2793.

Ball lightning, 1946.

Balloons, 347; balloon barrage in London in both World Wars, 1332; in meteorology, 2150; toys, 2836; in stratosphere, 3102.

Ballot, 351, 3330; introduced in Eng., 1470, 3279; John Bright, 570. *See also* Elections.

Ball race, grooved ring holding ball bearings, 386.

Ballroom dancing, *965*, 967.

Balm. A fragrant herb of the mint family, also a balsam. *See* Balsams.

Bal'mat, Jacques, mountaineer, climbed Mont Blanc, 127.

Balm of Gilead. An aromatic resin obtained from a small oriental evergreen tree belonging to myrrh family.

Bal'moral Castle, Aberdeenshire. A favourite residence of British Royalty, 351, 2893, 3320.

Balsa. A raft, *482.*

Balsa. Extremely light, pithy wood used in model aircraft construction, refrigerators, etc.; the balsa tree (*Ochroma lagopus*) is a native of tropical S. America; is also called corkwood.

Balsam fir, 1278.

Balsams, various mixtures of volatile oils and resins exuded by trees; Canada balsam, 1278; in perfumes, 2550; Peruvian, 2868.

Bal'sas River, in S. Mexico, flows 430 m. w. to Pacific, *map, 2157.*

Baltic Provinces. Collective name of former Rus. provinces of Courland, Livonia, Estonia; became separate states, and later republics of the U.S.S.R.; Estonia, 1226; Latvia, 1899; Lithuania, 1967.

Baltic Sea. Arm of North Sea, 351, *map, plate f. 1232, 2395*; amber, 138; coast, 1277, 1445, 3126; fisheries, 1233; navigation in winter, 3129; Russia gets a foothold, 2563.

Baltic-White Sea Canal, U.S.S.R. Opened 1933, linking Leningrad with Murmansk and saving voyage of 3,000 m. round Norway.

Baltimore, chief city of Maryland, U.S.A., pop. 859,100; 352; 2116; and Peabody, 2531.

Baltimore, George Calvert, 1st Baron (c. 1580–1632). Founder of Avalon colony of Newfoundland (1621); applied for charter for Maryland which was granted after his death to his son Cecilius.

Baluchistan (b*a*-lōōk-i-stahn'). Region in S. Asia on Arabian Sea, in extreme N.W. corner of Indian subcont., 134,000 sq. m.; pop. 858,000; former Brit. part joined Pakistan, 352; 1691; *map, 1702.*

Balzac, Honoré de (1799–1850). Fr. novelist, 352, 1381, 2404.

Bamako, Cap. of Fr. Sudan, 3110, 3367.

Bamberg, Ger. Bavarian city; pop. 48,000; 11th cent. cath.; large breweries, cotton and woollen mills.

Bamboo'. A tropical tree-like grass, 353, 3247; found in Burma, 623;

China, 809 ; India, 1701 ; Japan, 1797 ; bridge of, *565*.

Bamburgh. Village on coast of Northumberland, 2391 ; first lifeboat at, 1935.

Bamian. Valley and pass in Afghanistan 60 m. N.W. of Kabul ; colossal Buddhist idols carved in rock.

Bana'na. A tropical fruit, **354** ; Canary Isl., 690 ; Cent. Amer., 744 ; W. Indies, *354, 1793*.

Ban'at of Temesvar. Fertile dist. lying between Danube and Theiss rs. and Transylvanian Alps ; 11,000 sq. m. ; formerly part of Hungary, now divided between Rumania and Yugoslavia.

Banbury. Market tn. in Oxfordshire ; old " Banbury Cross " demolished in 1610, replaced by modern one ; famous for pasty cakes containing mincemeat, and as centre of Puritanism in 17th cent., whence " cakes and zeal " (corrupted to " cakes and ale ") : aluminium manufactures, agricultural implements, surgical appliances, etc. ; pop. 18,500 ; 2466.

Bancroft, George (1800–91), American historian, 3294.

Bancroft, Sir Squire (1841–1926). Famous Eng. actor.

Bandages, used in first aid, *1292*.

Ban'da Islands. Part of Molucca Archipelago in East Indies ; pop. 9,500 ; nutmegs and mace, 2407.

Banda Sea, in Malay Archipelago, s. of Isl. of Ceram and N. of Timor ; *map, 1074*.

Banda″ Ab'bas, Iran. Spt. on Strait of Ormuz, Persian Gulf ; pop. 9,000 ; exports fruit, tobacco, wool, carpets, opium.

Ban'dicoot. A marsupial, 2111.

Bandoeng (ban-dung'). Tn. of Java, Indonesia ; seat of govt. and of Allied command after Jap. invasion ; in Jap. hands March 1942 to Aug. 1945 ; in 1948 centre of administration of W. Java, U.S.I.

Ban'don. R. of Eire, flowing to Kinsale Harbour ; 42 m. long ; 910.

Band saw, 2037.

Banff, Alberta. Famous resort situated amid magnificent scenery in the Canadian Rockies ; national park, *103*, 680.

Banffshire. Maritime co. in N.E. of Scot. ; area 630 sq. m., pop. 53,000 ; 355.

Bangalore. Chief city of Mysore, India ; pop, 248,300 ; textiles, 2270.

Bangkok'. Commercial cap. of Thailand (Siam), near mouth Menam r. ; Jap. base in 2nd World War ; pop. over 1,117,000 ; **355** ; Wat Arun temple. *2063*.

Bangor. Old Cath. city on coast of Wales, in Caernarvonshire ; pop. 12,500 ; seat of bishopric since 6th cent. ; University College of N. Wales ; slate quarries.

Bangweo'lo or Bangweulu Lake, in N. Rhodesia, 150 m. long, 2771 ; formed by head-streams of Congo ; discovered by Livingstone, 1970.

Banjermasin. Chief tn. in Dutch Borneo, built chiefly on piles ; pop. 70,000 ; exports spices, gold, precious stones, drugs.

Ban'jo. A stringed instrument, **356**.

Banket. A gold-bearing conglomerate.

Bank for International Settlements. Established at Basle, Switzerland. June 7, 1929, under the Young Plan, primarily to furnish means for the distribution of German reparations ; later acted as the foreign exchange reserve of central banks, and for the movement of funds in aid of temporary weak currencies.

Bank holidays, 323, 1635.

Banknote, 2202 ; replace gold, 1483. *See also* Coinage ; Money.

Bank of England, 356. *357*, 2010 ; guard, 356, *605* ; nationalized 1945, 356.

Bank Rate. Rate at which Bank of England lends money, 357.

Bankruptcy. Legal admission by a debtor that he is unable to pay his debts, **356**.

Banks, Sir Joseph (1743–1820). Eng. naturalist, 359. Fingal's Cave, 3071 ; and Kew Gardens, 1854.

Banks and banking, 356. Bankers' Clearing House, 357 ; credit money, 926, 2202 ; foreign exchange, 1699 ; gold standard, 1482 ; interest and discount, 2548 ; London's banking district, 2010 ; money, 2200 ; P.O. savings bank, 2662. *See also in Index,* **Economics ; Finance.**

Bankside. S. bank of Thames at Southwark ; power station, *2195*.

Banks Island, Canadian isl. in Arctic Ocean, 223.

Banks of Newfoundland. *See* **Newfoundland Banks.**

Bann. Rivers (Upper and Lower) of Northern Ireland. Valuable salmon fisheries. Upper Bann, 25 m. long, Lower Bann, 33 m. long.

Ban'nockburn, battle of (1314), **359**, 591, 2892.

Banns, of marriage, 2107.

Banque de France. Central bank of France, founded by Napoleon in 1800. Only the 200 largest shareholders could attend the annual meeting (see **"Two Hundred Families")** ; came under state control, 1936 ; nationalized, 1946.

Banqueting Hall, Whitehall, London : designed by Inigo Jones, *1836*.

Bantam. Spt. of Java, gave name to bantam fowls.

Bantam fowls, 2671.

Banting, Sir Frederick Grant (1891–1941). Brit. doctor who (in Canada) discovered insulin, a cure for diabetes; awarded Nobel Prize, 1923, shared with three other doctors, *2133*, 2375 ; killed in aeroplane crash, Feb. 21, 1941.

Ban'ting, William (1797–1878). Brit. dietician ; discovered a method of slimming ; his name gives " to bant," meaning " to slim by dieting."

Bantock, Sir Granville (1868–1946). Eng. composer (" Atalanta in Calydon " ; " Vanity of Vanities " ; " Omar Khayyam " ; " Hebridean Symphony ").

Bantry Bay. Inlet of co. Cork, Eire, noted for its beauty. In 1689 and 1796 it was the scene of French attempts to invade Ire., and in 1697 King William's troops landed here, 910.

Ban'tu. Group of tribes in Cent. and S. Africa, including Kaffirs, Zulus, Bechuanas, Basutos, 70.

Ban'yan tree, 359, 3246 ; India, 1707.

Baobab, or monkey-bread tree, 69, 3246.

Bao Lai, Emperor of Annam (1926–45). Invested as head of State of Viet-Nam, Indo-China, in 1949 ; 3323.

Baptism. The sacrament by which a person is made a member of the Christian community, 359.

Baptistery, part of church where baptisms take place ; of Florence, 1318 ; Ghiberti's doors for, 1460, *2905*.

Baptists. Protestant denomination which holds that baptism should be by immersion ; world membership about 12,000,000 ; 1390.

Barab'bas. A robber released by Pilate on demand of Jews when Jesus was condemned.

Barada (ba-rah'-da). Small river of Syria flowing through Damascus ; supposedly the Abana of the Bible.

Barbados (bah-bā'-dōz). Isl of Brit. W. Indies ; pop. 203,000 ; 166 sq. m. ; 360, 3368.

Barbara. Christian martyr of 3rd cent. ; was beheaded in public by her own father, who was immediately struck dead by lightning.

Barbarossa (" red beard "). Nickname for Frederick I, 1388 ; sacked Milan, 2172. *See* **Frederick I.**

Barbarossa, Khair-ed-Din. Turkish pirate who terrorized Mediterranean in 16th cent.

Barbary Coast, N. Africa, *map. 117*.

Barbary sheep, or **Aoudad,** 2940.

Barbary States. Region of N. Africa inhabited by Berbers ; includes Morocco, Algeria, Tunis, and Libya ; 118, 2227 ; centre for pirates, 746, 754, 2612.

Bar'bel. Fresh-water fish.

Barbels. The " feelers " of fish, 1296, 1297.

" Barber of Seville." Opera by Rossini, 2438.

Barberry. An ornamental shrub ; harbours wheat rust, 2857.

Barber-surgeons. Sign, *149*.

Barbette'. Armoured tower of warship, 2306.

Barbiroll'i, Sir John (b. 1899). Brit. musician ; conductor of the New York Philharmonic, 1937–42, and then the Hallé orchestra, Manchester ; knighted 1949 ; 2447.

Barbit'urate. Class of dangerous drugs, small doses of which steady the nerves and induce sleep.

Barbizon (bahr-bē-zawn') **school,** in painting, 914. *1374*, 1378, 2476 ; and Millet, 2176.

Barbour, John (*c*. 1316–95), Scots poet, 2894.

Barbuda. One of Leeward isls. in Brit. W. Indies, 63 sq. m. ; pop. 903 ; 3368.

Barbusse (bahr-büs'), **Henri** (1875–1935). Fr. novelist (" Under Fire," " Inferno "). 1382.

Barcelona. Spt. and chief mfg. centre of Spain : pop. 1,225.318 : 3•0, 3032 ; Govt. base in Civil War, 1936–39, 361, 3039.

" Barchester," in novels of Anthony Trollope, 3250.

Bard. A minstrel and poet, esp. Welsh ; *plate f. 3337*.

Bardia (bar-dē'-ah). Spt. in Libya, 12 m. from Egyptian frontier ; impt. base in N. African campaign of Second World War ; changed hands 5 times between 1940 and 1942 ; *map, 3421*.

Barebone's Parliament, 2524.

Bareilly, India. Trade centre in United Provinces ; pop. 192,600 ; massacre of Europeans in mutiny of 1857.

Bar'ents, Willem (d. 1597). Dutch explorer ; discovered Spitsbergen, 3067.

Barfrush' or Babal. A trading tn. in Iran, on Bahbul r. ; pop. 30,000 ; rice, cotton, silk.

Barge. Various forms of boat, *686, 687, 2953*.

Bargeboard. A board placed at a gable to conceal the roof timbers.

Barham, R. H. *See* Ingoldsby, Thomas.

Bari (bah'-rē). Spt. in s.E. It. on Adriatic ; pop. 196,000 ; anc. Barium ; broadcasting stn.

Bar'ing. Family of Eng. financiers and bankers. *See* Cromer.

Baring, Hon. Maurice (1874–1945). Journalist, airman, author of 70 books ; diplomatic service 1898–1904 ; war correspondent, Russo-Japanese War, 1905.

Baring-Gould, Sabine (1834–1924). Brit. divine and author ; wrote " Onward Christian Soldiers " ; 1678.

Barium (Ba). Dense metallic element of the alkaline earth metal group ; atomic weight, 137·36 ; occurs in the mineral sulphate-barytes ; in pitchblende, 2731 ; soluble salts a poison, 2638 ; properties, 777 ; in X-ray photography, name derived from the Greek, *barys*. heavy.

Bark, of shrubs and trees ; cork-oak, *909* ; function, 2622 ; lacking in palms, 3246 ; used in tanning, 1911. *See also* names of trees.

Barker, Sir Ernest (b. 1874). Brit. scholar ; liberal thinker ; wrote " Ideals of Brit. Empire," " Reflections on Govt."

Barker, Granville. *See* Granville-Barker, Harley.

Barker, Sir Herbert Atkinson (1869–1950). Specialist in manipulative surgery.

Barker, William George (d. 1930). Canad. air pilot of the 1st World War ; won V.C. in 1918 after fighting 60 enemy machines single-handed.

Barley, a cereal crop, 361, 745 ; attacked by rust fungus, *2857*.

Barleycorn. Ancient unit of measure.

Barleycorn, John. Personification of intoxicating liquors.

Barley sugar, 3116.

Bar magnet, *2060, 2061.*

Bar'low, Sir Montague (b. 1868). Min. of Labour 1922-24; author of Barlow Report, in 1940, advising decentralization of industry and population.

Barmecides. Persian family, powerful under early Abbassid caliphs (8th cent.); " Barmecides' feast," meaning an imaginary banquet, comes from the " Arabian Nights," where a Barmecide jests at a hungry man's expense by placing empty dishes before him.

Bar'men, Germany. *See* Wuppertal.

Bar'nabas. Fellow-labourer with the Apostle Paul, 189; Epistle of, 425.

" Barnaby Rudge." Dickens' novel based on the Gordon Riots (1780).

Barnacle. Crustacean which lives attached to ships' bottoms, piles, etc., 361, *362.*

Barnacle goose, 1486; and legend of barnacles, 362.

Barnard, Frederick (1846-96), Brit. artist; illustration for " Christmas Carol," *820*; illustrations of characters in " Pilgrim's Progress," *618, 619.*

Barnardo, Thomas John (1845-1905). Brit. philanthropist, founder of Dr. Barnardo's Homes, 362.

Barnes, Alfred J. (b. 1887). Brit. politician; chairman of Co-operative Party 1924-37 and 1945; app. Min. of Transport in 1946.

Barnes, Ernest William (b. 1874). Bishop of Birmingham from 1924; upholder of scientific outlook; wrote " Scientific Theory and Religion "; rebuked by Archbp. Fisher for his book " The Rise of Christianity " in 1947.

Barnes, William (1801-86). Dorset dialect poet, 1030.

Bar'net. Market tn. of Hertfordshire, 11 m. N. of London, pop. 22,000; scene of Yorkist victory over Lancastrians in 1471; important horse fair held annually.

Barnett, Rev. Samuel Augustus (1844-1913). British social reformer. Founder, and later president of Toynbee Hall. Originated Children's Country Holiday Fund and was associated with the formation of Hampstead Garden Suburb. Married Henrietta Octavia Rowland (1851-1936), who shared in his philanthropic work, and wrote, with him, " Practicable Socialism." She was made D.B.E. in 1924.

Barneveldt, Jan van Olden (1547-1619). Dutch statesman; secured Twelve Years' Truce with Spain, 1609; unjustly beheaded for treason.

Barns'ley. Mfg. tn. in Yorkshire; pop. 69,230; coal fields; iron, steel, looms, glass bottles, paper, linen, clothing.

Barnstaple Bay. Inlet on the north Devon coast. Also called Bideford Bay.

Bar'num, Phineas Taylor (1810-91), Amer. showman; called his travelling circus " The Greatest Show on Earth "; introduced Gen. Tom Thumb, Jenny Lind, etc., to the public.

Baro'da, India. Trade and rly. centre in E. cent. India. Pop. 153,300. Cap. of native state of same name, ruled by the Gaekwar of Baroda until his 1948 reforms were rejected, and Baroda state was merged in Bombay prov., 1949; (a. 8,164 sq. m.; pop. 2,855,000).

Baroja (bah-rō'-hah), Pio (b. 1872), Spanish novelist, 3051.

Barom'eter, 362; for measuring mts., 90; and heights, 2293; controlled altitude of flying bomb, 1332; in meteorology, 2149; principle of mercury type, 90; aneroid type, *363.*

Bar'on, a member of the lowest order in the Brit. peerage, 2536.

Bar'onet. An inheritab'e title in Gt. Brit. ranking next below that of baron; the highest degree of

honour borne by commoners; abbreviated Bt. or Bart.

Barons' Wars, in England, 1611, 2221.

Baroque (ba-rok'). Style in architecture, 220, 2854; in sculpture, 2906.

Barotseland. Native dist. of S. Africa, now part of N. Rhodesia.

Bar'ra. Isl. of Hebrides, 1602.

Barrage (bar'-ahzh), a form of dam, 958; in Nile, 1097; of anti-aircraft guns, *258*; balloons, 1332.

Barramun'da, a lung-fish, 2038.

Barranquil'la. Spt. of Colombia, on Magdalena 17 m. from mouth; pop. 202,760; terminus of river traffic; exports coffee, hides.

Barras (bar'-ah), Paul, Comte de (1755-1829). Fr. statesman, member (1795-99) of Directory.

Barren Lands, region in Canada, 676, 2392.

Barrès, Maurice (1862-1923). French novelist, 1382.

Bar'rett, Wilson (1846-1904). Brit. melodrama actor and dramatist. Staged " The Silver King " and " The Sign of the Cross."

" Barretts of Wimpole St.," play by Rudolf Besier, 589.

Barrias (bar'-i-ah), Louis Ernest (1841-1905). Fr. sculptor; " The First Funeral "; " Victor Hugo " monument in Paris.

Bar'rie, Sir James Matthew (1860-1937). Scot. novelist and dramatist, 364, 1215, 2895; novels, 2403; story of " Peter Pan," 364.

Barrier reefs. Off-shore reefs formed by corals, 307, 908.

Barrister. Qualified member of that branch of the legal profession which has the exclusive right to plead in the superior courts of law in England and Ireland. In Scotland he is termed an advocate; training for, 1903.

Barrow. Ancient burial mound. Long barrows are typical of the Stone Age, and round barrows of the Bronze Age.

Barrow, 2nd largest r. of Ire., in s.E. of Eire; flows into Waterford Harbour, 1744.

Barrow, Isaac (1630-77). Celebrated mathematician and divine, tutor to Sir Isaac Newton.

Bar'row-in-Fur'ness. Spt. in Lancashire; pop. 66,000; 367, 1890.

Barry. Spt. of Glamorganshire, with large docks, *3335.*

Barry, Sir Charles (1795-1860). English architect; designed Houses of Parliament at Westminster.

Barry, Gerald Reid (b. 1898). Eng. journalist and editor; editor of New Statesman and Nation, 1934-36; of News Chronicle, 1936-47.

Barrymore. Surname of a famous American theatrical family. Lionel Barrymore (b. 1878), John Barrymore (1882-1942), and Ethel Barrymore (b. 1879) all acquired a great reputation on stage and screen.

" Barsetshire novels " of Anthony Trollope, 3250.

Barter. Exchange of articles without use of money, 2200; in furs, 1412; Phoenicians, *1201.*

Barth, Karl (b. 1886). Swiss theologian. Professor of theology, Univ. of Basle, 1935. Works include " Das Wort Gottes un die Theologie " (Theology and the Word of God), " Die Auferstehung der Toten " (Resurrection of the Dead).

Bartholdi, Frederic A. (1834-1904). Fr. sculptor, 2906; Statue of Liberty, *2351.*

Bartholomew, St. One of Twelve Apostles; traditions of, 188.

Bartholomew's fair, 1257.

Bartholomew's Hospital, St. (Bart's), London, 1684.

Barthou (bahr'-tōō), Louis Jean Firmin (1862-1934). French prime minister (1913) and foreign minister (1934); murdered, 107.

Bartizan. In architecture, a small overhanging turret, with loopholes, projecting from the top of a tower.

Bart'ok, Bela (1881-1945). Hungarian composer and pianist, 2266. Works

include " Bluebeard's Castle " (opera), " The Woodcut Prince " (ballet), violin concerto, string quartets, concerto for orchestra.

Bartolommeo (bah-tol-om-ā-ō), Fra (1475-1517). One of the great painters of the Florentine Renaissance. Works include " St. Mark " now in Pitti Palace, " The Presentation in the Temple," at Vienna, etc.

Bartolozzi (bah-to-lot'-si), Francesco (c. 1727-1815). Italian engraver, 1180. One of the original painter members of the Royal Academy. Mainly adopted stipple method, and left over 700 engravings.

Baruch. Apocryphal book of Old Testament, 424.

Bar'uch, Bernard M. (b. 1870). Amer. economist; U.S. delegate to U.N. atomic energy commission; submitted proposals for international atomic control in 1946.

Barye, Antoine Louis (1796-1875). Fr. sculptor of animals; 2906. Bronzes include the celebrated " Jaguar Devouring a Hare " at the Luxembourg, " Lion Seated " in the Tuileries garden, etc.

Barysphere, of the earth, *1067.*

Basalt'. A fine-grained, heavy igneous rock, often soliuified into prismatic columns, 2795; Fingal's Cave, *3071*; in Giant's Causeway, *1461.*

Basan. *See* Bashan.

Bascule bridges, *567, 568.*

Base, in chemistry, term applied to the oxides or hydroxides of metals which combined with acids form new bodies known as salts, 20, 2148.

Baseball. America's national sport, 367, *368.*

Base Compound. Any base or alkali capable of neutralizing an acid, 20.

Basel. *See* Basle.

Ba'shan. Rich dist. in anc. Palestine, beyond the Jordan; famed for cattle of great size (" bulls of Bashan ").

Bashkir. Autonomous republic of the R.S.F.S.R. Lies between Tartar republic and s. Urals. Ufa cap. on Bielaya r. Rich oil deposits.

Bashkirtsev (bash - kĕrt' - sef), Marie (1860-84). Brilliant versatile Rus. painter and author; famed through her " Journal."

Basic English. System devised by C. K. Ogden to make English serve as an international language by restriction of vocabulary, 1210. In 1946 its copyright was assigned to the Brit. crown by its inventor for £23,000. Bible published in Basic, 1949.

Basidiomycetes (bas-id'-i-ō-mī-sē'-tēz). Class of fungi with spores borne on the outside of special cells, 1408; mushrooms, 2260; rusts and smuts, 2857; spores on basidia, *2918.*

Basil the Great (329-379). Early father of Gk. church, bishop of Caesarea in Cappadocia; founder of Eastern monasticism, 2212.

Basil'ica, in architecture, 214.

Bas'ilisk, hooded. A lizard, 1686, 1973.

Basin, in physiography, 2598.

Basket, 368.

Basket-ball. Team game, 369, *370.*

Basket shell, *2913.*

Basle (bahl), B.le, or Basel. Second largest city of Switzerland; pop. 162,000; *370.*

Basques. People inhabiting Basque provs. N.E. Spain and s.w. Fr., 1358, 3032; legend of Roland, 2797. *See* Euzkadi.

Basra or Basrah. Port of Iraq on Shat-el-Arab; pop. 85,000; airport; exports dates; occupied Nov. 1914 by Brit. troops; 1743, 2512.

Bas-relief (bas-ri-lēf'), or " low relief," 2903.

Bass (bās). The lowest part in musical compositions; the deepest male voice in a choir.

Bass (bas). A fish, 370, 1296; American, *1302.*

Bassein (bas-ān'), Burma. Trading tn. and port in delta of Irrawaddy r., 90 m. from sea; pop. 43,000; mills and exports rice.

Bas'senthwaite. Lake in the Eng. lake dist., 943.

Basse-Terre. Cap. of Guadeloupe ; pop. 9,000 ; 1551.

Basset hound, for hare hunting.

Bass horn, or tuba, 1644.

Bassoon'. Musical instrument, 2267, 3009, 3404.

Bass Strait. Channel between Australia and Tasmania ; 80 to 150 m. broad.

Basswood. Amer. linden tree.

Bastia (bas-tē'-a). Largest city of Corsica, on N.E. coast ; pop. 52,000 ; 914.

Bastille (bas-tēl'). Prison fortress in Paris, built in 1369 to protect palace of Charles V ; destroyed by mob at outbreak of Fr. Rev., *1395.*

Bastina'do. Method of torture by beating the soles of the feet.

Bastogne (bas-tōñ). Tn. of the Ardennes, Belgium, 5 m. from border of Duchy of Luxemburg ; held Dec. 18–26, 1944, by the U.S. 101st Airborne Div., against constant attack by superior forces and completely surrounded during Rundstedt's Ardennes offensive.

Basu'toland. Brit. protectorate, S. Africa, N.E. of Cape of Good Hope ; 11,716 sq. m. ; pop. 556,400 ; 3015.

Bat. A winged mammal, 370, *371, 372, 373* ; fly by sound " radar."

370 ; flying fox, 372 ; in flight, *2585.*

Bat, cricket, 928.

Bata, Thomas (1876–1932). Czech shoe manufacturer, 373.

Bataan (ba-tahn') Peninsula. Headland of W. Luzon, Philippine Is. ; attacked by Japanese Dec. 1941, held by Americans until April 9 ; retaken Jan. 9–Feb. 15, 1945 ; MacArthur's escape, 2045. *See also* Corregidor.

Bata'via (Djakarta). Spt. on N. coast of Java, cap. of United States of Indonesia ; exports coffee, sugar, tea, rice, spices, 1813 ; occupied by Japanese (1942–45).

SOME OF THE WORLD'S MOST IMPORTANT BATTLES

Agincourt (1415) : Exhausted Eng. force (mostly archers) under Henry V defeat Fr. army many times their strength.

Alamein, El (1942) : Decisive defeat of Axis in N. Africa.

Anzio Beaches (1944) : Landings north of Italian port of Anzio by Anglo-U.S. forces made possible Allied advance on Rome.

Arbela (331 B.C.) : Alexander the Great finally defeated Darius III of Persia, and became master of Asia.

Armada, Spanish (1588) : Flotilla of nimble Eng. ships defeated great Sp. war fleet in Eng. Channel.

Austerlitz (1805) : " Battle of Three Emperors " ; Napoleon defeated united forces of Russia and Austria.

Blenheim (1704) : Eng. and Austrians under Marlborough and Eugene defeated Fr. and Bavarians under Tallard in War of Sp. Succession ; dissipated Louis XIV's ambitions.

Borodino (1812) : Costly Fr. victory over Russians opened road to Moscow.

Britain (1940) : First great air-battle in history. R.A.F. defeated attempts by German air-force to put out of action the airfields of S.E. England and thus pave way for invasion of Britain. The " Battle of Britain " lasted three months.

Caen (1944) : A key town in the Allied invasion of Normandy, Caen fell to British and Canadian troops after fierce fighting and heavy casualties.

Cannae (216 B.C.) : Frightful battle in which Hannibal annihilated great Rom. army. Rome's existence threatened.

Cassino (1944) : One of costliest and most protracted of Second World War campaigns in Italy. A key position to the German Gustav Line, Cassino became scene of bitter street fighting and intense bombardment ; eventually captured by the Allies.

Chaeronea (338 B.C.) : Philip of Macedon gained mastery of all Greece.

Châlons (451) : Rom. and Visigoths checked Attila's advance in Fr., saving W. Europe from the Huns.

Coral Sea (1942) : A U.S. navy defeated a Japanese fleet, saving Australia from invasion.

Crécy (1346) : Edward III and Eng. longbowmen won victory over a vastly superior Fr. army of cavalry.

Crete (1941) : Island in Mediterranean defended by Allied troops against overwhelming German airborne forces, first example of an island captured entirely from the air.

Gettysburg (1863) : Union troops under Meade sharply defeated Lee, forcing his retreat from northern soil ; one of decisive battles of Amer. Civil War.

Hastings (1066) : William, Duke of Normandy, defeated Eng., their king, Harold, falling in battle ; originated Norman rule over England.

Jutland (1916) : Most important naval conflict of 1st World War, in North Sea ; after heavy losses on both sides, Brit. fleet, under Jellicoe and Beatty, forced retreat of Ger. vessels.

Kohima (1944) : A town in Assam garrisoned by British troops and besieged by Japanese. With its relief, the Japanese offensive towards India collapsed.

Leipzig (1631) : Swedes and Saxons under Gustavus Adolphus won brilliant victory over Cath. Imperialists, and saved Prot. cause in Thirty Years' War ; also called Breitenfeld.

Leipzig (1813) : " Battle of the Nations " ; overwhelming defeat inflicted upon Napoleon by allied forces ; marked end of Fr. rule in Ger. ; turning-point in Napoleonic wars.

Lepanto (1571) : Venetian and Sp. fleets under Don Juan of Austria decisively defeated Turkey in Gulf of Corinth, ending Turkish sea power.

Leyte Gulf (1944) : With defeat of a Japanese fleet by U.S. fleet off Leyte, Philippine Is., Japanese sea-power was smashed.

Marathon (490 B.C.) : Miltiades, with a small force of Athenians and Plateans, routed large Persian army, saving Greece from Asiatic conquest.

Marne, First Battle of the (1914) : Fr. and British forces under Joffre and French checked Ger. invasion in four-day battle and drove Ger. back to r. Aisne, where battle line remained nearly stationary for three years.

Marne, Second Battle of the (1918) : Counter-offensive launched by Foch with Fr. and Amer. troops ; placed Germans permanently on defensive.

Metaurus (207 B.C.) : Romans under the consul Nero defeated Hasdrubal (who was slain) and his Carthaginians, thus preventing union of Hasdrubal and Hannibal, saving Italy.

Midway (1942) : Defeat by a U.S. fleet of a Japanese force equipped for invasion of the Hawaiian Is. marked end of Japanese advance in the Pacific.

Nile (1798) : Naval battle in Aboukir Bay, Egypt ; Nelson destroyed Fr. fleet, cutting off Napoleon from Fr.

Normandy (1944) : Battle of Normandy ended with closing by the Allies of the Falaise " pocket " in which German 7th Army was trapped.

Orleans (1429) : Joan of Arc raised Eng. siege ; turning-point in Hundred Years' War.

Plassey (1757) : Brit. under Clive defeated forces of Suraj-ud-Dowlah, nawab of Bengal ; established Brit. rule in India.

Plevna (1877) : After long siege, surrender of this pivotal point by Turks, virtually concluded Russo-Turkish War.

Poitiers (1356) : Victory of Black Prince over King John of Fr. ; many prisoners taken, including John ; ended first period of Hundred Years' War.

Poltava (1709) : Peter the Great of Russia completely defeated Charles XII of Sweden, annihilating his army ; Rus. succeeded Sweden as the leading power of the N. at conclusion of the Great Northern War.

Quebec (1759) : Brit. under Wolfe stormed and took Quebec after gallant defence by Fr. general, Montcalm, securing Brit. domination of N. Amer.

Sadowa (1866) : Crushing defeat administered to Austria by Germans under Moltke ; led to exclusion of Austria from Ger. Confederation ; also called Königgrätz.

Salamis (480 B.C.) : Athenian fleet built by Themistocles almost annihilated Persian fleet ; forced withdrawal of Xerxes from Greece.

Saratoga (1777) : Surrender of Burgoyne and his Brit. army to Amer. general, Gates ; turning-point in War of Amer. Independence.

Sea of Japan (1905) : Japan destroyed Rus. navy and became a world power ; also called Tsushima.

Sedan (1870) : Prussians under Moltke defeated MacMahon and forced surrender of Napoleon III and 100,000 men ; caused fall of Fr. Empire and proclamation of Third Republic.

Somme (1916) : Eng. and Fr. took offensive for five months ; made small gain in territory at enormous cost, but relieved Verdun and aided Rus. in east.

Stalingrad (1942–43) : Russians prevented Germans crossing River Volga.

Syracuse (413 B.C.) : Syracusans with Spartan aid destroyed Athenian fleet, dealing a death-blow to Athens' naval supremacy and contributing to her defeat in the Peloponnesian War.

Tannenberg (1914) : Hindenburg stopped the Rus. invasion of E. Prussia.

Teutoburger Wald (A.D. 9) : Germans under Arminius (Hermann) annihilated Rom. army commanded by Varus ; established Rhine and Danube as northern Rom. frontier.

Thermopylae (480 B.C.) : Heroic effort of Leonidas and a small body of Spartans to check Persian hordes of Xerxes in their march on Athens ; Athens destroyed.

Tours (732) : Charles Martel and the Franks forced the retreat of the Saracens, saving W. Europe from Moslem invasion.

Trafalgar (1805) : Nelson destroyed the combined Fr. and Sp. fleets, firmly securing England's sea power, the chief menace to Fr. conquests.

Valmy (1792) : Fr. commanded by Dumouriez defeated troops of " First Coalition " under Brunswick, saving revolutionary govt. from destruction at hands of invaders.

Verdun (1916) : General Pétain retained fort in spite of supreme effort by Germans, thus keeping barred the road to Paris and increasing the confidence of the Allied forces.

Vicksburg (1863) : Grant cut Confederacy in two by its capture ; capitulation, with Gettysburg, decided Am. Civil War.

Waterloo (1815) : Eng., Prussians, and allies under Wellington and Blücher effected final overthrow of Napoleon.

Yorktown (1781) : Americans and Fr. under Washington forced surrender of Lord Cornwallis with 7,000 men, practically ending War of Amer. Independence.

Ypres, First Battle of (1914) : Brit. prevented Germans from reaching Calais and occupying Channel ports.

Bath. Famous watering place of Somerset; pop. 71,000, **373**; hot springs, 3070; object of "Baedeker" air raids, 374.

Bath, Order of the, 2449, 3369.

Bathing, 374. *See* Swimming and Diving.

Baths, in hygiene, 1675; Rom., 2802, 2804; *plate f.* 2805.

Bathsheba. Wife of Uriah the Hittite; David later married her (2 Samuel xi); mother of Solomon.

Bathurst. Spt. and cap. of Gambia, Brit. W. Africa; extensive trade; airport; pop. 6,000; 3366.

Bathurst Island, site of magnetic North Pole, 2390.

Bathysphere. Deep sea diving sphere, 1019, 2414.

Batik (bat-ēk') **dyeing.** Method of colouring fabrics, 1060.

Batoni (or **Battoni**), **Pompeo Girolamo** (1708–87). Italian painter; painted "Chiron and Achilles."

Batrachia (bat-rā'-kia). *See* Amphibia.

Batsman, in cricket, 930.

Batten, Jean (b. 1909). N.Z. aviator, **375**; in Oct. 1937, flew from Australia to England in 5 d. 18¼ hrs.

Bat'tenberg. Family name of medieval Ger. counts; revived 1851; Princess Victoria Eugenie married Alfonso XIII of Spain (1906); Eng. branch the Mountbattens.

Battersea. Met. bor. of s.w. London; pop. about 95,000; park, 185 acres; power station, 221, 222; Whistler's painting of old bridge, *1182*.

Battery. In artillery, unit of four or more guns.

Battery, electric, 375, 1131; accumulator, *376*; charging from mains, 2751; dry cell, 375; Leclanché cell, *375, 376*; radio, motor-car, 377; voltage, 376.

Battle cruisers, vulnerability, 2296.

Battle dress. Utility service uniform adopted for general use in Brit. Army (1939).

Battlement. In architecture, wall or rampart built round the top of a fortified building.

Battles, world's greatest, *see* list, 3724; of the 1st and 2nd World Wars. *See* World Wars.

Battleships, in modern navy, *2295, 2296, 2297, 2304*; armament, 2295.

Batu Islands, Small group in Indonesia off w. Sumatra; 445 sq. m.; inhabited by Malays; forest produce.

Batum (bat-ōōm'), or **Batumi,** Georgia, cap. of Adzharian A.S.S.R. Chief port on Black Sea; pop. 70,800; terminus of rly. and of petroleum pipe line from Baku; 733, 1443, *2847*.

Baudelaire (bō-de-lār) **Charles Pierre** (1821–67). French poet; 1381.

Baudet Multiplex, system of telegraphy transmission, 3167.

Bautzen (bowt'-zen). Tn. of Saxony, with textile and machinery mfrs.; pop. 40,000; here Napoleon won a success over the Prussians and Russians in 1813.

Baux (bō) or **Beaux.** A vil. in s. of Fr., near Arles; gives name to bauxite ore.

Bauxite (bō'zit). Chief aluminium ore, 135; aluminous cements, 740; electrolysis, 1137.

Bavaria. State in s. Ger.; pop. 7,000,000; 28,000 sq. m.; **377**, 1445, 1447; Danube in, 972; Munich, 2256; Nuremberg, 2406; peasant costumes, *377, 1447*; history, 1449, 2414. in U.S. zone of occupn.; self-govt. restored, 378.

Bax, Sir Arnold Edward Trevor (b. 1883). Eng. composer. Chief compositions, six symphonies; "The Garden of Fand"; "Tintagel"; "London Pageantry." Master of King's Musick, 1942; 2266.

Bax, Clifford (b. 1886). Eng. dramatist. Brother of Sir Arnold Bax (above). Plays include: "Midsummer Madness"; "The Rose Without a Thorn"; "Mr. Pepys"; "The House of Borgia."

Baxter, Richard (1615–91). Eng. Puritan preacher and scholar ("The Saint's Everlasting Rest").

Bay. An evergreen tree, *1900*.

Bayard, Pierre du Terrail, Chevalier de (1476–1524). Fr. military commander of time of Charles VIII and Francis I; pattern of chivalry.

Bayberry, or **Wax Myrtle.** A shrub; the wax is used in candles.

Bayern (bī'-yêrn). The Ger. form of Bavaria.

Bayeux (bī-yê'), Fr. Historic tn. in Normandy, famous for old cathedral, *379*, and for Bayeux tapestry, **378**, 2377. First tn. in w. Europe liberated, June 8, 1944, 2379.

Bayeux tapestry, *379*, 1153, 2377, 3153; death of Harold, *1196*.

Bay laurel, 1900.

Baylis, Lilian (1874–1937). English theatrical manager of Old Vic and Sadler's Wells, 1042.

Bayonne, Fr. Historic tn. and fortress 4 m. from Bay of Biscay; pop. 31,700; mfg. and export trade.

Bayreuth or **Baireuth** (bī'roit). City in Bavaria; pop. 35,000; home of the composer Wagner; noted for the Wagnerian musical festivals; 378, 1447, 3332.

Bay rum. A toilet preparation made by mixing oil of bay with diluted alcohol and adding oil of allspice and oil of orange peel.

Bazaar'. Oriental market place; African, 64.

Bazaine (baz-ān'), **François Achille** (1811–88). Fr. marshal; commander-in-chief of the main Fr. armies in Franco-Prussian War.

Bazan, Emilia Pardo (1851–1921), better known as Pardo-Bazan. Sp. novelist ("Los Pazos de Ulloa"; "La Madre Naturaleza").

Beachy Head. Chalk cliff (532 ft.) in Sussex, 3 m. from Eastbourne; famous lighthouse near by; *plate f. 1945*; Dutch and Eng. fleet defeated (1690) by Fr.

Beacon. Method of signalling; radio, 2291; by fire, 3164, *3165*.

Beacons, Belisha. *See* Belisha Beacons.

Bea'consfield, Earl of. *See* Disraeli, Benjamin.

Beads, as money, 2201; anc. Egypt, 1472.

Beagle. Hound used in hunting, 1658.

Beagle, H.M.S. Ship in which Darwin made five-year voyage round the world, 976.

Beak; duck, *plates f. 1052, 1053*; duckbill, 1053; flamingo, *plate f. 1312*; gannet, 1418; goosanders, 1053; mergansers, 1052; octopus, 945.

Beale, Benjamin. Inventor of bathing machine, 374.

Beale, Dorothea (1831–1906). Brit. educationist; with Frances Mary Buss, a pioneer of higher education for girls; principal of Ladies' College, Cheltenham; estab. first residential training college for women, St. Hilda's, Cheltenham, 1885, and St. Hilda's Hall, Oxford, 1893.

Beam, in building, *379*; of timber and steel, *380*. Beam-engine, form of steam engine, 3085, *3086*.

Beam-wireless. A system of sending wireless messages by short waves gathered into a beam by reflectors so that their direction is controlled; 3396; Marconi, 2099.

Bean. Fruit of various leguminous plants, chiefly of genus *Phaseolus*, 380, 2918; clover, 852; lucerne, 2034; peas, 2530; food value, 2174, 2694; geotropic and phototropic properties, 2622; Mexican bean or frijole, 2157; stages of growth, *381*.

Bear, 382; black, in N. Amer., *2382*; emblem of Berne, 418; in India, 1701; foot, *1343*; hibernation, 1623. Story: "Adventures of Blackie and Ginger," 3489.

Bearded Tit, rare Brit. bird, *Panurus biarmicus*; close relation of the commoner tits (blue, great, cole, etc.), but of family Panuridae; 3218.

Beardsley, Aubrey (1872–98). Famous Eng. black and white artist; work noted for its beauty of outline.

Bear garden, in 17th cent. London, 2035.

Bear, Great (*Ursa Major*) constellation, 894, 895.

Bearings, in machinery, 385; ball and roller, *386*; in navigation 2290; of wheel, 3375.

Beasley, John A. (1895–1949). Australian politician; Min. of Supply and Shipping (1941–45). Min. of Defence (1945–46); resident Austr. min. in London (1946–49); app. High Commissioner in Aug. 1946.

"Beat" (heterodyne), in wireless reception, 3394.

Beaton (bā'-ton) or **Bethune, David** (c. 1494–1546). Only Scot. cardinal; able but unscrupulous statesman, arrogant and cruel; death, 1871.

Beaton, Cecil (b. 1904). British designer and photographer. Designed décor and costumes for ballet, and Cochran revues. "Cecil Beaton's Scrapbook," "Indian Album," "Time Exposure."

Beatrice. In the "Divina Commedia," the "glorious lady" of Dante's mystic adoration, and his guide through Paradise; identified with a certain Beatrice Portinari (1266–90) whom he saw when they were both children, and but seldom thereafter; 969.

Beatrix, Princess (b. 1938). Daughter of Queen Juliana and Prince Bernhard of the Netherlands, 2323.

Beatty, David, 1st Earl (1871–1936). Commander of Brit. Grand Fleet in World War, 386. Memorial in Trafalgar Sq. unveiled Oct. 21, 1948.

Beauchamp. Eng. surname pronounced bē'-cham.

Beaufort (bō'-fort), Countess of Richmond, Margaret (1441–1509). Founded Cambridge colleges, 668.

Beaufort Scale; for measuring the strength of the wind at sea (e.g. 0=calm; 12=hurricane, wind 74–82 m.p.h.; scale in 1944 extended to 17 (wind 126–136 m.p.h.). Beaufort Letters (c=cloudy, q=squall, etc.) indicate the type of weather; invented in 1805 by Sir F. Beaufort.

Beauharnais (bō-ahr'-nā). Name of well-known Fr. family; Alexandre, Vicomte de (1760–94), married Josephine (later empress), 1838.

Beauharnais, Eugène (1781–1824). Son of Empress Josephine, 1839.

Beauharnais, Hortense (1783–1837). Daughter of Empress Josephine, and wife of Louis Bonaparte, 1839.

Beaulieu (bū'-li) **Abbey,** Hants, *1571*.

Beauly (bū'-li) **Firth.** Inlet of Inverness-shire, Scot., the upper basin of the Moray Firth, 7 m. long and 2 m. broad, *1738*.

Beaumarchais (bō'-mahr-shā), **Pierre Augustin Caron de** (1732–99). Fr. politician, dramatist, and satirist; chief works, "The Barber of Seville," "The Marriage of Figaro."

Beaumaris Castle, Wales, *717*, 718.

Beaumont, Francis (1584–1616). Eng. dramatist whose association with John Fletcher formed a "perfect union in genius and friendship"; ("Philaster," "The Maid's Tragedy"; "The Knight of the Burning Pestle"), 1040, 1211.

Beauvais (bō'-vā). Fr. cap. of Oise; pop. 17,250; Gobelin tapestry, textile mfrs.; famous cathedral begun in 13th cent.; R101 crashed near, 94; tapestry.

Beaver. An amphibious rodent mammal, 387; fur, 1412, 3287; instinct, 159, *160*; in N. America, *2382*; yields castor perfume, 2549.

Beaverbrook, William Maxwell Aitken, 1st Baron (b. 1879). Brit. politician and newspaper proprietor, 388.

Becerra, Gaspar (1520–70). Span. sculptor, 3040.

Bêche-de-mer (bāsh'-de-mār). A sea-cucumber, *2911*; 2472.

Bechuanaland, British. Dist. of Cape Colony, S. Africa, 697, 3016.

Bechuanaland Protectorate. Region of S. Africa under Brit. protection; 275,000 sq. m.; pop. 285,000; 3016.

Beck, Josef (1894–1944). Polish soldier and statesman. Foreign min. (1932–39), 3416.

Becke, Louis. Australian author, 315.

Beck'et, Thomas (c. 1118–70). Archbishop of Canterbury, **389** ; shrine in Canterbury, 692 ; murder, *389* ; plays by Tennyson, 3187 ; T. S. Eliot, 1042, *389.*

Beck'ford, William (1760–1844). Eng. author and politician ; eccentric personality ; wrote Oriental romance, " Vathek " ; spent lavishly on his estate at Fonthill, Wilts.

Becquerel (bek'rel), **Antoine Henri** (1852–1908). Fr. physicist ; Nobel prize winner in 1903 ; discoverer of radio-activity (Becquerel rays), 2731.

Bedaux (bĕ'-dō), **Charles Eugene** (d. 1944). Amer. industrialist ; Fr. by birth ; introduced system to simplify movements and speed up work in factories, etc. ; associated with Ribbentrop and Schacht ; intermediary between Vichy and Berlin ; committed suicide under detention in U.S.A., Feb. 1944.

Beddgelert (beth-gě-lărt). Parish and vil. on borders of Caernarvonshire and Merionethshire, Wales.

Beddoes, Thomas (1760–1808). Eng. scientist, 979.

Beddoes, Thomas Lovell (1803–49). Brit. dramatic poet ; has been called " a belated Elizabethan " ; " The Bride's Tragedy," " Death's Jest Book."

Bede, Beda, or Boeda (c. 673–735). Eng. monk known as " The Venerable Bede," and " Father of English History " (his " Ecclesiastical History of the English Nation " chief source of information for period covered), 423.

Bedford. Co. tn. of Bedfordshire on Ouse ; pop. 56,000 ; 390.

Bedford, John, Duke of (1389–1435). Son of Henry IV of Eng. and brother of Henry V ; regent of Fr., 1611 ; In Shakespeare's " Henry IV " he is Prince John of Lancaster.

Bed'fordshire. S. midland co. of Eng. ; 473 sq. m. ; pop. 275,000 ; 390.

Bed'lam. Bethlehem Royal Hospital, Eden Park, Beckenham ; founded in London in 1247 as a priory ; afterwards became lunatic asylum ; site of, in Lambeth, now Imperial War Museum.

Bed'uin. Wandering Arabs of Arabian, Syrian, and N. African deserts, 197, 265, *plate 793* ; in Egypt, 1097 ; horses, *1646* ; Sahara, 3860 ; Semitic race, 2920.

Bee. An insect, **390** ; *plates f. 392, 393* ; bumblebee, *392* ; carpenter bee, *394*, 1729 ; clovers, 852 ; drone, 391 ; Forel's researches, 1349 ; leaf-cutter bee, 394, *1729* ; eggs, *1094* ; life, *391*, *393* ; metamorphosis, 1728 ; miners, 394 ; pollen carriers, 391 ; queen, *391*, *392* ; social instincts, 159, 390 ; solitary types, 394 ; worker, *391.*

Bee'be, William (b. 1877). Amer. naturalist (" Our Search for a Wilderness " ; " Galapagos ") ; inventor of the bathysphere, 1019, 2414.

Bee-bread, 391, 394.

Beech. A shade tree, **395**, *3244.*

Beech'am, Sir Thomas, Bart. (b. 1879). Eng. musical conductor and composer, 3ʋ5, *396.*

Beecher, Henry Ward (1813–87). Amer. preacher, champion of abolition of slavery, woman suffrage, and other unpopular causes.

Beechnut oil, 395.

Beef. Best cattle for, 732 ; cuts of, *2125* ; food value, *2174.*

" Beefeaters," in Tower of London, **396**, 3ʋ31 ; costume, *plate f. 396* ; with Maundy Money, *plate f. 397.*

Beefsteak fungus. Edible bracket fungus, *Fistulina hepatica,* growing as parasite mostly on oak trees ; succulent, dark red, resembling a beef steak.

Bee Hawk. Small hawk moth with wings transparent except for brown margin. Often seen in spring on rhododendron flowers ; larva eats honeysuckle.

Beelzebub (bĕ-el'-zĕ-bub) or **Baalzebub.** In Old Testament heathen god (2 Kings i, iii, vi) ; in New Testament, prince of devils ; in Milton's " Paradise Lost," Satan's chief lieutenant.

Beer, or ale. Beverage made by boiling and fermenting barley, malt and hops, with water, 103 ; fermentation 3434 ; brewed at Burton, 627 ; gypsum and, 1559 ; from hops, 1641 ; malt for, 2071 ; from Munich, 2256.

Beerbohm, Sir Max (b. 1872). Eng. author and caricaturist (" Zuleika Dobson " ; " The Happy Hypocrite " ; " Seven Men " ; " And Even Now ").

Beershe'ba. Anc. vil. of Jerusalem ; referred to in Bible as southern limit of Palestine : " Dan to Beersheba."

Beerstraaten, Abraham, 17th cent. Dutch painter ; " Catwyck in Winter," 2331.

Beeswax, made by bees, 394, 3359.

Beet, comprising red and white varieties, 396.

Beet sugar. Any kind with high sugar content, 397 ; as commercial crop, 3114, *3115.*

Beethoven (bā'-tō-ven), **Ludwig van** (1770–1827). Ger. composer and musician, 397 ; birthplace, 500 ; influence on music, 2264 ; and the piano, 2602.

Beetle, 398, *401* ; eye, *1253* ; foot and claw, *1727* ; head, *1729* ; life, *399* ; lunar dungbeetle, *400* ; sexton beetle, *400* ; phosphorescent (fireflies), 1288 ; sacred scarab, 1427 ; stag beetle, *398* ; weevils, 3362 ; wings, 1732 ; wood tiger beetle, *398.*

Beeton, Mrs. Isabella Mary (1836–65). Eng. housewife ; compiled the famous " Beeton's Household Management."

Begbie, Harold (1871–1929). Eng. journalist and author, writer of many story books for children and novels (" The Priest " ; " Broken Earthenware " ; " An English Family " ; " The Mirrors of Downing Street ").

Beggar's Opera, The. Lyrical drama of thieves and highwaymen, written by John Gay in 1728. Revived, with much success, at the Lyric Theatre, Hammersmith, in 1920–23 ; notable revival Cambridge and London, 1948, music being newly scored by Benjamin Britten.

Begon (be-gawn'), **Michel** (1638–1710). Fr. patron of botany ; the begonia named after him, 402.

Bego'nia, a plant, 402.

Beguinage (beg'-in-ahzh). Cluster of cottages in which Beguines, a religious community, live.

Behaviourism. System of psychology which views animal and human behaviour objectively, and analyses action as response (conditioned or otherwise) to stimulus.

Behistun, Rock of, 2556.

Beira. Town and port of Port. E. Africa ; spt. outlet of Rhodesia, railway terminus and stop on Empire airway ; pop. 11,000. In 1948 the Brit. owned port was sold to Port. govt. for £3,500,000.

Beirut (bār-oot'). City of the Lebanese republic, pop. 233,970 ; exports silk, tobacco, cotton ; many Christian missions and schools. As H.Q. of French High Commissioner for Syria, it was occupied by Allies, July 15, 1941. Scene of disturbances, 1943, concerned with recognition of Lebanese independence ; 3146.

Beit, Alfred (1853–1906). Brit. financier ; in association with Rhodes, had control of diamond mines ; he and his brother, Sir Otto (1865–1930) were noted philanthropists.

Beith, John Hay. See Hay, Ian.

Bėk scsaba (bek-es'-chah-bah), Hungary. Market tn., rly. junction ; pop. 49,900 ; linen and hemp fabrics.

Bekonscot. Model town at Beaconsfield, Bucks, 2197.

Bel. One of the chief Babylonian gods ; identified with the Phoenician Baal.

Belas'co, David (1859–1931). Amer. dramatist and theatrical producer.

Belcher, George F. A. (1875–1947). Brit. painter and cartoonist ; many charcoal drawings of cockney charladies, etc., in " Punch."

Belem (bā'-lêm), Port. A suburb of Lisbon, contains one of the finest ecclesiastical buildings in the country, the Convento do Jeronymos de Belém, a convent (now an orphanage) and church founded in 1499 in honour of Vasco da Gama's discovery of the sea-route to India, and whose tomb is in the church.

Belem. Same as **Pará.**

Bel'fast. Cap. of N. Ire., pop. 438,000 ; mfrs. ships, aircraft, linen, rope ; 2nd World War shipping centre ; 402, *1747, 1748.*

Belfast Lough. Inlet of the Irish Sea between Counties Antrim and Down. It provides harbourage for Belfast, 402.

Belfort (bel'-fōr). Fortified tn. of E. Fr., cap. of Belfort Territory (a. 235 sq. m., pop. 99,500) ; important strategic position near Ger. and Swiss frontiers ; pop. 36,400.

Belfort Gap. Between Vosges and Jura Mts., 1842.

Belfry. In architecture, part of a tower or steeple in which the bell is hung ; sometimes called the bell-tower.

Bel'gian Congo. See Congo, Belgian.

Belgian hare, 2772.

Belgium (bel'-jum). Kingdom of w. Europe, bordering North Sea, between Netherlands and Fr. ; 11,775 sq. m., pop. 8,300,000 ; 403, 594 ; *map, 404* ; agriculture, 403 ; architecture, 405, 406, 407 ; army decorations, 2449 ; chief cities and mfs. ; 592, 594, 595, 1460, 1934, 2032 ; commerce, 404, 1460 ; dialects, 404 ; mineral resources, 404 ; people, *403*, *408.*—*History,* 407 ; medieval Flanders, 1313, 3153 ; Charles the Bold, 757 ; Hapsburg possession (1477–1797), 2568 ; Fr. acquires, 1396 ; union with Holland, 2323 ; independent, 2323 ; acquires Congo, 72, 73, 887 ; 1914–18 War, 407, 3409 ; Antwerp occupied, 182, 3409 ; Brussels occupied, 595 ; Liége falls, 1935 ; sack of Louvain, 2032 ; Ypres, *407*, 3409, 3436 ; peace (1919), 3414 ; overrun by Germans, May 1940, liberated, Sept. 1944, 1452, 3416. See also **Flanders,** Netherlands, and chief towns.

Belgrade (bel-gr d'). Cap. of Yugoslavia ; pop. 267,000 ; 408 ; Danube at, 972 ; in 1914–18 War, 3414 in German occupn. 1941–44.

Belial (bĕ'-li-al). Biblical name o: Satan ; " sons of Belial," wicked men

Belisarius (bel-i-sār'-i-us) (c. 505–565) Byzantine general to whom Rom Empire under Justinian I largely owed its safety against Persians Vandals, Goths, etc., 1844, 3304 Late legend represents him, blinded by Justinian's jealousy, begging ir Constantinople.

Belisha Beacons. Signs erected a either side of a pedestrian crossing Named after Leslie Hore-Belisha the Minister of Transport responsibl for their introduction ; *2782, plate f 2785.*

Belize (bā-lēz'). Cap. of Brit. Hon duras ; pop. 16,687 ; claimed, 1948 by Guatemala, 1638.

Bell, Alexander Graham (1847–1922) Scottish-Amer. scientist and inven tor, 408, *409* ; telephone, 3173, *317*

Bell, Dr. Andrew (1753–1832). Co founder with Joseph Lancaster an others of the National Society fo establishing Free National School 2884.

Bell, Sir Charles (1774–1842). Scottis anatomist, discoverer of distinctio between motor, sensory, and sensor motor nerves.

Bell, Charles Frederic Moberley (1847 1911). Brit. journalist, successivel correspondent, assistant manager, manager and managing-director of "The Times."

Bell, Currer, Ellis, and Acton. Pen-names of Charlotte, Emily and Anne Brontë.

Bell, Henry (1767–1830). Scottish engineer, builder of steamship Comet (1812).

Bell, Rev. Patrick. Inventor of reaping machine, 79.

Belladonna, a drug, 2369, 2370, 2638, 2639.

Belleek' Ware ; fine porcelain, biscuit ware, etc., also with a mother-of-pearl glaze ; made at Belleek, Co. Fermanagh, N. Ireland.

Belleau (bel'-ō) **Wood.** Fr., near Château-Thierry, bought by U.S.A. in 1918 for a national park ; battle in 1st World War, 3412.

Belle Isle, Strait of. Channel between Labrador and Newfoundland, N. entrance to Gulf of St. Lawrence ; open only in summer ; 10 to 15 m. wide, 2861.

Bellerophon (be-ler'-ō-fon). Gk. mythical hero, slew the fire-breathing Chimaera and all who sought his death ; having offended the gods, he took flight and ended his days in solitude ; and Pegasus, 2536.

Bellerophon. Battleship on which Napoleon surrendered.

Bell-flower. Popular name for members of genus *Campanula*, family *Campanulaceae*, including Canterbury bells ; harebell, 479, also in this genus.

Bell-heather, 1597.

Bellini (bel-ē'-nē), **Giovanni** (c. 1430–1516), and **Gentile** (1429–1530). Venetian painters, 1776, 3217. Giovanni was first great Venetian colorist and most important figure of early Venetian school, 1782.

Bellini, Vincenzo (1801–35). It. operatic composer ; " Norma."

Bell metal, 410.

Belloc, Hilaire (b. 1870). Prolific Eng. writer of essays, biography, history, fiction, 409.

Bellona (bel-ō'-na). In Rom. myth., goddess of war, described as wife or sister of Mars.

Bell Rock. Reef and lighthouse in North Sea off coast of Forfarshire, Scot., 1944.

Bells and Bell-ringing, 409 ; " Emperor of Bells " at Moscow, 411 ; foundry, 411 ; in orchestra, 2268 ; in ship's time, 3214.

Bell-tower, or campanile, 220, 410 ; in Belgium, 403, 592 ; Giotto's tower, 1319, 1464 ; leaning tower of Pisa, 2612, 2613 ; St. Mark's, 3310, 3311.

Bel'sen. Ger. concentration camp near Celle, Hanover ; taken by Brit. 2nd Army April 1945 ; contained nearly 40,000 men, women and children ; scene of appalling horrors, 3422 ; see **Kramer, J.** (f-i.).

Belshazzar (bel-shaz'-ahr). In the Book of Daniel, last king of Babylon, son and successor of Nebuchadrezzar ; warned of his doom by " handwriting on the wall," interpreted by Daniel, 332.

Belu'ga. Same as **White Whale.**

Belvedere (bel'-vi-dēr). In architecture, open structure or pavilion built on the top of a house.

Belvoir (bē'-ver). Dist. of Leicestershire famous for fox-hunting.

Benares (ben-ah'-rēz). City of India, in N.E., on r. Ganges ; pop. 263,000 ; 411, 412.

Ben Attow, Mt. (3,383 ft.) in Ross and Cromarty and Inverness-shire, Scot.

Benavente y Martinez, Jacinto (bā-nah-ven'-tā ē mahr-tē'-neth). Sp. dramatist ; 3051.

Benbow, John (1653–1702). Eng. admiral ; during his 2nd command in W. Indies (1702) fought his greatest battle against Fr.

Benc'kendorff, Alexander, Count (1849–1917). Russ. diplomatist ; as ambassador in London 1903–17 he encouraged friendly relations between Brit. and Russ.

Bend. In heraldry, 1614.

" Bends," a malady of divers, 1019.

Ben'digo. Australia, 4th city in Victoria ; pop. 30,779 ; large gold-field, 3321.

Benedict. Popes. For list see **Pope.**

Benedict XV (1854–1922). Pope, elected Pope in succession to Pius X, Sept. 3, 1914 ; observed strict neutrality in 1st World War, and made efforts to bring about peace.

Benedict, St., of Nursia (c. 480–543). It. monk, founder of the Benedictine order, 412, 2212.

Benedic'tines. Order of monks, 412 ; costume, 2214.

Benelux. Customs union of Be(lgium) Ne(therlands) Lux(emburg) ; took effect from Jan. 1, 1948 ; 2042.

Benes, Edvard (ben'-esh) (1884–1948). Czech president, 412, 2677, 3416.

Benevento (ba-na-ven'tō) (anc. Beneventum). It. ; pop. 37,800 ; arch of Trajan (114) ; battle of (1266). City badly damaged and cathedral almost destroyed in 2nd World War.

Beneven'tum, battle of (274 B.C.). Romans defeat Pyrrhus, 2710, 2807.

Bengal (ben-gawl'). Region of Indian sub-cont. ; pop. 62,000,000 ; 77,000 sq. m., 413 ; map, 1702 ; Brit. rule established, 842 ; Calcutta, 660 ; silk culture, 2972 ; partitioned, 1947, w. Bengal to India, E. Bengal to Pakistan.

Bengal, Bay of. Portion of Indian Ocean between India and Burma ; map, 1702 ; Ganges, 1417.

Bengal'i. One of chief modern languages of Hindustan, derived from Sanskrit ; 413 ; literature of modern development known through works of Tagore, 1713.

Bengal tiger, 3211.

Benghazi (beng-gah'-zē). Spt. of Libya ; pop. 64,600 ; taken by Italians (Oct. 1911) in Turco-It. War ; taken by British, Feb. 7, 1941 ; retaken Dec. 1941 ; finally occupied, Nov. 1942, 3418, 3420, map, 3421.

Benguela or **Benguella.** Spt. of Angola ; pop. 4,000 ; 3368.

Ben-Gurion, David (b. 1886). Israeli politician ; chairman from 1944 of executive of Jewish agency and world Zionist organization ; prominent in formation of Israeli state, in 1948 ; its first prime minister and min. of defence.

" Ben Hur." A Biblical novel. 3295; staged 1899 and 1902 ; filmed 1927, 1931 and 1937.

Beni-Hasan (bā'-ni has'-ahn). Village Upper Egypt ; rock tombs and paintings (about 3000 B.C.).

Benjamin. Youngest son of Jacob and Rachel, and ancestor of the tribe of Benjamin (Gen. xxxv. 18).

Ben Lawers. Mt. in Perthshire, Scot. ; 3,984 ft. high, 2558.

Ben Ledi. Mt. in Perthshire, Scot. ; near Callander, 2,875 ft. high.

Ben Lo'mond. Mt. (3,192 ft.) in N.W. of Stirlingshire, Scot. ; on shore of Loch Lomond, 2889 ; 3092.

Ben Lui. Mt. on Perthshire and Argyllshire borders, Scot. ; 3,708 ft. high.

Ben Macdhui (mak-do'-i). Mt. in Scot., on the borders of Aberdeenshire and Banffshire, 4,296 ft. high ; second highest mountain in Gt. Brit.

Ben More. Mt. in s.w. Perthshire, Scot., 3,843 ft. high, 2558.

Ben More Assynt. Mt. in Sutherlandshire, Scot., 3,273 ft.

Bennett, (Enoch) Arnold (1867–1931). Eng. novelist ; 414, 1215, 2403.

Bennett, Air Vice-Marshal Donald C. D. (b. 1910). Australian airman ; Commander of the Pathfinder Force of R.A.F. Bomber Command, 1944–45 ; pioneer in developing radar and Fido ; later in charge of British South American Airways, resigning 1948.

Bennett, James Gordon (1795–1872). Amer. journalist, b. Scot. ; originated detailed reporting of public events, practice of interviewing, use of telegraph in reporting, and system of distribution by carriers ; founder of the " New York Herald," started in 1835. His son, James Gordon

Bennett (1841–1918), was ed. and proprietor " New York Herald " ; sent Stanley to Africa.

Bennett, Richard Bedford, Vis. (1870–1947). Canadian politician ; Min. of Justice (1921) ; Min. of Finance (1926) ; Prime Min. (1930–35) ; Viscount, 1941.

Bennett, Sir William Sterndale (1816–75). Brit. musician ; composer of symphonies, music for pianoforte, and choral works.

Ben Nev'is. Inverness-shire ; highest peak in Scot. and Brit. Isles (4,406 ft.) ; a 15-mile tunnel supplying water power for an aluminium works passes through the mountain ; 414, 583, 1737, 2889.

Ben Nuis. Isl. of Arran, Scot., climbing on, 2247.

Benois, Alexandre (b. 1870). Russian artist and scene painter, 2855.

Benson, Arthur Christopher (1862–1925). Eng. essayist and literary critic ; eldest son of Archbishop Benson (" The Upton Letters," " From a College Window," " Beside Still Waters ").

Benson, Edward Frederic (1867–1940). Eng. novelist ; brother of above ; " Dodo," published in 1893, brought him to the front as a novelist.

Benson, Edward White (1829–96). Eng. churchman, Archbishop of Canterbury.

Benson, Sir Francis (Frank) Robert (1858–1939). Eng. actor ; founded the Benson Shakespearian repertory company, in 1884.

Benson, Robert Hugh (1871–1914). Rom. Cath. priest ; wrote much on religious subjects and several novels (" The Light Invisible " ; " Christ in the Church " ; " Come Rack ! Come Rope ! " ; " An Average Man ").

Benson, Stella (1892–1933). Brit. novelist ; " Tobit Transplanted," " Goodbye Stranger."

Bentham, George (1800–84). Brit. botanist ; author of " Handbook of Brit. Botany " ; revised by Hooker, 1892 ; Rendle, 1925.

Ben'tham, Jeremy (1748–1832). Eng. philosopher and jurist, 414 ; philosophy of, 2571, 2572.

Bentley, Edmund Clerihew (b. 1875). Brit. journalist, novelist, etc., inventor of the form of verse known as the clerihew.

Bentley, Richard (1662–1742). Famous Eng. classical scholar (" Dissertation on Epistles of Phalaris ").

Benue (ben'-wē). River of w. Central Africa, over 800 m., tributary of Niger. 2367. Now gives its name to a prov. of N. Nigeria, formerly Nassarawa.

Ben Vorlich. Scot. mt., Dumbarton, 3,092 ft., 1054.

Ben Vrack e, Scot. mt. ; infra-red photograph, 2584.

Benzaldehyde. The essential oil of almonds ; used in many flavouring substances and perfumes, and the manufacture of benzoic acid and dyes ; prepared from toluol or benzol, 857.

Ben'zene, known commercially as benzole or benzol. Product of the distillation of coal-tar ; many drugs and dyes, including aniline dyes, may be made from it as a starting-point ; often added to motor fuel, 2564; 699, 857 ; plant, 1406.

Ben'zine, or petroleum ether. A mixture obtained by the fractional distillation of petroleum ; not to be confused with benzene ; much used for cleaning purposes, 1289.

Benzo'ic acid. A bacteriostatic, used in tooth pastes, the seasoning of tobacco, manufacture of dyes and preservatives, 857 ; in food preservation, 1340.

Benzol(e). The commercial name for benzene. See **Benzene.**

Beowulf (bā'-ō-woolf). Hero of early Anglo-Saxon epic poem, which bears his name, 415, 1210.

" Be Prepared." Boy Scouts' motto, 542.

Béranger (bā-rahn'-zhā), **Pierre Jean de** (1780–1857). Fr. song-writer, poet of the people, and political satirist.

Berar (bā-rahr). Region of India forming since 1903 part of the Central Provinces, 741; area 17,808 sq. m., pop. 3,605,000; produces cotton, wheat, etc.

Berbera. Cap. and chief spt. of British Somaliland on Gulf of Aden; pop. about 20,000; 3000.

Berbers. Anc. white race of N. Africa; includes Kabyles and Tuaregs; gave name to Barbary states; 66, 2227; Algeria, 117; Morocco, 2231; Sahara, 2860; Tunis, 3254.

Berchtesgaden (bärkh'-tes-gaht-en). Village in S. Bavaria, and country resort of Hitler; here Hitler received Neville Chamberlain on his first visit to Germany, Sept. 1938; bombed and captured, 1945.

Berchtold (bärkh'-tolt), **Leopold, Count von** (1863–1942). Austro-Hungarian statesman who, as ambassador to Rus. and foreign minister (1912–15), vainly strove to further Austria's interests in the Balkans; in 1914 he favoured war with Serbia and tried to secure new Allies for Central Powers.

Berdichev (ber-dē'-chef). *See* Ossipevsk.

Ber'esford, Charles William, 1st Baron (1846–1919). Eng. admiral, member of Parl. and author; second son of 4th Marquis of Waterford; in command of Naval Brigade at Abu Klea; held all the highest naval commands; made a peer in 1916.

Beresford, John Davys (1873–1947). Eng. novelist ("Jacob Stahl"; "The Hampdenshire Wonder"; "Revolution").

Berg, Alban (1885–1935). Austrian composer; works include opera "Wozzeck."

Bergamo (bêr'-gah-mō), It. Picturesque tn. nr. Milan; pop. 86,000; notable old churches; silk and other textiles.

Bergen, Norway, chief port on S.W. coast: pop. 109,000; exports fish and fish products; ship-building, 2397; and Hanseatic League, 1575, 2393. Occupied by Germany 1940; here British and Norwegian naval mission received the surrender of German naval authority in Norway.

Bergius Process, for obtaining fuel oil from coal-tar, 857, 1674.

Bergner, Elisabeth (b. 1898). Austrian actress ("St. Joan," "The Constant Nymph," "Escape Me Never," "Catherine the Great," Rosalind in "As You Like It").

Bergson (bärg'-son), **Henri** (1859–1941). Fr. philosopher who denied claim of science to explain universe on mechanical principles ("Time and Free Will"; "Matter and Memory"; "Creative Evolution"; "Laughter"); awarded Nobel Prize for Literature in 1927; 1382.

Beri-beri, nervous disease resulting in paralysis, dropsy, and frequently death, 1458, 2775, 3326.

Bering (bär'-ing) or **Behring, Vitus** (1680–1741), Danish navigator, commissioned by Peter the Great to explore N.E. Asiatic coasts for Russia; discoverer of Bering Strait and Alaska, 415, 2644.

Bering Sea, arm of N. Pacific Ocean between Alaska and Siberia, 415, 2469; *map, 99*; seal fisheries arbitration, 415.

Bering Strait, channel separating Asia and N. Amer. and connecting N. Pacific with Arctic Ocean, 415; *map, 99*; route of Asiatic migration to N. Amer.

Berkeley, George (1685–1753). Ir. idealistic philosopher; maintained that matter has no existence independent of mind; political economist, writer and Anglican bishop.

Berkshire (bahrk'-shēr). Eng. co., a. 725 sq. m.; pop. 361,000; 415.

Berlichingen (bär'-lêkh-ing-en), **Götz von** (1480–1562), "Götz with the iron hand"; Ger. feudal knight

and soldier of fortune; subject of drama by Goethe.

Berlin. Former cap. of all Germany. E. Berlin is cap. of the Russian-sponsored E. German Democratic Repub.; W. Berlin, though economically dependent on W. Germany, has its own govt. Pop. 2,932,430; 416; Brandenburg Gate, 416; Tiergarten, 416; modern buildings, 417; Unter den Linden, 417; fell to Russians May 2, 1945, 3424; air-lift, 1453. *See* Potsdam.

Berlin, Irving (b. 1888). Amer. musician; composer of popular songs.

Berlin Conference (1884) and Africa, 72.

Berlin Congress (1878), Bosnia and Herzegovina, 345; Serbia and Bulgaria, 614; Serbia independent, 2922.

Berlin Decree. Issued by Napoleon, Nov. 12, 1806, beginning of "Continental System."

Ber'liner, Emil, inventor of gramophone, 1496.

Berlin Pact, or **Tripartite Pact.** Military, political and economic agreement, in 1940, between Germany, Italy, and Japan; to establish a "New Order in Europe and Greater Asia." *See* Axis.

Berlin Secession, in German art, 1455.

Berlin-to-Baghdad Railway, 339.

Berlin, University of, 416.

Berlioz (bär'-lē-ōz), **Hector** (1803–69), Fr. musical composer, brilliant romanticist, father of modern orchestration ("Damnation of Faust," "Symphonie Fantastique").

Ber'mondsey. Met. bor. of London; pop. 111,452. Extensive air raid damage during 2nd World War.

Bermu'da lily, parts in detail, *1323–28.*

Bermudas, group of Brit. isls. in Atlantic Ocean; 19 sq. m.; pop. 34,000; 418. Sites leased to U.S.A. as air and naval bases, 1940; in 1941 Tucker and Morgan islands opened to U.S.A. on 99-yr. lease as flying-boat base.

Bermudez. State in N. Venezuela, between Orinoco r. and Caribbean Sea.

Bermudez (ber-mū'-thāz), **Juan** (b. 1495). Span. sailor; discovered Bermudas, 418.

Bermudian rig, for racing yachts, 483.

Bernadette (bairn-ah-det) (1844–79). Fr. saint: at the age of 14 had visions of the Virgin Mary at the grotto of Massabieille; there a spring began to flow, now the waters of Lourdes; canonized in 1933.

Bernadotte (bêrn'-a-dot), **Folke, Count** (1895–1948). Swedish humanitarian; nephew of King Gustavus V; intermediary in Ger. offer of unconditional surrender to Gt. Brit. and U.S.A., April 1945, 3422; also between Arabs and Jews 1947–48; assassinated in Jerusalem by Jewish terrorists, Sept. 17, 1948; 2483.

Bernadotte (bêr-na-dot'-i), **Jean Baptiste Jules** (1764–1844). Fr. general, elected crown prince of Sweden, 3131. Ruled as King Charles XIV (1818–44).

Bernal', John Desmond (b. 1901). Brit. scientist; eminent crystallographer; important in Operational Research, Second World War; wrote "The Social Functions of Science."

Bernard (bär'-nahr), **Claude** (1813–78). Fr. physiologist, discoverer of digestive work of pancreatic juice, sugar-forming work of liver, and existence of vaso-motor and vaso-constrictor nerves.

Bernard, St., of Clairvaux (1090–1153). Fr. monk, one of most illustrious and eloquent preachers of Middle Ages; opposes Abelard, 11; preaches 2nd Crusade, 936; victory over Mahomedans, 128.

Berne. Cap. of Switzerland; pop. 130,000; 418, 419, 3142.

Berners, Dame Juliana. Perhaps first Eng. woman writer; wrote "Boke of St. Albans" (1486).

Bernese' Oberland or **Alps**, dist. in Switzerland, 3138, *3142, plate, 132.*

Bern'hard, Prince of the Netherlands (b. 1911). Prince of Lippe-Biesterfeld; consort of Queen Juliana of the Netherlands; in 1941 was liaison officer between Netherlands and Brit. forces (army, navy, and air force); at inauguration of Juliana, *2322.*

Bernhardi (bär-nahr'-dē), **Friedrich von** (1849–1930). Ger. general and author ("Germany and the Next War"; "World Power or Downfall").

Bernhardt (bär-nahr; Eng., bêrn'-hart), **Sarah** (1845–1923). Fr. actress, 419.

Bernina Alps. Mt. range bordering Switzerland and Italy (13,290 ft.).

Bernini (bêr-nē'-nē), **Giovanni Lorenzo** (1598–1680). It. architect, sculptor and painter; designed the colonnade of St. Peter's and a palace for Urban VIII; director of public works at Rome; *2631.*

Bernouilli (bairn-wē-yē), **Daniel** (1700–82). Swiss mathematician, member of a family of which nine others were well known scientists; prof. of maths. at St. Petersburg, of anatomy and physics at Groningen, and of anatomy, physics and botany at Basle; observations of flowing liquids, 2154.

Berruguete, Alonzo (1486–1561). Span. artist, 3040.

Bersaglieri (bêr-sal-yär'-i). Corps of It. sharpshooters.

Bertha or **Berthrada** (d. 783). Mother of Charlemagne.

Berthelot (bärt'-lō), **Pierre Eugène Marcellin** (1827–1907). Fr. chemist; founded synthetic chemistry and thermochemistry; proved organic compounds may be produced outside of living bodies.

Berthollet (bär-tol'-ā), **Claude Louis, Count** (1748–1822). Fr. chemist; first physical chemist; with Lavoisier contributed to modern chemical nomenclature.

Bertillon (bär'-tē-yawn), **Alphonse** (1853–1914). Fr. anthropologist; introduced system of measurements for identifying criminals.

Berwick-on-Tweed. Tn. at mouth of Tweed on Scottish border; pop. 12,000; 419, 420.

Berwickshire. Marit. co. of Scot. separated from Eng. by the r. Tweed; a. 457 sq. m.; pop. 26,000; 420.

Ber'wyn Mountains. Range of N. Wales, between Merionethshire and Montgomeryshire; 2,715 ft. high.

Ber'yl, a not uncommon mineral; source of beryllium; colour varies from blue to light green and yellow.

Beryllium (Be), hard white metallic element of the alkaline earth metal group; at. No. 4; at. weight 9·02; melts at 1280°C.; obtained from and named after beryl; 420; in atomic experiments, 298.

Berzel'ius, Jöns Jakob, Baron (1779–1848), Swedish chemist, discovered selenium thorium, and other elements; inventor of chemical symbols; 2919; and tellurium, 3185; isolated zirconium, 3444.

Besançon (bez-ahn'-sawn). Fr. fortified city on r. Doubs; pop. 65,000; watches and clocks; notable Rom. remains.

Besant (bez-ant'), **Annie** (1847–1933). Eng. theosophist; prominent in socialist and Indian nationalist movements.

Besant, Sir Walter (1836–1901). Eng. novelist, mostly in collaboration with James Rice ("All Sorts and Conditions of Men").

Bessara'bia. Territory of S.W. Russia, formerly in Rumania; partly in Moldavia S.S.R., and remainder in Ukraine S.S.R.; 17,146 sq. m.; pop. 2,865,500; incorporated in Soviet Union, Aug. 1940; 2841, 3418.

Bessborough, Vere Brabazon Ponsonby 9th Earl of (b. 1880). Brit. statesman; Gov.-Gen. of Canada, 1931–35; created Earl of U.K. in 1937.

Bes'sel, Friedrich Wilhelm (1784–1846). Ger. astronomer and mathematician, 3078 ; and Sirius, 3079.

Bes'semer, Sir Henry (1813–98), Eng. inventor, 420 ; Bessemer process of making steel, 421, 1756 ; works at Sheffield, 2941.

Be'ta, β, B (Rom. b, B). Second letter of Gk. alphabet ; in astronomy usually denotes the second brightest star in a constellation.

Be'ta Centau'ri, a star, 3078.

Beta rays, 298 ; of radium, 2731, 2733.

Be'tatron. Electron-producing machine used in atomic research, 422 ; form of cyclotron.

Betel (bē'-tl), nut of E. Indian palm ; a preparation of the nuts is chewed by the natives ; 2408.

Betelgeuse (bet'-el-gēz), fixed star, 3081.

Beth'any. Village near Jerusalem often mentioned in Gospels ; home of Mary, Martha and Lazarus ; modern village El-Azariyeh.

Bethel, Palestine. Village (" House of God ") 10 m. N. of Jerusalem (Gen. xii, 8 ; xxviii).

Bethes'da. Pool in anc. Jerusalem with miraculous healing qualities.

Beth'lehem, Palestine, birthplace of Jesus ; pop. 9,000 ; 422, 1821, 2480 ; people of, plates f. 2480, 2481.

Bethlehem, Pennsylvania, U.S.A. City on r. Lehigh ; noted for large iron and steel works ; pop. 57,892.

Bethmann - Hollweg (bāt-mahn hol'-vǎkh), **Theobald von** (1856–1921), Ger. statesman, imperial chancellor (1909–17).

Beth'nal Green. Met. and parl. bor. of E. London ; pop. 108,178 ; has branch of Victoria and Albert Museum.

Betrothal Customs, 2109.

Betty, William (1791–1874), Eng. actor, known as " Young Roscius " ; famous as boy actor (in " Hamlet," etc.) from 1803 to 1808.

Betulaceae (bet-ū-lā'-si-ē), the birch family, including birches, hazels, and alders, 3619.

Beur'ling, Flt.-Lt. G. F. (" Screwball ") (b. 1921). R.A.F. fighter ace ; shot down 28 enemy planes in siege of Malta, 1940–42.

Beuthen (boi'ten), Poland. Mining and industrial tn. in Silesia ; pop. 86,881 ; incorp. from Germany, 1945.

Bevan, Aneurin (b. 1897). Brit. Labour politician ; Minister of Health, 1945.

Bev'eridge, William Henry, 1st Baron (b. 1879). Brit. economist ; director of London School of Economics, 1919–37 ; master of University Coll., Oxford, 1937–45 ; author of Beveridge Report, 1942, recommending unemployment insurance for all, free medical and hospital treatment, child benefits, marriage and death grants ; many of its proposals became law as National Insurance Bill, in Jan. 1946, 2994.

Bevin, Ernest (b. 1881). Eng. Labour politician. Gen. Sec. Transport and General Workers' Union, 1922-46 ; Min. of Labour, 1940 ; Foreign Secretary, 1945 ; 422.

Bewick, Thomas (1753–1828). Eng. wood engraver ; illustrated many books (" British Birds" ; "Aesop's Fables").

Bey, hereditary title of native sovereign of Tunis ; also title of nobility in Turkish Empire until 1934.

Beyle (bāl), **Marie Henri.** See Stendhal.

Beyer-Garratt, type of locomotive, 1986.

Beziers (bāz'-yā). Cath. tn. and trade centre in S. France ; pop. 73,000 ; massacre of Albigenses in 1209.

Bhamo (bah'-mō). Tn. and dist. of Upper Burma, 40 m. from Chinese border and 300 m. N.E. of Mandalay ; head of navigation of Irrawaddy ; centre for China-Burma trade ; occupied by Japs, May 1942 ; last Jap. stronghold in Burma to fall, Dec. 1944.

Bharatpur (bah-rat-pōōr'). One of the four states forming the Matsya union, India ; scene of famous British charge against the Jats (1826).

Bhils (bēlz). Savage dark-skinned race of cent. India, 1701.

Bhil'sa, town of Bhopal, Central India. Carved gate of the Sanchi Tope, 1709.

Bhutan (boo-tahn'). State in E. Himalayas between Tibet and India ; a. 18,000 sq. m. ; pop. 300,000 ; agric., stock-raising ; map, 1702.

Biarritz (bē-ar-ētz'). Fr. watering place on Bay of Biscay near Bayonne ; pop. 22,955 ; summer residence of Napoleon III.

Bias, current applied to grid of thermionic valve, 3199.

Bible, 423 ; Abraham, 13 ; Apocrypha, 424 ; Apostles, 188 ; Bede's translation, 423 ; Borrow, 527 ; Caedmon's " Paraphrases," 650, 1211 ; Codex Sinaiticus, 424, 425, 511 ; Coverdale's translation, 426 ; Daniel, 968 ; David, 979 ; Douai version, 426 ; Erasmus's Edition of New Testament, 1221, 2758, 2764 ; Esther, 1225 ; French translation, 1380 ; Gothic translation, 1456 ; Jesus Christ, 1821 ; Jewish history, 1829 ; Job, 1832 ; King James' version, 427 ; Luther and, 2041, 2758 ; Mazarin, first book printed from type, 427, 2685 ; medieval manuscripts, 510 ; Moses, 2235 ; New Testament, 425 ; Old Testament, 425, 2692 ; Paul, 2529 ; Peter, 2562 ; " poor man's," 2686 ; Prophets, 2691 ; Psalms, 979 ; Ruth, 2857 ; Solomon, 2999 ; Tyndale's translation, 426, 3269 ; Ulfilas's translation, 1456 ; Wycliffe's translation, 3428 ; Ximenes' "Complutension Polyglot, 427. Published in Basic English, July 1949.

BOOKS OF THE BIBLE.

OLD TESTAMENT

Genesis	Ecclesiastes
Exodus	Song of Solomon
Leviticus	Isaiah
Numbers	Jeremiah
Deuteronomy	Lamentations
Joshua	Ezekiel
Judges	Daniel
Ruth	Hosea
1 Samuel	Joel
2 Samuel	Amos
1 Kings	Obadiah
2 Kings	Jonah
1 Chronicles	Micah
2 Chronicles	Nahum
Ezra	Habakkuk
Nehemiah	Zephaniah
Esther	Haggai
Job	Zechariah
Psalms	Malachi
Proverbs	

NEW TESTAMENT

Matthew	1 Timothy
Mark	2 Timothy
Luke	Titus
John	Philemon
Acts	Hebrews
Romans	James
1 Corinthians	1 Peter
2 Corinthians	2 Peter
Galatians	1 John
Ephesians	2 John
Philippians	3 John
Colossians	Jude
1 Thessalonians	Revelation
2 Thessalonians	

Bibliography. Methodical study of books, 427.

Bibliothèque Nationale (bē-blē-ō-tāk' nas-ē-ō-nahl'). National library of France, 1930.

Bi'ceps muscle, 2258.

Bicester (bis'-ter) **Hunt**, 1162.

Bichat (bē'-shah), **Marie F. X.** (1771–1802). Fr. anatomist and physiologist, founder of general anatomy.

Bichlo'ride of mercury, 2146, 2638.

Bicycles and motor-cycles. See Cycles and Cycling.

Bidault (bē'dō), **Georges** (b. 1900), Fr. politician ; leader of M.R.P. party in 1945 ; Premier June–Nov. 1946; For. Min. in successive govts. until 1948 ; Premier again Oct. 1949–June 1950.

Biela's (bē-lahz) **Comet**, 880.

Biely, Andrei (1880–1934). Rus. writer, 2856.

Bien'nial plants, 2624.

" Big Ben." The great bell in the clock tower at the Houses of Parliament, named after Sir Benjamin Hall, First Commissioner of Works, when it was hung in 1856 ; face, 844.

Big'amy. Having more than one spouse alive at the same time, 2108.

" Big Bertha." Ger. siege gun, 2518.

Big Bone Cave, Tennessee, U.S.A., 734.

Big Dipper. Constellation. See Great Bear.

Big'elow, Erastus Brigham (1814–79), Amer. inventor, 707.

" Big Five," in banking, 356.

Big Game. African, 59, 60.

Bighorn. Rocky Mt. sheep, 2795, 2940.

Bight, of rope, 1868, 1869.

Bihar (bē-hahr'). State of India, lying w. of Bengal ; a. 69,000 sq. m. ; pop. 36,000,000, 428.

Bikaner (bē-kah'-nēr), India. Cap. of state of Bikaner, Rajputana ; pop. 69,410.

Bikini (bik-ē'-nē) **Atoll**, in Marshall Islands, Pacific Ocean. Here on July 1, 1946, a U.S. navy-army force exploded an atomic bomb against 73 obsolete warships ; on July 24 another was exploded under water. Almost three years later the atoll was still uninhabitable because of radio-activity.

Bilbao (bil-bā'-ō). Chief spt. of N. Sp., on Nervion ; pop. 205,717 ; exports iron ore from near-by mines ; long famous for sword-blades (called " bilbos ") ; captured by insurgents in Civil War (1937) ; 3031.

Bilberry. A low shrub, 428.

Bile, 1017, 1470, 1968.

Bill, of birds. See in Index Beak.

Billiard balls, 428, 739.

Billiards, indoor game, 428, 429.

Billingham-on-Tees. Tn. of Durham ; pop. 23,000 ; petrol manufacture at, 2430, 2429.

Billingsgate. London's famous fish market, near London Bridge on left bank of r. Thames ; elec. installation, 1545.

Billion. A million millions. (In France and America, a thousand millions.)

Bill of exchange. A written order from one person to another directing him to pay to a third person a sum of money which is to be charged to the account of the writer, 1348 ; and credit system, 924.

Bill of lading. A written acknowledgment of goods received for transportation issued by the master of a ship ; acts as a contract to deliver the goods ; when issued by a railway such a bill is called a way bill.

Bill of Rights, in Eng., 429 ; and Parl. govt., 1489.

Bill of sale. A formal written statement of the sale of personal property ; necessary when the transfer of the property does not occur at once.

Biltong', kind of dried meat, 1340.

Bi-metallism. System in which two metals, usually gold and silver, are used as currency standards.

Binding machines, agric., 79.

Bindings, book, 515, 516, 517, 518.

Bindweeds. Various plants of the genus Convolvulus, 898.

Binet (bē'-nā), **Alfred** (1857–1914). Fr. psychologist ; devised intelligence tests.

Bingen (bing'-en). Ger. tn. on Rhine, 2769 ; pop. 10,200 ; noted for Mouse Tower.

Binh-Dinh (bin'-din). Largest tn. in Annam, Indo-China ; pop. 74,000.

Bin'nacle. A compass casing, 881, 882.

Binoc'ulars, field glasses, 3088, 3189 ; principle in microscopes, 2163, 2164.

Bino'mial theorem, in algebra, 115.

Binyon, Robert Laurence (1869–1943). British poet (" To the Fallen ") ; author of books on art.

Biochemistry. Chemistry of the life processes, 429 ; radio-active tracers in, 1760.

Biography. Personal history, a literature ; and autobiography, 430.

Biol'ogy. The science of life which deals with the properties, growth, conditions, etc., of living matter, 430 ; anatomy and morphology, 531 ; animal kingdom, 156 ; animals distinguished from plants, 156 ; botany, 531 ; cells as life units, 738, *739* ; chemistry of life processes, 1016, 1079 ; ecology, 1079 ; embryology, 1154 ; evolution and origin of life, 977, 1244 ; heredity, 1617 ; parasites, 2512 ; plant life, 2620 ; protoplasm, 2695 ; zoology, 3446. *See also* Reproduction and index entries on chief subjects listed above.

Bi'on. Gk. pastoral poet, 1541.

Bio-physics. Physics as applied to the life processes.

Bi'otite, brown variety of mica, 2160.

Bi'plane. Aeroplane with two supporting planes, 45, *47.*

Birch, 436 ; found farthest north of all trees, 3246.

Bird, Cyril Kenneth. Brit. humorous artist. *See* Fougasse.

Bird cherry, tree, 778.

Bird-eating spider, 3065, *plate f. 3064.*

Birds. Feathered vertebrate animals, **437** ; archaeopteryx, earliest known type, *437,* 2681 ; behaviour of, 159 ; classification, 448 ; coloration, 447, 2692 ; eggs, *plate f. 440,* 442, 1093 ; evolved from reptiles, 437 ; feathers, 1264 ; feet, *448* ; first appear in Jurassic period, 1433 ; geographical distribution, 440 ; incubation, 444, 1095 ; instinct, 159, 162 ; used as lamps, *1887* ; mating, 441 ; migration, 440, 2169, *2171* ; moulting, 1265 ; in Nature study, *2286,* 2289 ; nests, 442, *443,* 447, *3360* ; nesting boxes, *444,* 445 ; prehistoric, 437, 2681 ; skeleton, *438* ; vertebrate animals, 437 ; vocal organs, 441 ; wing, 437. *See also* names of the various birds.

"Birds, The," by Aristophanes, 231.

Bird's-nest soup, 3125.

Birds of Paradise, 2511 ; *frontis. Vol. 6.*

Birds of prey. Term used loosely to include all vultures, eagles, hawks, falcons, and even owls. Strictly speaking, should be reserved for the eagles, hawks, and falcons of the order *Accipitriformes.*

Bird'wood, William Riddell, 1st Baron (b. 1865). Brit. general ; commanded Brit. forces at Gallipoli in 1st World War, also 5th Army in Fr. (1918–19) ; com.-in-chief in India (1925–29) ; Field-Marshal (1925) ; Master of Peterhouse, Cambridge (1931–38) ; cr. baron, 1938.

Bireme (bī'-rēm) Anc. type of ship with two tiers of oars.

Biret'ta. Square cap worn by Rom. Cath. clergy ; white for pope, red for cardinal, purple for bishop, black for others, 1584.

Bir Hacheim (bēr hak-em'). Outpost in Libya, 50 m. s.w. of Tobruk, held by Fighting Fr. under Gen. Koenig from May 26 to June 10, 1942, against odds ; *map, 3421.*

Birkbeck, George (1776–1841). Eng. educationist ; founder of Birkbeck College, 457.

Birkenhead. Spt. and shipbuilding centre in Cheshire, on Mersey ; pop., 116,000 ; 457.

Birkenhead. Brit. troopship, 457.

Bir'kenhead, Frederick Edwin Smith, Baron (1872–1930). Brit. lawyer and politician ; b. at Birkenhead ; Unionist M.P., 1906 ; led Ulster M.P.s against Home Rule bill ; solicitorgen., 1915 ; lord chancellor and baron, 1919 ; signed Irish treaty, 1921 ; viscount, 1921 ; earl, 1922 ; secy. for India, 1924–28 ; famous orator and robust personality.

Birkett, Sir William Norman (b. 1883). Barrister-at-law. K.C., 1924 ; Liberal M.P. Nottingham 1923–24 ; 1929–31 ; Justice of High Court, 1941.

Birmingham. City of Eng. Pop. 1,020,000 ; **457,** *458, 1164,* 1165, 3341.

Birmingham, Alabama, U.S.A. Chief city of the state ; pop. 267,500, iron and steel manufactures.

Birmingham, George A. (1865–1950). Pen name of Canon James Owen Hannay, Irish clergyman and novelist ("General John Regan" ; "Spanish Gold ").

Birmingham, University of. Birmingham, Eng. ; established 1900 ; about 1,750 students, *frontis. Vol. 7.*

Bir'nam. Vil. in Perthshire, Scot., 15 m. N.W. of Perth ; remains of a vitrified fort near ; Birnam Wood mentioned in " Macbeth."

Bir'rell, Augustine (1850–1933). Eng. essayist and political leader ; chief secretary for Ireland 1907–16 (" Obiter Dicta " ; " Men, Women and Books " ; critical biographies of Charlotte Brontë, William Hazlitt, Andrew Marvell).

Bis'cay, Bay of, part of Atlantic Ocean, w. of Fr. and N. of Spain, *1359, 3030.*

Biscuit and Bread, 633.

Biscuit ware. Same as **Bisque.**

Bisharin (bish-ar-ēn'). African tribe, 70.

Bishop. In Christian Church, costume, 826.

Bishop, William Avery. Canad. air pilot; received V.C. 1917 ; victor of 72 air combats. Director of Recruiting, Royal Canad. Air Force, 1940.

Bishops' Bible, 426.

Bis'kra, Algeria. Winter resort and important military post in fertile oasis ; pop. 9,000.

Bisley. Vil. in Surrey ; rifle-range, *2961. See also* **King's Prize.**

"Bismarck." Ger. battleship of 56,200 tons ; on May 24, 1941, she sank the Hood and damaged the Prince of Wales and escaped ; hit by a torpedo from a Swordfish from aircraft-carrier Illustrious, she was finally sunk by a torpedo from cruiser Dorsetshire on May 27.

Bis'marck, Otto von (1815–98). Ger. soldier and statesman, creator of German empire ; as Prussian chancellor waged war against Denmark, 1864, for Schleswig-Holstein ; against Austria, 1866, and against France, 1870 ; 2696 ; Ems dispatch, and Franco-Prussian War, 1384 ; and German Empire, 1449 ; and William I, 3378.

Bismarck Archipelago. Group of isls. N.E. of New Guinea ; New Britain, New Ireland, Admiralty Isls., etc., 2470, *2471* ; acquired by Ger. ; assigned to Australia, 2473 ; Japanese occupied part, 1942–45 ; sea battle, 2474.

Bismuth (biz'-muth), **458** ; anti-magnetic, 2062 ; in pitchblende, 2731.

Bi'son, or " American buffalo," **459,** *460* ; Alberta herd, 103 ; in Canada, *677* ; European, in Poland, *1234.*

Bisque, or biscuit ware, 2666.

Bis'sing, Moritz von, Baron (1844–1917). Ger. military gov.-gen. of Belgium (1914–17).

Bithyn'ia. Anc. country of N.W. Asia Minor on Black Sea.

Bitlis (bit-lēs'). Trade centre in Asiatic Turkey ; pop. 15,000 ; occupied by Rus. (1916) in 1st World War.

Bitolj. *See* Monastir.

Bitter almonds, oil of, 124, 1263.

Bittern. Marsh bird, **461** ; heron a relative, 3100.

Bitter orange, 2444.

Bittersweet. Hedgerow plant, **462,** 2370.

" Bitter Sweet." Operetta by Noel Coward, first staged in 1929.

Bitu'men, 2426 ; asphalt, 272.

Bitu'minous or **soft coal,** 855 ; does not contain bitumen, 855.

Bi'valve. Mollusc with two-piece shell, 2199, 2942 ; cockles and mussels, 860 ; oysters, 2466 ; scallop, 2879.

Bizerta. Fortified spt. of Tunis, pop. 28,500 ; occupied by Axis 1942 ; retaken 1943, 3420.

Bizet (bē'-zā), **Georges** (1838–75). Fr. musical composer ; " Carmen," 2438.

Björnson, Björnstjerne (byernst'-yernā byērn'-son) (1832–1910). Norwegian writer, 462, 2403, 2880.

Björnsson (byērn'-son), **Sveinn** (b. 1881). Icelandic statesman ; regent in 1941, when Iceland became independent of Denmark ; pres. in 1944, when Iceland became repub.

Black. A " colour," 875, 876.

Black, Adam (1784–1874). Scot. publisher and politician ; founded A. and C. Black, who secured copyrights of " Encyclopaedia Britannica " and Scott's " Waverley Novels."

Black, Prof. Davidson, and Peking Man., 2078.

Black, Joseph (1728–99). Brit. chemist and physicist, b. in Fr. ; discovered latent and specific heat, 1901.

Black and Tans. Nickname given to a force raised in 1920 by the British Government for service in Ireland and disbanded in 1922. They wore a black beret with a khaki uniform and were attached to the Royal Irish Constabulary.

Black ant. Insect, *165.*

Black ash. Calcium sulphide, 2997.

Blackball, 351.

Blackberry. Fruit-bearing shrub, 463 ; *plate f. 1401.*

Blackbird, 447, **463** ; egg *plate f. 440* " featherwear " instead of moulting 447.

Black'burn. Cotton mfg. tn. in Lan cashire ; pop. 105,000 ; **463.**

Blackcap, a warbler, 3340.

Blackcock. Species of grouse, 1551.

Black Country. Coal-mining and mfg dist. in Midlands of Eng. between Birmingham and Wolverhampton 1165, 3072, 3407.

Black currant, 944.

Black Death. An epidemic that swep Europe in the 14th cent., 463 ; in Edward III's reign, 1091 ; and English agriculture, 85 ; carried b rats, 2746.

Black earth belt, in Rus., 2844.

Blackett, Patrick Maynard Stuar (b. 1897). Eng. physicist, 2594 Awarded Nobel prize for physics 1948.

" Blackface meets his neighbours," story, 3481.

Blackfeet or **Blackfoot.** Tribe of Plain Indians of Algonquian stock, 275 *2755,* 2756.

Black Forest. Ger., 464 ; mts., 3330 peasant costume, *464* ; source o Danube, 972.

Black Friars. Same as **Dominica** **Friars.**

Blackfriars Bridge, London, 2012.

Black-headed gull, *1556.*

Blackheath. Open common and res dential dist. in s.E. London ; scer of many historic gatherings ; rallyin place of Wat Tyler and Jack Cade Rectory Field is headquarters o famous Blackheath Rugby Footba Club.

" Black Hole " of Calcutta, 660. T illus. on page 661 shows the memori erected in 1902 ; the site is near.

Black Market. The illicit selling rationed goods in short supply a prices higher than the legal maximu or the usual market price.

Black Marten. Trade name for skur fur, 2980.

Black Monks. Same as **Benedictine**

Blackmore, Richard Doddridge (182 1900). Eng. novelist, author " Lorna Doone," one of the mc popular novels of the 19th cent.

Blackpool. Popular watering place Lancashire on Irish Sea. Pc about 142,800, 1890.

Black poplar, 2655.

Black powder, or gunpowder, 1558.

Black Prince. *See* Edward, the Bla Prince.

Black race, 2723, 2725.

Black Sea. Between s.E. Europe a. Asia Minor, **464** ; *map,* 465. B porus outlet, 528 ; receives 4 gr rivers, 1232.

Blackshirts. Name given to membe of the former Fascist party in Ita by reason of their uniform.

Blacksmith, English, *1173.*

Blackstone, Sir William (1723–80). E jurist ; wrote " Commentaries the Laws of England," foundati of legal training.

Blackstrap, final molasses in sug refining, 3113.

Black swan, 3125.

Blackthorn, or sloe, 2630.

Black vulture, 3330.

Blackwall Tunnel, 3257.

Blackwater, r. of Eng., 40 m., flowing to North Sea ; 1225.

Blackwater, r. of Eire, chiefly in Cork Co. ; flows E. and S. 100 m. to sea at Youghal Bay, 1744.

" Black widow," spider, 3065.

Blackwood, Algernon (b. 1869). Brit. novelist ; tales of fantasy and horror. (" The Centaur " ; " A Prisoner in Fairyland " ; " Day and Night Stories ").

Blackwood, William (1776–1834). Founder of the Scot. publishing house of William Blackwood and Sons ; started " Blackwood's Magazine," April 1817.

Bladder, 1855.

Bladderwort. An insect-eating plant, 3624, plate f. 2621.

Bladder-wrack. The common brown seaweed which has small bladders on its fronds. These pop when trodden on.

Blade, of a leaf, 1914.

Blaeberry. See Bilberry.

Blairgow'rie and Rattray. Scot. tn. in Perthshire ; noted for fruit ; jute mfrs. ; pop. 5,000 ; 2558.

Blake, Robert (1599–1657), Eng. admiral, 465, 466 ; greatest feat, defeat of Spanish fleet off Canary Islands in 1657.

Blake, William (1757–1827), Eng. poet, painter and engraver, 466, 467, 1182, 1213 ; Swinburne on, 3138.

Bla'mey, Field-Marshal Sir Thomas A. (b. 1884). Australian soldier ; in 1940 C.-in-C. of Australian forces in Egypt ; in 1942 C.-in-C. Allied Land Forces S.W. Pacific ; reconquered New Guinea ; resigned command in Sept. 1945. Created F.-M. in 1950.

Blanc (blahn), **Jean Joseph Louis** (1811–82), Fr. socialist, 2996.

Blanc, Mont (" white mountain "), highest peak of Alps (15,782 ft.), 127, 1360, 3138 ; first ascent, 127 ; at sunset, 1144.

Blanchard (blahn'-shahr), **Jean Pierre** (1753–1809), Fr. aeronaut, first to cross Channel in balloon, 349.

Blanche of Castile (1188–1252), Sp. princess, queen of Louis VIII of Fr. ; regent during minority of Louis IX, mother of St. Louis, 2028.

Blanching, of celery, 738.

Blank verse, defined, 2636 ; Shakespeare's, 2933.

Blarney. Vil. in co. Cork, Eire ; castle contains Blarney Stone, 910.

Blasco, Ibañez, Vicente. See Ibañez, Vicente Blasco.

Blast furnace, 467, 468, 469, 868, 1754.

Blasting gelatine. An explosive ; invented by Nobel, 1060.

Blatch'ford, Robert (1851–1943). Brit. author and journalist ; assumed pseudonym of " Nunquam " and wrote largely on socialism, founded " Clarion " in 1891 ; series of newspaper articles in 1910 on the Ger. menace attracted considerable notice (" Merrie England " ; " Tommy Atkins ").

Blattnerphone. Method of recording sound electro-magnetically on a steel tape and of reproducing it by the same means ; takes its name from inventor, Dr. L. Blattner, 3013.

Blavat'sky, Helena Petrovna (1831–91). Rus. founder of Theosophical Society.

Bleaching, of fabrics, 469 ; chlorine used in, 1567 ; of silk, 2972.

Bleeding, how to stop, 1295.

Blende, or sulphide of zinc ; crystal, 939.

Blenheim (blen'-im). Ger., Bavarian village on Danube ; battle of, 470 ; Marlborough at, 2106.

Blenheim Palace, Woodstock, Oxfordshire, 2466.

Blenkinsop, John (1783–1831), Brit. inventor of a cog rly. (1812) used at a Yorks colliery ; Geo. Stephenson modelled his first locomotive on Blenkinsop's, 2734.

Blennerhassett. Isl. on Ohio r., U.S.A.

Bleriot (blār'-ē-ō), **Louis** (1872–1936), Fr. aviator, 470 ; first Channel flight, 45, 46.

Bles, Hendrik. Flemish painter, 2324.

Bligh, William (1754–1817). Eng. admiral ; capt. of H.M.S. Bounty, the crew of which revolted (1787) and set him adrift in an open boat.

Blights. Various plant diseases : mildews and moulds, 2173 ; rusts and smuts, 2857.

" Blimps," non-rigid dirigibles, 94, 95.

Blind, education of, 470 ; Braille books and maps, 471 ; careers for blind, 472 ; guide dog, 160 ; pensions, 2564 ; sense of touch, 2231.

" Blind Spot," of the eye, 1252.

Blind-worm. A legless lizard, 1973, 2985.

Bliss, Sir Arthur (b. 1891). Eng. composer. " Rout " (1920) ; " A Colour Symphony " (1922) ; " Morning Heroes " (1930) ; " Viola Sonata " (1933) ; ballet " Checkmate " (1937) ; ballet, " Adam Zero " (1946) ; opera, " The Olympians " (1949). Chairman of Brit. Council music committee in 1946. Knighted in 1950.

Blister-beetle, 400, 401.

Blisters. Treatment of, 1295.

Blitzkrieg (blitz'-krēg ; Ger. Blitz, lightning flash ; Krieg, war). A rapid and annihilating military attack, e.g. the Ger. invasions of 1939–41 ; also applied popularly to air raid attacks on Gt. Britain, e.g. the London raids of Sept. 7, 1940–May 10, 1941.

Blizzard. Storm of wind and snow having velocity of 40 m. or more per hour.

Bloater, or smoked herring ; preparation at Yarmouth, 1426.

Bloch (blokh), **Ernst** (b. 1880). Swiss-American composer ; orchestral works and chamber music ; later experiments in quarter-tones.

Bloch, Jean Richard (1884–1947). Fr. writer, 1382.

Blockade, 473 ; in 1st World War, 2293.

Block-and-Tackle, a set of pulleys, 2701.

Blockships. Vessels sunk in harbours, etc., to prevent their use ; part of Mulberry harbours, 2253.

Block books, 512.

Block printing. Method in use before invention of movable type, 511, 701, 2684, 2686.

Bloemfontein (bloom'-fon-tān). Cap. Orange Free State, S. Africa ; pop. 64,000 ; Boer stronghold in Boer War ; 2444, 2445.

Blois (blwah). Fr. historic tn. on Loire ; pop. 24,600 ; trade and mfg. centre ; splendid castle, once seat of powerful counts of Blois, 2765.

Blok, Alexander (1880–1921). Russian symbolist poet, 2856.

Blomfield, Sir Reginald (1856–1942). Eng. architect, past president, R.I.B.A. Architect of many London buildings, and designed R.A.F. monument on the Embankment and English church at Ypres. " History of Renaissance Architecture in England," " Studies in Architecture."

Blondel de Nesle (blon'-del de nāl). Fr. troubadour, friend and attendant of Richard I, 2776.

Blon'din, Charles (1824–97). Fr. acrobat ; 473 ; Niagara feat, 473, 2363.

Blood, 473 ; in birds, 437 ; formed in bone marrow, 2977 ; circulation, 1592, 2600 ; disease germs in, 1458 ; groups, 476 ; in fish, 1296 ; Leonardo's work on, 1927 ; plasma, 475 ; pressure, 1593, 1856 ; pulse, 2701 ; specific gravity test, 1674 ; transfusion, 476 ; withdrawn from brain in sleep, 2983.

Blood, Thomas (c. 1618–80). Called " Colonel," notorious Irish adventurer, 477.

Bloodhound, 1026, plate f. 1024.

Blood orange. Same as Maltese orange.

Blood-poisoning. Bacteria of, 1458.

Bloodstone. A semi-precious stone, 2713.

Blood transfusion, 476.

Blood-vessels, 474, 1591.

Bloody Assize, after Monmouth's rebellion, 1794.

" Bloody Mary," epithet given to Mary I, Queen of England.

Bloomsbury. District of west-central London, contains the British Museum and the London University buildings, 2021.

Blow-fly. Alternative name of bluebottle fly.

Blowlamp, 477 ; principle in bunsen burner, 616 ; in stove, lamp, and heater, 478.

Blowpipe, oxyacetylene, 18 ; use in Borneo, 526.

Blubber, of whale, 3372.

Blücher (blū'-khêr), **Gebhard Leberecht von** (1742–1819). Prussian field-marshal, leader of patriot Prussian party during Napoleonic period ; his intervention helped to defeat Napoleon at Waterloo, 3354, 3364.

Blue. A primary colour, 876 ; place in spectrum, 875 ; pigments, 2478.

" Blue." A man who has the right to wear the light blue cap and blazer of Cambridge, or the dark blue of Oxford, blues and half-blues being awarded for most inter-university sporting contests.

Bluebeard. Story-book monster who forbids his wife to open a locked door behind which her curiosity discovers the bodies of her murdered predecessors ; timely rescue saves her from sharing their fate.

Bluebell. Flower, **479** ; not a true hyacinth, 1663.

" Blue Bird." Campbell's racing motor-car having world record for speed in 1935 ; also name of his racing motor-boat, 485.

" Blue Bird, The," story of Maeterlinck's play, 3465.

Blue Books. Name given to parliamentary publications, which are usually bound with blue paper covers.

" Blue Boy." Painting by Gainsborough, 1187.

Blue butterfly, Large. Caterpillar in ants' nest, 168 ; plate f. 632.

Blue Coat School. Same as Christ's Hospital.

Blue Cornflower, 910.

" Blue Danube," waltz by J. Strauss, 3102.

Blue Grotto. Cave at Capri (It. isl.), 734, plate f. 733.

Blue gum. Kind of eucalyptus ; in Tasmania, 3156.

Blue Mts. Australia, 307, 2343.

Blue Nile. R. in Africa, rises in Abyssinia, unites with White Nile near Khartum, 2370, map, 13.

Blue Peter. Blue flag with white square in centre, hoisted in a ship about to sail.

Blue-print, coating for, 947 ; mfr. a photo-chemical process, 2574.

Blue Riband. Formerly the " blue riband," awarded for the fastest crossing of the Atlantic by a liner, was merely a term of honour. In 1935 a trophy was presented by Mr. H. K. Hales, M.P. Rules and regulations under which this trophy is to be awarded have also been drawn up.

Blue Ridge Mts. Easternmost range of Appalachian Mts., U.S.A., from Hudson r. s.w. to Georgia ; 190, 3326.

Blue shark, 2939.

Blue-stocking. Term applied to learned, pedantic woman. In the 18th century a literary circle of men and women was established in London, among whom was a certain Mr. Benjamin Stillingfleet, who regularly wore blue stockings.

Blue tits, 3218.

Blue vitriol. Copper sulphate, 3116.

Blum (bloom), **Léon** (1872–1950). French politician : elected to Chamber 1919 ; leader of Popular (Socialist) Front ; formed first Socialist Cabinet in France in 1936, 1368 ; again Premier 1938 ; liberated from German prison, 1945 ; again Premier, Nov. 1947. Served as vice-premier in Marie govt. July–Aug. 1948.

Blunden, Edmund Charles (b. 1896). English poet and biographer, winner of Hawthornden Prize in 1922.

Boabdil (bō-ab'-dēl) or **Abu Abdullah.** Last Moorish king of Granada (d. c. 1495).

Boa constrictor. Snake, S. Amer., sometimes 12 ft. in length, 2990, *2991*, *3025*.

Boadicea (bō-*a*-dis-ē′-*a*) or **Boudicca** (d. A.D. 62). Brit. warrior queen, **479**; statue, *480*; burns London, 2016.

Boanerges (bō-*a*-nêr′jēz). " Sons of thunder," name given by Jesus to the disciples James and John; applied to any loud-voiced orator.

Boar, **480**; Adonis myth, 28; ivory, 1788.

Board of Education. See **Education**.

Board of Trade. See **Trade, Board of.**

Board Schools, foundation, 2884.

Boater, straw hat, 1584.

Boat Race. Between Oxford and Cambridge Universities, held annually between Putney and Mortlake, *483*; first race rowed in 1829; recent winners—1935 and 1936, Cambridge; 1937 and 1938, Oxford; 1939 and 1940, Cambridge; 1943, 1944, Oxford; 1945 Cambridge; 1946 Oxford; 1947 Cambridge; 1948 Cambridge; 1949, 1950 Cambridge.

Boats and Yachts, **481**; basketwork, 369; coracles in Wales, *plate f. 3337*; Doggett's Coat and Badge, *1027*; " drifters " at Yarmouth, *1305*; Egypt, *1097*, *plate f. 1121*; fire float on Thames, *1887*; gondolas, Venice, *1774*; ice-breaker at work, 351; India, 1704; kayaks, Eskimo craft, *1223*; mahogany, 2065; motor, *485*; reed boats of Bolivia, *492*; sailing, *484*, *486*; trawler in North Sea, 1304. See also in Index **America Cup**; **Ships.**

Boaz (bō′-az) (Bible). Husband of Ruth, 2857.

Bobbin lace, or pillow lace, 1877, *1879*, *plate f. 1881*; bobbin-net machine, 1876.

Boccaccio (bok-ah′-chō), **Giovanni** (1313–75). " Father of Italian prose "; author of the " Decameron," a storehouse of characters and plots used by Chaucer, Shakespeare, and many others; *1786*, 2764.

Bochum (bokh′-*um*). Ger. industrial city in Westphalia; pop. 303,000; coal mines, iron and steel works.

Bode (bō′-dê), **Johann Ehlert** (1747–1826). Ger. astronomer, formulator of Bode's law.

Bo′den, Sweden. Tn. in N. on Lule r., near Lulea, 3129.

Bodiam Castle, in Sussex, *715*.

Bodleian (bod-lē′-*a*n) **Library,** Oxford, Eng. Public library of the Univ., named after Sir Thomas Bodley who restored and re-opened it in 1602, 1930, 2465. Extension, New Bodleian, completed 1939, opened by King George VI, 1946.

Bod′min. Co. tn. of Cornwall; bootmaking; pop. 5,526; 912.

Boehme (bê′-mê), **Jakob** (1575–1624). Ger. peasant who became a noted philosopher and mystic; " Aurora," his first published work, and many of his other writings have been extensively translated.

Boeotia (bē-ō′-shi-*a*). Dist. of anc. Greece, N.W. of Attica, 3197.

Boers. Dutch farmers of S. Africa; Great Trek and early relations with the British, 486, 2445, 3017, 3019, 3240; Smuts, 2987.

Boer War (1899–1902), **486**, 3019, 3240, 3279; leaders, 487, 533, 1863, 2771, 2789, 2987.

Boethius (bō-ê′-thi-*us*) (about 480–524). Rom. statesman and philosopher (" Consolations of Philosophy," trans. by King Alfred and Chaucer).

Bo′fors Gun. Mobile anti-aircraft and anti-tank gun of Swed. design; fires 2-lb. shells to height of 6,000 ft. ; 257, 258.

Bog, or swamp, peat in, *1405*, 2534; " quaking," 2239; vegetation, 3355.

Bogey, in golf, 1484.

Boghazkeui, Asiatic Turkey; Hittite archaeology at, 208.

Bogie, locomotive, *plate f. 1980*, 1981, 1982.

Bogotá (bog-ō-tah′). Cap. of Colombia, near centre; pop. 434,200; 874. Rioting during Pan-American conf.

March 1948, when capitol was devastated, and Liberal leader assassinated.

" **Bohème, La** " (lah bō-ām′). Opera, by Puccini, 2438.

Bohe′mia. Country in Cent. Europe, prov. of Czechoslovakia; a. 20,060 sq. m. ; pop. 7,000,000; **487**, 953; *maps*, *320*, *954*; glass industry, 633, *953*, 954; peasant costumes, *487*; Prague, 2677. See also **Czechoslovakia.**—*History*: in Holy Roman Empire, 1637, 2041; Huss and Hussite War, 1660; Thirty Years' War, 3202; revolt against Austria (1848), 319; gains independence, 3414.

Bohemians, 487. See also **Czechs.**

Bohemian Forest (Böhmerwald). Chain of mts. between Bohemia and Bavaria; highest peak Arber; 487.

Bohemond (bō′-hem-ond) (*c.* 1056–1111). Norman crusader, 936.

Bohr, Niels (b. 1885). Danish scientist, **487**; work on the atomic theory, *295*, 298; electron theory, 1137; and quantum theory, 2711.

Bohum, Sir Henry de. English knight who, at battle of Bannockburn, sought to kill Robert Bruce, King of Scotland, but paid for the attempt with his life.

Boileau (bwah′-lō), **Nicolas** (1636–1711). Fr. poet, satirist, and critic, called " Law-giver of Parnassus "; chief works, 1380.

Boiler, 488; autoclave, 488; domestic, 489, 1600; injector, 2704; of locomotive, 489, 1981, *plate f. 1980*; in power station, 2613, *2675*; of ships, 489; smoke and, 2986; steam-engines, 3085; thermostatic control, 3201; Trevithick's high pressure, 3247; hard water in, 3351.

Boiling, in cookery, 902; sterilization by, *179*; destroys vitamin C, 3327.

Boiling point : of water, 3084; on the thermometer scales, *3200*.

Boils. Inflammation of the skin and underlying tissue, accompanied by accumulation of pus.

Bois de Boulogne (bwah de bōō-lō′-nye), Paris, 2514.

Bois-le-Duc (bwah - le - dook′) or **'s Hertogenbosch.** City of Netherlands; pop. 47,000; noted cath., mfg., shipping.

Bojer (bō-′yer), **Johan** (b. 1872). Norwegian novelist (" The Great Hunger "; " The Power of a Lie "); 2403, 2881.

Bokhara (bok-ah′-ra), former khanate of Cent. Asia, lying N. of Afghanistan, now city of Uzbek S.S.R. ; 3267.

Bo′lan Pass. Defile 60 m. long in N. Baluchistan.

Boldrewood, Rolf. Pen name of Thomas Alexander Brown (1826–1915), Anglo-Australian novelist; 315.

Boleyn, Anne (1507–36). 2nd Queen of Henry VIII of Eng., **490**, 1612.

Bolingbroke, Henry St. John, Viscount (1678–1751). Eng. statesman and essayist, **490**.

Bolivar, Simon (1783–1830), " the Liberator." S. Amer. general and statesman, 490, 3025; and Bolivia, 491; and Ecuador, 1083; in Peru, 2560.

Bolivia. Inland country of S. Amer. ; estimated area, 506,000 to 562,000 sq. m. ; pop. 3,500,000, **491**; *map f. 3024*; climate, 491, 3742; Indians, *493*, *494*, 3025, *3026*; minerals, 492, 3024, 3215; war with Chile, 805; war with Paraguay, 2512; Villaroel, Bolivian dictator, deposed and killed, July 1946.

Boll-weevil, *921*.

Bologna, It. Rly. centre of N. It. ; pop. 270,000; **494**. Leaning Towers, *494*; by Bonington, *3353*.

Bologna (bol-ō′-nyah), **Giovanni da** (1524–1608). Italianized name of the Fr.-born Jean Boulogne, a great sculptor, 2906.

Bologna, University of. Bologna, It., one of oldest European universities; founded 1088, 494, 3296.

Bolom′eter, type of thermometer, 1722.

Bol′shevism, in Rus., **495**, 2849, 3411; leaders, 1922, 3072, 3251.

Bolting. In flour milling, 2973.

Bolton. Cotton-mfg. tn. in Lancashire ; pop. 153,000; **495**; home of Samuel Crompton, 933.

Bo′ma. Late cap. of Belgian Congo ; pop. 6,000.

Bombardier (bom-bar-dēr′) **beetle,** 399 ; gas attack, 1728.

Bombay. 2nd largest city of India, on w. coast; pop. 1,500,000, **495**, 1692; univ., 1714; new floating dock completed 1947.

Bombay. A State of India on w. coast ; pop. 20,850,000; 76,000 sq. m. ; 496, 1692.

Bombers. British bombing aircraft, *36*, *37*, *38*, *39*.

Bom′bidae. Bumble-bee family, 395.

Bombyc′idae. Family of moths, 2970.

Bon, Cape, Africa. On N.E. coast of Tunis, 2136. Figured in N. Africa campaign of 1942–43.

Bonampak. Anc. Maya city in Yucatan, excavated in 1947; 208.

Bo′naparte. Famous Corsican family, **497.**

Bonaparte, Carlo (d. 1785). Father of Napoleon I, 497.

Bonaparte, Caroline (1782–1839). Sister of Napoleon I; married Murat; 497.

Bonaparte, Elise (1777–1820). Sister of Napoleon I, 497.

Bonaparte, Jerome (1784–1860). Youngest brother of Napoleon I; king of Westphalia, 497.

Bonaparte, Joseph (1768–1844). Eldest brother of Napoleon I; *497*; king of Naples, later of Sp., 2275.

Bonaparte, Letizia (1750–1836), called **Madame Mère.** Mother of Napoleon I, *497*.

Bonaparte, Louis (1778–1846). Brother of Napoleon I, king of Holland, 497, 1839, 2278.

Bonaparte, Lucien (1775–1840). Prince of Canino, brother of Napoleon I, 497.

Bonaparte, Napoleon. See **Napoleon.**

Bonaparte, Pauline (1780–1825), sister of Napoleon I, 497.

Bonaventura (bō-n*a*-ven-too′-ra), **Giovanni de Fidanza, St.** (1221–74). It. Franciscan, professor of theology at Paris, where he was known as the " Doctor Seraphicus," Became general of his Order (1256). Made a cardinal by Pope Gregory X (1272); canonized by Pope Sixtus V.

Bond. Interest-bearing security, **498** ; building term, 498.

Bond′field, Margaret Grace (b. 1873). Brit. politician; the first woman-chairman of the General Council of the Trades Union Congress, and the first woman member of a British Cabinet; Minister of Labour, 1929–31; made C.H. 1948.

Bone, **498**. Broken, first aid, 1294; composition, 2977; of ear, 1065; growth affected by parathyroid, 1471; promoted by fluoride, 1567; in bird structure, 437; of horse's food, *1342*; marrow produces red corpuscles, 474; skeleton, 2977; in button mfr., 633; yields gelatine, 1426; phosphorus, 2574.

Bone, Henry (1755–1834). Brit. enamel painter, the most famous of his day.

Bone, Sir Muirhead (b. 1876). British etcher and painter. Official artist, Western Front and with the Fleet 1916–18; also 1940–43; specialist in etchings of buildings, docks, wharves, and all symbols of commercial life. His brother James (author and journalist) made C.H. 1947. Former's son, Stephen Bone (b. 1904), also well-known artist.

Bone-black, or animal charcoal, preparation and uses, 753.

Bone-char, as sugar filter, 3114.

Bone porcelain, 2670.

Bone-tar, 3154.

Bonheur (bon-êr′), **Marie Rosalie,** or **Rosa** (1822–99). Fr. artist, **499**. " Horse Fair," 499.

Bonhomme Noël. French name for Father Christmas, 820.

Bonhomme Richard. Ship of John Paul Jones, 1837.

Bon′iface, St. (680–755). Converted Germans to Christianity, **500**, 1449.

Bon'iface. Name borne by nine popes, 500. For list *see* Pope.

Bonifacio (bon-i-fah'-chō) Strait of, between Sardinia and Corsica, 914.

Bonin (bō-nēn') Islands. Group of 20 small volcanic isls. in the Pacific; 40 sq. m.

Bonington, Richard Parkes (1801–28). Eng. artist; has been called " the Keats of Eng. painting," 1182, *3353.*

Boni'to. A fish of the mackerel family.

Bonn. City of W. Germany, cap. of W. German Federal Republic from Sept. 1949; pop. 100,000; much damaged by air raids; 500. Beethoven's birthplace, 397.

Bonn, University of. At Bonn, Ger.; faculties of law, medicine, philosophy, theology; ranked 2nd among leading Ger. univs., 500.

Bonnard, Pierre (1867–1947). Fr. artist, *1378.*

Bon'ner, Edmund (*c.* 1500–69). Bishop of London and chaplain to Cardinal Wolsey; notorious for his persecution of Prot. martyrs.

Bonnet (bon-ā), Georges (b. 1889). Fr. politician; foreign min. at time of Munich agreement, 1938; in 1941 member of Vichy govt.

Bonnet monkey, or macaque, 2211.

Bony labyrinth. Inner ear chamber, 1065.

Boodle's Club. Adam style, *23.*

Book-keeping. Systematic method of recording all the transactions in goods and money of a person, business, etc.; 518.

Book-lice. Insects, 1733.

Bookplate. Label denoting ownership of a book, 519.

" Book of the Dead." Anc. Eg. work, containing prayers, 1116.

Books and their making, 509. Bibles, 423; binding, 514, *515, 516*; for children, 1964; library, 1930; manuscripts, *424, 509, 510, 2090*; printing, 512, 2684; steps in production, 512; reading, *426,* 2750; care of, 2750. *See also under* Literature; Stories.

Bookworms, 520.

Boom. An obstruction made of timber lashed together and placed at the entrance to harbours and rivers to prevent entry of enemy ships.

Boom. A spar attached to a ship's mast for the purpose of fixing a sail.

Boom'erang. Curved wooden missile, the weapon of Australian natives, 520.

Boötes (bō-ō'-tēz). Northern constellation containing the bright star Arcturus; near the Great Bear; name means " the ploughman."

Booth, Edwin (1833–93). Amer. actor; foremost Amer. tragedian of his day.

Booth, Evangeline Cory (b. 1865). English-American religious leader; daughter of William Booth; Commander of Salvation Army, U.S.A. (1904); " general " 1934–46, 520.

Booth, John Wilkes (1839–65). Amer. actor, assassinated Lincoln, 1952.

Booth, William (1829–1912). Eng. religious leader; founds Salvation Army, 520, 2868.

Booth, William Bramwell (1856–1929). Eng. religious leader, son and successor of William Booth as " General " of Salvation Army, 1912–28, 520, 2868.

Boothby, Guy Newell (1867–1905). Australian novelist (" Dr. Nikola "), *565.*

Boothferry, Yorks; swing bridge at, *565.*

Boothia (bōō'-thi-*a*) Felix. Northernmost peninsula of Amer. mainland; North Magnetic Pole, 2644.

Bootle, Lancashire. At the mouth of the Mersey; great docks are part of dock system of Liverpool, of which Bootle is virtually a suburb; pop. est. 59,100. Severely damaged during German air raids of 1941.

Boots and shoes, 521; anc. Saxon, *522*; and hygiene, 1676, *1677*; leather and its preparation, 1910; manufacture, *523*; Roman sandals, *521*; rubber, 2836; history, *522.*

Bopp, Franz (1791–1867). Ger. philologist, 2570.

Boracic acid. Same as Boric acid.

Borage (bu'-rij). Type plant of family *Boraginaceae,* hairy or bristly herbs with usually bright blue flowers.

Borax, sodium tetraborate, used in metallurgy as flux, in mfr. of enamel, porcelain and glass, as food preservative, detergent and water-softener, and as antiseptic.

Bordeaux (bōr-dō'). Fr., port on W. coast; pop. 253,000; **524,** 1359.

Bordeaux mixture. Fungicide of copper sulphate and milk of lime; preventive or remedy for potato blight, etc.

Borden, Sir Frederick William (1847–1917). Canadian statesman; Minister of Defence 1896–1911; responsible for Canadian Regt. in Boer War.

Borden, Sir Robert Laird (1854–1937). Prime minister of Canada, 1911–20, 524.

Borders, The, territory on both sides of boundary between Eng. and Scot.; border battles, 2892.

Bordighera, winter resort, It., on the Riviera; pop. 5,750.

Bore, of firearms, 1285.

Bore, or tidal wave, 525, 1573, 3210.

Bor'eas. The god of the north wind in Gk. myth.

Borer. *See* Boring animals.

Borghese, noble family of It.; Prince Camillo (1775–1832), 497; palace, 2800.

Borgia (bōr'-j*a*) family. Powerful house of Renaissance It., 525.

Borgia, Caesar (1476–1507), *525,* 1926.

Borgia, Francis (1510–72). Member of the Sp. Borgias; famous general of the Jesuits, 525.

Borgia, Lucrezia (1480–1519), Duchess of Ferrara, 525.

Boric or boracic acid, a crystalline substance found in Tuscany; a mild antiseptic widely used, chiefly in powder or ointment form.

Boring animals, insects, 1732; sponge, 3068.

Boring machines, *2428.*

Boris III (1894–1943). King of Bulgaria from 1918 to 1943, 614.

Boris Godunov (*c.* 1550–1605). Rus. Tsar; gained throne 1598; while regent, bound peasants as serfs to the soil (1587); subject of play by Pushkin, opera by Moussorgsky.

Bormann, Martin (1900–45 ?) Hitler's deputy from 1941, and head of Nazi Chancellory, 2282; death assumed, 1945. War criminal, tried in his absence at Nuremberg and sentenced to death.

Borneo (bōr'-ni-ō). Isl. in East Indies; 4th largest inhabited is. in world; 290,000 sq. m.; pop. 3,000,000; *map, 1074*; **525,** *plates f. 524, 525*; children, *plate f. 788*; Dyaks, 525; occupied by Jap., 1941–45, 527, 2473, 3420; political divisions, 527; resources, 527; rubber, 2833.

Bornholm. Isl. of Denmark, 991; fortress church. *Map, 992.*

Bornu. Country of the Central Sudan, former Negro kingdom; split up between Gt. Brit., Fr. and Ger. at end of 19th cent. The trib. state of Zinder and part of N. Bornu are in French West Africa; and the S.W. portion is in the Cameroons under a British trusteeship from U.N.

Bor'o Bu'dor. Buddhist temple in Java, 1813, *1814.*

Borodin (bor-ō-dēn'), Alexander (1834–87). Rus. composer (" Prince Igor," opera; symphonies, string quartets, and songs).

Borodino. Rus. vil; scene of fierce but indecisive battle (1812) between Napoleon and Russians.

Boron (B). Non-metallic element of the aluminium group; atomic weight, 10·8; occurs in boric acid and borax; properties, 776.

Borotra, Jean (b. 1898). French lawn-tennis player. Winner of Singles championship at Wimbledon, 1924 and 1926; Men's Doubles championship, 1932, 1933. Member of the French team which won the Davis Cup from U.S.A. in 1927.

Borough. An incorporated vil., tn., or city; of London, 2016.

Borough council, local governing body.

Borromeo (bor-ō-mā'-ō), St. Carlo (1538–84). Cardinal and Archbishop of Milan; chief figure in last years of Council of Trent.

Borrow, George Henry (1803–81). Eng. traveller and author, 527.

Bors, Sir, one of knights of Round Table; quest for Grail, 1414.

Bor'zoi. A Rus. wolfhound, 1026; *plate f. 1024.*

Bose, Sir Jagadis Chandra (1858–1937). Indian scientist; invented cresco-graph for recording life movement of plants.

Bosnia (boz'-ni-*a*) and Herzegovina (hêrts'-ă-gō-vē'-n*a*). Part of Yugoslavia, 528; *map, 320*; annexed by Austria, 343.

Bosniaks. People of Bosnia, 528, 2983.

Bos'porus or Bosphorus. Strait, 16 m. long between Sea of Marmara and Black Sea, 528; Constantinople on, 1761; Turkey, *3263*; origin of name, 529.

Bossuet (bos-wā), Jacques Bénigne (1627–1704). Fr. preacher, called greatest ecclesiastical orator in history, 1380.

Boston. Spt. tn., Lincolnshire; pop. 21,000, 529; a notable landmark is the tower of St. Botolph's church, known as Boston Stump, *529.*

Boston, Massachusetts, U.S.A. State cap.; pop. 771,000, **529,** 2118.

Boston Massacre, 529.

Boston Tea Party, 144, 529.

Boswell, James (1740–95), Scot. author; friend and biographer of Dr. Johnson, 529, *530,* 1836.

Bosworth Field, battle, 530, 2828.

Botanic garden, 531.

Botany, 531, *532*; anatomy and morphology, 531; bulbs, tubers and rootstocks, *612*; classification, 531, 2620; ecology, 531, 1079; flowers, 1322; fruits, 190, 191, *1270,* 1401; leaves, 1914; life story of flowering plant, *1323–28*; Linnaeus's work, 531; *1954, 1955*; Nature study, 2283, *2288*; plant life, *2288,* 2620; reproduction, 1266, 2238; roots, 2825; seeds and spores, 1402, 2916; trees, 3245.

Botany Bay. Inlet on E. coast of Australia, 310; so named by Cook (1770) because of variety of flora.

Botha (bō'-tah), Louis (1862–1919). Boer leader, later prime minister of Union of S. Africa, 533, 2988, 3411.

Both'nia, Gulf of. Arm of Baltic Sea, between Finland and Sweden, 352, 1277, 3126.

Both'well, James Hepburn, Earl of (1536–78). Third husband of Mary Queen of Scots; died after eight years' imprisonment in the castle of Draxholm, Denmark; 2116.

Botticelli (bot-i-chel'-i), Sandro (*c.* 1444–1510), Florentine painter, with poetic feeling and decorative style, 1775; " Christ's Nativity," *1779*; " The Birth of Venus," *186.*

Bottle tree, 533.

Bottles, blown by machines, 1472; how corks are made, 910; bottling of fruits and vegetables, 1341.

Bottom. Clownish rustic in " Midsummer Night's Dream," *2169.*

Bottom-fishing, 1309.

Boucher (bōō-shā), François (1703–70). Gay, brilliant Fr. painter of Pompadour era, styled " Anacreon of painting," *1372,* 1378.

Boucicault (bōō'-si-kō), Dion (1822–90). Celebrated Irish actor and writer of many plays (" Colleen Bawn," and " The Shaughraun").

Boucicault, Nina (b. 1867). Eng. actress, daughter of Dion B.; the first " Peter Pan."

Boudicca. *See* Boadicea.

Bougainville (bōō-gan-vēl). Largest and most N. of Solomon Is.; since 1947 administered by Australia under U.N. trusteeship; exports copra; area 3,880 sq. m.; pop. 49,067; in Jap. occupn. 1942–45.

Bougainville, Louis Antoine de (1729–1811). Fr. navigator, 534, **3472.**

Bough'ton, George Henry (1834–1905). Eng.-Amer. painter ; "Milton and Marvell," *2177*.

Boughton, Rutland (b. 1878). Eng. composer ; co-founder of Glastonbury Festival Players ; music drama includes "The Immortal Hour."

Bouillon (boo-ē-yon'). Anc. duchy in the Ardennes ; possession of Godfrey de Bouillon, leader of First Crusade ; now comprised in Belg. prov. of Luxembourg.

Boulanger (boo-lahn'-zhā), **Georges** (1837–91). Fr. general, anti-republican popular idol and Royalist plotter ; convicted of treason ; committed suicide.

Boulder Dam, on r. Colorado, *960*, *2335* ; hydro-electric installation, 1669.

Boulders, left by glaciers, 1680.

Boulogne (boo-lō'-nye), or **Boulogne-sur-Mer**. Fr. fortified spt. on Eng. Channel ; pop. 52,000 ; Rom. lighthouse, *1943* ; occupied by Germany, 1940–44, 3417.

Boult, Sir Adrian (b. 1889). English musical conductor ; of Royal Philharmonic Society (1918–19) ; City of Birmingham Orchestra (1924) ; musical director of B.B.C. (1930–1942) ; conductor of B.B.C. Symphony Orchestra (1930–1950) ; knighted 1937 ; *2446*, 2447.

Boulton, Matthew (1728–1809). Eng. manufacturer and engineer, 3357 ; and William Murdock, 2256 ; Watt's partner, 3357.

Boundary, in cricket, 930.

Bounty, mutiny on H.M.S., 2473.

Bourbon (boor-bawn), **House of**, younger branch of Fr. royal (Capet) family, figuring in history from 9th cent. and occupying various European thrones after 16th cent., **534** ; in Fr., 2028, 3149 ; in Sicily, 2968 ; Sp., 3036.

Bourchier (bow'-chêr), **Arthur** (1864–1927). Brit. actor ; became joint-manager of the Criterion and later manager of the Garrick, both London theatres ; translated and adapted many plays.

Bourgeois (bĕr-jois'), type, 3270.

Bourgeoisie (boor-zhwah-zē'). Fr. term applied to commercial or middle class.

Bourges (boorzh). Fr. historic city, mfg. and trade centre ; pop. 45,000 ; magnificent cath. ; govt. arsenal.

Bourget (boor-zhā), **Paul** (1852–1935). Fr. novelist and critic. ("Sensations d'Italie" ; "Cosmopolis" ; "Outre-Mer" ; "Le Disciple"), 1382.

Bourget, Le. *See* Le Bourget.

Bourne, Francis (1861–1935). Rom. Cath. Archbishop ; Bishop of Southwark (1897–1903) ; Archbishop of Westminster (1903) ; Cardinal (1911).

Bournemouth. Hampshire watering place and winter resort ; pop. about 127,400, 1571.

Bournville. Town in the vicinity of Birmingham, Warwicks. Established by George Cadbury, of cocoa and chocolate fame, as a garden city for employees of the firm, but since made over to trustees as a garden suburb.

Bourse (boors). In Europe ; a stock exchange or money market ; 3094.

Bovary, Emma. In Flaubert's novel "Madame Bovary," irresponsible, selfish, extravagant young woman who, involved in debt and intrigue, finally poisons herself.

Bovidae (bō'-vi-dē). Family of hoofed, hollow-horned animals, such as cattle and sheep, 752.

Bow. Dist. in E. London ; potteries, 2670.

Bow and arrow, In medieval warfare, 209 ; for fishing in New Guinea, *2340* ; use in sport, 210.

Bowdler (bowd'-ler), **Thomas** (1754–1825). Eng. editor of the "Family Shakespeare," which excluded all passages that might cause offence ; from his name came the verb "to bowdlerize."

Bo'wen, Elizabeth D. C. 20th cent. Irish novelist and critic ; characters

drawn with subtle delicacy ; "The Last September" ; "The Death of the Heart" ; "The Heat of the Day."

Bo'wen, Marjorie (b. 1888). Pen-name under which Margaret G. V. Long wrote historical romances ; "The Viper of Milan" ; "The Netherlands Displayed."

Bower Bird, of Australia and New Guinea, 534.

Bowery, New York City, 2353.

Bowline, knot, *1869*.

Bowling, in cricket, 928, 930.

Bowls, Eng. game, 534.

Bow Street. London thoroughfare in which stands the chief police court of the metropolis. Built in 1881, it replaced a court established in 1749 which gave its name to the Bow Street Runners, who served writs and acted as detectives until superseded in 1829, 2647.

Box. Small evergreen tree found on chalk hills in England, whence Box Hill. Wood used for engraver's blocks.

Box calf leather, 1914.

Boxer Rebellion, in China (1900), 812.

Box Hill. Hill on N. Downs, Surrey, 3123.

Boxing. "The noble art of self-defence," **535**, *536*. Recent world heavyweight champions : 1934, M. Baer ; 1935, J. J. Braddock ; 1937–48, J. Louis. Brit. heavyweight champions : 1933, L. Harvey ; 1934, J. Petersen ; 1936, B. Foord ; 1937, T. Farr ; 1938, L. Harvey ; 1944, J. London ; 1945, B. Woodcock. *See* Olympic Games.

Box wood, in wood engraving, 1219.

Boy'cott, Charles Cunnigham (1832–97). Agent for Irish estates, driven out of Ire. (1880) through "boycotting," 537 ; film of, *831*.

Boyd-Carpenter, William (1841–1918). Eng. divine, bishop of Ripon, 1884–1911, and canon of Westminster, 1912–18.

Boyd Orr. *See* Orr.

Boyle, Robert (1627–91). Eng. scientist, 537 ; association with Hooke, 1640.

Boyle's law, in physics, 537, 1419.

Boyne, r. in E. of Eire (Irish Republic) flowing about 80 m. into Irish Sea ; battle of (1690), 537, *1746*, 1745, 2125.

Boys' Brigade. An organization founded in 1883—the oldest of its kind—by Sir William A. Smith ; its object is to train both mind and body with the aid of discipline and religious teaching ; physical training is an important feature.

Boy Scouts, 538, *539–41*. Badges, *plate f*. *542*, *543* ; founded by Baden-Powell, 337 ; Lord Rowallan, Chief Scout, 542.

Boz. Pen-name sometimes used by Charles Dickens.

Bozzaris (bot'-sah-rēs), **Marcos** (c. 1789–1823). The "Leonidas of modern Greece," hero of Gk. war of independence ; killed at Missolonghi.

"Brabançonne" (bra-ban-son'). Belg. national anthem, 2283.

Brabant'. Medieval duchy of Netherlands ; now N. Brabant (Nether.) and Antwerp and S. Brabant (Belg.).

Brab'azon. Long-range Brit. air-liner of immense size ; eight-engined monoplane ; span 230 ft., length 177 ft. ; first flown in 1949, 53.

Brabazon, Hercules Brabazon (1821–1906). Eng. painter, 3353.

Brabazon of Tara, John T. C. Moore-Brabazon, 1st Baron (b. 1884). Brit. airman and politician ; the first British aviator ; Min. of Aircraft Production, 1941–42 ; chairman of cttee. on Gt. Brit.'s post-war civil aircraft.

Brachycephalic (brak-i-se-fal'-ik). "Short-headed," term in anthropology, 2724.

Brack'en. A type of fern, 542, *543*, 1266.

Bracken, Brendan (b. 1901), Brit. politician, Min. of Information 1941–45.

Bract. A modified leaf which protects or supports a bud or flower.

Brad-awl, small piercing tool ; origin of name, 2271.

Brad'bury, John Swanwick Bradbury, 1st Baron (b. 1872). Brit. civil servant ; as chief cashier of the Bank of England, his name appeared on the currency notes issued in 1914 ; often referred to as "Bradburys."

Brad'dock, Edward (1695–1755). Brit. general, defeated and killed during Seven Years' War, 3342 ; 2925.

Brad'don, Mary Elizabeth (1837–1915). Eng. authoress, wrote more than sixty novels of the melodramatic type ("Lady Audley's Secret" ; "Aurora Floyd" ; "The Infidel" ; "Ishmael").

Bradford. City of Yorkshire ; pop. 289,600 ; 543, 1168, 3435.

Brad'ford, William (1589–1657). Mayflower pilgrim, 2nd gov. of Plymouth Colony ; wrote "History of the Plymouth Plantation," 2122.

Bradlaugh (brad'-law), **Charles** (1833–91). Social reformer, lecturer, free-thinker, and politician ; founded "The National Reformer."

Brad'ley, James (1693–1762). Eng. astronomer ; discoverer of the aberration of light ; became astronomer-royal 1742.

Bradley, Omar Nelson (b. 1893), Amer. general, c.-in-c. U.S. forces in N. Africa, 1943, and invasion of W. Europe, 1944 ; succeeded Eisenhower as U.S. army chief of staff, 543.

Bradman, Sir Donald George (b. 1908). Australian cricketer, 543 ; captain of many Australian test match sides ; retired 1948 ; knighted 1949.

Braemar, vil. of Aberdeenshire ; Highland gathering, *2893*.

Braga (brah'-gah), Port. city. Pop. 29,900 ; Rom. and medieval ruins.

Bragan'za or **Bragança, House of.** The reigning family of Port. 1640–1853, and of Brazil 1822–89.

Bragg, Sir William Henry (1862–1942). British scientist ; Cavendish professor at Leeds 1909–15 ; Quain prof. of physics London University 1915 ; awarded O.M. 1931 ; chief work concerned with X-rays, crystals and radiography ; use of ionization chamber, 1739 ; X-ray analysis, 3056. His son, **Sir William Lawrence Bragg** (b. 1890) awarded (with his father) the Nobel prize 1915, for work on X-rays ; 940, 3056, 3431.

Bragi (brah'-gē), god of poetry in Norse myth., 2881.

Brahe (brah'-he), **Tycho** (1546–1601), early Danish astronomer, 544 ; and Kepler, 1852.

Brahma, Hindu god regarded by Hindus as creator of the world, 1626.

Brahma, a breed of fowls.

Brah'manas, 1626.

Brah'manism, 1626, 1628.

Brahmans, priestly caste of Hindus, *1626*.

Brahmaputra (brah'-ma-poo-tra), r. of India ; rises in Tibet and flows E 800 m., bending S. breaks through Himalayas and flows S.W. to Gange 1,800 m., 1417, 1691, 2479, 3208.

Brahms, Johannes (1833–97). Ger pianist and composer, 544 ; chief works, 545 ; influence, 2264.

Braid, James (b. 1870). Scot. golfer won Open Championship 1901, 1905 1906, 1908, and 1910.

Braila (brah-ē'-lah). Rumanian por on Danube, *2840* ; pop. 97,300 former Turkish fortress ; seized b Ger. 1916.

Braille (brah'-ē), **Louis** (1809–52). F educator and organist, inventor o Braille (brāl) system of printin for the blind, *471*.

Brain, 545, and the eyes, 1252 connected with the ear, *1065* ; o Java "ape-man," 2079 ; man compared with ape's, 184 ; an involuntary muscles, 2258 ; an nerves, 2316 ; in prehistoric animal 1354 ; of Peking man, 2079 ; an senses, 1066, 1252, 3157 ; sleep an dreams, 2983. *See also* Psychology

Brains Trust. Team of experts wh broadcast impromptu answers t listeners' questions ; the first regula team, in 1941, comprised Juli

Huxley, C. E. M. Joad, and A. B. Campbell, with Donald McCullough question master. The term was originally used in 1932 of the team of specialists who advised Pres. F. D. Roosevelt.

Brakes, 547 ; hydraulic, 1665 ; ejector, 2704 ; locomotive, *548, plate f. 1980* ; motor-car, 2243, 2788 ; for electric trams, 3235.

Bramah (brah'-mah), **Joseph** (1749–1814), Brit. inventor of hydraulic press and other machines, and of a type of lock, 1979.

Bramante (bram-ahn'-tā), **Donato** (1444–1514). It. Renaissance architect, reconstructed Vatican and St. Peter's, 2766.

Bramble. *See* **Blackberry.**

Bramble, H.M.S., minesweeper, *2301.*

Brambling, a finch. Winter visitor to Britain from Scandinavia. White on back, 1272.

Bran, husk of wheat grains, 1320.

Brand, peasant priest and rebel against the world's conventions ; hero of Ibsen's drama of that name, 1679.

Bran'denburg, nucleus of modern Prussia, 2696 ; Thirty Years' War, 3203. Entered by Russians Jan. 1945.

Brandenburg Gate, Berlin, *416* ; 1871, procession through, *1450.*

Brandes (bran'-des), **Georg** (1842–1927), Danish author and literary critic (" Main Currents of the 19th Century ").

Brandy, 103, 3066.

Brandywine Creek, U.S.A. Tributary of Delaware in Pennsylvania and Delaware ; Howe, the English commander, defeated Washington at Chadd's Ford (1777).

Brangwyn, Sir Frank (b. 1867). Eng. painter and etcher ; combined most effectively rich colouring with breadth of design ; decorative works include panels in Royal Exchange (London), Rockefeller Centre (New York), etc., 1183.

Branly (brahn-lē), **Édouard** (1846–1940). Fr. scientist ; his invention of the Branly coherer, a method of detecting Hertzian waves, greatly assisted Marconi.

Branting, Hjalmar (1860–1925). First Socialist Prime Minister of Sweden, 1920, again 1921 ; Nobel peace prize, 1921.

Braque (brahk), **Georges** (b. 1881). Fr. painter of still-life studies in which abstract pattern and design are all-important.

Bras d'Or (brah dōr) **Lakes,** Cape Breton Is., 695.

Brasenose College, Oxford, *2462,* 2464.

Brasov (brah'-sof), Rumania. Formerly Kronstadt ; has anc. 14th cent. fort ; banking and commercial centre ; pop. 85,200.

Brass, an alloy of copper and zinc, 549. 3443 ; lacquer for, 1882 ; pins, 2609.

Brassica (bras'-i-ka). Genus of family *Cruciferae,* including cabbage, turnip, mustard, etc. ; 639, 3619.

Brassie, a wooden golf club, with a brass plate on the sole.

Brass instruments, in orchestra, 2267, 2446.

Bratislava (Ger. Pressburg). Cap. and chief spt. of Slovakia, on Danube ; pop. est. 139,000 ; occupied by Ger. Mar. 1939. Liberated April 1945.

Brauchitsch (brow'-khitz), **Field-Marshal Walther von** (1881–1948). Ger. soldier ; c.-in-c. Ger. Army, 1938–41 ; commanded in Poland, 1939, and later on Western front ; led ops. against Russ. 1941, but after reverses dismissed by Hitler, who took command himself ; died while awaiting trial for war crimes.

Bray, tn. of cos. Wicklow and Dublin, Eire, 3377.

Brazil, Angela (d. 1947). Eng. author of fifty children's books, mostly about girls' schools, and an Autobiography, 1925 ; 1966.

Brazil, republic of S. Amer. ; 3,300,000 sq. m. ; pop. 45,300,000, **550** ; *maps, 551, plate f. 3024* ; Amazon, *136,* 550, animals, *550 ;* cities, 554, 2779 ;

coffee, 553, 864, *865 ; history,* 2659, 2660, 3025 ; Indians, 332, 3026 ; jungle, *136 ;* minerals, 551, 1009 ; stamp, *3075.*

Brazil nut, 2408, *3023.*

Brazilwood, for making red ink, 1724.

Brazing, a form of welding, 3362.

Brazzaville (brat'-za-vēl). Tn. of Fr. Equatorial Africa ; cap. of Middle Congo Colony ; in Aug. 1940 declared for De Gaulle ; became African h.q. and training centre for Free French colonial troops.

Bread and Biscuit, the " staff of life," 554 ; biscuit-making, 557 ; flour, 1320 ; food value, 1338, *1339 ;* unleavened, 555 ; ceremonial use, 2527 ; cooking of, 901 ; wheat, 3372 ; ultraviolet ray treatment, 2730 ; yeast, 3433.

Breadalbane Range, Scotland, 2891.

Bread-fruit, tree of Pacific Isls., **557,** *558.*

Breakfall, movement in jujitsu, 1840.

Break rolls, a process in milling grain, 1320.

Breakspear, Nicholas. *See* **Adrian IV.**

Breakwater, 558, 1576 ; at Dover, *1031 ;* for harbours, 1576 ; for Mulberry harbours, 2251.

Bream, fish, 558, *559.*

Breasted, James Henry (1865–1935). American archaeologist ; professor of Egyptology (" Ancient Times : the History of the Early World ").

Breast stroke, in swimming, 3135, *3136.*

Breathing, in hygiene, 1676 ; for swimmers, 3135.

Brecknockshire, Wales. S. co. ; a. 733 sq. m. ; pop. 58,000 ; 559.

Brec'on, Wales. Co. tn. of Brecknockshire ; textiles, lime ; also called Brecknock ; pop. 5,334 ; 559.

Brecon Beacons, mts., Wales, 559.

Breda (brā'-da), Netherlands. Tn. pop. 50,800 ; once important frontier fortress, repeatedly taken by Sp. and Fr. ; residence of Charles II during exile ; surrender of, by Velazquez, *3050.*

" Breeches Bible," 427.

Breeches-bouy, sling apparatus used in saving life from wrecks.

Breech-loading rifle, invention of, 1283.

Breeding : of cattle, 730 ; of fish, 1300 ; of foxes for fur, 1412 ; of horses, 79 ; of plants, 79, 533.

Brege, r. in S. Ger., 972.

Breitenfeld (brī'-ten-felt), Ger. Village of Saxony ; Swedish victories (1631, 1642) in Thirty Years' War ; Gustavus Adolphus at, 1558.

Bremen (brā'-men). Ger. city ; free state, 1871–1933 ; a Hansa town ; pop., 1939 (city), 295,000 ; (state) 323,000 ; enclave of Amer. zone in Brit.-occupied Ger., 559.

Bremerhaven (brā'-mer-hah-fen). Ger. spt. on Weser ; pop. 24,500 ; 559.

Bren (from name of Czech town, Brno, and Enfield). Army light machine-gun, 2050 ; Bren carrier. 244, *249.*

Bren'nan, Louis (1852–1932), Irish engineer, invented Brennan torpedo and gyroscope monorail ; 1562.

Bren'ner Pass, lowest pass over Alps (4,500 ft.), between Germany and Italy ; 3215.

Brennus. Chief of Gauls ; led invasion and sack of Rome in 390 B.C.

Brent'ford. Co. tn. of Middlesex, 559. 2168 ; with Chiswick, Brentford became a borough in 1931, pop. 62,000.

Brentford of Newick, 1st Viscount (1865–1932). Brit. politician ; as William Joynson-Hicks was Minister of Health (1923) and Home Sec. (1924–29).

Brent (or brant) goose. Species of wild goose, 1486.

Brera (brā'-ra) **Palace,** Milan, 2172.

Brer Rabbit. Hero of Joel Chandler Harris's " Uncle Remus " ; constantly outwits the stronger animals, his enemies.

Brescia (bresh'-ya), It. Anc. city at foot of Alps ; pop. 123,000 ; Rom. remains ; firearms, textiles, paper. Many historic buildings destroyed by bombing in 2nd World War.

Breslau (bres'-low). Ger. name of Silesian city under Polish admin. since 1945. *See* **Wroclaw.**

Breslau, Peace of (1742), ended first Silesian War ; Austria to grant Silesia to Frederick of Prussia.

Bressey, Sir Charles Herbert (b. 1874). Eng. engineer ; Principal Technical Officer to Ministry of Transport (1928–35) ; prepared Highway Development Survey of Greater London, 1938.

Bress'umer, form of building beam, 380.

Brest. Fr. spt. of Brittany ; pop. 79,000 ; **560,** 586, 1359 ; occupied by Ger. 1940–44, *292* ; almost two-thirds of rebuilt city devastated when Norwegian nitrate ship exploded in harbour, July 28, 1947.

Brest-Litovsk, Poland. Fortified tn. on r. Bug ; pop. 30,000 ; rly. and mfg. centre ; taken by Ger. in 1915 ; scene of meeting of Ger. and Russ. forces Sept. 1939 ; awarded to U.S.S.R. in treaty ; fell to Germans 1941, 3419 ; again in Russian hands 1944, 3424.

Brest-Litovsk, Peace of (1917), 2849, 3412.

Brétigny (brā-tēn'-yē), **Treaty of** (1360), 1653.

Breton, André, Surrealist writer, 3122.

Bretons, People of Brittany, 585, *586* ; language, 740.

Bretton Woods. Town in New Hampshire, U.S.A., where in July 1944 U.N. representatives set up an International Monetary Fund to grant loans to member nations ; 1348, 1483, 2203.

Breuer (broi'-er), **Josef** (1842–1925). Austrian nerve specialist ; associated with Sigmund Freud in development of psycho-analysis.

Breughel. *See* **Brueghel.**

Breviary (brē'-vi-ĕr-i). Book used in Roman Catholic Church containing daily service for the canonical hours.

Brevier (bre-vēr') type, 3270.

Brewing, of beer, 103 ; yeast in, 3434.

Brewster, Sir David (1781–1868). Scot. scientist, 560 ; kaleidoscope, 1845 ; stereoscope, 3088.

Brewster, William (c.1560–1664). Mayflower Pilgrim leader ; one of the founders of Plymouth, U.S.A., 2122.

Brezina (bzhez'-ē-nah), **Otokar.** Pen name of Vaclav Jebavy (1868–1929). Czech poet ; wrote symbolic and mystical verse of great beauty.

Brian Boru', or **Brian of the Tribute** (926–1014). " High king " of Ireland, 1002–14 ; victor over Danes at Clontarf, where he was slain.

Briand (brē'-ahn), **Aristide** (1862–1932). Fr. politician ; premier eleven times, 560.

Brian de Bois-Guilbert (bwah-gēl'-bār). Knight in " Ivanhoe " ; 2900, *2901.*

Briard, French herding dog.

Briareus (bri-ar'-ioos). In Gk. myth., hundred-handed giant, 3298.

Bricklaying, 564.

Bricks and Tiles, 561, *563* ; arch. *205* ; in building, *610.*

Brick tea, 3162.

Bridewell. Originally royal palace in London, named after St. Bride's Well in the vicinity ; afterwards for 300 years used as reformatory.

Bridge, 564, *566, 567* ; " Auld Brig," Ayr, *324* ; Bailey, *250,* 569 ; bascule, 567 *(see* **Tower Bridge)** ; Brisbane, *571* ; cables for suspension, 2827 ; caisson for, 654 ; cantilever, *565,* 568 ; Coalbrookdale, 565 ; Cologne, 872 ; Forth bridges, *567,* 568 ; Kiel Canal, *1856* ; London bridges, 2012 ; longest, 569 ; Menai Suspension, *155,* 568, *2128,* 3336 ; Montreal, *2862* ; New York City, 565, 568, 2353, *2355,* 3289 ; Palladio and, 565 ; pontoon, 569 ; Quebec, 2716 ; Saltash, 568 ; San Francisco, *567,* 569, 2872 ; Stephenson and, 565 ; suspension, *155,* 568, 2127 ; Sydney, *567, 1576,* 3144 ; Tay, *1055* ; Tower, London, *567, 568, 2017* ; truss types, *565* ; Venice, *6310, 3311* ; new Waterloo bridge, *2011* ; Westminster, *2520* ; over r. Witham, 1953 ; Zambezi, 3441.

First aluminium alloy bridge, weighing 54 tons, opened at Sunderland, Nov. 26, 1948.

Bridge of Sighs. Covered bridge in Venice ; so called because condemned prisoners formerly passed over it from the judgement hall to execution, 3310, *3311* ; similar bridge at Cambridge, *667*.

Bridge, Sir Frederick (1844–1924). Eng. musician and composer, organist Manchester Cath. (1869–75) ; deputy organist (1875–82) and organist (1882–1918) Westminster Abbey.

Bridgeport, Conn., U.S.A. 2nd city of state ; spt. on Long Island Sound ; important mfrs. ; pop. 147,121.

Bridges, Robert (1844–1930). Eng. poet and dramatist ; Poet Laureate (1913–30) ; awarded O.M. in 1929 ; 1216 ; spelling reform proposals, 3058.

Bridget, Brigit, or **Bride, St.** (A.D. 452 ?–523). One of the three great saints of Ire. ; founded church and monastery of Kildare.

Bridget of Sweden, Birgitta, or **Brigitta, St.** (1303 ?–73). Founder of Brigittines, order of nuns ; patroness of Sweden ; festival Oct. 8.

Bridgetown. Cap. of Barbados, Brit. W. Indies ; pop, 14,000 ; 360.

Bridgewater Canal, 569 ; Brindley and, 570 ; construction, 686, *688*.

Bridgman, Laura Dewey (1829–89). American blind deaf-mute, 470.

Bridgwater. Spt. tn. in Somersetshire, on Parret ; pop. 17,139.

Bridie, James (b. 1888). Pen-name of Scottish dramatist O. H. Mavor ; made C.B.E. 1946 ; plays include "Tobias and the Angel " ; " The Sleeping Clergyman " ; " The Black Eye " ; " John Knox " 1947 ; " Dr. Angelus " 1947 ; " Daphne Laureola " 1949.

Bridlington, Yorkshire. Believed to have been the site of a Roman encampment ; Bridlington Bay has fine sands and lovely gardens ; pop. 21,460.

Bridport. Tn., Dorset ; rope, sailcloth mfrs., pop. 5,917 ; 1030.

Brie (brē). Anc. dist. of Fr. between rivers Seine and Marne ; noted for cheese.

Brienz (brē-ents'), **Lake.** In Switzerland, 3140.

Brieux (brē-ē'), **Eugène** (1858–1932). Fr. dramatist noted for sensational treatment of social subjects.

Brigach (brē'-gahkh), **River.** In S. Ger., 972.

Brigade. A sub-division of an army (armoured, cavalry or infantry) under the command of a brigadier ; its composition varies in different countries.

Bright, Sir Charles Tilston (1832–88). Eng. engineer ; first transatlantic cable, 642.

Bright, John (1811–89). Eng. Liberal statesman and brilliant orator, 569.

Brightlingsea, Essex. On Colne estuary ; pop. 4,145 ; oysters, 2466.

Brighton. Popular seaside resort in Sussex, pop. 133,000 ; 570 ; elec. supply, 1545 ; George IV in, *1441*.

Bright's disease, of kidneys, 1856.

Bril, Paulus (1554–1626). Painter ; one of the " Italianized " Flemings, 2324.

Brimstone, or sulphur, 3116.

Brimstone butterfly ; *plate f. 632*.

Brindisi (brin'-diz-i), Italy. Anc. Brundisium, chief Rom. spt. on Adriatic ; stop on Empire airway ; Rom. ruins ; pop. 41,700.

Brindley, James (1716–72). Eng. engineer ; builder of Bridgewater Canal. 569, 570.

Brine, 2866 ; in refrigeration, 1392.

Brisbane, Australia. Cap. of Queensland, on r. Brisbane, 15 m. above mouth ; pop. 384,000 ; exports wool, hides, gold ; 571, 2718 ; Test Match at, *930*.

Briseis (brī-sē'-is), 19.

Brissot (brē-sō'), **Jean** or **Jacques Pierre** (1754–93). French revolutionist ; leader of the Girondists, who were

originally called Brissotins ; for opposing the trial of the king, he was arrested by Robespierre and executed.

Bristles, 1565 ; porcupine, 2656.

Bristol, seventh city of England. Important spt., pop. 416,000 ; **571,** 1168, 1477.

Bristol Channel. Arm of Atlantic between Wales and England, 572.

Britain (Rom. Britannia), **572,** *1431*. History (to 829), 572 ; history (829 to 1707, Act of Union), 1193 ; prehistoric remains, *323, 3095, 3096* ; Caesar's visit, 651, 1193 ; Celtic people and religion, 740 ; Rom. conquest, 651, 1193 ; *2009, 2391, 2810, 2811, 2812* ; Anglo-Saxon conquest, 255, 1194, 1209 ; Arthurian legends, 255 ; Christianity introduced, 302, 1194 ; Phoenicians, 1193, *1201* ; battle of, in 1940, **575.** For geography and later history, *see* **British Isles ; England ; Great Britain ; Scotland ; United Kingdom ; Wales.**

Britain, Battle of, 1940 ; 575, *576*, 1452, 3417 ; memorial in Westminster Abbey, *577* ; " the few," **577.** Annual Battle of Britain " fly-past " takes place on Sept. 15, and the memorial services on the nearest Sunday to that date.

Britannia. Latin name for Britain ; figure on coins, **578.**

Britannia metal, alloy of tin, antimony, copper, and sometimes zinc ; proportions vary according to use.

British Academy, 17.

British and Foreign Bible Society, Borrow and, 527.

British Army of the Rhine (B.A.O.R.). On Aug. 26, 1945, the Brit. Liberation Army (B.L.A.) became the occupation forces of the Brit. zone of Ger.

British Association, for the advancement of science in all its branches ; was founded by Sir David Brewster and others in 1831. Chief function is the holding of an annual conference, at which an address is delivered by some eminent man chosen President for the year.

British Broadcasting Corporation (B.B.C.). Public corporation, created by Royal Charter in 1927 ; is controlled by a Director-General and five Governors ; 3398, 3399 ; studios, *1497*, 2446, *3183*, *3399* ; television, 3182, 3184 ; transmitter, *3399*.

British Columbia. Westernmost prov. of Canada ; 359,000 sq. m. ; pop. 1,082.000 ; 578, *map. plate f. 680* ; Vancouver, 3303 ; Victoria, 3321.

British Commonwealth of Nations, 580, *map,* **581** ; in Africa, *map f. 68,* 69, 70, 72 ; in Asia, 268 ; 271 ; decorations of honour, *see* **Orders and Decorations** ; flags and badges, *frontis. Vol. 8* ; government, 1488. *See also* **Crown Colonies ; Dominions.**

British Council. Organization for spreading knowledge of Brit. culture and life in foreign countries.

British Courts, 921.

British East Africa, largest territory in centre of E. coast incl. Kenya, Tanganyika, and Uganda and isls. of Zanzibar and Pemba. *See* **East Africa.**

British Empire, Order of the, 2449.

British Expeditionary Force (B.E.F.). Army which, under Gen. Gort, moved into France and Belgium from Sept. 1939, and was finally evacuated from Dunkirk in May 1940 ; 1056, *f. 1057*.

British Guiana, a crown colony on N.E. coast of S. Amer. ; 89,500 sq. m. ; pop. 367,000 ; *1552*, 1553 ; boundary dispute, 203 ; rare stamp, *3075*.

British Honduras. *See* **Honduras, British.**

British Industries Fair (B.I.F.), *1257*.

British Isles, name popularly applied to Gt. Brit., Channel Isls., Ire., Isle of Man, and numerous surrounding islands ; 121,633 sq. m. ; pop. 49,200,000 ; **582** ; *map, plate f. 584. See also* **England ; Gt. Britain, Ireland, Scotland,** etc.

British Legion, organization founded in 1921 ; membership is open to ex-Service men and women, and certain others who served with the forces in the World Wars ; 1919.

British Liberation Army (B.L.A.), 1944–45. 21st Army Group (Brit. 2nd Army and 1st Can. Army), commanded by Montgomery.

British Medical Association (B.M.A.). Organization estab. 1832 ; publishes the " British Medical Journal " and looks after interests of profession.

British Museum, London, **584,** *plate f. 585* ; library, 1930 ; mummies in, 2255 ; Parthenon sculptures, 22 ; reading room, *585* ; Rosetta stone, 2828.

British New Guinea. *See* **Papua.**

British North America Act, 683.

British North Borneo, Crown Colony in N. Borneo ; 29,500 sq. m. ; pop. 270,200 ; cap., Sandakan, pop. 13,800 ; timber, tobacco, 527 ; *map f. 264* ; in Japanese hands 1941–45, 527.

British Overseas Airways Corporation (B.O.A.C.). Public corporation formed 1939 under Govt. control to operate Imperial Airways and British Airways ; responsible for Commonwealth and N. Atlantic services.

British Red Cross Society, 2752.

British Somaliland, protectorate in N.E. Africa bordering Gulf of Aden ; 68,000 sq. m. ; pop. est. 700,000 ; chief tn., Berbera ; *maps f. 68, 1072. See under* **Somaliland.**

British South Africa Company, 2771, 3019.

British Thermal Unit (B.Th.U.), definition, 1596, 2154, 3350.

Brit'omart. A maiden knight, representing chastity, in Spenser's " Faerie Queene."

Britons, early Celtic inhabitants of Brit. Isles, 740, 1193 ; baskets, 368. *See* **Britain.**

Brittany, old province of N.W. France, **585,** 1359, 1360 ; oysters, 2466 ; people, 1358.

Britten (Edward) Benjamin (b. 1913). Brit. composer ; operas, " Peter Grimes," *2437*, " Albert Herring " ; string quartets, songs, etc. ; " Spring Symphony."

Brno (br-nō), or **Brünn.** 2nd city of Czechoslovakia ; cap. of Moravia. Fell to French in 1809 ; under Austro-Hungary till 1918 ; occupied by Germans March 15, 1939, and became German arms centre during 2nd World War until liberated by Russians April 26, 1945 ; gives its name to Bren gun ; pop. (1938) 264,900.

Broad Bean, 380.

Broadcasting, Marconi and, 2098 ; studios, *1497*, 2446, *3399. See also* **Radio ; Television ; Wireless.**

Broadcasting House, Portland Place, London, headquarters of Brit. Broadcasting Corp. ; control panels, *3399* ; studios, *1497*, 2446, *3399*.

Broadlaw, mt. in Peeblesshire, Scot., 12 m. s.w. of Peebles ; 2,723 ft. high, 2535.

Broad-leaved trees, one of the two great groups into which trees are divided as opposed to the conifers, with needle-like leaves ; 3245, 3246.

Broads, The. Dist. in Norfolk and Suffolk, consisting of a number of shallow lakes and reed marshes ; attracts many visitors for sailing ; 2375, 2376.

Broadway, vil. of Worcestershire, with Tudor stone houses and old inn.

Broadway. Famous thoroughfare of New York, centre of the city's night life, 2352, *2354, plate f. 2353*.

Brob'dingnag, in " Gulliver's Travels," 3134.

Brocade', a cloth, 850.

Brocade Moth, eggs, *629*.

Broche (brōsh), implement used in tapestry weaving, 3152.

Brock, Sir Thomas (1847 – 1922). Notable Eng. sculptor ; among his most famous works is the Queen Victoria Memorial in front of Buckingham Palace.

Brock. Old English name for the hedger.

Brocken, highest peak in Harz Mts., (3730 ft.), 1581.

Broderie Anglaise, 1154.

Broglie (brō-lē), **Prince Louis de** (b. 1892). Fr. physicist; author of wave mechanics theory, 2711; Nobel prize for physics (1929), and electron microscope, 2165.

Broken Bones, how to set, 1294; bandages, 1292.

Broken Hill, Australia, mining tn. in w. of New South Wales; pop. 26,500; 2344. There is also a mining town of this name in N. Rhodesia, 2772.

Broker. One who buys or sells on behalf of another; 3094.

Brom'berg. Ger. name for the Polish city **Bydgoszcz** (q.v.).

Bromide, a compound of bromine; silver bromide in photography, 2973.

Bromine (Br), a non-metallic gaseous element of the halogen group, 1567; atomic weight, 79·9; used in the manufacture of coal-tar dyes; freezes at 19° F.; properties, 777, 816; the name is derived from the Greek *bromos*, a stench.

Brompton Oratory, London, s.w., built in the style of the Italian Renaissance; the Oratory of St. Philip Neri was founded by F. W. Faber, the hymn-writer; a statue of Cardinal Newman, one of the founders of the Oratory, faces the building.

Bronchi (brong'-kī) (sing. bronchus), the two main branches of the windpipe, or trachea, 2039.

Brontë. Name of English literary family who lived at Haworth Parsonage, Yorks. Charlotte (1816–55) wrote " Jane Eyre," " Shirley " and " Villette "; Emily (1818–48), wrote " Wuthering Heights "; Anne (1820–49) wrote " Agnes Grey." Their brother Branwell (1817–48) was a painter. Their father was Rev. Patrick Brontë (1786–1861). 586, 587, 2402.

Brontosaur'us, prehistoric reptile, 2678.

Bronx, a borough of New York City, U.S.A., 2353.

Bronze, alloy of copper and tin, 122, 587, 3215; Japanese work, 1810; metallic paint, 2478; statuary, 2904.

Bronze Age, period in history characterized by use of bronze, 587.

Bronze turkey, 3261.

Brooke, Sir Basil S. (b. 1888). Prime min. of N. Ireland 1943 and 1949.

Brooke, Frances (1724–89), Canadian novelist, 684.

Brooke, Sir James (1803–68), rajah of Sarawak, Borneo; wealthy retired Eng. soldier; suppressed piracy and head-hunting and introduced civilization; 527, 2873.

Brooke, Rupert Chawner (1888–1915), Eng. poet of great promise, who died in 1st World War, 587, 588.

Brooke, Stopford Augustus (1832–1916). Brit. preacher and author; appointed chaplain to Queen Victoria (1872); became Dissenting minister (1880); (" Primer of Eng. Literature "; " History of Early Eng. Literature ").

Brooking, Charles (1723–59). Eng. marine painter, 2956.

Brooklands. Former motor racing track near Weybridge, Surrey.

Brooklyn, N.Y., U.S.A. A borough of New York City on Long Isl.; pop. (1944) 2,742,000; 2351, 2353.

Brooklyn Bridge, 568, 2355.

Broom. Shrub of the pea family, emblem of the Plantagenets, 1609.

Brotherton, Edward Allen, 1st Baron (1856–1930). Brit. pioneer in chemical industry; established his first works for manufacture of ammonia sulphate in 1878; benefactor of Univ. of Leeds.

Brougham (brō'-am or brōōm), **Henry, Baron** (1778–1868). Brit. lord chancellor and Liberal reforming statesman; counsel for Queen Caroline in defence against divorce from George

IV: his unique private carriage was forerunner of the brougham.

Brouwer, Adriaen (c. 1606–38). Flemish artist, 2333.

Brown, Sir Arthur Whitten (1886–1948). Eng. engineer; received knighthood for having first flown the Atlantic with Alcock in June 1919; 47.

Brown, Douglas Clifton (b. 1879). Deputy speaker of Brit. House of Commons 1938–43; Speaker, 1943.

Brown, Ernest (b. 1881). Eng. politician; Min. of Labour, 1935–40; Sec. for Scotland, 1940; Min. for Health, 1941; Chan. Duchy Lancaster, 1943–45.

Brown, Ford Madox (1821–93). Eng. painter; realistic treatment of historical subjects; inspired Pre-Raphaelite movement; 2476; " Danes expelled from Manchester," 1203; " The Last of England," 2682.

Brown, John (1800–59). Amer. abolitionist, 588; (" John Brown's body . . .").

Brown, John (1810–82). Scot. physician and writer (" Rab and His Friends "; " Pet Marjorie "; little masterpieces of keen, kindly, humorous character-drawing).

Brown, John (1826–83). Scot. gillie; for 34 years the personal servant of Queen Victoria.

Brown, Robert (1773–1858), Brit. botanist, discoverer of Brownian movement, 589.

" **Brown Bess** " musket, 1282.

Browne, Sir Thomas (1605–82). Eng. physician and author; unrivalled master of stately rhythmic, but highly artificial and latinized prose style (" Religio Medici "; " Urn-Burial ").

Brownian movement, 588.

Brownie. In Scot. folklore, good-natured goblin who milks cows, sweeps floors, and does other household drudgery for the family to which he attaches himself.

Brownies. Junior Girl Guides, 1466, 1467.

Browning, Elizabeth Barrett (1806–61). Eng. poet, wife of Robert Browning, 589, 1215.

Browning, Lt.-Gen. Sir Frederick A. M. (b. 1896). Brit. soldier; deputy commdr. of Allied Airborne Army (1944) at time of airborne invasion of Holland (see Arnhem); app. Comptroller and Treasurer of Princess Elizabeth's Household in 1947.

Browning, Robert (1812–89). Eng. poet, 590, 1215.

Brownists. Early dissenters, 1390.

Brown race, 2723, 2725.

Brown rat, 2746.

Bruce, Charles Granville (1866–1939), son of 1st Lord Aberdare; leader of Mt. Everest expeditions of 1922 and 1924 (" Twenty Years in the Himalayas," " The Assault on Mt. Everest," " Himalayan Wanderer ").

Bruce, James (1730–94). Scot. explorer, 590.

Bruce, Robert (1274–1329), king of Scot., victor at Bannockburn, 359, 590, 591.

Bruce, Stanley Melbourne, Viscount (b. 1883). Australian statesman, 591.

Bruch (brōōkh), **Max** (1838–1920), Ger. violinist and composer (" Kol Nidrei " and four concertos).

Brucine (brōō'sin). An alkaloid found with strychnine in nux vomica and false angostura bark.

Brueghel (brū-khel), **Jan** (1568–1625). Flemish artist, son of Pieter Brueghel, 592, 2324.

Brueghel, Pieter the Elder (d. c 1570), Flemish painter, 592, 2324; two sons **Pieter the Younger** (1564–1637), and **Jan** (above), also celebrated painters.

Bruges (brōōzh), Belgium. Old Flemish tn.; pop. 51,000, 592; famous belfry, 592; market, 403; in Ger. occupn. 1940–44, 593. As from 1939 official name is Brugge.

Bruises, treatment for, 1295.

Brum'mell, George Bryan (1778–1840). " Beau Brummell," Eng. dandy, dictator of fashion, early friend of Prince of Wales (King George IV).

Brunei (brōō-nā'-ē). Brit. protectorate in N.W. Borneo; 2,226 sq. m.; pop. 30,000; chief tn., Brunei (12,000); 527.

Brunel', Isambard Kingdom (1806–59). Brit. engineer, son of Sir Marc Brunel, 593; designed Great Eastern, 593; Great Western Rly., 594.

Brunel, Sir Marc Isambard (1769–1849). Brit. engineer; 593.

Brunelleschi (brōō-nel-es'-kē), **Filippo** (1377–1446). It. architect, called founder of Renaissance architecture; and Ghiberti, 1460.

Brunetière (brūn-tyär), **Ferdinand** (1849–1906). Fr. critic, editor of the " Revue des Deux Mondes."

Bruneval (brūn-val). Fr. village 12 m. N. of Le Havre; Ger. radar centre here demolished by Brit. combined ops. attack, Feb. 27–28, 1942.

Brunhild (broon'-hild) or **Brunhilda.** In Scandinavian myth., valkyrie whom Odin punishes for disobedience by placing her inside a ring of fire, there in a charmed sleep to await the hero destined to waken her; in " Nibelungenlied," 2363; in Wagner's operas, 2440.

Brunhilde (d. A.D. 613), queen of Austrasia, daughter of Athanagild, king of the Visigoths.

Brüning, Heinrich (b. 1885), Ger. statesman; Chancellor 1930–32.

Brünn. Ger. name for Czech city of Brno (q.v.).

Brunner, Sir John Tomlinson, Bart. (1842–1919). Brit. industrialist; with Dr. Mond founded alkali works.

Bru'no, Giordano (1548–1600). It. Renaissance philosopher; attacked orthodox Aristotelian doctrine.

Bruno, St. (c. 1030–1101), founds Carthusians, 2213.

Brunswick. Republic in w. Ger., duchy until 1918; 1,425 sq. m.; pop. 599,200. Also its cap., pop. 201 000; extensive mfts.

Brunswick or **Hanoverian dynasty** (Eng.), 1574.

Bru'sa. See Bursa.

Brush, Charles Francis (1849–1929). Amer. inventor; invented type of dynamo; developed arc light.

Brush. Commutator contacts in generators or motors, 1061.

Brush turkey, of Australia, 1095.

Brusilov (broos'-i-lof), **Alexei** (1856–1926). Rus. general; brilliant successes in Galicia 1914–15 and 1916; after revolution of 1917 was in supreme command for short time, later accepting Bolshevik regime.

Brussels. Cap. of Belgium; pop. (with suburbs) 900,000; 594, 404; in Ger. occupn. 1914–18 and 1940–44; 595, 3417, 3422.

Brussels carpet, 706, 707.

Brussels lace, 1880, plate f. 1880.

Brussels sprouts, Small sprouts, each a miniature cabbage, springing from a certain species of cabbage, 594.

Bru'tus, Lucius Junius. Legendary Rom. patriot; one of first 2 consuls of the Rep. (509 B.C.); 595, 596, 2804.

Brutus, Marcus Junius (85–42 B.C.), one of Caesar's assassins; 596; and Caesar's death, 653.

Brutus the Trojan. Mythical first king of Brit., grandson of Ascanius, the son of Aeneas.

Bruxelles (brū'-sel). Fr. name for Brussels.

Bruyère, Jean de la. See La Bruyère.

Bry'ant, Arthur W. M. (b. 1899). Brit. historian; " Charles II," " Pepys," " The Years of Endurance "; appointed official naval historian of Second World War.

Bryant, William Cullen (1794–1878), " father of Amer. poets " (" The Embargo," " Lines to a Waterfowl," " The Battlefield "), 597, 3293.

Bryce, James, Viscount (1838–1922). Brit. statesman and historian, ambassador to U.S.A. (" The Holy Roman Empire "; " The American Commonwealth," a classic; " Modern Democracies "; " A Study of American History.")

Brynmawr (brin-mawr'), Wales. Tn. in Brecknock ; ironworks ; pop. 6,489 ; 559.

Bryol'ogy. Science of mosses, 533.

Bryony, white : *Bryonia dioica*, fam. Cucurbitaceae ; climbs by tendrils ; flowers greenish-white, berries red ; leaves lobed and hairy : black bryony *Tamus*, fam. Dioscoreaceae, also a climbing plant, has simple, heart-shaped, shiny leaves, and is not related to white bryony.

Bryophytes (brī'-ō-fītz), plant group, 2620.

Bryozoa (brī'-ō-zō-*a*). Name given by Ehrenberg to a class of molluscoid animals, called moss plants.

Brython'ic languages. Group of Celtic languages including Welsh and Breton.

Bry'um. Genus of mosses.

Bubonic plague. Epidemic disease, causing swollen glands, fever, and rapid death (the Black Death), 463 ; carried by fleas and rats, 1459, 2746 ; great epidemics, 757.

Buccaneers'. Piratical adventurers (chiefly Eng. and Fr.) who in 17th cent. plundered Spaniards along coasts of W. Indies and S. Amer., 701. *See also* **Pirates.**

Buccleuch (bu-klōō), **Henry Scott, 3rd Duke of** (1746–1812), friend of Sir Walter Scott, 2898.

Bucephalus (bū-sef'-*a*-lus). War horse of Alexander the Great.

Buchan (buk'*an*), **Alexander** (1829–1907). Scottish meteorologist. He discovered that there were certain periods when temperatures, instead of rising, fall or remain stationary, while at others, instead of falling, temperatures would tend to rise ; " Buchan's Cold Spells."

Buchan, John (1875–1940), Scot. author, made Gov.-Gen. of Canada 1935, when created Baron Tweedsmuir, 597, 2895.

Buchan'an, Jack (b. 1891). Brit. actor, manager, producer, of musical comedies and revues.

Buchanan, Robert Williams (1841–1901). Scot. poet, novelist, and playwright. (" London Poems," "Shadow of the Sword," " God and the Man.")

Bucharest (bōō-kar-est'). Cap. of Rumania, 30 m. N. of r. Danube ; pop. 985,000 ; 597, 2840 ; in Ger. occupn. 1916–18 ; Allies bombed in 2nd World War, 598.

Bucharest, Treaty of. Ended 2nd Balkan War (1913), 345, 598, 3202.

Bucharest, Treaty of (1918). Made between Germany and her allies and Rumania, May 7, 1918.

Buchenwald (bōōk'-*en*-valt). Ger. concentration camp near Weimar, Thuringia ; overrun by U.S. forces April 12, 1945, 3422 ; its horrors seen by Brit. and U.S. parl. delegations.

Buchman, Frank Nathan Daniel (b. 1878). American evangelist. Founder of the Group and Moral Re-Armament Movements.

Buck, or male deer, 984.

Buck, Pearl. Amer. novelist. (" The Good Earth," " The Patriot "). Awarded Nobel prize 1938 ; 3295.

Buckingham. Tn. in Bucks, on r. Ouse ; agric. centre ; pop. 3,000, 600.

Buckingham, George Villiers, 1st Duke of (1592–1628). Eng. courtier, unscrupulous favourite of James I and of Charles I ; 598.

Buckingham Palace, London, 599, 2015, *3283* ; bombed in 2nd World War, 599.

Buckinghamshire or **Bucks.** Southmidland co., Eng. ; 749 sq. m. : pop. 271,000 ; 599, *1162.*

Buckle, Henry Thomas (1821–62). Eng. historian (" History of Civilization in England ").

Buck'master, Stanley Owen, 1st Baron (1861–1934). Brit. politician and lawyer ; Solicitor-General (1913–15) ; Lord Chancellor (1915–16).

Buckskin. Leather ; tanning, 1914.

Buckthorn. Flowering shrub of genus *Rhamnus* ; alder buckthorn, thornless, 5 ft. to 10 ft., has broad leaves on which brimstone butterfly caterpillars feed ; purging buckthorn, taller, is thorned at branch ends. Sea buckthorn, no relation, found on E. coast.

Buckwheat. Cereal crop of N. Amer. ; grain used for poultry and buckwheat cakes.

Bucolics (bū-kol'-iks) (from Gk. word for " cowherd "). Pastoral poems of Gk. and Rom. poets, partic. Virgil.

Bud, of flower, *532,* 1322.

Bu'da, Hungary, now **Budapest.**

Budapest (boo'-d*a*-pest'). Cap. of Hungary on Danube ; pop. (1943) 1,217,000 ; 600, 1656 ; more than half destroyed in 2nd World War, 600.

Budenny (bōōd-yon'-i), **Simeon Mikhailevitch** (b. 1876). Russian soldier ; as cavalry gen. defeated Denikin's White Army, 1920 ; prominent in defeating Finns in 1940 ; pursuing " scorched earth " policy, blew up the Dnieper Dam, Aug. 1941.

Buddha (bood'-*a*) (about 568–488 B.C.). Hindu prince Siddhattha Gotama, or Gautama ; founder of Buddhism, 600 ; in Tibet Temple, *269* ; statues (Canton), 695.

Buddh Gaya. Vil. of Bihar, India ; traditional resting place of the Buddha and a famous pilgrimage centre, 428 ; shrine at, *601.*

Buddhism. Oriental religion, 600, 1706, *1708, 1709* ; Burma, 625 ; China, 809 ; distinguished from Hinduism, 1628 ; influence on architecture, 1708 ; in India, 1703 ; Japan, 1796 ; 1798, *1801, 1805* ; Java, 1813, *1814*: Siam, 2964.

Budge (John) Donald (b. 1916). Amer. tennis player ; won singles at Wimbledon in 1937 ; repeated his success in 1938. Turned professional after winning all the principal championships of that year.

Budgerigar. Small Australian long-tailed parrakeet, *2526.*

Budget. Name given to the annual statement of the country's finances made by the Chancellor of the Exchequer in the House of Commons.

Buea (bū-ā'-*a*). Cap. of Brit. Cameroon, *map, 3366.*

Buenaventura (bwā-na-ven-tōōr'-*a*). Colombia port on Pacific at mouth of Dagua ; destroyed by fire in 1931 but since rebuilt ; important trade centre ; pop. 30,000.

Buenos Aires (bwā'-nōs-ī'-rēz). Cap. of Argentina, harbour on Rio de la Plata ; 80 sq. m. ; pop. 2,500,000 ; 601, *602* ; 228, *map, 3417.*

Buffalo, N.Y., U.S.A. At E. end of L. Erie, 2nd largest city of state ; univ. ; pop. 575,900 ; 2357.

Buffalo. Animal of Asia and Africa, *71, 602* ; water, 1352 ; in India, *1701* ; in S. Africa, instinct, 160. Name also given to amphibious tank, 244, *247. See also* **Bison.**

" Buffalo Bill " (William Frederick Cody) (1846–1917). Noted Amer. frontiersman and Indian fighter, 603.

Buffalo bird, 602.

Buffer states. Areas strategically or economically important, whose independence is sanctioned by great powers as checks or " buffers " on rival nations.

Buffon (bū'-fon), **George Louis Leclerc, Comte de** (1707–88). Fr. naturalist and writer (" Natural History ") ; 603, 3446.

Buff Orpington, breed of domestic fowl, *435.*

Bug. Two rivers of Europe ; one, also called Western Don, rises in Poland, flows N. 440 m. into Vistula at Novo Georgievsk, 3326, 3424 ; the other, in s.w. Ukraine, flows about 450 m. to Black Sea.

" Bug Bible," 427.

Bugs. Insects with sucking beaks, 1730 ; cochineal, 859 ; " green " or aphis, 185, 1733.

Building construction, 604, *605–608* ; aluminium, 604, 611 ; brick, 561, *610;* cantilever principle, 604 ; kit-

chen, *123,* 612 ; prefabrication, 611 ; reinforced concrete, 604 ; roof, 2821 ; and atom bombs, *609. See also* **Architecture.**

Building Societies. Companies lending money on mortgage to house-purchasers.

Builth (bilth) **Wells,** Wales. Tn. and health resort in Brecknockshire ; mineral springs ; pop. 1,663 ; 559.

Bukovina (bōō-kō-vē'-n*a*). Rumania ; former crownland of Austria : 4,030 sq. m. ; pop. 800,000 ; N. Bukovina incorporated in Soviet Union, August 1940 ; 2840, 2841.

Bulama. *See* **Bolama.**

Bulawayo (bōōl-*a*-wī'-yō). Tn., gold-mining centre and commercial cap. of S. Rhodesia ; former cap. of the Matabeles ; pop. 29,000 ; 2772, *2773.*

Bulb. In electric lighting, 1134, *1135.*

Bulb. Of plants, **612** ; cultivation in Holland, 2320, 2321.

Bul'bul. A Persian bird, 2367.

Bulgaria. Balkan state ; 39,825 sq. m. ; pop. 7,021,000 ; *map, 344,* **612** ; in Balkan Wars, 343 ; and Macedonia, 2049 ; people, *613* ; cap. Sofia, 2997 ; former cap. Trnovo, *614* ; attar of roses, 2549 ; 1st World War, 3410, 3414 ; 2nd World War, 614.

Bull or Taurus. A constellation, 3444.

Bull (papal), 2495.

Bulldozer, a mechanical excavator, *1248,* 1249.

Bull, Golden, 1449, 1637.

" Bull, John." Nickname for typical Englishman, 2366.

Bull, Ole (1810–80). Norwegian violinist, largely self-taught.

Bulldog, *plate f. 1024.*

Bul'len, Frank Thomas (1857–1915). Eng. writer of sea stories (" The Cruise of the Cachalot " ; " Sea Wrack " ; " The Call of the Deep ").

Bul'ler, Sir Redvers Henry (1839–1908). Eng. general ; commander-in-chief of Brit. forces in the Boer War ; was superseded by Lord Roberts ; relieved Ladysmith after several reverses.

Bullet, as ammunition, 1283, 1908 ; physics of, 2793.

Bull fighting, in Spain, *3036.*

Bullfinch. European song-bird of the finch family, **614,** 1272.

Bull moose, *2228.*

Bull Run, battle of (1861). First battle of American Civil War ; Jackson at, 1789 ; in second battle (1862) Lee defeated Pope.

Bull Terrier, *plate f. 1024.*

Bülow (bü'-lof), **Bernard von, Prince** (1849–1929). Ger. statesman and diplomat, imperial chancellor 1900–09.

Bülow, Hans Guido von (1830–94). Ger. pianist and conductor, one of the greatest of his time.

Bulrush, 615.

Bulwer Lytton. *See* **Lytton.**

Bumble. Fat pompous beadle who terrorizes workhouse inmates in Dickens' " Oliver Twist."

Bumble-bee or **humble-bee,** 390, 394 ; *plate f. 392.*

Buna. Syn. rubber ; first made from *butadiene* and *natrium* (soda) ; from petroleum, 2430.

Bunbury. Spt. of W. Australia, on Koombanah Bay ; pop. 5,700.

Bundesrat (boon'-des-raht'), federal council of the former Ger. empire ; replaced in 1918 by the Reichsrat ; name revived for upper house of Fed. Ger. Rep., Sept. 1949.

Bundestag. Name given to lower house of Fed. Ger. Rep., Sept. 1949.

Bunker Hill, battle of, 1775, first battle of War of Amer. Independence, 144.

" Bunkum." Origin of term, 615.

Bunsen, Robert Wilhelm (1811–99), Ger. chemist ; developed spectrum analysis, *plate f. 3057* ; isolated elements caesium and rubidium ; explained geysers, 1459 ; and gas lighting, 1424 ; invented Bunsen burner, 615.

Bunsen Burner. Gas-air burner, **615,** *616* ; in gas fire, 1598 ; in linotype machine, 1958. *See also* **Blowpipe.**

Bunt, form of smut fungus.

Bunting, bird of finch family, 616.

Bun'yan, John (1628–88). Eng. Puritan leader and author of "Pilgrim's Progress," **617,** 1211, 2401 ; " Pilgrim's Progress," story of, 618.

Buonarroti (bwō-nah-rot'-ē). *See* **Michelangelo.**

Buoy. A navigation aid, **620.**

Buoyancy. Archimedes's principle, 210.

Bur'bage or **Burbadge, Richard** (*c.* 1567–1619). Eng. actor, famous for impersonation of Shakespearian characters ; associated with Shakespeare, 2933.

Burbank, Luther (1849–1926). Amer. experimenter with plants, **621.**

Burdekin. R. of Queensland, rises on E. slope of Great Dividing Range and flows 350 m. into Pacific.

Burdett-Coutts (bêr-det-kōōts'), **Angela Georgina, Baroness** (1814–1906). Eng. philanthropist.

Burdock, seeds, 2622, *2623.* This plant, of order *Compositae,* is very common by roadsides in Britain. Has heads of purplish florets.

Bure. River in Norfolk flowing into the Yare, 50 m. long ; 2375.

Bur'gesses, House of. The first Amer. representative legislative body, called in Virginia in 1619 ; name continued until time of War of Independence.

Burgh (bu'-ro). Scot. equivalent for borough ; there are three kinds, royal burghs, police burghs, and parl. burghs, 2894.

" **Burghers of Calais,**" Rodin's group, *2796,* 2797.

Burghley, David George Brownlow Cecil, Lord (b. 1905). Eng. athlete ; son of the Marquess of Exeter ; won hurdles in 1928 Olympic Games ; pres. A.A.A. ; on Nat. Fitness Council ; Gov. of Bermudas (1943–45) ; Chairman of Olympic Games committee in 1948. Elected Rector of St. Andrews Univ. in 1950.

Burghley (or Burleigh), William Cecil, Baron (1520–98), Eng. statesman, for 40 years chief adviser of Queen Elizabeth ; obtains Elizabeth's signature to Mary's death warrant, *1148.*

Burglar Alarm, automatic, 322 ; photoelectric cell, 2575.

Burgos (bōōr'-gos), Sp. Former cap. of old Castile on r. Arlanzon, 130 m. N. of Madrid ; pop. 62,474 (est. 1931) ; 3030 ; In Spanish Civil War, H.Q. of Nationalist forces, 3039 ; cath., *3035, 3041.*

Burgoyne (bêr-goin'), **John** (1722–92). Eng. general in War of Amer. Independence ; northern campaign and defeat at Saratoga, 146.

Burgundy (bêr'-gun-di). Former kingdom and duchy in E. cent. France, now included in 4 depts.

Burial and funeral customs, anc. Egypt, *1109, 1120* ; Hindu, 411.

Bur'iat-Mongol Region, autonomous Asiatic republic of U.S.S.R. ; pop. 542,000 ; cap. Ulan-Ude.

Buriats, branch of Mongols, 2207.

Bu'rin. An engraving tool, *1218.*

Burke, Edmund (1729–97). Brit. statesman, orator, and writer, **621,** *622* ; literary associations, 1213.

Burleigh. *See* **Burghley.**

Burma (bêr'-ma). Republic on E. side of Bay of Bengal ; over 262,000 sq. m. ; pop. 14,660,000 ; **623** ; *map, 1702* ; alphabet, *126* ; elephants, 1142 ; independence, 3283 ; natives, *624* ; cap. Rangoon, 2744 ; ricegrowing, 2775 ; teak, 1142, 3162 ; tungsten, 3254 ; in 2nd World War, 2473, 3420, 3424 ; Lord Alexander and, 107.

Burma Road. Highway from Lashio, Burma, to Chungking on the Yangtze built by Chinese native labour in 1939 ; closed by Brit. Govt. July 1940 ; re-opened Oct. 1940.

Burma-Siam Rly. So-called " Death Railway," 282 m. long, built by

forced labour of Brit. and Allied prisoners in Jap. hands Oct. 1942–Nov. 1943 ; of 54,000 whites, over 13,000 died ; connects rly. lines through Bangkok and Moulmein.

Burma star. Medal for service in Burma campaign from Dec. 11, 1941.

Burmese Wars. Fought between the Brit. and the Burmese ; first war, 1824–6 ; second, 1852 ; third, 1885–6 ; in the last of these King Theebaw was made prisoner ; Rangoon captured, 2745.

Burn'aby, Frederick Gustavus (1842–85). Eng. traveller, soldier, and war correspondent ; chiefly remembered for his journeys on horseback to Khiva and through Asia Minor and Amer.

Burnand, Sir Francis Cowley (1836–1917). Eng. journalist, who was editor of " Punch " for about 25 years ; author of many stage burlesques (" Black-eyed Susan ").

Burne-Jones, Sir Edward (1833–98). Eng. painter noted for highly decorative design ; and William Morris, 2232.

Bur'net, Gilbert (1643–1715). Brit. bishop and historian (" History of My Own Time ").

Burnett, Frances Hodgson (1849–1924). Amer. novelist, b. in England. (" Little Lord Fauntleroy " ; " The Secret Garden " ; " A Lady of Quality.")

Burney, Sir Charles Dennistoun (b. 1888). Brit. sailor ; designed R100 airship, 94 ; invented paravane device for severing mooring-line of sea-mines.

Burney, Edward Francis (1760–1848). Eng. painter, *3380.*

Bur'ney, Fanny (Frances) (1752–1840), also known by her married name Mme. D'Arblay. Eng. novelist ; her first novel " Evelina " (1778) made her famous, and her " Letters and Diaries " are very valuable.

Burn'ham, Edward Lawson, 1st Baron (1833–1916). Eng. journalist, son of Joseph Moses Levy, founder of " Daily Telegraph," of which he became managing proprietor and editor in 1855.

Burnham, Harry Lawson, 1st Viscount (1862–1933). Eng. journalist and politician, son of Baron Burnham.

Burnley. Tn. in Lancashire, 22 m. N. of Manchester ; pop. est. 77,900 ; cotton and worsted weaving, iron mfrs.

Burns, John (1858–1943). First Labour member of Eng. House of Commons (1892–1918) ; pres. Local Govt. Board 1905–14, of Board of Trade 1914 ; opposed Brit. entrance into 1st World War and retired into private life ; had a notable library.

Burns, Robert (1759–96), Scotland's greatest poet, **625,** 1214, 2895 ; " Auld Brig " of Ayr, *324.*

Burns and scalds, treatment of, 1295.

Bur oak, 2409.

Burr. Spiny fruit, esp. of burdock, 2917.

Burrinjack Dam, N.S.W., *1672.*

Burroughs, Edgar Rice (1875–1950). Amer. writer of fanciful adventure stories (" Tarzan of the Apes ").

Burroughs, William Seward, invents calculating machine, 656.

Burrow, of chipmunk, 815 ; mole, 2196, *2198* ; rabbit, 2721.

Bursa, or **Brusa,** city of Turkey ; pop. 86,000 ; silk manufactures.

Burslem. Famous pottery dist., in Staffordshire, part of Stoke-on-Trent ; birthplace of Josiah Wedgwood.

Burton, Sir Richard Francis (1821–90), Eng. explorer and writer, **626** ; discovers L. Tanganyika, 3150.

Burton, Robert (1577–1640). Eng. author (" The Anatomy of Melancholy," curious fantastic book, beloved by Lamb and Samuel Johnson), 1211.

Burton-on-Trent. County bor. in Staffordshire ; pop. 45,000 ; seat of enormous brewing industry ; **627,** 3072.

Buru (bōō'-rōō), Isl. of Molucca group, East Indies, *map, 1075.*

Bury (bûr'-i), **John Bagnell** (1861–1927). Irish historian, author of histories of Greece and Rome.

Bury. Tn. in Lancashire ; pop. 56,660 ; cotton and woollen mfrs.

Burying beetles, 400.

Bury St. Edmunds or **St. Edmundsbury.** Tn. in w. Suffolk ; pop. 18,000 ; named from Saxon King Edmund ; ruins of old Benedictine abbey, **627.**

Busby, Richard (1606–95). Eng. schoolmaster, head of Westminster School (1638–95) ; notorious for unsparing use of the birch.

" **Bush** " in S. Africa, 3013.

Bushel, a unit of measure. *See* **Weights and Measures,** *f-i.*

Bushey Park, Royal park in Middlesex ; adjoins Hampton Court. Here was H.Q. of U.S. forces in U.K. during 2nd World War.

Bushmen. People of S. Africa, 70, 3017, insect superstition, 2270.

Business terms. *See* list pp. 3740–41.

Bus'kin, shoe worn by Gk. actors, 3194.

Buso'ni, Ferruccio Benvenuto (1866–1924). Ger.-It. pianist and composer.

Buss, Frances Mary (1827–94). With Dorothea Beale (*q.v.* in *f-i.*), one of the pioneers of higher education for girls ; a founder of the North London Collegiate School.

Bus'tard. European and Asiatic bird, 441.

Butadi'ene. A hydrocarbon used in making artificial rubber. *See* **Buna.**

Butcher, Samuel Henry (1850–1910). Brit. classical scholar ; translated (with Andrew Lang) Homer's Odyssey.

Butcher-bird, *see* **Shrike.**

Butcher's Broom. Small perennial, evergreen plant of lily family, remarkable for its " cladodes," leaf and flower stalks flattened to look like, and act as, leaves, the latter being absent. Flowers whitish, minute ; large red berries at Christmas-time.

Bute, John Stuart, 3rd Earl of (1713–92). Brit. statesman, supporter of royal autocracy ; prime minister (1762–63), 3276 ; influence on George III, 1441.

Bute. Isl. of the Inner Hebrides, Argyllshire. Scot., 627.

Buteshire, Scot. Western co., consisting of Bute, Arran, and several smaller isls. ; a. 218 sq. m., pop. 16,000 ; **627.**

Butler, Lady Elizabeth (1850–1933). Brit. artist. (" Defence of Rorke's Drift," " The Dawn of Waterloo," " Steady the Drums and Fifes," " The Remnant of an Army," " The Roll Call.")

Butler, Joseph (1692–1752). Eng. bishop, philosopher and theologian. (" Analogy of Religion.")

Butler, Nicholas Murray (1862–1947). Amer. educationist and politician ; president of Columbia Univ., 1902–47 ; pres. of Pilgrims' Society 1928–46 ; received New York City award, 1945, for distinguished and exceptional public service ; and was first recipient, 1947, of Alexander Hamilton medal.

Butler, Richard Austen (b. 1902). Brit. politician ; Cons. ; Min. of Education 1941–45 ; in 1944 introduced the Butler Education Act, 2886.

Butler, Samuel (1612–80). Eng. satirist, author of " Hudibras."

Butler, Samuel (1835–1902). Eng. satirical novelist and critic. (" The Way of All Flesh " ; " Erewhon.")

Butlin, William E. (b. 1900). Brit. business man ; in 1921 had one hoop-la stand at a fair ; in 1936 opened holiday camp at Skegness, and later all round the coast, accommodating 100,000 holiday makers ; in 1944 opened N.A.A.F.I. recreation centres for Brit. army in Belgium.

Butt, Dame Clara (1873–1936). Eng. singer ; first professional appearance in London, 1892 ; foremost contralto singer in the country.

Butte, Montana, U.S.A. Largest city in state ; pop. 39,532 ; in rich copper, silver and gold mining region and site of famous Anaconda mine, 2218.

Butter. Fatty portion of milk or cream solidified by churning, 627, 955, 2174 ; butter-fat, 955, 2174 ; Denmark, 991 ; food value, 2174 ; 1338, *1339* ; no melting point, 1391 ; substitutes, 864 ; 2100 ; vitamins, 3327.

Butterbur. Plant of order *Compositae,* producing enormous leaves and growing in damp places ; flowers, which appear in March, before leaves, are very small, very numerous, purplish in colour.

Buttercup. A plant, **628.**

Butterflies and Moths. Insects of the order *Lepidoptera,* **628,** *plates f. 628, 629, 632, 633* ; caterpillars, 720, 1728 ; chrysalis stage, 1728 ; eggs, *629, 630* ; life history, *630, 631* ; protective coloration, 630 ; *See also* **Moth.**

Butterfly orchid, 2448.

Butterine, or margarine, 2100.

Buttermere. Lake in Cumberland ; 1¼ m. long.

Buttermilk, 2174.

Butterwort. Insect eater, *2624.*

Buttonholes. How to make, *2928.*

Buttons, 632 ; sewing on, 2928 ; of " vegetable ivory," 2408.

Button's, coffee-house, **28.**

But'tress, in architecture, 218, *1236.*

Buxton, Sydney, 1st Earl (1853–1934). Brit. politician and author ; became Postmaster-General (1905) ; Pres. of Board of Trade, (1910) ; gov.-gen. of S. Africa (1914–20).

Buxton. Tn. in the Peak Dist., Derbyshire ; noted for its springs and natural hot baths ; pop. 15,353 ; 995.

Buys-Ballot, Christoph (1817–90). Du. meteorologist, discoverer of the law named after him, 2150 ; that, in the N. hemisphere, a person with his back to the wind has lower pressure on his left and higher on his right hand, and the converse in the S. hemisphere.

Buz'zard (turkey-buzzard), 634.

Buzzard hawk, 633, 634.

Byal'ystok. Tn. of Poland ; on Byaly r. ; wool, linen, silk, and hats ; grain and lumber ; at division of Poland, 1939, it went to the Russians ; taken by Germans June 1941 ; liberated by Russians July 1944 ; pop. (1938) 107,000.

Bydgoszcz (bid'-gōshch), formerly Ger. Bromberg. Tn. of Poland ; iron goods, locomotives, furniture, paper ; on Vistula–Oder Canal ; German 1772–1919 ; Polish 1919–

39, when captured by Ger. ; retaken by Russ., Jan. 1945 ; pop. 140,000.

Bye, in cricket, 930.

Byelorussia, or **White Russia.** Republic of Soviet Russia, formed out of the six E. districts of Minsk prov. ; a., 81,000 sq. m. ; pop. 10,500,000 ; cap. Minsk ; 2849, 2983 ; includes Western White Russia annexed from Poland Sept. 1939 ; occupied by Germany 1941–44.

By-laws, made by local authorities, 2651.

Byng, John (1704–57). Eng. vice-admiral ; son of Admiral Byng, 1st Viscount Torrington ; sent in 1756 to engage the Fr. off Minorca, his conduct was unsatisfactory and he was court-martialled and shot.

Byng of Vimy, Julian Hedworth George, 1st Viscount (1862–1935). Brit. general ; served in Sudan expedition, Boer War and 1st World War, gov.-gen of Canada (1921–26) ; Chief Commissioner of Metropolitan Police (1928–31).

Byrd, Richard Evelyn (b. 1888). Amer. explorer and Rear-Admiral, **634.**

Byrd, William (*c.* 1542–1623). Eng. musical composer ; pupil of Tallis ; organist of Chapel Royal, London.

Byrnes, James Francis (b. 1879). U.S. jurist and statesman ; to Yalta con-

---

A LIST OF TERMS COMMONLY USED IN BUSINESS

Above par. When the price of stocks or shares, etc., is higher than that at which they were issued, they are said to be **above par.**

Acceptor. One who agrees to pay a cheque, draft, or other written order. The **drawee** of a Bill of Exchange is called the **acceptor** after he has written his name across it, so engaging to pay it when due.

Accrued dividend. Dividend accumulated, but not paid, since the last dividend payment ; shares are often sold " plus accrued dividend," which means that the accrued dividend is added to the price.

Accrued interest. Amount accumulated on shares and other evidences of indebtedness, since the preceding interest date.

Ad valorem. A tax levied according to value ; particularly customs duties, expressed in per cent.

Amortization. The liquidation or reduction of debt through a fixed scale of payments ; usually a sinking fund.

Arbitrage. Simultaneous buying of stocks or shares in one market and selling them in another where the rate is more favourable.

At sight. On demand.

Audit. Examination of records, usually by independent accountants, to show that the accounts are correct.

Average. In marine insurance, the calculation of the proportions of a loss among several insurers is called **average.** The person calculating such amounts is called an **average adjuster.** In stock exchange dealings **averaging** is the act of increasing or decreasing transactions in securities with fluctuations in the market, to secure the desired average price.

Backwardation. The charge for postponing settlement of a " bear " transaction until next settlement day.

Balance of trade. Difference between the value of exports and imports.

Balance sheet. Statement of assets and liabilities of a business made out at regular intervals.

Bank rate. Rate per cent charged by Bank of England for discounting approved Bills of Exchange ; determines rate charged by other banks for loans and interest paid on deposits.

Bear. One who believes that prices of commodities or securities will go down ; he may work to that end either by selling securities he actually owns or by " selling short " ; term is supposed to come from the bear's practice of holding down his victim ; opposite of " bull."

Below par. When the price of stocks or shares, etc., is lower than that at which they were issued, they are said to be **below par.**

Bill of Exchange. A written order from one person (the drawer) to another (the drawee) to pay a certain sum at sight or on a given date to the drawer, or to a third person (the payee). (*See* **Acceptor).** Persons engaged in the sale and purchase of Bills of Exchange are known as **bill brokers.**

Bond. A deed whereby a person, company or government agrees to pay a sum of money at fixed time under certain conditions. Bonds are either **registered** or to **bearer.** Bonds to bearer have **coupons** attached for presentation when dividend is due.

Bonus. Amount given in addition to regular salary or wages ; extra dividend paid to shareholders when profits are above normal.

Books closed. Time when stock transfer books of a business are closed to permit checking of shareholders to whom dividends are due ; a company cannot transfer shares from one holder to another while the books are closed.

Book value. The net worth of a business, etc., as indicated by the company's books ; book value may be either greater or less than par value or market value.

Boom. A period of activity on the stock exchange with demand for all classes of security, causing a general rise in prices. A short period of this kind is called a " boomlet."

Broker (stock). One who acts between buyer (or seller) of securities and the jobber ; **outside broker**—one not member of Stock Exchange.

Bucket Shop. The office of an unscrupulous outside broker is called a bucket shop.

Bull. One who buys commodities or securities in expectation that they will advance in price ; term is supposed to come from the bull's method of attack,

which is to toss upward on his horns ; the opposite of " bear."

Carrying charges. Interest charged by brokers for money advanced to carry accounts of their customers for whom they have bought securities on margin.

Cheque. An order in writing to a banker to pay a certain sum on demand. If paid to individual or **bearer,** no endorsement required ; otherwise must be endorsed. **Crossed cheques** are payable only *via* a banking account.

Commercial agencies. Organizations which ascertain the financial standing of individuals and firms and furnish this information to their subscribers.

Commission house. An agency which buys and sells for others on a fee or percentage basis, without assuming any liability for prices.

Consols. Abbreviation of **Consolidated Funds**—the stock of British funded National Debt.

Contango. Interest charged by jobbers for carrying over a " bull " transaction to the next settlement.

Corner. The condition of the market when the available supply of a commodity or a security has been concentrated ; a corner is the ultimate result of bullish operations.

Cum-div. With the accrued dividend.

Cumulative shares. On these any dividend not paid one year is carried forward to the next as a liability.

Current assets. Possessions such as cash and inventory, which can be converted into cash without depreciation in value.

Current liabilities. Obligations which are payable in a short time, usually not over twelve months ; distinguished from funded obligations or funded debt.

Days of grace. Bills of Exchange are usually payable 3 days after due date— these being **days of grace.**

Debenture. Sealed bond issued by a company acknowledging it has borrowed a certain sum on which interest is payable. A debenture holder is a **creditor,** not a shareholder ; his claims must be satisfied before any dividend is paid.

Deferred stock, or bonds. Interest on these is payable only after the preferred stock has received its share.

ference with F. D. Roosevelt, Feb. 1945, Truman's first Sec. of State, 1945; resigned Jan. 1947.

By'ron, George Gordon, 6th Lord (1788–1824). Eng. poet, **634**, 1214.

Byssus (bis'-us). Name used formerly for a fine flax fibre and fabric; hence applied to the flax-like filaments of the mussel and other molluscs.

By'townite. Greenish mineral resembling feldspar, so called from its having been first found at Bytown (Ottawa).

Byzan'tine art and architecture, 213, 635, 636, 638; mosaic, 637, 1844.

Byzantine Empire, also called Eastern or Greek Empire (A.D. 395–1453), **635**; endured until Turks took Constantinople in 1453, 3262; division of the Rom. Empire (A.D. 395), 635; 2812; Justinian, 637; 1844; rise and fall, 2166; silk weaving, 3191; Venice and, 3310.

CHIEF BYZANTINE RULERS

395–408	Arcadius
408–450	Theodosius II
450–457	Marcianus
457–474	Leo I
474–491	Zeno
491–518	Anastasius I
518–527	Justinus I
527–565	Justinian I
565–578	Justinus II
578–582	Tiberius II
582–602	Mauricius
602–610	Phocas
610–641	Heraclius
642–668	Constans II
668–685	Constantine IV
685–695	Justinian II
695–697	Leontius
697–705	Tiberius III, Apsimarus
705–711	Justinian II (restored)
711–713	Philip
713–715	Anastasius II
715–717	Theodosius III
717–740	Leo III, the Isaurian
740–775	Constantine V, Copronymus
775–779	Leo IV
779–797	Constantine VI
797–802	Irene
802–811	Nicephorus I
811–813	Michael I, Rhangabe
813–820	Leo V, the Armenian
820–829	Michael II
829–842	Theophilus
842–867	Michael III
867–886	Basil I, the Macedonian
886–912	Leo VI, the Wise
912–958	Constantine VII, Porphyrogenitus
958–963	Romanus II
963–1025	Basil II, Bulgaroktonos
1025–28	Constantine VIII
1028–34	Romanus III, Argyrus
1034–42	Michael IV, the Paphlagonian
1042–55	Constantine IX, Monomachus
1055–57	Theodora
1057–59	Isaac I, Comnenus
1059–67	Constantine X, Ducas
1067–78	Michael VII
1078–81	Nicephorus III
1081–1118	Alexius I, Comnenus
1118–43	John II, Comnenus
1143–80	Manuel I, Comnenus
1180–83	Alexius II, Comnenus
1183–85	Andronicus I, Comnenus
1185–95	Isaac II, Angelus
1195–1203	Alexius III, Angelus
1203–04	Isaac II (restored) jointly with Alexius IV
1204	Alexius V
1204–22	Theodore I, Lascaris
1222–54	John III
1254–59	Theodore II
1259–82	Michael VIII, Palaeologus
1282–1328	Andronicus II, Palaeologus
1328–41	Andronicus III, Palaeologus
1341–91	John V, Palaeologus
1391–1425	Manuel II
1425–48	John VI
1448–53	Constantine XI
[1453	Capture of Constantinople by the Turks and fall of the Byzantine Empire.]

Byzantium (bĭ-zan'-ti-um). Anc. Gk. city on whose site Istanbul (Constantinople) was built, 1761, 2812.

TERMS COMMONLY USED IN BUSINESS (contd.)

Deflation. Decrease in the means of exchange, causing increase in its value and general fall in prices.

Demurrage. Compensation charged by a railway or other carrying agency for delay in releasing a freight, a vessel, or other conveyance.

Depreciation. Decrease in the value of assets, due to wear and tear of equipment, to decline in market price, or other causes; depreciation is a loss recognized on the company's books while the assets are still retained.

Earnest money. Part of the purchase price, paid by the buyer to the seller, for the purpose of binding the contract.

Ex dividend. Meaning "without dividend." Dividends are declared due to shareholders of record on a specified date. Between the record date and the date on which the dividend is payable, the stock is sold "ex dividend," the dividend accruing to the seller and not to the buyer.

Firm. The term used in grain and stock exchanges to describe binding options granted by a seller to a prospective buyer; when a security is offered "firm" the seller obligates himself to deliver the amount specified at the agreed price.

Fiscal year. The twelve months period for which the accounts of a government are figured.

Fixed charges. Interest on debt, sinking funds, sometimes rentals and similar items which cannot be reduced, as distinguished from dividends which may be changed by a corporation at its discretion.

Funding. The conversion of current liabilities into long-term obligations.

Futures. Securities or commodities sold or bought with the assumption of delivery at a later date.

Holding company. Corporation controlling subsidiaries by the ownership of shares, now common in public utility companies.

Inflation. Increase in the means of exchange, causing decrease in its value and general rise in prices.

Inventory. A report or statement listing the merchandise on hand and other assets of a business.

Invoice. A statement sent to a purchaser listing the item or items bought and their purchase price.

Jobber. A stock dealer who is a member of the Stock Exchange and deals with the public only through the medium of brokers.

Joint stock company. An association whose funds or capital are divided into shares.

Limited liability company. A partnership whose liability is limited to its stated capital, distinguished from the ordinary partnership where all the property of the partners may be seized for the debts of the partnership; usually indicated by the abbreviation "Ltd."

Option. The privilege of buying or selling some specified property or commodity at a given price within a stated time; to be legally binding, an option must state a consideration.

Ordinary shares. Shares on which dividend is paid only after debenture interest and preference dividend.

Par. At face value, or at the value at which stocks or shares were issued.

Preference shares, or **preferred stocks.** Shares bearing a stated fixed dividend which must be paid out of earnings before ordinary or common dividends are declared; ordinarily they are non-voting shares.

Prospectus. Document giving certain prescribed particulars of a new company.

Proxy. A person who is authorized to act for another; also the document conferring this authority.

Pump-priming. The pouring by a government of public money into business with the aim of stimulating activity, mainly by increasing the purchasing power of the working classes.

Receiver. A person or firm appointed by a court to manage the property or assets of another while adjustment of debt is being made according to statute.

Recession. A slump of minor intensity.

Refunding. The replacement of an old loan by a new one, perhaps at a lower rate of interest.

Rent. The payment made for the use of property, fixed or movable such as real estate or machinery.

Reserves. Profits set aside, in the operation of a business, to meet possible future losses or contingent expenses; dividends in poor years may be paid out of reserves set aside in earlier good years.

Rights. The privilege to subscribe, usually to stocks and bonds, at a price which makes the privilege valuable.

Secured creditor. One who has property pledged to secure the payment of debt.

Settlement. On Stock Exchange, Settling Day or Pay Day is last day for payment of an account or claim.

Shareholder or **stockholder.** One who owns shares in a corporation or limited liability company; a shareholder is liable only to the extent of unpaid shares.

Short selling. A sale made in anticipation of a decline in price, by a seller who does not own the securities or commodities sold; the broker who executes the sale borrows securities or commodities from another customer or broker and makes delivery to the buyer; when the seller "buys in," to take his profit or loss, he is "covering" his short position.

Sinking fund. Money set aside, out of earnings, at stated intervals, for the purpose of reducing funded debt.

Slump. A period of business inactivity marked by absence of demand for securities and fall in their prices.

Speculation. Trade in securities or other commodities in order to make a profit, distinguished from investment, which is purchased to obtain income.

Stag. Speculator in first issues of shares of new companies, who applies for allotments intending to sell them immediately the shares are quoted at a higher price on the Exchange.

"Ticker." The tape-machines on which stock exchange transactions are recorded are known as "tickers." At periods of great activity the machines are unable to record all transactions immediately, and the "ticker" is said to be ten minutes, or two hours, etc., behind the market. The lagging of the ticker is a sign of a "boom."

Underwriter. One who insures another on life, health, or property in a policy of insurance; also one who guarantees a new issue of capital.

Winding up. Voluntary or compulsory dissolving of a company.

IN the hieroglyphic writing of ancient Egypt C was a throne ⌂. In its simplified form it looked more like a camel with its hump 🐪. The Phoenicians and Hebrews called it *Gimel*, which was their word for "camel," and wrote it **7**. Among the Greeks *Gimel* became *Gamma*. By this time the camel had turned round and the hump had become a right angle, so that it looked like this **Γ**. Then gradually it became transformed into the rounding letter C. Its sound was a hard *g* (as in "go"), but the Romans afterwards gave it the sound of *k*. In Anglo-Saxon or Old English, *c* had the sound of *k*, but it was gradually changed to *ch* before *e* and *i*. In the English of today it still has the sound of *k* before *a, o, u,* and before any consonant other than *h*. Before *e, i,* or *y* we give it the *s* or *sh* sound. In fact C is not really needed in the alphabet nowadays, since all its various sounds can be represented by other letters.

Cabal (ka-bal'). Unpopular Eng. ministry (1667–73) under Charles II composed of Clifford, Ashley, Buckingham, Arlington, and Lauderdale, whose initials formed the word.

Cabala (kab'-a-la). Mystical interpretation of Scriptures, 1601.

Caballero, Francisco Largo (1869–1946). Spanish labour leader. Became Chairman of Spanish Socialist Party; Premier of Spanish republic in 1936 at the head of a Popular Front ministry; resigned, May 1937, 3039.

Cabanel, Alexandre (1823–89). French painter.

Cabbage. Well-known vegetable, native of Britain; cultivated varieties include cauliflower, broccoli, kales, **639**; vitamins, 3326, 3327.

Cabbage butterfly, life history, *630, 631.*

Cabell, James Branch (b. 1879). American writer, 3295; works include "Chivalry."

Cabinet, in govt., **640,** 1490.

Cable railway, mechanism, 3235.

Cables, Telecommunication and Power, **640**; Atlantic lines, *290, 291*; Kelvin, 641, 643, 1849; Morse, 641, 2232; Pacific, 643; Telegraph Plateau, 291, 643; coaxial, 644; electric light and power, 644, *645, 1548*; Ferranti, 644; plastic, 645; manufacture, *646,* 647; telephone, 3174.

Cable tramway, 3235.

Cabot, John (*c.* 1450–98). It. explorer sailing under Eng. flag, 142, **647**; discovers Newfoundland, 681, 2337; Labrador, 1876; lays foundation of Brit. claims to N. Amer., 1612.

Cabot, Sebastian (1474–1557). Explorer, son of John, 648; explored Paraguay, 2512; discovers Prince Edward Isl., **2684**; his map, *142.*

Cabral or Cabrera, Pedro Alvarez (*c.* 1460–1526). Port. navigator; bound to E. Indies, accidentally carried out of course to Brazil (1500), 139, 554.

Cabrera. Isl. of Balearic group, 342.

Cacao (ka-kā'ō). Tropical Amer. tree whose seeds yield chocolate and cocoa, **648**; where grown, 648, 873.

Cachalot (kash'-a-lot). A sperm whale, 3372.

Cacique (ka-sēk'). An official of the Aztecs, 326.

Cactus. Leafless desert plant, **648**, *1915, 2288, 3024*; African, *plate f. 73*; "thornless," *621.*

Cad'bury, George (1839–1922). Eng. business man and philanthropist; chief proprietor of the cocoa manufacturing firm of Cadbury Brothers at Bournville, where, with his brother Richard, he founded the well-known model suburban town of this name; prominently associated with the Society of Friends.

Cad'dis fly. Insect of order *Trichoptera.* Caddis grubs live on the bottom of streams and ponds, in cases made of pieces of stick, sand, or even tiny shells. In these they move about and pupate, finally emerging as 4-winged, rather moth-like creatures. There are many species in Britain, 1733.

Cade, Jack (d. 1450). Eng. peasant rebel, character in Shakespeare's "King Henry VI," **649**; leads rebellion, 1611.

Cader Idris, Wales. Extensive mt. ridge in Merionethshire; Pen-y-gader, 2,927 ft., its highest peak, is the fifth highest mt. of Wales, 2146.

Cadets, air force, *2832*; army, *251*; merchant navy, *2144*; naval, 2306, *2307.*

Cadi (kā'-di). A judge in a Mahomedan court; in Algeria, 117.

Cadiz. Sp. spt. and naval station on Atlantic, 50 m. N.W. of Strait of Gibraltar; pop. 93,000; exports wine, fruit, oil, 3032; founded by Phoenicians, 2573; Drake attacks, 236, 1037.

Cadman, John, 1st Baron (1877–1941). Eng. industrialist: chairman of Anglo-Iranian Oil Co. and Iraq Petroleum Co.; head of Committee that prepared Report on Civil Aviation in 1938.

Cadmium (Cd). A metallic element of the zinc group; atomic weight 112·4; used in the Weston standard electric cell; found in zinc ores and as Greenockite; melts at 609·6° F.; named after cadmia, the Latin name for the zinc ore calamine, 777; in electro-plating, 1139.

Cadmus. In Gk. myth., founder of Thebes, 649, 3197.

Cadogan (ka-dug'an), **Sir Alexander G. M.** (b. 1884). Brit. diplomatist; perm. Under-Sec. of State for Foreign Affairs, 1938–46; in 1946 app. perm. representative of the U.K. on the Security Council of the U.N.

Cadorna, Luigi, Count (1850–1928). It. general, chief of general staff 1914–17, commander-in-chief of It. armies in field 1915–17; replaced by Diaz following defeat at Caporetto.

Caduceus (ka-dū'si-us). In Gk. myth., magic wand of Hermes, 1619.

Cædmon (kad'-mon) (d. *c.* 675). Earliest Eng. Christian poet, **650,** 1210, *1211*; Bible of, 425, *1194.*

Caen. City of N.W. France; pop. 61,000; trade in Caen stone; makes leather and gloves, 2377; battle of, in 1944, 2379, 3422.

Caerleon. Town in Monmouthshire, on r. Usk; as Isca Silurum, Rom. station; traditional site of Camelot, seat of King Arthur's court.

Caernarvon. Co. tn. of Caernarvonshire, Wales; pop. 9,500; 650; castle, *716,* 718; investiture of Prince of Wales, *3337.*

Caernarvonshire, Wales. Mountainous co. in N.W.; 569 sq. m.; pop. 121,000; 650.

Caesar (sē'zar), **Gaius Julius** (102–44 B.C.). Rom. general, statesman, and author, 651, 1895, 2811; in Britain, 573, 1193; Brutus and, 596; reforms calendar, 662; Cleopatra and, *838*; Gallic wars, 1365; place in Latin literature, 1895; and Mark Antony, 2105; and Pompey, 2654.

"Caesar and Cleopatra." Play by Bernard Shaw, pub. 1901; filmed 1945.

Caesarea (sē-za-rē'-a) or **Caesarea Mazaca.** Anc. town in Asia Minor; cap. of kings of Cappadocia; destroyed by Persians A.D. 260; pop. then 400,000; modern town, Kaisarieh (*q.v.* in *f-i*).

Caesarea or Caesarea Palestina. Spt. in anc. Palestine on Mediterranean 55 m. N.W. of Jerusalem; built by Herod; modern village, Qisaraya, has many Rom. ruins.

Caesarea Philippi. Anc. town in Palestine on r. Jordan at foot of Mt. Hermon; here Jesus gave his charge to Peter (Matt. xvi. 13).

Caesium (sē'-zi-um) (Cs). Metallic element of the alkali metal group; atomic weight, 132·9; found in the rare mineral lepidolite; melts at 82·4° F.; properties, 777, 1943; named from the Latin *caesius*, bluish grey, owing to the colour it gives to a flame.

Caffeine (kaf'-ē-in). Alkaloid in tea and coffee, 21, 866, 3160.

Cagliari (kahl'-yah-rē). It., cap. of Sardinia, on S. coast; pop. 106,600; Rom. amphitheatre, tombs, and other remains of antiquity, 2873; Italian seaplane base during 2nd World War, and target for devastating Allied bombing raids; evacuated by civilians, May 1943; Allies in control of seaplane and air bases Sept. 1943.

Cagliostro (kahl-yōs'-trō), **Alessandro** (1743–95). Assumed name of Giuseppe Balsamo, It. charlatan, implicated in the Diamond Necklace affair.

Cagoulards (ka-gōō-lahr) (Hooded Men). French secret political organization (the "Comité Secret d'Action Révolutionnaire "), charged with engineering bomb outrages in Paris, Sept. 1937.

Caiaphas (kī'-a-fas). Jewish high priest, before whom Jesus was arraigned before the crucifixion (Matt. xxvi, 3, 57; John xviii, 13–14, 24, 28); and who figured at the examination of Peter and John (Acts iv, 6); after the raising of Lazarus (John xi, 49).

Caillaux (kah'-yō), **Joseph Marie Auguste** (1863–1944). Fr. premier 1911–12; imprisoned 1917–20; banished for five years (1920–25) for treasonable communication with the Germans; Min. of Finance (1935) for 6th time; his wife killed (1914) Gaston Calmette, editor of "Figaro," for printing attacks against Caillaux.

Cain. Adam and Eve's first-born son, slayer of his brother Abel (Gen. iv.).

Caine, Sir Thomas Henry Hall (1853–1931). Eng. novelist and dramatist; stories melodramatic with strong religious tone (" The Manxman "; " The Christian "; " The Eternal City "; " The Prodigal Son "; " Master of Man "; " The Woman of Knockaloe ").

Cainozo'ic Era, in geology, 1433.

Cairngorm. Range and peak (4,084 ft.) of Grampians, Scot.; gives name to a yellow or brown variety of quartz found here and elsewhere. The stones are used in Scot. for setting in brooches, dirk-handles, etc.

Cairn Terrier. Small Scottish long-haired dog, *plate f. 1024.*

Cairo (kīr'-ō). Cap. of Egypt. Largest city in Africa; pop., 1,312,000, 653, *plates f. 652, 653*; Saracen culture, 2067; children, 801; Holy Carpet, *2068*; Nile, 2371; H.Q. Allied Middle East Forces, 1939–45, 654, *3421.*

Caisson, in building, 654; " Mulberry " Harbour, 2251.

Caithness, Scot. Co. in extreme N.E.; a. 685 sq. m.; pop, 26,000; 655

Caius (kēz), **John** (1510–73). Eng. physician; attended Edward VI, Mary and Elizabeth. In 1557 refounded Gonville Hall, Cambridge, as college of Gonville and Caius.

Cakes, the cooking of, 902.

Cal′abash. African gourd. The fruits are enclosed in a shell used by the natives for drinking cups and other domestic utensils.

Calabria (ka-lā′-bri-a). Name, until 11th cent., of S.E. It. (the heel); now dept. in S.W. (the toe); a. 5,819 sq. m.; pop. 1,907,900; people, 1763.

Cala′dium. Ornamental plant of S. Amer. with large " arrow-head " leaves and air-passages in stem.

Calais (kal′-ā). Fr. spt. on Strait of Dover; pop. 50,000; **655**; Burghers of (statue by Rodin), *2796*; in Hundred Years' War, 1611, 1652, 1653; Eng. loses, 2114; Ger. objective in 1914–18 War, 3409; Mary I and, 2114; siege by Edward III; fighting in 2nd World War, resulting in almost complete destruction, 655, 3417.

Cal′amine. A zinc ore, a translucent brittle mineral, carbonate of zinc; also applied to a zinc silicate found associated with the carbonate (by some writers the latter is termed smithsonite).

Cal′amus. A split-reed pen, 2539.

Calamus. Rattan palms, 2485.

Calcarea. Class of sponges with limy skeletons.

Calceolar′ia. Garden plant of the *Scrophulariaceae*, with yellow, red and brown bell-like flowers; named from Lat. *calceolus*, small shoe.

Calcite (kal′sīt). Calcium carbonate. Crystal refracts light doubly, so is used in Nicol prisms for the polarization of light; Iceland spar, 655, 1684.

Calcium (kal′-si-um) (Ca). White metallic element of the alkaline earth metal group, atomic weight, 40·08; melts at 1,490° F., **655,** 776; carbide, 18, 1420, 2374; carbonate, 1948, 2977, 3351; in bones, 498, 2977; chloride, *plate f. 3057*; essential to plant growth, 2998; in food, 655, 1338; in milk, 2174; " hard " water, 3351; hydroxide, 1949; oxide, 1948; permanganate, 2792; sulphate, 742, 2977; and sleep, 2983; and Vitamin D, 2978.

Calculating machines, for mathematical computations, **656**; " Ace," 660; accounting machine, 17; adding machine, 17, 656; Babbage, 656; cash register, 712; census recording, 742; counting by photo-electric device, 2575; " Eniac," 660; " electric brain," 659; meter, 2152; number-printing, *657*; punched cards, 658, 660; slide rule, 2985.

Cal′culus. Branch of higher mathematics, 1512, 2120; Newton's method, 2349.

Calcutta (kal-kut′-a). Largest city of India; in w. Bengal; pop., with Howrah, 2,488,000; 413, **660**; famous banyan tree, 359; jute industry, 1844; 17th cent. trading post, 1714; university, 1714.

Calcutta Cup. Trophy awarded to the winning country in the annual England v. Scotland International Rugby football match; presented by the Calcutta R.F.C. in 1879.

Caldecote, Thomas Walter Hobart Inskip, 1st Viscount (1876–1947). Brit. lawyer and politician; Minister for Co-ordination of Defence (1936–39); Lord Chancellor, 1939–40; Dominions Secretary, May–Oct. 1940; Lord Chief Justice, 1940–46.

Calder. R. in Lancashire and Yorkshire, trib. of the Aire; 45 m. long.

Calderon, Philip Hermogenes (1833–87). British painter of Spanish descent; his " Ruth and Naomi," *2858*.

alderón (kahl-dā-ron′) **de la Barca, Pedro** (1600–81). Span. dramatist, 1040, *3051*.

aledo′nia. Name given by Romans to Scotland; now used poetically.

Caledonian Canal, Scot, 1737, 2889

Caledonians, people, 2892.

Calendar, in reckoning time, **661,** *662*; Aztec, 326; Babylonian, 330; day, 980; ancient Egyptian, 1114; determining time, 3212; changes during Fr. Revolution, 1396; Gregorian, 662; Julian, 662; Jewish New Year, 2350; mistake in dating birth of Christ, 661; Mahomedan, 661, 2066; month, 2223; New Year's Day, *2350*; Red Indian, *2754*; week, **3361.** *See* Time; *also* Month.

Calender, for glazing paper, 2500; for rubber, 2836.

Calf. Young of ruminants; moose and caribou, 984.

Calfskin, 1913; parchment and vellum, 2496.

Calgary (kal′ga-ri). Alberta. Leading inland city of Canadian North-West; pop. 88,000; 103, **663**.

" Calgon," a water-softening phosphate, 3351.

Cali, Colombia. Commercial centre in s.w. on branch of Cauca; pop. 121,300; rly. to Pacific port Buenaventura.

Caliban (kal′-i-ban), in Shakespeare's " Tempest," deformed savage son of a witch and a devil, enslaved by Prospero, 3185.

Calico. A cloth, 850, 920; printing, 2684.

Calicut, India. Port on s.w. coast; pop. 82,334; gave name to calico, 850; visited by Vasco da Gama, 3306.

California. A Pacific state of U.S.A., 158,693 sq. m.; pop. 6,907,000, **663**; chief cities, 2026, 2871; citrus oils, 2549; film industry, 828, 2026; gold, *1047*, 1479; orange growing, 1403, 2443; sequoia trees, **2921,** *2921*; Yosemite National Park, *663*.

California, Gulf of. Arm of Pacific Ocean 710 m. long between Lower California and mainland of Mexico, *2157*, 2469.

California, Lower. Peninsula of Mexico between Pacific and Gulf of California and Colorado r., 55,000 sq. m.; pop. 95,000.

Caligula (kal-ig′-ū-la) (" Little Boot "). Nickname of Gaius Caesar (A.D. 12–41); Rom. emperor, **664**, 2811.

Caliper (kal′-i-per). Adjustable gauge for measuring small objects.

Cal′iper beetle, *401*.

Caliph (kā′-lif) or **calif.** Civil and religious head of a Mahomedan state, 2067; office abolished by Turks, 3265.

Calix′tus II (d. 1124). Pope, concluded Concordat of Worms with Henry V (1122).

Calix′tus III (d. 1458). Pope, 525.

Cal′la lily, 1948.

Callao (kal-ah′-ō). Chief port of Peru, 6 m. w. of Lima; pop. 84,400; excellent harbour; exports sugar, cotton, minerals, wool; 1948, 2560.

Callimachus (ka-lim′-a-kus). Gk. lyric poet of 3rd cent. B.C., 1541.

Calliope (ka-lī-o-pē). In Gk. myth., muse of epic poetry, 2259.

Callisto (kal-is′-tō). Nymph changed to constellation by Zeus, 894.

Cal′omel. Mercurous chloride, beneficial in liver complaints, 2146.

" Calorgas," an illuminating and heating gas, 1424.

Calor′ic. Fluid once assumed to be cause of heat, 1593; theory disproved, 1593.

Calorie (kal′-o-ri). The scientific unit of heat; heat required to raise one gramme of water one degree Centigrade, 1338, 1596; as measure of food value, 1338.

Calpur′nia. Last wife of Julius Caesar, who married her 59 B.C. She pleaded with him not to attend the senate (following a disturbing dream) on March 15, 44 B.C. She appears in Shakespeare's play.

Caltanissetta. City in Sicily; pop. 50,500.

Calumet. The " peace-pipe " of N. Amer. Indians; tobacco-pipe with stone bowl and long reed stem ornamented with eagles' feathers;

smoked on ceremonial occasions, especially in making treaties of peace.

Calusari, Rumanian dance, *plate f. 2841*.

Cal′vary or **Golgotha.** The place where Jesus was crucified, 1820.

Calvé (kahl′-vä), **Emma** (1864–1942). Fr. operatic singer of great dramatic power; famous " Carmen."

Cal′verley, Charles Stuart (1831–84). Eng. humorous poet and barrister (" Fly Leaves ").

Calvin, John (1509–64). Swiss theologian and reformer, 664, 819, 2758; in Geneva, 1428; and Knox, 1871; and Reformation, 2758, *2759*; influence on Fr. literature, 1380.

Calydon (kal′-i-don). Ancient city of Aetolia, Greece; scene of legendary hunt for the monstrous Calydonian boar which Artemis sent to ravage the country because she had been neglected in a sacrifice by the king of Calydon.

Calypso (ka-lip′-sō). In Gk. myth., nymph who detained Odysseus for seven years, 2422. In West Indies a ballad or broadsheet with a political or topical bias.

Calyx (kā′-liks). Collective term for the sepals of a flower, 531.

Cam. River in Cambridgeshire; 40 m. long, emptying into Ouse; Cambridge on, 666, *667*.

Cam. Projection on a wheel, or eccentric wheel, for turning circular into to-and-fro movement; in internal combustion engines, 1736; in sewing machine, *2929*.

Camaguey (kah-mah′-gwä). Largest inland city of Cuba; pop. 138,300; exports cattle products.

Camalodunum. Rom. Colchester, 869.

Cam′berley. Dist. in Surrey. It is the seat of the Staff College for training staff officers for the British Army. Near here is Sandhurst, the Royal Military Academy.

Camberwell. Met. bor. of S. London, Camberwell Green once celebrated for fairs. Pop. (1939) 251,300.

Camberwell Beauty butterfly. *Plate f. 632.*

Cam′bium. Growing layer between bark and wood of trees, etc., 3245.

Cambo′dia. Autonomous state in Indo-China within French Union; 67,550 sq. m.; pop. over 3,000,000; **664,** *665*, 1718; Angkor Vat, 270, 665, *666*. A French protectorate 1863–1946.

Cambrai (kahm′-brā) or **Cambray.** Fr. city; pop. (1946) 26,130; linen goods, especially cambric, to which it gave name; in 1st World War, 3411, 3413.

Cam′brian Mts. Highlands of Wales, **666.**

Cambrian period, in geology, 1432; *plate f. p. 1432, 1433.*

Cambric. A fine linen fabric; now also kind of cotton cloth made to imitate linen.

Cam′bridge. Co. tn. of Cambridgeshire; seat of Cambridge Univ., on r. Cam; pop. 104,000; *666*, *667*, *668*; Polar Research Institute, 2896.

Cambridge, Massachusetts, U.S.A.; pop. 110,900; seat of Harvard Univ.; 669, 2118.

Cambridgeshire. Agric. co. in E. Eng.; 864 sq. m.; pop. 217,700; **669**.

Cambridge University. Famous centre of learning, Cambridge; secured charter from Henry III (1231); **666,** 3296; arms and hoods, *frontis.,* *Vol. 7*; Boat Race, *483*; library, 1930; observatory, 3024. From 1948 women admitted to matriculation and degrees on same terms as men; thus Girton and Newnham became recognized colleges of the university.

Cambunian Mts., Greece. Range in N. Thessaly intersecting the Pindus Mts. on the w. and culminating in Mt. Olympus on the E.

Cambyses (kam-bī′-sēz) (d. 522 B.C.). Son of Cyrus the Great; king of Medes and Persians 529–522 B.C.; conquers Egypt, 2554.

Camden Town. District of N.W. London, 2015.

Camden Town Group. Artists, 1184.

Camel. Ruminant desert animal, 669, 670, 671, 2074 ; Bactrian, 670 ; in Arabia, 198, 199, 201, 670 ; in Australia, 314, 315 ; caravans, 314, 841 ; story of a young, 3497 ; for transport, 314, 1100.

Camelidae. The camel family, includes camels, 669 ; alpaca and vicuña, 124 ; llama, 1975.

Camellia (kam-ĕl'-i-a). A shrub, 671.

Camelopard. Anc. name for giraffe, 1465.

Camelot (kam'-e-lot). Legendary seat of King Arthur's court, 2830.

Camembert (kam-om-bār) **cheese,** 766.

Cameo. Engraved gem or sea shell bearing design cut in relief, 671, 2942.

Camera, 672 ; choice of, 2578, 2580 ; moving picture, 829 ; lens, 1924 ; miniature, 2579 ; stereoscopic, 3088 ; television, 3182, 3184. See also Photography.

Camera obscura, mechanism, 672.

Cameroons or **Kamerun'.** A region in w.-cent. Africa (190,000 sq. m.), formerly a Ger. protectorate, 72, 672 ; Brit. and Fr. mandates ; in 2nd World War, 673. Pop. 3,400,000.

Cam'eron, Basil (b. 1885). Brit. orchestral conductor ; promenade concerts, 1942–44, with Sir Hy. Wood ; from 1945 with Sir Adrian Boult ; excelled in interpreting the classical symphonists.

" Camille " (ka-mēl'). Eng. version of play by the younger Dumas (" Dame aux Camélias "), 1054.

Camil'lus, Marcus Furius (d. c. 365 B.C.). Rom. general, dictator in war against Veii 396 B.C.

Cammaerts, Emile (b. 1878). Belgian poet and author who settled in England. Translated Ruskin into Fr. (" Treasure House of Belgium " ; " Discoveries in England " ; " The Child of Divorce " ; " The Flower of Grass ").

Camoens (kam'-ō-ens), **Luis Vaz de** (1524–80). Greatest Portuguese poet ; largely fixed language ; developed lyric poetry and greatly influenced national drama (" The Lusiads," great national epic of discovery) ; 2659.

Camomile (kam'-ō-mīl) or **chamomile.** Hardy perennial plant, 673.

Camor'ra. It. secret organization for robbery, blackmail, etc.

Camouflage (kam'-oo-flahzh). Art of disguising or concealing in warfare, 673, 674 ; camouflaged sniper, 674 ; warship, 673 ; principles from animals, 2692, 2693 ; insects, 1728. See also Protective Coloration.

Campagna (kahm-pah'-nya) **di Roma.** Large uncultivated plain around Rome, once malarial owing to Tiber floods and marshes ; now largely reclaimed ; 1772, 2799.

Campania (kahm-pahn'-i-a). It., dept. on s.w. coast ; chief city, Naples ; 5,214 sq. m. ; pop. 3,991,400 ; delightful climate and scenery ; very fertile ; 1763.

Campanile (kam-pa-nē'-le). See Belltower.

Campanula (kam-pan'-ū-la), 479.

Campbell, Sir Colin (Lord Clyde) (1792–1863). Brit. general ; served in Peninsular War, Crimean War, and Sepoy mutiny ; recaptures Lucknow, 2035.

Campbell, Sir Malcolm (1885–1948). Brit. racing motorist, 485, 674, 1828.

Campbell, Mrs. Patrick (1865–1940). English actress (Paula in " The Second Mrs. Tanqueray "). In 1914 created part of Eliza Doolittle in Shaw's " Pygmalion."

Campbell, Dr. Reginald John (b. 1867). Pastor of City Temple, London, 1907–15 ; entered Church of England, 1916 ; canon and chancellor of Chichester, 1930–46.

Campbell, Roy Dunnachie (b. 1902). S. African poet, 3020. Works include " The Flaming Terrapin " ; " Taurine Provence " ; and " Flowering Rifle."

Campbell, Thomas (1777–1844). Scottish poet known for his stirring lyrics (" Hohenlinden " ; " Ye Mariners of England " ; " Lord Ullin's Daughter ").

Campbell, William Wilfrid (1861–1918). Canadian poet. (" Sagas of Vaster Britain "), 685.

Campbell-Bannerman, Sir Henry (1836–1908). Brit. Liberal leader ; premier (1905–08) ; 1976 ; premiership, 3279.

Campbell Islands. Small uninhabited group s. of New Zealand, 2358, 2360.

Campeche or **Campeachy,** Mexico. State on w. side of Yucatan peninsula ; 19,670 sq. m. ; pop. 84,000 ; cap. Campeche (pop. 20,000) ; 3437.

Cam'perdown, Netherlands. Vil. on North Sea ; Brit. naval victory over Dutch (1797), 3277.

Camphor. An aromatic gum, 674 ; Borneo, 526 ; in celluloid mfr., 2625 ; in surface tension experiment, 3122 ; tree related to laurel, 1900.

Camping, for Boy Scouts, 540, 541 ; for Girl Guides, 1466.

Campion. Eng. flower, Lychnis dioica, not dioicia ; 674, 675.

Campo Formio. It., market tn. ; treaty of (1797), 2275.

Camp olive shell, 2943.

Campo Santo. Name meaning " holy field " applied to burial grounds in It. ; Campo Santo of Pisa severely damaged by shell fire and fire in July 1944.

Camp'us Martius (mar'-shi-us). Large field on Tiber near anc. Rome used for military drills and assemblies, 2799.

Camrose, William Ewert Berry, 1st Viscount (b. 1879). Brit. journalist and newspaper proprietor, 675.

Camshaft, of motor-car engine, 2244.

Cana, of Galilee. A village in Palestine near Nazareth ; here Jesus Christ turned the water into wine at the marriage feast.

Canaan. Pre-Israelite Palestine.

Canada. Brit. Dominion in N. Amer., 3,800,000 sq. m. ; pop. 13 million, 676 ; map, 677, plate f. 680 ; canals, 1515, 1516, 3363 ; cities, 2223, 2458, 2714, 2861, 3217, 3223, 3224, 3303, 3388 ; flag, frontis. to Vol. 8 ; French Canadians, 680 ; immigration, 680 ; Indians, 2757 ; national emblem, 2092 ; national game, 1882 ; national parks, 103 ; national song, 681, 2282 ; police, 2650 ; provinces, 102, 578, 2088, 2336, 2392, 2400, 2434, 2684, 2714, 2874, 3440 ; railways, 678, 2336 ; reindeer, 2760. Geography and Industries : agriculture, 679, 2088 ; Arctic regions, 223 ; climate, 677, 2384 ; dairying, 2435 ; fruit, 1401, 1649 ; furs and fur trade, 680, 1649 ; geological history, 1680, 2384 ; Hudson Bay, 1649 ; lumber and forestry, 579, 678, 2035 ; minerals, 678, 858, 1479, 2973, 2974, 3440 ; mountains, 2795 ; rivers and lakes, 677, 1515, 2050, 2088, 2861, 3440 ; tobacco, 3221 ; water-power, 2361, 2458. See also Canadian history ; Canadian literature.

Canada, Lower. See Quebec.
Canada, Upper. See Ontario.
Canada balsam, 1278.
Canada goose, 1486.
Canada House, London, 2019.
Canadian history and government, 681 ; early days, 143 ; Cabot, 648, 681 ; Cartier, 681, 712 ; Champlain, 751 ; Hudson's Bay Company formed, 1650 ; Marquette and Joliet, 2107 ; La Salle, 1894 ; Montreal founded, 2224.
 Development of self-government (1763–1867), 683 ; loyalist immigration, 683, 2435 ; Mackenzie, explorer, 2050 ; Selkirk settlement, 3388 ; Great Lakes neutralized, 1516 ; rebellion of 1837, 683 ; Dominion govt. established (1867), 683.
 Under Dominion government, 683 ; administrations of Sir John Macdonald, 2048 ; Red River rebellion, 2089, 3102 ; Brit. Columbia joins federation, 683 ; Canadian Pacific Rly. built, 678, 2089, 3102 ; Yukon organized, 3440 ; under Sir Robert Borden, 524 ; in 1st World War, 525, 678 ; in League of Nations, 525 ; in 2nd World War, 684, 3416, 3422.

Canadian literature, 684.

Canadian lynx, 2043.
Canadian Mounted Police. See Royal Canadian Mounted Police.
Canadian National Rlys. (C.N.R.), 678.
Canadian Pacific Rly. (C.P.R.), 678, 2089 ; locomotive, 1994.
Canadian pondweed, in experiment in photo-synthesis, 2589.
Canadian Sable, 2112.
Canaigre (ka-nā'-ger). A variety of dock ; root used in tanning.
Canal. Artificial waterway, 686 ; to relieve floods, 1318 ; Belgium, 689 ; Bridgewater, 569, 570, 688 ; Caledonian, 2889 ; Canada, 1515, 1516, 2861 ; China, 686, 802 ; Corinth (reopened July 5, 1948), 689 ; Eng., map, 686, 687 ; 3194 ; Europe, 972 ; Fr., 1360, Göta (Sweden), 3128 ; Holland, 686, 2319 ; Kiel, 352, 1607 ; Manchester Ship, 688, 1577, 2084 ; Panama, 2486 ; Russia, 2844, 3329 ; Suez, 3110, 3111 ; Sweetwater, 1104 ; Venice, 3310, 3311 ; Welland, 1515, 3363.

GREAT CANALS OF THE WORLD

Name	Country or State	Length, Miles
Albert	Belgium	80
Baltic-White Sea (Stalin)	Rus.	141
Erie	N.Y.	340
Göta	Sweden	115
Grand Union	England	255
Juliana	Netherlands	21
Kiel	Ger.	62·1
Manchester	Eng.	35·5
Moscow-Volga	Rus.	79
Panama	Canal Zone	50·7
Rhône-Marseilles	Fr.	50·3
St. Lawrence	Can.	46
Sault Ste. Marie	Can.	1·3
Sault Ste. Marie	Mich.	1·6
Suez	Eg.	104
Welland	Can.	27

Canal du Midi, 1360.
Canaletto (Canale), Antonio, (1697–1768) ; architectural painter of Venetian school, famed for his rendering of buildings by waterside, e.g. Venice, London, 1776.
" Canals " of Mars, 2617.
Canal Zone. Territory on both sides of Panama Canal leased by U.S.A., map, 2487.
Canary (ka-nār'-i). A songbird of finch family, 689.
Canary Islands. Group of Span. isls. about 60 m. off N.W. coast of Africa ; 2,894 sq. m. ; pop. 761,000 ; 690 ; bananas, 354, 690 ; serious volcanic eruptions on La Palma isl., July 1949.
Canberra (kan'-be-ra). Cap. of Australia, 312, 690, 691, 2344. Name of Federal Capital Territory changed (1938) to Australian Capital Territory.
Cancer. Constellation, 895, 3444.
Cancer, genus of crabs, 924.
Cancer. A malignant spreading growth on the human body ; diagnosis by radio-active tracers, 1761 ; of the liver, 1968 ; neutron ray treatment, 951 ; radium treatment, 2733.
Cancer, Tropic of, 1898 ; winds, 3385. So named because sun is in " Cancer " sign of zodiac when over Tropic.
Can'dia (or Heraklion). Spt., largest city, and former cap. of Crete, on N. shore ; pop. 33,400, 927. Also It. name of Crete.
" Candida." Play by G. B. Shaw.
" Candide." Story by Voltaire ridi culling optimism, 3330.
Candle, 691 ; for lighting, 1887 ; unit of illumination, 692.
Candleberry. Same as Bayberry.
Can'dlemas. Church festival, Feb. 2 in commemoration of presentation of Christ in Temple.
Candle-nut, 2408.
Candle-power. Light given by a specified type of candle, used as unit of illuminating power, 692.
Candolle (kahn-dol'), **Augustin de** (1778–1841). Swiss botanist ; introduced natural as opposed to artificial or Linnaean system of classification.
Can'dour, Mrs. In Sheridan's " School for Scandal," a slanderer who affects great frankness.
Candy, Ceylon. Same as Kandy.

Can'dytuft. Garden flower of genus *Iberis*, some short rock plants, some tall, white to purple ; name taken from Candia (Crete).

Canea (kan-nē'a). Seaport and cap. of Crete, on N.W. shore ; pop. 27,000 ; 927.

Cane sugar, 3112.

Canidae (kan'-i-dē). The dog family, 1027.

Canine teeth, 3163.

Canis (kā'-nis). The dog genus ; includes dogs, 1025–27 ; jackals, 1789 ; wolves, 3400.

Canis major (" Great Dog "). A constellation, *chart, 895.*

Canis minor (" Little Dog "). A constellation, *chart, 895.*

Canker. Various plant diseases.

Cankerworm. Caterpillar destructive to trees.

Canna. A member of the *Scitaminaceae* family, once a weed, but now cultivated with immense and dazzlingly beautiful flowers.

Can'nabis. Genus of hemp plants, 1609.

Cannae (kan'nē). Anc. vil. near S.E. coast of It. where Hannibal annihilated Rom. army (216 B.C.) ; battle, 1574.

Cannes (can). Fr. seaport and fashionable winter resort on Riviera ; pop. 45,500.

Cannibalism, among Aztecs, 326 ; origin of, 2057 ; in Pacific isls., 1271, 2340.

Canning, George (1770–1827). Brilliant Eng. statesman and orator ; as foreign secretary, supported liberal tendencies ; recognized independence of revolted Span. colonies in S. Amer. ; d. four months after becoming prime minister.

Canning industry, 692. In California, 2871 ; peas, 2577 ; why tin cans are used, 3215.

Can'nock Chase, coalfield, Staffordshire, Eng., 3072.

Cannon. *See* **Artillery** ; in billiards, 428, 429.

Cano, Alonzo (1601–67). Span. architect, painter, and sculptor ; chief architect of Granada cathedral ; religious paintings characterized by bold design and pure flesh-tints ; for variety of his talents dubbed " Span. Michelangelo."

Canoes and canoeing, 481, 482, 486.

Canon. Inspired books of Bible, 424.

Canon. A dignitary of the Church, receiving a stipend out of the estate of a cath. or collegiate church, 825.

Canon, in music, 2263.

Canonical hours, 2213.

Canonization. Roman Catholic ceremony at which a deceased person is formally declared by the Pope to be a saint. It is preceded by (1) declaration that the person is " venerable," (2) lengthy inquiry into sanctity and proof of miracles performed resulting in " beatification," (3) another long period during which proof of performance of two miracles since beatification is shown. The " Devil's Advocate," or Promoter of the Faith, cross-examines all witnesses.

Canon law, defined, 1903.

Cano'pus, a star, 3078, 3080.

Canossa. It. ruined castle 12 m. s.w. of Reggio ; here the emperor Henry IV did penance before Pope Gregory VII (1077), 1609.

Canova (kah-nō'va), **Antonio** (1757–1822). It. sculptor ; great influence as leader of classic revival, 2906.

Can'so, Strait of, or Gut of. Passage between Nova Scotia and Cape Breton Isl.

Canta'brian Mts. Range extending W. from Pyrenees across N. Spain over 300 m., bordering Bay of Biscay ; highest pt. 8,743 ft. ; *map, 3030.*

Cantaloup, rock-melon, 2137.

Canta'ta, a musical composition, 2264.

Canter. Horse's pace, 2779.

Can'terbury, Kent. Cathedral city ; pop. 19,500 ; **692** ; cathedral, *724* ; Marlowe's monument, *2107* ; miracle play in cathedral, *2118* ; pilgrims at,

9000 ; shrine of Thomas Becket, 189, 692 ; air raids, 1940–42, 693.

Canterbury, Archbishop of. Chief dignitary of the Church of Eng. ; the Primate of all Eng., the Archbishop of York being the Primate of Eng., 692, 825 ; at Coronation, 912.

Canterbury bells. Species of Bell-flower.

Canterbury Pilgrims, *763.*

Canterbury Plains, in New Zealand, 693.

" Canterbury Tales," by Geoffrey Chaucer, 692, 761 ; stories from, 762.

Cantilever bridge, *565, 567, 568* ; principle in beam, *380* ; in roof, 2822.

Cantlie, Sir James (1851–1926). Scot. surgeon, who did valuable work during the cholera epidemic in Egypt in 1883, and in the World War of 1914–18 ; author of important works on surgery and tropical diseases.

Canton, China, 693. Cap. of Kwangtung province and commercial centre of S. China ; pop. 1,500,000 ; occupied by Communists Oct. 1949.

Canton River. Also called **Shu-kiang** (" Pearl River "), main channel of the delta formed by the Si-kiang ; at Canton, 694 ; Hong Kong, 1639.

Cantons. States of the Swiss Confederation.

Canute (ka-nūt') (c. 994-1035). Great king of Danes and Norwegians, ruler of Eng. 1017–35 ; **694,** 1194.

Canvas-back, a sea-duck, 1052.

Canyon or **Cañon** (kan'-yon). Deep river channel with precipitous sides ; Grand Canyon, 1498, *plates f. 1496, 1497.*

Caoutchouc (kow'-chōōk). Rubbery juice of the caoutchouc tree, 2833 ; also term for rubber.

Capablanca (kap-a-blang'-ka), **José Raoul** (1888–1942). World-famous chess-player, a native of Cuba ; gained world title in 1921.

Capacity, electrical, 1132 ; of wireless aerial, 3319.

Cape Breton Island, Canada. Separated from Nova Scotia by Strait of Canso ; 3,975 sq. m. ; pop. 150,000 ; **695** ; Cabot discovers, 648 ; coal, 2401.

Cape Cod, Massachusetts, U.S.A. L-shaped peninsula between Nantucket Sound and Cape Cod Bay ; length 65 m., width 1 to 10 m.

Cape Colony or **Province.** *See* **Cape of Good Hope.**

Cape Dutch. Another name for Afrikaans, 73.

Cape Horn. *See* **Horn, Cape.**

Capek, Karel (1890–1938). Czech author and playwright, 953, 2983 ; his plays include " The Insect Play," " R.U.R." and " The Mother."

Capel'la. A fixed star, 3078 ; *chart, 895.*

Cape of Good Hope. Promontory near southern tip of Africa, 695, *696* ; route to India, 3016 ; rounded by Vasco da Gama, 3306.

Cape of Good Hope. Formerly Cape Colony, prov. in the Union of S. Africa ; 277,113 sq. m. ; pop. 4,016,800 ; 697 ; 3014 ; cap. Cape Town, **697** ; Cecil Rhodes, 2771 ; stamp, *3075.*

Capernaum (ka-pêr'-nā-um). Anc. tn. of uncertain position ; perhaps on N. coast of Sea of Galilee ; often visited by Jesus.

Ca'pers. A condiment, 3061.

Capet (kah-pā), **House of.** Reigning family of France from 987 to 1328 ; 1365, 2027, 2567 ; France unified, 1238.

Capet, Hugh (c. 939–996). King of France, elected by nobles and prelates to succeed Louis V, last of the Carolingians ; founds Capetian dynasty, 1365.

Cape-to-Cairo Railway, planned by Rhodes, 2771.

Cape Town. Cap. of Cape of Good Hope province ; largest city in S. Africa ; pop. 383,890 ; *696, 697, 698, 3020* ; van Riebeeck statue, *plate f. 3017* ; Dutch settlement, 69.

Cape Verde Islands, Port. colony in Atlantic, 350 m. w. of Cape Verde, Africa ; 1,516 sq. m. ; pop. 181,300 ; **698** ; Portugal colonizes, 1613, 2659.

Cap'illary. Minute blood vessel, 474.

Capillary attraction, in liquids, **698.**

Capital, in architecture, 215.

Capital, in economics, 1081 ; Marxian doctrine, 2113, 2996.

" Capital," by Karl Marx, 2113, 2996.

Capitalism. Economic system in which the means of production are privately owned and run for profit.

Capital punishment, 2687 ; during 2nd World War reintroduced in Norway and Netherlands for collaboration with the enemy, and in Italy for crimes of violence ; in U.K. in 1948 an amendment to Criminal Justice Bill proposed suspension for 5 years, except as penalty for murder of police and prison officers and for espionage ; it was defeated,

Capitol, Washington, U.S.A., 3344 ; *3343, 3344.*

Capitoline (kap'-i-to-līn) **Hill.** Smallest but most famous of 7 hills of Rome, 2799, *plate f. 2804, 2806* ; statue of Jupiter, 1841.

Caporet'to, battle of, (1917), 3411.

Cappadocia (kap-a-dōsh'-i-a). Anc. inland country in Asia Minor w. of r. Euphrates ; conquered by Persians and by Alexander the Great ; reduced to Rom. prov. by Tiberius A.D. 17.

Cappelle, Jan van de (c. 1624–c. 1675), Dutch painter, 2335.

Capra (kap'-ra), the goat genus, 1478, 1679.

Caprera (ka-prā'-ra). It. isl. ; Garibaldi's home, 1419.

Capri (kah'-prē), beautiful isl. s. of Bay of Naples. It. ; 5½ sq. m. ; resort of tourists and artists, 2274 ; the Blue Grotto, 734, *plate f. 733.*

Cap'ricorn, Tropic of, 1898 ; winds, 3385. So named because sun is in " Capricorn " sign of zodiac when over the Tropic.

Capricor'nus, " The Goat " in zodiac, 3444.

Caprifica'tion of figs, 1270.

Capri fig, 1270.

Caprifolia'ceae, the honeysuckle family.

Caps and Hats, 1582.

Capsians, cave-men, wall paintings, *plate f. 736.*

Cap'sicum, a genus of peppers, 2547, 3061.

Captain, in Services, 699 ; *plate f. 2292.*

" Captains Courageous," story by Kipling dealing with life on the Newfoundland fishing-grounds.

Captive balloon, in war, 349, *350.*

Capua (kap'-ū-a). It. city on site of anc. Casilinum ; pop. 10,000 ; cathedral seriously damaged during 2nd World War ; anc. Capua, 3 m. distant, was luxurious city under Romans, 3053.

Capuchin (kap'-ū-chin) **monkey,** 2208.

Capuchins. Branch of the Franciscan friars ; extreme vows of poverty, and much attention to learning.

Capulet, noble family of Verona ; feud with the Montagues forms basis for tragedy of Shakespeare's " Romeo and Juliet," 2821.

Capuzzo (kah-poots'-ō), **Fort.** Ital. stronghold in Libya, s. of Bardia, on Egyptian frontier ; occupied successively by Italians, Brit. (in 1940), and Gers. before the 8th Army captured it Nov. 21, 1941.

Capybara, the largest rodent, found in S. America.

Carabobo, Venezuela. Plain 20 m. s.w. of Valencia ; victory of Bolivar over Spaniards (1821) established Colombian independence.

Caracal (kar'-a-kal), a species of lynx, 699, 2043.

Caracalla (kar-a-kal'-a), nickname of Bassianus (A.D. 188–217), Rom. emperor ; succeeded 211 ; brutal madman, 2816 ; baths, 2804, *plate f. 2805.*

Cará'cas (ka-rah'-kas), Venezuela, cap., 6 m. from spt. La Guaira, on Caribbean Sea ; pop. 269,000 ; *3026, map, 3309.*

Caracci. *See* **Carracci.**

Carac'tacus, King of Britain ; opposed Romans ; defeated A.D. 51 after 8 years' war, imprisoned at Rome ;

Tacitus ("Annals," Bk. XII, chap. 37) quotes noble speech he made before Rom. emperor, 574.

Car'apace. Shell-like cover of crustacean, 2942.

Car'at, unit of weight for gems, 200 milligrams, or 3·1 grains; also measure of purity of gold, 1481.

Caravaggio (kah-rah-vah'jō), **Michelangelo Merigi da** (1569–1609). It. painter of religious and genre subjects, founder of the naturalistic school, 1785, 3667.

Car'away, herb of the parsley family, 3061; essential oil from, 1263.

Carbajal (kar-bahr'-hal), **Francisco de** (1464–1548). Sp. soldier; with Cortes in Mexico and Pizarro in Peru; his extraordinary valour gave him nickname "Demon of the Andes."

Carberry Hill, 7 m. s.e. of Edinburgh; Mary Queen of Scots taken prisoner (1567), 2116.

Carbide, compound of carbon and metallic element; calcium carbide, 18, 655, 1420, 2374.

Carbohy'drates, compounds containing hydrogen and oxygen (in proportions of two to one) with carbon, 699; cellulose rayon, 2749; in food, 1338, 1339; sugars, 3114.

Carbolic acid, or phenol, **699,** 2638; base of certain plastic materials, 699; distilled from coal-tar, 857; in nylon mfr., 2749; a poison, 699.

Carbon (C), a non-metallic element closely related to silicon; occupies a unique position in the periodic table; contained in all organic compounds; atomic weight, 12·0, 699, 776; amorphous and crystalline forms, 940; arc welding, 3363; charcoal, 753; coal, 857; diamonds, 940, 1009; in dry cell, 376; graphite, 940, 1500, 1908; microphone, 2162; in paints, 2478; proportions in iron and steel, 1756; essential to plant growth, 2998; in protoplasm, 2695; in smoke, 2986; spectrum, *plate f.* 3057; use in electric light filaments, 1134; in ink, 1725.
Compounds: carbides, 2374; disulphide, 3117; hydrocarbons, 699, 1263, 1423; oxides, 699, 1423. *See also* Carbohydrates; Carbonates; Carbon dioxide; Carbon monoxide.

Carbonari (kar-bō-nahr'-ē) ("charcoal burners"). It. secret society, 1769; and Mazzini, 2124.

Carbonated water, how made, 700.

Carbonates, of ammonia, 146; calcium (chalk and limestone), 749, 1950, 2097; lead (white lead), 1908, 2478; sodium (soda), 2997.

Carbon dioxide, 699; in air, 88, 1598; as anaesthetic, 149; in beet sugar refining, 3114; makes bread rise, 3434; in combustion, 2673, 2986; forms "dry ice," 1341, 1391, 1420; fire extinguisher, 700; generated by volcanoes, 3328; generated by yeasts, 1266, 3434; in human blood, 1591; in illuminating gas, 1423; lime, 1948, 1949; in natural gas, 1420; as plant food, 699, 1915, 2589, 2601, 2621; in respiration, 2039, 2601; in rusting, 2856; in smoke, 2673, 2986; and sleep, 2983; in Solvay process, 2997; dissolves in water, 1420.

Carbonic acid gas. *See* Carbon dioxide.

Carboniferous period, or "Coal Age," *plate f. 1432, 1433,* character of vegetation, 855; giant insects, 1733; in. N. Amer. 2384; petroleum formation, 2428; primitive fish, 1298; cockroaches, 861.

Carbon monoxide, poisonous gas, 700; in blast furnace, 1754; from coke, 1597, 1674; in illuminating gas, 1423; petrol from, 1674, 2430; poisonous effect, 700, 1420, 2638.

Carborun'dum, hard, artificial compound, chemically a silicon carbide, 2970; formed in bluish- or yellowish-green crystals by intensely heating a mixture of carbon, finely ground coke, salt, and sand.

Car'buncle. Acute inflammation of tissue beneath the skin; resembles boil in early stages, but much more

painful and often accompanied by constitutional disturbances such as chills or fever.

Carbuncle. A garnet cut with a convex surface and flat or concave below in order to lighten the colour; name applied by ancients to all red and fiery stones, including ruby.

Carburetter, in petrol engine, 1737, 2244.

Carcassonne (kahr-ka-son'), Fr. city on r. Aude; pop. (1946) 38,140; wine market; medieval fortress, wall attributed to Visigoths, 1365.

Carchemish (kahr'-kem-ish). Anc. Hittite cap. on Upper Euphrates, *1633.*

Car'damom, a spice, 3060.

Cardan (kahr-dahn'), **Jérome (Hieronymus Cardanus,** also **Girolamo Cardano)** (1501–76), Italian mathematician, physician, and astrologer; among his ideas was his indication of method of teaching the blind to read and write by sense of touch, and use of signs in teaching the deaf; invented a type of lamp, 1887.

Cardboard, how made, 2500.

Cardenas (kahr'-dā-nas), **Lazaro** (b. 1895). President o Mexico 1934–40; Min. of Nat. Defence 1943–45; C.-in-C. Mexican Army 1945 retired; his decree of 1937 aiming at oil nationalization led to rupture of dip. relations with Britain.

Car'diff, Wales, coal and iron shipping port on Taff, just above Bristol Channel; pop. about 242,100; 700; castle presented to city by Lord Bute in 1947, 700; Llandaff cathedral bombed in 1941, 700; *map. 3334.* 1470.

Cardigan, Wales. Co. borough and spt. of Cardiganshire; extensive docks, iron and copper works, flour milling, engineering; pop. 3,609; 701.

Cardigan, James Thomas Brudenell, Earl of (1797–1868). Commander in "Charge of the Light Brigade" at Balaclava, 1854, celebrated in Tennyson's poem.

Cardiganshire, Wales. Southern co. bordering Cardigan Bay; a. 692 sq. m.; pop. 55,000; 701.

Cardinal. Highest dignitary of Rom. Cath. church next to Pope; the College of Cardinals is advisory body to Pope; 70 in number, appointed by Pope and hold office for life.

Cardinal bird. Red-feathered bird of finch family, found in N., Cent., and S. America.

Cardinal flower. A tall perennial plant (*Lobelia cardinalis*) with alternate, oblong, slightly toothed leaves, and bright red irregular flowers clustered in leafy terminal spikes.

Cardinal numbers. Simple names of the numbers (1, 2, etc.) as opposed to ordinals (first, second, third, etc.).

Cardinal points of compass. Four chief directions (N., S., E., W.); 882.

Cardinal virtues. The 4 chief virtues, viz. justice, prudence, temperance, fortitude, on which all others hinge (Lat. *cardo,* a hinge).

Carding, cotton, 919, 920; wool, 3406.

Cards, playing, 701.

Card sliver, 920.

Carducci (kahr-dōō'-chē), **Giosuè** (1836–1907). It. poet, greatest of later 19th cent. and liberator of It. poetry from hitherto fashionable sentimental romanticism, 1787.

Cardwell, Edward, Viscount (1813–86). Brit. statesman who, when Sec. of State for War, made drastic reforms in the army system (1871–2), among them being the institution of short service and the establishment of the army reserve.

Carew, Thomas (c.1598–c.1638). Eng. poet; earliest of "Cavalier poets"; famous for love lyrics; for a time at Court of Charles I.

Carey, Henry (.1690–1743). English poet and composer of musical farces and songs; best known for "Sally in Our Alley"; also reputed author of "God Save the King."

Carey, William (1761–1834). Eng. oriental scholar and first Baptist missionary to India; leader in 19th cent. Prot. missionary movement; translated Bible into many oriental languages.

Caria. Anc. country in s.w. corner of Asia Minor; contained Gk. tns. of Miletus and Halicarnassus.

Car'ib. S. Amer. Indians; "cannibal" derived from name (Caribal).

Caribbean Sea. Arm of Atlantic, 750,000 sq. m., enclosed by e. coast of Cent. Amer., n. coast of S. Amer. and crescent of W. Indies, **701;** hurricanes, 1551; "Spanish Main," 872; *map, 3309.*

Caribou (kar'-i-bōō). Wild reindeer of N. Amer., **702,** 984; antlers, 984; Hudson Bay herds, 676.

Caricature, in line drawing, 1046.

Carillon (kar'-il-yon), or **glockenspiel** (glok'-en-spēl). Set of bells or metal bars arranged so that tunes may be played upon them, 410, 2446.

Carin'thia. Dist of S. Austria; mining (especially lead) and mfg.; pine forests; chief city Klagenfurt, 316, *317.*

Car'isbrooke Castle. Norman edifice, at Carisbrooke, Isle of Wight, in which Charles I was imprisoned for more than a year; the parish gives the title to the Marquess of Carisbrooke.

Carleton, William (1794–1869). Irish novelist, author of several powerful stories; best remembered for his "Traits and Stories of the Irish Peasantry."

Car'line thistle. Grows in poor soils of Europe; so named because of supposed medicinal use by Charlemagne; seeds, 2917.

Carlisle (kar-līl'). Co. tn. of Cumberland, near Scot. border; pop. 65,000; **702,** 943; Rom. wall, 1168.

Car'lists. Sp. political party, supporters of the descendants of Don Carlos, claimants to the throne of Spain; waged civil war in which they were defeated in 1840; later attempts to secure the throne ended in their subjection in 1876; they played a part on the Nationalist side in the Civil War of 1936.

Carlos I (1863–1908). King of Port.; succeeded 1889; suspended constitution 1907; assassinated while driving in Lisbon.

Carlos, Don (1545–68). Son of Philip II of Spain; vicious weakling about whose disappointment in love (his father married Carlos's fiancée, Elizabeth of France) and mysterious death Schiller and others have woven romances.

Carlos, Don (1788–1855). Uncle of Isabella II of Spain and first Carlist pretender to Sp. throne; called Charles V by followers.

Carlos, Don (1848–1909). Claimant to the Sp. throne; he took the field in an effort to effect his claim in 1872 and, failing, spent the remainder of his life in Fr. and It.

Carlot'ta (1840–1927). Empress of Mexico; wife of Maximilian and daughter of Leopold I of Belgium became insane after execution of husband, and lived in retirement near Brussels.

Carlow, Eire. Second smallest co. of Ire.; a. 346 sq. m.; pop. 34,000 702.

Carlton Club. London club, in Pall Mall; headquarters of Conservatism since its foundation by the Duke of Wellington, in 1832.

Carlton House. Old London mansion in Pall Mall, where the Duke of York's Column stands; built by Henry Boyle, Baron Carleton, who left it to the Prince of Wales (afterwards George IV). It was pulled down in 1827, and the columns were used for the National Gallery. The name was perpetuated in Carlton House Terrace, now also demolished.

Carlyle, Jane Welsh (1801–66). Witty, brilliant, sharp-tempered, but devoted wife of Thomas Carlyle, 702.

Carlyle, Thomas (1795–1881), Scot. essayist and historian, 702, 703, 1215, 1224 ; friendship with Emerson, 1156.

Carman, Bliss (1861–1929). Canadian poet and essayist (" Ballads of Lost Haven " ; " Daughters of Dawn "), 685.

Carmar'then, Wales. Old spt. tn. in s. on r. Towy ; pop. 10,600 ; co. tn. of Carmarthenshire, 703.

Carmarthenshire, Wales. Maritime and largest co. ; a. 919 sq. m. ; pop. 179,000 ; 703.

Car'mel, Mt. Ridge in Cent. Palestine, near Mediterranean ; associated with the prophets Elijah and Elisha ; Carmelite order founded there by hermits.

Car'melite Friars. Mendicant order of " Our Lady of Mount Carmel," founded 1207 ; called White Friars in Eng. because of white mantle ; 2214.

Car'men. Fickle fascinating gipsy heroine of Mérimée's story ; Bizet's opera " Carmen " founded thereon ; 2438.

Carmen Sylva (1843–1916). Pen-name of Elizabeth, queen of Carol I, King of Rumania.

Carnac, France. A Breton village famous for ancient stone monuments in vicinity, 3095.

Carnavon. See Caernarvon.

Carnar'von, George Edward, 5th Earl of (1860–1923). Educated Eton and Trinity Coll., Cambridge ; in his later years he took a keen interest in Egyptology, and, aided by Howard Carter and other assistants, made the great discovery of the tomb of Tutankhamen, 1118, 1120.

Carnat'ic or **Karnatak.** Region in Madras State, extending along E. coast of S. India, 1714.

Carnation. Cultivated variety of pink, 703.

Carnauba, vegetable wax, 3359.

Carnegie (kar-neg'-i), **Andrew** (1835–1919). Scot.-Amer. ironmaster and philanthropist, 703, 203.

Carn Eige. Peak in Ross and Cromarty, 2828.

Carne'lian or **Cornelian**, or red chalcedony. Semi-precious form of quartz, 2713.

Carniola. Former prov. in s.w. Austria-Hungary ; following 1st World War included in Yugoslavia, except small strip to It.

Carnivora (kar-niv'-o-ra). The order of flesh-eating mammals, 2077 ; evolutionary position, 158.

Carnivorous plants, 2624 ; pitcher plant, 2613, plate f. 2621 ; Venus's fly trap, 3313.

Carnot (kahr-nō), **Lazare Nicolas Marguerite** (1753–1823). Fr. statesman, general, mathematician, and military author ; member of Committee of Public Safety and of Directory.

Carnot, Marie François Sadi (1837–94). Fourth pres. of Fr. (1887–94) ; assassinated ; grandson of L. N. M. Carnot.

Carnot, Sadi Nicolas Léonard (1796–1832). Fr. physicist, formulator of " Carnot's principle," or the second law of thermodynamics ; son of L. N. M. Carnot.

Car'notite, ore of radium and uranium, 3297.

Carnsore Point, promontory in s.e. of co. Wexford, Eire (Irish Free State); the extreme s.e. point of Ireland.

Car'ob tree (Ceratonia siliqua), a native of the Levant ; an evergreen, its pulp is used as a food for horses and sometimes for human beings, and called St. John's bread.

Carol I, of Rumania. See Charles I.

Carol II (b. 1893), King of Rumania, renounced succession to throne (1925), his son Michael becoming King under a regency council (1927) ; proclaimed King in 1930, following a dramatic return from exile, 2841 ; in 1937 became virtual dictator ; abdicated Sept. 6, 1940, when his son Michael became King ; married Mme. Lupescu, 1947.

Carolina, States of U.S.A., 704. See also **North Carolina** and **South Carolina.**

Caroline Islands. Coral group in Pacific E. of Philippines ; includes Ponape (pop. 11,000) ; Yap (6,000) ; formerly Ger. ; Jap. mandate (1919) ; 2470, 2473 ; shells, 2942 ; U.S. bombed and shelled, 1944–45 ; placed under U.S. administration by U.N. in 1947.

Caroline of Anspach (1683–1737), queen of George II of Eng. ; d. 1441.

Caroline of Brunswick (1768–1821). Queen of George IV. of Eng.

Carolin'gians, Frankish rulers, 751–987, descendants of Charles Martel, 1365.

Carols, Christmas, 820.

" Caro'nia." Cunard White-Star luxury liner of 34,000 tons ; dual-purpose passenger ship for Atlantic crossing and cruising ; maiden voyage, Jan. 1949.

Car'otene. Vitamin-A-containing substance in carrots, etc. ; in dried grass, 1510.

Carot'id artery. One of the two great arterial trunks of the neck (l. and r. sides) that convey blood to the brain.

Carp, a fish, 704 ; goldfish, a species of, 1481 ; varieties, 2781.

Carpaccio (kahr-pah'-chō), **Vittorio** (c 1450–c. 1522). Venetian painter, among greatest of early Renaissance (" Life of St. Ursula "), 1776.

Carpal bones of wrist, 1572.

Carpathian Mts., in Cent. Europe, 704, 1232, 1233, 2844 ; resources, 2839.

Carpatho-Ukraine. Another name of former Czech province of Ruthenia (q.v.). Incorporated in U.S.S.R., 1945.

Carpel. That part of a flower which comprises the female organs. See Flowers.

Carpenter, Edward (1844–1929). Brit. social reformer. Books include " Towards Democracy," " Civilization : Its Cause and Cure."

Carpenter bee, 394, 1729.

Carpenter wasps, 3346.

Carpentier (kahr-pahn'-tyā), **Georges** (b. 1894). Fr. boxer ; won world's "white" heavyweight championship in 1914 ; defeated by Dempsey in U.S.A. (1921).

Carpetbaggers, northern U.S.A. politicians who settled in the south, after Civil War. Term used in Gt. Brit. for a candidate for Parl. who is entire stranger to the constituency.

Carpets and rugs, 705, 3361. See also Spinning ; Weaving.

Carracci (kahr-rah'-chē), **Annibale** (1560–1609). It. painter, greatest of the three Carraccis, 1785.

Carracci, Ludovico (1555–1619). The founder of the Bolognese or eclectic school of painting, 1785.

Carrageen (kar'-a-gēn), or Irish moss, 2239, 2916.

Car'rantuo'hill, loftiest mt. in Ire., part of the Macgillicuddy Reeks ; also called Carntual and Carrantual; it is 3,414 ft. high.

Carranza (kah-rahn'-zah), **Venustia'no** (1859–1920), pres. of Mexico (1917–20).

Carrara (kahr-ahr'-a), It., city 60 m. N.w. of Florence ; pop. 52,000 ; famous marble quarries, 1763, 2097.

Carrickfer'gus. Historic Irish spt. in N. Ire., 9 m. N.E. of Belfast ; pop. 6,200 ; 12th cent. castle.

Carrier pigeons, 2606.

" Carriers " of disease, 1459.

Carrier wave, in wireless, 3393, 3394.

Carrion crow, 935.

Carroll, Lewis (1832–98), pen-name of Charles L. Dodgson, Eng. mathematician and story-writer for children, 707," story of " Alice in Wonderland," 708.

Carroll, Sydney Wentworth (b. 1877), Brit. theatrical manager, editor and critic ; ed. Daily Sketch 1938–42 ; estabd. open-air theatre in Regent's Park, London, 3197.

Carron, ironworks at, 3092.

Carron oil, constituents, 1949.

Carrot. Root vegetable of the Umbelliferae, related to parsley, parsnip, and hemlock ; introduced by Dutch in 16th cent. ; root, 2825.

Carson, Edward, Baron (1854–1935), Irish Unionist leader and great criminal lawyer ; head of Ulster rebellion against Brit. government's Home Rule Bill for Ireland (1912–13) ; Brit. attorney-gen., June–Oct. 1915, in Asquith coalition cabinet ; First Lord of the Admiralty (1916–17) ; member War Cabinet (1917–18).

Cartagena (kahr-ta-jē'-na), Colombia. Spt. on Caribbean Sea ; pop. 84,980 ; exports cattle, hides, woods, tobacco ; founded in 1533.

Cartagena, Spain, spt., mfg. city, and mining centre in s.E. on Mediterranean ; pop. (est.) 117,100 ; naval station ; founded 3rd cent. B.C. by Carthaginians ; 3030. Blake destroys royalist fleet, 465.

Carte, Richard D'Oyly (1844–1901). Eng. theatrical manager, producer of Gilbert and Sullivan operas ; failed in an effort to found the Grand English Opera House, but achieved great success with touring opera companies, 2438.

Carter, Howard (1873–1939). Eng. Egyptologist, carried out exploration work in Egypt on behalf of Lord Carnarvon during 1907–23, and amongst his discoveries was the tomb of Tutankhamen, 206, 1118, 1120.

Cartesianism, the philosophy of Descartes, 995.

Carthage (kahr'-thaj), anc. city and state in N. Africa, 710, 711 ; founded by Phoenicians, 2573, 3254 ; allied with Etruscans, 1230 ; in Libya, 1931 ; Cato's denunciation, 712 ; conquers Sardinia, 2874 ; colonizes Spain, 3033 ; Punic Wars, 1574, 2808 ; Vandals in, 3304.

Carthu'sian monks, 2213.

Cartier (kahr-tyā), **Sir George Étienne** (1814–73). Fr.-Canadian statesman, premier 1858–62 ; active in promoting Canadian federation.

Cartier, Jacques (1494–1557). Fr. explorer of Canada, 143, 712 ; discovers St. Lawrence, 1534, 2715, 2861 ; and Montreal, 2224.

Cartilage, or gristle, a tough elastic animal tissue, 2977 ; changed into bone, 498 ; thyroid, 3327.

Carton de Wiart (vē'-art), **Lt.-Gen. Sir Adrian, V.C.** (b. 1880). Brit. soldier ; V.C. of First World War, when he was wounded 8 times and lost an eye and an arm ; commanded Brit. forces in cent. Norway in 1940 ; during 1941–43 a prisoner in Ital. hands ; in 1944 Churchill's military and personal representative in China ; in 1947 retired.

Cartoons, humorous sketches, 1046 ; film, 829 ; Disney's work, 829.

Cartouche (kahr-tōōsh'), in architecture, an ornament in the form of an unrolled scroll ; on Egyptian monuments it is an oblong device with oval ends, containing the name or title of a famous person.

Cartridges, as ammunition, 1283, 1284.

Cartwright, Edmund (1743–1823), inventor of power-loom, 712, 3361.

Caruso (ka-rōō'-zō), **Enrico** (1873–1921). It. dramatic tenor, greatest of his time ; gifted with extraordinarily powerful and beautiful voice.

Caryatides (kar-i-at-i'-dēz), in architecture, figures of women draped in long robes, serving to support porches or entablatures.

Caryatides, or **Maidens, Porch of the**, Athens, 285.

Casabianca (ka-za-bē-an'-ka), **Louis de** (1755–98). Fr. naval officer, commander of Napoleon's flagship, L'Orient, which caught fire at Aboukir ; his son Giacomo, aged 10, was the boy who " stood on the burning deck " in Mrs. Hemans's poem ; both father and son perished.

Casablanca (ka-sa-blan'-ka) or **Darel Beida.** Spt. of Morocco, on Atlantic ; pop. 257,000 ; wool, leather, grain ; 2231, 3420 ; Allied conference, Jan. 1943.

Casals (kah-zahlz), **Pau** (b. 1876). Spanish violoncellist and conductor ; one of the world's greatest 'cellists.

Casanova (ka-sa-nō'-va), **Giovanni Jacopo** (1725–98). Venetian adventurer and writer; famous for "Memoirs" of his amazing and eventful life, which led him to all the capitals of Europe.

Cascade Mts., range in Canada and U.S.A., extending from Brit. Columbia to California; highest peak Mt. Shasta (14,440 ft.); 3285, *3287*.

Case, in grammar, 2399.

Case, printer's, 3270.

Casein (kā'-sē-in), protein compound found in milk, 2174, 2500; fibre from, 2749; plastics, 2625.

Case'ment, Roger (1864–1916). Irish conspirator; knighted (1912) for investigation of Congo and Putumayo atrocities; hanged (Aug. 3, 1916) for high treason (being degraded from his knighthood when found guilty), for anti-British activities in Germany and his part in organizing the "Easter Rebellion" in Ireland; 887, 1051, 1746.

Cash. A Chinese coin, worth less than one-tenth of a penny.

Cashel. Town of Tipperary, 3215.

Cash'ew. A nut, 2408.

Cashmere. *See* Kashmir.

Cashmere (Kashmir) goat, 1478.

Cash register, 712.

Casimir-Perier (ka-zē-měr pā-ryā), **Jean Paul Pierre** (1847–1907). Fifth president of France (June 1894–Jan. 1895).

Casino (ka-sē'-nō). A gambling house; at Monte Carlo, 2219.

Casket Letters. A celebrated collection of letters, supposed to be the correspondence between Bothwell and Mary Stuart.

Caslon, William (1692–1766). First of a famous family of Eng. typefounders; name is given to typefaces still much used.

Cas'pian Sea. Salt sea on borders of Europe and Asia, largest inland body of water in world; 760 m. long, 120 to 300 m. wide; **712,** 1232, 1885, 2563, 2844.

Cassaba (ka-sah'-ba) **melon,** 2138.

Cassandra (ka-san'-dra). Daughter of Priam king of Troy; prophetess of woe, doomed never to be believed; in vain warned against keeping Helen and admitting the wooden horse; became Agamemnon's captive; slain with him by Clytemnestra.

Cassava (ka-sah'-va), or manioc, 3153.

Cassel. *See* Kassel.

Cassia, spice, 3061.

Cassino. Tn. of It. prov. of Naples, at foot of Monte Cassino (*q.v.* in *f-i.*); key position of Gustav Line in 2nd World War, as Monte Cassino commanded road to Rome; Allies vainly assaulted Jan. 30–Mar. 14, 1944; dropped 1,400 tons of bombs on tn., Mar. 14, and destroyed Monte Cassino monastery, Mar. 15; finally took tn. and mt., May 18; 3422.

Cassiopeia (kas-i-ō-pē'-ya), in Gk. myth., Ethiopian queen, mother of Andromeda.

Cassiopeia, constellation, *chart, 895.*

Cassiterite, or tinstone; ore of tin, 3215.

Cassivellau'nus. Brit. king, conquered by Julius Caesar (54 B.C.).

Cas'son, Sir Lewis (b. 1875). Brit. actor and producer; m. Sybil Thorndike in 1908; for services with theatre, as director of C.E.M.A., was knighted in 1945.

Cas'sowary. Large flightless bird of Australasia, related to ostrich, emu, and rhea; distinguished from emu, 1157.

Caste, in India, 1626, 1628, 1707; Japan, 1799.

Castelar y Ripoll, Emilio (1832–99). Span. Liberal statesman; dictator of Spanish republic (1873).

Castellón de la Plana (kas-tel-yon' dä lah plah'-nah), Spain. Mfg. and trade city near Mediterranean; pop. 46,876.

Castiglione (kas-tē-lyō'-nā), **Baldassare** (1478–1529). It. writer and diplomat, employed on many important missions; called "the perfect courtier," portrait by Raphael, *2745.*

Castile (kas-tēl'), former kingdom of N. cent. Sp., 1238, 1760, *map, 3030.*

Castil'ian. Chief literary dialect of Sp. language, 3050.

Casting. Process of moulding molten metal; of bells, *411*; iron, 1756; pottery, 2665; sculpture, 2904; type, 3270.

Cast iron. A cast alloy of iron, carbon, and other elements, 1756.

Castle, *713–716,* **717,** *718,* 1268. *See also* Balmoral, *351*; Bosporus, 528; Caernarvon, *3337*; Cardiff, *700*; Chateau de Chenonceaux, 1363; Chillon, 1429; Edinburgh, 1087; Glamis, *155*; Hurstmonceux, *218*; Kenilworth, *1851*; Lewes, *3123*; Rhine, 2769; Stirling, 3902; Tower of London, 3231, *3232, plate f. 3232*; Windsor, *3381.*

Castle Coombe. Village of Wilts, Eng., *1164.*

"Castle of Otranto," by Horace Walpole, 3338.

Castlereagh, Robert Stewart, Viscount (2nd Marquess of Londonderry) (1769–1822), Brit. statesman; Sec. for Ireland (1798–1800); Sec. for War (1805–06, 1807–09); Foreign Sec. (1812–22); committed suicide.

Castle Rising, Norfolk, *714.*

Castor. Secretion of beaver, 2549.

Castor and Pollux. Famous demigods of Gk. myth., twin sons of Zeus, **718,** *2801,* 2804; constellation, *3078, 3080*; temple of (Rome), *2801, 2803.*

Castor bean. Fruit of castor plant, from which castor oil is obtained, 1263.

Castor oil. Medicine obtained by crushing seeds or beans of the castor oil plant (*Ricinus*) grown in tropical and semi-tropical countries; oil is also used for waterproofing leather, in perfumes and dyes, as lubricant, and in mfr. of varnish, ink, rubber, soap, linoleum, etc., 1263.

Castro, Cipriano (1858–1924), Venezuelan revolutionary leader and pres.

Cat. Animal of the genus *Felis,* **718,** *719*; eye, 1252, *1253*; and flycatcher, *2289*; foot, 1342; resembles the lion, 1959; mummies, 2256; tongue.

Catabolism (ka-tab'-o-lizm), or **Katabolism,** chemical process by which energy is produced from food in the body.

Catacombs of Rome, *817,* 2476, 2802.

Catalo'nia. Former principality and prov. in E. Sp.; granted partial autonomy in 1932; stronghold of Government forces in Spanish Civil War (1936–39), 3040; Barcelona the cap., 361.

Catalysis (ka-tal'-i-sis). Chemical change brought about by an agent which remains unchanged, 720; example in mfr. of sulphuric acid, 3117.

Catalyst (kat'-a-list). An agent which causes catalysis, **720**; in hydrogen mfr., 1674; platinum as example, 2628; selenium compounds, 2920.

Catamaran (kat-a-ma-ran'). A sailing craft, *482,* 486.

Cat'amount ("cat of the mountain"). The puma, 2702.

Catania (ka-tah'-ni-a). It. spt. on E. coast of Sicily near Mt. Etna; pop. 245,000; 1228.

Catapult. Original military "engine" invented by Archimedes; modern aircraft, type on warship, *2301*; Roman, *2807.*

Cataracts, of Nile, 2371.

Catch-as-catch-can wrestling, 3426.

Catchfly. Species of campion, 674.

Catenary (kat-ē'-nari). Curve assumed by a flexible rope or chain hanging naturally between two points; such curves, inverted, may be used as models for arches, 205.

Caterpillar Club, of airmen forced to save their lives from the enemy by parachuting, 2510.

Caterpillars. Larvae of moths and butterflies, *630, 631,* **720**; destroy vegetation, 729; kept down by birds, 438, 943; kept down by other insects, 3346; larval nature, 1729, 1893; metamorphosis into pupae, 729, 1729; silkworm, 2970.

Catesby, Robert (1537–1605). One of the chief "Gunpowder Plot" (Nov. 5, 1605) conspirators; fled on discovery of plot and was shot dead by his pursuers.

Cat family, the *Felidae,* 719; feet, 1342.

Catfish. Smooth-skinned fish, with barbels, **729.**

Cathay- (kath-ā'). Poetic name for China; originated with Marco Polo; used vaguely in Middle Ages for regions in Far East, 810.

Cathays Park, Cardiff, 700.

Cathedral (ka-thē'-dral). Principal church of a diocese, containing the seat or chair of the bishop (or archbishop), 219, *721–728,* **729.** *See also* Amiens, *1362*; Antwerp, *182*; Burgos, *3035*; Canterbury, *724*; Chelmsford, *1224*; Chichester, *784*; Cologne, *872*; Exeter, *1249*; Florence, *1319*; Gloucester, *1476*; Hereford, *1617*; Mexico City, *2159*; Milan, *2173*; Notre Dame, Paris, *2519*; Ripon, *2781*; St. Mark's, Venice, *1762,* *3311*; St. Paul's, London, 219, 2020, *2863*; St. David's, *2539*; St. Peter's, Rome, *2802*; Salisbury, *219, 721*; Santiago de Compostela, 3034; Segovia, *3038*; Seville, *2926*; Winchester, *3384*; Worcester, *3407.* Separate articles are devoted in the main text to Eng. cathedral cities.

Cather, Willa Sibert (1876–1947). American novelist, 2403, 3295. Works include "A Lost Lady" (1923); "Death Comes to the Archbishop" (1927); "Shadows on the Rock" (1931).

Catherine I (1683–1727). Empress of Russia, wife and successor of Peter the Great (1725), 2563.

Catherine II, the Great (1729–96). Empress of Russia; murdered her husband Peter III and seized his throne (1762), 2847; founds Odessa, 2420; partition of Poland, 2642.

Catherine de' Medici (med'-i-chi) (1519–89), queen of Henry II of Fr., 758, 870, 2131.

Catherine Howard (c. 1522–42), 5th queen of Henry VIII, 1612.

Catherine of Alexandria, St. (4th cent. A.D. ?). Virgin martyr, tortured on a toothed or "Catherine" wheel; patroness of scholars, theologians, and virgins.

Catherine of Aragon (1485–1536), daughter of Ferdinand and Isabella of Spain, and first queen of Henry VIII of Eng.; divorced, 1612; buried at Peterborough, 2563.

Catherine of Braganza (1638–1705), wife of Charles II, 757.

Catherine of Siena, St. (1347–80). It. ascetic and mystic, a dyer's daughter; persuaded Pope Gregory XI to return from Avignon to Rome.

Catherine Parr (1512–48), 6th queen of Henry VIII, 1612.

Cath'ode, 1136; electro-plating, 1139; in ionization, 1739; in thermionic valve, 1138, 3198, *3199*; of steel, *1137.*

Cathode rays, 1138, 2731, 3430.

Cathode Ray Tube; in radar, 2726; television, 3182.

Catholic Church. *See* **Roman Catholic Church.**

Catholic Emancipation Act, 2535; O'Connell and, 2420.

Catiline (kat'-i-lin). (Lucius Sergius Catilina) (c.108–62 B.C.), Rom. conspirator; Cicero and, 827.

Cation (kat'-ion). Ion flowing to cathode, or negative pole; in electrolysis, 1136, 1739.

Catkin. Type of inflorescence characteristic of the class *Amentiferae,* 3619.

Cato (ka'-tō), **Marcus Porcius** (234–149 B.C.), **the Censor** ("the Elder"), Rom. statesman and orator; **730**; and Carthage, 712; prose writings, 1895.

Cato, Marcus Porcius (95–46 B.C.), of Utica ("the Younger"). Rom. statesman and Stoic philosopher.

Cato Street Conspiracy. Political plot to kill Lord Castlereagh and other members of Cabinet, Feb. 23, 1820; conspirators hanged or transported.

"Catrio'na," by R. L. Stevenson, 3089.

Catroux, Georges (b. 1879). F.F.I. Leader, 1941–45 ; Ambassador to U.S.S.R., 1945–46.

Cat's Cradle. Children's game ; in New Guinea, *801*.

Cat's-eye. A form of quartz, greenish gold in colour ; it is a semi-precious stone used in jewelry.

Catskill Mts. Part of the Appalachian Mts., U.S.A., 190.

Cat's Whisker, in crystal wireless receivers, 3394.

Cattaro. *See* **Kotor.**

Cattermole, George (1800–68). Notable Eng. water-colour artist ; illustrator of Scott's "Waverley Novels," and several of Shakespeare's plays.

Cattle, 730. Bison, 459 ; buffalo, 459 ; dairy breeds, 732, *956* ; meat, 2124 ; as money, 2201 ; sacred cow in India, *1703* ; yak, 3433.

Cattle raising, 3394.

Cattle raising, in Australia, *312* ; India, *1701*, 1708 ; S. Africa, 3014.

Cat'tleya. An orchid, 2447.

Catullus (*ka*-tul'-*us*), **Gaius Valerius** (c. 84–54 B.C.), Roman lyric poet, 1896.

Caucasia (kaw-kā'-zha) or **Caucasus.** Former division of Russia between Black and Caspian Seas, **732**, 2845, *2846, 2849, 2849* ; a. 181,173 sq. m. ; pop. about 14,000,000 ; divided into N. Caucasia and Transcaucasia, latter including Georgia, Azerbaijan and Armenia ; rug-making, 706 ; in 2nd World War, 1452, *3073*, 3420.

Caucasian race ; origin of name, 732 ; Polynesians, *2469*, 2471.

Caucasian tiger, 3211.

Caucasus (kaw'-*ka*-sus), **Mt.,** in Gk. myth., scene of Prometheus' punishment.

Caucasus Mts., range between S.E. Europe and Asia ; extending from Sea of Azov to Caspian Sea ; 732 ; *map f.* 264 ; 1232 ; avalanche in, 322 ; peoples, 732.

Caudillo. Title assumed by Gen. Franco as leader of Sp. govt. in 1939.

Caudine Forks. Mt. pass in Samnium, 25 m. N.E. of Naples, where 40,000 Romans surrendered (321 B.C.) in 2nd Samnite War.

Cauliflower. Vegetable of cabbage type, introduced into Gr. Brit. from Mediterranean countries, *639*.

Caustic potash, 2664 ; soap-making, 2993.

Caustic soda, hydrogen a by-product, 1674 ; in paper-making, 2497 ; in rayon mfr., 2748 ; in reclaiming rubber, 2838 ; soap-making, 2993.

Cavaliers'. Royalists in Eng. Civil War, 755.

" Cavalleria Rusticana " (ka-val-lā-rē'-*a* roos-tē-kah'-na). Opera by Mascagni, 2438.

Cavalli, Francesco (1602–76). It. composer ; influence on opera, 2435.

Cavalry. Mounted troops, 244, 246.

Cavan (kav'-an), **Frederick, 10th Earl of** (1865–1946). Brit. soldier ; comd. Guards Division in 1st World War, and later the 14th Army Corps, which went to the assistance of the Italians ; chief of the Imperial General Staff (1922–26) ; Field-Marshal (1932).

Cavan. Inland agric. co. in Eire ; 730 sq. m. ; pop. 72,000 ; **733.**

Cave, George, 1st Viscount (1856–1928). Brit. lawyer and politician ; Home Secretary 1916–19 ; Lord Chancellor in 1922 and 1924.

Cave, 733, *plates f. 732, 733* ; Fingal's Cave, *3071* ; Mammoth Cave, *733* ; temple at Ellora, *1664*.

Cave Dwellers of the Old Stone Age, **734**, *735, 736, plate f. 737*, 2080 ; paintings of, 736, *plate f. 736 ; plates f. 2080, 2081* ; 1646, 2057.

Cavell', Edith Louisa (1865–1915). Eng. nurse, matron of a Brussels hospital, shot by Germans for helping Allied soldiers to escape into Holland. Oct. 12, 1915 ; buried, 1919, in Norwich Cathedral ; memorial in S. Martin's Place, London ; her last recorded words : " I realize that patriotism is not enough."

Cav'endish, Lord Frederick Charles (1836–82). Brit. politician ; shortly after appointment as Chief Secretary for Ire. in 1882 was murdered in Phoenix Park, Dublin.

Cavendish, Henry (1731–1810). Eng. chemist and physicist, 736, 1512.

Caviare (kav-i-ahr'). A preparation of sturgeon roe, 1095, 3104 ; Russian production, 717.

Cavour (kav-ōōr'), **Camillo Benso, Count di** (1810–61). It. statesman, 737, 3319 ; work for It. liberty, 1769.

Cavy. *See* **Guinea-pig.**

Cawnpore, India. Industrial city in United Provs., on Ganges ; pop. 487,324 ; massacre in Sepoy mutiny, 1714, *3284* ; Ram Lilla at, *1697*.

Caxton, William (c.1422–91). First Eng. printer, 1210, 2686 ; woodcut from " The Game and Play of Chess." *511.*

Cayenne (kah-yen'). Cap., chief tn. and spt. of Fr. Guiana ; pop. 11,704 ; formerly Fr. penal settlement, *map f. 1552*, 1553.

Cayenne canary. Canary with reddish feathers.

Cayenne pepper, 2547.

Cayley, Sir George (1773–1857). Eng. aeronautical pioneer, 44, 1735.

Cay'man. Reptile of crocodile type, 932.

Cebu (sā-bōō'). One of Philippine Isls. ; 1,703 sq. m. ; pop. 1,066,000 ; occupied by Japanese 1942–45 ; captured by U.S. forces Mar. 28–April 22, 1945, thus ending battle for central Philippines ; cap. and chief spt. Cebu on E. coast ; pop. 155,100 ; important trade centre, 2568 ; Magellan at, 2056.

Cec'il. Great Eng. family ; most famous members, William Cecil, Lord Burleigh (Queen Elizabeth's great minister) ; and Marquess of Salisbury, Victorian Premier.

Cecil, Robert, Viscount (b. 1864). Brit. statesman ; son of Marquess of Salisbury ; Minister of Blockade (1916–18) ; outstanding figure, representing S. Africa, at first meeting of Assembly of the League of Nations at Geneva (1920) ; received a peerage in 1923 and took as his title Viscount Cecil of Chelwood ; Pres. League of Nations Union, 2531 ; awarded Nobel peace prize, 1937.

Cecil'ia, St. Christian martyr, supposed to have perished in Sicily about A.D. 180 ; patron saint of musicians ; festival celebrated on Nov. 22.

Cecrops (sē'-krops). Mythical founder of Athens and first king of Attica ; represented as half man, half dragon.

Cedar, 737 ; essential oil from, 1263 ; wood used for pencils, 2541.

Celandine (sel'-*an*-dīn). Derived from Lat. *chelidonium*, Gk. *chelidon*, swallow ; the lesser celandine (*Ranunculus ficaria*), a member of the buttercup family, has starry yellow flowers ; roots, 2825 ; The much less common greater celandine (*Chelidonium majus*) is no relation, being a kind of poppy with soft, hairy leaves ; this grows in old walls ; both are supposed to flower with the arrival of swallows.

" Celanese." Form of rayon ; manufacture, 2749.

Celebes (sel'-e-bēz). Isl. in Indonesia ; a., with dependent is., 72,000 sq. m. ; pop. 4,230,000 ; **738** ; *map, 1074*, 1076 ; in Jap. occupn., 1942–45, 738.

Celery. Plant with edible stems, **738** ; blanching, 2623.

Celesta (se-les'-*ta*). A musical instrument containing steel plates backed by wooden resonators, played with keyboard, 2268, 2446.

Cell. Unit structure of living organisms, **738**, *739* ; division, *431* ; of brain, 546 ; grow after death, 739 ; how differentiated for higher life, 112 ; in embryology, 1154 ; protoplasm, 2695 ; in reproduction, 1154 ; single-celled animals, 738 ; single-celled plants, 112 ; spore, 2918.

Cell, electric. Device for changing chemical energy into electric current, 375, 377, 1131 ; invented by Volta, 376.

Cellini (chel-lē'-nē), **Benvenuto** (1500–71). It. goldsmith, sculptor ; brawling, braggart soldier of fortune, and mirror of his time (" Autobio-graphy ") ; 2766, 2906 ; Poseidon and Aphrodite salt-cellar, *1784*.

Cello (chel'-lō) or **violoncello** (vē-ō-lon-chel'-ō). A stringed instrument, 3009, 3324.

" Cellophane." A transparent product of a sodium compound and cellulose, extensively used as a wrapping, 1477, 2749.

Cell theory, 738.

Cel'luloid. Ivory-like artificial substance, 739.

Cel'lulose. Stiffening substance of plants, 739, 2709, 2748 ; acetate, 2749 ; cotton, 3404 ; formed by leaves, 1915 ; in explosives, 1250 ; lacquer, 1882 ; nitrate, 2748 ; in paper-making, 2496 ; rayon, 2748 ; in trees, 3245.

Celsius (sel'-si-*us*), **Anders** (1701–44). Swedish astronomer ; devised Centigrade (" Celsius ") thermometer.

Celtic languages and literature, 1209. Arthurian legends, 1210 ; in Ireland, 1750 ; in Wales, 3334.

Celts (kelts), or **Kelts**, 572, **740** ; in Britain, 1193 ; enamel ware, *1158* ; in France, 585, 1365 ; in Ireland, 1744 ; in Wales, 3333.

Cement (sē-ment') **and Concrete.** Building materials, 740, *741* ; in building construction, 640 ; pneumatic mixers, 2633 ; quarrying for, 2713.

Cenis (se-nē). Mountain and pass of Alps on border of France and Italy.

Cenotaph (sen'-ō-taf). Monument erected to commemorate the dead who are buried elsewhere ; the best-known example is the Cenotaph in Whitehall, London, *239*.

Censors, in anc. Rome, 2805.

Census. Enumeration of the population, 742.

Cent. A coin of the U.S.A., weighing 48 grains (95 per cent copper, 5 per cent tin and zinc) and valued at the hundredth part of a dollar ; first issued in 1787 ; Brit. equivalent, about halfpenny.

Centaur (sen'-tawr). Fabled monster, half man, half horse, 742 ; Theseus slays, 3202.

Centau'rus. A southern constellation ; brightest star, Alpha Centauri, 3078.

Cen'tigrade thermometer, 3200.

Centigram. Unit in metric system (0·154 grains), 2155.

Centilitre. Unit in metric system (0·338 fluid oz.), 2155.

Centime. Fr. coin, 100th part of a franc.

Cen'timetre. Unit in metric system (0·3937 in.), 2155 ; centimetre-gramme-second (C.G.S.) system of units, 2155.

Centimetric waves, in wireless, 3397.

Cen'tipedes. A type of many-legged arthropod, 742, 3065 ; evolutionary position, *158* ; not an insect, 1730.

Central African Council, 2772.

Central America. Extending from Mexico to Colombia ; 220,000 sq. m. ; pop. 8,000,000 ; **743** ; *map, 743* ; history, 744 ; Mayas, 3428. *See also* **America,** and names of separate countries.

Central Criminal Court, Old Bailey, 922.

Central Hall, Westminster, London ; U.N. assembly *3284*.

Central heating, 1599 ; in Korea, *1873*.

Central Powers. Countries (Germany, Austria, Hungary, Bulgaria, Turkey) opposed to the Allies in 1st World War.

Central Provinces and Berar (Madhya Pradesh), India ; 131,686 sq. m. ; pop. 17,000,000. 744 ; *map, 1702*.

Centre of gravity, explanation, 1513, 2128.

Centrif'ugal force, 744, *745* ; in fan, 1260 ; against gravity, 1512 ; in locomotives, 1986 ; in mechanics, 2127 ; in water-wheels, 1672.

Centrifugal machinery, 745 ; cream separator, 955 ; pump, 2704 ; in sugar-making, *3114*, 3115.

Cen'trifuge. Machine using centrifugal force ; 745 ; in laundry, 1900.

Centrip'etal force. Force operating on a body moving in a curve, tending to draw the body to the centre, 744.

Centrosphere, of earth, *1067*.

Century plant. *See* **Agave.**

Cephalic (se-fal´-ik) **index,** 2724.

Cephalonia (sef´-*a*-lo´-ni-*a*). Mountainous Gk. isl. w. of mainland ; second largest of Ionian group ; 260 sq. m. ; pop. 72,140.

Ceph´alopods. A class of molluscs, 2199. *See also* **Cuttle-fish; Octopus; Squid,** etc.

Cepheids. Variable stars, 3080.

Cepheus (sē´-fūs). In Gk. myth., king of Ethiopians, father of Andromeda ; Cassiopeia was his queen, 2554.

Cephis´sus. River of an. Attica, flowing into Saronic Gulf just s. of Athens.

Ceram (se-ram´). Second largest isl. in Moluccas, Indonesia, w. of New Guinea ; 6,625 sq. m. ; pop. 98,744 ; mountainous, thick forests ; sago palm agricultural products, etc.

Ceramics. *See* **Bricks ; Clay ; Pottery,** etc.

Cerberus (sēr´-ber-*us*). In Gk. myth., many-headed watchdog, guardian of entrance to infernal regions ; Hercules captures, 1615.

Cer´dic (d. 534). Founder of w. Saxon kingdom.

Cereals. Edible grain, **745.** *See also* **Barley, Wheat,** etc.

Cerebel´lum. The " little " or " back " brain, 545, *546.*

Cerebro-spinal nerves, 2317.

Cer´ebrum. The " big " or " front " brain, 545, *546.*

Ceres (sēr´-ēz). Rom. goddess of agriculture ; 745, 989.

Ceres. An asteroid.

Cereus. A cactus genus, 649.

Cerigo. Southernmost Gk. isl. of Ionian group, 10 m. s.e. of Mainland ; 116 sq. m. ; anc. Cythera, sacred to Aphrodite.

Cerium. A metallic element of the rare earth group, 777, 3187, 3188 ; in monazite sand, 2871. *See* **Rare Earth.**

Cernauti (formerly Czernowitz). City in Bukovina on Prut ; pop. 110,000 ; strategic point in 1st World War ; with rest of Bukovina annexed in 1940 by U.S.S.R. ; taken by Rumanians 1941 ; regained by 1st Ukrainian army 1944 and incorp. in Ukraine S.S.R.

Cerro del Merca´do. Iron hill near Durango, Mexico, 2157.

Cerro de Pasco. Peru mining tn. ; pop. 14,000 ; 2560.

Cervantes Saavedra (ser-van´-tēz), **Miguel de** (1547–1616). Greatest of Span. writers, 745, *746,* 3051 ; story of " Don Quixote," 746.

Cetacea (se-tā´-si-*a*). An order of aquatic mammals, 2077 ; dolphins, 1027 ; whales, 3371.

Cetewayo (set-*e*-wā´-yō) (d. 1884). Zulu chief, 70, 3019, 3448.

Cetinje. Town of Yugoslavia ; pop. 6,400 ; situated in high mountain valley e. of Kotor ; several times destroyed by Turks ; former cap. of Montenegro, 2219. Occupied 1941–44 by Italians or Germans, liberated by Marshal Tito's Yugoslav forces Nov. 1944 ; regional govt. for Montenegro set up here, 1945.

Cette (set). Fr. spt. on s. coast ; pop. 35,400 ; trade in wine, salt, fish.

Ceuta (sū´-t*a*), Morocco. Span. port, military station, and penal settlement on n. coast opposite Gibraltar ; pop. 59,115 ; long a Moorish stronghold, 1613.

Cevennes (sā-ven´) **Mts.** Chief range in s. Fr., extending n.e. to s.w., w. of r. Rhône ; highest point Mt. Mézenc (5,754 ft.) ; scene of Stevenson's " Travels with a Donkey " ; 1360.

Ceylon (sē-lon´). Isl. s.e. of India ; Dom. of Brit. Commonwealth ; 25,330 sq. m. ; pop. 6,700,000 ; **748,** *map, 1702 ;* Buddhism, 601 ; Colombo the cap., *874 ;* dancers of, *plates f. 748, 749 ;* dominion status, 3283 ; ebony, 1077 ; gems, 1427 ; graphite, 1500 ; pearl fisheries, *2468 ;* rice, *79, 2775 ;* rubber, 2833 ; tea culture, 3159 ; 2nd World War, 749.

Cézanne (sā-zan´), **Paul** (1839–1906). Fr. portrait, landscape, and figure

painter, **749,** 2477 ; river scenes, *1375.*

Chaco (chah´-ko´), **El Gran.** Vast alluvial plain of cent. S. Amer. between Paraguay and Paraná rivers and Andes Mts., 2511 ; wars, 2512.

Chad, Lake, in w.-cent. Africa, 68, 3109.

Chadband. A hypocritical clergyman in Dickens's " Bleak House."

Chadwick, Sir James (b. 1891). Brit. physicist ; during research on atomic energy discovered the neutron ; shared in the experiments that led to the atomic bomb ; 297, 2594.

Chaeronea (kēr-ō-nē´-*a*). Anc. tn. in Boeotia ; birthplace of Plutarch ; battle of (338 B.C.), 1524, 3198.

Chaetopods (kē´-tō-podz). Sub-class of annelid worms with bristles.

Chaf´ers. An immense family of beetles, including scarab group, cockchafer, rose chafer, leaf chafer, etc., 398.

Chaffinch. A well-known Brit. bird of the finch family, noted for its beauty of voice, 454, *1272 ;* nest, 442.

Chagall, Marc (b. 1887). Russ. painter ; at first cubist and surrealist, later attacked the waywardness of " modern " art ; lived in Paris ; 3122.

Chagres (chah´-gres) **River.** Flows across Isthmus of Panama into Caribbean Sea ; supplies water for locks of Panama Canal ; dammed to form Gatun Lake, 2488, *map, 2487.*

Chaillu (shī-ū), **Paul Belloni du** (1835–1903). French explorer who described pygmies and gorillas of Central Africa, 72.

Chain. Unit of measurement in surveying (22 yds.). *See* **Weights and measures.**

Chain, Ernest Boris (b. 1904). Anglo-Ger. bio-chemist ; worked with Prof. Florey in isolating penicillin ; with Florey and Fleming received Nobel prize in 1945 ; 2544.

Chalcedon (kal-sē´-don). Anc. spt. in Asia Minor on Bosporus, opposite Byzantium ; Kadiköi now occupies site ; 4th council of Christian Church held here in A.D. 451.

Chalcedony (kal-sed´-o-ni). A variety of quartz, 2713.

Chalcidice (kal-sid´-i-sē). Anc. name of peninsula in n.e. Greece with 3 smaller peninsulas projecting into Aegean Sea.

Chalcis (kal´-kis) or **Khalkis,** Greece. Chief tn. of isl. of Euboea ; Aristotle flees to, 232.

Chaldean (kal-dē´-an) **Empire** (606–538 B.C.), 331, 1830, 2371 ; sculpture, 2904.

Châlet. Alpine cottage, 3141.

Chal´font St. Giles. Vil. in Bucks, Eng. ; Milton's cottage, *2177,* 2178.

Chal´grove Field, battle of. In Oxfordshire (1643) ; Royalists under Prince Rupert defeated Parl. army.

Chaliapin (shal´-ya-pēn), **Feodor** (1873–1938). Celebrated Russian bass opera singer (" Boris Godunov ").

Chalk. A soft limestone, **749,** 1353, 1948, 1950, 2795 ; Dover cliffs, 1030 ; formations of Cretaceous period, 1433 ; foraminifera, 2695.

Challenger Expedition. Famous Brit. expedition to study physical and biological conditions in deep sea (1872–76) ; results fill 50 vols.

Chal´mers, Thomas (1780–1847). Scot. preacher and political economist ; one of chief promoters of Free Church of Scotland.

Châlons-sur-Marne (shah-lawn´ sür mahrn). City in n.e. Fr. ; pop. 32,300 ; exports champagne ; taken by Germans 1870, 1914 and 1940 ; liberated by U.S. troops Aug. 29, 1944 ; scene of famous battle of A.D. 451.

Chalon-sur-Saône. Fr. city 80 m. n. of Lyons on r. Saône ; pop. 32,530 ; occupied by Germans 1940–44 ; iron mfrs. ; large ordnance works.

Chamberlain (Arthur) Neville (1869–1940). Brit. statesman, younger son of Joseph Chamberlain ; **750** ; 3416 ; 3282 ; Prime Minister, 1937–40 ; negotiated Munich agreement, 1938 ; announced Britain's declaration of

war against Germany Sept. 3, 1939 ; Lord President of the Council in Churchill's Cabinet, May–Oct., 1940.

Chamberlain, Joseph (1836–1914). Eng. statesman, 458, **749,** *750,* 3019.

Chamberlain, Sir (Joseph) Austen (1863–1937). Eng. statesman, elder son of Joseph Chamberlain, **750.**

Chamber music, 2264.

Chamber of Deputies, Fr., 1362, 251*7.*

Chambers, Raymond W. (1874–1942). A.S. scholar ; Quain prof. of English, London Univ., 1922–41 ; studies on " Beowulf " and " Widsith " ; " Sir Thomas More," " Man's Unconquerable Mind."

Chambers, Robert (1802–71). Scot. publisher ; joint editor " Chambers's Journal " ; Au." Vestiges of Creation," partner in the Scot.publishing firm of W. and R. Chambers.

Chambéry. Fr. Historic tn. 55 m. s.e. of Lyons ; pop. 29,980 ; cap. former duchy of Savoy.

Chambord (shahm-bōr), **Henri,Comte de** (1820–83). Fr. prince, son of the Duc du Berry and grandson of Charles X.

Chameleon (ka-mē´-lē-on). A type of lizard, **750,** 1974 ; *plates f. 752, 753.*

Chaminade (sham-ē-nahd), **Cécile Louise Stéphanie** (1861–1944). Fr. pianist and composer.

Chamois (sham´-wah). A fleet goat-like antelope, **750,** *751,* 1237 ; leather (sham´-i), 1477, 1914.

Chamonix (sha-mō-nē) or **Chamouni.** Beautiful valley and village in s.e. Fr. at foot of Mont Blanc, *127.*

Champagne (shahn-pan). Former prov. in n.e. Fr. ; chief city, Troyes ; *map,* 1359 ; celebrated wines 1360, 3388 ; 1st World War battles, 3410.

Champaigne (shahn-pān), **Philippe de** (1602–74), French artist, *1369,* 1377.

Champ de Mars (shahn de mars). Large square in Paris on Seine, 2517.

Champlain, Samuel de (1567–1635). Fr. explorer, founder of Quebec, 681, **751,** 2862 ; explorations, 143, 2380, *2381.*

Champlain, Lake. Between Vermont and New York, U.S.A., discovered by Champlain ; length 110 m.

Champlevé enamel, 1158.

Champollion (shahn-pol-yon), **Jean François** (1790–1832). Fr. scholar, founder of Egyptology ; deciphered the Rosetta Stone, 2828.

Champs Elysées (shahnz-ā-lē-zā). Celebrated boulevard, Paris, *2515,* 2517.

Chan´cellor. Title given to high state officials in many countries, e.g. in Gt. Brit., Chancellor of the Exchequer, Chancellor of the Duchy of Lancaster, Lord Chancellor ; chancellor of university, 3296.

Chancellorsville, battle of (1863). The Federal forces under Hooker were defeated by the Confederates led by Lee ; Stonewall Jackson was mortally wounded ; 1790.

Chan´cery, High Court of, Eng., 922.

Chancery, Papal, 2495.

Chanctonbury Ring, on S. Downs, Sussex ; dew-pond at, *1000.*

Chandernagore. Former prov. of Fr. India on r. Hoogli, 22 m. above Calcutta ; since June 1949 a part of the Indian Union ; 3 sq. m. ; pop. 38,284 ; 1692.

Changchun. Capital of Manchuria ; pop. (1939) 415,264.

Change, automatic machine for giving, 867.

Changsha, China. City 350 m. n. of Canton on Hsiang r. ; cap. Hunan prov. ; pop. 606,972 ; silk mfrs. ; matches ; tinplate ; trade in timber ; large native trade. After several attempts, between Sept. 1940 and 1944, the Japanese seized Changsha June 1944, holding it until Aug. 1945.

Channel, English. *See* **English Channel.**

Channel Islands. Brit. possession off coast of Fr. ; pop. 93,000 ; 75 sq. m. ; **751,** *752 ;* cattle-breeding, 732 ; tomato cultivation, 3223 ; in Ger. occupn. 1940–45, 752.

Channel Tunnel. Submarine tunnel to connect Eng. and Fr., originally projected by M. Matthieu to Napoleon I ; a beginning was made in 1876 at Dover and at Sangatte, near Calais; mooted many times since; 3258.

" Chanson de Roland " (" Song of Roland "), 2797.

Chant, in music, 2261.

Chanticleer (chan'-ti-klēr) (Fr. *chante-clair*, " clear singer "). The cock in " Reynard the Fox."

Chantilly (shahn-tē'-yē). Fr. Anc. tn. 20 m. N. of Paris; splendid château; art collection; once noted for Chantilly lace; famous race-course; 2670.

Chantrey (chahn'-tri), **Sir Francis Legatt** (1781–1841). Eng. sculptor. The bulk of his fortune, forming the Chantrey Bequest, was bequeathed to the trustees of the British Museum for the furtherance of the fine arts; first exhibition of the entire collection held by R.A. in 1949.

Chanute (shan-ewt), **Octave** (1832–1910). Fr.-Amer. aeronaut; experimented with gliders from 1896, writing on the theory of flight, and helped the Wright bros. in their early work on aeroplanes; 1474. A city in Kansas is named after him.

Chaplain. Clergyman attached to the court, army or navy, etc., 248.

Chaplin, Charles Spencer (b. 1889). Film comedian, b. London; went to U.S.A. in 1910 and achieved worldwide fame from 1913 (The Kid, 1920; The Gold Rush, 1925; City Lights, 1931; Modern Times, 1936; The Great Dictator, 1938; Monsieur Verdoux, 1947); *828*.

Chapman, George (c. 1559–1634). Eng. poet and dramatist. Translator of Homer.

Chappe silk, 2973.

Chapter House. Meeting place in cath., etc., where dean and chapter or abbot and monks conduct their business.

Charade. Syllable-puzzle game, 752.

Charcoal, 752; activated, 753; manufacture of, 499, *1405*; as fuel, *1405*, 1406; in gunpowder, 1588; in smelting, 1754; spontaneous combustion, 1280.

Charcot (shahr'-kō), **Jean Baptiste** (1867–1936). Fr. Antarctic explorer; commanded expeditions in 1903–05 and 1908–10; mapped Graham Land, Alexander Land, etc.; Charcot Land was named after him.

Charcot, Jean Martin (1825–93). Fr. physician; one of the first to employ hypnotism to treat mental disorders.

Chard. A beet with edible top.

Chardin (shahr-dan), **Jean Siméon** (1699–1779), French artist, 1378; " La mère laborieuse," *1373*.

Chardin, Teilhard de, and Peking Man, 2078.

Chardonnet (shahr'-do-nā), **Hilaire de, Count** (1840–1924), French chemist; inventor of the nitrate process of making rayon, 2748.

Charge, in heraldry, 1614.

Charge, electric, 1127.

Chargé d'affaires. Diplomatic agent acting as deputy to an ambassador or representing his country at a court of minor importance.

Charged water. How made, 700.

" Charge of the Light Brigade." Poem by Tennyson, 931.

Charing (chār'-ing) **Cross.** Rly. station, etc., in London on site of former village of Cheringe, where Edward I erected great cross in memory of his queen Eleanor, 2009, *2016*; present cross is a copy; rly. bridge, *1290*.

Charioteer' or **Auriga.** A constellation, chart, *895*.

Charity, Sisters of. Name of several Rom. Cath. orders and branches of orders, whose members are devoted to care and education of sick and poor; oldest order founded in Paris in 1633 by St. Vincent de Paul.

Charlemagne (shahr'-le-mān), (742–814), Charles the Great, King of the Franks and Holy Rom. emperor, 753, 757; reign, 1365, *1366*; conquers Lombards, 2000; buried at Aachen, 9; founds Hamburg, 1568; founds Holy Rom. Empire, 1238, 1636, 2167; and Roland, 2797.

Charleroi (shahr-lė-rwäh), Belgium, rly. and iron-mining centre, 30 m. s. of Brussels; pop. 28,200; occupied by Germans in both World Wars.

Charles of Edinburgh, Prince (b. 1948). Son of Princess Elizabeth and the Duke of Edinburgh, Charles Philip Arthur George was born Nov. 14, 1948, at Buckingham Palace, 1150.

Charles (b. 1903), **Prince.** Brother of Leopold III; joined Resistance forces while Leopold was in Ger. hands; Belgian prince-regent from Sept. 21, 1944 to July 21, 1950.

Charles I, Holy Rom. emperor. Same as **Charlemagne**.

Charles II, the Bald (823–77). Holy Rom. emperor and (as Charles II) king of Fr., 757.

Charles III, the Fat (832–88), Holy Rom. emperor.

Charles IV, Holy Rom. emperor (1316–78); Golden Bull, 1449, 1637.

Charles V (1500–58). Holy Rom. emperor, king of Sp. and the Netherlands, **754**, 3036; Reformation, 1449, 2040, 2759; wars with Fr., 1383, 1769, 2759; abdicated, 755.

Charles VI, Holy Rom. emperor (1685–1740); 2101.

Charles VII, Holy Rom. emperor (1697–1745).

Charles I (1887–1922). Emperor of Austria-Hungary (1916–18), succeeded Francis Joseph; abdicated on collapse of Central Powers; exiled to Madeira, 1383.

Charles I (1600–49), king of Eng., **755**, *756*, 1196; Cromwell and, 933; execution, 1206; Hampden and, 1571; with Harvey, *476*; in House of Lords, *1199*; statue, *2904*; and Vandyck, 3305. Date of accession 1625 (not 1600 as in page 1489).

Charles II (1630–85), king of Eng., **756**, *757*; 1198; escape from England, 1198; return to England, *1199*; Pepys and, 2547; and Wren, 3426.

Charles II, the Bald, king of Fr. *See* **Charles II** (Emperor).

Charles III, the Simple (879–929), Fr., 757, 2376, 2388.

Charles IV, the Fair (1294–1328), Fr., youngest son of Philip IV; succeeded brother Philip V as king of Fr. and Navarre. 757.

Charles V, the Wise (1337–80), Fr., 757; and Hundred Years' War, 1653.

Charles VI (1368–1422), Fr., 757.

Charles VII (1403–61), Fr., 757, *758*; and Hundred Years' War, 1653; Joan of Arc, 1831.

Charles VIII (1470–98), Fr., 757, 1238, 1764, 2876.

Charles IX (1550–74), Fr., 758, 870.

Charles X (1757–1836), Fr., last of Bourbon rulers, 758, 2031; Lafayette helps to depose, 1884, 2031.

Charles (Carol) I, (1839–1914). King of Rumania; elected prince 1866, crowned first king 1881; married Elizabeth of Wied (" Carmen Sylva "); 2841.

Charles IX (1550–1611), king of Sweden.

Charles X (1622–60), Sweden.

Charles XI (1655–97), Sweden.

Charles XII (1682–1718), Sweden; 758, 916, 2563, 3131.

Charles XIV (1763–1844), Sweden. *See* Bernadotte.

Charles Albert (1798–1849), king of Sardinia; succeeded 1831; began struggle for It. independence; 1769, 3319.

Charles Edward (1720–88), " the Young Pretender," 2682; and Flora Macdonald, 2047; and the Jacobites, 1790.

Charles the Bold (1433–77), duke of Burgundy, 759; and Louis XI, 2028.

Charles, Jacques Alexandre César (1746–1823), Fr. physicist; Charles's Law, 1419; first hydrogen balloon, 348.

Charles Martel (688–741), Frankish ruler, defeated Saracens at Tours, 759, 2067.

Charleston, South Carolina, U.S.A. Most important harbour of S.E. U.S.A.

Charlock, wild mustard, 2270.

Charlotte, grand duchess of Luxemburg (b. 1896), succeeded 1919, on abdication of sister, 2041; escaped to England May 1940; returned April 1945.

Charlottetown, Prince Edward Is., 2684.

Charm. An incantation or object believed to bring good luck, 2058, 2757.

Charnock, Job, and Calcutta, 660.

Charon, in Gk. myth., ferryman of r. Styx.

Charpentier (shahr-pahn'-tyā), **Gustave** (b. 1860), Fr. composer. His opera " Louise " is his most popular work.

Char'ter, a written deed or instrument granted by a sovereign or parl. conferring privileges on the recipient; boroughs, corporations, companies, institutions, etc., often receive charters; the most famous charter in Brit. history is Magna Carta.

Char'terhouse. A Carthusian monastery in London, after 1611 used as a hospital for old men and a school for boys; the Great Hall was severely damaged by German incendiary bombs, Dec. 29, 1940; the school was transferred to Godalming, Surrey, in 1872.

Chartism. Radical movement in Eng., culminating between 1840 and 1848; sought reform in parl. representation and universal adult male suffrage, 1875, *3279*.

Chartres (shahtr), Fr. Mfg. city; pop. 26,400; famous cathedral; occupied by Germans in 1870, and again 1940 44.

Chartreuse (shahr-trēz'), **La Grande.** Original mother-house of Carthusian monks, near Grenoble, 2213.

Charybdis (kɑ-rib'-dis), in Gk. myth., whirlpool, Straits of Messina, 2422.

Chase, in printing, 2346.

Chassis (shas'-ē), of motor-car, *2242*.

Château (shah-tō), 718.

Chateaubriand (sha-tō-brē'-ahn), **François René, Vicomte de** (1788–1848), Fr. author and politician; exquisite prose stylist, one of first romanticists (" René " ; " Atala " ; " The Genius of Christianity ").

Château d'If, off Marseilles, 2110.

Château Gaillard (gī-yahr). Famous castle on Seine, now in ruins, 2777.

Chatfield, Alfred Ernle Montacute, 1st Baron (b. 1873). Eng. admiral. First Sea Lord (1933–38). Awarded O.M. Jan. 1939; Minister for the Co-ordination of Defence, Jan. 1939–April 1940.

Chatham, William Pitt, 1st Earl of (1708–78). Brit. statesman, **759**; and Amer. Independence, 144; Seven Years' War, 2924.

Chatham. Spt. in Kent, on Medway, adjoining Rochester; pop. 37,000, **759**, 1852; H.M.S. Victory built at, 3321.

Chatham Islands, group belonging to New Zealand, 550 m. E.; 372 sq. m.; pop. 700; sheep grazing, 2360.

Chattanoo'ga, Tennessee, U.S.A. Rly. and industrial city; pop. 128,160; cotton, grain, coal, lumber and iron.

Chat'terton, Thomas (1752–70). Eng. poet and literary forger, **760**.

Chaucer (chaw-ser), **Geoffrey** (c.1340–1400). Early Eng. poet, **761**, 1210; stories from " Canterbury Tales," 762, 2608; tomb, *2635*, 3369.

Chauvinism (shō'-vin-izm). Term used to denote exaggerated patriotism or " jingoism "; derived from a character in play, " La Cocarde tricolaire " (1831), by T. and H. Cognard, which in turn came from Nicolas Chauvin, a veteran of Napoleon's who was devoted to his memory.

Chaux-de-Fonds (shō-de-fon), **La,** Switzerland. Tn. N.W. of Berne in Jura valley; watch and clock making.

Chavannes (sha-van'), **Puvis de** (1824–98). French painter, 1378; decorated Paris Pantheon with pictures of St. Geneviève.

Cheapside. Historic London thoroughfare, extending between St. Paul's Cathedral and Poultry, which is a continuation leading to the Mansion House.

Checkmate, in chess, 779.

Ched'dar. Vil. in Somersetshire; gives name to Cheddar cheese; caves, 733, *plate f. 732*; gorge, *1163*.

Cheddar pink, 2611.

Cheese, 765; use of bacteria in, 336; from milk, 2174.

Chee'tah. "Hunting leopard" of Asia, *1928*.

"Chef de l'Hôtel Chatham, Le." Painting by Sir Wm. Orpen, *1183*.

Chefoo or Chifu, China, spt. on N. coast of Shantung; pop. 250,000; one of first ports captured by Japan in summer of 1937; liberated Sept. 1945; Jan. 1943 Gt. Brit. signed treaty with China renouncing extra territorial rights in Chefoo and other treaty ports; 2938.

Cheka (chă-kah), Soviet Russian secret police.

Chekhof. See Tchekhov.

Chekiang. Fertile maritime province of China on Pacific; 39,486 sq. m.; pop. 21,776,000; cap. Hangchow; silk, tea, cotton, fruit, are among the chief products.

Cheliabinsk (chel-yah-binsk'). Town of U.S.S.R. on Trans-Siberian railway. It has distilleries and tanneries. Pop. 273,000 (1939 census).

Chelmsford, Frederick John Napier Thesiger, 1st Viscount (1868–1933). Brit. politician. Viceroy of India (1916–21) and First Lord of the Admiralty in Labour Government (1924).

Chelmsford. Co. tn. of Essex; pop. 33,000; brewing industry, trade in agric. produce, 1225; cathedral, *1224*.

Chelo'nia. Turtle sub-class of reptiles, 2767; tortoises and turtles, 3229.

Chelsea. Parl. and met. bor. of s.w. London, on right bank of the Thames; pop. 42,000; contains Chelsea Hospital for pensioned and disabled soldiers, in the gardens of which the annual Flower Show is held; formerly had noted porcelain works; Stamford Bridge football ground; heavy air raid damage and casualties, 1940–45; Chelsea Old Church destroyed in 1941; 2015, 2670.

Chelsea porcelain, *2669*.

Chel'tenham. Watering place, in Gloucestershire; pop. 58,000; 766.

Chelyuskin (chel-yoos-kĕn'), Cape, N. Siberia, 263.

Chemi-luminescence, in insects, etc., 2574.

Chemin des Dames ("Ladies' Road"). Fr. road running from point near Soissons along ridge between rs. Aisne and Ailette to Reims; objective of repeated "battles of the Aisne."

Chemistry (kem'-is-tri), 766; acids, 20, 2148; in agric., 80; alcohols, 774; aliphatic, 774; allotropes, 770, 2466, 2574; alloys, 122; analysis, 773; aromatic, 774; atoms, 294, 766, 1137, 2733; bases, 2148; catalytic action, 771, 2628; coal-tar derivatives, 857; colloids, 773; compounds, 766, 770; combustion, 1280, 2466; crystals and crystallization, 939, 940; cyanides, 947; detergents, 998; of digestion, *1016*, 1017; dyes, 857, 1059, 1060; electrolysis, 771, 1136, *1137*; electron theory of matter, 1137; elements, 766; periodic table, 768, 769; characteristics, 775–778; enzymes, 1220; equation, 767; the "ethers," 1227; explosives, 1250, *1251*; fats and oils, 1263; food, 1338, 1340; food preservation, 1340, *1341*; formulae, 767; halogens, 1567; human, 429, 1016, 1017, 2601; infra-red rays, 1724; ions, 772, 773; isomers, 774; isotopes, 296, 769, 1760; metals, 2148, 2180; minerals, 2180; molecules, 769; nitrogen, fixation of, 2374; oxidation, 771; of plant life, 429, 2621; organic, 774; polymerisation, 775; proportions, laws of, 767; photochemistry, 2574; proteins, 1338, *1339*, 2693; radicals, 767; radioactivity, 2731; reduction, 771; salts, 2865; spectroscope and spectrum analysis, 281, 3055; symbols, 767; valence, 770; of tanning leather, 1913; X-ray spectra, 3431.

History: Arab contributions, 2068; Boyle, 537; Cavendish, 736; Davy, 979; Faraday, 1260; Lavoisier proves "oxidation theory" of combustion, 1280, 2466; Priestley, 2683; radium upsets old theories, 2731; Ramsay, 2744; of watersoftening, 3351; of waxes, 3359.

Chemistry and Industry: alloys, 122; artificial silks, 2748; coal-tar products, 857; industries based on salt, 2866; detergents, 998; synthetic substances, 699, *850*, 2478, 2625, 2838.

Chemnitz, Ger. mfg. and commercial city, in Saxony; pop. 350,700; textiles, gloves, locomotives, machinery, leather, chemicals; in Russian occupied zone from 1945; 2878.

Chemother'apy. Use of synthetic chemical drugs and antiseptics, 179.

Chemot'ropism, 2623.

Che'nab. R. of Pakistan, 2479.

Chengtu. City in w. China on Min R.; pop. 600,000; agricultural and mining centre.

Chénier (shā'-nyā), André de (1762–94). Fr. poet, one of greatest of 18th cent.; guillotined during Reign of Terror for his opposition to the excesses of the Convention.

Chenille (she-nēl') carpets, 707.

Chenonceaux, Château of, *1363*.

Cheops (kē'-ops). See Khufu.

Chephren. See Khafre.

Chepstow. Small port in Monmouthshire on r. Wye; pop. 5,144; fortress remains, 2215; tides, 3210.

Cheque, in banking, 357.

Chequers (chek'-erz). Historic mansion in Buckinghamshire, 778.

Cher (shār), river in Cent. Fr., tributary to Loire, 200 m. long.

Cherbourg (shār'-bŏŏr). Fr. Atlantic port and naval harbour on English Channel. Pop. 39,760; fortified arsenal, 1359, 2377; breakwater, 558. Germans occupy 1940; U.S. forces liberate 1944, 2378.

Cherokees'. Indian tribe of s.E. U.S.A.; originally lived in mountain region of Virginia, the Carolinas, Georgia, Alabama, and Tennessee, before moving to Indian territory.

Cherrapunji. India, vil. of Assam, in Khasi Hills; rainfall, *841*, 1701, 2741.

Cherry, 778, *779, back of plate f. 1401*, 1403; origin, 265.

Cherry-laurel, poisonous plant, *2639*.

Chersonesus (kĕr-so-nē'-sus). Gk. word for peninsula, applied especially to Thracian Chersonesus (modern Gallipoli), Tauric Chersonesus (Crimea), and Cimbrian Chersonesus (Jutland).

Cherubini (kā-roo-bē'-nē), Maria Luigi (1760–1842). It. composer and author; "link between classic idealism and modern romanticism" ("Requiem in C Minor"; work on counterpoint still a standard).

Cher'well. R. in Northamptonshire and Oxfordshire, joining the Thames at Oxford; 30 m. long, *2463*.

Cher'well, Frederick A. Lindemann, 1st Baron. Brit. physicist; prof. of Experimental Philosophy at Oxford from 1919; personal and scientific adviser to Winston Churchill in 1940–41.

Chesapeake Bay. Largest inlet on Atlantic coast of U.S.A.; scene of indecisive naval action between Eng. and Fr. during War of American Independence in 1781.

Ches'ham. Tn. of Buckinghamshire; mfrs. chairs; noted for watercress beds and trout; pop. 8,809.

Cheshire. Co. in N.W. Eng. bordering on N. Wales and Irish Sea, 1,019 sq. m.; pop. 1,087,500; 779; gypsum, 1559; salt, 2866.

Cheshire, Group Capt. Geoffrey L., V.C. (b. 1917). Brit. airman; master bomber and pioneer of R.A.F. Pathfinders.

Cheshire cheese, 766, 779.

Cheshire Cheese, famous tavern off Fleet Street, London, having associations with Dr. Johnson.

Ches'il Bank. Gravel and shingle ridge on coast of Dorset, 1030, 2657.

Chess (game), 779, *780*; Caxton illustration, *511*.

Chester. Picturesque old city, co. tn. of Cheshire, on r. Dee; pop. 43,100; mfg. and rly. centre; 779, 781, 1165.

Ches'terfield, Philip Dormer Stanhope, 4th Earl of (1694–1773). Eng. statesman, author, and patron of literature; name used as a synonym for courtly manners; letters to his son full of worldly wisdom.

Ches'terfield. Tn. in Derbyshire; has Gothic church with curious crooked spire; ironworking, coalmining; pop. 63,430.

Chesterton, Gilbert Keith (1874–1936). Eng. novelist, critic, and brilliant satirist, 781, 1216.

Chestnut, 782; burs, 2918; as food, 914; structure of nut, *2408*. See *also* Horse Chestnut.

Chetniks. Group of Yugoslav partisans under Mihailovitch in the Second World War. See Mihailovitch (f-i).

Chetwode, F.-M. Sir Philip Walhouse, 1st Baron Chetwode (1869–1950). Brit. soldier; served in Burma (1892–93); Boer War (1899–1902); 1st World War (1914–18); C.-in-C. India (1930–35); O.M. in 1936; Constable of Tower (1943–48).

Chevalier (she-val'-yā), Albert (1861–1923). Eng. character comedian, especially noted for coster studies.

Chevalier, Maurice (b. 1889). Fr. actor; famous on stage and films as comedian, dancer, and romantic "lead."

Cheviot Hills, range 35 m. long, forming part of Eng.-Scot. boundary; famous for sheep, 2391, 2889.

Chevreul, Michel Eugène (1786–1889). Fr. chemist, 2993.

Chevron. In architecture, a zigzag moulding, characteristic of Norman architecture; a variety of fret ornament; in heraldry, a bent bar rafter-shaped, according to some a third, and according to others a fifth, of the field; also the distinguishing mark on the coat sleeves of non-commissioned officers.

"Chev'y Chase." Famous Eng. ballad celebrating battle of Otterburn (1388) in which Scots defeated English.

Chewing gum. Sweetmeat made from chicle, the sap of the Cent. Amer. sapodilla tree.

Chi (khī), χ, X. Twenty-second letter of Greek alphabet; in Eng. words of Gk. origin, e.g. chloral, the χ is spelt "ch" and pronounced "k."

Chiang Kai-shek (b. 1888). Chinese general and statesman, 782, *783*; resigned presidency Jan. 1949. When Communists overran China in late 1949 he continued fighting from Formosa.

Chiang, Mme. Chinese sociologist; daughter of the influential Soong family; married Chiang Kai-shek in 1927; indefatigable worker for Chinese unity in war, for the betterment of war victims, and for the emancipation of her country-women; director-gen. of New Life movement; in Feb. 1943 addressed the U.S. Congress; in Nov. 1948 went to U.S.A., *783*.

Chiapas (chē-ah'-pahs), Mexico. State in s. on Isthmus of Tehuantepec, on Pacific; 28,729 sq. m.; pop. 679,885; cap. Tuxtla Gutiérrez.

Chiari. It. city, 36 m. E. of Milan; Austrians under Prince Eugene defeated Fr. and Sp. troops in 1701.

Chiaroscuro (kyahr-ō-skŏŏ'-rō). In drawing, 1046.

Chicago, Illinois. 2nd largest city in U.S.A.; pop. 3,396,808; 783, 1687.

Chicherin (chē-chăr'-ĕn), Georgy Vassilievich (1872–1936), Russian politician. In early life was attached to the diplomatic corps of the Tsar; banished (1908); returned (1917);

expelled from England (1918); people's commissar for foreign affairs (1918–29).

Chichester. City in Sussex; pop. 16,000; **784**, 3123.

Chick, embryology of, *1154, 1155.*

Chicken pox. Highly contagious disease, chiefly of children; characterized by skin eruptions and fever; no relation to smallpox and seldom dangerous.

Chickweed. Common garden weed, *Stellaria media,* of fam. *Caryophyllaceae;* good feed for chicks.

Chicle (chěk'-lā or chik'-el). Sap of the sapodilla tree of Cent. Amer., basis of chewing gums.

Chic'ory. Plant related to dandelion, largely cultivated for its root, which is ground and roasted for mixing with coffee.

Chiff-chaff, a warbler, 3341.

Chifley, Joseph Benedict (b. 1885). Australian politician; leader of Labour party, 1945; prime min. of Australia during 1945–1949.

Chig'ger or **chig'oe.** A skin parasite.

Chihli. *See* Hopei.

Chihuahua (chě-wah'-wah), Mexico, State in N. bordering on Texas, U.S.A.; 94,000 sq. m.; pop., 613,944; cap. Chihuahua.

Chihuahua, Mexico. City in silver-mining and stock-raising dist.; pop. 57,456.

Chilblains. An inflammation of the feet (sometimes of the hands or other parts of body) caused by exposure to extreme cold or by rapid changes in temperature; accompanied by painful swelling, burning, and itching.

Child, care of, 1338, 3326; heredity, 1617; hygiene, 1676; teeth, 3164.

"Childe Harold's Pilgrimage," poem by Byron, 635.

Children, 801, plates *785–800*; Aztec, 326; in China, 807; Red Indian, 2754, 2756, *plate f. 2757*; in Japan, *789*; and sleep, 2983; in anc. Sparta, 3052.

Children, literature for, 1964, 2750.

Children's Act, 2688.

Children's Courts, 923, 2688.

Children's Crusade, 937.

Child training; Froebel, 1398; literature for children, 1964; Montessori method, *2220*; music in schools, 2265; nature study, 2283; physical exercise, 2589; reading, 2750; schools, 2883.

Chile (chil'-i). Republic on w. coast of S. America, 286,000 sq. m.; pop. 5,348,000; **802**; *map, 227,* 3025; chief cities, 2872, 3302; Easter Island, 1074, *1075*; mountains, 153, 802; nitrates, *803,* 2374, 3022; war with Peru, 2560.

Chile saltpetre, 2374, 2868.

Chil'koot Pass. In S.E. Alaska, 60 m. N.W. of Juneau, used by gold-seekers in rush of 1896–98; superseded by rly. through White Pass.

Chillianwal'la, Pakistan. Vil. in the Punjab; scene of battle in the second Sikh War in 1849.

Chillingham. Vil. in Northumberland. There is a famous herd of pure-bred white cattle in the park, which was enclosed probably early in the 13th century.

Chillon (shě'-yon), **Castle of,** on Lake Geneva, 1429.

Chil'tern Hills, Eng. A range of low chalk hills 40 m. N.W. of London; once densely forested, 600, 1621.

Chiltern Hundreds. Three districts in Buckinghamshire, Eng., whose stewardship is a nominal Crown office. As the acceptance of a Crown office disqualifies a member of Parliament (who by law may not resign his seat) the stewardship of Chiltern Hundreds has become an avenue of escape for members who wish to leave the Commons.

Chimborazo (chim-bō-rah'-zō). Volcanic (extinct) mt. in Ecuador 100 m. s. of Quito; 20,702 ft.; one of the highest peaks in Andes, 153, 1081.

Chimaera (ki-měr'-a). In Gk. myth., fire-breathing monster with lion's head and serpent's tail; killed by Bellerophon, 2536.

Chimes, how rung, 410.

Chimney. Purposes of, 1597; of power station, 2675.

Chimney swallow, 3124.

Chimpanzee'. The most intelligent of the anthropoid apes, dwelling in Africa; 68; *183, 184, 805, 2075,* 2207, *3446.*

China. Country in E. Asia; 4,300,000 sq. m.; pop. 458,000,000; *807*; *map, 808*; art, 810, 811, 812, 1158, 1219; children, *785, 807, 809*; festivals, 808; Great Wall, *806,* 810; kite-flying, 1863; language, 808, 2571; people, *plates f. 808, 809*; religions, 809; river-dwellers, *694*; treaty ports, 810, 3211; writing, 808.

Geography and industries: agriculture, 266, *808*; bamboo, 353; chief cities, 693, 1573, *1639,* 2273, 2536, 2937, 3211; fisheries, *814,* 1299; foreign commerce, 809, 1639, 2938; lacquer, *1881*; manufactures, 706, 1640, *1881,* 2250, 2273, 2938; minerals, 810, 1573, 2938; porcelain from, 2665, *2668*; rice, 2775; rivers and canals, 686, 810, 1662, 3433; silk industry, 2250, 2938, 2972; stamp, *3075*; tea, 809, 3159.

History and government, 807, 810; early civilization, 268, 807, 1558, 1724; early Man, 2078, *2079*; Communists, 814; Confucius, 809, 886; Govt. at Chungking, 814; Manchu dynasty founded, 2087; Marco Polo's visit, 2652; Mongols, 2205; Opium War, 2442; Revolution (1927), 814; Treaty ports opened, 810, 3211; Taiping rebellion, 813; war with Japan, 814, 1800; new constitution set up in 1946; first national election in Nov. 1947; Communists successful in civil war in 1949. *See also* **Manchuria**; **Mongolia**; **Shantung**; **Tibet**; **Turkistan,** and names of chief rivers and towns.

China aster. 274. 275.

China clay, or kaolin, 814, **836,** *912,* 2836.

China grass, 1424.

China Sea, 2470, *map, 808.*

China silk, 2973.

Chinaware. *See* **Porcelain**; **Pottery.**

China wood oil, 1263.

Chinchilla. Small fur-bearing rodent of Peru and Chile, **815.**

Chinchilla fur, 1412.

Chin'dits. Brit. special force in Burma, 1941–45; **815.**

"Chinese Gordon," 1486, *1487.*

Chinese language, 808, 2571; alphabet, 125.

Chinese Turkistan, 264, 3266.

Chingachgook (chin-gach'-gook). Indian chief of James Fenimore Cooper's tales, "Last of the Mohicans," "Pathfinder," "Deerslayer," and "Pioneer"; *903.*

Chinghai. Second largest prov. of China. In N.W. Area 269,187 sq. m.; pop. 1,513,000; cap. Sining. Produces wool, hides, salt, gold.

Chingford, tn. of Essex, Eng.; Humphrey pump of reservoir, 1421, *1423.*

Chinkiang (chin-kě-ang'), China. Former treaty port on Yangtze Riv. 150 m. from mouth; pop. 199,776; 3443.

Chinook winds. Warm dry winds which descend from E. slopes of Rocky Mts., in N. U.S.A. and Canada, bringing great relief in cold weather.

Chinquapin. Nut of dwarf type of chestnut; also water-lily seeds.

Chins. Tribe of Upper Burma, 623.

Chintz (Hindu "spotted"). Printed cotton fabric, usually with vari-coloured patterns, and with highly calendered surface.

Chios (kī'-os). Fertile isl. in Aegean Sea, w. of Smyrna, modern Scio 320 sq. m.; pop. 32,914; reputed birthplace of Homer; ceded to Greece by Turkey in 1913; anc. Gk. colony. Cap. Chios or Castro.

Chip'munk, or ground squirrel, **815.**

Chip'pendale, Thomas (d. 1779). Famous Eng. cabinet-maker; best work produced 1735–60; "mar-

vellous for beauty of proportion, comfort in use, strength, and durability"; 1409, *1411.*

Chirico (kē'-ri-kō), **Giorgio di,** painter of modern Fr. school; and Surrealism, 3122.

Chiron (kīr-on). In Gk. myth., famous centaur noted for his learning and wisdom, 742; tutor of Achilles, 19.

Chiropodist (ki-rop'-o-dist). Person skilled in the care of the feet.

Chiroptera (kir'-op-te-ra), 2077.

Chisinau. *See* Kishinev.

Chita (chě'-ta), town of East Siberian prov. of Asiatic U.S.S.R.; on Trans-Siberian Rly.; pop. 102,555; *2967.*

Chitin (kī'-tin). Stiffening material in skins of arthropoda; in insects, 1727; overlaid with lime in crustaceans.

Chiton (kī'-ton). Gk. garment.

Chiton. Mollusc with a "coat-of-mail" shell, 2199, 2943.

Chitral (chit-ral), Pakistan. Former native state, tn. on riv., N.W. Kashmir; the fort of Chitral was besieged for several weeks in the spring of 1895 and relieved by Colonel Kelly.

Chittagong'. Spt. of E. Bengal, Pakistan, 2479; near s. terminus of Assam-Bengal rly.; rice, jute, tea, hides exported; pop. 36,031; supply centre for Brit. 14th army in Burma campaign, 1942–45.

Chiv'alry. The knightly class of feudal times, and hence also the qualities of the ideal knight—gallantry, a high sense of honour, and courtesy; spirit expressed in romances, 2798; burlesqued by Cervantes, 746. *See also* **Knighthood.**

Chive. Plant allied to onion, 2434.

Chkalov. New name of territory and town (prev. Orenburg) in Middle Volga area of U.S.S.R.; pop. of tn. 172,900.

Chlamys (klam'-is). Gk. garment.

Chlo'ral, a drug, 1048.

Chlo'rate. Salt containing a metal with chlorine and three atoms of oxygen; of potassium, 2119.

Chloride (klōr'-īd). A compound of chlorine with an element, 815; of ammonia, 146, 2997; cobalt, 1724; gold, 1481; lime (bleaching powder), 469; potassium, 2664; silver in photography, 2579; sodium (common salt), 2865.

Chlorina'tion process, 815.

Chlorine (Cl) (klōr'-in). Dense green gaseous element of the halogen family; atomic weight, 35·5; named from the Greek, *chloros,* greenish yellow; many industrial uses, 815; mfr. by electrolysis, *1137*; a halogen, 1567; isotopes of, 1760; properties, 776; poison, 1420, 2638; from hydrochloric acid, 1667; purifies water, 3349; specific gravity, 3054.

Chlo'roform. A colourless volatile liquid with a pungent odour; an anaesthetic, 1048, 2135.

Chlorophyll (klōr'-ō-fil). Green colouring matter of plants, 88, 112, 1915, 2574, 2589, 2621; in algae but not in fungi, 1932; the basic "food maker" for all life, 112; withdrawal in autumn, 1917; in oil, 2426.

Chloro-wax, 3359.

Choc'olate and cocoa, 861; made from cacao bean, 648, 2918.

Chodowiecki, Daniel Nikolaus (1726–1801). Polish artist who worked in Germany; a master of small engravings.

Choir (kwīr). In architecture, part of church occupied by singers.

Choke. In electricity, 1133; in internal combustion engine, 1736.

Choke-boring, of shot guns, 1285.

Choke damp. Miner's term for carbon dioxide, 700.

Choking, first aid for, 1295.

Cholera (kol'-e-ra). Dangerous epidemic disease; caused by bacteria, 1458, 2132; in Naples, 2274.

Cholest'erol, a constituent of protoplasm, 2695.

Cholmondeley (chum'li). Eng. surname.

Cholon ("great market"). Largest commercial centre of Cochin-China; pop. 145,250; rice mills.

Chopin (shō'-pan), **Frédéric François** (1810–49). Polish pianist and composer), **816**.

Chord, in music, 2263.

Chorda'ta (chordates). All animals, including vertebrates, with spinal cords, *158.*

Chorley. Manuf. tn. of Lancs; pop. 32,500 ; site of new arsenal.

Choroid. Middle layer of the eyeball, *1252.*

Chorus, in Gk. drama. 1037.

Chosen (chō'-sen). Former Japanese name for Korea, 1872.

Chosroes I (koz'rō-ēz). King of Persia A.D. 531–79 ; sacks Antioch, 177.

Chosroes II. Ruler of Persia A D. 591–628, 2555.

Chough (chuf). A small crow with red beak and feet, native of the western shores of Brit.

Chow, dog ; *plate f. 1024.*

Christ, the Messiah. Title of Jesus. *See* **Jesus Christ.**

Chris'tabel. The gentle, pious heroine of Coleridge's fragmentary poem of that name.

Christchurch. Tn. in Hampshire, s. coast, 30 m. w. of Portsmouth, at confluence of Avon and Stour rivs. ; great medieval church; pop. 9,183 ; 1571.

Christchurch, New Zealand, city on South Isl. 7 m. from port Lyttelton on E. coast ; pop. 149,741 ; trade in timber, mutton, wool, 2357.

Christ Church, Oxford, 2464 ; " Great Tom " bell, 410 ; " Tom Tower," 2462.

Christian, hero of Bunyan's " Pilgrim's Progress," 618.

Christian, ten Kings of Denmark, **816.**

Christian II (1481–1559), king of Denmark and Norway ; conquered Sweden (1520) ; he fled to the Netherlands following his massacre of the nobles and spent most of his remaining years in prison.

Christian IV (1577–1648), king of Denmark and Norway ; in Thirty Years' War, 3202.

Christian V (1646–99), king of Denmark and Norway ; weak but despotic ruler ; waged unsuccessful war against Sweden.

Christian IX (1818–1906), king of Denmark, 816.

Christian X (1870–1947), king of Denmark, 816.

Christian Era, miscalculation, 661.

Christiania, Former name of capital of Norway. *See* Oslo.

Christianity, 817 ; art of, 2476 ; Bible, 423 ; Orthodox Church, 2846. *History* : doctrines formulated by Paul, 2529 ; spread by apostles, 188 ; early persecutions, 2316 ; Constantine legalizes, 893 ; spread by Rom. Empire, 2811, 2812 ; in N. Africa, 3254 ; in Brit. Isles, 1193, 1745, 2528 ; Iona an early centre, 1602 ; Gauls and Franks converted, 854, 1238, 1365 ; spread by Charlemagne, 2878 ; conversion of Northmen, 2388 ; spread in Asia, 809, 3429 ; in India, 1707 ; in Japan, 1798 ; in Pacific isls., 2473. *See also* Church, Christian.

Christian Science and Mrs. Eddy, 1390.

Christie, Agatha (Mary Clarissa). Anglo-Amer. writer of detective stories ; " The Murder of Roger Ackroyd," " Ten Little Niggers," etc. ; her second husband, Dr. Mallowan, an archaeologist.

Christie's. Popular name for the firm of Christie, Manson and Woods, auctioneers. Firm was founded by James Christie the elder in 1766 ; perhaps the most famous sale-rooms in the world.

Christina (kris-tē'na) (1626–89). Queen of Sweden ; brilliant, erratic daughter of Gustavus Adolphus ; succeeded in 1632 ; abdicated 1654 in favour of her cousin, Charles X.

Christmas, 819 ; circus, *plate f.* 820 ; customs, *plate f. 821* ; mistletoe, 2194 ; holly at, origin, 1636 ; tree, history of, 820.

" Christmas Carol," by Dickens, story of, **820.**

Christmas Island. Name of two small isls., one in the Indian Ocean 190 m. s. of Java, the other in the Cent. Pacific near Fanning Isl. ; both are Brit. possessions.

Christmas rose, plant of genus *Helleborus,* of buttercup family. Flowers in winter, vary in colour from white to pink. Wild, greenish-flowered species are setterwort and stinking hellebore, both of which are uncommon.

Christmas tree, the spruce, *3070.*

Christophe (krēs-tof'), **Henri** (1767–1820), King of Haiti ; freed Negro slave, rose to be lieutenant of Toussaint and Dessalines and life president ; proclaimed king in 1811 ; killed himself during rebellion provoked by his revolting cruelties.

Christopher, St. (3rd cent.). Christian martyr ; said to have been a giant who carried people across a stream ; given the name Christophorus, " Christ Bearer," by the Christ Child, whom he unwittingly carried across ; by Titian, *1780.*

Chris'topher III (d. 1448), king of Denmark, Norway and Sweden.

Christopher Robin, name of the little boy featured in A. A. Milne's " When We Were Very Young," and " Winnie-the-Pooh."

Christ's College, Cambridge, 668.

Christ's Hospital, school, formerly in London, 1886, 2883. Now the " Bluecoat School " at Horsham ; Coleridge Memorial, *869.*

Chro'mate, a salt containing chromium and oxygen ; poisoning, 822.

Chromat'ic aberration, 1925 ; in telescopes, 3178 ; correction in microscope, 2163.

Chromatic, in cells, *431.*

Chrome tanning, 1913.

Chrome Yellow, a pigment, 2478.

Chro'mite. Ore of chromium ; lining for furnaces, 822.

Chromium (Cr.) (krō'-mi-um), a silvery blue metallic element of the tungsten group ; atomic weight, 52·01, 821 ; in alloys, 123 ; properties, 776 ; in electroplating, 1139 ; in rustless steel, 2856 ; sesquioxide in paints, 2478 ; in tanning, 1913.

Chro'mosome of cell, 738.

Chro'mosphere of sun, 3120.

Chron'icle, Anglo-Saxon, 111.

Chronicles. Two Books of the Old Testament (originally one), supplementing history given in Books of Samuel and Kings.

Chronol'ogy. *See* **Calendar ; Time.**

Chronom'eter, type of clock, 822, *823* ; John Harrison's, 822, *823* ; in navigation, 2290 ; used on ships, 1898, 2210.

Chronos. Same as **Kronos.**

Chrysalis (kris'-a-lis) of butterfly, 630, *631,* 729.

Chrysanthemum (kris-an'-the-mum), cultivated flower of aster family, **823**, *824.*

Chryseis (kri-sē-is). In Homer's Iliad, captive daughter of a Trojan priest of Apollo ; Agamemnon refused the ransom offered by her father until Apollo sent pestilence to the Gk. camp.

Chrysler (krīz'-ler) **Building,** New York. Has 68 storeys and is 1,046 ft. high, with a needle-like spire, 2353.

Chrysoberyl (kris-ō-ber'-il), semi-precious stone, 1427.

Chrysoprase (kris'-ō-prāz), a form of quartz, 2713.

Chrysostom (kris'-os-tom), **John, St.** (*c.* 357–407). " The golden-mouthed," a monk of Antioch, most famous of Gk. Fathers, called the greatest orator of anc. Church.

Chub, a freshwater fish, 1310.

Chubb lock, 1979.

Chukker or chukka. Period of play in the game of polo, 2652.

Chulalongkorn (1853–1910), king of Siam ; succeeded to throne in 1868 ; introduced many reforms and improved condition of country.

Chungking, China. Port in Szechwan on Yangtze ; pop. 1,900,000 ; seat of Chinese Govt. 1938–45 ; emergency Nationalist Cap. Oct. 1949.

Church, Christian, 817 ; architecture, *see* Church Architecture ; art. 2476 ; baptism, 359 ; drama, 1039 ; ecclesiastical organization, 2495 ; festivals, 819, 1073 ; hymns, 1678 ; monks and monasticism, 2212 ; music of, 2261 ; Papacy, 2495, 2562 ; formation, 2758 ; of Scotland, 2892. *See also* Christianity, Church of England, Free Churches, Papacy, Pope, Protestantism, Reformation, Roman Catholic Church.

Church Architecture, 219 ; Byzantine, 213, 638 ; early Christian, 216 ; Gothic, 216 ; Renaissance, 2766 ; Romanesque, 216, 2612. *See also* Cathedral.

Church Army. Church of Eng. organization, founded in 1882 by the Rev. Wilson Carlile ; among its objects are care of waifs and strays and assistance of the poor ; established a number of homes ; did splendid work in World Wars.

Church Assembly, 825.

Churchill, Charles (1731–64). Eng. poet and satirist ; his " Rosciad " exposed faults of actors of the day.

Churchill, Lord Randolph (1849–95). Brit. statesman, third son of 7th Duke of Marlborough ; brilliant but erratic Conservative free-lance ; Sec. for India (1885–86) and twice leader of the House of Commons.

Churchill, Winston (1871–1947), Amer. novelist (" Richard Carvel," " The Crisis " ; " Con's on " ; " Mr. Crewe's Career " ; " The Inside of the Cup ").

Churchill, Winston Spencer, O.M. (b. 1874). Brit. statesman and author ; son of Lord Randolph Churchill, 824, *2386, 3417, 3283* ; First Lord of Admiralty (1911-15 and 1939-40 ;) Prime Minister, May 1940 to July 1945 ; leader of Conservative Party, Oct. 9, 1940 ; Warden of Cinque Ports 1941 ; Leader of Opposition, July 1945 ; O.M., 1946 ; French Médaille Militaire in 1947. Hon. R.A. Extraordinary in 1948. Books include : " My Early Life " ; lives of Marlborough and Lord Randolph Churchill ; " The World Crisis " ; 2nd World War memoirs.

Churchill, formerly **Fort Churchill,** Manitoba, Trading station and port on Hudson Bay, 1649.

Churchill River, in Cent. Canada ; rises in w. Saskatchewan ; flows E. and N.E. about 1,100 m. to Hudson Bay, 2874.

Churchill tank, 3152.

Church Missionary Society (C.M.S.). An organization, founded 1799, for undertaking missionary work in the East and Africa ; it has several thousand missionaries and has opened up countless schools, in addition to a training college and other institutions.

Church of Christ Scientist. *See* **Christian Science.**

Church of England (C.E.), the Established State Church, **825** ; home, 692 ; under William Rufus, 3380 ; John, 1834 ; Henry II and Becket, 389, 1611 ; Wycliffe, 3427 ; Henry VIII becomes head of, 1612 ; Elizabeth reforms, 1146 ; King James Bible, 426 ; disestablishment in Ire., 1746 ; confirmation, 886.

Church of Jesus Christ of Latterday Saints. *See* **Mormons.**

Church of the Holy Sepulchre, Jerusalem, 1820.

Churchwarden, duties, 825.

Chuvashia. Autonomous republic of Soviet Russia, comprising parts of Kazakstan and Simbirsk ; area 7,192 sq. m. ; pop. 894,475.

Chuz'zlewit, Martin. Hero of Dickens's novel " Martin Chuzzlewit " ; emigrates to America but returns to Eng. completely disillusioned.

Chyme (kīm). Food partly digested by stomach, 1017.

Ciano (chah'-nō), **Count Galeazzo** (1903–1944). It. statesman ; married Signor Mussolini's daughter in 1934 ; appointed Minister for Foreign Affairs in 1936 ; supervised invasion of Albania, 1939 ; executed Jan. 1944 ; parts of diary published in 1947.

A LIST OF COMMON CINEMA TERMS

Action. Director's signal for " begin the scene." Also " movement " in a film.

Adaptation. Alteration of book, play, or story so as to form basis of a film.

Animation. Process of making moving cartoons, apparent motion of inanimate objects, and the like.

Arc. Powerful carbon light

Back Projection. Showing actors in front of scene separately filmed.

" Blimp." Sound-proof box in which the camera-head is placed so that the working of the mechanism shall not be picked up by the sound microphone.

Breakaway. A bottle, club, or other object, made of wax or some light material, which breaks when the victim is struck. Breakaway furniture is commonly made of yucca wood.

Cameraman. The lighting and photography expert.

Cast. Characters in a film.

Casting Director. One who selects and arranges cast of a film.

Chemical fade. Chemical treatment of negative to give a fade-in or fade-out effect.

Chips. The carpenter.

Climax. Chief dramatic moment in a film.

Close up. Close view of an artist on screen.

Continuity. Succession of scenes, theme running through picture.

Continuity Girl. Script girl, who watches the action.

Credit titles. Names shown on screen at beginning of film.

Crowd artist. An extra or super, one who works in crowd scenes.

Cut ! Director's command to stop the scene ; the camera and sound motors are " cut " and the scene stops.

Cutter. A film editor.

Decor chief. Person responsible for the " grooming " of players.

Dialogician. A film dialogue writer.

Diffusion disk. A disk placed over camera lens to tone down hard lines of the photography.

Director. Person chiefly responsible for the making of a film.

Dissolve. The melting of one scene into another, or the merging of one image, such as a young actor dissolving into an older person.

Dolley. A small cart on which camera can follow or move about the set.

Double. An actor who takes the place of a star in a hazardous bit of action.

Double exposure. The photographing of two separate images on one film.

Dubbing. The sound effect is sometimes " dubbed " in, or added, after the completion of the photographing of a scene.

Dupe negative. A negative film, secured by printing from a positive. News reels are printed from several " dupes," in order to gain speed in distribution.

Exteriors. Scenes which are taken out of doors, or outdoor scenes staged in the studio.

Extra. A crowd player or super.

Fade. A gradual darkening or lightening of the whole scene. Accomplished in professional cameras by the shutter, which closes or opens a slight bit over each successive exposure, thus gradually and progressively decreasing or increasing the exposure.

Fade in. To start with a black screen and build up the picture to full brilliance.

Fade out. To reverse the preceding effect.

Feature player Artist either supporting a star or sharing the honours with other artists. (*See* Star).

Film editor. A person who edits or cuts the film.

Flash 'em " Put the lights on."

Flicker. The intermittent fluttering of light and dark on the screen. May be due to slow speed of the projecting machine, or faulty adjustment.

Floor (The). Studio where picture is being filmed.

Flop. A failure.

Follow focus. To adjust the focus of the camera lens as the subject moves nearer to or farther away from the camera, during the filming of a scene.

Frame. One picture of a moving-picture film.

Gag. Comedy situation in a film.

Gate. The part of the film track where the film is exposed ; or the corresponding place in the projector where the picture is projected to the screen.

" Get-over." To register satisfactorily.

Gripps. Labourers who move heavy objects in the studio.

Halation. The glare of light on a film, especially on glaring white clothes and bright metals.

Ham (A). A poor actor.

Hard lighting. Use of undiffused light to create a certain mood in the lighting of a set. An example is the prowling of a burglar, where the effect is wanted of weird lighting and shadows.

Heavy (The). The villain.

High Spot. Big dramatic or comic moment in a film ; a climax.

Iris in. } Gradual fading or illuminating of a scene on the screen
Iris out. } through a widening or decreasing circle.

" Kick 'em." Command to light the lights.

" Kill 'em." Command to turn off the lights.

Lens Lizard. Artist who continually tries to get his face before the camera.

Location. Filming in actual or out-of-door setting of incident.

Mac goo pie. A custard pie used in slapstick comedies.

Make-up (a) Disguise for players to alter their appearance.
(b) Application of preparations to the faces for better filming purposes.

Master negative. The final arrangement of the negative. From this will be printed the positive prints for distribution throughout the country, and also from one of these positives may be printed a number of dupe negatives.

Meg (To). To direct.

Mike. A microphone.

Mixer. Man who controls the volume of voice and sound—sound recordist.

Mixing panel. The electrical equipment for effecting the proper relation between sounds in making records.

Monitor. An operator who listens to all sounds being recorded, to ensure correct balance and effect desired.

Montage. A word used to denote quick cutting climaxing in a mood or effect.

Multiple exposure. More than three exposures on one frame or series of frames.

" Non-flam." Safety or non-inflammable film. This type of film is always used for home projectors.

O.K. for sound. The scene all right for recording—no sound flaws.

Pan. To swing the camera slowly about to follow a moving scene.

Panned (to be) or receive a panning. A bad criticism.

Play-back. After each rehearsal of a scene, the sound is played through for actors and directors to hear. This is done from a wax negative, another exactly similar one being recorded simultaneously and kept as the master negative if the particular scene is accepted.

Positive. The film printed from the negative and used in the course of the actual projection.

Pre-view. A picture " tried out " at a theatre to see how the audience likes it.

Projection box. The small room in a cinema where machines are situated that " project " the film on to the screen.

Projection theatre. A small theatre where a picture is shown at the studios.

Prop. Contraction of " property " ; any object which is used in the action of a story or play. Not to be confused with the furnishings of a set, which are not handled by the actors.

Quickie. A cheap and hurriedly-made production.

Reel. Special spool on which film is wound.

Release. The finished picture, available for rental, on and after a certain date, the " release date."

Reserve motion. Comedy effects secured by means of running the camera backwards, or turning it upside-down.

Running shot. A scene secured with the camera on a platform on the front of a locomotive, or car, or other vehicle. Used to show action taking place while the subject moves along, as in driving a car.

Rush. Quickly prepared film of scenes made during the day, and shown to director at end of day's work.

Scenario. The actual film story complete and written in sequences suitable for filming.

Scenarist. One who writes scenarios.

Script. The director's working scenario. Contains all directions and changes made in the original scenario.

Sequence. A series of scenes which tie together in a more or less logical order.

Set. A representation of a room or any other place in which action takes place. May be indoors, or otherwise.

Slapstick. Very broad comedy.

Slow motion. The grotesque and interesting effect in which the action is very slow. Secured by running the camera many times normal speed, usually eight times faster than normal. Projected at normal speed, the action is thus slowed down.

Splice. The place where two pieces of film are joined together.

Spool. A reel on which film is wound.

Star. Player whose name is given greater prominence than the title of the film, and is considered a greater box-office draw than either the story or the direction.

Still. A picture taken with an ordinary camera, usually for advertising purposes.

Stop motion. The method by which animated effects are secured. A special shaft on the camera allows one frame to be exposed for each turn of the crank. Between each exposure the object being animated is moved slightly.

Sub-title. A title occurring in the course of the story or film.

Super. A giant production. Also an artist playing a crowd part.

Synopsis. Brief outline of a story.

Synchronism. The proper running of cameras and sound recording machines, so that the sound shall occur at the right moment when the picture is projected.

Take. As each scene is photographed, perhaps over and over until action and sound are correct, it is given a number. Each of these attempts is called a " take."

Technical Adviser. A person who advises a film company on technical data, e.g., for a military film, an Army officer.

Tempo. The timing and mood of a film.

Test. A brief film made of artists to test their suitability for a part.

Trade show. A special performance of a film given to members of the trade, cinema owners, and critics, before it is shown to the public generally.

Trailer. Short extract from a film exhibited in cinemas as an advertisement.

Zoom up. When camera moves up quickly to an object.

Cibber (sib'-er), **Colley** (1671–1757). Eng. actor and dramatist ; hero of Pope's " Dunciad " ; wrote " Apology," amusing autobiography ; poet laureate, 2634.

Cicada (si-kā'-da). An insect, **826.**

Cicatrization. Formation of scar tissue ; as method of tattooing, 3158.

Cicero (sis'-e-rō), **Marcus Tullius** (106–43 B.C.). Rom. statesman, orator, author, and philosopher, **827** ; his prose, 1895.

Cid, The (Arabic, *El Seid*, the lord). Popular name of Rodrigo Ruy Diaz (c.1040–99) ; called also *El Campeador*, the Champion, Sp. national hero, 3036 ; epic poem, 3050 ; subject of play by Corneille, 910.

Ci'der. Apple juice, 191, **828.**

Cienfuegos (sē-en-fwā'-gōs). Cuba, on s. coast ; centre for sugar and tobacco trade ; pop. 92,258.

Cierva, Juan de la (1895–1936). Span. engineer ; inventor of autogiro, 1605, *1606.*

Cigarettes, 3221.

Cigars, 3221 ; Havana, 1584 ; Paraguay cigar-makers *3026.*

Cig'oli, Lodovico Cardi da (1559–1613). It. painter, famed for his beautiful colouring.

Cilia. Hair-like projections of cells ; moss sperms, 2238 ; water snails, 2989.

Cilia'ta. Class of protozoan animals with vibratory hairs, or cilia.

Cilicia (si-lish'-ia). Anc. country of Asia Minor, on N.E. coast of Mediterranean, N. of crest of Taurus Mts. ; noted for forests, grain, and wine ; Rom. prov. 64 B.C. ; now part of Adana.

Cilician Gates (Gulek Bo'ghaz). Famous pass through Taurus Mts. from Cappadocia to Cilicia.

Cimabue (chē-mah-bōō'-ā) (1240–1302). Florentine painter, whose real name was Giovanni Gualtieri ; credited with revival of painting in It. after Dark Ages ; teacher of Giotto, 1775.

Cima da Conegliano. 16th cent. It. painter, 1776.

Cimaro'sa (chē-mah-rō'-zah), **Domenico** (1749–1801). It. musical composer ; worked at Courts of Empress Catherine II of Russia and the Emperor Leopold II. " Il Matrimonio Segreto " is his masterpiece.

Cimbri (sim'-bri). A Germanic tribe ; Marius defeats, 2809.

Cimmer'ians. In Gk. (Homeric) myth., far western of northern people who lived in perpetual (" Cimmerian ") darkness ; also certain anc. historical inhabitants of the Crimea.

Ci'mon (c. 504–449 B.C.). Athenian statesman and leader in wars against Persians ; son of Miltiades ; fought at Salamis ; drove Persians out of Thrace, Caria, and Lycia ; banished 461 B.C. through influence of Pericles, but promptly recalled and restored to command of fleet.

Cinchona (sin-kō'-na). Tree from whose bark quinine is obtained, 748, 2718 ; in E. Indies, 1813 ; S. Amer., 1083, 2559.

Cincinna'ti, Ohio, U.S.A. Rly. and mfg. centre on Ohio R. ; pop. 455,610 ; mfrs. boots, clothing, machinery.

Cincinna'tus, Lucius Quintius (c. 519–439 B.C.). Dictator of Rome, **828.**

Cinderel'la. Household drudge who marries a prince in an old fairy tale of many lands.

Cinema. The art of the moving picture, **828,** *830, 831* ; cartoons, 829 ; Charlie Chaplin, 829 ; early cinema, 2761 ; Hollywood, 2026 ; nature films, 833 ; news reels, 833 ; sound track, 832, 2576, *3012. See also* Photography ; list of terms, 3755.

Cinera'ria. Familiar garden plant, which came originally from the Canary Isls.

Cinna, Lucius Cornelius (d. 84 B.C.). Rom. noble ; consul 87–84 B.C. ; one of principal supporters of Marius against Sulla ; his daughter Cornelia married Julius Caesar.

Cin'nabar. Sulphide of mercury, 2145, 3117.

Cin'namon. A spice, 3060 ; essential oil from, 1263.

Cinnamon stone. Gem stone allied to the garnet ; orange-red in colour ; obtained chiefly in Ceylon.

Cinquefoil. Common weed, with leaves divided into five leaflets (*Potentilla reptans*), having bright yellow flowers.

Cinque Ports. Five Eng. Channel ports (Hastings, Sandwich, Dover, Romney, Hythe) ; granted charter by Edward I ; special privileges for defending coast ; Winchelsea and Rye added later, **834.**

Cintra. Mountainous mass of jagged grey peaks (highest 1,772 ft.) near Lisbon, Portugal, 1962.

Cipango. Name given by Marco Polo to Japan, 1799.

Cipher. Origin of word, 233.

Cippolino. Kind of marble, *2097.*

Circassia (sĕr-kash'-ya). Region of N.W. Caucasus ; originally independent but added to Russia by treaty of Adrianople (1829).

Circassians. Noted for beauty, 732 ; in Macedonia, 2049.

Circe (sĕr-sē). In Gk. myth., a sorceress who could turn men into beasts, **834.**

Circle, in geometry, 1435. Parallels of earth, 1898.

Circuit, electric. Path followed by an electric current, 1128 ; series and parallel, *1129* ; in telegraph 3166 ; compared with water *1129.*

Circuit, of Justices, 922.

Circulation, of blood, 476, 1581 ; Harvey's discovery, 1581 ; why sap flows in plants, 2621 ; of air, 1598.

Circumference, in geometry, 1435.

Circus (Latin for " ring "). Originally a place for chariot races, etc. ; now used with various derived meanings ; at Olympia, *plate f. 820* ; circular open space, as Piccadilly Circus, 2015.

Cir'cus Max'imus (Greatest Circus). Huge circular building in Rome, used for chariot races and gladiatorial combats, 651, 3194.

Cirencester. Market tn. of Gloucestershire ; the Rom. Corinium.

Cirl bunting. Bird, 617.

Cirrho'sis. Diseased condition of the liver, 1968.

Cir'rus clouds, 852, *853.*

Cisalpine (sis-al'-pīn), **Gaul** (" Gaul this side of Alps "). Portion of N. It., bounded on N. by Alps, on S. by Rubicon ; conquered by Rome.

Cisalpine Republic. Former state in N. It., organized by Napoleon, 2275.

Cistercians (sis-tĕr'-shanz) or **Grey** or **White Monks.** An offshoot of the Benedictine order, 2213.

Cithae'ron. Mt. range in Greece, now called Elatea ; famous in Gk. myth., especially in connexion with Dionysus.

Cith'ara or lyre. Fabled invention by Hermes, 1619 ; of Orpheus, 2454.

Citrate. A salt of citric acid.

Citric acid. Complex organic acid obtained from citrus fruits, 1922.

Citrine, Baron Walter McLennan (b. 1887). English labour leader ; gen. sec. T.U.C. in 1926 ; elevated to peerage, 1946.

Gitroën, André Gustav (b. 1878). Fr. motor-car mfr. ; known as the " French Ford."

Cit'ron. Large lemon-like fruit of semitropical tree, *Citrus medica,* and provides candied peel.

Cit'rus fruits. Fruit of trees, belonging to *Citrus* genus ; grape-fruit, 1499 ; lemon, 1922 ; oranges, 2442.

City. Large town, usually with a cathedral ; oldest in world, 961.

WORLD'S LARGEST CITIES

		Pop.	Year
1. London ..	..	8,282,217	1948
2. New York ..	..	7,782,000	1946
3. Tokyo ..	..	6,778,804	1940
4. Moscow ..	..	4,137,000	1939
5. Shanghai ..	..	3,599,000	1946
6. Chicago ..	..	3,396,808	1940
7. Osaka ..	..	3,252,300	1940
8. Leningrad ..	..	3,191,300	1939
9. Berlin ..	..	3,199,938	1946
10. Paris ..	..	2,725,000	1946

N.B.—The first four include what are

known as the " Greater " areas ; the year given is that of the last census or reliable estimate.

City Cross, Edinburgh, *1086.*

City Guilds. *See* **Livery Companies.**

City of London, 2009. *See* **London.**

" **City of Palms,**" 2480.

" **City of the Seven Hills,**" 2799.

" **City of Steel,**" 2614.

City States. In Ger., 1449 ; of Greece, 1518 ; Rom. republic, 2807.

Ciudad Bolivar (sē-ōō'-dad bō-lē'-vahr), Venezuela. City on Orinoco r. ; pop. 25,000 ; 2452.

Ciudad Rodrigo. Fortified frontier tn. in w. Sp. ; pop. 8,700 ; taken by Fr. under Ney in 1810 ; retaken (1812) by Brit. under Wellington.

Ciudad Trujillo (troo-hē-yō). Formerly Santo Domingo, cap. of Dominican Rep., W. Indies ; pop. 114,300 ; 1029.

Civet (siv'-et) or **civet cat.** Animal between cats and hyenas ; fierce and active ; perfume, 2549.

Civics. *See* **Government.**

Civilization. The opposite state to savagery ; 2078 ; Aegean, 29 ; Bronze Age, 587 ; cave dwellers, 734, 2078 ; Celts, 740 ; domestication of animals, 735 ; fire, 1278 ; geographical influences, 1430 ; Gk. influence, 1517 ; iron, 1753 ; Roman influence, 2812 ; Stone Age, 3094.

Civil law (Roman), 1902 ; and government, 1490.

Civil List. Sum of money voted by the Government on the accession of a new sovereign for the regular and domestic expenses of the Crown ; pensions, 2546.

Civil Service. General name given to those depts. concerned in the administration of the civil affairs of the State ; **835,** 1490 ; address of Commission, 835.

Civil War, American. *See* **American Civil War.**

Civil War, England (1642–49), 1196, 1198, 755 ; Hampden, 1571 ; Charles I, 755 ; Cromwell, 933 ; Milton, 2176.

Clackmannanshire. Smallest Scottish co., bordered by Firth of Forth ; a. 55 sq. m. ; pop. 33,000 ; **835.**

Clacton-on-Sea. Seaside resort of Essex ; pop. est. 15,000 ; severely damaged in air raids of 2nd World War.

Clairvoy'ance (Fr. " clear seeing "). The psychic power to observe things not actually visible to the eye.

Clam, a bivalve mollusc, 860, 2199 ; giant, 861, 2942.

Clan, 835 ; origin of, 1259 ; assembly, *2893.*

Clapham. Dist. in south-west London, forming part of the borough of Wandsworth. Clapham has a common of 220 acres, and a rly. junction (one of the largest in the world) which is actually in Battersea.

Clare, St. (1194–1253). It. nun, follower of St. Francis, 1384.

Clare. Marit. county in N.W. of prov. of Munster, Eire ; 1,230 sq. m. ; pop. 86,000 ; **836.**

Clare College. One of the colleges of Cambridge Univ. ; founded 1326 as University Hall, it was rebuilt and given present name in 1338 ; *668.*

Clar'endon, Edward Hyde, Earl of (1609–74), Eng. historian, 756.

Clarendon, George Herbert Hyde Villiers, 6th Earl of (b. 1877). Under-Secretary for Dominions (1925–26) ; chairman B.B.C. (1927–30), Governor General of Union of S. Africa (1931–37) ; appointed Lord Chamberlain in 1938.

Clarinet, musical inst., *2267,* 2446, 3009, 3404.

" **Clarissa ; or the History of a Young Lady,**" novel by S. Richardson, 2402.

Clark, Francis Edward (1851–1927). Cong. minister in U.S.A. ; founder and president of United Society of Christian Endeavour.

Clark, Mark Wayne (b. 1896). Amer. soldier ; commander of U.S. ground forces in Europe in 1942 ; C.-in-C. U.S. 5th Army and later Allied 15th group in Italy, 1943–45 ; 1947 comm. U.S. 6th Army h.q., San Francisco.

Clarke, Marcus (1846–81), Australian novelist, 315.

Clarkson, Thomas (1760–1846), Eng. philanthropist ; active worker in the cause of anti-slavery.

Clary sage oil, a vegetable fixative for perfumes, 2550.

Class, in biology, 434.

Classical literature, influence in Renaissance, 2764. *See* **Greek literature** ; **Latin literature.**

Classics. As school subjects, Latin and Greek.

Classification, of animals, 434 ; of birds, 448, 3446 ; of crystals, 940 ; of human races, 2723 ; of insects, 1733 ; of languages, 2570 ; of minerals, 2180 ; of plants, 434, 2620 ; principles of animal classification, 434 ; of rocks, 1432.

Claudel′, Paul (b. 1868). Fr. poet and dramatist (" The Tidings Brought to Mary," drama of amazing beauty in guise of medieval folk legend).

Claude Lorrain. *See* **Lorrain, Claude.**

Clau′dius I (10 B.C.–A.D. 54). Rom. emperor, nephew of Tiberius, 2811 ; conquers Britain, 1193 ; poisoned, 2315 ; subject of historical novels by Robt. Graves.

Claudius, Appius. Rom. decemvir 451–449 B.C., whose attempt to abduct Virginia, beautiful daughter of a plebeian centurion, caused revolution and abolition of the decemvirate ; story told in Macaulay's " Lays of Ancient Rome."

Claudius, Caecus, Appius. Rom. patrician chosen to censorship 312 B.C., builder of Appian Way and Claudian aqueduct.

Clausen, Sir George (1852–1944). English artist of figure and landscape ; R.A. in 1908.

Claverhouse, John Graham of (1649–89), **Viscount Dundee,** Persecutor of Scottish Covenanters and Jacobite rebel, " bonny Dundee " to Jacobites and " bloody Claver′se " to Covenanters.

Clav′ichord, forerunner of the piano, 333, 2601, *2602.*

Claws in mammals, 2074.

Clay, Henry (1777–1852), Amer. orator and political leader.

Clay, Gen. Lucius Dub (b. 1897). Amer. soldier ; C.-in-C. European command and military gov. of (U.S.) Germany, 1947–49.

Clay, 836 ; for brick-making, 561 ; in cement mfr., 740 ; " clay minerals," 2181 ; source rock of oil, 2426 ; for pottery, 2665, 2670 ; soil, 2998.

Clayton, Philip Thomas Byard (b. 1885). Eng. chaplain ; founder padre of Toc H.

Clear, Cape. The southernmost point of Eire, in s.w. of Clear Isl., co. Cork.

Clearing House, Bankers', 357.

Cleddau. Two rivs. of Pembrokeshire, Wales. The East Cleddau (15 m. long) and West Cleddau (20 m. long) ; both flow into Milford Haven, 2539.

Clee Hills. Range in Shropshire, 14 m. long ; highest point, Brown Clee Hill, 1792 ft. ; stone is quarried.

Cleek. An iron golf club, 1484.

Clem′atis, a flowering climbing plant, 836.

Clemenceau, Georges Eugène Benjamin (1841–1929). Fr. prime minister in 1st World War, 837.

Clem′ens, Samuel Langhorne (1835–1910). *See* **Twain, Mark.**

Clement, popes. For list *see* **Pope.**

Clement IV (d. 1268), elected Pope 1265 ; befriends Roger Bacon, 334.

Clement V (1264–1314). First Avignon Pope, elected 1305, abolished order of the Templars.

Clement VII (Giulio de' Medici) (*c.* 1480–1534), Pope besieged in Castle of St. Angelo during Sack of Rome by Constable de Bourbon in 1527 ; refused to divorce Henry VIII of England from Catherine of Aragon, and thus caused separation of Church of England from Rome ; 1612.

Clement VII (d. 1394), first anti-pope of the Great Schism ; elected 1378 ; 3298.

Clement XIV (1705–74). Elected Pope 1769 ; suppressed the Jesuits.

Cleon (d. 422 B.C.). Athenian politician, opponent of Pericles, and leader of the democracy.

Cleopatra (klē-ō-pat′ra) (69–30 B.C.), beautiful queen of Egypt, **837**, *838* ; and Mark Antony, 2105.

Cleopatra's Needle, 838, *839,* 110.

Clepsydra (klep′-si-dra), a water clock, *843.*

Clerestory (klēr′-staw-ri), in architecture, 216.

Clergy. Term used to denote all ordained ministers in Christian Church ; costume, 825, 826; in Middle Ages, 818.

Cler′ihew. Form of comic verse in two irregular couplets invented by Edmund Clerihew Bentley in " Biography for Beginners " (1905).

Clerk, Sir Dugald (1854–1932). Brit. engineer, pres. of the socy. of Brit. gas industries, 1906–08, and member of several 1st World War cttees. ; knighted 1917 ; invented a 2-stroke gas engine (the Clerk cycle), 1421, 1736.

Clerk-Maxwell, James (1831–79), famous Scot. physicist, **839,** *840,* 2594, 2728, 3391.

Clermont, first Amer. steamship, built by Fulton, *1407.*

Clermont-Ferrand, Fr. City w. of Lyons ; pop. 108,090 ; 13th cent. cathedral.

Cleveland, Stephen Grover (1837–1908), 22nd president of U.S.A. in 1885–89 and 1893–97.

Cleveland. Moorland dist. of Yorkshire ; important for iron deposits, the industry centring in Middlesbrough.

Cleveland, Ohio, U.S.A., on L. Erie, at mouth of r. Cuyahoga ; largest city in Ohio and 6th largest in U.S.A. ; pop. 878,336 ; iron and steel ; clothing, motor-car mfrs. ; 2426.

Cleves, Ger. Tn. in Rhine prov. of Prussia, near frontier of Holland ; formerly cap. of duchy of Cleves ; pop. 20,000 ; castle associated with the legend " Knights of the Swan," immortalized in Wagner's " Lohengrin." Captured by Brit., Feb. 1945 ; heavily damaged in earlier fighting.

Click beetle, 399.

Cliff Dwellers. Prehistoric race of s.w. U.S.A. ; ancestors of Pueblo Indians, 2698, *2699.*

Clifford, John (1836–1923). English Baptist minister and politician, who started active life as a worker in a lace factory ; from 1877 to 1915 was pastor of Westbourne Park chapel ; strongly opposed Education Act (1902) ; wrote many religious works.

Clifford's Inn. The oldest of the Inns of Chancery, in Fetter Lane, London.

Cliffs, at Dover, *plate f. 1165* ; of Sussex, 2777.

Clifton. Suburb of Bristol, Eng. ; college is a noted public school ; suspension bridge.

Climate. Typical atmospheric conditions of a region, **840** ; altitude causes cold, 840, 2156 ; continental type, 677, 840 ; effect on civilization, 1430 ; and ecology, *f. 1080* ; evaporation, 1243 ; forests maintain even moisture, 1349, 3245 ; Gulf Stream, 1554, 2419 ; hail, 1564 ; modified by mountains, 840 ; oceanic, 1232, 2419 ; rainfall, 2741 ; distinguished from weather, 2149 ; winds, 3384. *See also* **Weather.**

Clinical thermometer, 3200.

Clinton, Sir Henry (*c.* 1738–95). Brit. general in War of Amer. Independence, commander-in-chief of Brit. land forces (1778–82).

Clio (klī-ō). In Gk. myth., muse of history, 187, 2259.

Clippers, sailing ships, 2947, *2958* ; name also used for trans-oceanic aircraft of Pan-American Airways.

Clisthenes (klīs′-the-nēz) or **Cleisthenes** (6th cent. B.C.). Athenian statesman, democratic reformer ; founded political organization of the Athenian Golden Age ; 1522.

Clitus (klī′-tus) (d. 328 B.C.). Macedonian general and friend of Alexander the Great, 106.

Clive, Robert, Baron Clive of Plassey (1725–74), founder of Brit. Empire in India, **842,** 1714, 2925 ; captured Calcutta, 660 ; Warren Hastings, 1581 ; and Chatham, 759.

Cloaca Maxima, 2804.

Clocks and watches, 843, *845* ; chronometer, 822 ; early devices, 843, 1414 ; electric, 1125, *1126, 1127,* 3214 ; escapement, *848, 849* ; grandfather, *847* ; Harrison's chronometer, 2290 ; Hooke's inventions, 1640 ; piezo-electric control, 2605 ; pendulum, 844, *plate f. 1513,* 2543 ; Switzerland, 418, 3412 ; synchronous, *1126* ; time switch, 3215 ; wheel, 3375 ; 24-hour clocks, 3214.

Clodd, Edward (1840–1930). Eng. Rationalist (" Story of Creation " ; " The Story of Primitive Man ").

Cloete, Stuart, S. African novelist, 3020.

Clogs. Wooden-soled shoes, worn in Holland, Belgium and by mill operatives, etc., in N. Eng. ; alder for soles of, 105.

Cloisonné (klwah-zon′-nā), enamel, 1157, 1158, *1159,* 2271.

Cloister. Covered walk in monastery, 2213.

" Cloister and the Hearth, The." Novel by Charles Reade, 2764.

Close (klōs). Land and buildings within the precincts of a cathedral, reserved for the private use of the bishop and canons.

Cloth, 850 ; asbestos, 262 ; cotton, 920 ; felt, 1265 ; glass, 1474 ; hemp, 1609 ; Jacquard loom, 1790 ; jute, 1844 ; lanital, *850* ; linen, 1313, 1953 ; loom, 2024 ; silk, 2972 ; spinning, 2024, 3065 ; weaving, 3360 ; wool, 3404.

Clothes, 851. *See also* **Dress.**

Cloth Hall, Ypres. *407,* 3436.

Clotho. One of the Fates in Gk. and Rom. myth., 1262.

Clotilda, Saint (d. 544), wife of Clovis, 854.

Clouded Yellow butterfly, *plate f. 632.*

Clouds, 851 ; chief types, *853* ; and aircraft, *40* ; electricity in, 1945 ; and elec. consumption, 1548 ; height of, 2149 ; highest levels, 89.

" Clouds, The." Title of a play by Aristophanes, the great comic dramatist of ancient Athens, 231.

Clouet (klōō′-ā), Jean and François. French artists, *870,* 1377.

Clough (kluf), **Arthur Hugh** (1819–61). Eng. poet, typical, in his scepticism and introspection, of middle 19th cent. (" Say Not the Struggle Nought Availeth ").

Clove hitch, *1870.*

Clovelly. Devon village, *1000.*

Clove pink. A flower, 2611.

Clover, 852 ; fertilized by bumble-bees, 394 ; has nitrogen-fixing bacteria, 1509.

Cloves, spice, **854,** 3060, *3061* ; essential oil from, 1263 ; Zanzibar, 3441.

Clo′vis (A.D. *c.*470–511), King of Franks, **854,** 1365 ; becomes Christian, 2167 ; first " Louis," 2027.

Club moss, species of family *Lycopodiaceae* of mosses.

Clubs, for golf, 1484.

Cluj. City of Rumania, formerly Kolozsvar ; pop. 110,956 ; univ. ; varied mfrs.

Cluny. Tn. in E. cent. Fr. ; remains of Benedictine abbey (910) ; seat of Cluniacs or Congregation of Cluny.

Cluny lace, 1881.

Cluster pine, or pinaster, 2610.

Clutch, in motor-car, 2244 ; fluid fly-wheel, 1667.

Clyde. R. in s.w. Scot., flows N. and N.W. 106 m. to Firth of Clyde ; great shipbuilding centre ; **854,** 1471, 1577, 1890.

Clyde, 1st Baron. *See* **Campbell, Sir Colin.**

Clyde, Firth of. Scot. estuary of r. Clyde, which expands into bay ; 65 m. long, 1 m. to 37 m. wide ; part of Greenock near head of the estuary ; Ayr is on E. shore ; isls. of Arran, Bute, Cumbrae, 855.

Clyde′bank. Tn. in Dumbartonshire, on r. Clyde, 5½ m. N.W. of Glasgow ; pop. 48,200 ; busy ship-building centre, where the Queen

Mary, Queen Elizabeth, etc., were built, *854*, 1472 ; shipyards, *2948*, *2950*.

Clydes'dale horse, 1647.

Clymene (klim'-e-nē). In Gk. myth., mother of Phaeton.

Clynes, John Robert (1869–1949). Brit. Labour politician ; worked in a cotton mill as a boy ; succeeded Lord Rhondda as Food Controller during 1st World War ; Lord Privy Seal and deputy leader of the House of Commons in first Labour Government in 1924 ; Home Secretary (1929–31).

Clytemnestra (klī-tem-nes'-tra). In Gk. myth., sister of Helen and wife of Agamemnon, whom she murdered, and mother of Iphigenia, Electra, and Orestes, 75.

Clytie (klī'-ti). In Gk. myth., maiden beloved and deserted by Helios, the sun, after whom she gazed till the pitying gods changed her into a sunflower.

Cnidus (nī'-dus). Anc. Gk. city on promontory in Caria, Asia Minor ; contained famous statue of Aphrodite by Praxiteles.

Cnossus. Anc. cap. of Crete. *See* **Knossos.**

Cnut. *See* **Canute.**

Coagulation, of the blood, 475.

Coahuila (kō-ah-wē'-la). Mex. state in N. bordering on Texas, U.S.A. ; 58,000 sq. m. ; pop. 436,000 ; cap. Saltillo.

Coal, 855 ; not a mineral, 2181 ; anthracite, 855 ; bituminous, 855 ; Brit. Isls., *1165*, 2336, 3333 ; coke from, 856, 868 ; energy from, 855, *1160* ; flame, 1280 ; formation, *855*, 856 ; 2384 ; Fr., 133, 1361 ; as fuel, 1165, 1405, *1406* ; gas from, 1423 ; geology, 856 ; Ger., 1447 ; how it produces heat, 1595 ; hydrogenation of, 1674 ; lignite, 856 ; mining, *2182*, *2183* ; developed from peat, 2535 ; petrol from, 2430 ; at power station, 2673 ; reserves, 857 ; spontaneous combustion, 1280 ; steam coal, 855 ; "stored sunlight," 1161 ; sun and, 3118 ; trees forming,

Coal Age. *See* **Carboniferous period.**

Coal Board, National. The Coal Industry Nationalisation Act came into force on Jan. 1, 1947, when Brit. mines were taken over by the govt. The Nat. Coal Board was formed to direct the workings of the mines.

Coal Gas. Illuminating gas obtained by distilling coal, 1405, 1423 ; in gas engine, 1420.

Coalition. Lit. a process of fusion. Applied to a temporary union of forces by political parties of divergent opinions for some particular purpose ; of govt., 1491.

Coal oil or **kerosene**, 2426.

Coalport, Shropshire. China from, 2693.

Coal-tar and its products, 857, 868 ; artificial indigo, 1718 ; carbolic acid, 699 ; creosote, 927 ; dyes, 1059, 1060 ; explosives, 1250 ; drugs, 1048 ; in nylon mfr., 2749 ; pitch, 3154 ; plastics, 699, 2626 ; resins, 1882 ; saccharin, 3116.

Coal-tit, *3218*.

Coastguard, 857.

Coatbridge. Scot. mfg. tn., Lanarkshire ; iron-smelting, 1890.

Coates, Albert (b. 1882). English musician, born in Russia, conductor Russian Imperial Opera, London Symphony Orchestra, Royal Philharmonic Society and Philharmonic Orchestra, N.Y.

Coates, Eric (b. 1886). English composer ("Countryside Suite," "London Suite" from which "Knightsbridge" march **was** chosen to introduce B.B.C.'s ' In Town Tonight.'').

Coat of Arms, 1614.

Coats. Scot. family of threadmakers at Paisley ; George Coats (1849–1918) was made Baron Glentanar.

Co-axial cable, 3177.

Cobalt (Co). A hard white metallic element of the iron group ; atomic weight, 58·9 ; most cobalt salts are red in solution and blue when dried,

and so are used for testing for moisture ; also used in "invisible inks" ; metal melts at 2731° F. ; 857, 1724 ; in alloys, 123 ; properties, 776 ; "trace" metal in diet, *2149* ; named after the gnomes or kobolds. Compounds : aluminate, 2478 ; chloride, 1724 ; nitrate, 1724.

Cobb, Irvin Shrewsbury (1876–1944). American humorist.

Cobb, John R. (b. 1899). Brit. racing motorist ; on Sept. 16, 1947, made new speed record at Bonneville Salt Flats, Utah, for measured mile at 394·196 m.p.h., driving a Railton Mobile Special.

Cobbett, William (1762–1835). Brit. politician and reformer 858.

Cobden, Richard (1804–65). Eng. Liberal statesman, "apostle of free trade," 858 ; anti-corn law campaign, 3278.

Cobh (formerly Queenstown). Spt. in co. Cork, Eire. It stands on Great Isl. in Cork Harbour ; noted yachting centre ; pop. 10,000 ; 859.

Cobham, Sir Alan John (b. 1894). British aviator ; active in stimulating popular interest in aviation ; flew London-Australia and back (1926), London-Cape Town and back (1925–26) ; afterwards organized air "circuses."

Coblenz or **Koblenz** (kō'-blents), Germany. City at confluence of Rhine and Moselle ; pop. 65,000 ; opposite is the fortress of Ehrenbreitstein ; *2991* ; taken by U.S. March 1945.

Cobra. Venomous snake of Asia and Africa, 859.

Coburg, Ger. Mfg. town in Bavaria ; formerly one of the caps. of duchy of Saxe - Coburg - Gotha ; pop. 24,700.

Cobweb, 3062.

Coca. Cocaine-yielding shrub of flax family, 2559.

Cocaine (kō-kān'). A narcotic drug, 1048, 2559 ; an alkaloid, 21.

Coccus. A round bacterium, 336, 1458.

Coccyx (kok'-siks). The small bone in the adult skeleton forming the tip of the spinal column below the sacrum.

Cochet (kō-shā), **Henri** (b. 1901). Fr. lawn tennis player. Won French championship 1926 ; with Brugnon won Men's Doubles at Wimbledon same year. With Borotra won Davis Cup for France in 1927. Same year he won U.S. national singles title and won Men's Doubles at Wimbledon with Brugnon. Singles champion at Wimbledon in 1927 and 1929 ; later became a professional.

Cochin-China. S. part of Viet-Nam, Indo-China ; 26,000 sq. m. ; pop. 4,616,000 ; cap. Saigon ; 1718, 1719, 3323. *map f. 264.*

Cochineal (koch-i-nel'). Red dye obtained from scale insects, 859, 1059, 2879 ; in ink, 1724.

Cochlea (kok'-lē-a). Part of the ear, 1066.

Cochran, Sir Charles Blake (b. 1872). Eng. theatrical manager and impresario ; knighted 1948.

Cockaigne (ko-kān), **Land of.** An imaginary land of luxury, joy, and delightful feats ; applied in lit. to London.

Cockatoo (kok-a-tōō'). Crested, parrot-like bird, 859, *860*, 2526, *3445*.

Cockchafer. A large beetle (1 to 1½ in. long), very common in some parts of the continent of Europe, and very destructive to the foliage of fruit and forest trees.

Cockcroft, Sir John Douglas (b. 1897). Brit. physicist ; worked on development of radar and of the atomic bomb in Second World War ; in 1945 made director of the experimental station for atomic energy, Harwell, Berks ; 298, 2594.

Cocker, Edward (1631–75). Celebrated Eng. arithmetician, whose "Arithmetick" ran into 112 editions ; this work gave rise to the saying "according to Cocker," *i.e.* correct.

Cockles and mussels. Molluscs, 860.

Cockney. Term applied to Londoners and their peculiar accent, **861.**

Cockpit, of aeroplane, *43.*

Cockroach. An insect, 861, 1732.

Cocksfoot, a grass, 1509.

Cocoa and chocolate, 861, *862.*

Cocoa butter, 862.

Coconut palm, 862, *863*, *2484*, *2485* ; how it spreads seeds, 2917 ; oil, 1263 ; value to Pacific islanders, 2472.

Cocoon (ko-kōōn'), 630, 631, 729, 1729 ; of caterpillar, 729 ; of silkworm, *2970.*

Cocos (kō'-kos) or **Keeling Islands.** About 20 small coral isls. S. of Java ; annexed to Singapore, Strts. Settlmts. 1903 ; Emden captured (1914). Incorp. in Singapore Colony, 1945.

Cocteau (kok'-tō), **Jean** (b. 1891). French poet, essayist, novelist and playwright ; strikingly original ; has greatly influenced young writers of his time ("Plain Chant"; "Enfants Terribles"; "The Infernal Machine"; "The Eagle Has Two Heads"), 1383.

Cod. A food fish, 864 ; fisheries, 681, *1876*, 2393 ; fishing dangers, 1299 ; food value, 2174.

Cod, Cape, Massachusetts, 2118.

Code (laws), of Hammurabi, 1902 ; of Justinian, 1844, 1902 ; of Napoleon, 2276.

Code. Signalling, 3164 ; Five-unit, *3166* ; Morse, 2232, *3166.*

Codex Sinaiticus. Greek manuscript of the Bible assigned to early part of 4th century ; discovered by Tischendorf in monastery at Sinai in 1859 ; purchased from Soviet Russia by Brit. Museum for £100,000 in 1933, *424*, 425, 511.

Cod-liver oil. Vitamin content, 3327.

Cody (kō'-di), "**Colonel**" **Samuel Franklin** (1861–1913). British aviator. Born in U.S.A., but became naturalized Englishman in 1896 ; first man to fly in Great Britain, and maker of the first practical British flying-machine.

Cody, William Frederick. *See* "**Buffalo Bill.**"

Co-education. School and college system of educating boys and girls together, 2886.

Coefficient. In algebra, a number or known quantity which is used as a multiplier with a known or unknown quantity, 115.

Coelenterates (sēl-en'-te-rāts). Large group of invertebrate animals (*Coelenterata*), 156 ; corals, 908, *plates f. 908*, *2104*, *2105* ; hydra, 1664 ; jelly-fish, 1817.

Coello, Claudio (1630–93). Spanish artist, 3049.

Coercive Acts, 144.

Coffee, 864, *865* ; Brazil, 551, *553* ; Costa Rica, *916*, 917 ; caffeine, 3160.

Coffee-houses, 864.

Coffer dam. A temporary dam built so that the enclosed space may be pumped dry to permit work, 654, 958.

Cog, an ancient ship, 2946 ; of wheel, 3375.

Cognac (kō-nyak), France. Old town in s.w., famous for brandy which bears its name ; pop. 17,500 ; on r. Charente.

Coherence, of molecules, 3121.

Coher'er. A radio detector. *See* Detector.

Cohune, a nut, 2408.

Coil. Induction, 1720 ; in dynamo 1061 ; magnetic effect, 2063 ; in radio apparatus, 3393 ; in transformer, 3257.

Coimbra (kō-ēm'-bra). Tn. in Beira prov., Portugal ; univ. 2659 ; pop. 27,000.

Coinage, 1482, 2201 ; alloys, 1481 first use, 2201 ; gold, 1479 ; Lydian first to use, 2201 ; minting process 2187 ; Royal Mint, 2187 ; new Irish, *1750* ; silver, 2973. For list of the world's chief coins, se **Money.**

Coin-Slot Machines, 866 ; hot sand wiches from, 1625 ; ticket-issuing (diagrams), *866*, *867.*

Coir. Coconut husk fibre, 864, 248. 2826.

Coke, 868 ; in blast furnace, 468 as fuel, 1405, 1406 ; hydrogen from

1674 ; used in making iron and steel, 1754 ; petrol from, 2430 ; smokeless, 2986.

Coke, Sir Edward (1552–1634). Eng. judge and politician ; held the offices of Speaker of the House of Commons, Attorney-General, and Chief Justice ; showed great brutality in prosecuting Sir Walter Raleigh.

Cola, or **Kola**, a nut, 2408.

Colbert (kŏl'-bār), **Jean Baptiste** (1619–83). France's greatest financial statesman, **868** ; quoted on taxation, 3158.

Col'chester. Port on r. Colne, Essex ; pop. 45,000 ; **869** ; oysters, 2466 ; damaged in 2nd World War ; here was sounded the last air raid siren, March 29, 1945.

Colchis (kol'-kis). Dist. in Caucasia at E. extremity of Black Sea ; in myth., land of Golden Fleece ; 229, 265.

Cold. Lack of heat ; how sensed, 3231 ; produced artificially, 1391 ; by evaporation, 1243.

Cold Front, in meteorology, 2150.

Colds, 2132 ; causes of, 1676.

Cold storage. Preserving foodstuffs by refrigeration, 1341, 1391 ; fruit industry, 1401 ; meats, 1393.

Coldstream. Scot. historic border vil. on Tweed, near famous ford ; celebrated Coldstream Guards raised by Gen. Monk in 1659.

Cold welding, 3363.

Cole, George D. H. (b. 1889). Brit. economist ; Chichele prof. of Social and Political Theory, Oxford Univ., from 1944 ; director of Nuffield Coll. Social Reconstruction survey, 1941–44 ; wrote " Guild Socialism," 1920 ; " The Intelligent Man's Guide to Post-War World," 1947 ; also detective stories, with his wife, M. I. Cole.

Coleoptera (kol-e-op'-te-ra). The beetle order, 1733 ; weevils, 3362.

Coleridge, Hartley (1796–1849). Eng. poet and essayist, eldest son of Samuel Taylor Coleridge ; as a poet, best known for a number of beautiful sonnets.

Coleridge, Samuel Taylor (1772–1834). One of England's " Lake Poets," **869**, 1214 ; his " Ancient Mariner," 101 ; Charles Lamb, 1886 ; Southey, 3028 ; Wordsworth, 3408.

Coleridge-Taylor, Samuel (1875–1912). Brit. musical composer, whose early death ended a most promising career ; set to music Longfellow's " Hiawatha."

Colet (kol'-et), **John** (c. 1467–1519). Eng. theologian, dean of St. Paul's, **870**, 2229, 2758 ; founded St. Paul's School, 2883.

Coligny (kŏ-lē-nyĕ), **Gaspard de, Admiral** (1519–72). Fr. Huguenot leader, **870** ; and Henry of Navarre, 1613.

Colijn, Hendrik (1869–1944). Dutch statesman ; Prime Minister, 1925–26 and 1933–39.

Colima (kol-ē-ma), Mexico. State on cent. w. coast ; 2,000 sq. m. ; pop. 78,800 ; cap. Colima.

Col'in Clout. Poetic name for a shepherd or countryman, used esp. by Spenser.

Collar-bone. How to give first aid to, 1294.

Collat'eral. Property pledged as security for fulfilling financial obligations.

Collective nouns, 2399.

Collective Security. A principle based upon Article 10 of the Covenant of the League of Nations, which sought to discourage aggressor nations by forming a united front with guarantees of mutual assistance, among the members of the League.

Colleges. At the universities, 3296.

Collie, Scotch, plate f. 1024.

Collier, Jeremy (1650–1726). Eng. nonjuring clergyman, writer of many controversial pamphlets ; denounces theatre, 1040.

Collier, John (1850–1934). Eng. artist ; among his best-known paintings are " The Last Voyage of Henry Hudson," " The Laboratory," " The Cheat," and " Sentence of Death " ; 1661.

Col'limator, of spectroscope, 3055.

Collingwood, Cuthbert, Baron (1750–1810). Brit. admiral ; **870** ; at Trafalgar, 3234.

Collins, Michael (1890–1922). Irish statesman ; Sinn Fein member of House of Commons (1918–22) ; became head of provisional govt. of Irish Free State in Jan. 1922 ; killed in ambush Aug. 22, 1922.

Collins, Wilkie (1824–89). Eng. novelist ; friend of Dickens, for whom he contributed much of his best work to " Household Words " and " All the Year Round " ; his stories hold the interest by reason of their excellent plots (" The Woman in White " ; " The Moonstone " ; " No Name ").

Collins, William (1721–59). Eng. poet (" The Passions " ; " To Liberty " ; " To Evening ") ; d. insane ; 1213.

Collinson, James (c. 1825–81). Eng. painter, one of the original seven of the Pre-Raphaelite brotherhood, 2681.

Collo'dion. Clear, colourless, gummy and highly inflammable liquid prepared by dissolving cellulose nitrate (pyroxylin) in equal parts of alcohol and ether, 2709 ; used in surgery ; made from cellulose, 740 ; and rayon, 2748.

Col'loids. Substances whose molecules gather into large, non-crystalline clusters, **871**, 773 ; protoplasm, 2695 ; in tanning leather, 1913.

Col'mar, Fr. Tn. of Alsace, at the base of the Vosges Mts. ; pop. 46,000 ; cotton, brewing, metal industries.

Colne, r., in Essex, flows to North Sea, 35 m. long, oyster beds ; 1225.

Col'ney Hatch. District of N.E. Middlesex, containing the L.C.C. mental hospital referred to as Colney Hatch, in 1937 renamed Friern hospital for nervous and mental disorders ; accom. for 2,000.

Colobus. White-tailed monkey, 2209.

Cologne (ko-lōn'), Ger. Cath. city on Rhine ; pop. (1935) 756,600 ; **871**, 2769 ; cathedral, 872 ; 85 per cent destroyed in 2nd World War, 872 ; 1,000-bomber raid, 3420 ; captured by Allies, 3422.

Cologne, eau de. A perfume made of alcohol scented with aromatic oils ; originally made in Cologne, 872.

Colombia. Republic, northernmost country of S. Amer. ; pop. (est.) 9,700,000 ; a. 440,000 sq. m., **872** ; map, 873 ; history, 874, 2480 ; physical features, 873.

Colombo (ko-lom-'-bō), Ceylon. Cap. and chief spt. ; pop. 284,000 ; **874**, 748.

Colon, Panama. Spt., N. terminus of Panama Canal and rly. ; pop. 44,400 ; 2487, 2489.

Co'lon. Mark of punctuation, 2705.

Colon, Cristobal. Sp. name for Christopher Columbus (q.v.).

Colonel (kêr-nel) ; badge of rank in Brit. Army, 245.

Colonial Office, headquarters of Brit. Colonial administration, 1492. See also **Crown Colony.**

Colonna, Vittoria (1490–1547). Marchioness of Pescara ; It. poet, friend of Michelangelo ; one of most beautiful characters of It. Renaissance.

Colonnade (ko-lo-nād'). In architecture, 216.

Col'onsay. One of the Hebrides, 1602.

Coloph'ony, or rosin, 2767.

Colorado (kol-o-rah'-dō). A Rocky Mountain state of U.S.A., **874** ; 104,000 sq. m. ; pop. 1,123,300 ; Grand Canyon, 1498, plate f. 1496, 1497 ; Rocky Mts., 2795 ; uranium in, 3297.

Colorado Beetle (Leptinotarsa decemlineata). Pest of the potato crop ; notifiable if found ; yellow in colour, with long black stripes on wing cases ; common in the U.S.A. and Europe, its presence in the U.K. is kept in check by severe measures ; rate of increase, 438.

Colorado Desert, 3285.

Colorado Plateau, 3285.

Colorado River, in s.w. U.S.A., remarkable for the famous Grand Canyon ;

flows to Gulf of California ; with its chief headstream it flows for 2,000 m., 874, 3190, 3285, 3287 ; Boulder Dam, f. 960 ; Grand Canyon, plate f. 1496, 1497, 1498.

Coloration, of birds' eggs, plate f. 440, 442 ; of feathers, 447, 1265 ; protective, 1550, 1551, 2692.

Colossae (ko-los'-ē). Anc. city in Phrygia, Asia Minor ; early Christian Church.

Colosseum (kol-o-sē'-um). Amphitheatre in Rome, 2800, 2802, 2803.

Colos'si of Memnon, 1118.

Colos'sians, Epistle to the. The 12th book of the New Testament, addressed by Paul to the Christians at Colossae.

Colos'sus of Rhodes. 2924, plate f. 2924, 2770.

Colour, 875 ; plates f. 876, 877, 1942 ; effect in factories, 2478 ; in paints, 875, 2478 ; of flowers, 1321 ; of rly. signals, 2739, 2740 ; rainbow, plate f. 2740, 2741 ; in spectra, plate f. 3056 ; in television, 3184.

Colour-blindness, 1254.

Colour photography, 876, plates f. 2576, 2577, 2580.

Colour printing, 876 ; in process engraving, 2689, plate f. 2688 ; Japanese, 1810.

Colour, Trooping the. Annual military ceremony on King's birthday, 877, 878.

Colours, of sports team, 877 ; of regiment, 877.

Colquhoun. Scot. surname. Pron. ko-hōōn'.

Colt, Samuel (1814–62). Amer. mfr., inventor of revolver, 1282, 1283.

Colt's-foot. Plant (Tussilago furfura) of order Compositae ; used in medicine as remedy for coughs ; yellow flowerheads appear in Feb., enormous broad leaves in summer.

Colum, Padraic (b. 1881). Irish author notably of children's books. 1966.

Colum'ba or **Colum, Saint** (521–597). Irish missionary to Picts and Scots, also called Columkille (" Colum of the churches "), because of the great number of churches and monasteries he founded ; at Iona, 1602.

Columbia (from Columbus). The feminine personification of the U.S.A.

Columbia, South Carolina, U.S.A. Cap. and seat of state univ., on r. Congaree ; pop. 62,400.

Columbia, District of (U.S.A.). See District of Columbia.

Columbia River. Formerly Oregon r., one of the largest rivers of N. Amer., 1,400 m. long, 3285 ; Canada, 578.

Col'umbine. Dancer courted by Harlequin in pantomimes, 878.

Columbine, spring flower with five-spurred blossoms, 878.

Columbium (Cb) or **Niobium** (Nb). An unimportant hard white metallic element of the tantalum sub-group ; atomic weight, 93·3 ; closely resembles tantalum, 777, 3152.

Colum'bus, Christopher (c. 1451–1506), discoverer of America, 139, **878**, 879 ; Colombia named after, 872 ; exploration in Central Amer., 744 ; Hispaniola (Dominican repub.), 1029 ; Jamaica, 1793 ; North Amer., 2379 ; Puerto Rico, 2698 ; Trinidad, 3248 ; and Red Indians, 2753 ; and West Indies, 3368 ; Isabella of Castile and, 1760 ; knowledge of navigation, 2290 ; voyages, 139, 141, 872, 916, 941.

Columbus, Ferdinand (1488–1539). Son of Christopher Columbus, whom he accompanied on 4th voyage ; wrote biography of father.

Columbus, Ohio, U.S.A. State cap. ; pop. 306,087 ; in cent. part of state on Scioto r. ; one of most important rly. centres in U.S.A. ; 2426.

Column, in architecture, 215.

Colville, Sir David John (b. 1894). Brit. politician. Sec. for Scotland 1938–40 ; Gov. of Bombay, 1943.

Colvin, Sir Sidney (1845–1927). Eng. literary and art critic, keeper of prints and drawings in Brit. Museum (1884–1912). (Lives of Landor and Keats ; Edinburgh edition of R. L. Stevenson's works).

Colza, an oil used in lamps, 1888.

Combat, trial by, 1844.

Combination lock, 1980.

Combined Operations, in 2nd World War ; army landings, 247 ; Mountbatten chief of, 2248.

Combing machine, wool, *3406*.

Combustion, 1280, 2244 ; in Bunsen burner, 616 ; explosives, 1250 ; internal combustion engine, 1735 ; oxygen in, 2466 ; phlogiston theory, 1280 ; smoke, 2986 ; spontaneous, 1280.

Comédie Française (ko'-mä-dē-frahn-säz'). Famous Paris theatre,founded in 1680 ; also called Théâtre Français ; home of the highest form of drama from the days of Molière ; rebuilt after destruction by fire in 1900.

" Comédie humaine (ko'-mä-dē-ū-mǎn') La " (" The Human Comedy "), series of novels by Balzac, 353.

Com'edy. Eng., 1049 ; Greek, 1038, Latin, 1038, 1895 ; Molière's comedy of manners, 2198 ; origin of word, 1037.

" Comedy of Errors." Play by Shakespeare in which an amusing series of mistakes arises from likeness between twin brothers and likeness between their two servants.

Comet. Astronomical phenomenon, 880, 280, *plates f. 880, 881* ; meteors, 2151.

Comet. Early passenger steamship, built for Henry Bell at Port Glasgow on the Clyde (1811–12).

Comfrey. A coarse brookside plant whose flowers vary from pale yellow to red and purple ; belongs to the order *Boraginaceae.*

Comic opera, 2436 ; Gilbert and Sullivan, 1463.

" Coming of Christ, The," by Masefield, *2118.*

Comino. Isl., 2072.

Com'inform. *Communist Information* Bureau, set up secretly at Warsaw, Oct. 1947, by Communist parties of U.S.S.R., Bulgaria, Czechoslovakia, Poland, Rumania, Yugoslavia ; the Dutch communist party joined in Dec. ; in 1948 Yugoslavia was expelled and h.q. moved from Belgrade to Bucharest.

Comintern. Shortened form of " Communist International," and applied to the 3rd international (International Working Men's Association), set up at Moscow in 1919 ; dissolved in 1943 ; 2852.

Comitadji (kom-i-tah'-jē). Lawless bands of Bulgarian fighters ; during the 1st World War they acted with the Bulgarian army in the Balkan operations.

Comi'tia centuria'ta. Rom. assembly, 2805.

Comitia tribu'ta. Rom. assembly, 2805.

Comma. Mark of punctuation, 2705.

Comma butterfly, *plate f. 632.*

Commander. Brit. naval officer whose rank is next below captain, *plate f. 2292.*

Commander-in-Chief (C.-in-C.). Formerly the highest position in the Brit. army, abolished in 1904 ; during times of war the officer commanding an army in the field receives the title.

Commandments, The Ten, 2235.

Commando (kom-ahn'-dō). Swift moving mounted troops used by Boers in S. African War ; from 1940 the term was used for shock troops of exceptional physique, specially trained in amphibious warfare ; for combat unarmed, or with small arms, knife, bayonet, etc., also for demolition work, and able to live off the country. Disbanded in 1945.

Command Performance. Theatrical performance given at the express request of, and in the presence of, the Sovereign.

Commen'sal. A living organism which forms partnership with another. *See* Symbiosis.

Commerce, beginnings in barter, 2200 ; customs and tariffs, 944 ; modern fairs 1256, *1257*, 2846 ; geographical influences, 1232, 1517, 1576 ; guilds, 1553 ; Hanse, 1575 ; railways, 2734 ;

ships and ocean routes, *2136*, 2945. *History*: *see* under each country, ancient, medieval, and modern ; and names of chief commercial cities and products.

Commines (ko-mēn'), Philippe de (*c.* 1445–*c.* 1511). Fr. historian called " first truly modern writer " (" Memoirs," one of classics of history).

Committee of Public Safety. Fr., 2789.

Commodore. Temporary rank in Brit. navy, between rear-admiral and captain ; in merchant navy, rank given to senior captain of a line ; in air force (air commodore), rank between group captain and air vice-marshal.

Com'modus, Lucius Aelius Aurelius (A.D. 161–192). Rom. emperor 180–192, son of Marcus Aurelius ; a brutal tyrant, he was assassinated.

Common, land, 880.

Common Denominator, in fractions. 1356.

Common Entrance. Examination, 2886.

" Commoner, The Great." Nickname of William Pitt the elder.

Common law, origin of, 1902.

Common Pleas, Court of, 922

Commons, House of. In Brit. Parl. : debating chamber, *2523* ; foundation, 1489 ; hat etiquette, 1584 ; origin of, 2521, *2522*, 2221 ; in Canadian Parl., 684.

Commonwealth, The. In Eng. (1649–59), 1198, 2177.

Com'mune of Paris (1871), 1385, 2518.

Commu'nion. *See* Eucharist.

Com'munism. Form of social organization, 881 ; Marx and, 2113, 2996 ; in Russia, 2849 ; Bulgaria, 614 ; China, 814 ; Czechoslovakia, 954 ; Hungary, 1657 ; Poland, 2643 ; Rumania, 2841 ; Yugoslavia, 3440, 345.

Com'munist Manifesto, 881, 2113, 2996.

Com'mutator. In electric motors, 2239 ; in dynamo, *1061.*

Como (kō'-mō). Beautiful lake in N. It. at foot of Alps, 55⅓ sq. m., city of Como (pop. 53,200) at s. extremity, 1763.

Companion of Honour (C.H.). Order, 2449.

Company. Unit in an army ; it now consists of three platoons in the Brit. army.

Comparative anatomy, 1245.

Comparison. Of adjective, 27 ; of adverb, 29.

Compass, mariner's, 881, 2290 ; aero, *882*, 2293 ; gyroscopic, 1560 ; a magnet, 2061.

Compensating pendulum, 2543.

Compiègne (kom-pyän). Fr. historic tn. in N. on Oise, pop. 18,200 ; Joan of Arc taken prisoner by Eng. in, 1831 ; 1918 ; Armistice signed in Forest of, 3414 ; also Fr.-Ger. armistice of 1940, 3417.

" Compleat Angler," by Izaak Walton, 3339.

Complex sentence, 2921.

Compline. A prayer, 2213.

Compluten'sian Polyglot Bible, 427 ; the work of Cardinal Ximenes de Cisneros and produced 1502–1517.

Compositae (kom-poz'-i-tē). Family of plants with composite flowers, 1321, 1322.

Composite Aircraft, Short-Mayo. A flying boat and seaplane linked together for the take-off, 51.

Composite Order, in architecture, *213.*

Composition. In painting, 1274.

Compositor. In printing, 2346.

Compound. In chemistry, 766.

Compound engines, 3084.

Compound eye. An eye composed of numerous simple eyes, *1253*, 1730 ; of dragon-fly, 1034.

Compound leaves, 1916.

Compound microscope, 2163.

Compound motor, electric, *2239*, 2240.

Compound sentence, 2920.

Compressed air, 90, 1016 ; in brakes, 2246 ; in diving apparatus, 1020 ; in gas turbine,1425 ; in glass-blowing, 1473 ; pneumatic appliances, 2633 ; spray-gun, 2478 ; in tunnel construction, 3257.

Compressed air appliances, 2246, 2478, 2632.

Compressor ; of fuel in i.c. engine, 1736 ; in gas turbine, 1425 ; of refrigerator, *1392.*

Comp'ton, Denis Charles Scott (b. 1918). Eng. all-round cricketer ; scored 1,000 runs when 18, in first season with Middx. ; on Australian tour 1946–47 scored century in each innings of Adelaide test ; in 1947 his aggregate, 3,816, with 18 centuries, broke all records, and he took 73 wickets with slow left-arm bowling ; an Arsenal footballer from 1935–36 season.

Compton, Edward (1854–1918). Eng. actor, son of Henry Compton ; first appeared in London, in 1877 at Drury Lane ; founded the Edward Compton Company which toured the country for about 30 years ; Fay Compton, actress, is his daughter, and Compton Mackenzie, author, his son.

Compton, Henry (1805–77). Eng. actor, most successful as a Shakespearean clown.

Compton Wynyates. Manor-house in Warwickshire ; magnificent example of Tudor domestic architecture.

Compulsory Service. See Conscription.

Compurga'tion, trial by, 1843.

Comte (kawnt), Auguste (1798–1857). Fr. philosopher, founder of Positivist school of philosophy.

Comus (kō'-*mus*). In late Gk. myth., god of revelry ; in Milton's great poem, enchanter, son of Circe, who offers a brutalizing draught to travellers to accomplish their ruin.

" Comus." Poem by Milton, 2176.

Concave lens, 1925.

Concave mirror, 2191.

Concepcion (kon-sep-si-ōn), Chile. City on Bio-bio r., 8 m. from Bay of Concepcion ; pop. 92,364 ; trade centre for agric. region ; 5 times destroyed by earthquake, including 1939.

Concerto (kon-chär'-tō). Musical composition, 2264.

Conch (kongk) or concha. In architecture, term for the concave ribless surface of a vault ; also an apse or the dome of an apse.

Conciergerie (kon-syär-zhe-rē). Prison in Paris, 2102.

Concord, New Hampshire, U.S.A. Cap. of state, on Merrimac r. ; pop. 27,170 ; granite, silverware, electrical appliances, 2341.

Concor'dat. A type of treaty, 3240 ; Fr. (1801), Napoleon's work, 2276 ; of 1929, 3307.

Concord Bridge. Battle, 144.

Concorde, Place de la (plahs de lah kon-kord), Paris, *2515.*

Concrete, 883, 604, 2713 ; and Cement, 742 ; mixer, 885, 2633 ; moulding, 885 ; mulberry harbours, 2251 ; reinforced, *883, 884* ; Roman, 883.

Condé (kawn'-dä), Louis I de Bourbon, Prince of (1530–69), Fr. general and Huguenot leader, 870.

Condé, Louis II de Bourbon, Prince of (1621–86), called " The Great Condé." Fr. general ; won victory of Rocroy, 1643, which ended Span. and began Fr. military predominance.

Con'dell, Henry (d. 1627), Eng. actor associated with Shakespeare, 2933 ; 2936.

Condensa'tion of water vapour, 851.

Condensed milk, 2174.

Condenser. In electricity, 1132 ; for high-frequency currents, 1624 ; in induction coil, 1721 ; Leyden jar a form of, 1929 ; microphone, 2162 ; at power station, *2673*, 2676 ; variable, 1132 ; wireless, 3392.

Condensing steam engines, 3085.

Condillac (kawn-dē-yak), Étienne Bonnot de (1715–80). Fr. philosopher member of French Academy.

Con'diments and spices, 3060.

Condor. Large Andean vulture, 885 3330 ; young, 446.

Condorcet (kawn-dor-sä), Marie Jean Caritat, Marquis de (1743–94). Fr mathematician, philosopher, and revolutionist ; as member of Legislative Assembly laid foundation of Fr educational system.

Condottieri (kon-dot-tyä'-rē). Mercenary forces, 13th to 15th cents., 251

Conduction of heat, *1594*, 1595, 1597, *1598.*

Conductiv'ity, electrical, 1128 ; silver, 2973 ; skin effect in, 1624.

Conductor, electrical, 1128 ; in electric motor, 2239 ; magnetic field, 2063.

Conductor, of orchestra, 2446.

Cone, of coniferous trees, *2610.*

Cone, of volcano, 3328.

Cone shell, *2943.*

Coney Island, seaside resort of New York City, of which it is a part, 2353.

Confec'tionery, chocolate bars, 862 ; use of glucose in, 1477.

Confederate States of America. Name by which those states which broke from the union in 1860–1 were known ; S. Carolina was the first to act.

"Confessions of an English Opium Eater," by De Quincey, 994.

Confirmation. Church sacrament by which one is admitted into full Church membership, 886.

Confu'cianism, commonly called a religion. System of ethics taught by Confucius, 886, 809 ; in Japan, 1798.

Confucius (kon-fū'-shŭs), (551–478 B.C.), Chinese philosopher, founder of Confucianism, 886 ; tomb of, *887.*

Conger eel. A large salt-water type, 1093.

Congo, Belgian. Colony of equatorial Africa ; 909,000 sq. m. ; pop. over 10,000,000 ; 887, 72 ; map, *888* ; formed, 3077, 72 ; jungles, 68 ; Leopold II, 1928 ; rubber, 2833 ; uranium, 3297.

Congo, French. Colony of equatorial Africa ; 960,000 sq. m. ; pop. over 3,000,000 ; 888.

Congo, Portuguese. *See* Angola.

Congo, River, Africa. One of the longest r. in the world ; length. 3,000 m. ; 887, 68, 72 ; basin, *map, 888*, 68, 72 ; peoples, *889* ; Stanley's explorations, 72, 3077 ; upper course discovered by Livingstone, 72, 1970.

Congrega'tionalism. A religious denomination ; membership in Brit. over 1,000,000 ; 1390, 2707.

Congregations, Roman. Administrative commissions to aid Pope, 2495.

Congress. The legislative branch of the govt. of U.S.A., composed of Senate and House of Representatives, 3290 ; Capitol, 3344 ; library, *3343*, 3344.

Congress Hall, Philadelphia, 2566.

Congressional Medal, in United States, 2249.

Con'greve, William (1670–1729). Eng. dramatist, one of greatest writers of comedy ; plots are intricate, characters often gross and heartless, but brilliant (" The Double-Dealer " ; " Love for Love," *1041* ; " The Way of the World ") ; 1040.

Congreve, Sir William (1772–1828). Brit. soldier, inventor of military rockets, 2794.

Conic Projection, of maps, 2094.

Con'ifers. Cone-bearing trees, 890, *891*, 3245 ; classification, 2620 ; world distribution, 3246.

Coningham (kun'-ing-ham), Air Marshal Sir Arthur (1895–1948). Australian airman ; joined N.Z. Expeditionary Force, 1914 ; his record flight Cairo to Kano won him A.F.C. in 1925 ; in 1941 A.O.C. Western Desert ; A.O.C.-in-C. 2nd Tactical Air Force in Nov. 1944 ; Aug. 1945, A.O.C.-in-C. Flying Training Command ; retired from R.A.F. 1947 ; lost life in Tudor IV Star Tiger disaster on Azores to Bermuda flight, Jan. 1948.

Con'iston. L. in Lancashire, 4 m. w. of Hawkshead ; about 6 m. long ; on its shores are houses where Ruskin and Tennyson resided, 1890.

Conjuga'tion, of verbs, 3314.

Conjunc'tions, in grammar, 891, 1494, 2921.

Connacht (or Connaught). Smallest province of Ire., in w. Eire. Area 6,611 sq. m. ; pop. 500,339.

Connaught (kon'-awt), Arthur, Duke of (1850–1942). Eng. prince, 3rd son Queen Victoria ; Gov.-Gen. of Canada (1911–16) ; Field-Marshal of Brit. Army (appointed 1902) ; father of Lady Patricia Ramsay, and of

Prince Arthur of Connaught (1883–1938), who was Gov.-Gen. of S. Africa (1920–24).

Connecticut (ko-net'-i-kut), southernmost of New England states, U.S.A., 5,009 sq. m. ; pop. 1,710,000 ; mfg. region ; 891.

Connecticut River, U.S.A. Largest stream in New England ; 370 m. long ; 2118.

Connecting rod, *3086.*

Connemar'a. Picturesque mountainous dist. in Galway, Eire ; has many fine bays and lakes.

Connor, Ralph. The pen-name of Charles W. Gordon (1860–1937), Canadian missionary and novelist (" The Sky Pilot," " Corporal Cameron "), 685.

Conrad. Holy Roman Emperors. For list *see* Holy Roman Empire.

Conrad II (c. 900–1039), emperor, founder of Salian line.

Conrad III (1093–1152), emperor. Founder of Hohenstaufen line ; leads 2nd crusade, 936.

Conrad IV (1228–1254), emperor, son of Frederick II ; became king in 1237.

Conrad, Joseph (1857–1924). Eng. novelist, b. in Poland, 891, *892*, 1215, 2403 ; 2641.

Conscription. Compulsory military service ; the modern army, 250, 3416 ; Bill (1916), 3410.

Conservation of energy, 1160, 2592.

Conservatives. Brit. political party, 892, 1490 ; primrose as emblem, 2684.

Consis'tory, meeting of cardinals.

Consols. Short for Consolidated Stock. Originally applied to the 3 per cent consolidated annuities, certain perpetual and lottery annuities consolidated by an Act of 1731. Long looked upon as the standard security of the London market. Term has of late years been applied to other securities.

Con'stable, John (1776–1837), Eng. landscape painter, called founder of modern school ; 893, 1181, 2476 ; " The Cornfield," *1188* ; " The Hay Wain," *892* ; water-colours, 3353.

Constable, police officer, *2649.*

Con'stance or Konstanz, Ger. city of Baden on L. Constance at efflux of Rhine ; pop. 31,000.

Constance, Council of (1414–18), *818, 1661.*

Constance, Lake (Bodensee), on N.E. frontier between Switzerland and Germany, formed by the Rhine ; divides into two arms, the Untersee and the Ueberlingersee ; 3140.

Constanta, Rumania. Port on Black Sea ; pop. (est. 1945) 79,700 ; Anc. Tomi or Constantiana, Ovid's place of exile ; taken by Central Powers in 1st World War ; 2839, 2840. Occupied by Germany 1940–44.

Constant Combining Weights, Law of, 295, 767.

Con'stantine I (1868–1923), king of Greece ; succeeded in 1913 ; abdicated in 1922 ; his consort was Sophie, elder daughter of Frederick III of Germany, who died in 1932 ; 1525.

Constantine XIII (1394–1453), last Byzantine emperor.

Constantine the Great (c.288–337). Rom. emperor, 817, 893, *894* ; founded Constantinople, 894, 1761 ; Jerusalem, 1821 ; rebuilds Byzantium, 635, 2812.

Constantine, Algeria. Fortified city on natural citadel in N.E. ; pop. 106,830 ; leather, woollens ; Rom. remains ; rebuilt A.D. 313 by Constantine, 117.

Constantine, Arch of, 2819.

Constantinople. City of Turkey, was cap. of former Turkish Empire ; now known as Istanbul ; during Byzantine Empire, 635, 637 ; fall of, 1238 ; Justinian and, 1844 ; and Renaissance, 2764 ; origin of name, 894 ; Turks take, 3264.

Constan'tinus (c.250–306), Rom. emperor ; father of Constantine the Great, 893.

Constella'tion, 894, *895*, 3079 ; also name for U.S. air liner, put on trans-

Atlantic service in 1946, 315 m.p.h., four 1,800 h.p. engines.

Constitution. Organic law or principle of govt. of a nation or society, usually in written document ; Brit., 1490 ; U.S.A., 3290.

Constitutional Law, 1903.

Constrictors, snakes, 2990.

Con'sul, Rom. magistrate, 2805.

Contact lens, spectacle lens worn under eyelid, *3055.*

Continent. Great land mass of the globe, 896 ; origin of, 2596.

Continental climate, 840.

Continental Divide. Watershed in Rocky Mt. region between streams flowing to Atlantic and those flowing to Pacific.

Continental shelf, 2596, 2413.

Continental system, of Napoleon I, 2276.

Contour map, *2096.*

Contract Bridge. Card game, development of the game of bridge, introduced in 1912.

Controls, of aeroplane, 41, *42, 43* ; car, *2242.*

Convec'tion of heat, 1597, *1598.*

Convention. A form of treaty, 3240.

Convention, The National. Fr. assembly (1792–5), 1396 ; condemns Louis XVI, 2030 ; and Robespierre, 2789. *See* French Revolution.

Conversation piece, in English art, 1182.

Converter, in copper smelter, *907* ; Bessemer, *421.*

Converter, electric. Device for changing alternating current to direct.

Convex lens, 1925.

Convex mirror, 2191.

Conveyors. Moving belts or platforms carrying work past operatives in factories, 896, *897* ; in motor vehicle mfr., 2242 ; at power station, 2673.

Convicts, 2687.

Convolvulus. Genus of twining plants, 898.

Con'voy. *See* Atlantic, Battle of.

Con'way or Aberconway, Wales. Spt. tn. in Caernarvonshire, 13 m. N.E. of Bangor ; pop. 8,769 ; famous castle ; suspension bridge, *3336.*

Conway, William Martin Conway, 1st Baron (1856–1937). English traveller, scholar and explorer ; Himalayas, Alps, Andes (Aconcagua, 23,000 ft., 1898).

Co'ny. Rabbit fur, 2722.

Cook, Captain James (1728–79). Eng. explorer and navigator, 898 ; at Botany Bay, *308*, 310 ; British Columbia, 580 ; circumnavigates Antarctic Continent, 2645 ; death, *899* ; explores Australian coasts, 310, 581 ; in Hawaiian Isls., *899*, 1587 ; discovered New South Wales, 2344 ; New Zealand, 2360 ; Pacific exploration, 2472 ; Victoria, 3321.

Cook, Thomas (1808–92). Famous English travel agent.

Cook, Mt. In Alps of the South Island, New Zealand ; highest peak in Australasia (12,349 ft.).

Cooke, Sir William (1806–79). Eng. electrical engineer ; built first Eng. telegraph line ; 3164.

Cookery, 900 ; bread baking, 554 ; by dielectric heating, 1625 ; at high altitudes, 3084. *See also* Food.

Cook Islands or Hervey Archipelago. In s. Pacific ; 111 sq. m. ; annexed to New Zealand in 1901 ; 2473 ; *map, 2358.*

Cook Strait. Between N. and S. Isls., N.Z., 2357, *897.*

Coolgardie. Tn. in w. Australia, in important gold-mining region ; 3368.

Coolidge (kōō'-lij), Calvin (1871–1933). Thirtieth President of U.S.A., 3292.

Coolidge, William David (b. 1873), Amer. scientist, researched at Massachusetts Institute of Technology and General Elec. Co.'s labs. on X-rays, cathode rays, etc. ; invented X-ray generator, 3432, *diag. 3056* ; invented tungsten filament lamps, 3253, 3432 ; gave name to the Coolidge tube, *3056.*

Coolie. Chinese labourer, 902.

Cooling towers, at power station, *2676.*

Coon or racoon, 2722 ; fur, 1412.

Cooper, Sir Alfred Duff (b. 1890). English politician. Sec. of State for War (1935); First Lord of Admiralty (1937); resigned from Cabinet in Oct. 1938, as protest against Munich agreement; Min. of Information in Churchill's Cabinet, May 1940; Chancellor of Duchy of Lancaster 1941 and 1943; Resident Min. for Far Eastern Affairs at Singapore 1941–42; Brit. ambassador to Paris, Sept. 1944–47; made K.C.M.G. in 1948. Wrote Lives of Talleyrand and Earl Haig.

Cooper, Sir Astley Paston (1768–1841). Brit. anatomist and surgeon, *2134*; surgeon at Guy's Hosp. from 1800; pres. of Coll. of Surgeons 1827 and 1836; operated on George IV in 1820; the Cooper Prize Essay at Guy's commemorates him.

Cooper, Gladys (b. 1888). Eng. actress; graduated from musical comedies to more serious plays (" The Last of Mrs. Cheyney," " Cynara "); films, (" The Eleventh Commandment," " The Iron Duke ").

Cooper, James Fenimore (1789–1851). Amer. novelist, famed for vivid Indian and sea tales, **902**, 2403, 3293.

Cooper, Samuel (1609–72). Eng. miniaturist, *933*, 1177.

Co-operative Societies. Associations of consumers or producers for economical buying or selling, **903**; origin, 2996.

Coorg. Province of India adjacent to Mysore; a. 1,500 sq. m.; pop. 168,000.

Coot. Water-bird common in Eng.; black, with white bar across wings, and white bald spot on forehead; toes are edged with a scalloped membrane; 2734.

Coote, Sir Eyre (1726–83). Brit. gen., 1582.

Copais. Former lake in Boeotia, Greece, 1526.

Co'pal. A resin, 1558, 2768; African sources, 2367.

Copan (kō-pahn'). Ruined city of W. Honduras, with remains of Mayan civilization.

Cope, Charles West (1811–90). Eng. painter : "The First Trial by Jury," *1843*.

Copenha'gen. Cap. of Denmark; pop. 890,000; **904**, *991*, *993*; Hans Andersen in, 152; in Ger. occupn. 1940–45, 904.

Copenhagen, battle of (1801), 905, 2313, 3277.

Copernicus (kō-per'-ni-kus), **Nicolaus** (1473–1543). Polish astronomer, **905**, 276; theory developed by Galileo, 1415; by Newton, 1512.

Cophetua (kō-fet'-ū-a). Legendary king. **905**.

Copley, John Singleton (1737–1815), one of the leading painters of the Anglo-American school; born Boston, U.S.A., settled in London; R.A., 1779; many fine historical paintings and, in America, portraits.

Coppée (kop'-ā), **François Edouard Joachim** (1842–1908). Fr. poet, dramatist, and novelist.

Coppélia (kop-ā-lya). Ballet to music by Delibes; choreographer Saint-Léon; prod. 1870; danced by Adeline Genée; a classic of the Diaghilev and Vic-Wells repertories.

Copper (Cu). A reddish metallic element, known from the dawn of history; atomic weight 63·57; found native near Lake Superior; melts at 1980° F.; the Romans obtained it from Cyprus and thus named it cuprum; **906**; alloys, 93, 135, 2365; copper-plating, 1140; in diet, 2149, 2468; first use, *2083*, 2084; origin of name, 952; oxide as rectifier, 2751; poison, 2638; properties, 776; in rayon mfr., 2748; refined by electrolysis, 1137; smelting, 906, 907; specific gravity, 3054; sulphate, 3116. *See under copper-producing countries, e.g.* Mexico, etc.

Cop'peras. Ferrous sulphate, 3116.

Copperfield, David. Hero of Dickens's novel, David Copperfield," 1012, 1013.

Cop'ra. Dried coconut meat, 864; Ceylon, 748; Pacific isls., 2472; 1272; *2869*; Zanzibar, 3441.

Coptic Church, 1098.

Copts. Native Egyptians descended from anc. stock, 1098; 3191.

Copy-book, Greek, *509*.

Copyright. The exclusive right of property of an author, composer, or artist. Duration is for life of author and 50 years after; of a photo., 50 years from making of negative. Berne international convention, 1886, covers all countries except U.S.A.

Coquelin (kōk'-lan), **Benoît Constant** (1841–1909). The greatest of modern Fr. actors; most famous role, " Cyrano de Bergerac."

Coquet (kok-et), r. in Northumberland, Eng., flowing to the North Sea; 40 m. long.

Cor'acle. Saucer-shaped boat used in anc. Brit., *482*, 484; in Wales, *plate f. 3337*.

Coral. Marine polyp with limy " skeleton," **908**. *plates f. 908, 909*; 2104; atolls of Pacific, 2471; in geology, 1433; Great Barrier Reef, 307; life history, 2104.

" Coral Island," novel by R. M. Ballantyne (1825–94).

Coral lily, 1947.

Coral Sea. Part of Pacific Ocean N.E. of Australia, named from numerous coral islands; Allied naval victory over Japan, May 1942, 2473, 3293.

Cor'am, Thomas (1668–1751). Brit. sea captain and philanthropist; estab. a Hospital in Hatton Garden; in 1741 for foundling children; died poor.

Corbassi.re, Glacier de, Switzerland, *plate f. 3140*.

Corbel. A form of bracket used in Gothic architecture for supporting the ends of timbers, parapets, arches, floors, etc.

Corbière Lighthouse, Jersey, *752*.

Corbusier, Le. *See* Le Corbusier.

Corday, Charlotte (1768–93). Fr. revolutionary heroine; guillotined; murders Marat, 1396, 2096.

Corde'lia. In Shakespeare's " King Lear," the youngest and favourite daughter of Lear, 1858.

Cordeliers (kōr-de'-lyā) (Society of the Friends of the Rights of Man and of the Citizen). Fr. revolutionary club; first to demand a republic; popularized motto " Liberty, Equality, Fraternity "; leaders guillotined in 1794.

Cordillera (kor-dil-yā'-ra) (Span. " rope " or " chain "). Great mountainous mass in w. N. Amer. and S. Amer. extending from Alaska to Cape Horn, 153, 2380, 2384, 3285. Term applied originally only to the Andes.

Cordite. A brownish-yellow translucent explosive powder.

Cordoba (kōr'-dō-ba), Argentina. City in N. centre, on Rio Primero; pop. 287,598; univ. (founded 1613); exports livestock, wool, hides; observatory.

Cordouan (kor-dwahn), **Tour de, a** famous lighthouse, 1945.

Cordova (kor'-dō-va), or **Cordoba.** City in s. Spain, on the Guadalquivir; pop. 148,990; founded by Romans; makes textiles, silver filigree work, cordovan leather, 1914, 3776; mosque, *3787*.

Cordova, Caliphate of, in S. Spain; founded by Moors in 8th cent., with city of Cordova as centre and 8 other cities subject to its monarch, 2227.

Cordovan leather, 1914, *3032*.

Cor'duroy, ribbed cloth; used in mfr. of clothing.

Core, electrical; iron bar within windings of induction coil, 1720; in electro-magnets, 2063.

Corelli (ko-rel'-lē), **Marie** (1864–1924). Brit. novelist; numerous melodramatic romances with religious or ethical undertone (" Romance of Two Worlds "; " The Sorrows of Satan "; " The Master Christian "; " The Life Everlasting ").

Corfu (kor-foo') or **Kerkira** (anc. Corcyra), most northerly of Ionian

Isl., belongs to Greece; 277 sq. m.; pop. 114,620; *map*, *1518*; olives, fruit, wine, honey; cap. Corfu (pop. 32,000); bombarded and occupd. by It., Sept. 1–27, 1923; occupd. by It. and Ger. 1941–44.

Corian'der. A spice, 3062.

Corinna (ko-rin'-a) (about 500 B.C.). Gk. lyric poetess, famous for her beauty and victory over Pindar in five poetic contests.

Cor'inth or **Corinthus.** City of Greece, called New Corinth to distinguish it from anc. ruined city; almost destroyed by earthquake in 1928; pop. 6,000; 1523; burned by Romans, 1524; gives name to currants, 944.

Corinth Canal, *689*.

Corinth, Gulf of, 1517, 1526, *map*, *1518*.

Corin'thian architecture, *215*, 213.

Corinthians, Epistles to, 2529.

Corinto. Chief port of Nicaragua, 2364.

Coriolanus (ko-ri-ō-lā'-nus), **Gaius Marcius** (5th cent. B.C.). Rom. patrician who, legend says, sought revenge for slights by leading an enemy (Volscian) army against Rome but relinquished vengeance at plea of his mother and his wife; basis of Shakespeare's " Coriolanus," *1041*.

Cork. Bark of cork-oak trees, **909**; Portugal, 909, 2658; Spain, 3032; specific gravity, 3054.

Cork. Marit. co. of province of Munster, Eire; 2,885 sq. m.; pop. 346,500; **910**.

Cork. 2nd city of Eire, co. tn. of Co. Cork; pop. 81,000; 910, 1749.

Cork Harbour. Splendid landlocked basin of Eire; 1 m. wide at the entrance, with extreme breadth of 8 m.; contains Great Island, on which stands Cobh (Queenstown).

Corm. A bulb-like stem, 612; of crocus, 932.

Cor'morant. A web-footed bird related to pelican, *814*; 2931.

Corn. Name given in a general sense to cereals and the grain produced by them; in U.S.A. applied to maize in particular, 2068; cutting in Devon, *83*. *See* Cereals, Maize, Wheat, etc.

Corncrake, or land-rail, 2734.

Cor'nea. Part of the eye, 1252.

Corneille (kor-nā-ē), **Pierre** (1606–84). Dramatist, " father of Fr. tragedy," **910**, 1380; Racine compared with 2725.

Corne'lia (2nd cent. B.C.). Rom. matron, daughter of Scipio Africanus, mother of the Gracchi. " These are my jewels," she said, showing her children to a friend who asked to see her ornaments, 1493.

Cornelius (kor-nē'-li-us), **Peter von** (1783–1867). Ger. painter; revived mural painting and founded Munich school of art (" Last Judgement ").

Cornell University, at Ithaca, New York State. One of the leading univs. of U.S.A.

Cor'net. A musical instrument, *1644*, 2267.

Cornflower. Garden flower, **910**, *911*.

Cornhill. Street in London, 2010.

Cornish stone or **feldspar,** 1265, 2670.

Corn Laws. In Eng. history, a series of laws extending from 1436 to 1846 placing restrictions upon grain trade in Ireland, 1746; Peel repeals 2535, 3278.

Cor'no, Mt., in Apennines, 184.

Corn poppy, *2655*.

Corns. Horny thickening of epidermis

Corvette', a small warship; name revived for a type of escort vessel in 2nd World War, 2296.

Corn'wall. Co. in extreme s.w. Eng. 1,356 sq. m.; pop, 317,950; **911** china clay, *912*; granite, 1499 Phoenician trade with, *1201*; 3215 and titanium, 3216.

Cornwall, Duchy of. Crown property inherited by the eldest son of the King of Eng., situated in Cornwall Devon and London; the duchy was created in 1337; 911.

Cornwal'lis, Charles, Marquess (1738–1805). Brit. general whose surrender at Yorktown in 1781 ended Amer. War of Independence, 146.

Corn'well, John Travers (1899–1916). Heroic boy sailor, who, in spite of being mortally wounded, while serving on his ship Chester at the battle of Jutland (1916), gallantly continued at his post ; he died two days later in hospital, his bravery being recognized by the posthumous award of the Victoria Cross.

Corol'la. Petal structure of a flower, 1321.

Corol'lary, in geometry, 1438.

Coroman'del Coast, India. Part of the E. coast of S. India, 1691.

Coro'na, of sun, 3120, 1079.

Coronado (kōr-ō-nah'-dō), **Francisco Vasquez** (about 1500–45). Sp. explorer of s.w. U.S.A., 141.

Coronation, 912, 913.

" Coronation." British stream-lined express locomotives ; the " Coronation Scot " train, 1988, 1990.

Coronation Chair, in Westminster Abbey, 913.

Coronation robes, 913.

Coronation Stone, in Westminster Abbey, 913.

Coronel (kō-rō-nel'), Chile. Spt. 25 m. s. of Concepcion ; naval battle, Nov. 1, 1914, in which Brit. cruiser squadron under Admiral Cradock was defeated by Germans under Admiral von Spee, 3411.

Coroner's jury, 1843.

Cor'onet. Small crown, worn as a head-dress on state occasions by the nobility, and varying according to the rank of the wearer, 935.

Corot (kor'-ō), **Jean Baptiste** (1796–1875). Fr. landscape painter, 913, 1378 ; " Dance of the Nymphs," 1274, 1275 ; " The Pool," 914.

Coro'zo or tagua nuts, 632, 1788, 2408.

Cor'poral. Non-commissioned officer in Brit. army, ranking next below a sergeant, 245.

Corpora'tion. A body of persons (corporation aggregate) vested by law with the power to carry out certain acts ; examples are the B.B.C., municipal corporations ; there are also corporations sole, such as a bishop.

Corporative State, and Fascism, 1262.

Corps. A body of troops consisting of two or more divisions.

Corpus Christi College, Cambridge, 668 ; Oxford, 2464.

Corpus juris civilis (body of civil law), compiled by Justinian.

Cor'puscle, of blood, 474, 475.

Corpus'cular theory of light, 2349.

Correggio (kor-rej'-ō), **Antonio Allegri** (1494–1534). It. painter, master of use of light and shadow and of flesh painting, 1785, 2557, 2766.

Corregidor (kor-rej'-i-dōr). Philippine Isls. Fortified isl. in Manila Bay. Occupied by Japan 1942–44. Ceded by U.S.A. to republic of the Philippines in 1947.

Correspondence, good form in, 1228.

Corrib (kor-rib), **Lough.** Second largest lake of Ire., in cos. Galway and Mayo, Eire ; nearly 70 sq. m. in area ; contains numerous small isls.

Corrodentia (ko-rō-den'-sha). Order of insects.

Corrosion. The wearing away of metals or other materials by chemical agents, as in the formation of rust ; prevented by zinc, 3444. In some manufacturing processes acids are used as corrosive agents, as in the etching of copper plates with nitric acid, or of glass with hydrofluoric acid.

Corrosive poisons, 2638.

Corrosive sublimate, or bichloride of mercury, 2146, 2638.

Corsairs, or Barbary pirates, 2612.

Corsica. Fr. isl. in Mediterranean ; 3,367 sq. m ; pop. 268,000 ; 914, 915; map, 2136 ; Napoleon, 2275 ; in Ger. and It. occupn., 1940–43, 914.

Corsican pine, 2610.

Cort, Henry (1740–1800). Eng. inventor and ironmaster, 1758.

Corte-Real (kôr'-tā rä-al'), **Gaspar** (c.1450–c.1501). Port. explorer, 142.

Cortes (kôr'-tez). National legislative assembly of Sp., 3038.

Cortes, Hernando (1485–1547). Sp. explorer, conqueror of Mexico, 914, 141, plate f. 2158 ; conquers Aztecs, 325 ; Cent. Amer., 744.

Cor'tex. Any outer layer, such as the bark, rind, or outer coverings of plants, and the outer rind of any tissue or structure of the human or animal frame.

Cortot (kôr'-tō), **Alfred** (b. 1877). French pianist, born Switzerland ; foremost pianist of French school.

Corun'dum. An oxide of aluminium, 1157.

Corunna (ko-run'-na) or Coruña, Sp. Spt. on N.W. coast ; pop. 112,096 ; sailing port of " Invincible Armada," (1588) ; repulse of Fr. by Brit. under Sir John Moore in Peninsular War in 1809, 2227, 3031.

Corvidae (kôr'-vi-dē). Crow family, including raven, rook, jackdaw, magpie, jay.

Corvi'nus. See Matthias I.

Cor'vus. Crow genus of family Corvidae, 935, 2065, 2747.

Corybantes (kor-i-ban'-tēz). Mythical attendants of goddess Cybele whom they honoured by frenzied dancing in mountains and woodlands to the sound of flutes, tambourines, and cymbals.

Cosette (kō-set'). Little girl in " Les Misérables " cared for by Jean Valjean, the ex-convict who becomes a reformed character and prospers. Cosette eventually marries Marius whose life Valjean saves in the revolution of 1830.

Cos'grave, William Thomas (b. 1880). Ir. statesman ; took a leading part in Irish govt. and was appointed Pres. of Dail Eireann 1922, and re-elected 1927 and 1930. Leader of Opposition 1932–44.

Cosimo de' Medici (kō'-ze-mō dā med'-i-chē) (1389–1464). Florentine banker, politician, art patron, 2131.

Cosmati work. A decorative art created by the Cosmati family in Rome in 12th and 13th centuries ; inlay made by combining mosaics, porphyry, marbles, etc., found in ruins of Rome ; used in architecture, church interiors, and furniture.

Cosmic rays, form of radiation of unknown origin, 2729 ; wavelength of, 1942.

Cos'sack, H.M.S. Brit. destroyer ; under Capt. P. L. Vian rescued 299 Brit. seamen from the Altmark (see Altmark in f-i.) ; bombarded shore batteries at half mile range in second battle of Narvik in 1940 ; May 1940 in action against Bismarck ; on Nov. 10 torpedoed and sunk in Atlantic.

Cos'sacks. Rus. cavalrymen, renowned for daring and horsemanship, 916.

Cossettes, pieces of sugar beet, 3114.

Costa Rica (kos'ta rē-ka). Republic of Cent. Amer. ; 23,000 sq. m. ; pop. 725,000, 917; capital, San José; large coffee exports ; map, 743 ; conquered by Spaniards, 744 ; in Feb. 1948 the govt. and the president annulled the presidential election ; civil war followed, and country was governed by a revolutionary junta pending new constitution, and official army was disbanded.

Cos'tello, John Aloysius (b. 1891). Irish statesman ; member of Fine Gael party ; in Feb. 1948 prime min. of a coalition govt., 1749, re-placing De Valera, 998.

Cos'ter, Lourens (15th cent.), Dutch printer, 2686.

Costes, Dieudonné (b. 1892). Fr. airman. Made non-stop flight Paris-New York, the first in this direction, in Sept. 1930.

Cos'way, Richard (1742–1821). Most brilliant Eng. miniature painter of his day ; painted Mrs. Fitzherbert, Mme. Du Barry, and other ladies of fashion, 1177.

Cotentin. Norman peninsula of Fr., 2377.

Cot'man, John Sell (1782–1842). Eng. landscape painter ; 917, 1181, 3353 ; " Greta Bridge," 917, " Wherries on the Yare," 1189.

Cotopaxi (kō-tō-pak'-sē), **Mt.** Active volcanic peak, S. Amer., in the Andes, in Ecuador (19,613 ft.), 153, 1081.

Cotrone (kō-trō'-nă) (anc. Crotona); Spt. of s. It. on Gulf of Taranto ; pop, 10,000 ; exports oranges, olives, liquorice ; most famous medical school of anc. Gk. world ; home of athlete Milo ; Pythagoras at, 2710.

Cots'wold. A breed of sheep native to Cotswold Hills.

Cotswold Hills. Range in western counties, mainly in Gloucestershire, Eng., 1162, 1164, 1476, 3193, 3341.

" Cottar's Saturday Night," by Burns, 625, 626.

Cotton, 917. Barbados, 360 ; bleaching, 469 ; Bombay, 496 ; Brazil, 553 ; China, 809 ; close-up of weave, 3405 ; cloth introduced into Europe, 937 ; diseases and pests, 921, 3362 ; dyeing, 1060 ; E. Africa, 1072 ; Egypt, 1100 ; fabrics, 850, 920, 3404, 3405 ; India, 1708 ; miscellaneous products, 1263, 2709 ; nitrated, 2709 ; Peru, 2559 ; Russian Turkistan, 3267 ; South African, 3014 ; spinning, 919, 920, 3065 ; Sudan, 3110 ; thread, 3205 ; U.S.A., 2383, 2384, 3288 ; varieties, 921 ; weaving, 3192, 3360.

Cotton, (Thomas) Henry (b. 1907). Eng. golfer ; open golf champion in 1934, 1937, 1948.

Cotton, Sir Robert (1571–1631). Eng. antiquary ; manuscripts, 584.

Cotton boll weevil, 921, 3362.

Cotton gin. A machine to separate cotton fibre from the seed, 918.

Cotton manufactures, in England, 1165, 1890, 1968, 2084 ; India, 413, 496, 850 ; Japan, 1798 ; Korea, 1873 ; Lancashire, 1890 ; Spain, 360, 3032.

Cotton-seed meal, or oil cake ; as fertilizer, 1263.

Cotton-seed oil, 1263.

Cottony-cushion scale, 2879.

Cotyledon (kot-i-lē'-don). Seed leaf of plant, 2918.

Couchant, in heraldry, 1615.

Coué (kōō'-ā), **Émile** (1857–1926). Fr. physician ; specialized in auto-suggestion : " Every day in every way I get better and better."

Cougar (kōō'-gahr) or **puma**, 2702 ; belongs to cat family, 719 ; enemy of deer, 1080.

Coulomb (kōō-lawm'), **Charles Augustin** (1736–1806), Fr. physicist ; founded mathematical theory of electric and magnetic action ; practical unit of electric quantity was named after him ; enunciated " Coulomb's law " of electric attraction.

Coulomb. Unit quantity of electricity, defined as amount carried by current of one ampere flowing for one second.

Coumarin. Crystalline substance derived from sweet clover and other plants ; used in perfumes and flavours ; made artificially, 857.

Council of Europe. " Parliament " of W. Europe, consisting of (1) Cttee of Ministers and (2) Consultative Assembly ; reps. from Belgium, Denmark, France, Rep. of Ireland, Italy, Luxembourg, Netherlands, Norway, Sweden and U.K. ; first meeting at Strasbourg in Aug. 1949, 1242.

Council of Ten (1310–1797). Tribunal of 10, afterwards 17, which governed republic of Venice, 3312.

Council schools, 2886.

Councils, Church. See Church, Christian.

Coun'terfeiting. Crime of making imitations of coins or paper money, 2187 ; in the Middle Ages it was punishable by death.

Counterpoint, in music, 2263.

Counter-Reformation. In Rom. Cath. Church, 2760 ; Council of Trent, 2760 ; Loyola, 2034.

" Count of Monte Cristo." Novel by Dumas ; story of Edmond Dantès, sailor, who escapes from prison, gains buried treasure, returns to dazzle Paris ; 1053, 2110.

County. A subordinate political division into which the United Kingdom and certain other countries are divided ; some cities are counties in themselves—Belfast, for example ; in England, 1195. See also lists under **England ; Ireland, Northern ; Irish Free State ; Scotland ; Wales.**

County colleges. Institutions in U.K. for further education, age 16–18 years.

County council, in local government, 1491.

County court, Brit. court of law, 923.

County cricket, 928.

County Hall, London. H.q. of L.C.C., 2013, 2014 ; L.C.C. in session, 1491.

County schools. Secondary schools maintained entirely by a local Education Authority ; usually secondary grammar schools, 2886.

Coup d'état. Bold or brilliant stroke of statesmanship, usually unconstitutional and often accompanied with violence ; particularly Napoleon III's assumption of unlimited power in 1851, 2278.

Cou'perus, Louis (1863–1923). Dutch novelist, whose stories of human tragedies have an Aeschylean inevitability (" The Small Souls " ; " The Later Life " ; " The Twilight of the Soul " ; " Old People and the Things that Pass ").

Couplet (kup'-let). Two closely-connected lines in poetry, usually rhymed, and of the same length ; used by Pope, 1213 ; metre of, 2636.

Cou'pon. A dated certificate, attached to bond or other commercial instrument ; represents interest due and should be presented independently. Also a ration document.

Courbet (koor-bā), **Gustave** (1819–77). Fr. landscape, figure, and portrait painter, founder of modern realist school (" Burial at Ornans " ; " Combat of the Stags "), 1378.

Cour'land. A former Baltic prov. of Russ. ; became part of Latvia (1918). Incorp. in U.S.S.R. (1940).

Coursing. Pursuit of hares by greyhounds, not by scent but by sight ; chief annual event is the Waterloo Cup.

Courtauld, Augustine (b. 1904). Eng. explorer ; during 1930–31 Arctic Expedition in Greenland remained on ice plateau alone for five months ; 2646.

Courtauld, Samuel (1793–1881). Brit. manufacturer, born in U.S.A. ; founded the crêpe silk (rayon) manufacturing firm of Courtaulds, 2749.

" Court Circular." Daily publication in London containing an account of the movements of royalty and society people.

Court Martial. Court which tries offenders against military, air force or naval discipline. Courts-martial are divided into (1) District C.M.; (2) General C.M., (3) Field General C.M. Only a Field General C.M. of three officers can pass sentence of death, 923.

Court of Appeal. Brit. court of justice for appeals against verdicts given by lower courts, 922, 1490.

Court of the Lions, Alhambra, plate f. 120, 3040.

Courtois (koor-twah), **Bernard** (1777–1838). Fr. chemist, discoverer of iodine, 1738.

Court plaster. Sticking plaster made of silk gummed and mixed with a healing admixture ; so called from former use by ladies of the court as " beauty plasters."

Courtrai (koor-trā), Belgium. Fortified tn. on r. Lys ; pop. 40,000 ; fine linen and lace ; " Battle of Spurs " (1302), French vanquished by Flemings ; battle 1918 in Ypres campaign ; occupied by Germans 1940–44. In 1939, official name became Kortrijk.

Courtship, among birds, 441, 1397 ; spiders, 3065.

" Courtship of Miles Standish," poem by Longfellow, 2022.

Courts of Justice, 921, 1490 ; equity, in England, 1903 ; jury trials, 1842 ; medieval " Court of Pie-powder," 1257 ; reforms of Henry II of Eng., 1609.

Court (or **real**) **tennis,** an old form of lawn tennis, 1905, 3186.

Cousin (koo-zan), **Victor** (1792–1867). Fr. philosopher, greater as expounder of historical systems than as original thinker ; called greatest modern

---

eclectic ; important figure, 1830 to 1848, in reorganization of Fr. public-school system.

Cousins (kuz'-enz), marriage of, 1617.

Cousins, Samuel (1801–87). Eng. mezzotint engraver ; used mixed method of engraving and etching ; copied many paintings by Reynolds, Lawrence, Gainsborough ; work characterized by delicacy and versatility of treatment.

Coutts (kōōts), **Thomas** (1735–1822). Brit. banker, one of the founders of the great London banking business of Coutts and Co.

Covenant, Ark of the. Sacred chest of acacia wood which Israelites took with them into Palestine ; contained two stone tablets on which Ten Commandments were inscribed ; placed by Solomon in temple at Jerusalem.

Covenanters. In Scot., the dissenters who bound themselves by oath or covenant to maintain Presbyterian forms and doctrines ; first covenant signed 1557 at inspiration of John Knox ; covenant of 1638, signed at Greyfriars' Church, Edinburgh, to resist introduction of Laud's prayer-book.

Covent Garden, London, formerly " convent garden " of Westminster Abbey, now spacious square noted for its vegetable, fruit and flower market ; fruit hospital, 1403 ; Royal Opera House, opened in 1858, with seasonal performances of grand opera and ballet, 3196 ; cyclorama, 1043 ; in 1948 Ministry of Works proposed purchase of Royal Opera House on behalf of Treasury, to take over in 1950.

Coventry, mfg. city in Warwickshire ; pop. 221,300, 922, 923, 3341 ; heavily bombed, Nov. 14–15, 1941, 923.

Coventry, Sent to, origin, 923.

Cov'erdale, Miles (1488–1568), Augustinian friar, Bishop of Exeter, translator of first complete printed Eng. Bible (1535) ; helped to edit Henry VIII's " Great Bible " (1539), 426.

Cov'erley, Sir Roger de, simple, kindly whimsical country gentleman in the " Spectator " of Addison and Steele, 24, 1213 ; dance, 967.

Cow, female of various bovine animals, 732, 731, 956, 984, 2173, 2842.

Coward, Noel (b. 1899). Eng. actor, playwright and composer. (Plays, " Hay Fever," " Private Lives," " Bitter Sweet," " Cavalcade," " Blithe Spirit," " Present Laughter " ; films, " In Which We Serve," " This Happy Breed," " Brief Encounter.")

Cowdray, Weetman Dickinson Pearson, 1st Viscount (1856–1927), Eng. capitalist, head of Pearson oil interests.

Cowen, Sir Frederick Hymen (1852–1935). Eng. musical composer, producer of many cantatas, operas, oratorios, and anthems.

Cowes, spt. on N. coast of Isle of Wight ; headquarters of the Royal Yacht Squadron ; pop. 15,000 ; 483, 3377 ; Cowes Week, 483, 485.

Cowley, Abraham (1618–67). Eng. poet and essayist ; his sonorous lyric style was copied by Dryden and his successors of 18th cent. ; wrote " The Mistress," love verses ; " Davideis," a scriptural epic ; " Pindarique Odes."

Cow parsley, 2637.

Cowper, William (1731–1800), Eng. poet, author of " John Gilpin," 923, 1213 ; hymns, 1678.

Cow-pox, a mild form of smallpox, 3301 ; vaccination, 1818.

Cowrie Islands. Same as **Maldive Islands.**

Cowry or **cowrie,** a large genus of molluscs ; shells used as money, 2201, 2202, 2942, 2943.

Cow's eye, 1253.

Cowslip, flowering plant of primrose family, 924.

Cow trees, or milk trees, of family Urticaceae, closely related to breadfruit, 3246.

Cox, David (1783–1859). Eng. landscape painter, in water colour and oils ; 1181, 3353.

Cox'swain, or **cox,** one who steers rowing-boat.

Coyote (kō-yō'-tē or kī'-ōt), the prairie wolf.

Coypel, Noel (1628–1707). Fr. religious and historical painter ; much influenced by Poussin ; several other members of his family also became known as painters.

Coy'pu. S. Amer. rat, yields nutria fur.

Crab, a crustacean, 924 ; plates f. 924, 925; eye, 1253; hermit crab, 924, plate f. 925 ; king crab, 1354, plate f. 925.

Crab or **Cancer,** a constellation ; chart, 895.

Crab-apple (Malus). The wild apple, common in Britain in several forms ; the Siberian crab (M. baccata) is often grown in gardens.

Crabbe, George (1754–1832). Eng. poet ; his pen pictures of country life and scenes were most faithfully drawn ; was curate of Aldeburgh ; " Tales in Verse " ; " Parish Register "—little novels of homely realism in verse.

Crab-spider, 3065.

Cracking, in petroleum refining, 2430.

Cracow or **Krakow,** city in S. Poland on r. Vistula ; pop. 350,000 ; 925, 2640 ; temp. cap. of Polish " state," after German invasion in 1939 ; liberated Jan. 1945, 925.

Cradock, Sir Christopher (1862–1914). Eng. admiral ; commanded cruiser squadron which was defeated off Coronel, Chile, Nov. 1, 1914.

Craft guilds, 1553.

Craig, (Edward) Gordon (b. 1872). Eng. actor and author ; son of Ellen Terry ; founded school of theatrical art 1913 in Florence, Italy ; designs stage settings, 1043, 3197.

Craigavon, James Craig, 1st Viscount (1871–1940). Irish politician ; took part in the Boer War and 1st World War ; Premier of N. Ire. from 1921 ; created a Viscount in 1927.

Craigmyle, Thomas Shaw, 1st Baron (1850–1937). Scot. jurist ; Lord Advocate for Scotland (1905–09) ; Lord of Appeal (1909–29).

Craik, Mrs., pen-name of Dinah Maria Mulock (1826–87). Eng. novelist and children's story writer (" John Halifax, Gentleman ").

Craiova (krah-yō'-va), Rumania. Trading and mfg. tn. 100 m. w. of Bucharest ; pop. 74,786.

Crait or **krait,** a snake, 1701, 2991.

Cramp, muscular, 2258.

Crampons, for mountaineering, 2247.

Cranach or **Kranach** (krah'-nahkh), **Lucas** (1472–1553), Ger. painter and engraver ; founder of Saxon school ; portraits of Luther and all Ger. reformers and princes of Reformation period ; also painted scriptural and mythological subjects, 1454 ; " A Rest During the Flight into Egypt," 1454.

Cran'borne Chase, anc. forest in Wiltshire and Dorset, 3383.

Crane, Walter (1845–1915). Eng. artist, craftsman, designer, social idealist, and writer ; like William Morris in social creed and in devotion of art to everyday use of all classes of people.

Crane, bird, 3098, 3099, plate f. 3101.

Crane, machine, 605, 654, 1748, 2700, 2701 ; camera-crane in filming, 833.

Crane's-bill or **wild geranium,** 1444.

Craniom'etry, 2724.

Cra'nium, brain case of skull, 545.

Crank, steam-engine, 3086 ; sewing machine, 2930.

Crank case, in internal combustion engine, 1736.

Crank shaft, in engineering, 1736, 2243.

Cran'mer, Thomas (1489–1556). Eng. Church reformer, 925 ; declares divorce of Henry VIII, 1612.

Cranwell, vil. in Lincs, famous for R.A.F. college, 1953, 2832.

Crape or **crêpe,** a gauzy fabric, either silk or cotton.

Crashaw (krā'-shaw), **Richard** (1613–49). Eng. poet, whose poems, marked by a wonderful purity of thought and pronounced mysticism, greatly influenced Milton, Shelley, and Coleridge (" Steps to the Temple ").

Cras'sus, Marcus Licinius (c. 115–53 B.C.). Rom. general and statesman; called " the rich " because of his immense wealth; supported Sulla against Marius; suppressed Spartacan rebellion; in first triumvirate.

Craters, attributed to meteorite in Arizona (U.S.A.), *2152*; of moon, 2224, 2225, *2226*; of volcano, 3328, *plates f.* 3328, *3329*.

Craw'fish, salt-water crustacean; it is rather larger than the lobster, and is found round the coasts of Brit.; distinguished from crayfish, 926.

Crawford, Francis Marion (1854–1909). Amer. novelist, b. and lived much in It.; " Mr. Isaacs," story of Anglo-Indian life; later novels, almost exclusively It. in subject and setting (" A Roman Singer," " A Cigarette Maker's Romance "); 3294.

Crawley, Sir Pitt. Vulgar, miserly old baronet in Thackeray's " Vanity Fair."

Crawl stroke, in swimming, 3135, *3136*.

Cray'fish. A freshwater crustacean, 926.

Crayon, 749.

Cream, 955.

Cream of tartar, 1500, 3155.

Cream separator, 955.

Crease, in cricket, 928.

Creasy, Sir Edward Shepherd (1812–78). Eng. historian, chief justice of Ceylon (" Fifteen Decisive Battles of the World ").

" Creation, The," Oratorio by Haydn, 1590.

Crécy (krā'-sē). Fr. village 100 m. N.W. of Paris; battle of (1346), 926, 1652.

Credit. In business world, **926**; currency, 2202.

Creek Indians, *2753*.

Creeper. An insect-eating bird, 2407; egg, *1094*.

Crees. Tribe of Plains Indians, N. Amer., living mainly about l. Winnipeg and Saskatchewan r., 1875, 2874.

Creighton (krī'-ton), **Mandell** (1843–1901). Eng. clergyman and historian, appointed Bishop of London in 1896 (" The Age of Elizabeth "; " History of the Papacy ").

Cremo'na. It. city on r. Po; pop. 64,000; famous for 16th cent. school of painting; violins, 3324.

Creodont, a prehistoric animal, *2679*.

Creole (krē'-ōl). Name used in S. U.S. and Latin Amer. for pure-blooded descendants of early Fr., Sp., or Portuguese settlers; incorrectly used for a mulatto.

Cre'olin. Antiseptic derived from coal-tar.

Creon (krē'-on). In Gk. myth., king of Thebes, uncle of Antigone.

Creosote (krē'-ō-sōt). Distillate of coal-tar, preservative of wood, 927; also antiseptic oil distilled from beech-wood, 927.

Crer'ar, Gen. Henry D. G. (b. 1888). Canadian soldier; led 1st Canadian corps in Italy; from March 1944 led 1st Canadian army in Normandy and up Rhine—the first independent Canadian army to take field; retired in 1946.

Cre'sol. Antiseptic distilled from wood or coal-tar, 857.

Cress. Plant of mustard family. *See also* Water-cress.

Crested auklet, *304*.

Crested tit, 3218.

Creta'ceous period. In geology, 1433.

Crete (krēt). Gk. isl. in Mediterranean; 3,190 sq. m.; pop. 386,000; **927**, *map, 30*; annexed, 1525; architecture, 213; civilization, 29; in myth., 927, 3201; money, *2202*; navigation invented, 2290, 2945; in 2nd World War, 927, 3418, *map, 3421*.

Cre'tin. A type of imbecile dwarf.

Cretonne. A printed cotton fabric, usually thick and strong, woven in a ridged or other figure; it is used for curtains and furniture covers, but, unlike chintz, is rarely glazed or calendered; originally it was a white cloth produced in Fr. and named from its manufacturer.

Creusot (krē'-zō), **Le.** Tn. in E. cent. Fr., 75 m. N.W. of Lyons; pop. 24,106;

great Schneider munitions factory. Occupied by Germans 1940–44.

Crevasse (kre-vas'). In glaciers, 1469.

Crewe, Robert Offley Crewe-Milnes, 1st Marquess of (1858–1945). Brit. statesman. Liberal leader in House of Lords; Lord-Lieut. of Ire. (1892–5); Sec. of State for India (1910–15); Chairman of L.C.C. (1917); Sec. of State for War (1931).

Crewe. Important rly. tn. in Cheshire; pop. 47,500; locomotives, rails, and rolling stock.

Crichton (krī'-ton), **James** (1560–82). " The Admirable Crichton." Scottish scholar, adventurer, and swordsman of proverbial versatility.

Crichton-Browne, Sir James (1840–1938). Brit. physician; specialist on nervous disorders.

Cricket. Insect, **927**; ear, 1730; young, 1729.

Cricket. Summer game, **928**, *929*; Bradman, 543; champion county in recent years; 1932, Yorks; 1933, Yorks; 1934, Lancs; 1935, Yorks; 1936, Derbyshire; 1937–8–9, Yorks; 1946, Yorks; 1947, Middx.; 1948, Glamorgan; 1949, Yorks/Middx. *See also* Records.

Crieff (krēf), Scot. Tn. in Perthshire, 18 m. W. of Perth; noted as a health resort; has large hydropathic establishment; pop. 5,500; 2558.

Crimea (kri-mē'-a). Province of Soviet Rus.; comprises the peninsula jutting into the Black Sea; 23,300 sq. m.; pop. 2,150,000; **931**; in 2nd World War, 1452, 3419.

Crimean War (1854–56), **931**; Balkan Peninsula, 344: Napoleon III, 2278; Nicholas I, 2365; Florence Nightingale's work, *2368*; Russia, 2848; Turkey, 3265.

Criminal Appeal, Court of, 922.

Criminal Investigation Dept. (C.I.D.), 2648.

Criminal Law, 1903.

Crin'oid or **sea lily.** An echinoderm animal, early type of sea, life, 1433.

Crippen, Hawley Hervey (1862–1910), Anglo-Amer. criminal; arrest for murder notable for use of wireless.

Cripps, Sir (Richard) Stafford (b. 1889). Eng. lawyer, son of Lord Parmoor; Solicitor-General (1930–31); Labour M.P. in 1931; Ambassador to Moscow, 1940–42; mission to India, Mar. 1942; Lord Privy Seal, 1942; Min. of Aircraft Production, 1942; Pres. Board of Trade, July 1945; Min. of Economic Affairs, Oct. 1947; Chancellor of Exchequer, Nov. 1947.

Crispi (kris'-pē), **Francesco** (1819–1901). It. statesman, one of makers of modern Italy; premier 1887–96.

Cris'pin, St. Christian martyr of late 3rd cent.; patron saint of shoe-makers.

Cristobal, Panama Canal port at Atlantic end, 2488.

Cristofori (kris-tō-fōr'ē), **Bartolommeo** (1655–1731). It. harpsichord maker; invented piano, 2601.

Croatia-Slavonia (krō-ā'shi-a sla-vō'ni-a). Part of Yugoslavia, formerly of Hungary; 3438.

Croce (krō-chā), **Benedetto** (b. 1866). It. philosopher; wide influence on modern idealistic philosophy (" Philosophy of the Spirit "), 1787.

Crochet (krō-shī). A kind of knitting or lace-making done with silk, wool or cotton, by using hooked needle.

Crocket, in architecture. An ornament used to decorate the angles of spires, canopies, etc.

Crockett, Samuel Rutherford (1860–1914). Scot. novelist, for some time a Free Church minister (" The Stickit Minister ").

Crocodile (krok'-ō-dīl), **931**, *69*. Alligator distinguished, 121; classified, 2767; eggs, *1094*; largest reptile, 2767; in India, 1701.

Crocodile bird, 931.

Crocus. Plant of the iris family, **932**, *130*; bulb structure, 612.

Croesus (krē'-sus). King of Lydia 560–546 B.C., **932**, 55.

Crofts, Ernest (1847–1911). Eng. painter; his " Charles I on the Scaffold," *1206*.

Croix de Feu (krwah de fē). Fr. right-

wing organization, led by Col. de la Rocque; dissolved by the French government in 1936.

Croix de Guerre (krwah de gär). Fr. decoration, 2449.

Cro-Magnon (krō-man'-yon). Race of Stone Age men, 734, *735, 736*, 2080.

Cromarty (krum'-ar-ti), **Firth.** Arm of Moray Firth, Scot.; 19 m. long, average breadth 4 m.; 2828.

Crome (krōm), **John** (1768–1821). Eng. landscape painter and etcher often styled " Old Crome " to distinguish from his son John Bernay Crome (1794–1842); originally a house decorator; his " Mousehold Heath " is in the National Gallery, London, 1181; " Moonlight on the Marshes of the Yare," *1180*.

Cro'mer, Evelyn Baring, Earl of (1841–1917). Brit. statesman and diplomatist; as Brit. agent, 1883–1907 directed and reorganized Egyptian govt.; called maker of modern Egypt.

Cro'mer. Seaside resort in Norfolk, 25 m. N. of Norwich; the " Garden of Sleep " near by is noted for its profusion of poppies; pop. 4,177; 2376.

Crom'lech, group of huge stones set up by Stone Age men.

Cromp'ton, Richmal. Pen-name of Richmal Crompton Lamburn (b. 1890); Brit. author; creator of William, the schoolboy hero of " Just William," " William the Conqueror," etc.

Crompton, Samuel (1753–1827). Inventor of spinning mule, 933, 3361; spinning wheel, *1723*.

Cromwell, Oliver (1599–1658). Eng. Puritan soldier and statesman, Lord Protector of the Commonwealth, 933, 1658; battle of Dunbar, 933; Hampden, 1571; Ire. subdued, 1745; Rump Parliament, 933, *934*; Scot. conquered, 2893.

Cromwell, Richard (1626–1712). Son of Oliver Cromwell and Lord Protector (Sept. 1658—May 1659), 933.

Cromwell, Thomas (1485–1540). Earl of Essex, Eng. statesman; confidential servant to Cardinal Wolsey and agent of Henry VIII in effecting Eng. Reformation.

Cromwell tank, 3152.

Cronin, Archibald Joseph (b. 1896). British novelist. Author of " Hatter's Castle," " The Stars Look Down," " The Citadel," etc.

Cronje (kron'-ye), **Piet** (c.1840–1911). Boer general; captured Jameson raiders; surrender, 487.

Crookes, Sir William (1832–1919). Eng. chemist and physicist; invented Crookes tube, 3430; discovery of thallium, 3193; of Uranium X, 2732.

Crookes tube, 3430.

Crop. The first of a bird's three stomachs; stores food and prepares it for digestion by the other two; largest in grain-eating birds and missing in fruit- and insect-eaters.

Crop rotation, 80; clover, 852; lucerne, 2034; and nitrogen, 2374.

Croquet (krō'-kā), game, **934**, *935*.

Cros'by, Bing (Harry Lillis Crosby, b. 1904). Amer. singer of world-wide fame, and film actor; films " Road to Singapore," " Blue Skies," " Going my Way."

Cross, in biology. See Hybrid.

Crossbill. A type of finch, seen in Eng. in winter; named from the way its mandibles cross, 1272.

Crossbow. In medieval warfare, 76, 1864.

Cross Fell, Eng. Mt. (2,930 ft.) in Cumberland, one of the chief peaks in the Pennine Range, 10 m. N.E. of Penrith.

Cross-pollination, 1322.

Cross-staff. For determining latitude, 2290.

Cross stitch, embroidery, 1154.

Crotalinae, the pit viper family of snakes, including the rattlesnakes, 2991.

Croto'na. Anc. name of Cotrone (*q.v.*).

Croton oil. Purgative drug obtained from a plant of the spurge family.

Crouch. Small r. of Essex, 1225.

Crow, 935; related to birds of paradise, 2511.

Crow family, *Corvidae,* **935** ; includes jays, magpies, jackdaws and rooks ; ravens, 935, 2747.

Crow'borough Beacon. Sussex, 792 ft.

Crowfoot family, *Ranunculaceae,* includes buttercups, *628* ; clematis, *836* ; columbine, 878 ; larkspur, 1893.

Crown. An Eng. silver coin, worth 5 shillings, not minted since 1902.

Crown. Of tooth, 3163.

Crown colony. In Brit. Commonwealth, 1492.

Crown Colonies, Protectorates, etc., of Britain :

Aden	Malayan Federation
Ascension	Malta
Bahamas	Mauritius
Barbados	Nigeria
Basutoland	Nyasaland
Bechuanaland	Pacific Is.
Bermuda	Papua
British Guiana	Rhodesia, Northern
British Honduras	Rhodesia, Southern
British North Borneo	St. Helena
British Somaliland	Sarawak
Brunei	Seychelles
Cyprus	Sierra Leone
Falkland Is.	Singapore Colony
Fiji Is.	Sudan,
Gambia	Anglo-Egyptian
Gibraltar	Swaziland
Gold Coast	Trinidad
Hong Kong	Tristan da Cunha
Jamaica	Uganda
Kenya	Windward Is.
Leeward Is.	Zanzibar

Crown glass, 1474.

Crown Jewels (Gt. Brit.), **935,** *frontis.* *Vol. 2* ; Col. Blood attempts to steal, 477 ; at Coronation, 912 ; in the Tower, 3232.

Crowns and Coronets, *935,* **936.**

Croydon. Tn. in Surrey, 10 m. s. of London ; pop. (1947) 237,300 ; once residence of Archbp. of Canterbury ; bell foundries ; heavily bombed 1940–44, both H.E. and flying bombs.

Cro'zier. Pastoral staff carried by bishop, *826.*

Cru'cible. In glass-making, 1472 ; heated by high-frequency currents, 1624, 1625 ; in steel-making, 1756.

Cruciferae (krōō-sif'-e-rē) or *Brassicacea.* Cabbage or mustard family, including radishes and turnips, *639.*

Crucifix'ion. Of Jesus Christ, 1825.

Cruden, Alexander (1701–70). Compiler of " Biblical Concordance " (1737).

Cruikshank (krook'-shank), **George** (1792–1878). Eng. caricaturist, etcher, and illustrator ; illustrated some of Dickens's works.

Cruiser. In navies, 2296 ; tank, 3152.

Crum'mock Water. Lake in Cumberland among the mts., 2 m. long, ¾ m. broad.

Crusader's Scallop. Shell, *2943.*

Crusader tank, 3152.

Crusades, 936, *937* ; 1st, 2nd & 3rd, 936 ; 4th, 5th, 6th, 7th, 937 ; children's crusade, 937 ; effects on Europe, 638, 937 ; Richard I at, 2776 ; Saladin, 2864 ; and Renaissance, 2766.

Crusading orders, 2072.

Crusoe, Robinson. Hero of novel by Defoe, 804, 2402.

Crusta'cea. Class of heavily armoured arthropod animals, **937,** *938, 939, 986* ; distinguished from molluscs, 2199 ; includes barnacle, 361 ; crab, 924 ; crayfish, *926* ; lobster, 1977 ; shrimp, 2962.

Cry'olite. Mineral containing sodium, aluminium, and fluorine ; mined in Greenland, 223 ; used in electrolytic production of aluminium, 135, 1567.

Cryp'togams. Plant group, including all spore-reproducing types, 2918.

Crystal. In radio, 2751, 3394 ; microphone, 2163.

Crystal glass, 1472.

Crys'talline lens. Of eye, *1252.*

Crystalliza'tion of metals, 939.

Crystallog'raphy. Science of crystals, 940.

Crystal Palace. Building of iron and glass erected in HydePark,London,for great exhibition of 1851 ; re-erected at Sydenham, S.E., and opened in 1854 ; burned down in 1936 ; grounds used for motor-racing, etc. Requisitioned by War Office in 1939 ; *3563.*

Crystals, 939 ; diamonds, 940 ; 1680 ; and ionization, 1739 ; and polarization of light, 1942 ; in piezo-electricity, 2604 ; snow, *2992.*

Ctesiphon (tēs'-i'fon). Anc. city of Babylonia, on Tigris, 45 m. N.E. of Babylon ; cap. of Parthian kingdom ; battle between Brit. and Turks (1915) ; arch of Chosroes I.

Cuba (kū'-ba). Largest and richest isl. of W. Indies ; 44,160 sq. m. ; pop. 4,777,000 ; 940, *map, 940* ; cap. Havana, 1584 ; discovery, 941 ; tobacco, 941, 3221 ; U.S.A. liberates, 3291.

Cubbing. Form of hunting, 1657, *1659.*

Cube. In geometry, 1437 ; finding cube and cube root, *2984.*

Cubic foot, a measure of gas, 2154.

Cubic measure. *See in Index* **Weights and Measures.**

Cubists. In painting, 2477; Picasso, 2604.

Cubit. *See in Index* **Weights and Measures** (Old).

Cuchulain (koo-hōō'-lin). Legendary Irish hero, 1750.

Cuckoo (kook'-ōō). European bird notorious for laying eggs in nests of others, **941,** *942* ; with meadow pipit, *2612* ; eats hairy caterpillars, 943.

Cuckoo-pint. *See* **Wake-robin.**

Cucujo. A S. Amer. firefly, 1288.

Cu'cumber, 943 ; marrow's relation, 2109.

Cucumber, sea, 2911.

Cucurbitaceae (kū-kêr-bi-tā'-se-ē). Plant family including cucumbers, **943** ; melons, 2137 ; pumpkins, 2704.

Cud-chewing animals, 732.

Cuddalore', Rep. of India. Spt. on Bay of Bengal, nr. Madras ; pop. 50,500 ; 1692.

Cudworth, Ralph (1617–88). Eng. philosopher, one of Cambridge Platonists (" True Intellectual System of the Universe " ; " Treatise on Eternal and Immutable Mortality ").

Cue, mining township in the Murchison goldfield of Western Australia.

Cue, in billiards, 428.

Cuenca (kwen'-ka). Third city of Ecuador in s.w. ; pop. 45,000 ; mfg. and trade centre.

Cuffley. Vil. of Herts ; here, on Sept. 3, 1916, Lt. W. L. Robinson attacked with his aeroplane and brought down the first raiding airship in the 1st World War, for which he was awarded the V.C.

Cuirass (kwi-ras'), armour protecting the trunk of the body, *244.*

Culebra, or **Gaillard, Cut,** in Panama Canal, 2490.

Cul'linan diamond, *1009,* 1012.

Cullo'den Moor. Famous Scottish battlefield in Inverness-shire near Moray Firth ; battle of (1746), 1738, 1790, 2682.

Cultured pearls, 2534.

Cumae (kū'-mē). Anc. city on coast of Campania, w. Italy ; oldest Gk. colony in Italy ; supposed home of Cumaean Sibyl.

Cumaean (kū-mē'-an) **Sibyl.** Prophetess who offered nine books of prophecies to the Roman King Tarquin the Proud, who refused to pay the price demanded, but after she had destroyed six his curiosity prompted him to buy the remaining three at the price asked for the whole nine.

Cumer'a, a nut, 2408.

Cum'berland, William Augustus, Duke of (1721–65). Third son of George II of Eng. ; commanded at Culloden Moor, 2682.

Cumberland. Extreme N.W. co. of Eng. ; 1,520 sq. m. ; pop. 263,151 ; includes part of Lake District ; **943,** *1166* ; *plate, 1169* ; granite, 1499.

Cum'brian Hills, in N.W. Eng. Part of Cumberland, Westmorland, and Lancashire ; joined to Pennine Range by Scafell Pike (3,210 ft.), highest mountain in Eng. ; **943** ; Lake District, *1166* ; *plates, 1169, 1175.*

Cum'in. Spice from a plant of the parsley family, *3062.*

Cumulus (kū'-mū-lus) **clouds,** 852, *853* ; hail formed in, 1564.

Cunae'us. Dutch physicist ; invented Leyden jar, 1929.

Cunard (kū-nard'), **Sir Samuel, Bart.** (1787–1865). Eng. shipowner, b. Nova Scotia ; founder of Cunard steamship line.

Cunard-White Star Line. Brit. line of ocean steamers, with headquarters at Liverpool ; owns the Queen Elizabeth, Queen Mary, Caronia, Aquitania, and other great liners, 2947 ; ships, *2948, 2949, 2950, 2958, 2960.*

Cunaxa. Plains in Iraq, on Euphrates, 60 m. N. of Babylon ; def. at and death of Cyrus the Younger in battle against his brother Artaxerxes Mnemon 401 B.C. ; 3429.

Cuncta'tor (" The delayer "). Nickname of Quintus Fabius Maximus, 1574.

Cundall, Charles, R.A. (b. 1890). Brit. painter, an official 2nd World War artist ; " The Withdrawal from Dunkirk " *plate f. 1056.*

Cuneiform (kū'-nē-i-form) **writing.** Anc. system of writing used by Babylonians, Assyrians, and Persians, *329, 331.*

Cuneo (koo-nā'-ō). It. tn. in Piedmont. 50 m. s. of Turin ; pop. 35,321.

Cunningham, Admiral Viscount Andrew (b. 1883), C.-in-C. Mediterranean 1939–42 ; C.-in-C. Allied Naval Forces, Medit. ; Admiral of the Fleet in 1948.

Cun'ningnam, Admiral Sir John H. D. (b. 1885). Brit. sailor ; in 1938 viceadmiral, commanding 1st cruiser squadron ; in 1943 C.-in-C. the Levant, promoted admiral, and C.-in-C. Mediterranean, retiring 1946, and becoming 1st Sea Lord, succeeding Visct. Cunningham (above).

Cunninghame-Graham, Robert Bontine (1852–1936). Brit. author and politician ; M.P. 1886–92 ; works dealt largely with Spain and South America ; had ranches in Mexico.

Cupar. Co. tn. of Fife, Scot. ; pop. 7,110 ; 1269.

Cup Final. Football Association. Held annually at Wembley Stadium ; recent winners : 1933, Everton ; 1934. Manchester City ; 1935, Sheffield Wednesday ; 1936, Arsenal ; 1937. Sunderland ; 1938, Preston North End ; 1939, Portsmouth ; 1946. Derby ; 1947, Charlton ; 1948, Manchester United ; 1949. Wolverhampton Wanderers ; 1950, Arsenal.

Cupid (kū'-pid). In Rom. myth.. same as Gk. Eros ; god of love, 943, 186.

Cu'pola. Spherical cup-shaped roof ; also a revolving shell-proof turret.

Cupro-nickel, an alloy for coins, 2187 ; replaced silver in the U.K.

Curaçao (koo-rah-sah'-ō) or **Curaçoa.** Isl. in Netherlands W. Indies ; 210 sq. m. ; pop. 75,587 ; exports salt. phosphate ; peculiar variety of oranges used in Dutch liqueur Curaçao ; colony of Curaçao also includes neighbouring isls. ; total area, 384 sq. m. ; pop. 133,800.

Curd. Of milk, 765, 2174.

Cur'few, 410 ; rung at Oxford, 410.

Curia Regis (kū'-ri-a rē'-jis) (Latin " King's court "). Instituted by William the Conqueror as the supreme central judicial body of Eng. ; ceased to function in 1268 under Henry I and II, 1609.

Curia Romana. Collective body of administrative organizations which aid the Pope in governing Rom. Cath. Church, 2495.

Curiatii (kū-ri-ā'-ti-ī). In Rom. legend three brothers of Alba Longa who fought their three cousins, the Horatii, 2864.

Curie, Marie Sklodowska (1867–1934). Fr. physicist, born in Warsaw Poland ; discovered radium, 944. 296, 2731.

Curie, Pierre (1859–1906). Fr. physicist with his wife found radium, 2731 and piezo-electricity, 2604.

Cur'ium (Cm). Element, atomic number 96 ; unknown in nature, but produced by artificial radio-activity discovered 1946 by Glenn T. Seaborg, U.S.A.

Cur'lew. Largest native British wader *3331.*

Curling. An ice game, **944.**

Curragh (kur'-ra), **Tne,** Ire. Extensive plain in Kildare, Eire ; formerly military camp for Brit. soldiers ; a. about 8 sq. m. ; 1856.

Cur'ran, John Philpot (1750–1817). Irish lawyer, patriot, and orator ; defended Wolfe Tone and other Irish rebels of 1798 ; bitterly opposed union with Gt. Brit.

Currant. Fruit of bush related to gooseberry, **944** ; in Greece, 1527 ; red, *rev. of f. 1401.*

Currency. *See* **Money.**

Current, electric. Flow of electricity along a conductor, 1128 ; primary and secondary cells, 375, 377 ; consumption of, *1546* ; dynamo, 1060 ; electrolysis, 771, 1136 ; in lights, 1134 ; magnetic effects, 2063 ; tramcars, 3235 ; transformers, 3237. *See also* **Electricity.**

Currents, air. *See* **Wind.**

Currents, ocean, 2419. In Atlantic, 291 ; Gulf Stream, 1554 ; Japan current, 98, 2419 ; Labrador current, 291, 1333. *See also* **Tide.**

Curricle. A two-wheel chaise with a pole for a pair of horses.

Currie, Sir Donald (1825–1909). Scot. shipowner and politician ; founder of the Castle Line which merged with the Union Line in 1900 to form the Union-Castle Steamship Co.

Currier (ku'-ri-er). One who dresses and colours leather after it has been tanned ; 1913.

Curry. A spiced condiment, 3062.

Curtana (kêr-tah'-na). Blunted and edgeless sword carried at Eng. sovereign's coronation as emblem of mercy.

Cur'tin, John (1885–1945). Australian statesman ; became leader of Federal Labour party in 1935 ; prime min. 1941 to his death in 1945.

Curtiss, Glenn Hammond (1878–1930). Amer. inventor and pioneer aviator ; designer of many flying craft and flying boat types ; inventor of seaplane.

Curtis turbine, 3260.

Curtius, Ernst (1814–96). Ger. archaeologist, scholar and historian (" History of Greece ").

Curtius, Marcus (kêr'-shi-us). Legendary Roman hero ; an earthquake chasm in the Forum which soothsayers said would not close until it had received Rome's greatest treasure, was closed when Curtius, declaring that Rome had no greater treasure than a brave citizen, rode his horse into it.

Curule chair (kū-rūl). An ivory chair, in shape like a modern camp-stool, used by Roman magistrates.

Curzola. Isl. of Yugoslavia in Adriatic off coast of Dalmatia ; 107 sq. m. ; pop. 28,000 ; boat-building, fishing ; *map, 1764.*

Curzon of Kedleston, George Nathaniel, 1st Marquess (1859–1925). Brit. Conservative statesman ; Gov.-Gen. of India (1899–1905) ; Member of Imperial War Cabinet (1916) ; Secretary of State for Foreign Affairs (1919) ; Leader of the House of Lords (1916–24) and again in 1924, when he became Lord Pres. of the Council ; travelled extensively in Central Asia, Persia, Afghanistan, etc.

Cusp. In architecture, a spear-shaped ornament with sharp, rigid point.

Custard apple. A tropical fruit, native of the West Indies, but also cultivated in India and the neighbouring countries ; it is dark brown in colour, and netted all over, 1401.

Custom House. Public building in E. London where the duties on goods entering the Port of London have to be paid ; the present building was erected in 1814 and repaired 1852, but the Custom House as an institution dates from 1385.

Customs and Tariffs, 944 ; indirect tax, 3158.

Custozza (koos-tot'-sah). It. vil. 11 m. s.w. of Verona ; Italians defeated by Austrians in 1848 ; also in 1866.

Cutch or Kutch. State in Dominion of India ; 8,249 sq. m. ; pop. 514,000 ; cap. Bhuj.

Cut glass, 1474.

Cuthbert, St. (c. 635–687). Eng. bishop, hermit, and missionary ; life by Bede.

Cuticle or epidermis, 2979.

Cutlory. Birmingham, 457 ; Sheffield, 2941.

Cuts. First aid for, 1291.

Cuttack. Capital of Orissa, Rep. of India, pop. 74,291 ; 2453.

Cutter. Vessel with one mast, having fore and aft sails ; the spars are a mast boom, gaff, and bowsprit ; usually small, but sometimes as large as 460 tons ; *484.*

Cutting, of gems, 1011, 1427.

Cuttle-fish. A ten-armed cephalopod mollusc, **945, 946,** 2199 ; eggs, *1094* ; sepia, 945, *1725.*

Cutty Sark. Famous clipper-ship, built on the Clyde in 1869 and formerly engaged in the China tea trade. Now a training ship at Greenhithe, *2144, 2958.*

Cuvier (kū'-vyā), **Georges, Baron** (1769–1832). Fr. naturalist, pioneer in palaeontology, **946,** 150, 3446.

Cuxhaven (kooks'-hahfn). Ger. port on North Sea ; pop. 17,600 ; 1570. Heavy air raids in 2nd World War ; taken May 1945.

Cuyp (koip), **Albert** (1620–91). Dutch landscape painter, 2334.

Cuza (kōō'-za), **Alexander John** (1820–73). Prince of Rumania (1859–66) ; harsh methods led to abdication.

Cuzco (koos'-kō). Peru, mfg. and trade city in s., 11,380 ft. above sea-level ; pop. 40,000 ; univ. ; anc. cap. empire of Incas, *1690,* 2560.

Cyanamide (sī-an'-am-īd). Radicle containing carbon and nitrogen in the ratio of one to two.

Cyanides (sī'-an-īdz). Salts of hydrocyanic, or prussic, acid ; poisonous properties, **947** ; used in refining ores, 1480.

Cyanogen (sī-an'-ō-jēn). A poisonous gas with pungent odour, much used in organic synthesis, 947.

Cyaxares (sī-aks'-a-rēz). King of Media about 624–584 B.C. ; founder of Median empire ; destroyed Nineveh 606 B.C.

Cybele (sib'-e-lē). The " Great Mother of the Gods." Asiatic goddess identified by Romans with Rhea, mother of Jupiter; her worship became one of the three great cults under Rom. Empire.

Cycad (sī'-kad). A gymnosperm tree, 3246, 3247.

Cyclades (sik'-la-dēz). Group of Gk. isls. in Aegean Sea, S.E. of Greece ; pop. 130,000 ; *map, 1518* ; excavations, 1527.

Cyclamen (sik'-la-men). Plants of primrose family, native to mts. of central Europe, popular as pot-plants in Eng. ; kidney-shaped leaves, white, rose or purple flowers with reflexed petals.

Cycle. A series of events which repeats itself ; in electricity, 1130 ; " four-cycle " and " two-cycle " engines, *1736, 1737.*

Cycles and Cycling, 947 ; bearings, 386 ; motor-cycle diag., *948* ; bicycle pump, 2704 ; safety rules, 2788 ; signals, 2788. *See also* **Records.**

Cyclolith (sī'-klō-lith). Circle of stones such as are seen at Stonehenge in Wiltshire ; popularly, but possibly erroneously, regarded as Druidic.

Cy'clone, **949** 3100 ; rainfall, 2741.

Cyclops (sī'-klops). In Gk. myth., a one-eyed giant, **949** ; story, " How Odysseus Outwitted the Cyclops," 949.

Cyclorama (sī-klor-ah'-ma). Wall or stiff sheet at back and sides of stage on to which lighting and scenic effects are projected ; in stage production, 1043.

Cyclostomata (sī-klō-stom'-a-ta). Class of animal kingdom containing the lampreys and hag-fishes ; most primitive type of craniate vertebrates ; 1886.

Cyclotron (sī'-klō-tron). Apparatus used in atomic research for accelerating electrified particles, **950, 951** ; invention and devpmt., 952 ; beta-tron a .orm, 422.

Cygnet. A young swan, *3126, 449.*

Cygnus or Swan. A constellation, across the Pole Star from the Great Bear.

Cyl'inder. In bridge building, 654 ; in dynamo, *1061* ; in internal combus-

tion engine, 1736, 1737, *1734* ; in dams, *plate f. 760* ; in steam-engine, 3085, *3086.*

Cylinder press, 2686.

Cym'bals. Pair of plate-like musical instruments played by clashing together, 2267, 2268, 2446.

Cymbeline (sim'-be-lēn) or **Cunobeline** (d. c. A.D. 43). Brit. king, whose half-mythical history is used by Shakespeare as a basis for his drama " Cymbeline."

Cymothoidae (sī-mō-thō'-i-dē). Family of parasitic crustaceans, order Isopoda, with hooked legs to enable them to cling to the tails of fish.

Cymric. Welsh language, 3334.

Cynics (sin'-iks). School of anc. philosophers, forerunners of the Stoics, whose aim was to encourage virtue and simplicity of manners, 1017.

Cynoscephalae (sī-nō-sef'-a-lē). battle of (197 B.C.), 1524.

Cy'press. Conifer tree yielding durable timber, 952.

Cyprian (sip'-ri-an), **St.** (c. 200–258), A leader of African Church, converted to Christianity in middle life ; became Bishop of Carthage ; beheaded by Emperor Valerian.

Cypripedium. *See* **Lady's slipper.**

Cyprus (sī'-prus). Brit. isl. colony in Mediterranean ; 3,584 sq. m. ; pop. 462,000 ; **952** ; in myth., 186.

Cypselidae (sip-sel'-i-dē). The swift family of birds.

Cyrano de Bergerac (sē'-rah-nō de bär-zhär-ak) (1620–55). Fr. soldier, writer, and dramatist ; subject of play (1897) by Edmond Rostand.

Cyrenaica (sī-rē-nā'-ik-a). Dist. in former It. colony of Libya, 1770 ; in 2nd World War, *map, 3421.*

Cyrena'ic school of philosophy, founded by disciple of Socrates.

Cyrene (sī-rē'-nē). Anc. Gk. city, cap. of Cyrenaica.

Cyril (sī'-ril), **St.** (c. A.D. 376–444). Bishop of Alexandria noted for zeal against heretics ; said to have instigated murder of Hypatia.

Cyril, St. (A.D. 827–69). " The Apostle of the Slavs," to whom is attributed Cyrillic alphabet.

Cyril'lic alphabet, 126 ; used by Russians, 2855 ; by E. Slavs, 2983.

Cyrtarachne. Genus of orb-weaving spiders, widely dist.

Cy'rus the Great (c. 600–529 B.C.). Founder of the Persian Empire, 2554 ; conquers Lydia, 932 ; restores Jews to Jerusalem, 1830.

Cyrus the Younger (d. 401 B.C.). King of Persia, 3429.

Cythera (si-thēr'-a). *See* **Cerigo.**

Cytherea (sith-e-rē'-a). Name given to the goddess Aphrodite from her island of Cythera.

Cytol'ogy. Science of cell organism.

Cy'toplasm, of cell, 2695.

Czar. *See* **Tsar.**

Czarniecki (char-nyet'-ski), **Stephen** (1599–1665). Polish general ; drove Swedes under Charles X from Poland, and restored kingdom to King John Casimir (1655–57).

Czechoslovakia (chek'-ō-slo-vak'-i-a). State of Cent. Europe created in 1918 ; **953** ; *map, 954* ; Bata shoe works, 373 ; Benes, *413* ; Bohemia, 487 ; Carpathian Mts., 704 ; children, 799, *plate f. 952* ; Ger. invasion, 3416 ; history, 487, 954 ; Masaryk, 2117 ; people, 953, *plate f. 953* ; cap. Prague, 954, 2677 ; in 2nd World War, 3424.

Czechs. People, 953 ; in Bohemia, 487 ; language and Huss, 1660.

Czenstochowa (chens-tō-hō-fa). Polish holy city, 65 m. N.W. of Cracow ; pop. 120,000 ; in Ger. occupn., 1939–45.

Czernin (chêr'-nin), **Ottokar, Count** (1872–1932). Austro-Hungarian statesman ; at outbreak of 1st World War made vain effort to win over Rumania to Central Powers ; as Minister of Foreign Affairs (1916–18) sought to save Austria-Hungary.

Czernowitz. *See* **Cernauti.**

Czerny (tsêr-nē), **Karl** (1791–1857). Austrian pianist and composer ; teacher of Liszt and Thalberg ; exercises for pianoforte still widely used.

IN Egyptian picture-writing the symbol corresponding to our letter D was a hand ⬠. When conventionalized, it looked like this ⬠, and later among the Phoenicians became a triangle with a short tail **4**, the tail in time being dropped. The Phoenicians called it *Daleth*, which means " door " (remember the primitive house was a tent and the door simply a triangular curtain hung in front of the opening). The name and form of this letter were adopted by the Greeks with slight variation, and thus *Daleth* became *Delta* △. The delta of a river gets its name from its resemblance to the Greek letter *Delta*. For a long time its form did not change greatly, but it showed a tendency to turn over. Thus in one form we find it standing on its head, and in another its apex is turned to the right. When the sides which met at the right were written at one stroke, it became the D with the rounded back adopted by the Romans and used today.

Dab'chick. Another name for the lesser grebe ; common in Britain, 1516.

D'Abernon, Edgar Vincent, 1st Viscount (1857–1942). Eng. diplomat ; ambassador in Berlin (1920–26).

Dacca. City of Pakistan in E. Bengal on Boor Gunga r. ; pop. 550,000 ; muslins, gold and silver ware, 2479.

Dachshund (daks'-hoond or dash'-). Short-legged, long-bodied dog, *plate f. 1024*, 1027.

Dace, coarse fish, *2781.*

Dachau (dakh'-ow). Market tn. of Bavaria, 10 m. N.N.W. of Munich ; paper mills ; site of Ger. concentration camp, estab. 1933 ; overrun by U.S. troops, Ap. 30, 1945, who discovered revolting conditions of squalor and disease, and evidence of torture ; 3422.

Dacia (dā'-si-a). Anc. country of central Europe N. of Danube, 2840.

Dactyl. In poetry, 2635.

Da'daism. Short-lived aesthetic movement in the arts and literature, founded by J. Miró in Zürich in 1916 ; forerunner of Surrealism in painting ; explored the possibilities of incoherence and madness.

Daddy-long-legs, or crane-fly. A large fly of the family *Tipulidae*, with very long thin legs and a narrow, pale brown body. Its larva is the " leather-jacket " so destructive to lawns and grasslands, 1732.

Daedalus (dē'-da-lus). In Gk. myth., the first man to fly, **955**, 1680.

Daf'fodil, 955, 2279.

Dagenham. Tn. in Essex, on Thames ; pop. est. 105,000 ; severe German flying-bomb and rocket damage 1944–45 ; power lines at, 1547.

Daghestan (dah-ges-tahn'). Autonomous republic of Soviet Russia formerly the prov. of Daghestan ; a. 11,470 sq. m. ; pop. 930,000 ; cap., Makhach-Kala on the Caspian.

Da'gon. A Philistine god, worshipped at Gaza ; he had the head and hands of a man and the body and tail of a fish.

Daguerre (da-gãr'), **Louis Jacques Mandé** (1789–1851). Fr. painter and physicist ; inventor of daguerreotype, 2580.

Daguerre'otype. An early kind of photograph, 2580.

Dahlia (dāl'-ya). Garden flower, **955** ; roots, 2825.

Dahomey (da-hō'-mi). Fertile colony of Fr. W. Africa, former Negro kingdom ; 43,232 sq. m ; pop. 1,458,000 ; 70 m. coast ; chief city Porto Novo, pop. 27,000 ; 3368.

Daibutsi, or Great Buddha. Famous bronze image in Japan, 600, 1810.

Dail Eireann (dawl ãr'-an). Lower House of the Irish Legislature, *3281.*

" Daily Express." London newspaper, 2348 ; Lord Beaverbrook, 388.

" Daily Herald." London newspaper, 2348.

" Daily Mail." London newspaper, 2348 ; Lord Northcliffe founds, 2386.

" Daily Mirror." London picture newspaper, 2348 ; founded by Lord Northcliffe, 2386.

" Daily Graphic." London illustrated newspaper, 2348.

" Daily Telegraph and Morning Post." London newspaper, 2348 ; Lord Camrose, 675 ; offices, 2012.

Daimio (dī-mē-ō), Jap. feudal baron, 1799.

Daimler, Gottlieb (1834–1900), Ger. inventor, pioneer in development of motor-car engine, 1737, 2241.

Dairen (dī-ren') or **Dalny.** Customs port in S. Manchuria, on Kwantung Peninsula ; pop. 101,850 ; outranked only by Shanghai among Chinese spts. ; exports soya beans and coal ; founded by Russia (1899) ; " leased " to Japan (1905), 2087 ; *3029* ; free port under Chinese administration (1945).

Dairying, 955. Butter, 627 ; cattle, 79, 730, *956* ; cheese, 765 ; cream separator, 745, 955 ; goats, 1478 ; margarine, 2100 ; milk, 955, 2173 ; New Zealand, 2358 ; Switzerland, 3141.

Dais, in architecture. Raised portion of floor at end of a hall.

Daisy. Small field plant having white, yellow-centred flowers, **956** ; " Shasta," 621.

Dakar (da-kahr). Fortified naval station, airport, and rly. terminus, in Senegal at tip of Cape Verde ; pop, 182,000 ; cap. of Fr. W. Africa, 3367. Under Vichy France June 1940 ; Gen. de Gaulle unsuccessfully attempted to land his expeditionary force in Sept., 1426 ; Nov. 1942 Fr. W. Africa declared for Allies when Dakar became important air, military and naval base.

Dako'ta. Two States of the U.S.A. (N. and S. Dakota) lying in the Missouri basin, 957.

Dakota. U.S. transport plane largely used by U.S.A.A.F. and R.A.F. in Second World War for troops and cargo ; converted for use as civil airliner after the war.

Dakotas. Tribe of N. Amer. Indians of Sioux stock ; inhabited Mississippi plains ; now few in number.

Dal (Swedish *Dal-Elf*), river in S. Sweden. Rises on Norwegian frontier, flows S.E. and N.E. 250 m., forming several lakes and enters Gulf of Bothnia ; *map, 2395.*

Daladier (da-lad-yã), **Édouard** (b. 1884). Fr. premier (1933, 1934, 1938–40). After outbreak of war in Sept. 1939 became also Foreign Min. and Min. for War ; resigned premiership, March 1940 ; Min. for Nat. Defence under Reynaud ; Foreign Min., May-June 1940 ; arrested by Vichy Govt., removed to Germany 1943 ; released by Allies, 1945.

Dalai Lama (dal'-ī lah'-ma). Chief priest of Lamaism, the religion prevalent in Tibet. He has supremacy in all temporal as well as spiritual matters ; 3208.

Dalcroze, Émile Jaques- (1865–1950). Swiss composer ; inventor of eurhythmics, 1231.

Dale, Sir Henry H. (b. 1875). Brit. physiologist ; shared Nobel prize for medicine, 1936 ; P.R.S. 1940–45 ; from 1942 director of Scientific Advisory cttee. to Brit. war cabinet ; director of Royal Institution Labs. 1942–46 ; one of team who helped produce atom bomb ; Pres. Brit. Ass., 1947.

Dalecarlia (dah-le-kahr'-li-a) (" the valleys "), picturesque region in Sweden ; iron, copper, silver, lead ;

peasant costumes, 3126, *3128, plate f. 3128.*

D'Alembert, Jean de Rond. *See* Alembert.

Dalhou'sie, George Ramsay, 9th Earl of (1770–1838). One of Wellington's generals in Peninsular War ; gov.-gen. of Canada (1820–28).

Dalhousie, James Ramsay, 10th Earl and 1st Marquess of (1812–60). One of the master-builders of Brit. Indian Empire ; gov.-gen. (1849–56) ; annexed Punjab and other native states ; established imperial telegraph and postal systems ; built first rly., completed Ganges canal.

Dali (dah'-lē), **Salvador** (b. 1904). Spanish Surrealist painter ; expressing the irrationalism of dreams, he influenced greatly ballet décor, decorative arts, film technique ; 3122.

Dallas, Texas, U.S.A., leading mfg. city and rly. centre of state ; agric. trade ; pop. 294,700.

Dalmatia (dal-mā'-sha). Part of Yugoslavia, bordering Adriatic ; 4,900 sq. m. ; pop. 620,000 ; **957**, 2983, 3438.

Dalton, Hugh (b. 1887). Min. of Economic Warfare (1940–42). Pres. Board of Trade (1942–45). Chancellor of Exchequer (1945–47) ; Chancellor Duchy of Lancaster in 1948 ; became Min. of Town and Country Planning in 1950.

Dalton, John (1766–1844). Eng. chemist and physicist ; **957** ; atomic theory, 294, 767 ; Law of Multiple Proportions, 767 ; " Daltonism," 958.

Dalziel (dē'-el), **Henry James, 1st Baron** (1868–1935). Brit. newspaper owner and politician ; formerly had controlling interest in " Pall Mall Gazette " and was chairman of the company owning " The Daily Chronicle " and " The Sunday News."

Dam. Barrier built across watercourse to store water, **958**, *plate f. 961* ; beavers, 387 ; to control floods, 1318 ; hydroelectric installations, 1669 ; famous dams and barrages (table), 961 ; Ankara, *3263* ; Assuan, *959*, 1097, *1102* ; Boulder, 959, *plate f. 960* ; Burrinjack, N.S.W., *1672* ; Dnieper, 961, *plate f. 961* ; Gatun, *2490* ; Genissiat, 2774 ; Grand Coulee, 960 ; Lloyd, 960, *plate f. 961* ; Sardinia, *2873* ; Sennar, 3110 ; Sukkur, same as Lloyd.

Damanhur. Tn. in Lower Egypt, rly. centre ; pop. 61,000 ; textiles ; anc. Timenhor (tn. of Horus), known to Greeks as Hermopolis Parva.

Damão or **Daman.** Port, spt., and settlement on w. coast of India at entrance to Gulf of Cambay, 1692.

Dam'ar. A resin, 2768.

Damascene (dam-a-sēn'). Ornamentation of metal by inlaying with other metals, 963, *1809*, 1810.

Damascus (da-mas'-kus). Chief city of Syria ; pop. 286,300, **961** ; captured in 1st World War, 3414 ; centre of Saracen culture, 2067 ; damask cloth, 963 ; swords, 963 ; in 2nd World War, 963.

Dam'ask cloth, 850, 963, 3191.

Damien (da-mē-ahn), **Father** (1840–89). Belgian priest, missionary to lepers of Molokai, Hawaiian Isls., **963**.

Damietta (dam-i-et'-a). Port and trade centre in Lower Egypt on delta of

Nile ; pop. 40,332 ; anc. city bulwark of Egypt against Crusaders ; 1098.

Damocles (dam'-ō-klēz), 963.

Damon and Pythias, 963, 964.

Dampier (dam'-pēr), **William** (1652–1715), Eng. buccaneer and explorer, 310, 964.

Dampier Archipelago. Group of high rocky isls. off N.W. coast of Australia.

Damson, plum, 2630.

Dan. Son of Jacob and Bilhah, ancestor of Hebrew tribe of Dan (Gen. xxx. 6).

Dan. Anc. tn. in N. Palestine, at head of the Jordan, settled by descendants of Dan ; " from Dan to Beersheba," from one end of Palestine to the other.

Da'na, Charles Anderson (1819–97). Amer. journalist ; editor and part-proprietor of New York " Sun."

Dana, Richard Henry, Jr. (1815–82). Amer. jurist and author (" Two Years Before the Mast," classic sea story, describing voyage as common seaman to California).

Danaë (dan'-ā-ē), in Gk. myth., mother of Perseus, 2552.

Danaides (dan-ā'-i-dēz). In Gk. myth., the 50 daughters of Danaüs, king of Libya, doomed to fill sieves with water throughout eternity for killing their husbands at their father's command.

Dance music, provided by jazz, 1815.

" Dance of the Nymphs," or " Morning," painting by Corot, 1274, 1275.

Dancing, 965 ; Bali, 967 ; ballet, 345 ; ballroom, 965, 967 ; eurhythmics, 346, 1231 ; folk dances, 966, 1334, 1335 ; among Red Indians, 2756 ; Japanese, *plate f. 964* ; Javanese, *backs of plates f. 964, 965* ; Mongolian, *plate f. 965* ; nautch girls, 1699 ; Scottish, 965 ; Siamese, 967, 2964 ; Swedish, 3128.

Dan'delion, flowering weed of *Compositae* family, 967, 968.

Dandie Dinmont. In Scott's " Guy Mannering," a rough, shrewd, humorous Scotch farmer from whose dogs are named the " Dandie Dinmont " breed of Scotch terriers.

Dandolo (dan-dō'-lō), **Enrico** (c. 1120–1205). Doge of Venice, 1193–1205 ; leader of Crusaders in capture of Constantinople during 4th Crusade, 3312.

Danegeld (dān'-geld). A tax levied in Eng., 10th to 12th cents. ; originated as tribute to Danes.

Dane-law or **Danelagh.** Territory in E. Eng. ruled by Danes in 9th and 10th cents., 2388.

Danemora (da-ne-mōr'-a) or **Dannemora.** Vil. in Sweden 30 m. N. of Uppsala ; iron mines.

Danes (Northmen), 992, 2387 ; in Eng., 110, 694, 1194, 1195, 1203 ; costume, 991. *See* Northmen.

Daniel. Hebrew prophet, central figure of the Book of Daniel, 332, 968, 2691, 2692.

Danish language and literature, 2880.

Dan'necker, Johann Heinrich von (1758–1841), Ger. sculptor, friend of Schiller ; his work a constant struggle between classic and naturalistic schools.

D'Annunzio, Gabriele (da-noont'-si-ō) (1864–1938). It. poet, dramatist and airman, 1770, 1787.

Dante (dahn'-tā) **Alighieri** (1265–1321). Greatest It. poet, 969 ; at Bologna, 494 ; " Divine Comedy," story of, 970 ; influence on It. language, 1786 ; " Dante's Dream " by Rossetti, 1190.

Dantès (dahn-tes), **Edmond.** Hero of Dumas' " Count of Monte Cristo " ; sailor who, condemned through conspiracy to life imprisonment, escapes, gains buried treasure, and returns to dazzle Paris as the fabulously wealthy Count of Monte Cristo.

Danton (dahn-tawn), **Georges Jacques** (1759–94). Fr. Rev. leader, 971, 972, 1396 ; leads Jacobins, 1790 ; and Robespierre, 2790 ; and Madame Roland, 2798.

Danube (dan'-ūb). 2nd r. of Europe ; extends 1,780 m. from s.w. Ger. to Black Sea ; **972**, 316, 464, 600 ; 1232, 3322 ; Hungary, 1656 ; northern boundary of Rom. Empire, 1237, 1447 ; Rumania, 2840.

Danzig (dant-sik) or **Gdansk**, Poland. Former free city and state under League of Nations, on the Vistula ; under Nazi control from Aug. 1939 to Mar. 1945 ; pop. 94,000 ; **973** 1451, 2643, 3326, 3416.

Daphne (daf'-nē). A nymph in Gk. myth., turned into laurel tree, **974**, 1900 ; grove at Antioch, 177.

D'Arblay, Frances. *See* Burney, Fanny.

Darby and Joan. John Darby (d. 1730) and his wife Joan, originals of hero and heroine of Henry Woodfall's ballad " Darby and Joan," or " The Happy Old Couple," illustrating conjugal felicity.

Dardanelles (dahr-da-nelz') (anc. Hellespont). Narrow strait separating Europe from Asia, **974** ; refortified, 3266 ; in 1st World War, 3265, 3410.

Dar-es-Salaam (dahr-es-sa-lahm'). Spt. cap. of Tanganyika Territory, E. Africa ; pop. 74,000 ; 3150.

Darfur. Westernmost division of Anglo-Egyptian Sudan. Area 153,000 sq. m. ; pop. est. 1,000,000.

Darien (dār'-i-en), **Isthmus of.** Another name of Isthmus of Panama ; sometimes applied only to lower portion.

Darien Scheme. Unsuccessful attempt to establish Scottish colony on Isthmus of Panama (Darien), headed by William Paterson ; settlement begun in 1698 ; Sp. opposition, starvation, and disease led to abandonment in 1700.

Dario (dah-rē'-ō), **Ruben** (1867–1916). South American poet, 3027.

Darius (da-ri'-us) **I the Great** (c. 558–485 B.C.), King of Persia, 2554, 2555 ; attempts to conquer Greece, 2554.

Darius III (c. 380–330 B.C.). Last king (336–330 B.C.) of Persian Empire, conquered by Alexander the Great, 105, 2555.

Darjeeling (dar-jē'-ling). Resort and centre of tea-growing dist. N. Bengal, India, 413, 1626.

" Dark Continent," 65.

Dark line spectrum, *plate f. 3057.*

Darlan, Admiral Jean (1881–1942). French Gov. N. Africa ; resisted Allied invasion Nov. 1942, capitulated and joined Fighting French ; assassinated Dec. 1942, 3420.

Darling, Charles John, 1st Baron (1849–1936). Eng. judge, noted for wit and graceful light verse. He retired in 1924.

Darling, Grace Horsley (1815–42). Eng. heroine, **974**, 975.

Darling Range. Low mts. in w. Australia, running parallel with coast for nearly 250 m.

Darling River, Australia, rises in Queensland, flows s.w. through New South Wales, joins Murray ; length 1,160 m. ; 307.

Darlington. Industrial tn. of Durham, on r. Skerne, 18 m. s. of Durham city ; large rly. workshops, iron works, engineering works ; the rly. to Stockton was the first passenger line to use steam locomotives ; pop. est. 77,910 ; 1059.

Darmstadt (dahrm'-shtat). Ger. mfg. city and rly. centre, cap. of state of Hesse, 20 m. s. of Frankfort ; pop. (1939) 115,000 ; heavily damaged by air raids in 2nd World War.

Darning, 2928.

Darn'ley, Henry Stuart, Lord (1545–67). Scottish noble, 2nd husband of Mary Queen of Scots, 2115, 2116.

D'Arsonval. Galvanometer, 1134.

Dart. R. of Devonshire, flows to Eng. Channel ; 46 m. long ; 999.

D'Artagnan (dahr-tan-yawn), **Charles.** Gascon adventurer, hero of Dumas' " The Three Musketeers," " Twenty Years After," " Le Vicomte de Bragelonne " ; 1054.

Dartford. Town of Kent, road tunnel under Thames to Purfleet ; 3256.

Dart'moor. Rugged tableland in s.w. Devonshire ; about 20 sq. m. ; convict prison at Princetown, 1000 ; druidi-

cal and other remains ; 999 ; river Dart, 1311 ; post bridge, 566.

Dartmouth. Spt. in Devonshire, near mouth of r. Dart ; pop. 6,707 ; castle ; shipbuilding and engineering industries ; here Crusaders embarked for Holy Land (1190) ; Royal Naval College, 1000, 2306.

Darts, the game, 975.

Darwen. Industrial tn. of Lancashire, 3 m. s. of Blackburn ; cotton and paper mills ; pop. 36,010.

Dar'win, Sir Charles Galton (b. 1887). Brit. physicist ; grandson of Charles Darwin ; director of National Physical Lab. from 1938 ; chief of the Brit. cttee. of scientists advising on the atomic bomb.

Darwin, Charles Robert (1809–82). Eng. biologist, **975**, 976 ; developed theory of organic evolution, 1244, 1617 ; effects of theory on zoology, 3447 ; " cats and clover " in ecology, 1079 ; on cruise of the Beagle, 977, 2472 ; relations with Huxley, 1661.

Darwin, Erasmus (1731–1802). Eng. physician, naturalist, and poet, grandfather of Charles Darwin, 975.

Darwin, Sir Francis (1848–1925). Eng. botanist, 3rd son of Charles Darwin, whose biography he wrote.

Darwin, Sir George Howard (1845–1912). Eng. geologist and astronomer, 2nd son of Charles Darwin ; made estimate of earth's age ; study of the moon, 2225.

Darwin, Australia. Spt. and chief tn. of Northern Territory on N.W. coast ; airport on main Empire airway ; bombed by Japs in 1942.

Darwinism. The evolutionary theory of Charles Darwin, 977, 1244, 1245.

Dash. Mark of punctuation, 2705.

Dashboard, motor-car, 2242.

Dashur, Eg. Place s. of Great Pyramids ; noted for pyramids.

Dashwood, Elinor and **Marianne.** Two sisters who represent " Sense and Sensibility " in Jane Austen's novel of that name.

Date Line, International. *See* International Date Line.

Date palm, 978, 2484, 2485.

Dates, food value, 978, 1339.

Daubigny (dō-bē-nyē), **Charles François** (1817–78). Fr. landscape painter and etcher of Barbizon school.

Daudet (dō-dā), **Alphonse** (1840–97). Fr. novelist, 979.

Daugavpils, or **Dvinsk.** City of s.E. Latvia ; pop. 45,000 ; former Rus. fortress ; linen, flax, sawmills ; in German occupation 1941–44.

Daumier (dō-myā), **Honoré** (1808–79). Fr. caricaturist and painter, inspired by inexhaustible genius for mockery of social and political life ; drew about 4,000 lithographs, 1967 ; as a painter was a pioneer of naturalism, 1378.

Dau'phin (Fr. " dolphin "). Title borne first by rulers of certain Fr. territories, called the Dauphiné ; later, when the Dauphiné became crown land (1364), borne by the Fr. king's eldest son ; Charles VII, 758 ; 1653 ; 1831 ; Louis XVII, the " Lost Dauphin," 2030.

Dauphiné Alps. A range of the Alps in former Dauphiné prov. in s.E. Fr. (13,462 ft.).

Davenant (dav'-en-ant), **Sir William** (1606–68). Eng. poet and dramatist ; became poet laureate in 1660, following Ben Jonson ; his heroic poem " Gondibert " was written while he was in prison for a political offence.

Daventry. Town in Northants. Famous for B.B.C. radio station (1925–47), 2385.

Da'vid (c. 1030–990 B.C.). King of Israel (about 1000 B.C.), **979**, 1829 ; birthplace, 422 ; descended from Ruth, 2858 ; conquers Jerusalem, 1820 ; statue by Michelangelo, 2161.

David I (1084–1153). King of Scotland, 1123–53. Son of Malcolm Canmore and St. Margaret of England ; called " maker of Scotland " ; reformed courts, established many towns ; promoted trade, shipping, and manufactures.

David II (1324–71). King of Scotland. Crowned king in 1331 at death of father, Robert Bruce ; began to rule in 1341 ; weak and incapable.

David (dah-vēd), **Félicien César** (1810–76). Fr. composer, called " the musical orientalist " ; wandered for years in East and expressed oriental melodies in gorgeous orchestral colours ; wrote symphonic ode, " The Desert " ; oratorio, " Moses on Sinai " ; operas, " Herculaneum," " Lalla Rookh."

David, Jacques Louis (1748–1825). Fr. portrait and historical painter, active revolutionist, zealous Jacobin, later court painter to Napoleon ; 1378 ; painted " Coronation of Josephine," *1839* ; " Mme. Récamier," *1372.*

David, St. (d. *c.* 601). Patron saint of Wales, who established several monasteries ; his festival day is March 1.

" David Copperfield," novel by Charles Dickens, his own favourite, *2402.*

Davidson, John (1857–1909). Eng. poet ; thoroughly pessimistic, best known for ballads ; wrote " Bruce," " Scaramouch in Naxos," fantastic plays ; " Fleet Street Eclogues " ; " Perfervid," a prose romance.

Davidson, Randall Thomas, Baron (1848–1930). Archbishop of Canterbury, 1903–28 ; previously Bishop of Rochester, 1891–5, and Bishop of Winchester, 1895–1903.

Davies, Benjamin Grey (1858–1943). Welsh singer, better known as Ben Davies, one of the leading concert platform tenors of modern times.

Davies, Sir (Henry) Walford (1869–1941). Eng. musician ; appointed Master of the King's Musick in 1934.

Davies, William Henry (1870–1940). Brit. poet ; tramp and pedlar in England and America for several years. ("Autobiography of a Super-tramp.")

Da Vinci. *See* **Leonardo da Vinci.**

Davis, Henry William Carless, (1874 1928). Eng. historian ; " England under the Normans and Angevins."

Davis, Jefferson (1808–89). U.S.A. soldier and statesman ; president of the Confederate States on outbreak of Civil War.

Davis, Joe (b. 1901). Brit. billiards player ; won billiards championship 10 times ; world snooker champion from 1927 ; on Feb. 9, 1948, his snooker break of 180 was a world record.

Davis or **Davys, John** (*c.* 1555–1605). Eng. navigator and early Arctic explorer ; discovered (1587) Davis Strait, 142.

Davis Cup. International lawn-tennis team competition, instituted by Dwight Davis in 1900.

Davis Strait. Between Greenland and Baffin Island ; connects Baffin Bay with Atlantic ; width 180 to 500 m.

Davitt, Michael (1846–1906). Irish political leader and founder of the Irish Land League (1879) ; bitterness that marked his entire career sprang from eviction of parents for non-payment of rent during his childhood ; several times returned to Parliament ; ardent " Home Ruler," but opposed to Parnell.

Davos (dah-vos). Winter resort in Switzerland lying in canton of Grisons.

Davout (da-vōō), **Louis Nicolas, Duke of Auerstädt and Prince of Eckmühl** (1770–1823). One of Napoleon's marshals ; distinguished himself by brilliant victories at Auerstädt and Eckmühl, turned tide at Wagram ; minister of war during " 100 days."

Davy, Sir Humphry (1778–1829), Eng. chemist and physicist, **979** ; developed theory of heat, 1593 ; magnesium, 2060 ; potassium, 2662 ; and Faraday, 1260 ; safety lamp, *979*, 980, *1889* ; sodium, 2997.

Davy Jones. Sailors' colloquial name for the devil or bad spirit of the sea ; " Davy Jones's Locker," place where men and ships go when lost at sea.

Dawes, Charles Gates (b. 1865). Amer. statesman ; head of committee that framed the " Dawes Plan" for the payment of German reparations (1923) ; vice-president of U.S.A. (1924) ; ambassador to Gt. Brit. (1929–32).

Dawson of Penn, Bertram Edward Dawson, 1st Viscount (1864–1945). Brit. physician, specialist in diabetes and gastric diseases ; physician to Edward VII, George V, Edward VIII, and George VI ; first physician in practice to be raised to peerage ; president R.C.P. in 1931 ; Viscount in 1936.

Dawson City, Canada. Cap. of Yukon Territory and centre of Klondike mining region on Yukon river ; pop. at time of gold rush, 20,000, now 1,040 ; 3440.

Day, 980.

Day, Thomas (1748–89). Eng. writer, author of " The History of Sandford and Merton" (1783–89), one of the earliest children's books.

Daylight Saving, 980.

Days of grace. Extension of time allowed for settlement of bills after they become legally due.

Day'ton, Ohio, U.S.A. Mfg. city ; home of Wright brothers, the airmen ; pop. 210,720 ; 2426.

Daytona Beach. City of Florida ; popular winter resort ; pop. 22,580 ; sands used for motor racing.

D-day. Code name for day, June 6, 1944, on which Operation Overlord (the Normandy Invasion of Second World War) took place, 2377, 3422.

D.D.T. (Dichloro-diphenyl-trichloro-ethane), insecticide invented in 1874, came into use in 2nd World War against typhus-carrying lice and other noxious insects, 179.

Deadly nightshade, or belladonna, *2369,* 2370, 2637, *2639.*

Deadly upas-tree, or anchar, a member of fig family, chiefly in Java, 3246.

Dead nettle, 2335, 3207.

Dead Sea. Salt lake in s.E. Palestine, 340 sq. m. ; 263, **981,** 2480.

Dead stars, 3080.

" Deadwood Dick." Nickname of Richard Clark (d. 1930), an Englishman who was one of the pioneer drivers of the pony express across the American prairies in the days of the Sioux Indians ; alias taken from Deadwood, South Dakota, U.S.A.

Deaf, 981 ; Abbé de l'Epée founds first school for, 981 ; disabled persons, 982 ; Helen Keller, 471 ; Laura Bridgman, 470.

Deák (dā-ak'), **Francis** (1803–76). Hungarian statesman, one of ablest political leaders in Europe ; chief organizer (1867) of Austro-Hungarian dual monarchy ; 1874.

Deakin (dē'-kin), **Alfred** (1856–1919). Australian statesman, three times prime minister ; called most brilliant orator of Brit. Empire, reconciling influence between Labour and Conservative parties.

Deakin, Arthur (b. 1890). Brit. trade union leader ; in 1946 succeeded Ernest Bevin as gen. sec. of Transport and Gen. Workers' Union ; pres. of W.F.T.U.

Dean, of cathedral, status, 730.

Dean, Forest of. District (25,000 acres) in w. Gloucestershire, between the Severn and Wye ; anc. royal forest ; 1476.

Deans, Jeanie. The heroine of Scott's " Heart of Midlothian " ; a simple Scottish peasant girl who refuses to testify falsely to save her sister Effie from conviction of child murder, but walks alone most of the way from Edinburgh to London to win her pardon from Queen Caroline ; one of Scott's strongest and noblest characters.

Death penalty, 2687.

Death Valley, U.S.A., desert region of s. California.

Death watch beetle, *Xestobium rufovillosum,* insect whose larva bores in old oak beams, often doing immense damage, 399.

Debenture stock, 3093.

Debits, in book-keeping, items shown on the debit side, indicating money owing. 518.

Deb'orah. Hebrew heroine, prophetess, and judge who helped to deliver Israelites from Canaanites, 1829.

Debreczen (deb'-ret-sen), Hungary. City 135 m. E. of Budapest ; pop. 122,500 ; centre of Hungarian Protestantism ; here Kossuth (1849) proclaimed deposition of Hapsburgs ; varied mfrs. and trade.

Debrett'. List of peerage of the U.K., pub. under the name of an early compiler, John Debrett (*c.* 1752–1882).

Debt, bankruptcy laws, 356 ; Greek law, 2999 ; Roman law, 2805.

Debussy (de-boo-sē), **Claude Achille** (1862–1918). Fr. composer, leader of a new school ; produced music of elusive and subtle beauty by use of " whole-tone " scale ; (" Pelléas et Mélisande," " L'Après-Midi d'un Faune ") ; 2266, 2436.

Debye, P. J. W. (b. 1884). Du. scientist, Nobel prize for chemistry, 1936; prof. in U.S.A. from 1940 ; research on molecular structure ; and ionization, 1739.

Dec'agramme. The 10 gramme unit in metric system (0·353 oz.), 2155.

Decalitre or **centistere.** The 10 litre unit of metric system (22 gallons, 0·77 pints), 2155.

Dec'alogue (" ten words "). The Ten Commandments, 2235.

" Decam'eron." A famous collection of stories by Giovanni Boccaccio, 1786, 2764.

Dec'ametre. The 10 metre unit in metric system (10·936 yards), 2155.

Decay, caused by bacteria, 336 ; of rock into soil, 336.

" Decca " navigation aids, *2292,* 2293 ; radar, 2727.

Deccan, or **Dekkan.** The whole peninsula of India s. of the r. Narbada, 1692, 1701, *map, 1702.*

Decem'ber. 12th month in the year, got its name from being the tenth month of the old Roman calendar, 2223.

Decemvirs (de-sem'-vērz) (" ten men "). Rom. commission appointed 451 B.C. to draw up code of laws, 2805.

Decibel. The logarithmic scale for the comparison of sound energies is graduated in units of " 1 bel " subdivided into 10 decibels. An increase of 1 decibel represents an increase in sound of 26 per cent, the smallest change that the average person can appreciate ; the noise of a pneumatic drill 20 ft. away is about 90 decibels. Replaced in 1937 by the Phon. *See* Phon.

Deciduous (de-sid'-ū-us) **plants.** Those which shed their leaves periodically and are bare in winter, 1244, 3245 ; autumn coloration, 1917.

Decigramme. The 1/10th of a gramme unit of metric system (1·543 grains), 2155.

Decilitre. The 100 cubic centimetre unit of metric system (0·176 pints), 2155.

Dec'imals. In arithmetic, **982** ; Arabic numerals, 2405 ; percentage, 2548.

Decimal system, of weights and measures, 2154.

Dec'imetre. The 1/10th of a metre unit of metric system (3·937 in.), 2155.

Decius (dē'-si-us) (A.D. *c.* 201–251). Rom. emperor (249–51), remembered chiefly for Christian persecutions ; killed fighting Goths.

Declaration of Independence, American 144, 3291.

Declaration of Paris (1856), 3240.

Declaration of the Rights of Man (1791), 1394.

Declar'ative sentence, 2921.

Decien'sion of nouns, 2399 ; of pronouns, 2690.

Dec'lination, of a star, the angle made between an imaginary line from the observer to the star and the plane of the earth's Equator, used in pointing telescopes, 2411.

Declination or **variation,** of compass, angle between magnetic north and true north, 882.

" Decline and Fall of the Roman Empire," by Gibbon, 1461.

Decorations and Orders, 2448, 1864.

Deduc'tion, in logic, 2572.

Dee. R. 70 m. long in Eng. and Wales, 1165.

Dee. R. in Scot., famous for salmon ; flows 87 m. to North Sea at Aberdeen. 11.

Dee. R. in Scot., flows to Kirkcudbright Bay ; 45 m. long, 1862.

Deep-sea crab, plate f. 925.

Deep-sea diving, 1019.

Deep-sea fish, 2103, 2416.

Deer, 984, 2842, 2285 ; antlers, 985 ; caribou, 702 ; foot structure, 1342, 2976 ; leathers, 1477, 1914 ; moose, 2228 ; prehistoric, 2680 ; reindeer, 2760, 2847 ; photographed at night, 2285 ; "White Tail and the Old Stag's Lesson," 3493.

Deerhound, plate f. 1024.

Deerslayer. Nickname of Natty Bumppo, hero of J. Fenimore Cooper's novel, "The Deerslayer."

Defence Medal. Brit. medal issued during the Second World War to some 7,000,000 persons for military, naval, air force, or civilian service ; ribbon flame-coloured edged with green and with two black stripes.

Defender of the Faith. Title borne by all Eng. sovereigns since Henry VIII ; origin, 1612.

Definite Proportions, Law of, 767.

Deflation. Diminution in volume of currency, causing money units to rise in value and prices of commodities to fall.

Defoe (de-fō'), Daniel (c. 1659–1731). Eng. novelist and journalist, author of "Robinson Crusoe," 937, 985, 986, 1213.

De Forest, Lee (b. 1873). Amer. inventor of wireless valve, 3198.

Deforesta'tion. Effects of, 3246 ; in Britain, 1350 ; Sp., 3030 ; U.S.A., 1350. See Forests.

Degas (dā-gah). Hilaire Germain (1834–1917), Fr. impressionist painter of the ballet, etc., 346, 1378.

Degaussing (dē-gow'sing). Method of protecting steel ships against magnetic mines ; through an insulated cable which encircles the ship high above water-line is run an electric current of strength to neutralize the natural magnetic field of the ship, 2065, 2185–86. Named after K. F. Gauss. See Gauss.

Degenera'tion. In biology ; barnacles, 361 ; parasites, 2513 ; penguins, 2544.

Degree, the 360th part of a circle ; in geometry, 1435 ; of latitude and longitude, 1898.

Degree, a division of a scale ; of temperature, 1594, 3200 ; of water hardness, 3351.

Degree. Title of honour or mark of distinction conferred by colleges and univs. on students, such as B.A., bachelor of arts, M.A., master of arts, B.Sc., bachelor of science, 3296. See Abbreviations.

De Havilland, Sir Geoffrey (b. 1882). Brit. aircraft designer, director of the De Havilland Aircraft Co., Ltd. Made first ascent 1908 in plane designed by himself ; in 1934 awarded first British Gold Medal for Aeronautics ; produced 1912 Mosquito all-wood fighter-bomber, 1945 Vampire jet fighter, 1949 Comet jet airliner. D.-H. aircraft, 38, 47, 53.

de Hooch. See Hooch, Pieter de.

Dehydrated food, food from which the water has been removed, 1340 ; milk, 2174 ; prunes, 2696.

Deianira (dē-i-a-nīr'-a), wife of Hercules, 1651.

Deiphobus (dē-if'-o-bus), brother of Hector in Gk. myth, 1603.

Deira (dē'-i-ra). Anc. kingdom in Eng. ; united with Bernicia as Northumbria.

Deirdre (dēr'-dre). In anc. Celtic myth., a beautiful woman fated to cause misfortune, heroine of most famous of Ulster cycle of old Irish tales, the "Death of the Sons of Usnech," one of the "Three Sorrows of Story-Telling" ; basis of dramas by "Æ," Yeats, and Synge, 1751.

De'ism. System of belief which admits the existence of a God, but denies the existence or even the necessity of a divine revelation.

Dek'ker or Decker, Thomas (c. 1570–1641). Eng. dramatist of Shakespeare's time ; "the Dickens of the Elizabethan period" ; pictured London life of shop and tavern ("The Shoemaker's Holiday, or the Gentle Craft").

Delacroix (de-lah-krwah), Eugène (1798–1863). Fr. painter, great colourist, leader of Romantic school ("Barque of Dante" ; "Massacre of Chios" ; "The Barricade" ; "Baron Schwiter") ; 1377, 1378.

Delafield, E. M. (1890–1943). Eng. authoress of light, humorous prose ("The Diary of a Provincial Lady" ; play, "To See Ourselves"). Real name, Elizabeth M. Dashwood.

Delago'a Bay. Inlet of Indian Ocean in Port. colony of Mozambique in s.E. Africa, 986 ; fine harbour, 1073.

De la Mare, Walter John (b. 1873). Eng. poet and novelist; "Peacock Pie" ; "Henry Brocken" ; "On the Edge" ; "The Three Mulla Mulgars" ; "Memoirs of a Midget" ; "The Listeners," and much excellent children's verse ; C.H. in 1948.

Delane (de-lan'), John Thadeus (1817–79). English editor. Edited "The Times," 1841–77.

Delarey (de-lah-rā'), Jacobus (1848–1915). Prominent Boer general, who was assistant commandant-general of the Transvaal army in the S. African (Boer) War (1899–1902) ; victor of several engagements, in one of which he took Lord Methuen prisoner, 487.

De la Roche, Mazo. See Roche, Mazo de la.

Delaroche (de-lah-rosh), Paul (real name Hippolyte) (1797–1856). Fr. historical and portrait painter ; "The Princes in the Tower," 1090 ; "Laud Blessing Strafford," 1899.

De Laval, Carl Gustaf Patrik (1845–1913), Swedish inventor of cream separator (1879), first successful steam turbine (1883) and flexible shaft ; 3259.

Del'aware, or De La Warr, Thomas West, Baron (1577–1618). Brit. soldier and administrator ; colonial governor of Virginia (1609–18) ; Delaware state and r. named after him ; 986.

Delaware, 2nd smallest state in U.S.A. ; in South Atlantic group ; 2,057 sq. m. ; pop. 267,000 ; 986.

Delbos, Yvon (b. 1885). Fr. statesman. Minister of Education (1925) ; of Justice (1936) ; Foreign Minister (1936–38).

Del'brück, Hans (1848–1929). Ger. historian ("History of Warfare in Relation to Political History") ; member of Delegation to Peace Conference of 1919.

Delcassé (del-kas-ā), Théophile (1852–1923). Fr. statesman instrumental in cementing Triple Entente and Fr. alliance with Russia ; minister for Foreign Affairs (1898–1905), and for several brief periods between 1911 and 1915 ; ambassador to Russia (1913).

Deledda, Grazia (b. 1873). It. author of over 20 novels, many dealing with her native Sardinia ; Nobel prize for lit., 1927 ; 2403.

De Lesseps, Ferdinand. See Lesseps.

Delft, Netherlands. Dutch pottery tn., pop. 58,000 ; 986, 2320 ; painting by Vermeer, 3315.

Delft pottery, 986, 2666.

Delhi (del'-i). New Delhi is cap. of Republic of India and chief city of Delhi prov. ; pop. (city) 522,000, (prov.) 918,000 ; 987 ; Jama Masjid (Great Mosque), 987, 1706 ; Lutyens' designs, 987, 2041 ; Mogul palace, plate f. 989 ; observatory, 1713 ; Pearl Mosque, plate f. 988 ; peacock throne, 987, 2532.

Delian Confederacy, 231, 286, 1522.

Delibes (dā-lēb), Clément Philibert Léo (1836–91). Fr. composer ("Coppélia").

Delilah (de-lī'-la). Philistine woman loved by Samson, whose downfall she caused by cutting his strength giving locks (Judges xvi.), 2870.

Delius (dē'-li-us), Frederick (1863–1934), Eng. composer of Ger. parentage, 988, 2266.

Della Robbia, Andrea (1435–1523). Florentine sculptor, 2765, 2906.

Della Robbia, Luca (1399–1482). Uncle of Andrea ; marble reliefs, Singing Gallery at Florence Cathedral ; 2670, 2906.

Delos (dē'-los). Gk. isl. in Aegean ; smallest but most famous of Cyclades, 1527 ; birthplace of Apollo, 187 ; excavations at, 1527 ; treasury of Delian League, 1522.

Delphi (del'-fī). Anc. town, site of famous oracle on Mt. Parnassus, Greece, 186, 188, 988 ; excavations at, 1522, 1527 ; oracles, 21, 188, 649, 2043, 3202.

Delphinium. See Larkspur.

Del Rio, Andres Manuel (1765–1849). Span. mineralogist who in 1801 in Mexico discovered vanadium, 3303.

Del'ta, δ, Δ (Rom. d, D). Fourth letter of the Gk. alphabet.

Delta. Tract of land formed by earth deposited by rivers at mouth, 2598 : of Amazon, 136 ; Ganges, 1417 ; Indus, 1721 ; Mississippi, 2191 ; Nile, 1098.

Delta metal, an alloy of zinc, 3444.

Deluge, The. Flood which overwhelmed the earth in time of Noah (Gen. vii.) ; Babylonian story, 332, 2374.

Demarca'tion, Line of. Imaginary line from North to South Pole 100 leagues w. of Azores ; fixed in 1493 by Pope Alexander VI ; all new lands discovered to E. were to belong to Port. and all w. to Sp.

Demavend, Mt., Iran. Extinct volcano, 18,549 ft.

Demesne (de-mān) or domain, of a lord in feudal system, 86.

Demerar'a. River and tn. of British Guiana ; gave name to brown sugar, 3113.

Demeter (dē-mē'-ter). Goddess of agric. in Gr. myth., 989, 1921.

Demetrius (dē-mē'-tri-us) or Dmitri (dmē'-trē). Russian pretender ; appeared in 1603, took name of heir to the throne who had been secretly killed by the usurping Tsar Boris Godunov, reigned with vigour and ability until his murder (1606) ; followed by a series of less able "false Dmitris."

Demetrius I (337–282 B.C.). Called Poliorcetes ("besieger") ; besieged Rhodes with elaborate machinery 305–204 B.C. ; established supremacy over Macedonia and Greece, seizing throne 294 B.C. ; expelled by Pyrrhus and died a prisoner of Seleucus.

Democ'racy. Form of govt. in which the sovereign power is retained by the people and exercised by their chosen representatives ; 989, 2651 ; beginnings in anc. Greece, 1519, 2999.

Democrat'ic party (U.S.A.), 3290.

Democritus (dē-mok'-ri-tus) (c. 460–357 B.C.). Gk. philosopher ; called "Aristotle of 5th century," also inappropriately styled the "Laughing Philosopher," as Heraclitus was the "Weeping Philosopher" ; advanced theory of the mechanical formations of the universe by atoms in action, 294.

Demonstrative adjectives, 27.

De Morgan, William (1839–1917), Eng. novelist ; for 30 years an artist-potter ; began to write at 65, for amusement after illness ; excels in naturalness of dialogue, but characters often more important than plot ; "Joseph Vance", "Alice-for-Short" ; "Somehow Good."

Demosthenes (dē-mos'-the-nēz) (c. 383–322 B.C.). Most famous Gk. orator, 990, 1524, 3198.

De.np'sey, Gen. Sir Miles C. (b. 1896). Brit. soldier ; commanded Brit. 2nd Army from Normandy landings (June 1944) to disbandment, June 1945 ; C.-in-C. Allied Land Forces, S.E. Asia, 1945 ; C.-in-C. Middle East, 1946 ; retired 1947.

Dempsey, William Harrison ("Jack") (b. 1895). Amer. boxer. World heavyweight champion (1919–26).

Denain (de-nan'). Coal-mining and iron-mfg. tn. in N. Fr., 6 m. s.w. of Valenciennes; pop. 24,500; victory of Fr. over Allies under Prince Eugene (1712).

Denar'ius. A Rom. coin of silver, later one of copper, the "penny" of the New Testament; "denarius" was Latin name given to Eng. penny; hence its initial (d.) became sign for pence.

Denbigh (den'-bi), Wales. Co. tn. of Denbighshire; dairying, boot and shoe mfrs.; castle; pop. 8,100; 990.

Denbighshire, Wales. Northern co. bordering Irish Sea; a. 665 sq. m.; pop. 158,000, **990.**

Den'eb, a star, 3079.

Denham, Bucks. Vil. 15 m. w.n.w. of London; large film studios, 600.

Denikin (dye-ně'-kin), **Anton** (1872–1947). Rus. general on general staff in early part of 1st World War; after revolution followed Kornilov, later becoming anti-Bolshevik Cossack commander operating between Caspian and Black Seas (1919); completely routed in 1920. Died in U.S.A. Aug. 1947.

Denis (de-ně'), **St.** (Latin **Dionysius**), apostle to the Gauls (d. c. 275), first bishop of Paris, martyr and patron saint of France.

Denmark. One of the three Scandinavian kingdoms of N.W. Europe; pop. 4,024,000; 16,575 sq. m.; **991**; cap. Copenhagen; 904, *905*; *map, 992*; children, *800*; folk-dancing, *1334*; foreign trade, 991, 1541; Greenland, 1541; neolithic remains, 2083; physical features, 351; relations with Iceland, 991, 1685. *History*, 992, 2880; Northmen, 992, 2387; Canute, 694, 992; war with Hanseatic League (1368), 1575; union with Sweden (1397), 992, 3131; in Thirty Years' War, 3202; loses Norway, 992, 2398; loses Schleswig-Holstein, 992; occupied by Germans, 1940–45, 992, 1452, 3416.

RULERS OF DENMARK SINCE THE UNION OF KALMAR

DENMARK, SWEDEN and NORWAY
1397–1412	Margaret and Eric VII (XIII of Sweden)
1412–38	Eric VII (alone)
1438–40	[Interregnum]
1440–48	Christopher III
1448–81	Christian I
1481–1513	John
1513–23	Christian II (Sweden revolts and becomes independent 1523)

DENMARK AND NORWAY
1523–1533	Frederick I
1533–1559	Christian III
1559–1588	Frederick II
1588–1648	Christian IV
1648–1670	Frederick III
1670–1699	Christian V
1699–1730	Frederick IV
1730–1746	Christian VI
1746–1766	Frederick V
1766–1784	Christian VII
1808–1839	Frederick VI (regent 1784–1808); (Norway annexed to Sweden, 1814)

DENMARK
1839–1848	Christian VIII
1848–1863	Frederick VII
1863–1906	Christian IX
1906–1912	Frederick VIII
1912–1947	Christian X
1947–	Frederick IX

Density, specific, 1513, 3054.

Dent, Edward J. (b. 1876). Brit. musical critic and writer; translated many opera libretti; wrote "Mozart's Operas," "Life of Handel."

Dental Corps, in Brit. army, 248.

Dentil. In architecture, small block or projection in the bed-mouldings of cornices in Ionic, Corinthian, Composite, and occasionally Doric orders.

Den'tine, tooth substance, *3164.*

Dentistry. *See* **Teeth.**

Denver, Colorado, U.S.A. Cap. and largest city; pop. 322,000; rly. centre; univ.; trade in livestock; distributing point for surrounding gold, silver, and coal mines, 874.

Deodar. The Indian cedar tree, 737.

Department. Fr. govt. division, 1362.

Depew', Chauncey Mitchell (1834–1928). Amer. lawyer, politician, and orator.

Deposits, in banks, 357.

Depression, in meteorology, 2150.

Deptford (det'-ford). Met. and parl. bor. in s.e. London; Peter the Great worked in the dockyard, for long the most important in Eng.; pop. 106,890; elec. supply station, 1546.

Depth and Height, *89.*

Depth Charge. Anti-submarine weapon. Cylinder containing high-explosive charge, dropped overboard from ship or from aircraft and adjusted to explode at pre-determined depth.

Deputies, Chamber of, Fr., 1362.

De Quin'cey, Thomas (1785–1859). Eng. essayist and critic, 994, 1214.

Derain, André (b. 1880). Fr. painter and stage designer. Exhibition of works in London in 1934.

Derbend' or Derbent or Derben. Anc. Rus. city on Caspian in Daghestan A.S.S.R.; pop. 23,000, largely Mahomedan; 717, 733.

Derby, Edward Geoffrey Stanley, 14th Earl of (1799–1869). Eng. statesman, supporter of Reform Act of 1832, prime minister 1852, 1858–59, 1866–68; translated Iliad.

Derby, Edward George Stanley, 17th Earl of (1865–1948). Eng. statesman, Conservative leader, House of Commons (1892–1906), director-general of recruiting (1915–16), during which time he introduced the "Derby Scheme"; Sec. of State for War (1916–18, 1922–3), ambassador to Fr. (1918–20). Died Feb. 4, 1948; succeeded by grandson, Edward John Stanley, Lord Stanley (b. 1918).

Derby, Frederick Arthur Stanley, 16th Earl of (1841–1908). Eng. statesman and colonial administrator; held various offices in Disraeli and Salisbury cabinets, gov.-gen. of Canada 1888–92 (as Baron Stanley).

Derby. Co. tn. on Derwent; pop. 131,500; rly. workshops; noted for china; also motor-car, aero-engine, and silk mfrs.; 995, 2670.

Derby, The. The most famous horse racing event in Eng., 994, *995*. Recent winners : 1932, April the Fifth; 1933, Hyperion; 1934, Windsor Lad; 1935, Bahram; 1936, Mahmoud; 1937, Mid-day Sun; 1938, Bois Roussel; 1939, Blue Peter; 1940, Pont l'Evêque; 1941, Owen Tudor; 1942, Watling Street; 1943, Straight Deal; 1944, Ocean Swell; 1945, Dante; 1946, Airborne; 1947, Pearl Diver; 1948, My Love; 1949, Nimbus.

Derbyshire. A N. midland co. of Eng.; a. 1,012 sq. m.; pop. 757,000; 995, *1318*, 2941.

Derg Lough. Two lakes of Eire. One 24 m. long and 1–2 m. wide is a widening of the r. Shannon. The other, in co. Donegal, is 25 sq. m. in area.

Dermes'tid. Skin-devouring beetle, 400.

Dermis or derm, true skin, 1913, 2979.

Dermot Mac Mur'rough (c. 1110–71). King of Leinster, pivot of first Eng. intervention in Ireland (1135–71); dethroned because he had carried off another chieftain's wife : sought aid of Henry II.

Der'na. Small spt. of Cyrenaica, 100 m. w. of Tobruk; changed hands five times during the N. Africa campaign in 1941–42; *map, 3421.*

De Robeck, Sir John (1862–1928). Brit. admiral, who had charge of the landing at Gallipoli in the 1st World War.

De Rougemont, Louis (1847–1921). Swiss adventurer, real name Henri Louis Grin. In 1898 caused sensation in London by account of 28

years among Australian blacks. Story later discredited, but now believed true in part.

Déroulède, Paul (1846–1914). Fr. poet, dramatist and politician.

Derris powder. Insecticide made from roots of a tropical plant, *Derris elliptica.*

Derry. *See* **Londonderry.**

Dervish, a member of Mahomedan religious fraternity living in a monastery or wandering as a mendicant. In 1948 the last of the dancing Dervishes (Maulawiyeh) was reported to have died at Istanbul.

Derwent, river in Cumberland, flows into Irish Sea; 35 m. long, 943.

Derwent, river in Derbyshire, trib. of the Trent, 60 m. long, 995.

Derwent, r. in Northumberland and Durham, trib. of the Tyne; 30 m. long.

Derwent, r. in North Riding of Yorkshire, trib. of the Ouse; 70 m. long, 3435.

Derwentwater, small oval lake in Cumberland, noted for its scenic charm, *1175.*

Desaix (de-sā'), **Louis,** Fr. soldier (1768–1800); defended Kehl fortress in 1796 against the Austrians, and made possible Napoleon's success at Marengo, June 14, 1800, where he lost his life.

De Saussure, Horace Bénédict (1740–99). Swiss Alpine traveller and physicist; one of first to ascend to summit of Mont Blanc.

Descartes (dā-kart), **René** (1596–1650). Fr. philosopher and mathematician, 995, *996*; and spectrum, *plate f. 3056.*

"Descent from the Cross," famous painting by Michelangelo.

"Descent of Man," by Darwin, 978.

Deschanel (dā-shah-nel'), **Paul Eugene Louis** (1856–1922). Fr. statesman, orator, and writer; Liberal leader; president of France, 1920, but resigned the same year.

Desdemona (dez-de-mō'-na), heroine of Shakespeare's "Othello," *2457.*

"Deserted Village, The," poem by Oliver Goldsmith, 1482, 1213.

Deserts, 996; Arabian, 195; Asia, 263, 264, 265; Australia, 307; camels, 669; caravans, *314*, 997, 2204, *2205*; Chile, 802; Egypt, *1096*, 1095, 1097, *1103*; Gobi, 263, 264, 2204; Libyan, 996, 1097; mirage, 996, *2190*; Sahara, *997*, 2859; Turkistan, 3266; U.S.A., 3285.

Desert Rat. Name for the jerboa, common in N. Africa, adopted as badge by the 11th Hussars and later by part of the 8th Army stationed in N. Africa in the Second World War; 1819.

Deside'rius, last king of Lombards (ruled 756–774), 753.

Des Moines (dā moin'), cap. and largest city of Iowa, U.S.A.; pop. 159,800; univ.; flour, machinery.

Desmoulins (dā-mōō-lan), **Camille** (1760–94). Fr. politician and journalist; active, with Danton, in early days of Fr. Revolution; was guillotined in 1794.

De Soto, Hernando (c. 1496–1542). Span. explorer of s.e. U.S.A., and discoverer of Mississippi r., 2192.

Despen'ser, Hugh le, the Elder (1262–1326). Eng. nobleman, powerful, wealthy leader of the Barons' party opposing Edward II; almost alone opposed execution of Gaveston; later himself chief adviser of king; arrogance and rapacity of his son Hugh the Younger largely responsible for their fall.

Dessie (des'-yā). Tn. of Abyssinia, in prov. of Shoa; in the Abyssinian campaign, the It. army, retreating N. from Addis Ababa, halted at Dessie, a strong position astride the mts., to fight a fierce battle with pursuing S. African troops; Dessie fell April 26, 1941.

Destroyer, a war vessel, 2296, *2299.*

Detectives, in police force, 2648; "Sherlock Holmes," 1032.

Detec'tor, in radio apparatus, 3394.

Deterding, Sir Henri Wilhelm (1866–1939), Flemish financier, Director of Royal Dutch Petroleum Co., and Shell Transport and Trading Co. ; outstanding figure in the oil world.

Detergents (dē-ter′-jents). Cleansing agents, 998 ; petroleum products, 2430 ; soap, 2994 ; and surface tension, 3122.

Det′mold, Germany. Cap. of former principality of Lippe ; pop. 17,800 ; cloth mfrs. ; colossal statue of Hermann or Arminius, who defeated Romans, A.D. 9.

Detroit′, Mich., U.S.A., city on Detroit r. ; pop. 1,625,000, 998 ; "General Motors" building, 3288.

Detroit River, U.S.A., connecting l. St. Clair and l. Erie, 998.

Dettingen, vil. of Bavaria, on r. Main ; battle (1743) in which George II was last Eng. king to lead troops ; with Hanoverians, etc., he defeated Fr.

Deucalion (dū-kal′-ion). Son of Prometheus ; the "Noah" of Gk. myth., he built an ark and survived a flood sent by Zeus. From stones thrown by him and his wife Pyrrha sprang men and women respectively.

Deuterium (D), name given to the heavy isotope of hydrogen, mass 2, which has many physical properties very unlike hydrogen ; 998, 3351. *See* Heavy Water.

Deu′teron. The nucleus of a deuterium atom, which has twice the mass of the hydrogen nucleus ; much used in the transmutation of elements by bombardment, 951.

Deuteronomy, the fifth book of the Bible ; contains last injunctions of Moses to his people ; account of the death of Moses, 2235.

Deutschland, Ger. name for Germany. "Deutschland über Alles," Ger. song, 2282.

De Valera (dā-vah-lār′-a), **Eamon** (b. 1882), Irish statesman, premier, 1932–48 ; 998, 1749, 3281.

De Valois (de val′-wah), **Ninette** (b. 1898). Anglo-Irish choreographer ; director of the Vic-Wells ballet ; created "The Gods Go A-begging," "Job," "The Rake's Progress," "Promenade" ; 347.

Devaluation. Reduction of value of a currency in terms of other currencies, *e.g.* devaluation of £ sterling from 4·03 to 2·80 dollars, Sept. 1949.

Developing, in photography, 2580.

Deventer, Netherlands. Quaint old tn. on Ysel ; pop. 40,300 ; famous for "Deventer koek," a honey cake.

De Vere, Aubrey Thomas (1814–1902). Ir. poet, inspired by Gk. spirit and by Irish legends ("Irish Odes" ; "Legends of St. Patrick" ; "St. Peter's Chains").

Devia′tion, of compass, 882.

Devil or **Satan,** ruler of kingdom of evil, personification of spirit of evil ; in Faust legends, 1263 ; in "Paradise Lost," 2178 ; in Job, 1832.

Devil dancers, *plate f. 965* ; *plate f. 3208.*

Devil-fish or **sea-devil,** a ray, 2976 ; name applied to giant squid, 945.

Devil's Bible, 427.

Devil's coach-horse, a beetle, representative of family *Staphylinidae,* so called because when annoyed it raises the hind end of its body in a threatening manner. In summer small members of this tribe often swarm in thundery weather ; they are the countryman's "thunder-bugs."

Devil's Island, in Atlantic, 30 m. off coast of Fr. Guiana, former Fr. convict station.

Devis, Arthur (1711–87). Eng. artist ; early depicter of the "conversation piece," 1182.

Devi′zes, Eng. tn. in Wiltshire, on Kennet and Avon Canal ; important corn trade ; engineering and other industries ; pop. 6,058 ; 3383.

Dev′on, breed of cattle ; cows and bulls rather small ; oxen grow to great size and are prized for work, 732.

Devo′nian period, in geology, 1432, *plate f. 1432,* 1433 ; called "Age of Fishes."

Devonport, Hudson Kearley, 1st Viscount (1856–1934). Brit. politician and business man ; became chairman of the Port of London Authority (1909) and was first Food Controller during 1st World War.

Devonport. Tn. and fortified port on promontory in s.w. Devonshire ; formerly a borough, now part of Plymouth ; large dockyard and naval arsenal ; during 2nd World War the dockyard carried out extensive repairs to over 200 destroyers, and played major part in naval invasion preparations of 1944 ; heavy air raid damage made good by repair organization in swiftest possible time.

Devonshire, Elizabeth, Duchess of (1759–1824). One of the two beautiful duchesses of Devonshire painted by Gainsborough ; Elizabeth's portrait was the famous "Stolen Duchess," lost for 25 years.

Devonshire, Spencer Compton Cavendish, 8th Duke of (1838–1908). Eng. statesman, prominent in Victorian era ; a Liberal, but opposed Gladstone's Home Rule policy ; leader of Liberal Unionists ; developer of modern Eastbourne.

Devonshire, Victor Christian William Cavendish, 9th Duke of (1868–1938). In House of Commons (1891–1930) ; civil lord of the Admiralty (1915–16) ; gov.-gen. of Canada (1916–21) ; colonial secretary (1922–23).

Devonshire, Edward William Spencer Cavendish, 10th Duke of (b. 1895). Under-secretary for Dominions (1936–40) ; for India and Burma (1940–42) ; and secretary for the Colonies (1943–45). In 1948 installed as grand master of English freemasons.

Dev′onshire, co. in s.w. peninsula of Eng. ; 2,610 sq. m. ; pop. 732,000 ; 999, *1000, 1249.*

Dew, 1000.

Dewar, Sir James (1842–1923). Brit. physicist ; inventor of original vacuum flask ; investigated liquefaction of gases and properties of matter at very low temperatures ; with Sir Frederick Abel invented cordite.

Dewberry, bramble with fruit the bloom on which has a resemblance to dew.

De Wet (de-vet′), **Christian** (1854–1922), Boer general, commander-in-chief of Orange Free State forces in S. African (Boer) War (1899–1902), 487 ; rebelled at outbreak of 1st World War (1914), was defeated and taken prisoner.

Dewey, Admiral George (1837–1917). U.S.A. naval commander in Span.-Amer. War ; he completely destroyed the Spanish fleet in Manila Bay without the loss of a ship or man.

Dewey, John (b. 1859), Amer. philosopher and educator ; prof. of philosophy at Columbia Univ.

Dewey, Thomas E. (b. 1902). Amer. lawyer and politician ; Gov. of New York in 1942 ; unsuccessful Republican candidate for presidency in 1944 against F. D. Roosevelt, in 1948 against H. S. Truman.

De Windt (de vint′), **Harry** (1856–1933), Brit. traveller ; went by land from Peking to Calais ; rode to India from Russia through Persia ; visited mines and prisons of Siberia ; wandered over the Balkans, and spent two years in Sahara and Morocco ; his journeys are described in many books.

De Winter, Jan Willem (1750–1812). Dutch admiral, in command at the battle of Camperdown.

De Witt (de vit′), **Jan** (1625–72). Dutch statesman, grand pensionary for nearly 20 years ; in domestic politics supported republicans against House of Orange ; sought alliance with Louis XIV ; lost influence when Fr. designs against Netherlands became apparent ; killed by mob.

Dew-point hygrometer, 1677.

Dew ponds, *1000.*

Dews′bury. Town in Yorkshire, pop. 54,303 ; makes carpets, blankets, worsted ; 3435.

Dex′trin. A gum obtained from starch and so called because of its dextro-rotatory effect on polarized light, 3082.

Dextro-rotation of light, 3155.

Dextrose or grape sugar, 3114.

Dhole (dōl). Wild dog of India ; differs from wolf by hair between toes and shorter muzzle, 1701.

Dholpur (dōl-poor′). Native state of Rajputana, India ; 1,173 sq. m. ; pop. 286,900 ; cap. Dholpur (25,400).

Di′abase or **greenstone.** A granular igneous rock with lime-soda feldspar and pyroxene (augite) as its essential minerals ; generally crystalline throughout ; almost identical with basalt.

Diabetes (dī-a-bē′-tēz), 1471 ; inherited tendency, 1617.

Diadem, ancient Egyptian, *1116.*

Diaeresis (dī-ēr′-e-sis). Two dots placed on second of two consecutive vowels to indicate that it forms separate syllable from the first, e.g. naïve.

Diaghilev (dē-ah′-gi-lef), **Serge Pavlovitch** (1872–1929). Russian impresario ; through his presentation of Russian ballet to the world, Pavlova, Nijinsky, Karsavina, Massine, Lopokova and Serge Lifar became famous ; 345, 347, 2855.

Diagno′sis of disease, 2132.

Dial (automatic telephone), *3172, 3175,* 3176.

Dial, watch. How made, 843.

Dialysis. Process used in chemistry for separation of crystalloids from colloids, using a semi-permeable membrane, 773.

Dia-magnetic or anti-magnetic, 2062.

Diam′eter, of circle, 1436 ; of earth, 1067 ; as measure of magnifying power of lenses, etc., 3180.

Diamond, 1009, 1427, 2181 ; Brazilian mines, 551 ; consists of carbon 699, 1009 ; cutting, 1011, 1427 ; famous diamonds, *1011* ; Koh-i-Nur, *1011,* 1012 ; method of mining, *1010* ; S. African fields, 70, 73, 1009, *3017* ; S. America, *3023* ; synthetic and imitation, 1427 ; used as drill points, 1011, 2182 ; for wire dies, 1011, 3389.

Diamond Necklace Affair. Historic Fr. political scandal, involving Marie Antoinette, in whose name the necklace had been fraudulently ordered through certain swindlers.

Diamond Sculls. Principal sculling event in Brit. rowing calendar, held during Henley Regatta.

Diamond snake, 2710.

Diana (di-an′-a). Goddess in Rom. myth., identified with Gk. Artemis, 252 ; temple at Ephesus, *2923,* *plate f. 2924. See also* Artemis.

Diana monkey, 2211.

Diana Ver′non. Brilliant and beautiful heroine of Scott's "Rob Roy."

Diaphragm (dī′-a-fram), dome-shaped muscle between lungs and abdomen, 1591 ; vibrating disk in gramophone, 1496 ; in microphone, 2162 ; in telephone, 3011.

Diarbekr, Turkey. Tn. on Tigris ; pop. 43,260 ; silk goods, gold and silver filigree, 3212.

Diary (dī′-eri), day to day record of personal events, reflections, etc. ; famous diarists are Marie Bashkirtseff (1860–84), Fanny Burney, Creevey (1768–1838), Evelyn, Fulke Greville (1794–1865), and Pepys.

Diastase. A ferment in malt, 2071.

Diastrophism (dī-as′-tro-fizm). The process of change in the shape of the earth's crust, 2596.

Diathesis. Inherited predisposition to a disease, 1617.

Diatom (dī′-a-tom). A minute single-celled water plant, 2416 ; *plate f. 2620.*

Diavolo, Fra (frah dē-ah′-vō-lō) ("Brother Devil") (1771–1806). It. brigand and renegade monk ; subject of opera by Auber.

Diaz (dē-ahz), **Armando** (1861–1928). It. general, commander-in-chief of It. armies in 1st World War.

Diaz, or **Dias de Novaes, Bartholomew** (d. 1500). Port. navigator, discoverer of Cape of Good Hope; 69, 695, 2444, 2659, 3016.

Diaz, Narcisse Virgilio, (1807–76). Fr. landscape painter of Barbizon school, 1378.

Diaz, Porfirio (1830–1915). Pres. of Mexico; led successful rev. in 1871 and became pres. in 1877; in 1911 resigned in consequence of revolt by Madero; 2159.

Dib'din, Charles (1745–1814). Eng. poet, dramatist, and musical composer; wrote upwards of 50 plays and many popular sea-songs, the best known of the latter being " Tom Bowling " and " Poor Jack."

Dick, Sir William Reid (b. 1879). Scot. sculptor; pres. Royal Society of British Sculptors, 1933–38; designed many groups of statuary, including Roosevelt statue, Grosvenor Sq.

Dickens, Charles (1812–70). Eng. novelist, 1012, *1013*, 1215, 2402, 2791; " A Christmas Carol," 820; " Mr. Pickwick Goes to Dingley Dell," 1013.

Dickin, Mrs. Maria E. (b. 1870). Founder of P.D.S.A. (People's Dispensaries for Sick Animals of the Poor), in 1917; also of Dickin Medal (the Animals' V.C.) for animals recommended by military authorities for special war service; pigeons, 2606.

Dickinson, Emily (1830–86). Amer. poetess, 3295.

Dick'see, Sir Francis (1853–1928). Eng. artist, usually called Frank Dicksee; works include " Harmony " and " The Funeral of a Viking; " President of the Royal Academy in 1924.

Dicotyledons (dī-kot-i-lē'-donz). Plants with two-lobed seeds, 1322, 2918; include most trees, 3247.

" Dic'taphone." Sound-reproducing machine used in business houses for dictating letters, etc.; the words spoken into the mouthpiece are recorded on a wax cylinder, and reproduced to the typist by another machine, 3012.

Dicta'torship. Govt. by one man or one party, 2651; in anc. Rome, 2809, 2811; Cincinnatus, 828; Julius Caesar, 651; Franco, 1384, *3039*, 3040; Hitler, 1447, 1451, 1631; Kemal Ataturk, 1850; Lenin, 1923; Mussolini, 2268; Stalin, 3072.

Dic'tionary, 1015 ; Dr. Johnson's, 1835.

Dictys. In Gk. myth., 2552.

Diderot (dē'-de-rō), **Denis** (1713–84). Brilliant, witty, versatile and prolific " Encyclopedist," 1381.

Di'do or Elis'sa. Legendary Carthaginian queen; founder of Carthage, 711; and Aeneas, 32; opera by Purcell, 2706.

Diego Suarez (dyā'-gō swar'-ez). Pt. of Madagascar, near N. end of island; good harbour; pop. 12,237; Fr. naval base and military h.-q.; occupied by Brit. May 1942.

Dieppe (dē-ep'). Spt. of Normandy, N. France, with service to Newhaven; pop. 21,170; 2377; Commando raid, August 1942; port and harbour installations destroyed; liberated Sept. 1, 1944; 3422.

Diesel (dē'-zel) **engine.** Form of internal-combustion engine invented by Rudolf Diesel (1858–1913), 1015, 1736; fire-engine, *1287*; locomotive, *plate f. 1981*, 1987, 1988, *1995*; ships, 2949; submarines, 3105.

Diet. A formal assembly or meeting; name often applied to legislative assemblies of Cent. and N. European countries; also the formal meetings of councillors of Holy Rom. Empire; of Spires, 2759; of Worms, 2759.

Diet and Dietetics. Choice of diet, 1336. *See* Cookery; Food; Food Values.

Differen'tial gear, of motor-car, 2245.

Diffrac'tion, 1941; grating, of spectroscope, 3056, *plate f. 3057.*

Diffusion. The tendency of two liquids or two gases when brought into contact to mix; of gases, 1419. *See* Osmosis.

" Digest " of Justinian, 1844.

Digestion, 1016; action of enzymes, 1220, 1470; function of liver, 1968; of stomach, *1016*, 3094; in mouth.

3082; pepsin, 2547; tongue's part in, 3223; studied with X-rays, 3432.

Digger wasp. A sandwasp (*Ammophila*), *3346.*

Digita'lis, heart stimulant prepared from foxgloves, 2132.

Digitigrade (dij'-i-ti-grād) **animals, or** " toe walkers," 1342; horse, 1645.

" Dignity and Impudence," by Landseer, *1891.*

Di-he'dral angle, in aeroplane construction, 41.

Dijon (dē'-zhawn). Fortified tn. in E. France in dept. of Côte-d'Or; former cap. of Burgundy; pop. 100,664; mustard, wine.

Di'ka-nut. Seed of the wild mango, 2408.

Dikes or dykes. Earth embankments generally used to protect low lands from inundations of streams or of the sea; in Belgium, 403; in Holland, *1233*, 1234.

Dill, F.-M. Sir John G. (1881–1944). Brit. soldier; May 1940 C.I.G.S.; promoted F.-M.; went with Church-ill to Washington; there died and was buried in Arlington Cemetery, Nov. 1944.

Dime. In U.S. currency, a silver coin, tenth part of dollar or ten cent piece.

Dimity. A fine cotton fabric with a reversible stripe or bar which is raised on one side when it is depressed on the other; name originally applied to a heavy fabric of the same type made in Sp. for bed hangings.

Dinant (dē-nahn). Tn. in Belgium, in prov. of Namur, on Meuse; pop. 7,000; captured and burned by Germans in 1914.

Dinar'ic Alps. Mountains in w. Yugoslavia; highest point Dinara (6,008 ft.); *map, 344.*

D'Indy (dan-dē), **Vincent** (1851–1931). Fr. musical composer; pupil and follower of Cesar Franck; noted for rich and subtle instrumentation (" La Forêt Enchantée "; " Symphonie sur un air montagnard français ").

Dingle Bay. Inlet of co. Kerry, Eire. Dingle, a spt. and fisheries centre, lies on the north side.

Din'go. Australian wild dog; 309, *313.*

Dingwall, Scot. Co. tn. of Ross and Cromarty, on Cromarty Firth; trade in cattle and wool; pop. 2,600; 2828.

Dinosaurs (dī'-no-sawrz). Extinct reptiles of great size, *2678*, 2767; fossil foot-prints, 1354.

Di'ocese. A bishop's district; the name was first used in this sense at the beginning of the 4th cent.; 825.

Diocletian (dī-ō-klē'-shan) (A.D. 245–313). Rom. emperor (284–305), able soldier, and energetic ruler, under whom a memorable persecution of Christians took place, 817; division of empire, 2812.

Di'ode, of thermonic valve, 3198, *3199*; in electronic devices, 1138; form of rectifier, 2751.

Diodor'us Sic'ulus (d. about 20 B.C.). Gk. historian, 1541.

Dioecious (dī-ēsh'-us) **plants,** 1321.

Diogenes (dī-oj'-en-ēz) (412–323 B.C.), Gk. Cynic philosopher, **1017.**

Diomedes (dī-o-mē'-dēz). One of Gk. heroes of Trojan War, 3249.

Diomedes. In Gk. myth., king of Thrace; slain by Hercules, 1615.

Dionys'ius the Elder (430–367 B.C.) Tyrant of Syracuse; type of cruel despot; pardons Damon and Pythias, 963; and Plato, 2628; " sword of Damocles," 963.

Dionysus (dī-o-nī'-sus). In Gk. myth., god of wine and growing principle of Nature; Rom. Bacchus; **1018**; Gk. festivals, 1037; theatre of, 284, 3194; temple, *1529*; and Hermes, *1533.*

Diophan'tus. Gk. mathematician of 3rd or 4th cent. A.D., " father of algebra," 113.

Di'orite. A very hard rock, used in anc. Eng. for pottery ware. It has a higher specific gravity than granite, and is either green or grey.

Dioscuri (dī-os'-kū-rī). " Sons of Zeus," name of Castor and Pollux, 718.

Diphtheria (dif-thĕr'-i-α). An infectious disease; caused by bacteria, 1458; serum-therapy for, 180.

Diplod'ocus. A huge prehistoric reptile that was native to N. Amer.; it was some 60 ft. long from head to tail; head about 2 ft., tail about 25 ft.; 2678, 2680.

Dip'lopoda. A class of arthropods including millepedes ("thousand feet"); some authorities place millepedes in sub-class Diplopoda of class Myriapoda, which contains centipedes as well.

Dip needle. A magnetic needle used for measuring the vertical component of the earth's magnetism at different places; it is balanced beside a dial horizontally and dips towards a vertical position in proportion to the power of magnetism exercised; horizontal only at magnetic equator.

Dipneusti or Dipnoi. The lung-fish subclass, 2038.

Di'poles, in chemical solutions, 773.

Dipper. Constellation. *See* Great Bear.

Dipper. A small bird of the family *Cinclidae*; typical of N. streams; plumage black above, white breast, red beneath; earliest Brit. bird to nest in spring.

Dipper dredger, 1046.

Dip'tera. Insect order containing two-winged types, *1732*; includes flies, 1329; mosquitoes, 2236.

Direct current (D.C.). Electricity flowing continuously in one direction, 1128, 1129, 1130; derived from alternating current by rectifier, rectifying valve or rotary converter; dynamos, 1061; motors, 2239; transformed to A.C. by induction coil, 1720; rectifier, 2751; radio receivers, *3392*, 3393; used by tramcars, 3235.

Directory, French. Committee of 5 which held executive power in Fr. 1795–9, succeeding the Convention, 1396; appoints Napoleon commander, 2275; and Talleyrand, 3149; overthrown by Napoleon, *1367*, 1396, 2276.

Direction-finding, by wireless, 2291, 3397.

Direct tax, 3158.

Dire Dawa. Abyssinian town; pop. 30,000; 15.

Dirigible (dir'-ij-i-bl). *See* Airship.

Dirt Track Racing with motor cycles, 948.

Di-saccharide, sugar with the formula $C_{12}H_{22}O_{11}$, 3114.

" Discobolus " (dis-kob'-o-lus) or **" Discus Thrower."** Statue by Myron, 1528, *1532.*

Discovery. Name of two famous exploring ships, 2647, 2895.

Disease, 1458, *2132*; children's, 1675; defective teeth a cause, 3164; germ causes, 1458; of heart, 1593; and heredity, 1617; insect carriers, 1313, 1329, 1733, 3252; notification of, 1677; prevention, 2132; radio-activity in diagnosis, 1761, and treatment, 951. *See also* Germs in Disease; Medicine and Surgery.

Disinfectants. Substances used to destroy disease germs or prevent infection; antiseptics, 177.

Disney, Walt (b. 1901). Amer. film artist; originator of " Micky Mouse" and " Silly Symphony " films, 829. Disney's full-length films include " Snow White and the Seven Dwarfs," " Fantasia," " Make Mine Music," and " Melody Time."

Dispersion, of light, 1942.

Displaced Person (D.P.). Term first used in 1945 of those persons moved from their homes by Nazi, Fascist, Quisling, or Falangist regimes, of whom more than 7,500,000 then existed in Europe alone; 2170, 3296.

Displacement, of ship, meaning, 2951, 210.

Disraeli (diz-rā'-li), **Benjamin, Earl of Beaconsfield** (1804–81). Statesman and novelist, twice prime minister of Gt. Brit., **1018**; friendship with Queen Victoria, 1019; primrose day, 2684; rivalry with Gladstone, 1469.

D'Israeli, Isaac (1766–1848). Eng. author, of Jewish parentage ; father of Benjamin Disraeli, Earl of Beaconsfield (" Curiosities of Literature ").

Dissent'ers. Those who refused to comply with usages of Church of Eng. More recently the term has been superseded by " Nonconformists " or " Free Churchmen." *See* **Free Churches.**

Distaff. Staff used in hand spinning.

Distaff spindle, sea-shell, *2943.*

Distemper or **tempera.** Painting medium, 2478.

Distilla'tion, 1019 ; of alcohol, 103 ; camphor, 674 ; coal-tar, 857 ; of petrol, 2564 ; nature of process, 103 ; oil, 2426 ; sea water, *1019* ; wax, 3359.

Distinguished Conduct Medal (D.C.M.), Brit. decoration, 2448.

Distinguished Flying Cross (D.F.C.), Brit. decoration, 2448.

Distinguished Flying Medal (D.F.M.). Brit. decoration, 2448.

Distinguished Service Cross (D.S.C.), Brit. decoration, 2448.

Distinguished Service Medal (D.S.M.), Brit. decoration, 2448.

Distinguished Service Order (D.S.O.), Brit. decoration, 2448.

Dis'trene, a type of plastic, 2627.

Distressed, Special or **Development Areas.** Regions principally affected by the economic crisis of 1929–31—such as S. Wales, Tyneside, etc. New industries were established in " estates " therein, and surplus labour transferred elsewhere.

District nursing, 2407.

District of Columbia (D.C.). Federal district containing Washington, cap. of U.S.A. ; a. 60 sq. m. ; pop. 663,000 ; 2116, 3344.

Disulphide. A compound of two sulphur atoms with an element or compound ; of carbon, 3116 ; of iron (iron pyrites), 1753, 3117.

Ditch-digger, mechanical excavator, *1247.*

Diver. Bird of the order *Gaviiformes* ; Brit. species include Gt. Northern diver or loon, red- and black-throated divers.

Dives (di'-vēz) (Latin, " rich "). Popular name of rich man in parable of Lazarus (Luke xvi, 19–31).

Divide. In physical geography, ridge or height of land separating the head-streams of one drainage system from those of another.

Dividend. In arithmetic, 1021.

Div'i-div'i. Seed-pods of tree, 1912.

" Divine Comedy." Poem by Dante, 969, 1786.

" Divine right " of kings, 1794.

Diving, 1019, *1020*, 2414, 3137 ; dangers, 2413 ; greatest depth attained, *89*; for pearls, 2533 ; and swimming, 3135. Dr. Otis Barton reached the greatest depth ever, 4,500 ft., in his Benthoscope in 1949.

Diving beetles, *401*, 400.

Diving bell, 1020.

Diving-suit, *1020.*

Divining rod. A forked branch or rod, usually of hazel, used by a dowser to discover underground water-supplies.

Division. In arithmetic, 1021 ; algebra, 114 ; decimals, 982 ; fractions 1357 ; by slide rule, *2984.*

Division. An army unit, 249.

Divorce. Legal breaking of marriage bond, 2107.

Dixmude. Tn. of Belgium on Yser Canal.

Djakarta, formerly Batavia (q.v.).

Djibouti or **Jibuti** (ji-bōō'-ti), chief. spt and cap. of Fr. Somaliland ; outlet for Abyssinian trade ; pop. 10,421 ; 3000.

Dnieper (nē'-per). R. of S.W. Russia and Ukraine, rising in govt. of Smolensk, flowing 1,410 m. to Black Sea, 465, 2844, 3273 ; dam, 961, *plate f. 961* ; heavy Russo-German fighting 1941–44, 3419.

Dniepropetrovsk (formerly Ekaterinoslav). Tn. of the Ukraine, U.S.S.R., on the r. Dnieper ; in centre of great mineral region ; site of huge dam, blown up 1941 ; restored 1947 ;

---

town in Germans' hands 1918, again 1941–43.

Dniester (nēs'-ter). R. of S.E. Europe ; rises in Carpathian Mts., flows S.E. 865 m. to Black Sea ; rich in fish ; scene of fighting in 1914–18 war ; 465 ; heavy fighting around lower Dniester 1941 and 1944, 3424.

Dobbin, William. In Thackeray's " Vanity Fair," bashful kind-hearted officer, friend of Osborne, whose widow, Amelia, he eventually marries.

Dobell, Bertram (1841–1914). Eng. bookseller and writer. Shop in Charing Cross Road, London, became resort of bookmen.

Dobruja (dō-brōō'-ja). Agric. dist. now divided between Bulgaria and Rumania on Black Sea, S. Dobruja is Bulgarian, and N. Dobruja is Rumanian, by treaty of 1940 ; 8,900 sq. m. ; pop. about 700,000 ; 2811.

Dobson, Henry Austin (1840–1921). Eng. poet and essayist ; delicate satire and graceful handling of artificial Fr. verse forms (" Proverbs in Porcelain " ; " Old World Idylls"; " At the Sign of the Lyre ").

Dobson, Frank (b. 1887). Eng. sculptor ; for many years one of the most advanced sculptors of reputation, 2911 ; most celebrated work " Truth " stands outside the Tate Gallery.

Dock. A coarse weedy herb of the genus *Rumex*, from 2 to 4 ft. high ; flowers small and greenish, growing in panicles ; leaves usually long and lance-shaped.

Dock family (*Polygonaceae*). Includes rhubarb, 2774.

Docks, 1022. London, *1024* ; Southampton, 1023, *1024*, 3027 ; floating, *3111. See also* **Harbours.**

Doctor. One skilled or learned in any profession ; in general speech indicates a person qualified to practise in medicine (training, 2135) ; but there are also doctors of divinity, law, science, philosophy, etc.

" Dr. Jekyll and Mr. Hyde." Story by R. L. Stevenson of a man with dual personality.

Dod'der. A parasitic plant of the order *Convolvulaceae*, *2514.*

Dodec'anese (" 12 islands "). Small Isls. in Aegean Sea ; seized by Italy in 1911 ; Germans invaded in 1943 ; again Italian in 1945 ; ceded to Greece in 1947.

Dodgson, Charles Lutwidge. *See* **Carroll, Lewis**, his pen-name.

Do'do. An extinct bird of Mauritius, 1025.

Dodo'na. Anc. city of Epirus ; seat of ancient oracle of Zeus.

Dods'ley, Robert (1703–64). Eng. author and publisher, 1835.

Doe. A female deer, 984.

Doenitz, Karl (b. 1891). U-boat commander, 1916–1918, captured by British ; commander of cruiser Emden, 1929 ; organized secret U-boat construction before 2nd World War ; admiral 1942 ; grand admiral and C.-in-C. German navy, 1943 ; responsible for " pack " method of U-boat attack ; in May 1945 became Hitler's successor as leader of Germany. Tried as war criminal, Nuremberg, 1945–46 ; sentenced to 10 years' imprisonment.

Dog, 1025, *plate f. 1024* ; in Belgium, 404 ; breeding variations, *435* ; chief breeds, *plate f. 1024* (see also list in pp. 3766-3767); classification, 1027 ; dingo, *313* ; eye, 1253 ; first domesticated animal, 736 ; foot, 1342 ; guide for blind, *160* ; instinct, 159, 160 ; Landseer's paintings, 1890 ; licence, 1027 ; of St. Bernard's hospice, 128 ; sheep dog trial, *1026* ; sporting dogs, 1026, *1658*, *1659*; street control, 2787 ; transport, *2644* ; in war, 1025.

Dogberry. In Shakespeare's " Much Ado About Nothing," constable, type of official stupidity.

Dog Days. Period of hot weather in July and August, when the dog star Sirius rises with sun ; 895, 3079.

Doge (dōj). Elective duke or chief magistrate of the city-republics of

---

Venice and Genoa during Middle Ages, 3310 ; Leonardo Loredano, *1782.*

Doge's Palace. At Venice, 3310.

Dog family. The Canidae, 1027.

Dog-fish. A shark, 2938, *2939* ; egg, *1094.*

Dogger Bank. Extensive sandbank and fishing ground in North Sea, 2391 ; battle in 1st World War, 387.

Doggett's Coat and Badge. Rowing event, 1027.

Dogskin gloves, 1477.

Dog Star or **Sirius.** The most brilliant star, 895, 3079, *3080.*

" Dog teeth," or canines, *3163.*

Dog-tooth. In architecture, ornament used in medieval hollow mouldings, consisting of a series of tabs usually resembling teeth, but sometimes elaborate floral designs.

Dog violet, *3324.*

Dogwood. A hard-wooded shrub, *Cornus sanguinea*, distinguishable by bright red twigs, opposite leaves, and white flowers ; leaves dark red in autumn, berries black.

Doherty, Reginald (1872–1911) and **Hugh Lawrence** (1876–1919). British lawn-tennis players, 1907.

Doihar'a, Gen. Kenji (1883–1948). Jap. soldier ; head of Intelligence in Manchuria ; creator of the Kwantung Army ; hanged under sentence of Tokyo tribunal Nov. 1948.

Dol'drums. Belt of calms near equator, 3384.

" Dole." Colloquial term for unemployment benefit. In ancient Rome it really meant a free gift, but unemployed who receive it today have subscribed to it at least in part.

Dolgelley (dol geth'-li), Wales. Co. tn. of Merionethshire, near Cader Idris ; associations with Owen Glendower ; fellmongering and wool trade ; pop. 2,740 ; 2146.

Dolichocephalic (dol-i-kō-se-fal'-ik) (" long-headed "), in ethnology, 2724.

Dollar (sign $). The monetary unit in the U.S.A. and Canada, established as such in the U.S.A. by the Coinage Act of 1792 ; before that date Sp. dollars were used in the colonies ; in the 15th cent. large silver coins struck in Joachimsthal, Bohemia, were called " thalers," from which, through the low Ger. " daler," the word " dollar " came into use ; " dollar shortage," 1348 ; and gold standard, 1482 ; also monetary unit of China.

Dollfuss, Engelbert (1892–1934). Austrian chancellor and unofficial dictator (1932) ; defied Austrian Nazis ; assassinated in 1934 ; 318, 3416.

" Doll's House, A." Ibsen's drama, in which Nora, the " child-wife," finding her " doll's house " no longer a shelter for her ideals, leaves it to grow up.

Dolly Varden. In Dickens's " Barnaby Rudge," the locksmith's coquettish daughter, whose characteristic dress and hat gave name to goods so designed.

Dol'mens. Megalithic monuments, 3095.

Dolmetsch, Arnold (1858–1940). Fr. musician. An expert in the playing and construction of old musical instruments, he inaugurated at Haslemere, Surrey, in 1925, an annual music festival devoted to music of the 16th, 17th, and 18th centuries ; started in 1928 Dolmetsch foundation for training scholars and craftsmen to meet demand for Dolmetsch instruments ; and the harpsichord, 2601.

Dolomite (dol'-ō-mīt). A limestone, 1951 ; source of oil, 2426.

Dolomites (from mineral dolomite). Limestone mts. in S. Tirolese Alps ; highest peak Marmolata (10,972 ft.) 3215.

Dolphin (dol'-fin). Sea mammal related to whale, 1027 ; a cetacean, 3371.

Domagk, Gerhard, Gr. scientist who in 1935 discovered prontosil, the first of the sulpha drugs ; Nobel prize for med., 1939 ; *179*, 3116.

Domains, magnetic ; theory of magnetism, 2062.

Dome. In architecture, principle, 214 ; Byzantine, *213, 214* ; Florence, *1319*; Roman, 214, *2802* ; St. Paul's, London, *219, 2863* ; St. Peter's, Rome, *2802, 3306*.

Domenichino (dō-mä-ni-kē'-nō), **Zampieri** (1581–1641). It. painter, excelled in religious frescoes ; one of earliest landscape painters ; with Guido Reni most distinguished follower of the Carracci ; " Communion of St. Jerome," " Scourging of St. Andrew," and " Adam and Eve," his masterpieces ; 1785.

Domesday (or **Doomsday**) **Book.** William I's (" the Conqueror's ") statistical record of England, 742, **1027,** *1028*, 3379.

Dom'inic, St. (1170–1221). Sp. priest ; founded Dominican Order of Preaching Friars ; buried at Bologna, 494.

Dominica. Brit. colony in Windward group of West Indian Islands. *See also* **Dominican Republic.**

Dominican or **Black Friars,** 2214.

Dominican Republic, Dominica, or **Santo Domingo.** Occupies E. two-thirds of isl. of Santo Domingo or Hispaniola, West Indies ; a. 19,000 sq. m. ; pop. 1,850,000 ; **1028,** 1565, *map f. 1565*.

Dominion Day. Canadian national holiday, July 1, to celebrate anniversary of the formation of the Dominion, July 1, 1867.

Dominions. A general title for the self-governing territories (Canada, Australia, New Zealand, South Africa, Pakistan, and Ceylon) and peoples of the British Commonwealth.

Dominoes. A game, **1029.**

Domitian (dō-mish'-an) (A.D. 51–96). Rom. emperor (81–96) ; murdered for his cruelties ; the Apostle John was probably banished to Patmos during his reign, 1220, 2811.

Domrémy-la-Pucelle (dawn-rä-mē-lah-poo-sel). Vil. in N.E. Fr. on Meuse ;

birthplace of Joan of Arc, 1831, *plate f. 1833*.

Don. R. in S. Russia, rises in L. Tura, flows S.E. and S.W., 1,325 m. into Sea of Azov ; the ancient Tanais ; navigable for 800 m. ; valuable fisheries ; 37 m. canal connects with Volga ; 465, 2844 ; heavy fighting in 1941 and 1942–43.

Don, or **Dun.** R. in Yorkshire, tributary of the Ouse ; 70 m. long ; navigable for 39 m. ; 2941.

" Donald Duck." Character in Walt Disney's film cartoons, *829*.

Donatello (don-a-tel'-lō) (1386–1466). Florentine sculptor whose works are supreme expression of spirit of the early Renaissance, 2766, 2904.

Donati (dō-nah-tē), **Giovanni** (1826–73). It. astronomer ; became director of Florence observatory in 1864 ; discovered six comets, one of which was named after him.

Donati's Comet. Discovered by Giovanni Donati (above) in 1858 ; 45,000,000 m. long by 10,000,000

PRINCIPAL BREEDS OF DOGS

Abyssinian Sand Terrier.—Small, hairless dog with large, erect ears ; white skin ; very active.

Affenpinscher.—Toy breed ; small, wiry-coated, with hairy, snub-nosed, round face, erect ears.

Afghan Hound.—Long, fine-haired, long-eared coursing dog, bred for centuries in Afghanistan.

Airedale Terrier.—Large terrier with wiry coat ; tan with black or grizzled saddle ; excellent police- and watch-dog.

Alsatian.—Large dog with wolf-like head ; black, white, grey, or mixed ; very intelligent ; originally German shepherd-dogs ; excellent as guards and guide-dogs for the blind.

Australian Terrier.—Toy breed ; small, silky-haired, active dog ; long, flat head, with high-set ears.

Basset.—A small, short-legged, long-eared, smooth-coated hunting dog.

Beagle.—A small hound, sturdily built, with smooth coat and long ears.

Beauce. — Large, smooth-coated French sheep-dog.

Bedlington Terrier.—Wiry-haired terrier with long ears and silky topknot ; about 15 inches tall ; blue-grey, liver, or tan.

Black-and-tan, or **Rat Terrier.**— Smooth black coat marked with tan ; miniature of Manchester terrier.

Bloodhound. — Good-sized dog ; black and tan or red-brown and tan ; smooth hair and loose skin lying in folds on forehead ; long ears and chops, giving a mournful expression ; keen scent.

Border Terrier. — Small, wiry-haired terrier from the borderland of England and Scotland.

Borzoi.—Large, graceful, narrow-headed, long-snouted Russian hunting dog. Silky-coated and capable of great speed.

Boston Terrier.—Smooth coat, short head, with erect ears, brindle to black with white markings ; both

toy and medium-sized varieties. National dog of U.S.A.

Bulldog.—Low, heavy dog with undershot jaw and retreating nose.

Bulldog, French.—Small bulldog with upstanding " bat " ears.

Bull Terrier.—White or brindle, smooth-coated, medium size ; agile and courageous.

Cairn Terrier.—A small terrier from Scotland, having a long harsh coat.

Chow Chow, or **Chow Dog.**—Native of northern China, of medium size and sturdy build, with large broad head, short erect ears, blue-black tongue, thick hair and bushy up-curled tail ; usually reddish brown or black.

Collie.—Large, thick-furred, with long tapering nose ; golden brown with white mane, or tan, black, and white, or all white ; much used for herding ; the smooth-coated collie is rarer.

Corgi, Welsh.—Short-legged, smooth-coated, highly intelligent farm dog.

Dachshund.—Short-legged, long-bodied German dog with hound-like head.

Dalmatian.—Strong, muscular, with short, smooth hair ; white with small black or liver-coloured spots ; also called " plum-pudding " dog.

Dandie Dinmont Terrier, Scottish. —Long-bodied, short-legged, with rough coat, silky topknot, long ears ; pepper or mustard colour.

Deerhound, Scottish.—A large hunting dog, more heavily built than a greyhound, and with rough coat.

Dingo.—Wild dog of Australia, in danger of extermination because it kills sheep ; some have been domesticated.

Elkhound, Norwegian.—One of the wolf-like dogs from which shepherd breeds have been developed.

Eskimo Dogs.—Several kinds of wolf-like dogs used to pull sledges ; malamute, husky, and North Greenland Eskimo are varieties.

Foxhound.—An able hunting dog ; their chequered coats and baying voices are known wherever foxes are hunted.

Fox Terrier.—A small, sturdy, active dog ; one variety smooth-coated, the other wire-haired ; white with black-and-tan markings.

Great Dane.—A very large strong dog, agile and symmetrical, with head carried high ; hair short ; brindle, fawn, grey, black, white or white with black patches (harlequin).

Greyhound.—Fleet, slim, long-limbed coursing dog, used from ancient Egyptian days ; brindle, fawn, black, and white.

Griffon.—Rough-coated German or French hunting dogs.

Griffon, Brussels.—A small rough-coated toy dog, reddish brown ; pug nose ; heavy " moustaches."

Harrier.—Dog resembling fox-hound, but smaller : used to hunt hares.

Irish Terrier.—Medium size, rough hair of reddish colour ; noted for gameness.

Keeshond.—Chow-like dog, medium in size between chow and pomeranian. Also called wolf spitz or Dutch barge dog.

Kelpie. — Black-and-tan, prick-eared Australian sheep-dog, resembling dingo.

Kerry Blue Terrier.—Irish dog with soft coat of bluish tint ; V-shaped drooping ears ; water dog.

Lakeland Terrier.—Black or blue and tan, or grizzle or black, miniature Airedale. Used for fox-hunting in Fell country.

Maltese.—Active toy dog, of sharp terrier appearance, with long silky white hair.

Manchester Terrier. — Medium-sized, smooth-coated ; black with mahogany tan markings. (*See* Black-and-tan).

Mastiff.—Ancient breed, large powerful, from which many other breeds have been developed.

wide ; last seen in 1859 ; 880, *back of plate f. 881.*

Donbas. Contracted name for basin of the r. Donetz, s. Russia, an impt. industrial region of the Ukraine.

Don'caster. Tn. in West Riding of Yorkshire, on r. Don ; large rly. and machinery works ; racecourse, on which St. Leger is run ; pop. 71,000 ; 3435.

Donegal (don-ē-gawl'). Extreme N.W. co. of Eire ; 1,860 sq. m. ; pop. 136,000 ; 1029.

Donegal Bay. Inlet of Eire, 30 m. wide at entrance ; valuable fishing ground.

Donetz (do-nyets'). R. in S. Russia ; flowing S.E. 670 m. to join r. Don near Shakhati ; basin, minerals, 2845, 3273 ; great battles in 1942–43, 3419.

" Don Giovanni " (don-jō-vah'-nē). Mozart's opera of which Don Giovanni (Don Juan) is hero ; story, 2438.

Donington Park. Motor-racing road circuit in grounds of Donington Hall, near Castle Donington, Leics.,

opened in 1934. During the 1st World War Donington Hall was a place of internment for German officers.

Donizetti (dō-nē-dset'-tē), **Gaetano** (1797–1848). It. operatic composer ; wrote 70 operas ; combined an endless flow of melody with dramatic talent and power of humorous characterization, 2436 ; most popular operas are " Lucia di Lammermoor," 2439, " La Fille du Régiment," " Don Pasquale," " L'Elisir d'Amore."

Don'jon or **dungeon,** 717.

Donkey or **ass,** 273.

Donne (dun), **John** (1573–1631). Eng. poet and preacher ; in youth wrote metaphysical love poetry ; also brilliant " Satires," among the first use of rhymed couplets in English ; at 41 took orders, became dean of St. Paul's, and most popular preacher of his day.

Don'nybrook. A part of the city of Dublin, Eire ; famous for its fair, started 1204, held annually, notorious

for its attendant fighting and debauchery ; abolished in 1855.

Donoghue, Stephen (1884–1945). Irish jockey. At one time or another he rode the winners of all the classic flat races and rode the Derby winner on six occasions between 1915 and 1925. In 1920 he rode 143 winners.

" Don Quixote " (don kwiks'-ot ; Span. don kē-hō'-tā). Book by Miguel Cervantes, 745 ; story retold, 746.

Doon. River and loch of Ayrshire, Scot., flowing N.W. 30 m. into Firth of Clyde ; the riv. is immortalized by Burns (" The Banks o' Doon ") ; hydro-elec. installations on loch, 1670.

Doone valley, in Exmoor, made famous by R. D. Blackmore's " Lorna Doone."

Doorn. Vil. near Amerongen in the Netherlands ; 1920–41 the residence of ex-Kaiser William II.

Doppler effect. Law in physics discovered (1842) by Christian Doppler, Austrian scientist (1803–53) ; explains the apparently rising note of an approaching sound.

PRINCIPAL BREEDS OF DOGS *(contd.)*

Newfoundland.—Massive head and square muzzle ; long thick hair ; usually black, or black and white ; brave and devoted.

Old English Sheep-dog.—Moderate size, with broad head, thick-set body, and long shaggy hair which falls over face and eyes.

Otterhound.—Large, with head similar to bloodhound ; thick wavy greyish coat ; used purely for otter-hunting.

Papillon, or **Butterfly Dog.**—Toy dog with abundant silky coat ; long bushy tail and ear resembling a butterfly.

Pekinese.—Small lap-dog with long silky hair, broad head, short muzzle, large protruding eyes, squat legs ; reddish, fawn, black, sable and mixed.

Pinscher, Doberman. — Smooth, moderately large, muscular ; black-and-tan, or brown ; developed in last half-century in Germany ; used there as a police dog ; one miniature variety.

Pointer.—Excellent shooting dog developed from Spanish pointers and speedy foxhounds ; smooth coat ; white with black, liver or lemon markings.

Pomeranian.—T o y , long-haired dog, with fox-like expression ; sable and orange usual colours ; differs from Spitz chiefly in size.

Poodle. — Curly-haired, usually white or black ; often displaying intelligence, especially in learning tricks ; toy, curly, and corded varieties ; usually clipped in fantastic fashion.

Pug.—Small with round head and short blunt square muzzle ; fawn with black shading, or black.

Retrievers.—Dogs trained to retrieve dead or wounded game ; large, usually black or liver-coloured, resembling Newfoundland and setter ; varieties are the curly-coated, flat-coated and Labrador retrievers.

St. Bernard.—Very large, with massive head : either long and

rough, or smooth coat ; originally bred at the Hospice of St. Bernard in the Alps.

Saluki, or **Persian Gazelle Hound.**—One of the oldest historic breeds ; introduced into the West from the Orient ; large, speedy and graceful, like the greyhound, with silky coat ; hunts by sight and does not bark.

Samoyed.—A strong, medium-sized, thick-furred white dog from Asiatic Russia. Used as sledge dog.

Schipperke.—Small, black, with fox-like head, erect ears, square and firmly-built body, thick hair, docked tail ; name is Flemish for " little skipper," coming from its use in Flanders as watch-dog and ratter on barges.

Schnauzer.—Strongly built German dog ; pepper and salt colouring ; wire coat, bristling moustache and beard ; miniature, medium and giant, or *Riesenschnauzer* varieties ; also called wire-haired pinscher.

Scotch Terrier.—Long stocky body and short legs ; rough hair ; black, grey, sandy, or grizzled.

Sealyham Terrier.—Developed in Wales ; long body, short sturdy legs, wiry hair ; mainly white, with occasional markings of brown, tan or yellow.

Setter, English.—Sporting dog, medium size with long coat ; white with liver, tan, orange, or black blotches.

Setter, Gordon or **Black-and-tan.**—Similar to English setter ; coat black with mahogany-tan markings.

Setter, Irish.—Somewhat lighter in build than the English setter, with long, flat, glistening red-brown coat.

Shetland Sheep-dog. — A small collie.

Skye Terrier.—Small with long, hard hair falling to the ground ; Clydesdale terrier similar but with silky hair.

Spaniel, Blenheim. — White and chestnut, or all chestnut, variety of King Charles spaniel.

Spaniel, Clumber.—Medium height with massive head and frame ; white with lemon or orange markings.

Spaniel, Cocker. — Moderate-sized ; varied colour markings ; long drooping ears ; broad feet ; quick and alert.

Spaniel, English Toy.—Round head and pug face ; varieties : King Charles, black and deep brown ; Prince Charles, white with black-and-tan markings ; Ruby, mahogany bay ; Blenheim, white with chestnut markings.

Spaniel, Field.—Larger, heavier, and stronger than Cocker spaniel ; all black, or white with black or other markings.

Spaniel, Irish Water.—Curly liver-coloured coat, smooth face, and curly topknot ; excellent water dog.

Spaniel, Japanese.—Small, resembles Pekinese ; black or yellow and white.

Spaniel, King Charles.—Black-and-tan, or white, black, and tan, closely resembling Japanese.

Spaniel, Springer.—So named because it was formerly used to drive out or " spring " the game ; it now points ; English and Welsh varieties.

Spaniel, Sussex.—Massive muscular hunter with abundant golden-liver coat.

Spitz.—Medium-size ; heavy upstanding coat ; probably related to Samoyed.

Welsh Terrier.—Wire-haired, resembles fox terrier ; coloured like Airedale.

West Highland White Terrier.—Small with long active body and short, muscular legs ; white wiry coat.

Whippet.—Bred for racing ; a cross between the greyhound and terrier.

Wolfhound, I r i s h .—Resembles deerhound, but more massive ; with its high-held head, the tallest of all dogs.

Yorkshire Terrier.—A toy, long-haired terrier.

Dora. In Dickens's " David Copperfield," David's " child wife."

Dor'cas or **Tab'itha.** Disciple of Jesus at Joppa, a woman " full of good works " (whence the " Dorcas societies " of the Church), raised from the dead by Peter (Acts ix. 36–40).

Dorchester. Co. tn. of Dorsetshire; pop. 10,030; Prehist. (Maiden Castle) and Rom. remains, *207*; Jeffreys' " Bloody Assize " (1685), sentencing 292 to death after Monmouth Rebellion, 1030.

Dorchester. Vil. of Oxfordshire; beautiful old abbey with famous Jesse window.

Dordogne (dôr-dôn'-ye). R. in S.-cent. Fr., 305 m. long; unites with Garonne, *back of plate f. 1361.*

Dordrecht (dôr'-drekht) or **Dort,** Netherlands, port on Merwede; pop. 62,000; first assembly of independent states of Holland here; Synod of Dort (1618–19) upheld Calvinism; trade in wine and lumber; shipyards, 2320.

Doré (dôr'-ā), **Gustave** (1833–83). Fr. painter and illustrator, famous for vivid imagination and grotesque humour with which he illustrated the world's classics; among these Balzac's " Contes Drôlatiques," Dante's " Divine Comedy," Milton's " Paradise Lost," and the Bible; " Samson and the Lion," *2870.*

Doria (dôr'-ē-a), **Andrea** (1466–1560). Genoese admiral and patriot, soldier of fortune under Francis I of France and the Emperor Charles V; drove French from Genoa and set up republic of which he became perpetual censor; exercised predominant influence until his death.

Dor'ians. One of four great branches of Gk. people; took name from Dorus, son of Helen; came from N. or N.W. and invaded Corinth, then Crete; Spartans always regarded as representatives of unmixed Dorian blood, 1517.

Dor'ic. Dialect in anc. Greece, 1541.

Doric. Earliest of the three great Greek styles in architecture, *213.*

Dormant, in heraldry, 1615.

Dor'mouse. A small arboreal rodent, 1029.

Dornoch. Co. tn. of Sutherlandshire, Scot.; summer resort; Skibo Castle, the Scottish home of Andrew Carnegie, is near; pop. 725; 3124.

Dornoch Firth, arm of the North Sea, forming part of coast-line of Rossshire and Sutherlandshire; 22 m. long, average breadth 5 m.

Dorpat. *See* Tartu.

D'Orsay (dôr'-sā), **Count Alfred** (1801–52). Fr. dandy and wit, friend of Byron and Countess of Blessington; long arbiter of literary and artistic London society.

Dor'set, Thomas Sackville, 1st Earl of (1530–1608). Eng. statesman and poet, one of leading advisers to Queen Elizabeth; carried deathwarrant to Mary Queen of Scots; part author of "A Mirror for Magistrates," probably most important work between Chaucer and Spenser; helped write " Gorboduc " (" Ferrex and Porrex "), first Eng. tragedy.

Dorset or **Dorsetshire,** English co., on English Channel; 973 sq. m.; pop. 239,000; 1030; in Hardy's novels, *1577.*

Dort, Netherlands. Same as **Dordrecht.**

Dortmund, Ger. Largest city in Westphalia, in centre of coal basin; pop. (1939) 540,000; one of leaders of Hanseatic League. Heavily bombed, practically destroyed, taken by Allies April 13, 1945.

Do'ry. Flat-bottomed fishing boat, 481.

Dory or **John Dory.** Sea fish of the Zeidae family, found in Mediterranean, English Channel, St. George's Channel; valued for table use.

Dos Passos, John (b. 1896), Amer. author of novels, plays and essays (" Three Soldiers "; " Manhattan Transfer ").

Dostoievski (dos-tō-yef'-ski), **Feodor** (1821–81), Rus. novelist; **1030,** 2404, 2856.

Dou, Gerard, or **Douw** (1613–75). Dutch painter, 2334.

Douai (dōō'-ā). Mfg. tn. in N. Fr.; pop. 37,258.

Douai Bible, 426.

Douaumont (dōō-ō-mawn). Fortified hill and village near Verdun; 1st World War battle ground.

Double-bass violin. Stringed musical instrument, *2267,* 2445, 3325.

Double-crested humming bird, 1652.

Double refraction. Formation of two refracted rays. *See* **Polarization.**

Double Summer Time, a war-time measure, 980.

Doublet. A garment worn by men about 1600–1750.

Doughty, Charles Montagu (1843–1926). Brit. traveller, poet and scientist (" Travels in Arabia Deserta," " Dawn in Britain "), 1216.

Doug'las. A Scottish family famous in history, song, and legend. An earl of Douglas fell fighting against " Hotspur " Percy at Otterburn (1388). Douglas of Lochleven was jailer of Mary Queen of Scots (1567–68).

Douglas, Major Clifford Hugh (b. 1879), Brit. engineer and economist. Exponent of " Social Credit."

Douglas, Sir James (1286–1330), " the Black Douglas," 591.

Douglas, Lewis Williams (b. 1894). U.S. Ambassador to Gr. Britain 1947.

Douglas, Marshal of R.A.F. William Sholto Douglas, Lord (b. 1893). Brit. air force officer; A.O.C.-in-C. Fighter Command 1940–42; A.O.C.-in-C. Coastal Command 1944–45; air C.-in-C. Brit. Air Forces of occupation in Ger., 1945–46; C.-in-C. Brit. forces in Ger. and military Gov. of Brit. zone, 1946–47; Marshal of R.A.F. 1946; app. chairman B.E.A. in 1949.

Douglas. Cap. of Isle of Man; popular summer resort; pop. 20,000; 2084.

Douglas fir, in Brit. Columbia, 579.

Douglass, Sir James (1826–98). Eng. engineer; built the Eddystone Lighthouse that replaced the one constructed by Smeaton; 1084.

Doulton, Sir Henry (1820–97). Eng. inventor and manufacturer of pottery; developed pottery works at Lambeth founded by father, John D. Opened works at Burslem in 1877.

Doumer (dōō-mār), **Paul** (1857–1932), Thirteenth Pres. of Fr. Republic, elected 1931; Gov.-Gen. of Indo-China, 1897–1902; shot dead by half-crazy fanatic in May 1932.

Doumergue (dōō-mārg), **Gaston** (1863–1937). Fr. politician and lawyer; Pres. of the Council and Minister for Foreign Affairs (1913–14), and later became Foreign Minister again; President (1924–31); Premier 1934.

Douro (dōō'-rō). Riv. rising in N. Sp. and flowing w. then s.w. along Port. border and w. through N. Port. to Atlantic; 485 m.; *2660, 2658.*

Dove. *See* **Pigeons.**

Dove. Eng. r. in Derby and Stafford, trib. of the Trent; 45 m. long; 995.

Dovedale. Famous Derbyshire beauty spot, associated with Izaak Walton; purchased by National Trust, *2283.*

Dover. Port on Eng. Channel; pop. 32,000; 1030, 1851; breakwaters, 588; Caesar's landing, 1143; castle, 713; Charles II's landing, *1199,* *1207;* harbour, *1031,* 1576; Shakespeare Cliff, *plate f. 1165;* shelled and bombed in 2nd World War, 1031.

Dover. Capital of Delaware, U.S.A.; 35 m. s. of Wilmington in fruit-growing region; pop. 5,500, 986.

Dover, Strait of. Channel connecting North Sea with Eng. Channel and separating Eng. and Fr.; 21 to 27 m. wide; chalk cliffs on both sides.

Dovrefjeld (dō-vre-fyeld') or **Dovre Mts.** Range in cent. Norway; highest peak, Snehätten, 7,620 ft.; 2393.

Dowding, Air Chief Marshal Hugh C. T. D., 1st Baron (b. 1882). Brit. airman; A.O.C.-in-C. Fighter Command 1936–40, covering the Battle of Britain; retired 1942.

Dow'lais, Wales. Industrial area in Glamorgan; pop. 10,250; coal-mining, iron-working; lighter industries have been introduced; suburb of Merthyr Tydfil, 1470.

Down. Plumage, 1265.

Down. Coastal co., Northern Ireland; a. 951 sq. m.; pop. 211,000, 1031.

Downing College, Cambridge Univ.; founded 1800; 669.

Downing Street, London, **1032.**

Downpatrick. Co. tn. of Down, N. Ireland, 1031.

Downs. System of chalk hills in S.E. Eng.; North Downs in Surrey and Kent; South in Sussex; latter feeding ground for famous Southdown sheep, **1032,** *1033,* 3123.

Dowsing. Art of divining water, etc.

Doyle, Sir Arthur Conan (1859–1930). Brit. novelist, creator of famous detective character Sherlock Holmes, **1032,** *1033.*

Drac. R. in S.E. France, *backs of plates f. 1360, 1361.*

Drachenfels (drah-khen-felz). " Dragon's Rock," mtn. in Ger., 1,065 ft. high; castle, *2769.*

Drachm (dram) or **dram.** A fluid measure and weight (fluid, 1-8th of an ounce; weight 1-16th of an ounce). *See* **Weights and Measures.**

Drachma (drak'-ma). Gk. silver coin.

Draco (drā'-kō) (fl *c.* 620 B.C.). Compiler of first written code of Athenian laws, 1522, 1902.

Draft. A bill of exchange issued by one bank against another; often applied to all domestic bills of exchange. *See* **Bill of exchange.**

Draft. Term applied to a party of soldiers dispatched to join a unit of their regiment.

Draga (Mme. Draga Masin), d. 1903. Queen of King Alexander of Serbia; formerly lady-in-waiting to his mother Queen Natalie; murdered in Belgrade with her husband, 2922.

Drag hunt, 1658.

Dragon. Fabulous animal, **1033.**

Dragon. E. Indian lizard, also called Komodo, 1034, *plate f. 1973.*

Dragonet. Fish, **1034.**

Dragon-fly. Insect, **1034;** life story *1035; 1733.*

Dragon's Teeth. Story, 649.

Drais, Karl von. Invents velocipede, 947.

Drake, Sir Francis (*c.* 1545–96). Explorer and privateer, first English man to circumnavigate the globe **1036;** in Brit. Columbia, 580; in Calif., 663; monument at Plymouth 2631; a privateer, 2612; statue a Offenburg (Ger.), 1445; Spanish Armada, 236; voyages, 142.

Drake. A male duck, 1051.

Drakensberg or **Quathlamba.** Mtn range in S. Africa, *2279*

Dram. *See* **Drachm.**

Drama and dramatics, 1037; advice to amateurs, 1044; Sarah Bernhardt 419; career, 1044; Chinese actor *back of plate f. 809;* cinema, 828 English, 1039, 1211; Greek, 1037 1540; influence of Ibsen, 1040, 1679 Sir Henry Irving, 1759; music-dram (Wagner's), 3332; opera, 2435 recent development, 1043; producing a play, 1044; religious plays, 378 1039, 1211, 1244, 2189; Roman 1038, 1895; Shakespearian, *1039 1041,* 1211, 2933–2936; theatre 3194; wireless, 1038, 3398. *See als* **English Literature ; France ; Literature,** etc.; *also* list in p. 3779 and chief dramatists by name.

Drammen, Norway. Spt. at mouth o r. Drammen, on arm of Oslo Fiord pop. 25,500; exports timber; saw mills.

Draughts. A game, 1044.

Drave (drah'-ve). R. rising in Tirol flows s.e. between Hungary an Yugoslavia, joining Danube afte 450 m.

David'ians. A people of India, 1701

Drawing. The fundamental art, 104

Drayton, Michael (1563–1631). En poet laureate (" Polyolbion " " Ballad of Agincourt ").

FAMOUS NAMES IN THE HISTORY OF THE DRAMA

GREEK

Aeschylus (525–456 B.C.)—" Prometheus Bound " ; " Agamemnon " ; " Choëphori " ; " Eumenides."

Sophocles (about 495–406 B.C.)—" Antigone " ; " Oedipus Tyrannus."

Euripides (480–406 B.C.)—" Alcestis " ; " Medea " ; " Bacchae."

Aristophanes (c. 445–c. 388 B.C.)—" The Knights " ; " The Clouds " ; " The Frogs " ; " The Birds " ; " Lysistrata."

ROMAN

Plautus (c. 251–184 B.C.)—" Amphitruo " ; " Captivi " (The Captives) ; " Aulularia " (The Pot of Gold).

Terence (c. 194–159 B.C.)—" Andria " ; " Heauton Timorumenos " (The Self-Tormentor) ; " Phormio."

Seneca (3 B.C.–A.D. 65)—" Thebias " ; " Medea."

ENGLISH

Christopher Marlowe (1564–93)—" Tamburlaine " ; " Doctor Faustus " ; " The Jew of Malta."

William Shakespeare (1564–1616)—" Hamlet " ; " Macbeth " ; " Twelfth Night " ; " The Tempest," etc.

Ben Jonson (c. 1573–1637)—"Every Man in His Humour " ; " The Alchemist " ; " Volpone, or the Fox."

Francis Beaumont (1584–1616) and **John Fletcher** (1579 – 1625) — " Philaster " ; " The Maid's Tragedy " ; " The Knight of the Burning Pestle."

John Dryden (1631–1700)—" All for Love."

Oliver Goldsmith (1728–74)—"She Stoops to Conquer."

Richard Brinsley Sheridan (1751–1816)—" The Rivals"; " The School for Scandal " ; " The Critic."

Henry Arthur Jones (1851–1929)—" Michael and His Lost Angel " ; " The Hypocrites " ; " The Liars."

Sir Arthur Wing Pinero (1855–1934)—" The Second Mrs. Tanqueray " ; " His House in Order."

Oscar Wilde (1856–1900)—" Lady Windermere's Fan " ; " The Importance of Being Earnest."

George Bernard Shaw (1856–)—" Man and Superman " ; " Pygmalion " ; " Saint Joan " ; " Back to Methuselah " ; " The Apple Cart."

Sir James Matthew Barrie (1860–1937)—" Peter Pan " ; " The Admirable Crichton " ; " Quality Street."

John Galsworthy (1867–1933)—" The Silver Box " ; " Strife " ; " Justice " ; " Escape " ; " The Roof."

Harley Granville-Barker (1877–1946)—" The Voysey Inheritance " ; " Waste."

William Somerset Maugham (1874–)—" Our Betters " ; " The Circle " ; " The Constant Wife."

St. John Ervine (1883–)—" Jane Clegg " ; " The First Mrs. Fraser " ; " Anthony and Anna."

Noel Coward (1899–)—" Hay Fever " ; " Private Lives " ; " Cavalcade."

J. B. Priestley (1894–)—" Dangerous Corner " ; " Laburnum Grove " ; " Time and the Conways."

Terence Rattigan (1911–)—" French Without Tears " ; " While the Sun Shines " ; " The Winslow Boy."

IRISH (CELTIC LITERARY REVIVAL)

William Butler Yeats (1865–1939)—" The Land of Hearts' Desire " ; " The Hour Glass " ; " Deirdre."

John Millington Synge (1871–1909)—" Riders to the Sea " ; " The Playboy of the Western World."

Sean O'Casey (1890–)—" Juno and the Paycock."

AMERICAN

Bronson Howard (1842–1908)—" The Henrietta " ; " Shenandoah " ; " The Young Mrs. Winthrop " ; " Aristocracy."

William Gillette (1855–1937)—" Secret Service."

Clyde Fitch (1865–1909)—" The Climbers " ; " The Truth " ; " The Girl with the Green Eyes."

William Vaughan Moody (1869–1910)—" The Great Divide."

David Belasco (1854–1931)—" The Girl of the Golden West " ; " The Return of Peter Grimm."

Eugene O'Neill (1888–)—" Emperor Jones " ; " Anna Christie " ; " The Hairy Ape " ; " Strange Interlude " ; " Mourning Becomes Electra."

Elmer Rice (1892–1937)—" The Adding Machine " ; " Street Scene " ; " Judgement Day."

Marc Connelly (1890–)—" The Green Pastures."

Clifford Odets (1906–)—" Waiting for Lefty " ; " Golden Boy."

FRENCH

Pierre Corneille (1606–84)—" Le Cid " ; " Médée " ; " Polyeucte " ; " Oedipe " ; " Le Menteur."

Jean Racine (1639–99)—" Thébaïde " ; " Bérénice " ; " Phèdre."

Molière (Jean-Baptiste Poquelin) (1622 – 73) — " Tartuffe " ; " Le Bourgeois Gentilhomme."

Pierre Augustin Caron de Beaumarchais (1732–99)— " Le Barbier de Séville " ; " Le Mariage de Figaro."

Alexandre Dumas, the younger (1824–95)—" La Dame aux camélias " (The Lady of the Camellias).

Edmond Rostand (1869–1918)—" Cyrano de Bergerac " ; " L'Aiglon " ; " Chantecler."

Eugène Brieux (1858–1932)—" Les Avariés."

Maurice Donnay (1859–1945)—" Lysistrata " ; " Les Éclaireuses."

Paul Claudel (1868–)—" L'Annonce faite à Marie."

Henri René Lenormand (1882–)—" Les Ratés " ; " In Theatre Street."

Sacha Guitry (1885–)—" Pasteur."

Jules Romains (1885–)—" Dr. Knock."

Jean-Paul Sartre (1905–)—" Crime Passionel."

GERMAN

Gotthold Ephraim Lessing (1729–81)—" Minna von Barnhelm"; "Nathan der Weise" (Nathan the Wise).

Johann Wolfgang Goethe (1749–1832)—" Faust " ; " Egmont " ; " Iphigenie auf Tauris."

Johann Christoph Friedrich Schiller (1759–1805)— " Maria Stuart " ; " Wallenstein " ; " Wilhelm Tell."

Hermann Sudermann (1857–1928)—" Die Ehre " ; " Heimat."

Gerhart Hauptmann (1862–1946)—" Die Weber " (The Weavers) ; " Die versunkene Glocke."

Frank Wedekind (1864–1918)—" The Dance of Death."

Georg Kaiser (1878–1945)—" From Morn to Midnight."

Ernst Toller (1893–1939)—" Masse-Mensch."

SCANDINAVIAN

Henrik Ibsen (1828–1906)—" The Pillars of Society " ; " A Doll's House " ; " Peer Gynt " ; " Brand."

Björnstjerne Björnson (1832–1910)—" The Gauntlet."

August Strindberg (1849–1912)—" Master Olof " ; " The Father " ; " Lucky Peter " ; " To Damascus."

Hans Kinck (1865–1926)—" The Cattle Dealer."

SPANISH

Lope de Vega Carpio (1562–1635)—" Los cautivos de Argel " ; " El castigo sin venganza."

Pedro Calderón de la Barca (1600–81)—" El Mágico prodigioso " ; " La Vida es sueño."

José Echegaray (1833–1916)—" Mariana " ; " El gran Galeoto."

Jacinto Benavente y Martinez (1866–1939)—" La Malquerida " (The Passion Flower) ; " Princess Bebé."

Serafin and **Joaquin Alvarez Quintero** (1871–1938 and 1873–1944)—" The Lady from Alfaqueque."

Gregorio Martinez Sierra (1881–1947)—" The Kingdom of God " ; " The Road to Happiness."

ITALIAN

Vittorio Alfieri (1749–1803)—" Merope " ; " Virginia."

Gabriele D'Annunzio (1864–1938)—" La Gioconda " ; " Francesca da Rimini " ; " La Figlia d'Jorio."

Luigi Pirandello (1867–1936)—" Six Characters in Search of an Author."

RUSSIAN

Alexander Pushkin (1799–1837)—" Boris Godunov."

Nikolai Gogol (1809–52)—" The Government Inspector."

Anton Pavlovitch Tchekhov (1860–1904)—" The Sea Gull " ; " The Cherry Orchard " ; " Uncle Vanya."

Maxim Gorki (1868–1936)—" The Lower Depths " ; " The Children of the Sun " ; " The Barbarians."

Leonid Andreyev (1871–1919)—" King Hunger " ; " To the Stars " ; " He Who Gets Slapped."

BELGIAN

Maurice Maeterlinck (1862–1949)—" Pelléas et Mélisande " ; " Monna Vanna " ; " L'Oiseau bleu."

CZECHOSLOVAK

Karel Capek (1890–1938)—"R.U.R." ; "Insect Play"; " The Mother."

AUSTRIAN

Arthur Schnitzler (1862–1931)—" Anatol " ; " The Lonely Way " ; " The Green Cockatoo."

HUNGARIAN

Ferencz Molnár (1878–)—" Liliom " ; " The Swan " ; " The Devil " ; " The Guardsman."

Dream of Gerontius." Oratorio by Elgar, 1143.

Dreams, 2985.

Dredge-net. For fishing, 1299.

Dredgers, 1046, 1047; in gold mining, 1480; for other minerals, 2182.

Dreiser, Theodore (1871–1945). American novelist of intense realism; " Sister Carrie " (1900); " Jennie Gerhardt." (1910); " An American Tragedy " (1925); 3295.

Dreissensia. Fresh-water mussel, native of Russia; named after Belg. physician Dreyssen; first found in Eng., in Surrey Docks, London, in 1824, now common in Gt. Brit., Fr., and Belg.

Dresden. Ger. cap. of Saxony, on r. Elbe; pop. 454,000; 1048, 2878; largely destroyed in 2nd World War, 1048.

Dresden china, 1048, 2670; at Meissen, 1447, 2878.

Dress. Boots and shoes, 521; buttons, 632; gloves, 1477; hats and caps, *plate f. 1584*, 1582, *1583. See also* under separate countries.

Dreux (drê). Old tn. in N.W. Fr.; pop. 10,000; Huguenots defeated by Catholics under Duke of Guise (1562); taken by Germans (1870).

Drey, squirrel's nest, 3071.

Dreyfus (drā–*fus*), **Alfred** (1869–1935). Fr. (Jewish) military officer, centre of the famous " Dreyfus case " which convulsed Fr. political life (1894–99). Accused of espionage, he was sent to Devil's Is., 1895. Sentence was quashed, 1898, but he was re-tried by military court and again sentenced, 1899, but pardoned; declared innocent and reinstated in army in 1906, he won Legion of Honour in 1st World War.

Dribbling, in football, 1344.

Dri'ers, in paints, 2478.

Drift, in Transvaal, 3239.

Drift, glacial, 1469, 1682; in N. Amer., 2384–85.

Drill. A machine tool; diamond, 2182; oil well, 2428; pneumatic, 2632, 2633; artesian well, 253.

Drinks. Cider and perry, 828; spirits, 3066; wines, 3388.

Drinkwater, John (1882–1937). Eng. poet and playwright; studies of William Morris and Swinburne (" Cophetua "; " Rebellion "; " Abraham Lincoln "; " Oliver Cromwell "; " Bird in Hand "; " Pepys ").

Driscoll, Jem (James) (1880–1925). British boxer. Feather-weight champion 1910, and won Lonsdale belt outright for that weight.

Drive. In golf, 1483, *1485*; in lawn tennis, 1906.

Driver. A golf club, 1484.

Driver ants, 166.

Driving wheel, locomotive, *plate f. 1980*, *1988*.

Droeshout, Martin (fl. 1640). Eng. engraver of the famous portrait of Shakespeare, frontis. in the 1st Folio edn. of Comedies, Histories & Tragedies printed 1623; *2935*, 2936.

Drogheda (droi'-da). Town of Louth, Eire; spt. on Boyne; pop. 15,180; captured by Cromwell in 1649; taken by William III, 1690, after Battle of the Boyne, *1746*, 2032.

Droitwich. Tn. in Worcestershire, 20 m. s.w. of Birmingham, famous for salt mines and brine baths, 2866, 3407.

Dromedary (drum'-e-dãr-i). A one-humped riding camel, 669, *670*.

Drome, River. Tributary of Rhône, 2774.

Dromios (drō'-mi-ōz). Comic twins, attendants on the twins Antipholus of Ephesus and Antipholus of Syracuse in Shakespeare's " Comedy of Errors."

Drone bees, *391*, 392.

Drood, Edwin. Hero of Dickens's unfinished novel " The Mystery of Edwin Drood."

Dropwort, water. A poisonous plant, *2639*.

Dros'era. Sundew genus of plants, 3120.

Drought. Caused by deforestation, 3246.

Drugs, 1048; made from coal-tar, 857; containing nitrogen, 2373; opiates, 2442. *See also* names of individual drugs.

Drug-store beetle, 399.

Dru'ids. Priestly class among anc. Celts, 1048; Stonehenge, 3097.

Drum, of ear, 1065.

Drum. A musical instrument, 1049, 2267, 2446.

Drupa'ceous fruits, 1403.

Drury, Alfred (1857–1944). Eng. artist and sculptor; first academy exhibit " The Triumph of Silenus " (1885); in 1896 his bronze head of " St. Agnes " was bought for the Chantrey collection; R.A. in 1913.

Drury Lane. Dist. in w.-cent. London; present Theatre Royal, opened 1812, on site of 17th-cent. playhouse, since largely rebuilt; long famous for spectacular drama.

Druses (drōō'-sez). Religious sect of Syria, 3145.

Dryads (drī'-adz). In Gk. myth., wood nymphs, 2408.

Dryasdust. An antiquary invented by Scott as lay figure in various novels. The name, made more famous by Carlyle, is applied to a prosy writer.

Dryburgh Abbey, Berwickshire, Scotland; Scott's grave, *2899*.

Dry cell, in elec. battery, *376*.

Dry cleaning, and laundry, 1900.

Dryden, John (1631–1700). Eng. poet, critic, essayist, 1040, **1050**, 1212; poet laureate, 2634.

Dry Dock, 1024.

" Dry Ice " (solid CO_2). Carbon dioxide, liquefied at pressures above one atmosphere and cooled into a white solid at atmospheric pressure; used as a refrigerant and dropped by aircraft, to " make rain "; 700, 1420; in food preservation, 1341, 1391.

Drying oils, 1263.

Dry measure. *See* **Weights and Measures,** *f-i.*

Dry-point. Method of engraving, 1218.

Duala. Cap. and chief port, Cameroons, W. Africa; pop. 22,000; 672.

Dual Alliance. Union formed between Fr. and Rus. (1891) by secret treaty for common action in international matters.

Dual Monarchy (Austria–Hungary), 319, 1383, 1656. For complete history, *see* Austria.

Du Barry, Marie Bécu, Countess (1746–93). Fr. adventuress, favourite of Louis XV.

Dublin, Eire. Co. bordering Irish Sea; a. 342 sq. m.; pop., without city of Dublin (co. tn), 129,241; chief river, the Liffey; chief port, Dun Laoghaire (Kingstown); mts. in the s.; fisheries, agric., brewing, distilling.

Dublin (Baile-Atha-Claith), largest city of Ireland; formerly cap. of all Ireland, now of Eire; pop. (1946) 506,635; **1051**, 1749; 1916 Rebellion, 1746; Ger. bombs on, in 1941, 1750; zoo at, 3446.

Dublin, University of, or **Trinity College,** founded 1591; 1050.

Dublin Bay, Eire. An inlet of the Irish Sea, which penetrates the E. coast as far as Dublin; lightship at entrance, *1944*.

Dubois (dū-bwah), **Paul** (1829–1905), Fr. sculptor and painter; his greatest work, in Renaissance spirit, is tomb of Gen. Lamoricière at Nantes; also noteworthy are statues of Joan of Arc at Reims and Montmorency at Chantilly.

Dubrovnik. City in Dalmatia, Yugoslavia; large commerce in medieval times; centre of Serbian culture 15th–17th cents.; pop. 8,500; *3440*; became part of Yugoslavia after 1st World War; Italians occupied it 1941, until formation of Croatian kingdom; again occupied it Sept. 1941; liberated by Marshal Tito's forces Oct. 1944.

Duc'at. Coin formerly used by various European countries; probably first struck by Byzantine emperors 11th cent.; golden ducats varied in value from 7s. 5d. to 9s. 4d.; silver ducats were valued at about 3s. 4d.

Duce (dōō'-chā) (leader). Title applied to Mussolini, dictator of Italy; 1262, 2268.

Duck. A flat-billed waterfowl, **1051**, *plates f. 1052, 1053,* 2671; eider, *1053*; hatching period, 444; related to swan, 3125; letter z from shape of. *See*, in Index, letter A.

" Duck," in cricket, is scored by a player who is " out " without making a run.

Duckbill platypus. A mammal peculiar to Australasia, 309, *313*, **1053**, 2074.

Ducking stool, 2687.

Duck Mountain, Manitoba, Can., forest reserve, 2089.

Duckweed. A stemless water plant, 3355.

Duct, of body gland, 1470; bile, 1470.

Ductil'ity, 3389; of gold, 1481; of platinum, 2628; of silver, 2973.

Ductless glands, of body, function, 1470.

Dud'ley, Guildford (d. 1544), husband of Lady Jane Grey; executed for part in plot against Queen Mary, 1545.

Dudley. City in Worcestershire, 8 m. N.W. of Birmingham in "Black Country "; pop. est. 58,700; coal and iron mining; makes iron and brass products.

Duet (dū-et'), in music, composition for two instruments or voices.

Du Fay, Charles François de Cisternay (1699–1739). Fr. physicist; discovered " positive " and " negative " electricity.

Duff, Alexander (1806–78). First Church of Scotland missionary to India; initiated western education in India.

Duff Cooper. *See* **Cooper, Sir Alfred Duff.**

Duf'ferin and A'va, Frederick Temple Blackwood, 1st Marquess of (1826–1902). Brit. diplomat, gov.-gen. of Canada (1872–78), Viceroy of India (1884–88), and at various times Brit. ambassador to Russia, Turkey, Italy and France.

Du Gard, Roger Martin. French writer. Nobel prize for literature (1937) (" Jean Barrois "; " Les Thibault ").

Dug'out. Primitive boat, 486.

Du Guesclin (dū-gā-klan'), **Bertrand** (c. 1320–80). Fr. general, constable of France, 757.

Duhamel, Georges (b. 1884). French writer of poetry, novels and plays (" The Pasquier Chronicles "), 1382.

Duisburg. Ger. city in N. Rhine-Westphalia, between Ruhr and Rhine with which it is connected by canal; pop. (with Hamborn), 440,000; coal and iron.

Dukas, Paul (1865–1935). French composer (" L'Apprenti Sorcier "; " Ariane et Barbe-Bleue ").

Duke (Lat. *dux*), in Gt. Brit., a nobleman of the highest hereditary rank, except princes of the royal family, 2536; in Parliament, 2521.

" Duke of York," Brit. battleship, *2297*, *2304*.

Duke of York's School, founded at Chelsea, London, by Frederick Duke of York, second son of George III; transferred to Dover in 1909; the Queen Victoria School near Dunblane, Scot., is a similar establishment.

Duke of York's Theatre (1673), *3195*.

Dukeries. Dist. in Nottinghamshire covering an area of 100 sq. m. within the famous Sherwood Forest; so called from the ducal estates here 2399.

Dukhobors or **Doukhobors.** Russian religious sect in Canada, 2846, 2875.

Dulcinea (dul-sin'-ē-a). Romantic name given by Don Quixote to his peasant " lady "; hence, a sweetheart; 746.

Duluth'. Town of Minnesota, U.S.A., shipping centre at head of l. Superior; splendid natural harbour pop. 101,065; iron, steel, flour industries.

Dulwich (dul'-ij). Suburb to S.E. o London. D. College, founded by Edward Alleyn in 1606, is one of the important Eng. public schools, 121 ; picture gallery, built by Sir John Soane.

Dum or doom palm. A species of palm with fan-shaped leaves and a stem repeatedly forked, an unusual feature among palms ; native to Arabia, Egypt, and Cent. Africa ; fruit red-skinned with a sweet brown spongy centre used as food.

Duma (dōō-mah). Former Rus. national assembly, 2365, 2848.

Dumas (dū-mah), **Alexandre** (1802–70). Fr. novelist and dramatist ; author of " The Count of Monte Cristo " and " The Three Musketeers " ; **1053**, *1054*, 1381, 2404.

Dumas, Alexandre, the Younger (1824–95). Fr. dramatist, author of " La Dame aux Camélias, **1054**, 1381.

Du Maurier (dū-môr´-yā), **George** (1834–96). Brit. illustrator ; gay little pictorial satires on society, chiefly published in " Punch," also novelist (" Peter Ibbetson " ; "Trilby ").

Du Maurier, Sir Gerald (1873–1934). Eng. actor, son of George du Maurier ; appeared in " The Ad-mirable Crichton," " Peter Pan," " Raffles," " Bulldog Drummond," " The Last of Mrs. Cheyney." His daughter Daphne wrote " Gerald " (his life, a study of the Du Maurier family), and novels (" Rebecca ").

Dumbar´ton, Scot. Co. tn. of Dum-bartonshire, port at junction of rivers Leven and Clyde ; shipbuild-ing ; pop. 22,000 ; 1054.

Dumbar´ton Oaks. 18th cent. mansion near Washington, U.S.A. ; here representatives of the U.K., U.S.A., and U.S.S.R., and China drew up a draft of the new international league to avoid war, basis of U.N. organiza-tion ; 3283.

Dumbartonshire, Scot. Western co., a. 246 sq. m. ; pop. 159,000 ; **1054.**

Dum´-dum, India. Tn. in Bengal, 5 m. N.E. of Calcutta ; pop. about 30,000 ; first produced deadly dum-dum bullets.

Dum-dum bullet. Name given to bullets that expand on entering the body.

Dumfries (dum-frēs´), Scot. Tn. in Dumfriesshire, on r. Nith ; pop. 25,000 ; burial place of Robert Burns ; tweeds, hosiery, cattle markets ; 1055.

Dumfriesshire, Scot. Southern co. : a. 1,072 sq. m. ; pop. 82,000 ; **1054.**

Dumping. Export of goods to foreign markets at prices below those at which they can be economically produced in those countries.

Duna, also called Southern Dvina, river rising in w. Russia, near source of Volga (connected by canal) ; flows w. through Poland and Latvia into Gulf of Riga ; length 650 m. ; Riga, 2779.

Dunant (dū-nahn´), **Jean Henri** (1828–1910). Swiss author and philan-thropist, founder of Red Cross Society, *2752.*

Dunbar, William (c. 1460–c. 1520). Scottish poet ; disciple of Chaucer, but with wider humour and greater warmth (" Two Married Women and the Widow " ; " The Dance of the Deadly Sins "), 1210, 2894.

Dunbar, Scot. Spt. in Haddington-shire, on Firth of Forth ; pop. 5,062 ; historic old castle ; Cromwell de-feated Scots (1650) in battle of, 933, 2893.

Dunblane´, Scot. Tn. in Perthshire ; health resort ; the Queen Victoria School for sons of Scottish soldiers and sailors ; woollen mills ; pop. 4,421 ; 2558.

Duncan (d. 1040). Scottish king mur-dered by Macbeth ; a character in Shakespeare's tragedy " Macbeth."

Duncan, Adam, Viscount (1731–1804). Brit. admiral ; defeated the Dutch off Camperdown in 1797.

Duncan, Isadora (1878–1927). Amer. classical dancer, revived and popu-larized Gk. bare-foot dances with simple, free draperies ; wrote very frank memoirs ; 347.

Duncan, Sir Patrick (1870–1943). Brit. administrator. Appointed Governor-general of Union of S. Africa in Nov. 1936.

Duncansby Head. Promontory of Caith-ness, Scot., 210 ft. high ; the House of John o' Groat is 2 m. to the w.

Dundalk (dun-dawk´) **Bay,** Eire. Inlet of the Irish Sea, 7 m. wide at the entrance.

Dundee´, 3rd city in Scot., in Angus ; important spt. on Firth of Tay ; pop. 162,000 ; **1055,** 2890 ; jute industry, 1844.

Dundrear´y, Lord. Caricature of a Brit. nobleman in Tom Taylor's comedy " Our American Cousin " ; made famous by Edward A. Sothern, revived by his son, Edward H. Sothern ; at a performance of this play Abraham Lincoln was shot.

Dunedin (dun ē´ din), New Zealand. Cap. and chief spt. in S.E. of South Isl. ; pop. 87,700 ; woollen mfrs., gold mining ; Otago Univ. ; *2359.*

Dunes, sand, 2870 ; Denmark, 991 ; of Sahara, 996, 2859 ; of Takla-Makan desert, 997.

Dunferm´line, Scot., in Fifeshire, 16 m. N.W. of Edinburgh ; pop. est. 37,600 ; famous for damask table-linen, 1954 ; birthplace of Charles I and Andrew Carnegie, 703 ; burial-place of Rob-ert Bruce.

Dung-beetle, *399, 400, 401.*

Dungeness (dunj-nes´), Kent. A low marshy promontory on the s. coast, with lighthouse, Lloyd's signalling station, coastguard, etc. ; here Admiral Tromp defeated Blake in 1652.

Dun´kery Beacon, Exmoor, Somerset-shire. It is the highest hill on the moor, being 1,707 ft. high and 12 m. in circumference ; in " Lorna Doone " there is a fine description of the lighting of the beacon on Dun-kery, 3000.

Dun´kirk (Fr. Dunkerque). Fr. spt. on the Strait of Dover ; pop. 10,575 ; in Ger. occupn., 1940–45, 1055.

Dunkirk, Evacuation of. Withdrawal of B.E.F. and Allied troops, May 26–June 2, 1940, after surrender of Belgian army, **1056,** *plates f. 1056,* *1057,* 1452, 3417 ; organized by Gen. Alexander, 107.

Dun Laoghaire (dun-lēr´-i), Eire. See **Kingstown.**

Dunlop, John Boyd (1840–1921). Scot-tish inventor. Invented in 1887 inflated tire, from which developed his pneumatic tire, 2836.

Dunmore Head. Headland on coast of co. Kerry, Eire ; most westerly pt. of Ireland.

Dunmow Flitch. A flitch of bacon offered to any married couple who " will go to the priory (at Little Dunmow, Essex), and kneeling on two sharp-pointed stones, will swear that they have not quarrelled nor repented of their marriage within a year and a day after its celebration." Inst. 1244. Competition held at Dunmow annually on Whit Mon-day ; similar ones at West Wickham, Kent, and other places.

Dunne, John William (1875–1949). Brit. inventor and thinker. Invented tail-less type of aeroplane. Pub. " An Experiment with Time " (1927) ; " The Serial Universe " (1934).

Dunsa´ny, Edward Plunkett, 18th Baron (b. 1878). Irish story-writer and dramatist ; fantastic and imag-inative work (" The Gods of Pe-gana " ; " The Gods of the Mount-ain " ; " King Argimenes " ; " A Night at an Inn," " While the Sirens Slept ") ; several radio plays.

Duns Sco´tus, John (c.1265–1308). Scottish theologian and philosopher, one of the greatest of the School-men ; as destructive a critic as Thomas Aquinas was constructive ; his followers became bigoted op-ponents of the New Learning ; so the name of the learned " Subtle Doctor " came to mean a " dunce " ; *2572.*

Dunstable. Tn. of Bedfordshire ; for-mer centre of straw plaiting ; indus-

tries now include engineering, print-ing, rubber manufacture, and plastic products ; gliding centre ; pop. 16,500 ; *390.*

Dun´stan, St. (A.D. 924–988). Abbot of Glastonbury, Archbishop of Can-terbury and adviser to kings Ed-mund I and Edgar of England ; first of a long line of Eng. ecclesi-astical statesmen.

Dunsterville, Col. Lionel Charles (1865–1946). Hero of Rudyard Kipling's " Stalky and Co." ; in 1st World War he led a small Brit. force across Persia to Baku in attempt to save oil wells from Bolsheviks and Turks, 1918.

Dunwich (dun´-ij). Vil. in Suffolk ; has suffered much from sea en-croachments. From Anglo-Saxon times until the Middle Ages a pros-perous port with many churches and monasteries.

Duodec´imo, a book size (12 mo.), 512.

Duode´num. The first portion of the small intestine between the stomach and the jejunum, encircling the pancreas, *1016.*

Dupleix (dū-pleks´), **Joseph François, Marquis** (1697–1763). Greatest Fr. gov. in India ; failure as empire-builder due to lack of support by Fr. govt. against his Eng. rival Clive and Brit. East India Co. ; recalled to France (1754), died in obscurity and want ; 2925.

Duplex telegraphy, 3167.

Du Pont de Nemours (dū pawn de ne-mōōr´), **Pierre Samuel** (1739–1817). Fr. statesman and economist ; im-prisoned and property confiscated in Fr. Rev. ; emigrated to U.S.A. His son, Eleuthère Irénée (1771–1834), established the famous Du Pont powder works.

Duquesne (dū-kān´), **Abraham, Mar-quis** (1610–88). Fr. admiral ; gained two notable victories over the Dutch fleet in 1676.

Dural´umin. An alloy of aluminium, 124, 135 ; used in airship con-struction, 92.

Durance. R. of Fr., rises in Fr. Alps, flows 220 m. to Rhône, 2774.

Durango (dū-ran´-gō), Mexico. State in N.-centre ; 42,272 sq. m. ; pop. 483,800 ; cap. Durango (33,400).

Durazzo or Durres. Chief spt. and old cap. of Albania ; pop. 8,739 ; 100.

Dur´ban or Port Natal. Chief spt. in prov. of Natal, S. Africa ; pop. 338,817 ; **1057,** 2279.

Durbar. Indian term applied especially to great state ceremonies ; Imperial Durbar of 1911, 987.

Durendal. Sword of Roland, 2797.

Dürer (dür´-er), **Albrecht** (1471–1528). " Prince of Ger. artists," **1058,** 1454 ; " Charlemagne," 753 ; compared with Holbein, 1635 ; engraving of Nuremberg, *1217* ; home in Nurem-berg, 2406 ; Renaissance artist, 2766 ; " St. Jerome in his study," *1058* ; water-colours, 3352.

Dur´ham, John George Lambton, 1st Earl of (1792–1840). Brit. gov.-gen. of Canada (1838) ; his " Report on the Affairs of British North America " outlined scheme which later re-sulted in present Dominion of Canada ; helped to draft the Reform Bill of 1832.

Durham. Maritime co. of N.E. Eng. ; 1,015 sq. m. ; pop. 1,486,000 ; **1059.**

Durham. Co. tn. of Durham, on r. Wear ; pop. 19,000 ; castle built by William the Conqueror ; univ. ; 1059 ; cath., *723, 729* ; great hall, 718.

Durham cattle. A short-horned breed noted for beef quality.

Durham University. Consists of two parts, one in Durham and the other in Newcastle-on-Tyne ; it was founded in 1832 ; Codrington College, Barbados, and Fourah Bay College, Sierra Leone, are affiliated to it, 1059.

Du´rian. Tall forest tree resembling the elm ; spherical fruit 6 to 8 inches in diameter ; seeds, about the size of chestnuts, are roasted and eaten ; 2069.

Dur′ra. Grain of Indian millet. *See also* **Sorghum.**

Dur-Sargon. Anc. city near Nineveh, 2372.

Du′rum wheat, 2045.

Duruy (dü-rwē′), **Jean Victor** (1811–94). Fr. historian and educator ; minister of education (1863–69) ; wrote Histories of France, Rome, Greece.

Duse (dōō-zā), **Eleonora** (1859–1924). It. tragic and emotional actress of international reputation (" Juliet " ; " Francesca da Rimini "). Many of Gabriele D'Annunzio's plays were written for her.

Düsseldorf (dü′-sel-dorf), Ger. industrial city and port on Rhine ; in Westphalian coal region ; pop. (1939) 539,900 ; 1447 ; 2769 ; birthplace of Heine ; bombed, taken by U.S. April 1945 ; in 1946 made capital of new prov. of North Rhineland and Westphalia.

Dust. Effect on light rays, 88 ; fog formation, 1333 ; volcanic, 3328.

Dutch and Flemish Art, 2324.

Dutch East India Company, colonies in S. Africa, 697, 3016 ; sends Hudson to America, 1648.

Dutch East Indies. General name for the former Dutch possessions in the East Indies. *See* **Indonesia.**

Dutch Guiana (gē-ah′-na) or **Surinam.** Dutch colony on N.E. coast of S. Amer. ; 55,143 sq. m. ; pop. (1944) 191,628 ; .1553. 3022.

Dutch metal. A malleable alloy which simulates gold.

Dutch mill, type of windmill, *3386.*

Dutch New Guinea. *See* **Netherlands New Guinea.**

Dutch painting. *See* **Netherlands Art.**

Dutch West India Company. Established 1621 with monopoly of trade on Amer. and African coasts.

Dutch West Indies. Dutch Guiana and Curaçao. *See* **Curaçao ; Guiana.**

Duval (dü-vahl′), **Claude** (1643–70). Eng. highwayman, daring and polite; hanged at Tyburn, 1625.

Duveen, Joseph Duveen, 1st Baron (1869–1939). Eng. benefactor to art ; endowed galleries at the Tate and National Galleries.

Dvina (dvē-nah′). R. in N. Russia, formed by Sukhona and Jug ; flows 780 m. N.W. into White Sea ; scene of fierce battles between Russians and Germans in 1915 and 1916 ; 1232, 2779 ; also in 1941–44. Name Dvina sometimes given to Duna river.

Dvinsk. *See* **Daugavpils.**

Dvorak (dvŏr′-zhahk), **Antonin** (1841–1904). Bohemian musical composer (" New World " symphony, " Humoreskes," " Slavonic Dances ").

Dwarf elder. Flowering shrub, 1124.

Dwarfs, 1059. In Africa, 3017 ; Lilliputians, 3133.

Dyaks (dī′-aks). Aborigines of Borneo, 525, *plate f. 524.*

Dyce, William (1806–64). Brit. painter associated with Pre-Raphaelite school.

Dyes, 1059 ; alder tree, 105 ; alizarin, 857 ; aniline, 857, 1724 ; and chemical research, 766 ; coal-tar,

857 ; cochineal, 859, 2879 ; indigo, 1718 ; from nettles, 2335 ; containing nitrogen, 2373 ; controlled by photoelectric device, 2576 ; of rayon, 2750 ; of silk, 2972 ; Tyrian purple, 1059, 2573.

" Dying Gaul," or " Dying Gladiator," famous Gk. statue in the Capitoline Museum, Rome, *1538.*

Dyke. *See* **Dike.**

Dykhtau Mt., in Caucasus, 732.

Dynam′ics. Mechanics of motion, 2127.

Dy′namite and nitro-glycerine, 1060 ; for bridge demolition, 1250 ; invented by Nobel, 2375.

Dynamo, an electric generator, 1060, *1129* ; principle discovered by Faraday, 1260 ; and electric motors, 2239, 2740 ; in hydro-elec. installations, 1670 ; at power station, *2674,* 2676.

Dyne. A unit of force in physics ; the force which, acting on a gramme for one second, would give it an acceleration of one centimetre per second.

Dys′entery. Intestinal disease accompanied by fever and loss of blood ; amoebic form caused by protozoa, 1458.

Dy′son, Sir Frank (1868–1939). Brit. astronomer ; Astronomer Royal, Scot. (1905–10) ; Astronomer Royal (1910–33).

Dyspro′sium. A chemical element belonging to the rare-earth group. *See* **Rare-Earths.**

Dytiscus. Water beetle, 400, *401.*

OF all the letters in the English alphabet E is the one most used ; yet the Egyptians and the Phoenicians did not have it in their alphabets. Its ancestor, however, was the Egyptian ⎕, which was simply the sign of a 𓏤 breathing. When later it was written 𝕸 it looked like our E turned down. The Phoenicians called it *He* (pronounced *ha*), meaning " window," which seems a good name for a breathing sound, although it is hard to see its resemblance to a window in form

The Phoenicians and Hebrews changed the form of it still further, turning the stem up. But they wrote from right to left, and so they ⊒ faced it towards the left like this ⌐. The Greeks, who wrote from left to right just as we do, turned it round. They were the first to use it as a vowel. In English we give the name of the letter the long " ee " sound. But in the other languages using the Roman alphabet its name is pronounced " ay," which is its original long sound.

Eagle, bird of prey, **1063** ; eye, *1253* ; foot, *448* ; harpy eagle, *439* ; letter A derived from, *see,* in Index, letter A ; national emblem, 1063, 1787.

Eagre (ē′-ger). Ancient name, surviving locally, for tidal bore ; 3210.

Ealing. Boro. in Middlesex, became a bor. in 1901 ; pop. 163,650 ; 2168.

Ear, 1065, 2983 ; grasshopper, 1511 ; insects, 1730 ; rudimentary in fish, 1296.

Earhart, Amelia (1898–1937) (Mrs. Putnam), American airwoman. " Lady Lindy " (so called from her facial likeness to Charles Lindbergh) flew Atlantic solo in 1932, and crossed E. Pacific in 1935. She was lost in mid-Pacific on last lap of a round-the-world flight.

Earl. In Gt. Brit. a title and rank of nobility, third in the order of peerage, between marquess and viscount, 2563, 3084.

Earl Marshal, functions, *1614,* 1615, 3084.

Earls Barton, Northants. Church tower, *219.*

Earl's Court, London, S.W. Site of exhibitions held 1884–1914 ; new stadium for exhibitions, sporting events, etc., opened in 1937, *608.*

Ear shell, an abalone, *2943.*

Earth, one of the planets, **1067** ; *plate f. 1432* ; diagram, *1067* ; age of, 2732 ; atmosphere, 88, *1067* ; distance from sun, 3119 ; equinox and solstice, 1221 ; formation of physical features, *1068,* 2595 ; geography, 1430 ; gravitation, *1513* ; history revealed by geology, 1432, *plate f. 1432* ; ice

age, 1680 ; latitude and longitude, 1898 ; Magellan circumnavigates, 2056 ; mapping, 2093, 1898 ; moon's influence, 2225 ; motion and relativity, 2762 ; origin and evolution, 1067, 1244, 1432, 2620 ; planetesimal theory, 2619 ; quaint old ideas, 1431 ; rotation and revolution, 1067, *1561* ; size, 3119 ; in solar system, *276, 280, 3118,* 3078, 2617 ; tides, 3209 ; time zones, *3213* ; winds, 3384.

Earth, in brick-making, 561.

Earth, in radio apparatus, 3392.

Earthenware. *See* **Pottery and Porcelain.**

Earthquake, 1069 ; in Andes Mts., 3022 ; Cent. Amer., 744, 1552, 2868 ; France, 2364 ; Gt. Brit., *1070* ; Italy, 1770 ; Japan, 1796, 3435 ; Lisbon, 1962 ; Messina, 2968 ; Nicaragua, 2364 ; Philippines, 2568 ; San Francisco, 2871 ; Tokyo, 3221 ; part played by volcanoes, 3328 ; seismology, 1070. (*See* list in p. 3783).

Earthworm, or angleworm, **1070,** *1071* ; breathing, 2768 ; hibernation, 1623.

Earwig, an insect, **1071** ; method of defence, 1728.

East, Sir Alfred (1849–1913). Noted Eng. landscape painter ; his works are in many art galleries throughout Europe ; became R.A. in 1913.

East Africa, 1072 ; British, 1072 ; Italy's conquests, 1073 ; League of Nations mandate administered by Gt. Brit. of German E. Africa replaced by U.N. trusteeship in 1947 ; natives, *63, 69* ; *maps,* 1072, 1073 ; sunflower crop, 3121 ; ground-nut

scheme, 1550. *See also* **Abyssinia ; Rhodesia ; Zanzibar.**

East An′glia. Early kingdom in E. of Anglo-Saxon Britain, comprising present counties of Norfolk and Suffolk, 574.

Eastbourne. Fashionable watering place on the Sussex coast ; many schools, incl. Eastbourne College ; close by is Beachy Head ; pop. 42,210.

East Dudgeon lightship, 1944.

East End, district of London east of Aldgate Pump.

Easter, Christian Church festival, **1073.**

Easter Island. In S. Pacific Ocean ; 50 sq. m. ; belongs to Chile, **1074,** *1075,* 804, 2469 ; archaeological remains, 2469.

Easter Lily, 1947.

Eastern Empire. Same as Byzantine Empire.

Eastern Orthodox Church. *See* **Greek Orthodox Church.**

Eastern Question in European politics, the complicated problems arising out of European interference in the affairs of Turkey and the Balkan states formerly under Turkish rule ; in Balkans, 344 ; Crimean War, 931 ; Turkey, 3265.

Easter Revolt. Abortive attempt of Irish to throw off Brit. rule ; much of Dublin seized Easter Monday (1916) ; 1051, 1746.

East Ham. Tn. in Essex ; residential dist. for large working-class pop., many of whom find employment in the docks ; has large engineering works, soap and other factories ; heavy air raid damage in 2nd World War ; pop. 100,100.

East India Company, Dutch, 143, 697, 1648, 3016.

East India Company, English, a company founded for the purpose of trading with India and the E. Indies ; received its original charter from Queen Elizabeth in 1600 ; the growth of the company was the real foundation of Brit. dominion in India ; 1714 ; chartered, 142 ; Calcutta settled, 660 ; Clive's services, 842 ; French power in India, broken, 2925 ; power transferred to Crown, 3278 ; at Rangoon, 2745 ; ships of, 2946, 2956 ; Warren Hastings, 1581.

East Indies or **Malay Archipelago, 1075,** *map, 1074, 1075* ; bananas, 354 ; climate, 2742 ; coffee, 864 ; Malays, 2725 ; pepper, 2547 ; rubber, *2834* ; spices, 3060 ; Sumatra, 3117. See *also* Borneo ; Indonesia.

Eastlake, Sir Charles Lock (1793–1865). Eng. artist ; R.A., 1829 ; as first director of Nat. Gallery, 1855, did much to procure many of the finest works now owned by the Gallery.

East London, S. Africa. Important spt. on E. coast of Cape of Good Hope ; expansive harbour, obstructed by bar at low water ; pop. 78,530.

East Lothian or **Haddingtonshire.** Scot. co. ; area, 267 sq. m. ; pop. 48,800 ; **2027.**

Eastman, George (1854–1932). Amer. pioneer in photography ; invented the Kodak and roll film, 2580.

East Prussia. Until 1945 easternmost prov. of Prussia, on Baltic, separated from rest of country by Polish Corridor ; cap. was Konigsberg. Divided between Poland and R.S.F.S.R. in 1945 ; 3424.

East River, at New York, 2351, *2352.*

Eating, hygiene of, 1675.

Some Notable Earthquakes

1755. Lisbon, Portugal. Sea wave produced by quake destroyed the city with loss of about 40,000 lives.

1797. Ecuador. Quito and other towns destroyed ; 40,000 killed.

1891. Mino and Owari, Japan. Killed, 7,279 ; injured, 17,393 ; wholly destroyed 197,000 houses.

1900. San Francisco, California. Violent quakes, accompanied by surface movements ranging up to 23 feet, followed by fire ; about 700 killed.

1908. Calabria and Sicily. About 76,000 persons killed, 95,000 injured ; most of Messina destroyed.

1917. Guatemala. Repeated earthquakes over a week killed about 2,500.

1920. Kansu Province, China. Violent quakes ranging over 300 square miles ; 200,000 lives lost.

1923. Tokyo and Yokohama, Japan. One of the severest quakes in history ; nearly 160,000 killed.

1931. North Island, New Zealand. Destruction along 45 miles of coast ; Napier harbour level rose 18 feet.

1935. Quetta, India. Cities of Quetta, Kalat, and Mastung destroyed, including outposts ; 30,000 dead.

1939. Chile. Disastrous quake overwhelmed Concepcion, Chillan, and other towns. Over 20,000 killed.

Turkey. Vast area in Anatolia devastated ; 23,000 killed, 8,000 injured and 29,000 houses destroyed.

1942. Ecuador. Guayaquil devastated.

1943. Turkey. 25 m. railway wrecked. 4,000 killed.

1944. Argentine. San Juan destroyed in 40 secs. Over 2,000 killed.

1947. Japan. 60,000 sq. m. damage. 50 places destroyed. Over 1,250 killed.

1949. Ecuador. 5 tns. and many vills. in area between Chimborazo and Cotopaxi destroyed. About 10,000 killed.

Eau de Cologne (ō-de-ko-lōn'). Perfume made at Cologne, 872.

Eaves, in architecture. That part of the edge of a roof which projects beyond the face of the wall.

E'bal, Mt., in Palestine, opposite Mt. Gerizim, 3,077 ft. high, 2480.

Ebenezer (cb-o-nē-zer) (" stone of help "). Place in Judea where Samuel with divine assistance defeated Philistines (1 Sam. vii. 10–12).

Eberlein (ā'-ber-līn), **Gustav** (1847–1926). Modern Ger. sculptor.

Ebers (ā'-berz), **Georg Moritz** (1837–98). Ger. Egyptologist and novelist (" An Egyptian Princess " ; " Uarda ").

Ebert (ā'-bert), **Friedrich** (1871–1925). Ger. statesman, formerly a saddler, became leader of the Social Democratic party ; was elected first pres. of Ger. Republic (1919), 1451.

E-boat. Eng. name for Ger. and Ital. torpedo speed boats used in the Second World War.

Eb'onite, a form of vulcanised rubber, 2836.

Eb'ony. Tropical tree with black heartwood, **1076** ; Borneo, 526 ; burns with difficulty, 1280.

Eboracum. Roman name for York, 3435.

Éboué (ā-bōō-ā), **A. Félix S.** (1884–1944). Fr. administrator ; Negro governor of Lake Chad Territory in 1938, he declared for De Gaulle, Aug. 1940 ; governor of Fr. Equatorial Africa Nov. 1940.

Ebro. R. of N.E. Spain ; flows S.E. 465 m. from Cantabrian Mts. to Mediterranean, *map, 3030.*

Ecbatana (ek-bat'-a-na), Iran. Anc. cap. of Media ; modern Hamadan.

Eccen'tric of steam-engine, 3086.

Ecclefechan (ek-l-fekh'-an). Vil. in Scot., 14 m. E. of Dumfries ; birthplace of Thomas Carlyle ; pop. 988.

Eccles. Tn. in Lancashire, 4 m. w. of Manchester ; chiefly devoted to cotton and textile industries ; Eccles cakes are famous ; pop. 44,415.

Ecclesiastes (e-klē-zi-as'-tēz) (" the preacher "). A book of the Old Testament attributed by Jewish tradition to Solomon.

Ecclesiastical courts, 923.

Ecclesias'ticus. Book of Bible Apocrypha, 424.

Echegaray (ā-chā-ga-rī), **José** (1833–1916). Span. mathematician, statesman, and exceptionally popular dramatist ; sharer of Nobel prize in 1904 ; 3051.

Echidna (e-kid'-na). " Spiny anteater " of Australia, an egg-laying mammal, *313,* 1053.

Echinoderms (e-kī'-no-dêrmz). A group of marine animals, 156 ; sea-cucumber, 2911 ; starfish and sea-urchins, 3082.

Echo (ek'-ō), in myth., **1077,** 2278 ; and Narcissus, *1077,* 2278 ; an Oread, 2408.

Echo. A reflected sound, **1077.**

Echo organ, 2450.

Echo-sounding, for locating underwater objects ; in fisheries, 1300 ; navigation, 2291 ; mapping the oceans, 2413 ; radar a form of, 2726.

Eckener, Hugo (b. 1868). Ger. airship engineer ; successor of Count Zeppelin ; commanded " Graf Zeppelin " on world trip in 1929 ; trained all Germany's Zeppelin pilots in 1st World War.

Eck'ermann, Johann Peter (1792–1854). Ger. writer, friend and literary executor of Goethe (" Conversations with Goethe ").

Eckhardt (ek'-hahrt) or **Eckhart,** " the Faithful." Old man in Ger. legend who warned of evils those who followed Frau Holle or Holda (Venus); companion of Tannhäuser.

Eckhart, Johannes (" Meister Eckhart ") (c. 1260–1327). Ger. Dominican monk, father of Ger. mysticism.

Eclipse (e-klips'), in astronomy, **1077,** *plates f. 1076, 1077,* 2225, 3079.

" **Eclogues** " (ek'-logz). Pastoral poems by Virgil, 3325.

Ecology. Science of life in relation to environment, **1079,** *plate f. 1080,* 434, 531 ; distribution of birds, 440 ;

---

of trees, 3246 ; division between Australian and Asiatic life (" Wallace's line "), 264, 440, *1074* ; effect of climate on plant life, 841 ; peculiar mammals of Australia, 309, *313,* 1845 ; plant " societies," 531, 3355 ; primitive life forms precede the higher, 2239 ; protective coloration, 448, 1297, 1727 ; and zoology, 3447. See also **Adaptation.**

Economics, or political economy ; science of the production, distribution and consumption of wealth, **1080,** *plate f. 1081* ; Bankruptcy, 356 ; banks, 356 ; boycott, 537 ; child labour, 802 ; Communism, 881 ; co-operative societies, 903 ; customs and tariffs, 944 ; factories and factory laws, 802, 1722 ; fairs and markets, 1256 ; foreign exchange, 1347 ; gold standard, 1482 ; guilds, 1553 ; Hanseatic League, 1575 ; Industrial Revolution, 1721 ; labour organizations and legislation, 204, 3233 ; money, 2200 ; slavery and serfdom, 2981 ; Socialism, 2996, 2113 ; stamps, 3074 ; stocks and shares, 3093 ; taxation, 3158.

Écru silk, 2972.

Ecuador (ek'-wa-dōr). S. Amer. republic on Pacific coast ; 275,000 sq. m. ; est. pop. 3,200,000 ; **1081** ; *map, plate f. 3024* ; Andes, 152 ; cacao, 3022 ; Panama hats, 1584. Earthquakes in Aug. 1949 destroyed Ambato, Pelileo, other tns. and villages, and caused the loss of about 10,000 lives.

Edam (ā-dahm'), Netherlands. Tn. in N. Holland ; pop. 8,200 ; makes ships, rope, leather, cheese, 2320.

Edam cheese, 766.

Ed'das. Two collections of early Scandinavian literature, 2388 ; 2880.

Eddington, Sir Arthur Stanley (1882–1944). Brit. astrophysicist, awarded Order of Merit in 1938, **1083,** *1084.*

Eddy, Mary Baker (1821–1910). Founder of Christian Science. Born at Concord, N.H., she was three times married. Discovered Christian Science principles after a serious accident in 1866, publishing " Science and Health with Key to the Scriptures " in 1875 and founding the " Christian Science Monitor " newspaper in 1908. She organized the Church of Christ Scientist at Boston in 1879, remaining leader of the movement until her death.

Eddy currents (electrical) ; of dynamo, 1061 ; in high frequency heating, 1624.

Eddystone Lighthouse, off Plymouth, **1084,** 740, 1943, *plate f. 1944.*

Ede, James Chuter (b. 1882). Home Secretary from 1945.

Edelweiss (ā'-del-vīs). White flower of aster family, found in Alps ; now rare, except in inaccessible places.

E'den (Bible). Garden of paradise, home of Adam and Eve ; **1084,** *1085,* 1231, 2146 ; " Paradise Lost," 2178.

Eden, r., flows to Solway Firth ; salmon stream ; 65 m. long ; 943.

Eden, Robert Anthony (b. 1897). Brit. statesman ; Secretary for Foreign Affairs from 1935 to Feb. 1938 ; resigned over the Anglo-Italian Pact ; dominions sec., Sept. 1939 ; Sec. for War, May 1940 ; Foreign Sec., Dec. 1940–45, **1085.**

Edenta'ta. An order of toothless mammals ; anteater, 176 ; armadillo, 237 ; sloth, 2985.

Ederle, Gertrude (b. 1908). American swimmer, holder of many women's championships ; swam English Channel, Aug. 6, 1926, in 14 hrs. 34 mins.

Edessa (e-des'-a). Anc. city in Asia Minor ; became great centre of early Christianity and learning ; modern city Urfa (pop. 31,000).

Edfu (ed-fōō), Eg. Anc. tn. on Nile, 54 m. S.E. of Thebes ; Temple of Horus (3rd cent. B.C.), most perfect existing Eg. temple, *1121.*

Edgar (944–75). King of Eng. ; called " the peaceful," **1086.**

Edgehill. Ridge 12 m. s. of Warwick, 800 ft. high ; in 1642 scene of first battle of Civil War.

Edgeworth, Maria (1767–1849). Irish-Eng. novelist whose Irish stories ("Castle Rackrent" etc.) influenced Thackeray and Turgenev; her "Belinda" introduced the natural heroine, who did not faint and blush constantly, 1751, 1965.

Edict of Nantes (1598). Decree granting religious freedom to Fr. Huguenots, 1613, 1651, 2274; revocation of, in 1685, 1651.

Edinburgh (ed′-in-bur-o). Cap. and 2nd largest city of Scot.; pop. 475,000; **1086**; 2027; royal observatory, 2413.

Edinburgh, Duke of. Title given on Nov. 19, 1947. to Lieut. Philip Mountbatten. *See* **Philip, Prince.**

Edinburgh, University of, at Edinburgh. Scot.; co-ed.; arts, medicine, law, theology, music; 1087.

Ed′inburghshire. Now **Midlothian.**

Edirne. New name for **Adrianople.**

Edison, Thomas Alva (1847–1931). Amer. inventor and manufacturer, **1087**, *1088*; invents incandescent lamp, 1134; invents gramophone, *1495*; wireless pioneer, 3198.

Editor, of newspaper, 2344.

Ed′monton, Canada, cap. of Alberta; pop. 93,800; rly. and trading centre, especially for furs, 103.

Edmonton, Eng. Bor. in Middlesex; trade in timber; pop. est. 100,000.

Edmund (c. 922–46), Saxon king of Eng., grandson of Alfred the Great and son of Edward the Elder; warred with the Danes, conquered Cumbria.

Edmund Ironside (c. 981–1016). Saxon king of Eng., son of Ethelred "the Unready"; as ruler of Mercia, he led Saxon armies against Canute, who defeated him, drove his army back into Northumberland, and compelled division of Eng.; named "Ironside" for extraordinary strength and courage, 695.

Edom. Rugged country s. of Palestine, later called Idumaea; Edomites, enemies of Israelites, 1829.

Ed′red (d. A.D. 955). Saxon king of Eng., subdued Danes in Northumberland; guided chiefly by his intimate friend St. Dunstan.

Edsel Ford Mts., in the Antarctic, 2647.

Education, 1088; athletics, 287; Babylon, 328; of blind, 470; Boy Scouts, 531; broadcasts to schools, 3398; Charlemagne's interest in, 753, *754*; colour training, 875; examinations, 1246; Froebel, 1398; Girl Guides, 1465; Gt. Brit., 2883; of deaf and dumb, 981; how to study, 2139; India, 1691, 1713, 1714; Japan, 1798; kindergarten, 1378; medieval schoolroom, *1197*; memory training, 2138; Ministry of, 1089; Montessori method, 2220; Nature study, 2283; Negroes (U.S.A.), 2312; physical training, 2589; psychology in, 2697; road safety, 2787; schools, 2883; anc. Sparta, 3052; universities, 3296; Act of 1944, 2886. *See also* **Arithmetic** and other school subjects by name.

Education Acts, 2886, 3279.

Edward I (1239–1307), king of Eng., **1089**; built Caernarvon castle, 650, *716*, 718; on 7th Crusade, 937; in Elgin castle, 2228; victory at Evesham, 2221; "Model" Parl., *2522*; and Simon de Montfort, 2221; subdues Wales, 559, 3334; Eisteddfod, 3336; Eleanor Cross, 1124.

Edward II (1284–1327), Engl., **1089**; defeated at Bannockburn, 359; 2892.

Edward III (1312–77), Eng., **1091**, *1090*; besieged Calais, 655; claims Fr. throne, 1652; establishes Order of the Garter, 2449; in Hundred Years' War, 655, 1652, *1653*; and Philip VI, 2567; victory at Crécy, 926.

Edward IV (1442–83), Eng., first of the Yorkist kings, **1091**, *1090*, 2828.

Edward V (1470–83), Eng., **1091**, *1090*, 3232.

Edward VI (1537–53), Eng., **1091**, *1090*; grammar schools, 2883.

Edward VII (1841–1910), Eng., **1092**, *1091*; marriage, 108, 816.

Edward VIII (b. 1894), Eng., became Duke of Windsor on his abdication

in Dec. 1936; **1092**, 1091; as Prince of Wales, *1092*, 3334, *3337*.

Edward the Black Prince (1330–76) (so called because of his black armour), Prince of Wales, son of Edward III of Eng., and father of Richard II; victor of Poitiers (1356) and sharer in victory of Crécy (1346); great soldier and national hero, 524, 1652.

Edward the Confessor (c. 1005–66), last of Saxon kings of Eng., **1089**, 1194; begins Westminster Abbey, 2014, 3369; and William I, 3379.

Edward the Elder (d. 924), Saxon king of Eng., from 901 (sometimes given 899), **1089.**

Edward the Martyr (c. 963–978), Saxon king of Eng., **1089.**

Edwardes, George (1852–1915). Eng. theatrical manager; director at the Gaiety, London, for nearly 30 years, producing a series of famous musical plays.

Edwards, John Passmore (1823–1911). Eng. journalist and philanthropist; proprietor of the "Echo," a former London evening newspaper; devoted large sums of money to hospitals, art galleries and libraries.

Ed′wy or **Eadwig** (c. 940–959). Saxon king, eldest son of Edmund I; succeeded his uncle in 955; shared throne with brother Edgar.

Eel, elongated, snake-like fish, **1092**; electric, 1297; instinct, 159; migrations, *1093*, 2169.

Ef′ferent nerves, 2317.

E′gan, Pierce (1772–1849). "Father of Brit. sporting journalism"; wrote on races, prize-fights, cock-fights, cricket matches, executions, etc.; "Pierce Egan's Book of Sports and Mirror of Life."

Eg′bert (d. 839), king of Wessex; conquered Northumbria and Mercia; called "first king of the English"; 574.

Eger (ā′-ger), city in Czechoslovakia. *See* **Cheb.**

Egeria (ē-je′-ri-a), in Rom. myth., a nymph who inspired Numa Pompilius, 2804.

Egg, 1093, *1094*; albumen in (white of the egg), 2964; alligator, 121; beetle, 398; birds, 442, 443, *plate f. 440*, *442, 443*; butterflies and moths, *629*, *630*, 630; coloration of birds' eggs, 442; crocodile, 932; development into animal, *1154, 1155*; "dried," 1341; economic value of poultry eggs, 2671; fish, 1297; fly, 1329; food value, 1338, *1339*; 2174, 2694, 3327; frog, 1155, 1398; grasshopper, *1511*; how to cook, 902; incubating eggs, 2671; laid by mammalian duckbill and echidna, 1053; lizard, 1095, 1975; lobster, 1978; mosquito, 2236; ostrich, *2456*; poultry, 2671; protein, 2694; shark, 2938; shell, *1155*; snake, 2991; toads, 3219; tortoise, *plate f. 3229*; turtle, 3229. *See also* articles on various birds.

Egg-eater, a S. African snake, 2990.

Egg-plant, plant of nightshade family, with purplish edible fruit.

Egg plum, 2630.

Eginhard. Same as **Einhard.**

Eg′mont, Lamoral, Count of (1522–68). Flemish hero, gov. of Flanders and Artois under Philip II of Spain; his unjust execution for treason by Council of Blood gave impetus to the Netherlands revolt; theme of Goethe's "Egmont."

Egoists (eg′-ō-ists), or epicureans, in philosophy, 2571.

Egret (ē′-gret), member of the stork family, *3098.*

Egypt, ancient, 1113, *map, 1113*; agriculture, 87, 1115, 3374; alphabet, 125; army, 251; astronomy, 275; boats and ships, *plate f. 1121*; books and literature, 509; bread, 554; brickmaking, 561; canals and irrigation works, 686; enamelling, 1158; excavation, 206, 208; fisheries, 1298; furniture, 1409, *1410*; harp, *1579*; language and writing, 2496; mathematics, 113, 1434; painting, *1115*, *1119*, 2475; papyrus, 2500, 2496; Rosetta Stone, *1118*, 2828; sculpture, *1106, 1107, 1114, 1115, plates f. 1120, 1121*, 2904; ships, 2945;

slavery, 2981; spinning and weaving, 920, 3066, 3191; water-clock, 843. *Architecture*: 212; Memnon, 2138; pyramids, *212*, 1114, *2708*; Sphinx, 3058, *3059*; temples of Luxor and Karnak, *1105, 1106, 1107, 1111, 1112, 1116*; of Edfu, 1121. *Religion and mythology*: animal worship, 399, 719, 931, 1427, 2207; Isis, *1760*; mummies, *back of plate f. 1120*, 2255; Osiris, 2455; Tutankhamen's tomb, 206, 1118, *back of plates f. 1120, 1121*. *History*: chief events (*see also* History): influence on Mediterranean civilizations, 29, 30, 2573; conflicts with kingdom of Judah, 1829; Persian conquest, 2554; Alexander the Great conquers (322 B.C.), 105; under Ptolemies, 109, 1830, 1930; Cleopatra, 837; made Rom. prov. (30 B.C.), 303; rise of monasticism, 2212.

Egypt, modern, an independent country of N.E. Africa; 383,000 sq. m.; pop. 17,423,000; **1095**, 653; *map, 1096*; agriculture, 921, 978, *1098*, *1100*; air survey, 2096; chief cities, 109, 653; children, 801; first governed by Britain, 1101; foreign trade, 110, 654; irrigation, *959, 1098*; massacres of Europeans (1882), 1101; Napoleon's campaign, 2275; Nile, 1095, 1113, 2370; Palestine, 1104; people, *1097, 1099*; Sahara, 2859; Sudan, 3109; Suez Canal, 3110; in 2nd World War, 1102, *3421*; invaded by Jews in 1949, 2483.

Egyptian vulture, 3330.

Egyptology, archaeology, etc., in Egypt, 208, 1113.

Ehrenbreitstein (ār′-en-brīt′-shtīn), Ger. Tn. across the Rhine from Coblenz; fortress on rock 400 ft. high, taken by Fr. (1799), restored to Ger. by Congress of Vienna (1815), occupied by Amer. Army of Occupation (1918); 2769.

Ehrenburg, Ilya G. (b. 1891). Russ. writer; war correspt. in both World Wars; many stories and novels; "The Fall of Paris" won 1942 Stalin prize for lit.

Ehrlich (ār′-likh), **Paul** (1854–1915), Ger. bacteriologist, discovered drug salvarsan; Nobel prize winner (1908).

Eichendorff (ī′-khen-dorf), **Joseph, Baron von** (1788–1857), Ger. poet and story-writer; his poems are probably the finest lyric expression of Ger. romanticism.

Eiderdown, obtained from eider duck, 1052.

Eider duck, 1052, *1053*.

Eifel (ī′-fel), **The.** Barren plateau of Germany in Rhine Province s.w. Prussia; about 1,000 sq. m.; average elevation 1,500 to 2,000 ft.; of volcanic origin; crater lakes, 3328.

Eiffel (ī′-fel), **Alexandre Gustave** (1832–1923). Fr. engineer, builder of Eiffel Tower.

Eiffel Tower, Paris, 2517.

Eiger (ī′-ger), peak (13,042 ft.) in Bernese Oberland, Swiss Alps, 3924.

Eighth Army, 249; N. Africa advance, 3420, *map, 3421.*

"Eikon Basilike" (ī′-kon ba-sīl′-i-kē). Famous book which appeared immediately following execution of Charles I and professed to be the king's own account of his sufferings in prison; probably written by Bishop John Gauden (1605–62).

"Eikonoklastes" ("image breaker"). Milton's defence of the execution of Charles I written to counteract "Eikon Basilike"; at the Restoration it was ordered to be suppressed and burned by the hangman.

Einaudi (ā-now′-dē), **Luigi** (b. 1874). It. economist and second pres. of It. republic; exiled for opposing Abyssinian war in 1935; returned to It. in 1944; in 1947 app. Vice-premier and min. of finance; in May 1948 elected president.

Eindhoven. Tn. in Netherlands; rly. junct. and mfg. centre of Brabant; pop. about 136,000. Its huge radio factory, which became important German source of supply during 2nd

World War, made the town an Allied air-raid target.

Einhard (ĭn-hahrt) or **Eginhard** (c. 770–840). Secretary, biographer and son-in-law of Charlemagne.

Einsiedeln (ĭn'-zē-dĕln), Switzerland. Tn. 20 m. S.E. of Zürich ; famous pilgrim resort ; Benedictine abbey ; reputed birthplace of Paracelsus.

Einstein (ĭn'-shtĭn), **Albert** (b. 1879). Ger.-Swiss scientist of Jewish parentage, **1122** ; and gravitation, 1514 ; explained photo-electric effect, 2711 ; theory of relativity, 1122, 2728, 2760 ; theory of space, 3081.

Eire (ār'-e). Independent republic of S. Ireland, **1122**. See **Ireland** ; **Irish Free State**.

Eisenach (ī-ze-nahkh). Summer resort in cent. Ger. at N.W. end of Thuringian Forest ; pop. 43,385 ; birthplace of Bach, 333 ; refuge of Luther, 2041.

Eisenhower (ī'-zen-how-er), **Gen. Dwight David** (b. 1890). Amer. C.-in-C.

Allied Forces, N. Africa, 1942 ; Supreme Commdr. Allied Exped. Forces in Europe Dec. 1943–July 1945 ; Chief of Staff, U.S. Army, 1945–47, **1123** ; Normandy invasion, 2377, 3422 ; h.-q. at Reims, 2760, 3424.

Eisleben (īs'-lā-bĕn). Ger. tn. in Saxony, 20 m. N.W. of Halle ; pop. 25,000 ; cop. and sil. smelting ; in Russian occupied zone after 2nd World War ; Luther, 2041.

Eisner, Kurt (1867–1919). Bavarian (Jewish) Socialist politician ; took lead in overthrow of Bavarian monarchy. Pres. of revolut. govt. 1918.

Eisteddfod (ās-teth'-vod). National congress of Welsh bards and minstrels held annually , 1123, 3336, plate f. 3337.

Eka-caesium. Name first given to Element No. 87, now known as Virginium (q.v.).

Eka-iodine. Name first given to

Element No. 85, now known as Alabamine (q.v.).

Ekaterinburg. See **Sverdlovsk.**

Ekaterinodar. See **Krasnodar.**

Ekaterinoslav. See **Dniepropetrovsk.**

Ek'ron. One of five Philistine cities, 2507.

Elagabalus. Same as **Heliogabalus.**

Elaine (e-lān'). In Arthurian legend, the maid of Astolat who pines and dies for love of Sir Lancelot, 2830.

Elam (ē'-lam). Bible name for anc. Persian prov. of Susiana.

E'land. S. African antelope ; back of plate f. 72.

Elasmobranchii (ē-las-mō-bran'-ki-ī). Sub-class of cartilaginous fishes ; includes sharks, 2938.

Elastic'ity. Of gases, 1419 ; of rubber, 2831 ; of the skin, 2980.

Elba. It. isl. off w. coast ; 140 sq. m. ; pop. 26,200 ; map, 1764 ; Napoleon exiled to, 2278.

ELECTRICAL TERMS IN COMMON USE

A.C. Abbreviation for Alternating Current.

Accumulator. A group of secondary cells.

Alternating current (A.C.). A current whose direction of flow reverses at intervals (usually in Britain 50 times per second) called cycles.

Ammeter. Instrument for measuring current.

Ampere (amp.). Practical unit of current ; current passing through a conductor of resistance one ohm under a pressure of one volt.

Anions. Ions in a solution which during electrolysis move to the anode.

Anode. Electrode through which the current enters an electrical apparatus : positive plate of a cell.

Arc. Luminous discharge of electricity through a gas.

Armature. Central rotor of a dynamo or electric motor.

Battery. Two or more primary or secondary cells connected together.

Brush. Commutator contacts which transfer current in generators or motors.

Capacity. The ratio of the charge on a body to the potential due to that charge.

Cations (or **Kations**). Ions moving to the cathode.

Cathode. Electrode through which the current leaves an electrical apparatus ; negative plate of a cell.

Cell. Assemblage of dissimilar metal (or of metal and carbon) electrodes in an electrolyte, producing a current by electro-chemical means.

Charge. An excess or deficiency of electrons on a body.

Circuit. Conductor through which a current can flow from its source through some electrical device back to its origin.

Coil. A conductor wound in a number of turns so as to produce electro-magnetic effects.

Commutator. Rotating part of a generator or electric motor upon which the carbon brushes press.

Condenser. Two conductors separated by a dielectric, a device for obtaining large capacity effects.

Conductor. A substance possessing a large proportion of free electrons enabling it to carry a current.

Coulomb. Unit of electrical quantity, the amount of electricity conveyed per second by a current of one ampere.

Crookes tube. Vacuum tube highly exhausted, which under high voltages produces cathode rays and X-rays.

Current. The passage of electricity through a conductor.

Cycle. In alternating currents there is both reversal and rise and fall of the current and voltage values. One complete series of these events is termed a cycle and may occur many times per second. A.C. current is usually supplied in Britain at 50 cycles per second.

D.C. Abbreviation for direct current.

Dielectric. An insulating substance placed between the plates of a condenser.

Direct current (D.C.). A current that flows continuously and does not change its direction.

Dynamo. A machine that converts mechanical energy into electrical energy by the movement of conductors in a magnetic field.

Electrolysis. Chemical decomposition of a fluid by the action of a current.

Electrolyte. Solution decomposed by passage of electric current, e.g. in an electric cell or in a plating bath.

Electro-magnetism. Magnetic effects due to current in a coiled wire.

Electro-motive force (E.M.F.). Force (in volts) due to potential difference, producing current flow.

Electron. Fundamental unit of electricity ; particle of an atom.

Electronics. Science of and industrial applications of electron emission by cathode ray tubes, thermionic valves, etc., as in radio, television, automatic counting and control devices, radar, etc.

Electrostatics. Stationary electric charges and the forces due to them.

E.M.F. Electro-motive force.

Farad. Unit of electrical capacity ; the capacity of a condenser charged to one volt by one coulomb of electricity.

Frequency. The number of cycles which an alternating current completes per second.

Fuse. A wire or metal strip designed to melt and break a circuit when the maximum safe current is exceeded.

Galvanometer. Instrument for detecting and measuring small currents.

Grid. National system of power transmission lines in Great Britain.

Insulator. A substance having a very low conducting power.

Ion. An electrically charged atom or molecule.

Kilovolt (kV.). Practical unit of high-tension voltage (1,000 volts).

Kilowatt (kW.). Unit of electrical power (1,000 watts).

Kilowatt-hour (kWh.). The Board of Trade unit ; 1,000 watts for 1 hour.

Lines of force. Lines indicating the direction and intensity of a magnetic field.

Magnet. Piece of iron which exerts attraction or repulsion on other magnetic material, and produces a magnetic field.

Magnetic field. Area affected by a magnetic force. (See **Lines of force**).

Magnetism. Property of iron, steel, nickel, and a few other metals, due to electron movements within the metal, of exerting attraction or repulsion upon other magnets.

Microfarad. One-millionth part of a farad (q.v.).

Neutral. Conductor or electrical system in which no current flows.

Neutron. Particle in atom similar to proton, carrying no charge.

Ohm. Standard international unit of resistance ; the resistance of a circuit through which a current of one amp. at a pressure of one volt is passing.

Parallel. Method of connecting conductors so that the current flowing is equally divided between them ; if all the negative and all the positive terminals are connected the effect is obtained.

Photo-electric cell. Light-sensitive valve in which current varies directly with amount of light falling on it.

Pole. Part of magnet where lines of force converge ; also cell terminals.

Positron. Particle in atom similar to electron but positively charged.

Potential. Short for potential energy ; energy which causes a current to flow from a point at higher potential to one at a lower. (See **Electro-motive force**).

Proton. Atomic particle charged with one unit of positive electricity.

Rectification. Conversion of an alternating current into a direct current.

Rectifier. Any apparatus such as a radio valve, which converts A.C. to D.C.

Relay. Instrument employed to control heavy currents by weak currents.

Resistance. The property of a conductor causing it to absorb part of the energy of an electric current, converting this into heat.

Rheostat. Variable resistance for regulating the flow of current.

Rotor. The rotating part of an electric motor or generator.

Series. Method of connecting conductors so that a current flows from one to the other in turn ; connecting positive to negative poles alternately, produces the effect.

Short circuit. Connexion of two conductors through a low-resistance path, allowing a much larger current than usual to pass.

Switch. Device for cutting off or establishing a current flow.

Transformer. Apparatus which, by electro-magnetic induction, transforms alternating current in one circuit into a current of different voltage in another circuit.

Volt. The practical unit of electromotive force or potential difference ; defined as that E.M.F. which, when applied to a conductor of resistance one ohm, produces a current of one ampere.

Voltmeter. Instrument for measuring potential difference or voltage between any two points in a circuit.

Watt. Unit of electrical power ; work done by a current of one amp. flowing with a pressure of one volt.

X-rays. Electro-magnetic waves of same nature as light ; able to penetrate solid substances and affect photographic plates.

(Many other terms frequently used in electricity will be found in the Fact-Index and the list of wireless and television terms).

Elbe. Germany's second r. in importance, **1124,** 2878 ; at Hamburg, 1568, 1577 ; in 2nd World War, 1452.

Elberfeld-Barmen. Two tns. in w. Germany forming single community known as Wuppertal (*q.v.*).

Elbing, Poland. Spt. in former E. Prussia, 5 m. from the sea on r. Elbing ; shipbuilding, iron and tin works, textile mfrs. ; pop. 72,000 ; ceded to Poland from Germany in 1945 and given Polish name of Elblag.

Elbruz. Mt. peak of Caucasus Mts. in Transcaucasia, highest point in Europe (18,470 ft.) ; 732.

Elburz (el-bōōrz') **Mts.** Range of Iran along s. border of Caspian Sea ; highest point, Mt. Demavend (18,600 ft.).

Elchingen (el'-khing-en). Vil. in Bavaria on Danube, 75 m. N.w. of Munich ; victory of French under Ney over Austrians (1805).

Elder. Flowering shrub, **1124.**

Elderberry wine, 1124.

El Dorado (el-do-rah'-dō). Mythical region abounding in gold and precious stoѹes, believed by Sp. explorers to be somewhere in Amer. ; Raleigh seeks in Guiana, 1552, 2744.

El´eanor (*c.* 1122–1204). Duchess of Aquitaine, queen of Louis VII of France, and later of Henry II of England ; 1609, 2027 ; mother of Richard I, 2776.

Eleanor of Castile (d. 1290). Consort of Edward I of Eng., with whom she journeyed on a Crusade, **1124.**

Eleanor Crosses, 1124.

Elections. Ballot, 351 ; basis of democracy, 2651 ; how to vote, 351, 3330 ; Parliament (Eng.), 1490, 2522 ; in Russia, 2850.

Electors, of the Holy Roman empire, 1449, 1637.

Elec´tra. In Gk. myth., daughter of Agamemnon and Clytemnestra ; saved life of her brother Orestes to be their father's avenger ; subject of opera by Richard Strauss.

Electrical conductors, 1128, 1391. *See* Conductivity.

Electric arc. *See* Arc, electric.

Electric battery. *See* Battery.

Electric bell, 2062.

Electric clocks, 1125, 1547, 3214.

" Electric eye," the photo-electric cell, 2575.

Electric fire, 1598 ; fire prevention, 1289.

Electric fishes. Eel, 1297, 3228.

Electric furnace, 1409 ; artificial gems, 1427 ; calcium carbide, 18 ; steels, *1755.*

Electric heating, 1128, 1132, 1598.

Electricity, 1127 ; in agriculture, 79 ; submarine cables, 640 ; conductors, 1128, 1391, 940, 2973, 3389 ; consumption, *1546* ; for dairy work, 955–6 ; direct and alternating current, 1130 ; electro-magnets, 1132, 2064 ; galvanometers, 1134 ; generated by dynamos, 1060, 1132 ; heat from, 1132, 1134 ; grid system of transmission, 1545, 2673 ; high frequency, 1623 ; hydro-electric installations, 1669 ; induction coil, 1720 ; insulators, 1128, 2160, 2626 ; internal combustion engine ignition, 1736 ; 2246 ; Leyden jar, 1929 ; lighting, 1134, 1887, 3301 ; lightning, 1131, 1945 ; meters, *2152, 2153* ; motors, 2239 ; origin of name, 138 ; photo-electric cells, 1139, 2574 ; piezo-electric effect, 1127, 2604 ; positive and negative, 771, 1128 ; power from, 2673 ; radiation, radioactivity, 2731 ; rectifiers, 2751 ; refrigeration, 1392 ; " static " and " current," 1127, 1130 ; and telegraphy, 2232, 3164 ; telephone, 3173 ; television, 3182 ; electrical theory of matter, 296, 1137, 2731 ; thermionic valve, 3198 ; thermocouples, 1132 ; tramcars, 3235 ; transformer, 3237 ; welding, 3362 ; wire for, 3389, *3390* ; wireless, 3391 ; X-rays, 3430.—*Pioneers in Electrical Research;* Boyle, 537 ; Cavendish, 736 ; Clerk-Maxwell, 839 ; Davy, 979 ; Edison, 1087 ; Faraday, 1260 ; Franklin, 1386 ; Galvani,

1416 ; Hertz, 1622 ; Kelvin, 1849 ; Marconi, 2098 ; Morse, 2232. *See also* Ampère, Coulomb, Du Fay, Henry, Oersted, Ohm, Röntgen, Thales, Thomson ; list of terms, 3785.

Electric lamp, in lighting, 1135.

Electric lift, *1937.*

Electric light, 1134, 1887 ; carbon filament lamps, 699, 1134 ; construction of lamp, 1135, 3301 ; discharge lamps, 1135 ; Edison's invention, 1087, 1134 ; fluorescent, *1134* ; in lighthouses, 1945 ; power station, 2673 ; tungsten-filament lamps, 1135, 3253.

Electric locomotive, *plate f. 1981,* 1987, 1988, 2738, 3273.

Electric meter, 2752, *2153.*

Electric motor, 2239, 1424 ; clocks, *1127* ; locomotive, 1987 ; *plate f. 1981* ; tramcars, 3235.

Electric power : how made, 2673 ; how transmitted, 1545 ; alternating current, 1130 ; applied to lighting, 1134 ; generated by dynamos, 1060 ; by water-power, 1669, 3259, 3349 ; by windmills, 3387.

Electric railways, 1987, 2738, 2740.

Electric ray, or torpedo fish, 2976, *3228.*

Electric shock, 1721, 1929.

Electric tramways, 3235.

Electrification, of flue gases, 2675 ; of glass rod, 1128, 2972 ; of rlys., 2738 ; of vulcanite, sealing wax, 1127.

Electrocardiograph, instr. for examining the heart, 1593.

Electro-chemistry, 1136, 1738, 2574.

Electrocution, or killing by electric shock. A form of capital punishment practised in parts of the U.S.A.

Electrode. Point at which elec. current enters or leaves a solution or elec. device, 1136, *1137* ; in arc welding, 3362 ; in Crookes tube, 3430 ; in thermionic valve, 3198.

Electro-dynamics or **electro-kinetics.** Science of electricity in motion, 1127.

Electrolysis. Electrical decomposition of a compound in solution, 1136, *1137* ; in chemistry, 771 ; in electro-plating, 1140 ; in gold production, 1481 ; ionization, 1739 ; magnesium produced, 2060 ; measures elec. current, 1137 ; in metallurgy, 135, 908, 1137, 1481 ; rectifiers, 2751.

Electrolyte. A solution conducting a current and decomposed by electrolysis, 1136 ; in battery, 375.

Electro-magnet, 1132, 2064 ; in dynamos, 1062, 1132 ; in elec. clocks, 1126 ; in electron microscope, 2165 ; field of, *1134* ; Lodge's researches, 1997 ; in telephone, 3175.

Electro-magnetic waves, 2728 ; in ether, 1226 ; of heat, 1595, 1722 ; light, 1942 ; wireless, 3392. *See* Radiation ; Spectrum.

Electromotive force or **potential,** 1128.

Electron, 1137 ; in atom, *295, 296, 297* ; in chemistry, *771* ; in Crookes and X-ray tubes, 3430 ; in cyclotron, 950 ; development of theory, 296, 1129, 1137, 2732, 3430 ; in ionization, 1738 ; quantum theory, 2711 ; in radar, 2726 ; in rectifier, 2751 ; in television, 3182 ; in thermionic valve, 3198 ; from uranium, 3297 ; in wireless, 3392.

Electron´ic Devices, 1138 ; in amplifiers, 3012 ; for automatic control, 321 ; cathode-ray tube, 1138 ; cyclotron, *950,* 951 ; high frequency heating, 1624, *1625* ; ignitron, 1138 ; microscope, *2164,* 2165 ; photoelectric cell, 2574 ; radar, 2726 ; rectifier, 2751 ; television, 3182 ; thermionic valve, 3198 ; thyratron, 1138, 1139 ; time switch, 3215 ; welding, 3363.

Electron microscope, 2165.

Electro-plating. Coating with metal by electrolysis, 1139.

Electroscope. Device for detecting elec. charges, *1133.*

Electrostatics. Elec. charges at rest, 1127.

Electro-thermal processes, 1132.

Electro-typing. Method of duplicating type or engravings by electro-plating, 1140 ; gramophone records, 1496.

Elegiac (el-e-jī´-ak), poetry, 2637.

Elegy, defined, 2637.

" Elegy in a Country Churchyard," by Thomas Gray, 1213, 1514.

Element. In chemistry, 766, 768, 769, 775–778 ; classification, 768 ; " transmutation " of radioactive elements, 2733 ; 96 have been discovered, or made. They are given below with their symbols ; *a*=artificial. *See* elements by name and **Rare Earths.**

Element	Symbol	Element	Symbol
Actinium	Ac	Molybdenum	Mo
Alabamine	Ab	Neodymium	Nd
Aluminium	Al	Neon	Ne
Americium (*a*)	Am	Neptunium (*a*)	Np
Antimony	Sb	Nickel	Ni
Argon	A	Niobium	Nb
Arsenic	As	Niton or Radon	Nt
Barium	Ba	Nitrogen	N
Beryllium	Be	Osmium	Os
Bismuth	Bi	Oxygen	O
Boron	B	Palladium	Pd
Bromine	Br	Phosphorus	P
Cadmium	Cd	Platinum	Pt
Caesium	Cs	Plutonium (*a*)	Pu
Calcium	Ca	Polonium	Po
Carbon	C	Potassium	K
Cerium	Ce	Praseodymium	Pr
Chlorine	Cl	Protoactinium	Pa
Chromium	Cr	Radium	Ra
Cobalt	Co	Rhenium	Re
Copper	Cu	Rhodium	Rh
Curium (*a*)	Cm	Rubidium	Rb
Dysprosium	Dy	Ruthenium	Ru
Erbium	Er	Samarium	Sa
Europium	Eu	Scandium	Sc
Fluorine	F	Selenium	Se
Gadolinium	Gd	Silicon	Si
Gallium	Ga	Silver	Ag
Germanium	Ge	Sodium	Na
Gold	Au	Strontium	Sr
Hafnium	Hf	Sulphur	S
Helium	He	Tantalum	Ta
Holmium	Ho	Tellurium	Te
Hydrogen	H	Terbium	Tb
Illinium	Il	Thallium	Tl
Indium	In	Thorium	Th
Iodine	I	Thulium	Tm
Iridium	Ir	Tin	Sn
Iron	Fe	Titanium	Ti
Krypton	Kr	Tungsten	W
Lanthanum	La	Uranium	U
Lead	Pb	Vanadium	V
Lithium	Li	Virginium	Vi
Lutecium	Lu	Xenon	Xe
Magnesium	Mg	Ytterbium	Yb
Manganese	Mn	Yttrium	Yt
Masurium	Ma	Zinc	Zn
Mercury	Hg	Zirconium	Zr

Elementary schools, 2884.

Elephant. Largest of land animals, **1140** ; African, 60, 1141 ; Indian, *1142, 1696* ; drives, 1142 ; hyrax a relation, *2074* ; ivory, 1143, 1788 ; mammoth and mastodon related, *735, 1140,* 2077 ; in Siam, *plate f. 2965* ; and modified teeth, 3163 ; used in anc. warfare, 1573, 2710 ; white, in Siam, 2963.

Elephan´ta Isle. Small isl. between Bombay and mainland of India ; interesting for Hindu religious sculpture ; named from colossal statue of elephant found there.

Elephant beetle, *401.*

Elephantiasis (el-e-fan-tī´-*a*-sis), or "elephant skin," disease in which parts of body swell enormously and skin becomes discoloured and hardened.

Elephantine (el-e-fan-tī´-nē), Eg. Small isl. in the Nile opposite Assuan (Syrene) ; anc. monuments and nilometer (water-gauge).

Elephant seal, 2913.

El Erg. An oasis of Sahara, 2859.

Eleusin´ian mysteries. Religious rites of anc. Greece, 989.

Eleusis (e-lū´-sis). Anc. city in Attica, Greece, on coast opposite isl. of Salamis ; in early times a powerful rival of Athens ; Eleusinian mysteries in honour of goddess Demeter (Ceres) 989.

Elevated railways, 2353.

Elevator. Store for grain, *679. See also* Lifts.

Elevators. Aeroplane control surfaces, 42.

Elgar, Sir Edward, Bart. (1857–1934). Perhaps the greatest of recent Eng. composers, **1143,** 2266.

Elgin (el'-gin). Co. tn. of Morayshire; pop. 9,000 ; 2228.

Elgin, James Bruce, 8th Earl of (1811–63). Eldest son of 7th earl ; appointed gov. of Jamaica at 30 ; Gov.-Gen. of Canada (1846–54), one of the most popular holders of this office ; Viceroy of India (first appointed directly by the Crown), 1860 to his death.

Elgin, Thomas Bruce, 7th Earl of (1766–1841). Eng. diplomat and art collector, envoy to Belgium, Prussia, and Turkey.

Elgin, Victor Alexander Bruce, 9th Earl of (1849–1917). Brit. statesman ; viceroy of India 1894–99.

Elgin Marbles. Remains of Parthenon sculptures in Brit. Museum, **1143,** *1144, 1537,* 22, 584, 2098.

Elginshire. *See* **Morayshire.**

El Greco. *See* **Greco, El.**

E'li. Hebrew priest and judge, under whose care Samuel was brought up (1 Samuel).

Elia (ē'-li-a). Pen-name of Charles Lamb (" Essays of Elia "), 1886.

Eli'jah. Hebrew prophet ; denounced Ahab, king of Israel, for idolatry ; destroyed the 450 prophets of Baal ; was carried to heaven in a chariot of fire (1 Kings xvii.; 2 Kings ii.); 2691.

Eliot, George (1819–80). Pen-name of Mary Ann Evans, Eng. novelist, **1145,** 1215 ; novels. 2402 ; and Savonarola, 2877.

Eliot, Sir John (1592–1632). Eng. statesman. Parl. leader with Pym and Hampden against Charles I's encroachments ; promulgated theory of a responsible ministry ; imprisoned for 2 years and died in Tower of London.

Eliot, Thomas Stearns (b. 1888), Anglo-American poet ; naturalized Brit. subject (1927) ; awarded O.M. in 1948, and Nobel prize for literature, 1948 ; made his name by the poem " The Waste Land " (1922), 1042, 1216 ; " Murder in the Cathedral," *389* ; " Family Reunion " ; " Four Quartets."

E'lis. Dist. of anc. Greece in w. Peloponnesus (with Achaea forms nome or dept. of modern Greece) ; *map, 1518.*

Elis. Important city of anc. Greece on r. Peneus ; here all candidates for Olympic games trained for a month.

Eli'sha. Hebrew prophet, on whom fell the " mantle of Elijah," his master and predecessor in struggle against Baal worship (1 Kings xix. ; 2 Kings xiii).

Elis'sa. Phoenician name of Dido. *See* **Dido.**

Elizabeth (1709–62). Empress of Russia; daughter of Peter the Great and Catherine I ; seized throne (1741) ; sided against Prussia in Seven Years' War ; only her timely death saved Frederick the Great in his last extremity, 2924.

Elizabeth (1837–98). Austrian empress, wife of Francis Joseph, assassinated at Geneva by an anarchist.

Elizabeth (1533–1603). Queen of Eng. ; **1146 ;** death, *1149* ; Drake, 1037 ; literary and dramatic development, 1146, 1211, *1212* ; Mary Queen of Scots, 1146, *1148,* 2116 ; Raleigh, 2743 ; religious policy, 1146, 1872 ; Spanish Armada defeated, 237, 1146, 2946, 2568 ; in the Tower, 3232.

Elizabeth, Queen Consort (b. 1900), wife of George VI, **1149,** *1150, 3283* ; Glamis castle, *155* ; marriage to Duke of York, 1443 ; celebrated silver wedding Ap. 26, 1948 ; stamp, *3075.*

Elizabeth (1596–1662). Queen of Frederick of Bohemia, and daughter of James I of England, ancestress through her daughter, the Electress Sophia, of Hanoverian (Windsor) kings of England.

Elizabeth. Queen of Carol I of Rumania. *See* **Carmen Sylva.**

Elizabeth (b. 1876). Queen of Albert I of Belgium, former princess of Bavaria, 102.

Elizabeth Alexandra Mary, H.R.H. Princess (b. 1926), elder daughter of Geo. VI, heiress presumptive, **1150,** *3283* ; portrait on stamps, 3075. Married Nov. 20, 1947, Lt. Philip Mountbatten (created H.R.H. Prince Philip, Duke of Edinburgh, Nov. 19), *1151* ; Prince Charles born Nov. 14, 1948.

Elizabeth, St. (1207–31). Hungarian princess, landgravine of Thuringia ; according to legend bread she carried for poor, seized by her husband, was turned to roses.

Elizabeth Marie Hélène (1764–94), commonly called " Madame Elizabeth," sister of Louis XVI of Fr., executed by revolutionary tribunal.

Elizabeth of York (1465–1503). Daughter of Edward IV and queen of Henry VII of Eng., 1612.

Elizabethan Age. In Eng. literature, 1146, 1210, *1212* ; Bacon, 333 ; romances, 2401 ; Shakespeare, 1211, *1212,* 2932.

Elizabeth Bennet. Sensible, charming heroine of Jane Austen's " Pride and Prejudice " ; Elizabeth is " Prejudice " and Darcy, whom she finally marries, is " Pride."

Elk. *See* **Moose.**

Ellenborough, Edward Law, 1st Baron (1750–1818). Eng. judge ; chief counsel for Warren Hastings ; became lord chief justice.

Ellenborough, Edward Law, Earl of (1790–1871). Eng. administrator ; gov.-gen. of India ; annexed Sind.

Ellerman, Sir John Reeves (1862–1933). British shipowner ; left fortune of nearly £37,000,000.

Ellesmere (elz'-mēr) **Island.** N.W. of Greenland, almost covered by ice caps, *2644* ; explored by Brit. expedition in 1934–35.

Ellice (el'-is) or **Lagoon Islands.** Group of small coral isls. in Gilbert and Ellice Islands colony, belonging to Gt. Brit., in Pacific, N. of Fiji Isls. ; 14 sq. m. ; pop. 4,613 ; 2471.

Elliot, Walter Elliot (b. 1888). Brit. politician ; Minister of Agriculture (1932) ; Sec. for Scotland (1936) ; Minister of Health (1938–40).

Elliotson, John (1791–1868). Eng. physician, one of the first to urge clinical lectures in teaching medicine ; physician to both Dickens and Thackeray; " Pendennis " dedicated to him.

Ellis, Henry Havelock (1859–1939). Eng. writer on scientific-humanist subjects (" Studies in the Psychology of Sex," " The Criminal," " Affirmations," " The Dance of Life." etc.). Pioneer in sex-education.

Ellis Island. Small isl. in New York Bay, used as U.S.A. immigrant station, 2351.

Ellora (el-lōr'-a), India. Tn. in Hyderabad ; famous temples, *1664.*

Ellsworth, Lincoln (b. 1880). Amer. explorer ; in Antarctic, 2647.

Elm. A shade tree, **1152** ; 3247 ; leaf, *1152.*

El'man, Mischa (b. 1891). Rus. violinist and composer (" Humoresque ").

Elmo's fire, Saint, 1946.

Elohim (ē'-lō-hīm). God of the Hebrews.

El Paso (el-pah'-sō), Texas, U.S.A. Rly. centre and main distributing point for s.w. U.S., and main gateway between U.S. and Mexico ; important smelting industry ; pop. 96,000.

El'sa. In Ger. legend, wife of Lohengrin, 2000.

Elsinore (el-si-nōr') (Danish Helsingör), Denmark, spt. on N.E. coast of isl. of Zealand ; pop. 15,000 ; shipbuilding, commerce ; scene of Shakespeare's " Hamlet " ; now Helsingör, 991.

El'ster or **White Elster.** R. of Cent. Ger. emptying into Saale 3 m. s. of Halle ; 115 m.

Elstree. Tn. of Herts ; pop. 3,460 ; a centre of British film industry.

Elswick. Suburb of Newcastle-upon-Tyne, Eng. ; shipbuilding and armament manufacture.

Elver. Young eel, 1092.

Ely. City on Isle of Ely (a marshy plain) ; pop. 8,500 ; 1152 ; cath., 727, 1152; defence by Hereward, 1618.

Ely, Isle of. Eng. administrative co., part of the geographical co. of Cambridge, 1152, 669.

Elyot, Sir Thomas (c.1490–1546). Eng. diplomat and scholar ; friend of Sir Thomas More ; remembered for his books " The Castle of Health," and " Book Named the Governor."

Elysium (e-liz'-i-um), or **Elysian Fields.** In Gk. myth., a place to which the souls of the good depart at death.

El'ytra. Beetle wing-covers, 398.

Elzevir (el'-ze-vĕr). Family of Dutch 17th cent. printers famous for beautiful types and choice grade of paper ; Louis (1540–1617) began printing in 1583, his five sons carried on the work.

Emancipa'tion Act, Catholic (Gt. Brit.), 2420, 2535 ; 3278.

Emancipation Act (Rus.), 2848.

FLORAL EMBLEMS OF THE NATIONS

Abyssinia—arum lily
Argentine—kapok-tree flower
Australia—mimosa (wattle)
Austria—edelweiss
Belgium—azalea
Bolivia—Bolivian magic-tree flower
Brazil—Tecoma araliacea
British Commonwealth—daisy
Bulgaria—rose
Canada—maple leaf
Chile—Chilean bellflower
China—plum blossom
Colombia—triana cattleya (orchid)
Cuba—fragrant garland flower
Czechoslovakia—linden tree
Denmark—red clover
Dominican Republic—mahogany flower
Ecuador—red cinchona flower
Egypt—lotus
England—red rose and white rose

Finland—lily of the valley
France—Marguerite, poppy and cornflower (since Republic)
—fleur-de-lys (iris) (Royalist France)
Germany—cornflower
Greece—laurel leaf
Guatemala—white orchid
Hungary—tulip
India—lotus
Iran or Persia—red rose of Shiraz
Ireland—shamrock
Italy—marguerite
Japan—chrysanthemum
Lithuania—common rue
Mexico—dahlia
Netherlands—marigold
New Zealand—fern leaf
Nicaragua—fragrant garland flower
Norway—heather

Panama—Holy Ghost or dove flower
Paraguay—jasmine of Paraguay
Peru—Peruvian magic-tree flower
Poland—daisy, poppy, pansy, mallow
Portugal—lavender
Rumania—white rose
Russia—sunflower
Salvador—coffee flower
Scotland—thistle
South Africa—protea
Spain—carnation
Sweden—lily of the valley and the twin-flower
Switzerland—rose of the alps (rhododendron)
Turkey—tulip
Uruguay—kapok-tree flower
U.S.A.—wild rose
Wales—leek
Yugoslavia—linden tree

Emancipation Proclamation. Abolishing slavery in U.S.A. (Sept. 22, 1862), 1952.

Emanuel I, the Happy (1469–1521). King of Portugal, in whose reign, called "Portugal's golden age," Vasco da Gama opened sea route to India, Cabral took possession of Brazil, and Albuquerque established Port. rule in the E. Indies.

Embalming. In anc. Egypt, 2255.

Embankment, The. London thoroughfare, incl. (on the north of the Thames) the Victoria Embankment from Westminster Bridge to Blackfriars Bridge, Grosvenor Rd., and the Chelsea Embankment ; on the south side, between Westminster Bridge and Vauxhall, is the Albert Embankment, 2012, *2616.*

Embargo. In international law, 473.

Em'bassy. The person or persons sent as ambassadors or those entrusted with public messages to another state ; also the official residence of an ambassador, 138.

Embez'zlement. The fraudulent appropriation of money or other personal property by one employed in official capacity.

Emblems, National. *See* list of floral emblems in p. *3787.*

Embroidery, 1152, *1153* ; Japanese, *1810* ; machine, 2829.

Em'bryo. Young of plant or animal in earliest stages of development from seed or egg ; of flowering plants, 2918 ; formed by cell division, 738, *739, 1154,* 1155 ; growth in bean, 381.

Embryol'ogy. Science dealing with development of plant or animal from original germ cell, **1154,** 433 ; founded by von Baer, 1155, 3447 ; theory of evolution, 1244.

Em'den. A fortified spt. in N.W. Germany ; pop. 28,000 ; at mouth of r. Ems. Heavily bombed by R.A.F. and U.S.A.A.F. 1941–44 ; taken by Russians, May 1945.

Em'erald. A precious stone, **1156,** 1427 ; Columbia, 3024 ; eyeglass, 3054 ; phosphorescent, 2574.

Emerald Isle. Name for Ireland, 1744.

Emerson, Ralph Waldo (1803–82). Amer. philosopher, essayist, and poet, **1156,** 3294.

Em'ery. A very hard mineral, a form of aluminium oxide, **1156.**

Emigra'tion. Departure from one country to settle in another ; Ireland, 1746 ; Scandinavia, 2880. *See also* Immigration.

Emigrés (ā-mē-grā). Refugees from France during Fr. Rev., 1394.

Emil'ia. Division of N. It., s. of the Po and N. of Tuscany, pop. **3,339,000** ; 8,537 sq. m. ; 1763.

Emily. In Chaucer's "Knight's Tale," 762.

Emin Pasha (1840–92). Turkish name of Eduard Schnitzer, Ger. explorer and administrator in Africa.

Emission theory of light. Same as Corpuscular theory.

Emitron television camera. Consists of a lens system focusing the picture to be televised on to a mosaic of photo-electric cells at the broad end of a cathode ray tube, 3182.

Emmanuel College, Cambridge. Founded in 1583 ; 668.

Em'met, Robert (1778–1803). Irish revolutionist, who, after travel abroad, arranged a rising in Dublin for July 1803. Betrayed, he fled but was captured when visiting his sweetheart Susan Curran, daughter of John Philpot Curran. Guilty of treason, Emmet was hanged Sept. 20, 1803.

Emmett, Daniel Decatur (1815–1904). Amer. actor and song writer, originator of " Negro minstrel " performances ; author of " Dixie."

Emotion, 1157.

Empedocles (em-ped'-o-klēz) (*c.* 495–435 B.C.). Great Gr. philosopher, poet, statesman ; and matter, 2593 ; superhuman legendary character.

Emperor penguin, 2544.

Empire, British. *See* British Commonwealth.

Empire, Eastern. *See* Byzantine Empire.

Empire, Holy Roman. *See* Holy Roman Empire.

Empire Day. A day, in some places a holiday, May 24 (the birthday of Queen Victoria), which is observed throughout the Brit. Commonwealth, particularly in schools ; officially recognized in 1904.

Empire flying boat. Built by Short Bros. for Imperial Airways, 330.

Empire Society. *See* Royal Empire Society.

Empire State Building, New York ; 1,250 feet ; 104 storeys ; July 28, 1945, a U.S. bomber crashed into the 79th storey, when 13 people were killed and 26 injured ; *222,* 2351.

Empir'icists, in philosophy, 2572.

Ems or Bad Ems. Ger. health resort on r. Lahn 10 m. E. of Coblenz ; pop. 7,000 ; " Ems dispatch " sent from here, 1385.

Ems. R. in Westphalia and Hanover, Germany ; flows N.W. 200 m. to North Sea ; irrigates surrounding country by a series of canals ; 1445.

" Ems dispatch " (or telegram), 1385.

E'mu. Large Australian running bird, 1157, *313* ; egg, *1094.*

Emul'sion. A liquid mixture in which a fatty substance is suspended in minute globules ; of photographic plates and films, 877, 2579.

Enamel and enamelling. Coating metal, glass, or pottery with a glassy composition, **1157,** 2666 ; Celtic, *1158* ; cloisonné, 2271 ; Japanese, *1159,* 1810 ; paints, 2478.

Encaus'tic tiles, made in moulds, in which the pattern to be shown on the tile is made by small metal partitions.

Enc'ke's comet, 880.

Ency'clical Letters. Ecclesiastical letters sent on some important occasions by the Pope to his bishops. An Encyclical differs from a Bull in not dealing with any special case ; it indicates general principles to guide the bishops.

Encyclopedia. An alphabetically arranged book of reference, **1160.**

Encyclopedists. Writers of great Fr. Encyclopedia, including Diderot, d'Alembert and other distinguished thinkers of 18th cent. ; influence, 1160.

Enderby Land, Antarctica, 2647.

Endive (en'-div). An annual plant of the family *Compositæ ;* probably native of East Indies, but cultivated in Europe since 16th cent. ; curled or narrow-leaved varieties most used for salads.

En'docarp. Stone of a fruit, 1403.

Endocrine gland, 1470.

En'dolymph. Fluid in labyrinth of the ear, 1065.

En'dosperm. Nutritive material surrounding embryo in many seeds, 2918.

Endurance. Sir Ernest Shackleton's Polar ship, 2931.

Endymion (en-dim'-i-on). In Gk. myth., beautiful youth sleeping for ever in a cave on Mt. Latmos, beloved and nightly visited by Selene, moon goddess ; subject of poem by Keats, 1849.

Energy, 1160 ; atomic, 1161, 2733 ; chemical and radioactive compared, 2733 ; conservation of, 1160, 2592 ; derived ultimately from sun, 1161 ; electrical, 1128 ; kinetic, 1513 ; applied to machines, 1397 ; radiation, 3119 ; plants store "food energy," 2621, 2374 ; radio-active, 2733 ; released by explosives, 1250 ; steam-engine transforms, 1596, 3084.

Enfield. Tn. of Middlesex, 10 m. N. of London ; Edward VI and Queen Elizabeth lived here ; Government small-arms factory.

Engadine (en'-ga-dēn). Valley of r. Inn in E. Switzerland ; 60 m. long ; noted for picturesque scenery and health resorts, *133, 3140.*

En'gels, Friedrich (1820–95). Ger. Socialist, co-author with Marx of the " Communist Manifesto," 2113, 2996.

Enghien (an'-gyan), **Louis de Bourbon, Duc d'** (1772–1804). Fr. émigré prince, last of the Condés, seized on neutral land as conspirator and executed by Napoleon's order though proved innocent. " It was worse than a crime," said Fouché, " it was a blunder."

Engine. A machine that converts energy into mechanical power ; aeroplane, 41, 44, 1737 ; Diesel (oil), 1015, *1734,* 1737 ; gas, *1421* ; high pressure, *488* ; internal combustion engine, 1735 ; motor-car, 2243, *2244* ; railway (locomotive), *plate f. 1981* ; steam, 3085 ; turbine, 3249 ; water types, 3258 ; windmills, 3386.

Engineering. Aeronautical, 41 ; basic principles of all machines, 2127 ; bridge building, 564 ; building construction, 212, 604 ; canal construction, 686, 3110 ; compressed-air devices, 2632 ; dams, 958 ; docks, 1022 ; dredgers, 1046 ; electrical (*see* Electricity) ; harbours, 1576 ; hydro-elec. installns., 1669 ; mechanics, 2127 ; mines and mining, 2181 ; railways, 2734 ; road building, 2783 ; Rom. achievements, 214, 2799 ; shipbuilding, 2945 ; tunnels, 3255 ; water supply of cities, 214, 3347.

Engineering bricks, 562.

Engineers, Royal, in modern army, 246.

England. The southern part (not including Wales) of the isl. of Gt. Brit. ; area, 50,337 sq. m. ; pop. 37,916,000, 1161 ; *map f. 1164* ; Christmas customs, 819 ; co-operative societies, 903 ; crown jewels, *frontis.* Vol. 3, 935 ; flag, 1312 ; geological hist., *582,* 2391 ; John Bull the personification, *2366* ; first united under Egbert, 574 ; national anthem, 2282 ; origin of name, 1194 ; preservation of the countryside, 2283 ; religion, 302 (*see* Church of England) ; univs., 3296 ; foreign trade, 941 ; Kings and queens, 3790.

Counties : Bedfordshire, 390 ; Berkshire, 415 ; Buckinghamshire, 599 ; Cambridgeshire, 669 ; Cheshire, 779 ; Cornwall, 911 ; Cumberland, 943 ; Derbyshire, 995 ; Devonshire, 999 ; Dorsetshire, 1030 ; Durham, 1059 ; Essex, 1224 ; Gloucestershire, 1476 ; Hampshire, 1571 ; Herefordshire, 1617 ; Hertfordshire, 1621 ; Huntingdonshire, 1658 ; Kent, 1851 ; Lancashire, 1890 ; Leicestershire, 1919 ; Lincolnshire, 1952 ; London, 2016 ; Middlesex, 2168 ; Monmouthshire, 2215 ; Norfolk, 2375 ; Northamptonshire, 2385 ; Northumberland, 2391 ; Nottinghamshire, 2398 ; Oxfordshire, 2465 ; Rutland, 2858 ; Shropshire, 2963 ; Somerset, 3000 ; Staffordshire, 3072 ; Suffolk, 3111 ; Surrey, 3122 ; Sussex, 3123 ; Warwickshire, 3341 ; Westmorland, 3371 ; Wiltshire, 3383 ; Worcestershire, 3407 ; Yorkshire, 3435.

Geography and industries (*see also* under names of tns.) : *582,* 1161, *1166, 1167, 1169–71, 1174–76* ; chief tns. and mfrs., 1165 ; agriculture, 78, *81–84,* 730, 955 ; cap. London, 2009 ; climate, 1161, 1554 ; coal, *855, 856,* 1162, 1165, 1918, 2084, *2182,* 2336 ; fisheries, *plates 1172, 1176,* 1299, 1300, *1304–08* ; forests, 1165, 1351 ; grid transmission lines, *map, 1546* ; iron and steel, 458, 1165, 2941 ; oil, *2429* ; population, 1162, 2656 ; pottery and porcelain, 2670, 1165 ; ports and harbours, 572, *1023, 1024,* 1165, 1576, 2009 ; railways, 2734, *2735,* 2736, 2738 ; rivers and canals, 686, 1918, 2084 ; shipping, 2947 ; silk industry, *2971* ; textile mfrs., *919,* 920, 1165, 1918, 2084, 3191 ; tin, 3215 ; weaving, 3360. *Government :* general article, 1488 (*see also* chief govt. departments) ; banks, 356 ; Cabinet, 640 ; Civil Service, 835 ; common law, 1902 ; courts, 921, 1842, 1902 ; factory laws, 802 ; fire brigades, 1285 ; local government, 1491 ; Magna Carta, 2059 ; Parliament, 2521 ; police, 2647 ; postal system, 2661, *2663* ; telecommunications, 3164–77 ; trade unions, 3233. *See* English History ; Prime Ministers.

TWO THOUSAND YEARS OF ENGLISH HISTORY

55–54 B.C. Julius Caesar invades Britain.

A.D.
43–410. Romans rule Britain. Insurrection of Queen Boadicea put down (A.D. 62).
449–700. Anglo-Saxons conquer the land (" Angle-land," or England).
597. St. Augustine reintroduces Christianity.
829. England united under one king (Egbert of **Wessex**).
878. Alfred checks the raids of the Danes.
1016–1042. Danes rule England (Canute).
1066. Duke William of Normandy conquers England ; feudalism introduced.
1154–1189. Henry II (Plantagenet) rules over England, and holds Normandy, Anjou, Aquitaine, etc., in
France. Conquest of **Ireland** begun.
1199–1216. John loses Normandy and Anjou ; forced to grant **Magna Carta** (1215).
1282. Edward I conquers **Wales** ; calls Model Parliament (1295).
1314. Edward II defeated by Scots at Bannockburn ; attempt to conquer **Scotland** fails.
1338–1453. Hundred Years' War with France. Victories at Crécy (1346), Poitiers (1356), Agincourt
(1415) ; Henry V king of France as well as England, 1420 ; **Joan of Arc** turns the tide
against the English (1429–31).
1381. Revolt of peasants under Wat Tyler.
1399. Richard II overthrown by Henry IV (House of **Lancaster**).
1450. Jack Cade's Rebellion.
1455–1485. Wars of the Roses (red rose of Lancaster against the white rose of York).
1485. Henry VII (Lancaster) defeats Richard III (York) at Bosworth and ends the war. Strong
monarchy established under the Tudor dynasty.
1534. Henry VIII breaks the ties which linked the English Church to Rome.
1553–1558. Mary restores the Roman Catholic Church.
1558–1603. **Elizabeth re-establishes the Church of England ;** great development in industry, sea-power and
literature (Shakespeare).
1588. **Spanish Armada defeated.**
1603. **Scotland united with England** in personal union under **James I** (Stuart).
1642–1649. **Civil War between Parliament and King Charles I,** over religion and rights of Parliament ;
Charles beheaded, 1649 ; England becomes a Commonwealth (republic).
1653–1658. **Oliver Cromwell** rules England, Scotland and Ireland as " Lord Protector."
1660. **Stuart line restored in Charles II.**
1688–1689. **" Glorious Revolution "** drives James II from the throne and establishes the Protestant
succession with William III and Mary II as joint sovereigns.
1701–1713. **The War of the Spanish Succession.** Preserves the Protestant succession for England, curbs
the power of France, and paves the way for the increase of England's colonial empire (Marlborough's victory at Blenheim, 1704). Peace of Utrecht, 1713.
1707. **Union of England and Scotland** into the kingdom of **Great Britain.**
1714. **Hanoverian line** succeeds to the throne in George I. Supremacy of Parliament firmly established;
gradual growth of **Cabinet government.**
1745. Rebellion of Stuart adherents (" Jacobites ") in Scotland and England put down.
1756–1763. Seven Years' War. Canada conquered ; British supremacy in **India.**
1760. Accession of **George III** ; attempt to rule arbitrarily by means of party known as " the King's
Friends."
1764. **Industrial Revolution** begins with Hargreaves' invention of the spinning-jenny.
1775–1783. **Thirteen American Colonies revolt** and establish their independence with the aid of France.
1788. Colonization of **Australia** begun.
1793–1815. Wars with Revolutionary France and Napoleon (Trafalgar, 1805 ; Waterloo, 1815).
1801. Irish Parliament abolished and Irish members added to Parliament of Great Britain.
1806. Cape Colony conquered from the Dutch ; beginning of **British South Africa.**
1832. **Great Parliamentary Reform Act** gives control to the middle class. A large number of social
and political reforms follow (**slavery abolished,** 1833 ; numerous factory laws, etc.).
1846. " Corn laws " repealed and **Free Trade** established.
1853–1856. Crimean War with Russia in defence of Turkey.
1867. **Second Parliamentary Reform Act** extends the vote to working men.
1870. Beginning of **Irish Home Rule** agitation. Education made compulsory.
1882. British occupation of **Egypt** begun.
1899–1902. **Boer War** in South Africa. (Formation of Union of South Africa, 1909.)
1911. Power of **House of Lords** limited.
1914–1918. **First World War.** United Kingdom mobilized 6,211,427 men ; 743,702 killed ; 1,693,262 wounded.
1922. Irish Free State established ; independence of Egypt recognized.
1924. **First Labour Government ;** remains in power ten months.
1929. **Labour Party** returned to power.
1931. **National Government** formed under J. R. MacDonald. Gold standard abandoned.
1935. National Government returns under Stanley Baldwin. George V's Silver Jubilee.
1936. King George dies, succeeded by Edward VIII, abdicates in December in favour of George VI.
1939–1945. **Second World War.** Brit. Commonwealth and Empire Forces 452,504 killed and missing ;
475,057 wounded. Civilian casualties (U.K.) 60,595 killed, 86,182 injured.
1940. Coalition Government under Winston Churchill.
1945. Labour Government under C. R. Attlee.
1947. India, Pakistan and Ceylon granted dominion status ; Burma an independent republic.
1949. India a republic ; Republic of Ireland proclaimed.

KINGS AND QUEENS OF ENGLAND

SAXON LINE

802–839	Egbert.	924–940	Athelstan.
839–858	Ethelwulf.	940–946	Edmund I.
858–860	Ethelbald.	946–955	Edred.
860–866	Ethelbert.	955–959	Edwy.
866–871	Ethelred.	959–975	Edgar.
871–901	Alfred the Great.	975–979	Edward the Martyr.
901–924	Edward the Elder.	979–1016	Ethelred "the Unready."

DANISH LINE

1016–1035	Canute.	1035–1040	Harold I.
		1040–1042	Hardicanute.

SAXON LINE

1042–1066	Edward the Confessor.	1066	Harold II.

NORMAN LINE

1066–1087	William the Conqueror.	1100–1135	Henry I.
1087–1100	William II.	1135–1154	Stephen.

PLANTAGENET LINE

1154–1189	Henry II.	1272–1307	Edward I.
1189–1199	Richard I.	1307–1327	Edward II.
1199–1216	John.	1327–1377	Edward III.
1216–1272	Henry III.	1377–1399	Richard II.

HOUSE OF LANCASTER

1399–1413	Henry IV.	1413–1422	Henry V.
		1422–1461	Henry VI.

HOUSE OF YORK

1461–1483	Edward IV.	1483	Edward V.
		1483–1485	Richard III.

HOUSE OF TUDOR

1485–1509	Henry VII.	1547–1553	Edward VI.
1509–1547	Henry VIII.	1553–1558	Mary.
		1558–1603	Elizabeth.

HOUSE OF STUART

1603–1625	James I.	1625–1649	Charles I.
		1649–1660	Commonwealth.
1660–1685	Charles II.	1689–1702	William III.
1685–1688	James II.	1702–1714	Anne.

HOUSE OF HANOVER OR BRUNSWICK

1714–1727	George I.	1820–1830	George IV.
1727–1760	George II.	1830–1837	William IV.
1760–1820	George III.	1837–1901	Victoria.
		1901–1910	Edward VII.

HOUSE OF WINDSOR

1910–1936	George V.	
1936	Edward VIII.	
1936–	George VI.	

England, Church of. *See* **Church of England.**

"England expects that every man will do his duty," Nelson's signal, 2313.

English Art, 1177, *1185–1192*; architecture, 218, 219, 220, 221 (*see also* **Castle ; Cathedral**); engraving, 1219 ; Impressionists, 1689 ; painting, 2476 ; Pre-Raphaelites, 2681 ; sculpture, 2906, *2907–10* ; Surrealism, 3122 ; water-colours, 3352. (*See also* under names of chief artists.)

"English Bards and Scotch Reviewers." Satire by Byron, 635.

English Channel. Separates Eng. from Fr. ; breadth, 21 to 145 m. ; length, 350 m. ; *map, plate f. 584* ; Dover and Calais, 1030 ; importance, 1514 ; Blériot's crossing, 45, 470 ; balloon, *349* ; cables, *641* ; swimming, 3137.

"English Constitution," by Walter Bagehot (1867). A study in British politics, 338.

English History. General sketch, **1193,** *1201–1208* ; in outline, 3789 ; (*see also* History).

To Norman Conquest (1066), *1193* ; prehistoric life and remains, 208, *323, 572, 573,* 3094, 3096 ; Celtic people and religion, 572, 740 ; Phoenicians visit, 1193, *1201* ; Rom. conquest, 573, *574,* 1193 ; Teutonic conquest, 574, 1194 ; Arthurian legends, 255, 2830 ; Christianity introduced, 817, 1194, 1542 ; Danish invasions, 110, 694, 1089, *1195, 1202, 1203* ; Alfred's reforms, 110 ; end of Anglo-Saxon period, 1089.

Under Norman Kings (1066–1154): Norman conquest, 1194, *1204,* 1579, 1581, 3379 ; feudalism established, 717, 1268, 1864 ; serfdom, 2981 ; beginning of jury system, 1843 ; misgovernment of William II, 3380 ; Henry I, 1609 ; Stephen and Matilda struggle for crown, 3087.

Struggle for constitutional liberty (1154–1377), 1194 ; reforms of Henry II, 1609 ; Richard I and the Crusades, 936, 2776 ; Magna Carta, *1196,* 1205, 1834, 2059 ; Barons' Wars, 1611, 2221 ; rise of Parliament, 1089, 2221, 2521 ; Wales conquered, 1089, 3334 ; wars in Scotland, 1089, 2892.

Hundred Years' War and Wars of the Roses (1338–1485), 76, 926, 1611, 1652, 1831, 2567 ; Black Death, 85 ; Wat Tyler's rebellion, *1197,* 3269 ; serfdom ended, 2281 ; increase of Parliament's power, 1611 ; Wycliffe and the Lollards, 3427 ; Wars of the Roses, 1091, 2828.

Renaissance and Reformation (1485–1603): the new Tudor mon-archy, 1612 ; Cabot's voyages to the New World, 647 ; Renaissance, 1210, 2764 ; Flodden Field, 1315 ; Henry VIII and the Reformation, 1612, 2759 ; Wolsey, 3401 ; More, 2228 ; Mary and the Catholic reaction, 2114 ; Elizabethan Age, 1146 ; war with Spain (1588), 236, 1036, 1146 ; Mary Queen of Scots, 1146, *1148,* 2115 ; growth of sea-power, 1036, 1146, 1195 ; exploration and colonizing ventures, 1036, 1195, 2337, 2743.

From the Puritan Revolution to the Act of Union (1707): James I, *1198* ; Scot. and Eng. united, 2892, 2893 ; struggle between Parliament and the Stuarts, 755, 1196, 1794 ; Gunpowder Plot, 1264 ; Puritans, 2707 ; settlements in Amer., 2121, 2545 ; Civil War, 755, 1196, 1745, 2176 ; Charles I, *1199* ; beheaded, 756, *1206* ; Cromwell and the Commonwealth, 756, 933, 1198, 2177 ; Hampden, 1571 ; war with Dutch Netherlands, 465, 2323 ; Restoration, 756, 1198, *1199, 1207* ; coffee, tea, and chocolate introduced, 861 ; James II and the "Glorious Revolution" of 1688, *1200, 1207, 1208,* 1794 ; Bill of Rights, 429 ; wars with Louis XIV, 2029, 2105 ; Anne, *1200* ; union with Scot., 1200, *1208.* For history from 1707 to the present day *see* **United Kingdom, history of.** *See also* **Britain ; British Commonwealth** ; **England** ; **Great Britain ; Middle Ages ; Scotland, etc.**

English horn. A musical instrument, 3404, 2267, 2445.

English Language, 1209, 2750 ; alphabet, 125 ; Basic English, 1210 ; Bible translations, influence, 423, 1210, 3428 ; Chaucer's influence, 762, 1210 ; dictionaries, 1015, 3058, 1835 ; grammar, 1493 ; Greek words 1209, 1539 ; Latin words, 1209, 1894 ; origin of names, 2272 ; in Pakistan, 2479 ; rhetoric, 2769 ; spelling, 3057. *See also* **Grammar.**

English Literature, 1210 ; beginnings, 415, 650, 1210 ; Chaucer, 761, 1210 ; development of drama, 1040, 1211 ; Dryden and the 18th cent., 1050, 1212 ; essay, 1213, 1214, 1224 ; novel, 1213, 1214, 2401 ; Puritan influence, 1211, 2176 ; romance, 2401, 2798 ; Romanticism, 1213, 1214, 3408 ; Shakespeare and the Age of Elizabeth, 1146, 1211 ; Victorian Age, 1214, 2402 ; outstanding figures of the 20th cent., 1215, 1216. *See* chief authors ; list pp. 3791–3 ; **Literature. Children's.**

English setter, sporting dog ; "setts" by crouching ; *plate f. 1024.*

English sheep-dog, large, long-haired sheep-dog, *plate f. 1024.*

English type (printing), 3270.

Engraving, 1217 ; dry-point, 1218 ; Dürer's influence, 1058 ; etching, 1218 ; of gems, 1427 ; Japanese, *1810* ; line, 1218 ; lithography, 1218, 1967 ; wood, 1217, 1219, 1812, 2684. *See also* **Process Engraving.**

"Eniac," electronic calculating machine, *659.*

Enniskil'len or **Inniskilling.** Co. tn. of Fermanagh, Northern Ire. ; defeat of James II's forces at battle of Cromin 1689 ; famous cavalry regiment "Inniskilling Dragoons" formed by defenders ; 1266.

Ennius (en'-i-us), **Quintus** (239-169 B.C.). Latin epic poet, called "father of Rom. poetry," 1895.

Enoch (ē'-nok). Hebrew patriarch who "walked with God" and after 365 years "was not, for God took him" (Gen. v, 18-24).

"Enoch Arden." *See* **Arden.**

En'sa (Entertainments National Service Association). Organization formed in 1939 by Basil Dean which between 1939 and 1946 provided entertainment for Brit. and Allied forces, and civilian war workers, in the U.K. and all theatres of war.

Enschede (en-skä-de), Netherlands. Mfg. tn. near E. border ; pop. 90,289 ; cotton-spinning, weaving, etc.

En'sign. National flag flown on the ensign staff ; there are three Brit. ensigns, red, white and blue, each with the Union Jack in the upper corner next to the staff ; the red is for the merchant service ; white for the Navy and the Royal Yacht Squadron ; the blue for the Royal Naval Reserve.

En'silage, method of preserving green fodder for winter, 1510.

Entab'lature, in architecture, *215,* 213.

Entail. Law restricting inheritance to a particular heir or class of heirs.

Enteb'be. Cap. of Uganda Protectorate, Africa, on N.W. shore of Lake Victoria, 1072, 3321.

Entente Cordiale (ahn-tahnt' kor-dyahl'), between Britain and France, 1092, 1240.

Entolodonts, a class of prehistoric animals, *2679.*

Entomol'ogy. The science of insects, **1219,** 1726 ; services to agric., 80 ; work of Fabre, 659. For complete references *see* **Insects.**

Entrepreneur (ahn-tr-pre-nêr'), in economics, 1081.

Enver Pasha (1879–1922). Turkish politician and soldier, one of the leaders of the Young Turks ; helped to depose Abdul Hamid, and was largely responsible for bringing Turkey into the 1st World War ; died in action at Bokhara.

Envir'onment, and heredity, 840, 1617 ; climatic environment affects plants, 840 ; forms subject-matter of ecology, 531, 1079 ; effect upon evolution, 308, 1428 ; influences structure and life-processes of animals, 125 ; of plants, 648, 840, 3355 ; plant " societies " corresponding to environments, 1080, *plate f. 1080,* 3355. *See* **Adaptation ; Ecology ; Evolution.**

Enzymes (en'-zĭmz). Organic substances impt. in growth, digestion, and other life processes, **1220 ;** in alcohol formation, 103 ; in digestion, 1016, 1263, 1470, 3082 ; in fermentation, 1266 ; in jam, 1341 ; pepsin, 2547 ; and sleep, 2983.

Eocene (ē'-ō-sēn) **period,** in geology, *plate f. 1432,* 1432.

Eohippus (ē-ō-hip'-us). Ancestor of the horse, *1245,* 1645.

Eolithic Age, earliest age of mankind, 2080, 3094 ; flint implements, *1314.*

Eos (ē'-os). Gk. name for Aurora, 304.

Epaminondas (ē-pam-i-non'-das) (c. 418–362 B.C.). Theban general and statesman, 1524 ; *3197,* 3198.

Eph'edrine. Alkaloid extracted from sub-tropical herbs of genus *Ephedra* ; of general use in treatment of allergic diseases.

Ephemeroptera (e-fem-er-op'ter-a) An order of winged insects, comprising the may-flies, 1733, 2122.

Ephesus (ef'-e-sus). Anc. Gk. city, greatest of 12 on coast of Asia Minor ; Temple of Artemis (Diana), one of Seven Wonders of World, 252, 2923 ; *plate f. 2924.* Also seat of 2 notable Church councils in 5th cent. ; St. Paul laboured there 3 years (Epistle to the Ephesians).

Ephialtes (ef-i-al'-tēz). A Malian, traitor at battle of Thermopylae, 3201.

Ephors (ef'-orz). Spartan officials, 3053.

Ephraim (ē'-fra-im). Hebrew patriarch, younger son of Joseph ; ancestor of tribe of Ephraim (Joshua xvi.).

Ephraim, Mt. In Palestine, 25 m. N. of Jerusalem ; one of the many low peaks in the ridge extending s. from Lebanon Mts.

Epic poetry. Defined, 2637 ; Eng., 415, 1210, 2178 ; Fr., 1379, 2797 ; Ger., 1456, 2363 ; Gk., 1539, 1637 ; It., 969, 1786, 3157 ; Latin, 1895, 3325 ; Sanskrit, 1713 ; Span. (" Cid "), 3050.

Epic poetry, Muse of, 2259.

Epictetus (ep-ik-tē'-tus). Gk. Stoic philosopher of first cent. A.D., **1220.**

Epicure'ans, 1220, 2571.

Epicurus (ep-i-kūr'-us) (341–270 B.C.). Gk. philosopher, **1220.**

Epidaurus. Greek theatre at, *1540.*

Epidem'ic. A disease widespread for a time in certain region ; opposed to endemic disease, one continually prevalent in a region.

Epider'mis, of human skin, 2979, *2980 ;* of animals, 1913.

Epiglot'tis. Lid at base of tongue that covers the larynx during act of swallowing ; how it works, *2599.*

Epimetheus (ep-i-mē'-thūs). In Gk. myth., brother of Prometheus and husband of Pandora, 2494.

Epinephrin. Same as **Adrenalin.**

Epiphany (e-pĭf'-a-ni). A festival of the Christian Church kept on January 6 in commemoration of the showing (Gk. *epiphaneia*) of Christ to the Magi, 819.

Epiphytes (ep'-i-fīts). Plants which grow upon other plants but are not fed by them ; orchids, 2447.

Epirus (e-pīr'-us). Anc. dist. of N. Greece along Ionian Sea ; under Pyrrhus, 2709 ; *map, 1518.*

Epping Forest, Essex. 10 sq. m. of wild woodland once part of a huge oak-hornbeam forest ; fallow deer and many other creatures run wild ; bought by City of London in 1882 ; 1225.

Ep'silon, ε, E. Fifth letter (short e) of the Gk. alphabet.

Ep'som, Surrey. Borough 15 m. s.w. of London ; pop. est. 65,000 ; mineral springs from which Epsom salts were first obtained ; famous racecourse where Derby and other races are held ; 3123. *See* **Derby.**

FAMOUS NAMES IN ENGLISH LITERATURE

(Note : for dramatic works, *see* list under Drama).

Joseph Addison (1672–1719), poet and essayist—Sir Roger de Coverley Papers in " The Spectator."

W. Harrison Ainsworth (1805–82), historical novelist—" Old St. Paul's " and " The Tower of London."

Richard Aldington (1892–), poet and novelist—" Images Old and New " ; " Death of a Hero."

Alfred the Great (848–901), translator—Boethius' " The Consolation of Philosophy."

Matthew Arnold (1822–88), poet and essayist—" The Scholar-Gypsy " ; " Thyrsis " ; " Essays in Criticism."

Roger Ascham (1515?–68), scholar—" Toxophilus " ; " The Scholemaster."

Jane Austen (1775–1817), novelist—" Pride and Prejudice " ; " Mansfield Park " ; " Sense and Sensibility."

Alfred Austin (1835–1913), poet—" English Lyrics."

Francis Bacon (1561–1626), philosopher and essayist—" New Atlantis " ; " The Advancement of Learning " ; " Essays."

Roger Bacon (1214?–94?), philosopher—" Opus Majus."

John Barbour (1316?–95), poet—" The Brus."

William Barnes (1801–86), dialect poet—" Linden Lea."

Herbert Ernest Bates (1905–), novelist—" The Poacher," " Fair Stood the Wind for France."

Sir James M. Barrie (1860–1937), novelist—" The Little Minister " ; " Sentimental Tommy " ; " A Window in Thrums."

Bede (673?–735), historian—" Ecclesiastical History of the English Nation."

Sir Max Beerbohm (1872–), essayist and novelist—" The Happy Hypocrite " ; " Zuleika Dobson " ; " A Christmas Garland."

Hilaire Belloc (1870–), essayist, historian, biographer—" On Nothing " ; " Richelieu " ; " The Path to Rome."

Arnold Bennett (1867–1931), novelist—" The Old Wives' Tale " ; " Clayhanger " ; " Riceyman Steps."

E. F. Benson (1867–1940), novelist—" Dodo " ; " The Challoners " ; " The Osbornes " ; " David Blaize."

E. C. Bentley (1875–), novelist—" Trent's Last Case."

J. D. Beresford (1873–1947), novelist—" The Mountains of the Moon " ; " These Lynnekers " ; " Love's Pilgrim."

Laurence Binyon (1869–1943), poet and art historian—" The Four Years" ; " Poems of Nizami" ; " Flight of the Dragon."

R. D. Blackmore (1825–1900), novelist—" Lorna Doone."

William Blake (1757–1827), poet—" Songs of Innocence."

Edmund Blunden (1896–), poet—" Collected Poems " ; " Undertones of War."

George Borrow (1803–81), prose writer—" Bible in Spain " ; " Lavengro " ; " Romany Rye."

James Boswell (1740–95), biographer—" Life of Samuel Johnson."

Robert Bridges (1844–1930), poet—" The Growth of Love " ; " The Testament of Beauty."

Charlotte Brontë (1816–55), novelist—" Jane Eyre."

Emily Brontë (1818–48), novelist—" Wuthering Heights."

Rupert Brooke (1887–1915), poet—" Poems."

Sir Thomas Browne (1605–82), prose writer—" Religio Medici " ; " Hydriotaphia."

Elizabeth Barrett Browning (1806–61), poet—" Sonnets from the Portuguese " ; " Aurora Leigh."

Robert Browning (1812–89), poet—" The Ring and the Book " ; " Pippa Passes " ; " Rabbi Ben Ezra."

John Buchan (1875–1940), historian and novelist—" Montrose " ; " The 39 Steps " ; " Greenmantle."

John Bunyan (1628–88), prose writer—" Pilgrim's Progress."

Edmund Burke (1729–97), political philosopher—" Reflections on the Revolution in France " ; " On Conciliation with the Colonies " ; " Letters on a Regicide Peace."

Fanny Burney (Mme. d'Arblay) (1752–1840), novelist and diarist—" Evelina " ; " Diary and Letters of Madame d'Arblay."

Robert Burns (1759–96), poet—" The Cottar's Saturday Night " ; " Tam o' Shanter."

Sir Richard Burton (1821–90), prose writer and translator—" Pilgrimage to El Medina and Mecca " ; " The Arabian Nights " (trans.).

Robert Burton (1577–1640), prose writer—" The Anatomy of Melancholy."

Samuel Butler (1612–80), satirist and poet—" Hudibras."

Samuel Butler (1835–1902), satirical novelist and critic—" The Way of All Flesh " ; " Erewhon " ; " Notebooks."

Lord Byron (1788–1824), poet—" Childe Harold's Pilgrimage " ; " Don Juan " ; " Manfred."

Caedmon (died 680), poet—" Paraphrases " (of the Bible).

Sir T. H. Hall Caine (1853–1931), novelist—" The Deemster " ; " The Manxman " ; " The Prodigal Son."

Thomas Campbell (1777–1844), poet—" Hohenlinden " ; " Ye Mariners of England."

Thomas Carlyle (1795–1881), historian and essayist—" Sartor Resartus " ; " French Revolution."

Lewis Carroll (Charles L. Dodgson) (1832–98), children's writer—" Alice's Adventures in Wonderland " ; " Through the Looking-Glass."

George Chapman (1559?–1634), poet and translator—Homer's Iliad and Odyssey (trans.).

Thomas Chatterton (1752–70), poet—" Rowley Poems."

Geoffrey Chaucer (1340?–1400), poet—" Canterbury Tales."

Gilbert Keith Chesterton (1874–1936), poet, essayist, novelist and critic—" The Man Who Was Thursday " ; " Heretics."

Samuel Taylor Coleridge (1772–1834), poet and critic—" The Rime of the Ancient Mariner " ; " Kubla Khan."

William Collins (1721–59), poet—" The Passions."

William Wilkie Collins (1824–89), novelist—" The Woman in White " ; " The Moonstone."

Padraic Colum (1881–), poet and writer of children's stories—" Wild Earth " ; " The Adventures of Odysseus."

Joseph Conrad (1857–1924), novelist—" The Nigger of the Narcissus " ; " Almayer's Folly " ; " Youth " ; " Chance."

Abraham Cowley (1618–67), poet and essayist—" Pindarique Odes " ; " Davideis " ; " The Mistress."

William Cowper (1731–1800), poet—" The Task " ; " John Gilpin."

George Crabbe (1754–1832), poet—" The Village."

A. J. Cronin (1896–), novelist—" Hatter's Castle " ; " The Citadel."

(Cont. in next page.)

FAMOUS NAMES IN ENGLISH LITERATURE (contd.)

Cynewulf (8th or 9th century), poet—"Christ"; "St. Juliana."

Harvey Darton (1879–1936), topographical writer—"The Marches of Wessex"; "English Fabric."

Charles Darwin (1809–82), scientific writer—"The Origin of Species."

Daniel Defoe (1661–1731), novelist and journalist—"Robinson Crusoe"; "Moll Flanders"; "Journal of the Plague Year."

E. M. Delafield (Elizabeth M. Dashwood) (1890–1943), novelist—"The Diary of a Provincial Lady"; "Turn Back the Leaves."

Walter de la Mare (1873–), poet and novelist—"Memoirs of a Midget"; "The Listeners"; "Peacock Pie."

William De Morgan (1839–1917), novelist—"Joseph Vance"; "Alice-for-Short"; "Somehow Good."

Thomas De Quincey (1785–1859), essayist and critic—"Confessions of an English Opium Eater"; "On Murder Considered as One of the Fine Arts."

Charles Dickens (1812–70), novelist—"David Copperfield"; "The Pickwick Papers"; "A Christmas Carol"; "Oliver Twist."

Benjamin Disraeli, Earl of Beaconsfield (1804–81), novelist—"Vivian Grey"; "Coningsby"; "Sybil."

Austin Dobson (1840–1921), poet and essayist—"Proverbs in Porcelain"; "Old World Idylls"; "At the Sign of the Lyre."

John Donne (1573–1631), poet and preacher—"Poems."

Ernest Dowson (1867–1900), poet—"Cynara."

Sir Arthur Conan Doyle (1869–1930), novelist—"The Adventures of Sherlock Holmes"; "Sir Nigel."

Michael Drayton (1563–1631), poet—"Agincourt"; "Polyolbion."

John Drinkwater (1882–1937), poet, critic and biographer—"Collected Poems"; "The Lyric"; "Pepys"; "Cromwell."

William Drummond (1585–1649), poet and historian—"Flowers of Sion"; "The Cypresse Grove."

John Dryden (1631–1700), poet—"Astraea Redux"; "Alexander's Feast"; "Ode on St. Cecilia's Day"; "Absalom and Achitophel."

William Dunbar (1465?–1525?), poet—"Two Married Women and the Widow"; "The Dance of the Seven Deadly Sins."

Lord Dunsany (Edward Plunkett) (1878–), story writer—"The Sword of Welleran."

Maria Edgeworth (1767–1849), novelist—"Castle Rackrent."

"George Eliot" (Mary Ann Evans) (1819–80), novelist—"Adam Bede"; "The Mill on the Floss"; "Silas Marner."

T. S. Eliot (1888–), poet and critic—"The Waste Land."

Havelock Ellis (1859–1939), essayist and critic—"The Dance of Life"; "Impressions and Comments."

John Evelyn (1620–1706), diarist and writer—"Diary"; "Sylva."

Henry Fielding (1707–54), novelist—"Tom Jones"; "Joseph Andrews"; "Jonathan Wild."

Edward FitzGerald (1809–83), poet and translator—"Omar Khayyam" (trans.).

James Elroy Flecker (1884–1915), poet—"Golden Journey to Samarkand"; "The King of Alsander"; "Hassan."

Giles Fletcher (1588?–1623), poet—"Christ's Victorie . . ."

Ford Madox Ford (1873–1939), novelist and critic—"Some Do Not"; "No More Parades"; "Return to Yesterday."

Edward M. Forster (1879–), novelist—"A Passage to India."

James Anthony Froude (1818–94), historian—"The History of England from the Fall of Wolsey to the Defeat of the Spanish Armada"; "Short Studies on Great Subjects."

John Galsworthy (1867–1933), novelist and short story writer—"The Forsyte Saga"; "Caravan."

Elizabeth Gaskell (1810–65), novelist—"Cranford."

John Gay (1685–1732), poet—"The Shepherd's Week"; "Fables"; "Trivia."

Geoffrey of Monmouth (1110?–54), historian—"Historia Britonum."

Edward Gibbon (1737–94), historian—"Decline and Fall of the Roman Empire."

Sir Philip Gibbs (1877–), novelist and essayist—"The Street of Adventure"; "The Middle of the Road."

George Gissing (1857–1903), novelist—"The Private Papers of Henry Ryecroft"; "The Whirlpool"; "The New Grub Street."

William Godwin (1756–1836), political writer and novelist—"Inquiry concerning Political Justice"; "Caleb Williams."

Oliver Goldsmith (1728–74), novelist, poet and essayist—"The Vicar of Wakefield"; "The Deserted Village."

Sir Edmund Gosse (1849–1928), poet and critic—"Father and Son"; "History of Modern English Literature."

John Gower (1325?–1408), poet—"Confessio Amantis."

Kenneth Grahame (1859–1932), writer of children's stories—"The Golden Age"; "The Wind in the Willows."

Robert Graves (1895–), poet and critic—"Good-Bye to All That"; "I, Claudius."

Thomas Gray (1716–71), poet—"Elegy in a Country Churchyard"; "The Progress of Poesy."

J. R. Green (1837–83), historian—"Short History of the English People."

Robert Greene (1560?–92), poet—"Sweet are the Thoughts"; "Sephestia's Song to Her Child."

Lord Grey of Fallodon (1862–1933), nature-writer and essayist—"The Charm of Birds"; "Fly-Fishing."

Sir H. Rider Haggard (1856–1925), prose writer—"King Solomon's Mines"; "She"; "Allan Quatermain."

Richard Hakluyt (1552?–1616), historian—"Principal Voyages of the English Nation."

Thomas Hardy (1840–1928), novelist and poet—"Far from the Madding Crowd"; "The Return of the Native"; "Tess of the D'Urbervilles"; "Wessex Poems"; "The Dynasts."

William Hazlitt (1778–1830), essayist and critic—"Table Talk"; "Characters of Shakespeare's Plays."

William E. Henley (1849–1903), poet and critic—"London Voluntaries"; "Hospital Sketches."

George Herbert (1593–1633), poet—"The Temple."

Robert Herrick (1591–1674), poet—"Hesperides."

Maurice Hewlett (1861–1923), novelist and poet—"Richard Yea-and-Nay"; "The Queen's Quair"; "The Forest Lovers."

James Hilton (1900–), novelist—"Lost Horizon"; "Good-bye, Mr. Chips."

Thomas Hobbes (1588–1679), philosopher—"The Leviathan."

Ralph Hodgson (1871–), poet—"The Last Blackbird."

Thomas Hood (1799–1845), poet and humorist—"The Song of the Shirt"; "Miss Kilmansegg."

Richard Hooker (1553–1600), theologian—"Laws of Ecclesiastical Polity."

Anthony Hope (1863–1933), novelist—"The Prisoner of Zenda"; "Rupert of Hentzau"; "The Dolly Dialogues."

Alfred E. Housman (1859–1936), poet—"A Shropshire Lad."

Laurence Housman (1865–), poet—"Green Arras"; "Spikenard"; "Mendicant Rhymes."

William H. Hudson (1841–1922), nature-writer and novelist—"Green Mansions"; "A Shepherd on the Wiltshire Downs."

David Hume (1711–76), philosopher and historian—"Inquiry Concerning Human Understanding."

Leigh Hunt (1784–1859), essayist and poet—"Abou Ben Adhem"; "The Story of Rimini"; "Autobiography."

A. S. M. Hutchinson (1879–), novelist—"If Winter Comes"; "The Happy Warrior"; "This Freedom."

Aldous Huxley (1894–), poet and novelist—"Chrome Yellow"; "Antic Hay"; "Point Counterpoint."

William Ralph Inge (1860–), essayist—"Lay Thoughts of a Dean"; "God and the Astronomers."

James I of Scotland (1394–1437), poet—"The Kingis Quair."

Richard Jefferies (1848–87), nature-writer and novelist—"Wood Magic"; "The Story of My Heart."

Jerome K. Jerome (1859–1927), humorist—"Three Men in a Boat."

Samuel Johnson (1709–84), essayist and lexicographer—"A Dictionary of the English Language"; "The Lives of the Poets."

Ben Jonson (1573?–1637), poet—"Drink to Me Only with Thine Eyes."

James Joyce (1882–1941), poet and novelist—"Portrait of the Artist as a Young Man"; "Dubliners"; "Ulysses."

Sheila Kaye-Smith, 20th-century novelist—"Sussex Gorse"; "Joanna Godden"; "The History of Susan Spray."

John Keats (1795–1821), poet—"Ode to a Nightingale"; "Ode on a Grecian Urn"; "Endymion"; "La Belle Dame sans Merci."

Margaret Kennedy (1896–), novelist—"The Constant Nymph."

Charles Kingsley (1819–75), novelist—"Westward Ho!"; "Water Babies"; "Hypatia."

Henry Kingsley (1830–76), novelist—"Ravenshoe."

Rudyard Kipling (1865–1936), novelist, poet, and short story writer—"Kim"; "Barrack Room Ballads"; "Puck of Pook's Hill"; "Just So Stories"; "The Jungle Book."

Charles Lamb (1775–1834), poet and essayist—"Essays of Elia"; "Tales from Shakespeare" (with Mary Lamb).

Walter Savage Landor (1775–1864), poet and prose writer—"Imaginary Conversations"; "Hellenics."

Andrew Lang (1844–1912), poet and prose writer—"Ballades in Blue China"; "Blue," "Red," and other fairy books; "The Making of Religion"; "The Maid of France."

William Langland (1330?–1400?), poet—"Vision of Piers Plowman."

David Herbert Lawrence (1885–1930), poet, novelist, and essayist—"Sons and Lovers"; "Sea and Sardinia."

Thomas Edward Lawrence (1888–1935), prose writer—"The Seven Pillars of Wisdom"; "The Odyssey" (trans.).

Layamon (about 1200), metrical historian—"Brut."

Eric Linklater (1899–), novelist—"Juan in America"; "Poet's Pub."

John Locke (1632–1704), philosopher—"Essay Concerning Human Understanding."

William J. Locke (1863–1930), novelist—"The Beloved Vagabond"; "Joyous Adventures of Aristide Pujol."

Thomas Lodge (1558?–1625), poet and romance-writer—"Rosalynde."

Richard Lovelace (1618–58), poet—"To Althea from Prison."

FAMOUS NAMES IN ENGLISH LITERATURE (contd.)

Edward Verrall Lucas (1868–1938), essayist and biographer—"Listener's Lure"; "London Lavender"; "Life of Charles Lamb."

John Lydgate (1373?–1450?), poet—"Troy Book."

John Lyly (1553?–1606), novelist—"Euphues : The Anatomy of Wit"; "Euphues and his England."

Edward Bulwer-Lytton, Lord Lytton (1803–73), novelist—"Last Days of Pompeii"; "Harold"; "My Novel."

Lord Macaulay (1800–59), historian, poet, and essayist—"History of England"; "Lays of Ancient Rome"; "Critical and Historical Essays."

Sir Thomas Malory (died 1470?), translator—"Morte d'Arthur."

Katherine Mansfield (1890–1923), short story writer—"The Garden Party"; "Bliss"; "The Dove's Nest."

Christopher Marlowe (1564–93), poet—"Come Live with Me and Be My Love."

John Masefield (1875–), poet and novelist—"Salt-Water Ballads"; "The Daffodil Fields"; "Dauber"; "Reynard the Fox"; "Sard Harker."

W. Somerset Maugham (1874–), novelist and short story writer—"Of Human Bondage"; "Cakes and Ale"; "The Painted Veil"; "Rain."

George Meredith (1828–1909), novelist and poet—"The Egoist"; "The Ordeal of Richard Feverel"; "Love in the Valley."

Alice Meynell (1850–1922), poet and essayist—"Preludes"; "Renouncement"; "The Rhythm of Life."

John Stuart Mill (1806–73), philosopher and economist—"Principles of Political Economy"; "System of Logic"; "On Liberty."

A. A. Milne (1882–), novelist, essayist, and children's writer—"When We Were Very Young"; "Winnie-the-Pooh."

John Milton (1608–74), poet—"Paradise Lost"; "L'Allegro"; "Il Penseroso"; "Lycidas"; "Samson Agonistes."

Charles E. Montague (1867–1928), novelist and critic—"A Hind Let Loose"; "Right Off the Map"; "Dramatic Values."

George Moore (1852–1933), novelist—"Esther Waters"; "Héloïse and Abélard"; "Confessions of a Young Man"; "The Brook Kerith."

Sir Thomas More (1478–1535), prose writer—"Utopia."

Charles Morgan (1894–), novelist—"The Fountain."

William Morris (1834–96), poet—"The Earthly Paradise."

John Henry Newman (1801–90), essayist and poet—"Apologia pro Vita Sua"; "The Dream of Gerontius"; "Lead, Kindly Light" (hymn).

Alfred Noyes (1880–), poet—"Tales of the Mermaid Tavern"; "The Wine Press"; "Drake, an English Epic."

Walter Pater (1839–94) essayist—"Imaginary Portraits"; "Marius the Epicurean."

Thomas Love Peacock (1785–1866), poet and novelist—"Headlong Hall"; "Nightmare Abbey"; "Crotchet Castle."

Samuel Pepys (1633–1703), diarist—"Diary."

Alexander Pope (1688–1744), poet and translator—"Rape of the Lock"; "Essay on Criticism"; "Essay on Man"; Iliad and Odyssey (trans.).

John Cowper Powys (1872–), novelist and critic—"Visions and Revisions"; "A Glastonbury Romance."

Llewelyn Powys (1884–1939), prose writer—"Black Laughter."

Theodore Francis Powys (1875–), novelist—"Mr. Weston's Good Wine."

J. B. Priestley (1894–), novelist—"The Good Companions"; "Angel Pavement."

Sir Arthur Quiller-Couch ("Q") (1863–1944), poet, critic, and novelist—"On the Art of Writing"; "The Astonishing History of Troy Town."

Charles Reade (1814–84), novelist—"The Cloister and the Hearth"; "It's Never Too Late to Mend"; "Foul Play."

Samuel Richardson (1689–1761), novelist—"Pamela, or Virtue Rewarded"; "Clarissa, or the History of a Young Lady."

Christina Rossetti (1830–94), poet—"Sing-Song"; "Goblin Market."

Dante Gabriel Rossetti (1828–82), poet—"The Blessed Damozel"; "The House of Life."

John Ruskin (1819–1900), art critic and essayist—"Modern Painters"; "The Seven Lamps of Architecture"; "Sesame and Lilies."

George William Russell ("Æ") (1867–1935), poet and essayist—"Homeward"; "Gods of War"; "The Interpreters"; "The National Being."

Victoria Sackville-West (1892–), poet and novelist—"The Land"; "The Edwardians"; "All Passion Spent."

George Saintsbury (1845–1933), critic and historian—"A History of Criticism"; "A Short History of English Literature."

Siegfried Sassoon (1886–), poet and novelist—"Counter-Attack"; "Memoirs of a Fox-Hunting Man."

Dorothy L. Sayers (1893–), novelist—"Gaudy Night"; "The Nine Tailors."

Sir Walter Scott (1771–1832), poet and novelist—"The Lady of the Lake"; "Waverley"; "Ivanhoe"; "Kenilworth."

William Shakespeare (1564–1616), poet—"Sonnets"; "Venus and Adonis."

George Bernard Shaw (1856–), essayist and novelist—"The Intelligent Woman's Guide to Socialism and Capitalism"; critical prefatory essays to his many plays : "Cashel Byron's Profession."

Percy Bysshe Shelley (1792–1822), poet—"Ode to the West Wind"; "Prometheus Unbound"; "To a Skylark"; "Adonais."

Joseph H. Shorthouse (1834–1903), novelist—"John Inglesant."

Sir Philip Sidney (1554–86), poet—"Astrophel and Stella"; "Arcadia."

Edith Sitwell (1887–), poet and essayist—"Wheels"; "The Wooden Pegasus"; "The English Eccentrics."

Adam Smith (1723–90), economist—"The Wealth of Nations."

Tobias Smollett (1721–71), novelist—"Roderick Random"; "Humphrey Clinker."

Robert Southey (1774–1843), poet and historian—"Battle of Blenheim"; "Inchcape Rock"; "Life of Nelson."

Edmund Spenser (1552?–99), poet—"Faerie Queene."

Sir Richard Steele (1672–1729), essayist—Essays in "The Spectator" and "The Tatler."

James Stephens (1882–), poet, short story writer, and novelist—"The Hill of Visions"; "The Crock of Gold."

Laurence Sterne (1713–68), novelist—"Tristram Shandy"; "A Sentimental Journey."

Robert Louis Stevenson (1850–94), novelist, essayist, and poet—"Treasure Island"; "Kidnapped"; "Travels With a Donkey"; "A Child's Garden of Verses."

G. Lytton Strachey (1880–1922), biographer—"Eminent Victorians"; "Queen Victoria"; "Elizabeth and Essex."

L. A. G. Strong (1896–), novelist and poet.—"Dewer Rides"; "The Brothers"; "Sea Wall."

Jonathan Swift (1667–1745), satirist—"Gulliver's Travels"; "Tale of a Tub"; "Journal to Stella."

Algernon Charles Swinburne (1837–1909), poet—"Atalanta in Calydon"; "Songs before Sunrise"; "Poems and Ballads."

Frank A. Swinnerton (1884–), novelist—"Nocturne."

John Addington Symonds (1840–93), critic—"The Renaissance in Italy."

Alfred, Lord Tennyson (1809–92), poet—"Idylls of the King"; "In Memoriam"; "Locksley Hall."

William Makepeace Thackeray (1811–63), novelist—"Vanity Fair"; "Henry Esmond"; "The Newcomes."

Francis Thompson (1859–1907), poet—"The Hound of Heaven."

James Thomson (1700–48), poet—"The Seasons"; "The Castle of Indolence"; "Rule, Britannia."

James Thomson ("B.V.") (1834–82), poet—"The City of Dreadful Night"; "Vane's Story."

H. M. Tomlinson (1873–), essayist and novelist "Old Junk"; "Gallion's Reach"; "All Our Yesterdays."

George Macaulay Trevelyan (1876–), historian—"Garibaldi and the Thousand"; "English Social History."

Anthony Trollope (1815–82), novelist—"Barchester Towers"; "Framley Parsonage"; "Doctor Thorne."

William Tyndale (1492?–1536), translator and tract writer—The New Testament (trans.).

Horace Walpole (1717–97), novelist and letter writer—"Castle of Otranto"; "Letters"; "Memoirs."

Sir Hugh Walpole (1884–1941), novelist—"Fortitude"; "Rogue Herries."

Izaak Walton (1593–1683), essayist and biographer—"The Compleat Angler"; "Lives."

Evelyn Waugh (1903–), novelist—"Black Mischief"; "Edmund Campion."

Mary Webb (1881–1927), novelist—"Precious Bane"; "Gone to Earth."

Herbert G. Wells (1866–1946), novelist and historian—"Tono-Bungay"; "The Time Machine"; "Outline of History"; "The Shape of Things to Come."

Rebecca West (1892–), novelist, essayist, and critic—"The Judge"; "Harriet Hume"; "The Return of the Soldier"; "The Strange Necessity"; "The Thinking Reed."

Gilbert White (1720–93), naturalist—"Natural History and Antiquities of Selborne."

George J. Whyte-Melville (1821–78), novelist—"Digby Grand"; "Market Harborough"; "Katerfelto."

Oscar Wilde (1856–1900), poet and novelist—"The Ballad of Reading Gaol"; "The Picture of Dorian Gray."

Virginia Woolf (1882–1941), novelist and critic—"Mrs. Dalloway"; "The Lighthouse"; "Orlando"; "The Years."

William Wordsworth (1770–1850), poet—"Tintern Abbey"; "Intimations of Immortality"; "The Prelude."

Sir Thomas Wyat (1503–42), poet—sonnets and lyrics.

William Butler Yeats (1865–1939), poet and essayist—"The Wild Swans at Coole"; "Ideas of Good and Evil."

Charlotte M. Yonge (1823–1901), novelist—"The Dove in the Eagle's Nest"; "Unknown to History"; "Book of Golden Deeds."

Francis Brett Young (1884–), novelist—"Woodsmoke"; "The Dark Tower"; "The House Under the Water."

Israel Zangwill (1864–1926), novelist—"Children of the Ghetto"; "Dreamers of the Ghetto."

Epsom salts, magnesium sulphate, 2865, 2060.

Ep'stein, Jacob (b. 1880). Sculptor, b. New York ; **1221** ; " Rima," *1649* ; " Roma II.," *1221* ; Consummatum Est," " Adam," " Genesis," " Jacob and the Angel."

Ep'worth. Vil. in Lincolnshire, birthplace of John Wesley, 3365.

Equa'tion, in algebra, 112 ; in chemistry, 767.

Equa'tor, in geography, 1898 ; crossed by sun at equinoxes, 1221 ; heavy rainfall, 2741 ; region of little wind, 3384.

Equator'ial mounting of telescopes, 2411.

Equilib'rium. State of balance ; balancing organs of human ear, 1066 ; centre of gravity determines, 1514 ; gyroscopic stabilizers, 1562.

E'quinox. Time of year when the sun is equidistant from both poles, **1221** ; vernal equinox fixes date of Easter, 1074 ; and the seasons, 2914.

Equinoxes, precession of. Slow shift in time of year when poles are equidistant from the sun, 1221 ; illustrated by gyroscope, 1560 ; shifts relation of zodiac to calendar, 3444.

Equisetum. Genus of "horse-tails," related to ferns.

Equitation. The art of horse riding.

Eq'uity. In Eng. law, 921, 1903.

Equus (e'-kw*u*s). Animal genus including the ass, 273 ; horse, 1645–47 ; zebra, 3442.

Era, geologic, 1432.

Erard, Sebastien (1752–1831). Fr. maker of musical instruments ; perfected the harp and greatly improved the piano, 1579.

Erasmus (e-raz'm*u*s), **Desiderius** (1466–1536). Dutch scholar and theologian, **1221**, *1222* ; friends, 1635, 2228 ; influence on Zwingli, 3448 ; and the Reformation, 2758 ; and Renaissance, 2764.

Erato (er'-a-tō), Gk. myth., muse of love poetry, *187*, 2259.

Eratosthenes (er-*a*-tŏs'-the-nēz), **of Alexandria** (*c.* 284–204 B.C.). Gk. scientist, chief librarian of Alexandrian Library ; calculated earth's circumference ; first real maps, 1431.

Er'bium (Er). A rare-earth element. *See* **Rare Earths ; Terbium.**

Erckmann-Chatrian (êrk-mahn sha'-trē-ahn). Signature of Fr. literary collaborators, Emile Erckmann (1822–99) and Louis Gratien Charles Alexandre Chatrian (1826–90), writers of novels, short stories, dramas (" Madame Thérèse " ; " L'Ami Fritz ").

Er'ebus. In classical myth., the dark space between the earth and Hades.

Erebus, Mt., Antarctic volcano, 173.

Erechtheum (e-rek-thē'-*u*m). Temple on Acropolis, *21*, *22*, *285* ; *back of plate f.* 1524, *plate f.* 1525.

Erechtheus (e-rek'-thūs). Legendary king of Athens, 22.

" Erewhon." Book satirizing society written by Samuel Butler.

Erfurt. City in cent. Ger., 70 m. s.w. of Leipzig ; pop. 166,700 ; in flower- and vegetable-growing and seed-exporting region ; formerly had famous univ.

Erg. The unit of work on the C.G.S. system ; work done in moving one gramme against a force of one dyne ; 10⁷ ergs equal one joule, the practical unit.

Ergot, rye fungus, 2858.

Erica'ceae, the heath family, 1596.

Er'icson or **Ericsson, Leif** (11th cent. A.D.). Norse adventurer ; discovers N. Amer., *139*, 2290, 2388.

Ericsson, John (1803–89). Swedish-Amer. inventor and engineer, **1222 ;** hot air engines, 1735 ; screw steamships, *2903*.

Eric the Red (10th cent.). Norwegian navigator, father of Leif Ericson, colonizer of Greenland, 1542, 2388.

Eridu. Pre-Babylonian city of Mesopotamia, excavated 1947 ; *208*, 209.

Erie (ēr'-i), Pennsylvania, U.S.A. Lake port 88 m. s.w. of Buffalo, N.Y. ; pop. 115,964 ; largest harbour on L.

Erie ; steam-engines ; large fishing interests.

Erie, Lake. Shallowest and stormiest of the Great Lakes ; a. 10,000 sq. m. ; Detroit and other ports on its shores ; battle fought in 1813 ; 1515 ; size, 3287 ; Welland Canal, 3363.

Erie Canal, N.Y., U.S.A. Completed in 1825 ; connecting l. Erie with r. Hudson ; 1516.

Erigena (e-rij'-*e*-n*a*), **Johannes Scotus** (*c.* 810–877). Philosopher and theologian, native of Ireland (Scotia), later branded as heretic ; head, under Charles the Bald, of the palace school founded by Charlemagne.

Erin (ār'-in). Anc. name for Ireland (Eire), now used poetically.

Erinyes (e-rin'-i-ēz). Gk. name of the Furies.

Eris (e'-ris), in Gk. myth., goddess of discord.

Eritrea (e-ri-trē'-*a*). Former It. territory in N.E. Africa on Red Sea ; 15,754 sq. m. ; pop. 850,000 ; **1222**, *13*, 1073 ; *map*, *1074* ; conquered by British in 1941, 1222, 3418.

Erivan (er-i-van') or **Yerevan.** Cap. and largest city of Armenia, U.S.S.R., 110 m. s. of Tiflis ; pop, 200,000 ; on caravan route Russia to Iran ; 239.

Erl-king or **Erlkönig.** In Teutonic folklore, a malicious being who haunts the forest and carries away children ; subject of poem by Goethe and song by Schubert, 2887.

Er'mine. Fur-bearing animal of weasel family, **1222** ; fur, 1412.

" Ernani." Opera by Verdi.

Erne, r. and two loughs (Upper and Lower) in Northern Ire. ; the r. flows into Donegal Bay ; length of r. and lakes together 60 m.

Ernest Augustus (1771–1851). King of Hanover, 5th son of George III of Eng. ; succeeded to Hanoverian throne in 1837 (males alone being eligible), separating Eng. and Hanoverian crowns after personal union of over 100 years.

Ernst, Max (b. 1891), Ger. surrealist painter ; work banned by the Nazis ; 3122.

" Ero'ica " Symphony. Popular name of the symphony No. 3 in E flat by Beethoven (op. 55).

Eros (er'-os). Gk. name for Cupid, Aphrodite's son, 186, 943.

Eros. Popular name of Shaftesbury Memorial Fountain, Piccadilly Circus, London, *2017*, *2907*.

Ero'sion, glacial, 1680 ; mountains, 2597 ; by rivers, 2598, 3302 ; by winds, 3884.

Erse. Language of the Celts of Ire. and Scot., 740.

Erup'tions, volcanic, 3328. *See* **Volcanoes.**

Ervine, St. John Greer (b. 1883), Irish writer ; plays include " The First Mrs. Fraser," " Anthony and Anna."

Erymanthian boar. In Gk. myth., slain by Hercules, 1615.

Erysipelas (er-i-sip'-*e*-l*a*s). A skin disease ; caused by bacteria, 1458.

Erythi'a. In Gk. myth., isl. beyond Strait of Gibraltar, home of monster Geryon, 1615.

Erzberger (ärts'-bär-ger), **Matthias** (1875–1921). Leader of Democratic Catholic party in Ger. Reichstag ; sec. of state (1918) ; negotiated armistice terms ending 1st World War ; minister of finance (1919) ; assassinated.

Erzerum (ārz'-room) or **Erzurum.** Anc. city of Asiatic Turkey (pop, 52,500), and cap. of vilayet of same name (pop. 371,400) ; copper and iron wares ; capture by Russians in 1st World War (Feb. 1916) ended projected Turkish invasion of Egypt. The name means " the fortress of Rome " ; it was the chief fortress of the north-eastern frontier of the Roman Empire.

Erzgebirge (ärts'-ge-bēr'-ge) (" Ore Mountains "), low range between Saxony and Bohemia, *320*.

Esarhaddon (ē-sahr-had'-on) (d. 668 B.C.), king of Assyria (680–668 B.C.) ; son of Sennacherib and father of Assurbanipal ; brought Egypt un-

der Assyrian rule, rebuilt Babylon ; enlarged Assyrian Empire.

Esau (ē'-saw). Son of Isaac and Rebekah and elder twin brother of Jacob ; hairy hunter who sold his birthright to his brother for a mess of pottage and was cheated by the wily Jacob (Gen. xxv., xxvii.) ; founds Edomites, 1829.

Esbjerg (es'-byärg), Denmark. Spt. on w. coast of Jutland ; pop. 33,000 ; submarine cable connects with Calais ; 991.

Escalators. " Moving stairways," 1938 ; London Underground, 3275.

Escalette, a kind of marble, *2097*.

Escapement, of watch, *848*, *849* ; anchor, *848*, 1640.

Escarp'ment. In geology, the steep face of a cliff, usually caused by erosion or by prehistoric changes in water line.

Esco'rial or **Escurial,** Spain. Royal palace of Philip II near Madrid, 2054, *3042*.

Escort-carriers, small naval aircraft carriers, 2296.

Escuallin. Waterfall, Sutherlandshire, Scot., 3124.

Escutch'eon, in heraldry, 1614.

Esdraelon (ez-dra-ē'-lon), **Plain of.** The greatest plain of Palestine ; fertile, level, roughly triangular, bounded by Mt. Carmel on w., Mt. Gilboa on S.E., highlands of Galilee on N. ; scene of many battles in all ages ; 2481.

Eskimo. A race whose habitat is the Arctic regions, 1222, 224, *225*, 1875 in Alaska, 97 ; boats, *482*, 484, 1223 children, 800 ; in Greenland, 1541 in Labrador, *1875.*

Eskimo dog, 1026.

Esna or **Esneh,** in Egypt. Tn. on left bank of Nile, 25 m. s. of ruins of Thebes ; active trade post for caravans ; Nile barrage, 1097.

Espar'to. A fibrous grass, native to N. Africa and s. Spain ; long used for mats, baskets, rope, sandals ; paper 2497.

Esperanto (es-pe-ran'-tō). An international language, **1223.**

Espérey (es-pā-rā), **Louis Franchet d** (1856–1942). Fr. general of 1st World War ; created marshal of France in 1921 ; commanded 5th Army in First battle of Marne ; commander-in-chief at Salonika in 1918 overcame Bulgaria.

Esquiline (es'-kwi-līn) **Hill.** Highest of the seven hills of Rome, 2799.

Esqui'mault. British Columbia, naval station on Vancouver Isl. about 3 m w. of Victoria ; pop. 3,000 ; large harbour, naval yards, fortifications shipbuilding, salmon canning ; 3321

Es'quimaux. Same as **Eskimo.**

Essad Pasha (*c.* 1875–1920). Turkish soldier, bandit, and provisional president of Albania (1914) ; killed in Paris.

Es'say, in literature, **1224** ; Addison and Steele, 23, 1213 ; Bacon, 333 1211, 1224 ; De Quincey, 994, 1214 O. W. Holmes, 1636 ; Dr. Johnson 1214, 1224 ; Charles Lamb, 1886 1214, 1224 ; Macaulay, 2046, 1224 Môntaigne, 2218, 1224 ; Ruskir 2843 ; Stevenson, 3089.

" Essay on Criticism." Poem by Pope 1224, 2654.

" Essay on Man." Poem by Pope, 1224 2655.

Essen. Ger. industrial and rly. centre in N. Rhine–Westphalia ; pop (1939) 660,000, **1224** ; heavily bombed in 2nd World War, and taken by U.S. forces April 1945.

Essential oils, in perfumes, 2549.

Essequibo (e-se-kē-bō). Largest r. of Brit. Guiana, S. Amer. ; 600 m long ; flows into Atlantic by estuary 20 m. wide ; *maps, 1552, f.* 3024.

Es'sex, Robert Devereux, 2nd Earl (1566–1601). Eng. soldier and courtier ; won distinction in war with Sp. ; later fell into disfavour tried to excite insurrection, was executed for treason ; favourite of Queen Elizabeth, 1147 ; patron of Bacon, 333.

Essex, Robert Devereux, 3rd Earl of (1591–1646). Eng. general, son of preceding; commander of Parliamentary forces 1642–5 in Civil War.

Essex. Marit. co. in S.E. Eng.; 1,530 sq. m.; pop. 1,755,000; **1224.**

Es'sling. Vil. in Lower Austria, 7 m. E. of Vienna; between it and Aspern occurred bloody battle between French and Austrians in 1809.

Estate Duty, 3158.

Estates-General or **States-General.** Former representative assembly of France, 2567; meeting in 1789, 1393; Mirabeau in, 2189; Talleyrand, 3149.

Este (es'tā), **House of.** Old and illustrious family of Italy, capital at Ferrara; famous for political importance and splendid court; encouraged poets, painters and scholars; Alberto Azzo II (11th cent.) was common ancestor both of House of Este and of House of Guelf, to which royal family of England belongs; Alfonso of Este (1486–1534), Duke of Ferrara, husband of Lucrezia Borgia, was patron of Tasso.

Ester. Class of substances formed by the condensation of an alcohol and an acid with elimination of water; many are found in plants, some giving rise to their scents, 775, 1341; ester gums, 2768.

Esther (es-ter). Heroine of Old Testament book, **1225.**

Estienne, Robert and **Henri,** 16th cent. French printers, 2764.

Estivation. See **Aestivation.**

Estonia or **Esthonia** (es-tō'-ni-a). Republic of the U.S.S.R., on Baltic Sea; pop. 1,120,000; 18,353 sq. m.; **1226.** Independent republic, 1917–39; part of U.S.S.R. from Aug., 1940, 2850, 2852, 3418; in Ger. occupn., 1941–44, 1226.

Estremadura (es-trā-ma-dōōr'-a). Prov. of Portugal, in which Lisbon lies; 6,937 sq. m.; pop. 2,114,000; 2658.

Estuaries, wide river mouths, 1232.

Eta (ē̆'-ta), η, H. Seventh letter (long e) of Gk. alphabet.

Etah, Greenland. Eskimo settlement on Smith Sound; most northerly vil. in world.

Etana, in Babylonian myth., 332.

Etching, 1219; half-tones, 2688; photogravure, 2689; zinc, 2689.

Etchmiadzin (ech-mē-ad'-zin) or **Echmiadzin.** Vil. and convent in Armenia, 15 m. W. of Erivan; residence of the *Catholicos,* or head of the Armenian Church, 238.

Eteocles (et'-e-o-klēz). In Gk. myth., son of Oedipus and brother of Antigone.

Ete'sian winds, winds that are heated on their course, 840.

Ethane, a colourless gas; in natural gas, 1420.

Ethelbald or **Æthelbald.** King of Wessex, A.D. 858–860.

Ethelbert or **Æthelberht** (c. 552–616). King of Kent, bretwalda or overlord over all the English S. of the Humber, and author of the first written Eng. laws; converted by St. Augustine, 302.

Ethelfleda or **Æthelflæd** (d. A.D. 918). Eldest daughter of Alfred the Great, wife of the Earl of Mercia.

Ethelred or **Æthelred.** King of Wessex and Kent 866–871, brother of Alfred the Great.

Ethelred or **Æthelred, "the Unready"** (c. 968–1016), king of the Eng. 979–1016, in whose reign Danish invasions were renewed and policy of paying tribute (Danegeld) was begun; his marriage with the Norman princess Emma "opened a distinct policy which led to the Norman conquest of England"; 1089.

Ethelwulf or **Æthelwulf.** King of Wessex, 839–58. Father of Alfred the Great.

Ether (diethyl oxide). An anaesthetic, **1227,** 149; evaporation of, 1243.

Ether or **aether,** in physics, elastic medium sometimes supposed to pervade all space and transmit light, electric phenomena, etc., **1226,** 3358;

development of ether theory by Huygens, 1941; Clerk-Maxwell, 839; Einstein, 1122; Hertz, 1622; Lodge, 1988; radiation and, 2728; relation of light, heat, wireless, and X-ray waves, 2728; transmits heat, 1595; light, 1941, 2728; wireless, 3391; X-rays, 1942, 2728, 3430.

Eth'ics. A branch of philosophy dealing with morals, 2571.

Ethiopia (ē-thi-ō'-pi-a). Name given in anc. geog. to countries S. of Egypt; later applied to Abyssinia, **1227.** See **Abyssinia.**

Ethiopian or **African race,** 2725.

Ethio'pic language, 1601.

Ethnol'ogy. Science which deals with the races and classification of mankind, **1227;** branch of anthropology, 2723.

Eth'yl alcohol, 104.

Ethyl chloride. An anaesthetic resembling in its effects both nitrous oxide and ether; also used as a "local" anaesthetic for freezing the skin, 149.

Eth'ylene. A gaseous compound, 1424; from petroleum, 2430.

Etiquette (et'-i-ket), **1227.**

Et'na or **Aetna, Mt.,** volcano (10,750 ft.) on E. coast of Sicily, **1228,** 2968.

Eton. Tn. in Bucks, on Thames, opposite Windsor; pop. 4,000, **1229.**

Eton College. Famous Eng. public school; founded in 1441 by Henry VI; greatest sporting event is cricket match against Harrow; 1178, 1229, 2885, 3388; fives game, 1312; "calling absence" on Speech Day, 2885.

Etruria (e-trōōr'-i-a). Anc. country N.W. of Rome, inhabited by Etruscans; modern Tuscany, 1230.

Etrus'cans, 1230. Conflicts with Rome, 1230, 2804, 2805, 3207; gladiatorial shows, 1469.

Et'trick, Scot. Mt. on borders of Selkirkshire and Dumfriesshire; 2,269 ft.

"Et tu, Brute," 653.

Etty, William (1787–1849); R.A.; greatest Eng. painter of the nude; attended life-classes at R.A. schools till the end of his life; 1182.

Etymol'ogy. The science of words. 1209, 1230; of names, 2272.

Et'zel. Name of Attila in Ger. legend, 2363.

Euboea (ū-bē'-a). Largest isl. in Greek archipelago; 90 m. long, 4 to 30 m. wide; pop. 179,500; chief tn. Chalcis; minerals, oil, wine, farm products; map, 1518.

Eucaine (ū-kān'). A local anaesthetic used in place of cocaine, than which it is less dangerous.

Eucalyptol (ū-ka-lip'-tol). Oil from eucalyptus leaves, 1230.

Eucalyp'tus. Gum tree, native to Australia, **1230,** 309, 314, 3156; essential oil from, 1263.

Eucharist (ū'-ka-rist), or **Communion.** The offering of praise and thanksgiving in the Christian Church; it consists of partaking of the consecrated elements—the bread and the wine, representing the Body and Blood of Christ.

Eucken (oi'-ken), **Rudolf Christoph** (1846–1926). Ger. idealistic philosopher; urged the "application of a vital religious inspiration to the practical problems of society"; winner of Nobel prize for literature (1908).

Euclase. A rare mineral resembling aquamarine; a beryllium aluminium silicate; occurs in Urals and Brazil; colourless; sometimes cut as a gem.

Euclid (ū'-klid) or **Eucleides** (about 300 B.C.). Gk. mathematician, called "father of geometry" ("Elements of Geometry" long used as school text-book), 1434; his saying on learning, 2762.

Eudoxia (c. 393–460). Rom. empress; the daughter of Theodosius II, and wife of Valentinian III.

Euergetes I (ū-êr'-gē-tēz). Same as Ptolemy III.

Eugène (ē-zhän') **of Savoy, Prince** (1663–1736). Fr.-born Austrian general and statesman, one of great

captains of history, defeated Turks at Zenta (1697), helped Marlborough to win at Blenheim and Malplaquet; took Belgrade from Turks (1717).

Eugenics (ū-jen'-iks). Science of race improvement; **1230,** 1617. See **Heredity.**

Eugénie (ê-zhā-nē), **Empress** (1826–1920). Wife of Napoleon III, emperor of the French.

"Eugénie Grandet" (grahn'-dā). Novel by Balzac, one of the world's greatest stories; old Grandet, the miser, is probably the most terrible portrayal of the corroding influence of greed in any literature; his daughter, Eugénie, is Balzac's finest female character.

Eulenspiegel (oi'-len-shpē-gel), **Till.** Ger. folk-hero of 14th cent., about whose name have gathered popular tales of jests and pranks. Richard Strauss made him the subject of a brilliant symphonic poem.

Eumaeus (ū-mē'-us), in the Odyssey, swineherd of Odysseus, 2423.

Eumenides (ū-men'-i-dēz). Gk. name for the Furies, meaning the "well-disposed," "kindly" goddesses; drama, by Aeschylus, 53.

Eupat'rids. Hereditary aristocrats of anc. Greece, 1519.

Eupen (oi'-pen). Tn. and dist. in E. Belgium 20 m. E. of Liége; ceded with Malmedy by Ger. in 1919.

Euphonium (ū-fō'-ni-um). Musical instrument, 1644.

Euphrates (ū-frā'-tēz). The 2nd largest r. of W. Asia; flows S. and E. 1,700 m. to Persian Gulf; **1231;** Babylon on, 328; basket boats, 482, 484; Iraq, 1743, 2146.

Euphrosyne (ū-fros'-i-nē). In Gk. myth., one of the three Graces.

Euphues (ū'-fū-ēz). Name and hero of a romance (published 1578) by John Lyly, which made the affected artificial style of "fine language" called "euphuism" fashionable in Elizabethan Eng., 2401.

Eura'sia, 264.

Eura'sians. Term used in India to designate people of mixed Hindu and European extraction; also used of other persons born of mixed European and Asiatic blood.

Eureka (ū-rē'-ka) (Gk. for "I have found"). Expression used by Archimedes, 210.

Eurhythmics. Art of expressing harmony of music by gestures, **1231.** See also **Ballet; Dalcroze, E. J.; Dancing.**

Euripides (ū-rip'-i-dēz) (480–406 B.C.). Anc. Gk. tragic dramatist, **1231;** and Greek drama, 1038.

Euro'pa, in Gk. myth., daughter of a Phoenician king and sister of Cadmus; carried off to Crete by Zeus in form of a bull, 649; 2817.

Europe. Most densely populated of the continents; 4,000,000 sq. m.; pop. 500,000,000; **1232,** 896; map, plate f. 1232; canals, 686; climate, 840, 1232, 1237, 1554; coast-line and harbours, 1232, 1576; elevation, 263; fishing industry, 1233, 1298, 2391, 2136; forests, 464, 1237, 1350, 1445; former land connexion with Africa, 3030; ice age, 1469, 1680; languages, 2570; minerals, 704, 732, 855, 857, 1234, 1753, 3297; mountains, 126, 1233, 1234, 1235; population, 1234; races, 2725; railways, 2736; rainfall, 2741, 2742; rivers and lakes, 972, 1232.

European Countries: Albania, 100; Andorra, 2709; Austria, 316; Belgium, 403; Bulgaria, 612; Czechoslovakia, 953; Denmark, 991; Eire, 1122, 1749; Estonia, 1226; Finland, 1277; France, 1358; Germany, 1444; Gibraltar, 1462; Great Britain and Northern Ireland, 1514, 1747; Greece, 1517; Hungary, 1654; Iceland, 1684; Latvia, 1899; Liechtenstein, 1934; Lithuania, 1967; Luxemburg, 2041; Malta, 2072; Monaco, 2219; Netherlands, 2318; Norway, 2392; Poland, 2640; Portugal, 2658; Rumania, 2839; Russia (U.S.S.R.),

2844 ; San Marino, **2872** ; Spain, 3030 ; Sweden, 3126 ; Switzerland, 3138 ; Turkey in Europe, 3262 ; Vatican, 3306 ; Yugoslavia, 3438.

European History, **1237** ; chief events summarized, *see under* **History** ; prehistoric period, 734, 735, 740, *3095* ; beginning of European civilization, 29, 1237, 1517 ; Roman supremacy, 1193, 1365, 2811 ; Byzantine Empire, 635, 2812 ; barbarian migrations, 96, 740, 1237, 1487, 1657, 3304 ; Mahomedan invasion checked, 759, 2067 ; invasion of Northmen, 1238, 2387, 2376 ; Charlemagne's empire, 753 ; Holy Roman Empire, 1636 ; feudal system, 1268 ; Crusades, 936, 3310 ; medieval commerce, 1256, 1553, 1575, 3060, 3112, 3310 ; revolutionary inventions, 1558, 2684 ; Renaissance, 2764 ; Hundred Years' War, 1652 ; fall of Constantinople and Turkish invasions, 1761, 3264 ; exploration and discovery, 878, 1431, 1613, 2056, 2652, 3306 ; Portugal at its height, 2659 ; Hapsburg Empire at its height, 754 ; Reformation, 2040, 2758 ; Thirty Years' War, 3202 ; wars of Louis XIV, 2029, 2106 ; Seven Years' War, 2924 ; partition of Poland (1772–95), 2642 ; Industrial Revolution, 1721 ; French Revolution and Napoleon (1789–1815), 1239, 1366, 1393, 2275 ; colonial expansion in 19th cent., 70, 580, *581* ; revolutions (1830 and 1848), 1240, 1449, 2275, 1873 ; unification of It., 737, 1769, 3319 ; formation of Ger. Empire, 1449, 2696 ; Hague Peace Conference, 1240, 1563 ; Morocco incidents, 2230 ; Balkan Wars and " Eastern Question," 344, 345, 1240 ; 1st World War, and reconstruction, 1241, 3409 ; League of Nations formed, 1908 ; rise of the dictatorships, 1242, 1261, 1451, 1631, 1770, 1923, 2268, 2849 ; economic difficulties, 318, 1242, 1483 ; 2nd World War, 1242, 2371, 3416 ; spread of Communism, 1242, 3424 ; Western Union, 1242 ; United Nations, 3283. *See also* topics above and countries by name.

European Assembly. Name given to Consultative Assembly of the Council of Europe (*q.v.*).

European or **Caucasian race**, 732, 2725 ; Polynesians, 2471.

European Recovery Programme (E.R.P.). Plan evolved in 1947 for the economic restoration of W. European nations, largely financed by the U.S.A. ; also called the Marshall Plan, 1242, 2111, 3283.

Euro'pium (Eu). *See* **Rare Earths.**

Eurus (ūr'-*us*), in Gk. myth., east wind.

Eurydice (ū-rid'-i-sē), in Gk. myth., wife of Orpheus ; killed by serpent's bite, rescued from the underworld by Orpheus, but lost again ; *2454* ; subject of first opera, 2435.

Euryl'ochus, in Gk. myth., companion of Odysseus (Ulysses), 834.

Eurys'aces. Reliefs from tomb of, *555.*

Eurystheus (ū-ris'-thūs), in Gk. myth., cousin of Hercules, 1615.

Eusebius (ū-sē'-bi-*us*) **of Caesarea**, called Pamphili (*c.* 264–340). Christian theologian, most learned man of his age ; " History of the Christian Church," by far the most important anc. record of the Church ; chief figure at Council of Nicaea.

Eusebius of Nicomedia, called " the Great " (d. *c.* A.D. 341). Theologian, leading defender of Arius, and after death of Arius leader of his party ; Bishop of Nicomedia and Constantinople.

Eusta'chian tube of ear, 1065.

Eustachius (ū-stā'-ki-*us*) **(Bartolommeo Eustachio)** (d. 1574). Ital. anatomist, physician to Pope Sixtus V ; investigated structure of ear, heart, kidneys, teeth, muscles of head and neck, and other parts of body ; gave his name to Eustachian tube of ear, 1065.

Euston. London rly. terminus for the midlands and north.

Euterpe (ū-ter'-pē), in Gk. myth., Muse of lyric poetry, 187, 2259.

Euthanasia. Easy death advocated by some for those suffering from incurable and painful disease.

Euwe, Dr. Max. Dutch chess player, world champion (1935–38).

Euxine (ūk-sīn) **Sea.** Anc. name for Black Sea.

Euzkadi (ā-ooth-kah'-di). The Basque Country in the N.E. corner of Spain, including the provinces of Vizcaya, Guipuzcoa, Alava, and Navarre ; of these all but the last-named were under an autonomous govt., ratified by the Sp. Republican Govt. in Oct. 1936 ; a. 6,795 sq. m. ; est. pop. 1,350,000 ; conquered by the insurgent forces in the Civil War of 1936.

Eva. In H. B. Stowe's " Uncle Tom's Cabin," beautiful, affectionate, and supernaturally good child, daughter of Uncle Tom's master, who dies young.

Evangeline. Heroine of Longfellow's poem ; and dispersal of the Acadians, 17, 2022.

Evangelists, symbols of, 188.

Evans, Edith, D.B.E. (b. 1888). Eng. actress, brilliant characterizations ; (Nurse in " Romeo and Juliet," Rosalind in " As You Like It," Florence Nightingale in " The Lady with a Lamp," also Gwenny in " The Late Christopher Bean," Irela in " Evensong," The She-Ancient in Shaw's " Back to Methuselah," " Daphne Laureola " ; films, " Queen of Spades," " Last Days of Dolwyn ") ; D.B.E. 1945.

Evans, Petty-officer Edgar. One of heroic party of five who accompanied Capt. Scott in Antarctic and died on tragic journey from the South Pole, 2896.

Evans, Sir Arthur John (1851–1941). English archaeologist ; excavated Minoan palace of Knossos, Crete, 32, 208.

Evans, Edward Ratcliffe Garth Russell. Eng. naval officer, known as " Evans of the Broke." *See* **Mountevans.**

Evans, Mary Ann. *See* **Eliot, George.**

Evapora'tion, 1243 ; of ether, 1227 ; fog, 1333 ; Mediterranean, 2137 ; in plants, 1230, 1914 ; rainfall dependent on, 2741 ; refrigeration, 1392 ; in salt mfr., 2866, *2867* ; steam, 3084 ; sugar refining, *3113* ; in partial vacuum, 3302 ; water, 3349.

Evatt, Herbert Vere (b. 1894). Australian politician ; attorney-gen. and min. for External Affairs in 1941 ; Australian delegate to Paris Peace conf. ; in 1946 dep. prime min. of Australia ; attended Commonwealth conf. in London Oct. 1948 ; chairman of U.N. gen. assembly, Paris, in 1948.

Eve. In the Creation story of Genesis, first woman, formed out of Adam's rib, ancestress of human race ; in Milton's " Paradise Lost," 1085, 2178 ; in Shaw's " Back to Methuselah," *1042* ; by Rodin, 2796.

" Evelina." Fanny Burney's first and best novel ; told in form of letters ; early example (1778) of novel of domestic manners.

Evelyn, John (1620–1706). Eng. diarist of the Commonwealth and Restoration, **1243** ; discovered Grinling Gibbons, 1462.

Evening primrose. A flowering plant with yellow flowers that open in evening only ; genus *Œnothera* of fam. *Onagraceae.*

Evening Star. Usually Venus, first planet visible after sunset ; occasionally Mars, Jupiter, or Saturn.

" Eve of Saint Agnes, The." Poem by Keats, 1849.

Ev'erest, Sir George (1790–1866). Eng. surveyor and geographer ; superintended first survey of India ; located Mt. Everest. 1243.

Everest, Mt., in Himalaya Mts. (29,141 or 29,002 ft.) ; loftiest mountain on earth ; **1243** : 263, *1627, 3209.*

Evergreen, 1243 ; how it guards against overloads of snow, 2623 ; conifers, 890 ; laurel, 1900 ; oak, 2409.

Everlasting or **Perpetual League.** Foundation of Swiss independence, 3141.

" Everyman." Eng. morality play, **1244**, 1040.

Evesham. Market tn. in Worcestershire on Avon in vale of Evesham ; pop. 8,799 ; site of battle of Evesham ; centre of fruit-growing area ; 3407.

Evesham, battle of. Ended Barons' War, 2221, 1611.

Evesham, Vale of, 3407.

" Evil Eye," magic against, *2057,* 2058.

Evolution, 1244, *158* ; ancestral relationships of animals, 158, 1297, 1353 ; ancestry revealed by embryos and young, 1154, 1245 ; of birds from reptiles, 437, 442, *448,* 1975 ; chart of, 158 ; Darwin and Darwinism, 975, 1244, 3447 ; of earth, 1067, 1432, 2595, 2618 ; effect on zoology, 3447 ; elephant, *1140* ; evidence supporting theory, 1155, 1244, 1353 ; fish, 1297 ; foot, 1342 *1343* ; fossils as evidence, 1244 1353 ; and genetics, 1427 ; of higher plants from algae, 112 ; horse, *1245 1246, 1342* ; Huxley, 1661 ; o mammals, 2074 ; " natural selection," 978, 1245 ; nest-building instinct in birds, 442 ; of penguin 2544 ; planets, 2618 ; in plants 2620 ; relation between Man and apes, 182 ; of reptiles, 1975 " struggle for existence," 156, 1726 " survival of the fittest," 978, 1246 " transitional " forms of life, 1053 Wallace's theory, 978 ; of whales 3371. *See also* **Adaptation ; Environment ; Heredity,** etc.

Evora (ev'-o-ra), Port. The cap. of the dist. of Evora ; it is hilly, and slope E. and S., and forms the basin of number of small streams that flov into the r. Guadiana ; cork oak forests relieve the district from it barrenness.

Ev'zones. Gk. light troops whos uniform is a white kilt or *fustanello* wide sleeved white shirt, red-pointe shoes, and blue-tasselled red cap.

Ewald (ā'-vahlt), **Johannes** (1743–81 Denmark's greatest lyric poet, firs used in imaginative writing the anc history and mythology of Scan dinavia ; " Rolf Krage," first origina Danish tragedy ; " Balder's Death, an heroic opera ; " The Fishers, which contains the Danish nationa song, a lyrical drama.

Ewe (ū). A female sheep, 2940.

Ewer. In Brit. Museum, *plate f. 58.*

Ew'ing, Juliana Horatia Orr (1841–85 Eng. writer of books for children simple in style, quiet humour " The Story of a Short Life " an " Jackanapes " are the most popu lar. Many of her books are illus trated by Kate Greenaway an Randolph Caldecott.

Ew'ins, Arthur J. (b. 1882). Bri chemist ; with Dr. M. Phillips dis covered the sulpha-drug M & B 69 in 1932.

Examination, 1246, 2886.

Exarchate of Ravenna, 2748.

Excalibur (eks-kal'-i-bur) or **Escalibu** King Arthur's sword ; story of, 25. According to another account (Ter nyson's " Idylls of the King ") it wa given to him by the Lady of the Lak

Excavations, by archaeologists, 32, 20

Excavators, 1247, *1248* ; bucket-ladde dredger, *1047* ; bulldozer, *124* 1249 ; power shovel, *741.*

Exchange, bill of, 357.

Exchange, foreign, in finance, 1348 credit, 926 ; Gold Standard, 1482.

Exchange, telephone, *3170, 3171,* 371 automatic, *3172,* 3175.

Exchequer (eks-chek'-er), **Chancellor** the. In Gt. Brit. the actual head the Treasury and the official charge with the preparation of the Budget he must be a member of the Hou of Commons and holds a portfoli in the Cabinet.

Exchequer, Court of. A division of th Eng. High Court of Justice, 921.

Excise (ek-sīz'), or internal revenue ta 3158.

Exciter (for elec. generator), in dynam 1060.

Exclamation mark or **point,** use of, 270

Excommunica'tion, 1726.

Exe. R. of Somerset and Devon, flowing to Eng. Channel ; 55 m. long, 999.

Execu'tion, methods of, 2687.

Exercise, physical, 2589 ; athletics, 287 ; effect on health, 1675 ; "P.T." exercises, *2590* ; running, 2843. *See* **Sports**.

Ex'eter. Co. tn. of Devonshire on r. Exe ; pop. 69,000 ; 1000, **1249** ; "Baedeker" air raid in 1942, 1249.

Exeter College, Oxford, 2464.

Exeter, H.M.S. Brit. cruiser sunk by Japs. after the battle of the Java Sea, Feb. 26, 1942 ; took part in the battle of the r. Plate ; *see* **Plata, River, Battle of** ; 3417, *map, 3417,* 3421.

Exhaust, of motor-car, 2243.

Exhaust stroke, 1736.

Existen'tialism. A philosophy derived partly from Kierkegaard, who declared " every man is . . . planned to be a self . . . Truth is subjective " ; influenced post-war Fr. literature, e.g. Sartre, Camus.

Exmoor. Moorland and forest expanse, bordering Somerset and Devon, close to Bristol Channel ; made familiar by Blackmore's "Lorna Doone" ; highest point Dunkery Beacon, 1,707 ft. ; forest, 3,000.

Ex'mouth, Edward, 1st Viscount (1757–1833). Brit. admiral ; bombardment of Algiers, 118.

Ex'ocarp. Fleshy portion of a stone or drupaceous fruit, 1403.

Ex'odus (Gk. "going forth" or "departure"). 2nd book of the Old Testament and Pentateuch ; describes the giving of the divine law ; opens with the account of Moses leading Israelites out of Egypt ; 2235.

Experiment, as a scientific method, foreshadowed by Roger Bacon, 334 ; developed by Francis Bacon, 333 ; in plant breeding by Burbank, 621 ; in conquest of yellow fever, 2236.

Exploits. Longest r. (150 m.) in Newfoundland ; flows into bay on N.E. coast ; timber on, *2331.*

Exploration, 1431 ; in Arabia, 195 ; Baker, 340 ; Balboa discovers the Pacific, 341 ; Burton, 626 ; Cabots reach coast of N. Amer., 647 ; Columbus discovers New World, 878 ; Cook, 898 ; Drake circumnavigates globe, 1037 ; Mt. Everest, 1243 ; Henry the Navigator, 1613 ; Henry Hudson, 1649 ; Livingstone, 1970 ; Magellan circumnavigates the world, 2056 ; Marco Polo reaches China, 2652 ; Mungo Park, 2521 ; discoveries of the Northmen, 2387 ; ocean, 2414 ; Pacific discoveries, 899, 2469 ; Polar, 224, 2895, 2534, 2644 ; *maps, 173, 223* ; Stanley, 3076 ; Vasco da Gama, 3306.

Explosion, 1250 ; atomic bomb, *299* ; depth charge, *293* ; of gases, 1280 ; in internal combustion engine, 1736, 2244.

Explosives, 1250, *1251* ; atomic bomb, 299, 1251 ; dynamite, 1060 ; in fireworks, 1291 ; in flying bomb, 1330 , glycerine for, 1478 ; gunpowder, 1558 ; in mines, 2184 ; nitric acid for, 2372 ; nitro-glycerine, 1060 ; picric acid, 699, 857 ; powdered zirconium, 3444 ; in rockets, 2793 ; fulminating silver, 2973 ; T.N.T., 857 ; why nitrogen is needed, 1250, 2372.

Exposure Meters, in photography, 2576.

Expressionism. Art movement in Germany, 19th-20th cent., opposition to Impressionism ; led by Oscar Kokoschka (b. 1886) in Vienna and Max Pechstein (b. 1881) in Berlin ; less concerned with pictorial possibilities than with dramatic and romantic implications.

Extradition. The surrender by a govt. of fugitives from justice to the authorities of the country where the crime was committed.

Extragalac'tic ; in astronomy means distant from the Milky Way ; nebulae, 2310.

Extra-territorial rights. The privilege accorded by international law to foreign sovereigns and diplomatic representatives of freedom from compliance with the laws of the country in which they are stopping. By special treaty citizens of European powers have at times had similar rights in African and Asiatic countries ; in China, 812. Renounced in China 1942–47.

Extroverts, in psychology, 1840.

Eyck, Van. *See* **Van Eyck.**

Eye, the organ of vision, **1252,** *1253* ; "accommodation" discovered,3426 ; bird, 438, 1252 ; brain control, 546 ; cat, 718, 1252, *1253* ; chameleon, 750, *1253* ; colour-blindness, 1254 ; of crayfish, 926 ; cuttle-fish, 945 ; defects of vision, 1254, 3054, 3327 ; dislodging foreign body, 1295 ; of dragon-fly, 1034, 1252 ; drone bee, 392 ; eagle, 1063, 1253 ; fish, 1296 ; flat fish, *1298* ; insects, 1730 ; lens of, 1925 ; persistence of vision, 3182 ; sight and sleep, 2983 ; sight a photochemical process, 2574 ; of snail, *1253,* 2989 ; snakes lack eyelids, 2990 ; spectacles, 3054 ; of spider, *1253,* 3005 , "visual purple," 2574 ; Vitamin A and, 3327 ; whirligig beetle, *1253.*

Eye-glasses, or spectacles, 3054.

Eyepiece, of telescope, 3878.

Eye splice, of a rope, *1871.*

Eye tooth. *See* **Canine.**

Eyot (āt), or **ait.** Term applied to a small island, especially one in inland waters.

Eyre (ār), **Edward John** (1815–1901). Brit. colonial governor and explorer, **1254** ; in cent. Australia, 310.

Eyston (ē'-ston), **George Edward Thomas** (b. 1897), English racing motorist ; land speed record in Thunderbolt (1938).

Ezekiel (e-zē'-ki-el) (Hebrew, "God will strengthen"), one of the major Hebrew prophets (author of 26th book of Old Testament), who was carried prisoner to Babylonia in 597 B.C. and flourished about 592–570 B.C., *2691,* 2692.

Ez'ra, "the Scribe." Hebrew priest and reformer (books of Ezra and Nehemiah) ; sent to Palestine in 458 B.C. by Artaxerxes to investigate conditions of Jews ; brought back observance of Mosaic law ; **1830.**

THE letter F looks so much like E that some have thought it developed from the same form, but such is not the case. Long ago it was the Egyptian cerastes 🝔 or horned asp. The two bars are survivals of the two horns of this poisonous viper, while the vertical stroke represents the body. Written in a running hand it became ⌐ and then the Phoenician ⅄, which was called *Wau* or *Vau*, meaning a "hook" or "peg." The Greeks wrote it much like our Y and

called it *Digamma* from its fancied resemblance to two united gammas or G's, one above the other. We fail to find it in the modern Greek alphabet, for after a time it dropped out of general use. The western Greeks continued to use it for some time, and the Romans adopted it, giving it the form which we now use, as well as its sound, "ef." Its original sound, as you might guess from its Phoenician name, was that of our *w* or *v*, and it was sounded as *w* by the Greeks.

'aber, Frederick William (1814–63). English theologian and hymn writer ("Pilgrims of the Night").

Fabian Society," 1875, 2996.

'a'bius (Quintus Fabius Maximus) (d. 203 B.C.), Rom. general, 1574.

'ables. Usually stories in which animals are given the power of speech, and a moral is pointed ; Aesop, 54 ; La Fontaine, 1885.

'abliaux (fab'-li-ō). Medieval tales, forerunner of the novel, 2401.

'abre (fah'-br), **Jean Henri** (1823–1915). Fr. entomologist and author, **1255** ; on wasps, 3346.

'açade, in architecture, the front elevation or face of a building.

'acial angle, 2723.

'acing bricks, 562.

'acsimile transmission, by wireless, of pictures, etc., 3397, *3398.*

'actors, in mathematics, 1255.

'actories and factory laws ; hygiene, 1677 ; in Japan, 1798 ; Industrial Revolution, 1721 ; motor works, *896,* 2241 ; Shaftesbury and, 2931 ; shoe industry, 521 ; smoke, 2986. *See also* names of industries.

Fad'den, Arthur W. (b. 1895). Australian politician ; prime min. Aug.-Oct. 1941 ; led opposition 1941–43 ; became leader of Country party 1943.

Fading, in wireless reception, *3395.*

Faenza (fah-ent'-sa). It. city 19 m. s.w. of Ravenna ; 15th-cent. cathedral ; noted "faience" pottery ; used as German military base, late 1944, captured by N.Z. troops Dec. 16, 1944 ; several palaces and museums damaged.

"Faerie Queene." Allegorical romance by Edmund Spenser, 1211, 3058.

Faeroe Islands. Same as **Faroe Islands.**

Fagaceae (fa-gā'-sē-ē), the beech family ; includes beeches, 395 ; oaks, 2409.

Fa'gin. A crafty old Jew, thief-trainer and receiver of stolen goods, in Dickens's "Oliver Twist."

Fahrenheit (fah'ren-hīt), **Gabriel Daniel**, (1686–1736). Ger. physicist and instrument maker ; devised Fahrenheit scale for thermometers, 3200.

Fahrenheit thermometer, 4004, *3200,* 4005.

Faience (fī-ahns'), a variety of pottery, 2666.

Fainting, treatment, 1295.

Fairbairn, Sir William (1789–1874). Scottish engineer and inventor ; a pioneer builder of iron ships in Gt. Brit. ; with Robert Stephenson, built tubular bridge over Menai Strait.

Fairbanks, Alaska, on Tanana r., largest gold-mining tn. in interior ; pop. 7,500 ; 98, 99.

Fairbanks, Douglas (1883–1939), Amer. film actor ; dashing hero of such famous screen plays as "The Three

Musketeers," "Robin Hood,"; his son, Douglas Fairbanks, jun., also became a film star.

Fairbridge Schools. Farm-training schools in Australia and Canada; the first at Pinjarra, Australia, started in 1913 by Kingsley Fairbridge to help emigration of underprivileged children of the U.K.; voluntary finances helped by U.K. govt. and Dominion grants.

Fairey, Sir Charles Richard (b. 1887), Brit. aircraft designer and yachtsman; President, Royal Aeronautical Soc. (1930–31; 1932–33), being awarded its Wakefield gold medal for wing flap invention; apptd. dir.-gen. of Brit. air commission at Washington, 1942, and knighted; "Fulmar" fighter, *50*; "Gyrodyne" helicopter, *1605*, 1606; "Seafox" seaplane, *51*.

Fairfax, Thomas, 3rd Baron (1612–71), Eng. Parliamentary general; under Cromwell, victor at Naseby; helped to quell the royalist insurrection of 1648 that attempted to restore Charles II to the throne.

Fair Head, headland (636 ft. high), on N. coast of Antrim, Northern Ireland.

Fairs and markets, 1256; British Industries, *1257*; Leipzig, 1920; Oxford, *1256*; Russia, 2846.

Fairy, 1333, 2057; in "Midsummer Night's Dream," *2169*.—Stories: "Peter Pan," 364; "The Blue Bird," 3465.

Fairy-fly, instinct of, 160.

Fairy ring, 1257, *1258*.

Fairy tales, compared with myths, 2270; Hans Andersen, 152; Grimm, 1549. See also **Fairy**.

Fakir (fa-kēr'), India, 411.

Falaise (fa-lāz'). Tn. N.W. France; birthplace of William the Conq., 3379; captured by Allies Aug. 1944.

Falange. The Spanish Fascist party led by General Franco since 1938.

Falcon (fawl'-kon), bird of prey, 1258.

Falconry or hawking, 1258, 1587.

Faliero (fah-lē-ār'-ō) or **Falier, Marino** (1279–1355), Doge of Venice (1354–55), conspired to make himself sovereign; executed; subject of dramas by Byron, Swinburne, etc.

Falkenhayn, Erich von (1861–1922), Ger. general; Prussian minister of war (1913); succeeded von Moltke (1914) as chief of general staff of Ger. army; failure at Verdun caused his retirement in favour of von Hindenburg; served remainder of 1st World War in Rumania and in Caucasus.

Falk'enhorst, Nikolaus von (b. 1885). Ger. soldier; in 1940 C.-in-C. occupation forces of Norway; in 1941 commanded on N. sector of Russ. front; after reverses relieved of command; sentenced to death by Brit. war crimes court, Brunswick, Aug. 1946, but reprieved and imprisoned for life.

Falkirk (fawl'-kerk), Scot. tn. in Stirlingshire, 17 m. E. of Glasgow; pop. 38,400; iron-founding, cattle market; near by, at Westerglen, is the B.B.C. Scottish Regional transmitter. Here Wallace was defeated in 1298 by Edward I, 2892, 3092, 3338. Second battle of Falkirk (1746), Highlanders under Prince Charles defeated English under Gen. Hawley.

Falk'land, Lucius Cary, 2nd Viscount (c. 1609–43), Eng. soldier and politician, he supported the Parliamentarians, but later sided with the Royalists, and was killed in battle at Newbury (1643); was a friend of Clarendon.

Falkland Islands, in S. Atlantic Ocean; Brit. colony, a. 4,618 sq. m.; pop. 2,500; **1259**, 3022; naval battle, in 1st World War, 1259, 3411.

Falkland Island Dependencies. Brit. groups of islands in S. Atlantic Ocean, with part of Antarctic continent; including S. Shetlands, S. Orkneys, S. Georgia, and Graham-

land; mostly covered with snow and ice, and almost without plant life; formerly whaling centres; F.I.D. Survey has reported minerals, esp. copper; 173.

Falla (fah-yah), **Manuel de** (1876–1946). Spanish composer; music in Sp. manner; "Pièces Espagnoles"; "Nights in Gardens of Spain"; music for ballets, "The Three-Cornered Hat," *347*, "Love the Magician."

Fallières (fahl-yār'), **Armand** (1841–1931), Fr. statesman, prime minister (1883), pres. of Fr. Republic (1906–13).

Falling bodies, law of, 1512, 2129; Galileo's experiment, 1414.

Fallopius, Gabriello (1523–1562), Italian anatomist, 151.

Fall River, Mass., U.S.A. City taking its name from the r. upon which it stands; greatest textile centre in Amer.; 50 m. S.S.W. of Boston; pop. 115,400.

Falmouth, spt. and winter resort in Cornwall at mouth of r. Fal; pop. 15,500; Pendennis and St. Mawes castles.

False acacia, a tree. Same as **Locust**.

Falstaff, Sir John, genial, dissolute "fat knight," boon companion of wild Prince Hal in Shakespeare's "Henry IV" and comic butt in the "Merry Wives of Windsor," 2933.

"**Falstaff,**" opera by Verdi, 2438, 3315.

Fal'ster, Danish isl. 30 m. long, renowned for its orchards; chief crops fruit and sugar beet; now connected to Zealand by Storström bridge, 991, *992*.

Family. In zoology and botany, a group formed of related genera and itself a subdivision of an Order.

Family and tribal life, 1259.

Family names, origin of, 2272.

Famine, in Hebrides, 1603; in India, 1701; Ireland, 1746, 2664.

Fan, 1259; mechanical, 1260; in rectifier, 2751.

"**Fan,**" sports or film, 1260.

Fang, snake's, 2746, 2991, 3325.

Fan'nich, Loch. L. in centre of Ross and Cromarty, Scot.; 6½ m. wide, 1 m. long; used under N. of Scot. hydro-electric scheme as reservoir for power stn. at Grudie Bridge, Strath Bran.

Fanning Island, one of a group of British coral islands in Pacific near Equator; cable station, 643.

Fantail: variety of pigeon; of windmill, 3386.

Fantin-Latour, Ignace Henri Jean Théodore (1836–1904); French artist famed for his paintings of flowers, in many ways influenced by the Impressionists; also a master of lithography, 1967.

Fan vaulting, in architecture, 220.

Farad, a measure of electrical capacity equivalent to a charge of one coulomb at a pressure of one volt; a microfarad (one millionth of a farad) is a more practical unit; 1133.

Faraday, Michael (1791–1867). Eng. chemist and physicist, 1260, 772, 1127, 1132, 1133, 2594; Davy's tribute, 980; influence on Tyndall, 3270; named "ions," 1738.

Far East, term applied to countries of E. Asia—China, Japan, Manchuria, Siam, Siberia, etc.

Far Eastern Region. Asiatic territory of U.S.S.R., Siberia; timber, minerals, fisheries; in Kamchatka region, agriculture and cattle breeding; area 900,731 sq. m.; stretches from Vladivostok (Pacific ocean) to Bering Straits; and N. to the Arctic Ocean; pop. 1,593,400; cap. Khabarovsk, pop. 199,364.

Farel, Guillaume (1489–1565), Fr. reformer and preacher in Switzerland; and Calvin, 664, *2759*.

Farewell, Francis George, Brit. sailor; took possession of "the port or harbour of Natal" in the name of Gt. Brit. in 1824; was murdered in 1829.

Farman, Henry (b. 1874), French aviator, son of an Englishman; devel-

oped biplane known by his name; with his brother Maurice supplied many aircraft to Allies in 1st World War.

Farmers of taxes, in anc. Rome, 2808

Farming, and agriculture, 78. See **Agriculture.**

Farms, average size in Denmark, 991; France, 1360.

Farne Islands, a group of 17 islets and rocks off the Northumbrian coast, opposite Bamburgh; the isls. have two lighthouses and the remains of a Benedictine priory; i was here that Grace Darling made her famous rescue in 1838; noted sea-bird haunt; 2391.

Farnese (fahr-nā'-zā), great It. family including one Pope, Paul III, a great general, Alessandro Farnese (1547–92), and the dukes and prince of Parma (1545–1731). The Farnese name is connected with several works of anc. art, formerly owned by the family; palace at Rome 2800.

Farnol, (John) Jeffery (b. 1878), Eng novelist, writer of popular adventure stories: ("The Broad Highway," "The Amateur Gentleman," "Black Bartlemy's Treasure," "Another Day").

Faroe Islands ("Sheep Islands"), group of Danish isls., between th Shetland Isls. and Iceland; 54 sq. m.; pop. 24,200; fishing, sheep raising, 991; in 1948 local autonom granted by Denmark.

Farouk (b. 1920), king of Egypt; succeeded his father, Fuad, i 1936; married Farida Zulfikar i 1938; divorced 1949; 1102.

Farquhar (fahr'-kwar), **George** (1678–1707), Eng. comic dramatist ("Th Beaux' Strategem"), 1040.

Farrar, Frederic William (1831–1903 Brit. divine; assistant master a Harrow and headmaster of Marlborough (1871–6); Canon of Westminster (1876–95); Dean of Canterbury (1895); ("Life of Christ, "Life of St. Paul"; "Eric, or Littl by Little," and other school stories

Farson, Negley (b. 1890). Ame. journalist; autobiography "The Way of a Transgressor"; als "Behind God's Back," "Bomber Moon."

Farthing, an Eng. coin; value ¼ of penny.

Faruk. See **Farouk**.

Fasces, of Roman lictors, *1261*.

Fascism, political movement originating in Italy, 1261, *1262*, 1770, 226 2804; in Europe, 1242, 3415. Se **Mosley.**

Fasho'da, tn. in Anglo-Eg. Sudan, o upper Nile; occupation by F in 1898 angered Brit.; adjustmen led to mutual support of the tw countries in African affairs; r named Kodok in 1904.

Fata Morgana, a mirage, 2190.

Fates, in Gk. myth., *1262*.

"**Father Brown.**" Character in dete tive stories, by G. K. Chesterto 781.

Father of Algebra. Diophantus.

Father of Angling. Izaak Walton.

Father of Church History. Eusebius o Caesarea.

Father of Comedy. Aristophanes.

Father of English Poetry. Chaucer.

Father of Epic Poetry. Homer.

Father of Geometry. Euclid.

"**Father of his Country.**" Washingto

Father of History. Herodotus.

Father of Italian Prose. Boccaccio.

"**Father of Lies.**" Satan.

Father of Medicine. Hippocrates.

Father of Music. Palestrina.

Father of the English Navy. Alfred th Great.

"**Father of the Faithful.**" Sultan Turkey.

Father of Tragedy. Aeschylus.

"**Father of Waters.**" The Mississipp

Fathers of the Church. Early Christia teachers and writers of the 2nd t 5th cents. who are accepted as hi authorities on the Church faith; among the chief of these were Ambrose, Bishop of Milan; Basil, the promoter of monastic life; Jerome, translator of the Scriptures; and Augustine, Bishop of Hippo.

Fathom. A nautical measure of length, (6 feet); see **Weights and Measures.**

Fathom'eter, instr. for measuring ocean depths, 2413.

Fatigue, of muscles, 2258.

Fatima (fa'-ti-ma) (c. 606–632). Favourite daughter of Mahomet, wife of Ali, and ancestress of the Fatimite caliphs, 2067; burial place, 962.

Fatimite dynasty. Arabian caliphs who ruled Eg., Syria, and N. Africa 908–1171; claimed descent from Fatima, 2067.

Fats and Oils, 1262; in butter substitutes, 628; from coal-tar, 857; digestion, 1017; essential oils, 2549; as food, 1263; hydrogen in, 1673; hydrogenation of, 1674; in lamps, 1887; in tanning leather, 1913; in margarine, 2100; mineral oils, 2426; nickel in hardening, 2366; olive oil, 2431; in paints, 2478; palm oil, 2485; in soaps, 2993. See **Oil; Petroleum.**

Fat-soluble vitamins, 3327.

Fat-tailed sheep, 2940.

Fatty acids. Organic acids derived from " open chain " hydrocarbons; combined with glycerine in fats and oils, 1263, 1478; in soap-making, 998, 2993.

Faucit, Helena (1820–98). Eng. actress; the foremost of her time; played with great success the parts of Lady Macbeth, Portia, Juliet, and Rosalind, besides many others.

Faulkner, William (b. 1897). Amer. novelist; " The Sound and the Fury," " The Unvanquished," " Go Down, Moses"; 2403.

Fault, in geology, causes earthquakes, 1070.

Faun. In Rom. myth., goat-like creature corresponding to Gk. satyr, 1018, 2485; of Praxiteles (" The Marble Faun "), 1537.

Fau'na. All the animals of a region or division of geologic time.

Faunus (faw'-nus). In Rom. myth., rural god identified with Gk. Pan.

Faure (fōr), **Félix** (1841–99). Fr. statesman, pres. of Fr. republic (1895–9).

Fauré, Gabriel U. (1845–1924). Fr. composer; " Requiem," songs, chamber music.

" Faust " (fowst). Dramatic poem by Goethe, 1264, 1478.

" Faust." Opera by Gounod, 1264, 2441.

Faustina (faws-tī'-na). Wife of Marcus Aurelius.

Faust legends, 1263.

Fawcett, Henry (1833–84). Blind Eng. statesman, reformer, economist, member of parl., and postmaster-general; inaugurated parcel post and postal savings bank and insurance.

Fawkes, Guy (1570–1606). Leader in Gunpowder Plot, 1264, 1794.

Fawn. Name applied to young of deer, 984.

Fayal (fī-ahl'). One of the Azores Isls. belonging to Portugal; 69 sq. m.; pop. 19,000; chief tn., Horta, has best anchorage in the Azores; following treaty of Portugal with Gt. Brit. 1943, the R.A.F. maintained a radar station near Horta; also R.N. base for warships engaged on escort and anti-submarine duties in 2nd World War.

Fayolle (fah-yol'), **Marie-Emile** (1852–1928). Fr. general, marshal of Fr.; commanded Fr. forces in Somme offensive July–Nov. 1916; commanded central group of armies (1917), northern group (1918).

Fayum (fī-oom') or **Fayoum.** Prov. of upper Eg. on w. side of Nile; 670 sq. m.; pop. (1937) 602,000; noted for fertility; cap. Faiyum (Medinet el Fayum), pop. 63,700; market for fruits, rice, cotton; 1097.

Fealty, oath of. In feudal system, 1269.

Feathers, 438, 441, 446, 447, **1264,** 1265; egret, 3098; how coloured, 447; in owls, 2460; paradise birds, 2511, frontis., Vol. 6; peacock, 2532, plate f. 2532; protective coloration, 2693.

Feather-wing beetles, 398.

Feb'ruary. Second month of calendar, 2223.

Fechner (fekh'-ner), **Gustav Theodor** (1801–87). Ger. philosopher and physicist, founder of modern psychology and psychophysics.

Federal Bureau of Investigation (F.B.I.), a U.S. police force, members called G-men, 2651.

Federal Union. Plan for the formation of a " United States of Europe " devised by C. K. Streit (U.S.).

Federated Malay States (F.M.S.); former Brit. protectorate, consisting of federation of native states absorbed in new Federation of Malaya in 1948. See **Malaya.**

Feelers, of animals. Same as **Antennae.**

Fegen, Capt. E. S. Fogarty, V.C. (d. Nov. 5, 1940). Brit. sailor; commanded Brit. armed merchant cruiser Jervis Bay; wounded in fight against Ger. pocket battleship, he chose to go down with his ship. See **Jervis Bay.**

Feisal I (fī'-sal) (1883–1933). Arab Emir, son of Husein, Arab king of Hejaz; leader in Arab revolt (1916) and commander of N. Arabian forces in 1st World War; represented Arabia at Peace Conference; crowned King of Iraq in 1921.

Feisal II (b. 1935). King of Iraq, succeeded father. Ghazi in 1939.

Feldberg. Highest point of Black Forest, 464.

Feldspar. Potassium aluminium silicate, **1265;** 2180; for porcelain, 2670.

Felidae (fē'-li-dē). The cat family, 720; includes cheetahs, 1927; lynxes, 2043; and other members of genus Felis.

Felis. The cat genus; includes domestic cats, 720; jaguars, 1791, 1792, plates f. 1792, 1793; leopards, panthers, ocelots, 1927; lions, 1959, 1961; pumas, 2702; tigers, 3211.

Fe'lix, Antonius. Rom. procurator of Judea (A.D. 52–60), before whom the apostle Paul, arrested in Jerusalem, was sent to be judged.

Fo'lixstowe. Seaside resort on coast of Suffolk, at mouth of r. Orwell; R.A.F. station and marine testing base; pop. 12,037; 3112.

" Felix the Cat." Film cartoon character who " kept on walking "; introduced by Sullivan in 1917.

Fellahin. Egyptian labourers, 1095.

Fellowship. Foundation entitling the holder, who is called a fellow, to participate in the revenues of a certain college, and also conferring a right to rooms in the college and certain other privileges as to meals, etc.; its annual pecuniary value varies; formerly a fellowship was tenable for life or until marriage, but nowadays in many cases there is a limit to the period.

Felt. A fabric, **1265;** how made, 850; 3405; hats, 1583, 1584.

Felucca (fe-luk'-ka). Sailing boat used on the Nile.

Fencing. A sport, **1266.**

Fénelon (fā-ne-lon), **François de Salignac de la Mothe** (1651–1715). Fr. churchman and author; Archbishop of Cambrai and tutor to Louis XIV's eldest grandson the Duke of Burgundy; wrote " Télémaque," famous didactic tale, children's classic.

Fenians (fē-ni-anz). Irish revolutionary society which flourished about 1861–72; sought to end Eng. rule in Ireland; failure in direct results, but instrumental in convincing Gladstone and others of the need of ending such incitements to disaffection as the Irish Established (Protestant) Church; name derived from the Fianna, legendary band of heroes surrounding Finn MacCool.

Fenn, George Manville (1831–1909). Eng. author of numerous stories of adventure for boys; sometimes wrote in collaboration with G. A. Henty.

Fennec. Several species of small, desert-dwelling, fox-like animals of the Old World, characterized by large pointed ears.

Fen'nel. Herb of parsley family; small yellow flowers; seeds used for seasoning in many countries; leaves are used for flavouring; sweet fennel yields aromatic essential oil.

Fen'rir or **Fenris the Wolf.** In Scandinavian myth., monster, child of the evil god Loki; kept chained by magic till Ragnarök (Judgement Day), when he is destined to break loose, spread his jaws to heaven and earth, and, breathing fire, devour Odin.

Fens, The. Marshy, low-lying districts in E. Eng., in Lincoln, Huntingdon, Cambridge, and Norfolk counties; mostly reclaimed, very fertile, 1165; floods, 1318; skating on, 2977.

Feodo'sia (formerly Kaffa, Gk. Theodosia), Rus. Busy port and resort of s.e. Crimea; pop. 44,000; dist. famous for grapes; makes carpets, rugs, soap.

Ferber, Edna (b. 1887). American authoress (" Show Boat " and " Dinner at Eight "), 2403, 3295.

Ferberite, an ore of tungsten, 3254.

Fer-de-lance (fār-de-lahns). A snake, 2991.

Ferdinand I (1503–64). Holy Roman emperor; succeeded his brother Charles V (1558); 1239, 1656.

Ferdinand II (1578–1637). Holy Roman emperor; succeeded in 1619; and Thirty Years' War, 1558, 3202.

Ferdinand III (1608–57). Holy Roman emperor, active in terminating Thirty Years' War; distinguished for intellectual attainments.

Fer'dinand I (1793–1875). Emperor of Austria; succeeded 1835; was intermittently insane; informal regency headed by Metternich, governing in his name, provoked rebellion which led to his abdication (1848), 1383.

Ferdinand I (1861–1948). King of Bulgaria (1887–1918); a Ger. princeling, elected prince of Bulgaria in 1886; assumed title of king or tsar 1908; abdicated in 1918.

Ferdinand I (d. 1065). " The Great," King of Castile and Leon, celebrated for victories over Mahomedans, 2659.

Ferdinand I (1423–94). King of Naples; able but tyrannical, cruel, and treacherous.

Ferdinand I (1865–1927). King of Rumania; succeeded his uncle Charles (1914), 2841.

Ferdinand. Kings of Spain. For list see **Spain:** History.

Ferdinand II (1452–1516) **of Aragon,** " the Catholic " (Ferdinand V of Spain); first ruler of united Spain and patron of Columbus; 878, 879, 1760, 3036; married Isabella of Castile, 1760; Inquisition under, 1726, 1760.

Ferdinand VII (1784–1833). King of Spain; succeeded on abdication of father, Charles IV, in 1808; deposed by Napoleon same year; restored in 1814; vicious, cruel, incompetent ruler under whom Spain lost Amer. colonies on mainland.

Ferdinand I (1751–1825). King of the Two Sicilies; succeeded 1759; stupid, cruel, cowardly; twice dethroned as king of Naples; restored by foreign aid.

Ferdinand II (1810–59). King of the Two Sicilies; succeeded in 1830; cruel, treacherous tyrant; earned nickname " King Bomba " by bombarding rebellious cities.

Ferghana (fer-gah'-na). A fertile valley in Uzbek Repub., U.S.S.R.; coal, lead, graphite, oil, raw cotton; largest city Khokand; cap. New Marghelan.

Fer′guson, Sir Samuel (1810–86). Irish poet and antiquary ; pres. of Irish Academy (1882) ; his poetry deals with Gaelic myths and traditions, 1751.

Fergusson, Robert (1750–74). Scots poet, 2895.

Fermanagh (fêr-man′-a). A co. of Northern Ireland ; 653 sq. m. ; pop. 54,600 ; **1266.**

Fermenta′tion, 1266 ; alcoholic, 103 ; bacteria, 337 ; cacao beans, 862 ; caused by yeasts, 3434 ; cream of tartar, 1500 ; Pasteur's discoveries, 2528 ; putrefaction, 1266 ; tea, 3160 ; tobacco, 3221 ; vinegar, 3324.

Fermi, Enrico (b. 1901), Ital. physicist who first, in 1934, "split" the uranium atom ; Nobel prizewinner in 1938, he settled in U.S.A. and helped produce the atomic bomb ; 298.

Fermoy, Eire. Garrison tn. in Co. Cork ; pop. 4,500 ; market for agricultural produce and flour.

Fernandez (fer-nahn′-deth), **Juan** (c. 1536–1602). Spanish explorer and navigator ; Juan Fernandez Islands, which he discovered, were named after him ; Robinson Crusoe islands, 937.

Fernando Po. Span. isl. in Bight of Biafra off w. coast of Africa ; a., including adjacent isls., 795 sq. m. ; pop. 26,400 ; mountainous ; timber, sugar, coffee, tobacco, cacao, cotton, indigo.

Ferns, 1266, *1267, 1268* ; botanical classification, 2620 ; bracken, 542, *543* ; fossilized, *434* ; reproduced by spores, *2918.*

Ferozepore (fê-rôz-poor′) or **Firozepore.** Town and dist. in W. Punjab, Dom. of Pakistan ; pop., town, 72,000 ; dist., 1,423,000 ; scene of operations of first Sikh War (1845) ; now grain trading city ; largest arsenal in Pakistan.

Ferranti, Sebastian Zianide (1864–1930), Eng. scientist ; invented an alternator and an elec. meter named after him, and founded the Ferranti elec. co. in 1892 ; F.R.S., 1927 ; 644, 1546.

Ferrara (fer-rah′-ra). Commercial city of N. Italy ; pop. 119,200 ; in Po valley 30 m. N.E. of Bologna ; medieval seat of famous house of Este ; 11th-cent. cathedral and massive campanile ; 14th to 15th-cent. school of painting.

Ferrari (fer-rah′-rē), **Gaudenzio** (1484–1546). It. painter, one of masters of Milan school ; work uneven, but excels in heads and draperies ; colours bright, harmonious ; his paintings usually intensely dramatic ("Holy Family with Saints" ; "Life of Christ" ; fresco of "The Crucifixion").

Ferrero (fer-rār′-ō), **Guglielmo** (1871–1942). It. historian, disciple and son-in-law of Lombroso ("Greatness and Decline of Rome" ; "Ancient Rome and Modern America") ; brilliant rather than scholarly.

Fer′ret. A domesticated breed of pole-cat, **1268.**

Ferricyanide. Compound of hydrogen, iron, cyanogen and another metal, e.g. potassium $(K_3Fe(CN)_6)$; 947 ; salts used in blue-prints and dyeing, 947.

Ferro-concrete. Another name for "reinforced concrete," 883.

Ferrocyanide. Compound of hydrogen, iron, cyanogen and another metal, e.g., potassium $(K_4Fe(CN)_6)$; used in dyeing, 947.

Ferrol or **El Ferrol.** Spt. and naval station of N.W. Spain ; pop. 30,500 ; shipping, shipbuilding, fishing.

Ferro-magnetism, possession of very strong magnetic properties, 2062.

Ferro-man′ganese. An alloy of iron and manganese, 2087.

Ferrous alloys, 123.

Ferrous sulphate. Green vitriol or copperas, 3116.

Ferrum (Fe). Latin and chemical term for iron. *See* **Iron.**

Ferry, Jules (1832–93). Fr. statesman, opponent of the empire ; premier (1880–81, 1883–85) ; promoted free, compulsory, non-clerical education.

Ferry. A passage by boat across river or other narrow body of water ; jet propelled, 1826 ; New York, 2353, *2355.*

Fertile Crescent. Semicircle of fertile land fringing the Arabian desert, stretching from Iraq to Egypt, 330, *1113.*

Fertiliza′tion. In biology, accomplished by pollination in flowering plants, 531, 1322 ; mosses, 2238. *See also* **Flowers ; Reproduction.**

Fer′tilizers. Chemicals essential for plant growth ; bone as, 499 ; gypsum, 1559 ; importance in soil, 2998 ; nitrogenous, *803,* 2868 ; crushed oyster shells, 2466 ; potassium, 2664.

Fescue grass, valuable sweet grass of meadows and pastures of cold and temperate zones ; genus *Festuca* of fam. *Gramineae* ; includes sheep's, meadow, and hard fescues ; 1509.

Festiniog or **Ffestiniog,** Wales. Vil. in Merionethshire ; slate quarries in the dist. ; pop. 9,072 ; 2146.

Festival of Britain. A cultural exhibition demonstrating Britain's achievements in science, industry and the arts, planned for 1951, with chief centre (area 27 acres) in London, on the s. bank of the Thames.

Festival of the Three Choirs. Yearly musical festival held in the cathedrals of Gloucester, Worcester, and Hereford in turn.

Festivals and Holidays, 1635.

Fetishism and magic, 2058. Worship of object as dwelling-place of a spirit, 70.

Fet′lar, Scot. One of the Shetland Isls.

Fetlock. Of horse, 1645.

Fettes (fet′-tez) **College.** Scot. public school in Edinburgh, opened in 1870.

Feuchtwanger (foikht′-vahng-er), **Lion** (b. 1884). German writer of novels and plays, born in Munich of Jewish family ; wrote novels of great dramatic force and rich historic background ("The Ugly Duchess" ; "Power" ; "Jew Süss"), 1457.

Feudal System, 1268, 1488 ; castles, 717 ; in England, 1488, 2059 ; France, 1365, 1393 ; Froissart's chronicles, 1399 ; Germany, 1449 ; Japan, 1795, 1799 ; knighthood, 1863 ; romances of, 2797 ; survivals in Channel Isls., 751.

Feuds or **vendettas.** In Albania, 100 ; in Corsica, *915.*

Fez. City and northern cap. of Morocco, 125 m. s. of Strait of Gibraltar ; pop. 144,400 ; caravan trade centre and distributing city for N. Africa ; independent from 13th to 16th cent. ; gave name to cap. ; *2231.*

Fez. Brimless red cap formerly worn by Turks and still worn in Egypt and other countries of N. Africa and the Near East, plate f. *1584* ; abolition in Turkey, 3266.

Fezzan. A division of former It. colony of Libya, N. Africa ; cap. Murzuk ; dates, camels, and horses ; 1931, 2861.

Fian′na Fáil (foil) (Soldiers of Destiny). Irish political party of Eamon de Valera, formed in 1926 ; held power 1932–Feb. 1948 ; abolished oath of loyalty to Brit. crown and post of gov.-gen. ; introduced 1937 constitution and name of Eire.

Fi′at money. Irredeemable paper money made legal tender by law ; examples are assignats, 1395.

Fibres. Hair, 1564 ; muscle, 2258 ; nerve, 546.

Fibres, industrial uses ; agave, 75 ; asbestos, 261 ; banana plant, 355 ; China grass, 1424 ; in cloth, 850 ; coir (from coconut), 864 ; cotton, 850, 917 ; esparto, 2497 ; eucalyptus, 1230 ; flax, 850, 1313 ; glass, 1474 ;

henequen, 2158 ; jute, 1844 ; Manila hemp, 2569 ; Mexican, 2157, 2158 ; in paper, 2497 ; in rope and twine, 2825 ; silk, 850, 2970 ; sisal, 76, 1609, 2158, 2975 ; wool, 850, 3405. *See* **Furs ; Hair ; Wool.**

Fibrin. In blood, 475.

Fibroin. Silk-worm's silk, 2970, 2972.

Fibrous roots, 2825.

Fichte (fikh′-te), **Johann Gottlieb** (1762–1814). Ger. idealistic philosopher who built on the foundation of Kant's teaching ; "Addresses to the German Nation" stimulated patriotic resistance to Napoleon.

Ficus (fī′-kus). A genus of trees including figs and the India-rubber tree, 1270.

Fiddle, or violin, 3324.

"Fido" (Fog Investigation Dispersal Operation). Wartime method of clearing aircraft runways of fog ; first used operationally on Nov. 19, 1943 ; use limited by enormous oil consumption.

Fief (fēf), in feudal system, 1269.

Field, Cyrus West (1819–92). Amer. financier ; projector and promoter of the first submarine transatlantic cable, 641, 643.

Field, Eugene (1850–95), Amer. poet and journalist, noted for his child poems.

Field cricket, 928.

Fieldfare. Largest Brit. bird of the thrush tribe ; a winter visitor, breeding in Scandinavia ; grey-blue on back, blackish tail ; birds form noisy flocks in winter, feeding on berries and leaving in April, *2171, 3206, 3205.*

Field glass, 3180.

Field gun, 257.

Fielding, Henry (1707–54). Eng. novelist, 1269, 2402.

Field-magnet. Part of dynamo, *1061* of electric motor, 1062.

Field-marshal, in Brit. army, *245.*

Field-mouse, 2249, plate f. *2249* ; rate of increase, 439.

Field of the Cloth of Gold, plain in N. Fr., near Calais, so called from display on occasion of meeting of Henry VIII and Francis I, 1612.

Fields, Gracie (b. 1898). Eng. actress a native of Lancashire, famous on stage, screen and radio as comedienne and singer ; created C.B.E. in 1938.

Fieldsmen, or fielders, in cricket, *928.*

Fiesole (fē-ā′-zo-lā). A tn. in It. ; pop 10,400 ; home of Fra Angelico anc. Faesulae, important Etruscan city.

Fife or **Fifeshire,** Scot., marit. co. in E. bordered S. by Firth of Forth a. 500 sq. m. ; pop. 286,600 ; **1269** *2891.*

Fife. Musical instrument, 3404.

Fife Ness, Scot. A low headland, at the easternmost point of Fife ; there is lightship at Carr Reef, 1 m. out to sea.

Fifth Avenue. Famous street of New York City, U.S.A., 2353.

Fifth Column. Phrase first used of the siege of Madrid, in the Sp. civil war, 1936–39, when Franco's four besieging columns outside the city were helped by sympathisers, i.e. "fifth column," inside the city since used of those inside a country who work in collusion with enemies outside.

Figaro (fē′-gah-rō). The daring, witty roguish barber in Beaumarchais "Barber of Seville" and "The Marriage of Figaro" ; a brilliant Parisian periodical is named after him.

"Figaro, Marriage of." Opera by Mozart, 2250, 2439.

"Fighting Téméraire." Picture by Turner, *1275.*

Figs, 1270 ; wild in Africa, plate f. 72.

Figure eight knot, *1870.*

Figure of speech, 1270.

Fig-wasp, *1270.*

Figwort ; plant of order *Scrophula iaceae* ; several species common Britain ; 4-sided stems, opposi leaves, brownish, lipped flowers.

IMPORTANT FOOD FISHES OF BRITISH SEAS

Name	Description	Habits	Remarks
Cod	Sea-fish with long barbel under chin. Back and sides greenish with brown spots. May weigh as much as 100 lb.	Will apparently eat anything; largely predaceous. Abounds in British seas during the spawning season in January.	Apart from herring, the world's most important food fish. Cod fisheries are an important industry in many countries.
Haddock	Resembles cod, with smaller mouth, dark spot behind head. Black lateral line. Average size, 3 to 4 lb.; largest, 20 lb.	Found on cod fishing-grounds in large schools, feeds on bottom of the sea and, unlike cod, chiefly eats molluscs and crustaceans.	A valuable food fish; will keep on ice longer than most varieties. " Finnan haddie " (Finland haddock) is smoked haddock.
Halibut	Member of the flat-fish family, with both eyes on right side. Dark above and whitish below. Average weight, 50 to 75 lb., but grows to an enormous size.	Has about same geographical range as cod, showing a preference for cold water. Feeds on crabs, molluscs, and on other fish.	Important as a food supply; halibut liver oil has recently largely replaced cod-liver oil in medicine. Food value greater than cod and less than mackerel.
Herring	Well formed sea-fish, thin scales, blue-green above, silvery-white below. Average length 12 in.	Great schools come into shallow water to spawn. Principal food, shell-fish.	Most important food fish in world; not used so extensively in America as in Europe.
Mackerel	A perfectly proportioned sea-fish, varying in length from 10 to 20 in., in weight from $\frac{1}{2}$ to 3 lb. Bluish or green with wavy black stripes on top, silvery beneath.	Travel near the surface of the sea in great schools, sometimes so large as to cover 10 square miles. They feed on small ocean fish.	Caught in nets and on line. Highly prized for food, especially fresh. Spanish mackerel (found in both North and South Atlantic) are not so abundant.
Plaice	Flat-fish, darkish-brown with red spots on upper surface, eyes on right side; never a large fish, usually 10 to 13 in. in length.	Like other flat-fish, feeds on bottom, when adult eating shell-fish; in summer lives offshore, in winter inshore and in estuaries.	Most important flat-fish of British seas, though many small plaice are destroyed as unmarketable.
Salmon	Large fish living in salt and fresh water; nearly 100 species. Brownish above with silvery sides, black dotted; flesh reddish-orange.	Ranges northward of Spain in Europe, and of New York in N. America. Spends much of life in salt water, enters freshwater streams to spawn.	Salmon are caught in nets as well as on rod and line in Britain; season strictly limited by law. Among the most valuable food fishes.
Smelt	Small fish related to the salmon, and silvery in colour.	Found in some English rivers, including the Medway, and on the east and west coasts of Great Britain.	Prized as food because of delicate flavour. When fresh they have a smell resembling cucumbers.
Sole	Small flat-fish, of oblong form, brown, blotched above, whitish below; eyes on right side. Several closely related species. Lemon sole belongs to plaice genus, as also does the dab.	In common with plaice and other flat-fish, likes a clean, sandy bottom, and is chiefly caught in inshore waters.	The true sole is often considered finest-flavoured of all sea-fish, and is correspondingly valuable as a fishery. Lemon soles and other similar fish are often substituted for it.
Trout	Fresh-water fish akin to the salmon; includes large range of species from sea-trout which run up rivers from sea, like salmon, to lake trout, and other types in small streams and rivers. Minute scales with red or dark mottlings.	Trout live in cold, clear streams or lakes with gravelly bottom. Powerful fish, they possess voracious appetites.	Popular as food and game fish, much sought by anglers. Season is strictly limited by law, and, as in the case of salmon, a licence is necessary to fish for trout.
Turbot	Large sea-fish of the flat-fish family; brown above, whitish below, sometimes reaching weight of 70 lb.	Ranges from the Mediterranean to the coast of Scandinavia. Feeds on crabs, sea-urchins, and fish eggs.	Highly esteemed as food; one of the best of flat-fishes.
Whiting	Small member of cod and haddock family, distinguished by lighter colour and black spot at base of pectoral fin.	Common in shallow and medium waters from North Sea to Mediterranean.	Popular food fish, and one of the cheapest to buy.

Fishguard, Wales. Spt. of Pembroke-shire in N. on Fishguard Bay; rly. terminus on route to Ire.; pop. 2,900; excellent harbour; fisheries; "Fishguard Invasion" of French (1797); 2539.

Fishing, 1309, *1311. See also in Index* **Fisheries**; and under names of fish.

Fishing-wheel. For catching salmon, 1300.

Fis'sion; in biology, *431, 432*; atomic, 296.

Fitton, Mary. Maid of honour to Queen Elizabeth; supposed by some to be the "dark lady" of Shakespeare's Sonnets.

FitzGerald, Edward (1809–83). Eng. poet, whose famous translation of the "Rubáiyát" of Omar Khayyám is an almost unique instance of successful "transplantation" of a foreign poem.

Fitzroy River. One of the chief rivers of Western Australia, navigable about 100 m.; flows into Indian Ocean; 3368.

Fitzsimons, Robert (1862–1917). Eng. boxer; world's middle-weight championship (1890); heavy-weight (1897).

Fiume (fē-ōō'-mā), Yugoslavia. Spt., formerly It., on Adriatic sea; ind. city state 1920–24; 8 sq. m.; pop. (1939) 53,900; *map, 320*; seized by D'Annunzio, 1770.

Five-Power Conference, on naval disarmament, 2296.

Fives. Court game, **1312**.

Five-Unit code, replacing Morse code in telegraphy, *3166*.

Five Year Plan. Scheme introduced by Stalin in 1929 for the complete reorganization of the economic system of Russia; was followed by second and third Plans, and by post-war Plan, 2850, 2852, 2854, 3072, 3073.

Five Year Plans, in Turkey, 3266.

Fixation of nitrogen, 2373.

Fixed oils, 1263.

Fixed stars, 3077.

Fizeau (fē-zō), **Armand H. L.** (1819–96). Fr. physicist; measures speed of light, 1939.

Fjord. Same as **Fiord**.

Flak. Ger. name for anti-aircraft gunfire, from initials of *Flieger-abwehr-kanone*.

Flag. An iris, 1748, *col. plate f. 1748*.

Flag Day. Day on which flags and other emblems are sold for charitable purposes; the forerunner of flag days was Alexandra Day in June, on which imitation wild roses were sold.

Flagella. Same as **Cilia**.

Flagella'ta. Class of unicellular animals with tail or "flagellum."

Flags, **1312**; of admirals, *28*; of British Commonwealth, *frontis.*, *Vol. 8*; Union Jack, 1312; U.S.A., 1312.

Flam'borough Head. A cape on coast of Yorkshire, 18 m. S.E. of Scarborough; has lighthouse visible for 21 m.; 3435.

Flame, 1280, 1673; acetylene, 18; natural gas, *1406*; oxy-hydrogen, 1673.

Flame-thrower, tank, 244.

Flamin'go, **1312**; *plate f. 1312, 1313*; foot, *1343*.

Flamin'ian Way (*Via Flaminia*). Road from anc. Rome to Ariminum (modern Rimini) constructed by censor Flaminius (220 B.C.), 2799.

Flamininus (flam-in-ĭ'-nus), **Titus Quinctius** (*c.* 230–*c.* 176 B.C.). Roman general, victor of Cynoscephalae (197 B.C.) and "liberator of the Greeks."

Flammarion (fla-ma-rē-awn), **Camille** (1842–1925). Fr. astronomer and writer of popular scientific books ("Marvels of the Atmosphere").

Flamsteed, John (1646–1719). Eng. astronomer; King's astronomer, 1675, at new Greenwich Observatory; began first catalogue of fixed stars.

Flanders. Dist. in N.W. Europe, **1313**, 403; cities, 181, 592, 594, 1460, 1947, 2032; medieval tapestry, 3153; medieval trade, 403, 592; painting, 2324; poppies, 2656.

Flanders, battles of (Ypres and Passchendaele Ridge), in 1st World War, 1313, *3412*, 3436; in 2nd World War, 1313.

Flandin (flahn-dan), **Pierre E.** (b. 1889). Fr. politician; prime min. 1934–35; foreign min. 1936; favoured *rapprochement* with Ger.; after Fr. capitulation was foreign min. in Vichy govt.; Oct. 1944 arrested and interned; at trial March 1945 all property sequestrated.

Flannel. A loosely woven woollen fabric, with soft surface.

Flare, a form of firework, 1291.

Flash-butt welding, 3363.

Flash-gun, photography by, *2588*.

Flat fish, 1298.

Flaubert (flō-bār), **Gustave** (1821–80). Fr. novelist and literary artist, whose extraordinarily perfect and polished style was the result of tireless labour—sometimes a week to a page; ("Madame Bovary," "Salammbo"); 1381, 2404.

Fla'vian Amphitheatre. The Roman Colosseum. *See* **Colosseum**.

Flax. Plant cultivated for fibre, **1313**; linen fabrics, 850, 1953; Ireland, 1747. The botanical family to which flax belongs is *Linaceae*.

Flaxman, John (1755–1826). Eng. sculptor and designer, often charming but obsessed by classicism, 2906.

Flea. A parasite, **1313**, *1313, 1314, 1732, 1733, 2513*.

Fleabane. A common name for plants of the genera *Pulicaria* and *Erigeron* of the family *Compositae*, having a peculiar aromatic odour; they are considered obnoxious to fleas.

Flecker, James Elroy (1884–1915). Eng. poet; lyrical beauty is found in many of his verses ("The Golden Journey to Samarkand" and an Oriental play "Hassan").

Fleet. Stream in London flowing into Thames, now large sewer; gave name to Fleet Street and Fleet Prison.

Fleet Air Arm. *See* **Naval Aviation**.

Fleet Street, London. Temple Bar to Ludgate Circus; famous for newspaper offices, 2348.

Fleming, Sir Alexander (b. 1881). Brit. doctor, **1314**; discovered penicillin, 2544.

Fleming, Sir John Ambrose (1849–1945). Eng. physicist and engineer; inventor of thermionic valve, 2099, 3198, 3391.

Flemings, in Belgium, 404.

Flemish language, 404, 1313.

Flemish painting, 2324, 2838.

Flensburg. Spt. and mfg. city of Ger. in Schleswig-Holstein; pop. 66,000. 992.

Fletcher, John (1579–1625). Eng. dramatist, collaborator with Francis Beaumont, 1040, 1211.

Fleur-de-lis (fiêr-de-lē'). A white iris, 1748.

Fleurus. A small tn. in Belgium; scene of 4 important battles in Sp. and Fr. wars.

Flight. Bat, 371, *2585*; bee, *392*; birds, 437; flying-fish, 1332; human, 44; Leonardo's studies of, 1927; mosquito, 2236; theory of, 2127, 2128. For flying-machines *see* **Aeroplane**; **Airship**; **Balloon**; **Glider**.

Flinders, Matthew (1774–1814). Brit. sailor; explored coasts of N.S.W. and Tasmania (1795–99) and N. Australia (1801–03), 3028.

Flinders, r. in Queensland, Australia, flowing into Gulf of Carpentaria.

Flint, Michigan, U.S.A. City on r. Flint; pop. 156,492; motor vehicles and parts; centre of grain trade.

Flint, William Russell (b. 1880). Brit. artist; water-colourist famous for his Span. scenes and illustrations to Kingley's "Heroes" and other classics.

Flint. A mineral, **1314**, *1315*.

Flint and steel. In making fire, 1278, *1279*.

Flint (or crystal) glass, 1474.

Flint implements, 3095, *2080*.

Flint-lock. Musket, 1281, *1282*.

Flintshire, Wales. Northern maritime co.; a. 256 sq. m.; pop. 113,000, **1315**.

Float. For bottom-fishing, 1309.

Floating bodies, law of, 211.

Floating-dock. Used sometimes in place of stationary dry-dock, and consisting of great pontoons of wood or steel, forming a bed for the ship, *1024, 3111*.

Flodden or **Flodden Field**. In Northumberland; battle (in 1513), 1315, 2391, 2892.

Floods, 1316; caused by deforestation, 1318, 3246; England, *1316, 1318*; Ganges, 1418; Hwang-ho, 1662; legends of the Great Flood, 332, 2374; Mississippi, 1316, 2192; Nile, *1101, 2371*; tidal, 1316, 1573.

Flood control, in engineering, *1317*; reforestation, 3246; levees, 1318, *2192*; Nile, *1102*.

Flood plain, in physiography, 1316.

Flora. Rom. goddess of flowers and spring identified with Gk. Chloris.

Flora. All the plants of a region or division of geological time. For flora of a particular region *see* region by name.

Florence. City of cent. It.; pop. 322,000, **1318**; Mrs. Browning, 589; chained library at, *1931*; Dante, 969; Ghiberti's doors, 1460, *2905*; Giotto's works, 1464; Medici, 2131; Palazzo Vecchio, *1776*; Pisa, 2612; Savonarola, 2876; in 2nd World War, 1319.

Flores (flōr'-es). Is. of Indonesia, E. of Java; 8,870 sq. m.; pop. 430,000, mostly Papuan savages; exports sandalwood, rubber; *map, 1074*.

Flores. Westernmost isl. of Azores; 57 sq. m.; pop. 9,000; 324.

Flor'ey, Sir Howard W. (b. 1898). Australian pathologist; with E. B. Chain purified penicillin extract, from the mould *Penicillium notatum*, of poisonous characteristics; Nobel prizewinner 1945; 2544.

Florian (flōr-ē-ahn'), **Jean Pierre Claris de** (1755–94). Fr. poet whose "Fables" are part of every Fr. school child's education.

Flor'ida. A gulf state of U.S.A.; 58,560 sq. m.; pop. 1,897,000; **1319**; alligators, 121; coral reefs, *2104*; Spanish colonization, 140, 1319; sponges from, *3068*.

Florin (from Latin *flos*, "flower"). Florentine gold coin, first used in 13th cent.; so named because of lily on the obverse; also modern Dutch coin; Eng. 2-shilling piece also called florin.

Flor'izel. In Shakespeare's "A Winter's Tale," prince of Bohemia, lover of Perdita, the daughter of the king of Sicilia, whom he weds as a shepherdess, 3389.

Floss silk. The outside of cocoons, 2972.

Flotow (flō'-tō), **Friedrich von** (1812–83). Ger. composer of light opera ("Martha," "Alessandro Stradella"); pleasing melodies and lively dramatic action.

Flotsam, jetsam, and lagan. Eng. legal terms; flotsam means shipwrecked goods which float; jetsam, goods thrown overboard and lost; lagan, goods which sink but are fastened to a buoy so that they may be recovered. Flotsam and jetsam often used figuratively to refer to human wrecks.

Flounder. A flatfish of which there are some 500 species; similar to the plaice but smaller, 1298.

Flour and flour-milling, **1320**; banana, 355; barley, 361; bread and baking, 554; corn, methods of milling, 1320; potato, 2664; rye flour, 2858; wheat, 1320, 3372; windmills, *3386*.

Flowers, **1321**, 531, 532, 2620; composite type, 1321; in Japan, 1795. *colour plates 1802, 1803*; life story, 1322; Nature study, 2283; perfumes, 2549, 2827; pollen carried by insects, 391, *531*, 852, 1270, 1321, 1733, 2447. *See* the various flowers by name.

Flowers of sulphur, 3116.

Flue, of open fire, 1597 ; gases, 2986 ; thallium from dust, 3193.

Fluid flywheel. In motor-car design, 1667.

Fluid theory of electricity, 1128.

Fluores'cence and Phosphorescence, 2573 ; fluorescent screen in electron microscope, 2165 ; lighting, *1134*, 1135, 1136.

Flu'orine (F). Gaseous element of the halogen group, 816, 1567 ; used as an intense oxidising agent ; atomic weight, 19 ; has been liquefied and boils at − 300° F. ; properties, 776.

Flu'oroscope, 3431.

Flu'orspar or **fluorite.** A calcium fluoride ; a source of hydrofluoric acid, and used as a flux in smelting, 1567, 2573.

Flushing (Dutch **Vlissingen**). Fortified port in s.w. Netherlands on isl. of Walcheren ; pop. 22,500 ; formerly important naval station ; shipbuilding, iron and steel works ; its guns command mouth of r. Scheldt ; port completely destroyed in 2nd World War ; liberated Nov. 1944 ; rly. connexion with N. Netherlands restored autumn 1946.

Flute. A musical instrument, 2267, 4301 ; in orchestra, 2445.

Flux. A substance which promotes the fusing of metals ; limestone, 1950.

Flux'ions. Newton's name for calculus, 2349.

Fly. An insect, **1329**, 1732, 1733 ; dragon-fly, 1034, *1035* ; eggs, *1094* ; eye, *1253* ; fossilized in amber, *138* ; ichneumon, 1685 ; Spanish, 400.

Fly agaric. A poisonous toadstool, *plate f. 1408.*

Fly-catcher. Insectivorous birds of the family, in Britain, *Muscicapidae.* British species are the pied and spotted fly-catchers. American " fly-catchers " belong to the family *Tyrannidae,* **1330,** *2289.*

Fly fishing, 1309.

Flying boat. Sea-going aircraft with boat-like hull, *40, 51.*

Flying-bomb, 1330, *1331,* 3422 ; Spitfire attacking, *1332* ; on Antwerp, 182 ; jet-propelled, 1827.

Flying buttress. In architecture, 218.

Flying dragon. A Malayan lizard, 1973.

Flying Dutchman. A legendary Dutch sea-captain, doomed for a rash oath or as punishment for crime to sail round the Cape of Good Hope till Judgement Day ; subject of opera by Wagner.

Flying Fish, 1297, **1332.**

Flying-fox. Species of Malayan bat. *See* Bat.

Flying machine. *See* **Aeroplane ; Airship ; Balloon.**

Flying Scotsman, B.R. train, *2737.*

Flying-squirrel, 3071.

Fly River, of Papua, Brit. New Guinea ; rises near w. border and flows s.e., entering Gulf of Papua by a delta, 2339.

Flywheel. A heavy wheel mounted on a shaft that receives its turning impulses intermittently ; by virtue of its weight it resists sudden changes of velocity and stores up energy, thus ensuring uniform motion ; of gas engine, 1421 ; of steam-engine, *3086* ; of petrol engine, *2242* ; of sewing machine, *2929* ; " fluid flywheel," 1667.

Foal. Young of horse, *1645, 1646.*

Foam, in fire fighting, 1286.

Fo'cal length, in optical instruments, 1924, 3178.

Focal plane, of camera, 1925 ; found by focusing, *2578, 2579.*

Foch, Ferdinand (1851–1929). Fr. general and marshal of Fr., commander-in-chief of Allied armies in 1st World War, **1332** ; assumes command, 3412.

Fo'cus, from Lat. *focus,* a hearth ; in optics, 1924 ; camera lens, 1925, 2578 ; of eye, 1252, *1254* ; in telescopes, 3178, *3180.*

Fod'der. Coarse feed such as hay, vegetables, given to live-stock. *See* **Forage crops.**

Fog, 851, **1333** ; smoke a cause, 2987 ; radar guides through, 2727.

Fogazzaro (fō-gat-tsah'-rō), **Antonio** (1842–1911). It. novelist and poet ; his prose works depicted the life and thoughts of the It. people (" Miranda," " Leila," " Daniele Cortis ").

Foggia (foj'-ah). City in s. It. ; pop. 62,300 ; market for agric. produce of great Apulian plain ; Frederick II often a resident.

Fog signals, 1333.

Foil. A light sword used in fencing, *1266.*

Foix (fwah), **Gaston de,** duke of Nemours (1489–1512). Fr. general, 2748.

Fokker, Anthony H. G. (1890–1939), Dutch aeroplane designer ; inventor of Fokker machines used by Germans in 1st World War, and of outstanding aircraft since that time.

Fokine (fō-kēn'), **Mikhail** (1880–1942). Russ. dancer and choreographer ; created for Diaghilev the ballets " Les Sylphides," " Scheherazade," " Petrouchka," and other masterpieces, 347.

Folio, in book production, 512.

Folk-dances, *1334* ; in England, *966, 967* ; Red Indian, 2756 ; Spanish, *3037.*

Folkestone. Spt. and fashionable watering place in Kent, s.e. Eng. ; pop. est. 30,060 ; fishing and shipping trade. Leas, 1852 ; bombed and shelled 1940–44.

Folklore, 1333 ; cave superstitions, 734 ; Celtic, 740 ; dragon in, 1033 ; Faust legends, 1263 ; Grimm brothers' work, 1333, 1549 ; of India, 1713 ; legendary origin of fire, 1278 ; literature for children, 1964 ; magic, 2057 ; Mother Goose, 2239 ; nursery rhymes, 3501 ; in the Old Testament, Frazer's work, 1387 ; Scandinavian, 2880 ; willow pattern, 3382. *See* **Mythology ; Superstitions.**

Folk-songs, 1333, 1456, 2262.

Folk-tales, 1333 ; " Adventures of Robin Hood," 3469 ; " Song of the Nibelungs," 2363 ; " Siegfried," 2969. For other folk-tales, *see* **Stories.**

Follicle, of hair, 1565.

Fo'malhaut. A star in the constellation Southern Fish, *3078, 3079.*

Fonck, René (b. 1896). Fr. airman. During 1st World War brought down 75 enemy planes.

Fonseca, Gulf or **Bay of,** inlet of the Pacific bordering on San Salvador, Honduras, and Nicaragua ; 40 m. long.

Font (type), *see* **Fount.**

Fontaine, Jean de la. *See* **La Fontaine.**

Fontainebleau (fon-tăn-blō'). Forest-girdled tn. and resort of N. Fr., 35 m. s.e. of Paris, on Seine ; pop. 15,000 ; magnificent royal palace ; revocation of Edict of Nantes (1685) ; abdication of Napoleon (1814) ; Barbizon, on N.W. edge of forest, made famous by painters ; 499, 2176, 2476.

Font de Gaume (fon-de-gōm'). Palaeo-lithic cave in Dordogne, France ; paintings from, *plate f. 2084.*

Fontenoy (font-nwah'). Vil. in w. Belgium, 45 m. s.w. of Brussels ; Fr. defeated Allies (1745) in War of the Austrian Succession.

Fonteyn', Margot (b. 1919). Brit. prima ballerina of Vic-Wells ballet.

Foochow', China. Spt. on r. Min, opposite isl. of Formosa ; pop. 323,000 ; **1335.**

Food, 1336 ; canning industry, 692 ; carbohydrates, 1338, *1339* ; carbon the basis of, 699, 2621 ; cold storage and refrigeration, 1391 ; cooking, 900 ; a balanced dietary, 1340 ; digestion of, 1016 ; fats and oils, 1263, 1338, *1339* ; minerals, 1338, *1339* ; phosphorus compounds, 2574 ; plants the ultimate source of, 2621 ; preservation, 1340 ; proteins, *1339,* 2693 ; refrigeration, 1391 ; rules for eating, 1675 ; taste as guide to diet, 3158 ; vitamins, 1340, 3326.

Food and Agriculture Organization (F.A.O.). Body of the U.N., founded Oct. 1945, with 42 nations participating ; to collect information on food supplies, help fair distribution, advise on crops and methods of agriculture.

Food and Drugs Act, and bread, 557.

Food Preservation, 1340 ; canning, 692 ; freezing and refrigeration, 1391 ; jam, 1792 ; pasteurization, 956, 2528 ; resins lining tins, 2768.

Food Values, 1263, 1336, 2693 ; apples, 191, 1339 ; bananas, 355 ; barley, 361, 745 ; beans, 380 ; bread, 554, 1339 ; bread-fruit, 557 ; butter, 628, 1339 ; cereals, 745 ; cheese, 765 ; cocoa and chocolate, 861 ; coconut, 862, 864 ; currants, 944 ; eggs, 1095, 1339 ; fishes, 1300, *1306, 1307,* 1339 ; flour, 1320 ; fruits, 1402 ; grape-fruit, 1499 ; margarine, 2100 ; meat, 1338, *1339,* 2125 ; milk, 955, 2173, *2174* ; nuts, 2407, *2408* ; oats, 745, *1339,* 2410 ; olives and olive oil, 1338, 2431 ; oysters, 2468 ; peas, 2530 ; plantains, 354 ; potato, 2664 ; prunes, 2695 ; rice, 745, 2774 ; rye, 2858 ; salt, 2865 ; spices and condiments, 3060 ; sugar, 3112 ; tapioca, 3153.

Foolscap. Sheet of paper usually 17 in. by 13½ in. in size.

Fool's gold, or iron pyrites, 1753.

Foot (anatomy), **1342,** *1343* ; bear, 382 ; birds, *448* ; camel, 669 ; cat, 718 ; duck, 1051 ; fly, *1329* ; horse, 1645 ; hygiene, *1677* ; insects, *1727* ; monkeys, 2207 ; snail, 2989 ; spider, *plate f. 3065* ; starfish, 3083 ; walrus, 3339.

Foot. A division of a verse, 2635.

Foot. A unit of measure, 1342 ; *see* **Weights and Measures.**

Foot, Isaac (b. 1880). Sec. of Mines, 1931–32 ; pres. of Lib. party, 1947 ; his son Dingle (b. 1905), was parl. sec. to Min. of Economic Warfare, 1940–44 ; another son Michael (b. 1913), was Lab. M.P. for Devonport, 1945 ; editor of Evening Standard, 1942 ; of Tribune, 1948.

Foot and mouth disease. An infectious disease to which cattle and pigs are especially subject ; characterized by fever, with ulcers about the mouth and feet ; epidemics in Britain have resulted in great losses of livestock.

Football. Britain's national winter sports, **1344** ; Association, 1344, *1345* ; Rugby, 1345, *1346.* See also **Rugby Football.**

Football Association. Governing body of one code of Eng. football, 1344. *See also* **Cup Final.**

Football League. Principal competition for the first-class professional " Soccer " clubs, 1344.

Football Pools. *See* **Pools.**

Foot-binding in China, 807, *809.*

Foote, Samuel (1720–77). Noted actor and dramatist ; played both tragedy and comedy parts and wrote many plays, among them "The Mayor of Garratt."

"Footlight," for mounted police, *2648.*

Foot-pound. A unit used in physics ; the work done in raising one pound one foot.

Forage crops. Crops fed to livestock ; agave, 75 ; beans, 380 ; beets, 396, *397* ; clover, 852 ; hay, 1509 ; lucerne, 2034 ; mangel-wurzels, 397 ; millet, 2175 ; oats, 2410 ; peas, 2530 ; potatoes, 2664 ; soya bean, 3029.

Forain, Jean Louis (1852–1931). Fr. artist and caricaturist ; best known for his satirical black-and-white drawings in Paris journals.

Foraker, Mt., Alaska, *2380.*

Foraminif'era. An order of single-celled water-dwelling animals with limy outer coats, 2695 ; bodies make chalk, 749 ; limestone, 1950.

Forbes, Joan Rosita (b. 1893). Eng. explorer and author ; travelled extensively in China, N. Africa, and other parts (" The Secret of the Sahara-Kufara " ; " Quest "), 2861.

Forbes, Stanhope Alexander (1857–1947), R.A., Eng. artist. Known as painter of village life and similar genre in academic style.

Forbes-Robertson, Sir Johnston (1853–1937). Eng. actor ; first appeared with Irving and Mrs. Patrick Campbell ; later as star in own company in " Hamlet," and other Shakespeare plays, "The Light that Failed," " The Passing of the Third Floor Back " ; his daughter Jean (b. 1905) appeared in " Berkeley Square," " Peter Pan," etc.

" Forbidden City," Lhasa, 3208 ; Peking (Peiping), 2537.

Force ; centrifugal, 744 ; in physics, 2700.

Force pump, 2703.

Forces, Parallelogram of, 9197.

Forchheim, Ger. Historic tn. in Bavaria, 15 m. S.E. of Bamberg ; residence of Carolingians, including Charlemagne.

Ford, Edsel Bryant (1893–1943). Son of Henry Ford, 1347.

Ford, Edward Onslow (1852–1901). Eng. sculptor ; R.A. in 1885 ; among his finest work is the Queen Victoria Memorial at Manchester.

Ford, Henry (1863–1947). Amer. motor-car manufacturer ; **1346**, *1347* ; and the motor-car, 2241.

Ford, Henry (b. 1918). Grandson of the above, 1347.

Ford, John (1586–c.1639). Eng. dramatic poet ; work characterized by dramatic beauty and intensity of passion : " The Broken Heart," most enjoyable of his plays because, unlike most of them, there is nothing revolting in the central idea of the tragedy ; 1040.

Ford motor works (Eng.), at Dagenham, *1347*.

Foreign exchange. Relative value of legal tender money of two countries. **1347**, 1482 ; devaluation, 1349.

Foreign Legion, of France, 118, 1919.

Foreign Office. Brit. Govt. dept. in Downing Street, London, which attends to State affairs connected with foreign countries ; headed by Secretary of State and Under Sec. ; separate dept. since 1782.

Forel, August (1848–1931). Swiss psychologist, **1349**.

Foreshortening, in drawing, 1046.

Forest cantons, of Switzerland, 3140.

Forestry. The work of developing and maintaining forests, 1350 ; Canadian forest reserves, 678 ; control of lumbering, 1350 ; diploma in, 1351 ; fighting fires, *1350*.

Forestry Commission, Brit. govt. dept.; work of the, 1351.

Forests, 1349 ; conservation movement, 678, 1351 ; effects of deforestation, 1237 ; fires, *1350* ; improve soil, 3246 ; prevent floods and drought, 1318 ; *see also* Lumbering ; Timber, *also* names of countries and states.

Forfarshire, Scot. Now Angus.

Forget-me-not (Myosotis), flower, 1351, *1352*.

" Forked " lightning, *1946*.

Forks and knives, 1867.

Formal'dehyde. A gas, composed of carbon, hydrogen and oxygen, which will dissolve in alcohol or water ; used in making plastic materials, 2625 ; in resin mfr., 2768.

For'malin. A 30 or 40 per cent. solution of formaldehyde ; preserves rubber latex, 2834.

Forme, in printing, 512, 2346, 2686.

Formentera. Span. isl. in the Mediterranean, one of the Balearic group ; a. 38 sq. m. ; 342.

For'mic acid. Colourless pungent liquid ; in ant sting, 165 ; in nettles, 2335.

Formicary. Ants' nest, *168*.

Formosa. Isl. off E. China ; nearly 14,000 sq. m. ; pop. 6,500,000 ; **1352**; *map, 808* ; twice acquired by Japan ; camphor, 674 ; tea, 3160.

Forms of address. *See* Address, forms of.

For'mula, in chemistry, an expression denoting by means of letters and numbers, the number and arrangement of the atoms in a compound ; in mathematics, an expression of a general rule or principle in algebraic symbols.

Forrest, John, Baron (1847–1918). Australian surveyor, explorer, and statesman ; first premier and treasurer of W. Australia (1890–1901) ; pres. Australian Federal Council (1897) ; introduced free homestead system ; established Agricultural Land Bank ; first Australian to receive peerage.

Forster, Edward Morgan (b. 1879). British author (" A Passage to India," 1925) ; and English literature, 1216.

Forster, John (1812–70). Eng. biographer, essayist and historian of the mid-Victorian period ; his lives of Dickens and Goldsmith are among his best-known works.

Forster, William Edward (1818–86). Eng. Liberal statesman, member of House of Commons 1861 to his death ; active in educational interests ; secretary for Ireland in Gladstone's cabinet (1880–82) covering time of Phoenix Park murders ; Education Act (1870) ; 2884.

" Forsyte Saga, The." Series of novels by John Galsworthy, beginning with " The Man of Property," dealing with bygone middle-class life in England, 1215, 1415.

Fort Dearborn, U.S.A. Fort built in 1804 on site of Chicago, 783.

Fort de France. Cap. of Martinique ; pop. 52,000 ; port on w. coast ; 2112.

Fort Duquesne (dū-kān'). Fr. colonial fort in Pennsylvania, U.S.A., on site of present city of Pittsburgh, 2924, 2925.

Fortescue, Hon. Sir John (1859–1933). Eng. historian ; his monumental work, " The History of the British Army," in 13 vols., occupied him for 30 years ; librarian at Windsor Castle (1905–26).

Fort Frontenac (fron-te-nahk'). Fr. colonial fort on site of Kingston, Ontario.

Fort Garry, Canada. Now Winnipeg, 3388.

Forth. Scot. r. formed by two head streams rising near Ben Lomond ; it flows 53 m. to the head of the Firth of Forth.

Forth, Firth of, Scot. Estuary (50 m. long) of Forth r. on E. coast ; *map, plate f. 584* ; bridges, 567 ; construction, 654.

Fortifications, 717, 1688, 3034.

Fort Lamy (lah-mē), cap. of Chad territory, Fr. Equatorial Africa, at s. edge of Sahara ; pop. 6,000 ; from here Gen. Leclerc (q.v. in f-i.) marched to join 8th Army in Libya in Jan. 1943, 2861.

Fort Sum'ter, in Charleston harbour, South Carolina, U.S.A. ; scene of first engagement of American Civil War.

Fortu'na, in Rom. myth., goddess of fortune, **1352**.

Fortunate Isles, possibly the Canaries, 690.

Fortunatus (for-tū-nā'-tus). Hero of European folk-tale, possessor of proverbial inexhaustible " Fortunatus purse " and wishing-cap which would transport him wherever he desired to go.

Fortuny, Mariano (1838–74). Great Span. painter and etcher, dazzling colourist, dominant influence in Span. art until rise of Impressionism.

Fort Wayne, Indiana, U.S.A. Railway and trading centre in N.E. on Maumee r. ; pop. 118,400 ; steam-engines, trucks, machinery ; site of fort built by Gen. Anthony Wayne (1794).

Fort William. Brit. post in India founded 1696 to protect traders ; nucleus of Calcutta, 660.

Fort William, Ontario. Shipping centre at head of L. Superior ; pop. 26,200 ; products include flour and iron ware.

" Forty Immortals." Members of Fr. Academy, 16.

For'um. Open space in centre of a Rom. city used as market-place, for political assembly, amusements ; at Rome, *2801*.

Forward, in football, 1344, 1346.

Foscari (fos'-kah-rē), Francesco (1373–1457). Doge of Venice (1423–57) ; made war against Milan ; with son Jacopo forms subject of Byron's tragedy " The Two Foscari."

Fosse-way. Ancient Roman military road running from Lincoln to Exeter, 2783.

Fossil gums and resins, *138*, 1558.

Fossils. Organic bodies preserved in the strata of the earth's crust, **1353**, 1432, 2795 ; archaeopteryx, 437 ; evidence for theory of evolution, 1244 ; horse, 1645 ; insects in amber, *138* ; marine, 1432 ; prehistoric animals, *2678*.

Foster, Stephen Collins (1826–64). Amer. song-writer ; most famous works are " The Old Folks at Home," " Massa's in De Cold, Cold Ground," and " My Old Kentucky Home."

Foucault pendulum. A pendulum with a heavy bob hung on a long wire ; its direction of swing appears always to deviate to the right (N. hemisphere), thus showing that the earth is rotating ; first constructed by Leon Foucault (1819–68) ; 1561.

Fouché (fōō'-shā), Joseph (1759–1820), Duke of Otranto. Fr. politician, Chief of Police under Napoleon and Minister of Police under Louis XVIII ; with extreme severity he quelled the revolt in Lyons.

" Fougasse," pseudonym of Cyril Kenneth Bird (b. 1887), Brit. humorous artist. Art editor, and from 1949 editor, of " Punch." Published " Drawn at a Venture " (1922) ; " You Have Been Warned " (1935).

Foundling Hospital. Charitable foundation to rescue deserted children ; founded by Thomas Coram in 1741 in Hatton Gdn. ; in 1745 moved to Guilford str., Bloomsbury ; in 1935 to Berkhamsted ; in 1918 became a mixed county Modern Secondary School with 160 boarders.

Foundry. Establishment where metal is cast ; 1752.

Fount (type), 3270.

Fountain pen, 2541.

Fountains Abbey. Ruin in the W. Riding of Yorkshire, 3 m. S.W. of Ripon, largest and finest in Eng., the abbey was founded in 1132 ; *3435*.

Fouqué (fōō'-kā), Friedrich de la Motte, Baron (1777–1843), Ger. romantic poet and novelist, 1456, 2404.

Fouquet (fōō'-kā), Jehan (c. 1416–c. 1480). A skilful French miniature painter to the court of Louis XI, founder of a new school and famed for his illuminated " History of the Jews," and " The Book of Hours," 1377.

Fouquet, Nicolas (1615–80). Superintendent of finance, and procureur-général under Louis XIV ; patron of arts ; amassed great fortune and power ; put in prison for life.

Fouquier-Tinville (foo-kyā tan-vēl), Antoine Quentin (1747–95). Fr. revolutionist ; public prosecutor during Reign of Terror ; guillotined.

Fourah Bay College. Coll. of Sierra Leone, Africa, nr. Freetown ; pioneer of university education in W. Africa, founded 1828 ; affiliated with Durham Univ., 1876 ; has a university dept., a teacher training dept., and a technical vocational training dept. ; 73.

Fourdrin'ier machine for making paper, *2499*, 2500.

Four-eyed fish. A mud skipper, 2250.

Fourier (fōō'-ryā), François Charles Marie (1772–1837). Fr. Socialist and political economist ; originator of the co-operative community plan known as " Fourierism," tried unsuccessfully at Brook Farm and elsewhere ; 904, 2996.

Franche-Comté (frahnsh kon-tā'), old prov. in E. Fr., in Rhône basin, now depts. of Doubs, Haute-Saône, Jura, and part of Ain; conquered by Louis XIV in 1668.

Franchise, constitutional or political right of voting; Britain, 1489; reformed in England, 2522, 3280, 3330. See **Elections**.

Francia (frahn'-cha) (c. 1450–1517) (real name Francesco Raibolini), It. painter, chief master of the Bolognese school; though deficient in composition, his pictures charm by their peaceable lyric sentiment and lovely landscapes.

Francia, José Gaspar Rodriguez da (1757–1840), dictator of Paraguay (1813–40), austere, gloomy, ruthless despot, whose very name Paraguayans dared not pronounce.

Francis I (1708–65). Holy Roman emperor.

Francis II (1768–1835), Holy Roman emperor; resigns title, 1449.

Francis I (1494–1547), King of France, 1383; and Henry VIII, 1612; sent colonizing expedition to Canada under Cartier, 68.

Francis II (1544–60), France; married Mary Queen of Scots, 2116.

Francis de Sales (sahl), St. (1567–1622), Fr. churchman, Bishop of Geneva; his book, "Introduction to the Devout Life," has been translated into almost every modern language, and is probably more widely read than any devotional work except the "Imitation of Christ."

Francis Ferdinand (1863–1914), Archduke of Austria; assassination, 1383, 3409.

Francis Joseph I (1830–1916), Emperor of Austria and King of Hungary, 319, 1383.

Francis of Assisi (as-sē'-zē), St. (c.1182–1226), founder of Franciscan Order, 1383, 1384.

Francis, Sir Philip (1740–1818), Eng. politician, reputed author of the "Letters of Junius"; hostility to Hastings, 1582.

"Francis Smith," screw-driven ship, 2903.

Francis Wheel, a type of reaction turbine, 1670, 1671.

Franciscan Nuns, or Poor Clares, 1384.

Franciscans, Order of, also called Minorites, Rom. Cath. religious order founded by St. Francis of Assisi, 1383, 2214.

Franck, César (1822–90), Fr. (Belgianborn) composer; work as an organist influenced all his music; Symphonic Variations for piano and orchestra; symphony; and "Les Béatitudes," an oratorio.

Franco, Francisco (b. 1892), Sp. general, leader of insurgents in Spanish Civil War and dictator of Spain, 1384, 3416.

Franco'nia ("land of the Franks"). Medieval Ger. duchy chiefly E. of Rhine, in valley of Main; 1445.

Franco-Prussian War (1870–71), 1366, 1384; S. Ger. states join Prussia, 1449; siege of Metz and Napoleon III, 2155.

Frank, Hans (1900–46), Ger. Nazi leader, gov.-gen. of Poland 1939–45, where he ordered massacre of Poles and Jews; hanged at Nuremberg as war criminal, 2282.

Frank, Karl H. (1898–1946). Ger. politician; dep. Gauleiter for Sudetenland in 1938; state sec. for Ger. protectorate Bohemia-Moravia in 1939; responsible for Lidice massacre, June 1942; captured by Allies May 1945; tried by Czechs; hanged May 22, 1946.

Frank'enstein, student in Mary Shelley's novel "Frankenstein," who fashions a soulless man monster, repulsive yet yearning for sympathy, pursuing its creator from one land to another and complaining of its loneliness. Boris Karloff portrayed the monster in a film of same name in 1932.

Frankfort or **Frankfurt-am-Main**, Ger., in s. on r. Main; pop. (1935) 556,000, 1385, 1386, 1449; in 2nd World War much bombed, captured March 29, 1945; became h.-q. of U.S. zone of Ger., and in 1947 admin. centre of joint Anglo-U.S. zone, 1386.

Frankfort,Treaty of, terminating Franco-Prussian War (1871), 1385.

Frankfort-on-Oder, Poland. Former Ger. trade centre 50 m. s.E. of Berlin; pop. 75,000; on r. Oder and connected by canal with Elbe and Vistula; important mfrs. and rly. shops; captured by Russians Feb. 1945, 1385. Came under Polish control and admin. after 1945; name changed to Slubice.

Frankland, Sir Edward (1825–99), Eng. chemist and physicist, formulator of the doctrine of chemical valency and discoverer (with Lockyer) of helium.

Franklin, Benjamin (1706–90). Amer. scientist, statesman and diplomat, 1386; invented duplex lamp burner, 1888; described shock from Leyden jar, 1929; lightning experiments, 1945; "fluid" theory of electricity, 1128; invented closed stove, 1597.

Franklin, Sir John (1786–1847). Brit. admiral and Arctic explorer, discoverer of North-West Passage, 682, 1387, 2644.

Franks, Sir Oliver S. (b. 1905). Brit. diplomatist and philosopher; prof. of Moral philosophy, Glasgow Univ., 1937–45; provost of Queen's Coll., Oxford, 1946; perm. sec. Min. of Supply, 1945–46; in 1947 Brit. representative at Marshall Plan Talks in Paris and Washington; in 1948 Brit. ambass. to U.S.A.

Franks, group of tribes in Europe in 3rd cent.; overrun Gaul, 1237, 1365; united by Clovis, 854; repel barbarian invaders, 1488; defeat Mahomedans at Tours, 759.

Franz Josef, Emperor. See **Francis Joseph**.

Franz Josef Glacier, New Zealand, 1468.

Franz Josef Land. See **Fridtjof Nansen Land**.

Fra'ser River, Canada, chief r. of Brit. Columbia; two forks unite nr. Fort George, flowing s. 785 m. into Strait of Georgia; gold deposits.

Fraser of North Cape, Bruce Austin Fraser, Baron (b. 1888). Brit. sailor; in 1939 3rd Sea Lord; in 1943 C.-in-C. Home Fleet; on Dec. 26, 1943, sank the Ger. battleship Scharnhorst off North Cape; adm. in 1944; 1945–46 commanded Brit. Pacific Fleet; 1946 made baron; in 1948 1st Sea Lord and Adm. of Fleet.

Fraser, Sir (William Jocelyn) Ian (b. 1897). Brit. politician, blinded in the 1st World War; chairman of St. Dunstan's, 473; governor of B.B.C. 1937–39, and 1941–46.

Fraser, Marjorie Kennedy (1857–1930). Scottish writer and musician; collected and edited Hebridean folksongs.

Fraser, Peter (b. 1884). N.Z. statesman; emigrated to N.Z. in 1910; prime min. of N.Z. from March, 1940 to Dec., 1949; attended war cabinet in London 1941.

Fraunhofer (frown'-hō-fer), **Joseph von** (1787–1826), Ger. optician and physicist; discovered dark lines of absorption spectrum, plates f. 3056, 3057; spectroscope, 3055.

Fra'zer, Sir James George (1854–1941). Scot. anthropologist, 1387; "The Legend of the Golden Bough," 1387.

Fréchette, Louis Honoré (1839–1908), Fr.-Canadian poet, general acknowledged the greatest of his people; his lyrics are inspired by intense patriotism, love of nature, beauties of friendship and family ties ("Veronica," a tragedy; "Papineau" and "Félix Poutré," historical plays).

Frederick I, Barbarossa (c. 1124–90), Holy Rom. emperor, "in many respects the ideal emperor of the Middle Ages," 872, 1388; leads 3rd Crusade, 936; opens Charlemagne's tomb, 9.

Frederick II (1194–1250). Holy Rom. emperor, 1389; develops Sicily, 2968; crowned in Jerusalem, 937.

Frederick III (1415–93), Holy Rom. emperor, 1389.

Frederick III (1609–70), King of Denmark; he transformed Denmark into an absolute monarchy and made crown hereditary; unsuccessful wars with Sweden (1657–60).

Frederick VI (1768–1839). King of Denmark and Norway; succeeded 1808 (previously regent); joined Armed Neutrality of North and was punished (1801) by destruction of fleet by Eng.; suffered similarly for neutrality again in 1807; then allied self with Napoleon and was compelled by Allies (1814) to surrender Norway and Sweden.

Frederick VII (1808–63), Denmark. Succeeded 1848; in his reign Schleswig-Holstein troubles grew ripe for Bismarck's intervention in next reign.

Frederick VIII (1843–1912), Denmark, succeeded in 1906; father of Haakon VII of Norway, brother of King George I of Greece, and of Queen Alexandra of Eng., 816.

Frederick IX (b. 1899), Denmark. Succeeded in 1947.

Frederick I (1657–1713). First King of Prussia (1701), previously Elector of Brandenburg (1688–1701), and Duke of Prussia; patron of learned men, but vain and extravagant; gained title of king for aiding Emperor Leopold I in War of Sp. Succession.

Frederick II, the Great (1712–86). Prussia, 2696, 2878, 2924, 1389; Carlyle's biography, 703; Ger. literature in his reign, 1456; Germany under, 1449; and Maria Theresa, 2101.

Frederick III (1831–88). King of Prussia; Ger. emperor (March 9 to June 15, 1888); son of William I, first Ger. emperor, father of William II; commanded at Sedan and siege of Paris in Franco-Prussian War.

Frederick I, the Victorious (1425–76). Elector palatine (1451–76); tried to dethrone Emperor Frederick III; great military leader.

Frederick II, the Wise (1482–1556). Elector palatine (succeeded 1544); commanded imperial army at siege of Vienna in 1529; became Protestant through influence of Melanchthon.

Frederick III, the Pious (1515–76). Elector palatine (succeeded 1559); laid foundation for systematic Calvinism; aided Fr. Huguenots.

Frederick IV, the Upright (1574–1610). Elector palatine (succeeded 1583), noted for firm support of Protestantism.

Frederick V (1596–1632). Elector palatine and "winter king" of Bohemia; through his marriage with Elizabeth, daughter of James I of Eng., ancestor of the Windsor (Hanover) line of Eng. kings; King of Bohemia 1619–20, thereafter in exile.

Frederick III, the Wise (1463–1525). Elector and Duke of Saxony; refused imperial throne (1519) and suggested election of Charles V; friend of Luther and Melanchthon, whom he invited to teach at Univ. of Wittenberg founded by him.

Frederick Augustus I (1750–1827). King of Saxony; he was an ally of Napoleon, who made him King and Grand Duke of Warsaw.

Frederick Henry (1584–1647). Prince of Orange; youngest son of William the Silent and brother of Maurice of Nassau; ended the 80-year struggle with Sp. by the treaty of Münster (1648); his term as Stadtholder (1625–47) is accounted the golden age of the Dutch Republic.

Frederick William I (1688–1740). King of Prussia; succeeded in 1713; the real founder of modern Prussia ; trains Frederick the Great, 1389.

Frederick William II (1744–97). King of Prussia, succeeding his uncle, Frederick the Great, in 1786 ; reign saw a great decline in Prussia's power.

Frederick William III (1770–1840). King of Prussia ; succeeded in 1797 ; good, weak man under whom Prussia was almost effaced by Napoleon, but restored by Congress of Vienna and rehabilitated by the great ministers Stein and Hardenberg ; member of Holy Alliance ; his queen, Louisa, a heroine of modern Ger.

Frederick William IV (1795–1861). King of Prussia ; succeeded 1840 ; reactionary idealist ; reluctantly granted Prussian constitution following revolutionary risings of 1848 ; refused imperial Ger. crown, 1449.

Frederick William (1620–88). The " Great Elector " of Brandenburg and Duke of Prussia ; succeeded 1640 ; laid foundation of greatness of Prussia, previously ruined by Thirty Years' War ; 2696.

Frederick William (b. 1882). Crown Prince of Ger., abdicated in 1918 ; commander of Fifth Ger. Army in 1st World War, when he was known to the Allies as " Little Willie " ; 3412.

Fredericksburg, battle of. Important battle in American Civil War (1862), between Confederates under Lee and Federals under Burnside, ending in the victory of the former ; remarkable in military history as exhibiting the power of passive defence when time has been allowed for entrenching.

Fredericton, New Brunswick. Cap. and rly. centre on St. John r. ; pop. 10,000 ; makes boots and shoes, boats, lumber, cotton ; coal-mining ; provincial univ. ; 2336.

Frederikshald, formerly **Halden,** Norway. Fortified spt. on Idde Fiord ; pop. 11,000 ; timber trade ; Charles XII of Sweden was killed here during siege in 1718 ; 759.

Frederiksstad, Norway. Spt. and mfg. tn. at mouth of r. Glommen, 50 m. S.E. of Oslo ; pop. 14,000 ; export lumber trade ; Hanko, most fashionable Norwegian resort, near by.

Freeboard, of a ship, 2305.

Free Churches, 819, **1390.**

Free city. City with an independent govt. ; applied especially to Ger. free cities ; Bremen, 559 ; Danzig, 973 ; Hamburg, 1568.

Freedom of the seas, in international law, 1905.

Freehand drawing, 1045.

Freeman, Edward Augustus (1823–92). Eng. historian (" History of the Norman Conquest ").

Freemasonry, a secret fraternity, **1390.**

Free ports. Ports or specified areas within ports wherein imported goods may be stored, transferred from ship to ship, or used in manufacturing for export sale, without levy of customs duties ; Copenhagen an example, 904.

Freetown. Spt. of W. Africa, cap. of Brit. colony of Sierra Leone ; pop. 86,000 ; military station ; during 2nd World War used as naval and R.A.F. station and terminal of aeroplane ferry route across Africa ; exports rubber, palm oil, gums, nuts, ginger, 3266.

Free Trade, in Gt. Brit., 944, 2535 ; Richard Cobden, 858 ; Adam Smith, 2906.

Freezing and Refrigeration, 1391, *1392,* 1594 ; and food preservation, 1341 ; liquefaction of gases, 1419 ; heat pump a reversed refrigerator, 1600 ; fluorine compounds in refrigerators, 1567 ; in ships, 2951 ; water, 3350.

Freezing points, 1391, *3200.*

Freiberg (frī′-bêrg). Ger. mining tn. in Saxony ; pop. 34,742 ; famous mining academy ; silver and lead ; cath. has fine " golden door."

Freiburg-im-Breisgau (frī′-boorg ĕm brīz′-gow). Ger. univ. tn. in Baden

Gothic cath. ; pop. 111,860 ; cotton, silk industries.

Fre′mantle, W. Australia. Spt. tn. at mouth of Swan River, adjoining State cap., Perth ; sawmills and iron foundries ; port of call for mail steamers ; pop. 29,000 ; 3368.

Frémiet (frā′-myă), **Emmanuel** (1824–1910). Fr. classic sculptor noted for animal studies.

Frémont′, John Charles (1813–90). Amer. general and explorer ; demonstrated the practicability of a route over the Rocky Mts. ; made first scientific exploration of Pacific coast.

French, Sir John. *See* Ypres, Earl of.

French Academy, 16, 1380.

French-Canadians, 680, 2716.

French chalk, a kind of talc.

French Congo, Africa. *See* **French Equatorial Africa.**

French Equatorial Africa (French Congo.) Fr. colony in w.-cent. Africa ; includes most of former Ger. colony of Cameroons ; about 960,000 **sq.** m. ; pop. 3,127,700 ; cabinet woods, palm oil, rubber, ivory ; 888, *map, 888.*

French Guiana. Fr. dept. on N.E. coast of S. Amer., about 32,000 sq. m. ; pop. about 31,000 ; cap. Cayenne ; mining ; old penal settlement ; *1552,* 1553.

French Guinea. Territory forming part of Fr. W. Africa, on coast between Port. Guinea and Brit. Sierra Leone ; 89,436 sq. m. ; pop. about 2,125,000 ; cap. Conakry, pop. 32,000 ; 3367, *map, 3366.*

French horn, *1644,* 2446.

French Indo-China. *See* Indo-China.

French language and literature. *See* **France : language and literature,** 1379 ; *also* list in p. 3809.

French Revolution (1789–95), 1366, 1393 ; Carlyle's history, 702 ; Danton, 971 ; Declaration of Rights of Man, 1394 ; effects in Europe, 1239 ; Jacobins, 1790 ; Louis XVI, *2030* ; Marat, 2096 ; Marie Antoinette, 2102 ; the " Marseillaise," 2283 ; Mirabeau, 2189 ; Napoleon I, 2275 ; paper money, 1395 ; Reign of Terror, 1396 ; Robespierre, 2789 ; Madame Roland executed, 2798 ; Rousseau, 2831 ; States-General, 1393 ; Talleyrand, 3149 ; Voltaire, 3329.

French Somaliland. Territory in N.E. Africa bordering Gulf of Aden ; 8,490 sq. m. ; native pop. 44,000 ; chief tn. Djibouti, pop. 10,400 ; 1073, 3000.

French Union. Since 1946 the inclusive name for the French Republic, her over-sea departments, and associated states and territories, 1362 ; the president of the Republic is also pres. of the Union.

French West Africa. Collective name for w. Sahara and adjacent coastal colonies ; 1,815,000 sq. m. ; pop. 14,702,000 ; 2861, 3367.

" French " nails, 2271.

Frens′sen, Gustav (b. 1863). Ger. novelist ; " Jörn Uhl," strong novel of peasant life, made him famous.

Frequency. The number of crests of a wave passing a point in one second, 3358, 3393 ; of elec. current, 1547, 1549 ; high frequency, 1623 ; control by piezo-elec. effect, 2604 ; of radar, 2726 ; in radiation, 2729 ; sound, 3010 ; of telegraphy, 3167 ; of television, 3184 ; wireless, 3393, 3397.

Frequency Modulation, a system of wireless transmission, 3397.

Frere, Sir (Henry) Bartle (1815–84). Eng. administrator, nephew of John Hookham Frere ; gov. of Bombay (1862–7) ; as special commissioner to East Africa influential in abolishing slave trade in Zanzibar ; as gov. of Cape Colony (1877–80) attempted confederation of South Africa.

Frere, John Hookham (1769–1846). Eng. diplomat and author, minister to Port. (1800–02), to Sp. (1802–04 and 1808) ; his spirited verse trans-

lations of Aristophanes' plays remain unrivalled.

Fres′co. Method of painting on fresh plaster, 2476.

Fresh-water clam. A mussel, 860.

Fresh-water fishing, 1309.

Fresnel (frā-nel), **Augustin Jean** (1788–1827). Fr. physicist ; research on wave theory of light ; improvements in lamps and reflectors, 1945.

Freud (froid), **Sigmund** (1856–1939). Austrian neurologist and psychologist, **1396,** 2697 ; and Jung, 1840.

Frey (frā). In Norse myth., god of peace, prosperity, and fruitfulness.

Freyberg, Lt.-Gen. Sir Bernard, V.C. (b. 1890). won V.C. in 1st World War ; C.-in-C. N. Zealand Exped. Force, 1939–45 ; C.-in-C. Allied forces in Crete, 1941 ; Gov.-Gen. N. Zealand from 1946 ; famed for his fearlessness.

Freyja (frā′-a), **Freyia,** or **Freya.** In Norse myth., goddess of love.

Freytag (frī-tahg), **Gustav** (1816–95). Ger. novelist and playwright ; chief works, " The Journalists " and " Debit and Credit."

Friars. Distinguished from monks, 2214.

Frick, Wilhelm (1877–1946). Ger. politician ; magistrate in Bavaria, he supported Hitler from 1923 ; Reich min. of Interior from 1933 ; taken by U.S. troops Mar. 5, 1945 ; executed Oct. 16, 1946, for suppressing Jews, trade unions, and the press ; 2282.

Friction, 1396, 2127, *2592* ; coefficient of, 1397 ; creates electricity, 1127 ; and perpetual motion, *1396* ; and pulleys, 2700 ; produces heat, 123, 1397, 1594, 1595, 2842 ; in starting fire, 1278, *1280.*

Friday. Sixth day of week ; meaning of name, 980 ; Good Friday, 1074.

" Friday, Man." In Defoe's " Robinson Crusoe," savage rescued from cannibals by Crusoe, later his servant, *938,* 939.

Frideswide (frē′-des-wi-de), **Fritheswith,** or **Fredeswitha** (8th cent.). Eng. saint, 2462.

Fridtjof Nansen Land. Formerly Franz Josef Land ; Arctic archipelago of about 100 small isls. N. of Novaya Zemlya and E. of Spitsbergen, 223.

Friedland (frēd′-land). Former Ger. tn. n E. Prussia, on r. Alle, 27 m. S.E. of Königsberg ; now in U.S.S.R. ; battle of Friedland (1807) ; 2276, 2360.

Friendly Islands. *See* Tonga Islands.

Friendly Societies. Organizations formed for various benevolent objects, such as financial help and medical attention for the sick, death benefit, and old age relief.

Friends, Society of (or Quakers). Religious sect founded in Eng. about 1650 by George Fox ; among earliest opponents of slavery ; war they consider opposed to spirit of Christ ; refuse to swear oaths ; famed for international social relief work ; 1390.

Friese-Greene, William (1855–1921). Eng. inventor ; in 1889 he took out the first patent for a ciné camera and projector, 828.

Friesian (frē′-zhan), or **Frisian Islands.** Chain in North Sea off Dutch coast ; from former Zuider Zee E. and N. as far as Jutland ; 400 sq. m. ; cattle, *731,* 732.

Friesians or Frisians, 1237, 1447.

Friesland (frēz′-land). N.W. prov. of Netherlands, surface partly below sea-level, protected by dikes ; 1,286 sq. m. ; pop. 436,700 ; horses, cattle.

Frieze (frēz). In architecture, *215* ; of Parthenon, 22, *1143, 1144,* 1145.

Frig′ate, type of ship, 2296.

Frigate-bird, 1397.

Frigga (frig′-a), **Frigg,** or **Friia.** In Norse myth., wife of Odin and greatest of goddesses, 2881 ; mother of Balder, 341 ; Friday named after, 980.

Frilled lizard. *Plate f. 1972,* 1973.

Fringil′lidae, The Finch family
Fringing reefs, 909.
Frinton-on-Sea. Coast resort in Essex ; pop. 2,196 ; 1225.
Fripp, Sir Alfred (1865–1930). Eng. surgeon ; surgeon-in-ordinary to the King ; senior surgeon Guy's Hospital, London.
Frith, William Powell (1819–1909). Eng. artist ; he excelled in painting canvases containing many figures, notable examples being " Derby Day " and " The Railway Station " ; elected R.A. in 1853 ; 1182 ; work by, *1625.*

Fritillaria. Member of lily family, bearing pendent chequered purple and white flowers ; very beautiful in spring ; popularly known as snake's head.
Fritillary. Name of a number of butterflies of the order *Argynnidae* ; usually bright yellow-brown in colour ; black markings on upper surface, silvery underneath ; *plates f. 632, 633.*
Friuli (frē-ū′-li). Dist. of Italy on the Adriatic.
Frobisher, Sir Martin (*c.* 1535–94). Brit. navigator and naval hero, first to seek the North-West Passage ; 142, **1398, 2644.**

Frobisher Bay. Inlet of Davis Strait opening westward at S. end of Baffin Land.
Froebel (frê-bel), **Friedrich Wilhelm** (1782–1852). Ger. educator, founder of kindergarten, **1398.**
Frog, 1398, *1399* ; classification, 435 ; eggs, 1398, 1094, *1155* ; hibernation, 1623 ; life history, *1399* ; story, " The Tadpole Who Wanted to be a Frog," 3453.
Frog-bit. A water plant, 3356.
Frog-fish, 1297.
Frog′more. Royal mausoleum 1 m. S.E. of Windsor Castle, 3388.

GREAT FIGURES IN FRENCH LITERATURE

Geoffroy de Villehardouin (1160–1213)—" Histoire de la Conquête de Constantinople."
Jean de Joinville (1224–*c.* 1318)—" Histoire de Saint Louis IX."
Jean Froissart (1337–1410)—" Chroniques."
Philippe de Commynes (*c.* 1445–1511)—" Mémoires."
François Villon (1431–*c.* 1465)—" Petit Testament " ; " Grand Testament."
Clément Marot (*c.* 1497–1544)—" Les Epîtres " ; " Blasons."
François Rabelais (*c.* 1490–*c.* 1553)—" Gargantua " ; " Pantagruel."
Pierre de Ronsard (1524–85)—" Sonnets " ; " Amours."
Michel de Montaigne (1533–92)—" Essais."
François de Malherbe (1555–1628)—" Odes " ; " Stances."
Pierre Corneille (1606–84)—" Le Cid " ; " Horace " ; " Polyeucte."
François de la Rochefoucauld (1613–80)—" Maximes."
Jean de la Fontaine (1621–95)—" Fables " ; " Contes et Nouvelles."
Molière (Jean-Baptiste Poquelin) (1622–73)—" Tartuffe " ; " Le Bourgeois Gentilhomme " ; " Le Malade Imaginaire."
Blaise Pascal (1623–62)—" Pensées " ; " Lettres Provinciales."
Madame de Sévigné (1626–96)—" Lettres."
Nicolas Boileau (1636–1711)—" L'Art Poétique " ; " Satires."
Jean Racine (1639–99)—" Athalie " ; " Phèdre " ; " Britannicus " ; " Andromaque."
Jean de la Bruyère (1645–96)—" Caractères."
François de Salignac de La Mothe-Fénelon (1651–1715)—" Télémaque."
Voltaire (François Marie Arouet) (1694–1778)—" Candide " ; " Zadig " ; " Siècle de Louis XIV."
Georges Louis Leclerc de Buffon (1707–88)—" Histoire Naturelle."
Jean-Jacques Rousseau (1712–78)—" Le Contrat Social " ; " La Nouvelle Héloïse " ; " Émile " ; " Les Confessions."
Denis Diderot (1713–84)—" L'Encyclopédie " (editor) ; " Le Neveu de Rameau " ; " Jacques le Fataliste."
Bernardin de Saint-Pierre (1737–1814)—" Paul et Virginie."
Madame de Staël (1766–1817)—" Delphine " ; " Corinne."
Stendhal (Henri-Marie Beyle) (1783–1842)—" Le Rouge et le Noir " ; " La Chartreuse de Parme."
Alphonse de Lamartine (1790–1869)—" Méditations poétiques " ; " Jocelyn " ; " Histoire des Girondins."
Alfred de Vigny (1797–1863)—" Cinq-Mars " ; " Servitude et Grandeur Militaire."
Honoré de Balzac (1799–1850)—" Eugénie Grandet " ; " Le Père Goriot " ; " La Cousine Bette."
Victor Hugo (1802–85)—" Notre Dame de Paris " ; " Les Misérables " ; " Les Châtiments."
Prosper Mérimée (1803–70)—" Colomba " ; " Carmen."
Alexandre Dumas, the elder (1802–70)—" Les Trois Mousquetaires " (The Three Musketeers) ; " Vingt ans après " ; " Le Comte de Monte Cristo."
Charles-Augustin Sainte-Beuve (1804–69)—" Causeries du lundi."
George Sand (Lucile-Aurore Dudevant, née Dupin) (1804–76)—" La Mare au diable " ; " François le Champi " ; " Le Marquis de Villemer " ; " Consuelo."
Alfred de Musset (1810–57)—" La Confession d'un enfant du siècle " ; " On ne badine pas avec l'amour."
Théophile Gautier (1811–72)—" Émaux et Camées," poems ; " Mademoiselle de Maupin," novel ; " Le Capitaine Fracasse," novel.
Charles Baudelaire (1821–67)—" Les Fleurs du Mal," poems; " Les Paradis Artificiels."
Gustave Flaubert (1821–80)—" Madame Bovary " ; " Salammbô " ; " L'Éducation Sentimentale."
Edmond and Jules de Goncourt (1822–96, 1830–70)—" Renée Mauperin " ; " Germinie Lacerteux."
Ernest Renan (1823–92)—" Origines du Christianisme," which includes " La Vie de Jésus."
Alexandre Dumas, the younger (1824–95)—" La Dame aux Camélias."
Hippolyte Taine (1828–93)—" Histoire de la littérature anglaise " ; " Origines de la France contemporaine."
Émile Zola (1840–1902)—" Rougon-Macquart " series, including " L'Assommoir " ; " La Bête humaine " ; " La Débâcle."

Paul Verlaine (1844–96)—" Fêtes galantes " ; " La bonne Chanson " ; " Sagesse " ; " Romances sans paroles."
Anatole France (Jacques Anatole Thibault) (1844–1924)—" L'Ile des Pingouins " ; " L'Étui de Nacre " ; " Le Crime de Sylvestre Bonnard " ; " L'Histoire contemporaine " series, including " L'Orme du Mail " ; " Le Mannequin d'osier " ; " L'Anneau d'améthyste " ; " M. Bergeret à Paris."
Joris Karl Huysmans (1848–1907)—" Là-bas " ; " À Rebours"; " La Cathédrale."
Guy de Maupassant (1850–93)—" Bel-Ami " ; " La Maison Tellier " ; " Contes de la Bécasse " ; " Une Vie."
Pierre Loti (Louis Marie Julien Viaud) (1850–1923)—" Pêcheur d'Islande " ; " Madame Chrysanthème."
Paul Bourget (1852–1935)—" Le Disciple " ; " L'Émigré " ; " Un Divorce " ; " La Duchesse bleue."
Albert Samain (1858–1900)—" Au Jardin de l'Infante " ; " Le Chariot d'Or," poems.
Henri Bergson (1859–1941)—" L'Évolution créatrice " ; " Matière et mémoire."
Maurice Barrès (1862–1923)—" Le Culte du moi " ; " Les Déracinés " ; " Colette Baudoche " ; " Le Jardin sur l'Oronte " ; " La Colline inspirée."
Henri de Régnier (1864–1936)—" Tel qu'on songe " ; " La Sandale ailée " ; " Le Miroir des heures," poems ; " La Double Maîtresse," " La Pécheresse," novels.
Romain Rolland (1866–1944)—" Jean-Christophe " ; " Colas Breugnon " ; " Gandhi " ; " Au-dessus de la Mêlée."
Francis Jammes (1868–1938)—" Quatorze prières " ; " Le Roman du lièvre " ; " Quatrains."
Edmond Rostand (1869–1918)—" Cyrano de Bergerac " ; " L'Aiglon " ; " Chantecler."
René Boylesve (René Tardivaux) (1867–1926)—" Le Parfum des Iles Borromées " ; " L'Enfant à la Balustrade."
Paul Claudel (1868–)—" L'Otage " ; " L'Annonce faite à Marie."
André Gide (1869–)—" Nourritures terrestres " ; " Les Caves du Vatican " ; " Les Faux Monnayeurs " ; " L'Immoraliste."
Pierre Louÿs (1870–1925)—" Les Chansons de Bilitis " ; " Aphrodite " ; " Les Aventures du Roi Pausole."
Marcel Proust (1871–1922)—" À la recherche du temps perdu " series, including " Du côté de chez Swann " ; " À l'ombre des jeunes filles en fleurs " ; " Le Côté de Guermantes " ; " Sodome et Gomorrhe " ; " La Prisonnière."
Paul Valéry (1871–1945)—" La Jeune Parque " ; " Odes " ; " Fragments du Narcisse," poems ; " Variété," essays.
Henri Barbusse (1874–1935)—" Le Feu " (Under Fire).
Anna-Elisabeth de Noailles (1876–1933)—" La Nouvelle Espérance " ; " L'Honneur de souffrir " ; " Le Cœur innombrable " ; " Les Innocentes, ou la sagesse des femmes."
Roger Martin du Gard (1881–)—" Jean Barois " ; " Les Thibault."
Jean Giraudoux (1882–1944)—" Juliette au pays des hommes " ; " Bella " ; " Lecture pour une ombre " ; Siegfried," " Electre," plays.
Jean Richard Bloch (1884–1947)—" Et Cie." (& Co.); " La Nuit kurde " ; " Le dernier Empereur."
Georges Duhamel (Denis Thévenin) (1884–)—" Lettres au Patagon " ; " Deux Hommes " ; " Journal de Salavin."
François Mauriac (1885–)—" Le Baiser au lépreux " ; " Génétrix " ; " La Fin de la Nuit " ; " Thérèse Desqueynoux."
Jules Romans (Louis Farigoule) (1885–)—" Knock " ; " Les Hommes de Bonne Volonté " ; " Psyché."
André Maurois (Emile Herzog) (1885–)—" Ariel : The Life of Shelley " ; " Les Silences du Colonel Bramble " ; " Climats " ; " Édouard VII et Son Temps."
Paul Morand (1888–)—" Ouvert la nuit " ; " L'Europe galante " ; " Londres."
Jean Cocteau (1892–)—" Plain-Chant," a poem ; " Les Mariés de la tour Eiffel," a ballet ; " Les Enfants terribles"; " Le grand Écart " ; " Thomas, l'imposteur," novels.
Henri de Montherlant (1896–)—" Les Bestiaires " ; " Les Célibataires " ; " Les Jeunes Filles."
Jean-Paul Sartre (1905–)—" Les Chemins de la Liberté," novel ; " Huis-Clos," play.

Frogs, fable of the, 54.

"Frogs, The." Play by Aristophanes, 231.

Froissart (frwah'-sar), **Jean** (1337–1410 ?). Fr. chronicler and poet, 1379, *1380*, **1399**, *1400*.

Frome. River of Glos., flowing 20 m. into Avon, 1476 ; another, in Dorset, flows to Poole Harbour, 1030.

Fronde, The. A civil war in France during minority of Louis XIV (1649–52) and the consequent war with Spain (1653–59), so called (fronde, " sling ") from windows having been pelted by Paris mob ; its suppression contributed to the growth of absolutism under Louis.

Fronds. Leaves of ferns, *1268*.

" Front," in meteorology, cold, warm, etc., 2150.

Frontenac, Count Louis de (1620–98). Gov. of New France ; he was a French nobleman and served his country as a soldier with distinction ; he was a successful governor, but his haughty manner made him many enemies ; and Quebec, *2714*.

Frost, 1400 ; damage to fruit trees, 1402, *1403*.

Frost, Robert Lee (b. 1875). American poet, 3296.

Froude (frōōd), **James Anthony** (1818–94). Eng. historian, often prejudiced but a master of Eng. style (" History of England from the Fall of Wolsey to the Death of Elizabeth " ; " Reminiscences of Thomas Carlyle " ; " Life of Beaconsfield ").

Fructose, or fruit sugar, 3114.

Fruit (in botany). The matured seed-container of a flowering plant, 1402.

Fruit and Fruit Growing, *plates f. 1400*, *1401*, **1401** ; canning, 692 ; food value, 1340, 1402 ; grafting, 1401, *1402* ; pollination by bees, 394 ; protection against frost, 1402, *1403* ; scale insects, 2878 ; sprays and spraying, 1402. See also names of chief fruits and fruit-growing regions.

Fruit-bat. Same as Flying-fox.

Frun'ze, Russ. cap. of Kirghiz S.S.R. ; pop. 93,000 ; 3267.

Fry, Charles Burgess (b. 1872). Eng. athlete ; in 1893 led the Oxford University Association football, cricket, and athletic teams ; afterwards captained England at cricket and played for his country at football ; columnist in " Evening Standard."

Fry, Elizabeth Gurney (1780–1845). Eng. Quakeress, prison reformer, **1403**, *1404*, 2688.

Fry, Roger Elliot (1866–1934). Eng. painter and defender of modern tendencies, 2477.

Fry'att, Charles (1872–1916). Eng. captain of a Brit. merchant ship, in 1st World War court-martialled and shot by Germany on charge of having tried to ram a submarine.

Frying. Cookery process, 902.

Fuad (foo-ahd') I, **Ahmed Ali Pasha** (1868–1936). King of Egypt ; became sultan (1917), proclaimed king (1922), upon removal of Brit. protectorate, 1102.

Fuca, Juan de (d. 1602). Gk. navigator whose real name was Apostolos Valerianos ; served in Span. navy ; explored N.W. coast of N. Amer.

Fuchow, China. Same as Foochow.

Fuchsia (fū'-sha). An ornamental plant, **1404**.

Fu'cus. Genus of brown seaweeds, including bladder-wrack (*f-i.*) and saw-edged wrack.

Fuehrer, (Ger., leader). Title assumed by Adolf Hitler when Chancellor and dictator of Germany, 2281.

Fu'el, 1405 ; alcohol, 104, 1406, 2665 ; atomic energy, 299 ; charcoal, 753, *1405* ; coal, 855 ; coal gas, 1423 ; coke, 868 ; combustion, 1280 ; consists of carbon forms, 699 ; how it produces heat, 1595, 1736 ; and national greatness, 1406 ; oil, 2426 ; peat, 2534 ; petrol, 1736, 2564 ; **power stations,** 2673 ; smoke, 2986.

Fuel values, of food, 1338, *1339*, 2693.

Fuenterrabia (fwen-ter-rah-bē'-*a*), or **Fontara'bia,** Spain. Tn. on Fr. frontier, on r. Bidassoa ; famous fortress destroyed by French (1794) ; Wellington crossed Bidassoa in spite of opposition (1813).

Fugger (foo'-ger). Wealthy family of Ger. merchants and bankers famous in 16th cent. ; founded by Johann Fugger, a Bavarian weaver, in the 14th cent.

Fujiyama (foo-jē-yah'-m*a*), or **Fuji-San.** Sacred mt. of Japan, 70 m. s.w. of Tokyo ; 12,390 ft. high ; 1795, *1808*.

Fukien (fōō'ki-en), or **Fokien,** China. Maritime prov. in S.E. ; 61,000 sq. m. ; pop. 11,990,000 ; cap. Foochow ; 1335.

Fukuoka. Tn. of Japan on isl. of Kiushiu ; pop. 323,217 ; silk industry centre.

Fula. Dominant African people in the W. Sudan, est. number 8,000,000 ; light in colour, with well-marked features, and probably of Berber origin.

Ful'crum. Fixed point about which lever moves, 2128, *2130*.

Fulda (fool'-d*a*), **Ludwig** (1862–1939). Ger. dramatist ; wrote " The Talisman," " The Lost Paradise " ; translated works of Molière, Beaumarchais, and Rostand.

Fulda, Ger. tn. in Hesse, famous in Middle Ages for Benedictine abbey ; pop. 30,000 ; cattle market ; rly. workshops.

Ful'gurites. Tubes in sand or rock made by lightning passing through these materials and fusing them ; common in Alps and Pyrenees.

Fulham. Parl. and met. bor. of S.W. London on N. side of the Thames ; pop. 150,940 ; the Manor House became the palace of the bishops of London in 11th cent. ; seriously damaged in 2nd World War.

Fuller, Thomas (1608–61). Eng. clergyman and writer ; style vigorous and full of humour ; chaplain to Charles II (" History of the Worthies of England ").

Fuller's earth. A clay-like substance used in cleansing cloth and wool of grease, and in clarifying oil ; greenish, brownish or yellow.

Full moon, 2225.

Ful'mar. A petrel, 2564.

Ful'minate. A highly explosive salt of fulminic acid ; mercury, 1250 ; silver, 2973.

Ful'ton, Robert (1765–1815). Amer. inventor of steamship, **1407** ; steamship Clermont. *1407*.

Funchal (foon-chahl'). Cap. of Madeira ; pop. 55,000 ; picturesque and well built, with narrow steep streets ; sugar plantations and vineyards, *2052*.

Functional architecture, a recent development, 222.

Fundamen'tal, in music, etc., 3010 .

Fun'dy, Bay of. Large inlet of Atlantic between New Brunswick and Nova Scotia, remarkable for high tides.

Fü'nen or **Fyen.** Largest of Danish isls. after Zealand ; 1,133 sq. m. ; pop. 286,000 ; in German occupation 1940–45 ; with adjacent isls. forms prov. of Fünen ; cap. Odense, 991.

Fünfkirchen, Hungary. Same as Pecs.

Fungi. Primitive plants, **1407**, *2288*, 2620 ; *plate f. 1408* ; mildews and moulds, 2173 ; mushrooms, 2260 ; parasitic and saprophytic, 2514 ; rusts and smuts, *2857* ; spores, 2918 ; yeasts, 3433.

Funny-bone. Really not a bone, but the ulnar nerve, which is only slightly protected at the elbow ; pressure or blow on this nerve causes sharp pain.

" Fur," in kettles, 3351.

Fur-farming, 1412 ; in Canada, 679.

Fur felt, for hats, *1583*, 1584.

Furfurol, a volatile oil distilled from bran, wood, etc. ; in nylon mfr., 2749.

Furies or **Eumenides.** In Gk. and Rom. myth., goddesses who punished crime.

Furlong. A unit of length. See **Weights and Measures,** *f-i.*

Furnace, 1408 ; for heating houses, 1600 ; blast furnace, 467 ; open-hearth, *1753*, 1756 ; electrically heated. *135* ; boiler, *489* ; in copper-smelting, *906*, *907* ; in glass-making, 1472, 1473 ; in steel manufacture, *1755*.

Fur'ness, Christopher, 1st Baron (1852–1912). Eng. shipowner and politician ; founded the Furness line of steamers : represented the Hartlepools in Parl. ; raised to peerage in 1910.

Furness. Dist. of N.W. Lancashire, peninsula across Morecambe Bay from rest of co. ; hematite iron ore ; ruins of famous abbey.

Fur'niss, Harry (1854–1925). Irish caricaturist, author, lecturer ; for many years on staff of " Punch," for which he illustrated " Diary of Toby, M.P." ; Dickens drawings, *1014*.

Furniture, 1409, *1410*, *1411* ; influence of Morris, 2232.

Furniture beetle ; small beetle, *Anobium punctatum,* whose larvae are the " wood-worm " of furniture ; adult is about ¼ in. in length, cylindrical, brown in colour ; emerge in May making the " worm " holes, and fly to other furniture ; larval life is 2 to 3 years.

Fur'nivall, Frederick James (1825–1910). Eng. philologist ; founded Early English Text Society, Chaucer Society, and other societies for publication of texts ; supervised publication of 43 facsimiles of quartos of Shakespeare's plays.

Furs, 1412 ; from Alaska, 97 ; in Canada, 103, 679, 1649, 2088, 2392 ; felt-making, 1265 ; importance in settlement of N. Amer., 1412, 1875 ; list of chief furs, 1412 ; see also names of principal fur-bearing animals.

Furse, Charles Wellington (1868–1904). Eng. painter (" Diana of the Uplands ").

Fur seal, 2912.

Furtwängler (foort'-ven-gler), **Wilhelm** (b. 1886). Ger. conductor, Director of Berlin Philharmonic Concerts, 1922–1934 ; conductor of many famous orchestras, including Vienna Philharmonic. " Denazified " Dec. 1946.

Fusan (foo-sahn') or **Pusan.** Chief spt. of Korea, in S.E. ; opened to foreign trade 1876 ; pop. (1939) 249,734.

Fuse. In electricity, wire designed to melt when overloaded with electric current, 1130. In artillery, 258.

Fu'seli, Henry (1741–1825). Eng. painter and art critic, of Ger.-Swiss birth ; elected R.A. 1790 (" The Nightmare," " Titania and Bottom ") ; wrote valuable " Lectures on Painting."

Fu'sel-oil. A poisonous liquid formed in fermentation ; used in paints and varnishes.

Füssen (fü'-sen). Ger. historic tn. 58 m. s.w. of Munich ; peace signed here between Elector Maximilian III, Joseph of Bavaria, and Maria Theresa (1745).

Fust or Faust, Johann (d. 1466). Ger. money-lender, associated with Gutenberg in invention of printing, 2684, *2685*.

Fustel de Coulanges, Numa Denis (1830–89). Fr. historian. Best known for his ingenious and charmingly written " La Cité antique," showing influence of religion in anc. Rome and Greece.

Fus'tian. A cotton cloth, used in making hard-wearing clothes.

Fus'tic. A yellow dye, 1060.

Futurism, in It. art, 1785, 2477.

Fyfe, Sir David Patrick Maxwell (b. 1900). Brit. lawyer and politician ; solicitor-gen. 1942–45 ; attorney-gen. May–July 1945 ; Brit. acting chief prosecutor at Internat. Milit. Tribunal for major war criminals, Nuremberg, 1945–46.

Fyne, Loch. Herrings, 1621.

OUR capital G is derived from the Latin C, which, as we have learned, is a rounded form of the Greek *Gamma*. Until the middle of the 3rd century B.C. the letter C was used in Latin inscriptions to denote both the *c* and *g* sounds, and throughout the whole of Roman history C remained as the symbol for G in the abbreviations C. and Cn. for " Gaius " and " Gnaeus." But because of the inconvenience of not being able to distinguish between the two sounds of the character C, a slight modification was made for the *g* sound. Plutarch says that the symbol was invented by Spurius Carvilius Ruga, who spelled his family name R V G A instead of R V C A (the V still being used for the sound which we represent by U). At first G differed from C only in the lower lip of the crescent rising up in a straight line. In a later form this was curved inward, and in another had a sort of " beard " added, which became the little cross-bar of today's G.

Gable. In architecture, the triangular portion of the end of a building, bounded by the sides of the roof and a line joining the eaves, *2821.*

Gaboriau (ga-bŏr'-i-ō), **Emile** (1833–73). Fr. writer of detective stories; among the best are " Monsieur Lecoq," " The Slaves of Paris," " Other People's Money."

Gabriel (gā'bri-el). Archangel and heavenly messenger sent to the Virgin Mary (Luke i. 19, 26), the prophet Daniel and others; recognized by Mahomedans as well as Christians and Jews; and Mahomet, 2066.

Gabun' or **Gaboon'.** A territory of Fr. Equatorial Africa, 888; cap. and spt. Libreville; bounded w. by Atlantic, E. by Fr. Middle Congo, s. by Belgian Congo and Port Cabinda; rubber, palm kernels, cocoa; coast regions unhealthy; area 92,218 sq. m.; pop. 422,517.

Gad. Son of Jacob; ancestor of tribe of Gad.

Gadames. *See* **Ghadames.**

Gad'di. Family of Florentine artists. Most important was Taddeo (c. 1300–66), said to have continued Giotto's work on Florence campanile and to have built the Ponte Vecchio.

Gaddin, Johan (1760–1852). Finnish chemist, discovered rare earth group, 3187; gave his name to the ore gadolinite, 3437, and element gadolinium.

Gadolin'ium (Gd). A rare earth element. *See* **Rare Earths.**

Gadsden Purchase. Territory s. of Gila r. in Ariz. and N.M., U.S.A. bought from Mexico in 1853; sale negotiated by James Gadsden, U.S. minister to Mexico, 3291.

Gaea (jē'-a) or **Ge**, in Gk. myth., the anc. goddess " Mother Earth," 3298; intercedes for Daphne, 974; mother of Antaeus, 1615.

Gaede pump, 3301.

Gaelic (gā'-lik). Anc. language of Ire. and Scot., 1413, 740, 1750, 2894.

Gaelic League. In Ire., 1751.

Gaels. In Brit., 1413, 572.

Gaeta (gah-ā'-ta), It. Strongly fortified spt., 45 m. N.W. of Naples; refuge of Pope Pius IX when he fled (1848–50) from Rome; Francis II of Naples surrendered to Garibaldi (1861) after siege.

Gage, Thomas (1721–87). Brit. general, gov. Massachusetts, and military C.-in-C. in America at outbreak of War of Independence.

Gaillard Cut. In Panama Canal, 2490.

Gainsborough, Thomas (1727–88). One of greatest Eng. portrait painters, 1413, 1179; landscapes, 1180; " Blue Boy," 1187; portrait of Duchess of Cumberland, 1413; portrait of Pitt, 2614.

Gaitskell, Hugh Todd Naylor (b. 1906). Min. of Fuel and Power in 1947; Min. of State for Econ. Affairs, 1950.

Galac'tic. In astronomy, means in or near the Milky Way; 2310.

Galahad (gal'-a-had). Hero of Arthurian legends, **1413.**

Galapagos (ga-lah'-pa-gŏs) or **Tortoise Islands.** 600 m. w. of Ecuador; 2,868 sq. m.; pop. 1,500, **1414**; 2469; iguana, 1686; Darwin's visit, 977; giant tortoise, 3229.

Gala'ta. Chief business quarter of Istanbul, 1763.

Galatea (gal-a-tē'-a). Statue made by sculptor Pygmalion and endowed with life by Venus; also, nymph in classical legends; " Pygmalion and Galatea," comedy by Sir W. S. Gilbert, part of the statue played by Dame Madge Kendal.

Galatia (ga-lā'-shi-a). Anc. country in cent. Asia Minor; kingdom founded by Celts.

Gala'tians, Epistle to the. Ninth book of the New Testament, written by the Apostle Paul to the Galatian churches about A.D. 56.

Galatz (ga-lahts') or **Galati**, Rumania. Important Danube port in E.; 972; pop. 93,000 (1945); exports, 2840.

Gal'axy. The Milky Way, 3078.

Galba, Servius Sulpicius (3 B.C.–A.D. 69). Rom. emperor, successor of Nero, 2316.

Galdhöppigen. Peak in s. Norway, highest mt. in Scandinavia (8,400 ft.).

Ga'len, Claudius (c. A.D. 130–200). Gk. physician, most celebrated anc. medical writer; during Middle Ages held, like Aristotle, as infallible; as anatomist, 151; on the blood, 477.

Galena (PbS). Lead sulphide; the chief source of lead, 1908, 3117.

Galer'ius (Galerius Valerius Maximianus) (d. 311). Rom. emperor A.D. 305–311; rose from common soldier to be Diocletian's son-in-law and successor; and Constantine, 893.

Galicia (ga-lish'-i-a), Poland. Agricultural dist. on N. slopes of Carpathians, former Austrian crownland; has oil deposits; Russian defeat, 3410; part incorporated in U.S.S.R. in 1945.

Galicia. Dist. in N.W. corner of Sp., formerly kingdom; area, 11,255 sq. m.; pop. 2,586,000; inhabitants, Gallegos, resemble Portuguese; chief city, Corunna; *map, 3030*.

Gal'ilee (Hebrew " border " or " ring "). Rom. prov. in N. Palestine, land of Christ's boyhood and chief centre of his active work, 2480.

Galilee or **Gennes'aret, Sea of.** Large pear-shaped lake in between Palestine and Transjordan, traversed by Jordan; 64 sq. m.; frequented by Christ and disciples; also called Tiberias; 2481, *2481.*

Galileo (ga-li-lā'-ō), **Galilei** (1564–1642). Great It. mathematician, physicist, and astronomer, **1414**; discovers laws of falling bodies, 1513; invents microscope, 2163; laws of motion, 1513; and the pendulum, 2543; in Pisa, 2612; telescope, 1415, 3178; 276, 277; thermometer, 3199.

Gall. A swelling caused on some part —root, stem, leaf, or flower—of plant or tree, usually either by small insects, bacteria or fungi. " Witches' brooms " are typical examples; so are oak-apples and other oak-galls, 1730, 2410.

Gall or **Gallus, St.** (c. 550–645). Irish monk and missionary to European continent; founded monastery of St. Gall, Switzerland.

Gall, Franz Joseph (1758–1828). Ger. anatomist, founder of the pseudoscience of phrenology.

Gal'las. Powerful and most numerous of Hamitic peoples of E. Africa and Abyssinia, 70.

Gall-bladder, 1470.

Galle (gahl'-e), **Johann Gottfried** (1812–1910). Ger. astronomer, discoverer of 3 comets and the planet Neptune, 2618.

Galle (gal) or **Point de Galle.** Fortified spt. on s.w. coast of Ceylon; pop. 38,424.

Galleon (gal'-ē-on) (derived from galley). A three- or four-decked sailing vessel of 15th cent.; in Sp. Armada, 236; *plates f. 236, 237.*

Gal'leys. Ships propelled wholly or partly by oars, 2296. Also, first proofs of printed matter, 1958.

Gall-fly, 1725, 2410; eggs, 1095.

Galli-Curci (gal-lē-koor'-chē), **Amelita** (Mrs. Homer Samuels) (b. 1889). Ital.-Amer. coloratura soprano; famous roles were Dinorah, Lucia, Juliette, Gilda in " Rigoletto."

Galliéni (gal-yā'-nē), **Joseph Simon** (1849–1916). Fr. general and colonial administrator, pacificator of Madagascar (1896–1905), military gov. of Paris (1914–15).

Galliformes. Order of fowl-like birds, includes grouse, 1550; chicken, 2671; pheasant, 2565; turkey, 3261.

Gal'lio, Lucius Junius Annaeus (1st cent A.D.). Older brother of Seneca, Rom. proconsul of Achaea (A.D. 53), who " cared for none of these things " when Jews haled the Apostle Paul before him; " careless Gallio " has become a synonym for easy-going indifference.

Gallipoli (ga-lip'-o-lē) (anc. Chersonesus), peninsula, Turkey, separating the Dardanelles on E. from Gulf of Saros on w.; 55 m. long, 4 to 13 m. wide; seized by Ottoman Turks, 3262; in 1st World War, 974, 3411.

Gallium (Ga) (gal'i-um). An exceedingly rare metallic element of the aluminium sub-group; atomic weight, 69·7; found in minute quantities in aluminium and certain zinc ores; properties previously predicted by Mendeléev's Periodic Table, melts at 86° F.; properties, 777.

Gall-nut or **nut-gall.** On oak-trees, 2410; used in ink-making, 1724; in tanning leather, 1912.

Gal'lon. A unit of measure of liquid volume; *see* **Weights and Measures,** *f.-i.*

Gal'loway. Former division of s.w. Scot., comprising counties of Kirkcudbright and Wigtown, famous for breeds of horses and cattle; the Bruces were lords of Galloway; power scheme, 1670.

Galloway. Breed of beef cattle, 732.

Galloway, Mull of, Scot. A bold headland of Wigtownshire, the most southern point in Scot.; has lighthouse visible for 23 m.

Gal'lup Poll. Sample opinions taken from a representative cross-section of the public in an attempt to foretell accurately the opinion of the whole; named after Dr. G. Gallup, an American who established the technique.

Gall wasp, and its work, 1730.

Gals'worthy, John (1867–1933). Eng. novelist and dramatist; 1415, 1416,

1215 ; novels, 2403. Born Aug. 14, 1867, not Aug. 4, as stated in p. 1415.

Galt, John (1779–1839). Scottish novelist, whose sketches of Scottish life (" The Ayrshire Legatees " ; " The Annals of the Parish " ; " Last of the Lairds ") have given him a secure place in history of the novel ; 2895.

Gal'ton, Sir Francis (1822–1911). Eng. anthropologist and meteorologist, noted student of heredity ; made first attempt to chart weather on extensive scale and propounded anticyclone theory ; founder of eugenics, 1230 ; finger-prints, 1277 ; theory of heredity, 1617.

Galvani (gal-vah'-nē), **Luigi** (1737–98). It. physiologist, discoverer of electric phenomena called " galvanism," **1416** ; in Bologna, 494 ; frog's legs experiment, 1127.

Gal'vanized iron, zinc used, 2856, 3443.

Galvanom'eter. Device for measuring electric current, *1061, 1134.*

Gal'veston, Texas, U.S.A. One of greatest cotton-exporting ports ; pop. 60,000 ; 3190.

Galway (gawl'-wā). Largest co. of Connaught prov., Eire, in middle of w. coast ; a. 2,293 sq. m. ; pop. 166,000 ; **1416.**

Galway. Spt. (co. tn.) of Co. Galway, Eire, with flour mills, distilleries, and fisheries ; pop. 18,300, 1416.

Galway Bay, Eire. Inlet of the Atlantic on the w. coast between Galway and Clare ; 30 m. long, average breadth 10 m.

Gama, Vasco da. *See* **Vasco da Gama.**

Gamaliel (ga-mā'-li-el) (d. *c.* 52). A learned Pharisee. Paul's instructor in law (Acts xxii. 3) ; advocate in the Sanhedrin of moderate treatment of the Christian apostles (Acts v. 34–9).

Gambet'ta, Léon (1838–82). Fr. statesman and orator, anti-imperialist during Second Empire and Republican leader during and after Franco-Prussian War ; premier in 1881 ; 1385.

Gam'bia. Brit. colony and protectorate in W. Africa on both sides of lower r. Gambia ; 4,000 sq. m. ; pop. 200,000 ; 3366 ; cap. Bathurst, 3366 ; Bathurst market-place, 62.

Gambia. River flowing N.W. over 1,000 m. through Fr. Senegal and Brit. Gambia into Atlantic at Bathurst ; navigable for about 350 m.

Gamboge (gam-bōōzh'). Gum-resin, 2768.

Game, birds as, 439 ; shooting, 2961.

Game'cock, domestic fowl, *435.*

Gamelin (gam'-*e*-lan), **Marie Gustave** (b. 1872). French general. Supreme Commander of French forces Jan. 1938–May 1940, superseded by Weygand ; arrested by Vichy govt. Sept. 1940, indicted at the Riom trials and in Oct. 1941 imprisoned at Bourrassol ; moved to Germany 1943 by the Nazis, he was liberated May 1945 by Allied troops from a secret prison camp.

Gam'ma, γ, Γ (Rom. g, G). Third letter of Gk. alphabet.

Gamma rays. Exceedingly high frequency X-rays, emitted by radium, 2731 ; how formed, 2733 ; atom, 298 ; ionize gases, 1739.

Gander Lake, Newfoundland. Trans-atlantic air base, 2338.

Gandhara. Ind. art school, *1708.*

Gandhi (gahn'-dē), **Mohandas Karamchand** (1869–48). Indian leader of the " non-co-operation " (passive resistance and boycott) movement for Indian self-government, **1416,** *1417* ; and modern India, 1715.

Ganesa (ga-nā'-sa) or **Ganesh** (Sanskrit, " lord of the host "). Hindu god of wisdom and remover of obstacles, chief of the minor deities who attend Siva ; represented as a human figure with the head of an elephant.

Ganges (gan'-jēz), India. Sacred r. of the Hindus, rises in Himalaya Mts., flows 1,540 m. into Bay of Bengal, **1417,** 2479, *map, 1702* ; at Benares, 411, *412* ; at Calcutta, 660 ; vallсy, soil and population, 1691.

Gan'net or **Solan goose.** A sea bird, related to pelican, **1418,** 2538.

Gan'oids. A sub-class of fish with bony plates instead of scales, 1296.

Ganymede (gan'-i-mēd), in Gk. myth., beautiful youth carried off to be cup-bearer of Zeus ; sculpture by Thorwaldsen, *3205.*

Ga'per. A bivalve mollusc, 860.

Gaping Ghyll, Yorkshire, pot-hole, 734.

Gapon (gah-pōn'), **Father George** (*c.* 1870–1906). Rus. priest, revolutionary and govt. spy ; led strikers' march to Winter Palace on Red Sunday (Jan. 22, 1905) ; believed murdered by revolutionaries he had betrayed.

Gar'bett, Cyril F. (b. 1875). Eng. archbishop ; bishop of Winchester, 1932–42, in 1942 became Archbishop of York ; wrote " Physician, Heal Thyself."

Garbo, Greta. Stage name of Greta Gustaffson (b. 1906), Swedish-born American film actress. First film " The Atonement of Gösta Berling " (1925). Later films include " Queen Christina," " Anna Karenina," " Camille," " Marie Walewska," also " Ninotchka."

Garcia (gahr'-sē-a), **Manuel** (1805–1906). One of the most famous singing teachers of all time ; Jenny Lind was one of his pupils ; invented the laryngoscope.

Gar'da, Lake. Largest l. of N. It., extending from Lombard plain into Tirolean Alps, 1763, *map, 1764.*

Garde Mobile (gard mō-bēl), Fr. semi-military police, 2650.

Gardenia (gahr-dē'-ni-a). Genus of trees and shrubs of madder family (*Rubiaceae*), natives of tropical and sub-tropical regions.

Garden mint, 2185.

Garden warbler, *3340.*

Gardinas, Lithuania. Same as **Grodno.**

Gardiner, Alfred George (1865–1946). Eng. journalist and author ; edited " Daily News " from 1902 to 1919 ; (" Prophets, Priests and Kings ").

Gardiner, Samuel Rawson (1829–1902). Eng. historian, who dealt chiefly with the history of the period from James I to Cromwell ; his " History of England " is careful, non-partisan, and based on exhaustive study.

Gardiner, Stephen (*c.* 1493–1555). Eng. prelate and statesman ; succeeded Wolsey as Bishop of Winchester ; he was largely responsible for fall of Thomas Cromwell and inherited his power ; lord chancellor 1553–5.

Gareth (gār'-eth), **Sir.** Knight of the Round Table, 2831.

Garfield, James Abram (1831–81), 20th pres. of U.S.A. ; general in the Federal army, American Civil War ; shot by disappointed office-seeker.

Garga'no. Mountainous peninsula of s. It. extending about 30 m. into Adriatic, 1763.

Gargantua (gahr-gan'-tū-a). Giant hero of Rabelais's satire of that name, whose " Gargantuan " appetite is proverbial ; 2722.

Gargoyle, in architecture, a quaintly formed head of an animal or a man, used as a decorative spout for the rain-water from a roof.

Garibaldi (ga-ri-bahl'-dē), **Giuseppe** (1807–82). It. national hero, **1418,** *1419* ; Cavour and, 737 ; part in Italy's unification, 4170, 1769, and Sicily, 2969.

Gar'lic. A bulbous plant of the onion family ; of strong odour, it is largely eaten in S. European countries and is also used medicinally ; introduced into Europe, 937.

Gar'misch (-Partenkirchen), Bavaria. Small tn. 50 m. s.w. of Munich ; scene of Winter Olympic Games in 1936 ; *378.*

Gar'net. Semi-precious stone, 1427 ; crystal, *939.*

Garnett, David (b. 1892). Eng. author, grandson of Richard Garnett, works include " Lady into Fox," " A Man in the Zoo," " Pocahontas." His mother was Constance Garnett (1861–1946), famous translator from Rus.

Gar'nett, Richard (1835–1906). Eng. librarian and author, keeper of the printed books in Brit. Museum ; wrote lives of Carlyle, Emerson, Milton ; with Gosse wrote history of Eng. literature.

Garnier, Jean Louis Charles (1825–98). Fr. architect, designed Paris Opera House, *2516.*

Garonne (ga-ron'). Chief river in s.w. Fr., rises in Sp. Pyrenees, flows N. into Bay of Biscay ; length 357 m. ; 1360, 1234 ; at Bordeaux, 524 ; Canal du Midi, 1360.

Gar'rick, David (1717–79). Brit. actor and manager, introduced more natural style of acting ; inaugurated revival of Shakespeare's plays in their original form ; universally considered greatest Eng. actor of his age, equally at home in tragedy or farce ; associated with Dr. Johnson, 1213, 1836 ; born at Lichfield, 1934 ; portrait by Hogarth, *1185.*

Garstang, John (b. 1876). Eng. archaeologist, explored ancient Egypt, the Hittite sites of Asia Minor, and Jericho, 208.

Garter, Order of the, 2448 ; Windsor Castle, 3388.

Gar'vin, James Louis (1868–1947). Eng. journalist and publicist, ardent imperialist, most powerful champion of Joseph Chamberlain's tariff reforms ; editor of the " Observer " (1908–42) ; also edited " Pall Mall Gazette " (1912–15) and 14th edition of " Encyclopaedia Britannica ; wrote " Life of Joseph Chamberlain." C.H. 1941.

Gary, Indiana, U.S.A. World's greatest steel-producing centre ; at head of L. Michigan, about 25 m. from Chicago ; pop. 111,700.

Gas. Term invented by van Helmont (1577–1644), Belgian chemist ; he suggested " gas " and " blas," meaning *ghost* and *blow* , the former being adopted, **1419** ; air, 88 ; anaesthetic, 148, 1420 ; carbon dioxide and monoxide, 699 ; chlorine, 816 ; helium, 1607 ; hydrogen, 1673 ; ionization, 1136, 1739, 3396 ; liquefaction, 1391, 1419, 1594, 1826 ; methane, 1420 ; neon, 2314 ; nitrogen, 2372 ; oxygen, 2466 ; in pipes, 1397 ; poisonous kinds, 2638 ; solidification, 1391 ; specific gravity, 3054 ; steam a gas, 3084 ; no surface tension, 3121. *See also* **Liquefied Gases.**

Gas, natural, 1420 ; a bitumen, 2426 in Canada, 679 ; in U.S.A., 2614 yields helium, 1607.

Gas, water, 1424.

Gas black. A type of lamp black used in printing ink, 1725.

Gas burner, a form of Bunsen burner, *616*

Gas'cony. Former duchy in s.w. Fr. ; boundaries were Bay of Biscay, r Garonne, and the Pyrenees ; acquired by Eng. crown, 1609 ; people 1358 ; redemption of Landes, 2870

Gas Engine, 1420, 1016.

Gas'kell, Elizabeth Cleghorn (1810–65) Eng. novelist ; many of her book deal with the poor classes in Manchester ; " Cranford," her best work, is a delightfully humorous sketch of vi lage life ; she wrote an admirabl " Life of Charlotte Brontë," 2402.

Gas manufacture. Production of in flammable gases for heating an lighting, *1422,* **1423,** 856, 1887 ; fron coal distillation, 1423 ; acetylene 18 ; coal-tar industry, 857 ; cooke 3206 ; danger of asphyxiation, 2638 discovery and development, 1423 for heating houses, 1598 ; meter 2152 ; Murdock and, 1423, 2256 natural gas, 1420, 2426 ; in refriger ators, 1392 ; torch, in welding, 3362 water gas, 1424.

Gas meter, 2152, *2153.*

Gasoline. Another name, used espec ally in U.S.A., for petrol.

Gaspar'ri, Pietro (1852–1934). I cardinal, sec. of state under Po Benedict XV (1914–30).

Gas'peri, Alcide de (b. 1881). It. state man ; imprisoned 1926–30 for ant fascist activities ; worked in " u derground " movement during 2r World War ; in 1945 became I prime min.

Agate. A type of chalcedony or semi-precious quartz, with coloured bands, first found on banks of River Achates, hence the name agate. The markings of moss agates occasionally resemble natural objects, hence were much prized in the past. Most agates are naturally greyish and are artificially coloured.

Amethyst. A quartz found in Brazil, Ceylon, and Siberia. Heat turns it yellow. Worn by ancients to prevent intoxication; many wine-glasses were made of it in ancient Rome. Was formerly ten times as valuable as today.

Aquamarine. A sea blue or sea green beryl, of the same class as the emerald, but far less valuable.

Aventurine. A quartz spangled with yellow mica or other mineral. Also called goldstone.

Azurite. An azure-blue copper carbonate found in most copper mines, usually directly above a layer of green malachite. Pliny calls it caeruleum. Value not great.

Beryl. A silicate of low value, though related to the emerald. May be green, light blue, yellow, pink, or white.

Bloodstone. A quartz, dark green with blood-red spots, prized in Middle Ages for carvings of martyrs. Also called heliotrope. Found in Iran, Siberia, Colorado, U.S.A.

Cairngorm. Black or smoky yellow quartz, changed by heating to dark brown or yellow. National stone of Scotland; also called Scottish topaz. Often nearly opaque.

Carbuncle. A garnet cut en cabochon, that is, flat on the bottom, rounded above, without facets. In ancient times any red stone was called a carbuncle, and a mythical " carbuncle " was said to give out light in darkness.

Carnelian. Name given to brown and red chalcedony. Much used for engraved seals in ancient times.

Cat's-eye. The cheaper cat's-eye is of quartz, the more highly valued is of chrysoberyl. Colours range from apple-green to olive, from yellow to brown, but each has a streak or line through the middle, of varying brilliance, like a cat's eye. Hindus value the stone second to the diamond.

Chalcedony. A cryptocrystalline quartz, used by gem engravers in all ages. Called onyx, sardonyx, sard, and carnelian, according to staining.

Chrysoberyl. A rare, unusually hard stone. One variety, the alexandrite, green by day and red by lamplight, had a great vogue among Russian aristocrats.

Chrysolite. An olive-green vitreous magnesium iron silicate, also called olivine and peridot. It is crystalline and, when transparent, used as gem.

Chrysoprase. An apple-green type of chalcedony, found in U.S.A. and Silesia.

Cymophane. Same as cat's-eye.

Diamond. Pure crystallized carbon; hardest known substance, is fairly brittle and easily split, contrary to popular belief that a diamond may be pounded with a hammer and will not break. World's diamonds are said to be worth over £1,000,000,000. (*See* **Diamond, 1009**).

Emerald. When large, brilliant, and flawless, the emerald is the costliest of gems. Composed of silicate of aluminium and beryllium. Chief source of deep green emeralds is Colombia. Some of the most beautiful from North Carolina, U.S.A.

Garnet. A deep red stone, of two varieties, almandine or almandite, and pyrope or Bohemian garnet. When cut en cabochon, both are called carbuncles. The Bobrovka, or green garnet, resembles emerald, but is not hard. Olivine is erroneously called green garnet. Hyacinths are garnets.

Heliotrope. Same as bloodstone.

Jade. A name applied to jadeite, nephrite, and chloromelanite. Jewelry, cups, altar-pieces, and bells or sounding stones are made of it, and poems of emperors have been carved in priceless jade bowls. It does not occur naturally in China, but is imported from Burma. It is also found in Siberia, New Zealand, Mexico, and Europe.

Jasper. An opaque quartz, a variety of chalcedony, putty colour, red, or yellow, mined in Egypt and Russia, much used in Russia for vases, tables, mantels, and pillars.

Jet. A hard black lignite, or variety of fossil coal, mined in Great Britain, China, and elsewhere. Light in weight.

Lapis Lazuli. Mines in Afghanistan, worked for 6,000 years, probably world's oldest mines. Called " sapphire " by ancient world. Finest varieties are gold-flecked with iron pyrites. Cracked quartz stained blue is sold as " Swiss lapis."

Malachite. Colours range from dark to grass green, streaky, much used in Russia. Occurs large enough for table tops.

Marcasite. Metallic stone ranging from slate-grey to bronze-yellow, same composition as pyrites, often set as brilliants in modern costume jewelry.

Moonstone. A variety of translucent feldspar; has a moon-like flash; best specimens found in Ceylon.

Obsidian. A smoky natural glass of volcanic formation, abundant in Yellowstone Park, U.S.A. Used by early Mexicans and North American Indians to make mirrors, arrow-heads, and knives.

Olivine. Same as peridot and chrysolite, differing only in colour.

Onyx. The cameo carver's favourite material. Quartz, or chalcedony, with horizontal stripes of black and white, found in South America and India.

Opal. Harlequin opals have flashes of colour throughout, fire opals are yellow or red with a shifting glow, black opals are dark with coloured lights. Occur in Hungary, Australia, Mexico, and U.S.A. World's largest opal, size of half a brick, black with green and blue fire, found in Nevada. Reputation for ill luck may be due to fragility of stone and occasional loss of brilliance.

Pearl. Not truly a gem stone but the product of pearl oysters. (*See* **Pearls, 2533**).

Peridot. Same as olivine and chrysolite.

Rhodonite. A red or rose stone, streaked with black, of manganese and silica; much prized in Russia.

Rock crystal. A quartz much used for beads, vases, goblets, and crystal balls.

Ruby. A transparent red corundum valued according to shade of colour. Best grade found in Burma, others in Siam, Ceylon, U.S.A. Most valuable shade is " pigeon's blood." Fine rubies of 4 or more carats are worth from 2 to 5 times as much as diamonds of same size. Seldom weigh more than 8 or 10 carats.

Sapphire. A transparent corundum, or aluminium oxide, found mainly in Burma, Ceylon, Siam, and Kashmir; lesser qualities in Australia and U.S.A. Best shades " cornflower " and " velvet " blues. Largest known weighs 916 carats.

Sardonyx. A variety of chalcedony with brown and white stripes or layers of chalcedony and carnelian.

Spinel. Composed of magnesium and aluminium. Clear spinels are valuable; red ones called " spinel rubies."

Topaz. Scotch topaz is yellow quartz. Oriental is yellow sapphire. Brazilian is true topaz. When heated, yellow topaz turns pink. " World's largest diamond," among Portuguese crown jewels, may be colourless topaz. Topaz may be blue, green, brown, pink, white, or yellow.

Tourmaline. A silicate, either black, brown, blue, green, red, or colourless, various colours having different names. Found in Brazil, Siberia, and U.S.A.

Turquoise. An aluminium phosphate, from sky-blue to apple-green. Best grade from Persia, where it has been mined for 800 years. Also found in U.S.A. Heat and sunlight fade turquoise or turn it green. Turquoise matrix is mottled with natural rock.

Zircon. Has recently become fashionable in America. Is found in Ceylon, Australia, Europe, and South America. Natural colours are blue, brown, and green, but are frequently heat-treated to secure greater brilliancy, and colours have been known to fade. Closely related to the hyacinth (red), jacinth (yellow), and jargoon (white), differing only in colour.

Gas poisoning, 2638.

Gasquet (gas'-ket), **Francis Aidan, Cardinal** (1846–1929). Eng. historian; president of International Commission for the Revision of the Vulgate Version of the Bible; Prefect of the Vatican Archives. ("Henry VIII and the Suppression of the Eng. Monasteries"; "The Old English Bible"; "Monastic Life of the Middle Ages").

Gastric juice. Secreted in the stomach, 1016, 3094; contains hydrochloric acid, 816; contains pepsin, 2547; secretion, 1470.

Gas'tropods. A class of molluscs, 2199; snails and slugs, 2989.

Gas Turbine, in aircraft and industry, **1424,** *1425,* 1827, 2673.

Gas warfare, 1420, 1567, 2638.

Gates, Horatio (1728–1806). Amer. general, helped to bring about Burgoyne's surrender at Saratoga in 1777; was defeated at Camden in 1780.

Gateshead. Mfg. tn. in Durham; pop. 113,750; practically suburb of Newcastle on r. Tyne; important shipbuilding, engineering, glass industries; also large rly. workshops, and extensive export trade; here Defoe wrote "Robinson Crusoe."

Gath. Philistine city, 979, 2570.

Gatineau (gat'-i-nō), river in Canada, flowing s. 400 m. into s. Ottawa, 2458.

Gat'ling, Richard Jordan (1818–1903). Amer. inventor; invented machine-gun, 2050.

Gatling gun, 2050.

Gatun (ga-toon'). Tn. in Panama Canal Zone; dam and artificial lake in Panama Canal, *2490, 2491,* 2488, 2490.

Gauchos (gow'-chōz). Cowboys of Argentina, *228.*

Gau'den, John (1605–62). Eng. churchman and writer; reputed author of the celebrated "Eikon Basilike," a defence of Charles I purporting to have been written by the king himself; Bishop of Exeter and of Worcester.

Gauge, of railway track, 594, 2738; of wire, 3391.

Gauge, rain, 2742.

Gauguin (gō'-gan), **Paul** (1848–1903). Fr. painter, pioneer post-impressionist; 2477; portrait, *1689;* and Van Gogh, 3305.

Gaul (gawl) or **Gallia.** Latin name for districts of Celtic peoples; conquered by Romans, 1365; barbarian invasions, 1358, 1365, 3304.

Gaulle, Gen. Charles André de (b. 1890). Leader of Free and Fighting French Govts. and Armies, June 1940 to Aug. 1944; Head of Prov. Govt., Aug. 1944. Prime Min., 1945–46; founded Rassemblement du Peuple Français. 1947: 1426. 3417

Gauls, Celtic people; capture Rome, 2805, 2812; in Fr., 1358, 2518.

Gaur (gowr). Bison of India, 1701.

Gauss (gows), **Karl Friedrich** (1777–1855). Ger. mathematician and physicist, one of the most brilliant of modern times; founded mathematical theory of electricity; de-gaussing, 2186.

Gautama (gow'-tah-ma) or **Gotama.** Family name of Buddha, 600.

Gautier (gō'-tyā), **Théophile** (1811–72). Fr. poet, novelist, and critic, originator of the theory of "art for art's sake" in Fr.; a genius within narrow limits; "Émaux et Camées," his masterpiece, a collection of poems exhibiting his love of miniature effects; novel "Mlle. de Maupin," an attempt at self-analysis; "History of Romanticism," 1381.

Gavarni (ga-vahr-nē') (1804–66). Fr. caricaturist and illustrator; real name Guillaume Chevalier; prolific critic of Parisian life, especially of the poorest and somewhat disreputable classes.

Gaveston, Piers (d. 1312), Earl of Cornwall, arrogant, extravagant favourite of Edward II of Eng.; beheaded by Eng. barons.

Ga'vial or **Gharial.** Indian reptile of crocodile type, 931, *2767.*

Gavotte (ga-vot'). Originally a Fr. peasant dance, merry and light; after its introduction at court in 16th cent. became quieter and more dignified; very popular as a theatrical dance; special music for it written by Bach, Glück, Grétry, and others, 944.

Gawaine (ga'wān), in Arthurian legend, nephew of King Arthur and knight of the Round Table.

Gay, John (1685–1732). Eng. poet and dramatist; his "Beggar's Opera", a famous social satire, created a furore in its day, and since successfully revived.

Gaya. Tn. of Bihar, India, 428.

Gayford, Oswald Robert (d. 1945), Wing-Commander, R.A.F.; set up non-stop long-distance flight record in 1933, flying with G. E. Nicholetts from Cranwell to S.W. Africa; O.C. Long-Distance Flight (1938).

Gay-Lussac (gā-loo-sak), **Joseph Louis** (1778–1850). Fr. chemist and physicist, discoverer of important law that volumes of combining gases bear simple and constant ratio to each other; pioneer in scientific balloon observations.

Gaza, Palestine. Anc. tn. 50 m. s.w. of Jerusalem; most important of the 5 Philistine cities, 2570. Taken by Alexander the Great, became rival of Alexandria and Athens as centre of Hellenic culture; modern port and commercial centre; pop. (1943) 30,300; captured by Brit. in 1917; in Jewish-Arab conflict 1948.

Gazelle (ga-zel'). An antelope of N. Africa, *back of plate f. 72,* 176.

Gaziantep, Turkey. Tn. and trading centre with pop. of 50,000.

Gdansk'. Polish name for **Danzig.**

Gdynia. Polish port 12 m. N.W. of Danzig; pop. 120,000, *2643;* in Ger. occupn., 1939–45.

Gean. Common cherry, 778.

Gears. Motor-car, 2244; differential mechanism, 2245; fluid flywheel, *1667.*

Geatland. Perhaps same as Götaland, in "Beowulf," 415.

Geck'o. Lizard, 1974.

Ged, William (1690–1749). Scottish goldsmith and printer, inventor of stereotyping.

Geddes (ged'-ez), **Auckland Campbell, Baron** (b. 1879). Brit. ambassador to U.S.A., 1920–23; Director of Recruiting, 1916, and in Lloyd George cabinet, Minister of National Service, President of Local Government Board and Minister of Reconstruction; raised to peerage, 1942.

Geddes, Sir Eric (1875–1937). Brother of above. Brit. director-general of military railways and inspector-general of transportation in all theatres of war (1916–17); First Lord of the Admiralty and Controller of the Navy (1917–18); first Minister of Transport (1919); chm. of cttee. on nat. expenditure 1921–23 ("the Geddes axe"); afterwards chairman of Dunlop Rubber Co., Ltd., and Imperial Airways.

Geelong (jē-long'), Australia. Spt. in Victoria; pop. 44,561; woollen trade and mfrs.: quarrying, 3321.

Geffrye Museum, London, 2260.

Gehen'na, or Valley of Hinnom, in Palestine near Jerusalem, 1193.

Geiger-Müller counter. Instr. for detecting radioactivity, 1739; first devised by Hans Geiger (b. 1882).

Geikie, Sir Archibald (1835–1924). Celebrated Scottish geologist; appointed president of the Royal Society 1908; for several years director-general of the geological survey of the United Kingdom; ("Story of a Boulder"; "Text Book of Geology," "Class Book of Geology," etc.).

Geissler (gīs'-ler), **Henry** (1814–79). German maker of scientific instruments, after whom Geissler tubes were named, 3430.

Gel (jel). A colloidal substance that is semi-solid, 871.

Gel'atine or **gelatin.** A jelly obtained by boiling various animal tissues, **1426;** glue from, 1477; isinglass, 1760.

Gelée, Claude. Fr. painter. *See* Lorrain, Claude.

Gell'ius, Aulus (2nd cent. A.D.), Rom. writer of a miscellany, "Attic Nights"; story of Androcles and the Lion, 1960.

Gelmo, P., Ger. chemist, synthesized a sulpha drug in 1908; 3116.

Gelsenkirchen (gel'-zen-kêr-khen). Industrial tn., in Westphalia, Ger. 8 m. N.W. of Essen; pop. (1939) 313,000; town destroyed in 2nd World War; mines, iron and steel, chemicals.

Gemini (jem'-i-nī) or **Twins.** A constellation in the zodiac, 718, 3444; where situated, *chart 895.*

Gemma'tion. Reproduction of a cell by growth of a bud which develops into a new cell.

Gems, or precious stones, **1427;** artificial, 1427; cameo, 671; cutting 1427; diamonds, 1009. *See* list in page 3813.

Gendarmes (zahn'-darm). Members of a police force in France, 2650.

Gender, in grammar, of nouns, 2400; pronouns, 2690.

General, in Brit. Army, rank badge, *245.*

Generalife. Moorish palace in Granada.

General Post Office (G.P.O.), St. Martin's-le-Grand, London; headquarters of the Brit. postal service, 2662; damaged in air raid in 1940.

General Staff. An organized body of officers which assists the commander-in-chief or chief executive in controlling land or naval forces.

General Strike (1926), 3281.

Generator, in electricity. Same as **Dynamo.**

Genes, in heredity, 1427, 1617.

Genesis (jen'-e-sis) (Gk. "coming into being"). The first book of the Bible, sometimes called Book of Creation; it tells of the creation of the world, of the foundation of the Israelite nation, and of the nation's history down to deaths of Jacob and Joseph in Egypt.

Genet'ics. The scientific study of heredity, 433, 533, **1427;** Mendel's theory, 2140. *See also* **Biology.**

Geneva (je-nē'-va), Switzerland. City on L. Geneva; pop. 124,430; **1428,** 3142; centre of Calvinism, 664, 3142, *2759;* League of Nations headquarters. *1909;* Red Cross, 2752.

Geneva (Fr. Lac Léman). Largest lake in Switzerland, in s.w. bordering on France: 223 sq. m.: 45 m long: *1428,* 1885, 3140; fed by Rhône, 2774; geological formation, 1885.

Geneviève (zhen-vyāv) (*c.* 422–*c.* 512). Patron saint of Paris, said to have saved Paris from Attila's Huns by her prayers; caused church to be built over tomb of St. Denis.

Genghis (**Jenghiz** or **Jinghis**) **Khan** (jen'-gis kahn) (1162–1227). Mongol conqueror who first raised Mongol race to power, and swept over Asia, 2205, 1714.

Genie or **jinn.** A supernatural being of vast magical powers, 2057; in the "Arabian Nights," 3451.

Genissiat (zhen-ēs-yah), Fr. Vil. nr. Bellegarde, Ain dept., on Upper Rhône, nr. Swiss frontier; second largest European hydro-elec. installation with 320 ft. dam, to supply large part of Fr.; constructed 1938–49; 961, *plate f. 961,* 2774.

Genlis (zhahn-lēs'), **Stephanie, Comtesse de** (1746–1830). Fr. author and educator, tutor to Philippe Égalité's children, including Louis Philippe; anticipated many modern methods of teaching.

Gennes'aret, Lake or **Sea of.** *See* **Galilee, Sea of.**

Genoa (jen'-o-*a*). It. spt. on Mediterranean, gateway to N. It.; pop. 630,000, **1429;** birthplace of Columbus; Campo Santo, *1772;* bombed and shelled, 1940–1945; liberated April 1945, 1429.

Genoa, Gulf of. Large indentation of Mediterranean in N.W. Italy, with city of Genoa at its head; broad southern portion known as Ligurian Sea: *map, 1764.*

Gen'ocide or **Race Murder.** Any attempt "to destroy, in whole or in part, a national, ethnical, racial, or religious group, as such," was declared a crime by the U.N., Dec. 10, 1948.

Genre (zhahnr) **painting.** The depicting of scenes of everyday life.

Genseric (jen'-se-rik) or **Gaiseric** (A.D. c. 390–477). Vandal king; conquered N. Africa, including Carthage (429–39); plundered Rome (455), 3304.

Gentian (jen'-shan). Plants of fam. Gentianaceae, **1429.**

Gentiles. Term often used in Bible, especially in New Testament, to designate non-Jews.

Genus (jen'-us). A group of related species.

Geod'esy. Measurement of the earth or portions of the earth's surface.

Geode'tic surveying. Surveying in which the curvature of the earth is taken into account.

Geoffrey (jef'-ri) **of Monmouth** (c. 1110–1154), Welsh historian, bishop of St. Asaph; Arthurian legends, 1210.

Geoffrey Plantag'enet (1113–51), Count of Anjou, husband of Matilda, daughter of Henry I of England and father of Henry II, 1609.

Geoffroy-Saint-Hilaire, Étienne (1772–1844). Fr. naturalist, pre-Darwinian believer in mutability of species, founder of the science of teratology or study of monsters.

Geography. Science that describes the earth's surface, its natural products, its peoples, and their economic activities, **1430;** latitude and longitude, 1898; maps and map-making, 2093; physical geography, 2595, 3384. See also **Exploration;** the principal topics above; geographical features (climate, oceans, winds, etc.); and the continents and countries by name.

Geological Survey. Brit. govt. dept. which undertakes among other things the collection of information regarding the geological formation of the country, and the publication of geological maps and explanatory literature concerning them; it was established in 1832; headquarters and museum at S. Kensington, 2250; dioramas, plate f. 1433.

Geology. The science of the earth, its origin, evolution, materials, and physical structure, **1432,** plate f. 1432; earthquakes, 1069; fossils, 1353, 1432; Ice Age, 1469, 1680; idea of earth's evolution established by Lyell, 977; igneous rocks, 1432, 1498; metamorphic rocks, 1432; mountain formation, 2597; origin and evolution of earth, 1067; palaeontology, 1354; periods of geological time, 1432; related to physiography, 2596; sand, 2870; sedimentary rocks, 1432, 2795, 1950; soils, 2998; stratified rock, 2712; valleys, 2597, 3302; volcanoes, 2597, 3328; winds as geologic forces, 2595, 3384. See also **Earth; Physiography;** and the principal rocks and geological features by name.

Geom'etry. The science that treats of mathematical relations and measurements in space, **1434;** mensuration, 2141; non-Euclidean, 1440; Pythagorean contributions, 2710.

Geophyte. A plant with an underground root or tuber.

George I (1660–1727). King of Gt. Brit. **1440,** 1441, 2106, 3276.

George II (1683–1760). King of Gt. Brit. **1440,** 1441; and Chatham, 759.

George III (1738–1820). King of Gt. Brit. **1441;** 3476; bathing, 374; bought Buckingham Palace, 599; and Chatham, 759; and William Pitt, 2614; Seven Years' War, 2924.

George IV (1762–1830). King of Gt. Brit., **1441;** and Brighton, 570.

George V (1865–1936). King of Gt. Brit, **1442;** and Albert I, 102; silver jubilee, 3282; married to Princess May (Mary) of Teck, 2114.

George VI (b. 1895). King of Gt. Brit, **1442;** coinage, 2203; coronation, 912, 913; with Queen Eliza-

both and the Princesses, 3083; silver wedding stamp, 3075; marriage, 1150; in N. Africa, 118; and opening of Parliament, 2524; accession, 1614; relinquished title of emperor of India in 1947, when India and Pakistan were granted independent dominion status. See **Royal Family.**

George I (1845–1913). K. of Greece, 1525.

George II (1890–1947). King of Greece; proclaimed Sept. 1922, following abdication of his father, King Constantine; deposed (1924); returned (1935), 1526; when war broke out between Italy and Greece, 1940, he commanded his army, later when Germany over-ran country he moved with his govt. to Cairo and London. On outbreak of civil war in late 1944 he apptd. Archbishop Damaskinos as regent; king returned to Greece after plebiscite in 1947.

George, St. (d. 303). Patron saint of Eng., **1440;** how he slew the dragon, 1033.

George, David Lloyd. See Lloyd George.

George, Henry (1839–97). Amer. author and political economist; named "single tax" and made it a social creed ("Progress and Poverty"); also wrote "The Condition of Labour."

George, Walter Lionel (1882–1926). Eng. novelist and essayist; "Caliban" and "Blind Alley" are considered his best novels; also wrote "The Intelligence of Woman," "Woman of Tomorrow."

George Cross and **George Medal.** Decorations for civilian gallantry instituted by King George VI, Sept. 1940; G.C. ranks next to Victoria Cross, 2449; presentation to Malta, 2073.

Georgetown. Cap. of Brit. Guiana, on N. coast of S. Amer. at mouth of r. Demerara; pop. 72,000; tropical exports, 1553, 1552.

Georgetown or **Penang.** Cap. of Penang Isl., Straits Settlements, 2 m. from w. coast of Malay Peninsula; 2nd largest port in the Straits.

Georgia. A s. Atlantic state of the U.S.A.; 58,876 sq. m.; pop. 3,123,000; **1443.**

Georgia. Republic of Soviet Russia, bordering Black Sea, 27,000 sq. m.; pop. 3,542,000, **1443;** children of, 275; cap. Tiflis, 2844.

Georgian Period in architecture, 220; in furniture, 1411.

"Georgics." Poem by Virgil, 3325.

Geot'ropism. Tendency of plant structures, especially roots, to seek the earth, 2622; seen in bean rootlet, 381; and banyan branches, 359.

Geraldine the Fair. Lady Elizabeth Fitzgerald, celebrated in some of the Earl of Surrey's sonnets; in late romantic legend, object of Surrey's fantastic chivalrous devotion.

Ger'aldton. Tn., W. Australia, on Champion Bay, 305 m. N.W. of Perth; has an extensive harbour; exports gold, copper, lead and wool; pop. 4,627.

Gera'nium. Flowering plant, **1443,** 1444.

Gérard, François Pascal, Baron (1770–1837). Fr. painter.

Gerard, James Watson (b. 1867). Amer. lawyer and diplomat; ambassador to Germany 1913–17 ("My Four Years in Germany"); headed U.S. delegation to Coronation in 1937.

Gerbert (later Pope Silvester II) (d. 1003), tutor to Otto III, 2460; famous as statesman and scholar; a fine musician; built organs, also clocks, globes, and other instruments; fables clustered round his name; later regarded as a magician.

Géricault (zhā-rē-kō), **Théodore** (1791–1824). Fr. painter, leader of realistic school and revolt against David's classicism.

Gerizim, Mt., Palestine, 2480.

Gerlsdorfer. Mt. in the High Tatra,

loftiest peak in Carpathians (0.707 ft.), 704.

Germ. Popular name for a disease-producing bacterium and protozoan. See **Germs in Disease.**

Germ. The embryo, usually small, in a seed or egg. See **Embryo.**

German, Sir Edward (1862–1936). Eng. musical composer, **1444,** 1464.

German Art. See **Germany, painters and painting of.**

German Confederation, 1449.

German East Africa, now **Tanganyika Territory.**

German Empire. See under **Germany.**

Germanic or **Teutonic languages,** 1456, 2570; contribution to Eng., 1209.

German'icus, Caesar (15 B.C.–A.D. 19). Rom. general, nephew of Tiberius; had nearly conquered Ger. when jealousy of Tiberius led to his recall and transfer to Syria; believed to have been poisoned at instigation of emperor.

Germa'nium (Ge). An extremely rare, greyish metallic element of the carbon group; atomic weight, 72·6; before it was discovered, Mendeléev predicted its properties from the periodic table, naming it Eka-silicon; 777.

German or **Teutonic tribes,** 1456, 2725, 2880; converted to Christianity, 500, 1449; described by Tacitus, 1447; languages and literature, 1456; law, 921.

German silver, an alloy of zinc, 3444.

German South-West Africa, now **South-West Africa Protectorate.**

German-Volga. Autonomous Soviet republic of Russia proper, created in 1923 from parts of prov. of Saratov and Samara; German citizens evacuated to Siberia, 1941.

Germany. Country of cent. Europe; a. 180,000 sq. m.; pop. of German Repub. in 1939 was 69,622,480; **1444;** maps, 1446, 1448, 1453; universities, 1604, 1920; folk customs and costumes, 377, 820, 1447, 2256; gliding, 1476; opera, 2436, 2441, 3331; patriotic songs, 2282; religion, 2878; social insurance, 2994; government under the Nazis, 1451, 1632, 2281.

Geography and Industries: Berlin, 416; Bonn, 500; chief cities and manufactures, 871, 1568, 1574, 1920, 2256, 2696 (see also under names of cities); states, 377, 2696, 2878; foreign trade, 1059; forests, 464, 1581; minerals, 1581, 1753; mts., 1581, 404; oil from coal, 2430; rivers and canals, 686, 689, 972, 1124, 1856, 2769; sugar beet, 3112; toy manufactures. 378. 464.

Germany, History of. General sketch, chief events summarized, **1447.** See also **History.**

Beginnings and Middle Ages (to 1517): Christianity introduced, 500; under Charlemagne, 753, 2878; Holy Rom. Empire revived, 2459, 1637; Henry IV and investiture conflict, 1542, 1609; Frederick I, 1388; Frederick II, 937, 1389; Hanseatic League, 1575.

Reformation and Religious Wars (1517–1640), 1449, 2758; Luther, 2040; Charles V, 1383; Peasants' Revolt, 1449; Thirty Years' War, 1449, 3202.

Rise of Prussia (1640–1871), 2696; Frederick the Great, 1389, 2101, 2642; Seven Years' War, 2924; wars of Fr. Revolution and Napoleon, 1366; serfs freed, 2981; N. German Confederation formed, 1449; Franco-Prussian War, 2155, 1384.

Under the Empire (1871–1918), 1449; Triple Alliance, 1240, 3410; militarism and rivalry with Gt. Brit., 1240, 3378, 3409; 1st World War and peace settlement, 3414. For Kings and Emperors, see under **Prussia.**

Founding the Republic, 1450; William II abdicates, 3378, 3414; reparations payments, 1450, 3414.

The Third Reich: Nazi movement, 1450, 1632, 2281; Hitler as Chancellor and Fuehrer, 1451, 1632; absorption of Austria, 3323, 3416; of Sudetenland, 954, 1451, 3416; of

Bohemia and Moravia, 954, 1451, 3416 ; support for Franco, 3039 ; 2nd World War and after, 1452, 1453, 2222, 2296, 2377, 2794, 2882, 2982, *map 3073*, 3415 et seq., *map, 3419, 3423* ; occupn. stamp, *3075.* Fed. Repub. of W. Ger. formed, cap. Bonn, May, 1949, E. Ger. Repub. in Russian Zone Oct., 1949 ; 418 ; Dr. Adenauer, Chancellor of W. Ger., 1453 ; zones of occupation. 1445. *See also* chief events, states, and historical characters. For list of earlier rulers, *see* Holy Roman Empire ; Prussia.

Germany, language, 1456 ; number of people speaking, 2571.

Germany, literature, 1456 ; drama, 1040, 1042 ; Goethe's influence, 1478 ; novel, 2404 ; Heine, 1604 ; Kant, 1847 ; Schiller, 2882 ; Song of the Nibelungs, 2363.

Germany, painters and painting of, 1454 ; Dürer, 1058 ; Holbein, 1635.

Germination. Start of growth toward mature individual of a seed or egg germ ; seen in bean, *381.*

Germs in Disease, 1458 ; 2132 ; animal germs or protozoans, 2695 ; antiseptics, 177 ; antitoxins, 179 ; bacteria or vegetable germs, 335 ; disease carried by insects, 1313, 1329 ; Lister's work, 1963 ; para-

sitic character of germs, 2513 ; Pasteur, 2527 ; sleeping sickness, 3252 ; vaccination, 3301.

Gérôme (zhä-rōm'), Léon (1824–1904). Fr. painter and sculptor, noted especially for his spirited portrayal of oriental and classical scenes ; " Caesar and Cleopatra," *838* ; " Death of Caesar," *652.*

Gershwin, George (1898–1937). Amer. " jazz " composer ; " Rhapsody in Blue " ; also an opera, " Porgy and Bess."

Ger'yon. A monster in Gk. myth., 1615.

Gessler. A legendary Austrian official ; and William Tell, 3185.

Gestapo. Ger. Nazi secret police ; full name, Geheimnis Staatspolizei, 2282 ; R.A.F. raid on Hague h.q., 1564.

Gethsemane. Garden E. of Jerusalem ; scene of Christ's agony on night before crucifixion, 1820, 1825.

" Getter," a chemical used to complete formation of vacuum, 3301.

Gettysburg, Pennsylvania, U.S.A. Small tn. 35 m. s.w. of Harrisburg ; pop. 5,916 ; scene of decisive battle of American Civil War ; national cemetery, 1952 ; battle at, and Lincoln's speech, 1918, 1952.

Geyser (gā'-zer or gī'-zer). A hot spring, 1459 ; formation, *2596* ; in Iceland, *1685* ; in New Zealand, 2357.

Gezer or Gazara. Anc. royal city of Canaan 20 m. N.W. of Jerusalem ; important frontier post in Maccabean wars ; excavations of impt. material for history of Palestine.

Ghadames (ga-dah'-mes) or Rhadames. Tn. of Libya in an oasis of the Sahara Desert, about 300 m. s.w. of city of Tripoli, 2861 ; pop. 7000.

Gharial or Gavial. A crocodile, 931, *2767.*

Ghat (gawt). Tn. and oasis of Sahara desert in s.w. Tripoli, 2861.

Ghats. Two mt. ranges parallel with E. and w. coasts of peninsula of India, known as Eastern and Western Ghats, 495, 1691, 1701.

Ghats, burning, at Benares, 411, *412.*

Ghazi (1912–39). K. of Iraq ; succeeded his father Feisal in 1933. Killed in car accident April 1939.

Ghazni. Tn. in E. Afghanistan ; strategic position on route between India and Iran ; taken by Eng. 1839 and 1842.

Ghee (gē), in India, butter clarified by boiling, 628.

Ghent (gent), Belgium. Picturesque city famous for flowers, many bridges, and relics of Middle Ages ; in German occupn. 1940–44 ; pop. 161,000 ; 1460, 403.

PROMINENT WRITERS IN THE GERMAN TONGUE

Ulfilas (311 ?–383 ?)—Translation of Bible into Gothic.

Walther von der Vogelweide (1165 ?–1230 ?), minnesinger ; national poet of Middle Ages.

Wolfram von Eschenbach (1170–1220), poet of knighthood— " Parzival " ; " Titurel."

Martin Luther (1483–1546)—Translation of the Bible ; hymns.

Hans Sachs (1494–1576), mastersinger and dramatist— " Fastnachtsspiele " (Shrovetide Plays).

Friedrich Gottlieb Klopstock (1724–1803), classical poet— " Der Messias " (The Messiah) ; odes.

Gotthold Ephraim Lessing (1729–81), critic and dramatist —" Emilia Galotti " ; " Minna von Barnhelm " ; " Laokoön."

Christoph Martin Wieland (1733–1813), novelist and poet— " Der goldene Spiegel " (The Golden Mirror) ; " Agathon."

Johann Gottfried von Herder (1744–1804), critic—" Kritische Wälder " (Critical Forests) ; " Ideen zur Philosophie der Geschichte " (The Philosophy of History).

Johann Wolfgang Goethe (1749–1832), poet, critic, dramatist, and novelist—" Die Leiden des jungen Werthers " (The Sorrows of Young Werther) ; " Wilhelm Meister " ; " Faust " ; " Hermann und Dorothea."

Johann Christoph Friedrich Schiller (1759–1805), poet and dramatist—" Das Lied von der Glocke " (The Song of the Bell) ; " Wallenstein " ; " Maria Stuart " ; " Die Jungfrau von Orleans " (The Maid of Orleans) ; " Wilhelm Tell."

Johann Paul Friedrich Richter (" Jean Paul ") (1763–1825), humorous novelist—" Quintus Fixlein " ; " Siebenkäs " ; " Flegeljahre " (Wild Oats).

Friedrich de la Motte Fouqué (1777–1843), poet and novelist —" Undine " ; " Theodolf, the Icelander."

Heinrich von Kleist (1777–1811), dramatist and poet— " Penthesilea " ; " Der zerbrochene Krug " (The Broken Pitcher).

Jakob (1785–1863) and Wilhelm (1786–1859) Grimm—Fairy Tales ; works on philology.

Arthur Schopenhauer (1788–1860), philosopher—" Die Welt als Wille und Vorstellung " (The World as Will and Idea).

Franz Grillparzer (1791–1872), Austrian dramatist—" Sappho " ; " Das goldene Vliess " (The Golden Fleece).

Heinrich Heine (1797–1856), poet—" Die Lorelei " and many other poems ; " Reisebilder " (Travel Pictures).

August Heinrich Hoffmann (" Hoffmann von Fallersleben ") (1798–1874), poet and song writer—" Deutschland, Deutschland über alles."

Berthold Auerbach (1812–82), novelist—" Schwarzwälder Dorfgeschichten " (Black Forest Village Stories).

Richard Wagner (1813–83), writer of operas—" Lohengrin " ; " Tannhäuser " ; " Der Ring des Nibelungen " ; " Tristan und Isolde " ; " Die Meistersinger " ; " Parsifal."

Gustav Freytag (1816–95), novelist and dramatist—" Die Journalisten " (The Journalists) ; " Soll und Haben " (Debit and Credit).

Theodor Storm (1817–88), poet, novelist, and short story writer—" Immensee."

Gottfried Keller (1819–90), poet, novelist, and short story writer—" Der grüne Heinrich " (Green Henry) ; " Die Leute von Seldwyla " (Seldwyla Folk).

Theodor Fontane (1819–98), poet and novelist—lyric poems and ballads ; " Effi Briest."

Conrad Ferdinand Meyer (1825–98), Swiss poet and novelist —" Jürg Jenatsch " ; " Der Heilige " (The Saint).

Paul Heyse (1830–1914), poet, dramatist, novelist, and short story writer—" L'Arrabbiata " ; " Kinder der Welt " (Children of the World) ; " Im Paradiese " (In Paradise).

Friedrich Nietzsche (1844–1900), philosopher and essayist— " Jenseits von Gut und Böse " (Beyond Good and Evil) ; " Also sprach Zarathustra " (So Spake Zarathustra).

Detlev von Liliencron (1844–1909), poet—lyric poems.

Karl Spitteler (1845–1924), Swiss epic poet and novelist— " Der olympische Frühling " (The Spring of Olympus).

Hermann Sudermann (1857–1928), dramatist and novelist— " Es lebe das Leben " (The Joy of Living) ; " Heimat " (translated as Magda) ; " Frau Sorge " (Dame Care).

Clara Viebig (1860–   ), novelist—" Das tägliche Brod " (Daily Bread) ; " Das schlafende Heer " (The Sleeping Army).

Gerhart Hauptmann (1862–1946), dramatist—" Die Weber " (The Weavers) ; " Die versunkene Glocke " (The Sunken Bell) ; " Hannele."

Arthur Schnitzler (1862–1931), Austrian dramatist and novelist—" Anatol " ; " None but the Brave " ; " The Lonely Way."

Gustav Frenssen (1863–1945), novelist—" Jörn Uhl."

Frank Wedekind (1864–1918), dramatist—" Frühlings Erwachen " (The Awakening of Spring).

Ricarda Huch (1864–1947), novelist and poet—" Defeat " ; " Victory " ; " The Deruga Trial."

Stefan George (1868–1933), poet—" Das Jahr der Seele " (The Year of the Soul) ; " Die Lieder von Traum und Tod " (Songs of Dreams and Death).

Heinrich Mann (1871–1950), novelist—" Die Armen " (The Poor) ; " Mutter Marie " (Mother Mary).

Jakob Wassermann (1873–1934), novelist—" The World's Illusion " ; " Caspar Hauser " ; " The Maurizius Case."

Hugo von Hofmannsthal (1874–1929), Austrian dramatist— " Elektra."

Thomas Mann (1875–   ), novelist—" Die Buddenbrooks " ; " Der Zauterberg " (The Magic Mountain) ; " Der Tod in Venedig " (Death in Venice) ; " Lotte in Weimar."

Rainer Maria Rilke (1875–1926), poet—lyric poems.

Georg Kaiser (1878–1945), dramatist—" Gas " ; " Von Morgens bis Mitternachts " (From Morn to Midnight).

Emil Ludwig (1881–1948), novelist and biographer— " Napoleon " ; " Bismarck " ; " Lincoln " ; " Roosevelt."

Kafka, Franz (1883–1924). Austrian novelist—" The Castle," " The Trial."

Lion Feuchtwanger (1884–   ), novelist—" Jew Süss."

Arnold Zweig (1887–   ), novelist—" The Case of Sergeant Grischa."

Franz Werfel (1890–1945), Austrian novelist, poet, and dramatist—" Einander " (One Another) ; " Der Spiegelmensch " (Reflected Humanity) ; " Class Reunion " ; " The Pure in Heart " ; " The Forty Days of Musa Dagh."

Ernst Toller (1893–1939), poet, dramatist—" Massemensch " (Man and the Masses) ; " Die Machinestürmern " (The Machine Wreckers) ; " Die Wandlung " (Transition).

Vicki Baum (1896–   ), novelist—" Grand Hotel."

Erich Maria Remarque (1898–   ), novelist—" All Quiet on the Western Front " ; " The Road Back."

Erich Kästner (1899–1942), novelist—" Fabian " ; and children's writer—" Emil and the Detectives " ; " The 35th of May " ; " Annaluise and Anton."

Ghent, Treaty of. Ended War of 1812 between Gt. Brit. and U.S.A. (1814).

Gherkin (gêr'-kin). Type of cucumber used for pickling.

Ghetto (get'-ō). Jewish quarter of a city, 1830.

Ghibellines. *See* Guelfs and Ghibellines.

Ghiberti (gē-bêr'-tē), **Lorenzo** (1378–1455). It. sculptor, 1460, 2766, 2904 ; bronze doors for Florence Baptistery, *2905.*

Ghirlandaio (gēr-lan-dah'-yō), **Domenico** (1449–94). It. painter, greatest of a family of Florentine painters ("The Adoration of the Kings"), 1776 ; Michelangelo apprenticed to, 2160.

Giacosa (jah-kō'-sah), **Giuseppe** (1847–1906). It. dramatist.

Giant clam, an enormous mollusc found on Gt. Barrier reef, 861, 2942.

Giant Mts. (Riesengebirge). Highest range of Sudetic Mts. between Czechoslovakia and Silesia ; highest point the Schneekoppe (5,265 ft.).

Giants, 1461 ; Antaeus, 1615 ; of Brobdingnag, in "Gulliver's Travels," 3134 ; Cyclops, 949 ; Giant Despair in "Pilgrim's Progress," *619* ; in Norse myth., 2420 ; Prometheus, 2690 ; Titans, 3298.

Giant salamander, 2864.

Giant's Causeway. Natural formation of close-fitting prismatic columns of basalt rock on N. coast of Ire., 1461.

Giant Spider Crab, *plate f. 925.*

Gibbings, Robert John (b. 1889). Eng. engraver ; did fine work on wood, including much book illustration ; director of Golden Cockerel Press.

Gibbon, Edward (1737–94). Eng. historian, 1461.

Gibbon. A small E. Indian ape with very long arms, 1462, *183, 184.*

Gibbons, Grinling (1648–1720). Eng. sculptor and carver, 1462.

Gibbs, James Edward Allen (1829–1902). Amer. inventor ; invents chain-stitch sewing-machine, 2929.

Gibbs, Sir Philip Hamilton (b. 1877). Eng. journalist and author ; acted as war correspondent in Balkan Wars (1912–13) and 1st World War (1914–18). ("Street of Adventure," "Blood Relations," "European Journey.")

Gibral'tar. Brit. naval base at w. end of Mediterranean, 1462 ; siege raised (1782), *3277* ; caves, 734 ; ceded to Gt. Britain by Treaty of Utrecht, (1713) ; in 2nd World War, 1463.

Gibraltar, Strait of. Passage 40 m. long, to 15 m. wide between Sp. and Africa, connecting Atlantic with Mediterranean ; 1462, 3030.

"Gibraltar of the East," 26.

Gibson, Charles Dana (1867–1944), Amer. illustrator ; excelled as portrayer of society life ; creator of the "Gibson Girl."

Gibson, Wing-Commdr. Guy P., V.C. (1918–1944). Brit. airman ; led attack which breached the Möhne (*q.v.* in *f-i.*) and Eder dams and flooded Ruhr valley, May 16–17, 1943 ; was killed over Ger. in Sept. 1944.

Gibson, John (1790–1866). Brit. sculptor, b. Conway, Wales ; introduced colour after Gk. fashion in tinted "Venus" ; "Sleeping Shepherd"; "Mars and Cupid" ; statue of Queen Victoria for Houses of Parliament.

Gide (zhēd), **André** (b. 1869). Fr. novelist, 1382, 2404 ; D.Litt. (Oxon), 1947 ; awarded Nobel prize for literature in 1947.

Gideon (gid'-e-on). Hebrew judge and warrior ; called by Jehovah to deliver Israel from the Midianites.

Gielgud, John (b. 1904). English actor, member of the Terry family ; achieved great success in "Richard of Bordeaux," "Hamlet," "Romeo and Juliet," "Richard II," "Merchant of Venice," "Love for Love," "The Lady's Not For Burning."

Giffard', Henri (1825–82). Fr. engineer, invented airship run by steam, 92, *93.*

Gif'fen, Sir Robert (1837–1910). Famous Eng. statistician and political economist ; for 15 years controller-general

of the statistical and commercial departments of the Board of Trade ("Essays on Finance," "The Growth of Capital").

Gif'ford, William (1756–1826). Eng. journalist and author ; vehement critic of Keats, Shelley, and other poets when editor of "Quarterly Review" (1809–24).

Gigli (jēl'-yē), **Beniamino** (b. 1890), It. tenor singer ; operatic début at Rovigo (1914) ; Covent Garden début (1930).

Gijon (hē-hōn), Sp. Port for rich mining dist. in centre of N. coast on the Bay of Biscay ; pop. 102,000 ; watering-place ; last N. stronghold of Govt. forces in Civil War, fell to insurgents in Oct. 1937.

Gila monster, poisonous lizard, 1974.

Gil'bert, Sir Alfred (1854–1934). Eminent Eng. sculptor and worker in gold and silver metal, 2900 ; designed Shaftesbury Memorial Fountain (Eros), London, *2017, 2907.*

Gilbert, Sir Humphrey (c. 1539–93), Eng. navigator ; seeking the North-West Passage (1583), took possession of Newfoundland for Queen Elizabeth ; lost at sea on return voyage, 142, 580, 2338, 2743.

Gilbert, Sir John (1817–97), Eng. painter and illustrator ; great historic themes of vigorous design and colour ; "Charles I Sentenced," *756* ; "The Morning of Agincourt," *76* ; "Shylock, Salanio and Salarino," *2145.*

Gilbert, William (1540–1603). Eng. scientist ; coined word "electricity," 1127 ; first showed that the earth itself is a magnet, 2060.

Gilbert, Sir William Schwenk (1836–1911). Eng. humorist and playwright, 1463.

Gilbert and Sullivan, 1463, 2438.

Gilbert Islands, Brit. group of coral isls. on Equator in mid-Pacific, part of the Gilbert and Ellice Isls. Colony ; 166 sq. m. ; pop. 27,000 ; 2473 ; Japan occupied 1942–43, 2474, 3421.

Gil Blas, hero of one of the world's great picaresque novels, "The Adventures of Gil Blas" by Le Sage.

Gilbo'a, mt. range in Palestine, scene of battle in which Saul and Jonathan were slain, 979.

Gilds. Same as Guilds.

Gilead (gil'-e-ad), anc. name for mountainous but fertile dist. in Palestine, 2641.

Giles (jīlz), **St.** (b. c. 7th cent. A.D.). Patron saint of beggars and cripples ; hermit and Benedictine abbot of France.

Gil'gal, anc. city in Jordan valley between Jericho and river, where Israelites first encamped after crossing the Jordan (Josh. iv).

"Gilgamesh, Epic of," 332.

Gill (jil), a unit of dry and liquid measure : quarter of a pint.

Gill, (Arthur) Eric (Rowton) (1882–1940). Eng. sculptor ; carved figures on Broadcasting House and Underground building, London, 2911 ; evolved Gill Sans type, 2217 ; "Stations of the Cross," *2910.*

Gillette (ji-let'), **King Camp** (1855–1932), Amer. inventor of the safety-razor which bears his name.

Gillette, William (1855–1937), Amer. actor and playwright ; best known for his work in "Sherlock Holmes" and "The Admirable Crichton."

Gillies (gil'-ēz), **Sir Harold D.** (b. 1882). N.Z. surgeon ; plastic surgeon to the three services in Second World War ; wrote "Plastic Surgery of the Face."

Gillingham, tn. in Kent, on the Medway, E. of Chatham ; industries include making bricks and cement, while the dockyards of Chatham find work for many ; pop. 60,980.

Gill-net, for cod fishing, *1299.*

Gillott, Joseph (1799–1873), Eng. manufacturer of steel pens, 2539.

Gillray, James (1751–1815), Eng. caricaturist ; satirized all great figures of the era.

Gills (gilz), organs for breathing under water, 2768 ; in fish, 1296 ; in tad-

poles of frogs and toads, 1398, 3219 ; in embryo vertebrates, 3318.

Gilpin (gil'-pin), **John,** in Cowper's "John Gilpin's Ride," a linen-draper who has many ludicrous adventures on horseback, 923.

Gimbal (jim'-bal), in compass mountings, 882.

Gimson, Ernest (1864–1919). Eng. furniture-designer ; disciple of William Morris and re-creator of a tradition in Eng. furniture after stereotyped Victorian era ; 1412.

Gin, a liquor, 103 ; juniper berries for, 1841.

Gin, cotton, a machine, 918.

Ginger, a spice, **1464,** *3061*

Gingko, or **Ginkgo,** maidenhair tree, 1464, 3246.

Ginza, The. Centre of Tokyo's business quarter, 3222.

"Gioconda" (jō-kon'-da), **La,"** or **"Mona Lisa,"** painting by Leonardo da Vinci in the Louvre, *2033.*

Giolitti (jō-lē'-tē), **Giovanni** (1842–1928). It. statesman ; several times premier ; opposed Italy's participation in the 1st World War.

Giordano (jor-dah'-nō), **Luca** (1632–1705), Italian painter ; born Naples ; painted with astonishing speed ; called "Fa-Presto" (work fast) ; his works show influence of the great masters of painting ("Christ Expelling the Traders" ; "Francis Xavier" ; "Judgement of Paris").

Giordano, Umberto (1867–1948), Italian composer ; studied under Verdi "(Andrea Chénier" ; "Fedora" ; "Madame Sans-Gêne," and other operas).

Giorgione (jor-jō'-nā), or **Giorgio Barbarelli** (1478–1510). It. painter, 1776 ; portrait of Cesare Borgia, 2031.

Giotto (jot'-tō) **di Bondone** (c. 1266–1337), It. painter, sculptor, and architect, **1464,** 1775, 2766 ; tower in Florence, 1014.

Giovanni de' Medici (d. 1429), Florentine merchant ; founded greatness of de' Medici family, 2131.

Gipsies, nomad peoples ; Hungarian, 1655 ; Spanish, *plate f. 3032.*

Giraffe (ji-rahf'), long-necked animal, 1464 ; *plate f. 1464, 1465* ; in Africa, *back of plate f. 72.*

Giralda (hi-ral'-da), a bell-tower at Seville, *2926.*

Girard (zhē-rahr'), **Jean Baptiste** ("Le Père Girard") (1765–1850). Swiss educator ; entered Franciscan Order ; held all elements of study should serve to stimulate the ability to think.

Girard, Stephen (1750–1831). Amer. merchant, banker, and philanthropist.

Girasol (jir'-a-sol), a blue-white precious opal with red play of colour, used as a gem.

Giraud (zhē-rō), **Henri H.** (1879–1949). Fr. soldier ; in Sec. World War commanded Fr. 7th Army ; captured May 2, 1940, and imprisoned in Königstein, Saxony, but escaped April 1942 ; by Brit. submarine to N. Africa, where app. C.-in-C. (1942–Apr. 1944) by Darlan ; replaced Darlan as high commissioner of Fr. N. and W. Africa Dec. 1942 ; rival of De Gaulle in Free Fr. govt. in N. Africa ; retired May 1944 ; 1426.

Giraudoux (zhē-rō-dōo), **Jean** (1882–1944), French writer and diplomat ; graceful, impressionistic, original style ("Lecture pour une ombre," a novel of the 1st World War ; "Bella," a political novel ; "Juliette au pays des hommes"; "Siegfried"; "Suzanne et le Pacifique" ; play, "Amphitryon 38 ").

Girder, a form of beam, *380, 565, 605* ; bridge, 568.

Gir'ga, Eg. tn. and former cap. of Upper Eg., on Nile ; pop. 20,000, 1098.

Girgenti (jir-jen'-tē), city near S. coast of Sicily ; pop. 30,000 ; ruins of Gk. temples ; anc. Agrigentum, 2968.

Girl Guides, 1465, *1466, 1467* ; *plates f. 1468, 1469.*

Gironde (zhē-rond), estuary in S.W. France, 45 m. long ; *map, 1359*; route to Bordeaux, 524.

Girondists (ji-ron'-dists), political party of Fr. Rev.; advocated moderate republicanism, 524, 2798.

Girtin, Thomas (1775–1802), Eng. artist, founder of modern school of water-colour painting, 1181 ,3353; Kirkstall Abbey, *3352*.

Girton College, Cambridge, 666, 669; from 1948 full univ. degrees were granted by Cambridge Univ. to women students.

Girvan, Scot. Tn. in Ayrshire; fisheries; pop. 5,300, 324.

Gish, Lillian (b. 1896), American cinema actress; starred in "The Birth of a Nation"; "Way Down East"; "Broken Blossoms"; "Orphans of the Storm," with her sister Dorothy Gish (b. 1898), cinema star of "Nell Gwyn"; "Madame Pompadour."

Gis'sing, George Robert (1857–1903), Eng. realistic novelist who chiefly depicted the struggling life of the shabby-genteel and the conflict between education and circumstances ("The New Grub Street"; "Born in Exile"; "The Private Papers of Henry Ryecroft"; "The Odd Women").

Giuliano (joo-lē-ah'-nō) **de' Medici** (1453–78), younger brother of Lorenzo de' Medici, 2131.

Giulio Romano (jōō'-lē-ō rō-mah'-nō) (1492–1546). It. painter and architect (Fr. form of name Jules Romain); pupil, assistant, and successor of Raphael as head of Rom. school of painting; "Dance of Apollo and the Muses," *187*; "Battle of Milvian Bridge," *894*.

Giurgevo or **Giurgiu** (joor'-jōō), Rumania. Port of Bucharest on Danube; pop. 30,300; engagements in Russo-Turkish wars.

Giz. Classical Ethiopic, 16.

Gizeh (gē-ze), also **Giza.** Eg. tn. on Nile nearly opposite Cairo; pop. 37,800; Great Pyramid, *2708*; Sphinx, 3058, *3059*.

Gizzard. The last and most important of a bird's three stomachs; has muscular walls and grinds food with aid of gravel in seed and grain eaters; merely a membranous sac in carnivorous birds; discharges prepared food for absorption into intestine; 437.

Gjellerup (yel'-*e*-roop), **Karl** (1857–1919). Danish poet and novelist; early disciple of Georg Brandes; wrote "The Disciple of the Teutons," an anti-theological work, under his influence; later works showed deep spiritual and ethical strain; shared Nobel Prize 1917 with Pontoppidan ("The Mill").

Gjöa. Amundsen's ship, 148, 2645.

Glacial Period or **Ice Age**, 1680; in N. Amer., 2384.

Glacier. A moving ice field, **1468**, 2596, *2598*; Canada, 578; greatest of Europe, 2393; Greenland, 1541; icebergs, 1682; Switzerland, 126.

Glacier National Park. In Montana, U.S.A., 1,450 sq. m.

Glacier Park. Brit. Columbia, in the Selkirk Mts.; 468 sq. m.; series of caverns called Nakimu Caves.

Gladiator (glad'-i-ā-tor). Professional fighter in anc. Rome, **1469**.

Gladiolus (glad-i-ō'-lus). Flower belonging to the Iris family (*Iridaceae*); most of them are natives of S. Africa; flower in summer and autumn; red, white, or yellow blooms, extremely popular in Eng. as garden plant.

Gladkov (glahd'-kof), **Feodor Vasilievich** (b. 1883). Russian novelist of industrialism ("Cement").

Gladstone, Herbert, 1st Viscount (1854–1930). Brit. politician, youngest son of William Ewart Gladstone; was Home Secretary (1905–9) and Governor-General of S. Africa (1909–14).

Gladstone, William Ewart (1809–98). Brit. Liberal statesman, **1469**, 3278, 3279; rivalry with Disraeli, 1019; Irish question, 2525, 1746; Victoria and, 3320.

Glaisher, James (1809–1903). English aeronaut; founded Meteorological Society in 1860; helped to found Aeronautical Society (1866); made several balloon ascents, reaching 28,000 ft. with H. T. Coxwell in 1862.

Glamis (glahmz). Vil. in Angus, Scot.; Glamis Castle is the historic seat of the Earl of Strathmore, 155.

Glamorganshire. Southernmost co. of Wales; 813 sq. m.; pop. 1,225,000; **1470.**

Gland. In human body, **1470**; kidneys, 1855; liver, 1968; sebaceous, 2979; sweat, 2979.

Glanders. An infectious disease, common among horses and asses, less frequently attacking cattle and other livestock; ulcers, pus discharge from lungs, and high temperature are characteristics.

Glarus. Cap. of Swiss canton of same name, 43 m. from Zurich; pop. 5,200; cotton mills, breweries.

Glasgow. Largest city of Scot.; pop. 1,075,000; on Clyde; **1471**, 854, 1890, 2890.

Glasgow University. Founded 1451 by Bishop Turnbull; co-ed. since 1893; retains many medieval customs, including student election of rector; faculties of arts, science, medicine, divinity, law; *1472*, 2893.

Glass. A super-cooled liquid, **1472**, *plates f. 1472, 1473*, 1391; artificial, 2627; Czech, *953*; etching, 1567; fibres from, 2750; mirrors, 2190; optical instruments, 3178; safety glass, 2626; salt compounds used, 2866; sand and silica, 2871; specific gravity, 3054; telescope disk, *3178*; thallium compounds in, 3193.

Glasses, for eyes. *See* **Spectacles.**

Glass wool, 1474.

Glastonbury. Tn. in Somersetshire, on r. Brue; ruins of 12th-cent. abbey; "Glastonbury thorn," a variety which flowers once a year at Christmas, said to have sprung from the staff planted by Joseph of Arimathea, who was reputed to have built here first Christian church in Eng.; 1589, 3000.

Glauber (glow'-ber), **Johann Rudolf** (1604–68). Ger. chemist, discovered (1658) Glauber's salt; used medicinally.

Glauber's salt. Found in large quantities in Austria, It., and Sp.; small quantity in blood; 2865.

Glau'conite or **greensand.** A soft olive-green mineral.

Glaze. In pottery, 2666, 2667; enamelling, 1158.

Glazed bricks, 562.

Glencoe, Scot. Glen 60 m. N.W. of Glasgow; wild scenery; massacre of Macdonalds by royal troops in 1692.

Glendower (glen-dow'-er), **Owen** (c. 1359–c. 1416). Welsh chief, national hero; last independent Prince of Wales and leader of last war for Welsh independence; 3334.

Glider, 1474, *1475, plate f. 1513*; early expts., *44*, 45; Glider Pilot Regt., 245, 1476.

Glinka (glin'-ka), **Michael Ivanovich** (1803–57). Pioneer of modern Rus. school of national music.

Globe Theatre. Old playhouse in London, *1039, 2935*.

Glockenspiel. Same as **Carillon.**

Glommen, Norway. Largest of the rivers in Scandinavian peninsula; rises in Dovrefjeld tableland and flows s. 350 m. entering Skagerrak 50 m. s.e. of Oslo.

Gloos'kap. A demi-god in myth. of N. Amer. Indians.

Gloriana (glor-i-ah'-na). In Spenser's "Faerie Queene," representation of Queen Elizabeth.

Glossop. Mfg. tn. in Derbyshire; cotton, paper; dyeing, bleaching; pop. 20,000; 995.

Gloucester, Duke of (b. 1900). Henry, third son of George V; m. Lady Alice Scott, d. of 7th Duke of Buccleuch, in 1935; has two sons, b. 1941 and 1944; Gov.-General of Australia, 1943–47.

Gloucester (glos'-ter). Co. tn. of Gloucestershire, on Severn; pop. 52,900; has railway, eng., and aircraft works, flour mills and numerous other industries; canal joins tn. to Bristol; noted cath. of Norman-Gothic architecture, *1476*.

Gloucester, Massachusetts. Leading fishing port in U.S.A. and one of largest in world; on Cape Ann, 27 m. N.E. of Boston; pop. 24,000.

Gloucestershire. County in s.w. Eng. at head of Severn estuary; 1,243 sq. m.; pop. 786,000; **1476.**

Gloves, 1477; preparation of leather, 1914; rubber, 2836.

Glow-worms and fireflies, **1288.**

Glubb, John Bagot, "Glubb Pasha" (b. 1897). Brit. soldier; in Iraq, 1920–30; commanded Arab Legion, Transjordan, from 1939.

Glucinum (gloo-sī'-*num*) (Gl.) Another name for the metallic element beryllium (Be) of atomic weight 9·02. *See* Beryllium.

Gluck, Christoph Willibald (1714–87). Ger. composer; earliest of great modern opera writers, and first to make opera truly dramatic, suiting the music to the character by whom it is sung; 2264, 2436.

Glucose. A variety of sugar, also called grape sugar or dextrose, **1477**, 2589, 3082, 3114.

Glu'coside. A vegetable substance, yielding glucose when decomposed.

Glue. An adhesive substance for sticking together wood and other materials; **1477.**

Gluten (glōō'-ten). A tough, elastic albuminous substance; in bread, 555; in macaroni, 2045; a protein, 2694.

Glycerine (glis'-er-in) or **Glycerol.** A clear colourless sweet-tasting syrup, **1477**, 1263; base of nitro-glycerin, 1060; in resin mfr., 2768; in soap-making, 2993.

Glycogen (glī'-kō-jen). Formed by liver, 1968, 3052.

Glycol. Dihydric alcohol, with industrial uses, 1478, 2430.

Glyndebourne. Estate near village of Glynde in Sussex, 3 m. s.e. of Lewes. Famous for its summer seasons of opera; *2436*, 3123.

Glyp'todon (Gk. "fluted tooth"). A very large armadillo-like animal of S. Amer., now extinct; attained size of an ox; had very strong limbs with short broad feet; teeth were deeply grooved or fluted, *2679*.

G-men, detectives of the U.S. Federal Bureau of Investigation, 2651.

Gnat (nat). A popular term for various small two-winged insects, 1732; life story, 2236.

Gneisenau (nī'-zen-ow). Ger. battleship, second of name; completed 1938; 35,100 tons; after sinking about 20 merchant ships in the Atlantic with Scharnhorst, put into Brest to refit Mar. 28, 1941; joined by Prinz Eugen; bombed repeatedly by R.A.F. from Mar. 30, 1941, to Feb. 12, 1942, when the 3 ships slipped unseen up Channel; attacked by 6 Swordfish torpedo-carriers, which were shot down. Gneisenau was bombed at Kiel; moved to Gdynia, where Mar. 28, 1945, she was captured by Russians, and commissioned as floating battery.

Gneiss (nīs). An igneous rock, 1265.

Gnetales. Group of plants, found chiefly in warm regions, intermediate between Angiosperms and Gymnosperms; *Ephedra*, typical example, shows resemblances to conifers; *Gnetum* converges to flowering plants; reproductive organs cone-like, leaves scale-like.

Gnome, rotary aero engine, 46.

Gnosticism (nos'-ti-siz-m). Movement within early Christian Church (flourishing in 2nd and 3rd centuries) combining elements of Christian, Jewish, Greek, and Oriental philosophies; held knowledge, obtained from revelation, not faith, is key to salvation.

Gnu (nū). An antelope, 176.

Goa (gō'-*a*). Portuguese possession on Malabar coast of India; 60 m. long, 30 m. wide; conquered by Albuquerque in 1510; total pop. of colony (1940), 624,000; 1691; Xavier at, *3429*.

Goal, in football, 1344, 1345, 1346.

Goat. A domesticated ruminant, **1478,** 2842 ; ibex, 1679 ; milk, 2173 ; related to sheep, 2940.

Goat (Capricornus). A sign of the zodiac, 3444.

Goat, Rocky Mountain. An antelope, 176.

Goat fish, in coral reef, *2104.*

Goat Island, in Niagara r., 2361, *2362.*

Goat's-beard. Member of the *Compositae* order with large, yellow, dandelion-like flowers ; also known as Jack-go-to-bed-at-noon.

Goatskin, 1914.

Göbbels. *See* **Goebbels.**

Gobelin (gŏb'-lan). Famous French tapestries, made in Paris ; so named from a family of dyers of name of Gobelin who owned building in which tapestry industry was established in 16th cent. The industry is maintained by the French government ; 3153, 3192.

Gobi (gō'-bē) or **Shamo.** Desert region ; in cent. China ; 260,000 sq. m., elevation 3,000 to 5,000 ft. ; 2204, 263, 264, 265 ; driest place in world, *808* ; in Mongolia, 2204 ; wild camels, 671.

Goblins. Grotesque fairies, similar to gnomes and kobolds ; they are sometimes evil and malicious and sometimes only playful and tricky.

" Goblin " jet engine, *1828.*

Goby, or mud-skipper, an E. Indian fish, 2250.

Godard, Benjamin Louis Paul (1849–95). French composer ; works for orchestra, violin, piano, songs, chamber music, operas (" Jocelyn ").

Godavari. Large r. in s. India ; rises N.E. of Bombay in W. Ghats, flows 900 m. s.E., entering Bay of Bengal by 7 mouths : navigable for 300 m.

God'dard, Rayner Goddard, Baron (b. 1877). Brit. judge ; in 1946 Lord Chief Justice ; advised rejection of experimental suspension of death penalty for five yrs., in 1948.

Godfrey of Bouillon (boo-yon') (c. 1061–1100). Leader in First Crusade, and first Christian ruler of Jerusalem ; hero of Tasso's " Jerusalem Delivered " ; 936.

Godiva (gō-dī'-va), **Lady** (11th cent.). Legendary Eng. heroine ; at Coventry, *922.*

Godowsky (gō-dof'-ski), **Leopold** (b. 1870). Russian-American pianist and composer, born Vilna (Wilno) ; paraphrases of Bach, Chopin, Johann Strauss ; many original compositions.

Godoy, Manuel de (1767–1851). Sp. Duke of Alcudia and Prince of the Peace, favourite of Charles IV and his queen ; virtually dominated Sp. during the imbecile king's reign.

" God Save the King." Brit. national anthem, 2282.

Godthaab. Settlement in s.w. Greenland.

Godwin, Mary Wollstonecraft (1759–97). Eng. women's rights advocate (" Vindication of the Rights of Woman ") ; wife of William Godwin, a political philosopher and novelist ; mother of Shelley's wife, Mary.

Godwin-Austen. Second highest mt. in the world, 28,278 ft. high ; in Mustagh range on N.E. frontier of Kashmir ; also called Dapsang.

Goebbels (gě'-blz), **Paul Josef** (1897–1945). German politician ; appointed Reich minister for propaganda, 1933. Committed suicide May 1945 ; 2282.

Goering (gě'-ring), **Hermann Wilhelm** (1893–1946). German politician ; " ace " of German air force during 1914–18 War ; Pres. of Reichstag (1932), Reich min. for Air Forces (1933) ; supreme commander Air Forces (1934) ; 1937 superseded Schacht as economic dictator ; Field-Marshal Feb. 1938 ; Air Minister, etc., 1939–45 ; war criminal ; committed suicide Oct. 1946 ; 2282.

Goethals (gō'-thahlz), **George Washington** (1858–1928). Amer. army officer and engineer ; Panama Canal, 2488.

Goethe (gě'-te), **Johann Wolfgang** (1749–1832). Ger. poet, novelist and

philosopher ; the greatest figure in Ger. literature, **1478,** 1456, 2404 ; " Faust," 1263 ; friendship with Schiller, 2882 ; home in Weimar, 3362.

Gog and Ma'gog. Heathen prince and people (Ezek. xxxviii-xxxix) ; in Brit. legend, two giants whose effigies were kept in London Guildhall, until destroyed by bombing 1940.

Gogh, Van. *See* **Van Gogh.**

Go'gol, Nicholas Vasilievich (1809–52). Rus. novelist and dramatist ; called " father of modern Russian realism"; 2856, 2983 ; influence on modern novel, 2404.

Goitre (goi'-ter). An enlargement of the thyroid gland, 1470.

Golconda (gol-kon'-da), India. Ruined city 5 m. w. of Hyderabad ; famous as diamond-cutting centre in 16th cent. ; name hence used to mean a mine of wealth.

Gold (Au). A precious metallic element of the copper group ; atomic weight, 197·2 ; extremely malleable and ductile ; melting pt. 1,061° C., used as a standard for high temp. thermometers ; **1479,** 2148 ; Alaska, 97 ; alloys, 1481 ; Australia, 308, *310,* 2136, 3368 ; California, 1479 ; Canada, 1479 ; chemical and physical properties, 777 ; currency, 2201 ; dredging for, *1047* ; industrial uses, 947, 2541 ; mining and refining, 947, 1479, *1480, 2183* ; Russia, 2845 ; Siberia, 2967 ; S. Africa, 73, 1833, 3013, 3239 ; specific gravity, 3054 ; Transvaal, 3239 ; U.S.A., 3288 ; white gold, 1481 ; Yukon, 3444.

Gold-beating, 1481.

Gold chloride, 1481.

Gold Coast. Brit. colony in W. Africa extending 334 m. along Gulf of Guinea ; 91,843 sq. m., including Ashanti and N. Territories ; pop. (1942) 3,963,000 ; cap. Accra : 648, 3366 ; *map, 3366.* New constitution in 1946 led to serious riots in Accra in Feb.–March 1948.

Gold Coast University College. Opened Oct. 1948 ; at first sharing buildings of Achimota College, Gold Coast.

Gold-crest. A wren, 3425.

Golden Age, of Athens, 2551 ; of It. literature, 1786 ; of Latin literature, 1896 ; of Saturn, 2875.

Golden apple. Awarded by Paris to Aphrodite, 2514.

Golden apples of Hesperides. In Gk. myth., obtained by Hercules, 1615.

Golden Bough, legend of the, by Sir James Frazer, 1387.

Golden Bull. Originally any charter with golden seal or bulla ; especially edict issued (1356) by the Emperor Charles IV.

Golden Calf. Image made by Israelites from their earrings at instigation of Aaron while Moses was absent on Mount Sinai receiving the Ten Commandments.

Golden eagle, *1063, 1064.*

Golden Fleece. Sought by the Argonauts, 229 ; possible origin of legend, 2182.

Golden Fleece, Order of, 593.

Golden Gate. Channel about 2 m. wide at entrance to San Francisco Bay, California, U.S.A., 2871 ; bridge, 569, 2872.

Golden Hind. Drake's ship.

Golden Horde. Tartars who overran Rus. in 13th cent., 2205, 2847 ; effect on Rus. literature, 2855.

Golden Horn. Harbour of Istanbul, 529, 1761.

Golden Lion. Lord Thomas Howard's ship.

Golden oriole, *2452.*

Golden pheasant, 2565.

Golden plover, 2171, 2629, *2630.*

Golden-rayed lily, 1947.

Golden-rod. An autumn-flowering plant.

Golden Rose. A papal honour, probably established in the 11th cent. ; awarded to Queen of Italy by Pope Pius XI in 1937.

Golden Rule. " Whatsoever ye would that men should do to you, do ye even so to them ; for this is the law and the prophets " (Matthew vii. 12, and Luke vi. 31).

Golden syrup, how made, 3114.

" Golden Treasury," anthology of English songs and lyrical poems, compiled by F. T. Palgrave, 1966.

Goldfinch, or **wild canary,** 1272.

Goldfish. A small species of carp, **1481,** *1482.*

Gold lace. Manufacture, 1481.

Gold leaf. An extremely fine sheet of beaten gold.

Gold-leaf electroscope, 1133.

Goldoni (gol-dō'-nē), **Carlo** (1707–93). It. dramatist, founder of modern It. comedy ; " The Coffee House," " Pamela " and " La Locandiera " (Eng. adaption " Mirandolina ") are his best plays ; wrote several plays in Fr.

Goldsmith, Oliver (1728–74). Irish novelist, essayist, and poet, **1482,** 1213, 2402 ; and Dr. Johnson, 1836.

Gold standard. Use of gold alone for standard money, as opposed to bimetallic use of gold and silver, **1482,** 2203 ; re-adopted in 1925 in U.K., 1483 ; suspended in 1931.

Goldwyn, Samuel (b. 1884). American film magnate. With Jesse Lasky formed Lasky Co. in 1910. Formed Goldwyn Pictures Corporation, 1918, later absorbed in Metro-Goldwyn-Mayer Co.

Golf. Outdoor sport, **1483,** *1485.*

Golgotha (gol'-gō-tha) or **Calvary.** Place near Jerusalem where Christ was crucified.

Goli'ath. Philistine giant (1 Sam. xvii.), 979.

Goliath beetle, 398.

Goltz, Colmar von der (1843–1916). Prussian general and military writer ; reorganized Turkish army (1883–95) ; gov.-gen. of Belgium (1914) ; commanded Turkish army in Mesopotamia (1915–16) (" War History of Germany in 19th Century " ; " The Nation in Arms ").

Gomez (gō'-mās), **Estevan.** Port. sailor ; explored coast of N. America, 142.

Gomez, Juan Vicente (1859–1935). pres. of Venezuela for 26 yrs. ; successful in extricating Venezuela from foreign complications created by Castro.

Gompers, Samuel (1850–1924). Amer. labour leader ; one of the outstanding figures of the Labour movement ; pres. of the Amer. Federation of Labour for about 40 years.

Goncharov (gon-cha-rof'), **Ivan Alexandrovitch** (1812–91). Rus. novelist, wrote " Oblomov," " masterpiece that ranks with the best work of Tolstoy and Turgeniev," which gave Rus. the term " Oblomovism " as a synonym for diseased will and indolence.

Goncourt (gon-kōōr), **Edmond de** (1822–96). Fr. novelist and historian ; in collaboration with his brother Jules (1830–70) wrote minute valuable studies of Fr. society in 18th cent. ; novels continued naturalistic method of Flaubert and taught Zola (" Germinie Lacerteux," called " the clinic of love " ; " Renée Mauperin," a convincing story of young Parisian society girl).

Gondar. Religious centre of Abyssinia ; cap. of Amhara prov. ; in the N., 250 m. from Red Sea ; pop. 8,000.

Gondoko'ro. Eg. village on Upper Nile ; formerly centre of slave and ivory trade, 1095.

Gon'dola. Long narrow Venetian boat, 3310, *3312.*

" Gondoliers, The." Famous comic opera by Gilbert and Sullivan.

Gonds. An aboriginal race of India, who maintained independence until 18th cent., 1701.

Gon'eril. One of King Lear's two cruel daughters, in Shakespeare's tragedy, 1858.

Go'niatites. Fossil shells common in Devonian rocks ; forms of Cephalopoda now extinct ; resembling nautilus ; 1433 ; 2199.

Gonville and Caius (kēz) **College,** Cambridge, founded in 1348, 668.

Gonzales (gon-zah'-lez), **Manuel** (1833–93). Mex. general, close friend of

Diaz, whom he aided in rev. of 1876; succeeded Diaz as pres. 1880–84, when he resigned in his friend's favour.

Goodall, Frederick (1822–1904). Eng. artist. Member of a family of painters; did many pictures, very popular in reproductions. Many of his scenes are set in Egypt and the near East.

" Good Companions, The." Novel, subsequently dramatized and made into a film, by J. B. Priestley; deals with the fortunes of a touring concert party; 2683.

Good Friday. Day commemorating Our Lord's Crucifixion.

" Good Queen Bess." Queen Elizabeth, 1146.

Goodwin Sands. Dangerous shoals at entrance to Strait of Dover, separated from mainland by the Downs, a roadstead of Eng. Channel.

Goodwood. 3 m. N.E. of Chichester, seat of Duke of Richmond and Gordon. Near by is racecourse where races are held annually at the end of July. Principal event, the Goodwood Cup.

Goodyear, Charles (1800–60). Amer. inventor; discoverer of method of vulcanizing rubber, 2834.

Goofah. Circular basket-like boat, *482, 484.*

Goosander. A duck, 1053.

Goose, Elizabeth. Supposed original of " Mother Goose," 2239.

Goose, web-footed bird, **1484**, 2671; at Michaelmas, origin, 1580; barnacle goose, 361.

Gooseberry. A spiny shrub and its fruit, **1486.**

Gopher (gō-fer). A species of burrowing rodent; *Geomys*; the European variety is not unlike the squirrel, but the tufted tail and ears are absent.

Gorboduc (gor'-bŏ-duk). Mythical king of Brit.; subject of first Eng. tragedy. *See* **Dorset, Thomas Sackville, 1st Earl of.**

Gor'dian knot. Alexander and, 105.

Gordon, Adam Lindsay (1833–70). One of most popular and distinctive of Australian poets, 315.

Gordon, Gen. Charles George (1833–85). Brit. army officer (" Chinese Gordon "), **1486**; death, *1487*, 1102, 3279; at Khartum, 1855.

Gordon, Lord George (1751–93). Eng. agitator; headed anti-Catholic movement which resulted in " Gordon Riots " of 1780.

Gordon, Patrick (1635–99). Scot. military adventurer; fought in war between Sweden and Poland, first for one country and then the other; eventually rose to high and confidential position in the service of Peter the Great of Russia.

Gordon Riots. " No popery " riots in 1780, named after the leader, Lord George Gordon, who resented the withdrawal of certain restrictions on Rom. Catholics; described in Dickens's " Barnaby Rudge."

Gore, Charles (1853–1932). Eng. theologian; Canon of Westminster (1894–1902); Bishop of Worcester (1902–4); Bishop of Birmingham (1905–11); Bishop of Oxford (1911–19); author of many works on theological subjects.

Gorgas, William Crawford (1854–1920). Amer. army officer and sanitary engineer; he completely wiped out the yellow-fever plague in Havana during the Sp.-Amer. War, and waged a successful war against disease during the building of the Panama Canal; 2488, *2489.*

Gorge, formation, 2598.

Gorgias (gor'-gi-as) (about 480–380 B.C.). Gk. orator and sophist noted for florid eloquence; one of Plato's dialogues is named after him.

Gorgons (gor'-gonz). In Gk. myth., three female monsters, 2552.

Gorgonzo'la. Tn. in Lombardy, It., centre of cheese-producing district.

Gorgonzola cheese, 766.

Goril'la. The largest of the apes, **1487;** *183*, 184, 2207.

Göring. *See* **Goering.**

Gorizia (gō-rēt'-si-a) (Austrian Görz or Göritz), It., 20 m. N.W. of Trieste; pop. 46,600; ceded to Italy by Treaty of Rapallo (1920).

Gorki, Maxim. Pen-name of Alexei Maximovitch Pyeshkov (1869–1936), Rus. author, 2856.

Gorki or **Gorky,** formerly Nijhni-Novgorod, which was renamed by Soviet Govt. in honour of the author. Great trade centre of E. Russia; pop. 644,000; fairs, 2846.

Görlitz (gĕr'-lits), Poland. Wealthy industrial tn. of Silesia on r. Neisse; pop. 94,000; fine Renaissance architecture; under Polish admin. from 1945; Polish name, Zgorzelec.

Gorm the Old (*c.* 860–*c.* 935). King of Denmark, 992.

Gorse, Furze or **Whin.** Shrubby plant of genus *Ulex*, order *Leguminosae*, very conspicuous on heaths and commons with masses of yellow bloom, especially in March, though found all year. Autumnal and dwarf gorse are separate species; *4406.*

Gort, John Standish Surtees Prendergast Vereker, 6th Viscount (1886–1946). Eng. general who won V.C. in 1918; appointed C.I.G.S. 1937, and C.-in-C. B.E.F., Sept. 1939, 1056; Insp.-Gen. to Forces, July 1940; Gov. of Gibraltar, 1941; Gov. of Malta, 1942–44, *2073*; Fld.-Marsh., 1943; High Comm. Palestine, 1944–45.

Goschen (gō'-shen), **George, 1st Viscount** (1831–1907). Brit. statesman and financier; broke with the Liberal Party on Home Rule; First Lord of Admiralty (1871 and 1895–1900), and Chancellor of Exchequer.

Goschen, Sir William Edward, Bart. (1847–1924). Brit. diplomat and ambassador; brother of Lord Goschen, the Unionist statesman; he was attached to various embassies at different periods, and was ambassador at Berlin from 1908 till outbreak of war in 1914.

Goshen. The region in Egypt occupied by the Israelites, w. of modern Suez Canal (Gen. xiv. 10).

Goslar, Ger. Walled tn. in Hanover; celebrated millenary in 1922; pop. 21,000.

Gos'nold, Bartholomew (d. 1607), Eng. navigator, explorer of New England, leading colonist of Jamestown, Virginia, U.S.A.; died there; discovers Cape Cod, 142.

Gospels. Four books of New Testament (Matthew, Mark, Luke, John) giving account of life and teachings of Jesus Christ.

Gosse, Sir Edmund (1849–1928). Eng. poet, biographer, and critic, son of P. H. Gosse; wrote lives of Gray and Congreve, recollections of his father and his own early life in " Father and Son," and " History of 18th Century Literature," etc.

Gosse, Philip Henry (1810–88). Eng. naturalist of pre-Darwinian school; author of several works on marine life (" The Ocean "; " The Romance of Natural History ").

Göta (yĕ'-ta) **Canal.** In Sweden, 3128.

Götaland. A prov. of Sweden, 3128.

Gotama (gō'-tah-ma) or **Gautama.** Family name of Buddha, 600.

Göteborg (yĕ'-te-borkh), also **Gothenburg.** Second city, chief port, and important mfg. centre of Sweden, on s.w. coast at mouth of R. Göta; pop. about 337,000; 3128.

Gotha (gō'-tah). Ger. mfg. tn. on Leine canal, 80 m. s.w. of Leipzig; pop. 45,780; formerly joint cap. with Coburg of Duchy of Saxe-Coburg Gotha; Friedenstein Castle; gave name to type of large aeroplane which bombed Eng. during 1st World War.

Go'tham. A vil. in Nottinghamshire, inhabitants of which are said to have played the fool in order to dissuade King John from settling there and burdening them with expense of royal residence; hence called " Wise Men of Gotham." Also nickname of New York City from alleged pre-

tensions of its people to wisdom; first used by Washington Irving in " Salmagundi " (1807).

Gothenburg. Same as **Göteborg.**

Gotenhafen. Former Ger. name for Gdynia (*q.v.*).

Gothic alphabet, 1456.

Gothic architecture, 216, *598*, 729, *973*, *1236*, *2519*, 3040.

Goths, 1487, 1237; original home, 3128.

Gottland or **Gothland.** Largest isl. in Baltic Sea, E. of Sweden, to which it belongs; 1,220 sq. m.; pop. (1944) 59,600; *map, 2395.*

" Götterdämmerung " (gĕ-ter-dem'-e-roong), or " Twilight of the Gods." Opera by Wagner, 2440, 3331.

Göttingen (gĕ'-ting-en). Ger. tn. 60 m. s. of Hanover; pop. 47,000; noted univ., founded by George II.

Gottwald (got'-valt), **Klement** (b. 1896). Czechoslovak pres.; sec.-gen. Communist party 1929; in Moscow during Ger. occupation; in 1946 premier of left-wing coalition; Gottwald's Communist Constitution was rejected by Benes, who resigned and was succeeded by Gottwald as president, June 7, 1948.

Gough (gof), **Sir Hubert** (b. 1870). Brit. general, commanded Fifth Army during Ger. Somme offensive, March 1918, being recalled for his inability to prevent Germans breaking Brit. lines; later exonerated from personal liability for the defeat; in 2nd World War joined Home Guard as a private, later became a zone commander, resigned 1942.

Goujon, Jean (*c.* 1515–67). French Renaissance sculptor and architect; best known works are his " Diana " and the gallery for musicians in the Louvre.

Gould, Sir Francis Carruthers (1844–1925). Famous Eng. political caricaturist and journalist; much of his best work appeared in the " Westminster Gazette."

Gould, Jay (1836–92). Amer. self-made capitalist; early associate of Daniel Drew and James Fiske in manipulating Erie railroad stocks; gained mastery over what became the Gould system of railways.

Gounod (gōō'-nō), **François Charles** (1818–93). Fr. composer of sacred and dramatic music; opera " Faust," 1263, *2441*, 2437.

Gouraud (gōō'-rō), **Henri Joseph Eugène** (1867–1946). Fr. general in the 1st World War; commanded Fourth Army (1915–16, 1917 to end of war), in 1919 made high commissioner in Syria and commander-in-chief in the Levant.

Gourd family of plants, the *Cucurbitaceae*; cucumber, 943; melons, 2173; pumpkin, 2704.

Gourmont (goor'-mon), **Rémy de** (1858–1915). Fr. critic and poet, second only to Anatole France as an authority on contemporary Fr. literature; defender of naturalism of Huysmans and symbolism of Mallarmé; wrote several volumes of " symbolist " poetry.

Government, 1488, 2657; Brit. Commonwealth, 580; Communism, 881; courts, 921; customs and tariffs, 944; elections, 351; family and tribal systems, 1259; Fascism, 1261; feudal system, 1268; Gt. Brit., 1194, *1198*; international law, 1904; law, 1902; local government, 1491; nationalization, 1492; parliament, 2521; police, 2647; prisons and punishments, 2686; Socialism, 2996; taxation, 3158; U.S.A., 3290. *See* also under various countries, names of political parties, etc.

Government and public offices, 1492.

Governor, in hydro-elec. installations, 1672.

Governor-General. Appointed by the Crown to represent the King in a Dominion of the Empire; each Colony has a Governor.

Gower, John (*c.* 1325–1408). Eng. poet, called by Chaucer " moral Gower "; chief work, " Confessio Amantis," includes many moral stories for purpose of warning a lover against the vices of that day.

Gowrie, John Ruthven, 3rd Earl of (c. 1578–1600). Scottish nobleman killed, with his brother Alexander, in apparent attempt to assassinate King James VI of Scotland ; some evidence that " Gowrie's Conspiracy " may have been a story contrived to hide the king's fault in a personal quarrel which led to violence.

Gowrie, William, 1st Earl of (c. 1541–84). Scottish nobleman ; concerned in murder of Rizzio in 1566 ; custodian of Mary Queen of Scots at Lochleven ; captured James VI of Scotland. Executed for treason by order of James.

Goya (gō′-ya) **y Lucientes, Francisco** (1746–1828). Span. portrait painter and etcher of war scenes and bull-fighting, **1492**, 1967, 3049 ; snow scene and "The Parasol," *3047* ; " Duke of Wellington," *3363* ; portrait of Doña Isabel Cobos de Porcel, *1492*.

Goyen, Jan Josephszoon van (1596–1656). Dutch landscape painter, depicts typical landscapes with naturalistic truth unmixed with sentiment, 2334.

Gozo (got′só) or **Gozzo.** Brit. isl. in Mediterranean, incl. in the Colony of Malta ; 26 sq. m. ; pop. 23,000 ; Victoria chief town, 2072.

Gozzi (got′sē), **Carlo** (1722–1806). It. dramatist ; plays include satirical plays founded on fairy tales, and tragedies with a comic element. " Re Turandote " is the best known.

Gracchus (grak′-us), **Caius Sempronius** (153–121 B.C.). Rom. popular leader, son of Cornelia and brother of Tiberius Gracchus ; 1493, 2808.

Gracchus, Tiberius Sempronius (163–133 B.C.). Rom. tribune in 133 B.C. ; proposed agrarian laws and other reforms for relief of poor ; **1493**, 2808.

Grace, William Gilbert (1848–1915). Famous Eng. cricketer, entered first-class cricket at 15, and from then until he retired in 1899 scored over 54,000 runs ; highest score, 344 ; batted 126 three-figure innings in first-class cricket ; made ten double centuries, and three treble centuries, and thrice scored a century in each innings. As bowler, he took over 2,800 wickets, and once took all 10 wickets (against Oxford Univ.). In seven seasons he made over 1,000 runs and took over 100 wickets. Captain of Gloucestershire and England.

Grace. In religion, the enjoyment of God's favour ; spiritual gift of God by which man is able-to choose the right and find salvation ; in Roman Catholic Church the state of grace is held to be obtained through the sacraments. The term is also used for a prayer before or after a meal, asking a blessing or returning thanks.

Grace, days of. *See* Days of Grace.

Graces. In Gk. myth., three daughters of Hera and Zeus : Euphrosyne (joyfulness), Aglaia (brightness), and Thalia (bloom), goddesses of grace and charm.

Gracián (grah-thē-ahn′), **Baltasar** (1601–58), Sp. writer and Jesuit ; style concise and epigrammatic, but sometimes obscure ; best known for philosophical novel, " El Criticón " ; in " El Discreto " describes typical gentleman.

Grada′tion, in physiography, 2596.

Graeae (grē′-ē), in Gk. myth. " the grey ones," three sisters, Dino, Enyo, and Pephredo, daughters of Ceto and Phorcys, grey-haired from birth ; tell Perseus where to find Gorgons, 2552.

Graetz (grets), **Heinrich** (1817–91), German-Jewish historian ; most noted for his scholarly history of the Jews.

Graf Spee (grahf shpā), **Admiral.** Ger. pocket battleship of 14,000 tons ; scuttled on Dec. 17, 1939, in estuary of riv. Plate ; *see* Plata River, Battle of ; 3417, *3417*.

Grafting of fruit trees, *1402*.

Graf Zeppelin, German airship, *92*, *94*. Graf Zeppelin II launched Sept. 1938.

Graham, John, Viscount Dundee, Scot. soldier. *See* Claverhouse.

Graham, Robert Cunninghame. *See* Cunninghame-Graham, Robert.

Graham, Stephen (b. 1884). Brit. author ; has written a number of books on Rus., where he has travelled much.

Graham, Thomas (1805–69). Scot. chemist, originated term " colloids," and discovered " Graham's law " that diffusion rate of gases is inversely as square root of their densities, 1419.

Grahame, Kenneth, (1859–1932). Scot. writer, author of " The Wind in the Willows," " The Golden Age," and " Dream Days," 1967.

Grahame-White, Claude (b. 1879). Eng. aviator, early pioneer of flying ; rival of Paulhan in London-Manchester race of 1910, 46.

Graham Land, region of the Antarctic discovered by John Biscoe, captain of an Eng. sealing ship, in 1831, 2647.

Grahamstown. Tn. in Cape of Good Hope, S. Africa ; white pop. 8,000 ; ships ostrich feathers ; Rhodes Univ. College, St. Andrew's College.

Grail, Holy. Cup used by Christ at Last Supper ; Arthurian legends. 255, 256 ; quest of by Galahad, 1413, 2830.

Grain. Unit measure of weight, 1-16th dram, 1-4th carat, or 1-20th scruple. *See* Weights and Measures.

Grain elevators. Warehouses for storing grain, *679*.

Grain′ger, Percy A. (b. 1882). Australian composer and pianist ; collector of folk-songs ; composed " Shepherd's Hey," " Molly on the Shore," " Handel in the Strand."

Grain ship, on Great Lakes, *1516*.

Gramineae (gra-min′-e-ē). The grass family of plants, 1509.

Grammar, 1493 ; adjective, 27 ; adverb, 29 ; conjunction, 891 ; distinguished from rhetoric, 2769 ; noun, 2399 ; preposition, 2681 ; pronoun, 2690 ; punctuation, 2705 ; sentence, 1493, 2920 ; spelling, 3057 ; verb, 3313.

Grammar schools, 2886.

Gramme, or **gram.** The basic metric unit of weight (0·564 drams), 2155.

Gramophone, 1495, 3012 ; how it works, *1496* ; radiogram, *1497* ; records of heart sounds, 1593.

Grampian Mts. or **Hills.** Principal mt. mass in Scot., really a series of spurs ; 150 m. long ; 2889.

Grampus (from Lat. " large fish "), or black-fish, an inoffensive genus of the dolphin family. Name is also applied to the killer whale and to a genus of porpoises, 3371, *3373*.

Granada (gra-nah′-da). One of chief cities of Nicaragua ; pop. 35,000 ; univ. ; cacao-growing dist., *2364*.

Granada. Former Moorish kingdom in s. Sp. ; div. into 3 modern provinces. Granada (4,928 sq. m. ; est. pop. 776,400) is one ; history, 3036.

Granada, Sp., once cap. of Moorish kingdom, now cap. of prov. of the same name ; pop. 162,000 ; **1498,** 3032; Alhambra, 119, *plates f. 120, 121*; 3040.

Gran Chaco. *See* Chaco, El Gran.

Grand Alliance. League of European powers, 1240.

Grand Canal, China, 265, 686, 810; commerce, 2538.

Grand Canal, Venice, *3310, 3312.*

Grand Canary. One of the Canary group ; 640 sq. m. ; pop. 130,000 ; cap. Las Palmas.

Grand Canyon, of Colorado r., U.S.A., *plates f. 1496, 1497*, **1498.**

Grande Chartreuse (grahnd shahr′-trēz). Celebrated monastery in Fr., 2213.

Grand Coulee. Dam on the Columbia r. in State of Washington, 960, *plate f. 961.*

Grand Falls, of the r. Hamilton, Labrador ; water-power from, 1876.

" Grandfather clock " a weight-and-pendulum timepiece, 845, *847*, 848.

Grandi, Count Dino (b. 1895). Italian diplomat ; member of the Fascist

Grand Council, Ambassador in London in 1932–9, then Minister of Justice and Pres. of Chamber of Fascists and Corporations ; acquitted Dec. 1947 of all charges of Fascist activity.

Grandison, Sir Charles, hero of Richardson's novel of that name ; self-conscious prig, designed to represent ideal English gentleman ; 2402.

Grand jury, 1842 ; instituted in Eng., 1609.

" Grand Monarque," The, 2029.

Grand National. Steeplechase held annually at Aintree, nr. Liverpool ; water-jumps include famous Becher's Brook.

Grand piano, *2602*, 2603.

Grand Pré, Nova Scotia. Historic vil. ; pop. 400 ; famous as scene of Longfellow's " Evangeline."

Grand Prix (grahn prē) (Fr. " great prize.") Name given to many important sporting events, espec. the Fr. Grand Prix d'Endurance motor race.

Grand Rapids, Michigan, U.S.A. ; the " furniture capital of U.S.A." ; pop. 168,592.

Grand Remonstrance. Protest against misgovernment presented to Charles I (1641) by Eng. House of Commons ; the king's impeachment of and attempt to arrest the 5 leaders responsible for the Remonstrance were causes of the Civil War.

Grand Union Canal. Canal system of England. Formed in 1929, it is a union of the Grand Junction, Regent, and other canals, extended in 1932, altogether 240 m. long, *686*, *687*.

Grania (grā′-ni-a) or **Grainne.** In Celt. myth. the Helen of the Fenian cycle of old Irish tales, beautiful young bethrothed of the old Finn ; deserts him for Dermot, but finally weds him when Dermot is dead.

Granicus (gra-nī′-kus). Anc. name of small r. in N.W. Asia Minor where Alexander the Great won first victory over Persians, 334 B.C.

Granite. Hard stone, **1498,** 2795 ; from Aberdeen, 11 ; for roads, 2784 ; mica in, 2160 ; minerals in, 2180.

" Granite City," The. Name for Aberdeen.

Granny knot, *1868.*

Granson, battle of (1476). Charles the Bold at, 759.

Grant, Duncan James Corrowr (b. 1885). Eng. painter ; leading member of the London Group, 1184.

Grant, James (1822–87). Scot. novelist, author of stirring historical stories, chiefly dealing with Scottish life ; (" The Romance of War " ; " Bothwell " ; " The Yellow Frigate " ; " Scottish Soldiers of Fortune ").

Grant, Ulysses S. (1822–85) ; famous general of the Amer. Civil War, 1918 ; 18th pres. of U.S.A.

Grantham. Tn. in Lincolnshire ; pop. 22,500 ; **1499,** 1953.

Granville-Barker, Harley (1877–1946). Eng. dramatist and theatrical producer (" The Voysey Inheritance " ; " Waste " ; " Prefaces to Shakespeare ").

Grape aphis (phylloxe′ra). An insect which attacks grape-vines.

Grape-fruit. A citrus fruit, **1499.**

Grapes, the fruit of the vine, **1499,** *1500, back of plate f. 1401* ; brandy from, 3066 ; currants, 1499 ; Portugal, 2658 ; raisins, 2742 ; wines, 3388.

Grape-shot. An old type of artillery projectile.

Grape sugar, or dextrose. The commonest of the simple carbohydrates, 3114, 1477.

Graphite (graf′-īt). A soft, black allotropic form of crystalline carbon, **1500,** 940; crucible of, 1624 ; as " lead " in pencils, 2541 ; in atomic pile, 1500.

Gras′mere. Vil., dist. and lake in Westmorland, famous as a haven for poets and authors, *1169*, 3371 ; home of Wordsworth, 3408.

Grasse (grahs), **François J. P., Comte de** (1722–88). Fr. admiral, commanded Fr. fleet in operations before Yorktown in War of Amer. Independence.

Grasse, Fr., 18 m. w. of Nice ; winter resort ; marble quarries ; makes oil and conserves ; perfume industry, 2549.

Grass family, or *Gramineae*. A large family of monocotyledonous plants, 1509, *frontis. Vol. 4* ; includes bamboo, 353 ; barley, 361 ; bulrush, 615 ; ensilage, 1510 ; hay, *1509, 1510* ; maize, 2068 ; millet, 2175 ; oats, 2410 ; rice, 2774 ; rye, 2858 ; sugar-cane, 3112 ; wheat, 3372.

Grassholm. Isl. off coast of Pembrokeshire, famous for its colony of gannets ; a bird sanctuary since 1940 ; in 1947 purchased by the Royal Society for the Protection of Birds.

Grasshopper. An orthopterous insect, 1510, *1511* ; distinguished from locusts, 1511 ; egg, *1094* ; eye, *1253* ; larval stage, 1728 ; locust swarms, *plate f. 1512.*

" Grasshopper " steam engine, 3087.

Grasshopper warbler. Bird, one of the warblers, 3340.

Grassi (grahs'-sē), **Battista** (1854–1925). An It. zoologist, studied especially life and habits of white ants and eels, 2488.

Grass snake. One of the garter snakes, so called because it lives in the grass, 1512. 2991 ; eggs, *1094*.

Gratiano (grah-shi-ah-'nō). Character in Shakespeare's " Merchant of Venice," 2144.

Grattan, Henry (1746–1820). Irish patriot, orator, and statesman ; opposed parliamentary union of Ireland with Gt. Brit. ; in Brit. Parl. 1805 till death ; strove for Catholic emancipation ; conspicuous for probity of his character no less than for his ability.

Grätz. Same as Graz.

Gravelines (grahv'-lēn), Fr. Fortified spt. on r. Aa, 10 m. s.w. of Dunkirk ; fisheries, shipping, shipbuilding ; here Span. troops under Egmont defeated French under Marshal Thermes.

Gravelotte, Fr. Vil. 7 m. w. of Metz ; defeat (Aug. 18, 1870) of French under Bazaine by Prussians under Crown Prince Frederick.

Graves, Alfred Perceval (1846–1931). Irish poet ; wrote "Father O'Flynn."

Graves, Robert (b. 1895). Eng. author ; books include " I, Claudius " ; " The Golden Fleece " ; " King Jesus."

Gravesend, Kent. Tn. and r. port on Thames 22 m. s.e. of London ; pop. est. 400,000 ; airport ; customs and pilot station.

Gravimetric analysis. In chemistry, 773.

Graving dock, *1023*, 1024.

Gravita'tion, 1512, *1513* ; causes tides, 3209 ; controls comets, 880 ; Galileo's research, 1414 ; influence on earth, 1067 ; on moon, 1512, *1513*, 2225 ; how measured, 2543 ; Newton's theory, 2349 ; strength on different planets, 3119, 2617 ; speed of falling bodies, *2130*.

Gravity, centre of, 1513, *1514*, 2128.

Gravity, specific, 1513.

Gray, Asa (1810–88). Amer. botanist ; co-operated with Darwin, 1230 ; professor of natural history, Harvard Univ. ; prolific writer on botany and allied subjects, the most important of which was his admirable " Manual of the Botany of the Northern United States."

Gray, Elisha (1835–1901). Amer. electrician ; perfected various telegraphic devices ; invented telautograph and the telephone, 408, 3174.

Gray, Thomas (1716–71). Eng. poet (Gray's " Elegy "), 1514 ; birthplace, 2010.

Grayling. Fish of salmon family, but spawns in summer, its close season coinciding with that for coarse fish ; caught on fly ; prefers fast, clear streams, and found especially in w. and n. of England ; seldom exceeds 2 lb. in weight ; silvery grey in colour.

Grayling, butterfly, *plate f. 632.*

Graz (grahts), or **Grätz**. 2nd city of Austria ; iron and steel manufs. ; univ. and technical schools ; interesting medieval buildings ; pop. 152,000.

Graziani (grat-zē-ah'-nē), **Rodolfo** (b. 1882). It. soldier ; prominent in conquest of Abyssinia, 1935–36 ; commanded It. forces invading Egypt, 1940 ; recalled after Brit. recaptured Tobruk, 1941 ; surrendered to Amer. troops Apr. 29, 1945 ; illness stopped his trial as war criminal, May 1946.

Grazing. Pasturing of cattle on grass, 1509.

Great ant-eater, 176.

Great auk. Extinct bird, 303.

Great Australian Bight, 307, *map, f. 308.*

Great Barrier Reef. Off n.e. coast of Australia, longest coral reef in world (1,200 m.), 307, *map f. 308*, 908.

Great Basin. Region in w. U.S.A., about 200,000 sq. m. between Sierra Nevada on w. and Wasatch Mts. on e. ; streams have no outlet to sea, 3285.

Great Bear or **Ursa Major**. A constellation ; *chart, 895* ; Gk. legend, 894.

Great Bear Lake. In N.W. Canada ; 11,200 sq. m. ; uranium deposits, 3297.

Great Belt, Denmark. Strait separating isls. of Fünen and Zealand, 352, 991.

Great Bible, 426.

Great Bird of Paradise, 2511, *frontis. Vol. 6.*

Great Britain. Isl. separated from w. Europe by English Channel ; 88,745 sq. m. ; pop. 44,937,000 ; comprises England, Scotland, Wales and adjacent small isls., 1514, *map, pl. f. 584* ; air force, 91 ; army, 244 ; coinage, *2203* ; constitution, 1490 ; flag, 1312 ; forestry, 1351 ; govt., 1488, 2521 ; merchant fleet, 2144 ; motor vehicles, 2241 ; national songs, 2282 ; navy, 2293 ; oil wells, 2430 ; orders and decorations, 2448 ; postage stamps, 3074 ; railways, 2736, 2738 ; roads, 2784 ; schools, 2883 ; social insurance, 2994 ; tramways and buses, 3235 ; weaving industry, 3360. *See also* **British Commonwealth ; British Isles ; England ; English History ; Scotland ; United Kingdom ; Wales.**

Great Britain. Steamship designed by Brunel, 594.

Great Charter. Same as **Magna Carta**.

" Great Commoner " (Wm. Pitt the Elder), 759.

Great Council, in England, 2521.

Great crested grebe, *1516.*

Great Dane. Dog, *plate f. 1024.*

Great Divide. Same as **Continental Divide**.

Great Dividing Range, Australia, 307.

Great Eastern. Ship, designed by Brunel, *593*, 594 ; used in cable laying, *642*, 643.

" Great Elector." *See* **Frederick William**.

Greater Antilles, 3368.

Greater bindweed. Trailing weed, 898.

Greater celandine. *See* **Celandine**.

Greater spotted woodpecker, 3404.

Great Exhibition (1851) ; Prince Consort and, 102.

Great Falls of the Missouri, 2194.

Great Fire. Name given to the fire that destroyed a great part of London in 1666 ; among the buildings that suffered destruction were St. Paul's Cath., the Guildhall and the Royal Exchange ; more than eighty churches were razed ; 2016, 757, 3425, 4327.

Great Gable, mt. of Cumberland, Eng., 7 m. s. of Keswick, 2,950 ft. ; *1166.*

Great Harry. Ship built to order of Henry VIII, *2954.*

Greathead, Henry (1757–1816). Eng. boat-builder, inventor of the first lifeboat, 1935.

Greathead shield. In tunnel construction, 3258.

Greatheart. In Bunyan's " Pilgrim's Progress," guide of Christiana and her children to the Celestial City.

Great humming-bird, 1652.

Great Ice Barrier, in Antarctic region, 173, 2645.

Great Lakes. The 5 lakes (Superior, Michigan, Huron, Erie, and Ontario), lying on the borders of Canada and the U.S.A. ; total area about 94,000 sq. m. ; 1515, *1516* ; maps 1515, 677. *See* individual lakes by name.

Great Mogul. A famous diamond, *1011*, 1012.

Great Mosque, Delhi, 987, Mecca, 2125.

Great nebula, in astronomy, 2310.

Great organ. Manual of an organ, 2449.

Great Orme's Head. Peninsula on the coast of Caernarvonshire, N. Wales.

" Great Paul," bell of St. Paul's Cath., 411.

Great Plague. Name given to a terrible outbreak of bubonic plague in London in 1665, when nearly 70,000 deaths occurred, 757.

Great Plains, region in cent. U.S.A., 3285, 3289.

Great Primer type, *3270.*

Great Pyramid, at Gizeh, 1114, *2708.*

Great Rebellion, in Eng. (1642–49). *See* Civil War (England).

Great Russians, language, 2983, 2855.

Great Salt Lake, in N.W. Utah, U.S.A., 80 m. long ; large quantities of salt are obtained by evaporation ; scene of motor racing record attempts ; 3285.

Great Salt Lake Desert, 3300.

Great Schism (sizm). Division in Rom. Cath. Church (1378–1417) between two factions, each of which supported its own Pope, 818, 3298.

Great snipe, 2991.

Great Southern Ocean. *See* Antarctic Ocean.

Great tit, 438, 3218.

" Great Tom," bell, 411.

Great Trek of the Boers, 2445, 3017.

Great Wall of China, *806*, 810.

Great War. *See* World Wars, 3409.

Great Western, early steamship, 594, 2946, *2957.*

Grebe, diving bird, 1516 ; foot of, 448.

Greco, El (el-grä'-kō) (" The Greek "). Name given to Domenico Theotocopuli (c. 1544–1614). Cretan-Spanish religious painter, sculptor and architect. Well represented in National Gallery ; remarkable for weird use of colour, light, and shade ; 2476, 3049 ; " Burial of Count Orgaz," *3044.*

Greece, Ancient, 1517 ; *plate f. 1524* ; maps, *30*, *1518* ; athletics, 287, 2432 ; chief cities, 284, 3197 ; coins, 220, *2202* ; commerce, 1523 ; drama, 1037, 1540, 3194 ; food, 2431, 3112 ; games and festivals, 989, 1037, 2097 ; govt., 2999, 3052, 1518 ; life and customs, 3052, 1518, 1523 ; locks, *1979* ; Marathon, 2097 ; sculpture in, *1276*, 1528, 2904 ; ships, 2945 ; slavery, 1523, 2981, 3052 ; textiles, 3191.

History : chief events summarized, *see* History ; Aegean civilization, 29 ; Homeric Age, 1518, 3252 ; Trojan War, 3248 ; Persian Wars, 230, 2555, 3201 ; founding of colonies, 2968 ; Athenian Empire, 286, 2551, *1521*, 1522 ; Peloponnesian Wars, 1523 ; supremacy of Sparta, 3052, 1524 ; Theban leadership, 1524, 3197 ; Macedonian rule, 105, 990, 1524 ; Hellenistic Age, 109, 1524 ; Rom. conquests, 1524 ; Gothic invasion, 96.

Greece, Modern, kingdom of s.e. Europe ; 50,150 sq. m. ; pop. 7,335,000 ; 1525, *plates f. 1524, 1525* ; maps, *344*, *1518* ; cap. Athens, 284 ; national costume, *286*, 1525 ; olive industry, 2431 ; religion, 1525 ; Thessaloniki, 3202. *History*, 1525 ; Balkan Wars (1912–13), 2049, 344, 1525 ; union with Crete 927 ; 1914–18 War, 2049, 3415 ; return of monarchy, 1526 ; 2nd World War and after, 927, 1452, 1526, 3418.

Greek art, 1528, *1529–36* ; music, 2261 ; influence of Pericles, 2551 ; painting, 2475, 1528, *1536* ; Pheidias, 2566 ; sculpture, 1528, 2904, 3443. *Architecture, plates f. 212 and 213*, 1528, *1530* ; reconstructions, *1520*, *1521* ; remains at Athens, 284, 285, 21, *back of plate f. 1524, 1530* ; three orders, 213, 215.

Greek Empire. *See* Byzantine Empire.

Greek fire, 1558.

Greek language, 1539 ; alphabet, 2573 ; dialects, 1541 ; New Testament in, 425 ; relation to Latin, 1895.

Greek literature, 1539 ; Aesop's fables, 54 ; drama, *1520, 1521,* 3194 ; Hellenistic Age, 1541 ; historians, 2630. 3206, 1540, 1541 ; Homeric epics, 1637 ; influence on Latin, 1895 ; influence on Renaissance, 2764 ; novels, 1541 ; oratory and philosophy, 2628, 1540. *See also* chief Gk. authors, e.g., **Aeschylus** ; **Homer** ; **Sophocles**, etc.

Greek Orthodox Church, 1517, 1527.

Greek philosophy, 2571, 2572, 1278 ; Aristotle, 231 ; Diogenes, 1017 ; Epictetus, 1220 ; Epicurus, 1220 ; Plato, 2628 ; Pythagoras, 2710 ; Socrates, 2996.

Greeley, Horace (1811–72), Amer. journalist and politician ; founder and 1st editor of " New York Tribune."

Greely, Adolphus Washington (1844–1935). Am. explorer. Originally a soldier, he served many years in the Arctic and was a pioneer of laying telegraph lines in America and the East. Wrote on meteorology, electricity, geography.

Green. A secondary colour of pigment and a primary colour of light, 875 ; an intermediate colour, *plates f. 876, 877* ; paints, 2478 ; place in spectrum, *plate f. 3056.*

Green, John Richard (1837–83). Eng. historian. Famous for " History of the English People " (short and long editions) ; he also wrote " The Making of England," " The Conquest of England," and " Stray Studies from England and Italy."

Green, Thomas Hill (1836–82). Eng. philosopher ; chief Eng. representative of so-called Neo-Hegelian school of philosophy ; maintained the existence of a timeless intelligence as the essential principle of all knowing beings ; though never popular, wielded wide influence over other philosophers.

Green, Valentine (1739–1813). Eng. engraver, who became famous for his mezzotints after the Eng. and foreign masters.

Greenaway, Kate (1846–1901). Eng. artist, famous for quaint drawings of children, characterized by skilful colouring and humorous touches.

Greenbacks. U.S.A. currency notes of Civil War period, so called because back was printed in green.

Green Belt. A belt of open spaces round London on which building is forbidden, though agriculture is carried on.

Greene, Graham (b. 1904). Brit. writer ; " A Journey Without Maps," " The British Dramatists " ; novels, " Brighton Rock," " The Man Within," " The Power and the Glory."

Greene, Harry Plunket (1865–1936). Irish baritone singer of great merit ; took the lead in operas and oratorios.

Greene, Nathanael (1742–86). War of Amer. Independence general, who was in command of the Army of the South ; his successful campaign gained for him the name of " the man who saved the South."

Greene, Robert (c. 1560–92). Eng. dramatist and poet, remembered for a few charming lyrics and a derisive reference to Shakespeare in his " Groatsworth of Wit Bought with a Million of Repentance " ; 2932.

Greenfinch. A type of finch, 1272, 1955.

Green fly. *See* Aphis.

Greengage plum, 2630.

Greenland. Danish isl. N.E. of Canada ; almost wholly within Arctic Circle ; a. 826,000 sq. m. ; pop. 18,400 ; 1541, 2880 ; in Arctic Circle, 224 ; *maps, 1542, 2334* ; children, *plate f. 800* ; Eskimos, 1222 ; Hudson explores coasts, 1648 ; ice-cap, 1468, 2534 ; Northmen settle, 2388 ; crossed by Nansen, 2273 ; Peary's explorations, 2534 ; 2nd World War, 1542.

" Green Mansions," by W. H. Hudson, 1649.

Green monkey, 2211.

Green Mts. Range of Appalachian system, U.S.A., extending through Vermont ; highest peak, Mt. Mansfield (4,364 ft.).

Greenock (grin'-ok), Scot. Spt. 20 m. N.W. of Glasgow ; pop. 81,700 ; shipbuilding, sugar refining ; 3356, 2890.

Green Park, London, between Piccadilly and the Mall ; a. 54 acres.

Greensand. A clay or sand coloured green by glauconite.

Greensand marl. A marl containing greensand ; used as fertilizer.

Green tea, 3162.

Green turtle, 3229.

Green vitriol, ferrous sulphate, 3116.

Greenwich (grin'-ij). Met. bor. of London on Thames ; pop. 100,879 ; Naval Hospital and College ; famous Royal Observatory ; National Maritime Museum, 2260.

Greenwich mean time (G.M.T.), 3213.

Greenwich Observatory, *281,* 1898, 2015, 2413 ; time signals, *3212* ; transferred to Hurstmonceux, Sussex, from 1947.

Greenwich Tunnel, 3194.

Greenwich Village, N.Y.C., 2353.

Greenwood, Arthur (b. 1880). British politician. Labour M.P. since 1922 ; parl. sec. to Ministry of Health, 1924 ; Minister of Health, 1929–31 ; Minister without Portfolio 1940–42, presiding over Economic Policy Committee ; Lord Privy Seal, 1945–47 ; Minister without Portfolio 1947. Resigned Sept. 1947.

Greenwood, Frederick (1830–1909). Eng. journalist ; first editor of " Pall Mall Gazette " and founder of the " St. James's Gazette " ; on his information the Brit. govt. purchased Suez Canal shares.

Greenwood, Hamar, 1st Viscount (b. 1870). Brit. statesman ; Under-Sec. for Home Affairs 1919 ; Chief Sec. for Ire. 1920–22.

Green woodpecker, 3403, *plate f. 3404.*

Greet, Sir Philip Ben (1857–1936). Eng. actor and manager, known as Ben Greet ; presented Shakespeare's plays as they were done in Elizabethan times.

Greeting, New Year, 2350.

Gregg, John Robert (b. 1867). Amer. educator and author, b. Ire. ; founder of Gregg system of shorthand, 2961.

Gregg Shorthand, 2961, 2962.

Gregor, Rev. William (1761–1817), Eng. chemist, discovered, in Cornish sand, the element titanium in 1781 ; 3216.

Gregorian calendar, 662.

Gregorian chant, 2261.

Gregory, popes. For complete list *see* Pope.

Gregory I, the Great (c. 540–604). Pope, 1542 ; sends Augustine to Eng., 302 ; Church music, 2261.

Gregory VI (d. 1047), Pope, deposed in 1046.

Gregory VII, Hildebrand (c. 1025–85), Pope, 1542 ; investiture conflict, and Henry IV, 1449.

Gregory IX (c. 1145–1241), Pope, 1543.

Gregory XI (1331–1378), Pope, 1543.

Gregory XII (c. 1327–1417), Pope, 1543.

Gregory XIII (1502–85), Pope, 1543 ; calendar, 662.

Gregory XVI (1765–1846), Pope, 1543.

Gregory, Augusta, Lady (1859–1932). Irish dramatist and romance writer, associated with Yeats in Irish literary revival (" Gods and Fighting Men " ; " Irish Folk History Plays "), 1751.

Gregory, John Walter (1864–1932). English geologist. Author of " The Great Rift Valley " ; " The Rift Valleys of East Africa " ; drowned while exploring in S. America.

Gregory, the Illuminator, St. (c. 257–332). Reputed founder and patron saint of Armenian Church, 238.

Gregory of Nazian'zus, St. (c. 330–390). Churchman whose writings contain best statement of doctrine of Trinity in Gk. orthodox theology.

Gregory of Nys'sa, St. (c. 331–c. 396). Gk. churchman who anticipated doctrine of transubstantiation ; a constructive thinker.

Greg'ory, Sir Richard A. (b. 1864). Brit. scientist ; editor of " Nature," 1919–39 ; pres. of Brit. Ass., 1940–46 ; " The Vault of Heaven."

Gremial. Silk apron laid on the lap of a bishop ; originally intended to protect vestments from oil.

Grenada (gre-nah'-da). Southernmost of Windward Isls., Brit. W. Indies' 90 m. N. of Venezuela ; 133 sq. m. ; pop. 88,000 ; cap. St. George's ; cocoa, nutmegs, spices, fruit, and cattle ; health resort ; 3368.

Grenade (gre-nād'). An explosive missile, usually thrown by hand.

Grenadier (gren-a-dēr'). Name once given to soldier who threw handgrenades ; later each regiment had company of grenadiers ; name survives only in Grenadier Guards.

Grenadier Guards. The senior regiment of Foot Guards, *245.*

Grenadines. Group of about 600 small isls. in Brit. W. Indies.

Grenfell, Julian Henry Francis (1888–1915). English soldier and poet ; won D.S.O. in 1st World War ; died of wounds (" Into Battle ").

Grenfell, Sir Wilfred Thomason (1865–1940). Brit. medical missionary, 1543.

Grenoble (gre-nō'bl), Fr. Fortified city on r. Isère 60 m. S.E. of Lyons ; pop. 102,000 ; univ. ; kid gloves. Following German occupation in 1940, it became a centre of French resistance movement in 1942 ; latter destroyed an artillery park Nov. 1943, and De Bonne barracks in Dec. Liberated by Amer. troops on Aug. 23, 1944.

Grenville, George (1712–70). Eng. statesman ; prime minister (1763) ; secured passage of Amer. Stamp Act, one of the causes of War of Amer. Independence.

Grenville, Sir Richard (c. 1541–91). Eng. naval hero, 1543.

Grenville, William Wyndham, Baron (1759–1834). Eng. statesman, son of George Grenville ; as premier (1807) secured abolition of Afr. slave trade ; advocated Cath. emancipation.

Gresford. Vil. of Denbighshire, Wales ; scene of colliery disaster in 1934, in which 264 lives were lost, including some of the rescuers.

Gresh'am, Sir Thomas (c. 1519–79). Eng. merchant and financial agent of the govt. ; founder of Royal Exchange and Gresham's College ; formulator of " Gresham's law "— " bad " money tends to drive " good " from circulation.

" Greta Bridge " (vil. of Yorks), painting by J. S. Cotman, *917.*

Gretchen, heroine in Faust legends, 1264.

Gretel, in opera " Hansel and Gretel," 2438.

Gret'na Green. Vil. of Dumfriesshire in S.W. Scot. near Eng. border ; scene of runaway marriages from Eng. ; 2108, *2109* ; scene, in May 1915, of worst accident in British railway history.

Greuze (grēz), **Jean Baptiste** (1725–1805). Fr. genre and portrait painter, whose work in painting, like Rousseau's in literature, represents a sentimental return to Nature ; 1378.

Greville, Charles Cavendish Fulke (1794–1865). Eng. public official and diarist whose journals (published 1875–87) contain much valuable historical material for first half of the 19th cent.

Grévy (grā-vē'), **Jules** (1807–91). Fr. statesman, pres. of Fr. Assembly (1871–6), pres. of Chamber of Deputies (1876–9) ; pres. of Fr. Republic (1879–87) ; resigned owing to scandals involving his son-in-law in traffic in offices and decorations.

Grévy's zebra, 3442.

Grey, Charles, 2nd Earl (1764–1845). Eng. statesman ; premier (1830–4) ; forced passage of Parliamentary Reform Bill in 1832 ; 3278.

Grey, Lady Jane (1547–54). " Nine days' queen " of Eng., 1544, *1545.*

Grey, Zane (1875–1939). Amer. novelist ; " Desert Gold," " Riders of the Purple Sage," " Desert of Wheat," " Man of the Forest," and other tales of adventure in the West.

Grey Friars. Founded by St. Francis of Assisi, 1383.

Greyhound, *435,* 1026, *plate f. 1024.*

Greylag, a wild goose, *1486*.

Grey of Falloden, Edward Grey, 1st Viscount (1862–1933). Eng. statesman, **1544**.

Griboedov (grē-bo-yed'-of), **Alexander** (1795–1829). Rus. dramatic poet and statesman ; sent as minister to Persia, where he was killed by a mob ; famous for one comedy, " Misfortune from Intelligence," a satirical drama showing Rus. manners and social struggle between older and younger generation.

Grid, in thermionic valve, 1138, 3198, *3199*.

Grid, Electricity. Network of electricity supply transmission lines in the U.K., **1545** ; *map, 1546* ; control, *1547* ; power stations, 2673 ; transformer, 3237.

Grieg (grēg), **Edward Hagerup** (1843–1907). Norwegian composer, one of the greatest of the 19th cent. ; **1549**.

Griffin. A mythical creature, half eagle, half lion, supposed to guard hidden treasure.

Griffith, Arthur (1872–1922). Irish statesman ; organiser of Sinn Fein ; became pres. of Dail Eireann succeeding De Valera in 1922 on negotiation of peace with Gr. Brit.

Griffith, David Wark (b. 1880). **Amer.** pioneer film director.

Griffiths, James (b. 1890). Brit. politician ; pres. S. Wales Miners' Federation and member exec. cttee. Miners' Federation (1934–36) ; Min. of Nat. Insurance (1945–50) ; became Sec. of State for Colonies in 1950.

Griffon, Brussels, dog, *plate f. 1024.*

Griffon vulture, 3330.

Grigg, Sir (Percy) James (b. 1890). Brit. politician ; princip. Private Sec. to successive Chancellors of Exchequer, 1921–30 ; finance mem. of govt. of India, 1934–39 ; perm. Under-Sec. of State for War, 1939–42 ; Sec. of State for War, 1942–45 ; Exec. director Internat. Bank for Reconstruction and Development, 1946–47.

Grilling, cookery process, 901.

Grillparzer (gril'-pahrt-ser), **Franz** (1791–1872), greatest Austrian dramatic poet ; (" Die Ahnfrau," " Der Traum, ein Leben ").

Grilse. An immature salmon, 2865.

Grimaldi, name given to supposed prehistoric race of Man represented by skeletons found in grotto near Mentone.

Grimal'di, Joseph (1779–1837). Famous Eng. clown ; Charles Dickens edited his " Memoirs."

Grimm, Jakob (1785–1863). Ger. scholar ; founder with his brother Wilhelm (1786–1859) of science of folklore, **1549**, 1333 ; fairy tales, 1965 ; pioneer in philology, 2570.

Grims'by or **Great Grimsby.** Spt. on N.E. coast of Lincolnshire, near mouth of Humber ; pop. 78,000 ; shipbuilding works ; fisheries, 1299, 1953.

Grindelwald (grin'-del-valt). Swiss valley and tn. (pop. 3,000) overlooked by Wetterhorn and other lofty peaks of the Alps.

Grinding teeth, or molars, 3163.

Grindstones, 2871, 1156.

Griqualand (grē-kwa-land) **East.** A native territory of Cape of Good Hope Prov. ; 6,602 sq. m. ; pop. 1,118,000.

Griqualand West, S. Africa. Dist. of the Cape of Good Hope, to which it was joined in 1877 ; it contains some of the most valuable diamond mines in the world, including Kimberley ; pop. 85,000.

Grisel'da. Heroine of romance, famed for her patience ; Chaucer's story retold, 764.

Grisi (grē'-zē), **Giulia** (1811–69). Ital. dramatic soprano, greatest of her day.

Gris Nez (grē-nā) (" grey nose "), **Cape.** Headland of Fr. ; point of Fr. coast nearest to that of Britain.

Gri'son, a weasel, 815.

Grisons (grē-zon'). Easternmost and largest canton of Switzerland ; 2,746 sq. m. ; pop. 128,200 ; noted for superb Alpine scenery, especially in the Engadine ; language, 3141.

Grizzly bear, 384, 385.

Groat. A medieval Eng. silver coin, value fourpence.

Grock (b. 1880). Famous Swiss clown.

Grodno or **Gardinas.** City of White Russia. Formerly Lithuanian, then occupied by Poland ; on r. Niemen ; pop. 30,000 ; old buildings ; taken by Germans in 1st World War ; varied mfrs. ; trade in grain and timber ; ceded to U.S.S.R. in 1945.

Groin, in architecture, 216.

Gromyko (grom-ē'-kō), **Andrei** (b. 1909). Russ. diplomat ; ambass. to U.S.A., 1943 ; represented Russ. at Dumbarton Oaks and San Francisco Conferences, and at U.N. meeting in London, 1946, becoming perm. mem. of Security Council ; in Mar. 1949 replaced Vyshinsky **as** First deputy Foreign Min.

Groningen (grō'-ning-en). Spt. and cap. of Groningen prov., Holland ; pop. about 133,000 ; numerous canals ; large trade, various mfrs., shipbuilding ; univ.

Groote Schuur, nr. Cape Town. Residence built by Cecil Rhodes, 698, 2771, *3019.*

Gropius, Walter (b. 1883). German architect. Founded school of design named Staatliches Bauhaus, uniting art and industry.

Gros (grō), **Antoine Jean, Baron** (1771–1835). Fr. painter of military pictures, chiefly Napoleonic ; pupil of Louis David.

Grosbeak. Name given to the crossbill, of the finch family, 1272.

Groseillers (grō-sā-yār', **Menard Chouart, Sieur de** (1621–c.1684), intrepid Fr. explorer and fur trader, brother-in-law of his companion Radisson ; exploration, 681.

Grossmith, George (1847–1912). Eng. actor and entertainer, who came into prominence in 1877 when playing in Gilbert and Sullivan operas ; his humorous recitals were very popular in both Gt. Brit. and Amer.

Gross tonnage, 2951.

Grote, George (1794–1871). Eng. historian and banker ; his " History of Greece " is " one of the few great comprehensive histories."

Grotewohl, Otto (b. 1894). Became Premier of E. German Repub. in Oct. 1949.

Grotius, Hugo (1583-1645). Dutch statesman and jurist, " father of modern science of international law," 1904 ; tomb, 2320.

Grotto. Pilgrim custom, *2609*

Grouchy, Emmanuel, Marquis de (1766–1847). Fr. marshal, to whose delay at Waterloo Napoleon attributed his defeat, 3354.

Ground bait, for fishing, 1309.

Ground-beetles, *401*, 399.

Ground ivy, *Nepeta hederacea.* A trailing herb, with two-lipped, bluishpurple flowers ; a perennial plant of the order *Lobiatae*; not related to ivy.

Ground-nut, 1549, *1550* ; 1707 ; in E. Africa, 1073, 1550, 3151 ; fibre from, 2749 ; oil, 1263, 1674.

Groundsel, *Senecio vulgaris.* Plant of order *Compositae* ; a common garden weed, with small heads of tubeflorets ; flowers all year round ; used as canary food.

Ground squirrels. Several species of ground-living squirrels ; include chipmunk, 815.

Ground-water, 252.

Group Movement. Religious movement, sometimes called Oxford Group, founded by American, Frank Buchman, in 1921 ; chief feature, " sharing " of spiritual experiences by public confession.

Grouse. Game bird, **1550** ; courtship drumming, 441 ; egg of red grouse, *plate f. 440* ; ptarmigan, *1551.*

Growth, affected by glands in animals, 1470 ; cell division, 738 ; marked by " rings " in trees, 3245 ; rapid in bamboos, 353.

Groz'ny. Tn. of U.S.S.R. in Grozny Region, N. of the Caucasus Mts., on Zunzha riv., and on rly. connecting Rostov and Baku ; rich oil and

naphtha area ; oil-pipes to Tuapse (Black Sea), 509 m., and to Makhach-Kala (Caspian Sea), 94 m.

Grubs, 1893.

Grub Street. Name of a former street in London, where lived many poor literary men, hence the phrase " Grub Street authors."

Gru-gru, a nut, 2408.

Grundy, Mrs. The personification of society's judgements, generally " prudish " ; name originated in old play, " Speed the Plough," where a character asks continually, " What will Mrs. Grundy say ? "

Grünewald, Matthias (c. 1478–c. 1530). Ger. painter, 1454.

Gruyère (grū-yār'), Switzerland. Picturesque tn. perched on a high hill 16 m. s. of Fribourg ; pop. 2,000 ; famous for its cheeses ; 3142.

Gruyère cheese, 766.

Guadalajara (gwah - da - lah - hah'-ra). Second city of Mexico, and cap. of Jalisco ; pop. 227,730 ; centre of Mex. steel and glass industries ; Indian pottery ; silver mining and farming region ; severe earthquakes in 1875 and 1912 ; city founded in 1531.

Guadalajara. City of Sp., 35 m. from Madrid on main rly. ; pop. 14,000 ; scene of bitter fighting in Civil War (1936–8).

Guadalaviar (gwah-dah-lah-vē-ahr') (Arabic " white river "). A river in Sp., 150 m. long ; its waters irrigate fertile plain around Valencia and give city most of its water supply ; 3302.

Guadalcanal (god-al-kan-al'). Largest is. (area est. 2,500 sq. m.) of Brit. Protectorate, Solomon Is., s.w. Pacific ; h.q. of Brit. resident commissioner ; invaded by Japs. Jan. 1942 ; U.S. marines secured a position Aug. 7 ; Allied naval victory Nov. 13–16 ; Feb. 10, 1943, is. cleared of Japs. ; 3293, 3421.

Guadalquiver (gwad-dal-kē-vēr') (Arabic " great river "), river in Sp., 350 m. long ; rises in E. of prov. of Jaen ; flows s.w. through Seville and Cordova into Atlantic, 20 m. N. of Cadiz ; *map, 3030.*

Guadalupe (gah-dah-lōōp). Inhabited isl. in Pacific Ocean, 75 m. off coast of U.S.A.

Guadeloupe. Fr. colony in W. Indies ; 688 sq. m. ; pop. 304,000 ; with its dependencies, it became a dept. of France, Jan. 1, 1947 ; **1551,** 3368.

Guadiana (gwah-dē-ah'-na). One of the longest (520 m.) of the five great Span. rivers, but narrow and poor in volume ; flows into Gulf of Cadiz ; *map, 3030,* 2658.

Guam (gwahm). U.S. South Sea isl. at s. extremity of Mariana archipelago ; 225 sq. m. ; pop. 23,000 ; naval station ; air port ; 2056 ; Japan occupied, 1941–44, 3293 ; administered by U.S. Navy, but in 1946 civil commission recommended extension of citizen rights of U.S.

Guanaco (gwah-nah'-ko). Wild S. Amer. ruminant of the camel family, 124, 1975.

Guanajuato (gwah-nah-hwah'-tō).State in cent. Mexico ; 11,000 sq. m. ; pop. (1940) 1,046,000 ; cap. Guanajuato ; minerals, 2157.

Guanajuato or **Santa Fé de Guanajuato.** Historic city of Mexico ; pop. 40,000 ; gold and silver mining ; first battle in Mex. war of independence fought there in 1810.

Guanchos (gwahn-chōz). Hamitic people, natives of Canary Isls. ; originally tall, blond, athletic, but later mixture with Arabs changed these characteristics ; by language allied to anc. Numidians.

Guano (gwah'-nō). A fertilizer obtained from massed droppings of seabirds in their breeding haunts, certain islands off the coast of S. Amer. ; nitrogen in, 2374 ; penguin deposits, 2544.

Guantanamo (gwahn-tah-nah'-mō), Cuba. Tn. on r. Guaso near head of fine harbour on s. coast ; pop. 68,000.

Guarani (gwah-rah'-nē), native Indians of Paraguay ; their descendants also form bulk of population of Uruguay, and are important element in Bolivia and Brazil, 2512.

Guardafui (gwahr-dah-fwē'), **Cape.** Extreme eastern point of Africa ; promontory of Somaliland at entrance to Gulf of Aden.

Guardi, Francesco (1712–93). It. painter, 1776, *1781*.

Guards. The King's guards are divided into two groups : (1) Personal bodyguard, comprising Honourable Corps of Gentlemen-at-Arms ; Yeomen of the Guard and Royal Company of Archers (Scottish). (2) Regiments from the active army, comprising Household Cavalry and Foot Guards. The former are made up of Life Guards and Royal Horse Guards ; the latter of Grenadiers, Coldstreamers, Scots Guards, Welsh Guards and Irish Guards.

Guarini (gwah-rē'nē), **Giambattista** (1537–1612). It. poet ; wrote " Il Pastor Fido " ; like Tasso's " Aminta," on which it is patterned, it is a lyric conception of the ideal life ; identifies happiness with simple rustic life ; " Il Pastor Fido " and " Aminta " are the finest pastoral poems in It. literature.

Guarneri (gwah-nār'-ē), **Guarnie'ri,** or **Guarne'rius,** celebrated family of It. violin-makers of 17th and 18th cents., of whom most celebrated was Guiseppe Antonio (1687–1745) ; 3324.

Guatemala (gwah-te-mah'-lą), republic of Cent. Amer. ; 45,450 sq. m. ; pop. 3,451,000 ; **1551,** *743* ; *map 743*, 744 ; claims on Brit. Honduras, 1552 ; Yucatan, 3437.

Guatemala City, cap. of Guatemala, rly. and commercial centre ; pop. 186,000 ; 50 m. from Pacific coast ; makes textiles, earthenware, 1552 ; *map, 743* ; earthquakes, 1552.

Guava (gwah-vą), a small fruit grown in tropics, 1401.

Guaviare (gwah-vē-ah'-rā). River of Venezuela ; rises in Andes, flows E. 700 m.

Guayaquil (gwī-a-kēl'), only spt. of Ecuador, S. Amer., on estuary of the Guayas, at head of the Gulf of Guayaquil ; pop. 160,000 ; large foreign trade ; shipyards, 1081.

Guayaquil, Gulf of, large inlet of Pacific in Ecuador ; over 100 m. wide at its mouth ; narrows into estuary of r. Guayas ; 1081.

Guaymas (gwī'-mas), spt. of Mexico on Gulf of California ; rly. connexions with U.S.A. ; 2156.

Guayule (gwah-ū-lā) **shrub,** of the family *Compositae* ; yields rubber.

Gudbrandsdal (goo'-branz-dahl), cent. valley of Norway, 2393.

Guder'ian, Heinz (b. 1888). Ger. soldier, born in Poland ; staff officer in First World War ; formed Panzer divisions victorious in Poland, France, and Flanders, 1939–40 ; replaced Jodl as chief of gen. staff, 1944 ; supreme commdr. Russ. fronts ; captured by Allies May 1945 ; for 2 yrs. helped compile Ger. history of the war for U.S.A., then faced denazification court.

Gudgeon. Fish of carp family, distinguished by small size and by two " barbels " below mouth ; feeds on bottom in shallow, gravelly water ; caught in large numbers, gudgeon are good to eat ; 2783.

Gudrun (good'-roon). A Low German epic saga, taking the place of the Nibelungenlied in High German ; Gudrun, the heroine, is kidnapped by an admirer, but after being held prisoner for 14 years is rescued by her brother and Herwig, her true lover.

Guedalla (gwe-dal'-a), **Philip** (1889–1944). Eng. historian. Publications include " The Second Empire " ; " Palmerston " ; " Conquistador " ; " The Hundred Years."

Guelder-rose, small tree, *Viburnum opulus*, common in damp places in Britain ; bears flat clusters of white flowers, the outer ones in each cluster being large, consisting of perianth only and used to attract insects which fertilize the inner ones ; red berries in autumn ; leaves lobed. Variety of this is the snowball tree of cottage gardens. *V. lantana* is the wayfaring tree, common in hedges on limestone soils ; leaves entire, mealy above and below, flowers in rounded clusters, berries flattened, white, then red, finally black.

Guelf (gwelf), **House of,** Hanoverian rulers of Eng., 1440.

Guelfs and Ghibellines, political factions of medieval It. and Ger. (where they were called Welfen and Waiblingen, the latter being the Hohenstaufens) ; Dante, 969 ; Otto IV, 2460.

Guenevere. *See* **Guinevere.**

Guenon (ge-non'), an African monkey ; species commonly used by organ-grinders and as pets, 2211.

Guercino (gwār-chē-nō) (1591–1666), It. artist of the Bologna school, 1785 ; " Elijah fed by the ravens," *1785*.

Guericke (gā'-rik-e), **Otto von** (1602–86). Ger. physicist ; built early water barometer, 363, 2702 ; invented air pump, electrostatic machine, 1127, and the " Magdeburg hemispheres."

Guérin (gā-ran'), **Eugénie de** (1805–48). Fr. writer ; sister of Maurice, to whom she was devoted ; " Journals " and " Letters," imbued with religious mysticism.

Guérin, Georges Maurice de (1810–39). Fr. poet and prose writer ; wrote " The Centaur," prose poem of strange mystic beauty ; all his work characterized by passion for Nature ; " Reliquiae," his collected poems.

Guernica (gwēr'-ne-kah), tn. of Vizcaya, Spain, 17 m. E.N.E. of Bilbao. At one time capital and " holy city " of the Basque people. Aircraft of Franco's army dropped 4,000 bombs on this undefended tn. on April 17, 1937, in Sp. civil war, killing hundreds of civilians ; tn. restored by 1946.

Guernier'i or **Werner.** Mercenary captain of 14th cent. ; ravaged Tuscany and Lombardy ; when dismissed by Louis I, king of Hungary and Poland, sacked Anagni in 1358.

Guernsey (gērn-zi). 2nd in size of Channel Isls. ; 25 sq. m. ; pop. 40,600 ; dependencies include Sark, Herm, and Jethou ; St. Peter Port and St. Sampson chief towns ; Victor Hugo, 1650 ; occupied by Germany 1941–1945.

Guernsey cow, *731*, 732, 751.

Guerrero (gē-rār'-ō), Mexico. State in S. on Pacific ; 24,000 sq. m. ; pop. 732,900 ; cap. Chilpancingo ; agricultural and undeveloped mineral resources.

Guests. In ants' nest, 166.

Guiana (gē-ah'-na). A region N.E. of S. Amer., comprising Brit. Guiana (89,500 sq. m. ; pop. 373,600), Dutch Guiana (Surinam) (50,000 sq. m., pop. 191,000), Fr. Guiana (34,740 sq. m.; pop. 31,000), 1552 ; *map, 1552*.

Guide. Alpine, tests, 133.

Guido of Arezzo or Aretinus (c. 995–c. 1050), Benedictine monk ; introduced modern system of music notation, 2261.

Guido Reni (1574–1642). Bolognese painter, great master in a school beginning to decline into sentimental insipidity, 1785 ; " Aurora and the Hours," *304*.

Guidonia. It. aeronautical research establishment.

Guienne (gē-en'). Anc. Aquitania, former prov. of s.w. Fr. ; cap. Bordeaux ; acquired by Eng. crown, 1609 ; Hundred Years' War, 1652.

Guilbert (gēl-bār'), **Yvette** (1869–1944). A Parisian singer unsurpassed in her day for dramatic and humorous rendition of old ballads.

Guildford. Former co. town of Surrey ; pop. est. 43,000 ; remains of Norman castle ; cath. under construction, 730 ; agric. market trade, *3123*.

Guildhall. Old council hall near Cheapside, London, several times rebuilt ; in Great Hall were two giant wooden figures of Gog and Magog (destroyed Dec. 29, 1940) ; other features the crypt, the Common Council Chamber, and Aldermen's Rooms ; also Free Library ; heavily damaged by bombs and Museum and Art Gallery destroyed, Dec. 29, 1940.

Guilds or **Gilds.** Medieval organizations for protection of trade and industry, for social intercourse and religious fellowship, **1553,** *1554* ; London Livery Companies, 1970.

Guild Socialism. Movement led by G. D. H. Cole in decade of 1st World War, aiming at control of industry by " guilds " of people employed therein ; similar idea in Fascist " Corporations."

Guillaume (gē-yōm'), **Charles Édouard** (1861–1938). Swiss physicist, inventor of invar ; 1920 Nobel prize winner in physics.

Guillemot (gil'-e-mot). A bird of the auk family ; common species is dark above, whitish below, black guillemot almost entirely black ; 304 ; eggs, *plate f. 440, 1094*.

Guillotine (gil-o-tēn'). Fr. instrument of execution, 2687.

Guinea (gin'-i). Term loosely applied to w. coast region of equatorial Africa, from r. Senegal to Orange r., 3367, 3368 ; former slave trade, 68.

Guinea. A former Eng. gold coin so named because gold of which it was coined originally came from Guinea Coast ; first minted in 1673, recalled in 1776 ; term still used as money unit (21 shillings).

Guinea, Gulf of. The part of the Atlantic between Cape Palmas and Cape Lopez, on w. coast of Africa, 3366 ; *map, 3366*.

Guinea-fowl, 1554, 2671 ; in Africa, *plate f. 73*.

Guinea-pig, or cavy, **1554,** *1555*.

Guinevere (gwin'-e-vēr). In Arthurian romance, Arthur's beautiful but unfaithful queen, 255, 2830.

Guinness (gin'-is). Famous family of Irish brewers ; brewery at Dublin founded by Arthur Guinness in 1759 ; Edward Cecil Guinness (1847–1927) was created Earl of Iveagh in 1919.

Guiscard, Robert. *See* **Robert Guiscard.**

Guise (gēz). Fr. ducal family, branch of house of Lorraine, whose heads led extreme Cath. party and aspired to snatch crown from house of Bourbon. Title became extinct in 1688.

Guise, Henry, Duke of (1550–88). " Le Balafré " (the Scarred) ; incited murder of Coligny and Massacre of St. Bartholomew ; assassinated by order of Henry III of Fr.

Guise, Fr. Fortified tn. on R. Oise, 90 m. N.E. of Paris ; taken by Germans in 1914.

Guitar (gi-tahr'). A stringed musical instrument resembling the lute, much in use in It. and Sp. ; its six strings are played by the fingers of the right hand, the left-hand fingers pressing on the finger-board to control the pitch.

Guitry (gē'-trē), **Lucien Germain** (1860–1925). Fr. actor, considered the greatest Fr. interpreter of modern realistic drama ; his son Sacha (b. 1885) also became distinguished as an actor and writer of clever comedies.

Guizot (gē'-zō), **François** (1787–1874). Fr. statesman and historian ; head of ministry under Louis Philippe (" History of Civilization in Europe "), 2031.

Gujarat (gooj-raht). The Gujarat States in the State of Bombay, India, now merged in Bombay **State** ; Brit. defeated Sikhs in 1849.

Gules (gūlz). In heraldry, 1614.

Gulfs. How they originated, 2596.

Gulf Stream. A warm-water current flowing from the Gulf of Mexico, across the Atlantic to northern Europe, **1554** ; in Atlantic, 291 ;

how formed, 2419 ; touches Norway, 2302.

Gulf weed. A seaweed with air-bladder floats, 2914.

Gullet or **oesophagus.** Muscular tube from mouth to stomach, 3094, 1016.

" Gulliver's Travels." Satire by Swift ; story retold, 3133.

Gulls and terns. Long-winged sea-birds, 1555, *1556*, 1557.

Gum arabic. Soft gum obtained from acacias, 16, 1556 ; used in confectionery, 1556.

Gums. Substances obtained by drying various tree saps, **1556** ; camphor, 674 ; copal, 1558 ; distinguished from resins, 3767, 1556 ; kauri, 1558, 2357 ; in perfumes, 2550 ; tragacanth, 1558.

Gum senegal, from acacia, 16.

Gum tree or **eucalyptus**, 1230.

Guncotton. An explosive made by treating cotton with nitric and sulphuric acids, 1250, 740.

Gunga Din. In Rudyard Kipling's poem, faithful Hindu water-carrier, who dies succouring his master. " Though I've belted you and flayed you . . . you're a better man than I am, Gunga Din ! "

Gun'ny. Coarse cloth used as sacking, made of hemp and jute, 1844.

Gunpowder, 1558 ; explosive force, 1250 ; effect on feudal system, 1864 ; used in quarrying, 2712.

Gunpowder Plot. Eng. conspiracy (1605), 1264, 1794.

Gunpowder tea, *3162.*

Guns and rifles. *See* **Artillery ; Firearms ; Machine-guns.**

Gunter, Edmund (1581–1626). Eng. mathematician ; invented " chain " for land measurement ; first to observe variation of the compass.

Gunter chain. Measure of length used in surveying ; it is 66 ft. long and is divided into 100 links.

Gunther (goon'-ter). In " Nibelungenlied," king of Burgundians, 2363, 2969.

Gurkhas (goor'-kaz). Dominant race of Nepal, 2315 ; in Brit. army, 249.

Gur'nards. Medium-sized fish with bony-plated heads and several detached fin-rays used as feelers ; *frontis. Vol. 3.*

Gurney, Sir Goldsworthy (1793–1875). Inventor of steam-jet and Gurney stove.

Gusher. A spouting oil well, 2428, 3288 ; gas in, 1420.

Gusta'vus I, Vasa (1496–1560). King of Sweden, founder of Vasa dynasty ; made king (1532) by Swedish peasants on expulsion of Danes ; established Prot. Reformation in Sweden, 3131.

Gustavus II, Adolphus (1594–1632). King of Sweden, 1558, 3131 ; originates modern army, 251 ; and Thirty Years' War, 3202. He died Nov. 16, 1632.

Gustavus V (b. 1858). King of Sweden, 3131.

Gutenberg (gōō'-ten-berg), **Johann** (*c.* 1400–*c.* 1468). Ger. inventor of printing from movable types, 2685 ; house, *134.*

Guthrie, Tyrone (b. 1900), British theatrical producer, 3197.

Guthrum (gooth'-*rum*) (d. 890). Danish chief, king of E. Anglia ; defeated by Alfred, 111.

Gutta-percha (gut'-*a* pêr'-cha). Gummy substance resembling rubber, **1559** ; use in cables, 640.

Gutzkow (goots'-kō), **Karl Ferdinand** (1811–78). Ger. dramatist and novelist ; a leader in " Young Germany " school (" Uriel Acosta " ; " Die Ritter vom Geiste ").

Guy, Thomas (*c.* 1645–1724). Eng. bookseller, printer and philanthropist ; he amassed a large fortune and bequeathed £300,000 to found the London hospital that bears his name.

Guy Fawkes Day (Nov. 5), 1264, 1794.

Guynemer (gēn-mär), **Georges** (1894–1917). Fr. aviator, one of the most brilliant " aces " of 1st World War ; brought down more than 50 enemy machines before he was killed.

Guyot (gē-ō), **Yves** (1843–1928). Fr. journalist and economist, whose writings on political subjects have been widely read in Europe ; editor of " Le Siècle " 1892–1903, and became editor of " Le Journal des Economistes," 1909.

Gwalior (gwah'-li-or), India. Citadel and anc. city in Gwalior State ; pop. (with modern Lashkar, cap. of native state of Gwalior) 80,000 ; 1559.

Gwalior. Mahratta state in Madhya Bharat Union, India ; area 26,000 sq. m. ; pop. 4,000,000 ; **1559** ; maharajah's procession, *1704.*

Gwynn, Nell (1650–87). Eng. actress, favourite of Charles II ; her wit, generosity, and kindness endeared her to the Eng. public ; portrait by Lely, said to be of Nell Gwynn. *1178.*

Gyges (gī-jēz). In Gk. myth., hundred-handed giant flung into Tartarus for making war on the gods.

Gyges. King of Lydia (7th cent B.C.). Possessor, according to legend, of magic ring that made the wearer invisible ; with its aid he killed the reigning king and usurped his throne.

Gymkhana (jim-kah'-na). Anglo-Indian term for a miscellaneous sports or games meeting ; originally used for the place of such a meeting.

Gymnasium (jim-nā'-zium). Place for regular physical exercise, with apparatus and equipment ; from Gk. *gymnos,* naked. *See* **Athletics.**

Gymnosperms (jim'-nō-spermz). Flowering plants whose immature seeds are not protected by a seed-containing structure, 2620 ; trees, 3247.

Gypsies. *See* **Gipsies.**

Gypsum (jip'-sum). A soft mineral, usually white, used in making plaster of Paris, **1559**, 2180 ; crystal, *939* ; hardness, 2180.

Gyro-compass. Mechanism and use, 1561, *1562.*

" Gyrodyne," type of helicopter, built by Fairey aviation co., *1605,* 1606.

Gyroscope. Rapidly revolving flywheel maintaining a constant orientation in space, **1561** ; in aircraft, 1562 ; in automat. pilot, *see* **Pilot** ; compass, 2291 ; in flying bomb, 1331 ; in rocket bomb, *2792,* 2793.

THE sound of the letter H is a weakened form of the Phoenician *Cheth,* which was pronounced like the Scots or German *ch.* This Phoenician letter consisted of two uprights connected by two or three transverse bars ⊞ ⊟ and its name meant " fence." It was derived from the Egyptian hieroglyph representing a sieve ⊘, which developed into the form ⊘, and was finally transformed into the angular, ladderlike ⊟ character. The early Greeks wrote it ⊟ and later, omit-

ting the cross bars top and bottom, gave it the form of our H. Its sound ceased to be a guttural and became an aspirate, or breathing sound like our *h.* The eastern Greeks lost the aspirate and adopted the symbol to represent the long *e*-sound (like our " a "), calling it *Eta.* The western Greeks retained the aspirate, and the Romans took it over from them. But in vulgar Latin it disappeared ; hence the *h*-sound is virtually non-existent in languages derived from Latin.

Haakon (haw'-kon) **IV** (1204-63), " the old." King of Norway ; added Greenland and Iceland to Norwegian realm ; invades Scotland, 3203.

Haakon VII (b. 1872). King of Norway ; accepted Norwegian crown, 1905, on separation of Norway from Sweden, 2398 ; married a daughter of Edward VII of Gt. Brit. ; in June 1940, after German invasion, came with his govt. to England ; returned Sept. 1945.

Haarlem (hahr'-lem), Netherlands. Cap. of N. Holland ; pop. 159,000 ; cathedral ; various manufactures ; large flower industry ; 2320 ; Hals paintings, 1568.

Habakkuk (ha-bak'-kuk). A Hebrew minor prophet, probably of 7th cent. B.C. ; Book of Habakkuk, 8th of the minor prophets, 2692.

Habe tribe, Senegal, *3367.*

Habeas corpus (hā'-be-as kor-pūs). A writ requiring a person in custody to be brought before a court, **1563.**

Haber (hah'-ber), **Fritz** (1868–1934). German chemist ; with Carl Bosch invented industrial process for making synthetic ammonia, 1674 ; Nobel prize in 1919.

Habichtsburg. " Hawk's Castle," seat of Hapsburgs, on top of the Wüpelsberg (1,682 ft. high), N. Switzerland, 1575.

Habitant (ah'-bē-tahn). Name given to Fr.-Canadian peasant, 2716.

Hackbut. Early hand-gun, 1281.

Hack'ney. Met. and parl. bor. of N.E. London ; chiefly residential dist. ; severe air-raid damage in 2nd World War ; pop. (1945) 154,900.

Had'dingtonshire, Scotland. *See* **East Lothian.**

Haddock. A cod-like fish, 1563.

Had'don Hall. Famous old mansion in Derbyshire, England, 30 m. s.E. of Manchester ; seat of Duke of Rutland ; associated with Dorothy Vernon.

Ha'den, Sir Francis Seymour (1818–1910). Eng. etcher and surgeon ; in addition to distinguished career as surgeon, became foremost Eng. etcher, causing revival of etching in England ; 1219.

Hades (hā'-dēz). In Gk. myth., god of underworld ; also the underworld itself ; and Persephone, 989 ; Hercules' journey and return with Cerberus, the many-headed dog, 1615.

Hadramaut (hah-drah-mowt'). A region of S. Arabia ; included in Aden Protectorate, 195.

Hadrian, popes. For list *see* **Pope.**

Hadrian (hā'-dri-*an*). Publius Aelius (76–138). Rom. emperor, 2812 ; Adrianople named after, 29 ; builds wall in Britain, 1168, 1193, *2391* ; public works under, *2818* ; mausoleum (Castle Sant' Angelo), 2800, *2803.*

Hadrian's Wall. Rom. fortification across N. England between the Tyne and Solway Firth, *2391*; building, *574*, 1168.

Haeckel (hek'-el), **Ernst Heinrich** (1834–1919). Ger. biologist; advocated Darwinian views; aroused controversy by anti-theological attitude (" Natural History of Creation "; " The Riddle of the Universe ").

Haematite. *See* **Hematite.**

Haemoglobin (hē-mō-glō'-bin), the colouring matter of the blood, 2039.

Haemon (hē'-mon). In Gk. myth., son of Creon.

Haemophil'ia, tendency to bleeding, 476; inherited, 1427, 1617; use of snake venom to stop bleeding, 2991.

Haemorrhage (hem'-o-rij). Violent bleeding; first aid for, 1291; stopped naturally by clotting, 474.

Hafiz (hah'-fiz). Pen name of Shamsed-Din Mohammed (d. *c.* 1388), greatest Persian lyric poet; tomb near Shiraz, a celebrated place of pilgrimage.

Hafnium (Hf). A metallic element of the titanium group; atomic no. 72; atomic weight 178·6; discovered in 1922 by von Hevesy and Coster in 1922; found in ores of zirconium, to which it is closely related; 768, 777.

Haganah. Jewish army, illegally formed in Palestine, 1936–39, to resist the Arab revolt; trained and used in Second World War by Brit.; disarmed in 1943; finally disbanded May 1948, when Israeli State declared.

Ha'gar. Sarah's handmaid, mother of Abraham's son Ishmael (Gen. xvi, xxi).

Hagen (hah'-gen). In " Nibelungenlied," slayer of Siegfried, 2363, 2969.

Hagen, Walter (b. 1892). Amer. golfer; U.S. open golf champion (1914, 1919); British open golf champion (1922, 1924, 1928).

Hagenbeck (hah'-gen-bek), **Carl** (1844–1913). Ger. animal dealer and showman, first to train " happy family " groups of lions, tigers, dogs, cats, rabbits, mice, living or performing together; introduced many improvements in methods of caring for and exhibiting animals; zoological gardens, 1568, 3446.

Hagfish, or borer. An eel-like parasitic fish, 2513.

Haggai (hag'-ī). The 37th book of the Old Testament and 10th of the minor prophets. Haggai prophesied about 580 B.C.; appealed to his countrymen to restore the temple

Hag'gard, Sir Henry Rider (1856–1925). Eng. novelist and writer on land economics; spent early life in S. Africa, scene of many of his best novels, including " She," " King Solomon's Mines," " Alan Quatermain," and " Ayesha, or the Return of She," 3020.

Hagiographa (hag-i-og'-ra-fa), or "Holy Writings." Books of the Hebrew Scriptures which are not included in the Law and the Prophets, 2692.

Hague (hāg), **The.** Seat of govt. of the Netherlands; pop. 542,000; scene of many international conferences. **1563,** *1564,* 2318; Court of International Arbitration, *203*; in 2nd World War, 1564.

Hague Peace Conferences, 2531. Established Hague Tribunal, 203, 1563; determine international law, 1905; Nicholas II, 2365; Peace Palace, gift of Carnegie, 203, 704, 1910.

Hague Tribunal. A permanent court of international law, composed of not more than four delegates appointed from each state; created at first Internat. Peace Conference (1899), 203, 1563; trans. to U.N. in 1946.

Hahn, Otto (b. 1879). Ger. chemist and physicist; discovered the radioactive substances radiothorium, and mesothorium, and the element protoactinium; foremost in atomic research in Ger.; went to U.S.A. during Hitler's regime; awarded Nobe prize for chemistry in 1944;

pres. of Kaiser Wilhelm Gesellschaft, Göttingen, since 1946; atom, 298.

Hahnemann (hah'-ne-man), **Samuel C. F.** (1755–1843). Ger. physician, founder of homoeopathy.

Haider Ali or **Hyder Ali** (*c.* 1722–82). Indian ruler, formidable rival of British; ruler of Mysore, 1582, 1714, 2270.

Haifa (hī'-fa), Palestine. Spt. 70 m. N. of Jerusalem at foot of Mt. Carmel; pop. about 145,000; outlet of pipe-line from Iraq; magnificent new harbour, 2482; scene of many terrorist acts in 1946–47.

Haig of Bemersyde, Douglas, 1st Earl (1861–1928). Brit. soldier, **1564;** in 1st World War, 3410.

Hai Ho. R. of China, formed just above Tientsin by the confluence of the Pei Ho and three other rivers, 3211.

Hall. Pellets of ice formed during a thunderstorm, **1564.**

" Hail Columbia." Patriotic song of America, written by Joseph Hopkinson in 1798; tune from " President's March," by Philadelphia band director Fyles, to honour Washington.

Haile Selassie I (hī'-lē se-lah'-sē) (Ras Taffari) (b. 1892). Emperor of Ethiopia (1930); fled country when Italians invaded it in 1936; 14, 15; reinstated, 1941.

Haileybury College. Public school near Hertford, Eng.; originally college of East India Co.

Hailsham, Douglas Hogg, 1st Viscount (b. 1872). Brit. statesman and lawyer; Attorney-General (1922–24, 1924–28); Lord Chancellor (1928–29); Sec. of State for War (1931–35); Lord Chancellor (1935–38); Lord Pres. of the Council (March–Oct. 1938).

Hainan (hī-nahn'). Chinese isl. 10 m. S. of China in China Sea; area, 13,900 sq. m.; pop. est. 1,500,000; jungle-covered mts.; rich valleys; sugar-cane, cotton; occupied by Japan 1939–45; *808.*

Haiphong. Spt. of Tongking, republic of Viet Nam; pop. 74,000; 1713, 1720.

Hair, 1565; distinction from wool, 3405; of camel, 124, 670; care of, 1675; characteristic of mammals, 2074.

Hair-line micrometer, 2161.

Hairy or **woolly rhinoceros.** Extinct species, common in Europe during the Ice Age, *735.*

Haiti (hā'-tī). Negro republic in W. Indies; 10,200 sq. m.; pop. estimated 3,000,000; **1565;** *map, 1565.*

Hajji or **Hadji** (haj'-ē). Title gained by pilgrims to Mecca, 2127.

Hake. A large marine fish closely related to the cod, but not so popular as food; usually eaten fresh, occasionally smoked and dried; found round the Brit. coasts.

Hakluyt (hak'-loot), **Richard** (*c.* 1552–1616). Eng. geographer; the Hakluyt Society is named after him (" Voyages and Discoveries of the English Nation," called the " prose epic of the modern English nation").

Hakodate (hah-kō-dah'-tē), Japan. Fortified promontory in S. Hokkaido; pop. 207,000; exports fish products, charcoal, sulphur, timber; it had a naval school.

Halcyon. A kingfisher, 1858.

" Halcyon days," 1858.

Halcyone (hal'-si-o-nē, hal-sī'-o-nē) or **Alcyone.** In Gk. myth., daughter of Aeolus.

Haldane, (hawl'-dān), **John Burdon Sanderson** (b. 1892). Eng. scientist and author, Fullerian prof. of physiology of the R.I., and later prof. of genetics at U.C., London; a brilliant biologist and experimenter, he joined the Communist party, served in the Spanish civil war, and in both World Wars. Wrote " Daedalus," "Science and Ethics," " Causes of Evolution," " My Friend Mr. Leakey," " Science Advances."

Haldane, John Scott (1860–1936). Eng. scientist, father of the above; his experiments often involved his son when a child.

Hal'dane, Richard Burdon Haldane, 1st Viscount (1856–1928). Brit. statesman, lawyer, and philosopher; war minister 1905, establishing O.T.C., Territorial Army and Imperial General Staff; Lord Chancellor 1924; peerage and O.M. 1911 (" Philosophy of Humanism "; " Human Experience," etc.).

Hale, Edward Everett (1822–1909). Amer. preacher, social worker and writer, author of " The Man Without a Country," 3294.

Hale Observatory, Mount Palomar, Calif., 2413.

Halévy (ah-lā-vē), **Jacques** (1799–1862). Fr. (Jewish) composer (" La Juive " and " L'Eclair "); a master of fine effects of vocalization and instrumentation.

Halévy, Ludovic (1834–1908). Fr. dramatist and novelist (" L'Abbé Constantin," sweetly sentimental, immensely popular tale, classic for Fr. instruction).

Half-hitch. Knot, *1870.*

Half-tones. How made, 1218, 2688, *plate f. 2689,* 2689.

Hal'iburton, Thomas Chandler (1796–1865). Canadian humorist; penname " Sam Slick "; lawyer and judge in Nova Scotia, 684.

Halibut. Largest flat fish, **1566;** vitamins in oil, 3327.

Halicarnassus (hal-i-kahr-nas'-*us*), anc. Gk. city in Caria, Asia Minor; site of famed Mausoleum, 2923, *plate f. 2924;* Herodotus, birthplace, 1620.

Halidon Hill. Height N.W. of Berwick-upon-Tweed, Eng., where Eng. under Edward III defeated the Scots (1333), 2892.

Hal'ifax, Charles Montague, Earl of (1661–1715). Brit. statesman; introduced into Gt. Brit. national debt instead of annual taxation.

Halifax, Edward Frederick Lindley Wood, 1st Earl (b. 1881). Brit. statesman; Under-Sec. for Colonies (1921–22); Pres. of Board of Education (1922 and 1932) and Minister of Agric. (1924); Viceroy of India as Baron Irwin (1926–31); succeeded as Viscount 1934; Sec. for War (1935); Foreign Sec. (1938); Ambassador U.S.A. (1940–46). Created earl 1944.

Halifax, George Savile, 1st Marquess of (1633–95). Eng. statesman and author; supported the accession of James II, but later allied himself with William of Orange; great orator.

Halifax. Mfg. city in W. Riding of Yorkshire; pop. est. 94,540; textiles, iron products, chemicals, coal-mining, quarrying; 1168.

Halifax. Cap. of Nova Scotia; pop 70,000; 1563, 2401

Hall, Charles M. (1863–1914). Amer. inventor; invented electrolytic process for reducing aluminium, which made that metal, previously costly as silver, cheap enough for kitchen pots and pans.

Hall, George Henry, 1st Viscount (b. 1881). Sec. of State for Colonies 1945–6. 1st Lord of Admiralty 1946.

Hall, Joseph (1574–1656). Eng. divine and satirist; Bishop of Exeter in 1627; of Norwich in 1641; supported the ecclesiastical policy of Charles I and Archbishop Laud; imprisoned and expelled from his see during the Long Parl.

Hal'lam, Henry (1777–1859). Eng. historian; his writings are clear, graceful, and sound in judgement (" View of the State of Europe During the Middle Ages "; " Constitutional History of England "); father of Arthur Henry Hallam, subject of Tennyson's " In Memoriam."

Halle (hahl'-e), Ger. City in Saxony on r. Salle; pop. 220,300; salt works; noted univ.

Hallé (hal'-ā), **Sir Charles** (1819–95). Eng. musician of Ger. birth; founded famous Hallé orchestra in Manchester; his wife, formerly Mme. Normann Neruda (1839–1911), was one of the greatest violinists of her time.

Hallelujah (hal-e-lōō-ya). A Hebrew word meaning " praise the Lord."

Hal'ley, Edmund (1656–1742). Eng. astronomer ; predicted return of " Halley's comet," 880 ; a friend of Newton, 2349.

Halley's comet. A comet whose orbit makes it visible to earth every 75 years, 880, *plate f. 881*, named after Edmund Halley.

Halliford. Vil. of Middlesex on the Thames, *1171*.

Hall Mark. Official mark stamped on gold or silver plate at Goldsmiths' Hall, or at assay offices, to attest quality, 1481.

Hallowe'en. The evening of Oct. 31, the eve of All Saints' Day, **1566**, *1567*.

Hallstatt (hahl'-shtaht). Tn. of Upper Austria on L. Hallstatt ; old and famous salt mines ; anc. Celtic remains of Irona and Bronze Ages, dating back 3,000 years or more.

Halogens (hal'-ō-jenz). The closely related group of univalent non-metallic elements fluorine, chlorine, bromine, and iodine, 777, 816, **1567**, 1667, 1739 ; in antiseptics, 179.

Hal'ophytes. Plants which live in salt-water environment.

Hals (hahlz), **Frans** (c. 1580–1666), Dutch painter, **1568**, *1569*, 2333 ; " The Laughing Cavalier," *1569* ; "Portrait of Descartes," *996* ; "Nurse and Child," *2329*.

Hal'sey, William F. (b. 1882). Amer. sailor ; fought in both World Wars ; commdr. in S. Pacific Oct. 1942 ; commanding U.S. 3rd fleet in Pacific 1944, was victorious at Solomon Is., off Bougainville and Leyte Gulf, Oct. 1944, and Luzon invasion Jan. 1945 ; Jap. surrender signed on his flagship Missouri, Sept. 2, 1945.

Halter hitch. Knot, *1869, 1870*.

Ham. Son of Noah ; traditional ancestor of Hamites (Gen. vi., ix.), 2374.

Ham. Food value compared with milk, 2174.

Ham, East and **West.** See **East Ham ; West Ham.**

Hama (hah'-mah). City of Syria on the Orontes, 110 m. N. of Damascus ; pop. 71,300 ; the Hamath of the Bible.

Hamadan (ha-mah-dahn'), tn. in w. Iran ; pop. 104,000 ; 1741.

Hamadryad (ham'-a-drī-ad), or " king cobra," 859.

Hamadryad baboon, 2211.

Hamadryads. Wood nymphs in Gk. myth. ; 2408.

Haman (hā'-man). Chief minister of Persian king Ahasuerus, 1225.

Hambledon. Vil. of Hants. "Cradle of Cricket," 928.

Hambourg, Mark (b. 1879). Anglo-Russian pianist of great merit ; first public appearance in 1888.

Hamburg. City of Ger., on r. Elbe ; pop. (1948 est.) 2,000,000 ; 1124, 1445, **1568**, 1577 ; in Hanseatic League, 1575 ; heavily bombed ; taken by British, May 1945 ; h.-q. of Brit. Zone of Ger., 1945–47, 1569.

Hameln or **Hamelin.** Tn. in N.W. Ger., 25 m. S.W. of Hanover ; pop. 27,985 ; famed as scene of legend of the Pied Piper.

Hamilcar (ha-mil'-kahr) **Barca** (c. 270–228 B.C.). Carthaginian general, father of Hannibal and Hasdrubal, 361, 1573.

Ham'ilton, Alexander (1757–1804). Amer. statesman. On Washington's staff in war of independence, became first sec. of treasury, setting up a national bank and protective tariffs. One of the framers of the constitution, he was mortally wounded by Burr in a duel.

Hamilton, Emma, Lady (c. 1761–1815). Eng. beauty of lowly birth, who married Sir William Hamilton and exercised a great influence on the life of Lord Nelson, 1180, *2315*.

Hamilton, Sir Ian (1853–1947). Brit. general ; joined the army in 1872 and served until 1919 ; commanded Dardanelles expedition in 1st World War ; wrote poems, " Gallipoli Diary," etc.

Hamilton, James, 1st Duke of (1606–49) ; Scot. politician ; was adviser to Charles I ; led the forces that invaded Eng. with the object of securing the restoration of Charles and was defeated at Preston, being taken prisoner and executed.

Hamilton. Cap. of Bermuda Isls. ; pop. 3,000 ; 418.

Hamilton, Ontario. Mfg. centre and port ; pop. 166, 337, *2434*.

Hamilton, Scot. Co. tn. of Lanarkshire, 11 m. S.E. of Glasgow ; coal, ironstone, cotton mfrs. ; pop. est. 39,800 ; 1890.

Hamilton or **Grand River,** Canada. Chief r. of Labrador ; flows E. 600 m. into Melville L., extension of Hamilton Inlet on Atlantic coast.

Hamilton Inlet. Indentation of Labrador coast, estuary of Hamilton r.; potential water-power, 1876.

Hamites (ham'-ītz). Native race of N. Africa, 70.

" Hamlet." Shakespeare's greatest tragedy, 1211, **1570**, 2934 ; Hamlet's home at Elsinore, 904.

Hamm. Tn. of Westphalia, Ger., 19 m. N.E. of Dortmund ; on the Lippe, at E. end of Ruhr ; in industrial area ; the chief Ger. rly. centre, the marshalling yards were bombed by Allied aircraft 106 times during the Second World War ; Air Force, *91*.

Hammer, pneumatic, 2632 ; steam, 1758.

Hammerbeam. A beam in Gothic architecture which projects from the wall, forming a kind of bracket-support for the tie-beams of an ornamental roof.

Hammerfest, Norway. Port on Arctic Ocean ; pop. 2,300 ; northernmost tn. in world ; 2394.

Hammer-head shark. Species of shark so named from the hammer-like appearance of the head when seen from above, 2938.

Ham'mersmith. Western met. and parl. bor. of London, on Thames ; pop. est. 101,178 ; boat-building and other mfrs. ; Lyric and King's Theatres ; Kelmscott Press at, 2232.

Hammerton, Sir John Alexander (1871–1949). Brit. editor and writer. Among his books are " Stevensoniana " ; " George Meredith in Anecdote and Criticism " ; " Barrie : the Story of a Genius " ; " Other Things Than War " ; " Books and Myself " ; " Child of Wonder " (biography of Arthur Mee). Editor of " People of all Nations " ; " Countries of the World " ; " Universal Encyclopedia " and " New Universal Encyclopedia " ; " Universal History " ; " New Book of Knowledge " ; " Practical Knowledge for All " ; " Second Great War " ; " The War Illustrated " ; " World Digest," etc. See *frontispiece, Vol. 1.*

Hammond, Walter Reginald (b. 1903). Eng. cricketer. Played in Test matches against Australia, New Zealand, S. Africa and W. Indies ; became an amateur and captained England's team against Australians in 1938 and 1946–47 ; South Africa (1938–39) and W. Indies (1939).

Hammurabi (ha-moo-rah'-bē) (about 2100 B.C.), king of Babylonia, organizer of empire and codifier of laws, 329, 330 ; legal code, 1902.

Hamp'den, John (1594–1643). Eng. Puritan patriot and statesman, 1571 ; residence, 599.

Hampden Park, Glasgow. Chief Scot. Association football stadium.

Hampshire. Co. of Eng. on S. coast ; nearly 1,650 sq. m. including Isle of Wight ; pop. 1,102,000 ; 1165, *1168*, **1571.**

Hampshire. Brit. cruiser, 1863.

Hampstead. Met. bor. in N.W. of London ; pop. (1945) 83,400 ; formerly noted for mineral springs ; residence of many famous in art and letters, notably John Keats, *1849* ; *1309.*

Hampstead Heath. Open space of 240 acres in Hampstead ; famous fairground on Bank Holidays.

Hampton Court. Historic palace on Thames, 10 m. S.W. of London, built by Cardinal Wolsey in 1515 ; in the grounds is a famous maze ; portrait of Shakespeare, 2936 ; vine at, *1500* ; tennis court, *3186* ; *3402.*

Hampton Roads. Channel between James r. estuary and Chesapeake Bay, Va., U.S.A., scene of the encounter between the Monitor and the Merrimac during the Amer. Civil War.

Ham'sun, Knut (b. 1859). Norwegian novelist, 1920 Nobel prize-winner in literature (" Growth of the Soil " ; " Hunger " ; " Pan ") ; in 1947 fined over half his fortune as a member of former Quisling party ; 2881, 2403.

Han. Important dynasty of China 206 B.C.–A.D. 220, marked by increase in prosperity and advance in civilization, *810, 812.*

Hanau. Ger. industrial city of Hesse-Nassau on Main ; pop. (1939) 40,655 ; Napoleon defeated Bavarians in 1813 ; devastated in 1945.

Hand (anatomy), **1572** ; monkey's hand-like feet, 2207.

Hand. A unit of measure. See **Weights and Measures.**

Han'del, George Frederick (1685–1759). Ger.-Eng. composer, master of the oratorio, **1572**, 2264 ; his harpsichord, 2266.

Hand'ley, Tommy. Pioneer Brit. radio comedian ; moving spirit of verbal slap-stick radio show ITMA (It's That Man Again) ; died suddenly Jan. 9, 1949 ; aged about 56.

Hangchow', China, 100 m. S.W. of Shanghai ; pop. 507,000 ; in Jap. occpn., 1937–45 ; **1573.**

Hanging Gardens of Babylon. One of the Seven Wonders, 331, 2923 ; *plate f. 329,* 2924.

Han'gö. Fortified spt. of Finland, on peninsula at the entry to the Gulf of Finland ; leased to Russ. for 30 yrs. as military base by Treaty of 1940 ; Sept. 19, 1944, Russ. exchanged rights here for a sea and air base nr. Helsinki.

Hankey, Maurice Paschal Alers, 1st Baron (b. 1877). British civil servant ; Secretary Committee of Imperial Defence (1912–38) ; Secretary to Cabinet (1919–38) ; Clerk of the Privy Council (1923–38) ; retired in 1938 ; Director of Suez Canal Co. ; Minister without Portfolio, Sept. 1939 ; Chancellor of Duchy of Lancaster, May 1940 ; Paymaster-General 1941–42.

Hankow'. Second most important trading tn. of China, 600 m. up the Yangtze from Shanghai, **1573**, 3433 ; pop. Hankow dist., 778,000 ; in Jap. occupn. 1938–45.

Hannah. A pious Hebrew woman, wife of Elkanah and mother of Samuel.

Hannay, James Owen. See **Birmingham, George A.**

Han'nibal (c. 247–183 B.C.), Carthaginian general, **1573**, *1574*, 2808.

Hanoi (ha-noi'). Cap. of Viet-Nam and cap. and largest city of Tongking, in N. on Songka (Red) r. ; pop. 142,000 ; trade in silk, rice.

Han'over. Former Ger. prov. in N.W. Ger. ; a. 14,970 sq. m. ; pop. 3,367,000 ; **1574.**

Hanover. Cap. of new *Land* (state) of Lower Saxony, and former cap. of former prov. of Hanover ; pop. (1939) 443,000 ; 1574 ; captured Apl. 1945 ; in British zone of occupation, Oct. 1946.

Hanover, House of. Line of Brit. rulers ; becomes House of Windsor, 1442. List of rulers : see **England.**

Hansard. Popular name for the official record of Brit. parliamentary proceedings, so called after Luke Hansard (1752–1828), who printed the " Journals of the House of Commons." It has been a Government publication since 1909.

Hanseatic League. Medieval confederation of N. European cities for promotion of commerce, **1575** ; and merchant guilds, 1554 ; Bergen

1575, 2393 ; Danzig, 973 ; Hamburg, 1568.

"Hänsel und Gretel" (hen'-sel oont gret'-el). Ger. folk-tale, 1333 ; opera by Humperdinck, 2438.

Hansen, Gerhard Henrik Armauer (1841–1912). Norwegian physician, discoverer of leprosy bacillus.

Hansom cab. Vehicle popular in the latter half of the 19th century—invented by Joseph Aloysius Hansom (1803–82).

Hants. Shortened form of **Hampshire.**

Hanuman (han'-oo-man). An E. Indian monkey, *2210.*

Hanyang. China, city adjoining Hankow, *1573.*

Hapsburg or **Habsburg.** Famous Ger. princely family which supplied rulers for Austria, Spain, and Holy Rom. Empire ; **1575.** The last emperor (Charles) abdicated in 1918 and died in 1922, leaving a son, Francis Joseph Otto (born 1912). 1st World War brings downfall, 3414.

Hara, Takashi (1856–1921). First commoner to become prime minister of Japan (1918) and first prime minister directly responsible to parliament ; previously leader of Seiyu-Kai (Liberal) party and three times minister of home affairs ; assassinated.

Hara-kiri (hah-ra-kē'-rē). Form of suicide in Japan ; obligatory hara-kiri, formerly common, was abolished in 19th cent., but voluntary form is still sometimes practised out of loyalty to a dead superior, to avoid dishonour in battle, or as protest against a national policy.

Harar or **Harrar** (har-ahr'). Tn. in Abyssinia ; pop. 40,000 ; cap. of prov. in one-time Italian East African Empire, 15.

Har'bin or **Harphin,** Manchuria. Tn. and rly. centre on Sungari r. ; pop. 415,000 ; Rus. supply station in Russo-Japanese War ; 2085.

Harbour Grace, Newfoundland. Second spt. of the isl. on Conception Bay. connected with St. Johns, 25 m. w., by Newfoundland r. ; pop. 2,215 ; boots and shoes, cod-liver and seal oils, fish ; starting point of several Transatlantic flights.

Harbours 1022, **1576 ;** formed by "drowned coasts," 2596 ; importance to cities, 1430 ; Dover, *1031* ; London, 2010 ; "Mulberry," 2251. *See also* **Docks ; Floating Dock ;** and under great seaports.

Harcourt, Sir William Vernon (1827–1904). Brit. statesman and debater ; loyal lieutenant of Gladstone ; Home Sec. (1880–85) ; as Chancellor of Exchequer (1892–95) introduced graduated income tax.

Hardanger Fiord. Inlet 75 m. long on w. coast of Norway ; *map, 2395.*

Hardanger work. Embroidery, *1153,* 1154.

Hardenberg, Karl August, Prince (1750–1822). Prussian statesman ; with Stein, rebuilder of Prussia after Napoleonic wars ; abolished serfdom.

Hardicanute (c. 1018–42). King of Eng. Son of Canute ; succeeded brother Harold 1040 ; brief reign marked by cruelty and oppression.

Hardie, (James) Keir (1856–1915). Brit. Labour leader and politician ; a miner by trade ; worked for Independent Labour party ; first Labour member in Parliament 1892 ; chairman of Independent Labour party 1894–99 ; 1875.

Hardiman, Alfred Frank (1891–1949). Eng. sculptor ; works, statue of Earl Haig ; stone and bronze sculpture for Norwich City Offices.

Harding, Warren Gamaliel (1865–1923). 29th president of U.S.A., 3292.

Hardinge (har'ding) **of** Penshurst, **Charles, 1st Baron** (1858–1944). Viceroy of India (1910–16), Ambassador to France (1920–22) ; put into effect Morley-Minto reforms ; his grandfather, Henry Hardinge, 1st Viscount (1785–1856), was Gov.-Gen. of India (1844–48).

Hard water, how softened, 3351.

Hard'wicke, Sir Cedric Webster (b. 1893). Eng. actor ("The Apple Cart," "The Barretts of Wimpole Street," "The Late Christopher Bean," and films : "Dreyfus," "Nell Gwynn," "Tudor Rose," "The Winslow Boy.").

Hardwicke, Philip Yorke, 1st Earl of (1690–1764). Eng. lawyer ; became Solicitor-General (1720), Chief-Justice (1733), and Lord Chancellor (1737).

Hardy, Thomas (1840–1928). Great Eng. novelist and poet, noted for sombre view of life, **1577,** *1215,* 2402 ; and Dorset, 1030.

Hare, Sir John (1844–1921). Eng. actor and theatrical manager ; associated with the Bancrofts in Robertsonian plays ; a fine character actor, he took parts in "Caste," "School," "A Quiet Rubber," "A Pair of Spectacles," and other well-known plays.

Hare. Rodent of the *Leporidae* family, **1578 ;** hunting the, 1658 ; protective coloration, *2692.*

Hare or **Lepus.** A constellation ; situation, *chart,* 895.

Harebell. Bell-flower, *479.*

Harewood (har'-wood). **Henry George Charles Lascelles, 6th Earl of** (1882–1947). Served in 1st World War, winning D.S.O. and Croix de Guerre ; married Princess Mary, daughter of King George V, in 1922 ; two sons.

Harewood, George Henry Hubert, 7th Earl of (b. 1923). Served in 2nd World War ; in 1944 taken prisoner by Germans while serving with Grenadier Guards in It. ; liberated 1945 ; succeeded to title in 1947.

Harfleur (ahr'-flèr). Tn. in N. France, 4 m. E. of Havre ; pop. 3,500 ; formerly important spt. ; twice occupied by English in 15th cent.

Hargreaves, James (1730–78). Inventor of the spinning-jenny, 463, **1578,** 3361 ; and Arkwright, 235.

Haricot (ha'-ri-kō). The kidney or French bean, 380.

Har'ington, Sir Charles (1872–1940). Brit. general ; chief of staff to General Plumer in 1st World War 1914–18, became commander of the Black Sea army in 1920, and played an important part in the negotiations with Turkey up to 1923 ; Gov. of Gibraltar (1933–38).

Harington, or **Harrington, James** (1611–77). Eng. political writer, best known for his "Oceana," published 1656, which advocated an ideal form of government based on equality of forces and continuous change of offices.

Harlech (hahr'-lekh). Anc. spt. in Merionethshire, Wales ; ruins of Harlech Castle, captured by Yorkists in 1468 ; 718.

Harlech, William, 4th Baron (b. 1885). Eng. politician ; Under-Sec. for Colonies (as W. G. A. Ormsby-Gore) (1922–29) ; First Commissioner of Works (1931–36) ; Sec. for Colonies (1936–38) ; High Commissioner in S. Africa (1941–44) ; made a K.G. in 1948.

Harlem. Negro quarter, New York City.

Harlequin (hahr'-le-kwin). In old comedy and pantomime, conventional character in spangled motley, in love with Columbine.

Harlequins. Famous Rugby football club with headquarters at Twickenham, Middlesex, Eng.

Harmod'ius. Gk. youth, 1522.

Harmon'ics, 3010.

Harmo'nium. Musical instrument, 2450.

Har'mony. in music, 2263.

Harms'worth, Alfred. *See* **Northcliffe.**

Har'nack, Adolf (1851–1930). One of the most stimulating and prolific of modern Church historians, born in Russia, taught after 1889 at Univ. of Berlin ; claimed absolute freedom in study of Church history and New Testament ; preached practical Christianity as a religious life, not as a system of theology. His many works include "History

---

of Christian Dogma," "What is Christianity ?" and "The Sayings and Discourses of Jesus."

Harold I (d. 1040). King of Eng. ; son of Canute, upon whose death in 1035 he claimed and won crown in opposition to rightful heir, Hardicanute ; **1579.**

Harold II (c. 1026–1066). King of Eng., **1579 ;** killed in Battle of Hastings, 1194, *1196,* 1581 ; William I and, 3379.

Harold I (850–933). "Fair Hair," first king of united Norway, succeeded 872 ; conquered petty local kings, many of whom fled to harry and conquer elsewhere, as Rolf or Rollo the Ganger in Normandy ; 2388.

Harold III Sigurdson (1015–66). King of Norway, succeeded 1047 ; sought to conquer England with Tostig ; fell at Stamford Bridge, Yorks.

Haroun-al-Raschid (hah-roon'-ahl-ra'-shēd) (763–809). Abbasid caliph of Baghdad 786–809 ; scholar, poet, patron of learning, literature, and music, one of the greatest princes of his day, but a poor administrator ; hero of many stories in "Arabian Nights," 203 ; court at Baghdad, 339.

Harp. Stringed musical instrument, 1579, *2261,* 2267.

Harpagon (ahr'-pah-gon). The miser in Molière's "L'Avare," 2198.

Harper's Ferry, W. Virginia, U.S.A. Tn. at junction of Shenandoah and Potomac rivers ; pop. 766 ; scene of John Brown's raid, 588.

Har'pies. Bird monsters with the faces of old women, the ears of bears, and crooked talons, in Gk. and Rom. myth. ; the name means "the robbers," and they are supposed to be a personification of the storm winds. Harpy eagle, *439.*

Harpoon', spear-like missile, with a rope attached for catching large fish, seals, whales ; used by Eskimos, whalers, etc., 3372.

Harp shell, *2943.*

Harp'sichord, *2266,* 2601, 2602.

Harran (har-rahn'), also **Haran,** or **Charran.** In Bible times a thriving city in N. Mesopotamia ; ruins.

Har'rier. A dwarf foxhound, used to hunt hares, 1658.

Harrier. Type of hawk, 1588.

Harriman, Wm. Averell (b. 1891). U.S. diplomat ; Ambassador to U.S.S.R. 1943–46 ; to Gt. Britain, March–Oct. 1946 ; nominated ambassador-at-large for European Recovery programme 1948.

Harris. Peninsula in the Outer Hebrides ; famous for "Harris tweed," woven on hand looms. *See* **Lewis-with-Harris.**

Harris, Sir Arthur (b. 1892). Marshal of the R.A.F. ; Chief of Bomber Command 1942–1945 ; advocate of mass raids on Ger. industrial centres ; wrote "Bomber Offensive."

Harris, Joel Chandler (1848–1908). Amer. author ; unequalled Negro character and folklore tales ("Uncle Remus," "Brer Rabbit").

Harrisburg, Pennsylvania, U.S.A. State cap. and mfg. city ; pop. (1940) 83,900 ; rly. workshops, engineering works ; 2546.

Harrison, Benjamin (1833–1901), 23rd president of U.S.A., his period of office being 1889–1893 ; served with distinction in the Amer. Civil War ; 3291.

Harrison, Frederic (1831–1923). Eng. historian, jurist, literary critic, and Positivist philosopher ; voluminous writer ("The Meaning of History" ; "The Choice of Books" ; "Among My Books").

Harrison, John (1693–1776), Eng. clockmaker ; his chronometer, *822, 823,* 2290.

Harrison, William Henry (1773–1841), 9th president of U.S.A., elected 1840 ; served with distinction in the War of 1812.

Har'rogate. Fashionable inland watering place in North Riding of Yorkshire ; pop. 48,730 ; medicinal springs, 3435.

Harrow. A farm implement, having iron teeth that break up the soil when dragged over it ; there are various types ; use in Kent, *82*.

Harrow School. Famous Eng. school for boys at Harrow-on-the-Hill, 12 m. N.W. of London ; founded 1571 ; most famous sporting event is cricket match v. Eton at Lord's ; " Calling Bill " on Founder's Day, *2885*.

Hart, Sir Robert (1835–1911). Anglo-Chinese statesman ; inspector-general of imperial Chinese customs (1862–1907) ; placed Chinese national finance on solid footing.

Harte, Francis Bret (1839–1902). Amer. writer of poems and stories of western life, **1579**, *3294*.

Hart Fell, Scot. Mt. in Dumfriesshire and Peebleshire, 2,651 ft. ; *1054*.

Hartford, Connecticut, U.S.A. State cap. and mfg. centre ; pop. 166,300 ; mfrs. aero engines, machine-guns and other firearms, and typewriters.

Hart'land Point. Headland in N.W. Devonshire ; has a lighthouse.

Hartlepool. Spt. tn. in Durham ; pop. 20,545 ; West Hartlepool, lying to the w., is also a spt. ; pop. 61,300 ; exports coal, iron ores ; shipyards, iron and steel works ; *1059* ; German bombardment in 1st World War, Dec. 16, 1914, 113 civilian casualties.

Hart'mann, Karl Robert Eduard von (1842–1906). Ger. philosopher ; taught that existence is evil, and happiness an illusion (" Philosophy of the Unconscious ").

Harts'horn. Old name for ammonia water, *146*.

Harty, Sir (Herbert) Hamilton (1880–1941). Brit. composer and conductor, conductor of Hallé Orchestra from 1920 to 1933.

Harun-al-Raschid. *See* **Haroun-al-Raschid.**

Haruno'bu, Suzuki (c. 1760–80). Jap. painter, one of the first great masters of the colour print, *1812*.

Harvard, John (1607–38). Amer. clergyman ; b. in Eng., founder of Harvard Univ.

Harvard University. The oldest institution of higher learning in U.S.A., founded 1636 at Cambridge, Mass. ; *529*, *669*, *2118*, *2119*.

Harvest. The gathering in of the corn, *83*, *679*, *1580*.

Harvest festival. Ceremony which marks the close of the harvest, *1580* ; in Hungary, *plate f. 1656*.

Harvestman. A spider-like arachnid with unusually long legs.

Harvest mouse, *2249* ; *plate f. 2248*.

Har'vey, Sir John Martin. *See* **Martin-Harvey.**

Harvey, William (1578–1657). Eng. anatomist, who demonstrated circulation of the blood, *151*, *476*, *477*, **1581**, *1592*.

Har'well. Hamlet of Berkshire, Eng., 2 m. w. of Didcot ; site of first Brit. govt. controlled atomic research station ; director, Sir John Cockcroft.

Harwich (ha'-rij). Tn. on E. coast, chief spt of Essex ; 65 m. N.E. of London ; pop. 12,700 ; port for passenger ships to Flushing, the Hook of Holland, etc. ; during both World Wars, important naval base ; fisheries, shipbuilding, *1225*.

Har'wood, Sir Henry H. (1888–1950). Brit. sailor : commodore of the cruiser Ajax commanding the S. Amer. div. and H.M.S. Exeter, whose strategy led to retreat and scuttling of the Ger. battleship Adm. Graf Spee Dec. 1939 ; *see* **Plata, Battle of** ; retired as Adm. in 1945.

Harz (hahrts) **Mts.** In w. cent. Ger., *1445*, **1581** ; caves, *734*.

Hasa (hah'-sah), **El. Dist.** in E. Arabia on Persian Gulf ; combined with Nejd 1914 to form the Emirate of Nejd and Hara ; est. pop. 150,000 ; *197*.

Hasan (ha'-san) **and Husein** (hoo-sīn'). Grandsons of Mahomet, sons of Fatima and Ali ; killed A.D. 669 and 680 by adherents of the Ommayyad caliphs and revered as martyr saints by the Shiites.

Has'drubal (d. 207 B.C.). Carthaginian general, son of Hamilcar Barca and brother of the great Hannibal, slain at the Metaurus, *1574*.

Hashish (hash'-ēsh) or **hasheesh.** A narcotic drug, *1608*, *2768* ; " assassins " named from, *274*.

Has'sall, John (1868–1948). One of the best-known Eng. poster artists ; he also did much black-and-white, book cover and water-colour work ; much of his work is of a humorous kind.

Hassan Ibn Sabbah (d. 1124). Founder of the sect of Assassins, *274*.

Hastings. Port in Sussex, watering-place, one of the Cinque Ports ; pop. 65,000 ; *1581* ; *3123*.

Hastings, battle of (1066), **1581** ; Harold's death at, *1579* ; archers at, *210*.

Hastings, Sir Patrick (b. 1880). Eng. barrister and politician ; called to the Bar in 1906 ; became a K.C. in 1919 ; Labour M.P. (1922–1926) ; Attorney-General in first Labour govt. in 1924 ; author of plays, " Scotch Mist," " The Blind Goddess."

Hastings, Warren (1732–1818). First gov.-gen. of India, **1581**, *1582*, *1714* ; administration in Calcutta, *660* ; Burke impeaches, *622*, *1582*.

Hastings, Lord William (1430–83). Eng. soldier and confidential adviser to Edward IV ; executed, *2778*.

Hatay, The. New official name of Alexandretta (*q.v.*).

Hatfield House. Seat of the Cecil family in Hertfordshire, *1621*.

Hath'away, Anne (1556–1623). Wife of William Shakespeare, *3101* ; and Shakespeare, *2932*.

Hats and caps, **1582**, *plate f. 1584* ; " beaver," *388* ; manufacture, *1583* ; panamas, *1083*.

Hatshepsut (d. 1480 B.C.). Eg. queen ; temple and tomb, *1119*, *1119*.

Hat'to (d. A.D. 970). Archbishop of Mainz ; according to legend, devoured by mice in the Mouse Tower, *2769*.

Hauberk (haw'-bêrk). Coat of mail, *240*.

Hauptmann (howpt'-mahn), **Gerhardt** (1862–1946). One of greatest of modern Ger. dramatists ; runs the gamut from Zola-like realism to mystic symbolism, *1040*.

Hauraki Gulf, New Zealand, on which is situated the city of Auckland.

Hausas (how'-sas). African race of N. Nigeria, Brit. W. Africa ; among most intelligent of cent. Africa ; language widely spread through their activity as traders.

Haussmann (ōs-mahn'), **George Eugene, Baron** (1809–91). Fr. official, prefect of Seine (1853–70) ; famous for rebuilding Paris with wide boulevards, *2514*.

Haute-lisse (ōt-lēs'). A tapestry weave, *3153*.

Havan'a. Cap. of Cuba, largest and most important city in W. Indies ; pop. 783,000 ; *940*, **1584**.

Havelock, Sir Henry (1795–1857). Eng. general ; relieves Lucknow, *2035*.

Haverfordwest (haf'-ord-west), Wales. Co. tn. of Pembrokeshire, stands on the West Cleddau r., 8 m. N.E. of Milford ; has 12th cent. castle ; pop. 6,113 ; *2539*.

Havergal, Frances Ridley (1836–79). Eng. hymn writer (" Take my life and let it be ").

Havre (ahvr) or **Le Havre.** 2nd spt. of Fr. ; pop. 107,000 ; *1359*, **1585**, *2377* ; in both World Wars, *1585*.

Haw. Fruit of the hawthorn, *1589*.

Hawaiian (ha-wi'-an) or **Sandwich Islands**, or **Hawaii.** Group (of Polynesia) in Pacific Ocean ; 6,420 sq. m. ; pop. 502,000 ; **1585**, *1586* ; Cook at, *899*, *1587* ; Pearl Harbour, *1587*, *2533* ; U.S.A. and, *3291* ; volcanoes, *3329*.

Hawarden (haw'-den) **Castle**, Flintshire. Gladstone's home, *1470*.

Hawash. R. of S. Abyssinia, 500 m. long.

Hawfinch. Member of the finch tribe ; found in thickets, and remarkable for its very large beak adapted for cracking stones of fruits.

Hawk. Bird of prey, **1587** ; eats field mice, *439* ; eye, *1250* ; nest of sticks, *452* ; used in falconry, *1258*.

Hawkbill or **hawksbill turtle.** A sea turtle, *3230*.

Hawke, Edward Hawke, 1st Baron (1705–81). English admiral ; at Quiberon Bay, *2925*.

Hawke, Martin Bladen Hawke, 7th Baron (1860–1938). Eng. cricketer. Famous captain of Yorkshire from 1883 to 1910.

Hawker, Harry George (1891–1921). British airman, born in Australia. Rescued in mid-ocean on cross-Atlantic flight in 1919 ; killed on practice flight at Hendon.

Hawker Hurricane. Fighter plane, *34*, *50*.

Hawkins, Sir Anthony Hope. *See* **Hope, Anthony.**

Hawkins, Sir John (1532–95). Eng. adventurer and admiral, *142*, **1588** ; and Drake, *1036*.

Hawkins, Sir Richard (c. 1562–1622). Eng. admiral, son of Sir John H. ; commanded vessel in attack on the Sp. Armada.

Hawk-moth. Name given to the *Sphingidae* family of moths, found in Gt. Brit. ; the Death's Head is one of the species, *plate f. 633*.

Hawksmoor, Nicholas (1661–1736). Eng. architect ; worked so intimately with Wren that it is impossible to make exact division of credit for their work, *3371*.

Hawkweed. Plant of the family *Compositae*, having yellow flowers.

Haworth (hah'-wêrth). Eng. vil. in Yorkshire, home of Brontë family ; Brontë museum, *587*.

Ha'worth, Sir W. Norman (1883–1950). British scientist : apptd. Prof. of Chemistry, Univ. of Birmingham, in 1925 ; worked on release of atomic energy ; Nobel prize for chemistry in 1937 ; Royal Medal of Royal Soc. in 1942.

Hawthorn. An ornamental shrub, **1588** ; classified, *3247*.

Hawthorne, Nathaniel (1804–64). Amer. novelist, **1589**, *2403*, *3294*.

Hawtrey, Sir Charles (1858–1923). Eng. actor, playwright and theatrical manager ; he achieved considerable success in light comedy (" The Private Secretary ").

Hay. Dried grass or other plants as fodder for cattle, sheep and horses, *1509*, *1510* ; baling machines, *1510* ; spontaneous combustion, *2043* ; lucerne, *1280* ; harvest in Switzerland, *3140*.

Hay, Ian (b. 1876). Pen-name of John Hay Beith, Scottish author ; during the 1st World War (1914–18) he served with the Argyll and Sutherland Highlanders. (" A Safety Match " ; " A Knight on Wheels " ; " The First Hundred Thousand " ; " Carry On ") ; plays, " Tilly of Bloomsbury " ; " Orders are Orders " ; " The Sport of Kings " ; " The Housemaster," etc. Director of Public Relations to War Office 1938–41.

Hay, John (1838–1905). Amer. statesman and diplomat ; sec. to Pres. Lincoln ; sec. of state (1898–1905) ; negotiated Hay-Pauncefote treaty.

Hay, Will (1888–1949). Eng. " schoolmaster " comedian ; famous on films and radio ; also an astronomer.

Haydn (hī'-dn), **Franz Joseph** (1732–1809), Austrian composer, **1589** ; and the sonata, *2264*.

Hayes, Rutherford Birchard (1822–93). 19th pres. of U.S.A. ; elected pres. by one vote in 1876.

Hay fever. Irritation of the mucous membrane of nose and throat caused by pollens of grasses, dust, etc.

Hay-Pauncefote Treaty. Negotiated 1901 between U.S.A. and Gt. Brit. ; provided for construction of Panama Canal by U.S.A. and its permanent neutralization.

Hay'ter, Sir George (1792–1871). Eng. artist, painter of many historical scenes ; he was court painter during the reign of Queen Victoria, whose coronation and marriage formed two of his subjects ; portrait of Queen Victoria, *3320*.

Hay'ward, Thomas (1871–1939). Professional cricketer, played for Surrey co. and Eng.

Haze. Dispersal of light caused by suspension of fine particles in the air, making it less clear.

Hazel. Bushy shrub related to the birches, **1590** ; nuts, 2407.

Haz'litt, William (1778–1830). Eng. critic and essayist ; whatever his theme, he derives the essence of his commentary from himself, being in turn metaphysician, moralist, humorist, painter of manners and characteristics ; friend of Lamb ("Characters of Shakespeare's Plays" ; "Table Talk"), 1224.

"Head," pressure of water, 1669.

Head-dress, from Ur, 2147.

Head-hunters, of Borneo, 525 ; of Formosa, 1352.

Head louse, egg, *1094*.

Health. *See* Hygiene.

Health, Ministry of. Dept. of the Brit. Civil Service, **1590.**

Healy, Timothy Michael (1855–1931). Gov.-Gen. of the Irish Free State (1922–28) ; entered Parl. 1880 ; was private sec. to Parnell, whose leadership he afterwards opposed ; advocate of the Land League.

Hearing. *See* Ear.

Hearn (hêrn), **Lafcadio** (1856–1904). Writer of Eng. books on Japan, unique in combination of truthful insight with literary art ("Kotto" ; "Glimpses of Unfamiliar Japan" ; "In Ghostly Japan") ; cosmopolitan, b. Ionian Isls., son of Irish army doctor and Gk. mother ; married Japanese and became citizen of Japan.

Hearst, William Randolph (b. 1863). Amer. capitalist and journalist ; owner of " string " of newspapers from San Francisco to New York and of many magazines ; chief exponent of sensational journalism.

Heart. Organ of circulation, 474, **1591,** *2600*, 2701 ; diseases of, 1593 ; in insects, 1732 ; pulse, 2701 ; of spider, *plate f. 3065*.

Heartsease or wild pansy, 2494.

Heart-wood of trees, 3245.

Heat, 1593, 3084, 2593 ; of the body, 1599 ; causes emission of light, 1942 ; causes winds, 3384 ; effect on cloud formation, 851 ; electric current causes, 1128, 1130, 1133, 1134, 1623, *1624, 1625* ; energy, 3084 ; and fire, 1280 ; friction, 1397 ; highest temperatures produced, 1409, 1594 ; infra-red rays, 1722 ; Joule's research, 1839 ; latent, 3350 ; measuring high temperatures, 2709 ; melting points, 1391 ; quantity measured in calories, 1596 ; radiant, 1594, 1595 ; Rumford's researches, 2842 ; specific, 1596 ; of stars, 3080 ; of sun, 3119 ; thermometers, 1596, 3119 ; vacuum as insulator, 3302.

Heat engines. Machines which convert heat into mechanical energy, 1596 ; include internal combustion engines, 1735 ; steam-engines, 3085, 3258.

Heath. A sterile, acid area covered by heather, with pine and birch trees ; usually exhibits extremes of dry and wet soil.

Heath. A small evergreen shrub related to heather ; name often applied to heather, 1596.

Heather. An evergreen shrub, **1596.**

Heath family or *Ericaceae*. A large family of shrubs and vines, found on poor land, including heaths, cranberries, and rhododendrons, 1596.

Heathcoat, John (1783–1861). Brit. inventor of steam plough, salt purification process, and lace-making machine, 1876 ; M.P. for Tiverton, Devon (1832–1859).

Heathfield, Sussex, Eng. ; natural gas at, 1420.

Heath fires, prevention, 1289.

Heath Row, London airport, near Hounslow, and largest in Britain. Opened 1946, *48*.

Heating and ventilation, 1597, 1676 ; central heating, *1599,* 1600 ; humidity, 1243, 1598, 1677 ; high-frequency, 1623, *1624* ; in mines, 2184 ; by gas, 1423 ; by steam, 3084 ; thermostatic control, 3201.

Heat pump, 1600.

Heaven. The place or state of righteous souls after death ; Dante's, 971.

Heavenly Twins or **Gemini.** A constellation of the zodiac, 3444 ; location, *chart, 895.*

Heaviside, Oliver (1850–1925). Eng. scientist specializing in electrical research. Chiefly memorable for postulating existence of ionized layer in upper atmosphere which now bears his name. *See* **Heaviside Layer.**

Heaviside Layer. Upper region of atmosphere containing ionized air that reflects wireless waves ; named after its discoverer, 3395, 3396.

" Heavy " hydrogen. *See* **Deuterium.**

Heavysege, Charles (1816–76). Canadian poet, b. Eng. ; wrote "Saul," a poetic drama original in conception and containing many passages of striking beauty and power.

" Heavy " soil, 2998.

" Heavy " water. Contains one or more atoms of deuterium, the heavy isotope of hydrogen, per molecule. The deuterium atom contains two protons and an electron in its nucleus instead of single proton of hydrogen atom. Deuterium has chemical properties of hydrogen, since it has only one orbital electron, 998 ; 3351 ; in atomic heat ; atom, 296.

Heb'bel, (Christian) Friedrich (1813–63). Ger. poet and dramatist ; shows skill in characterization and true feeling for dramatic situations, but marred by occasional extravagances.

Hebe (hē-bē), in Gk. myth., goddess of eternal youth and joyousness ; **1600.**

He'ber, Reginald (1783–1826). Eng. churchman and hymn-writer, Bishop of Calcutta ("Holy, Holy, Holy, Lord God Almighty" ; "From Greenland's Icy Mountains ").

Hébert (ā'-bār), **Jacques René** (1757–94). Fr. revolutionist and atheist, 2790.

He'brew language and literature, 1600 ; alphabet, 126 ; belongs to Semitic group, 2571 ; Bible, *424,* 425, 1601, 2691. *See* Bible.

Hebrews. *See* Jews.

Hebrews, Epistle to the. The 19th book of the New Testament, a letter addressed to Christians of Hebrew birth, probably those living at Rome, about A.D. 65. The authorship is unknown but frequently attributed to Paul.

Hebrides (heb'-ri-dēz). Group of more than 500 isls. off the w. coast of Scotland ; divided by the Minch into the Inner and Outer Hebrides ; 2,812 sq. m. ; pop. 79,000 ; 230, **1601,** 2388 ; during 2nd World War chief northern minesweeping base at Stornoway, also base for R.A.F. flying-boats on Atlantic anti-submarine patrol ; also radar bases for detecting E-boats ; Staffa, *3071* ; Johnson's tour of, 529.

Hebron (hē'-bron). One of the oldest cities of Palestine. 18 m. s. of Jerusalem ; pop. 24,560 ; tombs of patriarchs, 2480.

Hecate (hek'-*a*-tē), in Gk. myth., goddess of moon, night and magic.

Hectare. A unit in metric system (2·471 acres), 2155.

Hec'togramme. A unit in metric system (1-10th of a kilogramme, 3·527 oz.), 2155.

Hec'tolitre. A unit in metric system (1-10th of a kilolitre), (22 gals.), 2155.

Hec'tometre. A unit in metric system (1-10th of a kilometre), (328 ft. 1 in.), 2155.

Hec'tor, in Gk. myth., Trojan hero, 19, **1603** ; death of, story retold from Homer, 1603.

Hector, Sir Knight in Arthurian legends, 255.

Hecuba (hek'-ū-ba), in Gk. myth., wife of Priam and mother of Hector, 1603, 2514.

" Hedda Gabler." Play by Ibsen ; its heroine is one of the most unscrupulous egoists of literature, 1680.

Heddle, part of a loom, 2025.

Hedgehog. A spiny, insect-eating animal of Europe and Asia, **1604** ; hibernation, 1600.

Hedges. Trees and shrubs used for ornament or division between fields and gardens ; privets, laurels, and whitethorns are often used.

Hedge-sparrow, *454,* 3052.

Hedin (hā'-dēn), **Sven Anders** (b. 1865). Swedish explorer, who made a number of journeys through Asia ("Through Asia" ; "Overland to India ", "Central Asia and Tibet " ; "Across the Gobi Desert ").

Hedjaz. Same as **Hejaz.**

Hedley, William. Brit. inventor ; designs the locomotive " Puffing Billy," 1981, 2736.

He'donists. A school of philosophers, 2571.

Heep, Uriah. In Dickens's " David Copperfield," a malignant hypocrite who calls himself " the 'umblest person going."

Hegel (hā'-gel), **Georg Wilhelm Friedrich** (1770–1831). Ger. philosopher, founder of the school of absolute idealism.

Heg'ira (hej'-i-ra) or **Hejira.** Mahomet's flight from Mecca (A.D. 622), from which Moslem dates are calculated, 661, 2066.

Heidelberg (hī-dl-berg). Ger., univ. tn. on Neckar ; pop. 84,000 ; 3296, **1604.**

Heidelberg Man. Type of man existing in prehistoric times, a reconstruction based on a primitive lower jaw found near Heidelberg in 1907.

Heidelberg Tun, 1604.

Heifetz (hī'-fets), **Jascha** (b. 1901). Rus. violinist ; made first public appearance at 5, and before he was 18 had won recognition throughout world as master of violin.

Height, of land, *89* ; of tree, how to find, *3246, 3248.*

Heil'bron, Sir Ian M. (b. 1886). Brit. scientist ; prof. of Organic Chemistry, Univ. of London, Imp. Coll. of Sc., from 1938 ; scientific adviser to Min. of Supply 1939–42 ; won Priestley medal of Amer. Chem. Soc. for synthetic penicillin in 1945.

Heilbronn (hīl'-bron). Industrial tn. in s. Ger. on r. Neckar ; pop. 60,308 ; fine Gothic church and Rathaus.

Heimwehr (hīm'-vār). Austrian military organization dissolved by Dr. Schuschnigg in 1936.

Heine (hī'-ne), **Heinrich** (1797–1856). Ger. poet, 1457, **1604.**

Heinkel (hīn'-kel). Series of Ger. aircraft used before and during 2nd World War ; He. 111 twin-engine monoplane bomber used in Battle of Britain ; later He. 177 heavy bomber and the jet-propelled He. 162.

Heir apparent. (a) The next in succession by law to property, which cannot, if he survives the actual holder, pass to anyone but him. (b) Next in descent to the reigning monarch of England, who is bound to succeed to the throne on the death of the latter.

Heir presumptive. One who at a given moment is actually the next in succession to property or title, but who may at any time cease to be so by the birth of a child nearer to, or more direct in descent from, original ancestor.

Heisenberg (hī'-zen-berg), **Werner** (b. 1901). Ger. physicist ; created system of quantum mechanics and did research on atomic energy ; awarded Nobel prize for physics in 1932.

Hejaz (hej-ahz') or **Hedjaz.** Part of the Kingdom of Saudi Arabia on Red Sea ; 150,000 sq. m. ; pop. est. about

3,500,000 ; independence from Turkey recognized by treaty of Sèvres (1920) ; cap. Mecca ; 197, 201 ; Mecca, 2125.

Hejira. *See* **Hegira.**

Hek′la or **Hecla.** A volcano in s.w. Iceland ; height 4,747 ft. ; becomes active at irregular intervals.

Hel′ena, St. (d. 328). Mother of Constantine the Great ; legendary discoverer of the Holy Cross ; 893.

Helen of Troy, in Homer's " Iliad," most beautiful woman in Greece, daughter of Zeus and wife of Menelaus, king of Sparta, 1638 ; cause of Trojan War, 3249, 3250.

Hel′frich, Conrad E. L. (b. 1886). Dutch sailor ; commanded Netherlands naval forces in E., 1939–42 ; supreme commdr. Allied naval forces in s.w. Pacific from 1942 ; C.-in-C. Netherlands land, air, and sea forces 1942–46 ; in 1945 C.-in-C. of Netherlands naval forces.

Helgoland. Same as **Heligoland.**

He′liades, in Gk. myth., daughters of Helios, god of the sun ; their tears at death of Phaëthon turned into amber.

Helian′thus. Sunflower genus of plants, 3121.

Helicon (hel′-i-kon). Anc. name of a peak or mt. range in Boeotia, Greece ; on the E. slope were a grove and temple sacred to the Muses, 2259.

Helicon. Brass wind-instrument resembling Fr. horn.

Helicopter (hel′-i-kopter), **1604,** *1605* ; for traffic control, 2787.

Heligoland. Ger. isl. in North Sea, 1606, *1607.*

Heliogabalus (hē-li-ō-gab′-*a-lus*) or **Elagabalus** (A.D. 205–222). Dissolute Rom. emperor, proclaimed A.D. 218 ; introduced into Rome worship of Syrian sun-god whose namesake and high priest he was ; assassinated.

Heliograph. A sunlight reflector used in signalling, *3165.*

Heliopolis (hē-li-op′-o-lis). Anc. city at head of Nile delta, Egypt ; once seat of sun-worship ; also anc. name of Baalbek, Syria.

He′lios, in Gk. myth., god of the sun ; Colossus of Rhodes, 3770, 2924, *plate f.* 2924.

He′liotrope. Flowering plant of the order *Boraginaceae* ; a native of Peru and other warm and temperate climates ; has fragrant smell ; colour of flowers gives name to purplish colour.

Heliot′ropism. The tendency to turn toward or away from light ; in plants, 2623, 2625.

Helium (He.) A gaseous element of the inert gas group ; atomic weight, 4·002 ; has been liquefied at −269°C. The name was given to it because of its discovery in the sun (Gk. *helios,* sun) ; 769, 775, 1161, **1607,** 2744 ; in atmosphere, 1420 ; discovered by spectroscope, *plate f. 3057* ; emanates from radium, 2731 ; and from thorium, 1607 ; fission product of boron, 296, 297 ; liquefaction, 1391 ; obtained from natural gas, 1420.

Hell, the Infernal Regions ; Dante's, 971 ; in Milton's " Paradise Lost," 2178.

Hel′las. Originally a small dist. in Thessaly ruled by Peleus, father of Achilles ; later applied vaguely to all anc. Greece.

Hel′lebore. Name given to various plants of the buttercup family. *See* **Christmas rose.**

Hellen. Mythical founder of the Greeks, son of Deucalion and Pyrrha, father of Dorus (from whom came Dorians), and grandfather of Ion (Ionians) and Achaeus (Achaeans) ; myth probably first current about 8th cent. B.C., when feeling of national unity developed among the Greeks.

Hellenes (hel′-ēnz). Name for anc. Greeks.

Hellen′ic languages, 2570.

Hellenistic Age, 1524 ; at Alexandria, 109 ; literature, 1541.

Hel′lospont. Anc. name for Dardanelles, 974.

Helmer, Nora. Heroine of Ibsen's " A Doll's House."

Helmet shell, 2942.

Helm′holtz, Hermann von (1821–94). Ger. physicist, physiologist, and mathematician ; invented the ophthalmoscope ; eminent in nearly every other branch of science.

He′loderm. A poisonous lizard, 1972, 1974.

Héloise (ā-lō-ēz′) (*c.* 1101–64). Talented Fr. abbess, celebrated for her devotion to Abelard, 11.

He′lots. Spartan serfs, 3053.

Help′mann, Robert M. (b. 1911). Australian dancer, choreographer, and actor ; *premier danseur* at Sadler's Wells Ballet from 1933 ; choreographer of " Comus," " Hamlet," " Miracle in the Gorbals," " Adam Zero," " Red Shoes " ; acted as Hamlet, Flamineo in " The White Devil," etc.

Helsingborg or **Halsingborg.** Spt. and 5th city of Sweden ; pop. 66,500 ; in s. opposite Elsinore, Denmark ; had important part in Scandinavian wars ; 3128.

Helsingfors. *See* **Helsinki.**

Helsingör, Denmark. Same as **Elsinore.**

Helsin′ki or **Helsingfors.** City and cap. of Finland ; pop. 355,000 ; frequently bombed 1939–44 ; 1277, **1607,** *1608.*

Helvellyn (hel-vel′-lin), Eng. Mt. in the w. of Cumberland, between Keswick and Ambleside, 3,118 ft. high ; 3371.

Helvetian (hel-vē-shan) or **Helvet′ic Republic.** Swiss republic formed by French, 1798 ; lasted until recognition of Swiss independence by Congress of Vienna (1814).

Helvetii (hel-vē′-shi-ē). Celtic tribe originally dwelling in what is now s.w. Ger. ; later, according to Caesar, they lived in what is now w. Switzerland ; Caesar defeated them, 58 B.C.

Helvetius, Claude Adrien (1715–71). Fr. philosopher ; his most famous book, " De l'esprit " (" Of the Spirit "), raised a storm, was condemned by the Sorbonne.

Hemans (hē′-manz), **Felicia Dorothea** (1793–1835). Eng. poet whose lyrics include household classics like " Casabianca " and " The Homes of England."

Hematite. A red iron ore, 1753.

Heminge, John (*c.* 1556–1630). Eng. actor, close friend of Shakespeare, 2936.

Hemingway, Ernest (b. 1898). American novelist (" Farewell to Arms " ; " Winner Take Nothing " ; " For Whom the Bell Tolls "), 2403, 3295.

Hemip′tera. The order of insects with sucking mouth parts, 1730, *1732* ; aphis, 185 ; cicadas, 826 ; scale insects, 2878, 2879.

Hemisphere. Half of the terrestrial or celestial globe or the geographical globe ; the former consists of northern and southern (above and below the Equator) and the latter of eastern and western (the Old World and the New World).

Hem′lock or **hemlock spruce.** Conifer with flat, blunt needles, 1608, 3289 ; bark used in tanning, 1911.

Hemlock or **poison hemlock.** A poisonous plant of the parsley family, **1608,** 2637 ; poison of Socrates, 2638.

Hemming, 2927.

Hemp. A herbaceous plant, **1608** ; Manila " hemp," 1609, 2825 ; rope and twine, 2825 ; sisal, 1609, 2975.

Hemy, Charles Napier (1841–1917). Eng. painter of marine subjects.

Hen (domestic fowl), 2671 ; embryology, 1155.

Henbane. A hairy, poisonous plant of the nightshade family ; gives the drug hyoscine ; flowers are pale yellowish with purple markings, *2639.*

Henderson, Arthur (1863–1935). Brit. Labour leader ; Home Sec. in first Labour Govt. (1924) ; Foreign Secretary (1929–31) ; presided over Disarmament Conference (1932–3) ; Nobel peace prizewinner for 1934.

Henderson, Arthur (b. 1893). Min. of State for Commonwealth Relations, Aug.–Oct. 1947 ; Secretary of State for Air 1947.

Henderson, Sir Nevile Meyrick (1882–1942). Brit. diplomat ; Ambassador in Berlin 1937 to outbreak of war 1939. Book, " Failure of a Mission," 1940.

Hendon. Bor. of Middx. 8 m. N.W. of London ; pop. (1942) 132,300 ; aerodrome famous for R.A.F. displays ; former Police College, 2650.

Hendren, Elias (" Patsy ") (b. 1889). English cricketer. From 1919–1933 regularly scored over 1,000 runs each season. Played for Middlesex and in many Test Matches.

Henequen (hen′-e-ken). A sisal plant, 2975 ; Yucatan production, 2158.

Hen′gist and **Hor′sa.** Chieftains of first Saxon settlers (*c.* 450) in Eng. legendary.

Henie, Sonja (son′-ya hen-ye) (b. 1913). Norwegian skater. Won World's Championship for Figure Skating on ten occasions ; Olympic Champion in 1928, 1932, and 1936 ; afterwards became film star, 2977.

Henlein (hen′-līn), **Konrad** (1901–45). Czech politician and head of Sudetic Germans ; in Mar. 1939 was app. Civil Administrator for Bohemia ; June 1939 Reichsstathalter of Sudetenland ; committed suicide June 1945.

Henley, William Ernest (1849–1903). Brit. poet, critic, and dramatist (" London Voluntaries " ; " Hospital Sketches ") ; author of the unforgettable lines : " I am the master of my fate, I am the captain of my soul " ; collaborated with R. L. Stevenson in several plays.

Henley-on-Thames, Oxfordshire. Tn. on r. Thames famous for its beautiful situation and its annual regatta ; chief events at regatta Diamond Sculls and Grand Challenge Cup ; pop. 10,000 ; 2466.

Hennepin, Louis (*c.* 1640–*c.* 1706). Fr. missionary and explorer, 2192.

Henner, Jean Jacques (1829–1905). Fr. painter, called " Modern Correggio " because of fondness for soft flesh tints and warm shadows.

Henrietta Maria (1609–69). Fr. princess, queen of Charles I of Eng. ; 755.

Henry, a measure of elec. inductance, 1133.

Henry I, " the Fowler " (*c.* 876–936). Holy Roman emperor.

Henry II (973–1024), emperor.

Henry III (1017–56), emperor, 1609.

Henry IV (1050–1106), emperor, **1609** ; and the Pope, 1449, 1542.

Henry V (1081–1125), emperor.

Henry VI (1165–97), emperor.

Henry VII (*c.* 1270–1313), emperor, **1609.**

Henry I (1068–1135), king of Eng., **1609** ; death, 1886 ; zoo at Woodstock, 3446.

Henry II (1133–89), Eng., **1609,** *1610,* 2776, and Thomas Becket, 389 ; conquers Ireland, 910, 1745.

Henry III (1207–72), Eng., reigned 1216–72 (not 1227–72 as in p. 1489). *1610,* **1611,** 2221, *3123.*

Henry IV (1367–1413), Eng., **1611** ; overthrows Richard II, 2777.

Henry V (1387–1422), Eng., 757, **1611** ; at Agincourt, 76 ; and Hundred Years' War, 1653.

Henry VI (1421–71), Eng., **1611** ; in Wars of the Roses, 2828 ; loses Fr. possessions, 1653 ; founds Eton College, *1229,* 2883, *2885* ; King's College, 668 ; murdered, 1091, 2777.

Henry VII (1457–1509), Eng., reigned 1485–1509 (not 1421–71 as in p. 1489) ; **1612,** 4078 ; at Bosworth, *530,* 2828 ; *2765, 3369.*

Henry VIII (1491–1547), Eng., reigned 1509–47 (not 1491–1547 as in p. 1489). **1612,** *1455, plate f. 1864,* 3253 ; 426 ; 2759 ; 490 ; shows favour to Holbein, 1635 ; Sir Thomas More, 2229 ; Wolsey, 3402.

Henry I (1008–60), king of France, **1613**.

Henry II (1519–59), France, **1613**.

Henry III (1551–89), France, **1613**.

Henry IV (1553–1610), France, called Henry of Navarre, 870, **1613**, 2568 ; issues Edict of Nantes (1598), 1651, 2274.

Henry FitzHenry (1155–83). Second son of Henry II, and subsequently heir to Eng. throne ; intrigued against father and died warring against brother Richard ; celebrated for knightly exploits.

Henry of Blois (1101–71), Bishop of Winchester and papal legate, brother of King Stephen ; quarrelled with latter upon refusal of primacy and for a time supported Matilda's claims to throne.

Henry of Navarre. *See* **Henry IV** (France).

Henry the Lion (1129–95). Duke of Saxony and Bavaria, son of Henry the Proud ; son-in-law of Henry II of Eng. ; by series of wars extended power of his duchies in face of opposition of Hohenstaufen emperors.

Henry the Navigator (1394–1460), **1613** ; and African exploration, 69 ; his tomb, 2653.

Henry Alexander, Canadian writer, 684.

Henry, Sir Edward, Bart. (1850–1931). Eng. police official, Com. of Met. Police, 1903–18 ; originated filing system of finger prints, 1276.

Henry, Joseph (1797–1878). Amer. physicist ; developed methods for weather forecasting ; gave name to

unit of inductance, 1133 ; discovered oscillatory nature of Leyden-jar discharge, 3391.

Henry, O., pen-name of William Sydney Porter (1862–1910). Amer. short-story writer (" The Trimmed Lamp " ; " The Furnished Room " ; " Options "), 3294.

Henry, Patrick (1736–99). Amer. rev. orator and political leader.

" Henry Esmond," hero of Thackeray's novel " Esmond," 3198.

Hen'schel, Sir George (1850–1934). Eng. musical director, composer, and singer.

Henson, Leslie (b. 1891). Eng. comedian and theatrical producer ; (" It's a Boy " ; " Funny Face " ; " Going Greek ").

Henson, William (1805–88). Brit. pioneer aircraft constructor, 44.

Hen'ty, George Alfred (1832–1902). Eng. author, soldier, and war correspondent ; **1613**.

Hepaticae. A class of primitive plants, including liverworts, 1970, 3617.

Hepat'ic artery, 1968.

Hephaestus (he-fẽs'-tŭs). In Gk. myth. god of fire and metal-working, **1613** ; makes armour of Achilles, 19 ; weds Aphrodite, 186 ; and Cyclopes, 949.

Hep'plewhite, George (d. 1786). Eng. furniture maker, whose delicate graceful chairs were lighter and smaller than Chippendale's and had typically straight, slender legs ; his pieces were characterized by simplicity and most refined elegance ; *1411*, 1412.

Heptam'eron (Gk. " seven days "). Collection of short stories made by various writers at court of Marguerite

of Valois (or Navarre), modelled on Boccaccio's " Decameron " ; often cynical but important in history of Fr. literature.

Heptane, a hydrocarbon used in testing petrol, 2564.

Heptateuch (hep'-ta-tūk). The first seven books of the Old Testament.

Hepworth, Barbara (b. 1903), Brit. sculptor in the abstract manner, 2911.

Hera (hẽ'-ra). In Gk. myth., queen of the gods, wife of Zeus ; **1614**, *3443* ; and Callisto, 894 ; hostile to Hercules, 1615 ; judgement of Paris, 3249.

Heracle'a, battle of (280 B.C.), 2710.

Heracles (hẽr'-a-klẽz) or **Herakles.** Same as **Hercules.**

Heraclitus (hẽr-a-klī'-tŭs) (c. 540–480 B.C.). Gk. philosopher, called founder of metaphysics ; taught that constant change from being to not being is fundamental principle of universe ; sometimes called the Weeping Philosopher.

Heraclius (hẽr-ak'-li-ŭs) (c. 575–642). A Byzantine emperor ; defeated Chosroes II, emperor of Persia.

Herald. A public official who, in anc. times, conveyed challenges to battle, proclaimed war or peace, etc. ; in mod. times the three Kings of Arms, six Heralds, and four Pursuivants are responsible for proclaiming a new sovereign, *1614*.

Heraldry. Art of armorial bearings, **1614** ; flag emblems from, 1312.

Heralds' College. *See* **Arms, College of.**

Herat (hẽr-aht'). Fortified city in w. Afghanistan, of strategic importance ; pop. about 85,000 ; caravan

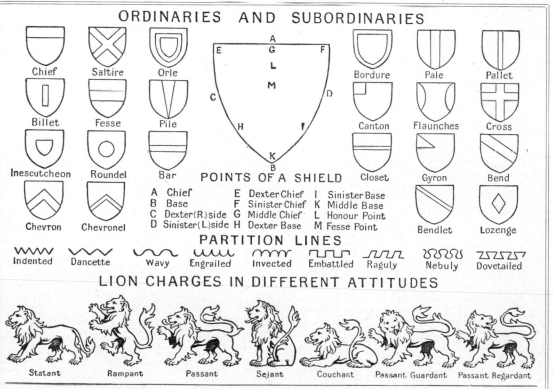

ORDINARIES AND SUBORDINARIES

Chief · Saltire · Orle · Bordure · Pale · Pallet · Billet · Fesse · Pile · Canton · Flaunches · Cross · Inescutcheon · Roundel · Bar · Closet · Gyron · Bend · Chevron · Chevronel · Bendlet · Lozenge

POINTS OF A SHIELD

A Chief   E Dexter Chief   I Sinister Base
B Base   F Sinister Chief   K Middle Base
C Dexter(R)side   G Middle Chief   L Honour Point
D Sinister(L)side   H Dexter Base   M Fesse Point

PARTITION LINES

Indented · Dancette · Wavy · Engrailed · Invected · Embattled · Raguly · Nebuly · Dovetailed

LION CHARGES IN DIFFERENT ATTITUDES

Statant · Rampant · Passant · Sejant · Couchant · Passant Guardant · Passant Regardant

SOME MYSTERIES OF HERALDRY EXPLAINED

To facilitate blazoning, the field or shield was plotted out into sections. In connexion with the points of a shield it should be noted that what is known as the dexter side (*dexter*, Latin for right) is the left side as you look at it, and the *sinister* (Latin for left) is the right, the terms applying to the wearer, not to the spectator. Among the great body of charges are certain conventional or geometrical figures, broad bands, crosses, whirls, etc. These are called ordinaries and subordinaries, and several of those most commonly met with are explained above. How the various metals, colours and furs are indicated is shown in page 1614.

centre ; once important city, cap. of Timur's empire ; 56.

Herbart, Johann Friedrich (1776–1844). Ger. philosopher, psychologist and educator.

Herbert, Sir Alan Patrick (b. 1890). Eng. author, wit, and politician ; joined staff of " Punch " in 1924 ; M.P. 1935, and introduced new divorce legislation ; novels include " Water Gipsies " and " Holy Deadlock " ; comic operas, " Tantivy Towers," " Derby Day," " Bless the Bride," " Tough at the Top." Cr. knight 1945.

Herbert, George (1593–1633). Eng. poet, saintly pastor of Bemerton, 1211. " The Temple " is full of quaint artificialities, but contains some of the most treasured Eng. sacred lyrics.

Herbiv′orous animals. Those adapted to vegetable food ; include ruminants.

Herb Robert, flowering plant of fam. Geraniaceae, 1444.

Herbs, flavouring, 2187, 3060.

Herculaneum (hêr-kŭ-lā′-nē-ŭm). Anc. Rom. city at foot of Mt. Vesuvius, buried with Pompeii in the eruption of A.D. 79 ; valuable antiquities revealed by excavations ; 207, 2654, 3319.

Hercules (hêr′-kŭ-lēz) or **Heracles.** Hero in Gk. and Rom. myth., **1615,** 1616.

Hercules, constellation, 894.

Hercules, Pillars of (Gibraltar), 1463.

Hercules beetle, 400.

Her′der, Johann Gottfried von (1744–1803). Ger. critic, philosopher, and poet ; influences Goethe, 1456.

Hérédia (ā-rā′-dē-ah), **Jose de** (1842–1905). Fr. poet, b. Cuba ; " the modern master of the Fr. sonnet," 3027.

Hered′ity. Transmission of qualities from parents to offspring, **1617,** 1427 ; and environment, 1428 ; Mendel's laws, 2140 ; " reversion to type," 1298, 1481.

Her′eford, Co. tn. of Herefordshire, on r. Wye ; cath. ; agric. trade, brewing ; pop. 30,500 ; 1617.

Her′eford. Breed of cattle, commonly red with white markings, 731, 732.

Herefordshire. Inland co. in s.w. Eng. on border Wales ; 842 sq. m. ; pop. 112,000 ; **1617,** 1316.

Herero (ha-rā′-rō). A Bantu people of the South-West Africa Protectorate ; chief occupation cattle-raising.

Her′esy. Teaching opposed to established religion or religious authority ; Huss burned for, 1661 ; Inquisition, 1726.

Hereward (her′-e-ward) **the Wake** (11th cent.). Eng. patriot outlaw at time of Norman Conquest ; **1618.**

Hergesheimer, Joseph (b. 1880). Amer. novelist ; given to psychological studies with complex social backgrounds (" The Three Black Pennies " ; " Java Head " ; " Cytherea " ; " Swords and Roses "), 3295.

Herkomer, Sir Hubert von (1849–1914). Naturalized Brit. artist, b. in Bavaria ; won speedy success as a portrait and subject painter ; R.A. in 1890 ; best-known works include " The Last Muster," " On Strike," and " The Lady in White."

Hermann or **Arminius** (17 B.C.–A.D. 21). Ger. chieftain, 1447.

Hermannstadt. Same as **Sibiu.**

" Hermas, Shepherd of." Apocryphal book of New Testament, 424.

Hermes (hêr′-mēz). In Gk. myth., messenger of gods, **1619,** 2146 ; conducts Persephone from Hades, 1921 ; head on coin, 2202 ; invented lyre, 1579 ; protects Odysseus against Circe's spells, 835 ; statue by Praxiteles, 1533, 1537.

Hermes Trismegis′tus (" Hermes the thrice greatest "). Gk. name of Eg. god Thoth ; reputed author of Hermetic Books, encyclopedic works on Eg. religion, art, and science.

Her′mia. In Shakespeare's " Midsummer Night's Dream," daughter of Egeus, in love with Lysander, 2169.

Hermione (hêr-mī′-o-nē). In Shakespeare's " Winter's Tale," wife of Leontes, 3389.

Hermit. Precursor of monks, 2212.

Hermit crab. A type that lives in an empty mollusc shell, 924, plate f. 925.

Hermon Mt., in Syria 30 m. s.w. of Damascus ; 9,380 ft. ; modern Jebeles-Sheikh ; 2480.

Hernandez, Gregorio (c. 1576–1636). Span. sculptor, 3040.

Hernani (ār-nah′-nē). Hero of tragedy of same name by Victor Hugo and opera founded on it by Verdi ; romantic outlaw, who, on point of honour, ends life just as love, wealth, and high dignities are his.

Hero or **Heron of Alexandria** (first cent. A.D.), Gk. mathematician and writer on mechanical and physical subjects ; and turbine, 2949, 3260.

Hero and Leander. Lovers in famous Gk. legend, **1619.**

Her′od I, the Great. King of Judaea 37–4 B.C., 422, **1620.**

Herod Antipas. Son of Herod the Great ; tetrarch of Galilee 4 B.C.–A.D. 39 ; **1620,** 1821.

Herodias (he-rō′-di-as). Wife of Herod Antipas, mother of Salome, and instigator of the beheading of John the Baptist, 1620.

Herod′otus (c. 484–424 B.C.). Gk. historian, the " father of history," 1540, **1620** ; on the Pyramids, 2709.

Hero′ic couplet. A verse form, 2636 ; used by Dryden, 1050.

Heroin (he-rō′-in). A derivative of opium.

Her′on. A long-necked, long-legged wading bird, **3097** ; in flight, 3099.

Her′onries. Nesting and breeding-places of herons, 3100.

Herostratus (he-ros′-tra-tus) (4th cent. B.C.). Ephesian who set fire to Diana's temple.

Herrera architecture, in Spain, 3040 ; named after Juan Herrera (c. 1530–1597) who built the Escorial, 3042.

Herrick, Robert (1591–1674). Eng. lyric poet ; regarded by Swinburne as the greatest of Eng. song writers ; " Corinna's Maying," " Night Piece to Julia," " Gather Ye Rosebuds," and other delicate, exquisite, unimpassioned verse, 1211.

Herring. The most important of all the food fishes, **1620** ; fisheries, 1299, 1308 ; girls gutting, 1306 ; at Yarmouth and Hull, 1307.

Herringbone. Sewing stitch, 2927.

Herring gull, 1557.

Herriot (er′-i-ō), **Edouard** (b. 1872). French statesman ; Prime Minister 1924–5–6 ; afterwards Pres. of Chamber of Deputies ; imprisoned in Germany 1944–45 ; apptd. Chairman of the Five-Power (Western Union) Committee, and member of European Unity Committee, 1948.

Herschel (hêr′-shel), **Caroline** (1750–1848). Eng. astronomer, b. Ger., assistant of Sir William Herschel.

Herschel, Sir John Frederick William (1792–1871). Eng. astronomer, son of Sir William Herschel ; discovered 525 star clusters and nebulae not recorded by his father, 2311 ; made first telescopic survey of southern heavens ; invented a process of photography on sensitized paper.

Herschel, Sir William (1738–1822). Eng. astronomer, b. Ger. ; developed study of fixed stars and discovered 5,000 star clusters ; proved motion of solar system through space ; and nebulae, 2311 ; discovered planet Uranus, 2618, 3298.

Herschel, Sir William (1833–1917). Brit. official, son of Sir J. F. W. Herschel and grandson of Sir William Herschel ; inventor of system of finger-print identification.

Herstmonceux. See **Hurstmonceux.**

Hertford (hahr′-ford). Eng. co. tn. of Hertfordshire ; pop. 11,300 ; 1622.

Hertford College, Oxford, 2464.

Hertfordshire. Inland co. in England, N. of London ; 632 sq. m. ; pop. 535,000, 1621.

Hertz (hârts), **Gustav** (b. 1887). Ger. physicist, son of Heinrich Hertz ; with J. Franck, carried out experi-

ments on the emission of spectral lines caused by electronic bombardment, which led to the proof of the quantum theory ; awarded Nobel prize 1926.

Hertz, Heinrich Rudolf (1857–94). Ger. physicist, 1622, 2594, 2728 ; confirmed Maxwell's theory concerning existence of ether (" Hertzian ") waves ; studied cathode rays, 3430 ; ether wave work led to radio telegraphy, 2098, 3391.

Hertzian waves. Wireless waves, similar to those of light, but varying from a few feet to several miles in length, in the ether of space, 2098, 2728 ; named after Heinrich Hertz, 1622.

Hertzog (hărt′-zog), **James Barry** (1866–1942). S. African statesman, 2988.

Hervey Archipelago. Same as **Cook Is.**

Herzegovina (her-tse-gō-vē′-na), and Bosnia, 528 ; annexed by Austria, 528 ; in Yugoslavia, 3439.

Herzen (hert-sen), **Alexander** (1812–70). Rus. author and publicist, whose political writings, secretly circulated in Russia, stirred up revolt against Rus. absolutism.

Herzl (hert′-zl), **Theodor** (1860–1904). Hungarian Jew, founder of modern political Zionism.

Hesiod (hē′-si-od) (8th cent. B.C.). father of Gk. didactic poetry, 1539

Hesperides (hes-per′-i-dēz). In Gk. myth., sisters, symbols of love and fruitfulness ; 1615.

Hess, Dame Myra (b. 1890). Brit. pianist ; from 1939 organized lunch hour musical concerts in National Gallery.

Hess, Rudolf (b. 1894). Leading Nazi Deputy to Hitler. Flew to England May 1941, held prisoner. Tried at Nuremberg, 1945–46 ; sentence, life imprisonment, 2282.

Hess, Victor F. (b. 1883). Austro-American physicist ; researches on cosmic rays won him the Nobel prize for physics 1936.

Hesse (hes′-e). State in s.w. Germany grand duchy until 1918 ; 2,970 sq. m. ; pop. 1,470,000. Incorp. into Land of Greater Hesse in 1946.

Hesse-Cassel or **Electoral Hesse.** Former Ger. landgraviate and electorate N. of Hesse-Darmstadt ; joined Austria in Austro-Prussian War (1866) incorp. with Prussia in 1866.

Hesse-Darmstadt. Name of Hesse until 1866.

Hes′sian fly. One of the worst pests of Amer. farms, doing many million of pounds worth of damage to grain in a year ; fossil ancestor found in amber, 138.

Hes′tia. Gk. goddess of hearth and home ; daughter of Kronos ; same as Rom. Vesta.

Heston. Borough (with Isleworth) of Middlesex, 12 m. w. of London pop. 95,600 ; important airport chief London centre for international air-lines and private flying.

Heterodyne, or " **beat,**" in wireless 3394.

Heuss (hois), **Theodore** (b. 1884). 1st pres. W. Ger. Fed. Repub., Sept 1949 ; formerly prof. of pol. econ.

Hev′esy, George von (b. 1885). Hungarian chemist and physicist ; with D. Coster discovered the element Hafnium in 1922 ; introduced application of isotopes as indicator or tracers in chemistry and biology.

Hew′art, Gordon, Viscount (1870–1943). Brit. lawyer and politician ; solicitor-general (1916) and attorney general (1919) ; Lord Chief Justice (1922–40) ; peerage in 1922, viscounty in 1940 ; taking oath, 1904

Hew′lett, Maurice Henry (1861–1923 Eng. romantic novelist ; " Forest Lovers " ; " Richard Yea and Nay " ; " The Queen's Quair " ; " Open Country " ; 1215, 2777.

Hex′apods or **Insecta.** The class of six legged arthropods, or insects.

Hex′ham. Market tn. in N. Eng. o r. Tyne, 20 m. w. of Newcastle here Yorkists defeated Lancastrian in 1464 ; pop. 8,888 ; ironworks coal-mining, etc., and trade in agricultural products.

Hexuronic Acid. A carbohydrate ; pure form of Vitamin C.

Heydrich (hī'-drikh), **Reinhard** (1904–42). Ger. Nazi police officer ; in 1935 chief of security police, incl. the Gestapo ; tried by terrorism and murder to stamp out resistance in Norway, Netherlands, and Sept. 1941, in Bohemia and Moravia ; died as result of bomb thrown May 1942, in Prague ; Lidice (q.v., in f-i.) obliterated in revenge.

Heye Foundation. Museum (2 million exhibits), research labs., and library completed 1922 in New York, for anthropological, etc., study of the American Indian ; founded in 1916 by Dr. G. G. Heye (b. 1874).

Heyse (hī'ze), **Paul** (1830–1914). Ger. poet, novelist, and short-story writer ; Nobel prize winner (1910) ; master of the novelette ; his stories usually consist of one incident polished and worked over till it stands out like a cameo ; a pessimistic but progressive, radical thinker.

Heysham (hē-sham), in bor. of Morecambe and Heysham, Lancs, Eng. ; harbour and steamship service to N. Ireland ; oil-from-coal plant, 2430.

Hezeki'ah (8th-7th cents. B.C.). Strong righteous king of Judah, in whose reign " the Assyrian came down like a wolf on the fold," as Byron tells in " Destruction of Sennacherib " ; (read 2 Kings xviii, xix, xxii) ; 1830.

Hiawatha (hī-a-wah'-tha). Legendary Indian chief, founder of the League of Six Nations (Iroquois), and promoter of the arts of peace, 2022 ; Longfellow's story retold, 2022.

Hiberna'tion. Passing the winter in sleep or torpor, 1622 ; among bears, 382 ; frogs, 1399.

Hibernia (hī-bêr-ni-a). Anc. Latin and poetical name of Ireland.

Hibis'cus. A large genus of plants of the mallow family, natives of warm climates, many with large flowers ; fibres used in the East for cordage and matting.

Hichens, Robert Smythe (b. 1864). Eng. novelist and playwright ; (" The Garden of Allah " ; " Bella Donna " ; " The Dweller on the Threshold " ; " Incognito " ; memoirs, " Yesterday").

Hick'ory. A N. Amer. tree of the walnut family ; nuts (known as pecan-nuts) are sweet and tasty, and the wood is used for making axe, pick and tool handles ; botanical classification, 3247.

Hicks, Sir (Edward) Seymour (1871–1949). Popular Eng. comedy actor, born in Jersey ; married Ellaline Terriss, with whom he took part in many plays ; for several years he was the leading actor in the Gaiety Theatre musical comedies (notable parts in " Sporting Life," " Catch of the Season," " Vintage Wine ") ; appointed war-time Controller of E.N.S.A. in 1939.

Hidalgo, Mexico. State in cent. part ; 8,000 sq. m. ; pop. (1940) 792,000 ; cap. Pachuca ; mining, textiles.

Hidalgo y Costilla, Miguel (1753–1811). Mex. patriot priest, venerated as a saint ; leader of revolt, 2158.

Hides, leather from, 1910, 1911, 1912, 1913.

Hierat'ic writing. A running form of Eg. hieroglyphic writing, 125.

Hieroglyphics (hī-er-ō-glif'-iks) or picture-writing. Term used by Greek and Latin writers to describe sacred characters of ancient Egyptian language, 125, 1623.

High, The. Popular name of the High Street in Oxford, 2465.

High Courts of Justice, Strand, London. Eng. courts of law, divided into three groups — Chancery ; King's Bench ; and Probate, Divorce and Admiralty ; bankruptcy and the winding up of companies are treated

in separate courts, but under the King's Bench division ; 1902, 1490.

Highest Common Factor (H.C.F.), in arithmetic, 1256.

High Frequency Currents, 1623, 1624 ; generated by thermionic valve, 3199 ; in wireless, 3393.

High German, language, 1456.

High Jump, in athletics, 288, 289.

Highlands. The part of Scotland N. of the Grampians, 582, 583, 2889, 2891.

High relief, 2903.

High Seas. Ocean waters 3 m. or more from shore not included in territorial limits of any nation.

High-speed tools, 123, 3253.

Highway Code. A code prepared by the Ministry of Transport for the instruction of all users of the King's highway, whether pedestrian or in wheeled vehicles ; 2787, plate f. 2785.

Highwaymen, 1625.

High Will'hays, Eng. Highest point of Dartmoor, Devon ; 2,039 ft.

High Wycombe (wik'-um), Eng. Tn. in Buckinghamshire, 34 m. N.W. of London ; chair-making ; pop. 27,987 ; 600.

Hil'ary (Hilarius). Bishop of Arles (403–449), organized his cathedral clergy into a band of workers devoted to social exercises of religion ; he had a high reputation for piety and learning, wrote various works, and the poem " De Providentia " is attributed to him.

Hilary (Hilarius). Bishop of Poitiers (c. 300–367) ; ranks highest among Latin writers of 4th cent. ; treatise on the Trinity ; called the " Hammer of the Arians " for his labours against Arianism.

Hilda or Hild, St. (614–680). Eng. abbess, descendant of royal Northumbrian line ; founded monastery of Whitby.

Hil'debrand. See Gregory VII.

Hill, David Octavius (1802–70). Scot. painter and pioneer of photography ; camera portrait by, 2583.

Hill, Sir Leonard Erskine (b. 1866). Brit. physiologist, prof. at London Hosp. ; invented kata thermometer, 1677, 1678.

Hill, Sir Rowland (1795–1879). Eng. administrator, author of uniform " penny " postal system, 2661, 3074.

Hilliard, Nicholas (1537–1619). Eng. artist ; goldsmith, carver and limner to Queen Elizabeth ; miniaturist, 1177.

Hilo. Hawaiian Isls., port on N.E. coast of Hawaii ; pop. 22,000 ; 1587.

Hilton, James (b. 1900). Eng. author. Books include : " Lost Horizon " ; " Goodbye, Mr. Chips " ; " We Are Not Alone " ; " Random Harvest " ; " So Well Remembered."

Himachal Union. Union, formed Apr. 1948, of 24 Punjab Hill States, Ind. Repub., formerly called the Simla Hill States ; area exceeds 11,000 sq. m., bounded N. by Tibet, s. by E. Punjab prov., E. by Jumna riv., w. by Kashmir ; cap. Simla ; pop. over 1,000,000.

Himalaya (hi-mah'-la-ya or him-a-lā-'a) **Mts.** The loftiest mountain system on earth, between India and Tibet ; 1,500 m. long ; 20,000 to 29,000 ft. high, 1626, 1627, map, 1702, 1691 ; Mt. Everest, 1243, 1627 ; plant life, 1701.

Himalayan bear, 385.

Himation (hi-mat'-i-on). Gk. garment.

Himmler, Heinrich (1900–45). Chief of Ger. Gestapo ; committed suicide after capture May 1945.

Hincmar (c. 805–882). Archbishop of Reims ; ecclesiastical and political leader in West Frankish kingdom.

Hind. A female deer, 984.

Hindemith, Paul (b. 1895). Ger. composer ; earlier works ultra-modern ; later compositions more classical.

Hin'denburg, Paul von (1847–1934). Ger. soldier and pres. of Ger. Republic ; in 1st World War, he stopped the Russian advance at

Tannenberg, and took chief command of Ger. armies, Aug. 1916, establishing the " Hindenburg line " of defences. President from 1925, he was too old to appreciate Hitler's intentions in 1933 ; he died in July 1934 ; 1631, 3415.

Hindenburg. Ger. airship, 94 ; crash of the, 1673.

" Hindenburg line." A strong defensive zone of trenches and strong points constructed by the Ger. army in 1916, from a point near Soissons N. over Vimy Ridge to Lille, 3411.

Hindi. Dominant language of India, 1703 ; proclaimed the official language of India in 1950.

Hinduism. Great Oriental religion, 1626. 1707 ; animals venerated, 1703, 2211 ; caste system, 1626, 1707 ; Ganges worshipped, 1417 ; in India, 1703, 1707 ; in Java, 1813, 1814 ; pilgrimages to Benares, 411 ; yoga in, 3434. Hindus drink milk, and eat meat other than beef (not as in pp. 1703, 1708).

Hindu Kush (hin-dōō' koosh) **Mts.** Range in cent. Asia w. of Himalayas ; highest point, 25,400 ft. ; 263.

Hindu literature, 1713.

Hindustan'. Persian name, meaning " land of the Hindus," for land N. of Vindhya Mts., or upper basin of Ganges.

Hindusta'ni. Language of N. India, 1703, 2571.

Hinkler, Herbert John Louis (1892–1933). Australian airman ; flew in 1st. World War, and afterwards a test pilot ; in 1928 flew to Australia in a light plane in 15 days ; lost on a similar flight in 1933.

Hinsley, Arthur (1865–1943). Roman Catholic Archbishop of Westminster from 1935 ; created a Cardinal in 1937.

Hipparchus (hi-pahr'-kus) (d. 514 B.C.). Tyrant of Athens ; murder, 1522.

Hipparchus (fl. c. 146–126 B.C.). Gk. astronomer and mathematician ; was founder of trigonometry ; also discovered precession of the equinoxes and invented method of fixing terrestrial positions by circles of latitude and longitude, thereby founding scientific geography.

Hip'per, Franz von (1863 1932). Ger. admiral in command at battle of Jutland.

Hip'pias (d. 490 B.C.). Athenian tyrant, 1522.

Hippocrates (hi-pok-ra tŏz) (c. 460–377 B.C.). Famous Gk. physician, called " father of medicine " ; first to dissociate medicine from superstition and to insist on scientific study of disease, 2132, 3123.

Hippol'yte. Queen of the Amazons ; wore famous girdle given her by father, Ares ; killed by Hercules, 1615.

Hippopot'amus (" river horse "). An amphibious mammal, **1628** ; plate f. 1628, 1629 ; found in Africa, 68 ; teeth yield ivory, 1788.

Hi'ram, King of Tyre about 1000 B.C. ; contemporary of David and Solomon; raised Tyre to leading position in Phoenician Confederacy ; subjugated Cyprus ; aids Solomon, 2573.

Hirohito (hē-rō-hē'-tō) (b. 1901). Emperor of Japan since 1926 ; abjured belief in his own divinity, and became secular and constitutional monarch 1945, **1629.**

Hiroshige (hē-rō-shē'-ge), **Ando Tokitaro** (1797–1858). Japanese artist ; finest work in colour printing from wooden blocks, 1812 ; print by, 1810.

Hiroshima (hē-rō-shē-ma). Port at s. end of Honshu Isl., Japan ; pop. (1945) 343,000 ; atom-bombed, Aug. 6, 1945, **1629,** 609, 2474.

Hirst, George (b. 1871). Eng. cricketer ; in 1906 scored over 2,000 runs, took 208 wickets ; played for Yorks.

Hirundinidae (hi-run-din'-i-dē). The swallow family of birds, 3124.

Hispania (his-pā'-ni-a). Rom. name for Sp. peninsula.

Hispanio'la (" Little Spain "). Name given by Columbus to Santo Domingo isl., now Haiti.

Hissarlik (his-ahr'-lik). Place in Asia Minor on site of anc. Troy, 3252.

Hist'amine. Chemical produced in the cells of the body as result of shock or by the action of substances such as pollen, white of egg, etc., on persons allergic to them ; by contracting plain muscle and dilating capillaries it is immediate cause of allergic diseases.

Histol'ogy. Science which studies body tissues microscopically, 344.

History. The record of past events, 1630 ; beginnings as a science, 1540, 1620 ; Macaulay's view of, 2046 ; Marx's economic interpretation, 2113 ; " Second Great War," 1630 ; Thucydides and, 3206. *See* also **England** and other countries, and charts beginning in page 3837.

Hitches and knots, 1868.

Hitler, Adolf (1889–1945). Ger. leader and dictator ; 1450, *1451*, **1631**, *1632*, 2281, 2697, 2852, 3415 ; autobiography (" Mein Kampf ") 430 ; in Munich, 2256 ; in Vienna, 3323. Officially stated to have committed suicide, April 30, 1945, in the Chancellery at Berlin, 3424.

Hittites (hit'-īts). Anc. people of Asia Minor, **1633.**

Hizen ware. Japanese pottery, 1809.

Hoang Ho. *See* **Hwang-Ho.**

Hoare, Sir Samuel. *See* **Templewood.**

Hobart. Cap. and largest city of Tasmania, on s. coast, 12 m. above mouth of R. Derwent ; pop. 76,567 ; **1633**, *3156*.

Hobbema (hob'-e-mah), **Meindert** (1638–1709). Dutch landscape painter, *2330*, 2334, 2476.

Hobbes, Thomas (1588–1679). Eng. philosopher ; developed his theory of sovereignty in a book called " Leviathan," in which he regards the State as a monster composed of men.

Hobbs, John Berry (b. 1882). Eng. professional cricketer, played for England 1907–1930 ; opening bat for Surrey ; surpassed W. G. Grace's record of 126 centuries in first-class cricket in 1925, when he scored 16 centuries in one season ; in 1930, beat Grace's aggregate record of 54,896 runs.

Hobby, A hawk, 1588.

Ho'boken, New Jersey, U.S.A. Port of entry, rly. and industrial centre opposite New York City on Hudson r. ; pop. (1940) 50,000.

Hobson's choice. Expression used to signify " this or nothing " ; arose from fact that Thomas Hobson (1544 –1630), a stable-keeper of Cambridge who said that customers could have any horse they liked, in practice insisted upon the hiring of the horse nearest the door.

Ho Chi-minh (b. 1892). Leader of Communist party Viet-Minh in Viet-Nam, 3323.

Hochkirch (hōkh'-kirkh), Ger. Vil. 35 m. N.E. of Dresden where Austrians defeated Prussians under Frederick the Great in 1758.

Höchstädt (hēkh'-shtet), Ger. Tn. in Bavaria on Danube 60 m. N.W. of Munich ; battle of Blenheim (1704).

Hoc'key. An outdoor sport, **1633**, *1637* ; ice, 1683.

Hock'ing, Joseph (1855–1937). Eng. author and Nonconformist minister ; among his numerous novels are " Jabez Easterbrook " ; " All Men are Liars " ; " Lest We Forget " ; " The Sword of the Lord."

Hocking, Silas Kitto (1850–1935). Eng. novelist, and for many years a Nonconformist minister ; most of his numerous novels have a religious interest (" The Flaming Sword " ; " The Silent Man " ; " The Third Man ").

" Hoc signo vince " (" By this sign conquer "), 893.

Hodeida (hō-dā'-i-dɑ). Fortified spt. of Yemen, Arabia, on Red Sea ; pop. 35,000 ; centre of coffee trade.

Ho'der. In Norse myth., blind god who slew Balder, 341.

Hodja, or **Hoxha, Enver Ahmed** (b. 1908). Pres. of Albanian Republic from 1916 ; head of guerrilla forces in 1942, and organized resistance movement which freed Albania ; in 1944 pres. of provisional govt. ; 101.

Hódmezö-Vásárhely (hod'-ⲙⲛā-zē-vah-sahr-hā-lē). Agricultural tn. in S.E. Hungary, 15 m. N.E. of Szeged ; pop. 61,700.

Hoe, Richard March (1812–86), Amer. manufacturer and inventor ; with his brothers Peter and Robert developed the web perfecting press ; their rotary press revolutionized newspaper printing, and improved machines printed both sides of the sheet, and cut and folded it.

Hoenir (hē'-ner). In Norse myth., god who with Odin and Loder created first men, Ask and Embla, from trees in Midgard ; from Odin they obtained life, from Hoenir mind, and from Loder blood ; and Rodmar, 2363.

Hof'burg. Palace in Vienna, 3322.

Ho'fer, Andreas (1767–1810). Tirolese patriot and popular hero, leader of insurrection against Bavaria ; betrayed, court-martialled and shot.

Hoffmann, Ernst Theodor Amadeus (1776–1822). Ger. novelist, leader in romantic movement ; " The Devil's Elixir " is his most famous novel.

Hoffmann, Heinrich (1809–94). Ger. writer ; his " Struwwelpeter," 1965.

" Hoffmann, Tales of." Opera by Offenbach, 2440.

Hofmann, August Wilhelm von (1818–92). Ger. chemist and teacher whose work helped to found Ger. coal-tar industry ; discovered benzol (benzene) in coal-tar.

Hofmann, Heinrich (1824–1902). Ger-historical painter ; popular for ideal conceptions of Biblical events ; " Christ in the Temple," *1822*.

Hofmann, Josef (b. 1877). Polish pianist ; an infant prodigy at six, made a successful concert tour of Europe at nine ; in his mature years, considered both as an interpreter and as a technician, had few rivals.

Hofmannsthal (hōf'-mahnz-tahl), **Hugo von** (1874–1929). Austrian neo-romantic dramatist and poet ; " The Death of Titian " ; " Elektra " and " The Rose Cavalier " used as libretti for operas by Richard Strauss.

Hog. *See* **Pig.**

Ho'garth, David George (1862–1927). Eng. archaeologist ; excavated in Cyprus, Egypt, Syria, Greece, Crete, etc. ; writings include " Wandering Scholar in the Levant."

Hogarth, William (1697–1764). Eng. painter and engraver, called the " Molière of painting," 1178, **1634 ;** portrait of Garricks, *1185* ; " Marriage à la Mode," *1635*.

Hogben, Lancelot (b. 1895). Eng. biologist ; Professor of Social Biology, Univ. of London (1930–37) ; Regius Professor of Natural History at Univ. of Aberdeen from 1937 ; works include " Mathematics for the Million," 1434 ; " Science for the Citizen."

Hogg, James (1770–1835). The " Ettrick Shepherd," Scottish peasant poet, helped Scott to collect his Border Minstrelsy (" Scottish Pastorals " ; " The Mountain Bard " ; " The Queen's Wake ").

Hogg, Quintin (1845–1903). Eng. philanthropist, best known as founder of the original Polytechnic. *See* **Polytechnic.**

Hogmanay (hog'-mɑ-nā). Scot. New Year's Eve festival ; " first footing," or being the first to enter another's house at midnight, is a part of the celebrations, 2350.

Hogshead. Unit measure of liquid; *see* **Weights and Measures.**

Hogue, La, battle of (1692), 1794.

Hohenfriedeberg (hō'-en-frē'-de-berg), Poland. Small tn. Silesia, 36 m. s.w.

of Breslau ; ceded from Ger. 1945 ; scene of victory of Frederick the Great (1745) in War of Austrian Succession.

Hohenheim, Theophrastus Bombast von. *See* **Paracelsus.**

Hohenlinden (hō-en-lin'-den), Ger. Vil. in Upper Bavaria, 19 m. E. of Munich ; Fr. gained victory over Austrians in 1800.

Hohenstaufen (hō'-en-shtow-fen). A noble Ger. family of Middle Ages ; the castle from which the family took its name was in Swabia ; Frederick Barbarossa was a member ; 1388, 1449 ; overthrown, 1388. For list of Hohenstaufen emperors *see* **Holy Roman Empire.**

Hohenzollern (hō'-en-tsol-ern). A noble Ger. family ; the castle from which it took its name was in Swabia, near the Danube ; Frederick II and William II are the most notable members ; 2696. For list of Hohenzollern kings *see* **Prussia.**

Hohe Tauern. A division of the Eastern Alps ; name also applied to a particular summit (8,080 ft.) lying s. of Hof-Gastein.

Hokkaido (hōk-kī-dō), or **Yezo.** Most northern large isl. of Japan ; with adjacent islands, 34,276 sq. m. ; *map, 1796.*

Hokusai (hō'-koo-sī), **Katsushuka** (1760–1849). Japanese artist of popular school ; on his deathbed at 89 he mourned that he had not lived long enough to become a great artist ; strongly influenced modern art ; remarkable for his industry ; 30,000 drawings known to be his ; *1273, 1807*, 1812.

Holbein (hol'-bīn), **Hans, the Elder** (c. 1460–1524). Ger. painter, best known for " The Basilica of St. Paul " and a " Passion " in 11 scenes ; later work shows It. influence grafted on Flemish of his youth ; 1454, 1635.

Holbein, Hans, the Younger (c. 1497–1543). Ger. painter, son of Hans the Elder, **1635**, 1454, 2476, 2766 ; " Anne Boleyn," *490* ; " Erasmus," *1222* ; " Duchess of Milan " (National Gallery), *2281* ; Henry VIII, *1455*.

Holberg, Ludvig, Baron (1684–1754). Norwegian-Danish dramatist, historian, and philosopher ; made Danish a literary language ; had vast influence over his countrymen (" Subterranean Journey of Niels Klim " ; " Letters " ; " Comedies ") ; 2880.

Holborn (hō'-born). Met. bor. in cent. part of London ; pop. 38,816 ; contains Lincoln's Inn and Gray's Inn and British Museum.

Holborn Viaduct, Holborn, London. Erected by the City Corporation in 1863–69 to avoid the steep gradient of Holborn Hill, and generally to improve this leading thoroughfare between the City and the west end.

Holden, Charles (b. 1875). Eng. architect ; gold medallist, R.I.B.A. ; vice-president Architectural Assn. ; works include new London University buildings, head offices Underground Railway, Bristol Central Reference Library.

Hole, William (1846–1917). Brit. artist ; specialist in Scottish subjects (" Bruce at Bannockburn," *591*).

Holidays and festivals. Days or periods given up to freedom from general work ; the word holiday originally meant " holy day " ; **1635 ;** " All Fools' Day," 191 ; Chinese, 808, *809*, 2350 ; Christmas, 819, *plate f. 821* ; Easter, 1073 ; Guy Fawkes' Day, 1264 ; Harvest festival, 1580 ; Japanese, 2350 ; Jewish, 2350, 2527 ; May Day, 2223 ; New Year's Day, 2350 ; Saint Patrick's Day, 2528.

Holinshed or **Hollingshead, Raphael** (c. 1520–80). Eng. chronicler, compiler of " Chronicles of England, Scotland, and Ireland " ; source book of Eliz. dramatists ; Shakespeare's debt to, 2933.

HISTORY SHOWN IN CHARTS

HISTORICAL CHARTS are to history what maps are to geography. They help us to visualize the facts—to fix them in *time* as maps do in *space*—and so aid both the understanding and memory.

A glance across these pages will enable you to see at once what was happening in the different countries in any period. Thus you will discover that about when the Greeks were besieging Troy, the great Empire in Egypt was already declining, Samuel was ruling in Israel, and Tiglath-Pileser I and his wandering armies were gazing out across the Mediterranean. You will learn that some of the Norman knights who invaded England with William the Conqueror lived to take part in the First Crusade, and that shortly before that Conquest the Northmen discovered America; and that in the same century that the Puritans were settling Plymouth and Boston, there was revolution and civil war in England, Huguenots were persecuted in France, a great religious war was fought in Germany, and the Dutch finally won their independence from Spain.

This graphic arrangement of contemporaneous events is particularly valuable in that it will lead you to regard history, not as a collection of disconnected incidents, but as a series of related movements, each contributing to the progress of civilization and the advancement of the human race.

PREHISTORIC PERIOD

125,000(?)–10,000(?) B.C. Old Stone Age.   25,000(?). Last Glacial Age Ends.   10,000(?). Neolithic (New Stone) Age Begins.

HISTORIC PERIOD—ANCIENT HISTORY

B.C.	EGYPT	PALESTINE AND SYRIA	BABYLONIA AND ASSYRIA	AEGEAN REGION AND GREECE	ITALY
	New Stone Age in Nile Valley. **Pre-dynastic period**; many little kingdoms. **4241. First fixed date in history**; Egyptian calendar established. **3400. Menes** unites Egypt into one kingdom; beginning of **dynastic period**.		5000–2750. **Sumerian city kingdoms** (non-Semitic). Early development of cuneiform writing.	New Stone Age in **Crete** before 4000.	New Stone Age in Italy.
3000	**3000–2500. PYRAMID AGE**; high cultural development under IVth Dynasty; capital at Memphis (Lower Egypt). Great Pyramid at Gizeh (2900). 2400. Removal of capital to **Thebes** (Upper Egypt). 2100. Hyksos (Shepherd) kings conquer Egypt.	2550–2000. **Phoenicians** (another wave of Semites) settle in Palestine. 2120. **Abraham** leaves Ur, in southern Babylonia; enters southern Palestine.	2750–2550. **Semites under Sargon of Akkad conquer Sumeria.** 2500–2200. Rule of Semitic kings of Sumer and Akkad; Babylonian Empire. 2120–2080). **Hammurabi of Babylon** conquers Akkad and Sumeria (**code of laws** issued).	3000–2800. Transition from Stone to Bronze Age. Dawn of European civilization in Crete. 2800–1200. **Minoan Age in Crete**; high civilization with capital at Knossos. 2500–2000. Second city of Troy flourished.	
2000	1800–1750. Hyksos kings expelled. 1580. Founding of New Empire (XVIIIth Dynasty). 1501–1447. **Tethmosis III** conquers Palestine, Phoenicia, and Syria; **greatest conqueror among Pharaohs.** 1411–1375. **Amenhotep III**; magnificent palaces and temples at Thebes. 1375. **Amenhotep IV (Akhnaton)** tries to reform old religion. 1350. **Rameses II** completes Great Hall at Karnak. 1150. Beginning of **Egyptian decline.**	1950. **Joseph** and his brethren go into Egypt. 1520. **Moses** leads Jews out of Egypt; the Ten Commandments. 1405–1095. Rule of Judges; **Samuel** the last judge. 1095. **Saul** becomes first king of the Jews.	1900. **Assyria** (north) **settled** by immigrants from Babylonia (south). Kassite immigrants from **Elam** gradually absorb power in Babylonia and establish Kassite dynasty (1780–1200). 1400. Babylonia has well-established diplomatic and commercial relations with Egypt. 1300. **Constant wars of Assyria with Babylonia.** 1100. **Tiglath-Pileser I** of Assyria conquers to the Mediterranean.	2000–1500. 3rd, 4th and 5th cities of Troy built. 1600–1100. 6th city of Troy built (Homeric city). **1500–1450. GOLDEN AGE OF CRETE.** 1500–1100. Greatness of **Mycenae**, Tiryns, etc. 1450–1200. **Hittite Empire** in Asia Minor. 1500–1000. Greek (Achaean) colonization of Greece and islands. Dorian and Ionian conquests and colonization follow. **1100. Fall of Troy** following siege by Greeks; gradual growth of hero songs about the siege.	2000. Lake dwellers occupy Italian lakes.
1000	945. Libyan rulers succeed line of priestly rulers of Thebes (XXIst Dynasty). 972. Sheshonk I plunders **Jerusalem** (XXIInd Dynasty).	1055. **David** becomes king; capital at Jerusalem. 1000–700. **Phoenician cities at height of their power.** 1015. **Solomon** becomes king; temple dedicated (1005). 975. Kingdom divided into **Israel** and **Judah**. 930. **Jerusalem** plundered by Egyptians.	930–626. **Brilliant period of Assyrian history** (great activity in architecture, literature, and sculpture, as well as in military conquests).	1000–900. **Greek colonization** of Aegean islands and Asia Minor extended.	1000. **Etruscans** come into Italy (probably from Asia Minor by sea). 1000. **Latin** villages established along Tiber.

B.C.	EGYPT	PALESTINE AND SYRIA	BABYLONIA, ASSYRIA, AND PERSIA	GREECE	ITALY AND ROME
900		Period of the Prophets (Elijah, Elisha).	885–860. Assurnazirpal restores the empire of Tiglath-Pileser I; marches to Mediterranean.	928–800. **Iliad** and **Odyssey** composed (by Homer ?). 820. **Lycurgus** frames laws for Sparta.	
800	800. Egypt again divided among **many small kingdoms** (XXIIIrdDynasty).	The Prophets: Amos, Joel, Hezekiah, Isaiah.		800–700. **Rise of aristocracies** in Greece. 776. **Traditional date of first record of Olympic games (1st Olympiad).** 750–650. Sparta conquers Messenia; becomes a military power.	
			750–606. **ASSYRIAN EMPIRE** at its height. 742–727. **Babylonia subjugated by Tiglath-Pileser III** of Assyria. Assyrian rule extended to **Egypt.**		753. (traditional date). **Rome founded.** 750. Etruscan kings invade Latin towns.
	722. **Ethiopian rulers** gain Egyptian throne (XXVth Dynasty).	722. **Israel destroyed**; people carried to **Assyria.** 701. **Assyrians besiege Jerusalem** (Isaiah's prophecies).	722–705. **Conquests of Sargon II** (palace of Nineveh). 722. Conquest of Israel; people made captive. 705–681. **Sennacherib**; walls and temples of **Babylon razed** following revolt.	734 (traditional date). **Syracuse** founded in Sicily. 707. **Tarentum** founded in Southern Italy.	
700	670–661. **Assyrians conquer Egypt**: plunder Thebes. 663. Egyptian rulers restored (XXVIth Dynasty); **revival of power and art.** 609–594. Necho II digs **canal from Nile to Red Sea**; Africa circumnavigated.	Prophet Jeremiah.	681–668. **Esarhaddon**; Assyria at its height. 640. Revolt of the Medes. 606–604. **Chaldeans move into Assyria from the desert; Nineveh destroyed**; end of Assyrian Empire. 606–539. **CHALDEAN (NEW BABYLONIAN) EMPIRE.** 604–561. **Nebuchadrezzar**; wars in Palestine and Syria; **Hanging Gardens of Babylon built.**	650–600. **Rise of tyrannies in Ionia**; established in Corinth, Megara, etc. 630. Cyrene founded in Africa. 621. Code of Laws for Athens issued by **Draco.**	700. **Greek colonies in Sicily and Southern Italy.**
600		586. **Jerusalem captured** by Babylonians; temple burned (**Babylonian captivity**). 539. **Return of Jews**; temple rebuilt; Palestine **subject to Persia** (until 332).	586. Capture of **Jerusalem**; Jews carried to Babylon. 539. **Babylon taken by Cyrus the Great**; becomes Persian province. 539–331. **MEDO-PERSIAN EMPIRE.** Lydia conquered (capture of Sardis, 546). 528–521. **Cambyses**; conquers **Egypt.** 521–485. **Darius I rules from Aegean and Egypt to India**; advances to Danube against Scythians (513); revolt of Greeks in Asia Minor (500); two expeditions against **Greece** (493, 490).	594–593. **Solon**, archon of Athens, **reforms Athenian constitution.** 560–527. **Peisistratus** tyrant of Athens. 514. Hipparchus, son of Peisistratus, slain by Harmodius and Aristogiton; his brother Hippias expelled, 510. 508. **Reforms of Cleisthenes** at Athens.	509 (traditional date). **Kings (Etruscans ?) expelled from Rome**; republic founded.
	525. Psammetichus III conquered; **Egypt a Persian province.**				
		Prophet **Zechariah.**			
500	**Frequent revolts against Persian rule.**	458. **Ezra** returns to Jerusalem. 445. **Nehemiah rebuilds Jerusalem. Malachi** last of the Old Testament writers. 414. Successful revolt re-establishes **Egyptian independence for 60 years.**	485–465. **Xerxes Great** expedition against Greece (480). Internal decay of Persian Empire; frequent revolts of Egypt, etc. 401. Unsuccessful revolt of Cyrus the Younger against his brother, Artaxerxes II; **retreat of Xenophon** and the 10,000 Greeks.	500. Athens aids Greeks of Asia Minor against Persia. 493–492. **Themistocles** archon of Athens. 493–479. **Persian Wars.** Darius sends expedition into Thrace and Macedonia (493); attacks Greece (**Marathon**, 490); Xerxes invades Greece (**Thermopylae and Salamis**, 480; **Plataea**, 479). 478. An **Athenian Empire** founded by Confederacy of Delos, against Persians; **Athens and Sparta at head of rival leagues.** 444–429. **AGE OF PERICLES**, height of Athenian culture, (Aeschylus, Sophocles, Euripides, Aristophanes, Herodotus, Thucydides, Pheidias, Ictinus, Socrates, Zeno). Acropolis developed; Parthenon built. 431–404. **Peloponnesian Wars** between Athenian and Spartan alliances; Athenian expedition to Syracuse unsuccessful (415–413); Spartans besiege Athens (413–404); Athenian fleet destroyed at Aegospotami (405); **surrender of Athens.**	494. Struggle between **Patricians** and **Plebeians; tribunes** created. 450. Roman laws made public (12 tables).

B.C	EGYPT	PALESTINE	SYRIA AND ASSYRIA	GREECE	ROME
400		Sidon chief city of Phoenicia.		399. **Socrates** put to death in Athens.	396. Romans take **Veii** after 10 years' siege; end danger from Etruscans.
			358–338. Artaxerxes III King of Persia; poisoned by his Egyptian favourite Bagoas.	379–362. War between Sparta and Thebes (**Epaminondas**); Leuctra (371); **leadership passes to Thebans.** 357–355. **Revolt of Athens' allies destroys Athenian Empire.** 359–336. **Rise of Macedon to power under Philip** (power of Thebes destroyed at Chaeronea, 338). **Macedonian supremacy in Greece.**	390. **Gauls plunder Rome** (Battle of the Allia). 365. Licinian laws passed to **equalize Patricians and Plebeians.**
	343. New Persian conquest of Egypt by Artaxerxes III.	346. Revolt of Sidon suppressed by Artaxerxes III with great cruelty.		336–323. **Alexander the Great** invades Asia and founds Greek (Hellenistic) power of far-reaching influence.	343–341. First war against Samnites (kindred mountain tribes south-east of Rome). 340–338. Revolt of Latins crushed; Latin League dissolved.

MACEDONIAN EMPIRE

334. **Alexander attacks Persian Empire** (Battle of the **Granicus**, 334; of **Issus**, 333; of **Arbela**, 331).
332. **Palestine** conquered by Alexander.
332. **Alexander conquers Egypt** from Persia and founds **Alexandria.**
331. Darius III slain while fleeing after Arbela; **end of Persian Empire.**
323–276. **Wars among the successors of Alexander** (Diadochi), who divide the Macedonian Empire.

326–304. Second Samnite War. Roman army defeated in the **Caudine Forks** and sent "under the yoke" (321). Victories of Romans at Vadimonian Lake (310) and Bovianum (305) end the war.

	EGYPT	PALESTINE	SYRIA AND ASSYRIA	GREECE	Rome becomes the **dominant power of Italy south of the River Rubicon.**
	323–30 B.C. Ptolemies (descendants of one of Alexander's generals) rule Egypt; great library at Alexandria.	323–276. Ptolemies rule Palestine. 312–281. **Seleucus,** son of one of Alexander's generals, **rules from Syria to the Indies** (his descendants called Seleucids).		323–146. Macedonia and Greece under Demetrius Poliorcetes and his descendants. 323–322. Greek states fail in revolt against Maccedonians.	
300	285–246. Ptolemy II (Philadelphus); brilliant court at Alexandria; Egypt's navy rules eastern Mediterranean.	276. Antiochus of Syria conquers Palestine from Egypt.	250. **Parthians** under Arsaces revolt. 233. **Antiochus the Great** defeated by Romans at **Magnesia** (190); Seleucid rule curtailed in west.	280–180. **Aetolian and Achaean Leagues** prevent Macedonia securing complete power in Greece.	282–272. War with Tarentum aided by **Pyrrhus** of Epirus. 265–241. **First War with Carthage** (over Sicily). Rome becomes a naval power, invades Africa and Sicily, and defeats Carthage in numerous battles at sea. **Rome gains Sicily.** 218–202. **Second War with Carthage. Hannibal** invades Italy over the Alps; defeats Romans at **Cannae** (216); Scipio carries the war into Africa (204), and defeats Hannibal at **Zama** (202). Carthage becomes a vassal state. 215–206. First Macedonian War.
200	Decline of Egypt; frequent wars of **Ptolemies** with the **Seleucids** of Syria.		175–136. **Mithridates I founds Parthian Empire** (Media, Persia, Babylonia, etc.).	197. Macedonians defeated at **Cynoscephalae** by Romans, and Greece freed from Macedonian rule.	200–197. Second Macedonian War; Greece freed. 191. Antiochus of Syria overthrown (western Asia Minor under Roman control). 171–168. Third Macedonian War; **end of Macedonian monarchy** 149–146. **Third War with Carthage**; Carthage destroyed. 146. Macedonia becomes a Roman province.
		167–130. **Maccabees** (kings) rule Palestine as Roman vassals.		146. Achaean League defeated by Romans and Corinth destroyed. Greece passes under Roman rule.	133. **Practically all Spain under Roman rule.** 133–123. Tiberius and Gaius **Gracchus** attempt to reform the land laws and are slain. 113–101. Cimbri and Teutones (Germanic invaders) defeated by **Marius.**

B.C.	EGYPT	PALESTINE	SYRIA AND ASSYRIA	ROME
100	Civil wars among degenerate Ptolemies pave way for fall.		88–64. Mithridates VI (the Great) defeated by Romans; Syria and Armenia submit to Rome.	90. Roman citizenship granted to all Latins and most other Italians, following revolt of Rome's allies ("Social War," 90–88).
				88–82. Civil War between Sulla (wealthy classes) and Marius (poorer classes). Reactionary reign of terror under Sulla as dictator.
		63. Pompey makes Jews tributary to Rome.		73–71. Revolt of gladiators and slaves under Spartacus.
				66–62. Catiline's conspiracy (Cicero's speeches).
				60. Caesar, Pompey, and Crassus form first Triumvirate.
	47. Cleopatra made ruler of Egypt under Roman supremacy.	40. Herod (the Great) recognized by Rome as dependent king of Judea.		58–51. Caesar conquers Gaul; two expeditions to Britain (55–54).
	31. Cleopatra and Antony defeated at Actium.			49–48. Civil War between Caesar and Pompey (battle of Pharsalus; Pompey slain). Under forms of the republic, Caesar gets all power into his own hands.
	Egypt becomes a Roman province.			44. Assassination of Caesar by Brutus, Cassius, and others.
TIME B.C.				43–42. Mark Antony, Octavian (Augustus), and Lepidus form second Triumvirate and defeat Cassius and Brutus at Philippi.
				31–30. War between Octavian and Antony; Antony and Cleopatra of Egypt defeated at Actium.
				31 B.C.–A.D. 14. Octavian rules as Emperor Augustus. Beginning of ROMAN EMPIRE. (Golden Age of Roman culture; Livy, Horace, Virgil, Seneca, Pliny the Elder).
TIME A.D.	Under Roman rule Egypt enjoys a period of industrial and commercial prosperity.	6. Judea becomes part of Roman province of Syria.		14–37. Tiberius emperor (stepson of Augustus).
				37–41. Caligula (great-grandson of Augustus).
				41–54. Claudius; Britain added to Roman Empire.
		70. Jerusalem destroyed by Titus following revolt. Dispersal of survivors.		54–68. Nero; his crimes and excesses: great fire in Rome: Christians persecuted.
				69–79. Vespasian proclaimed emperor by his troops in Syria; good rule.
				79–81. Titus (son of Vespasian).
				79. Eruption of Vesuvius destroys Pompeii and Herculaneum.
				98–117. Trajan, a Spaniard by birth and a great general (conquest of Dacia; defeat of Parthians in Syria; Empire reaches greatest extent).
100			114–116. Armenia, Mesopotamia, and Assyria made Roman provinces.	117–138. Hadrian adopted by Trajan; frontiers strengthened; Asia east of Euphrates given up; magnificent buildings.
		132–135. Revolt of Jews suppressed by Hadrian; survivors dispersed.		139–161. Antoninus Pius.
	Revolt of native troops begins decline of Egypt.			167–180. Marcus Aurelius, adopted son of Antoninus and a renowned Stoic philosopher. Wars with barbarians along Danube.
			193–211. Northern Assyria conquered by Rome.	193–284. Emperors elected by the army.
				193–211. Septimius Severus; war in Mesopotamia; northern Assyria conquered.
200			226–241. New Persian Empire under Sassanids.	212. All freemen in the Empire made citizens (to get more taxes).
	270. Egypt occupied by Zenobia of Palmyra.		267–273. Zenobia, queen of Palmyra, defeated by Aurelian.	270–275. Aurelian; recovers Palmyra and subdues revolt in Gaul; new walls about Rome.
	272. Egypt reconquered by Rome.			284–305. Diocletian (resides in East); empire divided into four administrative prefectures; great persecution of Christians; abdicates.
300	Quarrels between branches of the Christian Church lead to persecution of the Arians.			311. Christianity made legal.
				323–337. Constantine the Great sole ruler; capital removed to Constantinople; empire reorganized.
				325. Council of Christian Church at Nicaea.
				375. Beginning of TEUTONIC MIGRATIONS into the Empire.
				378. Visigoths defeat Roman army at Adrianople.
				379–395. Theodosius the Great, last ruler of united empire.
				395. Empire divided into Eastern and Western parts.
				395–476. WESTERN EMPIRE. / **395–1453. EASTERN OR BYZANTINE EMPIRE.** For nearly 1,000 years a defence against Asiatic invasions.
400				410. Alaric the Visigoth captures Rome.
				455. Vandals from Africa sack Rome.
				476. German leader Odoacer deposes last Roman emperor in West.

MEDIEVAL AND MODERN HISTORY

	WESTERN EUROPE	ENGLAND	EASTERN EUROPE AND OTHER COUNTRIES
400	383–394. Wars for power among claimants of Empire in West ended by recognition of Theodosius (*see* Eastern Europe). 395–423. Honorius receives Western Roman Empire on permanent division (Stilicho his minister).	Romans rule Britain since about A.D. 43–81; Christianity introduced; Hadrian's wall begun (121).	375. Visigoths cross Danube; defeat Romans at Adrianople (378). 395. Death of Theodosius the Great, last ruler of united Roman Empire. 395–1453. EAST ROMAN EMPIRE (Arcadius emperor, 395–408).

A.D.	WESTERN EUROPE	ENGLAND	EASTERN EUROPE AND OTHER COUNTRIES
400	410. **Sack of Rome** by Visigoths under **Alaric**; Visigoths move into Spain (414). 429. **Vandals** cross from Spain into Africa; under Genseric plunder Rome. 451. **Attila** the Hun defeated at Châlons (in Gaul). 476. Odoacer, German mercenary, displaces Roman emperor; **end of Western Roman Empire.** 481–511. **Clovis founds kingdom of Franks** in Gaul (Merovingians); becomes **Christian** (496). 493–555. **Ostrogoths (Theodoric the Great)** rule Italy.	410. Roman legions withdrawn. 449–700. **Angles, Saxons, and Jutes conquer Britain** ("Angleland" or England).	474–491. Zeno eastern emperor.
500	511–751. Decline of Merovingian kings of Franks and **rise of Mayors of Palace.** 568–774. **Lombard** kingdom in Italy. 590–604. **Pope Gregory I (the Great)**; Rome the head of Christendom.	577. Battle of Deorham; West Saxons reach Bristol Channel. 597. **Augustine reintroduces Christianity.**	527–565. **Justinian emperor**; Roman law codified; Vandals in Africa and Ostrogoths in Italy overthrown.
600	613. Queen **Brunhilde** of Austrasia (Eastern Frank-land) captured, tortured, and dragged to death by wild horses in Merovingian quarrels. 687. Pepin of Heristal becomes Mayor of Palace for whole Frankish kingdom (Battle of Testry).	607. Chester sacked and left desolate for 300 years.	622. Mahomet's flight from Mecca (the "Hegira"); **founding of Mahomedan religion.**
700	711. Mahomedans from Africa overthrow Visigothic kingdom in Spain. 732. Franks **(Charles Martel)** defeat Mahomedans at **Tours** (in France). 752. Pepin the Short (Mayor of the Palace) deposes last Merovingian king and takes the crown (Carolingian rule).	755–796. Offa king of Mercia.	750. Mahomedans rule all western Asia, northern Africa, and Spain — from River Indus to the Pyrenees.
800	800. **Charlemagne, king of the Franks,** and ruler of most of Western Europe (768–814), crowned emperor at Rome. 843. **Partition of Verdun.** Charlemagne's empire divided; separation of **France** and **Germany.**	827. Egbert of Wessex unites **England.** 871–901. **Alfred** rules southern England; Danes checked.	809. End of brilliant reign of **Haroun-al-Raschid,** caliph of Baghdad. 862. **Russian kingdom founded by Rurik the Northman** (Kiev, capital).

900	FRANCE	GERMANY AND ITALY	ENGLAND	EASTERN EUROPE AND OTHER COUNTRIES
900	911. Normandy ceded to Rolf (Rollo), the Northman; decline of Carolingians in France. 987. **Hugh Capet chosen king** (Capetian line); **Feudalism** at height of its power.	911–918 Conrad I (Franconian) first non-Carolingian king. 936–973. **Otto I, the Great** (Saxon), ends anarchy in Italy; defeats Hungarians (955); **revives Empire** (962).	910–954. Northern England ("**Danelaw**") reconquered from Danes. 980. Danish invasions renewed.	905–959 Constantine VII Porphyrogenitus ("Born in the Purple") emperor, patron of literature.
1000	1096. Council of Clermont; Pope Urban II calls First Crusade.	1002–24. Henry II (the Saint), last of the Saxon line. 1075. **Investiture conflict begun** by Pope Gregory VII (**Hildebrand**) and Emperor Henry IV (1056–1106).	1016–1035. **Canute** of Denmark king. 1042–66. Edward the Confessor king. 1066. **Norman conquest** (William I).	1000. **Northmen discover America** (Greenland colonized, 986).

PERIOD OF THE CRUSADES—TO RESCUE PALESTINE FROM MAHOMEDAN RULE—1096–1291

1096–99. **First Crusade. People's crusade** under Peter the Hermit fails. Crusade of nobles under Godfrey of Bouillon and others takes Jerusalem (1099) and establishes a feudal kingdom of Jerusalem.

A.D.	WESTERN EUROPE		ENGLAND	EASTERN EUROPE AND OTHER COUNTRIES
1100	1108–37. **Louis VI (the Fat)** establishes order in crown possessions.	1122. Concordat of Worms ends investiture conflict.	1110–35. Henry I ("the Lion of Justice"); a charter issued.	1145. **Edessa taken by** Mahomedans.
	1147–49. **Second Crusade.** Preached by St. Bernard of Clairvaux; led by Conrad III of Germany and Louis VII of France without results.			
	1180–1223. **Philip Augustus**; recovers Normandy, etc., from England.	1152–1190. **Frederick Barbarossa (Hohenstaufen)**; quarrel with Pope; defeated by league of Lombard towns.	1154–89. Henry II (Plantagenet) holds **Normandy, Anjou, Maine**, etc., in France. Conquest of **Ireland** begun.	1187. Capture of **Jerusalem by Saladin.**
	1189–91. **Third Crusade.** Led by Richard Cœur de Lion of England and Philip Augustus of France; Emperor Frederick Barbarossa drowned on way. Armistice with Saladin permits pilgrimages to Holy Places.			
1200	1209–29. **Albigensian crusade.** 1214. Battle of Bouvines; defeat of English and enemies of Frederick II. 1226–70. **Louis IX (St. Louis)**; good rule. Crusade to Egypt (1248–54); to Tunis (1270). 1285–1314. **Philip IV (the Fair).** Power of king increased; quarrels with Pope.	1200–1450. **Hanseatic League** between German cities promotes commerce. 1215–50. **Frederick II**; rules Naples and Sicily as well as Empire; quarrels with Pope; **Fifth Crusade** (1228–29). 1256–73. **Interregnum in Empire.** 1273–91. **Rudolph of Hapsburg** king of Germany. 1295. Marco Polo returns from 20 years' travels in China and the East.	1204–06. King John loses Normandy and Anjou; forced to grant **Magna Carta** (1215). 1272–1307. Edward I; conquest of **Wales** (1282); wars with **Scotland** begun. 1295. **Model Parliament** called.	1202–04. **Fourth Crusade** directed against **Constantinople** by Venetians. 1206–27. **Genghis Khan** conquers China, Persia, Turkistan, and Southern Russia. 1291–1499. **Growth of Swiss Confederation** (Battle of Morgarten, 1315; Sempach, 1386). 1291. Fall of **Acre**; end of Crusades.
1300	1302. First meeting of **States-General.** 1302. Battle of **Courtrai**; Flemish townsmen defeat French knights.	**PERIOD OF ITALIAN RENAISSANCE 1300–1500.** Dante, Petrarch, Boccaccio, Giotto, Michelangelo, Leonardo da Vinci, Raphael, Titian.	1314. Edward II defeated at **Bannockburn** by Scots under **Bruce.** 1327–77. **Edward III.**	

A.D.	FRANCE	GERMANY AND ITALY	ENGLAND	EASTERN EUROPE AND OTHER COUNTRIES
1300 (*continued*)	1305–77. "Babylonian captivity of Popes" (papal residence at Avignon, France). 1328. Philip VI (Valois) becomes king. 1333–1453. Hundred Years' War with England (Peace of Brétigny, 1360; war renewed, 1369). 1364–80. Charles V (the Wise). Most of English possessions in France won back by Du Guesclin.	1347–1437. Emperors of Luxemburg-Bohemian line. 1348. Black Death appears in Florence and spreads over Europe. 1356. Charles IV issues Golden Bull. 1377. Papacy returns from Avignon to Rome. 1378–1417. Great Schism (two, later three, claim to be Pope). 1380. Venice crushes Genoa at Chioggia.	1338–1453. Hundred Years' War with France. English victories at Crécy (1346) and Poitiers (1356). 1381. Peasants' revolt led by Wat Tyler and John Ball. 1399. Henry IV (Lancaster) overthrows Richard II.	1331–55. Stephen Dushan rules an extended Serbian empire. 1357. Ottoman Turks gain foothold in Europe (Gallipoli). 1389. Serbs defeated by Turks in great battle at Kossovo.

A.D.	FRANCE	GERMANY	ITALY AND PAPACY	GREAT BRITAIN	OTHER COUNTRIES
1400	1415. Hundred Years' War renewed in reign of Charles VI. 1429–31. Joan of Arc saves France. (War ends in 1453; England loses all her possessions in France except Calais). 1461–83. Louis XI strengthens France. 1477. Charles the Bold of Burgundy overthrown; his duchy annexed to France. 1494. Charles VIII invades Italy (Italian wars begun).	1410–37. Sigismund emperor. 1419–36. Hussite Wars. (Ziska blind leader against Germans.) 1440–93. Frederick III (Hapsburg) emperor. 1450. Invention of printing from movable types. 1493–1519. Maximilian I emperor.	1414–18. Council of Constance; schism ended; John Huss burned as heretic (1415). 1469–92. Lorenzo de' Medici rules Florence. 1494–98. Savonarola attempts reform in Florence.	1415. Henry V invades France (Agincourt, 1415). 1450. Jack Cade's rebellion. 1455–85. Wars of the Roses (Houses of York and Lancaster claim crown). 1485. Henry VII (Tudor) defeats Richard III (York) at Bosworth and ends war. Strong monarchy established.	1453. Turks take Constantinople; end of Eastern Empire 1492. Columbus discovers America. 1492. Conquest of Granada; Moors expelled from Spain. 1497–98. Vasco da Gama reaches India by sea.
1500	1515–47. Francis I; wars with Charles V over Milan; Renaissance encouraged in France. 1562. Huguenot Wars begun (St. Bartholomew's massacre, 1572). 1589–1610. Henry IV (Bourbon). Edict of Nantes ends Huguenot wars (1598).	1517. Luther begins Protestant Reformation; Diet of Worms condemns Luther (1521). 1519–56. Charles V rules Spain, Germany, Netherlands, parts of Italy and America. Opposes Luther; wars against Turks (1526–32); abdicates (1555–56). 1555. Religious peace of Augsburg (toleration of Lutherans). 1556–64. Ferdinand I. 1563. Council of Trent ends (beginning of Catholic recovery).	1503–13. Pope Julius II (Italian wars; patron of Michelangelo and Raphael). 1508. League of Cambrai (Pope, Austria, France, and Spain) against Venice. 1513–21. Pope Leo X (Medici) patron of arts and letters. 1542. Pope Paul III establishes the Inquisition in Rome. 1571. League of Papacy, Spain and Venice against Turks (Battle of Lepanto, 1571).	1509–47. Henry VIII; separation of English Church from Rome. 1547–53. Edward VI. 1553–58. Queen Mary restores Catholic Church. 1558–1603. Elizabeth establishes Church of England. Growth of sea-power; industrial development. Elizabethan period of literature (Shakespeare). 1588. Spanish Armada destroyed.	1518. Zwingli begins Reformation in Switzerland. 1536. Calvin begins Reformation at Geneva. 1540. Jesuit order founded by Loyola. 1556–98. Philip II succeeds his father Charles V in Spain, Italy, Netherlands, and the New World. 1568. Revolt of Netherlands against Spain; siege of Leiden (1574); Union of Utrecht (1579); declaration of independence by the Dutch (1581).
1600	1610–43. Louis XIII; political power of the Huguenots crushed. (Richelieu chief minister of the crown.) 1643–1715. Louis XIV; numerous wars of conquest; extravagant court at Versailles; brilliant period of French literature. 1685. Edict of Nantes revoked and toleration of Huguenots ended.	1618–48. Thirty Years' War. Imperialist (Catholic) generals, Tilly and Wallenstein; Gustavus Adolphus, Protestant king of Sweden, victorious at Leipzig (1631); Lützen (1632); Peace of Westphalia (1648). 1640–88. Growth of Prussia under the Great Elector 1683. Vienna besieged for last time by Turks; rescued by King John Sobieski of Poland.	1629. War over Mantua between Spain (which possessed Milan) and Austria. 1684. Venice joins Austria and Poland in attacks on Turks; makes conquests in Morea.	1603–25. James I (Stuart); personal union of England and Scotland. 1607. Virginia colony founded (Jamestown). 1620. Plymouth colony settled (Boston, 1630) by Puritans fleeing persecution in England. 1642–49. Civil war between Crown and Parliament; Marston Moor (1644); Naseby (1645). Charles I executed (1649). England a commonwealth. 1653–59. Cromwell rules England, Scotland, and Ireland as Lord Protector. 1660. Stuart restoration under Charles II. 1688. "Glorious Revolution" expels James II and brings in William and Mary; Protestant succession established.	1611–32. Gustavus Adolphus king of Sweden. 1644. Manchu rule begins in China. 1648. Spain recognizes independence of the Dutch Netherlands. 1672–1715. Peter the Great; introduction of western culture in Russia; St. Petersburg founded (1703). 1697–1718. Charles XII of Sweden.

A.D.	FRANCE	GERMANY	ITALY AND PAPACY	GREAT BRITAIN	OTHER COUNTRIES
1700	**1701–13. War of the Spanish Succession.** Treaty of Utrecht seats French prince (Philip V) on Spanish throne. **1715–74. Louis XV** ; lax morals at court ; Fr. aids Prussia in Austrian Succession War. **1756–63. Seven Years' War** ; France aids Austria against Prussia, loses Canada and India to British. **1774–93. Louis XVI** (Marie Antoinette of Austria, queen) ; reform measures defeated. **1789–95. French Revolution.** States-General becomes National Assembly (1789) ; constitution accepted by king (1791) ; kingship abolished (1792) ; **Louis XVI** executed (1793) ; Reign of Terror (1793–94) ; Directory established (1795). 1796–99 Rise of **Napoleon Bonaparte.**	1701. Elector of Brandenburg receives title of **King of Prussia.** 1701–13. Austria takes part in **War of Spanish Succession.** 1713–40. Frederick William I develops Prussian army. 1740–80. **Maria Theresa** queen of Bohemia and Hungary, archduchess of Austria ; **War of Austrian Succession** (1740–48). **1740–86. Frederick II (The Great)** seizes Silesia from Austria and retains it in **Seven Years' War** (Battles of Rossbach and Leuthen, 1757) ; builds up Prussia in peace time. 1765–90. **Joseph II** emperor ; attempts reforms in Hapsburg lands. 1790–92. Leopold II emperor.	1715. Milan, Naples, etc., given to Austria by treaty. 1715. Turks drive Venetians from the Morea and Crete. 1734. Spanish Bourbons established in Naples. 1738. Tuscany given to Francis of Lorraine (husband of Maria Theresa). 1796. **Napoleon** invades Italy ; siege of Mantua. 1797. Cisalpine Republic set up by Bonaparte.	1701–13. Eng. takes part in War of Spanish Succession (**Blenheim**, 1704). 1702–14. Anne queen. **1714. George I (Hanover) becomes king** ; growth of cabinet government. 1741–48. Eng. aids Austria in Austrian Succession War. 1745. Jacobite rebellion (Stuart supporters). **1756–63. Seven Years' War** ; England aids Prussia ; **Canada acquired** ; British supremacy established in India by Clive. **1764. Industrial Revolution begun** ; Hargreaves invents spinning-jenny. **1775–83. Revolt of the American colonies.** 1788. British colonization of **Australia** begun.	1709. Battle of Pultowa ; forces of Charles XII subdued by Russia. **1736–96. Catherine II** empress of Russia. **1772–95. Poland** partitioned among Russia, Prussia, and Austria.

WARS OF THE FRENCH REVOLUTION AND BONAPARTE : 1792–1815

1796. Bonaparte's **Italian Campaign.** 1798. Egyptian expedition fails (Battle of the Nile). 1800. Napoleon's victory at Marengo. 1805. Nelson victorious at **Trafalgar.**	1805. Bonaparte wins at **Austerlitz.** 1806. Prussia crushed at **Jena.** 1807. Napoleon defeats Austrians at **Wagram** and Russians at **Friedland.** 1807. **Peace of Tilsit** ; hard terms for Prussia. Alexander I of Russia becomes Napoleon's ally.	1812. **Napoleon invades Russia** ; sack of Moscow ; retreat with heavy losses. 1813. Napoleon defeated in three-day battle at **Leipzig.** 1815. Wellington victorious at **Waterloo.** 1815. Treaty of Vienna.

THE BRITISH EMPIRE TO 1783

1600. **East India Company** founded by Queen Elizabeth. 1604. **Port Royal (Annapolis, Nova Scotia),** first permanent French settlement, founded. 1607. **Jamestown (Virginia) founded** by English colonists. 1608. **Quebec settled** by French colonists led by **Champlain.** 1608. Capt. Hawkins obtained from Jahangir permission to build a factory at Surat. 1610. **Hudson** discovers Hudson Bay while searching for the North-West Passage ; England claims Hudson Bay region. 1611. **Capt. Hippon** founded the first English settlement (Pettapoli) in Bay of Bengal. 1613. English colonists from Virginia **capture Port Royal** ; Quebec captured by the British (1629) ; New France and Acadia restored to the French by the treaty of St. Germain (1632). 1614. Dutch trading post established on Manhattan Island (**New York**). 1615. Champlain explores Lake Huron. 1619 First Negro slaves introduced into Virginia. 1620. **Plymouth colony founded** by English Puritans (**Massachusetts**). 1623–32. War between English and French. English attack Acadia (Nova Scotia) ; capture Quebec. Canada restored to France by treaty. 1626. New Amsterdam founded. 1627. St. Lawrence valley granted to Richelieu's company of " One Hundred Associates " ; control New France (1627–63). 1632. Maryland granted to Lord Baltimore. 1634. **First colonists land in Maryland.** 1635. **Connecticut** (Hartford, Windsor, etc.) founded. 1636. Rhode Island settled. Roger Williams founds Providence. 1638. **Swedes settle along the Delaware.** 1639. Francis Day founded **Madras.** 1642. **Montreal** founded by Maisonneuve as a religious colony. 1647. Representative assembly established in Maryland.	1658–60. **Groseillers** and **Radisson** reach the Mississippi and Great Plains. 1661. **Charles II received Bombay** as part of the dowry of Catherine of Braganza. 1662. **Charter** granted to **Connecticut.** 1663. **Charter for Carolina** granted to **Lord Clarendon** and others. **Rhode Island** obtains a charter. 1663. Charter of the company of " One Hundred Associates " revoked ; **New France a royal colony.** 1664. **New Jersey** granted to **Lord Berkeley** and **Sir George Carteret. New Amsterdam** captured by English fleet ; becomes **New York.** 1666. **Allouez** founds a mission on Lake Superior. 1669. Fundamental constitution of Carolina drawn up by John Locke. 1670. **Hudson's Bay Company** founded in England to carry on trade in the new territory. 1672. **Frontenac** becomes governor of Canada. 1673. **Marquette** and **Joliet** discover the **Mississippi.** 1680. **New Hampshire** separates from Massachusetts. 1681. **Charter for Pennsylvania** granted to **William Penn.** 1681. **La Salle** descends the Mississippi and takes the country for France. 1683. First Assembly in New York. 1688. New York united to New England under Andros. 1689–97. " **King William's War** " ; Acadia captured by the British ; attack on Quebec fails ; conquest restored at the Peace of Ryswick (1697). 1690. **Job Charnock** founds **Calcutta.** 1691. Maryland becomes a crown colony. 1701. **Detroit** founded as French post ; Forts Frontenac and Duquesne, and other posts on the British frontier follow. 1701–13. " **Queen Anne's War.** " Unsuccessful attack on Quebec ; Acadia seized, France cedes Hudson Bay region, Newfoundland, and Acadia to **Great Britain** (Treaty of Utrecht, 1713). 1733. **Georgia settled** by Oglethorpe.	1743. The **Verendryans** reach the foothills of the Rocky Mountains. 1744–48. " **King George's War,** " Louisburg captured by English colonists (1745) ; restored to French by treaty of Aix-la-Chapelle. 1749. English settlement of **Halifax** founded ; colonization of Nova Scotia begins. 1751. Capture of Arcot by Clive. 1755–63. " **French and Indian War.** " French deported from Nova Scotia (1755) ; British under **Wolfe** capture Quebec (1759) ; **New France ceded to England** by Peace of Paris (1763). 1756. Black Hole of Calcutta. 1757. Clive won battle of Plassey and England gained Bengal and Behar. 1758. Massacre of Patna. 1763. British ministry adopts rigid colonial policy ; **Navigation Acts** restricting colonial commerce to England strictly enforced. 1675. Stamp Act resisted in colonies. Virginia resolutions. Stamp Act Congress protests against colonial policy ; Act repealed. 1773. " **Boston Tea Party.** " 1773. India Bill passed. 1774. Quebec Act passed to organize government for Canada. 1775–83. **American Revolution** ; Loyalists flee to Canada ; colonists' attack on Quebec repulsed. 1775. War of American Independence begins. Second Continental Congress. 1775–82. First Mahratta War. 1776. **Declaration of Independence** adopted. 1778. France recognizes independence of the colonies. 1779–84. First Mysore War. 1780–81. War in the South. Charleston captured by the British. Cornwallis retreats to the north. 1781. Siege of Yorktown ; surrender of Cornwallis. 1782. Evacuation of Savannah and Charleston ; hostilities cease. 1783. Treaty of Paris ; **Great Britain recognizes the independence of the American colonies.**

A.D.	FRANCE	GERMANY	AUSTRIA-HUNGARY	ITALY
1800	1804. **Napoleon made Emperor.** 1814 **Napoleon** abdicates ; returns from Elba (1815) ; **exiled** (1815). 1814. **Bourbons restored** under Louis XVIII. 1824–30. **Charles X ;** reactionary policy. 1830. French begin occupation of Algeria. 1830. **July Revolution ;** Charles X abdicates ; **Louis Philippe becomes king** (" citizen king "). 1840–48. Guizot ministry, conservative. 1848. **February Revolution;** Louis Philippe abdicates ; republic proclaimed. 1848–52. **Second Republic** (Louis Napoleon president). 1851. Coup d'état of Louis Napoleon : proclaimed emperor **(Napoleon III,** 1852–70). 1854–56. **Crimean War.** 1859. **War with Austria** in behalf of Italy. 1861–67. Attempt to found a monarchy in Mexico fails (Maximilian). 1870–71. **Franco-Prussian War ;** France loses **Alsace-Lorraine.** 1870. **Third French Republic** proclaimed. 1875. Republican Constitution adopted. 1881. **Tunis** occupied ; complications with Italy, Spain, and England. 1891. **Dual Alliance** of France and Russia announced. 1894–1906. Trials of Dreyfus for treason the centre of political scandal. 1896. Annexation of Madagascar.	1806. **Confederation of the Rhine** formed by Napoleon. 1806. **Holy Roman Empire dissolved.** 1819. **Carlsbad Decrees** passed by German Diet suppress liberalism. 1834. German Customs Union **(Zollverein)** formed. 1840–61 **Frederick William IV** king of Prussia. 1848. Liberal risings in Prussia and other German states. 1848–49. **Frankfort Parliament** to unite Germany fails. 1861–88. **William I** king of Prussia. 1862. **Bismarck** becomes chief minister. 1864. **Schleswig** and **Holstein** seized by Prussia and Austria. 1866. **Austro-Prussian War.** 1867–71. **North German Confederation** under Prussian leadership. 1870–71. **Franco-Prussian War ;** siege of **Metz** and battle of **Sedan** (1870) ; capture of **Paris** (1871). 1871. **German Empire** proclaimed ; **William I** emperor ; Bismarck chancellor (1871–90). 1882. Germany enters **Triple Alliance.** 1884. Germany begins African colonization. 1888–1918. **William II** emperor. 1898. Germany seizes Kiaochow. 1899. Germany obtains Baghdad railway concession from Turkey; other powers refuse to participate in work ; Great Britain begins obstruction. Growth of Turko-German friendship.	1806. **Holy Roman Empire dissolved ;** Francis II becomes Francis I of Austria. 1809. **Metternich** becomes minister of foreign affairs; reactionary leader of Europe (1815–48). 1815. **Congress of Vienna ;** treaty of Vienna signed ; " **Holy Alliance** " formed by Russia, Prussia, and Austria. 1835–48. **Ferdinand I ;** reactionary rule. 1848. Revolution expels Metternich ; liberal gains short-lived. **Francis Joseph I** begins long reign. 1849. Hungarian war for independence fails **(Kossuth).** 1859. War with France and Italy (battles of **Magenta** and **Solferino).** Austria loses Lombardy. 1866. War with **Prussia (Sadowa).** Austria withdraws from German Confederation and loses Venetia. 1867. **Dual Monarchy** of **Austria-Hungary** established. 1876–90. Count Tisza, liberal leader, pursues policy of " Magyarization " in Hungary ; economic development. 1882. **Triple Alliance** formed by Austria, Germany, and Italy.	1815. Italy a group of small states under Austrian domination. 1820. **Revolt** in **Naples** put down. 1821. **Revolt in Sardinia - Piedmont** fails. 1830. **Revolution in** Italy **suppressed** by Austria. 1848. **Revolution** headed by Sardinia - Piedmont **crushed by Austria.** 1849. **Victor Emmanuel II** becomes king of Sardinia-Piedmont. **Cavour** premier (1852–61). 1859. **War with Austria :** Austrian control in Italy broken. 1860. **Garibaldi** conquers Naples. 1860–61. **Italy** (except Rome) **united** under Victor Emmanuel ; kingdom of **Italy** proclaimed (1861). 1870. **Rome** taken from Pope and made **capital** of Italian kingdom. 1878–1900. **Humbert I** (assassinated by anarchist). 1882. Italy enters **Triple Alliance** with Austria and Germany. 1896. **War with Abyssinia ;** fall of Crispi as prime minister.
1900	1904. **Entente Cordiale** between France and Great Britain settles disputes over colonies. 1905. **Separation of Church** and **State.** 1905–06. Extension of French influence in **Morocco** challenged by Germany ; **Algeciras Conference** upholds French policy. 1911. Germany's attempt to protect its nationals during native rising in Morocco reopens **Moroccan question.** Moroccan and Congo Conventions guarantee economic opportunities to Germany and Protectorate to France ; part of French Equatorial Africa given to Germany.	1900. Great **naval development** begins. 1905–06. **First Moroccan Incident.** 1908. Germany upholds Austria **in Bosnia affair** 1911. **Second Moroccan incident.** 1911. **Enormous development** of Germany shown by increase of population and growth of foreign trade. 1911–13. German standing army increased from 515,000 to 866,000 men. 1912. Socialists elect 110 of 397 members of Reichstag.	1905–13. Struggle in Hungary over electoral reform ; **Magyars** retain political control. 1907–12. Reform measures in Austria blocked by racial quarrels. 1908. Austria annexes **Bosnia** and **Herzegovina ;** blow to Serbian nationalist movement. 1914. **Archduke Francis Ferdinand,** heir to Austrian throne, **assassinated** in Bosnia by subjects of Serbian blood.	1900. **Victor Emmanuel III** becomes king. 1911–12. **War with Turkey ;** Italy takes **Tripoli** from Turkey. 1912. **Universal suffrage** introduced.

WORLD WAR

	FRANCE	GERMANY	AUSTRIA-HUNGARY	ITALY
	1914. Aug. 1. **Germany declares war** on Russia ; 1st World War begins. 1914. Sept. 6–10. **Battle of Marne** halts German invasion of France and Belgium. 1915. **Gallipoli expedition** fails.		1915. **Italy and Bulgaria** enter the war. 1916. Germans fail to take **Verdun ;** first **battle** of the **Somme.** 1917. **United States** enters the war.	
	1919 **Treaty of Versailles** ratified. By this and subsequent peace treaties France obtains **Alsace-Lorraine,** parts of **Cameroon** and **Togo** (in Africa), mandate over **Syria,** etc., also economic reparations.	1918. German revolution; **William II abdicates.** 1919. June 28. **Treaty of Versailles** signed (ratified July 10) ; Germany loses overseas colonies ; **Alsace-Lorraine,** parts of **Posen** and **West Prussia,** etc., armament reduced ; reparations provided for. 1919. " **Spartacan** " (extreme Socialist) **revolt** suppressed. 1919. **Republican constitution** adopted.	1916. **Charles I** succeeds Francis Joseph. 1918. Oct. 21. Independence of Czechoslovakia proclaimed. 1918. Nov. 3. Austria **signs armistice.** 1918. Oct. 31. Hungary declares itself an independent republic. 1918. Nov. 12. **Republic of Austria** proclaimed ; Charles I abdicates.	1919. **Treaty of St. Germain ;** Italy gains **Trentino,** etc.

GREAT BRITAIN	RUSSIA	TURKEY AND THE BALKANS	OTHER COUNTRIES AND GENERAL PROGRESS
1801. **Irish Parliament abolished**; Irish members seated in British Parliament. **United Kingdom** of Great Britain and Ireland. 1806. **Cape Colony** conquered; beginning of British expansion in South Africa. 1807. **Abolition of slave trade** in British Dominions. 1812–14. **War** with the **United States**; Treaty of Ghent (1814). 1820–30. **George IV** king. 1827. English fleet participates in battle of **Navarino** against Turks. 1830–37. **William IV** king. **1832. Reform Bill**; political power to middle classes. Other legislation abolishing slavery, reforming labour conditions, etc. **1837. Victoria** begins her long reign. 1846. Repeal of corn laws; **free trade** established. **1854–56 Crimean War** with Russia in defence of Turkey. 1857. **Indian Mutiny**; **British government assume rule of India** (1858). 1867. Second parliamentary reform act; **political power** extended to **working men**; beginning of democratic rule. 1868–74. First ministry of **Gladstone** (Liberal); "Great Ministry." 1870. Beginning of **Home Rule** agitation. 1874–80. **Disraeli** ministry (Conservative). 1882. British occupy **Egypt.** 1887. First Colonial Conference. 1899–1902. **Boer War. Union of South Africa** formed (1909).	1801–25. **Alexander I** emperor. 1809. **Finland** ceded to Russia following war with Sweden (1807–09). 1815. Tsar grants a constitution to Poland. 1825–55. **Nicholas I** emperor. 1828–29. Russia wages **war against Turkey** on behalf of Greece. 1830–32. Revolution in Poland fails; **Poland** made a **Russian province.** 1854–56. **Crimean War**; Western powers against Russia (siege of **Sevastopol**, 1854–55). Peace of Paris formulates rules for naval warfare (1856). 1855–81. **Alexander II** emperor. 1861. **Tsar frees Russian serfs.** 1863. **Polish insurrection** suppressed vigorously. **1877–78. Russo-Turkish War.** 1881. Alexander II assassinated. 1881–94. **Alexander III** pursues strong reactionary policy. Persecution of Jews begins. **1891. Dual Alliance** with France. 1894–1917. **Nicholas II** exercises **absolutism**; suppression of intellectual progress. 1899. Finnish constitution abrogated.	1821–29. **War for Greek independence** (Philhellenic movement; Lord Byron). Greece gains independence (1829). 1828–29. **Russo-Turkish War** (Treaty of **Adrianople**; Greek Independence acknowledged; **Moldavia** and **Wallachia** partially independent). 1830. **Serbia** secures autonomy after long struggle (revolts of 1804, 1820). 1833–62. **Otto I** (House of Bavaria) king of Greece. **1854–56. Crimean War.** Western powers aid Turkey against Russia. 1866. **Rumania formed** as self-governing state by union of Moldavia and Wallachia (Charles I, 1866–1914). **1877–78. Russo-Turkish War** (siege of **Plevna**, 1877). Treaties of **San Stefano** and **Berlin** make Serbia, Montenegro, and Rumania independent; Bulgaria partly autonomous.	Application of steam-power, by James Watt, to spinning and weaving industries leads to **industrial revolution.** 19th century opens a new era. 1807 **Steamboat** service established by **Fulton.** 1812. **Rising in Spain** against **Napoleon** and adoption of Liberal Constitution. **Liberalism** later suppressed by **Ferdinand VII** (1814–33). 1820. **Revolutions** in Italy and Spain crushed by European Alliance (1821–23). 1830. **Revolutionary movements** in Italy, Poland, and Belgium. Independent monarchy established in **Belgium** (**Leopold I**, 1833–65). 1830. **Manchester and Liverpool railway opened.** 1837. Patent granted to S. F. B. **Morse** for electro-magnetic **telegraph.** 1840. British " **opium war** "; China opened to foreigners. 1854. **Japanese ports opened** to foreigners. 1858. **Transatlantic** telegraph **cable** laid (permanent from 1866). 1859. Publication of Charles **Darwin's** " **Origin of Species** " setting forth doctrine of evolution. 1864. **Geneva Convention**; beginning of **International Red Cross.** 1869. **Suez Canal** opened. 1883. **Congo Free State** formed, Leopold I of Belgium king; made Belgian colony (1908). **1884. Partition of Africa** among European powers. 1894–95. **War** between **China** and **Japan. Expansion of Japan** begins. **1899. First Hague Peace Conference.** Establishment of Court of International Arbitration. 1899. **Wireless telegraphy** established between France and England by **Marconi.**
1901. **Queen Victoria dies.** 1901–10. **Edward VII** king. 1901. **Commonwealth of Australia** formed. 1903. Irish land purchase act passed. 1907. **Anglo-Russian Agreement** to settle differences over Persia. 1908–16. **Asquith** prime minister (Liberal). 1910. **George V** becomes king. **1911. Power of House of Lords limited.** 1914. **Irish Home Rule Bill** passed and suspended. 1914. Bill passed for **disestablishing Anglican Church of Wales**; suspended.	1902. **Trans-Siberian railway** opened. 1904–05. **Russo-Japanese War.** 1905. **Russian Revolution** begins; first **Duma** meets (1906). 1907. **Anglo-Russian agreement** made.	1908–09. Successful **revolution in Turkey** by " **Young Turks.** " **1911–12. Turco-Italian War.** 1912–13. **Balkan Wars**; Balkan allies conquer most of Turkey in Europe; fight over new boundaries.	1900. European Powers intervene in **Boxer Rising** in China. 1903. First successful demonstration of **aeroplane** by Wright brothers in U.S.A. 1905. **Union of Sweden and Norway** dissolved. 1907. Nineteen women elected to Finnish Diet, **first women members** in a national legislature. 1907. **Second Peace Conference** at The Hague. 1909. **Peary** reaches **North Pole.** 1910. **Revolution in Portugal**; **republic** established. 1911–12. **Revolution in China**; **republic** proclaimed. 1911. Capt. Roald **Amundsen** reaches **South Pole.** 1914. **Panama Canal** opened to traffic.

OF 1914–18

1917. **Jerusalem captured** by the British.
1918. **Russia** (Mar. 3) and **Rumania** (May 6) sign **peace** with Central Powers.
1918. Mar. 21–July 18. **German drive** in the West **fails.**

1918. July 18–Nov. 11. **Allied counter-offensive successful**; Hindenburg line smashed.
1918. **Armistice** signed by Bulgaria (Sept. 29), Turkey (Oct. 31), Austria (Nov. 3), Germany (Nov. 11).

GREAT BRITAIN	POLAND	RUSSIA	TURKEY AND THE BALKANS	OTHER
1916. **Sinn Fein** revolt in Ireland crushed; Sir Roger **Casement** executed. 1916. **Lloyd George** becomes premier (Coalition Cabinet). 1918 **Suffrage** extended to women over 30. 1918. **Labour party** secures 75 seats in Parliament at general elections.	1917. **Poles** organize army and join **Allies.** 1918. **Republic of Poland** proclaimed.	1917. Mar. 15. **Revolution**; Nicholas II **abdicates**; **Kerensky** becomes dictator. **Republic** proclaimed, Sept. 17. 1917. Nov. **Bolshevik government** succeeds Kerensky regime.	1917. **Greece** joins **Allies** following abdication of Constantine I. 1918. **Kingdom of Serbs, Croats and Slovenes** (**Yugoslavia**) proclaimed. 1919–20. **Greece** obtains **Thrace, Smyrna**, etc., by treaties of Neuilly and Sèvres.	1919. **International labour conference** in Washington. *For full chronology of First World War see* **World Wars.**

FRANCE	GERMANY	CZECHO-SLOVAKIA	HUNGARY	AUSTRIA	ITALY
1920. **Clemenceau** resigns as premier. Millerand app. successor. French troops occupy **Frankfort** but withdraw upon protest of British government. 1921. Briand appointed premier and minister of foreign affairs. 1922. Poincaré premier and minister of foreign affairs. 1923–25. French occupation of **Ruhr**. 1924. Doumergue president. 1925. Painlevé and Briand premiers. 1926. Herriot and Poincaré premiers; 15 changes of ministry since 1920. 1931. Paul Doumer president. 1931. Laval premier. 1932. Briand dies; Doumer assassinated; succeeded by Lebrun. 1935. Laval premier. 1936. **Blum** premier; first Soc. cabinet. 1936. "Popular Front" formed. 1937. "Forty-hour week" law. 1938. Daladier premier; signs Munich Agreement.	1921. **Upper Silesia** vote for German union. 1924. Dawes reparations plan; Pres. Ebert dies; Hindenberg president. 1925. Locarno Treaty. 1926. Germany joins League. 1932. Reparations end. 1933. Nazi revolution; **Hitler** Chancellor; Germany leaves League. 1934. Hindenberg dies; Hitler president. 1935. Saar rejoins Germany. 1936. Locarno denounced; Rhine remilitarized. 1938. "Anschluss" with Austria; Munich Agreement. 1939. Bohemia, Moravia, Memel occupied; Non-aggression Pact with Russia.	1920. **Constitution** adopted. 1924. Treaty of **alliance with France**. 1918–35. Masaryk president. 1935. Benes president. 1937. Sudetens demand autonomy for German minority. 1938. Lost "minority" territories to Germany, Poland and Hungary. 1939. Slovakia proclaimed independent and rest of republic annexed by Germany and Hungary.	1919. Mar.–Aug. Soviet regime overthrown. 1920. **Treaty of Trianon**; Hungary loses territory to Czechoslovakia, Italy, etc. Monarchy again declared; Horthy regent. 1921. **King Charles I** exiled; dies 1922. 1936. Death of General Gömbös (premier); M. Daranyi appointed. 1938. Obtained territory from Czechoslovakia.	1919. **Treaty of St. Germain** reduces Austria to small area about Vienna. 1920. **Klagenfurt region** votes for union with Austria. 1921. Various districts vote for union with Germany. 1933. **Dollfuss** sets up anti-Fascist regime. 1934. Dollfuss assassinated; succeeded by Schuschnigg. 1938. Austria incorporated in Reich.	1919–20. **D'Annunzio** holds Fiume. 1920. **Treaty of Rapallo** with Yugoslavia secures **Istria** and **Gorizia**; Fiume free state. 1921. Struggle between Fascisti and Communists. 1922. Mussolini becomes premier. 1923. Reparation extracted from Greece for assassination of members of Epirus Frontier Commission. 1924. Treaty with Yugoslavia; Fiume annexed. 1929. Vatican State established. 1934. Corporate State formed. 1935–36. War with Abyssinia. 1937. "Axis" created. 1938. Signs Munich Agreement. 1939. Annexation of Albania.

FRANCE	GERMANY	CZECHO-SLOVAKIA	HUNGARY	AUSTRIA	ITALY
1939. War declared on Germany. 1940. Reynaud premier (March); Pétain (June). Armistice with Germany (June 22). 1940–44. German occupation. 1944. **Liberated by Allies**. Gt. Britain, U.S.A. and Russia recognize Gen. de Gaulle's Provisional Govt. 1946. New Constitution.	1939. Invasion of Poland; **War declared by Britain and France**. 1940. W. Europe invaded; Armistice with France. 1941. Invades Russia. 1943. Driven fr. N. Africa. 1944. Driven fr. France, Belgium and Russia. 1945. **Surrenders to Allies**. Occupied in four zones. 1946. Major war criminals sentenced. 1947. Economic union of Saar with France. 1949. W. German constitution.	1945. Freed by Russians and U.S.; Ruthenia ceded to U.S.S.R. 1948. Communist coup d'état.	1939. Occupied Ruthenia. 1940. Regained large part of Transylvania from Rumania. Joined Axis. 1944. Invaded by Russians. 1945. German population deported. 1946. **Republic proclaimed**. 1947. Peace Treaty. Communists seize power.	1945. Allies enter from E. and w. 1920 constitution restored. **Occupied in four zones**.	1940. War with Britain & France; Greece invaded. 1941. Driven from E. Africa. 1943. Allies invade. Mussolini resigns. Armistice (Sept.). 1944–45. German-Allies battlefield. 1946. **Republic proclaimed**. 1947 Peace Treaty.

THE BRITISH EMPIRE AND COMMONWEALTH FROM 1783

1783. First Colonial Empire ended by Treaty of Versailles.
1788. N.S. Wales a British possession.
1790–92. Second Mysore War.
1791. Canada divided into **Upper** and **Lower Provinces** by the **Constitutional Act** passed by British Parliament; popular assemblies established with limited powers.
1797. Trinidad occupied by British.
1799. Tippoo defeated at Seringapatam.
1802. Ceylon became a Crown Colony.
1812–15. Gt. Britain and U.S.A. at war.
1812–20. Earl of **Selkirk** founds settlement in Red River Valley.
1825–26. Burmese War.
1837–38. **Rebellions** against officialdom; French-Canadians led by **Papineau** attempt to found a republic in Lower Canada; **William L. Mackenzie** heads armed rebellion in Upper Canada.
1838. **Lord Durham's** report to Colonial Office leads to changes in Canadian policy.
1840. New Zealand ceded to Gt. Britain (Treaty of Waitangi).
1841. **Act of Union** joins the two provinces of Canada under a royal governor.
1841. Establishment of Melbourne.
1843. Annexation of Sindh.
1845–49. Sikh War.
1848. Lord Dalhousie Gov.-Gen. of Bengal.

1851. Second Burmese War.
1855. S. Australia received a constitution.
1856. Natal became a separate Colony. Annexation of Oudh.
1857. Outbreak of Indian Mutiny.
1858. Administration of East India Co. transferred to the Crown.
1858. Capital of Canada removed to **Ottawa**.
1859. Establishment of Queensland.
1866. Legislative Council established for Jamaica.
1867. **British North America Act** establishes **Dominion of Canada** (Confederation of Ontario, Quebec, New Brunswick, Nova Scotia).
1867. Conservative government organized in Canada by **Sir John Macdonald** (premier 1867–73, 1878–91).
1870. **Rebellion of Red River** half-breeds led by **Louis Riel**. Province of **Manitoba** formed.
1871. **British Columbia joins the Union**
1873. **Prince Edward Is. admitted** to Union.
1877. Queen Victoria Empress of India.
1885. Riel leads half-breed rebellion in Saskatchewan to obtain squatter rights.
1885. **Canadian Pacific Railway finished.**
1896–1911. **Sir Wilfrid Laurier** premier (Liberal) of Canada.
1898. Lord Curzon Viceroy of India.
1899–1902. Boer War.

1901. **Commonwealth of Australia** formed.
1905. **Alberta** and **Saskatchewan** organized as provinces.
1907. New Zealand became a Dominion.
1910. **Union of S. Africa** established.
1911. King George V's Coronation Durbar.
1911–20. **Sir Robert Borden** premier (Conservative) of Canada.
1912. Seat of Govt. in India transferred from Calcutta to Delhi.
1921. W. L. Mackenzie King, Liberal premier of Canada. Irish Free State formed.
1931. Earl of Clarendon Gov.-Gen. of S. Africa. Earl of Willingdon Viceroy of India.
1931. **Statute of Westminster.**
1936. Lord Linlithgow Viceroy of India.
1937. Sir Patrick Duncan Gov.-Gen. of S. Africa.
1945. Colonial Development Bill provides £120,000,000 for colonies.
1945–48. All W. African colonies receive new constitutions.
1946. Interim Govt. established in India.
1947. **Lord Mountbatten** Viceroy. India partitioned into Dominions of India and Pakistan. Burma independent.
1948. Ceylon a self-governing Dominion.
1949. **India** and **Eire independent republics.**

WORLD WARS

GREAT BRITAIN	POLAND	RUSSIA	TURKEY AND THE BALKANS	OTHER COUNTRIES AND GENERAL PROGRESS
1919. Anglo-Persian agreement signed.	1919. **Treaty of Versailles** recognizes Polish independence and restores G e r m a n, Austrian and part Russ. Poland.	1917–18. Russian provinces establish independence: **Finland, Ukraine, Estonia, Lithuania, Latvia.**	1920. **Turkey** loses by **Treaty of Sèvres : Smyrna, Adana, Syria, Palestine** and **Mesopotamia.** Straits internationalized.	1920. **League of Nations established ;** Assembly meets in Geneva, Nov. 17.
1919. **Irish declare independence.**		1918. Mar. 3. **Peace of Brest-Litovsk** with Germany.	1920. Turkish capital removed to **Angora.**	1921. **Limitation of Armament Conference** at Washington.
1919. Great Britain obtains **mandates** over much former German territory in **South Africa, Palestine, Mesopotamia.**		1919–20. Counter revolution crushed.	1921. Turks recover Smyrna.	1923. Progress in broadcasting. Tutankhamen's tomb discovered.
1921. King opens **Ulster Parliament.** Ireland given dominion status.	1920. Peace with Russia.	1922. Chief Soviet republics setting up a union of Socialist **Soviet Republics.**	1922. George II's accession in Greece.	1924. British Empire Exhibition. Olympic Games in Paris.
1923. Baldwin premier.	1921. Plebiscite in **Upper Silesia** gives Poland important districts.	1924. **Constitution of Union ratified.**	1923. Turkey regains many former possessions Becomes republic.	1926. Abd el Krim, leader of Moroccan revolt, surrenders.
1924. First Labour Govt.		1924. Lenin dies.	1924. Greece republic.	1931. Spain declared a republic.
1929. MacDonald premier.	1926. General **Pilsudski** dictator.	1928. Trotsky and other leaders banished for opposition.	1929. Carol again King of Rumania.	1933. Japan leaves League.
1931. **Coalition Govt.,** end of free trade ; gold standard dropped.	1933. **N o n-aggression** pact with Russia.	1931–32. **5-Year Plan** finished in 4 years; new Plan 1933.	1934. King Alexander of Yugoslavia assassinated. Peter II becomes king.	1936. Persia changes its name to Iran.
1932. De Valera president of Irish Free State.	1934. New Constitution.	1936. Mutual Assistance Pact with France.	1935. Greek monarchy restored (George II).	1936. Civil war in **Spain** begins.
1935. Baldwin premier ; new Indian Constitution.	1936. G e n. Smigly-Rydz Marshal of Poland.	1936. Revised Constitution adopted.	1936. Turkey re-fortifies **Dardanelles.**	1936. Arab outbreaks in Palestine
1936. **Death of King George V.** Accession and abdication of King Edward VIII ; **Accession of King George VI.**	1938. Teschen area (previously Czech) annexed.	1937. 2nd Five-Year plan completed, 3rd plan announced.	1937. Turkey institutes second Five-Year plan.	1937. Mexico nationalizes oil-fields.
1937. Neville Chamberlain premier ; new constitution of Eire.		1939. Non-aggression Pact with Germany.	1938. Kemel Atatürk dies ; Ismet Inönü president.	1937. Outbreak of Sino-Japanese War Egypt independent. Provincial autonomy in India.
1938. Anglo-Irish agreement signed ; Munich Agreement signed.			1939. Annexation of Albania by Italy.	1939. Spanish Civil War ends. Franco dictator of Spain.

—1945 AND AFTER

1939. War on Germany.	1939. Invasion by Germany. Country partitioned.	1939. E. Poland i n c o r p o r a t e d. War with Finland.	1941. Germans overrun Yugoslavia, Greece and Crete. Rumania and Bulgaria join Axis.	1940. Japan joins Axis.
1940. Churchill premier. Battle of Britain.	1941–44. Russo-German battlefield.	1940. Baltic States incorporated.	1944. Rumania joins Allies ; Bulgaria withdraws ; partisans liberate Yugoslavia.	1941. Syria liberated by British and Free French. Japan starts war on U.S.A.
1940–43. N. African campaign.		1941. **Invaded by Germany.**		1942. Japan occupies Malaya and Burma ; invades Dutch Indies.
1943–44. Invasion of Europe.	1945. Liberated. New frontiers agreed.	1944. Russians drive Germans out ; invade Balkans.	1945–46. **Civil War in Greece.** British troops intervene. Wide social reforms in most Balkan states. Many become republics.	1945. **Japan surrenders. United Nations created** at San Francisco. Civil War in China.
1945. **Victory over Axis.** 3rd Labour Govt. **Anglo-U.S.** loan of £1,100,000,000.	1945–46. Expulsion of G e r m a n population.	1945. **Victory (May). New Western frontiers.**		1946–47. Terrorism in Palestine. Jap. Emperor becomes secular constitutional monarch.
1946–48. Nationalization of Bank of England, coal mines, railways, electricity and gas.		1946. Fourth Five-Year Plan begins.	1947. Peace Treaties signed.	1948. State of Israel proclaimed.
1950. Fourth Labour Government				1949. Chinese Communists capture Nanking. North Atlantic Treaty signed. *For full chronology of Second World War see* **World Wars.**

THE UNITED STATES OF AMERICA

1787. **Federal Constitution** framed by Constitutional Convention.

1789–97. **George Washington** president.

1789. **First Congress** meets at New York.

1797–1801. **John Adams** president.

1801–09. **Thomas Jefferson** president.

1803. **Louisiana** purchased from France.

1809–17. **James Madison** president.

1817–25. **James Monroe** president.

1823. **Monroe Doctrine** advanced against the aggression of the Holy Alliance in U.S.A

1825–29. **John Quincy Adams** president.

1829–37. **Andrew Jackson** president.

1837–41. **Martin Van Buren** president.

1841. **William Henry Harrison** president

1841–45. **John Tyler** president.

1845–49. **James K. Polk** president.

1846–48. **Mexican War.**

1849–50. **Zachary Taylor** president.

1850–53. **Millard Fillmore** president.

1852. " **Uncle Tom's Cabin** " published.

1853–57. **Franklin Pierce** president.

1857–61. **James Buchanan** president.

1860. Abraham Lincoln elected president.

1861. **South Carolina secedes; other southern states secede to form a confederacy.**

1861–65. **Abraham Lincoln** president.

1861–65. **Civil War.**

1863. Lincoln issues **Emancipation Proclamation.**

1865. **Lee surrenders at Appomattox Court House.**

1865. **Lincoln assassinated.** [House.

1865–69. **Andrew Johnson** president.

1865. **Thirteenth Amendment prohibits** slavery.

1869–77. **Ulysses S. Grant** president.

1870. **Fifteenth Amendment extends franchise to the Negroes.**

1871. Treaty of Washington provides for arbitration of Alabama Claims."

1877–81. **Rutherford B. Hayes** president.

1881. **James A. Garfield** president ; assassinated the same year.

1881–85. **Chester A. Arthur** president.

1885–89. **Grover Cleveland** president.

1889–93. **Benjamin Harrison** president.

1893–97. **Grover Cleveland** president.

1897–1901. **William McKinley** president.

1898. **Spanish-American War.**

1898. Annexation of Hawaii ; division of Samoan Islands with Germany.

1901. President McKinley assassinated.

1901–09. **Theodore Roosevelt** president.

1901. Hay-Pauncefote treaty allows U.S.A. to build Panama Canal.

1909–13. **William Howard Taft** president.

1913–21. **Woodrow Wilson** president.

1917. War declared against Germany.

1919. Prohibition established.

1921–23. **Warren G. Harding** president.

1921. Bill passed to restrict immigration.

1923. **Calvin C. Coolidge** president.

1929. **Herbert C. Hoover** president.

1933. **Franklin D. Roosevelt** president.

1933. Volstead Act (Prohibition) repealed.

1934. Roosevelt introduces New Deal.

1937 and 1940. F. D. Roosevelt re-elected.

1941. Lease-Lend Bill passed (March). War declared on Axis (Dec.).

1944. F. D. Roosevelt re-elected president.

1945. **Death of Roosevelt ; Truman** president. **Victory.** End of lease-lend. Loan to Britain.

1946–49. Atomic bomb research continues. Financial and military aid to Greece and Turkey. " **Marshall plan** " gives economic aid to Europe. Anti-Communist action at home and abroad.

Holland, North and **South.** Chief provinces of the Netherlands, **1635.** *See* **Netherlands.**

Holland, John P. (1841–1914). American inventor of submarines, 3105.

Holland, Sidney G. (b. 1893). New Zealand politician. Became Prime Min. and Min. of Finance in 1949.

Hollander, Bernard (1864–1934). Eng. physician; developed theories on phrenology, based on " bumps " on the skull. not generally accepted.

Holland Line. Netherlands defence line in 2nd World War, 1636.

Hollar, Wenceslaus (1607–77). Bohemian engraver; worked largely in England and was drawing-master to Charles II; his views of London are notably fine.

Hol'les, Denzil, 1st Baron (1599–1680). Eng. parliamentary leader active in opposing Stuart autocracy; imprisoned in 1629; helped Pym to draw up Grand Remonstrance; participated in Civil War but opposed Oliver Cromwell and army policy.

Holly. Evergreen tree (*Ilex aquifolium*); used as a Christmas decoration, **1636**; botanical classification, 3247.

Holly Blue butterfly, 1636.

Hol'lyhock (*Althaea*). A garden plant of the mallow family, **1636.**

Hollywood, California, U.S.A. Section of Los Angeles; centre of film industry, 664, 828, 2026; the Bowl, 3197.

Holmenkollen. Hill near Oslo, Norway, 2392.

Holmes, Oliver Wendell (1809–94). Amer. poet and essayist, 1636, 3294; invents open stereoscope, 3088.

Holmes, Sherlock. In Conan Doyle's detective stories, marvellous amateur detective who unravels the most baffling mysteries, 1032.

Holmium (Ho), one of the rare earth elements; atomic weight, 163·5. *See* **Rare Earths.**

Holm oak. Same as **Ilex.**

Holocene (hol'-ō-sēn), in geology, the epoch of recent time, including the present.

Holofernes (hol-ō-fêr'-nĕz). Assyrian general slain by Judith; story told in apocryphal book of Judith.

Holothur'ian, or **sea-cucumber,** a worm-shaped marine animal related to starfish, 2911, 3626.

Holst, Gustav Theodore (1874–1934). Eng. composer. Works include: " The Planets " (orchestral suite); " The Perfect Fool " (opera); Choral Symphony. Music master at St. P. ul's Girls School.

Holstein (hōl'-stīn). Former duchy of Denmark; since 1866 s. part of Schleswig-Holstein. *See* **Schleswig-Holstein.**

Holstein. A breed of dairy cattle, 732.

Holy Alliance. League of European powers, promoted by the Tsar Alexander I, 1240.

Holy Carpet, in Mahomedanism, *2068.*

Holy Ghost, Island of the, 3093.

Holy Grail. *See* **Grail, Holy.**

Holyhead. Welsh port on Holy Isl., just w. of Anglesey, N. Wales; pop. 10,707; terminus of steamer service to Dun Laoghaire (Kingstown), Eire.

Holy Island or **Lindisfarne.** Isl. off N.E. coast of Northumberland, joined at low water to the mainland; remains of an 11th-cent. monastery; St. Cuthbert was bishop of the see; 2391. " Lindisfarne Gospel," Anglo-Celtic MS.

Holy Island, Wales. Isl. off Anglesey, 8 m. long and ½ m. to 3 m. broad; connected to mainland by causeway; also called Holyhead Isl.

Holy Land, Palestine, 2480.

Holy League. Formed 1511 by Pope, Venice and Ferdinand II of Spain to drive Fr. from It.; later joined by Emperor Maximilian and Henry VIII.

Holyoake, George Jacob (1817–1906). Eng. secular lecturer and author; a pioneer of the co-operative movement (" History of Co-operation in England ").

Holy Office, Congregation of the, 1726.

Holy Roman Empire, 1238, 1240, 1449, 1636; Charlemagne founds, 753; Saxon and Franconian emperors, 1609, 2459; Otto I revives, 1238, 1764, 2459; investiture conflict, 1542, 1609; under the Hapsburgs, 754; Thirty Years' War, effect, 1239; dissolved, 1449. *See also* **Austria; Germany;** and emperors by name.

RULERS OF THE HOLY ROMAN EMPIRE

800–814	Charlemagne
814–840	Louis the Pious
840–911	Later Carolingians
[911–918	Conrad I]

SAXON LINE

919–936	Henry I, the Fowler
936–973	Otto I, the Great
973–983	Otto II
983–1002	Otto III
1002–24	Henry II

FRANCONIAN LINE

1024–39	Conrad II
1039–56	Henry III
1056–1106	Henry IV
1106–25	Henry V
[1125–37	Lothair II of Saxony]

HOHENSTAUFEN LINE

1138–52	Conrad III
1152–90	Frederick I (Barbarossa)
1190–97	Henry VI
1198–1208	Philip of Swabia } rival
1198–1214	Otto IV } claimants
1215–50	Frederick II
1250–54	Conrad IV
[1256–73	Great Interregnum]

RULERS FROM VARIOUS HOUSES

1273–91	Rudolph of Hapsburg
1292–98	Adolf of Nassau
1298–1308	Albert of Austria
1308–13	Henry VII of Luxemburg
1314–47	Louis IV of Bavaria } rival
1314–30	Frederick the Fair } claimants

LUXEMBURG LINE

1347–78	Charles IV
1378–1400	Wenceslaus
[1400–1410	Rupert of the Palatinate]
1410–37	Sigismund

HAPSBURG LINE

1438–39	Albert II
1440–93	Frederick III
1493–1519	Maximilian I
1519–56	Charles V
1556–64	Ferdinand I
1564–76	Maximilian II
1576–1612	Rudolph II
1612–19	Matthias
1619–37	Ferdinand II
1637–57	Ferdinand III
1658–1705	Leopold I
1705–11	Joseph I
1711–40	Charles VI
[1742–45	Charles VII of Bavaria]
1745–65	Francis I
1765–90	Joseph II
1790–92	Leopold II
1792–1806	Francis II (after 1806 reigned as Francis I of Austria)
[1806	Title of Holy Roman Emperor abolished.]

EMPERORS OF AUSTRIA

1806–35	Francis I
1835–48	Ferdinand II
1848–1916	Francis Joseph
1916–19	Charles

Holyroodhouse, Edinburgh, 1086.

Holy Saturday, 1074.

Holy Sepulchre, Church of the, Jerusalem, 1820.

Holy Thursday, or **Maundy Thursday.** In commemoration of the washing of the disciples' feet by Jesus, 1074.

Holy Week, 1074.

Hom'age. In feudalism, *1269.*

Home counties. Name given to the counties around London—Middlesex, Essex, Kent, Surrey, Hertfordshire, Buckinghamshire and Berkshire.

Home economics. *See* **Household Science.**

Home Guard, Brit. defence force of 2nd World War, **1637,** 3417.

Homel' or **Gomel',** Soviet Russia. Mfg. centre and rly. centre and river port on branch of Dnieper, 350 m. s.w. of Moscow; pop. (1939) 144,000.

Home Office. Brit. govt. dept., **1637.**

Homer. Anc. Gk. poet, to whom is ascribed authorship of Iliad and Odyssey, 1539, 1541, **1637.**
Stories from: Achilles, 19; Adventures of the Great-Hearted Odysseus, 2421; Aphrodite in the Trojan War, 186; Death of Hector, 1603; How Odysseus and His Men Outwitted the Cyclops, 949; Odysseus and Circe, 834; Proteus, 2694; Wooden Horse, 3249.

Homer, Winslow (1836–1910). Considered most typically national of all Amer. painters; pictures the ocean and fisherfolk with uncompromising truth, 3353; " The Maine Coast," and " On a Lee Shore " considered his masterpieces.

" **Homer, The insects' " (Fabre),** 1255.

Home Rule, for Ireland, 1746; Gladstone's measures, 1469; 3279; O'Connell, 2420; Parnell, 2525.

Home Secretary. Head of Home Office, senior to other State Secretaries, 1637.

Home Security, Min. of. Brit. govt. dept. functioning Sept. 1939 to May 23, 1945; the Home Secty., as min., directed Civil Defence, Defence Regulations, and upheld home morale.

Homing instinct, birds, 159.

Homing or **carrier pigeon,** 2606, *2607.*

Homo (hō'-mō). Generic name for Man, 2079.

Homoeop'athy. A system of medicine founded by Hahnemann; guiding principle is that a drug causing certain symptoms in normal persons is the proper remedy for a disease showing the same symptoms (" like cures like ").

Homophones, in spelling, 3057.

Honan'. Inland prov. of E.-cent. China; 66,000 square miles; pop. 34,000,000; cap. Kaifeng; cereals, cotton, tobacco, indigo, hemp, minerals.

Hondecoeter, Melchior d' (c. 1636–95). Dutch artist. Famous for his paintings of birds and still-life, 2335.

Hondo. Same as **Honshu.**

Honduras (hon-dōō'-ras). Republic of Cent. Amer.; 46,322 sq. m.; pop. 1,200,000; 744, *map, 743,* **1638**; mahogany, 2065.

Honduras, British. Crown Colony in Cent. America; area 8,867 sq. m.; pop. 64,000; **1633,** 3437; Guatemalan claims on, 1552, 1638.

Honduras, Gulf of. Inlet of Caribbean Sea on E. coast of Cent. Amer.; *743.*

Hon'egger, Arthur (b. 1892). Swiss composer; symphonies; "Pacific 231" (description in music of a locomotive); music for films.

Honey. Produced by bees, *393, 390*; clover best source, 852; contains glucose, 1477; used for sweetening before sugar, 3112.

Honey-bee. Social bees, 390. *See also* **Bee.**

Honey-buzzard, 634.

Honeycomb. Waxy many-celled structure made by bees for holding honey, *393.*

Honeydew, from aphids, 155.

Honeysuckle. Various shrubs bearing fragrant trumpet-shaped flowers, **1639.**

Hong Kong, China. Isl. city and Brit. colony ; area (incl. Kowloon) 391 sq. m. ; pop. 1,100,000 ; **1639** ; in Jan. occupd. 1941-45, 2400.

" Honi soit qui mal y pense." Motto of the Order of the Garter, 2448.

Hon'iton pillow lace, 1881, *plate f. 1880.*

Honolulu (hon-ō-lōō'-lōō), cap. of Hawaiian Isls. ; pop. 200,000 ; *1585, 1586* ; pineapples, *2611.*

Honor'ius, Flavius. Rom. emperor of the West (395–423) ; son of Theodosius ; invasion of Goths, 96 ; suppresses gladiatorial contests, 1469.

Honourable Artillery Company (H.A.C.). Oldest Brit. regiment, founded 1537 ; in Territorial Army.

Honourable Corps of Gentlemen at Arms. King's bodyguard at State ceremonies within doors ; part of the Royal Household.

Honshu or **Honshiu.** Largest isl. of Japan ; 88,000 sq. m. ; 1795, *1798* ; *map, 1706.*

Honthorst, Gerard van (1590–1656). Dutch painter ; decorated Whitehall, London, with allegorical paintings, 2333 ; Buckingham family, *598.*

Hooch (hōkh), **Pieter de** (c. 1632–81). Dutch artist ; one of the greatest of all painters of interiors, *2334.*

Hood, Alexander, Viscount Bridport (1727–1814). Brit. sailor ; second in command of Channel fleet under Howe (1793) ; at glorious First of June ; vice-admiral of England (1796).

Hood, Samuel, Viscount (1724–1816). Brit. naval commander-in-chief in America (1767–71) ; distinguished in various battles 1780–83 with Fr. fleet under De Grasse ; commanded in Mediterranean in 1793 ; great tactician.

Hood, Sir Samuel (1762–1814). Brit. sailor ; distinguished himself in several naval engagements, notably against the Fr. in 1802 and 1804 ; previously served under Nelson at Santa Cruz (1797) and at battle of the Nile (1798).

Hood, Thomas (1799–1845). Eng. poet and humorist, **1640.**

Hood. British battle cruiser, largest warship in world prior to 1945 ; sunk by German battleship Bismarck using German equivalent of radar at range of 13 m. off coast of Greenland, May 24, 1941.

Hood, Mt., in Cascade Range of N. Oregon, U.S.A., 11,225 ft., 45 m. S.E. of Portland.

Hooded crow, 935.

Hoo'doo. A person or thing whose presence is supposed to cause bad luck ; derived from voodoo, 2057.

Hoof. A horny sheath encasing toes of many animals ; corresponds to finger-nail or toe-nail of Man ; 1342, 2076.

Hooghli. Same as Hugli.

Hook, Captain, in "Peter Pan," 366.

Hook, Theodore Edward (1788–1841). Eng. humorous author and dramatist ; he won popularity with " Gilbert Gurney " and " Jack Brag," both of which first appeared in the " New Monthly " ; he was a great practical joker.

Hoo'kah. Tobacco pipe used in the Orient.

Hooke, Robert (1635–1703). English scientist, **1640** : invented hair spring used in watches, 844, 848.

Hooker, Sir Joseph Dalton (1817–1911). Eminent Eng. surgeon and naturalist, **1640.**

Hooker, Richard (c. 1553–1600). Eng. author, wrote " Laws of Ecclesiastical Polity," a masterly exposition of philosophical and political principles.

Hooke's Law, 1640.

Hook of Holland. Vil. spt. of Netherlands ; point of land at mouth of r. Maas (Meuse), 18 m. from Rotterdam ; terminus of steamer services from Harwich.

Hooper, John (c. 1495–1555). Eng. martyr, bishop, and religious reformer ; burned as heretic in reign of Mary.

Hoopoe (hōō'-pōō). Bird, *Upupa,* common in most of Southern and Central Europe, about the size of a thrush ; has plumage of black, white, and pink mixed, a long-pointed bill, and a large erectile crest of two parallel rows of feathers. Once bred in Britain, now extinct ; nested in holes in willows.

Hoover, Herbert Clark (b. 1874). Amer. statesman and mining engineer ; food administrator during 1st World War, Sec. of Commerce in 1921 ; President of U.S.A. (1929–33) ; *3292.*

Hope, Anthony. Pen-name of Sir Anthony Hope Hawkins (1863–1933). Eng. novelist ; " The Prisoner of Zenda " and " Rupert of Hentzau " set fashion for romantic comedies involving noblemen of fictitious principalities.

Hopei or **Hopeh.** Prov. of N. China, formerly known as Chihli ; chief tns., Peking and Tientsin ; agric. wealth ; area 59,000 sq. m. ; pop. 28,644,000.

Hopis or **Mokis.** Tribe of Pueblo Indians in cent. Arizona, U.S.A., 235, 2698.

Hopkins, Sir Frederick Gowland (1861–1947). English b ochemist ; awarded Nobel prize in medicine, 1929, for discovery of Vitamin D. Professor of B ochemistry, Univ. of Cambridge, from 1914 ; 3326.

Hopkins, Gerard Manley (1844–89). Eng. poet ; works show a born love of Nature expressed in fine language.

Hopkins, Harry L. (1890–1946). Amer. administrator ; personal friend and adviser of F. D. Roosevelt, accompanying him to war-time conferences, signing of Atlantic charter, etc. ; personal adviser to H. Truman as pres., but resigned ; died Jan. 1946 ; his " White House Papers " pub. 1948.

Hoppner, John (1758–1810). Eng. portrait painter, rival of Lawrence, painted portraits of several members of the royal family (" Nelson " ; " Countess of Oxford "), 1180 ; " Abercromby," " Burke," *622.*

Hops and hop-picking, 1641, *1642.*

Horace (Quintus Horatius Flaccus) 65–8 B.C.). Latin lyric poet, **1641,** 1896.

Horae (hor'-ē) or **Hours.** Maidens in Gk. myth.

Horatii. Legendary Rom. heroes, 2804.

Horatio (hō-rā'-shi-ō). In Shakespeare's " Hamlet," devoted friend of Hamlet.

Hora'tius. Legendary Rom. hero, 2804, 3207.

Horder, Thomas Jeeves Horder, 1st Baron (b. 1871). English physician ; specializes in diagnosis and radiology ; Physician in Ordinary to H.M. the King.

Hore-Belisha, Leslie (b. 1893). Eng. politician. Minister of Transport in 1935 ; introduced special crossings (marked with yellow beacons) for pedestrians, 2789 ; *plate f. 2785* ; became War Minister in 1937, introducing many reforms. He resigned Jan. 1940.

Hore'hound. A genus of plants (*Marrubium*) of the family *Labiatae,* common in hedgerows, has opposite serrated leaves and white flowers. Another plant (*Ballota*), Black Horehound, has purple flowers.

Hori'zon, artificial, in aerial navigation, 2293.

Hormones (hor'-mōnz). Bodily secretions necessary for various processes such as growth, 1470.

Horn, of animals, **1641** ; permanent in antelopes, 176 ; renewed in deer, 984 ; yields gelatin and glue, 1426. Of a sea mine, 2185.

Horn, Alfred Aloysius (d. 1931). Travels in S. Africa, 3020.

Horn, Cape. Most southerly point of S. Amer., a steep, bare, black rock, 1,390 ft. high, on isl. of the Fuegian Archipelago ; *map, plate f. 3024.*

Hornbeam. A tree (*Carpinus*) of the birch family ; long male catkins conspicuous in spring ; leaves serrated, like those of elm, 1152 ; bark grey, corrugated but not furrowed ; hardest and heaviest English wood.

Hornbill. A tropical bird, **1643.**

Hornblende. A black or greenish-black mineral ; magnesium iron calcium silicate ; found in crystalline and granular masses ; a common constituent of granite and other igneous rocks.

Horn dance, *966.*

Horne of Slamannan, Robert Stevenson Horne, 1st Viscount (1871–1940). Brit. politician ; Minister of Labour (1919) ; Pres. of Board of Trade (1920) ; Chancellor of Exchequer (1921) ; Chairman of the Great Western Railway in 1934.

Horned toad, A lizard, 1974.

Horned viper, 3325.

Hor'net, a social wasp, **1643,** 3345.

Hornet-moth. The largest Brit. representative of the clearwing moths ; bears a striking resemblance to a wasp ; larvae burrow in trees.

Hornet Moth. Light aeroplane ; also 1945 fast Hornet fighter.

Horns and trumpets. Musical instruments, **1643,** *1644,* 2268.

Horn'sey. Bor. of Middlesex, 4 m. N. of King's Cross ; a residential dist., it includes Finsbury Park and Alexandra Palace ; pop. 96,584.

Hor'nung, Ernest William (1866–1921). Eng. writer of novels with a sensational interest, some of which were dramatized ; he created the celebrated character " Raffles " (" The Amateur Cracksman " ; " Mr. Justice Raffles " ; " The Crime Doctor ").

Hor'oscope. A chart indication of the position of the heavenly bodies at time of a person's birth, 3443.

Horowitz (hor'-ō-vits), **Vladimir** (b. 1904). Russ. pianist ; settled in U.S.A.

Horse. " The Friend of Man," **1645** ; in army cavalry, 244, 246 ; evolution, 1245, 1246 ; foot of, 1342, 1343 ; French breeds, 1360 ; in hunting, 1657, 1659 ; racing, 1648 ; riding, 2779 ; Wooden Horse of Troy, 3249.

Horse chestnut, 1647 ; botanical classification, 3247 ; daily growth, *3284* ; leaves, 1915, 1917.

Horse family or *Equidae.* A family of one-toed, hoofed animals with peculiarly ridged and hollowed teeth ; includes horse, 1645 ; ass, 273 ; zebra, 3442.

Horse-fly or gadfly. A short-bodied fly with horny pointed proboscis adapted for bloodsucking.

Horse Guards. A Household Cavalry regiment of the British Army ; in Whitehall, London, 244 ; Parade, *877.*

Horsehair, artificial, 2749.

Horse latitudes. A zone of light winds between the " trade wind " and " prevailing westerly " zones, *3385.*

Horse leech. Species of leech, 3425.

Horse mackerel or tunny, *3258.*

Hor'sens. Denmark. Spt. on Horsens Fiord ; pop. 32,400 ; iron products, ships, woodenware ; exports butter and bacon ; 991.

Horse of Troy. Story of, 3249–50.

Horse-power. Power required to raise 33,000 lb. one foot in one minute. Murdock's calculations, 2257.

Horse-racing. " The sport of kings," **1648** ; the Derby, 994. *See also* **Derby ; Grand National.**

Horseradish. An edible perennial whose white root is served with roast beef and used in sauces, 640.

Horse's head. Dark nebula, *2311.*

Horseshoe or king crab. A crab-like creature of uncertain zoological relationships, possibly descended from trilobites, 1354.

Horseshoe Fall. The Canadian portion of Niagara Falls, *2361* ; *map, 2362.*

Horseshoe magnet, *2060.*

Horses of St. Mark's. A famous bronze group adorning St. Mark's Cathedral in Venice, *1773.*

Horsetail. Primitive plant of genus *Equisetum*, only living member of large prehistoric group. Hollow, jointed stem, whorled simple leaves, primitive spore system of reproduction. Member of phylum *Pteridophyta*, 2620.

Hor'sham. Tn. in Sussex, near the head of the Arun ; at West Horsham is Christ's Hospital (the Blue Coat School) ; pop. 13,579.

Horst Wessel. *See* Wessel, Horst.

Hor'ta. A city of the Azores, cap. of Fayal.

Horten'sian law (*lex Hortensia*), in Rom. history, 2805.

Horthy (hor'-tě) **de Nagybanya, Nikolaus** (b. 1868). Hungarian admiral ; elected Regent of Hungary 1920 ; suppressed attempts of former King Charles to regain throne, 1656 ; resignation Feb. 1942 ; captured by Allies and released, 1657.

Horton, Bucks. Milton's home, 2176.

Horunger Mts., in Norway, *plate f.* 2393.

Horus (hor'-*us*), Eg. sun-god, 2455.

Hosea (hŏ-zě'-*a*) (8th cent. B.C.), Hebrew minor prophet ; wrote 28th book of Old Testament, 2691.

Ho'siery ; machine for knitting, 1867.

Hosoda Eishi. Jap. artist, *1806.*

Hos'pitallers (Order of the Hospital of St. John of Jerusalem), 2072, 2771.

Hospitals, 1648 ; Red Cross, 2752 ; state administration, 1590, 1648 ; training of nurses, 2406 ; work of Florence Nightingale, 2368, 2406.

Host, in biology, 2512.

Hot air engine, 1735.

Hot-bulb ignition in i.c. engines, 1737.

Hotch'kiss, Benjamin (1826–85), Amer. inventor of Hotchkiss machine-gun.

Hôtel des Invalides (ō-tel dā-zan-vah-lěd'), Paris, 2517.

Hôtel de Ville (de-vēl'), Brussels, *595.*

Hot Springs, 3070.

Hotspur. *See* Percy, Sir Henry.

Hot'tentots. Race of S. Africa now confined to w. Cape of Good Hope and adjoining territory ; 70, 3017.

Hot-tube ignition in i.c. engines, 1737.

Hot-water heating, *1599.*

Hot-wire ammeter, 1134.

Houdin (ōō-dan'), **Robert** (1805–71). Fr. conjurer, presided over a Theatre of Magic in Paris ; wrote " The Secrets of Conjuring and Magic."

Houdon (ōō-don'), **Jean Antoine** (1740–1828). Fr. sculptor, 2906 ; bust of Voltaire, *3329* ; of Rousseau, 2831.

Houghton, William Stanley (1881–1913). Eng. critic and dramatist, a leader in realistic movement (" Hindle Wakes ").

Hounds. Hunting dogs, 1026.

Hour. Why divided into 60 seconds, 329.

Hour-glass, or sand-glass, for time measurement, 843, 3212.

Houris (hōō'-riz). In Mahomedan religion, beautiful maidens who minister to the faithful in Paradise.

House. Building, *610* ; central heating, *1599* ; prefabricated, 611 ; roof, 2821.

House, (Col.) Edward Mandell (1858–1938). Amer. political leader ; confidential agent of Pres. Wilson to European govts. during 1st World War ; member Amer. Peace Commission in 1919.

House-boats. Chinese life on, *813.*

House cricket, 927.

House-fly, *1329* ; wing under microscope, *2165.*

Household science ; cloth and clothing, 850, 851 ; cookery, 900 ; electric devices, 1125, 1134 ; food and food values, 1336, 2693, 3326 ; furniture, 1409 ; heating and ventilation, 1597 ; laundry, 1900 ; lighting systems, 1134, 1939 ; paints and varnishes, 2477 ; rugs and carpets, 705 ; sewing, 2927 ; soap, 2993 ; *See also* Cookery, Food, Food values, Sewing, etc.

House martin, *3124.*

House of Commons. *See* Commons, House of.

House of Lords. *See* Lords, House of.

House of Representatives. *See* Representatives, House of.

Houses. Elizabethan manor houses, 220 ; Eskimo igloos, *1223* ; heating and ventilation, 1597 ; Malay, 2069 ; medieval castle, *715, 718* ; modern concrete house, *611* ; New Guinea tree dwellings, *2339* ; Red Indian, 2753 ; Roman (anc.), *2653. See also* articles on separate countries ; and **Housing problem.**

Ho ses of Parliament. *See* Parliament, Houses of.

House sparrow, 1272, *3052* ; how he gets his black throat, 447.

Housing problem. The consequence of intense industrialism of England, 3233 ; Ministry of Health and, 1591 : and modern building, 611.

Hous'man, Alfred Edward (1859–1936). Eng. poet and scholar ; professor of Latin, Cambridge ; best-known work " A Shropshire Lad "—lyric sequence of exquisite sensitiveness to life's beauty and cruelty, 1216 ; rhymes, 2635.

Housman, Laurence (b. 1865). Eng. writer and illustrator, brother of A. E. Housman ; distinguished by phantasy and mysticism (" Little Plays of St. Francis " " Victoria Regina ").

Houston, Sam (1793–1863). Amer. soldier and statesman, pres. of republic of Texas ; commanded Texan troops at battle of San Jacinto, 1836, which gained Texas independence.

Houston, Texas, U.S.A., important spt. and rly. centre of S. Tex. ; cotton, rice, lumber industries ; pop. 384,500, 3190.

Houyhnhnms (hoo-in'-mz), in " Gulliver's Travels," 3134.

Hov'as, tribe of Madagascar, 2051.

Hove. Tn. and watering-place of Sussex, immediately w. of Brighton ; pop. est. 66,730.

Hover fly, 1330 ; life history, *1731.*

Howard. Great Eng. Cath. family ; head is the Duke of Norfolk, first duke and Earl-Marshal of England, and whose branches hold many other peerages ; rose to greatness and met misfortune in Tudor reigns.

Howard, Catherine (*c.* 1520–42), 5th queen of Henry VIII of England ; beheaded, 1612.

Howard, Sir Ebenezer (1850–1928). Eng. social reformer ; devoted himself to garden city and town-planning development.

Howard, John (1726–90). Eng. philanthropist and prison reformer ; work remedied shocking abuses ; *2687.*

Howard, Leslie (1893–1943). Eng. actor, famous on stage and films (" Outward Bound," " Berkeley Square," " The Scarlet Pimpernel," " Romeo and Juliet," " First of the Few ").

Howard of Effingham, Charles Howard, 2nd Baron (1536–1642), created Earl of Nottingham 1596, lord high admiral, influential with Queen Elizabeth, his kinswoman ; and Span. Armada, 236.

How'dah. Seat for riding elephant, 1142.

Howe, Elias (1819–67). Inventor of the sewing-machine, 2929, *2930.*

Howe, H.M.S. Battleship, displacement 45,000 tons ; completed 1942 ; served in Pacific fleet against Japs. in 1945 ; in 1946 used as seagoing training ship.

Howe, Julia Ward (1819–1910). American writer and reformer ; pioneer of woman suffrage ; wrote " The Battle Hymn of the Republic."

Howe, Richard, Earl (1726–99). Eng. admiral, one of greatest Brit. naval commanders ; commanded Brit. sea forces in war of Amer. Independence ; relieved Gibraltar (1782) ; gained victory of " glorious first of June " (1794) over French off Ushant ; 3277.

Howe, Samuel Gridley (1801–76). Amer. educator and humanitarian reformer ; founder of the Perkins Institution for the Blind and of the first school in the U.S.A. for the mentally deficient, 470.

Howells, William Dean (1837–1920). Amer. novelist, essayist, and critic ; he had a masterly style, but his strength lay in his fidelity to truth (" Their Wedding Journey " ; " The Lady of the Aroostook " ; " The Vocation of the Kelwyns "), 2403, 3924.

" How Goldenwings Learned to Fly," story, 3485.

How'itzer. High-elevation artillery. 257, *259.*

Howler monkey, 2210.

How'rah. Industrial and rly. centre, suburb of Calcutta, India, separated from it by r. Hugli ; pop. 224,000 ; jute, cotton, iron, and machinery mfrs., 661.

" How Screecher Learned to Hunt," story, 3473.

Howth Head. A peninsula on the E. coast of Eire, forming the N. side of the Bay of Dublin.

Hoy (Norse " high island "). 2nd in size (53 sq. m.) of Orkney Isls., 2453.

Hoyle, Edmond (1672–1769). Eng. author of works on rules of whist and other games, long regarded as authoritative, so that " according to Hoyle " has become a proverbial phrase.

Hradcany Palace, Prague ; defenestration at, *3203.*

Hruod'land, Count, or **Roland,** 2797.

Hsinking. *See* Changchun.

Huber (ōō'-bär) **François** (1750–1831). Swiss naturalist, first to gain scientific knowledge of life of bees.

Hubert (hū'-bert), **Saint** (656–727). Apostle of the Ardennes and patron of huntsmen.

Hubertsburg, Peace of. Signed 1763, in château of Hubertsburg in Saxony, Ger., ending Seven Years' War, 2924.

Hüb'nerite. A tungsten ore.

" Huckleberry Finn." Story by Mark Twain, 3269.

Hud'dersfield. Eng. mfg. tn. in W. Riding of Yorkshire ; pop. 124,000 ; centre of wool and worsted cloth industry, 1168, 3435.

Hudibras (hū'-di-bras). Hero of a mock epic poem of that name by Samuel Butler (1663) ; satire on Puritanism, 1212.

Hudson, Henry (*c.* 1575–1611). Eng. navigator, 143, 682, 1648, 2357, 2644, 3067.

Hudson, William Henry (1841–1922). Eng. naturalist and writer on the countryside, 1649.

Hudson Bay, Canada. The 3rd largest land-locked sea in the world ; explored by Henry Hudson in 1610 and named after him ; a. over 500,000 sq. m., **1649** ; Hudson Bay sable, 2980.

Hudson River. Principal r. of New York state, and one of the most important highways of commerce in U.S.A. ; 350 m. long ; flows into New York Bay ; highway to the w., *2356* ; traffic, 2353.

Hudson's Bay Company. Brit. trading company in Canada, **1650** ; aids exploration, 682, 2644 ; fur trade, 1412 ; in Manitoba, 2089 ; North-West Territories, 2392 ; in Saskatchewan, 2875.

Hudson Strait. Connects Hudson Bay with Atlantic ; 500 m. long, ; extreme breadth, 138 m.

Hué (oo-ā'). Fortified city, cap. of Annam, Viet-Nam ; pop. 13,000 ; on Hué r., 10 m. from mouth ; 1719.

Hue and cry. Old Eng. common-law practice of pursuing criminal with " horn and voice " (" hue " from old Fr. word for cry or shout).

Huerta (wer'-ta), **Victoriano** (1854–1916). Mex. general, full-blooded Indian ; overthrew Madero administration and made himself pres. (1913) ; resigned (1914) ; arrested in U.S.A. for fomenting a revolution against Mexico ; died before trial.

Hug'gins, Sir Godfrey M. (b. 1883). Brit. statesman ; prime min. of S. Rhodesia from 1934.

Hug'gins, Sir William (1824–1910). Eng. astronomer, pioneer in spectroscopic astronomy ; introduced spectroscopic photography into astronomy.

Hugh Capet. *See* **Capet, Hugh.**

Hughes, Charles Evans (1862–1948). Amer. lawyer and statesman ; defeated for presidency by Woodrow Wilson (1916) ; Chief Justice of U.S.A. (1930).

Hughes, David Edward (1831–1900). Anglo-Amer. inventor, b. Eng. (printing telegraph, microphone, 2162, 3174, and induction balance).

Hughes, Hugh Price (1847–1902). Welsh Wesleyan minister and ardent social reformer ; he founded the " Methodist Times."

Hughes, Sir Sam (1853–1921). Canadian soldier and political leader ; as minister of militia and defence was responsible for raising and equipping a large part of the 600,000 men that Canada contributed in the 1st World War.

Hughes, Thomas (1822–96). Eng. author and social reformer ; entered parl. 1865 ; he was a co. court judge, but is best known for his books " Tom Brown's School Days " and " Tom Brown at Oxford."

Hughes, William Morris (b. 1864). Australian statesman. b. in Wales ; prominent labour leader ; Prime Minister of Commonwealth from 1915 to 1923 ; in Cabinets of 1934 and 1937, on latter occasion as Minister for External Affairs ; in War Cabinet (Sept. 1939) appointed Attorney-General and Minister for Industry ; C.H., 1941.

Hugh of Lincoln. Eng. boy said to have been put to death by Jews at Lincoln in 13th cent. in mockery of the death of Christ.

Hugli (hōō'-glē) or **Hooghli.** The westernmost arm of the r. Ganges, 660, 1417.

Hugo (hū'-gō). Victor Marie (1802–85). Fr. writer, author of " Les Misérables." 1381, 1650, 2404.

Huguenots (hū'-ge-nots). Fr. Protestants of 16th and 17th cents., 1366, 1650 ; Henry II begins persecution, 1613 ; Coligny, 870 ; St. Bartholomew's Massacre, 870, 2131 ; Henry of Navarre and the Edict of Nantes, 1613 ; Richelieu and, 2778 ; settlements in N. Amer., 1651.

Hulaku Khan (d. 1265). Mongolian leader, first independent ruler of Persia.

Hulbert, Jack (b. 1892). Eng. actor ; after successes in musical comedy and revue (" Clowns in Clover," " Folly to be Wise "), took to film acting (" Jack's the Boy," " Sunshine Susie," etc.) ; married Cicely Courtneidge ; later, producer of musical comedies.

Hull. City and spt. in E. Yorkshire on r. Humber ; pop. 287,300 ; official name Kingston-upon-Hull ; shipping and fishing industries, 1168, 1307, 1651 ; bombed 1940–41, 1651.

Hull, Cordell (b. 1871). Amer. politician ; became Secretary of State under Franklin Roosevelt in 1933 ; resigned Nov. 1944.

" Human Comedy." Series of Balzac's novels, 353.

Hu'manists. Classical scholars of the Renaissance, 2764.

Human Rights, Declaration of. International bill drawn up by a U.N. commission (chairman Mrs. E. Roosevelt) and adopted by the U.N. Dec. 10, 1948, stating in 31 articles the fundamental minimum rights of every human being.

Human torpedo, 3228.

Humber. Estuary formed by the Trent and Ouse in N.E. Eng., 1162, 1168. 1952.

Hum'bert I (1844–1900). King of Italy ; succeeded 1878 ; popularly called " Humbert the Good " because of courage and generosity in plague and earthquake ; fostered policy of colonial expansion ; assassinated, 3319 ; street in Rome named after, 2799.

Humble-bee or **bumble-bee,** *plate facing* 392 ; nest, 392.

Hum'boldt, Alexander, Baron von (1769–1859). Ger. naturalist, explorer, founder of modern science of physical geography, and contributor to nearly every branch of science (" Kosmos ").

Humboldt, Karl Wilhelm, Baron von (1767–1835). Ger. philologist, statesman, and writer, first to define philosophy of speech ; brother of Alexander von Humboldt.

Humboldt's woolly monkey. A spider monkey of Brazil, 2209.

Hume, David (1711–76). Scottish philosopher, historian, and political economist. (" A Treatise of Human Nature," 1737 ; " Essays—Moral, Social, and Political " ; first part of " A History of England," 1754, other parts in 1756, 1759 and 1762 ; " An Inquiry Concerning the Principles of Morals " ; a criticism of " Miracles.")

Hume Dam, Australia, 961.

Humidity, moisture content, 1243 ; of atmosphere, 2149 ; affected by trees, 3246 ; in houses, 1598 ; how measured, 1678.

Humming-bird, 1651, 1652.

Humpback whale, 3372, 3373.

Humperdinck (hoom'-per-dink), **Engelbert** (1854–1921), Ger. composer, chiefly known for his opera " Hänsel und Gretel."

Humphrey pump, a gas-explosion water pump, 1421, 1423.

Humus, soil, 2999.

Hunan'. An inland prov. of China ; 105,000 sq. m. ; pop. 28,092,000 ; cap. Changsha ; immense coal and iron deposits, also yields wolfram and antimony ; one of the chief tea-producing regions of the world ; during 2nd World War it was scene of Japanese offensives, 1941–45.

Hundred. A division of Eng. and Welsh counties, supposed to have contained a hundred families originally.

" Hundred Days," period between date of Napoleon's return to Paris from Elba, March 20, 1815, and the restoration of Louis XVIII, June 28 ; 2278.

Hundredweight (cwt.). A unit of weight. *See* **Weights and Measures,** *f-i.*

Hundred Years' War (1337–1453), between England and France, 1365, 1652, 2377 ; archers in, 210 ; battle of Crécy, 1652 ; battle of Agincourt, 76, 1653 ; capture of Calais, 1633 ; Joan of Arc, 1831 ; results, 1365, 1652 ; Froissart's " Chronicles," 1399 ; Philip VI, 2567.

" Hungarian Rhapsodies." Musical compositions by Liszt, 1964.

Hungary. A republic in cent. Europe ; 35,000 sq. m. ; pop. 9,320,000 ; 1654 ; plates f. 1656, 1657 ; map, 1654 ; agriculture, 1233, 1654, 2741 ; cap. Budapest, 320, 600, 1656 ; Carpathian Mts., 704 ; children, 798 ; r. Danube, 972 ; folk-dancing, 1334 ; minerals, 704 ; stamp, 3075 ; trade, 973 ; types, 1655.
History : Otto I defeats Magyars, 2459 ; becomes Hapsburg possession, 1656 ; Turks conquer, 1656, 3264 ; Revolution (of 1848), 319, 1656, 1874 ; Dual Monarchy, 1656 ; in 1914–18 War and Peace, 1656 ; joined Axis in 1940 ; surrendered Dec. 1944, 3424 ; communist coup d'état, 1657 ; trial of Cardinal Mindszenty, *f-i.*

Huns. Barbarian people of cent. Asia who invaded Europe in 4th and 5th cents., 1237, 1487, 1657.

Hun'stanton (hun'-ston). Watering place in Norfolk, on the E. side of the Wash ; pop. 2,700 ; 2376.

Hunt, Leigh (1784–1859). Eng. poet and essayist, friend of Byron, Keats, and Shelley ; sentenced to two years' imprisonment in 1813 for a libel on Prince Regent during which he wrote " The Story of Rimini " (" Abou Ben Adhem " ; " Wit and Humour," " Autobiography ").

Hunt, William Holman (1827–1910). Eng. painter, who, with Rossetti and Millais, founded the Pre-Raphaelite school or brotherhood as a protest against the Eng. art of his period ; 2476, 2681 ; " The Light of the World," 1825.

Hunter, John (1728–93). Brit. physiologist and surgeon, one of world's greatest anatomists, 151, 2134 ; introduced experiment into study of physiology ; bequeathed to the nation a valuable surgical museum, which is now part of the Royal College of Surgeons' Museum.

Hunter, William (1718–83), Br.t. anatomist and obstetrical surgeon, brother of John Hunter ; physician-extraordinary to Queen Charlotte ; 151.

Hunter, Sir William Wilson (1840–1900). Brit. historian, geographer and statistician ; organized the first Indian census in 1872 and produced the " Statistical Survey of India " (128 volumes), which formed the basis of the " Imperial Gazetteer of India."

Hunting, 1657 ; Assyrian (anc.), 106, 331 ; dogs, 1026 ; falconry or " hawking," 1258 ; fox-hunting, 1162, 1659 ; otter-hunting, 1658 ; horns used, 1644.

Hunt'ingdon, co. tn. of Huntingdonshire ; brewing, agric. trade ; birthplace of Oliver Cromwell, 933 ; pop. 5,290 ; 1658.

Huntingdonshire. A small inland co. in E. of England ; 366 sq. m. ; pop. 56,200 ; agric., grazing, brewing ; co. tn. Huntingdon ; 1658.

Hunting spider, 3065.

Huntington. West Virginia, U.S.A. Commercial and industrial city on Ohio r. ; pop. 78,800 ; Marshall College ; rly. workshops, foundries, lumber mills.

Huntsman, Benjamin (1704–76). Eng. inventor and steel mfr., 2941.

Hunyadi (hoon'-yah-dē), **Janos** or **John** (c. 1387–1456). National hero of Hungary, warrior and statesman ; his defence of Belgrade against Turks in 1456 made Hungary independent for 70 years ; 1656 ; and Turks, 3264.

Hupeh (hōō-pā). A cent. prov. of China ; 80,000 sq. m. ; pop. 24,659,000 ; cap. Wuchang ; chief city Hankow ; coal, iron.

Hurdling. Running and jumping races over short distances, in which a series of ten flights of hurdles is set, 289, 288.

Hurling. National game of Eire, 1660.

Hurlingham. Dist. and Sports Club of s.w. London ; club h.q. of Brit. polo, 2651 ; N. part taken over by L.C.C. as open space in 1948.

Huron, Lake. Second largest of the Great Lakes of the St. Lawrence system, 1515 ; map, 1515.

Hurricane. High wind with a velocity of over 75 m.p.h., 3100.

Hurstmonceux, Sussex. Castle, 218 ; home for Greenwich observatory since 1947, 2411, 2413.

" Huskies." Eskimo dogs, 1026.

Huss, John (about 1369–1415). Bohemian religious reformer and martyr, 1660, 1661.

Hussein or **Husein.** *See* **Hasan.**

Hussein ibn Ali (hoos-sīn'-ib'-n-ah'-li), (1856–1931). King of the Hejaz, 200.

Hussite Wars (1419–34), 487, 1661.

Hutchinson, Arthur Stuart Menteth (b. 1879). Eng. novelist. (" Once Aboard the Lugger " ; " The Happy Warrior " ; " If Winter Comes.").

Huth, Henry (1815–78). Brit. banker and book collector ; bequeathed part of his library to the British Museum.

Hutten, Ulrich von (1488–1523). Ger. humanist reformer and satirical writer, friend of Luther.

Hutton, James (1726–97). Scot. landowner and geologist ; propounded modern view that existing land forms were developed gradually by same processes that are at work today (" Theory of the Earth ").

Hutton, Leonard (b. 1916). Eng. cricketer ; opening batsman for Yorkshire and England ; in 1938 against Australia at the Oval broke world test match record by scoring 364 in 13 hrs. 20 mins. ; in 1949 made 3,429 runs, inc. 1,294 in June (record for one month).

Huxley, Aldous Leonard (b. 1894). English novelist and essayist ; (" Antic Hay " ; " Point Counter Point " ; " Brave New World " ; " Eyeless in Gaza " ; " Ends and Means" ; " Ape and Essence"). Play " The Gioconda Smile " at Wyndham's 1948 ; 1216, 1662.

Huxley, Julian Sorell (b. 1887). English biologist, 1662 ; first Director-General U.N. Educational, Scientific and Cultural Org., 1946–49.

Huxley, Leonard (1860–1933). Editor of " Cornhill Magazine," **1662.**

Huxley, Thomas Henry (1825–95). Eng. biologist and essayist ; **1661.**

Huygens (hī'-genz), **Christian** (1629–95). Dutch mathematician, astronomer, and physicist ; applied pendulum to the clock, 2543 ; improved the telescope ; theory that light consisted of ether vibrations, 1941, 2594.

Huysmans (ēs-mahn'), **Joris Karl** (1848–1907). Fr. realistic novelist (" À Rebours " ; " En Route " ; " La Cathédrale ").

Huysum (hī'-sum), **Jan van** (1682–1749). Dutch painter ; his " Vase with Flowers," 2332.

Hwang-Ho. 2nd largest r. in China (2,600 m.), **1662** ; Shantung built by, 2938 ; in China-Jap. War, 1662.

Hy'acinth. Plant of the lily family, **1663** ; bluebell and wild, 479 ; gem variety of zircon, 3444.

Hyacin'thus, in Gk. myth., youth accidentally killed by Apollo, 1663.

Hyades (hī'-a-dēz). A V-shaped constellation, situation, chart, 895.

Hy'att, John Wesley (1837–1920). Amer. inventor ; probably his greatest contribution to science was a method of purifying large bodies of water.

Hy'brid. A plant or animal produced by cross-breeding of different species or varieties, 621 ; in fruit-growing, 1401.

Hyde, Douglas (1860–1949). Irish historian and poet. Elected 1938 first President of Eire. Professor of Modern Irish, National Univ. of Ireland (1909–32). President of Gaelic League (1893–1915). To him revival of Gaelic is largely due.

Hyde, Edward. *See* **Clarendon, Earl of.**

Hyde Park. Open space in W. London, covering 361 acres ; the chief entrances are from Hyde Park Corner at the S.E. corner, and the Marble Arch at the N.E. corner ; site of 1851 Great Exhibition when Crystal Palace was here ; Park Lane on E. side, 2015 ; Rotten Row is used by riders, and " Speakers' Corner," in N.E., by impromptu orators, 2015.

Hyderabad (hī-da-ra-bahd'). Largest state of India ; 82,313 sq. m. ; pop. 16,330,000 ; **1663,** *map, 1702* ; occupied by Indian forces, 1664 ; Joined Indian Union in 1949.

Hyderabad. Cap. of Hyderabad state, India : pop. about 740,000 ; 1664.

Hyder Ali. *See* **Haider Ali.**

Hy'dra, in Gk. myth., nine-headed monster, slain by Hercules, 1664.

Hydra. A primitive water animal, **1664,** *1665.*

Hydrangea (hī-drān'-ja). A flowering shrub, **1665.**

Hydrau'lic cement. Any cementing substance which hardens after wetting.

Hydraulic dredge. One that excavates under water by suction, 1047.

Hydraulic lift. One that operates by hydraulic power. 1937.

Hydraulic machinery. Machinery which uses water as a power source or to apply power to work, **1665,** *1666* ; lifts, 1936.

Hydraulic mining. Excavation of surface ore by washing down with powerful streams of water ; practised in gold mining.

Hydraulic press. Machine using hydraulic power to apply pressure, *1666.*

Hydraulic ram. Form of water pump, 1667, 2703, *2704.*

Hydraulics. Science of liquids in motion, **1665** ; Archimedes' screw, 210.

Hydrocar'bons. Compounds consisting of hydrogen and carbon, 1673 ; fats and oils, 1263 ; in illuminating gas, 1423 ; paraffin wax, 3359 ; petroleum, 2429 ; rubber, 2838.

Hydrochlo'ric or **muriatic acid.** An acid composed of hydrogen and chlorine in equal parts, largely used in manufactures, 1667 ; gas produced by sunlight, 2574 ; Leblanc process, 2997 ; in vanadium process, 3303.

Hydrocyan'ic or **prussic acid.** A poisonous compound of hydrogen, carbon, and nitrogen in equal parts, 947 ; causes instant death, 2638, 2664.

Hydro-electric installations, 1669 ; power from, 135, 958, 2673 ; turbines, 3258 ; at Lake Victoria, 3321.

Hydro-extractor. A centrifugal drying machine used in laundries, 1900.

Hydrofluor'ic acid. A compound of hydrogen and fluorine in equal parts ; etches glass.

Hy'drogen. The lightest known chemical element ; the name hydrogen, meaning water producer, was given to the gas by Lavoisier ; the gas is colourless and odourless and non-poisonous, but highly explosive when mixed with air or oxygen ; **1673** ; in acids, 20 ; in atmosphere, 88 ; atoms in sun, 1161 ; in gas, 1423 ; " heavy," 998 ; industrial uses, 1674 ; liquefaction, 1419 ; in ionization of salt, 1738 ; from petroleum, 2430 ; for cooling alternators, 2677 ; essential to plant growth, 2995 ; isotopes of, 296 ; properties, 775 ; in thermometer, 3200 ; used in balloons, 347.

Hydrogenation. Process of hardening oils, and of obtaining oils from coal, etc., 857, 1674.

Hydrogen chloride. Same as **Hydrochloric acid.**

Hydrogen-ion concentration (symbol pH), 21.

Hydrogen peroxide. A compound of hydrogen and oxygen in equal parts ; bleaching properties, 470 ; in rocket bomb, 2792.

Hydrogen sulphide. A vile-smelling, gaseous compound of hydrogen and sulphur.

Hydrographic surveying. Surveying of oceans, lakes and rivers.

Hydrolog'ical cycle, 1316.

Hydrol'ysis. Reaction of a chemical compound with water so that it splits up to form two compounds, one with the hydrogen of the water, the other with the hydroxyl, 20 ; of starch, 3082.

Hydrom'eter. Instrument for determining specific gravity or density of liquids, **1674,** 3054 ; for testing spirits, 3067.

Hydrophobia (hī-drō-fō'-bi-a) or **rabies.** Disease caused by an unknown virus in saliva of infected animals, and inoculated by their bites ; prevented by Pasteur treatment, 2528.

Hy'drophone. Device for listening under water ; used to detect submarines.

Hy'drophytes. Plants which live in watery situations.

Hy'droplane. A type of motor-boat which skims lightly over the water ; the word is also sometimes wrongly used to signify " seaplane."

Hydropon'ics. The growing of crops in balanced chemical solutions, without soil ; suitable for cattle fodder, also fruit and vegetables ; used for Allied occupation troops in Japan after Second World War.

Hydrosphere, of earth, 1067.

Hydrostatics. Science of pressure and other phenomena in liquids at rest ; law of floating bodies, 211.

Hydrot'ropism. The tendency of plant structures to grow towards water, 2623.

Hydrox'ide. A compound containing one or more elements in combination with a hydroxyl group, 120 ; of potassium, 2664.

Hydrozo'a. A class of primitive coelenterate animals ; coral-forming types, 908 ; hydras, 1664 ; jellyfish, *1817, 1818.*

Hyena (hī-ē'-na). A dog-like carrion-eating animal, 1675.

Hygieia (hī-jē'-a). In Gk. myth., goddess of health.

Hygiene, 1675 ; athletics, 287 ; diet, 1338 ; exercise, 1675, 3589 ; heating and ventilation, 1597 ; humidity and health, 1243 ; physiology, 2598 ; public water supply, 3348 ; sanitation and sewerage, 1329 ; sleep, 2983 ; of teeth, 1675. *See also* **Medicine and Surgery ; Physiology ;** and chief topics above by name.

Hygrom'eter. Instrument for measuring moisture in air, 1677.

Hygrostat. Instrument controlling humidity, 1678.

Hyksos (hik'-sos), or **Shepherd Kings.** Dynasty of foreign rulers of Egypt, 1118.

Hymen. In Greek mythology, the god of marriage, from whose name the word " hymeneal " (meaning pertaining to marriage) derives.

Hymenop'tera. An order of membranous-winged insects, *1732* ; ants, 165 ; bees, 390 ; wasps and hornets, 3345 ;

Hymet'tus, Mt. Peak of Attica, 3,370 ft. ; famous for honey in anc. times ; 284.

Hymns, 1678.

Hynd, John Burns (b. 1902). Chan. of Duchy of Lancaster, 1945–47. Min. of Pensions, Apl. to Oct. 1947.

Hynd'man, Henry Mayers (1842–1921). Eng. Social Democrat (" Evolution of Revolution ").

Hyne, C. J. Cutcliffe (1866–1944). Eng. novelist (" The New Eden " ; " Adventures of Captain Kettle " ; " Further Adventures ").

Hypatia (hī-pā'-shi-a) (c. A.D. 370–415). A Gk. woman mathematician and philosopher of Alexandria, murdered by Christian mob ; the heroine of Kingsley's " Hypatia."

Hyperbola (hī-pêr'-bo-la). The name given in geometry to a curve so drawn that any point on it is distant from two fixed points called foci by a difference which is constant for all points.

Hyperbole (hī-pêr'-bo-li). A figure of speech, 1271.

Hyperbore'ans. In Gk. myth., people dwelling in land beyond north wind ; connected with worship of Apollo.

Hyperion (hī-pē'-ri-on). In Gk. myth., a Titan, father of Helios the sun god ; later, sometimes the sun god himself ; subject of poem by Keats.

Hypermetamor'phosis. The type of insect growth in which the larva undergoes more than one transformation before becoming a pupa, 398, 1729.

Hypermetro'pia, or far-sightedness, 1254.

Hyphen, use of, 2705.

Hyp'notism. A condition resembling normal sleep, except that the hypnotized subject may retain some of his waking faculties ; and psychoanalysis, 2697.

Hy'po. A commercial name for sodium thiosulphate, 3117 ; often sold under incorrect name of sodium hyposulphite (*see next entry*).

Hyposul'phite of sodium. A salt of sodium and hyposulphurous acid ; name often applied incorrectly to sodium thiosulphate (" hypo ") used in photography ; 2997.

Hyrax. A mammal, *2074.*

Hyssop. A garden herb with leaves from which a tea is made for use in the treatment of lung diseases. The hyssop mentioned in the Bible as a plant used for sprinkling purposes, is a different plant.

THE letter I is one of the simplest in form, but was not always so. The Egyptians represented it by two parallel lines ⳡ and the scribes wrote it like this ⳝ. The Phoenicians gave it the form ⳡ and called it *Yod*. As written by the Hebrews (ⳝ) *Yod* was such a little insignificant letter that its name came to be used for the smallest part, the least bit of anything (our word "jot"). Thus Christ is quoted as saying, "Till heaven and earth pass, one jot or one tittle shall in no wise pass from the law, till all be fulfilled " (Matt. v, 18). The Greek I (*Iota*) is used similarly and was first written as a zigzag like a thunderbolt, but it finally straightened to upright I, which the Romans adopted. *Yod* was first a consonant with a sound like our *y*; in Latin it was a vowel and a consonant. As a vowel, its name and its long sound rhymed with " bee," and it was not until the late 16th cent. that its long sound in English became *i*.

Iago (ē-ah'-gō). Villain in Shakespeare's " Othello," 2457.

Iambus (I-am'-*bus*), in poetry, 2635.

Ib'adan. Tn. and dist. of the w. prov. of Nigeria, Africa; fair pastoral and agricultural land; Ibadan is largest native tn. in w. Africa (pop. 327,284); 119 m. by rly. N.E. of Lagos; trade in ground nuts, palm oil and kernels, cotton products, hides.

Ibañez (ē-bah'-nyeth), **Vicente Blasco** (1867–1928). Sp. novelist; author of "The Four Horsemen of the Apocalypse," 2403, 3051.

Ibans, or Sea Dyaks. People of Borneo, 525, *788.*

Iberia (I-bē'-ri-*a*). Anc. dist. between Caucasus Mts. and Armenia, now part of Georgia; also anc. name of Spain.

Ibe'rian Peninsula. In s.w. Europe, 1232, *map, 3030.* See **Portugal**; **Spain.**

Iberian people. Anc. race, ancestors of modern Basques, 3032.

I'bex. A type of mountain goat, 1079.

I'bis. A wading bird (order *Herodiones*), 3007; sacred ibis of Eg., *plate f. 3100, 3099.*

Ibn Sa'ud (b. 1880). Arab. ruler; enlightened dictator of Nejd and Hejaz from 1926, he aimed at union of Arabia under one king and one faith; in 1932 became King of Saudi Arabia, 201; invited Brit. military mission Jan. 1947.

Ibrahim Pasha (ē-brah-hēm' pa-shah') (1789–1848). Egyptian general, adopted son of Mehemet Ali, viceroy of Eg.; Turkish commander (1826–28) in Gk. war for independence.

Ib'sen, Henrik (1828–1906). Norwegian dramatist, **1679**; contrasted with Björnson, 462; father of drama of protest, 1040; in Scandinavian literature, 2881.

Icarus (ik'-*a*-*rus*). In Gk. myth., son of Daedalus, 955, **1680**, *1681.*

Ice, 1680; artificial, 1392; crystals, 1564; physics of freezing and melting, 1391. See **Snow.**

Ice Age, 1680; Agassiz helps establish theory, 75; in Europe, *1682*, 2392; g ologic era, 1432; in N. Amer., **1680,** 2384.

Ice axe, for mountaineering, *2247.*

Ice Barrier, Great Antarctica, 173, *175.*

Icebergs, 1682, *170*; in Labrador current, 291.

Ice-cap. A type of glacier, 1468; Antarctic, 173.

Ice cream, value as food, 2174.

Ice hockey, 1683, *1684.*

Iceland. Isl. of N. Atlantic; 39,700 sq. m.; pop. 130,000; **1684**; *map, 1684*; cod fishery, 1299; geysers, 1459; union with Denmark, 2880; occupied by Allies during 2nd World War, independence declared in 1944, 1685.

Icelandic literature, 1685.

Iceland moss. A lichen, 1933, 2239.

Iceland spar, transparent calcite, 1684.

Iceni (I-sē'-nī). Anc. Eng. people, 479.

Ichneumon (ik-nū'-mon). Another name for the mongoose.

Ichneumon flies, 1685; egg-laying habits, 1095.

Ichthyology (ik-thi-ol'-*o*-ji). The science of fishes. See **Fish.**

Ichthyosaurs (ik'-thi-ō-sawrz). Prehistoric aquatic reptiles, 164, *2681,* 2767.

Icon. See **Ikon.**

Iconium. See **Konia.**

Iconoclast (I-kon'-ō-klast). Literally an image-breaker; in Church history 8th-9th cents., member of Byzantine party opposed to use of images in worship; today one who shatters tradition; 638.

Ictinus (ik-tī'-n*us*) (5th cent. B.C.). Gk. architect, designer of the Parthenon; temple at Bassae, *1530.*

Ida, Mt. range of Asia Minor, 30 m. S.E. of plain of Troy, 3252.

Ida, Mt., Crete, now called Psilorati. Fabled birthplace of Zeus, 927.

I'daho. One of the N.W. states of U.S.A., 83,557 sq. m.; pop. 524,800. **1685.**

Iddesleigh, H. Stafford Northcote, 1st Earl of (1818–87). Brit. statesman; as Chancellor of the Exchequer he introduced the national debt sinking fund; raised to peerage in 1885, in which year he became First Lord of the Treasury.

Ide alism. A philosophical school, 2572.

Ideographic (I-de-o-graf'-ik), or **picture writing,** 125; Chinese, 808; Jap., 1809.

Ides. In the Rom. calendar, 3rd "landmark day" in the month; in March, May, July, and Oct., ides fell on the 15th, other months on 13th; Caesar told to "beware the ides of March," 653.

Idiocy. Grade of mental deficiency.

Iduna or Idun (ē-dōō'-na). In Norse myth., goddess of youth and spring; "Apples of Iduna," story, 190, 2881.

'Idylls of the King.' Series of poems by Tennyson based on legends of King Arthur and his knights, 1413, 2830, 3187.

" If." Short poem with a stirring message to youth written by Kipling.

Igarka. Siberian spt. on r. Yenisei; pop. 20,000; 2967.

Igloo (ig'-lōō). Eskimo hut, 1223.

Igna'tius, St. (d. *c* A.D. 116). Bishop of Antioch, Apostolic Father, and eager martyr; legend says he was disciple of the Apostle John.

Ignatius of Loyola. See **Loyola, Ignatius de.**

Igneous (ig'-ni-*us*) **rocks.** Geological class of, 1432, 2795; granite, 1499.

Ignis fatuus (ig'-nis fat'-ū-us) (Latin "foolish fire "), or "will-o'-the-wisp," flickering pale-bluish light caused by marsh gas.

Igni'tion, electric, in internal combustion engines, 1736, 2243.

Ignition point. Temperature at which a substance will catch fire, 1278.

Ignitron, an electric device, 1138; in rectifiers, 2751.

Igorots. Mountain tribes of Philippines, *2568.*

Iguana (i-gwah'-na). A lizard, *1686*; as food, 1974; chameleon, 750; horned toad, 1974.

Igua'nodon. A prehistoric reptile, 2678.

Iguassu or Iguazú (ē-gwah-sōō'). River in s. Brazil; rises near Atlantic, flows w. 800 m. to Paraná r.; falls 20 m. above mouth 215 ft. high, broken into 20 or more falls separated by rocky isls., among finest in world.

Ijssel, r. of the Netherlands, 87 m. long; distrib. of the Rhine, flows

---

from Arnhem N. and N.E. to Ijssel-meer at Kampen; 3416.

Ijsselmeer or Ijssel Lake, or Ysselmeer. Fresh-water lake of the Netherlands, 470 sq. m.; remnant of the Zuider Zee; *960,* 2318, *2319.*

Ikhenaton or Akhenaton (Amenhotep IV) (reigned about 1367–1350 B.C.). Egypt. King of the XVIIIth dynasty, son of Amenhotep III.

Ikhwan. Arabian sect, the Puritans of the Moslem world, 201.

Ikon (I'-kon). An image; in the Gk. church a venerated image of a sacred person; Russian art and, *2855.*

I'lex. Name often given to holm oak, *Quercus ilex*; also generic name of holly, 1636, 2409.

" Il'iad, The." Gk. epic poem of Trojan War, 1637; stories from, 19, 1603, 1638.

Iliffe, Edward Mauger Iliffe, 1st Baron (b. 1877). Brit. newspaper proprietor, 1683.

Il'ium. Name for anc. Troy. See **Troy.**

Il'keston. Tn. in Derbyshire, 9 m. N.E. of Derby; coal-mining; lace hosiery; pop. 32,800; 995.

Illampu, Mt. See **Sorata.**

Illimani. Volcanic peak of Andes; in Bolivia about 30 m. S.E. of La Paz, 153.

Illinium (Il). A metallic element of the rare earth group; of unknown atomic weight. See **Rare Earths.**

Illinois (il-i-noi'). A cent. state of the U.S.A.; 56,400 sq. m.; pop. 7,900,000, **1687.**

Illinois River. Chief r. of Ill., U.S.A., flows 500 m. s.w. to Mississippi r.; exploration, 1894, 2192.

Illuminated manuscripts, 511, 1177, 2090.

Illusions, of motion in cinematography, 828; mirages, 2190; of touch, 3231.

Illyria (i-lir'-i-*a*). Indefinite region on eastern coast of Adriatic Sea.

Illyrians. Ancestors of modern Albanians, 100.

Ilmenite, an ore of titanium, 3217.

Iloilo (ē-lō-ē'-lō), Philippines. Spt., Panay Isl.; pop. 90,480.

" Il Pensero'so " (" the pensive man "). Ode by Milton to "divinest Melancholy," celebrating peace. leisure, contemplation, 2176.

" Il Trovatore " (ēl-trō-vah-tor'-ā) (" the troubadour "). Opera by Verdi, 2440, 3315.

I'lus. In Gk. myth., founder of Troy or Ilion; grandfather of Priam.

Images. Formed by lenses, 1924, 2163, 3178; in photography, 2577; in reflection and refraction, 1940.

Imago (i-mā'-gō). Term used to denote a mature insect.

Imari or Hizen ware. One of finest Japanese porcelains, 1809.

Imbecility. Grade of mental deficiency.

Imber Court, Surrey, Eng.; training estab. for mounted police, 2648.

Imbros. Greek isl. in Aegean Sea, near Dardanelles; 87 sq. m.; anc. Gk. colony, later Turkish possession until 1920; returned to Turkey in 1923.

" Immaculate Conception." Painting by Murillo, 2258.

Immaculate Conception. Dogma of. established by Pius IX, 2615.

Immanuel or **Emmanuel.** The divinely appointed deliverer foretold by Isaiah (vii. 14) and recognized by the Evangelist in Jesus (Matt. i, 23).

Immigra'tion. Entrance into a country for permanent residence; the opposite of emigration.

Immortal'ity. Egyptian belief in, 1114, 2904.

Immu'nity, from disease, 180.

Impeach'ment. The prosecution by a government of one of its civil officers; in England the House of Commons prosecutes before the House of Lords; an historic instance was the impeachment of Warren Hastings.

Impe'dance, in electricity, 1133.

Imperative mood, of verbs, 3314.

Impera'tor. Ger. ocean liner which became the Cunarder Berengaria.

Imperator. Rom. title of honour.

Imperial Airways. Brit. air transport company, 48; Empire flying boat, 33. In 1939 formed with British Airways public corporation known as British Overseas Airways.

Imperial bushel, dry measure (2,218·192 cubic inches).

Imperial Chemical Industries (I.C.I.); industrial combine formed in 1926; petrol from coal, 2429; development of antrycide (q.v. in f-i.).

Imperial College of Tropical Agriculture, Trinidad. Founded 1921 as W. Indian Agric. Coll., at St. Augustine, nr. Port of Spain, Trinidad; centre from 1929 for post-graduate training in tropical agriculture and research.

Imperial Conference, 1492.

Imperial gallon. A measure of capacity (4·546 litres).

Imperial Institute. London, s.w., erected as the national memorial of the jubilee of Queen Victoria; the work of the Institute is to display and illustrate the natural resources and industries of the Empire and to supply information about it.

Imperialism, in modern politics, policy of national territorial expansion; Disraeli, 1018; Ger. tendencies, 1447; Japan, 1800.

Imperial standard wire gauge, 3391.

Imperial War Graves Commission. Instituted in 1918 to maintain permanently the graves of British soldiers killed during the 1st World War. Continued for 2nd World War.

Imperial War Museum. In Lambeth, London, 2260.

"Implacable," H.M.S., an aircraft carrier, 2300.

Im'phal. Cap. of Manipur state, India; pop. 80,000; isolated by Jap. advance, but held as key point March to June 22, 1944, by Allied 4th Corps, provisioned by airlift; relieved by 33rd corps and became Allied milit., air, and supply base; 3424.

Impres'sionism, in painting, **1687,** 2476; Cézanne's work, 749; influence of Japanese art, 1812; in French art, 1378; in music, 1689, 2265, 2436.

Impulse turbines, 1670, 1671, 3258.

Incandescent lamp, 1134; tungsten, 3253; why vacuum is necessary, 3301.

Incanta'tions. Magic words, 2057.

Incas (ing'-kaz). Anc. S. Amer. race, **1689,** 1083, 2560; architecture, 1688, 1690; and Polynesians, 2471; domesticated llamas, 1975; Pizarro conquers, 3025.

In'cense. Aromatic mixtures which yield a pleasing perfume when burning; made of spices and resins, 2550, 3060.

Inch. Twelfth part of a linear foot.

Inch'cape, James Lyle Mackay, 1st Earl (1852-1932); shipping magnate; in 1919 he took over the Government's standard ships and sold them, realizing £35,000,000 for the Exchequer; baron (1911), viscount (1924), and earl (1929).

Inchcape Rock. Dangerous reef off Firth of Tay, Scot.; also known as Bell Rock; submerged at spring tides; lighthouse built here in 1807; formerly bell tolled to warn mariners; subject of Southey's poem.

Inci'sor teeth, 3163.

Inclined plane, in mechanics; probably used in building pyramids, 2128.

Income tax. A direct tax much used in modern countries, including Britain, as a means for defraying the increasing expenses of government with least hardship to individuals, 3949; P.A.Y.E. (" Pay As You Earn ") introduced April 1944.

Incuba'tion, of chickens, 2671.

In'cubator, 2671.

Incunabula (in-kū-nab'-ū-la). Term applied to very early printed books.

Indem'nity. Protection against or compensation for loss or damage; especially compensation paid by defeated power after war; Franco-Prussian War, 1384; Ger. after 1st World War, 1450, 3414.

Independence, Declaration of, signed in Philadelphia, 145, 2566; and United States, 3291.

Independence, War of American, 144; Franklin, 1386; Fr. aid, 1366, 1884; George III's attitude, 1441; Lafayette, 1884; Stamp Act, 1386; Washington, 3342.

Independence Day. See **Fourth of July.**

Independence Hall, Philadelphia, U.S.A., 2566.

Independent Labour Party (I.L.P.). British Socialist organization, founded in 1893 by J. Keir Hardie and others, 1875, 2996.

Independents. Older name of Congregationalists, Free Church denomination in which each local body is practically independent.

Index, cephalic or **cranial,** 2724.

Index Librorum Prohibitorum. Catalogue of prohibited books in Rom. Cath. Church.

Index number. Average of price, 2203.

India. The central of 3 peninsulas in s. part of Asia; 1,800,000 sq. m.; pop. 389,000,000; **1691,** 1693-1700; map, 1702; animals, 270, 1696, 1701, 1703; caste, 1626, 1691, 1692, 1707; children, 786, 802; Dominions, 1717 (see chief cities and political divisions below); Fr. possessions in, 1692; government, 1717; illiteracy, 1691, languages, 1703; literature, 1713; native states, 1716; nautch girls, 1699; painting and minor arts, 1708; people, 1626, 1701; population, 264; religions, 600, 1626, 1703 (see also Buddhism; Mahomedanism; Parsees); reverence for animals, 601, 859, 1703, 1708, 2211; sculpture, 1708, 1712.

Architecture: 269, 1709-1711, cave temples, 1712, 1664; Great Mosque (Delhi), 987, 1706; Hall of the Winds (Jaipur), 1711; Kutb Minar tower, 988; Mogul Structures at Delhi, plate f. 988; Taj Mahal, 3147. 3148.

Chief cities and states: Assam, 273; Benares, 411 Bengal 413; Bihar, 428; Bombay, 496-497; Calcutta, 660; Central Provinces, 744; Delhi, 987; Gwalior, 1559; Hyderabad, 1663; Karachi, 1848; Kashmir, 1848; Lucknow, 2035; Madras, 2052; Mysore, 2270; Orissa, 2453; Punjab, 2705; Sind, 2974; United Provinces, 3284.

Geography and industries: agriculture, 1707; Cashmere shawls and carpets, 705, 1848; climate, 1626, 1692; cotton mfrs., 413, 496, 920, 3066, 3192; the Deccan, 1692; gems, 1009, 1427; gold, 1479; Himalaya Mts., 1626; Hindustan, 1692; indigo, 1718; irrigation, 1417, 1721; jute, 1844; Khyber Pass, 55, 56; mfrs., 1708 (see also under chief cities and political divisions); mica, 2160; minerals, 1708; opium, 2442; polo, 2651; railways, 1708; rice, 2775; rivers, 265, 412, 1417, 1691, 1692, 1721; rugs, 706; silk, 2970, 2972; spices, 2547, 3060;

sugar, 3112; tea, 265, 3159, 3160, 3161; teak, 3162; vegetation, 1692, 1701.

History, **1714;** Aryan conquest and establishment of Hinduism, 1714; Alexander's invasion 106; Tamerlane's partial conquest, 2206; Mogul empire, 1714, 2206; rise and fall of Fr. power, 1714; Clive and the Seven Years' War, 660, 842, 2925; Hastings and establishment of Brit. rule, 1581; Mutiny of 1857 (Sepoy Rebellion), 1714, 2035, 3278; Victoria empress, 1019, 1715, 3320; 1914-1918 War, 1715, 1939-45 War 1716, 3420; partitioned, 1717, 3283, last viceroy, 2248; Ind. Imp; dropped from Brit. coins, 2203 Pakistan, 2479.

Art and letters, 1708.

India, Republic of, 1692; map, 1702; formation, 1716; first gov.-gen., 2248; changed from dominion to independent repub. in Jan. 1950. First president. Dr. Rajenda Prasad.

Indiana. A central state of U.S.A., 36,291 sq. m.; pop. 3,427,800; 1717.

Indianapolis, Indiana, U.S.A. Cap. of state; pop. 387,000; meat-packing industry; motor speedway; 1717.

Indian Archipelago or **Malay Archipelago.** Same as **East Indies.**

Indian cobra, 859.

Indian corn. See **Maize.**

Indian Empire, Order of the, 2449.

Indian ink, 1724; a colloid, 871.

Indian jungle fowl, 435.

Indian mutiny, of 1857; 1714; siege of Lucknow, 2035.

Indian Ocean. 3rd largest ocean, **1718;** area, 2413; trade winds, 3385.

Indian Order of Merit. Three orders of knighthood; the Star of India, with four grades; the Order of the Indian Empire, with three grades; the Imperial Order of the Crown of India for women.

Indian rhinoceros, 2770.

Indians, Central American, Aztec, 325.

Indians, North American. See **Red Indians.**

Indians, South American. 137, 552, 873, 1082, 2512, 2528, 2560; Incas, 1689.

Indian summer. (U.S.A.) Summerlike weather occurring in autumn.

India Office, Whitehall, London. Dept. of the British govt., abolished 1947, **1718.**

India-rubber. See **Rubber.**

Indicative mood, of verbs, 3314.

In'dic languages. Subdivision of Indo-European group.

In'digo, 1059, **1718.**

Indium (In). A soft white metallic element of extreme rarity and similar to gallium; atomic weight, 114·76; found in some zinc blendes in minute quantities; melting point 311°F.; spectrum has two strong indigo-blue lines; properties, 777.

Indo-China. S.E. projection of Asia, formerly a Fr. colony, now a federation of Viet-Nam, Cambodia, and Laos, within the French Union, **1718;** Cambodia, 664; children, 787; invaded by Siam in 1940, 2965; Japanese occupied 1941-1945; Viet-Nam Republic formed. 1720.

Indo-European languages, 261, 2570.

Indo-European peoples, 2170; enter Europe, 1517; first to tame horse, 1646.

'Indomitable," H.M.S., an aircraft carrier, 2300.

Indonesia. As a geog. term, equal to **East Indies.**

Indonesia, United States of. Comprising the former Netherlands E. Indies, with the exception of Dutch New Guinea; given independence by the Netherlands in 1949. Principal islands: Java, Sumatra, Madura, Celebes, Borneo, Moluccas; **1720.** See also names of individual islands. and map, 1074-75.

Indonesian Republic. Formed, 1946, by rebellion against the Netherlands, from the former Dutch colonies in Sumatra, Java and Madura; cap. Jogjakarta; **1720.**

Indore. State of cent. India now part of Malwa union ; 9,900 sq. m. ; pop. 1,513,900.

Indra. Deity in ancient Hindu belief, representing the air or the heavens ; in later mythology overshadowed by other gods.

Indri. Animal of Madagascar, known also as babakoto (" little old man ") ; belongs to lemur family.

Induc'tance. The capacity for electro-magnetic induction used as a means of " tuning " radio circuits, or the device used to cause the induction, 1133, 3393.

Induc'tion. A method of reasoning, 2572 ; Bacon's work, 334.

Induction, electro-magnetic. The process whereby an electric current of changing value, or a moving magnetic field, creates electric currents in near-by conductors, 1132 ; heating by, 1623 ; discovered by Michael Faraday in 1831, 1132, 1260 ; in microphone, 2163.

Induction, electrostatic. The process whereby an electric charge induces charges on near-by bodies, 1131.

Induction, magnetic. The process whereby a magnet or an electric current creates magnetism in near-by iron bodies, 1132, 2062.

Induction coil. A device for inducing high-voltage alternating current from low-voltage direct, 1720 ; in i.c. engines, 1736 ; principle discovered by Faraday.

Induction motor. Type of electric motor ; principle, 1133, 2240.

Indul'gences. In Rom. Cath. Church, remission of temporal punishment due to sins, after repentance has removed guilt ; Huss attacks granting of, 1660 ; Luther, 2040, 2759.

Indus. One of the chief rivers of India ; 1,800 m. long ; 1721, 1691 ; irrigation system, 960 ; in Pakistan, 2479 ; Sukkur dam, 960 ; in Tibet, 3208.

Indu'sium, cover encasing fern spores, 2918.

Industrial alcohol, 3067.
Industrial arbitration, 204, 3234.
Industrial chemistry, 766, 775.
Industrial hygiene, 1677.
Industrial psychology, methods, 2697.
Industrial Psychology, National Institute of. Trained group of psychologists who apply science to the increase of business and industrial efficiency.

Industrial Revolution, 1721, 1723. Agriculture revolutionized, 78, 85, 1722 ; child labour, 802 ; effects in England, 3278 ; machines introduced, 712, 933, 1578, 3361 ; in Russia, 2845 ; in Scotland, 2893 ; transport improved, 2734.

Industrial Workers of the World. A labour organization established in U.S.A. 1905–1924. Advocated " syndicalism "—seizure of power by industrial workers through strikes, organized by one great union.

Inertia and mass, 2592.
Infallibil'ity, papal, doctrine of, 2615.
Infan'te and Infan'ta. Titles of Sp. royal princes and princesses, respectively.

Infantile Paralysis, or acute anterior poliomyelitis. Infectious virus disease of nervous system attacking chiefly children of 2 to 4 years and young adults ; mild form resembles influenza ; severe form shows paralysis.

Infantry, or foot soldiers, 244.
Infectious diseases. See **Germs in Disease.**

Inferiority complex. Feeling of inferiority which the sufferer often over-compensates by boasting and aggressive behaviour.

Infer'no. In Dante's " Divine Comedy," 971.

Infin'itive, of verbs, 3314.

Inflation of currency. Creation of an artificial purchasing power by over-circulation of notes above the gold cover, 2203.

Inflected languages, 2571.
Inflec'tion, characterizes Indo-European languages, 2571 ; declension, 2400 ; conjugation, 3314.

Influen'za. Caused by a virus, 1458.
Information, Central Office of. Brit. peace-time information ·ervice carrying govt. publicity campaigns and overseas news, also films and exhibitions.

Information, Min. of. Brit. wartime govt. dept. which censored and distributed news 1916–18 and during 2nd World War ; terminated Mar. 31, 1946 ; published books and pamphlets in many languages and sponsored films " Desert Victory," " In Which We Serve," etc.

Infra-red photograph, 1596, 1724, 2579, 3584.

Infra-red rays, 1722, 1595. Place in spectrum, 1722, plate f. 3057, 1942 ; action, 2729 ; discovery, 2728 ; photography by, 1596 ; telescope, etc., 1596, 1724.

Infuso'ria, protozoa, 2695.
Infusorial earth. See **Kieselguhr.**
Inge (ing), **William Ralph** (b. 1800). Brit. divine ; dean of St. Paul's Cathedral (1911–1934) ; a profound thinker, his unconventional and pessimistic views on modern tendencies led to his being styled the " gloomy dean " ; wrote " The Church and the Age " ; " Outspoken Essays " ; " Christian Ethics and Modern Problems."

Ingelow (in'-je-lō), **Jean** (1820–97). Eng. poet and novelist, remarkably popular in her time (" High Tide on the Coast of Lincolnshire " ; "Songs of Seven ").

In'gersoll, Col. Robert Green (1833–99). Amer. lawyer, author, and orator ; served in Civil War ; chiefly remembered for his lectures and books violently assailing the Bible and Christianity.

In'gleborough. Mt. of the Pennine range, in Yorkshire (2,373 ft.), 3 m. from Settle ; underground lake, 1950.

In'goldsby, Thomas. Pen-name under which the Eng. humorist, the Rev. Richard H. Barham (1788–1845), wrote the whimsical " Ingoldsby Legends " ; " Jackdaw of Rheims," 1789.

Ingolstadt (ing'-ol-shtaht), Ger. Fortified tn. on Danube, 45 m. N. of Munich ; pop. 29,840 ; soap, brushes.

In'got. A mass of cast metal, 1754, 1755, 1757.

Ingres (an'-gr), **Jean Auguste Dominique** (1780–1867). Fr. portrait and historical painter, leader of classical school, in constant competition with Delacroix, leader of romantic school ; wonderful draughtsmanship (" Apotheosis of Homer " ; " Stratonice "); 1378.

Ini'tiative. Independent action in a self-appointed course of action ; in politics, it means the power to create new legislation.

Injunction. A writ issued by the court ordering a person or persons to do or not to do a certain thing.

Ink, 1724 ; for manuscript books, 510 : invisible, or sympathetic, 858, 1724: resin in, 2768.

Ink'erman, Rus. Spt. vil. in s. Crimea near E. extremity of Sevastopol harbour, where Brit. and Fr. in 1854 defeated Rus. in Crimean War ; 931.

Ink'pen Beacon. Chalk down in Wiltshire, Eng. ; 1,011 ft. high ; 3383.

Inman, Philip, 1st Baron (b. 1892). Chairman of B.B.C. 1946–47. Lord Privy Seal, 1947. Resigned 1947.

" In Memoriam." By Tennyson, 3187.
Inn. R. rising in E. Switzerland, one of chief tributaries of Danube ; 320 m. long ; 3140, map, 3140.

Inner Mongolia. The S.E. part of Mongolia, 2204.

Inniskil'ling. See **Enniskillen.**
In'nocent, popes, 1725. See **Popes.**
Innocent III (1161–1216). Pope, 1725 ; conflict with King John of Eng., 1834 ; and St. Francis, 1383.

Innocents, Massacre of the, 1822.
Innsbruck. Historic and picturesque city on r. Inn ; cap. of Austrian Tirol ; pop. 61,000 ; 1725, 3215.

Inns of Court. Corporate bodies having the power to call law students to the bar ; in London there are four : Inner Temple, Middle Temple, Gray's Inn and Lincoln's Inn.

Innuits. See **Eskimo.**
Inocula'tion. In medicine, 3301.
Inönü (in-én'-ü), **Ismet** (b. 1884), 2nd pres. of Turkish republic ; life-long friend of Atatürk, he served in 1st World War and against the Greeks, taking his surname from his victory at Inönü in 1922 ; foreign minister, in 1923, and premier until 1937 ; succeeded Atatürk as pres. (1938–1950). Celal Bayar became 3rd pres. in 1950.

Inouye (ē-nōō'-yā), **Kaoru, Marquis** (1835–1915). Japanese statesman, a leader in reform movement which culminated in rev. of 1867 ; for 30 years no great issue in affairs was settled without his advice.

In'quest. A judicial inquiry ; early form, 1843 ; coroner's, 1843.

In'quiline. An insect which lays eggs in nest of another insect, thus living as a parasite.

Inquisi'tion. In the Rom. Cath. Church, 1726, 1760 ; Galileo forced to recant by, 1415.

Insecta. Scientific name for insect or hexapod (six-legged) class of arthropods. See **Insects.**

Insec'ticide. Preparation for killing insects, 179 ; fluorides, 1567.

Insectiv'ora. An order of insect-eating mammals, 2077.

Insectivorous plants, plate f. 2621 ; sundew, 3120 ; Venus's fly-trap, 3313.

Insects. The six-legged arthropod animals, 1726 ; caterpillars, 720 ; classification, 1733 ; disease-spreading types, 1313, 1329, 1459 ; eaten by birds, 438 ; egg forms and hatching, 1095 ; Fabre's work, 1255 ; larvae, 720 ; metamorphosis, 720, 1664, 1665 ; parasites check, 2513 ; pollen carriers, 852, 1322 ; pupae, 1728 ; spiders not insects, 3065. See also the principal insects and insect orders by name.

Insects, beneficial and harmful, 1731 ; aphides, 185 ; bees, 390 ; beetle pests, 399 ; butterflies, moths, and caterpillars, 628 ; cicadas, 826 ; cochineal yields dyes, 859 ; grasshoppers and locusts, 1510, 1511 ; mosquitoes, 2236, 2237, 2238 ; scale insects, 2513, 2878, 2879 ; silkworm, 2970 ; wasps prey on insects, 3346 ; weevils, 3362.

Inside edge, in skating, 2976.
Instinct of animals, 159.
In'stitute of France, 17.
Institutes of Justinian, 1844.
" Institutes of the Christian Religion," 664.

Insufflator, a powder spray, 178.
In'sulators, electric. Substances which do not conduct electricity, 1128 ; cables, 641 ; gutta-percha and substitutes, 1559 ; mica, 2159.

Insulin. An extract of the pancreas discovered by Sir F. G. Banting, found successful in the treatment of diabetes ; 1470.

Insurance. The act of insuring or assuring against damage or loss, 1733 ; pensions, 2546 ; social insurance, 2996.

Insurance, National Health. See **National Health Insurance.**

Insurance, Unemployment. Introduced into Gt. Brit. in 1911 as Part II of the National Insurance Act ; it was compulsory insurance in certain grades and classes of labour against unemployment to which employers, employees, and the State contributed. Superseded in 1948 by National Social Insurance, covering both health and employment and compulsory for all, 1735.

Intaglio (in-tal'-yō). An incised carving or sunk design, 2903 ; distinguished from cameo, 671 ; printing, 1217.

Intel'ligence, in Man, 2601, 2697.
In'terdict, Church. Punishment by a Pope, bishop, etc., of a country, community or person ; now rarely exercised.

Interest. How to calculate, 2548.
Interest, in economics, 1081.

Interfer'ence, of light, 1941 ; of sound, 3394.

Interference (" static "), in wireless reception, 3397.

Interferom'eter, for measurement of the wavelength of light, 1941.

Interior decoration. A household science.

Interjection, in grammar, 1494.

Interlaken (int-ter-lah'-ken) (" between the lakes "), Switzerland. Popular pleasure resort in Alps between Lakes Thun and Brienz, 25 m. S.E. of Berne ; starting point for excursions to Lauterbrunnen and the Jungfrau ; 127.

Internal combustion engine, 1735 ; Diesel engines, *1734*, 1737 ; in motor-car, *2244*.

Interna'tional, The (in full, The International Working Men's Association). Three organizations which asserted rights of Labour and aimed at international socialism. First International formed by Marx in 1866, ended 1872 in disagreement with anarchists. Second (Social-Democratic) International formed 1882 to unite political and trade union activities. Failure of 2nd International to prevent 1st World War resulted in formation of 3rd International (Comintern) to co-ordinate world Communist parties ; disbanded in 1943 to strengthen co-operation against Axis. *See* **Comin-form.**

International Bank, 927.

International Brigade, in Spanish Civil War, 1919, 3639.

International Cloud Atlas, 852.

International Committee for Bird Preservation, 302.

International date line, 3214.

International Justice, Permanent Court of, 1910.

International Labour Office (I.L.O.) and League of Nations, 1910.

International Law. *See* **Law, International.**

International Meteorological Organization, 2149.

International Monetary Fund, 1348, 1483, 2203.

International telephone exchange, London, *3171*.

Interreg'num, Great. In Ger. history, the interval (1256–73) between the fall of the Hohenstaufen emperors and the election of the first Hapsburg.

Interrogative pronoun, 2690.

Intestines, 1017.

Intran'sitive verb, 3314.

Introduc'tions, etiquette of, 1228.

Introverts, in psychology, 1840.

Invalides (an-vah-lēd'), **Hotel des**, Paris, 2517.

Invar'. A hard alloy having a very low rate of expansion to heat, 2365 ; use in pendulum, 2543.

Inveraray. Co. tn. of Argyllshire ; famed for its forest ; market-cross ; memorial to Campbells hanged for share in rising of 1685 ; pop. 460 ; 230.

Inverchapel, Archibald John Kerr Clark Kerr, 1st Baron. Ambassador in U.S.S.R. 1942–46. Ambassador to U.S.A. 1946–48.

Inverlochy (in-ver-lokh'-i), Scot. Vil. and castle ruin in Inverness-shire ; here the Marquis of Montrose inflicted defeat on the Earl of Argyll's army, Feb. 2, 1645.

Inverness (in-ver-nes'). Chief city of N. Scot., spt. and resort of N.E. coast on r. Ness ; pop. 25,000 ; co. tn. of Inverness-shire, 1737.

Inverness-shire, Scot. Marit. co., extending from Moray Firth to the Atlantic ; a. 4,210 sq. m. ; pop. 82,000 ; sheep rearing, fisheries ; **1737.**

Invertase, yeast enzyme, 1220, 3434.

Inver'tebrates. Animals which have no jointed body or cartilaginous spinal column.

Inverted image, 2579 ; pictures, *1925* ; in eye, 1252.

Invert sugar, 3114, 3116.

Investiture conflict, in Eng., 3380 ; in Ger., 1542, 1609.

Invisible spectrum, *plate f. 3056.*

Io (I'-ō). In Gk. myth., maiden loved by Zeus and changed into a heifer to protect her from the jealousy of his wife, Hera ; Hera, however, was not deceived, and tormented Io until she was restored to her human form, 529 ; a name given to one of the moons of Jupiter.

Iodine (I) (I'-ō-dīn). A grey-black solid element with a metallic lustre ; atomic weight, 126·92 ; obtained from seaweeds and Chile nitrates ; melts at 237·2° F. ; the name iodine from the Greek *ioeides*, was given to it owing to the purple colour of its vapour, **1738** ; a halogen, 1567 ; in food, 1338 ; nitrogen iodide, an explosive, 1250 ; properties, 777 ; as radio-active " tracer," 2733 ; " iodised " salt, 2866.

Io'doform. An antiseptic consisting of carbon, hydrogen, and iodine.

I'on. An electrically charged atom, molecule, or radical in a gas or liquid medium, 1136, *1137*, **1738**, 772, *773* ; of acids and bases, 20 ; in Wilson cloud chamber, 2731, *2732.*

Iona (I-ō'-na) or **Icolmkill.** One of Inner Hebrides ; 5 sq. m. ; centre of Celtic Christianity, 1602.

Ion-exchange, in beet sugar refining, 3114 ; in water-softening, 3351.

Io'nia. In anc. geography, a dist. on the w. coast of Asia Minor and adjacent isls., settled by the Ionian Greeks.

Ionian Islands. Group of 7 chief isls. in Ionian Sea off w. coast of Greece ; *map, 1518* ; ceded to Greece, 1525.

Ionians. One of the four great branches of the Gk. people, 1517.

Ionian Sea. The part of the Mediterranean between Greece and S. It. ; *map, 1518.*

Ionic (I-on'-ik) dialect, 1541.

Ionic order, in architecture, *213, 215.*

Io'nium. Radio-active element (Io) having same chem. properties as thorium ; in uranium-lead series, 2732.

Ioniza'tion. Chemical process, 1136, **1738**, 20 ; by lightning, 1946.

Ion'osphere. Uppermost layer of the earth's atmosphere, extending from the higher limits of the stratosphere ; it is strongly ionised (hence its name) by solar rays and cosmic radiation, *89*, 3396.

Io'ta, ι, I (Rom. i, I). Ninth letter of the Gk. alphabet, the vowel i.

I'owa. A N. cent. state of U.S.A. ; the leading maize state of the Union ; also cattle and pig breeding ; coal ; 56,280 sq. m. ; pop. 2,538, 000 ; **1739.**

Ipecacuanha (i-pe-kak-ū-an'-a). S. Amer. plant of the madder family ; used as an emetic.

Iphigenia (if-i-je-nī'-a). In Gk. myth., daughter of Agamemnon, offered as a sacrifice in Trojan War ; 75, **1740.**

Iphitus (I-fi-tus). In Gk. myth., friend of Hercules, 1615.

Ips'wich. Spt. and mfg. city and co. tn. of Suffolk, on Orwell estuary ; pop. est. 102,450 ; engineering works, mfrs. agric. implements, boots and shoes ; 15th cent. school ; 1311.

Iquique (ē-kē'-kā). One of leading ports of Chile, in extreme N. ; pop. (1940) 39,300 ; exports nitrate.

Iquitos (ē-kē'-tos). Trade centre of N.E. Peru in R. Amazon, at head of navigation for ocean vessels, 2,500 m. from mouth ; pop. 40,000.

Irak. Same as **Iraq.**

Iran (ē-rahn'). Official name of Persia, kingdom in Asia ; a. 628,000 sq. m. approx. ; pop. 13,000,000 ; **1740**, *map, 1742* ; children, 801. For history *see* **Persia.**

Iranian Plateau. High tableland including Afghanistan, Iran, and Baluchistan ; 1741.

Iran'ic languages, 2571.

Iraq (ē-rahk'), formerly **Mesopotamia.** Arab kingdom in Asia, a. 116,600 sq. m. ; pop. est. 4,611,000 ; **1743**, 2146 ; *map, 1743* ; Baghdad, 339 ; children, 801 ; r. Euphrates, 1231 ; Kish, 1862 ; mandate, 581 ; oil-fields, 2426 ; r. Tigris, 3212. Treaty with U.K. Jan. 1948 occasioned Baghdad anti-Brit. and anti-Govt. riots.

History, 2146 ; early civilization, ~268, 3297 ; Arab rule, 195, 339 ; devastated by Mongols, 2206 ; 1st World War, 3410, 3411 ; 2nd World War, 1744, 3418. For anc. history *see* **Babylonia and Assyria ; Ur.**

Irawadi. *See* **Irrawaddy.**

Irazu, Mt., Costa Rica. Volcano near Cartago (11,200 ft.), 916.

Ireland, John (b. 1879). Brit. composer ; symphonic rhapsody " Maidun," " Concertino Pastorale " ; songs, " Sea Fever," " Land of Lost Content."

Ireland. The smaller of the two main Brit. Isles ; 32,586 sq. m. (excluding water area) ; pop. 4,230,000 ; **1744** ; *map, 1745* ; agriculture, 1744, 1746 ; cities, towns, and counties, *see* under Irish Free State (Eire), Ireland, Northern, and individual names ; emigration, 1746 ; flax, 1313 ; folk lore, 1330 ; Gaelic language, 740, 1413 ; Giant's Causeway, 1461 ; lace-making, 1877, *1878*, 1881 ; linen industry, *1954*, 3205 ; National University, 1050 ; peat cutting, 2535 ; people, 1744 ; physical features, 584 ; potato growing, 2664 ; St. Patrick, 2529.

History, 1744 ; monasteries established, 2212 ; cities founded, 2388 ; Eng. conquest, 1745 ; rebellion (1641) and Cromwell's reconquest, 933, 1745 ; battle of the Boyne, 1745, *1746*, 1794 ; rebellion (1798), 3277 ; union with Gt. Brit. (1801), 1746, 2524, 3277 ; Cath. Emancipation Act, 1746, 2420 ; Home Rule movement, 1470, 1746, 2420, 2525, 3279 ; great famine and repeal of corn laws, 1746, 2535 ; Church disestablished, 1470, 1746 ; land acts, 2525, 1470 ; Sinn Fein, 1746 ; Dublin Easter Revolt, 1051, 1746 ; separate parliaments established for Ulster and the Irish Free State, 1746, 2525. *See also* **Irish Free State (Eire) ; Ireland, Northern ;** and names in Irish history, e.g. **de Valera ; O'Connell.**

Ireland, National University of. Univ. of Eire, founded in 1908 to take the place of the Royal Univ. of Ire. ; it comprises the univ. colleges of Cork, Dublin, and Galway ; faculties include science, arts, medicine, surgery, engineering ; 1050.

Ireland, Northern. Div. of Ire., comprising the greater part of the prov. of Ulster ; a. 5,237 sq. m. ; pop. 1,280,000 ; **1747** ; parliament, 2525 ; cap. Belfast, 402. *Counties* : Antrim, 181 ; Armagh, 237 ; Down, 1031 ; Fermanagh, 1266 ; Londonderry, 2021 ; Tyrone, 3272. *See* **Ireland ; Irish Free State (Eire) .**

Ireland, Republic of. *See* **Irish Free State (Eire).**

Irenaeus (I-re-nē'-us), **St.** (*c.* 130–202). A Gk. Church father and martyr, Bishop of Lyons ; wrote a treatise in Greek against heresies.

Irene (I-rē'-ne) (752–803). Byzantine empress, first woman to rule Eastern Empire ; originally a poor orphan, seized power in 780, on death of her husband, Leo IV ; blinded and later murdered her son, Constantine VI ; planned to unite Eastern and Western Empires by marrying Charlemagne ; deposed (802) and exiled.

Ire'ton, Henry (1611–51). Eng. soldier ; son-in-law of Oliver Cromwell ; he was a general in the Parliamentary army and one of the judges who condemned Charles I to execution.

Ir'gun (Irgun Zvai Leumi). Jewish terrorist organisation ; active in the Arab troubles 1936–39 ; during 1945–May '48 committed outrages in attempt to force Brit. to set up Jewish state ; outlawed by Israel on estab. of State, May 1948 ; 2413.

Irides'cence. Rainbow-like play of colours ; how caused in shells, 2942.

Irid'ium (Ir). A hard, brittle, white metallic element of the platinum group ; atomic weight, 193·1 ; alloyed with platinum, used to tip fountain-pen nibs and for standard metre ; properties, 777 ; in compass, 881 ; found in Urals, 3297.

I'ris. In Gk. myth., rainbow goddess, messenger of gods.

Iris. Of the eye, 1252.

Iris. A flower, **1748**; in Japan, *1803*; orris root from, 1748 ; *plate f. 1748, 1749.*

Irish Free State (Eire since Dec. 1937). Independent republic of the British Isles ; a. 26,600 sq. m. ; pop. 3,000,000 approx. ; **1749** ; cap., Dublin, 1050, *1051* ; parliament, 2525, *3281. See also* Ireland.

Counties : Carlow, 702 ; Cavan, 733 ; Clare, 836 ; Cork, 910 ; Donegal, 1029 ; Dublin, 3780 ; Galway, 1416 ; Kerry, 1853 ; Kildare, 1856 ; Kilkenny, 1857 ; Leitrim, 1920 ; Leix, 1920 ; Limerick, 1949 ; Longford, 2024 ; Louth, 2032 ; Mayo, 2124 ; Meath, 2125 ; Monaghan, 2200 ; Offaly, 2425 ; Roscommon, 2827 ; Sligo, 2985 ; Tipperary, 3215 ; Waterford, 3354 ; Westmeath, 3369 ; Wexford, 3371 ; Wicklow, 3377. A measure severing all links, save certain aspects of citizenship, between Eire and the Brit. Commonwealth was passed by the Dail, Dec. 1948, and came into operation Apr. 18, 1949 ; 3283.

Irish Guards. A regiment of the Brigade of Guards.

Irish Home Rule. *See* **Home Rule.**

Irish Lace, 1877, *1878*, 1881.

Irish Land Acts, 1470, 3278.

Irish Land League, 537, 2525.

Irish language, 1750.

Irish literature, 1750 ; drama, 1040.

Irish moss, or carrageen. A seaweed used for food, 1426, 2239, 2916.

Irish Romanesque, illumination, 2092.

Irish Sea. Body of water, between England and Ireland, with North Channel at N. and St. George's at S.

Irish Setter. Large shooting dog ; fine, long coat, usually bright red-brown ; now seldom used for sport.

Irish terrier, *plate f. 1024.*

Irish Wolfhound. Largest of dogs, this breed resembles the deerhound.

Irkutsk (ir-kootsk'). Trade centre and largest city of Siberia near Chinese border and near S. end of L. Baikal ; pop. 243,000 ; on Trans-Siberian rly., 2967, *map f. 2844.*

Iron. A white metallic element known from about 3000 B.C. ; atomic weight 55·8 ; of enormous industrial importance ; melting point 1505° C. ; properties, 776, **1752,** 2148 ; carbonates, 2856 ; cyanides, 947 ; in diet, 2468 ; essential to plant growth, 2998 ; disulphide (pyrites), 1753, 3117 ; early use, 1753 ; in food, 1338 ; four kinds, *2143* ; in human body, 2598 ; magnetic properties, 2062 ; meteoric, 2151 ; ores, *469,* 1753, 2181 ; oxide (rust), 135, 1752, 2478, 2856 ; first bridge of, *565* ; used as money 2201. Geographical distribution, 1753 ; Czechoslovakia, 953 ; Europe, 1753 ; France 1361, 1753 ; Germany, 1447, 1753 ; Gt. Brit., 1165, 3333 ; Mexico, 2157 ; Russia, 1753, 2845 ; Sweden, 3128 ; U.S.A., 3290.

Iron, galvanized, 2856, 3443.

Iron Age. The 3rd and highest period of barbarism, separating the Bronze Age from the Stone Age ; so named from the use of iron implements by the people of the period, 1753.

Iron and steel, 1752 ; alloys, 122, 2087, 2365, 3303, 3444 ; armourplate, 240 ; Bessemer converter, 421 ; cast-iron, 1756 ; characteristics of iron, 1752, 1756 ; characteristics of steel, 1756, 3087 ; furnaces, various types of, 467, 1409 ; Gt. Brit., 2941 ; how welded, 3362 ; importance in modern life, 1752 ; mfg. processes, 1754, 1756 ; paint preservative, 2477 ; properties, 776 ; rusting, 1752 ; wrought iron, 1756.

Iron Cross. Ger. mil. decoration, 2449.

Iron Crown. Jewelled gold crown, 6 ins. in diam., embodying iron circlet beaten out of a nail used in the Crucifixion ; made for Agilulf, king of the Lombards, in 591 ; Charlemagne crowned with it, 2000 ; also subsequent emperors who were kings of Lombardy ; Napoleon crowned himself with it in 1805 ; presented to Victor Emmanuel by the Austrians at Turin in 1866.

Iron Curtain. Physical and ideological barrier between Communist-controlled areas and the rest of Europe ; term invented by Winston Churchill at Fulton, Mo., March 5, 1946 ; "From Stettin, in the Baltic, to Trieste, in the Adriatic, an Iron Curtain has descended across the Continent."

Iron Lung. Device for applying artificial respiration, particularly in infantile paralysis.

Iron Gates. Point on Danube between Rumania and Yugoslavia, nearly barricaded by mts., 912, 1233.

Iron Mask, Man in the. Mysterious Fr. state prisoner, **1758.**

Iron ores, *469,* 1753, 2181.

Iron pyrites (FeS) or "fool's gold," 1479, 1753, 3117.

Ironside, (William) Edmund, Baron (b. 1880). Eng. gen. ; C.-in-C. Allied Forces N. Russia (1918–19) ; Gov. Gibraltar (1938–39) ; C.I.G.S., Sept. 1939 ; C.-in-C. Home, May–July, 1940 ; Field-Marshal, July 1940 ; peer, 1941.

Iron-wood. Popular name for several tropical trees, especially certain members of myrtle and ebony families whose timber is very hard ; in Borneo, 526 ; in Eng., given to hornbeam.

Iroquois (ir-ō-kwoi') **Indians,** or **Five Nations.** Confederacy of N. Amer. Indians formerly living in cent. and w. N.Y. ; Hiawatha legends, 2022.

Irrawaddy (i-ra-wah'-di) or **Irawadi.** Chief r. of Burma ; rises in N., flows S. 1,500 m. to Bay of Bengal ; large delta ; 624, 625 ; rice-growing, 2775.

Irregular verbs, 3314.

Irrigation and reclamation ; artesian wells used, 252 ; in Australia, 308 ; in Ceylon, *2775* ; in China, 809, *2775* ; in Egypt, 1095, 1097, *1098,* 1100, *1102* ; in Holland, *2318, 2319* ; India, 1417, 1418 ; Iraq, 1231, 1743 ; Japan, 2774 ; S. Africa, 3014 ; Spain, 3032, 3302 ; Sudan, 3110.

Irritant poisons, 2638.

Irtish (er-tish'). Important river of Russian Central Asia, a trib. of the Ob ; length about 2,250 m.

Irving, Sir Henry (1838–1905). Most famous Eng. actor of the late Victorian period. First English actor to receive a knighthood, **1759.**

Irving, Henry Brodribb (1870–1919). Eldest son of Sir Henry Irving ; he played with George Alexander, and later took the name parts in "Hamlet" and "The Admirable Crichton" ; for a time was manager of the Shaftesbury Theatre.

Irving, Laurence Brodribb (1871–1914). Second son of Sir Henry Irving, with whom he acted ; among the plays in which he acted were "The Unwritten Law" and "Typhoon." Was drowned with his wife, when the Empress of India went down May 29, 1914.

Irving, Washington (1783–1859). Amer. essayist, historian, and story-writer, 1759, *3293.*

Irwell. River of Lancashire, enters the Mersey ; canal, 570.

Irwin. *See* Halifax, 1st Earl.

Irwin, Margaret. English writer. Historical romances include : "Royal Flush" (1932), "The Stranger Prince" (1937), "The Gay Galliard" (1941) and "Young Bess" (1944).

Isaac (I'-zak). Hebrew patriarch, son of Abraham and father of Jacob and Esau, 13, 1929.

Isaac I, Comne'nus (d. 1061). Byzantine emperor, 1057–59.

Isaacs, Rt. Hon. George Alfred (b. 1883). Min. of Labour and Nat. Service, 1945.

Isabella II (1830–1904). Queen of Spain ; succeeded 1833 ; abdicated 1870 ; mother of Alfonso XII.

Isabella of Castile (1451–1504), **1760,** 3036 ; aids Columbus, 879. *See* Ferdinand II of Aragon.

Isabel'la of France (1292–1358). Queen of Edward II of England and daughter of Philip IV of France.

Isabey (ē-zah-bā'), **Jean Baptiste** (1767–1855). Fr. portrait painter ; pupil

of David ; became court painter ("Review of Troops by the First Consul").

Isaiah (I-zī'-a) (8th cent. B.C.), one of greatest of Old Testament Hebrew prophets ; gives name to 23rd book of Old Testament, 2691.

Isandhlwana (ē-sand-lwah'-na). Hill in Zululand, S. Africa, on the Tugela r. ; here a gallant stand was made by a small force of British and native troops against an overwhelming number of Zulus in 1879.

Isar (ē-zahr). R. rising in Tirolese Alps in S. Bavaria, flows N.E. 219 m. to Danube ; total fall, 4,816 ft. ; 1447. 2256.

Ischia (is'-ki-a). Volcanic isl. of Italy 16 m. s.w. of Naples ; 26 sq. m. ; pop. 28,000.

Ischl (ēshl), Austria. Celebrated resort, 28 m. S.E. of Salzburg ; pop. 10,000.

Iseo (ē-zā'-ō), **Lake of.** In N. Italy at S. foot of Alps ; 15 m. N.W. of Brescia ; formed by r. Oglio ; 24 sq. m.

Isère (ē-zār'). River rising in Alps in S.E. France and flowing S.w. 180 m., 2774.

Iseult (ē-soolt'), **Yseult,** or **Isolde.** Heroine of medieval romance "Tristan and Iseult." *See also* **Tristan.**

Isfahan or **Ispahan.** City of Iran ; pop. 205,000 ; in 17th cent. cap. of Persia, and had a pop. of nearly a million ; 1740.

Isherwood, Christopher W. B. (b. 1904). Brit. poet and novelist ; collaborated with W. H. Auden in plays in verse, "The Ascent of F6," "On The Frontier."

Ishmael (ish'-mā-el). Son of Abraham and Hagar, Sarah's Egyptian handmaid ; ancestor of Ishmaelites (Arabs, according to Arab tradition) ; driven out with his mother and grew up in the wilderness ; 13.

Ish'tar. Chief goddess of Babylonia and Assyria, corresponding to Phoenician Astarte and Gk. Aphrodite ; and Adonis, 28.

Isidore (c. 560–636). Sp. writer ; became Bishop of Seville (599) ; author of an encyclopedia ; to him was falsely ascribed the authorship of the so-called Isidorian or False Decretals.

Isinglass, 1760, 1426.

Isis (I-sis). Chief goddess in Eg. myth. 1760.

Isis. Name given to Thames near Oxford ; 2462, 2466, 3194.

Is'lam. Arabic word meaning "pious submission to the will of God" ; another name for Mahomedanism, and therefore for the whole group of Mahomedan peoples. *See* **Mahomedanism.**

Islands. Coral, 908 ; volcanic, 3328.

WORLD'S LARGEST ISLANDS

	AREA IN SQ. M.
Australia (island-continent)	2,948,366
Greenland	826,000
New Guinea	311,000
Borneo	290,000
Madagascar	241,094
Baffin	231,000
Sumatra	165,000
Great Britain	88,745
Honshu (Japan)	87,500
Prince Albert Island	60,000
New Zealand (South Island)	58,093
Java (with Madura)	51,032
New Zealand (North Island)	44,281

Is'lay. Southernmost isl. of Inner Hebrides, Scot. ; 240 sq. m. ; 1602.

Is'lington. Met. and parl. bor. of N. London ; pop. 212,750 ; contains Royal Agricultural Hall.

Ismail (ēs-mah-ēl') **Pasha** (1830–95). Khedive of Egypt, son of Ibrahim Pasha ; succeeded his uncle Said as viceroy (1863) ; by aiding the Sultan of Turkey secured direct succession of his line and title of khedive : improved economic condition of Egyptians, but destroyed national credit : deposed (1879), 1101.

Is'may, Hastings L. Ismay, 1st Baron (b. 1887). Brit. soldier ; chief of personal staff to Winston Churchill from 1940 and liaison officer between the war cabinet and chiefs of staff in 2nd Great War.

Ismet Ineunu. *See* Inönü, Ismet.

Isobars (ī'-sō-bahrz). In barometric readings, lines connecting places with same barometric pressure; regions of pressure marked "low," and "high," 2150.

Iso'chronism, pendulum's property of taking equal times for successive swings, 2543.

Isocrates (ī-sok'-ra-tēz) (436–338 B.C.). Athenian orator and patriot; preached Gk. union to conquer Persia and was killed, according to Milton, by report of "that dishonest victory at Chaeronea, fatal to liberty."

Isomet'ric projection, a form of perspective, 2557.

Iso-octane, hydrocarbon used in testing petrol, 2564.

Isonzo (ē-zon'-zō). River in Yugoslavia and in N.E. Italy (formerly in Austria), rises in Alps and flows S. 75 m. to Gulf of Trieste; in 1st World War, 3410, 3411; peace treaty with Italy in 1947 gave upper reaches, N. of Gorizia, to Yugoslavia.

Isoprene, a constituent of rubber, 2838.

Isop'tera. Termite order, insects, 1733.

Isotherms (ī'-sō-thêrmz). Lines joining up points on the earth's surface at the same temperature, 841.

I'sotope. Atoms of same atomic no. and properties but differing at. wt. due to extra protons in nucleus, 1760; atom, 296; in chemistry, 769; of lead, 2732; radioactive, 2733; as "tracers" in biology, 2733; of uranium, 3297, 299; "heavy" water, 3351; separation of, 1419, 1759, 1760.

Ispahan. See **Isfahan.**

Israel (iz'-rā-el). Name borne by Hebrew patriarch Jacob, and by 12 tribes descended from him, 1829. For history of kingdom of Israel see **Jews.** The independent state of Israel, in Palestine, was declared May 14, 1948; 2483. See **Palestine.**

Israels, Josef (1824–1911). Dutch genre painter, the Millet of the fisher folk ("Toilers of the Sea,"), 2335.

Issachar (is'-a-kahr). Son of the patriarch Jacob, ancestor of the tribe of Issachar.

Issus (is'-us). Anc. spt. of S.E. Asia Minor, of great strategic importance because of its position on the pass leading from Syria into Cilicia; battle of (333 B.C.), 106.

Istanbul. Former cap. of Turkish Empire, and formerly known as Constantinople; pop. 845,000; 1761; plate f.3265; Bosporus, 528; melons in, 2138; relics of earlier empires, 636; Santa Sophia, 213, 636. For early history see in Index **Constantinople.**

Is'tria. It. dist. comprising peninsula in N. Adriatic Sea and Quarnero Isls.; acquired by Italy, 1770.

Itagaki (ē-ta-gah'-kē), **Taisuke, Count** (1837–1919). The "Rousseau of Japan"; helped to overthrow feudalism; established school to teach principles of govt. to the people; advocated constitutional govt. and founded first political party in Japan.

Italian language, 1786, 2570; origin, 2798; in Switzerland, 3141; Tuscan dialect, 1786.

Italian East Africa. Former Empire, incl. Abyssinia, Eritrea and It. Somaliland, 600,000 sq. m.; pop. (est. 8,000,000; 1073; fell to Allies in 1941.

Italian literature, 1786; Dante's influence, 969; novel, 2403. See list of authors below.

Italian Somaliland (Somalia). Colony of N.E. African coast, included in **Italian East Africa** before 1941; 3000.

Italic languages. Defined, 2570.

Italy. Republic in S. Europe; 116,000 sq. m.; pop. 45,637,000; 1763; plates, 1765–1768; map, 1764; children, 801; Christmas customs, 820; people, 1763.

Art: 1775, 1777–1784, 2476; architecture, 254, 256; influence on Flemish art, 2324; Milan cathedral, 2173; mosaic, 2233; music, 2261, 2264; painting, 2476; pottery, 2669, 2670, 2666; Renaissance period, 2764; sculpture, 2904–2906; Vatican, 2745, 3306. See also **Rome:** Painting and Sculpture and names of chief cities and artists.

Geography and industries: Cap. Rome, 2799; chief cities and products, 1319, 2171, 2274, 2612, 3310 (see also under names of cities); climate, 1763; fisheries, 908, 2968; foreign trade, 1429, 2968; laces, 1877, 1878, 1880, f. 1880; marble, 2097; mountains, 127, 184; Pompeii, 2653; rivers, 2633; Sardinia, 2873; Sicily, 2968; silk, 2972; Tirol, 3215.

History (medieval and modern), 1763; chief events summarized, see in Index under **History.** Barbarian invasions, 1237, 1487, 1763; development of monasticism, 2212; under Charlemagne, 753; Norman invasions, 2968; in Holy Roman Empire, 1636 (see also **Holy Roman Empire;** **Papacy**); Renaissance in, 2764, 2765, 2766, 2904 (see also **Renaissance**); in Napoleonic era, 2275.

Unification and recent events, 1769; Cavour, 737; Garibaldi, 1418; Mazzini, 2124; papacy, 2495, 3306; Victor Emmanuel II, 3319; colonies in Africa, 1931, 1932; in Triple Alliance, 1240; war with Turkey, 1770; 1914–1918 War and peace settlement, 1770, 3410, 3411, 3414, 3415, 3416; Fascism, 1261; Mussolini, 2268; Albania invaded, 1773, 3416; Abyssinian conquest, 14, 15, 3415; support for Franco, 3039; 2nd World War and after, 1452, 1773, 3417, map, 3419, 3421, 3422. For ancient history see **Rome.**

Italy Star. Brit. medal, instituted May 1945, for military service in Sicily or Italy between June 11, 1943, and May 8, 1945; medal ribbon of the It. colours, green, white, and red.

Itas'ca Lake. Small lake in Minn., U.S.A., source of Mississippi, 2191.

Ith'aca. Isl. of Ionian group, Greece; 40 sq. m.; legendary home of Odysseus.

Ithuriel (I-thū'-ri-el). Angel of truth in Milton's "Paradise Lost."

Ito (ē'-tō), **Prince Hirobumi** (1841–1909). Japanese statesman and leading reformer, 4 times premier; drafted constitution; assassinated.

Iturbide, Augustin de (1783–1824). Emperor of Mexico, 2158.

Ivan III, the Great (1440–1505). Grand Duke of Moscow, 1787.

Ivan IV, The Terrible (1530–84). Tsar of Russia, 1787.

"Ivanhoe." Novel by Sir Walter Scott, 2900.

Ivanov (ē-vahn'-of), **Vsevolod Viacheslavovich** (b. 1896). Russian novelist and short-story writer; work distinguished for brilliant descriptions ("The Armoured Train"; "Coloured Winds"), 2856.

Ivanovo-Voznesensk (ē-vah-nō'-vō-voz-ne-sensk'). Soviet Russia. Mfg. tn. on r. Uvod 160 m. N.E. of Moscow; pop. 285,000.

Ives, Frederic Eugene (1856–1937). Amer. inventor; originator of the half-tone process of photo-engraving and also of the three-colour process of colour printing.

Ivinghoe. Vill. of Bucks., Eng., in the Chilterns, 583.

Iviza (ē-vē'-thah). One of Balearic Isls.; a. 230 sq. m.; pop. 25,000; 342; map, 3030.

I'vory, 1788, 73; carving, 1698, 1788, India, 1698; Japan, 1810, 1812; from mammoth tusks 2078; vegetable, 1758, 2408; walrus tusks, 1788, 3339; Zanzibar, 3441.

Ivory coast, region in Fr. W. Africa between Liberia and Brit. Gold Coast; 180,000 sq. m.; pop. 4,100,000; dense forests; palm products, rubber; 3366; map, 3367.

Ivory-nuts or **vegetable ivory,** 632, 1788.

Ivory Palm, 2485

I'vy, 1788; poison ivy, 2638.

Iwakura (ē-wah-kōō'-ra), **Prince Tomomi** (1835–83). Jap. statesman; leader in movement to abolish feudalism.

Iwojima (I-wō-jē'-ma). Central is. of the three Volcano Is., Pacific Ocean, 775 m. from Japan; Jap. air base in Second World War; taken by U.S. marines during Feb. and March 1945 with great loss of life to both sides, 2474, 3424.

Ixion (iks-ī'-on). In Gk. myth., father of the Centaurs, who for impiously attempting to win the love of Hera was bound for ever to a rolling fiery wheel.

Izmir. Turkish name for **Smyrna.**

PROMINENT FIGURES IN ITALIAN LITERATURE

Dante Alighieri (1265–1321), epic poet—"Divina Commedia" (Divine Comedy); "Vita Nuova" (New Life).

Francesco Petrarch (1304–74), poet—Sonnets.

Giovanni Boccaccio (1313–75), poet and writer of prose tales—"Decameron."

Ludovico Ariosto (1474–1533), epic poet—"Orlando Furioso."

Torquato Tasso (1544–95), poet—"Aminta"; "Gerusalemme Liberta" (Jerusalem Delivered).

Giovanni Batista Marini (1569–1625), poet—"L'Adone."

Carlo Goldoni (1707–93), comic dramatist—"La Bottega di Caffè (The Coffee House).

Giuseppe Parini (1729–99), poet—"Il Giorno."

Carlo Gozzi (1722–1806), dramatist—"Turandot."

Vittorio Alfieri (1749–1803), dramatist—"Saul"; "Oreste"; "Virginia"; "Timoleone."

Vincenzo Monti (1754–1828), poet and dramatist—"Aristodemo"; "Bassevilliana."

Alessandro Manzoni (1785–1873), poet and novelist—"Il Cinque Maggio" (The Fifth of May); "I Promessi Sposi" (The Betrothed).

Giacomo Leopardi (1798–1837), poet—"La Ginestra."

Giosuè Carducci (1836–1907), poet—"Hymn to Satan"; "Odi Barbare" (Barbaric Odes).

Antonio Fogazzaro (1842–1911), novelist and poet—"Miranda"; "Leila"; "Daniele Cortis."

Giuseppe Giacosa (1847–1906), dramatist—"Come le Foglie" (Like Falling Leaves); "Tristi Amori" (Hapless Love).

Giovanni Pascoli (1855–1912), poet—"Poemmetti"; "Le Odi e gli Inni."

Matilde Serao (1856–1927), novelist—"Il Paese di Cuccagna" (The Land of Cockayne).

Roberto Bracco (1862–1943), dramatist and novelist—"Piccolo Santo" (Little Saint); "Donne"; "Maternità."

Alfredo Panzini (1863–1939), biographer and critic—"Le Fiabe della Virtù"; "Piccole Storie del Mondo Grande."

Gabriele D'Annunzio (1864–1938), poet, novelist, dramatist—"Fedra"; "Il Ferro"; "Forse che sì, forse che no"; "Canzoni della Gesta d'Oltremare."

Benedetto Croce (1866–), philosopher—"Problemi di Estetica."

Luigi Pirandello (1867–1936), dramatist—"Sei Personaggi in Cerca d'Autore" (Six Characters in Search of an Author).

Grazia Deledda (1875–1936), novelist—"La Madre" (The Mother).

Giovanni Gentile (1875–), philosopher—"Discorsi di Religione"; "Il Concetto del Progresso."

Giovanni Papini (1881–), critic—"Storia di Cristo" (Life of Christ); "Un Uomo Finito"; "Stroncature."

Ignazio Silone (1900–), politician and writer—"Fontamara"; "Bread and Wine."

LIKE C and G, and U and V, the letters I and J were originally forms of the same letter. The vowel sound *i* and the consonant sound *j* were both represented by I until about the 15th century. Then some of the monks who worked on the beautiful illuminated manuscripts of that time used to lengthen the letter I and curve it toward the left when it began a word, thus making of it an ornamental initial. Gradually this form came to be used entirely to represent the consonant

sound while the old form was retained for the vowel sound. This consonant sound was originally like our *y*. Thus *Julius* in Latin was pronounced as though it were spelt *Yulius*. The sound we give it in English, *dzh*, like our soft *g*, came to us from the Old French. In modern French it is pronounced with a still softer sound like *zh*. In German and some other languages it is still pronounced *y*, and we ourselves give it this sound in the word *hallelujah*.

Jabalpur. See **Jubbulpore.**

Jacinth, gem variety of zircon, 3444.

Jack'al. A dog-like animal. **1789.** Indian, 1701.

Jackdaw. A member of the crow family of birds, native of Gt. Brit., **1789.**

Jack-o'-lantern, or **Will-o'-the-wisp.** See **Ignis fatuus.**

Jacks, Lawrence Pearsall (b. 1860). Eng. theologian and philosopher; first editor of "Hibbert Journal," a review of ethics, etc.; brilliant literary sketches.

Jack-snipe, 2991.

Jackson, Andrew (1767–1845), 7th pres. of U.S.A.

Jackson, Sir Barry Vincent (b. 1879). Eng. theatre manager; founded repertory company in Birmingham in 1913, and staged such notable plays as "Abraham Lincoln," "Back to Methuselah," "The Farmer's Wife," etc.

Jackson, Thomas Jonathan (1824–63). "Stonewall," Confederate general. **1789.** *1790.*

Ja'cob. Hebrew patriarch, 2nd son of Isaac, supplanter of his brother Esau; husband of Leah and Rachel, and progenitor of Israelites (Gen. xxv. 1). 1829; burial place, 2480.

Jac'obins. Club of Fr. Rev. period, **1790**; Committee of Public Safety, 1396; Lafayette plots against, 1884; Robespierre leads, 2789.

Jacobites (jak'-ō-bīts). Adherents of James II or the direct Stuart line after the revolution of 1688; **1790, 1791**; and the Pretenders, 2682; and Stuart kings, 3104.

Jacobs, Helen Hull (b. 1908). Amer. tennis player; Wimbledon Ladies' Singles Champion, 1936, and reached final on 5 other occasions; 4 times Ladies Singles Champion of U.S.A.

Ja'cobs, William Wymark (1863–1943). Eng. novelist; celebrated for his quaintly humorous stories, many of which deal with seafaring characters ("Many Cargoes"; "The Skipper's Wooing"; "A Master of Craft"; "At Sunwich Port").

Jacquard (ja-kahrd') **loom.** Invented by Joseph Marie Jacquard (1752–1834), of Lyons, Fr.; **1790,** 321, 1877, 2025, 3361.

Jade. A semi-precious stone; in Burma, 623, carved in china, 809. See A B C of Gems, 3813.

Jael (jā'-el). Hebrew woman exalted in the "Song of Deborah" as "blessed among women" because she killed Sisera, leader of the Canaanites.

Jaffa (jaf'-*a*) or **Joppa.** Spt. of Palestine on Mediterranean; pop. 102,000, exports wool, wine, oil, and sesame. Jaffa oranges are reputed the finest in the world; captured by Brit. from Turks, Nov. 1917; 2482.

Jagannath (ju-gah-nahth'), **Juggernaut,** or **Puri.** Tn. on E. coast of India noted for temple to Jagannath (Vishnu); at annual festival idol is drawn on enormous car under which devotees were formerly supposed to cast themselves, 1693.

Jagellon (yah-gel'-on). Famous royal family whose members for two centuries ruled in Lithuania, Poland, Hungary, and Bohemia.

Jagger, Charles Sargeant (1885–1934). Eng. sculptor; his work included Royal Artillery Memorial, London; British Memorial to Belgium, Brussels; statue of King George V, Delhi, etc.; 2911.

Jag'uar. A wild cat, 719, *1791, plate 1. 1792, 1793.*

Jah. A variation of **Jehovah.**

Jainism (jān'-izm; jīn'-izm). Religious system in India, founded by Vardhamana Mahavira, a contemporary of Buddha, 601, 1703.

Jaipur (jī-poor') or **Jeypore,** repub. of India. It has responsible govt. and joined Rajasthan Union March 1949. 15,590 sq. m.; pop. 3,040,876; chiefly agricultural: some marble, copper, and cobalt found in the hills.

Jaipur. Mfg. and commercial city in N.-cent. India; pop. 175,800; cap. of state of Jaipur; 2743; "Hall of the Winds," *1711*; sacred monkeys, *2211.*

Jajce, Yugoslavia. Tn. 65 m. N.W. of Serajevo; chief outpost of E. Christendom from 1463 until captured by Turks in 1528.

Jal'ap. A perennial twining plant (*Ipomoea alapa*) with large flowers; grows in Mexico near the tn. of Jalapa, whence its name; the root contains a resin used in cathartics; relative of Morning Glory.

Jalisco (ha-lēs-kō), Mexico. State on cent. w. coast; 31,000 sq. m.; pop. (1940) 1,418,300; cap. Guadalajara; corn, wheat, tobacco; cattle; iron and silver; one of the wealthiest Mex. states.

Jam, 1792, 1341.

Jamaica (ja-mā'-ka). Largest isl. of Brit. W. Indies; 4,404 sq. m.; pop. 1,237,000; 1797; *map, 1792.*

Jamaica banana, 355.

Jamaica ginger, 1464.

Jamaica pepper. Same as **Allspice.**

Jamb, in architecture, the upright sides of an aperture, as a window, doorway, or fireplace, supporting the lintel, entablature, or mantel.

Jam'boree (U.S. slang, merry-making). Boy Scouts, 539, 542.

James, St. The Elder. Son of Zebedee; one of the 12 apostles, 188; shrine at Santiago de Compostella, *3034.*

James, St. The younger. Son of Alpheus: one of the 12 Apostles. 189.

James, the Lord's brother. Traditional author of Epistle of James.

James I (1566–1625). King of Gt. Brit. (James VI of Scotland): **1793,** *1794,* 1149, 2116, 2892, 3104; Bible translation under, 427; Gunpowder Plot, 1264; opposes use of tobacco, 3219; Raleigh and, 2744.

James II (1633–1701). King of Gt. Brit.. **1794;** battle of the Boyne, 537; capture of New Amsterdam, 2357; Charles II secures succession, 756; and the Jacobites, 1790; and Marlborough, 2105; Revolution (of 1688), *1207, 1208,* 2682.

James I (1394–1437). King of Scot., poet and constitutional reformer; succeeded in 1406, while captive in Eng., released in 1424; murdered by rebel nobles.

James II (1430–60). King of Scot., son of James I; succeeded to the throne at the age of seven; the Earl of Douglas, who was regent, was murdered by James, who was himself killed when besieging Roxburgh Castle, Aug. 3, 1460.

James III (1451–88). King of Scot.; a weak ruler, the nobles rose in arms against him, and he was murdered when fleeing from Sauchieburn, after his army had been defeated.

James IV (1473–1513). King of Scot.; succeeded in 1488; figures in Scott's "Lady of the Lake"; killed at Flodden, 1315.

James V (1512–42). King of Scot.; succeeded in 1513; father of Mary Queen of Scots.

James VI of Scotland. See **James I** (Gt. Brit.).

James (James Edward Francis Stuart) (1688–1766), "the Old Pretender," 1790, 2682.

James, Epistle of. Book of the New Testament, addressed by James the Lord's brother, from Jerusalem to twelve tribes of the Dispersion inculcating practical morality.

James, Henry (1843–1916). Amer. novelist and essayist; Brit. subject (1915); refined, subtle, and perceptive, but in later works becoming involved and artificial stylist ("Daisy Miller"; "The Portrait of a Lady"; "The Finer Grain"); brother of William James; 3295; work characterized, 2403, 3295.

James Tait Black Prizes. Two annual Brit. literary money prizes, for fiction and biography, first awarded 1919; founded by Mrs. Black to commemorate J. T. Black, publisher; won by E. M. Forster, J. B. Priestley, Graham Greene, P. A. Scholes, etc.

James, William (1842–1910). Amer. psychologist; brilliant, original and highly readable philosopher ("Principles of Psychology"; "Varieties of Religious Experience"; "Pragmatism"), 2572.

Jameson (jām'-son), **Sir Leander Starr** (1853–1917). Scot. physician, leader of "Jameson raid" on the Transvaal (1895); became leader of S. African Progressive party and prime minister (1904–08) of Cape Colony; 486, 3019; aided by Cecil Rhodes, 2771.

Jamestown, Virginia, U.S.A. First permanent settlement made by Eng. in Amer.; pop. 1,352; 3290, 3326.

Jammes, Francis (1868–1938). French writer, 1382.

Jammu. Winter cap. of Kashmir; pop. 36,500; 1848. Jammu and Kashmir is the full name of the state of Kashmir.

Jams and Jellies, 1792; food value, 1339.

Jane Eyre. Plain, shy governess, heroine of Charlotte Brontë's "Jane Eyre," 587.

Jane, Fred T. (1870–1916). Brit. naval writer and novelist; founded in 1898 the annual "All the World's Fighting Ships," in 1909 "All the World's Aircraft."

Janiculum (ja-nik'-ū-lum). Anc. name of hill in Rome. 2799.

Janina (yah'-nē-na) or **Yanina**. Tn. in N.W. Greece; pop. 20,000; taken from Turkey (1913); makes gold ware, silks.

Janizaries (jan'-i-za-riz) or **Janissaries**. A powerful military force of Turkish Empire; suppressed (1826) by Mahmud II, 3262.

Jan'sen or **Janse'nius, Cornelius** (1585–1638). Dutch theologian, Bishop of Ypres, founder of Jansenism.

Jan'senism. A doctrine intended to reform Catholicism, defended by Pascal but condemned by several popes as heresy; it rent France in 17th and early 18th centuries.

Jan'uary. First month of year, 2223.

Ja'nus. In Rom. myth., two-faced god.

Japan. Isl. kingdom of Asia; 144,000 sq. m.; pop. 79,000,000; **1795**, *plates, 1801–1808; map, 1796;* children, *789*, 802; costume, 1798, *1803, 1805;* dancing girls, *plate f. 964;* earthquakes, *1069;* education, 1798; embroidery *1810;* festivals, 1795, 2350; government, 1799, 1800; marriage customs, *2108;* former Pacific isl. possessions and mandates, 2473; religion, 1798; types, *267;* writing, 1809.
Geography and industries : agriculture, 1797, 2774, *2775;* cap. Tokyo, 3221; chief cities and manufactures, 1796, 1798, 1874, 2271, 2454, 3435; fisheries, 1299, 1797, 2912, 2931; foreign trade, 1798, 2454; lacquer work, 1881; mining, 1798; physical features, 1795; population, 265, 1795; porcelain, 2665; rice, 2774, *2775;* silk industry, 1797, 2972; tea cultivation, 3162; vegetation, 1797.
History, 1795, 1798; Xavier's mission, 3429; opened to foreigners, 3435; Chinese relations, 812, 814; Russo-Japanese War, 1800, 2848; 1st World War, 3409, 3411; Shanghai, 2937; Shantung, 2938; Hirohito, *1629;* Manchuria, 2087, 3415; invasion of China, 814, 3415; 2nd World War, 1800, 2473, 2474, 2965, 3419, *map, 3419,* 3424.

Japan, Sea of. Part of Pacific between Japan and Asia; *map, 1796.*

Japanese art, 1809, *plates 1806, 1807;* carved wood and ivory, 1809, *1812;* colour prints, *1273, 1806, 1807;* embroidery, *1810;* enamelling, 1158, 2271; Kyoto, centre of, *1874;* lacquerware, 1811, 1881; pottery, 1809, 2271, 2665, *2668.*

Japanese sika. A deer, 985.

Japan'ning or lacquering, 1881.

Japheth (jā'-feth) or **Japhet.** Third son of Noah.

Jaques (jā'-kwēz). Melancholy courtier in Shakespeare's " As You Like It "; 282.

Jargoon, a gem variety of zircon, 3444, 3813.

Jarrow. Tn. of Durham Co., on the riv. Tyne; grew with ship-building yards estab. by Sir C. M. Palmer (1822–1907); became a " special area " through distress caused by unemployment (80 p.c. of workers) during 1930–40; steel-rolling, asphalt preparation, etc., introduced; pop. est. 27,000; here are ruins of the monastery in which the Venerable Bede lived and died.

Jas'mine. A garden shrub, **1812**; and tea, 3160.

Ja'son. In Gk. myth., leader of Argonauts, 229.

Jasper. A yellow semi-precious stone; a form of quartz, 2713.

Jasper Park. In Alberta, on E. slope of Canadian Rockies (4,200 sq. m.), 680.

Jassy (yah'-si) or **Yassy,** Rumania. Trade centre of Moldavia, 200 m. N.E. of Bucharest; pop. 109,000, 2840.

Jats. A people of N.W. India numbering 8,377,000 in 1931.

Jaujard (zhō-zhahr), **Vice-Adm. R.** (b. 1896). Fr. sailor; in Oct. 1948 app. flag officer on the permanent milit. organization of Western Union (*q.v.* in *f-i*).

Jaun'dice. Malady of the liver, 1968.

Jaunpur (jawn-poor'). A city in United Provs., N.E. India, on r. Gumti, 34 m. N.W. of Benares; pop. 44,800; once a magnificent Mahomedan capital; famous for perfumes.

Jaurès (zhō-rez), **Jean** (1859–1914). Fr. Socialist, ardent defender of Dreyfus, strong opponent of militarism; assassinated by fanatic because of his opposition to 1914–1918 War.

Java (jah'-va). Isl. in Indonesia; a. (with Madura) 51,032 sq. m.; pop. 45,000,000. **1813** : *map, 1074;* prehistoric " ape-man " of, 2079; coffee industry, 864; fishing, *1076;* quinine, 2719; rattan palms, *2484;* rubber, 2833; volcanoes, *plate f. 3329;* 2nd World War and after, 1813, 2473, 3420.

Javelin, throwing the, in athletics, *289.*

Jaw. In birds, 437; fish, 1297; human, 3163; rodents, 2795; snakes, 2990.

Jaxartes (jaks-ahr'-tēz). Anc. name of Syr-Darya, r. in cent. Asia; flowing N.W. to Aral Sea; Alexander the Great at, 106.

Jay, John (1745–1829). Amer. jurist and statesman; in 1794 concluded the " Jay Treaty " between Gt. Brit. and U.S.A.

Jays. Bird group of crow family; native of Asia, Africa, Europe; the Brit. species is the common jay, **1815,** *455.*

Jazz. Music, 1815.

Jeanne d'Arc. *See* **Joan of Arc.**

Jeans, Sir James Hopwood (1877–1946). Brit. physicist, astronomer and mathematician, **1815,** 1816; tidal theory of planets, 2620; awarded O.M., Jan. 1939.

Jebb, Sir Richard (1841–1905). Brilliant Scot. classical scholar; he was professor of Greek at Glasgow Univ. and Regius Professor of Greek at Cambridge Univ. (" Sophocles ").

Jedburgh (jed'-bu-ro), Scot. Co. tn. of Roxburghshire, 50 m. S.E. of Edinburgh; has ruins of a magnificent Augustinian abbey founded by David I; from Jedburgh comes " Jeddart's Justice," meaning to hang first and try afterwards, 2832.

Jeep. Popular name of a general purposes (G.P.) U.S. army truck in 2nd World War.

Jefferies, (John) Richard (1848–87). Eng. essayist and naturalist, **1816.**

Jefferson, Thomas (1743–1826). 3rd pres. of U.S.A., **1816**; drafts Declaration of Independence, *145.*

Jeffrey, Francis Jeffrey, Lord (1773–1850). Scot. lawyer; co-founder and editor of Edinburgh Review; merciless critic of Romantic movement.

Jeffreys, George, Baron (1648–89). Eng. judge, chief justice and later lord chancellor under James II; notorious for brutality in " bloody assizes " following Monmouth's insurrection.

Jehol. Mongolian province lying between Great Wall of China and Manchuria. Occupied by Japanese 1933–45; 2087.

Jehosh'aphat. Son of Asa and king of Judah, 9th cent. B.C.

Jehoshophat, Valley of. A place mentioned in the Bible; supposed to be between Jerusalem and Mount of Olives.

Jeho'vah (more properly **Yahweh**) or **Jah.** Hebrew name for the God of Israel; means the " self-existent " or " unchangeable One "; in English versions generally rendered " the Lord."

Jehu (jē'-hū). King of Israel; killed Jezebel and massacred house of Ahab (2 Kings ix.-x.), enemy of Baal worshippers; furious driver (2 Kings ix. 20), 2481.

" Jekyll, Dr." The kindly reputable physician in R. L. Stevenson's " Strange Case of Dr. Jekyll and Mr. Hyde."

Jellicoe, John Rushworth, 1st Earl (1859–1935). Brit. admiral, 387, **1816,** 1817; national memorial unveiled in Trafalgar Sq. on Oct. 21, 1948.

Jelly, food, 1341, 1792.

Jelly-fish. A primitive coelenterate animal, **1817,** *1818.*

Jemappes (zhe-map'). Vil. in Belgium, 3 m. S.W. of Mons; decisive defeat of Austrians by Fr. Rev. Army in 1792.

Jena (yā'-na). Ger. Famous univ. tn. of Thuringia on r. Saale 45 m. S.W. of Leipzig; pop. 58,000.

Jena, battle of (1806), 2276, 2696; effect in Prussia, 1449.

Jena, University of. One of the chief Ger. univs., founded about 1547; noted for its many distinguished teachers, including Fichte, Schelling, Hegel, Schiller, Haeckel, and Eucken; identified with liberal movement in theology.

Jenghiz Khan. Same as **Genghis Khan.**

Jenkins's Ear, War of. Robert Jenkins, English merchant sea-captain, appeared before the House of Commons and alleged that the Spaniards had boarded his vessel and cut off his ear. The incident led to war between Eng. and Spain in 1742 and to the downfall of Walpole.

Jenner, Edward (1749–1823). Eng. physician, originator of smallpox vaccination, **1818,** *1819,* 3301.

Jennings, Sarah. *See* **Marlborough, Sarah, Duchess of.**

Jenny (spinning machine). *See* **Spinning Jenny.**

" Jenny Jones." Eng. folk-song, 1335.

Jenny-wheel, a large single pulley, 2698.

Jephthah (jef'-tha). Judge of Israel who, in fulfilment of a rash vow, sacrificed to the Lord the first creature that he met on return from victory—his only daughter (Judges xi.).

Jer'ba. Fr. isl. off E. coast of Tunis, N. Africa; 425 sq. m.; pop. 90,000, mostly Berbers; the lotus-eaters' isl. of Gk. and Rom. geographers.

Jerbo'a. A rat-like animal, **1819.**

Jeremi'ah (7th cent. B.C.). One of the major Hebrew prophets, last before the exile; Book of Jeremiah is one of the greatest and longest of the Old Testament prophetical books; prophesies disaster to Judah, 2691.

Jerez (or **Xerez**) **de la Frontera** (hā-rāth' dā lah fron-tā'-ra), Spain. Old city in S. 14 m. N.E. of Cadiz; pop. 93,000; famous for sherry, to which it gave the name; battle of, 3033.

Jericho (je'-ri-kō). Important city of anc. Palestine 7 m. N. of Dead Sea; miraculously captured and almost destroyed by Joshua (Josh. vi. 20-4); 2480; archaeological expedition to, 208.

Jerobo'am I, leader of revolting 10 tribes and first king of Israel (10th cent. B.C.) after separation from Judah (1 Kings xii, 20), 1829.

Jerome (je-rōm'), **Jerome K.** (1859–1927). Eng. humorist and dramatist, who won success originally with his " Three Men in a Boat "; with Robert Barr he founded " The Idler "; (" Idle Thoughts of an Idle Fellow "; " The Passing of the Third Floor Back ").

Jerome, St. (c. 340–420). Most learned of early Fathers of Latin Church; translated Bible, 425.

Jerome of Prague (d. 1416). Learned and eloquent Bohemian religious reformer and friend of John Huss, 1661.

Jer'rold, Douglas (1803–57). Eng. dramatist, journalist, and humorous author; contributed " Mrs. Caudle's Lectures " to " Punch " (" Black-eyed Susan ").

Jersey. Largest of Channel Isls., 20 m. from Fr. coast; 45 sq. m.; pop. 50,460; chief tn. St. Helier. Air services from London, Southampton, etc., 751, *752*. Occupied by Germany 1940–45,

Jersey cattle. Breed originating in isl. of Jersey, *731*, 732.

Jersey City, New Jersey, U.S.A. Mfg. city on Hudson r., opposite New York : pop. 301,170 ; rly. centre, with large trade in coal, iron, agric. ; extensive meat packing business.

Jerusalem (je-rōō′sa-lem), Palestine. The anc. cap. of the Hebrew nation and largest city of Palestine ; pop. (1946) 164,330 ; **1819,** 2480 ; scene of Christ's Crucifixion, 1820, 1825 ; Crusades, 936, **937,** 2864 ; captured by Nebuchadrezzar, 1830 ; captured by Pompey, 1830, destroyed by Titus, 1830 ; taken in 1st World War, 121, 936, 1821, 2480, 3411 ; in fighting of 1947–48, 1821, 2483. Proclaimed cap. of Israel in 1950.

"Jerusalem." Hymn with words by W. Blake and music by Parry, 467.

Jerusalem artichoke, 256.

"Jerusalem Delivered." Epic by Tasso, 1786, 3157.

Jervis (jar′-vis) **Bay, H.M.S.** Brit. armed merchant cruiser and escort vessel ; commander, Capt. E. S. F. Fegen (posthumous V.C.) ; sunk Nov. 5, 1940, on escort duty, while engaging Ger. pocket battleship Adm. Scheer so that the convoy might escape.

Jes′se. Father of David ; "the tree of Jesse," a favourite medieval Church emblem, represents Jesse as the root. and the Saviour or Virgin and Child as the supreme flower (Isaiah xi. 1, 10).

Jessop, Gilbert Laird (b. 1874). Eng. cricketer ; captained Glos. team and was particularly famous for his mighty hitting.

Jesuits (jez′-ū-its), or **Society of Jesus.** Religious order founded by Loyola, 2034 ; and Counter-Reformation, 2760 ; missions in N. Amer., 2107 ; spread use of quinine, 2719 ; Xavier one of the founders, 3429.

"Jesus, Sayings of." Anc. manuscript, 425.

Jesus Christ. Founder of Christianity, 817, **1821** ; Andes statue, 153, *228*, 229, *805* ; and the Apostles, 188, 1822, 1825, 2562 ; Ascension, 1825 ; home in Nazareth, 1822, *2309* ; reputed birthplace, 422 ; "The Last Supper," *189*, 1825, 2527 ; and Peter, 2562 ; bearing the Cross, *1184* ; Resurrection, 1825 ; sacred places in Jerusalem, 1820 ; sacred places in Palestine, 422, 2480, 2481 ; and the Wandering Jew, 3340.

Jesus College, Cambridge, 668.

Jesus College, Oxford, 2464.

Jet. A dense black lignite, sometimes used for jewelry.

Jet Propulsion, 1826, *49* ; flying-bomb, 1330 ; gas turbine, 1424 ; Gloster Meteor, 1827, *38* ; speed boat engine, *1828* ; rocket bomb, 2792, 2793 ; venturi in, 3312.

Jet-pump, 2704.

Jetty. A pier or embankment used to direct or strengthen current or shelter a harbour, 1577.

Jevons, William Stanley (1835–82). Eng. political economist and logician ; professor at Owens College, Manchester, and Univ. College, London.

Jew, the Wandering, 3340.

Jewels. *See* Gems.

"Jew of Malta." Marlowe's tragedy whose chief character, Barabbas, is believed to have contributed suggestions for Shakespeare's Shylock.

Jews, "the children of Israel," *1601*, **1829,** 2920 ; language and literature, 423, 1600 ; music (anc.), 2261 ; New Year, 2350 ; Passover, 2527 ; religion, 423 ; sabbath, 2859 ; Zionist movement, 1786, 2482.
History : Abraham founds nation, 13, 1829 ; Egyptian captivity, 1829, 2235 ; conquer Canaan, 1829, 2570 ;

wars with Philistines, 2570 ; reign of David, 979, 1829 ; Solomon, 2999 ; prophets, 1829, 2691 ; captivity in Babylon, 332, 1830, 2554 ; story of Esther, 1225 ; life and teachings of Jesus Christ, 1821 ; persecution, 1830 ; repression in Germany, in Austria, 1451, 1830, 2281 ; Jewish-Arab wars, 2483 ; state of Israel, 1831. *See* **Palestine.**

"Jew's Ear." An edible fungus (*Hirneola auricula-judea*) found on elder trees, named because it vaguely resembles a human ear in shape.

Jez′ebel. Idolatrous wife of Ahab, cursed by Elijah for treachery to Naboth (1 Kings xxi.) and murdered by Jehu (2 Kings ix. 30-7).

Jezreel (jez′-re-el). Anc. city in plain of Jezreel, 50 m. N. of Jerusalem ; cap. of Israel under Ahab ; modern tn., Zerin, has a few ruins of little interest ; 2481.

Jhelum (jā′-lum) or **Jehlam.** Anc. Hydaspes, flows s.w. from Himalayas into Chenab r., in Pakistan (450 m.), 2479 ; reached by Alexander, 1714.

Jibuti. *See* Djibouti.

Jig′ger, chigger, or **chigoe.** Small tropical flea ; causes irritation by burrowing under the skin.

Jigger. Mould used in pottery-making, 2665.

Jiménez. *See* Ximenes.

Jiménez, Juan Ramon. Spanish poet, 3051.

Jim′mu Ten′no or **"Son of Heaven"** (7th and 8th cent. B.C.). Legendary founder of the line of Jap. mikados, descendant of the sun-goddess and first ruler of Japan.

Jimson weed or **stinkweed,** *2639*. Amer. name of the thorn-apple, highly poisonous plant of nightshade family.

Jin′gle, Alfred. Character in "Pickwick Papers," *1014*.

Jin′go (2nd and 3rd cent. A.D.). Legendary warlike empress of Japan, on whose alleged conquest of Korea Japan based traditional claims of suzerainty over that country ; name not connected with modern "jingoes"—a term which was derived from a song popular in England in 1878 : "We don't want to fight, but by jingo, if we do——."

Jinn. Supernatural beings in Mahomedan belief.

Jinnah, Mahomed Ali (1876–1948). founder and first gov.-gen. of Pakistan, **1831.**

Jinrik′sha or **rickshaw.** Light man-drawn carriage said to have been invented in 1869 by a Baptist missionary in Japan, *67*.

Jiu-jitsu. *See* Jujitsu.

Joachim (yō′-a-kēm), **Joseph** (1831–1907). Hungarian violinist and composer, called "the king of violinists" ("Hungarian Concerto"). His grand-nieces, Adila Fachiri and Jelly d'Arányi, also attained fame as violinists.

Joad, Cyril E. M. (b. 1891). Brit. writer on philosophy and broadcaster ; prof. of philosophy at Birkbeck Coll., Univ. of London ; member of original B.B.C. Brains Trust ; wrote "Philosophical Aspects of Modern Science," "The Mind and Its Workings," "Is Christianity True ? "

Joan. Mythical woman pope supposed to have reigned about 855–858 as John VIII ; the story says she fell in love with a Benedictine monk and fled with him to Athens disguised as a man, afterwards going to Rome and becoming a priest.

Joan of Arc (1412–31). "The Maid of Orleans," 1365, 1653, **1831,** 2454, 2760 ; *plates f. 1832, 1833* ; and Charles VII, 757 ; heroine of Schiller's play, 2882 ; Shaw's play, 2940 ; museum at Orléans, 2454.

Joanna (jō-an′-a) (1479–1555). Queen of Castile, daughter of Ferdinand and Isabella, and mother of Emperor Charles V and Emperor Ferdinand

I ; did not actually rule, because partially insane.

Ju′ash or **Jehoash.** King of Israel, about 798–790 B.C. ; expelled the Syrians from kingdom, defeated and captured Amaziah, king of Judah, and plundered the temple at Jerusalem (2 Kings xiii.-xiv.).

Joash or **Jehoash.** King of Judah, about 837–797 B.C. ; slain by conspiracy of his own servants (2 Kings xi., xii. ; 2 Chronicles xxii.-xxiv.).

Job. Long-suffering hero of the Book of Job in the Old Testament, **1832.**

Jobber. Professional dealer on the Stock Exchange, who buys and sells securities (but not with the general public, who must act through a broker), 3094.

Jodhpur (jōd-poor′). Cap. of Jodhpur state, in the Rajasthan Union, repub. of India ; pop. of city 94,000, 2743.

Jodl (yō′-del), **Alfred** (1890–1946). Ger. soldier ; staff capt. in 1918 ; Hitler's personal adviser on strategy during Second World War, 2282 ; col.-gen. in 1942 ; signed Ger. surrender May 1945, 2760 ; found guilty at Nuremberg trials of conspiracy to wage aggressive war and executed Oct. 16, 1946.

Jo′el (5th cent. B.C.). Hebrew minor prophet, author of the Book of Joel, the 29th book of the Old Testament ; prophesied the judgments coming to Israel, and urged the people to repent and reform, 2692.

Joffre (zho′-fr), **Joseph Jacques Césaire** (1852–1931). Fr. general and marshal of France, **1832,** 3409.

Johan′nesburg, S. Africa. Largest city in Transvaal ; centre of one of world's greatest goldfields, pop. 762,910 ; 1479, **1833,** *73, 3017,* 3239.

John, St. One of the 12 Apostles, 188, 2562.

John, popes. For list *see* **Pope.**

John XXIII (c. 1370–1419), anti-pope during the Great Schism ; Pope ; called Council of Constance by which he was deposed (1415) : imprisoned in Germany.

John (1167–1216). King of Eng., **1833,** *1834* ; and Arthur, Duke of Brittany, 254 ; died at Newark Castle, *714* ; struggle with Pope Innocent III, 1725, 1834 ; grants Magna Carta, 1194, *1205,* 1489, 2059.

John (1296–1346). Blind king of Bohemia ; death, 926.

John (1319–64). King of France, called "the Good," succeeded 1350 ; at Poitiers, 1652.

John III, King of Poland. *See* **Sobieski, John.**

John I (1357–1433). King of Portugal, called "the Great" and "father of his country," chosen king in 1385, 2659 ; father of Henry the Navigator, 1613.

John II (1455–95), "the Perfect," King of Portugal ; under him Portugal reached height of its power ; and Columbus, 878.

John VI (1769–1826), King of Portugal ; succeeded 1816 (regent from 1799) ; accepted Port. constitution after insurrection (1821) and recognized independence of Brazil (1825) ; exile in Brazil, 554.

John, Don, of Austria (1545–78). Son of the Emperor Charles V and half-brother of Philip II of Spain, victor over Turks (1571) in famous naval battle of Lepanto.

John of Gaunt (1340–99), Duke of Lancaster ; 4th son of Edward III of Eng., ancestor of House of Lancaster ; character in Shakespeare's "Richard II" ; famous speech, 1161 ; built hall at Kenilworth castle, *1851*.

John of Leiden (c. 1510–36). Dutch religious (Anabaptist) fanatic and revolutionary leader ; for a year ruled "the Kingdom of Zion" in Münster ; executed by prince-bishop of Münster on capture of city.

John o' Groats. Locality on N. coast of Scot., in Caithness ; mistakenly regarded as the northernmost point of mainland of Gt. Brit. ; named from an eight-sided house built by a Dutchman named Groat or Groot at end of 15th cent. ; 655.

John the Baptist, 1620, 2480, 2562.

John, Augustus (b. 1879). Eng. painter, espec. famous for portraits, **1834** ; "The Orange Jacket," *1192*.

John, Epistles of. 23rd, 24th, and 25th books of New Testament, attributed to Apostle John ; first exhorts to Christian faith ; second and third are short notes, one to a church. the other to Gaius, a member of church ; authorship disputed.

John, Gospel of. 4th book of New Testament, attributed to Apostle John ; purpose to present life and works of Jesus so as to arouse faith in readers ; authorship disputed.

"John Brown's Body." Amer. Civil War song, 588.

"John Bull." Name commonly used to personify the Brit. people, supposed to have arisen from John Arbuthnot's "History of John Bull," 578, 2366, **1834.**

John Dory. Predatory fish, coloured yellow (whence the name, from Fr. *jaune*, yellow—and *dorée*, gilt), and with large dark spot on either side. Legend says that this is the mark of St. Peter's finger and thumb, the dory being the fish in whose mouth he found the piece of tribute money ; high, narrow body, large dorsal fins, front one with spiny rays.

"John Gilpin," poem by Cowper, 923.

"John Halifax, Gentleman." Novel by Miss Mulock (Mrs. Craik) ; the hero, an orphan, reared in poverty and obscurity, rises to wealth and marries a girl of gentle birth.

Johnson, Amy (1904–1941). British air pilot, **1834.**

Johnson, Andrew (1808–75). 17th pres. of U.S.A. ; he succeeded Lincoln, holding office from 1865 to 1868 ; he was impeached in 1867, but acquitted, 3291.

Johnson, Esther (1680–1728). Friend of Jonathan Swift, 3132.

Johnson, Samuel (1709–84). Famous Eng. man of letters, *1213*, **1835** ; birthplace, *1835*, *1934* ; and Boswell, 529, *530* ; Boswell's "Life," 1213, 1836 ; and Burke, 622 ; friendship with Goldsmith, 1482 ; quotations from "Dictionary," 1836 ; and Reynolds, 2768.

Johnston, Sir Harry Hamilton (1858–1927). Brit. administrator, African explorer ; originator of plan for Brit. "Cape-to-Cairo" route ; discoverer of okapi and other African animals ; author of books on Africa and of several novels.

Johnstown, Pennsylvania, U.S.A. Iron and steel mfg. city 7 m. E. of Pittsburgh on Conemaugh R. in softcoal dist. ; pop. 66,993.

Johore (jō-hor'). Sultanate and state of Malayan Federation under Brit. protection ; 7,500 sq. m. ; pop. 737,600 ; rubber principal product and export ; scene of bitter fighting early 1942 during Japanese advance on Singapore ; occupied by Japan 1942–45 ; 2069.

Joint Stock Company. Trading company incorporated under the Companies Acts, as distinct from a statutory or public company (such as a gasworks or waterworks company) created by individual Acts of Parliament.

Joinville (zhwan-vĕl'), **Jean, Sire de** (1224–1317). Fr. historian of Louis IX and his first Crusade.

Jókai (yō'-kī), **Mór** or **Maurice** (1825–1904). Hungarian novelist (" the Magyar Dumas ") and revolutionist of 1848 ; brilliant, prolific but uneven genius (" Timar's Two Worlds ").

Joliet (zhō'-lyā), **Louis** (1645–1700). Fr.-Canadian explorer, 143, 2192.

Joliot-Curie (zhol-yō kü-rē), **Frederic** (b. 1900). Fr. physicist ; married Irène Curie, daughter of Pierre and Marie Curie ; they researched together on radio-activity, turning aluminium to an isotope of phosphorus by alpha particle bombardment ; awarded Nobel Prize for physics in 1935 ; head of Fr. atomic energy research dept. ; and physics, 2595.

"Jolley," machine for making pottery. 2665.

Jolo. See **Sulu Islands.**

Joly (jō'-li), **John** (1857–1934). Irish physicist and geologist ; wrote scientific works, including "The Birth Time of the World."

Jo'nah. Hebrew prophet (? 8th cent. B.C.) ; as told in Book of Jonah, disobedient to divine summons, draws storm on ship in which he tries to escape ; is thrown into sea and swallowed by a great fish ; is saved by Jehovah ; delivers divine message to Nineveh, but resents city's preservation until taught compassion by the lesson of the gourd ; 2692.

Jon'athan. Son of Saul and beloved friend of David (1 Samuel xx. ; 2 Samuel i. 19-27), 979, 1829.

Jones, Arthur Creech (b. 1891). Colonial Under-Sec. in 1945. Sec. (1946–50).

Jones, Griffith (1683–1761). Welsh divine ; he was a pioneer in Welsh education, both religious and secular ; he set up many " circulating charity schools " with great success.

Jones, Sir Harold Spencer (b. 1890). Brit. astronomer ; from 1933 Astronomer Royal ; measured more accurately the distance from the earth to the sun.

Jones, Henry Arthur (1851–1929). Eng. dramatist ; among his chief plays are " The Silver King," which brought him into prominence, " Mrs. Dane's Defence," " The Liars," " The Hypocrites," " The Pacifists."

Jones, Inigo (1573–1652). Distinguished Eng. architect ; **1836**, *1837*.

Jones, John Paul (1747–92). Amer. naval hero, **1837.**

Jones, Robert Tyre (Bobby) (b. 1902). Amer. golfer ; frequent winner of championships in both America and England (British Open, 1926, 1927).

Jones, Sir William (1746–94). Eng. orientalist and linguist ; pioneer in Sanskrit ; 2570.

Jonescu (zhō-nes'-kōō), **Take** (1858–1922). Rumanian statesman ; as foreign minister in 1920 helped to create the Little Entente.

Jongkind (yong'-kint), **Johann Barthold** (1819–1891). Dutch painter ; born Lattrop, Holland ; forerunner of the Impressionists and distinguished as an etcher, 2335.

Jonson, Ben (c. 1573–1637). Eng. dramatist, lyric poet, epigrammatist, and scholar ; 1040, 1211, **1837**, *1838* ; burial place, 3369 ; and Shakespeare, 2932, 2936 ; poet laureate, 2634.

Jooss (yōs), **Kurt** (b. 1901). Ger. choreographer and ballet master ; his co., the Ballets Jooss, appeared in London, Paris, New York ; created " The Green Table," " Pandora."

Jordaens (yor-dahnz'), **Jakob** (1593–1678). Flemish painter ; **1838.**

Jordan. Sacred r. of Palestine ; rises in N., flows 200 m. s. in deep valley through lakes Merom (Huleh) and Galilee into Dead Sea ; *2481.*

Jordan, Hashimite Kingdom of the. Formerly Transjordan ; title changed in June 1949 when the country took over territory west of the R. Jordan ; **1838**, 3238.

Jordans. Vil. of Bucks, Eng., famous for its Quaker associations ; burial place of Wm. Penn, 2545.

Jo'seph. Hebrew patriarch, son of Jacob and Rachel ; father of Ephraim and Manasseh (Gen. xxxvii. 1) ; 1829, **1838.**

Joseph, St. Husband of Mary, the mother of Jesus (Matt. i. ii. ; Luke ii), 1821.

Joseph I (1678–1711). Holy Roman emperor, succeeded to throne 1705 ; vigorously prosecuted wars against France and Hungary, and forced pope to acknowledge his brother Charles as king of Spain ; a liberal ruler, especially in religion and matters relating to peasantry.

Joseph II (1741–90), Holy Roman emperor, son of Maria Theresa ; benevolent despot ; upset old customs and provoked discontent and revolt ; died disillusioned and brokenhearted.

Joseph, Father (1577–1638). Fr. Capuchin friar, Richelieu's secretary and confidential adviser, nicknamed, because of his influence, the " Grey Eminence " (" Eminence Grise ").

Joseph of Arimathae'a. Rich Israelite, who entombed the body of Jesus ; said to have brought the Holy Grail to Britain.

" Joseph Andrews." Novel by Fielding, 1269, 2402.

Josephine (1763–1814). Empress of the French, first wife of Napoleon I, **1838**, *1839*, 2275, 2276 ; birthplace, 2112.

Jose'phus, Flavius (c. A.D. 37 –c. 95). Jewish historian ("The Jewish War," 170 B.C.–A.D. 70 ; " Antiquities, of the Jews " from earliest time to reign of Nero), 1601.

Josh'ua. Leader of Israelites, successor to Moses, 1829.

Joshua. Sixth book of Old Testament, named after Joshua ; account of Jewish settlement in Canaan.

Josi'ah (7th cent. B.C.). King of Judah. Abolished idolatry and re-established worship of the Lord (2 Kings xxii-xxiii.) ; 1830, 2481.

Jotunheim (yō'-tun-hăm). In Norse myth., home of frost giants, 2421 ; Thor's visit to, 3204.

Jotunheim. Mountainous region of s. Norway, 2393.

Joubert de la Ferté (zhōō-bair), **Air Chief Marshal Sir Philip B.** (b. 1887). Brit. Air Force officer ; A.O.C.-in-C. Coastal Command 1936–37 and 1941–43 ; Air Chief Marshal 1941 ; Inspector-gen. of R.A.F. in 1943 ; Deputy Chief of Staff, Information and Civil Affairs, S.E.A.C., 1943–45 ; Director of Public Relations, Air Min., 1946–47.

Joubert, Petrus Jacobus (1834–1900). Boer general, commandant-general in first and second Boer wars ; repelled Jameson Raid.

Joule, James Prescott (1818–89). Eng. physicist ; formulated law of conservation of energy ; measured mechanical equivalent of heat (Joule's Law), 1593, **1839** ; and Rumford, 2842.

Joule (J). Unit of energy ; work done in forcing one ampere against resistance of one ohm for a second ; or 10^7 ergs ; named after J. P. Joule, 1840.

Jourdain (zhoor-dan'), **M.** Hero of Molière's " Le Bourgeois gentilhomme " (" The Tradesman Turned Gentleman "), 2198.

Journal of the Plague Year, by Defoe, 986.

Journeyman, in medieval trade guild, 1553.

Joust (jōōst). Knightly combat in which the contestants engaged each other singly, 1864, *plate f. 1864*, 2830.

Jove (jōv) or **Ju'piter.** Chief deity of the anc. Romans, identified with Gk. Zeus, 1841, 3443. See also **Zeus.**

Jow'ett, Benjamin (1817–93). Eng. scholar, theologian, and great teacher, master of Balliol College, Oxford ; translations of Plato, 2629.

Jowitt, William Allen, 1st Viscount (b. 1885). Lord Chancellor since 1945.

Joyce, James (1882–1941). Irish author ; remarkable for psychological analysis of character, realistic handling of themes, and a style verging sometimes on incoherence ("Dubliners," 1914 ; "Ulysses," 1922 ; "Anna Livia Plurabelle," 1928), 1216, 2401, 2403.

Joyce, William, "Lord Haw-Haw" (1906–45). Traitor, born in New York of Irish father, English mother ; came as child to England where, 1923–39, worked on fascist and national socialist propaganda ; went to Germany Aug. 1939 ; broadcast Nazi propaganda in English to the U.K. throughout 2nd World War ; naturalized a Ger. Sept. 1940 ; was captured May 28, 1945, tried at Old Bailey, and hanged as traitor Jan. 3, 1946.

Joyn'son-Hicks, William. See Brentford, 1st Viscount.

Joystick. Popular name for control column used in aeroplanes.

Juan (hwahn) or **Giovanni** (jo-vahn'-ē), **Don.** Profligate hero of Sp. legend ; subject of many works of art, including Mozart's opera, "Don Giovanni," and Byron's poem, "Don Juan."

Juan Fernandez. Group of small isls. in S. Pacific ; largest isl. Mas-a-Tierra ; 804, 2469 ; Alexander Selkirk, 804, 937.

Juarez (hoo-ahr'-eth), **Benito Pablo** (1806–72). Mex. statesman, sometimes called the "Mexican Washington," 2158.

Ju'bal. Hebrew inventor of musical instruments (Gen. iv. 21), 2261.

Ju'baland. Region in E. Africa, adjoining the r. Juba ; formerly a part of Brit. Kenya Colony, it was ceded to Italy in 1924, and became part of It. Somaliland, 3000.

Jubilee. An anniversary ; notable Brit. jubilees have been Queen Victoria's (Golden) Jubilee (1887), 50th anniversary of accession ; Victoria's Diamond Jubilee (1897), 60th anniversary ; and King George V's Silver Jubilee (1935), which marked the completion of 25 years on the throne.

Jubbulpore, India. Mfg. and trading city in Central Provs. ; pop. (1941) 178,300 ; cotton ; military centre, 744.

Judah (jōō-'da), Hebrew patriarch, 4th son of Jacob and Leah, traditional ancestor of tribe of Judah.

Judah, S. kingdom of Palestine after separation of Israel, 1829, 1830.

Judaism, religion of the Jews. See Jews·

Ju'das (Thaddeus), **the Apostle,** 188· 189.

Judas Iscar'iot. Disciple who betrayed Jesus for 30 pieces of silver (Matt. xxvi. 14–16, 25, 47–50) ; 188, 189, 1825.

Judas Maccabae'us. See in Index Maccabees.

Judas tree. The traditional tree on which Judas Iscariot hanged himself ; the species in question, *Cercis siliquastrum,* of the pea tribe, is found in southern Europe.

Jude, Epistle of. Twenty-sixth book of New Testament, doubtful authorship, often attributed to Jude, brother of Jesus, described as "brother of James" (Jude i. 1) ; exhortation to constancy in Christian faith.

Judea (joo-dē'-a) or **Judaea.** S. Palestine, 2480 ; under Roman rule, 1830.

Judge. One who presides in a court of judicature, 1490.

Judge Advocate-General. Minister of the Crown whose duty it is to advise in questions of military law, especially courts-martial.

Judges. Leaders of Israelites, 1829.

Judges, Book of. Seventh book of the Old Testament ; describes history of Israelites under the rule of the judges.

Judi'cial Committee of Privy Council. The final court of appeal in the British Commonwealth, being composed of a committee of members of the Privy Council, represented by the Lord Chancellor, previous lord chancellors, and others who hold or have held high judicial offices ; any matter under dispute affecting the Commonwealth (apart from Great Britain and Ireland, whose cases go to the House of Lords) comes before this committee who make a recommendation to His Majesty.

Judi'ciary, 1490. See also **Courts of Justice.**

Ju'dith. Jewish heroine, captivated Assyrian general Holofernes and slew him while he slept, thereby delivering the besieged Israelites ; story told in the apocryphal book of Judith.

Judo. See Jujitsu.

Jug'gernaut. See Jagannath.

Jugo-Slavia. See Yugoslavia.

Jugur'tha (d. 104 B.C.). Usurping king of Numidia ; defied Rom. power for several years, defeating and bribing opposing generals ; captured by Marius, 2809.

Jujitsu (jōō-jit'-sŭ) or **Ju-jutsu** or **Judo.** Form of wrestling, 1840.

Ju'lia (c. 83–54 B.C.). Daughter of Julius Caesar, 2654.

Ju'lian (Flavius Claudius Julianus) (A.D. 331–363). Rom. emperor, called "the Apostate" ; nephew of Constantine the Great ; brought up as Christian, became philosophic pagan; emp. A.D. 361 ; last pagan emperor.

Juliana (yoo-li-ah'-na), Queen of the Netherlands and Princess of Lippe-Biesterfeld (b. 1909). Only child of Queen Wilhelmina, and succeeded to throne on her abdication, Sept. 4, 1948, 2323, 3378. Married Prince Bernhard of Lippe-Biesterfeld (b. 1911), Jan. 7, 1937. Four daughters, Beatrix, born Jan. 31, 1938 ; Irene, born Aug. 5, 1939 ; Margriet, born Jan. 19, 1943 ; Maria Christina, born Feb. 18, 1947.

Julian calendar, 662.

Ju'liet. Heroine of Shakespeare's tragedy "Romeo and Juliet," 2821.

Julius I, St. (d. 352). Pope.

Julius II (1443–1513). Pope, 1503–1513, patron of art, started re-building of St. Peter's ; and Michelangelo, 2160.

Julius III (1487–1555). Pope.

July, 7th month of year, 2223.

Jum'bo. Name of largest captive elephant known (11 ft. 2 in. at death, then still growing); at London Zoo for many years and sold to P. T. Barnum in 1882.

Jum'na. Tributary of the r. Ganges, N. India ; rises in Himalayas, flows 860 m. S. and S.E. to Ganges r. ; 1417 ; at Delhi, 987.

Jumping. In athletics, 288, 289 ; on horseback, 2779.

Juncaceae (jun-kā'-sē-ē). Plant family incl. rushes.

June. 6th month of year, 2223.

Juneau, Alaska. Cap. and largest city ; on inlet of Pacific 100 m. N. of Sitka ; pop. 5,730 ; commerce in gold, furs, 98, 99.

Jung (yoong), **Carl Gustave** (b. 1875). Swiss psychologist, 1840 ; and psycho-analysis, 2697.

Jungfrau (yoong'-frow). Alpine peak (13,670 ft.), 128, 132, 3138, 3142.

Jungle. Name given to thick vegetation of tropical districts, in Africa, India, Amazon, etc., 3441.

"Jungle Books." Collections of animal stories by Rudyard Kipling, 1860 ; plates f. 1860, 1861.

Junior school, 2886.

Ju'niper. Various conifer trees or shrubs with dark-blue, berry-like cones, and whorled, needle or scale-like leaves, 1840.

Ju'nius. Pen-name of author of a famous series of scathing Eng. political letters attacking George III and his ministers (1769–72) ; real authorship never proved, attributed to more than 40 persons, but generally conceded to Sir Philip Francis.

Junk. Oriental boat (usually Chinese or Japanese).

Junkers (yoon'-kerz). Former Prussian nobles or squires, generally marked by reactionary views.

Junkers (yoon'-kerz), **Hugo** (1859–1935). Ger. aircraft designer ; in 1919 founded Junkers works at Dessau which produced bombers (Ju. 87, Ju. 88, etc.), and transports (Ju. 52) of the 2nd World War.

Juno (jōō'-nō). In Rom. myth., goddess identified with Gk. Hera, 1614, 1841. See also **Hera.**

Juno. An asteroid, 1841.

"Juno's bird." The peacock, 2532.

Ju'piter. In Rom. myth., god identified with Gk. Zeus, 1841, 3443. See **Zeus.**

Jupiter. Largest of the planets, 1841, 2617, 2618 ; satellites discovered by Galileo, 1415.

Jura (joo'-ra) ("deer island"), 4th largest of Inner Hebrides, 160 sq. m.

Jura Mts. On border of France and Switzerland, 1360, 1842, 3140 ; stock-raising, 1360.

Juras'sic period. In geology, 1432, 1433.

Jurua. Tributary of Amazon ; 1,200 m. from source in Peru, 551.

Ju'ry, 1842, 1843 ; established in Eng., 1609 ; in anc. Greece, 2999.

Jus gentium. "Law of nations," the beginning of international law, 1904.

Jusserand (zhü-se-rahn), **Jean Jules** (1855–1932). Fr. diplomat and scholar, became ambassador to U.S.A. in 1902 ; author of several works on Eng. literature and life, notably "English Wayfaring Life in the Middle Ages" and a "Literary History of the English People."

"Justice," play by John Galsworthy, 1416.

Justice, courts of. See Courts of Justice.

Justice of the Peace (J.P.). Local magistrate.

Justin I (450–527). Byzantine emperor ; an ignorant peasant, he rose to rank through army ; and Justinian I, 1844.

Justin'ian I (483–565). Byzantine emperor, 637, 1844 ; legal code, 1902 ; silk culture introduced, 2970 ; Vandals conquered, 3304.

Justinian II (669–711). Byzantine emperor.

Justin, Martyr (c. 100–165). An early Church Father ; one of foremost Christian apologists ; b. in Palestine of pagan parents ; said to have been beheaded at Rome.

Jute, 1844 ; in Bengal, 413, 2479 ; paper made from, 2497 ; used to insulate cables, 647.

Jutes. A Teutonic people who invaded Britain in 5th cent. ; generally believed to have come from Jutland, 574, 992, 1194, 2880.

Jut'land. Low flat peninsula of N. Europe, forming largest part of Denmark, 991, 2388 ; map, 992.

Jutland, battle of (1916), 2293, 3411 ; Beatty at, 387.

Ju'venal (60–140) (Decimus Junius Juvenalis). Rom. poet and satirist, whose writings express a burning hatred of the evils of his time, 1897.

Juvenile courts. Special courts in which child offenders are dealt with ; in former times children were tried just like older criminals, and sent to prison, but now they are usually sent to a special institution or approved school.

OUR letter K was once the Egyptian hieroglyph ⌐ which was the picture of a bowl. But when written it looked like this ⌐ and its modified form ⅄ in the ⌐ Phoenician alphabet ⅄ begins to look somewhat like our K, written backwards. The Phoenicians called it *Kaph*, which means " the palm of the hand," or perhaps the " bent hand." The Greeks gave it its present form, changing the name to *Kappa*. In Latin, C came to be used for *k* sound, K being used only in certain abbreviations; this influenced use of C for *k* sound in Anglo-Saxon and Early English, e.g. *cynig* (*king*). The practice of giving C the *s* or *sh* sound before certain vowels (as in *century, cinder, ocean*) led to confusion. Then K came to be used, particularly before e and i, for the hard sound, as in *kind, keg*, etc. The combination *ck* was originally *kk*, the double consonant being used after a short vowel when *ed, er*, or *ing* was added.

Kaaba (kah′-*a*-b*a*) or **Kaba.** Mahomedan shrine at Mecca ; contains famous sacred Black Stone, 2125, *2126*.

Kabul (kah-bool′). Afghanistan cap. and largest city, key to N. India ; pop. 80,000 ; in fruit dist. ; populace evacuated by R.A.F. aircraft in 1928–29, during civil war.

Kabyles (ka-bīlz). Berber tribes of Algeria, 70, 117.

Kachins. A marauding people of Indo-Chinese origin, living along border of Upper Burma ; Kachin State within Union of Burma formed 1948.

Kaf′fa. *See* Feodosia.

Kaff′ir corn. A variety of sorghum, often miscalled millet ; native to India and South Africa, and widely cultivated.

Kaffirs (kaf′-erz). A loosely defined group of Bantu tribes in S. Africa, 70.

Kaf′ka, Franz (1883–1924). Austrian novelist ; " The Verdict," " The Great Wall of China " ; " The Castle," " The Trial," " America " published posthumously ; great influence on literature, 2404.

Kagera River. In E. Africa, headstream of Nile, 69, 3321.

Kagoshima (ka-gō-shē′-m*a*), Japan. One of the chief cities of Kyushu Isl. ; pop. 181,700 ; home of the famous crackled Satsuma ware.

Kaieteur Falls. In British Guiana, on the Potaro river. The falls are 300 ft. wide, with a sheer drop of 740 ft.

Kaifengfu (kī-feng′-fōō) or **Kaifong,** China. Walled city, cap. of prov. of Honan, 450 m. s. of Peking ; pop. 200,000.

Kailasa (kī-lah′-s*a*). Temple at Ellora, India, 1663.

Kailyard School. Term applied to group of Scot. novelists who wrote of life of common people sentimentally, with copious use of dialect ; best represented by Ian MacLaren, Sir James Barrie, and S. R. Crockett.

Kain, Edgar, " Cobber " (1919–1940). N.Z. fighter pilot ; after many heroic air-fights and narrow escapes on Western front, was killed in flying accident, June 1940.

Kairwan (kīr-wahn′), Tunis. Sacred city of the Mahomedans ; contains beautiful Ukbah mosque, rebuilt in 827 ; one of the most holy places of Islam ; pop. 23,000 ; 3254.

Kaisar-i-Hind (kī-z*ar*-ē-hind′) **Medal.** Awarded for public services rendered in the Indian Empire ; given to any race and either sex—had two classes—1st, gold ; 2nd, silver ; instituted by Queen Victoria in 1900.

Kaisariyeh (kī-za-rē′-*a*) or **Kayseri,** Turkey. Trade centre in Asia Minor 160 m. S.E. of Ankara ; pop. (1945) 57,700 ; exports carpets, hides, fruit ; anc. Caesarea.

Kaiser (kī-zer). Official title of Ger. and Holy Rom. emperors ; origin, 653.

Kaiser, Henry J. (b. 1882). Amer. industrialist ; built Boulder Dam ; in 1941 introduced prefabricated ships, welded instead of riveted, a 10,000 ton vessel taking a month to build, to defeat Ger. submarine campaign of 2nd World War.

Kaiserslautern (kī′-zerz-low-tern), Germany. Industrial city in Bavaria

35 m. w. of Mannheim ; pop. 62,600 ; Frederick Barbarossa built castle here about 1152.

Kaiser Wilhelm Canal. Same as **Kiel Canal.**

Kaiser Wilhelm′s Land or **German New Guinea.** Administered by Australia under U. N. trusteeship. *See* **New Guinea.**

Kajar (ka-jahr′). Ruling dynasty of Persia, founded by Aga Mahommed, 2555.

Kalah or **Calah.** Anc. Assyrian city, built 1300 B.C. by Shalmaneser I ; abandoned, then rebuilt as royal residence city about 880 B.C. ; excavations revealed much monumental material, 2372.

Kalahari (ka-l*a*-hah′-rē) **Desert,** S. Africa. Chiefly in Bechuanaland ; about 120,000 sq. m. ; 69, 3016 ; *map, 3015* ; crossed by Livingstone, 72.

Kalat (ka-laht′) or **Kelat.** Cap. of native state of Kalat in Baluchistan ; pop. of state, 253,300 ; town, 18,000 ; trade centre, rapid growth since 1900.

Kale, vegetable of cabbage family, 639.

Kaleidoscope (ka-lī′-*do*-skōp), **1845** ; inventor, 560.

Kal′ends or **Calends.** First day of Rom. month, 662.

Kalevala (kah-lā-vah′-l*a*). Anc. Finnish epic ; Longfellow closely imitated its rhythm and spirit in "Hiawatha."

Kalgoor′lie. Tn. in W. Australia ; famous for the rich East Coolgardie gold mines ; pop. 11,900 ; 3368.

Kali (kah-li). In Hindu myth., the Black Goddess of murder, death, and plague, patroness of Thugs ; wife of Siva.

Kalidasa (kah-lē-dah′-s*a*) (*fl.* 500–550). Greatest dramatic and lyric poet in India (" Sakuntala ").

Kalinin, formerly **Tver,** Soviet Russia. Cotton mfg., and trade centre on Volga ; pop. 216,000 ; alternately held by Germans and Russians in late 1941.

Kalinin, Michael Ivanovitch (1875–1946). Rus. politician ; banished 1908 ; active in 1917 Revolution ; first president of Petrograd (Leningrad) Soviet 1923 ; chairman of Supreme Soviet of U.S.S.R. 1938–46.

Kaliningrad. *See* **Königsberg.**

Kalix River, Sweden. Flows S.E. 208 m. to head of Gulf of Bothnia, 3126 ; *map, 2395.*

Kal′mar or **Calmar,** Sweden. Port and cathedral tn. 200 m. S. of Stockholm ; pop. 24,400 ; castle dating back from 12th cent., the scene of many historic incidents.

Kalmar, Union of (1397), 992, 2880, 2398, 3131.

Kalmuck. Autonomous Soviet republic of Russia proper, at N.W. corner of Caspian Sea.

Kal′mucks. Branch of Mongols, 2207.

Kalmuck Steppes, S. Russia. Largely arid plains inhabited by nomadic Tartars engaged in livestock raising.

Kal′tenbrunner, Ernst (1901–46). Austrian Nazi ; chief of Gestapo in Austria ; after 1943 chief of Gestapo in Ger. Reich ; captured May 1945 by U.S. troops ; hanged after Nuremberg Trials for war crimes and crimes against humanity Oct. 16, 1946 ; 2282.

Kama (kah′-m*a*). In E. Russia, largest tributary of Volga ; over 1,000 m. long ; timber trade, 3329.

Kamakura (kah-m*a*-kōō′-r*a*). Japan, sea-coast vil. near Yokohama, long centre of feudal govt. ; colossal image of Buddha, 600, 1810.

Kamchatka (kam-chat′-k*a*). Peninsula of E. Siberia, Soviet Russia ; 105,000 sq. m. ; pop. under 10,000 ; **1845, 2966.**

Kamehameha (kah-mā-ha-mā′-hah) (1753–1819). Hawaiian king ; encouraged European commerce ; 1587.

Kamerun. Same as **Cameroons.**

Kamet. Highest peak of the Central Himalayas (25,447 ft.) ; ascended by F. S. Smythe expedition 1931.

Kamika′ze. Corps of Jap. " suicide " fighter pilots who crashed their planes loaded with explosives on aircraft-carriers, destroyers, etc., of the Allied Pacific Fleets ; active in Philippines sea battle, Oct. 1944, and off Okinawa, May–June 1945.

Kampen, Netherlands. Tn. near mouth of r. Yssel ; pop. 22,177 ; formerly a Hanseatic tn. ; 14th cent. tn. hall.

Kanak′as. Natives of Polynesia, 2471, *1586.*

Kanawha (kah-nah′-w*a*) or **Great Kanawha.** Large r. of W. Virginia, U.S.A., flowing N.W. to Ohio r. ; 400 m. long ; the Little Kanawha is 100 m. long.

Kanazawa (kah-nah-zah′-wah). City on w. coast of main isl. of Japan ; pop. 163,000 ; bronze and lacquer work, pottery, silk ; fine gardens ; heavy earthquake damage, June 28, 1948.

Kanchanjanga. *See* **Kinchinjunga.**

Kandahar (kan-d*a*-hahr′). Cap. of prov. of same name and trade centre in Afghanistan ; pop. 77,000 ; captured by Genghis Khan, Timur, and others ; prominent in wars between Brit. and Afghans ; *map, 55, 56* ; Roberts′ expedition, 2789.

Kandy (kan′-di), Ceylon. Highland tn. in centre of isl. on artificial lake ; pop. 52,000 ; cap. of former native kingdom of Kandy ; annexed by Britain in 1815 ; governor′s residence became h.q. of S.E.A.C. April 1944 to Nov. 1945 ; Buddhist and Brahman temples, 601.

Kangaroo′, 1845, 309, *313*, distinguished from other mammals, 2077 ; jerboa′s resemblance, *1819* ; name also given to a 2nd World War British armoured vehicle.

Kan′sas. A cent. state of U.S.A. ; 82,726 sq. m. ; pop. 1,801,000 ; **1846,** 588.

Kansas City, Kansas, U.S.A., largest city in state at junction of Kansas and Missouri rs. ; pop. 121,850 ; slaughtering and meat-packing centre.

Kansas City, Missouri, U.S.A., 2nd city of state, on Missouri r. ; pop. 399,750 ; slaughtering and meat-packing centre, 2194.

Kan′su. North-westernmost prov. of China ; 145,000 sq. m. ; pop. 6,705,000 ; cap. Lanchow ; dyes, gold, mercury, silks, musk, tobacco.

Kant (kahnt), **Immanuel** (1724–1804). Ger. philosopher, **1846,** *1847* ; influence on Ger. literature, 1457.

Kantara. Eg. tn. on Suez Canal ; rly. crosses on swinging bridge.

Kaolin (kah'ŏ lin). Clay used in pottery, known as China clay, 836, *912*, 1499, 1798, 2670.

"Kapital, Das," by Karl Marx, 2996.

Kapit'za, Peter (b. 1894). Russ. physicist ; assist. director in magnetism, 1924–32, at Cavendish Lab., Cambridge, and director Royal Soc. Mond Lab., 1930–35, where he researched on atomic physics ; in 1935 visited Russ., was held there, and made director of the Inst. for Physical Problems, Acad. of Sciences of U.S.S.R.

Kapok (kap'-ok). Fibre from pods of a tropical tree, **1847**.

Kappa, κ, K (Rom. k, K). Tenth letter of Gk. alphabet.

Karachi (ka-rah'-chē) or **Kurrachee**. Cap. of Pakistan, at w. end of Indus delta ; pop. 359,500 ; "gateway of cent. Asia" ; mfrs., fisheries, **1848**, 2479, 2974.

Karafuto, 1795. *See* Sakhalin.

Kara-George ("Black George") (*c.* 1766–1817). Nickname given by Turks to George Petrovitch or George Czerny, Serbian peasant, leader of 1st Serbian war of independence (1804–08) and founder of Kara-Georgevitch dynasty, 2922.

Karajich (ka-rah'-yich), **Vuk Stefanovich** (1787–1856). Father of modern Serbian literature ; bent efforts toward adoption of vernacular Serbian as literary language ; wrote Serbian grammar and dictionary.

Kara-Kalpak. Autonomous S.S.R., in Russian Turkistan.

Kara Kirghiz or **"Black" Kirghiz**. So called from colour of their tents ; Mongolian race inhabiting highlands of cent. Asia ; 263, 265.

Karakoram (ka-ra-kŏ'-ram) or **Mustagh Mts.** Range of cent. Asia N.W. end of Himalayas ; highest peak, Mt. Godwin-Austen (28,265 ft.) is 2nd highest mt. in world.

Karakul'. A breed of sheep, 2940.

Kara (kah'-ra) **Sea.** Arm of Arctic Ocean between Nova Zembla and N.W. coast of Siberia.

Kara Strait. At w. entrance to Kara Sea ; reached by Hudson, 1648.

Karelian Republic. Autonomous republic of Soviet Rus. situated between Finland and the White Sea.

Ka'rens. A people of Siamese-Chinese race, numbering about 1,000,000, who live in the hill regions of central Burma ; Karenni state within Union of Burma formed 1948 ; attempt to secure autonomy by force 1948–49.

Karikal (ka-rē-kal'). Fr. settlement on S.E. coast of India ; 53 sq. m. ; pop. (1941) 60,500, chief tn., Karikal (pop. 19,300) ; 1692.

Karli. Rock temple at, *1710*.

Karlsbad, Carlsbad, or **Karlovy Vary,** Czechoslovakia. Famous watering-place, 78 m. w. of Prague ; pop. 53,763 ; 3070. Karlsbad decrees issued here (1819) put univs. and press under strict censorship to suppress liberal agitation.

Karlskrona or **Carlscrona,** Sweden. Port on Baltic, 238 m. s.w. of Stockholm ; pop. 32,300 ; Swedish naval headquarters, fine deep harbour, arsenals, shipyards ; exports fish, stone, iron, lumber ; 3128.

Karlsruhe (kahrlz'-roo-e) or **Carlsruhe,** Ger. N.W. of Stuttgart. Cap. of Baden ; pop. 189,000 ; first target attacked by R.A.F. with 8,000 lb. "blockbuster" bomb, Sept. 2, 1942 ; taken Mar. 1945.

Kar'ma. Doctrine in Hinduism, that salvation can only be obtained by building up a fine record.

Karnak (kahr'-nak). Vil. on Nile in Upper Eg. on N. part of site of anc. Thebes ; remains of Temple of Ammon, greatest of all known temples ; 216, *1116*, *1117* ; sphinx avenue, *3060*.

Karna'tak or **Carnatic.** Region along E. coast of S. India, 1714.

Karolyi (kah'-rēl-yĕ), **Count Michael** (b. 1875). Provisional pres. of the Hungarian People's Republic

(Nov. 1918–March 1919) ; handed reins to Soviet govt. because of atorn Allied terms. Exile 1919–46. Hungarian Min. in Paris, 1947.

Karoo' or **Karro.** Tablelands in s. Africa, 3014.

Kar'rer, Paul (b. 1889). Swiss chemist ; for research on vitamins A and B received Nobel prize 1937 ; wrote textbook on Organic Chemistry.

Kars. Tn. of Armenia about 100 m. S.E. of Batum ; pop. 25,000 ; Mahomedan holy city, with 11th cent. "Cathedral of the 12 Apostles" ; cap. of a medieval Armenian principality ; several times besieged in wars between Rus. and Turks.

Karsavina (kar-sah'-vi-na), **Tamara** (b. 1885). Rus. dancer, leading member of Diaghilev company ; notable roles included The Fire Bird and Scheherazade.

Karshi (kahr'-shē) Commercial centre of Bokhara, cent. Asia, 96 m. S.E. of city of Bokhara ; pop. 14,000 ; meeting point of several important roads ; market where Turkomans and Uzbeks sell carpets, knives and firearms ; fine tobacco and poppies.

Karst. Limestone region of Yugoslavia where removal of forests and consequent washing away of surface soil has exposed bare limestone and led to formation of swallow holes ; the name is applied to similar regions in other countries.

Kashgar (kash-gahr'). Commercial centre in w. Chinese Turkistan ; pop. 80,000 ; textiles, 264 ; gold and silver articles, 3267.

Kashga'ria or **Chinese Turkistan,** 3267.

Kashmir (kash'-mēr). Mountain state N. India ; 82,258 sq. m. ; pop. 4,000,000, **1848,** *1704* ; ceded to India in 1947. scene of much fighting, 1848.

Kassai (kas'-si). R., rises in N.E. Angola and flows N.W. 1,000 m. to Congo, 887.

Kas'sel or **Cassel,** Ger. mfg. city on R. Fulda ; pop. (1939) 217,000 ; important industries made it target for heavy air attack during 2nd World War ; lower town flooded by breaching of Eder dam in 1943.

Kassites. Elamite tribe overran Babylonia 18th cent. B.C. ; founded dynasty.

Kästner (kest-ner), **Erich** (1899–1942). Ger. writer ; his children's book, "Emil and the Detectives," translated into many languages and filmed, 1457.

Kas'tro. Formerly Rhodes, cap. of isl. of Rhodes ; founded 408 B.C. ; walls and old stone houses preserve medieval appearance ; trade centre.

Kastro, isl. *See* Mytilene.

Kata thermometer, measures cooling effect of air on the body, 1677, *1678*.

Katanga. Prov. of the Belg. Congo, a great copper-mining area ; rail connexion with the Cape and W. Africa.

Kation. *See* Cation.

Kato (kah'-tō), **Takaaki, Viscount** (1860–1926). Japanese statesman, ambassador to Gt. Brit. (1894–99, 1908–13) ; four times foreign minister ; leader of the constitutionalist party.

Kato, Tomosaburo, Baron (1859–1923). Japanese admiral and statesman ; commanded fleet which attacked Germans at Tsing-Tao in 1914 ; delegate to Washington Limitation of Armament Conference (1921) ; premier (1922).

Katowice (kah-tō-vit'-se). Tn. of Silesia, Poland ; centre of industrial district ; pop. 132,000 ; taken by Russians, Jan. 1945.

Kat'rine, Loch. L. of Perthshire, Scot. ; 5 sq. m. ; noted beauty spot of Trossachs, 2889 ; *plate f. 2892*.

Katsura (kah'-tsoo-ra), **Taro, Prince** (1847–1913). Japanese statesman, gov. of Formosa, minister of war, then premier (1901–06) ; again premier (1908–11 and 1912–13) ; accomplished various financial reforms

annexation of Korea, revision of commercial treaties with western powers, Anglo-Japanese alliance ; advocated constitutional development of Japan.

Kat'tegat or **Cattegat.** Strait between Denmark and Sweden ; 150 m. long, greatest width 90 m. ; 2391, 991 ; *map, 992*.

Katzbach River. Tributary of Oder in Silesia, now Polish ; on its banks Prussians under Blücher defeated French under Marshal Macdonald (1813).

Kauai (kow-I). One of Hawaiian isls. ; 547 sq. m. ; 1587.

Kauffer, Edward McKnight (b. 1890). Anglo-Amer. designer ; an original and brilliant poster artist.

Kauffmann (kowf'-man), **Angelica** (1741–1807). Anglo-Swiss painter, whose beauty and charming personality enhanced the reputation of her graceful but poorly drawn portraits ; friend of Goethe, Reynolds, and other famous men.

Kaulbach (kowl'-bahkh), **Wilhelm von** (1805–74). Ger. (Munich) fresco and historical painter and book illustrator, first and most celebrated of a family of painters.

Kaunas or **Kovno.** Town of Lithuania, on r. Nieman ; pop. 152,000, 1968 ; in German hands 1941–44, 3419.

Kaunitz (kow'-nits), **Prince Wenzel Anton von** (1711–94) ; Austrian statesman, 2101.

Kauri (kow'-ri) **gum.** The resin, usually fossilized, of kauri pine, 1558, 2611 ; New Zealand supply, 2357.

Kava (kah'-va) or **ava.** A shrub of the pepper family from which an intoxicating beverage is prepared in the South Sea Isls.

Kay, John (1704–*c.* 1764), Eng. inventor of the flying shuttle in weaving, 3361 ; died poor.

Kayak (kī-ak), Eskimo skin boat, *482*, 484.

Kaye-Smith, Sheila. Brit. novelist ; author of many novels dealing mainly with life in Sussex villages.

Kazakstan. The Kazak Socialist Soviet Republic created in 1920, which includes that part of S. Siberia inhabited by the Kazaks ; a. 1,047,000 sq. m. ; pop. 6,145,000 ; cap. Alma-Ata ; 271, 2849.

Kazan (ka-zahn'). Mfg. and commercial centre in E. Russia, 430 m. E. of Moscow ; pop. 401,000 ; cap. of anc. Tartar Kingdom taken by Russians in 1552 ; univ.

Kaz'bek or **Kasbek, Mt.,** one of the highest peaks of Caucasus Mts., 90 m. S.E. of Mt. Elbruz, 732.

Kazvin (kaz-vēn'). Tn. in Iran, 92 m. N.W. of Teheran ; pop. (1940) 60,000 ; trade in rice, fish, raisins, silk ; remains of old walls and buildings shattered by earthquakes ; at outbreak of 2nd World War was terminus of a branch line of Trans-Persian rly. ; with Anglo-Soviet occupation in 1941, line extended to Tabriz and this became Allied supply route to Russia ; remained in Russian hands until March 1946.

Ke'a, a sheep-killing parrot, 2526.

Kean, Edmund (1787–1833). Eng. Shakespearian tragedian, one of the foremost of all time ; according to Coleridge, "seeing him act was like reading Shakespeare by flashes of lightning" ("Shylock"; "Othello"; "Richard III ").

Kearton, Cherry (1871–1940). Eng. naturalist ; produced several films of animal life ; wrote "Wild Life across the World," "My Animal Friendships," "Adventures with Animals and Men."

Kearton, Richard (1862–1928). Eng. naturalist, brother of the above, wrote "With Nature and a Camera," "Wonders of Wild Nature," "Our Bird Friends."

Keats, John (1795–1821). Eng. poet, **1849,** 1214, 2010 ; Shelley's elegy, "Adonais," 2944.

Keble, John (1792–1866). Eng. poet and clergyman ; professor of poetry at Oxford for 10 years ; Keble College, Oxford, built as a memorial to him (" The Christian Year ").

Kebnekaise (cheb′-ne-kī-se). Highest peak in Sweden, in Kiolen Mts. (7,005 ft.).

Kecskemet (kech′-ke-mät). Hungarian city 65 m. S.E. of Budapest ; pop. 83,732, mostly Magyars ; cattle market ; trade in apples, apricots, flour, wine ; captured by Russians Nov. 1944.

Ked. Sheep tick, 2513.

Ke′dah. Native state in w. of Malay Peninsula ; 3,660 sq. m. ; pop. (1940) 515,700 ; 2069.

Keel. The lengthwise timber or structure at the bottom of a ship ; 2952, 2947.

Keel, false. An extra keel, often weighted, below the true keel of a ship, to help strengthen and stabilize the vessel.

Keel′ing Islands. See Cocos Islands.

Keel Mts. See Kiolen.

Keelson. A timber or beam bolted over a ship's keel to help stiffen the vessel.

Keene, Charles Samuel (1823–91). Eng. pen-and-ink artist, for 40 years a contributor to " Punch " ; foremost among Eng. craftsmen in black and white, but work has never been popular because of its unconventionality.

Keep, of castle. Inmost and strongest part, 713, 718.

Keewatin (kē-wah′-tin). Former dist. of Canada, merged into Manitoba, Ontario, and N.W. Territories, 1912.

Keighley (kēth′-lē). Tn. in West Riding of Yorkshire, 9 m. N.W. of Bradford ; worsted, woollen, and machinery industries ; pop. (est.) 55,700.

Keitel, Wilhelm (1882–1946). Nazi war leader, signatory to German surrender. Tried as war criminal Nuremberg, 1945–46 ; hanged, Oct. 1946 ; 2282.

Keith, Sir Arthur (b. 1866). Brit. anthropologist ; conservator and professor at Royal College of Surgeons (1908–1933) ; " Antiquity of Man," " The Human Body " ; knighted (1921).

Keith, Francis Edward James (1696–1758). Scot. soldier, Jacobite adherent, field-marshal under Frederick the Great in Seven Years' War ; prompt in action, skilful in tactics.

Kekule (kā-koo-lā) or **Kekulé von Stradonitz, Friedrich A.** (1829–96). Ger. chemist ; devised " graphic formulae " for organic chemistry and suggested molecular structure of benzene ; chemistry of explosives, dye-stuffs, and coal-tar products based largely upon his researches.

Ke′lantan. State of Malayan Union, formerly Unfederated State under Brit. protection. 750 sq. m. ; pop. 395,000 ; 2069.

Kelim rugs, 705.

Keller, Gottfried (1819–90). Ger. poet and novelist ; b. Switzerland ; chief work " Der Grüne Heinrich " (" Green Henry ").

Keller, Helen (b. 1880). Amer. author ; blind, deaf and dumb from infancy, she studied at the Perkins Institute, Boston, Mass., learning to speak as well as read, write, type, etc. ; B.A. degree in 1904 ; LL.D. of Glasgow in 1932 ; received Roosevelt Medal in 1936 ; 471.

Kel′lermann, François Christophe de (1735–1820). Fr. Revolutionary general, marshal of France, victor of Valmy (1792) over Prussians ; father of François Étienne de Kellermann, one of Napoleon's ablest generals.

Kellogg, Frank Billings (1856–1937). Amer. Ambassador to Gt. Brit. (1923 –25) ; Secretary of State, U.S.A. (1925–29) ; was formerly a lawyer and a U.S.A. senator for Minnesota ; awarded Nobel Peace Prize (1930), 2531.

Kellogg Pact. Pact to outlaw war, signed by all the principal nations in 1928 ; initiated by Frank B. Kellogg, U.S.A. Secretary of State, in association with M. Briand of France ; official title, the Paris Pact of 1928, 2531.

Kells, Eire. Old tn. in Co. Meath, on the Blackwater ; noted for antiquities, especially St. Columbkille's (Colomba's) house ; anc. cross, 2125.

Kells, Book of ; Irish art, 1177, 510, 2092.

Kelly, Sir Gerald (b. 1879). British artist, became P. R. A. in 1949.

Kelmscott Press, 2232.

Kelp. Any large coarse seaweed ; chief source of iodine, 2914, 1738, 2915.

Kel′tie, Sir John Scott (1840–1927). Scot. geographer ; he became librarian to the Royal Geographical Society in 1885, and its secretary seven years later ; edited the " Statesman's Year Book " for many years (" The Partition of Africa " ; " The History of Geography ").

Kel′vin, William Thomson, 1st Baron (1824–1907). Brit. physicist, 1849, 1850 ; electrical engineer for first Atlantic cable, 642, 643.

Kemal Atatürk (1881–1938). Turkish nationalist leader and dictator, 1850, 162 ; and modern Turkey, 3265, 3266.

Kem′ble, Charles (1775–1854). Brit. actor, brother of Mrs. Siddons and John Philip Kemble ; appeared first at Sheffield in 1795 ; later played Macbeth in London and many other leading parts, chiefly comedy.

Kemble, Fanny (Frances Anne) (1809– 93). Eng. actress and author, daughter of Charles Kemble ; spent most of her later life in America (" Journals," interesting picture of Amer. life).

Kemble, John Philip (1757–1823). Brit. actor, son of a theatrical manager, brother of Charles Kemble ; first appeared in Wolverhampton in 1776, and made his debut in London at Drury Lane as Hamlet ; played in nearly all Shakespeare's tragedies.

Kem′pis, Thomas a (c. 1380–1471). Ger. monk and mystic, remembered for one book, the " Imitation of Christ," a classic of devotional literature.

Kemp-Welch, Lucy (b. 1869). Brit. painter ; specialized in painting animals, particularly horses.

Kemsley, James Gomer Berry, 1st Viscount (b. 1883). British newspaper proprietor, created baronet 1928 ; raised to peerage 1936, made Viscount 1945, 1851.

Ken, Thomas (1637–1711). Eng. bishop, one of the " fathers of modern hymnology " (" Praise God from Whom All Blessings Flow " ; " Awake, My Soul, and with the Sun ").

Ken′dal. Tn. in Westmorland, 20 m. N. of Lancaster, on r. Kent ; woollen and other mfrs. ; pop. (1942) 19,600 ; 3371.

Kendal, Dame Margaret (1849–1935). Eng. actress ; wife of W. H. Kendal (1843–1917), also an actor ; greatest successes at St. James's in " Diplomacy," " The Elder Miss Blossom," and other plays ; received the D.B.E. in 1926.

Kendall, Henry Clarence (1841–82). Australian poet (" Leaves from an Australian Forest " ; " Songs from the Mountains "), 315.

Ken′ilworth. Small tn. in Warwickshire ; ruins of castle given by Queen Elizabeth to Earl of Leicester ; scene of Scott's " Kenilworth " ; 1851.

Ken′mare Bay, Eire. Inlet of Atlantic, between counties of Kerry and Cork ; extends inland for 28 m. ; also known as Kenmare river.

Kennedy, Joseph Patrick (b. 1888). Amer. diplomat ; U.S. Ambassador to Gt. Britain, 1938–40.

Kennedy, Margaret. British novelist and playwright ; author of " The Constant Nymph," " Escape Me Never," and other works, 1216.

Ken′net. R. of Wiltshire and Berkshire ; flows 44 m. to join the Thames.

Kenneth I, MacAlpine (d. c. 860). King of the Scots and conqueror of the Picts, often called first King of Scot.

Kennington. Dist. of S. London opposite Kennington Park, which occupies part of the site of Kennington Common, is the Oval, famous Surrey cricket ground.

Ken′sington. Parl. and Royal bor. of W. London ; pop. (1945), 134,600 ; Kensington Palace and Gardens ; residence of Thackeray ; museums at S. Kensington include the Natural History, Science, Geological, and Victoria and Albert, 2014.

Kensington Gardens, London, adjoining Hyde Park ; originally laid out by William III and Queen Mary as the grounds of their new palace at Kensington ; they were enlarged and improved by Queen Caroline ; contains the Albert memorial and famous statues of Queen Victoria and Peter Pan ; other features are the Round Pond, the Long Water, the Broad Walk and a replica of G. F. Watts' sculpture " Physical Energy " ; a. 275 acres : 2015, 2908.

Kensington Palace, London, on the w. side of Kensington Gardens has long been the home of royalty and was the birthplace of Queen Victoria (1819) ; here she was christened, and here she received the news of her accession. In 1945 became temporary home of the London Museum.

Kent, Edward Augustus, Duke of (1767–1820). Eng. prince, 4th son of George III ; father of Queen Victoria, 3319.

Kent, George, Duke of (1902–1942). Eng. prince ; fourth son of King George V, 1442 ; married Princess Marina of Greece, daughter of Prince Nicholas of Greece, in 1934 ; three children—Edward (b. 1935), Alexandra (b. 1936), Michael (b. 1942), 2833.

Kent, S.E. co. of Eng. ; 1,525 sq. m. ; pop. 1,219,270 ; first landing place of Anglo-Saxon invaders ; 1851, 1194 ; Christianity introduced, 302, 692, 1194 ; Canterbury cap. of earliest kingdom, 692 ; hop-picking, 1642.

Kentish plover. Close relative of ringed plover, 2630.

Kentuck′y. An E.-cent. state of U.S.A. ; 40,395 sq. m. ; pop. 2,845,000 ; 1852.

Kentucky River. In Kentucky, U.S.A., formed by several forks, rising in Cumberland Mts. of S.E. ; flows 259 m. N.W. to Ohio r.

Kenya (kĕn′-ya), Mt. Volcanic peak in Kenya Colony, E. Africa (17,200 ft.) ; discovered in 1849 ; first ascended in 1899.

Kenya Colony, Brit. E. Africa ; formerly called Brit. E. Africa Protectorate ; 224,960 sq. m. ; pop. (est. 1942) 4,047,000 ; cap. Nairobi, chief sp. Mombasa ; 581, 1072, maps, 1072, 1073.

Kep′ler, Johann (1571–1630). Ger. astronomer who formulated laws of planetary motion, 1852, 1853.

Kepler's laws, 1853.

Ke′rak. See Transjordan.

Ker′atin, chief constituent of horn, hoofs, nails, hair and feathers ; in leather, 1913 ; wool, 3404.

Kerbela (kêr′-be-la) or **Karbala.** Tn. in S. Iraq, 60 m. S.W. of Baghdad ; pop. 55,000 ; sacred city and place of pilgrimage of Shiite Moslems ; tomb of martyr Husein.

Kerch. Russ. tn. and peninsula, at E. tip of Crimean peninsula ; twice taken by Ger. offensive in Crimea and Caucasus and twice retaken by Russ. between Nov. 1941 and April 1944. Pop. of tn. 16,000.

Ker′en. Tn. of Eritrea, on plateau of 6,000 ft. ; natural stronghold defended by Italian troops from Feb. 6 to Mar. 27, 1941, against Brit. and Indian assaults ; its fall opened the road to Asmara.

Keren′sky, Alexander Feodorovitch (b. 1881). Rus. revolutionary statesman, head of the provisional govt. of 1917, 2848 ; driven from office by

Bolsheviks in Nov. Rev.: since lived in Paris.

Kerguelen (ker´-ge-len) **Land.** A desolate uninhabited volcanic isl. 85 m. long on s. border of Indian Ocean, midway between Cape of Good Hope and Australia ; Fr. possession.

Kerman (ker-mahn´) or **Kirman,** Iran (Persia). in s.E. ; cap. of prov. of same name ; pop. 50,000.

Kermanshah (ker-mahn-shah´), Iran ; cap. of province of same name in ´w. Iran (Persia); pop. 89,000 ; on high road between Baghdad and Teheran ; ruined walls.

Kern, Jerome (1885–1945). Amer. composer ; wrote music for " Show Boat," " Cat and the Fiddle," "Music in the Air," "Swing Time,"etc.

Ker´osene. An illuminating oil distilled from coal or petroleum, 2564 ; distillation, 2429 ; first used, 2426 ; Priestman's engine, 1737.

Ker´ry. Co. in s.w. of Eire, in prov. of Munster ; 1,815 sq. m. ; pop. 136,000, *1853, 1751.*

Kerry Blue Terrier. Med. sized shaggy haired breed of terrier ; plucky and sagacious ; puppies born black, become blue later.

Kess´elring, F.-M. Albert (b. 1885). Ger. airman ; chief of staff to Luftwaffe in 1936 ; directed **air** operations against Poland, 1939, the Netherlands and France, 1940 ; in 1942 commanded Ger. air force and in Sept. 1943 all Ger. forces in It. ; captured by U.S. 7th Army in 1945 ; in 1947 Brit. court in It. condemned him to be shot for massacre of It. civilians in the Ardeatine caves ; sentence was commuted to life imprisonment.

Kes´trel. A bird of prey (*Tinnunculus tinnunculus*). Commonest hawk in Gt. Brit., even nesting in London ; distinguished by habit of hovering in one spot, whence name windhover ; *453, 1587.*

Kettledrum, *1049,* 2446.

Kew (kū). Dist. in Surrey on s. bank of the Thames ; contains Royal Botanic Gardens ; Kew Palace, rebuilt in 1631, became the palace of George III in 1781 ; meteorological observatory, 2413.

Kew Gardens. Botanic gardens at Kew, Surrey, **1853,** *1854,* 1640.

Key, C. W. Eng. politician. Labour M.P. since 1940 ; Reg. Commr. Ldn. Civil Def. ; Min. of Works (1947–50).

Key, Francis Scott (1780–1843). Amer. lawyer ; wrote " Star-Spangled Banner," 2283.

Keyes, Roger John Brownlow Keyes, 1st Baron (1872–1945). Brit. admiral ; commodore of submarine service, 1910–14 ; led historic naval raid on Zeebrugge, 1918 ; commanded battle-cruiser squadron of Atlantic Fleet, 1919–21 ; Admiral of the Fleet, 1930 ; M.P., 1934–43 ; Director of Combined Operations, 1940–41 ; cr. Baron, 1943.

Keynes (kānz), **John Maynard, 1st Baron** (1883–1946). British economist ; author of works on world finance, and economics ; created Baron, 1942 ; married (1925) Lydia Lopokova ; 2203.

Keys, House of, 2084.

Keys and locks, 1978.

Khabarovsk or **Habarovsk** (hah-bah-rofsk). Capital of Far Eastern Region of Asiatic Russia, at junction of Amur and Ussuri. Pop. 199,360.

Khadija (kah-dē-jah), wife of Mahomet, 2066.

Khafra (kah´-frah), also **Khafre** or **Chephren,** Egypt, king of 4th dynasty (c. 2800–2700 B.C.) ; pyramid of, 1114, 2707, *2708* ; Sphinx, 3058, *3059,*

Khaki (kah´-ki). Drab cotton or woollen material, for Army uniforms.

Khama (1835–1923). African chieftain ; in 1895 induced Britain to make a native reservation of his part of Bechuanaland.

Khan (kahn). In Orient, unfurnished inn for traders ; In Damascus, 961.

Khan, Liaqat Ali (b. 1895). Mahomedan politician ; first prime min. of Pakistan ; a leader of the Muslim League from 1936.

Kharkov (khar-´kôf). Industrial city of Ukraine ; pop. 833,430 ; **1854,** 3273 ; heavy fighting, 1941–1944, 1855, 3419, 3421.

Khartum (kahr-tōōm´) or **Khartoum.** Cap. of Anglo-Egyptian Sudan at union of Blue and White Niles ; pop. 61,800 (later figure than given in p. 1855) ; **1835,** 3110 ; General Gordon, 1102, *1487* ; siege of, 1102, 1487 ; Kitchener captures, 1862.

Khatmandu (kat-man-dōō). Cap. of Nepal ; pop. 108,000 ; 2315.

Khedive (ke-dēv´). Former Turkish viceroy in Egypt, 1101, 1487.

Kherson (ker-sōn). Port on R. Dnieper in Soviet Russia, 100 m. E. of Odessa ; pop. 97,000 ; grain, woollen mills, tobacco mfrs. ; Germans occupy 1012 1944.

Khingan (kin-gahn´). Mt. range in China ; Great Khingan in E. Mongolia and N.W. Manchuria ; continuation in N.E. Manchuria s. of the Amur, known as Little Khingan ; 2085.

Khiva (khē-va). Cap. of former state of Khiva, now part of Uzbek Repub., U.S.S.R. ; pop. 20,000.

Khmer (kmär) **Empire.** Anc. stone buildings, 666.

Khokand (kō-kahnd´) or **Kokand.** Trade centre in Rus. Turkistan 275 m. E. of Bokhara ; pop. 84,000.

Khorassan (kō-rah-sahn´) or **Khurasan.** Mountainous prov. of N.E. Persia ; a. 125,000 sq. m. ; pop. 1,000,000 ; fruits, cereals, silk, carpets ; cap. Meshed ; people of, 1742.

Khorezm (kor´-eshm). Included in the Uzbek Soviet Socialist Republic formed in 1924; formerly known as Khiva, it lies s. of Aral Sea ; cap. Khiva ; silk and cotton industries.

Khorsabad (kor-sah-bahd´). Vil. near site of anc. Nineveh ; remains of Assyrian art found in 1843–55.

Khotan. Chinese Turkistan, trade tn. in s.w. ; pop. 18,000 ; 3267 ; bazaars, 264.

Khufu (kōō´-fōō) or **Cheops** (about 2800 B.C.). Eg. king of 4th dynasty ; Great Pyramid, 1114, 2707, *2708, 2923.*

Khyber (kī´-ber) or **Khaibar Pass.** Narrow mt. pass between India (Pakistan) and Afghanistan ; length 33 m., narrowing to 15 ft. wide; great strategic importance for 2,000 years ; the rly. to the head of the pass was opened in 1925 ; 55, *56,* 1691.

Kiang (ki-ang´). Wild animal of Asia, resembling both ass and horse, 1646.

Kiangsi (ki-ang-sē´). An inland prov. of China ; 77,000 sq. m. ; pop. 13,794,000 ; cap. Nanchang ; coal, iron, copper, tea, tobacco, silk.

Kiangsu´. A maritime prov. of cent. China ; 41,000 sq. m. ; pop. 36,464,000 ; cap. Chenkiang ; chief city Shanghai ; one of China's richest and most fertile regions.

Kiaochow (ki-ow-chow´). Tn., bay, and dist. on E. coast of Chinese prov. of Shantung ; held by Japan, 2938, 1800 ; returned to China, 1800.

Kid. Goatskin leather, forms of, 1914, 1478 ; in glove mfr., 1478 ; in shoe mfr., 522, 1478.

Kidd, Benjamin (1858–1916). Eng. sociologist (" Social Evolution ").

Kidd, Captain William (c. 1650–1701). Brit. pirate, **1855.**

Kid´derminster. Tn. in Worcestershire on r. Stour ; pop. 34,670 ; noted for mfr. of carpets ; *3361,* 3407.

Kidderminster carpet, 706.

" Kidnapped." Adventure story by Robert Louis Stevenson, 3089.

Kidney bean. Kidney-shaped seed of any plant of the common bean type.

Kidney or **Brazilian cotton.** A type whose seeds grow in a kidney-shaped mass, 921.

Kidneys. In human body, **1855.**

Kido (kē´-dō), **Takayoshi** (1832–77). Japanese statesman, called " the pen of the revolution of 1868," advocate of western civilization and constitutional govt. ; founder of first real Japanese newspaper.

Kidron (kid´-ron), **Kedron,** or **Cedron, Valley of.** Deep depression E. of Jerusalem where brook flowed in anc. times ; several times referred to in Bible ; 1819.

Kief. *See* Kiev.

Kiel (kēl). Ger. chief naval port of Ger. on Baltic ; pop. 218,000 ; shipyards, iron mfrs. ; univ. ; terminus of Kiel Canal ; scene of Ger. naval mutiny in 1918.

Kiel Canal, 1856, 352 ; protected by Heligoland, 1607 ; in 1914–1918 War, 3411 ; bombed and blocked in 2nd World War, 1856 ; repaired and redredged by end of 1945, and again declared an international waterway.

Kieloe (kycl´-tse). Poland. City in mts. 95 m. s. of Warsaw ; pop. 58,000 ; formerly noted for copper mines, no longer worked ; mfrs. of hemp, brick, paint ; German-occupied in 2nd World War, liberated by Russians Jan. 1945 ; scene of pogrom July 1946.

Kier´kegaard, Sören Aaby (1813–55). Danish philosopher ; immense influence on Danish literature (" Either —or ").

Kieselguhr (kē-zel-goor). An absorbent earth used by Alfred Nobel in his early invention of dynamite.

Kiev (kē´-ef). Russian city, on r. Dnieper, cap. of Ukraine Republic ; pop. 846,000, 18.6, 3273, 2846 ; Germans occupy 1941–1943, 1856, 3419, 3421.

Kilauea. Volcano in Hawaii.

Kildare, Eire. Eastern co. ; a. 654 sq. m. ; pop. 64,500 ; **1856.**

Kildare. Old tn. in Eire ; pop. 2,000 ; originated in nunnery founded 5th cent. by St. Bridget ; co. tn. of co. Kildare ; round tower, *1857.*

Kilimanjaro (kil-i-man-jah´-rō). Double-peaked volcanic mt. (19,720 ft.) in N. of Tanganyika Territory (formerly Ger. E. Africa), 65 ; *map, 1073.*

Kilkenny, Eire. Co. in the s.E. ; a. 800 sq. m ; pop. 68,000 ; *1857.*

Kilken´ny. Tn. in Eire ; pop. 10,000 ; 2nd largest cath. in Ire. ; 1857.

Killarney, Eire. Small market tn. in s.w. in co. Kerry, near Killarney Lakes ; pop. 5,300.

Killarney Lakes, 1744, *1751.*

Kil´ler whale, *3373.*

Killiecrankie. Pass in Perthshire, Scot. Viscount Dundee, leader of Jacobite Highlanders, killed in victory over royal forces in 1689 ; *2558.*

" Kilmainham Treaty." Agreement between Gladstone and Parnell, signed at Kilmainham, suburb adjoining Dublin on the w. ; 2525.

Kilmarnock, Scot. Tn. on Kilmarnock Water, in Ayrshire ; pop. 41,100 ; textiles, machinery, cheese ; first edition of Burns' poems published here (1786).

Kiln. Oven for burning or baking industrial products ; brick, *563,* 564 ; cement-burners, 740 ; pottery, 2666, *2667.*

Kilocycle (kc.). Frequency of wireless waves are often expressed in kilo-cycles per second (kc/s), that is, thousands of cycles in one second ; one wave crest to the next represents the complete cycle of a wave ; 1623.

Kil´ogramme (kg.). A unit of weight in the metric system ; 1000 grammes (2·204 lb.), 2155.

Kilo´litre (kl.). A unit of volume in the metric system ; 1000 litres (220 gal.), 2155.

Kil´ometre (km.). A metric unit of length (3,281 ft.), 2155.

Kil´owatt (kW.). Practical unit of electric power, 1,000 watts, 1·34 horse-power, 1128 ; kilowatt-hour, 2153.

Kilt. Scot., *plate f. 2893.*

" Kim." Novel by Kipling in which the hero, nicknamed " Kim," a precocious little Irish vagabond, roams through India with a Tibetan priest, 1859.

Kim′berley. S. African diamond-mining centre, Cape of Good Hope prov.; white pop. 17,000; besieged in Boer War (1899–1900), 2771; diamond mines, *3017*, 3019.

Kim′berley. Gold-mining centre in W. Australia.

Ki′mono. Japanese garment, 1799, 1802, 1803.

Kincardineshire (kin-kar′-din-shīr). Scot. Eastern maritime co., bordering North Sea; fishing, agric.; a. 383 sq. m.; pop. 28,000; **1857.**

Kinchinjunga, Mt. Third highest peak in world (28,146 ft.); one of the E. Himalayas; on boundary between Sikkim and Nepal, 2315.

Kin′dergarten. *See* **Nursery School.**

Kinder Scout, Mt. in Derbyshire (2,088 feet), 2546.

Kindersley, Robert M. Kindersley, 1st Baron (b. 1871). Eng. banker; gov. of Hudson's Bay Co., 1916–25; director of Bank of Eng.; pres. National Savings Cttee., 1920–46.

Kinematograph. *See* **Cinema.**

Kinet′ics. Branch of mechanics treating of bodies in motion.

Kinetic theory, of gases, 1419.

Kinet′oscope, 828.

King, Ernest J. (b. 1878). Amer. sailor; served in Span.-Amer. war of 1898; in First World War chief of staff to C.-in-C. of U.S. Fleet; in Dec. 1941 C.-in-C. of U.S. Fleet; chief of Naval Ops. March 9, 1942; retired after war as Fleet Admiral.

King, (William Benjamin) Basil (1859–1928). Canadian poet and novelist; numerous romances with strong religious undertone ("The Inner Shrine"; "Wild Olive"; "The Street Called Straight"), 685.

King, (William Lyon) Mackenzie (1874–1950). Canadian statesman and economist; Minister of Labour (1909–11); economic research for Rockefeller Foundation (1914); Premier of Canada (1921–26, 1926–30, and 1935–48).

King Cobra, or hamadryad, a large cobra-like snake, 859.

King Crab. A crab-like creature, *plate f. 925*; possibly descended from trilobites.

Kingdom. The three primary and largest divisions in classification of all natural objects; *i.e.* the animal, the vegetable, and the mineral kingdoms.

King Edward VII Land, 2895.

Kingfisher. A fish-eating bird, **1857**; *plate f. 1856, 1857*; young, 446.

King George V, H.M.S. Battleship, second of name, completed 1940; laden displacement 44,650 tons; in action which sank the Bismarck in 1941; covered Allied landings in It.; served with Pacific Fleet against Jap. and Jap.-occupied islands.

King George VI Reservoir, Staines, Middx, 3194.

King George VI Sound, discovered in Antarctic in 1934; 2647.

King George's War. Name given by the Eng. colonists to the conflict in Amer. between Fr. and Eng. (1744–48) (War of the Austrian Succession).

King-Hall, Stephen (b. 1893). Eng. sailor and author; ret. from Navy in 1929 with rank of Commander; works include "Our Own Times," and plays "The Middle Watch," etc. (with Ian Hay); broadcasts to and writes for children.

King James (Authorized) Version of Bible, 426, 1794.

"**King John,**" drama by Shakespeare; Prince Arthur in, 254.

Kinglake, Alexander William (1809–91). Eng. historian, author of "Eothen," a splendid record of travel, and an exhaustive history of the Crimean War.

"**King Lear.**" Tragedy by Shakespeare, **1858**, 2934.

Kings, of Eng. and Gt. Brit. *See under* **England.**

Kings. Eleventh and twelfth books of the old Testament, usually written 1 Kings and 2 Kings, dealing with the period that embraces the reigns of all the kings of Israel except Saul and David.

King's Bench, Court of, in Eng., 922.

King's College, Aberdeen, *12.*

King's College, Cambridge, *668.*

King's College. College of Univ. of London, in the Strand, London; founded in 1829; has faculties of arts, laws, theology, science, medicine, engineering, and economics.

King's County, Eire. *See* **Offaly.**

King's Cross. Principal London terminus of British Rlys. (E. Region).

King's Cup. Principal Brit. air race; open to Brit. civil aircraft and pilots only; run on a handicap basis.

Kingsford-Smith, Sir Charles Edward (1897–1935). Australian airman, **1858.**

Kingsley, Charles (1819–75). Eng. clergyman and author, **1858.**

Kingsley, Henry (1830–76). Eng. novelist, younger brother of Charles Kingsley ("Ravenshoe").

King's Lynn. Spt. tn. of Norfolk, on the Great Ouse, 2 m. from the Wash; shipping trade and shipbuilding industry; pop. est. 25,500; 2376.

Kings of Cologne, The Three. Caspar, Melchior, and Balthasar, the wise men who visited Bethlehem at Christ's birth. Their bodies are said to have been taken to Cologne by the Emperor Frederick in 1162.

King's Police Medal. Decoration awarded to members of any official police force or fire brigade in Gt. Brit., Ireland, and Dominions for acts of exceptional devotion to duty; estab. 1909.

King's Prize. The principal award at the annual National Rifle Assocn. championship at Bisley; open to all past and present members of H.M. Forces.

Kingston, Canada, at N.E. end of L. Ontario, historic city commanding entrance to St. Lawrence r.; principally an educational and residential city, but has shipbuilding and engineering industries and extensive trade; pop. 29,500; 2434.

Kingston, Jamaica, on S. coast, cap. chief port and rly. centre; pop 109,000; 1792, *1793, map, 1792.*

Kingston-on-Thames. Royal borough and co. tn. of Surrey on S. side of the Thames, 12 m. S.W. of London; breweries, flour mills; scene of crowning of old Anglo-Saxon kings; pop. 39,900; 3123.

Kingston-upon-Hull. *See* **Hull.**

Kingstown (now **Dun Loaghaire**), Eire. Spt. and watering place in Co. Dublin, on S. shore of Dublin Bay, 7 m. S.E. of Dublin; port for steamers to and from Holyhead; pop. 39,760.

Kingsway. London thoroughfare; it extends from Holborn to the crescent of Aldwych; below the surface lies a tramway subway, and, lower still, a tube rly.; it was opened in 1905 by King Edward VII and Queen Alexandra.

Kingtehchen (king-tä-chen′). Large mart of S.E. China, in prov. of Kiangsi on r. Chang; pop. more than 300,000; great porcelain centre.

King William Land. In Greenland, 148, *map, 1542.*

King William's War (1689–97). Part of Anglo-French struggle for N. Amer.

Kinnaird′ Head, Scot. Promontory of Aberdeenshire, extending into the North Sea; has a lighthouse.

Kinross′-shire. One of the smallest Scottish cos., w. of Fife; a. 82 sq. miles; pop. 7,450; co. tn. Kinross, pop. 2,500; includes Loch Leven.

Kinsale, Eire. Spt. on Kinsale Harbour, 17 m. S. of Cork; important fisheries; pop. 2,800; 910.

Kintyre′, Mull of, Scot. Peninsula at the extreme south of Argyllshire; has a lighthouse.

Kin′zie, John (1763–1828). Amer. pioneer, b. Quebec, Canada; first white settler of Chicago, 784.

Kiolen, Kjölen, or **Keel Mts.,** between Sweden and Norway, 2392, *map, 2395.*

Kioto, Japan. Same as **Kyoto.**

Kip′ling, John Lockwood (1837–1911). Brit. artist and educator in India; father of Rudyard Kipling.

Kipling, Rudyard (1865–1936). Eng. writer; **1859**, 1215; Story of Mowgli, 1860; Nobel prize-winner, 2375; and S. African lit., 3020.

Kippered herring, 1233.

Kirchhoff (kērkh′-hof), **Gustav Robert** (1824–87). Ger. physicist; developed spectrum analysis (with Bunsen), *plate f. 3057.*

Kirghiz (kēr-gēz′). Nomadic people of cent. Asia, of Turko-Tartaric (Mongolian) race, ranging from borders of European Russia to w. China, 265, 271.

Kirghiz S.S.R. Self-governing republic of Soviet Russia, comprising most of the provs. of Akmolinsk, Semipalatinsk, Uralsk, and Turgai, and parts of the Astrakhan and Transcaspian provs.; a. 76,000 sq. m.; pop. 1,459,000; cap. Frunze; 3267.

Kirghiz steppes. Region in S.E. Russia.

Kirin (kīr-in′). Prov. of Manchuria; a. 101,000 sq. m.; pop. 4,504,000; traversed by r. Sungari, on which is Kirin (pop. 138,900); the capital; tobacco, wheat, maize, millet are grown.

Kirk, Sir John (1847–1922). English philanthropist; connected for over 40 years with Ragged School Union.

Kirkcaldy (ker-kaw′-di), Scot. Spt. tn. on S.E. coast of Fifeshire; called the "lang toon" from its 4-m. High Street; flax, paper, linoleum, dyeing and other industries; pop. 46,800.

Kirkcudbright (ker-kōō′-bri), Scot. Co. tn. of Kirkcudbrightshire, 30 m. S.W. of Dumfries; large and secure harbour; pop. 2,300; 1862.

Kirkcudbrightshire, Scot. Co. in S.W. bordering Solway Firth; a. 900 sq. m., pop. 30,000; **1862**; granite, 1499; hydro-electric installation, 1670, *1671.*

Kirke, Sir David (1597–1656). Captured Quebec, Canada, for England in 1629.

"**Kirke's Lambs.**" Regt. (now the Queen's Royal West Surrey Regt.), which from its colonel, Percy Kirke (*c.* 1645–91) and regimental badge, a lamb, won the nickname, often used in sarcastic reference to its brutalities committed against Monmouth's followers and sympathisers after the battle of Sedgemoor (1685).

Kirk-Kilitsch, also Kirk-Kilisse or Sarandeklisie. Tn. 25 m. N.E. of Adrianople (Edirne); pop. 16,000.

Kirkpatrick, Sir Ivone Augustine (b. 1897), became British High Commissioner for Germany in June 1950.

Kirk′stall Abbey, Leeds, England, 1918; by Girtin, *3352.*

Kirk′wall. Cap. of Orkney Isls., on Mainland, important Brit. base during the 1st World War; pop. 3,517; fine Norman-Gothic cathedral begun in 1138; air service to Inverness, etc.; 2453.

Kiruna, Sweden. Mining tn. N. of Arctic Circle, 3128.

Kirunavara, mt. in Sweden, 3129.

Kirunga. Volcano in Africa, 69.

Kish. Ruined city of Iraq, 100 m. S. Baghdad, between rivers Tigris and Euphrates, 1862, 2375.

Kishinev. Cap. of Moldavia S.S.R. Destroyed by Russians in "scorched earth" policy in 1941.

Kismayu. Spt. of ex-Ital. Somaliland, cap. of Jubaland; captured by Brit. in 1941; 3000.

Kissingen, Ger.; famous watering-place in Bavaria, 60 m. E. of Frankfort-on-Main; salt springs known from 9th cent.

Kisumu. Spt. of Kenya on Victoria Nyanza; pop. 1,350; also airport, 3321.

Kit-Cat Club. A London club named after Christopher (Kit) Cat, the proprietor of the tavern in which the members met; it flourished from 1703–20; Sir Godfrey Kneller painted the members' portraits, which, owing to the lowness of the room in which they were to hang, were half length, a size that became known as kit-cat.

Kitchen, a modern example, *123.*

Kitch'ener of Khartum,HoratioHerbert, Earl (1850–1916). Brit. general, **1862**; S. African War, 487.

Kite, A bird of prey, **1863.**

Kites, 1863; aeroplane compared with, 41; box, 1863; in China and Japan, 809, 1863; how and why they fly, 1863.

Kitool. A wood fibre, from India and Ceylon, used for making bristles of scrubbing brushes.

Kit's Coty House, dolmen, Kent, *3095.*

Kittiwake. One of the smallest gulls, common off N. of Britain; white plumage, pale blue-grey back; very graceful flight.

Kiushu, Japan. Same as **Kyushu.**

Kiwi. Same as **Apteryx.**

Kjöbenhavn (kyĕ' bĕn hah vn). Danish name of Copenhagen, 904.

Kjölen Mts. Between Norway and Sweden, 2392. *Map, 2395.* Same as **Kiolen Mts.**

Klagenfurt. Important mfg. city of Lower Austria; pop. 56,700; chief city of Klagenfurt region (800 sq. m.) which voted to remain in Austria after 1st World War. Absorbed in German Reich 1938–1945.

Klaipeda. *See* **Memel.**

Klang River. In Malay peninsula; flows by Kuala Lumpur, *2070.* Scene of fighting with Japanese, Dec. 1941.

Klaproth, Martin Heinrich (1743–1817). Ger. chemist, prof. at Berlin univ. from 1810; discovered titanium, 3216; uranium, 3297; zirconium, 3444.

Klar River. Short stream in S. of Scandinavian peninsula; flows into Lake Wenner; *map, 2395.*

Klausenburg. *See* **Cluj.**

Kléber, Jean Baptiste (1753–1800). Fr. Rev. general, one of greatest of epoch; assassinated while conquering Egypt.

Klee (klā), **Paul** (1879–1940). Swiss painter; under influence of Picasso became a Cubist; later an Abstractionist, using Surrealist imagery; works exhibited at Nat. Gallery in 1945; *3122.*

Kleist (klīst), **Heinrich von** (1777–1811). Ger. romantic dramatist and poet; chief works, " Penthesilea," " Der Zerbrochene Krug " (" The Broken Pitcher "), 2404.

Klemantans. People of Borneo, 525.

Klon'dike. A gold mining dist. in Yukon Territory, Canada, scene of great gold rush in 1897, 99, 3440.

Klopstock, Friedrich Gottlieb (1724–1803). Ger. epic, lyric, and dramatic poet; helped free Ger. literature from foreign, especially French, influence, 1456.

Kluck (klook), **Alexander von** (1846–1934). Prussian general and field-marshal, in command of Germans invading Belgium and France in 1011.

Kneller (nel'-er), **Sir Godfrey** (1646–1723). Court painter to Charles II and succeeding Eng. sovereigns to George I; the most famous of his time; b. Germany; buried in Westminster Abbey; portrait of Addison, *24*; Dryden, 1050; Marlborough, *2106*; Wren, *3426*; influenced by Van Dyck, and importance in English Art, 1178. *See also* **Kit-Cat Club.**

Knickerbocker, Diedrich. Pretended author of Washington Irving's burlesque history of New York City. The Knickerbockers were an old Dutch family, and the name is now commonly applied to descendants of the original Dutch settlers of New York.

Knight, Dame Laura. Eng. painter; specialized in scenes from circus and stage life; elected A.R.A. (1927) and R.A. in 1936; m. Harold Knight, portrait painter.

Knighthood and chivalry, 1863; *plates f. 1864, 1865*; armour, 240, *241*; King Arthur and the Round Table, 255, 2830; castle, 717; Froissart's chronicles, 1399; heraldry, 1614; orders of knighthood, 1864, 2449; list at foot of page; quintain, 2719; romances, 2798.

Knights Hospitallers of St. John, 2072, 2771.

Knights of Malta, 2072.

Knights of the Round Table, 1413, 2830; Tales of the Round Table, 2830; growth of legends, 255.

" Knight's Tale of Palamon and Arcite," retold from Chaucer's " Canterbury Tales," 762.

Knights Templars (crusading order), **1865**; Temple in London, 1865, 2012.

Knitted Goods, 850, 1865.

Knitting Machines, 1865; Jacquard attachment, 3361; adapted for lace, 1876.

Knives and forks, 1867.

Knoblock, Edward (1874–1945). Brit. dramatist; b. in New York; among his successful plays are " The Shulamite," " Kismet," and " Milestones," with Arnold Bennett.

" Knocking," a fault in petrol engines, 2564.

Knole. Seat of Lord Sackville, nr. Sevenoaks, Kent; fine mansion containing Great Hall and Galleries, built early in 17th cent.; earlier building taken by Henry VIII from Cranmer, and afterwards given to Thomas Sackville by Queen Elizabeth; National Trust property, part being leased to Lord Sackville; stands in large deer park.

Knossos or **Cnossus.** Ruined city of Crete; civilization, 29, 32; excavations at, 208, 927.

Knot. Small wading bird about 9 ins. in length, with long legs and long slender bill, and grey in colour. In winter vast numbers visit E. and S.E. coasts of Brit. from the Arctic where they breed in summer.

Knot. Nautical unit for measuring a ship's speed, 1997, 1998; used as equivalent of nautical mile (1·15 statute m.). *See* **Weights and Measures.**

Knotgrass. Small plant, *Polygonum aviculare,* fam. *Polygonaceae*; trailing recumbent, matted stems, small simple leaves at base of which are tiny pink and white flowers; grows as a weed in gardens and is common in waste places.

Knots, hitches, and splices, 1868; weavers', 706.

Knowles, James Sheridan (1784–1862). Brit. actor and dramatist; achieved greater renown as a playwright, among his best remembered productions being " Virginius," " The Hunchback," and " The Love Chase."

Knox, John (*c.* 1514–72). Scot. Protestant leader, **1871**; Edinburgh associations, 1087; and Reformation, 2759.

Knoxville, Tennessee, U.S.A. In E. on Tennessee r., mfg. city and distributing point for mineral and agricultural region; pop. 111,500.

Koala (kō-ah'-la). The tree-bear of Australia, **1872,** *313.*

Kobe (kō'-bā), Japan. Important spt. in s. of isl. of Honshu; pop. 788,000; great shipyard; 1796, 2454; devastated by U.S. raids in 1945.

Koblenz. *See* **Coblenz.**

Ko'bold or gnome. In Ger. folk-lore, a teasing, mischievous elf, 857.

Koch (kokh), **Robert** (1843–1910). Ger. physician and bacteriologist, 335, *2133*; studied tuberculosis, cholera, and tropical fevers; originated tuberculin treatment; 1905 Nobel prize-winner in medicine; discovers anthrax germ, 1458.

Kocher (kōkh'-er), **Emil Theodore** (1841–1917). Swiss surgeon, first to operate successfully for exophthalmic goitre; 1909 Nobel prize-winner in medicine.

Kodak. Popular make of camera, originated by George Eastman.

Kodiak or **Kadiak Island.** Off coast of Alaska, s. of Cook Inlet; 36,000 sq. m.; greatest salmon fisheries in Alaska; growing agric. and grazing industries, 98.

Kodok. *See* **Fashoda.**

Koenig (kēn-ig), **Gen. J. M. P.** (b. 1898). Fr. soldier; served in Narvik campaign, April 1940; fought in Brittany against invading Germans, escaped to Gen. de Gaulle in Eng.; defended Bir Hacheim (*q.v.* in *f-i*); in 1944 chief liaison officer between Eisenhower and the F.F.I. of which he became head; milit. gov. of Paris on its liberation, Aug. 1944; as C.-in-C. Fr. forces in Ger. was on Allied Control Commsn.

ORDERS OF KNIGHTHOOD

The Most Noble Order of the Garter—K.G. Ribbon, blue. Motto, *Honi soit qui mal y pense* (Evil be to him who evil thinks).

The Most Ancient and Noble Order of the Thistle—K.T. Ribbon, green. Motto, *Nemo me impune lacessit* (No one provokes me with impunity).

The Most Illustrious Order of St. Patrick—K.P. Ribbon, sky blue. Motto, *Quis Separabit* (Who shall separate ?). No new knights of St. Patrick have been created since 1921.

The Most Honourable Order of the Bath. This order has both military and civil divisions, and is further divided into G.C.B. (Knight Grand Cross), K.C.B. (Knight Commander) and C.B. (Companion). The ribbon is crimson and the motto, *Tria juncta in uno* (Three joined in one).

The Most Exalted Order of the Star of India. Divided into G.C.S.I. (Knight Grand Commander), K.C.S.I. (Knight Commander), and C.S.I. (Companion). The ribbon, light blue with white edges. Motto, Heaven's Light Our Guide. Creation of new members ceased in 1947.

The Most Distinguished Order of St. Michael and St. George. Divided into G.C.M.G., K.C.M.G., and C.M.G. Ribbon, blue and scarlet. Motto, *Auspicium melioris aevi.*

The Most Eminent Order of the Indian Empire—G.C.I.E., K.C.I.E., C.I.E. Ribbon, Imperial purple. Motto, *Imperatricis auspiciis.* Creation of new members ceased in 1947.

The Royal Victorian Order. Besides G.C.V.O. and K.C.V.O. there is a special grade, D.C.V.O., Dame Commander, while below C.V.O. comes M.V.O., Member of the Order. Ribbon, blue with red and white edges. Motto, Victoria.

The Most Excellent Order of the British Empire. In this order there are additional ranks such as D.B.E., Dame of the British Empire; O.B.E., Officer of the British Empire; M.B.E., Member of the British Empire; this order is further divided into Military and Civil divisions. Ribbon, purple (civil); purple with red centre (military). Motto, For God and the Empire.

Knights Bachelor. Though not an order, the Knights Bachelor are the survival of the State Orders of Knighthood of former times.

¶ There are other orders which convey neither title nor precedence upon their holders, such as the Order of Merit (O.M.) and the Order of the Companions of Honour (C.H.).

Koestler (kêst'-ler), **Arthur** (b. 1905). Hungarian-born Brit. author ; in 1931 went with Graf Zeppelin expedition to the Arctic ; 1932–33 travelled in Soviet Central Asia ; was News Chronicle correspondent in Sp. Civil War ; imprisoned by Franco and Vichy Fr. ; wrote " Spanish Testament," " Darkness at Noon," " The Yogi and the Commissar," " The Tragic and the Comic."

Kohima (ko-hē'-mah). Tn. of Assam, India, in dist. of same name ; fiercely defended hill station isolated by the Jap. onslaught of Apr. 1944, and held 14 days ; invasion of India averted after 40 days' fighting by relieving 14th Army ; 3424.

Koh-i-nur (kō-i-noor'). A famous diamond among Eng. crown jewels. 935.

Kohlrabi (kōl'-rah-bi). Vegetable of the cabbage type, 639.

Kokand. Same as **Khokand.**

Koko-Nor' or **Kuku-Nor.** Lake in cent. Asia in N.E. Tibet, 263.

Koksagyz, Siberian plant substitute for rubber, 2967.

Koksoak River, Quebec. Largest river in Labrador peninsula ; flows N. 500 m. to Ungava Bay ; many tributaries.

Kola Peninsula. A mountainous peninsula of Russia between the Arctic Ocean and the White Sea ; 50,000 sq. m. Its N. coast, called the Murman Coast, has several ice-free ports. See **Murman Coast.**

Kolchak, Alexis (1875–1920). Former imperial Rus. naval officer ; headed Omsk govt. (Nov. 1917 to Jan. 1920), recognized by the Allies as de facto Rus. govt. ; organized Siberian anti-Bolshevik army and held country nearly to Volga before 1919 summer campaign of Red Army forced retreat and collapse of his govt. ; executed by Irkutsk revolutionary commission, 2849.

Kolin (kō-lēn), Czechoslovakia. Tn. on r. Elbe, 30 m. E. of Prague ; pop. 16,000 ; Austrians defeated Frederick II of Prussia (1757), securing evacuation of Bohemia.

Kolin'sky fur, 1412.

Köln (kêln). Ger. name of **Cologne.**

Kol'okol, Tsar. The great bell in the Moscow Kremlin, 411.

Kolozsvar. See **Cluj.**

Koltsov, Alexis Vasilevitch (1809–42). Rus. lyric poet, called the " Russian Burns."

Komarno (kō'-mahr-nō) or **Komorn,** Czechoslovakia. Tn. on Danube. 50 m. S.E. of Bratislava ; pop. 21,000 ; surrendered to Austrians (1840) after brilliant defence in Hungarian rev. ; grain and timber trade.

Komi (Ziryansk). Autonomous republic of Soviet Russia proper, bordering the Arctic Ocean ; cap., Ust-Sisolsk.

Komisarjev'sky, Theodore (b. 1882) Brit. theatrical producer. Born in Russia, naturalized Brit. (1932). Wrote " Myself and the Theatre " ; " The Costume and the Theatre " ; " The Art of the Actor."

Komo'do dragon. A lizard, 1034. 1973 ; plate f. 1973.

Komura (kō'-moo-rah), **Jutaro, Marquis** (1855–1911). Japanese statesman and diplomat, minister to Russia and to U.S.A. ; plenipotentiary (1905) at Portsmouth Peace conference ; effected Anglo-Japanese Alliance (1905).

Konarak, Orissa. Animal sculpture at, 1712.

Kongwa, Tanganyika. Centre of Brit. govt.-sponsored Overseas Food Corp. scheme for large production of oil-seeds, especially ground-nuts (peanuts) and sunflower ; taken over from United Africa Co. April 1, 1948.

Ko'nia or **Konieh,** Turkey. City on Anatolian Rly., 280 m. S.E. of Istanbul ; pop. (1945) 58,800 ; anc. Iconium ; became Seljuk cap.

---

in 1097 ; taken by Frederick Barbarossa in 1100 ; annexed to Turkey in 15th cent. ; famous medieval orchards ; carpets, textiles.

Koniev (kon'-yef), **Ivan Stepanovitch** (b. 1897). Russ. Red army soldier ; fought Koltchak's White Russians ; led Moscow counter-offensive ; in Jan. 1945, leading the 1st Ukrainian Army, left bridgehead on Vistula and crossed r. Oder, in Mar. encircled Breslau, on Apr. 16 (with Zhukov) advanced on Berlin, April 23 encircling the city, where resistance ceased on May 2.

König (kê'-nig), **Frederick** (1774–1833). German inventor, who built the first real steam-printing machine ; on one of his machines " The Times " was printed for many years, starting from 1814.

Königgrätz (kê'-nig-grāts), Czecho-slovakia. Small city 65 m. E. of Prague ; 13th cent. cathedral ; varied mfrs. ; battle of Sadowa or Königgrätz (1866) in Austro-Prussian War fought near by ; 1449.

Königsberg (kê'-niks-bărg). Formerly fortified spt., cap. of E. Prussia, on r. Pregel ; large univ. ; bombarded in 1914 ; captured Jan. 1945 ; incorporated as Kaliningrad into U.S.S.R. in 1945.

Koninck, Philip de (1619–88). Dutch artist ; studied under Rembrandt ; landscapes and portraits ; 2334.

Konoye, Fumimaro, Prince (1891–1945) Jap. politician ; prime min. 1937–39 and 1940–41 ; after Jap. surrender he poisoned himself Dec. 15, 1945, on hearing he was to be arrested and tried as a war criminal.

Koo, Vi Kyuin Wellington (b. 1887). Chinese diplomat. Minister of Foreign Affairs, Peking (1922–24) ; Finance Minister (1926) ; Prime Minister (1926–27) ; Foreign Affairs (1931) ; Chinese minister to France (1932–35) ; ambassador to France (1936–40) ; amb. to Gt. Brit. (1941–46) ; ambassador to U.S. (1946).

Koo'doo. One of the largest of African antelopes, having a white stripe down the back and vertical stripes down the sides ; male has long horns twisted into an open spiral.

Kookaburra. The laughing jackass, 310, 313.

Köpenick (kê'-pe-nik), **Captain of.** Name by which Wilhelm Voigt, perpetrator of hoax at that German town in 1906, was known ; shoemaker and ex-convict, he donned a guards officers' uniform, arrested both burgomaster and treasurer and appropriated a large sum.

Koran'. Sacred book of Mahomedans, 1872, 2066.

Korda, Sir Alexander (b. 1893). Brit. film director. Hungarian by birth, but naturalized British. Films include : " Private Life of Henry VIII " ; " The Ghost Goes West " ; " Rembrandt." Knighted in 1942.

Kordofan (kor-dō-fahn'). A prov. in Anglo-Egyptian Sudan, Africa.

Kore'a or **Chosen.** Peninsula of E. Asia between the Sea of Japan and the Yellow Sea ; 1872, 1873, 268, 1795. On June 25, 1950, S. Korea was invaded by N. Korea. The U.N. Security Council pronounced this an act of aggression. The U.S.A. sent immediate armed aid to S. Korea. Fifty-one other nations endorsed the Security Council decision.

Korea, Strait of. Separates Korea from Japan and unites Sea of Japan with Eastern Sea.

Koritza. Tn. of Albania, nr. frontiers of Greece and Yugoslavia, 55 m. s.w. of Monastir ; It. base in Albania in Italo-Gk. war ; in Nov. 1940 Gks. stormed the heights dominating the tn. and held it until Ger. invasion, April 1941.

Körner (kôr'-ner)' **Karl Theodor** (1791–1813). Ger. poet and patriot ; roused his countrymen by his patriotic songs.

Kornilov, Laurus Georgievich (1870–1918). Rus. general, commanded in Galician campaign during 1st World War ; his abortive mutiny against Kerensky (1917) prepared way for later Bolshevik victory ; killed in battle against Red Army while leading Volunteer Army in " ice flight " in the Kuban.

Kosciusko or **Kosciuszko** (kos-i-us'-kō)' **Tadeusz** (1746–1817). Polish general and patriot, 1873.

Kosciusko, Mt., in Australian Alps, New South Wales (7,328 ft.), 2343.

Kosher (kō'-sher). Jewish term for food made ceremonially clean, especially applied to meat slaughtered in a way insuring complete bleeding of the body.

Koshtantau (kosh-tan-tow'). Mt. in Caucasus range, 732.

Kosice. Beautiful old city, and largest in the area to be ceded to Hungary in Oct. 1938 ; 130 m. N.E. of Budapest ; pop. 70,000 mostly Magyar and descendants of Germans who founded city before 12th cent. ; 14th cent. Gothic cath. ; restored to Czechoslovakia in 1945.

Kossovo (ko-sō'-vō). Plain in s.w. Yugoslavia, near Prisrend : battle (1389), 2922, 3264.

Kos'suth, Louis (1802–94). Hungarian patriot, 1874, 1656.

Kota Bharu. Cap. and spt. of Kelantan, Malayan Union ; nr. mouth of Kelantan r. ; pop. 14,843 ; here the Japs made their first landing in Malaya, Dec. 7, 1941. 2nd World War.

Koto (kō-tō). A Japanese harp consisting of a long box over which are stretched 13 strings, each with a bridge ; played with both hands and tuned by shifting the bridges.

Kotor, formerly **Cattaro.** Spt. of Yugoslavia ; a famous beauty spot of Montenegro ; pop. 5,000.

Kotzebue (kot'se-boo), **August Friedrich von** (1761–1819). Ger. playwright, extraordinarily prolific and popular over all Europe ; best known play translated as " The Stranger."

Koumiss. Mongolian drink of fermented milk, 2174, 2205.

Koussevitzsky (koo-se-vit'-ski), **Serge** (b. 1874). Russian conductor. Founded orchestra in Russia. After revolution left to work in London, Paris and Boston, U.S.A.

Kovno. See **Kaunas.**

Koweit (kō-wā-it') or **Kuweit.** Port. N.E. Arabia on Persian Gulf ; large transit trade ; 195, 200.

Kowloon'. Small peninsula of China opposite isl. of Hong Kong, 1639.

Kraals (krahlz). Native huts and villages in Africa, 67, 3018.

Krafft or **Kraft, Adam** (about 1455–1507). Principal Ger. sculptor of late Gothic period ; his masterpiece, pyramid 64 ft. high, remarkable for its rich and delicate decorations, figures and relief and its architectural beauty.

Krait (krāt). Venomous bluish snake, India, 2991, 1701.

Krajova. Same as **Craiova.**

Krakatoa (kra-ka-tō'-a). Small volcanic isl. in E. Indies between Java and Sumatra ; eruption of 1883, 3328.

Kra'ken. Norwegian name for sea serpent.

Krakow. Same as **Cracow.**

Kramer (krah'-mer), **Joseph.** " The Beast of Belsen " (d. 1945). German S.S. commandant of Belsen concentration camp ; before that on staff of Auschwitz camp ; hanged Dec. 14, 1945, at Hamelin, for his brutalities.

Kranach, Lucas. Same as **Cranach.**

Krasnodar. Tn. in Caucasia, U.S.S.R. ; centre of mfg. dist. ; pop. 204,000.

Krasnoyarsk krahs-nō-yahrsk'),Siberia, U.S.S.R. City on Yenisei r. and Trans-Siberian Rly. ; pop. 190,000 ; centre of gold washings of Yenisei dist.

Krefeld (kra'-felt) or **Crefeld**, Ger. mfg. tn. in Prussia, 30 m. N.W. of Cologne; pop. 165,000; famous technical school; mfrs., 1447.

Kreisler (kriz'-ler), **Fritz** (b. 1875). Austrian violinist and composer, generally conceded to be one of the greatest of modern violinists; works include " Caprice Viennoise."

Krem'lin. Citadel of Moscow, 2234; plate f. 2845; Tsar Kolokol bell, 411.

Kreutzer (kroit'-zer), **Rudolph** (1766–1831). Fr. violinist of Ger. extraction; friend of Beethoven, who dedicated to him his " Kreutzer Sonata."

Kriemhild (krēm'-hilt). In the Nibelungenlied, wife of the hero Siegfried, 2363, 2969.

Kris. Malay sword, with wavy blade.

Krish'na. A Hindu god, incarnation of Vishnu, 1626.

Kris Kringle or **Christ Child.** Name a corruption of Ger. Christ. Kindlein, " the little Christ Child "; supposed to bring gifts, 820.

Krivoi Rog. Tn. of Ukraine, U.S.S.R.; 90 m. s.w. of Dniepropetrovsk; industrial tn. with large iron ore mines; pop. 197,621; taken by Ger. advance Aug. 17, 1941, retaken by 3rd Ukrainian Army Feb. 22, 1944.

Kronborg Castle, Elsinore, 904.

Kron'feld, Robert (1904–48), Austrian-born British glider pilot; held many records (over Alps, double Channel crossing, etc.); sqdn.-ldr. R.A.F. in 2nd World War; killed in glider crash; 1476.

Kronos or **Cronos.** In Gk. myth., Titan ruler of universe, 3298, 2875.

Kronstadt. See Brasov.

Kronstadt, Rus. port and fortified city on isl. of Kotlin in Gulf of Finland 31 m. w. of Leningrad; pop. 43,800; founded 1710 by Peter the Great; in defence of Leningrad, 1941, used as base for raiding and interrupting communications behind Finnish and German lines.

Kropot'kin, Peter, Prince (1842–1921). Rus. geographer and revolutionary; first to show that structural lines of physical Asia run s.w.–n.e.; exiled and imprisoned.

Kruger (kroo'-ger), **Paul** (1825–1904). Boer patriot, known as " Oom Paul " (Uncle Paul); pres. of S. African Republic (Transvaal) (1883–1901); 487, 3019; and Smuts, 2987.

Kruger National Park. Game reservation in Transvaal, 3013, 3014, plate f. 3341, 3239.

Krupp (kroop), **Alfred** (1812–87). Ger. " cannon king," discoverer of method of casting steel in large pieces; made great guns used (1870–1) in the siege of Paris.

Krupp, Friedrich (1787–1826). Ger. ironmaster, founder of house of Krupp and of great Krupp works at Essen; introduced manufacture of cast steel into Ger.; died in poverty.

Krupp, Friedrich Alfred (1854–1902). Son of Alfred, grandson of Friedrich; left Krupps to daughter Bertha.

Krupp von Bohlen und Halbach, Bertha (b. 1886). Eldest daughter of Friedrich Alfred; inherited Krupps at 16.

Krupp von Bohlen U. H., Gustav (1871–1950). Head of Krupps with son Alfred (b. 1907), in 2nd World War; Gustav Krupp, indicted for war crimes in 1945, was found unfit in health to stand trial; Alfred Krupp, found guilty at Nuremberg of war crimes, July 1948, was sentenced to 12 yrs.' imprisonment with forfeiture of all property.

Krupp Steel Works, bombed by Allies 1941–1945; dismantled 1946–47.

Krypton (Kr). A rare gaseous element of inert gas group; atomic No. 36; atomic weight 83·7; composed of several isotopes; found in air in minute quantities by Ramsay and Travers, 88, 1420; liquefied at –148° F.; name is Greek for " hidden "; properties, 777, 2744.

Kshatriyas (kshut'-ri-ya). A Hindu caste, 1626, 1707.

Kuala Lumpur (koo-ah'-la lum-poor'). Cap. of Federation of Malaya; in Selangor state; bombed by Japanese Dec. 26, 1941, evacuated by Brit. Imp. troops Jan. 11, 1942; here on Sept. 13, 1945, were surrendered all Japanese forces in Malaya; pop. 141,660; 2070.

Kuban' River, 500 m. long, flows across w. half of N. Caucasia.

Kubelik (kŏŏ'-be-lik), **Jan** (1880–1940). Bohemian violinist; acquired extraordinary technique at early age and for a decade was the most popular concert virtuoso.

Kublai Khan (kŏŏ'-blī kahn) (1216–94). One of the greatest, most intelligent, and most cultured of Mongol rulers, grandson of Genghis Khan; completed conquest of China; 2205, 2652.

Kuching. Cap. of Sarawak, in extreme s.w.; pop. 30,000; in Jap. occupn. 1941–45; 2873.

Kuenlun (kwen'-lun) **Mts.** In cent. Asia on N. border of Tibet; highest peak estimated 20,000 ft.; map, 808.

Kufra. Group of 5 oases in Sahara, N. of Tropic of Cancer; tn. of Kufra on caravan route; 2859.

Kuh-fu', China. Confucius' tomb, 887.

Kuibishev, formerly **Samara.** City of the U.S.S.R., 525 m. s.e. of Moscow on r. Volga; pop. (1939) 390,000; in 2nd World War temp. capital during attack on Moscow, 3421.

Kuka (kŏŏ'-ka). Tn. in N.E. corner of Nigeria, Africa; est. pop. 60,000; slave mart previous to 1894.

Ku Klux (kū-kluks) **Klan.** Secret society in U.S.A., which at close of Amer. Civil War sought to counteract influence of dishonest politicians; originated in Tennessee in 1865, other societies formed, and in 1871–2 laws were passed for their suppression. In 1915 the name was revived for a society admitting only native-born, white, Protestant, American citizens; founded in Georgia, it spread to other states, northern as well as southern.

Kulaks. Well-to-do peasants of Russia, 2852.

Kum. Persian oasis town; 80 m. s.s.w. Teheran; sacred place of Shiah Mahomedans; pop. (1945) 30,000, 7741.

Kumasi (koo-mah'-sē). Cap. of Ashanti, Brit. W. Africa; pop. 43,413; exports cocoa, rubber, cattle, and other products; captured by Brit. in 1874, 1896, and 1900; chief distributing centre for Ashanti.

Kum'quat. A plum-shaped citrus fruit, 2444.

Kun, Bela (1886–1939). Hungarian Communist leader; while prisoner of war in Russia instructed by Lenin, and after collapse of Central Powers sent back to Hungary in 1918 to found Soviet Republic; after its fall, escaped in 1920 to Russia, where he became in 1921 a member of the International Communist executive; reported shot in Aug. 1939; 1656.

Kunersdorf (kŏŏ'-nerz-dorf). Vil. in Prussia, 4 m. N.E. of Frankfort-on-the-Oder; Prussians defeated by Russians and Austrians 1759 (Seven Years' War).

K'ung Fu-tsu, Chin. name of the philospher Confucius, 887.

Kunlun Mountains. See Kuenlun.

Kunzite (koonts'-īt). A semi-precious stone found in Madagascar and California; phosphorescent after exposure to radium.

Kuomintang (kwŏ-min-tang'). The National People's Party of China, founded in 1928 by Sun-Yat Sen, aiming at independent China and social reformation; 782, 813.

Kur. Principal r. of Transcaucasia, flowing s.w. 820 m.; navigable for 350 m. from mouth; 717.

Kurdistan'. Mountainous country in E. of Asia Minor and extending into Persia; peopled by the Kurds.

Kurds. Mahomedan tribes of Asia Minor, descended from the Carduchi; they number about 2,500,000.

Kuré (kŏŏ'-rā), Japan. Important naval port on Honshu Isl. and Inland Sea; pop. 231,000; former armament factory; in the bay the Japanese fleet surrendered to the Allies on Aug. 14, 1945.

Kuria Muria (kŭ'-ri-a mŭ'-ri-a) **Islands.** Group of 5 isls. off s. coast of Arabia; 28 sq. m.; part of Brit. colony of Aden; cable station.

Kurile (koo'-ril) or **Chishima Islands.** Group of volcanic isls., stretching N.E. from Hokkaido, Japan; 3,969 sq. m.; name comes from Russian kurit (" to smoke ") in allusion to active volcanoes; 1795; transferred to U.S.S.R. in 1945.

Kuroki (koo-rō'-kē), **Itei, Count** (1811–1923). Japanese general and samurai; distinguished in Chino-Japanese War of 1894–5; in Russo-Japanese War of 1904–5 commanded First Army, defeated Russians at r. Yalu.

Kuropatkin (koo-rō-pat'-kin), **Alexei Nikolaievich** (1848–1925). Rus. general; in supreme command in East during Russo-Japanese War, until after battle of Mukden; again commanded an army in 1916 in 1st World War.

Kutb Minar. Tower at Delhi, 988.

Kut-el-Amara (koot-el-a-mah'-ra), Iraq. Tn. on r. Tigris, 105 m. s.e. of Baghdad; rly. terminus; coaling point; strategic point in 1st World War; Brit. force under Townshend surrendered to Turks after severe siege, 3410.

Kuweit, Arabia. Same as **Koweit.**

Kwang'chow Wan or **Kwang Chau Wan.** Coaling station on s. coast of China between Hong Kong and the Island of Hainan, leased to France in 1898; now called Changkiang; 325 sq. m.; pop. 250,000.

Kwangsi. Inland prov. of S. China; 83,000 sq. m.; pop. 14,861,500; cap. Yungning; commercial centre Wuchow; cassia, grain, metals, gems.

Kwang-Su or **Kuang-Hsu.** Title assumed by Tsai T'ien (1872–1908), emperor of China; during his reign occurred the war with Japan, the Boxer rebellion and the occupation of Pekin by the United Powers; under domination of the Empress Dowager, Tsze-Hsi.

Kwang'tung or **Kwantung.** Prov. of S.E. China; 85,447 sq. m.; pop. 32,338,800; considerable mineral wealth (gold, coal, iron); large exports of silk; cap. Kwangchow; chief cities, Hongkong, Macao, Canton; 693.

Kwannon Tunnel. Rly. tunnel under Shimonoseki Straits, Jap.; linking pt. of Shimonoseki, Honshu Is., with Moji on Kyushu; 1½ m. under water; completed in 1941.

Kweichow (kwī'-chow). Prov. of s.w. China; 69,000 sq. m.; pop. 10,557,400; cap. Kweiyang; gold, silver, mercury, tin, coal and iron.

Kyd, Thomas (c. 1558–94). Eng. dramatist, one of most important predecessors of Shakespeare (" The Spanish Tragedy ").

Kyoto or **Kioto.** Former cap. of Japan; pop. 1,000,000, 1874, 1796, 1801.

Kyrie Eleison (kir-i-ā e-lā'-i-son). Gk. words, meaning " Lord have mercy," used as form of prayer in both Gk. and Rom. Cath. Churches, and also (translated) in Anglican Church.

Kyrle (kêrl), **John** (1637–1724). Eng. philanthropist, known as " the Man of Ross "; his family had lived long at Ross, Herefordshire, and he did everything he could to benefit the tn., spending all his money in good works; his memory perpetuated in the Kyrle Society.

Kyushu or **Kiushu** (kū-shŏŏ'). Southernmost of 4 large isls. forming Japan proper; 16,000 sq. m.; pop. approx. 9,000,000; mountainous and volcanic; map, 1796.

THE letter L is thought to be descended from the ancient Egyptian hieroglyph representing a lioness which became the symbol , or when written in a running hand. Here some resemblance to our letter is already visible. The Phoenicians wrote it like this ⎿ and called it *Lamed*, " ox-goad," from its resemblance to that object. The Greeks called it *Lambda* and turned it about so that it looked like our V upside-down, ⋀. The Romans straightened it out to the form it has today. The sounds *l* and *r*, known as the liquids, are very closely related. In fact, scholars tell us that in Egyptian, as in some other languages, no clear distinction was made between them, the signs for these sounds being used interchangeably. There are peoples, e.g. Chinese, who cannot sound the *r*, and these substitute *l* for *r*, as *velly* for *very*. This use of *l* for *r* is known as " lambdacism." The Japanese, on the other hand, substitute *r* for *l* ('rhotacism').

L33. Zeppelin of 1st World War; raided Eng., 94.

Laaland (law'land). Danish isl. in Baltic sea; 445 sq. m., 991: *map, 992.*

La'ban. Father-in-law of Jacob who served him 7 years for his daughter Rachel (Gen. xxviii–xxxi).

La Bassée (lah-bas-sā). Tn. of Fr. in dept. of Nord; practically destroyed during 1st World War; scene of fierce battle fought in 1914.

Lab'danum. Gummy secretion of leaves of several plants of rock rose family, used as fixative for perfumes, 2550.

Labiatae (lā-bi-ā'-tē). Plant family including dead-nettles, mint, cat-mint, and ground-ivy.

Labiche (la-bēsh'), **Eugène M.** (1815–88). Fr. dramatist (" Le Voyage de M. Perrichon ").

Labouchère (la-boo-shār'), **Henry Dupré** (1831–1912). Eng. journalist and radical politician; founder and editor of the weekly " Truth," noted for exposure of public frauds.

Labour, as an economic factor, 1081; arbitration of disputes, 204, 2358; and capital, Marxian doctrine, 2996; child labour, 802; division of, 1080; factory system, 521, 1722; slavery and serfdom, 2981; trade unions, 3233.

Labour and National Service, Ministry of, Whitehall, London, a Brit. Government department, **1875, 3234.**

Labour legislation, 1875; child labour laws, ̇2; compulsory arbitration, 2538.

Labour movement, in politics, **1875**; Attlee, 300; MacDonald, 2048; Socialism, 2996; unions, 3233.

Labour Party. Formed 1906, to represent organized labour and Socialists; at first cooperated with Liberals, later adopted Socialistic programme of reform; 300, 1875, 1929, 2048, 2996, 3281.

Labours of Hercules, 1615.

Lab'rador. Most easterly part of Brit. N. Amer.; a. est. 110,000 sq. m.; pop. about 5,000; **1875,** 2338, 2714; *map, plate f. 680;* discovered, 648; Eskimos, 1222; work of Sir Wilfred Grenfell, 1543.

Labrador current, 291, 1875: causes fogs, 1333.

La Bruyère (lah brē-yār'), **Jean de** (1645–96). Fr. essayist, one of best writers of classical French; 1380.

Labuan (la-boo-an'). Brit. isl. of Malay Archipelago, forming part of Brit. N. Borneo, 527; formerly in Straits Settlements; 35 sq. m.; pop. est. 9,000; Victoria Harbour; sago factories.

Labur'num. A small tree, fam. *Leguminosae,* native to cent. and S. Europe; cultivated for showy yellow flowers and glossy foliage; all parts poisonous; wood extremely heavy.

Lab'yrinth or cochlea, of the ear, *1066.*

Labyrinth. Name given by Greeks and Romans to buildings, entirely or partly underground, with intricate winding passages in which one easily became lost; at Crete, 927; in Gk. myth., 955.

Lac. Resinous substance, consisting of shellac and crimson colouring matter, secreted by scale insects, 1881, 2768, **2879.**

Laccadive (lak'-a-dīv) **Islands.** Brit. group of 14 coral isls. 200 m. w. of S. India in Indian Ocean; attached to Madras Province; pop. (1941) 18,300; coconut plantations.

Lace, 1876; *plates f. 1880, 1881;* mfrs. in Belgium, 404, *408;* gold, 1481; Jacquard loom, 1791, 1877, 3361; knitting machine, 1865.

Lacedaemon. *See* Sparta.

Lace-making machinery, 1876, *1880.*

Lacertil'ia. The lizard order of reptiles, 1974.

Lace-wing fly. Insect of the order *Neuroptera,* distinguished by its lace-like wings and most brilliant eyes; common Brit. species is bright pale green in colour; eggs, *1094.*

Lachesis (lak'-e-sis). In classical myth., one of the Fates, the goddesses who were supposed to control human destinies, 1262.

Lachish (lā'-kish). Anc. city in S. Palestine, often mentioned in Tel-el-Amarna tablets and in Bible; destroyed by Joshua (Joshua x, 31–3) and assigned to tribe of Judah (xv, 39).

Lac-insect. Scale insect which secretes the resinous substance lac 1881, 1882, 2879, 3359.

Lackey moth. Moth of family *Lasiocampidae* whose larvae form large colonies in tent-like masses of web on hawthorn and similar hedges; larvae striped red, black, blue, yellow (hence name, lackey); adult, dull brown. Eggs are laid in masses round twigs of trees, especially apple trees, where caterpillars if not destroyed are liable to become a pest.

Lackland. Nickname for King John of Eng., 1833.

Laconia (la-kō'-ni-a). In anc. Greece, S.E. dist. of Peloponnesus, 1518, 3053; *map, 1518.*

Lacoste, (Jean) **René** (b. 1905). Fr. lawn-tennis player; first became singles champion of Fr. 1925, and won at Wimbledon twice, in 1925 and 1928; perhaps the greatest player of France's " Four Musketeers."

Lacquer (lak'-er). Resinous varnish obtained from Japanese varnish-tree, **1881,** 2709; for metal work, 1882; cellulose-lacquer, 1882; contains pyroxylin, 2709.

Lacquer-ware, 1881; Japanese, 1811.

Lacrosse. A game, **1882,** 2756.

Lac sulphuris (milk of sulphur), 3116.

Lac'tic acid. A bitter hydroxy-acid present in sour milk; in buttermilk, 2174; in ensilage, 1510 caused by fermentation, 1266.

Lac'tose, or milk sugar, 2174, 3116.

Ladislaus (lad'-is-laws) **I, St.** (1040–95). King of Hungary (1077–95) and founder of national greatness; established Christianity and subdued heathen; most beloved of Hungarian kings.

Ladoga (lah'-dō-ga). Largest lake of Europe, in N.W. Rus.; 7,000 sq. m.; discharges into Gulf of Finland by r. Neva; icebound about half the year; centre of fierce fighting 1939–40 in Russo-Finnish war, following which land N. and W. of lake was ceded to Russia.

Ladrone (la-drōn') or **Mariana Islands,** in the Pacific; about 1,500 m. E. of the Philippines; 440 sq. m.:

formerly part of Ger. New Guinea 2470, 2473; mandated to Japa between World Wars, ex. Guam ceded to U.S.A.; under U.S.A. ad ministration, 1945.

Ladybird. A small spotted beetl mostly red or yellow; familia inhabitant of gardens, fields, an orchards, **1883,** *1731;* preys upo aphids, 186; scale insects, 2878.

Lady Finger, banana, 354.

Lady of the Lake. In Arthurian legen water fairy who reared Lancelot.

" Lady of the Lake, The." Poem b Scott, 2898, 2900.

Ladysmith, S. Africa, trade centre an rly. junction in N. Natal; po 9,700; besieged by Boers for 1 days (1899–1900) during Bo War; Roberts raises siege. 487. 278

Lady's Slipper, flower, 1883.

Lady's Smock (*Cardamine pratensis* the cuckoo flower or milkmaid watercress relative, 3354.

Lady's Tresses orchid, 2448.

Lae. Tn., with harbour on Huc Gulf, Brit. New Guinea; taken b Japs. Mar. 8, 1942, recaptured b Australian forces Sept. 16. 1943.

Laer'tes, father of Odysseus.

Laertes in Shakespeare's " Hamlet 1570.

Laevo-ro'tatory substances. Substanc which rotate the plane of polariz light to the left, 3155.

Laevulose (lē'-vū-lōz). Another nan for fructose or fruit sugar, referrin to the fact that this form of sug rotates polarized light to the le (Lat. *laevus,* left).

Lafayette (lah-fā-yet'), **Gilbert du M tier, Marquis de** (1757–1834). F general and patriot, **1884,** 146.

La Fontaine (lah-fon-tān'), **Jean d** (1621–95). Fr. fabulist, **1884,** *18*

Lagan (lā'-gan). R. of Northern Ire flowing 35 m. to Belfast Lough.

Lagash'. Anc. city-kingdom in Bab lonia, one of oldest centres Sumerian civilization.

Lagerlöf (lah'-ger-lēf), **Ottilia Loui Selma** (1858–1940). Swedish writ **1885;** in Scandinavian literatu 2881.

Lagoon. A pool or lake, especiall when connected with the sea; coral isls., 2471.

Lagoon Islands. Same as Ellice Islan

Lagos (lā'-gos). Cap. and chief spt. Nigeria, in W. Africa; on a small i close to the coast; pop. 174,200: 336

Lagrange (lah-grahnzh'), **Joseph Lo** (1736–1813). Fr. mathematicia one of greatest of 18th cent contributed to verification Newtonian theory.

La Guaira (lah-gwī'-ra). Chief spt. Venezuela, on N. coast; pop. 21,00 3309.

La Guardia (lah gar'-dia), **Fiorello** (1882–1947). Amer. politician; may of New York City 1933, 1937, 19 the first to hold three consecuti terms; put an end to " boss" cont in city govt.; directed civilian defe 1941–42; director-gen. of U.N.R.R from Mar. 29 to Dec. 31. 1946. wh it ended; 3296.

Lahn. River of Ger., joins Rhine af S.W. course of 133 m., 2769.

La Hogue (lah hōg) or **La Houg batlle of.** Fought in 1692 near N extremity of peninsula of Cotentin, Normandy, Fr.; Eng. and Dutch fleets under Admiral Russell defeated Fr. fleet under Tourville; 1794.

Lahore (la-hor'). Pakistan, anc. walled city on R. Ravi, largest city and cap. of Punjab; pop. about 950,000; rly. centre; makes silk and cotton cloths, carpets, vegetable oils; Punjab Univ.; 2479, 2705; boundary commission award in Aug. 1947 caused serious disturbances.

Laibach (lī-'bahkh). *See* Ljubljana.

Laid paper, 2500.

L'Aiglon (lā-glon'). Poetic name meaning " eaglet " given by Victor Hugo to Duke of Reichstadt, son of Napoleon I and Marie Louise.

Laing's Nek. *See* Lang's Nek.

Laissez-faire (lā-sā-fār') (" let it be "). The 18th cent. (Fr.) way of saying " less government in business "; in contemporary use means unrestricted industrial and commercial competition.

Laity. Word generally used to distinguish the people from the clergy; a layman is one who does not belong to a profession or is not an expert.

Laius. In Gk. myth., father of Oedipus and king of Thebes; killed by Oedipus, 2424.

Lake District or **Lake Country.** In N. Eng., containing principal Eng. lakes, 943, 1164, *1166, 1169, 1175,* 3371.

Lake-dwellers. Prehistoric inhabitants of Europe, 1886.

Lake-dwellings, of Europe, *1237*; Neolithic, 2083; in Switzerland, 208; *plate f. 2081,* 2083; in Venezuela, 3308.

Lake Poets. A group of poets—Coleridge, Wordsworth, and Southey —who lived in the Lake District of N. England.

Lakes, 1885, 2598; effect on climate, 1515; glacial origin, 1680; salt, 1885, 2480; volcanic origin, 3328.

WORLD'S GREATEST LAKES

NAME	APPROX. AREA IN SQ. M.
Caspian	170,000
Superior	31,800
Victoria	26,000
Aral Sea	26,000
Huron	23,010
Michigan	22,400
Nyasa	14,200
Baikal	13,350
Tanganyika	12,700
Erie	10,000

Lalique (lal-ēk), **René** (1860–1945). Fr. designer specializing in glassware; used delicate colours, and designs of birds, deer, fish, flowers, etc.

" Lalla Rookh." Oriental romance by Thomas Moore.

Lama (lah'-ma). Tibetan priest; *plate f. 3208.*

Lamaism. National religion of Tibet, 3208; *plate f. 3208.*

Lamarck (lah-mahrk'), **Jean de** (1744–1829). Fr. naturalist, who suggested (in 1801) the word " biologie " as name of new science to be devoted to study of all life considered as the same process whether in plants or animals; forerunner of Darwin, 1244, 1246, 1617, 3447.

Lamartine (la-mahr-tēn'), **Alphonse de** (1790–1869). Fr. poet, historian, statesman; unsuccessfully contested presidency in 1851 (" Meditations "; " History of the Girondins ").

Lamb, Charles (1775–1834). Eng. essayist, **1886,** 1966; and English literature, 1214; and the essay, 1224; Dissertation on Roast Pig, 900.

Lamb, Mary (1764–1847). Eng. writer, sister of Charles Lamb, **1886,** 1966.

Lamb. A young sheep, 2940; from Canterbury, N.Z., 693; skin used for gloves, *2149*; growth affected by metallic salts, *2149*; wool, 3405.

Lamballe (lahm-bal'), **Marie Thérèse de** (1749–92). Fr. princess, friend of Marie Antoinette; killed by revolutionary mob and her head carried past the queen's prison windows.

Lambda, λ, Λ (Rom. l, L). Eleventh letter of Gk. alphabet.

Lambert, Constant (b. 1905). English composer, conductor, and critic. Compositions include " Romeo and Juliet," " Horoscope " (ballet), " Rio Grande," for chorus, pianoforte and orchestra; musical director of Vic Wells ballet 1932–47; conducted at Promenade concerts; writings include " Music Ho ! " (1934).

Lambert, John (1619–94). Eng. general, who fought under Cromwell; distinguished himself at Marston Moor, Dunbar and Worcester.

Lambeth. Met. and parl. bor. of s. London; pop. (1945) 192,350; pottery mfrs.; Lambeth Palace, London, residence of Archbishop of Canterbury.

Lambeth Conference. A meeting of prelates of the Church of Eng. which takes place once in ten years; first held in 1867; postponed 1940 conference held in 1948.

Lamellibranchia. Class of molluscs, including oysters and cockles, 2199.

Lamentations. Book of Old Testament, traditionally ascribed to Jeremiah, bewailing destruction of Jerusalem.

Lamia (lā'-mi-*a*). In Gk. myth., a beautiful vampire; in Keats' poem " Lamia."

Laminated glass, manufacture, 1474; laminated plastics, 2626.

Lammergeier (lam'-er-gī-er). A member of the vulture family, also called bearded vulture from tuft of bristles at base of beak.

Lammermuir Hills. Scot., range of hills in Berwickshire and Haddingtonshire; highest summit, Lammer Law, 1,723 ft.

La Motte Fouqué. *See* Fouqué.

Lamp-black. A sooty form of carbon; in ink, 1724; in lead pencils, 2541; in paints, 2478.

Lampern. *See* Lamprey.

Lamprey. Primitive cartilaginous fishlike creature parasitic on fish, with sucker mouth; with hagfish comprise class *Cyclostomata*; **1886,** 2512.

Lamps, 1887; acetylene, 18; electric, *1134, 1135,* 1887; gas, 616, 1424; lighthouse, 1944, *1945*; mercury vapour, 2146; miner's safety lamp, *979,* 980, *1889*; neon, 2315; nickelsteel in, 2366; pressure, *478*; time switch, 3214.

Lamp shell. Creature resembling a mollusc, but sole surviving representative of phylum *Brachiopoda*; similar forms are among the oldest of fossils; *2943.*

Lamy (lah-mē), **Claude Auguste** (1829–78), Fr. glass-maker; discovered thallium (1862), 3193; produced a dense thallium glass (1867).

Lanark, Scot. Tn. of Lanarkshire; weaving, cattle and sheep trade; pop. 6,178; 1890.

Lanarkshire, Scot. Inland co. in s.w.; a. 879 sq. m.; pop. 1,643,000; **1890.**

Lancashire. Co. of N.W. Eng.; 1,875 sq. m.; pop. 5,039,500; **1890**; textile industry, 1165, 2084.

Lancaster, John of Gaunt, Duke of. *See* John of Gaunt.

Lancaster, Joseph (1788–1838). Brit. educationist; started a school for poor children in South London, where he set the elder pupils to teach the younger; it finally developed into the Royal Lancastrian Society; 2883.

Lancaster. Co. tn. of Lancashire, on r. Lune, 7 m. from sea; pop. 47,000; mfrs. linoleum, cotton goods, furniture; was anc. Rom. station; castle gate, *1890.*

Lancaster. The chief heavy class bomber aircraft of Second World War, designed for the R.A.F. by A. V. Roe & Co.; converted into civil airliner Lancastrian after war.

Lancaster, House of. Famous Eng. royal family, descended from Edmund, son of Henry III, who was created first earl in 1267; the Wars of the Roses saw the fall of the great house; founded, 1611, 2777; list of kings, *see page* 3790; in Wars of the Roses, 2828.

Lance-corporal. Lowest non-commissioned rank in Brit. army; badge, 245; in the artillery is lance-bombardier.

Lancelet. Amphioxus, sand-burrowing, marine animal classed as a very primitive vertebrate in group *Cephalochorda*; diagram, *158.*

Lancelot or **Launcelot of the Lake.** In Arthurian legend, the most famous and bravest of the Knights of the Round Table; on quest for Grail, 1414; wins the 9th diamond, story, 2830.

Lanchester, Frederick William (1868–1946). Eng. engineer and pioneer motor-car designer, 2241.

Lancing College. In the vil. of Lancing in Sussex; is the senior of the schools founded in 1848 by the Rev. N. Woodard; chapel is well-known landmark.

Land, as a factor in economics, 1081; commons, 880; destruction and formation, 1432; irrigation and reclamation, *960*; medieval system of tenure, 85, *86,* 1268; proportion of earth's surface occupied by, 1068, 2413; wealth production, 1081.

Landes (lahnd). Region of s.w. Fr., vast tract of sandy marshland bordered by dunes, 1360; reclamation, 2870.

Land League, National, in Ireland, 2525.

Land or **square measure,** units of. *See* Weights and Measures.

Land mines, dropped by aircraft as bombs, 2186.

" Land of Hope and Glory." Song by Elgar, 1143.

" Land of the Midnight Sun " (Norway), 2392.

" Land of the Rising Sun " (Japan), 1795.

Landor, Walter Savage (1775–1864). Eng. author, 1890.

Land-rail or corncrake, 2734.

Lands, public. Irrigation and reclamation, 1097, *1102.*

Landscape painting : Corot, 913, *914*; development, 2476; English painters, 1180, 1181; Millet, 2176; Turner, 3267.

Land'seer, Sir Edwin (1802–73). Eng. painter of animals, etc., 1890, *1891,* 1182; his lions in Trafalgar sq., *2019.*

Land's End. Promontory of Cornwall, westernmost point of England, 582, 911.

Landsteiner, Karl (1868–1943). Austro-Amer. pathologist; did research on infantile paralysis and haemoglobinuria; his discovery of the human blood groups invaluable to blood transfusion methods in both World Wars; Nobel prize for medicine in 1930.

Lane, Sir William Arbuthnot, Bart. (1856–1943). Brit. surgeon; founder of the New Health Society (1925).

Lane-Poole, Stanley (1854–1931). Eng. historian, archaeologist, and biographer; professor of Arabic, Trinity College, Dublin (1898–1904). (" Mahomedan Dynasties "; " Histories of the Moors in Spain ").

Lanfranc (c. 1005–89). Eng. prelate and scholar, b. in Italy, Archbishop of Canterbury (1070–89); as chief counsellor of William the Conqueror, whom he accompanied to England, played important part in fixing the Norman rule upon Eng. Church and people; rebuilt Canterbury Cath.

Lang, (Alexander) Matheson (1879–1948). Brit. actor of Canadian birth; played Shakespearean roles and was the original Mr. Wu and the Wandering Jew in the plays of those names.

Lang, Andrew (1844–1912). Brit. scholar, poet, and writer on many subjects; a graceful essayist, and vivid historian; collected many charming fairy tales (" Ballades in Blue China "; " Custom and Myth "; " History of Scotland "), 1966.

Lang, Cosmo Gordon, Baron (1864–1945). 95th Archbishop of Canterbury 1928–42; Bishop of Stepney (1901–08); Archbp. of York (1908–28); crowned King George VI and Queen Elizabeth, *912*; created Baron Lang of Lambeth, 1942.

Langenhoven, C. J. Afrikaans writer, 3020.

Langevin (lahnj-van), **Paul** (1872–1946). Fr. physicist; worked with Pierre and Marie Curie; at Cavendish Lab., Cambridge, discovered secondary rays of X-rays; also supersonic waves, which he used for submarine detection; imprisoned by Ger. troops of occupation; adviser to Fr. atomic energy commission.

Langland, William (c. 1330–1400). Eng. poet, supposed author of "Vision of Piers Plowman," a religious allegory attacking corruption in Church and State.

Langley, Samuel Pierpont (1834–1906). Amer. astronomer and physicist; inventor of early heavier-than-air flying machine, 44.

Langmuir, Irving (b. 1881). Amer. scientist, inventor of gas-filled tungsten elec. lamp, researched on electrons and on heavy hydrogen; Nobel prize for physics 1932; the Lewis & Langmuir theory, 295; Langmuir pump, 3301.

Langobards ("long beards"). See **Lombards.**

Langshan. Breed of fowl.

Lang's Nek. Scene in 1881 of a Boer victory over Brit. force commanded by Sir G. Colley, an engagement that preceded the battle of Majuba; it is a pass of the Drakensberg range in Natal, less correctly called Laing's Nek.

Langton, Stephen (c. 1150–1228). Eng. cardinal and Archbishop of Canterbury, usually credited with being the first to divide the Bible into chapters; in Eng. politics, 1834.

Langtry, Lily (Emily) (1852–1929). Eng. actress, noted for her beauty, b. in Jersey and known as the "Jersey Lily"; first great success in "She Stoops to Conquer."

Language and literature, 1891, 2570; distribution, 2570; philology, 2570; romance, 2798; slang, 2900; universal, 1223, 1894. See also the principal languages of the world under their own names; **Grammar.**

Languedoc (lahn-ge-dok'). Former prov. in s. Fr., whose cap. was Toulouse, 1358, 1360; how the name originated, 1379.

Langue d'oc. Fr. dialect, 1379.

Languedoc Canal or **Canal du Midi,** 686, 1360.

Langue d'oil (lahng-dō-ēl'). Fr. dialect, 1379.

Lanital. Artificial wool made from milk, 850, 2749.

Lankester, Sir Edwin Ray (1847–1929). Eng. biologist, widely known for his delightfully entertaining writings; pres. of Brit. Association (1906); founder of Marine Biological Association. ("Science from an Easy Chair"; "Extinct Animals.")

Lanoline. Wool wax, 3359.

Lansbury, George (1859–1940). Brit. socialist, politician and journalist; entered local govt., 1891, and House of Commons 1910–12 and from 1922; editor Daily Herald 1914–22; first Commr. of Works 1929–31; inaugurated "Lansbury Lido" on the Serpentine, Hyde Park; leader of the Labour party 1931–35.

Lansdowne, Henry Petty-Fitzmaurice, 3rd Marquess of (1780–1863). Eng. statesman, Chancellor of the Exchequer at 25, a liberal leader and advocate of parliamentary reform, abolition of slavery, Free Trade, and Cath. emancipation.

Lansdowne, Henry Petty-Fitzmaurice, 5th Marquess of (1845–1927). Eng. statesman, Gov.-Gen. of Canada (1883–8); Viceroy of India (1888–93); Sec. of State for War (1895–1900); Sec. for Foreign Affairs (1900–05); minister without portfolio (1915–16); Unionist leader in House of Lords (1905–16); advocate of peace with Germany by negotiation in 1917.

Lan'sing, Robert (1864–1928). Amer. lawyer and authority on international law; secretary of state in Wilson's cabinet during 1st World War (1915–20).

Lansing, Michigan, U.S.A. Cap. on r. Grand, 80 m. N.W. of Detroit; pop. 78,397; motor-cars, agricultural machinery, 2161.

Lantern. In architecture, a small tower on the roof of a building, admitting light and air.

Lantern, portable lamp, 1887; of lighthouse, 1944, 1945. See also **Lamps.**

Lantern, magic. A lamp and lens system for projecting transparent pictures on a screen for the benefit of large audiences.

Lan'thanum (La). A lead-grey metallic element, 768, 777; often classed with the rare earths which it closely resembles. See **Rare Earths.**

Lanuvium (la-nū'-vi-um) (modern Civita Lavinia). Anc. city of Latium, 19 m. s.E. of Rome; member of Latin League; conquered by Rome 338 B.C.

Laocoön (lā-ok'-ō-on). In Gk. myth., Trojan priest of Apollo; warns his countrymen against wooden horse, 3249; statue of, 1538, 3249.

Laodicea (lā-od-i-sē'-a) or **Laodicea ad Lycum.** Anc. city (modern Latakia), wealthy trade centre, 120 m. s.E. of Smyrna; one of 7 primitive churches of Asia; Synod of Laodicea in 4th cent. decided religious questions.

Laoighis, Eire. See **Leix.**

"Laokoön." A book by Lessing (1776), in which the functions of poetry and painting are defined and distinguished.

Laomedon (lā-om'-e-don). In Gk. myth., founder and king of Troy; father of Priam; engages Poseidon to build wall around Troy, 2660.

Laon (lah-on'). City in Fr., 80 m. N.E. of Paris; pop. 17,400; fortified by Romans; Blücher defeated Napoleon (1814); captured by Germans (1870 and 1914); recovered by Allies, 3413.

Laos (lah-ōz) or **Laotians.** A people of Indo-China; division of Thai or Shan race; 1718, 2963.

Laos. Country of Indo-China; 89,320 sq. m.; pop. 1,500,000; 1719–20; cap. Vientiane.

Lao-tse (lah'-ō-tse) (b. c. 570 B.C.). Chinese philosopher, founder of Taoism; it is recorded that he interviewed Confucius in 517 B.C., but death date is unknown; 809.

La Paz (lah pahz'). Largest city and seat of govt. of Bolivia, S. Amer.; pop. (1946) 300,000; commercial centre of agricultural and mining region; univ.; 491.

Lap'idary. A worker in precious stones, 1427.

Lapis lazuli. A semi-precious stone.

Lapithae (lap'-i-thē). In Gk. myth., race related to the Centaurs, dwelling in Thessaly; Centaurs battle, 742; and Theseus, 3202.

Laplace (lah-plahs'), **Pierre Simon, Marquis de** (1749–1827). Fr. mathematician and astronomer, called "Newton of France"; proved stability of solar system; formulated the nebular hypothesis, 2619. ("Mécanique céleste.")

Lap'land. Region in extreme N. of Norway, Sweden, Finland, and Russia; population about 31,000, mostly engaged in fishing, hunting and tending reindeer, 1891; map, 2395; in Norway, 2394; people, see **Lapps**; reindeer, 2760; school in, 2884; in Sweden, 3128.

La Plata (lah plah'-ta), Argentina. City 35 m. s.E. of Buenos Aires, 5 m. from port of Ensenada on La Plata estuary; pop. (1945) 200,000; National Univ.

La Plata, Rio de. See **Plata River.**

Lap'pa, or burdock, seeds, 2917.

Lap'pet moth. Moth of the silkworm family, so named because larvae have lobes or lappets at sides of bodies.

Lapps. Natives of Lapland, 1891, 1892; in Norway, 2394, 2397; in Sweden, 3128.

Lapu'ta, in "Gulliver's Travels." An isl. visited by Gulliver, 3134.

Lapwing. A plover-like bird, common in Brit., having lustrous plumage on upper parts, and crested head; noted for its wailing cry; its eggs are the "plovers' eggs" esteemed as delicacy, 2629; nest, 2630.

Larch. A conifer tree which sheds its leaves seasonally, 1892.

Lard. Rendered pork fat, 1263.

Lardner, Ringold Wilmer ("Ring") (1885–1933). American humorist.

Lares (lā'-rēz). In Rom. myth., protecting deities closely associated with the Penates.

Large copper butterfly, pl. f. 633.

Large heath butterfly, pl. f. 633.

Large skipper butterfly, pl. f. 633.

Large white butterfly, pl. f. 632.

Largo (lahr-gō). A slow musical movement (notably that by Handel); in the sonata, 2264.

Largs. Scot. watering-place in Ayrshire, on Firth of Clyde; yachting centre; scene of battle (1263) between Norse and Scots; pop. 10,000; 3203.

Laridae (lār'-i-dē). Bird family including gulls and terns, 1555.

Larissa (la-ris'-a), Greece. City in Thessaly on r. Salambria; pop. 23,900; transit trade, textile mfrs.; important city in anc. times; centre of mobilization in Balkan Wars; in 2nd World War occupied by Germans from 1941 to 1944 when recovered by Greek patriot forces.

Lark. Bird of family Alaudidae, typified in Britain by skylark and woodlark, 1893; courtship flights, 441.

Larkspur. Plant with spikes of blue flowers, 1893, 2639.

Larnaka (lahr'-na-ka) or **Larnaca.** Chief spt. of Cyprus on s.E. coast; pop. 14,746; on site of anc. Citium.

La Rochefoucauld (lah rosh-foo-kō), **François, Duc de** (1613–80). Fr. courtier, type of old noblesse, unrivalled maxim writer.

La Rochelle (lah rō-shel'). Spt. of w. Fr.; pop. 37,900; once great maritime city and centre of Fr. Protestantism; 1613; besieged by Richelieu, 2778; in 2nd World War a Ger. U-boat base June 1940 to May 1945.

Lars Porsena. Attempt on Rome, 2804.

Larva. Any young insect or other animal which attains adult form by going through a marked transformation, 1893, 1728; of bee, 391; of beetles, 399; caterpillars, 720; distinguished from insect nymphs, 1729; of fly, 1329; of mosquito, 2236; silkworm, 2970; tadpoles of frogs and toads, 1399, 3219; wasp, 3345.

Larwood, Harold (b. 1904). Eng. cricketer; his persistent and successful use of "leg-theory" fast bowling during the 1932–33 Test matches in Australia led to heated controversy; played for Nottinghamshire; retired in 1938.

Larynx (la'-rings). The voice organ, 3327; inflammation of, 3328.

La Salle, René Robert Cavalier, Sieur de (1643–87). Fr. explorer, 1894; founds Louisiana, 143; voyage down Mississippi, 2192.

Las Casas (lahs kah'-sas), **Bartolomé de** (1475–1566), Sp. historian and missionary to W. Indies; popularly known as "the Apostle of the Indians," because he spent his life trying to secure better treatment of the Indians governed by the Spanish.

Lascelles. See **Harewood, Earl of.**

Laskhar. Cap. of Gwalior, state in Malwa Union, India; Laskhar is modern city adjoining the ancient city and citadel of Gwalior; 1559, 1704.

Las Palmas (lahs pal'-mas). Important port on E. coast of Grand Canary Isl. (Sp.); pop. 151,000; largest city and joint cap. of the group; cable station.

Lassalle (lah-sahl'), **Ferdinand** (1825–64). Famous Ger. Socialist, founder of Ger. social democratic movement; his vivid paradoxical personality and life formed basis of George Meredith's "Tragic Comedians."

Last. In shoe-making, 522, 523.

"Last Days of Pompeii." Novel by Lord Lytton, 2044, 2654.

"Last Judgment, The." Painting by Michelangelo, 2161.

"Last of the Mohicans." Novel by Fenimore Cooper, 903.

"Last Supper, The." Painting by Leonardo da Vinci, 189, 1926.

Laszlo de Lombos, Philip Alexius (1869–1937). Anglo-Hungarian artist; famous as painter of royalty and Society.

Latakia (lah-tah-kē'-a), Syria. Mediterranean port 115 m. N. of Beirut ; pop., 36,687 ; produces famous Latakia tobacco ; anc. Laodicea ; capital of govt. of Latakia, pop. 432,500 ; 3221.

La'tent heat. Heat absorbed or released when matter changes state, as when ice melts, 3350.

Lat'eran, The. Palace in Rome, dating from 16th to 18th cents., now a museum ; on site of anc. palace of Lateranus family, appropriated by Nero ; later given by Constantine to Bishop of Rome and used by popes as residence until 14th cent., 2800.

Lateran Church, or church of St. John Lateran at Rome ; built originally in Lateran palace by Constantine, 729.

Lateran Councils. General councils held at Rome in the church of St. John Lateran ; in 1123 the Concordat of Worms was confirmed ; in 1139 the Papal schism was settled ; in 1179 the conflict between empire and papacy was ended ; in 1215 the doctrine of transubstantiation was formulated ; and in 1517 the superiority of Pope over councils was asserted.

Lateran Pact of Reconciliation, 2496, 2616.

Latex (lā'-teks). Milky juice secreted by various plants, 1559 ; yields rubber, 2834, 2835, 2837.

Latham (lā'-tham), **Charles Latham, 1st Baron** (b. 1888). Brit. administrator ; leader of L.C.C. 1940–47 ; chairman of London Transport Executive from 1947.

Latham, Hubert (1883–1912). Fr. air pilot ; in 1909 made unsuccessful attempt to cross Eng. Channel just before Blériot's triumph.

Lathe (lāth). A machine used in turning, by means of which a piece of wood or metal is rotated while the edge of a chisel is held against it.

Lat'imer, Hugh (c. 1485–1555). Eng. Protestant reformer and martyr, Bishop of Worcester, whose homely practical preaching largely drove the Eng. Reformation home to the people ; burned at stake at Oxford, exhorting his fellow-martyr, " Be of good cheer, Master Ridley, and play the man ; we shall this day light such a candle by God's grace in England as I trust shall never be put out."

Latin America. Collective name for Mexico and countries of S. and Cent. Amer.

Latin Empire, established by Crusaders in 1188.

Latin language, 1894 ; alphabet, 125 ; Bible translation, 423 ; common abbreviations, 10 ; effect of Renaissance on study of, 2764 ; influence on English language, 1209 ; pronunciation, 1897 ; romance languages derived from, 1379, 1786, 2570, 2798.

Latin League. Confederation of cities of Latium in cent. Italy, existing from earliest historic times till 338 B.C., 2805.

Latin literature, 1894 ; Cicero, 1895, 827 ; drama, 1038 ; Renaissance, 2764 ; Virgil, 3325 ; Livy, 1896.

Latin Quarter, Paris, 2516.

Latins, in anc. times inhabitants of Latium, in cent. Italy, 1763 ; early history, 2804.

Lat'itude. Distance in degrees from Equator, 1898 ; " horse latitudes," 3385 ; how found at sea, 2291 ; shown on maps, 1898.

Latium (lā'-shi-um). Anc. dist. in middle of w. coast of Italy, inhabited by Latins, 40, 2804.

Lato'na. In Rom. myth., mother of Apollo and Diana ; in Gk. Leto.

Latter-Day Saints. See Mormons.

Lat'via or **Lettland.** Republic of the Soviet Union on Baltic Sea ; pop. 1,950,000 ; about 25,000 sq. m. ; 1899, 351 ; Riga, 2779 ; in Ger. occupn. 1941–44, 1899 ; incorpd. in U.S.S.R., 2850, 2852, 3418.

Laud, William (1573–1645). Eng. prelate, Archbishop of Canterbury, 1899 ; as adviser of Charles I, 755.

Lau'danum. Alcoholic tincture of opium, 2442.

Lauder, Sir Harry Maclennan (1870–1950). Scot. variety actor, a great favourite for Scottish dialect songs composed and sung by himself.

Lauds. One of the canonical hours, 2213.

Laue (low'-e), **Max von** (b. 1879), Ger. physicist ; Nobel prize in 1914 ; first used crystal for X-ray diffraction, 940, 3056.

" Laughing Cavalier, The," Painting by Frans Hals, 1568, 1569.

Laughing gas, or nitrous oxide. An anaesthetic, discovered by Davy, 149, 979.

Laughing jackass. An Australian bird, 310, 313, 1858.

Laughton, Charles (b. 1899). Anglo-American actor, notable in character parts on stage and screen (" Henry VIII," " Mutiny on the Bounty," " Rembrandt ") ; 1041.

Launceston. Quaint old tn. in Cornwall 21 m. N.W. of Plymouth ; pop. 4,071 ; George Fox, the Quaker, imprisoned here in 1655.

Launceston. Second city of Tasmania in N.E. on R. Tamar ; pop. (with suburbs), 40,450 ; commerce with Victoria and S. Australia.

Laundry and dry-cleaning, 1900.

Launfal, Sir. Knight of the Round Table and steward to King Arthur, in the Arthurian legends ; hero of Lowell's " Vision of Sir Launfal."

Laura (1308–48). Lady loved by Petrarch and celebrated in his poems.

Lauraceae (law-rā'-sē-ē), or laurel family, of plants, 1900 ; includes camphor, 674 ; cinnamon, 3060, 3061 ; European laurel, or bay. 1900.

Lau'reate (poet laureate), 2634.

Laurel. Name given to various flowering shrubs, 1900 ; leaves sacred to Apollo, 974.

Laurence, Samuel (1811–84). English artist ; portrait of Thackeray, 3193.

Laurencin (lō-rahn-san), **Marie** (b. 1885). Fr. painter ; paintings in pastel blues and pinks, with figures of attenuated physique ; designed settings for Diaghilev ballets (" Les Biches ").

Lauren'tian Plateau. Highland area in Canada, 676.

Laurier, Sir Wilfrid (1841–1919). Canadian statesman,; first French-Canadian to hold premiership.

Lau'rium or **Laurion,** Greece. Hill range forming S.E. part of Attica 20 m. below Athens ; silver mines, 1523, 2973.

Lausanne (lō-zan'), Switzerland. Beautiful city 1 m. N. of L. Geneva ; pop. 92,000 ; 13th-cent. cath. ; univ. ; long the home of historian Gibbon ; treaty between Allies and Turkey ; 3142, 3415.

Lauterbrunnen (low-ter-broon'-en), vil., Bernese Oberland, Switzerland, 3142.

Lava (lah'-va). Melted rock discharged from volcanoes, 1900, 1901, plate f. 3328 ; forms igneous rock, 1432 ; Herculaneum buried, 2654 ; Vesuvius, eruptions, 3319 ; Etna, 1229.

Laval, Pierre (1883–1945). French politician ; premier 1931–32 and 1935–36 ; signed Franco-Soviet treaty 1935, 1724 ; Vice-Premier in Pétain's Govt. June 1940 ; dismissed Dec. 1940 ; chief of Vichy Govt. Apl. 14, 1942 ; tried for treason Oct. 4, executed Oct. 15, 1945.

Laval-Montmorency, François Xavier de (1622–1708). First Rom. Cath. bishop of Quebec ; remarkable influence on French colonial govt.

Lavater (la-vah'-ter), **Johann Kaspar** (1741–1801). Swiss poet and mystic, founder of " science " of physiognomy, which professes to read character by outward appearance.

Lav'ender. An aromatic shrub native to s. Europe, 1901 ; perfume, 2549, 2550, 2551.

Laveran (lah-ve-rahn'), **Charles** (1845–1922). Fr. physician ; awarded Nobel prize (medicine) in 1907 ; discoverer of malaria parasite, 2488.

Lav'ery, Sir John (1856–1941). Portrait painter of Glasgow school ; b. in Ireland, knighted 1918, became R.A. in 1921.

Lavin'ium. Anc. tn. of Latium, 17 m. S. of Rome ; said to have been founded by Aeneas and named after his wife Lavinia.

Lavoisier (la-vwah'-zyā), **Antoine Laurent** (1743–94). Fr. chemist ; founded modern theory of chemical compounds, and combustion, 1901, 767 ; oxygen research, 2466 ; research in fire, 1280 ; and Priestley, 2683.

Law, Andrew Bonar (1858–1923). Brit. statesman, Prime Minister (1922–23) ; 3281.

Law, John (1671–1729). Scot. financier ; controller-general of Fr. finance ; induced Fr. govt. to adopt a paper currency ; established the " Mississippi Scheme " which proved a failure, a large number of speculators losing their money.

Law, William (1686–1761). Eng. non-juring theologian and mystic ; his " A Serious Call to a Devout Life " was a most influential work.

Law, 1902, 2651 ; commercial, origin, 1257 ; Courts of Justice, 1921 ; in Gt. Brit., how made, 1902, 2521 ; Greek codes, 1519, 1522, 1902, 2999 ; Hammurabi's code, 329 ; Henry II reforms, 1609 ; international, 1904 ; Justinian's code, 1844, 1902 ; Mahomedan, 1872 ; Napoleon's code, 2276 ; Roman, 1902 ; Scots, 2894. See also **Government ; Labour Legislation ; Law, International, etc.**

Law, international, 1904 ; blockade, 473 ; piracy, 2612 ; privateering, 2612 ; Hague regulations for warfare, 1563 ; violated in World Wars, 1905 ; United Nations, 1905, 3283.

Law, The. Division of the Old Testament, 2692.

Law Courts, London. Situated in the Strand ; the Royal Courts of Justice, as they are correctly called, were opened in 1882 ; 1902, 1903, 1904, 2013.

Lawn. A bleached fabric of very fine cotton or linen.

Lawn. Type of grassland, 1510.

Lawn tennis, 1905 ; championships and great players, 1907. See also **Davis Cup.**

Lawrence, St. (d. c. 258). " The Deacon," Christian martyr ; called on by the judge to produce the Church's treasures, produced the poor people in his care ; said to have been roasted to death on a gridiron, 2112.

Lawrence, David Herbert (1885–1930). Eng. novelist and poet, with extreme views on woman and her position in the social structure. " Sons and Lovers," " Women in Love," " The Lost Girl," " Aaron's Rod," " The White Peacock," are among his best novels, 1216.

Lawrence, Ernest Orlando (b. 1901). Amer. physicist ; developed the cyclotron, first model 1928, 950 ; director of Radiation Lab., Univ. of California in 1936 ; helped create atomic bomb ; adviser to U.S. govt. on use of atomic energy in medicine and industry ; Nobel prize for physics in 1939.

Lawrence, Gertrude (b. 1898). Eng. actress of stage and screen ; successes in " Nymph Errant," with Noel Coward in " Private Lives " ; autobiography, " A Star Danced."

Lawrence, Sir Henry Montgomery (1806–57). Eng. brigadier-general and colonial administrator, mortally wounded at the siege of Lucknow ; 1715, 2035.

Lawrence, John Laird Mair, 1st Baron (1811–79). Brit. Viceroy and Gov.-Gen. of India, called " saviour of India " because his relief of Delhi during the Mutiny (1857) maintained Brit. dominion ; brother of Sir Henry Lawrence.

Lawrence, Sir Thomas (1769–1830). Eng. court painter ; flattering but often superficial likenesses of Eng. beauties and European sovereigns ;

the successor of Reynolds as the most celebrated portrait painter of his day ; president of Royal Academy from 1826 until he died, *1177*, 1180 ; portrait of Warren Hastings, *1582*, of Sir John Moore, *2227*.

Lawrence, Thomas Edward (1888–1935). "Lawrence of Arabia," British soldier, administrator and scholar, **1907**, 200, 1217.

Lawson's cypress. Conifer of the cypress group much grown in England, distinguished by its narrow cylindrical outline and very small cones.

Lawyers, 1902 ; training, 1903.

Lay'ard, Sir Austen Henry (1817–94). Eng. diplomat, archaeologist and writer ; excavated ruins of Nineveh ; he was appointed ambassador to Turkey in 1877 (" Monuments of Nineveh "), 2371.

Laycock, Gen. Robert E. (b. 1907). Brit. soldier ; commanded a special service battn. of 5 Commando groups known as " Layforce " which raided Bardia Apr. 1941, etc. ; chief of Combined Ops. 1943–47 ; at Casablanca and Quebec Conferences ; expert on amphibious warfare to planners of Allied invasion of France 1944.

" Lay of the Last Minstrel." Poem by Scott, 2898, 2900.

" Lays of Ancient Rome." Four ballads by Macaulay, 2047 ; " How Horatius Kept the Bridge," story, 3207.

Layton, Walter T. Layton, 1st Baron (b. 1884). Brit. newspaper proprietor and economist ; editor of " The Economist " 1922–38 ; chairman of News Chronicle and Star in 1930 ; director-gen. of programmes, Min. of Supply and member of Supply Council 1940–42 ; chief adviser on planning to Min. of Production 1942–43.

Laz'arus. Beggar in parable of the rich man and the poor man (Luke xvi. 19–31).

Lazarus. Brother of Martha and Mary ; raised from the dead by Christ (John xi).

Lea. R. joining the Thames near Blackwall ; 45 m. long, 1225, 1621 ; viaduct, *885* ; water supply, 3194.

Leacock, Stephen Butler (1869–1944). Canadian educator and humorist, b. Eng. ; professor of political economy at Univ. of Chicago and later at McGill ; won a new and wider public with his delightful nonsensical sketches ("Literary Lapses " ; " Behind the Beyond " ; " Moonbeams from the Larger Lunacy "), 685.

Lead (Pb.). A soft, heavy, blue-grey metal of the silicon group ; atomic weight, 207·2 ; known since time of the early Egyptians ; melting point, 327·4° C., **1908** ; in alloys, 124, 3270 ; isotopes, 1760 ; in paint, 2478 ; pencils, 2541 ; properties, 777 ; radio-active properties, 2732 ; specific gravity, 3054 ; in mfr. of lead pipe, 1661 ; tellurium strengthens, 3185 ; in type metal, 124, 3270 ; white lead, 2478. *Compounds* : acetate (sugar of lead), 1724, 2638 ; chromate, 2478 ; oxide, 2119, 2478 ; red oxide, 2119 ; sulphide (galena), 3117.

" Lead, Kindly Light." Hymn by Newman, 2342.

Lead pencils, 2541.

Lead poisoning, 1908.

Leaf. *See* Leaves.

Leaf, butterfly, 630.

Leaf-cutter bees, 394 ; eggs, *1094* ; mandibles, *1729*.

Leaf-insect. An insect of tropical regions with wings which are amazingly leaflike both in form and colour ; family *Phasmidae*.

League. An obsolete unit of measure used in calculating distances at sea (3 miles).

League football, 1344.

League of Mercy. Founded in 1899 to promote the welfare of hospitals by obtaining subscriptions for King Edward's Hospital Fund for London, etc.

League of Nations, 1908, 2531, 3414 ; compulsory arbitration, 203 ; and Danzig, 973 ; Saar basin, 1361 ; in Geneva, 1428, *1909* ; opium, 2442

Palestine, 2482 ; International Labour Office, 1910 ; Italy resigns, 1909 ; Germany resigns, 1451 ; Russia joins, 2852 ; Russia expelled, 3416 ; Woodrow Wilson, 3291, 3383 ; World Court, 1910 ; succeeded by United Nations (*q.v.*), 1910.

Le'ah. Elder daughter of Laban and first wife of Jacob (Gen xxix).

Leahy (lē'-hē)**, Fleet-Adm. William D.** (b. 1875). Amer. sailor and diplomatist ; served in Sp.-Amer. war ; chief of Naval Ops. 1937–39 ; retired 1939, and went as Ambassador to Vichy France 1940–42 ; in 1942 Chief of Staff to Pres. Roosevelt ; Fleet-Adm. 1944, and continued adviser to Pres. Truman.

Leamington (lem'-ing-ton). Health resort in Warwickshire ; pop. 29,662 ; mineral springs, 3341.

Lean'der. In Gk. legend, lover of Hero, **1619.**

Leaning tower of Pisa, 1513, 2612.

Leap year, 662.

Lear. Hero of Shakespeare's tragedy " King Lear," 1858, 2934, 2936.

Lear, Edward (1812–88). Eng. artist and writer, famous for nonsense verses and comic illus., **1910,** 1950.

Lease-Lend. System of mutual aid among United Nations in 2nd World War ; Act passed by U.S. Congress, March 11, 1941 ; U.S. aid during war totalled 40,000 million dollars, and British £2,000 million ; U.S. lease-lend ended Aug. 20, 1945 ; 3292.

Least Common Multiple (L.C.M.), in factoring, 1256.

Leather, 1910 ; chamois skin, 151, 1912, 1914 ; cordovan, 1914, 3032 ; crocodile, 932 ; goat skin, 1478 ; morocco, 1100, 1914, 2232 ; parchment and vellum, 2496 ; patent, 1914 ; pigskin, 2605 ; preparation for gloves, 1477 ; sewing of, 2929 ; shagreen, 2938 ; shoe-making, 522.

Leather-back turtle, *3230*.

Leather-jacket. Destructive grub of the daddy-long-legs.

" Leatherstocking Tales," by Fenimore Cooper, 903.

Leaven. Substance used to produce fermentation. *See also* **Yeast.**

Leavened bread, 554.

Leaves, 1914, 1322 ; autumn coloration, 1917 ; chlorophyll and its work, 1915, 2589, 2620 ; evaporation from, 1243, 3246 ; fern fronds, *1268* ; forerunners seen in algae, 112 ; insect-catching leaves, 2613, *2624, plate f. 2621* ; growth illustrated in chestnut, 1915 ; lacking in cactus, 649 ; palm, 2483, *2484* ; as respiratory organs, 2621 ; sensitive to light and touch, *2624, 2625* ; of waterlily, *3354* ; in water-plants, 3355.

" Leaves of Grass," Poems by Walt Whitman, 3376.

Lebanon. Rep. of s.w. Asia, between Syria and Palestine ; includes the mts. of Lebanon and Anti-Lebanon where grew the O.T. cedar forests, the valley between, also the coastal plain ; area 3,475 sq. m. ; pop. 1,186,845 ; tns., cap. Beirut ; Tripoli (terminus of Iraq oil-pipe line) ; ancient Tyre and Sidon ; silk, olive oil, wheat, wine, iron ; under Fr. mandate 1918–44 ; in June 1941 Allied troops under Gen. Catroux removed Vichy Fr. administration ; Allied forces withdrew in 1946 ; May 18, 1948, Lebanon joined Arab League invasion of State of Israel.

Lebanon Mts., Syria. N. of Palestine ; Lebanon on w., Anti-Lebanon on E. ; average height 7,000 ft. ; 314 ; famous cedars, *737*.

Lebensraum (lā'-bens-rowm). Ger. " living space " ; slogan of Nazi Ger. used to justify Ger. expansion into other peoples' lands, 1452.

Leblanc (*le*-blahn'), **Nicolas** (1742–1806). Fr. chemist, won prize offered (1775) by Fr. Academy for method of making soda from common salt ; lost property and patent rights in French Revolution, 2993, 2997.

Leblanc process, 2997.

Le Bourget (le boor'-zhā). Air port of Paris, 7 m. w. from the centre of the

capital ; greatly enlarged and rebuilt in 1937.

Le Bris (le brē'), **Jean Marie** (1808–72). French air pioneer and sea captain ; constructed glider in 1854 with which it was stated he flew 200 yards.

Lebrun (le brēn)', **Albert** (1871–1950). French statesman ; minister for colonies (1911–13 and 1913–14) ; senator (1920) ; president of republic (1932–40). Did not favour Pétain-Laval admin. ; imprisoned by Gers (1943–44).

Le Brun, Charles (1619–90). French artist ; first painter to Louis XIV ; helped to found Academy of Painting and Sculpture 1648 ; and French School in Rome 1666 ; first director of Gobelin factory, 1377, *2102*.

Lebrun, Elizabeth Vigée (1755–1842) Fr. painter of portraits and land scapes.

Lech River. Rapid stream rising in Vorarlberg Alps at height of 6,120 ft. flows N. through Bavaria 180 m. joining Danube below Donauwörth

Lecithin, white waxy fatty substance obtained from egg yolk, soya beans etc., 1478.

Leck'y, William Edward Hartpole(1838–1903). Irish historian and publicist was a member of Parl. and a opponent of Home Rule for Ireland (" A History of European Morals " " History of England in the Eighteenth Century ").

Leclanché cell, for generation of elec current, *375, 376*, 1131.

Leclerc (lê-klair)**, Gen. Jacques,** assume name of Philippe, Viscount of Haute cloque (1902–47). Fr. soldier escaped Ger. captivity in 1940, an joined de Gaulle ; went to Cameroons in 1942 marched Fr. and nativ troops 1,500 m. across Sahara from Ft. Lamy (Chad Territory) t Mareth Line (*q.v.* in *f.-i.*) ; 2861 commanded Fr. 2nd armoured div. first troops to enter Paris ; receive the Ger. surrender there, Aug. 2 1944 ; killed in aircraft accident 1947

Leconte de Lisle (le-kont-de-lēl') **Charles Marie** (1818–94). Fr. poe chief of modern Parnassian scho (" Poèmes antiques "). " Coldnes cultivated as a kind of artistic dis tinction seems to turn all his poetr to marble in spite of the fire at h heart."

Le Corbusier (le kor-bū'-zyā) (b. 1887 Swiss architect ; real name Charle Edouard Jeanneret ; most famous ex ponent of functionalist architecture Works include " Urbanisme " ; " Th City of Tomorrow."

Le Creusot (le krē'-zō). *See* Creusot.

Ledger. A book in which all cash tran actions of a business are entered, th debit amounts on one side and th credit amounts on the other.

Ledo Road. Milit. highway of 2 World War ; joined Ledo railhea N.E. Assam, to Burma Rd. (*q.v.* in *f.-i.*) at Mongyu, passing throug Maingkwan, Myitkyina, and Bhamo 478 m. long ; crossed 5,000 ft. Patk Hills ; built by U.S. army enginee under Gen. Stilwell as supply roa for ops. against Japs.

Lee, Nathaniel (*c.* 1653–92). Eng. drama tist and poet ; among his best-know tragedies were " The Rival Queens," " Nero," and " Theodosius."

Lee, Robert Edward (1807–70). U. Confederate general, **1917,** *1918.*

Lee, Sir Sidney (1859–1926). En author and educator ; foremo authority on Shakespeare ; professo of Eng. language and literature East London Coll. for 11 years editor of " Dictionary of Nation Biography " ; works include " Li of Shakespeare," " Life of Quee Victoria " " Edward VII."

Lee, William (d. 1610). Eng. clerg man ; invented knitting machin 1865.

Lee of Fareham, Arthur Hamilton Le 1st Viscount (1868–1947). Brit. po tician ; entered Parl. 1900 ; a pointed Director-General of Fo Production in 1917, he becar Minister of Agriculture in 1919, a

First Lord of the Admiralty in 1921 ; he presented his country seat, Chequers, to the nation for use by the Prime Minister, *778*.

Lee. Small r. in co. Cork, Eire, 910.

Leech, John (1817–64). Eng. caricaturist, whose Punch drawings were called by Ruskin " the finest definition and natural history of the classes of our society, the kindest and subtlest analysis of its foibles," *821*.

Leech. A blood-sucking ringed worm of the order *Hirudinea*, used for medicinal purposes ; inhabits pools and marshy places ; it has two suckers ; English species are small, but in the tropics some reach many inches in length ; 3425.

Leeds, Thomas Osborne, Duke of (1631–1712). Eng. statesman ; created Earl of Danby in 1674 ; he was highly esteemed by Charles II, but in 1678 was charged with bribery and confined in the Tower for five years ; on his release he espoused the cause of William of Orange.

Leeds. Sixth largest city in Eng. ; pop. 493,120 ; **1918**, 1168, 3435.

Leeds. Vil. of Kent, 4½ m. from Maidstone ; here is famous Leeds Castle, on a small isl. in a branch of R. Medway.

Leeds, University of. Eng. univ. founded in 1904 to replace Yorkshire College, founded in 1874, one of the colleges of Victoria Univ., Manchester ; besides usual faculties, it has textile, engineering and agric. departments.

Lees-Smith, Hastings Bertrand (1878–1941). Eng. politician ; first Liberal, then Labour M.P. ; postmaster-general (1929–31) ; pres. of Board of Education (1931).

Leeuwarden (lā′-var-den). Netherlands. Cap. of prov. of Friesland ; pop. 74,438 ; flourishing trade in cattle, grain, fish.

Leeuwenhoek (lā′-ven-hook), **Anthony van** (1632–1723). Dutch microscopist, 2163 ; work on bacteria, 335 ; discovers capillary blood-vessels, 477.

Leeward (lū′-ard). Away from the wind ; the opposite of windward.

Leeward Islands. Brit. colony in W. Indies, N. of Windward Isls., and S.E. of Puerto Rico, comprising Antigua, St. Kitt's, Nevis, Dominica, Montserrat, and part of Virgin Isls. ; 727 sq. m. ; pop. (est. 1946) 108,800 ; name sometimes applied to other W. Indian isls., also to chain W. of Trinidad ; 3368.

Left. Term used in European politics, to denote the party holding the more advanced views ; use arose from fact that in Continental legislative chambers members sit in semi-circle facing the Speaker—the Socialists and Communists being on left, Conservatives on the right.

Leg, human, *151, 2258, 2316* ; caterpillars, 720 ; duckbill platypus's poison spurs, 1053 ; first aid when broken, *1294* ; insects, 1730, *1726* ; mammals, 2074 ; spider, 3065.

Le Gallienne, Richard (1866–1947). Anglo-Amer. critic, essayist and poet, b. Liverpool, Eng. ; " Prose Fancies," " The Quest of the Golden Girl," " Pieces of Eight " are imaginative prose sketches ; " Odes from the Divan of Hafiz," " English Poems," and other volumes of poems include many graceful lyrics.

Legal tender. Money that may legally be offered in payment of debt ; bronze to one shilling, silver to £2, and gold and currency notes to any amount are legal tender.

Legaspi, formerly Albay, tn. on Luzon, Philippine Is., pop. 36,000.

Legend, *1918. See* Folklore.

Leghorn or **Livorno.** Third commercial port in It., in Tuscany on W. coast ; pop. (1944) 128,700 ; Leghorn straw hats, leather, glass, iron and copper products ; shipbuilding.

Leghorn. A breed of fowls, introduced into Eng. from It. ; good layers, table, and show birds, *2671*.

Legion. A complement of soldiers, 1919.

Legion of Honour. Fr. order of merit for services to State, 2449.

Legislative Assembly. Fr., 1395.

Legislature. The law-making body of any govt. unit, such as the King and the Houses of Parl. in the United Kingdom. For other law-making bodies *see* under their proper names, as **Congress** ; **Diet** ; **Parliament** ; *etc.*

Legnano (lā-nyah′-no). It. tn. 16 m. N.W. of Milan ; pop. 27,254 ; cotton and silk mfrs. ; Lombard League defeated Frederick Barbarossa.

Legros (le-grō′), **Alphonse** (1837–1911). Fr. painter and etcher, for nearly 30 years a teacher in London, where his severe yet dignified realism and simple technique exerted an exceedingly powerful influence on the development of Eng. art ; portrait of Browning, *590*.

Legumin(e). A protein obtained from leguminous plants, 2694.

Leguminosae. Plant order containing the peas, beans, and vetches and similar papilionaceous flowers ; mimosas are primitive examples ; bean, 380 ; lucerne, 2034 ; and nitrifying bacteria, 2373, 2624 ; peas, 2530 ; sweet clover, 854.

Lehar, Franz (1870–1948). Hungarian composer of light music (" The Merry Widow " ; " The Count of Luxembourg " ; " The Land of Smiles," etc.).

Le Havre. *See* Havre.

Leibniz (līb-nits), **Gottfried Wilhelm** (1646–1716), Ger. philosopher, mathematician and scientist, " the most universal scientific genius of modern times " ; invention of calculus, 2350.

Leicester (les′-ter), **Robert Dudley, Earl of** (c. 1531–88). Eng. statesman and soldier, favourite of Elizabeth, 1147, 3656. His supposed secret marriage to Amy Robsart is the theme of Scott's " Kenilworth."

Leicester, Simon, Earl of. *See* Montfort, Simon de.

Leicester. Co. tn. of Leicestershire, on R. Soar ; pop. 275,000 ; hosiery, boots and shoes, lace ; Rom. remains ; 1919.

Leicestershire, Eng. Midland co. ; 823 sq. m. ; pop. 567,000 ; **1919.**

Leicester Square, in London, N. of Trafalgar Square ; it contains a garden in which is a fountain surmounted by a statue of Shakespeare ; formerly called Leicester Fields.

Leiden or **Leyden.** City of the Netherlands. On the R. Oude, 9 m. N.E. of The Hague ; pop. 84,000 ; *2320*.

Leigh. Tn. in Lancashire, 11 m. N. of Manchester ; manufactures of silks and cottons ; iron foundries ; breweries ; pop. 46,450.

Leigh (lē), **Vivien** (b. Vivian Mary Hartley, in 1913). Brit. actress, wife of Sir Laurence Olivier ; brilliant in " The Doctor's Dilemma," " The Skin of Our Teeth " ; films, " Gone with the Wind," " Caesar and Cleopatra."

Leigh Mallory, Air Marshal Sir Trafford (1892–1944). A.O.C.-in-C. Fighter Command R.A.F. 1942. Allied Air C.-in-C. 1943–44, 2377. Apptd. to air command in S.E. Asia, Oct. 1944 ; while flying there crashed near Grenoble, Nov. 14.

Leighton, Clare (b. 1899). English engraver. One of leaders of 20th cent. revival in wood-engraving ; illustrated books incl. " The Farmer's Year," " Four Hedges."

Leighton, Frederick, Baron (1830–96). Eng. painter, 1919 ; paintings by, *1201, 1619, 1921*.

Leinster (lens′ter). One of 3 old provs. of Irish Free State (Eire).

Leipzig (līp-sik), Ger. city of Saxony ; pop. (1933) 714,000 ; **1920** ; fair, 1257 ; in Russ. zone of Ger., 1920.

Leipzig, battle of (1631). *See* Breitenfeld.

Leipzig, University of, 3rd in size and 2nd in age of the universities of Ger. ; established by 400 teachers and

students who seceded from univ. of Prague through Hussite agitations ; faculties of medicine, law, theology, and philosophy.

Leitch, Charlotte Cecilia (Cecil) (b. 1890). Eng. golfer. Won British open ladies' championship (1914, 1920, 1921, 1926), also won French ladies' championship five times.

Leit-motif, in opera, 2437.

Leith (lēth), Scot. Spt. incorporated with Edinburgh in 1920 ; on Firth of Forth ; shipbuilding.

Leith Hill. Highest point in Surrey, Eng. ; 965 ft. ; 3123.

Leitrim (lē′trim). Co. of Eire ; 589 sq. m. ; pop. 46,200 ; **1920.**

Leix (lēs) or **Laoighis,** formerly Queen's County. In S.E. of Eire ; 664 sq. m. ; pop. 49,950 ; **1920.**

Lejarraga, Maria de la O. Spanish poetess.

Leland, or **Layland, John** (c. 1506–52). Eng. antiquary : chaplain and antiquary to Henry VIII.

Lely (lē′-li), **Sir Peter** (1617–80). Eng. court painter, b. Ger., of Dutch family ; famous for portraits of beautiful women of court of Charles II ; Charles I and Cromwell were also his patrons ; " Nell Gwynn," *1178*.

Leman, Lake. *See* Geneva, Lake of.

Le Mans. Tn. of France on r. Sarthe, S.W. of Paris ; magnificent Gothic cath. ; famous for road-race circuit for sports cars.

Lemberg. *See* Lwow.

Lemming. A small rodent, common in Norway, remarkable for migrating periodically in enormous numbers.

Lemnos. Isl. in N. Aegean ; 150 sq. m. ; est. pop. 4,000 ; held in turn by anc. Greeks, Byzantine Empire, Italians, and Turks ; Gk. since 1st World War, during which it was a Brit. naval base. After fall of Greece, Germans held Lemnos from April 1941 till British landed in Oct. 1944.

Lemon, Mark (1809–70). Eng. journalist and dramatist ; he was one of the founders, and first editor, of Punch ; he produced upwards of fifty plays, operettas, etc.

Lemon. A citrus fruit, **1920**, *1922* ; essential oil from, 1263 ; introduced into Europe, 937 ; " sympathetic " ink, 1724 ; vitamin content, 3327.

Lemprière, John (c. 1768–1824). Brit. classical scholar, chiefly notable for his " Classical Dictionary " which has been added to by others.

Lemur (lē′-mur). A fox-faced monkey-like animal, *1922*.

Lena. R. of Siberia, rises in Baikal Mts. in S. ; empties into Arctic Ocean, forming vast delta ; length, 2,860 m. ; 265, 2966, *map, 2844.*

Le Nain brothers (le nan′). French painters of 17th cent., 1377 ; " The Card Players," *1371.*

Lend-Lease. *See* Lease-Lend.

Lenglen (lahng-lahn), **Suzanne** (1899–1938). French lawn-tennis player ; won ladies' singles championship, Wimbledon 1919–23 and 1925 ; became professional in 1926 ; 1907.

Lengua Indians, in Paraguay, *2512.*

Lenin (lyā′-nin), **Nikolai** (1870–1924). Rus. Bolshevist leader, **1922**, *1923*, 495, 2850 ; and Stalin, 3072 ; and Trotsky, 3251 ; tomb, *2851* ; Lenin Library, 1931.

Leninakan (formerly Alexandropol). Town in Armenia (U.S.S.R.) ; pop. 67,000 ; situated 80 m. S.W. Tiflis ; earthquake (1926), 239.

Leningrad (originally St. Petersburg, then Petrograd). City of the Soviet Union ; pop. 3,191,000 ; **1923**, 2845, 2848, 2852, *2854*, 3329 ; *maps, 2845, 2853*; architecture, 2854, *2854* ; Church of the Blood, *2854* ; founded by Peter the Great, 2847 ; New Year customs, 2350 ; under German siege, Sept. 1941–Jan. 1944, 1924, 2852, 3419, 3420.

Lenoir (le-nwahr′), **Etienne** (1822–1900). Fr. inventor, 1420, 1736.

Lens (lahns). Fr. coal-mining and iron-mfg. city 135 m. N.E. of Paris ; pop. 30,000 ; victory of Fr. under Prince of Condé over Sp., 1648.

Lens, in optics, **1924 ;** aberrations (spherical and chromatic), 1925, 2163, 3178 ; in camera, 2578, *2578* ; contact lenses, *3055* ; crystalline, of eye, 1252, *1254* ; focuses heat, 1596 ; in lighthouse, 1945 ; limits of magnification, 2164 ; manufacture, 1474 ; of microscope, 2163 ; periscope, 2552 ; special glass, 1474 ; of spectacles, 3034 ; of telescope, 3178.

Lent. In Christian Church, 1074.

Len'thall, William (1591–1662). Eng. politician, who held the office of Speaker in the famous " Long Parliament " ; he supported the Parl. in the Civil War, but became a Royalist at the Restoration.

Len'til. A leguminous plant ; the seeds have a great food value, containing starch, casein, fat and water, **1925**, 2694.

Leo, popes, **1926.** For list *see* Pope.

Leo I the Great (*c.* 390–461), Pope, 1657, 1926.

Leo III (*c.* 750–816), Pope, 638, 1926.

Leo IV (*c.* 800–855), Pope. Did much to repair the damage done to Rome by the Saracens ; he reigned from 847–55.

Leo X (1475–1521), Pope, 1926, 2131 ; Raphael's portrait, *2765.*

Leo XIII (1810–1903). Pope, 1926.

Leo or **Lion.** A sign of the zodiac, 3444.

Leofric (lē-of'-rik), Earl of Mercia (d. 1057), husband of Lady Godiva.

Leofric. Companion of Hereward the Wake, 1618.

Leominster (lem'ster). Tn. in Herefordshire ; brewing ; pop. 5,700.

Leon, Ponce de. *See* Ponce de Leon.

Le'on. Anc. kingdom and modern prov. of N.W. Sp., 1238, 1760, 3036 ; *map, 3030.*

Leon, Mexico. City 200 m. N.W. of Mexico City ; pop. (1940), 74,200 ; leather, textiles ; trade in cereals.

Leon, Nicaragua. Second largest city and former cap. ; pop. 50,000 ; founded 1610 ; large trade ; univ., 2364.

Leonardo da Vinci (lā-o-nahr'-dō dah vēn'-chē) (1452–1519). It. painter and scientist, **1926,** 1785 ; his " Mona Lisa," 2032, *2033* ; his " Last Supper," *289* ; drawings, 1046 ; cartoon, *1927* ; and Renaisance, 2766 ; scientific work, 1927 ; helicopter, 1604 ; lamps, 1887 ; parachutes, 2510.

Leoncavallo (lā-on-ka-val'-lō), **Ruggiero** (1858–1919). It. composer (" I Pagliacci ") ; in early years strongly influenced by Wagner.

Leonidas (lē-on'-i-das). King of Sparta (491–480 B.C.) killed at Thermopylae, 2556, 320.

Le'onids. Group of meteors, so called because they appear to radiate from a point in the constellation of Leo. They occur in greater brilliancy and profusion every 33⅓ years, 2152.

Leonov (lā-ō'-nof), **Leonid Maksimovich** (b. 1899). Russian novelist (" The Badgers " ; " Sot "), 2856.

Leontes (lē-on'tēz). In Shakespeare's " A Winter's Tale," king of Sicily, 3389.

Leopard (lep'-ard). Animal of the cat family, **1927,** *1928* ; family characteristics, 719 ; in India, 1701.

Leopard Shark, *2416.*

Leopardi (lā-ō-pahr'-dē), **Giacomo, Count** (1798–1837). It. lyric poet, prose-writer, and scholar, master of finished style and slave of pessimism ; " La Ginestra " gives full expression to his creed.

Le'opold I (1157–94), Duke of Austria. Succeeded 1177 ; went on Crusades 1182 and 1190 ; quarrelled with Richard I in Palestine, 2776.

Leopold I (1790–1865). King of the Belgians, Ger. prince, uncle of Queen Victoria of Eng. ; elected 1831 to Belgian throne ; able ruler, called " Nestor of Europe," **1928,** 407.

Leopold II (1835–1909). King of the Belgians ; succeeded in 1865, 407, **1928 ;** and Congo, 887, 888, 3077.

Leopold III (b. 1901). King of the Belgians ; succeeded Albert I in 1934 ; prisoner at Laeken 1940–44 ; in Germany, June 1944 ; not recalled to Belgium at end of war 407, **1928,** 102. Returned on July 22, 1950, after a referendum, but agreed ten days later to relinquish power to his son Baudouin, pending abdication.

Leopold I (1640–1705). Holy Roman emperor, elected in 1658 ; defeated Turks and French.

Leopold II (1747–92). Holy Roman emperor, elected in 1790 ; son of Maria Theresa and brother of Marie Antoinette.

Leopold, Order of. Belgian decoration, 2449.

Leopoldville. Capital of Belg. Congo on r. Congo ; pop. 40,000 ; on rlwy., and on air service to Belgium, 888.

Lepan'to, battle of (1571). Fought in Gulf of Corinth near Lepanto, Greece, *2294,* 2305, 3264 ; Cervantes wounded, 746.

Lepidolite, a form of mica, an impt. ore of lithium, 2160.

Lepidop'tera. The order of scaly-winged insects, 1733 ; includes butterflies and moths, 628.

Lep'idus, Marcus Aemilius (d. 13 B.C.). Wealthy Roman, triumvir with Mark Antony and Octavian (Augustus), 303.

Lep'rosy. A chronic disease of the skin and nerves for which no specific cure has been discovered ; caused by bacteria, 1458.

Lep'tis Mag'na or **Ma'jor.** Anc. spt. in Libya, N. Africa, founded by Phoenicians ; chief commercial entrepôt for interior, 1931.

Leptocar'dii. A group of primitive animals, just below true vertebrates ; includes lancelets.

Le'pus. The genus of hares and rabbits, 2721.

Lepus or **Hare.** A constellation, *895.*

Le Puy (le pwē), Fr. Tn. 140 m. N.W. of Marseilles ; pop. 22,700 ; 12th-cent. cath. ; famous in Middle Ages ; lace, textiles, chocolate, spirits.

Le Queux (le kē'), **William** (1864–1927). Eng. novelist, writer of many popular novels of a sensational and mysterious kind (" The Eye of Istar " ; " Fatal Fingers " ; " In White Raiment " ; " The Hand of Allah " ; " The Invasion of 1910 " ; " The Stretton Street Affair ").

Lerida (lā'-rē-dā), Sp. Walled cath. city 80 m. w. of Barcelona ; pop. 46,400 ; as Celtiberian Ilerda heroically resisted Romans ; leather, glass, textiles.

Lérins (lā-ran'), **monastery of.** On small isl. of Lérins in Mediterranean 3 m. off Cannes, Fr., 2212.

Ler'wick. Chief tn. of Shetland Isls., Scot., on S.E. coast of mainland ; pop. 4,600 ; fishing industry, 2945.

Le Sage (le sahzh'), **Alain René** (1668–1747). Fr. novelist and dramatist, author of a hundred plays ; a satiric realist (" Gil Blas," comic masterpiece of adventurous roguery).

Les'bos. Same as Mytilene, 2270.

Leslie, Charles Robert (1794–1859). English painter.

Les'lie, David (1601–82). Scot. gen. who fought with distinction for the Parliament at Marston Moor and helped to defeat Montrose at Philiphaugh ; he afterwards supported Charles II and was taken prisoner at Worcester ; Charles II, on his release, created him Earl of Newark.

" Les Misérables " (lā mē-zā-rah'bl). Novel by Victor Hugo, 1650.

Lesseps (les'-eps), **Ferdinand, Vicomte de** (1805–94). Fr. engineer ; builds Suez Canal, 3111 ; Panama Canal, 2487, 2488.

Lesser Antil'les. Isls. of W. Indies, also called Caribbean Isls. *See also* West Indies.

Lesser redpoll. A type of finch, 1272.

Lesser spotted woodpecker, *3404.*

Les'sing, Gotthold Ephraim (1729–81). Ger. critic and dramatist ; helped free Ger. literature from Fr. influ-

ence ; chief works, " Emilia Galotti," " Minna von Barnhelm," " Laoköon," 1456.

Le Sueur, Hubert (*c.* 1595–*c.* 1650), Fr. sculptor ; came to Eng., 1628, and made the bronze statue of Charles I that still stands in Charing Cross, London, *2904.*

" L'état, c'est moi," 2029.

Letch'worth. In Hertfordshire, 2 m. N.E. of Hitchin ; the first garden city to be laid out in Eng. (1903) ; pop. 20,000 ; 1622.

Lethe (lē-thē). In Gk. myth., r. of oblivion.

Le'to, in Gk. myth., mother of Apollo and Artemis ; known as Latona by the Romans.

Le Touquet, tn. of France, on coast S. of Boulogne ; a favourite pleasure resort, esp. among Eng. people ; resident pop. 5,000.

Letts. People of Latvia, 1899.

Lettuce (let'-is). An annual plant, native of E. and cent. Asia ; introduced into Eng. about 1520, it is cultivated chiefly as a salad plant.

Leucocytes (lū'-kō-sīts). White corpuscles in blood, 474.

Leuctra (lūk'-tra), Greece. Vil. in Boeotia ; battle of (371 B.C.), 1524, *3197,* 3198.

Leuna (loi'-na). Synthetic oil plant, 12 m. w. of Leipzig, largest in Ger. ; put out of action in 1945 by repeated bombing of Allied Air forces ; reconditioned by Russ. during occupn.

Leuthen (loi'-ten), Ger. Vil. in Lower Silesia, 9 m. w. of Breslau ; battle of (1757), 2924.

Levant (le-vant') (" rising (of sun)," hence, " east "). Term applied to E. Mediterranean and its coast-lands.

Levee'. An embankment. Mississippi r. system, 2192.

Levée. An afternoon reception by the Brit. sovereign attended by men only.

Level. Instrument used in surveying.

Levellers. Political faction in Puritan Civil War, 933.

Lev'en, Alexander Leslie, 1st Earl of (*c.* 1580–1661). Scot. soldier who distinguished himself fighting for Charles IX and Gustavus Adolphus of Sweden ; returning from Sweden he defeated Charles I's army at Newburn, and later fell a prisoner to Gen. Monck, and for a short while was imprisoned in the Tower.

Leven, Loch. Lake in Kinross-shire, Scot. ; a. nearly 6 sq. m. ; it contains Castle isl., with ruins of a castle that was the prison of Mary Queen of Scots, and is famed for its trout.

Le'ver, Charles James (1806–72). Irish novelist, born story-teller, with inexhaustible fund of boisterous extravaganza portraying humorous side of Irish life (" Charles O'Malley " ; " Harry Lorrequer "), 1751.

Lever. A mechanical device, *2136,* 2128 ; Archimedes, 211 ; pulley a form of, 2700 ; wheel a form of, 3375.

Leveret. Young hare.

Leverhulme (lē'-ver-hūm), **William Lever, 1st Viscount** (1851–1925). Successful Eng. manufacturer, founder of the well-known soap-making firm of Lever Bros., Ltd., at Port Sunlight.

Leverrier (le-ver'-yā), **Urbain Jean Joseph** (1811–77). Fr. astronomer ; discovery of Neptune, 2618.

Le'vi. Hebrew patriarch, 3rd son of Jacob and Leah, ancestor of tribe of Levi or Levites.

Leviathan (le-vī'-a-than). A huge aquatic monster, *e.g.,* that described in the Book of Job ; also title of a work by Thomas Hobbes (1588–1679).

Le'vites. Tribe of Israelites, 1829.

Levit'icus. The 3rd book of the Old Testament containing priestly laws.

Lewes. Co. tn. of Sussex ; pop. (1945) 12,400 ; *3123* ; battle of (1264), 2221.

Lewes, George Henry (1817–78). Eng. philosopher and critic ; founded and edited "Fortnightly Review" (" History of Philosophy "); " Problems of Life and Mind "); and George Eliot, 1145.

Lewis, Cecil Day (b. 1904). English poet. Works include " Collected Poems, 1929–33 "; " Noah and the Waters." Created C.B.E. in 1950.

Lewis, Clive Staples (b. 1898). Brit. writer on relig. subjects ("The Silent Planet " ; " The Problem of Pain " ; " The Screwtape Letters."

Lewis, D. B. Wyndham. Brit. writer and humorist (" Beachcomber," " Timothy Shy ").

Lewis, Isaac Newton (1858–1931). U.S. Army officer ; inventor of machine-gun, 2050.

Lewis, John Llewellyn (b. 1880). American labour leader. President of United Mine Workers ; took prominent part in labour disputes of 1936–37. Head of Committee for Industrial Organization, a federation of labour unions. Led big coal strikes in U.S. in 1945–46.

Lewis, Percy Wyndham (b. 1886). Eng. painter and author ; exponent of Vorticism in art, 2477.

Lewis, Sinclair (b. 1885). Amer. novelist ; master of the realistic method ; awarded Nobel literature prize 1930 (" Mantrap " ; " Main Street " ; " Babbitt " ; " Martin Arrowsmith " ; " Elmer Gantry " ; " Dodsworth "), 2403, 3295.

Lewis, Butt of, Scot. A promontory in N. of Lewis-with-Harris Is., rising to a height of 145 ft.

Lewisham. Parl. and met. bor. in S.E. London, bordering co. of Kent ; mainly a residential dist. ; pop. (est.) 208,370.

Lewis gun, 2050.

Lewis-with-Harris Island, in Outer Hebrides, Scot. ; Lewis a. 682 sq. m. ; pop. 30,000 ; Harris a. 176 sq. m. ; pop. 5,500 ; 1602.

Lewisian. Name of pre-Cambrian rocks, mainly granites and gneisses ; named after Is. of Lewis, in Hebrides, where they occur ; 583.

Lewisite, a poison gas, 1420.

Lexington, Kentucky. Agricultural and mfg. centre ; pop. (1940) 49,300 ; famous horse market and race tracks.

Lexington, Massachusetts, U.S.A. Tn. 11 m. N.W. of Boston ; pop. 9,500 ; scene of first battle of War of Amer. Independence, 114, 3276.

Leybourne (lā´-born), **Sir William** (d. 1309). First Eng. admiral, 28.

Leyden. See Leiden.

Leyden jar. An electrical condenser, 1929, 1127.

Leys (lēz) **School,** Cambridge. Eng. public school, founded by Wesleyans in 1874.

Leyte (lā´-tē), one of the Philippine Is. ; 2,785 sq. m. ; hemp, bananas, sulphur ; in Jap occupn. 1942–44 ; U.S. naval-air victory in Leyte gulf, Oct. 1944, 2293, 3293, 3424.

Lhasa (lah´-sah) or **Lassa.** Cap. of Tibet in S. ; seat of Dalai Lama ; pop. est. about 50,000 ; 3208, plate f. 3209.

Liakoura. Modern name for Mt. Parnassus, 1517.

Liao-ho (lē-ow-hō). R. of Manchuria ; rises in Great Khingan Mts., flows E. along Chihli border, then S. to Gulf of Liaotung.

Liaotung (lē-ow-tung´) **Peninsula,** Manchuria, projects S.W. into Yellow Sea between gulfs of Liaotung and Korea ; Dairen and Port Arthur on Kwantung Territory (formerly leased to Japan) at tip.

Liaoyang (lē-ow-yang´). City in Manchuria on rly. from Mukden to Port Arthur ; pop. 100,000 ; captured by Japanese (1904) in Russo-Japanese War.

Li´ard River, Canada. Rising in N. Brit. Columbia and flowing N.W. to Mackenzie ; 2050.

Libau. See Liepaja.

Liberals, 1929 ; Gladstone, 1469, 2525. Lloyd George, 1976.

Liberal Unionist party (Gt. Brit.), 1470.

Libe´ria. Negro republic on W. coast of Africa ; 43,000 sq. m. ; pop. est.

2–3,000,000 ; 1929, 3366 ; U.S. development, 1930.

Liberty, Statue of, in New York harbour, 2351.

Liberty Bell, rung in Philadelphia, U.S.A., to commemorate Independence Day (July 4, 1776), 3291.

" Liberty, Equality, Fraternity," 1393.

Liberty or **Bedloe's Island,** N.Y., 2351.

Li´bra, the Scales. A sign of the zodiac, 3444.

Library, 1930 ; Alexandrian, 109 ; Assyrian at Nineveh, 331 ; Bodleian, 2465 ; Brit. Museum, 585 ; Cambridge Univ., 669 ; Carnegie's contributions to Public Libraries, 704 ; earliest librarian, 511 ; in medieval monasteries, 2214.

Library of Congress, Washington, 3344.

Libret´to. Text or words of a musical drama or opera ; among famous British librettists are John Gay, Alfred Bunn, Edward Fitzball, and W. S. Gilbert.

Lib´ya, also **Libia** or **Tripoli.** Former It. colony in N. Africa ; 632,000 sq. m. ; pop. (1938) about 888,000 ; 1931 ; map, plate f. 68 ; bazaar, 64 ; girl of, 57 ; desert area, 2859 ; 2nd World War Campaigns, 1452, 1932, 3418, 3419, map, 3421.

Libyan Desert. Part of Sahara, s. of Tripoli and w. of Egypt, 1097, 2859 ; Fayum, 1097.

Licence. Form of taxation, 3158 ; for dog, 1027 ; for marriage, 2107 ; for wireless and television receivers, 3299.

Licensing laws. Term applied to laws relating to the restriction of the sales of intoxicants under licence.

Lichens (lī´-kenz). " Partnership " plants composed of algae within fungi, 1932, 2514, 2620 ; as soil-makers, 2998. See also in Study Outline, 3617.

Lichfield. City in Staffordshire ; pop. 11,000 ; 1934, 3072 ; cathedral, 726, 1168 ; Dr. Johnson's birthplace, 1835.

Lichnowsky, Karl Max von, Prince (1860–1928). Ger. Ambassador to Gt. Brit. (1912–14) ; his memorandum showing Ger. diplomatic responsibility for 1st World War was made public without his authority in 1917 and created sensation.

Licin´ian Laws. Six laws of anc. Rome passed B.C. 367 in tribuneship of Gaius Licinius ; practically ended the struggle between the patricians and plebeians ; 2805.

Licin´ius, Flavius Galerius Valerius (c. 250–324). Rom. emperor, defeated Maximinus and became sole ruler in East ; executed for treason ; 893.

Licorice. See Liquorice.

Lid´dell, Henry George (1811–98); Dean of Christ Church (1855–91). With R. A. Scott prepared " Greek Lexicon " (1843).

Liddell Hart, Basil H. (b. 1895). Brit. writer on milit. subjects ; " The Future of Infantry," " Dynamic Defence," " The Revolution in Warfare," " The Other Side of the Hill."

Lidgett, Rev. John Scott (b. 1854). Brit. Nonconformist. Founder of the Bermondsey Settlement 1891 ; for many years member of the London County Council ; first president of the United Methodist Church.

Lidice (lid-it´-sē). Mining vill. of Czechoslovakia in Kladno coalfield, 20 m. w. of Prague ; completely destroyed by command of Karl Frank (q.v. in f-i.) in June 1942 on pretext that it had sheltered the killers of Heydrich (q.v. in f-i.).

Lido (lē´-dō). Ital. for shore ; at Venice, 3310 ; " Lansbury's Lido," bathing beach in Hyde Park, London.

Lie (lē), **Trygve** (b. 1896), Norwegian statesman, apptd. first Secretary-General of United Nations, Jan. 30, 1946, 1934.

Liebermann (lē´-ber-mahn), **Max** (1847–1935). Well-known German artist, champion of Impressionism, 1455.

Liebig (lē-big), **Justus von, Baron** (1803–73). Ger. chemist and teacher ; established first laboratory course for teaching chemistry ; proved that " organic " substances are subject to same chemical laws as inorganic ones and synthesized many organic compounds ; proved animal heat the product of combustion of food ; his studies of plant chemistry and fertilizers founded agric. chemistry.

Liebknecht (lēp´-knekht), **Karl** (1871–1919). Ger. Socialist leader ; son of Wilhelm Liebknecht, friend of Marx and Engels ; only member of Reichstag to oppose 1st World War ; shot by soldiers while on his way to prison after Spartacist rising ; 3053.

Liechtenstein (lēkh´-ten-shtīn). Principality of Europe, formerly Austrian, but independent since 1918 ; 65 sq. m. ; pop. 11,100 ; 1934.

Liège (lē-āzh´). Chief mfg. city of Belgium ; pop. 152,500 ; 1931 ; 404 ; occupied by Germans, May 1940–Sept. 1944 ; damaged by flying-bombs 1944–45, 1935.

Liegnitz (lēg´-nits) or **Lignice,** Poland. Former Ger. mfg. and trade tn. in Silesia ; pop. 76,500 ; victory of Frederick the Great (1760).

Liepaja, formerly **Libau,** Latvia. S.S.R. Baltic port and mfg. city ; pop. 57,100 ; ice-free artificial harbour ; shelled by Ger. fleet in 1914–18 War ; captured by Germans 1941 ; by Russians 1945.

Lieutenant (lef-ten´-ant), in Brit. Army, commissioned officer next in rank below a captain ; 245.

Lieutenant, in Brit. Navy, officer ranking next below lieutenant-commander ; plate f. 2292.

Lieutenant-Colonel. In Brit. Army, officer ranking next below a colonel : 245.

Lieutenant-Commander. In Brit. Navy, officer ranking immediately above lieutenant ; plate f. 2292.

Lieutenant-General. In Brit. Army, officer ranking next below general : 245.

Life, biology the science of, 430 ; chemistry of life processes, 1076 ; earliest appearance on earth, 1067, 1432 ; evolution of living forms, 1244 ; heredity, 1617 ; usual length in animals, 156; origin on earth, 1067 ; on other planets, 2617 ; plant, 2620 ; protoplasm the basis of, 2695. See Biology ; Longevity.

Lifeboat, 1935 ; latest type, 1936 ; jet-propelled, 1826 ; dropped by parachute, 2509 ; sea water distillation, 3351.

Life Guards. Household Cavalry regiment of Brit. Army, 246 ; trumpeters, frontis., Vol. 5.

Life saving (how to rescue drowning person), 3137.

Liffey, r. of Eire, 70-mile long stream rising s. of Dublin and flowing w. and N. in a semicircle into Dublin Bay, 1744, map, 1745 ; in Dublin, 1050.

Lift bridge, at Middlesbrough, 567.

Lifts and escalators, 1936, 1937, 1938 ; hydraulic, 1667 ; safety devices, 1937, 2575.

Lig´ament. Connecting or binding tissue in the body.

Light, 1939 ; measuring brightness of, 2575 ; action in eye, 1252 ; chemical action in photography, 2577 ; colour, 875, 1942 ; corpuscular theory, 1941, 1943 ; ether waves, 1226, 3358 ; fluorescent, 2573 ; generation, 1942 ; gravitation bends rays, 1514 ; mirage, 2190 ; needed by plants, 1914, 2589, 2623 ; Newton's discoveries, 2349 ; phosphorescence of animals, 2574 ; polarized, 1942 ; rays scattered by air, 88 ; and relativity, 1122, 2762 ; refraction, 1529, 1940 ; spectra of, 3055 ; in solar spectrum, plate f. 3057 ; analysed by spectroscope, 3055 ; " split " by prism, plate f. 3056 ; studied in optics, 2591 ; in television, 3182 ; velocity, 1939 ; wave theory, 1941, 1943 ; Young's discoveries, 3436. See also Lamps.

Light Brigade, at Balaclava, 341.

Lighthouses and light-vessels, 1943, *plates f. 1944, 1945* ; Eddystone, 1084, 1943 ; Pharos of Alexandria, *plate f. 2924* ; Roman structure at Dover, 1031 ; Wolf Rock, *321* ; 2nd World War, 1944.

Lighting ; lamps, 1887 ; electric, 1134 ; gas, 1424 ; photo-electric switches, 2576 ; of theatre, 3197.

Lightning, 1945 ; electric nature, 1946 ; fixes atmospheric nitrogen, 2373 ; how it causes thunder, 1946.

Lightning rod, for protecting buildings from lightning, 1946.

"Light of the World," by Holman Hunt, *1825*.

Lightship, 1943.

Light soil. Soil that is easily worked, 2998.

Light-year. Distance travelled by light in a year, at 186,300 miles per second, i.e., 5,883,886,386,500 miles, 1939.

Lignite (lig′-nīt). Fuel midway between coal and peat, 856, 2535.

Lignum vitae (lig′-num vī′-tē). Wood used for bowls balls, 535.

Ligny (lēn′-yē). Vil. in Belgium 25 m. s.e. of Brussels ; victory of Napoleon over Prussians under Blücher (1815) prelude to battle of Waterloo.

Ligugé, monastery of, 2212.

Liguria (li-gū′-ri-a). In anc. Rom. days, that part of n. Italy which lay between the Po and the Mediterranean, and extended w. from the Gulf of Genoa to the Gaul border, or even at one time to the Rhône ; also dept. of modern Italy ; 2,000 sq. m. ; pop. 1,536,000 ; 1763.

Ligu′rian Republic. Name given to the democratic govt. instituted in Genoa 1797 by Napoleon I ; incorporated in France 1805.

Ligur′ians. A pre-Roman and pre-Tuscan people, organized in tribes, considered by some authorities the aboriginal inhabitants of N. Italy ; in France, 1358.

Li Hung-Chang (lē-hung-chang′) (1823–1901). Chinese statesman ; aided by Gordon's army, suppressed Taiping rebellion ; bore chief burden of Chino-Japanese War ; for many years " buffer " between China and outside world ; 3211.

Li′lac. Shrub of the olive family, with clustered purplish or white flowers, **1947** ; flower structure, 1321.

Liliaceae (lil-i-ā′-si-ē). Plant family including lilies, tulip, Solomon's seal, Star of Bethlehem, butcher's broom, garlic, asparagus, and onions, 1947.

Lilia′les. Order including the *Liliaceae, Iridaceae,* and *Amaryllidaceae.*

Lil′iencron, Detley von, Baron (1844–1909). Ger. soldier, lyric poet, and realistic novelist.

Lilienthal (lil′-i-en-tahl), **Otto** (1848–96). Ger. inventor ; one of the early experimenters in aviation ; attempted to imitate flight of birds, *44* ; 1474.

Lil′ium. The lily genus of plants, 1947; *Lilium longiflorum* a common species, 1947.

Liliuokalani (lē-lē-oo-ō-kah-lah′-nē) (1838–1917). Queen of Hawaiian Isls. (1891–93), 1587.

Lille. Mfg. city of N. France ; pop. 201,500 ; **1947** ; in both World Wars, 1947.

Lillibu(r)ler′o. Satirical ballad sung to ancient tune by the Protestant party of Ireland during the Revolutionary period 1688 ; march of Commando Units in 2nd World War.

Lilliputians (lil-i-pū′-shanz). In Swift's " Gulliver's Travels," tiny inhabitants of Lilliput, 3133.

Lilly, " the Euphuist." *See* **Lyly.**

Lily, 1947, *1948* ; Bermuda or Easter lily, 1947 ; water-lilies, *2624, 3354, 3354.*

Lilybaeum (lil-i-bē′-um). Anc. city on Promontory of Lilybaeum (Cape Boeo), w. extremity of Sicily, founded by Carthaginians ; starting point of Romans on African military expeditions ; modern Marsala ; pop. 30,000 ; famous for wine.

Lily of the Valley, common garden plant (*Convallaria majalis*), also found wild in Britain ; has drooping white bell-like flowers, growing in clusters, with a delightful fragrance, 1948.

Lima (lē′-mah), Peru. Cap. of Peru ; pop. 628,800 ; **1948** ; *2560, 2561* ; founded by Pizarro, 2616.

Liman von Sanders, Otto (1855–1929). Prussian general ; in command of Turkish army which defeated allied attack on Gallipoli peninsula 1915 ; in 1918 in command of army in Palestine which was crushed by Gen. Allenby.

Limbs, of mammals, 2074.

Lim′burger cheese, 766.

Lime. Citrus tree and fruit of the same name ; not to be confused with the lime tree or linden (*see* below), common in Britain ; 1949.

Lime or quicklime (CaO). Calcium oxide used in preparation of mortars and cements, making paper pulp, etc. ; obtained by burning chalk, **1948** ; industrial uses, 1949 ; shells, 2942.

Lime, slaked. A compound of lime with water, 1949.

Lime juice, 1949.

Limelight, or Drummond light, produced by means of an oxy-hydrogen flame, 1949.

Lime, milk of, used to soften water, 3351.

Lime phosphate, from Pacific Islands, 2472.

Lim′erick. Co. of w. Eire ; 1,030 sq. m. ; pop. 142,000, **1949,** *1950.*

Limerick. Co. tn. of co. Limerick, Eire, at head of estuary of R. Shannon ; most important port on w. coast ; pop. 42,500 ; 1749, 1950.

Limericks. Nonsense verses of five lines, **1950** ; by Edward Lear, 1910.

Lime-soda process, of softening water, 3351.

Limestone, calcium carbonate, **1950,** 2795 ; cave formation, 734 ; in cement, 740 ; chalky forms, 749 ; classed as sedimentary rock, 1432 ; marble a limestone, 2097 ; oil from, 2426 ; principal material of shells, 2942 ; quarrying, 2713 ; yields lime, . 1448.

Lime tree (Linden), **1949,** 4068.

Lime water. Solution of slaked lime in water, 1949.

Lim Fiord. Sea-inlet stretching across the N. of Denmark ; 100 m. long, 1 to 15 m. broad.

Limitation, Statutes of. Laws in Eng. and U.S.A. by which right of bringing action is limited to a fixed period after occurrence of events giving rise to cause of action.

Limited Liability Company. A company having its members' liability limited to the amount which the members respectively guarantee to contribute to the company's assets should the company be wound up.

Limited monarchy, 1489.

Limmat. R. of Switzerland ; rises at N. end of L. Zurich, flows N.W. 18 m. to Aar r. ; upper course called Linth, 3448.

Limoges (lē-mōzh′). Tn. in w. cent. Fr. on r. Vienne ; pop. 107,874 ; taken by Black Prince 1370 ; porcelain-mgf. centre, 1361 ; in medieval times, one of the headquarters of the art of enamelling, 1158.

Limon (lē-mōn′). Chief spt. of Costa Rica, on a bay of the Caribbean ; founded 1871 ; almost entire coffee and banana crops of Costa Rica exported from here ; pop. 17,000.

Limonite (lī′-mō-nīt). A yellowish iron ore (iron hydroxide), 1753 ; in paints, 2478.

Lim′pet. A gastropod mollusc which clings to rocks, 159, 2199.

Limpopo (lim-pō′-pō) or **Crocodile River.** In E. part of S. Africa ; rises near Pretoria, forms N. boundary of Transvaal, then flows s.E. through Port. E. Africa 1,000 m. into Indian Ocean ; 2772, 3014, 3239.

Lincoln, Abraham (1809–65) 16th president of U.S.A., **1951,** *1952,* 2982.

Lincoln (lin′-kun). Co. tn. of Lincolnshire, on r. Witham ; pop. est. (co. bor.) 66,200 ; **1953** ; cathedral, *219, 722,* 1168.

Lincoln. Cap. of Nebraska, U.S.A., in S.E. ; pop. 81,900 ; distributing point for farming dist., 2310.

Lincoln College, Oxford. Founded, 2464.

Lincolnshire. Agric. co. in E. England ; 2,665 sq. m. ; pop. 624,500 ; **1953** ; bulb-growing, 612 ; iron ore, 1753.

Lincolnshire Wolds, Eng. A range of hills in Lincolnshire extending from Spilsby to Barton-on-Humber.

Lincoln's Inn, London. Between Lincoln's Inn Fields and Chancery Lane ; third of the London Inns of Court, dating back to 1312 ; the New Hall has a library containing over 70,000 books and manuscripts.

Lincoln's Inn Fields, London. A large square with many old trees.

Lind, Jenny (1820–87). The " Swedish nightingale," famous and beloved soprano singer ; toured Europe and U.S.A. and settled in London.

Lindbergh, Charles Augustus (b. 1902). Amer. aviator, **1953** ; child kidnapped and killed, 1953.

Linden, another name for the lime tree. *See* **Lime Tree.**

Lindisfarne or **Holy Island,** off Northumberland, 2391.

Lindrum, Walter (b. 1899). Australian billards player ; after carrying all before him in his native country, came to Eng. in 1931 and in the following year set up world's record break of 4,137 ; became world's champion in 1933, and repeated his success in 1934.

Lindsay, Nicholas Vachel (1879–1931) Amer. poet, 4140.

Line, in geometry, 1434.

Line engraving, 1218.

Linen, 1953, 1313, *1313,* 850, *3405* ; Belfast manufactures, 1747 ; bleaching agents, 469 ; thread, 3205.

Line of force. Imaginary line along which magnetic pole would move between two points of opposite magnetism ; part of magnetic field *2060, 2061, 2063.*

Line spectrum, *plate f. 3057.*

Ling. *See* **Heather.**

Linklater, Eric (b. 1899). Scot. author novels incl. " Juan in America " " Poet's Pub," " Private Angelo " the last two were filmed.

Links, for golf, 1483.

Link trainer, for aircraft pilots, *52.*

Linlithgow, Victor Alexander, 2nd Marquess (b. 1887). Eng. administrator. Viceroy and Governor General of India, 1936–43.

Linlithgowshire. *See* **West Lothian.**

Linné (lin′-ā) or **Linnae′us** (lī-nē′-us) **Carl von** (1707–78). Swedish botanist and naturalist, **1954** ; founded systematic classification of animals 3446 ; of plants, 531 ; statue, *1955* ; Linnean Society. Brit. institution founded in 1788 " for the cultivation of the science of Natural History in all its branches " ; possesses the collections and library of Linnaeus of Linné, after whom it was named.

Linnell, John (1792–1882). Brit. artist painted first portraits and later landscapes, in oils ; friend of William Blake ; portrait of Peel *2535.*

Lin′net. Bird of finch family, **1955** 1272.

Lino′leum and oilcloth. Floor covering **1956** ; resin in, 2768.

Li′notype, 1956, *2345.*

Linseed (flaxseed) oil, 1263 ; in ink 1725 ; in paints, 2478.

Lint, cotton, 918.

Lintel, in architecture. A piece of stone or timber placed horizontally over a doorway or window.

Linz (lints), Ger. Danube port, 90 m. w. of Vienna ; pop. 218,195 ; former cap. of Upper Austria ; large trade by rail and r. ; makes tobacco products, farm implements, boats cloth, 972.

Lion, 1959, *1961* ; in Africa, *59,* 69 belongs to cat family, 719 ; in heraldry, 1614 ; in India, 1701 ; in

SOME BOOKS FOR THE CHILD'S OWN LIBRARY

Picture Books and Simple Stories for Little Children

The Little Children's Bible.
" Mother Goose Rhymes " (any good illustrated edition).
Kate Greenaway's Picture Books.
" The Story of Noah," Clifford Webb.
" Picture Tales from the Russian." Valery Carrick.
" Picture Tales from Many Lands." Valery Carrick.

" The Story of Peter Rabbit." Beatrix Potter.
" The Tailor of Gloucester." Beatrix Potter.
" Struwwelpeter." Heinrich Hoffmann.
" When We Were Very Young." A. A. Milne.
" The Little Boy and His House." Stephen Bone and Mary Adshead.

For Children who are Older and Love Fairy and Wonder Tales, and Stories of Animals and the Big Outdoors

The Children's Bible.
" Fairy Tales." Hans Christian Andersen.
" Fairy and Household Tales." J. and W. Grimm.
" English Fairy Tales." Joseph Jacobs.
" Celtic Fairy Tales." Joseph Jacobs.
" Japanese Fairy Tales." Lafcadio Hearn and others.
" King of the Golden River." John Ruskin.
" Water Babies." Charles Kingsley.
" A Little Boy Lost." W. H. Hudson.
" The Rose and the Ring." W. M. Thackeray.
" Alice in Wonderland." Lewis Carroll.
" Sylvie and Bruno." Lewis Carroll.
" Fairy Books." Andrew Lang.
" The Bluebird " (from the French). Maurice Maeterlinck.
" Arabian Nights " (a good selection is that by Andrew Lang).
" Wonder Book " and " Tanglewood Tales." Nathaniel Hawthorne.
" Fables." Aesop.
" Tales from the Panchatantra." Alfred Williams.
" Tales from the Norse." Sir G. W. Dasent.
" Heroes of Asgard." A. and E. Keary.
" Stories of King Arthur."
" Old Peter's Russian Tales." Arthur Ransome.
" The Turf-cutter's Donkey." Patricia Lynch.
" Pinocchio, the Story of a Puppet." Carlo Collodi.
" Doctor Doolittle " series. Hugh Lofting.
" The Cuckoo Clock." Mrs. Molesworth.
" Santa Claus in Summer." Compton Mackenzie.
" What O'Clock Tales." Laurence Housman.
" Stories from Everywhere." Rhoda Power.
" Johnny Crow's Garden." Leslie Brooke.
" Listen, Children ! " Stephen Southwold.
" Tales Quaint and Queer." Stephen Southwold.
" My Friend Mr. Leakey." J. B. S. Haldane.
" Peter and Wendy." Sir J. M. Barrie.

" Robinson Crusoe." Daniel Defoe.
" Pilgrim's Progress." John Bunyan.
" Gulliver's Travels." Jonathan Swift.
" Swiss Family Robinson." J. R. Wyss.
" Tales from the Travels of Baron Munchausen."
" The Little Duke." Charlotte M. Yonge.
" Bows Against the Barons." Geoffrey Trease.
" The Hostages." Naomi Mitchison.
" Little Lord Fauntleroy." Frances Hodgson Burnett.
" The Little Princess." Frances Hodgson Burnett.
" Rebecca of Sunnybrook Farm." Kate Douglas Wiggin.
" Emil and the Detectives." Erich Kastner.
" Swallows and Amazons," and others. Arthur Ransome.
Numerous books by Enid Blyton.
" What Katy Did." Susan Coolidge.
" Five Children and It." Edith Nesbit.
" The Amulet." Edith Nesbit.
" Uncle Remus." Joel Chandler Harris.
" Winnie-the-Pooh." A. A. Milne.
" Just So Stories." Rudyard Kipling.
" Jungle Books." Rudyard Kipling.
" Black Beauty." Anna Sewell.
" The Wind in the Willows." Kenneth Grahame.
" Bevis." Richard Jefferies.
" Wood Magic." Richard Jefferies.
" Wild Animals I Have Known." Ernest Thompson Seton.
" Lives of the Hunted." Ernest Thompson Seton.
" My Friend Toto." Cherry Kearton.
" Child's Garden of Verses." R. L. Stevenson.
" Poems of Childhood." Eugene Field.
" Songs of Innocence." William Blake.
" Hiawatha." H. W. Longfellow.
" Poems for Children." Walter De La Mare.
" Book of Nonsense." Edward Lear.
" Children's Treasury of English Song." F. T. Palgrave.

For Still Older Children, who Desire Stories of Heroes and Great Men, Tales of Adventure, Romances, Historical and Otherwise, and Stirring and Beautiful Poems

" The Heroes : or Greek Fairy Tales for My Children." Charles Kingsley.
" Story of the Iliad." Retold by Alfred J. Church.
" Odyssey." Retold by Alfred J. Church.
" Aeneid for Boys and Girls." A. J. Church.
" Lives." Plutarch.
" Don Quixote " (from the Spanish) Cervantes.
" Scottish Chiefs." Jane Porter.
" The Talisman." Sir Walter Scott.
" Quentin Durward." Sir Walter Scott.
" Ivanhoe." Sir Walter Scott.
" Guy Mannering." Sir Walter Scott.
" Westward Ho ! " Charles Kingsley.
" Hereward the Wake." Charles Kingsley.
" Vicar of Wakefield." Oliver Goldsmith.
" Harold." Lord Lytton.
" Last Days of Pompeii." Bulwer-Lytton.
" Lorna Doone." R. D. Blackmore.
" Mill on the Floss." George Eliot.
" Silas Marner." George Eliot.
" Christmas Stories." Charles Dickens.
" David Copperfield." Charles Dickens.
" The Old Curiosity Shop." Charles Dickens.
" Tale of Two Cities." Charles Dickens.
" Oliver Twist." Charles Dickens.
" The Cloister and the Hearth." Charles Reade.
" Esmond." W. M. Thackeray.
" The Newcomes." W. M. Thackeray.
" Old St. Paul's." Harrison Ainsworth.
" King Richard's Land," L. A. G. Strong.
" Shirley." Charlotte Brontë.
" Northanger Abbey." Jane Austen.
" Sense and Sensibility." Jane Austen.
" Cranford." Mrs. Gaskell.
" Treasure Island." Robert Louis Stevenson.
" Kidnapped." Robert Louis Stevenson.
" Count of Monte Cristo." Alexandre Dumas.
" Lavengro." George Borrow.
" Tom Cringle's Log." M. Scott.
" Mr. Midshipman Easy." Capt. Marryat.
" Children of the New Forest." Capt. Marryat.
" Coral Island." J. M. Ballantyne.

" Moby Dick." Herman Melville.
" Twenty Thousand Leagues Under the Sea." Jules Verne.
" From the Earth to the Moon." Jules Verne.
" Round the World in Eighty Days." Jules Verne.
" The First Men in the Moon." H. G. Wells.
" The Time Machine." H. G. Wells.
" Typhoon." Joseph Conrad.
" Mirror of the Sea." Joseph Conrad.
" The Call of the Wild." Jack London.
" White Fang." Jack London.
" King Solomon's Mines." Rider Haggard.
" Greenmantle." John Buchan.
" Captains Courageous." Rudyard Kipling.
" Kim." Rudyard Kipling.
" Two Years Before the Mast." Richard Henry Dana.
" Under Drake's Flag." G. A. Henty.
" With Clive in India." G. A. Henty.
" Life of Nelson." Robert Southey.
" The Last of the Mohicans." James Fenimore Cooper.
" Uncle Tom's Cabin." Harriet Beecher Stowe.
" Little Women." Louisa M. Alcott.
" Little Men." Louisa M. Alcott.
" Tom Brown's School Days." Thomas Hughes.
" Tom Sawyer." Mark Twain.
" Huckleberry Finn." Mark Twain.
" Green Mansions." W. H. Hudson.
" Nature in Downland " W. H. Hudson.
" Travels with a Donkey." R. L. Stevenson.
" The Animals Come to Drink." Cherry Kearton.
" Watchers of the Trails." C. G. D. Roberts.
" The Feet of the Furtive." C. G. D. Roberts.
" Lays of Ancient Rome." Lord Macaulay.
" Marmion." Sir Walter Scott.
" Idylls of the King." Alfred Lord Tennyson.
" Evangeline." H. W. Longfellow.
" Salt Water Ballads." John Masefield.
" Golden Treasury." F. T. Palgrave.
" Oxford Book of English Verse." A. Quiller-Couch.
" Poems of Today."
Plays of Shakespeare. Read first " Midsummer Night's Dream," " The Tempest," " The Merchant of Venice," " Julius Caesar," " As You Like It, " The Taming of the Shrew."

animal kingdom, 158; story "Androcles and the Lion," 1960.

Lion or **Leo.** A constellation; as sign of the zodiac, 3444.

Lion. Admiral Beatty's flagship, 387.

"**Lion**," early locomotive, *1990*.

Lion, Gulf of the. Wide bay of Mediterranean, washing most of S. coast of Fr.

"**Lion of Lucerne.**" Sculpture by Thorwaldsen, 2906.

Lions, Court of, in the Alhambra; *plate f. 120*, 3040.

Lipari (lip'-a-ri) or **Aeolian Islands.** It. group of volcanic isls. in Mediterranean, N. of Sicily; 45 sq. m.; pop. 16,200; largest, Lipari; fruit, olives, pumice-stone, alum, sulphur, nitre; volcanoes, 2136.

Lipoids. Organic fatty substances containing nitrogen and sometimes phosphorus; in protoplasm, 2695.

Lippe (lip'-e). Former principality and state in W. Ger.; 470 sq. m.; pop. 188,600; cap. Detmold, pop. 17,000; forests, in which beech predominates, cover 130 sq. m.; incorp. in N. Rhine-Westphalia in 1946.

Lippershey, John (Hans). Dutch spectacle maker; accidentally discovered the principle of the astronomical telescope, 276, 3178.

Lippi (lip'pē), **Fra Filippino** (1460–1504). Florentine painter, son of Fra Filippo Lippi and pupil of Botticelli; his work is more ornamental than his father's, more realistic and less poetical than Botticelli's; 1775.

Lippi, Fra Filippo (*c.* 1406–69). Florentine painter, probably the greatest colourist of his day; his pictures reveal a strong, naïve nature, with a lively and somewhat whimsical observation; 1775, 2052.

Lip-reading. Aid to deaf, 981.

Lipton, Sir Thomas (1850–1931). Eng. merchant and yachtsman; at one time a small grocer in Scot., he developed his business into firm of Lipton Ltd.; five times challenger for the America's Cup, but was unsuccessful.

Liquefied gases. Gases reduced to liquids by chilling under pressure, 1594; air, 2466; helium, 1607; hydrogen, 1673; gas rocket propellant, 1826.

Liquid. A substance in the fluid state; capillarity, 698; dew formation, 1000; distillation, 1019; electrolysis, 1136; evaporation, 1243; freezing, friction, 1397; hydraulics, 1665, *1666*; 1391, 3350; incompressibility, 1665; latent heat, 3350; surface tension, 3121; water, 3349.

Liquid Air. Air is made liquid when its temp. is lowered under pressure to 312° below zero F.; it then resolves itself into its constituent elements; in mfr. of oxygen, 2466.

Liquid measure, *see* **Weights and Measures,** *f-i.*

Liquorice, 1962.

Liquors, 103. *See also* **Beer; Spirits; Wine.**

Liriodendron. The tulip tree, *L. tulipifera*; native of U.S.A., where it reaches nearly 200 ft. in height; distinguished by its curious truncated leaves; has tulip-like yellow-green flowers; member of magnolia family, *Magnoliaceae*, 3619.

Lis'bon. Cap. of Port.; pop. 709,000; *1962, 2658, 2659*.

Lisle (lēl), **Claude-Joseph Rouget de** (1760–1836); composer of "Marseillaise," *1963*, 2283.

Lisle (lil). Twisted thread originally linen, now cotton; origin of name, 1947.

"**Listener, The,**" a B.B.C. publication, 3398.

Lister, Joseph, 1st Baron (1827–1912). Eng. surgeon; discovered antiseptic methods of surgery, *1963, 1964*, 2135, 178, 2528.

Listowel, W. F. Hare, 5th Earl (b. 1906). P.M.G. (1945–47); last Sec. for India in 1947, and for Burma (1947–48); Minister of State for Colonial Affairs (1948–50).

Lists. In medieval tournament, 1864.

Liszt (list), **Franz** (1811–86), Hungarian composer, **1964.**

Litchi (lē-chē), a nut, 2408.

Literature, Children's, 1964.

Literature and Language, 1891; books, how to choose and read, 2750; children's, **1964,** 2887; *see also* **Child's Own Library,** 3881; drama, 1037; English, 1210; essay, 1224; reading, 2750. *See also* the literature of each country and writers by name.

Lith'arge. Yellowish lead monoxide.

Lithium. (Li.) A soft white metallic element of the alkali metal group; atomic weight, 6·94; found in small quantities in tobacco ash; melts at 366·8° F., 120, 775; spectrum of chloride, *plate f. 3057*.

Litho'graphy, 1967, 1218.

Lith'opone. A paint consisting of barytes, zinc sulphide and zinc white, mixed with turpentine, 3443.

Lithosphere, of the earth, 1067.

Lithuania (lith-ū-ā'-ni-*a*). Republic of the Soviet Union on Baltic Sea; a. 22,959 sq. m.; pop. 2,879,000; **1967;** *map, plate f. 1232, 2641*; incorpd. in U.S.S.R., 2850, 2552, 3418; occupied by Germany (1941–45), **1968.**

Lit'mus. Made chiefly in Holland from lichens, and used as a test for acids and alkalis.

Litre (lē-ter). Unit in metric system of capacity equal to 1,000 c.c., the volume of 1 kg. of pure water (1·76 pints), 2155.

Little, Dorothy Edith (b. 1909). Eng. lawn tennis player; as Dorothy Round, won Ladies' singles at Wimbledon in 1934 and 1937.

Little auk, 304.

Little Bear or **Ursa Minor.** A constellation, chart, *895*; legend, 894.

Little Belt. Strait between Fünen Isl. and mainland of Denmark; Swedish army under Charles X marched across it on ice to Fünen in 1658; 991, *map, 992.*

"**Little Corporal.**" Napoleon's nickname.

Little Dog or **Canis Minor.** A constellation, *chart, 895.*

Little Entente. A defensive alliance comprising Rumania, Yugoslavia, and Czechoslovakia after 1st World War; it proved ineffective against Hitler's territorial claims.

Little John. Follower of Robin Hood, 2790, 3469.

Little Minch, Scot., Channel separating Skye from N. Uist; 14 to 20 m. wide.

Little Owl, *2460.*

"**Little Red Riding Hood,**" 1333.

Little Rock, Arkansas, U.S.A. Cap. and largest city, on Arkansas r.; pop. 88,300; business in cotton and by-products.

Little Russia, 2983. *See* **Ukraine,** *f-i.*

Little Sisters of the Poor. Founded in France in 1840, for relief and nursing of the aged and infirm poor.

Little theatres, 1043.

"**Little Women.**" Book by Louisa M. Alcott, 3294.

Littoria. Name given 1934 to new prov. of Italy constituted out of parts of provs. of Rome and Frosinone, including the reclaimed Pontine Marshes; pop. 220,000. Cap. Littoria, inaugurated in 1932; pop. 19,000. Prov. and cap. renamed Latina 1945; 1772.

Litvinov, Maxim (b. 1876). Russ. politician; member of Central Executive Committee of Soviet Union; People's Commissar for Foreign Affairs (1930–39). Ambassador to U.S.A. (1941–43). Dep. Comm. Foreign Affairs (1943).

Liukiu Islands. Same as **Nansei Is.**

Liver. In human body, **1968;** largest gland, 1470; makes glycogen, 3082; how it works, *2600.*

Liver fluke. A worm, 3425.

Liverpool, Charles Jenkinson, 1st Earl of (1727–1808). Brit. statesman who was successively Secretary of the Treasury, Secretary for War, and President of the Board of Trade; wrote "A Discourse on the

Conduct of Government Respecting Neutral Nations."

Liverpool, Robert Jenkinson, 2nd Earl of (1770–1828). Brit. statesman, son of the 1st Earl; held the posts of Foreign Secretary, Home Secretary and Secretary for War, and became Prime Minister on the assassination of the Duke of Portland in 1812.

Liverpool. Atlantic spt. in Lancashire; on estuary of Mersey; pop. 756,230; 1165, 1577, 1890, **1968;** cathedrals, *219, 730*; Mersey Tunnel, *457*, 3255; 2nd World War, 1969; first port in world to be fitted with radar, early 1947.

Liverpool, University of. Founded 1903; formerly one of the colleges constituting Victoria Univ., Manchester; besides the usual faculties it has depts. of engineering, commerce, and tropical medicine, and also museums and a valuable library.

Liverpool and Manchester Railway, *1723, 2735.*

Liverpool Mts. Range in E. of New South Wales, Australia; highest point, 4,500 ft.

Liverpool Street. London thoroughfare, in the east-cent. dist.; extending between Blomfield Street and Bishopsgate; contains two railway termini, Liverpool Street, one of the busiest in the world, and Broad Street.

Liverworts (*Hepaticae*). Flowerless plants related to the mosses, **1969,** 2238, 2620.

Livery Companies. The collective body of liverymen of the City of London, **1970.**

Livestock. Cattle, 730; horses, 1645; oil-cake, 920, 1263; pigs, 2605; sheep, 2940; *breeding*: cattle, 730, 956; horses, 1646; laws of heredity, 1617. *See* **Cattle; Dairying; Forage crops; Pig,** etc.; also various countries by name.

Livingstone, David (1813–73). Great missionary explorer of Africa, **1970,** 72; memorial, 2772; Congo exploration, 887; discovers Victoria Falls, 3321; Stanley's search for, 3077.

Livingstone Mts. Range in Tanganyika Territory bordering N.E. shores of L. Nyasa; highest point 9,600 ft.

Liv'ius, Titus. *See* Livy.

Livius Andronicus (3rd cent. B.C.). First Rom. poet, 1895.

Livo'nia. Dist. in Latvia.

Livorno. Same as **Leghorn.**

Livy (liv'-i). Anglicized name of Titus Livius (59 B.C.-A.D. 17), Rom. historian; **1972,** 1896.

Liz'ard, The, or **Lizard Head.** A bold promontory of Cornwall; the most southerly point of Gt. Brit.

Lizardi, Jose Joaquin de. S. American novelist, 3027.

Lizards. Scaly-bodied, four-legged reptiles, **1972,** 158; *plates f. 1972, 1973*; chameleons, 750; of Galapagos Isls., *1686*; green, *2767*; iguanas, 1686; prehistoric, 2678; varied reproduction, 1095; stealing egg, *1095*; slow-worm, 2985.

Ljubljana (lūb-lē-ah'-na), in German **Laibach.** City of Yugoslavia and cap. of federal region of Slovenia; old cath.; pop. 79,000; former cap. of Carniola; Axis-occupied during 2nd World War (1941–45).

Ljusne (lūs'-na) **River,** Sweden. Stream flowing 220 m. S.E. into Gulf of Bothnia.

Llama (lah'-ma). S. Amer. animal of camel family, **1976,** 2842, 2559.

Llandrindod Wells (thlan-drin'-dod), Wales. Tn. and watering-place in Radnorshire; had mineral springs; pop. 2,925; *2733*.

Llandudno (thlan-dud'-nō), Wales. Tn. and popular watering-place of Caernarvonshire; has hydropathic establishments; pop. 13,677; govt. depts. evacuated here in 2nd World War.

Llaneros (lyah-nā'-ros). Cattlemen of Venezuela.

Llanfair Pg. Vil. with longest name (52 letters) in Anglesey, 155.

Llangollen (thlan-goth'-len), Wales, Tn. in Denbighshire, on R. Dee ; noted for scenery ; brewing ; pop. 2,366 ; 990 ; valley near, *3336,*

Llanos Treeless or prairie lands ; in Colombia, 873.

Llanthony (thlan'-tho-ni) Abbey, Monmouthshire, 2215.

Llewelyn (thloo-el'-in). Name of two princes of North Wales, Llewelyn the Great, who ruled from 1194 to 1239, and his grandson, Llewelyn ap Gruffydd ; the latter succeeded David II in 1246 and spent much of his reign in warring with the English ; he was killed in battle in 1282 ; 559.

Llewellyn, Sir William (1860–1941). Brit. artist ; President of the Royal Academy (1928–38).

Lloyd, George Ambrose Lloyd, 1st Baron (1879–1941). Eng. administrator, High Comm. Eg. and Sudan (1925–29) ; Colonial Secretary, 1940.

Lloyd, Harold (b. 1893). American film actor ; a comedian who always appeared in spectacles ; films included " Safety Last " ; " Movie Crazy."

Lloyd Barrage. At Sukkur, India ; large irrigation dam, *960, plate f. 961,* 1721, 2974 ; serious constructional faults reported early 1949.

Lloyd George, David, 1st Earl (1863–1945). Brit. statesman, Prime Minister (1916–22), **1976.**

Lloyd George, Gwilym (b. 1894). Brit. politician, son of 1st Earl Lloyd George ; parl. sec. to Bd. of Trade 1931 and 1939–41 ; parl. sec. to Min. of Food 1941–42 ; Min. of Fuel and Power 1942–45.

Lloyd George, Lady Megan. Brit. politician, younger daughter of 1st Earl Lloyd George ; represented Anglesey in parl. since 1929 ; chairman Welsh Parl. Party 1944–45.

Lloyd's. London association of insurance companies undertaking the insurance of ships and cargoes ; **1976,** 1735 ; A1 sign at, 9 ; register, 1977.

" Load-shedding," in elec. supply, 1549.

Loam, combined sandy and clayey soi of good fertility, 2999.

Loanda (lō-an'-*da*) or **Luanda** (São Paulo de Loanda). Cap. and chief spt. of Angola ; pop. 23,000 ; former centre of slave trade ; 3368.

Loango (lō-ang'-gō), Port of Fr. Equatorial Africa, 100 m. N. of mouth of Congo r.

Lobbying. Term applied in Gt. Brit. and U.S.A. to activities of interested parties in influencing legislation ; so-called from use of Parliament lobbies for conferences with members.

Lobe'lia. A genus of plants of the family *Campanulaceae*, having red, white, or blue flowers, with very irregular corolla ; blue-flowered species is extremely popular as an edging plant.

Lobengu'la (1833–94). King of the Matabeles, succeeding in 1870 ; sought and received Brit. protection, but his constant attacking of the Mashonas led to fighting with Gt. Brit. in 1893, and he was defeated in battle near Buluwayo.

Lobito Bay. Spt. of Angola ; terminus of transcontinental rly. ; 3368.

Lob Nor. Shallow lake in Gobi Desert, 264.

Lobster, 1977.

Lobster pot, *1978.*

Lobworm. A very large earthworm ; these worms appear above ground in wet dewy grass in the early morning.

Local anaesthesia, method, 149.

Local government, 1491.

Local option. Right of local areas to have power to determine their own course of procedure on certain questions, particularly in matter of opening of public-houses.

Locarno. Swiss town, *3141.*

Locarno Conference (1925). A pact of mutual guarantees, 2531.

Lochinvar (lokh-in-vahr'). Hero of Scott's ballad " Young Lochinvar," " so faithful in love and so dauntless in war."

Lochinver. Sutherlandshire, Scot. ; scenery, *583.*

Lochy, Loch, w. Scot., 2889.

Lock. Artificial basin whereby boats are taken to a higher or lower level ; *687,* 688 ; Panama Canal, *2491, 2492, 2493. See also in Index* **Canals.**

Lock, in jujitsu, 1840.

Locke, John (1632–1704). Eng. philosopher and political economist, **1978,** 1212.

Locke, William John (1863–1930). Brit. novelist and playwright, native of Barbados (" The Beloved Vagabond " ; " The Joyous Adventures of Aristide Pujol)."

Lockhart, John Gibson (1794–1854). Scot. writer, author of masterly biographies of Burns, Napoleon and Scott ; son-in-law of Sir Walter Scott ; editor of " Quarterly Review " (1825–53) ; 2895, 2900.

Lockhart, Sir Robert Hamilton Bruce (b. 1887). Scot. author (" Memoirs of a British Agent " , " Return to Malaya ").

Lockjaw or tetanus, 1458.

Lock-out. Closing of factories by employers in cases of dispute.

Locks and keys, 1978.

Lock stitch, 2929, *2930.*

Lockyer, Sir Joseph Norman (1836–1920). Eng. astronomer and physicist ; explained sunspots ; between 1870 and 1905 conducted eight British expeditions for observing total solar eclipses ; discovered helium in sun (" The Chemistry of the Sun ").

" Locomotion No. 1." Stephenson's locomotive, *2735, 2736, 3087.*

Locomotive, 1981, *1989–96,* 3084, 2734 ; boiler, 489 ; Diesel-electric, *plate f. 1981, 1987* ; electric, *1987* ; inventions of George Stephenson, 1981, 1982, 2736, 3087 ; Murdock's steam carriage, *2256* ; Trevithick's, 3247 ; Pacific stream-lined, *1987* ; example of unbalanced pressure, 2129 ; pneumatic, 2632. *See also* **Railways ; Steam engine.**

Locust. An insect, 1511, *plate f. 1512,* 1732 ; immense number, 1511 ; metamorphosis, 1729.

Locust bean. Pod of the carob tree, *Ceratonia,* fam. *Leguminosae,* which is found in Mediterranean countries ; used as a sugar food when ground into meal ; is rich in carbohydrates and albuminoids.

" Locust " tree. False acacia, 16.

Lode mining, 1479.

Lode'stone, or **magnetite.** A natural magnetic oxide of iron, 881, 2062.

Lodge, Sir Oliver Joseph (1851–1940). Eng. physicist, exponent of psychic research, and author, **1988,** 2594.

Lodi (lō'-dē). It. tn. 18 m. S.E. of Milan ; pop. 24,000 ; scene of Fr. victory over Austrians (1796).

Lodz. Polish city 75 m. S.W. of Warsaw ; pop. 496,860 ; textile industry ; great damage in 1914–18 War ; 2641 ; passed to Germany 1939 ; in Russo-German war 1941–44.

Loeb, Jacques (1859–1924). Ger.-Amer. biologist ; fertilized sea-urchin eggs chemically (" artificial parthenogenesis ") ; developed theory that many so-called " intelligent " actions of animals are physical or chemical in nature (" tropisms ").

Loeffler (lĕf'-ler), **Friedrich** (1852–1915). Ger. bacteriologist ; in 1882 discovered bacillus of glanders, in 1884 that of diphtheria, named after him and his co-discoverer the Klebs-Loeffler bacillus.

Loess (lēs). A type of soil, 2999 ; in China, 809, 3384.

Loetschberg tunnel, Switzerland, S. of Interlaken, 9¼ miles, *3257.*

Lofo'ten or **Lofoden Islands.** Group of rocky isls. off N.W. coast of Norway ; 2393 ; Commando raid, March 1941.

Lofting, Hugh John (d. 1947), author of children's books ; after engineering work in Canada, Africa and W. Indies, became famous for his " Dr. Doolittle " series ; 1967.

Log, Ship's. Device for measuring a ship's speed, 1997 ; log-book, 1998 ; in navigation, 2000.

Logan, Mt. Highest mt. in Canada (19,850 ft.) in S.W. corner of Yukon Territory ; first climbed in 1925 ; 2795.

Loganberry. Plant grown originally by Judge Logan (U.S.A.), who successfully crossed the raspberry and blackberry.

Log'arithms. Tables of figures enabling multiplication and division to be performed by addition and subtraction ; **1998** ; *see* page 3884.

Log-book, 1998.

Log-ship, 1997.

Logic. Branch of philosophy, 2572 ; mathematics a form of, 2120.

Logwood (*Haematoxylon*). Tree of W. Indies, Mexico, and Cent. Amer. from 30 to 50 ft. high ; so named from being shipped in logs ; member of the *Leguminosae,* one of the hardest and most valuable woods known ; as a dye, 1060 ; in ink, 1724.

Lohengrin (lō'-en-grin). In Ger. legend, a knight of King Arthur's court ; opera by Wagner, **2000,** 2437, 2439, 3332.

Loire (lwahr). Longest r. in Fr. (610 m.), flowing to Atlantic Ocean, **2000,** 1360, 2274.

Loki (lō'-kē). In Norse myth., mischief-making god, 341, 2363, 2881.

Lol'lards. Followers of Wycliffe, 3428.

Lombards. Germanic tribe which settled in N. It. ; invade N., **2000,** 1237, 1763 ; and Gregory I, 1542 ; Charlemagne conquers, 753, 1764.

Lombard Street, London. Origin of name, 357, 359, 2000.

Lombardy. A division of N. It. ; agric., 1233, 1763 ; history, 1769 ; Iron Crown of, 2000 ; mfrs., 1763.

Lombardy poplar. Fastigiate form of the black poplar (*Populus nigra* var. *italica*) ; it grows fast rising to well above 100 ft. ; used for ornamental purposes, 2655.

Lombok'. Isl. of Indonesia, just E. of Java ; 3,136 sq. m. ; exports rice, coffee, indigo, sugar ; 1076, 440.

Lombroso (lom-brō'-sō), **Cesare** (1836–1909). Famous It. criminologist, founder of science of criminal anthropology, originator of theory that there is a " criminal type," midway between the lunatic and the savage, marked by physical signs.

Lo'mond, Loch. Largest and most beautiful l. in Scot., in counties of Stirling and Dumbarton ; 27 sq. m. ; length, 23 m. ; 1054, *2889.*

Lomonosov (lom-o-nō'-sof). **Michael Vasilievitch** (1711–65). Rus. poet and philologist ; established basic principle of latter-day Rus. language (" Ode on the Capture of Khotin ") ; 2855.

London, Jack (1876–1916). Amer. novelist, whose stories are largely drawn from his own adventurous career as sailor, tramp, stevedore, gold hunter, and war correspondent (" The Call of the Wild " ; " People of the Abyss," " White Fang ").

London, Eng. World's largest city, cap. of U.K. ; a. (with suburbs) nearly 700 sq. m. ; admin. co. and City, 117 sq. m. ; pop. (admin. co. and City) 4,863,000 ; (Greater London) 8,700,000 ; **2009,** *2017–2020* ; airport, *48* ; artesian wells, 253 ; art galleries, 2013, 2015 ; 3158 ; Bank of Eng., *357, 605* ; Battersea Power Stn., *221* ; Brit. Museum, 584, 1537, *1536,* 2015 ; Buckingham Palace, 599 ; circus, Olympia, *plate f. 820* ; Cockneys, 861 ; County Hall, *2013* ; docks, *1024,* 2010, 2012 ; Downing St., 1032, 2014 ; Earl's Court exhib. hall, *608* ; Fleet St., *2020* ; fogs, 1333 ; government, 2016 ; Home Office, 1637 ; international telephone exchange, *3171* ; Livery Companies, 1970 ; Lord Mayor at Guildhall, *frontis., Vol. 5* ; Ludgate Circus, *2787* ; Middlesex Guildhall, *2168* ; museums, 2260 ; National Gallery, 2280 ; Parl. bldgs., *2013, 2523, 2524* ; police, 2647, *2648* ; Pool of, 2012 ; Regent's Park, *3197* ; St. Paul's

TABLE OF COMMON LOGARITHMS

	0	1	2	3	4	5	6	7	8	9	D
10	0000	0043	0086	0128	0170	0212	0253	0294	0334	0374	42
11	0414	0453	0492	0531	0569	0607	0645	0682	0719	0755	38
12	0792	0828	0864	0899	0934	0969	1004	1038	1072	1106	35
13	1139	1173	1206	1239	1271	1303	1335	1367	1399	1430	32
14	1461	1492	1523	1553	1584	1614	1644	1673	1703	1732	30
15	1761	1790	1818	1847	1875	1903	1931	1959	1987	2014	28
16	2041	2068	2095	2122	2148	2175	2201	2227	2253	2279	26
17	2304	2330	2355	2380	2405	2430	2455	2480	2504	2529	25
18	2553	2577	2601	2625	2648	2672	2695	2718	2742	2765	24
19	2788	2810	2833	2856	2878	2900	2923	2945	2967	2989	22
20	3010	3032	3054	3075	3096	3118	3139	3160	3181	3201	21
21	3222	3243	3263	3284	3304	3324	3345	3365	3385	3404	20
22	3424	3444	3464	3483	3502	3522	3541	3560	3579	3598	19
23	3617	3636	3655	3674	3692	3711	3729	3747	3766	3784	18
24	3802	3820	3838	3856	3874	3892	3909	3927	3945	3962	18
25	3979	3997	4014	4031	4048	4065	4082	4099	4116	4133	17
26	4150	4166	4183	4200	4216	4232	4249	4265	4281	4298	16
27	4314	4330	4346	4362	4378	4393	4409	4425	4440	4456	16
28	4472	4487	4502	4518	4533	4548	4564	4579	4594	4609	15
29	4624	4639	4654	4669	4683	4698	4713	4728	4742	4757	15
30	4771	4786	4800	4814	4829	4843	4857	4871	4886	4900	14
31	4914	4928	4942	4955	4969	4983	4997	5011	5024	5038	14
32	5051	5065	5079	5092	5105	5119	5132	5145	5159	5172	13
33	5185	5198	5211	5224	5237	5250	5263	5276	5289	5302	13
34	5315	5328	5340	5353	5366	5378	5391	5403	5416	5428	13
35	5441	5453	5465	5478	5490	5502	5514	5527	5539	5551	12
36	5563	5575	5587	5599	5611	5623	5635	5647	5658	5670	12
37	5682	5694	5705	5717	5729	5740	5752	5763	5775	5786	12
38	5798	5809	5821	5832	5843	5855	5866	5877	5888	5899	11
39	5911	5922	5933	5944	5955	5966	5977	5988	5999	6010	11
40	6021	6031	6042	6053	6064	6075	6085	6096	6107	6117	11
41	6128	6138	6149	6160	6170	6180	6191	6201	6212	6222	10
42	6232	6243	6253	6263	6274	6284	6294	6304	6314	6325	10
43	6335	6345	6355	6365	6375	6385	6395	6405	6415	6425	10
44	6435	6444	6454	6464	6474	6484	6493	6503	6513	6522	10
45	6532	6542	6551	6561	6571	6580	6590	6599	6609	6618	10
46	6628	6637	6646	6656	6665	6675	6684	6693	6702	6712	9
47	6721	6730	6739	6749	6758	6767	6776	6785	6794	6803	9
48	6812	6821	6830	6839	6848	6857	6866	6875	6884	6893	9
49	6902	6911	6920	6928	6937	6946	6955	6964	6972	6981	9
50	6990	6998	7007	7016	7024	7033	7042	7050	7059	7067	9
51	7076	7084	7093	7101	7110	7118	7126	7135	7143	7152	8
52	7160	7168	7177	7185	7193	7202	7210	7218	7226	7235	8
53	7243	7251	7259	7267	7275	7284	7292	7300	7308	7316	8
54	7324	7332	7340	7348	7356	7364	7372	7380	7388	7396	8

	0	1	2	3	4	5	6	7	8	9	D
55	7404	7412	7419	7427	7435	7443	7451	7459	7466	7474	8
56	7482	7490	7497	7505	7513	7520	7528	7536	7543	7551	8
57	7559	7566	7574	7582	7589	7597	7604	7612	7619	7627	8
58	7634	7642	7649	7657	7664	7672	7679	7686	7694	7701	7
59	7709	7716	7723	7731	7738	7745	7752	7760	7767	7774	7
60	7782	7789	7796	7803	7810	7818	7825	7832	7839	7846	7
61	7853	7860	7868	7875	7882	7889	7896	7903	7910	7917	7
62	7924	7931	7938	7945	7952	7959	7966	7973	7980	7987	7
63	7993	8000	8007	8014	8021	8028	8035	8041	8048	8055	7
64	8062	8069	8075	8082	8089	8096	8102	8109	8116	8122	7
65	8129	8136	8142	8149	8156	8162	8169	8176	8182	8189	7
66	8195	8202	8209	8215	8222	8228	8235	8241	8248	8254	7
67	8261	8267	8274	8280	8287	8293	8299	8306	8312	8319	6
68	8325	8331	8338	8344	8351	8357	8363	8370	8376	8382	6
69	8388	8395	8401	8407	8414	8420	8426	8432	8439	8445	6
70	8451	8457	8463	8470	8476	8482	8488	8494	8500	8506	6
71	8513	8519	8525	8531	8537	8543	8549	8555	8561	8567	6
72	8573	8579	8585	8591	8597	8603	8069	8615	8621	8627	6
73	8633	8639	8645	8651	8657	8663	8669	8675	8681	8686	6
74	8692	8698	8704	8710	8716	8722	8727	8733	8739	8745	6
75	8751	8756	8762	8768	8774	8779	8785	8791	8797	8802	6
76	8808	8814	8820	8825	8831	8837	8842	8848	8854	8859	6
77	8865	8871	8876	8882	8887	8893	8899	8904	8910	8915	6
78	8921	8927	8932	8938	8943	8949	8954	8960	8965	8971	6
79	8976	8982	8987	8993	8998	9004	9009	9015	9020	9025	5
80	9031	9036	9042	9047	9053	9058	9063	9069	9074	9079	5
81	9085	9090	9096	9101	9106	9112	9117	9122	9128	9133	5
82	9138	9143	9149	9154	9159	9165	9170	9175	9180	9186	5
83	9191	9196	9201	9206	9212	9217	9222	9227	9232	9238	5
84	9243	9248	9253	9258	9263	9269	9274	9279	9284	9289	5
85	9294	9299	9304	9309	9315	9320	9325	9330	9335	9340	5
86	9345	9350	9355	9360	9365	9370	9375	9380	9385	9390	5
87	9395	9400	9405	9410	9415	9420	9425	9430	9435	9440	5
88	9445	9450	9455	9460	9465	9469	9474	9479	9484	9489	5
89	9494	9499	9504	9509	9513	9518	9523	9528	9533	9538	5
90	9542	9547	9552	9557	9562	9566	9571	9576	9581	9586	5
91	9590	9595	9600	9605	9609	9614	9619	9624	9628	9633	5
92	9638	9643	9647	9652	9657	9661	9666	9671	9675	9680	5
93	9685	9689	9694	9699	9703	9708	9713	9717	9722	9727	5
94	9731	9736	9741	9745	9750	9754	9759	9763	9768	9773	5
95	9777	9782	9786	9791	9795	9800	9805	9809	9814	9818	5
96	9823	9827	9832	9836	9841	9845	9850	9854	9859	9863	5
97	9868	9872	9877	9881	9886	9890	9894	9899	9903	9908	4
98	9912	9917	9921	9926	9930	9934	9939	9943	9948	9952	4
99	9956	9961	9965	9969	9974	9978	9983	9987	9991	9996	4

Those unfamiliar with logarithms should read the general principles, especially about the mantissa and characteristic, in the article on Logarithms before using this table.

Finding logarithms of numbers. Locate the first two figures in the left-hand column and the third in the top row. The corresponding four numbers in the table are the mantissa (mantissa of 151 is 1790). The characteristic is one **less** than the number of digits to the **left** of the decimal point. Thus the logarithm of 1·51 (usually written log 1·51)=0·1790; log 15·1 =1·790; log 151=2·1790; and so on.

For decimal fractions, the characteristic is one **greater** than the number of zeros between the decimal point and the first significant digit, and has a **negative sign above** the characteristic, with the mantissa in the table (log 0·151=$\bar{1}$·1790; log 0·0151=$\bar{2}$·1790; and so on).

To find the logarithm of a number having four significant digits proceed by interpolation as follows : obtain the difference between the mantissas for the next smaller and next larger three-digit numbers ; multiply this by the last digit of your number, divide by 10, and add the result to the logarithm for the first three digits of the number. Thus to find log 15·13. Log 15·2 (=1·1818)−log 15·1 (=1·1790)=·0028. $\frac{3}{10}$ × ·0028 =·00084. Adding : 1·1790+·00084=1·1798(4) (=log 15·13). The column marked D at the right gives the average value for the difference between any two mantissas on the line, and may

be used (remembering to multiply, then divide by 10 as above) if less accurate results will suffice.

To find a number from its logarithm. Locate in the table the mantissa next below the one you have, write the three corresponding digits from the side column and the top row and put in the decimal point as the characteristic requires. For remaining digits, reverse the interpolation process given above. Thus, to find the number for the logarithm 1·17984. The next lowest mantissa is 1790, and the number (with decimal point inserted for characteristic 1) is 15·1. The difference between mantissas, ·1790 and ·1818 is ·0028. Divide by the difference you have $\frac{·0028}{·00084}$ =3·3. Adding this **after** 15·1 (not **to** it) gives 15·13(3), the answer.

Computing with logarithms. When all characteristics are positive, the computations proceed as explained in the article on Logarithms. When negative characteristics appear treat the characteristics and mantissas separately, and at the end combine any characteristic resulting from the mantissas with the others. Thus, to find 151×0·151. To log 151 (= 2·1790) add log 0·151 (=$\bar{1}$·1790). Result : 1·3580 (=log of 22·8 approx.). To divide 0·151 by 151 : from log 0·151 (=$\bar{1}$·1790) subtract log 151 (=2·1790). Result $\bar{3}$·000 (=log of ·001). To find the 7th power of 0·151 : multiply log 0·151 (=$\bar{1}$·1790) by 7. Answer : $\bar{7}$+(7+·1790) = $\bar{7}$ + 1·2530 = $\bar{6}$·2580 (= log of 0·00000179 approx. (*See also* **Powers and Roots.**)

Cath., 729, 2000, 0003, 2020 ; Roman wall, 209 ; sculpture in, 2907–2910 ; South Africa House, 2013 ; Stock Exchange, 3094 ; The Temple, 2012 ; Thames, 2009, 2011, 2013, 2017, 3193 ; Thames Embankment, 2012 ; Tower, 3231, 2017 ; Tower Bridge, 567, 2017 ; Trafalgar Square, 2019, 2904 ; tramways, 3235 ; Underground rlys., 2575, 2738, 3274, 3275 ; University, see London University ; water supply in early times, 3347 ; Westminster Abbey, 3369, 2014 ; Westminster Hall, 2822 ; Zoological Gardens, 3445, 3447 ; history, 111, 2009 ; origin, 2009 ; charter granted, 1204 ; Wat Tyler's rebellion, 3269 ; Jack Cade's rebellion, 1611 ; great fire, 757, 2010 ; 17th century, 2935 ; Wren and, 3425 ; 2nd World War, 2016, 3417, 3418.

London, Canada, commercial centre of w. Ontario, on R. Thames ; pop. 78,000 ; rly. workshops, petroleum refineries : machinery, chemical mfrs.

London, Treaty of (1913), 345.

London, Treaty of (1915), secret treaty for Italy's entry into 1st World War, 3410.

London Airport, Heathrow, w. of Hounslow, 48.

London basin, 253.

London Company. Corporation chartered 1606 for purpose of planting colonies in America ; grant to Pilgrims, 2122.

London County Council (L.C.C.). Governing council of the co. of London, instituted in 1888 on the formation of the co., 2016 ; County Hall, its headquarters, is opposite New Scotland Yd., on the s. side of the Thames ; 1491, 2013 ; night schools, 2886.

Lon'donderry, 2nd Marquess of. See Castlereagh.

Londonderry, Charles Stewart Henry Vane-Tempest-Stewart, 7th Marquess (1878–1949). Brit. politician ; 1st Commissioner of Works (1928–29 and 1931) ; Air Minister (1931–35) ; Lord Privy Seal and Leader of the House of Lords (1935) ; Chief Commissioner of Civil Air Guard (1938).

Londonderry or Derry, Northern Ire. Port on r. Foyle ; pop. 47,800 ; chief tn. of co. of Londonderry (816 sq. m. ; pop. 142,700), 2021 ; besieged by James II in 1689, 1747, 2021.

London Fire Brigade (L.F.B.), 604, 1285, 1287, 1288.

London Gazette. First appeared in 1666. Records appointments, promotions in the armed forces ; Court announcements ; honours, decorations.

London Group. Group of British painters evolved from Camden Town group, 1184 ; members included Duncan Grant, Vanessa Bell, Ethelbert White ; from its ranks also evolved more advanced groups.

London Museum, Lancaster House, temporarily housed at Kensington Palace in 1948 ; 2015, 2260.

London Transport. An organization including the Underground railways, tramways, trolley bus, omnibus and Green Line coach services in the London area ; began as London Passenger Transport Board (L.P.T.B.) in 1933 ; nationalized (1947) under the London Transport Executive ; 2016, 3239, 3275 ; and Underground, 3275.

London pride, a saxifrage, 2878. Song by Noel Coward.

London University. Properly known as the University of London ; largest university in the British Isles, with 50,000 students ; headquarters at central buildings in Bloomsbury, 2021, 606, 607 ; Birkbeck College, 457 ; observatory, Mill Hill, 3119, 3181. See also Universities.

London Wall, a London thoroughfare, running w. from Old Broad Street to the N. of Wood Street ; was originally built in the 2nd century and rebuilt again in the Middle Ages ; Rom. remains are still to be seen, 209.

Long, Crawford Williamson (1815–78). American surgeon, performed first recorded surgical operation using an anaesthetic.

Long, Loch. Inlet, Scot., branch of Firth of Clyde, 17 m. long.

Long Beach, California, U.S.A. Seaside resort and industrial centre on s. coast, about 20 m. s. of Los Angeles ; resident pop. 164,000 ; chief industry shipbuilding.

Longbow, origin and use, 209 ; in Hundred Years' War, 926 ; influence on warfare, 240, 1864 ; Robin Hood's skill, 2790.

Longchamps or Longchamp (lawnshahn'), race-course w. of Paris, 2516.

Long-eared owl, 446, 2461.

Longev'ity, length of life ; of animals, 156 ; cicada, 826 ; connected with rate of reproduction, 156 ; plants, 2624 ; sequoias the oldest living organisms, 2921, 3245 ; trees, 2624.

Longfellow, Henry Wadsworth (1807–82), Amer. poet, 2022, 3294 ; "Courtship of Miles Standish," ; "The Story of Hiawatha," 2022.

Longford, Eire, Inland co. in Leinster ; a. 403 sq. m. ; pop. 37.000 ; 2024.

Longinus (lon-ji'-nus), Cassius (c. 213–273), Gk. critic, 1541.

Long Island, New York, U.S.A., isl. s. of Connecticut, forming s.E. portion of N.Y. state ; 1,682 sq. m. ; pop. 4,600,000 ; contains Brooklyn and Long Island City, 2351, 2357.

Longitude (lon'-ji-tūd) and Latitude, 1898 ; how found at sea, 1898 ; shown on maps, 2094 ; and time, 3212, 3213.

Long measure, lineal measure or measure of length. See Weights and Measures.

Long Parliament, 755, 2524 ; Cromwell dismisses, 934 ; Hampden, 1571.

Long primer type, 3270.

"Longshanks," nickname of Edward I of Eng., 1089.

Long-tailed field mouse, 2249.

Long-tailed tit, 3218.

Longwy (lon-vē'). Fortified frontier tn. in N.E. Fr. ; iron works ; taken by Prussians in 1792 and 1815, and by Ger. troops in 1871 and 1914.

Lonsdale, Frederick (b. 1881). Eng. dramatist ; author of modern comedies ("Aren't We All ?" ; "The Last of Mrs. Cheyney").

Lonsdale, Hugh Cecil Lowther, 5th Earl of (1857–1944). Famous patron of horse-racing, boxing and other sports; instituted the Lonsdale Belt for Brit. boxing champions.

Loo'fah, substitute for sponges, 3069.

Loom, 2024, 2025, 920, 3066, 3360 ; carpet, 3361 ; development, 3066 ; hand loom, 2024 ; Jacquard, 707, 1790, 1877 ; for rug weaving, 705 ; tapestry, 3153.

Looming. A form of mirage in which the image is magnified, 2190.

Loon. Scot. name for the Great Northern diver. See Diver.

Loop Head. Promontory of Eire (the Irish Free State) forming the N. shore of the Shannon estuary.

oos (lōs), small vil. in N. Fr. 1 m. N.W. of Lens ; in Sept. 1915 a battle was fought here during a Brit. attack.

Loosestrife. Leafy-stemmed perennial herbs embracing the genus Lysimachia of the primrose family ; common loosestrife is L. vulgaris, a tall coarse plant with large yellow flowers in terminal leafy panicles ; L. nummularia (moneywort, or creeping jenny) is a trailing plant with small yellow flowers often found on the banks of streams ; purple loosestrife (Lythrum salicaria) is no relation of the other species.

Lope de Vega. See Vega Carpio.

Lopez (lō'-pās), Carlos Antonio (1790–1862). Dictator of Paraguay.

Lopez, Franscisco Solano (1826–70). Dictator of Paraguay, 2512.

Lopez de Legaspi, Miguel (1524–72). Sp. soldier and navigator, conqueror of Philippines and founder of Manila.

Lopez de Villalobos, Ruy (1500–44). Span. navigator ; expedition to Philippines, 2569.

Lopokova, Lydia (b. 1892). Russ. dancer, leading member of Diaghilev company ; created parts of Marfucha in "The Good-humoured Ladies," and the can-can dancer in "La Boutique Fantasque" ; married, in 1925, J. M. (Lord) Keynes.

Lo'quat. A plum-like fruit, 1401.

Loraine, Robert (1876–1935). Popular Eng. actor and pioneer airman ; served in S. Africa War (1899–1902), and in the First World War (1914–18) in Royal Air Force ; one of his chief successes as an actor was in "Cyrano de Bergerac."

Lorca. Anc. city in s.E. Spain on r. Sangonera ; pop. 70,000 ; trade centre ; scene of many battles between Christians and Moors.

Lorca, Federico Garc a (c. 1898–1936). Sp. poet and dramatist ; his poems influenced the Sp. revolutionary movement ; in 1930 went to New York ; in 1930 assassinated by Fascists at Granada ; poems. "Romancero Gitano," "El Poeta en Nueva York" ; tragedy "Bodas de Sangre" (trs. into Eng. as "Blood Wedding") ; 3051.

Lord. A Brit. title borne by bishops, marquises, earls, viscounts, and barons : also borne as courtesy title by eldest sons of dukes, marquesses and earls, and younger sons of dukes and marquesses, 2536 ; as title of office borne by Lord Chancellor, Lord Mayor, etc.

Lord Advocate. Chief law officer of Crown, in Scotland.

Lord Chamberlain. The title given to an officer of the British Royal Household is second dignitary of the court ; he is in charge of all the household above stairs, and the symbols of his office are a white staff and a key.

Lord Chancellor. The title given to the highest judicial functionary of Gr. Brit. ; he relinquishes his appointment when new Government comes into power ; he is keeper of the Great Seal, a cabinet minister, and a privy councillor ; he is also Speaker of the House of Lords, and appoints county court judges and justices of the peace ; 1490, 3083.

Lord Chief Justice, second highest title in the Supreme Court of Judicature ; taking oath, 1904.

Lord Great Chamberlain, 3083.

Lord High Admiral, title obsolete since 1828 ; 3083.

Lord High Constable, 3083

Lord High Steward, 3083.

Lord High Treasurer, 3083.

Lord Mayor. Chief magistrate in certain English cities, including London, Leeds, Manchester, Birmingham, Liverpool, and Sheffield ; in connexion with the appointment of the Lord Mayor of London an annual procession, begun in 1215, takes place on Nov. 9, frontis., Vol. 5 ; Richard Whittington, 3377.

Lord President of the Council, 3083.

Lord Privy Seal, 3083.

Lord Protector. Cromwell's title as head of the Commonwealth, 933.

Lord's. London cricket ground, 928.

Lord's Supper or Eucharist. A sacrament. See Eucharist.

Lord Steward. The title given to the first dignitary of the Court, an official of the Royal Household ; receives his office from the sovereign personally, and is a peer, privy councillor, and a member of the ministry ; directs all the household below stairs, and has authority over all royal officers and servants other than those connected with the chamber, the chapel, and the stable.

Lords, House of. Upper house of Brit. Parliament, 2521, 2522, 2524, 1490 ; court of appeal, 1490 ; powers limited, 1976, 3282 ; Judicial Committee, 922 ; Charles I in, 1199.

Loreburn, Robert Reid, Earl (1846–1923). Brit. politician and lawyer ; Lord Chancellor (1905–12).

Loredano, Leonardo. Portrait by Bellini, 1782.

Lorelei (lō-re-lī). Fabled Rhine siren, said to lure boatmen to destruction; legend probably from an echoing rock of that name in the Rhine, 2769.

Lorenzo de' Medici (lō-rent'-sō dā med'-i-chē) (1449–92). "The Magnificent," *2131*; patron of art, 1926.

Loret'to School. Public school at Loretto, Scot., about 6 m. from Edinburgh.

Lorient (lō-rē-ahn'). Fr. Fortified naval port in N.W. on r. Scorff; pop. 11,838; shipyards, arsenal; fisheries; German U-boat base 1940–45, heavily bombed by R.A.F.

Loris. A lemur, 1922.

"Lor'na Doone." Novel by R. D. Blackmore which made Exmoor famous; the heroine is an heiress kidnapped by outlaws and brought up in their wilderness fortress.

Lorne, Firth of. Inlet of Atlant. Ocean, on w. coast of Scot., 2889, *map*, 2890.

Lorrain, Claude (1600–82), Fr. landscape painter; real name Claude Gelée; *2026*, *1370*, 1377, 2476. *See also* Study Outline, 3667.

Lorraine (lo-rān'). Dist. of N.E. Fr. (also called Lotharingia and Lothringen), 1449; history, 133; iron ore, 1753; Metz, 2155. *See also* Alsace-Lorraine, *and under* Lothair, King of Lorraine.

Lo'ry. A parrot, 2526.

Los Angeles (los an'-je-lēz), Calif., U.S.A. Largest city on Pacific coast; pop. 1,504,200; *2026*, 664; rare type of fossil bed, 1354; cinema industry in Hollywood dist., *2026*.

Loss of voice, how to treat, 3328.

"Lost Dauphin," 2030.

Lost-head, a type of nail, 2271.

Lot. Abraham's nephew, 13.

Lothair' I (795–855). Holy Roman emperor, grandson of Charlemagne; became joint ruler 817 when Louis I, his father, divided the Empire among his sons; after some years of strife with his brothers received Italy and imperial title together with lands along Rhine and Rhône (Partition of Verdun, 843), 1449.

Lothair II, "The Saxon" (c. 1070–1137). Holy Roman emperor 1133–37; created Duke of Saxony in 1106, and elected Ger. king in 1125; a strong, capable ruler, whose reign was regarded as a golden age for Germany.

Lothair (825–869). King of Lorraine, son of Lothair I; received as his kingdom dist. w. of Rhine between North Sea and Jura Mts., called after him Lotharingia or Lorraine (Ger. Lothringen).

Lotharin'gia. *See* Lorraine.

Lothario (lō-thār'-i-ō). In Rowe's tragedy "The Fair Penitent," handsome, perfidious libertine, the proverbial "gallant, gay Lothario."

Lothian, Philip H. Kerr, 11th Marquess of (1882–1940). Brit. politician and diplomatist; chancellor of duchy of Lancaster in 1931; Brit. ambass. in Washington, U.S.A., Apr. 1939–Dec. 1940, where he died suddenly.

Lothians, Scot. cos., 2027. *See* East Lothian; Midlothian; West Lothian.

Loti (lō'-tē), **Pierre.** Pen-name of Louis Marie Julien Viaud (1870–1923). Fr. novelist; exquisite stylist, whose studies of strange places are "log-books of sentiment," 1382; chief works, "Pêcheur d'Islande" (The Iceland Fisherman), "Madame Chrysanthème," and "Mon Frère Yves."

Lotto, Lorenzo. Italian painter, pupil of Vivarini, and probably a native of Venice; portrait of Columbus, *879*.

Lo'tus, 2027, 3354; in Gk. myth., 2421.

Lotze (lot'-se), **Rudolf Hermann** (1817–81). Ger. philosopher; opposed theory of "vital force" and was a founder and developer of physiological psychology.

Loubet (lōō-bā), **Émile** (1838–1929). Fr. statesman, 7th pres. of Fr. Republic (1899–1906); remitted Dreyfus's sentence.

Loud-hailer, used at sea, 3012.

Loud-speaker, 3011, *3012*.

Louis, kings of Bavaria. *See* Ludwig.

Louis I, the Pious (779–840). King of France and Holy Roman emperor, the youngest son of Charlemagne; 2027.

Louis II (c. 822–75). Emperor (crowned 850) and king of Italy (succeeded 839), son of Lothair I; fought Saracens and restored order in Italy.

Louis III, the Blind (880–928). Emperor (crowned 901) and king of the Lombards (chosen 900), grandson of Louis II; his eyes were put out 905 by Berengar, rival king of the Lombards; thereafter lived in exile in Provence.

Louis IV, the Bavarian (about 1287–1347). Emperor (crowned 1328) and king of Germany (elected 1314); warred with Pope; added to possessions.

Louis VI, the Fat (1078–1137). King of France, 2027.

Louis VII (1120–80). France, 2027.

Louis VIII (1187–1226). France, 2028.

Louis IX (1214–70). "Saint Louis," France, 1365, 2028; in Crusades, 937.

Louis X (1289–1316), France, 2028.

Louis XI (1423–83), France, 2028, 1365; private postal system, 2661.

Louis XII (1462–1515), France, 2028.

Louis XIII (1601–43), France, 2028, 2778.

Louis XIV (1638–1715), France, 2029; literature under, 1380; and Molière, *1381*; Man in Iron Mask, 1758; marriage, 3307; Versailles palace, 3317, 2029; William III and, 3380.

Louis XV (1710–74), France, 2030.

Louis XVI (1754–93), France, 2030, 1383; calls States-General, 2030, 1393; death, 1395; and French Revolution, 1393, 1395; Marie Antoinette, *2102*; and Mirabeau, 2189.

Louis XVII (1785–95), France, "the lost dauphin," 2030.

Louis XVIII (1755–1824), France, 2030; and Talleyrand, 3149.

Louis, the German (804–76). King of the East Franks; 3rd son of Louis the Pious and grandson of Charlemagne; his share of Charlemagne's empire after partition of Verdun (843) formed nucleus of modern Germany.

Louis I (1838–89). King of Portugal; succeeded in 1861; abolished slavery in Port. colonies.

Louis Napoleon. Same as Napoleon III.

Louis Philippe (fē-lēp') (1773–1850), "Citizen-king" of France, 2031, 1366.

Louis, Joe (J. L. Barrow, b. 1914). Amer. negro boxer; world heavyweight champion June 1937 to his retirement Mar. 1, 1949; defended title over 20 times.

Louisburg. Shipping port and fishing village on Cape Breton Isl., Nova Scotia; pop. 1,100; important fortress under French; captured in 1758 by British, 2401, 3401.

Louise (1776–1810). Queen of Frederick William III of Prussia; her beauty, goodness, and fortitude in misfortune made her a German heroine; Napoleon's rudeness to her after Eylau and Friedland hardened resolve of her son William I to humiliate France after Sedan.

Louise, Lake, Alberta, in Rocky Mts. Park, it lies 5,800 ft. above sea level at foot of Mt. Victoria.

Louisiade (lōō-ē-zē-ahd') **Archipelago.** Group of islands off S.E. coast of New Guinea, belonging to Papua; 2340.

Louisiana (lōō-ē-zē-an'-a). A Gulf state of U.S.A.; 48,523 sq. m.; pop. 2,363,880; **2031**; foundation, 143; New Orleans, 2342, *2343*; sulphur, 3116.

Louisiana Purchase. Extensive area of land in N. Amer. purchased by U.S.A. govt. from Napoleon in 1803; 1816, 3291.

Louisville. Cap. of Kentucky, U.S.A., on Ohio r.; pop. 319,000; univ.; important centre of trade, 1852.

Lourdes (loord). Tn. in s.w. Fr.; place of Cath. pilgrimage; famous Grotto with healing springs; described in Zola's "Lourdes"; pop. 14,000.

Lourenço Marques (loo-ren'-sō mahr-kes'). Cap. and spt. of Mozambique; pop. 38,000; 1073.

Louse. A wingless, parasitic insect; two sub-orders, *Mallophaga*, biting lice, and *Siphunculata*, sucking lice, 1733, 2513; the species parasitic on Man is *Pediculus humanus*; eggs of head louse, 1094.

Louse, plant. *See* Aphis.

Louth. Marit. and smallest co. of Eire; a. 317 sq m.; pop. 65,000; **2032**.

Louvain (loo-van'), Belgium; pop. (1940) 35,000; damaged in both World Wars, 2032; *map, 404*.

Louvain, University of, at Louvain, Belgium, founded 1425; leading scientific institution of medieval Europe, having 6,000 students in 16th cent.; active in Counter-Reformation; suppressed during Fr. Rev., re-established in 1817; library twice destroyed in World Wars, 2032.

L'Ouverture, Toussaint. *See* Toussaint.

Louvois (loo-vwah'), **François Michel Le Tellier, Marquis de** (1641–91). Fr. statesman, Louis XIV's war minister; wasted prosperity of Fr. and destroyed peace of Europe for military "glory."

Louvre (loo'-vr). Art museum in Paris, 2032, *2033*, 2517.

Louvre. In architecture a lantern or open turret on the roof of a building; also applied to a type of shutter with sloping, overlapping surfaces.

Lovat (luv'-at), **Simon Fraser, 11th Lord** (c. 1667–1747). Scot. Jacobite intriguer; outlawed for forcing the Dowager Lady Lovat to marry him, he fled to Fr.; returning to Eng. he supported the govt. in the Jacobite rising of 1715, but went over to the Jacobites in the rising of 1745 and was taken prisoner after Culloden and executed; the 14th Baron, Simon Joseph Fraser (1871–1933), raised the body known as Lovat's Scouts in the Boer War. 17th Baron, Simon C. J. F. (b. 1911), Commando leader 2nd World War.

Love-bird. Small parrot, 2526.

"Love for Love." Comedy, produced 1695, by Wm. Congreve; typically witty and coarse Restoration comedy; scene from, *1041*.

Lovelace, Richard (1618–58). Eng. Cavalier poet, immortalized by two lyrics ("To Lucasta, on Going to the Wars"; "To Althea, from Prison"); 1211.

Lover, Samuel (1797–1868). Irish novelist and poet; "Handy Andy," a roaring farce dealing with an Irish servant lad's buffoonery; "Rory O'More," with its brave, good-natured peasant hero, equally popular as novel and play; 1751.

"Love's Labour's Lost." Play by Shakespeare, 2936.

Low, David (b. 1891). Brit. cartoonist; a New Zealander, he joined London "Star," 1919, and "Evening Standard," 1927; a brilliant draughtsman; he created a number of satirical characters, e.g. "Colonel Blimp."

Low, Sir Sidney (1857–1932). Brit. journalist and historian ("The Governance of England"; "The Political History of the Reign of Queen Victoria").

"Low," an area of low atmospheric pressure in meteorology, 2150.

Low Archipelago, Polynesia, 2471.

Low Countries. Eng. equivalent of "Netherlands," formerly applied to Belgium, Holland, and Luxemburg.

Lowe, Sir Hudson (1769–1844). Brit. general, fought throughout Napoleonic wars, conspicuous in campaigns of 1813 and 1814; custodian of Napoleon on St. Helena.

Lowell, James Russell (1819–91). Amer. poet, essayist, and critic, 3294.

Lowell, Percival (1855–1916). Amer. astronomer; lived in Japan (1883–93); established Lowell Observatory at Flagstaff; believed Mars to be inhabited, 2617 ; predicted Pluto, 2618, 2631.

Lowell, Massachusetts, U.S.A. Great textile mfg. centre ; pop. 100,700 ; mfrs. textiles, boots and shoes ; 2118.

Lower California. *See* **California, Lower.**

Lower Canada. Name formerly given to prov. of Quebec, 2435, 2715.

Lowestoft. Spt. and summer resort of Suffolk ; pop. 40,430 ; important fisheries ; captured by Cromwell (1643) ; Dutch fleet defeated by Duke of York (1665) ; former porcelain mfrs. ; bombed 1940–43.

Low frequency, in wireless, 3393.

Low German. Language, 1456

Lowlands, of cent. Scot., 2889, *2891.*

Lowther Hills. Scot. mt. range in Dumfries-shire and Lanarkshire ; highest pt. 2,403 ft.

Loyalty Islands. Pacific group 60 m. E. of New Caledonia ; 800 sq. m. ; export copra and rubber, 2470.

Loyola (loi-ō′-la), **Ignatius de** (1491–1556). Founder of Jesuit Order, **2032,** *2034* ; and Counter-Reformation, 2758, 2760 ; converts Francis Xavier, 3429.

Lubber′s or granny knot, 1868.

Lub′bock, Sir John. *See* **Avebury, Lord.**

Lübeck (lū′-bek). Ger. free city on r. Trave, 12 m. from Baltic ; pop. 129,000 ; medieval buildings ; mfrs. and Baltic trade ; cap. of city-state of Lübeck (115 sq. m. ; pop. (1939), 153,600) ; as head of Hanseatic League, 1575 ; bombed by R.A.F. March 1942, with serious damage to port installations and U-boat building yards ; taken by British, May 1945.

Lublin (loo′blen), Poland. City 95 m. S.E. of Warsaw ; pop. (1939) 122,000 ; Rus. victory over Austrians in early part of 1st World War ; in German occupation 1939–44 ; Russians re-take, 3424 ; Provisional Govt. 1944–45.

Lu′bricants. Substances used to diminish friction, 1396 ; graphite, 1500 ; oil, 2426 ; excessive lubrication, 1396.

Luca della Robbia. *See* **della Robbia.**

Lu′can (Marcus Annaeus Lucanus) (A.D. 39–65). Rom. poet, author of the "Pharsalia," epic on civil war between Caesar and Pompey.

Lucarne, in architecture, a Fr. term for a garret window ; also for the lights or small windows inset in spires.

Lucas, Sir Charles Prestwood (1853–1931). Eng. historian of Brit. colonial development ("An Historical Geography of the British Colonies" ; "A History of Canada"; "The Partition and Colonization of Africa").

Lucas, Edward Verrall (1868–1938). Eng. essayist, novelist, and biographer ; "the modern Charles Lamb" ; widely popular for his genial humour and broad sympathies ("The Open Road" ; "Life of Charles Lamb" ; "London Afresh").

Lucas, John Seymour (1849–1923). Eng. painter ; R.A. in 1898 ; "Drake Receives the Spaniard's Sword," *1036* ; "Drake Plays Bowls," *236* ; "William I grants London's Charter," *1204.*

"Lucas Malet." Pen name of Mrs. Mary St. Leger Harrison (1852–1931), novelist, younger daughter of Charles Kingsley ("Colonel Enderby's Wife" ; "The History of Sir Richard Calmady" ; "The Wages of Sin").

Lucas van Leyden (Lucas Jacobsz) (*c.* 1494–1533). Dutch painter and engraver, friend of Dürer.

Lucca (look′ka). Old and picturesque city in N. Italy, 12 m. N.E. of Pisa ; pop. 82,000 ; many antiquities ; textiles ; large trade.

Lucerne (loo-sern′) or **Luzern,** Switzerland, cap. of canton of Lucerne, at N.W. end of L. Lucerne ; pop. (1941)

54,700 ; tourist resort : Thorwaldsen's "Lion," 2906.

Lucerne, or alfalfa, 110, 2983.

Lucerne, Lake of (Vierwaldstättersee), cent. Switzerland ; 24 m. long, 3140.

Lu′chu or **Loochoo Islands.** Same as **Nansei Islands.**

"Lucia di Lammermoor." Opera by Donizetti, based on Scott's "Bride of Lammermoor," 2139.

Lucian (lōō′-sh*a*n) (A.D. *c.* 120–180). Gk. satirist and humorist, 1541.

Lucifer (lōō′-si-fer). Name of Venus as morning star ; applied by Isaiah to king of Babylon ("How art thou fallen from heaven, O Lucifer, son of the morning !") and, through misunderstanding of this passage by later writers, to Satan.

Lucil′ius, Gaius (*c.* 180–103 B.C.), Rom. satirist, 1895.

Luck′now. Mfg. and rly. centre in United Prov., India ; famous for heroic defence in Indian Mutiny ; pop. 387,000 ; **2035,** 1692, 3284.

Lucretia (lōō-krē′-shi-a). Rom. matron whose suicide (510 B.C.) because of outrage inflicted by Sextus, son of King Tarquin the Proud, provoked expulsion of the Tarquins.

Lucretius (lōō-krē′-shi-us). (Titus Lucretius Carus) (*c.* 98–55 B.C.), Rom. poet-philosopher, 1896.

Lucrezia Borgia. *See* **Borgia, Lucrezia.**

Lucullus (lōō-kul′-us), **Lucius Licinius** (*c.* 110–57 B.C.). Immensely wealthy Rom. noble, conqueror of Mithridates ; "Lucullan luxury" has become proverbial.

Lucy, St. (It. **Santa Lucia**) (*c.* 283–304), noblewoman of Syracuse, Sicily ; two attempts at torturing her having failed, she was finally killed by sword ; festival December 13.

Lucy, Sir Henry William (1845–1924). Eng. journalist and author ; for many years contributed humorous accounts of Parl. proceedings to Punch as Toby, M.P.

Lucy, Sir Thomas (1532–1600). Eng. squire, justice of peace, said to have prosecuted Shakespeare ; 2932, *2933.*

Lud. Legendary king of Brit., after whom Ludgate Hill, etc., in London, are named, 2009.

Ludgate Circus, London ; traffic control at, 2787.

Lud′dites. Bands of workmen organized in Eng. to smash machinery, 1812–18, in protest against displacement of hand labour.

Lu′dendorff, Erich von (1865–1937). Ger. general ; in 1st World War he took Liége (1914), was Hindenburg's chief of staff at Tannenberg, and when Hindenburg took supreme command because first quartermaster-general ; he was largely responsible for the strategy and tactics of Germany's forces from 1916 and disagreed with the surrender of Nov. 1918 ; after the war he joined the Nazis and violently denounced Christianity.

Lud′low. Old tn. in S. Shropshire ; ruined castle, once stronghold against Welsh ; pop. 5,642 ; 2963.

Ludovico il Moro (Sforza) (1479–1500). Duke of Milan ; patron of Leonardo, 1926.

Ludwig I (lood′-vig) (1786–1868). King of Bavaria, munificent patron of art ; forced to abdicate by revolution in 1848 ; beautifies Munich, 2256.

Ludwig II (1845–86). King of Bavaria, grandson of Ludwig I ; patron of Richard Wagner, became insane and committed suicide.

Ludwig III (1845–1921). King of Bavaria ; crowned in 1913, abdicated in 1918.

Ludwig, Emil (1881–1948). Ger.-Swiss writer ; famous for his biographies of the great ; 1457.

Ludwig, Otto (1813–65). Ger. dramatist and novelist ; chief works, "Der Erbforster" ("The Hereditary Forester"), "Zwischen Himmel und Erde" ("Between Heaven and Earth").

Ludwigshafen (lood′-vigs-hah-fen). City of Bavaria, on Rhine opposite Mannheim ; chemical and other mfrs. ; large trade in coal, timber, iron ; pop. (1939) 143,400 ; almost destroyed by bombing in 2nd World War ; taken by U.S. troops, Mar. 1945.

Luftwaffe (looft′-vaf-e). Ger. air force (Ger. "air weapon"), 91 ; in b. of Britain, 575.

Lugano (lōō-gah′-nō), **Lake.** Deep, narrow l. enclosed by mts., partly in Switzerland, partly in N. It. between L. Maggiore and L. Como ; 20 m. long ; 3140.

Lugard of Abinger, Frederick John Dealtry, 1st Baron, Lord (1858–1945). Brit. administrator, soldier, and traveller ; served with distinction in Afghanistan, the Sudan, and Burma ; Governor of Northern and Southern Nigeria (1912–13) and Nigeria (after union) (1914–19).

Luini (loo-ē′-nē), **Bernardino** (*c.* 1470–*c.* 1535). Italian artist ; most noted as a fresco painter ; excelled at depicting sacred and mythological subjects.

Luke, St. Traditional author of the Third Gospel and of the Acts, 189.

Luke, Gospel of St. Third Gospel and 3rd book of New Testament, attributed to Luke.

Lu′kin, Lionel (1742–1834). Eng. coach-builder ; invented the first lifeboat in 1785 ; 1935.

Luktchun. A depressed basin in N.W. China, nearly 400 ft. below sea-level.

Lule (loo′-lä) or **Lulea,** a r. in N. Sweden ; 200 m. to Gulf of Bothnia ; *map, 2395.*

Lulea (loo′-lä-a), Sweden. Spt. on Gulf of Bothnia ; pop. 16,500 ; shipbuilding ; lumber and iron ; ice-bound in winter, 3129.

Lulli (lool′-lē), **Giovanni Battista** (French, **Jean Baptiste Lully**) (1632–87), celebrated composer, born Italy, called "father of French opera" ; taken to Paris as boy, worked as servant, rose to position of court musician to Louis XIV ; introduced lively ballets ; dominated French opera for almost a century, 2264, 2435.

Lullingstone Castle, Kent, Eng. ; silkworm farm at, *2971.*

Lully, Raymond (Raimon Lull, or Raymundus Lullius) (1235–1315), Catalan (Spain) scientist and missionary ; authority on Arabic ; founder of western orientalism ; alchemist.

Lumbering, 2035, *2337* ; *map, 677,* 676. *See* **Forestry** ; **Trees** ; **Woods** ; *also* names of countries and trees.

Lu′men. Unit of light power ; it is the power, measured at source, which is emitted by one international candle ; 621 lumens equal 1 watt ; 692.

Lumière (lūm′-yär), **Auguste Marie Louis Nicolas** (b. 1862), French chemist and industrialist ; brother of Louis-Jean ; joint inventor of the cinématographe (primitive moving picture machine), and system of colour photography ; researches on vitamins.

Lumière, Louis Jean (1864–1948). French chemist and industrialist ; in 1895 with his brother constructed the cinématographe.

Lump-sucker. A clumsily built fish (*Cyclopterus lumpus*), common in northern seas ; heavy body marked with tubercles and ridges, and on chest a sticky disk enabling it to fasten itself to rocks ; usually about 12 in. long ; *1303.*

Lu′na. In Rom. myth., the goddess of the moon and of months.

Lunacharsky (loo-nah-chahr′-ski), **Anatoly Vasilievich** (1875–1934). Russian politician ; of wealthy parents, became revolutionary in 1892 ; as people's commissar for education in Soviet government prevented destruction of books and works of art after Bolshevik revolution ; promoted instruction of people and development of the theatre.

Lunar caustic. Silver nitrate, 2974.

Lunardi, Vincenzo (1759–1806). It. aeronaut; made first hydrogen balloon ascent in Eng. (1784), *348*.

Lunar month, 2223.

Lundy. Isl. of Devonshire, off Barnstaple Bay, 1000.

Lune. R. flowing through Westmorland, Yorkshire, and Lancashire to the Irish Sea; 45 m. long.

Lüneberg (lū′-ne-boorg). Dist. of E. Hanover, Prussia; contains Lüneburger Heide (Lüneburg Heath), about 55 m. long; scene of the surrender of Ger. forces in N.W. Germany in 2nd World War, *3424*.

Lüneburg, Ger. Tn. of Hanover 22 m. S.E. of Hamburg; pop. 29,000; was prominent member of Hanseatic League; cement works, salt spring.

Lunenburg, Nova Scotia, *2400*.

Lunette, in architecture, anything shaped like a half-moon, generally used in fortifications.

Lunéville (lūn-ā-vēl). Tn. of N.E. Fr. 18 m. S.E. of Nancy; pop. 20,300; important cavalry school; treaty between Fr. and Austria (1801).

Lung-fish or mud-fish, any one of a number of primitive, strange fishes in which the gills are supplemented by organs similar in function to lungs, 2038, 1296.

Lungs. Organs for breathing air, 2039, 2768; in lung-fish, 1296; modified type in land crabs, 924; spider, *plate f. 3065*.

Lungwort. *Pulmonaria* of the order *Boraginaceae* with hairy white spotted leaves and blue cowslip-like flowers; grown in gardens, but very rare in wild state in Brit.

Lunn, Sir Henry Simpson (1859–1939). Eng. travel organizer; went to India as a Wesleyan medical missionary, and later pioneered Continental touring; his son Arnold (b. 1888) popularized ski-ing for English people, and became known as a controversial writer on religious and other subjects.

Lunt, Alfred (b. 1893). Amer. actor; famous on stage both in U.S.A. and Europe with his wife, Lynne Fontanne ("Reunion in Vienna"; "Idiot's Delight").

Lupercalia. Rom. spring festival in honour of anc. god Lupercus; and St. Valentine's Day, 2864.

Lupin. Garden flower of the bean family, with white, yellow, pink, or blue flowers on a central spike.

Lurçat, Jean. Surrealist painter, 3122.

Lurs. Nomadic people of Persia, probably of Aryan origin.

"Lusiad." Epic written by Camoens, 2659.

Lusitania (lū-si-tā′-ni-a). Anc. Rom. prov. comprising most of modern Port. and S.W. Sp.

Lusitania. Brit. ocean liner, torpedoed and sunk by German submarine, U20, May 7, 1915; 3412.

Lute. Anc. pear-shaped stringed instrument of Arabian origin, *2264*.

Lutecium (Lu). Extremely rare element of Rare-Earth group; atomic weight, 174·99. *See* **Rare-Earths.**

Lutetia (lū-tē′-shi-a). Anc. name of Paris, Fr., 2518.

Luther, Martin (1483–1546). Leader of Prot. Reformation, 2040, 2758, 2759, 1456; Charles V opposes, 755, 2040; Henry VIII opposes, 1612; hymns, 1678; translation of Bible, 1456; and Zwingli, 3448.

Lutheranism. Early spread of, 2759; in Scandinavian countries, 2394, 3131.

Lutine Bell. H.M.S. La Lutine was a French man-of-war. Captured, she became a frigate in the Brit. Navy. On Oct. 9, 1799, she foundered off the Vlieland Is. on the Dutch coast. Her bell, which was later recovered, now hangs in Lloyd's, and is rung whenever a ship is posted as missing, and on other important occasions, *1977*.

Luton. Tn. in Bedfordshire, 9 m. S.W. of Hitchin; formerly important centre of straw-plait industry; engineering and motor works; hats, 1584; pop. (est.) 108,000.

Lutterworth. Tn. in Leicestershire, 90 m. N.W. of London; John Wycliffe was rector here; pop. 3,000; 1919.

Luttrell Psalter, *2091*, 2092; cooking scene from, *900*.

Lutyens, Sir Edwin Landseer (1869–1944). Eng. architect, 2041; Cenotaph, *239*; New Delhi, *987*; R.C. Cath., Liverpool, 1968.

Lützen (let′-sen). Ger., tn. in Saxony; battle of (1632), 1559.

Lux. Unit of illumination, being the illumination produced by one international candle measured at a distance of one metre, 692.

Luxembourg Palace, Paris, 2517; gallery decorated by Rubens, 2838.

Lux′emburg, Rosa (1870–1919). Ger. (Jewish) socialist agitator, cripple, but a fiery orator; nicknamed "Red Rosa"; killed in Berlin riots.

Luxemburg or **Luxembourg.** Grand duchy of N.W. Europe; 999 sq. m.; pop. 281,570; 2041, *2042*; occupied by Germany, 1940–44, 3416; joined Benelux union in 1946, 2042.

Luxemburg. Cap. of grand duchy of that name; pop. 58,000, 2041.

Lux′or. Vil. in Upper Egypt on part of site of anc. Thebes, near Karnak; temple of Karnak, 1112; Tutankhamen's tomb, 1118, *1120*.

Luzon. Largest of Philippine Isl.; Manila cap. of isl., 2568; Japan occupied during 1942–45.

Lwow. Former Polish town, incorporated U.S.S.R. 1945 (formerly Lemberg); pop. 317,000; held by Russians (1914–15); in 2nd World War, 3419.

Lyautey (lē-ō-tā), **Louis H.** (1854–1934). Fr. soldier and administrator; served in Algeria, Tongking, Madagascar; Resident commissary-gen. Morocco 1912–16, 1917–25; marshal in 1921.

Lycabettus. Mt., near Athens, *plate f. 212, 284, 285*.

Lyceum. Aristotle's school, 231, 1540.

Lycia. Anc. division of S.W. Asia Minor on Mediterranean; conquered by Persia 6th cent. B.C., then subject in turn to Macedon, Egypt, Syria, and Rome.

"Lycidas." Poem by Milton in commemoration of the death of his friend, Edward King, drowned at sea, 2176.

Lycurgus (9th cent. B.C.). Lawgiver of anc. Sparta, 2042, 1522, 3053.

Lyd′da. Anc. city of Palestine, 10 m. S.E. of Joppa; modern vil. called Ludd; St. George said to have been born and buried here.

Lyd′deker, Richard (1849–1915). Eng. scientist; wrote extensively on natural history ("Phases of Animal Life"; "The Horse and His Relations").

Lyd′dite. An explosive derived from picric acid, 1250.

Lyd′ia. Anc. kingdom in Asia Minor; early seat of Asiatic civilization with important influence on Greeks; later part of Rom. prov. of Asia; under Croesus, 932; earliest known coins, 2201.

Lydia Languish. In Sheridan's comedy "The Rivals," a sentimental romantic heiress.

Lye (lī). Watery solution of an alkali; particularly potassium hydroxide; leached from ashes, 2664.

Ly′ell, Sir Charles (1797–1875). Brit. geologist; his studies and evidence established Hutton's "uniformitarian" theory of earth's evolution as foundation of modern geology; proof of inorganic evolution led, in hands of Darwin and others, to idea of organic evolution; Darwin's debt to, 977.

Lyly (lil′-i) or **Lilly, John** (c. 1554–1606). Eng. romancer and dramatist who introduced into Eng. literature the fantastic style of writing called "euphuism," 2401.

Lyme grass. A coarse grass which grows in poor soil in cold and temperate climates; called also wild rye.

Lyme Regis. Tn. of Dorset, on Lyme Bay; holiday resort; pop. 2,620; Mary Anning and, 164.

Lymph (limf). Body fluid resembling blood save in lack of red corpuscles; fills lymphatic system, 475; in bones, 474.

Lymphat′ic glands. Small glands scattered throughout lymphatic system, but especially in the neck, armpits, groin, thighs, and body organs; produce corpuscular elements of lymph, including white corpuscles, 474.

Lymphatic system. A double network of vessels and glands containing lymph, and permeating nearly all structures of body; superficial network underlies skin, deep network permeates organs; conveys back to blood lymph which has exuded from blood-vessels into tissues; portion called lacteals conveys chyle from intestines.

Lynch, Charles (1736–96). Amer. politician and soldier; gave name to "lynching."

Lynching. Summary punishment of suspected criminals by private individuals and without a regular trial; originated in U.S.A. during the War of Amer. Independence; victims usually Negroes accused of attacks on white women.

Lynx (links). A large cat-like animal with short tail and tufted ears, 2043; fur, 1412.

Lyons, Sir Joseph (c. 1847–1917). British caterer. Inaugurated in 1894 the firm of J. Lyons & Co., which now has teashops in almost every town in the United Kingdom.

Lyons, Joseph Aloysius (1879–1939). Australian statesman; Prime Minister in 1932–39.

Lyons or **Lyon.** 3rd city of Fr.; at junc. of Rhône and Saône; pop. 460,760; in Ger. occpn. 1940–44, 2043.

Ly′ra or **Lyre.** Constellation across North Pole from Little Bear.

Lyre (līr). Harp-like instrument of Greeks; legendary invention by Hermes, 1619.

Lyre-bird, 2043, *2044*, 309.

"Lyrical Ballads" (1798). Volume of poems by Wordsworth and Coleridge, 3408.

Lyr′ic poetry, 2637.

Lys (lēs) River. Rises in extreme N. of Fr. and flows N.E. 120 m. past Armentières and Courtrai to the Schelde in Belgium; commerce in Middle Ages, 403; *map, 404*; axis of 2nd Ger. offensive (Apr. 1918) in 1st World War.

Lysander (lī-san′-der) (d. 395 B.C.). Able unscrupulous Spartan admiral; defeated Athens at Aegospotami and terminated Peloponnesian War, becoming most powerful man in Greece; killed at outbreak of Boeotian War before he could make himself supreme.

Lys′ias (c. 459–378 B.C.), one of great Attic orators.

Lysicrates (lī-sik′-rat-ēz). Monument of, *1529*.

Lysippus (lī-sip′-us) (4th cent. B.C.), Gk. sculptor, 1537.

Lyte, Henry Francis (1793–1847). Eng. divine; wrote "Abide with Me," and other hymns and songs; 1678.

Lyttelton, Alfred (1857–1913). Brit. politician, youngest son of 4th Lord Lyttelton; Colonial Sec. 1903–05; one of a famous sporting family, played cricket and football for Eng.

Lyttelton, Oliver (b. 1893). Brit. politician; controller non-ferrous metals Min. of Supply, 1939–40; 1940–41 pres. of Bd. of Trade; Min. of Production 1942–45.

Lyt′ton, Edward Bulwer-Lytton, Baron (1803–73). Eng. novelist, playwright and politician; 2044.

Lytton, Edward Robert Bulwer-Lytton, 1st Earl of (1831–91). Eng. statesman and poet, son of the preceding; Viceroy of India (1876–80); better known under pen-name of "Owen Meredith" ("Lucile"), 2044.

Lytton, Sir Henry (1867–1936). Eng. actor (leading comic roles in Gilbert and Sullivan operas); knighted in 1930.

Lytton, Victor Alexander George Robert Lytton, 2nd Earl (1876–1947). Eng. statesman, Governor of Bengal 1922–27; Chairman of Manchurian Commission in 1932, 2044.

SIX thousand years ago our letter M was an owl, and to this day the owl's "horns" remain in those two peaks—and the beak between them, where it is in the real owl. It must have taken considerable time to draw the owl as it appeared in Egyptian picture writing and so a very much simplified form was developed by the Egyptian scribes who wrote on papyrus. The early Phoenicians, carving on stone, naturally gave the letter a more angular character. It is easy to see how this developed into the symmetrical Greek and Roman M which we use. In sound *m* is called a labial nasal. It is made by sending the breath through the nose while the lips are closed and the vocal chords are vibrating. Its pronunciation has changed but little since ancient times. Like *l*, *n*, and *r*, it may stand alone as a syllable without the aid of a vowel, as in the end of the word chasm, where no vowel sound is heard.

Maas. *See* **Mouse.**

Maastricht. *See* **Maestricht.**

Mab. "Queen Mab" in Celtic and Eng. folk-lore, a fairy presiding over dreams ; mentioned in Shakespeare's "Romeo and Juliet," I, iv ; originally a legendary queen Maev of Connaught.

Mabinogion (mab-i-nō'-gi-on). A collection of anc. Welsh bardic tales, particularly the collection of 12th-cent. knightly romances translated by Lady Charlotte Guest, 3336.

Mabuse (ma-bōōz'), **Jan.** Name adopted by the Flemish painter Jenni Gossaert (d. 1532), first of the "Italianized" Flemings, 2324.

McAdam or **MacAdam, John Loudon** (1756–1836). Scottish engineer and inventor, 2045, 3783.

Macadamized roads, 3783.

MacAlpine, Kenneth, King of the Scots, 2892. *See* **Kenneth I, MacAlpine.**

Macao (ma-kah'-o), China. Port. settlement and spt. on w. shore of Canton r. 40 m. w. of Hong Kong ; pop. of colony 374,700 ; Camoens here finished the "Lusiad."

Macaque (ma-kak'). Pig-tailed monkey, 2209.

Macaroni. It. wheat paste, made into long tubes, 2045, 1769.

MacArthur, Gen. Douglas (b. 1880). C.-in-C. Allied Forces, s.w. Pacific 1942–45 ; supreme Allied Comdr. Pacific, Aug. 1945, and of Allied forces occupying Japan, 2045, 2474. Supreme Commander of United Nations forces in Korea in 1950.

Macassar (ma-kas'-ar). Spt. and cap. of Celebes, Indonesia, on w. coast of s. peninsula of isl. ; pop. 86,662 ; 738 ; in Japanese occupation 1942–45 ; source of Macassar oil.

Macassar, Strait of. A channel separating isls. of Borneo and Celebes, uniting Java Sea and Celebes Sea, and marking a celebrated biological division. *See* **Wallace's Line.**

Macaulay, Rose. English writer. Works include : "Dangerous Ages"; "Told by an Idiot" ; "Crewe Train" ; "Personal Pleasures" ; "Fabled Shore."

Macaulay, Thomas Babington, Baron (1800–59). Eng. essayist and historian, 2046 ; story of Horatius, 3207.

Macaw, S. Amer. parrot, 2047, *plates f. 2048, 2049,* 2525.

Macbeth (d. 1057). King of Scot., hero of Shakespeare's tragedy ; 2047 ; 2934, 2936 ; quotations from play, 2047 ; Ellen Terry as Lady Macbeth, 2874.

MacBride, Sean (b. 1904). Irish politician ; patriot ; led I.R.A. brigade as a youth ; founded Clann na Poblachta party which in 1948 won 10 seats ; min. for external affairs under Costello.

Maccabees (mak'-a-bēz). Distinguished Jewish family, dominant in Jerusalem in 2nd cent. B.C., descendants of the brave priest Mattathias ; chief member Judas (d. 160 B.C.) ; story in apocryphal Books of Maccabees ; 1830.

MacCarthy, Desmond (b. 1877). Brit. author and literary critic ; contrib. to New Statesman, Sunday Times ; "Portraits," "Experience."

McCarthy, Justin (1830–1912). Irish historian, journalist, and Nationalist leader, in succession to Parnell ("History of Our Own Times" ; "Modern England ").

Macclesfield. Tn. in Cheshire, 12 m. s.e. of Stockport ; noted for silk mfrs. ; has also textile and brewing industries ; pop. 34,902.

McClintock, Sir Francis Leopold (1819–1907). Brit. admiral and Arctic explorer who made 4 expeditions in search of Sir John Franklin's expedition ; McClintock Channel is named after him.

McClure, Sir Robert John LeMesurier (1807–73). Brit. admiral and Arctic explorer, born in Ireland ; discoverer of North-West Passage, 2644.

McCormack, John (1885–1945). Irish tenor, made first London appearance at Covent Garden, and later became a citizen of the United States ; he was made a Count by the Pope in 1928.

McCormick, Arthur David (1860–1943). Irish artist and traveller ; 466.

McCormick, Cyrus. Invented the reaping machine, 79.

McCudden, James Byford (1895–1918). Brit. air pilot ; killed in action after accounting for 54 enemy aircraft and having been awarded the V.C.

McCulloch, Derek I. B., "Uncle Mac" (b. 1897). Brit. broadcaster and writer ; director of Children's Hour programme ; "Cornish Adventure."

Macdonald, Flora (1722–90). Scot. Jacobite heroine, 2047 ; and the Young Pretender, 2682.

Macdonald, George (1824–1905). Scot. poet, preacher, novelist, who depicted Scottish life and manners in a most faithful and realistic manner ("David Elginbrod" ; "Robert Falconer" ; etc.), and writer for children ("At the Back of the North Wind" ; and other fairy tales).

Macdonald, Jacques Étienne Joseph Alexandre (1765–1840). Marshal of France and Duke of Taranto ; broke Austrian centre and won victory of Wagram ; created marshal by Napoleon on that battlefield.

MacDonald, James Ramsay (1866–1937). Brit. statesman ; first Labour Prime Minister of Gt. Brit. ; 2048, 3281.

Macdonald, Sir John Alexander (1815–91). Canadian statesman, first Premier of the Dominion, 2048.

MacDonald, Malcolm (b. 1901). Brit. politician ; Secretary for Colonies (June-Nov., 1935) ; Dominion Sec. (1935–1938) ; Colonial Sec. again from 1938 ; High Commissioner for Canada (1941) ; Gov.-Gen. Malaya and spec. commr. S.E. Asia (1948) ; son of James Ramsay MacDonald.

Macdonnell, Archibald Gordon (1893–1941). Brit. author ("England Their England" ; "How Like an Angel" ; "Napoleon and his Marshals ").

M'Dougall, William (1871–1938). Brit. psychologist. Founder and leading exponent of "Normic" school of psychology, but worked principally in U.S.A. Works include "The Group Mind" ; "Outline of Psychology" ; "Psycho-Analysis and Social Psychology."

MacDowell, Edward Alexander (1861–1908). Amer. musician ; called greatest and most original of Amer. composers and "Wordsworth of music."

Mace. Spice obtained from nutmeg fruit, 2407.

Mace, in Parliament, 2524.

Macedonia (mas-e-dō'-ni-a). A region of S.E. Europe, once seat of empire under Alexander the Great ; most of it ceded to Greece by Turkey in 1913 ; modern Gk. Macedonia has a. of 13,000 sq. m. and pop. of 1,411,000 ; civil war from 1946 ; 2049, *344, 345 ; map, 1518.* Chief events of history summarized *see chart* under **History** ; rise of empire, 105, 1524 ; (*see also* **Alexander the Great**) ; Romans in, 1524.

Maceio (mah-sī-'ō) or **Macayo,** Brazil. Important port on Atlantic coast, 135 m. s.w. of Pernambuco ; pop. 129,000.

McEvoy, Ambrose (1878–1927). Brit. painter, well known for his portraits, 1184.

Macgill, Patrick (b. 1890). Irish novelist and poet, much influenced by his service in the 1st World War ("Red Horizon" ; "Story of Loos" ; "Soldier Songs" ; "Children of the Dead End" ; "The Diggers" ; "Songs of a Navvy ").

McGill College and University. A leading Canadian institution, at Montreal, opened in 1829 ; 2224.

Macgillicuddy (ma-gil'-i-kud-i) **Reeks,** Eire. Group of mts. in co. Kerry, to the w. of Killarney ; three of the summits are over 3,000 ft. high ; between the Reeks and Mangerton are the Lakes of Killarney ; 1751.

McGowan, Harry Duncan McGowan, 1st Baron (b. 1874). Brit. industrialist ; chairman Imperial Chemical Industries, Ltd., etc.

MacGregor, John (1825–1892). Scot. traveller. After various early travels, he started in 1865 in his canoe, the original "Rob Roy," and explored the rivers and lakes of W. and Central Europe. Later trips included one through the Red Sea and up the Jordan. Became himself known as Rob Roy also.

MacGregor, Robert. *See* **Rob Roy,** 2791.

Mach (mahkh), **Ernst** (1838–1916). Austrian physicist and psychologist ; strongly influenced modern scientific and philosophical thought.

Mach number. In aeronautics, the ratio between the speed of an aircraft and the speed of sound, under similar atmospheric conditions ; named after Ernst Mach, 1828.

Machete (mah-chã'-tā). Cleaver-like knife used as tool and weapon in Span.-Amer. countries.

Machiavelli (ma-kē-a-vel'-lē), **Niccolo** (1469–1527). Ital. diplomat and writer ; founder of modern science of politics ; 2049, 2766.

Machicolation. In architecture, an aperture between the corbels that support a projecting parapet ; formerly much used in castellated architecture, and intended to permit the hurling of missiles on assailants.

Machine-gun, 2049, *1283.*

Machinery. Examples : aeroplanes, *33, 41 ;* autogiro, *320, 321 ;* automatic control, 321 ; automatic devices, 322 ; calculating, *656–659* ; coin-slot, *866* ; census, 742 ; conveyor, 896 ; cycles, 947, *948* ; and civilization, 1721 ; Diesel engine, 1015 ; dredgers, 1047 ; electric motor, 2239 ; escalators, 1936 ; gas engine, 1420 ; gas turbine, 1424 ; hydraulic, 1665 ; hydro-electric, 1669 ; internal combustion engine, 1735 ; lifts, 1936 ; locomotives, 1981 ; micrometers, 2161 ; motor-cars, 2241 ; motor cycles, *948* ; pneumatic appliances, 2632 ; pumps, 2702 ; sewing, 2929 ; ships, 2945 ; steam-engine, 3085, *3357* ; turbines, 3258 ; typewriters, 3271 ; windmills, 3386.

Machines in Industry : agricultural, 78 ; book-making, 513-515 ; boot and shoe-making, *593* ; bottle-making, 1472, 1474 ; breadmaking, *556*, *557* ; cable-making, *646* ; cement, *741* ; centrifugals, 744 ; cheesemaking, *765* ; coal-mining, *2182*, *2183*, 2184 ; coin-making, 2187 ; copper-reducing, *906*, *907* ; cotton mill, *919* ; flour-milling, 1320 ; gem cutting, 1427 ; gramophone records, 1496 ; harvesting, *1550* ; hay-making, *1509* ; iron and steel mfg., 1752 ; knitting, *1866*, *1867* ; lace-making, *1877*, *1880* ; leather-making, 1910 ; linotype, *1957–1958* ; in lumbering, 2035 ; match-making, *2120* ; mining, *2183* ; monotype, *2217* ; nail-making, *2271* ; paper-making, 2497 ; pencil-making, *2541*, *2542* ; pen-making, *2540* ; pin-making, 2609 ; printing, *513*, 1956, 2684 ; quarrying, 2712 ; rayon-making, *2749* ; safety by photo-electric devices, 2575 ; soap-making, *2995* ; spinning, *919*, *2971*, 3065, *3407* ; stamp-making, *3074* ; tire-making, *2835* ; type-casting, 3270 ; weaving, *919*, *3361* ; wire-making, *1481*, 3389 ; wool-carding and combing, *3406*.

Machines (physics) : friction in, *1396* ; gyroscopic, 1561 ; pendulum, 2543 ; principles studied in mechanics, 2127–2130, 1160 ; wheel, 3375.

Machines, calculating, 656–660, 712, 742 ; slide-rule, *2984*, 2985.

Machu Picchu. Inca town, *1688.*

Maciejowice (mat-sē-ä-yō-vĕt′-sä), battle of (1794), 1874.

Mac′intosh, Charles (1766–1843). Scot. chemist, inventor of waterproof fabrics (hence "macintoshes") and various new chemical processes, 2833.

Mackail′, John William (1859–1945). Eng. scholar and critic ; professor of poetry Oxford Univ. (1906–11) ; translations of Gk. and Latin literature, with criticisms ; married daughter of Burne-Jones ; received O.M. in 1935.

McKay, Gordon (1821–1903). Amer. inventor ; his boot and shoe machinery revolutionized industry.

McKell, W. J. (b. 1891). Governor-General of Australia, 1947.

McKen′na, Reginald (1863–1943). Brit. statesman and financier, Liberal member House of Commons (1895–1918) ; First Lord of Admiralty (1908–11) ; Home Secretary (1911–15) ; Chancellor of the Exchequer (1915–16).

Mack′ensen, August von (1849–1945). Ger. general, associate of Ludendorff and Hindenburg in 1st World War ; commanded decisive offensives against Serbia, Rumania, and Russia. His son, **Everhard von Mackensen** (b. 1889), held commands in 2nd World War ; captured in It. in 1946, a Brit. tribunal sentenced him to death for complicity in murder of 335 It. civilians in Ardeatine caves ; sentence commuted to life imprisonment.

Macken′zie, Sir Alexander (1755–1820). Scottish explorer ; employee North-West Fur Co. ; discovered Mackenzie r., and was first white man to reach Pacific overland ; 682, 684. 2050.

Mackenzie, Alexander (1822–92). Canadian Liberal statesman, b. Scot. ; Premier (1873–78) ; administration

introduced vote by ballot, created supreme court of Canada and organized territorial govt. of North-West Territories.

Mackenzie, Compton (b. 1883). Eng. novelist and playwright, son of Edward Compton, the celebrated actor (" Sinister Street " ; " Sylvia Scarlett " ; " Poor Relations " ; " Carnival " ; " Gallipoli Memories"; " Greek Memories ").

Mackenzie, district of, Canada. Named after Alexander Mackenzie ; it was merged in the North-West Territories in 1911.

Mackenzie River, 2050 ; water route, 677.

Mack′erel. A N. Atlantic food fish, 2050, 1296.

Mackerel family, the *Scombridae,* a large and important family of spiny-finned fish with spindle-shaped bodies, 2050 ; tunny, 3258.

McKinley, William (1843–1901). 25th pres. of the U.S.A. ; assassinated, 2825, 3291 ; and Theodore Roosevelt, 2825.

McKinley, Mt., Alaska (20,464 ft.), 97, *2380.*

Mackintosh, Charles Rennie (1869–1928). Brit. architect ; inventor of " functionalist " architecture, a notable example of his work being the Glasgow Art School.

Mackintosh, Sir James (1765–1832). Eng. philosopher, lecturer, and lawyer.

MacLar′en, Ian. Pen-name of Rev. John Watson (1850–1907), Scottish clergyman and author, whose stories of Scottish life were widely read (" Beside the Bonny Brier Bush," one of earliest of " kailyard school " novels).

McLaurin, Dr. Charles. Australian writer, 316.

Maclean′, Kaid Sir Harry (1848–1920). Brit. soldier ; entered service of Sultan of Morocco ; captured by brigand Raisuli and ransomed for £20,000.

MacLeish, Archibald (b. 1892). Amer. poet ; " Conquistador " ; radio verse dramas, " The Fall of the City," " Air Raid."

Maclise (ma-klēs′), **Daniel** (1806–70). Brit. painter of portraits and historical compositions ; R.A. in 1840 ; " Coleridge," *869* ; " Harrison Ainsworth," 87 ; play scene in Hamlet, *1570* ; " William Cobbett," *858.*

MacMahon, Marie Edmé Patrice Maurice de (1808–93). Duke of Magenta and marshal of Fr. ; crushingly defeated at Sedan (1870) ; as 2nd pres. of republic (1873–9) pursued reactionary policy not sustained by people.

MacMillan, Harold (b. 1894). Brit. politician ; min. resident at Allied h.q. N.W. Africa 1942–45 ; Dec. 1944 went to Athens in vain effort to make peace between E.A.M. and Gk. govt.

Macmillan, Hugh Pattison Macmillan, Baron (b. 1873). Brit. lawyer ; chairman of series of Royal Commissions, including those on lunacy, coal-mining, finance and industry.

McMillan, Margaret (d. 1931). Brit. educationist ; successfully fought for medical inspection in schools ; founded Deptford health school clinic and Rachel McMillan Coll. for Infants' teachers.

Macnaught′an, Sarah (d. 1916). Brit. novelist ; Red Cross nurse, 1914–15 (" A Lame Dog's Diary ").

McNaughton, Gen. Andrew G. L. (b. 1887). Can. soldier ; in 1st Great War ; reorganized army on return ; led 1st. Can. div. to Gt. Brit. in Dec. 1939 ; commanded 1st Can. Army 1942 but resigned 1943 through ill health ; in 1944 min. of Nat. Defence, and Can. representative on U.N. Atomic Energy Commission.

MacNeice, Louis (b. 1907). Brit. poet ; from 1941 a writer of feature programmes for the B.B.C. : " Christopher Columbus " ; " The Dark Tower " ; with W. H. Auden, " Letters from Iceland."

McNeil, Hector (b. 1910). Under Sec. Foreign Office, 1945–46 ; Minister of State, 1946.

McNeile, H. Cyril. *See* " **Sapper.**"

Macpherson, James (1736–96). Scot. author, professed " translator " (now generally believed author) of the poems of Ossian, 1213.

Macrame (ma-krah′-mä) **lace.** A delicate lace trimming of knotted thread; Genoese macrame, used for trimming wedding trousseaux ; popular in Gt. Brit. as industry towards end of 19th cent.

Macready (ma-krē′-di), **William Charles** (1793–1873). Celebrated Eng. tragic actor, first appeared at Birmingham in 1810, playing Romeo ; acted with Mrs. Siddons, and made first appearance in London at Covent Garden in 1816 ; achieved great success as Richard III, Hamlet, and Coriolanus ; was leading actor at Drury Lane theatre from 1823 to 1836.

Macrocarpa. Type of cypress, *952.*

Macropod′idae. The kangaroo family of animals, 1846.

Mactan (mak-tan′). Small isl. of the Philippines, off E. coast of Cebu ; Magellan killed at, 2056.

MacWhirter (mak-wer′-ter), **John** (1839–1911). Scot. painter, noted for Highland landscapes ; became R.A. in 1893 (" The Lord of the Glen " ; " Loch Katrine ").

Madagas′car. Fr. isl. in Indian Ocean, off E. Africa ; 241,000 sq. m. ; pop. 4,000,000 ; **2051,** 72 ; occupied by Britain, 1942 ; serious native revolt March to July 1947.

" **Madame Butterfly.**" Opera by Puccini, 2439.

Madariaga, Salvador de (b. 1886). Sp. diplomat and scholar ; prof. of Sp. studies, Oxford, 1928–31 ; ambass. to U.S.A. in 1931, to France 1932–34 ; books " Shelley and Calderon," " Christopher Columbus," " Victors, Beware."

Madder family of herbs ; red dye from (now superseded by alizarin), 1059.

Madeira (ma-dēr′-a). Isl. group off coast of Africa ; 314 sq. m. ; pop. 250,000 ; **2051** ; Portugal colonizes, 1613.

Madeira River. Largest trib. of Amazon ; flows N.E. 900 m. from frontier of Bolivia through W. Brazil ; *maps,* 551 ; *plate f.* 3024.

Madeleine (mad-lān′). Church in Paris, 2515 ; *plate f.* 2517.

" **Mad Hatter,**" in " Alice in Wonderland," 709.

Madison, James (1751–1836), 4th pres. of U.S.A. ; elected Democ. pres. in 1808 and 1812.

Madison, Wisconsin, U.S.A. State cap. and summer resort in S. centre ; 75 m. W. of Milwaukee; pop. 67,400; univ. ; mfrs. boots and shoes; trades in tobacco ; 3400.

Madison River, one of headstreams of the Missouri, 230 m. long. ; rises in Rocky Mts., 2194.

Madonna, the Virgin Mary in religion and art, **2052** ; by Mestrovic, *2906* ; Raphael, *1777*, 2745 ; " Madonna of the Chair," *2053* ; " Sistine Madonna," 2052 ; Titian's " Assumption of the Madonna," **3218.**

Madonna Lily, *1948.*

Madras. State of the Republic of India, 126,166 sq. m. ; pop. 49,341,000, 2052, 1582, 1692.

Madras, India, Cap. of Madras state ; pop. 777,480 ; *2054* ; captured by Fr., 842, 2925, 3276.

Madrid′. Cap. and rly. centre of Sp. ; pop. 1,413,690 ; **2054,** 3030, *map, 3030* ; in Span. Civil War. 3039.

Madrid, University of. Largest in Sp. and one of the leading institutions of Europe ; founded in 1508, but did not become real univ. until 1836, when the U. of Alcala was moved to Madrid and combined with it ; most of the students are under the medical and law faculties, 2054.

Madrigals, part songs, 2263.

Madura (mä-dōō-ra). City in Madras India ; pop. 239,100 ; fine Hindu architecture, 1692.

Madura. Isl. in Indonesia N. of E. Java ; 2,189 sq. m. ; pop. 1,744,000 ; numerous hot springs and a mud volcano ; isl. is a plateau-like prolongation of the N. Java limestone range.

Maecenas (mē-sē'-nas), **Gaius** (c. 73–8 B.C.). Wealthy Rom. patron of Horace and Virgil, 3325 ; name proverbial as that of liberal patron of letters, 1641.

Maelstrom (māl'-strom) or **Malström.** Celebrated whirlpool or current N. of Norway, near s.w. end of Lofoten Isls., 2393.

Maes, Nicholas (1632–93). Dutch painter renowned for the delicacy of his work, 2334.

Maestricht (mahs'-trikht) or **Maastricht.** City on Meuse in Netherlands ; pop. (1939) 67,600 ; sandstone quarries ; makes beer, brandy, cigars, glass, earthonware. Heavy fighting in 1940. Liberated by U.S. Sept. 1944.

Maeterlinck (mah'-ter-lingk), **Maurice** (1862–1949). Belgian dramatist, 2055 ; the "Blue Bird," story, 3465 ; dramas, 1040 ; "Life of the Bee," 390 ; quoted, on bees, 390 , on dogs, 1025.

Mafeking (ma'-fe-king). Tn. in Cape of Good Hope prov., S. Africa ; trading centre for W. Transvaal and Bechuanaland ; Brit. under Baden-Powell besieged Oct. 12, 1899, to May 17, 1900, 337, 487 ; relief was celebrated as a great national triumph, and introduced the word "mafficking" into our language.

Mafia (mah'-fi-a). A Sicilian secret organization broken up by Mussolini.

Magallanes, formerly **Punta Arenas.** Port and coaling station of Chile, on N.W. shore of Strait of Magellan ; pop. 33,100 ; mining ; stockraising district ; exports wool, 3022.

Magazine, of rifle, 1283, 1284.

Magazines, periodicals, origin, 1213.

Magdala (mag-dah'-la). Fortified tn. in Abyssinia ; it was carried by storm by the Brit. under Sir Robert Napier (1868).

Magdalen (St. Mary Magdalen) **College** (mawd'-lin), Oxford, 2463.

Magdalene (mag-da-lā'-na). R. of Colombia, S. Amer. ; rises in Andes in s.w., flows N. 1,000 m. to Caribbean at Barranquilla ; chief route to interior, 873.

Magdalene College (mawd'-lin), Cambridge, founded in 1519, refounded in 1542.

Magdalenian Man. Prehistoric Man, 2078.

Magdeburg (mag-de-boorg). Ger. city on R. Elbe, 75 m. s.w. of Berlin ; pop. (1939) 334,300 ; sugar, textile, machinery mfrs. ; destroyed in Thirty Years' War, 1558 ; bombed, taken by U.S., Apl. 1945.

Magellan (ma-jel'-an), **Ferdinand** (Fernao de Magalhaes) (1480–1521). Port. navigator, 2056 ; discoveries, 2056, 140, 2472, 2528, 2569 ; "Victoria," 143.

Magellan, Strait of. Passage between mainland of S. Amer. and Tierra del Fuego, 3022 ; discovered by Magellan, 140, 2056.

Magenta (ma-jen'-ta). Tn. in N. It., 15 m. w. of Milan ; battle in 1859 in which French and Italians won great victory over the Austrians.

Magenta. An aniline dye of brilliant red-purple colour, discovered shortly after the battle of Magenta and named after it.

Magersfontein (ma-gerz-fon'-tīn), S. Africa. Scene, near r. Modder, Orange Free State, of defeat of Brit. force under Lord Methuen by the Boers in Dec. 1899.

Maggiore (mah-jor'-ā) **Lake.** In Switzerland and N. It., 83 sq. m. ; famous for scenery : map, 3140, 1764, 3140, 3141.

Mag'got, a fly larva, 1893.

Magi (mā'-jī). Priestly and learned caste of anc. Medes and Persians ; pay homage to Jesus, 1821.

Magic, 2056, plates f. 2056, 2057 ; African natives, 70 ; Australian

aborigines, 309 ; modern conjuring. 2059 ; among N. Amer. Indians, 2756, 2757 ; witchcraft, 3400.

"Magic Flute," Mozart opera, 2436.

Magic Lantern. See **Lantern, Magic.**

Maginot (ma'-zhē-nō) **Line.** Line of fortifications along the eastern frontier of France ; the conception of M. Maginot, Fr. War Minister, who died in 1932 ; 134, 3416, 3417.

Magistrate, one who administers the law, 2059.

Mag'na Car'ta, charter of Eng. liberties, 2059, 1489, 1490, 1563, 1609 ; John seals, 1194, 1196, 1205, 1834.

Magna Graecia. In anc. geography, name given to Gk. settlements in S. It. and Sicily.

Magne'sia (MgO) or magnesium oxide. A white powdery substance obtained by burning magnesium in air.

Magnesia, battle of (190 B.C.). Decisive victory of Romans over Antiochus the Great at anc. tn. of Magnesia, Asia Minor, 20 m. N.E. of Smyrna.

Magnesia, milk of. See **Milk** of **Magnesia.**

Magnesium (Mg). A silver-white metallic element of the alkaline earth group ; light and hard ; at. wt., 24·3 ; melts at 1202° F. ; 2060 ; in alloys, 123 ; in glass-making, 1474 ; essential to plant growth, 2998 ; properties, 776 ; and salt, 2866 ; in hard water, 3351.

Magnet, 2060. See **Magnetism.**

Magnetic compass, 881, 2061, 2291, 2293.

Magnetic deviation. Deflection of compass needle caused by near-by metal. 882. See **Magnetic variation.**

Magnetic Equator. See **Aclinic Line.**

Magnetic field. Space through which a magnet exercises magnetic influence, considered as composed of "lines of force," 2060, 2062, 2063 ; electric current induced, 1134 ; in electric motor, 2239.

Magnetic mine, 2185.

Magnetic pole. Point on a magnet where its magnetic powers are strongest, 2060.

Magnetic poles, of earth. Point near the N. and s. geographic poles towards which lines of earth's magnetism converge, 2061, 2390.

Magnetic variation. Deflection of compass needle from the north, due to difference in position of magnetic and geographic poles, 882, 2062, 2390. See **Magnetic deviation.**

Magnetism, 2060 ; attraction by electrified bodies, 2063 ; aurora borealis and earth's, 306 ; cathode rays deflected, 3430 ; in electric clocks, 1126 ; measurement of earth's, 881 ; electro-magnets, 1132, 2063 ; field magnet in dynamo, 1061 ; in motors, 1130, 2239 ; sound recording, 3013 ; in telephone receiver, 3011. See **Magnetic compass, field, poles,** etc.

Magnetite or lodestone. Iron ore with magnetic properties, 2062.

Magne'to. Small dynamo with steel field magnets, 2240 ; in internal combustion engine, 1736 ; induction coil a substitute, 1721.

Magnetom'eter. An instr. for measuring the strength, direction, dip, or all three, of the earth's magnetic field at any point.

Mag'nifying glass. Convex enlarging lens, 1925.

Magnitogorsk. Tn. of Siberia ; pop. (1939) 145,800 ; industrial city arisen since the launch of the Five-Year Plan, 2967.

Magno'lia. A flowering tree, 2064 ; distribution, 3246 ; named after Pierre Magnol, 2065.

Magnolia'ceae. The magnolia family of plants, with triple petals and sepals ; includes magnolias, 2064.

Magog. See **Gog and Magog.**

Magpie, 2065, 455.

Maguey (ma-gwā') plant. See **Agave.**

Magyar or Hungarian language, 1655.

Magyars (mag'-yahr ; Hung. mod'-yor). A Finno-Ugric race appearing in Europe in 9th cent., 2065 ; dominant race of Hungary, 1654, 1655, 1656 ; in Budapest, 600 : rev. of 1848–49, 1656, 1874.

Mahabharata (mah-hah-bah'-ra-ta). Hindu epic, a chronicle of the Delhi kings.

Mahaf'fy, Sir John Pentland (1839–1919). Irish scholar, Gk. and Rom. historian ("Social Life in Greece from Homer to Meander " ; "Silver Age of the Greek World ").

Mahan (ma-han'), **Alfred Thayer** (1840–1914). Amer. naval officer and author ("The Influence of Sea Power upon History ").

Mahdi (mah'-di). The Mahomedan Messiah ; various pretenders have claimed the title ; the Sunnites hold that the true Mahdi has not yet appeared ; name given particularly to Mahommed Ahmed (1848–85), 1102, 1487 ; revolt of, 3110, 3279.

Mahé. Fr. settlement on Malabar coast, India : 26 sq. m. pop. 14,100.

Mahler, Gustav (1860–1911). Austrian composer ; nine symphonies ; "Song of the Earth " (voices and orchestra); "Kindertotenlieder."

Mahmud I (mah-mōōd') (1696–1754). Sultan of Turkey, most of whose reign was spent in warfare with Austria and Russia ; he gained successes over the former, recovering Belgrade, but lost the Crimea to the Russians.

Mahmud II (1785–1839). Sultan of Turkey, succeeded in 1808 ; suppressed janissaries, 3262 ; forced to recognize independence of Greece.

Mahmud of Ghazni (971–1030). Afghan conqueror, sultan of Ghazni 997–1030 ; numerous invasions of India, commencing in his youth under the leadership of his father Subuktigin ; established rule over India, 1714.

Mahog'any, 2065 ; in furniture making, 1409, 1411, 1412.

Mahomedanism. Religion founded by Mahomet, 2066 ; practised by the Arabs, 195 ; in Africa, 70, 2227 ; in Asia, 268 ; Baghdad, anc. cap., 339 ; calendar, 661 ; Crusades, 936 ; in India, 1703, 1706, 1707 ; Koran, 1872 ; Mecca, holy city, 2125, 2126 ; in Persia, 2555 ; Saladin, 2864 ; Spain conquered by Moors, 2227, 3033 ; in Sumatra, 3118 : in Turkey, 3265.

Mahome't or **Mohammed** (c. 570–632). Founder of Mahomedanism, 2066 ; Koran, 1872.

Mahout'. Elephant driver, 1142.

Mahrattas (ma-rat'-az). Hindu tribes of cent. and w. India ; conquered and ruled many states, forming a powerful confederacy 17th and 18th cents. ; 1714 ; Wellington crushes, 3364.

Maia (mā'-a). In Gk. myth., mother of Hermes, 1619.

Maiden Castle. Earthworks near Dorchester ; excavations at, 207.

Maidenhead. Tn. in Berkshire, on the Thames ; favourite boating resort : pop. 25,950 ; 416.

Maidenhair fern. A fern, rarely found in Brit., with dark brown polished stem and tiny divided leaflets.

Maid of Orleans. Same as **Joan of Arc.**

Maidstone. Co. tn. of Kent : pop. 49,700 ; on r. Medway, 1851.

Maimonides (mī-mon'-i-dēz) o **Moses ben Maimon** (1135–1204). Jewish rabbi and philosopher ; one of the principal Jewish teachers, he wrote mainly in Arabic ("The Guide to the Perplexed ").

Main (mīn). R. in s. Ger. formed by Red and White Main ; has tortuous course w. for 310 m., joining Rhine opposite Mainz ; canal to Danube, 972 ; at Frankfort, 1386.

Maine. Old prov. in N.W. Fr. s. of Normandy ; chief city, Le Mans.

Maine. Northernmost of New England states, U.S.A., 33,215 sq. m. pop. 847,200 ; 2068.

Mainland or **Pomona.** Largest of the Orkney Isls., 2453.

Mainland. Largest of the Shetland Isls., 2945, map, 2890.

Mainz (mints). Commercial city and fortress in s.w. Ger. on Rhine opposite mouth of Main ; pop. 142,627 : in 18th cent. 1447, 2769 ; centre for early printing, 2684 ; heavily bombed, taken by U.S., Mar. 1945.

Maipo (mī-po) or **Maipu**. R. of Chile; rises in Andes, flows 120 m. w. to Pacific, just s. of Santiago.

Maisky, Ivan (b. 1884). Soviet Ambassador to Britain 1932–43. Ass. Comm. Foreign Affairs, 1943–46.

Maitland, Frederick William (1850–1906). Eng. jurist and historian ("History of English Law"; "Canon Law in England"); notable alike for sweetness of character, acuteness in criticism, and wisdom in counsel.

Maize, 2068; Italy, *1770*; oil from, 1263; attacked by rust fungus, *2857*; spirit from, 3067; starch from, 3082; U.S.A., 3287, 3288.

Majol'ica pottery, 2666, *2669*.

Major, in Brit. army, 245.

Majorca (ma-jor'-ka) (Span. **Mal-orca**). Largest of Balearic Isls. (Spanish); 1,330 sq. m.; pop. 272,450; cap. Palma; *342, map, 3030*.

Major-general, in Brit. Army, 245.

Majuba (ma-jōō'-ba). Hill in extreme N.w. of Natal, S. Africa, where Boers defeated British in 1881; battle, 3019, 3240, 486.

Makerere College, Kampala, Uganda, E. Africa; founded as Technical Coll.; in 1937 scheduled for development as Higher Coll. for all E. African territories; in 1948 220 students in residence; 73.

Malabar (mal'-a-bahr) **Coast**. Name often given to w. coast of India as far N. as Bombay; properly confined to s. part; scene of Mahomedan revolt in 1921–22; 1691, 1692.

Malabar Hill, Bombay, 496.

Malacca (ma-lak'-a). Brit. territory of Straits Settlements, Federation of Malaya, on w. coast between Singapore and Penang; 640 sq. m.; pop. 236,100; 2069.

Malacca, Strait of. Channel between Sumatra and w. coast of Malay Peninsula, 2069; *map, 1074–5, 2071*.

Malachi (mal'-a-kī). 39th book of Old Testament and last of minor prophets, written betw. 464 and 424 B.C.

Malachite (mal'-a-kīt). A bright green basic copper carbonate ore, commonly found massive though occasionally in stalactitic and other forms; it is found in the Ural Mts., in France and elsewhere; prized as an ornamental stone; in paints, 2478.

Maladetta or **Pic de Néthou.** One of the highest peaks in the Pyrenees (11,168 ft.), 2709.

Malaga (mal'-a-gah). Spain. Mfg. city and spt. on Mediterranean, pop. 287,080; taken from Moors by Christians in 1487; ships wine grapes, raisins, 2743, olives, etc.; in Spanish Civil War, captured by insurgents in Feb. 1937; *map, 3030*.

Malagasy (mal-a-gas'-i). Native of Madagascar, 2051.

Malan', Adolph G., "Sailor" (b. 1910). S. African airman; joined R.A.F. 1936; won D.F.C. at Dunkirk, D.S.O. in the Battle of Britain, and later bars to both; commanded Biggin Hill Fighter Stn. 1943; retired 1946.

Malan', Daniel F. (b. 1874). S. African statesman; min. of Interior in Nationalist govt. 1924; resigned 1933 to lead Nationalist Repub. party; Jan. 12, 1942, moved that Union should retire from war and leave the Commonwealth; as result of 1948 election became prime min.

Mä'lar, Lake. Sweden, extends inland from Baltic Sea at Stockholm; 450 sq. m.; of irregular shape, contains some 1,200 isls.; *3127, 3128*.

Malaria. Disease consisting usually of successive chill, fever, and "intermission" or period of normality; cause and prevention, 2036, *2037*; in Panama, 2486; mosquito, 2036.

Malaspina (ma-la-spē'-na) **Glacier.** Largest glacier in Alaska, w. of Yakutat Bay; covers 1,500 sq. m. and has front 70 m. long.

Malatya (ma-lah-tē-a), Asiatic Turkey. Important trade centre in E. Asia Minor 5 m. s.w. of anc. Malatya or Melitēnē; pop. 41,500; massacre of Armenians in 1895 by Turks.

Malay Archipelago, 738, 3117. *See also* **East Indies**; **Indonesia**.

Malayan or **honey bear**, 385.

Malay Peninsula or **Malaya**. S.W. extremity of mainland of Asia; comprising Malayan Federation and Singapore Colony (former Malay States and Straits Settlements); 51,000 sq. m.; pop. approx. 5,000,000; **2069**, 2963, *map, 2071*; life of natives, 263, 2069; tin, 3215; rice-growing, 2775; rubber, 2833; in Jap. occupn. 1941–45, 2069, 2473, 3420; formation of Federation, 2071.

Malays. Natives of Malay Peninsula and adjacent isls., 2069, *2070, 2723, 2724*, 2725; Celebes, 738; Java, 1813, 1815; Siam, 2964.

Malay tiger, 3211.

Malcolm (mal'-kom). Name of four kings of Scot.; the most noteworthy was Malcolm III (Canmore), who ruled from 1054–93; he several times invaded Eng., and was killed at Malcolm Cross, in Northumberland.

Mal'dive Islands. Group of 13 coral islets in the Indian Ocean, s.w. of India; pop. (1941) 93,000 (Mahomedan); ruled by a sultan, tributary to Ceylon govt.

Maldon (mawl'-don). Small port of Essex, on R. Blackwater, 40 m. N.E. of London; Danish victory over English in 991.

Malebranche (mal-brahnsh), **Nicolas** (1638–1715). Fr. philosopher, follower of Descartes.

Malherbe (mal-ärb) **François de** (1555–1628). Fr. poet and critic, 1380.

Malia, Cape. The s.E. extremity of Morea, the s. peninsula of Greece.

Ma'lic acid. An organic acid found in apple juice.

Malines (mah-lēn') or **Mechlin**, Belgium. Mfg. city 14 m. s. of Antwerp; pop. 61,000; ecclesiastical cap.; noble Gothic cath.; once famous for lace; largely destroyed in 1914 by Germans.

Ma'lin Head, Eire. The northernmost promontory of Ireland, 10 m. N. of Cardonagh.

Malinowski, Bronislaw (1884–1942). Polish anthropologist; famous for study of primitive peoples in Melanesia.

Mal'lard. The common wild duck, 1051, *plate f. 1053*.

Mallarmé, Stéphane (1842–98). Fr. poet; leader of the Symbolists (*q.v.* in *f.-i.*); "L'Après-midi d'un Faune," "Vers et Prose," "Divagations."

Malleabil'ity, of copper, 906; gold, 1481; silver, 2973.

Mallet, type of locomotive, 1986.

Mallophaga (ma-lof'-a-ga). Sub-order of insects including bird lice, 2513.

Mal'lory, George Leigh (1885–1924). Brit. mountaineer who, after making a record climb of 26,800 ft. up Mount Everest in 1922 was lost with Irvine during the expedition in 1924, when attempting the last few yards to the summit.

Mal'low. Commonest member of the Mallow family of plants or *Malvaceae*, 2071.

Malmaison (mal - mā' - zon) **Castle.** Château near Paris, home of Empress Josephine.

Malmberg. An iron ore mountain of Sweden within the Arctic Circle, 3129, *3130*.

Malmédy (mal-mā-dē'). Tn. and dist. in E. Belgium. 25 m. s.E. of Liége, ceded with Eupen by Ger. in 1919; *map, 404*.

Malmö (mahl'-mē). 3rd city of Sweden, spt., airport, and industrial centre on s. coast; pop. 181,000; 3128; ferry to Copenhagen.

Mal'ory, Sir Thomas (fl. 1469). Translator, compiler, and author (in part) of first notable Eng. prose romance, "Morte d'Arthur," 255, 1210, 2798.

Malpighi (mal-pē'-gē), **Marcello** (1628–94). It. physiologist, one of the first to apply the microscope to the study of animal and vegetable structure, 2163; and the first to attempt the anatomy of the brain; demonstrates blood circulation, 477.

Malplaquet (mal-plah'-kā). Fr. vil. near Belgian frontier, scene of Fr. defeat by Marlborough in 1709; 2106.

Malraux (mal-rō), **André** (b. 1895). Fr. writer; fought on Repub. side in Sp. Civil War, and in Fr. army in 2nd World War; min. of information in de Gaulle govt. 1945–46; novels include "Days of Hope," "Man's Fate."

Malt. Barley or other grain that has been artificially sprouted by moisture and heat; used in brewing, **2071**; and vinegar, 3324.

Malta (mawl'ta). Brit. Colony in Mediterranean; naval base; a. with Gozo and Comino, 122 sq. m.; pop. 241,620; **2072**; *map, 2072*; in 2nd World War, awarded George Cross, 2072, *2073*.

Malta, Knights of, 2072.

Malt'ase. Starch-digesting enzyme of saliva.

Malted milk, 2175.

Maltese, or **Blood Orange**, 2444.

Malthus, Thomas Robert (1766–1834). Eng. economist and author of "Malthusian" theory; 977, 1081.

Malthu'sianism. The theory advanced in Malthus's "Essay on Population" that population, increasing in geometrical ratio, tends, unless checked, to outrun subsistence, which increases in arithmetical ratio.

Malt'ose. A sugar, 3116.

Malva'ceae. *See* **Mallow.**

Mal'vern or **Great Malvern.** Resort in w. Eng.; pop. 22,778; on E. side of Malvern Hills, which extend N. and s. 9 m., 3407; famous public school; festival of modern drama, 1043.

Malvern Hills, Eng. Hill range extending about 9 m. between Herefordshire and Worcestershire; 1,400 ft. high; 1618, 3407.

Malwa Union or **Madhya Bharat.** Union of 20 Mahratta states, the chief being Gwalior, Indore, Dhar, Knilchipur, in Ind. repub.; cap. (summer) Gwalior, (winter) Indore; food-grains, hemp, sugar-cane; pop. 7,100,000.

Mam'elukes. Fighting slaves of Egypt who served the Sultan as mounted soldiers, and in 1240 overthrew the rule of the Caliphs and made one of their own number sultan.

Mammals, or **Mammalia.** Vertebrate animals which suckle their young, **2074**; bats, *371, 372, 373*; egg-laying types, 1053, 1095, 2074; evolutionary position, 156, 1249, 2074; evolved from reptiles, 2767; suckle their young, 2077; feet, 1342; first appearance in geological time, 1244, 1433; fossil, 1353; groups, 2077; hair a distinguishing mark, 1564; hibernation, 1622; marsupials and placentals, 1845, *1846*, 2442; migrations, 2169; rodents, 2795; whales and their relatives, 3371; young, 2074.

Mam'mon. Riches or the god of riches and cupidity; term used in the New Testament.

Mammoth. A hairy elephant-like animal, now extinct, **2077**, *735*.

Mammoth Cave. Kentucky, U.S.A., 75 m. s.w. of Louisville, *733*, 734.

Mammoth Hot Springs. Yellowstone National Park, U.S.A.; there are altogether about 70 springs.

Mammoth tree. Popular name of the *Sequoia gigantea*, 2921.

Man, 2078; *plates f. 2080, 2081, 2084, 2085*; classified in animal kingdom, 156; brain, 545, 546, 547; early home in Asia and Africa, 265, 2079; evolution theory, 182, 1067, 1154, 1244; laws of heredity, 1246, 1617; life and geographic conditions, 1430, 2597; physiology, 2598; prehistoric period, 734, 1682, 2079, *2082*; races, 2723; relation to apes, 182; skeleton, 2977; vertebrate stature, 2977. *See also* **Anthropology**; **Archaeology**; **Civilization**; **Economics**; **Physiology**; **Psychology**; **Races of Mankind**; **Sociology**, etc.

Man, Isle of. In Irish Sea; pop. 49,300; *map, f. 1164*; 221 sq. m., **2084**; parliament, 2084; people and language, 740.

Management, as a factor in production of wealth, 1081.

Managua (ma-nah'-gwa). Cap. and 2nd city of Nicaragua, Cent. Amer., 30 m. from Pacific coast; almost destroyed by earthquake in 1931; pop. 132,154; on L. Managua, 40 m. long; 2363, *2364*.

Manama. *See* **Bahrein**.

Manaos (ma-nah'-ōs). City in N.W. Brazil on Rio Negro, 10 m. from the Amazon; pop. 107,456; 554.

Manasseh (ma-nas'-e). One of Hebrew tribes descended from Manasseh, elder son of Joseph; occupied cent. Palestine E. and w. of r. Jordan.

Manatee', or sea cow. An aquatic animal, belonging to the order *Sirenia*, from 8 to 10 ft. long; has no hind limbs, but the front flipper-like limbs are used with great dexterity; found on w. coast of Africa and E. coast of Cent. and S. America; the very similar dugong is confined to Indian Ocean; this has a forked tail.

Manchester. Inland spt., city and textile mfg. centre in Lancashire; pop. 684,600; **2084**, *2085*, 1890; cotton, 1165; harbour, 1577; hat mfr., 1584; Danes expelled, *1203*; Peterloo Massacre at, *3278*; air raids 1940–41, 2085.

Manchester, New Hampshire, U.S.A.; largest city and mfg. centre in state; pop. 77,700; cotton mfrs.; 2341.

Manchester, University of. The original Owen's College was founded in 1851, and in 1880 became a constituent college of a new foundation, Victoria University, which in 1903 was re-organized; faculties include arts, commerce, law, science, music, theology, medicine; 3296.

Manchester Ship Canal, 686, *688*, 2084, 1165, 1577.

Manchu (man-chōō') **Dynasty**, 810, 807; rulers of China from 1644–1912.

Manchuria, from 1932 to 1945 **Manchukuo** or **Manchoukuo**. Part of Greater China; in 1932 it became an independent state under Japanese protection, with puppet emperor, Henry Pu yi; restored to China Aug. 1945; 503,000 sq. m.; pop. (est.) 43,233,000; **2085**, 264, 807; *map, 2086*; costume, *plates f. 808, 809*; Japanese influence, 1800, 2087; sika deer, 985; invaded by Japan, 3415; by Russia, 3424; under Communist control in 1948, 2087.

Manchurian tiger, 3211.

Manchus, a Tartaric people; 810.

Man'co (c. 1500–44). Inca leader of Peru, set up by Pizarro, 2616.

Mandalay (man'-da-lā), cap. of Upper Burma, on r. Irrawaddy; pop. 147,000; silk mfrs.; 623.

Manda'mus (Latin, " we command "). A writ issued by a superior court ordering an official, corporation, or inferior court to perform a public duty as required by law.

Mandarin duck, *plate f. 1052*.

Man'darin orange, 3444.

Mandarins, Chinese officials.

Man'datory or **mandated territories**, former Ger. colonies and parts of Turkish Emp. assigned at close of 1st World War to various powers to be held under mandates (treaties of trust) for League of Nations. These territories (total pop. 13,000,000) were assigned as follows :
To Gt. Brit.: Iraq (became independent in 1927), Palestine (mandate surrendered, 2483), Nauru Isl., parts of Togo, Cameroon, German East Africa (Tanganyika Territory).
To Union of South Africa: South-West Africa.
To France: Syria (became independent in 1943), parts of Togo and Cameroon.
To Belgium: small parts of German East Africa.
To Australia: German New Guinea and adjacent isls.
To New Zealand: German Samoa.
To Japan: All German isls. in Pacific N. of Equator (after 2nd World War admin. by U.S.A.).

To Greece: Smyrna which Turkey reconquered.

In 1946 Belgian, Australian, New Zealand, French and Brit. (African) Mandates were placed under U.N. trusteeship.

M and B. Initials of firm of manufacturing chemists, May and Baker, used as name of series of sulpha drugs, the best known being M & B 693 (sulphapyridine); 179.

Man'deville, Sir John (Jehan de Mandeville). Reputed writer of a 14th-cent. book of travels.

Man'dible, lower jaw, *3163*; of insects, *1729*, 1730.

Mandin'go. A large group of Negroes mixed with Hamites, dwelling in w. Africa from the r. Senegal to Monrovia and numbering millions.

Man'dolin, stringed musical instrument played by striking the metal strings with a piece of bone or metal called a " plectrum," a favourite in Spain and Italy, 2267.

Man'drake or **mandragora**, plant of the nightshade family found chiefly in the districts bordering the Mediterranean Sea; one of the most important plants in the folk-lore of Europe, and in the Herbals of the Middle Ages.

Man'drill, an African baboon, *2210*.

Man-eating shark, 1297, 2938.

Manet (mah-nā), **Edouard** (1832–83). Fr. painter, pioneer and most important master of impressionism (not to be confused with Claude Monet); called most original painter of later 19th cent., 1378, 2477; " Bar aux Folies-Bergère," *1687*.

Man'etho. Egypt. historian of 3rd cent. B.C.; fragments of his work survive in Josephus.

Man'gan, James Clarence (1803–49). Irish poet (" Romances and Ballads of Ireland " ; " The Nameless One," an autobiographical ballad); a morbid genius who sincerely expressed the tragedy of Irish aspirations, 1751.

Manganese (Mn) (man'-ga-nēz), a soft grey metallic element; at. wt. 54·9; melts at 2273°F.; **2087**; used in alloys, 123, *2087*, 2365; dioxide in matches, 2119; properties, 776; sources, 803, 941, 2087, 2845; " trace " metal in diet, 2149.

Man'gel or **mangel-wurzel**, root crop, 397.

Mangin (mahn-zhan), **Charles Marie Emmanuel** (1866–1925). Fr. general; in 1st World War was Corps Commander at Verdun (1916); 6th Army commander in Aisne offensive of 1917.

Man'go, fruit of the mango tree, which grows in the East Indies, **2087**.

Man'gosteen, a tropical fruit, 1401.

Mangrove, a tropical tree, **2088**, 3246; aerial roots, 2825.

Manhattan Island, in New York City, *33*, 143, 2351, *2352*, 2353, *map, 2352, 3289*.

Manil'a, cap. of Philippine Isls.; pop. 684,800; **2088**; cable, 643; in Jap. occupn., 1942–45, 2088.

Manila Bay, Philippine Isls., large inlet of China Sea in isl. of Luzon; 2088.

Manila hemp, 1609, 2497, 2569; made into rope and twine, *2826*.

Manila paper, 2497.

Manil'ius, Gaius. Rom. tribune of the people in 66 B.C., whose proposal to give Pompey supreme command and unlimited power in the war against Mithridates was supported by Cicero in the famous oration " De lege Manilia."

Man in the Iron Mask, The, 1758.

Manioc (man'-i-ok), or cassava, plant from which tapioca is obtained, 70, 3153.

Manipur. State of Ind. repub., in Assam; on Burmese border; cap. Imphal; area 8,638 sq. m.; pop. 512,069; limit of Jap. drive towards India, held at Kohima (*q.v.* in *f-i.*) and Imphal (*q.v.* in *f-i.*).

Manis'sa or **Manisa**. City in w. Asiatic Turkey; pop. 38,000; anc. Magnesia, where Rom. consul Scipio Asiaticus defeated Antiochus the Great 190 B.C.

Manitoba (man-i-tō'-ba), prairie prov. of Canada; 246,512 sq. m.; pop. 729,700; **2088**; cap. Winnipeg, 3388; colonization, 683; prairies, 676; rainfall, 2741. *See* **Canada**.

Manitoba, Lake, in s.-cent. Manitoba, Canada; length 110 m.; drains into L. Winnipeg, through Dauphin r.; 2088.

Manitou. Indian name for spirit or supernatural being, 2757.

Mann, Thomas (b. 1875), German writer who became an American citizen. Won Nobel prize for Literature in 1929. Works include " Buddenbrooks " ; " Death in Venice " ; " The Magic Mountain " ; 1457.

Mann, Tom (1856–1941). Eng. Socialist and labour leader; prominently associated with the organization of the dock labourers following the strike of 1889; took leading part in many strike movements.

Man'na. In Bible, food on which Israelites lived in wilderness; said to have rained from Heaven (Exod. xvi.), but probably the secretion of a species of tamarisk tree when attacked by a scale insect.

Manna Ash, a tree, *Fraxinus ornus*, exuding a sugary " manna," for which the tree is grown in Sicily and elsewhere.

Mannerheim, Gustavus Charles, Baron (b. 1869). Finnish F.-M. and pres.; planned Mannerheim Line of fortifications from Gulf of Finland to L. Ladoga and from Taipale to Sortavala; F.-M. in 1933, he led army against Russ. 1939–40 and in 2nd war, 1941–44; made pres. Aug. 1, 1944, and negotiated armistice with Russ. which gave Russ. the Mannerheim Line in 1944; resigned in 1946.

Mannheim, in Baden, s.w. Ger., commercial city on upper Rhine; pop. (1939) 283,800; makes machinery, etc., 2769. Heavily bombed, taken by U.S., Mar. 1945.

Manning, Henry Edward, Cardinal (1808–92). Eng. High Church leader; became Rom. Cath. (1851) and cardinal (1875); ardent supporter of doctrine of papal infallibility.

Mannock, Edward (" Mick ") (d. 1918), Brit. air pilot; perhaps the greatest of all our fighting airmen in the 1st World War; awarded V.C. posthumously after shooting down 73 enemy aircraft.

Manoel. Kings of Portugal. Manoel I, king (1495–1521); Manoel II (1889–1932), crowned in 1908, dethroned in 1910, 2660.

Manom'eter, instr. for measuring atmospheric pressure, 3301.

" Manon," opera by Massenet, 2439; by Puccini, 2439.

Man orchis (*Aceras*), 2448.

Manor house, architecture, *218*, 220.

Man-o'-war bird or frigate-bird, 1397.

Mans, Le. *See* **Le Mans**.

Mansard, in architecture, a style of roof, also called the Fr. curb, or hip-roof, to make the attics available for rooms.

Mansfield, Katherine (1890–1923), Brit. authoress b. in N. Zealand, 1216.

Mansfield. Tn. in Nottinghamshire, in important coal and iron-working dist.; mfrs. boots, hosiery; pop. 49,000; 2399.

Mansion House, London, official residence of Lord Mayor, 2010.

Manson, Sir Patrick (1844–1922). Eng. physician and writer on tropical diseases, *2133*; malaria research, 2236; mosquito research, 2236, 2486.

Manstein, Fritz Erich von, F.-M. (b. 1887). Ger. staff officer commanding troops of Crimea and Sebastopol in 1941; F.-M. in 1942 on S. Russian front; dismissed in 1944; taken prisoner by Allies in 1945; in 1949 tried by Brit. military court for crimes against humanity, and sentenced to 18 years imprisonment, later reduced to 12

Mansura (man-soo'-ra). Eg. tn. on Nile delta 70 m. N. of Cairo; pop. 69,000; cotton trade and mfrs.; battle between Crusaders under

Louis IX of Fr. and Eg. in 1250 ;
Louis imprisoned.

Mantegna (man-tä'-nya), **Andrea** (1431–
1506). It. painter (" Triumph of
Caesar " ; " Madonna della Vittoria ") ; influence on painting, 1776.

Mantilla, a Spanish shawl, *3037*.

Mantinea (man-ti-nē-a), battle of (362
B.C.), between Thebes and Sparta,
1524, 3198.

Man'tis, an orthopterous insect, **2090**.

Mantle, the shell-forming tissue of
molluscs, 2199 ; in cuttlefish, 945,
946 ; in nautilus, 2199 ; in oyster,
2466.

Mantua (man'-too-a) (It. **Mantova**).
Fortified tn. in N. It. 80 m. S.W. of
Venice ; pop. 40,000 ; home of
Virgil ; held by Fr. (1797–99,
1801–14), by Austria (1814–66) ;
in German hands 1943–45.

Man'u. The " Adam " of Hindu
myth. ; also traditional author of
anc. Hindu lawbook, 2043.

Man'ual. Organ, 2450.

Manuel. *See* **Manoel.**

Manuscripts, illuminated, 2090, 511 ;
anc. papyrus, 509 ; of Bible, 425 ;
Caedmon's, 650 ; in medieval
monasteries, 510, 1930 ; famous
collections, 584, 585, *1930* ; parchment used, 510, 2496 ; pen, 2539 ;
illustrations from, *510, 1197. See
also* **Books.**

Manutius (ma-nū'-shi-us). It. family
of printers, who flourished during
16th cent. ; their press called
Aldine, from Aldus, the founder,
2764 ; system of punctuation, 2705.

Manx. A Celtic language, 740, 1750.

Manx cat. Tailless cat of Isle of
Man, *719*.

Manzanares. R. running through
Madrid, 2054.

Manzoni (mant-sō'-nĕ), **Alessandro**
(1785–1873). It. poet and novelist
(" I Promessi Sposi," called " best
historical novel ever written "),
1787, 2403.

Maoris (mär'-iz). The aboriginal
people of New Zealand, 2358, 2360.

Mao Tse-Tung (b. 1894). Chairman o
Communist Repub. of China, 814.

Maple, 2092 ; seeds, *2917* ; tapping
for sugar. *2093* : sycamore. *3144*.

" Maple Leaf Forever, The." Canadian
song, 2092.

Maple sugar. Making of, in Canada,
2092.

Maps and map-making, 2093 ; of the
sky, 2411 ; from the air, *2095* ;
latitude and longitude, 1898 ; by
Ptolemy, 1431, *2698* ; " drawn " by
radar, *2727, 2728.*

Maquis (ma-kē). Originally extensive
thicket-covered areas resorted to by
Corsican brigands ; in 2nd World
War used of Fr. and Belg. resistance
movements against Ger. occupation ;
3422.

Marabou (mar'-a-bōō), species of stork,
3097. *See* **Adjutant.**

Maracaibo (ma-ra-kī'-bō). Chief port
of Venezuela, in N.W. on channel
between Gulf of Venezuela and L.
Maracaibo ; pop. 110,000 ; exports
coffee, cocoa, hides and skins,
cabinets and dye woods ; taken by
Morgan, 2229.

Maracaibo, Lake. In N.W. Venezuela
opening through a long neck into
Gulf of Venezuela ; S. half of lake
is fresh, but N. half, under tidal
influence, is brackish ; 3308.

Marais, Eugène (1872–1936). Afrikaans writer (" The Soul of a White
Ant "), 3022.

Maramuresh (mah-ra-moo-resh') or
Marmaros, dist. in N.W. Rumania,
formerly Hungarian co. ; 6,258 sq.
m. ; pop. 767,000.

Marañon (mah-rah-nyon') **River,** in
Peru, upper course of Amazon, 136,
2559.

Marat (mah-rah'), **Jean Paul** (1744–
93). Fr. revolutionist, 2096, *1394,*
1396 ; assassinated by Charlotte
Corday ; 1396, 971.

Mar'athon, 2097 ; battle, 2555 ;
Aristides at, 230.

Marathon race, 2432, 2843.

Marble. A rock, **2097,** 2795, 1951 ;
quarrying, 2712.

Marble Arch, London. At the north-
east corner of Hyde Park, *2014* ;
modelled on the Arch of Constantine
for George IV at a cost of £80,000,
and brought from Buckingham
Palace in 1851 ; the reliefs were
chiselled by Westmacott.

Marble galls. On oak trees, *2410.*

Marbled white, butterfly, *plate f.
632.*

Marburg (mahr'-boorg), Ger. Tn. in
former Prussian prov. of Hesse-
Nassau, famous for univ. (founded
1527, first univ. established without
papal privileges), 13th-cent. church
containing tomb of St. Elizabeth of
Hungary, and its 13th-cent. castle.
Pop. 28,000.

Marcanto'nio (c. 1488–c. 1527). Foremost It. engraver in the Renaissance,
first to copy on copper the work
of other artists (Dürer's " Little
Passion " and " Life of the Virgin " ;
countless drawings and paintings
by Raphael).

Marcel'lus, Marcus Claudius (c. 268–
208 B.C.). A Rom. general in 2nd
Punic War, conqueror of Syracuse ;
five times consul ; killed near
Venusia.

March. 3rd month of year, 2223.

March. Tn. in Cambridgeshire, 15 m.
N.W. of Ely ; mfrs. machinery ; pop.
11,000 ; 669.

Marchand, Jean Baptiste (1863–1934).
Fr. army officer, who came into
prominence in 1898 when he refused
to withdraw from Fashoda at the
request of General Kitchener, leaving
later on the order of the French
government ; served with distinction
in World War of 1914–18.

Marches, The. Territorial division on
E. coast of cent. It., formerly part
of Papal States, 1763.

Marches, Welsh. Counties in England
bordering on Wales, containing
remains of many castles built to
withstand raiders, 3334.

" March Hare." In " Alice in Wonderland," 709.

Marco'ni, Guglielmo (1874–1937). It.
inventor of wireless telegraphy,
2098, 2728, 3317, 3392.

Marco Polo. *See* **Polo, Marco.**

Marco Polo's sheep, 2940.

Marcus Antonius. *See* **Mark Antony.**

Mar'cus Aure'lius Antoni'nus (A.D. 121–
180). Rom. emperor, 2099, *2100,*
2812, 2813.

Mardi Gras (mahr'-dē-grah), or **Shrove
Tuesday.** Day of carnival with
battle of flowers and similar gaieties
in certain countries ; at New
Orleans, 2343.

Ma're claus'um. In international law,
sea or portion of sea which is under
the jurisdiction of one nation instead
of open to all.

Maree, Loch, Scot. A fresh-water
l. in Ross and Cromarty, 40 m. w.
of Dingwall ; 32 ft. above sea-level,
it is 12 m. long and more than
2 m. broad ; overhung by mountains 3,000 ft. high, *map, 2890.*

Maren'go. Vil. in N. It. 35 m. N.W.
of Genoa ; battle of (1800), 2276.

Mareth Line. Fr. system of defences
in E. of Tunisia, N. Africa ; about
20 m. long ; from coast nr. Zarat,
through Mareth tn. to Matmata
Hills ; defended by It. and Ger.
forces after fall of Fr. ; won by
Allies Mar. 28, 1943 ; 2222, 3420.

Marey, Étienne Jules (1830–1904). Fr.
physiologist ; devised photographic
methods of recording the motion of
wings of insects and birds.

Mar'garet or **Gretchen.** In Faust
legends, 1264.

Margaret (1353–1412). " Semiramis
of the North," queen (governing
as regent for nominal sovereigns) of
Denmark, Norway and Sweden ;
unites three Scandinavian countries,
992.

Margaret, St. (c. 1045–93). Queen of
Malcolm III, king of Scotland ;
daughter of the Eng. prince Edward,
son of Edmund Ironsides ; probably
b. in Hungary ; canonized in 1251
on account of her great benefactions
to the Church.

Margaret of Anjou (1430–82). Queen of Henry VI of Eng., died in exile, leads Lancastrians, 2828, 1611.

Margaret of Valois or **Angoulême** (1492–1549). Queen of Henry d'Albret, king of Navarre, and sister of Francis I of Fr., joint author of the "Heptameron," stories modelled on the "Decameron" of Boccaccio; patroness of Marot and other literary men, and protector of Protestants; sometimes called Margaret of Navarre to avoid confusion with her grandniece.

Margaret of Valois (1553–1615). Daughter of Henry II of Fr. and Catherine de' Medici, married to Henry (Bourbon) of Navarre (afterward Henry IV of Fr.) on eve of Massacre of St. Bartholomew; 1611.

Margaret, Princess (b. 1930). Younger daughter of King George VI and Queen Elizabeth, christened Margaret Rose, 2100, *3283*; portrait on stamps, 3075.

Margarine (mahr'-ga-rēn); substitute for butter, 2100, 628; hydrogenation, 1674.

Mar'gate. Popular summer resort in Kent, on North Sea, 74 m. E. of London; pop. 40,000; 1851.

Marggraf, Andreas Sigismund (1709–82), Ger. chemist; discovered (1747) sugar in beet, 3112.

Marguerite (mahr-ge-rēt'). Popular name of several familiar flowering plants, such as the China aster, ox-eye daisy, etc.

Maria II, de Gloria (1819–53). Queen of Port.; succeeded in 1826 on abdication of her father, Dom Pedro; reign troubled by rebellion of uncle, Dom Miguel, and insurrections.

Maria Theresa (ma-rē'-a te-rā'-sa) (1717–80). Empress of Austria, and queen of Hungary and Bohemia, 2101; in Seven Years' War, 2924.

Maria Theresa (1638–83), of Spain. Queen of Louis XIV.

Mariana Is. *See* Ladrone Is.

Marie (1875–1938). Queen of Ferdinand I and mother of Carol II of Rumania.

Marie Antoinette (ma-rē ahn-twah-net') (1755–93). Queen of Louis XVI, 3102, 2030; daughter of Maria Theresa, 2101; death, 1396; and French Revolution, 1395; flight to Varennes, 1395, 2030; influence on Louis XVI, 2102.

Marie Byrd Land, in Antarctic, 2647.

Marie Celeste (more correctly Mary Celeste). Amer. brigantine, the fate of whose crew remains the greatest mystery of the sea; she was found in mid-Atlantic in Nov. 1872, a month after sailing from New York; although in perfect order, and under full sail, there was not a soul on board.

Marie de' Medici (1573–1642), 2131.

Marie Galante (ga-lahnt'). Isl. of Fr. W. Indies; dependency of Guadeloupe; 60 sq. m.; pop. 14,927.

Marie José. Consort of Umberto II, Queen of Italy May–June 1946; daughter of Albert I of Belgians, 102.

Marie Louise (1791–1847). Second wife of Napoleon I, 2276; daughter of Emperor Francis I of Austria, 1838, 2276.

Marienbad (Marianske Lazne). A celebrated watering-place near w. border of Czechoslovakia; mineral springs; *map, 954.*

Marienburg. Former Ger. city in Border Prov. of Prussia on r. Nogat, and since 1945 in Masuria, Poland. Its pop. of 21,000 were expelled when Poles took over admin.; seat of Teutonic knights (1309–1457); machinery and cotton mfrs.

Mariette (ma-rē-et'), **Auguste Edouard** (1821–81). Fr. Egyptologist; author of several books about his explorations and discoveries.

Marignac (mar-ēn-yak), **Jean Charles Galissard de** (1817–94). Swiss chemist, prof. at Geneva; work on atomic weights, ozone, and rare earths; discovered ytterbium, 3437.

Marignano (ma-rē-nyah'-nō) or **Melegnana.** Tn. in N. Italy 10 m. S.E. of Milan; victory of Francis I over Swiss allies of Milan (1515), 1383.

Mar'igold. A plant of the order *Compositae*, 2102; no relation of the Marsh Marigold.

Mariiskaia. Autonomous republic of U.S.S.R. within Russia proper; fertile plain watered by the Volga; pop. 482,000.

Marina, Princess. *See* Kent, Duke of.

Marine life, 2103, 2414, 702; *plates f. 2104, 2105*; models of radiolaria, *plate f. 1473.*

Marine, mercantile. *See* Merchant Navy.

Mar'iner's compass, 881.

Marines. *See* Royal Marines.

Marini (ma-rē'-nē), **Giovanni Battista** (1569–1625). It. poet ("L'Adone"); style stilted and bombastic.

Marinus, St. Legendary founder of San Marino.

Marionettes'. *See* Puppets.

Mariotte (ma-rē-ot'), **Edmé** (c. 1620–84). Fr. physicist, independent discoverer of Mariotte's law or Boyle's law.

Maritime Museum, National. Greenwich, London, 2260.

Mar'itime Provinces, Canada, 676, 679.

Marius Gaius (c. 155–86 B.C.). Rom. general, 2809.

Marjoribanks (marshbanks). Eng. family name.

Mar'joram. A herb of the mint family, 3206, 3061.

Mark. A silver coin, the monetary unit of Germany, consisting of 100 pfennig; nominal value of the Reichsmark about 11½d.; after 1st World War greatly depreciated and in 1923 practically lost all value, many millions being obtainable for £1; later stabilized; lost value after 1945; June 1948 currency changes and cancellation of Reich debts altered value of mark; in Dec. the exchange rate of new D.M. was 12·35 to the £.

Mark, St. Traditional author of the Second Gospel, 189.

Mark An'tony (83–30 B.C.). Roman orator and statesman, 2105; and Cleopatra, 837; decrees Cicero's death, 827; and Augustus, 303.

Mar'ken. Netherlands isl. and vil. formerly in the Zuider Zee, 2320.

Market Drayton. Tn. in Shropshire, 18 m. N.E. of Shrewsbury, on r. Tern; agricultural centre; pop. 5,100; 2963.

Market Har'borough. Tn. in Leicestershire, 16 m. S.E. of Leicester; hunting centre; mfrs. boots and shoes; pop. 10,830; 1919.

Marketing Boards. Organizations in Britain set up by agricultural producers for large-scale organization; also official as Milk Mktg. Bd.

Markets. *See* Fairs, 1256.

Mark'ham, Sir Clements (1830–1916). Eng. geographer, for more than 60 years himself an active explorer and traveller, and instrumental in the exploration of uncharted areas; funds for Scott's South Polar voyage raised almost entirely by his efforts ("Franklin's Footsteps"; "Travels in Peru and India").

Markievicz (mar-ki-vich'), **Constance, Countess** (1884–1927). Irish politician, wife of a Polish count whom she married in 1900; took a prominent part in Irish industrial affairs and the rebellion in April 1916, for which she was sentenced to death, but pardoned; became first woman member of Brit. Parl. in 1918, but did not take her seat.

Marking ink, 1724, *1725.*

Marl. Soil consisting of clay and lime.

Marlborough (mawl'-bre), **John Churchill, 1st Duke of** (1650–1722). Eng. general and statesman, 2105, *2106*; at Blenheim, 470.

Marlborough, Sarah Jennings Churchill, Duchess of (1660–1744). Favourite of Queen Anne, 163, 2105.

Marlborough College, Wiltshire. Public school founded in 1843; originally for the sons of clergymen, 3383.

Marlborough Downs, Wiltshire. Hills lying in a valley of the chalk uplands on the skirts of Savernake Forest, traversed by the river Kennet; 3383.

Marlborough House. Royal residence in Pall Mall, London; built for the Duke of Marlborough in 1710 by Christopher Wren, it became the London residence of the Prince of Wales in 1863; for some years occupied by Queen Alexandra, to whom a memorial in a recess of the garden wall was unveiled in 1932; later residence of Queen Mary.

Marlowe, Christopher (1564–93). Great Eng. poet and dramatist, 2107; 1211, 1264; influence on Shakespeare, 2933.

Mar'malade. A preserve made of fruit, especially oranges, 2444.

Marmara (mahr'-ma-ra), **Sea of.** Anc. Propontis, sea between European and Asiatic Turkey, 528, 974.

"Marmion." By Scott, 2898.

Marmora. *See* Marmara.

Mar'moset. A small monkey, 2210.

Mar'mot. A burrowing rodent; fur, 1412.

Marne. R. in N.E. Fr.; scene of two battles of 1st World War, 3409, 3412, 3413; 2nd World War, 3417.

Mar'onites. Christian sect of Syria.

Marot (mah-rō), **Clement** (1496–1544). Fr. poet; introduced new grace into stiff forms of Fr. poetry; his translation of Psalms greatly advanced Reformation in France.

Marquand, H. A. (b. 1901). Parl. Sec. (Overseas) Board of Trade (1945–47); Paymaster Gen. in 1947; Became Min. of Pensions in 1950.

Marquesas (mahr-kā-sas) or **Mendaña Islands.** 11 volcanic Polynesian isls; in mid-Pacific, 4,000 m. w. of Peru; 480 sq. m.; 2471.

Marqueste (mahr-ket'), **Laurent Honoré** (1848–1920). Fr. sculptor; statue of Victor Hugo in Sorbonne.

Marquette (mahr-ket'), **Jacques** (1637–75). Fr. Jesuit missionary and explorer, 2107, 143, 2192.

Marquis or **mar'quess.** Eng. nobleman next in rank below a duke, 2536.

Marr, J. W. S. Boy Scout and Patrol Leader who accompanied Sir Ernest Shackleton on his Antarctic expedition in the Quest in 1921; book "Into the Frozen South."

Marrakesh or **Morocco City**, Moroccan city in Fr. zone; pop. 241,000; *2231.*

Marram-grass. For sand dunes, *2871.*

Marriage, 2107; by capture, 2108; polygamy, 2007, 3266; by service, 2109.

"Marriage of Figaro." Opera by Mozart, 2250, 2439.

Marriott, Sir John Arthur Ransome (1859–1945). Brit. historian; works incl. "Making of Modern Europe."

Marrow, of bones, 498; manufactures red corpuscles, 474, 2977.

Marrows, Vegetable, 2109.

Marryatt, Frederick (1792–1848). Eng. naval captain and novelist, 2109, *2110.*

Mars. In Rom. myth., god of war, father of Romulus and Remus, 2110.

Mars. A planet, 2110, 2617; *plate f. 280*; satellites, 2618.

"Marseillaise." Fr. national song, by Rouget de Lisle, *1963.*

Marseilles (mar-sālz') or **Marseille** (mahr-sā'-e), Spt. on Mediterranean, 2nd city of Fr.; pop. about 636,264, 2110, 1359; founding, 1519; Rove tunnel, *3255*; in Ger. occupn., 1942–44, 2111.

Marsh. A tract of low, wet land; dried by eucalyptus trees, 1230; peat, 2534.

Marshall, George Catlett (b. 1880). Amer. soldier and statesman; chief of Staff, U.S., 1939–45; U.S. Sec. of State, 1947–49; proposed "Marshall Plan" to aid Europe 1947, 2111; 927, 3293.

Marshall-Hall, Sir Edward (1858–1927). Eng. lawyer and politician, most famous criminal advocate of his time.

Marshall Islands. 24 Micronesian isls. in N. Pacific, E. of Caroline Isls.,

a. 160 sq. m., pop. 10,000 ; export copra ; 2470. Former mandatory of Japan; in 2nd World War, 2474, 3421 ; U.S.A. admin. under U.N. trusteeship in 1947.

Marsh gas. See **Methane.**

Marshmallow. Plant of mallow family ; sweetmeats were once made from it, and it is also used in medicine.

Marsh Marigold. Plant of crowfoot family, Caltha palustris ; conspicuous with its brilliant yellow flowers and heart-shaped, bright green leaves in wet places in spring.

Marsh Orchis, a common Brit. orchis, often found in moist meadows; large leaves, sometimes spotted, and spikes of bright purplish flowers ; several varieties.

Marsh tit, 3218.

Marston Moor. Plain in Yorkshire, Eng., 8 m. from York ; battle of (1644), 756, 933.

Marsu'pials. Mammals such as kangaroo, with pouch for young, 2111, 1845, 1846 ; Australian, 309, 313 ; in New Guinea, 2339 ; opossum, 2442 ; of Tasmania, 3157.

Marsyas (mahr'-si-as). In Gk. myth., a satyr, 187.

Martello Towers. Round towers once used in Eng. for coast defence ; some still remain on s. coast ; erected during scare of Napoleon's threatened invasion in 1804. Name derived from fort at Mortella Point, Corsica, from which they were copied.

Marten. Animals of the weasel family, 2111 ; fur, 1412 ; " black marten," 2980.

Martha. Sister of Lazarus and Mary, and friend of Jesus (Luke x. 38).

Martial (mahr'-shal). Anglicized name of Marcus Valerius Martialis (c. 43–c. 104), greatest Rom. epigrammatist, 1897.

Martial law, 1903.

Martigny (mahr-tēn'-yē). Switzerland, tn. 33 m. below E. end of L. Geneva; pop. 5,700, 2774.

Martin, popes. For list see **Pope.**

Martin, St. (316–400). Bishop of Tours, patron saint of Fr. and cities of Maine and Wurzburg ; founds monastery of Ligugé, 2212.

Martin, Gregory (d. 1582). Eng. scholar, translator of Douai version of Bible, 427.

Martin, Richard, " Humanity Dick " (1754–1834). Irish humanitarian ; sat in Irish parl., also in U.K. parl. 1801–26 where in 1822 carried first law in any country for protection of animals ; in 1824 founded R.S.P.C.A.

Martineau (mahr-tē'-nō), **Harriet** (1802–76). Eng. novelist and writer on miscellaneous subjects ; " Illustrations of Political Economy"; " Tales of the Poor Laws " ; " Society in America " ; " Letters on the Laws of Man's Social Nature."

Martineau, James (1805–1900). Prominent Eng. Unitarian minister and essay writer ; eminent philosopher ; brother of Harriet Martineau.

Martinez Sierra (mahr-tē-neth sē-ār'-a), **Gregorio** (1881–1947), Span. dramatist and novelist, collaborated with his wife, Maria de la Lejarraga (b. 1880) (" The Cradle Song " ; " The Kingdom of God "), 3051.

Martin-Harvey, Sir John (1867–1944). Eng. actor, played in company with Henry Irving and Mrs. Patrick Campbell ; his greatest success was as Sydney Carton in " The Only Way," a character he created.

Martini (mahr-tē'-nē), **Giovanni Battista** (1706–84). It. musician, famous as teacher of composition and theory.

Martinique (mahr-ti-nēk). Isl. of W. Indies ; Dept. of France ; 385 sq. m. ; pop. 247,000 ; 2112 ; volcano, Mont Pelée, 2112, plate f. 3329.

Martins. See **Swallows and Martins.**

Martyrs. Those wl. suffer death for their faith ; 2112.

Marvell, Andrew (1621–78). Eng. poet and satirist ; under Restoration attacked Charles II and advocated a republic ; remembered now for his lyrics ; quoted on death of Charles I, 756 ; and Milton. 2177.

Marx, Karl (1818–83). Ger. socialist, founder and leader of Marxian socialism, 2113 ; Socialistic theories, 881, 2996.

Marx Brothers. Amer. film actors ; originally four, later three, brothers famous for their films (" Monkey Business," " A Night at the Opera," etc.), which exhibited a curious surrealist humour.

Mary. Mother of Jesus, 1821, 1777, 1779. See **Madonna.**

Mary (1457–82). Duchess of Burgundy, restored lost rights to her Dutch subjects (thus paving way for Dutch independence) ; tomb, 593.

Mary (b. 1867), consort of George V of Eng. ; 2114, 1442 ; at Silver Jubilee, 3282.

Mary (b. 1897). Eng. princess, only daughter of King George V and Queen Mary ; married Viscount Lascelles, later Earl of Harewood (1882–1947) in 1922 ; created Princess Royal in 1932 ; has two sons, George, who became Earl of Harewood in 1947, and Hon. Gerald Lascelles ; 1442.

Mary I (1516–58). Queen of Eng., 2113, 1455, 2114 ; and Calais, 655 ; imprisons Elizabeth, 1146, and Lady Jane Grey, 1545 ; Knox opposes rule, 1872 ; death a blow to Philip II's ambitions, 2568.

Mary II (1662–94). Queen of Eng., and wife of William III, 2114, 3380, 1784.

Mary Magdalene (" Mary of Magdala"), convert and devoted follower of Jesus (John xx.).

Mary of Guise or **Lorraine** (1516–60). Queen of James V of Scot., later regent for her daughter, Mary Queen of Scots ; arranged Fr. alliance ; used Scot. to aggrandize Guise family ; opposes Protestant movement, 1871.

Mary Stuart (1542–87). Queen of Scots, 2115, 2892, 1146 ; Edinburgh associations, 1087 ; and Elizabeth, 1146, 1148 ; mother of James I, 1793 ; plays by Swinburne, 3138 ; and John Knox, 1872.

Maryland. A middle Atlantic state of U.S.A. ; a. 10,577 sq. m. ; pop. 1,821,240 ; 2116.

Marylebone (ma'-ri-bon) **Cricket Club** (M.C.C.), 928.

Masaccio (ma-sah'-chō) (1401–28). Nickname of Tommaso Guidi. It. painter ; first to appreciate aerial perspective, to show figures in bold relief, and to introduce lively action into painting ; 1775.

Masai (ma-sī). An E. African people of Negro-Hamitic stock, remarkable for their fine physique, 65, 70.

Masaryk (mah'-sah-rēk), **Jan Garrigue** (1886–1948), Czech politician, son of Thomas Masaryk, 2117.

Masaryk, Thomas Garrigue (1850–1937). Czechoslovak statesman, educator, and historian ; 2117.

Mascagni (mas-kah'-nyē), **Pietro** (1863–1945). It. composer ; wrote the opera " Cavalleria Rusticana," 2438.

Mascara (mas-kah-rah'). Fortified town in Algeria, about 45 m. s.e. of Oran, on slope of Atlas Mts. ; stands on site of Roman colony ; pop. 33,000.

Mas'cot, 2059.

Masefield, John Edward (b. 1875). Eng. poet and dramatist, 2117, 1216.

Maseru. Cap. of Basutoland ; pop. 2,500 ; 3016.

Mashie. A golf club, 1484.

Masho'naland. Region in S. Africa s. of R. Zambezi, now part of Rhodesia, 2772; occupied by British, 3319.

Mask, Lough, Eire, between counties of Galway and Mayo ; about 12 m. in length and 2 to 4 m. in breadth ; contains about 20 isls.

Maskelyne (mas'-ke-lin), **Nevil** (1732–1811). Eng. astronomer ; founder of the " Nautical Almanac," first published in 1767, and compiler of a catalogue of fundamental stars.

Maskelyne. Name of English family of " magicians " ; for many years gave regular performances at St. George's Hall, London.

Masks. Worn by Gk. actors, 3194 ; for New Guinea magic, 2058.

Mason, Alfred Edward Woodley (1865–1948). Eng. author and playwright ; his powerful novels gained a wide circle of readers (" The House of the Arrow " ; " The Four Feathers " ; plays, " At the Villa Rose " ; " Running Waters " ; " Fire Over England ").

Mason, Charles (1730–87). Eng. astronomer and surveyor ; fixed precise measure of a degree of latitude in America.

Masons or **Freemasons,** 1390.

Mason wasps. Types that make mud nests, 3346.

Maspero (ma-spe-rō), **Gaston Camille Charles** (1846–1916). French Egyptologist ; professor of Egyptology at Collège de France ; headed government archaeological mission to Egypt in 1880.

Masque. Form of drama in which actors originally wore masks, 3196.

Mass. The amount of matter, distinguished from the weight, 1513 ; in a physical object, 2592 ; comparative masses of planets, 2619 ; " conservation of mass," 2592.

Mass. In Rom. Cath. Church, the celebration of the sacrament of the Eucharist, commemorating the passion and death of Christ ; music, 2263.

Massachu'setts. One of New Eng. states, U.S.A., 8,257 sq. m. ; pop. 4,316,720 ; cap. Boston, 529 ; 2118, 1299 ; Plymouth founded, 2122.

Massachusetts Bay. Arm of Atlantic indenting E. coast of Mass., U.S.A., 40 m. long.

Massacre of the Innocents. Slaughter of the children of Bethlehem by Herod's soldiers, 1822.

Massage (ma-sahzh') (from Gk. word for " knead "), and manipulation of joints. Method of treatment, using the hands, for the alleviation of bodily conditions.

Massawa (ma-sah'-wa). Spt. and chief tn. of former It. colony of Eritrea in N.E. Africa, on Red Sea ; pop. 17,169 ; taken by British, Apl. 1941.

Massecuite (mas-ek-wēt), in sugar refining, 3112.

Masséna (ma-sā-nah), **Andre** (1758–1817). Duke of Rivoli and Prince of Essling, perhaps the greatest of Napoleon's marshals ; victorious in It., Poland, Ger. ; first serious defeat by Wellington in 1810 in Peninsular War ; thereafter saw no more active service.

Massenet (mas'-e-nā), **Jules Émile Frédéric** (1842–1912). Fr. composer ; his distinctive style appears best in love scenes of his operas ; chief works, " Thais," " Le Jongleur de Notre Dame," " Manon," ballet music to " Le Cid."

Massi'lia. Gk. name for Marseilles, Fr., 1358, 1519, 2110.

Massine (mya-sēn), **Leonide** (b. 1896). Russ. dancer and choreographer. Member of Diaghilev ballet and Ballets Russes de Monte Carlo. Ballets include " Good-Humoured Ladies," " La Boutique Fantasque," " Le Tricorne," 347, and " Les Présages."

Mas'singer, Philip (1584–1640). Eng. dramatist ; author of 15 plays and collaborator with Fletcher and others in many more ; most of his plays have an obvious moral intention, but his heroes are too good and his villains too wicked to be convincing, 1040.

Massingham, Harold John (b. 1888). Eng. author, known especially for books on the countryside (" English Downland," " Cotswold Country," " Chiltern Country," " Where Man Belongs ") ; son of following.

Massingham, Henry William (1860–1924). Eng. journalist and author. Edited the Star and Daily Chronicle and finally the Nation (1907–23).

Mass production, of motor-cars, 1347 ; conveyors in, 897.

Mass spectrograph, instr. used in investigations of isotopes, etc., by action of " positive rays " in a discharge tube, *1760*.

Master. Degree in arts, science, etc. *See* **Degree.**

Master-key, for unlocking many doors, 1980.

Masters, Edgar Lee (b. 1869). American poet, 3295.

Master singers (Meistersinger). Medieval guild of Ger. singers, 2262 ; Wagner's opera, 2439, 3332.

Mastersongs. In Ger. literature, 1456.

Mastiff. A huge Brit. dog with a large head and broad hanging ears ; smooth-coated ; colour buff or fawn, 1026, *plate f. 1024*.

Mas′todon. A hairy, elephant-like animal now extinct, 2077.

Mas′toid, 1066.

Masulipatam or **Bandar.** Spt. of republic of India in N. Madras on one of mouths of the Kistna ; pop. 59,146 ; weaving, bleaching, and cloth printing.

Masurian Lakes. A sickle-shaped group of lakes in the S. part of E. Prussia ; strategically important in German-Russian battles of both World Wars. Battles of 1914, 3410.

Masurium (Ma). Element of the manganese group ; discovered in 1925 and named after a district in Prussia, 777.

Matabeleland. Dist. of S. Rhodesia, S. Africa, 2772 ; Brit. conquer, 3019 ; native revolt of 1896, Rhodes and, 2771.

Mat′ador. In bull fights, the man who administers the fatal stroke to the bull.

Mat′ador. Name of a domino game, 1029.

Matamat′a. A S. Amer. turtle, 3230.

Matanzas. Spt. and rly. centre on N. coast of Cuba, 50 m. E. of Havana ; pop. 72,820 ; chief export, sugar.

Matapan, Cape, Battle of. Brit. sea-air victory, Mar. 28, 1941, over It. fleet, off C. Matapan, Greece ; 3418.

Matches, 2119 ; duty on, 3158 ; phosphorus used, 2574 ; primitive, *1279* ; why easy to blow out, 1280.

Matchlock. Early hand-gun, 1981.

Maté (Span. *yerba maté*) or **Paraguay tea.** A S. Amer. beverage ; in Brazil, 553 ; in Paraguay, 2511.

Materialists. In philosophy, 2572.

Mate′ria med′ica (Latin words meaning materials of medicine). That part of the study of medicine which deals with the source, preparation, and use of drugs.

Mathematics. The science of number and quantity, 2120 ; addition, 28 ; algebra, 112 ; Arabs' contribution, 2068 ; Archimedes, 210 ; arithmetic, 233 ; calculus developed by Newton, 2349 ; decimals, 982 ; division, 1021 ; factors, 1255 ; fractions, 1355 ; geometry, 1434 ; logarithms, 1998 ; mensuration, 2141 ; multiplication, 2253 ; Ptolemy, 2697 ; Pythagoreans, 2710 ; subtraction, 3107 ; trigonometry, 3248. *See also* **Symbols.**

Mather, Cotton (1663–1728). Amer. preacher and scholar, leader of conservative New England Puritans and of Salem witchcraft persecution,3293.

Mathew, Theobald (1790–1856). " Father Mathew," Irish priest and temperance reformer.

Matil′da (d. 1083). Queen of William I and daughter of Baldwin V, count of Flanders.

Matilda (1080–1118). Queen of Henry I of Eng. and daughter of Malcolm III and St. Margaret of Scot., 1609.

Matilda (1102–67). Queen of Eng. (crowned 1141), daughter of Henry I of Eng. and wife of Emperor Henry V, 1609 ; Stephen and, 3087 ; besieged at Oxford, 2462.

" **Matilda** " **tank,** in 2nd World War, 3151.

Mat′ins. One of the canonical hours, 2214.

Matisse (ma-tēs′), **Henri** (b. 1869). Fr. painter, one of the most influential of his time ; evolved new colour-harmonies and use of tones ; led the " Fauvist " group ; also a fine lithographer, 2477, 1379.

Mat′lock. Tn. in Derbyshire, 17 m. N.W. of Derby ; near by are Matlock Bath and Matlock Bank, well-known inland health resorts ; pop., Matlock, 10,599 ; Matlock Bath, 1,825 ; 995.

Matop′po Hills. Range of hills in Matabeleland, S. Rhodesia, where is the grave of Cecil Rhodes, 2771, *2773*.

Matriarchy. In tribal life, 1259.

Matriculation (matric). Examination, 2886.

Matrimonial Causes Act. Statute relating to divorce, which came into force on Jan. 1, 1938. Its passing largely due to efforts of A. P. Herbert, M.P., novelist and writer on the strange ways of the law. By this Act desertion and incurable insanity became grounds for divorce.

Ma′trix. In type-making, 2685 ; linotype, 1956 ; monotype, 2216, 2217 ; stereotype, 3088.

Matsuoka, Yosuke (1880–1946). Jap. diplomatist ; delegate to League of Nations ; for. min. in 1940, and in 1941 signed non-aggression pact with Russ., and improved Jap. relations with Ger. and It. ; in 1946 arrested as war criminal and died in hospital June 27.

Matsya. Name for 4 Rajputana states near Delhi, repub. of Ind. : Alwar, Bharatpur, Dholpur, and Karauli ; joined Rajasthan in 1949 ; pop. 1,800,000.

Matsys (mat-sīs) or **Massys, Quentin** (1466–1530). Flemish artist ; religious subjects, portraits, etc. (" Burial of Christ " in Antwerp museum), 2324.

Mattathi′as (d. 167 B.C.). Jewish priest, 1830.

Matte (mat). Impure metal produced by smelting ; in copper refining, *diagram, 006 007*.

Matter. Composed of atoms and electrons, 966, 1137 ; indestructibility and conservation of matter, 2592 ; motion of molecules causes heat, 1593 ; theory of its electrical nature, 2731.

Matterhorn (Fr. *Mont Cervin*). Peak in Alps on W. frontier between Switzerland and Italy ; 14,782 ft. ; first ascended by a party led by Edward Whymper, July 14, 1865 ; *131*, 2247, 3138.

Matthay, Prof. Tobias (1858–1945). English professor of the piano, taught at London Academy for 45 years. Founded " Matthay Method."

Mat′thew, St. (Hebrew " gift of God "). One of the Twelve Apostles, traditional author of First Gospel, 188, 189.

Matthew, Gospel of St. First book of New Testament and of the Four Gospels.

Matthews, Jessie (b. 1907). Eng. actress ; her singing and dancing brought her fame in " This Year of Grace " and " Ever Green."

Matthi′as. One of the Apostles (Acts i.), 188, 189.

Matthias I, Hunyadi (1440–90). King of Hungary. Also called Matthias Corvinus from the raven (*corvus*) on his escutcheon ; son of János Hunyadi ; elected king 1458, repeatedly defeated Emperor Frederick III, Turks, Poles, and became most powerful ruler in cent. Europe ; equally capable as soldier, administrator, orator, law-maker ; *1656*.

Mattioli. Supposed " Man in the Iron Mask," 1758.

Maubeuge (mō-bēzh). Fr. tn. near Belg. border, 50 m. S.E. of Lille ; pop. 20,859 ; taken by Germans 1914 and 1940.

Maude (1869–1938). Queen of Haakon VII of Norway, youngest daughter of Edward VII of Gt. Brit.

Maude, Cyril (b. 1862). Eng. actor and theatrical manager ; finished performer of many quietly humorous parts (" Grumpy," etc.).

Maude, Sir (Frederick) Stanley (1864–1917). Brit. general in 1st World War ; took part in Dardanelles and Kut relief expeditions ; captured Baghdad, 3411.

Maudslay, Henry (1771–1831). Eng. engineer. Famous as an inventor

and manufacturer of machine-tools, he was also the founder of a famous family of engineers.

Maufe, Edward (b. 1883). Eng. architect (A.R.A., 1938). Known especially as an architect for modern churches, he was the architect for Guildford Cathedral ; designed B.B.C. studio for religious broadcasts ; also Festival Theatre, Cambridge ; reconstruction of Gray's Inn, and Middle Temple, London.

Maugham (mawm), **Frederick Herbert, 1st Baron** (b. 1866). Eng. lawyer. Judge of High Court of Justice (Chancery Div.) during 1928–34 ; Lord Justice of Appeal 1934–35 ; Lord High Chancellor 1938–39, brother of Somerset Maugham.

Maugham, William Somerset (b. 1874). Eng. novelist and dramatist, distinguished by his smooth irony, sparkling wit and objective dissection of character (" Liza of Lambeth " ; " Of Human Bondage " ; " The Moon and Sixpence " ; " The Circle " ; " For Services Rendered " ; " East of Suez " ; " Our Betters " ; " Rain " ; " The Razor's Edge " ; " Catalina "), 1216.

Maui. One of Hawaiian Isls. ; 728 sq. m.

Mauna Kea (mow′-na kā-a) (Hawaiian " white mountain "). Extinct volcano on isl. of Hawaii ; highest peak in Pacific isls. (13,823 ft.) ; 1587.

Mauna Loa (" great mountain "). Active volcano on S. Hawaii Isl. ; 13,675 ft. ; crater of Kilauea on E. slope, 1587, 3329.

Maundy or **Holy Thursday,** 1074 ; maundy money, 2189, *plate f. 397*.

Maupassant (mō-pah-sahn), **Guy de** (1850–93). Fr. novelist, master of short story ; chief works " La Ficelle " (" The Piece of String "), " La Parure " (" The Necklace "), " Une Vie " (" A Life "), 1382.

Mauretania. Anc. name for N.W. Africa, comprising modern Morocco and W. Algeria, 2231.

Mauretania. Name of two Cunard liners, 2121.

Mauriac (mō-rē-ak), **François** (b. 1855). Fr. writer ; novels " La Chair et Le Sang," " Thérèse Desqueyroux " ; play, " Asmodée " (Eng. trans. " The Intruder ") ; criticism, life of Racine.

Maurice (1521–53). Duke, and by conquest of his cousin John Frederick, elector of Saxony ; one of foremost generals and most cunning diplomats of his day ; extorted from Emperor Charles V Treaty of Passau (1552), giving Protestants liberty of worship until Diet of Augsburg ; deserts Protestants, 2759.

Maurice of Nassau (1567–1625). Prince of Orange (son of William the Silent), Dutch general, one of ablest of his age ; opposed successful resistance to Span. domination ; shared guilt of Barnevelt's execution.

Maurier, du, *see* **Du Maurier.**

Mauritania, colony, French W. Africa. A. 323,000 sq. m. ; pop. 383,000.

Mauritius (mō-rish′-us). Brit. isl. in Indian Ocean ; 720 sq. m. ; pop. 424, 450 ; 2121 ; dodo, *1025* ; stamp, *3075*.

Mauritshuis (mah-rits-hīs), picture gallery, The Hague, 1564.

Maurois (mō′-rwah), **André** (b. 1885). Fr. writer ; famous for brilliant biographies cast almost in fictional form (" Ariel ") ; acute observer of Eng. character (" Les Silences du Colonel Bramble "), 1382.

Mausole′um, of Halicarnassus, 2923, *plate f. 2924* ; **of Hadrian,** 2803.

Mausolus (maw-sō′-lus) (4th cent. B.C.). King of Caria, whose wife Artemisia erected famous " mausoleum " to his memory.

Mavis. Name formerly in general use in Eng. for the song-thrush.

Maw′son, Sir Douglas (b. 1882). Eng. polar explorer ; he accompanied Sir Ernest Shackleton on his Antarctic expedition in 1907, and commanded the Australian Antarctic expeditions of 1911–14 and 1929, discovering

King George V Land, *2645*, 2647 ; estab. position of S. magnetic pole, 2390.

Max, Adolphe (1869–1939). Burgomaster of Brussels at beginning of 1st World War for 3 months until imprisoned in Ger. ; heroeially resisted efforts to break his moral and spiritual opposition to Ger. invaders.

Max of Baden, Prince (1867–1929). Ger. soldier and statesman ; as imperial chancellor (appointed Oct. 3, 1918) he began negotiations for armistice ; brought pressure on Kaiser and announced his abdication ; Nov. 10, 1918, handed govt. control to Ebert.

Maxen'tius, Marcus Aurelius Valerius (d. 312), elected Rom. emperor A.D. 306 ; defeated by Constantine, 893.

Maxil'la, upper jaw, *3163* ; of insects, *1729,* 1730.

Max'im, Sir Hiram Stevens (1840–1916). Brit. inventor, b. in U.S.A. ; 2050 ; inventor of Maxim automatic machine-gun, and a smokeless powder ; a pioneer of aeronautics, 1605.

Maxim gun, 2050.

Maximil'ian I (1459–1519), Holy Rom. emperor ; succeeded in 1493 ; called 2nd founder of House of Hapsburg, which, by marriages of himself, son, and grandson, gained Netherlands, Spain, Hungary, and Bohemia, thus creating vast empire of Charles V and his successors.

Maximilian I, the Great (1573–1651). Elector and Duke of Bavaria, helped form Catholic League which opposed Prot. Union in Thirty Years' War ; party to peace of Westphalia in 1648 ; considered ablest Cath. ruler of his time.

Maximilian I (1756–1825). First king of Bavaria ; succeeded as elector in 1799 ; aided Napoleon and received title of king as a reward.

Maximilian II (1811–64), Bavaria. Monarch of liberal tendencies ; succeeded to throne on abdication of his father (1848) ; opposed exclusion of Austria from Ger. confederation ; father of the mad kings Ludwig II and Otto.

Maximilian (1832–67), archduke of Austria and emperor of Mexico, 2159.

Maxton, James (1885–1946). Brit. politician ; M.P. for Glasgow division 1922–46 ; chairman I.L.P. (1926–31), and leader of I.L.P. in House of Commons.

Maxwel, James Clerk-. *See* **Clerk-Maxwell, James.**

May, Phil (1864–1903). Eng. black-and-white artist, famous for his skill in using the fewest possible lines ; chiefly depicted " low life " in London ; contributed to the Graphic and Punch.

May, 5th month of year, 2223.

May. Same as **Hawthorn.**

Mayakovski (mah-yah-kof'-ski), **Vladimir** (1894–1930). Russian poet and dramatist, 2856.

Mayas (mah'-yaz). Race of Indians inhabiting peninsula of Yucatan at time of Sp. conquest ; developed a remarkable civilization, *3437,* 3438.

May Day. Festival on first day of May, 2223.

Mayfair. Fashionable West End quarter of London, situated N. of Piccadilly ; gives its name to the more fashionable and gayer aspect of " Society " life.

Mayflower. Ship which carried Pilgrim Fathers to New England, 2121, *2123.*

Mayfly, 2122.

Mayo, Eire. 3rd largest co. in Ire. (2,084 sq. m.) in Connaught prov. bounded N. and W. by Atlantic : pop. 148,200, 2124.

May'or. Chairman of cities and boroughs in the United Kingdom, and chief executive municipalities in U.S.A., and other countries ; elected annually, he acts as chief magistrate ; in London and 26 other cities of Gt. Brit. and the Commonwealth he is known as the Lord Mayor ; the Scot. equivalent is Provost or Lord Provost.

Mayor of the Palace (*major domus*). Official in Frankish kingdom under Merovingian rule.

Mazarin (ma-zah-ran'), **Jules** (1602–61). Fr. cardinal and statesman, 2124, 2435 ; in Thirty Years' War, 2779, 3202.

Mazarin Bible, 427 ; first complete printed book, *2685,* 2686.

Maz'da. Same as **Ahura Mazda.**

Maze. *See* **Labyrinth.**

Mazeppa (ma-zep'-a), **Ivan** (1644–1709). Cossack chief, powerful in Rus. under Peter the Great ; deserted to Charles XII of Sweden ; 916.

Mazzini (mat-sé'-né), **Guiseppe** (1805–72), famous Italian revolutionary leader, 2124, 1769.

Mbabane. Capital of Swaziland, 3016.

Meadow-pipit, bird, *2612.*

Meadow-sweet. A species of *Spiraea,* native in England, in moist places ; small, creamy, fragrant flowers.

" Mealies," 2068.

Meals, etiquette at, 1228.

Mean'der or **Maeander.** A r. of Asia Minor (now called Menderes) famous for its many windings ; 240 m. to its mouth at Miletus ; *map, 1518.*

Mean solar day, 980.

Mean solar time, 3212.

Means Test. Name given to bill, passed in 1932, full title of which is The Transitional Payments (Determination of Need) Bill. After drawing benefit for 26 weeks, an unemployed man had to satisfy Public Assistance Committees before he could receive any further relief. Amended 1940.

Meares, John (*c.* 1756–1809). Eng. navigator ; explored coast of Alaska ; sailed to China by way of Hawaiian Isls.

Measles. A contagious disease common among children ; probably a germ disease, 1458.

Measurement. Mensuration, the science of, 2141.

Measures. *See* **Weights and Measures.**

Meat, 2124 ; food value, 1339, 2694 ; how to cook, 901 ; packing, 228, 783 ; refrigeration, 1393.

Meath, Eire. Marit. co. in Leinster ; a. 905 sq. m. ; pop. 65,300 ; 2125.

Meaux (mō). Fr. tn. on r. Marne 20 m. E. of Paris ; pop. 14,230 ; marked closest approach to Paris of opening Ger. campaign, in 1914–18 War ; held by Germans 1940–44 ; farming and milling centre.

Mec'ca. Holy city of Mahomedans in Saudi Arabia near Red Sea ; pop. about 130,000 ; 201, 202, **2125** ; home of Mahomet, 2127.

Mechanical drawing, 1045.

Mechan'ics. Branch of physics dealing with force and motion, **2127** ; gravitation, 1512 ; laws of falling bodies, 1513 ; gyroscope principle, 1559 ; pulleys, 2701 ; wheel, 3375.

Mechanics' Institution, Glasgow. Founded by George Birkbeck, 457.

Mechlin. *See* **Malines.**

Meck'lenburg. Until 1945 fifth largest state in Germany, brought about by the union of Mecklenburg-Schwerin and Mecklenburg-Strelitz in 1934 ; each was formerly a grand duchy ; it had an area 6,197 sq. m. ; became Ger. Land 1946 ; pop. 2,106,000.

Mecklenburg-Schwerin, Henry, Duke of (1876–1934). Husband of Queen Wilhelmina of the Netherlands, 3378.

Mecop'tera. Order of insects containing the scorpion-fly, 1733.

Médai'le Militaire (Fr.), 2449.

Medal of Honour, in U.S.A., 2449.

Medal play, in golf, 1483.

Medals, 2448.

Medea (mē-dē'-a). In Gk. myth., a famous enchantress.

Medellin. Second city of Colombia, S. Amer. ; gold and silver mining and mfg. centre, 150 m. N.W. of Bogota ; pop. 198,100 ; univ., school of mines.

Medes (mēdz). Anc. Indo-European people of Caspian region, closely akin to the Persians, 2131, 2371, 2554.

Me'dia. Anc. kingdom and country now comprised in N.W. Persia ; home of Medes.

Medici (med'-i-chē). Famous Florentine family, 2131, 2876. For individual members, *see* under Christian names.

Medicine and surgery, 2132 ; anaesthesia, 148 ; antiseptics and asepsis, 177 ; antitoxins, 180 ; Arab contribution, 2068 ; as a career, 2132 ; chemotherapy, 179 ; drugs, 1048 ; first-aid, 1291 ; germ causes of disease, 1458 ; nursing, 2406 ; Pasteur's work, 2527 ; penicillin, 2544 ; physiology, 2598 ; preventive, 2132 ; streptomycin, 3103 ; sulpha drugs, 3116 ; uses of X-rays, 3430 ; vaccination, 3301, 1818. *See also* **Disease ; Hygiene ; Physiology.**

Medicine Hat, Alberta. Industrial and agricultural centre in S.E. on S. Saskatchewan r. ; pop. 10,000 ; milling and mining interests, 102.

Medicine man. One who professes to cure disease by sorcery ; among Red Indians, 2756, 2757.

Medina (mā-dē'-na). Holy city in cent. Arabia, 110 m. E. of Red Sea ; much visited by Mahomedan pilgrims ; pop. 20,000 ; Mahomet at, *2066* ; *map, 197.*

Medinet el Fayum. *See* **Fayum.**

" Meditations." Work by Marcus Aurelius, 2100.

Mediterranean race, 2724 ; Aegean civilization, 29 ; Cro-Magnon cave men, 734 ; Irish, 1744 ; Italy, 1763, 2804 ; in Sardinia, 2874.

Mediterranean Sea. Arm of the Atlantic between Europe and Africa, 1,145,000 sq. m. ; **2135,** 1232 ; *map, 2136* ; Adriatic, 29 ; Aegean, 29 ; coral fisheries, 908 ; Cyprus, 952 ; early commerce, 2573 ; French Riviera, *1364* ; Gibraltar western gateway, 1462 ; Gk. colonies, 1519 ; influence on Gk. civilization, 1517 ; Malta, 2072 ; sponge fisheries, 3069 ; Suez canal, *1103* ; tides, 1232 ; tunny, 3258 ; 2nd World War, 3418, 3422.

Me'dium. In spiritualism, a person who is utilized in communicating with the " spirit " consulted.

Medlar, fruit tree, 2718.

Medul'la oblonga'ta. Lower part of the brain, 545.

Medullary rays. Bands of tissue separating the vascular bundles of plant stems ; they give much of the " figure " to woods.

Medusa (me-dū'-sa). In Gk. myth., one of the Gorgons, 2552 ; head on shield of Athena, 283, 2554.

Medusae. Jelly-fishes, 1817, *1818.*

Medway. Navigable r. in S.E. Eng., joining Thames at Sheerness, near mouth ; length, with estuary, 72 m. ; on its banks are Tonbridge, Maidstone, Rochester, Chatham.

Mee, Arthur (1875–1943). Eng. author and editor. Editor of " Children's Newspaper," " Little Folks," " Children's Encyclopedia," etc. Author of " The Children's Bible," " The Children's Shakespeare " ; " The King's England," etc.

Meer, Jan van der. *See* **Vermeer.**

Meerschaum (mēr'-sham). A clay-like mineral used chiefly for pipes ; found in Morocco, Asia Minor, and Fr., **2136.**

Meerut. Tn. in United Provs., India, 35 m. N.E. of Delhi ; pop. 169,290 ; cotton trade centre ; here Sepoy mutiny first broke out (1857).

Megachiroptera. One of the two orders into which bats are divided.

Megacycle. Term in elec. and wireless for a million cycles (per sec.).

Megaera (me-gē'-ra). In Gk. myth., one of the Furies.

Megalopolis (meg-a-lop'-o-lis). Anc. Gk. walled city in Peloponnesus ; founded by Epaminondas (370 B.C.) as cap. of Arcadian confederacy ; sacked by Spartans (222 B.C.).

Meg'alosaurus. An extinct reptile, 2678.

Meg'apodes, or mound birds. Family of Australian birds that do not incubate their eggs, 1095.

Megara (meg'-a-ra). Cap. of Megaris, small dist. of anc. Greece W. of Attica ; founded many colonies.

Mège-Mouries (māzh moo-rē), **Hippolyte.** Fr. chemist, inventor of margarine, 2100.

Meg Merrilies. In Scott's "Guy Mannering," half-mad old gipsy witch.

Mehadia. Tn. in s.w. Rumania, famous for Hercules baths, known to Romans.

Mehemet Ali (mä'-he-met ah'-lē) (1769–1849). Viceroy of Egypt; massacred Mamelukes (1811); conquered Syria but compelled by European powers to give it up in 1841; did much to develop Egypt, 1101.

Meighen (mē'-ɛn), **Arthur** (b. 1874). Canadian statesman, premier (1920–21 and July–September, 1926).

Meikle (mik'-l), **Andrew** (1719–1811). Scot. inventor; invented the first really successful threshing machine.

"Mein Kampf," autobiography of Adolf Hitler, 1632, 3415.

Meissen (mī'-sen). Ger. tn. in Saxony on Elbe 15 m. N.W. of Dresden; pop. 45,000; 13th cent. cath.; Dresden china; 1447, 2669, 2670.

Meissonier (mä-sō-nyā), **Jean Louis Ernest** (1815–91). Fr. military and genre painter ("The Quarrel"; "The Gamblers"; "The Brothers Adrian and William Vandervelde").

Meistersinger (mīs-ter-zing-er). "Master singers," 2262.

"Meistersinger von Nürnberg, Die." Opera by Wagner, 2439, 3332.

Mekong (mā-kong'), r. in S.E. Asia; rises in Tibet; flows 2,600 m. into China Sea; forms greater part of boundary between Siam and Fr. Indo-China; 664, 2963.

Melanchthon (me-lank'-thon), **Philip** (1497–1560). Ger. religious reformer, friend and ally of Luther, and through his broad-minded tolerance, learning, and clear thought, the peacemaker and scribe of the Protestant Reformation, 2758.

Melane'sia. Division of Pacific Isls., 2470, map f. 2472.

Mel'anism. An excess of pigment in the skin and its appendages, producing real or comparative blackness; opposite of, and less frequent than, albinism.

Melba, Nellie (Nellie Porter Mitchell) (1859–1931). Australian prima donna; coloratura soprano; created D.B.E. in 1918.

Melbourne. Cap. of Victoria, Australia; pop. 1,226,920; 2136.

Melbourne, William Lamb, 2nd Viscount (1779–1848). Eng. statesman; entered Parl. 1806; succeeded to peerage 1829; Home Secretary 1830; premier (1834, 1835–41); remembered as guide to Queen Victoria, 3320.

Melchett, Alfred Mond, 1st Baron (1868–1930). Brit. politician and chairman of Imperial Chemical Industries, Ltd.; son of Ludwig Mond; entered Parl. 1906, as Sir Alfred Mond; First Commissioner of Works (1916–21); Minister of Health (1921–2).

Melchisedek (mel-kiz'-e-dek). Priest-king (Gen. xiv. 18); taken as typifying Christ (Heb. vii. 1–21).

Melilla (mä-lēl'-lya). Sp. fortified station and penal settlement on N. coast of Morocco; scene of Spanish defeat by native tribesmen (1921); pop. 60,500.

Mel'inite. A picric-acid explosive, 1250.

Melk. Abbey on Danube, 972.

Mellon, Andrew William (1852–1937). Amer. financier; sec. of Treasury (1921–32); U.S. ambassador to Gt. Brit. (1932–33).

Melody, in music, 2263.

Melon family of plants, the *Cucurbitaceae*, 2137, 943; melons, 2137; pumpkins, 2704.

Meloria, battle of, 2613.

Melos (mē'-los) or **Milo.** Mountainous Gk. isl. 75 m. E. of S. Greece; 52 sq. m.; exports sulphur, manganese; Venus of Milo found here in 1820, 1535, 1537.

Melpomene (mel-pom'-e-nē). In Gk. myth., the muse of tragedy, 2259.

Melrose Abbey, Scot. Magnificent ruin in tn. of Melrose, Roxburghshire; heart of Bruce, 2832, 591.

Mel'ton Mowbray (mō'-brä), Eng. tn. in Leicestershire, 102 m. N.W. of London, in famous hunting dist.;

noted for pork pies; pop. 12,000; 1919.

Melun (me-lêñ') Fr. mfg. and rly. centre on isl. and on both banks of r. Seine, 28 m. S.E. of Paris; it manufactures leather, pottery, etc.; pop. 17,570; 2919.

Melville, Herman (1819–91). Amer. author ("Typee" and "Omoo"), earliest and among the best tales of the South Seas; "Moby Dick, or the White Whale"; "White Jacket," effected abolition of flogging in U.S. Navy, 3294.

Melville Island, Australia. Off centre of N. shore; 1,800 sq. m.; densely wooded, especially with eucalyptus trees, map f. 308.

Melville Island. Uninhabited Canadian isl. of Arctic regions N. of Victoria Isl.; 26,000 sq. m.

Melville Peninsula, Canada. 400 m. N. of Hudson Bay between Gulf of Boothia and Fox Channel; 25,000 sq. m.

Mem'branous lab'yrinth. Part of inner ear, 1065.

Memel (mä'-mel) **(Klaipeda),** Lithuania. Baltic fortified port 60 m. S. of Libau; pop. 50,000; old Hanse tn.; taken from Ger. by Peace Conference (1919), 1968; annexed by Germany in 1939, 3416; restored to Lithuania in 1945.

Memel River. *See* Niemen.

Mem'ling or **Memlinc, Hans** (c. 1430–94). Flemish painter of portraits and religious subjects, 595, 2333.

Memmi, Lippo (d. 1357). It. painter of Sienese School; worked with Simone Martini.

Mem'non. In Gk. myth., son of Eros and Tithonus; killed by Achilles, 2138.

Memnon, Colossi of. Two colossal statues in Egypt, 2138, 1098.

Memorial Hall, Farringdon St., London, occupying part of the site of the old Fleet Prison; built by Congregationalists to commemorate the 2,000 ministers who were ejected from their livings by the Act of Uniformity of 1662.

Mem'ory, 2138, 2697; racial, 2139.

Memphis (mem'-fis). Early cap. of Lower Egypt at apex of Nile delta S. of Cairo, now in ruins; huge statues of Rameses II; 1114.

Memphis, Tennessee, U.S.A. Largest city of state; pop. 293,000; trade in cotton, lumber, horses, various mfrs., 2192, 3186.

Menag'erie, collection of living animals, 3445.

Menai (men'-ī) **Strait.** Narrow channel separating isle of Anglesey from Wales; spanned by Telford's suspension bridge and the Britannia tubular bridge, 155, 2128, 3088, 3336.

Menam River. Chief r. of Siam, flowing S. from Burma 750 m. and entering Gulf of Siam, 2963.

Menan'der (342–291 B.C.), Gk. dramatist, 1038; the inventor of "New Comedy" as we now know it, opposed to "Old Comedy" of Aristophanes.

Mencius (men'-shi-us) or **Meng'tse** (c. 372–289 B.C.). Chinese sage, placed second only to Confucius.

Mencken, Henry Louis (b. 1880). American critic, 3296.

Mendaña Islands. Same as **Marquesas.**

Men'del, Gregor (1822–84). Austrian priest and biologist; discovered laws of heredity, 2139, 1617.

Mendeléev (men-de-lā'-ef), **Dmitri Ivanovitch** (1834–1907). Russian chemist, 2140; formulated Periodic Law of the elements, 295, 768.

Mendelssohn (Mendelssohn-Bartholdy) (men'-del-son), **Jakob Ludwig Felix** (1809–47). Ger. musician and composer, 2141; works, 3071.

Mendelssohn, Moses (1729–86). Ger. (Jewish) philosopher, original of Lessing's "Nathan the Wise" and grandfather of the musician Felix Mendelssohn.

Mendenhall Glacier, Alaska, 98.

Mendès (man-des'), **Catulle** (1841–1909). Fr. poet and novelist, one of Par-

nassian group; a versatile and accomplished writer ("Histoires d'amour"; "Le roi vierge," best known of his novels; "Sainte Thérèse" and numerous other plays).

Mendip Hills. Range 6 m. broad and 20 m. long in w. Somersetshire (1,068 ft.); stalactite caves; Rom. remains; 734, 1163; 3000.

Mendo'za, Pedro de (c. 1487–1537). Span. captain, colonizer of Plata r. region in Argentina, 228.

Mendoza, Argentina. Cap. of prov. of Mendoza, at foot of the Andes, 650 m. N. of Buenos Aires; chief centre for trade with Chile; pop. 103,800.

Menelaus (men-e-lā'-us). In Gk. myth., king of Sparta, brother of Agamemnon and husband of Helen; organizes war against Troy, 3249; recovers Helen, 9950; wrests secret from Proteus, 2694.

Men'elik II (1844–1913). Emperor of Abyssinia, elected 1889; able and enlightened ruler; forced recognition of Abyssinian independence from European powers, 14.

Menes (mē'-nēz). First of the historical kings of Egypt; united Upper and Lower Egypt, 1114.

Mengelberg, Willem (b. 1871). Dutch conductor; was for 50 years conductor of Concertgebouw Orchestra of Amsterdam.

Mengs, Anton Raphael (1728–79). Ger. artist; decorated the royal palace at Madrid, 1455.

Menhirs, prehistoric monuments, 3095.

Menin Gate. 1st World War memorial at Ypres, 403.

Mening'itis. Disease caused by inflammation of membranes surrounding the brain or spinal cord; due to bacteria, 1458.

Menkaura or **Myceri'nus, Pyramid of,** 2707.

Men'lo Park, New Jersey, U.S.A. Vil. 14 m. S.W. of Newark; Edison's laboratory, 1088.

Men'nonites. Protestant sect growing out of Anabaptist movement in 16th cent.; opposed to oath-taking, military service, and theological learning; hold to simplicity of life and worship, and often live in separate communities; named from Menno Simons (1492–1559), leader in Netherlands.

"Men of Harlech." Welsh song, 2282.

Men of the Trees. Organization created by H. St. Barbe Baker, to further interest in trees.

Mensheviks (men'-she-viks). Minority of Rus. Social Democrats, opposed to Bolshevism, 495.

Mensura'tion. Process of measuring or taking dimensions, 2141. *See* Mathematics.

Men'thol, a waxy substance used locally to relieve irritation or pain; distilled from peppermint oil.

Men'tor. In Gr. myth., friend of Odysseus, guardian of his son Telemachus; hence wise counsellor.

Menuhin, Yehudi (b. 1917). Amer. violinist. Début with San Francisco Symphony Orchestra, in 1924. London début in 1929. His sister, Hepzibah (b. 1921) is a remarkable pianist.

Menzel (men'-tsel), **Adolph** (1815–1905), Ger. artist; by his engraving on wood, established himself as one of the first illustrators of his day, 1967; as a painter, 1455.

Menzies (men'-zēz), **Robert G.** (b. 1894). Australian statesman; Commonwealth Attorney-Gen. (1935–39); Prime Min. (1939–41); Leader of Opposition in 1943; again Prime Min. in 1949.

Mep'acrine. Synthetic substitute for quin.ne; also called Atebrin.

Mephistopheles (mef-is-tof'-e-lēz), an evil spirit of the Faust legends, 1263, 1478.

Merano, It. cap. of Tirol in 12th–15th cents.; health resort; pop. 19,000; 3216.

Mercantile Marine. *See* Merchant Navy.

Mer'cantilists, in economics, 1081.

Mercator (měr-kā'-ter), **Gerard** (1512–94). Flemish geographer and mapmaker; originated " Mercator's projection " of the globe, 2094.

Mercator's projection, *2094.*

Mer'cer, John. Eng. chemist; discovered process of mercerizing, 2143.

Mercerizing. Process which gives silky finish to cotton, 2143.

Merchant guilds, 1553.

Merchant Navy, 2143 ; in 2nd World War, 2144, 3238.

" Merchant of Venice." Comedy by Shakespeare, 2144, 2936.

Merchant Taylor's School, London. Occupied the site of the old Charterhouse School in the Charterhouse until 1933 ; it was founded in 1561 by the Merchant Taylors' Company, and for three centuries had its home in Suffolk Lane ; new buildings at Sandy Lodge, Herts., were opened in 1933.

Mercia. An Anglo-Saxon kingdom in cent. England, 6th to 9th cents. ; during 8th cent. it was the most powerful of all the kingdoms.

Mer'cury or **Mercu'rius.** In Rom. myth., the messenger of the gods, and god of merchandise and merchants ; identified with Gk. Hermes, 1619, *1921*, 2146 ; identified with Odin, 2421. *See also in Index* **Hermes.**

Mercury. The smallest planet, 2146, 2617, *2618* ; *plate f. 281.*

Mercury (Hg) or quicksilver, a fluid metallic element of the zinc group ; atomic weight, 200·6 ; found as the native metal and as the sulphide ; very poisonous but used medicinally ; melts at 38°F., 2145 ; in barometers, *362*, 363 ; bichloride (corrosive sublimate), 2638 ; in compensating pendulum, 3171 ; freezing point, 2145 ; fulminate a violent explosive, 1250 ; properties, 777 ; mercury arc rectifier, 1138, 2757 ; separates gold in placer mining, 1480 ; sulphide (cinnabar ore), 2145, 2478, 3117 ; and surface tension, 3121 ; used for backing mirrors, 2190 ; vapour, 1135, 1136, 1391, 2315, 3055 ; why used in thermometers, 2145, 3200 ; why used in elec. apparatus, 2146.

Mercutio (měr-kū'-shi-ō). In Shakespeare's " Romeo and Juliet," witty friend of Romeo.

Mer de Glace (mår-de-glahs). Glacier on Mt. Blanc, 126.

Mer'edith, George (1828–1909). Eng. novelist and poet, 2146, 1215, 2402.

Meredith, Owen. *See* Lytton, Edward Robert, Earl of.

Merganser (měr-gan'-ser). A fish-eating type of duck, *1052* ; foot, *448.*

Mergenthaler (mer-gen-tahl-er), **Ottmar** (1854–99). Ger.-Amer. inventor of linotype, 1956.

Merida (mā'-rē-da). Cap. of Yucatan, Mexico, 23 m. s. of its port, Progreso, on Gulf of Mexico ; pop. 98,600 ; large commerce in sisal hemp.

Meridian. An imaginary N. and S. line on earth's surface, 1898, 3214 ; on maps, 2093, *3213.*

Mérimée (mā-rē-mā), **Prosper** (1803–70). Fr. novelist, historian, and critic, great master of style (" Colomba " ; " Carmen " ; " Lettres à une inconnue "), 1381.

Merino (mer-ē'-nō). A breed of sheep, 2940 ; wool, 3405.

Merion'ethshire, Wales. Marit. co. ; a. 660 sq. m. ; pop. 43,000 ; **2146.**

Merit, Order for, Ger., 2449.

Merit, Order of (O.M.), Brit., 2449.

Mer'lin. Legendary Brit. bard, prophet, and magician of Arthurian times, 255.

Merlin, hawk, *1588.*

Mer'maids. Mythical sea maidens, half human, half fish, **2146.**

Merovingians (mer-ō-vin'-ji-anz). Frankish royal line (ruled from 496 to 752), 1365.

Mer'rimac. Confederate ironclad warship in Amer. Civil War, defeated in engagement with the " Monitor," 240.

Merrimac River. U.S.A., rising in N.W. and flowing through Mass. to the Atlantic, 2118.

Mer'riman, Henry Seton (1862–1903). Name adopted by Hugh Stowell Scott, the Eng. novelist, who wrote many popular novels (" The Slave of the Lamp " ; " The Sowers " ; " Barlasch of the Guard ").

Merrivale, Henry Edward Duke, Baron (1855–1939). Brit. politician and lawyer ; chief secretary of Ireland (1916–18) ; President Probate, Divorce and Admiralty Division (1919–33).

Merry del Val, Raphael (1865–1930). Rom. Cath. prelate ; cardinal (1903) ; b. in London, of Sp. parentage ; papal sec. of state under Pius X.

" Merry Wives of Windsor." Comedy by Shakespeare, 1211.

Mer'sa Matruh'. Coast tn. of Egypt, 100 m. W. of Alexandria ; strongpoint of Egyptian defence in African campaign of 2nd World War until evacuated to Rommel, June 29, 1942; retaken by 8th Army Nov. 8 ; 3418, 3420, *3421.*

Mer'sen, Treaty of. Charles the Bald of Fr. and Louis of Ger. divided Lotharingia, the territory left by their nephew Lothair II (870).

Mer'sey. R. in N.W. England ; flows 70 m. W. to Irish Sea ; wide estuary forms Liverpool harbour ; 457, 1890, 1968 ; Manchester ship canal, 686, 2084 ; road and railway tunnels.

Mersey Tunnel (road). Opened in 1934 ; 457, 3255.

Mersin or **Icel.** Turkish town ; pop. 27,000 ; *3264.*

Merthyr Tydfil. Tn. in s. Wales on R. Taff ; pop. 59,600, chief seat of Welsh iron industry ; 1470, 3333.

Merton. Tn. in Surrey, on r. Wandle, 8 m. s.w. of London ; pop. (Merton, and Morden), 77,500 ; tapestries, 3153.

Merv. Oasis and anc. city of Rus. Turkistan, 120 m. N. of Afghanistan frontier, 264.

Méryon (mā'-ri-on), **Charles** (1821–68). Fr. artist ; among the greatest of etchers, he produced superb plates of Paris streets ; led a most tragic life and died in an asylum.

Mesa (mā'-sa). Tableland of s.w. U.S.A. ; site of pueblos, 2698.

Mesa'ba Range. Minnesota, U.S.A., famous iron-mining region : open pit mine, *1752.*

Mesa Verde (vēr'-dā) (Sp. " green table "). National park in s.w. Colorado, U.S.A. ; 77 sq. m. ; contains ruins of prehistoric cliff dwellings.

Mescal. Mex. beverage obtained from agave, 76.

Mesdag (mes'-dakh), **Hendrik Willem** (1831–1915). Dutch marine painter, distinguished for studies of North Sea (" Return of the Fishing Boats" ; " After the Storm "); gave collection to The Hague, 1564.

Meshed (mesh-ed') (" place of martyrdom "). Persia, cap. of prov. of Khorasan in N.E. : pop. 176,000 ; fine silks, carpets, sword-blades ; shrine of Imam Riza, famous Shiite leader of 9th cent. ; visited by many pilgrims ; occupied by Soviet troops 1941–46, it was scene of heavy fighting during Persian revolt of 1946.

Mes'mer, Friedrich Anton (1733–1815). Austrian physician and charlatan, author of theory of " animal magnetism " or " mesmerism," also called hypnotism.

Mesocephal'ic, in ethnology, 2724.

Mesolithic age, 2080, 3094.

Me'sophytes. Plants growing in moist but not wet localities.

Mesopota'mia, 2146, 2920 ; early civilization, 268, *1743*, 2146 ; for modern country *see* Iraq.

Meso-tartaric acid, 3155.

Mesozo'ic era. In geology, 1433 ; plant and animal life, 2678.

Messager (mes-ah-zhā), **André Charles Prosper** (1853–1929). Fr. composer ; studied under Saint-Saens ; Lght operas include " Véronique " and

" Monsieur Beaucaire " ; ballet " The Two Pigeons."

Messalina (me-sa-lě'-na), **Valeria** (d. A.D. 48). Profligate 3rd wife of Rom. emperor Claudius.

Messe'nia. Co. of anc. Greece in s.w. Peloponnesus ; cap. Messene ; *map, 1518.*

Messerschmitt, Wilhelm (b. 1898). Ger. aircraft designer of series of fighter planes (Me 109) and fighter-bombers (Me 110, 210, etc.), and rocket-propelled Me 163, fastest (550 m.p.h.) of 2nd World War, 1827.

Messi'ah. An Anointed One, an expected Saviour or Deliverer ; the Israelites looked forward to the coming of such a one, to deliver them as a divine agent, and Jesus was looked upon by the Christian Jews as the fulfilment of their many hopes.

" Messiah." Oratorio by Handel, 1573.

Messina (me-sě'-na). Spt. in N.E. Sicily on Strait of Messina between It. and Sicily ; pop. 192,000 ; 2190, 2968 ; earthquake, 1770 ; " Sicilian Vespers," 409. Fall of city ended 38-day campaign in Sicily in 1943 ; harbour wrecked.

Messina, Strait of. Between It. and Sicily, 2968 ; *map, 1764* ; Scylla and Charybdis myth, 2422 ; mirages, 2190.

Mestizos (mes-tē'-zōz). Persons of mixed blood in Sp.-Amer. countries, 3024 ; Chile, 804 ; Venezuela, 3309.

Mestrovic (mes'-trō-vich), **Ivan** (b. 1883). Yugoslavian sculptor of international fame ; work marked by boldness of execution and forcefulness of design, *2906.*

Meta. A r. of Colombia 600 m. long, trib. of r. Orinoco ; *map, 873.*

Metab'olism. Term for all the chemical changes which occur in living tissue, including anabolism, or building up of tissues, and catabolism, the breaking down of tissues into simpler substances, 2695.

Metacar'pal bones. In the palm of the hand, 1572.

Metallurgy (me-tal'-êr-ji). Science of metal extraction and refining, 2148 ; alloys, 122 ; electric furnace, 1409. *See also* under names of the metals.

Metals, 2148 ; alloys, 122 ; bell-casting, 409 ; conduct heat, 1595 ; conduct electricity, 1128 ; crystallization, 939 ; ductility, 1481, 2973, 2628 ; magnetism, *2062* ; earliest uses, 587, 1753 ; first used as money, 2201 ; rare earths, 3188 ; " trace " metals in diet, 2149 ; welding, 3362. *See also* **Minerals ;** and the principal metals by name.

Metal tape, sound recording on, *3013.*

Metal work. Damascus blades, 963 ; Japanese, 1810, *1811* ; silver, 2973.

Metamor'phic rocks. Those derived from older rocks by heat, pressure, or chemical change, 1432, 2795 ; marble, *2097* ; slate, 2981.

"Metamorphoses" (met-a-mor'-fō-sēz). Poem by Ovid, 1896.

Metamorphosis (Gk. " change of form"). In zoology, transformation of structure during growth ; ants, 165 ; bees, 391, *392* ; beetles, 399 ; butterfly and moth caterpillars, 720 ; cicada, 826 ; crab, larval stage, 924 ; dragon-fly, 1034, *1035* ; eels, 1093 ; extra larval stages of oil and blister beetles, 399 ; frog tadpoles, *1399* ; insects, 1728, 1893 ; locust, 1511 ; malaria parasite, *2237* ; mosquito, 2236 ; toad tadpoles, 3219.

Me'taphor. Figure of speech, 1271.

Metaphys'ics. Branch of philosophy, defined, 232, 2571.

Metasta'sio, Pietro Bonaventura Trapassi (1698–1782). It. poet and dramatist, court poet at Vienna for 50 years ; composer of many lyric dramas.

Metatar'sal bones, of the foot, *1342.*

Metatar'sus. Scientific name for instep, 1342.

Metaurus. Small r. in cent. It. emptying into Adriatic Sea ; scene of defeat and death of Hasdrubal in 207 B.C., **1574.**

Metaxas, Gen. John (1871–1941). Gk. statesman and soldier; in 1936 set up totalitarian regime in Greece; when It. attacked Albania, Oct. 1940, won first Allied victories against Axis.

Metazo'a. Animal group including all many-celled types, 156.

Metcalfe, Percy (b. 1893). Designer of Irish coinage, 1750.

Metchnikov (mech-ni-kof), **Elie** (1845–1916). Rus. bacteriologist, naturalized in Fr.; originated theory of phagocytosis, that inflammation is due to struggle between white corpuscles and disease germs; held that a diet of sour milk would lengthen human life; Nobel prize winner.

Metempsychosis (me-tem-si-kō'-sis), or transmigration of souls. 1628 · 2710.

Meteor, Gloster. Jet propelled aircraft, 38.

Meteorolog'ical observatories. Gt. Brit., 2149, 2411.

Meteorological office, 2149.

Meteorol'ogy. Science of weather and climate, 2149, 3360; barometers used, 363; measuring humidity, 1677; measuring rainfall, 2472; recording thermometers or thermographs, 3200, 3201; related to physiography, 2595; radio-sonde and balloons, 349, 2150; and stratosphere, 3102. See also Climate.

Me'teors and meteorites. "Shooting stars," 2151, 281, 3102; set on fire by air, 89, 90; in Saturn's rings, 2618; supposed to have helped build up Earth, 2619, 2620.

Meters. For measuring gas, electricity and water, 2152; measuring brightness of light, 2575; at power station, 2676; venturi in, 3312.

Meth'ane, or marsh gas, 699, 1420.

Meth'odism. A religious movement whose various bodies have a world membership of nearly 12,000,000, 1390; founded by Wesley, 3365; in Wales, 3334. Union of the Methodist Churches by Deed of Union, Sept. 20, 1932.

Metho'dius (d. 885). "Apostle of the Slavs"; brother and co-labourer with Cyril.

Methuen Treaty (1703) between Portugal and England, 2660.

Methuselah '(me-thōō'-ze-la). Son of Enoch and father of Lamech; Gen. v. 27 assigns him a lifetime of 969 years.

Meth'yl alcohol, wood alcohol, 104.

Methylated spirit, 104.

Metopes (met'-ō-pēz). In architecture, 215; of Parthenon, 22, 1145.

Metre (mē'-ter). In poetry, 2635.

Metre. A unit of the metric system (39·37 in.), 2154; applied to radio wavelengths, 3396.

Me'tric system of weights and measures, 2154.

Metric ton. Unit in metric system (2,204·6 lb.), 2155.

Met'ronome. Instrument for marking time in music; pendulum in, 2544.

Metropol'itan Museum of Art, New York City, 2353.

Metropolitan Police, 2647.

Metropolitan Railway, London, 3275; in 1863, 2735.

Metropolitan Water Board, 3194.

Metsu, Gabriel (1630–67). Dutch painter, 2334.

Metternich, Clemens, Prince (1773–1859). Austrian reactionary statesman and diplomat; influence over Congress of Vienna (1814–15) secured preponderance of Austria in European affairs; period 1815–48 "Age of Metternich"; 1240.

Metz, Fr. cap. of Lorraine, formerly held by Germany; pop. 70,100; 2155, 133; besieged by Germans in 1870, 1385; occupied by them, 1940–44, 2156.

Meunier (mê-nyā), **Constantin** (1831–1905). Belg. sculptor and painter.

Meuse (mēz), r. of w. Europe, 575 m. long; in Holland called Maas; 2156; commerce, 2829; delta, 2158; Liége, 1935; Germans cross, 1940. Allies cross, Sept. 1944, 2156, 3416, 3417, 3422.

Mev=1 million electron-volts; the unit of energy in atomic physics is the electron-volt, or the energy acquired by one electron in passing between two points with potential difference of 1 volt.

Mexican grass. A fibre obtained from several species of Mex. agaves.

Mexican War, between Mexico and U.S.A., 663, 2158.

Mexico. A republic of N. Amer., S. of U.S.A.; 763,944 sq. m., **2156**; pop. 22,178,000; map, 2157; cap. Mexico City, 2159; oil, 2426, 2428; rubber, 2833; Vera Cruz, 3313; Yucatan, 3437; History, 914, 2158; Aztecs, 325, 915; Mayas, 2159; Cortés conquers, 141, 915, 2158; revolt from Spain, 663, 2158; Germany and 1914–18 War, 3412; and U.S.A., 3291.

Mexico. State in n. cent. Mexico; 9207 sq. m.; pop. (1940) 1,146,000; cap. Toluca.

Mexico, Gulf of. Arm of the Atlantic Ocean, almost enclosed by the U.S.A., Mexico, and Cuba; a. 715,000 sq. m.

Mexico City. Cap. of Mexico; pop. with suburbs 1,468,400; **2159**; cathedral, 2159; Cortés captures, 915; site of anc. Tenochtitlan, 325.

Mexitli. Aztec name for Mexico City, 2159.

Meyerbeer (mī'-er-bār), **Jakob** (1791–1864). Ger. opera composer ("The Huguenots"; "Dinorah"), 2437.

Meynell (men'-el), **Alice** (1850–1922). Eng. poet and essayist; warmly appreciated by a limited public for the delicacy of her work ("Poems"; "The Rhythm of Life").

Meynell, Sir Francis (b. 1891). Eng. typographer, poet and publisher. Son of Alice Meynell, he wrote on typography and with his sister, Viola, ran the Nonesuch Press.

Mézières (mā-zyār'). Tn. in N. Fr., 125 m. N.E. of Paris; pop. 9,800; resisted Allies for 6 weeks after Waterloo in 1815; taken by Germans in 1871, 1914 and 1940; 226.

Mezokovesd. Vil. of Hungary; Christmas play at, plate f. 821.

Mezzanine (mets'-a-nēn). In architecture, low window in an attic, or a storey (e.g., in a theatre) between an upper and lower one.

Mez'zotint. Method of engraving, particularly used in the 18th cent.

Mi'ca. A mineral, 2159, 2180, 2845; from granite, 2160; in elec. condenser, 1132.

Micah (mī'-ka) (about 757–700 B.C.). One of Hebrew minor prophets, contemporary of Isaiah; author of 33rd book of Old Testament, 2692.

Mica schist. A metamorphic rock composed chiefly of mica and quartz; divides readily into slabs.

Micaw'ber, Wilkins. In Dickens's "David Copperfield," an unpractical optimist who is always waiting for "something to turn up"; supposed to be drawn from Dickens's father, 1012.

Michael (mī'-kel), warrior archangel (Rev. xii. 7); in Milton's "Paradise Lost," 2180; patron saint, 595.

Michael (b. 1921), ex-King of Rumania, 2841; proclaimed king 1927, left throne on accession of his father, Carol II, in 1930. Became king again on Carol's abdication in 1940. Abdicated Dec. 30, 1947. In 1948 deprived, with other members of royal family, of Rumanian nationality, and property confiscated. Married Princess Anne of Bourbon-Parma at Athens 1948; their daughter Marguerite born 1949.

Michaelmas (mik'-l-mas). The feast of St. Michael, Sept. 29; origin of goose at, 1580.

Michaelmas daisy, 274.

Michael Obrenovitch III (1823–68). Prince of Serbia; succeeded 1840, deposed 1842, restored 1860; secured withdrawal of Turkish troops from Serbia; assassinated by Karageorgevitch supporters.

Michelangelo (mī-kel-an'-je-lō), **Buonarroti** (1475–1564). It. sculptor,

painter, architect, and poet, **2160**, 1785, 2476, 2906; Adam, 2161; Adonis dying, 28; "La Pietà," 2765; Moses, 1783; method of work, 2904; and Renaissance, 3765, 3766; statue of David, 2161.

Michelet (mēsh'-lā), **Jules.** (1798–1874). Fr. historian, learned and interesting but partisan and uncritical ("Historie de France").

Michelson (mī'-kel-son), **Albert, Abraham** (1852–1931), Amer. physicist and educator, b. Ger.; investigator of light phenomena; head of dept. of physics at Univ. of Chicago; invented echelon spectroscope; interferometer, 3080; measures star diameter, 3080; the Michelson-Morley experiment, 2730.

Michigan (mish'-i-gan), a N.-cent. state of U.S.A., 58,216 sq. m.; pop. 5,256,000; 2101, map, 1315.

Michigan, Lake, 3rd largest of Great Lakes (22,400 sq. m.), 2161, 3287; map, 1515.

Michigan Boulevard, impt. street in Chicago, 783.

Michoacan (mē-chō-ah-kahn'), state in s. Mexico on Pacific; 23,000 sq. m.; pop. 1,182,000; cap. Morolia.

Mickey Mouse, invented by Walt Disney, 829.

Mickiewicz (mits'-kyā-vich), **Adam** (1798–1855), greatest of Polish poets; chiefly famous for epics based on the folk tales and legends of his nation, 2641.

Mickle Fell. Mt. in N. Riding of Yorkshire (2,591 feet), 2546.

Microbes. See Germs.

Microfarad, practical unit of elec. capacitance, one-millionth of a farad, 1133.

Microm'eter, 2161.

Mi'cron, a scientific unit of measurement (symbol μ), one thousandth of a millimetre, 335, 2161.

Micronesia, a collection of small isl. groups in Pacific, 2470.

Mi'cro-or'ganisms. See Bacteria; Germs; Protozoa.

Mi'crophone, 2162; in gramophone recording, 1497; crystal, 2604; directional, 2163; of telephone, 3011; wireless, 3393.

Mi'croscope, 2163; lenses, 1925; electron, 2165.

Micro-waves, very short radio waves, 30 cm. to 1 cm. (or less), with frequencies of 1,000 to 30,000 megacycles per sec. (or more), 2729, 3397.

Mi'das. In Gk. myth., changed all he touched into gold, 2166.

Middelburg. Dutch tn.; cap. of Zeeland; back of plate f. 2321, 2321. Taken by British, Nov. 1944.

Middle Ages, 2166, 1630; history chart, see pages 3840-3842; agriculture, 80, 85; architecture, 218, 220; armour, 240; books and libraries, 509, 1930; castles, 717, 713-16; growth of cities, 403; commerce, 403, 407, 1575; Crusades, 936; education, 2462; fairs and markets, 1256; falconry, 1258; farming, 80, 85; feudal system, 1268; footwear, 521; Froissart, 1399; guilds in, 1553, 1554; hats and caps, plate f. 1584; heraldry, 1614; house furnishings, 1409; knighthood, 1863, plate f. 1864; literature, 1210, 1379, 1456, 2401, 2798; miracle and mystery plays, 1039, 2189; monks and monasticism, 2212-14; ordeals and other forms of trial, 1843; painting, 2476; prisons and punishments, 2687; roads, 2783; Robin Hood, 2790; serfdom, 2981; ships, 2946; spice and condiment trade, 3060; superstitions, 1033; table utensils, 1867; tapestry, 3152, 3153; water supply, 3347. See also Feudal System; Guilds; Knighthood.

Middle English, 1209.

Middlesbrough. Spt. and mfg. city on Tees in N.E. Eng.; pop. 140,470; centre of large iron and coal dist., 3435.

Middlesex. Small inland county N. and W. of London; 233 sq. m.; 50 sq. m. now included in administrative co. of London; pop. 1,629,000; **2168.**

Middlesex Hospital, 2168.

Middle Temple, London, one of the Inns of Courts, close to Law Courts ; it is famous for its hall, which was completed in 1572 ; the carved oak roof was one of best specimens of Elizabethan work in London ; bombed by Germans in 1940 it was repaired, and was reopened in 1949.

Middleton-in-Teesdale. Small tn. of Durham ; pop. 2,000 ; nr. is High Force, finest waterfall in Eng.

Middleton, Thomas (c. 1570–1627), Eng. dramatist ; collaborated with William Rowley and others (" The Spanish Gipsy " ; " The Changeling " ; " A Fair Quarrel "), 1040.

Middlings, in flour milling, 1320.

Mid'gard. In Norse myth., the Earth.

Midgardsorm or **Midgard serpent**, in Norse myth., serpent encircling the earth.

Midges, small flies, 1329.

Midi, Canal du (mē'-dē) Fr., 686.

Mid-iron, a golf club, *1484*.

Midland counties or **Midlands.** A name applied collectively to most of the interior counties of England.

Midlo'thian, also known as Edinburgh-shire ; pop. (est.) 563,000 ; 370 sq. m. ; 2027.

Midnight sun, in Norway, **2168** ; *plates f. 2168, 2169*, 2392 ; in Antarctica, *172*.

Midshipman, in Brit. Navy, junior officer between cadet and sub-lieutenant, *plate f.* 2292.

Midsummer Day, June 24, feast of the nativity of St. John the Baptist.

" Midsummer Night's Dream, A," comedy by Shakespeare, **2169**.

Midway Islands, Hawaiian Isls. group (U.S.A.), midway between Asia and America ; on trans-Pacific air route ; U.S. naval victory, Jun. 1942, 2474, 3293.

" Mignon," opera by Thomas, 2439.

Mignonette (min-yon-et'), a flowering plant, **2169**.

Migration, animal, 2169 ; Arctic tern, 1555 ; birds, 438, 440, 2169, *2171* ; crabs, 925 ; cranes, 3098 ; eels, 1092, *1093*, 2169 ; goose, 1484 ; locusts, 1511, *plate f. 1512* ; salmon, 2865 ; swallows, 3124.

Migration, human, 2170.

Miguel (mē-gel'), **Dom Maria Evaristo** (1802–66). Portuguese prince and pretender, 3rd son of John VI, and uncle of Maria da Gloria, whose throne he usurped (1828–34).

Mihailovitch (mil-hīl'-o-vich), **Draza** (1893–1946). Yugoslav soldier ; on Ger. invasion of Yugoslavia 1941, he raised guerrilla forces, Chetniks, against invaders ; given money and equipment by Allies until May 1944 ; min. of war in exiled Yugoslav govt. ; accused by Tito of collaboration with Germans ; tried and shot as collaborator July 1946 ; 3440.

Mikado (mi-kah'-dō), emp. of Japan, 1798 ; palace at Tokyo, 3222 ; became constitutional monarch in 1946, 1629.

" Mikado," Gilbert and Sullivan opera.

Mikindani. E. African site, 230 m. s. of Dar-es-Salaam, for pt. to serve Kongwa groundnut scheme, Tanganyika.

Mikolajczyk (mik-ō-lī'-chik), **Stanislaw** (b. 1901). Pol. statesman ; head of Peasant party in 1947 ; defended Warsaw against Gers. 1939 ; escaped to London, succeeding Sikorski as prime min. 1943 ; in Warsaw in 1945 became vice-premier, but by 1947 in Opposition ; persecuted, he fled to Eng. and thence to U.S.A.

Milan Obrenovitch IV (1854–1901). Prince of Serbia ; succeeded (1868) ; secured Serbian independence and became king (1882) ; abdicated 1889 in favour of his son, Alexander I.

Milan, 2nd largest city of It. ; pop. 1,260,000 ; **2170** ; Ambrosian library, 138 ; cathedral, *1236* ; La Scala, 3196 ; war of Charles V and Francis I, 1383 ; 2nd World War, 2172.

Milan, Edict of (A.D. 313), 817.

Milanion, Atalanta's husband, 283.

Milazzo, spt. of Sicily ; pop. 16,000.

Mildenhall, R.A.F. stn., Suffolk.

Mildenhall Treasure. Hoard of Romano-British silverware found West Row, Suffolk, in 1942.

Mil'dews and moulds, **2173**, 1407 ; nitrifying action, 2374 ; penicillin, 2544 ; streptomycin, 3103.

Mile, a unit of measure. *See* **Weights and Measures.**

Miles Master, a Brit. training aircraft, *43*.

Miletus (mī-lē'-tus), great maritime city and republic on Aegean Sea in anc. Ionia, Asia Minor ; colonizer and centre of learning ; sacked by Persians, 494 B.C. ; *map, 30*.

Mil'ford Haven, Wales. Natural harbour on the coast of Pembrokeshire ; it extends inland for about 17 m. and is from 1 to 2 m. in breadth ; the Royal Dockyard of Pembroke is on an islet on the s., whilst the tn. of Milford is on the N. side ; 1576, 2538.

Military Academy. *See* **Royal Military Academy.**

Military Cross, Brit. (M.C.), 2448 ; Belgian, 2449.

Military Medal, Brit. (M.M.), 2449.

Militia (mi-lish'-a), civilian bodies who receive occasional military training ; in the United Kingdom they were superseded by the Territorial Force (now Territorial Army) in 1908 ; conscripts of 1939 were called militia men.

Milk, 2173 ; animals giving milk, 2077, 2173 ; casein, 2174, 2694 ; best cattle for, *731* ; certified, 955 ; cheese-making, 765 ; condensed, 2174, 1341, 3084 ; cows, 730 ; dairying, 955 ; evaporated, 2174, 1341, 3084 ; food value, 1338, *1339*, *2174* ; of goats, 1478 ; pasteurized, 955, *1341*, 2528 ; powdered, 2174, 1341 ; protein in, *2174*, 2694 ; puddings, 902 ; rationing in U.K., 2175 ; specific gravity, *1674* ; substitute fluid obtained from trees, 862 ; sugar in, 3116, 2174 ; vitamins, 3327 ; wool from, *850* ; yield of good cow, 956.

Milk of lime, softens water, 3351.

Milk of magnesia, milky solution of magnesium hydroxide in water.

Milk of sulphur, 3116.

Milk sugar, or lactose, 2174.

Milk teeth, 3163, 3164.

Milkweed butterfly, egg, *1094*.

Milky Way, 3078, *3080* ; nebulae, 2310 ; Galileo's telescope, 1415.

Mill, James (1773–1836). Eng. philosopher and economist, whose strong personality and brilliant conversation added to influence of his books (" History of British India " ; " Analysis of the Human Mind," his greatest work) ; father of John Stuart Mill.

Mill, John Stuart (1806–73), Eng. philosopher, economist, scholar, and enthusiastic democrat, **2175** ; and Carlyle, 702 ; George Eliot, 1145 ; Emerson, 1156 ; " Principles of Political Economy," 1081.

Millais (mil'-ā), **Sir John Everett** (1829–96). Eng. painter, one of the Pre-Raphaelites, 2476, 2681 ; Carlyle, *703* ; " Mercy—St. Bartholomew's Day," *1651* ; " St. Stephen," *2112* ; " Victory, O Lord ! " *2235*.

Mill'bank. Dist. in Westminster, London, on the left bank of the Thames, deriving its name from prison in existence 1812–93 ; here are the Tate Gallery, and vast new office blocks such as Thames House and Imperial Chemical House.

Millen'nium. The kingdom of Christ on earth, period of 1,000 years preceding the Last Judgement ; belief in it is based on Rev. xx. 1–5.

Miller, Hugh (1802–56). Scot. geologist and author ; became editor, and later owner, of The Witness, a Free Church organ ; began life as a quarry worker (" First Impressions of England and Its People " ; " The Testimony of the Rocks ").

Millerand (mēl-e-rahn) **Alexandre** (1859–1943), Fr. premier, later pres. (1920–24) ; former Socialist ; instrumental in securing much social legislation ; war minister 1914–15.

Miller's thumb. Small fish, *Cottus gobio*, common in fresh water, with large flat head and spiny fins ; known also as bull-head.

Millet (mē'-yā), **Jean François** (1814–75). Fr. painter of peasant life, **2176**, *1374*, 1378.

Mil'let. Any of various cereal grasses with small grains borne on spikes or panicles, **2175** ; in India, 1691.

Mill Hill. Dist. N.W. of London ; Mill Hill School is an important public school ; London University Observatory, *3119* ; clock at, *3212* ; telescope, *3181*.

Mil'ligram. Unit in metric system (0·015 grain), 2155.

Millikan, Robert Andrews (b. 1868), American scientist ; Nobel prize in 1923.

Mil'lilitre. Unit in metric system (0·27 fluid dram), 2155.

Mil'limetre. Unit in metric system (0·03937 inch), 2155.

Millin, Sarah Gertrude, contemporary S. African writer, 3020.

Milling, of flour, 1320.

Mil'lipede or " thousand feet." A many-legged arthropod, 3065.

" Mill on the Floss, The." Novel by George Eliot, 1146.

Mills, flour. *See* **Flour and flour-milling.**

Mills grenade. Hand bomb invented by Sir William Mills (d. 1932).

Millstones, 1320.

Millwall. Dist. of E. London, in the Isle of Dogs ; name derived from seven windmills which once stood on river-bank ; Millwall Docks centre of grain trade ; Thames tunnel.

Milman, Henry Hart (1791–1868). Eng. churchman, historian and poet ; dean of St. Paul's, London, from 1849 to death (" History of the Jews " ; " History of Christianity " ; " History of Latin Christianity ").

Milne, Alan Alexander (b. 1882). Brit. author and playwright, on staff of Punch from 1906. Published children's verse (" When We Were Very Young," " Now We Are Six ") and stories (" Winnie-the-Pooh," " The House at Pooh Corner ") ; and wrote plays (" Mr. Pim Passes By," " The Dover Road," " The Truth about Blayds ") ; 1966.

Milner, Alfred, Viscount (1854–1925). Brit. statesman and colonial administrator ; High Commissioner for S. Africa (1897–1905) ; Sec. of State for War (1918–19) ; Sec. of State for Colonies (1919–21).

Milner, Sir Frederick, Bart. (1840–1931). Brit. politician, known as " the soldiers' and sailors' friend."

Milo (mī'-lō) or **Milon** (6th cent. B.C.). Gk. athlete ; crowned 6 times at Olympic Games and 6 times at Pythian Games for wrestling ; carried an ox through stadium.

Milo. *See* **Melos.**

Milosh Obrenovitch (1780–1860). Prince of Serbia, born a peasant ; for services in freeing Serbia from Turkish rule called " father of his country " ; 2922.

Miltiades (mil-tī'-a-dēz) (d. c. 488 B.C.). Athenian general, victor over Persians at Marathon (490 B.C.), 2555, 230.

Milton, John (1608–74). Eng. poet, 2176, 1211, *1212* ; birthplace, 2176 ; cottage, *2177* ; story of " Paradise Lost," 2178 ; " Samson Agonistes," 2870.

Milvian or. **Mulvian Bridge.** Anc. bridge over Tiber on Flaminian Way where Maxentius was drowned following his defeat by Constantine, A.D. 312, *894*.

Milwau'kee, Wisconsin, U.S.A. Spt. and largest city of state, on w. shore of L. Michigan ; large general trade ; pop. 578,000 ; 3400.

Milyukov (mil-ū-kof'), **Paul** (1859–1943). Rus. historian and statesman, leader of Constitutional Democrats in rev. of 1917.

Mime (mīm), play without words, 1039.

Mim'icry, among animals. *See* **Protective coloration.**

Mim idae. Mocking-bird family.

Mimir (mē'-mer). Giant in Norse myth., 2421.

Minner'mus (7th cent. B.C.). Gk. elegiac poet, the first to make elegiac verse a vehicle for love-poetry.

Mimo'sa. Any of various shrubs or trees of the bean family, *Leguminosae*, with sensitive leaves ; bark used in tanning, 1911 ; name sometimes applied to wattles.

Mimosoidae, a sub-fam. of *Leguminosae*. Acacia a member, 16 ; false acacia is also a member of *Leguminosae*.

Min, r. of S.E. China, entering Formosa Strait ; part navigable.

Mi'na. Vil. near Mecca, Arabia, 2172.

Min'arets. Slender towers of mosque provided with balconies from which are issued the calls to prayer, *2066, 2067*

Minch. Strait separating Hebrides from N.W. coast of Scotland, 1601.

Mind. That which thinks, remembers, reasons, feels or wills ; the brain is the main seat of the mind, 2180 ; brain, 545 ; psychology, the science of, 2697. *See* Psychology.

Mindanao. Southernmost and 2nd largest isl. of Philippines ; 36,906 sq. m., 2568 ; *map, 1074–75* ; in Jap occupn., 1942–45.

Min'den, Ger. Old tn. in w. on the r. Weser near which English and Prussians defeated French (1759) in Seven Years' War, 2924.

Mindszen'ty, Jossef (b. 1891). Hungarian cardinal, and R.C. primate ; accused by the Hungarian govt., Dec. 1948, of anti-democratic activities and of violating currency regulations ; sentenced to life imprisonment.

Mine detector, 2185.

Mineral'ogy, 2180.

Mineral oils, 1262 ; petroleum and its derivatives, 2426–31.

Mineral paints. Pigments derived from minerals, 2478.

Minerals, 2180 ; crystalline and amorphous forms, 939 ; diamond the hardest, 1009 ; in water, 3351. *See also* Geology: Mines and Mining, *and* the various minerals and countries by name.

Mineral salts ; in food, 1338, *1339,* 1016 ; needed by plants, 2998.

Mineral springs, 3069.

Miner bee, 394.

Miner'va. In Rom. myth., goddess of wisdom, identified with Gk. Athena, 284. *See* Athena.

Mines and mining, 2181 ; child labour in, *802* ; "choke damp" or carbon dioxide, 700 ; coal, 855, *856, 2182, 2183* ; copper, 907 ; Davy's safety lamp, *979,* 980, *1889* ; deepest mine, *89* ; diamond, *1010* ; dredging, 1047 ; geologists, 1434 ; gold, 1473, *2183* ; hydraulic, 1480 ; iron, *1752,* 1753 ; machinery, *2183* ; placer mining, 1479; oil, 2426; sulphur, 3116.

Mines in warfare, 2184 ; magnetic, 3417 ; sown by submarines, 3107.

Minesweeper. Vessel equipped to clear or neutralize sea mines, 2186, *2301.*

Ming dynasty. The ruling dynasty in China 1368–1644 ; cap. and tombs, 810, 2538 ; art of, *811, 812.*

Minho (mē'-nyō). A r. forming part of N. boundary of Port., 170 m. long, 2658, *map, 3030.*

Miniature camera, 2579, *2580.*

Miniature painting, Eng., 1177.

Min'ion type, 3270.

Minister. One charged with the performance of a duty, such as the representative of the State, a Cabinet minister or ambassador ; also a clergyman or priest ; particularly applied to pastors of Free Church congregations.

Min'ium, or red lead, 1908.

Mink. Animal related to weasel, 2186.

Minneap'olis, Minnesota, U.S.A. Largest city in state, on Mississippi ; pop. 492,370 ; 2186.

Minnehaha (min-e-hah'-hah) (" Laughing Water "). Maiden loved by Hiawatha, *2023.*

Min'nesingers. Medieval Ger. lyric poets, 2262.

Minnesongs, in German lit., 1456.

Minneso'ta. A state in N.-cent. U.S.A.; 84,068 sq. m. ; pop. 2,792,300 ; **2186.**

Minnesota River, U.S.A. Tributary of Mississippi (450 m. long).

Minnow. Fish, 2783.

Mino'an Age, 30.

Minorca (mi-nor'-ka). Second largest of Balearic Isls. ; 290 sq. m. ; pop. 380,000 ; fine harbour at Port Mahon ; 342, *map, 3030.*

Minorca. A breed of fowls, *2671.*

Minorites. Same as **Franciscans.**

Minos (mī'-nos), in Gk. myth., king and lawgiver of Crete, son of Zeus and Europa, father of Ariadne, 30 ; after his death, judge in underworld ; legend of Cretan bull, 1615 ; and Daedalus, 955 ; name given to Minoan Age, 30 ; Minotaur myth, 3201, 955 ; palace ruins, 927.

Minotaur (mī'-nō-tawr). In Gk. myth., bull-headed man-monster, eater of human flesh ; imprisoned by Minos in Cretan labyrinth, 3201, 955, 927.

Minsk. Cap. of White Russia, U.S.S.R., on r. Svisloch, city 400 m. s.w. of Leningrad ; pop. 239,000 ; in Ger. occupn., 1941–44.

Minstrels. Medieval bards, 2262, 2363; romances, 2798.

Mint. A genus of herbs, 2187, 3061.

Mint, Royal, London, 2187, *2188.*

Mintha. Nymph in Gk. myth., 2187.

Min'to, Gilbert Elliot-Murray-Kynynmound, Earl of (1845–1914). Gov.-Gen. of Canada (1883–85) and Viceroy of India (1905–10).

Minuet (min-ū-et'). Old-fashioned dance, music in triple measure, 965 ; in sonata, 2264.

Minute (min'-it), in measurement of angles, 1436.

Minute. Why divided into 60 seconds, 329.

Miocene (mī'-ō-sēn) **period,** in geologic time, 1432.

Miquelon (mē-ke-lon). Fr. isl. group near s. coast of Newfoundland forming (with St. Pierre) an Overseas Territory ; 83 sq. m. ; cod fisheries.

Mir (mēr). Rus. vil. community, 2845.

Mirabeau, Honoré Gabriel Riqueti, Comte de (1749–91). Fr. Rev. statesman, 2189, *1394,* 1393.

Miracle plays. Religious plays of Middle Ages, **3189,** 1039.

Miraflores Locks, in Panama Canal, 2490.

Mirage (mēr'-ahzh), an optical illusion, 2190.

Miran'da, in Shakespeare's " Tempest," daughter of Prospero, 3185.

Mir'iam. Hebrew prophetess, sister of Moses (Exod. ii ; xv. 20).

Mir Jaffier or **Jafar.** Indian general and ruler, 842.

Miron (mīr'-on) (5th cent. B.C.). Gk. sculptor, 1528 ; " Discobolus," *1532.*

Mirrors, 2190 ; in studies of light, reflections, etc., 1939, *1940,* 2191 ; periscope, 2552 ; telescope, *3178,* 3180, 3181.

Misch metal, alloy of iron and rare earths ; use, 3188.

" Misérables, Les " (The Unfortunates). Novel by Victor Hugo, 1650.

Mishua. Part of Talmud, 1601.

Missel-thrush. *See* **Mistle-thrush.**

Missions, Christian, 817 ; apostles, 188 ; St. Boniface, 500 ; Celtic monasticism, 2212 ; Franciscan, 1384 ; Grenfell, 1543 ; Japan, 1798, 1799, 3429 ; Livingstone, 1970 ; Loyola, 2032 ; N. Amer, Indians, 2107 ; Pacific Isls., 2473 ; St. Patrick, 2528 ; St. Paul, 2529 ; St. Peter, 2562 ; St. Francis Xavier, 3429.

Mississippi. A gulf state of U.S.A., 46,716 sq. m. ; pop. 2,183,800 ; 2192.

Mississippi. Greatest r. of N. Amer. and, including Missouri, the longest in the world (4,200 m., or, without the passes and old meanders, 3,988 m.), 2191, *2193,* 3287 ; and American colonization, 2380 ; in Minnesota, 2186 ; discovery, 143 ; floods, 2192 ; Marquette and, 2017 ; levees, 2192.

Mississippi Valley, 3285, 2380.

Missolonghi (mis-ō-lon'-gē) or **Mesolonghi.** Tn. in W. Greece on Gulf of Patras ; cap. of Aetolia and Acamania ; pop. 9,200 ; brilliantly

defended against Turks in War of Liberation 1822–26 ; scene of Byron's death.

Missouri (mi-zoor'-i). A N.-cent. state of U.S.A. ; 69,674 sq. m. ; pop. 3,784,700 ; 2194 ; Mississippi r., 2191 ; Missouri r., 2194.

Missouri. Chief tributary of Mississippi (2,723 m.), **2194,** 3287 ; junction with Missis-ippi, 2194 ; the combined river, the Missouri-Mississippi, has a length, excluding the " passes " (delta) and meanders now cut off, of 3,988 m. ; including them, its length is 4,200 m.

Mist. How formed, 1333.

Mistle-thrush, 3205.

Mis'tletoe. A parasitic evergreen shrub, **2194,** 2514 ; how it spreads its seed, 2917 ; Norse legend, 341 ; legend of the Golden Bough, 1387.

Mist pools. Dewponds, *1000.*

Mistral, Frédéric (1830–1914). Fr. poet, leader of Provençal literary revival (" Mireio ") ; Nobel prize winner 1904 ; aids Fabre, 1255.

Mistral, Gabrielle (b. 1889). Chilean poet, 3027.

Mis'tral. A cold wind blowing from the Alps, 3355.

Mitch'am. Tn. in Surrey, 4 m. N.W. of Croydon, on R. Wandle ; pop. 65,000 ; formerly lavender and mint grown.

Mitchell, Mt. On boundary between N. Carolina and Tennessee, U.S.A., 190.

Mitchell, Margaret. Pen-name of Amer. novelist, Mrs. Margaret M. Mitchell Marsh, who in 1936 pub. record-breaking " best-seller," " Gone With the Wind," winning Pulitzer prize ; killed in road accident Aug. 1949.

Mitchison, Naomi M. (b. 1897). Scottish novelist, daughter of J. S. Haldane ; " The Corn King and the Spring Queen," " The Blood of the Martyrs," " The Bull Calves " (early history of the Haldane family) ; 1966.

Mites. Tiny parasitic animals related to spiders.

Mitford, Mary Russell (1787–1855). Eng. novelist (" Our Village ") ; charming unpretentious sketches from life.

Mithradates (mith-ra-dā'-tēz) or **Mithridates, the Great** (131–63 B.C.). King of Pontus, waged wars against Rome in Asia Minor, exalted in legend for his culture, courage, physical strength, and skill in use of weapons ; said to have poisoned himself, 2654, 2809.

Mithras (mith'-ras). Persian god of sun and truth, whose worship was last great Asiatic cult imported into Rome before establishment of Christianity ; Mithraism very prevalent in Roman army ; many striking resemblances to Christianity in doctrine and rites.

Mi'tral valve, of heart, 1592.

Mi'tre, bishop's and archbishop's ceremonial hat, 1584.

Mitscherlich, Eilhardt (1794–1863), Ger. chemist, established (1819) principle of isomorphism in crystals ; discovered nitro-benzene etc. and the optical activity of tartaric acid, 3155.

Mittelhorn. Peak of the Wetterhorn, in the Bernese Oberland.

Mit'tenwald. Tn. on the boundary between Austria and Bavaria ; a favourite holiday resort.

Mitylene. *See* **Mytilene.**

Mixture, in chemistry, 767.

Mizpah or **Mizpeh.** Name of several places in Palestine ; most important Mizpah of Gilead, where Jacob raised heap of stones and made covenant of peace with Laban (Gen. xxxi. 49).

Mjölnir (myēl'-nēr). In Norse myth., hammer of Thor, 3204.

Mnemosyne (nē-mos'-i-nē). In Gk. myth., daughter of Uranus and Gaea, and mother of the Muses, the personification of memory, 2259.

Mo'a. River in Cuba rising in E. end of Sierra Maestra Mts. ; flows into Guatanamo Bay ; 300-foot cascade, 941.

Moa. Extinct bird of New Zealand, similar to emu, flightless but with long and powerful legs ; remains of 20 species found,

Moab (mō'-ab) or **Mo'abites.** Semitic tribe living in anc. Palestine E. of Dead Sea and the Jordan, 1829 ; Ruth. the Moabite, 2857.

Moat. A ditch, often filled with water, round a castle, 717, 715.

Mo'bile (-ēl'), Alabama, U.S.A., spt. and 2nd city of the state ; pop. 78,700 ; trade in iron and steel products, cotton, lumber ; original city founded in 1702 by the French.

Moc'casin. Red Indian shoe, usually made of deerskin or other soft leather ; 2756.

Mocha (mō'ka) or **Mokka.** Fortified spt. in Yemen, S. Arabia, on Red Sea ; 130 m. w. of Aden ; pop. 5,000, 196 ; coffee, 864 ; gives name to Mocha gloves, 1477.

Mocking-bird. Bird of N. Amer., resembling the thrush ; imitates the notes of other birds.

Mod'der, r. of S. Africa. Left bank trib. of the Vaal, flowing through Orange Free State ; scene in 1899 of British check in S. African War, when Lord Methuen was wounded in his attempt to relieve Kimberley.

Model Parliament, 1089, 2521.

Models and **model-making, 2194** ; in film-making, 833 ; aeroplane and ship tests, 2196 ; of loom, 2025, 3360 ; of ship, 2952 ; of war targets, 2195.

Modena (mō'-dā-na). City in N. It., 100 m. E. of Genoa ; cap. of prov. of Modena ; pop. 96,300 ; fine Romanesque cath. ; famous campanile ; univ. founded 1683 ; joins United Italy, 3319, 1769.

Modern history, extent of, 1630. See also chart under History.

Modernism, in architecture, 221 ; art, 2477, 3122 ; binding, 518 ; literature, 1216, 3122.

Modern School, 2886.

Modigliani (mō-dēl-yah'-nē), Amadeo (1884–1920). It. painter, identified with modern Fr. school of art ; highly individual in style and technique.

Modjeska (mō-jes'-ka), Helena (1844–1909). Polish tragic actress on Eng.-speaking stage, best known for Shakespearian roles (Ophelia, Juliet, Desdemona), first in Polish translations, later in English, 2983.

Mo'dred, Sir. King Arthur's nephew and one of Knights of Round Table, 255.

Mod'ulation ; amplitude, 3393 ; frequency, 3397 ; of wireless waves, 3393.

Möen. Danish isl. in the Baltic Sea between Zealand and Falster ; 82 sq. m. ; pop. 16,000 ; very fertile ; agriculture and fisheries ; cliffs, 991.

Moeran (mō'ran), Ernest J. (b. 1894). Brit. composer, whose Irish extraction influenced his musical idiom ; Symphony in G minor, violin concerto, cello concerto, songs.

Moesia (mēsh-i-a). Anc. prov. S. of Danube corresponding to modern Bulgaria and E. Yugoslavia ; settled by Goths about A.D. 376 ; Slavic tribes settled in 6th cent.

Moffat, Robert (1795–1883). Brit. missionary in Africa ; a colleague of Livingstone.

Mof'fat, Scot. Watering-place in Dumfries-shire, 63 m. S.W. of Edinburgh ; mineral springs ; pop. 2,000 ; 1055.

Moffatt, James (1870–1944). Scot. scholar ; modern version of Bible, 427.

Mogadishu, Mogadiscio, or **Magadoxo.** Cap. and chief spt. of Somalia (former Italian E. Africa); pop. (est.) 37,000 ; 1073, 3000.

Mogul, Great. Popular European name of Indian emperors descended from Babar, the first Great Mogul (d. 1530).

Mogul Empire, in India, 2206 ; Agra, the cap., 77, 1714, 1715 ; and Clive, 842 ; Delhi, 987 ; peacock throne, 2532 ; Taj Mahal, 3147, 3148.

Mohacs (mō'-hach). Market tn. in N. Yugoslavia on Danube ; pop.17,230 ; coal and silk centre ; formerly in Hungary ; two battles, at the beginning and close of Turkish rule of Hungary, 1656, 3264.

Mo'hair. A cloth, 850, 1478, 3405.

Mŏham'med. See Mahomet.

Mohammed I. Sultan of Turkey (1413–21), 3264.

Mohammed II (c. 1430–81). Sultan of Turkey 1451–81 ; ambitious, ruthless ; gains Constantinople, 3264.

Mohammed V (1844–1918). Sultan of Turkey, 3265.

Mohammed VI (1861–1926). Sultan of Turkey, deposed 1922 by Nationalist Assembly, 3265.

Mohammedanism. See Mahomedanism.

Mohave Desert. A desert region lying principally in San Bernardino Co., California ; part of Colorado Desert.

Mohawks. Leading Red Indian tribe of Iroquois group, formerly living in lower Mohawk valley.

Mohenjo-daro. Site of Indo-Sumerian culture in Sind, India, 2974.

Mohicans (mō-hē'-kanz). Red Indian tribe and-confederacy of Algonquian stock originally living in Hudson valley, later in Massachusetts, Connecticut, and also Pennsylvania, U.S.A., where most of them were absorbed into the Delawares.

Möhne (mē'-ne) Dam, on Möhne riv., Westphalia, Ger. ; holds back 140 million tons of water to supply Ruhr industry ; breached, with Eder dam, by Wing-Comdr. G. P. Gibson (q.v. in f-i.) May 1943.

Mohs's Scale, measuring comparative hardnesses of metals, against standard metals, ranging from 1 to 10 (1=talc, 3=calcite, 7=quartz, 10=diamond) ; introduced in 1820 by F. Mohs (1773–1839) ; 176.

Moiseiwitsch (moi-zā-vich), Benno (b. 1890). Russ.-born Brit. pianist ; friend of Rachmaninov, whose works he interprets brilliantly.

Moissan (mwah-sahn), Henri (1852–1907). Fr. chemist ; Nobel prize for chemistry in 1906 ; developed electric furnace for laboratory use and simplified production of acetylene gas ; artificial diamonds, 1011.

Moisture. See Humidity.

Mokka. Same as Mocha.

Mola, Emilio. Nationalist general in Sp. Civil War, 3039.

Molar teeth, 3163.

Molas'ses. By-product of sugar ; 3114 ; from sugar-beet, 3114 ; spirits from, 3067.

Mold. Co. tn. of Flintshire, Wales ; pop. 6,200, 1315.

Moldau. See Vltava.

Moldavia. Dist. in Rumania between R. Pruth and Carpathian Mts. ; 14,000 sq. m. ; pop. over 2,000,000 ; 2840. Russians entered Mar. 1944 ; ceded to U.S.S.R. in 1945.

Moldavia. Autonomous republic of Ukraine, U.S.S.R. ; a. 3,300 sq. m. ; pop. 2,200,000 ; cap. Tiraspol.

Mole. A small insect-eating mammal, 2196, 2198 ; feet, 1572.

Mole, r. of Sussex and Surrey, flows 30 m. to the Thames, 3122.

Mole cricket, 928 ; foot and ear, 1727.

Molecular weight, 769.

Molecules (mol'-e-kūlz). Smallest possible particles of a chemical compound, 769, 771, 773 ; difference from atoms, 766 ; electrically charged, 1738, 1739 ; fluorescence, 2573 ; of liquid, 3084 ; motions cause heat, 1594 ; move freely in gases, 1419 ; of soap, 2994 ; speed, 1594 ; studied by infra-red rays, 1722 ; visible under electron microscope, 2165 ; in surface tension, 3121 ; of waxes, 3359.

Molière (mōl-yār'), (Jean - Baptiste Poquelin) (1622–73). Fr. comic dramatist, 2198, 1380, 1381.

Mollendo. Spt. in Peru ; pop. 10,000 ; 2559.

Mollison, James Allan (b. 1905). Scot. airman ; record solo fight from Australia (1931) ; solo flights across both N. and S. Atlantic and to and from the Cape ; married Amy Johnson, 1835.

Mol'luscs. A group of soft-bodied animals, usually shelled, of a definite primitive type, 2199, 156 ; appearance in geologic time, 1432 ; cockles and mussels, 860 ; cuttle-fish, 945 ; nautilus, 2199 ; octopus, 946 ; oysters

2466 ; yield pearls, 2533, 2534 ; shells, of, 2942, 2943.

Mollwitz (mōl'-vits), Poland. Vil. 25 m. S.E. of Breslau ; here Frederick the Great defeated Austrians under Marshal Neipperg (1741) in First Silesian War. Ceded from Ger. 1945.

Molnar, Ferencz (b. 1878). Hungarian dramatist ; comedies include " Liliom " and " The Guardsman," 1042.

Moloch (mō'-lok) or **Molech.** Semitic fire-god, whose worship included child-sacrifice.

Molokai. One of the Hawaiian Isls. ; 261 sq. m. ; pop. 5,340 ; has large leper settlement.

Molotov (mol'-ō-toff), Vyacheslav Mikhailovich (b. 1890). Russ. politician, 2199 ; in Mar. 1949 he became a deputy premier of the U.S.S.R.

Moltke (molt'-ke), Helmuth Johannes von (1848–1916). Ger. general, nephew of following ; chief of staff at outbreak of 1st World War ; superseded by Falkenhayn in Dec. 1914 ; afterwards appointed chief of the department dealing with the important task of organizing the reserves and the territorial army corps.

Moltke, Helmuth Karl, Count von (1800–91), Prussian field-marshal and chief of staff, greatest strategist of later 19th cent. ; reorganizer of Prussian army ; planned campaigns against Austria (1866) and France (1870–71) ; a strong reserved man, " silent in 7 languages " ; in Franco-Prussian War, 1385.

Moluc'cas or **Spice Islands.** Group of Indonesian isls. in Malay archipelago between New Guinea and Celebes ; 192,404 sq. m. ; pop. est. 893,400 ; export spices, sago, coconuts ; map, 1074-75 ; cloves, 854 ; discovered, 2056 ; Japanese held 1942–44 ; recognized by Netherlands govt. in Dec. 1946 as part of new state of E. Indonesia.

Mo'ly. Fabled flower with magic properties, 835.

Molybdenite (mo-lib'-de-nīt.) A soft grey sulphide of molybdenum ; crystals used as wireless detectors.

Molyb'denum (Mo). A silvery metallic element ; atomic weight, 96·0 ; with steel gives alloy that does not crack, 777 ; in elec. lighting, 1135 ; "trace" metal in diet, 2149. Molybdenite was confused with the lead ore, galena ; hence the name molybdenum from the Greek molubdos lead.

Mombasa (mom-bas'-sa). Chief tn. and spt. of Kenya, Brit. E. Africa on isl. connected by causeway with mainland ; pop. 102,500 ; rly. terminus ; coaling station.

Momen'tum. The power of a moving body to overcome resistance ; equals its mass multiplied by its velocity, 2592 ; of bullet, 2793.

Mommsen, Theodor (1817–1903). Ger. classical scholar and historian, called by Freeman " wellnigh greatest scholar of all times" ; " History of Rome " ; Nobel prize winner for literature in 1903, 1457.

Momotom'bo. Active volcano of Nicaragua on N.W. shore of L. Managua (4.250 ft.), 2364.

Momus. In Gk. myth., god of censure and mockery who found fault with everything and burst with spite, unable to find flaws in Aphrodite.

Monaco (mon'-ah-kō), Albert Honoré Charles, Prince of (1848–1922). Ruler of the principality of Monaco and oceanographer ; succeeded his father Charles III in 1889 ; served in Sp. and Fr. navies ; made a number of voyages to investigate deep-sea life and sea currents, 2219.

Monaco. The smallest state in Europe, on Mediterranean in S.E. France ; 8 sq. m. ; pop. 19,240 ; Monte Carlo in, 2219.

Mon'aghan. Inland co. of Eire on the border between Eire and N. Ireland. 498 sq. m. ; pop. 57,208 ; 2200.

" Mona Lisa " (mō-na lē'-za). Da Vinci's great portrait, also called " La Gioconda," 1926, 2032, 2033.

Monarchy (mon'-ar-ki). System of government in which supreme place is held by a king (or queen ruling in her own right), *e.g.*, Gt. Brit., Sweden, Netherlands ; in anc. Greece, 1519 ; Rome, 303, 2804.

Monasteries, suppression of the, by Henry VIII, 1612.

Monastir, formerly **Bitolj.** Commercial tn. of Yugoslavia ; pop. 32,000 ; former impt. Turkish garrison taken by Serbia in 1912.

Monazite sand, 2871, 3187, 3437, 3444.

Mönch (mênkh) ("the monk"). A peak of the Bernese Alps (13,465 ft.), 3138.

Mond, Ludwig (1839–1909). Ger. chemist ; naturalized Brit. subject, father of Sir A. Mond (*see* **Melchett, Lord**) ; one of the founders of the Brit. alkali firm of Brunner, Mond ; nickel process, 2366.

Monda'min. In Longfellow's "Song of Hiawatha," personification of Indian corn, 2023.

Monday. 2nd day of week ; meaning of name, 980.

Mondovi (mon-dō'-vē), It. City 55 m. w. of Genoa ; scene of Napoleon's victory over Sardinians (1796).

Monel metal, an alloy of nickel, 2365.

Monet (mō-nā), **Claude** (1840–1926). Fr. landscape painter, one of the chief originators (with Edouard Manet) of the Impressionist school, and therefore a most influential modern painter ; captured wonderful fleeting effects of light and atmosphere, *1375*, 1378, 2477.

Money, Sir Leo Chiozza (1870–1944). Brit. politician, economist and statistician ; b. in Genoa ; entered Parl. in 1906 ("Riches and Poverty").

Money, 2200 ; banks, 356 ; coinage, 2201 ; in economics, 1080 ; foreign exchanges, 1347 ; gold standard, 1483 ; "hard" and "soft" currencies, 1348 ; Royal Mint, 2187 ; shells, 2942 ; stocks and shares, 3093. *See also* **Economics.**

Money orders, postal, 2662.

Mongibello or **Monte Gibello.** Sicilian name for Mt. Etna, "mountain of fire," 1228.

Mongo'lia. Vast ill-defined region of E. Asia ; about 1,875,000 sq. m. ; pop. est. 2,000,000 ; **2204,** 264, 807. Consists of Mongolian People's Republic and Tannu-Tuva (Outer Mongolia), and Inner Mongolia (Chinese) ; devil-dancers of, *plate f. 965* ; *map, 2204.*

Mongolian Race, *2724, 2725, 3262* ; origin of name, 2205 ; physical characteristics, 2205 ; resemble N. Amer. Indians, 2753.

Mongols. A nomadic type originating in cent. Asia, 2205 ; conquer China, 810, 2205 ; India, 1714, 2206 ; in Mesopotamia, 2147 ; modern descendants, 1701, 2207, 2966, 3262 ; Russia, 2846, 2205 ; Tartars, 3155.

Mon'goose. A weasel-like animal of India, **2207.**

Monica, St. Mother of St. Augustine, 302.

Mon'ists. School of philosophers, which includes idealists, pantheists, and materialists, who refer all phenomena of the universe to a single principle, 2572.

Mon'itor. A warship of slow speed and light draught which carries on the open deck one or two revolving turrets containing big guns, 240.

Monitor. Ericsson's ironclad, 240, 1222.

Monitor lizard, *plate f. 1973,* 1973.

Monk or **Monck, George** (1608–70). Duke of Albemarle ; Eng. Cromwellian general, after Cromwell's death secured Stuart restoration without bloodshed through parliamentary action.

Monkey. A lower primate mammal, **2207** ; apes, 182, *183, 184* ; allied to lemurs, 1922.

Monkey-bread tree, or baobab. A huge tropical tree, 69, 3246.

Monkey-nut. *See* **Ground nut.**

Monkey-puzzle or **Chili pine** (*Araucaria imbricata*). Tree, native of the Andean region, representing a primitive group of conifers, 3246. Leaves are sharply pointed, scale-like, and cover branches completely, rendering tree unclimbable. Cones large, green, consisting of numerous pointed scales.

Monkey's dinner bell. Explosive seed-pod of the sand-box tree, *2917.*

Monks and monasticism, 2212 ; Benedictines, 412, 2212, *2214* ; in England, 1612, 2462 ; in Greece, 1527 ; libraries and books, 510, 511, 1930, 2214, *2539* ; Luther's attitude, 2759 ; St. Benedict and, 412 ; St. Botolph, monastery, *829* ; St. Francis founds Franciscans, 1383 ; St. Bernard, monastery, *128* ; in Tibet, 3208, *3209.*

Monkshood, or wolfsbane. A plant of the buttercup family, with hooded flowers, yielding aconite, *2639.*

Monmouth, James, Duke of (1649–85). Eng. pretender to the throne, the "Protestant Duke," illegitimate son of Charles II ; regarded as head of English Protestant party ; led rebellion against uncle, James II ; defeated at Sedgemoor, captured and beheaded, 1794.

Monmouth. Co. tn. of Monmouthshire ; agric. trade, tinplate and chemical works ; pop. 4,700 ; 2215.

Mon'mouthshire. Eng. co. bordering Wales ; 546 sq. m. ; pop. 434,900 ; sometimes considered as part of Wales, 2215.

Monoceros (mon-os'-e-ros) or **Unicorn.** A constellation ; position, *chart, 895.*

Monocotyle'dons. Plants with one seed leaf, as opposed to Dicotyledons, 1322, 2620, 2918.

Monoecious (mō-nē'-shus) **plants.** Those having both pistillate and staminate flowers, 1321.

MONEY OF BRITAIN AND OTHER COUNTRIES

GOLD COINS

	s.	d.
Sovereign	20	0
Half-Sovereign	10	0

Legal tender to any amount, though in practice they are superseded by Bank of England notes.

SILVER (Cupro-Nickel) COINS

	s.	d.
Crown	5	0
Double Florin	4	0
Half-Crown	2	6
Florin	2	0
Shilling	1	0
Sixpence		6
Groat		4
Threepence		3
Twopence		2
Penny		1

NICKEL ALLOY COIN

	d.
Threepence (12-sided)	3

Legal tender up to £2. The coinage of Crowns and Double Florins has been discontinued. The silver groat, twopenny-piece, and penny-piece are circulated only on special occasions. Gold coins of the value of Five Pounds and Two Pounds are also issued on special occasions.

COPPER (Bronze) COINS

	d.
Penny	1
Halfpenny	½
Farthing	¼

Legal tender up to 1s.

CHIEF IMPERIAL AND FOREIGN MONETARY UNITS

	Country
Baht (=100 Satangs)	Siam
Balboa (=100 Cents)	Panama
Belga (=5 Francs)	Belgium
Bolivar (=100 Centimos)	Venezuela
Boliviano (=100 Centavos)	Bolivia
Colon (=100 Centesimos)	Costa Rica
Colon (=100 Centavos)	Salvador
Cordoba (=100 Centavos)	Nicaragua
Crown or Koruna (=100 Heller or Haleru)	Czechoslovakia
Dinar (=1,000 Fils)	Iraq
Dinar (=100 Paras)	Yugoslavia
Dollar or Yuan (=100 Cents)	China
Dollar (=100 Cents)	U.S.A., Canada, Newfoundland, Liberia
Dollar (=100 Cents)	Malaya
Drachma (=100 Lepta)	Greece
Escudo (=100 Centavos)	Portugal
Florin or Gulden (=100 Cents)	Netherlands
Franc (=5 Lek)	Albania
Franc (=100 Centimes)	France
Franc (=100 Centimes)	Switzerland
Gourde (=100 Centavos)	Haiti
Krona or Crown (=100 Ore)	Sweden
Krone or Crown (=100 Ore)	Norway, Denmark
Kroon (=100 Sents)	Estonia
Lat (=100 Santimi)	Latvia
Lempira (=100 Centavos)	Honduras
Leu (=100 Bani)	Rumania
Lira (=100 Centesimi)	Italy
Lira (=100 Piastres)	Turkey
Litas (=100 Centas)	Lithuania
Mark or Reichsmark (=100 Pfennig)	Germany
Markka (=100 Penni)	Finland
Milreis (=1,000 Reis)	Brazil
Pengö (=100 Filler)	Hungary
Peseta (=100 Centesimos)	Spain
Peso (=100 Centavos)	Argentine
Peso (=100 Centavos)	Chile
Peso (=100 Centavos)	Colombia, Paraguay
Peso (=100 Cents)	Cuba
Peso (=100 Centavos)	Mexico
Peso (=100 Centesimos)	Uruguay
Pound (=100 Piastres)	Egypt, Sudan
Pound (=1,000 Mil's)	Palestine
Quetzal (=100 Centavos)	Guatemala
Rial (=100 Dinars)	Persia (Iran)
Rouble (=100 Kopecks)	Russia
Rupee (=16 Annas)	India, Ceylon
Sol (=100 Centavos)	Peru
Sucre (=100 Centavos)	Ecuador
Yen (=100 Sen)	Japan
Zloty (100 Grosz)	Poland

Monog'amy, among the birds, 441.

Mon'oplane. Aeroplane with one set of wings, 48.

Monop'oly. Exclusive right to carry on a particular business; medieval guilds, 1553; spice trade, 3060; Monopolies Act 1948, set up inquiry into monopolies in the U.K.

Mon'orail. Single-rail method of transport, 1562.

Mon'otheism. Belief in one God; Hebrew religion, 423; in Mahomed's teachings, 2066.

Monotrem'ata. The order of primitive egg-laying mammals, including duckbills, 2074, 2077.

Mon'otype. Type-setting machine, 2215.

Monroe Doctrine. Principle held by U.S.A.—"America for the Americans." First formulated in 1823 by Pres. Monroe (1758–1831): "The American Continents are henceforth not to be considered as subjects for future colonization by any European power"; "We should consider any attempt on their part to extend their system to any portion of this hemisphere as dangerous to our peace and safety," 3291.

Monrovia. Spt. and cap. of Liberia; pop. 10,000, 1929.

Mons. Mining and mfg. city in s.w. Belgium 35 m. s.w. of Brussels; pop. 26,400; battle (1914) in 1st World War, 3409; occupied by Germany 1940–44.

Monserrat. See Montserrat.

Mons Graupius, Agricola's victory, 78.

Monsoon. A seasonal wind of Asia, 2217, 2741, 3385; effect in India, 1692, 1701.

Montagu, Lady Mary Wortley (1689–1762). Eng. beauty, wit, letter-writer, and eccentric character; introduced inoculation against small-pox into England.

Mon'tague, in Shakespeare's "Romeo and Juliet," Romeo's family, at feud with Capulets, 3821.

Montague, Charles Edward (1867–1928). Eng. author; novels, which show fine sense of style, including "A Hind Let Loose," "Disenchantment," "Rough Justice."

Montagu House, London, museum, 584.

Montaigne (mon-tān'), Michel Eyquem de (1522–92). Fr. essayist, 2218, 1224, 1380.

Montan wax, 3359.

Montana (mon-tan'-a). State in N.W. U.S.A.; 147,138 sq. m.; pop. 559,000; Butte has pop. of 39,000, 2218.

Montanes, Martinez Juan (1568–1649). Sp. sculptor, 3040, 3046.

Montargis (mon-tahr-zhē'). Fr. tn. in dept. of Loiret, 63 m. s.E. of Paris; pop. 14,615; famous for "dog of Montargis," said to have revealed master's murderer by constantly following him. Mirabeau born at the Château de Bignon near by.

Mont Blanc. See Blanc, Mont.

Montcalm', Marquis Louis Joseph de (1712–59), Fr. general, 2218; monument, 2716.

Montebello. Vil. in N. It. 40 m. N. of Genoa, where French defeated Austrians in 1800 and 1859.

Monte Carlo. Tn. in principality of Monaco; pop. 10,680; 2219.

Monte Cassino. Mt., 1,703 ft. high, overlooking tn. of Cassino (q.v. in f-i.), 45 m. N.W. of Naples, and commanding Liri valley and route to Rome; on it stands a monastery, founded by S. Benedict in 529, which was destroyed in 589 by the Lombards, again by the Saracens and the Normans, and totally destroyed in 2nd World War by Allied bombing; new monastery foundations laid Mar. 1945.

Monte Cris'to. Small barren It. isl. in Mediterranean, about 25 m. s. of Elba; penal colony since 1874. See "Count of Monte Cristo."

Montefiore (mon-te-fē-ōr'-e), Sir Moses (1784–1885). Wealthy Jewish philanthropist in Eng.; amassed fortune on London stock exchange, and after his 43rd year devoted all his time to improving condition of Jews in any part of world where they were oppressed, particularly Russia and Turkey.

Montenegro (mon-te-nē'-grō). Prov. of Yugoslavia, in N.W. Balkan peninsula; 3,730 sq. m.; pop. 360,000; 2219, 2983; map, 344; in Balkan wars, 343; in both World Wars, 2219.

Montenevoso, Prince of. See D'Annunzio, Gabriele.

Montenotte (mon-tä-not'-tä). Vil. 25 m. w. of Genoa, It., where Napoleon won first victory (1796), defeating Austrians.

Monterey (mon-te-rā'), California, U.S.A. Resort on Monterey Bay, about 100 m. s.E. of San Francisco; pop. 10,000; has picturesque old Span. buildings; first cap. of Calif.; 663.

Monterey. Rly. and mfg. centre in N.E. Mexico, cap. of Nuevo Leon state; pop. 125,100.

Montesquieu (mon-tes-kyê), Charles Louis de Secondat, Baron de (1689–1755), Fr. political philosopher, 2219.

Montessori (mon-tes-sōr'-ē), Maria (b. 1870). It. educator and psychiatrist, inventor of the "Montessori system" of teaching, 2220.

Montessori method, 2220.

Monteverde, Claudio (1567–1643). It. composer; influence on opera, 2435.

Montevid'eo (Sp. mon-tä-vē-dā'-ō). Cap. of Uruguay; pop. 730,000; 2220, map, 3417, 3299.

Montezu'ma II (1466–1520). Last Aztec chief or "emperor" of Mexico, 325; Cortes captures, 915.

Mont'fort, Simon de (c. 1208–65), Earl of Leicester. Eng. statesman and soldier, 2221; first Parliament, 1489, 2521; leader in Barons' Wars, 1611.

Montgolfier (mon-gol-fyä), Jacques Étienne (1745–99) and Joseph Michel (1740–1810), sent up first really practical balloon, 348.

Montgomery, Field-Marshal Bernard Law, 1st Viscount (b. 1887). British soldier, renowned in 2nd World War, 2221, 2222; mil. chairman c.-in-c. committee Western Union 1948, 2322; D-day message, 2377; in command of 8th Army, 3420, map 3421; accepted Ger. surrender at Lüneberg, 3424.

Montgom'ery, James (1771–1854). Scot. poet; his "Wanderer in Switzerland" greatly admired by Byron.

Montgomery, Lucy Maud. Novelist, 685.

Montgomery, Alabama, U.S.A. Pop. 78,000; mfg. centre, cotton market; ships grain, fruit, and vegetables.

Montgomeryshire. Inland co. in cent. Wales; 797 sq. m.; pop. 48,000; 2223.

Month, in calendar 2223.

Montherlant, Henri de. Fr. writer; "Les Olympiques," "Les Célibataires," "Les Jeunes Filles"; 1382.

Montholon (mon-tō-lon'), Charles Tristan, Marquis de (1782–1853). Fr. soldier, devoted to Napoleon, whom he accompanied to exile at St. Helena; to him Napoleon dictated notes on his career.

Montmartre (mon-mahr'-tr). A district in Paris; a "Bohemian" quarter, 2517, 2518.

Montmoren'cy, Falls of, Canada. Beautiful cascade over 250 ft. high in r. Montmorency at confluence with St. Lawrence near Quebec.

Mont Pelée, dormant volcano in isl. of Martinique, plate f. 3329.

Montpe'lier, Vermont, U.S.A. Cap.; pop. 8,000; on Winooski r., in agric. region; granite, flour, lumber, wood-working machinery, and clothes pins; 3316.

Montpellier (mon-pel'-yä). City in s. Fr., 6 m. from Mediterranean; pop. 93,100; noted univ.; large trade in wine, fruit, and silk; makes soap, candles, leather, distilled liquors.

Montreal (mon-trē-awl'). Quebec, largest city of Canada; pop. 900,000; 2223; 2715; Cartier founds, 681, 712; St. Lawrence r., 2862.

Montreal, University of. At Montreal, Quebec; Cath.; men; established in 1876 as branch of Laval Univ., Quebec; practically independent after 1889, and reorganized under present name in 1919; arts, law, medicine, theology, social, political, and applied sciences.

Montrose, James, Duke of (d. 1742). Scottish leader, favoured union of Scot. and Eng.; regent of kingdom on death of Queen Anne; and Rob Roy, 2791.

Montrose', James Graham, Marquess of (1612–50). Scottish Jacobite general, 2224; wrote many poems (celebrated lyric, "My Dear and Only Love").

Monts, Pierre du Guast, Sieur de (1560–1611). Fr. courtier, founder of Acadia; sent out expedition under Champlain which founded Quebec.

Mont St. Michel (mon-san-mē-shel') ("St. Michael's Mount"), rocky isl. of w. Fr. a mile off coast of Normandy; famous for fortress-abbey, one of the noblest examples of medieval Gothic architecture.

Montserrat. In Brit. W. Indies, one of Leeward Isls.; 32 sq. m.; pop. 14,300, mostly Negroes; Soufrière, an active volcano.

Montserrat. Jagged mt. 30 m. N.w. of Barcelona, Spain; vast fissure, dividing it into two, said to have occurred at time of Crucifixion; famous monastery, in medieval legend the castle of the Holy Grail, now houses celebrated image of Virgin, visited by thousands of pilgrims yearly.

Monulph, St. (6th cent.), Bishop of Tongres; founds Liége, 1935.

Monument, The. Memorial in City of London of the Great Fire (1666), designed by Christopher Wren; erected 1671–7; it is 202 ft. high, and has a staircase of 345 steps.

Mood, in verbs, 3314.

Moodie, Mrs. Susanna (1803–85). Canadian author; contributed to periodicals and wrote poems and novels of Canadian life, 684.

Moody, Dwight Lyman (1837–99). Amer. evangelist; with Ira Sankey he several times visited Eng.

Moody, Helen Wills (b. 1905). Amer. tennis player; a Californian, she became supreme among women players after retirement of Mlle. Lenglen; won singles at Wimbledon in 1927–30, 1932, 1933, 1935, and 1938.

Moon, satellite of the earth, 2224; plate f. 2224, 2225; eclipses, 1077; and gravity, 1512, 1513; influence on earth, 1067; Jupiter compared to, 1841; in myth., 252; tides, 3209.

Moon, Mountains of the. Name given in anc. geography to African range identified in part with Ruwenzori Mts., 2370.

Moonstone, 1427.

"Moonstone, The," by Wilkie Collins (1868). A fine early detective story.

Moor. Waste land, either dry or swampy; vegetation of swampy type.

Moore, George (1853–1933). Irish novelist and dramatist, whose highly individualistic work is appreciated by only a limited public; most popular books the autobiographical trilogy "Ave," "Salve," and "Vale"; also author of "Esther Waters," "Sister Teresa," "Drama in Muslin," "Mummer's Wife," "Brook Kerith," 1216, 412, 2402.

Moore, Henry Spencer (b. 1898). Eng. sculptor, 2909, 2911.

Moore, Sir John (1761–1809). Brit. general, commander in Sp. against Napoleon at Corunna; 2227.

Moore, Mary (1861–1931). Brit. actress, wife of Sir Charles Wyndham, with whom she was associated in many theatrical ventures ("David Garrick"; "Mrs. Gorringe's Necklace"; "The Mollusc.")

Moore, Thomas (1779–1852). Irish poet, "Lalla Rookh," "Irish Melodies," and "National Airs," containing many still familiar songs, 1751.

Moore-Brabazon, J. T. C. *See* Braba-zon.

Moor-hen, 2734.

Moors. Mixed Berber-Arabian race of N. Africa 2227; architecture, 119, *plate f. 120, 3043*; civilization, 2227; in Morocco, 2227; in Spain, 3033; 1488.

Moose. The Amer. elk, 2228.

Moose Jaw, Saskatchewan. Industrial, rly., and grain distributing centre, 40 m. w. of Regina; pop. 22,600; flour, lumber, packing-house products; 3875.

Mop'lah. Fanatical Mahomedan sect of Malabar dist., India; revolted in 1921–2.

Mor, Antonis (1512–76). Dutch painter, known in Eng. as Sir Anthony More; became Court painter to Philip II of Spain, 2333, 3049.

Mora'ceae. The mulberry family of plants, including mulberries, hemp, figs, and bread-fruits.

Moraine (mō-rān'). A rock belt formed by a glacier, 1469.

Moral'ities, or morality plays. Allegorical plays of Middle Ages, 2189, 1039; " Everyman," 1244.

Morand, Paul (b. 1888). Fr. writer; graphic delineator of modern European " night life," 1382.

Morat. Tn. in w. Switzerland 15 m. w. of Berne; battle (1476), 759.

Moratin, Leandro Fernandez de (1760–1828), Sp. dramatist and poet.

Moratorium (mor-a-tōr'-i-um). A period of time during which the payment of debts and other liabilities is suspended.

Mora'via. Prov. of Czechoslovakia, formerly Austrian; 8,584 sq. m.; pop. 2,840,000; *maps, 320, 954*; people, 2983; German Protectorate 1939–45, 1451.

Moravians or **United Brethren.** Christian sect which arose in Bohemia and Moravia among followers of John Huss; noted for missionary work; Wesley influenced by, 3365.

Moray Firth, large bay on N.E. coast of Scot., 2889.

Morayshire or **Elginshire.** Co. of N. Scotland; area 476 sq. m.; pop. 44,000, 2228.

Mor'dant. An acid or " biting " substance, particularly one used to fix dye; antimony, 176; gum tragacanth, 1558.

Mordecai (mor-de-kā'-I), cousin of Esther, 1225.

More, Hannah (1745–1833). Eng. writer of verse and of plays and books on moral and religious subjects; later years devoted to philanthropy and encouragement of popular education (" Coelebs in Search of a Wife ").

More, Sir Thomas (1478–1535). Eng. statesman, scholar, and author, 2228; Erasmus and, 2764.

Morea (mō-rē'-a). Modern name for s. Greece, anc. Peloponnesus.

Moreau (mō-rō), **Jean Victor Marie** (1763–1813). Fr. Rev. general; victor of Hohenlinden (1800); exiled for alleged conspiracy against Napoleon (1813); killed on battlefield of Dresden.

Morecambe Bay, Eng. Inlet on the coast of Westmorland and Lancashire, extending 17 m. inland; from Fleetwood to Walney Island it measures 10 m. in breadth; Morecambe and Heysham, a seaside resort, seaport, and mun. bor. of Lancashire (pop. 42,000), stands on the s. shore.

Morehouse's comet, *plate f. 880.*

Morel', an edible fungus.

Morelia, Mexico. City 130 m. N.W. of Mexico City named from patriot Morelos; pop. 44,300; college of San Nicholas de Hidalgo; textiles, sugar, sweetmeats.

Morelos, Mexico. State in s.-centre; 1,916 sq. m.; pop. 182,700; cap. Cuernavaca.

Moreton Old Hall, in Cheshire, *218.*

Morgan, Charles Langbridge (b. 1894). Eng. writer; novels include " Portrait in a Mirror," " The Fountain," " Sparkenbroke," " The Voyage," " The Judge's Story "; play, " The Flashing Stream."

Morgan, Sir Henry (c. 1635–88). Brit. buccaneer, 2229.

Morgan, Lt.-Gen. Sir Frederick E. (b. 1894). Brit. soldier; as dep. chief of staff to supreme commander A.E.F. 1944–45, he planned D-day; chief of U.N.R.R.A. ops. in Ger. 1944–45.

Morgan, John Pierpont (1836–1913). Amer. banker, financier, and art collector, head of Atlantic shipping combine and of U.S. Steel Co.

Morgan, John Pierpont (1867–1943). Son of the preceding, succeeded to control of his father's banking business.

Morganat'ic marriage. Marriage of a member of a royal family to one of lesser rank; not unusual in European Court circles; neither wife nor children receive royal rank and title. In Great Britain morganatic marriage is not recognized, and Royal Marriages Act requires consent of sovereign to marriages of persons of blood royal.

Morgarten. Hill in N. Switzerland, 18 m. s. of Zürich, where Swiss mountaineers defeated Austrian army in 1315; first Swiss victory in struggle for freedom; 3141.

Morgen. Ger. word for morning. Used in Scan., Holl., Ger., and S. Africa as a measure of land—perhaps orig. the amount ploughed in a morning.

Morghen, Raffaello (1758–1833). It. engraver; copied paintings by Leonardo da Vinci, Raphael and other masters.

Moris'cos (" little Moors "). Mahomedans in Sp. who accepted baptism, and their descendants, 2227, 2568.

Morland, George (1763–1804). Eng. painter of animals and rustic scenes; many of his best paintings are familiar through engraved copies; 1182; " Visit to the Boarding School," *2883.*

Morley of Blackburn, John Morley, Viscount (1838–1923). Eng. statesman and man of letters, twice sec. for Ireland and once for India, Lord Pres. of the Council 1910 14. "Honest John," last of the philosophic Radicals, wrote " Life of Gladstone," and edited Fortnightly Review, Pall Mall Gazette, and " English Men of Letters " series (Macmillan); O.M. 1902.

Mor'mons or **Latter-Day Saints.** A religious community, 2230; in Utah, 3300.

Morning glory. Climbing plant, *Ipomoea purpurea,* popular in Eng. gardens; member of family Convolvulaceae, 3621.

Morning Post. Famous daily newspaper founded in 1722; absorbed by Daily Telegraph in 1937, 675.

" Morning star of song " (Tennyson on Chaucer), 762.

Morocco. Country, largely a French protectorate, in N.W. Africa; 231,000 sq. m.; pop. 9,000,000; 2230; Moors, 2227, *map facing p. 68*; Spain, 3030; Morocco " question," 2230; Allied landings (1942), 3420.

Morocco City. *See* Marrakesh.

Morocco leather, 1100, *1913,* 1914.

Moros. Malay race in Philippines, 2568.

Morot (mo-rō), **Aimé Nicolas** (1850–1913). Fr. historical and portrait painter; portraits of members of fashionable and artistic world of Paris, battle scenes, etc.

Morpheus (mor'-fūs). In Rom. myth., dream god, son of Somnus (sleep).

Morphine. The principal alkaloid of opium, 2442, 21.

Morphol'ogy. Science dealing with form and structure of living organisms, 150; of animals, 3447; of plants, 531.

Morris, Gouverneur (1752–1816). Amer. statesman, aristocrat by training and temperament, but ardent supporter of War of Amer. Independence because he believed in its justice; proposed decimal system of coinage and words *dollar* and *cent.*

Morris, William (1834–96). Eng. poet, artist, and social reformer, 2232; influence on furniture-making, 1412; printing press, 518; and Pre-Raphaelites, 2682; tapestries, 3153.

Morris car works, conveyor in, 896, 2405.

Morris dance. One of the reel variety of Eng. country dances; introduced into Eng. from Spain, *966,* 967.

Morrison, Herbert Stanley (b. 1888). Eng. politician. Leader of Labour party on L.C.C.; one-time errand-boy; Minister of Transport (1929–31); Minister of Supply, May 1940; Home Secretary Oct. 1940. Lord President of Council; also Leader of House of Commons from 1945; opening new Waterloo Bridge, *3565.*

Morrison, Robert (1782–1834). Eng. missionary, first Protestant missionary in China (1807); compiled monumental " Chinese Dictionary."

Morrison, Mt., in Formosa, 1352.

Morse, Samuel Finley Breese (1791–1872). Amer. artist and inventor of the electric telegraph, 2232, *2233*; telegraph, 3164; wireless, 3301.

Morse code, in telegraphy, 2233; 3164, *3166*; signalling apparatus, *3165.*

Mortar. Vessel in which substances are pounded with a pestle; also building material containing lime, 1949.

Mor'tar. Short gun, firing at high angles.

Mortar-board, scholar's hat, 1584.

Morte d'Arthur. Greatest collection of Arthurian romances, first printed by Caxton in 1485, 255, 1414.

Mortgage (mor'-gāj). The grant of an estate or other immovable properties in fee in security for the payment of money, and on the condition that if the money be duly paid the grant shall be void, and the mortgagee shall reconvey the property to the mortgagor.

Mort Homme (" dead man "). Hill in Fr. N. of Verdun; scene of heavy Ger. losses in attack, March 1916.

Mortimer, Roger (1287–1330). First earl of March; an adherent of Edward II; later his enemy.

Mortimer's Cross. Battle in Wars of Roses (1461), in Herefordshire, 40 m. s.w. of Birmingham; Edward, Duke of York, defeated Lancastrians.

Mort'lake. Tn. of Surrey, on Thames, 9 m. s.w. of London (Charing Cross); finishing point of University boat-race; pop. 23,879; tapestries, 3153.

Morton, Henry Vollam (b. 1892). Eng. descriptive writer; works include " In Search of England," " The Heart of London," " In the Steps of the Master."

Mosaic, 2233; early It., 1775; and painting, 2476.

Mosaic law, 2235.

Mosander, C. G. 19th-cent. chemist, researched on rare earths, discovering lanthanum (1839), erbium (1843), yttrium, etc.; 3437.

Moscheles, Ignaz (1794–1870). Austrian pianist and composer; teacher and friend of Mendelssohn.

Moschus (mos'-kus) (2nd cent. B.C.) Gk. pastoral poet (" Europa," a short epic), 1541.

Moscicki, Ignace (1867–1946). Polish statesman and scientist; Prof. of electro-chemistry at Lwow 1912; organizer of chemical research inst., 1920; with over 600 patents to his credit, he discovered whirling arc method of recovering nitric acid from free nitrogen; President of Poland 1926; re-elected 1933; resigned 1939.

Moscovitch, Maurice (b. 1871). Jewish actor; he achieved a great success when (as Jew portraying Jew) he played the part of Shylock at the Court Theatre, London, in 1919; also appeared in " Don Carlos " and " The Great Lover."

Moscow. Cap. of Soviet Russia; pop. 4,137,000; 2233, *2851, 2854*; *map, 2845, plate f. 2844*; climate, 2844; grand dukes of, 1787; Kremlin, *plate f. 2845*; Lenin's tomb, 1923, *2851*; Napoleon, 2277; Red Square, *2234*; St. Basil Cathedral, *2234,* 2235; " Tsar Kolokol " bell, *411*; 2nd World War, 2235, 3419.

Moseley, Henry Gwyn-Jeffreys (1887–1915). Brit. physicist; discovered relationship of atomic numbers of elements to their structure as revealed by X-rays, in 1913 ; showed promise of being a second Newton or another Einstein, but was killed in action at Gallipoli ; 1138. (*Not* Mosely as in p. 1138.)

Moselle (mō-zel'). R. in N.E. Fr. and S. Ger. ; flows 320 m. N.E. to Rhine at Coblenz ; valley noted for vineyards, 1360, 1444, 2769.

Moses. Leader and lawgiver of the Hebrews, **2235** ; and the Jews, 1829 ; by Michelangelo, 2160, *1783*.

Moses ben Mai'mon or Maimon'ides (1135–1204). Jewish philosopher.

Mosley, Sir Oswald Ernald, Bart. (b. 1896). Eng. politician ; Cons. M.P. 1918–22, Ind. M.P. 1922–24 ; joined Labour party and was chanc. of the Duchy of Lancaster 1929 ; founded New Party 1930, and Brit. Union of Fascists 1931 ; detained Holloway gaol 1941–43.

Mosques. Mahomedan places of worship, usually of Byzantine style of architecture. Great Mosque at Mecca, *2126* ; Santa Sophia, Istanbul (now a museum), 213, 1761 ; of Delhi, *plate f. 988, 1706.*

Mosquito. Two-winged fly of the genus *Anopheles*, **2236**, 1732 ; eggs, *1094* ; Panama Canal, 2488, *2489*.

Mosquito coast or Mosquitia. Strip of land occupied by Mosquito Indians on E. coast of cent. Amer. ; now part of Nicaragua, 744.

Mosquito, De Havilland. All-wood aircraft, *38*, 1564.

Moss. A flowerless plant, **2238** ; classed among plants, 2620 ; Iceland moss a lichen, **2239**, 1933 ; "Irish moss," 2239, 2916 ; reindeer moss a lichen, 1933.

Mostar, Yugoslavia. City 46 m. S.W. of Sarajevo ; pop. 20,300 ; former cap. Herzegovina ; fine Rom. bridge.

Mosul (mō-sool'). City in Iraq on R. Tigris, 220 m. N. of Baghdad ; pop. 80,000 ; caravan trade ; 3212 ; ruins of Nineveh, 2372.

Moszkowski (mosh-kof'-ski), **Moritz** (1854–1925). Polish composer and pianist.

Motacil'lidae. Bird family of wagtails and pipits, 2611, 3332.

Moth. A scaly-winged insect whose antennae are not knobbed, **628** ; *plate f. 633, 1728, 1732, 1733* ; caterpillars of moths, 720, 721 ; cloth-eating types, ₹29 ; distinguished from butterflies, 628 ; eye, *1253* ; do not attack rayon, 2750 ; silk-worm, *2970, 2971*.

Moth balls. Of naphthalene, 857.

Mother Carey's chickens, 2563.

Mother Goose, 2239.

"Mother Gunga," or Ganges River, 1417.

"Mother of Parliaments," British, 2521.

Mother-of-Pearl or nacre. In shellfish, 2533, 2942.

Mother of the Gods, the Great. See Cybele.

Motherwell, Scot. Tn. of Lanarkshire, 12 m. S.E. of Glasgow ; coal-mining, iron and steel and engineering works ; pop. (including Wishaw) 68,000 ; 1890.

Motilon Indian, of Colombia, *873*.

Motion, laws of, 2129 ; relativity of, 2761.

Motion, perpetual, 1160.

Motion pictures. See Cinema.

Motley, John Lothrop (1814–77). Amer. historian and diplomat (" The Rise of the Dutch Republic "), 4139.

Motor. Machine supplying mechanical power. Aeroplane, 44 ; electric, *2239*, 2739, 3215, 3235, 3236 ; internal combustion, 1735 ; motor-car, 2242–45 ; solar, 1594, 3119. See also Engine ; Steam-engine.

Motor-boats, 484, *485*.

Motor-car. See Motor Vehicles.

Motor-cycles, *948*, 948, *3169* ; in war, *250*.

Motor Scooters, used by airborne troops, *251*.

Motoring signs and signals, *plate f. 2785.*

Motor nerves, 2317.

Motor Vehicles, **2241** ; Austin, *306* ; Sir Malcolm Campbell, 674 ; chassis,

---

2242, 2246 ; coil ignition, 1721 ; engine, 1736, 2243 ; fire engine, *1286, 1287* ; Henry Ford, 1346 ; how they work, 2243 ; hydraulic machinery in, 1665, *1666, 1667* ; mass production, *896, 897*, 898, 1347 ; motor cycles, *948* ; Lord Nuffield, 2404 ; petrol, 1567, 2564 ; pumps in, *2704* ; roads, 2783 ; road safety, 2787 ; Sir Henry Segrave, 2919 ; tires, *2835, 2836* ; tractors, 78 ; in warfare, *242, 243, 246, 247, 248, 249*.

Motte, Henri Paul. Fr. artist ; his " The Capitoline Geese," *2806.*

Mottistone, John Edward Bernard Seely, 1st Baron (1868–1947). Eng. politician. Sec. for War from 1912 to 1914 ; served with distinction in the Boer War and the 1st World War, reaching rank of major-general ; Under-Sec. for Air in 1919 ; writings include " Fear and be Slain," " For Ever England," and " My Horse Warrior."

Mottled umber moth, *3388*.

Mottram, Ralph Hale (b. 1883). Eng. author ; a leading war novelist, his most famous book being " The Spanish Farm " (awarded Hawthornden prize).

Moufflon, a wild sheep, *2940*.

Mould, in brickmaking, 561 ; plastics, 2626.

Moulds. See Mildews and moulds.

Moulting, of birds, 446, 1265 ; caterpillars, 720.

Moulmein'. 2nd spt. of Burma, nr. mouth of Salween, exporting teak and rice ; pop. 65,506 ; held by Japs. in 2nd World War from Jan. 1942 to Sept. 1945 ; seized by rebel Karens 1948 and again 1949 in attempt to force Burmese govt. to grant them promised autonomy.

Mounet-Sully (moo-nā-sü-lē), **Jean** (1841–1916). Fr. actor (Oedipus, Hamlet, Hernani, Ruy Blas.)

" Mountain," Fr. Rev. party, 2789.

Mountain Ash. See Rowan.

Mountaineering, as a pursuit, **2247** ; in Alps, 127 ; Mt. Everest, 1243.

Mountain goats, or goat-antelopes. Animals intermediate between goats and antelopes ; include Rocky Mt. goat, 176. The term is often applied to any wild goat—such as the ibex —that lives in mountains.

Mountain lion. See Puma.

Mountains ; avalanche, 322 ; affect climate, 840, 2742 ; climbing, 2247 ; definition, 2596, 2597 ; effect on

---

spread of civilization, 3287, 1517, 2597 ; formation, 2597 ; measuring by barometer, 363 ; origin, 3328 , 2596 ; submarine, Atlantic, 290 ; " young," *2596. See also* table below and under continents, countries, and names of chief mountains and mountain systems.

Mountains of the Moon, Africa, 69, 2370.

Mountbatten of Burma, Admiral Louis, 1st Earl (b. 1900). British war leader and statesman, **2248**.

Mountevans, Edward Ratcliffe Garth Russell Evans, 1st Baron (b. 1881). Eng. naval officer known as " Evans of the Broke " ; entered navy 1897 ; joined Brit. Antarctic Expedition and returned in command in 1913 after death of Capt. Scott ; c.-in-c. the Nore 1935–39 ; Civil Defence commr. for London region in 2nd World War ; cr. baron 1945 ; and Capt. Scott, 2895.

Mount Palomar, Calif. ; observatory has world's largest telescope, *3179.*

Mount Rainier. National Park, Washington, U.S.A., 3345.

Mount Royal. On isl. of Montreal ; 900 ft. high ; 2223.

Mount-Stephen, George Stephen, Baron (1829–1921). Anglo-Can. financier ; with Strathcona completed Can. Pac. Rly., of which first pres.

Mount Vernon, Virginia, U.S.A., George Washington's home, *3342.*

Mount Wilson Observatory, Pasadena, California, *2412*, 2413, *3180.*

Mourne Mountains, Eire. Range of mts. in S. of co. Down ; highest summit Slieve Donard, 2,796 ft., *1031.*

Mouse. A rodent, **2248** ; *plates f.* 2248, 2249 ; gnawing teeth, 2795 ; dormouse, 1029.

Moussorg'sky, Modeste Petrovitch (1835–81). Russian composer ; works include " Boris Godounov " and " Khovantchina " (operas), 2983.

Mouth. Entrance to alimentary canal of animals ; of bee, 395 ; birds, 437, 444 ; fish, 1297 ; insects, 1727, *1729* ; teeth, 3163 ; tongue structures, 3223.

Mouth-organ, or harmonica, **2249.**

Moving coil, in loudspeakers, 3012.

Moving pictures. See Cinema.

Moyne, Walter E. Guinness, 1st Baron (1880–1944). Brit. politician ; Min. of Agric. 1925 ; Sec. of State for Colonies 1941 ; Resid. Min. in Middle E. 1944, assassinated in Cairo on Nov. 6 by Stern Gang.

Moynihan, Berkeley George Andrew Moynihan, 1st Baron (1865–1936). Eminent Brit. surgeon ; wrote books on abdominal conditions.

Mozambique (mō-zam-bēk') or **Portuguese East Africa.** A colony of Portugal on E. coast of Africa ; 297,654 sq. m. ; pop. 5,085,600 ; 1073, 72, *map, 1073.*

Mozart (mōt'-sahrt), **Wolfgang Amadeus** (1756–91). Austrian composer, **2249**, 2264 ; friendship with Haydn, 1590 ; and opera, 2436.

Mu, *μ*, M (Rom. m, M). Twelfth letter of Gk. alphabet ; the small *μ* is used as symbol for the microscopic measurement, the micron ($\frac{1}{1000}$ millimetre).

Mu'cilage. An adhesive solution ; made of vegetable gums, 1556.

Mucous membrane. A thin, sheet-like structure lining all passages by which internal organs of body communicate with outer world ; has certain cells which form a semi-fluid secretion called "mucus" to protect membrane from irritation.

Mudania (moo'-dã-ni-a). Tn. of Turkey, Sea of Marmora ; olive oil.

Mud-fish. See Lung-fish.

Mudjekee'wis. In Hiawatha story, the West Wind, 2022.

Mud-skipper, or goby. E. Indian fish, 2250.

Muezzin (mū-ez'-in). Crier who calls Mahomedans to prayer, *2067.*

Mufti. (a) An official expounder of Mahomedan law ; (b) Civilian dress as opposed to uniform. Turkish Grand Mufti was chief spiritual authority

---

GREAT MOUNTAINS OF THE WORLD	HEIGHT IN FEET
Aconcagua, Argentina (*highest in South America*)	23,081
Chimborazo, Ecuador Andes	20,517
Cotopaxi, Ecuador Andes (*world's highest active volcano*)	19,580
Elbruz, Russia (*highest in Europe*)	18,470
Etna, Sicily	10,750
Everest, Nepal (*highest in world*)	29,141 or 29,002
Fujiyama, Japan	12,395
Godwin - Austen, Kashmir	28,265
Kilimanjaro, Africa (*highest in Africa*)	19,325
Kosciusko, Australia (*highest in Australia*)	7,328
Logan, Canada (*highest in Canada*)	19,850
McKinley, Alaska (*highest in North America*)	20,464
Mauna Kea, Hawaiian Islands	13,823
Mont Blanc, France (*highest in the Alps*)	15,782
Nanda Devi, Himalayas (*highest summit climbed by Man*)	25,645
Orizaba, Mexico	17,400
Popocatepetl, Mexico	17,520

of the land, but office abolished by the Turkish Republic in 1924. The self-styled " Grand Mufti " of Jerusalem, Haj Mohammed Emin el Husseini, spiritual leader of Arabs in Palestine, inspired anti-Zionist disturbances during 1935–36 ; fleeing to Lebanon and Baghdad, and finally to Berlin (1941), he conspired with Hitler against U.K. ; in 1946 he got to Egypt in spite of Brit. precautions, and played important part in activities of the Arab League.

Mugad′zhar Mts. In Asia, range extending from Ural r. s. almost to Aral Sea ; 27,786 ft. highest peak.

Mugwumps, in U.S.A., political nickname applied to independent voters who do not support any particular party ; really means " great chief," after an Amer. Indian, so is essentially satirical and disparaging.

Muharra Island, Pers. Gulf, N.E. of Bahrein ; B.O.A.C. landing ground, 107.

Mühlberg (mēl′-bärg). Ger. tn. on Elbe r., 35 m. N.W. of Dresden ; Emp. Charles V. defeated Protestants under Elector of Saxony (1547).

Muir Glacier. Large and picturesque ice sheet of S.E. Alaska, discharging into Glacier Bay ; about 350 sq. m.

Mukden (mook′-den). Largest city of Manchuria, on Hun r., 400 m. N.E. of Peking ; in 1932 it became largest city of Japanese Manchukuo ; Russians occupied it 1945–46 ; later objective of Chinese Communists ; pop. 1,135,860 ; 2086, 2538.

Mulberry. Name of several trees with black, white, or red fruit, **2250,** 3247 ; bark in paper-making, 2497, 1798 ; in Japan, 1797 ; for silkworm, 2970, 2971.

Mulberry family, or *Moraceae.* Plant family including mulberries, hemp, figs, and bread-fruits.

Mulberry Harbours. Artificial harbours used in invasion of Europe, June 1944 ; **2251,** *2252* ; 654, 1577, 2377, 3028.

Mule. Offspring of ass and mare, **2253** ; in Switzerland, *3141.*

Mule. Spinning machine, 933, 3066.

Mulhacen (mool-ah-thän′). Highest summit in Sp., 11,420 ft.

Mülheim-am-Ruhr (mēl′-hīm-am-roor). Ger. coal and iron mining and mfg. tn. in Rhine Prov.

Mulhouse (mūl-ōz) (Ger. Mülhausen, mēl′-how-zen). Commercial centre in Upper Alsace, pop. 87,650 ; large textile mfrs. ; under Ger. rule 1871–1918, and Ger. occupation 1940–44 ; potash deposits, 133.

Mull. Isl. off w. coast of Scotland, traditional home of the clan Maclean ; 2nd largest of Inner Hebrides, 367 sq. m. ; pop. 3,389 ; chief tn. Tobermory, where a Span. galleon, said to contain great treasure, was sunk in 1588 ; 1602.

Mul′lah. Complimentary title given to Mahomedan priest, 411 ; the " Mad Mullah," 3000.

Mullein. Plants of the order *Scrophulariaceae,* genus *Verbascum.* Great mullein has large leaves covered with matted white hairs ; tall spike of yellow flowers. Other species also have yellow flowers, except white mullein, which is also less hairy.

Müller (mu′-ler) **(Frederick), Max** (1823–1900). Anglo-German orientalist, Sanskrit scholar and popularizer of comparative philology, 2570.

Müller, Hermann J. (b. 1890). Amer. geneticist ; did research on the effect of X-rays on the genes and chromosomes of living cells in causing changes in heredity ; awarded Nobel prize in 1946.

Müller, Paul (b. 1899). Swiss chemist ; discovered insecticidal properties of D.D.T. (*q.v.* in *f-i.*) ; received Nobel prize for it, 1948.

Müller, William James (1812–45). Brit. landscape painter, one of the most important of his period.

Mul′let. Name given to two excellent food fishes, the red mullet and the grey mullet ; the former is a bright red or golden colour.

Mullion. In architecture, a vertical bar separating the compartments of a window, especially used in Gothic and double-casement windows ; the horizontal bars are called transoms.

Mulock, Dinah Maria. *See* **Craik, Mrs.**

Mulready, William (1786–1863). Irish painter, many of whose subject pictures are familiar through reproductions ; he designed the first postal envelope for Rowland Hill, still known to collectors as a " Mulready envelope."

Multan (mool-tahn′), Pakistan. Rly. centre 190 m. s.w. of Lahore ; pop. 142,700 ; silk and cotton mfrs. ; captured by British in 1849.

Multiple proportions, law of, 295, 767.

Mul′tiplex telegraphy, 3167.

Multiplicand, 2253.

Multiplica′tion. In arithmetic, **2253** ; in algebra, 115 ; calculating machines, 657, *658* ; of decimals, 983 ; of fractions 1357 ; by slide rule, *2984* ; table, *2253.*

Mul′tiplier, 2253.

Mulvaney (mul-vā′-ni), **Terence.** In " Soldiers Three " and other tales by Kipling, a reckless, resourceful Irish private in India.

Mulvian Bridge. Same as **Milvian.**

Mumbles. Vill. and seaside resort on Swansea bay, Glam. ; lifeboat disaster in 1947 ; 1936.

Mummy. Body preserved by embalming, **2255** ; in Brit. Museum, 584, *plate f. 585* ; cats, 719 ; in Peru, 920.

Mumtaz Mahal. Wife of Shah Jehan ; tomb (Taj Mahal), 3147, *3148.*

Munch (moonk), **Edward** (1863–1944). Norwegian painter ; early works marked by gloomy subjects ; later by vigorous landscapes and paintings.

München. Ger. for **Munich.**

Münchausen (münsh′-how-zen), **Karl Friedrich Hieronymus, Baron** (1720–97). Ger. soldier, whose exploits formed the basis of a collection of stories ("Munchausen's Travels," published 1785).

Munich (mu′-nik). 5th city of Ger. and cap. of Bavaria ; pop. 828,000, **2256,** 378.

Munich Agreement. Concluded Sept.29, 1938, between Germany, Italy, Britain, and France, providing for cession to Germany of Sudeten dist. of Czechoslovakia, 2256, 3416.

Munic′ipal government, 1491. *See* **Local Government.**

Muninn (mōō′-nin). In Norse myth., one of ravens of Odin.

Munkacsy (moon′-kah-chē), **Michael** (1844–1900). Hungarian genre, religious, and historical painter (" Milton Dictating Paradise Lost," " Christ before Pilate "), *1824.*

Munnings, Sir Alfred J. (b. 1878). Brit. painter, excelling at horses ; pres. of Royal Academy 1944–49.

Munster. Eire (Irish Free State). Largest of 4 provs. of Ireland, in s.w. ; it was in anc. times a kingdom.

Münster (mēn′-ster). City in w. Ger., Dortmund-Ems Canal ; pop. (1939) 143,740 ; textile and leather ; univ. ; Peace of Westphalia, 1648 ; *1239.* Bombed, taken, April 1945.

Mün′sterberg, Hugo (1863–1916). Ger. Amer. psychologist ; a pioneer of industrial psychology.

Munthe (moon′-te), **Axel** (1857–1949). Swed. physician and writer ; physician to King of Sweden 1903 ; wrote autobiography " The Story of San Michele " about himself and his island home, Capri.

Munt′jac. " Barking deer " of India, 985.

Murad II (*c.* 1403–51). Turkish sultan, 3264.

Murat (mū rah), **Joachim** (1767–1815). Fr. Rev. cavalry leader and marshal of the empire ; husband of Napoleon's youngest sister, Caroline ; made king of Naples in 1807 ; dethroned and shot by Allies, 497.

Murchison. R., w. Australia, flowing into Cantheaume Bay, 3368 ; also an important goldfield.

Murcia, Spain. Industrial centre, cap. of prov. of same name in s.e.

on r. Segura ; pop, 221,209 ; silk industry.

" Murder in the Cathedral." Play by T. S. Eliot, *389,* 1042.

Murdock, William (1754–1839). Scot. engineer, inventor of coal-gas lighting, **2256,** 1423, 3375 ; and steam-engine, 3086.

Mu′rex. Genus of molluscs that secrete Tyrian purple shell, 3573.

Muriat′ic acid. *See* **Hydrochloric acid.**

Murillo (mū-ril′ō ; Sp., moo-rēl′-yō), **Bartolomé Esteban** (1617–82). Sp. painter, **2257,** 3049 ; " Annunciation," *2257* ; " Peasant Boy," *3040* ; " Immaculate Conception," 2258.

Mur′man Coast, Rus. Arctic coast of Kola peninsula, 2844.

Murmansk. Ice-free spt. of U.S.S.R. on Arctic Murman coast ; rly. connection with Leningrad ; fishing ; pop. 117,054 ; base for Allies 1918–19, against Bolsheviks, later base for Russ. Arctic fleet ; and 1939–40 for Russ. attack on Finnish Petsamo ; in 2nd World War, terminal port for Brit. munitions convoys to Russ. ; 3419.

Murray, George Gilbert Aimé (b. 1866). Brit. classical scholar, best known for translations of plays of Euripides in Eng. verse (" History of Ancient Greek Literature " ; " Rise of the Greek Epic " ; " Four Stages of Greek Religion ") ; a leading advocate of League of Nations and Chairman of League of Nations Union ; O.M. 1941.

Murray or **Moray, James Stuart, Earl of** (*c.* 1530–70). Half-brother of Mary Queen of Scots and her chief adviser on her return from France ; her chief enemy after her open break with Protestantism, and regent for the infant James after Mary's abdication ; 1872.

Murray, Sir James Augustus Henry (1837–1915). Brit. lexicographer ; Editor from 1879 of " New English Dictionary."

Murray. Chief r. of Australia, draining, with Darling tributary, entire s.E. quarter ; mouth on s. coast 40 m. E. of Adelaide ; *map f. 308.*

Murrayfield. Scotland's international Rugby football ground at Edinburgh.

Murry, John Middleton (b. 1889). Brit. literary critic and writer ; " Countries of the Mind," " Keats and Shakespeare," " Son of Woman " (about his friend D. H. Lawrence), " The Free Society."

Murzuk′. A caravan station in Libya (Tripoli) ; cap. of Fezzan ; 2861.

Mus (mŭs). The mouse and rat genus of rodents, 2248, 2746.

Musa (mū′-za). The banana genus of plants, 354.

Musaeus (mū-zē-us) (*c.* 6th cent. A.D.). Gk. grammarian and poet ; story of Hero and Leander, 1619.

Mus′ca. Insect genus including common flies.

Musca domestica. The housefly, 1329.

Mus′carine. A poison found in certain mushrooms, e.g. fly agaric, *Amanita muscaria,* etc., *plate f. 1408.*

Muscat. Spt. and cap. of independent state of Oman in E. Arabia ; pop. 4,500 ; chief export, dates ; name also given to Oman itself ; 196.

Mus′cat or **mus′catel.** One of several varieties of musk-flavoured grapes, usually light coloured, 2743.

Musci (mus′-kī). The moss class of bryophyte plants, 2238.

Muscles. Consisting of contractile fibrous tissue, **2258** ; of birds, 437 ; of bivalve molluscs, 860, 2467 ; of eye, *1252* ; give impression of weight and position, 3231 ; growth affected by pituitary secretion, 1471 ; of insects, 1732 ; of stomach, 3094.

Muscle Shoals. Alabama, U.S.A. ; rapids 37 m. long in Tennessee r., capable of developing enormous hydro-electric power ; Wilson Dam was completed in 1926.

Mus′covite or **muscovy glass.** A form of mica, 2160.

A LIST OF THE CHIEF MUSICAL TERMS

A capella. Unaccompanied singing by several voices in the manner of Church music.

Accelerando. Increase the speed.

Accent. The emphasis on certain notes or chords required by the rhythmic pattern of a composition. "Artificial" accent, indicated by a special sign, demands stress on a particular note or chord.

Accidental. A sharp, flat or natural not a part of the key in which the composition is written.

Adagio. Slow; 100-120 metronome beats to the minute. Also, a slow movement in a composition.

Ad libitum. At the pleasure of the performer.

After note. An unaccented note following an accented one.

Allegro. Quick, lively; 160-184 metronome beats to the minute.

Andante. Smooth, flowing, and rather slow in tempo; 126-152 metronome beats to the minute.

Animato. In a lively, spirited manner.

Answer. Repetition of a motif or theme by voices or instruments other than the one which introduced it.

Anticipation. The introduction of a note before the sounding of the chord of which it is a part.

Aria. Literally an air, or melody; in opera, an important lyrical solo with instrumental accompaniment.

Arpeggio. A chord, the tones of which are played separately but in quick and regular sequence, as on the strings of a harp.

A tempo. In strict conformity to the established time.

Ballet. The music for a dance performed by one or more persons, whose movements are descriptive of an idea or emotion.

Bar. A vertical line on the staff, used to separate measures; the music between two such lines.

Barcarole. A song of the Venetian gondoliers, or an imitation of such a song. It is usually in a smooth, swinging tempo, suggestive of the graceful motion of a small boat.

Berceuse. A lullaby.

Cadence. A succession of chords or notes bringing a composition to its conclusion.

Cantabile. Even and continuous like a song.

Cantata. A short composition for solo voices and chorus, usually setting forth a brief Biblical narrative.

Canzonetta. A simple, short song, bright and light in character.

Chant. A short form of Church music in which words, often from the canticles or the psalms, are intoned usually without rhythm on two reciting notes, each followed by a cadence.

Chord. Two or more tones heard at the same time; its varied structure and relationships are governed by the rules of harmony.

Chromatic. Progressing by half tones.

Crescendo. Increase the power or loudness of tone.

Degree. The step between two consecutive notes in a scale.

Diatonic. Progressing according to the diatonic scale; that is, the standard major or minor scale of eight notes.

Entr'acte. Music performed between the acts of a play or opera.

Finale. The last number in an opera, usually sung by soloists and chorus; or the concluding part of any musical composition.

Forte. Loud; *fortissimo*, very loud; *fortississimo*, extremely loud.

Gavotte. A gay round dance originated in France and resembling the minuet.

Grace Note. A short note introduced as an ornament and not an essential part of the melody.

Intermezzo or Interlude. A short piece played between the acts, stanzas, or movements of a longer work. It may be played as a separate composition.

Interval. The distance between any two notes.

Key. The pitch of all tones in a scale, the key-note of which gives the key its name, as major C is the key-note or first in the scale of the key of C Major.

Largo. Slow, stately, 40-70 metronome beats to the minute.

Legato. In a connected, flowing manner.

Libretto. The text of an opera or other musical composition.

Major. Literally, greater; used of intervals which are greater by a half-tone than minor or smaller intervals; used also of keys and of chords in which such intervals predominate.

Mazurka. A spirited Polish dance in 3-8 or 3-4 time.

Measure. The notes between two bars. The measure represents a unit of rhythm since each measure has but one principal accent.

Melody. A succession of notes forming a tune or air; the leading part in a harmonized composition.

Metre. The regular succession of accents which establishes the rhythm of a composition.

Mezzo. Literally, half, medium; often used with other words, as *mezzo forte*, moderately loud.

Minor. Literally, smaller; used of an interval which is a half-tone smaller than the corresponding major interval, of chords containing such intervals, and of scales in which such intervals predominate.

Minuet. A musical form in triple time to accompany the small, light steps of a dignified dance, also known by the same name. It is often a part of a suite.

Modulation. A transition from one key to another by a succession of related chords.

Motif. A distinguishing musical phrase which usually recurs frequently in a composition.

Natural. A note especially marked in a composition to nullify a sharp or flat indicated in the key.

Natural scale. A scale without sharps or flats; C major or A minor.

Nocturne. A composition, generally for the piano, in a tranquil and dream-like mood.

Obbliga'to. An accompaniment which is essential to the composition; usually written for a single instrument which supplements the leading part taken by another instrument or voice.

Octave. An interval of eight diatonic degrees.

Oratorio. A composition similar to an opera but often founded on a Biblical theme and usually given without action or scenery.

Overture. An introductory part to an opera or other musical work; a concert overture is an independent composition for band or orchestra.

Phrase. A short passage which is more or less complete in itself and expresses a musical idea or thought.

Piano. Soft in tone; *pianissimo*, very soft.

Polka. A gay Bohemian dance in 2-4 time.

Prelude. An introduction to prepare for succeeding parts of a composition; sometimes applied to independent pieces of a rather informal character.

Presto. Rapidly; 184-208 metronome beats to the minute.

Recitative. Musical recitation to set forth narrative portions, especially in the older oratorios and operas.

Rhythm. The metrical quality of music produced by regularly recurring accents.

Rondo. Musical form in which one principal theme is repeated three or more times, alternating with two secondary themes.

Scale. A series of tones proceeding upward or downward according to rules of musical composition.

Scherzo. A tuneful, vivacious movement, often a part of a sonata, concerto, or symphony.

Score. A printed copy of all the vocal and instrumental parts in a composition, the tones which are to be sounded simultaneously being placed one above the other.

Staff. Five horizontal lines which, with the four spaces, are used for the placing of all notes in the score.

Syncopation. A change in the regular rhythmic pattern by stressing a note that falls on an unaccented beat.

Tarantella. A very fast and emotional Italian dance in 6-8 time.

Tempo. The rate of speed at which a composition is to be performed. From the slowest to the fastest tempo, some of the commonest terms are: *largo, grave, lento, adagio, andante, moderato, allegro, presto, prestissimo.*

Theme. A musical phrase developed with variations and embellishments throughout a composition.

Tonic. The first tone in any scale; the key-note.

Triad. A chord of three tones arranged according to the laws of harmony.

Triplet. A group of three notes played in the time ordinarily required for two notes of the same length.

See also in Index Symbols and Signs.

Mus'covy. Former name for Russia.

Muscovy Company. Eng. company formed for trade with Russia and polar exploration, 1648, 2644.

Muselier (mū-zel-yay), **Émile H.** (b. 1882). Fr. sailor, in charge of naval defences, Marseilles 1938–39; joined de Gaulle in Eng. 1940, and commanded F.F. naval forces; in Dec. 1941 took S. Pierre and Mique-lon islands from Vichy govt. for de Gaulle; retired 1942.

Mu'ses. In Gk. myth., goddesses pre-siding over the arts and sciences, 2259; Apollo and, 187.

Museums, 2259; Brit. Museum, 584; Louvre (Paris), 2032.

Mushet, Robert F. (1811–91). Eng. metallurgist, 123.

Mush'room. An edible fungus (*Agaricus campestris*), 2260, 2918.

Music, 2261, 3010: Bach's influence, 333; Beethoven's influence, 397; early Christian, 2261; folk songs, 1680; gramophone, 1495; great names in musical history, 2264, and in table at foot of this page; impressionism in, 1689; jazz, 1815; modern, 2265, 2266; opera, 2435; orchestra, 2446; physical basis, 3010; relation to poetry, 2634; Richard Strauss's innovations, 3863; time, 3214; Wagner's influence, 3331. *See also* under names of great musicians, and Symbols.

Musical Comedy. Modern type, 2438.

Musical Instruments, 2266, 3009: bag-pipe, 339; banjo, 356; bells, 409; clarinet, 2267; clavichord, 2601; double bass, 2267; drum, 1049; harp, 1579; harpsichord, 2601; horns and trumpets, 1643; lute, 2264; mouth-organ, 2249; in or-chestra, 2445, 2446; organ, 2449; piano, 2601; recorder, 2265; spinet,

2601; tone or "timbre," 3010; violin, 3324; wood wind, 0404; xylophone, 2267.

Music-dramas, of Wagner, 2437, 3332.

Musk. A perfume obtained from glands of animals, especially musk-deer, 2268, 2549.

Musk beetle, 401.

Musk-deer, 2268, 984, 2549.

Musket, the first, 1281.

Musk-melon, 2137.

Muskogee (mus-kō'gē), Oklahoma, U.S.A. Mfg. city and distributing centre in E. near Arkansas r.; pop. 32,332; in agricultural and stock-raising region; oil and natural gas near by.

Musk-ox, 2268; code name for Can. army exercise in Arctic in 1946, 226.

Musk-rat, 2268; fur, 1412.

Muslim (or **Moslem**) **League.** Formed 1906 by Ind. Moslems, aiming at more power in Ind. affairs; weakened by dissensions until 1934; under pres. Mohamed Ali Jinnah it de-manded (1940) and obtained (1947) an independent Moslem state, Paki-stan, 1716.

Muslin. Name given to various kinds of cotton cloth, 850, 920.

Musquash, from musk rat, 2268.

Musschenbroek, Peter van (1692–1761). Du. scientist, inventor of the Leyden jar, 1929.

Mus'sel. A bivalve mollusc, 860, 2199; pearls, 2533–34; shell, 2942; shells made into buttons, 632.

Musset (mū'-sā), **Alfred de** (1810–57). Fr. dramatist, poet and novelist, early in life was a member of the circle of romantics of whom Victor Hugo was chief, 1381.

Mussolini (moos-sō-lē-nē), **Benito** (1883–1945). It. statesman and dictator, **2268,** 2269; and Fascist revolution,

1261, 1262; Forum of, 1774; and modern Italy, 1770, 2799, 2800; resignation and death, 2269, 3415, 3421, 3424.

Mus'-tangs, or Indian ponies, 1646.

Mustapha IV (moos'-tah-fah) (1779–1808). Sultan of Turkey, placed on throne by the Janissaries who rebelled against Selim III in 1807.

Mustapha Kemal Pasha. *See* **Kemal Atatürk.**

Mustard. Plant having pungent seeds used as condiment and in medicine, 2270, 639, 3062; in India, 1707.

Mustard gas. The popular name for an asphyxiating chemical introduced by the Germans towards the end of the 1st World War, and later adopted by the Allies; 1420.

Mustel'idae, or weasel family. Long bodied carnivorous animals, such as weasels, minks, and skunks, 338.

Muta'tion theory, of evolution; an attempt to explain the origin of species founded on experiments made by Hugo de Vries of Amster-dam and published in 1901; 1246.

Mutsuhito (moot-soo-hē'-tō) (1867–1912), emperor of Japan, 1799.

Mutton, meat of grown sheep, 2941; cuts of, 2125.

Muzaffar-ed-Din (moo-zaf'-ar ed-dēn') (1853–1907). Shah of Persia; came to throne in 1896; filled depleted treasury by loans; widespread dis-content forced grant of liberal con-stitution (1906).

Muz'iano, Girolamo (1528–92). It. painter; early known for his land-scapes, later for historical and re-ligious pieces (" Resurrection of Lazarus ").

Mvule, an African timber tree, 3150.

Mwadui. Locality of Tanganyika, Africa, where in 1940 Dr. J. T.

FAMOUS MUSICAL COMPOSERS & THEIR CHIEF WORKS

Bach, Johann Sebastian (1685–1750). German. Organ and piano works (" Passion Music," " Well Tempered Clavichord ").

Beethoven, Ludwig van (1770–1827). German. Sonatas, symphonies, quar-tets (" Pathétique," " Moonlight," and " Kreutzer " sonatas; " Eroica " and " Pastoral " symphonies; " Egmont ").

Berlioz, Hector (1803–69). French. Operas (" Damnation de Faust "), symphonies (" Fantastique ").

Bizet, Georges (1838–75). French. Operas (" Carmen," " Les Pêcheurs de Perles ").

Brahms, Johannes (1833–97). German. Songs, symphonies, concertos (" Re-quiem," " Hungarian Dances ").

Britten, Benjamin (1913–). English. Orchestral, chamber music, operas (" Peter Grimes," " Rape of Lucretia," " Albert Herring ").

Chopin, Frédéric François (1809–40). French-Polish. Waltzes, etc., for piano (" Funeral March," " Nocturnes," " Preludes," etc.).

Debussy, Claude Achille (1862–1918). French. Operas, piano and orchestral (" La Mer," " Pelléas et Mélisande ").

Delius, Frederick (1862–1934). English. Choral, orchestral, and chamber music. (" Koanga," " Brigg Fair," " First Cuckoo in Spring ").

Donizetti, Gaetano (1797–1848). Italian. Operas (" Lucia di Lammermoor ").

Dvorak, Antonin (1841–1904). Bohemian. Choral works, symphonies (" New World Symphony,"" Slavonic Dances ").

Elgar, Sir Edward (1857–1934). English. Oratorios (" Dream of Gerontius "), orchestral pieces, symphonies (" Wand of Youth " suite, " Nursery " suite).

Falla, Manoel de (1876–1946). Spanish. Songs, ballet music, etc. (" Three-cornered Hat," " Jota ").

German, Sir Edward (1862–1936). Eng-lish. Light operas, songs, orchestral works (" Merrie England," " Henry VIII, Dances ").

Glück, Christoph Willibald (1714–87). German. Operas (" Orfeo," " Alceste," " Iphigénie en Tauride ").

Gounod, Charles François (1818–93). French. Sacred works, operas (" Faust ").

Grieg, Edvard Hagerup (1843–1907). Norwegian. Songs, short pieces for orchestra and piano (" Peer Gynt Suite ").

Handel, George Frederick (1685–1759). German. Oratorios, suites (" Messiah," " Water Music ").

Haydn, Franz Joseph (1732–1809). Aus-trian. Symphonies, quartets, oratorios (" The Creation," " The Clock Sym-phony ").

Liszt, Franz (1811–86). Hungarian. Piano pieces, songs, orchestral works (" Faust " symphony, " Hungarian Rhapsodies," " Consolations ").

Mascagni, Pietro (1863–1945). Italian. Operas (" Cavalleria Rusticana ").

Mendelssohn-Bartholdy, Felix (1809–47). German. Oratorios, symphonies, piano pieces (" Songs Without Words," " St. Paul," " Elijah," " Midsummer Night's Dream ").

Mozart, Wolfgang Amadeus (1756–91). Austrian. Operas, symphonies, cham-ber music, sacred compositions (" The Marriage of Figaro," " Jupiter Sym-phony ").

Palestrina, Giovanni Pierluigi da (1524–94). Italian. Sacred works.

Puccini, Giacomo (1858–1924). Italian. Operas (" Tosca," " Madame Butter-fly," " La Bohème ").

Rachmaninov, Sergei (1873–1943). Rus-sian. Piano pieces, symphonies, con-certos (" Prelude in C Sharp Minor ").

Ravel, Maurice (1875–1937). French. Ballets, suites, piano pieces, etc. (" Mother Goose Suite," " Bolero," " La Valse," " Daphnis et Chloe ").

Rossini, Gioacchino Antonio (1792–1868). Italian. Operas (" William Tell," " The Barber of Seville ").

Rubinstein, Anton Gregor (1829–94). Russian. Piano pieces, songs, con-

certos, symphonies (" Melody in F," " Eroica Fantasia ").

Saint-Saëns, Charles Camille (1835–1921). French. Operas, orchestral works (" Samson et Dalila," " Danse Maca-bre ").

Schubert, Franz Peter (1797–1828). Aus-trian. Songs, symphonies, chamber music (" The Erlking," " Hark, hark, the lark," " Who is Sylvia ? ", " Unfin-ished " symphony).

Schumann, Robert (1810–56). German. Songs, piano pieces, orchestral works (" Carnaval," " Scenes of Childhood," " The Two Grenadiers ").

Sibelius, Jan (1865–). Finnish. Sym-phonies, tone-poems (" Finlandia," " Swan of Tuonela," " Romance "), and orchestral suites (" Karelia," " Scenes Historiques ").

Strauss, Richard (1864–1949). German. Operas (" Salome "), tone-poems (" Ti Eulenspiegel ").

Stravinsky, Igor (1882–). Russian. Ballet music (" Petrouchka," " The Rite of Spring," " Fire Bird "), and experimental orchestral novelties (" Fireworks," " Polka," " Galop," etc.).

Sullivan, Sir Arthur Seymour (1842–1900). English. Comic operas, songs, Church music (" The Mikado," " Pir-ates of Penzance," " Patience ").

Tchaikovsky, Peter Ilyitch (1840–93). Russian. Symphonies, songs, concertos (" Pathétique " symphony, " Francesca da Rimini," " Nutcracker Suite ").

Vaughan Williams, Ralph (1872–). Eng-lish. Symphonies, opera, folk-music (" London Symphony," " Hugh, the Drover," " Job," etc.).

Verdi, Giuseppe (1813–1901). Italian. Operas (" Rigoletto," " Il Trovatore," " La Traviata," " Aïda ").

Wagner, Wilhelm Richard (1813–83). German. Operas (" Lohengrin," " Tannhäuser," " The Ring ").

Walton, William Turner (1902–). English. Ballet music (" Façade "), oratorio (" Belshazzar's Feast "), chamber music, and one symphony.

Williamson found a great deposit of diamonds, causing very marked expansion of Tanganyika's diamond exports.

Mycale (mik'-*a*-lē). Mt. in anc. Ionia, Asia Minor, near which Greeks destroyed Persian fleet 479 B.C.

Myce'lium. Collective term for the hyphal threads of which a fungus is composed ; of rust, 2857.

Mycenae (mī-sē'-nē). Anc. Gk. city in Argolis, 50 m. N.E. of Sparta, destroyed 5th cent. B.C. by Argos ; early civilization, 30 ; ruins of, *1519* ; Schliemann's excavations, 2883.

Myceri'nus or **Menkaura.** King of Egypt, son of Khufu (Cheops) ; pyramid of, 2707.

Myce'tozoa. The slime moulds when classified as animals, 3622. *See also* **Myxomycetes.**

Mycol'ogy. Science of fungi.

Myd'delton, Sir Hugh (*c.* 1560–1631). Eng. contractor ; made money in various commercial ventures ; took over scheme for supplying city of London with water from Ware ; New River opened 1613.

My'ers, Frederic William Henry (1843–1901). Eng. poet and essayist (" Re-

newal of Youth ") ; co-founder of Society for Psychical Research (" Human Personality and its Survival of Bodily Death ").

Mygale (mig'-*a*-lē). Bird-catching spider, *plate f. 3064.*

Myitkyina (mich-in-ah'). Tn. of Burma, 250 m. N.N.E. of Mandalay, on upper Irrawaddy, at limit of navigation ; terminus of rly. from Mandalay ; pop. 20,000 ; held by Japs May 1942 to Aug. 1944, their last stronghold in Upper Burma.

Myo'pia. Scientific term used to denote short sight.

Myr'iagramme. A unit in metric system (22·046 lb.), 2155.

Myriap'oda. Former name of group including centipedes and millepedes, now classified separately, 3624.

Myr'midons. A warlike race of anc. Thessaly led by Achilles in the Trojan War ; term now used of devoted and unquestioning followers.

Myrob'alan. A prune-like fruit used in tanning, 1912.

Myron. *See* **Miron.**

Myrrh. A fragrant gum resin, in perfumes, 2768.

Myrtaceae. Family of trees and shrubs

such as myrtles and cloves, often with pungent oils in leaves or berries.

Myrtle. An evergreen shrub or tree, *Myrtus communis*, native of w. Asia and Mediterranean countries ; it was brought to Eng. towards the close of the 16th cent. ; perfumes are made from the leaves and berries.

Mysia (mish'-i-*a*). Anc. dist. of N.W. Asia Minor between Phrygia and Lydia, inhabited by the Mysi.

Mysore (mī'-sōr). State in S. India ; 29,458 sq. m. ; pop. 7,329,000 ; **2270,** *map, 1702* ; giant bull of Siva, *1707* ; Hastings crushes sultan, 1582, 1714.

Mysteries, Eleusinian, 989.

Mystery plays. Medieval plays depicting stories from Bible, 3196, 1039, 2189.

Mythology. The study of myths and legends, **2270** ; as literature for children, 1966.

Mytile'ne or **Mityle'ne.** Anc. Lesbos, Gk. (formerly Turkish) isl. in Aegean Sea off coast of Asia Minor, **2270.**

Myxoede'ma. Disease caused by lack of thyroid secretion, 1470.

Myxomycetes (miks-ō-mī-sē'-tēz). The slime moulds when classed as plants, 3617. *See* **Mycetozoa.**

THE series of little waves which formed the Egyptian sign called the " water line " www was the ancestor of our letter N. When written in running hand, the undulations tended to disappear and the character assumed the form ᔒ which looked more like a fish. The Phoenicians and Hebrews called it *Nun*, the word for " fish " in their language, but they still further modified ɥ it so that we might be inclined to ʃ say it looked more like a fish-hook than a fish.

The early Greeks and Latins straightened the lines and, making them of more even length, evolved our N. M is a labial or " lip " nasal, and N a dental or " tooth " nasal. The sound is made by bringing the end of the tongue in contact with the upper teeth, or gums, and sending the breath through the nose while the vocal chords are vibrating. The contrary is true of the French " nasal *n*," the nose passage being closed and the breath sent through the mouth.

Naafi (naf'-i ; Navy, Army, Air Force Institutes). Instn. catering for the leisure hours of the three services with food, entertainment, and some home comforts.

Nablus (nah-bloos'). Formerly **Shechem,** Palestine ; pop. 23,480 ; soap and olive-oil industries.

Na'bob. A term at one time used to describe anyone who, having made a fortune in the East, spent it ostentatiously at home ; also a title given to Indian governors and other higher personages.

Nabonas'sar. King of Babylonia 747–734 B.C. ; seems to have been vassal of Tiglath-Pileser IV, who permitted his defeated foe to remain in nominal independence.

Naboni'dus. Last ruler of Chaldean Empire, and father of Belshazzar ; succeeded to throne 556 B.C., but gave more time to building temples than to preparing for resistance to the Persians, who took him prisoner in 538 B.C.

Nabopolas'sar. King of Babylonia 625–605 B.C., founder of the Chaldean Empire ; aided by Medes he captured Nineveh in 606 B.C. ; father of Nebuchadrezzar.

Naboth (nā'-both). Owner of a vineyard coveted by Ahab, and obtained by Jezebel through murderous fraud (I Kings xxi).

Nacre (nā'-ker). *See* **Mother-of-Pearl.**

Nadir Shah (1688–1747). Ruler of Persia, 987, 1012.

Naevius (nē'-vi-*us*), **Gnaeus.** First Rom. epic poet (3rd cent. B.C.), 1895.

Nagana, carried by tsetse fly, 2352.

Nagasaki (nag-*a*-sah'-ki), Japan. Spt. on S.W. coast of Kyushu isl. ; pop. (1935) 211,700 ; exports ; shipbuilding ; atom bombed, *299,* 2474 3424.

Nagoya (na-gō-ya). City of Japan, one-third destroyed in 2nd World War ; pop. (1940) 1,320,000 ; (1948) 483,000 ; **2271,** *1798* ; pottery works, *1799.*

Nagpur (nag-poor'), India. Cap. city of Cent. Provinces, 450 m. N.E. of Bombay ; pop. 300,000 ; rly. centre ; cloth mfrs., manganese mines, 744, 1692 ; *map, 1702.*

Nagy-Varad. *See* **Oradea Mare.**

Nahas Pasha, Mustapha. Eg. statesman. Became leader of Wafdist party (*see* **Wafd**) in 1927. Premier 1928, 1930, 1936 and 1942. Dismissed by King, 1944. Attempts were made on his life in Dec. 1945, and in April and Nov. 1948.

Nahua nations. Indian tribes inhabiting Mexico in 15th cent., 326.

Nahum (nā'-hum) (7th cent. B.C.). Hebrew minor prophet ; his book, the 14th of the Old Testament, foretells the doom of Nineveh.

Naiads (nī'-adz). In Gk. myth., spirits of the springs and fountains, 2408.

Nails, of fingers and toes, 2074.

Nails, hardware, 2271.

Nairnshire (nārn-shir), Scot. Marit. co. bounded N. by Moray Firth ; a. 163 sq. m. ; pop. 8,700 ; **2272.**

Nairobi (nī-rō'-bi). Cap. of Kenya Colony, Brit. E. Africa ; pop. 51,600 ; centre for big-game expeditions ; important trade centre, 1072.

Names, 2272 ; superstitions, 2057.

Namur (na-moor'), Belgium. Fortified industrial tn. 35 m. S.E. of Brussels at junction of Sambre and Meuse rivers ; pop. 32,000 ; 2156 ; repeatedly besieged ; occupied by Germans, 1914 and 1940 ; liberated by U.S. forces in Sept. 1944.

Nana Sahib (nah'-n*a* sah'-ēb) (*c.* 1821–*c.* 1860). Hindu prince, leader of Indian Mutiny of 1857 ; 1714.

Nancy, France. Fortified city 175 m. E. of Paris ; pop. 113,470 ; noted univ. ; unsuccessfully besieged by Germans in 1916 ; battle (1477), 3141 ; Charles the Bold at, 759.

Nanga Parbat. Mt. of Kashmir, 26,182 ft. German expeditions of 1934 and 1937 met with disaster trying to reach the summit.

Nankeen. A cloth, 2273.

Nanking. City and many times cap. of China, on r. Yangtse ; pop. 1,100,000 ; **2273.**

Nanking, Treaty of (1842), 810.

Nankow Pass. In Great Wall of China, 2537.

Nansei Islands, Luchu, Liukiu, or **Ryukyu,** Japan. Group of small isls. N.E. from Formosa to Kyushu ; 941 sq. m. *See also* **Okinawa.**

Nansen, Fridtjof (1861–1930). Norwegian scientist and explorer, **2273** ; Arctic explorations ; *map, 223, 1542,* 2644.

Nantes (nahnt). Historic city and spt. of Fr. ; pop. 200,300 ; **2274** 2000.

Nantes, Edict of (1598). Decree granting religious freedom to Fr. Huguenots, 1613, 1651, 2274 ; revocation and textile trade, 3192.

Nanteuil (nahn-tē-i), **Robert** (1630–78). Fr. portrait engraver, whose heads show masterly modelling and precise draughtsmanship ; was one of the greatest engravers of all time.

Nantucket (nan-tuk'-et) **Island.** Off S.E. coast of Mass., U.S.A. ; near by is a famous lightship ; tn. of Nantucket, a summer resort.

Nao'mi. Mother-in-law of Ruth, *2858.*

Nap, of cloth, how raised, 3407.

Napaeads (nā-pē'-adz). In Gk. myth., nymphs of valleys.

Naph'tha. An oil distilled from petroleum, 2833.

Naph'thalene. A coal-tar product used in moth balls, 857.

Napier (nāp'-yer), **Sir Charles James** (1782–1853). Eng. general, fought in Sp. and France in Napoleonic wars; in 1841 in India commanded the army which conquered Sind, and for 6 years successfully governed the conquered territory.

Napier, John (1550–1617). Scot. mathematician, inventor of logarithms; his logarithm tables (or "Napier's bones," as they were called) were first published in 1614, 1998.

Napier. Port on E. coast of North Isl., New Zealand; pop. 20,300; wool and meat exports; a severe earthquake caused great damage in 1931.

Napier of Magdala, Robert Napier, 1st Baron (1810–90). Brit. soldier, took part in first and second Sikh wars, relief of Lucknow, and later Indian campaigns; commanded expeditions which stormed Pei-ho forts in China in 1860, and Magdala, cap. of Abyssinia, in 1868.

Naples. Second largest city of It.; pop. 967,700; **2274**; aquarium, 192, 2275; Pompeii, 2275, 2653; Bay, 1765; Mt. Vesuvius, 3318; history, 2275; Norman kingdom, 1238, 2376; Garibaldi and Italian unity, 1418, 1769; stamps, 3075; much destroyed in 2nd World War, 2275, 3421.

Naples, Bay of. Inlet of Mediterranean in s.w. It., famous for scenery, 1765, 2274.

Naples, University of. The largest univ. in It.; has over 12,000 students, 2275.

Napo (nah-pō). River rising in Ecuador; flows 700 m. s.E. to Amazon.

Napoleon I (na-pō'-lā-on) (1769–1821). Emperor of the Fr., **2275**, 1239, 1366; abdication, 3278; early life and rise to power, 2275; family, 2276; elected First Consul, 2276; governmental reforms, 2276; Great Britain and, 3277; marriage to Josephine, 1838, 2275; marriage to Marie Louise (in 1810, not 1809 as implied in page 2276); relations with Alexander I, 2276; and Paris, 2518; Portugal, 3331, and Prussia, 2696; Spain, 3036; relations with Talleyrand, 3149; return from Elba and final exile, 3278, 2278; and the Revolution, 1396; tomb, 2517; at Waterloo, 3354. For military campaigns see also **Napoleonic Wars**; and see also **Bonaparte.**

Napoleon II. See **Reichstadt, Duke of.**

Napoleon III (1808–73). Emperor of the French, **2278**, 1366; aids Sardinia-Piedmont against Austria, 737, 1418, 1769, 2752; beautifies Paris, 2518; Franco-Prussian War and surrender at Sedan, 1385; Mexican expedition, 2158; opposed by Victor Hugo, 1650.

Napoleon, Fr. gold coin, 1482.

Napoleonic code or **Code Napoléon,** 2276.

Napoleonic Wars (1796–1815), 2275; chief events summarized (see in Index, chart, History); Italian campaign (1796), 2275; Egyptian expedition and battle of the Nile, 2072, 2275, 2313; battle of Trafalgar (1805), 3234, 2276, 2313; battle of Jena, 2696, 2360; "Continental System," 2276; Peninsular War, 3363, 2660; Russian invasion and retreat from Moscow (1812), 2277, 2360; Waterloo, 3354. See **Vienna, Congress of.**

Nara. City in Japan; pop. 52,000; on site of ancient cap. of country.

Narba'da or **Nerbudda.** R. in India, rising in N. of Central Provinces, flowing 750 m. to Gulf of Cambay; held sacred by Hindus; map, 1702.

Narbonne (nahr-bon'). Tn. in S. France, 5 m. from Mediterranean; pop. 26,000; coopering, distilling; early Rom. colony Narbo Martius.

Narcissus (nahr-sis'-us). In Gk. myth., 2278; and Echo, 1077.

Narcissus, plant, 2278.

Nares (nārz), **Sir George Strong** (1831–1915). Brit. admiral and Arctic explorer; commanded the "Challenger" during early part of expedition (1873–76) and the Arctic expedition (1875–70).

Nares, Owen (1888–1943). Eng. actor; achieved successes in "Lady Windermere's Fan," "Milestones," "Peter Ibbetson," "Rebecca," etc.

Narghile (nahr'-gi-lā) or **hookah.** Oriental tobacco pipe.

Narses (nahr'-sēz) (c. 474–568). General of the Byzantine Empire, grand chamberlain to Justinian; in Italy, 1844.

Narva, Estonia. Spt. in Rus.; pop. 24,200; cotton and lumber trade; makes textiles; battle, 758.

Narvaez (nahr-vah'-eth), **Panfilo de** (c. 1480–1528). Span. soldier and adventurer, one of earliest explorers of Florida; perished on expedition.

Nar'vik, Norway. Port in far N. on w. coast; pop. 6,750; rly. terminus, 2393, 3129; scene of successful British naval actions in 1940; 2994, 3416.

Nar'whal. A cetacean, *Monodon monoceros*; remarkable for the long, single tusk projecting forwards from its head. At first there are two of these tusks (which are really teeth), but one of them fails to develop. The female has no tusks, 2657, 3371; ivory from teeth, 1788.

Naseby (nāz'-bi), **battle of** (1645), 933, 2892, 756.

Nash, John (1752–1835). Eng. architect; made many improvements in London West End, notably Regent Street; designed Marble Arch, 2014.

Nash, John Northcote (b. 1893). Eng. artist; a member of the London Group; well known as painter of landscapes and for his wood engravings, 1184.

Nash, Paul (1889–1946). Eng. artist, brother of above; official artist in France during 1st World War, and like John Nash noted for landscapes and engravings, 1184, 3122.

Nash, Richard (1674–1762). Eng. Society leader, popularly called "Beau" Nash; he made Bath a resort of fashion and ruled it like a monarch, 374.

Nashville, Tennessee, U.S.A. State cap. on Cumberland r.; pop. 167,400; educational centre; important livestock and wheat-grinding market; trade in hardwood, cotton, and tobacco.

Nasmyth (nā'-smith), **James** (1808–90). Scot. engineer and inventor; invents steam-hammer, 958, 1758.

Nasr-ed-Din (nahzr-ed-dēn') (1829–96). Shah of Persia; succeeded 1848; able ruler; introduced postal system and other reforms.

Nassau (nas'-ow). Cap. and spt. of Bahama Isls. (Brit.); pop. 12,975; on New Providence Isl. (pop, 29,391), 200 m. s.E. of Florida, 340.

Nassau, Germany. Since 1946 part of Land of Hessen.

Nasturtium (na-ster'-shum), **2279.**

Natal (na-tal'). Prov. of Union of South Africa; 35,284 sq. m.; pop. 2,182,700, **2279**, 3014; map, 3015; cap. Durban, 1057; citrus-farm, 3018; Howick Falls, 3021; r. Tugela, 3016.

Na'than. Hebrew prophet; rebuked David for treachery to Uriah (2 Samuel vii., xii).

Nathan, Harry L., 1st Baron (b. 1889). First Minister of Civil Aviation 1946–48.

"Nathan the Wise." Dramatic poem by Lessing, a monument to the philosopher Moses Mendelssohn; story based on tale of Melchisedec the Jew in the "Decameron."

Na'tion, Carry Amelia (1846–1911). Amer. militant temperance reformer who, with female followers, smashed saloon bar fittings with an axe to show her disapproval of alcohol; a visit to Eng. in 1908 for similar purposes proved unfruitful.

National Anthem. See **National Songs.**

National Arbitration Tribunal (U.K.), for industrial disputes, 3234.

National Assembly, of France, 1393.

National Book League. Educnl. soc. representing authors, publishers, booksellers, librarians, and readers; inaugurated 1944, superseding Nat. Book Council.

National Electricity Grid. See **Grid, Electricity.**

National Fire Service, war-time organization, 1286.

National Gallery, London, **2280**, 2012, 2013, 2019; mosaic, 2233.

National Government. Formed in Gt. Brit. in 1931, with Ramsay MacDonald as Premier, to deal with financial emergency, Cabinet of representatives of Conservatives, Liberal and National Labour parties.

National Health Insurance, 1735; Lloyd George and, 1976; new Act in force in 1948, 1590, 1735, 2996.

National Hunt Committee. Ruling body of steeplechasing, 1648.

National Insurance in U.K., 2006; ministry of, 1735.

Nationalization, 2996; of bank of England, 356; railways, 3239.

National Maritime Museum, Greenwich. Established in 1934; 2250, 2314.

National Parks. Region of great natural beauty, protected by the governments of Canada and U.S.A.; 680, 1498; 13 projected for Britain in 1947.

National Physical Laboratory (N.P.L.), Teddington. Govt. Dept. for testing materials and standards.

National Police College, at Ryton, Warwickshire, 2650.

National Portrait Gallery. Charing Cross Road, London; opened in 1896, it contains the portraits of over 2,000 famous Brit. men and women; **2281.**

National Rifle Association, (N.R.A.), 2961.

National-Socialist Party, Germany, **2281,** 1450; Hitler, 1632; Jews, 2483; socialism, 2996; 2nd World War, 3415; war criminals, 2282.

National Society Schools, foundation, 2884.

National Songs, 2282.

National Trust. For places of Historic Interest or Natural Beauty, **2283.**

Nativity, Church of the, at Bethlehem, 422.

Nativity Plays, 819.

Natron. Sodium carbonate crystallized with water, 1472.

Natterjack. A toad, 3219.

Nattier (na-tyā), **Jean Marc** (1685–1766). Fr. portrait painter; portraits of Peter the Great and Empress Catherine and of ladies of Louis XV's court; portrait of Buffon, 603.

Natufian. A people of the Middle Stone Age who probably settled in the Valley of the Caves at the western foot of Mount Carmel, Palestine, about 7000 B.C.

Natural gas, in Alberta, 1406; use, 1420.

Natural history. The study of plants, animals, and the outdoor world. See also **Botany; Nature Study; Zoology.**

Natural History Museum, South Kensington, London. A branch of the Brit. Museum; moved from Bloomsbury to South Kensington in 1880; 2258, 2260, 2922, 3245.

Naturalism, in drama, 1050; Fr. fiction, 3445.

Natural Selection. Darwin's theory of, 978; how it works, 1245.

Nature study, 2283, 2285–2288.

Nature worship, 2270; Hinduism, 1626; Japan, 1798. See also **Animal worship.**

Naucratis. Prosperous Gk. colony in 6th cent. B.C. in Nile delta, Egypt, 50 m. s.E. of Alexandria.

Nauheim, Bad, Ger. watering-place in Taunus Hills; pop. 9,390.

Nauru Island. Small coral isl. in Pacific, just s. of Equator; 8 sq. m.; pop. 2,321; Brit. mandatory; captured from Germans in 1st World War; during 2nd World War phosphate plant badly damaged by Germans; bombed by Japanese and occupied Aug. 1942; surrendered to Australians Sept. 1945 ; the deposits of guano are estimated to amount to 100,000,000 tons.

Nausicaa (naw-sik'-*a-a*). In the Odyssey, Phaeacian princess who befriends the shipwrecked Odysseus, 2422, *2423*.

Nautch girl, of India, *1699*.

Nautical mile, *see* **Weights and Measures**, *f.-i.* ; how measured at sea, 1998.

Nautilus (naw'-ti-l*u*s). Capt. Nemo's submarine in Jules Verne's " 20,000 Leagues Under the Sea," 4165 ; name also given to submarine used by Sir Hubert Wilkins to travel under the Arctic ice.

Nautilus, Pearly. A primitive mollusc, sole survivor of group *Nautiloidea*, *2943* ; not to be confused with paper nautilus or argonaut, 230, 2199.

Navajos (nah'-v*a*-hŏz) or **Navahos**, Indian tribe living in s.w. U.S.A., 2757 ; in Arizona, 235 ; blankets and rugs, 706.

Naval Aviation. Name adopted after 2nd World War for former Fleet Air Arm, *50, 2300, 2301*.

Navan or **An Uaimh.** Tn. of Co. Meath, Eire (Irish Free State) ; pop. 3,000.

Navarino (na-vah-rē'-nŏ), **battle of** (1827). In which Fr., Rus., and Eng. fleets, in defence of Greece, fought Turks in Bay of Navarino on s.w. coast of Greece ; *1525*.

Navarre (na-vahr'). Medieval kingdom on both sides of w. Pyrenees ; now divided between Fr. and prov. of Navarra in Sp. ; Henry IV of Fr., king, 1613 ; struggle with Moors, 3036.

Navas de Tolosa, battle of (1212), 2227, 3036.

Nave, in architecture, 216.

Navel orange, 2444.

Na'vicert. War-time permit issued by blockading powers allowing lawful cargoes bound for, and coming from, neutral ports, to pass through contraband control areas ; instituted by Brit. in 1915.

Navigation, 2290 ; aerial, 42, 43, 52 ; buoy, 620 ; charts and maps, *2291* ; compass, 881 ; latitude and longitude determinations, 1898 ; lighthouses and light-vessels, 1943 ; precautions against icebergs, *1683* ; radar, 2726 ; ship's log, *1997*, 1998 ; by stars, 275, 281 ; tides, 3210 ; tide tables, furnished by governments, 3210 ; time at sea, 3214 ; winds, 3385 ; use of wireless, 2099, 3397. *See* **Ships** ; and the principal topics above by name.

Navigation Acts. Laws which greatly increased Brit. shipping trade ; Cromwell's Navigation Act, 1651, not first but most important ; no goods might enter Eng. ports unless in Eng. ships or ships of the country the goods came from (i.e. aimed against Dutch carrying trade), while Eng. goods must be exported in Eng. ships ; Eng. colonies, including America, were forbidden, 1660 and 1663, to trade with any but Eng. ships ; all repealed in 1849.

Navigator Islands. Former name of Samoa Isls.

Navy, 2293, *2297–2304* ; Alfred the Great founds, 111 ; anc. and mod. battleships, *2294*, *2295* ; armour-piercing shells, 240 ; armour-plate, 240 ; badges, *plates f. 2292*, *2293* ; battleship development, 2306, 2308, *2954*, *2955* ; as a career, 2296 ; Fulton builds first steam warship, 1407 ; guns, 2305 ; mines, 2184 ; " naval train," 2296 ; oil as fuel, 2949 ; Portsmouth, 2657 ; ranks, *plates f. 2292*, *2293*, 2308 ; submarines, 3104 ; torpedoes, 3224 ; training, 2306, *2307* ; uniforms, *plates f. 2292*, *2293* ; H.M.S. Victory, 3321, *3322* ; in 1914–18 War, 3411 ; in 2nd World War, 2293, 2295, 3417, 3420, 3422, 3424.

Naxos (nak'-sos). Gk. Aegean isl., largest of Cyclades ; 163 sq. m. ; pop. 18,000 ; ravaged by Persians 490 B.C. ; seat of Venetian dukes (1207) ; captured by Turks (1566) 1527 ; emery, 1156.

Nayarit (nah-yah-rĕt), Mexico. State on cent.-w. coast ; 10,000 sq. m. ; pop. (1940) 216,690 ; cap. Tepic.

A LIST OF IMPORTANT NAUTICAL TERMS

Aback. Term used when a square-rigged sailing ship is headed towards the wind and the sails are pressed back on the mast.

Abaft. Towards the stern, behind, as abaft the main mast.

Aft. Anything at or near the ship's stern.

Amidships. In the centre of the ship.

Anchor. A heavy contrivance of iron or steel which holds a vessel in place in emergencies at sea, or when lying in a harbour and not moored to a wharf. The anchor is attached to the bow of the vessel by a hawser or chain fastened to a ring or shackle in its head. The lower end is a cross-piece ending in flukes, and just below the head there is another cross-piece called the shank.

Ballast. Anything used for a weight to keep a ship seaworthy when she is sailing or steaming without cargo ; she is then said to be " in ballast."

Bearings. The directions in which points lie relative to an observer. These directions are given in terms of angle from true north, or from a compass. An object bearing 90° true thus is due east of the observer.

Bilge. That part of a vessel's hull between the section of greatest curvature and the keel ; usually about half way between the keel and the water-line.

Binnacle. Pedestal, usually of brass, on which the compass used by the helmsman is mounted. At night the compass is illuminated by a light in the hood of the binnacle.

Bitts. A post, or usually a pair of posts, fastened to the deck of a vessel for attaching the mooring lines, or towing hawsers ; also a support to the windlass.

Block. A wooden or iron casing fitted with one or two grooved wheels, through which ropes are passed for hoisting sails, spars, or other heavy objects ; a pulley-block.

Bobstay. A part of the standing rigging of a sailing ship, being the stay which holds the bowsprit down to the stem.

Boom. A large spar used for holding the foot of a fore-and-aft sail, one end being movably fastened to the mast ; also a boom for hoisting cargo.

Bow. The forward part of a ship, especially that part which curves around to the stem ; also called bows.

Boxing the compass. Naming the 32 points of the compass backwards and forwards, in any sequence. A method of learning the various points and their relation to all the other points of the compass.

Bridge. A platform raised above the deck of a vessel athwartships for the use of the navigating officers.

Bulkhead. A partition in the hull of a ship, running either athwartships or fore and aft.

Bulwark. The side of a ship above the main deck, usually topped by a rail.

Bunker. That part of a vessel's hull where the coal or other fuel is carried.

Buntline. One of the lines fastened to the foot of a sail and used to haul the sail up to the yard.

Capstan. A vertical windlass used for hoisting the anchor or heavy sails, and in warping a vessel to her mooring ; manned by the crew with capstan bars or operated by steam.

Carvel-built. A boat built with the planking flush.

Cathead. A projection of wood or iron on the bow of a ship to which the anchor is drawn up and secured. The tackle by which the anchor is drawn up is called a " cat," and when the anchor is finally secured it is said to be " catted."

Centre-board. A plate or board on a sailing-boat, pivoted so that it will drop through a well in the bottom of the boat to act as a keel to prevent leeway.

Cleat. A timber or iron fitting fastened to the deck of a vessel with arms around which a rope may be hitched.

Clew. The clew in a square sail is the lower corner ; that of the fore-and-aft sail is the after lower corner. The loop and thimbles in the corner of a sail ; also to haul up a square sail for furling, as " clew up," or to lower a yard, as " clew down."

Clinker-built. A boat built with the planking overlapped.

Coaming. A vertical strip around the cockpit of a sailing boat to keep out the water ; also used around the skylights and hatches of a vessel.

Cockpit. A space in small vessels which is lower than the deck, usually aft, equipped with seats and giving easy access to the cabin.

Companion way. The steps leading from the deck of a ship to the saloon or other quarters below.

Cutter. A single-masted, fore-and-aft rigged sailing-boat. Also a boat with a square stern used for carrying passengers and supplies and propelled by oars, sail, or steam.

Davits. Vertical metal pillars, with the upper ends bent over, to which a small boat is attached. They turn to allow the boat to swing out clear of the side to be lowered.

Dead eye. A round, flat, wooden block pierced with holes and used for tightening the shrouds of a sailing ship. One dead eye is attached to the lower end of a shroud and another to the bulwarks, and a lanyard passing through the holes makes it possible to tauten the shrouds.

Dead reckoning. The deduction, by means of records of courses, time, wind, and distances, of a ship's position. Plotted on a chart or sailing sheet, the dot representing the estimated position is marked " Est." or " D.R."

Dinghy. A small rowing-boat used as a tender.

Fall. The part of a hoisting rope which hangs from a block or pulley, to which the power is applied ; the tackle on the davits by which the boat is lowered : boat-falls.

Falling off. When a vessel's bow drops away to leeward of her course.

Fiddle. A rim round the edge of a table on board ship to prevent plates and dishes falling off in a heavy sea.

Forecastle. Raised deck in the bow of a ship beneath which the crew is often housed.

Freeboard. That part of a ship's side measured vertically between the bulwarks and the water-line when she is loaded.

Galley. The ship's kitchen.

Gangway. An opening in the bulwarks of a vessel to allow people to enter and leave it.

Naz'areth. Palestine, tn. 65 m. N. of Jerusalem ; pop. 15,000 ; occupied by Israeli forces in 1948. **2309.**

Naze. A headland on the E. coast of Essex, 5 m. S. of Harwich ; Naze means nose or promontory.

Nazi. Contraction of National-sozialistische Deutsche Arbeiterpartei. (National Socialist German Workers' Party), **2310.** See National-Socialist Party.

Nazimuddin, Khwaja (b. 1894). Pakistan statesman ; succeeded Mahomed Ali Jinnah as gov.-gen. of Pakistan in 1948.

Ndola. Mining centre, N. Rhodesia, 2772.

Neagh, Lough (lokhnā). Lake in N.E. Ireland, near Belfast, largest in Brit. Isls. ; *1744 ; map, 1745.*

Neanderthal (nā-ahn'-der-tahl) **man,** member of a race of Stone Age men, *2079, 2080.*

Neapolis (nē-ap'-ō-lis) Anc. Gk. settlement on site of Naples, 2275.

Neap tide, *3210.*

Near East. Name applied to Egypt, Iran, Iraq, Palestine, area comprising Arabia, Turkey, and Syria.

Near-sightedness, or **myopia,** 1254 ; corrected by concave lenses, *3054.*

Neath, Wales. Tn. in Glamorganshire, 8 m. N.E. of Swansea ; in important mining dist. ; copper smelting, tinplate works ; pop. 33,340.

Neb'neb. An African acacia, 16.

Ne bo. A mt. in Palestine whence Moses saw the Promised Land ; perhaps the modern Jebel Neba (2,650 ft.) near N. end of Dead Sea.

Nebras'ka. A N.-cent. state of U.S.A. ; 77,237 sq. m. ; pop. 1,315,000 ; **2310.**

Nebuchadrezzar or **Nebuchadnezzar** (neb-ū-kad-nez'-ar). Babylonian king 604–561 B.C. ; restores Babylon, 331, 686 ; captures Jerusalem, 1830 ; favours Daniel, 2692 ; Hanging Gardens, 2923, *plates f. 2924, 328, 329.*

Nebulae (neb'-ū-lē), in astronomy, **2310,** *278, 280 ;* of Andromeda, *2310, 3080, 3081 ;* of Orion, *234.*

Neb'ular hypoth'esis. Theory that solar system condensed from a nebula, 2618.

Necho II (nē-kō) (d. c. 594 B.C.), King of Egypt.

Neck'ar, Ger. Tributary of Rhine rising in Black Mts., entering main stream at Mannheim, 464 ; Heidelberg on, 1604.

Neck'er, Jacques (1732–1804). Fr. financier ; father of Mme. de Staël ; director-general of Fr. finances, 1393.

Nec'romancer. Magician who claimed to predict the future by communicating with the dead, 2058.

Nec'taries, of flower, *531.*

Nec'tarine. A fruit, smooth-skinned like the peach ; more tender of skin

than the peach, it must not be touched by hand whilst growing, 2532.

Needle, gramophone, 1496.

Needle-gun, *1282, 1283.*

Needlepoint lace, 1877, *1878, plate f. 1880.*

Needles, 2311 ; primitive, *2312 ;* in surface tension experiment, 3121.

Needles, The. A group of chalk rocks off the W. end of the Isle of Wight ; the Needles lighthouse is 109 ft. high, and stands on the westernmost rock ; the name comes from a single pillar of chalk, 120 ft. high, which fell in 1764 ; *3377.*

Neerwinden (nār'-vin-den), Belgium. Village 30 m. E. of Brussels where French defeated English in 1693, and Austrians defeated French in 1793.

Negapatam (neg-a-pa-tam'). Port of Madras, S.E. India ; pop. 18,000 ; brisk trade with Ceylon and E. Indies ; point for coolie emigration ; vegetable oils ; exports rice, 1692.

Negative electricity, 1128 ; in thermionic valve, 3198.

Neg'ative, photographic, 2577.

Negatron. Alternative name sometimes given to the electron since the discovery of the positron, 294.

Negrin, Juan (b. 1889). Spanish statesman and biologist. Became premier of " Government " Spain, during

---

A LIST OF IMPORTANT NAUTICAL TERMS *(contd.)*

Gasket. A tapered line on a yard or sail for use in making the sails fast when they are furled.

Gunwale. Side of ship's boat above the thwarts.

Halyard. A rope for hoisting a sail, or yard, etc.

Hatch. An opening in the deck of a vessel through which cargo is loaded and discharged.

Hawser. A large cable or rope used for mooring, towing, etc.

Heave-to. To stop a vessel's headway, usually by bringing her " head on " into the wind.

Heel over. Said of a sailing-ship when she is running close-hauled to the wind which causes her to lay over at an angle.

Helm. The steering apparatus of a vessel, made up of the rudder, tiller, wheel, and tiller ropes.

Hold. The main cargo space below the lowest deck.

Jack staff. Small flagstaff at the stern of a ship from which the ensign is flown.

Keel. A timber or series of plates running the length of the bottom of a vessel from stem to stern on the centre line, to which the ribs are attached.

Keelson. A beam extending over the keel to strengthen it.

Lee board. A fin-like contrivance pivoted to the side of a ship which can be lowered to prevent the ship making too much leeway. It is now used chiefly on sailing barges.

Leeward. The opposite side to that from which the wind blows.

Leeway. The sideways motion of a ship caused by pressure of wind.

Marline. A small rope or cord of two strands, usually tarred, used for " whipping " or winding the ends of large ropes or cables.

Marline-spike. A tapered iron pin used for spreading the strands of a cable in making a splice.

Martingale. A stay used to hold down the jib-boom or the flying jib-boom.

Poop. A raised deck at the stern of a vessel, above the spar-deck.

Port. The left-hand side of the ship as seen when looking forward ; also a porthole or circular opening in the side of a ship.

Ratline. A small rope fastened between a vessel's shrouds to form the rungs of a ladder.

Reef. In strong winds the sail area of a ship is reduced or reefed by rolling up the lower part of a sail and securing it with small ropes (reef points) passing through eyelets in the sail.

Riding light. A white light hoisted on the mast of a vessel and visible from all directions. It is shown when she is at anchor in the open sea or moored to a buoy in harbour.

Running rigging. That part of the rigging of a ship which is used to hoist, lower or hold the sails.

Scuppers. Holes in the side of a vessel at the deck level for draining the water from the deck.

Shackle. A link used to lock a porthole, or to fasten a block to an eye-bolt, or the like.

Sheet. A rope attached to a sail to regulate its angle to the wind ; also the open spaces between the thwarts and the ends of a small boat as the fore-sheets and sternsheets.

Shrouds. Part of the standing rigging, consisting of two or more ropes, usually wire, from the masthead to the bulwarks of a ship ; they are generally fitted with ratlines making a rope ladder.

Spar. Term applied to any mast, yard, or boom used to support a sail.

Sprit. A small spar extending diagonally from the mast to the aft upper corner of a fore-and-aft sail to extend it. The sail is then called a spritsail.

Stanchion. A post or pillar placed upright in a ship.

Standing rigging. That part of the rigging of a ship which is used only to support the masts.

Starboard. The opposite of port. The right-hand side of a ship when looking forward.

Stay. A rope used in tension to brace a mast or yard.

Stern. The after end of a vessel.

Strake. One continuous line of planking or plates on a vessel's bottom or sides.

Tack. A ship is said to be on the starboard tack when she is sailing with the wind on her starboard beam, and on the port tack when she has the wind on her

port beam. When a ship " beats to windward," she tacks, sailing as close as she can to the wind on each tack. In tacking, a ship's head is thrown into the wind as she goes about.

Taffrail. The railing placed around the stern of a ship.

Top. A platform at the foot of each top-mast on a sailing-ship. Like the cross-trees, it anchors and spreads the shrouds. The tops are called foretop, maintop, and mizzentop.

Waist. That section of a vessel between the quarter deck and the forecastle ; the central portion of the ship.

Warping. When a vessel is shifted from one position to another by means of a cable around a mooring post on which tension is put from the ship she is said to have warped to her new berth.

Watches. The division of a crew of a vessel for deck duty, usually called port and starboard watches, which are on duty alternately ; also the periods into which the day is divided, usually of four hours each. The watches are : first watch, 8 p.m. to midnight ; mid-watch or middle watch, midnight to 4 a.m. ; morning watch, 4 a.m. to 8 a.m. ; forenoon watch, 8 a.m. to noon ; afternoon watch, noon to 4 p.m. ; first dog-watch, 4 p.m. to 6 p.m. ; second dog-watch, 6 p.m. to 8 p.m. The dog-watches alternate the periods when the port and starboard watches are on duty.

Wear round. A ship wears round when she turns her course, but instead of her head being thrown into the wind as in tacking, her head is turned away from the wind and she goes about with the wind following her.

Weather deck. A deck with no covering overhead, therefore exposed to the weather.

Windlass. Device used for hoisting the anchor. It is a long, horizontal barrel revolving on two supports, and in the old days was turned by handspikes placed in holes on the drum. On modern ships the windlass is actuated by steam or electricity.

Windward. The direction from which the wind is blowing.

Yard. A spar set athwartships on which a sail is bent.

Civil War in May 1937. Exiled in France to 1940, later Mexico.

Negri (or Nigri) Sembilan (nä'-grĕ sem-bē-lan'). State of the Federation of Malaya bordering Strait of Malacca ; composed of 9 lesser states ; 2,580 sq. m. ; pop. (est.) 296,000 ; largely agricultural ; exports tin ; 2069.

Negrito (ne-grē'-tō). Racial type resembling Negro, 2312 ; in Philippines, 2568 ; in Andaman and Nicobar Isls., 1692.

Negro. Black and dark brown native, 2312 ; in Africa, 70, *3366, 3367* ; in Barbados, 360 ; Brazil, 553 ; Guiana, 1553 ; Haiti, 1566 ; Jamaica, 1793 ; Liberia, *1930* ; numbers, 65 ; U.S.A., 2312, 2982. *See* Slavery.

Negroids, 2312.

Negros (nā'-grōs). Fourth largest isl. of Philippines ; 4,900 sq. m.

Ne'gus Ne'gusti. Title of Abyssinian emperor, 14.

Nehemiah (nē-he-mī'-*a*) (5th cent. B.C.). Gov. of Judea under Artaxerxes ; restored walls of Jerusalem, relieved condition of poor, and re-established temple service ; 1830.

Nehemiah, Book of. Book of Old Testament largely written by Nehemiah ; recounts events of his rule.

Nehru, Jawaharlal (b. 1889). Indian nationalist leader ; first Prime Minister of Dominion and Repub. of India, 2312, *1717.*

Neilson, Julia (b. 1868). Eng. actress ; wife of Fred Terry ; won successes as Hypatia in the play of that title, Nell Gwyn in " Sweet Nell of Old Drury," and Rosalind in " As You Like It " ; in partnership with her husband produced many plays, among them " The Scarlet Pimpernel," " Henry of Navarre," and several of Shakespeare's works.

Nejd or Nedjed. Desert region in cent. Arabia ; Emir expelled Turks from E. Hasa (1913) ; recognized (1915) as independent ruler of Nedjed and El Hasa by Gt. Brit. ; Nejd is now part of the Kingdom of Saudi Arabia, 195, 196, 198, 200, 201.

Nell, Little. Sweet, unselfish child-heroine of Dickens's " Old Curiosity Shop," who dies from privation.

Nelson, H.M.S. British battleship completed in 1927 and taken out of service in 1947.

Nelson, Horatio, Viscount (1758–1805). Eng. naval commander, 2313 ; battle of Copenhagen, 905, 2313 ; column in Trafalgar Sq., *2019* ; commemorated at Portsmouth, 2657 ; signal " England expects . . .", *2313*; Southey's life, 3028 ; H.M.S. Victory, 3321, *3322* ; Trafalgar, 2313, *3234.*

Nelson, British Columbia. City in S.E. on arm of L. Kootenay ; pop. 5,750 ; commercial centre of the mining, lumbering, and fruit-growing Kootenay dist.

Nelson River, Canada. Name given to lower course of Saskatchewan in Manitoba ; flows 400 m. N.E. from L. Winnipeg to Hudson Bay ; 677, 2088.

Nelson's Column, London, erected by voluntary contributions in centre of Trafalgar Square 36 years after Nelson's death ; built of granite, 200 ft. in height, Corinthian in style, with capital of gunmetal ; bronze low-reliefs on pedestal of metal from captured French guns ; lions modelled by Sir Edwin Landseer 1868 ; 2013, *2019.*

Nematodes, worms, 3425.

Neme'an lion, in Gk. myth., monster slain by Hercules, 1615.

Nem'esis, in Gk. myth., goddess of justice ; **2314.**

Nemi. Crater lake of Central Italy ; " The Golden Bough," 1387, *1388.*

Nene or Nen. R. of Northamptonshire, flowing into the Wash ; 90 m. long ; Peterborough on, 2563.

Neodym'ium (Nd), metallic element of the rare-earth group ; atomic weight, 144·3. *See* Rare Earths.

Neolith'ic or New Stone Age, 2081–2083, 3095, 3097 ; flint mine, *1315* ; camp, 735.

Ne'on (Ne), an element of the inert gas group, **2314,** 776, 2744 ; atomic weight 20·2 ; it has been solidified and melts at –409°F. ; used largely in neon lamps, 1135 ; in the air, 88, 1420.

" **Neoprene,**" a synthetic rubber, 2838.

Nepal (ne-pawl'). Kingdom between N.E. India and Tibet, on S. side of Himalayas ; 54,000 sq. m. ; pop. (est.) 7,000,000 ; **2315** ; Mt. Everest, 1243.

Nephin (nef'-in) **Beg,** Eire, a mt. in co. Mayo, 2,065 ft. high.

Nepos (nē'-pos), **Cornelius** (*c.* 99–24 B.C.) Rom. historian (" De viris illustribus," much used as school text).

Nep'tune, in Rom. myth., sea-god, corresponding to Gk. Poseidon, **2315,** *2660. See* Poseidon.

Neptune, planet, **2315** ; comparative size, *2618* ; discovery, 2618 ; distance from sun, 280 ; orbit, 280, *2619* ; satellite, 2618 ; size, 2315, *2618* ; and Uranus, 27, 3298.

Neptunium (Np), new element derived from uranium 239 and giving rise to plutonium, **2315,** 299, 3297.

Nereids (nēr'-ē-idz), in Gk. myth., 50 sea nymphs, 2408 ; Calypso, 2422.

Nereus (nēr'-ūs). In Gk. myth., a minor sea-god, father of the Nereids ; sometimes called " the old man of the sea ; he guided Hercules to the Garden of the Hesperides after changing his form in turn to fire, lion, water, and smoke in effort to escape from Hercules.

Ne'ro (A.D. 37–68). Rom. emperor **2315,** *2316,* 2811 ; persecuted Christians, 817 ; spectacles, 3054.

Ner'va (A.D. 32–98). Rom. emperor, kindly but feeble ; adopted Trajan as colleague and successor ; 2811.

Nerves, 2316 ; auditory, 1066 ; and brain, 545 ; cells of cerebrum, 546 ; fibres of cerebrum, 546 ; grey and white matter, 546 ; controlling heart, 1593 ; injury, 2317 ; optic, 1252 ; derived from skin, 2317 ; in sleep, 2985 ; smell, 2986 ; teeth, 3163 ; touch, 3231.

Nesbit, Edith (1858–1924). Eng. poet, novelist, and author of children's books including " Five Children and It," and " The Amulet," 1966.

Ness, Loch. Lake in Scotland ; 23 m. long, average width one mile ; discharges into Moray Firth by R. Ness, 8 m. long ; at various times, espec. in 1933–34, it was said to harbour a monster of strange shape and enormous size, 1737.

Nes'sus. In Gk. and Rom. myth., centaur slain by Hercules ; shirt of, 1615.

Nes'tor. In the " Iliad," wise old warrior and counsellor of Greeks in the Trojan War, 3249. The " Nestor " of an organization or group means the oldest and most experienced member.

Nesto'rians. Christian sect named after Nestorius (d. about 440), patriarch of Constantinople ; centred in Persia ; " catholicus " or chief bishop had seat at Baghdad from 762 to 1258 ; in 6th and 7th centuries spread over much of Asia, evangelizing India and China ; adherents now number about 150,000 in Turkey and Iran (mod. Persia).

Nests ; of alligator, 122 ; ants, 165, 166, *168* ; birds, 441, 442, *443, 3360*; fish, 1297 ; of insects, 1729 ; termite, *3188, 3189, 3190* ; wasps and hornets, 3345, *3346.*

Netball. Team game, 2317.

Netherlands, Kingdom of (Holland), in N.W. Europe ; 13,550 sq. m. ; pop. over 10 million ; **2318** ; *plates f. 2320, 2321, map, 404* ; cap. Amsterdam, 147 ; The Hague, seat of govt., 1563 ; 3300, 2318, 2320, 2321 ; reclamation, 2318 ; former E. Ind colonies, 1075, 1720, 1813, 2335 ; government, 2323 ; people, *797, plates f. 2320, 2321, 2322* ; rivers and canals, 2156, 2318, 2319, 2769 ; stamp, *3075* ; tulip-growing, 612, 2320. *Art :* **2324,** *2325– 2332* ; Brueghels, 592 ; influence and work in Eng., 1178 ; Hals, 1568 ; 19th cent., 2335 ; oil painting invented, 2324 ; Rembrandt, 2762,

1219 ; Rubens, 2838 ; Van Dyck, 3304 ; Van Gogh, 3305 ; Vermeer, *3315.—History :* under Charles the Bold, 759 ; Renaissance, 2764 ; struggle for independence, 2321 ; early spice trade, 3060 ; wars with England, 2323 ; wars with Louis XIV, 2029 ; Louis Bonaparte king, 497 ; loss of colonies in S. Africa, 3017 ; under William the Silent, 3381 ; union with Belgium, 407 ; Queen Wilhelmina, 3378 ; Queen Juliana, 3378 ; 2nd World War, 2323 ; overrun by Ger., 1452, 3416.

Netherlands East Indies, 2335. *See* East Indies ; Indonesia.

Netherlands, New Guinea. *See* New Guinea.

Netherlands, Princess of. Title taken by Queen Wilhelmina after her abdication in 1948 ; 3378.

Nethou (nä-tōō'), **Pic de.** Highest mt. of the Pyrenees, 2709.

Nets, fish, *1304, 1308,* 1299.

Netsukes (nā'-tsoo-kĕz). Japanese carvings, 1809.

Nettle. A herb with hairs which exude a stinging juice when broken, **2335** ; poison, 2638 ; dead nettles, 3207.

Neuchâtel (nē-sha-tel'). Rly. and industrial centre in w. Switzerland on L. Neuchâtel ; pop. 23,800 ; univ. ; manufactures, 3142.

Neuchâtel. Lake in w. Switzerland, 18 m. N. of L. Geneva ; 93 sq. m. ; traversed by r. Thièle, 3140.

Neuilly (nē-yē') or **Neuilly-sur-Seine,** Fr. mfg. and residential tn. and N.W. suburb of Paris on r. Seine ; pop. 60,170.

Neuilly, Treaty of, and Bulgaria, 614.

Neukölln (noi'kĕln). Suburb of Berlin ; Karstadthaus, *417.*

Neurath (noi'-rahth), **Baron Constantin von** (b. 1873). Ger. statesman. Ambassador in London (1930–32) ; Min. for Foreign Affairs (1932–38). Appointed Reich Protector of Bohemia and Moravia 1939, after Nazi conquest of Czechoslovakia. Resigned 1941. Tried as war criminal, Nuremberg 1945–46 ; sentenced to 15 years, imprisonment.

Neurop'tera. An order of net-veined insects, such as ant-lions, 1733.

Neutralization. Chemical process, 20.

Neutron. A proton and an electron combined to form a neutral particle. In atom, *295–298* ; bombardment, *951* ; in uranium isotope, 2315.

Neuve-Chapelle (nēv-sha-pel'). Fr. vil. 25 m. S. of Ypres ; 1915 battle.

Ne'va. R. in N.W. Russia, flows 40 m. from L. Ladoga to Gulf of Finland 10 m. below Leningrad ; connected by canal with Volga system ; 1923, 1924.

Nevada (ne-vah'-da). State in w. U.S.A. ; 110,540 sq. m. ; pop. 110,200 ; **2335.**

Nev'ern, Wales. R. of Pembrokeshire, entering Cardigan Bay close to Newport ; 10 m. long, 2539.

Nevers (ne-vār), Fr. mfg. tn., 140 m. S.E. of Paris ; pop. 34,000 ; fine cathedral.

Neville. Great Eng. family ; the most famous member was Warwick " the Kingmaker " (Richard Neville). *See* Warwick.

Nevinson, Christopher Richard Wynne (1889–1946). Eng. artist ; famous for expressionistic work as official artist in 1st World War, *1183,* 1184.

Nevinson, Henry Woodd (1857–1941). Eng. author, father of C. R. W. Nevinson ; famous special correspondent, and champion of many reform movements.

Nevis, Ben. *See* Ben Nevis.

Nev'is. Isl. of British W. Indies, 3368.

Nevison, Nick. Highwayman, 1625.

Nevsky Prospekt. Famous avenue in Leningrad, later called the Prospekt of the 25th of Oct. 1924.

New Amsterdam. Name of New York City under Dutch rule, 2353.

Newark (nū'ark) or **Newark-on-Trent.** Old tn. in Nottinghamshire, 16 m. S.E. of Manchester ; pop. 23,120 ; once fortress of great strength and called " key to North " ; here Charles I was besieged in 1646 by the Scots, to whom he finally surrendered ; 2399 ; castle, *714.*

Newark, New Jersey, U.S.A. Largest city of state ; pop. 429,760 ; chief jewelry mfg. centre in the country, and has important leather, button, and hat industries ; airport for New York City ; 2341.

New Bedford, Massachusetts, U.S.A. Mfg. city on Buzzards Bay ; pop. 110,340 ; for long the chief whaling port in the world, and now the principal cotton-yarn and cloth centre in the U.S.A. ; 2118.

Newbery, John (1713–67). Eng. publisher, associated with Dr. Johnson and Goldsmith, 1964.

Newbolt, Sir Henry John (1862–1938). British writer. Works include : " Admirals All " and " Drake's Drum " (verse) ; " The Old Country " (novel) ; official Naval historian of 1st World War.

New Britain. Largest isl. in Bismarck Archipelago, part of Mandated Territory of New Guinea ; about 10,000 sq. m. ; native pop. 90,350 ; formerly the Ger. isl. of New Pomerania ; 2740 ; magic in, *plate f. 2056* ; Japan occupied 1942–45, 3421 ; Kokopo selected as administrative cap. in 1947 ; Rabaul, former cap. of mandated Australian New Guinea.

New Brunswick. A maritime prov. of Canada ; 27,895 sq. m. ; pop. 457,400 ; 2336 ; chief city, Saint John, 2861 ; joins Confederation, 683 ; United Empire Loyalists, 683.

Newburgh. Tn. of Fife, Scot. ; oilcloth mfg. ; *2891.*

Newbury. Market tn. in Berkshire on Kennet and Avon Canal ; agric. trade ; two battles were fought here in Civil War (1643, 1644) ; pop. 17,490 ; 416.

New Caledonia. Fr. isl. 850 m. E. of Queensland, Australia ; 8,500 sq. m. ; pop. 53,200, 2470, 2472 ; nickel, 2366.

New Castile. The S. part of Castile, including old Moorish kingdom of Toledo ; chief cities Madrid, Toledo, Ciudad Real ; fertile river valleys, sterile high plateaux, *map, 3030.*

Newcastle. City in New S. Wales, Australia, 100 m. N. of Sydney ; pop. 127,600 with suburbs ; coaling port ; ships wood, mutton ; 2344.

Newcastle-under-Lyme. Tn. in Staffordshire, 30 m. S. of Manchester ; pop. 63,850 ; important potteries and collieries in neighbourhood ; mfrs. chemicals.

Newcastle-upon-Tyne. Great coal-shipping centre of Northumberland, on Tyne ; pop. 291,000 ; 2336, 2391 ; first industrial gas turbine, *1425.*

Newchwang (nū-chwang') or **Niuchwang.** Also called **Yingkow** ; port of Manchuria, 300 m. N.E. of Peking; pop. 82,000 ; taken by Russians in 1900 and by Japanese in 1904 and 1932.

New College, Oxford, 2464.

Newcome, Colonel. In Thackeray's " The Newcomes," a gallant, simple-hearted gentleman ; 3193.

Newcomen, Thomas (1663–1729). Eng. mechanic ; first practical steam pumping engine, 3085, 3357.

New Deal. Programmes of legislation designed by Pres. F. D. Roosevelt in 1932 to promote national recovery, 2823, 3292.

New Delhi. *See* Delhi.

Newdigate, Sir Roger (1719–1806). Eng. politician and antiquary ; he was donor of the Oxford Univ. poetry prize bearing his name.

New Economic Policy (N.E.P.), in Russia, 2850.

New England. Collective name for states of Maine, New Hampshire, Vermont, Massachusetts, Connecticut, and Rhode Isl., U.S.A. ; settled by Pilgrims, 2122. *See also* separate states and cities.

New Forest. Wooded region in S.W. Hampshire, Eng., used as public pleasure ground, 1571, *3244.*

Newfoundland. Isl. in Gulf of St. Lawrence ; a prov. of Canada ; 42,734 sq. m. ; pop. (with Labrador) 321,170 ; 2337 ; *map f. 680* ; discovered, 580, 648 ; acquired by Britain, 580; fogs, 1333, 2337 ; Labrador, 1875.

Newfoundland Banks or **Grand Bank.** Submarine plateau off coast of Newfoundland, famous fishing ground, 2338 ; fogs, 1333, 2337.

Newfoundland dog, *plate f. 1024.*

New France. Name for Canada, under Fr. rule, 2715. For history, *see* **Canada.**

Newgate. Prison in London, built about 1200, several times rebuilt and remodelled and finally demolished in 1903, making room for the Central Criminal Court (" Old Bailey ") ; until 1868 public executions took place outside Newgate, and vast crowds assembled to see them.

New Granada. Original Sp. name for Colombia, 874.

New Guinea. Largest isl. of Malay archipelago, now three territories : 1. Australian Territory of Papua ; 2. Australian Trusteeship Territory of N.G. ; 3. Netherlands N.G. ; 311,000 sq. m. ; pop. (est.) 1,178,500 ; 2338, 1076, *map, 1075* ; magic in, *2058* ; pygmies, 2707 ; Allied-Jap. battlefield in 1942–44, 2340, 2474, 3420. *See also* **Papua.**

New Hampshire. New England state of U.S.A. ; 9,304 sq. m. ; pop. 491,500 ; 2341.

New Haven, Connecticut, U.S.A. Chief city of state, seat of Yale Univ. ; pop. 160,600 ; distributing centre for coal, cement, lumber ; mfrs. firearms, clocks, hardware.

Newhaven. Spt. on Eng. Channel at mouth of R. Ouse, 50 m. s. of London ; terminus of steamer line to Dieppe, Fr.

New Hebrides. Group of isls. E. of N. Australia, under joint control of Britain and France ; 5,700 sq. m. ; pop. (est.) 41,000 ; export coffee, copra, cotton, 2470, 2473.

New Holland. Former name of Australia.

New Ireland. Second largest isl. of Bismarck Archipelago ; Australian mandatory ; 4,600 sq. m. ; formerly New Mecklenburg ; 2470, *map, 1075* ; betrothal customs, 2109.

New Jersey. A cent. Atlantic state of U.S.A.; 7,836 sq. m.; pop. 4,160,200 ; 2341.

New Jerusalem Church, 3132. *See* Swedenborg.

New Lanark. Tn. in Lanarkshire, Scot., 25 m. S.E. of Glasgow ; Robert Owen's community, 2996.

Newlyn School, of painters, 1183.

Newman, John Henry, Cardinal (1801– 90). Eng. churchman, 2342 ; wrote hymn " Lead Kindly Light," 1678.

Newmarket. Tn. 14 m. N.E. of Cambridge ; pop. 9,753 ; h.q. of horse-racing in U.K.

New Mecklenburg. *See* New Ireland.

New Mexico. State of S.W. U.S.A. ; 121,666 sq. m. ; pop. 531,000 ; 2342.

New Netherlands. Dutch colony established in Amer. in 1614 ; afterwards New York.

Newnham College. Women's college at Cambridge, 666, 669.

New Orleans, Louisiana, U.S.A. Port on Mississippi ; pop. 494,500 ; 2342 ; ceded to Sp. by Fr., 2343.

New Place. Shakespeare's house at Stratford-upon-Avon, 2934.

New Plymouth, New Zealand. Spt. and rly. terminus on w. coast of North Isl. ; pop. 20,640 ; flour mills, leather mfrs. ; trade in dairy products.

New Pomerania. *See* New Britain.

Newport, Eng. Port in Monmouthshire on Usk ; pop. (est.) 100,000 ; coal, iron, cattle trade ; shipbuilding ; iron products ; was the scene of a serious Chartist riot in 1839 in which many thousands of miners took part.

Newport. Tn. in Isle of Wight, of which it is the cap. ; Carisbrooke Castle and Parkhurst Prison are near by ; pop. 20,000 ; 3377.

Newport, Rhode Island, U.S.A. Resort on S.W. coast of Rhode Island ; pop. 27,600 ; venue of America's Cup yachting races ; 2770.

Newport News, Virginia, U.S.A. Spt. and shipbuilding centre on James r., at entrance into Hampton Roads ; pop. 37,060.

New Radnor, Wales, Vil. in Radnorshire ; anciently a bor. ; fragments of a castle destroyed by Owen Glendower remain ; 2733.

New Scotland Yard, Whitehall, London. H.q. of Police Force, 2014, 2647.

New Siberia. Group of isls. in Arctic Ocean N. of Siberia ; largest Kotelnoi (116 m. by 100 m.) ; uninhabited except for hunters.

New South Wales (N.S.W.), Australia. State in S.E., 309,432 sq. m. ; pop. 2,912,800 ; 2343 ; cap. Sydney, *3144*; founded, *308* ; Burrinjack dam, *1672.*

Newspapers, 2344 ; Beaverbrook, 388 ; Camrose, 675 ; historical development, 985, 1213, 2347 ; Iliffe, 1686 ; Kemsley, 1851 ; linotype, 1956 ; monotype, 2215 ; Northcliffe, 2385 ; paper, 2497 ; printing, 2684 ; process engraving, 2688 ; stereotype, 3088 ; transmission of pictures by wire, 2577 ; transmitted and printed by wireless, 3398.

New stars, or *novae,* 3080.

New Sweden. Swedish colony in U.S.A., on Delaware r. , 15 m. S.W. of Philadelphia, Pa. ; founded in 1638.

Newt. A long-tailed animal typical of the order *Urodela* of class *Amphibia.* British species include smooth, crested, and palmate newts ; hibernate in mud, breed in ponds in spring. *4369* ; tadpole stage as in frogs. Evolutionary position, 2767.

New Testament (N.T.), of Bible, contents, 423 ; Epistles of Paul, 2530 ; Epistles of Peter, 2562 ; Gospels,188.

Newton, Sir Isaac (1642–1727). Eng. physicist and mathematician, 2348, 2593 ; determines compound character of colour, *facing* 3056 ; invented colour disk, 876 ; and the echo, 1077 ; and gravity, 1512–14, 2349 ; and Robert Hooke, 1640 ; studies of light, 1929, 2728, 2730 ; invents reflecting telescope, 3178 ; laws of mechanics, 2127 ; laws of motion, 2130 ; and modern astronomy, 276 ; and the Quantum Theory, 2711 ; and spectrum, *facing* 3056 ; his Third Law, 2793 ; and tides, 3209.

Newton, John (1725–1807). Eng. clergyman and poet ; collaborated with Cowper, 923.

New Year's Day, as festival, 2350.

New York City, in New York State, U.S.A. 2nd largest city of world : pop. (greater N.Y.) 7,454,995, (N.Y. proper) 6,930,000 ; 2351 ; *plates f. 2352, 2353* ; *map, 2382* ; bridges, 568, 2351, 2353, 2355, 3289 ; economic depression in, 3292 ; foreign population, 2353 ; harbour and islands, 2351, *2352* ; history, 2353 ; Manhattan, *2352* ; museums, 2260 ; skyscrapers, 222, 2351, *2354, 2355, back of plate f. 2352, 2353* ; Statue of Liberty, *2351* ; Stock Exchange, *3094* ; subways, 2353 ; transport, 2353, 3237.

New York State. Middle Atlantic state of U.S.A., 49,204 sq. m., pop. 13,479,000 ; 2353, *2356* ; Dutch settlement (New Amsterdam), 2357 ; England acquires, 757, 1552, 2357.

New Zealand. Brit. dominion comprising a group of isls. in S. Pacific Ocean ; 103,935 sq. m. ; pop; 1,823, 000 ; 2357, *2359* ; *map, 2358* ; Canterbury Plains, 693 ; cities, 301, 2357, 3364 ; government, 2358 ; hydro-electric installn., *1668* ; Cook's explorations, 898, 2360 ; German colonies captured in 1914–18 War, 2360, 3411 ; Maoris, 2358, *2360* ; rainfall, 2741 ; social insurance,2994.

Nexo, Martin Andersen (b. 1869), Danish novelist, 2881.

Ney (nā), **Michel** (1769–1815). Fr. marshal, 2360, 3355.

Niagara escarpment, 2362.

Niag'ara Falls. Most famous falls in the world, 2361 ; *maps, 1515, 2362* ; harnessing its power, 2363 ; Welland Canal, 1515, 3363 ; whirlpool, *2362,* 2363.

Niagara Falls, N.Y., U.S.A. Resort and industrial city on Niagara r. ; pop. 78,030 ; enormous water-power ; electro-chemical works ; Niagara University.

Niagara Falls, Ontario. City and port opposite Niagara Falls, N.Y., U.S.A.; pop. 20,589; enormous hydro-electric plant; cereals, iron products, carborundum, hats, silverware.

Niagara Gorge, 2363.

Niagara River. Outlet of L. Erie flowing N. to L. Ontario, 33 m., 1516, 2363.

Nib, of cacao bean, 862.

Nib, of pen, 2539.

" Nibelungs (nē'-be-loongz), **Song of the,"** or **" Nibelungenlied."** Ger. epic of 13th cent., 2363, 1456; Siegfried legend, 2969; Wagner's operas, 3332.

Nib'lick. A golf club, 1484.

Nicaea (nī-sē'-a) or **Nice** (modern Isnik). Important anc. city of Bithynia, Asia Minor, on L. Ascania; declined under Turkish rule (14th cent.); famous Church Council (A.D. 325), 817, 893.

Nicaragua (nik-a-rag'-wa). Largest of cent. Amer. republics; 57,143 sq. m.; pop. 1,389,000; 2363; map, 743.

Nicaragua, Lake. Largest lake in cent. Amer., in s.w. Nicaragua; drained by San Juan r.; 2364.

Nicaria (nē-kah-rē'-a). Anc. Icaria, Gk. isl. in Aegean Sea; 83 sq. m.; produces charcoal, sponges.

Niccoli (nē'-kō-lē), **Niccolo de'** (1363–1437). It. humanist, 2764.

Nice (nēs), France. Resort on Riviera; pop. 211,000; 2364, 1364; ceded to France, 1769, 4170; occupied by Italy 1940–45.

Ni'cene Creed, 817, 893; adopted by Church, 817.

Niche (nich). In architecture, a cavity or hollow place in the thickness of a wall for placing a statue, figure, vase, or other ornament.

Nicholas, St. (d. c. 342). Bishop of Myra, Asia Minor; in many legends, bountiful patron of children; his feast day (Dec. 6) is near Christmas; hence he comes to be the Christmas gift-bringer, " Santa Claus."

Nicholas I. Pope 858–867; one of the most vigorous of the early popes, uncompromising in upholding his claims to universal jurisdiction; first Pope of whom it is recorded that he was formally crowned.

Nicholas II. Pope 1059–61; he restricted election of popes to College of Cardinals; Hildebrand (later Gregory VII) was leading spirit of his pontificate.

Nicholas III. Pope 1277–80; materially strengthened temporal power of the Church; man of strict morals and considerable learning.

Nicholas IV. Pope 1288–92; General of the Franciscans in 1274 (first Franciscan Pope); tried to rouse Christian world against advancing Moslems.

Nicholas V. Pope 1447–1455; founded valuable library and manuscript collection; extended wide patronage to classical scholars of Renaissance; 2764.

Nicholas I (1796–1855), Tsar of Russia, 2365, 2848.

Nicholas II (1868–1918), Tsar of Russia, 2305, 2848, 2849, 3411.

Nicholas, Grand Duke (1856–1929). Grandson of Tsar Nicholas I; appointed commander-in-chief of Rus. army in 1914; failed to check Austro-German offensive of 1915; later Commander-in-Chief in Caucasus where he carried out successful offensive.

Nicholas (nik'-ō-las) or **Nikita** (1841–1921). Last hereditary prince and king of Montenegro; deposed in 1918 when Montenegro became merged in Yugoslavia.

" Nicholas Nickleby." Novel by Charles Dickens in which the evils of cheap schools are disclosed; the hero began his career at Squeers' school, Dotheboys Hall, Yorkshire.

Nicholas of Pisa. See Pisano, Niccolo.

Nichols, (John) Beverley (b. 1898). Eng. author; many popular works include " Crazy Pavements," " Evensong," " Down the Garden Path "; 430.

Nichols, Robert (1893–1944). Eng. poet (" Ardours and Endurances "; " The Flower of Flame "); 1216.

Nicholson, John (1821–57). Brit. soldier and administrator; served in East India Company; killed while at head of storming party at Delhi (1857).

Nicholson, Sir William (1872–1949). Eng. artist; one of the " Beggarstaff Brothers," founder of poster art, 1184; his son Ben is eminent surrealist painter, 3122.

Nichrome, an alloy of nickel, 2365.

Nicias (nish'-i-as) (d. 413 B.C.). Athenian statesman and general in Peloponnesian War; became leader of aristocrats on death of Pericles; arranged Peace of Nicias (421 B.C.) between Athens and Sparta, which terminated first decade of Peloponnesian War.

Nickel (Ni). A metallic element of the iron group; atomic weight, 58·7; used as a catalyst and in electro-plating; meteoric iron contains 20 per cent of the metal; melts at 2646° F.; 2365; in alloys, 122, 2365; Canadian resources, 678; electro-plating, 1139; in New Caledonia, 2472; in Siberia, 2967; in white gold, 1481.

Nickel, U.S. coin, value 5 cents or 1/20 of a dollar.

Nicknames, given to countries, peoples, etc., 2366.

Nicobar (nik-ō-bahr') **Islands.** Group of Brit. isls. in Bay of Bengal to the s. of the Andamans; chief product coconuts; 1692; occupied by Japan during 1942–45.

Nicode'mus. In New Testament, a prominent Pharisee, who visited Jesus by night as an inquirer (John iii.).

Nicol, John Pringle (1804–59). Inventor of the calcite nicol prism used in the polariscope and polarimeter.

Nic'oll, Sir William Robertson (1851–1923). Scot. man of letters; editor of The British Weekly and The Bookman, and wrote also under the pen-names of " A Man of Kent " and " Claudius Clear "; was a Presbyterian minister in Scot. before coming to London.

Nicolson, Harold (b. 1886). Brit. author, diplomat, and politician; parl. sec. to Min. of Information 1940–41; gov. of B.B.C. 1941–46; joined Labour party in 1947; wrote lives of Lord Carnock (his father), " Lord Curzon: the Last Phase," " Verlaine," " Dwight Morrow "; " Some People," " Public Faces," " Diplomacy."

Nicomedia or **Actia Nicopolis.** Anc. city of great splendour on E. arm of Propontis (Sea of Marmara); cap. of Bithynia; Constantine died here and Hannibal committed suicide near by; modern Ismid.

Nicopolis (ni-kop'-ō-lis). Important anc. city, now in ruins, in Epirus on w. coast of Greece; founded 31 B.C. by Emperor Augustus to commemorate his naval victory of Actium; Epictetus's school, 1220.

Nicopolis or **Nikopoli,** Bulgaria. Tn. in N. on Danube, at junction with Osem; pop. 6,000; Turks win, 3264.

Nicosia. Cap. of Cyprus; also called Levkosia; mfrs. silk and leather goods; pop. 34,460; 953.

Nicot (nē-kō), **Jean** (1530–1600). Fr. diplomat, brought tobacco seeds from Lisbon to France, 3219.

Nicotia'na. The tobacco plant genus, named after Jean Nicot, 3219.

Nic'otine. Poisonous alkaloid in tobacco, 21, 2638, 3221.

Nictheroy, tn. of Brazil; pop. 125,000; 2780.

Niebuhr (nē'-boor), **Barthold Georg** (1776–1831). Ger. historian and classical scholar, pioneer in modern historical methods (" Roman History," " epoch-making " work).

Niemen (nē'-men). R. 500 m. long, dividing Lithuania from Russia and Poland in s., and flowing N. and w. through Lithuania to Baltic; highway for lumber and farm

products; called Memel at mouth; internationalized by Treaty of Versailles; scene of Peace of Tilsit, 2276.

Niemöller (nē'-mêl-er), **Martin** (b. 1892). Ger. theologian. During 1st World War famous as U-boat commander. Later turned to theology and became pastor of Dahlem, western suburb of Berlin. Opposed Nazi control of religion. Arrested in 1937; 7 months' confinement 1938; imprisoned during 1939–45 war.

Niepce (nē-eps'), **Joseph Nicéphore** (1765–1833). Fr. physicist, one of inventors of photography, 2580.

Nietzsche (nēch'-e), **Friedrich Wilhelm** (1844–1900). Ger. philosopher exalted self-assertion, the " will to power," as the final self-justifying good in life; denounced Christian virtues of pity and humility as " slave morality "; died insane, 1457.

Nieuwveldt (nyê'-velt) or **Nieuwveld Mts.** Division of main range in prov. of Cape of Good Hope, S. Africa, 69.

Niflheim (nif'-l-hām). In Norse myth., land of eternal cold and night.

Niger (nī'-jer). 3rd largest r. of Africa (2,500 m.), 2367, 68, 72, 2861, 3109; Mungo Park, 2521.

Nigeria (nī-jēr'-i-a). Brit. colony in lower basin of r. Niger, in W. Africa; about 372,674 sq. m.; pop. 21,826,389; chief port Lagos; exports palm products, cocoa, hides; tin mines, 3367; map, 3366; betrothal customs, 2109; children of, 792; native dancers, 63.

" Nigger-toe," or Brazil nut, 2408.

Night-blindness, an inheritable condition of the eye, 1427, 3327.

Nighthawk, or nightjar, 2369.

Nightingale. A song-bird, 2367; at nest, 450.

Nightingale, Florence (1820–1910). Eng. war nurse, 2368; influence on nursing and hospitals, 1648, 2406.

Nightjar. Various large-mouthed insect-eating birds, including night-hawks, 2369; foot, 448.

Night School, 2886.

Nightshade, Deadly. A plant with poisonous properties, 2370, 2637, 2638, 2639.

Nightshade family, or Solanaceae, family of plants with small flowers, and usually containing poisonous alkaloids, 2637, 2638, 2639; includes European bitter-sweet, or woody nightshade, 462; potatoes, 2637; tomato, 3223.

" Night Watch, The," painting by Rembrandt, 2763.

Nigre, impure soap, 2993.

Ni'grosine. A black aniline dye, 1724.

Nihilists (nī'-hil-ists). Rus. revolutionaries, 2856, 3260.

Nihonbashi. Famous Tokyo bridge, 3222.

Nijinsky (ni-zhin'-ski), **Vaslav** (1892–1950). Russian dancer and choreographer. Member of Diaghilev's Russian Ballet Ill-health cut short his career in 1917. Choreographer of " L'Après-midi d'un faune " and " Le Sacre du Printemps."

Nijmegen (nī-māg-en). Tn. of Netherlands, in Gelderland prov., on the R. Waal, 10½ m. s. of Arnhem; brewing, leather and tobacco mfrs.; pop. 103,609; occupied by Ger. May 1940; here Allied airborne troops were dropped Sept. 17, 1944, to prevent destruction of bridges, in attempt to cross Lower Rhine 2769 2320. See Arnhem

Nijni-Novgorod, town in Russia, now known as Gorki.

Nike (nī'-kē). In Gk. myth., goddess of victory, 1276.

Nike Apteris or **Wingless Victory, Temple of,** 285.

Nikisch (nē'-kish), **Arthur** (1855–1922). Hungarian orchestral conductor, especially noted for interpretations of Wagner.

Nikho (nē'-kō). Religious centre in Japan, noted for Shintoist and Buddhist temples, 1804.

Nikolaiev (nē-kō-lī′-ef). Fortified grain port in Ukraine on Black Sea near mouth of r. Bug; pop. 167,100.

Nile, battle of (1798). Fr. fleet destroyed by Nelson in Aboukir Bay, 2276, 2313, 3277.

Nile, longest r. of Africa (3,500 m. from L. Victoria to mouth), **2370,** 1095, *1097, 1099, map, 1096*; Alexander the Great and, 107; Assuan dam, 958, *959,* 1097, *1102*; James Bruce, 590; crocodiles, 931; delta, 1098, *map, 1096,* 2371; early canals, 686; in flood, *1101*; irrigation, 1100; mud for bricks, 561; Sennar dam, *3110*; source, 3321, 2370; explored by Speke, 72, 3321; Suez Canal, 3110, *1103*.

Nil′gai, an Indian antelope, 176.

Nilgiri (nil′-gi-rē) **Hills.** Plateau in s. India; highest point 8,760 ft.; formed dist. of Madras Presidency, 2054.

Nim′bus, a rain cloud, 852.

Nimegen. *See* Nijmegen.

Nîmes (nēm). City s. Fr.; pop. 93,000; silk, wine market; Rom. ruins, *1363,* 1365; Pont du Gard, *194*.

Nimitz, Adm. Chester (b. 1885), C.-in-C. U.S. Pacific Fleet 1941–45; Victor of Coral Sea 1942; U.S. signatory of Jap surrender in 1945, *2474*.

Nim′rod. In Genesis x. 8–9, a mighty hunter and founder of the Babylonian and Assyrian empires.

Nimrod, Shackleton's ship, 2931.

Nina (nēn′-ya). One of three caravels of Columbus on his first voyage to America.

Ninety-five Theses, of Luther, 2040, 2759.

Nineveh (nin′-e-ve). Cap. of anc. Assyrian Empire, 2371; Sennacherib's city, 330.

Ningpo (ning-pō′), China. Former treaty port on r. Ningpo; pop. 218,770; commerce in tea, silk, cotton, carpets, fish, and sugar.

"Ninth Diamond, The." Story of Sir Lancelot, 2830.

Niobe (nī′-ō-bē). In Gk. myth., woman whose children were slain because of her pride, 2372.

Niobium (Nb). *See* Columbium.

Niort. Tn. in w.-cent. Fr.; pop. 32,750; mfrs. gloves, 1477.

Nipkow, Paul (b. 1860). Ger. scientist, inventor (1884) of the whirling disk method of television scanning, 3184.

Nip′pon. Native name for Japan; means "land of the rising sun"; Dai Nippon, "Great Nippon."

Nippur (nip-poor′). Anc. city of Mesopotamia (Iraq); flourished 4000 B.C.; excavated by Univ. of Pennsylvania; library, 1930.

Nirvana (nir-vah′-na), in Buddhism, 601.

Nish (nēsh), Yugoslavia. Serbian tn.; pop. 35,460; anc. Naïssus, birthplace of Constantine the Great; held by Turks 1456–1878; strategic value of the place due to converging road and railways; occupied by Germans during 1941–44.

Nissan. Isl. in Bismarck Archipelago, off New Guinea, 2471.

Nith, Scot. R. flowing to Solway Firth; 55 m. long, 1054.

Niton. *See* Radon.

Nitrates, 2373; bacteria produce, 2373, *2374,* 2624; Chile deposits, 803, 2374, 2868; invisible inks, 1724; obtained by plants, 2373, *2374,* 2624; of potassium, 2868; saltpetre, 2868; silver, 2190, 2974; of sodium, 2868; used in explosives, 1250, 1558. *See* **Nitrogen.**

Ni′tre. *See* Saltpetre.

Nitric acid, 2372; in *aqua regia,* 1481; dissolves nickel, 2366; in explosives manufacture, 1250.

Ni′trifying bacteria, 2373; in nitrogen cycle, *2373*; partnership with legumes, *2374,* 2624.

Nitro-cel′lulose, an explosive, 2372, 739, 2748; action in smokeless powder, 1250.

Nitrogen (N), an inert gaseous element of the phosphorus group; atomic weight, 14·0; has been solidified; melts at −646°F.; called "azote" by Lavoisier; **2372**; in

atmosphere, 2372; cycle, *2373*; electric furnace fixation, 2374; in electric light bulbs, 1135; in explosives, 1250; "fixed" by bacteria, 337, 1509, 2373, *2374,* 2624; in illuminating gas, 1423; in plant food, 2498, 2624; properties, 776; in proteins, 2693; in "room" air, 1598; in saltpetre, 2868.

Nitrogen peroxide, a very poisonous brown gas, soluble in water, giving nitrous and nitric acids, 2372.

Nitro-glyc′erine, and dynamite, **1060.**

Nitrous Oxide or "laughing gas"; Davy discovers anaesthetic properties, 979, 1420, 2372.

Nivelle, Robert Georges (1856–1924). Fr. general; rose from colonel in 1914 to commander-in-chief of the Fr. armies in Dec. 1916; succeeded by Foch, May 1917, after failure of spring offensive; commander-in-chief of Fr. army in N. Africa, Dec. 1917–19.

Nizam (nī-zahm′). Ruler of Hyderabad, India, 1663, 1664.

Nizhni-Novgorod. *See* Gorki.

Noah (nō′-a) and his Ark, story of, 2374; Babylonian version, 332; landing-place, 265.

Noailles (nō-ī′-ē), **Adrien Maurice, 3rd Duke of** (1678–1766). Fr. general at battle of Dettingen.

Noailles, Anna, Comtesse de (1876–1933). Fr. poetess, 1382.

Nobel (nō-bel′), **Alfred Bernhard** (1833–96). Swedish chemist and engineer, 3131; invents dynamite, 1060; founds Nobel prizes, 2375, 3131.

Nobel Prizes, 2375.

Nobile (nō′-bē-lā), **Umberto** (b. 1885). Italian airship designer, aviator, and Arctic explorer; designed airships Norge and Italia; with Amundsen, 148; in Arctic flights, 2646.

Nocera (nō-chē′-rah) **Inferiore,** It. City 20 m. S.E. of Naples; pop. 20,000; linen and woollen mfrs.; anc. Nuceria Alfaterna, reduced by Hannibal 216 B.C.

Noc′tule. A British bat, *371, 373*.

Noctuoidea. Family of moths, incl. tiger, ermine, footmen, etc., 3625.

Node. Central point or point at rest in vibrating body; 3010.

Noel-Baker, Rt. Hon. Philip J. (b. 1889). Sec. for Air (1946–47); Sec. for Commonwealth Relations (1947–1950); Min. of Fuel and Power in 1950.

Noel (nō-el′), **Bonhomme** (Father Christmas), 820.

Nogi (nō′-gē), **Ki-Ten Marosuke, Count** (1849–1912). Japanese general, victor of Port Arthur and Mukden in Russo-Japanese war.

Noise. *See* **Sound**; for units of measurement of noise, *see* **Decibel; Phon.**

Noko′mis. In Hiawatha story, 2022.

Nola (nō′-lah), It. City 16 m. N.E. of Naples; pop. 17,000; prominent in Rom. times; Augustus died there A.D. 14.

No′mad. One who wanders about looking for new pastures, game, etc. applied chiefly to pastoral tent-dwellers or van-dwellers such as gipsies.

Nombre de Dios (nom′-brā dā dē′-os). Port of Panama, on Caribbean Sea; in 1502 Columbus went along the coast from Almirante Bay to Porto Bello Bay, where he planted a colony under this name; it was immediately destroyed by Indians, but re-established by Diego de Nicuassa, governor of Castilla del Oro in 1510.

Nome (nōm). Alaska, gold-mining tn. and spt. in centre of w. coast on Seward peninsula; pop. 1,550; 20,000 during rush of 1899–1900; ships reindeer; 99.

Nomenclature, of animals, 158.

Nominative case, of nouns, 2400.

Non-commissioned officers (N.C.O.s.). In Brit. army, all soldiers of ranks above private and below warrant officer, as corporal and sergeant, 245.

Nonconform′ists, 1390.

None. A canonical hour, 2213.

Nones. In anc. Rom. calendar the 9th day before the ides, falling in March, May, July, and Oct. on 7th of month, in other months on 5th.

Non-Euclid′ean geometry, 1440.

Nonpariel (non-pa-rel′) **type,** 3270.

Noot′ka Indians. Tribe of N. Pacific area, dwelling on Vancouver Isl. and in S. British Columbia. Indians gave name to sound and isl. on w. coast of Vancouver Isl.

No′pal. A cactus of the Opuntia or prickly pear genus.

Noranda. Tn. in Quebec, Canada; gold and copper smelting, *678*.

Nor′bert, St. (d. 1134). Ger. ecclesiastic, archbishop of Magdeburg; founds Premonstratensians, 2213.

Nordau (nor′-dow), **Max** (1849–1923). Jewish author and philosopher, b. Hungary; leader in European Zionist movement ("Degeneration," criticism of modern civilization and art; critic of politics and social science).

Nordenskjöld (nor′-den-shёld), **Nils Adolf Erick, Baron** (1832–1901). Swedish Arctic explorer, first to accomplish (1878–80) the North-East Passage from Atlantic to Pacific, *map, 223*.

Nordfiord, Norway, *2393*.

Nordic race, of mankind, 2725.

Nördlingen (nêrt′-ling-en). Tn. in Bavaria, s. Ger.; in Thirty Years' War, scene of Imperialist victory over Swedes (1634) and defeat by Fr. (1645).

Nore, The. Sandbank at mouth of R. Thames, marked by lightships. Near here occurred the Nore Mutiny of 1797.

Norfolk, Duke of, Bernard Marmaduke Fitzalan-Howard, 16th Duke (b. 1908). Hereditary Earl Marshal of England, 3084.

Nor′folk. Large marit. co. in E. of Eng., bounded N. and E. by North Sea; 2,054 sq. m.; pop. 504,000; 2375; the Broads, *1168*; Norwich the co. tn., *2398*.

Norfolk, Virginia, U.S.A. Spt. on Elizabeth r. opposite Portsmouth; pop. 144,430; large trade in lumber, coal, peanuts, fruit, etc.

Norge. Amundsen's airship, *148*.

Norilsk. Siberian town, 2967.

Normal, in reflection of light, 1940.

Normal solution, in chemistry, 20.

Norman. Montagu Collet, 1st Baron (1871–1950). Eng. banker, governor of Bank of England 1920–44; had much influence on financial policy of Gt. Britain. Cr. baron in 1944.

Norman Conquest (of Eng.), 1194, 3379, 2376; battle of Hastings, 1581; effect on Eng. language, 1209.

Normandie, S.S. French Atlantic liner. Burnt out in 1932.

Normandy. Anc. prov. of Fr. on English Channel, 2376; cider, 1360; cotton and lace manufactures, 1361; history, 1609, 2376, 2388, 3379; mountains and rivers, 1366; Northmen in, 2388; peasant girl of, *plate f. 1361*.

Normandy Invasion. D-day operation of 2nd World War, June 6, 1944; 2377, *maps, 2378*; 1123, 1368, 1453, 2222, 2251, 3422.

Normans. Northmen who founded Normandy, 1368, 2376, 2388, 2892.

Norns. In Norse myth., the three Fates (Urd, personifying the past; Verdandi, the present; Skuld, the future); Asgard was their home.

Norrköping (nor′-chê-ping), Sweden. Spt. on S.E. coast; pop. 82,000 trade and manufactures, 3128.

Norr′land. N. prov. of Sweden, 3126, 3128, 3129.

Norse. *See* **Northmen; Scandinavia.**

North, Christopher. *See* Wilson, John.

North, Frederick, Baron (1732–92). later Earl of Guilford (better known as Lord North), Brit. statesman; as king's agent (disclaimed title of Prime Minister) supported George III's policies which led to Amer. Rev.

North, Sir Thomas (1535–1601). Eng. translator of Plutarch (first edition 1579); vigorous style greatly influenced Eng. prose.

North America. The 3rd largest continent ; 9,400,000 sq. m. ; pop. (est.) 185,000,000 ; **2379** ; *maps, plates f. 2384, 2385, 2742* ; agriculture, 2384 ; Arctic regions, 223, 2384 ; climate, 840, 2385 ; coastline and harbours, 2379, 2385 ; elevation, *plate f. 2385* ; fisheries, 1299, *1300* ; fur trade, influence on colonization, 1412 ; geographic influences on settlement, 2379, 2384 ; geological history, *1353,* 2384 ; Ice Age, 1680, 1682, 2384 ; lakes and rivers, 1515, 2379, 2384 ; mountains, 2380, 2384, 2385, 2795 ; native races, 2753, 1222 ; products and resources, 2384 ; rainfall, 2385, *plate f. 2385. Exploration* : 139 ; Cabot, 647 ; Cartier, 712 ; Champlain, 751, 2380 ; Columbus, 878, 2379 ; Drake, 1036 ; Hudson, 1648 ; La Salle, 1894 ; of Mississippi, 2192 ; along Pacific coast, 663 ; polar, 223 ; Raleigh's expeditions, 2743 ; *map, 141. See* **America** ; **Canada** ; **United States** ; and other physical features by name.

Northampton. City on r. Nene, pop. 104,000 ; shoe mfrs. ; co. tn. of Northamptonshire ; battle in 1460 in which Yorkists captured Henry VI ; 2385.

Northamptonshire. An east-midland co. of Eng. ; 998 sq. m. ; pop. 361,300 (inc. Soke of Peterborough) ; **2385** ; iron ore, 1753.

"Northanger Abbey." Novel by Jane Austen ; deals with the life of commonplace people at the abbey and at Bath, 306.

North Atlantic Treaty. Pact signed Apr. 4, 1949, at Washington, U.S.A., by 12 nations : the U.K., Fr., U.S.A., Canada, Belgium, Netherlands, Luxemburg, Norway, Denmark, Italy, Iceland, Portugal ; aimed at maintaining friendly relations and economic co-operation, with help from all if any signatory became a victim of aggression ; 1242, 3240, 3283, 3293, 3424.

North Cape, Norway. Northernmost point of Europe, 2394, *map, 2395.*

North Carolina. S. Atlantic state of U.S.A. ; a. 52,420 sq. m. ; pop. 3,571,600 ; 704.

North Channel. Separates Ire. from Scot. and connects Irish Sea and the Atlantic Ocean.

Northcliffe, Alfred Harmsworth, Viscount (1865–1922). Eng. newspaper proprietor, **2385,** *2386.*

North Dakota. A plains state of N.W. U.S.A. ; a. 70,000 sq. m. ; pop. 641,930 ; 957.

North Downs, Eng. *See* **Downs.**

North-East Passage. Name of route round N. of Europe and Asia to the Pacific. The Eng. travellers Willoughby and Chancellor attempted it in 1533, and the Dutch navigator Barents in 1594–5, but all failed. First accomplished successfully in 1878–80 by Nordenskjöld.

Northern Ireland. *See* **Ireland, Northern.**
Northern lights. *See* **Aurora Borealis.**
Northern Rhodesia. Brit. territory in S. Africa ; a. 290,300 sq. m. ; pop. 1,423,000 ; cap. Lusaka ; 2771.

Northern Territory. A division occupying the N. cent. part of Australia, directly administered by the Commonwealth Govt. ; 523,620 sq. m. ; pop. 10,866 ; gold, tin, copper ; cattle-raising ; *map, 310.*

Northern War (1699–1721). Between Charles XII of Sweden and Denmark, Russia, and Poland ; 758, 2563.

Northfleet. Tn. of Kent ; pop. 18,785.
North Foreland. Headland, on the N.E. coast of Kent.
North German Confederation (1866–70). Alliance consisting of 22 sovereign states, which succeeded the German Confederation in 1866.

North Holland. A prov. of the Netherlands, 1635.

North Island. 2nd largest isl. of New Zealand ; 44,000 sq. m. ; 2357, *map, 2358, 2359.*

North Magnetic Pole. *See* **Magnetic Poles.**

Northmen or **Vikings, 2387,** 1238, 2880 ; discover America, 139, 2388 ; ancestors of Danes, 992 ; in England, 110, 694, 1089, 1194, *1195,* 2388 ; in Greenland, 224 ; settle Iceland, 1685, 2388 ; in Ireland, 910, 2388 ; in Italy, 2812 ; in France, 2388 ; invade Scotland, 1602, 2945 ; ships, 2305, 2387, *2388,* 2946 ; in Sicily, 2968 ; in Sweden, 3131, 2388 ; voyages, 2290.

North Pole. The N. extremity of earth's axis, **2390** ; discovered by Peary, *2534* ; exploration of, 2644, 2646 ; latitude and longitude, 1898 ; R.A.F. flights over, 2646 ; Russian scientists at, 224. *See* **Polar Exploration.**

North Sea. The part of the Atlantic between Gr. Brit. and continent of Europe, **2390,** 1232 ; amber, 138 ; fisheries, 1233, *1304, 1305, 1308.*

North Somerset. Large isl. of Arctic Amer., directly N. of Boothia ; a. about 10,000 sq. m.

North Star or **Polaris.** Star nearest in line above North Pole, 3079, *map, 3080* ; located by the Plough, *895,* 896 ; not visible S. of Equator, 3022.

Northum'berland, John Dudley, Duke of (1502–53). Eng. statesman, an unprincipled and subtle intriguer ; executed for high treason, following discovery of plot to put Lady Jane Grey on throne ; 1091, 1545.

Northumberland. Co. in extreme N.E. of Eng. ; a. 2,018 sq. m. ; pop. 756,780 ; **2391.**

Northumbria (north-um'-bri-*a*). Anc. kingdom of Brit., extending between the Forth and the Humber ; most powerful in 7th cent. ; made tributary to Wessex in 827.

North - West Frontier Province (N.W.F.P.). Northernmost prov. of Pakistan ; a. (with native agencies and tribal dists.) 39,000 sq. m. ; pop. (est.) 4,700,000 ; cap. Peshawar ; Khyber Pass leads to Afghanistan ; cereals chief products ; 1691.

North-West Mounted Police. *See* **Royal Canadian Mounted Police.**

North-West Passage, 142, 681 ; Amundsen, 148 ; Cartier, *712,* 143 ; discovery, 141, 682 ; Hudson, 143 ; McClure, 2644.

North-West Territories, Canada, **2392,** 676.

North'wich. Tn., 20 m. S.E. of Liverpool ; pop. 20,820 ; brewing, salt, alkali, and boat-building ; 2866.

Norton, Charles Eliot (1827–1908). Amer. scholar and author ; foremost Amer. Dante scholar (prose translation of " Divina Commedia ").

Norway. A kingdom of N.W. Europe in W. part of Scandinavian peninsula ; a. 125,000 sq. m. ; pop. **3,123,900 ; 2392** ; *plates j. 2392, 2393* : 2880 · *map, 2395* : cap. Oslo, 2455 ; Christmas customs, 820 ; fiords, 1234, 2392, *2393, 2596* ; language and literature, 462, 1679, 2880 ; Midnight Sun, 2168, *plates f. 2168, 2169* ; people, *plate f. 2392, 2394, 2396, 2397* ; ski-ing, *plate f. 2392* ; Spitsbergen, 3067. *History* : Northmen, 2387 ; Canute, 694 ; Greenland colonized, 1542 ; Iceland colonized, 1685 ; Union of Kalmar, 3131, 992 ; Charles XII, 759 ; Sweden, 2398 ; Haakon VII, 2398 ; in Ger. occupn. 1940–45, 1452, 2398, 3416 ; raid on heavy water estabs., 998.

Norway maple, 2092.
Norway spruce, 3070.
Norwich (nor'-ij). Mfg. centre, co. tn. of Norfolk ; pop. 114,700 ; **2398,** 2375 ; heat pump at, 1600.
Nose. Organ of smelling : breathing, 1676.
Nose bleeding. Treatment for, 1295.
Nota'tion, in arithmetic, 233.
Notation, in music, 2261, *2262, 2263.*
Note. A musical sound, 2262 ; physical nature of, 3009.
Note. Short-term security ; companies sometimes issue certificates called notes, promising to repay principal within a short period—usually five years or less—without any mortgage ; bonds secured by mortgage are also called notes.

Note, Promissory. A paper acknowledging a debt and promising to pay, 2202.
Notification, of disease, 1677.
Notre Dame (nōtr dahm'). Fr. for " Our Lady." Name of cath. at Antwerp, 182 ; at Marseilles, *2110.*
Notre Dame de Paris. Cath., 218, *plate f. 2516,* 2516, 2519.
Notre Dame Mts., Quebec, 2714.
Not'tingham, Eng. City 110 m. N.W. of London, on r. Trent, co. tn. of Nottinghamshire ; pop. 290,300 ; centre of lace and hosiery mfr., 1876, *1877, 2399* ; Hargreaves, 1578 ; housing estate near, *3233.*
Nottingham, Sheriff of, and Robin Hood, 3470.
Nottinghamshire or **Notts.** Co. in cent. Eng. ; a. 844 sq. m. ; pop. 712,700 ; **2398.**
No'tus. In Gk. myth., the south wind.
Nought, 2253, 2405.
Noun, in grammar, **2399,** 1494 ; participle as, 3314 ; phrase or clause as, 2920 ; relation to verb, 3313, 2920.
Novac'ulite. Fine-grained rock made of quartz particles ; used for hones.
Novae (nō-vē). New stars, 3080.
Novalis (nō-vah'-lis). Pen-name of Friedrich Leopold Freiherr von Hardenberg (1772–1801), German romantic poet and novelist (" Hymns to Night ").
No'var, Ronald Munro Ferguson, 1st Viscount (1860–1934). Scot. politician ; Governor-General and Commander-in-Chief of Australia in 1914 ; Sec. for Scot. in 1922.
Novara (nō-vah'-ra). Rly. centre in N. It. ; pop. 62,500 ; textile mfrs. ; battle of, 1769.
Nova Scotia (nō'-va skō'-sha). A maritime prov. of Canada ; a. 21,068 sq. m. ; pop. 612,000 ; **2400** ; 682 ; Acadia its original name, 17 ; Cape Breton Isl., 695 ; cap. Halifax, 1566 ; fisheries, 2400 ; legislature, 683 ; Leif Ericsson, 2388.
Novaya Zemlya or **Nova Zembla** (" new land "), two isls. in Arctic Ocean, belonging to Rus., 171.
Novel, 2401, 2798 ; growth from old romances and fabliaux, 2401 ; American. 2403 · Cervantes' contribution (" Don Quixote "), 745 ; Defoe, 985 ; English, 1215, 2402 ; French, 1381, 2404 ; German, 1457, 2404 ; historical, created by Scott, 2402, 2899 ; Italian, 1786, 2403 ; Russian, 2404, 2855 ; Spanish, 2403, 3051. *See also* under names of chief novelists.
Novello, Ivor (b. 1893). Eng. actor-dramatist ; has written many successful comedies (" Fresh Fields ") and spectacles (" Glamorous Night," " Crest of the Wave," " The Dancing Years," " Perchance to Dream," " King's Rhapsody "), composed popular music (" Keep the Home Fires Burning ") ; romantic actor on stage and film (" The Rat," " The Lodger ").
Novem'ber, 11th month, 662, 2223.
Novgorod (nov'-go-rod), historic tn. in w. Russia, 100 m. s. of Leningrad, pop. 31,000 ; old fortress ; great trade centre in Middle Ages ; conquered by Ivan the Great, 1787 ; Germans occupied 1942–44.
Novibazar (no-vi-ba-zahr'), or **Yenipasar,** also **Novi Pasar,** Yugoslavia. Tn. in s.w. Serbia ; pop. 13,000.
Novi Sad, city of Yugoslavia ; pop. 64,000 ; 3438.
Novitiate (nō-vish'-i-āt), in Rom. Cath. Church, state or time of probation of one who has entered a religious house as a novice, but has not yet taken vows.
Novocaine, a local anaesthetic, extensively used by surgeons in Gt. Brit. and other countries.
Novorossisk', Rus., spt. in Caucasia, on N.E. of Black Sea ; pop. (1939) 95,280 ; 733 ; held by Germans in 1942–43.
Novosibirsk. Cap. of w. Siberia, in Soviet Russia ; formerly Novo-Nikolaevsk ; on R. Ob, and important rly. junction on Trans-Siberian Railway ; pop. 278,000.

Noyes, Alfred (b. 1880). Eng. poet (" Tales of the Mermaid Tavern " ; " The Wine Press ; " Drake an English Epic " ; " The Elfin Artist " ; " The Torch-Bearers ") ; shows technical skill in different metres ; virile, patriotic note in his work. Also wrote " A Study of Voltaire " and " The Edge of the Abyss."

Noyon (nwah-yawn'), Fr. Historic tn. 60 m. N.E. of Paris ; pop. 7,300 ; Charlemagne crowned king in 768 ; birthplace of Calvin ; ruined in 1st World War ; scene of fighting in 1940 and 1944 in 2nd World War.

Nu, ν N, (Rom. n, N). Thirteenth letter of Gk. alphabet.

Nu'bia, region in Africa, s. of Egypt, including Nubian desert.

Nubian Desert, great desert in Anglo-Egyptian Sudan between Red Sea and w. bend of r. Nile.

Nuclear Physics. See Study Outlines, 3679 ; **Atom ; Cyclotron , Electron ; Radium.**

Nucleoplasm, form of protoplasm, 2695.

Nucleus (nū'-klē-us), (from Lat. word for " kernel "). A minute body within a cell, 738, 2695 ; also of atom, 295-298, 1137, 2733.

Nuevo Leon (nwā'-yō lā-ōn), Mexico. State in N.E. ; a. 25,000 sq. m. ; pop. 541,140 ; cap. Monterey.

Nuffield, William Richard Morris, 1st Viscount (b. 1877). Eng. motor manufacturer and philanthropist, **2404** ; benefactor of Oxford University, 2464 ; and Royal College of Surgeons, in 1948.

Numa Pompilius, Roman ruler, 2804.

Numbers, 233 ; Pythagorean doctrine of, 2710. See **Arithmetic.**

Numbers, Book of. Fourth Book of Old Testament, so called because it begins with account of census ; includes part of history of Israelites during their wanderings.

Nu'merals, 2405, 233. See **Decimals.**

Numidia (nū-mid'-i-a). Anc. kingdom and Rom. prov. in N. Africa corresponding nearly to Algeria.

Numismat'ics. The science of coins and medals. See **Coinage ; Medals.**

Nun'cio, a diplomatic representative of the Pope, of lower rank than a legate ; his powers are limited by his instructions ; if a nuncio is a cardinal he is called pronuntius.

Nuneaton. Tn. in Warwickshire, on the R. Anker, 9 m. N. of Coventry ; has cotton, woollen, brick, tile, and iron industries ; pop. 52,000.

Nunez (noo'-nyeth) **de Ar'ca, Gaspar** (1834-1903). Span. writer and statesman ; governor of Barcelona (1868) ; cabinet minister (1882-90) ; noted for his lyrics.

Nuns, orders of, 2214.

Nureddin, Nurredin or **Nur-ed-din** (noor-ed-dēn), **Mah'mud** (1116-74), sultan of Syria and Egypt, 2864.

Nuremberg (nū-rem-berg), mfg. city of Bavaria ; pop. (1939) 430,800 ; **2406,** 377, 378 ; Dürer's engraving, 1217 ; air raid damage, captured by U.S. forces Apl. 1945, 2406 ; trials of war criminals, 2282, 2406.

Nurmi, Paavo (b. 1897). Finnish runner ; one of the greatest long-distance runners of all time.

Nurse-hound, a shark, 2939.

Nursery Rhymes, 3501.

Nursery School, 2886.

Nursing, 2406 ; first aid, 1291 ; influence of Florence Nightingale, 2368 ; Red Cross, 2752 ; training, in hospitals, 2406 ; registration, 2406.

Nut (noot), Egypt. goddess, 2455.

Nut butter, butter substitute largely composed of nut oil.

Nutcracker, bird of crow family.

Nut-gall, ink from, 1724, 1725.

Nuthatches, a family of small tree-climbing birds, **2407.**

Nutmeg and Mace, 2407, seed of nutmeg tree ; used as spice, 3061.

Nutmeg or **netted melon,** 2138.

Nutrition (nū-trish'-on), processes and function in man and in animals, 2601 ; in plants, 2601, 2621. See also **Digestion ; Food.**

Nuts, hard-shelled fruits, usually of trees, **2407** ; almond, 124 ; chestnuts, 782 ; coconuts, 862, 863 ; fats and oils, 1263 ; ground nuts, 1550.

Nux vomica (nuks vom'-i-ka), poisonous seed of an E. Indian plant, yielding strychnine,

Nyasa (nya'-sa), large lake on E. boundary of Nyasaland ; 14,200 sq. m. ; surrounded by mts., 69 ; discovered by Livingstone, 1970.

Nya'saland, Brit. protectorate in E. cent. Africa ; 37,373 sq. m. ; pop. 1,685,000 ; cotton, tobacco, rubber, coffee ; associated with Rhodesia, 2772 ; maps, facing 68, 1073.

Nye, Edgar Wilson (" Bill Nye ") (1850-96). Amer. humorous writer.

Nylon. Synthetic plastic material used for fabrics, stockings and other purposes, 2627, 2749 ; contains nitrogen, 2373 ; parachutes, 2509 ; rope, 2827.

Nymph (nimf), of insects, 1729, 1034.

Nymphs, in Gk. myth., **2408.**

Nystadt, Finland, small port on Gulf of Bothnia, 40 m. N.W. of Turku ; peace signed between Russia and Sweden (1721), 2563.

A S far back as we can trace the letter O, it has undergone little change. Its first appearance seems to be in the Phoenician alphabet as a slightly irregular circle. It was supposed to represent an eye and was called *Ayin,* the Phoenician word for " eye." In the Greek alphabet are two O characters, great O (*Omega,* Ω) and little O (*Omicron,* O), but originally there was only one. Such departures from the perfect circle as we find in ancient inscriptions were due to the

difficulty of inscribing a circle on stone. Thus sometimes its form is that of an ellipse, sometimes it is square, and sometimes it is nearly a diamond. The form of the letter suggests its pronunciation. The sound of " long " O is pronounced while the mouth is rounded, and the back part of the tongue is raised and somewhat rounded. In English O has many uses, alone and in combination with various sounds—short, long, unstressed, *oo* sound (e.g. *move*); *u* sound (e.g. *above*).

Oahu, isl. of Hawaii ; Honolulu stands on it ; 1587.

Oak, a hardwood tree, **2409** ; acorns, 2409 ; bark used in tanning, 1910, 2410 ; classified, 3247 ; forests, 1349 ; gall-nuts, 1724, 1730 ; held sacred in primitive faiths, 500 ; heliotropism, 2623 ; timber for ships, 3321. Oak-apples are galls.

Oak-galls, a big growth of the surface tissues of the oak brought about by gall-wasps ; oak-galls are used in dyeing, and were at one time employed in the manufacture of ink ; 2410.

Oakham. Co. tn. of Rutland, 95 m. N.W. of London ; boot and shoe mfrs. ; public school ; pop. 3,200 ; 2858.

Oakland, Calif., U.S.A., residential and industrial city on San Francisco Bay, connected to San Francisco by world's longest bridge ; pop. 284,000 ; shipping centre for agric. and fruit-growing region, 664.

" **Oak moss,**" a vegetable fixative for perfumes, 2550.

Oaksey, Geoffrey Lawrence, Baron (b. 1880). Brit. judge ; as Judge Lawrence was pres. of Internat. Tribunal in the Nuremberg trials,

1945-46 ; made a peer and lord of appeal in ordinary in 1947.

Oasis (ō-ā'-sis), fertile spot in a desert, 996, 997 ; Libyan desert, 1097 ; Sahara, 2859.

Oast house, kiln for hop roasting.

Oastler, Richard (1789-1861). Eng. reformer ; called " The Factory King," because of energetic advocacy of the factory-workers' cause ; with Lord Shaftesbury and others he worked for child-labour laws.

Oates, Lawrence Edward Grace (1880-1912), Eng. army officer and polar explorer ; heroism on Scott's last journey, 2896, 2897, 2898.

Oates, Titus (1649-1705). Eng. conspirator who falsely accused the Catholics of a " popish plot " (1678-80) to restore Catholicism.

Oath of the Tennis Court, 1393.

Oatmeal, how obtained, 2410.

Oats, a cereal crop, **2410** ; as cultivated grasses, 1509 ; " animated," 2411 ; classification, 2411 ; husks in nylon making, 2749 ; fungus, 2857.

Oaxaca (wah-hah'-kah) or **Oajaca,** Mexico, state in s. of Isthmus of Tehuantepec, on Pacific ; 36,000 sq. m. ; pop. 1,192,800 ; cap. Oaxaca.

pop. 36,000 ; produces sugar, coffee, cotton, coal.

Ob or **Obi,** great navigable r. of w. Siberia rising in govt. of Tomsk ; flows N.W. and N. 2,500 m. to Gulf of Ob, bay of Arctic Ocean ; chief tributary, Irtish ; 2966, 265.

Obadiah (ō-ba-dī'-a) (6th cent. B.C.). Hebrew minor prophet, author of the 31st book of the Old Testament, which bears his name, 2692.

Oban, spt. and holiday resort of Argyllshire, Scotland ; pop. 5,800 ; 230.

O'bed, in Old Testament, son of Ruth and Boaz, 2858.

Ob'elisk, a four-sided tapering shaft with a pyramid top, a favourite form of monument of the anc. Egyptians ; Cleopatra's Needle, 110.

Oberammergau (ō-ber-am'-er-gow). Vil. in Upper Bavaria, Ger. ; Passion Play, given as thank-offering for deliverance from plague in 1633, 378, 2190.

Oberhausen (ō'-ber-how-zen). Germany. Mfg. tn. in Rhine prov., 35 m. N. of Cologne ; pop. 191,300 ; iron and chemical works.

Oberon (ō'-be-ron). King of the fairies, 2169.

Obey (ō-bā), **André** (b. 1892). Fr. novelist and dramatist; plays "Noé" (" Noah "), " Le Viol de Lucrèce," " Don Juan."

Objec'tive. A type of lens; ordinary magnifying glass, *1924*, *1925*; in microscopes, 2163; in telescopes, 3180.

Objective case. Of nouns, 2400.

Oblong sunfish, 3120.

Oboe (ō'-bō). Musical instrument, 3404, 2445, 3009.

Obrenovitch (ō-brā'-nō-vich). Ruling Serbian family; held power (not continuously) from accession of Milosh Obrenovitch to assassination of Alexander (1903); 2922.

Obser'vatory. Astronomical, **2411**, 281, *3179*, *3181*; spectroscopes, to analyse stars, 3057; telescopes, 3178; transit instrument, *3214*; world's largest telescope, 3179.

Obsid'ian. A glassy volcanic rock, 1901, 2795.

O'Casey, Sean (b. 1884). Irish dramatist; " Juno and the Paycock " was awarded the Hawthornden Prize in 1926; other plays are " The Plough and the Stars," " The Silver Tassie," 1040.

Ocean, 2413, 2103; affects climate, 840, 1232, 2419; animals, *see* plant and animal life below; in Antarctic regions, *173*; Arctic, *223*; area and depth, 2413, *2414*; Atlantic, 290, 2413, 2419; Baltic Sea, 351; Black Sea, 465; bottom forms, 2598; cables, 640; Caribbean Sea, 701; contained first life on earth, 111, 1069, 1432; continental shelf, 2596; corals, 908; divers and diving, 1019, 2414; greatest depths, *89*, 2469 (for 1949 record dive, *see* Diving); 2417. Gulf Stream, 1554, 2419; icebergs, 1682; Indian, 1691, 2413; Mediterranean Seas, 1232, 1233, 2135, *map, 2136*; mirages, 2190; mountains, 701, 2413; North Sea, 2390; origin, 2413; Pacific, 2413, 2419, 2469; phosphorescence, 2414, 2573; plant and animal life, 701, 2103, *2104, 2105, 2413, 2416, 2417, 2418*; Red Sea, 2419, 2758; salt in, and from, 2866; sea-level changes, 1433; statistics, 2419; storms, 3100; tides, 3209; water-spouts, 3356; waves, *3358*; winds, 3384; 2419. *See also* **Navigation**, and the principal topics above by name.

Ocean currents. Antarctic, 1081; Atlantic, 290; Gulf Stream, 1554, 2419; Labrador, 1333, 1554, 1875.

Ocea'nia. Isls. of Pacific Ocean divided into Polynesia, Micronesia, Melanesia, 2470. *See also* chief isls. and groups by name.

Ocean'ic climate, 840, 1232.

Oceanides (ō-si-an'-i-dēz). In Gk. myth., ocean nymphs, 2408.

Oceanog'raphy. The science of ocean phenomena, includes hydrographic surveying, 2413.

Oceanus (ō'sē'-a-nus). In Gk. myth., eldest of the Titans, personification of the all-encircling ocean.

Ocelli (ō-sel'-ī). " Simple " eyes of insects, 1730.

Ocelot (ō'-se-lot). A leopard-like cat, 720, 1928.

O'chil Hills. Hill range of Scot., chiefly in Perthshire, but extending into Clackmannan, Fife, and Kinross counties; Ben Cleuch, the loftiest, is 2,363 ft. high; 2558.

Ochre (ō'-ker). A clay coloured yellow or reddish-brown with oxide of iron, used as a paint pigment, 2478.

O'Connell, Daniel (1775–1847). Irish lawyer and political leader, **2419**.

O'Connor, Feargus Edward (1794–1855). Chartist leader, *3279*.

O'Connor, Thomas Power (" Tay Pay ") (1848–1929). Irish Nationalist leader and journalist; entered Parl. 1880; founded and edited The Star, T.P.'s Weekly, etc.

Octane number. For fuel tests, 2564.

Octave. In music, the 8th full tone above or below any given note; also the interval between a note and its octave.

Octavia (ok-tā'-vi-a) (d. 11 B.C.). Sister of the Rom. emperor Augustus, and faithful wife of Mark Antony; deserted by him for Cleopatra, *2816*.

Octavia (A.D. 42–62). Rom. empress, wife of Nero, 2315.

Octa'vian (originally Gaius Octavius). Family name of Augustus Caesar. *See* **Augustus**.

Octa'vo. A book size, 512.

Octo'ber. 10th month of calendar year, 2223.

Oc'topus. Relative of the cuttle-fish, 945, 946, 2105; a cephalopod mollusc, 2199.

Oc'ulist, work of, 1252.

Odaena'thus or **Odenathus** (d. A.D. 271 or 266). General and ruler of Palmyra; husband of Queen Zenobia; 2485.

Ode (ōd). A form of stately and elaborate lyric poetry; originally a poem intended to be chanted or sung, 2637. Dryden, 1050; Horace, 1896; Keats, 1849; Pindar, 1539.

Odense (ō'-then-sā), 3rd city in Denmark, on isl. of Fünen at mouth of r. Odense; pop. 88,000; splendid cath.; comm. centre; 992.

" Ode on a Grecian Urn." Poem by Keats, 1849.

Oder (ō'-der). Important r. of Ger., rises in N.-cent. Czechoslovakia, flows N.E. 560 m. and enters Baltic by 3 arms; in 2nd World War, 3424.

Odes'sa. Spt. of Ukraine on Black Sea, pop. 604,200; **2420**; in Ger. occupn., 1941–44.

O'din or **Woden.** In Norse myth., father of the gods, **2420**, 980, 991, 2363, 2881.

O'do or **Eudes** (d. 898). King of the Franks, crowned 888 after deposition of Charles the Fat; son of Robert the Strong; fought Normans and his rival Charles III for Fr. throne; defence of Paris.

Odoacer (ō-dō-ā'-ser) (c. 435–493), Ger. leader who overthrew the Western Rom. Empire in 1488, 1763, 2812.

Odona'ta. Dragon-fly order of insects, 1733, 1035.

Odontoglos'sum. One of the genera of orchids most frequently grown in hothouses.

Odysseus (o-dis'-ūs). In Gk. myth., king of Ithaca and Trojan War hero, **2421**; combat with Ajax, 96; in Homer's Odyssey, 1637, 1518; Poseidon and, 2661; summons Achilles to war, 19, 2421. Stories: " Homer's Story of Odysseus and Circe," 834, 835; " How Odysseus and His Men Outwitted the Cyclops," 949, 950; " Some Adventures of Odysseus," 2421; " How the Wooden Horse Came to Troy," 3249.

Odyssey (od'-i-si). Gk. epic poem relating adventures of Odysseus on return from Trojan War, 1637, 1518, 2421; Latin translations, 1895; place in literature, 1539. *See* **Homer**.

Oedipus (ē'-di-pus). In Gk. myth., king of Thebes, **2424**; on Greek vase, *1528*; with Sphinx's riddle, *2425, 1528*, 3060.

Oenone (ē-nō'-nē). In Gk. myth., river nymph, wife of Paris, 2514. Story told in Tennyson's " Oenone."

Oersted (ēr'-sted) or **Orsted, Hans Christian** (1777–1851). Danish physicist, established connexion between electricity and magnetism, 1127, 1132, 2063, 3164.

Oesophagus (ē-sof'-a-gus), or gullet, muscular tube from mouth to stomach, 1016, 3094.

O'Faolain (o-fawl'-len), **Sean** (b. 1900). Irish writer; novels " Midsummer Night Madness," " A Nest of Simple Folk "; biographies, " Constance Markievicz," " The Great O'Neill."

Of'fa (d. 796). King of Mercia; defeated Wessex and the Welsh, wresting part of territory from the latter and building great fortifications along whole border between Eng. and Wales known as " Offa's Dyke," 2963.

Offaly. Inland co. of Eire (Irish Free State). Formerly King's County; a. 772 sq. m.; pop. 52,000, **2425**.

Offenbach (of-en-bahkh), **Jacques** (1819–80). Fr. composer, originator of opéra bouffe, b. Ger. (" Tales of Hoffmann ").

Officer. Anyone serving under a commission granted by the sovereign in the Services; in the army a man is either a private or an officer of some grade; there are also warrant-officers and non-commissioned officers. *See* under various ranks.

Off-set process, in lithography, 1967.

Oflag, abbreviation of Ger. *Offizierlager*. Ger. prisoner-of-war camp for officers.

O'Flaherty (ō-flah'-er-ti), **Liam** (b. 1897). Irish author; works include " The Informer " (James Tait Black Prize); " Famine "; " Life of Tim Healy."

Ogden, C. K. (b. 1889), Brit. scholar and teacher of languages; with I. A. Richards invented Basic English, of which copyright was assigned to the Crown, 1946; founded the Basic English Foundation, 1947; 1210.

Ogee (ō-jē') or **ogive** (ō'-jīv), in architecture, a wave-like moulding, with an inner and outer curve, something like the letter **s**.

Oglethorpe, James Edward (1696–1785). Eng. general and philanthropist, founded Georgia, U.S.A., 3290.

Ogpu. Rus. secret police, originally known as the Cheka; in 1935 it became the State Security Dept.

Ogygia (ō-jij'-i-a). In Gk. myth., the isl. of Calypso, 2422.

O'Higgins, Bernardo (1778–1842). Chilean patriot and dictator, leader in war for independence; head (1818–23) of first national govt.

Ohi'o. A N.-cent. state of U.S.A.; 41,222 sq. m.; pop. 6,907,600; 2426.

Ohio. R. of the U.S.A. which flows over 1,000 m. to join Mississippi at Cairo, **2425**.

Ohm (ōm), **George Simon** (1787–1854). Ger. mathematician and physicist; ohm, unit of electrical resistance, named after him; discovered " Ohm's law," 1128.

Ohm. Unit of electrical resistance; 1 ohm represents the resistance of a conductor when a pressure of 1 volt is needed to get a current flow of 1 ampere; 1128.

Ohm's law. For calculating the properties of electrical circuits, 1128.

Oil, 2426; Alaska, 97; asphalt from, 272; Baku fields, 341, 717, 2426; Burma, 2426; Canada, 679, 2430; from coal, 856, 2429; cracking process, 2430; drilling, 2427, *2428*; E. Indies, 1076; England, 2430; fractional distillation, 1019, 2429; as fuel, 1405, 1987, 2429, 2987; a gusher, 2428; Iran, 1742; Iraq, 1743; Mexico, 2426; molecules, *3121*; N. Amer., *2383*, 3288, 3289; nature, 1262, 2426; and photosynthesis, 2589; pipeline, *1742*; in politics, 2431; Rumania, *2841*, 2426; S. Amer., 3024; and surface tension, 3122; synthetic rubber from, 2838; for tanning, 1912, 1913; on water, *3122*; wax, 3359. *See also* **Petrol**; **Petroleum**; **Fats and Oils**.

Oil-beetles. Types which exude oil when alarmed, *401*.

Oil-cake. Seeds from which oil has been pressed, 1263; cotton-seed, 920; flax, 1313.

Oilcloth and linoleum, 1956.

Oil engine (Diesel), 1016, 2246.

Oil'ets, in architecture, openings or loopholes made in the battlements and walls of medieval fortifications so that arrows could be shot at besieging parties.

Oil of vitriol. Same as **Sulphuric acid**.

Oil painting. Process discovered, 2476; paints used, 2477. *See* **Painting**.

Oils. *See* **Fats and Oils**; **Petroleum**.

Oil stove, pressure type, 478.

Oil varnishes, 2478.

Oise (wahz). R. of N. Fr., rises in s.w. Belgium; flows s.w., receiving Aisne at Compiègne and joins Seine, 15 m. N.W. of Paris; length 187 m.; important strategic line in 1st World War.

OLYMPIC GAMES—RESULTS 1948

Athletics (Men)

		H.	M.	S.
100 Metres	H. Dillard, U.S.A....	0	10	3/10
200 Metres	M. E. Patton, U.S.A..	0	21	1/10
400 Metres	A. S. Wint, Jamaica...	0	46	1/5
800 Metres	M. G. Whitfield, U.S.A.	1	49	1/5
1,500 Metres	H. Eriksson, Sweden..	3	49	4/5
5,000 Metres	G. Rieff, Belgium	14	17	3/5
10,000 Metres	E. Zatopek, Czechoslovakia	29	59	3/5
110 Metres Hurdles	W. F. Porter, U.S.A. .		13	9/10
400 Metres Hurdles	R. B. Cochran, U.S.A.		51	1/10
3,000 Metres Steeplechase	T. Sjoestrand, Sweden	9	4	3/5
400 Metres Relay	U.S.A. (H. N. Ewell, L. C. Wright, H. Dillard, M. E. Patton)		40	3/5
(4 × 100 metres)				
1,600 Metres Relay	U.S.A. (A. H. Harmden, C. F. Bourland, R. B. Cochran, M. G. Whitfield)	3	10	2/5
(4 × 400 metres)				
10,000 Metres Walk	J. F. Mikaelsson, Sweden	45	13	1/2
50,000 Metres Road Walk	J. A. Ljunggren, Sweden	4 41	52	
Marathon	D. Cabrera, Argentina	2 34	51	1/2

		FT.	IN.
High Jump	J. L. Winter, Australia	6	6
Long Jump	W. S. Steele, U.S.A..	25	8
Hop, Step and Jump	A. Ahman, Sweden ..	50	6 1/4
Pole Vault	O. G. Smith, U.S.A...	14	1 1/4
Putting the Shot	W. M. Thompson, U.S.A.	56	2
Throwing the Discus	A. Consolini, Italy ...	173	2
Throwing the Javelin	K. T. Rautavaara, Finland	228	10 1/2
Throwing the Hammer	I. Nemeth, Hungary..	183	11 1/2
Decathlon	R. B. Mathias		
Modern Pentathlon	Capt. W. O. G. Grut, Sweden		

Athletics (Women)

		S.
100 Metres	F. E. Blankers-Koen, Holland	11 9/10
200 Metres	F. E. Blankers-Koen, Holland	24 2/5
80 Metres Hurdles	F. E. Blankers-Koen, Holland	11 1/5
400 Metres Relay	Holland (X. Stad de Jong, J. J. M. Witziers-Timmer, G. J. M. Van der Kade, F. E. Blankers-Koen)	47 1/2
(4 × 100 metres)		

		FT.	IN.
High Jump	A. Coachman, U.S.A...	5	6 1/4
Long Jump	V. O. Gyarmati, Hungary	18	8 1/4
Putting the Shot	M. O. M. Ostermeyer, France	45	1 1/2
Throwing the Javelin	H. Bauma, Austria ..	149	6
Throwing the Discus	M. O. M. Ostermeyer, France	137	6 1/2

Boxing

Flyweight	P. Perez, Argentina
Bantamweight	T. Csik, Hungary
Featherweight	E. Formenti, Italy
Lightweight	G. Dreyer, South Africa
Welterweight	J. Torma, Czechoslovakia
Middleweight	L. Papp, Hungary
Lightheavyweight	G. Hunter, South Africa
Heavyweight	R. Inglesias, Argentina

Cycling

		H.	M.	S.
1,000 Metres Time Trial	J. Dupont, France ..		1	13 1/2
4,000 Metres Team Pursuit	France		4	57 1/2
Road Race, 120 m. 914 yds.	J. Beyaert, France ..	5 18	12 1/2	
1,000 Metres Scratch	M. Ghella, Italy			
2,000 Metres Tandem	Italy			
Road Race : Team	Belgium			

Fencing

Epée (Individual)	L. Cantone, Italy
Epée (Team)	France
Foils (Individual)	J. Buhan, France
Foils (Team)	France
Sabres (Individual)	A. Gerevich, Hungary
Sabres (Team)	Hungary
Foils (Women)	A. Elek, Hungary

Gymnastics

Team (Men)	Finland
Individual	V. A. Huhtanen, Finland
Team (Women)	Czechoslovakia

Hockey	India
Association Football	Sweden
Basketball	U.S.A.
Water Polo	Italy

Rowing

		M.	S.
Single Sculls	M. Wood, Australia .	7	24 2/5
Double Sculls	Great Britain	6	51 1/5
Pairs (Coxwainless)	Great Britain	7	21 1/10
Pairs (Coxwained)	Denmark	8	0 1/2
Fours (Coxwainless)	Italy	6	39
Fours (Coxwained)	U.S.A.	6	50 1/5
Eights	U.S.A.	5	56 1/10

Swimming (Men)

		M.	S.
100 Metres Free-style	W. Ris, U.S.A.		57 1/5
200 Metres Breast-stroke	J. Verdeur, U.S.A. ...	2	39 1/5
400 Metres Free-style	W. Smith, U.S.A.	4	41
100 Metres Back-stroke	A. Stack, U.S.A.	1	6 2/5
1,500 Metres Free-style	J. McLane, U.S.A.	19	18 1/2
800 Metres Relay	U.S.A.	8	46
High Diving	S. Lee, U.S.A.		
Springboard Diving	B. Harlan, U.S.A.		

Swimming (Women)

		M.	S.
100 Metres Free-style	G. Andersen, Denmark		66 1/5
200 Metres Breast-stroke	N. Van Vliet, Holland	2	57 1/5
400 Metres Free-style	A. Curtis, U.S.A.	5	17 1/2
100 Metres Back-stroke	K. Harup, Denmark .	1	14 1/2
400 Metres Relay	U.S.A.	4	29 1/2
High Diving	V. Draves, U.S.A.		
Springboard Diving	V. Draves, U.S.A.		

Wrestling (Free-style)

Flyweight	V. Viitala, Finland
Bantamweight	N. Akar, Turkey
Featherweight	G. Bilge, Turkey
Lightweight	C. Atik, Turkey
Welterweight	Y. Dogu, Turkey
Middleweight	G. Brand, U.S.A.
Lightheavyweight	H. Wittenberg, U.S.A.
Heavyweight	G. Bobis, Hungary

Wrestling (Graeco-Roman)

Flyweight	P. Lombardi, Italy
Bantamweight	K. Petersen, Sweden
Featherweight	M. Oktav, Turkey
Lightweight	K. Freij, Sweden
Welterweight	G. Andersson, Sweden
Middleweight	R. Gronberg, Sweden
Lightheavyweight	K. Nilsson, Sweden
Heavyweight	A. Kirecci, Turkey

Shooting

Rapid Fire Pistol (25 metres)	K. Takacs, Hungary
Free Pistol (50 metres)	E. Vasquez Cam, Peru
Free Rifle (Smallbore 50 metres)	A. Cook, U.S.A.
Free Rifle (300 metres)	E. Grunig, Switzerland

Riding

3 Days' Test (Individual)	Capt. B. M. Chevallier, France
3 Days' Test (Team)	U.S.A.
Dressage (Individual)	Capt. H. Moser, Switzerland
Prix des Nations (Individual)	H. M. Cortes, Mexico
Prix des Nations (Team)	Mexico

Weightlifting

Bantamweight	J. N. de Pietro, U.S.A.
Featherweight	M. Fayad, Egypt
Lightweight	I. Shams, Egypt
Middleweight	F. Spellman, U.S.A.
Lightheavyweight	S. A. Stanczyk, U.S.A.
Heavyweight	A. Davis, U.S.A.

Yachting

6 Metre Class	U.S.A.
Dragon Class	Norway
Star Class	U.S.A.
Swallow Class	Great Britain
Firefly Class	Denmark

Canoeing

		H.	M.	S.
10,000 Metres.				
1-Seater Kayak	G. Fredriksson, Sweden		50	47 1/10
2-Seater Kayak	Sweden		46	9 2/5
1-Seater Canadian	J. Holecek, Czechoslovakia	1	2	5 1/4
2-Seater Canadian	U.S.A.		55	55 2/5
1,000 Metres.				
1-Seater Kayak	G. Fredriksson, Sweden		4	33 1/2
2-Seater Kayak	Sweden		4	7 1/10
1-Seater Canadian	J. Holecek, Czechoslovakia		5	42
2-Seater Canadian	Czechoslovakia		5	7 1/10
500 Metres, 1-Seater Kayak (Women)	K. Hoff, Denmark ...		2	31 1/10

Ojib'wa or **Chippewa Indians.** Large and important Algonquian tribe once living about upper Great Lakes and extending w. into Minnesota, U.S.A. ; *plate f. 2757.*

Oka (ō-kah'). R. of cent. Russia ; though rapid, is navigable for almost entire length of 950 m. ; joins Volga.

Okano'gan or **Okan'gan.** A lake in s. British Columbia, 60 m. long.

Okanogan River. A tributary of the Columbia in British Columbia and Washington, rising in L. Okawogus ; 300 m. long.

Okapi (ō-kah'-pi). A giraffe-like animal, *71.*

O'Kelly, Sean T. (b. 1883). Irish statesman ; with A. Griffith founded Sinn Fein party ; fought in Easter Rising, 1916, and consequently imprisoned ; under De Valera min. for local govt. and public health 1932–39 ; 1938 vice-premier ; from 1939 min. of finance ; June 1945 pres. of Eire.

Okhotsk, Sea of, 1845.

Okinawa. Largest is. of Riukiu group, Pacific Ocean, 325 m. from Jap. mainland, and belonging to Japan before 2nd World War ; area 485 sq. m. ; Jap. air base, opposing U.S. air attacks on Japan based from Marianas ; its capture by U.S. 10th army took 82 days, Apr. 1–June 21, 1945, costing the U.S. 47,000 casualties, and the Japs. almost the whole 60,000-strong garrison ; *2474, 3424.*

Oklahoma (ō-kla-hō'-ma). State of s.-cent. U.S.A. ; 69,919 sq. m. ; pop. 2,336,400, **2431.**

Oklahoma City, Oklahoma, U.S.A. State cap. ; pop. 204,400 ; in centre of rich agric. and stock-rearing region ; has cotton and flour mills, ironworks, etc.

Okubo (ō-koo-bō), **Toshimitsu** (1830–78). One of 5 great Japanese nobles who led revolution (1868) against shogunate ; one of the Mikado's chief advisers.

Okuma (ō-koo-mah), **Shigenobu, Marquess** (1838–1922). Organizer and leader of progressive party in Japan ; early advocate of abolition of feudal system and reform leader ; founder of Japanese Women's Univ. ; premier in 1895, 1898 and 1914–16.

Olaf (ō-lahf) (b. 1903). Crown Prince of Norway, son of Haakon VII ; married Princess Martha of Sweden in 1929.

Olaf I, Tryggvesson (969–1000). King of Norway ; began Christianization of Norway ; leaped into sea after defeat by Danes and Swedes ; heroic deeds recounted in Longfellow's " Saga of King Olaf."

Olaf II, St. (995–1030). King and patron saint of Norway ; conquered throne in 1016 ; united kingdom and continued its Christianization, 2390.

Oland (ō'-lahnt). Swedish isl. in Baltic Sea across Kalmar Sound from s.e. extremity of Sweden ; 519 sq. m. ; cap. Borgholm on w. coast ; pop. 130,000.

Old age pensions, 1976, 2546, 2994.

Old Bailey. London street, at the n. end of which is the Central Criminal Court.

Old Castile, Sp. ; n. part of Castile, an elevated plateau walled in by mountains ; *map, 3030.*

Oldenburg (ōl'-den-boorg). State (former grand duchy) of n.w. Ger. on North Sea ; 2,480 sq. m. ; pop. 585,000 ; cap. Oldenburg (pop. 66,950).

Old English or **Anglo-Saxon** language, 1209.

Oldfield, Anne (" **Nance** ") (1683–1730). The most brilliant actress of her time ; played both comedy and tragedy roles, among her successes being Jane Shore and Lady Jane Grey.

Old Guard. Popular name of noted body of troops in army of Napoleon I ; made last Fr. charge at battle of Waterloo.

Oldham. Important cotton mfg. tn. in Lancashire, 6 m. n.e. of Manchester ; pop. (est.) 118,280 ; coal mines ; 1165.

" Old Lady of Threadneedle Street." The Bank of England, *357.*

Old Man of the Mountain. Head of the Assassins, 274.

Old Man of the Sea. In " Arabian Nights," the little old man who begs Sinbad the Sailor to carry him across a brook and then will not be dislodged from his back ; hence, a bore or burden.

Old Man's Beard. The wild clematis, *1036,* 1037.

Old Pretender. Son of James II, 1794, 2682.

Old Régime (rā-zhēm'). In Fr., 1366, 1393.

" Old St. Paul's," by Ainsworth, 87.

Old Sarum. Parish in Wiltshire, 2 m. n. of Salisbury ; former city, deserted by 16th cent., sent members to Parliament until 1832 ; proverbial " rotten borough," 2864.

Old Testament (O.T.). Division of the Bible, 424 ; divisions, 2692 ; language, 1601.

Old Vic. Theatre in Waterloo Rd., S.E., famous for productions of Shakespeare and opera, *1041,* 1043; bombed 1940.

" Old Wives' Tale," by Arnold Bennett, 414.

Oleaceae (ō-le-ā-si-ē) or olive family. Plant family including olives and lilacs, ash and privet ; distributed over temperate and tropical regions.

Olean'der. Flowering shrub of order *Apocynaceae,* found in Mediterranean countries, lance-shaped leaves with clusters of rose-like flowers.

Olein (ō-le-in). Compound found in fats and oils.

O'leo oil, oleo-stock, oleostearin, 1263 ; oleo-resins, 2767.

Oléron. Fertile isl. off w. coast of Fr. at mouth of R. Charente ; included in dept. of Charente-Inférieure ; 66 sq. m. ; chief tn. St. Pierre.

Oligarchy (ol'-i-gahr-ki). Form of govt. in which power is held by small group.

Ol'igocene period, in geology, 1432, 1433.

Oliphant, Marcus L. E. (b. 1901). Australian physicist ; prof. of physics at Birmingham, 1937 ; researched on electricity in gases, and nuclear physics ; helped develop the atomic bomb ; nat. univ. of Australia, 1948.

Oliphant, Margaret Oliphant (1828–97). Scottish novelist and historical writer (" Life of Mrs. Margaret Maitland ").

Olive. Tree from which oil and other products are obtained, **2431.** The cultivated variety is named *Olea europaea* var. *sativa.*

Olive family. Same as Oleaceae.

Olive oil, 1263, 2431 ; food value, 1338, *1339.*

Oliver. One of Charlemagne's paladins, friend of Roland, 2797.

Oliver, James (1823–1908). Amer. inventor and manufacturer, b. Scot. ; revolutionized plough-making.

" Oliver Twist." Novel by Dickens ; relates adventures of workhouse orphan who asks for more gruel ; runs away and becomes innocent pupil of Fagin the pickpocket and tool of Bill Sykes the burglar.

Olives, Mount of. Historic ridge E. of Jerusalem ; favourite resort of Christ and Disciples ; contains " Hill of Offence," reputed scene of Solomon's idolatry ; *1820.*

Oliv'ia. Countess beloved by the duke in Shakespeare's " Twelfth Night."

Olivier, Sir Laurence Kerr (b. 1907). Brit. actor, film star and producer. Stage successes include Romeo and Juliet, Hamlet, Henry V, Macbeth ; productions include screen version of Henry V when he achieved international fame in 1944 as director and star ; directed and played lead in film of Hamlet 1948 ; knighted 1947 ; as Coriolanus, *1041.* Married Vivien Leigh.

Olmedo, José Joaquin de (1780–1847). S. American poet, 3027.

Olney. Tn. in Buckinghamshire, 12 m. s.e. of Northampton ; William Cowper, the poet, lived here ; pop. 2,400 ; 923, 600.

Olomouc, or **Olmütz,** Czechoslovakia. Moravian tn. on r. March ; coal mining ; pop. 61,240 ; occupied by Swedes in Thirty Years' War ; besieged by Frederick the Great (1758) ; conference to settle Prussian affairs (1850).

Oltenitza (ol-tā-nēt'-sa), Rumania. Tn. on Danube : Turks defeated Russians in Crimean War ; large grain and lumber trade.

Olym'pia, Greece. Plain in anc. Elis on r. Alpheus (modern Ruphia) ; scene of Olympic games, *2432* ; excavations at, 1526 ; temple and statue of Zeus, *1520,* 1528, *plate f. 1524,* 284, *plate f. 2924.*

Olympia, London, near Addison Rd. station ; a large hall, where the Royal Tournament, horse shows, and exhibitions, such as Radiolympia, are held ; British Industries Fair, *1257* ; Bertram Mills Christmas Circus, *plate f. 820.*

Olym'piad. Interval of 4 years between celebrations of Olympic Games, formerly used by Greeks for dating events, 776 B.C. being first year of first O.

Olym'pias (d. 316 B.C.). Fierce, ambitious Epirote princess, wife of Philip II of Macedon and mother of Alexander the Great.

Olympic Games, 2432 ; at Athens, 287, 2097 ; 1948 Games in Britain, *2433,* 2434 ; results in p. 3923. *See* Athletics.

Olympic Register, and Gk. calendar, 661.

Olympieum (o-lim-pi-ē'-um). Temple of Zeus at Athens, 284, *285.*

Olym'pus, Mt., ridge in n. Greece, separating Thessaly and Macedonia, 1517 ; fabled home of gods, 3443. Name also applied in anc. times to several other peaks, especially one in Asia Minor.

Omagh. Co. tn. of Tyrone, N. Ireland ; pop. 6,000 ; 3772.

Omaha (ō'-ma-hah), Nebraska, U.S.A., known as the " Gate City of the West " ; dairy produce, maize and livestock ; pop. 223,000, 2310.

Oman (ō-mahn'). Independent state of s.e. Arabia on Persian Gulf, Gulf of Oman, and Arabian Sea ; 82,000 sq. m. ; pop. 500,000, chiefly Arabs ; exports dates ; cap. Muscat ; 196.

Oman, Sir Charles (1860–1946). Brit. writer and historian ; Prof. Mod. Hist., Oxford University 1905–1946.

Oman, Gulf of, arm of Arabian Sea s. of Persia ; connected with Persian Gulf by Strait of Ormuz.

Omar (ō'-mahr) (c. 581–644), 2nd Mahomedan caliph, organizer of Mahomedan power from warring sect to empire ; founds Cairo, 653.

Omar, Mosque of, Jerusalem. Built over rock supposed by Jews to be scene of the sacrifice of Isaac and, by Mahomedans of the Prophet's ascension.

Omar Khayyám (kī-yahm'), **Hakim.** (1071–1123). Persian mathematician, astronomer, and poet ; his wonderful " Rubáiyat " (collection of epigrams) was translated into Eng. by Edward FitzGerald, 1740, 1741.

Omdurman (om-door-mahn'). Anglo-Eg. Sudan, city on Nile, opposite Khartum ; pop. 116,200 ; ivory, ostrich feathers, gum-arabic ; *3109* ; captured by Kitchener, 1862, 3110.

Omega, ω, Ω. Twenty-fourth and last letter (long o) of Gk. alphabet.

Omicron, o, O. Fifteenth letter (short o) of Gk. alphabet.

Ommiads (ō-mī'-adz), **Omayyads,** or **Umayyads.** Dynasty of caliphs or successors of Mahomet who asserted rule over Mahomedan empire from death of Ali, 4th caliph, to rise of Abbasids (661–750), and ruled in Spain (756–1031).

Omsk. Distributing point for w. Siberia, on Irtish r., and Trans-Siberian Rly. ; pop. 281,000 ; seat of unsuccessful anti-Bolshevik govt. established by former Kerensky supporters, headed by Gen. Kolchak ; 2967.

Oña, Pedro de. Chilean poet, 3027.

Onager (on'-*a-ger*). A wild ass, 273.

One'ga, Lake. In N.W. Rus., 2nd largest l. in Europe ; 3,700 sq. m. ; indented rocky shores ; outlet to White Sea, canal connexion with Volga and Dvina ; fisheries, timber trade.

O'Neill, Eugene (b. 1888). Amer. playwright ; his plays, mystical in outlook, include " Emperor Jones," " Anna Christie," " Strange Interlude," and " Mourning Becomes Electra," 1042.

On'ion. A biennial food plant, **2434** ; bulb structure, 612.

On'nes, Heike Kamerlingh (1853–1926). Dutch physicist, winner of Nobel prize for physics in 1913 ; low temperature experiments.

Ontario. Cent. prov. of Canada ; 412,582 sq. m. ; pop. 4,107,000 ; **2434** ; 676, *map, plate f. 680* ; apples and peaches, 2435 ; cities and mfrs., 3223, 2435 ; grain elevators, 679 ; Great Lakes, 1515 ; minerals, 2974 ; Niagara Falls, 2361 ; Ottawa, 2458 ; Parl. building, *3224* ; St. Lawrence r., 2861 ; cap. Toronto, 3223 ; Welland Canal, 3363.

Ontario, Lake. Smallest of Great Lakes ; 7,540 sq. m. ; 1515, 1516, *map, 1515* ; Welland Canal, 3363.

On'yx. A form of quartz in coloured layers, 2713.

Onyx marble, 2097.

Oolitic (ō-ō-lit'ik) **limestone,** *plate f. 1432* ; 1950.

Oolitic period, in geology, a period when the continents of Europe and Asia were to a large extent covered by the ocean. Oolite deposits are chiefly limestone, rich in fossil remains of marine animals.

Oolong (oo-long'). A dark Formosan tea, 3162.

Oo'miak. Eskimo woman's boat, 486.

O'ospore. Fertilized egg-cell in primitive plants.

Ooze. Slimy mud on sea bottom, 2103, 2419.

O'pal. A precious stone, 1427.

Open air theatre, 3197.

Open-door policy. Term used in international politics to designate equality of commercial opportunity to all nations.

Open-hearth process of steel manufacture, *1753*, 1756.

Opera (op'*-e-ra*). A music-drama, **2435**, 2264 ; Wagner's influence, 2437, 3331 ; stories of some well-known operas, 2438.

Opéra bouffe, origin, 2436.

Opéra comique, rise of, 2436.

Opera glass, 3180.

Operations, surgical, 2135 ; anaesthetics, 148.

Ophelia (ō-fē'-li-*a*), in Shakespeare's " Hamlet," daughter of Polonius, beloved by Hamlet, *1570*, 1571.

Ophid'ia. Snake order of reptiles, 2990.

Ophthal'moscope, 3055.

Opiates (ō'-pi-*ats*), 2442.

Opie, John (1761–1807). Brit. painter ; became known as the " Cornish Wonder " for his portraits and somewhat theatrical historical compositions.

O'pitz Martin (1597–1639). Ger. poet ; head of so-called First Silesian School ; called " father of modern German poetry."

O'pium. A drug, **2442** ; trade in China, 2442.

Opium poppy, 2655.

Opium War (1840–42), 810, 2442 ; Hong Kong ceded to Gt. Brit., 1639.

Oporto (ō-por'-tō), 2nd city of Portugal, spt. and commercial centre of Douro, 2 m. from sea ; pop. 262,300 ; textiles, port wine, 2658.

Opos'sum. Amer. marsupial, **2442** ; fur, 1412.

Oppenheim, Edward Phillips (1866–1946). Eng. novelist, writer of over 150 novels and books of a dramatic and sensational character (" The Mysterious Mr. Sabin " ; " The Mischief Maker " ; etc.).

Ops. In Rom. myth., goddess of plenty, 2875.

Op'sonin. Germ-fighting substance in the blood.

Optical glass. Any kind used in optical instruments, 1474. *See* **Glass.**

Optical illusions. *See* **Illusions.**

Optical instruments ; lenses, 1924 ; microscope, 2163 ; spectroscopes, 3055 ; telescopes and field-glasses, 3180.

Optic nerve, 1252 ; grows inward toward brain, 2317.

Op'tics. The science of light, 2591. *See* **Light.**

Opuntia (ō-pun'-shi-*a*). A genus of cacti, 049.

Or, in heraldry, 1614.

Oracle (o'-ra-kl), **Delphic,** 988, 186 ; responses of, 21, 650, 932, 3202.

Oradea Mare or **Nagy-Varad.** City in w. Rumania ; pop. 92,940 ; old Hungarian tn. founded by St. Ladislaus (1080) ; potteries and agricultural trade ; ceded to Hungary, 1940–45.

Oradour-sur-Glane. Vill. of Fr., Haute-Vienne dept. in Ger.-occupied Fr., it was totally destroyed and nearly all the 750 inhabs. killed, June 1944, as mistaken reprisal for resistance by the people of a vill. of similar name ; the ruins remain as memorial.

Oran (ō-rahn'), Algeria. Prosperous city on N. coast of Africa, 230 m. s.w. of Algiers ; pop. 194,700 ; Britain attacked French Fleet July 3, 1940, 118, 3418 ; U.S. troops occupied it in Nov. 1942.

Orange. Principality in s.e. Fr. ; fell to House of Nassau in 1531, under Nassau-Orange family until 1702, annexed to Fr. in 1714, 3380.

Orange, House of. Princely family whose heads were sovereigns of Orange (s.e. Fr.) ; also held large possessions in the Netherlands and thus became defenders of Dutch liberty against Sp. oppression, and ancestors of present Dutch royal line, 2323 ; William the Silent, 3381 ; William III of England, 3380.

Orange, a citrus fruit, **2442** ; California production, *2443* ; in Florida, 1319 ; introduced into Europe, 937 ; perfume, 2549 ; seedless, 2444 ; vitamins, 3227.

Orange. A colour, 876 ; position in spectrum, *plate f. 3056.*

Orange Free State. Prov. in the Union of S. Africa ; 49,647 sq..m. ; pop. 875,550 ; *2444* ; Boer War, 480, 3019.

Orangemen. Members of Orange Society of Irish Protestants (essentially political) originating in Ulster ; name derived from King William III (Prince of Orange), 1746.

Orange Pekoe tea, *3162.*

Orange River. Large r. in S. Africa ; rises in Drakensberg Mts. ; flows 800 m. into Atlantic, 2444, 69.

Orang-utan (o-rang'-oo-tan'). An anthropoid ape, 2445, *183*, 184.

Orator'io. Dramatic composition for voices, 2264 ; developed by Handel, 1573 ; the first, 2264.

Oratory, 2769 ; Greek, 1540 ; Roman, 1895.

Orb. In Eng. regalia, 935, *frontis., Vol. 2.*

Or'bit. Path of heavenly body ; of comets, 880 ; planets, 1853.

Orcagna or **Andrea di Cione.** 14th cent. Italian painter, sculptor, and architect, one of Giotto's principal followers, 1775.

Orchard, management of, 1401, *1403*. *See* names of fruits.

Orchardson, Sir William Quiller (1835–1910). Brit. artist ; built up a great reputation as a portrait painter ; his other works include " On Board the Bellerophon."

Orchestra (or'-kes-tra), **2445**, *2446* ; *2265* ; B.B.C.'s, 3398 ; development, 2264 ; musical instruments, *1644*, 2267.

Orchestra. Part of theatre, 3194.

Orchid (or'-kid). Any member of plant family *Orchidaceae* family of flowering plants, **2447** ; lady's slipper, *1883* ; in India, 1701 ; man orchis, 2445.

Orchomenus (or-kom'-e-nus). Anc. Gk. city in Boeotia ; great continental and marit. power in prehistoric times, cap. of the Minyae, a seafaring race from Thessaly ; superseded by Thebes.

Orczy (or'-chē), **Emmuska, Baroness** (1865–1947). Brit. novelist and playwright, b. in Hungary ; " The Scarlet Pimpernel," presented on stage and screen, " The Elusive Pimpernel," " I Will Repay," and other of her works were very popular ; her memoirs " Links in the Chain of Life " appeared in 1947.

Ord. R. of W. Australia.

Or'deal, trial by, 1843.

Order. Division of a class of living organisms.

Order in Council. In Gt. Brit., any order issued by the sovereign on advice of the privy council.

Order of Mercy. Established in 1899 in connexion with the League of Mercy to promote the welfare of hospitals by obtaining subscriptions for King Edward's Hospital Fund for London.

Order of Merit (O.M.). British honour, 2449.

Orders, religious, 2213. *See* names of various orders.

Orders and decorations, 2448 ; orders of knighthood, 1864.

Orders of architecture, Gk., 213, *215.*

Or'dinance. An established rule, rite, law, custom, or ceremony ; often used among Presbyterians for the sacraments.

Ordina'tion of clergy. The act or rite of investing with priestly or ministerial functions.

Ord'nance. Heavy firearms, such as mortars and cannon. *See* **Artillery.**

Ordnance Survey. The official survey of Gt. Brit. and N. Ire. ; came into existence in 1784 ; headquarters at Chessington, Surrey ; mapping, 2094.

Ordovician (or-dō-vish'-*a*n) **period,** in geology, 1432.

Ordre pour le Mérite, in Germany, 2449.

Oreads (o'-rē-adz). In Gk. myth., nymphs of mts. and grottoes, Echo being one of the most famous, 2408.

Orebro (ê-rā-brō), Sweden. Mfg. tn. on R. Svarta, near w. end of L. Hjelmar ; pop. 59,880 ; diet of 1540 declared crown hereditary ; diet of 1810 elected the French marshal Bernadotte crown prince.

Or'egon. A N.W. state of U.S.A. ; 96,981 sq. m. ; pop. 1,090,000, 2449.

O'Rell, Max (1848–1903). Pen-name of Paul Blouet, French author ; French master of St. Paul's School (" John Bull and His Island," similar books on Scotland, U.S. and France).

Ore Mts. Same as **Erzgebirge.**

Orenburg. Now Chkalov. Town in s.e. Russia on R. Ural ; pop. 172,920.

Ores. Natural substances containing metals, 2145, 2148, 2182 ; reduction processes, 906. *See also* under metals.

Orestes (o-res'-tēz). In Gk. myth., son of Agamemnon and Clytemnestra ; killed his mother because she had killed his father, 75.

Orford, Earl of. *See* **Walpole, Horace** ; **Walpole, Sir Robert.**

Organ. A musical instrument, **2449**, *2451*, 2264, 2268 ; how sound is produced, 3009, *3010.*

Organ'ic chemistry. Branch of chemistry dealing with the compounds of carbon, 774. *See* **Chemistry.**

Organic evolution. Evolution of living organisms, 1244. *See* **Evolution.**

Or'ganzine. A silk thread, 2972.

Oriel (or'-i-el). In architecture, a projecting window, of polygonal or semi-cylindrical form, and divided by mullions and transoms into different bays and other proportions.

Oriel College, Oxford, founded, 2464.

O'rient, the East, 268.

Orient Line. Line of steamships plying between London and Australia, etc.

Origen (or'-i-jen) (c. 185–254). Early Christian theologian, native of Alexandria, Egypt ; his authority waned as Augustine's waxed ; sought to reconcile Platonism and Christianity.

"Origin of Species." Book by Darwin ; 978, 1244 ; effect, 978.

Orinoco (o-rē-nō-kō). 3rd largest river in S. Amer., **2452,** 3308 ; betrothal customs, 2109 ; llanos, 3308 ; Raleigh's expeditions, 2452, 2744.

Oriole (or'-i-ōl). A passerine bird, **2452.**

Orion (o-rī'-on). In Gk. myth., **2453.**

Orion. A very large and conspicuous constellation, represented as a hunter with belt and sword, 2453 ; position, *chart, 895* ; nebula, *2311.*

Orissa (o-ris'-a). Prov. of the Rep. of India ; a. 32,000 sq. m. ; pop. 8,728,000 ; **2453** ; temple, *1710* ; gigantic animal sculpture, *1712.*

Orizaba (ō-rē-zah'-bah), **Mt.** Highest peak in Mexico ; 175 m. s.e. of Mexico City ; 2156.

Orkhan (1326–59). Sultan of Turkey, 3262.

Ork'ney Islands. Group of isls. forming a co. of Scot., 375 sq. m. ; pop. 21,400 ; **2453,** 2889.

Orlan'do. Lover of Rosalind in " As You Like It," 282.

Orlando, Vittorio Emmanuele (b. 1860). It. statesman ; favoured intervention in 1st World War in advance of his party ; Prime Minister (1917–19) ; owing to his failure to secure a settlement in Paris, his cabinet fell June 1919. Retired on advent of Fascism.

" Orlando Furioso," by Ariosto, 1786.

Or'leanists. Fr. political party in 15th cent., supporters of the house of Orleans as opposed to that of Burgundy, 757 ; also in 19th cent., a party led by the house of Orleans ; sought to establish constitutional monarchy ; Louis Philippe, 1366.

Orléans (or-lā-ahn), Fr. historic city ; pop. 70,200 ; 2000, **2454** ; relieved by Joan of Arc, 1653, 1831 ; 2nd World War damage, 2454.

Orléans, dukes of. Heads of a younger branch of Fr. royal house of Bourbon.

Orléans, Louis Philippe, Duke of (1747–93). " Philippe Égalité," the regent's great grandson ; as " Citizen Equality " was elected Paris deputy to Convention in 1792 ; voted for death of Louis XVI ; executed under the Terror. His son was Louis Philippe, king of the French.

Orléans, Philip, Duke of (1674–1723). Regent of Fr. during minority of Louis XIV ; able but dissolute and corrupt ; supported " Mississippi Bubble " scheme.

Orlov. A famous diamond, *1011,* 1012.

Ormuz. A small barren isl. at entrance to Persian Gulf ; in Middle Ages headquarters of trade between Persia and India ; red ochre and rock salt ; also known as Hormuz ; pop. 1,000.

Orne. R. in Normandy ; flows N. 95 m. to Eng. Channel ; in Normandy invasion, 2378.

Ornithol'ogy. Division of zoology dealing with the study of birds.

Ornithosauria. An extinct order of flying reptiles.

Oropesa float, mine-sweeping apparatus, *2186.*

Orpah (or'-pah). In Bible, sister-in-law of Ruth, 2857.

Orpen, Sir William (1878–1931). Irish painter ; one of the foremost portrait painters of the 20th cent. ; elected R.A., 1919 ; official War artist ; many of his finest pictures in Imperial War Museum ; " Signing of the Versailles Treaty," 1241 ; " Le Chef de l'Hôtel Chatham," *1183.*

Orpheus (or'-fūs). In Gk. myth., musician of marvellous powers, **2454,** 2261.

Or'pington. A breed of fowls, *2671.*

Orr, John Boyd, 1st Earon (b. 1880). Brit. physiologist and dietician. Orr Report " Food, Health and Income," pub. 1936. Dir.-Gen. World Food and Agric. Org. (1945–48). Created baron (1949) ; Nobel peace prize (1949).

Orris-root, 1748.

Orsay, Comte D'. *See* **D'Orsay.**

Orsini (or-sē'-nē). A noble Rom. family, champions of Guelfs against their hereditary enemies, the Colonna ; first prominent in 12th cent.

Orta, Lake, N. It., *1767.*

Orthez (or-tez'), Fr. Small tn. in Basses Pyrénées dept., 40 m. E. of Bayonne ; here the Fr. under Soult were defeated by Wellington, Feb., 1814.

Or'thoclase. A glassy, variously coloured silicate of potassium and aluminium.

Orthodox Greek Church. *See* **Greek Orthodox Church.**

Orthoptera (or-thop'-te-ra). An order of insects, 1733 ; cockroaches, 861 ; crickets, 927 ; grasshoppers and locusts, 1510, *1511,* 1512, *1513* ; mantises, 2090 ; " stick " and " leaf " insects, 1728.

Ort'ler. Highest point in Tirol and in E. Alps (12,802 ft.).

Or'tolan. A bunting, with plumage of reddish-brown, the throat being yellow and the breast and head green ; found in Africa and Europe, numbers were netted in s. Europe and fattened for the table.

Orwell. R. of Suffolk, extending from Ipswich to the Stour estuary at Harwich ; 10 m. long.

Oryx. Abyssinian antelope, *plate f. 72.*

Osage. R. of U.S.A., a tributary of the Missouri in Kansas and Missouri 500 m. long.

Osage orange. N. Amer. tree with inedible fruit, resembling a large orange ; wood bright yellow, fine grained and very elastic.

Osaka (ō-zah'-kah). 2nd largest city and chief mfg. centre of Japan ; pop. 3,252,340 ; **2454** ; textile mfrs., 1796 ; bombed by U.S.A. 1945, 2455.

Osborne. Estate near E. Cowes, Isle of Wight, now seat of convalescent home for army and navy officers ; Royal Naval College, transferred to Dartmouth in 1921 ; home of Queen Victoria, 3320.

Osbourne, Lloyd (b. 1868). Amer. author, stepson of R. L. Stevenson, with whom he collaborated in " The Wrecker," and " The Ebb Tide," 3089.

Os'car I (1799–1859). King of Sweden and Norway, son of Bernadotte (Charles XIV), succeeded to throne in 1844.

Oscar II (1829–1907). King of Sweden and Norway, 3131.

Osceola (c. 1804–38). Seminole Indian chief, leader of 2nd Seminole War, precipitated by seizure of his wife as fugitive slave ; himself seized under flag of truce, died in captivity.

Os'cillating currents, electric, 3199. 3393 ; in broadcasting, 3393.

Osiers. Willow twigs used in basket-making, *369,* 3382.

Osiris (ō-sī'-ris). Anc. Egypt deity, **2455** ; and Isis, 1760.

Os'ler, Sir William (1849–1919). Canadian physician ; professor of medicine at Johns Hopkins Univ. (1889–1904); became regius professor of medicine at Oxford in 1905 ; author of many medical works.

Oslo. Cap. and chief spt. of Norway ; pop. 427,000 · **2455** 2392 *2397* ; aurora at, *plate f. 305* ; in Ger. occupation, 1940–45, 2456.

Osman. Same as **Othman.**

Osmanli. Ottoman Turks. *See* **Turkey.**

Osmium (Os). A metallic element of the platinum group ; atomic weight 191·5 ; found alloyed with iridium ; used as a catalyst and filament for electric light bulbs ; most dense substance on earth ; melts at 4,288° F. ;

properties, 768, 777 ; found with platinum, 2627 ; specific gravity, 3054.

Osmo'sis. Passage of a solvent through a membrane in order to dilute a solution on the other side.

Osnabrück. Industrial tn. of Hanover, Germany, on R. Hase, 30 m. N.E. of Münster ; pop. 94,000 ; iron and steel mfrs. ; member of Hanseatic League ; until 1815 seat of a prince-bishop ; bombed, taken by British, Apl. 1945.

Os'prey. Large bird of prey, feeding on fish ; extinct in Britain.

Osprey feathers, from egrets, *3098.*

Os'sa. Mt. in anc. Thessaly (modern Kissovo). *See* **Pelion.**

Ossawatomie, Kansas, U.S.A. City 45 m. s.w. of Kansas City ; pop. 4,772 ; attack by pro-slavery men (1856) resisted by John Brown and followers ; latter finally overpowered and tn. practically destroyed ; 588.

Ossein. Toughening material in bones, 498.

Ossian or **Oisin** (3rd cent. A.D.), legendary Irish bard, son of Finn ; supposed author of Macpherson's " Poems of Ossian," 1213.

Ossipevsk'. Mkt. tn. of Ukraine S.S.R., formerly Berdichev ; 120 m. w.s.w. of Kiev ; grain, cattle, horses ; pop. 66,306 ; in 2nd World War held by Gers. 1941–Jan. 1944.

Ostade (os-tah'-de), **Adriaen van** (1610–85). Dutch painter, pupil of Hals ; vigorous treatment of rustic life, 2334.

Ostade, Isaac van (1621–49). Dutch painter, brother of Adriaen, 2334.

Ostend, Belgium. Spt. and resort on North Sea ; pop. 47,520 ; repeatedly shelled in 1914–18 War, harbour closed by Brit. by sinking of ships, May 10, 1918 ; in Ger. occupn., 1940–44 ; 404, *405.*

Osteop'athy. A system of treating bone disorders by manipulation. It is accepted that adjustment of misplaced bones, ligaments or cartilages may alleviate or cure many pathological conditions.

Ostia (os'-tē-a). Port of Rome at mouth of Tiber ; Roman theatre at, 1038 ; foundation, 2804, 3207.

Os'tiaks. Tribe of Finno-Ugric group inhabiting Ob valley in w. Siberia.

Östmark. Ger. name for state of Austria during annexation, 1938–45.

Ostracism (os'-tra-sizm), in anc. Greece, banishment by popular vote ; of Aristides, 231.

Os'trea. Oyster genus of molluscs, 2466, *2467.*

Os'trich. A flightless running bird, the largest of living birds, **2456** ; farming, 3014, *3018* ; egg, 444, *1094, 2456* ; foot, 448.

Os'trogoths, or East Goths, 1487, 1237.

Ostwald (ōst'-vahlt), **Wilhelm** (1853–1932). Ger. chemist ; leader in physical chemistry ; Nobel prize winner in chemistry (1909).

Os'westry. Tn. in Shropshire, 17 m. N.W. of Shrewsbury ; rly. carriage works, tanning and brewing industries ; pop. 9,750 ; 2963.

Otaru, Japan. Chief tn. on w. coast of Hokushu Isl. on s. shore of Ishikari Bay ; pop. 154,000 ; marine experiment station ; fisheries ; large trade.

" Othel'lo." Opera by Verdi, 2439, 3315.

" Othel'lo." Tragedy by Shakespeare, 2457, 2934 ; quotations from, 2458.

Oth'man or **Osman I** (c. 1259–1326). Turkish sultan, founder of Ottoman empire, 3262.

Otho. *See* **Otto.**

O'tis, Elisha Graves (1811–61). Amer. inventor ; invented lift safety device.

Otranto (ō-tran'-tō). Spt. on S.E. coast of Italy, 46 m. S.E. of Brindisi ; pop. 3,152 ; during Middle Ages chief Adriatic port of Italy ; sacked by Turks (1480).

Otranto, Strait of. Passage connecting Adriatic and Ionian seas and separating Italy from Albania ; minimum width about 45 m.

O'Trigger, Sir Lucius. In Sheridan's comedy "The Rivals" fortune-hunting, duel-loving Irishman.

Ottar or **Ohthere** (9th cent. A.D.). Norwegian explorer; rounded North Cape and discovered White Sea.

Ottawa (ot'-a-wa). Ontario. Cap. of Dominion of Canada, pop. 154,000; 24·8, 2434; Houses of Parliament, 683.

Ottawa River, Canada. Chief tributary of St. Lawrence; rises in Quebec, flows W., then S.E., forming boundary between Quebec and Ontario; length 685 m.; enters St. Lawrence by 2 channels enclosing isl. of Montreal; 2458; lumbering, 2037.

Ottawa, University of. At Ottawa, Ontario; men; Cath.; founded 1849 (univ. since 1889); arts, science, theology, law, commerce.

Ottawa Conference. Agreements between U.K. and Dominions were signed at Ottawa in 1932 relating to mutual preferential tariffs.

Ot'ter. Aquatic animal, our largest member of weasel family, *Mustelidae*, 2459; fur, 1412; hunting the, 1658.

Ot'terburn. Vil. in N.E. Eng., near Scottish border; Scots under Douglas defeated English under Percys (1388); battle celebrated in ballad of Chevy Chase, 2391.

Ot'to I (1848–1916). King of Bavaria; insane throughout reign (1886–1912); his uncle, Prince Luitpold, acted as regent, and on his death Otto was deposed.

Otto I (1815–67). King of Greece, very unpopular, forced to grant constitution and appoint ministry of Greeks (1843); 1525.

Otto I, or **Otho** (912–973). Holy Roman emperor, 2459, 1449, 1764, 1238; extent of empire, 1449, 1637.

Otto II, or **Otho** (955–983), emperor, 2460.

Otto III, or **Otho** (980–1002), emperor, 2460; at tomb of Charlemagne, 9.

Otto IV, or **Otho** (1175–1218), emperor, 2460.

Otto, Nicholas (1832–91). Ger. engineer, inventor of Otto four-stroke cycle, 1420, 1421, 1736.

Ot'toman Empire. *See* Turkey.

Ot'toman Turks. Branch of Turks which founded Turkish Empire; named from Othman, first sultan (reigned 1288–1326); 3262.

Ot'tos, or essential oils, in perfumes, 2551.

Ottringham, Yorks., Eng.; B.B.C. transmitter, 3399.

Otway, Thomas (1652–1685). Eng. dramatist. A master of tragic pathos, he wrote numerous plays, of which "The Orphan" and "Venice Preserved" were the finest and remained for nearly 200 years stock pieces on the English stage.

Oudenarde, Belgium. Town on r. Schelde, 18 m. S. of Ghent; victory of the Allies over French (1708), 2106.

Oudh (ōōd). Region of India, in N. centre; part of United Provinces of Agra and Oudh; chief city, Lucknow, 1692, 3284.

Ouida (wē'-da). Pen name of Louise de la Ramée (1839–1908). Eng. novelist ("Under Two Flags," "Moths"; and children's stories, "The Nürnberg Stove"; "A Dog of Flanders").

Oulton Broad, Eng. Shallow lake in Suffolk, frequented by yachtsmen.

Ounce. The snow leopard, 1928.

Ounce (oz.). A unit of weight in the avoirdupois, troy and apothecaries systems, and a unit of fluid measure. *See* Weights and Measures.

Oundle. Market tn. in Northamptonshire; public school founded under the will of Sir W. Laxton, lord mayor of London, who died in 1556 and left property to the Grocers' Company for that purpose; famous recent headmaster (1892–1922), F. W. Sanderson; pop. of tn. 3,100; 2385.

Ouricuri wax, 3359.

"Our Mutual Friend." Novel by Charles Dickens (1865); plot centres around Lizzie Hexam, the bargeman's daughter, and Eugene Wrayburn, her lover.

Ourthe (oort). R. of Belgium, flows N. 100 m. to Meuse.

Ouse (ōōz). R. of Yorkshire, Eng., joining the Trent to form the Humber; length 60 m.

Ouse. R. of Sussex, flowing 30 m. to the Eng. Channel, 3435.

Ouse, Great. R. in E. of Eng. flowing into Wash near King's Lynn; length 160 m.; 1658, 2375.

Outboard motor-boat, 484.

Outer Mongolia. N.W. part of Mongolia, a high plateau, 2204.

Outlanders or **Uitlanders,** in S. Africa, 3019.

Outram (ōō'-tram), **Sir James** (1803–63). Eng. general, at Lucknow, 2035.

Outrigger. Boat with rowlocks supported by projecting brackets, 481, 482; in New Guinea, 481.

Outside edge, in skating, 2977.

Oval, Kennington, S.E. Surrey county cricket ground.

Oval window. Membrane of inner ear, 1065.

O'vary, in plants. The receptacle in which fertilized ovules develop; in flowers, 1321, 1327, 1328, 531.

Oven, bakery, 555, 557; coke, 868; thermostatic control, 3201. *See also* Kiln.

Ovenbird. Family of S. Amer. birds which build nests shaped like bakers' ovens.

Over, in cricket, 930.

Overcasting, in sewing, 2927, 2928.

Overhand knot, 1868.

Overlord, Operation. Code name for the D-day invasion of Normandy, June 6, 1944; 2377.

Oversewing, 2927.

Overtones, sound; nature of, 3010.

Ov'id (Publius Ovidius Naso) (43 B.C.–A.D. 18). Rom. poet, author of "Metamorphoses," etc., 1892.

Oviedo (ō-vē-ā'-dō). Prov. of N. Spain, a. 4,205 sq. m.; pop. 862,345.

Oviedo. Industrial city of N. Sp. 16 m. S. of Bay of Biscay; pop. 86,724; univ.; held successfully by insurgents against a siege in Civil War (1936).

Ovip'arous animals, those which lay eggs, 1093; insects, 1729.

Ovipos'itor. Egg-laying organ of insects, 1732; of grasshopper, 1511.

O'vis. The sheep genus.

Ovule. Female body which when fertilized becomes the "germ" of the seed, 1322, 1327.

O'vum. *See* Egg.

Owen, Goronwy (1722–69). Welsh poet, 3336.

Owen, Sir Richard (1804–92). Eng. biologist, conservator of museum, Royal College of Surgeons; superintendent Natural History department British Museum ("Odontography").

Owen, Robert (1771–1858). Brit. Utopian socialist; turned his cotton mills into a kind of philanthropic trust; advocated Factory Acts, inspired many kinds of social reform, and established communistic colonies in Brit. and U.S.A.; 1875, 2996.

Owl. A nocturnal bird of prey, 2460, 439, 446, plates f. 2460, 2461; eggs, plate f. 440; eye, 1252; eats field-mice, 439; foot, 448; incubation of eggs, 444. "How Screecher Learned to Hunt," 3473.

Ox'alis. A genus of plants including the wood sorrel; oxalic acid a poison, 2638.

Ox'en (plural of ox). *See* Cattle.

Oxenham, John (d. 1941). Pen-name of the Eng. novelist and poet W. A. Dunkerley (novels: "God's Prisoner," "Broken Shackles"; verse: "Bees in Amber").

Oxenstierna (ōks'-en-shêr-na), **Count Axel Gustafsson** (1583–1654). Noted Swedish statesman; became chancellor in 1612; exercised great diplomatic ability in directing foreign policy of Sweden and in conducting government at home; held absolute control in central Germany during Thirty Years' War; guardian of Queen Christina of Sweden, who opposed him.

Oxeye. Same as **Great Tit.** Also large white daisy.

Ox family, or **Bovidae.** A sub-family of hollow-horned ruminant mammals, including cattle, etc.

Ox'ford, Eng. Famous univ. tn. pop. 103,600; 2462, 1256, 2466, 3296.

Oxford and Asquith, Herbert Henry Asquith, 1st Earl of (1852–1928). Brit. statesman, 2405, 1746.

Oxford and Asquith, Margot, Countess of (1864–1945), English writer, wife of first Earl of Oxford and Asquith; ("The Autobiography of Margot Asquith"; "Places and Persons"; "Octavia"; "More Memories"), 2465.

Oxford Group. *See* Group Movement.

Oxford Movement. A movement begun in 1833 by some Oxford clergy to revitalize the Church of Eng., also called Tractarianism; Newman and, 2342.

Oxford Reformers, More and, 2229.

Ox'fordshire. Inland co. of Eng.; 748 sq. m.; pop. 209,600; 2465.

Oxford University, 4140; boat race, 483; Radcliffe Camera, part of Bodleian Library, 2464; religious restrictions removed (1872); Rhodes scholarships, 2464, 2771. In 1948 anonymous French gift of £1,500,000 to found St. Anthony's post-graduate college for 51 students; £250,000 of it to be used on existing Colleges.

Oxidase. A ferment that produces oxidation.

Oxida'tion. Chemical union with oxygen or other electronegative radicles similar to oxygen; causes fire, 1280.

Oxides (ok'-sidz), compounds with oxygen, 2466; calcium (lime), 655, 1948; carbon, 699; copper, 907; iron, 1752, 1753, 2856; lead, 1908; nitrogen, 2372; in paints, 2478; reduced by heated aluminium in thermite process, 135; sulphur, 3116; tin, 3215; zinc, 3443.

Oxlip, a species of Primula, 924.

Ox'us. Anc. name of r. Amu, 264.

Oxy-acet'ylene. Used in cutting and welding metal, 18, 3362.

Oxygen (oks'-i-jen). A gaseous element of the sulphur group, atomic weight 16·00, taken as standard for all atomic weights, 769; most widely distributed and commonest element; when solidified melts at 372°F.; 2466, 1420; affinity for aluminium, 135; air, 88, 1598; in blood, 474, 1591, 2258; in breathing, 474, 1420, 2039, 2786; in Bunsen burner, 616; combined with hydrogen, 1673; in explosives, 1250; in combustion, 1280, 1595; and iron, 1752; named by Lavoisier, 1902; liquefied, 2792; mfr., 2466; speed of molecules, 1594; ozone, 2466; properties, 776; in plant breathing, 1915, 2998; Priestley's work, 2684; specific gravity, 3054. *See also* Oxides.

Oxy-hydrogen flame, 1673.

Oyama, Iwao, Prince (1842–1916). Japanese field-marshal.

Oyster-catcher, shore bird, 456, 3331.

Oyster plant. Same as Salsify.

Oysters, Bivalve shell-fish, 2466; bed, 2467; evolutionary position, 158; pearls, 2533, 2534; preyed upon by starfish, 3083.

Ozaka, Japan. Same as Osaka.

Ozea, Mount. Formerly Parnes, in Greece, 15 m. N. of Athens; 4,600 ft.

Ozokerite (ō-zok'-er-ĭt), or mineral wax, 3359.

Ozone (ō'-zōn). Allotropic form of oxygen, 2466.

ONE of the Egyptian hieroglyphs was a shutter ▣. This developed into the character ⚏ which was borrowed by the Phoeni ⚏ cians. They called it *Pe*, "mouth," perhaps because it looked like a mouth with teeth. When they themselves wrote it, they simplified it so that it is hard ⟩ to see the resemblance to a mouth ⟩ but they still kept the name. The Greeks used the same form, but turned the hook to the right. They afterwards squared the top thus ⌐ and finally made the two legs of equal length, in the character ⊓ which became the modern Greek letter *Pi*. The Romans adopted the rounded form ⎛ which they curved more and more, until finally the semi-circle was closed exactly as in our letter P. Its name has changed very little, nor has its sound, formed by closing the lips for an instant, and then allowing the breath to escape through them explosively. In certain words in English, e.g. *psalm*, *psychic*, *p* is mute.

Paar'deberg. Locality on R. Modder, Orange Free State, S. Africa, where General Cronje surrendered to the Brit. on Feb. 27, 1900, after a short siege.

Paasikivi, J. K. Finnish statesman; negotiated with U.S.S.R. in 1920 and 1939; prime min. 1944–46; pres. of repub., Mar. 1946.

Paccard, M. Climbed Mont Blanc, 127.

Pacheco (pah-chā'-kō), **Francisco** (1571–1654). Sp. artist, 3040.

Pachmann (pahkh'-mahn), **Vladimir de** (1848–1933). Rus. pianist, especially noted for brilliant interpretations of Chopin's works and for his platform eccentricities.

Pachomius (pa-kō'-mi-*us*), **Saint** (*c.* 292–*c.* 346), Egypt. monk; established first monastery, 2212.

Pachuca (pah-chōō'-ka), Mexico. City 55 m. N.E. of Mexico City; altitude 8,000 ft.; pop. 52,452; cap. state of Hidalgo.

Pacific. Locomotive class, *1987.*

Pacific Islands, *2469*; bread-fruit, 558; canoes, *482*; coconut palm, 862; political control, 2473; superstitions of natives, 2056. *See also* under chief islands and groups.

Pacific Ocean, largest of the oceans, **2469**, 2413; *map*, *plate f. 2469*; area, 2413; Balboa discovers, 341; Bering Sea, 415; cables, 643; Drake sees, 1036; explorations, 142, 899, 1037, 2056, 2472; greatest depth, 2413; Japan current, 2419; salmon fisheries, 1300; 2nd World War in, 2473, 3420.

Packaging. Photo-elec. devices in, 2576.

Packet, a class of ship, 2951

Pacto'lus. Anc. r. in Lydia, the present Sarabat, rises in Mt. Tmolus; flows N.W. to r. Hermus.

Padang (pah-dang'), Sumatra, Indonesia. Tn. on w. coast; pop. 52,000; air attacks in 1944 and 1945 while under Japanese occupation; 3890.

Pad'dington. Metropolitan bor. of w. London; pop. 109,050; formerly noted for picturesque rural scenery; London terminus of W. Region (Brit. Rlys.); "newspaper special" at, *2347.*

Paddle-wheel steamers, *2946*, 2947.

Paddy. Rice in the husk whether gathered or in the field. *See Rice.*

Paderewski (pad-e-ref'-ski), **Ignace Jan** (1860–1941). Polish musician and statesman, **2474**, 2641, 2983.

Padua (pad'-oo-*a*) (It. *Padova*). It. educational and art centre and trade and mfg. city on r. Bacchiglione, 22 m. w. of Venice; pop. 138,000; univ. (13th cent.) one of the oldest in Europe. Frescoes by Mantegna in the Eremitani church were lost when latter was destroyed by bombing in March 1944.

Paestum (pēs'-*tum*) (originally Posidonia). Gk. city on w. coast of It. on Gulf of Salerno; founded 6th cent. B.C.; conquered by Romans, 273 B.C.; destroyed by Saracens in 9th cent.; ruins of 3 Doric temples among most remarkable of antiquity; Poseidon's temple,*plate f. 213.*

Paganini (pa-gah-nē'-nē), **Nicolo** (1784–1840). It. violinist, called "most extraordinary executant ever known"; great power and control of tone, intense passion of style.

Page, Frederick Handley (b. 1885). Brit. aeroplane designer; founded firm that bears his name in 1909; invented in 1927 slotted wing that increases stability of aeroplanes in flight.

Page, Gertrude (d. 1922). Rhodesian novelist, 3020; "The Edge of Beyond," "The Rhodesian," etc.

Page, Walter Hines (1855–1918). Amer. editor and diplomat; ambassador to Gt. Brit. (1913–18).

Page. How trained for knighthood, 1864.

Paget (paj'-et), **Sir Bernard C. T.** (b. 1888). Brit. soldier; in 1940 commanded Brit. land forces at Trondhjem, Norway; C.-in-C. Home Forces 1942–43; trained home defence troops and introduced battle schools; in 1944 C.-in-C. Middle E., retiring 1946; principal of Ashridge 1946–49.

Paget, Sir James (1814–99). British surgeon, prof. of anatomy at Royal Coll. of Surgeons, 1847–52; pres. of R.C.S., 1875; wrote text-book on anatomy, *2134.*

"Pagliacci" (pah-lē-ah'-chē). Opera by Leoncavallo, 2439.

Pago'da. An oriental sacred tower-like structure, *1801*, *2537*; at Kew gdns., *1854.*

Pago Pago, Samoa. Seat of govt. and U.S. naval station, 2869.

Pahang (pah-hang'). State of Malayan Federation; 13,820 sq. m.; pop. 221,800; agric.; tin and gold, 2069.

Pahlevi, Riza Khan. *See* **Riza Khan Pahlevi.**

Pai'force. Allied forces in Persia and Irak (giving initials P.A.I.) from Aug. 1942; chief task, to guard Persian oilfields.

Pain, Barry (1864–1928). Brit. journalist and humorous author ("In a Canadian Canoe"; "Eliza"; "Memoirs of Constantine Dix," etc.).

Paine, Thomas (1737–1809). Brit. author and reformer, **2474.**

Painlevé (pan-le-vā), **Paul** (1863–1933). Fr. statesman; minister for war (1916 and 1926–29); premier in 1917 and 1925; minister for air in 1932; also eminent in science and philosophy.

Painted Desert, in Arizona, U.S.A., 234.

Painted Lady butterfly,*plate f. 632.*

Painting, history of, **2475**; anc., *1523*, *1524*, *1528*, *1536*, *1115*, *1119*; cave men, 736, *plate f. 736*; *plate f. 2080*, *plate f. 2084*; Chinese, *812*, *1881*; composition, *1274*; Dutch and Flemish, 2324, 2476; early Christian, 2052; Eng., 1177, *1185–92*, 2476; Fr., *1369–1376*, 1377; Ger., 1454; Gk., 1528; Impressionism and post-impressionism, 1687, 2476, 2477; Indian, 1708; It., 1775; Japanese technique, 1809, 1881; Pre-Raphaelite, 2232, 2476; paints, 2479; processes, 2476; Renaissance, 2476, 2766; Roman, 2812, *2817*; Russian, 2854; Spanish, 3040; Surrealism, 3122; watercolours, 3352. *See also* **Fine Arts**, **Drawing**; **Perspective**; tables in 3930–31; and chief artists by name.

Paints and varnishes, **2477**; aluminium, 2478; cellulose, 740; gums, 1556; gypsum base, 1559; lacquer, 1881; lead in, 1908, 2478, 3284;

luminous, 2574; pyroxylin, 2709; resins, 2478, 2767; turpentine, 2478, 3268; zinc salts in, 3443.

Paisley. Scot. mfg. centre in Renfrewshire, 7 m. s.w. of Glasgow; pop. 92,700; cotton thread and textiles; 2767, 2890.

Pak'enham, Francis A. Pakenham, 1st Baron (b. 1905). Brit. politician; personal asst. to Sir W. (later Lord) Beveridge 1941–44; under-sec. for War 1946; min. of Civil Aviation 1948.

Pakistan. Moslem Dom. of N.W. and N.E. India created by partition of 1947; a. 360,935 sq. m. (W. Pakistan 306,920 sq. m.; E. Pakistan 54,015 sq. m.); pop. est. 80 million; **2479**, 1692; *map, 1702*; formation, 1716, 3283; Karachi proclaimed cap. in May 1948.

Palaeobot'any, 533.

Palaeolith'ic Age. The Old Stone Age, before the use of metals; culture survived in recent times, 3095; cave dwellers, 734, 2080.

Palaeontol'ogy. The science of fossils, 434, 1354, 2678; evidence of evolution, 1244.

Palaeozo'ic Era, in geology, 1432, 1433.

Palamedes (pal-a-mē'-dēz). In Gk. myth., Trojan War hero, 2421.

Pal'amon and Arcite. Chaucer's story of, retold, 762.

Palanquin (pal-an-kēn'). Covered litter for carrying passengers.

Palate. The roof of the mouth; it consists of the hard palate in front and the soft palate behind; the former has a bony framework, while the latter is composed of muscular fibres, enclosed by a movable fold of mucous membrane, *3163.*

Palat'inate, The, or Rhenish Palatinate (Ger. *Rheinpfalz*). Prov. of Bavaria, Ger., lying w. of Rhine; Heidelberg former cap., 1604; laid waste by Louis XIV, 2029.

Palatine (pal'-*a*-tīn) **Hill.** Central and earliest settled of the 7 hills of Rome; its rectangular shape gave name *Roma quadrata* to primitive city founded, according to legend, by Romulus; 2799, 2804.

Palawan (pa-lah'-wahn). Westernmost of the larger isls. of the Philippines; 4,500 sq. m.; 2568.

Pale, in heraldry, 1614.

Pale, The, in Ireland, 1745.

Palembang. Port of Sumatra, Indonesia. pop. 109,000; on r. Musi, 45 m. from its mouth; export trade; makes silk, gold articles and weapons; 3118. Heavy fighting and air raids during Japanese occupation 1942–45.

Palermo (pa-ler'-mō). Spt. and largest city of Sicily on N.W. coast; pop. 452,400; military post; exports fruit, sulphur; univ.; *2968*, 2969; silk-weaving, 3191. Occupation by U.S. forces, July 1943.

Palestine. Country of the E. Mediterranean, s. of Syria; about 10,000 sq. m. pop. 1,933,670: **2480**: *plates f. 2480*, *2481*; *map*, *2136*; agric., *2431*; Beth'ehem, 422; Hebrew language, 1600; Jerusalem, 1819, *1820*; Jesus Christ in, 1822, 2480; Jews, 1829; named from Philistines, 2480, 2570; Nazareth, *2309*, 2480. *History*, 1829; wars between Philistines and Israelites, 2570; David, 979;

Solomon, 2999 ; Assyrian conquest,
330 ; Crusades, 000 ; in 1st World
War, 121, 3411, 3414 ; Brit. mandatory, 581, 2482 ; Zionism, 2482
Arab-Jewish war, 2483, 3146, 3238 ;
formation of state of Israel, 2483.

Palestrina (pa-les-trē'-na), **Giovanni
Pierluigi da** (1524–94). It. composer
and master of sacred music, reformer
of Rom. Church music, 2263.

Paley, William (1743–1805), Eng.
clergyman and philosopher, chiefly
remembered for his " argument from
design " to prove the existence of
God (" Evidences of Christianity " ;
" Natural Theology ").

Palgrave, Francis Turner (1824–97).
Eng. critic and poet (anthology,
" Golden Treasury of English Songs
and Lyrics ").

Pali (pah'-lē) (Sanskrit " sacred text ").
An anc. language of N. India, surviving in Burma, Ceylon, and Siam ;
language of Buddhism, 601.

Palimpsests (pal'-imp-sests) (Gk.
" scraped again "). Manuscripts,
425.

Paling, Rt. Hon. Wilfred (b. 1883).
Postmaster-General 1947.

Palissy, Bernard (c. 1510–89). Fr.
artist, potter, naturalist and writer ;
one of first men in Europe to formu-
late correct theory of fossils (" Autobiography ") ; discovers new enamelling process, 2666, 2669.

Palladian architecture. Gk. origin,
1538 ; Inigo Jones and, 1837.

Palladio (pa-lah'-dē-ō), **Andrea** (1518–
80). It. architect of late Renaissance
from whom the classical It. style
called " Palladian " is named.

Palladium (pa-lā'-di-um). An image
of Pallas Athene, especially the
one (said to have fallen from heaven)
which was kept at Troy and believed
to be a safeguard of the city.

Palladium (Pd.). Rare white metallic
element of the ruthenium group ;
atomic weight 106·7 ; found alloyed
with gold ; melts at 2,822° F. ; used
as a catalyst and absorbent for
hydrogen ; properties, 777 ; in
white gold, 1481 ; found with
platinum, 2627.

Pallas (pal'-as). In Gk. myth. *See*
Athena.

Pall Mall (pel-mel). London street
famous for clubs, between Pall Mall
East and St. James's Palace.

Pall-mall. Old Fr. game, brought to
Eng. in reign of Charles I ; balls
were driven with mallets through
iron hoops fixed in a long alley of
about 800 yards ; gave name to the
London street.

Palm (pahm). A tropical tree, 2483,
2484, 1931 ; coconut, 862 ; date,
978 ; monocotyledon, 3247 ; nuts,
2408 ; oil, 1263 ; royal, 941 ;
trunk, 3246 ; vegetable ivory, 632,
1788.

Palm. From sallow willow, 3382.

Palma, Jacopo or **Giacomo** (c. 1480–
1528). It. painter of Venetian
school ; called Palma Vecchio (" The
Elder ") ; strongly influenced first
by Bellini, later by Giorgione ; work
characterized by rich colouring and
brilliant lighting.

Palma, Jacopo (c. 1544–1628). Venetian painter, called " the Younger "
to distinguish him from his great-
uncle.

Palma. Sp. port and cap. of Majorca,
largest of Balearic Isles, at head of
Bay of Palma ; pop. 131,950 ; lively
trade ; numerous mfrs. ; Gothic
cath. with tomb of James II (d.
1311), chief naval and air base of
insurgents in Spanish Civil War
(1936 onwards) ; 342.

Palmaceae (pal-mā'-sē-ē). The palm
family of plants, 2485.

Palma dum. Nuts of doom (*not* door)
palm, 633.

Palmas (pahl'-mas), **Cape.** On w.
coast of Africa ; *map f. 68.*

Palmate leaves, 1916.

Palm Beach, Florida, U.S.A. Fashionable winter resort on S.E. coast, on
a peninsula ; cut off from mainland
by L. Worth, an arm of Atlantic ;
residential pop. 3,740.

Palm cabbage. Terminal bud of
various palms, 804.

Palmers. Pilgrims returning from
Palestine, who carried with them
palm branches as evidence of their
pilgrimage.

Palmerston (pahm'-er-ston), **Henry
John Temple, 3rd Viscount** (1784–
1865). Eng. statesman ; War
min., 1809-28 ; Foreign Sec., 1830–
41 and 1846–51 ; Prime Minister,
1855–58 and 1859–65 ; a forcible
champion of Brit. rights and a
champion of the oppressed ; premiership, 3278.

Palmetto. A type of fan palm.

Palm oil, 2485, 1263.

Palm Sunday. Last before Easter, 1074.

Palmyra (pal-mū'-ra), Syria. Anc.
city ; cap. of former kingdom ; **2485.**

Palomar, Mt., California. Telescope,
2191, 3178, 3179, 3180.

Palos. Sp. tn on w. coast 55 m.
s.w. of Seville ; pop. about 1,900 ;
Columbus sails from, 879.

Paludrine. Valuable anti-malarial drug
discovered and used 2nd World War.

" Pam'ela, or Virtue Rewarded." Novel
by Richardson ; 1213, 2402.

Pamir (pa-mēr'). Plateau in cent. Asia
at convergence of Hindu Kush,
Himalaya, Kuenlun, and Tien Shan
Mts. ; 267.

Pam'pas. Argentine plains ; cattle
and sheep are extensively reared and
wheat is largely cultivated ; 226.

Pampas deer, 985.

Pamphylia (pam-fil'-i-a). Anc. moun-
tainous region on s. coast of Asia
Minor ; successively under rule of
Lydia, Persia, Macedon, Syria, and
Rome ; chief cities were originally
Gk. colonies.

Pan. In Gk. myth, god of flocks and
pastures, **2485.**

Panama City (pan-a-mah'). Cap. and
chief Pacific port of Republic of
Panama on Gulf of Panama at s.
terminus of Panama Rly. ; pop.
111,000 ; 2486 ; Morgan sacks, 2229.

Panama, Isthmus of. Strip of land
connecting N. and S. Amer. ; runs
E. to W. in form of an **S** ; usually
regarded as co-extensive with Republic of Panama ; average width 70
m. ; 2486.

Panama, Republic of. The southernmost of the Cent. Amer. states ;
28,576 sq. m. ; pop. 622,600 ; **2486** ;
map, 743 ; tagua nuts, 633.

Panama Canal, 2486, 2491, 689 ; locks,
2492, 2493 ; mosquito pest, 2236,
2489 ; S. Amer. and, 3024 ; U.S.A.
and, 3291.

Panama hats, 1584, 1083.

Pan-American Conference or **Congress.**
Name given to meetings of delegates
from countries of N., S., and Cent.
Amer. to consider questions of
mutual interest.

Pan-American Union. Official organization of the Republics of N. and S.
Amer. maintained at Washington
since 1890 for development of commerce and friendship, 2531, 3027.

Panathenaea (pan-ath-e-nē-a). Oldest
and most important of anc. Athenian
festivals in honour of goddess
Athena, 284.

Panay. Isl. nearly in centre of Philippine group, 6th in size ; 4,448 sq.
m. ; pop. 800,000 ; in Japanese
occupation 1942–45 ; Iloilo chief
city, 250 m. from Manila ; sugar,
rice, and copra chief crops.

Panay, U.S. gunboat, sunk in Chinese
waters by Japs in 1937.

Panchromatic film, in photography,
2579.

Pancreas (pan'-krē-as). A gland in the
abdomen, 1470 ; function in digestion, 1017.

Panda. Bear-like animal, **2494.**

Panda'nus tree. Tropical tree or shrub.
also called screw-pine, 2471.

Pan'dects, of Justinian, 1844.

Pando'ra. In Gk. myth., the first
woman, **2494.**

Panel. In architecture, an area on a
wall, etc., sunk below the general
surface of the surrounding work ;
also a compartment in a sunken
ceiling, bay or wainscot.

Panel. A register of doctors in a dist.
attending persons under the National
Health scheme.

Pan-Germanism. A movement, fostered by the Nazis, which conceived
Ger. people wherever situated as
forming one nationally ; others
proclaimed ultimate dominion of
Ger. race.

Panhard. Fr. engineer, and the motor-
car, 2241.

Pan'icle. A compound flower-cluster,
1321 ; of oats, 2411.

Panicum. A genus of grasses including
millets.

Pank'hurst, Dame Christabel (b. 1880).
Eng. militant suffragette ; helped her
mother in " suffragette " movement ;
imprisoned several times ; edited
" The Suffragette."

Pankhurst, Emmeline (1858–1928). Eng.
militant suffragette leader ; founded
in 1903 Women's Social and Political
Union, and, with her daughters,
Christabel and Sylvia, led campaign
of " suffragette " violence ; 3280.

Pankhurst, Sylvia (b. 1882). Eng. militant suffragette ; joined extreme
Socialist party ; edited " Worker's
Dreadnought," and imprisoned in
1921 for articles in it.

Panning, method of obtaining minerals,
2182.

Pannonia. Prov. of Roman Empire,
lying s. and w. of Danube ; Illyrians
were probably original inhabitants.

Panopticon. Bentham's invention, 415.

Pansa, house of, 2653.

Pan-Slavism. Movement toward political and cultural union of nations
of Slavic descent ; influenced Austro-
Hungarian politics, N. and S. Slavs
tending toward united action against
Magyars and Germans ; congresses
held in 1848 at Prague, in 1867 at
Moscow, and in 1908 at Prague ;
formation of Czechoslovakia and
Yugoslavia was a partial realization
of Pan-Slavism.

Pansy or **Heartsease.** Various species
of viola, both wild and cultivated ;
2494.

Pantag'ruel. Giant in Rabelais' satire,
" Gargantua and Pantagruel " ; son
of Gargantua and the last of a giant
race, he is boisterous and, as his
name is thought to imply, all-
thirsty ; the book is an amazing
medley of buffoonery, learning, and
philosophy ; 2722.

Pantelleria (pan-tel-la-rē'-a) or **Pan-
talaria.** Volcanic isl. in Mediterranean, 62 m. s.w. of Sicily ; belongs
to prov. of Trapani, Sicily ; 45 sq. m. ;
exports wine, raisins, fortified naval
base ; chief tn. Pantelleria (pop.
9,000) ; taken by bombing, June
1943.

Pan'theism. Belief that the universe
as a whole is God ; in Brahmanism,
1626.

Pantheon (pan-thē'-on), Rome, 2802.

Panthéon (pahn-tā-awn), Paris. Formerly church of Ste. Geneviève,
begun in 1764 ; secularized at Revolution and dedicated to great men
of nation ; later again used as
church, but finally secularized by
decree of 1885 ; 1650, 2517.

Pan'ther. The leopard, 1927 ; also
type of Ger. tank, 3152.

Panther. Ger. warship which visited
Agadir in 1911, 2230.

Pan'tomime, old and modern, **2495.**

Pan'zer (Ger. " iron-clad "). Ger.
armoured div. of 2nd World War.

Papacy. Office and dignity of the
Pope, **2495** ; origin, 2495, 2562 ;
early growth of papal power, 1238 ;
and Charlemagne, 753 ; investiture
conflict, 1449, 1542, 1609, 3380 ;
Crusades, 936 ; submission of John
of England, 1834 ; struggle with
Frederick II and overthrow of
Hohenstaufens, 1389 ; conflict with
Henry II of England, 389 ; dominated by France during "Babylonian
Captivity," 1543 ; Great Schism,
1660, 3298 ; Inquisition, 1726 ;
Luther attacks, 2040 ; Reformation,
2759 ; relations with Henry VIII,
1612 ; Counter-Reformation, 2760,
2034 ; and Italian unity, 1769 ;

MASTERS OF THE PAINTER'S ART

		NETHERLANDS	ITALY	FRANCE
Pre-1200	NOTE.—This chart gives a bird's-eye view of the Schools of Painting in the West through seven centuries. It is divided vertically into countries, horizontally into periods. The heavy lines indicate the main periods. Some small schools (e.g., Spanish and American) have been compressed to give due space to the greater ones (Italy, France, Britain). The Modern Continental and Modern British schools will be found in the two right-hand columns of the chart.		**Early Christian** (Catacomb frescoes) **Byzantine** (Mural decorations)	
1200–1400		**Flemish** Jan van Eyck (1370–1441) Hubert van Eyck (1390–1426)	**Trecento (Florence)** Cimabue (1240 ?–1300) Giotto (1266–1336) Agnolo (d. 1348) Orcagna (1308–58) **(Sienese)** Taddeo Gaddi (c. 1300–66) Lippo Memmi (d. 1357) Simone Martini (1389–1443) **Quattrocento (Florence)** Ucello (1397–1475) Fra Angelico (1387–1455) Andrea del Castagno (1390–1457)	
1400–1500	**GERMANY** Conrad Witz (1400–47) Wolgemuth (1434–1519) Martin Schongauer (c. 1445–91). Holbein the Elder (1462–1524) Dürer (1471–1528) Cranach (1472–1553) Holbein the Younger (1497–1553) Grünewald (1483–1529)	Van der Weyden (c. 1410–67) Memling (1430–94) Van der Goes (c. 1420–82) Hieronimus Bosch (1450–1516) Gerard David (c. 1460–1523) Quentin Matsys (1466–1530) Patinir (1485 ?–1524) Van Orley (c. 1490–1542) Lucas van Leyden (1494–1533) Mabuse (c. 1470–1532)	Masaccio (1400–28) Filippo Lippi (1406–69) Verrocchio (1435–88) Botticelli (1446–1510) Ghirlandaio (1449–94) **(Umbria)** Piero della Francesca (c. 1423–92) Perugino (c. 1450–1524) Pinturicchio (1454–1513) **(Padua)** Mantegna (1431–1506) **(Venice)** Jacopo Bellini (c. 1400–70) Gentile Bellini (c. 1429–1507) Giovanni Bellini (c. 1430–1516) Carpaccio (c. 1460–1520) **Cinquecento (Florence)** Fra Bartolommeo (1475–1517) Andrea del Sarto (1486–1531) **(Milan)** Leonardo da Vinci (1452–1519) **(Rome)** Michelangelo (1475–1564) Raphael (*also* **Umbrian**) (1483–1520) **(Parma)** Correggio (1494–1534) **(Venice)** Titian (1477–1576) Giorgione (1478–1510) Palma Vecchio (1480–1528)	Jehan Fouquet (c. 1415–85) François Clouet (c. 1510–70) Vouet (1590–1649) Nicholas Poussin (1594–1665) Claude Lorrain (1600–82) P. de Champaigne (1602–74) Le Nain (brothers) (c. 1600–77)
1500–1700		Pieter Brueghel (c. 1526–69) Jan Brueghel (1568–1625) Pieter Brueghel the Younger (1564–1638) Rubens (1577–1640) Van Dyck (1599–1641) Jordaens (1593–1678) Lely (*see* Britain) David Teniers (1610–90) **Dutch**		Gaspard Poussin (Dughuet) (1613–75) Le Sueur (1617–55) Charles Le Brun (1621–57) Mignard (1606–68) Largilliére (1650–1746)
	Kneller (1646–1723) (worked in England)	Hals (1584–1666) Rembrandt (1606–69) Steen (c. 1626–73) Ter Borch (1608–81) Gerard Dou (1613–75) De Hooch (1630–77) Metsu (c. 1630–67) Vermeer (1632–75) A. van Ostade (1610–85) I. van Ostade (1621–49) Cuyp (1605–91) Paul Potter (1625–54) Van Goyen (1596–1656) Koninck (1616–89) Ruysdael (c. 1628–79) Hobbema (1638–1709) Backhuysen (1631–1708) W. van de Velde (1633–1707) A. van de Velde (1639–71)	**Seicento (Venice)** Tintoretto (1518–94) Veronese (1528–88) **(Bolognese Eclectics)** Carracci (1560–1609) Guido Reni (1574–1642) Domenichino (1581–1641) Guercino (1590–1666) Sassoferato (1609–85) **("Naturalists") (Spanish-Neapolitan)** Caravaggio (1569–1609) Salvator Rosa (1615–73) **Baroque** Giordano (1632–1705) Tiepolo (1693–1770) **Venice, last period** Canaletto (1697–1768)	Rigaud (1659–1745) Watteau (1684–1721) Nattier (1685–1766) Pater (1690–1736) Lancret (1690–1743) Chardin (1699–1779) Boucher (c. 1703–70) La Tour (1704–88) Vernet (1714–89) Greuze (1725–1805) Fragonard (1732–1806) Vigée-Lebrun (1755–1842) **Classicists** David (1748–1825) Prud'hon (1758–1823) Gros (1771–1835) Ingres (1781–1867) Géricault (1791–1824) **Romantics** Delacroix (1798–1863)
1700–1800	Mengs (1728–79) Angelica Kauffman (1741–1807) (worked in England)	Wiertz (1806–65) Israels (1824–1911) Rops (1823–90) Maris (1837–99) Mauve (1838–88)	Longhi (1702–82) Guardi (1712–93)	**Barbizon School** Corot (1796–1875) Rousseau (1812–67) Millet (1814–75) Courbet (1819–77) Daumier (1808–79) Boudin (1824–98) Puvis de Chavannes (1826–98) Fantin-Latour (1834–1903)

BRITAIN	SPAIN	MODERN CONTINENTAL	MODERN BRITISH
Illumination Irish-Romanesque Books of Kells Lindisfarne Gospels Winchester School (Anglo-Saxon)	Rodrigo Esteban (c. 1290) Starnina (1354 ?–1408 ?) Berruguete (1480–1561)	**Impressionists : French** Pissarro (1830–1903) Manet (1832–83) Degas (1834–1917) Sisley (1840–99) Monet (1840–1926) Berthe Morisot (1841–95) Renoir (1841–1919) Seurat (1859–71) "Douanier" Rousseau (1844–1910)	**Impressionists** Clausen (1852–1944) Wilson Steer (1860–1942) Sickert (1860–1942) Tonks (1862–1938) Lucien Pissarro (1863–1944) **Glasgow School** Lavery (1856–1941) Crawhall (1861–1913) D. Y. Cameron (1865–1945)
Bury St. Edmunds (Anglo-Norman) Matthew Paris Bedford Book of Hours **Mural Decorators (Religious)** Chichester Canterbury Hardham Easby, etc. Eton College Paintings	Morales (1509–68) Vargas (1502–68) El Greco (c. 1548–1614) Ribalta (1551–1626) de las Roelas (1558–1625) Hernandez (c. 1576–1636) Ribera (1588–1656) Zurbaran (1598–1661) Velazquez (1599–1660) Murillo (1617–82) Coello (1630–93) Goya (1746–1828)	**Dutch** Jongkind (1819–91) **German** Menzel (1815–1905) Liebermann (1847–1933) Corrinth (b. 1894) Slevogt (1868–1932) **Scandinavia** Munch (1863–1944) Zorn (1860–1920) **Spain** Sorolla (1863–1923) Zuloaga (1870–1945) **Post-Impressionists** Cezanne (1839–1906) Gauguin (1849–1903) Van Gogh (1853–90) Toulouse-Lautrec (1864–1901) Matisse (b. 1869)	Arnesby Brown (b. 1856) Tuke (1858–1936) Strang (1859–1921) Brangwyn (b. 1867) Rothenstein (1872–1945) William Nicholson (b. 1872) McEvoy (1878–1927) Orpen (1878–1931) John (b. 1879) Munnings (b. 1878) **Camden Town (later London) Group** Roger Fry (1866–1935) Gilman (1876–1919) Ginner (b. 1879) Gore (1878–1914) Vanessa Bell (b. 1879) Wyndham Lewis (b. 1884) Duncan Grant (b. 1885) Paul Nash (1889–1946) John Nash (b. 1893) Roberts (b. 1895) Ethel Walker (b. 1867) Laura Knight Mary McEvoy
Miniaturists Hilliard (1547–1619) Isaac Oliver (c. 1567–1617) Peter Oliver (1594–1647) J. Hoskins (d. 1664) Cooper (c. 1609–72) Samuel Gibson (1615–90) Nathaniel Hone (1718–84) Smart (1741–1811) Cosway (1742–1821) Englehart (1750–1829) Andrew Plimmer (1763–1837) **Portraits (Flemish)** Gheeraerts (c. 1561–1635) Mytens (c. 1590–1642) Cornelius Jonson (1593–1664) Lely (1618–80) **Portraits (British)** Walker (c. 1600–c. 1660) Dobson (1610–46) Riley (1646–91) Hogarth (1697–1764) Thornhill (1675–1734)	**AMERICA** Copley (1737–1815) Benjamin West (1738–1820) Gilbert Stuart (1754–1828) George Inness (1825–94) **Impressionists** Whistler (1834–1903) Winslow Homer (1836–1910) Mary Cassatt (1845–1926) Sargent (1856–1925) A. B. Davies (1862–1928) Bellows (1882–1925) Rockwell Kent (b. 1882) Childe Hassam Theodore Robinson Jonas Lie Gifford Beal Alexander Brook Georgia O'Keefe Grant Wood	**Cubists** Picasso (b. 1881) Gris (1888–1927) Braque (b. 1881) Utrillo (b. 1883) Vuillard (1868–1940) Vlaminck (b. 1876) Derain (b. 1880) Rouault (b. 1871) Soutine (b. 1894) **Italian Futurism** Carra (b. 1881) Severini (b. 1883) **Other Modern (Surrealists, etc.)** Joan Miro Dali Pierre Roy Chirico Beaudin (b. 1895) Ozenfant Bonnard (1867–1947) **German Moderns** Kandinsky (1866–1944) Klee (1879–1940) Marc (1880–1916) Ernst (b. 1894)	Lamb (b. 1885) Nevinson (1889–1946) Stanley Spencer (b. 1892) Ben Nicholson (b. 1894) Wadsworth (b. 1889) Henry Moore (b. 1898) Graham Sutherland (b. 1903) John Piper (b. 1903) John Armstrong (b. 1893) Edward Burra (b. 1905)
Hudson (1701–79) Devis (1711–87) Ramsay (1713–84) Reynolds (1723–92) Gainsborough (1726–88) Romney (1734–1802) Raeburn (1756–1823) Hoppner (1759–1810) Morland (1763–1804) Lawrence (1769–1830) Etty (1787–1849)	**Landscape and Watercolour** Alex. Cozens (c. 1698–1786) Samuel Scott (1710–72) Richard Wilson (1714–82) Sandby (1725–1809) John R. Cozens (1752–97) Blake (1757–1827) Crome (1769–1821) Girtin (1775–1802) Turner (1775–1851) Constable (1776–1837) Cotman (1782–1842) Cox (1783–1859) de Wint (1784–1849) Copley Fielding (1787–1855)		
Landseer (1802–73) Alfred Stevens (1817–75) Watts (1817–1904) Ford Madox Brown (1821–93) Holman Hunt (1827–1910) Rossetti (1828–82) Millais (1829–96) Leighton (1830–96) Burne-Jones (1833–98) Alma-Tadema (1836–1912)	Lear (1812–88) Brabazon (1821–1906) Birket Foster (1825–99) A. W. Rich (1856–1922) Holmes (1868–1936) C. A. Hunt (b. 1873) Russell Flint (b. 1880)		NOTE.—During the 20th century, painters have tended more and more to form small groups, often very ephemeral, each following one or two "innovators" (as the **Cubists** followed **Gris** and **Picasso**), rather than definite schools. In each country, however, there has been the steady undercurrent of Academism with its single, popular appeal.

loses and regains temporal power, 1769, 2615 ; Vatican State, 3306. *Church Councils* : Constance, 1660 ; Nicaea, 1074, 893 ; Trent, 2760. For lists of Popes *see* **Pope.**

Papal States, 2496 ; origins, 2748, 1238 ; joined United Italy, 1769. *See also* **Papacy ; Vatican City.**

Papa'ver. The poppy genus, 2655.

Papaw. Tropical tree with orange-coloured fruit, 1401.

Papeete (pa-pā-ē'-tē). Cap. of Tahiti and other Fr. isls of E. Pacific.

Papen, Franz von (b. 1879). German politician ; Chancellor in 1932 ; Ger. Min. in Vienna ; ambass. to Turkey (1939–44) ; tried by Allies as war criminal at Nuremburg (1945–46) and acquitted, but sentenced by Germans to 8 yrs. in a labour camp.

Paper, 2496 ; anc. and medieval writing materials, 509, 510, 2496, 2500 ; from bamboo, 353 ; variety of materials used, 739 ; from mulberry, 2250 ; from papyrus, 2500 ; sizes of, 512 ; titanium in mfr., 3217.

Paper birch. A species of birch from which birchbark canoes are made.

Paper measure. *See in Index* **Weights and Measures.**

Paper money, 2202.

Paper mulberry. A bushy mulberry used in paper-making, 2497, 2250 ; in Japan, 1798 ; on Pacific isls., 2472.

Paper nautilus. The argonaut, 230.

Paphlagonia (paf-la-gō'-ni-a). Anc. country of Asia Minor on Black Sea ; subdued by Croesus ; later became part of Rom. prov. of Galatea and Bithynia ; made separate prov. by Constantine.

Paphos (pā'-fos). Name of 2 anc. cities on w. coast of isl. of Cyprus ; Old Paphos, founded about 10th cent. B.C., was chief seat of worship of Aphrodite ; New Paphos was cap. of isl. in Rom. times.

Papier mâché (pa'-pyā ma'-shā). Paper product resembling wood, made by mixing glue, paste, oil, and resin with paper pulp and compressing it in a mould ; boxes, buttons, vases, trays, and other articles are made with it ; also lacquerware, 1881.

Papil'lae, of skin, 1572, 2980 ; taste buds, 3157, *3223.*

Papin (pah-pan'), **Denis** (1647–1712). Fr. physicist, greatly improved air-pump, conceived idea of pneumatic transmission of power, invented the steam digester, 3084, 3085 ; constructs piston engine, 3085.

Papineau (pa-pē-nō'), **Louis Joseph** (1786–1871). Leader of Fr.-Canadian rebellion of 1837 ; his ideas of reform aimed at the complete independence of Fr. Canada ; results of rebellion, 2715.

Paprika (pap'-rē-ka). A red pepper, 2547.

Papua (pap'-ū-a), **Territory of,** S.E. New Guinea and neighbouring isls. ; 90,540 sq. m. ; est. pop. 338,800 ; admin. by Australia ; formerly called Brit. New Guinea ; name also applied to New Guinea as a whole ; 2340 ; natives, *2339, 2340, 2341* ; 2nd World War, 3421. *See also* **New Guinea.**

Papyrus (pa-pī'-rus). A plant and the paper made from it, **2500,** *509,* 2496 ; Bible manuscript, *424* ; manuscripts at Pompeii, 2654.

Pará (pa-rah') (official name Belem), Brazil. Spt. in N. on R. Pará, 55 m. from Atlantic ; pop. 293,000 ; rly. connexions with Braganza ; rubber, 554, 3022.

Pará. R. in Brazil ; estuary of the Tocantins and also one of mouths of the Amazon.

Parabol'ic reflector, 1945.

Paracelsus (par-a-sel'-sus). Assumed name of Theophrastus Bombastus von Hohenheim (1493–1541), German-Swiss physician and chemist ; scientific theories were advanced for his age ; hero of Browning's poem " Paracelsus."

Parachute (pa'-ra-shōōt). The airman's " lifeboat," **2509 ;** ejector parachutes, 2510 ; Leonardo's work on, 2510 ; troops dropped by, *251.*

Paradise, in Dante's " Divine Comedy," 971.

Paradise, birds of, 2511 ; *frontis., Vol. 6.*

" Paradise Lost." Epic poem by Milton, 1211, 2178 ; story of, 2178, *2179.*

Paraffin oil or kerosene. A fuel oil distilled from petroleum, 1888, 2426, 2429 ; in blowlamps, 477 ; engine, 1737 ; in picnic stoves, etc., 1289 ; in jet propulsion, 1828.

Paraffins, a group of hydrocarbons named after paraffin oil which is a mixture of several paraffins, 3687.

Paraffin wax. A white wax obtained from petroleum, coal-tar, and shale oils, 3359 ; process of obtaining, 2429 ; used in candles, 691.

Paragonite, one of the mica group of minerals, 2160.

Paraguay (par'-a-gwā). A country of S. Amer. ; a. (excl. Gran Chaco), 61,647 sq. m. ; pop. (est.) 1,141,400 ; **2511 ;** *map, plate f. 3024* ; disputes with Bolivia, 491 ; products and industries, 2512 ; war with Brazil, 554 ; war with Uruguay, 3299 ; women cigar-makers, *3026* ; yerba maté, 3160.

Paraguay River. Chief tributary of the Parana ; rises in s.w. Brazil, flows s. through Paraguay ; length about 1,500 m. ; chief commercial outlet for Paraguay, 552, 2511.

Paraguay tea, 2511. *See* **Maté.**

Par'allax, of stars, 3078.

Parallel, form of elec. circuit, *1129,* 3235.

Parallelepi'ped, in geometry, 1437.

Parallel'ogram, in geometry, 1437.

Parallelogram of forces, in mechanics : diagram for finding resultant of two forces, *2127.*

Par'allels, in geometry, 1437 ; of latitude, 1898, 2093.

Parallel-veined leaf, 1915.

Paralysis ; some causes, 2259. *See also* **Infantile Paralysis.**

Para-magnetic, weakly magnetic, 2062.

Paramaribo (par-a-ma'-ri-bō). Cap. and trade centre of Dutch Guiana, S. Amer. ; pop. 60,720 ; on estuary of R. Surinam, 17 m. from sea ; good harbour, 2 forts, 1553.

Parana (pa-ra-nah'), 2nd largest r. of S. Amer. ; rises in s.-cent. Brazil ; flows s.w. nearly 2,000 m., 552, 2511.

Parana pine, tree, 2611.

Par'apet, in architecture, a wall raised breast-high ; the upper part of a wall, bridge, balcony, or terrace ; the upper part of a house which is above the springing of a roof and guards the gutter.

Parasites (par'-a-sītz). Animals or plants living at expense of other organisms, **2512,** 432 ; barnacles, 361 ; fleas, 1313 ; flies, 1329 ; fungi, 1407, *plate f. 1408,* 1932, 2514, 2620 ; ichneumon flies, 1685 ; mildews and moulds, *2173* ; mistletoe, *2194* ; mosquitoes, 2236 ; rusts and smuts, 2857 ; scale insects, 2878, *2879.*

Parasol ants, the leaf-cutting ants of tropical America ; genus Atta : *166.*

Parathy'roid, a gland, 1471.

Par'avane, device to protect ships from mines, consisting of a serrated wire and oropesa float, 2186.

Parcae (pahr'-sē). Latin name for the three Fates who ruled the destiny of man.

Parcel post, 2261.

Parchment, writing material made of goat, sheep, or calf skin, 2496 ; in bookmaking, 510.

Pardon, for prisoners ; in Gt. Brit. this right rests solely with the sovereign, who is advised by the Home Secretary.

Paré, Ambroise (1510–90), Fr. surgeon to four kings ; saved Charles IX at St. Bartholomew's Eve ; first to use artery ligatures after amputations ; *2134.*

Parenchyma (pa-ren'-ki-ma). Parent tissue of plants.

Paren'thesis (brackets). Use of, 2705.

Pareto (pa-rā'-tō) **Vilfredo** (1848–1923). sociologist, and author of " Manuel d'économie politique."

Pargeting (pahr'-je-ting). In architecture, various kinds of plaster-work, notably decorative plaster-work in raised ornamental figures, largely used in internal and external decoration of 16th and 17th cent. houses. Also smooth chimney lining.

Pariahs (pah'-ri-az). Outcasts among
► Hindus.

Parini (pa-rē'-nē), **Giuseppe** (1729–99). It. poet, criticized society in beautiful blank verse.

Paris. Trojan warrior, **2514,** 3249.

Paris. Cap. of Fr. ; pop. 2,725,000 ; **2514,** 1360 ; *plates f. 2516, 2517* ; history, *1367,* 1385, 1394, 1395, 2518, 3347 ; Bastille, *1395* ; Louvre, 2032, *2033,* 2517 ; La Madeleine, *plate f. 2517* ; Notre Dame, *2519, plate f. 2516,* 2567 ; Opera House, *2516* ; Place de la Concorde, *2515, 2516* ; Seine, 2919, 2514, *2515, plate f. 2516* ; siege (in 1870), 1385 ; university, 3296 ; Versailles, 3317, *3318* ; in both World Wars. 2518, 3417 ; liberation in 1944, 1453, 3422.

Paris, Declaration of (1856), 3240 ; and blockade, 473.

Paris, Treaties of : (1763), 1366, 2925 ; (1783), 146 ; (1856), 2841.

Paris, University of. One of the largest and oldest universities in the world ; important in Middle Ages, gradually declined until abolished at Fr. Rev. ; re-established in 1896 ; faculties of letters, science, theology, law, medicine ; early years, 2518 ; early postal system, 2661.

Par'ish, unit of local govt., originally ecclesiastical ; several parishes are combined into rural or urban dists.

Parish Council. Formed in parishes of 300 pop. and upwards ; if under, **parish meeting** (which cannot levy a rate) usually performs local business.

Parity of exchange, 1349.

Park, Air Chief Marshal Sir Keith R. (b. 1892). N.Z. air ace of 1st World War ; in 1940 provided air cover for Dunkirk evacuation ; commanded No. 11 fighter group in Battle of Britain ; 1942–43 A.O.C. Malta ; Allied A.O.C.-in-C. S.E. Asia Command 1944–46.

Park, Mungo (1771–1806). Scot. explorer of Africa, **2521.**

Parker, Sir Gilbert (1862–1932). Brit. novelist and politician, b. in Canada ; entered Parl. in 1900 ; among his best-known books are " Pierre and His People," " The Right of Way," " The Seats of the Mighty," 685.

Parker, Sir Hyde (1714–82). Brit. vice-admiral ; had a distinguished career ; fought a fierce and indecisive battle with the Dutch off Dogger Bank in 1781.

Parker, Sir Hyde (1739–1807). Eng. admiral, second son of above ; fought in the War of Amer. Independence ; he was in command of the bombardment of Copenhagen in 1801, when Nelson's victory, following his refusal to act on Parker's signal to withdraw (the famous blind eye incident), led to the latter's recall.

Parker, Joseph (1830–1902). Eng. Congregational preacher ; built the City Temple, London, in 1874.

Parker, Louis Napoleon (1852–1944). Eng. dramatist and producer of pageants.

Parkes, Alexander (1813–90). Brit. chemist and prolific inventor ; first to make celluloid in 1855 ; 2625.

Park Lane. Fashionable thoroughfare in London, extending between Piccadilly and Marble Arch, bordered on w. by Hyde Park and E. by Mayfair ; once notable for its many palatial mansions, now mostly hotels ; Thornycroft fountain demolished in 1949.

Parkman, Francis (1823–93). Amer. historian, author of " The Oregon Trail," " The Conspiracy of Pontiac," " Montcalm and Wolfe," " A Half-Century of Conflict."

Park Row. Famous street of New York City, U.S.A., 2351.

Parlement of Paris. Supreme royal tribunal of Fr., originating in medieval court ; through registration of laws exercised considerable influence over king ; abolished in 1790.

Parliament, Gt. Brit., 2521, 2520, 1290, 1194, 1489, 2013, 2168, 2651 ; origin, 1194, 2221, 2521 ; growth of power, 1611, 1089, 2777 ; conflicts with Stuart kings, 755, 1794 ; House of Commons, 1489, 2523 ; House of Lords, 2520 ; Long Parliament, 755, 1571 ; Model Parliament, 2521, 2522 ; Rump Parliament, 933, 2524 ; Bill of Rights (1689), 429 ; Reform Bill (1832), 2522 ; Catholic disabilities removed, 1746, 2420 ; later electoral reforms, 2522, 2525 ; power of Lords limited, 1976, 2522, 3282 ; voting for, 3330 ; women admitted, 2522, 3330 ; House of Commons destroyed in 1941, 2525.

Parliament, Houses of, 2014, 2013, 1290, 2520, 2523.

Parliament, in France. See **Parlement ; National Assembly.**

Parliament, Icelandic, 2521.

Parliament, Irish, 1746, 1748, 1750, 2524.

Parliament Act (1911), 2522, 3280 ; Lloyd George and, 1976.

Parliament Buildings, Ottawa, Canada, 683, 2458 ; Melbourne, Australia, 2136.

Parma. It. tn. 88 m. N.W. of Florence on r. Parma ; pop. 71,000 ; varied mfrs., farming trade ; famous art works ; univ. ; home of Correggio ; joins United It., 1769, 3319.

Parmentier (pahr-mahn'-tyā), **Antoine** (1737–1813). Fr. scientist ; promotes cultivation of potato, 2664.

Parmesan (pahr-me-zan') **cheese,** 766.

Par'moor, Charles Alfred Cripps, 1st Baron (1852–1941). Brit. politician and lawyer, Lord Pres. of the Council in Labour Govt. in 1924 and 1929 ; father of Sir Stafford Cripps.

Parnas'sus, Mt. (modern Liakoura), in cent. Greece, 1517, 1526 ; oracle of Delphi, 988 ; sacred to Apollo and Muses, 188, 2259.

Parnell, Charles Stewart (1846–91), Irish political leader, 2525.

Parnell, Thomas (1679–1718). Eng. poet, b. in Dublin ; most of his poems, written in a charming and easy style, were translations (" The Hermit " ; " Hymn to Contentment ").

Par'nes Mount. Modern Ozea, in Greece, 15 m. N. of Athens ; 4,600 ft. ; 284.

Paros (pär'-os) or **Paro.** Gk. isl. of Cyclades group in Aegean Sea just w. of Naxos ; 96 sq. m. ; formed by Mt. Elias (2,500 ft.) ; celebrated white marble quarries ; 1527, 2098.

Parr, Catherine (1512–48). 6th and last queen of Henry VIII of Eng., tactful, kindly woman to whose influence her stepchildren, the future sovereigns Edward VI, Mary, and Elizabeth, owed much ; 1612.

Parr. A young salmon, 2865.

Par'rakeet. A small parrot, particularly certain species with long, wedge-shaped tail ; budgerigars, 2526.

Parratt, Sir Walter (1841–1924). Eng. musician ; organist of St. George's Chapel, Windsor, for more than half his lifetime ; also " Master of the King's Musick."

Par'ret. R. in Dorset and Somerset, flowing 35 m. to the Bristol Channel, 3000.

Parrhasius (pa-rā'-si-us). Gk. painter of 4th cent., first master of correct drawing, and first to use light and shade to express round form ; won contest with Zeuxis ; 1528.

Parrots, Macaws, and Cockatoos, 2525, 2047, plate f. 2048 ; African home, 68 ; cockatoos, 860.

Parry, Sir Charles Hubert Hastings, Bart. (1848–1918). Eng. composer ; series of great choral works with orchestra ; 2266.

Parry, Sir William Edward (1790–1855). Eng. Arctic explorer ; made three attempts to cross North-West Passage ; in 1827 tried to reach North Pole, attaining latitude 82° 45' N., which remained for 49 years the " farthest north " reached by explorers.

Parsec. Unit used in astronomy for measuring stellar distance ; one parsec = 3·26 light years, or 19·2 million million miles.

Parsees (pahr-sēz'). Followers of Zoroaster in India, 496, 1703, 3447.

Parsifal (pahr-si-fal). Father of Lohengrin ; subject of opera by Wagner, 3332.

Parsley. A herb with aromatic leaves ; several kinds grow wild in Britain ; all have deeply cut leaves and umbels of very numerous, very small white flowers, 3061.

Parsley family, or **Umbelliferae.** A family of herbs with umbrella-shaped clusters of small flowers ; includes carrots, celery, parsley and parsnip.

Parsnip. A vegetable, 2526, 2825.

Parsons, Sir Charles Algernon (1854–1931). Eng. engineer ; creator of the steam turbine, 2949, 3259, 3260 ; developed the searchlight ; improved manufacture of optical glass ; O.M. (1927).

Parsons turbine, 3260.

Parthenogen'esis. Reproduction from unfertilized egg cells.

Par'thenon, on the Acropolis at Athens, 21, 22, 284, 286, 1144 ; Elgin marbles, 1143, 1144, 1537 ; frieze, 22, 1537, plate f. 585 ; meaning of name, 284 ; Pericles, 2551, 1528 ; Pheidias' sculptures, 1537 ; and reconstruction, plate f. 212.

Parthia (pahr'-thi-a). Anc. country of Asia, S.E. of Caspian Sea ; most extensive sway under Mithridates I ; Parthians' favourite tactics were to discharge arrows as they retreated —hence " Parthian shot " ; map, 2808.

Par'ticiple, in grammar, 3314.

Partition. In arithmetic, a process of division, 1021.

Partridge, Sir Bernard (1861–1945). Eng. artist, famous contributor to Punch.

Partridge. Name of various birds of the grouse family ; 2526, 2527.

Parts of speech, 1494. See also under separate names, as **Adjective, Noun,** etc.

Party government, 1490.

Pasade'na, Calif., U.S.A. Residential city and winter resort, 8 m. N.E. of Los Angeles ; pop. 81,860 ; founded in 1882 ; fruit-growing and mfg. interests ; California Institute of Technology ; Mount Wilson Observatory, 3180, 2412.

Pasargadae (pa-sahr'-ga-dē). Anc. cap. of Persia, said to have been built by Cyrus the Great on site of his great victory over Astyages (6th cent. B.C.) ; contained tomb of Cyrus.

Pascal, Blaise (1623–62). Fr. philosopher, mathematician, and physicist (" Thoughts " ; " Provincial Letters," best example of " polite, controversial irony " since Lucian) ; 1380 ; invents first calculating machine, 656 ; states law of fluid pressure, 1666.

Pascoe Knot. Section of Andes, 153.

Pasig, Philippines. Short river in s. end of Luzon ; flows 15 m. from Laguna de Bay through Manila into Manila Bay, 2088.

Pasque-flower, anemone, at one time used for colouring Easter eggs, 154.

Pass'ant. In heraldry, 1615.

Passau (pa'-sow). Old town of Bavaria, Ger., at junction of Danube, Inn, and Ilse, and at border of Austria ; pop. 25,150 ; Treaty of Passau (1552) granted religious freedom to Lutherans.

Passchendaele (pahs'-ken-dah'-le) **Ridge.** Height 6 m. N.E. of Ypres ; 1st World War battles, 3412.

Passeres (pas'-e-rēz). Perching birds.

Passfield, Baron. See **Webb, Sidney.**

Passion flower, Passiflora. A shrubby, climbing plant chiefly found in the hotter parts of America ; the solitary flowers are blue, purple, red, or white and about 2 in. across ; the extraordinary form of the corolla and stigmas accounts for the flower's name ; the roots of some are poisonous.

Passionists (Congregation of the Discalced Clerks of the Most Holy Cross and Passion of our Lord Jesus Christ). Religious order founded in It. about 1730.

Passion Play. Dramatic representation of sufferings of Christ ; first given by villagers of Oberammergau in 17th cent. in gratitude for escape from plague of 1633 ; 378, 1456, 2190.

Passion and Holy Weeks, 1074.

Passover. Jewish festival, 2527 ; influenced Easter customs, 1073.

Passy (pa-sē). Fr. suburb of Paris on w. adjoining Bois de Boulogne ; artesian well, 252.

Paste. Use in imitation diamonds, 1427.

Pasternak, Boris (b. 1890), Russ. poet, 2856.

Pasteur (pahs-tēr'), **Louis** (1822–95). Fr. chemist and bacteriologist, 2527, 2135 ; and antiseptics, 178 ; Lister and, 1963 ; and the Panama Canal, 2487 ; and silkworm disease, 2972 ; study of tartrates, 3155.

Pasteuriza'tion, 2528, 956.

Pastry, cooking of, 901.

Pasture lands, 1509.

Patago'nia. The S. part of the continent of S. Amer., mainly in the Argentine but also partly in Chile ; the Argentine portion has an area of about 300,000 sq. m. ; 2528, 3022, 227 ; map f. 3024 ; Andes Mts., 226 ; native superstition, 2056.

Patala (pa-tah'-la). In Hinduism, the abode of evil spirits.

Patching. In sewing, 2928.

Pâté de foie gras (pa-tā de fwah grah), 1486.

Patent leathers. How prepared, 1914.

Pater, Walter (1839–94). Eng. essayist, refined and subtle stylist (" Marius the Epicurean " ; " Imaginary Portraits "), 1215.

Paterson, A. B. (1864–1941). Australian writer, 315.

Paterson, William (1658–1719). Scottish financier, founder of the Bank of England ; promoter of a disastrous attempt to colonize Darien (Panama) in 1698, 356.

Paterson, New Jersey, U.S.A. Chief silk-mfg. city of New World ; locomotives, aeroplanes, and other textiles are also large industries ; pop. 139,650.

Pathans. Iranian tribes of E. Afghanistan and N.W. Frontier Prov., India, 1695.

Pathé Frères (Émile, Charles, and Théophile Pathé). Fr. originators of the cinema news reel.

"Pathétique " (pat-ā-tēk). Name given popularly to Beethoven's Sonata in C minor (op. 13) and to Tchaikovsky's 6th Symphony in B minor (op. 74).

Pathfinder. In James Fenimore Cooper's novel " The Pathfinder," nickname of Natty Bumppo, the hero, 903.

Pathol'ogy. Science dealing with disease, 2132 ; of plants, 533. See also **Disease ; Germs in Disease.**

Patiala and E. Punjab States Union. Union of predominantly Sikh states in repub. of India, formed in 1948 ; area, 10,119 sq. m. ; pop. 3,424,000.

Patient Griselda. Clerk's Tale in Chaucer's " Canterbury Tales," 764.

Patinir, Joachim de (c. 1475–1524). Flemish artist, 2324.

Patio (pah'-tē-ō). Inner court of a Sp. or Sp.-Amer. dwelling, 2872.

Pat'more, Coventry (1823–96). Eng. poet and critic (" The Angel in the House " ; " The Unknown Eros "— odes of exalted thought expressed in rich, dignified melody).

Pat′mos. Bare volcanic isl., one of the Sporades in Aegean Sea ; here St. John (the Evangelist) lived for 18 months in exile, and here he is said to have written the Apocalypse.

Patna. Rep. of India, chief city of Bihar prov. (now merged with Orissa prov.) on Ganges ; pop. 175,706 ; rice, opium, indigo ; univ. (founded 1917) ; massacre of Patna (1763), and Indian Mutiny (1857) ; 428.

Patras (pah′-trahs), Greece. Fortified spt. and trade centre on w. coast of Gulf of Patras ; pop. 61,280 ; one of 12 Achaean cities ; early centre of Christianity ; cradle of Gk. revolution in 1821, *1527*.

Patriar′chal system, 1259.

Patricians. Aristocratic class of Rome, 2805.

Patrick, Order of St., 2449.

Pat′rick, St. (d. 461 or 493). Apostle to Ireland and its patron saint, *2528*, 1745, 2212 ; and the shamrock, 2936.

Patroclus (pa-trok′-lus). Hero of Trojan War in Gk. myth., friend of Achilles, 19 ; killed by Hector, 1603.

Patronym′ics (" father-names "). Origin of, 2272.

Pattern, in poetry, 2636 ; in weaving, 3361.

Patterson, Elizabeth (1785–1879). First wife of Jerome Bonaparte, 497.

Patti, Adelina, Baroness Cederström (1843–1919). Operatic soprano celebrated in many countries for her wonderfully pure voice, which kept its freshness even in her later years ; made debut as " Lucia " in New York City at 16.

Pat′tison, Mark (1813–84). Eng. scholar and author ; the history of classical scholarship his special study ; (" Learning in the Church of England " ; " Life of Casaubon " ; " Life of Milton ").

Patton, Gen. George Smith (1885–1945). Commanded U.S. 7th Army in N. Africa 1942–43, and in Sicily 1943 ; led U.S. 3rd Army's advance across France and Germany 1944–45. Victor of Bastogne.

Pau (pō). Winter health resort of s.w. Fr. ; pop. 46,160 ; anc. cap. of Navarre.

Paul, St. (d. about A.D. 67). " The Apostle of the Gentiles", first great Christian missionary (name originally Saul), *2529, 2530*, 817, 189 ; in Athens, 286 ; converted at Damascus 963 ; shipwreck, 2946 ; Epistle to Thessalonians, 3202.

Paul, popes. For list *see* Pope.

Paul III (Alexander Farnese) (1468–1549). Pope, elected 1534 ; excommunicated Henry VIII of England ; commissioned Michelangelo to paint the " Last Judgement " ; and Inquisition, 1726.

Paul IV (Giovanni Pietro Caraffa) (1476–1559). Pope, elected 1555 ; opposed Reformation and made breach between Churches of England and Rome impassable.

Paul I (1754–1801). Tsar of Russia ; succeeded his mother, Catherine II in 1796 ; cruel despot and madman ; assassinated by conspiracy of nobles.

Paul I, King of Greece (b. 1901). Succeeded to throne, April 1947.

Paul, Prince (b. 1893). Regent of Yugoslavia 1934–41 during the minority of King Peter ; overthrown Mar. 1941 by coup d'état, having signed an agreement with Hitler ; fled to Athens and later Kenya.

aul, Epistles of. Books in New Testament comprising 13 letters attributed to St. Paul, though authorship of some doubtful, 2530.

Paul, Jean. *See* Richter, Johann Paul.

Paul, Lewis (d. 1759). Brit. inventor ; roller-spinning machine, 235.

Paul of Thebes (3rd cent.). A hermit 2212.

Paulhan, Louis (b. 1884). Fr. aviator ; one of the pioneers of flying ; in 1910 won " Daily Mail " £10,000 prize for London to Manchester flight.

Paulus (powl′-oos), **Friedrich von** (b. 1890). Ger. soldier ; commanded 6th army at Stalingrad, and was taken prisoner with staff Jan. 1943 ; denounced Nazis from Russ. and appealed to Ger. to end war ; remained in Russ. after war.

Paul Veronese. *See* Veronese, Paolo.

Pausanias (paw-sān′-i-as) (d. c. 471). Spartan general and regent ; led Gk. forces to victory at Plataea 479 B.C. ; ambition then led him to treason ; after vain attempt to provoke a revolt, he took refuge in a temple, where he was walled up to starve to death ; in order to prevent temple's pollution by death he was removed at last moment.

Pausanias (2nd cent. A.D.). Gk. traveller, geographer, and writer on art, 1541 ; visits Acropolis, 22.

Pavia (pa-vē′-a) (anc. Ticinum). City of N. Italy, 18 m. s. of Milan on r. Ticino ; pop. 51,700 ; univ. ; cap. of Lombard kingdom ; taken by Charlemagne in 774 ; Charles V here defeated and took Francis I of France prisoner (1525), 1383.

Paving materials, 2783 ; bricks, 962.

Pavlov (pahv′-lof), **Ivan Petrovich** (1849–1936). Russ. psychologist ; devoted much time and thought to behaviour of animals (" conditioned reflex ") in order to apply knowledge to human beings.

Pavlova (pahv′-lo-va), **Anna** (1885–1931). Russian dancer ; debut London 1909 ; unexcelled in classical style of ballet-dancing ; most famous dance " Le Cygne," 345.

Pavonazzo (pav-ō-nat′-sō), a kind of marble, 2097.

Pax Romana, " Roman Peace," 2811.

P.A.Y.E. (Pay as you earn), 3158. *See* Income Tax.

Pay′ens, Hugh de. Burgundian knight who in 1118 undertook with Godfrey de St. Omer the work of protecting the pilgrims who, after the first crusade, flocked to the Holy Land ; thus originated the Knights Templars, one of the three great military orders founded in the 12th cent. ; the Knights Templars' first home was near the Temple in Jerusalem.

Paymaster-general. Brit. unpaid Govt. official ; office dates from Restoration, but was reorganized in 1835 and 1848 ; pays out money required by Govt. depts. ; member of the Govt., but not in Cabinet.

Payne, John Howard (1791–1852). Amer. actor and dramatist ; remembered as author of " Home, Sweet Home."

Pea. Plants of family *Leguminosae*, **2530** ; food value compared with milk, *2174* ; rich in protein, 2694.

Pea, Sweet, 2530.

Peabody, Elizabeth Palmer (1804–94). Amer. educator and writer ; studied Gk. under Emerson, taught under Amos Bronson Alcott ; introduced Froebel's methods into U.S.A.

Peabody, George (1795–1869). Amer. merchant, banker, and philanthropist, 2530.

Peace Conferences, of 1919, at Versailles, 3317, 3414 ; Clemenceau, 837 ; Lloyd George, 1976 ; Smuts, 2988 ;

Peace conferences, Hague, 203, 1563.

Peace movement, 2531 ; arbitration, 203 ; Hague conferences, 203, 1563 ; League of Nations, 1908 ; United Nations, 3283. The U.N. charter was signed June 26, 1945.

Peace pipe or **cal′umet.** Tobacco pipe presented by Red Indians to those with whom they wish to be on good terms ; 3219.

Peace Pledge Union. Movement founded in 1934 by the Rev. " Dick " Sheppard.

Peace River, in Alberta, Canada, rises in w. of Rocky Mts. and flows E. through range to junction with Slave r. ; more than 1,000 m. long, 2050.

Peace treaties. *See* Treaties.

Peach, 2531, *back of plate f. 1400,* classification, 1403 ; nectarine, 2532 ; original home, 2650.

Peacock, 2532, *plates f. 2532, 2533.*

Peacock, Thomas Love (1785–1866). Eng. satirical novelist and poet, friend of Shelley and father-in-law of George Meredith (" Nightmare Abbey " ; " Crotchet Castle ").

Peacock butterfly, *plate f. 632.*

Peacock Throne, Delhi, 987, 2532.

Pea-crab, 924.

Peahen, a female peacock, 2532.

Peak District. Mt. dist. of Derbyshire, forming S. end of Pennine Chain ; lies N. of Buxton ; highest point Kinderscout (2,088 ft.) ; 995 ; Dovedale, *2283.* Projected National Park.

Peanut. *See* Ground-nut.

Pear, favourite fruit, **2532,** *plate f. 1400,* 1401.

Pear, prickly, 649.

Pearl buttons, 632, *633,* 2942.

Pearl Harbour, Hawaiian Isls., **2533,** 1585 ; attacked by Japan, Dec. 1941, 2473, 3292, 3419, 1800.

Pearl Mosque, Agra, 77.

" Pearl of the Desert," a name given to Damascus, 961.

Pearl River, or Shu-kiang, China. Same as Canton River.

Pearls, 2533 ; Australian fisheries, 308 ; Ceylon fisheries, 749 ; cultured in Persian Gulf, 2557 ; diving for, in ancient Greece, *1524* ; pearl oyster, *2468, 2534.*

Pearly nautilus, shell, *2943.*

Pearson, Sir Cyril Arthur, Bart. (1866–1921). Prominent Eng. journalist and newspaper proprietor ; he founded " Pearson's Weekly " and many other periodicals and started the " Daily Express " ; later he acquired the " Standard " and the " Evening Standard " ; he became blind and subsequently devoted much of his attention to the welfare of those similarly afflicted, taking a great interest in " St. Dunstan's Hostel " for the blind ; succeeded as 2nd Baronet by his son Sir Neville Pearson (b. 1898) ; 473.

Pearson, Weetman Dickinson. *See* Cowdray.

Peary, Robert Edwin, Rear-Admiral (1856–1920), discoverer of North Pole, 2534, 2645 ; Polar exploration, 2645 ; *map, 1542.*

Peasants' Revolt, in Eng. (1381), 3269, 2777, 2981, 3428.

Peasants' Revolt, in Ger. (1525), 2758, 2759, 1449.

Peat. Partly carbonized vegetable material, 2534 ; as fuel, *1405* ; by-products, 2535 ; changed to coal, 857 ; formed by moss, 2239 ; in glaciated areas, 1682 ; yields wax, 3359.

Pe′brine, a silkworm disease, 2972.

Pecan. A N. Amer. tree of the hickory family producing nuts.

Pec′cary. Small wild hog of N. and S. Amer. ; the northern, collared peccary is about 3 ft. long and the southern white-lipped peccary a few ins. longer, *3025.*

Pechora. R. of N. Russia, rising in Ural Mts. and flowing 970 m. to N. coast, 1232.

Peck. A fourth part of a bushel. *See* Weights and Measures.

Pecksniff, Seth. In Dickens's " Martin Chuzzlewit," a canting hypocrite who posed as an architect and made his apprentices do all his work.

Pecos. R. of the U.S.A., chief tributary of Rio Grande ; rises in New Mexico at base of Baldy Peak ; flows s. and s.e. 800 m. entering Rio Grande on Texas-Mexican border.

Pécs (pāch) (Ger. *Funfkirchen*), Hungary ; pop. 70,000 ; fine medieval cathedral ; makes woollens, leather, paper, porcelain ; surrounding vineyards produce famous wine.

Pectin. Gelatinous substance allied to sugars and gums, 1792 ; 1341.

Pedals, organ, 2450 ; piano, 2603.

Pedersen, Christiern (1480–1554). " Father of Danish literature " ; his translation of the Bible, called " Christian III's Bible," is landmark in Danish literature.

Ped′estal. In architecture, an insulated basement or support for a column, a vase, or a statue.

Ped′iment. In classic architecture, triangular-shaped portion of wall above the cornice, corresponding to gable in Gothic architecture ; of Parthenon, 22.

Ped'ipalp. Grasping claw of arachnids.

Pedro III (1236–86). King of Aragon ; called " the Great " because of success in conquering Sicily.

Pedro I (1798–1834). Emperor of Brazil, son of John VI of Portugal, crowned in 1822 ; succeeded to Port. crown in 1826, and at once resigned it to his daughter Maria da Gloria ; abdicated Brazilian crown in 1831 ; died after restoring his daughter to Port. throne ; 554.

Pedro II (1825–91). Emperor of Brazil ; succeeded in 1831 ; compelled to abdicate in 1889 ; prosperous reign notable for emancipation of slaves, and war (1864–70) with Paraguay ; 554.

Pedro I, the Cruel (1333–69). King of Castile and Leon ; succeeded 1350 ; provoked rebellion of his brother Henry, by whom he was killed.

Pedro V (1837–61). King of Portugal ; succeeded in 1853 ; reign marked by freedom from civil strife and by economic improvement.

Pedro Miguel locks on Panama Canal, 2490.

Peeblesshire, Scot. Inland co. in S.E. ; a. 347 sq. m. ; pop. 15,100 ; **2535.**

Peel, Arthur Wellesley, 1st Viscount (1829–1912). Youngest son of Sir Robert Peel ; he entered Parl. and became Speaker, occupying that post from 1884 to 1895.

Peel, John (1776–1854). Eng. huntsman ; a renowned hunter of the fox in his native Cumberland ; immortalized in the song " D'ye ken John Peel ? "

Peel, Sir Robert (1788–1850). Brit. statesman, **2535, 3278** ; Disraeli on, 1019 ; police system, 2647.

Peel, William Robert Wellesley, 1st Earl (1867–1937). British lawyer and politician ; called to the Bar in 1893 ; chairman of the London County Council in 1914, he was Under-Secretary of State for War (1919–21), Minister of Transport (1921–22), and Secretary of State for India in 1922–4 and 1928–9.

Peele, George (1558–98). Eng. dramatist and poet (" The Old Wives' Tale " ; " The Love of King David and Fair Bethsabe ") ; shares with Marlowe credit for improving English dramatic diction and making blank verse smoother.

" Peeler." Former Eng. nickname for police, 2535, *2536.*

Peenemunde (pä'-ne-mōōn-de). Ger. research station on Baltic Sea, 60 m. N.W. of Stettin, specializing in radio-location, pilot-less planes, rocket-bombs, etc. ; heavily bombed by Allies 1943 and 1944 ; occupied May 1945 by Russ., who continued researches.

Peeping Tom, 923.

Peerage, 2536.

" Peer Gynt " (pär gunt). Ibsen's poetic drama, whose hero, a character derived from Norwegian folklore, is a kind of Norse Faust, 1680.

Peer Gynt Suite, music by Grieg, 1549.

Peet, Thomas Eric (1882–1934). Eng. Egyptologist ; an acknowledged authority whose works include " Stone and Bronze Ages in Italy and Sicily," and " A Comparative Study of the Literatures of Egypt, Palestine, and Mesopotamia."

Pee'wit. Same as **Lapwing.**

Pegasus (peg'-a-sus). In Gk. myth., winged horse of Muses, **2536** ; figurehead of Phoenicians' ships, 2945.

Peg'gotty. Family in Dickens's " David Copperfield," who lived at Yarmouth ; Clara Peggotty, David's loyal nurse, marries Barkis, the shy carrier (" Barkis is willing ").

Pégoud, Adolphe (1887–1915). Fr. airman ; first man to fly upside-down and to loop the loop (1913).

Peiho (pä-hō'). Important r. of N. China ; rises N. of Peking, flows S.E. 350 m. to Gulf of Pechili.

Peiping. Name given to city of Peking during the period 1368–1421 and from 1928. *See* Feking.

Peipus. Large lake of U.S.S.R., 120 m. S.W. of Leningrad on E. Estonian boundary ; centre of German attacks on Estonia and Leningrad during 2nd World War ; drains into Gulf of Finland through r. Narova ; 1,356 sq. m. ; rich fisheries.

Peisistratus or **Pisistratus.** Greek tyrant, 1522.

Peking', or **Peiping.** Capital of China ; pop. (est.) 2,000,000, **2536** ; Japanese occupation, 814 ; Boxer rebellion, 812 ; Ming tombs, 2538 ; Mongols capture, 2205.

Peking Man, *2079.*

Pelagosa. Is. of Adriatic, midway between Gargano and Dalmatia ; ceded by It. to Yugoslavia under peace treaty of 1947 ; 3440.

Pelargo'nium. The so-called " geranium," most popular of pot-plants, 1444.

Pelecypods (pe-les'-i-podz). Class of molluscs more usually known as *Lamellibranchia*, 2199, 3626.

Pelée, Mont. Volcano in Martinique, 2112 ; *plate f. 3329.*

Peleus (pē'-lūs). In Gk. myth., husband of Thetis and father of Achilles ; marriage feast, 3248.

Pelew (pe-lū) or **Palau Islands.** Group of 26 small fertile isls. in Pacific E. of Philippines ; discovered by Spanish (1543) ; sold to Ger. (1899) ; seized by Japan in 1914 ; fertility, 2470 ; in 2nd World War taken by U.S., 2474.

Pel'ias. In Gk. myth., son of Poseidon and king of Iolcus ; sends Jason in search of Golden Fleece.

Pel'ican. A fish-eating water bird, **2538** ; foot, 448.

Péligot, Eugène. Fr. scientist who in 1842 first isolated uranium, 3297.

Pelion (pē'-li-on), **Mt.** Lofty mt. range in Thessaly, Greece, celebrated in myth. ; had temple to Zeus and cave of Centaur Chiron ; giants are said to have attempted to pile Pelion on Ossa to scale summit of Olympus, the abode of the gods ; ship Argo built from wood on its slopes.

Pel'la. Cap. of Macedon under Philip II and Alexander the Great, 105.

Pella'gra. A deficiency disease, causing severe nervous and physical disturbances, common in It. and U.S.A., 1458, 3327.

" Pelléas et Mélisande." Opera, by Debussy, 2438.

Pelopidas (pe-lop'-i-das) (d. 364 B.C.). Theban statesman and general, friend and associate of Epaminondas and his aid at Leuctra.

Peloponne'sian Wars, 286, 1523, 3053 ; 3197 ; 3206 ; Pericles, 2551.

Peloponnesus (pel-o-pon-nē'-sus). Anc. name of S. Greece (modern Morea), 1517 ; Sparta wins control, 1524, 3053.

Pelops (pel'-ops). In Gk. myth., son of Tantalus, king of Phrygia, and father of Atreus and Thyestes ; Pelops' line was cursed by Myrtilus, the charioteer to whom he refused to pay a promised bribe ; " Pelops' Island," 1517.

Pelorus Jack. Famous dolphin, 160.

Pelton wheel, type of impulse turbine, 1670, *1671,* 3259.

Pelusium (pe-lū'-shi-um). Anc. fortified city of Eg. at N.E. extremity of Delta of Nile ; gave name to E. mouth of Nile ; important point in wars between Eg. and Sennacherib, Cambyses, Antiochus, and other Eastern monarchs.

Pel'vis. In human skeleton, 2977.

Pem'ba. Isl. of the Zanzibar Protectorate, off the E. coast of Africa ; about 380 sq. m. ; pop. 100,000 ; 3441, 1072, *map, 1073.*

Pem'berton, Sir Max (1863–1950). Eng. novelist and playwright ; author of many successful adventure romances (novels, " The Iron Pirate," " Kronstadt," " The Man of Silver Moor," plays, " The Dancing Master," " The Finishing School ").

Pembroke, Mary Sidney, Countess of (1561–1621). Sister of Sir Philip Sidney, for whom he wrote " The Countess of Pembroke's Arcadia " ; subject of Ben Jonson's famous epitaph on " Sidney's sister, Pembroke's mother."

Pembroke, Richard de Clare, Earl of. *See* Strongbow.

Pembroke, Wales. Tn. of Pembrokeshire, in S. on estuary, Milford Haven ; pop. 12,000 ; chief industries connected with Pembroke Dock, fortified naval dockyard near by ; ruined 11th cent. castle, reputed birthplace of Henry VII.

Pembroke College, Cambridge, founded, 668.

Pembroke College, Oxford, founded, 2464.

Pembrokeshire. Co. of Wales ; a. 614 sq. m. ; pop. 87,000, **2538.**

Pem'mican. An Amer. Indian food, 459.

Pen, 2539 ; ball-pointed, 2541 ; ink, 1724 ; fountain pen, *2540,* 2541 ; steel pen, 2539 ; stylo pen, 2541.

Pen. Female swan, 3125.

Pen'ance. A self-imposed punishment as an expression of repentance for a sin committed ; one of the sacraments of the Rom. Cath. Church.

Penang (pē-nang'). Isl. at N. end of Straits of Malacca, off the W. coast of Malay Peninsula ; 110 sq. m. ; pop. 247,460. With Province Wellesley, made one of Straits Settlements. Incorp. into Malayan Federation in 1946.

Penates (pe-nāt'-ēz). Rom. gods of the storeroom ; each family worshipped its own Penates, which seem to have varied in different families ; worship connected with that of Vesta, 3318.

Pencil, 2541 ; mfr. of " leads," *2542.*

P.E.N. Club. Working literary club, with centres in many countries. Concerned with friendliness between writers all over the world, regardless of race, politics, and religion. First President, H. G. Wells. The initials indicate Poets and Playwrights, Editors and Essayists, and Novelists, to whom the Club is open.

Pend'ant. In architecture, an ornament suspended from the roof of a Gothic or Tudor building ; the hanging ornaments of a vaulted ceiling, uniting solidity with richness ; also a hanging keystone, the lower face of which projects beyond the intrados of the arch.

Penden'nis, Arthur. The unheroic but human and likeable hero of Thackeray's " History of Pendennis."

Penden'tive. In architecture, 214.

Pendle Hill, Lancashire. 3 m. S.E. of Clitheroe (1,800 ft.), 1890.

Pen'dulum, 2543 ; applied to clocks, 844, *plate f. 1513* ; in electric clocks, *1125* ; Foucault's, 1560, *1561* ; laws discovered by Galileo, 1414.

Penelope (pe-nel'-o-pē). In the " Odyssey," wife of Odysseus ; proverbial for faithfulness, 2024, 2421, 2423.

Pene'us or **Peneios** (modern Salamyria). Chief r. of Thessaly ; 100 m. long ; *map, 1518* ; turned through Augean stables by Hercules, 1615.

Pengö. Monetary unit of Hungary, adopted in 1925.

Pen'guin. An Antarctic sea-bird, **2544,** *170, 174, plates f. 2544, 2545* ; maternal instinct, 162.

Penicillin, 2544, 180, 2132 ; found by Sir A. Fleming, 1314 ; how discovered, 429 ; for lung diseases, 2040 ; from a mould, 2173 ; and streptomycin, 3103.

Penicillium. Genus of mould fungi, including *P. glaucum,* the common blue-green saprophytic mould that grows on moist bread, etc., and *P. notatum,* from which the antibiotic penicillin is obtained ; 2544, 3155.

Penin'sula. In physiography, 2596.

Peninsular and Oriental Steamship Line (P. & O.). Line of steamships plying to Egypt, India and Australia ; celebrated its centenary in 1937.

Peninsular War (1808–14). War in which Gt. Brit. assisted Sp. and Portugal to free Iberian Peninsula from domination of Napoleon, 2277, 2660, 3036, 3277, 3364.

Penknife. Origin of name, 2539.

Pen'ley, William Sydney (1851–1912). Eng. actor and theatrical manager ; an excellent comedian, he achieved his greatest successes in " The Private Secretary " and " Charley's Aunt."

Penn, Sir William (1621–70). Eng. admiral ; home, 572.

Penn, William (1644–1718). Founder of Pennsylvania, 2544, 2545 ; house in Philadelphia, 2566.

Pennell, Joseph (1860–1926). Amer. etcher, lithographer, and author, 1967.

Pennillion (pen-ith'-lyon) singing, plate f. 3337.

Pennines (pen'-īnz) or **Pennine Chain**, Eng., 2546, 1161, 1164 ; coal, 1165 ; map, plate f. 584.

Pennine Way. Footpath along the length of the Pennine Chain, 2546.

Pennsylvania (pen-sil-vā'-ni-a). A middle Atlantic state of U.S.A. ; a. 45,000 sq. m. ; pop. 9,900,000, 2546 ; founded, 2546 ; oil, 2428.

Pennsylvania, a U.S. battleship, 2533.

Pennsylvania, University of, at Philadelphia ; established in 1740 as a charitable school ; made an academy in 1751 through the efforts of Benjamin Franklin, and became a college in 1755, 2556 ; electric calculating machine, 659.

Penny. An Eng. bronze coin worth one-twelfth of a shilling or 4 farthings ; before the time of Edward I halfpence and farthings were not coined, but the penny was deeply indented with a cross, so that it could be broken into two or four pieces, 2203.

Penny postage, introduction, 2661.

Pennyroyal. A mint-like herb or its oil, 2187.

Pennyweight. A unit of measure. See Weights and Measures.

Pensaco'la, Florida. U.S.A. port on Pensacola Bay ; pop. 37,350 ; fish, lumber, and shipbuilding interests ; large naval air station.

Pensions. Grant or payment made for services rendered ; usually a fixed periodical payment, 2546 ; defined by Dr. Johnson, 1836 ; granted to literary men in Eng., 1836, 2634 ; industrial, 704 ; contributory pensions, old-age, 2996, 1976, 312, 2358.

Pensions, Ministry of. Brit. Govt. dept. formed in 1916 to deal with the payment of pensions of soldiers, sailors, and their dependents, 2546 ; the head office is at Gt. Smith St., Westminster, London.

Penstocks, for water-power, plate f. 960, 1669, 1670.

Pentateuch (pen'-ta-tūk). First five books of Bible, 2235.

Pentathlon (pen-tath'-lon). " Five-in-one " contest in Olympic Games in which each competitor must ride, fence, shoot, swim, and run a cross-country race.

Pen'tecost. See Whitsunday.

Pentel'icus, Mt. (modern Mendeli), marble from, 2098.

Penthesilea (pen-thes-i-lē'-a). Daughter of Ares and queen of the Amazons ; aided Trojans against Greeks ; slain by Achilles.

Pent'land Firth. Channel separating Orkney Isls. from mainland of Scot., and connecting Atlantic Ocean with North Sea.

Pent'land Hills. Scot. A range running through counties of Edinburgh, Peebles, and Lanark, s.w. for 16 m. ; Scald Law is the highest summit, being 1,898 ft. high.

Pentothal, an anaesthetic, 149.

Penum'bra, of eclipse. The partial shadow between the umbra, or region of total eclipse, and the region entirely free from eclipse.

Penyghent (pen-i-gent'), Eng. Mt. in the West Riding of Yorkshire ; 2,273 ft. high ; 2546.

Penzance'. Tn. and sept. in Cornwall ; the westernmost tn. in Eng. at the head of Mount's Bay ; chief industry fishing ; pop. 20,000 ; special trains from Paddington, 2347.

Pe'ony. Plant of the buttercup family, 2546.

People's Palace, Mile End, London. Owes its origin to a bequest by Barber Beaumont which was supplemented by the Drapers' Company and certain individual donors ; provides facilities for education, recreation and amusement ; its chief feature is the Queen's Hall. This was burnt down in 1931, rebuilt, and new building opened in 1936.

Peo'ria, Illinois, U.S.A. Mfg. and rly. city in N.-centre on Illinois r. ; pop. 105,000 ; formerly great distilling centre ; agric. implements, paper, motor-cars.

Pep'in or **Pippin the Short** (d. 768). First Carolingian king of the Franks, son of Charles Martel and father of Charlemagne, 753, 759.

Pepin II (sometimes called Pepin of Heristal) (d. 714). Duke of the Franks ; as leader of nobles of Austrasia gained great victory over Neustria which made him master of almost entire Gaul ; subdued Frisians and Alamanni ; father of Charles Martel.

Pepper, 2547, 3061.

Peppermint, 2187 ; essential oil from, 1263.

Pep'sin. Protein-digesting ferment in gastric juice, 2547, 1016, 1220.

Pep'tone. Product of pepsin action upon a proteid, 2547.

Pepys (pēps or pep'-is), **Samuel** (1633–1703). Eng. diarist and Admiralty official, 2547, 2548 ; home in London, 2010.

Pera (pā'-ra) part of Istanbul, 1763.

Perak (pā-rahk'). State of Malayan Federation, formerly northernmost of Fed. States ; a. 7,900 sq. m. ; pop. (including Dindings) 992,690 ; rice, tin, rubber ; 2069.

" Perbunan," a synthetic rubber, 2838.

Percentage and interest, 2548.

Per'ceval or **Percival, Sir,** knight of Round Table, 255, 2830, 1414.

Perch. A fresh-water fish, 2549.

Perch (Rod or Pole). A unit of measure, 5½ yards. See Weights and Measures.

Perch, climbing, 1297.

Percheron (per'-she-ron). A heavy type of horse.

Percus'sion cap, 1281.

Percussion instruments, 2267 ; in orchestra, 2446.

Percy. English family, 1611.

Percy, Sir Henry (1365–1403). " Harry Hotspur," Eng. warden of Scottish marches and hero of Chevy Chase (1388) ; killed in rebellion against Henry IV ; 1611.

Percy, Thomas (1720–1811). Brit. bishop ; ballad collection, " Reliques of Ancient English Poetry," 1213.

Perdita (pêr'-di-ta). In Shakespeare's " Winter's Tale," 3389.

Pereda (pā-rā'-da), **José Maria de** (1833–1906). Sp. novelist, 3051.

" Père Goriot," (pär gōr-yō). Novel by Balzac, in which an indulgent father is made the victim of his daughter's social ambition and pride.

Peregrine falcon (pe'-ri-grin). Bird of prey now chiefly confined in Brit. to cliffs of south-west and west, famed for its speed, strength and ferocity ; in hawking, the most important of all falcons, 1258 ; feeds chiefly on fair-sized birds such as ducks, pigeons, etc.

Perekop, Isthmus of, 931.

Père-Lachaise (pär lah shāz'). Famous cemetery in N.E. Paris ; contains 20,000 monuments and 800,000 graves, including many of great figures in Fr. history.

Peren'nial plants, 2624.

Pèrez Galdós (pā'-reth gal-dōs), **Benito** (1843–1920). Sp. novelist and dramatist (" Doña Perfecta "), 3051.

Perfumes, 2549 ; animal fixatives, 2549, 932 ; eau de Cologne, 872 ; essential oils, 1263 ; synthetic, 2550 ; vegetable fixatives, 2550.

Pergamum (per'-ga-mum) or **Pergamus.** Celebrated anc. city of N.W. Asia Minor, cap. of kingdom of Pergamus and later of Rom prov. of Asia ; fine sculptures, many of them were exhibited in Berlin's Pergamon Museum which was severely damaged during the 2nd World War, and the exhibits dispersed ; parchment, 2496.

Peri, Jacopo (1561–1633). It. composer, 2435.

Perian'der (c. 665–585 B.C.). Gk. sage.

Per'ianth. Name for petals and sepals of a flower when taken together.

Pericar'dium. A cone-shaped membraneous sac which encloses the heart and about two inches of the great blood vessels ; attached at its base to the diaphragm ; the inner surface, a serous membrane, secretes a thin fluid which lubricates the heart.

Per'icarp. Pulpy seed-envelope of fruits such as apples, 1403.

Pericles (c. 490–429 B.C.). Athenian statesman, 2551 ; Athens under, 1523 ; Greek art under, 1528 ; Pheidias, 2566 ; beautifies Athens, 21, 1528 ; in 2nd Peloponnesian War, 1523.

Per'igon, in geometry, 1435.

Per'ilymph. Fluid filling bony labyrinth of ear, 1065.

Perim. Small Brit. isl. at s. end of Red Sea, included in colony of Aden, 26.

Period (full stop). Mark of punctuation, 2705.

Period, in mechanics. The time taken by a recurring event ; in geology, 1432.

Period'icals. Name given to magazines or journals that come out regularly at stated intervals.

Periodic Law, in chemistry. A law enunciated by Mendeléev in 1869 stating that : " The elements, if arranged according to their atomic weights, exhibit an evident periodicity of properties." This enabled him to predict the properties of elements hitherto undiscovered ; they were proved to be true within his lifetime, 769, 3686.

Perioeci (per-i-ē'-sī). Free labourers of Sparta, 3053.

Peripatet'ic philosophy, 232.

Per'iscope, 2551, 2553, 672, 3104, 3105, 3106 ; home-made, 2552.

Peristal'sis, 1017.

Peritone'um. A serous membrane which encloses all the organs lying in the abdominal and pelvic cavities ; inflammation of the peritoneum is called peritonitis.

Per'iwinkle. A sea-snail with top-shaped shell, 2199, 2942.

Periwinkle. Various creeping plants of family Apocynaceae with opposed evergreen leaves ; the lesser periwinkle, Vinca minor, is native to the Brit. Isles ; it has violet or lilac flowers which appear early in the year ; great periwinkle, V. major, has much finer flowers and is larger in every way.

Perkin, Sir William Henry (1838–1907). Eng. chemist ; discoverer of the first aniline dye, aniline purple, and founder of the coal-tar dye industry, 1059.

Perkins, Frances (Mrs. Paul C. Wilson) (b. 1882). Amer. politician ; app. sec. of Labour by Roosevelt 1933, she carried out Labour policies of the New Deal, and was the first woman min. in U.S. cabinet, retiring 1945 ; wrote " The Roosevelt I Knew."

Perkins, Jacob (1766–1849). Amer. inventor and physicist ; he came to Eng. with a plan for engraving banknotes on steel, which proved successful ; inventor of freezing machine.

Perlis. Northernmost state of Malayan Fedn., formerly northernmost of Unfederated States on w. coast of peninsula ; rubber, rice, coconuts, and tin are produced ; a. 316 sq. m. ; pop. 57,770 ; in Japanese hands 1941–45 ; 2069.

Perm. Cap. of Perm dist. in Sverdlovsk region of E. Soviet Rus. on r. Kama ; pop. 255,196 ; iron, copper, smelting, machinery mfr.

Permanent Court of International Justice, at The Hague, 1563.

Permanent magnets, 2062.

Permanganate (pêr-man'-ga-nǎt). Salt of permanganic acid, 2087.

Permeabil'ity, in magnetism, 2063.

Per'mian period, in geology, 1432.

"Permutit," water-softening process, 3351.

Pernambuco (pêr-nam-bōō'-kō) or **Recife**. Brazil spt.; mfg. centre, and cap. of state of Pernambuco on Atlantic coast at easternmost point of S. Amer.; pop. 472,760; 554.

Perón, Juan D. (b. 1895). Argentine statesman; took part in 1943 revolution; pres. of nat. dept. of labour; in 1944 sec. for war and vice-pres.; his popularity with working class made him suspect as possible dictator and he resigned Oct. 1945; Feb. 1946 elected pres.; introduced wide social reforms; women given vote in 1947; his wife, Dona (Maria) Eva, played a political part.

Péronne (pā-ron'), Fr. Fortified tn. on Somme; Charles the Simple and Louis XI imprisoned here; unsuccessfully besieged by Imperialists (1536); taken by Ger. in 1871.

Perox'ide of hydrogen. A mild antiseptic; bleaching properties, 470.

Perpendic'ular, in geometry, 1436.

Perpendicular style, in architecture, 219, 220; Canterbury Cath., 724.

Perpet'ual Calendar. A system of reckoning time by means of a calendar which enables one to find the day of the week for any date in any year; dominical letters are used for the purpose of showing on what day of the year the first Sunday comes.

Perpetual or **Everlasting League**, Swiss, 3141.

"Perpetual motion" machines, 1396, 1397, 1398.

Perpignan (pār-pē-nyahn), Fr. Fortified city in s. on R. Têt, 7 m. from Mediterranean; pop. 75,000; 14th-cent. cath.; commands passage by E. Pyrenees from Sp. into Fr.

Perrault (pe-rō), **Charles** (1628–1703). Fr. author who gave literary form to many old fairy tales, 1964, 2239.

Perry, Frederick J. (b. 1909). English lawn tennis player. One of the world's leading players, winning the singles at Wimbledon in the years 1934–36; afterwards turned professional; 1907.

Perry, Matthew Calbraith (1794–1858). Amer. commodore; expedition to Japan, 1795.

Perry and cider. Types of drink made from juice of pears and apples respectively, 828.

Perseids, 2152.

Persephone (pêr-sef'-o-nē) or **Proserpina**. In Gk. and Rom. myth., daughter of Demeter (Ceres), 989, 1921, 2631; origin of mint plant, 2187.

Persepolis (pêr-sep'-o-lis). Anc. cap. of Persian Empire, in s.w., 35 m. N.E. of modern city of Shiraz; 1741; tomb of Cyrus, 2554.

Perseus (pêr'-sūs), in Gk. myth., hero who slew Medusa, 2552.

Perseus. A northern constellation, chart, 895.

Pershing, John Joseph (1860–1948). Amer. general, commanded Amer. army in 1st World War.

Persia. Country of s.w. Asia also known as **Iran**; History, 2554, 1522; Cyrus the Great, 2554; wars against the Greeks, 2555; Alexander conquers, 106, 2554; Assassin sect, 274; Mongols conquer, 2206. For geography, etc., see Iran.

Persian cat, 719, 720.

Porcian Gulf. Arm of Indian Ocean, separating Persia from Arabia, 2556, 195, map, 197.

Persian lamb, fur, 1412, 275.

Persian rugs, 705, 706.

Persian Wars (493–479 B.C.), **2555**, 1522; and defence of Acropolis, 21; effect on Gk. art, 1528; Marathon, 2097, 230; Salamis, 2556, 230; Thermopylae, 2556, 3201.

Persim'mon. A tree of the ebony family; a native of N. Amer., it yields a hard wood used for shoe lasts and handles; the Japanese persimmon is an important fruit tree.

Person, in grammar, 3314.

Personal names, 2272; superstitions about, 2057.

Personal pronoun, 2690.

Personifica'tion, figure of speech, 1271.

Perspec'tive, 2557.

"Perspex," a transparent plastic, 2627; lenses of, 1925.

Perspira'tion, 2979, 1243.

"Persuasion." Novel by Jane Austen, 306.

Perth, James Eric Drummond, 16th Earl of (b. 1876). Brit. diplomat. Sec. General to League of Nations (1919–33); Ambassador to Italy (1933–1939); succeeded 15th earl in 1937.

Perth. Cap. of Western Australia, **2557**; pop. with Fremantle 272,586; 3368.

Perth, Scot. Co. tn. of Perthshire on Tay; pop. 39,700; rope and twine, textiles, dyes; stock market; scene of murder of James I (1437); 2558.

Perthshire, Scot. Co. noted for its scenic grandeur; a. 2,493 sq. m.; pop. 120,000; co. tn., Perth; 2558.

Peru. Republic on Pacific coast of S. Amer.; max. est. 524,000 sq. m.; pop. (est.) 7,023,000, **2558**; 2561; map, 2559; Andes Mts., 152; cap. Lima, 1948, 2560, 2561; Chile and, 805; minerals, 2559, 3024; money, 2202; mummies, 2256, 921; population, 2560, 3026; quinine, 2559, 2718; surface features, 2559; transport, need of improved, 2560; weaving, in early times, 3191; History, 2560, 3025; Pizarro's conquest, 2560, 2616; Incas, 1689, 1690; independence gained, 491; war with Chile, 805, 2560.

Perugia (pe-rōō'-jah), It. Historic city on R. Tiber, 84 m. N. of Rome; pop. 82,400; cath. and other interesting buildings; Etruscan gateways, frescoes by Perugino; old univ. (13th cent.); anc. Perugia was one of 12 principal cities of Etruria; taken by Romans 310 B.C.; centre of Umbrian school of painting (15th cent.).

Perugino (pā-roo-jē'-nō). "Easel name" of painter Pietro Vannucci (1446–1524), of Perugia; created classic type of Madonna and moulded early style of Raphael, 1775, 2745.

Peru'vian balsam, 2868.

Peru'vian bark. See Cinchona.

Pesaro (pā'-zah-rō). It. spt. on Adriatic at mouth of r. Foglia; pop. 44,000; several palaces; silk, ships, ironware, earthenware; founded by Romans 184 B.C.

Pescadores (pes-ka-dō'-rez), ("fishers' isles"). An isl. group (50 sq. m.) between China and Formosa; Jap. ceded to China 1945. Name also given to isl. group off coast of Peru.

Peseta (pā-sā'-tah). A silver coin, the unit of the Sp. monetary system; consists of 100 centesimos.

Peshawar (pe-shah'-war) or **Peshawur**. Cap. of N.W. Frontier Prov., Pakistan, on R. Bara, 19 m. E. of Khyber Pass; pop. 275,000; centre of trade with Afghanistan and Central Asia; military and air base; manufactures scarfs; rly., 56.

Pest, Hungary. Old tn., now part of Budapest, 600.

Pestalozzi (pes-ta-lot'-sē), **Johann Heinrich** (1746–1827). Swiss educational reformer, 1398.

Pétain (pā-tan), **Henri Phillippe** (b. 1856). Fr. soldier and statesman, 2560, 1452, 3417.

Petals, of flowers, 531, 1321, 1917.

Peter, St. One of the Twelve Apostles, 2562, 188, 817, 818, 2495.

Peter, Epistles of. Two books of New Testament ascribed to Apostle Peter, addressed to scattered Christians urging them to conduct themselves in an exemplary manner and avoid false teachings.

Peter I, the Great (1672–1725). Tsar of Rus., 2562, 2563, 2847, 2855; Bering's explorations, 415; conquers Baltic provinces, 1899; founds St.

Petersburg (Leningrad), 1022, 2847; war with Charles XII, 758.

Peter II (1715–30). Grandson of Peter the Great, who became Tsar of Rus., in 1727, on the death of Catherine I.

Peter III (1728–62). Emperor of Russia, imbecile grandson of Peter the Great; after 6 months' rule deposed in July 1762 by his wife, Catherine II, and probably murdered; makes peace with Prussia, 2924.

Peter I, Kara-Georgevitch (1846–1921). King of Serbia, 2922, 3410.

Peter II (b. 1923). King of Yugoslavia, 3439, 3440. In 1947 deprived of his nationality and his property confiscated.

Peterborough. City of Northants; pop. 52,000; burnt by Danes; 2563, 2385, 1618; cath., 2385; "soke" of, pop. 61,000, 2563, 2385; sugar beet factory, 397.

"Peter Grimes." First opera of Benjamin Britten, based on Crabbe's poem "The Borough"; prod. Sadler's Wells, June 1945, 2437, 2439.

Peterhouse, Cambridge (also called St. Peter's College), 666.

Peter Lombard (c. 1100–60). It. theologian and teacher; bishop of Paris 1159 ("Four Books of Sentences," famous theological text-book).

Peterloo massacre. Name given to dispersal by military of a meeting at St. Peter's Field, Manchester, in 1819, when several lives were lost, 3278.

"Peter Pan." Statue in Kensington Gardens, London, the work of Sir George Frampton; there is a replica in Brussels, 2906, 2908.

"Peter Pan." Fairy play by Sir James Barrie, 364; story retold, 364.

"Peter Simple." Novel by Frederick Marryat, published in 1834.

Peter's Pence. A tax levied in England by the pope in 8th or 9th century. Abolished by Henry VIII in 1534 during quarrel with Papacy.

Peter the Hermit (d. 1115). Fr. monk, preacher of First Crusade, 936.

Pethick-Lawrence, Frederick William, 1st Baron (b. 1871). Secretary for India and Burma 1945–47.

Petiole (pet'-i-ōl), of leaves, 1914.

Petitgrain oil, 2152.

Petition of rights, 1196, 1489.

Petit-point, embroidery, 1133.

Petkov, Nikola (1889–1947). Leader of Bulgarian Peasants' party, executed Sept. 23, 1947, for opposition to Communist govt.

Petra (pet'-ra). Anc. city in mts. of N.W. Arabia; once important caravan centre; cap. of Nabataeans; absorbed into Rom. empire A.D. 106; remarkable remains, especially cliff temples and dwellings.

Petrarch (pē'-trahrk) (**Francesco Petrarca**) (1304–74). It. lyric poet, scholar and patriot, second to Dante alone in It. poetry, 1786, 2764.

Pet'rel. A sea bird, 2563.

Petrie, Sir (William Matthew) Flinders (1853–1942). Eng. Egyptologist; author of many works on Egyptian history and antiquities, 208.

Petrified forests, 234.

Pet'rograd. See Leningrad.

Pet'rol. Volatile liquid distilled from petroleum, **2564**, 1619; "antiknock," 1567, 3185; extracted from coal, 856, 1674, 2429; engine, 1016; internal combustion engine, 1736; danger of fire, 1289.

Petroleum, 2564; with natural gas, 1420; in lamps, 1887, 1945; products 998, 1674. See Oil.

Petro'nius Arbiter. Rom. writer of age of Nero, 1897.

Petruchio (pe-trōō'-chi-ō). Hero of Shakespeare's "Taming of the Shrew," who tames Katharina "the shrew" into a model wife.

Petsamo. Ice-free pt. of Murmansk region, R.S.F.S.R., on Arctic; ceded by Russ. to Finland in 1920; changed hands several times in Russo-Finn. war; ceded to Russ. Sept. 1944; 3419.

Pettie, John (1839–93). Scot. artist, became R.A. in 1873; picture by, 1791, plate f. 1865.

Petty jury, 1842 ; developed by Henry II, 1609.

Petty officer. In the Royal Navy ranks below an officer just as a N.C.O. does in the army.

Petunia. A perennial plant introduced into Brit. from S. Amer. in the 19th cent. ; plants 6 in. to 2 ft. high, funnel-shaped flowers, usually shade of blue, red, or purple.

Petun'tse. Chinese name for variety of feldspar, 2670.

Pew'ter, an alloy, originally of tin and lead ; now sometimes of tin, copper and antimony.

Pfalz. Ger. name for **Palatinate.**

Pforzheim (pforts'-hīm). Ger. mfg. tn. in Baden, 16 m. S.E. of Karlsruhe ; pop. (1939) 79,800.

Phaeacians (fē-ā´-shanz), in Gk. myth., people who inhabited isl. of Scheria (probably Corfu) ; entertain Odysseus, 2422.

Phaethon (fā-e-thon), in Greek myth., the son of Helios, 2564.

Phagocytes (fag´-ō-sīts). Body cells that destroy bacteria and other cells ; white blood cells (leucocytes), 474.

Phalan'gers. Various five-toed marsupials.

Phalanges (fa-lan´-jēz) (plural of phalanx), scientific name for toes or fingers, 1342, 1572.

Phalanx (fal´-anks). Order of ranks in battle ; finger bones named from, 1572 ; Macedonian, 106 : of Sparta and Thebes, 3197.

Phalarope (fal´-a-rōp). A small wading bird ; grey phalarope is common winter visitor ; red-necked breeds in far N. of Brit. ; males hatch the eggs, 447.

Phalerum (fa-lēr´-rum). One of anc. harbours of Athens, chiefly used before Persian Wars ; superseded by port of Piraeus.

Phan'erogams. In the Linnaean classification, all flowering plants, 2918.

Pharaohs (fār´-ōz). Kings of anc. Egypt.

Pharisees (fa´-ri-sēz). Most powerful and exclusive Jewish sect at time of Christ ; especially exact in observance of traditions and ceremonies, 1830.

Pharmacopoeia (fahr-ma-kō-pē´-a). An official publication issued by the General Medical Council containing the list of drugs of the Materia Medica, with directions for the preparation of medicines.

Pharos (fā´-ros). Isl. at mouth of Nile, 110, 1943.

Pharos. Lighthouse, one of Seven Wonders of World, 109, 1945, 2924, *plate f. 2924.*

Pharpar (fahr´-pahr). One of the two famous "rivers of Damascus." *See* Abana.

Pharsalus (fahr-sā´-lus) (now Pharsala). Gk. city of S. Thessaly ; battle fought between Caesar and Pompey (48 B.C.), 652, 2654.

Pharynx (far´-inks). Lined passage running from nostril above and behind the mouth to the oesophagus.

Phases of moon, 2225.

Pheasant (fez´-ant). A long-tailed, fowl-like bird, **2565** ; belongs to family *Phasianidae,* which also includes chickens, 2671 ; peacocks, 2532 ; turkeys, 3261.

Pheidias (fī´-di-as) (490–432 B.C.). Greatest Gk. sculptor, **2566,** 21, 1537 ; sculptures, *1143, 1144* ; statue of Athena, 284 ; statue of Zeus, 2923, 3443, *plate f. 1524.*

Pheidippides (fī-dip´-i-dēz). Athenian runner, 2097.

Phelps (felps), **Samuel** (1804–78). Famous Eng. Shakespearian actor, playing chiefly tragedy but also comedy roles ; at Sadler's Wells Theatre, London, he produced upwards of thirty of Shakespeare's plays.

Phenacetin (fe-nas´-e-tin). A fever-allaying drug ; obtained from coal-tar, 1048.

Phenobarbitone, a sedative drug, poison and antidote to poisons, 1048. 2638.

Phe'nol. *See* **Carbolic Acid.**

Phenol-formaldehyde, in rayon mfr. 2749 ; in synthetic resin, 2768.

Phenolphthalein (fe-nol-thal´-ē-in). A laxative drug obtained from coal-tar.

Phi (fī), ψ, Φ. Twenty-first letter of Gk. alphabet.

Phi Beta Kappa (fī bē´-ta kap´-a). The name of the oldest college or literary society in the U.S.A. ; the first society was founded at William and Mary College, Virginia, in 1776.

Philadelphia (fil-a-del´-fi-a), Pennsylvania, U.S.A. Chief city of state and 3rd city of the country ; pop. 1,931,000 ; **2566, 2545** ; **Liberty Bell,** *3291.*

Philae (fī´-lē). **Temple of.** On isl. of Philae in R. Nile ; erected by Egyptians to goddess Isis, 4th cent. B.C.

Philately (fi-lat´-e-li). Stamp-collecting. *See* Stamps.

Philby, Harry St. John (b. 1885), British explorer ; crosses Ruba-el-Khali desert of Arabia, 195.

Phile'mon, Epistle to. Book of New Testament ; written by Paul during first captivity at Rome explaining the return of a runaway slave who had been converted to Christianity.

Philibert (fē-lē-bār´), **Emmanuel,** Duke of Savoy 1553–80.

Philip. One of the Twelve Apostles, 188.

Philip I (1052–1108). King of Fr. ; seized advantage of quarrels among his powerful vassals to enlarge crown holdings ; ancestry, 2567.

Philip II, Augustus (1165–1223). King of Fr., 2567, 1611 ; quarrels with Richard I, 2567, 2776 ; Crusade, *937* ; wins Normandy from Eng., 2377.

Philip IV, the Fair (1268–1314). King of Fr., **2567,** 500.

Philip VI (1293–1350). King of Fr., **2567,** 1652.

Philip II (382–336 B.C.). King of Macedonia, father of Alexander the Great, and conqueror of Greece, 105, 1524 : Demosthenes denounces. 990.

Philip I (1478–1506). King of Sp. ; son of Maximilian I and Mary of Burgundy ; right to Castile and Aragon through wife Joanna disputed by his father-in-law Ferdinand ; father of Charles V.

Philip II (1527–98). King of Sp., **2567,** Armada defeated, 237 ; battle of Lepanto, 746, 3264 ; makes Madrid royal capital, 2054 ; marries Mary of Eng., 2114 ; revolt of Netherlands, 2321, 3381 ; seizes Portuguese crown, 2660.

Philip III (1578–1621). King of Sp., succeeding on the death of Philip II, his father, in 1598 ; a pious but weak ruler, Sp. continued to decline during his reign.

Philip IV (1605–65). King of Sp., incapable administrator ; reign marked by rapid decline of Sp. power ; honours Velazquez, 3307.

Philip V (1683–1746). King of Sp., grandson of Louis XIV, founder of Bourbon dynasty, 2029, 2567.

Philip, King. The Indian chief Metacomet (c. 1639–76), sachem of Wampanoags in Mass., U.S.A. ; son of Massasoit ; leader of "King Philip's War" (1676) against New Eng. colonists.

Philip, Prince, Duke of Edinburgh (b. 1921), husband of Princess Elizabeth ; formerly a prince of Greece, son of Prince and Princess Andrew of Greece, he served in the R.N. as Lt. Philip Mountbatten, being a nephew of Lord Mountbatten ; betrothed to Princess Elizabeth July 1947, married Nov. 1947, when he was created Duke of Edinburgh and a prince of the Royal house ; on wedding day, *1151.*

Philip "the Good" (1396–1467). Duke of Burgundy ; signed treaty of Troyes for Fr. ; later aided Eng. against Fr., gaining considerable territory ; patron of commerce and industry ; founded Order of Golden Fleece.

Philip of Swabia (c. 1177–1208). Youngest son of Frederick Barbarossa, Duke of Swabia ; succeeded brother Henry VI as emperor (1198).

murdered while disputing claims of his rival, Otto IV.

Philippa. Queen of Edward III, *1653.*

Philippe Égalité. *See* **Orleans, Louis Philippe, Duke of.**

Philippi (fi-lip´-ī). Anc. city of N.E. Macedonia ; battle of (42 B.C.), 303.

Philip'pians, Epistle to. Book of the New Testament ; letter from Paul to Christians at Philippi reassuring them of his prospects of release and appealing for unity in their church : probably written at Rome A.D. 63.

Philip'pics, of Demosthenes, 990 ; of Cicero, 827.

Philippine Islands. Archipelago between China Sea and Pacific Ocean, since July 1946 an independent republic, formerly Sp. then U.S.A. possession ; a., with the Sulu isls., 114,830 sq. m. ; pop. 16,971,000 ; **2568,** 1076 ; cable connexions, 643 ; cap. Manila, 2088 ; coconuts, *863* ; Manila hemp, 1608, *2826* ; sugar, 3112 ; water buffalo, 602. *History :* Magellan discovers, 2056 ; as U.S. possession, 2569 ; independence, 2569 ; Japs occupy 1942–45, 2569, 3293, 3420 : liberated, 2473, 2474, 3424.

Philippopolis (fil-i-pop´-o-lis) or **Plovdiv.** Second largest city of Bulgaria, S.E. of Sofia ; pop. 99,880 ; anc. Thracian city ; heavily bombed during 2nd World War ; trade in silk, cotton, attar of roses.

Phil'istines. Tribe of anc. Canaan, **2570** ; David defeats, 979.

Phillip, Arthur (1738–1814). Eng. naval officer who became governor of Botany Bay, and helped in the colonization of Australia ; he arrived in Botany Bay in 1788 ; 3144.

Phillips, Stephen (1868–1915). Eng. poet ("Marpessa " ; " Paolo and Francesca"; "Herod": "Ulysses": " Nero ").

Philology (fi-lol´-o-ji), **2570** ; Eng. language, 1209 ; personal names, 2272 ; slang, 2980 ; universal language, 1223.

Philomel (fil´-ō-mel) or **Philome'la.** Poetic name for nightingale. Philomela, in Gk. myth., was sister of Procne, wife of Tereus, king of Thrace ; in revenge for their wrongs they killed Itys, Tereus' son, and served him as food to his father ; the gods punished them by turning Procne into a swallow and Philomela into a nightingale.

Philosophy (fi-los´-o-fi), **2571** ; work of Aristotle, 231 ; Epictetus, 1220 ; Epicurus, 1220 ; in Germany, 1456 ; Greek, 1540 ; Marcus Aurelius, 2099 ; natural, 2591 ; Plato, 2628 ; Pythagoras, 2710 ; Socrates, 1540, 2996, 2997.

Philpotts, Eden (b. 1862). Eng. novelist and playwright, born in India ; novels with a rural Devonshire background include "Children of the Mist " and " Widecombe Fair " ; and his plays, "The Farmer's Wife " and " Yellow Sands."

Phiva or **Thivae,** Greece. Modern name for Thebes ; pop. 3,500.

Phlogiston (flō-jis´-ton). Theoretical "fire substance" supposed in 17th and 18th cents. to exist in combustible bodies and be lost upon combustion, 2589 ; theory overthrown by Lavoisier, 1280.

Phlox (floks). A favourite garden flower, **2572.**

Phobos (fō´-bos). Satellite at Mars, 2619.

Phocion (fō´-si-on) (d. 317 B.C.). Athenian general. opponent of Demosthenes and the anti-Macedonians, virtual ruler of Athens for a time after Chaeronea ; finally forced to drink hemlock for alleged treason.

Phocis (fō´-sis). Anc. dist. in cent. Greece ; chief mt., Parnassus ; took part in Sacred War (357–346 B.C.) and was conquered by Philip of Macedon ; contained Delphic oracle. 988.

Phoenicians (fē-nish´-anz). Semitic race inhabiting narrow strip along Mediterranean coast of anc. Syria.

2573, 2920 ; alphabet, 125, 2573 ; colonies, 711, 2072, 2573, 2968, 3032 ; glass-making, 1472 ; bring grape to Europe, 1499 ; language, 1601 ; aid Solomon, 2573, 2999. *Exploration and commerce*, 1431, 2573 ; Africa, 65, 711 ; Britain, 1193, *1201*, 2573 ; ships, 2945 ; Sicily, 2968 ; Spain, 3033.

Phoenix (fē'-niks), Arizona, U.S.A. Cap. and popular winter and health resort in s. centre ; pop. 65,400 ; trade centre of rich farming dist. created by great Roosevelt dam ; 235.

Phoenix. Fabulous sacred bird of anc. Egyptians, said to come out of Arabia every 500 years to Heliopolis, where it burned itself on altar and rose again from its ashes young and beautiful ; regarded as symbol of rising sun and immortality.

Phoenix Park, Dublin, 1050 ; murders, 2525.

Phon. The unit of the National Scale of Loudness, based upon the decibel scale with an arbitrary zero corresponding to an acoustical pressure of 0·0002 dynes per sq. cm., using a 1,000-cycle source of sound as a standard. *See* **Decibel ; Noise.**

Phonography. A form of shorthand, 2961.

Phonopticon. Device for converting light impulses into sound to enable the blind to read through hearing.

Phorcys (for'-sis). In Gk. myth., a sea-god, father of the Gorgons, the Graeae, and other monsters.

Phosphate (fos'-fāt). A salt of one of the phosphoric acids, used as fertilizer ; in human body, 498, 2601.

Phosphate rock, 2574, 2845 ; in Pacific isls., 2472.

Phos'phor-bronze, 587.

Phosphorescence and Fluorescence (fos-for-es'-ens, flŏŏ-or-es'-ens). Emission of light without heat, 2573 ; luminescence among insects, 1288 ; of sea creatures, 2414, *2418* ; in radar receiver, 2727 ; of zinc sulphide, 2731.

Phosphor'ic acids. Compounds of hydrogen, oxygen, and phosphorus.

Phosphorus (P) (fos'-fo-*rus*). An element of the nitrogen group, **2574** ; atomic weight, 31·0 ; exists in several allotropic forms of different colours ; red phosphorus, used in matches, is harmless and melts at 1135°F., 2119 ; white phosphorus is highly poisonous and catches fire at 90°F. ; antidotes, 2574 ; in bones, 498 ; in fluorescent lighting, 1136 ; in food, 1338 ; in iron and steel, 1756 ; needed by plants, 2998, 2621 ; properties, 776 ; sulphide in matches, 2119.

"Phossy Jaw." Disease of jawbone which attacked persons engaged in manufacture of matches, 2119.

Phot. Unit of illumination ; one phot=1,000 milliphots=10,000 lux.

Photo-chemistry. Study of chem. reactions in which light has impt. part, **2574** ; photography, 2577 ; photo-synthesis, 2589.

Photo-electric Cell. A light-sensitive elec. valve of great use in many automatic devices, 1138, 1943, 2574, 2711 ; in photo-telegraphy, 2577 ; in television, 3182.

Photo-electric Devices : burglar alarms, calculating machines, in canning, control of doors and lift gates, in dyeing, exposure meters, packaging, picture transmission, pyrometer, smoke detection, sound films, "speaking clock," street lighting, **2574** ; the Emitron, 3182 ; in facsimile transmission, 3398 ; selenium in, 2920 ; sound on film, 3012 ; thallium compound in, 3193.

Photog'raphy, *plates f. 2576, 2577*, **2577**, *2581–2588* ; 1924 ; from the air, 2096 ; in archaeology, 208 ; in astronomy, 281, 2413 ; bromine in, 1567 ; camera, 672 ; cinematograph, *833* ; colour, *plates f. 2576, 2577* ; exposure meters, 2574 ; infra-red, *1596, 1724* ; lens, 1924 ; of Nature, *2285–88*, *2289*, 2290 ; a photo-chemical process, 2574 ; plates at

low temps., 1391 ; and process engraving, 1218, *plates f. 2688, 2689* ; time switches in, 3215.

Photo-engraving, 1218.

Photogravure' process, 1219, 2689.

Photo-lithog'raphy, 2690.

Photom'eter. For measuring intensity of light ; in Bunsen's photometer a screen of paper, with a spot of grease, is placed between two lights to be compared, which are then moved until the spot is invisible from either side. Intensities of two lights differ as squares of distances from screen. Modern photometers use photo-electric cell, 2575 ; " thalofide " cell, 3193.

Photomi'crograph. Photograph taken through a microscope, *532*.

Photon. Unit of radiation energy ; a light particle or quantum, 2711 ; 1227, 1943.

Pho'tosphere. Light-giving layer of sun, 3120.

Photo-syn'thesis, in plants ; transformation by sunlight and chlorophyll of carbon dioxide and water into carbohydrates, **2589**, 2621, 434, 1915 ; carried out by chlorophyll in leaves, 1914 ; a photo-chemical process, 2594.

Photo-telegraphy. Sending pictures by telephone or wireless, 2577.

Phototr'opism, among plants, 1914, 2622, *2624*.

Phrase, in grammar, 2920.

Phrenol'ogy. Pseudo-science purporting to discover talents and mental characteristics from a study of the shape and irregularities of the skull.

Phrygia (frij'-i-a). Anc. country of w. Asia Minor ; extent varied at different periods ; overrun by Cimmerians 7th cent. B.C. ; later ruled by Lydia, Persia, Macedon, and Rome ; music and orgiastic rites influenced Greeks.

Phumiphon Aduldet (b. 1928), king of Siam, succeeded his brother in 1946 ; 2965.

Phycomycetes (fī-kō-mī-sē'-tēz). A class of fungi, 1408 ; includes some of the lower mildews and moulds, 2173.

Phylloxera (fil-oks-ēr'-a) or grape aphid. An insect parasite.

Phylogeny (fī-loj'-e-ni). Ancestral history of a species or race ; of plants, 531 ; rehearsed in animal embryos, 1156.

Phy'lum. A major division in biological classification, the first sub-division of a Kingdom and itself divided into Classes.

Physical chemistry. Physics and chemistry, 2591, 3672 ; electro-chemistry, a typical study, 1136.

" Physical Energy." Statue by G. F. Watts, in Rhodes Memorial, Groote Schuur (S. Africa), *697* ; a replica is in Kensington Gardens, London.

Physical geography. *See* Physiography.

Physical training, **2589** ; athletics, 287 ; field-dances, *1334*, 1335 ; hygienic value of exercise, 1657 ; influence on Gk. sculpture, 1528 ; why violent exercise after meals is harmful, 1593 ; correct posture in sitting and walking, *1676* ; in standing, *2591*.

Physician, work of, 2132, 2598.

Physicians, Royal College of. Corporation founded by Henry VIII, in 1518, under presidency of Linacre. Has fine building and library in London.

Physics. Science of matter and energy, **2591**, 1512 ; air, 88 ; Aristotle's contributions, 232 ; and the atom, 294 ; capillary attraction, 698 ; how it affects our lives, 2593 ; centrifugal force, 741 ; conservation of energy, 1160 ; development of, 2593 ; Einstein theory of light deflection, *1514* ; electricity, 1127 ; ether theory, 1226 ; Faraday's discoveries, 1260 ; friction, 1396, *2592* ; Galileo, 1414 ; gases, 1419 ; gravitation, 1512 ; heat, 1593 ; hydraulics, 1665 ; hydrometer, 1674 ; hygrometer, 1677 ; light, 1939 ; lightning, 1945 ; liquefying gases, 91, 1411, 1391, ammonia, 1392 ; magnetism, 2060 ; mechanics, 2127 ; Newton's work, 2348 ; nuclear, 296 ; pneumatics, 2632 ; quantum

theory, 2711 ; radiation, 2728 ; radium and radio-activity, 2731 ; relativity, 1512, 2760 ; sound, 3009, *3010* ; spectrum and spectroscope, 3055, *f. 3056* ; Tyndall's contributions, 3270 ; vacuum, 3301 ; wave motion, 3358, *3009*, *3010* ; X-rays, 3430. *See also* under the leading physicists ; **Atom ; Symbol ; Telegraphy ; Telephone ; Telescope ; Television ; Wireless ; and lists of Electrical Terms ; Wireless and Television Terms.**

Phys'iocrats. School of 18th cent. French economists, 1081.

Physiog'raphy. The science dealing with the form of the earth's surface, **2595** ; avalanches, 322 ; canyons, 1498 ; factors affecting climate, 840, 3246 ; continents, origin of, 1433, 2384 ; coral reefs and atolls, 908 ; the Earth, 1067 ; earthquakes, 1069 ; geysers, 1459 ; glaciers, 1469 ; icebergs, 1682 ; lakes, origin, 1885 ; land, *plates f. 1432, 1433* ; oceans, 2413, *2414* ; relations with geology, 1432 ; sand dunes, 2870 ; soil formation, 2998 ; springs, 3069 ; valley formation, 3302 ; volcanoes, 3328 ; work of winds, 3384.

Physiology (fiz-i-ol'-o-ji), and anatomy, **2598**, 434 ; bio-chemistry, 429 ; blood and circulation, 474, 1591, 2701 ; body heat, 2466 ; bones, 498, 2977 ; brain, 545–547 ; cells the units of body structures, 738 ; digestion, 1016, 3094 ; ear, 1065 ; eye, 1252, *1254* ; foot, 1342 ; glands and their work, 1470 ; hair, 1564 ; hand, 1572 ; heart, 1591, 2701 ; hygiene, 1675 ; jaws, *3163* ; kidneys, 1855 ; liver, 1968 ; lungs, 2039 ; muscles, 2258 ; nerves, 2316 ; pulse, 2701 ; respiration, 2039 ; skeleton, 2977 ; skin, 2979 ; sleep, 2983 ; smell, 2986 ; stomach, 1016, 3094 ; taste, 3157 ; teeth, 3163, *3164* ; tongue, 3223 ; touch, 3231 ; voice, 3327. *See* **Disease ; Food ; Food Values ; Germs ; Hygiene ; and the** chief topics by name.

Physiology, of plants, 533, 2589, 2601, 2620.

Phytoflagella'ta. Group of unicellular animals containing chlorophyll.

Pi (pī), π, Π (Rom. p, P). 16th letter of Gk. alphabet ; used as symbol representing the ratio of the length of circumference of a circle to the length of its diameter = 3·14159 ; 1436.

Piacenza (pē-ah-chent'-sa). Fortified tn. in N.-cent. Italy on R. Po ; pop. 79,670 ; founded by Romans as Placentia 218 B.C. ; a leading tn. of Lombard League in Middle Ages.

Piano (pē-a'-nō), 2601, 2264 ; how made, *2603*.

Pianola or **Player-piano.** Apparatus by means of which the piano can be played automatically with music rolls, 2603.

Piat (Projector, Infantry, Anti-Tank). Brit. gun, introduced in 1943 ; weighs 33 lb., fires 2¼ lb. bomb, from shoulder, to pierce 4 ins. of armour.

Piave (pē-ah'-vă). R. of N.E. It. ; rises in Carnic Alps and joins Adriatic 20 m. N.E. of Venice ; length 130 m. ; *map*, *1764* ; scene of desperate fighting in 1st World War, 3411.

Piazzi (pe-at'-si), **Giuseppe** (1746–1826). It. astronomer ; discovered Ceres, largest of the asteroids (diam. 485 m.) on Jan. 1, 1801.

Picardy (pik'-ar-di). Old prov. of N. Fr. ; contained towns of Amiens (cap.) and Boulogne, and battlefields of Agincourt, Crécy, St. Quentin ; 1st World War battle, March–April 1918.

Picaresque (pik-*a*-resk') novel, 2401.

Picasso (pē-kas'-sō), **Pablo** (b. 1881). Sp. painter, **2604**, 2477, 3050 ; ballet décor, *347*.

Pic'cadilly, Manchester, *2085*.

Pic'cadilly Circus, London, *2017*, 2015 ; Eros statue in, *2907*.

Piccard (pē'-kahr), **Auguste** (b. 1884). Swiss scientist ; investigated action of cosmic rays by balloon ascents into the stratosphere (1931 and 1932) ; in 1945 investigated disintegration of sunlight at ocean depths, and in 1947 built a bathyscaphe or submarine chamber in which he made descents in the sea off the N.W. African coast.

Pic'colo. A small flute, 2445, 3404.

Picea (pis'-ē-*a*) The spruce genus of trees, 3070.

Pichincha (pē-chēn'-ch*a*). Volcano on W. slope of Andes near Quito, Ecuador (highest peak 15,918 ft.); battle between patriots and Spaniards which freed Ecuador was fought on its slopes May 24, 1822.

Picidae (pis'-i-dē). The woodpecker family, 3403.

Pick'ering, Edward Charles (1846–1919). Amer. astronomer; devoted particular attention to the study of light and spectra of stars; invented meridian photometer.

Pickford, Mary (b. 1893). Canadian film actress; born at Toronto; real name Gladys Mary Smith; appeared on stage as child, but achieved fame as "the world's sweetheart" in films; later entered business management of films.

Pickle, in brine and vinegar, 1340.

Pick-up, in radiogram, 1497.

"Pickwick Papers." Novel by Dickens; story, "Mr. Pickwick Goes to Dingley Dell," 1013, *1014*.

Pico Mt. On isl. of Pico, Azores (7,612 ft.), 325.

Picric acid, 699, 1250.

Picts. People of disputed origin, early inhabitants of Scot., 2558, 2892; invade Brit., 1193, 1194, 574; in Shetland Isls., 2945.

Picture Writing. *See* **Hieroglyphics; Ideographic writing.**

Pid'dock. Bivalve mollusc which bores in soft rocks.

Pie. A copper coin of sub.-cont. of India.

Pied fly-catcher, *1330*.

Piedmont (pēd'-mont). Division of N.W. It.; comprises provinces of Turin, Novara, Alessandria, and Cuneo; 11,331 sq. m.; pop. 3,602,720; 1763, 1769; cap. Turin, 3261; annexed by Napoleon I, 2276; united It., 2874, 1769, 737, 1418, 3261.

KINGS OF PIEDMONT AND SARDINIA AND OF UNITED ITALY

1720–30	Victor Amadeus I
1730–73	Charles Emmanuel I
1773–96	Victor Amadeus II
1796–1802	Charles Emmanuel II
1802–06	Victor Emmanuel I
(1805–13	Sardinia part of the kingdom of Italy under Napoleon I)
1814–21	Victor Emmanuel I (restored)
1821–31	Charles Felix
1831–49	Charles Albert
1849–78	Victor Emmanuel II (King of Italy, 1861)
1878–1900	Humbert I
1900–1946	Victor Emmanuel III
1946 (May–June)	Humbert II

Piedmont region, a name (means "at the foot of the mountains") used for that part of the Atlantic coast plain between the Appalachian Mts. and the coastal plain.

Pied Piper of Hamelin. Magician in Ger. legend who, by his piping, charmed the rats of Hamelin into following him into the r.; because he was not paid he lured the children of the city away; story used by Browning in poem of same name.

Pienaar, A. A. Afrikaans writer, 3022.

Fiepowder, Court of, 1257.

Pier. In architecture, a detached pillar or wall supporting the ends of adjoining trusses or spans; or the springers of adjacent arches.

Pier, Palace, at Brighton, *570*; Admiralty, at Dover, 1031; of Mulberry harbour, 2251.

Pierce, Franklin (1804–69). 14th pres. of U.S.A., from 1853 to 1857; regarded as one most incompetent to hold presidency.

Pierian (pī-ēr'-i-*a*n) **Spring.** In Gk. myth., fountain of the Muses in Pieria, a region of Macedonia; supposed to give poetic inspiration.

Pierrot (pyă'-rō). Idealized clown in Fr. pantomime, similar to It. Harlequin.

Piers Plowman. *See* **Langland, William.**

Pietermaritzburg (pē-ter-ma'-rits-bêrg). Cap. of Natal, 40 m. N.W. of Durban; has various industries, including brewing, tanning; pop. 63,160; 2279, 3020.

Piezo-electricity. Generation of electric current by compression of crystals, **2604**; in electric clocks, 1127; microphone, 2163; quartz in, 2713.

Pig, a domesticated mammal of the swine family, **2605**; lucerne as feed, 2034; and rattlesnake, 2747; lard, 1263.

Pigafetta (pē-gah-fet'-*a*), **Antonio** (1491–c. 1534). Companion of Magellan, 2056.

Pigeons and doves, 2605, *2607*; care of young, 444; courtship, 441; dodo, a relative, 1025; homing instinct, 2606.

Pig iron, 123, 469, 1753.

Pigments, in paints, 2478.

Pigmies. *See* **Pygmies.**

Pigmy grass, 1509.

"Pig-sticking," 1658.

Pig-tail ape, *2209*.

Pigtails or queues; in China, 807, *809.*

Pike, Zebulon Montgomery (1779–1813). Amer. general and explorer, 1431; first to view mtn. called after him "Pike's Peak."

Pike. A voracious freshwater fish, **2606.**

Pike's Peak. Famous peak of Rocky Mts. near Colorado Springs, Colo., U.S.A., 14,108 ft.; discovered 1806 by Zebulon Pike; vegetation, 2795.

Pilas'ter. In architecture, a square column, generally attached to a wall, as an ornamental support to an arch, etc., and seldom projecting more than one-fourth or one-third of its breadth from the wall.

Pilate (pī'-l*a*t), **Pontius** (first cent. A.D.), Rom. gov. of Judaea; gives up Jesus to be crucified, *1824*, 1825.

Pilatus (pi-lah'-t*u*s), **Mt.,** Switzerland (6,996 ft.); railway up, *2736.*

Pil'chard, an edible fish which resembles a small herring, found chiefly on the coasts of Devon and Cornwall, 1620, *1621.*

Pilcomayo (pēl-kō-mah'-yō), r. of Bolivia and Paraguay; flows 1,000 m. from the Andes to the Paraguay r., 2512.

Pile, atomic. *See* **Atomic pile.**

Pile-driver, in dam construction, *958*; worked by gravity, *plate f. 1513.*

Pil'grimage of Grace, insurrection in N. England, on behalf of the monks (1536), 1612.

Pilgrim Fathers, who sailed to America in the Mayflower (1620), **2606,** *2608*; 2118, 2122, *2123.*

Pilgrims, 2608; Canterbury, 389, 692, 761; and Crusades, 936; Mahomedan, 2066; pilgrimage centres in Asia, 2125, *2126*; scallop shell a badge, *2609,* 2879.

"Pilgrim's Progress." Allegory by John Bunyan, 617, 2401; story retold, 618.

Pilgrim's scallop, *2943.*

Pilgrim's Way. Anct. road, stretching from Winchester to Canterbury, and passing foot of North Downs, and through N. Kent. Pilgrims to the shrine of St. Thomas Becket at Canterbury followed this road, *1852.*

Pilgrim Trust. Founded in 1930 by Mr. Edward Stephen Harkness, a citizen of U.S.A., in appreciation of the sacrifices made by Great Britain in the 1st World War. It is administered by trustees for charitable purposes.

Pilica. R. of Poland, 3326.

Pillar. In architecture, a kind of irregular column, round and insulate, but deviating from the proportion of a just column; the form is more generally applied to Gothic architecture than to Classical; pillars are used for support or ornament, or as a monument or memorial.

Pillars of Hercules. In anc. geography, the two promontories, Gibraltar in Europe and Abyla in Africa, at E.

extremity of Strait of Gibraltar, 1463; legendary origin, 1615.

Pil'lory. Instrument of punishment, 2687.

Pillow, or **bobbin lace,** 1877, *plate f. 1881.*

Pilnyak (pēl-nyak'), **Boris** (b. 1884). Pen-name of Boris Andreyevich Vogou, Russian short story writer and novelist ("The Naked Year," "Machines and Wolves"), 2856.

Pilot. In shipping, person taken on board ship to conduct it through a difficult channel or river, or into or out of port.

Pilot, automatic. Gyroscope and compass control of aircraft keeping it on predetermined course; called "George" in R.A.F.; 41, 1562.

Pilotless plane. Skymaster made 8,000 m. full automatic control flight, including landing, Ohio and Newfoundland, to England and back, Sept. 26–Oct. 8, 1947.

Pilsen or **Plzen.** The 3rd city of Czechoslovakia; pop. 122,750; fine buildings; breweries; steel, machinery, and guns; bombed by Allied aircraft during 2nd World War.

Pilsudski (pil-sood'-ski), **Josef** (1867–1935). First provisional president of Poland (1920) and commander of army. Becoming leader of a student organization, he was banished to Siberia by Russia, and during the 1st World War started guerrilla operations. Germans interned him in the fortress of Magdeburg; after the War was virtual dictator, becoming Premier and Minister of War in 1926; 2643.

Piltdown skull. Fossil skull discovered in 1911 in Pleistocene gravel at Piltdown, Sussex.

Pimen'to. Same as **Allspice.**

Pimpernel. Name of several small plants, especially the scarlet pimpernel, *Anagallis arvensis*, a common garden weed, also known as "Poor Man's Weather Glass" because it closes its flowers on the approach of rain. It has simple, opposite leaves from whose axils appear the single scarlet flowers. Other species are bog pimpernel (*A. tenella*), a creeping form with very pale pink, delicate flowers, and tiny leaves; and yellow pimpernel (*Lysimachia nemorum*), which is really a species of loosestrife.

Pin, 2608.

Pinaceae. Family of coniferous trees which contains the pines. *See* **Pine.**

Pinar del Rio (pē-nahr' del rē-o), Cuba. Inland city 85 m. S.W. of Havana; pop. 64,000; tobacco centre.

Pin'dar (c. 522–443 B.C.), Gk. lyric poet, master of "the grand style in simplicity," *1539*, 105.

Pindar'ics. Loose and irregular odes, in imitation of Pindar, fashionable in Eng. at close of 17th and beginning of 18th cent.

Pin'dus Mts., main range of Greece, running from N.W. to S.E.; source of principal rs. in Greece; 343; *map, 344.*

Pine, a cone-bearing tree found chiefly in northern hemisphere; 2609, *2610*, 890; cones and needles, *890*; woodtar, 3154.

Pine, Chili. *See* **Monkey Puzzle.**

Pin'eal body or **gland,** in the human brain; may be vestige of a third eye; in lizards, 1974.

Pineapple, 2611; Hawaiian industry, *1586*, 1587.

Pine marten, *2111.*

Pinero, Sir Arthur Wing (1855–1934). Eng. playwright, one of most skilful dramatic craftsmen of his day; chief works, "The Second Mrs. Tanqueray," "His House in Order," "Trelawny of the Wells."

Pines, Isle of. Fertile isl. belonging to Cuba, about 40 m. S. of W. coast; 1,180 sq. m.; pop. 5,000; cap. Nueva Geronna; *map, 940*; also island 58 sq. m., S. Pacific, S.E. of New Caledonia.

Pingyang' or **Heijo-fu,** Korea. Walled city, 40 m. from W. coast; pop. 285,960; great strategic importance.

Pink, a flower, **2611** ; carnation, **703**. Pink coral, 908.

Pin'kerton, Allan (1819–84). Amer. detective, b. Glasgow, Scot. ; organized (1861) Federal secret service and founded a famous private detective agency.

Pin'nate leaves, 1916.

Pin oak, 2409.

"Pinocchio." Story for children about a naughty wooden puppet ; by C. Collodi, pen-name of Carlo Lorenzini (1831–90) ; made into a film by Walt Disney.

Pinsk. Town of White Russia, S.S.R. (Polish until 1945) ; pop. 40,000 ; on the R. Pripet, 105 m. E. of Brest-Litovsk ; formerly cap. of separate principality ; captured by Germans in 1915 and in June 1941.

Pint. A unit of measure. *See in Index* **Weights and Measures.**

Pin'ta. One of the 3 caravels used by Columbus on his first voyage to America.

Pin-tail duck, 1052.

Pinto, Fernão Mendes (1509–83). Portuguese adventurer ; companion of Francis Xavier on mission to Japan ; his description of unknown Japan, long regarded as a sort of Munchausen tale, " did for prose of Portugal what Camoens did for poetry."

Pinturicchio (pēn-too-rĕk'-yō) (" little painter "), **Bernardino.** " Easel name" of Bernardino di Betti (1454–1513), It. artist, one of the foremost painters of Umbrian school.

Pinwheels or **catherine wheels.** Revolving fireworks, 1291.

Pinzon (pēn-thōn'). Family of Sp. navigators, three of whom, Martin Alonzo, Francisco, and Vicente Yañez (brothers), were companions of Columbus in discovery of Amer. ; Vicente discovers Brazil, 554.

Piom'bo, Sebastiano del. *See* **Sebastiano del Piombo.**

Piozzi (pē-ot'-si), **Hester Lynch**, friend of Dr. Johnson. *See* **Thrale, Hester.**

Pipefish. Long slender fishes with tubular snouts belonging to family *Syngnathidae*, which also includes sea-horses, 2911.

Pipe-lines. For petroleum, laid above or below ground ; steel piping generally used for conveying oil from wells to reservoirs ; system, 1742. *See also* **Pluto.**

Pipe organ, 2268, *2450.*

Piper, John (b. 1903). Brit. painter ; in 2nd World War commissioned to paint ruins of famous buildings, incl. House of Commons ; series of water-colours of Windsor Castle ; illustrated books (Sir O. Sitwell's autobiography) and designed décor for ballets ; pub. " Brit. Romantic Painters."

Pip'it. A passerine bird, **2611**, *2612.*

Piraeus (pī-rē'-us), 2nd largest city and chief port of Greece, 5 m. s.w. of Athens ; pop. 284,000 ; 284, 287 ; in German hands 1941–44 ; anc. fortifications and long walls, 284, 1522, 1524.

Pirandello (pī-ran-del'-lō), **Luigi** (1867–1936). It. dramatist ; wrote a number of plays having as their main theme the power and prevalence of illusion in people's lives ; most famous, " Six Characters in Search of an Author," " As You Desire Me " ; Nobel Prize for Literature in 1934 ; 1787.

Pirates and piracy, 2612 ; Caribbean Sea, 701 ; Captain Kidd, 1855 ; Morgan, 2229 ; Northmen, 2387 ; Pompey drives from Mediterranean, 2654 ; Vandals, 3304.

Pirithoüs (pī-rith'-ō-us). King of Lapithae, friend of Theseus, 3202 ; battle of centaurs at marriage feast, 742.

Pirna. Tn. of Saxony, Ger., on Elbe ; pop. 31,215. Prussians defeated Saxons in 7 Years' War in 1756.

Pisa (pē'-za). City of N. It. ; pop. 82,000 ; famous for leaning tower ; **2612** ; history, 2874 ; leaning tower ; 1513, *2613.*

Pisa, Council of (1409). Church council which deposed rival popes Gregory

XI and Benedict XIII ; Alexander V elected.

Pisano (pē-zah'-nō), **Andrea** (" Andrew of Pisa ") (c. 1270–1349). It. sculptor, pupil of Giovanni Pisano ; made bronze doors on south side of Baptistery at Florence.

Pisano, Giovanni (" John of Pisa ") (c. 1250–1330). It. sculptor, one of greatest of Renaissance, founder of It. Gothic style ; son of Niccolo Pisano.

Pisano, Niccolo (" Nicholas of Pisa ") (c. 1206–78). It. sculptor and architect, " first great precursor of the Renaissance."

Pisces (pis'-ēz). The fish class of vertebrate animals.

Pisces. A sign of the zodiac, 3444.

Pisgah (piz'-gah). Mt. in Palestine from which Moses saw the Promised Land ; identified with Nebo (Deut. xxxiv. 1).

Pisidia (pī-sid'-i-a). Anc. dist. of S. Asia Minor ; mountainous, with wild and warlike inhabitants who kept independence against all successive rulers of Asia Minor until reduced by Rome.

Pisistratus (pī-sis'-tra-tus) or **Peisistratos** (c. 605–527 B.C.) " tyrant " of Athens, 1522 ; in Aesop's fable, 54.

Pissarro, Camille (1831–1903). Fr. painter and etcher of impressionist school, 1379, 2477 ; his son Lucien (1863–1944) worked in Eng., being a naturalized Brit. subject.

Pistachio (pis-tah'-shi-ō) nut, 2408.

Pis'til. Seed-developing structure in flowers, 1321.

Pis'tol. In the " Merry Wives of Windsor," " Henry IV," and " Henry V," a swaggering, cowardly bully, companion of Falstaff.

Pistol. A small firearm, *1282* ; evolution, 1283 ; X-ray of, *3432.*

Pis'ton. In gas engine, 1420, *1421* ; hydraulic press, 1666 ; internal combustion engine, 1736 ; steam-engine, 3085, *3086.*

Pistons, or valves, of musical instruments, 1644.

Pi'sum sati'vum. The garden pea, 2530.

Pit'cairn, John (1740–75). Brit. army officer, commanding Gage's troops in expedition to Lexington and Concord ; killed at Bunker Hill.

Pitcairn Island. Brit. possession in S. Pacific Ocean ; story of settlement, 2472, 2473.

Pitch (angle) ; of roof, 2821 ; of screw, 2902.

Pitch (sound), 3010 ; how ear perceives it, 1066 ; of voice, affected by vocal cords, 3327.

Pitch (substance), 3154, 855.

Pitch, mineral, or asphalt, 272.

Pitch-blende. An ore, source of radium, 2731 ; and of uranium, 3297.

Pitcher. In baseball, 367.

Pitcher plants, **2613**, 2624, *plate f. 2621.*

Pitch Lake, Trinidad, 272.

Pitch pine, 2610.

Pith. Spongy core of many plant stems.

Pithecanthro'pus erec'tus. The " missing link," 182, 2079.

Pitiscus, Bartholomaeus (1561–1613). Inventor of decimal point, 984.

Pitman, Sir Isaac (1813–97). Eng. inventor of Pitman system of shorthand, and a keen advocate of simplified spelling, 2962.

Pit props, timber for, 1350.

Pitt, William, the Elder. *See* **Chatham, Earl of.**

Pitt, William, the Younger (1759–1806). Eng. statesman, **2614.**

Pit'tacus (c. 652–569). Statesman of Mytilene ; hero of war against Athens ; restored order following civil strife ; one of 7 sages.

Pitt or **Regent diamond.** Famous Fr. crown jewel, *1011*, 1012.

Pitti (pit'-tē) **Palace.** In Florence, designed as a residence for Luca Pitti, chief magistrate of Florence in 1449 ; became home of famous picture collection ; severely damaged in 2nd World War.

Pittsburgh, Pennsylvania, 10th city of U.S.A., pop. 665,400 ; **2614.**

Pituitary gland, 1471.

Pit vipers. A sub-family of poisonous snakes, 2991 ; moccasin, 2991 ; rattlesnake, 2764.

Pius, Popes, 2615.

Pi'us I (d. A.D. 154), Pope, 2615.

Pius II (1405–64), Pope, 2615.

Pius III (1439–1503), Pope, **2615.**

Pius IV (1499–1565), Pope, **2615.**

Pius V (1504–72), Pope, 2615, 2131.

Pius VI (1717–99), Pope, 2615.

Pius VII (1740–1823), Pope, 2615.

Pius VIII (1761–1830), Pope, 2615.

Pius IX (1792–1878), Pope, 2615, 1769.

Pius X (1835–1914), Pope, 2615.

Pius XI (1857–1939), Pope, 2615.

Pius XII (b. 1876), Pope, 2615.

Pixie Cup. Lichen found on heathland, 1933.

Piz Palu. In Swiss Alps, 3139.

Pizarro (pī-zar'-ō), **Francisco** (c. 1475–1541). Sp. conqueror of Peru, **2616**, 1690, 1948, 3025.

Place de la Concorde (plahs de la kon'-kord), Paris, *2515*, 2516.

Place de l'Étoile (lā-twahl'), Paris, *2515*, 2516.

Place de l'Opéra, Paris, 2516.

Place-names, 2272.

Placer mining, 1479, 2181, 2182, 1047.

Plague. In Athens, 1524 ; in London, 2016. *See also* **Bubonic plague.**

Plaice, or flounder. A flatfish, 1298 ; eyes of, *1298.*

Plains, defined, 2596, 2597 ; North Sea a drowned plain, 1234.

Plains of Abraham, Quebec, 2716.

Plain Song. Also called Gregorian Chant. System of music used in R.C. churches for the greater part of the liturgy. Said to have been systematized by St. Gregory the Great.

Planck, Max (1858–1947). Ger. physicist ; devised " Planck's constant " ; quantum theory, 2728, 2594, 2711.

Plane, focal, of lenses, 1924.

Plane, inclined, in mechanics, 2128, *2129.*

Plane geometry, 1434.

Plane tree, 2616.

Planetarium. Construction and use, *2619.*

Planetes'imal theory, that planets were made of meteorites (planetesimals), 2619.

Plan'etoids. Same as **Asteroids.**

Planets, **2617**, *plate f. 276, 3118* ; earth, 1067 ; gravitation, 1512 ; Kepler's laws of motion, 1852 ; nebular theory, 2618 ; planetesimal theory, 2619 ; tidal theory, 2620.

Plank'ton. The microscopic organisms found in ocean water, 2416 ; of Antarctic, 174 ; of Newfoundland Banks, 2338.

Plant. *See* **Plant Life.**

Plantagenet (plan-taj'-e-net), **House of.** Line of Eng. kings ruling 1154–1399 ; also called House of Anjou ; founded by Henry II, 1609 ; list of kings, *see* **English History.**

Plantain. Genus of wild plants, growing as weeds, esp. the greater plantain, perennial herb with low-growing, tough, ribbed, flat leaves ; and a spike of inconspicuous flowers ; other species are the lamb's-tongue, with pink flower spikes, sea plantain, etc. ; water varieties, 3356.

Plantain. A type of banana tree or its fruit, 354 ; in India, 1701 ; yields Manila hemp, 1609, 2569, 2868.

Plant breeding, 79, 533 ; asparagus, 271 ; Burbank's work, 621 ; carnation, 703 ; celery, 738 ; chrysanthemum, 823 ; dahlia, 955 ; date palms, 978 ; grafting fruit trees, *1402* ; grapes, 1499 ; lemon, 1920 ; Mendel's work, 2139 ; oranges, 2444 ; pansies, 2494 ; potato, 2664 ; roses, 2827 ; sugar beet, 396.

Plantigrade animals. Those whose heels touch the ground, 1342 ; bear, 382 ; raccoon, 2723.

Plantin (plahn-tan), **Christophe** (1514–89). Fr. printer ; his house and printing office in Antwerp is now the Plantin-Moretus Museum, where his tools may still be seen ; printed Polyglot Bible, 182.

Plant lice. Same as **Aphis.**

Plant life, 2620 ; *plates f. 2620, 2621* ; the " Adams " of the plant world (algae), 111 ; adaptation to surroundings, 648, *plate f. 1080* ; affected by altitude, 840, 2795 ; alternation of generations, 1266, 2238 ; animal life depends upon plants, 2373 ; of Arctic regions, 174 ; Australia's strange forms, 308 ; autumn coloration, 1917 ; bacteria, 335 ; breathing in plants, 1914, 2621 ; bulbs and tubers, 612 ; cells, the structural units, 738, 1155 ; cellulose, 739 ; chemistry of plant life, 2589, 2373, 699, 738 ; in desert regions, 648, 996 ; elements needed for growth, 2374, 2998 ; flowers, life of the, 1322, *532, 2288* ; forest life, 1341 ; fossil plants, 1353, 1433 ; fruits, 1401 ; fungi, 1407, *plate f. 1408*, 1932, 2514, 2260, 2637, 2857 ; germination, illustrated by bean, *381* ; grasses as land makers, 1509 ; how to study, 2283 ; hybridization, 621 ; insect-eating (carnivorous) types, 2613, *2624* ; leaves, 1243, 1914, *1916*, 3245 ; legumes and nitrifying bacteria, 2373, 2034 ; length of life, *3245* ; moisture affects form and life, 1243, 2741, 648, 841 ; in ocean, 2914 ; origin of higher plants, 111 ; parasites and parasitism, 2513, 2194 ; " partnerships " (symbiosis) among plants, 1932, 2374 ; physiology of plants, 2601 ; photo-synthesis, 2589 ; poisonous plants, 2637 ; protoplasm the " life substance," 738 ; reproduction, 738, 1322, *1324–28*, 1266, 2238 ; roots, 2825 ; seaweeds, 2914, *2915* ; seeds and spores, 1323, 1403, 2916 ; snow, 2992 ; as soil makers, 2239, 2998, 3246 ; trees, 1349, *3241–3244*, 3245 ; water plants, 3355 ; yeasts, 3433. *See* **Botany ; Ecology ; Nature Study ; Plant Breeding ;** and the chief topics above by name.

Plant societies, *plate f. 1080*, 3355.

Plant surgery, 3246 ; grafting, *1402*.

Plasma. The fluid of the blood, 474.

Plasmo′dium. Genus of unicellular animals containing malaria parasite.

Plassey or **Plassi,** small town of India, 75 m. N. of Calcutta ; battle (June 23, 1757), 842, 660, 3276, 1714.

Plaster of Paris, 1559 ; pottery moulds, 2665 ; use in sculpture, 2903.

Plastics. Inorganic substances capable of being moulded readily under heat and pressure, **2625,** 836, 857 ; acetylene in, 18 ; in cables, 645 ; cellulose, 2709 ; waterproof cement, 742 ; glycerine in mfr. of, 1478 ; lenses, 3055 ; contain nitrogen, 2373 ; from petroleum, 2430 ; pyroxylin for, 2709 ; rayon, 2748 ; synthetic resins, 2768 ; synthetic rubber, 2838 ; welding, *1624*, 1625.

Plataea (pla-tē′-a). Anc. city of Boeotia ; assisted Athenians at battle of Marathon, 230 ; battle of (479 B.C.), 2555.

Plata River. Great estuary on E. side of S. Amer. formed by junction of Paraná and Uruguay rs. ; at Buenos Aires, 601, *602*, 228 ; at Montevideo, 2220, 3298.

Plata River, Battle of. Fought Dec. 13, 1939, between Ger. pocket battleship and Atlantic raider Adm. Graf Spee and Brit. cruisers Achilles, Ajax and Exeter which lay in wait 150 m. off Plata esty. ; after 1¼ hrs.' fight Graf Spee fled, disabled, into estuary nr. Montevideo pt., and after 4 days scuttled herself ; 3417, *map, 3417*.

Plate (pottery) ; mfr. of, *2667*.

Plate armour, 240.

Plateau, Joseph (1801–83). Belgian physicist ; though blind, studied properties of liquids from soap bubbles.

Plateau. A land formation, 2596, 2597.

Plate glass, 1473.

Plateresque architecture, in Spain, 3040.

Plating, 1139.

Plat′inite. Iron-nickel alloy, copperplated and used in electric lamp connexions, 1135, 2628.

Plat′inum (Pt.). White metallic element of the osmium group ; atomic weight 195·2 ; used in jewelry ; melts at 3190°F. ; **2627,** *2628*, 2845 ; and gold, 1481 ; in pyrometers, 2709 ; properties, 777 ; spectrum, *plate f. 3057*.

Plato (plā-tō) (427–347 B.C.), Gk. philosopher, pupil of Socrates, **2628,** 1540, 2572, 2997 ; and Aristotle, 232 ; description of Atlantis, 294 ; his academy, 16, *17* ; account of magnetism, 2060.

Platoon′, in Brit. army ; subdivision of a company ; further subdivided into sections.

Platte River. Largest tributary of Missouri, U.S.A. ; length of main stream 200 m.

Plat′ypus. The duckbill, an egg-laying mammal ; **1053,** *313*.

Plauen (plow′-en). Town of Saxony, Ger. ; pop. 110,300 ; chief centre in Ger. for mfr. of white cotton goods ; lace mfrs., 1877.

Plautus (plaw′-*tus*), **Titus Maccius** (c. 251–184 B.C.). Rom. comic dramatist, 1038, 1897 ; chief works, " Amphitruo," " Captivi " (" The Captives "), " Aulularia " (" The Pot of Gold ").

Player-piano, mechanism, 2603.

Playfair, Sir Nigel (1874–1934). Eng. actor and theatrical manager ; gave new life to Eng. drama by his productions at the Lyric Theatre, Hammersmith.

Playing cards, 701.

" Playing Possum," meaning, 2442.

Plays. *See* **Drama.**

Plebiscite (pleb′-i-sit). Vote by all electors on an urgent question of the day (= referendum).

Plebs (plebs) or **plebeians** (ple-bē′-anz). The lower order of citizens of anc. Rome, 2805.

Plecop′tera. An insect order including stone-flies, 1733.

Pleiades (plī-′a-dēz). In Gk. myth., the seven daughters of Atlas ; pursued by Orion, they were changed into doves by the gods, 2629.

Pleiades. In astronomy, the constellation of Taurus, a conspicuous star cluster, popularly regarded as the Seven Stars, though six stars are as a rule visible, 2629, *895* ; nebulae, 2310.

Pleistocene (plīs′-tō-sēn) **epoch,** in geology, 1432, 1433.

Plenipotentiary ministers. Ambassadors to foreign courts invested with full powers to act for their countries.

Plesiosaur (plē′-si-ō-sawr). Type of extinct marine reptile, 2767, *2678*, 2680, *2681*.

Plev′na or **Pleven.** Tn. in N. Bulgaria ; pop. 31,500 ; celebrated for gallant resistance of Turks during siege in Russo-Turkish War (1877).

Plim′soll, Samuel (1824–98). Eng. politician ; he caused to be passed the Merchant Shipping Act (1876) which prevented vessels deemed unsafe from sailing ; the Plimsoll mark, indicating the safety line of loaded vessels, is named after him, 2951.

Plinlimmon. *See* **Plynlimmon.**

Plinth. In architecture, a square member forming the lower division of the base of a column, etc. ; in Gothic architecture, the plinth is occasionally divided into two stages, the tops of which are either splayed or finished with a hollow moulding, or are covered by the base mouldings.

Pliny (plin′-i) the **Elder** (**Gaius Plinius Secundus**) (A.D. 23–79). Rom. historian and naturalist, 191, 1897 ; glass, 1172 ; soap, 2993 ; as zoologist, 3446.

Pliny the Younger (**Gaius Plinius Caecilius Secundus**) (61–c. 113). Nephew of the elder Pliny ; letters, 1897.

Pliocene (plI-ō-sēn) **period.** In geologic time, 1432, 1433, 1298.

" Pliofilm," a type of plastic, 2627 ; made from rubber, 2838.

Ploegsteert. Small tn. and wood in w. Flanders, Belgium ; known to " Tommies " in the 1st World War as " Plug Street."

Ploësti. Tn. of Rumania 40 m. N. of Bucharest ; pop. 105,100 ; petroleum centre. After 1941 it became Germany's chief source of natural oil, hence the objective of heavy Allied air attacks in the 2nd World War.

Plotinus (plō-tī′-nus) (c. 205–270). Rom. philosopher, founder of Neo-Platonism ; his philosophy is a development of the Platonic theory of Ideas, combined with Oriental mysticism, etc.

Plough. Agricultural implement, **2629,** 78, *81*, 87, 2775.

Plough, or the Dipper constellation, 894, *895*.

Ploughing, 79, 80, 81, 87.

" Ploughman Poet," name given to Robert Burns, 625.

Plomer, William C. F. (b. 1903). Brit. author, b. in S. Africa ; " I Speak of Africa " ; " Cecil Rhodes " ; " Selected Poems " ; " The Dorking Thigh."

Plovdiv. *See* **Philippopolis.**

Plover (pluv′-er). A shore bird, **2629,** *2630*, 443 ; foot, *448* ; migrations of golden plover, 2170 ; nests on ground, 443 ; ringed, *443*.

" Plug Street." *See* **Ploegsteert.**

Plum. A tree of the rose family, **2630,** *back of plate f. 1400* ; Burbank, 621 ; classified, 1403. *See* also **Prunes.**

Plumage, of birds, 446.

Plumba′go. Same as **Graphite.**

Plumbing. Trade originally confined to working in lead (Latin, *plumbum*), but now embracing the installing and repair of pipes, gutters, and other domestic fittings ; earthenware drain pipes, 2666 ; lead pipes, 1908.

Plumb-line. Device used for measuring depths and checking perpendicularity of objects, 2413, 2414.

Plumcot. A Burbank fruit, 621.

Plu′mer, Herbert, 1st Viscount (1857–1932). Brit. soldier ; he served in the South African War (1899–1902), and during the 1st World War (1914–18) commanded the 2nd Army in France and later the Italian Expeditionary Force ; Governor of Malta 1919, and High Commissioner and Com.-in-Chief of Palestine (1925–28).

Plumule (plōō′-mūl). First bud of an embryo ; of bean, *381*.

Plunkett, Sir Horace Curzon (1854–1932). Irish publicist, perhaps the foremost advocate of compromise in the settlement of the Irish question ; founded Irish Agricultural Organization in 1894, and 1899–1907 was vice-president of Irish Agriculture Dept., through which he constantly laboured to improve condition of Irish farmer.

Plur′al, of nouns, 2399, 3058 ; of verbs, 3314.

Pluralists, in philosophy, those philosophers to whom the distinction and separateness between things seem most important, 2572 ; also applied to persons who hold a large number of posts at the same time.

Plush. A fabric, 850.

Plutarch (plōō′-tahrk) (c. A.D. 48–122). Gk. biographer, **2630,** 1541 ; story of Lycurgus, 2042.

Pluto or **Hades,** in Gk. and Rom. myth., god of underworld, **2631.**

Pluto (Pipe Line Under The Ocean). Code name for supply pipes on sea bed carrying petrol to Allied armies in France 1944 ; 2631.

Pluto. Outermost planet ; discovered in 1930, 2631, 279, *2619*, 3119.

Plutonium. Element (Pu), atomic no. 94, produced by the bombardment of uranium 238 which gives rise to neptunium, 2315, the latter decaying to plutonium, 299, 778 ; first produced in Britain at Harwell in Mar. 1949.

Plymouth. Devonshire spt. and naval base ; pop. 180,400 ; **2631,** 558.

Plymouth, Massachusetts, U.S.A., mfg. tn., first New England settlement ; Pilgrims settle at, 2606.

Plymouth Brethren. Sect founded at Plymouth, Devonshire, in 1830.

Plymouth Hoe, Eng. ; ridge on which Plymouth partly stands ; *2631* ; Drake plays bowls on, *236*.

Plymouth Rock. Breed of fowls, *2671*.

Plynlim′mon. Mt. in Wales ; 2,465 ft. high ; *1167*, 2223.

P.M. (Lat. *post meridiem*), 3214.

Pneumatic (nū-mat′-ik) **appliances, 2632,** 90 ; air brakes, 549 ; dredgers,

1047 ; tunnelling "shield," 3257 ; vacuum cleaner, 3301.

Pneumatics. A branch of physics, 2632.

Pneumatic tire, *2835*, 2836.

Pneumogastric nerve. Same as **Vagus.**

Pneumonia (nū-mō'-ni-*a*). A lung disease ; caused by bacteria, 1458 ; treated with sulpha drugs, 3116.

Pnom-Penh. Commercial centre and cap. of Cambodia, Indo-China, on R. Mekong ; pop. 102,680 ; 666.

Pnyx (niks). A hill in Athens, 286.

Po. Chief r. of N. It., 420 m. long ; rises in the Cottian Alps and flows E. through Piedmont and Lombardy into the Adriatic ; **2633**, 29 ; *map, 1764* ; valley, 1233, 1763.

Pocahontas (pŏ-ka-hon'-tas) (*c.* 1595–1617). Indian "princess," traditional ancestress of many Virginia families by her marriage to John Rolfe, a Jamestown settler ; and Capt. John Smith, 2754.

Pocket borough, 2522.

Pocket compass, 881.

Poe, Edgar Allan (1809–49). Amer. writer, **2633**, 3293.

Poet laureate, 2634.

POETS LAUREATE

Ben Jonson	.. ..	1619
Sir William Davenant		1637–1668
John Dryden	.. ..	1670
Thomas Shadwell	..	1688
Nahum Tate	.. ..	1692
Nicholas Rowe	.. ..	1715
Laurence Eusden	.. ..	1718
Colley Cibber	.. ..	1730
William Whitehead	..	1757
Thomas Warton	..	1785
Henry James Pye	..	1790
Robert Southey	..	1813
William Wordsworth	..	1843
Alfred Tennyson	..	1850–1892
Alfred Austin	..	1896
Robert Bridges	.. ..	1913
John Masefield	.. ..	1930

Poetry, 2634 ; beginnings in Greece, 1539 ; Chaucer "father of English poetry," 761 ; Dryden's theory, 1050 ; for children, 1965 ; Longfellow as the children's poet, 2022 ; medieval minstrels and romances, 2798 ; Wordsworth's theory, 3408. *See* **English literature ; France : literature,** etc.

Poets' Corner, Westminster Abbey, 3369, *2635*.

Poggio Bracciolini (poj'-ō brah-chō-lē'-nē) (1380–1459). It. scholar of Renaissance, discovers MSS. of Cicero and Lucretius, 2764.

Poi (pō'ē). A food used in the Pacific isls., 2472.

Poilu (pwah'-lū). Name given to the Fr. soldier during 1914–1918 War.

Poincaré (pwan-ka-rā), **Raymond** (1860–1934). Fr. statesman, premier and foreign minister 1912 and thrice after the 1st World War ; pres. of France 1913 ; ordered Fr. occupn. of the Ruhr 1923, and stablized the franc 1926 ; 1367.

Point Barrow, Alaska. The northernmost cape of N. Amer. ; whaling station ; school for natives ; average pop. about 500, 2646.

Point d' Alençon (pwan-da-lahn-son) lace, 1880.

Point de Galle. *See* **Galle.**

Pointe-à-Pitre (pwant-ah-pētr'). Guadeloupe, chief spt. ; pop. 43,550 ; ships cocoa, sugar, vanilla ; 1551.

Pointer. A dog, *plate f. 1024*, 1026.

Point system, of type sizes, 3270.

Poison gas, in warfare, 1420, 1567, 2638, 3409.

Poisoning, antidotes, 2638, 1295.

Poisonous animals : centipedes, 743 ; duckbill, 1053 ; among fish, 1297 ; Gila monster, *1974* ; hydras, 1664, *1665* ; scorpions, 2888 ; snakes, 2990 ; spiders, 3065 ; tarantula, 3154 ; wasps, 3345.

Poisonous plants, 2637, *2639* ; bittersweet, 462 ; fruit stone kernels, 947 ; hemlocks, 1608 ; mushrooms, 2260 ; nightshades, *2369* ; upas tree, 3246 ; yew, 3434.

Poisons, 2638 ; antidotes, 1295, 2638 ; antimony salts, 177 ; bichloride of mercury, 2146 ; carbolic acid, 699 ;

carbon monoxide, 799 ; chlorine, 815 ; copper compounds, 907 ; hydro-cyanide acid and cyanides, 947 ; lead compounds, 1908 ; phosphorus, 2574 ; thallium compounds, 3193.

Poitiers (pwah-tyā). Fr. tn. 60 m. s.w. of Tours; pop. 48,500 ; old churches, Rom. remains ; Charles Martel defeated Moors near by (732) ; victory of Black Prince over French (1356), 1652.

Poitou (pwah-tōō). Old prov. of w. Fr., part of Aquitaine ; former cap. Poitiers ; acquired by Eng. crown, 1609.

Pola, Yugoslavia. Fortified tn. with one of finest harbours in Europe, on peninsula of Istria on Adriatic Sea ; pop. 48,000 ; before 1914 chief naval station of Austria-Hungary ; then It. ; transferred to Yugoslavia 1947, when about 25,000 Italians left the city.

Poland. Republic of N. Europe, 119,700 sq. m. ; pop. 23,911,000 ; **2640** ; *map, 2641* ; cap. Warsaw, 3341 ; cities, 925, 2640 ; racial characteristics, 2983.

History : 2641, 1239, 1241 ; Sobieski, 925, 3264 ; Sweden, 758 ; partitions, 2640 ; shrinking boundaries, *2642* ; Kosciusko, 1873, 925 ; in 1914–18 War, 3410, 3414 ; Danzig, 973 ; Paderewski, 2474 ; Pilsudski, 2643 ; and Russia, post-war, 3415 ; Polish Corridor, 3416 ; invaded by Ger., 1452, 3416 ; by Russia, 2852 ; fourth partition in 1939, 2641 ; liberated by Russians in 1945, 2643, 3416.

Polar bear, *383, 385, 3446.*

Polar exploration, 2644 ; *map, 173* ; Amundsen, 147 ; Andrée's balloon attempt, 154 ; Byrd, 2646, 2647 ; James Cook, 898 ; Franklin, 1387 ; Hudson, 1648 ; Nansen, 2273 ; Peary, 2534 ; Russian (Schmidt), *224*, 2646; Scott, 2895 ; Shackleton, 2931. *See also* **Antarctica ; Arctic Regions.**

Polar'iscope. An optical instrument for exhibiting and analysing polarized light or objects in polarized light.

Polariza'tion, of light, by double refraction, 1942 ; of tartrates, 3155. Of voltaic cell, 376.

Polar regions defined, 1898. *See* **Antarctica ; Arctic Regions ; Polar exploration.**

Polder. Land reclaimed by diking, 2319.

Poldhu, Cornwall, Eng. ; site of transmitter of Marconi's first transAtlantic radio message, *3391.*

Pole, Reginald (1500–58). Eng. cardinal and Archbishop of Canterbury ; opposed divorce of Henry VIII and compelled to leave England ; a leader at Council of Trent ; returned on accession of Mary.

Pole, rod, or **perch.** Unit of measure. *See* **Weights and Measures.**

Pole, barber's. Origin of the sign, 149.

Pole, magnetic. *See* **Magnetic pole.**

Polecat. A small weasel-like animal, noted for its unpleasant odour ; usually of a dark brown colour ; more or less extinct as a wild animal in Britain ; domesticated as the ferret.

Polen'ta. A noble family of It. ; Francesca da Rimini was born a Polenta.

Pole Star or **Polaris.** Star nearest in line above North Pole, 3078, 3079, *3080* ; located by Dipper or Plough, *895* ; not seen s. of Equator, 3022.

Pole vaulting, in athletics, 288, *289.*

Police, 2647, *2649* ; fingerprint identification, 1276 ; founded by Peel, 2535, *2536* ; traffic control, 2784, *2787* ; wireless for, 3396 ; women police, 2648.

Poliomyeli'tis. *See* **Infantile Paralysis.**

Polish Corridor, 3416.

Politian (po-lish'-i-*a*n), **Angelo** (1454–94). It. scholar and poet ; the greatest of his time.

Political economy. *See* **Economics.**

Political parties, 2651 ; in Eng., 755 ; in U.S.A., 3290. *See* under names of separate parties.

Political science. *See* **Economics ; Government ; Law ; Sociology.**

Politics, 2651 ; the art of government, 1488 ; Communism, 881 ; Con-

servatives, 892 ; democracy, 989 ; Labour movement, 1075 ; Liberals, 1929 ; local government, 1491 ; parliament, 2521 ; Socialism, 2996.

Polk, James Knox (1795–1849). 11th pres. of U.S.A., from 1844 to his death.

Polka. A round dance, of Bohemian origin, in two-four time. Very popular during the latter half of the 19th century, 965.

Pol'len. The fertilizing element of flowers, 1322, *1324-25* ; carried by bees, 391, *plate f. 392* ; how distributed for water-plants, 3355.

Poll tax. A tax on every poll or head, introduced into Eng. in 1377, but abolished by William III in 1689 ; a cause of Peasants' Revolt in Eng., 3269.

Pollux (pol'-uks). Twin of Castor, **718**. *See* **Castor and Pollux.**

Pollux. A star, 3079, *3080* ; where situated, *895.*

Polo. A game played on horseback, **2651**. *See also* **Water Polo.**

Po'lo, Maffeo, 2652.

Polo, Marco (*c.* 1254–*c.* 1324). Venetian traveller, **2652**, 131 ; tales of Kublai Khan, *2205* ; first reports about Japan, 1799 ; visits China, 810.

Polo, Nicolo, 2652.

Polonium (Po). Radioactive metallic element of the oxygen group ; found in minute traces with tellurium, 778 ; discovery, 2731.

Polonius (po-lō'-ni-*us*). In Shakespeare's "Hamlet," vain, garrulous old chamberlain, father of Ophelia ; "full of wise saws and modern instances " ; accidentally killed by Hamlet, 1570.

Polperro. Fishing vil. of Cornwall, *1176.*

Poltava (pol-tah'-v*a*), Soviet Rus., in Ukraine, 220 m. s.E. of Kiev ; pop. 130,300 ; trade in cattle, grain ; battle of, 758, 2563, 3131 ; countryside, 3273. Captured by Germans Sept. 1941 ; recaptured by Russians Sept. 1943.

Polyandry. Form of marriage in which a woman has two or more husbands.

Polybius (po-lib'-i-*us*) (*c.* 204–125 B.C.). Gk. historian of Rome, 1541.

Polycarp (pol'-i-karp) (*c.* 69–*c.* 155). Christian martyr, Bishop of Smyrna ; called on to revile Christ, replied, " Eighty and six years have I served Him, and He hath done me no wrong. How can I revile my Lord and Saviour ? " ; martyred by Romans.

Polyclitus (pol-i-klī'-t*us*) (5th cent. B.C.). Gk. sculptor ; " Doryphorus " or Spear-Bearer, described, 1528, 1614.

Polydec'tes. In Gk. myth., king who sent Perseus to kill Medusa, 2552.

Polygamy (po-lig'-*a*-mi). Form of marriage ; among birds, 441 ; Mahomedanism, 2067 ; in tribal life, 1259.

Polygno'tus. Gk. painter of 4th cent., 1528.

Polygon (in geometry). A plane figure with more than four sides.

Polygonaceae (pol-i-go-nā'-si-ē). The dock family of plants.

Polyhymnia (pol-i-him'-ni-*a*). In Gk. myth., Muse of sacred songs, 2259.

Polymerization. The joining of two or more molecules to form one, 775 ; in oil, 2430 ; in plastics mfr., 2626 ; rubber, 2838.

Polynesia (pol-i-nēzh'-i-*a*). A division of the Pacific isls., in a belt chiefly within 30 degrees on each side of the Equator, 2471.

Polynesians. *See* **Malays.**

Polynices (pol-i-nī'-sēz). In Gk. myth., son of Oedipus, king of Thebes, and brother of Eteocles ; tradition had it that the two brothers should rule by turn, a year at a time ; at the end of the first year, however, Polynices' brother refused to give way, and war followed in which both were killed.

Polyp (pol'-ip). Coral, 908, *plate f. 908* ; evolutionary position, 158 ; of jellyfish, 1817.

Polypet'alae. Division of the Angiosperm group of plants.

Polyphase current, in elec., 1130, *1131.*

Polyphemus. In the Odyssey, Cyclops from whom Odysseus escaped by putting out his eye ; legend, 949.

Polyphon'ic music, 2263

Polypody (pol'-i-pō-di). A common British fern, often seen growing in the moss of old oak trees or similar situations. Distinguished by its simply pinnate fronds.

Poly-saccharide, starch, 3082.

Polystyrene, a type of plastic, 2627.

Polytechnic Schools (Gk. "many arts"). Applied to schools with a varied curriculum of practical instruction in applied arts and sciences. First in England was the Regent St. Polytechnic, London, founded by Quintin Hogg in 1882. French École Polytechnique, at Paris, established in 18th century.

Pol'ytheism (Gk. "many gods"). The belief in and worship of many gods, as opposed to monotheism, the belief in one God; the belief, still extant, has been common among the eastern peoples since the dawn of history.

Polythene, a type of plastic, 2627.

Polyvinyl chloride (PVC), a type of plastic, 2627.

Pombal, Sebastião José de Carvalhoe Mello, Marquis of (1699–1782). Premier of Portugal under King Joseph, called the "Great Marquis"; expelled Jesuits, rebuilt Lisbon after great earthquake 1775, reorganized army, education, and freed Indian slaves in Brazil.

Pomegranate (pom'-gran-at). Tree of myrtle family, 2652.

Pom'elo, or grape-fruit, 1499.

Pomera'nia. Former agric. prov. of Prussia on Baltic Sea; chief r., Oder; large sea trade, of which Stettin was centre; largely incorporated in Poland in 1945.

Pomeranian dog, 1025, plate f. 1024.

Pomo'na. Rom. goddess of fruit and fruit trees.

Pomona. Another name for Mainland, largest of Orkney Isls., 2453.

Pompadour, Jeanne Antoinette Poisson, Marquise de (1721–64). Favourite and powerful political adviser of Louis XV of Fr., 1372.

Pompeii (pom-pā'-ē), It. Anc. Rom. city destroyed by an eruption of Mt. Vesuvius A.D. 79, 2653, 3319, 2820; painting from, 2817; excavations, 207.

Pompey. Colloquial name for Portsmouth.

Pompey the Great (106–48 B.C.). Rom. general and statesman, 2654; and Caesar, 651; takes Jerusalem, 1830.

Pompey's Pillar, Alexandria, 109.

Ponce (pōn'-thā). 2nd city of Puerto Rico, 3 m. from S. coast; pop. 105,000; tobacco mfrs.; exports coffee and sugar from port at Playa de Ponce.

Ponce de Leon (pōn'-thā dā lā-ōn'), Juan (c. 1460–1521). Sp. explorer, accompanied Columbus to America in 1493, was governor of Puerto Rico in 1510, and discovered Florida in 1513; was killed in 1521 whilst trying to establish his colony; 1319, 140.

Poncho (pon'chō). Cloak worn by men in Peru, Chile, Argentina, and other parts of S. America; a wide strip of cloth with a slit in the middle, through which the head is passed; part of equipment of Brit. army from 1949.

Pondicherry. Fr. settlement in S.E. on Coromandel coast of India, dating from 17th cent. and still cap. of few remaining Fr. possessions in India proper; pop. 53,100; several times taken by Eng.; 1692.

Pond-lily. See Water-lily.

Pond-scum. A massed green alga (Spirogyra), 112.

Pond snail, shell, 2943.

Pondweeds, 3355.

Pongee' silk, from "wild" silkworms, 2973.

Pon'iard. Term used for a small slender dagger.

Poniatowski (pō-nyah-tof'-ski), Joseph Anton (1763–1813). Polish prince, commander under Napoleon, and marshal in aid of Fr.; died fighting to cover retreat from Leipzig.

Ponta Delgada. Tn. on St. Michael's Isls., Azores; pop. 21,000.

Pont de Bordeaux, 524.

Pont du Gard. Roman structure carrying aqueduct across the valley of the R. Gard, France, 194.

Pon'tiac (c. 1712–69). Ottawa Indian chief, organizer of "conspiracy of Pontiac" (1763–65) against Brit.

Pon'tifex Max'imus, 2495.

Pontine Marshes. Former swampy region in w.-cent. It., near Rome; the malarial atmosphere prevented cultivation; reclaimed under Fascist regime, and became new prov. of Littoria, developing into one of Italy's richest wheat growing districts; 1772.

Pontius Pilate. See Pilate.

Pontoon bridge, 568; and Mulberry harbour, 2251.

Pon'tus. Anc. region in N.E. Asia Minor on Black Sea; originally part of Cappadocia; kingdom founded 4th cent. B.C.; subdued by Pompey, 2654.

Pontypridd, Wales. Tn. in Glamorganshire, at the junction of rs. Rhondda and Taff, about 12 m. N.W. of Cardiff; chief industries tin plate and iron goods, and brass founding; pop. 38,000.

Pony, Shetland, 1646, 1647, 2945.

Pony Express. Early overland mail route in U.S.A., 603.

Pool, The, London, 2012, 3194.

Poole. Spt. tn. in Dorsetshire, 113 m. S.W. of London; isl.-studded harbour; Branksea or Brownsea Isl. has 16th-cent. castle; coasting trade and shipbuilding; potters' clay worked; potteries, iron foundries, agric. implement works; mfrs. cordage, sailcloth; oyster beds; pop. 80,000.

Pools. Popular form of competition in which the entrant attempts to forecast the results of football matches.

Poo'na, India. Agric. tn. of Bombay Province, healthful climate; pop. 258,200; summer seat of Bombay govt.

Poor Clares. Rom. Cath. religious order for women, 1384.

"Poor Richard's Almanac," 1386.

Popcorn. Any kind of Indian corn, which, by reason of the oil it contains, will explode when subjected to great heat.

Pope, Alexander (1688–1744). Eng. poet, 2654, 1213; birthplace, 2010.

Pope. Election, 2496; infallibility, 2615; origin of office, 2495, 2562; primacy, 2495. See also Papacy; list, 3945; and individual popes by name.

Pope, or ruffe. Small Eng. freshwater fish with spiny fin-rays.

Popish Plot. Between 1678 and 1680 Titus Oates made repeated efforts to prove by false testimony and forged papers that the Queen and some of the leading Eng. Catholics were plotting to murder Charles II and restore Catholicism as the state religion; popular feeling ran high; a number of Jesuits and other Catholics were executed.

Pop'lar. A genus of trees, 2655; leaf, 1915; classified, 3247, 3618.

Pop'lin. A fabric with a warp of silk and a heavier filling of worsted, cotton, or linen, which gives the material a corded surface; name may come from "Pope," for fabric was first manufactured at Avignon when that was a papal residence.

Popocatepetl (pō-pō-ka-tā'-petl), Mt. Volcano about 40 m. S.E. of Mexico City; one of the highest peaks in N. Amer. (17,520 ft.); crater yields sulphur; violent eruptions in 1921 2156, 2158.

Poppaea Sabina (pop-ē'-a sa-bī'-na) (d. A.D. 65), second wife of Nero, 2315.

Popping crease, in cricket, 928.

Poppy, 2655; opium poppy, 2442.

Poppy Day. Day preceding Remembrance Day, Sunday before Nov. 11, when artificial poppies are sold in the street in aid of Earl Haig's fund for disabled soldiers.

Population, 2656; census, 742. For population of continents and other political divisions see Africa; Asia, etc.

Poquelin, Jean-Baptiste. See Molière.

Porbeagle, a shark, 2939.

Porcelain and chinaware, 2665; Chinese, 810, 2670; Copenhagen ware, 905; Dresden, 1048; English, 3407; Japanese, 1809; Sèvres, 2670. See also Pottery.

Porch. In architecture, a covered entrance to a building; a covered approach or vestibule to a doorway. See also Portico.

Por'cupine. A rodent with quill-like spines, 2656; story, "Prickles Learns to Like His Quills," 3477.

Pore. Minute opening in the skin through which gland secretions reach the surface.

Porif'era. The sponge group of animals, 156, 3067, 3623.

Pork. Meat of the pig, 2125.

Pork-fish, in coral-reef, 2104.

Porphyry (por'-fi-ri). An igneous rock, 1901.

Porpoise (por'-pos). A marine mammal, 2657; distinguished from dolphin, 1027; evolutionary position, 158.

Por'sena, Lars. In Rom. legends, king of Clusium and Etruria, 3207.

Porson, Richard (1759–1808). One of the greatest Eng. classical scholars of all time; notes and emendations on Aeschylus, Aristophanes, and other Gk. authors.

Port. "Wheel to port," since Jan. 1933, has meant that a captain wishes his vessel to turn to the left.

Port, wine, origin of name, 2658, 2660.

Porta, Giambattista della (1538–1615), It. scientific experimenter, who dabbled in alchemy, biology, magnetism, etc.; described early camera obscura; and first steam engine, 3085.

Portal, of Laverstoke, Wyndham R. Portal, 1st Viscount (1885–1949). Brit. industrialist and politician; chairman coal production council 1940–49; as min. of works and planning, 1942–44, gave name to Portal prefabricated house.

Portal of Hungerford, Marshal of the R.A.F. Charles F. A. Portal, 1st Viscount (b. 1893). Brit. airman; A.O.C.-in-C. Bomber Command, 1940; Chief of Air Staff, 1940–45; head of min. of supply dept. concerned with work on atomic energy; awarded O.M. 1946.

Portal vein, 1968.

Port Arthur (Ryojun). Naval base on Liao-tung pen., Manchuria; pop. 145,000; placed under joint Sino-Soviet control in 1945; 1800.

Port Arthur, Ontario. City on L. Superior, grain and coal-shipping centre of w. Canada; pop. 24,420; 679.

Port Augusta, S. Australia. Spt. on Spencer Gulf; 3028.

Port-au-Prince. Cap. and principal spt. of Haiti, W. Indies, on w. coast; pop. 115,000; 1565.

Port Churchill. Terminus of Hudson Bay railway, 677.

Port Colborne, on Welland Canal between Lake Erie and Lake Ontario, 3363.

Portcul'lis, 717.

Port Darwin, Australia. See Darwin.

Porte. See Sublime Porte.

Porte du Palais, Bordeaux, 524.

Port Elizabeth. 2nd city of Cape of Good Hope, S. Africa, spt. 400 m. E. of Cape Town, on Algoa Bay; pop. 147,544; ostrich feathers, jam boots and shoes.

Porter, Cole (b. 1892). Amer. composer and song writer: "Night and Day," "The Still of the Night," "Begin the Béguine"; also musical plays "Gay Divorce," "Anything Goes."

Porter, Gene Stratton (1868–1924). Amer. author; keenly interested in animal life ("A Girl of the Limberlost"; "The Harvester"; "Her Father's Daughter").

Porter, Jane (1776–1850). Eng. novelist who had a great success with "Scottish Chiefs" in 1810, with patriot William Wallace as hero.

Porter, William Sydney. *See* Henry, O.

Port Glasgow, in Renfrewshire; pop. 19,000; 2767.

Porthos. One of the "Three Musketeers" of Dumas' novel; noted for size, strength, and fondness for display; 1054.

Portia (por'-shi-*a*). Heroine of Shakespeare's "Merchant of Venice"; and Shylock, 2144.

Portico, in architecture. Covered walk, supported by columns and usually vaulted; a porch before the entrance of a building fronted with columns. *See also* Porch.

Port Jackson. Harbour in New South Wales, Australia; is a naval station, and on its south shore is the prosperous city of Sydney, 3144.

Portland, Maine, U.S.A. Largest city and chief spt. in state on Casco Bay, 50 m. s.w. of Augusta; pop.

13,040, ocean ships, machinery, lumber products, fish; burned by British in 1775.

Portland, Oregon, U.S.A. Largest city of state; pop. 305,394; important lumber mfg. and shipping centre; large trade in wheat, and extensive furniture, flour, and paper industries, 2449.

Portland, battle of. Fought Feb. 18–20, 1653, between the Eng. and the Dutch; the Dutch under Tromp attacked the Eng. fleet under Blake, but were driven off and lost many ships.

Portland, Isle of. Peninsula on s. coast of Dorsetshire; noted for building-stone, 1030; break-waters, 558.

Portland Bill. Promontory on the E. coast of Dorsetshire, the tip of the isle of Portland, extending into the English Channel, 2657.

Portland cement, 740, *741*.

Portland stone, quarrying for, 2657; 2713.

Portland vase. Beautiful dark-blue glass urn with figures in white; found in tomb near Rome; broken by a madman in 1845 but skilfully repaired; now in British museum; *plate f. 585.*

Portlaoighise (port-lē'-sha), or **Maryborough,** co. tn. of Leix, Eire; pop. about 12,000; 1920.

Port Louis. Cap. of Mauritius; pop. 66,800; *2121.*

Port Mahon. Spt. and cap. of Minorca, one of Balearic Isls., *342.*

Port Moresby. Admin. centre of New Guinea, 2340; during 2nd World War, after U.S. naval victory of Coral Sea, became advance base for Australian forces in New Guinea, 3421.

A LIST OF THE POPES FROM ST. PETER

(Names of doubtful Popes and antipopes are in square brackets)

died 67?	Peter	625–638	Honorius I	984–985	Boniface VII	1316–34	John XXII
67–79?	Linus	638–640	Severinus	985–996	John XV	[1328–30	Nicholas V]
79–90?	Anacletus	640–642	John IV	996–999	Gregory V	1334–42	Benedict XII
90–99?	Clement I	642–649	Theodore I	[997–998	John XVI]	1342–52	Clement VI
99–107?	Evaristus	649–655	Martin I	999–1003	Silvester II	1352–62	Innocent VI
107–116?	Alexander I	654–657	Eugenius I	1003	John XVII	1362–70	Urban V
116–125?	Sixtus I	657–672	Vitalianus	1003–09	John XVIII	1370–78	Gregory XI
	(Xystus)	672–676	Adeodatus II	1009–12	Sergius IV	1378–89	Urban VI
125–136?	Telesphorus	676–678	Donus	1012–24	Benedict VIII	[1378–94	Clement VII]
136–140?	Hyginus	678–681	Agathon	1024–32	John XIX	1389–1404	Boniface IX
140–154?	Pius I	682–683	Leo II	1032–45	Benedict IX	[1394–1423	Benedict XIII]
154–165?	Anicetus	684–685	Benedict II	[1045	Silvester III]	1404–06	Innocent VII
165–174	Soter	685–686	John V	1045–46	Gregory VI	1406–15	Gregory XII
174–189	Eleutherius	686–687	Conon	1046–47	Clement II	1409–10	Alexander V
189–198	Victor I	687–701	Sergius I	[1047–48	Benedict IX]	1410–15	John XXIII
198–217	Zephyrinus	701–705	John VI	1048	Damasus II	1417–31	Martin V
217–222	Calixtus I	705–707	John VII	1049–54	Leo IX	[1424	Benedict XIV]
222–230	Urban I	708	Sisinnius	1055–57	Victor II	[1424–29	Clement VIII]
230–235	Pontianus	708–715	Constantine I	1057–59	Stephen IX	1431–47	Eugenius IV
235–236	Anterus	715–731	Gregory II	[1058–59	Benedict X]	[1439–49	Felix V]
236–250	Fabian	731–741	Gregory III	1059–61	Nicholas II	1447–55	Nicholas V
251–253	Cornelius	741–752	Zacharias	1061–73	Alexander II	1455–58	Calixtus III
[251–258?	Novatianus]	752	Stephen	[1061–64	Honorius II]	1458–64	Pius II
253–254	Lucius I	752–757	Stephen II	1073–85	Gregory VII	1464–71	Paul II
254–257	Stephen I	757–767	Paul I	[1084–1100 Clement III]		1471 84	Sixtus IV
257–258	Sixtus II	767–768	Constantine II	1086–87	Victor III	1484–92	Innocent VIII
259–268	Dionysius	768–772	Stephen III	1088–99	Urban II	1492–1503	Alexander VI
269–274	Felix I	772–795	Adrian I	1099–1118 Paschal II		1503	Pius III
275–283	Eutychianus	795–816	Leo III	[1105–11	Silvester IV]	1503–13	Julius II
283–296	Gaius	816–817	Stephen IV	1118–19	Gelasius II	1513–21	Leo X
296–304	Marcellinus	817–824	Paschal I	[1118–21	Gregory VIII]	1522–23	Adrian VI
308–309	Marcellus I	824–827	Eugenius II	1119–24	Calixtus II	1523–34	Clement VII
309	Eusebius	827	Valentine	1124–30	Honorius II	1534–49	Paul III
310–314	Melchiades	827–844	Gregory IV	[1124	Celestine II]	1550–55	Julius III
314–335	Silvester I	844–847	Sergius II	1130–43	Innocent II	1555	Marcellus II
336	Marcus	847–855	Leo IV	[1130–38	Anacletus II]	1555–59	Paul IV
337–352	Julius I	[855	Anastasius]	[1138	Victor IV]	1559–65	Pius IV
352–366	Liberius	855–858	Benedict III	1143–44	Celestine II	1566–72	Pius V
[355–365	Felix II]	858–867	Nicholas I	1144–45	Lucius II	1572–85	Gregory XIII
366–384	Damasus I	867–872	Adrian II	1145–53	Eugenius III	1585–90	Sixtus V
384–398	Siricius	872–882	John VIII	1153–54	Anastasius IV	1590	Urban VII
398–401	Anastasius I	882–884	Marinus I	1154–59	Adrian IV	1590–91	Gregory XIV
402–417	Innocent I	884–885	Adrian III	1159–81	Alexander III	1591	Innocent IX
417–418	Zosimus	885–891	Stephen V	[1159–64	Victor IV]	1592–1605	Clement VIII
418–422	Boniface I	891–896	Formosus	[1164–68	Paschal III]	1605	Leo XI
422–432	Celestine I	896	Boniface VI	[1168–78	Calixtus III]	1605–21	Paul V
432–440	Sixtus III	896–897	Stephen VI	[1179–80	Innocent III]	1621–23	Gregory XV
440–461	Leo I	897	Romanus	1181 85	Lucius III	1623–44	Urban VIII
461–468	Hilarius	897	Theodore II	1185–87	Urban III	1644–55	Innocent X
468–483	Simplicius	898–900	John IX	1187	Gregory VIII	1655–67	Alexander VII
483–492	Felix II (III)	900–903	Benedict IV	1187–91	Clement III	1667–69	Clement IX
492–496	Gelasius I	903	Leo V	1191–98	Celestine III	1670–76	Clement X
496–498	Anastasius II	903–904	Christopher	1198–1216	Innocent III	1676–89	Innocent XI
498–514	Symmachus	904–911	Sergius III	1216–27	Honorius III	1689–91	Alexander VIII
514–523	Hormisdas	911–913	Anastasius III	1227–41	Gregory IX	1691–1700	Innocent XII
523–526	John I	913–914	Lando	1241	Celestine IV	1700–21	Clement XI
526–530	Felix III (IV)	914–928	John X	1243–54	Innocent IV	1721–24	Innocent XIII
530–532	Boniface II	928	Leo VI	1254–61	Alexander IV	1724–30	Benedict XIII
533–535	John II	928–931	Stephen VII	1261–64	Urban IV	1730–40	Clement XII
535–536	Agapetus I	931–936	John XI	1265–68	Clement IV	1740–58	Benedict XIV
536–538?	Silverius	936–939	Leo VII	1271–76	Gregory X	1758–69	Clement XIII
538?–555	Vigilius	939–942	Stephen VIII	1276	Innocent V	1769–74	Clement XIV
556–561	Pelagius I	942 946	Marinus II	1276	Adrian V	1775–99	Pius VI
561–574	John III	946–955	Agapetus II	1276 77	John XXI	1800–23	Pius VII
575–579	Benedict I	955–964	John XII	1277–80	Nicholas III	1823–29	Leo XII
579–590	Pelagius II	963–965	Leo VIII	1281–85	Martin IV	1829–30	Pius VIII
590–604	Gregory I, the Great	964	Benedict V	1285–87	Honorius IV	1831–46	Gregory XVI
		965–972	John XIII	1288–92	Nicholas IV	1846–78	Pius IX
604–606	Sabinianus	973–974	Benedict VI	1294	Celestine V	1873–1903	Leo XIII
607	Boniface III	[974	Boniface VII]	1294–1303	Boniface VIII	1903–14	Pius X
608–615	Boniface IV	974–983	Benedict VII	1303–04	Benedict XI	1914–22	Benedict XV
615–618	Adeodatus I	983–984	John XIV	1305–14	Clement V	1922–39	Pius XI
619–625	Boniface V					1939–	Pius XII

Port Natal'. *See* **Durban.**

Porto Alegre (por'-tõa-lã'-grã). Port and cap. of state of Rio Grande do Sul, Brazil, near N. extremity of L. Patos; pop. 321,600; Ger. colony handled most of the commerce before 1st World War; exports, 554.

Portobel'lo. Port of Atlantic coast of Isthmus of Panama 20 M. N.E. of Colon; pop. 9,900; long the shipping point for Spanish treasure from Peru.

Port of entry. Any point, whether on the frontier or not, designated by the customs authorities as a place where merchandise or persons may enter or pass out of a country.

Port of London Authority (P.L.A.). Controls the Docks of London with all its varied trading; its jurisdiction extends 40 m. below London Bridge with the exception of the Surrey Commercial Docks; 2010, 3194.

Port of Spain. Cap. of Trinidad; pop. 107,500; 3248.

Porto Grande. Spt., Cape Verde Isls., 698.

Porto Rico. *See* **Puerto Rico.**

Porto San'to. Mountainous isl. of Madeiras; about 20 sq. m.; 2052.

Port Pirie, S. Australia, 3028.

Portraiture, in Eng. art, 1179, *1185–87*; Fr. art, *1369, 1372, 1377*; It. art, 1776; photographic, *2582, 2583*; in Roman art, 2812, *2814, 2816*.

Port Royal. Spt. and naval station of Jamaica; headquarters of the Brit. naval forces in the w. Indies; has dockyard, barracks, arsenal and military hospital.

Port Royal, Nova Scotia. Former name of Annapolis; founded, 2401.

Port-Royal des Champs. Celebrated Fr. nunnery about 8 m. s.w. of Versailles, established in 1204; transferred to Paris in 1626, it became a prominent Jansenist and educational centre, but in 1709 the nuns were expelled, and the following year the nunnery was demolished.

Port Said, Egypt. At N. end of Suez Canal; pop. 124,750; founded as coaling station in 1859; exports cotton; *1098, 1103*; *maps, 1096, 3110*.

Ports and harbours, 1576.

Portsmouth. Important fortified spt. and great Eng. naval station and arsenal in Hampshire on the Eng. Channel; pop. 157,580; **2657,** 1571; H.M.S. Victory, *3322*; bombed 1940–41, 2657.

Portsmouth, Virginia, U.S.A. Twin city of Norfolk; pop. 50,750; Norfolk Navy Yard.

Port Sunlight. Tn. of Cheshire, 3 m. s.e. of Birkenhead; laid out in 1888 by Messrs. Lever Bros. as a model industrial tn.

Portugal. Republic of s.w. Europe; a. (incl. isls.) 35,490 sq. m.; pop. 8,500,000; **2658;** *map, 3030*; Azores, 324; cap. Lisbon, 1962, *2659*; colonial possessions, 70, 72, 698, 1073, 1714, 3368; cork, 909; language and literature, 2798; Madeira, 2051; millet harvest, *2175*; olive industry, 2431; uranium, 3297. *History*: African explorations, 69, 139, 887; Brazil, 554; Far East, 1076, 1799, 1813, 2069; Henry the Navigator, 69, 1613; Vasco da Gama, 3306; revolution of 1910, 1962; Salazar's dictatorship, 2660; in 2nd World War, 2660.

Portugal laurel, 1900.

Portuguese East Africa. *See* **Mozambique.**

Portuguese Guinea. Colony on w. coast of Africa enclosed on land side by Fr. territory; includes adjacent Bissagos or Bijagoz Isls.; 13,948 sq. m.; pop. 351,000; chief tn. Bissao; 3368.

Portuguese language and literature, 2659, 2798.

Portuguese man-of-war, a jelly-fish, *1817*, 1818.

Portuguese West Africa. *See* **Angola.**

Port Weller, on Welland Canal, 3363.

Poseidon (po-sī'-don). In Gk. myth. god of the sea, **2660,** 2315; and Athena, 283; Cretan bull, 1615; Odysseus, 950; Temple of, Paestum, *plate f.213.*

Po'sen (Polish **Poznan**). Former Prussian prov.; 10,240 sq. m.; pop. 2,180,000; cap. Posen (Poznan); ceded to Poland in 1919.

Posen (or **Poznan**), Poland. Tn. 170 m. s. of Warsaw on R. Warthe; pop. 267,962; important medieval trade centre; held by Prussia 1793–1918; bitter battles in 2nd World War.

Positive electricity, 1128, 3198.

Pos'itivism. System of philosophy founded by Auguste Comte, which organized all knowledge to form a basis for a science of society and a religion of humanity.

Positron. Fundamental particle of positive electricity in atom, equal and opposite to the electron, 297.

Post, Wiley (1900–35). Amer. airman, a Texan, who after farming, drilling for oil, and losing an eye, in 1924 took up flying and parachute jumping; in 1931 flew round world with H. Gatty in 8 days 15 hrs. 51 mins.; in July 1933, flying solo, did it again in 7 days 18 hrs. 49½ mins.; in Aug. 1935 he and Will Rogers killed in flying from Alaska to Siberia.

Postage, rates of, 2662.

Postage stamp. *See* **Stamps.**

Postal orders, 2662.

Postal Union, Universal, 2662.

Poste restante, 2662.

Postern gate, 717.

Posters, lithographic printing of, **1967.**

Post-impressionism, in painting. Name covering the work of a group of painters who followed the Impressionists; Cézanne, Gauguin, Van Gogh were chief of these, 1687, 2477; in French art, *1375*, 1378; Van Gogh and, 3305.

Postmaster-General (P.M.G.). The political chief of the Post Office department of Gt. Britain, 2661.

Post mill, type of windmill, *3386*.

Post Office, 2661, *2663*; cable ship, *643*; helicopter delivers mail, 1605, *1606*; "speaking clock," *2576*, 3013; stamps, 3074; telegraphy, 3164, *3169*; telephone system, 3173, *3170, 3171, 3172*; and broadcasting, 3398.

Post Office Savings Bank (P.O.S.B.), 357, 2662.

Posture, and hygiene, 1676; and physical fitness, *2591*.

Potash or **potassium carbonate,** 2664; in Alsace, 133; caustic potash (potassium hydroxide), 2664; from seaweed, 2916.

Pot'ash feldspar, 1265.

Potas'sium. Element of the alkali metal group; atomic weight 39·1; isolated by Davy in 1807; melts at 143·6°F.; **2662;** in baking powder, 3155; cyanide used in gold extraction, 947, 1480; nitrate used in gunpowder, 1558; essential to plant growth, 2998; properties, 776; feebly radio-active, 2732; and salt, 2866; salts used in soap-making, 2993, 2994; in tartrates, 3155. *Compounds*: chlorate, 2119, 2664; cyanide, 947, 1480, 2664; hydroxide, 2664; nitrate (saltpetre), 1558, 2664, 2868; permanganate, 179. *See* **Potash.**

Pota'to, 2664; Burbank, 621; in France, 1360; in Germany, 1445; Ireland, 1745; spirit from, 3067; starch, 3082; structure of tuber, 612, 2825; vitamins, 3326.

Potato-beetle. *See* **Colorado Beetle.**

Potato starch, 3082.

Potemkin (po-tyom'-kin), **Gregorei Alexandrovitch, Prince** (1739–91). Rus. statesman, most famous favourite of Catherine the Great.

Poten'tial. Electric voltage or "pressure," 1128, 1129.

Pot-holes, in Derbyshire and Yorkshire, 734; in limestone country, 1951.

Po'ti. Spt. of Georgia on Black Sea, 35 m. w. of Batum; pop. 17,000; unhealthy climate; commerce, 733.

Potiphar (pot'-i-far). An Egypt. official, whose wife tempted Joseph, his slave (Gen. xxxix, 1).

Potomac (po-tō'-mak). A r. of E. U.S.A., flowing 450 m. into Chesapeake Bay, 3328, 3343.

Potomac Park, Washington, U.S.A., 3344.

Potosi (pō-tō-sē'). Silver and tin-mining city of Bolivia on N. slope of Cerro de Potosi, 47 m. s.w. of Sucre (14,350 ft.); pop. 40,000, 491.

Potsdam. Ger. city and cap. of Brandenburg on R. Havel, 16 m. s.w. of Berlin; pop. 73,676; observatory; palace of Sans Souci.

Potsdam Conference, July 1945. Held in the Cecilienhof Palace, between Pres. Truman, Mr. Churchill (later replaced by Mr. Attlee) and J. Stalin, to decide how Germany should be occupied.

Potter, Beatrix Helen (1866–1943). Brit. author of children's stories, **2665,** 1965.

Potter, Paul (1625–54). Foremost Dutch animal painter and etcher; in Nat. Gallery, London, 2334.

Potteries, The. Name given to dist. of N. Staffordshire, chief seat of china and earthenware industry; includes several towns united in 1910 as one county borough (Stoke-on-Trent), 3072.

Pottery and porcelain, 2665; Aegean, 30, *31*; Chinese, *2668*; clay, 2665; anc. Egyptian, 1116; Gk. vases, *1523, 1524, 1528, 1536*; Portland Vase, *plate f.* 585; Japanese, *1809*, 2271; Stone Age invention, 2082. *See also* **Porcelain** and **chinaware.**

Pouishnoff (pwēsh'-noff), **Leff** (b. 1891). Russ.-born Brit. pianist; exponent of Chopin.

Poulsen, Valdemar (b. 1869). Danish inventor of the Poulsen arc, producing continuous radio-frequency oscillations; recorded sound on magnetized wire, 3013.

Poultry, 2671; Buff Orpington, *435*; duck, 1051; egg production, 444; food value of chicken compared with milk, *2174*; gamecock, *435*; goose, 1484; guinea fowl, 1554; Indian jungle fowl, *435*; oyster shells as feed, 2466; turkeys, 3261; chickens, 1245.

Pound, Adm. Sir Dudley (1877–1943). Brit. sailor; in bat. of Jutland; 2nd Sea Lord 1932; C.-in-C. Med. fleet in 1936; 1st Sea Lord and Chief of Naval Staff just before 2nd World War; went to conferences of Churchill and Roosevelt and died Oct. 1943 while at U.N. staff talks.

Pound, Ezra Loomis (b. 1885). Amer. poet and critic, lived in Europe from 1907; ("Canzoni"; "Exultations"; "Cathay"; translations of Japanese and Chinese drama and poetry); a leading exponent of "free verse," 3296; indicted for treason by U.S.A. 1943; captured in Italy 1945 declared mentally unsound in 1946.

Pound (lb.). A unit of weight (*see* **Weights and Measures**); and of steam pressure, 3085.

Pound. Brit. monetary unit (£); in full the pound sterling, 20 shillings; now represented by a Bank of England note; sovereigns are not now in circulation; their gold value is considerably more than £1.

Pounds, Charles Courtice (1862–1927). Eng. actor; in early days played various parts in Gilbert and Sullivan operas; one of his chief successes was as Ali Baba in "Chu Chin Chow," which ran for five years.

Pounds, John (1766–1839). Eng. teacher, philanthropist, and founder of the ragged schools; crippled as a shipwright when young, he took up the work of shoemaking, and gave free education to poor children; many schools were opened in his memory in various parts of the country after he died.

Poussin (poo-san'), **Nicolas** (1594–1665). Fr. painter, originator of Fr. classical style; court painter to Louis XIII 1640–43 ("The Triumph of Pan"; "The Arts"; "The Labours of Hercules"), *1371*, 1377; repr. in Nat. Gallery, London.

Pouter pigeons, *2607*; courtship antics, 441.

Powder, explosive, 1250.

Powdered egg, 1341.

Powdered milk, 1341.

Powder Metallurgy. Process for working metals, also making alloys, without smelting, by compression of metals in powder form at temps. below their melting point, 122.

Powell, John Wesley (1834–1902). Amer. geologist; exploration of Grand Canyon, 1498.

Power. Electric, 1060, 1128, 1545, 1549, 2673; steam, 3085; water, 1669; watt, 1128; wind, 3384; atomic, 299.

Power-loom. Cartwright's invention, 712.

Power Station, for generating electricity, 2673; boilers, 489; dynamo, 1060; supply the Grid, 1545; in hydro-electric installations, 1669; smoke from, 2986; transformer in, 3238.

Powers and roots, in mathematics, 2671; logarithms and, 1998; slide rule and, 2984.

Pownall, Sir Henry R. (b. 1887). Brit. soldier; chief of gen. staff, B.E.F., 1939–40; C.-in-C. Far East 1941–42; G.O.C., Ceylon, 1942–43; C.-in-C. Persia-Iraq 1943; Chief of Staff to Mountbatten, S.E. Asia com., 1943–44; retired 1945.

Powys (pō'-is), **John Cowper** (b. 1872). Brit. writer; known for his imaginative fiction, philosophical works, and critical essays; his brothers, Llewelyn (1884–1939) and Theodore Francis (b. 1875), are also notable modern authors, 1217.

"Poy." Pseudonym of Brit. cartoonist Percy Hutton Fearon (1874–1948); creator of Dilly and Dally, etc.

Poy'nings, Sir Edward (1459–1521). Lord-deputy of Ire.; proclaimed traitor for his part in the rising against Richard III in 1483, he fled to Fr., returning in 1485 with the forces of Henry, Earl of Richmond; he passed the Acts, known as the Statutes of Drogheda, or " Poynings' Law," which provided that no Acts of an Irish Parl. were valid unless first sanctioned by the Eng. Privy Council.

Poynter, Sir Edward John (1836–1919). Eng. portrait and classical painter, director of National Gallery, London (1894–1904); designs for Houses of Parl., St. Paul's Cath.; " Atalanta's Race," *283*; " Catapult before Carthage," *2807*.

Poynting, John Henry (1852–1914). Eng. scientist; " weighed " the earth by an ingenious experiment carried out with a small and a large lead ball hung in a very fine balance.

Poznan. *See* Posen.

Pozzuolana, form of cement from Pozzuoli, Italy, 740.

Prado, Madrid. Picture gallery, 2054.

" Praeterita," Ruskin's autobiography, 2844.

Praetorian (pre-tor'-i-an) **Guard.** In Rom. history, imperial bodyguard, founded by Augustus, suppressed by Constantine; frequently made and unmade emperors, *2815*.

Prae'tors, Rom. judges, 2805.

Pragmat'ic Sanction. A term applied to several imperial decrees of fundamental importance, especially that of Charles VI (1713).

Prag'matism, in philosophy, 2572.

Prague (prahg). Cap. of Czecho-slovakia; pop. 924,000; **2677**, 954; cap. of old Bohemia, 487; city of toys, 801; defenestration of, *3203*; university of, 487; in 2nd World War, 2677.

Praia (prī'-ah). Cap. of Cape Verde Isls.; pop. 4,000; cable station; 698.

Prairie (prăr'-i). Tract of level or rolling land destitute of trees and covered with coarse, tall grass, interspersed with varieties of flowering plants; of Argentina, 227; Canadian, *679*; steppes of Rus., 2844; the " prairie province," 2089.

Prairie chicken, courtship antics, 441.

Prairie-dog. A New World rodent closely related to the marmot; and rattlesnake, 2747.

Prairie Provinces, of Canada, 676.

" Praise of Folly." Satire by Erasmus, 2764; Holbein illustrates, 1635.

Prajadhipok (1893–1941). King of Siam 1925 to 1935, 2965.

Prasad, Dr. Rajendra (b. 1884). Indian politician. First pres. of the Indian republic, in 1950.

Praseodymium (Pr.) (prā-se-ō-dim'-i-um). A metallic element of the rare-earth group; atomic weight, 140·92 properties. 768. *See* Rare Earths.

Prawn. Shrimp-like crustacean, 2962.

Praxiteles (praks-it'-e-lēz) (fl. 360–340 B.C.). Gk. sculptor, greatest of his age, 1537; statue of Hermes, *1533*.

Prayer Book, in Church of Eng., 819, 825.

Praying mantis. An insect, *2090*.

Pre-Cambrian era, in geology, 1432.

Precession of the equinoxes, 1221, 3080; illustrated by gyroscope, 1560.

Precious metals. Term usually restricted to gold and silver, but sometimes also including platinum and mercury. *See* names of those metals.

Precious stones. *See* Gems; list, 3813.

Precipita'tion. Chemical procedure, 773; clouds, 851; dew, 1000; rainfall, 2741; snow, 2992. *See* Climate; Rainfall.

Pred'icate. In grammar, part of sentence, 1494, 2920.

Predictor. Instrument used in anti-aircraft defence which predicts the course of hostile aircraft for the guns, 257.

Prefabrication. Factory production of standardized parts of houses, ships, etc., for erection or assembly on sites; economizes labour; largely employed in recent years; 611.

Preference shares, 3093.

Prefixes, in Eng., 1209.

Pregl, Fritz (1869–1930). Austrian chemist; famous for his method of quantitative micro-analysis; Nobel prize in chemistry in 1923.

Prehistoric Age, 1630. *See* Civilization; Stone Age.

Prehistoric animals, 2678, *2679, 735*; archaeopteryx, *437*, 2681; bison, *459*; dinosaurs, 2678, 2767; extinct horse types, 1645; fossil reptiles classified, 2707; ichthyosaurs, *2680, 2681*; mammoth and mastodon, 2077; pterodactyls, 2680; tuatara, " the living fossil," 1974.

" Prelude, The." Poem by Wordsworth, 3408.

Pre'mium. In insurance, a sum periodically paid by the person insured in order to get a stated sum of money from the society to whom the premium is paid in case of death, fire, etc., 1733.

Pre'molars or bicuspids, teeth, 3163.

Preposition, in grammar, 2681; use, 1495.

Pre-Raphaelites. Group of painters of 19th cent., 2681, 2476; in Eng. art, 1182; Morris, 2232.

Presbyterian Church. A free church, 1390; Calvin's influence, 664; in Scot., 3894, 1871.

Prescott, William Hickling (1796–1859). Amer. historian; achieved great results in face of invalidism and partial blindness (" Conquest of Mexico " : " Conquest of Peru "), 2394.

Preseley or **Prescelly Top.** Highest peak in Pembrokeshire, Wales, 1,760 ft.; 2538.

Preservation of food, 1341.

President. One who presides over a corporation or an assembly; in a republic it is the highest office; the chief officer in a society, univ., or club; 1488; of France, 1362; of the U.S.A., 3291. *See* lists under **France**; **United States of America**.

Press, Hydraulic, 1665, *1666*.

Press, freedom of. Milton's " Areopagitica," 2177.

Pressburg. *See* Bratislava.

Press photography, 2587.

Pressure. Atmospheric, 3301; and freezing water, 1392; " electric " (potential or voltage), 1128, *1133*; in gases, 1419; in gas mains, 1424; in liquids, 1665, *1666*, 3674; of sap in plants, 2621; in venturi tube, 3312; in water mains, 3348; of water in ocean depths, 1019, 2414.

Pressure cooker, 900; how it works, 3084.

" Pressure " microphone, 2163.

Presteign (pres-tān'), Wales. Co. tn. of Radnorshire, on r. Lugg; pop. 1,102; 2733.

Prester John. King and priest of a mythical land which had no poor, no thieves, no lies, no vices; legends of 12th and 13th cents., 13.

Preston. Tn. and port of Lancashire situated at mouth of R. Ribble; pop. 116,440; brass and iron products, ships, beer, exports coal; cotton mfg. centre, 1165; has famous Association football club, Preston North End.

Prestonpans, Scot. Vil. in E. Lothian on Firth of Forth; victory of Jacobites under Prince Charles Edward over royal army Sept. 21, 1745.

Prestwich, Sir Joseph (1812–96). Eng. geologist, 2078.

Pretender. Name applied to son and grandson of James II of Eng., who claimed Brit. throne, 2682, 1790; Jacobite risings, 2682, 1440. *1791*.

Pretor'ia. Cap. of Transvaal and joint cap. of Union of S. Africa; pop. 167,649; 2682, 3239, 3013, 3020; in Boer War, 487.

Prevailing westerlies, *3385*. Effect on rainfall, 2741.

Prevention of Cruelty to Animals, Royal Soc. for (R.S.P.C.A.). Formed 1824 by R. Martin (*q.v.* in *f-i.*).

Prevention of Cruelty to Children, Nat. Soc. for (N.S.P.C.C.). Movement founded by the Rev. B. Waugh, 1884; Royal charter 1895.

Preventive medicine, 2132.

Prévost d'Exiles (prā-vō' dek-sēl'), **Antoine François** (1697–1763) (Abbé Prévost). Fr. monk and novelist (" Manon Lescaut," " one of the greatest novels of the century ").

Priam (prī'-am). In Gk. myth., king of Troy, 3252, 1603.

Pribilof Islands, Alaska. Group of isls. in Bering Sea, abounding in fur seals, 98; seals, *2913*.

Prichard, Katherine S. Australian writer, 316.

Prickly pear. A flat-stemmed cactus and its pear-shaped fruit, 648; Burbank's thornless, 621.

Pride, Thomas (d. 1658). Parl. officer in Eng. Civil War; carried out order (1648) to expel by force Royalist and Presbyterian members from House of Commons (" Pride's Purge ").

" Pride and Prejudice." Novel by Jane Austen, 306, 1214, 2402.

Priestley, John Boynton (b. 1894). Eng. author and playwright, 2683, 1216. 2403.

Priestley, Joseph (1733–1804). Eng. chemist, discoverer of oxygen, 2683. 2466; and photo-synthesis, 2589; named rubber, 2833.

Primary, in elec.: cell which generates electric current without previous charging, 375, 1131, 1132; winding of induction coil, 1720.

Primate of All England. The Arch-bishop of Canterbury, 692, 825.

Primate of England. The Archbishop of York, 825.

Primates (prī-mā'-tēz). The order of nailed mammals, including man, 2077, 2079.

Prime Minister. In Eng., 1490; First Lord of the Treasury, 3240; in Canada, 684.

PRIME MINISTERS OF GT. BRITAIN

1721–42	Sir Robert Walpole.
1742–43	Earl of Wilmington.
1743–54	Henry Pelham.
1754–56	Duke of Newcastle.
1756–57	Duke of Devonshire.
1757–62	William Pitt, aft. Earl of Chatham, and Duke of Newcastle.
1762–63	Earl of Bute.
1763–65	George Grenville.
1765–66	Marquess of Rockingham.
1766–67	Earl of Chatham (2nd time).
1767–70	Duke of Grafton.
1770–82	Lord North, aft. Earl of Guilford.
1782	Marquess of Rockingham (2nd time). [*contd. in next p.*]

Primo de Rivera, José, and Spanish Fascism, 3038.

Primo de Rivera, Miguel (1870–1930). Spanish statesman and soldier ; in 1923 seized power, setting up a military directorate ; introduced in 1925 a civilian administration of which he became premier ; 3037, *3039.*

Primogen′iture. Right of eldest son (Latin, *primus genitus,* first-born) to inheritance.

Primrose. A flowering plant, **2684.**

Primrose League. Conservative party organization in Brit., **2684.**

" Prince, The." By Machiavelli, 2049.

Prince Albert, Saskatchewan. Distributing city for farming region on N. Saskatchewan r. ; pop. 14,290 ; lumber, livestock, and fur interests ; packing houses, gov. dockyards ; 2875.

Prince Edward Island (P.E.I.). The smallest of the Canadian provinces, in Gulf of St. Lawrence ; 2,184 sq. m. ; pop. 95,000 ; cap. Charlottetown ; **2684.**

Prince of Wales. Title given to eldest son of Sovereign of England, 3334, *3337,* 1089 ; crest, 926.

Prince of Wales, H.M.S. Battleship of King George V class, displacing 35,000 tons ; in chase of Bismarck (*q.v.* in *f-i.*) ; on board her Churchill and Roosevelt discussed Atlantic Charter, 1941 ; torpedoed by Jap. aircraft with H.M.S. Repulse Dec. 10, 1941, while intercepting Jap. convoy off Malay coast ; 3420.

Prince of Wales Island ; in the Malayan Fedn. *see* Penang ; in the Arctic, 2390.

Princess Elizabeth Land, in Antarctic, *2645.*

Princes Street, Edinburgh, *1086,* 1087.

Princeton University. At Princeton, New Jersey, U.S.A., men ; nonsect. ; chartered as College of New Jersey in 1746 ; arts and science, civil and electrical engineering ; 3296.

Princip, Gavrilo (1894–1918). Serbian revolutionary ; shot Francis Ferdinand, 3409.

Principal. Money upon which interest is paid, 2548.

" Principia." Treatise by Newton, 2349.

Pringle, Thomas (1789–1834). S. African poet, 3020.

Prin′sep, Valentine Cameron (1838–1904). Anglo-Indian artist and author ; pupil of G. F. Watts ; R.A. in 1894 ; he exhibited many historical and genre paintings at the Royal Academy and wrote " Imperial India " and several novels.

Printing, 2684 ; from blocks, 701, 1217, *1218,* 1811 ; books, 509, *513, 514, 515* ; on cloth, 850 ; colour-printing, 1811, 2689, *plate f. 2688* ; electrotyping, 1140 ; engraving, 1217 ; importance of invention, 3457 ; inks, 1724 ; linotype, 1956 ; lithography, 1218, 1967 ; monotype, 2215 ; newspapers, 2344 ; paper, 2496 ; postage stamps, *3075* ; process engraving, 2687 ; and Renaissance, 2764, 2766 ; sterotyping, 3088 ; type, 2685, 3270 ; typesetting machines, 1956, 2215 ; by wireless, 3398.

Printing, in photography, 2580.

Printing press, 2686 ; Japanese, 1811.

Prinz Eugen (oig′-gen). Ger. cruiser ; escaped to Brest when Bismarck was sunk 1941 ; up Eng. Channel with Scharnhorst and Gneisenau 1942 ; damaged in U.S. navy atomic bomb tests at Bikini Atoll (*q.v.* in *f-i.*) and sank there Dec. 16, 1946.

Prior, Matthew (1664–1721). Eng. poet and diplomat, best remembered for his light humorous verse ; served the govt. long in various capacities ; from his share in the negotiations the treaty of Utrecht was popularly labelled " Matt's Peace."

Prior. Monastic superior, 2213.

Priory. A monastic house presided over by a prior or prioress.

Pripet (pré′-pet). R. in w. Rus. ; rises in group of lakes and marshes in White Russia, S.S.R. ; flows E. and S.E. 400 m. to Dnieper ; during both World Wars scene of fighting between Ger. and Russians.

Prism. Effect on light, *plate f. 3056* ; in field-glass, 3180 ; in periscope, 2552 ; of rock-salt, 2866 ; in spectroscope, 3055, *plate f. 3056* ; in telescope, 3178 ; Newton's, *2349.*

Prism spectroscope, 3055.

Prison reform, 2687 ; Elizabeth Fry, *1404.*

Prisons and punishments, 2686.

Privateer, 2612 ; Sir Francis Drake, 1036.

Priv′et. A hardy shrub *Ligustrum,* of olive tribe, very popular for hedges. Several species are common, of which one, *L. vulgare,* is wild in limestone and chalk districts of Brit. Simple green leaves and white sickly-smelling flowers, succeeded by purple-black berries.

Priv′y Council, Eng. Originally the sovereign's body of advisers, **2688 ;** was final court of appeal for Canada, 684.

Prizend or **Prizren,** Yugoslavia. Serbian tn. ; pop. 18,952 ; numerous mosques ; once Turkish city ; many bazaars, active trade.

Probability, in statistics. The likelihood of an event, measured by the ratio of the favourable cases to the total number of possible cases ; probability of drawing a red ball first from a bag containing 3 red balls and 7 white, is 3–10.

Probate, Divorce and Admiralty, Court of, 922.

Probation. System by which a prisoner, on the score of youth or for other considerations, is given a chance to reform without going to prison.

Proboscis, of butterfly, magnified, *629* ; trunk of elephant, 1141.

Proboscis monkey, *2207,* 2211.

Process engraving, 2688 ; *plates f. 2688, 2689.*

Procne (prok′-nē). *See* Philomel.

Procrustes (prō - krus′ - tēz) (" the stretcher "). In Gk. legend, robber slain by Theseus ; placed guests on a bed and stretched short men and chopped off tall ones to fit ; " bed of Procrustes " has become proverbial.

Procter, Adelaide Ann (1825–64). Brit. poet ; wrote many well-known lyrics, including " The Lost Chord," and a number of popular hymns.

Procter, Bryan Waller (" Barry Cornwall ") (1787–1874). Eng. poet ; friend of Lamb, Keats, Scott, Dickens, Tennyson.

Procyon (prō′-si-on). A star, 3078, *chart, 895.*

Producer gas, 1406 ; from peat, 2535.

Production, in economics, 1080, 1081 ; stage, *1043* ; mass, 1347, *897.*

Profits, in economics, 1081.

Progreso, Mexico. Port for Mérida, Yucatan, on N.W. coast ; exports sisal, 2156.

Prohibition. Term used specially for prohibiting sale of intoxicating liquors in U.S.A. 1919–33, 3292 ; also tried in Iceland, Sweden, Greenland, Finland and the Indian subcontinent.

Projec′tiles, for artillery, 257.

Projection, of maps, *2094.*

Projective geometry, 1440.

Prokofief (pro-kôf′-yef), **Sergei** (b. 1891). Rus. composer ; works include " Loves of the Three Oranges " (opera) ; " Chout " (ballet) ; " Scythian Suite " (for orchestra). Famous for film music, " Ivan the Terrible," " Alexander Nevsky."

Prokopievsk. Siberian tn. ; pop. 107,000 ; 2967.

Proletariat (prō-le-tār′-i-at). In modern usage, working men as a class.

Promenade Concerts (Proms.). Series of orchestral concerts given at Queen's Hall, London, until 1941, then at Albert Hall ; instituted in 1895, and conducted until 1944 by Sir Henry Wood ; now broadcast by the B.B.C.

Promethean, an early kind of match, 2119.

Prometheus (prō-mē′-thŭs). In Gk. myth., hero who championed man and defied Zeus, **2690 ;** and Hercules, 1615 ; and Pandora, 2494.

" Prometheus Bound." Tragedy by Aeschylus, 53, 2690.

Prominences, of sun, 3120.

Promised Land, of the Jews, 1829.

Promissory note. *See* Note, promissory.

Pronoun, 2690 ; use, 1494, 2920.

Pron′tosil, an aniline dye from which sulpha drugs were derived, 179.

Pronunciation, key, 8.

Proof, geometrical, 1438.

Proof spirit. Alcohol weighing $\frac{13}{16}$ of an equal measure of distilled water at 51°F. ; 103, 3067.

Propaganda. Organized dissemination of information in attempts to influence the minds of the people ; in Germany, 1451.

Propagation of the Faith, Congregation of the, 2495.

Propel′ler, aeroplane, 44, 50, 2903 ; screw, 2902, *2903,* 2947 ; of torpedo, 3224 ; type of water turbine, 1670, *1671.*

Propertius, Sextus (*c.* 49–16 B.C.). Greatest Rom. elegiac poet, 1896.

Property tax, 3158.

Prophets, Hebrew, **2691,** 1829.

Propontis. *See* Marmara.

Propylaea (prō-pi-lē′-a). Monumental gateway to Acropolis, *21,* 22.

Proscenium (prō-sē′-ni-um), in theatre, 3194.

Proserpina. *See* Persephone.

Prospecting, and mining, 2181, 2182.

Pros′pero. In Shakespeare's " The Tempest," banished Duke of Milan. 3185.

Protagoras (prō-tag′-ō-ras) (490–415 B.C.). Gk. philosopher, first to call himself sophist and to teach for payment ; taught that " man is the measure of all things."

Protection, in economics. System of protecting the industries of a country from foreign competition by taxing foreign commodities and granting bounties to home products, 945.

Protective coloration and resemblance, 2692 ; among animals, 2692 ; birds, 448, 2692 ; cephalopods, 2199 ; chameleon, 750 ; fish, 1297, 2692 ; flat-fish, 1298 ; giraffe, 1465 ; grouse, *1550* ; hare, *2692* ; insects, 1726, *2693* ; leaf butterfly, 630, *1728* ; principles applied in camouflage, 673 ; ptarmigan, *1551, 2693* ; tiger, 2692, 3211 ; weasel, *2693*. See **Camouflage.**

Protec'torate, in Eng. (1653–59), 933, 1198 ; also name given to a territory in Brit. Commonwealth under protection of Crown. See list under **Crown Colony.**

Proteins. Complex amino-acid foodstuffs containing nitrogen, **2693,** 1338, *1339,* 1340 ; abundant in beans and peas, 2530 ; and allergy, 429 ; cookery of, 902 ; digestion of, 1017, 2547 ; hydrogen in, 1673 ; leather, 1913 ; nitrogen a part of, 2373 ; in potatoes, 2664 ; rayon and silk, 2749 ; in soya bean, 3029.

Proterozoic era, in geology, 1432.

Protestant Episcopal Church. A religious sect in Amer. ; separated from the Church of Eng. in 1789.

Protestantism, branch of Christian Church, 819 ; origin of term, 2759 ; Germany, 1449 ; Ireland, 402, 1747 ; Sweden, 3126. For history, *see* **Reformation, Protestant.**

Proteus (prō'-tūs). A sea-god in Gk. myth., **2694.**

Proteus, or cave-newt, a blind tailless amphibian, **2694.**

Prothall'us, of spore-bearing plants, *2918,* 2919.

Prothrom'bin. Element of bloodstream concerned with clotting, 475.

Protoactinium (Pa). Radioactive element of the actinium series and vanadium group ; atomic weight 231 ; properties, 778.

Protohip'pus. An evolutionary ancestor of the horse, coming between Eohippus and the modern horse.

Proton. Unit of positive electricity forming part of nucleus of atom, 295, 296, 297, 2732.

Pro'toplasm. The basic material of all cells and living organisms, **2695,** 1069, 738 ; in respiration, 2768.

Protozo'a. The single-celled animals as a group, **2695,** 156 ; as disease producers, 1458 ; as parasites, 2513 ; in termites, 3189.

Protrac'tor. An instrument for measuring and constructing angles, 1436.

Proust (prōost), **Marcel** (1871–1922). French author ; produced in 1913 the first of a series of novels published under the collective title " A la Recherche du Temps Perdu," all characterized by its discursive style and psycho-analytical methods ; 1382, 2404.

Prout, Samuel (1783–1852), Brit. painter of landscape and architecture, 1967.

Prout, William (1785–1850). Eng. physician and worker in physiological chemistry ; suggested that all the elements were compounds of hydrogen ; this view (" Prout's hypothesis ") stimulated inquiry and some recent discoveries have appeared to confirm it.

Provençal (pro-vahn-sahl'). Old Fr. dialect, spoken in Provence, 2798.

Provence (pro-vahns'). Old prov. in S.E. Fr. ; annexed by Fr. in 1486 ; literature and language, 2798; racial character, 1358.

Proverbs, Book of. Twentieth book of the Old Testament, containing a collection of the sayings of the sages of Israel ; a large proportion ascribed to Solomon.

Providence. Cap. and chief city of Rhode Island, U.S.A., at head of navigation of Providence r. ; pop. 253,500 ; famous for mfr. of jewelry and silverware, etc., 2770.

Prunes, 2695, 2630,

Prussia. Formerly the largest and most powerful state of Ger., abolished 1946 by the Allies, **2696,** 1449 ; *maps, 1446, 1448, 2696* ; cap. Berlin, 416 ; history, 2696 ; Teutonic knights, 1238 ; Frederick the Great, 1389, 2696 ; Silesia, 1389 ; Poland, 2696 ; in Seven Years' War, 2924 ; in Fr. Rev. and Napoleonic Wars, 1396, 1449, 2696, 2878 ; serfs freed, 2981 ; Rev. of 1848, 1449, 3378 ; Bismarck's work, 1449, 2696 ; war with Denmark, 992 ; Seven Weeks' War with Austria, 1574, 1449, 2878 ; N. German Confederation, 1449 ; Franco-Prussian War, 1384 ; German Empire proclaimed, 1449, 2696, 3317, 3378 ; dominant in German Empire, 1449. See also **Germany.**

KINGS OF PRUSSIA AND EMPERORS OF GERMANY

1701–13	Frederick I
1713–40	Frederick William I
1740–86	Frederick II, the Great
1786–97	Frederick William II
1797–1840	Frederick William III
1840–61	Frederick William IV
1861–88	William I (Emperor of Germany, 1871)
1888	Frederick III
1888–1918	William II
(1918	Republic proclaimed)

Prussia, East. See **East Prussia.**

Prussia, West. See **West Prussia.**

Prussian blue, 2478.

Prussic acid. *See* **Hydrocyanic acid.**

Pruth (prōōt), **Prut** or **Prutul.** Trib. of Danube ; 380 m. ; after 1945 frontier between Rumania and U.S.S.R. ; *map, 344.*

Przemysl (pshcm'-ĕsl), Poland. Tn. 50 m. w. of Lwow ; pop. 51,000 ; timber and grain trade ; besieged in 1914–18 War ; in 2nd World War, liberated by Russians July 1944.

Przevalsky's horse. Wild horse, 1646.

Psalms (sahmz). The 19th book of the Old Testament ; contains 150 psalms about the Exile, New Jerusalem, and the period of David ; attributed to David, 979 ; originally sung, 2261.

Psammetichus (sam-met'-i-kus). Name of 3 kings of the 26th dynasty of Egypt ; under the first (664–610 B.C.) Egypt recovered its prosperity after internal wars and the Assyrian invasion ; Psammetichus III reigned but 6 months, being dethroned 525 B.C. by the conquering Persians.

Pseudopo'dia (" false feet "), part of amoeba, 2695.

Psi, ψ, Ψ. Twenty-third letter of Gk. alphabet.

Psiloriti Mt., Crete. Formerly called Mt. Ida, 927.

Psittaci (sit'-a-kī). The parrot order of birds, 2525.

Psittacosis. Parrot disease, 2526.

Pskov. Soviet Rus. Old city near Estonian border ; pop. 59,900 ; free town and Hansa city in Middle Ages ; conquered by Moscow (1510) ; Germans occupy 1941–44.

Psyche (sī'-kē). In Gk. and Rom. myth., beautiful maiden, beloved of Cupid, *943.*

Psychical Research, Society for. Founded in 1882 for study of spiritualistic phenomena.

Psycho - analysis (sī'-kō - a-nal'i-sis). Name given to method of psychotherapy based on the theory that many nervous and mental disorders are due to repression of desires, 2697 ; and dreams, 2985 ; Freud and, 1396.

Psychology (sī-kol'-ō-ji). The science of the mind, **2697,** 2180 ; animal behaviour, 159 ; Aristotle, 232 ; brain, structure and function of, 545 ; Freud, 1396 ; Kant's study, 1846 ; memory, 2139 ; mind, 2180 ; nerves, 2316 ; psycho-analysis, 2697 ; sleep and dreams, 2985 ; how to study, 2139 ; suppressed memories, 2139.

Psychrom'eter. A type of hygrometer, 1677.

Ptah. Anc. Egypt, creative deity, patron of artisans, worshipped at Memphis ; represented as a shrouded figure holding a sceptre or as a clumsy dwarf, then corresponding to Hephaestus of Gk. myth.

Ptarmigan (tahr'-mi-gan). The " snow grouse," 1550, *2693* ; foot, *448.*

Pteran'odon. Prehistoric flying reptile, *2680.*

Pteria (tē'-ri-a). Anc. cap. of " White Syrians " (probably Hittites) of Cappadocia, Asia Minor ; according to Herodotus, captured and ruined by Croesus of Lydia (6th cent. B.C.) ; ruins at Boghazkeui.

Pter'idophytes. The fern-like plants as a botanical group, 2620 ; include ferns, 1266.

Pterodactyl (ter-ō-dak'-til). A prehistoric flying reptile, *2680* ; Mary Anning and, 164.

Pter'osaur. Extinct sub-class of flying reptiles, 2767.

Ptolemies (tol'-e-miz). Line of Gk. rulers of Egypt, 1121.

Ptolemy I, Soter and **Lagi** (367–283 B.C.). General of Alexander the Great and founder of the line of " Ptolemies," 1121 ; founds Alexandrian library, 109.

Ptolemy II, Philadelphus (308–246 B.C.). Gave chief care to encouragement of commerce and culture, and internal administration of Egypt ; built Pharos of Alexandria, 1943, 2924.

Ptolemy III, Euergetes (" benefactor ") (281–221 B.C.). Became ruler of Egypt on death of his father, Ptolemy II ; his armies invaded Syria and India, and his fleets conquered shores of the Hellespont and Thracian coast ; under him Ptolemaic Egypt attained greatest prosperity at home and widest dominion abroad.

Ptolemy XIII (Auletes) (95–51 B.C.). Father of Cleopatra and Ptolemy XIV, to whom he left the kingdom, 837.

Ptolemy XIV (61–47 B.C.). Brother of Cleopatra. Defeated by Julius Caesar on the Nile and drowned in retreating ; Cleopatra made queen.

Ptolemy XV (d. 43 B.C.). Last of the Ptolemies, youngest son of Ptolemy XIII ; put to death by his sister Cleopatra to make room for her son Caesarion.

Ptolemy or **Ptolemaeus, Claudius.** Astronomer, geographer, mathematician, **2697,** *276,* 2094, 2766, 1431 ; his map of Britain, *1431* ; formulates idea of gravity, 1512.

Ptomaines (tō'-mānz). Poisons found in food, 2638 ; poisoning, treatment for, 1295.

Ptyalin (tī'a-lin). Starch-digesting enzyme of saliva, 1016, 1220, 1470.

Publicani. Rom. tax-farmers, 2808.

Public health, 2132, 1677 ; the fly menace, 1329 ; waterworks, 3347, *3349, 3350.*

Public Safety, Committee of (Fr. Rev.), 1396, 2789.

Public school. Name applied to certain large boys' schools in Brit., 2883, *2885.*

Public trustee. An Eng. official appointed under the Official Trustee Act of 1906, whose duty it is to see that the funds of trusts put into his care are not lost in speculation or embezzled, as sometimes happens when left to a private trustee ; the Act does not apply to Scotland.

Publishing. The business of issuing books and other literary matter, music, maps, etc., for sale to the public ; at Leipzig, 1920. See **Books and Book-making ; Printing.**

Puccini (poo'-chē-nē), **Giacomo** (1858–1924). It. operatic composer ; chief works " La Bohème," 2438 ; " Madame Butterfly," 2439 ; " Turandot."

Puck. Mischievous sprite in English folklore who appears in " Midsummer Night's Dream," 2169.

Puddling. In iron mfr., 1754.

Pu'du. Smallest known deer, 985.

Puebla (pwä'-blah). State in S.-centre of Mexico ; 13,000 sq. m. ; pop. 1,294,600 ; cap. Puebla.

Puebla. Third city of Mexico, rly. and mfg. centre ; pop. 137,930 ; textiles, glass, straw hats ; onyx quarries near by ; headquarters of Carranza in 1914.

Pueblo (pweb'-lŏ), Colorado, U.S.A. 2nd city in state and one of most important industrial centres w. of Missouri r. ; on Arkansas r. ; pop. 52,160 ; iron and steel.

Pueblo Indians, 2698, 2757.

Puerto Barrios. Chief Atlantic port of Guatemala, 1551.

Puerto Cortez, Honduras. Port on N.W. coast on Gulf of Honduras ; pop. 7,000.

Puerto Principe, Cuba. Same as **Camaguey.**

Puerto Rico or **Porto Rico** (rē'-kō). Isl. of W. Indies, ceded to U.S.A. by Spain in 1898 ; 3,423 sq. m. ; pop. 1,869,000 ; **2698,** 3368.

Puff-adder. A viper, *2767,* 3325.

Puff-ball. A group of fungi, some edible ; 1407, *plate f. 1408.*

Puffin. A sea bird of the auk family, remarkable for its huge beak, which during the breeding season is striped blue, yellow, and red ; plumage is black above, white beneath, feet orange ; a diving bird, the puffin feeds on fish and lays its single whitish egg in an old rabbit burrow or similar hole ; 304.

" Puffing Billy." An early locomotive, built by W. Hedley, 1981, 2736.

Pug-dog, 1025, *plate f. 1024.*

Puget Sound. Large inlet of Pacific Ocean entering state of Wash., U.S.A., at N.W. corner ; begins at junction of Straits of Juan de Fuca and Georgia and extends south.

Pug-mill. Machine, 561.

Pulaski (poo-las'-ki), **Casimir** (1748–79). Polish count and Amer. Revolutionary hero ; fought for native freedom against Russia and became commander-in-chief of the Polish troops ; when he fell into disfavour he went to America, and took a distinctive part in the War of Independence.

Pulci (pool'-chē), **Luigi** (*c.* 1432–87). It. poet remembered for " Il Morgante Maggiore," an epic based on the adventures of Roland ; said to have been one of the authors read by Shakespeare.

Pu'lex irritans. Scientific name of common flea, 1314.

Pulitzer, Joseph (1847–1911). Amer. journalist and newspaper proprietor " New York World," pioneer in use of " human interest " stories. In his will provided for a series of annual prizes for authors, known as the Pulitzer Prizes.

Pulley. A mechanical device, **2698,** *2129* ; Archimedes, 211 ; in lifts, 1937 ; wheel, 3376.

Pullman, George Mortimer (1831–97). Amer. inventor ; originator, with Henry Wagner, of the Pullman sleeping-car.

Pul'monary artery, 1591, *1592.*

Pulmonary circulation, 1592.

Pulmonary valve, *1592.*

Pulmonary veins, *1592.*

Pulque (pool'-kā). Mex. beverage from agave, 76.

Pulse. Collective name for leguminous plants (peas, beans, etc.), or their edible seeds. *See* **Leguminosae.**

Pulse. Rhythmic beating of the arteries, **2701,** 1951.

Pultusk (pool'-toosk), Poland. Mfg. and trading tn. on r. Narey, 30 m. N. of Warsaw ; pop. (est.) 20,000 ; Charles XII of Sweden defeated Saxons and Poles (1703), and Fr. fought Rus. (1806).

Pu'ma. Animal of cat family, **2702,** *2382.*

Pum'ice (stone). A spongy form of lava, **2702,** *2795.*

Pump, 2702, *2703,* 1665 ; air pressure in, 90 ; artesian well, 252 ; hydraulic press, 1666 ; hydraulic ram, 1667 ; mercury vapour, 3301 ; motor-pump, *1287,* *1288* ; " perpetual " *1398* ; steam, in jet-propulsion, *1826* ; suction, 90 ; vacuum, 90, 3301 ; worked by windmills, 3387.

Pum'pernickel. Peculiar kind of coarse Ger. bread ; very doughy and of an acid taste, it is still largely eaten in some districts.

Pump'kin, 2704, 2109, belongs to same family as the vegetable marrow.

Punch and Judy. A puppet show, 2705, 2706.

Punch work. In embroidery, *1153,* 1154.

Punched cards, in automatic machines, 659 ; in Jacquard loom, 1791, 3361 ; in telegraphy transmission, 3166.

Punctuation, 2705, 1493.

Pu'nic Wars. Conflicts between Rome and Carthage (264–146 B.C.), 711, 2808 ; Hannibal, 1573, *1574.*

Punishment, of criminals, **2686.**

Punjab (pun'-jahb'). Region of N.W. India ; West Punjab (Pakistan), a. 62,261 sq. m. ; pop. 16,000,000 ; State of Punjab (repub. of India), a. 37,428 sq. m. ; pop. 12,500,000 ; **2705,** 1691, 1721, *map, 1702. See* **Himachal Union** ; **Patiala and E. Punjab States Union.**

Punta Arenas, Chile. *See* **Magallanes.**

Puntarenas or **Punta Arenas.** Port of Costa Rica ; cap. dept. of Punta Arenas ; pop. 8,868.

Pu'pa, 3rd stage in life of insect, 1728 ; honey-bee, 392 ; beetles, 398, *399* ; butterflies and moths, 630, *631* ; fly, 1329 ; mosquito, 2238, *2236.*

Pupil of the eye, 1252.

Puppets, 2706.

Puranas (poo-rah'-naz), Sanskrit religious writings, 1628, 1713.

Purbeck stone, 1030.

Purcell, Henry (1658–95). Eng. musical composer, called " father of English melody " ; **2706.**

Purchase Tax. Imposed in Oct. 1940 on sale of certain classes of goods in U.K., to restrict buying of all but necessities.

Pur'gatory. In Dante's " Divine Comedy," 971.

Puri (pu'rē), India. Juggernaut festival at, *1693.*

Puritans and Puritanism, 2707 ; Calvin's influence, 664 ; and Charles I, 755 ; Cromwell, 933 ; festivals prohibited, 819 ; hats, 1584 ; influence on Eng. literature, 1211, 2177 ; and James I, 1794 ; Milton champions, 2177 ; Plymouth settlement, 2122 ; theatres closed, 1041. *See also* Civil War (Eng.) ; **Commonwealth.**

Purlin, a roof timber, 2822.

" Purple and fine linen," 1953.

Purple of Cassius. A pigment, colloidal gold chloride and tin chloride, 1481.

Purpura. A shellfish, *1094.*

Purpure. In heraldry, 1614.

Purse-net, use, 2414, *2415.*

Purus. One of chief southern tributaries of the Amazon ; navigable for 800 m. of its 1,850 m. course ; *map, 551.*

Pusey, Edward Bouverie (1800–82). Eng. theologian, leader in Oxford Movement ; suspended from preaching for two years for a sermon delivered before Univ. 1843 ; Pusey House at Oxford named after him.

Pushkin (poosh'-kin), **Alexander** (1799–1837). Greatest Rus. poet ; his gentle humour and keen wit produced some of the best epigrams in any language ; originally imitative of Byron, his later work was entirely original in character and method (" Eugene Onegin "), 2855, *2856.*

" Puss in Boots." Source of story, 1333.

Puss moth. Moth whose caterpillar is common on willow and poplar trees ; it is green and purplish in colour and front view looks like a face ; in rear end are two long red filaments which can be protruded when caterpillar is alarmed. Moth, grey and white brindled, emerges from iron-hard cocoon of bark, made by larva, in mid-summer.

Putnam, Mrs. G. P. *See* **Earhart, Amelia.**

Putter. A golf club, used for holing the ball on the green, *1484.*

Putty. A compound of whiting and linseed oil used in glazing, 2478.

Putumayo. R. of S. Amer., rises in Andes in S.W. Colombia, flows S.E. about 800 m. to Amazon, 873.

Puvis de Chavannes (pü-vē de sha-van'), **Pierre** (1824–98). Fr. painter, restored mural painting to its proper function of decoration (Panthéon, Paris ; and in Lyons, Marseilles, Amiens, and Rouen Museums).

Pu-Yi, Henry (Hsuan-Tung) (b. 1906). Last emperor of China, succeeded 1908 ; dethroned 1911 ; temp. restoration 1917 ; Jap. puppet Emperor of Manchukuo 1934–45 ; in Russian custody in 1947 ; 814, 2087.

Puzta. Hungarian steppes, 1655.

Pydna (pid'-na). Gk. tn. in anc. Macedonia on Thermaic Gulf ; subdued by Macedonian kings ; victory of Romans under Aemilius Paulus over Perseus (164 B.C.).

Pye, Henry James (1745–1813). Eng. poet, succeeded Warton as Poet Laureate, perhaps as reward for supporting Pitt ; his works were very dull, 2634.

Pygmalion (pig-mā'-li-on). In Gk. legend, a sculptor who fell in love with an ivory image he had made ; Aphrodite heard his prayers and granted life to the image, so that Pygmalion might marry her ; story, told in Ovid's " Metamorphoses," used in Gilbert's comedy, " Pygmalion and Galatea," and G. B. Shaw's modern play.

Pygmies or **pigmies, 2707** ; African, *67* ; New Guinea, 2339 ; Philippines, 2568.

Py'gostyle. Tail-bone of birds, 437.

Py'lon. A gateway ; in Eng. architecture one having truncated pyramidal form.

Pylon. In electrical engineering, a steel tower, used to support heavy electric cables, 1547, *1548.*

Pylor'us, of stomach, *1016,* 3094.

Pym, John (1584–1643). Eng. statesman, parl. leader, conspicuous in struggle against Charles I ; and John Hampden, 1571.

Pyorrhoe'a. A disease of the sockets of teeth.

Pyramid, The Great, Gizeh, Eg. World wonder, 2707, *2708,* 1114, 2923.

Pyramids. Famous tombs in Eg., **2707** 654, 1095, 1114 ; architecture, 212.

Pyramids, Aztec, 327.

Pyramids, battle of the (1798) (or battle of Aboukir). Victory gained near Eg. pyramids by Fr. under Napoleon over Mamelukes, 2275.

Pyramus (pi'-ra-mus). Hero of the classic story of Pyramus and Thisbe, parodied in the interlude of " Midsummer Night's Dream," 2169.

Pyr'enees Mts. Between Fr. and Sp. ; highest peak 11,168 ft. ; **2709,** 1234, 3030, *map, 3030* ; Andorra, 2709 ; cave sculpture, *2082.*

Pyre'thrum or **Feverfew.** Several species of chrysanthemum, one wild in U.K. ; grown as crops in Kenya and Tanganyika for use in insecticides.

Py'ridine. Derivative of coal-tar, with pungent smell ; put into methylated spirits to make it unpalatable ; a solvent in rubber and paint industries ; remedy for asthma.

Pyrites (pī-rī'-tēz) **of iron,** " fool's gold," a sulphur compound, 1753, 2845 ; thallium from, 3193.

Pyrom'eter, 2709, 2577, 3200.

Pyrosulphuric acid, in smoke screens, 2987.

Pyrotechnics (pī-rō-tek'-niks). Making or using fireworks, 1289.

Pyrox'ylin. A nitro-cellulose, **2709,** basis of celluloid, 739.

Pyr'rha. In Gk. myth., wife of Deucalion, 2807.

" Pyrrhic (pir'-ik) **victory,"** 2710.

Pyrrhus (pir'-us). King of Epirus (318–272 B.C.), **2709.**

Pytchley (pīch-li). Vil. of Northants, famous for hunt, 2385.

Pythagoras (pī-thag'-ō-ras) (*c.* 582–500 B.C.). Gk. philosopher and mathematician, **2710,** 1434.

Pythagorean theorem, in geometry, 1434, 2710.

Pyth'eas. Massilian navigator of 4th cent. B.C. ; 1431.

Pyth'ia. Priestess of Delphi, 988.

Pyth'ian games, 187, 989.

Pyth'ias, Damon and, 963.

Py'thon. In Gk. myth., slain by Apollo, 186.

Python. A snake, **2710** ; egg, *1094.*

Pyx, Trial of the, 2189.

THE Egyptian picture sign Δ from which our Q is descended represents either an angle or a knee which, of course, forms an angle when bent. In the Egyptian script this sign takes a form which begins to look a little like our Q. The Phoenicians formed it like this ꝙ and named it *Qoph*. Some scholars say this means " ape " and that the character represents an ape with its tail hanging down. Another theory is that it represents an aperture of some kind, the

eye of a needle, perhaps. Others think it is the picture of an ear, and still others that of a knot. The Phoenicians and Hebrews gave it a sound similar to that of *Kaph* (the Phoenician K), but sounded farther back in the throat. We do not find the letter Q in classic or modern Greek, for it was dropped (except as a numeral) at a very early date. The Romans kept it and gave it its present form, using it as we do, with *u*, the combination *qu* having the sound of *kw*.

Qisaraya. *See* **Caesarea Palestina.**
" Q-ships." Decoys for submarines in 1st World War.
Quad′rant. In geometry, 1434.
Quadrant. Instrument at one time used for fixing the position of a vessel at sea by taking angles ; now superseded by the sextant, 2290. Also a type of electrometer invented by Lord Kelvin for measuring small quantities of electricity.
Quadriga. Chariot with four horses abreast ; sculpture by Adrian Jones on Wellington Arch, Green Park, London.
Quadruplets. Four children born at the same birth.
Quad′ruplex telegraphy, 3167.
Quaes′tors. Officials of anc. Rome, 2805.
Quag′ga. A zebra-like animal, 3442.
Quai d'Orsay (kā-dor-sā′). The Fr. Foreign Office, so named from the quay on the s. bank of the Seine in Paris where its buildings stand.
Quail. A fowl-like game bird, 2711.
Quakers. *See* **Friends.**
Quaking bog, 2239.
Quaking grass, *Briza media* or **Tottergrass.** A conspicuous grass of the early summer found mainly in the s. and midlands ; has fine silky stems that quiver in the slightest breeze ; *frontis.*, *Vol. 4.*
Qualitative analysis, in chemistry. The analysis of an unknown substance to find the radicles present, 773.
Quantitative analysis, in chemistry. The analysis of a mixture to find the percentage of each constituent present, 773.
Quantity theory, of money, 1081.
Quan′tock Hills. Range in Somersetshire, 8. m. long ; highest point, 1,262 ft. ; 3000.
Quantum theory, 2711, 1138, 1943, 2593.
Quar′antine (from old Fr. word meaning 40 days). Period during which ships suspected of carrying infectious or contagious disease or coming from an infected port are isolated from the shore ; any similar isolation.
Quarles, Francis (1592–1644). Eng. poet who wrote much religious verse, including the well-known " Emblems."
Quar′rying, 2712. *See* **Granite** ; **Limestone** ; **Marble** ; **Slate.**
Quart. A unit of measure, of capacity (2 pints). *See in Index* **Weights and Measures.**
Quarter. A measure of weight, the fourth part of a hundredweight. *See* **Weights and Measures.**
Quarter days. Days appointed for payment of house and land rent. In England and Ireland : Lady day, March 25 ; midsummer day, June 24 ; Michaelmas day, Sept. 29 ; Christmas day, Dec. 25. In Scotland : Feb. 2, May 15, Aug. 1, and Nov. 11.
Quartering. In heraldry, 1614.
Quar′termaster (Q.M.). In Brit. army, an officer with the honorary rank of lieut. or capt. ; his chief duties concern the clothing and feeding of his regiment or battalion.
Quartermaster-general (Q.M.G.). Brit. general officer in charge of supply departments of the army ; his assistants are A.Q.M.G.

Quartern. Old English measure of capacity (¼ pint) ; a 4-lb. loaf is termed a quartern loaf. *See in Index* **Weights and Measures.**
Quarterstaff. Staff much used as weapon in the olden days in England, six to eight feet long, shod with iron at both ends and swung with the two hands from its middle.
Quartet′. In music, a score written for four voices or instruments ; also applied to a party of singers or players of that number.
Quar′to. A book size, 512.
Quartz. Silica or silicon dioxide ; a hard mineral, 2713, 2181 ; for porcelain, 2670 ; flint a variety, 1314 ; gold found in, 1479 ; made into fire-resisting glass, 1474 ; in piezo-electricity, 2605 ; relative hardness, 2181 ; sand a form, 2870.
Quartz′ite. A metamorphic rock, 2713, 2795.
Quasimodo. A dwarf, one of chief characters in Victor Hugo's " Notre Dame."
Quassia (kwosh′-a). Several small tropical trees and shrubs of the *Simarubaceae* family. The white wood of the bitter ash or Jamaica quassia (*Picraena excelsa*) of South America is used in medicine and as a substitute for hops in beer making.
Quater′nary period. In geological time, 1432.
Quat′rain. In poetry, 2636.
Quatre-Bras (katr-brah′). Vil. 19 m. s.e. of Brussels ; indecisive battle between Brit. and Germans under Wellington and French under Ney, on June 16, 1815, 2 days before battle of Waterloo.
Quebec (kwe-bek′). Oldest and largest of provinces of Canada, 2714 ; a. 594,860 sq. m. ; pop. 3,331,000 ; education, 2224 ; history, 2715 ; legislature, 683, 684 ; Montreal, 2223. *See also* **Canadian History.**
Quebec, City of. Cap. of prov. of Quebec on St. Lawrence r. ; pop. 150,000 ; 2714, 2715, 2862 ; Champlain founds, 751, 2381 ; Montcalm at, 2218 ; captured 1759 by Brit. under Wolfe, 3277, 3401 ; memorial to Wolfe, 2716 ; Conferences of 1943–44, 2824.
Quebec Act. Passed by British Parlt. 1774, extending province of Quebec to Ohio and Mississippi rivers, establishing French civil law, and withholding representative institutions ; resentment among English colonists helped bring on Revolutionary War.
Quebracho (kā-brah′-chō). S. Amer. tree of the sumach family with exceedingly hard, heavy wood ; yields tannin, 1912.
Queen. Title given to a woman sovereign of a state ; queen regnant, queen in her own right ; queen consort, wife of a king ; queen dowager, widow of a king ; queen mother, mother of a king.
Queen, among social insects ; ant, 165 ; bee, 390 ; termite, 1733, 3189 ; wasp, 3345.
Queen Anne, Age of. In Eng. literature, 1213 ; architecture in Queen Anne's Gate, London, 163.
" Queen Anne is Dead." Origin of saying, 164.

Queen Bee (aeroplane). For naval target practice, 2301.
Queen Charlotte Islands. Part of British Columbia, 100 m. off coast and 135 m. above Vancouver Isl. ; 5,100 sq. m. ; coal and other minerals ; pop. about 2,000, mostly Indians.
Queen Charlotte Islands, Melanesia. *See* **Santa Cruz.**
Queen Elizabeth, R.M.S. Cunard White-Star liner ; sister ship to Queen Mary ; launched in 1938 ; troopship in 2nd World War ; maiden voyage as liner in 1946 ; gross tonnage 84,000 ; 2949 ; building, 2948.
Queen Mary. Cunard White-Star liner of 81,235 tons, launched in 1934 ; 2950, 2960 ; entering Southampton graving dock, 1023 ; model tested, 2197 ; at New York, *plates f. 2352–53* ; speed, 2949.
Queen of Sheba, 2999.
Queens, Borough of, New York City, 2352.
Queensberry rules, of boxing, 535.
Queensberry, John Sholto Douglas, 8th Marquess of (1844–1900). English statesman and sportsman ; represented Scotland in Parliament, 1872–1880 ; best known as a patron of boxing ; took part in formulating " Queensberry Rules."
Queens′ College, Cambridge. Founded, 666.
Queen's College, Oxford. Founded, 2464.
Queen's County. Now **Leix.**
Queen's Hall, Langham Place, London. Opened in 1893, and long regarded as the chief concert-hall in London ; could comfortably accommodate 3,000 people ; famous for its broadcast symphony and promenade concerts, 2266 ; destroyed by fire bombs, May 10, 1941.
Queen's Institute for Nurses, 2407.
Queensland. A state in n.e. of Australia ; 670,000 sq. m. ; pop. 1,106,300 ; 2716, 2717 ; *map, plate f. 308* ; dance of natives, *plate f. 2057* ; sunflower crop, 3121 ; Brisbane the cap., 571.
Queenstown. *See* **Cobh.**
Queen's University, Belfast. Northern Ireland. Formerly Queen's College (established in 1849, and one of the three colleges in the Royal Univ. of Ireland), it was founded in 1909 when the Royal Univ. was dissolved ; arts, science, medicine, law, commerce.
Queensway. Mersey Tunnel, 1968.
Queen Victoria Memorial, London. In front of Buckingham Palace ; surrounded by a colonnade is a lofty column on top of which is a winged figure of victory, with a statue of Queen Victoria below, and several symbolical figures ; 599.
Queen wasp, 3345.
" Quentin Durward." Hero and title of a historical novel by Sir Walter Scott ; scene laid in France during reign of King Louis XI.
Quercus (kwêr′-kus). The oak genus of trees, 2409.
Querétaro (kā-rā′-ta-rō), Mexico. State in centre ; 4,432 sq. m. ; pop. 244,700 ; cap. Querétaro.
Querétaro, Mexico. Cap. of state of Querétaro, 110 m. n.w. of Mexico City ; pop. 33,600 ; large cotton mills.

Quern. A primitive grain mill, worked by hand, *1320*.

Quest. Shackleton's last ship, 2931.

Question mark, or interrogation point, 2705.

Quetelet (ket-lā), **Lambert Adolphe Jacques** (1796–1874). Belgian astronomer, mathematician, and statistician ; director Royal Observatory ; published numerous works on statistical researches, astronomy, meteorology, etc.

Quet'ta. An important fortified frontier tn., cap. of Baluchistan (Pakistan) at end of Bolan Pass ; terminus of rly. from India ; former Brit. garrison ; pop. 900,000 ; 352 ; earthquake destruction (1935), *1070*.

Quetzal (ket-sahl'). A beautiful bright green crested bird, a species of Trogon ; tail feathers 2 or 3 ft. long ; plumage used as decorations for priests and royalty among Aztecs and Mayas ; also used as national emblem of Guatemala.

Quetzalcoatl (ket-sal-kō-at'l). A hero-god of the Aztecs ; represented as author of their civilization ; Aztec remains, *327*.

Queues (kūz) or **pigtails,** in China, *809*.

Queuille (kê-yē), **Henri** (b. 1884). Fr. statesman ; held numerous ministerial offices ; in 1940 de Gaulle's dep. in London ; prem. and finance min. Sept. 1948 to Oct. 1949.

Quevedo y Villegas (kā-vā'-dō ē vēl-yā'-gahs), **Francisco Gomez de** (1580–1645). Spanish man-of-letters, took part in political and diplomatic affairs until imprisoned by Philip IV ; wrote poetry, satire and a picaresque novel (" Historia de la vida del Buscón ").

Quiberon (kē-be-ron'). Fr. Historic tn. on Bay of Quiberon 22 m. S.E. of Lorient ; defeat of French Royalists by Republicans (1795).

Quiberon Bay. Small arm of Bay of Biscay E. of Quiberon ; scene of Brit. naval victory under Admiral Hawke over French under Conflans Nov. 20, 1759, *2925*.

Quichuas (kē-chwahz). A family of S. Amer. native tribes in Peru, Ecuador and Bolivia ; formed greater part of anc. Inca Empire ; *494. See* **Incas.**

Quick-freezing. Method of preserving fruit and vegetables, 1393.

Quicklime. Calcium oxide produced by the consuming of limestone and coal in a kiln, 655, 1949 ; from oyster shells, 2466.

Quickly, Mistress. Character in three of Shakespeare's plays—in both parts of " King Henry IV " and in " King Henry V," hostess of a tavern ; in " The Merry Wives of Windsor," servant to Dr. Caius.

Quicksands, 2870.

Quicksilver. *See* **Mercury.**

Quickswood, Hugh R. H. G. Cecil, 1st Baron (b. 1869). Brit. politician ; 5th s. of 3rd Marquess of Salisbury ; provost of Eton, 1936–44 ; protagonist of Church of England ; wrote " Conservatism," " Nationalism and Catholicism."

Quill. Part of feather, 1265.

Quiller-Couch (kōōch), **Sir Arthur Thomas** (1863–1944). Eng. writer known under pseudonym of " Q " ; professor of Eng. literature at Cambridge ; edited " Oxford Book of English Verse " ; author of many volumes of verse, criticism, and romance (notably " On the Art of Writing," " On the Art of Reading ").

Quill pens, 2539.

Quilter, Roger (b. 1877), Eng. composer. Works include music to the fairy play " Where the Rainbow Ends " ; " A Children's Overture ' ; " Seven Elizabethan Lyrics " and " Three Shakespeare Songs."

Quilting. A form of decorative needlework in which the stitches are worked to make patterns standing in some relief. It is done with an ordinary sewing needle in running-stitch or back stitch over a layer of wadding interposed between layers of thin material. When used to decorate down quilts, used for bed coverings, the stitching is usually done by machinery.

Quince and medlar. Fruit trees of the apple family, *2718* ; *plate f. 1400.*

Quincentenary (Latin *quinque*, five, and *centum*, hundred), relating to a period of 500 years, as an anniversary.

Quinet (kē'-nā), **Edgar** (1803–75). French author, professor of literature at the Collège de France ; banished from France for agitation against Napoleon III, after whose fall he returned to Paris ; wrote historical and philosophical works as well as poetry (" Ahasuerus," a prose poem).

Quinine (kwi-nēn'). A drug from cinchona bark, *2718*, 2132 ; from Ceylon, 748 ; Ecuador, 1083 ; Java, 1813 ; Peru, 2559 ; sulphate, 2573 ; substitutes, 2719.

Quin'oline. Colourless liquid distilled from coal-tar, 857.

Quintain. Old Eng. sport, **2719.**

Quintal. A metric unit of weight, 100 kilogrammes, or 1·968 cwt., 2155.

Quintero (kĕn-tā'-rō), **Serafin Alvarez** (1871–1938), and brother **Joaquin** (1873–1944). Sp. dramatists ; collaborators in brilliant comedies ; 3051.

Quintet, in music, composition for five voices or instruments.

Quintil'ian (Marcus Fabius Quintilianus). (A.D. *c.* 35–97). Famous Roman teacher of oratory ; wrote " Institutio Oratoria," a complete treatment of the art of rhetoric, 1897.

Quintuplets. Five children born at the same birth ; notably the Dionne " quins " born at Callender, Ontario (Canada), in 1934.

Quippus (kē'-pōōs). Anc. Peruvian device for keeping records, 1690.

Quir'inal (Lat. *Collis Quirinalis*). One of the seven hills of Rome ; situated in the N.E. quarter of the city, 2799.

Quirinal palace, Rome, 2800.

Quirinus, the deified Romulus, 2821.

Quirites (kwi-rē'-tēz). Name applied to citizens of ancient Rome in their civil or domestic capacity, Romani being reserved for military or foreign affairs.

Quisling (kwiz'-ling), **Vidkun A.** (1887–1945). Norwegian traitor who collaborated with the Germans at and after their invasion of Norway, 2720. The name " quisling " was applied to any similar traitor during the 2nd World War.

Quito (ke-to). Capital of the Republic of Ecuador in N., about 15 m. S. of the Equator ; university ; northern cap. of Incas until taken by Spaniards in 1534 ; 1081, *1083* ; climate, 841 ; railway, 1081.

Quixote, Don. *See* **Don Quixote.**

Quoin (koin). In architecture, an external angle of a wall ; especially **an** ashlar or brick corner projecting beyond the general faces of the walls which meet at the angle.

Quoits (koitz). Game in which rings have to be thrown over a pin, **2720.**

Quorn. Famous hunt in Leicestershire.

Quor'um. The number of members of an organized body whose presence is necessary for the legal transaction of business.

Quotation marks (quotes, or inverted commas), use of, 2705.

Quotient (kwō'-shent), in arithmetic, 1021.

" Quo Vadis ? " (kwō-vah'-dis) (Lat. " Whither Goest Thou ? "), novel by Polish writer, Sienkiewicz, originally published in 1895.

OUR letter R is generally traced back to the old Egyptian hieroglyph ◠ representing a mouth. Written in a running hand (the so-called hieratic form) it became ◿. The Phoenicians, writing on stone, gave it a more angular form **4** and called it *Resh*, meaning " head," from its fancied resemblance to the head supported by the neck. The Greeks turned it round and then later rounded it so that it looked just like our P. We should have had two

letters with exactly the same form had they not added a little tail, which made the letter R as we have it today. The Romans kept this form, but the Greeks, who had developed the form ⊓ for P, dropped the tail again, so their R (*Rho*) is still written **P**. No other consonant shows so many variations in pronunciation. In France and Germany it is rolled. In England and North America it varies according to locality. The close relationship of *l* and *r* is told in the story of L.

R, Brit. rigid airship. R.34 first airship to fly across the Atlantic (1919), 94, *95* ; R.38 was wrecked during its third flight in 1921, 94 ; R.100 flew from England to Canada and back (1930) but was broken up in 1931, 94 ; R.101 wrecked in Fr. with great loss of life in flight from Eng. to India (1930), 94, *95*.

Ra (rah) or **Re,** Eg. sun-god. *See* **Ammon.**

Raab (rahb) or **Györ** (gyĕr), Hungary. Tn. at confluence of Raab and Little Danube rs. ; pop. 50,900 ; machinery, cutlery, oil ; farm trade.

Raabe (rah'be), **Wilhelm** (1831–1910).

Ger. novelist ; eccentric character ("Christoph Pechlin"; "Horacker").

Rabaul. Cap. of Mandated New Guinea until 1938 ; Japanese base 1942–45. So badly damaged during 2nd World War that it was not rebuilt.

Rabbits, 2721 ; in Australia, 310.

Rabelais (ra-be-lā), **François** (*c.* 1490–1553), celebrated Fr. satirist and humorist ; his sole book, a medley of wit, wisdom, and the coarsest buffoonery, recounts the amazing exploits of two giants—Gargantua and Pantagruel ; **2722**, 1380.

Rabies, Pasteur and, 2528. *See* **Hydrophobia.**

Raccoon (ra-kōōn'), **2722,** *2382* ; " Blackface Meets His Neighbours," 3481 ; fur, 1412.

Raceme (ra-sēm'). A type of inflorescence, 1321.

Racemic acid, 3155.

Races of Mankind, 2723, 2656 ; African races, 70 ; Aryans, 261, 2570 ; Caucasian, origin of name, 732 ; Celts, 740 ; classification, 2723 ; by hair, 1565 ; by language, 2570 ; distribution in Asia, 263, 265, *plate f. 265* ; in Europe, 1237 ; Eskimos, 1222 ; Finns,

1277 ; Hamitic, 70, 2312 ; of India, 1701 ; Red Indians (N. Amer.), 2753 ; Jews, 1829 ; Magyars, 1656 ; Malays, 2069 ; Mongols, 2205 ; Negro, 2312 ; prehistoric, 2078 ; how related to one another, 2724 ; Semitic, 70, 2573 ; South Sea isl. types, 2339, 2469 ; Slavs, 2982 ; Tartars, 3155 ; Turks, 3262. *See also* races by name.

Ra'chel. Favourite wife of Jacob, for whom he served 14 years ; mother of Joseph and Benjamin.

Rachel. Stage name of Elizabeth Rachel Félix (1821–58), Fr. tragic actress ; unequalled in such roles as Racine's "Phèdre."

Rachmaninov (rakh-mah'-ni-nof),**Sergei** (1873–1943). Rus. composer and pianist, after Paderewski the greatest of contemporary pianists ; composed the popular " Prelude in C♯ Minor," and numerous more important works.

Racine (ra-sēn), **Jean Baptiste** (1639–1699). Fr. dramatist, **2725**, 1040, 1380.

Racine, Wisconsin, U.S.A., industrial city and port on L. Michigan 50 m. N. of Chicago ; pop. 67,200 ; mfrs. carriages, motor-wagons, rly-wagons, boots and shoes.

Racing ; athletics, 287 ; boats and yachts, *481, 483, 485* ; cycle, 947 ; horse, 994, 1648 ; motor-boat, *485* ; motor-cycle, *948* ; running, 2843 ; skating, 2976 ; ski-ing, 2978 ; swimming, 3135. *See also* **Records.**

Rack. Instrument of torture on which the victim was stretched.

Racket, tennis, *1906.*

Rackets. A court game, 3071. *See also* Squash Rackets.

Racket-tailed humming-bird, 1652.

Rackham, Arthur (1867–1939). Eng. artist ; noted for his delicate and fantastic illustrations to " Peter Pan," " A Midsummer Night's Dream," many books of fairy-tales, etc.

Raclawice (raht-slah-vět'-se), battle of. Fought at vil. of Raclawice N. of Cracow 1794 ; Rus. defeated by Poles under Kosciusko, 1874.

Racquet. *See* **Racket.**

Radar (rā'-dahr). Direction finding and ranging of objects by ultra-short-wave radio, **2726** ; in anti-aircraft guns, *260* ; " Decca " charts, *2292* ; in fisheries, 1300 ; in meteorology, 2150, 3360 ; naval operations, 2295 ; navigation by air, 2293 and sea, 2292 ; and television, 3183 ; thermionic valve in, 3198 ; similar direction-finding in bats, 370 ; wavelength, 2729.

Radcliffe Camera, Oxford, *2464.*

Radcliffe Observatory ; at Oxford 1772–1929 ; moved to Pretoria, S. Africa, in 1935.

Radiant heat, 1595, 2729.

Radiation, 2728, 1595 ; and ether, 1226 ; of heat, 1595, 1597, *1598*, 1722 ; from human body, 1600 ; of light, 1942 ; radar, 2726 ; beyond solar spectrum, *plates f. 3506, 3507* ; of uranium, 3297 ; wireless, 3392.

Radiator : in house heating, *1599,* 1600 ; in refrigerator, *1392.*

Radical or **Radicle.** In chem., an element (simple radical) or group of elements (compound radical) forming the base of a compound and remaining unaltered during ordinary chem. changes, 20, 767 ; electrically charged, 1738.

Radio. *See* **Wireless.**

Radio-active elements, 2731.

Radio-activity. *See* **Radium and radio-activity.**

Radio-frequency, 3394.

Radiogram, combined gramophone and wireless receiver, *1497.*

Radiograph, X-ray photograph, 3431.

Radiolaria. Order of unicellular animals with silica spines, *433, plate f. 1473.*

Radio Link, in long-distance telephony, 3174, 3396.

Radiolocation. *See* **Radar.**

Radio-sonde, wireless transmitter dispatched to upper air and broadcasting weather information, 2150, 3102, 3360.

" Radio Times," journal of the B.B.C., 3398.

Radish. Plant of cabbage family ; root is eaten raw as salad or relish, *639.*

Rad'issen Pierre Esprit, Sieur de (17th cent.). Fr. Canadian explorer and fur trader, 681.

Raditch or **Radic', Stephan** (1871–1928). Yugoslav statesman ; leader of Croatian Peasant party ; worked for Croatian autonomy ; several times imprisoned ; died from effects of a bullet wound inflicted by a government deputy.

Radium (Ra). A radio-active metallic element of the magnesium group ; atomic weight, 226·05 ; melts at 1292° F., **2731** ; detection of, 1739 ; discovery, 944 ; generates helium, 1607 ; properties, 778.

Radium and radio-activity, 2731 ; and Becquerel, 2731 ; fluorescence, 2574 ; isotopes, 1760 ; and Marie Curie, 944, 2594 ; uranium parent of all radio-active elements, 3297.

Ra'dius. In geometry, 1435.

Radnor Forest, Wales. Mountainous tract in Radnorshire ; highest point, 2,163 ft., 2733.

Radnorshire, Wales. Inland co. in s., a. 471 sq. m. ; pop. 21,300, 2733.

Radon (Rn), **Niton** (Nt), or **Emanation** (Em). A radioactive gaseous element of the inert gas group ; produced by radium, 2732 ; atomic weight, 222·0 ; used extensively in medical work ; properties, 778.

Ra'dula. Tongue-like rasping structure in snails ; means " little file," 2989.

Raeburn, Sir Henry (1756–1823). Scot. portrait painter ; produced forcible, telling likenesses, frank, sincere, 1180.

Raeder, Grand Admiral Erich (b. 1876), C.-in-C. German Navy 1935–1944 ; tried as war criminal, Nuremberg, 1945–46. Imprisoned for life.

Raemakers, Louis (b. 1869). A Dutch cartoonist who won world reputation by his powerful, often bitter, anti-Ger. cartoons during 1914–1918 War ; 1967.

Raff, Joseph Joachim (1822–82). Ger. composer ; friend of Liszt ; produced great number of works, including compositions for piano, violin (" Cavatina "), orchestra ; operas ; chamber music.

Raffles, Sir (T.) Stamford (1781–1826). Brit. administrator ; from a clerk in E. India Co., he became Lieut.-Gov. of Java 1811 ; founded settlement of Singapore 1819 ; naturalist and collector, founding Zoological Soc. in 1826.

Raft spider, 3064.

Rafters of roof, 2821.

Ragtime, and Jazz, 1815.

Ragusa. *See* Dubrovnik.

Ragwort, *Senecio jacobaea.* One of the commonest British weeds, known for its upright growth and masses of yellow flower-heads ; blooms in late summer often covering large areas. Several species of ragwort sprang up profusely on bombed sites of London. Members of family *Compositae.*

Raikes, Robert (1735–1811). Eng. philanthropist ; founds first Sunday school, 2883.

Rail. A water bird, **2733**, *2734.*

Railways, 2734 ; in Africa, 72, 117, *map, 3366* ; air-brake, 549 ; Alpine, *133* ; " atmospheric," 2632, *2633* ; Australian, 308, 3028 ; Brit. groups, 3726 ; buffet car, *2627* ; in Canada, 678, *1994*, 2738, 3102 ; electrification, 1987, *1994*, 2738, 2740, 2751, 2738 ; gauges, 2738 ; in India, 1708 ; Liverpool-Manchester, *1723* ; locomotives, 1981 ; models, 2194, *2197* ; nationalized, 2736, 3239 ; northernmost, 2393 ; permanent way, 2738 ; P.O. trains, 2661, *2662, 2663* ; P.O. tube, *2662* ; example of relativity, 2760, *2761* ; signals, *2738, 2739* ; speeds, 2737 ; traffic control, 2784 ; Trans-Andean, 153, 804 ; Trans-Siberian, 2736, 2967 ; Trevithick's, 3247 ; Turkish, 2736, 3262 ; underground railways, 2016, 2353, 2518, 3273 ; tunnels, *3257* ; in U.S.A., *1995*, 2736, 2738, 3289.

Rainbow, 2741, *plates f. 2740, 2741.*

Rainbow trout, 3251.

Rainfall, 2741, 2149 ; affected by mts., 152, 840, 1626 ; affects land forms, 2597 ; Africa, *plate f. 69* ; Asia, *plate f. 265* ; Australia, *plate f. 309*, 2344 ; clouds, 851 ; desert regions, 996 ; and ecology, *plate f. 1080* ; floods, 1316 ; gauge, 2742 ; Indian monsoons, 1701 ; N. Amer., 2384 ; *plate f. 2385* ; " rain-makers," *plate f. 2057* ; S. Amer., *plate f. 3025* ; thunder showers, 3101 ; world's wettest town, *841.*

Rain gauge, 2742.

Rainier or **Tacoma, Mt.** Glacier-capped volcano in Cascade Range, Wash., U.S.A., 50 m. s.e. of Tacoma ; 14,400 ft. ; National Park, *3287,* 3345.

Raisins, 3742.

Raisuli. Moroccan bandit, 2230.

Rajagopalachari, Chakravarti (b. 1879). Ind. statesman ; a Brahmin, he was gen. sec. of Nat. Congress 1921–33 ; prime min. of Madras 1937–39 ; gov.-gen. of India after Ld. Mountbatten until Ind. repub. estab. 1949 ; 2248.

Rajasthan. Union of Rajput states in the rep. of India, 2743. In May 1949 the 4 states of the Matsya Union (Alwar, Bharatpur, Dholpur, Karauli) joined Rajasthan Union, making it the largest single unit of rep. of India.

Raj Pramukh. Title of chief executive of constituent union of Repub. of Ind. ; equal to Provincial Gov. ; elected or apptd. for life.

Rajput (rahj-poot'). A people of India, 1701, 1703, 2743 ; art of, 1708.

Rajputana (rahj-poo-tah'-na). Large inland region in N.W. India, including 21 native states ; 132,500 sq. m. ; pop. over 13,000,000 ; **2743**, 1691 ; architecture, *1700.*

Raleigh, Sir Walter (*c.* 1552–1618). Eng. soldier, sailor, and historian, **2743** ; establishes first Eng. colonies in N. Amer., 704 ; describes Orinoco r., 2452 ; introduces tobacco into England, 3219 ; and the potato 2664 ; in Tower of London, 3232 ; voyages, 142.

Raleigh, Sir Walter (1861–1922). Eng. man of letters ; professor of Eng. literature at universities of Glasgow, Liverpool and Oxford (" The History of the War in the Air," Vol. 1).

Raleigh, North Carolina, U.S.A. Cap. of state ; pop. 46,800 ; important cotton and tobacco market.

Ram. A male sheep, 2940 ; an ancient naval weapon, 2296.

Ram (Aries). A sign of the zodiac, 3444.

Ram, hydraulic, 1666 ; 2703, *2704.*

Rama (rah'-ma). In Hindu myth., one of incarnations of the god Vishnu, hero of great Hindu epic Ramayana.

Ramadan (ram-a-dan'). Ninth month of Mahomedan year, kept as strict fast among Mahomedans, 2067.

Ramayana (rah-mah'-ya-na). Hindu epic, describing the adventures of Rama, an incarnation of Vishnu.

Rambaud (rahm-bō), **Alfred Nicolas** (1842–1905). Fr. historian (" History of Russia " ; " History of French Civilization ").

Rambler rose, 2828.

Rambouillet (rahm-bwē-yā), **Catherine de Vivonne, Marquise de** (1588–1665). Founder of first great Fr. literary salon (satirized by Molière in " Les Précieuses Ridicules ").

Ramée, Louise de la. *See* Ouida.

Ram'eses II, the Great. King of Egypt (13th cent. B.C.), famous as a builder, some of his temples still remain ; warred with Hittites, 1121 ; colossi at temple of Abu Simnel, *1107.*

Rameses III. King of Egypt (12th cent. B.C.) ; founded 20th dynasty ; famed for his military exploits ; remarkable tomb at Thebes.

Ramie or **China grass.** Fibre of Asiatic plant belonging to nettle family, 1424, 2497.

Ramillies (rah-mē-yē'). Vil. in cent. Belgium 28 m. s.e. of Brussels where Marlborough defeated French (1706) in Seven Years' War, 2106 ; severe fighting in 1st World War.

Ram Lilla. Indian play, *1697*.

Ramon, Gaston (b. 1886). Fr. bacteriologist; his vaccination serum giving immunity against diphtheria and tetanus in one injection widely used.

Ramoth-gilead. In Biblical times, city in Palestine E. of R. Jordan.

Ram'pant. In heraldry, 1615.

Ramsay, Allan (1686–1758). Scot. pastoral poet and publisher; best remembered for his "Gentle Shepherd," *2894*; his son Allan (1713–84) was a successful portrait painter whom George III patronized; *1179*.

Ramsay, Sir Bertram H. (1883–1945). Brit. sailor; served in 1st World War, retiring 1938; rejoined 1939, and withdrew Brit. army from Dunkirk 1940; planned amphibious ops. for Allied landings in N. Africa, Sicily, and It.; had naval command at D-day 1944, *2377*; killed in flying accident in Fr., Jan. 1945.

Ramsay, Lady Patricia (b. 1886). Formerly Princess Patricia of Connaught; patroness of famous Princess Pat's regiment of Canada; resigned royal title upon marriage to Rear-Adm. Sir Alexander Ramsay.

Ramsay, Sir William (1852–1916). Brit. chemist; discovered helium, neon, krypton, and xenon, **2744**; Nobel prize in 1904, *2375*; discovery of argon, 88; of neon, 2315.

Rams'gate. Seaside resort of Kent; pop. (est.) 35,000; coasting, fishing trade; St. Lawrence College; 1852.

Rand or **Witwatersrand.** Gold-mining, Johannesburg, 1479, 3019.

Randall's Island, N.Y., U.S.A., 2351.

Randers, Denmark. Tn. in N. Jutland; pop. 30,254; glass and other mfrs.; exports, grain, dairy products, wool, 992.

Range-finder. Instrument used in the army, navy, and air service for finding the distance of any object; also called a telemeter; the Barr and Stroud instrument is generally in use in the Brit. services, partly superseded by radar, 2552; also small instrument adapted for use with cameras to ensure correct focusing.

Rangers, in Girl Guides, *1466*.

Rangoon (ran-gōōn)'. Chief port and mfg. centre of Burma on Irrawaddy; pop. 400,400; exports rice, teak; in Jap. occupn. 1942–45, *3424*; **2744,** 625.

Ranjitsinhji (ran-jit-sin'-ji), **Kumar Shri** ("**Ranji**") (1872–1933). Indian prince and cricketer; Cambridge blue, played for Sussex and England; one of greatest batsmen ever known; Duleepsinhji (b. 1905) is his nephew.

Rank, J. Arthur (b. 1888). Brit. financier and film magnate; head of organization owning Gaumont-British, Ealing Studios, Odeon Theatres, Gainsborough, Two Cities, and Eagle-Lion film cos.

Ranke (ran'-ke), **Leopold von** (1795–1886). Ger. historian, founder of modern critical methods of historical study; 1457.

Ransome, Arthur. Modern English writer for children; works include "A History of Story-Telling"; "Old Peter's Russian Tales"; "Swallows and Amazons"; "Peter Duck"; "Secret Water"; "Great Northern?"

Ranunculaceae (ra-nun-kŭ-lā'-si-ē). The buttercup family containing, besides the buttercups, the delphinium, anemones, clematis, columbine and many other common wild and cultivated plants.

Rapallo (ra-pal'-lō). It. Small winter resort on Bay of Genoa, 16 m. E. of Genoa; treaties between It. and Yugoslavia (1920) and Ger. and Rus. (1922), signed here.

Rapallo, Treaty of, between It. and Yugoslavia (1920), settling disputed Adriatic territory.

Rapallo, Treaty of. Signed 1922, between Germany and Russia; annulled treaty of Brest-Litovsk and restored diplomatic relations; cancelled indemnity claims and pre-war debts.

Rape. Plant of cabbage tribe, also known as wild navew (*Brassica campestris*); cultivated forms grown for forage and oil, 1707.

"Rape of the Lock, The." Poem by Pope, 2655.

Raphael (raf'-ā-el), **Santi** (1483–1520). One of the greatest of the It. painters. **2745,** *1777, 1785, 2375*; and the Renaissance, *2765*, 2766; "St. Paul at Athens," *2530*; his Madonnas, 2052, *2053*, 2745; "St. George and the Dragon," *1440*.

Raphael, An angel; in Milton's "Paradise Lost," 2179.

Rapids, St. Lawrence r., 2861.

Rappahan'nock. R. of Virginia, U.S.A., source in Blue Ridge Mts.; flows S.E. to Chesapeake Bay.

Rare earths. A group of metallic elements of remarkably similar properties in the aluminium group; atomic weights 138·9 up to 175·0 inclusive; found together in minute quantities in several minerals; a list is given at the foot of the table in p. 768; 777, 3187, 3437; use in gas mantles, 1424.

Rashid Ali (b. 1889). Iraqui politician; prime min. to Feisal I in 1933 and again in 1940; by a *coup* established himself April 3, 1941, as premier of Iraq supporting the Axis; fled to Persia after month's fighting with Brit. troops, then to Berlin; received by Ibn Saud in Saudi Arabia after the war.

Ras'mussen Knud (1879–1933). Danish Arctic explorer, b. in Greenland; made five important expeditions to Greenland, including a remarkable trip across the island, 1912–14; route, *map*, *1542*. In 1922 he discovered relics of the Franklin expedition.

Raspberry, a fruit, **2745,** 463; *plate f. 1401.*

Rasputin (ras-pōō'-tin), **Gregory Efimovitch** (1871–1916). Rus. fanatic; uncouth peasant who deserted family for religious life in 1904; gained vast influence through fanatical teachings and personal magnetism; interference in politics led to his murder by Rus. nobles, 2365.

Ras'selas. Prince of Abyssinia, in Samuel Johnson's philosophical romance of that name, seeker for happiness, at last disillusioned.

Ras Taffari. *See* **Haile Selassie.**

Rastatt. Tn. in Baden, S. Ger.; pop. 14,000; treaty between Fr. and Austria (1714) ending War of Spanish Succession.

"Raster," scanning pattern in television, *3182*.

Rat, 2746; a rodent, *2075*; ship's disk, *2746*.

Rates, local taxation, 3158.

Rat flea, 1313.

Rathenau (rah'-te-now), **Walther** (1867–1922). Ger. economist and industrialist; controller of raw materials during 1st World War, and one of outstanding figures of Ger. post-war industrial reconstruction; foreign minister, 1922; assassinated June 1922.

Rathbone, Eleanor (1873–1946). Brit. politician; worked for women's suffrage and family allowances; helped found dept. of social science, Liverpool univ.; wrote "The Disinherited Family," "The Case for Family Allowances."

Ratio (rā'-shi-ō), in geometry, 1436.

Ra'tionalists, in philosophy, 2572.

Ratisbon or **Regensburg,** Ger. commercial and mfg. tn. in Bavaria on Danube; pop. 83,580; stormed by Napoleon in 1809; once free imperial city; 377, 972, 1447.

Ratites (ra-tī'-tēz). Sub-class of birds without a "keel" breastbone, including the ostrich, emu, etc.

Rattan' palm, 2483, *2484*.

Rattigan, Terence M. (b. 1912). Brit. dramatist; among his many plays are "French Without Tears," "Flare Path," "While the Sun Shines," "The Winslow Boy," "Adventure Story," "The Browning Version."

Rattlesnake, 2746; a pit viper, 3325; action of poison, 2991.

Rauch (rowkh), **Christian Daniel** (1777–1857). The greatest Ger. sculptor of his time; most famous works, the monument to Queen Louise at Charlottenburg and the bronze equestrian statue of Frederick the Great in Berlin.

Ravel (ra-vel'), **Maurice Joseph** (1875–1937). Fr. composer. Works include "L'Heure Espagnole" (comic opera); "Daphnis et Chloe" (ballet); "Bolero" (orchestral); Piano Concerto.

Raven. Large bird of crow family, **2747.**

"Raven, The." Poem by E. A. Poe, 2633, 2747.

Raven-Hill, Leonard (1867–1942). Eng. artist, for many years known as a cartoonist for "Punch."

Raven'na, It. Old city celebrated for its churches; 75 m. S. of Venice; pop. 81,000; **2747**; Dante's burial-place, 969; in 2nd World War, 2748.

Ravenna, battle of. Victory of Fr. over united Sp. and papal armies in 1512, 2748.

Ravenna, Exarchate of. Territory ruled by Byzantine exarch or governor in It. 6th–8th cents.; cap. Ravenna; conquered by Pepin and given to Pope, 2748.

Ravensbrück. Nazi concentration camp for women, nr. Berlin; extermination by lethal injections, experimental operations, and gas chambers practised; 11 camp attendants sentenced to be hanged, Feb. 1947.

Ravi, r. of Punjab, boundary in part between India and Pakistan; 450 m.; passes Lahore and joins Chenab 35 m. N. of Multan; 2479.

Rawalpindi, S.S. Brit. armed merchant cruiser; sunk by Ger. battleship Scharnhorst Nov. 23, 1939, in first naval engagement of 2nd World War.

Rawlinson, Sir Henry Creswicke (1810–95). Eng. soldier, diplomat, and orientalist; first successful decipherer of Persian cuneiform inscriptions; discovered Behistun rock recording triumphs of Darius the Great in Persian, Babylonian, and Susian, *2556*.

Rawlinson, Henry Seymour, 1st Baron (1864–1925). Brit. soldier; served with distinction in Sudan, S. Africa, and France, where he commanded the 4th army; raised to peerage in 1919; commander-in-chief in India (1920–25).

Rawsthorne, Alan (b. 1905). Brit. composer; variations for two violins; symphonic studies; concerto for piano, another for violin; songs.

Ray, Cape. S.W. point of Newfoundland, 2861.

Rayleigh, John William Strutt, Baron (1842–1919). Brit. physicist; 1904 Nobel prize winner, 2375; discovery of argon, 88, 2744; of neon, 2315.

Raymond of Toulouse (d. 1105). Powerful count of Provence; a leader in First Crusade, 936.

Rayon. Artificial textile fibre, mainly resembling silk, **2748,** 2709, 3069, 3217.

Rays. *See* **Atom; Light; Radar; Radiation; Radium and Radio-Activity; Wireless; X-rays.**

Rays. Various primitive flattened fish; including the skates, 1298, 2976; egg, 1094; evolutionary position, 1298; torpedo-fish, *3228*.

Rays, of the sun, power from, 1594, 3119.

Rays, of the sunflower, 1321.

Razorbill. A bird of the auk family, 304, *3530*.

Re. Eg. deity, the sun god, father of gods and men. *See* **Ammon.**

Ré (rā). Fr. isl. in Bay of Biscay; 33 sq. m.; mainly sand dunes; salt, oysters.

Reac'tance, in elec., 1133.

Reaction turbine, 1670, 3258, *3259*.

Read, Herbert (b. 1893). Brit. critic and poet; "English Prose Style," "Poetry and Anarchism," "Education through Art," "In Defence of Shelley," "The Grass Roots of Art";

story, " The Green Child " ; poetry, " Thirty-five Poems," " The World Within a War."

Reade, Charles (1814–84). Eng. novelist and reformer ; " It's Never Too Late to Mend," directed at prison abuses ; " Foul Play," an attack on over-loading and over-insuring of ships ; " The Cloister and the Hearth," 2764.

Reading (red′-ing), **Rufus Isaacs, 1st Marquess** (1860–1935). Brit. jurist, first Jewish Lord Chief Justice of Eng. (1913–21) ; special ambassador to U.S.A. (1918) ; Viceroy of India (1921–26) ; Sec. for Foreign Affairs in National Govt. (1931) ; Lord Warden of the Cinque Ports (1934).

Reading, Stella, Dowager Marchioness of. Brit. founder and chairman of W.V.S. from 1938 ; gov. of B.B.C. 1946, vice-chairman 1947.

Reading. Co. tn. of Berkshire, 36 m. w. of London, on R. Kennet, near junction with Thames ; pop. 117,800 ; biscuits, aircraft ; Univ. ; 416.

Reading, Pennsylvania, U.S.A. Mfg. city 50 m. N.W. of Philadelphia ; pop. 110,500 ; mfrs. iron- and steel-ware, etc.

Reading, 2750. How to judge books, 2751 ; how to use the public library, 1930 ; literature for children, 1964. *See* **Literature, Children's ; English Literature** ; etc.

Reading Room, British Museum, 584, *585.*

Realism, in the fine arts ; beginning of, in painting, 2476, *2332* ; in the Eng. novel, 2401.

Reaping machines. Devices for harvesting standing grain, *83* ; invention, 79 ; wheat, 3374.

Rear-admiral, in Brit. Navy, 28, *plate f. 2292.*

Reason. Faculty which distinguishes men from animals. *See also* **Mind ; Psychology.**

Réaumur (rā-ō-mūr′), **René Antoine de** (1683–1757). Fr. physicist and naturalist ; showed corals to be animals, not plants ; discovered method of tinning iron ; thermo-meter, 3200 ; artificial silk, 2973.

Rebec′ca. A Biblical character ; wife of Isaac and mother of Esau and Jacob (Gen. xxiv.).

Rebecca. Character in Scott's " Ivan-hoe " ; beautiful Jewess, daughter of Isaac of York.

Rebecca (Becky) Sharp. Character in Thackeray's " Vanity Fair."

Re′bek. Arab musical instrument, 3324.

Rebellion, The Great. *See* **Civil War** (in Eng.).

Recall, in memory, 2139.

Récamier (rā-kah′-myā), **Madame Julie** (1777–1849). Fr. society leader, famed for beauty and intelligence ; friend of Chateaubriand and Madame de Stael ; opponent of Napoleon, who exiled her ; portrait by David, *1372.*

Reconnaissance Corps (Recce). Unit of Brit. army ; formed 1941 and trained on Commando lines ; one battn. with mechanized transport attached to each infantry div. as vanguard, to reconnoitre ; absorbed in R.A.C., Jan. 1944.

Receiver ; in radio apparatus, *3392,* 3393, 3394, 3295, 3397 ; television, 3183.

Receiver, telephone, 3011.

Recife, Brazil. Same as **Pernambuco.**

Recip′rocating engine, 1735, 3258.

Reciprocating saw, 2037.

Recitative (res-i-ta-tēv′). Musical recitation, 2436.

Reclus (ra-klŭ), **Jean Jacques Élisée** (1830–1905). Fr. geographer ; remarkable scientific knowledge and literary style (" The Earth and Its Inhabitants ").

Recognition, and memory, 2139.

Record, gramophone, *1496,* 3012.

Recorder, at Quarter Sessions, 922.

Recorder, musical instr., *2265.*

Record Office. Building situated between Fetter Lane and Chancery Lane, London, in which are pre-served state papers, etc., among

them Domesday Book, numerous royal charters, and other historic documents.

Records. The shortest known times in which races have been run, the best performances in athletics and other branches of sport. *See* list of records in pages 3956 to 3959.

Rectangle, in geometry, 1435.

Rectified spirit, 104.

Rectifier, for converting A.C. to D.C. current, **2751** ; in radio apparatus, 3394 ; silenium in, 2920 ; thermi-onic valve as, 3198.

Rector, in church, 825 ; of University, 3296.

Recurring decimals, 984.

Red, a primary colour of pigments, 875 ; in paints, 2478 ; in spectrum, *plate f. 3056.*

Red Admiral butterfly, *plate f. 032.*

Redbreast, the Eng. robin, 2790.

Red-breasted merganser, a diving duck with long, hooked beak adapted to gripping fish, *1052.*

Red cedar, used for pencils, 2541.

Red clover, 854.

Red coral, 908.

Red corpuscles, in blood, 474, *475.*

Red Crescent. Emblem used by Turkey corresponding to the Red Cross.

Red Cross societies, 2752.

Red currant, 944, *back of plate f. 1401.*

Red deer, 984.

Redditch. Tn. of Worcestershire ; pop. 19,000 ; formerly noted for needles, 3407.

Red fox, 1355.

Red grouse, 1550.

Red gum, species of eucalyptus, *1230.*

Red gurnard. Fish, commonest of the English gurnards.

Red Indians. Name given to native aborigines of N. Amer., though they are not red, **2753** ; *plates f. 2756,* 2757. Alaskan, 97, 1222 ; and ex-plorers, 143 ; Eskimos, 1222 ; Labra-dor, *1875* ; languages, 2754 ; Pueblo, 2698 ; tribal divisions, 2753, 2757 ; Canadian reservations, 2757 ; U.S. reservations, 2757 ; basketry, 369 ; blankets, 706 ; canoes, 436, 481 ; dwellings, 2753, 2755, 2756 ; hunt-ing and trapping, 459, 2756 ; lacrosse, 1882 ; legends, 2754 ; signalling system, *3165* ; tobacco, 3219 ; totems, 97, 2753 ; wampum beads, 2201 ; position of women, 2754 ; *History* ; 2753, 2757 ; origin of name, 2753 ; William Penn's treaty, 2545.

Red lead. Minium ; an ingredient of mineral paint, 1908.

Red′manol. An artificial plastic material.

Redmond, John Edward (1851–1918). Irish parl. leader who secured passage of Home Rule Bill of 1914 ; its operation, however, was sus-pended until after his death.

Red pepper, 2547.

Redpoll, linnet relation, 1955.

Red Polled cattle, a beef breed, 732.

Red race, *2723, 2724* ; classification, 2725.

Red River. The southernmost of the great tributaries of the Mississippi, U.S.A., rises in Staked Plains of Texas ; 1,200 m. long.

Red River. R. of N. America. Rises near source of Mississippi in Minne-sota, and flows finally N. into Lake Winnipeg in Manitoba, 700 m. long, 2088. In flood time enables vessels to pass from Hudson Bay to Gulf of Mexico. Red River district famed for wheat.

Red River Settlement. Former colony of Canada, now part of Manitoba. Founded 1811 by Earl of Selkirk. In 1869 half-breeds in district rose against Canadian govt. as protest against annexation, but suppressed by Can. and Brit. force under Sir G. Wolseley.

Red Sea. Arm of Indian Ocean be-tween Arabia and Africa connected with Mediterranean by Suez Canal ; 1,200 m. long ; **2758,** 3109 ; redness caused by algae, 2620 ; Suez Canal, 3110.

Redshank, a wader, *3331.*

Red Snow, formed by algae, 2620.

Red Squirrel, how it hibernates, 1623.

Redstart. Bird, relative of the robin, seen locally in most districts in Eng-land, but not common ; migratory. Distinguished by its brilliant chest-nut-red patch at base of the tail ; rest of plumage is white (on head) and slate-coloured (back) ; *2171.*

" Reductio ad Absurdum " (Lat.). Method of proof, which begins by assuming that what has to be proved is wrong, and then shows that this assumption results in an absurdity, that consequently the assumption is not true, and hence that the proposition is true.

Reduction. Chemical union with hydrogen, or other electro-negative radicle similar to hydrogen ; opposite to oxidation.

Redwing, species of thrush, 3205.

Redwood, a giant tree, 2921 ; section, *3245.*

Ree, Lough, Eire. L. traversed by R. Shannon ; 16 m. long, from 1 m. to 7 m. broad.

Reed, of a loom, 2025 ; in organ pipe, *3010.*

Reed, Ezekiel (18th cent.). Amer. inventor ; first nail-making machine, 2272.

Reed, Talbot Baines (1852–93). Eng. writer of boys' books. Best-known works : " Fifth Form at St. Dominic's " ; " Adventures of a Three-guinea Watch."

Reed, Walter (1851–1902). Amer. army surgeon and bacteriologist ; discovers cause of yellow fever, 2236, 2488.

Reedbuck, an African antelope, 176.

Reed bunting, 617.

Reed instruments, 2267.

Reed mace, plant, *615.*

Reed organ, 2450.

Reeds, various tall hollow-stemmed grasses, *frontis., Vol. 4,* 3355 ; used for pens, 2539.

Reed warbler, *443,* 3340–41.

Reefs, coral, 908 ; atolls of Pacific, 2469 ; Great Barrier, 307 ; in Red Sea, 2758.

Reel, cotton manufacture, 3205.

Reel, fishing, *1309.*

Reeves, John Sims (1818–1900). Eng. tenor singer, the most famous of his period ; sang chiefly in oratorio, but also achieved success as a ballad singer.

Referee′. An arbitrator or umpire ; in certain games and sports, the official who controls the contest and whose decision is final.

Referen′dum. Referring a measure passed by a legislative body to a public vote ; system most highly developed in Switzerland ; also used in Australia and some states of American Union.

Refining, of metals. *See* **Metallurgy.**

Refining, of petroleum, 2429.

Reflecting telescope or **reflector,** 3178.

Reflection, of light, 1939, *1940* ; in lighthouses, 1945 ; of sound, 1077 ; of wireless waves, 3396.

Reflex actions, 545.

Reflex camera, *2578,* 2579.

Reform Acts, in Eng. (of 1832), 1489, 2522, 3278, 3364 ; (of 1867, 1884–85), 570, 2522.

Reformation, Protestant, **2758,** 2040 ; Counter Reformation, 2759 ; Eras-mus and, 1221 ; Huss a forerunner, 1660, *1661* ; in Netherlands, 2568 ; in Scotland, 1871, 2892 ; in Switzer-land, 664, 3448 ; Wycliffe's influence, 3428. *In England,* 1195, 2759 ; Henry VIII begins, 1612 ; More opposes, 2228 ; under Edward VI, 1092 ; Elizabeth supports, 1146 ; Puritans, 933, 2707 ; Stuarts and Puritan Revolution, 755, 933, 1794 ; King James's Bible, 426 ; reflected in literature, 1210 ; *see* **England, Church of.** *In France,* 1366, 1650, 870 ; *see* **Huguenots.** *In Germany,* 1449, 2758 ; Luther begins, 2040 ; and Charles V, 754. *See* **Thirty Years' War.**

Reformatory school. Former name of institution for young offenders, now called " approved " school ; 2688.

RECORDS IN AMATEUR ATHLETICS AND OTHER SPORTS

Abbreviations : d., day(s) ; h., hour(s) ; m., minute(s) ; s., second(s).

Note : Records are given as in mid-1950.

ATHLETICS

Flat Racing

	World record	*Brit. (all-comers) record*	*Brit. national record*
100 yds.	9·3 s. M. E. Patton (U.S.A.), 1948. 9·4 s. M. E. Patton (U.S.A.), 1947. C. Jeffery (U.S.A.), 1940. J. C. Owens (U.S.A.), 1935.	9·6 s. E. Conwell, 1947.	9·6 s. E. McD. Bailey, 1947.
220 yds.	20·3 s. J. C. Owens (U.S.A.), 1935.	21·1 s. E. McD. Bailey, 1950.	
440 yds.	46·0 s. H. McKenley (Jamaica), 1948.	47·2 s. A. S. Wint, 1948.	
880 yds.		1 m. 49·2 s. S. C. Wooderson, 1938.	
1 mile	4 m. 01·4 s. G. Haegg (Sweden), 1945.	4 m. 6·4 s. S. C. Wooderson, 1937.	
3 miles	13 m. 32·4 s. G. Haegg (Sweden), 1942.	13 m. 53·2 s. S. C. Wooderson, 1946.	
6 miles	28 m. 30·8 s. V. Heino (Finland), 1949.	29 m. 22·4 s. V. Heino (Finland), 1947.	29 m. 33·6 s. F. Aaron, 1950.
10 miles	49 m. 22·2 s. V. Heino (Finland), 1946.	50 m. 30·8 s. W. E. Eaton, 1936.	
1 hour	12 miles 29 yds. V. Heino (Finland), 1945.	11 miles 1,137 yds. A. Shrubb, 1904.	
Marathon .. .. (26 miles 385 yds.)		2 h. 30 m. 57·6 s. H. W. Payne, 1929.	

Hurdle Racing

120 yds.	13·6 s. H. Dillard (U.S.A.), 1948. 13·7 s. F. Wolcott (U.S.A.), 1941.	13·9 s. W. F. Porter (U.S.A.), 1948.	14·4 s. D. O. Finlay, 1949.
440 yds.	52·2 s. R. B. Cochran (U.S.A.), 1942.	52·7 s. R. B. Cochran (U.S.A.), 1939.	53·4 s. H. Whittle, 1949.

Relay Racing

	World record	*British (all-comers) record*
4 × 110 yds. ..	40·5 s. U.S.A., 1938.	41·8 s. British Empire, 1948.
4 × 440 yds. ..	3 m. 09·4 s. U.S.A., 1941.	British Empire, 1936.
4 × 880 yds. ..	7 m. 34·6 s. U.S.A., 1941.	7 m. 35·8 s. U.S.A., 1936.
4 × 1 mile ..	16 m. 55·8 s. Sweden, 1948.	17 m. 07·2 s. U.S.A., 1936.

Track Events over Metric Distances (world records):

Flat Racing

100 metres	10·2 s. J. C. Owens (U.S.A.), 1936. H. Davis (U.S.A.), 1941.	3,000 metres ..	7 m. 5·8 s. G. Reiff (Belgium), 1949.
200 metres	20·3 s. J. C. Owens (U.S.A.), 1935.	5,000 metres	13 m. 58·2 s. G. Haegg (Sweden), 1942.
400 metres	45·9 s. H. McKenley (Jamaica), 1948.	10,000 metres ..	29 m. 27·2 s. V. Heino (Finland), 1949.
800 metres	1 m. 46·6 s. R. Harbig (Germany), 1939.	20,000 metres ..	1 h. 03 m. 01·2 s. A. Csaplar (Hungary), 1941.
1,000 metres ..	2 m. 21·4 s. R. Gustafsson (Sweden), 1946.	25,000 metres ..	1 h. 20 m. 14 s. M. Heitanen (Finland), 1948.
2,000 metres ..	5 m. 7 s. G. Reiff (Belgium), 1948.	30,000 metres ..	1 h. 40 m. 46·6 s. M. Heitanen (Finland), 1948.

Hurdle Racing

110 metres	13·7 s. F. G. Towns (U.S.A.), 1936. F. Wolcott (U.S.A.), 1941.	400 metres	50·6 s. G. Hardin (U.S.A.), 1934.
200 metres	22·3 s. F. Wolcott (U.S.A.), 1940.		

Relay Racing

4 × 100 metres ..	39·8 s. U.S.A., 1936.	4 × 800 metres ..	7 m. 29 s. Sweden, 1946.
4 × 200 metres ..	1 m. 25 s. Stanford Univ. (U.S.A.), 1937.	4 × 1,500 metres ..	15 m. 34·6 s. Sweden, 1947.
4 × 400 metres ..	3 m. 8·2 s. U.S.A., 1932.		

Field Events

	World record	*British (all-comers) record*	*British national record*
High Jump	6 ft. 11 ins. L. Steers (U.S.A.), 1941.	6 ft. 7½ ins. A. Paterson, 1947.	
Long Jump	26 ft. 8¼ ins. J. C. Owens (U.S.A.), 1935.	25 ft. 8 ins. W. Steele (U.S.A.), 1948.	24 ft. 9¼ ins. T. Bruce, 1948.

Field Events—(continued)

	World record	British (all-comers) record	British national record
Pole Vault	15 ft. 7¾ ins. C. Warmerdam (U.S.A.), 1942	14 ft. 3 ins. C. Warmerdam (U.S.A.), 1938.	13 ft. 6 ins. V. W. Pickard, 1938.
Hop, Step and Jump	52 ft. 5⅞ ins. N. Tajima (Japan), 1936.	51 ft. 3½ ins. J. P. Metcalfe (Austr.), 1934.	47 ft. 4 ins. J. Higginson, 1938.
Putting the Weight..	58 ft. ⅜ in. C. Fonville (U.S.A.), 1948.	56 ft. 2 ins. W. Thompson (U.S.A.), 1948.	51 ft. 11½ ins. J. A. Savidge, 1950.
Throwing the Hammer	195 ft. 5¼ ins. I. Nemeth (Hungary), 1949.	183 ft. 11½ ins. I. Nemeth (Hungary), 1948.	178 ft. 3 ins. D. Mc. D. Clark, 1950.
Throwing the Javelin	258 ft. 3½ ins. Y. Nikkannen (Fin.), 1938.	237 ft. 3½ ins. J. Varszegi (Hungary), 1938.	222 ft. 9 ins. S. A. Lay (N.Z.), 1928.
Throwing the Discus	186 ft. 11 ins. F. E. Gordien (U.S.A.), 1949.	173 ft. 2 ins. A. Consolini (Ita.), 1948.	154 ft. 6½ ins. J. A. Savidge, 1950.

CYCLING
(British records)

1 mile (standing start unpaced) ..	2 m. 1·2 s. E. V. Mills, 1937.	50 miles (paced) ..	1 hr. 37 m. 34·4 s. E. V. Mills, 1937.
1 mile (standing start paced) ..	1 m. 47·6 s. F. W. Southall, 1931.	1 hour (motor paced)	41 miles 1,634 yds. H. Oxley, 1938.
1 mile (flying start, unpaced) ..	1 m. 59·8 s. F. W. Southall, 1927.	1 hour (human paced)	31 miles 1,457 yds. F. W. Southall, 1929.
10 miles (paced) ..	18 m. 42·8 s. F. W. Southall, 1929.	1 hour (unpaced) ..	26 miles 1,020 yds. C. Marriner, 1947.
25 miles (paced) ..	47 m. 4·8 s. F. W. Southall, 1929.		

WALKING

	World record	British (all-comers) record	British national record
2 miles	12 m. 45 s. V. Hardmo (Sweden), 1944.		13 m. 11·4 s. G. E. Larner, 1904.
7 miles .	48 m. 15·2 s. V. Hardmo (Sweden), 1945.		50 m. 11·2 s. R. Hardy, 1950.
10 miles ..	1 h. 10 m. 55·8 s. J. F. Mikaelsson (Sweden), 1945.		1 h. 14 m. 30·6 s. F. J. Redman, 1934.
20 miles ..	2 h. 41 m. 7 s. H. Olsson (Sweden), 1943.		2 h. 43 m. 38 s. A. E. Plumb, 1932.
1 hour ..	8 miles 1,025 yds. J. F. Mikaelsson (Sweden), 1945.		8 miles 474 yds. A. H. G. Pope, 1932.
2 hours ..	15 miles 1,521 yds. O. Andersson (Sweden), 1945.		15 miles 701 yds. R. Bridge, 1935.

SWIMMING
(Men's free-style)

	World record	British record
100 yds.	49·4 s. A. Ford (U.S.A.), 1944.	51·8 s. B. Bourke (Australia), 1947.
220 yds.	2 m. 7·1 s. W. Smith (U.S.A.), 1944.	2 m. 13·1 s. A. Jany (France), 1946.
300 yds.	3 m. 4·4 s. J. Medica (U.S.A.), 1935.	3 m. 13·2 s. N. Wainwright, 1937.
440 yds.	4 m. 38·5 s. W. Smith (U.S.A.), 1941.	4 m. 54·4 s. N. Wainwright, 1937.
500 yds.	5 m. 16·3 s. J. Medica (U.S.A.), 1935.	5 m. 44·8 s. J. I. Hale, 1946.
880 yds.	9 m. 54·6 s. W. Smith (U.S.A.), 1942.	10 m. 26·6 s. N. Wainwright, 1937.
1000 yds.	11 m. 37·4 s. J Medica (U.S.A.), 1933.	12 m. 26·6 s. N. Wainwright, 1933.
1 mile	20 m. 29 s. K. Nakama (U.S.A.), 1942.	21 m. 25·2 s. J. I. Hale, 1946.

Over Metric Distances (world's records):

100 metres ..	55·9 s. A. Ford (U.S.A.), 1945.	800 metres	9 m. 50·9 s. W. Smith (U.S.A.), 1941.
200 metres ..	2 m. 5·4 s. A. Jany (France), 1946.	1,000 metres ..	12 m. 33·8 s. T. Amano (Japan), 1938.
300 metres ..	3 m. 21·6 s. J. Medica (U.S.A.), 1935.	1,500 metres ..	18 m. 58·8 s. T. Amano (Japan), 1938.
400 metres ..	4 m. 33·2 s. H. Furuhashi (Japan), 1950.	4 × 100 metres relay	3 m. 50·8 s. Yale Univ. (U.S.A.), 1942.
500 metres ..	5 m. 56·2 s. R. Flannagan (U.S.A.), 1938.	4 × 200 metres relay	8 m. 24·3 s. Yale Univ. (U.S.A.), 1936.

MOTOR RACING
(World records)

Flying mile	394·2 m.p.h. J. R. Cobb (G.B.), 1947.	12 hours	170·21 m.p.h. A. Jenkins (U.S.A.), 1939.
1 hour	182·51 m.p.h. A. Jenkins (U.S.A.), 1939.	24 hours	161·18 m.p.h. A. Jenkins (U.S.A.), 1939.

MOTOR-CYCLE RACING	MOTOR-BOAT RACING
(World record)	(World record)
Flying mile .. .. 150·89 m.p.h. R. Free (G.B.), 1948.	Flying mile.. .. 160·32 m.p.h. Stanley Sayers (U.S.A.), 1950.

CRICKET

Highest Individual Scores
Australia, D. G. Bradman, 452 not out for New South Wales *v.* Queensland, 1920–30.
England, A. C. MacLaren, 424 for Lancashire *v.* Somerset, 1895.

Highest in Any Class of Cricket
A. E. J. Collins, 628 not out, for Clarke's House *v.* North Town in a junior house match at Clifton College, 1899.

Century in Each Innings
W. R. Hammond scored two hundreds in a match on seven occasions ; J. B. Hobbs on six ; C. B. Fry on five. In 1938 A. Fagg scored a double century in both innings for Kent *v.* Essex.

Centuries in One Season
D. Compton in 1947 scored 18 separate hundreds ; J. B. Hobbs 16 in 1925 ; W. R. Hammond 15 in 1938 ; H. Sutcliffe 14 in 1932.

Most Centuries in One Innings
In 1946, Holkar State against Mysore scored six centuries. In 1900–01 five separate hundreds were scored for New South Wales *v.* South Australia.

Highest Partnership
First wicket : H. Sutcliffe and P. Holmes, 555, for Yorkshire *v.* Essex, 1932.
Last wicket : A. F. Kippax and J. E. H. Hooker, 307, for New South Wales *v.* Victoria, 1928–29. In England : S. Banerjee and C. T. Sarwate, 249, for India *v.* Surrey, 1946.

Highest Individual Aggregate for Season
D. Compton (1947), 3,816. W. J. Edrich (1947), 3,539.

Highest Batting Average in an English Season
D. G. Bradman (Australia) in 1938 : average 115·66 ; H. Sutcliffe (Yorks), in 1931 : average 96·96.

Most Individual Centuries
J. B. Hobbs, 197 ; E. Hendren, 170 ; W. R. Hammond, 167 ; C. P. Mead, 153.

Four Wickets with Consecutive Balls
Twenty-three bowlers have taken four wickets with consecutive balls in first-class cricket. R. J. Crisp did so twice.

Two Hat Tricks in Innings
A. E. Trott, in his benefit match, Middlesex *v.* Somerset, at Lord's in 1907, took four wickets with four balls, and also three with three balls.

Two Hat Tricks in Match
A. Shaw, for Notts *v.* Gloucestershire, in 1884 ; T. J. Matthews, for Australia *v.* South Africa, in 1912 ; C. W. L. Parker, for Gloucestershire *v.* Middlesex, in 1924 ; and R. Jenkins, for Worcestershire *v.* Surrey, in 1949.

All Ten Wickets
All ten wickets in an innings have been taken by 51 bowlers 56 times.

200 Wickets in a Season
Twenty-six bowlers have taken 200 wickets in a season 55 times. A. P. Freeman's 304 wickets in 1928 is the record.

2,000 Runs and 200 Wickets
Only G. H. Hirst has performed this feat, in season 1906.

3,000 Runs and 100 Wickets
In 1937 J. H. Parks (Sussex) scored 3,003 runs and took 101 wickets.

1,000 Runs and 100 Wickets
W. Rhodes (Yorkshire) scored 1,000 runs and took 100 wickets in a season 16 times ; G. H. Hirst completed 14 " doubles," eleven in succession.

200 Wickets and 1,000 Runs
A. E. Trott (twice), A. Kennedy (once), and M. W. Tate (three times) are the only players to accomplish this feat.

2,000 Runs and 100 Wickets
F. E. Woolley four times scored 2,000 runs and took 100 wickets in a season.

1,000 Runs in May
W. G. Grace (1895), W. R. Hammond (1927), C. Hallows (1928), D. G. Bradman (1930 and 1938), and W. J. Edrich (1938) each scored 1,000 runs by May 31st.

Most Runs in any Month
L. Hutton (June 1949) scored 1,294 runs in 16 innings (including three successive " ducks ").

Innings Aggregate
The 1,107 runs scored by Victoria *v.* New South Wales in 1926–27 is the greatest number of runs ever scored in one innings. Victoria's next innings totalled 36 !
Yorkshire's 887 against Warwickshire in 1896 is the highest county innings.
Most runs in a day were scored by Australia against Essex in 1948—721.

Wicket-keeping
L. Ames in 1929 caught 79 and stumped 48—127 victims.

County Championship
Yorkshire have won the County Championship 23 times (once jointly) ; Nottinghamshire 12 times (4 times jointly) ; Lancashire 11 times (thrice jointly).

Test Cricket
Highest Innings
England 903 for 7 wickets, *v.* Australia at the Oval (1938) ; Australia *v.* England, 729 for 6, at Lord's, 1930.

Lowest Innings
South Africa, 30, *v.* England at Port Elizabeth (1895–96) and *v.* England at Birmingham (1924).

Record Partnerships
First wicket : 359 by L. Hutton and C. Washbrook, *v.* South Africa at Johannesburg, 1948. Last wicket : 130 by R. E. Foster and W. Rhodes *v.* Australia at Sydney in 1903–04. Highest partnership for any wicket : 451 by W. H. Ponsford and D. G. Bradman *v.* England at the Oval in 1934.

Record Individual Scores
364 by L. Hutton *v.* Australia at the Oval (1938) ; 336 not out by W. R. Hammond *v.* New Zealand at Auckland (1932–33) ; 334 by D. G. Bradman *v.* England at Leeds (1930).

Most Individual Centuries
D. G. Bradman 28, W. R. Hammond 22, H. Sutcliffe 16, J. B. Hobbs 15, G. Headley 10.

Two Centuries in a Match
H. Sutcliffe (twice), D. Compton, W. R. Hammond, E. Paynter, A. C. Russell, for England ; W. Bardsley, A. Morris, D. G. Bradman, for Australia ; G. Headley for West Indies ; A. Melville, B. Mitchell, for South Africa ; V. Hazare for India.

Hat Tricks
W. Bates, J. Briggs, J T. Hearne, M. J. C. Allom, T. W. Goddard for England ; F. R. Spofforth, H. Trumble (twice), T. J. Matthews (twice in same match) for Australia.

FOOTBALL

Football Association Cup
Winners Most Times
Aston Villa and Blackburn Rovers have won the Cup 6 times, and The Wanderers (amateurs) won it 5 times.

Biggest Win in Final Tie
Bury 6 goals, Derby County nil, in 1902–03.

Greatest Number of Goals in Final Tie
Seven : Blackburn Rovers 6 ; Sheffield Wednesday 1 ; in 1889–90.

Highest Score in Any Tie
In 1887 Preston North End beat Hyde in a F.A. Cup Tie by 26 goals to nil.

Medals
Lord Kinnaird, C. H. R. Wollaston, and J. Forrest each won 5 F.A. Cup winners' medals.

Cup and League
Preston North End in 1888–89, and Aston Villa in 1896–97 won both the Cup and the League (First Division) in the same season.

No Goals Against
When Preston North End won the Cup and League in 1888–89 they did so without a goal being scored against them in the Cup competition and without losing a League match.
Bury won the Cup in 1903 without a goal being registered against them in any of the ties.

Record Attendance
In 1922–23, 126,047 spectators (official return), saw Bolton Wanderers (2) beat West Ham United (0) at Wembley.

Record Gate Receipts
£27,776 was taken at Wembley in 1922–23 when Bolton Wanderers met West Ham United (*see Record Attendance* above).

RECORDS IN AMATEUR ATHLETICS AND OTHER SPORTS—(*continued*)

Football—(*continued*)

Successive Wins

The Wanderers and Blackburn Rovers each won the Cup in three successive years, the former in 1875–76, 1876–77, 1877–78, and the latter in 1883–84, 1884–85, and 1885–86.

The Football League

Championship Record

Aston Villa, Sunderland and Arsenal have won the League (Division I) Championship most times—six.

Individual Goal-scoring Record

" Dixie " Dean, of Everton, in season 1936–37 passed Stephen Bloomer's long-standing record of 352 goals in League football ; his total at his retirement in 1939 was 379 ; in 1927–28 he scored 60 goals.

League and Cup

Winners of both in one season—see above under *Cup and League.*

International Football

Record Attendance

In 1937, 149,547 spectators were admitted by ticket to see Scotland beat England 3—1 at Hampden Park, Glasgow.

Caps

W. Meredith (Wales) gained 51 International Caps ; R. Crompton (England) 34 ; E. Scott (Ireland) 31 ; and A. Morton (Scotland) 30. Including both International and Amateur International matches, V. J. Woodward was capped 60 times. Including war-time (1939–45) games, Stanley Matthews played 57 times for England.

Miscellaneous

No Goals

During the first seven years of their existence Queen's Park (Glasgow) did not have a goal scored against them.

Record Score

36 goals to nil scored by Arbroath against Bon Accord in a Scottish Cup Tie, Sept. 5, 1885 ; on the same day Dundee Harp defeated Aberdeen Rovers in the same competition by 35 goals to nil.

Won Every Match

In 1898–99 Glasgow Rangers won all their matches in the Scottish League.

AVIATION

The following is a list of some of the more important achievements in recent years :

In *1927* Charles Lindbergh flew alone in a monoplane (" Spirit of St. Louis ") from New York to Paris, 3,600 miles, in 33½ h. ; Clarence Chamberlin and Charles Levine (the first passenger to cross the Atlantic in an aeroplane) flew from Roosevelt Field (New York) to Helfta (Germany), 3,905 miles.

In *1928* Lady Heath made the first light aeroplane flight from Cape Town to Cairo ; Sqn.-Ldr. Bert Hinkler made the first solo flight from England to Australia in 15 d. 2 h. ; H. Koehl and 2 others flew from Baldonnel to Greenly Island (Labrador), the first from east to west.

In *1929* the " Graf Zeppelin " airship flew round the world in 21 d. 7½ h. (actual flying time 11 d. 23½ h.) ; the Duchess of Bedford, Capt. C. D. Barnard, and R. Little flew from Croydon to Cape Town and back (18,500 miles) in a monoplane in 21 d., the total flying time being about 105 h. ; a Royal Air Force monoplane made the first non-stop flight to India (over 4,130 miles) in 50½ h. ; Sqn.-Ldr. A. H. Orlebar flew in a seaplane at a speed of 365·1 m.p.h.

In *1930* Lt. A. Soucek (U.S.A.) reached a height of 43,166 ft. in an aeroplane ; Wing-Commander Kingsford-Smith flew from England to Australia (10,400 miles) in 10 d. 2 h., and from Portmarnock (near Dublin) to Harbour Grace (Newfoundland) in 30½ h. ; Miss Amy Johnson flew alone from Croydon to Australia in 19½ d.

In *1931* C. W. A. Scott flew from England to Australia in 9 d. 4 h., and from Australia to England in 10 d. 23 h. ; Wiley Post and Harold Gatty flew round the world in 8 d. 16 h. ; Flt.-Lt. J. N. Boothman won the Schneider trophy at a speed of 340·08 m.p.h. ; Flt.-Lt. G. H. Stainforth reached an average speed of 407·5 m.p.h., Clyde Pangborn and Richard Herndon (U.S.A.) made the first Japan to U.S.A. non-stop flight (some 4,465 miles) in 41 h. 31 m. ; C. A. Butler flew from England to Australia in 9 d. 2 h.

In *1932* J. A. Mollison flew from Lympne to Cape Town (6,255 miles) in 4 d. 17 h. ; Miss Amelia Earhart (Mrs. G. P. Putnam), the first woman to fly the Atlantic alone, flew from Newfoundland to Ireland ; Mrs. James A. Mollison (formerly Miss Amy Johnson) flew from Lympne to Cape Town in 4 d. 7 h.

In *1933* Sqn.-Ldr. Gayford and Flt.-Lt. Nicholetts flew from Cranwell to Walvis Bay (5,309 miles) ; K. Schmidt glided for 36½ h. ; MM. Codos and Rossi (France) flew from New York to Rayak, Syria (about 5,500 miles), in 55 h. ; an air fleet of 23 Italian flying boats commanded by Gen. Balbo made a double crossing of the N. Atlantic.

In *1934* Miss Jean Batten flew from Lympne to Port Darwin (Australia) in 14 d. 24 h. ; C. W. A. Scott and T. Campbell Black flew from England to Melbourne (11,300 miles) in 2 d. 23 h. ; Lt. Agello, in a seaplane, reached a speed of 440 m.p.h. ; Sir Charles Kingsford-Smith and P. G. Taylor flew from Australia to California (6,525 miles) in 52½ h., thus being the first to fly across the Pacific from west to east.

In *1935* Miss Amelia Earhart flew solo across the Pacific from Honolulu to Oakland in 18 h. ; in a landplane H. Hughes reached a speed of 352 m.p.h. ; A. Stevens and O. Anderson reached an altitude of 73,395 ft. in a balloon ; R. Oeltzschner glided a distance of of 310 miles ; Miss Jean Batten flew from Australia to England in 17 d. 16¼ h., she was thus the first woman to complete the double journey ; Miss Batten was also the first woman to fly the South Atlantic (Lympne to Port Natal), her time being 62 h. ; H. Broadbent flew from England to Port Darwin in 6 d. 21 h.

In *1936* Mlle. Hilsz reached an altitude of 48,714 ft. ; T. Rose flew from England to Cape Town in 3 d. 17¾ h. and from the Cape to England in 6 d. 6¾ h. ; Mrs. Mollison flew from England to Cape Town and back in 7 d. 22¾ h. ; the " Hindenburg " airship flew from Germany to Lakehurst, U.S.A., in 61½ h. ; Sqn.-Ldr. F. Swain reached an altitude of 49,967 ft. ; Miss Jean Batten flew solo from England to Port Darwin in 5 d. 21 h. ; J. A. Mollison crossed the Atlantic from Harbour Grace, Newfoundland, to Croydon (2,300 miles) in 13½ h.

In *1937* M. J. Adam broke world's altitude record by reaching 53,937 ft. ; M. Gromov and crew of two covered record distance of 6,305 m. non-stop from Moscow to San Jacinto, U.S.A.

In *1938* A. E. Clouston and V. Ricketts flew from England to New Zealand in 4 d. 8 h. and back in 6 d. 12 h. ; P. A. Wills glided 209 miles from Heston to St. Austell ; H. Hughes and three others circled N. Hemisphere (14,874 miles) in 3 d. 19½ h. ; Mercury, upper component of Mayo Composite, crossed N. Atlantic in record E. to W. time (Foynes to Montreal) in 20¼ h.).

In *1939* Fritz Wendel with Messerschmitt Me109R raised world's air speed record to 481·4 m.p.h. ; in Aug. 1939 Imperial Airways inaugural trans-Atlantic weekly flight was made between Foynes and Botwood.

In *1940* Caproni-Campini (first jet-plane) flown near Milan.

In *May 1941*, I. Sikorsky flew helicopter for 1 h. 32 m. ; in Mar. 1941 first Gloster jetplane flown.

In *June 1942* Liberator flew Atlantic five times in 9 days.

In *1944* 70-ton Martin Mars flying-boat test flown 32 h. 17 m.

In *1945* R.A.F. started Canada–New Zealand transport service ; in May 1945 Avro Lancaster " Aries " flew 17,720 miles in North Polar regions ; in Nov. 1945 Group-Capt. H. J. Wilson set world's air speed record at 606 m.p.h. with jet-propelled Meteor.

In *1947* Capt. Odom (U.S.A.) made round-the-world record of 73 hrs. 5 mins. in a Douglas Invader. U.S. Navy pilot set new record of 650·6 m.p.h.

In *1947*, U.S. Army C82 fighter, Batty Jo, flew from Honolulu to New York (4,978 miles) non-stop in 14 h. 31 m. ; in May B.S.A.A. Lancaster flew non-stop London to Bermuda, refuelling in the air ; in Sept. U.S. Army pilotless Skymaster landed in Britain from Newfoundland, the first trans-Atlantic automatic flight.

In *March 1948* Group-Capt. J. Cunningham reached record altitude of 59,446 ft. in jet-propelled fighter at Hatfield ; in May Flying Officer G. Archibald set up new British gliding record of 194 m. in 5 h. 41 min. ; in June U.S. Air Force rocket aircraft flew faster than sound, and prototype helicopter set up international record at Maidenhead for rotor aircraft of 124·3 m.p.h. ; in July Vickers-Viking jet air liner flew from London to Paris in 34 m. 7 secs. In Sept. Maj. R. Johnson in a U.S. jet fighter reached 670·98 m.p.h. (world record).

In *March 1949*, the first non-stop round-the-world flight was completed by Lucky Lady II (U.S. Superfortress), which refuelled four times in mid-air on flight of 23,452 m. ; in Sept. " Brabazon I," largest landplane yet built, made first flight, and a R.A.F. jet fighter climbed 40,000 ft. in 4 mins.

In *Oct. 1949* Group-Capt. J. Cunningham, in the world's first four-engine jet airliner, the de Havilland Comet, flew from London Airport to Castel Benito, in Tripolitania, Africa, and back (total distance just under 3,000 miles) in 8¾ hrs.

In *May 1950* J. Cooksey in a Gloster Meteor VIII won for Britain the international air-speed record for the 1,000 kilometres closed circuit, covering the distance in 1 hr. 12 mins. 58·2 secs., average speed 510·925 m.p.h.

Refracting telescope, 3178.

Refrac′tion of light, *1940*, 1939 ; law of, 1941, 1925 ; by lenses, 1924 ; by prisms, 3055, *plate f. 3056* ; rainbows, 2741 ; of wireless waves, 3396.

Refractive index. When a light ray passes through a transparent material the direction of its path is bent. The sine of the angle of incidence bears a constant ratio to the sine of the angle of refraction. This constant is known as the refractive index for that substance.

Refrigeration. *See* **Freezing and Refrigeration.**

Refrigerator, home, *1392* ; how it works, 1392 ; in ships, 1393.

Rega′lia. Decorative symbols of royalty ; British, 935, *frontis., Vol. 2.*

Re′gan. One of King Lear's two cruel daughters, in Shakespeare's tragedy. 1858.

Regeneration of lost parts. The renewal or replacement of parts or organs of living animals ; of hydra, 1664 ; lizard's tail, 1973 ; in snails, 2990.

Regeneration, natural. One of the systems of forestry, in which trees are allowed to sow themselves in order to produce a continuous crop, instead of felling a whole area completely and re-planting it.

Regenerative furnace, 1756.

Regensburg. *See* **Ratisbon.**

Regent. Person acting for a sovereign who is absent or otherwise incapable of ruling ; Prince Regent in Britain, 1441 ; Ad. Horthy in Hungary, 1656 ; Belgium, Prince Charles from 1946.

Regent or Pitt diamond, *1011*, 1012.

Regent's Park, London. An area of 470 acres in N.W. London, originally laid out as grounds of suggested palace during Regency of King George IV ; contains the Zoological Gardens and Bedford Coll. for Women, 2015 ; Open-Air Theatre, *282*, 3197.

Regent Street, London. A famous mile-long street laid out by John Nash in 1813–20 to connect the Prince Regent's (George IV) residence with Regent's Park, since rebuilt and now a fine shopping thoroughfare.

Reger (rā′-ger), **Max** (1873–1916). Ger. composer, wrote much for organ, 300 songs, and numerous orchestral and choral pieces.

Reggio di Calabria (rej′-ō-dē-ka-lah′-bria). Spt. of s. It. on Strait of Messina ; pop. 136,580 ; silk, perfume, olive-oil ; earthquakes in 1783 and 1908 ; ancient Gk. city Regium ; mirages, 2190 ; Allied landing Sept. 3, 1943, *3422.*

Reggio nell' Emilia. Commercial and mfg. city of N. It., on branch of R. Po ; pop. 105,600 ; cath., works of art.

Regicides (rej′-i-sīdz). In Eng. history those persons directly responsible for execution of Charles I ; especially the 67 members of High Court of Justice who voted for the death penalty.

Regillus (re-jil′-*us*). Anc. l. near Rome, now disappeared ; battle of, 2804 ; Twin Brethren at, 718.

Reg′iment. In Brit. Army, a regiment of infantry of the line consists of a number of battalions, *e.g.*, the Royal Warwickshire Regiment ; in the cavalry (now mechanised), a unit of four squadrons.

Regin (rā′-yin). In Norse and Ger. myth., dwarf smith who rears Siegfried, 2969.

Regina (rē-jī′-na). Cap. of Saskatchewan ; pop. 58,000 ; railway and trade centre *2875*

Regional Planning, 3233.

Regional stations, of the B.B.C., 3399.

Register Office. Office of registrar of births, marriages and deaths ; marriage at, 2107.

Régnier, Henri François Joseph de (1864–1936). Fr. poet and novelist, 1382.

Regular clergy. Distinction from seculars, 2214.

Regular verbs, 3314.

Regulus (reg′-ū-lus), **Marcus Atilius** (3rd cent. B.C.). Rom. general and consul in first Punic War ; he took part in the destruction of the Carthaginian fleet at Ecnomus, and was later made prisoner ; according to tradition, tortured to death for dissuading Romans from) king peace.

Regulus, a star, 3079.

Re′han, Ada (1860–1916). Amer. actress, b. Limerick, Eire ; as leading lady for Augustin Daly and later as star, won high rank both in comedy and farce (Rosalind in " As You Like It " ; Katharina in " Taming of the Shrew ").

Rehobo′am (*c.* 953–*c.* 937 B.C.). King of Israel, 1829.

Reich. Ger. word for empire or realm ; the name Deutsches Reich was applied to Germany, and the govt. during the Nazi regime (1933–45) was known as the Third Reich.

Reichenbach (rīkh′-en-bahkh). Tn. in E. Ger., 30 m. s.w. of Breslau ; pop. 16,560 ; Prussian victory over Austrians (1762) ; convention (1790) guaranteeing integrity of Turkey ; alliance against Napoleon (1813).

Reichenberg (rī′-ken-bärg), or **Liberec,** Czechoslovakia. City N.E. of Prague ; pop. 67,000 ; cloth mfrs.

Reicher (rīkh′-*er*), **Emanuel** (1849–1924). Ger. actor, considered foremost interpreter of Ibsen, Strindberg and Björnson.

Reichsrat (rī-khs′-raht). Ger. imperial council, established in 1919 to consider all Bills before they were introduced into the Reichstag ; it comprised 66 members, Prussia supplying 26 and Bavaria 10 ; also name of Austrian parl. down to 1918.

Reichstadt (rīkh′-shtaht), **Duke of,** title given by European powers to Napoleon II (1811–32) ; son of Napoleon and Marie Louise ; called L'Aiglon (" little eagle ").

Reichstag (rīkhs′-tahg). Ger. legislative assembly, 1449 ; part of the Reichstag building in Berlin was burnt out by the Nazis in 1933.

Reid, Thomas, (1710–96). Scottish philosopher (" Inquiry into the Human Mind," etc.) ; distinguished for his assertion of certain irresistible convictions due to intuitions.

Reid, Thomas Mayne (1818–83). Irish writer of tales of adventure and hunting romances ; lived in U.S.A. (1840–49) ; traded with Indians, fought in Mexican War. (" The Scalp Hunters " ; " White Chief " ; " The Rifle Rangers " ; " The Boy Tar " ; " Afloat in the Forest ").

Reigate. Tn. in Surrey ; about 21 m. s. of London ; sand used in glassmaking is obtained ; pop. (including Redhill, an important rly. junc.), 40,500.

Reign of Terror, in Fr. history, 1393 ; in Bordeaux, 524 ; Danton, 971 ; executions, 2030, 2102, 2516, 2797, 1280 ; Robespierre's share, 2789.

Reims (rēmz ; Fr. rans). Fr. city in N.E. 100 m. from Paris ; pop. 110,800, 2760 ; in World Wars, 2760 ; Ger. surrender at, on May 7, 1945, 1453, 3424.

Reincarna′tion, or transmigration of souls, Buddhist teachings, 600.

Reindeer, 2760 ; caribou of N. Amer., 702 ; females have antlers, *985* ; in Stone Age, *735, plate f. 736.*

Reindeer moss. A lichen most abundant in arctic and sub-arctic regions ; large starch content, *1932*, 1933.

Reinecke Fuchs. *See* **Reynard the Fox.**

Reinforced concrete, *611*, 742.

Reinhardt (rīn-hahrt), **Max** (1873–1943). Ger. theatrical director, whose chief aim was to bring the audience into the action of a play, side by side, as it were, with the actors ; especially notable were " The Miracle," " Oedipus Rex," and " A Midsummer Night's Dream " ; 3197.

Reis, Johann P. Ger. inventor, 3174.

Reith, John Charles Walsham Reith, 1st Baron (b. 1889). Brit. engineer ; director-general British Broadcasting Corporation from its foundation until 1938 ; Chairman of Imperial Airways 1938 ; Minister of Works and Buildings 1940–42 ; chairman Commonwealth Communications Council 1946.

Reitz (rīts), **Deneys** (1882–1944). S. African politician ; fought against Brit. in Boer war ; in 1st World War served under Botha in Ger. W. Africa campaign and in Flanders ; min. of Lands under Smuts ; 1938–43 dep. prime min., and in 1942 high commissioner for S. Africa in London.

Reitz, F. W. (1844–1934), Afrikaans poet, 3020.

Réjane (rā-zhahn′), **Gabrielle** (1857–1920). French emotional actress ; " Madame Sans Gêne " and " Zaza " brought her fame in both Europe and America.

Relative pronoun, 2690.

Relativ′ity. Theory of physics formulated 1905–29 by Albert Einstein, **2760**, 1122 ; and gravitation, 1514.

Relay, in automatic signalling, 2739 ; in automatic telephone exchange, 3175 ; in telegraphy, 3166.

Relief, in sculpture, 2903.

" Religio Medici " (" Religion of a physician "). Contemplative soliloquy and religious treatise written by Sir Thomas Browne, 1212.

Religions : animal worship, 2270 ; Asiatic origin, 268, 269 ; Aztec, 326 ; Buddhism, 600, 1798 ; Christianity, 817, 2528 ; Confucianism, 886, 1798 ; fetishism, 2058 ; fire-worship, 3448, 1278 ; Hebrew, 1829 ; Hinduism, 1626, 1703 ; influence on drama, 1037, 1039 ; Jainism, 601 ; relation to magic, 2056 ; Mahomedanism, 2066 ; monks and monasticism, 2212 ; mythology, 2270 ; Nature worship, 2270, 2756, 1626, 1798 ; papacy, 2495, 2562 ; reformation, 2758 ; Shintoism, 1798 ; sun worship, 1798 ; war against, in Russia, 2846 ; Zoroastrianism, 3447. *See also* chief religions and sects, and articles on each country.

Religious orders. Monks, friars, nuns, 2212. *See also* chief orders by name, as **Franciscans, Jesuits,** etc.

Remagen, Rhine bridge, taken by Allies in Mar. 1945 ; 2769, 3422.

Remarque (re-mark), **Eric Maria** (b. 1898). Ger. novelist (" All Quiet on the Western Front "), 1457.

Rembrandt (rem′-brahnt), **Harmenz van Rijn** (1606–09). Dutch painter, **2762**, 2333, 2476 ; as etcher, *1219* ; " Man in Golden Helmet," *2328.*

Remembrance Day. In the U.K., Sunday preceding Nov. 11 (unless Nov. 11 or 12 falls on a Sunday), on which the dead of both World Wars are remembered ; replaced Armistice Day (Nov. 11) in 1946 ; *239.*

Remington typewriter, 3271.

Remizov (rä′-mē-zof), **Alexis Mikhailovich** (b. 1877). Russian novelist, 2856.

Remus (rē′-mus). Twin brother of Romulus, mythical founder of Rome.

Remus, Uncle. In Joel Chandler Harris's " Uncle Remus's Tales," old plantation Negro with a fund of Negro songs and stories of Brer Rabbit and Brer Fox.

Renaissance (re-nä-sahns), **2764** ; architecture, 220 ; 3040, *1776* ; effect of Crusades, 937 ; Dante, 969 ; drama, 1040 ; Dürer, 1058, 2476 ; and education, 2883 ; in Eng, 1612, 1210, 2228 ; in France, 1383 ; furniture-making, 1409 ; Ghiberti, 1460 ; It. literature affected, 1786 ; Leo X, 1926 ; Leonardo da Vinci, 1926 ; Medici, 2131 ; Michelangelo, *2160* ; More and, 2228 ; painting, 2475, 2766 ; philosophy influenced, 2572 ; Pius II, 2615 ; Raphael, 2745 ; and the Reformation, 2758 ; Rubens. 2838 ; Savonarola, 2876 ; Sculpture. 2904.

Renaissance work, in embroidery *1153.*

Renan (re-nahn'), **Ernest** (1823–92). Fr. author, philosopher, religious historian, and Biblical critic; studied for Catholic priesthood, but became exponent of scepticism; 1381.

Rendering, of oils, 1263.

Ren'frewshire, Scot. Co. in s.w., bordered by r. Clyde; a. 240 sq. m.; pop. 322,700; **2766**; r. Clyde, 854.

Reni, Guido. See **Guido Reni.**

Renner, Karl (b. 1870). Austrian statesman; led Austrian delegation to Peace Conference after 1st World War; chancellor 1919–20; 1st pres. of Austrian parl. 1931, but imprisoned for high treason 1934 when Dolfuss struck at the Socialists; premier in 1945, then pres.

Rennes (ren). Mfg. city 190 m. w. of Paris on Vilaine and Ille rivers; pop. 113,780; cathedral, univ.; in Ger. occupn. 1940–44; 586.

Rennet, 765.

Rennie, John (1761–1821). Celebrated Scot. civil engineer, who was responsible for the construction of Southwark, old Waterloo, and London Bridges, the Kennet and Avon and other canals, and Sheerness and Chatham Dockyards; his second son, John (1794–1874), was knighted on the completion of London Bridge in 1831.

Ren'nin. Casein-digesting enzyme of gastric juice, 1016.

Re'no, Nevada, U.S.A. Largest city in state; pop. 21,500; state univ.; trade in farm produce, lumber, flour, etc.; notorious for the ease with which divorce is granted here; 2336.

Renoir (re-nwahr'), **Pierre Firmin Auguste** (1841–1919). Fr. painter, a leading impressionist, 1378, 2477; "Les Parapluies," 1376.

Rent, 1081.

Repeater, telegraph, 1088.

Repertory Movement, and modern drama, 1043.

Reporter, on newspaper, 2344.

Representation of the People Act, and female suffrage, 3330.

Represen'tatives, House of, U.S.A., 3290. See also **Congress.**

Reproduction, of living organisms, cells the reproducing units, 738; embryology, 1154; genetics, 1427. Of plants: algae, 112; bacteria, 336; caprification of figs, 1270; ferns, 1267, 1268; flowering plants, 1322, 2622; mosses, 2238; mushrooms, 2260; by seeds and spores, 2916; yeast, 3433. Of animals: birds, 442, 444; corals, 908; by eggs (oviparous), 1093; fish, 1093, 1297, 3091; frogs, 1398; insects, 185, 720, 1728, 1729, 1893, 391; jelly-fish, 1817; kangaroo, 1845; by living young (viviparous), 1729, 1095; rate connected with longevity, 156; reptiles, 122, 3229.

Reptiles, 2767; alligators, 121; crocodiles, 921; eggs, 1095; evolution, 1244, 1974; lizards, 1972; parent form of birds, 437; prehistoric, 1433, 2678, 2680; results of being coldblooded, 437; snakes, 2990; tortoises and turtles, 3229.

Reptiles, Age of, 1433.

Repton. Vil. in Derbyshire, near Burton-on-Trent; chiefly noted for its famous public school, founded in 1557.

Repub'lican party, U.S.A., 3290.

Repulse, H.M.S. Brit. battle-cruiser, completed 1916; torpedoed by Jap. aircraft off Malaya with H.M.S. Prince of Wales (q.v. in f-i.), Dec. 1941; 3420.

Repul'sion, electrical, 1128.

"Requiem," by R. L. Stevenson, 3090.

Requiem Mass, by Mozart, 2250.

Res'ervoir. See **Dam;** **Water-works.**

Resht. Chief silk-making and exporting tn. of Iran (Persia), near Caspian Sea; pop. 122,000.

Resid'ual soils, 2999.

Res'ins, 2767; amber, 138; distinguished from gums, 1556; kauri, 2357; in soaps, 2994; in varnish, 3305.

Resis'tance, electrical, 1128; resistance microphone, 2162.

Resistance-welding, 3362.

Resonance, of molecules, 1724; in wireless, 3393.

Respiration or breathing, 2768; artificially induced, 1294; in caterpillars, 720; correct breathing, 1676; firemen's respirators, 1286; fishes, 1296; insects, 1732; lungs, 2039; plants, 1914, 2621; snails, 2989; sponges, 3069; water-plants, 3355; whales, 3371.

Restoration, in Eng. (1660–88), 756, 1198; effect on literature, 1212; reflected in drama, 1040.

Resurrec'tion of Christ, The, rising from the dead, 1825.

Resurrection plant. Same as **Rose of Jericho.**

Reszke (resh'-kā), **Jean de** (1850–1925). Polish operatic tenor, the greatest of his time; brother of the dramatic bass, Edouard de Reszke (1856–1917).

Ret'ina. Inner layer of the eyeball, 1252, 1254; retinoscope, 3055; "visual purple" in, 2574.

Retort, in gas industry, 1422, 1423.

Retrie'ver. A sporting dog, plate f. 1024, 1027.

Retting, of flax, 1953; of hemp, 1609.

Reuben (rōō'-ben). Eldest son of Jacob, ancestor of the tribe of Reuben.

Reuchlin (roikh'-lin), **Johann** (1455–1522). Ger. scholar, pioneer of the "new learning" and of study of Hebrew and Greek in Ger.; made famous struggle against bigots who wished to burn or confiscate all Jewish books except Bible; 2758.

Réunion (rā-ū-ni-on') (formerly Bourbon.) Volcanic isl. in Indian Ocean, 400 m. E. of Madagascar; former French colony, became Dept. of France in 1947; a. 970 sq. m.; pop. 221,000; sugar, rum, coffee, vanilla, spices.

Reuss (rois). A dist. of Thuringia, Ger.; formerly two principalities, Reuss-Greiz and Reuss-Schleiz-Gera.

Reuter (roi'-ter), **Paul Julius, Baron von** (1821–99). Ger.-Eng. capitalist; founder of famous world-wide newscollecting service (1849); Reuters building, London, 2020.

Reval. See **Tallinn.**

Revela'tion, Book of, or Apocalypse. The 27th and last book of the New Testament; date and authorship disputed, but generally attributed to Apostle John.

Revenge. Drake's flagship, 1036; Grenville's flagship, 1543, 1544.

Revenue, internal, 3158.

Reverbera'tion. Reflection of sound as echo, 1077.

Reverberatory furnace. Furnace with vaulted ceiling that deflects flame and heat, 1409, 907.

Revere (re-vēr'), **Paul** (1735–1818). Amer. patriot; a Boston goldsmith he took part in the Boston Tea Party; in the night of April 18, 1775, he rode from Boston to Lexington on horseback warning the colonists of the approach of Brit. soldiers; subject of a poem by Longfellow.

Reverse gear, in motor-car, 2243.

Rever'sion to type. Return of domesticated plant or animal to ancestral type; of goldfish, 1297.

Revised Version of the Bible (R.V.), 427.

Revi'val of Learning. See **Renaissance.**

"Revolt in the Desert," by T. E. Lawrence, 1908.

Revolution, in the internal-combustion engine, 1736.

Revolution, American. See **American Independence.**

Revolution, French. See **French Revolution.**

Revolution, Russian. See **Russia.**

Revolution of 1688. in Eng., 1794.

Revolution of 1830, in Europe, 1240; in France, 758, 1366, 1884; in Italy, 1769, 2124.

Revolution of 1848–49, in Europe, 1240; in France, 2031; in Germany, 1449; in Hungary, 1383, 1656, 1874, 2365; in Italy, 1418, 1769, 2124, 3312.

Revol'ver. Small firearm with revolving chambered cylinder; mechanism, 1285.

Rewa, in Central India. Largest and chief of the 35 states forming Vindhya union; the maharaja was elected first president of union in 1948. Executioner in traditional costume, 1694.

Rexists. Belg. pro-German and Fascist party under Léon Degrelle (b. 1906); collaborated with Ger. during occpn. of Belg. 1940–45.

Reykjavik (rā-kyah-vēk'). Cap. and spt. of Iceland on s.w. coast; pop. 46,570; univ.; port icebound in winter, 1685. During 2nd World War it became h.q. of Allied occupation forces.

Reymont, Wladislaw Stanislaw (1867–1925), Polish novelist, 2983 ("The Peasants," "The Promised Land," "The Storm"); Nobel prize for lit., 1924.

Reynaud (rā-nō), **Paul** (b. 1878). Fr. statesman; prime min. 1940; resigned after Paris occupied by Germans; favoured removing govt. to N. Africa; arrested Sept. 1940; transferred 1942 to Oranienburg (Tirol) prison camp and released by Allied troops May 1945; min. of finance July-Aug. 1948; 3417.

Reyn'olds, Sir Joshua (1723–92). Eng. portrait painter, **2768;** association with Dr. Johnson, 1213, 1836; "The Age of Innocence," 1186; and Gainsborough, 1413; portraits of John Hunter, 2134; Nelly O Brien, 3462; Sheridan, 2944.

Rezonville. Vil. in Fr., scene of battle in Franco-Prussian War (also called battle of Gravelotte).

Rhadamanthus (rad-a-man'-thus). In Gk. myth., brother of Minos, king of Crete, made with him judge in underworld because of his "Rhadamanthine" inflexibility.

Rhadames. See **Ghadames.**

Rhaetian Alps, Switzerland, spring in, 130.

Rhea (rē'-a). In Gk. myth., sister and wife of Kronos, and mother of the chief gods.

Rhea. S. Amer. flightless bird, 3025.

Rhea Silvia. In Rom. myth., vestal mother of Romulus and Remus.

Rheims. See **Reims.**

Rheinfels (rīn'-felz). Ger. castle, 13 m. s. of Coblenz; built in 13th cent.; 2769.

"Rheingold, Das." Wagner's opera, 2440.

Rhein'stein. Castle, 17 m. w. of Mainz, Ger.; owned by Prince Henry of Prussia; 2769.

Rhen'ish Palat'inate. See **Palatinate.**

Rhenium (Re). Metallic element of the manganese group; atomic weight 186·31; discovered in 1925 and named after the Rhine; melts at c. 6000° F.; properties, 777.

Rhe'ostat. A variable resistance for controlling amount of electric current; in tram-cars, 3235.

Rhesus Factor. Substance missing from the blood of 15 per cent of the population (known as the Rhesus negative blood group); first discovered in the blood of the Rhesus monkey; necessitates, in case of blood transfusion, the use of blood of the same group; birth of a child to Rh. negative mother and Rh. positive father (or vice versa) calls for special precautions.

Rhe'sus (rē'-sus) or **Bengal Monkey,** of N. India; 2 ft. long, tail 6–8 ins., fur brown with greenish tinge; semisacred and found in precincts of Hindu temples; eats fruit and seeds, also insects; in its blood the Rhesus Factor (see above) was found.

Rhetoric, 2769; Aristotle, 232; Demosthenes, 990; figures of speech, 1270; Gk. orators, 1540.

Rheumatism. Inflammatory disease attacking joints, muscles, or heart, either in acute or chronic form; and diseased teeth, 1459; inherited tendency, 1617; infra-red treatment, 1722.

Rhine (rīn). R. of w. Europe, rising in Swiss Alps and flowing 820 m. N. to North Sea, **2769,** 1444, 3138; map, 1446, 3140; cities on, 370, 792, 2769; delta, 2318; Alpine tributary,

126 ; wines, 3388 ; crossed by Allies in Mar. 1945, 1453, 2769. 3433, *3423*.

Rhine Province, Rhenish Prussia, or **Rhineland.** Most w. prov. of Prussia bounded on w. by Holland, Belgium and Luxemburg ; chief Ger. mineral dist. ; cap. Coblenz ; chief city, Cologne, 871 ; re-militarization by Germans, 1451, 3415.

Rhinns of Galloway, Wigtownshire, 3377.

Rhinoceros (rī-nos'-*e*-ros), **2770** ; *plate f. 73* ; prehistoric type, *1682, 735*, 736.

Rhinoceros beetle, 400, *401* ; method of defence, 1728.

Rhinoceros iguana, 1686.

Rhi′zoid. Root-like organ of attachment in primitive plants.

Rhizome. A root-like stem, 2825.

Rhi′zopoda. Class of unicellular animals with " false feet " (pseudopodia), 3622.

Rho, ρ, P (rom. r, R). Seventeenth letter of Gk. alphabet.

Rhode Island. New Eng. state, smallest in U.S.A. ; 1,214 sq. m. ; pop. 713,300 ; **2770**.

Rhode Island Red. A breed of fowls, *2671*.

Rhodes, Cecil John (1853–1902). Brit. S. African financier and statesman, **2771**, 3019 ; his home, *3019* ; memorial, *697*.

Rhodes, Wilfred (b. 1877), Eng. cricketer ; played for Yorks. and many times for England ; one of the greatest all-rounders.

Rhodes. Easternmost of Aegean Isls. ; a. 545 sq. m. ; pop. 61,900 ; **2770** ; *map*, 2136 ; in 2nd World War, 2771.

Rhodes, Colossus of, world wonder, 2770.

Rhodesia (rō-dē′-zi-*a*). Brit. territory in S. Africa N. of Transvaal, **2771**, *2773* ; divided into Southern Rhodesia and Northern Rhodesia ; total a. 440,600 sq. m. ; pop. 3,200,000 ; *map f. 68* ; early man in, 2079 ; named after Cecil Rhodes, 2771 ; tobacco cultivation in, *3220* ; Zambezi, 3441 ; Victoria Falls, 3321, *plate f. 3016*.

Rhodesian man, 2079 ; skull found at Broken Hill, 2772.

Rhodes Scholarships, at Oxford, 2464.

Rho′dium (Rh.). White metallic element of the palladium group ; atomic weight 102·9 ; used in thermocouples, alloys, and high-class plating ; melts at 3463° F. ; found in platinum ores, 2627 ; 777.

Rhododen′dron. Flowering shrub, **2772**, *plate f. 1472* ; on Himalayas, 1701.

Rhodope (rod′-ō-pe) **Mts.** A southern arm of the Balkans in Macedonia and Thrace, *2998*.

Rhondda. Tn. in Glamorganshire, Wales. Coal mining centre ; pop. 111,800

Rhondda, David Alfred Thomas, Viscount (1856–1918). Brit. food controller in the 1st World War ; for 22 years member of Parliament ; made immense fortune from coal mines.

Rhondda, Viscountess (b. 1883). Daughter of preceding ; prominent in women's movements ; directs and edits weekly " Time and Tide."

Rhône (rōn). R. of Europe rising in Swiss Alps and flowing through S.E. Fr. 500 m. to Mediterranean, **2773**, 1360 ; in France, 1360, 2043 ; at Geneva, *1428* ; Genissiat dam, 2774 ; Hannibal crossing, *1574* ; in Switzerland, 3140 ; in 2nd World War, 3422.

Rhu′barb. An edible plant, **2774**.

Rhyme, in poetry, 2634.

Rhythm, in music, 2263 ; in poetry, 2635.

Rial′to. Bridge in Venice, *3310, 3312*.

Rib. In architecture, a timber arch supporting a plastered ceiling ; applied to ornamental roof mouldings.

Ribalta, Francisco (1551–1628). Spanish painter, 3049.

Ribbentrop, Joachim von (1893–1946). Ger. politician. Member of Reichstag in 1933 ; Ambassador Extraordinary to Reich (1935–36) ; Ambassador in London (1936–38) ; Foreign Minister 1938 ; War criminal Nuremberg 1945–46 ; hanged, 2282.

Rib′ble, r., Eng. Flows through Yorkshire and Lancashire to the Irish Sea ; 74 m. long.

Ribbon Development Act (**1935**), 3233.

Ribbon-fish. Any of various deep-sea forms with long ribbon-like bodies ; the oar-fish is an example.

Ribera (rē-bã′-r*a*), **Jusepe** or **Jose de** (1588–1652). Span. painter ; a leader of Neapolitan school in Italy ; called Lo Spagnoletto, " Little Spaniard," 3049.

Riboflavin, Vitamin B₂ ; found in eggs, meat, esp. liver, cheese, wheat germ, and yeast.

Ribot (rē-bō), **Alexandre Félix** (1842–1923). Fr. statesman who was prime minister in 1892, 1895, 1914 (for 2 days only), and 1917.

Ribs, in human skeleton, 2977 ; of snakes, *2990*.

Ricardo (ri-kahr′-dō), **David** (1772–1823). Eng. (Jewish) political economist, 1081.

Riccio (rē′-chō). *See* **Rizzio.**

Rice, Alice Hegan (1870–1942). Amer. novelist (" Mrs. Wiggs of the Cabbage Patch," humorous tale of a ragged optimist, one of the first and most popular of its kind).

Rice, Elmer (b. 1892). Amer. dramatist (" Street Scene," " The Adding Machine," " Judgement Day ").

Rice, James (1843–82). Eng. novelist; wrote many successful novels in collaboration with Sir Walter Besant.

Rice. A cereal, **2774**, 745 ; crops in Burma, 625 ; Ceylon, *79* ; China, 807, 809 ; cultivation, 79, *2775* ; food value in, 1336 ; introduced into Europe, 937 ; Japan, 2774, 1797 ; in Malay Peninsula, 2069 ; production in Philippines, *2568, 2569* ; in Sumatra, 3117 ; in Siam, 2964.

Rice-bird or **Bobolink.** Found in N. Amer. during summer months ; noted for its beautiful song.

Rice-paper, a delicate paper made from the pith of a Formosan shrub, *Fatsia papyrifera.*

" Riceyman Steps," by Arnold Bennett, 414.

Rich, Alfred William (1856–1922). Eng. water-colour painter, known esp. for views of Sussex and N. counties of Eng. ; ptgs. in Brit. Mus., V. & A., Tate, and other galleries.

Richard I, the Lion-Hearted (1157–99). King of England, **2776** ; conspires against Henry II, 1833 ; leads 3rd Crusade, 936, *plate f. 937* ; and Philip Augustus of France, 2567 ; and Saladin, 2864 ; sells claim to Scotland, 2892.

Richard II (1367–1400). King of England, **2777**, 1611 ; Wat Tyler's rebellion, *1197*, 3269.

Richard III (1452–85). King of England, **2777** ; at Bosworth, 530 ; in Wars of Roses, 2828.

Richard of York. *See* York, Richard, Duke of.

Richards, Gordon (b. 1904). English jockey, champion from 1925 (except in 1926, 1930, 1947). He rode his 4,000th winner at Chester in May 1950

Richardson, Henry Handel, pen-name of Henrietta Richardson (d. 1946). Australian novelist, 315.

Richardson, John. Canadian novelist, 684.

Richardson, Sir Owen Willans (b. 1879). Eng. physicist ; professor of physics at Princeton University (1906–14) ; at King's College, London, after 1914 ; Nobel prize in physics 1928 (" Electron Theory of Matter" ; "The Emission of Electricity from Hot Bodies ").

Richardson, Sir Ralph D. (b. 1902). Brit. actor, joint director of Old Vic. Co. at New Theatre ; Shakespearian parts ; Peer Gynt ; Uncle Vanya ; knighted 1947.

Richardson, Samuel (1689–1761). Eng. novelist ; made first literary effort when fifty years of age ; introduced entirely new style (" Pamela " ; " Clarissa " ; " History of Sir Charles Grandison ") ; 2402.

Richardson, Thomas (1870–1912). Eng. cricketer ; played for Surrey and England ; famous fast bowler.

Richelieu (rēsh′-lyê), **Cardinal** (1585–1642). Fr. churchman and statesman, **2778** ; portrait by de Champaigne. *1369* ; founded French Academy, 17 ; Louis XIII supports, 2028 ; in Thirty Years' War, 3202.

Richelieu work, in embroidery, 1154.

Richepin (rēsh-pan′), **Jean** (1849–1926). French poet, dramatist, and novelist ; vigorous, outspoken style (" Les Caresses," " Les Blasphèmes," verse ; " Grandes amoureuses," " Flamboche," novels ; " Nana Sahib," " Le Chemineau," " Don Quichotte," plays.

Richmond, Duke of. *See* **Henry VII,** Eng.

Richmond, George (1809–1896). Eng. painter, son of an artist ; worked chiefly as a portrait painter and excelled in pastel and water-colour ; well represented in Nat. Portrait Gallery.

Richmond, Sir William Blake (1843–1921). Eng. painter of portraits and historical pictures ; an adherent of the pre-Raphaelite school, he was responsible for much of the interior decoration of St. Paul's Cathedral.

Richmond, Eng. Residential borough in Surrey, 9 m. S.W. of London, situated on the R. Thames ; Chaucer, Bacon, Pope and other eminent men lived in the town ; here are the gateway of Richmond Palace, where Queen Elizabeth died, and Richmond Park ; pop. 40,000 ; 3123.

Richmond, Eng. Tn. in N. Riding of Yorkshire, on the R. Swale ; ruins of famous castle built about 1071 ; pop. 4,770.

Richmond, Virginia, U.S.A. State cap., pop. 193,900, *3326*.

Richmond Park, Surrey. Area 2,358 acres ; includes White Lodge, where the Duke of Windsor was born ; famed for its red and fallow deer ; created by Charles I.

Richter (rikh′-ter), **Hans** (1843–1916). Austrian musical conductor, born Hungary ; conducted in Vienna, Bayreuth, London, and other cities ; authority on Wagner.

Richter, Johann Paul Friedrich (1763–1825). Ger. novelist and humorist ; commonly called " Jean Paul " ; 2404 ; chief works " Quintus Fixlein," " Flegeljahre " (" Wild Oats ") ; 1457.

Richthofen (rikht′-hō-fen), **Manfred, Baron von** (1892–1918). Ger. airman ; famous for his aerial victories in 1st World War (80 in all) when leading the Richthofen " circus."

Rick, building, *84*.

Rickets. Disease in childhood, due to vitamin deficiency ; bones remain soft, producing deformities, 2977, 3327.

Ricketts, Charles (1866–1931). English painter, designer and printer ; born Geneva, Switzerland ; edited " The Dial " (1889–97) ; designed types used by his private (Vale) press (1896–1904) ; famed for his theatrical designs.

Rick′shaw. Same as Jinriksha.

Riddarholm, Church, Stockholm, 3093.

Rideau (rē-dō) **Canal,** Canada, 2458.

Rideau Lake, Ontario. At summit level of Rideau Canal ; 21 m. long.

Rideau River, Ontario. Stream flowing N. to Ottawa r., 2458.

Ridge, William Pett (1860–1930). Popular Eng. humorous author, many of whose stories deal with the poor classes of London (" Mord Em'ly " ; " A Son of State " ; " Telling Stories " ; " 'Erb " ; " Thanks to Sanderson " ; " The Bustling Hours " ; " The Amazing Years " ; " Richard Triumphant ").

Ridge. In photography, 2597.

Riding, or horsemanship, **2779**.

Riding Mountain, a natural park in Manitoba, Can., 2089.

Ridings, of Yorkshire, 3435.

Ridley, Nicholas (*c.* 1500–55). Eng. Protestant reformer and martyr.

Bishop of Rochester ; burned for heresy.

Riebeeck, Johann van. Dutch colonizer, founded Cape Town, 697 ; at Table Bay, 3016 ; statue, *plate f. 3017.*

Riel (rē-ĕl'), **Louis** (1844–85). Canadian half breed, leader of Riel and Saskatchewan rebellions.

Rienzi (rē-ent'-sē), **Cola di** (*c.* 1313–54). Rom. revolutionist ; overthrew aristocracy and attempted to re-establish Rom. republic and world rule ; hero of Bulwer-Lytton's " Rienzi, The Last of the Roman Tribunes."

" **Rienzi.**" Opera by Wagner, 3331.

Rievaulx (riv'-erz) **Abbey**, Yorkshire, Eng., 3435.

Riffs. Berbers of the Riff Region of Morocco, 2231.

Rifles, firearms, 1283 ; automatic, 1283 ; how a modern army rifle works, *1284* ; variety and use, 2961.

Rifling, in artillery, 260 ; in firearms, 1283.

Rift Valley. Formation, 3302.

Riga (rē'-ga). Cap. of Latvian S.S.R. ; Baltic port of Dvina ; pop. 393,200 ; 2779.

Riga, Gulf of. Inlet of Baltic Sea between Latvia and Estonia, 100 by 60 m. ; receives Duna r. ; named after city 7 m. above.

Riga, Treaty of. Treaty between Russia and Poland signed March 18, 1921, by which Poland gained about 44,000 sq. m. with a population of 3,685,000.

Rigel. A fixed star, 3078 ; *chart, 3080.*

Rigging. Of sailing ships, *484, 2946, 2947, 2953, 2954, 2955, 2956.*

Riggs, Mrs. Kate Douglas. *See* **Wiggin, Kate Douglas.**

Right angle, 1435.

Rights, Bill of. *See* **Bill of Rights.**

Rights of Man, Declaration of (1791), 1394.

" **Rights of Man, The.**" By Thomas Paine, 2474.

Right whale, 3371, *3373.*

" **Rigoletto** " (rē-gō-let'-tō). Opera by Verdi, 2439, 3315.

" **Rigsthula.**" An Edda song, 2388, 2880.

" **Rig-Veda** " (rig-vă'-da). Hindu epic, 1713, 1714.

Riiser-Larsen, Hjalmar (b. 1890). Norwegian polar explorer, 2647.

Riksdag. Swedish Parliament, 3131.

Ri'ley, James Whitcomb (1853–1916). Amer. poet, noted for child and dialect poems.

Riley, William (1646–91), Eng. painter, 1178.

Rilke, Rainer Maria (1875–1926). Poet, Czech by birth, who wrote in German ; " Note-book of Malte Laurids Brigge " (prose account of terrors of his childhood), " Duino Elegies," " Sonnets to Orpheus."

Rimbaud (ram-bō), **Jean N. A.** (1854–91). Fr. poet ; friend of Verlaine ; his influence gave rise to the Symbolist movement ; wrote most of his poetry before he was 20 ; " Le Bateau Ivre," " Les Illuminations."

Rimini (rē'-mē-nē), **Francesca da.** *See* **Francesca da Rimini.**

Rimini, It. Historic tn. on Adriatic Sea, 65 m. s.E. of Bologna ; pop. (est.) 60,000 ; bathing resort, fisheries ; anc. Ariminum. During 2nd World War it was E. bastion of German Gothic line, and in 1944 scene of bitter fighting ; taken by Allies Sept. 21.

Rimsky-Korsakov (rim'-ski-kor'-sah-kof), **Nicholas Andreievich** (1844–1908). Russian composer of symphonies and other orchestral pieces ; chief works, " Le Coq d'Or " (opera), " Scheherezade."

Rin'derpest. An infectious disease, believed to be caused by bacteria, affecting cattle, sheep, goats, etc.

Rine'hart, Mary Roberts (b. 1876). Amer. novelist and playwright ; especially successful in detective and mystery stories (" The Bat ").

" **Ring and the Book.**" Poem by Browning, 590.

" **Ring der Nibelungen.**" A series of music dramas by Wagner based on the Nibelung legends, 2439.

Ring dove. *See* **Wood pigeon.**

Ringed plo'ver, 2629, *443.*

Ringed snake. *See* **Grass-snake.**

Ringed worms or **annelids.** Worms with round, segmented bodies, 3623 ; include earthworms, 1071.

Ringhals. Spitting cobra, 859.

Rings, annual. In tree trunks, *3245.*

Rings of Saturn, 2618.

Ringstrasse. Street in Vienna, 3322.

Ring-tailed lemur, *1922.*

Rink. For curling, 944 ; ice hockey, *1684.*

Riobamba or **Bolivar.** Historic city of Ecuador ; Inca palace remains ; cath. ; pop. 19,500.

Rio de Janeiro (rē-ō' dă zha-nă'-rō). Cap. of Brazil and 2nd largest city of S. Amer. ; pop. 2,000,000 ; **2779,** *2780* ; 554, 3022.

Rio de Janeiro. State, Brazil ; produces coffee, rice, sugar, etc. ; a. 26,627 sq. m. ; pop. 2,070,660 ; cap. Nictheroy ; 551.

Rio de la Plata. *See* **Plata River.**

Rio de Oro. Sp. colony on w. coast of Africa s. of Morocco ; a. with Adrar 109,200 sq. m. ; European pop. 840 ; arid sandy plateau ; 2861, *map f. 68.*

Rio Grande. R. of N. Amer. forming part of boundary between U.S.A. and Mexico ; 2,000 m. from source in Colorado to Gulf of Mexico ; boundary between U.S. and Mexico, 2156 ; length, 3287.

Riom (rē-awn). Tn. of Fr., in Puy-de-Dôme dept., 8 m. N. of Clermont-Ferrand ; tobacco, linen mfrs. ; corn, wine trade ; pop. 12,975 ; here, Feb. 1942, Vichy Fr. staged a trial of soldiers and politicians of time of fall of France (Daladier, Blum, Gamelin, Reynaud, and others) in Nazi-instigated attempt to fix responsibility for 2nd World War on France ; evidence produced showed the guilt to be German, and trials " suspended."

Rio Muni or **Spanish Guinea.** Sp. colony in W. equatorial Africa on E. coast of Gulf of Guinea ; 10,036 sq. m. ; pop. 139,000 ; chief tn. Bata ; cap. Sta. Isabel on Fernando Po Isl., 3368.

Rio Negro. One of chief tributaries of Amazon ; rises in Colombia, flows E. 1,000 m. through N. Brazil ; *map, 551.*

Rio Negro. River in cent. Argentina flowing E. 700 m. from Andes in Chile to Atlantic, 226, *map, 227.*

Rio Negro. R. in cent. Uruguay flowing w. 300 m. to Uruguay r., 3299.

Rip cord, of parachute, 2509.

Ripon. City in West Riding of Yorkshire ; pop. 9,200 ; *2780* ; cathedral, *2781.*

Ripsimé, Saint. Early Christian martyr put to death, according to tradition, A.D. 301, 237.

" **Rip van Winkle.**" Washington Irving's story of a lovable good-for-nothing, who, while hunting in the Catskill Mts., drinks liquor offered him by Hendrik Hudson's legendary crew, falls asleep, and wakes 20 years after ; 1759 ; dramatized version made famous by Joseph Jefferson.

Ristori, Adelaide (1822–1906). It. tragic actress, rival of Rachel (" Mary Stuart " ; " Medea " ; " Queen Elizabeth ").

Rit'ter, Karl (1779–1859). Ger. geographer, founder of comparative geography.

Ritty, J. Inventor of cash register, 712.

Riukiu Islands (or **Ryukyu**). *See* **Nansei** ; **Okinawa.**

" **Rivals, The.**" By Sheridan, 2944.

Rivera, Miguel Primo de. *See* **Primo de Rivera.**

River-hog. Pig of genus *Potamochoerus* found in the swampy forests of W. Africa ; is responsible for much damage to plantations.

Rivers. Of Africa, 68, 1095, 2370 ; Asia, 263, 265 ; Australia, 307 ;

bores, 525, 3210 ; canyons, 1498 ; dredging and dredgers, 1047 ; Europe, 1232 ; geological action, 2597, 2598 ; N. Amer., *2193,* 2379, 2425 ; rate of discharge into ocean, 2413 ; S. Amer., 3022 ; subterranean, *733* ; valleys, 3302. *See also* Alluvial Soil ; Dam ; Delta ; and chief rivers by name.

WORLD'S LONGEST RIVERS.

Name	Continent	Length in m.
Missouri-Mississippi	N. Amer	3,988
Nile	Africa	3,500
Yangtze	Asia	3,400
Amazon	S. Amer.	3,350
Congo	Africa	3,000
Yenisei	Asia	3,000
Amur	Asia	2,920
Lena	Asia	2,860
Hwang-ho	Asia	2,600
Mekong	Asia	2,600
Niger	Africa	2,500
Mackenzie	N. Amer.	2,500
Ob	Asia	2,500
Volga	Europe	2,500

Riveting, pneumatic, 2632 ; in ship-building, 2952 ; welding replaces, 3362.

Riviera (ri-vē-ă'-ra). Picturesque dist. bordering Mediterranean coast between Nice, France, and Spezia, Italy ; favourite winter resort ; 2364 ; French, *1364* ; perfume farms, 2549 ; Monte Carlo, *2219.*

Riviere (rē-vyăr'), **Briton** (1840–1920). Eng. painter ; portrayed animals in their relation to mankind ; " Daniel in the Lions' Den," *968* ; " Androcles and the Lion," *1960* ; " Circe and the Swine," *834.*

Rivoli (rē'-vō-lē). Vil. in N. Italy 75 m. w. of Venice, noted for Napoleon's victory over Austrians in 1797.

Riyadh. Cap. of Nejd, Arabia, 196.

Riza Khan Pahlevi (1877–1944). Shah of Iran (Persia) 1926–41 ; *1742.*

Rizzio (rēt'-sē-ō) or **Riccio, David** (*c.* 1533–66). Ital. musician and secretary of Mary Queen of Scots, 2115, 2116 ; place of assassination, 1087.

" **R.L.S.**" *See* **Stevenson, Robert Louis.**

Roach. Fish of the carp family, 2781.

Road races. Events for cars, motorcycles or cycles, run on normal roads as opposed to specially banked tracks. Many road courses (*e.g.* Donington Park, Leics.) are built to re-produce road conditions in a confined space, esp. in Eng. where all racing on normal (public) roads is illegal.

Road Safety, 2787, 2788 ; *plate f. 2785.*

Roads and Streets, 2782, **2783** ; *plate f. 2784* ; Alpine, 127, *128* ; asphalt, 272, *273,* 2784 ; concrete, 883, *plate f. 2784* ; crushed stone, 2713 ; It. autostrade, 1772, 2804 ; macadam, 2045, 2783 ; under Ministry of Transport, 3238 ; road making, 883 ; Roman, *plate f. 2784,* 2799 ; rule of the road, 2787 ; and development of wheel, 3375.

Road signs, 2788, *plate f. 2785.*

Roanne (rō-an'), Fr. Mfg. and rly. centre 40 m. N.W. of Lyons ; pop. 44,500 ; head of navigation on R. Loire.

Roanoke (rō'-a-nōk), Virginia, U.S.A. Industrial city in s.w. on Roanoke r. ; pop. 69,300.

Roanoke Island. Isl. 10 by 2 m., off coast of N. Carolina, U.S.A. ; unsuccessful colony founded by Raleigh (1585–87).

Roaring Forties. Region between 40th and 50th parallels in S. Atlantic Ocean ; characterised by strong westerly winds ; 3385.

Roasting. Cookery process, 900.

Robarts, Emma. Founded Y.W.C.A.

Robb, Air Marshal Sir J. M., Brit. airman ; A.O.C. No. 2 Bomber Group 1940 ; A.O.C. N.W. Africa 1943–44 ; dep. Chief of Staff (air) at S.H.A.E.F. in 1944–45 ; A.O.C.-in-C. R.A.F. Fighter Command 1945–47 ; C.-in-C. Air forces, Western Europe, in perm. milit. organization of Western Union,

Robber Crab, a tree-climbing species, 924, *plate f. 924.*

Robber-fly. Large fly of the family *Asilidae,* seen in dry, heathy places; orange and blue, pointed body, brownish-tinged wings; a predaceous, useful insect.

" Robbers, The," by Schiller, 2882.

Robbia, della. *See* **Della Robbia.**

Robert I (c. 865–923). King of Fr., son of Robert the Strong and younger brother of Odo; permitted Charles III to succeed his brother, but revolted 921 and was crowned king 922; his grandson was Hugh Capet.

Robert I, the Bruce. King of Scot. *See* **Bruce.**

Robert II (1316–90). King of Scot. grandson of Robert Bruce; founds Stuart line, 3104.

Robert III (c. 1340–1406). King of Scot.; came to the throne in 1390; a weak ruler, his reign was an unhappy one, and he died broken hearted.

Robert I, the Devil (d. 1035). Duke of Normandy. Father of William the Conqueror; his great strength and ferocity subject of medieval legends; aided Edward the Confessor in exile.

Robert II, Duke of Normandy (c. 1054–1134). Son of William I, succeeded to Normandy, 3379; claims Eng. throne, 1609; leads First Crusade, 936.

Robert Guiscard (gēs-kahr) (" the resourceful ") (1015–85). Norman soldier of fortune; began conquest of Sicily from the Saracens (completed by his brother Roger I and consolidated by his nephew Roger II), becoming Duke of Apulia and Calabria; aids Pope against Henry IV, 2388.

Robert of Molesme, St. (d. 1108). Founder of Cistercians, 2213.

Robert the Strong (d. 866). Count of Anjou and Blois; at first rebelled against Charles the Bald, but later earned his surname and won king's confidence by defence of the Seine and Loire valleys; his two sons, Odo and Robert I, became kings of France.

Robert-Fleury, Joseph Nicolas (1797–1890). Fr. historical painter of vigorous talents (" Scene of St. Bartholomew "; " Triumphal Entry of Clovis at Tours "; " Children of Louis XVI in the Temple ").

Robert-Fleury, Tony (1837–1911). Fr. painter, taught many of the best-known painters of 19th cent.; like his father, Joseph, excelled in historical paintings.

Roberts, Bartholomew (d. 1722). Famous pirate, 2612.

Roberts, Sir Charles George Douglas (1860–1943). Canadian poet and author of animal stories, 685.

Roberts of Kandahar, Frederick Sleigh Roberts, Earl (1832–1914). Brit. soldier, **2789**; in Boer War, 487; and 2nd Afghan War, 56.

Roberts, William (b. 1895). Eng. artist, painter of lower class life, 1184.

Robertson, Gen. Sir Brian Hubert (b. 1896). Brit. soldier. United Kingdom High Commissioner in Germany (1947–1950).

Robertson, John Mackinnon (1856–1933). Brit. author; M.P. for Tyneside 1906; parl. sec. to Board of Trade 1911–15; wrote much on economic questions and free thought; also " Modern Humanists," " The Shakespeare Canon," etc.

Robertson, William (1721–93). Scot. historian; his " History of Scotland" and " Reign of Charles V " set new standard in historical writing and research.

Robertson, Sir William Robert (1860–1933). Brit. field-marshal who rose from the ranks; in 1915 was Gen. French's chief of staff; Dec. 1915 to Feb. 1918 chief of imperial general staff; commander-in-chief of Brit. Army on the Rhine (1919–20); Field-Marshal (1920).

Robeson, Paul (b. 1898). Negro stage and film actor and singer; won fame in " Emperor Jones," as Othello, and

in " Show Boat "; interpreter of Negro spirituals.

Robespierre (rōbs-pyär), **Maximilien** (1758–94). Fr. Rev. leader, **2789**, 1396; and Danton, 972; leads Jacobins, 1790; and Mme. Roland, 2797.

Robey, George (b. 1869). Eng. comedian famous on music-hall stage and in revue as the " Prime Minister of Mirth "; later appeared in films; real name George Edward Wade.

Rob'in, 2790; egg, *plate f. 440*; food required, 439; hatching period, 444; nest and eggs, 2790.

Robin Goodfellow, or **Puck, 2169.**

Robin Hood. Famous English outlaw, **2790**; story, " Robin Hood and His Merry Men," 3469.

Robin Hood's Bay. Seaside resort in N. Riding of Yorkshire, 7 m. S.E. of Whitby.

Robinson, Edwin Arlington (1869–1935). Amer. poet, 3296.

Robinson, Henry Crabb (1775–1867). Eng. journalist and diarist; friend of Lamb, Wordsworth, Coleridge, and Southey (" Diary "; " Reminiscences "; " Correspondence ").

Robinson, James Harvey (1863–1936). Amer. historian and educator; a pioneer in teaching the " new history " which draws on anthropology, sociology, and natural science, as well as on war and politics (" The Mind in the Making ").

Robinson, John (c. 1575–1625). Eng., nonconformist, pastor of Leiden congregation of Pilgrim Fathers, organized Mayflower colony, but died at Leiden, 2122.

" Robinson Crusoe." Novel by Defoe, 937, *939*, 240; basis in fact, 937, 986.

Robles (rōb'-les), **(José Maria) Gil.** Span. politician; Catholic right-wing leader of C.E.D.A. (Spanish Confederation of Autonomous Rights) and the " Accion Popular," 3038.

Robot (rō'-bot). Term derived from Czechoslovak word meaning "work." Came into common use in England after the production of Karel Capek's play " R.U.R." (Rossum's Universal Robots) in 1923; applied to various kinds of mechanisms which perform work previously performed by manual labour. *See* **Automatic Control; Electronic devices; Photo-electric devices.**

Rob Roy (Robert MacGregor or Campbell) (1671–1734). Celebrated Scottish outlaw, **2791**; not to be confused with John MacGregor, also called Rob Roy, who invented the canoe. *See* **MacGregor, John.**

Rob Roy canoe, 486.

Robsart, Amy (c. 1532–60). The wife of Robert Dudley, afterwards Earl of Leicester, who was suspected of having caused her sudden death in order that he might be free to marry Queen Elizabeth; story told in Scott's " Kenilworth."

Robson, Mt., British Columbia. One of highest peaks of Canadian Rocky Mts. (12,972 ft.).

Roc (rok). A monster bird in Arabic legend, said to have its home in Madagascar; so large that it could carry off elephants, and Sinbad the Sailor tells of an egg which was " 50 paces in circumference."

Roca, Julio Argentino (1843–1914). Argentine soldier and statesman, rose to general in war with Paraguay (1865–70); suppressed rebellion (1880) and elected president (1880–90), again (1898–1904); greatly strengthened national administration and patriotic spirit.

Rochambeau (rō-shahn-bō), **Jean Baptist Donatien de Vimeur, Count de** (1725–1807). Fr. soldier, served in Bavaria, Bohemia and on the Rhine, later fought against the English under Washington; finally commanded Northern Army in French Revolution.

Rochdale. Mfg. tn. in Lancashire, 10 m. N.E. of Manchester; pop. 91,600; cotton and woollen goods; " Rochdale Pioneers," first Eng. co-operative society founded in 1844;

birthplace of John Bright and Gracie Fields.

Roche, Mazo de la (b. 1885). Canadian novelist (" Whiteoaks " series), 685.

Rochefort (rōsh'-for), **(Victor) Henri, Marquis de Rochefort-Luçay** (1830–1913). Fr. journalist and politician, bitter opponent of Napoleon III. supporter of the Commune, several times exiled and imprisoned for his fearless attacks on persons and projects he believed wrong.

Rochefort, Fr. Fortified naval harbour 75 m. N. of Bordeaux near mouth of R. Charente; pop. 25,000; near by Napoleon surrendered to British in 1815.

Rochefoucauld, François de la. *See in Index* **La Rochefoucauld.**

Rochelle (rō-shel'), **La,** Fr. *See* **La Rochelle.**

Rochelle salt (sodium-potassium tartrate). An ingredient of Seidlitz powders, 3155; in piezo-electricity, 2605.

Roch'ester. Spt. in Kent adjoining Chatham and Strood; pop. 41,000; **2791**, 1852; castle, 718.

Rochester, New York, U.S.A., mfg. city in w. of state; pop. 325,000; univ. and various industries, including machinery, flour, boot and shoe, and camera mfrs.; 2357.

Rock, classification of, 1432, *plate f. 1432*; 2795.

Rock-climbing, 2247, *2248.*

Rock-cress, hairy, 3354.

Rock crystal, 2713.

Rock-dove. Ancestor of domesticated pigeons and doves, 2606.

Rock'efeller, John Davison (1839–1937), Amer. capitalist, founder of Standard Oil Company, **2791**; his son, John D. (Jr.), born 1874, was a noted philanthropist.

Rockefeller, William (1841–1922), Amer. capitalist, 2791.

Rockefeller Foundation, 2791.

Rockefeller Medical Institute, 2791.

Rockefeller Range. Mts. in the Antarctic, 2647.

" Rocket," Stephenson's locomotive, 1981, *1990,* 2736, 3088.

Rocket. Firework, 1291; principle, 2793; jet propulsion, 1826.

Rocket-bomb, Ger. weapon of 2nd World War (V2), **2791**, *2792,* 3422; on Antwerp, 182; post-war experiments, 2793; reached stratosphere, 3102; venturi in, 3312.

Rockets in warfare, 2793; as artillery, *258*; fired by tanks, 3152.

Rockford, Illinois, U.S.A., mfg. city 75 m. w. of Chicago on Rock r.; pop. 84,600; Rockford College.

Rockhampton. Port in Queensland, on Fitzroy r. near E. coast; pop. 34,000; trade in gold, meat.

Rockingham, Charles Watson-Wentworth, 2nd Marquess of (1730–82). Eng. statesman; as prime minister 1765–66 tried to conciliate Amer. colonies by repealing Stamp Act; again prime minister for 3 months in 1782; and Burke, *622.*

Rock-melon, a cantalupe, 2137.

Rock oil or **petroleum,** 2426, 2564.

Rock pipit, 2611.

Rocks. Three main classes, **2795.**

Rock salmon, name given in fishmongering to a variety of poorer quality fish, esp. those used for " fish and chip " trade, and including catfish, 729, and dogfish, 2939.

Rock-salt, 2866; in Carpathian Mts., 704.

Rocky Mountain goat, an antelope, 176.

Rocky Mountain Park, in Colorado, U.S.A., 50 m. N.W. of Denver; 359 sq. m.; has many high peaks.

Rocky Mountains. Chain of ranges extending along E. side of N. Amer. Cordilleras from Mex. to Alaska, **2795**; in Canada, 102, 578, 676, early explorers, 2050; Gates of, 2194; Grand Canyon, 1498, *plate f. 1496*; in Mexico, 2156; Mount Rainier, *3287*; shale oil reserves, 2430; in U.S.A., 3285.

Rococo (rō-kō'-kō), in architecture, a florid debased kind of ornament which succeeded the style adopted by Louis XIV and XV and which exaggerated the main features and peculiarities of that fashion; sometimes a term employed to denote bad taste in design and ornament generally; 220.

Rocroi (rō-krwah), Fr. Tn. near Belgian frontier, 50 m. N. of Reims; great Fr. victory over Sp. 1643 in Thirty Years' War.

Roc'ta. A stringed musical instrument used in the 13th cent.; resembled modern violin.

Rod, pole, or perch, a unit of measure. *See in Index* **Weights and Measures.**

Ro'dents. The order of gnawing animals, **2795,** 2077, 3629; evolutionary position, 158; kept down by hawks and owls, 439; structure of gnawing teeth, 387. The sub-order *Duplicidentata* which hares and rabbits is by some modern authorities made into a separate order, called *Lagomorpha.*

Rodeo (rō-dā'-ō). Sp.-Amer. term for the driving together of cattle for branding, counting, etc.; a roundup; also the enclosure into which they are driven.

Rodin, (rō-dan'), (François) **Auguste** (1840–1917). Fr. sculptor, **2795,** *2796, 2797*; influence, 2906.

Ro'ding, Eng., r. in Essex, trib. of the Thames; length 34 m.; 1225.

Rodney, H.M.S. Brit. battleship (33,900 tons), launched in 1925; sister-ship of the Nelson. Mined after D-day; at Rosyth to be scrapped, 1947.

Rodney, George Brydges, 1st Baron (1719–92). Brit. admiral; somewhat vain and boastful, but a skilful seaman, he was the victor of many naval encounters; he defeated the Sp. off Finisterre and St. Vincent and relieved Gibraltar in 1780 and then set off for the W. Indies, where he won a great victory over the Fr. off St. Lucia in 1782, for which he received a peerage and a pension of £2,000 a year.

Rodo, José Enrique. Uruguayan essayist, 3027.

Rodrigues (rō-drē'-ges). Isl. in Indian Ocean; dependency of Brit. Mauritius; 42 sq. m.; pop. 11,900; Mathurin is the principal tn. and port.

Roe. Fish eggs used as food, 1095; of sturgeon, 3104.

Roe, A. V. *See* **Verdon-Roe, Sir Alliott.**

Roe, Sir Thomas (c. 1581–1644). Ambassador to India, *1715.*

Roebuck, or **roe-deer.** A small deer (*Capreolus caprea*) of Europe and W. Asia.

Roedean School. Famous Eng. girls' school, near Brighton, in Sussex.

Roemer (rĕ'-mer) or **Römer, Ole** (1644–1710). Danish astronomer; measures speed of light; 1939.

Roeskilde (rĕs-kil-de) or **Roskilde,** Denmark. Old tn. 16 m. w. of Copenhagen on Zealand Isl.; cap. until 1443; cath. with tombs of early Danish kings.

Roger de Coverley, dance, 967.

Roger de Coverley papers, 1213.

Rogers, John (c. 1500–55). Eng. martyr, burned at stake for preaching against Catholicism, 426.

Rogers, Samuel (1763–1855). Eng. banker, poet, art patron; published at his own expense several volumes of poems which, if not brilliant, showed care and taste ("Italy"; "Poems"; "Pleasures of Memory"); declined laureateship after death of Wordsworth.

Rogers, Capt. Woodes. Eng. navigator; and Alexander Selkirk, 938.

Roget, Peter Mark (1779–1869). English scientist and philologist of Huguenot descent; discovered phenomenon of persistence of vision, on which cinema is based; helped to establish Univ. of London, and published the famous "Thesaurus of English Words and Phrases."

Rog'geveen, Admiral Jacob. Dutch explorer, 1075, 2472.

Rogue elephant, 1141.

Rohan (rō-ahn'), **Henri, Duke of** (1579–1638). Fr. Huguenot general, leader

of Prot. party after death of Henry IV; secured confirmation (1623) of Edict of Nantes.

Rohan, Louis René, Prince de (1734–1803). Fr. cardinal, ambassador to Austria (1772–74) and grand almoner of Fr.; imprisoned 1785–86 for his connexion with the Diamond Necklace Affair.

Rohlfs, Friedrich Gerhard (1831–96). Ger. explorer; travelled in Morocco in guise of Mahomedan; explored Sahara, visiting many regions unknown to Europeans ("Travels in Morocco"; "Across Africa").

Rokossov'sky, Konstantin (b. 1887). Russ. soldier; commander of Army of the Don, distinguished himself at Stalingrad (1942–43), 2852; led 1st, then 2nd White Russ. armies, in Poland and in conquest of E. Prussia 1944–45; marshal 1944; *2222.* In 1949 appted. Marshal of Poland, def. min. and chief of the Polish armed forces.

Ro'land. Hero of Charlemagne's army, celebrated in medieval song and verse, **2797.**

Roland, Jean Marie (1734–93). Fr. politician, 2798.

Roland, Madame (1754–93). Social leader in Fr. Rev. days, **2797,** *2798.*

Rolf. *See* **Rollo.**

Rolland (ro-lahn'), **Romain** (1866–1944). Fr. novelist and uncompromising idealist and anti-militarist; called (in vain) on Ger. authors to join him in opposing 1st World War ("Jean Christophe"; "Liluli"; "Colas Breugnon"; "Pierre and Luce"); was Nobel prize winner in 1915; 1382.

Rolled gold, 1481.

Roller. A bird of the crow family found chiefly in tropical countries, which tumbles like a tumbler pigeon; only one species in Europe.

Roller bandage. In first aid, 1291.

Roller-skating, 2977.

Rolling mill, in iron and steel manufacture, *1757, 1758.*

Rollo, Rolf, or **Rou** (c. 860–932). Norse conqueror of what became Fr. duchy of Normandy (911–912), 2376, 2388.

Rolls, Hon. Charles Stewart (1877–1910). Eng. motorist and aviator. Joint founder, with Henry Royce, of the firm of Rolls-Royce, Ltd. First Englishman to be killed while flying in an aeroplane (at a Bournemouth meeting), 46.

Rolls, bread, 554, 557.

Roll sulphur, 3116.

Romagna (rō-mah'-nya). Former prov. of Papal States, now divided into It. provs. of Bologna, Ferrara, Ravenna, and Forlì, 1763; joins united It., 1769.

Roma'ic. Modern Gk. dialect, 1541.

Romain, Jules. Same as **Giulio Romano.**

Romains (ro-man'), **Jules** (b. 1885). Pen-name of Louis Farigoule, French novelist and playwright. Principal works: "Dr. Knock" (play); "Men of Good Will" (series of novels).

Roman alphabet, 126.

Roman candles. Fireworks, 1291.

Roman Catholic Church (R.C.). Bible, 426; in Canada, 2714; confirmation in, 886; Easter and Holy Week, 1074; emancipation, 3278; in Fr., 1361, 2276; in Ger., 377, 1445; in Gt. Brit., Emancipation Bill, 2419, 2535; in Ire., 1744, 1745, 1746, 1748, 2419; monks and monasticism, 2212; music, 2261; Nicene creed, 817; papacy, 2495, 2562. *See also* **Papacy; Reformation; Vatican City;** and countries by name.

Romance, 2798, 3014; Arthurian legends, 255, 2830; burlesqued by Cervantes, 746; "Song of Roland," 2797. *See also* **Novel.**

Romance languages, 2798, 1894, 2570.

Roman Congregations. *See* **Congregations, Roman.**

Romanes (rō-mah'-nes), **George John** (1848–94). Brit. naturalist ("The Philosophy of Natural History before

and after Darwin"); founded Romanes Lecture at Oxford.

Romanesque (rō-man-esk') **architecture,** 216, 3040; Pisa cath., 2612.

Rumania. *See* **Rumania.**

Romania (rō-mah-nē'-a), **Cape.** Headland at S.E. extremity of Malay Peninsula, 263.

Roman law, 1902; jus gentium, 1904; Justinian codifies, 1844.

Roman numerals, 233, 2405.

Romano, Giulio. *See* **Giulio Romano.**

Romanov (ro-mah'-nof). Family name of Tsars of Russia from 1613 to downfall of the empire, 2365, 2847.

Romanov, Michael (1596–1645). Tsar of Russia; elected in 1613, 2847.

Romans, Epistle to. Book of the New Testament; letter written by Paul to the Christians at Rome; deals with justification by faith and relations of Jews and Christians.

Romansch (rō-mansh'). Dialect in Switzerland, since 1938 the 4th national language of that land, 3141.

Roman'ticism. In literature, the tendency to emphasize the imaginative, emotional, and natural, as opposed to the restraint and formality of classicism and the matter-of-fact attitude of realism; applied especially to movement in later 18th and early 19th cents.; in Eng. literature, 1214; in Fr. literature, 1381, 1650; in Ger. literature, 1457; in It. literature, 1787.

Roman Wall. *See* **Hadrian's Wall.**

Romany. The language of gipsies.

Rome (Ancient), 2799, *plate f. 2805*; agriculture, 80; aqueducts, 194, *2801, 2803, 2818, 3347*; Arch of Constantine, *2819*; army, 251; art, *see* **Rome: Painting and Sculpture**; bakeries, 554, *555*; and Bath, 373; baths, 2802, *plate f. 2805*; calendar, 661, *662*; Capitol, 2800; catacombs, 2802; cement, 740; census, 742; citizenship, 2805; coins, 2202; Colosseum, 2800, 2802, 2803; drama of, 1038; family names, 2272; festivals, 1018; food, 3112; Forum, 2799, 2800, *2801, 2802*; furniture in, 1409, *1410*; geographical knowledge, 1431; gladiators, 1038, 1469; houses, *2653, 2820*; lamps, *1887*; language and literature (*see* **Latin Language; Latin Literature**; libraries, 509, 510; life of people, 2653, 2654; lighthouses, *1943*; locks and keys, *1979*; money, 2202; numerals, 233; Pantheon, 2802; poor relief, 2811; Phoenicia, 2573; postal system, 2661; religion and myths, 3318; roads, 2783, *plate f. 2784,* 2799; St. Angelo Castle, 2803; and bridge, *565*; sewerage system, 2804; ships, 2946; slavery, 2805, 2811, 2981, 3053; theatres, 3194; R. Tiber, 3207; tools, instruments and utensils, *2809*; trade, 1298, 2485, 2970; water-clock, 843; water-supply, 3347; writing and writing materials, 509, 2496, 2539. For history *see* **Rome, History of.**

Rome (Modern). Cap. of It.; pop. 1,874,000; 2799; forum, *1774*; history, 1418, 1769, 2804; improvements, 2799, *2800*; St. Peter's, 2160, 2800, *2802*; Vatican, 2799, 2800, *2802*; Victor Emmanuel Mon., 2800, *plate f. 2804*; under Fascism, 2799, 2800, 2804; in 2nd World War, 453, 2804. *See also* **Vatican State and City.**

Rome, History of (to A.D. 476), 2804, 1237; chief events summarized, *see chart under* **History**; peoples of Italy, 1763; legendary period, 2821; influence of Etruscan culture, 1229; Gk. colonies, 1524. *The Republic* (509–27 B.C.), 2804; Cincinnatus dictator, 828; development of govt., 2805; conquest of It., 2805; war with Pyrrhus, 2807; Punic Wars, 711, 1573, 2808; siege of Syracuse, 211; conquest of Sp., 3033; conquest of Greece, 1524; Marius and Sulla, 2809; Spartacan rebellion, 3053; conquests in Asia, 1830, 2654; conquest of Gaul, 1365, 1447; Caesar and fall of the republic, 759–762, 2811; invasion of Brit., 572, 573, *574,* 1193; Catiline's conspiracy,

827. *The Empire*, 2811 ; rule of Augustus, 303 ; defeat in Ger., 1447 ; Brit. conquered, 373, 574, 1193, *2009* ; rule of Nero, 2315 ; destruction of Pompeii, 2653 ; empire reaches greatest extent, 2811, *map, 2808* ; Marcus Aurelius, 2099, *2100* ; decline of Empire, 2166, 2812 ; Rome and Palmyra, 2485 ; Constantine and the separation of East and West, 1237 ; Gothic invasions, 29, 96, *1238*, 1487 ; invasions of Huns, 1657 ; and the Scots, 2892 ; Vandals, 3304 ; and Vienna, 3323. For later Roman History *see* Byzantine Empire ; Italy ; Rome (Ancient).

Rome : painting and sculpture, 2812 ; enamels, 1158 ; influence of Etruscans, 1229 ; portrait sculpture, *2813, 2814, 2816*. *Architecture*, 213, 2799, 2800, 2801, 2802, 2803 ; *plates f. 2804, 2805 ; 2810, 2818, 2819, 2820* ; aqueduct of Nimes, *194* ; arch and dome, 214 ; mosaics, 2233. *See also* Rome (Ancient) ; Pompeii.

"Ro'meo and Juliet." Tragedy by Shakespeare, 2821, 2933, 2936.

Römer, Ole. *See* Roemer.

Romford. Tn. in Essex, 12 m. N.E. of London ; brewing, engineering ; pop. 72,500, 1225.

Rom'mel, F.-M. Erwin E. J. (1891–1944). Ger. soldier ; led Panzer div. in Fr. 1940 ; in Libya, successful against Brit. 8th army until defeated at Alamein, 250 ; 1452, 2377.

Rom'ney, George (1734–1802). Eng. portrait painter, chiefly famous for his portraits of Lady Hamilton, *2315*, who was also his model for a large number of other paintings ; excelled as a painter of women and children, 1180.

"Romola" (rom'-o-la). George Eliot's novel based on Savonarola's life ; Romola, the heroine, is the beautiful and noble-minded daughter of an aged Florentine scholar.

Romsey, tn. of Hants, Eng., on the R. Test ; pop. 6,500 ; famous Norman abbey, *214*.

Rom'ulus and Remus. Twin brothers, the former being the mythical founder of Rome, 2821, 2804.

Romulus Augustulus. Last Rom. emperor, 2812.

Ron'ald, Sir Landon (1873–1938). Eng. musician ; conductor of Royal Albert Hall Concerts, New Symphony Orchestra, etc. ; wrote a large number of popular ballads ; from 1910 to 1937, Principal of the Guildhall School of Music.

Roncesvalles (rŏn-thä-vah'-yäs). Vil. in N. Sp. near pass in W. Pyrenees where Charlemagne's rearguard was defeated and Roland slain, 2797.

Ronda. Tn. of Spain ; pop. 32,600 ; *plate f. 3033*

Rondebosch. Near Cape Town, Rhodes's house at, 698, *697, 3019*.

Ronsard (rawn-sahr), Pierre de (1524–85). Fr. "prince of poets" ; leader of the Pléiade, a group of writers who sought to remould Fr. language and poetry on classical lines, 1380.

Röntgen (rönt'-gen), Wilhelm Konrad (1845–1923). Ger. physicist ; Nobel prize winner in 1901 ; discovers X-rays, *3430*.

Röntgen rays. Same as X-rays.

Rood. *See in Index* Weights and Measures.

Roof, of buildings, 2821, 213, 216, 218, 610.

Roofing Tiles, 562.

"Roof of the World." The Pamir Plateau, 263.

Rook. Bird of the crow family, 2823, *451* ; harm to farming, 1079.

Rookery. Originally a breeding-place or colony of rooks, *451* ; also applied to those of penguins, 2544, and of seals, *2913*.

Roosevelt (rō'ze-velt), Franklin Delano (1882–1945). Amer. statesman elected President of U.S.A. in 1932, re-elected in 1936, 1940 and 1944 ; 2823, *2824*, 3292, 3293 ; and Atlantic Charter, 3283 ; in Second World War, 2824, 3416.

Roosevelt, Theodore (1858–1919), 26th President of U.S.A., 2824, *2825*.

3291 ; recognizes Panama, 2486 ; intervenes in Russo-Japanese War, 2825.

Roosevelt Dam, near Phoenix, Arizona, U.S.A., on the Salt River.

Root, Elihu (1845–1937). Amer. lawyer and statesman ; sec. of war (1899–1905) ; sec. of state (1905–09) ; U.S.A. senator from N.Y. (1909–15) ; member of various arbitration tribunals and commissions ; headed mission to Russia (1917) ; Washington limitation of armament conference (1921–22).

Root, of plants, 2825, *2623*, 1322 ; air plants, or epiphytes, 2447 ; barley, 361 ; chemotropism, 2623 ; clover taps the subsoil, 852 ; forerunners seen in algae, 112 ; function, *2621, 2622* ; lucerne or alfalfa, 2034 ; pressure, 2998 ; in water-plants, 3355.

Root, of tooth, *3164*.

Root crops. Those grown for their edible roots, 2825 ; beets, 396 ; first introduced in agriculture, 85.

Roots and powers, 2671 ; logarithms and, 1998 ; found by slide rule, 2984.

Rope, 2825, *2826, 2827* ; bridge of, *565* ; coir fibre, 864 ; hemp, 1608 ; jute, 1844 ; knots, hitches and splices, 1868 ; sisal fibre, 2975.

Roper, Margaret, 2229.

Rops (rŏps), Félicien (1833–98). Belgian illustrator and etcher, whose work, though sometimes too decadent and cynical to be pleasing, is almost unique in power of execution.

Roquefort (rŏk'-for) cheese, 766.

Rorke's Drift, Natal, S. Africa. On Tugela r., the scene of a gallant stand by a small Brit. force under Lieuts. Chard and Bromhead against some 4,000 Zulus, Jan. 22, 1879, following the Isandhlwana disaster ; the Zulus failed in their attack and withdrew.

Rorqual (ror'-kwal). A whale, 3372, *3373*.

Rosa, Carl (1842–89). Ger. operatic impresario, who came to Eng. and founded the Carl Rosa Opera Company, which familiarized the public of Gt. Britain with opera in English.

Rosa, Salvator (1615–73). It. painter, chief master of Neapolitan school, wild and romantic in life and art.

Rosa, Monte (15,217 ft.). Alpine peak, 3138.

Rosaceae (rō-zā'-si-ē). Rose family of plants, 2828, 3245 ; almond, 124 ; pear, 2532.

Rosales (rō-zā'-lēz). The rose order, including roses, "pitted" fruits, apples, and the bean family.

Ros'alind, in Shakespeare's "As You Like It," 282.

Rosamond, Fair. In Eng. legend, beloved of King Henry II, hidden away by him in a bower at heart of a labyrinth in Woodstock ; found by jealous Queen Eleanor and forced to drink poison.

Rosario (rō-sah'-rē-ō). The 2nd city of Argentina, rly. centre and port on Parana r., 214 m. above Buenos Aires ; est. pop. 518,500 ; large foreign trade.

Rosas (rō'-sahs), Juan Manuel (1793–1877). Argentine dictator (1835–52) ; cruel despot ; overthrown by combination of foreign and domestic enemies.

Roscoe, Sir Henry (1833–1915), Brit. chemist, prof. at Manchester univ. ; M.P. 1885–95 ; author of textbooks ; and spectrographic analysis, *plate f. 3057*.

Roscom'mon, Eire. Co. in Connaught, bounded on E. by the Shannon ; 951 sq. m. ; pop. 74,000 ; 2827.

Rose. Genus of flowering plants, 2827 ; blackberry a relation, 463 ; cultivation in Bulgaria, 612, *613* ; wax in petals, 3359.

Roseate tern, 1557.

Rose-bay, a willow-herb, *3382*.

Rose'bery, Archibald Philip Primrose, 5th Earl of (1847–1929). Eng. Liberal statesman, orator, and writer ; premier in 1894–95, and long thereafter a power in politics, though he held no office, 3279 ; wrote biographies of Pitt, Peel, Cromwell, Napoleon, and Lord Randolph Churchill ; won the Derby three times (in 1894, 1895, and 1905).

Rose-chafer. Beetle, *Cetonia aurata*, closely related to the cockchafer, bright bronze-green all over, often found in roses whose petals it eats. Larva lives in soil for several years. 399.

Rose diamond. Diamond cut with small facets, 1012.

Rose family. See Rosaceae.

Ro'senberg, Alfred (1893–1946). Russ.-born Ger. writer and politician; early Nazi; in newspaper Völkischer Beobachter, from 1921, and in many writings developed Nazi " philosophy," anti-Semitism, Teutonic mythology; head of Nazi press and foreign policy office; min. of Occupied E. Territories; hanged Oct. 1946 as war criminal, 2282.

" Rosenkavalier, Der," Richard Strauss's opera, 2440, *2441*, 3103.

Rose of Japan, the camellia, 671.

Rose of Jericho. Plant of Syria and N. Africa; after the fruits are formed it dries up, becomes detached from ground, the stems curve inward, and the plant is rolled by the wind like a ball to a moist place, where it opens again and discharges its seeds.

Rose of Sharon. Name given to an ornamental shrub (*Hibiscus syriacus*), and also to the Great St. John's Wort, *Hypericum calycinum*, popular in English gardens for its big, bright yellow flowers. Biblical rose of Sharon was probably a kind of narcissus.

Roses, attar of. See Attar of Roses.

Roses, War of the. Contest between rival houses of York and Lancaster for Eng. throne, 2828; battle of Wakefield, 3332; Edward IV, 1091; Henry VI and, 1611; Henry VII and Bosworth Field, 531, 3253; Richard III, 2777. See also Lancaster, House of; York, House of.

Rosetta (rō-zet'-*a*). Eg. tn. on Rosetta mouth of Nile r.; pop. 25,000; formerly of commercial importance; Rosetta Stone found near by; Nile r., 1098, 2371.

Rosetta Stone. The name given to an inscribed slab of stone discovered near Rosetta on the Nile in 1799; 2828, *1118*; Young's work on, 3436.

Rosewood. Hard, close-grained, fragrant wood of Brazilian tree of the pea family; prized in cabinet-making; in perfumes, 2549.

Rosicrucians (rō-zi-krōō'-sh*a*nz). Ger. society said to have been founded by a monk named Rosencreutz in the middle of the 15th cent.; it was supposed to be a secret society, whose members were said to possess the secrets of alchemy. A modern Rosicrucian Order, known as " The Ancient Mystical Order Rosae Crucis " throughout the world, is a non-sectarian fraternity; its h.q. is in San José, California, U.S.A.

Ros'in, 2767; in soap, 2994.

Rosinante (roz-i-nan'-te). Don Quixote's famous raw-boned steed, 746.

Ros'kilde, Denmark. See Roeskilde.

Rospigliosi. Noble Rom. family; Pope Clement IX is its most famous member.

Ross, Betsy (1752–1836). Traditional maker of first Amer. flag.

Ross, Sir James Clark (1800–62). Brit. admiral and polar explorer; nephew of another Brit. admiral and polar explorer, Sir John Ross; Antarctic explorations, 2645; he (*not* Capt. John Ross) reached North Magnetic Pole in 1831, 2644.

Ross, Sir John (1777–1856). Brit. admiral and Arctic explorer, uncle of Sir James Ross; he wrote an account of his 1829–33 expedition under the title, " Narrative of a Second Voyage in Search of a North-West Passage "; commanded an expedition in search of Sir John Franklin in 1850; 2644.

Ross, Martin. Pen-name of Violet F. Martine (d. 1915), Irish novelist who collaborated 1887 to 1915 with Edith O. Somerville (*q.v.* in *f-i.*).

Ross, Sir Ronald (1857–1932). Brit. physician, discoverer of life-history of malaria parasite in mosquitoes; Nobel prize for medicine (1902), 2236, 2648.

Ross and Cromarty, Scot. Co. on N.W. coast; a. 3,089 sq. m.; pop. 60,700; 2828.

Rossbach (rōs'-bahkh). Ger. vil. 25 m. w. of Leipzig; battle (1757), 2924.

Rossetti, Christina Georgina (1830–94). Sister of Dante Gabriel Rossetti; a lyric poet of distinction; excelled in religious and mystical verse (" Goblin Market "; " A Pageant ").

Rossetti, Dante Gabriel (1828–82). Eng. poet and painter; leading spirit of Pre-Raphaelite Brotherhood, 1182, 2232, 2681; " Dante's Dream," *1190*.

Ross Ice Cap or **Great Ice Barrier,** in Antarctic region, 173, 2645.

Rossini (rōs-sē'-nē), **Gioacchino Antonio** (1792–1868). It. operatic composer (" The Barber of Seville "; " William Tell "; " Stabat Mater "; music of ballet, " Boutique Fantasque ").

Rosslare, Co. Wexford, Eire; harbour for cross-Irish Sea traffic from Fishguard, 3371.

Ross Sea, in Antarctic region, 173; discovered by Sir James Ross, 2645; Amundsen's base, 2645.

Rostand (ros-tahn'), **Edmond** (1868–1918). Fr. dramatist; wrote " Cyrano de Bergerac " and " Chantecler," 1382.

Rostock, Ger. Largest city of Mecklenburg and one of chief Baltic ports; pop., including Warnemünde, 122,400; univ.; an old Hanse tn.; heavily bombed by R.A.F. in 2nd World War.

Rostov-on-Don. Commercial centre of Soviet Russia, 20 m. from Sea of Azov; pop. 520,700; grain, flour, iron, annual fair; scene of heavy fighting in 2nd World War, 1452, 3419, 3420.

Rosyth (rōs'-ith). Naval base and important dockyard in Fife, on Firth of Forth, Scot.; construction was begun in 1903 and was just about completed at the outbreak of the 1st World War, during which it was the headquarters of the cruiser squadron and a repairing base for the ships of the Grand Fleet; later breaking-up yards; in 2nd World War assembly port for 1940 expedition to Norway, and a fitting-out base.

Ro'tary International. Organization which seeks to found all business transactions on a basis of service, peace and good fellowship. First Rotary Club started in America in 1905. Motto is " Service Above Self."

Rotary printing press, *2345*, 2686.

Rotary pump, 2704.

Rotation of crops, 85, 2374.

Rothamsted. Pioneer agricultural experimental station, nr. Harpenden, Herts, founded 1843.

Rothenstein, Sir William (1872–1945). Eng. artist; known at first for his paintings and portrait drawings (many in Tate Gallery); head of the Royal Coll. of Art 1920–35; 1183. His son, John Rothenstein (b. 1901), a writer on art, became in 1938 keeper of the Tate Gallery.

Rother. Name of 3 rs. in Eng.; (1) flowing 21 m. through Derbyshire and Yorkshire, where it joins the Don; (2) flowing 31 m. through Sussex and Kent to the Eng. Channel; (3) a 24-m. trib. of the Arun, flowing through Hants and Sussex, 3123.

Rotherham. Mfg. tn. 6 m. N.E. of Sheffield at junction of r. Rother with R. Don; pop. 80,890; iron and steel products, glass, pottery.

Roth'erhithe Tunnel, London. Deep cutting 1 m. 440 yds. long, of which 1,530 ft. is beneath the Thames; opened in 1908, it connects Union Road, Rotherhithe, with Commercial Road, Stepney; 3257; also another from Rotherhithe to Wapping completed 1843, used as rly. tunnel. 3255.

Roth'ermere, Harold Harmsworth, 1st Viscount (1868–1940). Eng. newspaper proprietor, younger brother of Viscount Northcliffe; chief proprietor of " Daily Mail," " Evening News," " Sunday Dispatch," and " Sunday Pictorial "; director-general of Royal Army Clothing Dept.

1916; first Air Minister 1917; endowed chairs of Eng. Lit. and Naval Hist. at Cambridge and of American Hist. at Oxford.

Rothesay, co. tn. of Buteshire and holiday resort, on the Firth of Clyde, 627; pop. 9,346.

Rothschild (roths'-chïld). Great Jewish banking family of Ger. origin with unprecedented international influence; total fortunes estimated in 1915 as £400,000,000; 2829.

Rothschild, Mayer Anselm (1743–1812). Ger. merchant and money-lender, in whose charge the elector of Hesse Cassel, fleeing from Fr. Rev. armies, left his treasures and thus laid foundation of Rothschild fortune.

Rothschild, Nathan Mayer, Baron (1777–1836). Third son of first Rothschild; head of the firm's London branch and founder of its unique international greatness; staked all on Napoleon's overthrow and financed Brit. govt. in crisis of 1813.

Roti'fera. The microscopic " wheel animalcules," so called by reason of the peculiar wheel-like " cilia " used for locomotion; commonly found in ponds; there are some marine species.

Rotogravure. Picture printing process in which the impression is imparted by a rubber surface upon a cylinder.

Ro'tor, a rotating mechanism; in elec. clock, *1126*, *1127*; of helicopter, 1605; of induction motor, 2240.

Rot'te. Small r. of Holland, 2829.

Rotten boroughs, in Eng. politics, 2522.

Rotten Row. Track in Hyde Park, London, reserved for horse riders. Name said to be a corruption of " Route du Roi " (The King's Way).

Rot'terdam, Spt. of Holland; pop. 653,000; 2829, 2769; bomb devastation, 2829, 3417.

Rouault (rōō-ō), **Georges** (b. 1871). Fr. painter; apprenticed to painter of stained glass, with effect on the style and colour of his paintings, which show great power; of Expressionist school; book illustrations for " Danse Macabre," " Les Fleurs du Mal."

Roubaix (roo-bā). Fr. mfg. tn. in N. near Belgian border; pop. 101,000; woollen and linen goods, carpets.

Rouble (rōō'-bl). Rus. monetary unit formerly gold; it consists of 100 kopecks.

Rouen (roo-ahn'). Fr. mfg. and trading city on Seine, 75 m. N.W. of Paris; pop. 107,700; 2829, 2376, 2919; 1359, 1361, 1365; Joan of Arc imprisoned and burnt at, 1832; Seine dredged, 2919; in 2nd World War, 2830.

Rouget de Lisle, Claude. See Lisle, Rouget de.

Roughage, in diet, 1340; in farm diet, 732.

Roumania. See Rumania.

Round, Dorothy. See Little, Dorothy.

Rounders, baseball derived from, 367.

" Roundheads," nickname for Puritans, 755.

Round Table, in the Arthurian legends, 2830; King Arthur and, 255; at Winchester, 3383; Tales of, 2830. See also Arthurian legends.

Rousseau (roo-sō), **Jean-Jacques** (1712–78). Fr. philosopher, 2831, 1380; " Confessions," 430; " Emile," 1964; influence on Ger. literature, 1456; isl. at Geneva named after him, 1428.

Rousseau, Théodore (1812–67). Fr. painter, a leader of Barbizon school, *1374*.

Rove-beetle. Beetles of family *Staphylinidae.* See Devil's coach-horse.

Rover Scouts, 538.

Roving, cotton yarn, 920.

Rowallan, Thomas Godfrey Polson Corbett, 2nd Baron (b. 1895). Chief Scout from 1945.

Row'an tree. Another name for mountain ash, 262; whitebeam, 3376.

Rowe, Nicholas (1673–1718). Eng. poet, 2634.

Rowe'na. Heroine of Scott's " Ivanhoe," the ward of the Saxon Cedric, who desires her to marry his friend

Athelstane ; Rowena, however, falls in love with Cedric's son, Ivanhoe, whom she eventually marries.

Rowing, *483.* *See also* **Boat Race ; Diamond Sculls.**

Row'landson, Thomas (1756–1827). Eng. artist, whose work included landscapes, portraits, and humorous caricatures, **2832.**

Rowley Manuscripts, by Chatterton, 760.

Rowntree, Benjamin Seebohm (b. 1871). Brit. social worker ; director of family chocolate co. and chairman 1925–41 ; trustee of Nuffield Trust ; chm. of Nat. Inst. of Industr. Psychology ; "Poverty, a Study of Town Life," "How the Labourer Lives," "Human Factor in Business," "Poverty and Progress."

Roxburghshire. Border co. of S.E. Scot. ; a. 666 sq. m. ; pop. 45,200 ; **2832.**

Royal Academy of Arts, London. Founded in 1768 " for the purpose of cultivating and improving the arts of painting, sculpture, and architecture " ; Royal Academicians (R.A.) are elected by vote, subject to the approval of the King. The Academy occupies the greater part of Burlington House, Piccadilly, 17 ; an early meeting, *2477* ; Reynolds and, 1179, 2769.

Royal Academy of Music, York Gate, Marylebone Rd., London. Originally founded in 1822, exists for instructing pupils in music. Successful students may take Licentiate's, Associate's, or Fellow's diploma, (L.R.A.M., A.R.A.M., F.R.A.M.).

Royal Air Force (R.A.F.). Britain's third fighting service, **2832,** 245 ; ranks, 2833 ; slang, 2981.

Royal Air Force Regt., 2833, 245.

Royal Albert Hall. *See* **Albert Hall.**

Royal and Ancient Golf Club (R. & A.), St. Andrews, 1484.

Royal Armoured Corps. Formed 1939, amalgamating mechanized Regular cavalry regiments and the Royal Tank Corps, 246.

Royal Army Dental Corps, 248.

Royal Army Educational Corps, 248.

Royal Army Medical Corps (R.A.M.C.), 248 ; badge, *54.*

Royal Army Ordnance Corps (R.A.O.C.), 248.

Royal Army Pay Corps, 248.

Royal Army Service Corps (R.A.S.C.), 246.

Royal Army Veterinary Corps, 248.

Royal Artillery (R.A.), 245.

Royal Astronomical Society. Brit. society, founded in 1820. Sir William Herschel was the first pres. ; granted Royal Charter by William IV in 1831 ; h.q. at Burlington House, Piccadilly, London.

Royal Automobile Club (R.A.C.). Club founded in 1897 on behalf of the interests of the motorist.

Royal Botanic Gardens, Kew, *1853.*

Royal Canadian Mounted Police (R.C.M.P.), "the Mounties." Were formerly known as the Royal N.W. Mounted Police ; with h.q. at Ottawa, responsible for maintaining order, esp. in remote parts of the Dominion ; *2650.*

Royal College of Music, S. Kensington, London. Founded in 1882 ; incorporated by Royal Charter in 1883 ; present building erected in 1894. Successful students at the college may sit for the diploma, A.R.C.M.

Royal Corps of Military Police, 249.

Royal Corps of Signals, 246, *250.*

Royal Electrical and Mechanical Engineers (R.E.M.E.). 248.

Royal Empire Society (formerly Royal Colonial Institute), Northumberland Avenue, London ; founded in 1868.

Royal Engineers (R.E.), 246.

Royal Exchange. London building between Threadneedle Street and Cornhill ; third on the present site ; first, founded by Sir Thomas Gresham, opened in 1566 and destroyed by the Great Fire of 1666 ; second, opened 1669, burnt in 1838 ; present building opened in 1844.

Royal Family, 2833, *3283.*

Royal Flying Corps (R.F.C.), and R.A.F., **2832.**

Royal Humane Society. Founded in 1774 by Dr. William Hawes and Dr. Thomas Cogan for rendering first aid in cases of drowning ; awards medals and certificates to persons saving life ; h.q. York Bldgs., London, W.C.2.

Royal Institution of Great Britain. Scientific institution founded in 1799 and chartered in 1800 to further research and spread knowledge ; famous workers and lecturers, 980, 1260, 2842 ; Tyndall succeeds Faraday, 3270.

Royalists. In Eng. history, the partisans of Charles I and II ; also called Cavaliers ; 933.

Royal jelly, for queen-bee, 392.

Royal Marines (R.M.), function of, 2306.

Royal Marriage Act, 2833.

Royal Meteorological Society. Founded in London (1850) ; incorporated under Royal Charter (1866) ; promotes the study of the weather and regular recording of observations ; Fellows are elected by ballot (F.R.Met.Soc.).

Royal Military Academy (R.M.A.), Sandhurst, Berks ; formed 1947 by combining former R.M.A. at Woolwich with R.M.C., Sandhurst ; 251.

Royal Military College (R.M.C.), Sandhurst, became in 1947 part of Royal Military Academy, Sandhurst, 251.

Royal Mint, London. *See* **Mint.**

Royal National Lifeboat Institution (R.N.L.I.). Founded in 1824 ; has splendid record of life-saving ; dependent upon voluntary contributions, 1935.

Royal Naval Air Service (R.N.A.S.), and R.A.F., 2832.

Royal Naval College, Dartmouth, founded in 1905 ; cadets trained for officership in Royal Navy ; 2306.

Royal Naval College, Greenwich, founded in 1873 ; here Brit. naval officers study for the higher examinations.

Royal Naval Volunteer Reserve (R.N.V.R.). The "territorial" branch of the Navy, 2308 ; Royal Naval Reserve, R.N.R., consists of officers and men who have served in the Navy.

Royal Navy (R.N.). *See* **Navy.**

Royal Oak, H.M.S. Battleship, displacing 33,500 tons ; completed 1916 ; in batt. of Jutland ; reconditioned in 1934 ; on Oct. 14, 1939, while anchored in Scapa Flow, was torpedoed and sunk, losing 800 lives, by Ger. submarine, commanded by Prein, which penetrated defences.

THE BRITISH ROYAL FAMILY

The Sovereign

	Born
His Majesty King George VI	Dec. 14, 1895
Succeeded his brother, King Edward VIII, Dec. 11, 1936. Married, April 26, 1923, Lady Elizabeth Bowes-Lyon, b. Aug. 4, 1900, daughter of 14th Earl of Strathmore, and had issue :—	
Princess Elizabeth Alexandra Mary, of York ..	Apr. 21, 1926
Married, Nov. 20, 1947, Prince Philip, Duke of Edinburgh, and has issue :—	
Prince Charles Philip Arthur George ..	Nov. 14, 1948
Princess Margaret Rose, of York	Aug. 21, 1930

Mother of His Majesty

Her Majesty Queen Mary	May 26, 1867
Married, July 6, 1893 (as Princess Victoria Mary of Teck), Prince George, Duke of York, who succeeded as King George V, May 6, 1910.	

Brothers Living

Edward Albert Christian George Andrew Patrick David (Duke of Windsor)	June 23, 1894
Succeeded his father, King George V, Jan. 20, 1936 ; abdicated Dec. 11, 1936. Married, June 3, 1937, Mrs. Wallis Warfield.	
Prince Henry William Frederick Albert (Duke of Gloucester) ..	Mar. 31, 1900
Married, Nov. 6, 1935, Lady Alice Montagu-Douglas-Scott, b. Dec. 25, 1901, 3rd daughter of 7th Duke of Buccleuch ; has issue :—	
Prince William Henry Andrew Frederick	Dec. 18, 1941
Prince Richard Alexander Walter George	Aug. 26, 1944

Widow Living of Brother

Princess Marina (Duchess of Kent)	Dec. 13, 1902
Youngest daughter of late Prince Nicolas of Greece. Married, Nov. 29, 1934, Prince George Edward Alexander Edmund (Duke of Kent), b. Dec. 20, 1902 : died Aug. 25, 1942, and left issue :—	
Prince Edward George Nicholas Patrick (Duke of Kent)	Oct. 9, 1935
Princess Alexandra Helen Elizabeth Olga Christabel	Dec. 25, 1936
Prince Michael George Charles Franklin	July 4, 1942

Sister Living

Princess Royal (Victoria Alexandra Alice Mary)	Apr. 25, 1897
Married, Feb. 28, 1922, Viscount Lascelles (Earl of Harewood, d. May 24, 1947), and has issue :—	
George Henry Hubert (Earl of Harewood)	Feb. 7, 1923
Hon. Gerald David Lascelles	Aug. 22, 1934

Other Members of the Royal Family

Princess Marie Louise	Aug. 12, 1872
Daughter of Princess Helena, granddtr. of Queen Victoria.	
Princess Alice, Countess of Athlone	Feb. 25, 1883
Daughter of Prince Leopold, granddaughter of Queen Victoria. Married, Feb. 10, 1904, Earl of Athlone (brother of Queen Mary).	
Princess Patricia of Connaught (Lady Patricia Ramsay) ..	Mar. 17, 1886
Daughter of Duke of Connaught. Married, Feb. 27, 1919, Admiral Sir Alexander Ramsay.	
Marquess of Carisbrooke, son of Princess Beatrice	Nov. 23, 1886
Ex-Queen Victoria Eugenie	Oct. 24, 1887
Daughter of Princess Beatrice. Married, May 31, 1906, King Alfonso XIII of Spain.	
Princess Arthur of Connaught (Duchess of Fife)	May 17, 1891
Daughter of Princess Louise and Duke of Fife. Married, Oct., 1913, Prince Arthur of Connaught (d. Sept. 11, 1938).	
Earl Mountbatten of Burma	June 25, 1900
2nd son of 1st Marquess of Milford Haven, great-grandson of Queen Victoria. Married, July, 1922, Edwina Cynthia Annette Ashley.	

Royal Observ′atory, Greenwich ; founded in 1675 ; directed by Astronomer Royal ; unbroken continuity of observations, 281, *2411* ; zero meridian of longitude reckoned from here, *1898* ; observatory sends out time signals, 3213 ; transfer to Hurstmonceux, Sussex, began 1946.

Royal Observer Corps, 2833.

Royal palm. A tall species with feathered leaves ; uses in Cuba, 941.

Royal Pioneer Corps, 248.

Royal Red Cross (R.R.C.) founded in 1883 ; British order conferred on ladies, usually nurses, for acts of mercy and bravery in tending sick or wounded soldiers or sailors in time of war.

" Royal Scot.'' Brit. railway train of L.M. region, 2737 ; locomotives, 1988.

Royal Scots. British Army regiment. Known as " the first regiment of the line,'' is descended from Sir John Hepburn's regiment, raised in 1662. Its long history is responsible for its soubriquet " Pontius Pilate's Bodyguard.''

Royal Society. Oldest scientific society in Gt. Brit. ; foreign membership limited to 50 ; founded, 756, 1212 ; Newton president, 2350 ; Wren and, 3426.

Royal Sovereign. Brit. battleship at Trafalgar, 3234.

Royal Standard. May only be hoisted over a building or on a ship or vehicle in which is the King, and never when Their Majesties are passing in procession ; *frontis., Vol. 8.*

Royal Tank Corps (R.T.C.). Merged in R. Armoured Corps, 246.

Royal Tournament. Spectacular armed services pageant, held annually at Olympia, London.

Royal Ulster Constabulary, 2650.

Royce, Sir (Frederick) Henry, Bart. (1863–1933). Eng. engineer. His first motor-car built in 1904, and he joined forces with Hon. C. S. Rolls, to found the Rolls-Royce Co., 2241.

Rozier (rō-zē-ā′), **Jean Pilâtre de,** first to ascend in balloon, *348.*

R.S.F.S.R., or **Russian Soviet Federal Socialist Republic.** A constituent republic of the Soviet Union in both Europe and Asia ; 6,368,000 sq. m. ; pop. (1939) 110,000,000 ; 2849.

Ruba-el-Khali. Desert of Arabia, 195.

" Rubáiyát '' (roo-bī-yaht′). Collection of poems by Omar Khayyám (rubáiyát, plural of rubai, means " quatrains,'' four-line poems) ; freely trans. into English by Edward Fitz-Gerald.

Rubber, 2833 ; in Africa, 2367 ; in Amazon basin, 3022 ; in Bolivia, 492 ; in Brazil, 551, 3022 ; in Colombia, 873 ; collecting rubber sap, *2834* ; differs from gutta-percha, 1559 ; Ecuador, 1083 ; india-rubber tree, a species of fig, 1270 ; making rubber goods, *2835, 2836, 2837* ; Macintosh invents water-proofed garments, 2833 ; New Guinea, 2340 ; in Peru, 2559 ; reclaimed, use, 2836 ; synthetic, 2838, 2430.

Rub′bra, Edmund (b. 1901). Brit. composer, pianist, and music critic ; five symphonies, Sinfonia Concertante (piano and orchestra), " The Dark Night of the Soul '' (choir and orchestra), Four Medieval Latin Lyrics (baritone and orchestra), "The Buddha'' (flute, oboe, and string trio).

Rubens (rōō′-benz), **Peter Paul** (1577–1640). Flemish painter, 2838, 2333, 2476 ; " Cadmus and Athena,'' *649* ; " Dance of Peasants,'' *2327* ; paintings at Antwerp, 182 ; at Brussels, 595 ; painting of Loyola, *2034* ; self-portrait, *2838* ; Van Dyck, pupil of, 3305 ; " Xavier preaching,'' *3429.*

Rubiaceae. Family of plants, which includes coffee, madder, and cinchona (quinine).

Rubicon. Anc. name of river emptying into Adriatic, 25 m. s. of Ravenna, formerly N.E. boundary of It. ; Caesar crosses, 651, 2654.

Rubid′ium (Rb). An extremely rare element of the alkali metal group, 120, 777 ; atomic weight, 85.44 ; very similar in its properties to the

metal potassium ; melts at 100.4° F. ; discovered by Bunsen and Kirchhoff spectroscopically in 1861 ; they named it after two dark-red lines in its spectrum (Lat. *rubidus,* red) ; slightly radioactive, 2732.

Rubinstein, Anton Gregor (1829–94). Russian composer and pianist.

Rublyov, Andrea. Russian artist, 2855.

Ru′bus. A genus of the rose family ; includes blackberry, loganberry, and raspberry.

Ruby. A precious stone, 1427, 2181 ; Burma, 623 ; phosphorescent, 2574.

Ruby-throat, a humming-bird, 1652.

Ruby type, 3270.

Ruby wasp, *1728.*

Rudd, fish, *2781.*

Rudder, device for steering ship, 486 ; of aeroplane, *42* ; of helicopter, 1605.

Rude, François (1784–1855). Fr. sculptor, 2906.

Ru′dolf, Lake, in Brit. E. Africa and Abyssinia, N.E. of Lake Victoria.

Rudolph (Fr. *Raoul*) (d. 936). King of the Franks and Duke of Burgundy ; succeeded his father-in-law, Robert I, in 923 ; most of his reign devoted to wars with the Normans and with Charles III.

Rudolph I of Hapsburg (1218–91). Ger. king and Holy Roman emperor (1273–91) ; founder of Imperial House of Austria, 319, 1449.

Rudolph II (1552–1612). Ger. king and Holy Roman emperor ; a weak ruler, he persecuted the Protestants, and was deposed in favour of his brother, Matthias, to whom most of his dominions were made over.

Rue. A herb with bitter leaves, formerly used in medicine ; also used in magic rites.

Ruff, wading bird ; female known as a reeve.

Ruffe, fish. *See* **Pope.**

Rufus, William. *See* **William II, King.**

Rug′by. Tn. in Warwickshire, on R. Avon ; pop. 45,000 ; famous public school, founded in 1567 ; has Post Office radio-telegraphy transmitter.

Rugby, fives, 1312.

Rugby football, 1345, *1346.*

Rugby Union. Governing body of Rugby football in Eng., 1346.

Rügen. German isl. in Baltic, N. of Pomerania ; in Russian zone of occup. in Ger. after 2nd World War ; a. 373 sq. m. ; pop. 54,000 ; cap. Bergen.

" Rugger.'' *See* **Rugby football.**

Rugs and carpets, 705. *See also* **Spinning ; Weaving.**

Ruhr. Dist. of Germany, on both sides of the R. Ruhr ; coal and iron fields, **2839.**

Ruhr. Chief German tributary of the Rhine, (145 m.), **2839.**

Ruisdael. *See* **Ruysdael.**

Ruiz (roo′ēth′), or **Azorin, José Martinez** (b. 1874). Sp. writer, 3051.

Ruiz de Alarcon, Juan (c. 1581–1639). Mexican poet, 3027.

" Rule, Britannia.'' Brit. national song, 2282.

Rule of the Road, for cars, 2784, 2787.

Rum, island of the Hebrides, 1602.

Rum, a liquor, 103, 1792, 3066.

Rumania, country of S.E. Europe ; 88, 715 sq. m. ; pop. 16,400,000 ; **2839 ;** *plate f. 2840, 2841* ; *map, 344* ; cap. Bucharest, *597,* 598 ; Carpathian Mts., 704 ; Danube, 972 ; language, origin, 2798 ; people, 2840 ; petroleum, 2426 ; *2841* ; plains of, 343 ; surface, 343, 2839. *History :* Balkan Wars, 344, 2841 ; 1st World War, 2841, 3410 ; King Carol, 2841 ; in 2nd World War, 2841, 3419, 3424.

Rumelia. Name of former Turkish lands in Balkans ; espec. cent. Albania and w. Macedonia ; E. Rumelia, autonomous prov. 1878 ; united with Bulgaria in 1885.

Rumford, Benjamin Thompson, Count (1753–1814). Scientist, soldier, and political adventurer, **2841.**

Ru′minants. The cud-chewing animals such as the ox, sheep, goat, **2842,** 732.

Rump Parliament, in Eng. history, 933, *934,* 2524.

Runciman, Walter, Viscount (1870–1949). Brit. politician ; Pres. of Board of Education (1908–11), of Board of

Agriculture (1911–14), and of Board of Trade (1914–16 and 1931–37) ; cr. Viscount 1937 ; Lord President of the Council 1938–39, examining Sudeten Ger. crisis in Czechoslovakia ; his father, Walter Runciman (1847–1937), a millionaire shipowner, was created Baron Runciman of Shorestone in 1933.

Rundstedt (roond′-shtet), **Karl R. G. von** (b. 1875). Ger. soldier ; 1938 organized invasion of Sudetenland ; took Warsaw, Sept. 1939 ; in 1940 made F.-M. for breaking Fr. lines in Ardennes and on Meuse ; defeated at Rostov 1940, transferred to supreme command on W. Front 1942–44 ; counter-attacked in Ardennes, Dec. 1944 ; relieved of command, Mar. 1945 ; captured nr. Munich in May, and interned 3 yrs. at Bridgend, Glam. ; repatriated to Ger. 1949, where he was judged unfit to stand trial ; 2377.

Runic stones, 2387.

Runic writing, of Northmen, 2387.

Running, 2843. *See* **Athletics ; Olympic Games ; Records.**

Running, sewing-stitch, 2927.

Runnymede, or **Runnimede.** Plain in Surrey, on s. bank of Thames, 20 m. s.w. of London ; Magna Carta sealed, *1205,* 1834, 2059.

Runt pigeons, *3607.*

Runyon, Damon (1884–1946). Amer. humorist (" More than Somewhat ''), 3296.

Rupee (rōō-pē′). Coin of India and Pakistan ; consists of 16 annas.

Rupert (Rupprecht) of Bavaria, Prince (1619–82). Nephew of Charles I of Eng. ; obtains charter for Hudson's Bay Co., 1650.

Rupert of Bavaria, Prince (b. 1869). Eldest son of Louis III, King of Bavaria ; took part in 1st World War ; according to legitimist ideas the rightful Brit. sovereign as head of the House of Stuart.

Rupert's Land. Former name of large territory around Hudson Bay, Canada, named after Prince Rupert, now called Saskatchewan, 2875, 1650.

" R.U.R.'' (Rossum's Universal Robots). Play by Karel Capek, *1042.*

" Rural Rides,'' by Cobbett, 858.

Ru′rik the Oarsman (d. 879). Norse leader, founds Rus. kingdom, 2388, *2389.*

Rushcliffe, Henry B. Betterton, 1st Baron (1872–1949). Brit. politician ; chm. of cttee. which produced in 1943 the Rushcliffe scale of salaries for nurses and midwives.

Rushes. Plants of the family *Juncaceae,* of the lily order ; leaves grass-like, flowers usually small, dull, and inconspicuous ; found principally in moist places, marshes, or acid moorlands.

Rushlight. Manufacture and use, 691, *1887.*

Rushworth, John (c. 1612–90). Eng. historian ; he was for some time sec. to Oliver Cromwell and represented Berwick in parl.; for several years he was confined in a debtors' prison, where he died (" Historical Collections '').

Rusk. Biscuit or cake crisped and browned in oven.

Ruskin, John (1819–1900). Eng. writer, art critic, and social reformer, **2843,** 2682, 1224, 1275.

Russell, Bertrand Arthur William, 3rd Earl (b. 1872). Distinguished philosopher, mathematician and author, also an advanced thinker on social questions and political theorist ; " The ABC of Atoms,'' " Problems of Philosophy,'' " Roads to Freedom,'' " On Education,'' " History of Western Philosophy,'' "Human Knowledge, its Scope and Limits.'' Awarded O.M. in 1949.

Russell, George William. *See* **Æ.**

Russell, Sir (Edward) John (b. 1872). Brit. agriculturist ; director of Rothamsted Experimental Station 1912–43 and of Imp. Bureau of Soil Science 1928–43 ; chm. Agric. Sub.-cttee. of U.N.R.R.A., 1941–45 ; wrote much on soil chemistry and plant nutrition.

Russell, John, 1st Earl (1792–1878). Brit. statesman ; a Whig leader, he introduced the Reform Bill of 1831 and was prime min. 1846–52 and 1865–66 ; his second Reform Bill of 1866 failed and he resigned the Liberal leadership to W. E. Gladstone ; 3278.

Russell, Lord William (1639–83). Eng. patriot ; tried to exclude Catholic successor to Charles II ; executed after mock trial as accomplice in Rye House plot.

Russell of Killowen, Charles, Baron (1832–1900). Brit. lawyer and politician ; in the Gladstone govts. of 1886 and 1892 he was Attorney-General ; defended Parnell in 1889 ; in 1894 appointed Lord Chief Justice.

Russell's viper, a snake whose venom is used to cause blood to clot, 2991.

Russia (Union of Soviet Socialist Republics). A vast country of E. Europe and Asia ; area, 8,708.000 sq. m. ; pop. 193,000,000 ; **2844**, *map plate f. 2844* ; cap. Moscow, 2233, *2234, plate f. 2845* ; agriculture, 2844 ; alphabet, 126 ; Arctic exploration, *224*, 2646 ; ballet, 345 ; importance of Black Sea to, 464 ; calendar, 662 ; Caucasia, 732 ; chief cities and mfrs., *2234*, 1856, 2420, 2844 ; climate, 2741, 2844 ; Communism in, 881, 2996 ; Cossacks, 916 ; Dnieper dam, *plate f. 961* ; electric power, 2845 ; emancipation of serfs in, 2981 ; fisheries, 717, 2845, 3104 ; forests, 1349, 2845 ; present govt., 495, 881, 2852 ; in Ice Age, 1680 ; land tenure, 2845 ; language, 2855 ; in Manchukuo, 2087 ; minerals, 732, 1479, 2426, 2428, 2845, 2852, 3297 ; mountains, 732, 3297 ; national song, 2283 ; oil, 2426, 2428, 2845 ; people, 2846, 2982, 3155 ; population, 2844, 2845, 2846 ; religions, 2846 ; rivers and canals, 686, 688, 3329 ; Slavs in, 2983 ; surface features, 2844 ; Siberia, 2966, *map, plate f, 2844 (see also Siberia)* ; transport facilities, 2844, 2845 ; Turkistan, 3266 ; Ukraine, *3273* ; Ural Mts., 3297 ; vegetation, 2844 ; water boundaries, 351, 717, 2844 ; women warriors in, 138.
  History, 2845, 2846 ; chief events summarized, *see* chart under **History** ; origin and early history, 1856, 2387, 2846 ; Mongol invasion, 2205, 2846 ; modern state founded by Ivan III and Ivan IV, 1787 ; progress under Peter the Great and Catherine II, 2562, 2847 ; Petrograd (Leningrad) founded, 1923, 2847 ; war with

Sweden, 758, 2563 ; Seven Years' War and partition of Poland, 2101, 2398 ; Alexander I and the Napoleonic Wars, 1240, 2276, 3131, 2848 ; under Nicholas I, 931, 2365, 2848 ; Alexander II, 2848 ; war with Turkey (1877–78), 344, 1019, 2848, 3265 ; nihilist movement, 2856 ; Alexander III, 2848 ; Nicholas II, 2365, 2848 ; Russo-Japanese War (1904–05), 1800, 2848 ; *1st World War and After*, 1241, 3265, 3409–12 ; Nicholas II. 2365 ; Kerensky establishes government, 2848 ; Bolsheviks overthrow the provisional government (on November 7 1917). 495. 1923. 2849, 3411 ; Lenin, 1922 ; disruption of empire, 1226, 1278, 1899, 1968, 2849 ; effect in Leningrad, 1924 ; counter-revolution in Siberia, 2849 ; war with Poland, 3415, 3642 ; war in the Ukraine, 3273 ; Soviet republics, 2844, 2849, *2850* ; Stalin, 2850, 3013 ; Five-Year Plans, 2850 ; part in Sp. Civil War, 3039 ; non-aggression pact with Ger., 3416. *2nd World War*, 2852 ; attack on Finland, 1278, 2852, 3416 ; invades Poland, 3416 ; new republics incorporated, 1226, 1899, 1967, 2852 ; German campaigns, 1452, 2852, 3418, *maps, 2853, 3073* ; Stalingrad, 3073 ; dec. war on Jap., 3424 ; post-war spread of Communism, 1242, 3283.

RULERS OF RUSSIA
HOUSE OF RURIK
1462–1505	Ivan III, the Great
1505–33	Vassili Ivanovitch
1533–84	Ivan IV, the Terrible
1584–98	Feodor Ivanovitch
1598–1605	Boris Godunov
1605–13	The Troublous Times

HOUSE OF ROMANOFF
1613–45	Michael
1645–76	Alexis
1676–82	Feodor Alexievitch
1682–89	Ivan V } jointly
	Peter the Great }
1689–1725	Peter the Great (alone)
1725–27	Catherine I
1727–30	Peter II
1730–40	Anna Ivanovna
1740–41	Ivan VI
1741–61	Elizabeth
1762	Peter III
1762–96	Catherine II
1796–1801	Paul
1801–25	Alexander I
1825–55	Nicholas I
1855–81	Alexander II
1881–94	Alexander III
1894–1917	Nicholas II
1917–	Soviet republic

Russia : Art and Architecture, 2854.

Russia leather, 1914.

Russian Church. *See* Greek Orthodox Church.

Russian language, 126, 2272, 2855.

Russian literature, 2855 ; drama, 1040 ; novels, 2404 ; Tchekhov, 3159 ; Tolstoy. 3222 : Turgenev. 3260.

Russian Soviet Federal Socialist Republic. *See* R.S.F.S.R.

Russian or Western Turkistan, 264, 3267.

Russian wolfhound, 1026, *plate f. 1024.*

Russo-Japanese War (1904–05), 1800, 2848 ; effect on China, 813 ; effect on Rus., 2848 ; Roosevelt's mediation, 2825.

Russo-Turkish Wars (1828–29), 1525, 344, 2365 ; (1877–78), 344, 528, 1019, 2922, 3265.

Rust. Oxidized iron, **2856**, 1752 ; removal, 2477.

Rust Fungus. Various fungi parasitic upon plants, **2857**, 1407, 3374 ; spores, *2918.*

Rustchuk or Ruschuk, Bulgaria. Tn. on Danube ; pop. 49,000 ; formerly important Turkish frontier fortress.

Rustless Alloys, 122.

Ruth. Heroine of Book of Ruth in Old Testament, **2857**, *2858*, 422.

Ruthe'nia. Former Czech province ceded to U.S.S.R. in 1945 ; 4,800 sq. m. ; pop. 3,800,000 ; 954.

Ruthenians. A branch of the Slavs, 319, 954, 3273.

Ruthe'nium (Ru). Hard grey brittle metallic element of the palladium group ; atomic weight 101·7 ; like palladium it absorbs gases ; melts above 3,540° F. ; found in platinum ores, 2627 ; properties, 777.

Rutherford, Ernest, Baron (1871–1937). Brit. physicist, 2858, *2594* ; and the atom, 319 ; quantum theory, 2711 ; radium research, 2732 ; Nobel prize, 2375.

Rutherford, Mark (1831–1913). Brit. novelist ; real name Wm. Hale White ; won fame with " The Autobiography of Mark Rutherford."

Rutile, ore of titanium, 3216.

Rutland. Smallest of the Eng. counties, between Leicestershire, Northamptonshire, and Lincolnshire ; 152 sq. m. ; pop. 17,400 ; **2858.**

Rutland, Vermont, U.S.A., 2nd city of state, near centre, on Otter Creek ; pop. 17,082 ; greatest marble industry in U.S.A.

Ruttledge, Hugh (b. 1884). Indian Civil Servant ; leader of British Mt. Everest expeditions 1933 and 1936.

PRINCIPAL NAMES IN RUSSIAN LITERATURE

Mikhail Lomonosov (1711–65), poet and grammarian ; " father of Russian literature."

Basil Zhukovski (1783–1852), critic and translator.

Alexander Griboiedov (1795–1829), dramatic satirist—" The Misfortune of Being Clever."

Alexander Pushkin (1799–1837), poet, dramatist, and short story writer—" The Prisoner of the Caucasus " ; " The Gipsies " ; " Eugene Onegin " ; " The Fisherman and the Fish."

Alexis Koltsov (1809–42), greatest Russian folk poet, author of numerous songs and ballads.

Nikolai Gogol (1809–52), realistic novelist and dramatist— " Taras Bulba " ; " Dead Souls."

Visarion Belinsky (1810–48), critic and essayist, author of powerful essays and reviews

Mikhail Lermontov (1814–41), lyric poet and novelist—" The Demon " ; " A Hero of Our Time " ; " The Angel."

Ivan Turgenev (1818–83), novelist—" A Sportsman's Sketches"; " Father and Sons " ; " Virgin Soil."

Feodor Dostoievski (1822–81), psychological novelist—" Crime and Punishment " ; " The Brothers Karamazov " ; " The Idiot."

Alexander Ostrovski (1823–86), dramatist—" The Thunderstorm " ; " Poverty Not a Vice."

Leo Tolstoy (1828–1910), novelist and philosopher—" War and Peace " ; " Anna Karenina " ; " Kreutzer Sonata " ; " Master and Man."

Anton Tchekhov (1860–1904), dramatist and short story writer —" Peasants " ; " The Cherry Orchard."

Maxim Gorki (Alexei Pyeshkov) (1868–1936), novelist and short story writer—" Comrades " ; " Lords of Life " ; " Humble Folk " ; " Mother."

Leonid Andreyev (1871–1919), dramatist and short story writer—" Judas Iscariot " ; " The Crushed Flower " ; " Anathema."

Alexis Remizov (1877–   ), novelist—" The Pond " ; " The Clock " ; " The Sisters of the Cross " ; " The Fifth Pestilence " ; " The Cockerel."

Alexander Blok (1880–1921), poet—" The Scythians " ; " The Twelve " ; " The Earth Under Snow " ; " Hours of the Night."

Andrei Biely (Boris Bugaiev) (1880–1934), poet and novelist— " The Silver Dove " ; " Moscow " ; " Petersburg " ; " The Urn."

Alexis K. Tolstoy (1817–75), novelist, dramatist, poet—" The Childhood of Nikita " ; " Prince Serebrany," historical romance ; " Death of Ivan the Terrible," drama.

Alexei N. Tolstoy (1882–1945), novelist, "The Road to Calvary."

Feodor Gladkov (1883–   ), novelist—" Cement."

Lydia Seifullina (1889–   ), short story writer and novelist— " Virineya " : " Humus."

Vladimir Maiakovski (1894–1930), poet and dramatist—" The Cloud " ; " Left March " ; " Mysteria-Bouffe " ; " Lenin."

Boris Pilnyak (1894–   ), short story writer and novelist— " The Naked Year " ; " Leather Jackets " ; " Machines and Wolves."

Isaac Babel (1894–   ), short story writer—" Stories of the Red Cavalry " ; " Tales."

Valentin Kataev (1897–   ), novelist and dramatist—" Lonely White Sail " ; " Squaring the Circle."

Mikhail Sholokhov (1905–   ), novelist—" And Quiet Flows the Don."

Ruwenzori (roo-wen-zō'-rē). Mt. group in Uganda Protectorate, E. cent. Africa, just N. of equator ; highest point 16,800 ft. ; 69.

Ruysdael or **Ruisdael** (rois'-dahl), **Jakob van** (c.1628–82). Great Dutch landscape painter, 2334, 2476.

Ruyter (roi'-ter), **Michael Adriaanszoon de** (1607–76). Dutch admiral ; redoubtable adversary of Fr. and Eng., 465, 2029.

Ry'dal Water. Lake in Westmorland, Eng. ; ½ m. long, rather less in breadth, 3371 ; Wordsworth's home, 3408.

Ryde. Tn. of the Isle of Wight, connected to Portsmouth and Southsea by steamer and air services ; pop. 19,624.

Ryder Cup. Trophy held by the winners of professional golf team competition between Gt. Brit. and U.S.A. ; first held in 1927.

Rye. A cereal grain, **2858** ; bread, 555 ; cultivated in Ger., 1445 ; rust fungus, 2857 ; grass, 1509 ; in Sweden, 3131.

Rye. Anc. tn. in Sussex, on R. Rother, Cinque Port ; trade in corn, wool, etc. ; pop. 3,950 ; 3123 ; lifeboat tragedy, 1936.

Rye House Plot. Conspiracy (1683) of extreme opponents of Eng. Catholic succession to assassinate Charles II and his brother, the Duke of York, afterwards James II ; used as pretext for execution of innocent political opponents including Alger-non Sidney and Lord William Russell.

Ryks museum, Amsterdam, 147.

Rylands, John (1801–88). Brit. merchant ; with father and brothers founded well-known Midlands firm, which became one of the largest textile concerns in Gt. Brit. ; John Rylands Library, Manchester, erected to his memory by his wife, 2085.

Ry'mill, John Riddock (b. 1905). Australian polar explorer, in Greenland, in 1930–31 and 1932–33 ; led Brit. Graham Land expedn. to Antarctic, 1934–37 ; wrote "Southern Lights" ; 2647.

Ryswick. Holland, vil. near The Hague ; Peace of Ryswick (1697), 3380.

THERE was a time when the letter S looked more like our W. Turn the W on its side and cut off the bottom line and you get something that looks very much like our S. The story of S begins, in Egyptian picture-writing, with the hieroglyph, known as the "inundated garden," representing papyrus or lotus plants growing out of the water. When it came to be written in the Egyptian running hand like this it no longer looked like a garden, and the Phoenicians called it *Shin*, which means "teeth." If you look closely, you can see the outline of the lower teeth, and the chin and beard as well. But the Phoenicians themselves made it *w*, like a squat W. The Greeks took it and, standing on its side, made it into their letter Σ (*Sigma*). Later the last stroke was omitted, and then, when the Romans rounded the points, it was our letter S. The swishing sound of water among reeds is still heard in the letter today.

Saale (zahl'e). R. of cent. Ger., flows N. 250 m. to R. Elbe, 1124.

Saalfeld (zahl'-felt). Old Ger. tn. on R. Saale, 60 m. S.W. of Leipzig ; pop. 17,960 ; ruined Sorbenburg castle said to have been built by Charlemagne ; Fr. defeated Prussians here in 1806.

Saar (zhar) **Basin.** Valley of R. Saar in W. Ger. along Lorraine boundary ; a. 738 sq. m. ; pop. 812,000 ; after 1st World War administered by League of Nations ; plebiscite decided its re-union with Germany March 1935 ; became autonomous state of Saar, in economic union with France, Oct. 1947 ; 1361.

Saarbrücken (zahr'brü-ken). City on R. Saar, 40 m. N.E. of Metz ; pop. 135,000 ; in Saar Basin ; first action in Franco-Prussian War ; coal-mining ; bombed, and taken by U.S. Mar. 1945.

Sabatier, Paul (1858–1928). Fr. historian ; "Life of St. Francis of Assisi."

Sabbath. 7th day of the week, Saturday ; kept holy by the Jews ; Sunday, the first day of the week, is the Christian Sabbath, **2859.**

Sabbath, Witches', 3400.

Sabine. R. of U.S.A., a stream flowing 500 m. to Gulf of Mexico, forming greater part of boundary between Texas and Louisiana.

Sabines (sab'-īnz). An anc. people of cent. It., 2804.

Sable, in heraldry, 1614.

Sable, a fur-bearing animal, 2112.

Sable antelope, 176.

Sable fur, 1412, 2112 ; imitated, 1412.

Sabotage (sa'-bo-tahz). A Fr. word denoting the infliction of personal violence ; violence or obstruction caused by men in industrial disputes ; also in enemy occupied-countries, as in 1940–45.

Saccharin (sak'-a-rin). An artificial sweetening substance, 3116 ; duty on, 3158 ; obtained from toluol, 857.

Sacculi'na. A parasite living upon crabs, 2513.

Sacheverell (sa-shev'-er-el), **Henry** (c.1674–1724). Eng. preacher, who created a sensation by his attack on Dissenters and the Whig party, for which he was brought before the House of Lords on a charge of high treason and suspended from preach-ing for 3 years ; his sermons were publicly burned by the hangman.

Sachs (sahks), **Hans** (1494–1576). Ger. shoemaker-poet, greatest of the master-singers, ardent adherent of Luther ; hero of "Die Meistersinger," 2539, 3332.

Sackville, Thomas. *See* **Dorset.**

Sackville-West, Victoria (b. 1892). Eng. poet and novelist ; daughter of the 3rd Baron Sackville, she brought Knole Park, the family seat, into "The Edwardians" ; poetry includes "The Land," (1927) ; "The Garden," (1946).

Sacramen'to, California, U.S.A. State cap. and a leading mfg. city ; on Sacramento r., about 90 m. N.E. of San Francisco ; pop. 105,958.

Sacramento River, California, U.S.A. Rises on Mt. Shasta in N., flows 400 m. s. to Suisun Bay, 50 m. above San Francisco ; 1047.

Sac'raments, in Christian Church. Rites ordained as outward and visible signs of inward and spiritual grace ; in the R.C. Church are seven in number ; in the Church of England, baptism and Holy Communion ; Luther's attitude, 2759.

Sacré Coeur (sah-krā' kēr'). Church at Montmartre in Paris, 2517.

Sacred ibis, of Egypt, 3097, 3099 ; plate f. 3100.

Sacred lotus. An Egyptian water-lily, found on the Nile, 2027.

Sacred Wars. In Gk. history, series of wars waged (600–338 B.C.) in defence of Apollo's shrine at Delphi by members of Amphictyonic League.

Sacsahuaman. Inca stronghold, 1688.

Sad'duces. Anc. Jewish sect, composed largely of the priestly aristocracy ; opposed to Pharisees ; rejected traditions of the elders, holding only to observances of the written law ; sceptical in doctrine, 1822, 1830.

Sadi (sah'-dē) or **Saadi** (c. 1184–1291). Assumed name of Muslih Ad-din, greatest Persian didactic poet ("Gulistan" or "The Rose Garden").

Sadi-Carnot. *See* **Carnot, M. F. Sadi.**

Sadler's Wells Theatre, London, 1043 ; ballet school, 347.

Sadowa (sah'-dō-vah), Czechoslovakia. Vil. 4 m. N.W. of Königgratz ; decisive engagement of Seven Weeks' War (1866), 1449.

Saeters (sä'-terz). Mountain pastures of Norway, 2393.

Saetersdal. Region in Norway, 2393.

Safed', Palestine. City 8 m. N.W. of Sea of Galilee ; pop. 10,900 ; important fortified place during Crusades ; repeated earthquakes in 19th cent. ; modern rabbinical school.

Safety-bicycle, evolution, 947.

Safety First, on the roads, 2787.

Safety-Lamp. Invented by Davy, 979, 980, 1889.

Safety matches, 2119.

Safety Pin, 2609.

Saffron. A yellow colouring matter and drug obtained from crocus, 932.

Saff'ron Wal'den. Tn. in Essex, 44 m. N.E. of London ; brewing ; anc. remains ; pop. 7,000.

Sa'gas. Old Scandinavian tales, 2880, 3388.

Sage. A plant of the mint family ; used as spice, 3061.

Saggar. Box of fire-clay in which pottery is baked, 2666.

Saghalin. Same as **Sakhalin.**

Sag'inaw, Michigan, U.S.A. Mfg. and trading city on Saginaw r. ; pop. 82,800 ; centre of Michigan coal fields ; glass, beet sugar, salt, lumber, iron and steel.

Sagittarius (saj-i-tār'-i-us). A sign of the zodiac, 3444.

Sa'go. Starchy foodstuff made from the soft inner portion, or pith, of the trunk of some palms, **2859,** 2484, 2485.

Sagres (sah'-gres). Small spt. of Port., home of Henry the Navigator, 1613.

Sagua'ro or **giant cactus.** In Arizona, U.S.A., 648.

Sagun'tum, modern **Sagunto** or **Murviedro,** Spain. Anc. Iberian city near Mediterranean, 20 m. N. of Valencia ; Rom. ally ; heroic resistance to siege of Hannibal 219 B.C. immediate cause of 2nd Punic War.

Sahara. Great desert region (3,500,000 sq. m.) in N. Africa, **2859,** 65, 996, 997 ; maps f. 68, 3366 ; caravans, 2861 ; children, 791 ; date palms, 979 ; dunes, 996, 2860 ; exploration, 2861 ; rainfall, 2859 ; trade, 2861.

Saida (sī'-dē) or **Saidi,** Syria. Tn. on w. Mediterranean coast, 25 m. s. of Beirut ; pop. 10,000 ; on site of anc. Sidon, 2573.

Saigon (sī-gon'). Port and trade centre of S.E. Fr. Indonesia and cap. of Cochin-China on R. Saigon, 35 m. from sea ; pop. 695,000 ; exports fish, *1719*, 1720 : occupied by Japan (1940–45).

Sailing vessels, 481, *482*, *484*, *485*.

Sailplane. High-performance type of glider, 1474.

Saint, Thomas. Invented sewing machine, 2929.

St. Abb's Head. Small promontory on Scot. coast in Berwickshire ; named after St. Elba, who founded monastery here in 7th cent. ; fine lighthouse, 310 ft. above sea-level.

St. Albans. City of Herts, 20 m. N.W. of London, pop. 42,500 ; **2861**, 1622 ; and Alban, 100 ; near old Rom. Verulamium, *2810* ; fine Norman abbey church, now cath., *724* ; battle (1455), 2828.

St. Andrews, Fifeshire, Scot. Small port 40 m. N.E. of Edinburgh ; univ. ; castle and cath. ruins, 1269 ; famous gold club and links, 1484.

St. Andrews, University of. At St. Andrews, Scot. ; co-ed. ; founded in 1411 ; faculties of philosophy, law, medicine, theology.

St. Andrew's cross, 188. On Union Jack, 1312.

St. Anthony. Falls of, Mississippi, 2191.

St. Augustine, Florida, U.S.A., on E. coast. Oldest permanent European settlement in U.S.A. ; pop. 12,000.

St. Bartholomew, Massacre of. Massacre of Huguenots beginning in Paris Aug. 24, 1572 ; 870, 1650, 2131.

St. Bartholomew's Hospital, London (" Bart's ") ; history, 1648.

St. Bees Head. Promontory in Cumberland, about 2½ m. N. of St. Bees ; lighthouse (erected 1867), with light visible for 25 m.

St. Bernard dog, *128*, 1025 ; *plate f. 1024*.

St. Bernard Pass, Great. Famous Alpine pass (8,100 ft.) connecting Rhône valley with Aosta, It. ; monastery, *128* ; *map*, *3140*.

St. Bernard Pass, Little. Alpine pass (7,180 ft.) in It. s. of Mont Blanc ; connects valleys of Dora Baltea and Isère.

St. Bride's Bay, Wales. Inlet of St. George's Channel, on w. coast of Pembrokeshire ; 9 m. wide at mouth, and extends some 8 m. inland ; sea encroaches here.

St. Bride's Church. One of Wren's City churches, in Fleet St., London, *2010* ; burnt out in 1940.

St. Catharine's College, Cambridge, 668.

St. Catherine's Point. Most southerly point of Isle of Wight, about 5 m. w. of Ventnor ; lighthouse one of the finest on Eng. coast.

St. Christopher or **St. Kitts.** A mountainous isl. of Brit. W. Indies, separated by narrow channel from Nevis ; one of Leeward Isls. ; a. 68 sq. m. ; pop. 29,800 ; 3368.

St. Clair, Lake. N. Amer., on Michigan-Ontario border, between L. Huron and L. Erie ; a. 396 sq. m.

St. Clement Danes. Church in Strand, London. Burnt out in 1940 ; reconstruction begun early 1949.

Saint-Cloud (săn-klŏŏ). Fr. tn. 5 m. w. of Paris ; pottery factories ; Napoleon's palace.

St. Croix (kroi) or **Santa Cruz.** One of Virgin Isls., W. Indies (U.S.A.) ; a. 85 sq. m. ; pop. 16,200 ; chief tn., Christiansted ; raises cane and cattle.

Saint-Cyr-l'Ecole (san-sēr-lā-kōl)'. Fr. vil. N.W. of Versailles ; famous for military school established (1806) in convent which housed Mme. de Maintenon's girls' school (1686–1793).

St. Davids, Wales. City in w. of Pembrokeshire ; cath. of SS. Andrew and David completed in 1198, *2539* ; pop. 1,600.

St. David's Head, Wales. Precipice (about 100 ft. high), 3 m. N.W. of St. Davids ; most westerly point of Wales.

Saint-Denis (san-de-nĕ'). Fr. suburb of Paris on R. Seine ; pop. 78,000 ; abbey church (12th cent.) ; metallurgical and chemical industries.

St. Denis, Michel (b. 1897), Fr. theatrical producer, 3197.

St. Dunstan's. Training institute for the blind, Regent's Park, London ; established for war-blinded sailors, soldiers, and airmen, under the supervision of Sir C. Arthur Pearson in 1915 ; it is maintained by voluntary contributions ; tuition in various occupations is given ; 473.

Ste. Anne de Beaupré (sant ahn de bō-prā'). Vil. and pilgrim resort in Quebec on St. Lawrence R. 20 m. below Quebec ; pop. 2,500 ; famous shrine of St. Anne, which thousands visit annually ; church burned and rebuilt in 1922.

Sainte-Beuve (sant-bĕv'), **Charles-Augustin** (1804–69). Fr. literary critic, exceptionally able and fair (" Causeries du Lundi ").

Sainte-Chapelle (sant sha-pel'). Church in Paris, 2517.

St. Elias, Mt., Alaska. Snow-clad peak (18,024 ft.) in St. Elias Range, near Pacific coast, 325 m. N.W. of Sitka ; Malaspina Glacier on s. slope ; *map*, *99*.

St. Elmo's Fire, 1946.

Saint-Etienne. Fr. industrial city 3 m. S.W. of Lyons ; pop. (1946) 178,000 ; near rich coal fields ; firearms, iron products, silks.

St. Eustatius or **Eustache.** Volcanic isl. in Dutch W. Indies ; 7 sq. m. ; pop. 1,403 ; chief tn., Orangetown ; source of supplies for Continental army in War of Amer. Independence ; captured by Brit. fleet (1781).

St. Francis River. A tributary of the Mississippi in S.E. Missouri and Arkansas, U.S.A. ; 450 m. long.

Saint-Gall or **St. Gallen.** Mfg. tn. in N.E. Switzerland, 40 m. E. of Zürich ; pop. 63,947 ; famous embroideries, laces ; celebrated library.

Saint-Gaudens, Augustus (1848–1907). Amer. sculptor, b. in Ireland ; works include " Puritan " at Springfield, Massachusetts, and " Lincoln " at Chicago, a replica of which stands in Parliament Sq., London.

St. George and the Dragon, 1440.

St. George's Channel. Strait 100 m. long and 60 to 100 m. wide connecting Atlantic and Irish seas and separating Ire. from Wales.

St. George's cross, 1312.

Saint-Germain, Treaty of, between Allies and Austria (1919), 316, 3216, 3323.

Saint-Germain-en-Laye. Fr. summer resort on R. Seine, 11 m. w. of Paris ; pop. 22,013 ; treaty between Allies and Austria signed here after 1st World War.

St. Giles Church, Edinburgh, 1087.

St. Gothard (got'-ahrd). Group of Alps, Switzerland ; highest points over 10,000 ft. ; 3138.

St. Gothard Pass. Over Swiss-Italian Alps ; long the chief route from N. Europe to It. ; 127 ; *map*, *3140*.

St. Gothard Tunnel, 3138.

St. Helena. Brit. volcanic isl. and colony in Atlantic 1,200 m. w. of Africa ; a. 47 sq. m. ; pop. 4,710 ; declining importance as port of call ; Napoleon exiled to, *2277*, *2278* ; tortoise from, *3230*.

St. Helens. Tn. in Lancashire, 10 m. N.E. of Liverpool ; pop. 105,880 ; chemicals, plate glass, copper products, bottles, patent medicines ; coal trade.

St. Helier, Cap. of Jersey ; pop. 30,000 ; 752 ; lifeboat, *1937*.

St. Hyacinthe, Quebec. City 35 m. N.E. of Montreal on Yamaska R. ; pop. 17,800 ; knitted goods, organs, agric. machinery.

St. Ives. Spt. and winter resort in Cornwall, 57 m. s.w. of Plymouth ; pop. 9,000.

St. Ives. Town in Huntingdonshire, on R. Ouse ; cattle trade ; pop. 3,100 ; home of Oliver Cromwell, 1660.

St. James's Palace, London. Original palace built in 1532, for Henry VIII. Much of it destroyed by fire in 1809. Though no longer the sovereign's official residence, foreign ambassadors and ministers are still accredited

to the " Court of St. James's," and from the palace balcony each new sovereign is proclaimed, 1614, 2014.

St. James's Park (93 acres). One of the oldest and perhaps the most beautiful of London's many parks ; enclosed by Henry VIII. Takes its name from St. James's Palace near by ; the lake (5 acres) is the haunt of several kinds of wild fowl, *2011*.

Saint-Jean, Isle of. Fr. name of Prince Edward Isl., 2684.

"Saint Joan," by Bernard Shaw, 2940.

Saint John, New Brunswick. Chief winter port of Canada, on Bay of Fundy ; pop. 51,000 ; **2861**, *2336*.

St. John. One of the Virgin Isls., West Indies (U.S.A.) ; a. 19 sq. m. ; pop. 765 ; sugar-cane, cotton, tobacco ; noted for bay oil.

St. John, Knights Hospitallers of, 1865, 2072 ; in Rhodes, 2771 ; in Tripoli (Libya), 1931.

St. John Lateran. Church in Rome, first built 3rd cent. ; destroyed by earthquake and fire and subsequently rebuilt 4 times, the last time in 14th cent. ; in part reconstructed and modernized several times since , 729.

Saint John River, New Brunswick, rises on boundary between Maine, U.S.A., and Quebec, flows across New Brunswick 550 m. to Bay of Fundy, 2861.

St. John's, Newfoundland. Prov. cap. and shipping point on E. coast ; nearest point in Amer. to Europe ; pop. 56,000 ; large export and import trade and various mfrs. ; founded in 1582 ; captured by Fr. in 1696 and during Seven Years' War ; ceded to British in 1713 ; *2338* ; cable, 642 ; first Atlantic wireless station, *2098*, *2099*.

St. John's College, Cambridge, founded, *667*, 668.

St. John's College, Oxford, founded, 2464.

St. John's Day, in Latvia, *1899*.

St. Joseph, Missouri, U.S.A., 48 m. N. of Kansas City, on Missouri R. ; live-stock market, immense yards and packing-houses ; pop. 75,700.

Saint-Just (san-zhŭst'), **Antoine de** (1767–94). Fr. revolutionist, associate of Robespierre and Danton ; organizer of the Reign of Terror ; denounces Danton, 972 ; arrested and guillotined, 2990.

St. Kilda, Scot. Isl. of Outer Hebrides ; numerous sea-fowl ; vacated by its inhabitants in 1930.

St. Kitts. See St. Christopher.

St. Laurent, Louis S. (b. 1882). Can. statesman ; Fr.-Can. by birth ; min. of external affairs 1946–48 ; premier Nov. 1948.

St. Lawrence, Gulf of. Inlet of N. Atlantic at mouth of St. Lawrence R., 2861.

St. Lawrence Island. An Alaskan isl. in Bering Sea, inhabited by Eskimos ; 100 m. long.

St. Lawrence River. One of the chief rivers of N. Amer., outlet of the Great Lakes ; nearly 2,000 m. long ; **2861**, *2862* ; Cartier's explorations, 712 ; Champlain, 751 ; commerce, 2224, 2435 ; early exploration, 2380, *2381* ; Great Lakes, 1515 ; " lakes to ocean " route, 1516 ; Montreal on, *2223*, *2862* ; Quebec on, *2715* ; water-system, 677.

St Louis, Missouri, U.S.A. Largest city of state and chief market for Mississippi valley ; pop. 816,000 ; 2194.

St. Lucia. Largest of the Windward Isls., a. 238 sq. m. ; pop. 73,770 ; sugar, cocoa, lime-juice, molasses, bay oil, 3368.

Saint-Malo (san-ma-lō). Fortified spt. and bathing resort of Fr. on Eng. Channel ; steamer service to Southampton ; shipbuilding and other mfrs. ; pop. 12,000 ; associated with Cartier, 712.

St. Mark's. Cath. in Venice, *1762*, 3310, *3311*, 214 ; bell-tower, 409.

St. Martin. An isl. of the Lesser Antilles ; the N. portion (20 sq. m.) belongs to Fr. and the S. portion (17 sq. m.) to the Dutch colony of Curaçao.

St. Martin-in-the-Fields. Church in Trafalgar Square, London ; the bells and services are often broadcast ; " down-and-outs " find refuge in the crypt ; " Dick " Sheppard was vicar from 1914 to 1927 ; *2012, 2280.*

St. Marylebone (ma'-ri-bon). Met. and pari. bor in N.W. London ; pop. (1945) 66,300 ; contains Lord's cricket ground, the headquarters of the Marylebone Cricket Club (M.C.C.).

St. Mary Redcliffe. Famous old church in Bristol, Eng., 572.

St. Mary's Strait or River. N. Amer. channel connecting L. Superior and L. Huron, 1515, *map, 1515.*

St. Michael and St. George, Order of, 2449.

St. Michael's Island. Largest of Azores ; a. 300 sq. m. ; pop. 126,000 ; chief city, Ponta Delgada ; 325.

St. Michael's orange, 2444.

St. Moritz, Switzerland. Loftiest vil. in Upper Engadine, on L. Moritz ; winter sports ; 3142 ; *map, 3140.*

Saint Nazaire (san-na-zār'). Fr. spt., 40 m. N.W. of Nantes, at mouth of R. Loire ; shipbuilding ; base in 1914–18 War ; pop. 35,000 ; 2000 ; Commando raid Mar. 1942 ; besieged by Allies 1944–45 ; surrendered May 12, 1945.

St. Neots (nêts). Tn. of Huntingdonshire, pop. 4,700 ; 1658.

Saint-Nicolas (san-nê-kō-lah'), Belgium. Trade and mfg. centre, 12 m. s.w. of Antwerp ; pop. 43,400.

St. Omer (san-tō-mâr'), **Godfrey de.** Fr. knight, joint founder, with Hugh de Payens, of the Order of Knights Templars, 1865.

St. Omer, Fr. Tn. in Pas-de-Calais dept., 25 m. s.e. of Calais ; headquarters of Brit. army during early part of 1st World War ; scene of Lord Roberts's death in Nov. 1914.

Saint-Ouen (san-twahn'), Fr. Suburb N. of Paris on R. Seine ; pop. 45,465 ; r. port and mfg. centre.

St. Pan'cras. Met. and parl. bor. of N.W. London ; pop. 140,000 ; contains University College and terminal rly. stations Euston, St. Pancras, and King's Cross.

St. Pat'rick, Order of, 2449.

St. Patrick's cross, 1312.

St. Patrick's Day (Mar. 17), 2528.

St. Paul, Minnesota, U.S.A., state cap. on Mississippi ; pop. 271,600 ; important meat-packing industry ; 2187.

St. Paul or St. Paul's Rocks, tiny isl. in cent. Atlantic, N. of Equator, 290.

St. Paul de Loanda. *See* **Loanda.**

St. Paul's. Cath. in London, 2862, *2863* ; *2020, 219,* 729, 2010 ; famous bell, *410,* 411 ; mosaic, 2233 ; Wellington's tomb, 2906 ; Wren and. 3425 ; air raid damage, 2862.

St. Paul's Bay on N.W. coast of Malta *2072.*

St. Paul's School, London. Public School in Hammersmith Road to which it was transferred from St. Paul's Churchyard in 1884 ; it was founded by John Colet, Dean of St. Paul's, in 1509 ; 870, 2883.

St. Peter Port. Cap. of Guernsey. pop. 18,000 ; 752.

St. Peter's. Cath. in Rome, 3506, *2802, 3306* ; dome designed by Michelangelo, 2161 ; " La Pietà," *2765.*

St. Petersburg. *See* **Leningrad.**

St. Peter College of Peterhouse, Cambridge, 666.

Saint-Pierre (san pyâr'), **Bernardin de** (1737–1814). Fr. writer, 1381.

Saint-Pierre. Formerly the chief tn. of Martinique, *plate f. 3329.*

Saint-Pierre and Miquelon. Fr. overseas terr. of barren rocky isls. 10 m. off S. Newfoundland ; 93 sq. m. ; pop. 4,350 ; important cod-fishing centre.

Saint-Quentin (san-kahn-tan'). City in N. Fr. on R. Somme, 95 m. N.E. of Paris, scene of several fierce battles in 1st World War ; Ger. attack on Brit. 5th Army, March 21, 1918, often called Battle of St. Quentin ; pop. 49,000.

Saints, Battle of the. Fought on April 12, 1782. Rodney gained a notable

victory over the Fr. under Comte de Grasse ; the battle is named after Les Saintes isls., W. Indies.

Saint-Saëns (san-sahn'), **Charles Camille** (1835–1921). Fr. musical composer and pianist ; works include the opera " Samson and Delilah " and the " Danse Macabre."

Saintsbury, George Edward Bateman (1845–1933). Eng. literary critic and historian, a great authority on Fr. literature (" A History of Criticism " ; " A History of English Prosody ").

Saint-Simon (san-sē-mon'), **Claude Henri de Rouvroy, Comte de** (1760–1825). Founder of Fr. socialism ; advocated a new organization of society on an industrial basis, ruled by industrial chiefs ; popularity chiefly due to his disciples (" The Industrial System " ; " The New Christianity ") ; 2996.

St. Sophia (sō-fē-a). Famous mosque at Constantinople (Istanbul), now a museum ; *1761, 213,* 214 ; Justinian I builds, 637, 1844.

St. Swithin's Day (July 15), 2862.

St. Thomas. One of Virgin Isls. (U.S.A.); 32 sq. m. ; pop. 11,200. *See* **Virgin Isls.**

St. Thomas (formerly Charlotte Amalie). Chief port of Amer. Virgin Isls., at head of St. Thomas Harbour, Isl. of St. Thomas ; pop. 9,000.

St. Thomas (tō-mah'). or **São Tomé.** Port. isl. in Gulf of Guinea, 270 m. s. of mouth of R. Niger ; forms prov. (384 sq. m.) with isl. of Principe ; pop. 60,500 ; exports coffee, cacao, rubber, cinchona.

St. Valentine's Day, Feb. 14. Festival of St. Valentine, long observed by sending love-tokens, 2862.

St. Valéry-en-Caux. Coast tn. of Fr., 20 m. w. of Dieppe ; fishing pt. ; pop. est. 3,000 ; intended embarkation pt. for Brit. troops retreating from Somme, June 1940, but s. position abandoned by Fr. and over 5,000 men of 51st Highland div. B.E.F. taken by encircling Gers. after fierce fighting ; tn. liberated Sept. 1944 by 51st Highland div.

Saint Vin'cent, John Jervis, Earl (1735–1823). Brit. admiral, who fought with distinction off Ushant in 1778 and at Gibraltar in 1780–2, and gained a brilliant victory over the Spaniards off Cape St. Vincent in 1797 ; he became Admiral of the Fleet in 1821.

St. Vincent. Brit. isl. off Windward group, W. Indies, a. 150 sq. m. ; pop. 61,600 ; cap. Kingstown, on s.w. coast, 3368.

St. Vincent. Port. isl. of Cape Verde group, off N.W. coast of Africa ; a. 75 sq. m. ; cable station ; 698.

St. Vincent, Cape. Promontory on s.w. extremity of Portugal extending into Atlantic Ocean ; Brit. fleet under Jervis and Nelson defeated Sp. fleet in 1797 ; 3277.

Sakais (sah'-kīz). A race of the Malay Peninsula, 2069.

Saké (sah'-kē). National drink of Japan.

Sakhalin (sah-kah-lēn'). Long mountainous isl. near E. coast of Siberia ; a. 27,800 sq. m. ; pop. 339,000 ; s. part (Karafuto) a. about 14,000 sq. m., held by Japan from Russia 1905–45 ; large forests, fisheries ; 1797 ; *map, 1796.*

Saki (sah'-kē). A S. Amer. monkey, *2209,* 2210.

Sakkara (sak-kah'-ra). Eg. vil. near Nile R. 15 m. s.w. of Cairo ; noted for Step Pyramid and other tombs, *212,* 2708.

Sala (sah'-la), **George Augustus** (1828–95). Eng. journalist ; a friend of Dickens, to whose " Household Words " and " All the Year Round " he was a regular contributor ; special foreign correspondent for the Daily Telegraph.

Sal'adin (1138–93). Chivalrous Mahomedan leader, sultan of Eg. and Syria, 2864 ; and Crusaders, 936, 3145 ; and Richard I, 2776.

Salaman'ca. Old Sp. city 110 m. N.W. of Madrid ; pop. 91,000 ; anc. Sal-

mantica, captured by Hannibal ; beautiful medieval buildings ; Wellington defeated Fr. in Peninsular War ; 3030.

Salamander. An amphibian, 2864.

Salamis (sal'-a-mis), Greece. Barren mountainous isl. in Gulf of Aegina ; 36 sq. m. ; famous for defeat of Persian fleet by Greeks in strait between isl. and Attic coast (480 B.C.) ; 2556, 1522, 2999, 230.

Sal-ammo'niac, or ammonium chloride. 146, 375.

Salamvri'a or Salambria River. Same as **Peneus.**

Salandra, Antonio (1853–1931). It. statesman ; prime minister (1915–16.)

Salayer (sah-li'-er) or **Saleyer Islands.** A fertile group in Indonesia s. of Celebes ; a. 270 sq. m., of which 250 sq. m. are occupied by Salayer Isl. ; pop. of group 63,000 ; timber, tobacco, potatoes, indigo, and cotton.

Salazar, Antonio de Oliveira (b. 1889). Portuguese statesman ; Prime Minister of Portugal from 1932 ; 2660.

Sa'lem, Mass., U.S.A. City 13 m. N.E. of Boston on Atlantic ; pop. 41,200 ; in 1692 many tried for witchcraft and 20 put to death ; Nathaniel Hawthorne a native of, 1589.

Salem. Cap. of Oregon, U.S.A. ; pop. 31,000 ; 2449.

Salerno (sa-ler'-nō). It. port on Gulf of Salerno ; pop. 67,000 ; textiles ; medieval univ., 4140. Site of Allied invasion, Sept. 1943, 3421.

Sal'ford. City of s.e. Lancashire, suburb of Manchester ; pop. 175,230 ; cotton, iron, chemicals ; 1890.

Sa'lian line of Ger. emperors, 1449.

Salicin (sal'-i-sin). Drug obtained from willow and used in preparation of aspirin ; also synthetic.

Salic law. In popular usage, a code debarring succession to females and to those tracing descent from a woman ; instigated by Salic or Salian Franks of the 5th cent. A.D.

Salicylic (sal-i-sil'-ik) **acid.** A drug 1048, 2132.

Salisbury (sawlz'-be-ri), **Frank O.** (b. 1874). Eng. portrait painter ; first exhibited at Royal Academy in 1899 ; portraits of King George V and Queen Mary, George VI's Coronation, and other State pictures.

Salisbury, James Hubert Gascoigne Cecil, 4th Marquess of (1861–1947). Brit. politician ; Lord Privy Seal (1903–05) ; Pres. of Board of Trade (1905) ; Lord Pres. of the Council (1922–24) ; Lord Privy Seal (1924–29).

Salisbury, Robert Arthur Talbot Gascoigne Cecil, 3rd Marquess of (1830–1903). Brit. conservative statesman ; Sec. of State for India, as Lord Robert Cecil, 1866 ; For. Sec. 1878 ; premier 1885, 1886, and 1895–1902 ; cautious, but forceful when necessary, he was the greatest diplomatist of his generation ; 3279.

Salisbury, Eng. Co. tn. of Wiltshire on R. Avon ; pop. 31,600 ; agric. centre, 2864, 3383 ; cath., 219, 721 ; Georgian house at, 220.

Salisbury. Cap. of S. Rhodesia ; pop. 69,000 ; 2865, 2772.

Salisbury Plain. High rolling plain in Wiltshire, N. of Salisbury, 3383 ; Avebury, 323 ; Stonehenge, 3096.

Sali'va, 1470 ; function in digestion, 1016, 3082.

Sal'lust (Caius Sallustius Crispus) (86–34 B.C.). First Roman historian as distinguished from annalists, 1895.

Salmon (sam'-on). A food fish, 2865, 1300, *1308* ; in Alaska, 97, *1300* ; in Brit. Columbia, 579 ; eggs, *1094* ; in Gt. Britain, 2391, 1310 ; U.S.A. fisheries, 1300.

Salmond, Sir John Maitland (b. 1881). Eng. airman, Marshal of the Royal Air Force (1933) ; was Chief of the Air Staff during 1930–1933. His brother, Sir William Geoffrey Hanson Salmond (1878–1933), became the Commander-in-Chief of the Air Defence of Gt. Brit. in 1931, and reached the rank of Air Chief Marshal.

Salmonidae (sa:-mon'-i-dē). The salmon family of fishes, 3627.

Salome (sa-lō'-mē). Daughter of Herodias, who bade her ask of Herod the head of John the Baptist ; Byzantine mosaic, 637.

" Salome." Opera by R. Strauss, 3103.

Salonika, Saloniki or Salonica. See **Thessaloniki.**

Salop. Abbreviation for Shropshire, from Sloppesbury, old Saxon of Shrewsbury.

Sal'sify or oyster plant. Purple-flowered composite plant similar to goatsbeard.

Salt, Sir Titus (1803–76). British manufacturer ; founded woollen business in Bradford that grew to such an extent that the town of Saltaire was erected for it in 1853.

Salt, or sodium chloride. Common salt, **2865** ; associated with gypsum, 1559 ; atomic structure, 295 ; Carpathian deposits, 704 ; chemical formation, 20 ; chlorine in, 815, 1567 ; crystal, 772, 939 ; in electrolysis, 1131 ; in food preservation, 1340 ; essential to life, 2149 ; freezing point of salt solution, 1392 ; in glazing pottery, 2666 ; and halogens, 1567 ; in human body, 2601 ; ionized compound, 1738 ; in Leblanc and Solvay sodamaking processes, 2997 ; in sea water, 2413, 3351 ; mine, 2183 ; production, 2867 ; associated with oil, 2428 ; under spectroscope, 3055 ; sodium in, 2997 ; in water softeners, 3351.

Salt, in chemistry. A compound formed from an acid by replacement of part or all of its hydrogen by a metal or basic radicle, **2865**, 20 ; mineral salts in food, 1338 ; of potassium, 2262 ; in soap-making, 2993 ; of sodium, 20, 2865, 2997. For salts of the important elements see the element by name.

Salt cake. Sodium sulphate (Na₂SO₄), 2997.

Saltcoats, Scot. Spt. and wateringplace in Ayrshire, 30 m. s.w. of Glasgow ; coalmining ; pop. 10,200 ; 324.

Saltillo (sal-tēl'-yō). Trade centre in N.W. Mexico, cap. of Coahuila state ; pop. 75,721 ; textile mfrs., flour ; alt. 5,200 ft.

Salt Lake City, Utah, U.S.A. State cap. and leading commercial city ; pop. 150,000 ; founded by and headquarters of the Mormons ; state univ.; distributing centre for minerals and agric. produce of the surrounding region, 3300, 2230.

Salto, Uruguay. City on Uruguay r., 250 m. N.W. of Montevideo ; pop. 30,000 ; shipping point for stockraising dist.

Saltpetre or nitre. Potassium or sodium nitrate, **2868** ; Chilean industry, 803 ; in gunpowder, 1250 ; preparation, 803.

Salvador (sal-vah-dor'), **El.** Smallest of Cent. Amer. republics ; a. 13,173 sq. m. ; pop. 2,000,000 ; **2868**, map, 743.

Salvation Army, 2868 ; founded, 520.

Salvator Rosa. See **Rosa.**

Salvini (sal-vē'-nē), **Tommaso** (1829–1915). It. tragedian, a great " Othello " ; played with Ristori and Booth.

Sal volatile. Ammonium carbonate ; used for smelling salts as a stimulant in fainting. 146.

Salween or Salwin. R. of S. Asia ; rises in S.E. Tibet and flows 1,750 m. S. principally through Burma, to Gulf of Martaban.

Salzburg (zahlts'-boorg). Austrian city beautifully situated in Salzburg Alps, near Bavarian border ; pop. 106,900 ; cap. of prov. of Salzburg ; 316, map, 320 ; cath. and many other fine buildings ; home of Mozart and scene of annual Mozart music festival, 2249.

Samara. See **Kuibishev.**

Samaria (sa-mār'-i-a). Anc. city of Palestine, 35 m. N. of Jerusalem ; became cap. of Israel 9th cent. B.C. ; captured by Assyrians, 1829. Name also applied to surrounding region.

Samar'itans. A people of Palestine, 2483, 1829.

Sama'rium (Sm.). Metallic element of the rare-earth group, 768 ; atomic weight, 150·43. See also **Rare Earths.**

Samarkand (sa-mahr-kand'), U.S.S.R. Important trading city of Uzbekistan, Soviet Central Asia ; pop. 154,000 ; anc. Marcanda ; medieval centre of learning, 3267.

Sambre (sahn'-br). R. in N.E. Fr. and Belgium ; rises 120 m. N.E. of Paris and flows 100 m. N.E. to Meuse at Namur, 2156.

Sam Browne. Uniform belt worn by officers in Brit. army. Designed by Gen. Sir Samuel Browne (1824–1901). It consists of a belt and two straps which pass over the shoulders and cross at the back.

Sam'nites. Anc. warlike tribes, inhabiting mountainous portions of S. half of It. ; wars with Rome, 2805.

Samoa (sa-mō'-a). Chain of isls. in S. Pacific in a direct line between San Francisco and Australia ; formerly called Navigator Isls. ; over 1,000 sq. m. ; est. pop. 82,000 ; **2869** ; rainfall, 2741 ; Stevenson in, 3089.

Samos (sā'-mos). Small Greek isl. in Aegean near coast of Asia Minor ; pop. 77,800 ; flourished 6th cent. B.C. ; famous temple of Hera ; exports wines, raisins ; colonized by Greeks.

Sam'othrace. Small mountainous Gk. isl. in N. Aegean ; " Winged Victory " found here 1863, now in Louvre, 1276 ; colonized by Greeks.

Samothracian rings, in magnetism, 2060.

Sam'pans. Chinese house-boats, 694.

Sam'son. Hebrew judge and hero ; **2870.**

" Samson Agonistes." Tragedy by Milton, 2178, 2870.

" Samson and Delilah." Saint-Saëns' opera, 2440, 2870.

Samsun. Turkish spt. on Black Sea ; famed for tobacco ; pop. 38,400 ; 3266.

Sam'uel. Last of Hebrew judges ; anointed Saul and David (1 Samuel) ; gave name to 9th and 10th books of Old Testament, which contain the history of Israel from the birth of Samuel to the death of David ; 1829.

Samuel, Herbert Louis, 1st Viscount (b. 1870). Brit. Liberal politician and philosopher ; Home Sec. 1916 and 1931, resigning in the following year ; High Commissioner for Palestine (1920–25).

Samurai (sa'-moo-rī). Feudal warriors of Japan.

Sana. Capital of Yemen (Arabia), 197.

San Anto'nio, Texas, U.S.A., largest and oldest city of state ; pop. 253,800 ; mfrs.

Sanchez, Florencio. Argentine dramatist, 3027.

San'chi. Small vil. in India on Bombay-Baroda rly. famous for old Buddhist memorial mounds (topes), 1708, 1709.

Sancho (san'-kō) **Pan'za.** Squire in Cervantes' " Don Quixote," 746.

Sancti Spiritus, Cuba. City 20 m. from S. coast ; pop. 92,300 ; founded in 1515.

Sand, George. Pen name of Amandine Lucile Aurore Dupin, Baroness Dudevant (1804–76), Fr. novelist and feminist, 1381 ; and Chopin, 816.

Sand, 2870 ; carried by wind, 3384 ; desert, 996, 997 ; in glass-making, 1472 ; titanium in black, 3217 ; in water filtration, 3348, 3349. See Index **Deserts ; Dunes.**

Sandal, 521, 522 ; Roman, 521.

Sandalwood. Fragrant E. Indian tree, used for making boxes and also as a source of perfume and incense.

Sandarac (san'-da-rak). A resin, obtained from the sandarac tree which grows in N. Africa ; employed in varnish making.

Sanday. One of Orkney Isls., 2453.

Sand-bags. Used in war for defence, 2871.

Sandblast, 2871.

Sand-box tree. See **Monkey's dinner bell.**

Sandby, Paul (1725–80). Eng. watercolour painter, and one of the finest artists of this school, 3353.

Sand-dollar. A sea-urchin.

Sand dunes. See **Dunes.**

Sanderling. A wading bird (Calidris arenaria) about 8 in. long, distinguished by having only 3 toes ; winter visitor to Britain ; plumage white underneath, bluish grey above in winter and chestnut in summer.

" Sandford and Merton," by T. Day, 1965.

Sand-glass. For time measurement, 843.

Sandhurst. Vil. in Berkshire ; the Royal Military College, transferred from Gt. Marlow in 1812, and combined in 1947 with Royal Military Academy, Woolwich, trains at Sandhurst candidates for commissions in all branches of arms in Brit. Army, 251.

San Diego (san-dē-ā'-gō), California, U.S.A. Spt. and Pacific naval base ; 126 m. S.S.E. of Los Angeles ; splendid harbour ; also a notable watering-place ; mfrs. wagons and carriages ; pop. 203,340 ; 664.

Sand martin, 3124, 3125.

San Domin'go. See **Santo Domingo.**

San'dow, Eugen (1867–1925). Physical culturist, b. at Königsberg, Ger. ; was at one time famous as a wrestler and in 1897 was awarded the world's championship belt for weight-lifting ; (" Strength and How to Obtain It ").

Sandpiper. A shore bird, 447, 3331.

Sandringham House, Sandringham, Norfolk ; built in 1870 ; favourite residence of King Edward VII ; was considerably damaged by fire in 1891; country residence of Royal Family ; 2376.

Sandstone. Sand cemented into rock. 1432, 2795, 2871 ; source rock of oil, 2426.

Sand viper, 3325.

Sand wasp, 3345, 3346.

Sandwich, John Montagu, 4th Earl of (1718–92), Eng. politician, notorious for his personal and political vices ; First Lord of the Admiralty (1771–82) ; invented sandwich, 1209.

Sandwich. Small spt. in Kent, on R. Stour ; one of Cinque Ports ; important in Middle Ages ; pop. 3,800 ; famous golf course.

Sandwich Islands. See **Hawaiian Islands.**

Sandy Hook. Narrow sandy peninsula in U.S.A., on New Jersey coast extending 6 m. N. and partly enclosing New York Bay.

San Francisco, California, U.S.A., most important Pacific port of the country and world's greatest land-locked harbour ; pop. 634,000 ; **2871**, 2872 ; new bridges, 567, 569 ; earthquake and fire of 1906, 2871 ; United Nations Conference, May 1945, 2872, 3283.

San Francisco River. See **São Francisco River.**

Sanger, George (1827–1911). Eng. showman ; inaugurated travelling circus (1854) ; in 1871 purchased Astley's amphitheatre and menagerie, London, and also ran circuses.

San Giulio, isl., It., 1767.

Sangster, Charles. Canadian poet, 685.

San'hedrin. The supreme judicial council of the anc. Jews.

San Joaquin (wah-ken') River, California, U.S.A., rises in Sierra Nevada near Yosemite National Park, flows W. and N. to meet the Sacramento r. near its mouth ; 350 m. long.

San José. Cap. and largest city of Costa Rica ; pop. 77,000 ; centre of agric. region ; coffee trade ; port on Pacific coast, 917.

San José Scale, pest, 2879.

San Juan (hoo-ahn'). Cap. and chief port of Puerto Rico, on N. coast ; pop. 222,840 ; 2698.

San Juan River, Colombia, 873.

San Juan Teotihuacan. Aztec remains at, 327.

Sankey, Ira David (1840–1908). Amer. singer, hymn-writer (" The Ninety and Nine "), and evangelist, long associated with D. L. Moody.

Sankey, John Sankey, 1st Viscount (b. 1866). Brit. lawyer ; judge of high court (1914) ; presided over Sankey

Commission (1919), on labour conditions in coal mines ; Lord Chancellor (1929–35) ; prominent in Indian Round Table Conference.

San Luis Potosi, Mexico. State in E. centre ; a. 24,000 sq. m. ; pop. 678,780 ; cap. San Luis Potosi ; silver, 2157.

San Luis Potosi. Commercial and rly. centre in Mexico, 225 m. N.W. of Mexico City ; pop. 77,100 ; mining region ; immense silver-lead reduction works, 2157.

San Mar'co, Venice. *See* **St. Mark's.**

San Marino (ma-rē'-nō). Small republic in N. It., near Adriatic coast ; 38 sq. m. ; pop. 14,500 ; **2872.**

San Martin (mahr-tēn'), José de (1778–1850). S. Amer. patriot, general, and statesman ; led famous expedition across Andes (1817) ; drove Spaniards from Chile ; captured Lima, Peru, and proclaimed Peruvian independence (1821), 229, 3025.

San Remo (rā'-mō), It. Winter resort on Riviera, 75 m. S.W. of Genoa ; pop. 21,000 ; famous for mild climate ; conference of Supreme Council of allied premiers (1920), which awarded mandates for Near East, *1766* ; modern city suffered severe damage during 2nd World War.

San Sal'vador. Cap. of El Salvador, Cent. Amer., 25 m. from coast ; pop. 123,000 ; industrial and trade centre, 2868.

San Salvador or **Watling's Island.** One of Bahamas ; first Amer. land seen by Columbus, 339, 880 ; pop. 693.

Sansculotte (sahn-kū-lŏt'). Name given to the revolutionaries of 1790 by the Fr. aristocrats and afterwards adopted by them as a title of honour ; the term means " without breeches," and was applied to the revolutionaries because they forsook knee breeches for trousers.

San Sebastián. Sp. spt., mfg. city, and fashionable watering-place on Bay of Biscay, 12 m. from Fr. ; it has suffered many sieges, notably in 1719, 1808, 1813, 1836, and 1936 ; pop. 124,892 ; *3032.*

San'skrit. Anc. Hindu language ; literature, 1713 ; relation to other languages, 261, 1703, 2570.

Sans Souci (sahn-soo-sē'). Palace and royal park in Potsdam, near Berlin, built by Frederick the Great.

San Stefano (stă-fah'-nō). European Turkey, port on Marmara Sea ; treaty ending Russo-Turkish War (1878), 344, 3265.

Santa Ana. 2nd largest city of Salvador, Cent. Amer., 40 m. N.W. of San Salvador ; pop. 98,942.

Santa Anna, Antonio Lopez de (1795–1876). Mexican general and intriguing politician, alternately dictator and banished rebel ; abolished Mex. constitution, causing Texan revolt, 2158.

Santa Clara. City in cent. Cuba ; cap. of Las Villas prov. ; pop. 99,500 ; exports asphalt, graphite, tobacco.

Santa Claus, origin, 820.

Santa Cruz (san'-ta krooz), **Andres** (1794–1865). Bolivian patriot, general in war of independence, pres. 1829–39 ; failed in attempt at forcible federation of Peru and Bolivia.

Santa Cruz, Virgin Isls. *See* **St. Croix.**

Santa Cruz or **Queen Charlotte Islands,** Melanesia. Isl. group in Pacific Ocean, incl. in Brit. Solomon Is. group ; a. about 360 sq. m. ; discovered in 1595, 2470 ; feather money, *2202* ; outrigged canoe, *482.*

Santa Cruz de la Sierra, Bolivia. Tn. on E. slope of Andes ; pop. 33,000 ; rubber centre ; wireless station.

Santa Cruz de Teneriffe (tă-nă-rē'-fă). Cap. and port of Canary Isls. on isl. of Teneriffe ; pop. 79,928 ; coaling station, 690 ; attacked by Nelson, 2313.

Santa Fé (fā), Argentina. City on arm of Parana r., 95 m. N. of Rosario ; pop. 154,100 ; trade in hides, timber ; shipbuilding ; univ.

Santa Fé. Cap. of New Mexico (U.S.A.); pop. 20,300 ; 2342.

Santa Isabel. Cap. of Spanish Guinea, on the isl. of Fernando Po ; pop. of district 15,000 ; 3368.

Santal. Primitive tribe of N. India, a remnant of the pre-Aryan pop., retaining many early customs.

Santa Maria (ma-rē'-a). Columbus's flagship, *878.*

Sant' Ambrogio (am-brŏ-ji-ŏ). Church in Milan, 2172.

Santander, Sp. Important spt. on Bay of Biscay ; pop. 114,348 ; fisheries, shipyards ; fine harbour ; exports iron ore, paper, wine.

Sant' Angelo (sant-ahn'-je-lŏ), **Castle of** or Hadrian's Tomb, Rome, *2803.*

Santa Sophia, mosque. *See* **St. Sophia.**

Santayana, George (b. 1863). Amer. philosopher and author (" The Sense of Beauty," " The Life of Reason ") ; influence on Eng. literature, 1217.

Santi, Raphael. *See* **Raphael.**

Santiago (san-tē-ah'-gō). Cap. of Chile, and largest S. Amer. city on w. of Andes ; pop. 1,001,850 ; **2872,** 804.

Santiago Bay. Excellent landlocked harbour on S.E. coast of Cuba ; Sp. fleet destroyed in Sp.-Amer. War.

Santiago de Compostela, Sp. City in extreme N.W. ; pop. 28,000 ; univ. ; hospitals ; 11th-cent. cath. over shrine of Apostle St. James, *3034,* 3040.

Santiago de Cuba. Port on S.E. coast of Cuba ; pop. 120,827 ; mining dist. ; extensive export trade ; founded by Sp. (1514), early cap. of Cuba ; badly damaged by earthquake (1932) ; stormed by U.S.A. (1898), 941.

San'to Domin'go or **Hispaniola.** Isl. of the W. Indies ; 28,000 sq. m. ; *maps, 1565 and f. 2384* ; divided politically into **Dominican Republic ; Haiti.**

Santo Domingo (City). *See* **Ciudad Trujillo.**

Santorin (san-tō-rēn') (corruption of St. Irene). Volcanic isl. in Aegean Sea southernmost of Cyclades ; a. 27 sq. m. ; important remains of prehistoric Aegean civilization ; anc. Thera, powerful commercial state.

Santos, Brazil. Port 200 m. S.W. of Rio Janeiro ; pop. 190,000 ; good harbour ; port for São Paulo ; greatest coffee-shipping port in world, *553,* 554, 3022.

Santos-Dumont, Alberto (1873–1932). Aeronaut, b. Brazil ; built first airship propelled by internal-combustion engine, also first aeroplane to make public flight, 45.

San Vicente (vē-sen'-tă). City of republic of Salvador, 30 m. E. of San Salvador ; on Acahuapa r. ; pop. 35,500 ; large commerce, various mfrs.

São Francisco River. Chief r. in E. Brazil ; rises N.W. of Rio de Janeiro, flows 1,800 m. N. and E. to Atlantic, *maps, 551, f. 3024.*

São Luiz. Tn. of Brazil, cap. of state of Maranhão ; pop. 70,000.

Saône (sŏn) **River.** In E. Fr., rises just w. of Vosges Mts., flows 300 m. s. to Rhône ; connected with Loire and Seine by canals, 1360, 2043, 2774.

São Paulo (sow pow'-lŏ). Seaboard state of s. Brazil ; a. 91,000 sq. m. ; est. pop. 7,230,100 ; cap. São Paulo ; coffee, 554.

São Paulo. 2nd city in Brazil, 210 m. s.w. of Rio de Janeiro and 25 m. from coast ; pop. 1,120,400 ; industrial and trade centre ; greatest coffee market, 554.

São Paulo de Loanda. *See* **Loanda.**

São Salvador, Brazil. *See* **Bahia.**

São Tomé. *See* **St. Thomas.**

Sap, in plants, 2621 ; in trees, 3245.

Sapajou (sap'-a-jōō) or **Capuchin monkey,** 2208.

Saponifica'tion. The formation of soap, 2993.

" Sapper " (Lt.-Col. Cyril McNeile) (1888–1937). Eng. author ; creator of " Bull-dog Drummond," who appeared in a series of thrillers.

Sappers. The Royal Engineers, 246 ; 2184.

Sapphi'ra. *See* **Ananias.**

Sapphire (saf'-Ir). A precious stone, 1156, 1427 ; in Burma, 623.

Sappho (saf'-ō) (7th-6th cent. B.C.). Gk. poetess, b. isl. of Lesbos ; called " Flower of the Graces " ; known today by few exquisite fragments of verse ; legend says she flung herself from Leucadian rock for unrequited love ; 1540.

Saprophytes (sap'-rō-fIts). Plants which live on dead organic matter, 2621 ; among fungi, 1407 ; yeasts and fermentation, 1266.

Sap-wood, of trees, 3245.

Sar'aband. A slow and stately Spanish dance with music in triple time ; probably originated among Saracens.

Sar'acens. Name applied to Mahomedans in Middle Ages, 2067. *See also* **Arabs ; Mahomedanism ; Moors.**

Saragossa or **Zaragoza.** Sp. rly. and commercial centre on Ebro, 175 m. N.E. of Madrid ; pop. 262,042 ; taken by Fr. after heroic resistance in Peninsular War (1808–09) ; former capital of Aragon ; 3030

Sarah (Sarai), wife of Abraham, 13.

Sarajevo or **Serajevo.** Tn. of Yugoslavia, cap. of Bosnia, 528 ; pop. 78,000 ; Francis Ferdinand assassinated here ; 3409.

Sarasate (sa-rah-sah'-tă), **Pablo de** (1844–1908). Sp. violinist and composer ; noted for lively dance music.

Saratoga, battles of (Sept. 19 and Oct. 7, 1777), fought at Stillwater, 12 m. S.E. of Saratoga Springs, N.Y., U.S.A. ; Burgoyne surrenders (Oct. 17), 169.

Saratov, U.S.S.R. Important city on Volga, 450 m. S.E. of Moscow ; pop. 376,000 ; rly workshops, mfrs. ; exports grain ; extensive river trade.

Sarawak (sa-rah'-wak). Brit. colony in Borneo ; a. 50,000 sq. m. ; pop. 500,000 ; **2873,** 527 ; *map, 1074* ; in 2nd World War, 3420.

Sarcophagus (sahr-kof'a-gus). A stone coffin.

Sardanapalus (sahr-da-na-pā'-lus). Gk. name of last great Assyrian king, Assur-bani-pal. According to legend he burned himself, his wives and treasures, to avoid falling into rebel power. *See* **Assur-bani-pal.**

Sardines or **pilchards.** Small food fish which belong to the herring family, so called because they were once caught chiefly off coast of Sardinia, 2136, 2873 ; Brest fisheries, 560 ; important to anc. Greece, 1517 ; confusion with sprat, 1621.

Sardin'ia. It. isl. in Mediterranean w. of It. ; a. 9,302 sq. m. ; pop. 1,196,000 ; **2873,** *map, 1764* ; people, 1769. For history of kingdom *see* **Piedmont.**

Sardis or **Sardes.** Cap. of anc. Lydia, Asia Minor ; flourished under Croesus ; destroyed by Timur (A.D. 1402) ; important recent excavations ; 932.

Sardonyx (sahr'-do-niks). A variety of sardonyx.

Sardou (sahr-dōō'), **Victorien** (1831–1908). Fr. dramatist, dextrou and prolific ; chief works, " Fédora," " Madame Sans-Gêne," " La Tosca."

Sargas'so Sea. Region in N. Atlantic, *map, 294,* 2914.

Sargent, Sir Harold Malcolm Watts (b. 1895). Musician and orchestral conductor, 2447. Became conductor of B.B.C. Symphony Orch. in 1950

Sargent, John Singer (1856–1925). Anglo-Amer. painter, b. It., **2874,** 1183 ; Ellen Terry as Lady Macbeth, *2874* ; " Frieze of the Prophets," *2961* ; water-colours, 3353.

Sar'gon I (about 2750 B.C.). Founder of first great nation in w. Asia, 329.

Sargon II (reigned 722–705 B.C.), king of Assyria, 330, 1633 ; his city, 2372.

Sarikol Mts., cent. Asia, 263.

Sark. One of the Channel Isls. ; 3 m. long ; famous cliffs and caves ; 751 ; Germans occupy, 1940–45.

Sarong (sah'-rong). A garment, 2069.

Saron'ic Gulf. Arm of Aegean Sea, separating Peloponnesus from N.E. Greece, 689.

Saroy'an, William (b. 1908), U.S. novelist, short-story writer and playwright, 3295.

Sarpedon (sahr-pě'-don). Trojan War hero, 3249.

Sarsaparil'la. A cooling drink made from the dried roots of smilax and woody vines; it is prepared by boiling the roots in water.

Sar'to, Andrea del (1487–1531), Florentine artist, great draughtsman and colourist, 1620, 2766.

Sarto'rius muscle, 2258.

" Sar'tor Resar'tus," book by Carlyle, 703.

Sartre, Jean-Paul (b. 1905). Fr. novelist, dramatist, and Existentialist; mobilised 1939, taken prisoner 1940, worked for resistance movement; plays " Huis-Clos " (performed London and New York as " Vicious Circle " and " No Exit "), " Les Mouches," " La Putain Respectueuse "; novel (trilogy) " Les Chemins de la Liberté."

Sa'rum. See **Old Sarum ; Salisbury.**

Saskatch'ewan. A prairie prov. of Canada, greatest wheat-growing dist. of Dominion; a. 251,700 sq. m.; pop. 896,000; **2874,** 676; *map f. 680*; cap. Regina, *2875*; wheat-growing, 676.

Saskatchewan River, Canada. A river formed by union of N. and S. Saskatchewan branches near Prince Albert, Saskatchewan; flows 240 m. E. to L. Winnipeg; 2874, 678.

Saskatoon'. Second city of Saskatchewan; distributing point for grain and cattle; pop. 43,000; flour, cereals, foundry products, machinery; Univ. of Saskatchewan, 2875.

Sas'safras. A tree, native of N.E. Amer.; is used in medicine; makes fine yellow dye; also sassafras tea; belongs to laurel family.

Sas'sanid dynasty. Last native dynasty of anc. Persia (226–637), 2555.

Sassari (sas'-sah-rē), It. Prov. in Sardinia; name also of its cap. (pop. 60,000); *2873.*

Sassoon, Sir Philip Albert Gustave David, Bart. (1888–1939). Eng. politician; Under-Sec. for Air (1924–29 and 1931–37); 1st Commissioner of Works (from 1937); a generous patron of art, becoming chairman of Trustees of Brit. Museum in 1932.

Sassoon, Siegfried Loraine (b. 1886). Eng. poet and author, (" Memoirs of a Fox-hunting Man "; " Memoirs of an Infantry Officer "; " Collected War Poems "; " Sherston's Progress "), 1216.

Satan. See **Devil.**

Satellites (sat'-e-līts), of planets, 2618.

Sat'in. A glossy closely woven silk (or cotton and silk) fabric; introduced into Europe, 937.

Satinwood. A tree yielding fine cabinet wood; in Ceylon, 748.

Satire (sat'-īr). A type of literary composition in which vice and folly are ridiculed; Dryden, 1050; in Eng. literature, 1212; in Latin literature (Horace and Juvenal), 1897; Pope, *2654*; Swift, 3132.

Sat'suma ware. A kind of earthenware made in Japan; named from the prov. of Satsuma in S.W. of Kyushu; 1809.

Satura'tion point, in physics, 1000.

Sat'urday, 7th day of week; meaning of name, 980.

Sat'urn. In Rom. myth., god of agri., identified with Gk. Kronos, 2875; gave name to Saturday, 980.

Saturn, a planet, 2617; length of day, 2617; orbit, speed, and size, 279; rings, 2618; satellites, 2618.

Saturna'lia. Rom. festival, in honour of the god Saturn, held in the middle of December each year; the festival was marked by a general holiday, and was to the Romans what Christmas is to the Englishman, 1636, 2875.

Satyrs (sat'-erz). In Gk. myth., woodland deities, 1018, 2485.

Sauckel, Fritz (1894–1946). Ger. Nazi leader; in 1927 gauleiter of Thuringia; as Hitler's importer of slave labour to the Reich from occupied territories he deported 5,000,000 people; major war criminal at Nuremberg trials; hanged Oct. 16, 1946; 2282.

Saudi Arabia. Kingdom formed in 1932 by the union of Hejaz and Nejd, with an area of some 800,000 sq. miles and a pop. of about 4,500,000. Ruled by King Ibn Saud; 195.

Sauerkraut (sour'krout). A food popular in Ger.; it consists of shredded cabbages which have been salted and allowed to ferment.

Saul (sawl). First king of Israel (1030 B.C.), 1829, 2481; and David, 979.

Saul of Tarsus. See **Paul, St.**

Sault Sainte Marie (sō-san Ma-re'). The rapids of St. Mary's River or Strait, between ls. Superior and Huron, N. Amer.

Sault Sainte Marie (" Soo ") Canals, 1516, *map, 1515.*

Saurashtra, United States of. Union of 217 Kathiawar States in repub. of India; pop. 3,500,000; inaugurated Feb. 15, 1948; important constituent states are Nawanagar, Bhavnagar, Gondal, Porbandar, Rajkot.

Sau'ria. Sub-class of reptiles, 1972.

Saussure, Horace Benedict de. See **De Saussure.**

Sava. See **Save.**

Savage, Michael Joseph (1872–1940). New Zealand statesman. National Secretary of N.Z. Labour Party and its leader since 1933. In 1935 he became first Labour Prime Minister of the Dominion.

Sav'age, Richard (1696–1743). Eng. poet and playwright; works include a comedy, " Love in a Veil "; a tragedy, " Sir Thomas Overbury," in which he took the leading part; and his masterpiece, " The Wanderer," a poem; died in a debtors' prison at Bristol.

Savaii (sah-vī'-ē) or **Sawaii.** Largest of Samoan Isls.; a. 700 sq. m.; legendary home of Polynesian race.

Savan'nah, Georgia, U.S.A. Important Atlantic spt. and 2nd largest city of state, on Savannah r.; mfrs. machinery, cotton goods, and fertilizers; pop. 96,000.

Savannah, r. of U.S.A.; rises in Blue Ridge Mts., flows S.E. 450 m. to Atlantic Ocean; 1443.

Savannah. First steamship to cross Atlantic, 2946.

Savannas. Tracts of treeless grass land; African, *map facing p. 69,* 69.

Savart (sav-ahr), **Félix,** Fr. physicist and surgeon; research on liquids, polarization, capillary action; invented toothed-wheel apparatus to determine sound frequency; and worked on electro-magnetic currents, 3391.

Save (sahv). One of chief tributaries of the Danube; rises in Carniola and flows 500 m. across Yugoslavia; scene of fierce fighting in 1st World War; 408, *map, 344.*

Sav'ernake Forest, Wiltshire, 2 m. from Marlborough; about 16 m. in circumference, famous for avenues of beeches and fine deer park; 3383.

Sa'very, Thomas (1650–1715). Eng. inventor; steam pumping engine, 3085.

Savings banks, 357, 2662.

Savona (sa-vō'-na). City on Italian Riviera, 25 m. s.w. of Genoa; pop. 64,000; good harbour; important iron industries; large potteries.

Savonarola (sa-vō-nah-rō'-la), **Girolamo** (1452–98). Florentine priest and reformer, 2876.

Sa'vory. Labiate plant grown as a potherb; chief characteristics, narrow leaves and purple flowers; found in Europe.

Savoy (sa-voi'). Dist. of London lying between the Strand and the river; includes noted hotel and theatre of that name; the Savoy Chapel is all that now remains of palace built in 1245, by Peter, Earl of Savoy and Richmond; drawing by Rowlandson, *2832.*

Savoy. Former duchy lying between It. and Fr. in w. Alps; chequered history under House of Savoy after 11th cent.; ceded to Fr., 3319, 1769; and Geneva, 1428; obtains Sardinia, 2874.

Savoy, House of. Ancient royal family of Europe, a branch of which reigned over Italy until 1946; founded by Humbert the White-handed in first half of 11th cent. and ruled over Savoy and Piedmont for 9 centuries.

Savoy cabbage. A wrinkled-leaf variety, largely cultivated in Eng.

Saw, machine types, *2037.*

Sawfish. A long-snouted, ray-like fish, 2877.

Saw-flies, 2877, *2693.*

Sawmill, 1350, 2037.

Saw-tit, the great tit, 3218.

Sawyer beetle. One of the longhorn beetles living in rotten or decaying wood; mandibles, 1726.

Sax, Antoine Joseph (known as Adolphe) (1814–94). Belgian maker of musical instruments, and inventor of saxophone and saxhorn; 1643.

Saxe, Maurice (1696–1750). Illegitimate son of Augustus the Strong of Saxony and Poland; marshal of Fr., one of the greatest generals of his age; victor of Fontenoy.

Saxe-Altenburg. Former Ger. duchy, since 1919 part of Thuringia.

Saxe-Coburg-Gotha. Former Ger. duchy; Prince Albert, consort of Queen Victoria, was the younger son of the 1st Duke of; Coburg was added (1919) to Bavaria, but remainder of duchy is part of Thuringia.

Saxe-Meiningen. Former Ger. duchy, since 1919 part of Thuringia; on N. boundary of Bavaria.

Saxe-Weimar (vī'-mahr). Former Ger. grand duchy, since 1919 part of Thuringia; dukes of Saxe-Weimar were famous as patrons of art and literature, and Weimar became home of Goethe, Schiller, Herder, and other men of letters.

Sax'horn, musical instrument, 1643.

Sax'ifrage. A favourite garden plant, 2877.

Sax'ons. A Teutonic people of N. Ger. appearing in history in 2nd cent., 1237, 1449, 2878; Charlemagne conquers, 753; invasion of Britain, 574, 1194; rulers in Eng., see **England.** See also **Anglo-Saxons.**

Saxony. State (former kingdom) of s. Ger., a. 5,785 sq. m.; pop. 5,560,000; with part of Silesia became a *Land* (province) in 1946, **2878**; cap. Dresden, 1048, 1447; industrial dist. 1447; Leipzig, 1920; Saxon emperors, 1447; in Seven Years' War, 2924; Thirty Years' War, 3203; 2nd World War, 2878.

Sax'ophone. A musical instrument, 1643, 2267.

Sayce, Archibald Henry (1846–1933). Eng. scholar, Orientalist and historian; Prof. of Assyriology at Oxford Univ. (1891–1919).

Saye and Sele, Lord (d. 1450). Lord Chamberlain and Lord Treasurer to Henry VI; was beheaded by rebels under Jack Cade.

Sayers, Dorothy Leigh (b. 1893). Eng. author; famous for detective novels introducing Lord Peter Wimsey (" Murder Must Advertise," " Nine Tailors," " Gaudy Night," " Busman's Honeymoon"); also religious plays, " Man Born To Be King," etc.

Sayes Court. John Evelyn's estate at Deptford; occupied by Peter the Great in 1698; pulled down 1729; residence of Tudor Duke of Sussex.

Scabious. Name of several plants of family *Dipsacaceae,* common on dry hills and heaths in Eng. Field scabious (*Scabiosa arvensis*) is a tall plant with fine pale blue-lilac flower-heads, each head consisting of a large number of small, irregular flowers; other species are devil's-bit (*S. succisa*) so-called because of its truncated rootstock, said to have been bitten off by the devil (bluish flowers, very common on dry pastures), and small scabious (*S. columbaria*), with smaller flowers, found in heathy wastes and dry pastures; the stem leaves of the small scabious are pinnate, those of devil's-bit entire. All these plants flower in late summer and autumn.

Scaevola (sĕv'-ō-la), **Gaius Mucius.** Legendary Rom. hero ; captured by enemy and threatened with death by torture unless he would betray comrades, thrust right hand into fire and held it until consumed.

Scafell Pike. Mt. of Cumberland, Eng. ; is the highest mt. in Eng., attaining height of 3,210 ft. ; *583*, *1166*, 943 ; **Scafell** (Scaw Fell) is a separate peak, 943.

Scalding, relief for, 1295.

Scale, computing, 233.

Scale insects. Small bugs parasitic on trees and fruit, **2878** ; cochineal, 859 ; lac-insect, 1726.

Scales (Libra). Sign of the zodiac, 3444.

Scaliger (skal'-i-jer), **Joseph Justus** (1540–1609). Fr. scholar, called " Father of chronological science " ; first showed that chronologies of different nations must be compared ; son of the philosopher J. C. Scaliger (1484–1558).

Scal'lop. A bivalve mollusc, **2879**, 2199.

Scan'derbeg (**George Kasiriota**) (1403–67). National hero of Albania, 100, 3264.

Scandin'avia. Collective name applied to Denmark, Sweden and Norway, **2880** ; *map*, *2395* ; story, " The Apples of Iduna," 2881. *See also* **Denmark ; Norway ; Sweden.**

Scandinavian Deep, part of the North Sea, 2390.

Scandinavian languages and literature, 2880 ; English words derived from, 1209 ; folk-songs, 1335 ; Icelandic, 1685 ; myths, 2270, 2420 ; novel, 2403.

Scandinavian Peninsula, 1234, 2392, 3126 ; *map*, *2395*.

Scan'dium, (Sc.). Rare metallic element of the aluminium group ;

atomic weight, 45·10 ; found in tungsten ores ; 3437.

Scanning, in television, 3182, 3398.

Scapa (skah'pa) **Flow.** Channel in Orkney Isls., chief Brit. naval base in 1st World War, 2293, 2453 ; chief base of Home Fleet in 2nd World War.

Scar'ab, a beetle, 399, *401* ; Eg. seals, 1427.

Scarborough. Popular seaside resort in Yorkshire ; pop. 44,000 ; fisheries ; bombarded (1914) ; 3435.

Scarf skin, the epidermis, 2979.

Scarlatti, Alessandro (1659–1725). It. composer ; and opera, 2435.

" **Scarlet Letter.**" Novel by Hawthorne, 1589.

" **Scarlet Pimpernel.**" Character who appears in the series of novels (subsequently dramatized and filmed) by Baroness Orczy with a Fr. Revolutionary background.

Scarlet, Will. One of Robin Hood's men, 2790.

Scarlet runner, a bean-plant, 380, *381.*

Scarlet tanager. American bird, *3150.*

Scar-tattooing, 3158.

Scaw Fell. *See* Scafell Pike.

Sceptre, in regalia, 935 ; *frontis. Vol. 2.*

Schacht (shahkat), **Dr. Hjalmar Horace Greeley** (b. 1877). Ger. economist. On the collapse of the mark (1923) introduced " Rentenmark " to stabilise currency. First Pres. of Reichsbank in 1924. Minister of Economic Affairs 1934–37, afterwards Minister without portfolio. Tried as war criminal, Nuremberg, 1945–46 ; released. Tried by Ger. denazification court and sentenced ; released on appeal.

Schaffhausen (shahf-how'-zen), Switzerland. Cap. of canton of same name, 24 m. N. of Zurich ; pop.

21,118 ; *plate f. 3141* ; celebrated falls of Rhine, 2769.

Scharn'horst, Gerhard Johann David von (1755–1813). Prussian general, one of founders of Prussian military system (1809–13) ; fatally wounded at battle of Lützen.

Scharnhorst. Ger. battleship, second of name ; completed 1939, displacing 26,000 tons ; sank armed merchant cruiser Rawalpindi (*q.v.* in *f-i.*), Nov. 23, 1939 ; damaged by aircraft, she was driven from Brest (where the Gneisenau was being repaired) to La Pallice, returning later ; both ships escaped up the Channel Feb. 12, 1942, Scharnhorst being later bombed at Kiel and Altenfjord, Norway ; on Dec. 26, 1943, she put to sea to attack a Russ. bound Brit. convoy, was intercepted by 3 cruisers and hit below water by the Duke of York, and later torpedoed and sunk by the cruiser Jamaica.

Schaumburg-Lippe. State in N. Ger. formerly principality ; a. 131 sq. m. ; pop. 50,000 ; merged into new *land* of Lower Saxony.

Scheele, Karl Wilhelm (1742–86). Swedish chemist ; discovered chlorine, 816 ; discovered oxygen as well as Priestley, 2466.

Schee'lite, a tungsten ore, 3254.

Scheer, Reinhard von (1863–1928). Ger. admiral ; commander-in-chief of Ger. battle fleet in latter part of 1st World War (inc. Battle of Jutland).

Schef'fel, Joseph Viktor von (1826–86). Ger. poet and novelist (" Der Trompeter von Säckingen " ; " Ekkehard ").

Scheffer, Ary (1795–1858). Fr. classical painter of historical and religious pictures ; " Dante and Beatrice," *969.*

LEADING WRITERS OF SCANDINAVIA

Carl Ludwig Emil Aarestrup (1800–56). Denmark. Poems : " Samlede Digte."

Hans Christian Andersen (1805–75). Denmark. Fairy tales, poems, novels, travel sketches ; " The Ugly Duckling " ; " The Tinder Box " ; " Big Claus and Little Claus," etc. ; " The Dying Child " ; " Only a Fiddler " ; " In Spain."

Anders Christensen Arreboe (1587–1637). Denmark. " Hexaëmeron " (a poem in six books on the six days of creation).

Jens Immanuel Baggesen (1764–1826). Denmark. Poems : " Comical Tales " ; " The Labyrinth " ; " Parthenais."

Björnstjerne Björnson (1832–1910). Norway. Stories of peasant life. " Synnöve Solbakken " ; " Arne " ; " A Happy Boy " ; " The Fisher Maid." Novels : " Flags are Flying in Town and Port " ; " In God's Way." Plays : " Lame Hulda " ; " King Sverre " ; " Sigurd the Bastard " ; " Sigurd the Crusader " ; " The Editor " ; " Beyond Our Powers " ; " Laboremus " ; " Dagelannet."

Georg Brandes (1842–1927). Denmark. Criticism. " Main Currents of Nineteenth Century Literature " ; " Study of Shakespeare."

Olof von Dalin (1708–63). Sweden. Poems : " Saga om Hasten " (" Tale of the Horse ") ; " Svenska Friheten " (" Swedish Freedom ").

Johannes Ewald or **Evald** (1743–81). Denmark. Poems : " Balder's Death " ; " Adam and Eve " ; " The Fishermen."

Arne Garborg (1851–1924). Norway. Dialect stories : " At Home with Mother " ; " Weary Folk."

Nikolai Frederik Severin Grundtvig (1783–1872). Denmark. Theology : " The Church's Reply " (a protest against the rationalistic tendency of the day). Miscellaneous : " Northern Mythology " ; " Roskilda Rhymes " ; " Roskilda Saga " ; " Northern Verses " ; " A Handbook of Universal History."

Per August Leonard Hallström (b. 1866). Sweden. Novels and short stories : " Wild Birds " ; " An Old Story " ; " Spring, a Novel of the Nineties " ; " New Tales."

Knut Hamsun (b. 1859). Norway. Novels : " Hunger " ; " Growth of the Soil " ; " August."

Sven Anders von Hedin (b. 1865). Sweden. Travel books : " Adventures in Tibet " ; " Overland to India " ; " My Life as an Explorer " ; " Mount Everest " ; " Jehol, die Kaiserstadt."

Carl Gustav Vernher von Heidenstam (1859–1940). Sweden. Novels : " Endymion " ; " Hans Alienus." Historical works : " The Carolins " (Eng. translation, " A King and his Campaigners ") ; " The Pilgrimage of St. Bridget " ; " The Swedes and their Chieftains."

Henrik Hertz (1798–1870). Denmark. Poetical dramas : " Svend Dyring's House " ; " King René's Daughter."

Ludvig Holberg (1684–1754). Denmark. Mock-heroic poem : " Peder Paars." Comedies : " The Pewterer turned Politician " ; " The Waverer " ; " The Fidget " ; " Henrik

and Pernille." History : " History of Denmark " ; " Biographies of Famous Men."

Henrik Ibsen (1828–1906). Norway. Plays : " Pillars of Society " ; " A Doll's House " ; " Ghosts " ; " An Enemy of the People " ; " The Wild Duck " ; " Rosmersholm " ; " The Lady from the Sea " ; " Hedda Gabler " ; " The Master Builder " ; " Little Eyolf " ; " John Gabriel Borkman " ; " When We Dead Awaken." Dramatic poem : " Peer Gynt."

Ellen Key (1849–1926). Sweden. " The Century of the Child " ; " Ideas " ; " Lines of Life."

Selma Lagerlöf (1858–1940). Sweden. Novels and short stories. " Gösta Berling's Saga " ; " Jerusalem " ; " The General's Ring " ; " Anna Svörd."

Jonas Lauritz Edemil Lie (1833–1908). Norway. Novels : " The Visionary " ; " The Commodore's Daughters " ; " Niobe." Play : " Grabow's Cat."

Fridtjof Nansen (1861–1930). Norway. Travel and history : " The First Crossing of Greenland " ; " Esquimo Life " ; " Farthest North " ; " In Night and Ice " ; " Norway and the Union with Sweden " ; " Spitzbergen " ; " Sporting Days in Wild Norway."

Adam Gottlob Oehlenschläger (1779–1850). Denmark. Plays : " The Eve of St. Agnes " ; " Aladdin " ; " Hakon Jarl " ; " Palnatoke."

Christiern Pedersen (d. 1554). Denmark. A pioneer of Danish literature. Stories of Ogier the Dane and Charlemagne. Trans. " Christian III's Bible."

Henrik Pontoppidan (1857–1943). Denmark. Novels : " Soil " ; " The Promised Land " ; " Lucky Peter " ; " A Winter's Journey." Drama : " Storeholt."

Johan Ludvig Runeberg (1804–77). Swedish-Finnish poet. " The Elk Hunters " ; " King Fjalar " ; " The Tales of Ensign Stål," containing " Our Land, our Land," the national song of Finland.

Saxo Grammaticus (12th century). Denmark. History : " Historia Danica."

Snorri Sturlason (1179–1241). Iceland. Poems and histories : " The Younger or Prose Edda " ; " Heimskringlasaga " (Lives of the Kings).

Georg Stjernhielm (1598–1672). Sweden. Didactic poem : " Hercules."

August Strindberg (1849–1912). Sweden. Novels : " The People of Hemsö " ; " The Life of the Skerry Men." Plays : " Gustavus Vasa " ; " Christmas " ; " The Dance of Death."

Sturla Thordarson (1214–84). Iceland. " The Islendinga Saga."

Esaias Tegner (1782–1846). Sweden. Poems : " Svea " ; " Frithiof's Saga."

Sigrid Undset (1882–1949). Denmark. Novels. " Kristin Lavransdatter " ; " The Master of Hestviken " ; " Ida Elizabeth " ; " Saga of Saints."

LANDMARKS IN THE HISTORY OF SCIENCE

B.C.

*c.*600 Thales of Miletus discovers that rubbed amber attracts light bodies.

*c.*500 The relationship between the tension in a wire and the note it emits when plucked discovered by Pythagoras.

*c.*400 Hippocrates, the first practising physician and surgeon.

*c.*300 The law of Reflexion of Light proved by Euclid. Theophrastus studies the germination of seeds.

290 The nervous system of Man investigated by Erasistratus.

260 Law of Moments and principle of the lever known to Archimedes.

220 The force of buoyancy in liquids discovered by Archimedes.

212 Archimedes said to have used the sun's heat reflected from a concave mirror to set the Roman fleet on fire.

130 A crude steam turbine invented by Hero.

A.D.

*c.*77 " Natural History "—a monumental encyclopedia published by Pliny the elder.

127 Earliest physics experiment on record, made by Ptolemy.

*c.*180 Anatomy and physiology brought to a high standard by Galen.

1000 America discovered by Leif Ericsson.

1200 Preparation of " oil of vitriol " or sulphuric acid, " aqua fortis " or nitric acid, aqua regia, and caustic alkalis described by Geber.

*c.*1280 Magnifying glass and gunpowder invented by Roger Bacon.

1450 Printing press invented by Gutenberg.

1500 First pistol invented.

1582 The time of swing of a pendulum is shown to be constant even though the amplitude diminishes, by Galileo.

1590 Galileo discovers that all bodies fall with the same rate of acceleration.

1600 The term " electricity " used for the first time by Gilbert, who also discovered that the earth is a magnet. Magic lantern invented by Kircher.

1608 The telescope invented by Lippershey.

1609 Jupiter's moons discovered by Galileo.

*c.*1609 Air thermometer invented by Galileo.

1610 Sun spots discovered by Harriott, Fabricias, and Scheiner.

1615 Circulation of the blood discovered by Harvey.

1620 Scientific method defined by Francis Bacon.

1621 Law of Refraction of Light discovered by Snell but not published.

*c.*1630 A system of philosophy applied to science developed by Descartes.

1637 Law of Refraction of Light published by Descartes.

1640 The word " gas " coined by van Helmont.

1643 First barometer made by Torricelli.

1648 Pascal shows that the barometric pressure is less on top of a mountain.

1649 " Spirit of salt," " muriatic acid," or hydrochloric acid prepared by Glauber.

1657 Pendulum clock invented by Huygens.

1660 The microscope invented by Leeuwenhoek.

1661 Boyle conceives the modern idea of the chemical element.

1662 Boyle's Law relating the pressure and volume of a gas at constant temperature, stated.

1663 Pascal shows that the pressure in a liquid depends upon its depth and density.

1665 Law of Gravitation discovered by Newton. Interference of light observed by Hooke. Diffraction of light observed by Grimaldi.

1666 Newton investigates the spectrum of light.

1669 Double refraction of light by Iceland spar discovered by Bartholinus.

1670 The " Phlogiston Theory " of combustion developed by Becher and Stahl.

1676 Law relating the stress and strain in a body stated by Hooke. The velocity of light determined by Römer.

1678 Wave Theory of light developed by Huygens.

1680 " Salt " in chemistry defined by Boyle.

1687 Laws of Motion of bodies stated by Newton.

1702 ": Volatile sulphurous acid " or sulphur dioxide prepared by Stahl, who burnt sulphur in air.

1704 Newton shows that diamonds will burn in air.

1709 Alcohol thermometer invented by Fahrenheit.

1720 Mercury thermometer invented by Fahrenheit.

1734 Two-Fluid Theory of electricity put forward by Du Fay.

1736 Classification of plants by Linnaeus.

1742 Centigrade thermometer scale devised by Celsius.

1745 Leiden jar discovered by Musschenbroek.

1747 One-Fluid Theory of electricity stated by Franklin.

1750 Industrial revolution or era of machines begins.

1752 Franklin obtains electricity from a thundercloud and invents the lightning conductor.

1754 Alkalis, earths, metals, and bases defined by Rouelle.

1755 " Fixed air " or carbon dioxide prepared from chalk by Black.

1760 Latent Heat of fusion and vaporization, and Specific Heat discovered and named by Black.

1766 " Inflammable air " or hydrogen prepared by Cavendish.

1769 First steam motor-car built by Cugnot.

1770 India-rubber given this name by Priestley.

1772 Priestley discovers " nitrous air " (called nitrogen in 1791 by Chaptal) in air, also " diminished nitrous air," the anaesthetic now known as nitrous oxide and called laughing gas by Davy in 1799.

1774 " Dephlogisticated marine acid air " or chlorine prepared by Scheele. Priestley discovers oxygen. Scheele also discovers oxygen independently, but does not publish his work until 1777.

1776 " Inflammable air," or carbon monoxide, prepared by Lassone.

1777 Oxygen theory of combustion put forward by Lavoisier.

1781 Water synthesized by Cavendish, who exploded hydrogen with oxygen. Uranus discovered by Sir William Herschel.

1782 Prussic acid prepared by Scheele.

1783 The hot air balloon invented by the Montgolfiers.

1784 Inverse Square Law of magnetism announced by Coulomb.

1785 Horse-power as a unit of work introduced by Watt. Power loom invented by Cartwright.

1787 " Method of Chemical Nomenclature " published by Lavoisier. Charles' Law of the expansion of gases enunciated.

1789 Classified list of 30 elements published by Lavoisier.

1790 Sewing machine invented by Saint.

1791 Effect of electricity on the muscles of a frog's leg published by Galvani.

1792 Gas lighting invented by Murdock.

1793 Photometry investigated by Rumford.

1794 Ethylene prepared and examined by a group of Dutch chemists.

1796 Vaccination first performed by Jenner.

1798 Mass of the earth determined by Cavendish. Rumford discovers that heat is due to molecular motion.

1799 Laws of Chemical Affinity announced by Berthollet. The Law of Fixed Proportions of combining weights of elements announced by Proust.

2,500 YEARS OF DISCOVERY AND INVENTION

1800 Electric cell invented by Volta. Nicholson and Carlisle electrolysed water. Infra-red portion of spectrum discovered by Sir William Herschel.

1801 Ultra-violet portion of spectrum discovered by Ritter. " Energy " defined by Young.

1802 Davy takes a photograph, but it fades.

1803 First practical steamer constructed by Fulton.

1808 Law of Multiple Proportions discovered by the chemist Dalton, but not published until 1810 by Berzelius. Atomic Theory of matter published by Dalton.

1809 Law of Volumes of Combining Gases stated by Gay-Lussac.

1811 Avogadro's Hypothesis first put forward. Iodine discovered by Courtois.

1813 Oxygen used as the standard of atomic and molecular weights (16) by Thomas Thomson. Fluorine discovered by Davy.

1814 Stephenson's first railway engine built.

1815 Prout suggests that the atomic weights of the elements are exact multiples of the atomic weight of hydrogen.

1817 Selenium discovered by Berzelius, who also lays down his theory of radicals.

1818 Davy invents the safety lamp. Dulong and Petit state a law that the product of the specific heat and atomic weight of elements is always the same.

1819 A list of 50 elements published by Berzelius.

1820 The magnetic effect of an electric current is discovered by Oersted. The diamond, graphite, and charcoal are described as " allotropes " by Berzelius.

1822 Velocity of sound determined by Arago.

1825 First steam railway opened—between Stockton and Darlington.

1826 Ohm announces his Law of Resistance in electrical circuits. Bromine discovered by Balard.

1827. Aluminium prepared by Wöhler. Brown observes the movements in liquids due to molecular motion.

1828 First synthesis of an animal product—urea—by Wöhler.

1830 Biology and geology related by Owen and Lyell's studies of fossils.

1831 Dynamo invented by Faraday. North magnetic pole discovered by Ross.

1832 Reaping machine invented by McCormick.

1834 Faraday states his Laws of Electrolysis of solutions. Dumas announces the three Laws of Substitution in organic chemistry. Peltier discovers the thermo-electric effect.

1837 Photography invented by Daguerre. Morse invents the telegraph.

1842 Ether used as an anaesthetic in the U.S.A. Law of Conservation of Energy announced by Mayer.

1843 Typewriter invented by Thurber. Joule overthrows the caloric theory of heat by his experiments on converting motion into heat, and thus helps to establish the law of conservation of energy. Faraday performs his famous Ice Pail Experiment on static electric induction.

1846 Neptune discovered by Adams.

1851 Second Law of Thermodynamics described independently by Kelvin and Clausius.

1852 Steam-driven airship invented by Gifford. Fluorescence studied by Stokes.

1854 Nursing revolutionized by Florence Nightingale.

1856 Aniline dye first made accidentally by Perkin.

1858 Theory of Evolution announced by Darwin. Cannizaro takes hydrogen (1) as the standard of atomic and molecular weights, and restates Avogadro's Law, which gains universal recognition.

1860 Forerunner of the gramophone invented by Reis. Bunsen and Kirchhoff discover rubidium and caesium spectroscopically.

1865 Wireless waves foreseen by Clerk-Maxwell. Kekulé suggests a structural formula for benzene. Antiseptics introduced by Lister.

1869 Periodic Law of the properties of the elements stated by Mendeléeff.

1873 Photo-electric cell invented by May.

1875 Telephone invented by Bell.

1876 Phonograph (now gramophone) invented by Edison.

1877 Pasteur proves the germ theory of anthrax and other diseases. Liquid oxygen obtained by Pictet and Cailletet independently.

1878 Microphone invented by Hughes.

1879 Law of Radiation of black bodies stated by Stefan and used as the basis of optical pyrometry.

1880 Still pictures transmitted over considerable distances by Carey.

1882 Tuberculosis shown by Pasteur to be due to a bacterium.

1884 Steam turbine invented by Parsons.

1885 Safety bicycle invented by Starley.

1887 Wireless waves demonstrated by Hertz. Daimler builds the first petrol-driven car. Panhard and Levassor patent the clutch and gearbox of the type now used in cars. Michelson and Morley fail to show the existence of the ether.

1889 Artificial silk manufactured by Chardonnet.

1895 The first wireless message sent by Marconi. X-rays discovered by Röntgen. Argon found in the air by Rayleigh and Ramsay.

1896 Radioactivity discovered by Becquerel. Zeeman discovers the effect of magnetism on polarized light.

1897 The electron discovered by J. J. Thomson.

1898 Cause of malaria discovered by Ross. Pierre and Marie Curie discover radium.

1899 The alpha, beta, and gamma rays (radioactive) discovered by Rutherford.

1900 Planck propounds Quantum theory.

1903 First flights in a power-driven aeroplane. Cosmic radiation first studied by Kohlhörster and Millikan.

1904 Wireless valve invented by Fleming.

1905 Einstein publishes his Theory of Relativity.

1906 Vitamins discovered to be a necessary part of diet by Hopkins. Tungsten filaments replace carbon filaments in electric light-lamps. Bakelite invented by Baekeland.

1908 South magnetic pole discovered by members of Shackleton's expedition.

1909 Einstein publishes his Special Theory of Relativity.

1911 A vitamin is isolated for the first time by Funk. Helium liquefied and low temperature (−436° F.) attained by Onnes.

1912 X-rays are found by von Laue to be a form of radiation.

1913 Atoms with the same chemical properties but different atomic weights are termed " isotopes " by Soddy.

1914 Einstein publishes his General Theory of Relativity.

1920 Aston shows that many elements are mixtures of isotopes, each of atomic weight a multiple of 1, see A.D. 1815.

1926 Television demonstrated by Baird.

1930 Pluto, planet, discovered by Tombaugh.

1931 Heavy hydrogen (deuterium) and heavy water discovered by Urey.

1932 Positron discovered by Anderson. Neutron discovered by Chadwick.

1939 Atom split by Joliot.

1940 Penicillin (discovered by Fleming, 1928), medical value established by Florey.

1941 First British (Whittle turbine) jet-propelled aircraft flew.

1945 First atom bombs dropped.

Scheherazade (she-hă-ră-zah'-de) in the "Arabian Nights," wife of the sultan and narrator of the tales, 203 ; also title of symphonic suite by Rimsky-Korsakov. to which was designed a ballet.

Scheidemann (shī'-de-mahn), **Philipp** (1865–1939). Ger. Socialist leader, first chancellor of Ger. republic (1919).

Scheldt or **Schelde**. An important navigable r. of Belgium rising in Fr. and flowing 250 m. to North Sea ; *map, 404* ; Antwerp, 181 ; delta, 2318.

Schelling (shel'-ing), **Friedrich Wilhelm Joseph von** (1775–1854). Ger. philosopher, 1457.

Schenectady (ske-nek'-ta-di), New York, U.S.A. Industrial city on R. Mohawk, about 18 m. N.W. of Albany ; manufactures include motors, machine-shop products and electrical apparatus ; wireless stations ; pop. 87,500.

Scheria (skē'-ri-a), **Island of**, in "Odyssey." Home of Phaeacians ; probably Corfu, 2422.

Scherl, Richard. Designer of a monorail.

Scherzo (skärt'-sō). In music, 2264.

Scheveningen (skā-vening-en). A fishing port and watering place of the Netherlands on North Sea, 1564, 2320 ; costume, *2322.*

Schiaparelli (skyah-pah-rel'-li), **Giovanni** (1835–1910). It. astronomer, first to detect the "canals" on Mars.

Schick test, for diphtheria, 180 ; method discovered in 1913 by Bela Schick, Hungarian bacteriologist. Generally used.

Schiedam (skē-dahm'), Netherlands. River port near mouth of Meuse ; pop. 62,624 ; numerous canals ; distilleries, trade in gin, grain.

Schiller (shil'er), **Ferdinand Canning Scott** (1864–1937) ; Eng. philosopher, leading Eng. exponent of pragmatism ("Riddles of the Sphinx," "Humanism").

Schiller, Johann Christoph Friedrich (1759–1805). Ger. poet and dramatist , **2882** ; friendship with Goethe, 1457, 1479 ; in Weimar, 3362.

Schipperke (skip'er-ke), dog, *plate f. 1024.*

Schirach, Baldur von (b. 1907). Ger. politician ; joined Nazi party 1924 ; by 1930 head of Nazi youth associations ; in 1932 Führer of Hitler youth ; anti-Christian propagandist ; in 1940 Gauleiter of Vienna ; recanted his Nazism at Nuremberg trials ; sentenced to 20 yrs.' imprisonment.

Schism. *See* **Great Schism.**

Schizomycetes (skī'-zō-mi-sēt-ēz). Plant sub-phylum, including bacteria and blue-green algae.

Schlegel (shlā'-gel), **August Wilhelm von** (1767–1845). Ger. critic poet, and translator.

Schlegel, Karl Wilhelm Friedrich von (1772–1929). Ger. critic, scholar and poet, "real founder of romantic school" ; brother of above.

Schleiermacher (shll'er-mah-kher), **Friedrich Ernst Daniel** (1768–1834). Ger. theologian and philosopher.

Schleswig-Holstein or **Slesvig-Holstein** (shlez'-vig-hol'-shtīn). Former Prussian prov. in Danish peninsula ; former Danish duchies of Schleswig, Holstein and Lauenburg forcibly annexed by Prussia (1866) ; N. Schleswig returned to Denmark following plebiscite after 1st World War, *map, 992*, 992, *993*. Until 1945 Prussian, when it came within British occupied zone bordering Denmark. Pop. 2,650,480.

Schleyer, Johann Martin (1831–99). Ger. priest, inventor, in 1879, of Volapuk, an international language.

Schliemann (shlē'-mahn), **Heinrich** (1822–90). Ger.-Amer. archaeologist, **2883** ; excavations at Troy, 3252.

Schmalkalden (shmahl-kahl'-den). Tn. of Hesse-Nassau, Prussia ; iron and steel mfg. centre ; here Protestant princes of Ger. formed Schmalkaldic

League, 1530, to resist efforts of Charles V to stamp out Protestantism.

Schmalkal'dic War (1546–47), 2759.

Schmidt (shmit), **Otto J.** Arctic explorer and professor. Organized Soviet North Pole expedition of 1937, 2646.

Schnabel (shnah-bel), **Artur** (b. 1882). Austrian pianist. Début in Vienna, 1896 ; world-renowned in particular for his masterly playing of Beethoven's works.

Schneider Trophy. International trophy, open to seaplanes of all nations. Presented in 1913 by Jacques Schneider, a Fr. patron of aviation ; discontinued after 1931 event, the trophy being won outright by Gt. Britain at 340 m.p.h.

Schnitzler (shnits-ler), **Arthur** (1862–1931). Austrian dramatist and novelist ; light, deft, psychological comedy and satire ; "Anatol" ; "Liebelei" ; "Professor Bernhardi."

Schnör.kel. Ger. device for submarines ; two air shafts, extendable to sea surface, allow submerged submarine to run electric motors and charge accumulators without robbing sub, of air and fouling atmosphere with exhaust ; standard Brit. equipment after 2nd World War, 3107.

Scholas'ticism. Medieval system of philosophy, 2572.

Schönberg (shēn-bärg), **Arnold** (b. 1874). Austrian composer. Best-known works "Gurrelieder" (for orch. and chorus) ; "Pelléas et Mélisande" (symphonic poem) ; "Pierrot Lunaire" (song cycle), 2266.

Schönbrunn (shēn'-broon). Imperial palace near Vienna, Austria ; treaties signed here between Napoleon and Prussia (1805) and Austria (1809) deprived these two countries of much territory.

Schöngauer (shēn'-gow-er), **Martin** (1446–91). Ger. painter and engraver, who attained, especially in his engravings, a firmness in modelling, delicacy in shading, and picturesqueness in landscape background exceeding any previous Ger. artist, 1454.

School, 2883 ; colours, 877 ; examinations, 1246 ; in Gt. Brit., 1089 ; medieval, *1197* ; Montessori system, 2220 ; open-air lessons, *2595* ; physical training, 2589 ; school-room, *1591* ; wireless lessons, 3398. *See also* **Education** ; **Universities.**

School Boards, 2884.

School Certificate. Examination taken in Public and secondary schools before leaving.

Schoolcraft, Henry Rowe (1793–1864). Amer. ethnologist ("Indian Tribes of the U.S.A." 6 large volumes published by order of Congress, which provided background for Longfellow's "Hiawatha"). Indian agent in L. Superior region for nearly 20 years ; discovered Mississippi's source.

"School for Scandal, The." One of R. B. Sheridan's popular comedies, first produced in 1777 ; the action deals chiefly with the scandal-mongers who frequented Lady Sneerwell's house, 2944.

School leaving age, 2886.

Schoolmen, in Middle Ages, learned doctors, versed in scholasticism, 2572.

School stories, 2887.

Schooner, a sailing vessel, 484.

Schopenhauer (shō' - pen - how - er), **Arthur** (1788–1860). Ger. philosopher, who taught the pessimistic doctrine that the only ultimate "reality is one universal will" ; but will or impulse is not rational, therefore Man's permanent redemption can be obtained only by moral unselfishness and resignation, 1457.

Schreiner (shrī'-ner), **Olive** (1862–1920). S. African author ; used pen name "Ralph Iron" ; wrote "Story of an African Farm" (a spiritual autobiography, showing a development from rigid Calvinism to hopeless atheism) ; "Women and

Labour" (an expression of her strong feminist views), 3020.

Schreiner, William Philip (1857–1919). S. African statesman, brother of the above. Prime Minister of Cape Colony 1898–1900 ; High Commissioner of S.A. Union in London from 1914.

Schubert (shōō'-bärt), **Franz Peter** (1797–1828). Austrian composer, world's greatest song-writer, **2887** 2265.

Schumann (shōō'-mahn), **Clara** (1819–96). Ger. musician, one of the great concert pianists of her time ; after her husband's death she wrote numerous charming songs and some instrumental music, largely in her husband's style, 2887.

Schumann, Robert (1810–56). Ger. composer, **2887**, *2888*, 2265.

Schuschnigg (shoo'-shnig), **Kurt von** (b. 1897). Austrian statesman ; Minister of Education and then of Justice in 1932, under Dr. Dollfuss. Founded the Sturmscharen, a military organization of Catholic youth. Succeeded Dollfuss as Chancellor of Austria in 1934, and remained in office until the annexation of Austria by Ger. in March, 1938. Arrested for high treason after the "Anschluss" ; 318, 3416. Released by Allies, May 1945.

Schwann (shvahn), **Theodor** (1810–82). Ger. physiologist ; discovered pepsin, investigated nerve structure ; founded histology, 3447.

Schwarzburg (shvahrts'-boorg). Name of two former principalities in Ger., now part of Thuringia.

Schweinfurth (shvīn'-foort), **Georg** (1836–1925). Ger. explorer, botanist, and archaeologist ; pioneer African explorer and discoverer of the river Welle.

Schweitzer (shvīts'-er), **Albert** (b. 1875). Ger. doctor of medicine, philosophy, divinity, and music, and a famous organist ; founded and conducted a medical mission at Lambarene in French Equatorial Africa (1913).

Schwerin (shvä-rēn'), Ger. Cap. of Mecklenburg - Schwerin, on L. Schwerin, 60 m. E. of Hamburg ; pop. 53,863 ; handsome ducal palace ; makes pianos, furniture, dyes.

Schwyz (shvēts). Swiss canton, a. 351 sq. m. ; pop. 65,000 ; in medieval times a free community ; gave name to Switzerland ; in Swiss confederacy, 3140 ; *map, 3140.*

Sciatic (sī-at'-ik) **nerves.** Two mixed nerves, rising in nerve plexus in pelvis ; great sciatic, the largest nerve in the body.

Science. *See under* **Astronomy, Chemistry, Physics,** and other sciences by name.

Science Museum. S. Kensington, London, 2015, 2260 ; Foucault pendulum in, 1561 ; models in, 2196 ; Parson's turbine in, *3259*, 3260 ; Trevithick engine in, *3247.*

Scilla or **Squills.** Genus of about 100 species, bulbous perennials of fam. *Liliaceae* ; 3 Brit. species ; bluebell (*S. nutans*), 479, the sea onion (*S. verna*), and the autumnal squill (*S. autumnalis*) ; the drug squills comes from a Mediterranean species.

Scilly (sil'-i) **Islands.** A group of 140 small granite islands off Cornwall ; pop. 1,450 ; **2888**, 911.

Scim'itar. A curved oriental sword.

Scio. *See* **Chios.**

Scion (sī-'on), in fruit grafting, *1402.*

Scipio (sip'-i-ō) **Africanus, the Elder** (237–c. 183 B.C.). One of greatest Rom. generals ; defeated Hannibal at Zama 202 B.C. ; father of Cornelia, mother of the Gracchi invasion of Africa, 1574.

Scipio Africanus, the Younger (c.185–129 B.C.). Rom. general, adopted by the son of the elder Scipio Africanus ; captured and destroyed Carthage (146 B.C.).

Scissorbill. *See* **Skimmer.**

Scitaminales (sī-tam-i-nā'-lēz). Plant order containing banana, canna, and ginger families.

Sciurus (sĭ-ûr'-*us*). The squirrel genus.

Sclerotic (skle-rot'-ik). Outer coat of the eye, 1252, *1252.*

Scombridae (skom'-bri-dē), mackerel family. Spiny-finned fish with spindle-shaped bodies ; mackerel, 2050 ; tunny and other members, 3258.

Scone (skōōn), Scot. Parish N. of Perth ; historic abbey ; Stone of Scone, still used at Coronations, is now in Westminster Abbey, 2558.

Sco'pas. Gk. sculptor of 4th cent. B.C. ; said to have sculptured part of Mausoleum of Halicarnassus ; 1537.

Scopolamine (skō-pō-lam'-in) or **hyoscin.** An alkaloid found in deadly nightshade, thorn-apple and henbane ; used as anaesthetic, 149.

Scoresby, William (1789–1857). Eng. Arctic explorer and scientist ; made his first trip to Greenland at the age of 11, and after 1810 made the voyage annually ; published " An Account of the Arctic Regions," in 1820 ; two years later abandoned the sea to continue his scientific studies, and in 1856 went to Australia ; published " Magnetical Investigations."

Sco'ria or **Scoria'ceous** lava, 1901.

Scor'pio or **Scorpion.** A sign of the zodiac, 3444.

Scorpion. An arachnid, **2888.**

Scorpion fly or **panorpa.** An insect, 1733 ; foot, *1727.*

Scotch blackface sheep, *2941.*

Scotch collie, 1025.

Scotch fir. *See* **Scots pine.**

Scotch mahogany or **Alder, 104.**

Scotch pine. *See* **Scots pine.**

Scotch terrier, *plate f. 1024.*

Scotch thistle, 3203.

Sco'ters. A genus of sea ducks noted for diving powers, 1052.

Scotland. Country occupying N. part of isl. of Gt. Brit. ; a. 30,405 sq. m. ; pop. 5,129,600 ; **2889 ;** *plates f. 2892, 2893 ;* maps, *2890, 1431, plate 1. 584 ;* cap. Edinburgh, 1086 ; Balmoral Castle, 351 ; bagpipes, *plate f. 2893,* **339 ;** bluebells of, *479 ;* clans, 835, *2893 ;* Courts of Justice, 923 ; education, 2893 ; games and sports, 944, 1483 ; Forth bridge, *567 ;* grid, *1546 ;* hydro-electric

scheme, *1671 ;* in Ice Age, 1680 ; language and literature, *see* **Scotland, language and literature of ;** marriage, 2108 ; national song, 2282 ; New Year's festival, 2350 ; Parliament, 2524 ; religion, 1871, 2892 ; scenery, *2889, 2891, plate f. 2892 ;* thistle emblem, 3203.

Counties : Aberdeenshire, 12 ; Angus, 155 ; Argyllshire, 230 ; Ayrshire, 324 ; Banffshire, 355 ; Berwickshire, 420 ; Buteshire, 627 ; Caithness 655 ; Clackmannanshire, 835 ; Dumbartonshire, 1054 ; Dumfriesshire, 1054 ; East Lothian, 2027 ; Fifeshire, 1269 ; Inverness-shire, 1737 ; Kincardineshire, 1857 ; Kinross-shire, 3868 ; Kircudbright, 1862 ; Lanark, 1890 ; Midlothian, 2027 ; Morayshire, 2228 ; Nairnshire, 2272 ; Orkney, 2453 ; Peebleshire, 2535 ; Perthshire, 2558 ; Renfrewshire, 2766 ; Ross and Cromarty, 2828 ; Roxburghshire, 2832 ; Selkirk, 3983 ; Shetland, 2915 ; Stirlingshire, 3092 ; Sutherlandshire, 3123 ; West Lothian, 2027 ; Wigtownshire, 3377.

Geography and Industries : agriculture, 2410, 2889 ; cities and mfrs, 11, 1055, 1086, 1471, 2890, 3092 ; fisheries, *1310,* 1298, *1306 ;* heather, 1596 ; Hebrides, 1601 ; highlands, *583 ;* Orkney Isls., 2453 ; people, 740, 2890 ; physical features, 582, 583 ; Shetland Isls., 2945.

History, 2892 ; Edinburgh, 1086 ; Northmen invade, 2388, 2945 ; Wallace leads rebellion, 3337 ; Bruce secures independence, 591 ; Shetland Isles, acquired, 2945 ; Reformation, 2892 ; reign of Mary Stuart, 2115, *2115, 2116 ;* crown united with England's, 3104 ; in Eng. Civil War, 756, 2892 ; Charles II, 756 ; union with England, 1200, 2524, 2893, 3276 ; Jacobite rebellions (1715 and 1745), 2682.

Scotland, Church of. Presbyterian body dating from 1560 ; the Church of Scot. (founded 1843) and the United Free Church of Scot. (formed 1900) were reunited in 1929 ; episcopacy several times revived, penal laws against it having been removed in 1792 ; 2894.

Scotland, language and literature of, 2894, 1210, 1214.

Scotland Yard, London. *See* **New Scotland Yard.**

Scots Guards. Formation dates from 1660 ; in 1713 title changed to " 3rd Regt. of Foot Guards " ; in 1831, altered to " Scots Fusilier Guards " ; in 1877, once more given original title of " Scots Guards."

Scots pine, 2609.

Scott, Charles Prestwich (1846–1932). Eng. journalist ; editor of " The Manchester Guardian " from 1872 to 1929.

Scott, Charles William Anderson (1903–1946). Brit. airman ; made record solo flights, England to Australia and back in 1931 and 1932 ; with Campbell Black won Melbourne race (1934) ; with Giles Guthrie won Portsmouth to Johannesburg race (1936).

Scott, Cyril Meir (b. 1879). Eng. musical composer, pianist, and author ; compositions for violin and piano, songs ; discovered and scored many Eng. folk-songs.

Scott, Elizabeth Whitworth (b. 1898). Brit. architect ; became A.R.I.B.A. ; designed Shakespeare Memorial Theatre, Marie Curie Hospital, and Newnham College, *3101.*

Scott, Sir George Gilbert (1811–78). Eng. architect, responsible for much of the work done on Eng. cathedrals and churches in early and mid-Victorian fever of " restorations " ; designed Albert Memorial in 1864.

Scott, Sir Giles Gilbert (b. 1880). Eng. architect, grandson of above ; responsible for restoration of Chester Cath. ; designed Liverpool Anglican Cath. and new debating chamber of House of Commons ; knighted in 1924 ; President R.I.B.A. (1933–35).

Scott, Hugh towell. *See* **Merriman.**

Scott, Michael (1175–1234). Scot. mathematician, scholar, magician, and astrologer, attached to the court of Emperor Frederick II ; legends associated with his name are current in the Scot. Borders and also on the Continent.

Scott, Michael, (1789–1835). Scot. author ; was estate manager in

---

FAMOUS SCULPTORS AND THEIR MASTERPIECES

Barye, Antoine Louis (1796–1875). French. (" Lion and Snake," " Centaur and Lapith ").

Bernini, Giovanni Lorenzo (1598–1680). Italian. (" Apollo and Daphne," " St. Theresa," etc.).

Bologna, Giovanni da (1524–1608). Italian. (" Fountain of Youth," " Flying Mercury ").

Canova, Antonio (1757–1822). Italian. (" Amor and Psyche," " Venus," " Perseus with the Head of Medusa").

Carpeaux, Jean Baptiste (1827–75). French. (" Ugolino and His Sons").

Cellini, Benvenuto (1500–71). Italian. (" Perseus ").

Clodion (Claude Michel) (1738–1814). French. (" Nymph and Satyr ").

Colombe, Michel (*c.* 1430–*c.* 1512). French. (" St. George and the Dragon ").

Coysevox, Charles Antoine (1640–1720). French. (" The River Dordogne," " The River Garonne ").

Dobson, Frank (1887–   ). English. (" Truth," Portrait Busts).

Donatello (1386–1466). Italian. (" David ").

Epstein, Jacob (1880–   ). English. (" Night," " Rima," " Weeping-Woman," " Dolores ").

Flaxman, John (1755–1826). English. (" St. Michael," " Marpessa ").

Frampton, Sir George (1860–1928). English. (" Peter Pan ").

Frémiet, Emmanuel (1824–1910). French. (" Gorilla and Woman ").

Gaudier-Brzeska, Henri (1891–1915). French. (" The Dancer," " The Embracers ").

Ghiberti, Lorenzo (1378–1455). Italian. (Doors of Baptistery, Florence).

Gilbert, Sir Alfred (1854–1934). English. (" Eros ").

Gill, Eric (1882–1940). English. (Figures at Broadcasting House, London).

Goujon, Jean (*c.* 1520–66). French. " Diana and the Stag ").

Houdon, Jean (1740–1828). French. (" Voltaire," " Button," " Napoleon").

Jagger, Charles Sargeant (1885–1934). English. (Royal Artillery Memorial, London).

Lysippus (*c.* 330 B.C.). Greek. (" Heracles ").

Maillol, Aristide (1861–1944). French. (" Baigneuse Accoudée ").

Mestrovic, Ivan (1883–   ). Yugoslav. (" Self-portrait " ; " Annunciation ").

Michelangelo Buonarroti (1475–1564). Italian. (" David," " Tomb of Medici," " The Captive," " Moses," etc.).

Montànes, Juan (1570–1649). Spanish. (" Virgin of the Immaculate Conception ").

Myron (*c.* 500–410 B.C.). Greek. (" Disk Thrower ").

Pheidias (*c.* 490–432 B.C.). Greek. (" Statue of Zeus ").

Pigalle, Jean Baptiste (1714–85). French. (" Mercury ").

Pisano, Giovanni (1250–1320). Italian. (' Madonna and Child ").

Polyclitus (*c.* 480–412 B.C.). Greek. (" Spear Bearer ").

Pollaiuolo, Antonio (1429–98). Italian. (" The Young Warrior ").

Praxiteles (*c.* 360 B.C.). Greek. ("Hermes Bearing Infant Dionysus").

Puget, Pierre (1620–94). French. (" Milo of Crotona ").

Quercia, Jacopo della (1371–1438). Italian. (" Creation of Eve ").

Rauch, Christian Daniel (1777–1857). German. (" Joseph Maximilian ").

Robbia, Andrea della (1435–1525). Italian. (" St. Francis and St. Dominic ").

Robbia, Luca della (1399–1482). Italian. (" Singing Boys ").

Rodin, Auguste (1840–1917). French. (" The Kiss," " The Thinker ").

Rude, François (1784–1855). French. (" Jeanne d'Arc ").

Saint-Gaudens, Augustus (1848–1907). American. (" Lincoln ").

Sansovino, Jacopo (1486–1570). Italian. (" Apollo ").

Scopas (*c.* 370 B.C.). Greek. (" Demeter ").

Stevens, Alfred (1818–75). English. (Monument of Duke of Wellington, St. Paul's Cathedral).

Thornycroft, Sir William Hamo (1850–1925). English. (" Oliver Cromwell ").

Thorwaldsen, Bertel (1770–1844). Danish. (" Adonis ").

Torrigiano, Pietro (1472–1522). Italian. (Tomb of Henry VII, Westminster Abbey).

Verbruggen, Henrik (1655–1724). Dutch. (Pulpit in Brussels Cathedral).

Verrocchio, Andrea del (1435–88). Italian. (Colleoni Monument, Venice).

Jamaica in early life, and later published his W. Indian experiences in "Blackwood's Magazine" under the title of "Tom Cringle's Log"; also wrote "The Cruise of the Midge."

Scott, Peter (b. 1909). Brit. painter, ornithologist, and naval officer; son of Polar explorer R. F. Scott.

Scott, Robert Falcon (1868–1912). Polar explorer, **2895**, *2897*, 2645; "Triumph and Tragedy in Scott's Last Venture," 2896; route, *map*, *2896*; at South Pole, 173, 2645; Shackleton with, 2931.

Scott, Sir Walter (1771–1832). Scot. novelist and poet, **2898**; Abbotsford, 10; and Perthshire, 2558; Edinburgh monument, 1086; Glasgow statue, *1471*; influence on Scottish literature, 2894; novels, 1214, 2402; poetry, 1214; Richard I, 2777; Robin Hood, 2791; Tournament at Ashby, 2900; "Rob Roy," 2791; Saladin, 2564; "The Talisman," 2864.

Scottish National War Memorial. In Edinburgh Castle, 1086.

Scottish Office, 2894.

Scott-Paine, Hubert (b. 1890). Eng. motor-boat designer; in 1920 designed and constructed the first "Miss England" racing motor-boat, and later "Miss Britain I"; in 1933 reached 100 m.p.h. and in 1934 111 m.p.h. in a single engined boat of his own design.

Scotus Erigena. *See* **Erigena.**

Scotus, John Duns. *See* **Duns Scotus.**

Scouts, Boy. *See* **Boy Scouts.**

"Scrambling," of telephone and radio messages for secrecy, 3177.

Scranton, Pennsylvania, U.S.A., 3rd city of state; coal-mining and mfg. city on Lackawanna r.; pop. 143,400; centre of chief anthracite region of U.S.A.; 2546.

Scraper board. Specially prepared thin board covered with kaolin, used for certain kinds of engraving.

Screech owl, 2460.

Screw. A fastening, **2902**; in Nov. 1948 agreed to standardise the thread of British, Canadian and U.S. machine screws, nuts, and bolts.

Screw. In mechanics, **2901**; used in micrometer, 2161.

Screw, Archimedes'. A water-raising device, 210.

Screw propeller, of ships, 2902, 2947, *2949*; applied to aeroplane, 41; invention by Ericsson, 1222.

Scriabin (skrē-ah'-běn), **Alexander** (1872–1915). Rus. composer and pianist, in his youth a concert virtuoso, later one of the most extreme innovators in composition; in his last work, "Prometheus," he attempts to prove relationship between music and colour by using a "colour-keyboard."

"Scribbling Lark." Country name for bunting, 617.

Scribe (skrēb), **Augustin Eugène** (1791–1861). Prolific Fr. dramatist, wrote some 400 plays noteworthy for sparkling dialogue and mastery of stage technique ("Adrienne Lecouvreur," his best); wrote libretti for operas by Auber and Meyerbeer.

Scriptor'ium. Room used for writing in medieval monastery, *510*.

Scroggs, Sir William (1623–83). Eng. lawyer, Lord Chief Justice; his reputation is even worse than that of Judge Jeffreys; would have been impeached for his conduct during the Popish Plot, but removed from the bench.

Scroll of the Law (or Sefer Torah), 1829.

Scroo'by. Vil. in Nottinghamshire, 20 m. E. of Sheffield; Eng. home of John Robinson, Brewster, and other Pilgrim Fathers, 2122.

Scrooge. Old miser in Dickens's "Christmas Carol," 821.

Scudé·ry (skū-dā-rē), **Madeleine de** (1607–1701). Fr. novelist, one of the leaders of Mme. de Rambouillet's brilliant salon; "The Grand Cyrus," a romance in 10 volumes, paints Fr. contemporary aristocracy under a classic disguise.

Sculling. Rowing by one man (or occasionally two) with a pair of sculls,

the blades of which differ from ordinary racing oars, 483. *See also* **Diamond Sculls.**

Sculpins. Amer. name for fish with warted bodies, long spiny fins, and huge mouths; family *Cottidae*; most of them inhabit rocky coast in N. regions and prey voraciously on small sea animals.

Sculpture, 2903; Aegean, 29; Babylonian and Assyrian, *328*, *329*, *331*, 2904; Brit. Museum, 584, *plate f. 585*, 1143; cave-dwellers, *2082*; classic revival (18th cent.), 2906; Easter Is., 1074; Eg., *1121*, *1106*, 1114; *plates f. 1120*, *1121*, 2904; in England, *2907–2910*; French, *2796*, 2906; Gk., *1276*, 1143, 1537, 1531, 2812; Hindu, 1708; Hittites, 1633; in ivory, 1788; Renaissance, *2765*, 2766, *2905*, 2906; Roman, 2812. *See also* names of famous sculptors, and list in page 3981.

Scur'vy. Disease in which blood spots appear under skin, gums bleed, and sufferer is prostrated by general weakness; cause and prevention. 3327.

Scu'tage, in feudalism, 1609.

Scutari (skōō'-tah-rī) or **Shkoder.** Tn. of Albania, on L. Scutari; pop. 29,200; fell to Montenegrins after siege in Balkan Wars; taken by Austrians in 1st World War.

Scutari (or **Uskudar**), Turkey. Suburb of Istanbul on E. shore of Bosporus, pop. 124,356; barracks of Selim III; hospital used by Florence Nightingale; 1761, *2368*; *plate f.* 3264.

Scylla (sil'-a). In Gk. myth., a sea monster, 2422.

Scyros (sī'-ros). Small rocky isl. in Aegean off coast of Thessaly, connected in legend with Theseus and Achilles, 3302.

Scythia (sith'-i-a). Name applied by Greeks to steppes N. of Black Sea inhabited by a nomadic people who disappear from history about 2nd cent. B.C.; Romans gave name to little-known region of N. Asia.

Sea, life in the, **2103**, 432, 432, *2416*; phosphorescence, 2574; salt in and from, 2866. *See* **Ocean.**

Sea-anemone. Name given to the class *Anthozoa*, of the sub-kingdom *Coelenterata*, from their flower-like form, *2105*, **2911**, *924*.

Sea angling, 1310.

Sea-aster, 275; common flower near the sea; purplish disk florets, yellow ray florets, show it belongs to order *Compositae.*

Seaborg, Glenn T. (b. 1912). Amer. chemist; worked on nuclear chemistry, experimented with plutonium, and in 1945 identified two new elements, Americium and Curium, artificial products of radio-activity.

Sea-bottom, configuration, 2598.

Sea cow or **manatee.** Evolutionary position, 158. *See also* **Manatee.**

Sea-cucumber or **holothurian.** Animal related to starfish, **2911.**

"Sea-devil" or **skate.** *See* **Rays.**

Sea-ducks, 1052.

Sea Dyaks, 525, *788.*

Sea-eagles, 1063.

Sea-elephant, *2913*, 2913.

Seaforth Highlanders (the Duke of Albany's Ross-shire Buffs). Famous Highland regiment, which had its origin in "Fraser's Highlanders," raised for service in the Seven Years' War.

Sea-horse, 2911.

Sea-island cotton, 921.

Seal, **2912**, 2105; in Antarctica, *175*; Bering Sea fisheries, 98; evolutionary position, 158; fur, 1412; fur imitated, 1412.

Sea-level. The level of the oceans taken at mean tide; changes in, during geological time, 1433.

Sealing wax, 3359.

Sea-lion, *2912*, 2913.

Sea lizard, prehistoric reptile, *2680.*

Seals. Engraved gems, 1427.

Seaman, in Royal Navy, 2308.

Seaman, Sir Owen (1861–1936). Eng. author, journalist and poet; joined the staff of "Punch" in 1897,

and became editor-in-chief in 1906; knighted in 1914.

Sea-moss. Name sometimes given to Irish moss and to certain moss-like animals. *See* **Bryozoa.**

Seam welding, 3363.

Séance (sā-ahns'). Fr. for "sitting"; used to denote a meeting, especially one of spiritualists for consulting spirits.

Sea of Japan, battle of, also called Tsushima, principal naval encounter of Russo-Japanese War, off isl. of Tsushima in Korea Strait (1905); the Russian fleet which had sailed from the Baltic was destroyed.

Sea-otter, 2459.

Sea-parrot. Same as **Puffin.**

Sea-perch. Common bass, 370.

Seaplanes, 51, *2301.*

Sea Rangers. Girl guides, *1467*, 1468.

Searchlights. Powerful lights mounted so that the rays are collected almost in a single beam, for throwing light on distant places, used in military and naval operations, etc.; searchlights are also an essential part of anti-aircraft defence; infra-red, 1596, *1722*, 1724.

Sea-scorpion, 2888.

Sea Scouts, 538, *542.*

Sea-snakes, 2990.

Seasons, 2914; equinox and solstice, 1221.

Sea-swallows. Same as **Terns.**

"Seat Perilous." In Arthurian legend, 2830.

Sea-trout. Term given to those trout which breed in rivers, spending rest of their time at sea like salmon, and also known as salmon-trout; 3251.

Sea turtle, prehistoric reptile, *2680.*

Seattle (sē-at'-l). Largest city of the state of Washington, U.S.A. Spt. and mfg. city on Puget Sound; pop. 368,300.

Sea-urchin. Spiny animal that lives in the sand, among the rocks or on the bottom of the sea, 3082, *3083*, 2911; evolutionary position, 156.

Seaweed, **2914**, *2915*, 2620; lime-forming, in coral isls., 909; evolution, 111; gelatine made from, 1426; iodine from, 1738; as water-plant type, 3355.

Seba'ceous glands, 2979, *2980.*

Sebas'tian (1554–78). King of Port. (succeeded 1557). Religious fanatic; killed in crusade against Moors; superstitious Portuguese awaited his return down to present cent.

Sebastian, St. (255–288). Rom. soldier and Christian martyr; patron against the plague; shot by archers, but recovered and later beaten to death, 2112.

Sebastiano del Piombo (1485–1547). It. painter, b. Venice, friend of Michelangelo; some portraits attributed to Raphael now recognized as Sebastiano's.

Sebas'topol or **Sevastopol.** Russian naval station on Black Sea in s.w. Crimea; pop. 112,000; 465; in Crimean War, 931. Taken by Germans after siege, June 1942; liberated May 1944.

Second, in time, the sixtieth part of a minute or 1-86,400th of a mean solar day, *see* **Weights and Measures; in** geometry, 1436.

Secondary. In elec., cell which generates electric current after "charge," 377, 1132; secondary winding, 1720.

Secondary colours. Mixtures of primary hues, 875.

Secondary schools, 2886.

Second Empire., in Fr., 1366.

Secretary, 2916.

Secretary bird, 2916.

Secretary of State. Chief officer of a department of the Brit. Govt. and a member of the Cabinet; 2916; in U.S.A. the Sec. of State is equivalent of foreign affairs minister.

Secre'tions. In physiology, 1470, 2979.

Sec'ular clergy, 2924.

Sedan'. City in N. Fr.; pop. 17,000; decisive battle in Franco-Prussian War (1870), 1385; reached by Americans in 1st World War just before armistice (1918). In German hands during 1940–44.

Sedan chair. A kind of enclosed chair carried by bearers by means of poles ; invented at Sedan ; *1810.*

Sedbergh (sed′l ê g). Small tn. in West Riding of Yorkshire, 10 m. E of Kendal ; has famous grammar school, which was founded in 1525.

Sed′don, Richard John (1845–1906). New Zealand statesman ; b. in Eng. ; he reached New Zealand in 1866, and entered Parliament in 1879 ; he became premier in 1893, and held the post until his death.

Sedgemoor. Barren tract near Bridgwater, Somersetshire, where troops of James II defeated Monmouth (1685) ; called "last battle in England."

Sedges. Members of the family *Cyperaceae*, of the grass order ; distinguished from grasses by triangular, not cylindrical, stem ; usually of stiff, erect growth, and found in cool, damp places ; Eng. examples include true bulrush, *Scirpus lacustris, 615,* and members of genus *Carex* ; the papyrus sedge is *Cyperus papyrus, 2500.*

Sedge warbler, 3340.

Sedimen′tary rocks. Those deposited from water, 1432, 2795 ; source of petroleum, 2426.

Sedimenta′tion. In geology, 1432.

Sedimentation process. In water purification, 3348.

Seeds and spores, 2916 ; ferns, 1266 ; fertilization, 1322 ; in fruits, 1401 ; germination of bean, *381,* 2622 ; maize, 2068 ; oil content in cotton, 918 ; scattering devices, 2622, *2623* ; seed selection in agriculture, 2625 ; spores are fore-runners, 111 ; of water plants, 3355 ; of yeast, 3434.

Seeland. *See* **Zealand.**

See′ley, Sir John Robert (1834–95). Eng. historian and essayist ; professor of Latin in University College, London, in 1863, and professor of modern history at Cambridge in 1869 ; all his writing was designed to bring history into contact with national life (" Ecce Homo " ; " Natural Religion " ; " Expansion of England " ; " Growth of British Policy ").

See′ly, John Henry Bernard. *See* Mottistone, 1st Baron.

" Seger cones." Devices for estimating temperatures by observing melting of various substances of which cones are composed.

Segovia (sä-gō′-vē-a). Sp., small city 40 m. N.W. of Madrid ; pop. 16,500 ; medieval religious centre and seat of Castilian court ; aqueduct, *194* ; cathedral, *3038.*

Segrave, Sir Henry O'Neal Dehane (1896–1930). Brit. racing motorist, **2919.**

Segu or **Segeou.** Tn. of Fr. Sudan on R. Niger, formerly cap. of native Mahomedan kingdom ; pop. 22,150 ; 2367.

Segura (sä-gōō′-ra). A r. of s.e. Sp. ; 150 m. to the Mediterranean.

Seidlitz powders. Laxative medicine composed of tartaric, or other solid acid, and a bicarbonate, which effervesce when mixed in water (named from Seidlitz, a vil. in Bohemia).

Seine (sän). A fish-net.

Seine. A chief river of Fr. ; flows N.W. 482 m. to English Channel ; **2919,** 1360 ; at Havre, 1585 ; Paris, 2514, *2515, plate f.* 2516 ; at Rouen, *2376* ; in 2nd World War, 3422.

Seismograph (sīz′mo-graf). Instrument for detecting earthquake vibrations, *1070* ; pendulum in, 2544.

Seja′nus, Lucius Aelius (d. A.D. 31). A Rom. courtier, favourite of Tiberius ; executed for plot to seize imperial power.

Selachians (se-lā′-ki-anz). An order of scaleless fish with gristly skeletons ; includes sharks, 2938 ; structure, 1296.

Selah. Term in Hebrew music, 2261.

Selangor. State of Malayan Federation, formerly Fed. State ; a. 3,160 sq. m. ; pop. 701,500 ; 2069.

Sel′borne, Roundell Palmer, 1st Earl of (1812–95). Brit. lawyer ; called to

the bar in 1837 ; he was Attorney-General (1863–66) and Lord Chancellor (1880–85) ; he framed the Judicature Act in 1873 ; was an authority on hymns and wrote " Defence of the Church of England against Disestablishment."

Sel′borne, William Palmer, 2nd Earl of (1859–1942). Brit. statesman ; Under-Secretary for the Colonies in 1895, and First Lord of the Admiralty in 1900 ; in 1905 he succeeded Lord Milner as High Commissioner for South Africa ; Minister of Agric. (1915–16).

Selborne. Vil. of Hampshire ; birthplace of Gilbert White, author of "The Natural History of Selborne"; 3376.

Selborne Society. Formed in 1885 as the Selborne League, for the preservation of birds, plants, and pleasant places.

Selden, John (1584–1654). Eng. lawyer and scholar ; active in political life but chiefly remembered for his " Table Talk," an entertaining miscellany in essay form.

Selene (se-lē′-nē). Gk. moon-goddess, later identified with Artemis.

Sel′enite. A translucent gypsum, 1559.

Sele′nium (Se). Non-metallic element of the oxygen group ; atomic weight, 78·96 ; similarly chemically to sulphur ; melts at 422·6° F. ; one crystalline form of selenium conducts electricity well when exposed to light, but very feebly in the dark ; this enabled it to be used in photo-electric cells ; **2919** ; properties, 777 ; uses, 2751, 3184.

Seleucia (se-lū′-shi-a), Babylonia. Anc. city on Tigris, s. of Baghdad ; centre of Gk. culture in Babylonia ; destroyed by Romans (2nd cent. A.D.) ; founded, 329.

Seleucia. Spt. of Turkey, near Antioch; *map, 3145.*

Seleucid dynasty, Syria (312–64 B.C.) ; founded by Seleucus Nicator, son of one of Alexander's generals.

Self-heal. Perennial herb (*Prunella vulgaris*) of the natural order *Labiatae* ; formerly supposed to heal wounds, etc.

Self-induction. In electricity, 1133.

Selfridge, Henry Gordon (1857–1947). Anglo-Amer. business man, founded in 1909 firm of Selfridge & Co. in London, which became one of the largest stores in Europe.

Se′lim I (1467–1520). Sultan of Turkey ; conquered Persians and Armenians ; annexed Egypt in 1517, 3264.

Selim II (1524–74). Sultan of Turkey ; the grandson of Selim I, he ruled from 1566 ; in his reign occurred the utter defeat of the Turkish fleet off Lepanto, Greece (1571).

Selim III (1762–1808). Sultan of Turkey ; administrative and military reformer ; dethroned and killed by janissaries.

Sel′juks. Group of Turkish dynasties, descended from a chieftain named Seljuk, which ruled most of w. Asia 11th to 13th cent. ; rule in Persia marked by literary and artistic revival ; superseded by Ottoman dynasty about 1300.

Seljuk Turks. Crusades against, 936, 2864.

Sel′kirk, Alexander (1676–1721). A Scot. sailor, the original of " Robinson Crusoe," 804, 937 ; and Dampier, 964.

Selkirk, Thomas Douglas, 5th Earl of (1771–1820). Scot. nobleman interested in colonization of Canada ; founded Red River Settlement, Manitoba, 2089.

Selkirk Mts. Range in Canadian Rockies, Brit. Columbia ; highest peak 10,645 ft. ; scenery, 578.

Selkirkshire. Inland co. of s. Scot. ; a. 267 sq. m. ; pop. 22,100 ; hilly country celebrated in lit. (notably Scott and James Hogg) ; sheep-raising ; co. tn. Selkirk (pop. 5,600) ; Galashiels (13,000), a centre of the woollen industry, is the most populous tn. ; the Tweed and its tribu-

taries—Ettrick and Yarrow—traverse the co. ; also in Selkirkshire are Ettrick Forest and St. Mary's Loch.

Selous (se-lōō′), **Frederick Courteney** (1851–1916). Brit. explorer of S. Africa, ethnologist, and daring big-game hunter ; secured Mashonaland territory for Brit. in 1890 ; captain in 1st World War ; killed in action ; 72.

Selsey Bill. Promontory in s.w. Sussex, stretching for 6 m. s. of Chichester ; off Selsey town, at tip of Bill, are remains of older town and cathedral washed into sea.

Sel′wyn, George Augustus (1809–78). Eng. divine ; became first bishop of New Zealand in 1841 ; on a visit to Eng. in 1868, appointed Bishop of Lichfield ; Selwyn College, Cambridge, erected by public subscription to his memory (1882).

Selwyn College, Cambridge. Founded (1882) in memory of George Augustus Selwyn, 669.

Semangs′. Aboriginal people of Malay Peninsula, 2069.

Semaphore signalling, *3165.*

Semele (sem′-e-lē). In Gk. myth., mother of Dionysus, 1018.

Semicir′cular canals. Organs of equilibrium in ear, 1066.

Semico′lon (;). Use of, 2708.

Sem′inoles (" Separatists "). Tribe of N. Amer. Indians, originally part of Creeks ; separated from tribe and settled in Florida, U.S.A.

Semiramis (se′-mi′-ra-mis). Assyrian queen, in legend, half-divine wife and successor of Ninus, founder of Nineveh ; herself great conqueror and ruler.

Semitic Languages, 2920 ; represented by Hebrew, 1600.

Semitic Races, 2920 ; in Africa, 70 ; Jews, 1829 ; Phoenicians, 2573 ; Syrians, 3145 ; in Tigris-Euphrates valley, 329.

Semliki, r. of cent. Africa, 69.

Sempach. A small tn. 10 m. N.W. of Lucerne, Switzerland ; battle (1386), 3141.

Sena, on Zambesi, bridge at, 3441.

Sen′ate. Anc. Rome, 2805, *827.*

Senate, Canadian, 684.

Senate, Fr., 1362.

Senate, U.S.A., 3290. *See also* **Congress.**

Sen′ators, Palace of the, Rome, *2803.*

Sendai, Japan. City near E. coast of Honshu Isl. 100 m. N.E. of Tokyo ; pop. 219,545 ; silk and lacquer mfrs.

Sen′eca (sen′-e-ka), **Lucius Annaeus** (c. 4 B.C.–A.D. 65). Rom. statesman, philosopher, and dramatist, 1897, 2315.

Senefelder (zā′-ne-fel-der), **Alois** (1771–1834). Inventor of lithography, 1967.

Seneffe (se-nef′). Belgian tn. 25 m. s. of Brussels ; Fr. defeated William of Orange near by (1674).

Senegal (sen-e-gawl′). Territory in Fr. W. Africa, bordering Atlantic ; a. 74,000 sq. m. ; pop. 1,720,000 ; cap. St. Louis ; exports peanuts, hides, gums ; *3367.*

Senegal. R. in Fr. W. Africa ; flows 1,000 m. N. and w. to Atlantic ; first r. for 1,300 m. s. of Morocco ; *map f. 68* ; rly. connexion with Niger, 2367.

Senegam′bia. Indefinite territory in French West Africa between the Senegal and Gambia rivers, extending from the Guinea coast ; 70, *map, 3366.*

Senigalia. Same as **Sinigaglia.**

Sen′lac. *See* **Hastings, battle of.**

Senlis (sahn-lē), Fr. Small city, 25 m. N. of Paris ; Gaulo-Rom. walls, medieval cath. ; captured by Germans in September 1914.

Sennacherib (sen-ak′-e-rib). Assyrian king (reigned 705–681 B.C.), great builder and warrior, 330, 1830 ; captures and razes Babylon, 330 ; builds Nineveh, 330, 2371.

Sennar Dam. On the Blue Nile, Anglo-Eg. Sudan, 3 m. above the tn. of Sennar, 2371, *3110.*

Sens (sahns), Fr. Industrial city on R. Yonne, 65 m. s.e. of Paris ; pop. 17,300 ; Rom. remains ; cath. of St. Étienne.

"Sense and Sensibility." Novel by Jane Austen, 306.

Senses. Hearing, 1065 ; sight, 1252 ; smell, 2986 ; taste, 3157, 3223 ; touch, 3231 ; and sleep, 2983.

Sensitive plants. Species the leaves of which, as in some of the mimosas, close on being touched, 2623, 2625.

Sentence. In grammar, 2920, 1493 ; importance of verb, 3313.

Sentinum (sen-ti'-num), It. Anc. city (modern Sentino), 37 m. s.w. of Ancona ; battle (295 B.C.), 2807.

Senus'sites. A fanatical ascetic Mahomedan sect centring in the oasis tns. of the eastern Sahara ; founded in 1837 by the Sheik es Senussi.

Seoul (sā-ool') or Keijo-fu. Cap. of Repub. of S. Korea, near R. Han, 19 m. from Yellow Sea ; pop. 1,141,766 ; 1873. N. Korea invaded S. Korea in 1950 and captured ·eoul June 28.

Se'pals, of flowers, 1321, 1323.

Sep'aratists, Eng., 2707 ; founded Plymouth Colony, 2122.

Sep'arator, cream, 745, 955.

Se'pia. Dark brown pigment obtained from cuttlefish, squid and octopus, 945 ; ink, 1724, 1725.

Se'poy Rebellion (Indian Mutiny) of 1857, 1714.

Sepsis, the presence of germs, 177.

September, 9th month, 2223.

Septic tank. A receptacle for sewage in which the organic substances are decomposed by the action of bacteria.

Septim'ius Sever'us. See Severus, Lucius Septimius.

Septuagint (sep'-tū-a-jint). A Gk. version of Hebrew Bible, made according to tradition in 3rd cent. B.C. by about 70 translators (Lat. septuaginta, " seventy "), 425.

Sepulchre (sep'-ul-ker), The Holy. In Jerusalem, 1820.

Sequoi'a. Genus of giant evergreen trees, 2921 ; oldest living organisms, 3246.

Sequoia National Park, Calif., U.S.A. In Sierra Nevada Mts., 160 m. N. of Los Angeles ; a. 161,597 acres ; established to preserve sequoias (1890).

Sequoy'a (c. 1760–1843). Amer.-Indian scholar (George Guess), after whom the " big trees " are named ; invented Cherokee alphabet, 2922.

Seraglio (se-rahl'-yō). The old palace of the sultan of Turkey at Constantinople ; name also used as synonymous with " harem."

Seraing (se-ran'), Belgium. Tn. on R. Meuse, 4 m. s.w. of Liége ; pop. 43,000 ; mfrs. machines.

Serajevo. See Sarajevo.

Serao (sā-rah'-ō), Matilda (1856–1927). It. novelist, 1787, 2403.

Seraph, H.M.S., a Brit. submarine, 3105.

Seraphim (se'-ra-fim) or seraphs. Guardians of the threshold of the Most High (Isa. vi. 2–6) ; in later Christian and Jewish lore, highest angelic order.

Serapis (se-rā'-pis). Eg. god worshipped in Gk.-Rom. towns of Egypt, 2455.

Serapis. Brit. warship, 1837.

Serbia. A Balkan country now part of Yugoslavia, 2922, 343, map, 344 ; people, 2927, 2983. History, 343, 2922 ; Balkan Wars, 345 ; in 1914–18 War, 3409, 3410, 3414.

Serfdom, in Middle Ages, 1268, 2981 ; in Russia, 2848 ; in anc. Sparta, 3053.

Sergeant (sar'-jent). In Brit. Army, a non-commissioned officer ranking above corporal ; badge, 245.

Sergeant-major. In Brit. Army, a warrant-officer rank, badge, 245.

Ser'icin, gummy secretion of silkworm, 2970, 2972.

Sericulture. The breeding, rearing, etc. of silkworms. See Silk.

Series. Type of elec. circuit, 1129 ; series-wound motor, 2239, 2240, 3235.

Sering'apatam. Tn. in Mysore, India, on an isl. 3 m. long, 8 m. N. of Mysore city ; from 1610 to 1799 the cap. of Mysore ; the fort was built by Tippoo Sahib, who was killed in defending it against the British in 1799 ; Tippoo routed, 2270.

Serous membranes. Membranes forming closed sacs and moistened with a serous fluid which line certain cavities of the body ; they are said to be reflected over the organ or organs contained in the cavity ; the portion lining the cavity walls is called the parietal portion and the reflected portion, the visceral ; the pleurae, the peritoneum, and the pericardium are examples.

Serpent. Constellation, 895.

Ser'pentine. A mineral consisting of hydrated magnesium silicate, ranging in colour from green to brown and sometimes yellow or red.

Serpentine. Artificial lake in Hyde Park and Kensington Gardens, London. Used for boating, and, since 1930, for mixed bathing.

Serpents. See Snakes.

Serpent worship, 859 ; goddess, 31.

Serrano Suñer (sōōn-yer), Ramón (b. 1901). Sp. politician ; leader of Falangists, min. of Interior 1937, also 1938–40 ; min. of Press and Propaganda 1939–40 ; of Foreign Affairs 1940–42 ; became pres. of political Junta and mem. of Falange Nat. council in 1942.

Serum. Colourless, watery fluid from tissues or organs of the body ; esp. used of blood serum—the watery substance which remains after blood has clotted ; blood serum of immune animals used as protection against disease in vaccination, etc., 180, 1459.

Serval. A large long-legged S. African wild cat (Felis serval) 3 ft. or more long, with yellow fur spotted and barred with black ; the tail is 15 in. in length ; 720.

Servetus, Michael (1511–53). Sp. physician (approached discovery of circulation of blood) and theologian (Unitarian, odious to Catholics and Protestants alike) ; burnt in Geneva as heretic, with Calvin's approval ; 664.

Servia. Same as Serbia.

Service, Robert William (b. 1874). Anglo-Canadian poet ; sometimes called the Canadian Kipling (" The Spell of the Yukon," " Rhymes of a Rolling Stone," ; autobiography " Ploughman of the Moon " ; 685.

Ser'vius Tul'lius (578–534 B.C.). 6th king of Rome, 2804.

Ses'amum or ses'ame. Herb producing oil-seeds, 1707, 1724.

Sesostris (se-sos'-tris). Gk. name of legendary Eg. king and world-conqueror.

Ses'tos. Anc. tn. in Thrace on Hellespont ; w. terminus of Xerxes' bridge ; home of Hero, 1619.

Set. In lawn tennis, 1906.

Set. In Eg. myth., god of evil ; brother and murderer of Osiris, 2455.

Seti (sā'-tē) I (c. 1300 B.C.). Eg. pharaoh of 29th dynasty ; built much of temple of Karnak.

Seto (sā'-tō), Japan. Tn. near Nagoya, famous for pottery, 2271.

Se'ton, Ernest Thompson (1860–1946). Canadian naturalist and author, b. Eng. (" Wild Animals I Have Known " ; " Lives of the Hunted " ; " Animal Heroes "), 685.

Sett. Of the badger, 337.

Setter. A hunting dog, plate f. 1024, 1026.

Settlement, Act of, 164.

Setubal. Port. spt. and 3rd city, 20 m. S.E. of Lisbon ; pop. 47,000 ; exports wine, fruit, salt, cork.

" Seven cities contend for Homer dead," 1637.

" Seven Pillars of Wisdom," by T. E. Lawrence, 1908.

Seven Sisters. On Sussex coast, 1170.

Seven Sleepers. In medieval legend, 7 Christian youths of Ephesus who during persecution under Emperor Decius in 3rd cent. hid in cave and there fell into a miraculous sleep that lasted nearly 200 years.

Seventh Day Adventists. Christian sect believing in the second coming of Christ in person and observing the seventh day as Sabbath.

Seven Weeks' War (1866), 1574.

Seven Wonders of the World, 2923, plate f. 2924. See also each of the seven by name.

Seven Years' War, between Prussia and other European powers (1756–63), 2924, 3276 ; Frederick the Great precipitates, 1389 ; in Amer. (Fr. and Ind. War), 144 ; in India, 1714 ; Pitt's policies, 759.

Severn. R. of Eng. and Wales ; rises in cent. Wales and winds S.E., then S.w. through S.w. Eng. 200 m. to Bristol Channel ; 2963, 3407 ; bore on, 525 ; salmon netting at, 1308.

Severn. R. of N.W. Ontario ; flows 350 m. through L. Severn to S.w. side of Hudson Bay.

Severn Tunnel. Rly. tunnel partly beneath R. Severn, linking Bristol and Cardiff ; constructed between 1873 and 1886 ; 3258.

Severus (se-vēr-us), Alexander. See Alexander Severus.

Severus, Lucius Septimius (146–211). Rom. soldier-emperor, raised to throne by provincial legions in 193 ; spent reign chiefly in warfare ; rebuilt Hadrian's wall in Britain ; arch in Rome, 2801.

Sévigné (sā-vē-nyā), Madame de (1626–96). Fr. writer.

Seville (sev'-il). Sp. Sevilla (sā-vēl'-ya). Sp. spt. on Guadalquivir, 60 m. from S. coast ; pop. 375,060 ; 2925 ; Alcazar, 3033 ; dancers, 3037 ; cath., 2926.

Sèvres (sā'vr). Fr. suburb of Paris ; pop. 15,240 ; treaty between Allies and Turkey in 1920 ; famous for porcelain, 2670.

Sèvres, Treaty of (1920), 3266, 3415.

Seward, William Henry (1801–72). Amer. statesman, sec. of state under Lincoln and Johnson ; active Abolitionist ; a founder and leader of Republican party ; wounded by a fellow-conspirator of the assassin of Lincoln, 97.

Sew'ell, Mary (1797–1884). Eng. authoress ; her children's books and poems, especially the ballad " Mother's Last Words," very popular ; her daughter Anna (1820–78) wrote " Black Beauty," the autobiography of a horse.

Sew'erage. System of collecting and removing waste water supply of a community, 1459.

Sewing, 2927 ; embroidery, 1152.

Sewing-machine, 2929 ; adapted to shoe-making, 521.

Sex. See Reproduction.

Sext, one of the canonical hours, 2213.

Sex'tant, in navigation, 2290, 2291.

Sextet', in music, six singers or players. or a composition for six parts.

Seychelles (sā-shel'). Archipelago of 90 isls. in Indian Ocean, with tributary groups Brit. colony of Seychelles ; est. a. 156 sq. m. ; est. pop. 33,600 ; largest isl. Malé (55 sq. m.) cap. Victoria ; coconuts, vanilla, rubber, etc.

Seymour or St. Maur. Noble Eng. family ; heads became dukes of Somerset.

Seymour, Jane (c. 1509–37), 3rd queen of Henry VIII, 1612.

Seymour, Robert (c. 1800–36). Illustrator, drew first 7 plates of original edition of " Pickwick Papers."

Seyss-Inquart, Arthur von. Gauleiter of Austria and Comm. for Holland, 1940–45 ; war criminal, Nuremberg, 1945–46 ; hanged Oct. 1946 ; 2282.

Sfax. Important spt. of Tunis ; pop. 43,000 ; 3254 ; taken by Germans in 1942, by Allies in 1943.

Sforza (sfort'-sa). Famous It. family ; founded by a peasant condottiere whose son, Francesco Sforza (1401–66), conquered duchy of Milan and founded line of Sforza dukes ; 2172.

Sforza, Count Carlo (b. 1873). It. statesman ; Min. Foreign Affairs, 1921–22 ; ambassador, France, 1922 ; anti-Fascist exile (1926–43) ; Min. Foreign Affairs 1947.

'sGravenhage (skrah'-ven-hah-ge). Dutch name of The Hague, 1563.

Shabwa. " Hidden city " of Arabia, reputed capital of Q. of Sheba, 195.

Shackleton, Sir Ernest Henry (1874–1922). Brit. sailor and Antarctic explorer ; 2931, 173, 2645.

Shad. A fish of the herring family, the two European species of which are the allis and the twaite ; formerly common in the Thames, 1620.

Shad'dock. A citrus fruit.

Shadoof (shah-doof'). Eg. water-raising device, 1095, 1098.

Shadwell, Thomas (c. 1642–92). Eng. poet laureate and playwright, chiefly remembered for quarrel with Dryden who satirized him in " MacFlecknoe " ; 2634.

Shaft. In architecture, the body of a column between the capital and the base ; in engineering, means of transmitting power, 2701.

Shaftes'bury, Anthony Ashley-Cooper, 1st Earl of (1621–83). Eng. statesman ; in Civil War fought first for king, then for Parl. ; member of famous Cabal ; lord chancellor.

Shaftesbury, Anthony Ashley-Cooper, 3rd Earl of (1671–1713). Celebrated moral philosopher, grandson of preceding ; (" Characteristics of Men, Manners, Opinions, and Times ").

Shaftesbury, Anthony Ashley-Cooper, 7th Earl of (1801–85). English politician, philanthropist, and social reformer, 2931 ; and child labour laws, 802.

Shag. A sea-bird, 2931.

Shagreen'. A leather ; from sharks, 2938.

Shah Jehan (shah ye-hahn') or **Jahan** (d. 1666), Mogul emperor of Delhi ; founder of modern Delhi ; dethroned (1658) by his son Aurungzebe ; built Taj Mahal, 77, 1713, 3147, 3148.

Shakers. Name given, originally in derision, to religious sect (offshoot of Eng. Quakers) officially called " United Society of Believers in Christ's Second Appearing " ; founded by Ann Lee, who emigrated to Amer. with followers in 1774.

Shakespeare, William (1564–1616). The greatest of Eng. poets and dramatists, 2932 ; and the English drama, 1040, 1211, 1212 (the artist, Eduard Ender, b. 1824, misnamed this picture, as Queen Elizabeth was dead when Macbeth was written) ; Bacon theory of authorship, 334 ; chronology of plays, 2936 ; development as dramatist, 2933 ; early life, 2932 ; friend of Jonson, 1837 ; Globe Theatre, 1039, 1837 ; home at Stratford-on-Avon, 2932, 3101 ; plots from Plutarch, 2630 ; portraits, 2935, 2936 ; quotations from, 1147 ; sonnets, 2636 ; on stamp, 3075 ; and Stratford-on-Avon, 3101 ; theatres of his time, 1039, 3196. *Chief plays* : " As You Like It," 282 ; " Coriolanus," 1041 ; " Hamlet," 1570 ; " King Lear," 1858 ; " Macbeth," 2047 ; " Merchant of Venice," 2144 ; " Midsummer Night's Dream," 2169 ; " Othello," 2457 ; " Richard II " and " Richard III," 2777 ; " Romeo and Juliet," 2457 ; " The Tempest," 3185 ; " Winter's Tale," 3389.

Shakespeare's Cliff, Dover, Eng., *facing p. 1165.*

Shale. A stratified rock, 836, 1432 ; in oil-yielding formations, 2426, 2427 ; shale oil, 2430.

Shallot'. An onion-like vegetable, 2434.

Shallow, Justice. In Shakespeare's " Merry Wives of Windsor," a self-important, foolish, ignorant country magistrate.

Shamanism (shah'-man-izm). A primitive religion of various cent. Asiatic peoples ; teaches that all good and evil come from spirits, which can be influenced by priests called " shamans " ; in Siberia, 2207.

Shameen, isl. of, Canton, 694.

" Shammy " leather, 751 ; tanning process, 1910.

Shamo'. Same as Gobi.

Sham'rock. Species of clover, adopted as the badge of Ire., said to have been used by St. Patrick to illustrate the Trinity ; 2936, 2529.

Shang'hai, China. Chief spt. of N. China, at mouth of R. Yangtze ;

pop 7,100,000 , 2531, 3433 ; entirely under Chinese control after 1945, 2938 ; surrendered to Communist forces May 27, 1949.

Shan'non, r. in Eire ; longest in the British Isles ; rises in s.w. Ulster and flows 224 m. s.w. to Atlantic, traversing series of lakes ; 1749 ; hydro-elec. plant, 1749.

Shans. A group of tribes of Burma, Siam, and China, 623.

Shansi. A N.-cent. prov. of China ; a. 60,000 sq. m. ; pop. 11,601,000 ; cap. Yangchu ; coal, iron, copper, salt, fruit.

Shantung'. Prov. in E. coast of China ; large coal and iron deposits ; a. 69,000 sq. m. ; pop. 38,099,700 ; 2938 ; birthplace of Confucius, 887 ; Japanese rights given up, 1800 ; 1st World War and after, 2938, 1800 ; 2nd World War, 2938.

Shantung silk, 2973, 2938.

Shap Fells. Upland tract in Westmorland, between mts. of Lake Dist. and Pennine Chain ; traversed by road and main rly. line.

Shari, r. in Africa, chief trib. of L. Chad ; with its windings, 1,400 m. long, 68.

Sharks, 2938, 1301 ; eggs, 1094, 1095 ; evolutionary position, 158 ; greatest length of, 1297 ; leopard shark, 2416 ; skates and rays related, 1298.

Shar'on, Plain of. Fertile plain in w. Palestine lying along Mediterranean between Joppa and Caesarea, 2480.

Sharon, Rose of. See Rose of Sharon.

Sharp, Cecil (1859–1924). Eng. composer, famous for his collections of folk songs, country dances, etc. Works include : " Morris Dance Tunes " ; " Folk Songs of England " ; " English Folk Song."

Sharp, Rebecca (" Becky "). See Rebecca Sharp.

Sharp, William (1856–1905). Scot. poet and novelist ; wrote many poetical and critical works under his own name ; best known as author of stories and sketches of the primitive Celtic world under the name of " Fiona Macleod," the secret of whose authorship he kept until his death (" Silence Farm " — Sharp ; " Pharais," " The Mountain Lovers " — Fiona Macleod).

Shas'ta, Mt., Calif., U.S.A., peak in Sierra Nevada Mts., near N. boundary ; 14,380 ft.

Shasta daisy, 621.

Shatt-el-Arab. Name of the Euphrates after its junction with Tigris ; flows s.E. 120 m. ; 1231, 3212.

Shaw, Anna Howard (1847–1919). Amer. suffrage leader and minister (first woman ordained by Methodists), credited with large share in passage of U.S.A. suffrage amendment ; b. Eng.

Shaw, George Bernard (b. 1856). Brit. dramatist, critic, and essayist, 2939, 2940 ; 1040, 1042, 1215, 1216 ; awarded Nobel Prize for Literature in 1925, 2375 ; and spelling reform, 3058.

Shawcross, Sir (William) Hartley (b. 1902). Brit. lawyer and politician ; attorney-gen. 1945 ; chief prosecutor for Brit. at Nuremberg trials, also at treason trials of Joyce and Baillie-Stewart.

Shawenegan or Shawinigan Falls, Quebec, tn. on St. Maurice r. 20 m. above Three Rivers ; pop. 24,750 ; falls, 150 ft. high, furnish water-power for mfrs. of aluminium, manganese, carbide.

Shawls, Kashmir, 1478, 1848.

Shawnee or Shawano Indians. Tribe of N. Amer. Indians of Algonquian stock ; originally lived in Wisconsin, U.S.A., but in 17th and 18th cents. were several times defeated by Iroquois and driven principally to S. Carolina and Tennessee ; now in Oklahoma.

Shay, type of locomotive, 1986.

Shays' Rebellion. Rising in Massachusetts, U.S.A., in 1786–87, headed by Daniel Shays, due to oppressive taxation and weak govt.

Shearing, of sheep, 3405.

Shear steel, 1756.

Shearwater. A petrel, 2564.

Sheath-bill. A white wading bird of Antarctic, with horny sheath over nostrils, 2544.

She'ba, Queen of. Queen of great beauty, mentioned in Bible (1 Kings, x.) ; frequently regarded as ruler of Sabaeans in s. Arabia ; visits Solomon, 196, 2999.

Shechem (shē'-kem). Anc. city of Palestine, 80 m. N. of Jerusalem ; connected with traditions of Abraham, Jacob, and later Hebrew history ; modern Nablus ; pop. 23,200 ; 2480.

" Shed," in weaving, 3360.

Shee, Sir Martin Archer (1769–1850). Brit. portrait painter, P.R.A. 1830–50 ; also painted many subject pictures ; portrait of William IV, 3381.

Sheep, 2940 ; anthrax immunization, 1458, 2528 ; in Australia, 308, 311, 312, 2717 ; breeding, 79 ; Brit. breeds, 2941 ; dogs as herders, 161, 1026 ; leathers, 1447, 1910 ; milk, 2173 ; New Zealand, 2359 ; parasites of, 2513 ; a ruminant, 2842 ; Scotland, 2941 ; S. Africa, 3014 ; U.S.A., 3289 ; wool, 3405.

Sheep, Rocky Mountain. Same as Bighorn.

Sheepdogs, 161, plate f. 1024, 1026.

Sheepshank. A hitch used for shortening rope, 1869.

Sheepskin, 1910, 1447 ; sold as chamois, 751 ; parchment, 2496.

Sheerness. Port and naval arsenal in Kent on Isle of Sheppey at confluence of Thames and Medway ; pop. 16,700.

Sheet lightning, 1946.

Shef'field. Steel mfg. city of Yorkshire on R. Don ; pop. 500,400, 2941 ; university, 2942, 3296.

Sheffield Steel, 1758.

Sheik (shēk). Arabian tribal leader, 197.

Shek'el. Anc. unit of weight and coin of same weight, used by Babylonians, Phoenicians, and Jews.

Sheldon, Gilbert (1598–1677). Eng. prelate ; Bishop of London (1660) and Archbishop of Canterbury (1663) ; chancellor of Oxford University, where he built and endowed the Sheldonian Theatre, 2465.

Sheldrake. A duck inhabiting sand-dunes, 456, 1052.

Shelf, continental. See Continental shelf.

Shell. Artillery projectile, 257–260 ; shell crater, 3412.

Shell, of animals, 2942, 2943 ; in button mfr., 632 ; chalk formation, 749 ; of crab, 924 ; crayfish, 926 ; egg, 1093 ; of gastropods, 2199 ; made into cameos, 671 ; of nautilus, 2199 ; oyster, 2467 ; pilgrim badge, 2608, 2879 ; of protozoans, 2695 ; snail, 2989.

Shell. A racing boat, 181.

Shellac'. The purified resin-like secretion (lac) of scale insects, 1733, 2768, 2879 ; in hat-making, 1584 ; in varnish, 3305.

Shelley, Mary Wollstonecraft (1797–1851). Eng. author, 2nd wife of P. B. Shelley ; daughter of Mary Wollstonecraft Godwin ; wrote " Frankenstein," the story of a monster, in 1818.

Shel'ley, Percy Bysshe (1792–1822). Eng. poet, 2942 ; leader in literary revolt, 1214 ; poetry, 1214, 2690.

Shellfish. See Crustacea ; Molluscs.

Shell money, 2942.

Shelsley Walsh. Vil. in Worcestershire, site of motor hill-climbs.

Shem. Eldest son of Noah ; traditional ancestor of Semitic peoples (Gen. x.).

Shenandoah (shen-an-dō'-a). R. of Virginia and W. Virginia, U.S.A., tributary of Potomac, 200 m. long.

Shenandoah Valley, Virginia, U.S.A. Picturesque valley between Blue Ridge and Alleghany Mts. ; scene of important fighting in Amer. Civil War.

Shennung. Emperor, said to have discovered tea, 3159.

Shensi. Prov. in N. China ; a. 72,000 sq. m. ; pop. 9,389,000 ; fertile plateau in N. ; cent. plain drained by Wei r. ; mts. in s.

Shepard, Ernest Howard (b. 1879). Eng. artist; famous contributor to " Punch "; illustrated A. A. Milne's and Kenneth Grahame's children's books, also " Everybody's Pepys," etc.

Shepherd Kings. *See* Hyksos.

" Shepherd of Hermas." Apocryphal book of Bible, 425.

Shepherd's Purse. A garden weed, 2944.

Sheppard, Hugh Richard Lawrie (" Dick ") (1880–1937). Eng. divine; vicar of St. Martin-in-the-Fields, London (1914–27); dean of Canterbury (1929–31); C.H. (1927); canon and precentor of St. Paul's cathedral (1934); a prominent Pacifist, he founded the Peace Pledge Union in 1934.

Sheppard, " Jack " (1702–24). Eng. highwayman; in 1724 Jonathan Wild gave him up to justice; after twice escaping from Newgate, was hanged at Tyburn.

Shep'stone, Sir Theophilus (1817–93). Eng. statesman; secretary for native affairs in Natal (1856–77); proclaimed annexation of Transvaal at Pretoria in 1877; acted as administrator till 1879, and retired in 1880.

" Sherardizing." Coating with zinc, 3444.

She'raton, Thomas (1751–1806). After Chippendale most famous Eng. furniture designer, *1411*, 1412.

Sherborne. Tn. of Dorset; magnificent church once belonging to an abbey; pop. 6,000; Sherborne School, a public school, dates from 1550.

Sher'brooke, Canada. Port and mfg. city at confluence of Magog and St. Francis rivers in Quebec; pop. 38,000; ships, asbestos, lumber, wood, machinery, textiles.

Shore Ali, Khan (1825–79). Amir of Afghanistan; defeated in war with Gr. Brit. (1878) and dethroned.

Sher'idan, Philip Henry (1831–88). Amer. general; prominent in Amer. Civil War; made commander-in-chief of U.S.A. army (1883); a stern and ruthless soldier.

Sheridan, Richard Brinsley (1751–1816). Brit. wit, dramatist, and statesman, 2944; and Dr. Johnson, 1836.

Sheriff. In Eng., public official in a county and in certain cities and boroughs, whose duties include the execution of writs, preparing panel of jurors for assizes, etc.; the two sheriffs of the City of London are elected annually by freemen who are liverymen of the City companies; in U.S.A., county officer with certain judicial functions, esp. those of keeping the peace.

Sheriffmuir, battle of. Indecisive battle fought between Jacobites and Royalists, in 1715.

Sherman, John (1823–1900). Amer. financier and statesman, younger brother of Gen. W. T. Sherman; as sec. of treasury (1877–81) under President Hayes, provided for resumption of specie payments in 1879; the Silver Purchase Act of 1890 is named after him.

Sherman, William Tecumseh (1820–91). Amer. general; joined the North on outbreak of Civil War; distinguished himself at Bull Run and Shiloh; with Grant at Vicksburg and Chattanooga; famous " march to the sea " from Atlanta to Savannah; commander-in-chief of U.S. army (1869–84).

Sherman tank, 3152; firing rockets, 2794.

Sherriff, Robert Cedric (b. 1896). Eng. dramatist (" Journey's End," 1929).

Sherry, wine (named from Jerez in Spain), 3032.

Sherwood, Robert Emmet (b. 1896). American playwright (" The Road to Rome," " Reunion in Vienna," " Idiot's Delight ").

Sherwood Forest. Hilly dist. in Nottinghamshire; former royal hunting forest; retreat of Robin Hood, 2398, 2790; story, 3469.

She'shonk or Shi'shak I (10th cent.B.C.). Egyptian king of 22nd dynasty, invaded Palestine and plundered

Solomon's Temple; monument at Karnak.

" She Stoops To Conquer," Comedy by Goldsmith, 1482.

Shet'land Islands. Group N.E. of Scot., constituting a Scottish co.; a. 550 sq. m.; pop. 20,200; 2945, 2889, *map, 2880*.

Shetland pony, *1646*, 2945.

Shibam. Arabian " city of skyscrapers," *196*.

Shield, armour, 240, *241*; heraldic devices, 1614.

Shield, Greathead. Device used in tunnel construction, 3258.

Shields, North. Port on N. bank of Tyne, near mouth, opposite S. Shields; incorporated with Tynemouth; industries include shipbuilding and the mfr. of ships' cables and anchors; trade in coal.

Shields, South. Port on S. bank of Tyne; pop. 102,930; iron and shipbuilding centre, supplemental shipping industries; enormous docks; exports coal; 1059.

Shi-Hwang-ti (shē-wang-tē') (259–210 B.C.). " First emperor " of China; king of Ts'in who overthrew feudal system and established centralized govt. over all China; to break opposition to reforms, ordered burning of all historical books; Great Wall, *806*, 810.

Shiites. Mahomedan sect, 1742, 2067.

Shikoku (shē-kō'-koo). One of principal isls. of Japan; a. 7,248 sq. m.; *map, 1786*.

Shillibeer, George (1797–1866). Eng. coach-builder; invented omnibus.

Shilling. An Eng. silver coin worth 12 pence, *2203*; new design of reverse, as for other British coins, struck in 1949, omitted the title Ind. Imp.

Shillong, Cap. of Assam; pop. 17,000; 274.

Shiloh (shī'-lō). Anc. tn. 20 m. N. of Jerusalem; contained sanctuary of ark of the covenant.

Shimonoseki or Akamagaseki, Japan. Fortified port on S.W. end of main isl.; pop. 133,000; rly. terminus and shipping point; bombarded by foreign vessels (1864); treaty ending Chino-Japanese War (1895).

Shin, Loch, Scot. Lake in Sutherlands., about 16¼ m. long and 1 m. broad, 270 ft. above sea, 3124.

Shi'nar, Plain of. Anc. name of Babylonia, 329.

Shin'toism or shinto. Primitive religion of Japan, 1798, *1800, 1804*; abolished as state religion, 2046.

Shinwell, Emanuel (b. 1884). Min. of Fuel (1945–47); Sec. for War (1947); became Min. of Defence in 1950.

" Ship-in-bottle " model; how made, *2195*.

Ship'ka Pass, Bulgaria. Pass through Balkan Mts. N.E. of Philippopolis; forced by Russians in Russo-Turkish War (1877–78).

Ship-money. Old Eng. tax imposed on maritime counties to pay for ships in time of war; attempt of Charles I to levy it upon all England as regular tax was a contributing cause of Civil War; 1571.

" Ship of the Desert," camel, 669.

Ships and shipbuilding, 2945, *2953–2960*; ancient Eg., *plate f. 1121*; armour-plate, 240, *242*; barnacles, 361, *362*; Belfast, 402, 1747, *1748*; boiler, 489; Brunel, 593; camouflage *673, 674*; Clydeside yards, 854, 2890; marine Diesel engine, *1734*; docks, 1022; early history, 2945, 3104; Fulton, 1047; Great Lake freighters, *1516*; gyroscopic stabilizers, 1562; Hamburg, 1568; harbours and ports, 1576; lighthouses, 1943, *plate f. 1944*; merchant navy, 2143; models, *2195*, 2196; modern shipbuilding, 854, 2947, 2948, 2950, 2951; motor-boats, 484, *485*; navigation, 2290; Navy, 2293; Nile boats, 2370; ocean commerce, 1232, 2945, 2949; oil-fuel, 2949; radar, 2726; rat disk, 2746; rigging, 2946; sailing vessels, *481, 482, 484, 485*, 2946, *2953–2955*; screw propeller, 1222, 2947, *2949*; speed, 2949; steamships, 2946, *2957*; steel construction, 2947; time on board, 3214; turbine engines, 2949, 3258; 3260, use of spruce timber,

3070; H.M.S. Victory, 3321, *3322*; warships, 2294, 2295, 2297, 2298, 2299, *2300*; how affected by waves, *3358*; early wireless receiver, *3392*; wireless control, 2304; *See also* specific ships' names and **Boats**; **Navigation**; **Navy**; **Ocean**.

Ship's log, for measuring speed, 1997; also a journal or record book kept by the commander.

Shipton, Mother (1488–1561). Eng. prophetess or witch, lived near Dropping Well, Knaresborough, where her cave is still to be seen; her maiden name was Ursula Southill; she is said to have prophesied the Fire of London, and the deaths of Cromwell, Wolsey, and others; she also foretold the invention of the steam-engine and the electric telegraph.

Shipworm or teredo, a bivalve mollusc.

Shiraz (shē-rahz'), s. Persia (Iran); trade centre 120 m. N.E. of Bushire in valley; pop. 129,000; home of Hafiz, Sadi, and other Persian writers.

Shire. Administrative division in Gt. Brit., usually corresponding to the county but sometimes small districts, such as Norhamshire in Northumberland.

Shire. A heavy type of horse, *1646*.

Shire (shē'-rā). R. of Brit. E. Africa, from end of L. Nyasa, s. 370 m. to Zambesi r.; only tributary of Zambezi navigable from sea.

Shirley, James (1596–1666). Eng. dramatist, link between Elizabethan and Restoration periods; wrote about 40 plays—(" The Traitor ", " Hyde Park ").

Shiva. Same as **Siva.**

Shkoder, Albania. *See* Scutari.

" Shock-headed Peter " (" Struwelpeter "), by H. Hoffmann, 1965.

Shoddy, 3404.

Shoe-bill stork, 3097, *3098*.

Shoes. *See* Boots and Shoes.

Shogun (shō'-goon). Former commander-in-chief of Japanese armies and virtual ruler, 1799.

Sholokhov, Michel (b. 1905). Russ. novelist; " And Quiet Flows the Don "; 2856.

Shooting, 2961.

Shooting Stars, 2151.

Shore, Jane (d. c. 1527). Favourite of Edward IV of Eng.; accused by Richard III of witchcraft; imprisoned; died in want.

Shore crab, 924.

Shore'ditch. Met. and parl. bor. of N.E. London; chief industries, furniture, cabinet, and boot and shoe making; pop. 45,000.

Short, Hugh Oswald. Eng. aircraft designer, one of three brothers. Began by building balloons, and later (1908) aeroplanes. Short Bros. (Rochester, and Belfast), is oldest est. aircraft concern in Gt. Britain, famous for marine aircraft; Empire flying-boat, *33*; Mayo Composite, *51*; Shetland, *40*; Sunderland, *39*.

Short circuit, in elec., 1129.

Short-eared owl, *2461*.

Shorter, Clement King (1857–1926). Eng. author and editor; founded " The Sketch," " The Sphere," and " The Tatler "; first editor of " The Sphere "; also well known as an authority on the Brontë family and George Borrow.

Shorter, Dora Sigerson (1872–1918). Irish poetess and authoress, wife of Clement King Shorter; (" Verses "; " Ballads and Poems "; " Through Wintry Terrors ").

Shorthand, 2961; in secretarial work, 2916; blind shorthand typist, *472*.

Shorthorn, breed of cattle, *731*, 732.

Short Parliament, in Eng. history, Parliament sitting from April 13 to May 5, 1640; followed by Long Parliament in November.

Short waves, in wireless, 3396.

Shoshone Falls (shō-shō'-nē). Cataract in Snake R., s. Idaho, U.S.A.; 190 ft.

Shot, 1908; in weaving, 3360.

Shot-gun, evolution, 1285.

Shoulder. Region where the arm joins the body; bones, 2977; muscles, 2258.

Shovel, Sir Cloudesley (1650–1707). Eng. admiral ; he led the attack on the shipping in the harbour of Tripoli in 1675, and distinguished himself at the battle of Bantry Bay in 1689 ; in 1705 he brought about the reduction of Barcelona, and on the journey home his ship was lost with all hands on board.

Shoveller duck, 1051.

Shreve′port, Louisiana, U.S.A. 2nd city of state ; pop. 98,100 ; on Red r. in N.W. ; rly. and distributing centre for oil, gas, and farming region ; cotton, foundry products, lumber.

Shrew. Small mammal resembling a mouse but with a long pointed muzzle, actually member of group *Insectivora* ; three species are found in Gt. Brit. ; one of them, the pygmy shrew, is our smallest mammal. Others are the common shrew often picked up dead by the roadside, and the water shrew.

Shrews′bury, John Talbot, 1st Earl of (1388–1453). Eng. soldier ; after service in Ireland he took part in the French Wars ; he was checked by Joan of Arc at Orleans and taken prisoner in 1429 at Patay ; his last fight was in Castillon in 1453, where he was killed.

Shrewsbury (shrōz′-be-ri). Old city, co. tn. of Shropshire, on R. Severn ; pop. 44,430 ; school founded by Edward VI ; Henry IV defeated and killed Hotspur (1403) ; 2963.

Shrike. A carnivorous bird, found in almost all parts of the world. 2962.

Shrimp. A small crustacean, 2962.

Shropshire or **Salop.** Eng. co. on Welsh border ; a. 1,347 sq. m. ; pop. 244,200 ; 2963.

Shrove Tuesday, or **Mardi Gras,** the day preceding Ash Wednesday, first day of Lent.

Shu-kiang or **Chu-kiang** (" Pearl River "). Same as **Canton River.**

Shunt. Type of connexion in elec. motor, 2239.

Shu′shan. Same as **Susa.**

Shuttle, in weaving, 920, 2025, 3360 ; Cartwright's, 712 ; " flying," 3361.

Shuttlecock. Weighted cork, with feathers projecting in a ring from one end, struck to and fro across a net in the old game of battledore and shuttlecock, and by a racket in mod. badminton, 338.

Shwe Dagon Pagoda, Rangoon, 2744.

Shylock, in Shakespeare's " Merchant of Venice," avaricious Jewish money-lender, 2145.

Siam (sī-am′) (also called **Thai** or **Thailand).** Ind. kingdom of south-east Asia ; a. 200,000 sq. m. ; pop. 17,256,000 ; **2963** ; 1718, *plates f. 2964, 2965* ; *map, f. 264* ; cap. Bangkok, 355 ; costume, *2964* ; gems, 1427 ; monsoons, 3385 ; people, 2964 ; Temple dancers of, *967* ; in both World Wars, 2965, 3420.

Siam, Gulf of. Arm of Pacific Ocean partly enclosed by Indo-China and the Malay Peninsula, 264.

Siamese cat, *719.*

Siamese Twins. Twins joined together at birth ; applied esp. to Eng and Chang (1811–74) twins born in Siam of Chinese father and Siamese mother ; joined together by carti-laginous band, 2965.

Sianfu (sē-an-fōō′), **Singanfu,** or **Siganfu,** China. Walled city on R. Wei 400 m. N.W. of Hangkow ; pop. 750,000 ; famous Nestorian tablet ; important trade centre for cent. Asia.

Sibelius (sē-bā′-li-us), **Jean Julius Christian** (b. 1865). Finnish composer, **2965,** 2266.

Sibe′ria. Part of Asiatic Russia, extending from Ural Mts. to Pacific ; a. over 4,000,000 sq. m. ; pop. over 14,000,000 ; **2966,** 265, *map, 223* ; Arctic regions, 225 ; climate, 2741, 2742, 2966 ; Cossacks, 916 ; Eskimos, 1222, *1223* ; history, 1787, 2967 ; Kamchatka, 1845 ; people, 2207, 2966 ; prehistoric animals, 2077 ; reindeer, 2760 ; rivers, 265, 2966 ; steppes and forests, 265 ; transport, 2845, 2966, 2967 ; Trans-Siberian Rly. 268, 2845, 2966, 2967 ; tundra, 265 ; Turk-Sib. Rly., 2967 ; Ural Mts., 3297 ; Vladivostok, 3327 ; 2nd World War, 2967. See also **Turkistan.**

Siberian mammoth, 2078.

Sibiu (sē′-bi-ōō). Rumania. Industrial tn., 132 m. N.w. of Bucharest ; 12th cent. Saxon settlement ; pop. 63,700.

Sib′ylline books, 2804, 2967.

Sibyls (sib′-ilz). Prophetesses in Gk. and Rom. legend, 2967.

" Sic et Non." Book by Abelard, 11.

Sicil′ian Vespers. Massacre of Fr. in Sicily (1282), 2968.

Sicilies, Kingdom of the Two, 2275, 2968. See also **Naples.**

Sicily. Isl. belonging to It., separated from mainland by Strait of Messina ; a. 9,925 sq. m. ; pop. 4,400,000,

2968 ; *map, 1764* ; early silk culture, 2970 ; earthquake of 1908, 2968 ; Mt. Etna, 1228 ; Gk. temple art, *3443* ; people, 1763 ; sulphur production, 3116. *History,* 2968 ; Pyrrhus in, 2710, 2807 ; in Punic Wars, 711 ; Rome conquers, 2808 ; Norman kingdom, 1238, 2275, 2376 ; under Frederick II, 1389 ; taken by Garibaldi, 1418, 1769 ; joins united It., 3319 ; captured by Allies in 1943, 2969, 3421. See also **Syracuse.**

Sickert, (Walter) Richard (1860–1942). Eng. artist ; R.A. in 1934 ; 1183, 2477.

Sickness, social insurance against, 2994.

Siddhattha Gautama (Buddha), 600.

Sid′dons, Sarah (1755–1831). Eng. tragic actress, greatest of the Kemble family and school ; unequalled "Lady Macbeth " ; painted by Reynolds as the " Tragic Muse " ; birthplace, 559.

Sidereal (sī-dēr′-i-al) time, *3214.*

Sid′erite, an iron ore, 1753.

Side stroke, in swimming, *3136,* 3137.

Side′winder, the horned rattlesnake, 2747.

Sidg′wick, Henry (1838–1900). Eng. philosopher ; from 1883 professor of moral philosophy at Cambridge univ. ; " Methods of Ethics " (1874).

Sidi Barrani. Vill. of Egypt, on Mediterranean, 60 m. E. of Bardia ; taken by Graziani's It. forces Sept. 1940, 3418, and recaptured by Brit. and Free Fr. forces Dec. 11 ; in June 1942 taken by Rommel's It. and Ger. troops, and recaptured after Alamein victory by Brit. on Nov. 10 ; *map, 3421.*

Sid′law Hills, Scot. Range of hills forming the S. boundary of Strath-more and extending N.E. from Kinnoull Hill in Perthshire to Stone-haven in Kincardineshire, highest point 1,493 ft. ; 2558.

Sidney, Algernon (1622–83). Eng. rev. leader ; beheaded for supposed complicity in Rye House Plot.

Sidney, Sir Philip (1554–86). Eng. poet, statesman, and soldier, mortally wounded at Zutphen, where, it is said, he gave his last cup of water to a dying soldier, saying, " Thy necessity is yet greater than mine."

Sidney Sussex College, Cambridge, 668.

Sidon (sī′-don) or **Zidon.** Anc. Phoenician city on Mediterranean (modern Saida), 25 m. S. of Beirut ; noted for glass ; commerce ; 1576, 2573, 3146.

Siege, in Middle Ages, 717 ; famous sieges, see list below.

SOME OF THE WORLD'S MOST FAMOUS SIEGES

Name	Date	Duration	
Adrianople	1912–13	155 days	Turks besieged by Bulgarians. Fell.
Antwerp	1584–85	14 months	Belgians besieged by Spaniards under Prince of Parma. Fell.
Arcot	1751	50 days	120 British and 200 Sepoys under Clive besieged by 150 French and 10,000 Sepoys. Raised.
Candia	1667–69	2 years	Venetians besieged by Turks. Fell.
Carthage	148–146 B.C.	2 years	Carthaginians besieged by Romans. Fell.
Constantinople	673–677	5 years	Byzantines besieged by Saracens. Raised.
	717–18	1 year	Same as above.
	1453	54 days	Byzantines besieged by Turks. Fell.
Delhi	1857	131 days	Indian mutineers besieged by British. Fell.
Gibraltar	1779–81	3 yrs. 7 mos. 12 days	British garrison besieged by Spaniards. Raised.
Jerusalem	637	4 months	Mahomedans led by Omar invested Byzantine forces. Fell.
Kut-el-Amara	1915–16	149 days	British under Townsend besieged by Turks. Fell.
Ladysmith	1899–1900	118 days	Boers besieged British. Relieved.
La Rochelle	1627	1 year	Richelieu besieged French Huguenots. Fell.
Leiden	1574	4 months	Spaniards besieged Dutch. Raised after Dutch cut dikes.
Leningrad	1941–44	29 months	Russians besieged by Germans. Raised.
Lucknow	1857	149 days	British besieged by Indian mutineers. Relieved.
Mafeking	1899–1900	217 days	Boers besieged British garrison under Baden-Powell. Relieved.
Orleans	1428–29	10 months	French besieged by English. Relieved by Joan of Arc.
Ostend	1601–04	3 years	Flemish besieged by Spaniards. Surrendered.
Paris	1870–71	135 days	Besieged by Germans. Surrendered.
Plevna	1877	144 days	Turks besieged by Russians and Rumanians. Surrendered.
Port Arthur	1905	241 days	Russian garrison surrendered to Japanese.
Richmond, U.S.A.	1864–65	287 days	Confederates besieged by Federals. Evacuated.
Sevastopol	1856	335 days	Russians besieged by Allies. Fell.
	1941–42	8 months	Russians besieged by Germans. Evacuated.
Stalingrad	1942–43	6 months	Russians completely destroy German 6th Army. Raised.
Syracuse	214–212 B.C.	2 years	Besieged by Romans under Marcellus. Fell.
Tobruk	1941	242 days	Besieged by Rommel's Afrika Korps. Relieved.
Troy	12th or 13th cent.(?) B.C.	10 years	Greeks besieged Trojans. Fell.
Verdun	1916	10 months	French besieged by Germans. Raised.
Vicksburg	1862–63	186 days	Confederates invested by Federals under Grant. Fell.

"Siege Perilous," in Arthurian legend, 2830.

Siegfried (sēg'-frēd). Hero of "Nibelungenlied," **2969**, 2363 ; Wagner's opera, 2440.

Siegfried Line, Ger. 2nd World War fortifications along w. frontier, facing Maginot line of France ; breached by Allies in 1944 ; *3423*.

Siemens (sē'-menz), **Ernst Werner von** (1816–92). Ger. inventor ; suggested use of gutta-percha in insulating underground and marine cables ; inventor of many electrical improvements and pneumatic tube system.

Siemens, Sir William (1823–83). Brit. inventor, b. Ger., younger brother of preceding ; with Werner von Siemens invented Siemens armature ; with Frederic, another brother, invented Siemens regenerative furnace.

Siemens-Martin or **open-hearth process,** 1756.

Siena (sē-en'-*a*) or **Sienna.** It. mfg. and trade city 30 m. s. of Florence ; pop. 48,000 ; famous Gothic cath. ; Sienese school of art ; univ. ; taken by French July 1944.

Sienkiewicz (shen-kyä'-vĕch), **Henryk** (1846–1916). Polish novelist, 1905 Nobel prize winner in literature (" Quo Vadis ? " most famous novel, tale of Rome under Nero, translated into more than 30 languages ; "With Fire and Sword," "The Deluge," "Pan Michael"—great historic trilogy of 17th-cent. Poland), 2403, 2641, 2983.

Sienna. Earth used as pigment ; brownish-yellow if raw, and reddish-brown if burnt. The name is derived from the town of Siena, where it was produced.

Sierra, Gregorio Martinez (1881–1947), Spanish novelist, 3051.

Sierra de Gata (si-er'-*ra* dā gah'-tah). Chain of mts. in Sp. and Port. separating the valleys of the rivers Tagus and Douro ; 5,690 ft.

Sierra de Gredos. Mt. range of cent. Sp. ; 8,730 ft. ; *map, 3030*.

Sierra de Guadarrama. Mt. range of cent. Sp. separating Old and New Castile ; 7,900 ft. ; *map, 3030*.

Sierra Leone (si-er'-*ra* lā-ō'-nā). Brit. colony and protectorate on w. coast of Africa ; colony, 2,500 sq. m. ; pop. 121,000 ; chief tn., Freetown ; protectorate, inland, 27,669 sq. m. ; pop. est. almost 2,087,000 ; exports ginger, palm nuts and oil, kola nuts, 3366 ; *map, 3366*.

Sierra Madre, Arizona, U.S.A., 3285.

Sierra Madre, Mexico. Name of two mt. ranges forming the eastern and the western walls of the great cent. plateau, 2156.

Sierra Maestra, Cuba, *map, 940*.

Sierra Morena. Low mt. range of s. Sp. ; rises slightly above Iberian plateau to the north and drops sharply on the s. to valley of the Guadalquivir ; *map, 3030*.

Sierra Nevada ("Snowy range"). Loftiest mt. range in Sp. ; extends about 60 m. E. and w. through Andalusia and Granada near Mediterranean coast ; highest peak, Mulahacen, 11,420 ft. ; vineyards and orchards on s. slopes.

Sierra Nevada. Loftiest mt. range in U.S.A., in E. part of California, 3285 ; contains the wonderful Yosemite valley ; E. slope caused by " fault," 1070 ; Mt. Whitney, 14,502 ft., highest peak in U.S.A. ; sequoias, *2921*.

Sieyès (syä-y-es'), **Emanuel Joseph** (1748–1836). Phrase-maker of the Fr. Rev. ; published in 1788 celebrated pamphlet beginning with the words, " What is the Third Estate ? Everything. What has it been ? Nothing."

Sigel (sē'-gel), **Franz** (1824–1902). Amer. soldier, b. Ger. ; major-general in Amer. Civil War, active in keeping Missouri in Union and fought at Pea Ridge, 2nd battle of Bull Run, Shenandoah valley campaigns.

Sigeum (si-jē'-um), **Cape.** Anc. lighthouse, 1943.

Sighs, Bridge of. *See* **Bridge of Sighs.**

Sight. *See* **Eye.**

Sigismund (sig'-is-mund) (1368–1437). Holy Rom. emperor, succeeded in 1410 ; caused convocation of Council of Constance, which ended the Great Schism in 1417 ; Huss and Hussite War, 1660.

Sigma, σ, ς (used at end of words), Σ (Rom. s, S). 18th letter of Greek alphabet.

Signalling, 2784 ; automatic, 321 ; electric telegraph, 3164 ; fireworks, 1291 ; old methods, *3165* ; on railways, 2739, *2740* ; on underground, 2740.

Signals, Royal Corps of, Brit. Army, 246.

Signatu'ra, Apostolic. Supreme tribunal of Rom. Cath. Church, 2495.

Sig'nature, of a book, 512.

Signs, for roads, *plate f. 2785*, 2788 ; Chinese shops, 3211 ; also table in pages 4004–05.

Signs of zodiac, *3444*.

Sigurd (sē'-goord). Norse hero who plays in the Volsunga Saga the part taken by Siegfried in the Nibelungenlied, 2390.

Si-hu. L. near Hangchow, 1573.

Sika (sē'-ka). Japanese species of deer, 985.

Sikes, Bill. In Dickens's " Oliver Twist," brutal thief ; kills Nancy and maltreats Oliver.

Sikhs (sēks). A religious sect of India, 1703 ; in Kashmir, 1848 ; defeated, 1714.

Sikh Wars (1845–46 and 1848–49). Indian campaign between Brit. and Sikhs ; the death in 1839 of Ranjit Singh was followed by anarchy, and Brit. territory was invaded ; the Sikhs were defeated at Mudki, Aliwal, and Sobraon ; in 1846 Brit. annexed the dist. between the Sutlej and Beas ; after the capture of Multan in 1848, the Punjab was annexed in 1849.

Si-kiang (" West River "). Largest stream in s.w. China ; 1,250 m. long ; enters China Sea through delta near Canton, 807. *See also* **Canton River.**

Sik'kim, state, India, formerly under Brit. protection ; adjoins Nepal ; a 2,818 sq. m. ; pop. 121,500.

Sikorski, Wladyslaw (1881–1943). Pol. soldier and statesman ; served in 1st World War and Pol.-Russ. war of 1919–20 ; in 1922 premier ; gathered army of exiled Poles in Fr. when Ger. attacked Poland ; prime min. and C.-in-C. in exiled govt. ; visited N. Amer. 1941 and 1942 to get help for Poland ; in Moscow (1941) signed short-lived treaty with Russia ; killed in air accident at Gibraltar, July 1943.

Sikorsky, Igor (b. 1889). Russ.-Amer. aircraft designer of first multiengined plane (1913), amphibian, and helicopter, 1605.

Si'lage. *See* **Silo.**

"Silas Marner," novel by George Eliot, 1146.

Silastics, a class of artificial rubbers, 2970.

Silchester. Vil. in Hants., site of the Roman tn. of Calleva Atrebatum. Excavations from 1890 onwards have revealed many remains, including the foundations of a church, probably 4th cent., described as the first Christian church in Britain.

Sile'nus, a satyr, 1018.

Silesia (sī-lēsh'-ya). Region in cent. Europe ; taken by Prussia from Austria in 1740–45 ; in 1914 a. was 18,000 sq. m., pop. 6,000,000. After 1914–18 war, Germany retained Lower Silesia (10,270 sq. m. ; pop. 2,000,000), Czechoslovakia received 1,707 sq. m. (pop. 738,000), which became the Czech prov. of Slezsko, and Poland received Upper Silesia (1,630 sq. m. ; pop. 1,315,000) after a League of Nations plebiscite in 1921. After 1939–45 War all of German Silesia E. of Oder went to Poland, the Ger. pop. being expelled ; Ger. pop. of Slezsko also expelled. Coal, iron, chemicals, glass, textiles ; impt.

agric. ; spas in Sudeten mts. of Czech portion ; 1444, 1447, 3415 ; seized by Frederick the Great, 1389, 2101, *map, 2696*.

Silesian Wars, 2101.

Silica (sil'-i-ka). Silicon dioxide (SiO_2) occurs in nature as sand, flint, rock of crystal, quartz, etc., 2970 ; in clay, 836 ; in flint, 1314 ; as furnace lining, 1472 ; gel, 871 ; in quartz, 2713.

Silicates, salts of silicic acid, 2970, 2180 ; of aluminium, 1265, 2160 ; asbestos, 261 ; contain bulk of world's potassium, 2664 ; in felspar, 1265 ; in mica, 2160.

Silicic acids. Weak polybasic acids of the formulae H_4SiO_4 and H_2SiO_3 ; silicic acid gels which are capable of absorbing large quantities of water are obtained by treating water-glass with hydrochloric acid, 2970.

Silicon (Si) (sil'-i-kon). Non-metallic element of the carbon group ; atomic weight 28·06 ; the second most abundant element in the earth's crust ; melts at 2588°F. ; **2970** ; dioxide, 2713 ; used in invar, 2365 ; properties, 776 ; in smoke screens, 2986.

Silicones, lubricating and waterproofing compounds of silicon, 2970.

Silistra or **Silistria.** Town on Danube in N.E. Bulgaria, ceded by Rumania in 1940 ; pop. 17,000 ; Rom. Durostorum ; former fortress, frequently besieged.

Silk, 2970 ; fabrics, 850, 2748 ; Japan, 1797 ; Jacquard loom, 1790 ; Lyons, France, 2043 ; mulberry, food of silkworms, 2250 ; parachutes of, 2509 ; rayon, 2748 ; Sp., 3032, 3302 ; from spider-threads, 3065 ; weaving, 3191 ; wild silks, 2938, 2973.

Silk, artificial. *See* **Rayon.**

Silk hats, manufacture, 1584.

Silkin, Lewis Silkin, 1st Baron (b. 1889). Min. of Town and Country Planning (1945–50). Peerage in 1950.

Silkworm, 631, 2970, 2972 ; cocoon, 729 ; moth from, *2970* ; mulberry food, 2250.

Sil'liman, Benjamin (1779–1864). Amer. chemist and geologist ; professor at Yale Univ., U.S.A. ; founded " American Journal of Science."

Silo (sī'-lō). Chamber or pit for preserving green fodder by excluding air and water, 1510.

Siloam (sī-lō-'-am). Pool in Jerusalem, part of anc. water supply ; fed from " Fountain of the Virgin " ; in wall oldest known Hebrew inscription.

Silt. Earth deposited by water (alluvial deposits), 2598 ; from floods, 1316. *See* **Alluvial soil.**

Silu'rian period, in geological time, 1432.

Silver. Precious metallic element of the copper group, atomic weight, 107·88 ; found native and as the sulphide ; melts at 1762°F. ; **2973** ; anc. Gk. mines at Laurium, 1523 ; electroplating, 1139 ; in Andes, 3024 ; in the sea, 2413 ; Mexico, 2157 ; ingots, **2973**, **2974** ; money, 2201 ; N. Amer., 2384 ; properties, 777 ; Russia, 2845 ; salts used in photography, 2574, 2577 ; S. Amer., 3024 ; sulphide, 3116.

Silver Age, of Latin literature, 1896.

Silver birch, 436.

Silver bream, 559.

Silver fir, 1278.

Silver fox, 1355, 1412.

Silver fulminate. An explosive, 2973.

"Silver," German, an alloy of zinc, 3444.

Silver Jubilee, of King George V, *3282*.

"Silver Jubilee." Streamline train, which reached a record speed of 113 m.p.h. on a trial run in 1936 ; 1988, *1993*, 2737.

Silver maple, 2092.

Silver nitrate, an antiseptic, 2974 ; used for backing mirrors, 2190.

Silver pheasant, 2565.

Silverware, 2973 ; electroplating, 1139 ; Ger. silver, 2365, 3444.

Silver Y moth. Commonest of Brit. moths, often seen on wing in daytime. Distinguished by Y-shaped markings on forewings.

Sim'coe, John Graves (1752–1806). Eng. soldier and first lieut.-gov. of Upper Canada (1792–96) ; memorial, *3224.*

Simcoe Lake, Canada, 30 m. long, 18 m. wide ; 160 sq. m. ; empties into L. Huron through Georgian Bay.

Simenon, Georges (b. 1903). Belgian novelist ; wrote many stories, inventing detective called Maigret.

Sim'eon. Second son of Jacob ; traditional ancestor of tribe of Simeon.

Sim'eon Stylites (stī-lī'tēz) (4th–5th cent.) Syrian monk, first and most famous of the " Pillar Saints," who lived on high pillars, 177.

Simferopol (sim-fer-ō'-pol). Russian tn. in s.w. Crimea, U.S.S.R. ; pop. (1939) 142,000 ; famous for fruit ; in Ger. occupn., during 1941–44.

Simile (sim'-i-li). Figure of speech, 1270.

Simla. In Punjab, India, summer cap., 170 m. N. of Delhi ; in Himalaya, 7,000 ft. up ; pop. (winter), 25,000 ; (summer) 92,000.

Simon of Wythenshawe, Ernest Darwin, 1st Baron (b. 1879). Eng. administrator, Chairman of B.B.C. 1947.

Si'mon, John Allsebrook, Viscount (b. 1873). Eng. lawyer and statesman ; Solicitor-Gen. 1910 ; Home Sec., 1915–16 ; leader of "Asquithian" liberals from 1922 ; chairman of Royal Commn. on home rule for India (Simon report, 1930) ; Home Sec. in Nat. Govt. 1931, For. Sec. 1931–35, Chancellor of Exchequer 1937–40, leader of " Nat.-Lib." party ; visct. 1940 ; Lord Chancellor 1940–45.

Simonides (sī-mon'-i-dēz) (c. 556–468 B.C.). Gk. lyric poet, a finished craftsman, but not a great imaginative poet ; celebrated the heroes of his own day in a great variety of metrical structure.

Simon Magus (sī'-mon mā'-gus). Samaritan sorcerer, converted to Christianity, who offered Peter and John money for the power o. the Holy Ghost (Acts viii.).

Simon Peter (St. Peter), 2562, 188, 189.

Simon's Town. Naval spt. of S. Africa, harbour berths the largest warships ; 22 m. s.E. of Cape Town.

Simony (sī'-mo-ni). Purchase of spiritual benefit or Church preferment.

Simon Zelo'tes, the apostle, 188, 189.

Simple leaves, 1916.

Simple microscope, 1925, 2163.

Simplified spelling, 3058.

Simplon Tunnel, 3138, 3257.

Simpson, George Gaylord (b. 1902). American zoologist, curator of fossil mammals and birds in the Amer. Mus. of Nat. Hist., N.Y.C. ; led expedns. in N. and S. Amer. to collect fossil animals ; author of a classification of mammals now widely adopted.

Simpson, Sir James Young (1811–70). Scot. physician ; aroused historic storm of religious and medical censure by using anaesthetic in child-birth ; invented acupressure in haemorrhage ; discovered chloroform, 149, *2133,* 2135.

Sims, William Sowden (1858–1936). Amer. naval officer ; commanded fleet of Brit. and U.S.A. ships in Irish Sea during 1st World War.

Sinai (sī-na-ī) or **Horeb Mt.** Biblical locality often identified with group of peaks in Sinai peninsula at head of Red Sea ; Moses receives Ten Commandments, 2235 ; singing sands, 2871.

Sinai peninsula. Between Gulf of Suez and Gulf of Akabah, 2758.

Sinait'ic manuscript, 425.

Sinaloa (se-na-lo'-a), Mexico. State in N.W. on Pacific ; a. 22,580 sq. m. ; pop. 560,000 ; cap. Culiacan ; mining and agriculture.

Sinbad the Sailor. Hero of a story in " Arabian Nights," 202, 3497.

Sinclair, Sir Archibald, Bart. (b. 1890). Eng. politician ; leader of Liberal party in House of Commons 1935–45 ; previously (1931–32) Sec. of State for Scotland ; Sec. for Air, 1940–45.

Sinclair, Upton Beall (b. 1878). Amer. novelist and social reformer ; " The Jungle " led Theodore Roosevelt to order investigation of meat-packing industry ; wrote numerous novels and books on social and economic problems (" King Coal," a novel of the Colorado strike ; " The Profits of Religion " ; " The Brass Check," an exposure of Amer. journalism), 3295, 2403.

Sind. Prov. of W. Pakistan. a. 47,000 sq. m. ; pop. 4,500,000 ; **2974,** 1721 ; temperature, 1701.

Sindbad. *See* Sinbad.

Sinding, Christian (1856–1941). Norwegian composer ; works strongly Norwegian in spirit (" Frühlingsrauschen," " Marche Grotesque ").

Singapore (sing-ga-por'). Brit. island city, Malay Peninsula, commercial centre and naval base of S. Asia, became cap. of Singapore Colony, 1945 ; pop. (whole isl.) 976,839 ; **2974,** 2069 ; in 2nd World War, 2975. 3420.

Singapore Colony. Brit. colony formed 1945 out of former Straits Settlements, Singapore, Cocos-Keeling Is. and Christmas I., 2974.

Sing'er, Isaac M. (1811–75). Amer. inventor ; sewing machine, 2930.

Singing, 2261–63 ; how vocal organs function, 3327.

Singing sands, 2871.

Sinhalese' or **Cingalese,** natives of Ceylon, 749.

Sinigaglia (sē-nē-gah'-lya) or **Senigalia.** It. port on Adriatic N. of Ancona ; pop. 12,000 ; anc. Rom. Sena Gallica.

Sinkiang (sin-kē-ang'). Prov. of w. China, including Chinese Turkestan ; a. 705,000 sq. m. ; pop. 4,360,000 ; cap. Tihua ; dry region, but fruit, cereals, and cotton raised by irrigation ; 3267.

" Sink-lakes," 1885.

Sinn Fein (shin fān). Irish revolutionary party, 1746.

Sino-Japanese War (1894–95), 812, 1800.

Si'non. Friend of Odysseus, 3250.

Sinope (sin-ō-pē) or **Sinop.** Port of Turkey ; best harbour on S. shore of Black Sea ; pop. 32,000 ; anc. Gk. colony ; Russians destroyed Turk. fleet (1853) ; exports timber, dried fruits, skins, and silks, 465, 1017.

Sion (zi'-on) **College.** London institution founded in 1623 under the will of Thomas White, vicar of St. Dunstan's in the West, as a college, parochial clergy guild, and almshouse ; now only a college and guild ; fine theological library ; moved from London Wall to Victoria Embankment (1886).

Siouan (sōō-an) **Indians.** One of the largest and most widely extended linguistic stocks of N. Amer. Indians, occupying chiefly the great plains area ; often called the Plains Indians.

Sioux (sōō) or **Dakotahs.** An Indian tribe of Siouan stock, with possible exception of Ojibwa the largest tribe in U.S.A., 2753 ; costume, *plate f.* 2756 ; risings, 603.

Sioux City, Iowa, U.S.A. Mfg. and commercial city on w. border on Missouri and Big Sioux rs. ; pop. 79,183 ; packed meat, flour, sashes and doors, brick and tile.

Si'phon. Strong vessel fitted with centre tube and tap ; when filled with aerated water under pressure this can be released as required ; the action is not that of a true hydraulic siphon.

Siphon. In hydraulics, a bent tube, with one limb longer than the other, by which a liquid can be drawn over the side of a receptacle to a lower level, 2975.

Siphon, of cockle, 860 ; of cuttle-fish. 945.

Siphonap'tera or **Aphaniptera.** The flea order of insects, 1313, 1733.

" Sir Charles Grandison." Novel by Richardson, 2402.

Sir'enia. An order of aquatic mammals such as the manatee, 2077.

Sir'ens. In Gk. myth., sea nymphs who lured mariners to destruction, 2422.

Sirex. Generic name of species of wood-wasp, or horntail, members of saw-fly group, 2877, of insect order *Hymenoptera* ; principal is *S. gigas,* giant horntail, large, bright, orange and bluish creature, whose grub does much damage in pine and larch woods ; it is attacked by ichneumon fly, *Rhyssa, 1685.*

Sirius (sir'-i-us). The dog star, 3079 ; *chart, 895.*

Sirius. Early transatlantic steamship, *2946.*

Sirocco (si-rok'-ō). A wind, 3385.

Sisal (sis'-al or sī'-sal). A Mexican fibre, **2975,** 2158, 2826, 1609 ; plant belongs to agave genus, 76.

Sis'kin. A type of finch, 1272.

Sisters of Mercy. R.C. order, founded in Dublin in 1827 by Catherine McAuley, devoted to visiting the sick, protecting women in distress, and instructing poor girls.

Sistine (sis'-tēn) **Chapel.** Private papal chapel in Vatican built by Pope Sixtus IV ; Michelangelo's frescoes, 2160, *2161.*

" Sistine Madonna." Painting by Raphael, 2052.

Sisyphus (sis'-i-fus). In Gk. myth., king condemned to roll stone up hill for ever, **2975.**

Sitka spruce, 97.

Sit'tidae. Nuthatch family of birds.

Sitting Bull (c. 1837–90). Sioux Indian chief, leader of band which massacred Custer and his forces (1876).

Sitwell. Name of family of Eng. writers ; works include : Edith Sitwell (b. 1887) : " Collected Poems " ; " Alexander Pope " ; " The English Eccentrics." Osbert Sitwell (b. 1892) : " Miracle on Sinai " ; " Penny Foolish " ; " Collected Poems and Satires " ; " Left Hand Right Hand " ; " The Scarlet Tree " ; " Great Morning " ; " Laughter in the Next Room " (autobiog. vols.). Sacheverell Sitwell (b. 1899) : "Southern Baroque Art" ; "Mozart" ; " Life of Liszt " ; 1216.

Siva (sē'-va). Hindu god, 1626 ; Giant Bull of, *1707.*

Siwa (sē'-wa) or **Siwah.** Oasis in Libyan Desert ; in anc. times seat of the oracle of Jupiter Ammon.

Siwash Indians, *2756.*

Six Nations. Confederation of Amer. Indians ; name given to the Iroquois ; towards the close of the 16th cent. a league was formed comprising 5 tribes or nations—the Mohawks, Oneidas, Onondagas, Cayugas, and Senecas—and in 1715 the Tuscaroras were added.

Six'tus IV (Francesco della Rovere) (1414–84). Pope, elected in 1471 ; built famous Sixtine or Sistine Chapel ; a party to the stabbing of Giuliano de' Medici.

Sixtus V (Felice Peretti) (1521–90). Pope, elected in 1585 ; reformed abuses in Rome, limited number of cardinals to 70, and re-established discipline in the Church.

Sizing. In paper making, 2500.

Skagen. Denmark, town and cape at N. tip of Jutland, *map, 992.*

Skag'erak. Arm of North Sea between Denmark and Norway, 991, 2391, 2392, 3126, 352, *map, 992.*

Skate. Fish of the ray family, **2976.**

Skating. Sport, **2976,** *2588* ; science of, 1392.

Skeat, Walter William (1835–1912). Eng. philologist, authority on Middle English, edited Chaucer and " Piers Plowman " (" Etymological English Dictionary ").

Skeleton. The framework of an animal's body, **2977** ; birds, 437 ; bone tissue, 498 ; human, 150 ; insects, 1727 ; molluscs, 2199 ; prehistoric animals, 2678, 2681 ; sharks, 1296 ; sponge, 3068 ; vertebrates, 3318.

Skelleftea. R. of Sweden flowing into Gulf of Bothnia ; *map, 2395.*

Skelton, John (c. 1440–1529). Eng. poet and satirist ; tutor to Henry VIII ;

satirized Wolsey and clerical and social abuses ; the "Skeltonic" metre of some of his verses is entirely irregular and unconventional (" Why come ye not to Courte ?," attacking Wolsey, and "Colin Clout," attacking the clergy).

"Sketch Book, The," by Washington Irving, 1759.

Skibbereen', Eire. Tn. in Co. Cork, on R. Ilen near coast.

Skiddaw. Mt. in Cumberland, 3,054 ft., 943.

Ski-ing (shē'-ing or skē'-ing). Winter sport, 2978 ; in Alps, 131.

Ski-joring, 2979 ; in Norway, plate f. 2392.

Skim'mer or scissorbill. A family of sea-birds in which the lower mandible is much longer than the upper and is used to skim the surface of the water for food.

Skin. Covering tissue of an animal, 2979, 2980 ; hygiene, 1676 ; leather, 1913 ; senses, 3231 ; of spider, plate f. 3065 ; tattooing, 3158 ; skin effect, in elec., 1624.

Skink. A lizard, 1974.

Skip'jack. A click beetle, 399.

Skittles, 2980.

Skoda works. Great armaments firm of Czechoslovakia near Pilsen, taken over by Czech government in 1936 ; Fr. armament firm of Schneider-Creusot at one time held half Skoda shares ; works seized by Germans for own arms production in 1939 on invasion of Czechoslovakia ; repeatedly bombed by Allies in 2nd World War ; rebuilt in 1946.

Skoplje. See Uskub.

Skull. Bony parts of the head, 2977 ; basis for classification of mankind, 2079, 2723 ; modified in birds, 437.

Skunk. Animal of the weasel tribe with an overpowering odour, 2980 ; fur, 1412.

Skutari. Same as Scutari.

Sky. Why it is blue, 88 ; clouds, 851, 853 ; personified by Greeks, 3298 ; rainbow, 2741.

Skye. Largest of Inner Hebrides ; a. 643 sq. m. ; 1602 ; fine scenery.

Skye terrier, plate f. 1024, 1027.

Sky'lark, 1893 ; care of young, 444 ; courtship flights, 441 ; foot, 448.

Skymaster. Transport aeroplane, C-54, used by U.S.A.A.F. in 2nd World War ; could carry 26 passengers 3,900 m.

Sky-rockets. Fireworks, 1291.

Skyscraper. Name for very tall building, 2352 ; in Alexandria, 1104 ; architectural value, 222 ; in New York City, 222, back of plates f. 2352, 2353.

Slag. Waste matter formed in metal smelting, 1754 ; "foamed," 2702 ; pumice from, 2702 ; in elec. welding, 3362.

Slaked lime. Calcium hydroxide, produced by sprinkling calcium oxide with water, 1949.

Slang, in language, 2980.

Slate. A rock that splits into thin slabs, 2981, 2795 ; formation, 836.

Slatin, Sir Rudolph Karl von (1857–1932). Austrian soldier ; joined Gordon in Egypt (1878) ; kept prisoner by the Mahdi (1883–95) ; made Pasha by the Khedive and served under Kitchener ; inspector-general under British in Sudan (1900–14).

Slave Coast. On Gulf of Guinea, Africa ; formerly resort for slave traders. Now forms the coast of Nigeria and Dahomey.

Slave or Great Slave Lake. In N.W. Canada ; a. 10,000 sq. m. ; 2050, 677.

Slave or Great Slave River. Portion (300 m.) of Mackenzie r. of Canada, 2050.

Slavery and serfdom, 2981 ; Africa, 3017, 68, 70, 118, 1613, 1970 ; Algeria, 118 ; Babylonia, 330 ; John Bright, 570 ; Cameroons, 673 ; Egypt, 216 ; Greece, 1523 ; and Hawkins, 1588 ; in ant world, 168 ; Liberia, 1929 ; Rome, 2805, 2808 ; S. Amer., 1553, 2312 ; Sparta, 3053 ; and Spartacus, 3053 ; United States, 588, 1951, 3291, 2312 ; West Indies, 1793 ; in 2nd World War, 2982.

Slavo'nia. See Croatia-Slavonia.

Slavon'ic or Slav languages, 2855, 2570, 2983.

Slavs. A racial division of E. Europe, 2982, 2725 ; Bulgaria, 613 ; Czechs, 487, 953 ; Yugoslavia, 3438 ; Poland, 2640 ; Russia, 2846 ; Serbs, 2922.

Sleep, 2983 ; and enzyme, 1220 ; and hibernation, 1622.

Sleepers, railway. Creosote treatment, 927.

Sleeping sickness. Carried by tsetse fly, 3252 ; caused by protozoa, 1458 ; in Congo basin, 68.

Sleepy Hollow, 1759.

Sleet. Hail or snow falling mixed with rain.

Slesser, Sir Henry (b. 1883). Brit. judge ; Solicitor-Gen. 1924, in 1st Labour govt. ; Ld. Justice of Appeal 1929–40 ; wrote "Trade Union Law," "The Pastured Shire" (verse) ; "Order and Disorder."

Slide rule, 2984, 2985.

Slide valve, in steam-engine, 3086.

Slieve Bloom, Eire. Range of mts. part of boundary between Co. Leix and Co. Offaly ; 1,733 ft. high.

Sli'go, Eire. Marit. co. in prov. of Connaught ; a. 694 sq. m. ; pop. 62,000. 2985.

Slim, F.-M. Sir William J. (b. 1891). Brit. soldier ; at head of Brit. 14th Army in Burma ; C.-in-C. Allied Land forces S.E. Asia (1945–46) ; Commandant Imp. Defence Coll. (1946–47) ; in 1948 chm. of rly. executive ; in Oct. 1948 apptd. C.I.G.S. ; Field-Marshal in 1949 ; created G.C.B. in 1950 ; 3424.

Slime moulds. A type of primitive organisms found on decaying wood.

Sling, use of, 1292, 1294.

Slip. Potter's clay, 2665.

Slip dock, 1024.

Slip knot, 1869.

Slipper animalcule, 2695.

Slipper shell, 2943.

Slip stitch, in sewing, 2927.

Slipstream, of aeroplane, 2903.

Slivers (sliv'erz). Textile fibres in loose strands ; cotton, 920 ; rope, 2826 ; wool, 3406.

Sloane, Sir Hans (1660–1753). Brit. collector and physician ; F.R.S. (1685), pres. (1727–41) ; went to Jamaica as physician to the governor in 1687, and there collected a variety of plants and other curiosities which he catalogued and published in 1696 ; purchased manor of Chelsea (1712) ; Hans Place, Sloane Street, Sloane Square, etc., named after him ; left his collections to the nation, and these, with another collection, were opened as the British Museum in 1759 ; 584.

Sloe. Name given to the fruit and tree of the blackthorn ; acid fruit used in the making of sloe gin.

Sloop. A sailing vessel, 484 ; in modern navy, 2296.

Sloth. A tree-living mammal, with hook-like feet and long claws, by which it clings to branches upside-down, 2985, 2077 ; prehistoric, 2679.

Slough (slow). Tn. in Buckingham shire, 2 m. N.E. of Windsor ; here the Herschels made astronomical discoveries ; pop. 64,240 ; 600.

Slough of Despond, in "Pilgrim's Progress," 618.

Slovak'ia. Prov. in E. Czechoslovakia ; a. 18,902 sq. m. ; pop. 3,400,000 ; 953, 2985, map, 954 ; puppet state of Germany 1940–45.

Slovaks. A Slavic people, 953, 2983.

Slovenes. A Slavic people, 2983.

Slovenia (slō-vē'-ni-a) or Slovinia. Constituent part of Yugoslavia, includes portions of former Austrian territory of Carniola, Carinthia, Styria, and Istria, 3438 ; Germans occupied 1940–44.

Slow-worm. Legless lizard common in Britain ; also known as blindworm, but neither a worm, nor slow, nor blind, 2985.

Slug, linotype, 1956.

Slugs and Snails, 2989.

Slum clearance, and town planning, 3233.

Sluys (slois) or Sluis, battle of. Fr. defeated off Dutch coast by Eng. and Flemish fleets under Edward III (1340), 1652.

Small, James. Maker of first iron plough, 79.

Small arms. See Firearms.

Small Copper butterfly ; plate f. 632.

Small Heath butterfly ; plate f. 633.

Small pox. A disease caused by germs, 1458 ; vaccination, 1818 ; 3301.

Smalt (smawlt). A cobalt blue pigment, 858, obtained from ore Smaltite.

Smart'weed, or water-pepper. Annual herb (genus Polygonum) which grows in wet places ; so called from acrid juice which will inflame tender skin.

Smeaton, John (1724–92). Eng. engineer ; started as a maker of mathematical instruments, but later turned to engineering ; designed the third Eddystone lighthouse ; built some bridges in Scot. ; surveying engineer for the Forth and Clyde Canal ; improved steam engine, 3085 ; 1084.

Smed'ley, Francis (Frank) Edward (1818–64). Eng. novelist ("Frank Fairleigh," which ranks with "Tom Brown's Schooldays" ; "Lewis Arundel" ; "Harry Coverdale's Courtship").

Smell, sense of, 2986 ; in cats, 718 ; contributes to taste, 3157.

Smelting, copper, 906, 907 ; iron, 1754 ; zinc, 3443.

Smet'ana, Bedrich (1824–84). Bohemian (Czech) composer and pianist, called the "Czech Beethoven" ("The Bartered Bride" ; "Vltava"), 2983.

Smethwick (smeth'-ik). Mfg. centre 3 m. N.W. of Birmingham ; pop. 76,700 ; mfrs. iron products, machinery, glass, chemicals.

Smike. In Dickens's "Nicholas Nickleby," half-witted, half-starved boy at Dotheboys Hall, befriended by Nicholas.

Smi'lax or greenbrier. A shrubby climbing or trailing plant related to lilies ; one type yields sarsaparilla.

Smiles, Samuel (1812–1904). Scot. biographer and didactic essayist ("Self-Help" ; biographies of Watt, Stephenson, Wedgwood, etc.).

Smith, why a common surname, 1753.

Smith, Adam (1723–90). Scot. political economist ; 2886, 1081, 2895 ; on taxation, 3158.

Smith, Sir Francis Pettit (1808–74). Eng. inventor of ship's screw, 2903.

Smith, Sir George Adam (1856–1942). Brit. Orientalist ; appointed professor of Hebrew and Oriental Literature in the Free Church College, Glasgow 1892, and 1909 principal of Aberdeen Univ. ; moderator of General Assembly of United Free Church (1916–17).

Smith, Sir Grafton Elliot (1871–1937). Australian anatomist and archaeologist. Fullerian Professor of Physiology at the Royal Institution (1933). Author of "The Evolution of Man," "The Diffusion of Culture," etc.

Smith, Horace (1779–1849) and James (1775–1839). Brit. wits and parodists ; achieved fame by vol. of parodies "Rejected Addresses," of contemporary poets Wordsworth, Byron, Southey, Crabbe, etc.

Smith, Sir Ross Macpherson (1892–1922) and Sir Keith Macpherson (b. 1890). Australian airmen. These brothers made the first flight from Eng. to Australia, Nov.-Dec. 1919, winning the prize of £10,000 offered by Australian Government.

Smith, Gipsy (Rodney) (1860–1947). Eng. evangelist ; special missionary of Nat. Free Church Council (1897–1912) and toured Australia and America ; served with Y.M.C.A. in France during 1914–18 ; brilliant orator.

Smith, Captain John (1580–1631). Eng. colonial adventurer, 2754, 142 ; writings, 3293.

Smith, Joseph (1805–44). Founded Mormons, 2230.

Smith, Sydney (1771–1845). Eng. clergyman and author ; firm friend of religious toleration, and a famous wit ; called Macaulay a " book in breeches," and compared House of Lords rejecting Reform Bill of 1831 to Mrs. Partington trying to mop up the Atlantic Ocean ; a founder of the " Edinburgh Review."

Smith, Walter Bedell (b. 1895). U.S. soldier and diplomat ; served in 1st World War ; chief of staff to Eisenhower 1942–44 ; for supreme Allied command signed Ger. surrender document, July 1945, at Reims ; Mar. 1946 became U.S. ambass. to the U.S.S.R.

Smith, William Henry (1825–91). Brit. business man and politician ; developed the rly. bookstall and circulating library ; First Lord of the Admiralty (1877), Sec. for War (1886), followed Lord R. Churchill as leader of House of Commons.

Smith, William Robertson (1846–94). Scots. scholar ; removed from professorship of Aberdeen on account of his articles on Biblical subjects in " Encyclopaedia Britannica " (1881) ; joint editor and afterwards editor-in-chief of the " Encyclopaedia Britannica " ; professor of Arabic at Cambridge.

Smith, Sir William Sydney (1764–1840). Eng. sailor. In 1799 defended Acre against Napoleon. Sank Turkish fleet at Abydos (1807).

Smith-Dorrien, Sir Horace Lockwood (1858–1930). Brit. soldier ; served in Zulu War, in Egypt, Sudan, South Africa and India ; in 1st World War commanded 2nd Corps and later 2nd Army ; C.-in-C. East Africa (1915–16) ; Governor of Gibraltar (1918–23).

Smith'field. Historic square in London, N. of St. Paul's, formerly jousting field and place of public executions ; chief central meat market ; *1197*, 1257. Hit by rocket in 1945.

Smith'son, James (1765–1829). Eng. scientist, son of first Duke of Northumberland ; F.R.S., founder of Smithsonian Institution at Washington, U.S.A.

Smock, wooden covering of upper part of windmill, 3386.

Smoke and smoke abatement, 2886 ; smoke as food preservative, 1340 ; detection, 2577.

Smoke-screen, as military weapon, 1291, *2987.*

Smokeless fuels, 2986.

Smoke'less powder, 1250, 1558.

Smolensk (smô-lensk'). One of the oldest Rus. cities on Dnieper ; pop. (1939) 156,000 ; strategic key to Russia ; taken by Fr. (1812) ; occupied by Germany 1941–44, 3419, 3421.

Smol'lett, Tobias George (1721–71). Brit. novelist (" Humphrey Clinker," " Roderick Random ") *2895*, 2402.

Smolt. Young salmon, 2865.

Smooth snake, 2991.

Smut, a fungus disease of plants, 2857.

Smuts, Jan Christian, O.M. (b. 1870), Brit. S. African soldier and statesman, **2987,** *2988* ; on British Empire, 580 ; philosophy, 3020 ; and 1st World War, 3411.

Smyrna (or Izmir) (smer'-na). Chief spt. of Asia Minor ; pop. 200,000 ; **2988** ; cession to Greece, 1526 ; Turkish re-occupation, 3265, 1526.

Smyrna fig, 1270.

Smyth, Dame Ethel (1858–1944). Brit. composer ; vigorous figure in Feminist movement, **2989.**

Smythe, Francis Sydney (1900–1949). Eng. mountaineer and author ; on expeditions to Kinchinjunga (1930), Kamet (1931), and Everest (1933, 1936 and 1938) ; books " Kamet Conquered," " The Spirit of the Hill," " The Valley of Flowers," etc.

Snae Fell. Highest mt. in Isle of Man ; 2,034 ft.

Snails and Slugs, 2989 ; 2199 ; eggs and egg baskets, *1094* ; eyes, *1253* ; hibernation, 1623 ; tongue, 3223.

Snake bird. Name often given in England to the wryneck, and in America to the darter. *See* **Wryneck.**

Snake-charmers, in India, *859.*

Snake dance. A ceremonial dance of the Hopi Indians in which the dancers carry live snakes in their hands and mouths.

Snake fly. Insect of order Neuroptera, fam. *Raphidiidae* ; named from its long flexible " neck " ; found in Europe and Pacific coast states of U.S.A. ; eggs, *1094.*

Snake goddess, Cretan, *31.*

Snake River, U.S.A. Chief tributary of Columbia r. ; rises in Yellowstone Park, flows through s. Idaho, then to Columbia in s. Washington ; length, 1,000 m.

Snakeroot. A name given to various plants which are or were supposed to cure snake bites ; among these the black snakeroot (*Cimicifuga racemosa*), and Seneca snakeroot (*Polygala senega*) of the milkwort family are common in the U.S.A. ; Canada snakeroot is the wild ginger.

Snakes, 2990, 2767 ; Australian, 310 ; cobra, 859 ; eggs, *1094* ; glass snake a lizard, 1973 ; hibernation, 1623 ; lizards, relationship, 1972 ; preyed upon by secretary bird, 2916 ; python, 2710 ; rattlesnakes, 2746; vipers, 3325.

Snapdragon. Popular name of flowers of genus *Antirrhinum,* family *Scrophulariaceae* ; simple, opposite, leaves, and brightly-coloured flowers ; lower lip of large tubular corolla snaps shut if opened ; *plate f. 392.*

Snapping turtle, *3230.*

Snell, Henry Snell, 1st Baron (1865–1944). Eng. Soc. politician ; Under-Sec. for India (1931) ; chairman of L.C.C. 1934–1937 ; P.C. 1937.

Snipe. A type of wading bird, **2991** ; " drumming," 441.

Snoek. S. African fish (*Thyrsites atun*) fam. *Gempylidae,* belonging to the same order as perch ; may be 4 ft. long ; weighs up to 16 lb. ; much tinned snoek exported to U.K. in food shortages after 2nd World War.

Snooker Pool. Game played on an ordinary billiard table with 22 balls. It consists exclusively of winning hazards, cannons being ignored; 428.

Snorkel. *See* **Schnörkel.**

Snorri Sturluson (stoor'-lu-son) (1179–1241). Icelandic historian and official ; author of " Heimskringla " (sagas of Norwegian kings) and collector and editor of Younger or Prose Edda.

Snow, 2149, **2992** ; avalanche, 322 ; and floods, 1316 ; glaciers and icecaps, 1449 ; red snow caused by algae, 2620 ; snowball, 1372.

Snow apple, from Quebec, 2715.

Snow'ball tree. Cultivated variety of the guelder rose (*var. sterilis*), in which all the flowers are of the sterile type, forming showy, balllike masses. *See* **Guelder rose.**

Snow'berry. Ornamental shrub with clustered white berries ; belongs to honeysuckle family, 1639 ; seed dissemination, *2917.*

Snow'den of Ickornshaw, Philip Snowden, Viscount (1864–1937). Eng. Labour leader ; crippled from youth, he became Labour M.P. 1906, and was Chancellor of the Exchequer in 1924 and 1929–31 ; Lord Privy Seal in Nat. Govt. ; visct. 1931.

Snow'don. Mt. in Wales, 3,560 ft. high, 584, 650, 666, 3333, *3335* ; *map, 3334.*

Snow'drop. A small low plant with bulbous roots, 2992.

Snow grouse or **ptarmigan** (tahr'-migan), 1551.

Snow leopard, *2075.*

Snow line, 2992.

" Snow of the Penitents," 2992.

Snow plough, in ski-ing, 2978.

Snow'y owl, *2461.*

Snuff. Tobacco prepared for inhaling ; also made from acacia, 16.

Soane, Sir John (1753–1837). Eng. architect ; designed Bank of England ; founded Soane Museum.

Soap, 2993 ; a detergent, 998 ; agave juice used, 76 ; molecule of, *3121* ; olive oil, 2431 ; from petroleum oil, 2430 ; and surface tension, 3122 ; and hard water, 3351.

Soap flakes and powders, 2994.

Soap nut. Fruit of the tropical or subtropical soapberry tree ; found chiefly in W. Indies, but also in s. Florida, U.S.A.

Soapstone. *See* **Talc.**

Soar, Eng. River rising just within Warwickshire and flowing through Leicestershire and Nottinghamshire to the Trent ; 40 m. long.

Sobieski (sō-bi-es'-ki), **John** (1624–96). King of Poland (John III) elected 1674 ; freed Hungary, and became hero of Poland; defeats Turks, 3264 ; burial-place, 925.

Sobre'ro, Ascanio. It. chemist, 1060.

" Soccer." *See* **Association Football.**

Sociability of alkali metals, 120.

Social Credit, an economic theory advocating periodical additions to purchasing power to prevent " underconsumption " causing " slumps " ; a similar principle is actually employed to implement a " full employment " policy by budgetary means.

Social insects. Ants, 165 ; bees, 390 ; wasps, 3345.

Social Insurance, 2994, 3283 ; pensions, 2546.

Socialism, 2996 ; Bolsheviks, 1923, 495, 2849 ; co-operative societies, 903 ; in France, 2996 ; in Germany, 1450, 1451 ; Karl Marx, *2113*, 2996 ; William Morris, 2232 ; in Russia, 2850 ; Tolstoy's doctrines, 3223. *See also* **Communism,** etc.

Social War, 2809.

Societies, Friendly. *See* **Friendly Societies.**

Society of Friends ; known as **Quakers.** Nobel Peace Prize, 1947. *See* **Friends.**

Society Islands. Group of 11 Fr. isls. in s. Pacific, nearly midway between Australia and S. Amer. ; volcanic, mountainous (highest peak 7,000 ft.), surrounded by coral reefs ; 2471 ; most important Tahiti (*q.v.*) and Moorea ; joint pop. over 25,000.

Sociol'ogy, the study of human society ; family and other social groups, 1259 ; personal names, 2272 ; prisons and punishments, 2686 ; slavery and serfdom, 2981 ; socialism, 2996 ; tattooing, 3158. *See also* **Civilization ; Economics ; Education ; Law ; Superstitions.**

Socks, how made, 1865, *1866,* 1867.

Socotra (sō-kō'-tra) or **Sokotra.** An island under Brit. control off E. coast of Africa at entrance to Gulf of Aden ; a. 1,382 sq. m. ; est. pop. 12,000 ; dates, gums, livestock, butter.

Socrates (sok'-ra-tēz) (*c.* 470–399 B.C.), Gk. philosopher, **2996,** 1540 ; hemlock poison, 2637 ; influence on Plato, 2628 ; Xenophon's " Memorabilia," 3429.

So'da, 2997 ; Le Blanc mfg. process, 2997, 3117 ; soda ash, 2997 ; Solvay process, 2997.

Soda. Process in paper-making, 2497.

Soda water. Water charged with carbon dioxide, 700.

Soddy, Frederick (b. 1877). Eng. scientist ; authority on radium and radioactivity. Writings include " Chemistry of Radioactive Elements " ; " Cartesian Economics " ; " Money Versus Man " ; " Interpretation of the Atom." Awarded Nobel Prize for Chemistry in 1921 ; originated theory of atomic disintegration, 296 ; isotopes, 1760 ; and radioactivity, 2732 ; and Lord Rutherford, 2858.

Söderblöm, Lars Olof Jonathan (Nathan) (1866–1931). Swedish divine ; Archbishop of Upsala (1914–31) ; awarded Nobel Peace Prize (1930) ; did much to promote the unity of the Christian churches and was an authority on Persian religion (" Religious Culture " ; " General History of Religion ").

Sodium. Soft silver-white element of the alkali metal group ; atomic weight 22·997 ; reacts violently with

water ; melts at 207·5° F. ; **2997** ; atom, *295* ; cyanide used in gold extraction, 947 ; hydroxide used in soaps, 2993 ; phosphate used in making silks, 2972 ; in Rochelle salts, 3155 ; properties, 776 ; sulphate used in paper-making, 2497 ; yellow light in spectrum, 3055, *facing* p. 3057, in water softening, 3351.
Compounds : bicarbonate (baking soda,) *1289* ; bromide, 2638 ; carbonate (soda), 3117 ; chloride (table salt), *1137*, 1567, 1738, 2149, 2865 ; cyanide, 947 ; glutamate, 3114 ; hydroxide, 20 ; nitrate (Chile saltpetre), 2372, 2868 ; permanganate, 2087 ; sulphate, 2497, 2748, 2865 ; thiosulphate ("hypo"), 2580.

Sodium chloride. *See* Salt ; Sodium.

Sodium hyposulphite. *See* Hyposulphite of sodium.

Sodium Light. Wave-length, 1941.

Sodium vapour lamp, 1135.

Sod'om, Apple of. Name of various prickly or spiny weeds of the nightshade family.

Sod'om and Gomor'rah. In Biblical geography, cities in Palestine destroyed for wickedness, 13.

Soeraba'va, Indonesia. *See* Surabaya.

Soest (zêst), Ger. City 25 m. E. of Dortmund, pop. 20,000 ; important Hansa tn. ; early code of municipal laws, *jus susatense*, model for other free cities.

Sofia (sō-fē'-*a*). Cap. of Bulgaria, centre of Balkan peninsula ; pop. 401,000 ; **2997**, 614.

"Soft" currency, 1348.

Soft Paste Porcelain, 2670.

Soft water, 3351.

Sogne (sōg'-nä) **Fiord,** Norway. Long, deep, narrow inlet of s.w. coast ; rugged scenery ; *map*, *2395*.

So'ho. Foreign quarter in w. London, 2015.

Soil, 2998 ; acidity corrected by limestone, 1950 ; alluvial, 2999 ; bacteria as soil-makers, 2373 ; clay, 836 ; effects of clover, 852 ; elements necessary for plant growth, 2621, 2624 ; erosion, 1318 ; fertilizers, 2373, 2916, 2998 ; glacial deposits, 1469 ; how moisture travels, 698 ; legumes as soil-builders, 2373 ; lichens as soil-makers, 1933 ; loess, 2999 ; mosses as soil-makers, 2239 ; nitrification by lucerne, 2034 ; nitrifying bacteria inoculations, 2374 ; nitrogenous material obtained, 2373 ; trees as soil-makers, 3246 ; volcanic, 743 ; work of grasses, 1509 ; work of earth-worms, 1070 ; work of roots, 2825 ; work of winds, 3384. *See* Alkaline Soils ; Alluvial Soil ; Fertilizers.

Soissons (swah'-sawn). Historic tn. of N. Fr., 55 m. N.E. of Paris on Aisne r. ; pop. 18,174 ; fine 13th-cent. cathedral shattered by Ger. shells 1918 ; restored and reconsecrated 1937 ; scene of desperate fighting (1914–15 and 1918) ; occupied by Germans 1940–44.

"Soke," defined, 2385.

Sokol. Organization of Czechoslovak youth, founded in 1862, utilizing the idea of a gymnastic society for furthering not only the physical but the moral well-being of the nation, *953*. "Sokol" is the Czech word for a falcon, and the motto of the movement is "Let us be strong."

Sokolovsky, Vasilij D. (b. 1899). Russ. soldier ; under Koniev's command liberated S. Poland, Jan. 1945, and crossed Oder in Mar. ; made Marshal 1946 ; C.-in-C. of Soviet forces occupying Germany Apr. 1946– Mar. 1949 ; as Soviet member of Allied Control Council in Berlin enforced road, rail, and canal blockade of Western powers' sectors in Berlin when on June 18, 1948, the U.K., U.S.A., and Fr. announced a currency reform ; 1st Dep. Min. of Armed Forces in U.S.S.R., Mar. 1949.

Soko'tra. *See* Socotra.

Sol. In chem., a colloid in solution, e.g. an emulsion, 871.

Solana'ceae. Nightshade family.

Solan'der, Dr. Daniel Charles (1736–82). Swedish botanist ; assistant librarian to Brit. Mus. ; accompanied Sir Joseph Banks on expedition, 359.

So'lan goose. *See* Gannet.

Sola'num. A genus of plants including common nightshades and potato, 2369, 2664.

So'lar corona, 1079.

Solar engines, 1594.

Solar plex'us. One of chief nerve centres, situated behind stomach.

Solar prominences, *plate f. 1076*, 1079. *plate f. 3120*.

Solar spectrum, *facing p. 3056*.

Solar System, 3318, *280* ; asteroids, 2617 ; comets, 880 ; eclipses, 1077, *plates f. 1076, 1077* ; earth, 1667 ; equinox and solstice, 1221 ; gravitation, 1512, 2349 ; Kepler's laws of planetary motion, 1853 ; meteors and meteorites, 2151, 2152 ; movement through space towards Vega, 3078 ; origin, 2619 ; planets, 2617 ; sun, 3318.

Solar time, 3212 ; day, 980 ; month, 2223 ; year, 662.

Solder. Composition of, 1391 ; solidification, 1391 ; and welding, 3362.

Soldier. *See* Army.

Sole. A flatfish, 1298.

Sole, of shoe, 522, 523.

Sole Bay. Alternative name of Southwold Bay, Suffolk.

Sole Bay, Battle of. Naval encounter in 1672 during the third Dutch war ; whilst the Eng. and Fr. fleets were in Sole Bay they were attacked by the Dutch, who withdrew on the appearance of Brit. reinforcements.

Solenhofen or **Solnhofen.** Vil. of Bavaria, 40 m. s. of Nuremberg ; lithographic stone, 1967.

Solenoid. *See* Electro-magnet.

So'lent. Channel, between w. Hampshire and the Isle of Wight, 8 m. s. of Southampton ; famous yachting waters.

"Sol-fa" singing, 2262.

Solferino (sol-fā-rē-nō). It. vil. 20 m. N.W. of Mantua ; Austrians defeated (1859), 2752, 1769.

Solicitor. Officer of the Supreme Court of Judicature, admitted to practise law on behalf of clients by advice and in the briefing of barristers, but allowed to plead only in the lower courts ; 1903.

Solic'itor-General. A law officer of the Crown ; his position is immediately below that of the attorney-general ; he acts as a legal adviser to the govt.

Solid. One of the three physical states of all bodies.

Sol'id, in geometry, 1437.

Solingen (zō'-ling-en). Ger. mfg. city in North Rhine-Westphalia ; pop. 132,600 ; 1447.

Solis (sō-lēs'), **Juan Diaz de** (1470 ?– 1516). Sp. navigator, 228.

Solitaire (sol-i-tār'). An extinct bird of the flightless pigeon family ; not unlike the dodo ; inhabited tropical islands ; also indoor game with marbles ; also ring with one stone.

Sollum. Small pt. and gulf of Egypt, nr. w. border with Tripoli ; in 1st World War Brit. base in ops. against Senussi ; in 2nd World War changed hands 5 times, the last being occupied by Brit. 8th Army after Alamein victory ; 3418, 3419, *map, 3421*.

So'lo. In music, formerly an unaccompanied performance by a voice or instrument ; term now used to denote any important or prominent passage of a solo nature.

Sologub (sō-lō-goob'), **Feodor** (1863– 1927). Pen-name of Feodor Kuzmich Teternikov, Russian novelist and poet, 2856.

Sol'omon. King of Israel (d. c. 937 B.C.), **2999** ; Phoenician workmen, 2573 ; and ships, 2945.

Solomon. Professional name of Solomon Cutner (b. 1902). Brit. pianist, excelling in the playing of Brahms and Beethoven.

Solomon, Temple of, 1819, 2999.

"Solomon, Wisdom of." Apocryphal book, 424.

Solomon Islands. Groups of Pacific volcanic isls. 1,000 m. N.E. of Australia ; N. group under Australian mandate, s. group Brit. protectorate ; a. 17,000 sq. m. ; pop. 132,000 ; 2470 ; in 2nd World War, 2474, 3293, 3420, 3421.

"Solomon of England," 1612.

Solon (sō'-lon) (about 638–558 B.C.). Athenian reformer, law-giver, and poet, 2999, 1522 ; and Croesus, 933 ; legal code, 1902.

So'lo organ, 2450.

Solstice (sol'-stis). Time when sun is nearest either Pole and farthest from the other, 1221.

Solute. Substance dissolved in a solvent forming a solution, 3683, 3688.

Solu'tion, in chemistry ; crystallization, 940 ; broken up by electricity, 1137.

Solutrean Man, 2081.

Solvay, Ernest (1838–1922). Belgian industrial chemist, called "Belgian Carnegie" for his philanthropies ; inventor of ammonia-soda or Solvay process of making soda, 2997 ; paid huge indemnity to save Brussels from destruction by Germans.

Solvent. Liquid or solid in which a gas or solid is dissolved forming a solution.

Sol'way Firth. Inlet of Irish Sea, between Eng. and Scot., 32 m. wide at entrance and nearly 50 m. long.

Solway Moss. Place in Eng. on Scot. border near Carlisle ; battle (1542).

Sol'yman I (or **Suleiman**) **the Magnificent** (c. 1495–1566). Greatest of the Ottoman sultans, 3264 ; rebuilds wall of Jerusalem, 1819.

Somali (sō-mah'-lē). Africans, 70.

Soma'liland. E. peninsula of Africa between Gulf of Aden and Indian Ocean ; comprises former Italian Somaliland, again under administration of Italy after March 1950 ; Somaliland Protectorate (Brit.) 68,000 sq. m. ; French Somali coast 9,071 sq. m. ; 2999, 72, 1073, *map, 1072* ; Italian war, 14 ; in 2nd World War, 3000, 3418.

Somers (sum'-erz), **Sir George** (1554– 1611). Eng. navigator. 418.

Somers or **Bermuda Islands,** 418.

Som'erset, Edward Seymour, Duke of (c. 1506–52). Protector of Eng. in early part of Edward VI's reign, 1091.

Somerset House. Brit. Govt. building in London, situate between Strand and Victoria Embankment ; built 1776–86, the east and west wings being added at later dates ; King's College occupies the east wing, but the rest of the house is given over to govt. work—audit, registration, inland revenue and wills and probate ; wills, once proved, can be seen here ; also birth and marriage certificates etc. ; 2108 ; damaged by bomb in 1940.

Somerset Island, magnetic N. pole in, 2390.

Somerset or **Victoria Nile,** 2370.

Som'ersetshire. Co. in s.w. Eng. ; a. 1,613 sq. m. ; pop. 475,000 ; **3000**, *1163*, 3365.

Somervell, Sir Arthur (1863–1937). Eng. composer, best known for settings of song-cycles drawn from Tennyson's "Maud" and Housman's "Shropshire Lad."

Somerville, Massachusetts, U.S.A., mfg. and residential suburb, N.W. of Boston ; pop. 102,000.

Somerville, Edith Oenone (d. 1949). Irish novelist and artist ; with her cousin "Martin Ross" (Miss Violet Martine), wrote many novels of Irish life, full of verve and racy Irish humour, some illustrated by herself ; "The Real Charlotte," "Some Experiences of an Irish R.M.," "Dan Russel, the Fox," "Mount Music."

Somme, r. of N. Fr., 150 m. long, 1360 ; touches Amiens and Saint-Quentin ; in 2nd World War, 3417.

Somme battles, 3410, 3412, *3413* ; first use of tanks, 3151.

Somnam'bulism. The act of walking while asleep.

Sonata (sō-nah'-ta). In music, 2961 ; Beethoven develops, 398.

Song birds or *Oscines* (os-i-nēz). Vocal organs, 441.

"Song of Solomon." Book of Old Testament, called also " Song of Songs " and " Canticles " ; authorship formerly ascribed to Solomon.

"Song of the Shirt," by Hood, 1640.

Songs, 1333 ; national, 2282 ; Schubert, 2887.

Son'net. Poem of 14 lines with a definite rhyme scheme, 2636 ; Petrarch's, 1786, 2636 ; Shakespeare's, 2636, 2936.

"Sonnets from the Portuguese," 589.

Sonnino (sō-nē-nō), Sidney, Baron (1847–1921). It. statesman and financier ; minister of finance (1893–94), of Treasury (1894–96) ; premier (1906 and 1909–10), minister for foreign affairs (1914–19).

Sonora (sō-nōr'-a), Mexico. State on Gulf of California bordering Arizona, U.S.A. ; a. 70,477 sq. m. ; pop. 364,000 ; cap. Hermosillo.

Soochow' or **Suchow**, China. Wealthy silk-mfg. city on Grand Canal 55 m. w. of Shanghai ; founded 500 B.C. ; pop. 260,000 ; almost destroyed by Taipings (1860).

Soong Family. Chinese family ; the father Soong Yao-ju (1863–1918) owned one of world's largest printing presses in Shanghai ; 4 children educated in U.S.A. ; eldest daughter Eling (b. 1890) married Kung Hsiang-hi, who became min. of industry and min. of defence ; the son Tse-ven (b. 1891) became prime min. (exec. Yuan) 1944–47, represented China at San Francisco Con., and became gov. of Kwantung in 1947 ; second daughter, Chingling, married Sun Yat-sen ; third, Meiling, became Mme Chiang (q.v.).

Sooth'sayer. One who claims to have supernatural foresight, 2058.

Sophia (sō-fī-a) (1630–1714). Electress of Hanover, heiress of Eng. crown by Act of Settlement of 1701 (because nearest Protestant heir) ; mother of George I and ancestress of Hanover-Windsor line of Brit. sovereigns.

Sophia. *See* **Sofia.**

Sophists (sof'-ists), in anc. Greece. A class of teachers of rhetoric and practical philosophy ; and Socrates, 2997.

Sophocles (sof'-ō-klēz) (495–405 B.C.). Gk. tragic dramatist ; **3000**, 2425 ; and Greek drama, 1038, 1540 ; supplants Aeschylus, 53.

Sopwith, Thomas Octave Murdoch (b. 1888). British sportsman ; pioneer airman and aeroplane constructor. In 1911 founded Sopwith Aviation & Engineering Co., and built many machines used in 1st World War. A yachtsman, he vainly endeavoured to wrest America's Cup from U.S.A. in 1934 and 1937. Head of Hawker Aircraft Co. (Hurricane, Tempest, etc.).

Sorata or **Illampu**. Mt. peak in Bolivia, after Aconcagua highest in S. America, 153.

Sorbonne (sor-bon'). Paris institution of theology, science, and letters ; founded in 13th cent. ; incorporated in Univ. (1852) ; 2517, 3296.

Sor'cery. *See* **Magic.**

"Sordel'lo." Poem by Browning, 590

Sore'dia of lichens, 1933.

Sorghum (sor'-gum). A tall cereal grass.

Sori (sōr'-ī) (plural of " sorus "). Spore cases of ferns, 2918.

Sorolla y Bastida (sō-rōl'-yah ē bas-tē'-dah), **Joaquin** (1863–1923). Sp. impressionist painter, leader of modern Sp. artists ; excels in marine compositions with brilliant sunlight effects.

Sor'rel. A species of biennial or perennial herb of the genus *Rumex* ; two kinds are found in Eng. in the form of common weeds ; oxalic acid, 2638.

Sorrel tree. Same as **Sourwood.**

Sorrento (sor-ren'-tō). It. resort on Bay of Naples ; pop. 7,000 ; anc. Surrentum, famous for wine ; birthplace of Tasso ; taken by Allied 5th Army

from Germans, undamaged, Sept. 1943.

S O S. Morse signal sent out by ships in distress, usually by radio : the letters are not abbreviations but chosen because distinctive and easy to transmit.

Sosnowiec (sos-nō-vě'ets), Poland. City in Upper Silesian coal field, 40 m. N.W. of Cracow ; pop. 121,000 ; textile centre.

Sothern (suth'ern), **Edward Askew** (1826–81). Eng. actor ; made part of " Lord Dundreary " famous ; father of E. H. Sothern.

Sothern, Edward Hugh (1859–1933). Amer. actor ; in early years played romantic parts ; later one of foremost Shakespearean actors (as Hamlet, Macbeth, Shylock).

Soto, Hernando de. Discovered Mississippi, 2192, 141.

Souchong (soo-shong') **tea**, *3162*.

Soul, Eg. beliefs, 2255, 2904 ; transmigration, 601, 1628, 2710.

Soult (soolt), **Nicholas Jean de Dieu, Duke of Dalmatia** (1769–1851). Marshal of Fr. ; led decisive attack at Austerlitz ; commanded in Sp. against Sir John Moore and Wellington.

Sound, 3009, 1495 ; echo, 1077 ; how the ear hears it, 1066 ; recording, 1497, 2576, 3011, 832 ; reproduction, 1495, 3011 ; speed, 1828, 3010, 1077 ; transmitted by telephone, 2162, 3173 ; voice, 3327 ; waves, 3358 ; ways of producing music, 2266 ; ultrasonic waves, 2713 ; in wireless, 3392, et seq. *See* **Decibel ; Phon.**

Sound, The. Strait between Sweden and Zealand, 352, *992.*

Souple silk, 2972.

Sour'wood or **sorrel tree.** A tree of the heath family with clustered white flowers and acid-tasting leaves.

Sousa (soō'-za), **John Philip** (1856–1932). Amer. bandmaster and composer ; leader U.S. Marine Band 1880–92, thereafter Sousa's Band. (" Washington Post " ; " Liberty Bell " ; " Stars and Stripes Forever " ; " El Capitan " ; and other marches).

Soutar, Andrew (1879–1941). English novelist (" Chosen of the Gods," " Green Orchard ").

South Africa, Union of. Brit. Dominion occupying S. peninsula of African continent ; a. (incl. S.W. Africa) 790,219 sq. m. ; pop. 11,418,350 ; **3014**, *map*, *3015* ; Afrikaans, 73 ; Afrikander, 74 ; air mail development, 2662 ; agriculture and grazing, 2279, 2444 ; animals, *3014*, *3018* ; climate, 3013 ; Cape of Good Hope, 695 ; Cape Town, 696, 697, 3019, *plate f. 3017* ; diamond mines, 1009, *1010*, *3017* ; Durban, 1057 ; gold mines, 1479, *1480*, 1833, 3239 ; Johannesburg, *1833*, *3017* ; kraals, 3018 ; mineral resources, 3013, 3239 ; Natal, 2279 ; *3021* ; natives, *3016* ; Orange Free State, 2444 ; ostrich farming, *3018*, 2457 ; physical features, 3014 ; population, 3020 ; Pretoria, 2682 ; railways, *2740* ; stamps, *3075* ; Transvaal, *3239* ; Victoria Falls, 3321, *plate f. 3016* ; Zambezi r., *3441* ; Zulus, 3448. *History* : Transvaal (1877–81), 3016 ; Cecil Rhodes, 2771 ; Boer War, 486, 3019 ; Botha, 533 ; Union of S. Africa formed, 2988, 3019 ; 1st World War, 533, 2988, 3019 ; 2nd World War, 2988 ; Smuts, 2987, 3020. *See also* **Rhodesia ; Southwest Africa.**

South African Literature, 3020.

South America. Southern continent of New World ; a. 7,310,800 sq. m. ; pop. about 90,000,000 ; **3022** ; *maps f. 3024*, *3025* ; Amazon, 136, 3022 ; climate, 3022 ; coast line and harbours, 3022 ; coffee, 864, *865* ; commerce, 3022 ; Incas, *1688*, 1689, 1690 ; languages, 228, 554 ; people, 2312, 3024, *3026* ; physical features, 152, 3022 ; population, 2312, 3022, *plate f. 3025* ; products and resources, 153, *3023*, 3024 ; revolt of Sp. colonies, 874, 3025 ; rubber, 2833 ; transport, 152, 153, 1975, 3024. *Exploration and conquest*,

141, *142* ; Columbus, 878 ; Vespucius, 3318 ; Magellan, 2056 ; Sebastian Cabot, *142*, 647 ; Pizarro's conquests, 2616 ; Raleigh, *2744. See also in Index* **America**, and chief cities and countries.

South American literature, 3027.

Southamp'ton, Henry Wriothesley, 3rd Earl of (1573–1624), friend and patron of Shakespeare, 2936.

Southampton. Snt. of Hampshire ; pop. 170,000 ; **3027**, 1571 ; docks, *1023*, *1024*.

Southampton Water. Inlet and harbour extending from Spithead and the Solent 11 m. into Hampshire.

South Australia. State in s.-cent. Australia ; a. 380,000 ; sq. m. ; pop. (est.) 646,000 ; **3028** ; *map f. 308* ; cap. Adelaide, 26.

South Bend, Indiana, U.S.A. Farm centre and industrial city in N., 75 m. E. of Chicago ; pop. 101,270 ; motor-cars, ploughs, machinery ; Univ. of Notre Dame, near by.

South Caroli'na. A s. Atlantic state of the U.S.A. ; a. 30,495 sq. m. ; pop. 1,900,000 ; 704.

South Dako'ta. A N.-cent. state of U.S.A. ; a. 76,868 sq. m. ; pop. 564,000 ; 957.

South Downs, Sussex, 3123 ; dewpond, *1000.*

South'down sheep, *2941.*

Southend-on-Sea. Popular watering-place in Essex at mouth of Thames ; pop. 144,350 ; bombed in 1915 and 2nd World War, *1165*, 1225.

Southern Cross. A constellation ; not visible in N. Hemisphere, 3022.

Southern Rhodesia. Self-governing Brit. territory in S. Africa ; 150,300 sq. m. ; pop. 1,837,000 ; cap. Salisbury ; 2772 ; tobacco, *3220.*

Southey (suth'-i), **Robert** (1774–1843). Eng. poet and prose writer, **3028**, 470 ; and Landor, 1890 ; poet laureate, 2634.

South Fore'land. A promontory on the coast of Kent ; has lighthouse visible for 26 m., 1945.

South Georg'ia. Brit. isl. in S. Atlantic, 900 m. S.E. of Falklands ; Shackleton's burial-place ; a. 1,000 sq. m. ; whaling station ; 1259 ; Shackleton, 2931.

South Island. Largest isl. of New Zealand ; a. 58,093 sq. m. ; 2357.

South Magnet'ic Pole. *See* **Magnetic poles.**

South Orkney Islands. Brit. group in Antarctic Ocean, 200 m. E. of South Shetlands, 1259.

South Platte. A r. rising in cent. Colorado, U.S.A., uniting with the N. Platte in Nebraska ; 550 m. long.

South Pole. The s. extremity of earth's axis, **3028**, *map*, *173* ; first reached by Amundsen, 147, *148*, 2645 ; independent discovery by Scott, 2895. *See also* **Polar exploration.**

South pole of magnet, *2060*, *2061.*

South'port. Watering-place in Lancashire at mouth of Ribble estuary ; pop. 84,240 ; 1890.

South River. Old name of Delaware r., 2351.

South Sea Bubble. Name given to collapse (ruining thousands) of project of South Sea Co. in Eng. (1711–20) for assuming national debt in return for annual payments and monopoly of trade with S. Amer. and Pacific isls. ; 3339.

South Seas. *See* **Pacific Ocean.**

South Shet'land Islands. Chain of mountainous isls. belonging to Gt. Brit. on border of Antarctic region, 500 m. s.E. of Cape Horn, 1259.

South Shields. *See* **Shields, South.**

South Victor'ia Land, Antarctica. Vast, ice-covered continental plateau S. of New Zealand and extending to South Pole ; Ross claims for British, 2645.

Southwark (suth'-ark). Central met. bor. of London, on the S. side of the R. Thames ; varied industries ; fine cath. ; pop. 96,000 ; Tabard Inn starting point of " Canterbury Tales," 761.

Southwark Cathedral, London. Chiefly Early English style ; it is cruciform and possesses a fine central tower ; built on site of an old Augustinian priory.

South-West Africa. Territory once a German colony ; a. 317,725 sq. m. ; pop. est. 352,000 ; administered by Union of S. Africa, 3029, 3411, 581, 2988, 4316, *map, 3015.*

South'wold, Eng. Watering-place in N. Suffolk, 12 m. s.w. of Lowestoft.

Southwood, Julius Salter Elias, 1st Baron (1873–1946). Chairman and managing director Odham's Press, Ltd. (owners of " The Daily Herald," etc.).

Sovereign (sov'er-in). An Eng. gold coin equivalent to 20 shillings ; Henry VIII, *2202.* Though no longer in circulation still the standard of the British coinage ; 1482.

Soviet (so-vyet') **government.** In Rus., 2848, 2850 ; Lenin, 1922, *1923* ; Stalin, 3072 ; Trotsky, 3251.

Soya bean, 3029 ; fibre from, 2749 ; oil, 1263 ; in Manchuria, 2086.

Soy sauce or **shoyu.** Made from soy beans which have been boiled with wheat or barley meal and salt ; it is served in the fermented state ; largely used in Japan.

Spa (spah), Belgium. Watering-place 16 m. s.e. of Liége ; pop. 8,000 ; medicinal springs ; Ger. general headquarters in 1st World War and scene of William II's abdication ; here Ger. delegates first met Supreme Council (1920) ; occupied by Germans 1940–44.

Spaak, Paul H. (b. 1899). Belgian statesman ; min. for foreign affairs and trade, 1936–38 ; worked for Belgian neutrality in case of war ; premier May 1938–Feb. 1939 ; foreign min. in exiled govt. in London ; in 1944 dep. prime min. in Belgium, then prime min. ; in 1946 elected pres. of U.N. Gen. Assem. ; prime min. again, 1947–June 1949 ; pres. of European Consultative Assem. Aug. 1949.

Space, 1227 ; curvature of, 1514 ; problem in metaphysics, 2571 ; and relativity, 2762.

Space charge, in thermionic valve, 3198.

Space-time continuum, 2762.

Spaghetti, 2045.

Spagnoletto (span-yō-let'-tō), Lo. *See* Ribera.

Spain. State of s.w. Europe occupying most of Iberian peninsula ; a. 190,112 sq. m. ; pop. about 27,729,000 ; **3030,** *plates f. 3032, 3033* ; *map, 3030* ; agric., 3030 ; Balearic Isles, 3032 ; Canary Isls., 690 ; cap. Madrid, 2054, 3030 ; chief cities and mfrs., 1498, 3650, *4148,* 2054, 3030 ; climate, 3032 ; education, 2054 ; government, 3038 ; leather, 1914 ; lemon culture, 1922 ; minerals, 1753, 2973, 2974, 3032 ; money, *2202* ; orange-growing, 2444 ; people, 3032, *plate f. 3032, 3037* ; population, 3030 ; Pyrenees, 2709 ; raisins, 2742 ; surface features, 3030.

　History, 3033 ; barbarian invasions, 1488 ; Mahomedan conquest, 2067 ; united under Ferdinand and Isabella, 1760, 1238 ; Inquisition, 1726 ; under Charles V, 754, Columbus discovers America, 139, 880, 1760 ; Magellan sails round the world, 140, 2056 ; New World explorations and conquests, 139–143, 744, 914, 2616 ; power declines under Philip II, 2567 ; wars with Eng., 1036, 1146, 1462 ; Philippines conquered, 2569 ; Port. independent, 2659 ; War of the Spanish Succession (1701–13), 3300, 2106, 2567 ; Gibraltar lost, 1462 ; War of the Austrian Succession, 2101 ; Seven Years' War, 2925 ; Joseph Bonaparte king, *497* ; Peninsular War (1808–14), 3036 ; insurrections in Cuba, 941 ; war with U.S.A. (1898), 3291, 941 ; under Alfonso XIII, 110 ; becomes a republic (1931), 3037 ; Civil War (1936–1939), 3039, 3416 ; 2nd World War and after, 3040. *See also* names of chief events and persons.

RULERS OF SPAIN (FROM 1479)

HOUSE OF ARAGON

| 1479–1504 | Ferdinand and Isabella (Union of Castile and Aragon) |
| 1504–16 | Ferdinand, King of all Spain |

HOUSE OF HAPSBURG

1516–56	Charles I
1556–98	Philip II
1598–1621	Philip III
1621–65	Philip IV
1665–1700	Charles II

HOUSE OF BOURBON

1700–46	Philip V
(1724	Louis I six months)
1746–59	Ferdinand VI
1759–88	Charles III
1788–1808	Charles IV
1808	Ferdinand VII

HOUSE OF BONAPARTE

| 1808–13 | Joseph Bonaparte |

BOURBON RESTORATION

1814–33	Ferdinand VII
1833–68	Isabella II
(1868–70	Provisional Government)

HOUSE OF SAVOY

| 1870–73 | Amadeo I |
| (1873–74 | Republic) |

HOUSE OF BOURBON

1874–85	Alfonso XII
1885–86	Maria-de-la-Mercedes
1886–1931	Alfonso VIII
(1931–1936)	Republic
(1939)	Dictatorship
(1947)	Monarchy (without King)

Spalato (spa-la-tō), or **Split.** Yugoslavia port on Adriatic, 75 m. s.e. of Zara ; pop. 43,710 ; wine and oil.

Spalding. Eng. tn. on R. Welland, Lincs., in centre of fen district ; pop. 13,500.

Spandau, Ger. Fortified suburb of Berlin ; pop. 100,000 ; state munitions works ; military school.

Span'dril. In architecture, the space over the haunch of an arch and between it and the outscribing rectangle ; between the estrados of an arch and the square head or dripstone over it ; also the space between the outer mouldings of two arches and the strong-course above them.

Span'iel. A long-haired, long-eared dog, *plate f. 1024,* 1027.

Spanish-American War (1898), 4136, 941 ; U.S.A. territorial gains, 2569.

Spanish Arma'da. *See* Armada.

Spanish Art and Architecture, 3040, *3041–3048* ; Alcazar, Seville, 3033 ; Alhambra, 119 ; Cordoba mosque, *3043* ; El Greco, 2476 ; Goya, 1492 ; Murillo, 2257 ; Picasso, 2604 ; Velazquez, 3307.

Spanish bay'onet. A yucca plant.

Spanish-fly. A blister-beetle, 400.

Spanish Guinea. *See* Rio Muni.

Spanish language, 3050 ; origin, 2798 ; in S. Amer., 3024.

Spanish literature, 3050 ; Cervantes, 745 ; drama, 1040, 1042 ; novel, 2403 ; prominent figures in, *see* list in page 3995.

Spanish Main, 701.

Spanish Netherlands. Prov. in the Low Countries left to Sp. after Holland secured her independence ; ceded to Austria 1713 ; corresponds in general to modern Belgium.

Spanish onion, 2434.

Spanish Succession, War of (1701–13). 3036, 2029, 2106 ; results, 3300, 2567.

Spanish Town. Old cap. of Jamaica, 1793.

Spark gap, in induction coil, 1712.

Sparking plug. In internal combustion engines, 1736, 2243.

Sparling, Scot. name for common smelt, small fish of salmon family.

Spar'row. A member of the finch family, 3052, 1272 ; black throat of the house sparrow, *437, 447* ; egg, *facing 512* ; food, 438 ; nest, *442.*

Sparrow-hawk, 1587 ; nest and young, *452.*

Spar'ta. City-state of anc. Greece, 3052, 1522, 1524, 2042 ; laws of Lycurgus, 2042 ; at Battle of Thermopylae, 2556 ; becomes rival to Athens, 1522 ; conquers Athens, 1524 ; supremacy, 1524, 3053 ; war with Thebes, *3197* ; modern tn., 3053.

Spart'acists. Extreme Socialist Ger. party, 3053, 1450.

Spartacus (spahr'-ta-kus) (d. 71 B.C.). Leader of slave revolt in It., **3053.**

Spartiates (spahr'ti-āts). Spartan citizens, 3053.

Spat, of oysters, 2467.

Spathe (spāth). A leaf-like envelope protecting certain kinds of flower bud, 3333.

Spawn. Eggs of fishes, amphibians, molluscs, and other animals, especially in masses, 1095 ; fishes, 1297 ; frogs, 1398 ; salamanders, 2864 ; toads, 3219.

Spawn, of fungi. Same as Mycelium.

Speaker. The presiding officer in various legislative assemblies. In Brit. House of Commons the Speaker is elected, but upon taking chair loses all political identity ; he may not take part in the debates, and votes only in case of a tie ; because of non-partisan character he is frequently re-elected in spite of change of party majority, and upon retirement customarily receives a peerage. In U.S.A. Congress he is elected by members for one Congress and is leader of party in power ; he is free to take part in proceedings (by calling another member to the chair), and by rulings wields tremendous political power, 2522, *2523.*

Speaking Clock, how it works, 2576, 3013.

Spear'mint. A perennial herb (*Mentha spicata*) found in various parts of Europe ; extensively used for culinary purposes ; has a pungent odour ; essential oil from, 1263.

Spear thistle, *3204.*

Special licence, for marriage, 2107.

Species (spē'-shēz). In biology, that which retains recognizable characteristics despite the course of time.

Specific dens'ity. *See* Specific Gravity.

Specific grav'ity, 3053, 1513, *1674,* 3351.

Specific heat, 1596 ; of water, 3349.

Speckled Wood butterfly, *plate f. 632.*

Spec'tacled bear. A small bear of the Andes Mts., (*Ursus ornatus*), with yellowish goggle-like rings about its eyes ; it is thought by some scientists to be a sub-species of the Amer. black bear.

Spectacled snake. Same as Cobra.

Spec'tacles, 3054 ; lenses, 1924.

" Specta'tor, The." A daily periodical issued from March 1711 to December 1712 ; 24, 1213.

Spectroheliograph, 2411.

Spectroscope and Spectrograph, 3055 ; used in astronomy, 281, 2411, 3080, 3119 ; discovery of thallium, 3193.

Spectrum, 3055, *plates f. 3056, 3057* ; colour, 875 ; in rainbows, 2741 ; infra-red rays in, 1722 ; " X-ray spectra," 4331.

Speculum, of reflecting telescope, 3178.

Spee (shpā), **Count Maximilian von** (1861–1914), Ger. admiral ; victor at Coronel ; went down with his ship Scharnhorst off Falkland Isls. ; 1259.

Speech, organs of, 3328.

Speed ; aeroplane, *38, 49* ; depicted by camera, *2585* ; electronic control, 1139 ; in physics, 2591 ; of earth, *2618* ; light, 1939 ; solar system, *3118* ; of trains example of relativity, 2760, 2761 ; sound, 3010.

Speedometer, 656.

Speedwell, Pilgrim Fathers' ship, 2122.

Speedwell. Name given in Brit. to herbaceous members of genus *Veronica* of fam. *Scrophulariaceae* ; common species are Germander speedwell, or bird's eye, and Brooklime, a species found in ditches ; other species are mostly small, inconspicuous weeds ; all have bright bluish flowers and opposite, simple leaves.

Spei'or, Ger. *See* Spires.

Speke (spēk), **John Hanning** (1827–64). Eng. explorer, discoverer of the source of the Nile, 72, 3150, 3321.

Spelling, 3057 ; formation of possessives and plurals, 2399 ; rules, 3057.

Spells. *See* Magic.

Spel'ter, refined zinc ore, 3443.

Spelt wheat, 3374.

Spen'cer, Herbert (1820–1903). Eng. philosopher ; attempted to organize all knowledge into a system on scientific and especially evolutionary lines (" Synthetic Philosophy " ; " Data of Ethics " ; " Education " ; " Principles of Biology " ; " Social Statics ") ; other works inc. " Study of Sociology "—penetrating analysis of various biases—and his " Autobiography " ; 2572, 1145.

Spencer, John Charles, 3rd Earl (1782–1845). Eng. Liberal politician. As Lord Althorp, Chancellor of Exchequer under Grey.

Spencer, John Poyntz, 5th Earl (1835–1910). Brit. statesman ; he acted as Lord-Lieutenant of Ire. (1868–74), and was twice Lord Pres. of the Council ; later was leader of the Liberals in the House of Lords.

Spencer, Stanley (b. 1891). Eng. painter. Famous as painter of mystical subjects, showing sacred and angelic characters in contemporary dress and settings. His " Christ Bearing the Cross," 1184, and " The Resurrection " are in the Tate Gallery ; elected A.R.A. (1932), but resigned in 1935 when two of his pictures were refused ; re-elected A.R.A. and elected R.A. in 1950 ; C.B.E. in 1950 ; 1184.

Spencer Gulf, South Australia, 3028.

Spen'der, Edward Harold (1864–1926), Eng. journalist and author ; was at various times on staff of the " Echo," " Pall Mall Gazette," " Daily Chronicle," " Manchester Guardian," and " Daily News." He was the father of Stephen Spender.

Spender, John Alfred (1862–1942). Eng. journalist and author ; brother of above, edited " Eastern Morning News," Hull (1886–90), and " Westminster Gazette " (1896–1922) ; C.H. 1937 ; (" The Comments of Bagshot" ; " The Foundations of British Policy " ; " The Life of Sir Henry

Campbell-Bannerman " ; " Great Britain : 1886–1935 ").

Spender, Stephen Harold (b. 1909). Eng. poet and critic, son of E. H. Spender. Works include : " The Burning Cactus," " Forward from Liberalism," " Trial of a Judge."

Spengler, Oswald (1880–1936). Ger. philosopher. His best-known work " Der Untergang des Abendlandes " (The Decline of the West) aroused much controversy on account of its revolutionary pessimism. In " Jahre der Entscheidung " he attacked the new rulers in Germany in spite of the fact that he favoured dictatorship.

Spen'ser, Edmund (c. 1552–99). Eng. poet, among greatest Elizabethans and master of melodious verse ; 3058 ; and English literature, 1211 ; tomb, 3369.

Spermaceti, from whales, 3359, 3372.

Spermatophyta (spẽ·'-ma-to-fīta). The group of seed-producing plants, 2620, 2918.

Sperm-whale, 3372, 3373 ; commercial " ivory," 1788.

Sper'ry, Elmer Ambrose (1860–1930). Amer. electrical engineer and inventor ; held over 400 patents ; perfected gyro-compass.

Spey (spā). Second largest r. in Scot. ; rises in the hills near Lochs Lochy and Laggan and flows to Moray Firth.

Speyer, Ger. Same as Spires.

Spezia (spãt'-si-a). Spt. and pleasure resort of Italy ; one of the chief Italian naval stations ; near here Shelley was drowned ; pop. 121,000 ; taken by Allies, April 1945.

Sphagnum (sfag'-num) moss, 2239.

Sphecoidea (sfe-koi'-dē-a), a family of solitary wasps, containing the muddaubers.

Sphe'nodon or tuate'ra, a reptile, 1974, 1975, 2767.

Sphere, in geometry, 1437.

Spher'ical aberration, 2163.

Sphinx (sfinks), Eg., 3058, 1114 ; the Great Sphinx, 3059, 830 ; Oedipus answers riddle, 2425.

Spi'ca, a star in the constellation Virgo, 3079.

Spice Islands, 1076. See Moluccas.

Spices and condiments, 3060 ; cloves, 854 ; ginger, 1464 ; mustard, 2270 ; nutmeg and mace, 2407 ; pepper, 2547 ; trade in, 3060, 1076.

Spicules (spik'-ūlz), of sponges, 3067.

Spider-beetle, 399.

Spider crab, plate f. 925.

Spider monkey, 2210.

Spiders, 3062 ; plates f. 3064, 3065 ; Bruce and the spider, 590 ; egg-laying habits, 1095 ; eyes, 1253 ; instinct, 159 ; mythical origin, 284 ; tarantulas, 3154, 3155 ; thread used in optical instruments, 2411.

Spider silk, 2973.

Spiegeleisen (shpē'gel-I-zen), a cast iron containing manganese, 2087.

Spike'nard or nard. A costly perfume produced from a plant native to the mts. of N. India ; used by the ancients in baths and at feasts ; the ointment of spikenard mentioned in the Bible was probably an oil or fat scented with the perfume ; in the U.S.A. a herb (Aralia racemosa) with large spicy aromatic roots is called spikenard. Ploughman's spikenard is a common Eng. wayside plant of family Compositae, with yellow flower-heads.

Spillway, of dams, 2490.

Spilsbury, Sir Bernard Henry (1878–1947). British pathologist. Gave evidence in numerous criminal cases in his capacity as honorary pathologist to the Home Office.

Spinach (spin'-ij). Garden vegetable, extremely nutritious and valuable for children and invalids. Member of family Chenopodiaceae.

Spi'nal cord. The nerve trunk in the spine ; in Man, 2316.

Spinal nerves, 2317.

Spindle, 3066 ; of sewing machine, 2929.

PROMINENT FIGURES IN SPANISH LITERATURE

" El Cantar de mio Cid " (Poem of the Cid), about 1140.
" El Auto de los reyes magos " (Mystery of the Magian Kings), 12th century.
Juan Manuel (1282–1347), short story writer—" El Conde Lucanor."
Juan Ruiz (14th century), poet and prose fiction writer—" El Libro de buen amor."
Gil Vicente (1470?–1536), dramatist—" Amadís de Gaula " ; " Ignez Pereira."
Mateo Alemán (1547?–1614?), novelist—" Guzmán de Alfarache."
Miguel de Cervantes Saavedra (1547–1616), novelist, dramatist—" Don Quixote," novel ; " La Numancia," play ; " Novelas exemplares," stories.
Luis de Góngora y Argote (1561–1627), poet—" Lloraba la niña " ; " Angélica y Medoro " ; " Soledades."
Lope Félix de Vega Carpio (1562–1635), dramatist—" Los Tellos de Meneses " , " Porfiar hasta morir " ; " El Acero de Madrid " ; " Las Bizarrias de Belisa " ; " La hermosa fea " ; " La Gatomaquia."
Guillén de Castro (1569–1631), dramatist—" Las Mocedades del Cid."
Gabriel Tellez, known as Tirso de Molina (1571-1648), dramatist —" El Burlador de Sevilla."
Juan Ruiz de Alarcón (1580?–1639), dramatist—" La Verdad sospechosa " ; " Las Paredes oyen."
Francisco de Quevedo y Villegas (1580–1645), philosopher, poet, novelist—" Historia de la vida del Buscón," picaresque novel.
Pedro Calderón de la Barca (1600–81), dramatist—" La Dama duende " ; " El Alcalde de Zalamea " ; " El Mágico prodigioso " ; " La Vida es sueño " ; " La Cena del rey Baltasar."
Baltasar Gracián (1601–58), novelist—" El Criticón."
Diego de Torres Villarroel (1696–1770?), autobiographer— " Vida."
Mariano José de Larra (1809–37), satirist—" El pobrecito hablador," periodical written entirely by Larra.
Antonio Garc a Gutiérrez (1813–84), dramatist—" El Trovador," inspired opera " Il Trovatore."
Juan Valera (1824–1905), novelist—" Pepita Jiménez."
José Echegaray (1833–1916), dramatist—" El Gran Galeoto."
Pedro Antonio de Alarcón y Ariza (1833–91), novelist— " El Sombrero de tres picos " (The Three-Cornered Hat).
José María de Pereda (1833–1906), novelist—" Sotileza " ; " Peñas arriba."

Rosalia de Castro (1837–85), poet—" Cantares gallegos " ; " En las orillas del Sar."
Benito Pérez Galdós (1843–1920), novelist—" Doña Perfecta " ; " La Corte de Carlos IV " ; " Zaragoza."
La Condesa Emilia Pardo Bazán (1852–1921), novelist—" Los Pazos de Ulloa " ; " La Madre naturaleza."
Armando Palacio Valdés (1853–1938), novelist—" Marta y María " ; " José " ; " La Espuma."
Miguel de Unamuno (1864–1936), philosopher, novelist, poet— " Niebla " (Mist), novel ; " Del sentimiento trágico de la vida en los hombres y en los pueblos " (The Tragic Sentiment of Life), philosophical treatise.
Ganivet, Angel (1865–98), novelist and essayist—" La Conquista del Reino de Maya " ; " Idearium Español."
Jacinto Benavente (1866–1939), dramatist—" Gente conocida " ; " Señora ama " ; " La Malquerida."
Rubén Dario (1867–1916), poet—" Azul " ; " Cantos de vida y esperanza."
Vicente Blasco Ibáñez (1867–1928), novelist—" Los cuatro jinetes del Apocalipsis " (The Four Horsemen of the Apocalypse) ; " La Catedral " ; " Mare Nostrum " ; " Sangre y arena."
Pio Barója (1872–   ), novelist—" Camino de perfeccion " ; " La Busca " ; " Mala hierba " ; " Aurora roja."
Ramón Maria del Valle-Inclán (1870–1936), novelist— " Sonatas" ; " La Guerra carlista " ; " Cofre de sandalo."
Joaquin (1873–1944) and Serafin (1871–1938), Alvarez Quintero, dramatists—" Los Galeotes " ; " El Centenario."
José Martinez Ruiz (" Azorín ") (1874–   ), critic and novelist—" Los Valores literarios," criticism ; " La Voluntad," novel ; " Los Hidalgos " ; " El Alma Castellana."
Ramón Pérez de Ayala (1881–   ), poet and novelist—" El Sendero innumerable," poem ; " La Pata de la raposa," novel.
Juan Ramón Jiménez (1881–   ), poet—" Arias tristes " ; " Piedra y cielo."
Gregorio Mart nez Sierra (1881–1947) and his wife, Maria de la O Lejárraga (1880–   ), poets, novelists, dramatists, under signature Martínez Sierra—" Flores de escarcha," verse ; " Tú eres la paz," novel ; " Canción de cuna," play.
Salvador de Madariaga (1886–   ), poet and novelist—" La Girafa sagrada," novel ; " Romances de Ciego," poem.
Garcia Lorca (1897–1936), poet—" Yenna," " Llanto por Ignacio Sanchez Mejias " and many short lyrics.
Ramon Sender (1901–   ), novelist—" Seven Red Sundays."

Spindle tree. Small tree, *Euonymus europea*, so-called because wood was formerly used for spindles. Rarely exceeds 20 ft. in height; grows on limestone soils; twigs bright greenish, leaves narrow, simple, flowers yellowish; distinguished by fruits, bright pinkish-purple and four-angled, containing brilliant orange aril, *3533*.

Spine. The vertebrate "backbone," 2977; evolution seen in fishes, 1297; modified in birds, 437; in snakes, 2990.

Spines. Stiff pointed projections; in fins of fish, 1296; of sea-urchins, 3083.

Spin'et, forerunner of piano, 2601.

Spin'neret, of silkworm, 2970; of spider, 3063; *plate f. 3065*; in rayon mfr., *2748*, 3152.

Spinning, 3065; 850; Arkwright's spinning frame, 235; cotton, *919*, 920; Crompton's "spinning mule," 933; Hargreaves' jenny, *1578*, 235; kinds of fabrics, 850; lace, 1876; linen, 1953; primitive methods, *238*; silk, 2970; thread, 3205; and weaving, 3360; wool, *3407*.

Spinning frame, *235*.

Spinning glands, of spider, *plate f. 3065*.

Spinning jenny. Invented by Hargreaves, *1578*, 235; improved by Crompton, 933.

Spinning mule, 933.

Spinning wheel, *238*, 3066.

Spinoza (spi-not'-*sa*), **Baruch** or **Benedict** (1632–77). Dutch (Jewish) philosopher, called by Novalis the "God-intoxicated man"; belonged to no school and founded none, yet influenced poets and thinkers like Goethe, Lessing, Wordsworth.

Spinthar'iscope. An instrument invented by Sir Wm. Crookes for detecting radio-activity.

Spiny ant-eater (Echidna), an egg-laying mammal of Australia, 1053, 176, 309, *313*.

Spiny Frog Shell, *2943*.

Spi'on Kop. Hill near the R. Tugela, Natal, S. Africa, where the Brit. were repulsed by the Boers in Jan. 1900, whilst attempting to reach and relieve Ladysmith, 176.

Spir'acle. Breathing orifice of an insect, 1732.

Spiral nebulae, 2310.

Spire'a or **spiraea.** Large genus of flowering plants found in N. temperate regions of the earth; in Eng. meadowsweet belongs to this genus.

Spires (Ger. **Speyer** or **Speier**). Tn. in Bavaria on Rhine; pop. 25,000; Romanesque cathedral begun in 1030; bishopric one of oldest in Ger.; 2769; in Diet of (1529), 2759.

Spires, in architecture, *219*.

Spiril'la (plural of *spirillum*). Corkscrew-shaped bacteria, 336.

Spirit of hartshorn, 3067.

Spirit of salt, 3067.

Spirits (drink), **3066.**

Spirogy'ra, a genus of green algae, 112.

Spit, in cookery, 900, *901*.

Spitfire. Brit. fighter aircraft, designed by R. J. Mitchell and made by Vickers-Armstrong Supermarine; first milit. version in 1936; impt. role in battle of Britain; later adapted to many purposes; wing span, 36 ft. 10 ins.; naval version called Seafire; *1332*.

Spithead'. Roadstead between Isle of Wight and E. Hampshire; it is about 4 m. wide and joins with the Solent and Southampton Water; scene of Jubilee Naval Review (1935) and Coronation Review (1937).

Spitsbergen. Called **Svalbard** by the Norwegians; group of isls. on Arctic Ocean, 500 m. N. of Norway; a. 24,294 sq. m.; **3067,** 2393, 223, 2644, 2646.

Spitz'kop. Mt. in Prov. of Cape of Good Hope, S. Africa; battle in Boer War, 487.

Spleen. A bean-shaped, pulpy organ to the left of the stomach; 474.

Spleen'worts. Various small ferns of the family *Polypodiaceae*; found in Europe, W. Asia and N. and S. Africa; are commonly seen growing among rocks, on walls, etc.

Splices, *1870*.

Split. See **Spalato.**

Spode, Josiah (1754–1827). Eng. potter. Popularized and improved the Willow Pattern and introduced the famous Spode Ware; his china is held in high esteem by connoisseurs.

Spofforth, Frederick Robert (1853–1926). Australian cricketer. Regarded by many as the greatest bowler who ever lived. Member of first Australian team to visit England.

Spohr, Louis (1784–1859). Ger. composer and violinist; wrote 200 works, including operas, oratorios, symphonies, chamber music; "The Violin School" is still a standard of instruction.

Spokane (spō-kan'). 2nd city of Washington State, U.S.A., on Spokane r. near Idaho border; mfrs. include foundry products, machinery, furniture, and brushes; pop. 122,000.

Spoleto (spō-lā'-tō). It. tn. 60 m. N.E. of Rome; pop. 18,000; Rom. ruins; Fr. besieged by Italians (1860) Taken by Allies, June 17, 1944.

Spoleto, Aimone, Duke of. See **Aosta, Aimone, Duke of.**

Spon'dee, metrical foot, 2635.

Sponges. A division of primitive animals or their skeletons, **3067;** Bahamas, 340; evolutionary position, 158.

Spon'gin. Fibrous stiffening matter in sponges.

Sponta'neous combus'tion, 1280.

Spontaneous generation. Doctrine that living forms sometimes arise from inorganic matter; the theory is discredited, 1244.

Spoon, a golf club, *1484*.

Spoon, utensil, 1867.

Spoonbill. Bird of stork and heron group, once bred in East Anglia, now seldom seen; *3100*; name sometimes given to Shoveller-duck. *See also* **Shoveller duck.**

Spooner, William Archibald (1844–1930). Eng. scholar; noted for inverted expressions, called "spooner-isms"—e.g. "a half-warmed fish" for "a half-formed wish."

Sporades (spor'-*a*-dēz) **Islands.** Group in Aegean Sea off coast of Asia Minor.

Sporan'gia (plural of *sporangium*). Spore bearing organs of lower plants, 2918; in mosses, 2238.

Spores and seeds, 2916; of algae, 111; in bacteria, 336; ferns, 1266; moss, 2238; mushrooms, 2260; rusts or smuts, 2857.

Spo'rophyte. A plant or plant structure which reproduces by unfertilized spores; in moss, 2238.

Sporozo'a. Class of unicellular animals parasitic upon higher animals.

Sport, in biology. A young organism markedly unlike its parent; in mutation theory of evolution, 1246.

Sports, games, and pastimes; angling, 1309; archery, 209; athletics, 287; badminton, 338; baseball, 367; basket-ball, 369; billiards and snooker, 428; boating, 481; bowls, 534; boxing, 535; cards, 831; charades, 752; chess, 779; cricket, 928; croquet, 934; curling, 944; cycling, 947; dancing, 965; darts, 975; draughts, 1044; dominoes, 1029; falconry, 1258; fencing, 1266; fives, 1312; football, 1344; gliding, 1417; golf, 1483; gymnastics, 2589; hockey, 1633; horse-racing, 1648, 994; hunting, 1657; hurling, 1660; ice hockey, 1682; kite-flying, 1863; lacrosse, 1882; lawn tennis, 1905; limericks, 1950; motor-boat racing, *485*; motor-cycle racing, 948; mountaineering, 2247; netball, 2317; Olympic Games, 2433; photography, 2577; polo, 2651; quoits, 2720; riding, 2779; rowing, 483; running, 2843; sailing, 484; sculling, 483; 1027; shooting, 2961; skating, 2976;

ski-ing, 2978; skittles, 2980; squash rackets, 3070; stamp collecting, 3074; swimming and diving, 3135; table tennis, 3147; tennis (real), 3186; water polo, 3356; wrestling, 3426; yachting, 483, *484, 485, 486*. *See also* **Athletics; Olympic Games; Records.**

Spotted fly-catcher, 1330.

Spotted hyaena, 1675.

Spotted sal'amander, *2864*.

Spotted woodpecker, Greater and Lesser, *3404*; *plate f. 3405*.

Spottsylva'nis Court House. Vil. of Virginia, U.S.A., scene of battles in Amer. Civil War in 1864, between the armies of Lee and Grant.

Spot welding, 3363.

Sprague, Frank Julian (1857–1934). Amer. inventor and engineer; he built one of the early electric street rlys.

Sprat. A small herring (*Clupea sprattus*) 6 in. long, abundant in the N. Atlantic off the European coast; dry-salted or cured in brine it forms a tasty and nourishing food, *1621*.

Spraying, 1402.

Spraying tools. Pneumatic appliances, 2478, 2633.

Spree (sprā). R. of Germany, rises in Saxony near Bohemian border, flows N.W. 227 m., joining Havel at Spandau; connected by canals with Oder and Elbe, 417.

Spreewald (sprā'-valt). Ger. low marshy dist. dotted with lakes and canals in Spree valley, about 50 m. S.E. of Berlin, about 106 sq. m.

Spring. The first season of the year, 2223; characteristics, 2914; Demeter myth, 989; Gk. festivals, 1037; Nature study, 3572; Scandinavian legend, 2882; vernal equinox, 1221.

Spring, in clocks and watches, 843, 846; in locomotives, *plate f. 1980*.

Spring, of water, **3069;** artesian wells, 252; geysers, 1459. *See also* **Mineral springs.**

Spring, or shear steel, 1756.

Spring, Howard (b. 1889). Brit. novelist; "O Absalom" (repub. as "My Son, My Son!"), "Fame is the Spur," "Hard Facts"; autobiog., "And Another Thing."

Springbok or **springbuck,** an African antelope, 176.

Spring'er, in architecture. The impost or place where the vertical support to an arch terminates and the curve of the arch begins.

Springfield, Illinois, U.S.A. State cap. near centre on Sangamon r.; it is a great mfg. centre, producing woollen goods, flour, engines, and boilers; soap also made in large quantities; pop. 71,864; 1687.

Springfield, Massachusetts, U.S.A. Important industrial centre of New Eng.; it is a noted seat of learning; its chief mfrs. are electric vehicles, engines, and general machinery; pop. 149,554.

Springfield, Ohio, U.S.A. Industrial and rly. city, 45 m. W. of Columbus, pop. 70,662; makes machinery, foundry products, etc.; printing and floral industries; Wittenberg College (Lutheran).

Springfield rifle, *1282*.

Spring tail. Small insect which leaps by using its tail as a spring; 3624.

Spring tide, *3210*.

Spring Usher moth. Member of the winter moth group which has a wingless female.

Spruce. A type of conifer tree, **3070,** 890; in Alaska, 97.

Spun glass, 1474.

Spun silk, 2973.

Spur, of flower; in larkspur, 1893; in nasturtium, 2279; in orchid, 2447.

Spurge. Name of plants of family *Euphorbiaceae*, characterized by strange, usually yellow and green inflorescence, and white juice. Many old-world forms assume same forms, live in same situations as new-world cacti. Commonest English species is wood spurge, typical member of oak-wood flora, tall green plant with yellowish inflorescence, 2638.

Spurgeon, Charles Haddon (1834–99). Eng. Nonconformist (Baptist) preacher, built Metropolitan Tabernacle in south London and filled its 6,000 seats; his forceful sermons, translated into many languages, had wide circulation.

Spurn Head. Promontory on the N.E. coast of Yorkshire; here are two lighthouses, 3435.

Spurs, battle of, the, fought near Thérouanne, in Flanders, between the Eng. and the Fr. on Aug. 16, 1513; during an Eng. cavalry charge the Fr. knights spurred away—hence the name.

"Spy." Famous Victorian political cartoonist (real name Sir Leslie Ward) (1857–1922). Known for his drawings of contemporary celebrities in "Vanity Fair."

"Spy, The," novel by James Fenimore Cooper, 903.

Squab, a young pigeon, 2607.

Square, in geometry, 1437.

Square, a unit of measure in building, 100 square feet.

Square knot, 1868.

Square measure. See **Weights and Measures,** f-i.

Square root, 116, 2672; by slide rule, 2984.

Squash (skwosh), a vegetable of the pumpkin family, 2704.

Squash rackets, a game, 3070.

Squeers. In Dickens's "Nicholas Nickleby," brutal, ignorant schoolmaster who flogged and starved pupils at Dotheboys Hall.

Squid. Mollusc, of the **Decapoda,** noted for ability to escape in a cloud of inky secretion; 945, 946; evolutionary position, 158; secretes sepia, 1724, 1725, 946.

Squinch, in architecture, a small pendentive arch formed across the angle of a square tower to support the side of a superimposed octagon; also called a sconce.

Squire, knight's attendant, 1864.

Squire, Sir John Collings (b. 1884). Eng. man of letters. Founded "The London Mercury" (1919) and edited it until 1934. Works include "Steps to Parnassus"; "Collected Parodies"; "Outside Eden."

Squir'rel, 3071; fur, 1412.

Squirrel, Ground. See **Chipmunk.**

Squirrel monkey, 2210.

Srinagar (srē-nug'ar), India. Cap. of Jammu and Kashmir, in N. on R. Jhelan, in famous Vale of Kashmir; pop. 207,787; makes paper, papier mâché, silver and copper ware, leather, 1704, 1848. Occupied by Dom. of India troops, Nov. 1947, to keep out invading hillmen in Kashmir fighting.

Stab'ilizing devices, 1559.

Stable fly. A blood-sucking fly, frequenting stables and often entering houses; egg, 1094.

Stac'poole, Henry de Vere (b. 1865). Brit. novelist; wrote "The Blue Lagoon"; "The Pools of Silence," and "The Beach of Dreams."

Stadacona (stah-dah'-kō-na), Canada. Vil. near Quebec; Cartier at; 712.

Sta'den, part of Stockholm, 3093.

Stadium (stā'-di-um). Gk. measure of length (equal to about 606 ft.); term applied to race-course at Olympia, which was exactly a stadium in length, and later to similar places for holding athletic contests; at Athens, 287; Olympic Games at Wembley Stadium, London, 2433.

Stadt'holder, former title of chief magistrate of the Netherlands.

Stae'dal Art Institute, Sachsenhausen, Ger.

Staël (stah'-el), **Madame de** (Anne Louise Germaine Necker, Baronne de Staël-Holstein) (1766–1817). Fr. novelist, daughter of financier Necker; enjoyed enormous reputation in her day; banished by Napoleon; chief works, "Delphine," "Corinne," 1428.

Staff, in army. See **General Staff.**

Staff, in music, 3002.

Staf'fa, tiny isl. of Scot., off w. coast, 7 m. from Mull, 3071.

Staf'ord, Henry, Duke of Buckingham (c. 1454–83); rendered great services to Richard III, but went over to side of Henry Tudor, and raised revolt in Wales; was captured and executed.

Stafford, William Howard, Viscount (1614–80), Eng. nobleman, executed on charge of complicity in the "Popish Plot" of Titus Oates.

Stafford. Co. tn. of Staffordshire, on R. Sow; important rly. centre of the "Black Country"; mfrs. boots and shoes and other leather goods; pop. 36,528; 3072.

Staff'ordshire. Eng. midland co.; a. 1,153 sq. m.; pop. 1,431,400; coal, iron, clay deposits; iron and steel mfrs.; 3072; pottery, 1165.

Stag, 984, 985.

Stag beetle, 398, 400; foot and claw, 1727; mandibles, 1729; method of defence, 1728.

Stage, of theatre, 1038, 1039, 3196.

Stage-coach introduced into England, 2783.

Stagira (sta-jī'-ra). In anc. geography, tn. on coast of Chalcidice, Macedonia; birthplace of Aristotle, who was called from it "The Stagirite," 231.

Stag's horn coral, 908.

Staghounds, 1658.

Stag-hunting, 1658.

Stahl, Georg Ernst (1660–1734). Ger. chemist, enunciated the phlogiston theory of combustion. See **Phlogiston.**

Stahlhelm. German movement of ex-Service men founded on military lines by Franz Seldte in 1918; the name means Steel Helmet; was totally dissolved by Hitler on Nov. 8, 1935.

Stainer, Sir John (1840–1901). Eng. composer. Organist of St. Paul's, London (1872–88); became prof. of music, Oxford, in 1889. Wrote oratorios, "Crucifixion" (1887), etc.

Staines, Eng. tn. of Middx., on Thames; pop. 37,670; reservoir, 3194.

Stainless alloys, 123.

Stainless steel, manufacture, 1758.

Stair, Earl of (1673–1747). Scot. soldier; served under Marlborough.

Stakhanovite (sta-kah'-nō-vīt). Name given to "champion" Russian industrial workers under Soviet; from Alexei Stakhanov, who evolved a system of increasing coal production.

Stalactites (sta-lak'-tīts) and **stalagmites** (sta-lag'-mīts), 733, plate f. 732.

Stalag (Ger. Stamlager, prison camp). Name in 2nd World War for Ger. camps for n.c.os. and men prisoners of war.

Stalin, Joseph Vissarionovitch (b. 1879). Rus. statesman, 3072, 2850; defence of Tsaritsyn, 3073.

Stalinabad, cap. of Tajikstan, 3267.

Stalingrad, formerly Tsaritsyn, Soviet Russia. Tn. and port on R. Volga; pop. (1935) 445,500; great tractor works; German siege Sept. 1942–Feb. 1943; 3073, 1452, 2852, 3420.

Stalinsk, Siberian tn., 2967.

"Stalky and Co.," by Kipling, 1859.

Stamboul (stahm-bool'). Mahomedan quarter, 1763.

Sta'men. Organ of plants, 531, 1321, 1324, 1325.

Stam'ford Bridge. Place in Eng. about 8 m. N.E. of York, where Harold II defeated Norse invaders (Sept. 1066).

Stamp, Josiah Charles, 1st Baron (1880–1941). Brit. economist. Elected a director of Bank of England in 1928; chairman of L.M.S. Rly. from 1927. Killed in air raid, April 1941.

Stamp Act (1765), 3276, 3290; Franklin secures repeal, 1386; Pitt opposes, 759.

Stamp album, 3076.

Stamping coins, 2188.

Stamps and stamp-collecting, 3074; first used, 2661; methods used in post office delivery, 2661, 2662, 2663.

Stance, in golf, 1485.

Stan'dard, battle of the, fought at Standard Hill in N. Riding of York-shire, in 1138, when David of Scot. was defeated by the northern barons.

Standard gauge, of railways, 2738, 594.

Standard Oil Company, 2791.

Standard time. A system by which time becomes uniform over given areas; the areas have a breadth of 15° and the difference in time between two adjacent areas is taken as 1 hour; the world receives its time from the Royal Observatory; time zones, 3213. See **Summer Time.**

Stand'ish, Miles (c. 1584–1656). Eng. soldier, military leader of Plymouth colonists (Pilgrim Fathers).

Stanford, Sir Charles Villiers (1852–1924). Brit. composer. Born in Dublin, he was professor at the R.C.M., London, and later at Cambridge; wrote opera ("Shamus O'Brien"), ballads and religious music, and was a noted organist.

Stan'ford, Leland (1824–93). Amer. capitalist and philanthropist, founder of Leland Stanford Jr. Univ., at Palo Alto, California, U.S.A.

Stan'islaus, Saint (1030–79). Bishop of Cracow and patron saint of Poland, slain by King Boleslaus.

Stanislavsky, Constantin (1863–1938). Russ. theatrical producer, 3197.

Stanley, Arthur Penrhyn (1815–1881). Eng. divine; Dean of Westminster (1864).

Stanley, Edward Montagu Cavendish Stanley, Lord (1894–1938). Eng. politician. Son of 17th earl of Derby; Parliamentary and Financial Sec. to Admiralty (1931–35; 1935–37); Parlty. Under-Sec. for India and Burma (1937–38); Sec. for Dominions (1938).

Stan'ley, Sir Henry Morton (1841–1904). British explorer, 3076; explores Congo basin, 72, 887; explores Victoria Nyanza (Lake Victoria), 3321; search for Livingstone, 1972.

Stanley, Oliver Frederick George (b. 1896). Eng. politician; younger brother of Lord Stanley, Minister of Transport (1933–34); Min. of Labour (1934–35); President of Board of Education (1935–37); Pres. of Board of Trade (1937); War Minister (1940); Colonial Secretary, 1942–45.

Stanley, cap. of Falkland Isls.; pop. 1,246; 1259.

Stanley Falls, cataract in R. Congo; map, 888.

Stanley Pool, expansion of R. Congo above Leopoldville; map, 888.

Stan'leyville. Trading and administrative station of Belgian Congo on Congo, at Stanley Falls.

Stanovoi (stah-nō-voi') **Mts.,** Siberia. Range running 2,400 m. N.E. Mongolia to Bering Strait; 3,000 to 5,000 ft.; s. portion heavily forested.

Stan'ton, Edwin McMasters (1814–69). Amer. statesman and noted lawyer; became leading member of the Amer. Bar in 1847; sec. of war under Lincoln and Johnson.

Staphylococc'us, bacteria occurring in irregular clusters, 3116.

Star, in astronomy, 3077; constellations, 894, 895; nebulae, 2310; observatory, 2411, 2412; planets not stars, 2617; "shooting stars," 2151. See also **Astronomy.**

Star apple, W. Ind. fruit, 1401.

Starboard. The right-hand side of a vessel, looking from aft forward.

Starch, 3082; animal (glycogen), 1968, 3082; changed into glucose, 1477; food value, 1338; formed by leaves, 1915, 2589; how it is digested, 1016; in potatoes, 2664; in rice, 2775; in wheat flour, 1320.

Star Chamber. Former Eng. court, 1612.

Starfish. An echinoderm animal, 3082; attacks oysters, 2468.

Starhemberg, Ernst Rudiger, Prince (b. 1899). Austrian statesman; leader of Heimwehr in 1930; Vice-chancellor 1934; dissolution of Heimwehr by Schuschnigg 1936 brought his fall; served with Allies in 2nd World War.

Stark, Freya Madeline. Eng. explorer ; awarded Burton Memorial Medal (1934) ; Mungo Park Medal (1936) ; books include " The Valley of the Assassins " (1934) ; " The Southern Gates of Arabia " (1936) ; " In the Hadhramaut " (1938) ; " East is West " (1945).

Stark, Adm. Harold R. (b. 1880). U.S. naval officer ; commander of U.S. naval forces in Europe 1942–45.

Starley, James Kemp (1831–81), invented safety bicycle, 947.

Star'ling, 3083, *446* ; egg, *plate f. 440.*

Star of Bethlehem. A genus of plants of the lily family, native of Europe, named from their star-shaped flowers ; the hardy common star of Bethlehem (*Ornithogalum umbellatum*) has racemes of from 6 to 9 white fragrant flowers which close late in the afternoon.

Star of India, Order of the, 2449.

Star of Africa. Famous diamond, 1012.

Star of the South. Famous diamond, *1011.*

Stars and Stripes. Origin of U.S. flag, 1312.

" Star Spangled Banner." Amer. national song, 2283.

Start Point. Promontory on Devon coast, 8 m. s. of Dartmouth ; lighthouse visible 20 m.

Stassfurt, Ger. Tn. 20 m. s. of Magdeburg ; pop. 16,000 ; salt works and famous potash deposits, 2866.

State. A political community organized under a govt. recognized by the people ; a state may be independent, subject to other states, or a unit in a federation (e.g., U.S.A.).

State, Great Officers of (Eng.), 3083.

State, Papal Secretary of, 2495.

State bank. Any bank that is under govt. control ; in U.S.A. state banks are those which secure their charter from the states in which they are situated and conduct their business according to state laws.

State governments, in U.S.A. ; represented in Senate, 3290.

Stat'en Island, N.Y., U.S.A. At entrance to New York bay, 2351.

States-general. Dutch parliament.

States-General, in France. *See* **Estates-General.**

States of the Church. *See* **Papal States.**

Stat'ic electricity, 1131, 1929.

Stat'ics. A branch of mechanics, 2127 ; a cause of wireless interference, 3397.

Stationer. Original meaning, 511.

Stationery Office, His Majesty's. Official govt. publishers, with h.q. in Oxford Street, London, 1492.

Stator, non-rotating part of elec. apparatus ; in dynamo, 1062 ; elec. clock, *1126, 1127* ; induction motor, 2240.

Statue of Liberty, N.Y., U.S.A., 2351.

Stat'ute. *See* **Act of Parliament.**

Statute law, 1702.

Staubbach (shtowb'-bahkh). Waterfall in Switzerland, s. of Lauterbrunnen ; height 980 ft. ; *3142.*

Stavanger (sta-vang'-er). Spt. on s.w. coast of Norway ; pop. 49,000 ; textiles, soap, preserves, iron, fisheries, 2393. Occupied by Germans during 1940–45.

Stavropol (stavro-pol'). Now **Voroshilovsk.** Trading and agric. centre in s. Russia, 275 m. N. of Tiflis ; pop. 61,400 ; 732.

Stead (sted), **Robert James Campbell** (b. 1880). Canadian author ; " Dennison Grant," and other popular novels, 685.

Stead, William Thomas (1849–1912). Eng. journalist ; opponent of social evils, advocate of international peace, took keen interest in psychical research ; founded " The Review of Reviews " ; drowned in " Titanic."

Steam, 3084, 3085 ; latent heat of, 3351.

Steam-engine, 3084, 3085 ; compound, 3085 ; first marine, 2946 ; importance to civilization, 1722, *1723* ; locomotive, *plate f. 1980,* 1981 ; driving looms, 3361 ; Newcomen's, 3085 ; power station, 2673 ; pump, 2704 ; Stephenson, 1981, *2735, 2736.*

3086 ; railway development, 2734 ; turbines, 3258 ; Trevithick's, *3247* ; Watt improves, 3356, 3357 ; Watt's perfected model, *3086, 3357.*

Steam-hammer, and steel manufacture, 1758.

Steam-heating, 1600, 3084.

Steaming, in cookery, 902.

Steamships, 2946 ; building, 2947, 2949 ; Brunel, 593 ; Fulton, 1407 ; turbines, 2949, 3260. *See also* **Ships.**

Steam turbine, 3258, 3084.

Stearine. The organic salt of glycerine and stearic acid ; soap from, 2993.

Ste'atite. *See* **Talc.**

Sted'man, Edmund Clarence (1833–1908). Amer. banker, poet, critic, and editor (" The Nature and Elements of Poetry " ; " Victorian Poets " ; " An American Anthology ").

Steed, Henry Wickham (b. 1871). Brit. journalist, correspondent of " The Times " at Berlin (1896), Rome (1897–1902), Vienna (1912–13) ; foreign editor of " The Times " (1914–19), and editor (1919–22) ; in 1st World War, engaged in propaganda work abroad.

Steel, Flora Annie (1847–1929). Brit. novelist ; lived long in India (" On the Face of the Waters," a stirring tale of the Indian Mutiny ; " The Potter's Thumb ").

Steel, 3087, 1752, 2087 ; alloys, 123, 2087, 2365, 3253 ; Bessemer process, 420, 1756 ; Damascus blades, 963 ; heat treatment, 1624 ; in modern architecture, 220, 221, 222 ; of needles, 2311 ; Sheffield, 2941 ; stainless steel, 1758, 2856 ; wire, 3389. *See also* **Iron and Steel.**

Steel construction. Bridges, 564–569 ; buildings, 220, 221, 222, 604, *884* ; door, *358* ; girders and joists, *380.*

Steele, Sir Richard (1672–1729). Brit. essayist, associate of Addison on the " Spectator," 24 ; essays, 1213.

Steel-Maitland, Sir Arthur (1876–1935). Brit. politician, entered parl. (1910) ; chairman of the Unionist Party Organization (1911) ; under-sec. for the Colonies, (1915–17) ; head of Dept. of Overseas Trade (1917–19) ; Minister of Labour (1924).

Steel pens, 2539.

Steelyard. Headquarters in London of Hanse merchants from 1250–1597, near present Cannon St. Station.

Steelyard. Type of simple weighing machine ; hence also the district of London where weighing took place (*see above*).

Steen (stān), **Jan Havicksz** (1626–79). Dutch genre painter (" Feast of St. Nicholas " ; " Music Master "), 2334.

Steenkerke (stān-ker-ke). Belgium. Vil. 20 m. s.w. of Brussels where Dutch and English under William III of Eng. were defeated by Fr. (1692).

Steeple. Tower or turret of a church or other public building, ending in a point, and usually intended to contain a bell or bells.

Steeplechases, 1648.

Steer, Philip Wilson (1860–1942). Eng. artist ; renowned for his mastery of atmosphere ; his works are in, among others, the following galleries : Uffizi, Florence ; British Museum ; Tate Gallery ; Metropolitan Museum, New York ; awarded Order of Merit (1931) ; 1183, *1191.*

Steevens, George Warrington (1869–1900). Eng. journalist and war correspondent ; went to Amer. in 1897, as special correspondent for the " Daily Mail," and later to Thessaly, Egypt, the Sudan, India, Germany, and S. Africa, where he died of enteric at siege of Ladysmith (" With Kitchener to Khartum " ; " From Cape Town to Ladysmith ").

Stefansson (stā'-fans-son), **Vilhjalmur** (b. 1879). Arctic explorer, b. Canada ; on 2nd expedition (1908–12) discovered " blond " Eskimos who had never seen a white man ; on 3rd expedition (1913–18) discovered three large and several small isls. ; also revolutionized Arctic research by living for months without supplies, killing seals, and deer for food (" The Friendly Arctic ") ; author of

" The Northward Course of Empire " and " Hunters of the Great North," 225, 2646.

Stegomy'ia, a mosquito, 2486.

Steg'osaur. Prehistoric reptile, 2678.

Stein (shtīn), **Heinrich Friedrich Karl, Baron von** (1757–1831). Prussian statesman ; abolished serfdom, reformed army, and laid foundation of Prussia's power.

Stein, Sir (Mark) Aurel (1862–1943). Asiatic explorer. After researches in Indian archæology, began in 1906 famous series of explorations in Cent. Asia, results of which he published in numerous books.

Steinbeck, John E. (b. 1902). Amer. novelist and playwright ; " Tortilla Flat," " Of Mice and Men," " The Grapes of Wrath," " The Moon is Down " (the last three filmed and dramatized) ; " The Russian Journal."

Steinbok. An African antelope, 176.

" Stella." Swift's friend, Esther Johnson, 3132.

Stelvio Pass. Alpine pass in Italy, on the great highway from Milan to Innsbruck, connects Meran and the valley of the upper Adige with Bormio, in the valley of the Adda, and carries the highest road in Europe ; *128.*

Stem, of plants, 1322, *2621* ; modified in water-plants, 3355 ; potato an underground stem, 2664 ; structure of tree-trunk, 3245 ; why sap rises, 2621.

Stem duchies, in Germany, 1449.

Stem rust. A grain parasite, 2857.

Stendhal (stahn-dahl'). Pen-name of Marie Henri Beyle (1783–1842). Fr. writer and critic, whose famous novels, " Le Rouge et Le Noir " and " La Chartreuse de Parme," had tremendous influence on the development of the Fr. novel ; a profound interpreter of the human soul, 1381.

Sten gun, automatic rifle of 2nd World War, *1283,* 2050.

Sten'ograph, 2962.

Stenog'raphy or **shorthand,** 2961.

Sten'otype, 2962.

Sten'tor. In the " Iliad," Gk. herald whose voice was as loud as that of 50 men.

Stephen (stē'-ven) (c. 1097–1154). King of Eng., 3087 ; besieges Matilda at Oxford, 2462.

Stephen, St. (977–1038). First king of Hungary, crowned in 1000 ; Christianized and civilized kingdom ; the " Crown of St. Stephen " was age-long symbol of Hungarian monarchy.

Stephen, St. First Christian martyr ; stoned to death (Acts vi.-vii.) ; *2112.*

Stephen, Sir Leslie (1832–1904). Eng. biographer and essayist ; editor of " The Dictionary of National Biography " ; wrote lives of Samuel Johnson, Pope, Swift, and numerous essays and sketches on 18th and 19th cent. literature.

Stephen Bathor (1522–86). Second elected king of Poland, succeeded Henry of Valois in 1575 ; seized Livonia from Russia, and organized first Cossack regiment.

Stephens, Alexander Hamilton (1812–83). Amer. statesman, vice-pres. of the Confederate States of Amer. during the Civil War ; governor of Georgia (1882–83).

Stephens, James (b. 1882). Irish poet, short-story writer, and broadcaster ; subtle humour and delicate fancy are tied to a keen appreciation of Irish character (" Insurrections " ; " The Hill of Visions " ; " Songs from the Clay " ; " The Crock of Gold " ; " Deirdre ").

Stephenson, George (1781–1848). Eng. engineer, 3087, 1981 ; first successful locomotive, 1981, 2736, *2735* ; and Ericsson, 1222 ; invented miner's lamp, 1889.

Stephenson, Robert (1803-59). Eng. engineer, son of George Stephenson, 3088 ; builder of Britannia tubular bridge over Menai Straits and Victoria tubular bridge over St. Lawrence at Montreal ; assists father, 1981, 3086.

Step′ney. Met. bor. of E. London ; a. 1,700 acres ; pop. 100,000 ; includes Whitechapel, Limehouse, and Mile End, Tower of London and Royal Mint.

Stepniak, Sergius (1852–95). Russ. writer ; banished from Russia owing to Nihilist tendencies and later settled in England ; wrote " Underground Russia " (1882), etc.

Steppes, in Asia, 2966 ; of Hungary, 1655 ; in Russia, 1234, 2844.

Ster′eoscope. Optical device, **3088.**

Ster′eotyping, in printing, 3088, 2345 ; contrasted with electrotyping, 1140.

Steriliza′tion. The act of making sterile, or freeing from living germs, 179, 1341.

Ster′let. A sturgeon, 3104.

" Sterling " silver. Composition, 2187.

Stern Gang. Terrorist organization in Palestine, formed in 1940 by Abraham Stern when Irgun made a truce with the U.K. ; co-operated with Axis, murdered Ld. Moyne (q.v. in f-i.) and Bernadotte (q.v. in f-i) ; outlawed by Israeli govt. and on Sept. 30, 1948, the leader, Nathan Yellin, captured ; 2483.

Stern, Gladys B. (b. 1890). Brit. writer ; among many novels, "Tents of Israel " (as a play, " The Matriarch "), " Mosaic," " Oleander River," " Another Part of the Forest," " No Son of Mine."

Sterne, Laurence (1713–68). Brit. novelist, humorist, and sentimentalist (" Tristram Shandy " ; " Sentimental Journey ") ; contribution to the novel, 1213, 2402.

Steth′oscope, medical instr. for listening to heart, lungs, etc., 1593.

Stettin (now Szczecin). Former German chief Baltic port on R. Oder, 17 m. above mouth ; pop. 270,747 ; shipyard ; clothing mfrs. ; Russians take April 26, 1945. Ceded to Poland 1945.

Stettinius, Edward R. (1900–49). Amer. politician ; chm. of U.S. Steel corp. ; in 1940, mem. of advisory commission to council of national defence ; Sec. of State 1944–45 ; U.S. representative on Security Council of U.N. 1945–June 1946.

Steu′ben, Frederick William, Baron von (1730–94). Ger. officer, served in Seven Years' War ; assisted Amer. colonies in War of Independence.

Steu′benville, Ohio, U.S.A. City on Ohio r., 35 m. s.w. of Pittsburgh, in coal, natural gas, and oil region ; pop. 37,650 ; iron and steel products, soap, tin-plate, clay, pottery, glass.

Stevenage. Mkt. tn. of Herts, 28 m. N. of London ; annual fair held in main str. in Sept. ; pop. 6,330 ; in 1946 chosen as site of new tn. with 60,000 pop., and first of chosen sites to be developed.

Stevens, Alfred (1818–75). Eng. sculptor and painter ; worked nearly 20 years at Wellington monument and tomb in St. Paul's Cathedral ; 1181, 1182, 2906.

Stevens, Alfred (1828–1906). Belgian painter, whose finished technique and careful execution greatly influenced many of his contemporaries ; particularly successful in portraits of ladies of fashion.

Stevens, John (1749–1838). Amer. engineer and inventor ; helped to secure Amer. patent system ; built steamboat Phoenix in 1807, which ran successfully on Delaware r.

Stevenson, Mrs. Fanny van de Grift Osbourne. Wife of Robert Louis Stevenson, 3089.

Stevenson, Robert (1772–1850). Scot. engineer, inventor of intermittent lights for lighthouses ; built Bell Rock and some other lighthouses on Scot. coast ; grandfather of Robert Louis Stevenson.

Stevenson, Robert Louis (1850–94). Scot. story-writer, poet, and essayist, **3089,** 1215, 1224, 2402, 2895 ; in Samoa, 2869.

Stevinus (ste-vē′-nus), **Simon** (1548–1620). Dutch mathematician ; invented decimal system.

Stewart. Scottish royal house. Same as **Stuart.**

Stewart, Dugald (1753–1828). Scottish philosopher of the " commonsense " school ; immensely popular lecturer at Univ. of Edinburgh (" Elements of the Philosophy of the Human Mind," " Outlines of Moral Philosophy ").

Stewart, Sir Herbert (1843–85). Brit. soldier ; served in Zulu War, Boer War (1881) and took part in attempt to relieve Gordon.

Stewart, Robert. See **Castlereagh.**

Stewart Island. One of New Zealand group ; a. 670 sq. m. ; pop. 350 ; 2360.

Stewing, in cookery, 902.

Steyn (stīn), **Marthinus Theunis** (1857–1916). S. African statesman, elected pres. of the Orange Free State in 1896 ; had many narrow escapes during the Boer War (1899–1902) and played a statesman's part at the conference in 1908–09 which brought about union in S. Africa.

Stib′nite. An ore of antimony, 177.

Stick-insect. Various insects resembling branches and twigs of trees, 1728, 2693.

Stickleback. A fish, **3091.**

Stig′ma. The pollen-catching structure in flowers, 531, 532, 1321, 1326.

Stig′mata of St. Francis, 1384.

Stikine or **Stickeen.** R. rising in N. British Columbia ; flows 500 m. to Alaskan coast.

S′ilicho (stil′-i-kō), **Flavius** (c. 359–408). Rom. general and statesman of Vandal birth ; as guardian of feeble Emperor Honorius was virtual ruler of W. Empire ; 96.

Stilt. A long-legged wading bird of the sandpiper group.

Stilted. In architecture, term applied to a form of the arch which does not spring immediately from the imposts, but from a vertical piece of masonry resting on them, so as to give the arch the appearance of resting on stilts ; frequently seen in medieval buildings.

Stilton cheese, 766.

Stilwell, Joseph W., " Vinegar Joe " (1883–1946). Amer. soldier ; won D.S.M. in 1st World War ; after Pearl Harbour U.S. milit. representative in China, and made chief of staff and commander of Chinese armies in Burma by Chiang Kai-shek ; in 1942 led retreat through jungle to India and built Ledo Rd. (q.v. in f-i.) ; diaries and letters pub. as " The Stilwell Papers."

Stimson, Henry L. (b. 1867). Amer. politician and lawyer ; as attorney-gen. of N.Y. prosecuted powerful trusts (sugar, etc.) ; sec. of war 1911–13 and 1940–45 ; sec. of state 1929–33 ; judge of perm. court of internat. justice at The Hague 1935 ; memoirs pub. 1947.

Sting, of insects, 1295, 1727, 1732 ; of scorpion, 2888 ; of wasps, 3346.

Stinging-nettle. See **Nettle.**

Sting-Ray. A fish of the family Battoidae ; the tail is armed in its middle portion with a sharp, flattened bony spine, sawlike on both sides, which is capable of inflicting a severe wound.

Stinkhorn. Fungus, Phallus phalloides of Basidiomycete group, so called on account of its exceedingly powerful and unpleasant smell ; common in shady places in woods, shrubberies etc., and distinguished by columnar shape with small pointed spore-cap ; smell attracts flies and these disperse the spores.

Stin′nes, Hugo (1870–1924). Ger. industrial manager and financier ; leading figure in post-war reconstruction ; organized a gigantic interlocking business based on the mining industry and including many subsidiary enterprises.

Stipen′diary. A paid magistrate.

Stipple engraving, 1218.

Stip′ules. Scale- or leaf-like bodies at bases of plant leaves, 1914, 1916.

Stirling, Scot. Historic mfg. city on R. Forth ; pop. 28,500 ; 3092.

Stirling Bridge, battle of, between Scots and English (1297), 2892, 3092, 3337.

Stirling Castle, 2892 ; battle of Bannockburn, 359.

Stirlingshire, Scot. Co. bounded N. by R. Forth ; contains part of Lochs Lomond and Katrine ; a. 450 sq. m. ; pop. 186,000 ; 3092.

Stitch welding, 3363.

Stitchwort. A plant, 3092.

Stoat, the ermine, 1222.

Stock. In fruit grafting, 1402.

Stock. Popular garden flower of order Cruciferae ; usually white, red, pink or purple with double flowers ; several species grow wild (rare) on cliffs in Britain.

Stock-breeding, heredity, 1617.

Stock-dove, 2606.

Stock Exchange. A place where stocks, shares and negotiable securities are bought and sold ; London and New York stock exchanges are the most important in the world, 3094.

Stock′holm. Cap. and commercial centre of Sweden, on E. coast ; pop. 703,000 ; 3092, 3126, 3127 ; city hall, 3127.

Stockholm tar, 3154.

Stockings, how made, 1865, 1866, 1867.

Stockport, Eng. Mfg. tn. of R. Mersey 5 m. S.E. of Manchester ; pop. 137,680 ; cotton mills, hat factories, foundries, breweries.

Stock-raising ; in Australia, 307, 308, 311, 312. See also **Live-stock.**

Stocks. Form of punishment, 2687.

Stocks and Shares, 3093.

Stockton, Frank Richard (1834–1902). Amer. humorist (" The Lady or the Tiger ? " ; " Rudder Grange "), 3295.

Stockton and Darlington Railway, 1981, 2736, 3087.

Stockton-on-Tees. Spt. in N.E. Eng. near mouth of R. Tees ; pop. 71,600 ; large iron and steel works, shipyards, potteries.

Stockyard. Place in which cattle are kept before being slaughtered. See also **Meat packing.**

Stoddard, Richard Henry (1825–1903). Amer. poet, critic, and editor ; (" Abraham Lincoln " ; " The Book of the East " ; " Songs of Summer ").

Stoddart, Andrew Ernest (1864–1915). Eng. sportsman ; brilliant Middlesex and England cricketer and international Rugby footballer.

Stoicism (stō′-i-sizm). School of philosophy ; Epictetus. 1220 ; Marcus Aurelius, 2099.

Stoke Newington. Met. bor. of N. London ; 3 m. N.E. of St. Paul's ; contains New River Waterworks and reservoirs ; pop. 46,900.

Stoke Poges. Eng. vil. in Buckinghamshire, 20 m. w. of London ; Gray's " Elegy," 599, 1514.

Stokes, Sir George Gabriel (1819–1903). Irish physician ; devoted himself to the mathematical investigations of physical problems and published his researches on the dynamical theory of diffraction ; one of his discoveries is known in science as Stokes's law.

Stokes, Sir Wilfrid (1860–1927). Brit. engineer ; invented the Stokes gun in 1915, when it was first used in the battle of Loos.

Stoke′say Castle, in Shrop., 715, 2963.

Stoke-upon-Trent. Centre of " Potteries " dist., in Staffordshire ; pop. 273,500 ; formed by union of Stoke-upon-Trent with neighbouring towns ; porcelain and pottery mfr. ; 3072.

Stokowski, Leopold (Antoni Stanislaw Boleslawowicz) (b. 1882). Amer. conductor ; b. in London of Polish parents ; conductor of Cincinnatti Orchestra 1909–12 ; of Philadelphia Symphony Orchestra 1913–36.

Stolzenfels (shtŏlts′-en-fels), castle 4 m. s. of Coblenz, Ger., founded 13th cent., 2796.

Stomach, 3094, 1016 ; of birds, 437 ; digestion, 1016 ; nerves, 2317 ; of ruminants, 2842 ; of starfish, 3082.

Sto'mata (plural of **stoma**). Minute openings in tissue, 2621 ; in leaves. 1914 ; in water-plants, 3355.

Stone, Frank (1800–59). Brit. painter ; entirely self-taught ; became A.R.A. in 1851.

Stone. See **Building construction.**

Stone. A unit of weight. See **Weights and Measures,** *f-i.*

Stone Age, 3094 ; giant bison, *459* ; bread, 554 ; cave-dwellers, 734, *735,* 736 ; dogs domesticated, 1025 ; horn implements, *1643, 2083* ; Neolithic peoples, 2081, 2082 ; painting in, *plates f. 736, 2084,* 2475.

Stonechat. A small European bird (*Pratincola rubicola*), so named from its clicking note ; its plumage is black above and dark reddish underneath, 3374.

Stone Circles, at Avebury, *323.*

Stone-fly, 1733.

Stonehaven. Co. tn. of Kincardineshire ; pop. 4,550 ; 1857.

Stonehenge. Celebrated pre-historic monument on Salisbury Plain, about 8 m. N. of Salisbury ; **3096,** 3383.

Stone pine, 2610.

Stone River, Tennessee, U.S.A. Tributary of Cumberland r., which enters 5 m. above Nashville ; gives name to a Federal victory over the Confederates in the Civil War (1863).

Stones, precious. See **Gems.**

"Stones of Venice." Book by John Ruskin in which he expounds his theories of the relation of architecture to all other human activities, 2843.

"Stonewall Jackson." Name given to Thomas Jackson, Amer. general, 1789.

Stoney, George Johnstone (1826–1911). Brit. physicist who named electron.

Stony Point, N.Y., U.S.A. Vil. on promontory on Hudson r., 35 m. N. of New York City ; taken by Clinton (1779) ; stormed and recaptured by Anthony Wayne.

Stool ball, game, 928.

Stop, in organ, 2449.

Storage battery or **accumulator.** See **Battery.**

Stories. "Adam and Noah in Babylonian Story," 332 ; "Adventures of Blackie and Ginger," 3489–92 ; "Adventures of the Great-Hearted Odysseus," 2421 ; "Adventures of the Great Hercules," 1615 ; "Adventures of Robin Hood and His Merry Men," 3469 ; "Aladdin and the Wonderful Lamp," 3450 ; "Alice in Wonderland," 708 ; "Androcles and the Lion," 1960 ; "The Apples of Iduna," 2881 ; "Arabian Nights," 202 ; "Blackface meets his Neighbours," 3481 ; "The Bluebird," 3465 ; "Canterbury Tales," 762 ; "A Christmas Carol," 820 ; "Death of Hector," 1603 ; Dante's "Divine Comedy," 970 ; "Don Quixote's Adventures," 746 ; "The Golden Bough," 1387 ; "The Greek Hero Who Slew the Medusa" (Perseus), 2552 ; "Gulliver's Travels," 3133 ; "The Story of Hiawatha," 2022 ; "How Golden Wings Learned to Fly," 3485 ; "How Horatius Kept the Bridge," 3207 ; "Odysseus and the Cyclops," 949 ; "How Screecher Learned to Hunt," 3473 ; "The Jewish Maiden who became Queen of Persia" (Esther), 1225 ; "King Arthur's Round Table," 255 ; 2830 ; "Mowgli," 1860 ; "Odin," 2420 ; "Odysseus' Adventures," 2421 ; "Paradise Lost," 2178 ; "Perseus," 2552 ; "Peter Pan," 364 ; "Pickwick at Dingley Dell," 1013 ; "Pilgrim's Progress," 618 ; "Prickles and his Quills," 3477 ; "Robin Hood and His Merry Men," 3469 ; "Robinson Crusoe in Fact and Fiction," 937 ; "The Shield of Achilles," 19 ; "Siegfried and the Dragon," 2969 ; "The Story of Two Little Bears," 3489 ; "The Tadpole Who Wanted to be a Frog," 3453 ; "Theseus," 3201 ; "The Tournament at Ashby," 2900 ; "Treasure Island," 3090 ; "The Trojan War," 3248 ; "Twenty Thousand Leagues under the Sea," 3316 ; "What Sinbad Found in the Desert," 3497 ; "White Tail and the Old Stag's Lesson," 3493 ; "How the Wooden Horse came to Troy," 3249. See also **Literature for Children.**

Stork. A large wading bird, 3097. *plates f. 3100, 3101.*

Stork's-bill. Plant of genus *Erodium,* and a close relative of the crane's-bills, family *Geraniaceae.* Several Brit. species, with pinkish flowers, pinnate leaves and beak-like fruits.

Storm, Theodor (1817–88). Ger. novelist and poet, master of the short story, 1457.

"Storm and Stress." Movement in Ger. literature, 1456.

Stormcock. See **Mistle Thrush.**

Storm-petrel, 2563.

Storms, 3100 ; in Caribbean Sea, 701 ; cyclonic, 949, 2741 ; equatorial thunder showers, 2741 ; equinoctial, 1221 ; forecasting, 363 ; lightning, *1945, 1946* ; wind, 3384.

Storm Troops (S.A., abbrev. of Ger. *Sturmabteilung*), armed and uniformed members of Nazi party, 2281.

Storting. Name of the parliament, or legislative body, of Norway, 2390, 2398.

Story, Joseph (1779–1845). Amer. jurist ; 34 years associate justice of U.S.A. Supreme Court ; with Chief Justice Marshall established powers of Supreme Court and with Chancellor Kent moulded Amer. equity jurisprudence.

Story, William Wetmore (1819–95). Amer. sculptor and poet ; son of Joseph Story ("Cleopatra," enthusiastically described in Hawthorne's "Marble Faun") ; many fine statues and portrait busts) ; his studio in Rome for 45 years a social centre for Amer. and Eng. artists and authors.

Stoss (shtos), **Veit** (*c.* 1440–1533). Ger. sculptor and one of the greatest Ger. wood carvers ; carved altars and tombs in churches at Nuremberg and Cracow.

Sto'thard, Thomas (1755–1834). English painter and engraver, noted for the uniform grace and distinction with which he illustrated "Robinson Crusoe," "Pilgrim's Progress," "The Vicar of Wakefield," and many other works, *763.*

Stour, name of several small Eng. rivers ; in Dorset and Hants, 1030 ; in Essex and Suffolk, 1225, 3111 ; in Kent, 692.

Stoves and fireplaces. Closed, 1597 ; cooking, 900 ; heating efficiency, 1597–1600 ; slow combustion, 1598 ; on blowlamp principle, *478.*

Stow, John (*c.* 1525–1605). Eng. chronicler and antiquary ; was a tailor till a few years before his death ("Summarie of English Chronicles" ; "Annales of England" ; "Survey of London").

Stowe, Harriet Elizabeth Beecher (1811–96). Amer. novelist, author of "Uncle Tom's Cabin," 3294.

Stowe. House, now a Public school, 599.

Strabo (strā'-bō) (*c.* 63 B.C.–A.D. 19). Gk. geographer and historian ; wrote first general treatise on geography with collection of all geographical knowledge attainable ; 1541.

Strachan (strawn), **John** (1778–1867). Canadian clergyman ; first Bishop of Toronto ; first pres. of Univ. of Toronto and founder of Trinity Univ.

Strachey, Rt. Hon. E. John St. Loe (b. 1901). Min. of Food (1946–50) ; became Sec. of State for War in 1950.

Strachey (strā'-chi), **Giles Lytton** (1880–1932). Eng. essayist and biographer ("Eminent Victorians" ; "Queen Victoria" ; "Books and Characters" ; "Elizabeth and Essex"), 430.

Strachey, John St. Loe (1860–1927). Eng. journalist, proprietor and editor of "The Spectator" ; originally a barrister, he became a journalist in 1884 ; sometime editor of "The Cornhill Magazine" ("From Grave to Gay" ; "The Problems and Perils of Socialism" ; "A New Way of Life" ; "The Adventure of Living"). Son E. J. Strachey.

Stradivari or **Stradivarius** (strad-i-vār'-i-*us*), **Antonio** (1644–1737). It. (Cremona) violin-maker, greatest that ever lived ; pupil of Nicolo Amati, 3324.

Strafford, Thomas Wentworth, Earl of (1593–1641). Eng. statesman, strong believer in absolute royal power ; advised Charles I to resist Parliament ; executed for treason by Long Parliament, 755, *1899.*

Straits Settlements. Former Brit. crown colony in Malay Peninsula, now part of Singapore Colony ; great strategic value ; free ports, immense transit trade ; 2069 ; Singapore, 2974.

Stralsund (shtrahl'-zoond). Ger. Baltic port ; pop. 38,000 ; important member of Hansa League ; Wallenstein's siege in Thirty Years' War ; captured by Russians May 1945, it came within Russian zone of occupation.

Stramo'nium. A drug, *see* **Jimson weed.**

Strand. Business thoroughfare in London, extending between Charing Cross and Temple Bar ; formerly led from city to Westminster along marshy bank of Thames, hence the name ; Law Courts in, *1902.*

Strang, William (1859–1921). Eng. painter and editor (etched portraits of Kipling, Thomas Hardy, Stevenson ; illustrated "Pilgrim's Progress," "Sinbad the Sailor," "Baron Münchausen") ; 1183.

Strasbourg (strahs-boor). Ger. **Strassburg**). Fr. city in Alsace ; pop. 175,500 ; *134,* 2769 ; taken by Germans 1940 ; recovered by French 2nd armoured division Nov. 1944.

Stratford, Ontario. Industrial city and farming centre on Avon r., 85 m. s.w. of Toronto ; pop. 17,742 ; rly. shops ; makes furniture, iron and brass products, textiles, machinery, electrical appliances, flour, cheese.

Stratford-upon-Avon. Tn. in Warwickshire ; pop. 13,550 ; **3101,** 3341 ; Shakespeare, 2932 ; portraits at, 2936.

Strathclyde. Anc. Brit. kingdom extending from Clyde to Derwent r. ; stronghold of original Celt inhabitants against Anglo-Saxons (7th–11th cents.), 943.

Strathco'na and Mount Royal, Donald Alexander Smith, 1st Baron (1820–1914). Canadian financier and railway builder, **3102.**

Strathcona's Horse, 3102.

Strat'ified rocks. Those occurring in layers, *2712.*

Stratosphere, the outer layer of the atmosphere, **3102,** 88, *89* ; and weather, 2150.

Stra'tus clouds, 852, *853.*

Straus, Oscar (b. 1870). Austrian composer. Chief works : "The Chocolate Soldier" ; "A Waltz Dream." Naturalized as Frenchman in 1939.

Strauss (shtrows) **David Friedrich** (1808–74). Ger. theologian whose "Life of Jesus" explains gospel narratives as essentially mythical.

Strauss, George Russell. Parl. Sec. Min. of Transport 1945–47 ; Min. of Supply 1947.

Strauss, Johann (1825–99). A popular Austrian composer, the "Waltz King" ; son of Johann Strauss the elder, also eminent composer ; **3102,** 967.

Strauss, Richard (1864–1949). Ger. composer and conductor, **3103,** 2265, 2440, *2441.* He died Sept. 8, 1949.

Stravin'sky, Igor (b. 1882). Rus. composer, noted for music for ballets ("L'Oiseau de Feu"; "Petrouchka"; "Le Sacre du Printemps").

Straw. From oats, 2410 ; in paper-making, 2497 ; rye, 2858.

Strawberry. A fleshy fruit, **3103,** *plate f. 1401.*

Strawberry tree, 204.

Strawboard, 2500.

Straw hats, 1584.

Streamline. In aeronautics and hydrodynamics, to shape a body in such a way that the natural fluid stream is impeded as little as possible, 2952.

Street, Robert, invents oil engine, 1736.

Street railways. *See* **Trams and Trolley-buses.**

Streets and roads, 2783 ; lighting by electricity, 1134.

Streicher, Julius (1885–1946). Ger. Nazi politician ; in Hitler's 1923 *putsch* ; in 1924 started a Jew-baiting wkly. paper which brought him huge fortune ; Gauleiter of Franconia under Hitler ; major war criminal at Nuremberg trials, and hanged for crimes against humanity, Oct. 16, 1946 ; 2282.

Strelt'si or **Strel'itz.** Household troops of the Tsars, instituted by Ivan the Terrible ; backbone of Rus. army in 16th and 17th cents. ; frequent mutinies led to abolition by Peter I.

Streptococcus (strep-to-kōk-*us*), bacteria occurring in chains, 3116, *1459*.

Streptomy'cin, antibiotic drug from an earth-mould, **3103**, 180.

Stresa (strā′*za*). It. vil. and Alpine resort on L. Maggiore ; scene of Three Power Conference in 1935.

Stresemann (strā′-ze-mahn), **Gustav** (1878–1929). Ger. statesman ; entered Reichstag 1906 ; became leader of National Liberal Party ; after 1st World War became head of the newly-founded German People's Party. Chancellor and Foreign Minister (1923) ; awarded Nobel peace prize in 1926 ; one of the authors of the Locarno pact, 1450.

Stretcher, in first aid, *1293*.

Strickland, Agnes (1796–1874). Eng. historical writer who wrote in collaboration with her sister, Elizabeth, though published in her own name alone (" Lives of the Queens of England," ; " Seven Bishops " ; " Tales and Stories from History ").

Strikes. Cessation of labour by employees to enforce their demands upon their employer, or to protest against his actions ; sympathetic strike is one called by workers without a grievance in behalf of strikers in another field ; general strike is one carried out in all fields of labour simultaneously ; " unofficial " strike is one called against the advice of trade union officials ; arbitration of, 203, 2358.

Strindberg, August (1849–1912). Swedish novelist and dramatist ; chief plays, " Master Olof," ; " The Father," " Lucky Pehr " ; 2881.

Stringed instruments, 2266, *2267* ; in orchestra, 2445. *See also* **Harp** ; **Piano** ; **Violin,** etc.

Stringfellow, John (1799–1883). Brit. inventor of first model aeroplane to fly, in 1848, using supporting wings and screw to provide motive power ; 44.

Striped hyena, 1675, 1701.

Striped maple. Seeds, *2917*.

Strobila, of jelly-fish, *1268*.

Stroboscopic effect. In cinematograph pictures of moving wheels the spokes sometimes appear to revolve slowly the wrong way. If the pictures were taken at the rate of 30 per second, and during the thirtieth of a second each spoke has moved into the position occupied by the previous one, they appear to be at rest. If they have not moved quite so far they appear to be slipping backwards.

Stromboli (strom′bō-lē), **Mt.** Active volcano 3,000 ft. high on Stromboli, one of Lipari Isles., 2136.

Stromness, Orkney Islands, 2453.

Strongbow. Nickname of Richard de Clare, Earl of Pembroke (d. 1176). Eng. noble who at appeal of Dermot of Leinster began Eng. conquest of Ireland.

Strong verbs, 3314.

Stronsay. One of Orkney Isles, 7 m. long, 2453.

Stron'tium (Sr.). Element of the alkaline earth metal group ; atomic weight, 87·63 ; first isolated by Davy in 1808 ; melts at 1652° F. ; properties, 777 ; chloride spectrum, *plate f. 3057*.

Strood, Dist. of Rochester, Kent, 2791.

Strowger selector, in automatic telephone exchange, 3175.

Strozzi (strot′-sē) **Palace,** Florence. Built 15th cent. ; willed to state (1907).

Strube, Sidney (b. 1891). Brit. cartoonist ; on Daily Express 1912–48 ; creator of the " little man."

Structural steel, 604.

" Struggle for Existence." Competition among living organisms for means of livelihood ; character and consequences among animals, 156 ; among fish, 1298 ; among insects, 1726 ; among plants, 2622, 2623 ; protective coloration a factor, 2692 ; results in " survival of the fittest," 978, 1246.

Strutt, Jedediah (1726–97). Brit. inventor of ribbed hosiery machine, *c.* 1755 ; partner of Arkwright in cotton mills ; ancestor of Lord Rayleigh ; 1865.

Strychnine (strik′-nin). A poisonous drug in the form of a crystalline powder ; in small quantities it is used in medicine, 2132, 2638.

Strych'nos nux-vom'ica. A tree yielding poisons strychnine and brucine.

Stu'art. Royal family in Scot. and Eng., **3104**, 755, 1793, 2115 ; attempts to regain throne, 2682. *See also* **Jacobites.**

Stuart, Lady Arabella (1575–1615). Cousin of James I ; centre of Eng. political intrigue because a possible heir to throne ; imprisoned for life after making forbidden marriage.

Stuart, Charles Edward (1720–88). The Young Pretender, 2682.

Stuart, James. *See* **Murray, James Stuart, Earl of.**

Stuart, James Ewell Brown (1833–64). Amer. soldier ; Confederate Civil War general, great cavalry raider.

Stuart, James Francis Edward (1688–1766). The Old Pretender, 2682.

Stubbs, George (1724–1806). Eng. painter ; one of the finest of English sporting painters ; much of his work is in the National Gallery and Victoria and Albert Museum. Published (1766), famous work " The Anatomy of the Horse," with plates drawn and engraved by himself : " Phaeton and Pair," *1179*.

Stubbs, William (1825–1901). Bishop of Oxford and one of the foremost historians of his time (" Constitutional History of England " is still the standard authority).

Studland, Dorset. Singing sands at, 2871.

Sturdee, Sir Frederick Charles Doveton, Bart. (1859–1925). Brit. admiral who sank Ger. squadron in battle of the Falkland Isls. Dec. 8, 1914, and commanded a battle squadron at Jutland ; promoted Admiral of the Fleet (1921) ; 1259.

Stur'geon, William (1783–1850). Eng. physicist ; inventor of electro-magnet, 2064.

Sturgeon. A large fish, **3104**, 1298 ; source of gelatin, 1426 ; isinglass made from, 1760.

Stuttgart (shtŏŏt′-gahrt). Former Ger. cap. of state of Württemberg ; pop. 414,070 ; fine collections of art and antiquities ; publishing centre. Heavily bombed in Second World War. Since 1946 cap. of new *Land* (province) of Württemberg-Baden.

Stuyvesant (stī-ve-zant), **Peter** (1592–1672), last Dutch colonial gov. of New York, became governor of Curaçao (1635) ; established better relationship with Amer. Indians.

Style. Stem which supports the stigma of a flower, *1321*, *1326*.

Style, literary, 2769.

Stylites, Simeon. *See* **Simeon Stylites.**

Stylograph'ic pen, 2541.

Sty'lus, *1897*, 2541.

Stympha'lian birds, in Gk. myth., 1615.

Sty'rene. An aromatic hydrocarbon, vinyl benzene, base of many polymers used in plastics mfr. for moulded coloured articles, insulation, dentures, paint-like coatings, synthetic rubber ; 2627.

Styria (stir′-i-a). Mountainous dist. in S.E. Austria and N.W. Yugoslavia ; formerly Austrian crown-land ; a. 8,600 sq. m. ; forests, valuable minerals (iron).

Styx (stiks), in Gk. myth., r. over which dead were ferried ; and Achilles, 19.

Suakin (soo-ah′-kin). Port in Anglo-Eg. Sudan, on Red Sea ; pop. 8,000 ; partly built upon a coral islet and partly on the mainland.

Subcon'sciousness. A state of mental activity unaccompanied by consciousness, e.g., in dreams ; activity in memory, 2139.

Sub'ject, of a sentence, 1494, 2920.

Subjunc'tive mood, 3314.

Sublima'tion, of camphor, 674.

Sublimed sulphur, 3116.

Sublime Porte, The ; Turkish govt., so called from high gate of building containing state dept. offices.

Sub-machine gun, *249*.

Submarine, 3104 2296 ; Fulton's experiments, 1407 ; greatest depth reached, *89* ; influence on naval warfare, 473 ; periscope, 2551, *2553* ; torpedoes, *3226* ; World Wars, 3411, 3417, 3419, 291.

Submarine cables, 640.

Subor'dinate conjunctions, 891.

Subotica (soo-bō′-ti-kah) or **Maria-Theresiopel,** city of Yugoslavia ; pop. 100,000 ; agric. and mfg. centre.

Subpoena (su-pē′-na) (Latin, " under penalty "). A judicial writ requiring a person to appear at a certain time and place ; commonly used to compel attendance of witnesses at court trials ; penalty imposed for failure to comply.

Sub rosa (Lat.), privately, in confidence ; origin of phrase, 2827.

Sub-species. *See* **Biology.**

Substantive. *See* **Noun.**

Substitution, in organic chemistry, 3687.

Subtrac'tion, 3107 ; in algebra, 112, 113 ; of decimals, 982 ; of fractions, 1356, 1357.

Subway. *See* **Tunnel.**

Succes'sion, Act of (1701), in Eng. history, a law providing that the crown should pass, after Queen Anne's death without heirs, to the nearest Protestant branch of the Stuart family.

Suchow. Same as **Soochow.**

Suckling, Sir John (1609–42), Eng. " cavalier poet," whose gay, charming lyrics are full of oft-quoted lines, especially the " Ballade upon a Wedding," 1211.

Sucre (soo′-krā), **Antonio José de** (1793–1830). S. Amer. soldier, who served under Bolivar ; first pres. of Bolivia (1826–28) ; drove Spanish from Upper Peru (Bolivia) in 1824, in brilliant battle of Ayacucho.

Sucre. Nominal cap. of Bolivia ; pop. 30,000 ; on high Andean plateau in s.-cent. part ; formerly called Ciudad de la Plata, it became Sucre upon declaration of independence (1825) ; 491.

Su'crose. Cane or beet sugar ; it differs from fructose and maltose in structure of molecule, 3114, 3687.

Suction pump, 90, 2702, *2703*.

Sudan or **Soudan** (soo-dahn′). A vast region (over 2,000,000 sq. m.) in cent. Africa, between Sahara Desert and Congo basin ; pop. between 30 and 40 millions ; **3109** ; 70, *map, plate f. 68* ; natives, 70, 801.

Sudan, Anglo-Egyptian. African territory under joint Brit. and Egypt. control ; a. 969,000 sq. m. ; pop. 7,547,500 ; *1855,* 3110, *maps, plate f. 68*, *1096* ; Gordon in, 1487 ; Kitchener, 1862 ; in 2nd World War, 3418.

Sudan, French. French Overseas Territory, W. Africa ; includes w. part of Sudan ; a. 360,330 sq. m. ; pop. 3,778,370 ; 3367 ; *map, 3366*.

Sudan grass. A hay grass found valuable in semi-arid regions ; it has no perennial root-stock ; it is treated as an annual, but it becomes a perennial in frostless regions ; in the island of Hawaii it has been found the most valuable grass ever introduced.

Sudbury, Ontario. Tn. 30 m. N. of Georgian Bay ; pop. 32,200 ; smelters, planing mills, machine shops, large creosoting plant, govt. school of mines, Jesuit College ; nickel deposits, 2366, 2435.

Sudd. Floating weed, etc., forming barrier on Nile. Also temporary dam, *959*.

Sudermann (zōō'-der-mahn), **Hermann** (1857–1928), Ger. dramatist and novelist, 1457.

Sudeten Germans. Germans inhabiting the Sudeten mt. region of Czechoslovakia who in 1938–39 demanded national recognition and full autonomy ; the Munich agreement, 3416, gave the area to Germany. In 1945, after Germany's defeat, the Czechs recovered the area and expelled the Sudeten Gers. into S. Germany.

Sudeten Mts., range along N.E. border of Moravia and Bohemia ; *map, 320.*

Su'dras. Hindu caste, 1626, 1707.

Sue, Eugène (1804–57). Fr. novelist, popular and sensational (" The Wandering Jew " ; " The Mysteries of Paris ").

Suède (swäd) **leather,** 1914 ; gloves, 1477.

Suetonius (swē-tō'-ni-us) **Tranquillus, Caius,** Rom. historian, 1897.

Suevi (swē'-vī) or **Suebi.** Anc. Germanic people, 1237, 3033.

Suez (soo'-ez), Egypt. Port on Red Sea at S. end of Suez Canal ; pop. 108,250 ; 3110.

Suez Canal. Connecting Mediterranean and Red Sea, 3110, 686, 689, 996, *1103*, 2758, 2829 ; Gt. Brit. obtains control, 1019, 3279 ; World Wars, 3111, 3410.

Suf'fixes, in Eng., 1209.

Suffoca'tion. 1420.

Suffolk (suf'-ok). Eng. co. on E. coast ; a. 1,482 sq. m. : pop. 416,000 : divided for administrative purposes into E. and W. Suffolk ; *1311*, **3111.**

Suffolk Punch. Breed of horse, 1647.

Suffrage. *See* **Parliament ; Government ; Vote.**

Sufi (sōō'-fē) **dynasty,** Persia, 2555.

Sugar, 3112 ; chemistry of sugars, 3114, 3687 ; contains carbon, 699 ; Cuba, 941 ; digestion, 1220 ; fermentation, 103 ; as food, 1338, 3112 ; in food preservation, 1341 ; formed by leaves, 1915, 2589 ; glucose a substitute, 1477 ; in raisins, 2742 ; introduced into Europe, 937 ; ion exchange process, 3351 ; ionization experiment, 1738 ; Jamaica, 1792 ; maple, 2092 ; minimum which taste can detect, 3158 ; and polarized light, 3114 ; refining, *3115* ; resembles starch, 3082 ; saccharine a substitute, 3116 ; centres of production, 3112 ; Barbados, **360** ; Bolivia, **491** ; Brazil, 551 ; Cuba, 941 ; Hawaiian Isls., 1587 ; India, 1708 ; Puerto Rico, 2698. *See also* **Sugar Beet.**

Sugar beet, 396, *397*, 3114, *3115*.

Sugar cane, cultivation and preparation, 3112, *3113*, 2717.

Sugar Loaf, Rio de Janeiro, *2780*.

Sugar maple, 2092.

Suggia (soo'-ja), **Guilhermina** (b. 1888). Portuguese musician ; world reputation as 'cellist ; painted by Augustus John (1921).

Suite (swēt), in music, 2264.

Sukkur, on the Indus ; Lloyd barrage at, *960*, *plate f. 961*, 1721, 2974.

Suleiman. Same as **Solyman.**

Sul'la, Lucius Cornelius (138–78 B.C.). Rom. general ; conquered Mithridates (84) ; died as dictator, extinguishing Marian party in cruel proscriptions ; 2809.

Sullivan, Sir Arthur Seymour (1842–1900). Eng. composer of both popular and artistic standing ; develops comic opera, **1463,** 2436.

Sullivan, John Lawrence (1858–1918). American pugilist. In 1889 won heavy-weight championship of world by defeating Jake Kilrain in 75 rounds. Beaten by Jim Corbett (1892).

Sully, Maximilien de Béthune, Duc de (sū'lē), (1560–1641). Fr. statesman and financier, great minister of Henry IV, 1613.

Sully-Prudhomme (sū-lē-prü-dom), **René François Armand** (1839–1907). Fr. poet. Awarded Nobel Prize for Literature (1901). Works include " Les Solitudes " ; " Vaines Tendresses " ; " Le Bonheur."

Sulpha Drugs. Series of drugs, bacteriostatic in action, derivatives of sulphonamide ; include sulphapyridine (M & B 693), sulphanilamide, sulphacetamide, sulphathiazole, etc. ; **3116,** 179, 2132 ; in lung diseases, 2040.

Sulphate (sul'-fāt). A salt of sulphuric acid ; of aluminium, and potassium (alum), 3117 ; of ammonia as fertilizer, 146 ; of calcium (gypsum), 1559 ; copper (blue vitriol), 3116 ; iron (green vitriol or copperas), 1724, 3116 ; sodium thiosulphate, 3116, 2997 ; sodium sulphate, 2997 ; sulphate process, in paper-making, 2497.

Sulphide. A compound of sulphur with an element or another compound ; of iron, 3686 ; of lead, 3117.

Sulphite. A salt of sulphurous acid ; sulphite process in paper-making, 2497.

Sulphur (S). Non-metallic element of the oxygen group ; atomic weight 32·06 ; occurs in three allotropic forms ; melts at 235° F. ; **3116** ; essential to plant growth, 2998 ; fumes, poisonous, 2638, 3328 ; in gunpowder, 1558 ; in Japan, 1798 ; in rubber mfr., 2836 ; in Russia, 2845 ; in volcanoes, 3328 ; from Mt. Etna, 1229 ; properties, 776, 3116. *See in Index* **Disulphide ; Sulphate ; Sulphide ; Sulphite ; Sulphuric acid ; Sulphurous acid.**

Sulphur dioxide, 3116 ; in beet sugar refining, 3114 ; in food preservation, 1340 ; in heat pump, 1600 ; liquefaction, 1419 ; in refrigerator, *1392* ; and discovery of thallium, 3193.

Sulphuretted hydrogen, 3116.

Sulphuric acid, 3117, 20 ; in making nitric acid, 2372 ; in Le Blanc soda process, 2997 ; in matches, 2119 ; in rayon mfr., 2748.

Sulphurous acid. An unstable compound decomposing readily into sulphur dioxide and water ; in making isinglass, 1426.

Sultan. Mahomedan sovereign, 3266.

Sultana (sul-tah'-na) **raisins,** 2743.

Sulu (sōō-lōō) or **Jolo Islands.** Group of isls. forming S.W. portion of Philippine Archipelago ; *map, 1074* ; Moros in, 2568 ; pearl fisheries, 2534.

Sumach (sū-mak). Any of several small trees or shrubs with feathery leaves, of the genus *Rhus* ; leaves used in tanning, 1914 ; poisonous, 2638.

Sumatra (soo-mah'-tra). Indonesia. 6th largest isl. in world and 3rd largest isl. of Malay Archipelago ; a. 165,000 sq. m. ; pop. 8,000,000 ; **3117,** 1076, *map, 1074* ; coffee, 864 ; orang-utan, 2445 ; rubber, 2833 ; occupied by Japan 1942–45, 2473, 3118, 3420.

Sumer (sū'-mer). Anc. name of Babylonia, used in cuneiform inscriptions together with "Akkad," each probably referring to whole country.

Sumerians. Predecessors of Babylonians in Tigris-Euphrates valley, 329, 2146 ; cuneiform writing, 328, *331* ; eagle symbol, 1063 ; engraved seals, 1427.

Summer. Second season of the year, 2914 ; solstice, 1221, 2914.

Summer Time Act (1916 and 1925). Brit. Act of Parl. by which official time is advanced one hour at 2 o'clock G.M.T. in the morning of the day following the third Saturday in April or, if that day is Easter Day, the day following the second Saturday, and put back to Greenwich mean time at 2 o'clock in the morning of the day next following one of the Saturdays in October (November in 1947). Double Summer Time was in operation in 1940–47. *See* p. 980.

Summerskill, Edith C. (b. 1901). Brit. politician ; on Middx. County Council (1931–41) ; parl. sec. Min. of Food (1945–50) ; became Min. of National Insurance in 1950.

Sumner, Charles (1811–74). Amer. statesman ; a strong supporter of anti-slavery and for some time a vehement opponent of the policy of Grant.

Sumter, Fort. *See* **Fort Sumter.**

Sun, 3118, 278, 280, 1942 ; a id aurora borealis, 304, *305* ; Copernican theory, 905 ; diameter, 278 ; eclipse, *plates f. 1076, 1077, 1078* ; energy

from, 1161 ; heat given off, 1594 ; halo round, *plate f. 2740* ; hydrogen in, 1673 ; influence on earth, 1067, 1594 ; latitude determined by, 1898 ; light analysed by spectroscope, 3055, *plate f. 3057* ; time of light to reach earth, 1939 ; midnight sun, 2168, 2392, 2394, 3128 ; from the moon, *plate f. 2224* ; motor, 1594, 3119 ; necessary for life, 432 ; origin of, 2619 ; photographing, 2411 ; in photo-synthesis, 2589 ; power from, 1594 ; recording sunshine, *1595* ; size, *280* ; source of light, 1942 ; temperature, 1594 ; and tides, 3209, 3210 ; source of all energy, 1161 ; passage through zodiac, 3444 ; sun-spots, *plates f. 3120, 3121.*

Sun and planet gear. An epicyclic system of gears revolving within a large outer gearwheel ; invented and used by James Watt in 1781, 3086 ; now used in certain makes of car gear boxes and in bicycle two-speeds.

Sun-animalcule, a protozoon, 2695.

Sun'da Islands. Group in E. Indies extending from Malay Peninsula to the Moluccas ; includes Sumatra, Java, Borneo, Celebes, and smaller isls. near.

Sundanese. Division of Malayan race, 1813.

Sunda Strait. Between Sumatra and Java, *map, 1074.*

Sunday. First day of the week, the Christian Sabbath ; meaning of name, 980.

Sunday schools, founded, 2883.

" Sunday Times," Sunday newspaper, founded 1822 ; owned by Allied Newspapers, Ltd. ; Lord Kemsley editor-in-chief, 675.

Sunderbans or **Sundarbans.** Region of Bengal, India and Pakistan ; S. part of Ganges-Brahmaputra delta ; jungle-covered and malarial ; 2479.

Sun'derland. Spt. on N.E. coast at mouth of Wear ; pop. 178,500 ; great coal-shipping port ; shipbuilding, 1059.

Sundew. A carnivorous plant found in most parts of the world, usually in marshy or boggy ground, **3120.**

Sundial. Device for measuring time, 843 ; invented by Babylonians, 843.

Sun-fish, 3120.

Sunflower. A large plant of the aster family, **3120** ; structure of flowers, 1322.

Sungari. R. of Manchuria, tributary of the Amur. ; 800 m. long ; *map, 2086* ; Harbin on, 2087.

Sung (soong) **dynasty** (960–1280). One of the great Chinese dynasties under which arts and letters flourished.

Su'nium. Promontory of S.E. Attica, Greece ; modern Cape Colonna.

Sun or **solar motor,** 3119.

Sun'nites. Members of the orthodox Mahomedan sect, predominating in Arabia and Turkey, 2067.

Sunspots, 306, *plates f. 3120, 3121.*

Sun Yat-sen (1867–1925). Chinese revolutionary leader ; chosen provisional pres. of Chinese Republic (1911) ; resigned 1912 in favour of Yuan Shih-kai ; elected pres. 1921 by Southern Parl. and led military campaign against Peking, *813* ; tomb, Nanking, *2273*.

Superb bird of paradise, 2511.

Supercharger. Device, in the form of a rotary pump fitted to motor-car and aircraft engines, for increasing the cylinder charge beyond that normally taken in at existing atmospheric pressure, 1736.

Super-conductor, of elec., 1391, 1594.

Superheater, in steam engines, *489*, 1981.

Superheterodyne, in wireless, 3395.

Superior, Wisconsin, U.S.A. One of two most westerly ports of Great Lakes, at head of L. Superior, opposite Duluth, Minnesota ; pop. 35,100 ; three connecting harbours, *1515*, *map.*

Superior, Lake. Most northern of Great Lakes of N. Amer. ; largest body of fresh water in the world ; a. 31,800 sq. m., 1885, 3287, *map, 1515*, 1516

Superphosphate, of calcium, 655.

Supersonic speed, greater than the speed of sound, 1828.

Super-steel. An alloy, 122.

Superstitions, 2059 ; comets, 880 ; eclipse, 1077 ; horoscopes, 3444 ; mistletoe, 2194 ; Pacific islanders, 2471 ; petrel, 2563 ; Red Indian, 2756 ; snakes, 2991 ; *See also* **Fairy ; Folklore ; Magic.**

Suprare′nal gland, above kidney, 1471.

Supremacy, Acts of, 819.

Supreme Council. Allied councils convened during and following both World Wars ; existed for the purpose of promoting united action and co-operation upon agreed points.

Supreme Court. In U.S.A., duties defined by Constitution, 3290.

Supreme Court of Judicature. Principal law court of Eng. and Wales, comprising the High Court of Justice, which consists of several divisions, and the Court of Appeal, 922, 1490.

Suppressor, of radio and television interference, 3397.

Sur. Syrian tn. ; pop. 5,000 ; 2573.

Surabaya (soo-ra-bah′ya) or **Soerabaya.** Largest city of Java, naval base of Indonesia ; pop. 250,000. In Japanese hands 1942–45 ; heavily raided by Allies from the air in 1943 and 1944.

Suraj-ud-Dowlah (soo-rahj′-ood-dow-lah) (*c.* 1732–57), Nawab of Bengal, who perpetrated the Black Hole massacre, 660, *661,* 842.

Surat (soo-raht′). Rep. of India. Spt. 160 m. N. of Bombay ; pop. 171,443 ; trade centre 16th to 18th cents.

Surcouf. Giant Fr. submarine, 350 ft. long, displacing at surface nearly 3,000 tons, submerging for 60 hrs. ; entered service in 1934 ; at fall of Fr., June 1940, taken by Brit. ; in Apr. 1942 reported lost by Free Fr.

Surface, Joseph. In Sheridan's " School for Scandal," an artful, malicious hypocrite ; brother of Charles, and nephew of Sir Oliver Surface.

Surface tension, 3121 ; in colloids, 871 ; and detergents, 998.

Surf-bird. A plover-like shore bird, found on the Pacific coast of Amer.

Surf-riding, *1585.*

Surgeons, Royal College of, founded 1460 ; exists for the advancement of surgical knowledge ; grants the diplomas of M.R.C.S. and F.R.C.S.

Sur′gery. *See* **Medicine** and **Surgery.**

Surgery, plant, 1401, 1402, 3246.

Surinam′. *See* **Dutch Guiana.**

Surinam toad, 3219.

Surnames, origin, 2272.

Surrealism, in art and literature, **3122.**

Surren′tum. *See* **Sorrento.**

Sur′rey, Henry Howard, Earl of (*c.* 1517–47). Eng. poet, soldier, and courtier who introduced blank verse into Eng., and, with Wyatt, the sonnet ; beheaded on trumped-up charge of treason.

Surrey, Thomas Howard, Earl of (1443–1524). Eng. soldier ; at battle of Flodden, 1315.

Surrey. Agricultural and residential co. in S.E. Eng. bordered on N. by Thames and adjoining London ; a. 722 sq. m. ; pop. 1,180,900 ; **3122.**

Surrey Commercial Docks, London, 3193, 3194.

Sur′tees, Robert (1779–1834). Eng. antiquary and topographer ; his chief work, " History of Durham " deals with the place of his birth ; he contributed to Scott's " Border Minstrelsy " two original ballads of his own.

Surtees, Robert Smith (1803–64). Eng. novelist ; at one time a solicitor, he made a great success with his sporting novels " Jorrocks's Jaunts and Jollities," " Handley Cross," and " Ask Mamma."

Surveying : maps and mapping, 2093, 2094 ; ocean bed, 2414 ; pendulums to determine latitude and altitude, 2543.

" Survival of the fittest," in biology, 1245, 1246 ; birth of Darwin's idea, 977. *See* **" Struggle for existence."**

Sus (soos). A genus of pig-like animals ; domestic hogs, 2605 ; wild boars, 480.

Su′sa. Anc. city (Biblical Shushan) of Persia near Shuster ; excavations

of ruins have revealed interesting objects ; taken by Alexander, 106.

Susa, now **Sousse.** Spt. in Tunis ; pop. (1936) 28,400 ; 3254.

Susiana. *See* **Elam.**

Suspension, of solids in liquids or gases, 3689 ; colloidal, 871.

Suspen′sion bridges, *567,* 568 ; mechanics of, 2127, *2128.*

Susquehanna (sus-kwe-han′-a), r. of U.S.A., rising in L. Otsego, N.Y., and flowing 500 m. s. through Pennsylvania to Chesapeake Bay.

Sus′sex. A co. in S.E. Eng. on the Eng. Channel ; a. 1,457 sq. m. ; pop. 769,900 ; **3123** ; historic interest, 1168 ; tannery in *1911, 1912.*

Sut′cliffe, Halliwell (1870–1932). Eng. novelist ; all his best work deals with the moors and fells and the people of Yorkshire (" A Man of the Moors " ; " Ricroft of Withens " ; " Under the White Cockade " ; " A Bachelor in Arcady ").

Sutcliffe, Herbert William (b. 1894). Eng. cricketer ; great opening batsman for Yorkshire and England, who set up several records in partnership with Hobbs, P. Holmes, etc.

Sutherlandshire, Scot. marit. co., bounded by Moray Firth on the S.E. and by the Atlantic on the N. and W. ; a. 2,028 sq. m. ; pop. 14,400 ; 3123.

Sut′lej or **Satlej,** r. of Pakistan and India ; largest of " five rivers " which give name of Punjab ; rises in Tibet and flows 1,000 m. to Indus ; 2479, *map, 1702.*

Su′tras, Hindu poems, 1713.

Su′tro, Alfred (1863–1933). Brit. author and dramatist ; his plays include " The Walls of Jericho " and " John Glayde's Honour " ; also published translations of works by Maeterlinck.

Suttee. Indian practice by which widows, especially of high caste Brahmans, burned themselves on their husbands' funeral pyre. Made illegal (1829) but continued to be practised until late 19th cent.

Suttner, Bertha, Baroness von (1843–1914). Secretary to Alfred Nobel before becoming Austrian author ; awarded in 1905 Nobel prize for promotion of world peace.

Sutton Coldfield. Tn. in Warwickshire, 8 m. N.E. of Birmingham ; pop. 46,226 ; television station, 3341.

Suva (soō-va), cap. of Fiji Isls., 1272.

Suwanee (soo-wah′-nē) **River,** stream in U.S.A., flowing from S. Georgia to Gulf of Mexico ; the " Swanee River " of " The Old Folks at Home."

Svalbard. Geog. term for Norway's northern colonial possessions. *See* **Spitsbergen.**

Svealand (svä′-a-land), prov. of Sweden, 3126.

Svengali (sven-gah′-li). In Du Maurier's novel, " Trilby," a sinister Jew who hypnotizes Trilby and makes her a great singer.

Sverdlovsk, formerly **Ekaterinburg** ; pop. 425,500 ; mining centre of U.S.S.R. on R. Iset at E. foot of Ural Mts. ; contested between Bolshevists and anti-Bolshevists in 1918–19 ; place of imprisonment and execution of Tsar Nicholas II and family ; 2849.

Swabia. Medieval duchy of S.W. Ger. ; flourished under Hohenstaufens ; disintegrated into small states in 1268 ; great Swabian League for mutual protection (1488–1534) ; now name of Bavarian prov.; 1445, 1449 ; Peasants' War, 1449.

Swahili (swah-hē′-li). An African people of Bantu stock, with some mixture of Semites ; they are Mahomedans and are noted as traders ; number less than 1,000,000.

Swale. Eng. r. rising on border of Westmorland and flowing 60 m. through N. Riding of Yorkshire to join the Ure.

Swallows and **Martins.** Long-winged, fork-tailed birds of family *Hirundinidae,* **3124** ; migration, 440.

Swallow, sea. Same as **Tern.**

Swallow-tail butterfly, *plate f. 632* ; caterpillar, *720.*

Swamp. Low land saturated with water; dried by eucalyptus trees, 1230.

Swan, goose-like bird, **3125** ; and cygnets, *449.*

Swan, Sir Joseph (1828–1917). Brit. inventor of carbon process (photog.), carbon filament elec. lamp, 1134 ; and of rayon, 2748.

Swanage. Tn. of Dorset ; pop. 6,276.

Swan River, W. Australia. A short r. rising as the Avon ; flows N.W. entering Indian Ocean 12 m. below Perth ; gave name to first colonial settlement in W. Australia, founded in 1829 ; 3368.

Swansea. Important pt. in S. Wales, on Bristol Channel ; pop. 158,800 ; copper-smelting centre, tin-plate trade ; **3126,** 1470, 3333.

Swan-upping, *3125.*

Swarming, of bees, *391* ; of locusts, 1511, 1512, *plate f. 1512.*

Swastika, ancient sign of good luck, adopted as symbol of Ger. (Nazi) govt.

Swatow. Treaty port in prov. of Kwangtung, S.E. China, on Han r. near mouth ; pop. 119,168 ; exports sugar.

Swaziland (swah′-zi-land). Brit. protectorate in S. Africa at S.E. corner of Transvaal ; a. 6,705 sq. m. ; pop. 186,880 ; exports tin ; cap. Mbabane ; 3016.

Sweat gland, 2979.

Sweden. Country of N. Europe occupying the E. part of Scandinavian peninsula ; a. 173,000 sq. m. ; pop. 6,842,000 ; **3126,** 2880 ; *map, 2395* ; agric., 3131 ; cap. Stockholm, 3092 ; climate, 3126 ; costume, 3126, *plates f. 3128, 3129* ; education, 3131, 3093 ; fisheries, 3129, 1299 ; foreign trade, 1753, 3129 ; forests and forest products, 3129 ; language and literature, 2880 ; manufactures, 3093, 3129 ; merchant marine, 3126 ; minerals, 3129 ; money, *2203* ; physical features, 3126, 1234. History, 3131 ; Northmen, 2387 ; Finland conquered, 1277 ; Union of Kalmar, 992 ; Gustavus Adolphus, *1558,* 3202 ; in 17th cent., 1239 ; Charles XII and War with Russia, 2563 ; in Seven Years' War, 2924 ; union with Norway dissolved, 2398 ; 2nd World War, 3131.

RULERS OF SWEDEN (FROM 1523)
HOUSE OF VASA

1523–60	Gustavus I, Vasa
1560–69	Eric XIV
1569–92	John III
1592–1604	Sigismund III
1604–11	Charles IX
1611–32	Gustavus II, Adolphus
1632–54	Christina

HOUSE OF PLALZ

1654–60	Charles X
1660–97	Charles XI
1697–1718	Charles XII
1718–20	Ulrica Eleanora

HOUSE OF HESSE

1720–51	Frederick I

HOUSE OF HOLSTEIN-GOTTORP

1751–71	Adolphus Frederick
1771–92	Gustavus III
1792–1809	Gustavus IV
1809–18	Charles XIII

HOUSE OF PONTE CORVO

1818–44	Charles XIV, John
1844–59	Oscar I
1859–72	Charles XV
1872–1907	Oscar II
1907–	Gustavus V

Swedenborg, Emanuel (1688–1772). Swedish scientist, philosopher, mystic and religious leader ; **3131.**

" Swedish Nightingale." *See* **Lind, Jenny.**

Sweep, windmill sail, 3386.

Sweetbread, or pancreas, 1470.

Sweet briar, a wild rose, 2828.

Sweet chestnut, 782, *2408.*

Sweet clover, 854.

Sweet-flag. Same as **Calamus.**

Sweet gum or **liquidambar.** Tree of witch-hazel family ; exudes a resinous gum.

Sweet laurel, 1900.

Sweet pea, *531,* 2530.

Sweet potato. A native perennial herb of S. America, of great food value.

SYMBOLS AND SIGNS IN COMMON USE

Algebra and Arithmetic

+ (plus)   addition, positive
− (minus)   subtraction, negative
±   plus or minus
+ve   positive
−ve   negative
=   equal
≠   not equal
≡   identically equal
×   multiplied by
ab a multiplied by b
b(a + b) $a + b$ multiplied by b
÷   divided by
a/b or $\frac{a}{b}$ a divided by b
%   per cent
‰   per thousand
√   square root
∛   cube root
a^n a multiplied by itself n times
a^{-n} $1/a^n$
∴   therefore
∵   because
∶   divided by
∷   equals, as
∝   is proportional to
→   gives
>   greater than
≯   not greater than
<   less than
≮   not less than
∞   infinity
$\jmath$ factorial

Astronomy

●   new moon   ♃   Jupiter
☽   first quarter   ♄   Saturn
○   full moon   ♅   Uranus
☾ or ☽   last quarter   ♆   Neptune
☉   sun   ☌   conjunction
☿   Mercury   ☍   opposition
♀   Venus   ☊   ascending node
⊕   earth   ☋   descending node
♂   Mars   *See* **Zodiac** *below.*

Biology

♂ or ☉   male
♀   female
♂♀   dioecious
☿ or ⚥   hermaphrodite
×   hybrid
♃   perennial
♄   tree

Chemistry

The use of symbols in chemistry is described in page 3685 and a list of them will be found in page 3786.

Geometry

□   square   ‖   parallel to
□″   square inches   A or a   area
□′   square feet   D or d   diameter
∧ or ∠   angle   H or h   height
∠rt   right angle   L or l   length
△   triangle   R or r   radius
⊙   circle   V or v   volume
                            π (pi)   *See* **Trigonometry**

Morse

The signs used in the Morse Code are depicted in page 3166.

Music

clefs

Treble or Soprano

Middle C

Bass

single bar   double bars

method of indicating various rhythms

$\frac{2}{4}$ $\frac{3}{4}$ $\frac{4}{4}$ or ($\mathbb{C}$) $\frac{6}{8}$

note values and their equivalent rest signs each half the value of that on its left

Breve	Semibreve	Minim	Crotchet	Quaver	Semiquaver	Demisemiquaver

♭   flat   ♭♭   double flat

♯   sharp   ×   double sharp

♮ (♮♯, ♮♭)   natural (and natural of double sharps and double flats)

⌒   pause   slur

∧ V or >   sforzando

crescendo   decrescendo

repeat

stave

4004

SYMBOLS AND SIGNS (contd.)

Pharmacy

℔	pound
℥	ounce
℥i or ℥j	one ounce
℥ij	two ounces
℥iss or ℥jss	one ounce and a half
f ℥	fluid ounce
ʒ	drachm
ʒi or ʒj	one drachm
℈	scruple
℈ i	one scruple
O	pint
♏	minim
Ṁ	mix
℞	recipe

Physics

Å	Angström unit
A	ampere
a	acceleration
c	velocity of light
d	distance
E	electro-motive force
F	force
f (or ∼)	frequency
g	force of gravity
h	height
I	current
kW	kilowatt
kWh	kilowatt hour
kc/s	kilocycles per second
l	length
m	mass
P	power, pressure
R	resistance
s	speed
t	time (seconds), temperature (°C)
V	volt, velocity, volume
v	velocity
W	watt
Wh	watt hour
λ (lambda)	wavelength
ω (omega)	ohm
Ω (omega)	megohm
⊣⊢	one cell
⊣ ⎮⎮⊦----⊣ ⊢	battery of cells
+ −	positive, negative poles, etc.

See also lists of **Electrical Terms in Common use; Terms used in Wireless and Television.**

Punctuation, etc.

@	at	/	fraction line
&	and (ampersand)	.	full stop (point)
'	apostrophe	-	hyphen
{ }	braces	( )	parentheses
[ ]	brackets	%	percentage
:	colon	£	pound (sterling)
,	comma	?	question mark
. . . .	ellipsis	" "	quotation marks
* * * *	ellipsis	;	semi-colon
!	exclamation mark	₨	rupee
		$	dollar

Reference Marks

Footnotes are referred to by small numbers or the following signs in order, and then repeated in duplicate:

*	asterisk
†	dagger or obelisk
‡	double obelisk
§	section mark
‖	parallel mark
¶	blind P or paragraph mark
**	
††	
☞	fist

Trigonometry

°	degrees
′	minutes
″	seconds
π (pi)	ratio of circumference of circle to diameter = 3.14159265

Zodiac

♈	Aries (ram)
♉	Taurus (bull)
♊	Gemini (twins)
♋	Cancer (crab)
♌	Leo (lion)
♍	Virgo (virgin)
♎	Libra (scales)
♏	Scorpio (scorpion)
♐	Sagittarius (archer)
♑	Capricornus (goat)
♒	Aquarius (water carrier)
♓	Pisces (fishes)

See also page 3444.

Sword of Damocles, 963.

Syb'aris. Anc. city of S. It., proverbial for luxury (hence " sybarite "), destroyed 510 B.C.

Sybrita, city of Crete ; money, *2202.*

Sycamore (sik'-*a*-mor). A very hardy and quick-growing tree, **3143,** 2092.

Syd'enham, Thomas (1624–89). Eng. physician ; served in the Civil War with the Parl. forces ; began to practise in London in 1660, and introduced a new method of treating smallpox ; published " Methodus Curandi Febres" in 1666 (augmented as " Observationes Medicae " in 1676) ; the Sydenham Society was named after him.

Syd'ney, N.S.W. Largest city of Australia ; pop. 1,484,000 ; **3144,** 307, 567, 2344; harbour, *1576;* university, 2344.

Sydney, Nova Scotia. Chief port of Cape Breton Isl. ; pop. 28,305 ; 695.

Sydney, North, Nova Scotia, headquarters of fishing fleet, pop. 6,836.

Syene. *See* **Assuan.**

Sykes, Sir Percy Molesworth (1867–1945). Brit. administrator. Authority on Persian history and culture. Wrote " Ten Thousand Miles in Persia " ; " History of Persia."

Sylhet. Dist. and tn. of E. Bengal, Pakistan ; a. 5,478 sq. m. ; pop. (dist.) 3,116,000 ; (tn.) 19,000 ; rice ; tea, 2479.

Sylt. Ger. isl. of N. Frisian group, off Slesvig, in N. Sea ; a narrow bank, 22 m. long and less than 1 m. wide except in centre ; occupied by Brit., May 11, 1945.

Sylves'ter (Silvester) II, Pope (999–1003) ; tutor to Otto III, 2460.

Sylviidae (sil-vī'-dē). Bird family which comprises the warblers.

Symbiosis (sim-bĭ-ō'-sis), in biology. Partnership between dissimilar plants or animals, 2374, 1932, 2514.

Symbol. A visible thing which represents an invisible object, or a whole idea ; all religions use symbols extensively ; use of in chemistry, 767. *See also* **Elements** and page 3685.

Symbolists. School of Fr. poets of late 19th cent., in reaction against classical Parnassian school ; leaders Mallarmé, Rimbaud.

Symington, William (1763–1831). Scottish engineer, inventor of marine steam-engine.

Symonds (sim'-ondz), **John Addington** (1840–93). Eng. critic, author of the monumental " History of the Renaissance in Italy."

Symons, Arthur (1865–1945). Eng. critic and poet ; greatly influenced by Fr. literature, especially the Symbolist School (" The Symbolist Movement in Literature" ; " Studies in Seven Arts ").

Sympathetic or **Invisible ink,** 858, 1724.

Sympathetic nerves, 1593, 2317.

Sympet'alous flowers. Flowers having united petals ; term used in botany.

Symphony. Musical composition, 2264 ; Beethoven develops, 397.

Syncar'pous flowers. Flowers whose pistils are joined together.

Synchronous motor (elec.), 2240, 3215.

Synchrotron. A modification of the cyclotron, 950, used to accelerate protons or electrons in atomic bombardment.

Syn'cline. A fold of rock with the point down.

Syn'dicalism. A labour movement closely allied to trade unionism.

Syn'dicate, in finance. A body of persons which meets to discuss and carry out some business enterprise.

Synge (sing), **John Millington** (1871–1909). Irish playwright, 1751 ; chief plays, " Riders to the Sea," " The Playboy of the Western World."

" Synnöve Solbakken," novel by Björnson, 462.

Synod, in Ch. of Scotland, 2894.

Synod'ic or **lunar month,** 2223.

Synthesis, in chemistry. The building up of a compound from its elements, or other compounds ; as opposed to analysis, 766.

Synthetic Products. Artificially made compounds, e.g. camphor made from turpentine, 674 ; from coal-tar, 857 ; drugs, 1048 ; dyes, 1059 ; gems, 1427 ;

indigo, 1718 ; perfumes, 2550 ; plastic materials, 739, 857, 2625 ; rayon, 2748 ; rubber, 2838 ; waxes, 3359.

Syracuse (sĭr'-*a*-kus). City on S.E. coast of Sicily, 2968 ; founded 734 B.C. ; Etruscan fleet, 2805 ; Athenian expedition (415–413 B.C.), 1524 ; Pyrrhus, 2710 ; taken by Rome (212 B.C.) ; modern city pop. 53,000 ; old coin, *2202.* Occupied by British, July 1943.

Syr-Darya (sir-dah'-ri-*a*). A great r. (anc. Jaxartes) of cent. Asia, flowing 1,500 m. from Tien-Shan range to Sea of Aral ; much used for irrigation.

Syria (si'-ri-*a*). State of w. Asia bordering the Mediterranean ; a. 66,046 sq. m. : pop. 3.006.000 : established in 1920 under Fr. mandate, became independent in 1946 ; **3144** ; *map, 3145;* Aleppo, *3145;* children, 801; cap. Damascus, *961;* Palmyra, 2485; rugmaking, 705 ; people, 3145 ; tobacco, 3221. *History* : general sketch, 3145; chief events summarized, *see chart* under **History** ; early history, 271, 329, 331 ; Phoenicians in, 2573 ; relations with Judea, 1830 ; Crusades, 936 ; Saladin, 2864 ; World Wars, 3145, 3414, 3418. *See also* **Palestine.**

Syrian Desert, 996.

Syringa (si-ring'-ga). Bot. name for lilac genus of shrubs of family *Oleaceae,* containing the garden lilacs, 1947.

Syringa or **mock-orange.** A shrub of the saxifrage family, not a lilac.

Syrinx (si'-ringks), in Gk. myth., maiden loved by Pan, 2485.

Syrinx. The vocal structure in singing birds, 441.

Systematic zoology, 3447.

Szechwan (sā-chwahn'). Prov. of W. China ; a. 166,000 sq. m. ; pop. 45,845,800 ; cap. Chengtu ; cereals sugar, tobacco, silk, coal, iron, salt.

Szegedin (se'-ge-dĕn) or **Szeg'ed.** The 2nd city of Hungary ; commercial centre on r. Theiss 100 m. S.E. of Budapest ; pop. 136,700 ; captured by Russians Oct. 1944.

Szeklers (sek'-lerz). A people of Rumania.

Szigetvar. Turks take, *3264.*

THE original form of T in the Egyptian hieroglyphics ⌐ is the picture of a noose or a lasso, Ø or, as some scholars think, that of a tongue. The Phoenicians made it in the form of a cross X + with the four arms of equal length. They and the Hebrews used it as a sign for marking the ownership of animals and for other identification purposes. It is this kind of mark that is probably referred to in Ezekiel ix, 4. The early Greeks moved the horizontal to the top and so made the T we have today. Examine the small form of the letter (t) as it is printed today; notice that the upper left angle of the t-bar is rounded, whilst the right is sharp. This originated in the old manuscripts when the t was not crossed after the vertical had been formed, but the horizontal bar was made first, from right to left, and the vertical stroke added without taking the pen off the paper. In all our small letters the printed follows the written form of the old scribes.

Taal. Volcano on Luzon Isl., Philippines ; crater 7,650 m. across.

Taal. South African Dutch language, also called Afrikaans, 73.

Tab'ard Inn, Southwark, 761.

Tabasco (t*a*-bas'-kō), Mexico. State in N. of Isthmus of Tehuantepec, on Gulf of Mexico ; a. 9,782 sq. m. ; pop. 285,600 ; oil field, 2157. Also name of species of pepper, 2547.

Tabernacle (" tent "). Tent-like portable structure erected by Israelites in wilderness as place of worship ; name later applied to the Temple, and hence to other houses of worship.

Tabernacles, Feast of. Annual autumn harvest festival of the Jews, commemorating dwelling in tents in the wilderness.

Tab'itha. *See* **Dorcas.**

Table Bay. Harbour of Cape Town, S. Africa, *696,* 697, 3016.

Table Mountain, near Cape Town, S. Africa, *696,* 697, 3016, *plate f. 3017.*

Table Tennis, an indoor sport, **3147.**

Tablet tea. Same as **Brick tea,** 3162.

Ta'bor, Mt. (Jebel Et-Tûr). Famous mt. of Palestine ; height 1,840 ft.

Tabriz (tab-rēz'). 2nd city of Iran, in extreme N.W. ; pop. 214,000 ; repeatedly devastated by earthquakes ; commercial importance, 1741.

Tabu (tab-ōō') or **taboo.** Among primitive races, the sacred prohibition of certain acts or the use of certain things, *2058.*

Tacamahac. N. Amer. native name for poplars, especially the balsam poplar (*P. balsamifera*).

Tachometer (t*a*k-om'-i-ter). A form of speed-indicator used in testing petrol and steam engines.

Tacitus (tas'-i-t*u*s), **Cornelius** (*c.* A.D. 55–*c.* 119). Rom. historian, great Latin stylist, concise and epigrammatic, 1897, 1447.

Tack, a small nail, 2271.

Tacking, in sailing, 484.

Tacking, sewing stitch, 2927.

Tacna (tak'-nah). Formerly province of N. Chile, since 1929 province of Peru ; rich nitrate beds ; 805, 2560.

Taco'ma, Washington, U.S.A. 3rd city of state, spt. on Puget Sound ; pop. 109,400 ; mfrs. include flour and foundry, lumber, and machine-shop products.

Tacoma, Mt. *See* **Rainier, Mt.**

Tac'tile papillae, 2980.

Tad'mor. Biblical name for Palmyra, 2485.

Tadpoles. The larval young of amphibians, 1398 ; evolution, *1399,* of salamander, 2864 ; of toads, 3219 ; story : The Tadpole Who Wanted to be a Frog, 3153.

Tadzhikistan. *See* **Tajik Republic.**

Taff, Wales. R. in Glamorganshire, entering the Bristol Channel at Cardiff ; 40 m. long.

Taf'feta. A somewhat general term used for plain, smooth silk with a lustre, or for silk woven in lines so fine as to appear plain woven ; in the 16th cent. it applied to a heavy, costly dress fabric and later to a soft, thin silk.

Taff'rail log, *1997.*

Taft, Robert A. (b. 1889). U.S. politician, son of Pres. W. H. Taft; senator in 1939; in 1940 and 1944 unsuccessful candidate for pres.; Republican and isolationist; influential in passing Taft-Hartley Labour Act against the trade union " closed shop " in 1947.

Taft, William Howard (1857–1930). 27th pres. of U.S.A., for many years a noted lawyer; was Secretary of War in Theodore Roosevelt's cabinet; Pres. U.S.A. 1909–13.

Tagliacozzo (tahl-yah-kot'-sō), It. Small tn. 45 m. N.E. of Rome; Charles of Anjou defeated Conradin of Hohenstaufen (1268).

Tagore (ta-gōr'), **Sir Rabindranath** (1861–1941), Hindu poet, philosopher, and educator, 1713.

Tagua (tah'-gwah), the " vegetable ivory " palm, 1788, 2485; in Ecuador, 1083; made into buttons, 632. *See* **Corozo Nut.**

Ta'gus, largest r. in Spanish peninsula, 550 m. long; flows across Sp., emptying into Atlantic at Lisbon, Portugal, 1962, 2658, 3030; *map, 3030*; Roman bridge, 2818.

Tahiti (tah-hē'-tē) or **Otaheite.** Largest of society Isls. in S. Pacific; a. 600 sq. m.; pop. 23,100; chief tn. Papeete; 2471; Capt. Cook's landing, 899.

Tail, of animals: beaver, 587; birds, 437; fish, 1296; lizards, 1973; mammals, 2076; fat-tailed sheep, 2940.

Tailings, in flour milling, 1320.

Tailor bird. A native of Asia, so named from the way it builds its nest, using its bill as a needle.

Taine (tān), **Hippolyte Adolphe** (1828–93). Fr. literary and art critic, philosopher, and historian; analysed art and literature scientifically as products of race and environment, 1381.

Taiping (tī-ping') **Rebellion,** in China (1850–64), 1487.

Taipoi or **Taipei.** Cap. of Formosa; pop. 340,000; 1352.

Taiwan (tī-wahn'). Same as **Formosa.**

Tajik Socialist Soviet Republic (or **Tajikstan** or **Tadzhik**). In central Asia; a. 55,700 sq. m.; pop. 1,485,900; cap. Stalinabad; 3267, 2849, *map, 2850.*

Taj Mahal (tahzh ma-hahl') (" gem of buildings "). Beautiful tomb of Agra, India, **3147,** *3148*, 77, 1713.

Takla Makan. Desert in cent. Asia, *997, map, plate f. 265,* 264.

Takoradi, Gold Coast spt., 3366.

Taku. China. Strongly fortified spt. guarding approach to Tientsin and Peking; captured by Brit. and Fr. fleets (1860) and by allied troops (1900) during Boxer uprising, 3211.

Talavera de la Reina (tal-ah-vār'-a-dä lah-rā-ē'-na) (Rom. *Coesobriga*). Tn. of cent. Spain on R. Tagus; pop. 14,500; victory of Wellington over French (1809), 3364.

Talbot, Edward Stuart (1844–1934). Eng. divine; bishop of Rochester (1895–1905), of Southwark (1905–11), of Winchester (1911–23).

Talbot, Gilbert (1891–1915). Son of the above, was killed in action in 1915; in his memory Talbot House (Toc H) was founded at Poperinghe.

Talbot, William Henry Fox (1800–1877). Eng. inventor. Shares with Niepce and Daguerre the honour of creating photography; a photograph made by his Calotype process in 1835 is the oldest direct photograph in existence; 2580.

Talc, magnesium silicate, 2181; in rubber mfr., 2836; slates, 2981.

Talca, Chile. Cap. of prov. of Talca on Rio Claro; pop. 56,700; makes blankets.

Talcahuana (tal-kah-wah'-na), Chile. Spt. and naval station on Bay of Concepcion; pop. 41,530; important wheat exporting point.

Talent. An anc. weight and denomination of money: Attic talent equal to about £240; great Rom. talent about £100; small Rom. about £75; Hebraic, Assyrian and Babylonian from £310 to £400.

" Tale of Two Cities." Novel of the Fr. Rev. by Charles Dickens (1859), in which Sidney Carton takes the place of Charles Darnay on the scaffold, while Darnay flees to Eng. with his family.

" Tales from Shakespeare," by Chas. and Mary Lamb, 1966.

" Tales of Hoffman," opera by Offenbach, 2440.

Talien Wan (tah-lē-en' wahn). Bay on E. coast of Liaotung Peninsula, Manchuria; leased to Russia by China (1898); surrendered to Japan (1905); returned to China (1945).

Talisman, 2058.

" Tal'isman, The," novel by Scott, 2777, 2864, 2900.

Tallahas'see, Florida, U.S.A. Cap. of state; pop. 18,100; 1319.

Talleyrand-Périgord (tal'-ä-rahn pā'-rē-gōr), **Prince Charles Maurice de** (1754–1838). Fr. statesman, **3149.**

Tallien (tal'-yan), **Jean Lambert** (1767–1820). Fr. Revolutionist, leading Terrorist; he was chiefly responsible for fall and execution of Robespierre.

Tallinn or **Reval.** Cap. of Estonia S.S.R.; spt. on Gulf of Finland; pop. 146,300; taken by Ger. 1918, 1226; occupied by Gers. 1941–44.

Tallow, 1263.

Tallow tree. Tree of China, India, and other warm countries, having seeds covered with greasy white substance used by Chinese in making candles, soap, etc.; also butter or tallow tree of W. Africa, yielding yellow greasy juice.

Tal'ma, François Joseph (1763–1826). Fr. tragedian; introduced practice of dressing in costume appropriate to time and country of play.

Tal'mud. Body of Jewish law, 1601; accumulation of centuries of study.

Ta'lus. In architecture, the slope or inclination of any work, as of a wall inclined on its face, either by decreasing in thickness towards the summit, or by leaning it against a bank, as a retaining or breast-wall.

Ta'mar. R. flowing between Devon and Cornwall to Eng. Channel; 60 m. long; 911.

Tam'arack. The Amer. larch, 1892.

Tam'arind. A pod-bearing tropical tree, 1401.

Tamarisk, 3149.

Tamatave (tam-a-tah'-vā), Madagascar. Pop. 21,000; meat-preserving plant; rly. to Antananarivo; 2051.

Tamaulipas (tam-ah-ū-lē'-pas), Mexico. State in N.E. on Gulf of Mexico; a. 30,731 sq. m.; pop. 458,800; cap. Ciudad Victoria.

Tambourine (tam'boor-ēn'), 1049, *2267.*

Tambov (tahm-bof'), Rus. Cap. of prov. of same name; pop. 121,300; founded in 1636 as fortress to keep out Tartars; centre of rich agricultural region.

Tamerlane, Timer Leng, or **Tamburlane.** Mongol emperor, 1714, 2206, 3264, 3267.

Tam'ils. A people of India and Ceylon, *plate f. 749,* 749, 1701, 1702, 2069.

" Taming of the Shrew." One of the most popular of Shakespeare's comedies; Petruchio, the hero, tames Katharina, his shrewish wife; first published in 1623.

Tam'many. Political organization of New York City, U.S.A., founded in 1789 by William Mooney, an ex-soldier, as a non-political, patriotic and benevolent secret society; it later became notorious as one of the most powerful political " machines " in the world.

Tammerfors or **Tampere.** Third city of Finland; pop. 87,123; water-power from near-by falls; mfrs. cotton, paper; sawmills and iron mills; locomotive works and shipyards.

Tam'muz. The Babylonian Adonis, for whom women worshippers wept yearly (Ezek. viii. 14).

Tam O'Shanter. In Burns's poem of that name, a drunken, good-natured farmer, who, returning from a night of revelry, surprises a witches' dance and is pursued by them.

Tam'pa, Florida, U.S.A. Commercial city, port, and winter resort on w. coast on inlet of Tampa Bay; pop. 124,470; cigars, naval stores.

Tampere. *See* **Tammerfors.**

Tampico (tam-pē'-kō), Mexico. Spt. on Pánuco near Gulf of Mexico; pop. 84,000; in rich oil region; 2156.

Tamworth. Tn. of Staffordshire on r. Tame; pop. 12,500.

Tana (tah'-nah). R. of Kenya Colony, E. Africa, rising on Mt. Kenya; flows 500 m. S.E. to Indian Ocean; *map, 1073.*

Tan'ager. A bird, **3150.**

Tanagra (tan'-a-gra), Greece. Anc. tn. of Boeotia; 457 B.C. Spartans defeated Athenians; famous necropolis with terra-cotta statuettes (Tanagra figurines).

Tananarivo (tan-an-ar-ē'-vō), Madagascar. Same as **Antananarivo.**

Tancred (tan'-kred) (d. 1112). Norman-Sicilian hero of the First Crusade, subsequently prince of Antioch; nephew of Robert Guiscard, cousin and companion-in-arms of Bohemond; portrayed by Tasso (" Jerusalem· Delivered ") as a brilliant, blameless hero.

Tan'ga. Spt. of Tanganyika Territory, E. Africa; estimated pop. 18,000 (300 white); *map, 1073.*

Tanganyika (tan-gan-ye'-ka), **Lake.** In E.-cent. Africa, one of longest freshwater lakes in the world; **3150,** 69, 2771, *map, 1073*; Livingstone, 1970; Burton, 626.

Tanganyika Territory (formerly Ger. E. Africa). A. 360,000 sq. m.; pop. 5,706,000; mainly Bantus, 3151, *63, map f. 68, map, 1073*; groundnut scheme, 1073; sunflower crop, 3121.

Tan'gent. In geometry, line touching a circle or curve at only one point, 1439; tan. in trigonometry, 3248.

Tangerine'. A kind of orange, 2444.

Tangier (tan-jēr'). International spt. of Morocco, on Strait of Gibraltar; pop. 100,000; **3151.** Occupied by Spain 1940–45, 3040.

Tango. Argentine dance, now very popular in Europe. A derivative of the Habañera, it is a slow dance with a marked rhythm, 967.

Tanjore', India. Literary and religious centre in Madras; pop. 68,702; cap. of anc. Hindu dynasty of Cholas.

Tanker, oil-carrying ship, 2431, 2949.

Tanks. Armoured motor vehicles with mounted guns and caterpillar tractors, **3151,** *242, 243,* 2185, *2794, 3423*; first use, 3410; first used on large scale, 3411; tank-landing craft, 247.

Tan'nenberg. Vil. in E. Prussia; centre of Ger. line in 1st World War battle by which Hindenburg stopped Rus. invasion (1914), 3410.

Tannhäuser (tan-hoi'-zēr). Knight in Ger. legend; opera by Wagner, 2440.

Tannin or **tannic acid.** An amorphous solid acid; in tanning, 1911; from African acacia, 16; from eucalyptus, 1230; in ink, 1724; in oak bark, 2410; oak galls, 2410; pomegranate, 2653; tea, 3160.

Tanning, *1912,* 1913; in Egypt, 1100; gloves, 1477.

Tannu-Tuva (Tuvian People's Republic). Independent republic under Soviet protection to the N.W. of Mongolia; formerly known as Uryankhai; 2204.

Tansy. Tall herb of the aster family with bitter aromatic flavour; used for garnishing and flavouring.

Tan'tah or **Tan'ta,** Egypt. Tn. and rly. centre; pop. 139,800; noted for fairs and Moslem festivals held every 3 years; 1098.

Tan'talite. A tantalum ore, 3152.

Tantalize. Origin of word, 3152.

Tan'talum (Ta). A silvery metallic element of the vanadium group; atomic weight, 180·88; occurs in tantalite and columbite; melts at 5000° F.; **3152**; properties, 777.

Tan'talus. In Gk. myth., **3152**.

Taoism (tow'-izm). A religion originating in China, 8090.

Taormina (tah-ōr-mē'-nah), Sicily. Winter resort on E. coast, 2968.

Taos (tah'-ōs) **Indians.** Pueblo tribe of S.W. U.S.A., 2698.

Tao Te King (" Book of the Way and Virtue "). The sacred book of Taoism written by Lao-Tse.

Tapa (tah'-pah) **cloth,** 2250.

Tapajos (tah-pah-zhōsh'). A r. of Brazil, flows N. 1,040 m. to join Amazon; navigable about 200 m. above its mouth; *map, 551.*

Tape machine, in newspaper office, *2346; 3167.*

Tapestry, 3152, 3191; Bayeux Tapestry, *379, 1196,* 2377; carpets, 705; embroidery, 1152; loom for, *2025.*

Tapeworm. A parasite flatworm, 3425; evolutionary position, 158.

Tapioca, 3153.

Ta'pir. Animal related to rhinoceros and horse, **3154.**

Tapiro pygmies, *2707.*

Tap-root, 2825.

Tar. Dark oily liquid resulting from destructive distillation of wood or coal, **3154**; no melting pt., 1391; coal-tar products, 857; tarred rope, 2826.

Tara, in Co. Meath, Eire, 2125; St. Patrick at, 2529.

Tarantel'la. An Italian dance, 3154.

Taran'to. Spt. of s. It. on Gulf of Taranto; pop. 180,850; large arsenal; oysters; textile mfrs.; 1763, *map, 1764.* Italian fleet attacked by air, Nov. 12, 1940, 3418; on Sept. 9, 1943, British troops landed and it became one of chief Allied bases in Italian campaign.

Taran'tula. Any of several large hairy spiders, **3154,** 3346, 3065.

Tarantula-killer. A wasp, 3346.

Tarapacá (tar-ah-pak-ah'). Maritime prov. of N. Chile, 805, 2560.

Tarascon'. Historic tn. of s.E. Fr. on Rhone; pop. 9,000; Rom. ruins and medieval church and castle.

Tarbes (tahb). Tn. of s.w. Fr.; pop. 44,850; horse-breeding; Wellington defeated French (1814).

Tardieu (tahr'-dyě), **André** (1876–1945). Fr. statesman; High Commissioner to U.S.A. (1917–19); plenipotentiary at Peace Conference (1919–20); Premier in 1929–30, and again in 1932.

Tare. Weight of a vessel, case or other object in which goods are packed; most usually seen on rly. wagons, when it refers to the weight of the wagon without load. Wagon and load together are " gross " weight, load alone is " net " weight.

Taren'tum. Chief anc. Gk. city in s. It.; modern Taranto; 1895, 2710.

Tarifa (tah-rē'-fah), Spain. Spt. on Strait of Gibraltar, southernmost tn. in Europe; pop. 12,100; anchovy and tunny fisheries.

Tar'iff. A list or table of goods giving the rates of customs duty to which they are liable; the term is also applied to the duty itself; and Customs, **944.** *See also* **Free Trade.**

Tarik (d. c. 720). Mahomedan chief, leader of first Moslem invasion of Sp., 1463.

Tarim (tah-rěm'). Chief r. of Chinese Turkistan; flows E. about 1,000 m. into group of lakes and marshes known as Lob Nor, 264; *map, 808.*

Tar'kington, Booth (1869–1946). Amer. novelist (" The Gentleman from Indiana "; " Penrod "; " Monsieur Beaucaire ", " Alice Adams "), 3294.

Tarn, r. of France; *back of pla'es f. 1360, 1361.*

Tarno'pol. Tn. of Ukraine S.S.R.; pop. 30,000; formerly in Austria, later in Poland; suffered from Rus. occupation in 1914–18 War; ceded to Russia in 1945; flour mills, distilleries, breweries.

Tarnow (tahr'-nov). Polish city; farm implements, glass, chicory; occ. by Ger. 1939–44.

Tarpe'ian Rock. Cliff of Capitoline Hill, Rome, from which condemned criminals were thrown.

Tarpon. A large herring-like fish found in the S. Atlantic; it affords good sport to anglers on the coast of Florida.

Tarpon Springs, Florida, U.S.A. Tn. and port of w. coast of Florida; pop. 3,414; sponge fisheries, *3068.*

Tarquin'ii. An anc. Etruscan city, 45 m. N.W. of Rome; site, near modern Corneto Tarquinia, marked by many remains, especially tombs; war with Rome, 2804.

Tarquin'ius Priscus. 5th legendary king of Rome, 2804.

Tarquinius Superbus (" The Proud "). 7th and last legendary king of Rome, 2804, 2967.

Tarragon. A plant with aromatic leaves; belongs to the family *Compositae* and is found in the s. of Europe; its leaves are used for the purpose of flavouring pickles and salads.

Tarrago'na, Spain. Spt. tn. on Mediterranean at mouth of r. Francoli; pop. 34,000; exports wine, oil; anc. Tarraco, captured by Romans 218 B.C. in Second Punic War.

Tarsus. Splendid anc. city of s.E. Asia Minor, cap. of Cilicia; birthplace of St. Paul; modern Tersous (pop. 74,000).

Tarsus. The ankle, 1342; elongated in birds, 438.

Tartar. Partly purified wine crust (argol), 3155.

Tartar, cream of, 3155, 1500.

Tartar emetic. Antimony potassium tartrate, a highly poisonous white powder, used as a mordant in dyeing; 3155.

Tartaric acid, 3155; crystals, *939.*

Tartarin (tahr'-tar-an). The vain, boastful Quixotic hero of Daudet's humorous masterpieces, " Tartarin of Tarascon," " Tartarin on the Alps," and " Port Tarascon."

Tartar (or Tatar) Republic. Autonomous republic of the R.S.F.S.R., consisting of a great part of Kazan prov. and portions of Ufa, Samara, Simbirsk, and Vyatka provs.; a. 25,950 sq. m.; pop. 2,500,000; cap. Kazan; 3155.

Tartars. Group of Cent. Asiatic tribes, **3155**; and Russian literature, 2855; Crimea, 931; Great Wall of China, *806,* 810; invade India, 1714; Mongols absorb, 2205; over-run Rus., 2846, 2847; in Siberia, 2966.

Tar'tarus. In Gk. myth., place of punishment in the underworld, 3298.

Tartary. Old name for Cent. Asia, 3155.

Tartu or Dorpat. Tn. of Estonia S.S.R.; pop. 50,000; founded in 1030; member Hanseatic League; famous for univ. founded by Gustavus Adolphus in 1632.

" Tartuffe " (tahr-tüf'). Play by Molière, 2198.

Tashkent or Tashkend. Cap. of the Uzbek Republic, U.S.S.R.; pop. 585,000; 3267.

Tasman, Abel Janszoon (c. 1602–59). Greatest of Dutch navigators, 310, 2358, 3156, 2472.

Tasmania. An isl. state of the Australian Commonwealth; a. 26,215 sq. m.; pop. 257,117; cap. Hobart; **3156**; *map f. 310*; duckbill, *1053.*

Tasmanian devil. A marsupial, *3157.*

Tassigny (Tass-sēēn-yē), **Jean de Lattre de** (b. 1890). Fr. soldier; 4 times wounded in 1st World War; in 1942, sentenced to 10 yrs. imprisonment by Gers., but escaped Sept. 1943, and joined de Gaulle; liberated Elba, Marseilles, Toulon, invaded W. Germany; inspector-gen. of Fr. army 1945; C.-in-C. land forces Western Europe after Oct. 1948.

Tas'so, Torquato (1544–95). It. poet, 3157, 1786.

Taste, sense of, **3157**; areas of tongue, *3223*; confused with smell, 2986; weak in cats, 718.

Tata, Jamsetjee Nasarwanjee (1839–1904). Indian industrialist; his son Sir Dorabji Jamsetjee Tata (1859–1932), carried on his work and founded great Tata steel works.

Tate, Maurice W. (b. 1895). Eng. professional cricketer of all-round talent; during 1924–30 played in every test match against Australia; fast-medium bowler, with world record of 38 wickets in one series of tests, 1924–25. *See* **Records, Cricket.**

Tate, Nahum (1652–1715). Brit. poet laureate and playwright; b. Dublin; 2634.

Tate Gallery. The National Gallery of Brit. Art, Millbank, London, built with money given by Sir Henry Tate and opened in 1897; **3159,** 2281.

" Tatler, The." Periodical published by Sir Richard Steele, 1213.

Tatra (tat'rah) **Mts.** Central and loftiest group of Carpathians, on border between Poland and Czecho-slovakia; highest pt., 8,737 ft.; 704.

Tattoo, military. Display or pageant, performed, usually at night, to a musical accompaniment.

Tau, τ, T (Rom. t, T). 19th letter of Greek alphabet.

Tauber (tow'-běr), **Richard** (1893–1948). Austrian-born tenor; first appeared in England in 1931 in " The Land of Smiles "; films include " Blossom Time "; became Brit. subject 1940.

Tauchnitz (towkh'-nits), **Christian B.** (1816–95). Ger. publisher; in 1841 he began publication of the famous " Tauchnitz edition " of Brit. and Amer. authors.

Taun'ton. Co. tn. of Somersetshire; pop. 31,200; here Monmouth assumed title of king, Jeffreys held bloody assizes; 3000; defended by Blake in Civil War, 465.

Taupo Lake. Largest l. of North Isl., New Zealand.

Taurus or Bull. A constellation of the zodiac, 3444; *chart, 895.*

Taurus Mts. Series of ranges in Asia Minor, extending w. from Euphrates; highest peaks over 10,000 ft.; N.E. extension sometimes called Anti-Taurus; 263, 1231, 3262; *map, 3262.*

Tavistock. Market town of Devon; pop. 6,000; sacked by Danes, *1203.*

Taw. R. in Devonshire, 50 m. long, 999.

Tawny owl; *plates f. 2460, 2461.*

Taxation, 3158; Eng. (modern), 1100; feudal system, 1269; Gt. Brit., 1976, 3158; income tax, 3158; Fr., " old regime," 1393; U.S.A., 3290. *See also* **Stamp Act; Customs and Tariffs.**

Tax'idermy, preserving and mounting animal specimens.

Taximeter. Automatic device for working out the fare due from a hirer of a taxi-cab, invented by Lazare Weiller (d. 1928).

Taxon'omy. Science of plant or animal classification; in botany, 533; branch of biology, 434.

Tay. Largest r. of Scot.; rises near borders of Perthshire and Argyllshire, flows E. 117 m., expanding into estuary at Firth of Tay, 2558; the rly. bridge across the Tay is 2 m. long; there are important salmon fisheries; 567, 1055, 2890.

Tay, Loch, Scot. L. in w. Perthshire; 15 m. long and about 1 m. broad.

Taylor, Ann (1782–1866) **and Jane** (1783–1824). Eng. writers for children (" Rhymes for the Nursery," containing " Twinkle, Twinkle, Little Star," " marked an epoch in young people's literature ").

Taylor, Sir Henry (1800–86). Eng. poet; for 48 years a confidential official in the Colonial Office, for which he wrote innumerable state papers; his best work is " Philip van Artevelde," a poetic tragedy performed with success by Macready.

Taylor, Jeremy (1613–67). Clergyman and author, called for his golden eloquence and rich fancy, the " Eng.

"Holy Dying "—popular devotional manuals).

Taylor, J. E. Excavations at Ur, 3297.

Taylor, Zachary (1784–1850). 12th pres. of U.S.A. (1848) ; he spent much of his life fighting against the Indians.

Tbilisi. *See* Tiflis.

Tchad Lake. Same as Chad.

Tchaikovsky (chĭ-kof′-skĭ), **Peter Ilyitch** (1840–93). Rus. composer, 3158, 2266.

Tchekhov (or **Chekhov**), **Anton Pavlovich** (1860–1904). Rus. dramat.st and novelist, 3159, 1040, 2983, 2856.

Tea, 3159, 265 ; Assam (India), 273 ; Ceylon, 748 ; China, 808 ; Japan, 1874, 1797 ; preparation for market, *3161* ; varieties, *3162.*

"Teaching of the Twelve Apostles." Apocryphal book of the New Testament, 425.

Teak. An E. Indian tree with dark, oily wood, **3162** ; chief producing regions, 526, 623, 1701, 2964, *2965.*

Teal. A small river duck, *1052.*

Tea rose, 2828.

Teasel or **teazel.** A plant with barbed burrs, **3163.**

Teaselling, of textiles, 3407.

Teazle, Sir Peter. In Sheridan's "School for Scandal," testy but good-hearted old aristocrat, jealous of his lively, pretty young wife.

Technetium. Alternative name for the chem. element **Masurium.**

Technical schools, 2886.

Tecumseh (tek-um′-sĭ) (1768–1813). Shawnee Indian chief. In 1804 he originated a scheme whereby Indians might unite to extirpate the whites ; he became a brigadier-general in the British army, leading the Indians in the War of 1812.

Tedder, Marshal of R.A.F. Arthur W. Tedder, Baron (b. 1890). Brit. air officer ; in charge of research and development of air force in 1939 ; as A.O.C.-in-C. of R.A.F. in Middle East 1941–43, he organized air offensive supporting 8th army in N. Africa ; dep. supreme commander, A.E.F. 1943–45 ; Marshal of R.A.F. 1945 ; chief of Air Staff (1946–50) ; a governor of B.B.C. in 1950 ; apptd. chairman Brit. Services Mission in Washington in 1950.

Teddington. Part of borough of Twickenham, Middlesex, Eng. ; the National Physical Laboratory was established here in 1902.

Tee, in curling, 944 ; in golf, 1483.

Tees. R. of N. Eng. that rises in Cumberland flowing along the Durham boundary to North Sea ; 81 m. long ; *567*, 1059, 3435.

Teeth, 3163, *2599* ; of beaver, 387 ; bears, 382 ; birds lack, 437 ; in fossil birds, 437 ; care of, 1675 ; cattle, 732 ; fluoride prevents decay, 1567 ; horse, 1645 ; mammals, 2076 ; rodents, 2795 ; ruminants, 2842 ; sharks, 2938 ; whales, 1245, 3372.

Tegea (tē′-ji-*a*), Greece. Anc. city in Arcadia, near Tripolitza ; many wars with Sparta, subdued abt. 550 B.C.

Tegner′, Esaias (1782–1846). Swedish poet (" Frithjofs Saga " best known of all Swedish poems), 2880.

Tegucigalpha (tā-gn̄-si-gal′-pah). Cap. and chief city of Honduras ; pop. 55,715 ; old Aztec city ; 1638.

Teguexin (tē-gweks′-ĭn). Lizard, 1973.

Teheran (ta-hēr-ahn′). Cap. of Persia in prov. of Teheran ; pop. 699,100 ; large caravan trade ; *1741 ; confer-ence of war, during which Churchill handed to Stalin the Stalingrad sword of honour.

Tehuantepec (tā-wahn′-tā-pek). Mexico. City in state of Oaxaca, 18 m. from Pacific ; pop. 12,300 ; oil field.

Tehuantepec, Isthmus of. Narrowest part of Mexico, between Gulf of Campeche and Gulf of Tehuantepec.

Teifi (tī′-vē), Wales. R. flowing 50 m. to Cardigan Bay ; 2539.

Teign. R. in Devonshire flowing to English Channel ; it is 30 m. in length, 999.

Teith. R. of Perthshire ; has its source near Loch Lomond ; flows to R. Forth.

Tel-Aviv, Palestine. Spt. and largest city ; founded in 1909 near Jaffa ; pop. 183,200 ; *2482.*

Telecommunications, *3169–3172* ; group-name for telephone, telegraph, radio, etc. ; high-frequency currents in, 1623. *See* **Telegraphy** ; **Telephone** ; **Wireless.**

Teleg′raphy, 3164, *3169–3172* ; Edison repeater and stock quotation apparatus, 1088 ; evolution, *3165* ; invented by Morse, *2233* ; Post Office control, 2662 ; submarine cables, 640 ; of pictures, 2577. *See also* **Wireless.**

Telegraph Plateau of Atlantic Ocean, *map*, *290*, 643.

Tel el-Armarna. Letters, discovery, 1120.

Tel el-Kebir, battle, 1102.

Telemachus (tel-em′-*a*-kus). In the " Odyssey " ; son of Odysseus and Penelope, 2421, 2423.

Telemachus. Asiatic monk, 1469.

Telemark, in ski-ing, 2979.

Telemeter. *See* **Range-Finder.**

Tel′eosts. Sub-class of fish with well-developed skeletons.

Telepathy. The power to transmit ideas from one person to another, even at a great distance, without using the ordinary channels of sense.

Telephone, 3173, 3009, *3011* ; Bell, 408, *3173*, *3174* ; cable, *645* ; Post Office control, 2662 ; automatic exchange systems, *3172*, *3175*, *3176* ; microphone, 2162 ; switchboard, *3170*, *3171* ; and thermionic valve, 3198. *See also* **Telegraphy.**

Teleprinter, *3167*, *3168*, *3169*, 3173.

Telescope, **3178**, 2411, *2412* ; collimating, 3055 ; construction of, 3180 ; Galileo's, *1415*, 3178 ; how astronomical telescope works, *diagram*, *3180* ; importance in astronomy, 276 ; infra-red, 1596, *1722*, 1724 ; invention, 276, 281 ; lenses, 1474, 1924 ; Mt. Palomar, *3179* ; Mill Hill, *3181* ; mirror, *3178* ; Newton's, *2349* ; in periscope, 2552, *2553* ; tower telescope, *3180* ; types, 3178 ; Yerkes observatory, 3181.

Telescope fish, *1482.*

Teletypesetter. 1958.

Television, **3182**, 3399 ; fluorescence in, 2574 ; history, 3184 ; thermionic valve, 3198. List of terms, 4043.

" Telex," rentable teleprinter service, 3173.

Telford, Thomas (1757–1834). Scottish engineer, builder of canals and roads ; **3184**, 2783 ; his Menai bridge, *2128.*

Tell, William. Legendary Swiss hero, **3185**, 3141 ; hero of Schiller's play, 2882.

Tellez, Gabriel. Sp. dramatist, 3051.

Tellur′ium. (Te). Widely distributed semi-metallic element of the oxygen group ; atomic weight, 127·61 ; found only in minute quantities ; its position in the periodic table does not correspond to its atomic weight, which is more than that of iodine ; melts at 845·6° F. ; **3185** ; assoc. with gold, 1479 ; properties, 777.

Teme. R. of Eng. and Wales ; flows 60 m. to join Severn, 2733, 2963.

" Téméraire, The Fighting," 3234 ; Turner's picture, *1275.*

Temesvar (tem′-esh-vahr) or **Timisio-ara.** City of w. Rumania ; pop. (1945) 108,200 ; has suffered many sieges, especially by Hungarian insurgents in 1849 ; tobacco, textiles, paper, leather.

Tem′me, Edward H. Eng. swimmer ; the first man to swim Channel both ways,

Tempelhof. Airport of Berlin, and among the largest airports of Europe ; near the centre of the city.

Tem′pera painting, 2476.

Temperature, 88, 1594 ; altitude variation, 840, 3084 ; climate, 840 ; compensation, 3201 ; effect on bridges, 568 ; most healthful, 1599 ; highest and lowest attained, 1391, 1594, 1607 ; of human body, 3200 ; pyrometers for measuring, 2709 ; recording, *3201* ; and speed of sound, 3010 ; of stratosphere, 3102 ; of sun, 1594, 3119 ; effect on radio-activity, 2733 ; thermostatic control, 3201 ; thermo-

meter measures, 3199 ; boiling water, 3084. *See also* **Air** ; **Climate** ; **Heat** ; for the temperatures at which the various elements melt, see under the respective elements.

Temperature, sense of, 3231.

Tempering, steel, 1756.

Tem′pest, Dame Marie (1866–1942). Eng. actress of great versatility, celebrated her jubilee on the stage in 1935 ; created D.B.E. in 1937.

" Tempest, The." Comedy by Shakespeare, **3185** ; 1211.

Tem′plars, Knights. *See* **Knights Templars.**

Template, or **templet,** in engineering. A mould of a certain figure to test or direct the conformation of a timber or other object ; a perforated piece or strip, by which a line of rivet-holes is marked on a plate to be punched ; one of the wedges in a building-block.

Temple, Frederick (1821–1902). Eng. divine ; in 1858 accepted headmastership of Rugby ; Bp. of Exeter 1869, Bishop of London in 1885, and Archbishop of Canterbury 1896.

Temple, Shirley (b. 1928). Amer. film actress ; appeared as a child in " The Littlest Rebel," " Curly Top," " Wee Willie Winkie," etc. ; also adult roles.

Temple, William (1881–1944). Eng. divine ; son of Frederick ; Bp. of Manchester (1921–28) ; Arch. of York (1928–42) ; Arch. of Canterbury (1942–44).

Temple, The, London, 2012, 1865, 1903 ; birthplace of Lamb, 1886 ; damaged by bombs 1940–45.

Temple of Heaven, Peking, 2537.

Temple of Solomon, 2999, 1819, *1820.*

Temple of the Sun, at Palmyra, 2485.

Temples. *See* **Architecture.**

Templewood, Samuel J. G. Hoare, 1st Viscount (b. 1880). Brit. politician ; Sec. for Air (1922, 1924) ; for India (1931) ; For. Sec. (1935–36), when party to Hoare-Laval pact for ending Abyssinian war and resigned ; 1st Lord Admiralty (1936) ; Home Sec. (1937) ; Privy Seal (1939–40) ; Ambass. to Spain (1940–44) ; peerage (1944).

Temu′co, Chile. Tn. 140 m. S.E. of port of Concepcion ; pop. 84,700 ; tanneries, breweries.

Ten′by. Small watering-place and spt. of Pembrokeshire, on Carmarthen Bay ; pop. 4,108

Tench. A fish, 2781.

Ten Commandments, 2235.

Tender, of locomotive, *plate f.* 1980.

Tendons, 1572, 2258 ; Achilles tendon, *1342*, 19.

Teneriffe′. Largest of Canary Isls. ; a. 782 sq. m. ; pop. 401,283 ; 690.

Teneriffe. Volcanic peak, 690.

Teniers (ten′-yērz), **David** (1610–90), the Younger. Noted genre painter of Flemish school ; son of David Teniers the Elder (1582–1649), also an important Flemish painter, 2333.

Tennessee′. A s-cent. state of U.S.A. ; a. 42,000 sq. m. ; pop. 2,915,840 ; **3185.**

Tennessee River. Largest tributary of Ohio r. ; 800 m. long.

Tennessee Valley Authority (TVA), 3185.

Tenniel (ten′yel), **Sir John** (1820–1914). Eng. political cartoonist, on staff of " Punch " for 50 years ; noted for grace and dignity of conception combined with powerful satire ; illustrated " Alice in Wonderland," 709.

Tennis. The " royal " game, **3186.** *See also* **Lawn Tennis.**

Tennis Court Oath. In Fr. Rev., 1393.

Ten′nyson, Alfred, 1st Baron (1809–92). Eng. poet, **3186**, 1214 ; use of Arthurian legends, 255.

Tennyson, Hallam (1852–1928), 2nd Lord Tennyson and son of the above; Gov. of South Australia (1899–1902) ; Gov. Genl. of Australia (1902–1904).

Tenochtitlan (tā-noch-tĕt-lahn′). Aztec city, 326.

Tension (elec.), 1128.

Tense, in grammar, 3314.

Tentacles. Long, flexible grasping organs ; of cuttle-fish, 945, 2199 ; "feelers" of coral, 908 ; of hydra, *1665* ; jelly-fish, 1817, *1818* ; nautilus, 2199 ; octopus, 946 ; snails, 2989 ; squids, *945, 946.*

Ten Thousand, Retreat of the, 3429.

Tent. A portable shelter, usually made of canvas ; Arab, 199.

Ten Years' War, in Cuba, 941.

Te′pee. Tent of Amer. Indians, *2755,* 2756.

Tepic (tā-pěk′), Mexico. *See* **Nayarit.**

Ter′bium (Tb), metallic element of the Rare Earth group ; atomic weight, 159·2 ; **3187** ; and ytterbium, and yttrium, 3437.

Ter Borch. Dutch painter, 2334.

Terebella. A seaworm, *3425.*

Ter′ebinth. A tree · of the genus Pistacia, which also includes pistachio nut ; resembles the ash, but smaller ; original source of turpentine.

Tere′do or **shipworm.** A crustacean or worm-like mollusc which bores into wood, causing extensive damage to piles, etc.

Terek (tā′-rek), r. in s. Rus., rises in glaciers on N. slope of Caucasus Mts. ; flows E. 400 m. ; outlet, 717.

Ter′ence (Publius Terentius Afer) (c.194–159 B.C.). Rom. dramatist, b. Carthage, Africa, 1038, 1895, 1897. Chief works, "Andria," "Heauton Timorumenos" ("The Self-Tormentor"), "Phormio."

Teresa (tā-rā′-zah), **St.** (1515–82). Sp. nun ; famous mystic, 2nd patron saint of Sp. monarchy and founder of the Barefooted (discalced) Carmelites.

Ter′eus. *See* **Philomel.**

Ter′mites. The so-called "white ants," **3188,** 1729 ; nest, *plate f.* 73 ; queen, *1733.*

Termonde′, Belgium. Fortified tn. on Schelde r. ; pop. 10,000 ; taken by Germans in drive on Antwerp and destroyed Sept. 1914 ; rehabilitated after 1st World War.

Ter′ni (anc. Interamna). It. mfg. city ; pop. 68,890 ; near famous falls of Terni ; govt. arsenal, iron, steel, textile mfrs. ; Neapolitans defeated by Fr. 1798.

Terns. Gull-like ·birds, **1555,** *1557* ; migrations, *2171.*

Terpsichore (terp-sik′-or-ē). In Gk. myth., muse of dancing, 2259, *186.*

Terracina (ter-a-chē′-na) (Lat. Tarracina). It. historic tn. ; pop. 8,000 ; remains of anc. forum and temple.

Terra cotta. Unglazed earthenware of a reddish-yellow colour.

Terra Nova. Capt. Scott's ship, *169,* 2896.

Ter′rapin or **mud-turtle,** 3230, *plate f. 3228.*

Terrestrial Magnetism, or magnetism caused by the earth, 2062.

Ter′rier. A burrowing type of dog (from Fr., *la terre*, the earth), 1027, *plate f. 1024.*

Terriss, William (1847–97). Eng. actor, whose real name was William Charles James Lewin ; his greatest triumphs were in "Olivia" and "Black-eyed Susan" ; assassinated by an insane actor.

Territorial Army. Brit. military organization of citizen soldiers, originally called the Territorial Force (dating from 1907) ; reorganized in 1947 ; in addition to other duties, has entire charge of Britain's anti-aircraft and coastal defences, 250. The T.A. is one of the formations in which a man may do his four years' compulsory part-time service after his 18 months' full-time service.

Territorial Decoration (T.D.). Founded 1908, awarded to commissioned officers of twenty years' faithful service in the Territorial Army.

Ter River, Sp. Rises in the Pyrenees in the N.E. corner, flows S. and E. 110 m., entering the Mediterranean by several mouths s. of the Gulf of Rosas.

Terror, The. *See* **Reign of Terror.**

Terry, Dame Ellen (1847–1928). Eng. Shakespearean actress, long associated with Sir Henry Irving ; she had few rivals in the grace and intellectual grasp with which she portrayed characters such as Portia, Lady Macbeth, Desdemona, and Cordelia ; Sargent's portrait, *2874.*

Tertiary (ter′-shi-ar-i) **period.** In geology, 1432, 1433 ; period of petroleum formation, 2428.

Tertul′lian (A.D. c. 155–c. 230). One of great fathers of the Latin Church, b. Carthage, called creator of Christian Latin literature.

"Terylene," a synthetic rayon, 2750.

Tesch′en, Czechoslovakia ; pop. 25,000 ; chief city in region which supplied only available coking coal to Poland and Czechoslovakia ; most of area awarded to Czechoslovakia by council of Allied Ambassadors, but Poland received part of coal output. Occupied by Poland 1938–39 ; by Germany 1939–45.

Teschen, Peace of. Treaty signed at Teschen, May 13, 1779 ; it ended the war of the Bavarian succession.

Tes′la, Nikola (1857–1943). Amer. inventor and electrician, b. Croatia ; discovered principle of rotary magnetic field, which made possible the alternating-current motor.

Tes′selated mosaics, 2233.

Test. R. of Hampshire ; flows almost due s. into Southampton Water, 3028.

Test Matches. Cricket matches played between specially chosen teams representing England, Australia, S. Africa, New Zealand, India, and West Indies, 928, *930* ; term is also applied to Eng.-Australia speedway matches.

Testu′do (Lat., tortoise). Military formation in anc. Roman army by soldiers' overlapping shields for protection.

Tet′anus or **lockjaw,** 1458. Antitoxin for, 180.

Tethmosis. *See* **Thothmes III.**

Te′ton Mts. A range of the Rocky Mts. in N.W. Wyoming, U.S.A.

Tetrazzini (tet-rat-sē′-nē), **Luisa** (1874–1940). It. coloratura soprano (famous roles in "La Traviata", "Rigoletto" ; "Lucia di Lammermoor").

Tetra-ethyl lead, in motor-car spirit, 2564.

Tetuan. Tn. of Span. Morocco ; pop. 49,535 ; 2231.

Tetzel, Johann (c. 1455–1519), Dominican friar, 2040.

Teufelsdröckh (toi′-felz-drěck), **Diogenes.** In Carlyle's "Sartor Resartus," its fictitious author, professor of Things in General at Weissnichtwo.

Teutoburger (toi′-tō-bür-ger) **Forest,** Ger. Series of wooded hills on Westphalia-Hanover border extending 70 m. from N.W. to S.E. ; battle of (A.D. 9), 1447.

Teutones (tū-tō′-nāz). Ger. tribe, defeated by Marius, 2809, 3190.

Teuton′ic Knights. Christianize Baltic regions, 973, 1899.

Teutonic languages. *See* **Germanic languages.**

Teu′tons. Group of European peoples, **3190** ; in Scandinavia, 2880. *See also* **German tribes.**

Teviotdale. *See* **Roxburghshire.**

Tewfik Pasha, Mohammed (1852–1892). Eg. ruler. He succeeded Ismail Pasha, his father, as Khedive in 1879, but was deposed after the revolt of Arabi Pasha in 1882, when the British took over ; 1101.

Tewkesbury. Historic tn. in N. Gloucestershire on the Avon ; pop. 4,401 ; remains of famous Benedictine abbey, 1447 ; Yorkists defeated Lancastrians (1471) in Wars of the Roses, 2828.

Tex′as. A state in s.w. U.S.A., largest in the Union ; a. 263,644 sq. m. ; pop. 6,786,740 ; 3190, 3291 ; *map f. 3285* ; sulphur deposits, 3116.

Texel, battle of, *2294.*

Textiles, 3191 ; of China, 808 ; Eng., 1165, 1168, 2084 ; Fr., 1361 ; Japan, 1798 ; linen centres, 1954. *See* **Loom, Spinning, Weaving,** etc.

Thackeray, William Makepeace (1811–63). Eng. novelist, **3192,** 1215, *2403* ; birthplace, 661 ; as essayist, 1224.

Thailand. Same as **Siam.**

Thakin Nu. Burmese politician ; imprisoned for seditious activities 1940, released by Japs 1942 and made foreign min. ; in 1945 formed "anti-fascist people's freedom league" against Japs. ; after Aung San's assassn., July 1947, became leader ; first premier of Union of Burma.

Thales (thā′-lēz) of **Miletus** (c. 640–c. 550 B.C.). Gk. philosopher, one of the "seven wise men," 1434 ; noted electric properties of amber, 1127 ; regarded water as primal substance.

Thalia (tha-lī′-a), in Gk. myth., one of the three Graces, muse of Comedy, 2259, *187.*

Thal′lium (Tl). Bluish-white metallic element of the gallium group ; atomic weight, 204·39 ; soft and malleable like lead ; obtained from the flue dust of pyrites burners ; melts at 575·6° F. ; **3193** ; properties, 777 ; salts, 3193.

Thal′lophytes. Great plant group containing the most primitive types, algae and fungi ; 3616.

Thalofide cell, a photometer, 3193.

Thame (tām). R. in Buckinghamshire and Oxfordshire, trib. of r. Thames ; 30 m. long.

Thame. Tn. in Oxfordshire, on r. Thame ; has fragments of 12th-cent. abbey ; 2466.

Thames (temz). R. in Ontario, 160 m. long, flowing into L. St. Clair.

Thames. R. of Gt. Brit. ; with windings said to be longer than ·Severn ; **3193,** 1168, 2465 ; at London, *1290, 2009, 2011, 2013, plate f. 3232* ; at Halliford, *1171* ; the "Doggett's," 1027 ; fire float on, *1287* ; oysters, 2466 ; radar map, *2727* ; Surrey boundary, 3122 ; "swan-upping," *3125* ; tunnels, *3256,* 3257, 3258 ; University boat race, *483* ; water supply, 3347.

Thames Conservancy Board, 3194.

Thames Embankment, London, 2012.

Thar Desert, N. India, embracing part of Sind and Rajputana ; climate, 1701.

Thasos. Gk. isl. in N. Aegean, off coast of Thrace ; pop. 8,000 ; *map, 30.*

Theatre, 3194 ; cinema, 828 ; anc. Greek, *1540* ; Elizabethan, *1039,* 2932 ; Greek ·"orchestra," 2446 ; Roman, *1038. See also* **Drama.**

Theba′is. Eg. desert region near Thebes, 2212.

Thebes (thēbz). Eg., anc. cap. of Upper Eg., on Nile, on site of modern villages of Karnak and Luxor ; famous temples, 1098, *3060* ; colossi at, *2138* ; sculpture, *1121. See also* **Luxor.**

Thebes, Greece, **3197,** 1524 ; razed by Alexander the Great, 105 ; Cadmus legend, 649 ; modern tn., 1526 ; in Trojan War, 1518.

Theiss (tīs) or **Tisza** (tē′-za). R. of S.E. Europe ; rises in Carpathian Mts. ; flows S. with many windings 870 m. ; 1654 ; *map, 344.*

Them′is. In Gk. myth., one of the Titans, goddess of eternal law and order ; by Zeus she became mother of the Hours and the Fates ; in art she is usually pictured with cornucopia and scales.

Themistocles (thē-mis′-tok-lēz) (c. 514–449 B.C.). A great Athenian general and statesman ; and Aristides, 231 ; lays foundations of Athenian Empire, 1522 ; long walls, 21.

Theobromine. Alkaloid in cocoa and chocolate ; 861.

Theocritus (thē-ok′-ri-tus) (3rd cent. B.C.). First and greatest of Gk. pastoral poets, 1541, 109.

Theod′olite. An instrument for measuring angles, used in surveying.

Theodor′a (d. A.D. 547). Consort and colleague of the Byzantine emperor Justinian I ; originally dancer and actress ; harsh and cruel, but able ruler ; 637, 1844 ; mosaic of, *2233.*

The′odore III (1818–68). Emperor of Abyssinia ; succeeded his uncle as chief of Kwara and after many conquests was proclaimed emperor in 1855 ; 14.

Theodoric (thē-od'-or-ik) **the Great** (c. 454–526). King of the Ostrogoths, greatest Gothic ruler ; in Ger. legend became the hero Dietrich of Bern ; 1488, 2747 ; tomb, Ravenna, 2747.

Theodosia, Rus. Same as **Feodosia.**

Theodo'sius the Great (346–395). Rom. emperor, succeeded (379) ; conquered frontier barbarians ; prohibited heathen worship ; recognized orthodox Catholicism ; accepting penance prescribed by St. Ambrose for Thessalonica massacre.

Theophras'tus (c. 372–288 B.C.). Gk. philosopher, successor of Aristotle as head of Peripatetic School, 1541.

Therapeutics (ther-α-pū'-tiks) or **therapy.** Part of medical science which relates to treatment and remedies for disease. See **Medicine and surgery.**

Therapy, mental, 2697 ; chemo-therapy, the administration of chemicals to cure disease, 2132 ; radium, 2733 ; serum, 180 ; X-ray, in the cure of cancer, 3432.

Theresa, St. See **Teresa.**

Theresiopel (tā - rā - si - ō' - pel). See **Subotica.**

Thermae (ther'-mē). Rom. baths, 2804, plate f. 2805, 2654.

Thermal unit, British (Therm or B.Th.U.), 1593, 1594, 1596, 2154.

Thermionic valve, 3198, 1138 ; as amplifier, 3012, 3393 ; in calculating machine, 659 ; in gramophone recording, 1497 ; generate high-freq. currents, 1623 ; as rectifier, 2751, 3393 ; in television, 3184 ; in wireless transmission, 3393 ; for X-ray set, 3432.

Thermit or **thermite.** A metallic mixture, used in welding, and sometimes in the preparation of metals such as the rare-earth metals.

Ther'mo-couple. Device for converting heat energy into electric current and vice-versa, 1132.

Thermo-couple pyrometers, 2709.

Thermodynamics. Branch of the study of heat and the principles underlying the action of all heat engines, 1593 ; applied to refrigerators, 1392.

Thermograph. A temperature-recording instrument, 3200.

Thermometer, 3199, 1722, 2149, 1596 ; deep-sea, 2415 ; for measuring high temperatures, 2709 ; kata type, 1678 ; use of mercury, 2145.

Thermopile, 1132.

Thermo-plastic, plastic becoming soft when heated, 2625.

Thermopylae (thêr-mop'-il-ē). Pass leading from Thessaly into cent. Greece, where Spartans heroically attempted to check Persian invasion (480 B.C.), **3201,** 2556.

"Thermos." A type of vacuum flask, 3302.

Thermo-setting, plastic becoming hard when heated, 2625.

Thermostat. Device for regulating temperature, 3201 ; mercury in, 2146 ; in refrigerators, 1392.

Thersites (thêr-sī'-tēz). In Homer, the one ugly, hateful, slanderous brawler among the Greeks before Troy.

Theseum (thē-sē'-um) or **Temple of Theseus,** Athens, 286, 3202.

Theseus (thē'-sūs). Gk. legendary hero, slayer of Minotaur, **3201,** 742 ; character in Chaucer's "Canterbury Tales," 762.

Thespiae (thes'-pi-ē). Anc. Gk. city of Boeotia near foot of Mt. Helicon ; enemy of Thebes ; served national cause against Persians.

Thes'pis (6th cent. B.C.). Gk. poet, called the inventor of tragedy ; hence "thespian," an actor ; 1037.

Thessalo'nians, Epistles to the, in New Testament, two of St. Paul's epistles dealing with second coming of Christ.

Thessaloniki (formerly **Salonika**). City and spt. of Greece ; pop. 236,000 ; **3202** ; massacre, 138.

Thes'-saly. Dist. in Greece, s. of Macedonia ; largest division of anc. Greece ; added to modern Greece, 1525 ; Vlachs, 1527.

Theta, θ, Θ. 8th letter of Gk. alphabet.

Thet'ford. Old tn. in Norfolk ; pop. 4,540 ; Castle Hill, anc. mound, 1,000 ft. in circumference and 100 ft. high.

Thetford Mines, Quebec. Tn. 55 m. s. of Quebec ; pop. 12,716 ; extensive asbestos mines.

Thetis (thet'-is), in Gk. myth., sea nymph, one of Nereids and mother of Achilles, 2408, 19 ; marriage feast, 3248.

Thiassi (tyah'-sē). A giant in Scandinavian myth., 2882.

Thibault (tē-bō'), **J. A.** See **France, Anatole.**

Thibet. Same as **Tibet.**

Thiers (tyār), **Louis Adolphe** (not Alphonse, as in p. 1385) (1797–1877). Fr. statesman and historian, first pres. of Fr. republic, 1385.

"Thinker, The" ("Le Penseur"), statue by Rodin, 2796, 2797.

Thinners, in paint, 2478.

Thiosul'phate, of sodium ("hypo"), 3116.

Third Estate, 1393, 2180.

Third International. Extreme Socialist organization in Russia that attempted to unite all Communists of the world ; dissolved June 1943.

Third Reich. See **Reich.**

Third Republic, France, 1366.

Thirl'mere. Lake in Cumberland, supplies water to Manchester, 943.

Thirty-nine Articles, establishment, 819.

Thirty Years' War (1618–48), **3202,** 1449, 1456, 1558, 2878 ; political results, 1239, 3203 ; Richelieu, 2791 ; rise of modern armies, 251 ; rockets in, 2794.

Thisbe (thiz'-bi). Maiden loved by Pyramus in the classic tale of "Pyramus and Thisbe," 2169.

Thistle, 3203 ; seeds, 2917.

Thistle, Order of the, 3203.

Thivai (thē'-vē) or **Phiva,** modern name for Thebes, Greece, 3197.

Thlingits. Same as **Tlinkits.**

Thomas, Albert (1878–1932). Fr. politician ; Minister of Munitions 1916–17 ; director of the International Labour Office at Geneva from 1920 until his death.

Thomas, Bertram Sidney (b. 1892). British explorer, 1925–30 Wazir and finance minister to Muscat and Oman. Explored many of the unknown parts of Arabia. Wrote "Alarms and Excursions in Arabia" ; "Arabia Felix" ; 195.

Thomas, Brandon (1849–1914). Eng. actor and playwright ; impersonator of Dickens's characters ; most successful play "Charley's Aunt," which enjoyed a record run ; other of his plays were "Comrades," "The Swordsman's Daughter," and "Women are So Serious."

Thomas, Sir George A. (b. 1881). Brit. chess and badminton player ; Brit. chess champion 1923 and 1934 ; All-Eng. Badminton champion, singles, 1920–23, doubles 9 times.

Thomas, James Henry (1875–1949). Brit. politician and labour leader ; general sec. of the National Union of Railwaymen (1916–31) ; Secretary for the Colonies (1924) ; Sec. of State for Dominion Affairs (1930 to 1936) ; resigned his seat in the Cabinet and Parl. following the Report of the Budget Leakage Tribunal.

Thomas (Philip) Edward (1878–1917). Eng. poet ; wrote extensively up to his death whilst fighting in France in 1917 ("The Woodland Life" ; "Horae Solitariae" ; "Rest and Unrest" ; "Light and Twilight" ; "Poems" ; and "Last Poems").

Thomas, St. One of Twelve Apostles, 188.

Thomas à Becket. See **Becket.**

Thomas à Kempis. See **Kempis.**

Thomas the Rhymer (c. 1220–97), Scot. poet, also known as Thomas of Erceldoune ; many prophetic statements associated with his name ; 2894.

Thompson, Benjamin. See **Rumford.**

Thompson, Francis (1860–1907). Eng. poet and mystic ; "for glory of inspiration and natural magnificence of

utterance he is unique among the poets of his time" ("The Hound of Heaven," intensely beautiful religious lyric).

Thompson, Silvanus Phillips (1851–1916). Eng. physicist ; for nine years held the chair of experimental physics in University College, Bristol, and in 1885 became principal and professor of physics in the London City and Guilds Technical College, London ("Electricity and Magnetism," "The Electro-Magnet," "Dynamo-electric Machinery" ; also "Michael Faraday," and "Life of Lord Kelvin").

Thompson sub-machine-gun. Automatic rifle, weighing 11 lb. 6 oz., with 12¼ in. barrel, firing ·45 shot ; invented in 1921 by J. T. Thompson, a Chicago police officer, 1283.

Thomson, Sir Basil Home (1861–1939). Brit. colonial servant ; was Assist.-Commsr. of the Metropolitan Police 1913–19 ("Diversions of a Prime Minister" ; "The Discovery of the Solomon Islands" ; "Queer People").

Thomson, Christopher Birdwood, Baron (1875–1930). Brit. soldier and politician ; served in Boer War 1899–1902, and was on staff of 1st Army Corps in France during 1st World War ; his brigade was the first to enter Jerusalem ; created baron 1924; Sec. of State for Air (1924 and 1929) ; perished in wreck of airship R.101.

Thomson, Sir George Paget (b. 1892). Brit. physicist, son of Sir J. J. Thomson ; prof. of physics, Imp. Coll. of Science, since 1930 ; chm. 1st Brit. cttee. on Atomic Energy 1940 ; scientific adviser to Brit. delegate of U.N. atomic energy commsn. 1946–47 ; received Nobel prize for physics 1937, for discovery of interference phenomena in irradiation of crystals by electrons ; 298, 2594.

Thomson, James (1700–48). Scot. poet, pioneer of romantic movement in Eng. literature ("The Seasons" ; "Rule, Britannia"), 1213.

Thomson, James (1834–82). Brit. poet and journalist ; profoundly melancholy and pessimistic ("The City of Dreadful Night").

Thomson, Sir John Arthur (1861–1933). Brit. zoologist, author of many interesting works, including "The Wonder of Life" ; editor of "The Outline of Science."

Thomson, Sir Joseph John (1856–1940). Eng. physicist, awarded O.M. (1912), developed electron theory, 296, 1137, 2594, 3430 ; and beta rays, 2731 ; and isotopes, 1760 ; Nobel prize, 2375.

Thomson, Robert William. Invented the pneumatic tire, 2836.

Thomson, William. See **Kelvin, William Thomson, Baron.**

Thor, in Norse myth., god of thunder, 3204, 2881, 980.

Thor'ax. Part of the body between head or neck and the abdomen, 1591 ; of crabs, 924 ; of insects, 1732, 1726 ; of lobsters, 1977 ; of spiders, 3065.

Thoreau (thôr'-ō), **Henry David** (1817–62). Amer. naturalist and writer, 3204, 3294.

Thorez, Maurice (b. 1900). Fr. communist politician ; in Moscow 1939–44 ; held govt. offices 1945–47.

Thor'finn, Karlsef'ni. Scandinavian explorer, who led expedition to N. Amer., 2388.

Thor'ium (Th). Iron-grey metallic element of the titanium group ; atomic weight, 232·12 ; melts at c. 3,100° F.; 3187 ; slightly radioactive, 2731, 2732 ; oxide used in gas mantles, 1424 ; in monazite sand, 2871 ; properties, 778 ; gives off helium, 1607 ; isotopes, 1760 ; Curies' experiments, 2731.

Thorn (tōrn) or **Torun,** Poland. Fortified tn. on Vistula, formerly in W. Prussia, Germany ; pop. 39,500 ; birthplace of Copernicus.

Thorn apple. Poisonous plant (Datura stramonium) of fam. Solanaceae, 2639.

Thorn'dike, Dame Sybil (b. 1882). Eng. actress, *1041* ; in Shakespearean repertory, played as many as 100 parts in 25 plays ; other notable successes in " St. Joan " and " Lottie Dundas " ; D.B.E. (1931) ; her brother (Arthur) Russell Thorndike (b. 1885), actor, wrote the novels " Dr. Syn " and " The Slype."

Thorne, Will (1857–1946). Brit. politician and labour leader ; founded with others the National Union of General Workers in 1889, and became general secretary.

Thorns. Why plants grow them, 2622.

Thornycroft, Sir John Isaac (1843–1928). Brit. engineer ; builder of internal combustion engines for road vehicles, also high-speed launches and torpedo craft.

Thornycroft, Thomas. Eng. sculptor ; Boadicea statue, *480*.

Thornycroft, Sir (William) Hamo (1850–1925), Eng. sculptor, son of above ; 2906 ; King Alfred statue, *111*.

Thorwaldsen (tŏr'-wald-sen), **Bertel** (1770–1844), Danish sculptor, greatest 19th-cent. classicist (" Night " ; " Morning " ; " Lion of Lucerne ") ; 3205, 2906.

Thoth (tŏt). Egyptian god of wisdom ; identified by Greeks with Hermes.

Thothmes III (*c.* 1501–1447 B.C.). Eg. king or pharaoh, " the Napoleon of Egypt." Sole ruler after death of Hatshepsut ; in 33 years conquered all W. Asia to Euphrates ; 1119.

" Thought," by Auguste Rodin, *2796, 2797.*

" Thousand and One Nights." *See* **" Arabian Nights."**

Thousand Isls., in St. Lawrence r., 2861.

Thrace. Region in E. of Balkan Peninsula varying in extent at different periods ; held by Turkey from 1453 to 1878 when N. part, by Treaty of Berlin, was placed under separate administration as Eastern Rumelia, later a part of Bulgaria ; scene of heavy fighting in 1st World War ; *map*, *344* ; chief city Adrianople, 29, part ceded to Greece, 1526 ; regained by Turkey, 3265, 3415.

Thrale, Hester (1741–1821). Eng. woman, wife of Henry Thrale, a brewer ; after his death married an It. musician named Piozzi ; wrote delightful letters and was central figure of a charming literary and artistic circle ; friend of Dr. Johnson, *1836.*

Thread, 3205 ; silk, 2970, *2971, 2972* ; spinning, 920 ; weaving, 920, 3360 ; wool, *3407.*

Threadneedle Street, London, 2010 ; the " Old Lady of Threadneedle St." is the Bank of Eng., *357.*

Three-field system of agriculture, *86.*

Three Kings of Cologne, 872.

Three-mile limit, in international law, 1905.

" Three Musketeers, The." Novel by Dumas, 1054.

Three Rivers, Quebec. Port on St. Lawrence and St. Maurice rivers ; pop. 44,500 ; exports lumber, grain, cattle ; wood, paper, and pulp industries ; founded in 1634 ; surrendered to Americans in 1775, taken by the British following year.

Three-toed woodpecker, foot, *448.*

Thresher shark, 2938.

Threshing (thrash'-ing). Agric. process by which grain is separated from the ears in crops, 3374 ; primitive methods, 79.

Thrift, or **Sea-pink,** 2611 ; a perennial herb, popular for borders and rock gardens.

Throat. Larynx and vocal cords, *3327* ; windpipe, *2039.*

Thrombo'sis. Clot of blood formed in blood-vessel, usually a vein ; caused by injury, inflammation, thickening of arteries, or drop in high blood pressure.

Throttle. Motor-car, 2244 ; steam-engine, 3085.

Throwing. In jujitsu, 1840 ; in pottery-making, 3339 ; silk, 2972.

" Thrums," in Barrie's works, 364.

Thrush. Name of two of our commonest resident birds, the song thrush and mistle or missel thrush,

3205, 161 ; thrush family, *Turdidae,* also contains blackbird, ring ouzel, redwing, fieldfare, as well as robin, redstart, nightingale and many other song birds, 3628.

Thrust, of aeroplane engines, 1828.

Thucydides (thū-sid'-id-ēz) (*c.* 464–*c.* 404 B.C.). Gk. historian, greatest of antiquity, 3206, 1540.

Thugs. An organization of professional murderers in India who strangled their victims in honour of the goddess Kali, wife of Siva ; killed 30,000 natives a year ; suppressed by Brit. govt. in 1840.

Thule (thū'-lē). Old name for Shetland Isls., 2945.

Thu'lium (Tm). Metallic element of the rare earth group ; atomic weight, 169·4. *See* **Rare Earths.**

Thumb, 1572 ; of monkey, 2210.

Thun (toon), Switzerland. Tn. on r. Aar ; headquarters of the Swiss artillery.

Thun, Lake of. Lake in canton of Bern, Switzerland, w. of Interlaken, an expansion of R. Aar, 10 m. long by 2 m.

Thunder, 1564, 2150, 1946, 3100 ; timing the sound, 3010 ; god, 980.

" Thunderbolt." Racing motor-car used by Capt. G. E. T. Eyston in breaking the land speed record, Nov. 1937.

Thunder showers, 2741, 3101.

Thuringia. State in cent. Ger. formed in 1919 by union of eight former states ; with part of Saxony formed new *Land* (province) of Thuringia in 1946 ; a. 4,540 sq. m. ; pop. 2,293,000 ; cap. Weimar, 3362.

Thuringian Forest (Thüringer Wald). Range of hills in Ger. from Werra r. near Eisenach, S.E. to Bavarian frontier ; magnificent pine forests, 1445.

Thurlestone. Devon vil., *1174.*

Thursday. 5th day of week ; origin of name, 980.

Thurston, Ernest Temple (1879–1933). Eng. novelist and dramatist (" The Apple of Eden " ; " The City of Beautiful Nonsense " ; " The Garden of Resurrection " ; " The Forest Fire " ; plays, " The Greatest Wish " ; " The Wandering Jew "), 3340.

Thutmose III. Same as **Thothmes III.**

Thyestes (thī-es'-tēz). *See* **Aegisthus** ; **Atreus.**

Thyme (tīm). Plant of the *Labiatae,* used for seasoning, 3206.

Thyratron, form of triode valve, 1138, 1139 ; in rectifiers, 2751 ; as time switch, 3215.

Thyroid gland, 1470, 1738.

Thyrox'in. Secretion of the thyroid gland, 1470.

Thysanu'ra. An order of wingless insects.

Tiahuanaco (tē-*a*-wah-nah'-kō). Vil. in Bolivia 38 m. N.W. of La Paz ; ruins, 492.

Tian Shan. Same as **Tien Shan.**

Tib'bu or **Te'bu.** A nomadic people of the Sahara, 2860.

Ti'ber. Famous r. of cent. It., **3207** ; Rome on, 2799, 2804 ; story, " How Horatius Kept the Bridge," 3207.

Tiberias (tī-bēr'-i-as). Tn. in Palestine on w. shore of Sea of Galilee, N.E. of Nazareth ; modern Tabarīya ; school of rabbis, 425.

Tiberias, Sea of. *See* **Galilee.**

Tiberius (tī-bēr'-i-*u*s), Claudius Nero (42 B.C.–A.D. 37). Rom. emperor, 2811 ; palaces on Capri, 2274.

Tibet or **Thibet.** Country in cent. Asia, nominally a Chinese dependency ; a. 470,000 sq. m. ; pop. 3,722,000 ; **3208,** *plates f. 3208, 3209,* 263, 807 ; *maps,* 808, *1702* ; climate, 840, 1626, 2742 ; Himalaya Mts., 1626 ; religion, *601,* 3208 ; yaks, *3433* ; Yangtze r., 3433.

Tibetan lynx, 2043.

Tibullus (ti-bul'-*u*s), **Albius** (50–18 B.C.). Rom. poet, 1896.

Ticino (tē-chē'-nō). Canton in S. Switzerland ; a. 1,086 sq. m. ; pop. 161,800 ; language, 3141.

Ticino. R. of Switzerland and northern Italy, 150 m. long ; flows into Po, 3140.

Tick. A minute parasite of the arachnid type, 2513, name also applied to various parasitic insects, such as the sheep tick.

Tick, sheep. A blood-sucking parasite, *2513.*

Ticker. Stock quotation telegraph receiver, invented by Edison.

Ticket-machine, *866, 867.*

Ticonderoga (tī-kon-der-ō'-ga), New York, U.S.A. Vil. on outlet from L. George to L. Champlain ; fort taken by British (1759).

Tidal waves, in rivers, 1573, 3210.

Tide, 3209 ; bores, 525 ; double tide at Southampton, 3028 ; harbours of Europe, 1232.

Tidworth. Village of Wilts. An important military camp of the Southern Command.

Tieck (tēk), **Johann Ludwig** (1773–1853). Ger. author and critic ; a leader of the German Romantic movement ; visited Eng. in 1817 ; translated the plays of Shakespeare.

Tien Shan. Mt. range in cent. Asia, 263, *map*, *808,* 3267.

Tientsin (tē-ent-sēn'). Spt. in N. China ; pop. 1,718,000, **3211** ; port for Peking, 2538.

Tiepolo, Giovanni Battisti (1696–1770). It. painter ; one of the greatest of the later Venetian school, being especially famous for his mural decorations in the Baroque manner ; 1776, 3666.

Tierce (tērs). One of the canonical hours, 2213.

Tierra del Fuego (tē-er'-a del fōō-ā'-gō) (" land of fire "). Archipelago at s. extremity of S. Amer., 802, *804,* 3022 ; Andes, 152.

Tierras frias (" cold lands "), 2156.

Tiflis (now **Tbilisi**). Cap. of Soviet rep. of Georgia at s. base of Caucasus Mts., between Black and Caspian seas ; distributing centre for Transcaucasia ; pop. 519,100 ; univ. ; rly. connexions, 732.

Tiger, 3211, 158, 719, *plates f. 3212, 3213* ; at Whipsnade, *3447.* Name of a type of Ger. tank, 3152.

Tiger beetle, 399, *399, 401,* 1729.

Tiger cowry shell, *2943.*

Tiger lily, *1948.*

Tiger moth, caterpillar of, *720,* 729.

Tiger top shell, *2943.*

Tig'lath-Pile'ser I, reigned about 1120–1105 B.C. One of the greatest Assyrian conquerors and builders ; claimed to have conquered 42 countries.

Tiglath-Pileser III, reigned *c.* 745–727 B.C. Assyrian king, usurper, who subdued Babylonia, Syria, and Media.

Tigranes (tī-grā-nēz) (about 121-55 B.C.). King of Armenia, defeated by Pompey, 2654.

Ti'gris. Great r. of w. Asia, flowing 1,150 m. to Persian Gulf, **3212,** 2146, *2147,* 1913 ; basket boats, *482* ; in 1st World War, 3410.

Til'burg, Netherlands. Mfg. tn. 38 m. S.E. of Rotterdam ; pop. 113,090 ; textiles, leather, iron products.

Tilbury Docks, Essex, 23 m. S.E. of London ; used by P. & O. and many other liners, 3193.

Tilden, William Tatem (b. 1893). Amer. lawn-tennis player ; won many championships between 1918 and 1927 and later turned professional, 1907.

Tiles and Bricks, 561.

Til'lett, Benjamin (1860–1943). Eng. politician and labour leader ; entered Parl. in 1917 ; had been sec. of the Dock, Wharf Riverside and General Workers' Union of Great Britain and Ireland since it was first started.

Til'lotson, John Robert (1630–94). Eng. ecclesiastic, appointed Archbishop of Canterbury in 1691 ; his sermons, published in 3 vols., are regarded as a model for ministers and lovers of English.

Til'ly, Johann Tserklaes, Count of (1559–1632), commanding general of Catholic League in Thirty Years' War, 3202, 1558.

Til'sit. City on R. Memel. Formerly in E. Prussia, incorp. in U.S.S.R., 1945 ; pop. 57,000 ; Peace of (1807), 2276.

Timber, *1340*; **bridge** of, *500*, *600*, commercial varieties, 2035; creosote treatment, 857, 927; pine most useful to Man, 2609; in Brit. Columbia, *579*; in Canada, 678; lumbering, 2035; in Queensland, *2717*; in roofs, 2821; in U.S.A., 3289. *See also* **Forestry**; **Wood**; and under names of countries and trees.

Timber wolf, 3400.

Timbre, in music, 2268.

Timbuktu or **Timbuctoo,** Fr. W. Africa; famous trading-post 9 m. N. of R. Niger at edge of Sahara; pop. 6,000; 2861, 2367.

Time, 3212, *3081*; calendar, 661; clocks and watches, 843; daylight-saving, 980; geological, 1432; local, 3212; and relativity, 2762.

Time base, in radar, 2726; in television, 3183.

Time lock, 1980.

" Times, The." London daily newspaper founded in 1785 under title of " The Daily Universal Register." Assumed title of " The Times " in 1788; 2348; elec. installn., 1545.

Timo switch, 3214; traffic lights, 2784.

Timisioara (tē-mē-shwah'-rah). *See* **Temesvar.**

Ti'mon of Athens. Famous misanthrope, living during Peloponnesian War; at first rich and generous, later soured by abandonment of friends when fortune failed; subject of play "'Timon of Athens " supposedly by Shakespeare.

Timor (tē-mōr). Isl. of Malay Archipelago, easternmost and largest of Lesser Sunda Isls.; a. 12,500 sq. m.; N.E. half belongs to Portugal, s.w. half to Netherlands; *map, 1075*; in Japanese hands 1942–45, 3420.

Timoshenko, Marshal Semyon (b. 1894). Russian marshal; app. C.-in-C. Red Army on W. front, July 1941; in 1942 led Kerch peninsula offensive; commanded N. front 1943; took charge of 2nd and 3rd Ukrainian fronts in 1944.

Tim'othy. Disciple and assistant of St. Paul (Acts xvi. 1, xvii. 14), who addressed to him the two epistles Timothy 1 and 2; the first of these is a letter upon Church order meant for the Asiatic Christian communities around Ephesus, while the 2nd is letter of counsel.

Timothy grass, 1509.

Timur Leng. *See* **Tamerlane.**

Tin (Sn). Metallic element of the silicon group; atomic weight, 118·7; occurs in cassiterite, a dioxide; melts at 449·6° F.; **3215**; alloys, 122, 124, 587, 1908; Bolivia, 492; cans, 692; Malaya, 2069; Phoenicians, 1193; properties, 777; Queensland, 2716; Siam, 2964; used to " weight " silk, 2972; in Wales, 3333.

Tinctures, in heraldry, *1614*.

Tindale, William. Same as **Tyndale.**

Tinstone, an ore, 3215.

Tintagel. Vil. in Cornwall; near by are the ruins of the so-called King Arthur's castle, which is actually of Norman date (c. 1100).

Tin'tern Abbey, Monmouthshire, 2215.

Tintoretto (tin-tor-et'-ō), " Little Dyer," popular name from his father's trade, of the great Venetian painter Jacopo Robusti (1518–94), 2766, 1776.

Tiny Tim, in Dickens's " Christmas Carol," 820.

Tipperar'y, Eire. Agric. co. in s.; a. 1,643 sq. m.; pop. 136,000, **3215**.

" Tipperary." Popular song written shortly before the 1st World War which became the favourite marching song of the troops. Its author was Jack Judge (d. 1938).

Tippermuir, battle of, fought in 1644 in Perthshire; first battle between Montrose and the Covenanters.

Tippett, Michael K. (b. 1905). Brit. composer; oratorio " A Child of Our Time," 3 quartets for strings, concerto for double string orchestra, symphony.

Tippoo Sahib (c. 1753–99). Indian potentate, son of Hyder Ali, whom he succeeded as sultan of Mysore in

1782; fought Brit. invasion, but defeated and slain in his cap. of Seringapatam, 2270.

Tirah (ti-rah'). Brit. expedition organized by Sir William Lockhart against the Afridis and the Orakzais in the Tirah Valley on the N.W. Indian frontier (1897–8); will always be remembered for the ascent and capture of Dargai by the Gordon Highlanders.

Tirana (tē-rah'-nah). Cap. of Albania since 1921; pop. 30,000; 18 m. E. of Durazzo, 100. In Axis hands 1939–44.

Tires (pneumatic), rubber for, 2835; 2836; rayon in, 2749.

Tirida'tes (238–314), king of the Armenians, 237.

Tirol (tir'-ol). Dist of Austria (prov. of Tirol) and N. Italy (Trentino); famous for scenery; **3215**, *316*; *map, 316*; Austrian Alps in, 127, *129*; cap. of Austrian Tirol Innsbruck, 1725; of Ital., Bolzano, 3216.

Tirpitz (tēr'-pits), **Alfred von** (1849–1930). Ger. lord high admiral 1911–16; active in advocating and creating powerful Ger. navy; supported policy of ruthless submarine warfare in 1st World War; rejection of certain recommendations brought his resignation in March 1916.

Tirpitz. Ger. battleship, sister ship of Bismarck, completed 1940; in Ger. invasion of Norway; attacked Allied convoys to Russia from her base in Alten Fjord; sunk by Lancasters of R.A.F. in Tromsö Fjord, Nov. 12, 1944; 2296.

Tir'so, r. of Sardinia; dam, *2873*.

Tiryns (tir'-ins), Greece, city in Argolis; destroyed 468 B.C.; excavations of Schliemann revealed finest palace of Mycenaean Age in Greece; 30, 2883.

Tishri (tiz'-ri) or **Tisri,** month in Jewish calendar, 2350.

Tisiphone (tis-if'-ō-nē), in Gk. myth., one of Furies.

Tisquan-tum, Indian chief. Same as **Squanto.**

Tissot (tē'-sō), **James Joseph Jacques** (1836–1902). Fr. painter and illustrator; " Life of Christ " series portraying with minute realism scenes of Palestine, *1838*.

Tissue. An organized mass of cells, defined, 738, 739; connective (bone, cartilage, and ligaments), 498, 2980; muscular, 2258.

Tissue, of plants, 1917, 3245; composed of cells, 738, 739.

Tissue paper, 2497.

Tisza, River. *See* **Theiss.**

Titania (tit-ā'-ni-a) in Eng. folklore, queen of the fairies, 2169.

Titanic. White Star liner which struck an iceberg on maiden voyage in 1912; *1683*.

Tita'nium (Ti). Metallic element of the thorium group; atomic weight, 47·9; prepared by the thermite process; melts at 3,640° F.; **3216**; and aluminium, 135; properties, 776.

Titanothere, prehistoric animal, *2679*.

Ti'tans, in Gk. myth., rebellious giant children of Uranus, 3298; dethroned by Zeus, 3443; Prometheus, 2690.

Tithe. Tax on one-tenth, usually on land; levied, especially for religious purposes, from anc. times; an Act for the abolition of Queen Anne's bounty (tithe rents) was passed in England in 1936.

Titho'nus, in Gk. myth., mortal husband of the goddess Aurora (Eos), the Dawn, 304.

Titian (tish'-an) (Tiziano Vecellio) (1477–1576). It. painter, **3217**, 2476, 1776, 2766, 3312; work by, *1780*, 2567, *3217*.

Titicaca (tē-tē-kah'-kah). Lake. Largest lake of S. Amer., bet. Peru and Bolivia; 130 m. by 30 m.; *492*.

Titles, knighthood, 1864; in the peerage, 2536.

Titmouse. Bird of tit family. *See* **Tits.**

Tito, Marshal. Popular alias of Josip Broz (b. 1891). Yugoslav guerrilla leader, who became Prime Min. and Min. of Defence Mar. 1945; de-

nounced by Cominform 1949; 1452, 3440.

Titration, chemical process, 20.

Tits, birds of family *Paridae*, **3218**; long-tailed, *443*.

Ti'tus. Gk. disciple of the Apostle Paul (Gal. ii, 1, 3) (N.T.).

Titus, Flavius Sabinus Vespasianus (A.D. 40–81). Rom. Emperor; succeeded Vespasian A.D. 79; humane and able ruler; captures Jerusalem, 1830; gladiatorial show, 1469; triumphal arch, *2803*.

Tiumen, Siberia. Same as **Tyumen.**

Tivoli (tē'-vol-ē), Italy. Picturesque walled tn. 18 m. N.E. of Rome at falls of r. Anio; pop. 16,000; many antiquities.

Tjerimai, volcano of Java, *plate f. 3329*.

Tlaxcala (tlas-kah'-lah), Mexico. State in S.E.; a. 1,555 sq. m.; pop. 224,000; cap. Tlaxcala.

Tlemçen (tlem'-sen), Algeria. Trading tn. near frontier of Morocco; pop. 71,400; former centre of Moorish art and culture.

Tlinkits or **Thlingits** (tlin-gītz), group of N. Amer. Indian tribes, 99.

T.N.T., trinitrotoluol, or **trinitrotoluene,** 1250, 857.

Toad, 3218; evolutionary position, 158; reproduction, 1246.

Toad, horned, a lizard, 1974.

Toadflax, ramsted, or **butter and eggs.** A genus, *Linaria*, of herbaceous plants native to Europe and Western Asia; the flowers of the common toadflax, grown in racemes, are pale yellow, except for an orange ridge on one lobe of the corolla, and have a short spur. Fam., *Scrophulariaceae*.

Toadstools, 1407.

Tobacco, 3219; France, 1360; as money, 2201; Puerto Rico, 2698; Raleigh popularizes, 2744; Rhodesia, *2773*; Sumatra, 3117; Syria, 3145; U.S.A., 3219, 3290, 3326.

Toba'go or **Tabago.** One of Brit. W. Indian Isls.; a. 116 sq. m.; pop. 25,300; exports sugar, coffee, rubber, tobacco, cacao; 3248.

" To be or not to be," from " Hamlet," 1570.

To'bit, apocryphal book of Old Testament, 425.

Tobolsk. Tn. in Ural area of U.S.S.R., on R. Irtysh; founded 1587 by Cossacks; pop. 25,000; cap. of Tobolsk, Prov. of W. Siberia.

Tobruk. Spt. of Cyrenaica, N. Africa, 60 m. w. of Bardia; excellent harbour; occupied Oct. 1911 by It.; taken Jan. 1941 by Imp., Brit. and Free Fr. under Wavell with 30,000 prisoners, 3418; in Apr. Ger. counter attack by-passed Tobruk whence Axis communications; held and used to land stores and ship men to Egypt during 8 mths.; during Brit. retreat towards Egypt 1942, Tobruk lost to Ger. counter-attack by S. African and Brit. garrison when 28,000 men taken, 3420; recaptured with little resistance by S. Africans after Alamein victory; 3420, *map, 3421*.

Tocantins (tō-kahn-tēnz'). Large r. in cent. Brazil, flowing N. 1,700 m. to Atlantic Ocean, *map, 551*.

Toc H. (Talbot House), social service institution founded, in memory of Gilbert Talbot, by his brother Neville and Rev. P. B. Clayton, at Poperinghe, near Ypres, in 1915; now international, with branches, groups and " Marks " in many places.

Tocqueville (tōk'-vēl), **Alexis, Comte de** (1805–59). Fr. statesman and political philosopher; wrote " Democracy in America," first analysis of democratic institutions in U.S.A.

Todt, Fritz (1891–1942). Ger. engineer; built the *Autobahnen* and Siegfried Line; as min. of munitions 1940, his orgn. conscripted workers from Ger. and occupied countries; killed in air accident, Feb. 1942.

Toe, 1342; mammals, 2074.

Toggenburg goat, 1478.

Togo, Heihachiro, Count (1847–1934). Japanese admiral, c.-in-c. of Jap. fleet in Russo-Japanese War ; destroyed Russ. fleet at Port Arthur in 1904.

Togo, Shigenori (b. 1882). Jap. Min. Foreign Affairs, 1941–42 ; war criminal, sentenced Nov. 1948 to 20 years' imprisonment.

Togoland. Territory in W. Africa on Gulf of Guinea ; a. 46,000 sq. m. ; pop. 1,310,000 ; became Ger. colony 1884 ; divided between Fr. and Gt. Britain under mandate from League of Nations ; in 1946, admin. by Fr. and Gt. Brit. under U.N. trusteeship ; *map f. 68,* 72, 3366 ; *map, 3366* ; 1st World War, 3410.

Tojo, Hideki (1884–1948). Jap. soldier and statesman ; war. min. in Konoye cabinet, and prime min. Oct. 1941 just before Jap. entered 2nd World War ; was also chief of gen. staff in 1944, but resigned both posts when his cabinet fell in July ; arrested by U.S. army Sept. 1945 and hanged Dec. 23, 1948, with 6 other Jap. war criminals.

Tokay (tō-kā'), Hungary. Tn. 130 m. N.E. of Budapest ; pop. 6,000 ; famous for wines.

Tokelau (tō'-kĕ-low) or **Union Islands.** Small group in Polynesia, 2471.

Tokugawa (tō-kŭ-gah'-wah). Family name of the Japanese shoguns or " mayors of the palace " (1600–1868) ; made Tokyo capital of Japan ; fall, 1799.

Tokugawa, Prince Yoshinobu (1837–1913). Jap. statesman, last of the shoguns ; after a year he resigned (1867) ; thus opening the way for friendship with European powers.

Tokyo (tō'-kē-ō), Japan. Cap. and largest city of Japan ; pop. (1940) 6,778,800 ; **3221,** 1796 ; earthquakes, *1069,* 1796 ; air raid damage, *3221.* Here were held, from May 3, 1946, the trials of 28 leading Jap. military and political leaders of the 2nd World War designated as war criminals by the U.N. War Crimes commission ; sentences promulgated Nov. 12, 1948.

Tolbukhin (tol-bū'-kin), **Fyodor I.** (1884–1949). Russ. soldier ; in 2nd World War defended Stalingrad and led offensive that regained Taganrog and Melitopol ; commanded in Crimean drive, isolated Budapest and marched through Rumania into Bulgaria 1944 ; in Apr. 1945 led offensive into Austria and captured Vienna ; made marshal of Soviet Union in 1944.

Tole'do, Ohio, U.S.A. Important Great Lakes port, near mouth of Maumee at w. end of Lake Erie ; pop. 282,350 ; has a fine harbour ; second largest mfg. city of state ; mfrs. include motor-cars, bicycles and electrical appliances.

Toledo, Sp. Former cap. of kingdom on Tagus ; pop. 27,443 ; medieval Gothic art and architecture, 3030 ; Alcazar besieged by govt. forces in Civil War (1936), 3039.

Toledo, Mts. of (Montes de Toledo). A rugged group of cent. Sp., s. of city of Toledo ; highest point 4,750 ft.

Toleration Act. Name given to a statute passed in 1689, under which freedom of worship was granted to Protestant dissenters from the Church of England.

Tol'fa. Tn. in S. Italy ; pop. 4,500.

Toll, for upkeep of roads, 2783.

Toll calls, on telephone, 3177 ; switchboard, *3171.*

Toller, Ernst (1893–1939). Ger. writer. His best-known works are his plays " Masse-Mensch " (Masses and Men), and " Maschinensturmer " (The Machine Wreckers). " National-socialismus " was a scathing indictment of Nazis, 1042, *1457.*

Tolo'sa, battle of (1212), 3036.

Tolpuddle Martyrs. Six labourers of Dorset village, who in Mar. 1834 were transported to Botany Bay for 7 years for forming a society (an offence against the Combination Acts) through which they hoped to press for a weekly wage of 10s. Many

protests caused the remission of the remaining sentence in 1836.

Tolstoy, Alexis (1882–1945). Russ. journalist and novelist ; short stories from 1910 ; trilogy " The Road to Calvary " (Stalin prize, 1942) ; play " Ivan the Terrible," 1944.

Tolstoy, Count Leo (1828–1910). Rus. writer and social reformer, **3222,** 2404, 2856.

Toltecs, pre-Aztec race of Mexico, c. 6th cent. A.D. ; 326.

To'luol or **toluene,** obtained from coal-tar, 857. *See also* **Trinitrotoluol.**

Tomato (to-mah'-to), **3223** ; food value, *2174* ; vitamins in, 3327.

" Tom Brown's Schooldays." Story of Eng. public school life, by Thomas Hughes (1857) ; *1966,* 2887.

" Tom Jones." A novel by Henry Fielding, 1213, 2402.

Tomlinson, George (b. 1890). Minister of Education, 1947.

Tomlinson, Henry Major (b. 1873). Eng. author ; " All Our Yesterdays," " Gallion's Reach," etc.

" Tommy Atkins." Nickname for the Eng. soldier, popularized by Kipling.

" Tommy gun." *See* **Thompson sub-machine-gun.**

Tompion, Thomas (1638–1713). Eng. clockmaker ; brought watch and clock making to a fine art ; made watch for Charles II, and a clock for William III which still strikes the hour.

" Tom Sawyer." Novel of a boy's life on Mississippi, by Mark Twain, 3269.

Tomsk, Siberia. Cap. and centre of agricultural and mining area in s.w. ; pop. 141,200 ; 2967.

Tomsky (1880–1936). Russian revolutionary ; real name, Michael Pavlovitch Efremov ; member of original executive of U.S.S.R.

Tom Thumb. Name given to various dwarfs, the best known being the one exhibited by Phineas T. Barnum, the Amer. showman ; his real name was Charles Sherwood Stratton, *1059* ; the name of Tom Thumb was first given to a dwarf in Charles Perrault's fairy story of that name.

Tom-tit. Popular name of the blue tit, commonest Brit. species of tit, known by its blue and yellow plumage. *See* **Tits.**

Ton (tun), unit of weight. *See* **Weights and Measures** ; metric, 2155.

Tonbridge. Tn. in Kent, on the r. Medway ; famous for its public school, founded in 1553 ; tanning, cricket ball mfg., brewing, wool-stapling ; pop. 20,000.

Tone, Theobald Wolfe (1763–98). Irish patriot ; formed soc. of United Irishmen in 1790 ; persuaded the Fr. to send, 1796 and 1798, small expeditions against England on one of which he was captured ; sentenced to hang, he cut his own throat, Nov. 19, 1798.

Ton'ga or **Friendly Islands.** Chain of isls. in s. Pacific E. of Fiji Isls. ; under Brit. protection ; a. 385 sq. m. ; pop. 40,600 ; chiefly Polynesians ; export copra ; 2471.

Tongking. Prov. of Fr. Indo-China ; a. 40,530 sq. m. ; pop. 9,920,000 ; cap. Hanoi ; 1718, 1720.

Tongland, Galloway, Scot. ; site of hydro-elec. installn., 1670, *1671.*

Tongue, 3223 ; of chameleons, 750, *plate f.* 752 ; fly, *1329* ; moth, *629* ; sense of taste, 3157 ; of snail, 2989 ; spider, *plate f.* 3065 ; taste buds, *3157* ; of woodpecker, 3403.

Ton'ka bean. A Guiana tree (*Dipteryx odorata*) of the fam. *Leguminosae* ; its seeds or beans are used for making perfumes and snuff.

Tonkin. *See* **Tongking.**

Tonks, Henry (1862–1937). Eng. painter. As professor of painting at the Slade School, London, he did much to introduce the ideas of French impressionism into Brit. and its practice was evident in his delightful " Conversation pieces " of life in Chelsea ; 1183.

Tonlé Sap (ton-lā sahp). Lake in Cambodia, 664.

Tonnage, of ships, 2951 ; and Archimedes, 211.

Tonsils, 1676.

Ton'sure. The shaving of the crown of the head in a circle, the distinguishing mark of clerics in the Roman Catholic Church ; the method of shaving differed ; in the Rom. style only a circle of hair was left, in St. Paul's method the shaving was entire, while in the Celtic style the head was shaved in front of a line drawn from ear to ear.

Tonty or **Tonti** (tawn'-tē), **Henry de** (c. 1650–c. 1704). Fr. explorer, b. Italy. La Salle's companion on explorations down Mississippi r.

Tooke, John Horne (1736–1812). Eng. politician ; entered Parl. in 1801 ; published a defence of Wilkes, and later became his opponent.

Toole, John Lawrence (1832–1906). Eng. actor ; played many comedy parts, his last being in " Walker, London " ; he acted altogether for nearly 50 years.

Tools ; agricultural, 78 ; anc. Roman, *2809* ; high-speed alloys, 123 ; pneumatic, 2632 ; steam engine, 3085 ; Stone Age, *2080,* 2082, 3095, used by digger wasp, 3346.

Toothache, caused by decay, 3958.

Toothed whales, 3372.

Toothwort. A leafless European herb parasitic upon roots of other plants, *2621.*

Top, gyroscopic, 1559.

To'paz. A semi-precious stone, 1427.

Tope, a dogfish, *2939.*

Tope'ka, Kansas, U.S.A. State cap., on Kansas r. ; pop. 67,800 ; headquarters of Sante Fé Rly. ; Washburn College ; one of " Free Towns " settled 1854 by eastern anti-slavery men ; rly. workshops, flour mills, etc.

Toplady, Augustus Montague (1740–78). Eng. clergyman, author of hymn " Rock of Ages," 1678 ; he also wrote " The Historic Proof of Doctrinal Calvinism of the Church of England."

Topsy. In Mrs. Stowe's " Uncle Tom's Cabin," mischievous, ignorant little imp of a slave girl ; asked if she knows who made her, replies " Nobody. I 'specs I jest growed."

Torah (tōr'-ah) (Heb. " law "). First five books of Bible, 2235.

Tordesillas (tōr-dā-sēl'-yas), **Convention of.** Treaty between Sp. and Port., regulating their rights of discovery and conquest ; signed June 7, 1494, at Tordesillas, Sp., because of dissatisfaction of Port. with " Line of Demarcation " ; by its terms Brazil later fell to Portugal.

Torgau (tōr'-gow). Ger. Historic tn. on Elbe, 30 m. N.E. of Leipzig ; prominent in Reformation ; victory of Frederick the Great over Austrians 1760 (Seven Years' War) ; in 1814 taken by Germans after siege of 3 months ; U.S. and Russian Armies meet Apr. 28, 1945.

Torii (tōr'-i-ē), Jap. sacred gateway, usually entrance to Shinto temple, *1797.*

Torino (tor-ē'-nō). It. name for **Turin.**

Tormes (tōr'-mās) r. of Sp. ; rises in mts. of cent. Sp., flows N.W. 150 m. to Douro ; Salamanca on, 3030.

Torna'do, *3100,* 3101 ; causes water-spouts at sea, 3356.

Tornio or **Tornea,** r. Rises in Swedish Lapland and flows S.E. 250 m. to Gulf of Bothnia, 3126, *map,* 2395.

Toron'to, Canada. Cap. of Ontario ; pop. over 660,000 ; **3223,** 2434.

Toronto, University of, at Toronto, Ontario ; co-ed., non-sect. ; founded 1827 (present name since 1849) ; arts, science, engineering, medicine, dentistry, law, agric., forestry, etc., 681, 3223.

Torpedo boat destroyer, *2296.*

Torpedoes. Naval explosive devices, **3224,** *2303* ; " human," *3228* ; use by submarines, *3106,* 3107.

Torpedo-fish, 3228 ; electric eel, 1297.

Torquay. Spt. and watering-place on S.E. coast of Devonshire ; pop. 59,250.

Torquemada (tŏr-kä-mah'-dah), **Tomás de** (1420–98). Span. Dominican friar, organizer of Inquisition in Spain ; became inquisitor-general ; incited expulsion of Jews from Spain, 1726.

Torrens system. System for transfer of real estate by registration in place of cumbersome method of deeds ; titles to all property accepted for registration guaranteed by state, and transfer effected by simple registration of fact with proper official ; first used in Australia (1857) ; adopted in parts of Brit. Empire and in U.S.A.

Tor'res, Luis de. Span. explorer, 310, 2340.

Torres, Strait, between Cape York Peninsula, Australia, and isl. of New Guinea, 310.

Torres Vedras (tor'-es vä-dras). Tn. of Portugal, 26 m. N. of Lisbon ; here in 1810–11 Wellington defended himself against Massena ; pop. 8,700.

Torricelli (tor-i-chel'-i). **Evangelista** (1608–47). It. physicist ; inventor of mercurial barometer, 363.

Tor'ridge. R. in Devonshire ; rises near Hartland Point and flows S.E. into Barnstaple Bay ; 36 m. long. 999.

Tor'ridon, Loch, Scot. Inlet of W. coast of Ross and Cromarty.

Torrid zone. See Tropics.

Tor'rington, George Byng, 1st Viscount (1663–1733). Eng. naval officer ; he was largely responsible for the fleet going over to the Prince of Orange ; he was prominent at Beachy Head in 1690, and at the capture of Gibraltar in 1703, and totally defeated the Spaniards off Cape Passaro in 1718.

Tortoise Islands. See Galapagos.

Tortoises and **Turtles, 3229,** 2767, *plates f. 3228, 3229* ; classified, 2767 ; . prehistoric, *2679.*

Tortoiseshell, actually usually the shell of a turtle, 3229.

Tortrix. Any moth of family *Tortricidae* ; the best known of these small moths is the green oak tortrix (*T. viridana*), a destructive pest of oak trees.

Torture, as punishment for crime, and to extract confessions, 2687.

Tory Party (England). Catholic Emancipation Bill, 2535. For later history see **Conservatives.**

Toscanelli dal Pozzo (tos-ka-nel'-ē dal pot'-sō), **Paolo** (1397–1482). It. astronomer ; suggested western route to the Indies to Columbus.

Toscanini (tos'-ka-nēn'-ē), **Arturo** (b. 1867). It. conductor, principal conductor at La Scala Opera House, Milan 1898–1908 and 1920–29 ; 1908–15 Metropolitan Opera House, New York City ; N.Y. Philharmonic Symphony Orch. 1926–36 ; N.B.C. Symphony Orchestra 1937–48.

Tosti, Sir Francesco Paolo (1846–1916). Anglo Ital. composer ; (" Goodbye " ; " Ask Me No More " ; " For Ever," etc.).

Totalisator (Tote). A machine for registering bets ; the sums paid out are regulated by the amounts invested.

Totalitarian State. One with a highly centralized form of government (*e.g.,* Nazi Germany, Fascist Italy, and Communist U.S.S.R.) under control of a single party, based on the theory of the State as the supreme expression of all forms of national life ; in Ger., 2281 ; Italy, 1772 ; Russia, 2850.

Totemism, 835 ; in Alaska, 97 ; among Red Indians, 2753.

To'tem Pole, *97.*

Tot'tenham. Tn. in Middlesex ; N. suburb of London ; famous Hotspur (" Spurs ") assoc. football club ; brewing and other industries ; pop. 129,000.

Toucan. Amer. bird, **3230,** *3231, 3025.*

Touch, sense of, **3231** ; Montessori method of training, 2220 ; nerve endings, 2980.

Touchstone, clown in " As You Like It," 282.

Toul (tōōl). Strongly fortified tn. in N.E. France ; pop. 10,000 ; important in Middle Ages ; taken by Germans (1870) and threatened by them in 1914.

Toulon', France. Important spt. and naval station on Mediterranean ; pop. 125,700 ; in 1707 unsuccessfully besieged by Prince Eugene ; in 1744 Brit. fleet defeated by French and Spanish ; in 1793 Napoleon defeated England and Spain ; French Fleet scuttled Nov. 28, 1942 ; 1359, 2275.

Toulouse (tōō-lōōz') (anc. Tolosa), France. Cathedral city, commercial and mfg. centre in s.w., on Garonne ; pop. 264,400.

Toulouse-Lautrec (tōō-lōōz' lō-trek'), **Henri de** (1864–1901). Fr. Impressionist painter, lithographer, and caricaturist ; famous for paintings of theatre and circus life.

Touquet, Le. See Le Touquet.

Touraine (tōō-rǎn'). Former prov. of France corresponding to present dept. of Indre et Loire ; cap. Tours ; united with Eng. crown, 1609.

Tourcoing (tōōr-kwan'), France. Mfg. tn. 8 m. N.E. of Lille ; pop. 76,000 ; woollens, carpets, upholstery ; occupied by Germans 1914–18 and again 1940–44.

Tour'maline, a semi-precious stone, 1427.

Tournai or **Tournay** (tōōr-nä'). Mfg. city of s.w. Belgium on Schelde, near Fr. border ; pop. 31,500 ; carpets, textiles, porcelain ; devastated by Ger. invasion 1914, and by German bombers 1940 ; *map, 404.*

Tour'nament in Middle Ages, 1864, *plate f. 1864* ; at Camelot, story, 2830 ; quintain, 2719.

Tourniquet (tōōr'ni-kā). Bandage applied very tightly above cut on limb to stop bleeding.

Tours (tōōr). City in w. cent. France, on Loire, pop. 80,000 ; makes silk stuffs, chemicals, iron and steel ; occupied by Germans in 1871 ; formerly cap. of Touraine, 759, 2067, 2000.

Tours, battle of (A.D. 732), 759, 2067.

Toussaint L'Ouverture (tōō-san lōō-vär-tūr'). **Pierre Dominique** (1746– 1803). Haitian Negro rebel and liberator ; threw off Fr. rule and became pres. and dictator of Haitian republic (1801) ; captured by treachery ; died in Fr. prison.

Tovey (tuv'-i), **Sir Donald F.** (1875– 1940). Leading Brit. mus. scholar of his day ; authority on Bach.

Tovey, Ad. of the Fleet Baron John (b. 1885). C.-in-C. Home Fleet 1940–43 ; C.-in-C. the Nore 1943–46 ; led chase and sinking of Bismarck May 1941.

Tow, fibre, 1313, 1844.

Tower, in architecture, 220, 409 ; leaning " tower " of Pisa, 2612, *2613* ; cooling tower at power station, 2676. See also **Bell-tower.**

Tower Bridge, London, 2012, *plate f. 3232, 567, 568.*

Tower mill, type of windmill, *3386.*

Tower of London. Anc. fortress and palace in E. London, **3231,** *3232* ; *plates f. 3232, 3233,* 718, 2009 ; beefeaters, 396, *plates f. 396, 397* ; Henry VI murdered, 1612 ; Raleigh in, 2744.

Towers of Silence, near Malabar Hill, Bombay, India, 496.

Town and Country Planning, Ministry of, establd. 1943 ; 3233.

Town Council, a governing body elected by local ratepayers to control municipal affairs ; its members look after borough property and impose rates for public purposes ; they are elected for 3 years and may be asked to serve on various committees ; the chairman is known as the Mayor in Eng., and provost in Scot., 1491.

Town planning, 3223.

Townshend, Charles (1725–67). Eng. politician ; Chancellor of the Exchequer under Pitt ; author of Townshend duties.

Townshend, Sir Charles Vere Ferrers (1861–1924), Brit. general ; entered Royal Marines (1881) ; served with distinction in the Sudan, on the Nile, and in S. Africa ; defended Kut in 1916, when he was taken prisoner by the Turks, 3410.

Township and town. The name applied to the earliest known form of territory belonging to a rural community, and sometimes applied to the community itself ; the term town is applied to any collection of houses, etc., larger than a village.

Townsville. Spt. and city of N. Queensland, Australia, 830 m. N.W. of Brisbane ; pop. 34,000 ; exports sugar ; twice raided by Jap. aircraft in 1942 ; *2718.*

Towton. Vil. in Yorkshire ; decisive victory of Yorkists, under Edward IV, over Lancastrians 1461 (Wars of the Roses).

Towy. R. of Cardiganshire, rises in N.E. and flows 66 m. into Carmarthen Bay.

Towyn. Watering-place in Merionethshire ; pop. 3,800 ; 2146.

Tox'in. Poisonous organic substance, formed by bacteria, 1458. See **Antitoxin.**

Toxophilites (archers). See Archery.

Toyn'bee, Arnold (1852–83). Eng. pioneer in social settlement work ; Toynbee Hall in Whitechapel, London, is named after him.

Toyoku'ni (1769–1825). Japanese artist, 1812.

Toys, 801 ; balloons, 2836 ; gyroscope, 1559 ; kaleidoscope, 1845 ; kites, 1863.

Trabzon. See Trebizond.

Trace metals, of which minute amounts are essential in diet, 2149.

Tracer, radio-active. Isotype of element, used in med. research and treatment, 1761, 2733.

Tracery. In architecture, the species of pattern work formed or traced in the head of a Gothic window by the mullions being continued, but diverging into arches, curves, and flowing lines enriched with foliations.

Trachea (trā'-ki-*a* or tra-kē'-*a*). Air passage or windpipe of an animal ; in caterpillars, 720 ; in insects, 1732.

Trachodon (trā'-kō-don). A prehistoric monster reptile ; remains have been discovered in N. Amer.

Track athletics, *289.*

Track circuit, in automatic rly. signalling, 2739.

Tractarianism. See Oxford Movement.

Trac'tor. In agriculture, *80, 85.*

Trade. See Commerce.

Trade, Board of, 3233.

Trade-mark. A symbol affixed by a manufacturer or merchant to special goods or classes of goods which is protected by law ; a register of such trade-marks is kept at the Patent Office.

• **Trade routes.** Atlantic, *map, 290* ; Asia (anc.), 263 ; Caribbean Sea, 701 ; Great Lakes, *map, 1515* ; Khyber Pass, 55 ; Mediterranean, *2136* ; Panama canal, 2490 ; Phoenician, 2573 ; sea route to India, 695, 1718 ; spice trade, 3060.

Trade union. An organized body of workmen in any trade or industrial occupation associated together for the protection of their common interests ; **3233,** 1875.

Trades Union Congress (T.U.C.), 3224.

Trade winds, *3385* ; affect rainfall, 2741.

Trafalgar. Cape of S. Spain at N.W. entrance to Strait of Gibraltar ; battle of (1805), **3234,** 3277, 2305, *870,* 2276, 2313, *2314,* 3321.

Trafalgar Square, London, 2013, *2019.*

Traffic control, 2784, *plate f. 2785.*

Traffic lights, automatic, 322, *2785– 2787* ; linked with fire-alarms, 1287. *See also* **Traffic Control.**

Tragacanth. A gum, 1558.

Tragedy. Eng., 1040 ; Gk., 1037, 1540 ; Latin, 1897.

Train. See Locomotive ; Railways.

Traitor's Gate, Tower of London, *3231.*

Trajan (Marcus Ulpius Trajanus) (A.D. 51–117). Rom. soldier-emperor ; adopted son of Nerva ; humane, able ruler, great builder, conqueror of Dacia, Armenia, and Parthia ; 2812 ; empire reaches greatest extent, *map, 2808.*

Trajectory. Curved path of missile from source to target ; of stone dropped from aeroplane, 2130.

Tralee, Co. Kerry, pop. 9,982 ; 1853.

Tramp steamers, 2949.

Trams and Trolley-buses, 3235 ; dynamos, 1060 ; electric motor, 2239.

Tram silk, 2972.

Trans-Ande′an railways, 153, 804, 3024.

Transcaucasia. *See* Caucasia.

Tran′sept. In architecture, 216.

Transformer. Device for changing voltage of electric current, **3237** ; grid substation, 1548 ; induction coil, 1720 ; compared with asynchronous elec. motor, 2240.

Transfusion of blood, 476.

Transit instrument. A telescope mounted to rotate vertically ; in astronomical observations, 2411, *3214.*

Transjordan became the Hashimite Kingdom of the Jordan in 1949, an independendent Arab kingdom on both sides of the R. Jordan. Transjordan was under Brit. mandate from 1923 to 1946 ; 3233, 1838.

Transmigra′tion of the soul. Buddhist doctrine, 601 ; Hindu, 1628 ; taught by Pythagoras, 2710.

Transmitter. In wireless, 3392, *3394, 3399* ; telegraph, 3165–67 ; of radar 2726 ; telephone, *3175* ; television, 3182.

Transmuta′tion. In chemistry, the changing of one element into another; usually achieved by bombarding it with swiftly moving particles such as neutrons, protons, etc., 2731, 2733 ; of nitrogen into oxygen, 2733.

Transom. In architecture, a term applied to horizontal stone bars or divisions of windows ; seldom seen prior to the 15th cent.

Transpiration. Process of evaporation of water from the stomata in the leaf surfaces of plants ; probably assists the movement of water up the stem, 2621.

Transport : aeroplane, 41 ; airship, 92 ; cycles and cycling, 947 ; canals, 686 ; caravans, *2860* ; locomotive, 1981– 96 ; mono-rail, 1562 ; motor-car, 2241–16 ; railways, 2734 ; refrigeration, 1393 ; roads and streets, 2783 ; ships, 2945 ; tramcar, trolley-bus, 3235 ; tunnels, 3255. *See* chief topics above by name.

Transport Commission, British, 3239.

Transport, Ministry of, 3238.

Trans-Siberian Railway, 2736, 2845, 2967, 3327.

Transubstantia′tion. In theology, doctrine of the change of the whole substance of the bread and wine, by consecration at the celebration of the Holy Eucharist, into the Body and Blood of Christ, only the appearance of the bread and wine remaining ; it is a dogma of the R.C. Church.

Transvaal (trahns-vahl). Prov. of Union of S. Africa ; a. 110,450 sq. m. ; pop. 4,183,800 : **3239**, *1833* ; *map, 3015* ; Boer Wars, 486, 3019 ; Botha, 533 ; Smuts, 2987, 2988.

Transver′sal. In geometry, 1438.

Transylva′nia. Region in N.W. Rumania, formerly part of Hungary ; a. 22,312 sq. m. ; pop. 3,399,000 ; 2839, *2840, plate f. 2840,* 2841 ; *maps, 320, 344.*

Transylvanian Alps. Range of Carpathian Mts. in cent. Rumania, formerly on Hungarian boundary, 2839, 1233, *maps, 320, 344.*

Trapani (trah′-pah-nē). Spt. and industrial centre on N.W. coast of Sicily ; pop. 63,540 ; anc. Drepanum, important Carthaginian naval station in First Punic War ; Rom. fleet defeated 250 B.C.

Trap-door spiders, 3064.

Trappists. Cistercian monks, *2213.*

Trasimene (tras-i-mē′-nē), **Lake.** In cent. Italy ; battle (217 B.C.), 1574.

Travancore. Indian state in extreme S.W. of Deccan ; a. 7,660 sq. m. ; pop. 6,000,000 ; tea, spices, rubber, coconuts ; mfrs. pottery, rubber,

glass, chemicals ; cap. Trivandrum ; monazite sands in, 3187.

Traveller's joy. The usual name for *Clematis vitalba,* climbing plant very common in Brit., known also as " Old Man's Beard," from long, silky threads attached to fruits, *836.*

Trawler, for fishing, 1299, *1304.*

Trawl-line. A fishing device, 1299.

Trawl-net, for fishing, *1299.*

Treason. Treachery or breach of faith, especially by a subject against his sovereign ; punishment for, 2687.

" Treasure Island." Story by Stevenson, 3090.

Treasury, Whitehall, London. Dept. of Brit. Govt. responsible for the national revenue ; the Prime Minister holds the office of First Lord, **3240.**

Treaties, 3240. For list of famous treaties, *see* facing page.

Treaty Ports, in China, 810.

Treb′ia (modern Trebbia). Tributary of Po ; battle (218 B.C.), 1574.

Treb′izond or **Trabzon** (anc. Trap′ezus). Turkey. Spt. on Black Sea ; pop. 50,000 ; varied mfrs. ; former centre of transit trade between Europe and Persia ; cap. of empire of Trebizond (1204–1461) ; taken by Russia (1916), recaptured by Turks (1918) ; *map,* 465.

Tree, Sir Herbert Beerbohm (1853–1917). Eng. actor-manager, half-brother of Max Beerbohm ; made his first London appearance in 1878 ; famous for elaborate revivals of Shakespeare's plays and for his creation of the part of Svengali in Du Maurier's " Trilby."

Tree-dwellers. In Ceylon, 749 ; in New Guinea, *2339.*

Tree-ferns, *1267,* 3247 ; in Ceylon, 748 ; in New Zealand, *2359.*

Trees, *3241–3244,* 3245, 2622 ; eucalyptus dries swamps, 1230 ; forests, 1349 ; giant redwoods and sequoias, 2921 ; leaves and their work, 1914, 1243 ; longevity, 2624 ; root, 2825 ; tallest, 1230. *See* **Forests ; Lumbering ; Timber ; Plant Life ;** and the various trees, as **Ash, Birch,** by name.

Tree sparrow, 3052.

Tree surgery, 3246 ; grafting, *1402.*

" Tree wool," cotton, 920.

Tre′foil (" three-leaved "). A name applied to the clovers (*Trifolium*) and other plants having compound leaves in three parts ; the birds'-foot trefoil (*Lotus corniculatus*) is so called because it has clusters of pods resembling a bird's foot ; other species are hop trefoil, hare's-foot, and strawberry-headed trefoil, all so called from the appearance of the bunches of flowers.

Trefoil. In architecture, an ornament used in the Gothic style, formed by mouldings so arranged as to resemble the trefoil.

Treitschke (trītsh-kêr), **Heinrich von** (1834–96). Ger. historian.

Trelawny, Edward John (1792–1881). Eng. traveller.

Trenail, a wooden nail, 2271.

Trench, Richard Chenevix (1807–86). Archbishop of Dublin, poet and philologist (" The Study of Words ").

Trench, in 1st World War, 3409 ; mechanical diggers, 1247.

Trenchard, Hugh Montague Trenchard, 1st Viscount (b. 1873). Eng. administrator ; chief of air staff (1918–29) ; Marshal of R.A.F. (1927) ; Commissioner of Metropolitan Police (1931) ; established Police College, Hendon.

Trengganu (treng′-ga-noo). State of Malayan Union ; a. 5,050 sq. m. ; pop. 226,426 ; 2069.

Trent, Jesse Boot, 1st Baron (1850– 1931). Eng. business man, founder of the extensive multiple shop business, Boots the Chemists.

Trent. R. of cent. Eng. flowing s. and N.E., 170 m. to Humber, 995, 2398, 3072 ; bore in, 525.

Trent, Council of (1547–63), 2760.

Trentino (tren-tē′-nō). Dist. in It. Tirol, 3215, 3410, 1770.

Tren′ton, New Jersey, U.S.A. State cap. ; pop. 124,700 ; 2946 ; stands on Delawere R. ; greatest pottery centre in the U.S.A.

Trepang′ or **sea-cucumber.** An animal related to starfish, 2911.

Trepan′ning or **trephining.** Surgical operation consisting in removal of disk from skull for purpose of relieving pressure, removing tumours, etc. Practised by prehistoric man.

Trevel′yan, George Macaulay (b. 1876). Eng. historian, a son of Sir G. O. Trevelyan ; Regius prof. of Mod. Hist. at Cambridge from 1927 ; O.M. in 1930 ; Master of Trinity in 1940 ; became Chancellor of Durham Univ. in 1950. Works include histories of England and mod. Italy, and a life of John Bright.

Trevelyan, Sir George Otto (1838–1928). Brit. statesman and author ; he was Chief Sec. for Ire. (1882–84) ; Chancellor of the Duchy of Lancaster (1884–85) ; and twice served as Secretary for Scotland ; a nephew of Lord Macaulay, whose " Life " he wrote ; he also published " The Early History of Charles James Fox " and " The American Revolution."

Treves, Sir Frederick (1853–1924). Eng. surgeon ; was consulting surgeon to the forces in the Boer War (1899–1902), and acted as surgeon-extraordinary to Queen Victoria ; he operated on King Edward VII for appendicitis ; he was one of the founders of the Red Cross Society.

Treves or **Trier.** Anc. city in west Germany, on Moselle ; pop. 76,700 ; imperial residence under later Rom. Empire ; fine Roman amphitheatre, basilica, baths, and other remains were badly damaged, and cath. ruined, during 2nd World War ; archbishop an imperial elector, 1637 ; bombed, taken by U.S. March 3, 1945.

Treviso (trā-vē-zō) (anc. Tarvisium). It. city, 16 m. N. of Venice ; pop. 53,900 ; textiles, metal ware ; art centre ; city republic under Lombard League.

Trev′ithick, Richard (1771–1833). Eng. engineer and inventor ; builds first moving steam-engine, **3247,** 2734, 1981.

Trial, by jury, 1609, 1842 ; courts, 921 ; medieval forms, 1843.

Trian′a. Suburb of Seville, 2926.

Triangle, in geometry, 1435, 1437, 1438.

Triangle. Percussion instrument, 2268, 2446.

Trianon (trē′-ah-nawn). Palaces at Versailles, 3317.

Trianon, Treaty of (1920), between Hungary and the Allied Powers.

Trias′sic period, in geological time, 1432, 1433.

Tribe, origin of, 1259.

Trib′unes. Roman magistrates, 2805.

Tricer′atops. A three-horned prehistoric reptile, 2678, 2680.

Trichina (trik-ī′-na). A parasitic worm. sometimes found in the muscles of a man ; though more commonly occurring in pigs and rats.

Trichinopoli (trik-in-op′-o-li). Tn. of Madras, India, on R. Cauvery ; pop. 159,500 ; cheroots, woven fabrics, hardware, jewelry ; 2054.

Trichop′tera. Insect order including caddis flies, 1733.

Tricolour, French. Originated by Lafayette, 1884.

Tricus′pid valve, of heart, *1592.*

Tri-dent. Three-pronged spear carried by Neptune ; borne by Britannia and symbolic of sea power.

Trier (tri-ār′). Same as **Treves.**

Trieste (trē-est′). Most important city on Adriatic ; pop. 270,000 ; 29 ; in 1914–18 War, 3410, 3411 ; occupied by Yugoslavia in 1945 ; formerly Italian, was made " Free Territory " by U.N. 1947 ; 1577.

Trifo′lium. Genus of plants, 852, 854.

Triglyph, in architecture, *215.*

Trigonom′etry. A branch of mathematics dealing primarily with the relations between the sides and angles of triangles, **3248** ; Ptolemy and, 2697.

Trilobite (trī'-lo-bīt). An extinct crab-like animal, 1354 ; abundant in Cambrian times, 1432.

Trinidad. Is. of Brit. W. Indies ; a. 1,860 sq. m. ; pop. 500,000 ; **3248** ; *map f. 3024*; asphalt, 272; sugar, *3113*.

Trinitrotol'uol or **trinitrotoluene** (T.N.T.) ; 857, 1250.

Trinity, doctrine of. In theology, belief that there are three persons in God or the divine nature, the Father, Son, and Holy Ghost.

Trinity Church, New York, 2352.

Trinity College, Cambridge, *668.*

Trinity College, Dublin (T.C.D.). *See* **Dublin University.**

Trinity College, Oxford, 1554.

Trinity House, London, **3248,** 621, 1945.

Trinity River, Texas, U.S.A. Flows 550 m. s.w., entering Galveston Bay 40 m. N. of Galveston.

Trio. In music, a composition written for three voices or three instruments ; the term is also used to denote a subsidiary movement in 3–4 time, common in certain styles of composition.

Triode, type of thermionic valve, 1138, *3199.*

Triomphe, Arc de (ahrk dē trē'-omf), Paris, *2515,* 2516.

Triple Alliance. Formed 1883 between Germany, Austria-Hungary, and Italy, 1240, 3240, 3410.

Triple Entente (ahn-tahnt'). Agreement between France, Russia, and England completed in 1907 ; 1092, 1240.

Triple expansion engine, 3085.

Tripoli, Port on N. coast of Africa, cap. of Libya ; pop. 108,240 ; taken by British Jan. 23, 1943 ; *map, 3421.*

Tripoli, Tripolis, or **Tarabulus,** Lebanon. Anc. tn. near coast ; pop. 71,500 ; captured in 1109 by Crusaders ; 3146.

Tripolitania. Former It. colony. *See* **Libya.**

Tripolitza or **Tripolis,** Greek tn. ; pop. 14,400 ; cap. of Morea under Turks ; taken in 1821 by Gk. insurgents ; destroyed in 1825 by Ibrahim Pasha.

Tri'pos. Term applied to the final honours examination at Cambridge University, so called from the three-legged stool upon which sat the M.A. who delivered the satirical Latin speech at degree-giving on Ash Wednesday.

Trireme (trī'-rēm). Anc. galley, with three banks of oars.

Tristan da Cunha (tris-tahn dah koon-yah). Mountain islet in S. Atlantic,

SOME HISTORIC TREATIES AND ALLIANCES

Adrianople (1829) : Treaty following Russo-Turkish War of 1828–29, recognizing the independence of Greece.

Aix-la-Chapelle (1748) : Terminated War of Austrian Succession.

Amiens (1802) : Treaty between England and France, which gave a breathing spell in the wars of the French Revolution.

Augsburg, Religious Peace of (1555) : Charles V granted toleration to Lutheran princes and cities in Germany.

Berlin, Congress of (1878) : Revised in Turkey's favour treaty of San Stefano which ended Russo-Turkish War, 1877–78. Montenegro, Serbia, and Rumania made independent of Turkey ; Bulgaria, while remaining under its rule, was given a Christian government, but with less territory than provided at San Stefano.

Brest-Litovsk (1918) : Peace treaty forced upon Bolshevik Russia by victorious Germany, requiring the surrender of border states and the payment of an enormous indemnity.

Brétigny (1360) : Afforded break in the Hundred Years' War between England and France. Edward III renounced his claim to the French crown, and received southern provinces in full sovereignty.

Brussels (1948) : Gt. Britain, France, Belgium, Netherlands, and Luxemburg pledged for 50 years to help each other if attacked.

Bucharest (1913) : Ended second Balkan War.

Cambrai, League of (1508) : Formed against Venice by the Pope, the Empire, France, and Spain.

Campo Formio (1797) : Between France and Austria, after Napoleon Bonaparte's first campaign in Italy.

Clayton-Bulwer (1850) : Between Great Britain and the United States, providing that neither power should have exclusive control over any canal built across Panama isthmus or Nicaragua.

Frankfort (1871) : Definitive treaty at end of Franco-Prussian War ; France forced to surrender Alsace and much of Lorraine to Germany and pay an indemnity of £200,000,000.

Ghent (1814) : Between United States and Great Britain, ending War of 1812.

Hay-Pauncefote (1901) : Between United States and Great Britain, setting aside Clayton-Bulwer agreement, and allowing the United States to build and fortify the Panama canal, although maintaining its neutrality.

Holy Alliance (1815) : Declaration of impractical Christian brotherhood signed by Russia, Austria, Prussia, and other European powers (except Pope, Turkey, and Great Britain).

Lausanne (1923) : Treaty defining the European boundaries of Turkey and in part her frontiers in Asia.

Locarno (1925) : A pact of mutual guarantees regarding territory signed by Great Britain, Germany, Belgium, France, and Italy, and of arbitration between Germany and Belgium, France, Poland, and Czechoslovakia.

London (1913) : Ended first Balkan War.

Lunéville (1801) : Treaty between France and Austria, following Bonaparte's second Italian campaign.

Neuilly (1919) : Treaty between Allies and Bulgaria at end of First World War, ceding Bulgarian territory to Rumania, Serbia, and Greece.

North Atlantic (1949) : Defensive alliance between U.S.A., Canada, Gt. Britain, France, Belgium, Netherlands, Luxemburg, Norway, Denmark, Italy, Portugal and Iceland.

Nystadt (1721) : Peace between Russia and Sweden, involving cession to Russia of territory conquered by Peter the Great, along the Gulf of Finland.

Paris (1763) : Terminated Seven Years' War (French and Indian War in America). France lost all her American possessions to Great Britain.

Paris (1783) : End of War of American Independence.

Paris (1856) : End of Crimean War.

Paris (1898) : End of Spanish-American War ; Cuba liberated and Porto Rico, Guam, and Philippines ceded to United States in return for £4,000,000.

Paris (1928) : "To renounce war as an instrument of national policy" ; originally signed by fifteen nations, including Great Britain, France, and U.S.A., afterwards by many others.

Paris (1947) : End of Second World War ; treaties signed with Italy, Finland, Rumania, Hungary and Bulgaria.

Portsmouth (1905) : Termination of Russo-Japanese War.

Pressburg (1805) : Peace between France and Austria, after the latter had been defeated for the third time by Napoleon.

Pretoria (1902) : Ended Boer War. Transvaal and Orange Free State lost their independence, becoming British colonies.

Rapallo (1920) : Settled controversy between Italy and Yugoslavia over Fiume, giving it status of a sovereign city contiguous to Italy.

Riga (1921) : Russia ceded to Poland 44,000 square miles of territory with 3,685,000 inhabitants.

Russo-German Pact (1939) : Pact of non-aggression concluded between Germany and the Soviet Republics.

Ryswick (1697) : Treaty of peace between France and England, Spain, and Holland.

St. Germain (1919) : Treaty with Austria at end of First World War, breaking up the Dual Monarchy into Austria, Hungary, Czechoslovakia and Yugoslavia, and ceding territory to Poland and Rumania.

Sèvres (1920) : Treaty of peace with Turkey at end of First World War, depriving it of over half its population and two-thirds of its territory.

Shimonoseki (1895) : Treaty of peace ending Chino-Japanese War of 1894.

Tilsit (1807) : Treaty of peace and alliance between Napoleon and the Tsar of Russia.

Trianon (1920) : Treaty of Allies with Hungary at close of First World War ; established boundaries with cessions to border states.

Triple Alliance (1882) : A defensive alliance created when Italy joined the Dual Alliance of Germany and Austria, formed in 1870.

Triple Entente (1907) : Diplomatic union of Great Britain, France, and Russia to counterbalance the Triple Alliance, concluded when agreement between England and Russia (1907) and England and France (1904) was added to the Dual Alliance of France and Russia (1891).

Troyes (1420) : Treaty interrupting Hundred Years' War between England and France. Henry V of England was to marry Catherine of France and succeed to French throne on death of Charles VI.

Utrecht (1713) : Peace treaty after the defeat of the French in the War of the Spanish Succession, giving Spain, Naples, and Sicily, and the Spanish colonies to the French claimant and territorial concessions to Austria, England, and Holland.

Verdun, Partition of (843) : Treaty among the three sons of Louis the Pious, dividing Charlemagne's empire into three parts, the western third of which later developed into France and the eastern third into Germany.

Versailles (1910) : Treaty of peace with Germany following First World War. Germany lost territory in Europe amounting to almost 48,000 square miles, and more than 1,000,000 square miles of colonial possessions ; reparations of many million pounds to be paid.

Vienna, Treaties of (1815) : Division of Europe following overthrow of Napoleon. Russia annexed a large part of Poland, and northern Italy was given to Austria ; Austrian Netherlands were given to Holland, and part of Saxony to Prussia.

Washington (1871) : Between Great Britain and United States, referring the Alabama claims and the north-west boundary dispute to arbitration.

Washington (1922) : A series of treaties signed at the conference of nine great powers at Washington, 1921–22 ; the most important were (a) Five-Power Naval Treaty providing for a reduction in naval armament ; (b) Five-Power Treaty restricting the use of submarines and prohibiting use of poison gas ; (c) Four-Power Treaty, between United States, Great Britain, France, Japan, providing for maintenance of existing conditions in Pacific ; (d) Nine-Power Treaty relating to China.

Webster-Ashburton (1842) : Between Great Britain and United States, settling the north-east boundary dispute.

Western Hemisphere Defence (1947) : Between 19 American nations, for defence against aggression. Signed at Petropolis, Brazil.

Westphalia (1648) : Ended Thirty Years' War.

midway between Buenos Aires and Cape of Good Hope ; claimed by Gt. Brit. ; 44 sq. m. ; pop. 222 ; 290. Commissioned in 1942 as H.M.S. Atlantic Isle ; radio and meteorological station.

Tristan or **Tristram of Lyonesse.** Hero of Celtic legend, sent to bring Iseult (Isolde), bride of his uncle, king of Cornwall ; drinks by mistake of a love potion which makes him Iseult's lover ; ivy legend, 1788.

" Tristan and Isolde," by Wagner, 2440.

Tritium. Isotope of hydrogen, of atomic weight 3, not found in nature but produced in nuclear reactions ; 296.

Triton (trī-ton). In Gk. myth, son of Poseidon and Amphitrite, personification of roaring waters ; blows a twisted seashell to calm or raise the waves ; tritons sometimes appear with the torso of a man, the tail of a dolphin, and the forefeet of a horse.

Triton. A gastropod mollusc ; trumpet-shaped shell, *2943.*

Trium'virate. In Rom. history ; first (Caesar, Pompey and Crassus), 651, 2654 ; second, 303.

Trobriand Islands. Group of islands off New Guinea, inhabited by a primitive race, whose beliefs and customs have been made known by Prof. Malinowski, 2340 ; U.S. occupy June 30, 1943.

Trochee (trō-kē). Metrical foot, 2635.

Trochilidae (trō-kil′-i-dē). The humming bird family, 1651.

Troczen (trē′-zen). Anc. city of Peloponnesus, Greece ; prominent in Persian wars, later ally of Sparta.

Troglodytes. Name given by ancient Greek writers to various tribes of cave-dwelling savages of debased habits ; best known lived along Red Sea.

Troglodytidae (trog-lō-dīt′-i-dē). The wren family of birds.

Tro′gon. A family of tropical forest birds, noted for their gorgeous plumage ; they occur in Africa, Asia, S. and Cent. Amer. *See also* **Quetzal.**

Troilus (trō′-il-us). In Gk. legend, son of Priam, king of Troy ; in medieval legend, hero of the love story which forms basis of Shakespeare's tragedy " Troilus and Cressida," and Chaucer's poem of same name.

Trojan War, 3248 ; Achilles, 19 ; Ajax, 95 ; Amazons, 137 ; Aphrodite, 186 ; Athena aids Greeks, 283 ; Hector, 1603 ; legends collected in Homeric poems, 1637 ; Odysseus, 2421 ; Paris, 2514 ; Poseidon aids Greeks, 2661 ; Wooden Horse, Story of the, 3249. *See also* **Homer ; Troy.**

Trolley bus, 3236.

Trollhättan Falls, Sweden, of R. Göta, 3129.

Trollope, Anthony (1815–82). Eng. novelist, keen-sighted chronicler of Eng. middle-class life, **3250,** 1215, 2402.

Trolls, in Norse myth, the " hill people," underground elves.

Trom′bone. A musical instrument, *1644,* 2267, 2446, 3009.

Tromp, Cornelius van (1629–91). Dutch sailor, son of following. Opposed Engl. with much bravery.

Tromp, Martin Harpertzoon (1597–1653). Dutch admiral ; defeated Sp. and Port. fleets (1639) ; fought against English fleet (1652–53).

Tromsö (trŏm-sŏö). Tn. of N. Norway ; pop. 10,785 ; 2394 ; German seaplane base 1940–45 ; German battleship Tirpitz sunk here by British bombers, Nov. 12, 1944.

Trondhjem (tron′-yem) or **Trondheim.** Norway spt. on w. coast ; pop. 56,400 ; timber, fish, copper, iron ; *map, 2395* ; cath., 2393 ; used by Germans 1940–45, as U-boat base, and target for frequent Allied air attack ; 3416.

Troon, Watering-place and spt. in Ayrshire ; famous golf links ; shipbuilding ; pop. 10,270 ; 324.

Trooping the Colour. Ceremony of escorting the colour through the regiment on parade, especially annual carrying the King's colour, in celebration of King's birthday on Horse Guards' Parade ; *877, 878.*

Tropaeolum. Genus of plants including the garden nasturtium, 2279.

Trope or **figure of speech,** 1270.

Trop′ics or **torrid zone.** Region of greatest heat, bordering the Equator, 1898. *See* **Cancer, Tropic of ; Capricorn, Tropic of.**

Trop′osphere. Lower belt of ordinary air, in which life exists, 88, *89,* 2150.

Troppau (trŏ′-pow) or **Opava,** Czechoslovakia. Former cap. of Austrian Silesia, on Oppa ; pop. 30,105 ; makes cloth, beet sugar, machinery.

Tros. In Greek mythology, king of Phrygia ; gave name to Troy, which his son Ilus founded.

Trossachs (tros′-aks). Pass of, Perthshire, Scot., 2558, 2889 ; *plate f. 2892* ; *map, 2890.*

Trot′sky, Leon (1879–1940). Rus. revolutionary leader and Minister of War 1917–1924 ; **3251,** 2850, 3072 ; and Lenin, 1923.

Trotwood, Betsy. In Dickens's " David Copperfield," David's eccentric but good-hearted great-aunt.

Troubadours (trōō′-ba-dōōrz). Fr. minstrels, 2262.

Trout. A food fish, **3251,** 1300, *1310.*

Trouvères (trōō-vâr′). Minstrels of N. Fr.

" Trovatore, Il." Opera by Verdi, 2440, 3315.

Troy or **I′lium.** Anc. city in N.W. Asia Minor, famous in Gk. legend ; scene of Trojan War, 3248 ; **3252,** 1638 ; centre of Aegean civilization, 30 ; excavation, 2883 ; wooden horse, story, 3249, *1896. See also* **Homer ; Trojan War.**

Troy, New York, U.S.A. ; pop. 70,300 ; mfrs. include shirts, collars and cuffs, also laundry and other machinery.

Troyes (trwah). Fr. tn. on Seine ; pop. 58,800 ; makes hosiery ; medieval fair, 1257 ; Treaty of (1420), 1653.

Troyon (trwah-awn′), Constant (1810–65). Fr. painter, by many critics considered the foremost animal painter of modern times ; his rich and glowing landscapes include animals as an integral part.

Troy weight. *See* **Weights and Measures,** *f-i.* ; origin, 1257.

Truce, 239.

Truce of God. In feudal times, prohibition by Church of private war on holy days and seasons, and certain week-days.

Trudgeon. A popular stroke used in swimming. Though less usual, the more correct form of spelling is " trudgen," after the swimmer, J. Trudgen, who popularized it, 3137.

Truf′fle. A fungus, 1408.

Truman, Harry Shippe (b. 1884). President of U.S.A. 1945 and 1948 ; **3252,** 3293.

Trumbull, Jonathan (1710–85). Amer. colonial statesman, gov. of Connecticut ; nickname " Brother Jonathan " said to come from Washington so calling Trumbull.

Trumper, Victor Thomas (1877–1915). Australian cricketer, one of the finest Australian batsmen. During 1902 tour scored 2,570 runs.

Trumpet. A musical instrument, **1643,** 2267, 2446.

Trumpet narcissus, 2279.

Trumpet shell, *2943.*

Trunk, of elephant, 1141.

Trunk calls, on telephone, 3177.

Trunk roads, 2784.

Truro. City of Cornwall ; mod. cathedral ; exports kaolin ; pop. 13,400.

Truss, of bridge, *565* ; of roof, 564, 2822.

Trusts, business. Organizations for the control of several companies or corporations under one director.

Trypanosomes (trip′-a-nō-sōmz). Various single-celled parasitic animals ; carry sleeping-sickness germ.

Tryp′sin. A proteid-digesting enzyme.

Tsar. Title of Rus. emperor taken by Ivan IV, 1788.

Tsarina (zah-rē′-na). Title of Rus. emperor's wife.

Tsaritsyn. *See* **Stalingrad.**

" Tsar Kolokol." Bell, 411.

Tschaikovsky. *See* **Tchaikovsky.**

Tsetse. Fly, carrier of sleeping-sickness, **3252,** 160 ; in Congo, 68 ; in Rhodesia, 2771.

Tsien-tang. R. of China in prov. of Chekiang ; enters Bay of Hangchow ; 1573.

Ts′in. Anc. Chinese dynasty ; most important ruler Shi Hwang-ti, " first universal emperor " ; 810.

Tsinan or **Tsinanfu,** China. Cap. of Shantung 3 m. from Yellow r. ; pop. 512,686 ; silk, precious stones, glass ; univ. ; on Tsinan-Tsingtau, rly ; 2938.

Tsingtao (tsing-tow′), China, treaty port in Shantung on Bay of Kiaochow ; pop. 756,000 ; 2938.

Tsushima (tsōō-she′-ma). Isl. of Japan in Korean Strait ; battle of Sea of Japan fought off its coast (1905).

Tsze-Hsi. *See* **Tze-Hsi.**

Tuamo′tu or **Low Archipelago.** French group of 80 atolls in Pacific s. of Marquesas ; a. 366 sq. m. ; pop. 4,000 ; 2471.

Tuaregs. Nomadic tribe of cent. and w. Sahara, 70, 2860.

Tuat′. Group of oases in w. part of Algerian Sahara, N. Africa, 2859.

Tuata′ra or **Tuatera.** A reptile, 2767, 1974, *1975.*

Tu′ba or **bass horn.** A musical instrument, 1644, 2267.

Tube. Term applied to underground electric rlys. in London, 2738, 3275, *3274. See* **Underground, London's.**

Tuberculo′sis (T.B.) or **consumption.** Bacterial disease, 1458 ; of bones, 2977 ; inherited tendency, 1617 ; streptomycin used against, 3103.

Tu′bers. Underground storage organs of plants, 612 ; potato, 2664, 2825.

Tubes, pneumatic, 2632.

Tubiflorales. An order of flowers with tubular corollas.

Tubina′res. Tube-nosed order of seabirds that nest in rocks and feed on small water creatures ; includes albatross. 101 ; petrel, 2563.

Tübingen (tu′bing-en). Ger. tn. on Neckar ; univ. ; pop. 28,686 ; sustained damage during 2nd World War ; since 1946 cap. of *Land* (province) of Württemberg-Hohenzollern.

Tubuai (tū-bū-I) or **Austral Islands,** in s. Pacific ; French ; a. 115 sq. m. ; pop. 3,900 ; 2471.

Tuck, Friar. Vagabond friar in Robin Hood legends ; appears in " Ivanhoe " as the " holy clerk of Copmanhurst " ; 2790.

Tucson (tū-son′ or tuh′son), Arizona, U.S.A., 69 m. N. of Mex. border ; pop. 36,800 ; farming, cattle-raising, and mining dist. ; copper mines, rly. shops ; state univ.

Tucuche Peak, Trinidad, 3248.

Tucuman (tōō-kōō-mahn′) or **San Miguel de Tecuman,** Argentina. Cap. of prov. of Tucuman, in N. ; pop. 158,000 ; commercial and rly. centre ; univ. ; declaration of independence from Spain signed by Plata provinces in 1816.

Tu′dor, House of. Eng. royal family, **3253** ; Henry VII founds, *1612* ; lists of rulers, *see* **England.**

Tuesday, 3rd day of week, 980.

Tufted duck, *1052.*

Tugela (tōō-ge′-la). R. of Natal, S. Africa ; length 300 m. ; *3016.*

Tuileries (twēl′-rē). Royal palace in Paris, 1395, 2517 ; gardens now a public park.

Tuke, Henry Scott (1858–1929). Eng. artist ; elected R.A. in 1914 ; painter of portraits and sea-life.

Tula (tōō-lah). Cap. of govt. of Tula in cent. Russia ; pop. 272,000 ; mfr. of firearms, samovars ; German defeat Dec. 1941.

Tu′lip. Flower of lily family, **3253** ; bulb structure, 612 ; Holland, 2320.

Tulip tree. Tree of magnolia family, *Liriodendron tulipifera* ; one of finest hardwoods ; native of N. Amer., it was introduced into Eng. in the 17th cent. ; known by its curiously truncated 4- or 6-sided leaves and greenish, tulip-like flowers.

Tull, Jethro (1674–1741). Eng. farmer and writer ; inventor of planting drill, 79.

Tulle (tōōl). Picturesque tn. in s. Fr. ; pop. 10,000 ; fine 15th-cent. cath. ; from Tulle first came fabric of that name.

Tullius, Servius. *See* Servius.

Tul'liver, Maggie. Heroine of George Eliot's " Mill on the Floss " ; her spiritual struggles are largely auto-biographical.

Tul'lus Hostil'ius. Rom. king, 2804.

Tul'sa, Oklahoma, U.S.A. Rly. and mfg. city in N.E. on Arkansas ; pop. 142,157 ; heart of important oil field ; more than 300 oil and refining companies ; natural gas and coal for manufacturing ; farming and stock-raising centre.

Tumbler luck, *1980.*

Tumbler pigeon, *2607.*

Tummel. R. in Perthshire, flowing 29 m. to join the Tay ; also a lake, 2¾ m. long. In 1945 scheme made to divert its waters with R. Garry, Loch Tummel, Briar Water and Errochty Water for hydro-electric power.

Tumour, 739.

Tu'na fish. *See* Tunny.

Tunbridge Wells. Inland watering place on Kent and Sussex border ; pop. 37,560 ; medicinal springs.

Tundras. Arctic plains ; in Asia, 223 ; Europe, 1234, 2966.

Tung oil, or China wood-oil, 1263, 2408.

Tungsten (W.). Exceedingly hard, dense metallic element of the chromium group ; atomic weight 184·0 ; found in the ores wolframite and scheelite ; melts at 6,100° F. ; named from the Swedish *tung,* heavy, and *sten,* stone ; **3253** ; in Alaska, 97 ; in alloys, 122 ; in Bolivia, 491 ; as electric-light filament, 1135, 3432 ; in electron microscope, 2165 ; in Portugal, 2658 ; properties, 777 ; in Siam, 2964.

Tungsten steel, 123, 3253.

Tunguses. Ural-Altaic people of Siberia and Mongolia, including the Tunguses proper and the Manchus.

Tunic. Gk. garment, 1325.

Tunicates. Sub-phylum of animals resembling primitive vertebrates.

Tuning circuit in radio, 3393.

Tuning-fork. A steel fork giving a definite pitch when struck, *3009,* 3394.

Tu'nis or **Tunis'ia.** A Fr. protectorate in N. Africa, E. of Algeria ; pop. 2,608,000 ; *maps f. 68, 117* ; Carthage, 711 ; Allies-Axis battle-field in 1942–43, 1452, 3254, 3420.

Tunis. Cap. of Tunis ; **3254** ; Allies captured May 7, 1943, 3420.

Tunnard, John (b. 1900), Brit. artist, designer of fabrics and carpets ; abstract and surrealist works ; 3122.

Tunnels, 3255 ; Alpine, 3138 ; in mining, 2182 ; in London, 3194, 3255 ; on " Underground," *3257,* 3275. *See also* Aqueducts.

Tun'ny or **tu'na.** Large fish of mackerel family, 3258, 1297, 1300, 1310, 1517 ; in Mediterranean, 2136, 2968.

Tupper, Sir Charles (1821–1915), Canadian statesman ; Prime Minister (1896) and one of the fathers of the Confederation of 1867 ; High Commissioner in London 1884–87 ; 1888–1896 ; leader of Opposition (1896–1900).

Tupper, Martin Farquhar (1810–89). Eng. author " Proverbial Philosophy " (moralizing in blank verse), " The Crock of Gold."

Turbine, 3258 ; gas, 1424 ; in hydro-elec. installns., *plate f. 960, 1668–1672* ; in jet engines, *1828* ; locomotive, 1988 ; at power stations, *2673, 2674* ; steam, 3184 ; in rocket bomb, 2792 ; in steamships, 2947, 2949.

Turbine, gas. *See* Gas Turbine.

Turbinia. Turbine-propelled ocean liner, 2949, 3260.

Turbit. Breed of domestic pigeons.

Turbo-alternators, for production of electric current, 2674.

Turbot. A large flatfish.

Turenne', Henri de la Tour d'Auvergne, Vicomte de (1611–75). Marshal of France, one of the great captains of history whose campaigns Napoleon advised soldiers to " read and re-read " ; commanded Fr. armies in many of wars of Louis XIV.

Turgeniev (tōōr-gen'-yef), **Ivan** (1818–83). Rus. novelist, **3260,** 2404, 2856.

Turgot (tōōr-gō), **Anne Robert Jacques, Baron de Laune** (1727–81). Fr. statesman and economist, comptroller-general of France (1774–76) attempted to abolish feudal privilege, 1393, 2102.

Turin' (It. Torino), 4th largest city in It. ; pop. 712,983 ; centre of motor industry ; **3260.**

Turkestan. *See* Turkistan.

Turkey. Country of Europe and Asia : a. 296,000 sq. m. (excluding marshes and lakes) ; pop. 18,860,222 ; **3262,** *plate f. 3264, 3265* ; Ankara, 162, Bosporus, 465 ; Dardanelles, 974 ; government, 3265 ; Istanbul, 1761 ; new alphabet, 125 ; people, 3262 ; religion, 2066 ; rug-making, 705, *706* ; Smyrna, 2988 ; surface features, 263, 3262. *History :* 3262 ; Byzantine Empire overthrown (1453), 638 ; conquests extended, 927, 953 2771 ; Greece gains freedom, 344, 1525 Crimean War, 344, 931, 2368 ; Serbian revolts, 2922 ; Rumania independent, 2841 ; war with Russia (1877–78), 344, 3265, 2922 ; Young Turk rev., 344, 3265 ; war with Italy, 3265 ; Balkan Wars (1912–13), 1525, 344 ; Armenian massacre, 237 ; 1st World War, 2480, 3410, 3414 ; Treaty of Sèvres and after, 974, 1526 ; reconstruction, 1850, 3265 ; neutral in most of 2nd World War, 3266.

Turkey. Bird, **3261,** 2671 ; Australian turkey, 1095.

Turkey-buzzard, 634 ; a North-Amer. member of the vulture group.

Turkey oak, 2409.

Turkey red oil, a detergent, 998.

Turkish language, classified, 2571, 1655.

Turkish rugs, 706.

Turkistan. Region in Asia between the Caspian Sea on the w. and desert of Gobi on the E., corresponding largely to Soviet Central Asia ; **3266,** 265 ; camels, 671 ; conquered by Mongols, 2205 ; Great Pamir, 263 ; rugs, 706 ; Tartars, 3155.

Turkistan-Siberian (Turksib) railway. Opened May 1, 1930 ; 906 m. long ; links Aris to Novo-Sibirsk ; 2736, *2967.*

Turkoman Republic (or Turkmenistan). Soviet Socialist Republic in Asiatic Russia, E. of Caspian Sea area 189,370 sq. m. ; pop. 1,254,000 ; formed 1924 from w. parts of Bokhara and Khiva ; cap. Ashkhabad (Polterask), 2844, 3267.

Turks. People, 3262 ; in Balkans, 343, 528 ; besiege Vienna, 3323 ; conquer Syria, 3145 ; crusades against, 936, 2864 ; in Russia and Siberia, 2966 ; in Turkistan, 3266.

Turk's cap lily, 1947.

Turk's cap shell, *2943.*

Turksib railway. *See* Turkistan-Siberian railway.

Turku (Abo). Tn. and archiepiscopal see of Finland ; a former cap. ; pop. 77,000.

Tur'meric. A plant yielding spice and yellow dye, 1464, 3060, 3062.

Turner, Joseph Mallord William (1775–1851). Eng. landscape painter, **3267,** 1181, 2476, 3353 ; " The Fighting Téméraire," *1275* ; " The Golden Bough," *1388* ; " Ulysses deriding Polyphemus," *1189* ; " Venice," *3268.*

Turner Valley, oil region of Alberta, Can., 102.

Turnip. Cabbage-like vegetable with edible root, said to have come to Eng. from Holland in 1550 ; early shoots boiled as greens, 640.

Turnpike or **toll-road,** 2783.

Turnspit, 900.

Tur'pentine. Pine sap or oil distilled from it, **3268,** 1263, 2611, 2478 ; in varnish, 3305 ; yields resin, 2768.

Turpin, Dick (1706–39). Eng. highwayman, subject of many legends and stories, including Harrison Ainsworth's novel " Rookwood." Hanged for horse-stealing, 87.

Turquoise (tēr'-kwahz). A precious stone.

Turret. In architecture, a small tower attached to and forming part of another tower, or placed at angles of church or public building.

Turtle. An armoured reptile, **3229;** evolutionary position, 158.

Turtle dove, 2606.

Tus'can dialect, Italy, 1786 ; used by Dante, 1786.

Tuscan or **Tyrrhenian Sea,** 1230.

Tuscany. Dist. in w. Italy, corresponding roughly to anc. Etruria ; fertile, rich in minerals ; chief port Leghorn, 1763 ; history, 1230, 1769, 3319 ; language and literature, 1786.

Tus'culum. Anc. city of Latium, 15 m. S.E. of Rome, near modern Frascati ; favourite residence of Cicero and other noted Romans.

" Tusitala." R. L. Stevenson, 3089.

Tusk. An elongated tooth ; elephant, *1142* ; walrus, *3339* ; wild boar, 480.

Tussah or **Tussore silk,** 2973.

Tussaud (tōō'-sō), **Marie** (1760–1850). Wax modeller, b. in Switzerland ; she learned the art of wax modelling in Paris ; was imprisoned during the Revolution ; came to England in 1802, and later opened her world-famous exhibition of waxworks in Baker Street, London.

Tussock moth. A leaf-eating type ; antenna, *629.*

Tutankhamen (*fl. c.* 1350 B.C.). Egyptian pharaoh, 1118, 1119 ; consort, *1108* ; tomb, 206, 1118, *1120, backs of plates f. 1120, 1121.*

Tutt'lingen, Ger. Tn. in Württemberg-Hohenzollern ; pop. 16,000 ; victory of Austrians and Bavarians over French in 1643 (Thirty Years' War).

Tutuila (tōō-tū-ē'-lah). Principal isl. of Amer. Samoa ; a. 44 sq. m. ; pop. 13,900 ; exports copra ; 2869.

Tver. *See* Kalinin.

Twain, Mark (Samuel Langhorne Clemens) (1835–1910). American humorist and novelist, **3269,** 1966, 3295.

Tweed. River rising in Peeblesshire, and flowing E. 97 m. to Berwick ; gives name to tweed cloth, 2391.

Tweedsmuir, 1st Baron. *See* Buchan, John.

Twelfth Day or **Epiphany,** 820.

Twelfth Night. End of Christmas celebration, 819.

" Twelfth Night." Play by Shakespeare, dealing with complications which arise when the shipwrecked Viola disguises herself as a boy, takes service with Duke Orsino, and is charged with the duty to win the Countess Olivia for him ; sub-plot concerns trick played on Malvolio, Olivia's steward, by Sir Toby Belch, Sir Andrew Aguecheek, and Maria, 2936.

Twelve Labours of Hercules, The, 1615. *1616.*

Twelve Tables of the Law. The earliest codification of the Roman Law ; based on old custom ; engraved or painted on wood, and placed in the Forum ; originally ten in number.

Twenty-four-hour clock, 3214.

" Twenty Thousand Leagues Under the Sea." Novel by Jules Verne. Highly imaginative story of adventures in an under-sea boat, written before the first submarine was built, 3316.

" Twenty Years After." Novel by Dumas, 1054.

Twick'enham. Residential tn. of Middlesex on Thames ; stadium, h.q. of Eng. Rugby Football Union ; pop. 92,400 ; residence of Alexander Pope, Horace Walpole, Louis Philippe.

Twilight of the Gods or **Ragnarök.** In Norse mythology, a time when the world of the Gods was to be destroyed. Wagner's opera " Götter-dämmerung " is based upon the myth, 2440.

Twilight sleep. Method of relieving pain in childbirth by administration of scopolamine and morphine.

Twill. Textile fabric in which the weft is carried over one and under two or more warp threads, thus producing diagonal lines.

Twiller, Wouter (or Walter) van (*c*.1580–*c*. 1650). Governor of New Netherlands 1633–37 ; amassed a personal fortune but was much criticised for incompetence in administration ; despite his protests English colonists settled in Connecticut valley.

Twine. *See* Rope and Twine.

Twin Falls, Idaho, U.S.A., near Snake r. ; pop. 11,800 ; flour mills, creameries.

Twins or **Gemini.** Sign of Zodiac, 3444.

Twite. Mountain linnet, 1955.

" Two Hundred Families." Financial oligarchy, the plutocracy of France, who had power to appoint the regents of the Banque de France prior to its nationalization in 1936.

Two Sicilies. Kingdom formed by union of Sicily and Naples (1130) and at times other parts of S. Italy ; history, 2275, 2968, 1418.

Two-stroke cycle, in internal combustion engine, 1736 ; in gas engine, 1421.

" Two Years Before the Mast." Classic sea story by Richard Henry Dana, Jr. (1840).

Ty'burn. Chief place of execution in London prior to 1783 ; near N.E. corner of Hyde Park ; named from small tributary of Thames.

Tyche (tī'kē) or **Fortuna.** In myth., goddess of fortune, **1352.**

Tycho Brahe. *See* Brahe.

Tychonic (tī-kon'-ik) **system.** In astronomy, 544.

Tyler, John (1790–1862). 10th pres. of U.S.A. ; elected vice-pres. in 1840 and pres. in 1841 on the death of Harrison ; his veto of the tariff bill of 1842 caused most of his cabinet to resign ; Texas was annexed whilst he was in office.

Tyler, Wat (d. 1381). Leader of Peasants' Revolt in England, **3269,** *1197, 1400* , Froissart quoted, 1400.

Tylor, Sir Edward Burnett (1832–1917). Eng. anthropologist (" Primary Culture " ; " Natural History of Religion ").

Tym'pani. *See* Kettledrum.

Tympan'ic membrane. The ear-drum, 1065.

Ty'nan, Katherine (1861–1931). Irish novelist and poetress ; published her first book of verse in 1885, and her first prose work in 1887 (" The Wind in the Trees," poems ; " Three Fair Maids " and " A Daughter of the Fields ").

Tyn'dale, William (*c*. 1492–1536). Eng. translator of New Testament and most of Old ; **3269,** *426,* 427, 1210.

Tyndall, John (1820–93). Eng. physicist, **3270.**

Tyne (tīn). R. of N. Eng., rising in Northumberland Hills, flowing E. through coalmining and mfg. region into North Sea, 1059, 1161, 1162, 1165, 1168, 2336, 2391.

Tynemouth. Spt. and watering-place in Northumberland at mouth of R. Tyne ; pop. 65,000 ; large export trade in coal and coke ; fisheries, shipyards.

Tynwald. Name for the old parliament of the Isle of Man. Tynwald Hill is the hill where the laws of the island are promulgated after receiving the royal assent, 2084.

Type. Printing, **3270** ; beginnings of modern printing, 512, 2684. *See also* Printing.

Type-casting machines, 3270.

Type metal, *122,* 124 ; antimony in, 176, 3270.

Type-setting. Linotype, 1956 ; Monotype, *2217.*

Typewriter, 3271 ; early type, *3272* ; used by blind, 472, 3271 ; as accounting machines, 17.

Ty'phoid fever. A bacterial disease, 1458, 2132 ; carried by flies, 1329.

Typhoon'. Asiatic name for cyclone, 3100.

Ty'phus or **spotted fever,** 1459.

Typist. Training in shorthand, 2961.

Typog'raphy, 512, 3270. *See also* Books ; Printing.

Tyr. Teutonic god of war, 980.

Tyran'nosaurus. Huge prehistoric reptile, 2678.

Tyr'anny. Form of govt. in Gk. city-states, 1519.

Tyre. Famous city of anc. Phoenicia on Mediterranean coast, 1576, 2573, 3146.

Tyres (rubber). *See* Tires.

Tyr'ian purple. Dye obtained from shellfish, 1059.

Tyrol. *See* Tirol.

Tyrone, Northern Ireland. Inland co. ; a. 1,200 sq. m. ; pop. 127,000 ; produces potatoes, oats, flax, cattle, **3272.**

Tyrrhenians. Same as Etruscans.

Tyrrhenian or **Tuscan Sea,** 1230.

Tyrtaeus (têr-tē'-us) (7th cent. B.C.). Gk. martial poet ; legend says, a lame schoolmaster derisively sent by Athenians to Sparta in response to request for a general in 2nd Messenian War ; his warlike songs inspired them to victory.

Tyrwhitt (tī'-rit), **Sir Reginald Yorke** (b. 1870). He commanded destroyer flotillas during the 1st World War, at Heligoland, Dogger Bank, etc. ; awarded D.S.O. 1915 ; later was C.-in-C. of China Squadron and at the Nore ; appointed Admiral of the Fleet in 1934.

Tyumen or **Tiumen,** Ural Area, Russia. Commercial centre on Tura ; pop. 50,000 ; at junction of several great routes.

Tze-Hsi (tsē-shē) (1835–1908). The " Great Empress Dowager " of China and its virtual ruler for half a century ; encouraged Boxer rising, 810, 812.

Tziganes (tsig'-*a*-nēz). Gipsies of Hungary, 1655.

LIKE C and G, and I and J, the letters U, V, W, Y were originally only variations of the same letter. They were all descended, like F, from the Phoenician *Wau* or *Vau*, which was once the horned asp of Egypt (*see* the story of F). In Latin for a long time the forms V and U were used without distinction. In most Latin inscriptions up to the end of the 2nd century A.D. no distinction is made between the two. But in the course of time the form V came to be used by

preference at the beginning of a word and the form U elsewhere. As the consonant sound more commonly occurred at the beginning, the form V finally came to denote the consonant and the form U to represent the vowel. The letter has several sounds in English, the *u* of " pull," like *oo* in " good " ; short *u* in " but " ; *yu* in " tube," " suit," " feud." It is also often used to modify the sound of another vowel that precedes it, especially *a* and *o*, as in *fraud* and *taut*, *rout* and *stout*.

Ubangi (ū'-bang'-gi) or **Mbangi.** Chief N. tributary of Congo, formed by junction of Mbomu and Welle ; flows s.w. and w. 700 m., forming boundary between Fr. Equatorial Africa and Belgian Congo.

Ubangi-Shari. Dist. of Fr. Equat. Africa, between Sudan and Cameroons ; a. 238,000 sq. m. ; pop. 1,000,000 ; cap. Bangui ; 888.

U-boat. Eng. name for Ger. submarine (Unterseeboot), 291–94, 3411.

Ucayali (ū-kah-yah'-le). R. of S. Amer., one of main headstreams of Amazon, rising in cent. Peru ; flows N. 1,000 m. to join Marañon ; *map, 2559.*

Uccello (utch-el'-ō), **Paolo** (1397–1475). Ital. painter, 2476, 1775, *1778,* 2557.

Udaipur (ū-dī-pōōr') or **Mewar.** Native state of the Republic of India in Rajputana ; a. 13,170 sq. m. ; pop. 1,926,700 ; 2743.

Udall (ū'-dawl), **Nicholas** (*c*. 1504–56). Eng. schoolmaster, author of earliest extant Eng. comedy, " Ralph Roister Doister."

Udine (ū-dē'-nā). Cap. of Udine prov.,

N. Italy ; pop. 63,100 ; makes silk, velvet ; trade in flax and hemp ; It. military base 1915–18 ; occupied by Austrians in 1917.

Uffizi (oof-ēt'-sē) **Palace,** Florence, Italy (erected 1560–76) ; a former palace of the Medici ; its art gallery contains a priceless collection of paintings ; damaged in 2nd World War.

Uganda. Brit. protectorate in E. Africa, N. of Lake Victoria ; a. 93,000 sq. m. ; pop. 3,930,700 ; chief product, cotton ; cap. Entebbe ; 1072 ; *maps, 1072, 1073* ; Lake Albert, 1072 ; Lake Victoria, 3321.

Uhlan. Name given to German lancers in 1st World War.

Uhland (ōō'lahnt), **Johann Ludwig** (1787–1862). Ger. romantic lyric-poet, literary historian, and philologist, wrote many ballads in the spirit of old folk songs.

Uist (wist), **North** and **South.** Isls. of Hebrides, 1602.

Uitlanders (oit'-land-êrz). Boer name for foreign immigrants in S. Africa, 486, 3019.

Ujiji (ōō-jē'-jē) or **Kavele.** Tn. in Tanganyika Territory, E. Africa ; pop. 29,000 ; 3150, *map, 1073* ; Stanley finds Livingstone, 3077.

Ujjain (ōō-jīn'), India. Historic tn. of Gwalior on Sipra ; pop. 72,729 ; opium trade ; one of 7 sacred cities of Hindus ; marks first meridian of longitude in Hindu geography.

Ukraine (ū-krān'). Soviet republic in s.w. Russia ; pop. about 40,000,000 ; **3273,** 2849 ; *map, 2853, facing 2844* ; Kharkov, 1854, *2853, 2845,* 3419, 3421 ; cap. Kiev, 1856, 3419 ; Cossacks, 916 ; language, 2855 ; Odessa, 2420 ; people, 2983.

Ukulele (ū-ke-lā-lē). A small four-stringed guitar-shaped musical instrument ; used in Hawaiian Isls.

Ulan Bator Hoto. *See* Urga.

Ulfilas (ool'-fil-as). " Little Wolf " (*c*. 311–*c*. 383). Apostle to the Goths, 1487, 1456 ; Bible of, 1456.

Ulianov, Vladimir Ilvich. Real name of Lenin. *1922, 1923.*

Ullswater, James William Lowther, 1st Viscount (1855–1949). Brit. politician ;

entered Parl. 1883 ; in 1905 became Speaker of the House of Commons ; retired in 1921, when he was raised to the peerage.

Ulls'water. Lake on borders of Cumberland and Westmorland ; second in size in the Lake District ; over 7 m. long ; 943, 3371.

Ulm. Fortress city of Württemberg-Baden, Ger., and river port on Danube ; pop. 62,500 ; Gothic cathedral ; varied mfrs. ; Austrians under Mack surrendered to Napoleon (1805).

Ul'mus. The elm genus, 1152.

Ul'nar nerve. Nerve from brachial plexus in neck to various muscles of forearm and fingers, 2316.

Ulster. Prov. in N. Ire. ; a. 8,000 sq. m. ; pop. 1,280,000 ; the name is sometimes used as an alternative for Northern Ireland, although three counties of Ulster are in Eire ; 1746, 1747, 1748 ; cap, Belfast, 402.

Ul'tima Thu'le. Rom. name for Shetland Isls., 2945.

Ultramarine, pigment, 2479.

Ultra-mi'croscope, 2164. Electron microscope, *2164.*

Ultra-short waves, in wireless, 3396, *3397.*

Ultrasonics. Branch of physics dealing with waves resembling sound waves but of very high frequencies (beyond the hearing of man) propagated in air, liquids, and solids ; such waves, passed through milk, kill all bacteria, passed through metal castings detect flaws, and show up faults in coal seams, etc. ; also used in the cleaning of fabrics ; 3010.

Ultra-violet rays, 1942, 2729 ; as antiseptic, 178 ; Hertz's discovery, 1622 ; from mercury vapour lamps, 1136 ; microscope, 2165 ; spectrum, *plate f. 3057.*

Ulundi, battle of, 3448.

Ulysses, (ŭ'-lis-ĕz). *See* **Odysseus.**

" Ulysses," by James Joyce, 1216.

Umbal'la, India. Same as **Ambala.**

Umbellif'erae or **Apiaceae.** The parsley family of plants; have flowers radiating in umbrella-shaped clusters.

Um'bra. A Latin word, meaning shadow ; in astron. the darkest part of a shadow in a lunar eclipse or the dark portion of a sunspot is sometimes called the umbra.

Um'bria, dist. in cent. It., until 1860 part of Papal States, 1763.

U'me or **Umea,** r. of Sweden. Rises in N. in mts. on the Norway border, flows S.E. more than 200 m. forming several lakes, and enters the Gulf of Bothnia.

Umpire, in baseball, 367 ; cricket, *930.*

Unamu'no, Miguel de (1864–1936). Sp. philosopher, poet, and novelist, 3051–52.

Unau'. The two-toed sloth, 2985.

" Uncle Sam." Nickname for U.S.A. ; it was first used during the War of 1812 ; 2366.

" Uncle Tom's Cabin." Novel by Harriet Beecher Stowe ; an indictment of Negro slavery in the U.S.A.

Underground railways, 3273, 2016 ; in Moscow, 2235 ; counting and timing trains, *2575* ; escalators, *1938, 3275* ; ticket machines, *866, 867* ; tunnel construction, 3255–58, 3275.

Undershot waterwheel, *1669.*

Undine (un-dēn'). In Fouqué's romance of that name, water nymph who wins a soul by marrying a mortal.

Undset, Sigrid (b. 1882). Norwegian novelist ; Nobel Prize Winner; " Kristin Lavransdatter " ; " The Master of Hestviken " ; " Jenny." Works show great psychological power and unusual ability to recapture the feeling of another age, 2881.

Unemployment, insurance against, 2994.

U.N.E.S.C.O. (United Nations Educational, Scientific, and Cultural Orgzn.). Subsid. body of the U.N. set up in Nov. 1945, with representatives of 44 nations including all major powers except Russia, to encourage friendship and understanding among nations by exchange of students, teachers, educational methods, etc.

Ungava (oon-gah'-va). Former dist. of Canada, including all of Labrador

peninsula except coastal strip ; a 351,000 sq. m. ; annexed to Quebec, 2714.

Unguicula'ta. Term first used by J. Ray in 1693 for a group of clawed, four-footed mammals ; in the modern classification of Simpson, the Order *Carnivora* is excluded and the Order *Primates* included.

Ungula'ta. The group of hoofed mammals, 2077.

U'niates. Eastern Christians who follow rites of Greek Catholic Church, but acknowledge supremacy of Pope.

Unicel'lular organisms, 738 ; animal types, 2695, 156 ; plant types, 111.

U'nicorn. Fabulous beast,. usually having head and body of a horse, hind legs of an antelope, tail of a lion, and a long, sharp, twisted horn in the middle of its forehead.

Unicorn or **monoceros.** A constellation, *chart, 895.*

Uniformita'rianism. Modern geologic teaching that existing land forms were created gradually by processes the same as those still at work.

Uniforms : Army (Brit.), 244 ; Boy Scouts, 538 ; Girl Guides, *1466, 1467*; Navy (Brit.), *plates f. 2292, 2293.*

Unimak' Island, Alaska. Largest of the Aleutians, 98.

Union, Acts of. *See* **Act of Union.**

Union - Castle Line. Shipping line formed in 1900 by amalgamation of the Union (1853) and Castle (1872) lines. Mail and passenger service between Eng. and South Africa.

Union Islands. Same as **Tokelau.**

Union Jack or **Flag.** Flag of Gt. Brit., 580, 1312, 1515 ; *frontis., Vol. 8.*

" Union " materials, mixed wool and cotton, 3405.

Union of South Africa. *See* **South Africa, Union of.**

Union of Soviet Socialist Republics. *See* **Russia.**

Unit. *See* **Units.**

Unita'rianism. A system of Christian belief that rejects the doctrine of the Trinity, fixed creeds, and all authority in religion ; first appeared as organized movement in England in 1773 ; widely influential in New England from middle of 18th cent.

United Brethren. *See* **Moravians.**

United Brethren in Christ. Evangelical Christian sect founded in U.S.A. under leadership of Philip William Otterbein (1726–1813) and Martin Boehm (1725–1812).

United Empire Loyalists, 682 ; in Nova Scotia, 2435.

United Kingdom, History of the, 3276. Development of Empire (1707–63) ; house of Hanover, 3276 ; Jacobite risings, 2682 ; Seven Years' War, 759, 2924 ; expansion of empire, 3276 ; India, 842 ; Walpole, the first prime minister, 3338, 3276.—*Revolutionary Epoch* (1763–1815) : Board of Trade founded, 3233 ; Reaction under George III, 1441 ; Stamp Act, 1386 ; Amer. Rev., 3291 (*see also* **Independence, War of American**) ; battle of Copenhagen, 905 ; Burke, 621 ; Pitt, 759, 2614 ; wars with Fr. and Napoleon, 1396 ; Peninsular War, 3364 ; Nelson and naval supremacy, 2313 ; Trafalgar, 2313, 3234 ; Wellington, 3363 ; colonial expansion, 3277. *Reform and the Victorian Era* (1815–1901) : Catholic Emancipation Act, 2420, 2535 ; Reform Bill (1832), 2522 ; slaves emancipated, 2981 ; railways, 1981–96, 2734, 3238 ; postal system developed, 3074 ; Corn Laws repealed, 2535 ; Crimean War, 931, 3265 ; Queen Victoria's influence, 3319 ; rival policies of Disraeli and Gladstone, 1018, 1469 ; Indian Mutiny, 1714 ; slave trade abolished, 2982; War of 1812 with U.S.A., 3291 ; Industrial Revolution, 1721, *1723* ; Waterloo, 3354 ; Canadian confederation, 683 ; Irish Home Rule, 1746, 2525 ; occupation of Egypt, 1101 ; Boer War, 486, 3019.—*The twentieth century* : Lloyd George's reforms, 1976 ; socialism, 2996 ; naval power threatened by Germany, 3378: 1st

World War and peace settlement, 3409 ; separate parliaments for Ire., 1746 ; National Govt., 1488, 3281 ; rearmament, 3282 ; Fascist and Nazi threats, 3415 ; abdication of Edward VIII, 1092, 3282 ; 2nd World War, 3416, 3282 ; 3rd Labour Govt., 1875, 3282 ; economic crisis, 3283 ; United Nations, 3283, 3424 ; Western Union, 3293 ; North Atlantic treaty, 3293 ; 4th Labour Govt., 3283. Prior to 1707 *see under* **English History.** (*See also* **British Commonwealth ; England ; Great Britain ; Ireland ; Royal Family ; Scotland ; Wales ; World Wars.**)

United Nations, 3283, 3424, 2531 ; first session, 3284 ; forestry division, 1351 ; and Palestine, 2483 ; Spain excluded, 3040 ; registers treaties, 3240 ; UNRRA, 3296.

United Nations Organizations :

AEC	Atomic Energy Commission.
ECE	Econ. Comm. for Europe.
ECOSOC	Econ. and Social Council.
GA	General Assembly.
ICJ	Int. Court of Justice.
ILO	Int. Labour Organization.
IMF	Int. Monetary Fund.
IRO	Int. Refugees Organization.
ITO	Int. Trade Organization.
MSC	Military Staff Committee.
SC	Security Council.
TC	Trusteeship Council
UNESCO	U.N. Educational, Scientific and Cultural Org.
UNFAO	U.N. Food and Agric. Org.
UNRRA	U.N. Relief and Rehabilitation Assn. (June 1943– June 1947).
WFTU	World Fed. of Trade Unions (Associated).
WHO	World Health Org.

United Provinces (Uttar Pradesh), N.W. India ; a. 106,247 sq. m. ; pop. 55 million ; 1692 ; chief cities ; Lucknow, 1692, 1714, 2035 ; Agra, 77, 1692, 1713 ; Benares, 411, 1692 ; Allahabad, 1692 ; cereals, sugar, indigo. opium ; **3284.**

United Service Museum, Whitehall, London, *1836, 2015.*

United States of America (U.S.A.). A republic of N. Amer. ; a. 3,022,387 sq. m. ; pop. (continental U.S.A.), 131,669,000 ; States ; maps *f. 3285, 3286, plate f. 2384* ; arbitration treaties, 203 ; architecture, 222, 2351, *2354–55, plate f. 2352* ; broadcasting, 3399 ; cap. Washington, 3343 ; children, *791* ; constitution, 3290, 3443, 1488, 2566 ; education, 704, 2312, 2353, 2887 ; finance, 2353 ; flag, 1312 ; forestry service, 1351 ; fossils, 1706, 1708 ; government, 1488, 3290 ; literature, *see* **United States Literature** : national song, 2283 ; navy, 2293, 2295, 2296 ; Negroes, 2312 ; Panama Canal, 2486–94 ; parl. buildings, *3343, 3344*; postage-stamps, 3075 ; railways, 2736, 2738, *1995,* 1986, 1987, 1988 ; Red Indians, 2753 ; tramways, 3237; water-power resources, 3288. *Foreign trade,* 3289 ; Argentina, 226 ; Brazil, 553 ; cotton, 918 ; Cuba, 1584 ; Mexico, 2156 ; New York City, 2353 ; Panama Canal, 2486 ; San Francisco, 2871 ; wheat, 3289. *Geographic features, 3286, 2379–85* ; States : *see under* each name, **Alabama, Georgia,** etc. ; chief cities, *see* **New York, Washington,** etc. ; climate, 840, 1515, 2379, 2384 ; coast-line, 3285, 2379, 2385 ; forests, 1350, 1351, 3289 ; geological history, 2384–85 ; Great Lakes, 1515 ; other lakes and chief rivers, 1885, 2191, 2194, 3287, 2379, 2425 ; mountains, 190, 3285, 2795, 2379–80, 2384 ; rainfall, 2741–2. *plate f. 2385. Industries and products,* 3288 ; agriculture, 3288, 79 ; asbestos, 261 ; asphalt, 272 ; cotton, 3288, 918 ; fisheries, 97, 1299, 3289 ; fruit, 3289, *2443,* 1401, grape fruit, 1499 ; gypsum, 1559 ; hay and forage crops, 2035 ; helium, 1607 ; iron, *1752* ; livestock, 3289 ; lumber and forest products, 3289, 1350–51 ; maize, 3288 ; manufactured products, 3289 ; meat-packing,

3288 ; mercury, 2145 ; metals, 3289 ; mica, 2160 ; minerals, 3289 ; motor vehicles, 2241, 3288 ; natural gas, 1420 ; oil, 2426, 2428, 2430 ; pork, 3288 ; rice, 2775 ; salt, 2866 ; silver, 2974 ; sugar, 3112, 3114, 3288 ; sulphur, 3116 ; tobacco, 3219, 3288 ; wheat, 3289.

United States : History, 3290 ; chief events summarized, *see chart under* History ; geographic influences, 3285, 2379 ; for period of discovery and exploration, *see* America : its Discovery ; North America. *Colonial period* (to 1763), 3290 ; Jamestown settled, 3290 ; Dutch settle New York, 2353, 2357 ; Plymouth founded, 2122 ; Puritan immigration to New England, 2606 ; New England Confederation (1643), 3290 ; British retain New Amsterdam (1664), 757, 2357 ; Penn founds Pennsylvania, 2545 ; Oglethorpe settles Georgia, 3290, 1443 ; Appalachian barrier checks expansion, 2380 ; tobacco trade, 3219 ; *see also* separate colonies by name. *Revolution and formation of the Union* (1763–89), 3291 ; Stamp Act, 1386 ; Continental Congress and Articles of Confederation, 3291 ; Washington's work, 3342 ; Constitution framed and adopted, 3291 ; *see also* American Independence, War of. *National beginnings* (1789–1817), rise of political parties, 3291 ; beginnings of industrial development, 3288 ; settlement of the West, 3291 ; steamboat revolutionizes water transport, 1407. *Western expansion and an*

nexation (1817–54), 3291 ; Florida purchased, 3291, 1319 ; Jacksonian epoch, 3291 ; Mexican boundary dispute, 3291, 203 ; Gadsden Purchase, 3291. *Civil War and Reconstruction* (1854–77) ; slavery question, 1951 ; Civil War, 3291, 1952 ; Alaska purchased, 3291, 97 ; French forced to leave Mexico, 3291, 2159 ; Alabama claims arbitrated, 203. *Business expansion and world influence :* Spanish-American War (1878), 3291, 941, 3037 ; island possessions acquired, 3291, 2869–70 ; Panama Canal built, 3291, 2486–94 ; 1st World War and peace settlement, 3412, 3291, 3383 ; slump, 3292 ; Roosevelt and his " New Deal," 2823, 3292 ; 2nd World War, 3292, 3419, 2533 ; H. S. Truman, 3252, 3293 ; Marshall Aid to Europe, 2111, 3293. *Foreign relations :* policy of arbitration extended, 203 ; Samoan controversy, 2870 ; in Hawaii, 1587 ; Mexican relations, 3291, 2158–59 ; Philippines, 2569, 3291 ; Haiti, 1565 ; in Cuba, 941 ; League of Nations, 1908, 3383, 3292, 204 ; Lease-lend to Europe, 3292 ; United Nations, 3283, 3424 ; North Atlantic Treaty, 3293. *See also* chief topics above by name.

United States : literature, 3293, 2403.

PRESIDENTS OF U.S.A.

1789–1797 George Washington
1797–1801 John Adams
1801–1809 Thomas Jefferson
1809–1817 James Madison
1817–1825 James Monroe
1825–1829 John Quincy Adams
1829–1837 Andrew Jackson
1837–1841 Martin Van Buren
1841–1841 William Henry Harrison
1841–1845 John Tyler
1845–1849 James Knox Polk
1849–1850 Zachary Taylor
1850–1853 Millard Fillmore
1853–1857 Franklin Pierce
1857–1861 James Buchanan
1861–1865 Abraham Lincoln
1865–1869 Andrew Johnson
1869–1877 Ulysses Simpson Grant
1877–1881 Rutherford Birchard Hayes
1881–1881 James Abram Garfield
1881–1885 Chester Alan Arthur
1885–1889 Grover Cleveland
1889–1893 Benjamin Harrison
1893–1897 Grover Cleveland
1897–1901 William McKinley
1901–1909 Theodore Roosevelt
1909–1913 William Howard Taft
1913–1921 Woodrow Wilson
1921–1923 Warren Gamaliel Harding
1923–1929 Calvin Coolidge
1929–1933 Herbert Hoover
1933–1945 Franklin D. Roosevelt
1945– Harry S. Truman

Units, in science the fundamental units are those of length (metre), mass (kilogramme), time (second) ; all the units are compounded of these ; C. G. S. system, 3672 ; electrical, 1128, 3682 ; force, 3672 ; heat, 1593, 1600, 3350, 3675 ; illumination, 3679 ; metric weights and measures, 2154 ; metric conversion tables, 2155 ; power, 3673 ; work, 3673. *See* Weights and Measures.

FAMOUS NAMES IN U.S.A. LITERATURE

Louisa May Alcott (1832–88), novelist and short story writer— " Little Women " ; " Little Men " ; " Moods."
Sherwood Anderson (1876–1941), novelist and short story writer— " Poor White " ; " Dark Laughter."
Gertrude Atherton (1857–1948), novelist—" The Conqueror " ; " Black Oxen " ; " The Jealous Gods."
Irving Babbitt (1865–1933), critic—" Rousseau and Romanticism " ; " Democracy and Leadership."
Ray Stannard Baker (1870–), journalist and essayist—" Our New Prosperity " ; " Adventures in Contentment."
George Bancroft (1800–91), historian—" History of the United States."
Rex Beach (1877–), novelist—" The Spoilers " ; " The Barrier."
Charles Beard (1874–1948), historian—" Rise of American Civilization " ; " American Government and Politics."
William Beebe (1877–), Nature writer—" Galápagos ; World's End " ; " Arcturus Adventure " ; " Jungle Days."
Robert C. Benchley (1889–1945), humorist—" Of All Things."
Stephen Vincent Benét (1898–1943), poet and novelist—" Five Men and Pompey " ; " John Brown's Body."
Ambrose Bierce (1842–1914 ?), short story writer—" In the Midst of Life " ; " Can Such Things Be ? "
William Cullen Bryant (1794–1878), poet and travel writer— " Thanatopsis " ; " Letters of a Traveler."
Frances Hodgson Burnett (1849–1924), novelist and children's author—" Little Lord Fauntleroy " ; " The Secret Garden " ; " Sarah Crewe."
John Burroughs (1837–1921), naturalist—" Wake Robin " ; " Signs and Seasons " ; " My Boyhood : An Autobiography."
James Branch Cabell (1879–), novelist and short story writer— " Jurgen " ; " Beyond Life " ; " Straws and Prayer-books " ; " The Cream of the Jest."
Willa Cather (1876–1947), novelist and short story writer—" O Pioneers ! " ; " My Antonia " ; " A Lost Lady " ; " Death Comes for the Archbishop " ; " Shadows on the Rock."
Robert W. Chambers (1865–1933), novelist—" Cardigan."
Winston Churchill (1871–1947), novelist—" Richard Carvel " ; " The Crisis " ; " Coniston " ; " The Inside of the Cup."
Irvin S. Cobb (1876–), short story writer and humorist—" Some United States " ; " Roughing It De Luxe."
James Fenimore Cooper (1789–1851), novelist—" The Pilot " ; " The Last of the Mohicans " ; " The Spy " ; " Deerslayer."
Stephen Crane (1871–1900), novelist—" The Red Badge of Courage " ; " The Little Regiment."
Francis Marion Crawford (1854–1909), novelist—" Saracinesca " ; " Sant' Ilario " ; " Fair Margaret " ; " Mr. Isaacs."
Countee Cullen (1903–46), poet—" Color " ; " Copper Sun."
James Oliver Curwood (1878–1927), novelist—" The Wolf Hunters " ; " Baree, Son of Kazan " ; " The Alaskan."
Richard Henry Dana, Jr. (1815–82), novelist—" Two Years Before the Mast."
Floyd Dell (1887–), novelist—" Moon-Calf " ; " The Briary-Bush " ; " Janet March " ; " This Mad Ideal."
John Dos Passos (1896–), novelist—" Rosinante to the Road Again " ; " Manhattan Transfer."
Theodore Dreiser (1871–1945), novelist—" Sister Carrie " ; " Jennie Gerhardt " ; " The Genius " ; " An American Tragedy."

Peter Finley Dunne (1867–1936), humorist—" Mr. Dooley in Peace and in War " ; " Mr. Dooley's Philosophy."
Jonathan Edwards (1703–58), theologian—treatises on " Freedom of the Will " and " Nature of True Virtue."
Edward Eggleston (1837–1902), novelist and historian—" Hoosier Schoolboy " ; " Hoosier Schoolmaster."
Ralph Waldo Emerson (1803–82), poet and essayist—" Self-Reliance " ; " Compensation."
John Erskine (1879–), essayist and novelist—" The Moral Obligations to Be Intelligent " ; " Private Life of Helen of Troy."
Edna Ferber (1887–), short story writer and novelist—" So Big " ; " The Girls " ; " Show Boat " ; " Cimarron."
Eugene Field (1850–95), poet and short story writer—" A Little Book of Western Verse."
John Fiske (1842–1901), historian—" The Critical Period of American History."
Stephen Collins Foster (1826–64), song writer—" My Old Kentucky Home " ; " Old Black Joe " ; " Suwanee River."
John Fox, Jr. (1863–1919), novelist—" The Trail of the Lonesome Pine."
Benjamin Franklin (1706–90), prose writer—" Autobiography " ; " Poor Richard's Almanac."
Mary E. Wilkins Freeman (1862–1930), novelist and short story writer—" A New England Nun " ; " Madelon."
Robert Frost (1875–), poet—" A Boy's Will " ; " North of Boston " ; " West-Running Brook."
Ellen Glasgow (1874–1945), novelist—" Barren Ground " ; " The Romantic Comedians " ; " The Shadowy Third."
Susan Glaspell (1882–), dramatist and novelist—" The Inheritors " ; " Fidelity " ; " Brook Evans."
Zane Grey (1875–1939), novelist—" The Last of the Plainsmen " ; " The Young Forester " ; " The Lone Star Ranger."
Edward Everett Hale (1822–1909), novelist—" The Man Without a Country."
Frank Harris (1856–1931), critic—" Contemporary Portraits."
Joel Chandler Harris (1848–1908), short story writer—" Uncle Remus " ; " On the Plantation."
Francis Bret Harte (1839–1902), short story writer—" Luck of Roaring Camp " ; " The Outcasts of Poker Flat."
Nathaniel Hawthorne (1804–64), novelist and short story writer— " The Scarlet Letter " ; " The House of the Seven Gables " ; " Tanglewood Tales."
Ernest Hemingway (1898–), novelist and short story writer— " Farewell to Arms " ; " Men Without Women."
" O. Henry " (Sydney Porter) (1862–1910), short story writer— " The Four Million " ; " The Voice of the City."
Joseph Hergesheimer (1880–), novelist—" The Three Black Pennys " ; " Balisand " ; " Java Head " ; " The Limestone Three."
Oliver Wendell Holmes (1809–94), poet and essayist—" The Autocrat of the Breakfast Table " ; " The Last Leaf."
Edgar Watson Howe (1854–1937), novelist—" The Story of a Country Town " ; " A Moonlight Bay."
Julia Ward Howe (1819–1910), poet and biographer—" Battle Hymn of the Republic " ; " Margaret Fuller."
William Dean Howells (1837–1920), novelist—" A Modern Instance " ; " The Rise of Silas Lapham."

Universalists. Christian denomination started in U.S.A. about 1770 ; central doctrine is belief in final triumph of good and salvation of all mankind.

Universal languages, 1223 ; Latin as, 1894.

Universal Postal Union, 2662.

Universe, visible, 278; expansion of,2311.

Universities, 3296 ; Cambridge, 666 ; Harvard, *2119* ; hoods and coats of arms, *frontis., Vol. 7* ; London, *2021* ; medieval, 2462 ; Oxford, 2462 ; Witwatersrand, *1833*.

University Boat Race, 483, 3999.

University College, Oxford, *2462* ; founded, 2464.

University College, South Wales, 700.

Unknown Warrior. Typical representative of the soldiers of the Allies who were killed in the 1st World War— an unidentified body taken from a French war cemetery, whose burial in a national temple of fame or other place of honour formed the nation's tribute to the fallen ; the idea arose in Britain, where the Unknown Warrior was buried in Westminster Abbey on Armistice Day (Nov. 11, 1920) ; France's Unknown Warrior lies under the Arc de Triomphe, Paris ; the U.S.A.'s in the national cemetery at Arlington, Virginia (near Washington) ; other countries followed the example ; British, 3371.

U.N.R.R.A. (United Nations Relief and Rehabilitation Administration), **3296.**

Unst. Isl. in N. Shetland ; most northerly of British Isles ; 12 m. long, 2 to 6 m. broad; pop. 1,820; fishing, knitting.

Unter den Linden, street in Berlin, *417*.

Untermeyer (oon′-têr-mī-êr), **Louis** (b. 1885). Amer. poet, critic, and parodist (" The Younger Quire " ; "—and other Poets ").

Unterwalden (oon′-têr-vahld-*en*), Swiss canton, 3141.

" Untouchables," India, 1707.

Unwin, Sir Raymond (1863–1940). Eng. architect ; designed first garden city at Letchworth, also Hampstead ; pres. of R.I.B.A. (1931–33).

Unwritten Law, 1902.

Upan′ishads, Hindu poems, 2206, 1713.

U′pas tree. Tropical tree of the mulberry family 3246.

Upland cotton, 921.

Uplands, region in Scotland; 2889.

Upolu (ōō′-pō-lōō). 2nd largest of Samoan Isls. ; a. 600 sq. m. ; 2869 ; Stevenson's grave, *3089*, 3090.

Upper Austria. A prov. in N.W. of Austria ; a. 4,600 sq. m. ; pop. 927,700 ; cap. Linz.

Upper Avon, River in England. *See* **Avon.**

Upper Canada, former name of Ontario, 2435, 2715.

Upper Egypt, 1095, *map, 1096*.

Upper Silesia. A region embracing the S.E. portion of former Prussian prov. of Silesia ; a. 7,000 sq. m. Incorp. in Poland 1945. *See* **Silesia.**

Upper Volta. Area in French West Africa, which ceased to be a colony in 1933, when territory and population were distributed to Niger, French Sudan, and Ivory coast.

Up′pingham. Tn. of Rutlandshire ; general trade in agric. ; has noted public school ; pop. 1,703 ; 2858.

Upsala (up-sah′-la) or **Uppsala.** A cathedral city of Sweden, on R. Fyris ; univ. ; pop. 48,725 ; 3128, *3219*, 2388.

Upsilon, *v,* ϒ (Rom. u, U). 20th letter of Gk. alphabet.

Ur. Anc. city of S. Babylonia near R. Euphrates ; **3297** ; site marked by ruin mounds ; original home of Abraham, 13 ; excavations, *207*, 2147.

Ural-Altaic, 2571.

U′ral Mts. Low range in Russia, forming part of boundary between Europe and Asia ; 1,600 m. long ; **3297**, 1233, 2627, 2845.

Ural River, in S.E. Russia ; rises in Ural Mts. and Orenburg ; flows W. and S. 1,485 m. into Caspian Sea.

Ura′nia, in Gk. myth. Muse of astronomy, *187*, 2259.

Ura′nium (U.). White metallic radioactive element of the chromium group ; atomic weight 238·07 ; 2731–32 ; **3297** ; atoms, *298* ; energy from, 1161 ; fission products, 3187 ; fluorescent, 2573 ; heat from, 1595 ; melts at *c.* 3,300° F. ; properties, 778 ; isotopes, 299, 1739, 1760 ; decays to lead, 2732 ; neptunium from, 2315.

U′ranus, in Gk. myth. The first ruler of the world, **3298.**

Uranus. Seventh planet from the sun ; 2618, **3298** ; and discovery of Neptune, 2315, 2618 ; distance, speed, diameter, etc., *279*, *2618*, *3118* ; gave name to uranium, **3297.**

Ur′ban I, Pope 222–230.

Urban II (*c.* 1042–99), Pope 1088–99, **3298.**

Urban III, Pope 1185–87.

FAMOUS NAMES IN U.S.A. LITERATURE—*(contd.)*

James G. Huneker (1860–1921), critic and essayist—" Ivory, Apes and Peacocks " ; " Steeplejack " ; " Iconoclasts."

Fannie Hurst (1889–), novelist and short story writer—" Humoresque " ; " Lummox " ; " Five and Ten."

Washington Irving (1783–1859), historian, essayist, and story writer—" Knickerbocker's History of New York " ; " The Alhambra " ; " The Sketch Book."

Henry James (1843–1916), novelist—" Daisy Miller " ; " What Maisie Knew " ; " The American " ; " The Portrait of a Lady."

William James (1842–1910), psychologist and philosopher— " Principles of Psychology " ; " Pragmatism " ; " Varieties of Religious Experience."

Ring Lardner (1885–1933), humorist and short story writer—" You Know Me, Al " ; " How to Write Short Stories."

Sinclair Lewis (1885–), novelist—" Main Street " ; " Babbitt" ; " Arrowsmith " ; " Dodsworth."

Vachel Lindsay (1879–1931), poet—" The Congo " ; " General William Booth Enters Into Heaven."

Walter Lippmann (1889–), social philosopher—" A Preface to Morals " ; " A Preface to Politics."

Jack London (1876–1916), novelist—" The Call of the Wild " ; " The Sea Wolf " ; " The Iron Heel " ; " John Barleycorn."

Henry Wadsworth Longfellow (1807–82), poet—" Hiawatha " ; " Evangeline " ; " The Courtship of Miles Standish."

James Russell Lowell (1819–91), poet, critic, and essayist—" Biglow Papers " ; " Among My Books."

Don Marquis (1878–1937), humorist and poet—" The Old Soak " ; " Archy and Mehitabel."

Edgar Lee Masters (1869–1950), poet and novelist—" Spoon River Anthology " : " Children of the Market Place."

Cotton Mather (1663–1728), theologian—" Wonders of the Invisible World " ; " Magnalia Christi Americana."

Herman Melville (1819–91), novelist—" Moby Dick " ; " Typee " ; " Omoo " ; " White Jacket."

Henry Louis Mencken (1880–), essayist and critic—" Prejudices " ; " The American Language."

Edna St. Vincent Millay (1892–), poet—" Renascence " ; " Second April " ; " The Harpweaver."

Christopher Morley (1890–), essayist, poet, and novelist— " Romany Stain " ; " Shandygaff " ; " Thunder on the Left."

Gouverneur Morris (1876–), novelist and short story writer— " If You Touch Them They Vanish."

John Lothrop Motley (1814–77), historian—" The Rise of the Dutch Republic."

Charles G. Norris (1881–), novelist—" Salt " ; " Bread."

Frank Norris (1870–1902), novelist—" The Octopus " ; " The Pit."

Dorothy Parker (1893–), writer of short stories and humorous verse—" Laments for the Living."

Francis Parkman (1823–93), historian—" The Oregon Trail " ; " A Half-Century of Conflict."

Josephine Preston Peabody (1874–1922), poet and dramatist— " The Wayfarers : A Book of Verse " ; " The Piper."

Edgar Allan Poe (1809–49), poet, critic, and short story writer— " Annabel Lee " ; " The Poetic Principle " ; " Tales of the Grotesque and Arabesque."

Gene Stratton Porter (1868–1924), novelist—" Freckles " ; " A Girl of the Limberlost " ; " The Harvester."

Ezra Pound (1885–), poet and critic—" Lustra " ; " Pavannes and Divisions."

William Hickling Prescott (1796–1859), historian—" Conquest of Mexico " ; " Conquest of Peru."

Alice Hegan Rice (1870–1942), novelist—" Mrs. Wiggs of the Cabbage Patch " ; " The Honourable Percival " ; " Quin."

Edwin Arlington Robinson (1869–1935), poet—" The Man Who Died Twice " ; " Tristram " ; " Cavender's House " ; " Merlin."

James Harvey Robinson (1863–1936), historian—" The Mind in the Making " ; " The Ordeal of Civilization."

Anne Douglas Sedgwick (1873–1935), novelist—" The Little French Girl " ; " Dark Hester."

Upton Sinclair (1878–), novelist—" The Jungle " ; " Oil " ; " Sylvia " ; " Wet Parade."

John Smith (1580–1631), historian—" True Relation of Virginia " ; " General History of Virginia."

Frank L. Stanton (1857–1927), poet—" Songs from Dixie Land " ; " Little Folks Down South " ; " Up from Georgia."

Frank R. Stockton (1834–1902), novelist and short story writer— " Tales Out of School " ; " The Lady or the Tiger."

Harriet Beecher Stowe (1811–96), novelist—" Uncle Tom's Cabin."

Booth Tarkington (1869–1946), novelist and short story writer— " Penrod " ; " Monsieur Beaucaire " ; " Seventeen."

Henry David Thoreau (1817–62), essayist—" Walden, or Life in the Woods " ; " Excursions " ; " Cape Cod."

" Mark Twain " (Samuel L. Clemens) (1835–1910), humorist— " Adventures of Tom Sawyer " ; " Huckleberry Finn " ; " The Innocents Abroad."

Louis Untermeyer (1885–), poet and critic—" Burning Bush " ; " This Singing World " ; " American Poetry Since 1900."

Hendrik Van Loon (1882–1945), historian—" The Story of Mankind " ; " The Story of the Bible."

Carl Van Vechten (1880–), novelist and critic—" Peter Whiffle " ; " The Blind Bow-boy " ; " The Merry-Go-Round."

Lew Wallace (1827–1905), novelist—" Ben Hur " ; " The Fair God " ; " The Prince of India."

" Artemus Ward " (Charles Farrar Browne) (1834–67), humorist —" Artemus Ward : His Book."

Edith Wharton (1862–1937), novelist and short story writer— " Ethan Frome " ; " The Custom of the Country " ; " The Age of Innocence " ; " The House of Mirth."

Walt Whitman (1819–92), poet—" Leaves of Grass " ; " Drum Taps " ; " November Boughs."

John Greenleaf Whittier (1807–92) poet—" Maud Muller" ; " Snow-Bound " ; " The Barefoot Boy " ; " Barbara Frietchie."

Kate Douglas Wiggin (1859–1923), short story writer and novelist— " Rebecca of Sunnybrook Farm " ; " Mother Carey's Chickens " ; " The Bird's Christmas Carol."

Thornton Wilder (1897–), novelist—" The Bridge of San Luis Rey " ; " The Cabala " ; " The Woman of Andros."

John Winthrop (1588–1649), diarist—" Journal."

John Woolman (1720–72), diarist—" Journal."

Urban IV, Pope during 1261–64.

Urban V (1309–70), Pope 1362–70.

Urban VI (1318–89), Pope 1378–89, **3298**.

Urban VII (1521–90), Pope.

Urban VIII (1568–1644), Pope 1623–44.

Urbino (êr-bē′-nō). Tn. in cent. Ital.; pop. 20,500; cap. of former duchy of Urbino; celebrated centre of art and literature in 15th and 16th cents.; birthplace of Raphael, now a museum; beautiful palace.

Ur′du. A language of India, 1703.

Ure. R. of Yorkshire; has its source in the Pennines; joins the Swale to form Yorkshire Ouse; 50 m. long.

U′rea. Principal solid in mammalian urine; the first organic substance ever to be synthesized (in 1828 by Wöhler) which completely revolutionized this science; excreted by kidneys, 1856; formed by liver, 1968; in plastics mfr., 2626.

Urey, Harold Clayton (b. 1893). Amer. scientist. Professor in chemistry at Columbia Univ., New York (1929). His work there led to the isolation of the isotope of hydrogen and the preparation of "heavy" water. Nobel prize for chemistry in 1934.

Ur′ga. Chief tn. of Outer Mongolia; since 1924 known as **Ulan Bator Hoto**; pop. 100,000; 2204.

Uri (ōōr-′ē), Swiss canton, s. of Lake Lucerne, 3140–41.

Uriah (ū-rī′-a). Officer in David's army, husband of Bathsheba; sent by David to the front line to be killed (2 Sam. xi. 15).

U′rim and Thum′mim. Obscure term applied to a mode of divination among the anc. Hebrews; perhaps two pebbles or bone tablets of contrary import used in casting lots; sometimes mentioned as being carried in a pouch on the high priest's breast.

U′rine. The excretion of the kidneys; contains nitrogenous substances including urea, 1855.

Urk, Dutch island, *plate f. 2321*.

Ur′mia or **Urumi′ah.** Tn. of N.W. Persia; near L. Urmia; pop. 35,000; traditional birthplace of Zoroaster; Armenians massacred by Turks (1915); raisins exported.

Urmia Lake, Iran. Shallow l. without outlet; its water is salt; a. 1,800 sq. m.

Urquhart (êr′-kêrt), or **Urchard, Sir Thomas** (c. 1611–c. 1660). Scot. writer and soldier; fought against the Covenanters and then fled to Eng. where Charles I knighted him in 1641; taken prisoner by the Round-

heads. ("Epigrams"; "The Jewel"; "The Pedigree"; "An Introduction to the Universal Language"; translation of "Rabelais").

Ur′sa Major or **Great Bear.** A constellation; legend, 894; location, *chart, 895.*

Ursa Minor or **Little Bear.** A constellation; legend of, 894; location, *chart, 895.*

Ur′sula, St. (3rd or 5th cent. A.D.). Legendary virgin martyr; said to have been massacred with 11,000 companions by the Huns.

Ur′sulines. Rom. Cath. religious order founded by St. Angela Merici of Brescia (1470–1540) primarily for education of girls and care of sick; patron St. Ursula.

Ur′sus. The bear genus of carnivores, 382.

Ursus horribilis, grizzly bear, 382, 385.

Urticacae (êr-tik-ā′-sē-ē) or **nettle family.** Family of herbs and vines with hairy stems and primitive flowers; includes nettles, 2335.

Uruguay (ūr′-a-gī). Smallest in size and 2nd smallest in pop. of the S. Amer. republics; a. 72,153 sq. m.; pop. 2,202,936; **3298**, *maps, 3298, f. 3024*; cap. Montevideo, *2221.*

Uruguay. A river of S. Amer. rising in S.E. Brazil and flowing 1,000 m. to the R. Plata; boundary between Argentina on w. and Brazil and Uruguay on E.; *map, 3298.*

Urumchi (ōōr-ōōm′-chi). Cap. of Sinkiang prov., China, N. of Tien Shan Mts. on caravan route from Peking; pop. about 30,000.

Ush′ant (Fr. ouessant). Fr., fortified, rocky, often fog-bound island; off coast of Brittany; 4½ m. long; pop. 3,000; indecisive naval action off Ushant between English and French (1778).

Usk. R. of Carmarthenshire, Brecknockshire and Monmouthshire; flows 70 m. to Bristol Channel; beautiful scenery; salmon and trout fishing.

Uskub′ or **Skoplje,** Yugoslavia. Serbian trade tn.; pop. 64,000; formerly Turkish; captured by Serbs in Balkan Wars, by Bulgarians in 1st World War; leather, dye-stuffs, textile mfrs.

Uspallata (us-pal-ah′-ta)**Pass,** Andes, 152.

Ussh′er or **Usher, James** (1581–1656). Author of a Biblical chronology printed in margins of Authorized Version.

U.S.S.R. Union of Soviet Socialist Republics (Russia), **2844**; and Armenia, 237.

Usti (ōō′-stē). *See* **Aussig.**

U′tah. A w.-cent. state of U.S.A.; a. 84,000 sq. m.; pop. 550,310; settled by the Mormons, **3300**; uranium in, 3297.

Utah, Lake. Largest fresh-water lake in Utah, U.S.A.; 23 m. long.

Utamaro (ōō-tah-mah′-rō), **Kitagawa** (1754–1806). Japanese designer of colour-prints; called by contemporaries "great master of the Popular School."

Uta-Napishtim, the Babylonian Noah, 332.

Uther Pendragon, King, in Arthurian legends, 255.

U′tica. Anc. Phoenician city on N. coast of Africa; sided with Rome in Third Punic War and succeeded Carthage as leading city of Africa; scene of last stand of Pompeians against Caesar and of suicide of younger Cato (46 B.C.).

U′tica, New York, U.S.A. City on Mohawk R. and Erie Canal; pop. 100,500; centre of dairy farming region; diversified mfrs., including textiles, clothing, iron and steel products.

Utilitar′ians, in philosophy. Those whose maxim was "the greatest happiness of the greatest number"; also called Benthamites, after Jeremy Bentham, 414.

"Utopia." Romance by Sir Thomas More, describing an ideal commonwealth, 2229, 1210. Similar imaginary States have been described by Plato in the "Republic" (c. 375 B.C.), by St. Augustine in "The City of God" (c. A.D. 415), by Bacon in his "New Atlantis" (c. 1625), by James Harrington in "Oceana," by Samuel Butler in "Erewhon," and by H. G. Wells in "A Modern Utopia."

Uto′pian socialism, 2996.

Utrecht (ū-trekht′), Netherlands. Historic Dutch city on Rhine; pop. 187,000. 3370. 2320

Utrecht, Treaty of (1713), 2106, 2320, 1947.

Utrecht, Union of, 2321.

Uxbridge. Tn. of Middlesex. Brewing, brick-making, iron-founding, and market gardening. Depot of the R.A.F. Pop. 50,980.

Uxmal (ōōz-mahl′), Mexico. Anc. ruined city in N.W. Yucatan; remarkable remains of Maya architecture.

Uz, home of Job, 1832.

Uzbek Soviet Socialist Republic (Uzbekistan), cent. Asia; a. 143,000 sq. m.; pop. 6,282,450; **3267**, 2849; communal farm, *2851.*

IN inscriptions on stone, on memorial tablets and public buildings, U is even today very frequently made in the shape of a V. This gives the inscription an air of antiquity, for the U was originally made in that way on Greek and Roman inscriptions, since it was easier to cut with the chisel. The story of how the two letters V and U developed is told under U. The characters V and U were used for the same sound in Latin, Norman-French, and English as late as the Elizabethan period and were counted as one in alphabetic arrangements. V was commonly called "single U" as W was "double U" until the early 17th cent. The sound of *v* in Latin was like our *w*. Our *v* sound seems to have been wanting in Greek and Latin. V is pronounced in English with the upper teeth touching the lower lip. In Spanish, and to some extent in German, V is pronounced with lips stiffened and brought together, the teeth not being involved.

Vaagso. Is. of Norway, 100 m. N. of Bergen; Ger. radio station and refuelling base in 2nd World War; combined British and Norwegian forces landed Dec. 27, 1941, and destroyed installations and Ger. shipping.

Vaal (Vahl) (Dutch, "yellow"). R. in S. Africa, rises on w. slope of Drakensberg; flows w. 500 m. to Orange r., of which it is chief tributary, 2444, *map, 3015, 3239.*

Vaccination (vak-si-nā′-shon) or **vaccine therapy.** Preventing or treat-

ing disease with vaccines, **3301**, 2132; discovery, 1818.

Vaccine (vak′-sin or vak′-sēn), 3301, 180.

Vac′cinium, cranberry and bilberry genus of plants, of family *Ericaceae;* 3621.

Vach′ell, Horace Annesley (b. 1861). Eng. novelist and dramatist; published his first novel in 1894, and has a big list to his credit ("The Hill"; "John Charity"; "Quineys"; "The Face of Clay").

Vac′uum (vak′-ūm), **3301**; causes thunder, 1946; how it "lifts" an

aeroplane, 41; in thermionic valve, 3199.

Vacuum or **air-pump,** 90, 2704, 2702; experiments with, 91.

Vacuum or **Crookes tube,** 3430.

Vacuum or **pneumatic appliances,** 90, 2632.

Vacuum cleaner, 3301.

Vacuum flask, 3302.

Vacuum lamps, 1135.

Vacuum pan, 3084, 3112; in sugar-making, 3115.

Vacuum valve or **audion,** 294. *See* **Valves.**

UNIVERSITIES AND COLLEGES OF THE BRITISH ISLES

England

Oxford

All Souls (1438).
Balliol (1263).
Brasenose (1509).
Christ Church (1546).
Corpus Christi (1520).
Exeter (1314).
Hertford (1740).
Jesus (1571).
Lincoln (1427).
Magdalen (1458).
Merton (1264).
New College (1379).
Oriel (1326).
Pembroke (1624).
Queen's (1340).
St. John's (1555).
Trinity (1554).
University (1249).
Wadham (1612).
Worcester (1714).
St. Edmund Hall (1317).
Keble (1870).
Nuffield (1937).
St. Catherine's Society (1868).
Campion Hall.
St. Benet's Hall.
St. Peter's Hall (1928).

Women's :

Lady Margaret Hall (1878).
Somerville (1879).
St. Hugh's (1886).
St. Hilda's (1893).
St. Anne's (1879).

Cambridge

Christ's (1505).
Clare (1326).
Corpus Christi (1352).
Downing (1800).
Emmanuel (1584).
Gonville and Caius (1348).
Jesus (1496).
King's (1441).
Magdalene (1542).
Pembroke (1347).
Peterhouse (1284).
Queens' (1448).
St. Catharine's (1473).
St. John's (1511).
Sidney Sussex (1596).

Trinity (1546).
Trinity Hall (1350).
Selwyn (1882).
Fitzwilliam House (1869).

Women's :

Girton (1869).
Newnham (1875).

London

University College (1826).
King's College (1829).
Birkbeck College (1823).
Queen Mary College.
Bedford College for Women (1849).
Royal Holloway College (Women).
Westfield College (Women).
Wye College.

Imperial College :
   Royal College of Science.
   Royal College of Mines.
   City and Guilds Engineering College.
Goldsmiths' College.
London School of Economics.
King's College of Household Science.
Institute of Education.
Courtauld Institute of Art.
Institute of Advanced Legal Studies.
Institute of Archaeology.
Institute of Historical Research.
Brown Animal Sanitary Institution.
School of Slavonic Studies.
School of Oriental Studies.
School of Pharmacy.
South-Eastern Agricultural College.

Theological :

New College.
Richmond College.
St. John's Hall.

University Observatory, Mill Hill (1929).

Durham

University College, Durham.
King's College, Newcastle (1832).
Armstrong College, Newcastle (1871).
Hatfield's College, Durham.
St. Chad's College, Durham.
St. John's College, Durham.
St. Mary's College, Durham.
Bede College.
St. Hild's College.
Neville's Cross College.

Manchester (Victoria) (1850).
Birmingham (1900).
Liverpool (1903).
Leeds (1904).
Sheffield (1905).
Bristol (1909).
Reading (1926).
Nottingham (1948).

UNIVERSITY COLLEGES

Bristol—Merchant Venturers' College.
Exeter (1901).
Hull (1928).
Leicester (1921).
Manchester (College of Technology).
Southampton (1850).

Wales

University College of Wales (**Aberystwyth**) (1872).
University College of N. Wales (**Bangor**) (1885).
University College of S. Wales and Monmouthshire (**Cardiff**) (1883).
University College of **Swansea** (1920).
Welsh National School of Medicine (Cardiff).
St. David's College, Lampeter (1827).

Scotland

St. Andrews (1411).
United College of St. Salvator and St. Leonard.
College of St. Mary.
University College, Dundee.
Conjoint Medical School, Dundee.
Glasgow (1451).
Aberdeen (1494).
Edinburgh (1583).

UNIVERSITY COLLEGE

Glasgow Royal Technical College (1886).

Northern Ireland

Queen's University of Belfast (1849).
Magee University College, Londonderry (1865).

Eire

University of **Dublin** and **Trinity College** (1591).
National University (1908).
University College, Cork (1845).
University College, Galway (1849).
University College, Dublin (1909).

Vaea, Mt. Samoa, 2869 ; R. L. Stevenson's grave, *3089.*

Vagus (vā′-*gus*) or **pneumogastric nerve.** Mixed nerve descending from medulla oblongata through the carotid sheath and branching to the various internal organs ; also called the tenth cranial nerve.

Vailima (vī-lē′-m*a*). Stevenson's Samoan home, 2869, 3089.

Vaisyas (vī′-si*az*). Farmer caste among Hindus, 1626, 1707.

Valais (val′-ā). Canton of s.w. Switzerland ; a. 2,000 sq. m. ; pop. 148,300 ; great Alpine peaks ; tourist resorts ; many minerals, and wines well-known, but most of area is pastoral.

Valdai (val′-dī) **Hills,** Rus. Groups of low hills and plateaus midway between Leningrad and Moscow ; form watershed for chief river systems of country ; 800 to 900 ft. ; *map, 2845.*

Valdemar Atterdag (1320–75). King of Denmark.

Valdés (vahl-dās′), **Juan de** (1500–41). Sp. author, one of foremost Sp. writers of prose ; dealt with problems of Biblical interpretation and their bearing on devout life.

Valdez, Pedro de. Sp. naval officer, *1036.*

Valdivia (val-dē′-vi-*a*), Chile. City on R. Valdivia ; pop. 49,480 ; coasting trade.

Valence (val-ahns′), Fr. (Rom. Valencia). Historic tn. on Rhône ; pop. 26,000 ; printed fabrics, flour, tinned foods ; vineyards ; 2774.

Valen′cia. Prov. of Sp. on E. coast ; a. 4,239 sq. m. ; pop. 1,419,184 ; agriculture, grazing, fisheries, silk ; cap. Valencia ; 3032.

Valencia, third largest city of Spain ; pop. 520,213 ; **3302,** *3035,* 3039.

Valencia, Venezuela. City 24 m. s. of Puerto Cabello ; pop. 50,000 ; trade in sugar, coffee, cacao, hides ; cotton mills.

Valenciennes (val-ahn-syen′), Fr. Industrial tn. on R. Schelde in coal district ; pop. 38,684 ; famous lace no longer made here ; taken by Germans in 1914 and 1940.

Valenciennes lace, 1881, *plate f. 1880.*

Va′lency (vā-len-si). Combining power of a chemical element ; the ratio of the atomic weight to the combining weight of the element ; indicated by the number of hydrogen atoms with which the atom can combine or which it can replace ; if one, called monad ; if two, dyad ; if three, triad, and so on, *770,* 3685 ; of antimony, 177.

Va′lens (c. 328-378). Byzantine emperor, chosen in 364 by his brother Valentinian I to rule East ; warred with Persians and Goths ; defeated at Adrianople, 1487.

Valen′tia Island. Off s.w. coast of Eire ; terminus of cables between Amer. and Gt. Brit.

Val′entine, St. Christian martyr of 3rd cent., whose feast day falls on February 14 ; 2862.

Valentin′ian I (321–375). Rom. emperor, son of humble parents, who rose to high rank in army and was elected emperor in 364 ; a firm, impartial ruler.

Valentinian II (A.D. 371–392). Rom. emperor ; ruled over It., Illyria and Africa, while his brother Gratian ruled the Gallic provs. ; on assassination of Gratian in 383, Valentinian governed the whole empire of the West, assisted by Theodosius ; assassinated at Vienne.

Valentinian III (c. 419–455). Rom. emperor, succeeded in 425, during whose reign Africa, Sicily, Gaul, and Britain were lost ; murdered Aetius and was himself murdered following year.

Valentino, Rudolph (1895–1926). Italo-Amer. film actor ; " The Four Horsemen of the Apocalypse," " The Sheik," " Monsieur Beaucaire," etc.

Valera, Eamon De. *See* De Valera.

Valera (vah-lār′-*a*), **Juan** (1824–1905). Sp. statesman and eminent man of letters ; his " Pepita Jiménez," marked the renaissance of the modern Sp. novel.

Valer′ian (Publius Licinius Valerianus). Rom. emperor 253–260, elected by army when he was over 60 ; zealous worker but overwhelmed by constant fighting with barbarians and Persians ; defeated by Persians A.D. 260 and held prisoner until his death.

Valerianos, Apostolos. *See* **Fuca, Juan de.**

Valerian Way. A principal highway of anc. It. ; continued Tiburtina Way (Rome to Tivoli) N.E. to Adriatic.

Valéry, Paul (1871–1945). Fr. writer, leader of mod. Fr. school, 1382.

Valet′ta. *See* **Valletta.**

Valhalla (val-hal′-*a*). In Norse myth., hall of slain warriors in heaven, 2421, 2881.

Valjean (val-zhahn′), **Jean.** Hero of " Les Misérables," by Victor Hugo.

Valkyries (val-kīr′-ēz) or **Valkys,** " choosers of the slain," in Norse myth., maidens who conduct souls of slain heroes to Valhalla, 2421.

Valladolid (vah-lyah-thō-lēth′), Sp. Former cap., 95 m. N.W. of Madrid ; est. pop. 135,780 ; Columbus died here ; home of Cervantes, birthplace of Philip II ; varied mfrs. ; univ.

Valle-Inclan, Ramón Maria del. Sp. writer, 3051.

Vallet′ta. Chief tn. and port of isl. of Malta ; pop. 22,700 ; winter resort, 2072, *2073.* Harbour heavily damaged during 2nd World War.

Valley, 3302, *2596,* 2597 ; dew, 1000.

Valley Forge, Pennsylvania, U.S.A. Vil. on Schuylkill r., 20 m. N.W. of Philadelphia ; winter quarters of Washington's army (1777–78), 146.

Valley of the Kings, tombs of Egyptian kings.

Vallombro′sa. It. summer resort in Apennines ; Vallombrosian order of monks, founded 11th cent., now extinct ; monastery occupied by Royal School of Forestry.

Valmy (val′-mē), Fr. Vil. ; battle between army of Fr. Rev. govt. and First Coalition (1792), 1396.

Valois (val′-wah), **Margaret of.** *See* **Margaret of Valois.**

Valois, House of. Fr. dynasty, branch of Capetian family ; reigned 1328–1589 ; began with Philip VI, 2567. *See also* list of rulers of France under **France.**

Valois. Old dist. of N.-cent. France, now comprised in departments of Oise and Aisne ; countship in Middle Ages ; later united to crown ; home of House of Valois.

Valona, Albania. Same as **Avlona.**

Valo′nia. Acorn cup of valonia oak, used in tanning, 1912.

Valorization, the fixing or maintenance of price of a commodity by govt. aid.

Valparaiso, Chile. Chief Pacific port S. of San Francisco ; pop. 215,600 ; 3302, 804 ; bombarded, 805.

Valtelline (vahl-tel-ē′-nā). Fertile upper valley of R. Adda in N. It., much fought over by anc. and medieval powers ; wines and honey ; mineral springs ; ruled by Austria, (1814–59).

Valve gear, locomotive, 1981.

Valve gear, motor-car, 1736, 2244.

Valve, Thermionic. *See* **Thermionic Valve.**

Valves. Of heart, 1592, *1592* ; in internal combustion engine, 1736 ; in pumps, 2703 ; slide-valve of steam engine, 3086 ; thermostatic control, 3201. For wireless valves, *see* **Thermionic Valve.**

Vampire. Legendary demon supposed to suck the blood of sleeping persons.

Vampire bats, 372.

Van. Town in Asia Minor (Turkey) near L. Van. ; pop. 22,000 ; Amer. missions and schools ; scene of massacre by Turks.

Van, Lake. Large salt lake of Turkey ; a. 1,400 sq. m. ; no outlet.

Vana′dium (V). Very hard, brittle, grey-white metallic element of the tantalum group ; atomic weight, 50·95 ; melts at c. 3090° F. ; 3303 ; properties, 776 ; sources, 2157, 3024.

Vanbrugh (van′-brêr), **Dame Irene** (1872–1949). Eng. actress ; won fame in " The Gay Lord Quex " ; acted in social comedies (" Admirable Crichton," " Mr. Pim Passes By," " All The King's Horses," " King Maker," etc.).

Vanbrugh, Sir John (1664–1726). Eng. dramatist and architect, one of leading wits of his day ; designed Blenheim Palace and other mansions.

Vanbrugh, Violet (1867–1942). Eng. actress, sister of Irene ; played in Shakespeare and later portrayed society women, farcical and otherwise.

Vancouver (van-kōō′-vêr), **George** (c. 1758–98). Eng. navigator, served under Cook on 2nd and 3rd voyages ; explored Vancouver Isl. ; 3304.

Vancouver. Chief city of Brit. Columbia ; pop. 275,000 ; **3303.**

Vancouver Island. Brit. Columbia, largest Is. off w. coast of Amer. ; a. 12,400 sq. m. ; 3304, 578, 683 ; Victoria, 3321 ; *map, plate f. 680.*

Van′dals. Ger. tribe, **3304** ; in Africa, 2231 ; sack Rome (A.D. 455), 3802 ; in Spain, 3033.

Vandenberg, Arthur H. (b. 1884). Amer. senator 1928–46 ; Roosevelt's delegate to U.N. conference at San Francisco 1945 ; supported Truman's foreign policy and Marshall Aid ; U.S. delegate to U.N. meeting in Paris 1948.

Van′derbilt, Cornelius (1794–1877). Amer. capitalist and financier ; founder of the Vanderbilt fortune ; nicknamed " Commodore " for his early steamboat activities ; acquired control of New York Central Railroad, to which his son, W. H. Vanderbilt, and grandsons added others.

Van Der Goes, Hugo (1440–82). One of the greatest of early Flemish painters ; brilliant colour and strong draughtsmanship.

Van Diemen's (dē′-menz) **Land.** Former name of **Tasmania.**

Van Druten, John William (b. 1901). Brit. dramatist and novelist (plays, " Young Woodley " ; " After All " ; " London Wall " ; " Behold We Live " ; " The Voice of the Turtle " ; " I Remember Mama ").

Van Dyck (dīk) or **Van Dyke, Sir Anthony** (1599–1641). Greatest of Flemish portrait painters, **3304,** 2333 ; pupil of Rubens, 2839 ; portrait of Gustavus Adolphus, *1558.*

Vane, Sir Henry (1589–1655). Eng. statesman ; one of the principal advisers of Charles I, he was made Sec. of State (1640) ; played a leading part in impeachment of Strafford ; suspected of betraying the King's cause, supported the parliament.

Vane, Sir Henry (1613–62). Eng. Puritan statesman, son of the preceding ; gov. of Massachusetts 1636–37 ; returned to England ; active Parliamentarian ; imprisoned at Restoration and beheaded for treason.

Väner or **Wener Lake** (vānêr). Largest in Scandinavian peninsula and 3rd largest in Europe ; a. 2,000 sq. m. ; 3128.

" Vanes′sa." Poetical name given by Swift to Esther Vanhomrigh (1692–1723), 3132.

Van Eyck (īk), **Hubert** (c. 1366–1426), Flemish portrait and landscape painter, who with his brother Jan (c. 1385–1440) introduced aerial perspective and landscape backgrounds ; Jan was also the perfecter of oil painting technique, the brothers being among the most important figures in the history of painting ; 2766, 2324, 2476, 1460 ; portrait of Arnolfini and wife, *2324.*

Van Gogh, Vincent (1853–90). Dutch painter, one of the most important and influential modern masters ; belonged to no school but ranked as a post-impressionist ; **3305,** 2335, *1687,* 1689, 2477.

Vanguard, H.M.S. Brit. battleship, built 1941–45 ; 50,000 tons ; length 814 ft., beam 107 ft. Earlier Vanguard blew up in 1917 at Scapa Flow, with loss of 627 lives.

Vanil'la. A substance derived from the perennial herb *Vanilla planifolia*, an orchid, native of Cent. Amer. ; **3305**, 3060, *3061* ; coal-tar substitute, 857.

Vanity Fair. In " Pilgrim's Progress," 620.

" Vanity Fair." Novel by Thackeray. 2402, 3193.

Van Loon, Hendrik Willem (1882–1945). Dutch-Amer. historian and illustrator, b. Rotterdam, Netherlands. (" The Story of Mankind " ; " The Home of Mankind " ; " The Arts of Mankind " ; " Ships ").

Vannes (van), France. Quaint old tn. 67 m. N.W. of Nantes ; pop. 28,180 ; anc. cap. Veneti, taken by Caesar 56 B.C. ; rich prehistoric remains.

Van Rensselaer (ren'-se-lãr), **Killian** (1595–1644). First patroon (proprietor under old Dutch grant) of New York, one of founders of New York and Albany.

Vansittart, Robert Gilbert, 1st Baron (b. 1881). Eng. diplomat and author ; Asst. Under-Secretary of State for Foreign Affairs and Private Sec. to prime minister (1928–30) ; Permanent Under-Secretary Foreign Affairs (1930–38) ; Chief Diplomatic Adviser to Foreign Sec. 1938–41 ; created baron in 1941.

Van't Hoff (vahnt hõf'), **Jacobus Hendricus** (1852–1908). Dutch chemist and physicist, founder of stereochemistry and first Nobel prize winner (1901) in chemistry.

Vanua Levu (vah'-nū-*a* lã'-*vu*). One of Fiji Isls. ; a. 2,130 sq. m. ; 1271.

Vaphio cup, *31.*

Va'pour. Gaseous form of a substance normally solid or liquid, 1420 ; water vapour in air, 1243 ; oil vapour in lamps, 1887, 1889.

Vapour heating systems, 1600.

Varanger (vahr-ahng'-gêr) Fiord. Inlet in Norway.

Varan'gians. Slav. name for the Norse invaders of Russia (9th cent.) ; Varangian guard.

Vardon, Harry (1870–1937). British golfer ; winner of Eng. Open Championship 1896, 1898, 1899, 1903, 1911, 1914 ; published " The Complete Golfer," " How to Play Golf," and " My Golfing Life."

Varennes-en-Argonne (var-enz'-ahn-ahr-gon'). Small tn. of France, on Aire r. ; taken by Americans on first day of Meuse-Argonne offensive, Sept. 1918 ; Louis XVI and family captured, 1759.

Variable star, 3080.

Variation of compass, 882.

Var'na. Chief port of Bulgaria, on Black Sea ; pop. 69,944 ; anc. Odessus ; cotton mills ; exports cattle, grain.

Varnhagen von Ense (fahrn'-hah-gen fon en'-sê), **Rahel** (1771–1833). Ger. author remembered for her letters and for her influence on A. von Humboldt, Goethe, Carlyle, and other literary men ; her salon in Berlin was the most important in Germany ; her husband, Karl (1785–1858), wrote historical and literary sketches of permanent value.

Varnish. Solution made from resins or drying oils which, when used as a paint, produces a hard, shiny and transparent protective surface, **3305**, 2478, 2709. *See also* Paints.

Varro (var'-ō), **Marcus Terentius** (116–28 B.C.). Rom. historian and soldier, " most learned of the Romans " ; most of writings lost. Only his works on the Latin language and on agriculture now exist.

Var'us, Publius Quintilius (d. A.D. 9). Rom. general whose defeat by Arminius in the Teutoburg Forest (A.D. 9) limited Rom. empire to the Rhine. Varus killed himself in despair, and the Emperor Augustus cried in anguish at the news ; " Varus, Varus, give me back my legions ! "

Vasa (vah'-*sa*). Swedish royal house beginning with Gustavus I 1523, and ending with Christina 1654. For list *see* Sweden.

Vasari (vas-ah'-ri), **Giorgio** (1511–74). It. author, painter, and architect (Uffizi Palace, Florence), biographer and " father of modern art, history and criticism." (" Lives of the Most Eminent Painters, Sculptors, and Architects," a classic despite inaccuracies).

Vasco da Gama (*c.* 1460–1524). Port. explorer ; **3306**, 69, 2279, 695, 3016.

Vas'cular or **circulatory system,** of human body, 1591, 474 ; palms, 3246 ; plants, 1322 ; trees, 3245.

" Vase'line." Proprietary brand of petroleum jelly, 2429 ; used as a salve, liniment, etc.

Vases, 2665, *2667, 2668, 2669* ; Aegean, *31* ; Chinese, *810* ; famous example in the Louvre, 2033 ; Greek, *1523, 1524, 1528, 1528, 1536* ; Portland, plate *f. 585.*

Vash'ti. Queen of Ahasuerus, king of Persia, put aside for disobedience (Book of Esther).

Vas'sals. In feudal system, 1268.

Vatican, City and State. The Papal See at Rome, including St. Peter's Ch., the Vatican Palace, etc. ; pop. 1,000 ; **3306**, 2495, 2615, 2800, *2802* ; art treasures, 2745 ; library, 1931 ; official residence, 1769. *See also* Sistine Chapel.

Vatican Council. Church council of 1870, which proclaimed the Pope's infallibility in questions of faith and morals.

Vatican manuscript of Bible, 425.

Vätter or **Wetter** (vet'-êr). 2nd largest lake in Sweden ; a. 733 sq. m. ; 3128.

Vauban (vō-bahn'), **Sebastien le Prestre de** (1638–1707). Marshal of France, most celebrated of military engineers.

Vaucanson, Jacques de (1704–82), Fr. inventor of automatic pattern weaving, 1791.

Vaudeville. Origin of pantomime, 2495.

Vaudois (võ'-dwah). Same as **Waldenses.**

Vaudreuil-Cavagnal, Piérre François, Marquis of (1698–1765). Last Fr. Gov.-Gen. of Canada, succeeding Duquesne in 1755 ; his father, Philippe (*c.* 1641–1725), was appointed Gov.-Gen. in 1703.

Vaughan, Henry (1622–95). Welsh metaphysical poet, known as " The Silurist " ; devotional poems, "Silex Scintillans," later influenced Wordsworth.

Vaughan (vawn), **Herbert** (1832–1903). Eng. Rom. Cath. prelate, Manning's successor as cardinal and archbishop of Westminster ; responsible for erection of Westminster R.C. Cathedral.

Vaughan Williams, Ralph (b. 1872). Eng. composer ; works, intensely English (influenced by folk-music), and entirely individual, include : " London Symphony " ; " Hugh, the Drover " (opera) ; " Mass in G. minor " ; " Job " (ballet) ; O.M. (1935).

Vault. Room or passage with arched roof, 214 ; Roman, 214, fan vaulting, *214,* Gothic, 216 ; Romanesque, 218.

Vauxhall (voks'-hawl) **Gardens,** S.W. London. On Surrey side of Thames, built 1661 ; fashionable resort ; closed 1859 and site built over.

Vecht (vekht) **River.** Arm of the Rhine, 18 m. long, 3300.

Vectis, Rom. Isle of Wight, 3377.

Vedas (vã'-das). Sacred writing of Hindus, 1626, 1713.

Ved'dahs. A people of Ceylon, *748,* 749.

Vega (vē'-ga). A fixed star, 3078, 3080 ; sun moving towards, 2762.

Vega Carpio (vã'-gah kahr'-pē-ō), **Lope Felix de** (1562–1635), generally called Lope de Vega. Sp. dramatist and poet, 3051.

Vegetable ivory. *See* Tagua.

Vegetable marrow, 2109.

Vegetable oils, 1263.

Vegetables. Edible plants or plant parts ; canning, 692, 1340 ; cooking, 902 ; digestion of, 1017 ; food value, *1339,* 1340. *See* under names of different vegetables.

Vegetation, desert, 996, *997,* 998, 1243 ; ocean, 2103, *plate f. 2104* ; rainfall, 2741.

Vehicles. *See* Motor Vehicles.

Veii, It. Anc. Estruscan stronghold, 2805.

Veile (vī'-lē). Picturesque tn. of Denmark ; pop. 23,000 ; 991.

Veins, of body, 474 ; how to stop bleeding, 1295 ; portal, 1968 ; pulmonary and vena cava, 1592.

Veins, in plants, 1915

Velazquez (vã-lath'-heth), **Diego** (1465– *c.* 1522), Sp. soldier ; accompanied Columbus to W. Indies on 2nd voyage ; founded Havana.

Velazquez, Diego Rodri'quez de Silva y (1599–1660). Sp. painter, **3307**, 2476, 3040, " Las Meninas " (the dwarfs), *3045,* " The Surrender of Breda," *3050* ; and Murillo, 2257.

Veld (velt) or **veldt.** Plains in S. Africa, 69, 3014.

Vella Gulf, battle of, in 2nd World War, 2474.

Vel'lum. A fine parchment, 509 ; 2496 ; drum heads, 1049.

Veloc'ipede. Form of bicycle, 947.

Velocity, in physics, 2591, 3673, 3676, 3678.

Velocity, of light, 1939 ; of sound in various substances, 3676 ; velocity microphone, 2163 ; in venturi tube, 3312.

Velvet. A silken fabric with short, thick pile ; introduced, possibly from the Far East, into Europe before the end of the 13th or at the beginning of the 14th century ; 937, 2973.

Velvet, of deer antlers, 984.

Velveteen. A cotton fabric having the appearance of velvet, from which it differs only in respect of the material.

Ve'na ca'va, 1592.

Vend'e (vahn'-dã). Maritime dept. of w. France ; a. 2,600 sq. m. ; pop. 393,800 ; centre of royalist revolt (1792–93) against Fr. republic.

Vendet'ta. A blood-feud, in Corsica, 915.

Vendôme (vahn-dõm'). Fr. tn. ; pop. 10,300 ; ruins of 11th cent. castle of Counts of Vendôme ; birthplace of Rochambeau.

Vendôme Column, in Paris, 2516.

Veneer'. A thin slip of wood or ivory glued or cemented to a piece of other material for which it forms an ornamental covering ; of mahogany, 2065.

Venetia (ven-ē'-shi-*a*). Dist. in N. It. between Alps and Adriatic ; anc. Rom. prov. ; long ruled by Venice ; ceded to Austria (1797) ; 1763, 1769.

Venezia (vã-nã'-tsi-*a*). It. for Venice.

Venezia Giulia. Region of Yugoslavia and Italy, along Gulf of Venice and incl. Trieste ; all Ital. before 2nd World War, it was partitioned under the Ital. peace treaty (1947), 183 sq. m. remaining Ital. and 3,274 sq. m. going to Yugoslavia ; 3440. *See also* Trieste.

Venezuela (ven-e-zwē'-la). A republic of S. Amer., on the Caribbean Sea ; a. 352,143 sq. m. ; pop. 3,850,770 ; **3308** ; *maps, 3309, f. 3024* ; asphalt, 272 ; Brit. Guiana boundary dispute, 203 ; Orinoco r., 2452 ; people, *795* ; petroleum, 3024. *History,* 3309 ; Bolivar leads insurrection, 491 ; disputes with Gt. Brit., 203 ; new constitution in 1947, 3309.

Venezuela, Gulf of, or **Gulf of Maracaibo.** Inlet of Caribbean Sea in N.W. Venezuela ; *map, 3309.*

Venice. It. city built on 117 small isls. in a bay of the Adriatic Sea ; pop. 303,260 ; **3310**, *1762, 1771, 1773, 1774, 1781* ; architecture, 212 ; Bridge of Sighs, *3311* ; Campaniles, *3311* ; Doge's Palace, 3310 ; first commercial bank, 358 ; Grand Canal, *3310, 3312* ; medieval trade and industry, *1472,* 1312, 3060, 2766 ; Turner, *3268* ; Renaissance, 2766 ; St. Mark's Cathedral, 638, 214, *3311* ; painters, 1776 ; scenes, Titian, 3217 ; ships, 2946 ; textiles, 3191 ; " wedding the Adriatic," 29.

Venizelos (vã-nē-zã'-lōs), **Eleutherios** (1864–1936). Gk. statesman ; several times Prime Minister and during 1st World War virtual dictator ; in 1935 engineered an unsuccessful revolt from his birthplace, the Isle of Crete ; 1525, 1526, 3414.

Vennachar (ven'-a-kahr) **Loch.** L. of Perthshire ; about 4 m. long and 1½ m. broad.

Ven'om, snake poison ; clots blood, 2991.

Venous blood, 474.

Ventilation and heating, 1597, 1260.

Ventricle. Cavity in an organ ; of heart, 1592.

Ventspils, formerly **Windau.** Spt. of Latvia, S.S.R. ; pop. 15,000. Captured by Germans July 1941, and held until after general surrender in May 1945.

Venturi, " bottleneck " passage for air or gas, **3312** ; in jet engines, 1331 ; law, 2154 ; in rocket bomb, 2792.

Ventur'imeter. Device for measuring the flow of water ; used in power-houses ; named after an It. physicist.

Ve'nus. Rom. goddess of love and beauty, identified with Gk. Aphrodite, **3312** ; and Psyche, 638.

Venus. A planet, 3313 ; 276, 279, *280*, 2617 ; *diagram, 2618* ; orbit, shape and size, 280, 2617.

Venus de Milo, statue, *1535*, 1537, 2032, *2033*.

Venus's flower-basket. A kind of sponge, 3068.

Venus's fly-trap. An insect-eating plant, 3313.

Vera Cruz (vā'-rah krooz), Mexico. State in E. on Gulf of Mexico , a. 27,000 sq. m., pop. 619,300 ; cap. Jalapa ; chief port, Vera Cruz.

Vera Cruz, Mexico. Principal port on the Gulf of Mexico ; directly E. of Mexico City ; pop. 76,000 ; 3313, 2156.

Verb, in grammar, 3313, 2920, 1494.

Vercingetorix (ver-sin-jet'-or-iks) (d. 46 B.C.). Chief of the Arverni in Gaul ; leader of the great rebellion against Caesar ; beheaded by Caesar's order ; 651.

Verde, Cape. Westernmost point of Africa, 65.

Verden (fär'-den). Tn. of Lower Saxony (formerly Hanover), Germany, on Aller r. ; pop. 10,000 ; Saxons executed by Charlemagne (782).

Verdi (ver'-dē), **Giuseppe** (1813–1901). It. composer, 3315 ; " Aïda," 2438 ; " Simone Boccanegra," *2437*.

Ver'digris. Poisonous green pigment known to the anc. Romans and produced largely in the wine districts of France ; it is a basic copper acetate made by the action of acetic acid on copper plates ; it is used in paints, especially with white lead, in dyeing and calico printing, and as a medicine in the form of liniment ; causes the green colour of copper and of brassware when exposed to the weather.

Verdon-Roe, Sir Alliott (b. 1877). Eng. aircraft des'gner ; a pioneer of the tractor type of aeroplane, he founded, with his brother Humphrey (1878–1949), the company of A. V. Roe & Co., Ltd., for the construction of Avro planes.

Verdun (vär-d'ŭn), France. Fortified city in N. ; pop. 14,600 ; in 1st World War, *3410* ; in 2nd World War, 3417, 3422.

Verdun, Partition of (A.D. 843), 1238, 1447.

Vereeniging (fer-ā'-nig-ging), **Peace of** (1902), 2988, 3240.

Verendrye. Family name of two Fr. Canadian explorers, sons of a fur trader ; first white men known to have visited North Dakota ; founded Winnipeg ; reached Rockies, 681.

Vereshtchagin (ver-es-chah'-gin), **Vasili** (1842–1904). Rus. painter ; sought by pictures of horrors of war to promote peace.

Verge. In architecture, the shaft of a column ; also name of a small ornamental shaft.

Vergil. Same as **Virgil.**

Verhaeren (vĕr-här'-en), **Emile** (1855–1916). Belgian poet and critic ; in his early work applied pictorial method to psychological studies ; later poems marked by patriotic fervour and by attempt to individualize

towns and fields of Belgium (" Les Flamandes " ; " Les Débâcles " ; " Villages Illusoires " ; " Les Aubes ").

Verkhoyansk, Siberia ; lowest recorded temperature at, 174.

Verlaine', Paul (1844–96). Fr. lyric poet, the exquisite cadence of whose verses expresses his delight in the fine shades of sensation (" Poèmes saturniens " ; " Sagesse," a collection of religious poems ; " Amour " ; " Bonheur ").

Vermeer (ver-mār'), **Jan** (1632–75). Dutch genre and landscape painter ; 3315, *2325*, 2334.

Ver'mes. Term formerly used to cover large number of primitive or lowly members of animal kingdom, grouped together as " worms " ; 156, 3425.

Vermicel'li, 2045.

Vermiform appendix. *See* **Appendix, Vermiform.**

Vermilion. Red sulphide of mercury ; poisonous red pigment used in sealing wax and paints, 2146, 2478.

Vermont'. A New Eng. state of the U.S.A. ; a. 9,609 sq. m. ; pop. 359,230 ; 3315.

Vernal equinox, 1221, 2223 ; determines date of Easter, 1074.

Verne, Jules (1828–1905). Fr. novelist, specializing in the romance of semi-scientific extravaganza ; **3316**, 3104 ; story, " Twenty Thousand Leagues under the Sea," 3316.

Vernier. Device applied to scale of accurate reading instruments to give readings of fractions of the smallest divisions of the scale ; consists of an auxiliary scale of ten divisions, together equal to nine divisions of the scale.

Vernier, Pierre (1580–1637). French inventor after whom the above device is named.

Vernon, Dorothy (16th cent.). Daughter and heiress of Sir George Vernon ; eloped with Sir John Manners and became ancestress of dukes of Rutland ; heroine of Charles Major's novel, " Dorothy Vernon of Haddon Hall."

Vernon, Edward (1684–1757). Eng. admiral ; captured (1739) Porto Bello, Panama, with a fleet of 6 ships ; Mt. Vernon named after him.

Verona (vār-ō'-nah). It. fortified city 62 m. w. of Venice on Adige r. ; pop. 153,700 ; art centre in Middle Ages ; famous art collections and Rom. remains ; Congress of European powers (1822) ; bombarded 1914–18 War ; *map, 1764* ; taken by Allies April 28, 1945.

Veronese (vār-on-ā'-sā), **Paolo** (1528–88). Last great painter of Venetian school ; real name Paolo Cagliari ; 1776, 1781.

Veronica (vĕr-on'-ik-a), **St.** Legendary woman of Jerusalem, on whose kerchief used by Jesus to wipe the bloody sweat from His brow on way to Golgotha, His portrait was said to have been miraculously imprinted.

Verrazano (ver-ah-tsah'-nō), **Giovanni** (c.1480–c.1527). It. explorer of New World in Fr. service, 2357, 143.

Verrocchio (ver-ok'-ē-ō), **Andrea del** (1435–88). It. sculptor, goldsmith, and painter, great early Renaissance artist, 1775, *1776, 1784*, 2906 ; teacher of da Vinci ; 1926.

Versailles (vĕr-sālz' ; Fr., vär-sī) ; France. Suburb of Paris ; pop. 73,000 ; **3317** ; court of Louis XIV, 2029 ; palace, 3317.

Versailles, Treaty of (1783), 146.

Versailles, Treaty of (1919) ; *1241*, 2841, 3414, 3326, 3317 ; covenant of League of Nations, 1908 ; provisions affecting Fr., 1367 ; Ger., 1450 ; Poland, 2642 ; rejected by U.S.A., 3414 ; Ger. denounces, 1451.

Verse. *See* **Poetry.**

Vers libre (vär-lē'-br) or free verse, 2637.

Vert. In heraldry, 1614.

Ver'tebrae. The segments of the backbone, 2977.

Vertebrates. Term applied to all animals which possess backbones ; there are over 30,000 known species ;

3318, 156 ; evolution, 158, 1297, 1244, 2767 ; first appear on earth, 1433 ; variations in skeleton, 2977. For subordinate groups *see* **Birds ; Fish ; Mammals ; Reptiles.**

Verula'mium. Anc. Rom. cap. of Southern Britain, outside modern St. Albans, 1622, 2861, *2810* ; Boadicea destroys, 480 ; excavations, *206.*

Verviers (vār'-vyā), Belgium, tn. ; pop. 40,300, woollen goods, dyes, glass ; suffered severely during Ger. occupation, 1914–18.

Vesa'lius, Andreas (1514–64). Belg. anatomist, 151, 3446.

Ve'sicant, blister-producing substance ; gas, 1420.

Vesle (vel). R. of N.E. Fr. ; rises N. of Châlons-sur-Marne, flows 80 m. past Rheims to Aisne ; in 1st World War, 3413.

Ves'pa. A genus of wasps, including the common wasp and hornet, 3345.

Vespa'sian (Titus Flavius Sabinus Vespasianus) (A.D. 9–79). Rom. emperor, father of Titus and Domitian ; in his reign Titus captured and destroyed Jerusalem, the Colosseum was begun, and Agricola extended Rom. sway in Britain : 2811.

Vespers. One of the canonical hours, 2213.

Vespers, Sicilian, name given to a massacre of their French oppressors by the Sicilians, on Easter Monday 1282 ; 2968.

Ves'pidae. Family containing the social wasps, 3345.

Vespu'cius, Americus (1451–1512), (or **Amerigo Vespucci**). Florentine navigator after whom Amer. was named, 3318, 139.

Ves'ta, in Rom. myth., goddess of the hearth, 3318.

Vestal Virgins, 3318.

Vestig'ial structures, in body, 1245.

Vesu'vius, Mt., 3318, *1765*, 3328, *1901*, 185 ; buries Pompeii, 2653.

Veta Madre (vā'-ta mah'-drā) **silver mine,** Guanajato, Mex., 2157.

Vetches. Various bean-like plants, grown largely for fodder.

Ve'to. A power possessed by a king or body to check proposed legislation ; curtailing of Lords' power of veto, 2522 ; Brit. crown, 2524. In the U.N., 3284.

Vevey (vev'-ā), Switzerland. Tn. on L. Geneva ; tourist resort ; pop. 12,600.

Vézelay (vāz'-lā). Fr. vil. noted for the Madeleine (12th cent.) ; one of largest and finest basilicas in Fr.

Vézère (vā-zār'). R. of S. Fr. ; flows 120 m. to the Dordogne ; prehistoric remains, 734.

Via dell' Impero, Rome, *2800.*

Vian (vī-an), **Adm. of Fleet Sir Philip** (b. 1894). Brit. sailor ; as capt. of the destroyer Cossack (*q.v.* in *f-i.*) he rescued Brit. sailors from Ger. prison ship Altmark ; was adm. in charge of convoys running Malta blockade in 1942 ; and covered the landings in Sicily and Salerno in 1943 ; commanded 1st aircraft carrier squadron in Pacific 1944–45 and became 2nd in command of Brit. Pacific fleet ; 5th Sea Lord in 1946 ; in 1948 Adm. of Fleet ; in 1949 c.-in-c. Home Fleet.

Viaud (vyō), **Louis Marie Julien.** *See* **Loti, Pierre.**

Vibra'tion. *See* **Wave Motion.**

Vicar, in Ch. of Eng., 825.

Vic'ar of Christ, 2495.

" Vicar of Wakefield." Novel by Goldsmith, 1482.

Vice-admiral of Royal Navy, 28.

Vicenza (vē-chen'-tsah). It. Tn. on Bacchiglione r. 40 m. w. of Venice ; pop. 69,380 ; produces silk goods.

Viceroy of India, 1715 ; the last Viceroy of India was Earl Mountbatten, in 1947.

Vichy (vē'-shē). Tn. in cent. Fr. on Allier R., famous mineral springs. Seat of Pétain's gov. after French capitulation (1940).

Vickers machine-gun, 2050. Army abolishes, 1947.

Vickers Viking airliner, *1826*.

Vickers Vimy aeroplane crosses Atlantic (1919), *47*.

Vicks'burg, Mississippi, U.S.A. Mfg. and cotton trading city on Mississippi ; pop. 24,400 ; decisive battle in Amer. Civil War, 1863.

" Vicomte de Bragelonne." Novel by Dumas, 1054.

Victor Emman'uel II (1820–78). King of It., 3319, 1769–70 ; and Cavour, 737 ; and Garibaldi, 1418 ; monument, *2801, plate f. 2804*.

Victor Emmanuel III (1869–1947). King of It., 3319.

Victoria (1819–1901). Queen of Gt. Brit. and Ire., 3319 ; Emp. of India, 1715 ; Balmoral built for, 351 ; Disraeli's ministries, 1018 ; Gladstone, 1469 ; Glasgow monument, *1471* ; literature, 1214 ; married Albert, 101 ; memorial, 599 ; postage stamps, *3075, 3075, 3076*.

Victoria, Australia. State in S.E. ; 87,884 sq. m. ; pop. 2,031,000 ; 3321, *map f. 308* ; cap. Melbourne, 2136 ; State parl., *2136*.

Victoria, Brit. Columbia. Cap. and commercial centre of prov. ; on Vancouver Isl. ; pop. about 44,000 ; 3321, 3304.

Victoria or Hong Kong, 1639.

Victoria, Lake, or **Victoria Nyanza**, in E.-cent. Africa, 2nd largest freshwater lake in world ; a. 26,000 sq. m. ; 3321, 69 ; *map, 1073*.

Victoria, Mt., Canada, in S.W. Brit. Columbia, overlooking L. Louise ; height 11,500 ft.

Victoria and Albert Museum, London, under the Min. of Education ; contains the finest collection of applied art—decorative and ornamental—in the world ; founded as the Museum of manufacturers in 1852, sometimes known as the South Kensington Museum, *2014*, 2260.

Victoria Cross (V.C.). Brit. decoration, 2448.

Victoria Falls. World's largest cataract ; on Zambesi, Rhodesia ; 3321, 69, 2772, *plate f. 3016*, 3441.

Victoria Island, Canada. Large isl. in Arctic Ocean, in Mackenzie dist., North-West Territories.

Victoria Land, Antarctica. See **South Victoria Land**.

Victorian Age, in Eng. literature, 1214.

Victoria Nile or **Somerset Nile**, 2370.

Victorian Order, 2449.

Victoria Nyanza. See **Victoria, Lake**.

Victoria regia. A giant water-lily, 1552, *1854*, 3354.

Victoria River. Rises in the W. of Northern Territory, Australia, and flows N. and W., entering the Indian Ocean by a wide estuary called Queen's Channel.

Victoria Tower, Houses of Parliament, London, *2013*.

Victoria University, Manchester. See **Manchester, University of**.

" Victor of the Marne," 1832.

Victory, H.M.S., Nelson's flagship, 3321, *3322*, 2313, 3234.

Vicuña (vĭ-kū'-na : Sp. vē-kōon'-yah). An animal of S. Amer., 125 ; vicuña cloth, 125.

Vienna (vē-en'-a). Cap. of Austria on Danube ; pop. 1,548,100 ; 3322, 316 ; besieged by Turks, 3264 ; taken by Russians in 1945, and occupied by Allies, 3323, 3324.

Vienna, Congress of (1815), 1240, *1240*, 3323 ; Ger., 1449 ; Netherlands independent, 2321 ; Scandinavian countries, 2800 ; Swiss neutrality, 3143 ; Talleyrand's influence, 3149.

Vienne (vē-en'), Fr. Anc. tn. on Rhône ; pop. 22,000 ; varied mfrs. ; large trade ; fortified by Caesar 47 B.C. ; Roman aqueducts ; many antiquities, 2774.

Viet-Minh. Organization in Indo-China led by Dr. Ho Chi Minh, 3323.

Viet-Nam. Repub. of S.E. Asia, comprising the former French protectorates of Annam, Tonking and Cochin-China ; 3323.

composed of the former protectorates of Northern Annam, Tongking, and Cochin China. See **Indo-China**.

Viewfinder, of camera, 672.

Vigny (vē-nyē), **Alfred de** (1797–1863). Fr. poet and dramatist ; though he wrote relatively little, his fame is secure ; some of his most famous poems (" Eloa" ; " Dolorida " ; " Moïse ") greatly influenced Hugo and the Romanticists.

Viipuri (Swed. Viborg). Town of Karelo-Finnish S.S.R. ; on Gulf of Finland, 75 m. N.W. of Leningrad ; founded by Swedes in 1293, cap. of Karelia ; taken by Peter the Great in 1709 ; Finnish after 1st World War, it became Russian in 1940 ; pop. est. 30,000.

Vi'kings (" pirates "). See **Northmen**.

Vilayet (vē-lah-yet') or **Il**, Turkish governmental unit, governed by a vali ; its sub-divisions are called sanjaks, 3266.

Villa (vē'-yah), **Francisco** or **"Pancho"** (1872–1923). Mex. revolutionist and bandit ; made peace 1902 with Mex. govt.

Villa Conception. Same as **Concepcion**.

Villa Franca (vē'-lah frahn'-kah), Azores, 324.

Villafranca. It. tn. ; pop. 12,000 ; preliminary treaty of peace ending war between Fr. and Austria signed here (July 11, 1859), 1418.

Villa Rica (vēl'-yah rē'-kah). City of Paraguay in agric. region ; pop. 31,000 ; large trade in tobacco and Paraguay tea, 2512.

Villars (vē-lahr'), **Claude Louis Hector, Duc de** (1653–1734). Marshal of France, one of greatest Fr. generals ; commanded against Eugène and Marlborough in War of the Sp. Succession.

Villeins or **serfs**, 1268.

Villiers, George. See **Buckingham, George Villiers**.

Villon (vē-yawn'), **François** (1431–c 1462). Greatest of Fr. medieval poets, a vagabond rascal who escaped hanging only by great luck, 1380 ; chief works, " Petit Testament," " Grand Testament."

Vilnius (formerly **Vilna** or **Wilno**). Cap. of Lithuanian S.S.R., occupied by Poland 1920–1939 ; pop. 207,750 ; formerly Rus. city ; captured by Germans in 1914–18 War ; rly. centre; grain and timber ; 1968 ; Germans occupied 1941–44 ; 3419, 3424.

Vimeiro. Wellington's victory, 3364.

Vim'inal Hill, Rome, 2799.

Vimy (vē'-mē) **Ridge**. A high ridge 4 m. N.E. of Arras, Fr. ; Canad. war memorial to Canad. troops who stormed the height in the third battle of Arras, in 1917 ; unveiled by King Edward VIII in 1936.

Viña del Mar. Resort and suburb of Valparaiso, Chile, pop. 70,000 ; 3303.

Vincennes (van-sen'), France. Military tn. adjoining Paris on S.E. ; pop. 49,200 ; celebrated castle begun 1164, now a fort, arsenal and barracks.

Vincent de Paul (van'-sahn der pōl), **St.** (1576–1660). Fr. priest, founder of the Sisters of Charity of St. Vincent de Paul and other orders devoted to " social service."

Vinci (vin'-chē), **Leonardo da.** See **Leonardo da Vinci**.

Vindhya. Range in cent. India ; highest point, 5,000 ft.

Vindhya Pradesh. Union of 35 Bundelkhand and Bagelkhand States within Indian repub. ; pop. 3,500,000.

Vindo'bona. Celtic vil. on site of Vienna, 3323.

Vine, Grape. See **Grapes** ; **Wines**.

Vin'egar. An impure acetic acid, 3324.

Vines, H. Ellsworth (b. 1911). Amer. lawn-tennis player. Won U.S. championship 1931 and 1932 ; also successful at Wimbledon in latter year. Became a professional in 1933.

Vinland or **Wineland**. Norse name for N. Amer, 2388, 139.

Vinyl Compounds, used in making synthetic substances; synthetic

rubber, 18 ; plastics, 2697 ; " Vinyon," a synthetic rayon, 2749.

Viola (vi'-o-la). Heroine of Shakespeare's " Twelfth Night " ; wrecked on coast of Illyria, in page disguise enters service of Duke Orsino, with whom she falls in love.

Vi'ola (vī-o-la). Genus of plants including violet and pansy.

Viola (vi-ō'-la). Stringed musical instrument, 3325, 2267 ; in orchestra, 2445.

Vi'olet. Flower, 3324.

Violin'. Stringed musical instrument, 3324, 2264, 2267, 3009 ; in orchestra, 2445.

Viollet-le-Duc (vē-ō-lā' lêr dūk'), **Eugène Emmanuel** (1814–79). Fr. architect, archaeologist, critic, scientist, chief prophet of the Gothic revival in architecture, who revealed to the modern world the logic and beauty of the despised " barbarous " medieval construction.

Violoncello (vē-ō-lon-chel'-ō). Stringed musical instrument, 3325, 2267 ; in orchestra, 2445.

Vi'pers, family of venomous snakes, 3325, *2990*.

Virchow (fêr'-khō), **Rudolph** (1821–1902). Ger. pathologist, anthropologist and archaeologist ; established doctrine that disease is a phenomenon of the body-cells primarily ; directed notable improvements in sanitation of Berlin. (" Cellular-pathalogie ").

Virgil (vêr'-jil) (Publius Vergilius Maro) (70–19 B.C.). Rom. poet, 3325, *1895*, 1896 ; in Dante's " Divine Comedy " 971 ; " Story of the Wooden Horse," 3249.

Vir'gin (*Virgo*). A sign of the zodiac, 3444.

Virginia. In Rom. legend, daughter of centurion Virginius, who killed her to prevent her falling into hands of Appius Claudius the decemvir (499 B.C.).

Virginia. A middle Atlantic state of U.S.A. ; a. 42,620 sq. m. ; pop. 2,677,000 ; 3326, 142 ; Raleigh, 2744 ; expeditions, 2711 ; Jamestown settled (1607), 3326 ; John Brown's raid, 588 ; battle of Chancellorsville, 1790 ; tobacco, 3219.

Virginia creeper. A creeping or climbing plant of the family *Vitacaea*.

Virginia deer. A white-tailed species of deer, 984.

Virginia juniper or **red cedar** ; species of juniper much used in N. America for cabinet making, etc.

Virginian nightjar, 2369.

Virgin Islands, in the Leeward Islands group, W. Indies, 50 m. E. of Puerto Rico ; owned by Gr. Brit. and U.S.A. ; 3368 ; there are over 100 isls. ; exceptionally mountainous ; inhabitants chiefly Negroes ; a. 190 sq. m. ; pop. 22,000 ; purchased by U.S.A. in 1917.

Virginium (Vi). Chemical element, also called Francium ; atomic no. 87 ; a solid, stated by Allison, in 1930, to be present in certain micas ; the authenticity of this element has been questioned ; 768, 778.

Virgin Mary, 1821, 2052, *2053*. See also **Madonna**.

Virgin's bower. A clematis, 837.

Virgo (vêr'gō), or **Virgin**. A sign of the zodiac, 3444.

Virus. Agents causing disease in plants and animals, and so minute as to pass all filters ; invisible under microscope, but have been photographed by ultramicroscope and electron microscope, 2165 ; cause foot-and-mouth disease, distemper, cattle plague, etc. ; mumps, chickenpox, smallpox, infantile paralysis, colds ; potato-leaf-curl, mosaic, etc.

Visby or **Wisby**, Sweden. Spt. city on w. coast of Gottland ; of anc. origin, it was a member of the Hanseatic League ; pop. 13,000 ; 2387, 2388.

Visch'er, Peter (1455–1529). Ger. sculptor, 2406.

Viscon'ti. Celebrated It. family ; ruled Milan 1277–1447.

Visconti, Gian Galeazzo (d. 1402). Ruler of Milan.

Vis'cose, 2748, *2749*, 739.

Viscount (vī'-kownt). British title of nobility, ranking between earl and baron ; 2521.

Vishinsky, Andrey J. (b. 1883). Russ. lawyer and politician ; prof. of jurisprudence at Moscow 1925–27 ; dep. pub. prosecutor 1933–39, figuring prominently at the treason trials 1936–38 ; in 1940 dept. commissar for foreign affairs ; at U.N. conferences from 1945 ; Mar. 4, 1949, took Molotov's place as Min. for For. Affairs.

Vish'nu. 2nd of the Hindu supreme triad of gods, 1626.

Vis'igoths or **West Goths**, 1487, *1238* ; Alaric, 96 ; in Sp., 3033.

Vision. *See* **Eye.**

Vis'tula, R. of Cent. Europe, flowing 650 m. to Baltic Sea, **3326**, 2640 ; *map*, 2641 ; at Danzig, 973 ; in Germany, 1445 ; at Warsaw, 3341.

Vitaceae (vī-tā-sē-ē). The grape family of plants.

Vitamins (vī-t*a*-minz or vit'-*a*-minz). Substances necessary in human diet, **3326**, 1458, 1340 ; in butter fat, 628 ; with calcium, 2978 ; in dried grass, 1510 ; in rice husk, 2775 ; in milk, 2174 ; in soya beans, 3029.

" Vita Nuova " (vē-tah nwō'-vah) (" New Life "), Work by Dante ; prose interspersed with short poems ; 969, 970.

Vitebsk (vē'tebsk). Tn. in Soviet Russia, on Dvina ; pop. 167,400 ; rly. centre ; in flax-raising dist. ; Germans occupied during 1941–44.

Viterbo (vē-tār'-bō). It. Historic walled tn. 88 m. N.W. of Rome ; pop. 36,000 ; Gothic cathedral and churches with tombs of several popes ; celebrated sulphur springs, Etruscan antiquities near by. Heavy air raid damage during 2nd World War.

Viti Levu (vē-tē lā'-vōō). Largest of Fiji isls. ; a. 4,053 sq. m. ; 1271.

Vitoria (vē-tōr'-i-*a*). Sp. city in N. centre 32 m. S.E. of Bilbao ; pop. 56,700 ; varied mfrs. ; decisive victory of Wellington (1813), freeing Sp. from Fr. dominion.

Vit'reous humour, of the eye, 1252, *1252.*

Vit'riol, or oil of vitriol. *See* **Sulphuric acid.**

Vitriol, blue. Copper suiphate, 3116.

Vitriol, green. Iron sulphate (copperas), 1724, 3116.

Vitriol, white. Zinc sulphide, 3443.

Vittorio Veneto, Battle of. Oct. 24–Nov. 4, 1918 ; Anglo-Italian advance on the line of the Piave, which brought about the rout of the Austrian forces.

Viviani (vē-vyah'-nē), **René** (1863–1925). Fr. Socialist statesman, premier (1914–15) on outbreak of 1st World War ; delegate to Limitation of Armament Conference at Washington 1921–22.

Vivip'arous animals. Those bearing living young ; among fish, 1297 ; insects, 1729 ; among reptiles, 1975.

Vlaardingen (vlahr'-ding-*en*). Holland. Old tn. and river port on Maas, 6 m. w. of Rotterdam ; pop. 41,500 centre of herring and cod fisheries.

Vlachs (vlakhs). A Latin race widely scattered through S.E. Europe, N. and S. of the Danube from R. Bug, to Adriatic ; in Greece, 1527 ; Macedonia, 2049 ; in Rumania, 2840.

Vladimir (vlad'-ē-mēr), **St.** (d. 1015), " the Great," grand duke of Kiev, first Christian sovereign of Rus. ; married a Byzantine princess and introduced Gk. Orthodox Church ; 1856.

Vladivos'tok. Chief spt. of Siberia and term. of Trans-Siberian Rly. ; pop. 206,000 ; **3327** ; *map f. 2844.*

Vltava. River of Czechoslovakia ; rises near Austrian frontier in Bohemian Forest and flows generally N. through Prague, joining Elbe at Melnik.

Vocal organs, 3327 ; of birds, 441.

" Vocoder," instr. for " scrambling " telephone messages, 3177.

Vod'ka. Rus. beverage, usually made from potatoes, corn, and rye malt, 2845.

Vogelweide, Walther von der. *See* **Walther von der Vogelweide.**

Voice, 3009, **3327.**

Voice, of verb, 3314.

Voice-frequency telegraphy, 3167.

Voile. A fabric of cotton or wool or silk.

Volcan'ic islands, 3328, *plate f. 3329*, 2472.

Volcanoes, 3328, *plate f. 3328*, *3329*, *2597* ; Andes, 153, 3022 ; in Cent. Amer., 2868, 743, 744, 2364 ; cause earthquakes, 1070 ; in E. Indies, 1076 ; Etna, 1228 ; formation, *2597* ; Fujiyama, 1795, *1808* ; Hawaiian Isls., 1585, 1586, 3329 ; Iceland, 1684 ; Java, *plate f. 3329* ; Kirunga in Africa, 69 ; of Kamchatka, 1845 ; lava, 1900 ; of Mediterranean isls., 2136 ; Mexico, 2156 ; of moon, 2224 ; Mt. Pelée, *plate f. 3329*, 2112 ; in Philippines, 2568 ; S. Amer., 3022 ; submarine volcanoes and tidal waves, 2472, 2598 ; Vesuvius, 3318.

Vole. General term for a group of small rodents, including the Water Vole ; word formed from " arvicole " (Lat. *arvicola*), meaning "field dweller."

Vol'ga, R. in Russia. Greatest r. of Europe, **3329**, 717, 1232, 2844, *map f.* 2844 ; battle of Stalingrad on right bank, 3073, 3420.

Vol'khov. R. of N.W. Russia ; issues from L. Ilmen near Novgorod, flows N.E. 130 m. to L. Ladoga ; 2846.

Volscians (vol'-shi-*a*nz). Anc. Italic tribe ; inhabited dist. S. of Latium ; Romans war against, 2805.

Volstead, Andrew J. (1860–1947). American politician ; became famous as author of the 18th amendment to the American Constitution, known as the " Volstead Act," prohibiting sale of intoxicating liquors. Act passed 1919 and repealed 1933.

Vol'sungs. In Norse myth., heroic race descended from Odin, from which sprang Sigurd ; story told in the " Volsunga Saga " and William Morris's " Story of Sigurd the Volsung."

Volt. The unit of electric potential or electro-motive force (pressure) ; named after Alessandro Volta ; 1127, 1128, 3681.

Volta. R. of W. Africa ; rises in the Fr. Sudan in two headstreams and flows to the Bight of Benin ; total length about 900 m. ; *map, 3366.*

Vol'ta, Alessandro (1745–1827). It. physicist ; invented voltaic cell, 1127, 1131.

Volt'age. " Pressure " of an electric charge or current ; measure in volts, 1128 ; of cell, 376, 1132 ; of dynamo, 1061 ; of grid, 1545 ; of elec. rlys., 2941 ; in series and parallel circuits, 1129 ; of tramways, 3235 ; changed by transformers, 3237 ; of wireless current, 3393.

Volta'ic pile. Device for producing electric current chemically, 376, 1131 ; invention, 1127.

Voltaire (vol-tār') **(François Marie Arouet)** (1694–1778). Fr. philosopher and writer, **3329**, 1380 ; characterizes Holy Rom. Empire, 1637 ; influence, 1393, 1456.

Volter'ra (anc. Volaterrae), Italy. Pop. 17,000 ; alabaster objects, salt, chemicals ; once powerful Etruscan city ; Etruscan antiquities.

Volt'meter. An instrument for measuring the pressure, electromotive force, or difference of potential between two points in a circuit ; electrostatic, 1133 ; for high voltages, 3238.

Voltur'no. R. in S. Italy, rises on w. slope of Apennines ; flows s.w. 100 m. to Tyrrhenian Sea. Allied crossings against German defensive in 1943.

Volume. A book ; origin of word, 509.

Volume. Of gases (Boyle's law), 537 ; in geometry, 1437 ; units, *see* **Weights and Measures.**

Volumetric analysis, 773.

Voluntary Aid Detachments (V.A.D.). Civilian bodies, of women and men, registered at War Office, organized by Red Cross and St. John Ambulance Assoc., etc., to help in emergencies.

Voluntary muscles, 2258.

Volute, in architecture, a kind of spiral scroll used in Ionic, Corinthian, and Composite capitals, of which it is a principal ornament ; the number of volutes in the Ionic order is four ; more in the Corinthian and Composite orders.

Volvoca'les. A group of unicellular organisms classed variously as animals or as plants ; found in colonies in ponds ; they move with the aid of " cilia " or vibrating hairlike organs.

Vol'vox. A greenish fresh-water organism, composed of similar cells gathered into a spherical colony, classified sometimes as an animal, sometimes as a plant ; sphere rotates incessantly ; *432* ; evolutionary position, 158.

Voo'doo, 2057.

Vorarlberg (fōr'-ahrl-bārkh), Austria, province in w. corner, adjoining Germany and Switzerland ; a. 1,005 sq. m. ; pop. 183,260 ; Alpine region ; pastoral region ; makes cotton fabrics ; 316.

Vor'onov, Serge (b. 1866). Rus. surgeon who experimented with a glandular treatment designed to overcome or postpone old age.

Voroshilov, Klementy Efremovich (b. 1881). Russian soldier ; appointed Commissar of War and C.-in-C. of the army and navy (1925) ; President of Revolutionary Military Council of U.S.S.R. ; of new Defence Committee (1940).

Voroshilovsk (formerly Stavropol). Trading and farming town in S. Russia, 250 m. S.W. of Stalingrad ; pop. 85,000. Held by Germans in Caucasian campaign 1942–43.

Vorticism, in modern art, 1184 ; 2477.

Vosges (vōzh) Mts., of E. France, **3330**, 1360 ; in Alsace-Lorraine, 133.

Vote, or suffrage, 3330 ; ballot, 351, 1488, 1490.

Voting machine. A mechanical contrivance for casting and counting votes, operated similarly to calculating and tabulating machines.

Vought-Sikorsky helicopter, 1605.

Voussoir (vōō'-swahr'), of arch, *204.*

Vow'el. A sound constituting a syllable or capable of being sounded alone ; an open and unimpeded sound as opposed to a closed, stopped, or mute consonant ; simple vowels, *a, e, i, o, u.*

Vries, Hugo de. Theory of evolution, 1246.

Vul'can, in Rom. myth., god of fire and metal-working ; identified with Gk. Hephaestus, 1613. *See also* **Hephaestus.**

Vulcanism. Volcanic activity, 2596. 3328.

Vulcanizing, pneumatic tire, 2836, 2834, *2835*, *2837.*

Vul'gate. Latin Bible, 425.

Vul'pes. The fox genus, 1355.

Vulture. A large carrion-eating bird, **3330** ; buzzards, 633, 634 ; condor, 885 ; related to secretary bird, 2916.

V-weapons. Ger. terror weapons in 2nd World War, 3422 ; V1, the flying bomb, 1330 ; V2, the rocket bomb, 2791.

Vyrn'wy Lake, Wales. Artificial lake in Montgomeryshire ; really the upper valley of the r. of that name which has been made into a lake by the construction of a dam ; holding more than 12,000 million gallons, it supplies Liverpool with water, and on the mountains around it is one of Britain's largest planted forests ; 2223.

THE twenty-third letter of the English alphabet is formed of two V's, but we call it "double u." The stories of U and V explain why this is so. The letter was originally written UU or VV in the days when U and V were forms of the same letter. But in this case the VV form, which became W when the letters were crossed, was the one that survived. In sound it remains an ambiguity, half vowel and half consonant. It is usually pronounced as in we, with the lips rounded as for the oo in pool, but without the resonance and fullness of a genuine vowel. The same sound is represented by u in quilt. In such words as which, when, or what, the spelling reverses the pronunciation, which is hw, a curious whisper peculiar to English today, though also occurring in the dead Gothic language. In whole the W is silent, and the W once sounded in write and wrong has quite disappeared. W is pronounced as v in German, the V being sounded as f.

Waal (vahl), r. in Netherlands, the southern arm of Rhine, 2156, *map*, *404*; in 2nd World War, 3422.

Wabash, tributary of Ohio r., U.S.A., rising in w. Ohio and forming part of Ill.-Ind. boundary; 550 m. long.

Waddington, Mt. *See* **Mystery, Mt.**

Wade, George (1673–1748). Brit. soldier; after the Jacobite rebellion (1715) held command in the Highlands, and built a series of fine military roads, 2893.

Waders. Birds of order *Charadriiformes*, 3331.

Wadham College, Oxford, founded, 2464.

Wadi or **wady**, dry river bed, 2859, 1097.

Wadsworth, Edward (1889–1949). Eng. artist of the London Group, 1184.

Wady Halfa or **Halfa**. Tn. on Nile, 150 m. below Assuan, 1097.

Wafd movement. Movement in favour of complete Egyptian independence, organized by Zaghlul Pasha, head of the nationalist party in Egypt, 1102.

Wages, 1081.

Wagner (vahg'-ner), **Charles** (1852–1918). Fr. pastor and author (" The Simple Life ").

Wagner, Cosima (1841–1930). Daughter of Liszt and 2nd wife of Richard Wagner, directing spirit of Bayreuth Theatre after Wagner's death.

Wagner (vagh'-ner), **Wilhelm Richard** (1813–83). Ger. composer, creator of the modern music-drama, 3331, 2264, 2437, 2446; on Beethoven, 398; and Liszt, 1964; and Lohengrin legend, 2000; and the Nibelungs' Song, 2363; " Siegfried," 2363.

Wagram (vah'-grahm), Austria, vil. 12 m. N.E. of Vienna; battle (1809), 2277.

Wagtail. Any one of a group of small birds with long tails which jerk incessantly, 3332.

Wailing Wall, Jerusalem; remains of old Temple, 1819, *1820*.

" Waiting for Master," *2586*.

Wake. Isl. of Pacific Ocean, one of group of 3; 3,000 m. E. of Hong Kong and 2,000 m. w. of Hawaii; area 1 sq. m.; in U.S. possession from 1898, but uninhabited until in 1935 Pan-American Airways made it a flight stage; taken by Japs. in 2nd World War in Dec., 1941; Jap. base until Sept. 4, 1945; 3293.

Wakefield, Charles Cheers Wakefield, 1st Viscount (1859–1941). British business man and philanthropist; founded (1899) firm of lubricating oil mfrs.; purchased and endowed Talbot House at Poperinghe (Belgium) and presented portraits by Sargent and Orpen to the National Portrait Gallery; took an active interest in aviation and motoring, being financially responsible for many speed records.

Wakefield. Mfg. tn. of Yorkshire, on Calder; pop. 58,000; battle (1460); 2828, 3332.

Wake-robin. Name of plant, also cuckoo-pint or lords-and-ladies, 3332.

Walcheren (vahl'-khĕr-en). Westernmost isl. of Netherlands, in prov. of Zealand; costume, *2322*; scene of unsuccessful Brit. expedition in 1809; British landing Nov. 1, 1944;

flooded and devastated in 2nd World War; later, rapidly drained and rebuilt.

Waldeck (vahl'-dek), former republic of w. Ger. absorbed by Prussia in 1929.

Waldeck-Rousseau (rōō'-sō), **Pierre Marie** (1846–1904). Fr. statesman, premier 1899–1902.

" Walden," book by Thoreau, 3204.

Waldenses (wawl-den'-sēz) or **Vaudois**, religious sect in Fr. Alps; founded 12th cent. by Peter Waldo, merchant of Lyons; persecuted until 18th century.

Wales. An historical division of Gt. Brit., a. 7,466 sq. m.; pop. (including Monmouthshire), 2,553,000; 3333, *map*, *3334*; Cardiff, 700; Celts in, 740; costume, *plate f.* 3336; Counties: Anglesey, 155; Brecknockshire, 559; Caernarvonshire, 650; Cardiganshire, 701; Carmarthenshire, 703; Denbighshire, 990; Flintshire, 1315; Glamorganshire, 1470; Merionethshire, 2146; Montgomeryshire, 2223; Pembrokeshire, 2538; Radnorshire, 2733; customs, *plate f. 3337*; history, 3334; language and literature, *see* **Wales, language and literature**; monasticism, 2212; physical features, 583; Swansea, 3126.

Wales, Church of. The Welsh Church Disestablishment Bill passed 1914, came into operation March 31, 1920, 3334; dioceses: Bangor, Llandaff, St. Asaph, St. Davids and Monmouth.

Wales, language and literature, 3334, 1123, 1209.

Wales, Prince of, 3334.

Wales, University of. Welsh national university, founded in 1893, has colleges at Cardiff, Bangor, Aberystwith, and Swansea; arts, science, medicine, law, music, applied science, and teaching, 701.

Walfisch Bay. *See* **Walvis Bay**.

Walker, Frederick (1840–75). Eng. artist; first known for book and magazine illustrations; pastorals based on Greek design (" The Harbour of Refuge ").

Walker Cup. Trophy competed for by amateur golfers representing Gt. Britain and U.S.A. Founded in 1922, and played for alternately in Gt. Britain and America.

" Walkie-talkie," wireless transmitter and receiver, *3396*.

Walking, in athletics, *see* **Records**.

Walking leaf insect, 1727, *1728*.

Walking stick. A long, slender insect; egg, *1094*.

" Walküre, Die " (the Valkyries), Wagner's opera, 2440.

Wal'laby. A small kangaroo.

Wallace, Alfred Russel (1823–1913). Eng. traveller and naturalist, codiscoverer with Darwin of natural selection theory of evolution, 978; in the Pacific, 2472. *See* **Wallace's Line**.

Wallace, Edgar (1875–1932). Eng. novelist, journalist, and playwright, 3337.

Wallace, Henry A. (b. 1888). Amer. politician; edited " Wallace's Farmer " (founded by his grandfather) (1924–29); sec. of Agriculture under Roosevelt (1933–40); Roosevelt's vice-pres. (1940–44); sec. of commerce (1945–47); attacked U.S.

foreign policy, especially towards Russ.; formed Progressive Party and stood for presidency in 1948, polling 1,116,379 votes out of 47 million.

Wallace, Lewis (1827–1905). Amer. Civil War general and author (" Ben Hur "; " The Fair God "); 3295.

Wallace, Sir William (c. 1270–1305). Scot. hero, 3337, 2892; memorial nr. Stirling, *2894*.

Wallace Collection. Superb collection of pictures, furniture, porcelain, miniatures, enamels and European and Oriental arms and armour bequeathed to the nation by Lady Wallace. The collection is in Hertford House, Manchester Square, London.

Wallace's Line. Imaginary line dividing regions of Australian and Asiatic life, first traced by Alfred Russel Wallace, 264, 440, *1074*.

Wallachia (wol-ā'-ki-a). Dist. of w. Rumania; a. 29,960 sq. m.; pop. 3,500,000; once a principality; becomes autonomous, 2841, 589.

Wal'lasey. Mfg. tn. on Mersey estuary; pop. 98,920; has immense dock formed from Wallasey Pool, former marsh.

Wallenstein (val'-en-shtīn), **Albrecht Wenzel Eusebius von, Duke of Friedland** (1577–1634). Ger. general, b. Bohemia; commanded imperial army in Thirty Years' War until 1630; recalled to command after Tilly's death; suspected of treason; assassinated; subject of drama by Schiller; 3202, *3203*, 1558.

Waller, Lewis (1860–1915). Brit. actor, b. in Sp.; first appeared at Toole's Theatre, London, in 1883; played leading Shakespearean parts; popular hero in " Monsieur Beaucaire "; " The Three Musketeers," etc.

Wallflower (*Cheiranthus cheiri*). Fragrant cruciferous perennial, best treated as a biennial. Some beautiful varieties are obtainable, with yellow, red and variegated flowers.

Wall-game, at Eton College, 1229.

Wallingford. Tn. in Berkshire, on R. Thames; castle; pop. 3,500; 416.

Wallingford, Treaty of (1153), 3087.

Wallis, Samuel (1728–95). Brit. navigator who discovered Tahiti and other Pacific isls. on voyage round the globe 1766–68.

Wallis Islands or **Uvea.** Group N.E. of Fiji; a. 40 sq. m.; 2473.

Walloons'. A people of Belgium, 404.

Wall painting, 2476.

Wallsend. Tn. in Northumberland; on R. Tyne, 4 m. E. of Newcastle; marks E. end of Hadrian's wall; collieries; shipbuilding; pop. 46,980.

Wall Street, New York City. Financial centre of U.S.A., 2351, *2355*.

Walnut. Tree of family *Juglandaceae*, 3338, 2407, *2408*; classified, 3247; for furniture, 1409, *1410*, *1411*; husks contain tannin, 2917; American species differs from the European in several details.

Wal'pole, Horace (1717–97), **4th Earl of Orford.** Eng. author and wit, called best of Eng. letter-writers; son of Sir Robert Walpole; his " Castle of Otranto," a mystery tale, initiated romantic movement, 3338.

Walpole, Sir Hugh (1884–1941). Eng. novelist ("Fortitude"; "The Cathedral"; "Harmer John"; "The Dark Forest"; "Rogue Herries" series; "Wintersmoon"), 1216.

Walpole, Sir Robert (1676–1745), **1st Earl of Orford.** First Eng. prime minister, **3338**, *3276*, 1440.

Walpurgis (vahl-pêr´-gĕs) or **Walburga, Saint** (c. 754–779). Eng. nun, missionary to Germany, regarded as protectress against witchcraft; hence May-Day eve, the time of witches' carnival according to Ger. legend, is called Walpurgis night.

Walrus. A marine seal-like animal, **3339**; ivory from teeth, 1788.

Walsall. Mfg. tn. in Staffordshire; pop. 111,150; leather goods, spirits, iron and brass products.

Walschaert gear, for locomotives, 1982.

Wal'singham, Sir Francis (c. 1530–90). Eng. statesman and diplomat; sec. of state under Elizabeth; maintained army of spies in foreign courts; exposed Babington plot and influenced Elizabeth to sign Mary Stuart's death warrant.

Walter, Bruno (b. 1876). German-born American musician. Conductor Vienna Opera (1901–12); Munich (1913–22); Berlin Opera (1925–29); Conductor of New York Philharmonic Orchestra (1933); also noted pianist.

Walter, John (1739–1812). In 1784 started printing business in Printing House Square, London, and in 1785 started, as "The Daily Universal Register," the newspaper which three years later became "The Times." His grandson, John Walter (1776–1847), transformed the small journal into a newspaper supreme in Britain and respected abroad.

Walter the Penniless. Fr. knight, leader of early crusade, 936.

Waltham Abbey or **Waltham Holy Cross,** Eng. Market tn. in Essex on R. Lea, 12 m. N. of London; named after abbey founded by King Harold; govt. armament factory; pop. 7,000; architecture, *219*.

Walther von der Vogelweide (vahl'-tär fon dĕr fō-gel-vī-dĕr) (c. 1168–c. 1230). Ger. minnesinger, one of greatest Ger. lyric poets.

Walton, Frederick. Invented linoleum, 1956.

Walton, Izaak (1503–1683). Eng. writer, author of "The Compleat Angler," a quaint, delightful embodiment of the pleasures of outdoor life, **3339**, 1212.

Walton, William Turner (b. 1902). Eng. composer. Works include a setting of Edith Sitwell's poems, "Façade"; an overture, "Portsmouth Point," a choral fantasia "Belshazzar's Feast," viola concerto, violin concerto, and music for films of "Henry V" and "Hamlet," 2266.

Waltz. Dance in three-four time, introduced on the Continent early in the 19th century, 965, 967.

Walvis Bay. Harbour on coast of South-west Africa, 3029; rainfall, 2741.

Walworth, Sir William (d. 1385), Lord Mayor of London, who killed Wat Tyler, *1197*.

Wam'pum. Shells used by N. Amer. Indians as money, 2942, 2201, 2754.

Wan'amaker, John (1838–1922). Amer. merchant, one of first to employ extensive advertising to build enormous dept. store; U.S. postmaster-general (1889–93).

Wandering Jew. Legendary character (sometimes called Ahasuerus), **3340**.

Wandiwash, battle of, 3276.

Wandsworth. Met and parl. bor. of S.W. London; has dye and paper works; oil mills, calico printing works; pop. 338,000.

Wantage. Tn. in Berkshire; birthplace of King Alfred; trade in agric. produce; pop. 5,350; 416.

Wapiti (wop´-i-ti). A deer closely allied to Eng. red deer but much larger; is found in N. Amer., being there called elk, *2382*.

War. *See* **Warfare.**

"War and Peace," by Tolstoy, 3222.

War'beck, Perkin (1474–99). Eng. pretender, claimed to be Richard, younger of the two princes murdered by Richard III; started several unsuccessful revolts, captured and executed by order of Henry VII.

Warbler. Bird of family *Silviidae,* but term also used for other song-birds such as nightingale, robin, etc., **3340**.

War Crimes and Criminals, of 2nd World War; German, 2282, 2406; Japanese, *see* in Index **Tojo**; Tokyo.

Ward, Artemus. Pen-name of Charles Farrar Browne (1834–67), American humorist. ("Artemus Ward: His Book" one of most popular series).

Ward, Dame Geneviève (1837–1922). Brit. actress, born in New York; after gaining distinction as an operatic singer made her first appearance on the dramatic stage as "Lady Macbeth" at the Theatre Royal, Manchester (1873); in 1879 produced "Forget-me-Not," in which she played the part of Stephanie; acted with Henry Irving and F. R. Benson; created D.B.E. (1921).

Ward, Mrs. Humphry (Mary Augusta Arnold) (1851–1920). Eng. novelist, daughter of Thomas Arnold of Rugby. ("Robert Elsmere," problem novel of the "battle of belief" became "talk of the civilized world" through review by Gladstone; "Marcella"; "Lady Rose's Daughter").

Ward, John Quincey Adams (1830–1910). Amer. sculptor ("Indian Hunter"; "General Thomas"; "George Washington").

Ward, Sir Joseph (1857–1930). Prime minister of N.Z. (1906–1912, 1928–1930).

Ward, Sir Leslie. *See* **"Spy."**

Ward. An electoral division as in a parish; the election of guardians is effected by wards.

Warded Lock, 1979.

Ward's Island, New York, U.S.A., 2351.

Warfare. Aeroplane, 43; airship, 92; armistice, 239; armour, 240; army, 244; artillery, 257; balloon, 347; camouflage, 673, *674*; courts-martial, 923; dogs, 1025; flying-bomb, 1330; guns, *3413*; poisonous gases, 1420; laws of, 1905; machine guns, 2049; mines, 2184; navy, 2293; rocket-bomb, 2791, *2792*; rockets, 2793, *2794*; submarines, 3104; tanks, 3151, *242*, *243*; torpedoes, 3224; trench, 3409.
Development: in anc. Greece, *3197*, 3198; siege in the Middle Ages, 717; developed in Hundred Years' War, 1652; artillery at Battle of Ravenna (1512), 2748; Gustavus Adolphus, 1558; revolutionized in 1st World War, 3409; 2nd World War, 3409, 3422; *see also* **Army**; **Artillery**; **Firearms**; **Navy**; **Royal Air Force**, etc.

Warham, William (1450–1532). Last Roman Catholic Archbishop of Canterbury.

Warlock, Peter (1894–1930). Eng. musician (real name Philip Heseltine); notable as song writer and for editing much Elizabethan music.

Warner, Sir Pelham ("Plum") **Francis** (b. 1873). Eng. cricketer. Captained Middx. (1907–20) and M.C.C. teams touring Australia (1903 and 1911) and S. Africa (1905). Pres. of M.C.C. in 1950. Wrote many books on cricket history and was founder-editor of "The Cricketer."

War Office, The, Whitehall, London, *2018*. Headquarters of British Army Staff and Council; controlled by Secretary of State for War, who is pres. of the Army Council.

War of 1812, between Gt. Brit. and U.S.A., 3291.

War of the Austrian Succession. *See* **Austrian Succession.**

Warp, in weaving, 2024, 3360, 3153.

Warp knit fabrics, 1865.

Warrant. A judicial writ ordering competent officers to make arrests, search houses, and seize property; warrant of arrest, search warrant.

Warrington. Mfg. tn. in Lancashire, on R. Mersey; pop. 77,300; varied iron products.

Wars. *See* names of various wars; *also* list of wars in page 4033.

Warsaw, Poland. Cap. and largest city, on R. Vistula; **3341**, 2640, 2643; Kosciusko defends, 1874; bombed, shelled, occupied and reduced to rubble in 2nd World War, 3341, 3416, 3424.

Warships. *See* **Navy**; **Ships.**

Wars of the Roses. *See* **Roses, Wars of.**

Wartburg (vahrt´-bōōrkh). 11th cent. castle near Eisenach, Saxe-Weimar, Ger.; scene of minstrels' contest; immortalized in Wagner's "Tannhäuser"; Luther hides in, 2041.

Warthe (vahr´-tê). Chief tributary of R. Oder; rises N.W. of Cracow, Poland, flows N. and W., entering E. Ger., and joins Oder after course of 445 m.

Wart hog, an African wild hog, **3341**, *plate f. 3340, 3341.*

Warton, Thomas (1728–90). Eng. poet and historian of poetry ("The History of English Poetry"), 2634.

Warwick, Richard Neville, Earl of (1428–71). Eng. statesman and soldier, called "The Kingmaker"; hero of Bulwer-Lytton's "Last of the Barons," and appears in Shakespeare's "Henry VI"; 2828.

Warwick. Co. tn. of Warwickshire on R. Avon; pop. 14,500; castle with many art treasures (vase from Hadrian's villa); Rom. station later fortified by Ethelfleda (915), woman ruler of Mercia; 3341.

Warwickshire. Midland co., a. 976 sq. m.; pop. 1,535,000; **3341**; Shakespeare's country, 3101.

Wasatch (waw´-sach) **Mts.** Range of Rocky Mts. in U.S.A., beginning in S.E. Idaho and running through Utah to S.W. corner; average height 10,000 ft.

Wash, The. Shallow bay of North Sea between Lincolnshire and Norfolk, Eng.; 1952.

Washing, and hygiene, 1675.

Washing Soda, sodium carbonate, 2997.

Washington, Booker Taliaferro (c. 1859–1915.) Negro educator; he was at one time a plantation slave working in a coal mine; wrote "Up from Slavery" and "Working with the Hands."

Washington, George (1732–99). Amer. patriot and soldier, first president of U.S.A., **3342**; War of Independence, 144; and Lafayette, 1884; and U.S.A. Gov., 3291.

Washington, Martha Dandridge Custis (1732–1802), married George Washington (1759), 3342.

Washington. A Pacific coast state of the U.S.A.; a. 68,000 sq. m.; pop. 1,736,000; **3345**.

Washington, District of Columbia. Cap. of U.S.A.; pop. 663,000; **3343**; Capitol, *3344*, White House, 3344; Pentagon, 3344.

Washington Conference (1921). Called to consider limitation of armaments; Brit. Empire, U.S.A., France, Italy, Japan, China, Belgium, Netherlands, and Portugal represented. Treaties signed: Five-Power (first five powers listed), limiting number and tonnage of capital ships in navies; Five-Power, regulating use of poison gas and submarines; two Four-Power (Italy omitted), pledging respect for rights of each in Pacific insular possessions, acceptance of mediation in case of dispute, and termination of Anglo-Japanese Alliance; two Nine-Power, outlining a policy towards China to secure her actual independence; Chinese-Japanese, for restoration of former Ger. leasehold in Shantung; U.S.A.-Japanese, securing Amer. cable and radio connexions in Yap isl.; Six-Power, allocating Ger. cables in Pacific; and naval power, 2296.

Wasps, 3345, 1727, *1728*, 1729, *1730*, 1733; fig wasp, 1270, *1270*; hornets, 1643.

"Wasps, The," by Aristophanes, 231.

Wastwater, Eng. Lake of Cumberland, 3 m. long, under ⅓ m. broad ; one of the beauty spots of the Lake District, *1166.*

Watch, on shipboard, 3214.

Watches. *See* **Clocks and watches.**

Water, 3347; in boilers, *488, 489;* chemical composition, 2466, 3351 ; density, 1674, 3351 ; dew formation, 1000 ; in diet, 1340, 1675 ; effect on climate, 840 ; Egyptian carriers, *1099;* compared with electricity, 1127, *1129–31;* evaporation, 1243, 3349; freezing, 1391, 1680, 3350; in gas engine, *1423;* heavy water, 298, 3351 ; how it changes earth's surface, 2596, 2598, 3349 ; in hydroelec. installns., 1669, *1669–72;* and hydrostatics, 3674 ; incompressible, 1665 ; latent heat of, 3350 ; marine life, 432 ; molecules, 769 ; oxygen in, 2466 ; in plant life, 2589, 2621, 2623, 2624 ; transmits pressure, 1666; purification, 3348; hard water and soap, 2994 ; softening of hard water, 3351 ; soda, 700 ; and sound, 3009; specific gravity, 3054; stalactites and stalagmites, 733, *plate f. 732, 733;* steam, 3084. *See also* **Deuterium; Hydro-Electric Installations ; Ice ; Water-power ; Water Supply.**

"Water Babies," by Charles Kingsley, 1859.

Water Bearer *(Aquarius).* A sign of the zodiac, 3444.

Water-beetles, 400, *401.*

Water boatman. An aquatic insect with stridulating disk, **3352.**

" Water-break-its-Neck." Waterfall, near New Radnor, Wales, 2733.

Waterbuck. An African antelope, 176.

Water-buffalo, 602, *2964.*

Water-bug. Aquatic insect of the *Hemiptera* family, 1728.

Waterbury, Connecticut, U.S.A. Mfg. centre ; pop. 99,300 ; watches : leads U.S.A. in brassware mfr. ; has other metal products.

Water-clock or **clepsydra,** *843.*

Water-colour painting, 2478, **3352,**

Watercress. A perennial aquatic herb common in ponds, ditches and swampy places, 2279, **3353.**

Water crowfoot, *3355.*

" Water Cycle," 3349.

Water deer, type native to China, 984.

Water-divining. *See* **Dowsing.**

Water dropwort. A poisonous plant, *2639.*

Waterfalls, *2598;* created by glaciers, 1682 ; in hydro-elec. installns., *1668,* 1669 ; important falls incl. Kaietur (Brit. Guiana) ; Niagara, 2361, *2362,* 2380 ; Ottawa, 2458 ; Rhine, 2769 ; Staubbach, *3142;* Trollhättan, 3128 ; Venezuela (highest), *3309;* Victoria, 3321, *plate f. 3016.*

Water-finders. *See* **Divining Rod ; Dowsing.**

Water-flea, a minute crustacean.

Waterfoot. Village of Antrim, *181.*

Waterford, Eire. Southern marit. co. ; bounded N. by R. Suir ; a. 713 sq. m. ; pop. 76,000 ; **3354.**

Waterford, Eire. Spt. co. tn. of co. Waterford, on estuary Waterford Harbour ; pop. 28,000 ; stronghold of Danes ; captured by Strongbow (1171) ; attacked by Cromwell (1649), taken by Ireton (1650), 3354.

Waterford Harbour (Eire). Inlet between cos. Waterford and Wexford ; receives waters of rivers Barrow and Suir.

Waterfowl. Term usually employed to include birds of order *Anseriformes,* e.g. : ducks, *plates f. 1052, 1053;* geese, 1486 ; swans, 3125.

Water gas, 1424, 2430.

Water-glass, sodium silicate. So named on account of its appearance ; used in the preservation of stone and eggs ; it is also used in the manufacture of soap.

Water hemlock. A poisonous perennial herb found in marshes.

Water-hen. Same as **Moor-hen.**

Water-hole. African afternoon scene, *plate f. 72, 73.*

Water-lily, 3354, 3355, *2288, 2624;* leaves, 3355 ; sacred lotus, *2027;* stems, 3354 ; Victoria regia, *1854, 3354.*

GREAT WARS IN THE HISTORY OF THE NATIONS

American Independence (1775–83) : Successful revolt of the Thirteen English Colonies in America against British rule.

Austrian Succession (1741–48) : Concerted action of Continental powers to appropriate desirable pieces of Hapsburg lands from Maria Theresa, whose cause was championed by Great Britain ; war ended with mutual restoration of conquests, except Silesia, which was retained by Prussia.

Austro-Prussian (1866) : " Seven Weeks' War," arising out of differences over Schleswig-Holstein question ; resulted in overwhelming defeat of Austria at Sadowa, and subsequent exclusion from German federation.

Balkan (1912) : Attempt of Balkan allies to expel Turkey from Europe ; remarkable successes were minimized by subsequent quarrels between allies over newly-won territory, enabling Turkey to retain her hold on Constantinople and surrounding territory.

Boer (1899–1902) : Spirited but futile resistance of Boer settlers in S. Africa to extension of British claims ; Transvaal and Orange Free State made British colonies.

Chinese-Japanese War (1894–95) : Occasioned by rival pretensions in Korea ; a complete victory of Japan's modern military machine over China's antiquated forces ; Japan forced by European powers to restore all conquests except Formosa.

Civil War in England (1642–49): Struggle between the Crown and Puritan Parliament over distribution of ecclesiastical and civil jurisdiction ; Marston Moor and Naseby ; execution of Charles I and establishment of Commonwealth.

Civil War in the United States (1861–65) : Between Union government and Southern Confederacy over latter's attempt to secede from Union ; Vicksburg, Gettysburg.

Crimean (1854–56) : Undertaken by Great Britain with aid of other powers in defence of Turkey against Russian aggressions ; siege of Sevastopol ; Turkey left intact.

Crusades (1096–1291) : Romantic military expeditions of western princes and prelates to recover Holy Sepulchre from Saracens ; capture of Antioch, Jerusalem, and Acre ; later Crusades were diverted to other ends, and Holy Land lapsed into Mahomedan control.

Dutch Independence (1568–1648) : Led by William of Orange ; Dutch threw off oppressive Spanish rule and established independent government ; siege of Leiden.

Franco-Prussian (1870–71) : Clash between Prussia's imperialistic aspirations and the jealousy of Napoleon III, resulting in humiliating defeat of France, downfall of the Second Empire, and proclamation of German Empire.

French Revolutionary (1792–99) : Great Britain headed coalition of Prussia, Austria, and other countries against France in contest that was last phase of long wars between England and France for colonial and maritime supremacy and also clash between two political systems ; Valmy, Italian campaign ; peace made with all allies except England.

Great Northern (1700–21) : Undertaken by Russia, aided by Denmark and Poland, to secure Baltic port at expense of Sweden ; siege of Narva, Poltava ; Russia secured provinces about Gulf of Finland and Sweden sank to second-rate power.

Hundred Years' (1337–1453) : Series of conflicts between rulers of France and England over disputed titles to French throne and territories ; Crécy, Poitiers, Agincourt, Orléans ; England lost French possessions except Calais ; French monarchy firmly established.

Napoleonic (1799–1815) : Determined resistance of Allied European powers to aggression of Napoleon, ending in his downfall ; Austerlitz, Leipzig, Trafalgar, Waterloo.

Peleponnesian (431–404 B.C.) : Between Athens and Sparta for economic and political control of Greece ; Athenian expedition to Syracuse, Aegospotami ; Athenian supremacy ended.

Persian (493–479 B.C.) : Expeditions of Persian emperors against Greece to punish Athens for aiding revolting Persian colonies in Asia Minor, and to extend empire ; Marathon, Thermopylae, Salamis, Plataea ; Greece maintained independence and control of Aegean.

Punic Wars (264–241, 218–202, 149–146 B.C.) : Death struggle of Rome and Carthage for domination of Mediterranean world ; Hannibal's invasion of Italy, Cannae, Zama, Metaurus ; Carthage taken and destroyed.

Russo-Japanese (1904–05) : Blow dealt by Japan to Russian aggression in Far East; siege of Port Arthur, battle of the Sea of Japan ; Japanese interests in Korea recognized as paramount, and Japan established as a first-rate power.

Russo-Turkish (1877–78) : Arose directly from Mahomedan uprising against Balkan Christians ; fall of Plevna ; power of Turkey in Europe practically destroyed, only to be resuscitated by Congress of Berlin.

Seven Years' (1756–63) : Resulted from alliance formed against rapidly expanding Prussia by Austria, Russia, France, and other powers ; Great Britain allied with Prussia ; Rossbach, Leuthen, Quebec ; Prussia established as great nation, and foundation of British Empire laid.

Spanish Succession (1701–14) : Attempt of England, Austria, and allies to prevent establishment of a French prince on Spanish throne ; Blenheim ; Bourbon House established in Spain, but Austria and England gained extensive French and Spanish possessions.

Thirty Years' (1618–48) : Struggle between Catholics and Protestants of Germany in which Gustavus Adolphus of Sweden played a brilliant part ; Leipzig, Lützen ; religious and territorial differences settled at price of devastation of Germany.

Trojan (c. 1100 B.C.) : Semi-legendary war waged by Greek princes against King Priam to avenge abduction of Helen, wife of Menelaus : siege and fall of Troy.

Wars of Alexander the Great (334–323 B.C.) : Persian Empire overthrown in battles of the Granicus, Issus and Arbela ; conquest of Syria, Palestine, and Egypt ; invasion of Media.

Wars of the Roses (1455–85) : Waged by Houses of Lancaster and York, rival claimants to English throne, until royal marriage united the two lines ; Bosworth Field.

War of 1812 (1812–14) : Between United States and Great Britain, caused by Great Britain's claims to right of search of American vessels on high seas and impressment of seamen : treaty adjusted boundaries, etc.

First World War (1914–18) : A world-wide struggle between Central Powers and Allied and Associated Powers, arising indirectly from clash between two rival systems of commercial imperialism, and directly from tangle following murder of Archduke of Austria by a Serb ; Central Powers crushed.

Second World War (1939–45) : A world-wide struggle between the Allies and the Axis powers, arising mainly out of the clash between the ideas of Democracy and Dictatorship as political systems. Axis powers utterly defeated.

Waterloo, battle of (1815), **3354**, 3278 ; Napoleon, 2278 ; Wellington, 3364.

Waterloo Bridge, London. The old bridge, demolished in 1936, was built by Sir John Rennie between 1811 and 1817. New bridge, to design of Sir Giles Gilbert Scott, has a width of 80 ft. and consists of five 238-ft. spans. Formally opened Dec. 1945 by Mr H. Morrison ; *566, 2011.*

Waterman, L. E., Amer. inventor, 2541.

Water-melon, 2137 ; introduced into Europe, 937.

Water meter. A mechanical device by which the consumption of water may be measured ; it works on the same principle as a gas meter, 2154.

Water plantain, 3356.

Water-plants, 3355.

Water polo, 3356.

Water-pot shell, *2943.*

Water-power, *1669, 1669–72*, 2673 ; Canada, 677, 2434, 2458 ; and electricity, 1669 ; in Italy, 1772 ; Niagara, *2361*, 2434 ; originally derived from sun, 1161 ; in Sweden, 3129 ; types of turbines used, 3259. *See* **Dams ; Hydraulics and Hydraulic Appliances ; Hydro-Electric Installations.**

Waterproofing, of garments, 1263, 2833.

Water-rail, 2733 ; at nest, *2286.*

Water scorpion. Belonging to the family of water-bugs ; breathes through its tail ; found in ponds. 3352.

Water-skater, 3352.

Water-softeners, 3351.

Water spider. A spider which nests under water, 3064 ; habits, *2287.*

Waterspout, 3356 ; cause, 3101.

Water supply, 3347 ; artesian well, 252 ; chlorine and fluoride in, 1567 ; Humphrey pump, 1421, *1423* ; meters, *2154* ; hard water and soap, 2994 ; soft water in lead pipes, 2638 ; from Thames, 3194.

Water table, 3349.

Water transport. *See* **Canals ; Ships.**

Water turbine, 1670, *1672*, 3258 ; runners, *1671.*

Waterwheels, *plate f. 1513* ; overshot and undershot, *1669*; world's largest, 1669.

Waterwitch, H.M.S., Brit. jet-propelled gunboat of 1866 ; 1826.

Waterworks, 3347, *3349, 3350* ; aqueduct, 194 ; artesian well, 252 ; pump, 2702–2704.

Watford. Tn. in Hertfordshire ; brewing, printing, silk mfrs. ; pop. 73,330 ; 1622.

Watkins, Herbert George (" Gino ") (1907–32). Eng. explorer ; leader of British Arctic Air Route Expedition (1930–31, 1932) ; of expedition to Edge Island, Spitsbergen (1927) ; and to Labrador (1928) ; drowned off Greenland ; 2646.

Watling Island. Small is. of Bahamas, Brit. W. Indies, 339.

Watling Street. Great Rom. road from Canterbury to London and past St. Albans to Chester, 2385, 2783 ; in Middlesex, 2168.

Watson, Sir William (1858–1935). Distinguished Eng. poet, classical and dignified in tone (" Wordsworth's Grave " ; " The Purple East ") ; 1216.

Watt, James (1736–1819). Eng. inventor of steam-engine, 3356, 2734, 3085, 3086 ; beam engine, *3086* ; centrifugal governor, 745 ; Soho factory, near Birmingham, 458. *See also* **Sun and Planet gear.**

Watt, unit of electric power, 1128, 3357. *See also* **Kilowatt.**

Watteau (wot´-ō), **Jean Antoine** (1684–1721). Fr. painter of gay pageants of the frivolous artificial 18th cent. which his poetic imagination endows with strange pathos (" Embarkation for Cythera "), 1377, 2476.

Wattle. An acacia tree, *16*, 309 ; bark used in tanning, 1911, 3014.

Watts, George Frederick (1817–1904). Eng. portrait and allegorical painter and sculptor, 1182 ; " Orpheus and Eurydice," *2454*; " Physical Energy," *697* ; portrait of John Stuart Mill, *2175* ; portrait of Shaftesbury, *2931.*

Watts, Isaac (1674–1748). Eng. clergyman, author of some of most famous hymns and most familiar lines in Eng. language (" O God our help in ages past " , " How doth the little busy bee " ; " Let dogs delight to bark and bite ") ; 1678.

Watts-Dunton, Walter Theodore (1832–1914). Brit. critic, poet, and author ; trained first as a solicitor, but turned to literary work ; critical work appeared in The Athenaeum 1875 to 1898 (" The Coming of Love" ; " Aylwin " ; " The Renascence of Wonder "), 3138.

Wat Tyler's Rebellion, 3269, 2777.

Waugh (waw), **Alec** (b. 1898). Eng. author (" The Loom of Youth " ; " Love in These Days " ; " The Balliols "). His brother Evelyn (b. 1903) wrote " Decline and Fall," " Vile Bodies," etc.

Wauters (vō´-tär), **Emile** (1846–1933). Belgian painter (" The Madness of Hugo van der Goes ").

Waveguide, in ultra-short wave wireless, *3397.*

Wavelength. Distance between two adjacent crests (or troughs) of a train of waves, 3358 ; times frequency = velocity, 2729 ; in wireless, 1942, 3392 ; in television, 3184 ; of various types of radiation, 1722, 1941, 1942, 2726, 2729, 3184, 3393, 3679.

Wavell, F.-M. Archibald, 1st Earl (1883–1950). G.O.C. Middle East (1940–41), 3418, *map 3421* ; C.-in-C. India (1941–43) ; Viceroy (1943–47). Created Earl in 1947. Constable of the Tower of London (1948–50).

Wave-mechanics, 2711.

Wave Motion, 3358 ; cosmic rays, 1942, 2729 ; in ether, 1226, 1941, 2729, *f.* 3057 ; Hertzian waves, 1942, 2098, 2728 ; Leonardo's study of, *1927* ; light, 1941 ; *f.* 3057, 3678 ; radar, 2726 ; radiant heat, 1722, 1942, 1595, *1594* ; sound, *3009,* 3676 ; television, 3182 ; transverse, 3358 ; ultra-violet, 1942, 2729 ; wireless, 3393 ; X-rays, 1942, 2728, 3430.

Waveney. River of Norfolk and Suffolk ; 50 m. long ; *1311*, 2375.

Waverley Novels, by Scott, 2899.

Waves. *See* **Wave Motion.**

Wax. A solidified fatty substance of vegetable or animal origin, 33⁻9 ; no melting pt., 1391 ; in pencil, 2543 ; mineral, 2426 ; produced by bees, 391, *393.*

Wax calf leather, 1914.

Waxwing. Passerine bird, of genus *Bombycilla*, occasionally seen in Eng. ; so named from wax-like scales on wing-feathers.

Weak verbs, 3314.

Weald, The. Dist of S.E. Eng., between N. and S. Downs ; formerly forested ; populated by S. Saxons in 5th cent.

Wealth, in economics, 1080, 2986 ; measured by money, 2200.

Wear. R. of Durham ; has its source near Cross Fell, whence it flows s. for over 65 m. to the North Sea at Sunderland, 1059.

" **Wearing o' the Green**," 2282.

Weasel, a long-bodied carnivorous animal, 3359, *2693.*

Weasel family, the *Mustelidae*, 3359, 338 ; badger, 338 ; ermine, *1222.*

Weather, 3360 ; atmosphere, 88 , chart, 2149 ; clouds, 851, *853* ; cyclones, 949, 3100 ; dew formation, 1000 ; distinguished from climate, 840, 2149 ; and elec. consumption, 1548 ; fog, 1333 ; forecast, 2149 ; frost, 1400 ; hail, 1564 ; lightning, 1945, *1946* ; meteorology, 2149 ; observations, 2413 ; radar, 2728 ; radio-sonde, 2150 ; rain, 2741, *2742* ; report, 2149 ; snow, 2992 ; storms, 3100, 3356 ; winds, 3384. *See also* **Climate**, and the principal topics above.

Weatherly, Frederick Edward (1848–1929). Eng. song writer (" Nancy Lee," " The Holy City," " Roses of Picardy ").

Weather-ship, 3360.

Weaver. River in Ches., trib. of Mersey ; 46 m. long.

Weaver-bird, 3360.

Weaver's knot, *1868.*

Weaving, 3360, *706, 920* ; carpets, 705 ; Cartwright, Edmund, 712 ; cloth, 850 ; Jacquard loom, 1790 ; loom, 2024, 2025 ; spinning, 3065 ; textiles, 3191 ; thread, 3205.

Webb, Sir Aston (1849–1930). Eng. architect ; designed Victoria and Albert Museum, *2014*, Admiralty Arch, *2018*, new front of Buckingham Palace, *599*, also Royal College of Science and Technology, 599.

Webb, Mary (1881–1927). Eng. novelist (" Precious Bane " and others).

Webb, Matthew (1848–83). First to swim English Channel, 3137.

Webb, Maurice (b. 1904). Brit. politician, became Min. of Food in 1950.

Webb, Philip Speakman (1831–1915). Eng. architect. With his friend William Morris he founded (1877) the Society for the Protection of Ancient Buildings.

Webb, Sidney James (1859–1947) or **Lord Passfield.** Brit. politician and economist, entered parl. 1922 ; Fabian Socialist, collaborator with his wife, Beatrice Potter Webb (" History of Trade Unionism " ; " Industrial Democracy" ; " Soviet Communism") ; Pres. Board of Trade (1924) ; created Baron Passfield (1929) ; Sec. State for Colonies (1929–31) ; 2996. Re-interred in Westminster Abbey.

Weber (vā´-ber), **Carl Maria von** (1786–1826). Ger. composer, founder of romantic school of Ger. opera (" Der Freischutz " ; " Invitation to the Waltz " ; " Oberon ") ; 2436.

Webster, Daniel (1782–1852). Amer. orator and statesman ; Sec. of State in 1841–3 and again in 1850–2.

Webster, John (*c.* 1580–1625). Eng. dramatist ; chief works, " The Duchess of Malfi " ; " The White Devil," 1040.

Webster, Noah (1758–1843), compiler of first Amer. dictionary of Eng. language, 3058.

Webster, Tom (b. 1890). Eng. cartoonist, whose drawings, mostly on sporting topics, were widely popular.

Weddell, James (1787–1834). British Antarctic explorer ; discovered Weddell Sea in 1823, 173.

Wedding, Chinese, *plate f. 808.* *See also* **Marriage.**

" **Wedding the Adriatic**," 29.

Wedekind (vā´-de-kint), **Frank** (1864–1918). Ger. dramatist (" Spring's Awakening ") ; many of his plays deal with problems of sex, and have caused great controversy.

Wedge, a mechanical device, 2128 ; screw a form of, 2901, *2902.*

Wedgwood, Josiah (1730–95). Most famous Eng. potter ; originator of " Wedgwood ware " and " queen's ware " (named in compliment to Queen Charlotte) ; *2669*, *2670* ; grandfather of Charles Darwin, 975.

Wednesday, origin of name, 980, 2421.

Week, *3361* ; day, 980.

Weeping Philosopher. *See* **Heraclitus.**

Weeping willow, *3243*, 3382.

Weevils, beetles with snouts, 3362, 399, *921*, *1728.*

Weft, or woof, in loom or fabric, 850, 2024, 360.

Weichsel (vīkh´-sel). Same as **Vistula.**

Weight, defined, 1513, 2127, 2592 ; of the air, *90* ; and specific gravity, 3054.

Weights, in boxing, 535.

Weights and measures, foot, 1342 ; liquid, 3054 ; metric system, 2154 ; origin of Troy weights, 1257. *See also* **Units** ; and Tables in pages 4036–39.

Weihaiwei (wē-hī-wē´). Port and naval coaling station on N.E. coast of Shantung, China ; a. 285 sq. m. ; pop. 178,900 ; leased by G. Brit. (1898) ; restored to China (1930), 2938.

Wei-ho (wī-hō´). In N. China, largest trib. of Hwang-ho (Yellow r.) ;

flows E. 500 m. and joins Hwang-ho at point where it turns from S. to E. ; trade route from interior.

Weimar (vī'-mahr). Ger., cap. of Thuringia ; pop. 52,000, **3362** ; intellectual centre in Goethe's time, 1479, 2882 ; taken by U.S. April 14, 1945 ; in Russian occupation zone.

Weimar Republic, 1450, 3362, 3415.

Weingartner, (Paul) Felix (1863–1942). Austrian composer and conductor.

Weinsberg (vīns' bărkh). Tn. of Würt-temberg, Ger., 28 m. N.E. of Stutt-gart ; victory of Ger. king Conrad III over Count Welf of Bavaria (1140) ; once free imperial city.

Weir, type of dam, 958.

Weismann (vĭs'-mahn), **August** (1834–1914). Ger. biologist ; advanced theory that changes in the charac-teristics of a species are due to changes in germ-plasm, 1246, 1617.

Weizmann, Chaim (b. 1874). First President of Israel (1948) ; Russian biochemist ; for many years Presi-dent of the World Zionist Organiza-tion.

Welbeck Abbey. Picturesque country seat of the Duke of Portland, in Nottinghamshire, 2399.

Welch, James (1865–1917). Eng. actor ; made first appearance in London in 1887 in some of G.B. Shaw's plays but later took comic parts ; played Sir Guy de Vere in " When Knights were Bold " for several years.

Welding, the process of uniting two pieces of a fusible material together, **3362** ; by acetylene, 18 ; atomic hydrogen, 3363 ; electric, 3362 ; in ship-building, 2952 ; " spot," " stitch," " seam," " flash-butt," 3363 ; cold welding, 3363.

Welfs. See **Guelfs and Ghibellines.**

Well, 3347, 3349, 3375 ; artesian, 253 ; deepest, 2428 ; oil, 2427, 2428.

Welland. English r. in the E., flowing 70 m. to the Wash, 2385.

Welland Canal, Canada, connecting L. Erie with L. Ontario, **3363,** 2435.

Weller, Sam, in Dickens's " Pickwick Papers," 1074.

Welles, Sumner (b. 1892). Amer. politician and diplomat ; under-sec. of state 1937–43 ; deleg. at Con-ference of Amer. repubs., Panama 1939, and Rio de Janeiro 1942 ; special represent. of Roosevelt re-porting on European conditions 1940 ; with Roosevelt at Atlantic meeting with Churchill Aug. 1941.

Wellesley, Richard Colley, Marquis of (1760–1842). Brit. statesman, one of greatest Eng. colonial administra-tors, gov.-gen. of India (1797–1805) ; " found the (Brit.) East India Co. a trading body, left it an imperial power " ; elder brother of Duke of Wellington.

Wellington, Arthur Wellesley, 1st Duke of (1769–1852). Brit. soldier and statesman, **3363,** 3354 ; in Mysore, 2270 ; and Napoleon, 3278 ; in Portugal, 2660 ; tomb, 2906 ; and Queen Victoria, 3320 ; Waterloo, 3354.

Wellington. Port and cap. of New Zealand on E. coast of North Isl. ; pop. 183,100 ; large trade ; varied mfrs. ; Victoria College of Univ. of New Zealand, **3364,** 2357.

Wellington College, Berkshire. Founded by public subscription in honour of the Duke of Wellington and incorporated in 1853 ; provides for the education of sons of officers of the army.

Wellingtonia, name sometimes applied to *Sequoia gigantea,* 2921, *3241.*

Wellman, Walter (1858–1934). Amer. explorer ; made two unsuccessful attempts (1907 and 1909) to reach North Pole by airship ; first to try to cross the Atlantic by dirigible (1910).

Wells, Charles Jeremiah (1798–1879). Eng. poet famous for Biblical drama " Joseph and his Brethren," written in 1823.

Wells, Herbert George (1866–1946). Eng. novelist, historian and socio-logist, **3364,** 1215, 2403.

Wells, Dr. Horace, and anaesthetics, 149.

Wells. City in Somersetshire ; impor-tant Saxon tn. ; made bishops' see in 905 ; pop. 5,900 ; **3365,** 3000 ; 13th cent. cath., *219, 845, 728.*

Welsbach (vels'-bahkh), **Karl Auer von** (1858–1929). Austrian chemist and inventor, discoverer of rare elements and inventor of Welsbach light and osmium incandescent electric light, 616, 1424, 1887. See **Rare Earths.**

Welsbach mantle, 1424.

Welsh language, 3334, 740, 1123, 1209.

Welwyn Garden City (pron. wellin). Between Welwyn and Hatfield in Hertfordshire ; a planned town, laid out in 1920, taken over by ministry of Town and Country Planning in 1948.

Wem'bley. Tn. in Middlesex, 8 m. N.W. of London ; 2168 ; in 1924–25 scene of great British Empire Exhibi-tion ; stadium used for F.A. Cup Final, Rugby League Final, grey-hound and speedway racing ; 1948 Olympic Games, *2433* ; Empire Pool and Arena opened in 1934.

Wemyss (wĕms), Scot. name.

Wenceslaus, Wenceslas (or Vaclav) (d. c. 929). Bohemian patron saint, commemorated in the carol " Good King Wenceslas," 2677.

Wen'dover. Tn. in Buckinghamshire ; near by is Chequers, the country home of Brit. prime ministers ; pop. about 5,000 ; 600.

Wends. Name given by Germans to W. Slavic tribes, 2983.

Wener Lake, see **Väner Lake.**

Wen'sum. R. of Norfolk ; rising in the N. of the co., it joins the Yare near Norwich ; 30 m. long ; 2375 ; heat pump, 1600.

Wentworth, Thomas, Earl of Strafford. See **Strafford.**

Wentworth Place, Hampstead, Keats's home, *1849.*

Wenzel (vent'sel) or **Wenceslaus** (ven-ses-lows) (1361–1419). King of Bo-hemia and Holy Roman emperor ; attempt to settle Great Schism an-tagonized Archbishop of Mainz, who persuaded the Imperial electors to depose him.

Werfel, Franz (1880–1945), Austrian novelist and poet : " Verdi " (1924), " Paul among the Jews " (1926), " The Song of Bernadette " (1942) ; *1457,* 2404.

Werner (vār-ner), **Zacharias** (1768–1823). Ger. romantic dramatist ; " Martin Luther," " Der 24 Februar ;" his best plays, are typical of the lurid " fate tragedy " ; became a Cath. priest (1814).

Wesel (vā'-zel). Tn. of Ger., at Rhine-Lippe confluence ; destroyed by bombing in 2nd World War ; Rhine bridge blown up in 1945 ; airborne operation, 2770, *3423* ; pop. (1935) 25,000.

Weser (vā'-zer). R. of Germany rising in S. Hanover ; flows N. 280 m. to North Sea ; 559, 1445.

Wesley, Charles (1707–88). Eng. preacher and hymn-writer (brother of John) ; 1390, 1678, 3365.

Wesley, John (1703–91). Eng. preacher and founder of the Methodists, 3365.

Wessel, Horst (1907–30). German Nazi ; composed the party song known as the Horst Wessel song.

Wes'sex. Anc. kingdom of W. Saxons in S. Britain ; founded by Cedric and Cynric in 519 ; Egbert became king 802, and later ruled all Britain ; in Thomas Hardy's novels, 1577.

West, Benjamin (1738–1820). Amer. historical painter ; Cromwell and the Mace, *934* ; Death of Nelson, *2314* ; Death of Wolfe, *3401* ; Penn and the Indians, *2545* ; William III at battle of Boyne, *1746.*

West, Rebecca (b. 1892). Pen name of Mrs. Henry Maxwell Andrews, Eng. writer (" Henry James " ; " The Strange Necessity " ; " Harriet Hume " ; " The Thinking Reed ").

West Africa, 3366 ; Congo, 887 ; Liberia, 1929 ; Niger, 2367.

West Bromwich. Mfg. tn. in Birming-ham in Staffordshire ; pop. 83,900 ; coal and iron ; 3072.

Westchester Cup, for polo, *2651.*

Westerly winds, *3385* ; effects upon rainfall, 2741.

Westermarck, Edward Alexander (1862–1939). Finnish anthropologist and author, professor of sociology at Lon-don Univ. (" Origin and Develop-ment of the Moral Idea " ; "History of Human Marriage " ; " Marriage Ceremonies in Morocco ").

Western Australia. Largest state of Australia, comprising w. third of continent ; a. 975,920 sq. m. ; pop. 502,000 ; **3368** ; sponge fisheries, *3069* ; *map f. 308.*

Western Isles or Hebrides, 1601.

Western Union. Economic milit., and cultural alliance between the U.K., Fr., Belgium, Netherlands, Luxem-burg ; entered into Mar. 17, 1948, in 50-yr. treaty signed at Brussels ; 5 bodies set up : 1, perm. consultative ctte. ; 2, diplomatic representatives ; 3, military ctte., with Western Union representatives F.-M. Visct. Montgomery (U.K.) as milit. chm., Gen. de Lattre de Tassigny (Fr.), C.-in-C. land forces, Air Marshal Sir J. Robb (U.K.), air forces, and Vice-Adm. R. Jaujard (Fr.), flag officer ; 4, finance ctte. ; 5, ctte. to promote European unity ; 3283, 3424, 1242.

West Ham. Tn. in Essex, E. suburb of London, on the Thames ; has large docks, and railway workshops ; pop. 174,390 ; *see also* **East Ham.**

West Hartlepool. See **Hartlepool.**

West Indies. Isl. group in Atlantic Ocean, N. and E. of Caribbean Sea ; a. 100,000 sq. m. ; pop. 13,000,000 ; **3368,** 832 ; Bahamas, 339 ; Bar-bados, 350 ; coffee introduced, 864 ; Columbus discovers, 880 ; Cuba, 940 ; ebony, 1077 ; Guadeloupe, 1551 ; Haiti, 1565 ; Jamaica, 1792 ; land crabs, 924 ; Martinique, 2112 ; Negro population, 2312 ; monkey's dinner bell, 2916, *2917* ; Puerto Rico, 2698 ; sponges, 3069 ; Trinidad, 3248 ; U.S. bases, 3369.

West Indies University College, Mona, Jamaica ; faculty of Medicine insti-tuted Oct. 1948, and others to follow.

Westinghouse, George (1846–1914). Amer. engineer, inventor of the air-brake, 549.

Westland-Sikorsky, a type of helicopter, 1606.

West Lothian, Lowland co. of Scot., formerly Linlithgowshire ; pop. 83,900 ; 120 sq. m. ; 2027.

West'meath, Eire. Inland co. in Leinster ; a. 681 sq. m. ; **3369.**

Westminster. City and met. bor. of London ; pop. 103,440 ; royal pal-aces, Westminster Abbey, Houses of Parliament, R.C. Cathedral, National and Tate Galleries, Govt. offices, Whitehall ; 2013.

Westminster Abbey. Famous church in London, 3369, 3370, 2014 ; beefeaters at, *plate f. 397* ; Edward the Con-fessor begins, 1089 ; George VI's Coronation in, *912, 913* ; Henry VI's tomb, *2765* ; Henry VIII's Chapel, *3369* ; organ, 2450 ; Poet's Corner, *2635* ; Coronation Stone and Chair *913* ; Battle of Britain Memorial Chapel, *577,* 3371.

Westminster Bridge, London, *2520.*

Westminster Cathedral. Chief Roman Catholic church in England, near Victoria Street, London ; built of red brick in early Byzantine style, and has lofty campanile ; consecrated in 1903 ; 730, *2910.*

Westminster Hall, London. Adjoins Houses of Parl., built in 11th cent. by William II ; Charles I was tried here ; scene of lying-in-state of Edward VII and George V ; former scene of Coronation Banquets, 2014 ; hammer beam roof, *2822* ; damaged by bombs ; repaired 1947–48.

Westminster School, London. Public school, formerly associated with Westminster Abbey ; refounded by Henry VIII later by Q. Elizabeth ; built round Little Dean's Yard.

WEIGHTS AND MEASURES IN COMMON USE

Long Measure
12 inches = 1 foot (ft.)
3 feet = 1 yard (yd.)
5½ yards (16½ ft.) = 1 rod, pole, or perch
40 rods = 1 furlong
8 furlongs (1760 yds.) = 1 mile
3 miles = 1 league (obsolete)

Square Measure
144 square inches (sq. in.) = 1 square foot (sq. ft.)
9 square feet = 1 square yard (sq. yd.)
30¼ square yards = 1 square rod, pole, or perch
40 square rods = 1 rood
4 roods = 1 acre
640 acres = 1 square mile

Cubic Measure
1728 cubic inches (cu. in.) = 1 cubic foot (cu. ft.)
27 cubic feet = 1 cubic yard (cu. yd.)
277·27 cubic inches = 1 British imperial gallon
A cubic foot of water weighs about 62·5 pounds.

Avoirdupois Weight
16 drams (dr.) = 1 ounce (oz.)
16 ounces = 1 pound (lb.)
14 pounds = 1 stone
2 stones = 1 quarter
4 quarters = 1 hundredweight (cwt.)
20 hundredweights = 1 ton

Troy Weight
4 grains = 1 carat
6 carats = 1 pennyweight (dwt.)
20 pennyweights = 1 ounce
12 ounces = 1 pound

Apothecaries' Weight
20 grains = 1 scruple
3 scruples = 1 drachm
8 drachms = 1 ounce
12 ounces = 1 pound

Dry Measure
4 gills = 1 pint
2 pints = 1 quart
4 quarts = 1 gallon
2 gallons = 1 peck
4 pecks = 1 bushel
8 bushels = 1 quarter
36 bushels = 1 chaldron

Liquid Measure
60 minims = 1 drachm
8 drachms = 1 ounce
20 ounces = 1 pint
2 pints = 1 quart
4 quarts = 1 gallon
9 gallons = 1 firkin
4 firkins = 1 barrel
2 barrels = 1 puncheon

Paper Measure
24 sheets = 1 quire
516 sheets = 1 ream
2 reams = 1 bundle
5 bundles = 1 bale

Surveyors' Measure
7·92 inches = 1 link
25 links = 1 rod
4 rods = 1 chain
10 chains = 1 furlong
8 furlongs = 1 mile

Nautical Measure
6 feet = 1 fathom
120 fathoms = 1 cable length
8·444 cable lengths = 1 nautical mile
3 nautical miles = 1 marine league
1·15 statute miles = 1 nautical mile
NOTE.—A geographical mile is one minute of the arc on the earth's surface at the equator. A knot is a speed of one nautical mile per hour.

Angular Measure
60 seconds (") = 1 minute (')
60 minutes = 1 degree (°)
360 degrees = 1 circumference
1 radian = 57°·296

Measures of Time
60 seconds = 1 minute
60 minutes = 1 hour
24 hours = 1 day
7 days = 1 week
4 weeks = 1 lunar month
12 calendar months = 1 year
365 days = 1 year
366 days = 1 leap year

Counting
12 things = 1 dozen (doz.)
13 things = 1 baker's dozen
12 dozen = 1 gross
12 gross = 1 great gross
20 things = 1 score

Bread Weight
1 quartern of flour = 3½ lb.
1 quartern loaf = 4 lb. 5 oz. 8½ dr.
1 half peck loaf = 8 lb. 11 oz. 1 dr.
1 peck loaf = 17 lb. 6 oz. 2 dr.

Common Household Measures
3 teaspoons = 1 tablespoon
1 tablespoon = ½ fluid ounce
16 tablespoons = 1 cup
1 cup = 8 fluid ounces
1 cup granulated sugar = ½ pound
1 cup flour = ¼ pound
1 cup chopped meat = ½ pound
1 cup lard = ½ pound
1 cup rice = ⅛ pound
1 cup raisins = 6 ounces
1 cup currants = 6 ounces
1 cup dry crumbs = 2 ounces

Some Miscellaneous Units
1 atmosphere (pressure) = 14·7 lb. per sq. in.
1 atmosphere = 34 ft. head of water
1 atmosphere = 760 mm. of mercury
absolute zero = −273°C. = −459°·4 F.
1 degree C. = $\frac{5}{9}$ (F. −32)
1 degree F. = ($\frac{9}{5}$ C.) +32
1 horse-power (H.P.) = 550 foot-pounds per second
1 horse-power = 746 watts = 0·746 kilowatt
1 kilowatt (kw) = 1·34 horse-power
1 international carat = 200 milligrams (gem weight)
1 point (type size) = $\frac{1}{72}$ inch = 0·01389 in.
1 light year = 5·88 × 10¹² miles
1 span = 9 inches (cloth measure)
1 ell = 45 inches
1 hand = 4 inches (measuring horses)
1 cubit (Biblical) = 18 inches
1 board foot = 144 cubic inches

METRIC AND BRITISH WEIGHTS AND MEASURES

Tables of Conversion Equivalents

BRITISH—METRIC	METRIC—BRITISH

Long Measure

1 inch = 2·54 centimetres	1 centimetre = 0·394 inch
1 foot = 3·048 decimetres	1 decimetre = 0·328 foot
1 yard = 0·914 metre	1 metre = 1·094 yards
1 mile = 1·6093 kilometres	1 kilometre = 0·621 mile

Square Measure

1 sq. inch = 6·452 sq. centimetres	1 sq. centimetre = 0·155 sq. inch
1 sq. foot = 9·29 sq. decimetres	1 sq. decimetre = 0·108 sq. foot
1 sq. yard = 0·836 sq. metre	1 sq. metre = 1·196 sq. yards
1 acre = 0·405 hectare	1 hectare = 2·471 acres
1 sq. mile = 2·591 sq. kilometres	1 sq. kilometre = 0·386 sq. mile

Cubic Measure

1 cu. inch = 16·387 cu. centimetres	1 cu. centimetre = 0·061 cu. inch
1 cu. foot = 28·317 cu. decimetres	1 cu. decimetre = 0·035 cu. foot
1 cu. yard = 0·765 cu. metre	1 cu. metre = 1·308 cu. yards

Avoirdupois Weight

1 grain = 64·799 milligrammes	1 milligramme = 0·015 grain
1 grain = 0·065 gramme	1 gramme = 15·432 grains
1 dram = 0·177 decagramme	1 decagramme = 5·644 drams
1 ounce = 0·284 hectogramme	1 hectogramme = 3·527 ounces
1 pound = 0·454 kilogramme	1 kilogramme = 2·205 pounds
1 quarter = 1·27 myriagrammes	1 myriagramme = 0·787 quarter
1 hundredweight = 0·508 quintal	1 quintal = 1·968 hundredweights
1 ton = 1·010 tonnes	1 tonne = 0·984 ton

Troy Weight

1 grain = 64·799 milligrammes	1 milligramme = 0·015 grain
1 carat = 0·259 gramme	1 gramme = 3·858 carats
1 pennyweight = 0·156 decagramme	1 decagramme = 6·431 pennyweights
1 ounce = 0·311 hectogramme	1 hectogramme = 3·215 ounces
1 pound = 0·373 kilogramme	1 kilogramme = 2·681 pounds

Apothecaries' Weight

1 grain = 6·48 decigrammes	1 decigramme = 0·154 grain
1 scruple = 1·296 grammes	1 gramme = 0·772 scruple
1 drachm = 0·389 decagramme	1 decagramme = 2·572 drachms
1 ounce = 0·311 hectogramme	1 hectogramme = 3·202 ounces
1 pound = 0·373 kilogramme	1 kilogramme = 2·668 pounds

Dry Measure

1 gill = 14·2 centilitres	1 centilitre = 0·07 gill
1 pint = 5·682 decilitres	1 decilitre = 0·176 pint
1 quart = 1·136 litres	1 litre = 0·879 quart
1 gallon = 0·455 decalitre	1 decalitre = 2·2 gallons
1 peck = 0·909 decalitre	1 decalitre = 1·1 pecks
1 bushel = 0·364 hectolitre	1 hectolitre = 2·75 bushels
1 quarter = 0·291 kilolitre	1 kilolitre = 3·434 quarters

Liquid Measure

1 minim = 0·059 millilitre	1 millilitre = 16·94 minims
1 drachm = 0·355 centilitre	1 centilitre = 2·817 drachms
1 fluid ounce = 0·284 decilitre	1 decilitre = 3·521 fluid ounces
1 pint = 0·568 litre	1 litre = 1·76 pints
1 quart = 1·136 litres	1 litre = 0·88 quart
1 gallon = 0·455 decalitre	1 decalitre = 2·2 gallons

FOREIGN WEIGHTS AND MEASURES

Brazil
1 libra = 1·012 pounds
1 arroba = 32·28 pounds
1 quintal = 129·54 pounds
1 oitava = 55·34 grains

India
1 ungul = 0·75 inch
1 guz = 33 inches
1 koss = 2,000 yards
1 bigha (Bengal) = 0·625 acre
1 cawny (Madras) = 1·33 acres
1 tola (rupee wt.) = 180 grains
1 chittak = 2·057 ounces
1 seer (80 tolas) = 2·057 pounds
1 maund (40 seers) = 82·284 pounds
1 maund (Bombay) = 27·864 pounds
1 maund (Madras) = 24·68 pounds
1 candy = 500 pounds
1 catty (Singapore) = 1·333 pounds
1 pikul (100 catties) = 133 pounds
1 seer (liquid) = 1·76 pints
1 dangali = 3 pints
1 parah = 15 gallons

China
16 taels (liang) = 1 catty
1 catty (kin) = 1·333 pounds
1 picul (tan) = 100 catties
1 li = 2,115 feet
1 ch'ih = 1·175 feet
1 chang = 11·75 feet
1 ts'un = 1·41 inches

Egypt
1 dira baladi = 29·83 inches
1 dira mamari (pic) = 29·53 inches
1 qasaba = 11·65 feet
1 qirat = 209·3 sq. yards
1 feddân = 1·038 acres
1 kêla = 0·454 bushel
1 ardeb (12 kêlas) = 5·444 bushels
1 rotl = 0·099 pound
1 oke = 2·75 pounds
1 qantar (100 rotls) = 99·05 pounds

Greece
1 Ionian pound = 1 pound
1 Venetian pound = 1·058 pounds
1 oka = 2·822 pounds

Mexico
1 libra = 1·014 pounds
1 arroba = 25·357 pounds
1 vara = 32·9 inches

Paraguay
1 cuadra = 97 yards
1 square cuadra = 2 acres
1 square legua = 7·5 sq. miles

Peru
1 ounce = 1·014 ounces
1 libra = 1·014 pounds
1 quintal = 101·44 pounds
1 arroba = 6·7 gallons
1 arroba = 25·36 pounds
1 vara = 33·37 inches

Russia
16 vershok = 1 arshin
1 arshin = 28 inches
3 arshin = 1 sajen
1 sajen = 7 feet
500 sajen = 1 verst
1 verst = 3,500 feet
1 sq. vershok = 3·063 sq. inches
1 sq. arshin = 5·444 sq. feet
1 sq. sajen = 5·444 sq. yards
1 sq. verst = 0·439 sq. mile
1 zolotnik = 65·831 grains
3 zolotnik = 1 loth
32 loth = 1 funt
1 funt = 0·903 pound
40 funt = 1 pood
1 pood = 36·113 pounds
10 poods = 1 berkovatz
1 tcharka = 0·216 pint
10 tcharkas = 1 shtoff
1 shtoff = 1·082 quarts
10 shtoffs = 1 vedro
1 vedro = 2·705 gallons
1 chetvert = 5·771 bushels

Siam
1 niu = 0·83 inch
1 ru'p = 10 inches
1 sen = 44·4 yards
1 röeneng = 2·525 miles
1 tael = 936·25 grains (troy)
1 chang = 2·675 pounds

Spain
1 quintal = 220·4 pounds
1 libra = 1·014 pounds
1 arroba (wine) = 3·5 gallons
1 arroba (oil) = 2·75 gallons

Turkey
1 oke = 2·826 pounds
1 batman (6 okes) = 16·958 pounds
1 cantar (44 okes) = 124·362 pounds
1 cheki (195 okes) = 551·148 pounds
1 muscal = 74·171 grains
1 kileh = 0·912 bushel
1 arshin = 26·96 inches
1 endaze = 25·555 inches
1 deunum = 1098·765 sq. yards
1 djerib = 2,470 acres

United States
1 long ton = 2,240 pounds
1 short ton = 2,000 pounds
1 bushel = 2,150·42 cu. inches
1 gallon = 268·8 cu. inches
1 gallon (8 pints) = 0·833 imperial gallon
1 pint = 16 fluid ounces

The following countries use the metric system : Argentina, Belgium, Bolivia, Brazil, Bulgaria, Chile, Czechoslovakia, Denmark, Dominican Republic, Ecuador, Egypt, Finland, France, Germany, Haiti, Honduras, Hungary, Italy, Japan, Malta, Mexico, Netherlands, Nicaragua, Norway, Paraguay, Portugal, Rumania, Russia, South Africa, Spain, Sweden, Switzerland, Uruguay, Venezuela. Some of them have other weights and measures, a few of which are given above.

N.B.—For British Weights and Measures *see* *pages* 4036–37.

OLD WEIGHTS AND MEASURES

Britain
1 hand = 4 inches
1 cubit = 18 inches
1 ell = 45 inches
1 Cheshire acre = 10,240 sq. yards
1 yard ($\frac{1}{4}$ hide) = 30 acres

Ancient Rome
1 digitus = 0·73 inch
1 Roman foot = 0·973 foot
1 gradus = 2·42 feet
1 actus = 116·4 feet
1 Roman mile = 4,865 feet
1 as = 0·72 pound
1 uncia = 420 grains
12 unciae = 1 libra
125 librae = 1 talent
1 bes = 0·48 pound
1 denarius = 60·16 grains
1 obolus = 8·77 grains
1 scrupulum = 17·53 grains

South Africa
1 morgen = 2·117 acres
1 Cape lineal foot = 1·033 feet
1 short ton = 0·892 ton
1 leaguer = 128 gallons
1 half aum = 15·5 gallons
1 anker = 7·5 gallons
1 muid = 3 bushels

Malta
1 palmo = 10·313 inches
1 canna = 6·875 feet
1 sq. canna = 47·20 feet
1 tumulo = 72·6 sq. feet
1 mondello = 10 misure
1 misure = 0·166 acre

Greece
3 palms = 1 span
2 spans (1 cubit) = 18·24 inches
4 cubits = 1 fathom
400 cubits (1 stadium) = 600 feet
1 talent = 93·65 pounds

Channel Islands
	Jersey	Guernsey
1 vergee =	0·44 acre	= 0·4 acre
1 bushel =	8·9 gallons	= 5·8 gallons
1 pound =	7,561 grains	= 7,623 grains
1 cwt. =	112·3 pounds	= 108·9 pounds

Japan
1 sun = 1·93 inches
1 shaku = 11·931 inches
1 ken = 1·988 yards
1 ri = 2·44 miles
1 sq. ri = 5·955 sq. miles
1 cho = 5·423 chains
1 sq. cho = 2·451 acres
1 tsubo = 3·954 sq. yards
1 liquid koku = 39·703 gallons
1 dry koku = 4·963 bushels
1 capacity koku = 0·1 ton
1 liquid sho = 1·588 quarts
1 dry sho = 0·199 peck
1 kin = 1·323 pounds
1 kwan = 8·267 pounds

Palestine
1 talmud cubit = 21·914 inches
1 Egyptian cubit = 18·24 inches
1 cubit of Ezekiel = 25·26 inches
1 reed = 151·6 inches
1 kikkar (talent) = 3,000 shekels
1 shekel = 0·5 ounce
1 bath (epha) = 6·477 gallons
1 cor (10 ephas) = 8·351 bushels

France
1 toise = 6 feet
1 foot = 12·789 inches
1 aune = 46·777 inches
1 league = 3·6 miles
1 perch = 23·44 feet
1 arpent = 1·26 acres
1 pound = 7,554 grains
1 setier = 34·317 gallons
1 boisseau = 2·86 gallons
1 pinte = 1·76 pints

Germany
1 morgen = 0·63 acre

Westminster, Statute of (1931), 580, 3281.

West'morland. Co. in N.W. England; a. 789 sq. m.; pop. 65,400; **3371**, *1169*; Wordsworth's home, *3408*.

Weston, Dame Agnes E. (1840–1918). Eng. philanthropist; known as the Sailor's Friend; in 1876 opened a Sailor's Rest at Devonport and later at Portsmouth.

Weston-super-Mare. Watering-place of Somerset, 18 m. s.w. of Bristol; pop. 39,590; 3000.

Westpha'lia. Formerly Prov. of W. Prussia; forests, coal and iron mines, extensive mfrs.; cap. Münster; 1840–1; Allies entered Feb. 1945.

Westphalia, Kingdom of, 497.

Westphalia, Treaty of (1648), 3141,3203.

West Point, New York, U.S.A. Military post on Hudson r. 52 m. from New York City; U.S. Military Academy; important in War of Amer. Independ.

West Prussia. Former prov. of Ger. on Baltic; a. 9,800 sq. m.; by Treaty of Versailles larger part went to Poland; remainder incorporated in Border Prov. (Grenzmark) until 1945, when it became part of Poland.

Wes'tray, Orkney Isl., 10 m. long, 2453.

West Riding. *See* Yorkshire.

West Virginia. A middle Atlantic state of the U.S.A.; a. 24,200 sq. m.; pop. 1,901,970; 3326.

West Wall. Ger. defences on Eng. Channel coast in 2nd World War, 2377.

" Westward Ho ! " by Charles Kingsley, 1859.

Westwood, Rt. Hon. Joseph (b. 1884). Sec. of State for Scotland 1945–47.

Wet, Christian de. *See* De Wet.

Wethered, Joyce (b. 1901). Eng. golfer; the greatest woman golfer in the history of the game; her brother Roger Henry (b. 1899) was also a noted golfer.

Wetter, *see* Vetter.

Wet'terhorn. Mt. in Swiss Alps, 128.

Wewak. Harbour and airfield on coast of N.E. New Guinea; taken by Japs. Mar. 1942, and used as supply base; its airfield was a target for Allied air attack; retaken by Australian troops June 5, 1945.

Wexford, Eire. Marit. co. in Leinster: a. 900 sq. m.; pop. 92,000; **3371**.

Wexford, Eire. Spt. and co. tn. of Co. Wexford, in S.E. on Wexford Harbour; pop. 12,300; 3371; Danish settlement; taken by Cromwell (1649); headquarters of rebels (1798).

Wey. River of Surrey, flows 35 m. to the Thames at Weybridge; 3122.

Weyden (vī'-den), **Roger van der** (originally Roger de la Pasture) (c. 1400–64), Flemish painter, 2324.

Weygand (vā̃'-gahn), **Maxime** (b. 1867). Fr. general; chief of Foch's staff during 1914–18 War; High Commissioner of Syria (1923); chief of staff (1930); called in as C.-in-C. in place of Gen. Gamelin in 1940; his property sequestered for collaboration Sep. 1945; 1056.

Weyler, Valeriano (1859–1930). Sp. colonial officer; captain-general of Cuba (1896–97); nicknamed "Butcher" Weyler for ruthless methods of repressing rebellion.

Weyman, Stanley John (1855–1928). Eng. novelist; achieved much success with his historical romances. ("The House of the Wolf"; "A Gentleman of France". "Under the Red Robe").

Weymouth, George, exploration, 142.

Weymouth, Dr. R. F. New Testament in modern speech, 427.

Weymouth. Spt. and watering-place in Dorsetshire on Weymouth Bay; pop. 35,550; shipping and passenger trade ; shipbuilding, stone quarrying ; 1030.

Whale, 3371, *3373,* 2074, in Antarctic, 174 ; dolphin related, 1027 ; ivory from, 1788 ; length of life, 156 ; porpoise related, 2657 ; teeth, lost before birth, 1245.

Whalebone, 3371.

Whale-headed stork or shoebill, 3097, *3098.*

Whale Island, Portsmouth, Eng., 2657.

Whale oil, 1263, 1674, 3372.

Whaling, 1406, 2394, 3372.

Whal'ley, Edward (d. *c.* 1678). One of Cromwell's generals, signed death warrant of Charles I. After restoration fled to America.

Wharfe. R. of Yorkshire, flows 60 m. to join the Ouse.

Wharton, Edith (1862–1937). Amer. novelist, 2403, 3294.

Wheat, 3372, 745 ; Australia, *80,* 308 ; bread and baking, 554 ; Canada, 676, *679,* 2088, 2874 ; Chile, 803 ; developed from grass, 2625 ; Egypt, 1100 ; Europe, 1234 ; flour milling, 1320 ; food value, 1337, 1338, 2694 ; France, 1360 ; Hungary, 1656 ; macaroni, 2045 ; Mexico, 2156 ; N. Amer., *2383,* 2384 ; pests, 2857 ; Rumania, 2839 ; Russia, 2845 : rusts, fungus, *2857* ; Siberia, 2966 ; starch content, 3082 ; structure of grain, 1320 ; Uruguay, 3299 ; United States, 3289.

Wheatear. A bird, **3374.**

Wheatley, John (1869–1930). Brit. politician ; worked in a coal mine for 10 years ; entered parl. in 1922 ; Minister of Health in first Labour Govt. (1924).

Wheatley, John (b. 1908). Solicitor-Gen. for Scotland, Mar. 1947 ; Lord Advocate, Oct. 1947.

Wheat rust, 2857.

Wheatstone, Sir Charles (1802–75). Eng. physicist ; invents early telegraph system, 3164, 3166 ; invents stereoscope, 3088.

Wheel, 3375 ; a mechanical device, 2128 ; form of lever, 2700 : of locomotives, arrangement, *1988* ; motorcar, 2242, *2243.*

Wheel, potter's, 2665, *2667.*

Wheel and axle. A mechanical device, 2128, *2129,* 3375.

Wheel animalcules. Same as **Rotifers.**

Wheel bug. Insect of s. U.S.A., with semi-circular elevation on thorax like toothed wheel ; eggs, *1094.*

Wheeler, Charles Thomas (b. 1892). Brit. sculptor ; war memorials, reliefs and figures on Bank of England, S. Africa House, etc. ; became R.A. in 1940 and pres. Royal Soc. of Brit. Sculptors in 1944 ; his bronze " Spring," *2910.*

Wheeling, W. Virginia, U.S.A. Shipping and industrial centre and largest city in state, in extreme N. on Ohio r. ; pop. 61,100 ; iron and steel, pottery, glass, tobacco.

Wheel turbine, *3260.*

Whelk. A marine mollusc, 2199 ; eggs, *1094* ; shell, 2942.

" When Adam delved and Eve span," 3269.

Whern'side. Mt. of Yorkshire ; one of highest peaks of Pennine range, forms conspicuous landmark where Yorks., Westmorland, and Lancs. converge ; 2,414 ft. high.

Whewell (hū'-el), **William** (1794–1866). Eng. scientist and philosopher ; a great scholar, he was professor of mineralogy and of moral philosophy at Cambridge, and later Master of Trinity College (" History of the Inductive Sciences ").

Whey, of milk, 765.

Whig Party (Eng.), 757 ; Gladstone, 1469 ; origin of name, 893. *See also* **Liberal Party.**

Whinchat. Bird that visits Brit. in summer ; related to wheatear, 3375.

Whip. In British politics, an official whose duty it is to see that the members of his party vote as they should. The Chief Whip is also guardian of the party funds ; 2524.

Whip'-poor-will, N. Amer. species of nightjar, 2369.

Whipsnade. A country " zoo " belonging to the Zoological Society. It is an area of 500 acres on the Chiltern Hills, developed as a park for wild animals and also as a sanctuary for British wild birds and plants, 3446 ; polar bears at, *3446* ; tigers at, *3447.*

Whipsnake, *2990.*

Whirl'igig Beetle. A water-beetle, 400.

Whirlpool, in water. An eddy or vortex consequent upon the meeting of two contending currents ; Charybdis, 2422 ; Maelstrom, 2393 ; Niagara, 2363.

Whirlpool Rapids. Niagara r., N. Amer., 2363.

Whirlwind. A funnel-shaped column of air moving spirally round an axis, which at the same time has a progressive motion ; it is purely local.

Whisky, 103, 3067.

Whispering gallery. A gallery built along the side of a building so shaped that a whisper produced at any one point may be heard with great distinctness in a distant part of the gallery ; that in the dome of St. Paul's Cathedral, London, is famous, 2862.

Whistle, principle of, 3009.

Whistler, James McNeill (1834–1903). Amer. artist ; great portrait painter, " master among masters " as etcher, ranking with Rembrandt, Van Dyck, Méryon ; an arrogant eccentric, whose quarrels and sarcastic wit made him notoriously a past-master in " the gentle art of making enemies," the title of one of his own lectures ; 1967, 1182, 2477 ; " Old Battersea Bridge," *1182.*

Whistler, Rex John (1905–44). Eng. artist. Well known as a book illustrator and designer of stage scenery, 1178. Killed in action.

Whistling swan, 3125.

Whitby. Seaport and resort of N. Yorkshire ; pop. 11,700 ; Synod of Whitby (664) established time for Easter ; 3435 : home of Caedmon, 650.

White, Andrew Dickson (1832–1918). Amer. diplomat and educator ; first pres. of Cornell Univ. (1867–85); minister (1879–81) and ambassador (1897–1902) to Ger. ; ambassador to Rus. (1892–94).

White, Gilbert (1720–93). Eng. country parson, naturalist, and author, **3376** ; quoted, 1070.

White, John. First Brit. water-colour painter, 3352.

" White ants," or termites, **3188,** 168, *1733.*

White Aylesbury. A duck, 1052.

Whitebait. The young of herrings and sprats ; a table delicacy.

Whitebeam. A tree, **3376.**

White Canons, or Premonstratensian monks, 2213.

White-capped tanager, 3150.

Whitechapel. Dist. of the E. end of London.

White City. Name given to the buildings erected at Shepherd's Bush, London, for the Franco-British Exhibition of 1908 ; planned in 1919 to become B.B.C. television h.q. The stadium is used for greyhound racing, boxing, and athletic events, 288.

White clover, *852.*

White Coomb. Mt., Dumfriesshire, Scot., 1054.

White corpuscles or **leucocytes,** in blood, 474.

White currant. Fruit of bush related to gooseberry, 944.

Whitefield (whit'-fēld), **George** (1714–70). Eng. evangelist, founder of Calvinistic Methodists ; said to have preached 18,000 sermons ; made 7 voyages to America, preaching in many parts ; 1213, 3365.

Whitefish. Various fresh-water fishes of genus *Coregonus,* rare in Brit. : members of salmon family.

Whitefish Bay. L. Superior, 1515.

White Friars. Same as **Carmelite Friars.**

White frost, 1400.

White gold, platinum-gold alloy, 1481.

Whitehall. Former royal palace, London, 2013.

Whitehall. London thoroughfare containing most of the Govt. offices, the Cenotaph, Horse Guards ; *1836,* 2013, *2018.*

Whitehaven. Spt. and coal- and iron-mining centre in Cumberland, on Irish Sea ; pop. 21,140 ; shipyards, iron foundries.

Whitehead, Alfred North (1861–1947). Eng. philosopher. Professor of philosophy at Harvard Univ. from 1924. Professor of mathematics at London Univ. (1914–24). Works include : " Science and the Modern World " ; " Adventures of Ideas."

Whitehead, Robert (1823–1905). Invented torpedo, 3224.

Whitehead, William (1715–85). Eng. poet ; best work in verse tales in the style of La Fontaine ; 2634.

Whitehead torpedo, 3224.

White Horse, Berkshire, *416.*

White House. Official residence of pres. of U.S.A., Washington, *3343,* 3344.

" White Knight, The." By Chesterton, 781.

White lead. Basic lead carbonate ; use in paints, 2478.

White or Cistercian monks, *2213.*

White Mountain. A hill near Prague, Czechoslovakia ; battle (1620), 3202.

White Mts. Group of peaks and hills of Appalachian system, U.S.A. ; highest point, Mt. Washington in New Hampshire (6,293 ft.) ; 190.

White Nile. Main confluent of the Nile, 2370.

White oak, 2409.

White Pekin. A duck, 1052.

White pine, 2610 ; importance in U.S.A., 3289.

White poplar, 2655.

White Rabbit," In " Alice in Wonderland," 708.

White race. Same as **Caucasian race.**

White River. Arkansas, U.S.A. Rises in Boston Mts. near w. border ; semicircular course 400 m. long, when it divides, one channel flowing into Arkansas r. and other directly into Mississippi.

White Russia. *See* **Byelorussia.** People, 2983.

White Scar Cavern. Cave in Ingleborough, Yorkshire.

White Sea. Arm of Arctic Ocean (36,000 sq. m.) extending s.w. into N. Russia between Kola and Kanin peninsulas, 2844 ; discovered by Ottar, 2644.

White stork, 3097.

White-tailed deer or **Virginia deer,** 984.

Whitethroat. A small songbird, 3340.

White Tower. Part of the Tower of London, *plate f.* 3232.

White vitriol, zinc sulphate, 3443.

Whitewash, 2478.

White water-lily, *3354.*

White whale or belu'ga. An Arctic cetacean closely related to the narwhal, pure white in colour, 12 to 18 ft. long ; valuable food and oil source.

Whiting. A form of chalk, 749.

Whiting. Fish of the cod family related to the haddock.

Whit'ley, John Henry (1866–1935). Brit. politician ; entered Parl. in 1900 and was Junior Lord of the Treasury and Govt. Whip during 1907–10 ; speaker of the House of Commons (1921–28) ; his name is associated with the Whitley Councils which were organized to deal with trade disputes by a committee over which he presided in 1917 ; chairman of the British Broadcasting Corporation (1930–35).

Whit'lock, Brand (1869–1934). Amer. municipal reformer, diplomat, and author ; minister to Belgium (1913–17) ; his handling of Cavell case, relief work, and difficulties due to Ger. occupation won wide notice.

Whitman, Walt (1819–92). Amer. poet, **3376,** 2637, 3294.

Whitney, Eli (1765–1825). American inventor, 918.

Whitney, Mt., Calif. Loftiest summit in U.S.A. outside of Alaska (14,502 ft.) ; 190, 663.

Whitstable. Tn. in Kent, 6 m. N. of Canterbury ; has small harbour ; pop. 17,000 ; oysters, 2466.

Whitsunday or **Pentecost.** A feast day of the Christian Church, 7th Sunday and fiftieth day after Easter ; commemorates descent of Holy Spirit on disciples.

Whit'tier, John Greenleaf (1807–92). Amer. poet, 3294.

Whit'tington, Richard (d. 1423). London merchant and lord mayor, 3377.

Whittle, Air Comdre. Sir Frank (b. 1907). Brit. airman and inventor ; applied jet propulsion to aircraft ; the engine first used in operational (Gloster) aircraft in 1941 ; in 1948 awarded £100,000 by govt. ; technical adviser to B.O.A.C. ; 1424.

Whooper. Same as Whistling swan.

Whooping cough. Cause of, 1458.

Whortleberry. See Bilberry ; Vaccinium.

Whyalla. Industrial tn. on Spencer's Gulf, S. Australia ; rly. terminus, 145 m. N.W. of Adelaide ; blast furnaces, shipyards, iron and steel works, and pipe-line ; development largely dates from 1941.

Whymper, Edward (1840–1911). Eng. mountaineer and explorer ; ascended Mt. Pelvoux in 1861 ; the Pointe des Écrins, one of the highest peaks in the Dauphiné Alps, in 1864 ; and the Matterhorn the following year. (" Scrambles Among the Alps," " Chamonix and Mont Blanc," and " Zermatt and the Matterhorn ").

Whyte-Melville, George John (1821–78). Brit. novelist ; served in the Crimean War ; his books deal with hunting and other country pursuits. (" Digby Grand " ; " The Gladiators " ; " Katerfelto " ; " Black but Comely ").

Wich'ita, Kansas, U.S.A. Industrial city and wholesale trade centre on Arkansas r. 47 m. N. of Oklahoma border ; pop. 114,900 ; livestock and grain market ; large mills and packing plants ; motor-cars, tractors, trucks.

Wichitas. Tribe of Plains Indians in U.S.A. Originally living in Wichita Mts. of Oklahoma ; roamed N. and E. to Kansas r.

Wick. Cap. of Caithness, 655.

Wicked Bible, 427.

Wicket. In cricket, 928.

Wickham, Sir Henry Alexander (1846–1928). British explorer and pioneer planter in tropics, 2833.

Wicklow, Eire. Marit. co. in Leinster ; agric., sheep-rearing, and mining of some copper and lead are carried on ; a. 780 sq. m. ; pop. 60,340 ; co. tn. Wicklow ; 3377.

Wicklow Mountains. In co. Wicklow, Eire ; highest summit Lugnaquilla, 3,039 ft.

Wiclif. Same as Wycliffe.

Widgeon. Name of a migrant duck (*Mareca penelope*), which breeds occasionally in the N. parts of Gt. Britain ; 1051.

Widnes, Eng. Tn. of Lancs, 12 m. S.E. of Liverpool ; pop. 45,000 ; alkali ; foundries, copper-smelting, asbestos, cement, and timber works ; salt mine at, 2866.

Widor, Charles Marie (1845–1937). French organist and composer. Considered one of the greatest of church organists. Works include ten symphonies, and many suites, concertos and chamber pieces. Wrote " Technique of the Modern Orchestra."

Wieck (vĕk), **Clara.** See Schumann, Clara.

Wieland (vĕ'lant), **Christoph Martin** (1733–1813). Ger. epic poet and novelist, 1851 ; chief works, " Der Goldene Spiegel " (" The Golden Mirror "), " Agathon," " Oberon."

Wieliczka (vyā-lich'-kah). Polish tn. 9 m. S.E. of Cracow ; pop. 6,000 ; famous salt mines.

Wien (vēn). Same as Vienna.

Wiesbaden (vēs'-bah-den), Germany. Beautiful watering-place on S. slopes of Taunus range 3 m. N. of the Rhine ; pop. 182,000.

Wife of Bath. In " Canterbury Tales," 761.

Wig'an. Mfg. tn. of Lancashire, 15 m. S. of Preston ; pop. 84,750 ; collieries, iron and cotton industries.

Wiggin, Kate Douglas (Mrs. Riggs) (1859–1923). Amer. novelist and playwright. (" The Birds' Christmas Carol " ; " Rebecca of Sunnybrook Farm ").

Wight, Isle of (I.O.W.). Isl. off S. coast of Eng. in Eng. Channel in Hants ; a. 147 sq. m. ; pop. 88,400 ; 3377, 1571, 2584.

Wightman Cup. Trophy competed for annually since 1923 by women lawn-tennis players in Gt. Britain and U.S.A. Played alternately at Forest Hills, U.S.A.,and Wimbledon.

Wigram, Clive Wigram, 1st Baron (b. 1873). Eng. soldier. Private Sec. to King George V (1931–36).

Wigtownshire. Scot. marit. co. in the S.W., almost divided into two by Loch Ryan and Luce Bay ; a. 487 sq. m. ; pop. 31,200 ; 3377.

Wig'wam. Indian tent, 2755.

Wilamowitz-Möllendorff, Ulrich von. Ger. historian, 1457.

Wil'berforce, Samuel (1805–73). Eng. clergyman ; position as Bishop of Oxford (1845–69) made difficult by Oxford Movement which he did not support, although he was a high churchman ; prominent in House of Lords and as opponent of Thomas Huxley ; facility in speaking earned nickname " Soapy Sam."

Wilberforce, William (1759–1833). Eng. philanthropist and statesman ; entered parl. (1780) and took foremost part in agitation for abolition of slavery ; 2982.

Wilcox, Ella Wheeler (1855–1919). Amer. writer of popular verses.

Wild, Frank (1874–1939). Eng. explorer ; with Capt. Scott (1901–04) ; with Shackleton (1907–09, 1914–17) ; with Mawson (1911–13) ; second in command of the Quest (1921) ; (" Shackleton's Last Voyage ").

Wild, Jonathan (c. 1682–1725). Eng. criminal ; blackmailer and receiver of stolen goods ; hanged at Tyburn. Fielding wrote a satirical " Life."

Wild boar, 408, 2605.

Wild cat, 719, 720.

Wilde, James (b. 1892). British boxer ; won outright the Lonsdale belt for flyweights ; one of the greatest ever known at that weight.

Wilde, Oscar (1856–1900). Brit. poet and playwright, leader of the " aesthetic " movement ; chief plays " Lady Windermere's Fan," " The Ideal Husband," " The Importance of Being Earnest " ; also wrote " The Ballad of Reading Gaol."

Wilder, Thornton (b. 1897). U.S. novelist and playwright ; " The Bridge of San Luis Rey." (novel) ; " The Skin of Our Teeth " (play) ; 3295.

Wilhelm (vil'-helm). See William.

Wilhelmina (vil-helm-ē'-na) (b. 1880). Queen of the Netherlands, 1890–1948 ; 3378.

" Wilhelm Meister " (mī'-ster). Novel by Goethe, 1479.

Wilhelmshaven (vil'-helms-hah'-fen) or **Wilhelmshafen.** Ger. spt. and naval station on North Sea 40 m. N.W. of Bremen ; pop. 25,000 ; 1607 ; heavily bombed ; taken by Allies May 7, 1945.

" Wilhelm Tell." See " William Tell."

Wilkes, John (1727–97). Eng. politician and journalist ; entered Parl. 1757 ; imprisoned in the Tower 1763 for criticizing the King's speech in the " North Briton " ; expelled from House of Commons for an impious libel 1764 and outlawed ; M.P. for Middlesex 1768 but expelled in 1769 ;

after being several times re-elected and rejected amid a popular outcry of " Wilkes and Liberty," became alderman for the City of London 1769 and in 1774 Lord Mayor ; M.P. for Middlesex (1774–90).

Wilkes-Barre (-bar'-i), Pennsylvania, U.S.A. Commercial and mfg. city 98 m. N.W. of Philadelphia, on Susquehanna r. ; pop. 86,000 ; shipping centre for greatest anthracite coal region in U.S.A. ; lace, silk, hosiery, locomotives.

Wilkie, Sir David (1785–1841). Scot. genre and historical painter, especially noted for scenes from village life (" Pitlessie Fair " ; " Village Politicians ").

Wilkins, Sir (George) Hubert (b. 1888). Australian Polar explorer, 2646, 2647.

Will, or last testament, 3378.

Willard, Frances Elizabeth (1839–98). Amer. temperance leader and educationist.

Willcox, J., Amer. inventor, 2929.

Willesden. Bor. of Middlesex, forming a great N.W. suburb of London ; rly. junct. ; mfs. foodstuffs, engineering ; pop. 187,000.

Willett, William (1856–1915). Eng. reformer ; builder of distinctive houses in Kensington ; promoter of first bill for daylight saving, 981.

William I, The Conqueror (c. 1027–87). King of England, 3379, 1194, 1579, 2376 ; at battle of Hastings, 1581 ; grants London its charter, 1204 ; defeats Henry I of France, 1613 ; builds Tower of London, 2009, 3232.

William II, Rufus (c. 1056–1100). King of Eng., 3380.

William III (of Orange) (1650–1702), King of Eng. and stadtholder of Holland, 3380, 1208, 1794, 2114 ; Bill of Rights, 429 ; at battle of the Boyne, 537, 1745, 1746 ; and Marlborough, 2106.

William IV (1765–1837). King of Eng., 3380, 1442, 3278, 3381.

William I (1797–1888). First German emperor, 3378, 2606.

William II (1859–1941). Ger. emperor, 3378, 1450 ; abdication, 3414, and 1st World War, 3409.

William I (1772–1844). First king of Netherlands, proclaimed king (1814) after revolt against Fr. ; harsh measures provoked revolt and loss of Belgian prov. (1830) ; abdicated (1840).

William II (1792–1849). King of the Netherlands, succeeded in 1840 ; gave Netherlands constitution in 1848, and averted revolution.

William III (1817–90). King of the Netherlands, succeeded 1849 ; father of Queen Wilhelmina, 2323, 3378.

William I, the Silent. Prince of Orange (1533–84), 3381, 2319, 2320.

William II. Prince of Orange (1626–50). Grandson of William the Silent, married Mary, princess royal of Eng., daughter of Charles I.

William I, the Lion (1143–1214). King of Scot. ; succeeded his brother Malcolm IV in 1165 ; invaded Eng. in 1174 ; was captured and forced to do homage to Henry II.

William and Mary, of Eng. See William III ; Mary II.

William of Wied (vēd), Prince (b. 1876). King of Albania, Feb. to Sept. 1914 ; 2nd cousin of William II of Ger. ; 100.

William of Wykeham (1324–1404). Eng. statesman and prelate, Bishop of Winchester, twice Chancellor of Eng. ; founded Winchester School and New College, Oxford ; 2883, 2885, 3383.

Williams, Emlyn (b. 1905). Welsh playwright, actor, and producer ; plays, " Night Must Fall," " The Corn is Green," " The Morning Star," " The Wind of Heaven," " Trespass " ; film, " The Last Days of Dolwyn," in which E. Williams played with Edith Evans.

Williams, Sir George (1821–1905). Eng. merchant, founder (1844) of Y.M.C.A.

Williams, Ralph Vaughan. *See* Vaughan Williams.

Williams, Rt. Hon. Tom (b. 1888), Min. of Agriculture 1945.

Williamsburg Bridge (New York), 569.

Williamson, Henry (b. 1897). Eng. author; works include "Tarka the Otter" and "Salar the Salmon."

Williamson, J. G. Submarine photography, *1301*.

"William Tell." By Schiller, 2882.

Wil'librod or **Willibrord, Saint** (657–738). Eng. missionary to the Frisians.

Willingdon, Freeman Freeman-Thomas, 1st Earl (1866–1941). Gov. of Madras 1919–24; Gov.-Gen. of Canada 1926; Viceroy of India 1930–36.

Will-o'-the-Wisp. *See* Ignis fatuus.

Willow, 3382; classified, 3247; "farthest north" among trees, 3246; used in basket-making, *369*.

Willow Beauty. Typical moth of the *Geometrid* group, whose caterpillars are of "stick" or "looper" type. Mottled brownish wings, with wavy markings. Larvae feed on willow.

Willow-herb. A tall plant with willow-like leaves and bunched flowers, **3382**.

Willow pattern, legend of the, **3382**.

Willow warbler, *3340, 3341*.

Wills. Name of family of Eng. manufacturers. Henry Overton Wills (1761–1826) founded the famous tobacco business; succeeded by sons William Day (1797–1865) and Henry Overton (1800–71) and firm became known as W. D. & H. O. Wills. In 1901 became a leading branch of the Imperial Tobacco Company.

Wills, Helen. *See* Moody, Helen Wills.

Will's Coffee House, in London, favourite resort of Dryden and Pope.

Wilmington, Spencer Compton, Earl of (*c.* 1673–1743). Eng. statesman; prime minister in 1742.

Wilmington, Delaware, U.S.A. Largest city and chief mfg. centre on Delaware R.; pop. 112,500; shipbuilding yards, machine-shops.

Wilmot, John (b. 1895). Min. of Supply, 1945–47, 1739.

Wilson, Allen B. (1824–88). Amer. inventor, 2930.

Wilson, C. T. R. (b. 1869), Eng. scientist; "cloud chamber," 2731, *2732*.

Wilson, Dr. F. A. Explorer, 2896.

Wilson, Harold (b. 1916). President of the Board of Trade 1947.

Wilson, Sir Henry Hughes, Bart. (1864–1922), Brit. soldier; served in Boer War (1899–1902), and 1914–16, field-marshal in 1910; assassinated in London by two Irishmen.

Wilson, F.-M. Lord Henry Maitland (b. 1881). G.O.C. 9th Army 1941–43; Supreme Allied Commander Medit. 1943–44; Sen. Brit. Rep. at Washington Nov. 1944; Field Marshal 1944; Baron 1946.

Wilson, John (1785–1854). Scot. author, the famous "Christopher North" of "Blackwood's Magazine" ("Noctes Ambrosianae"); became professor of moral philosophy at Edinburgh.

Wilson, Richard (1714–92). Eng. painter; first a portrait painter, later famous for landscapes in classical manner esp. Wales; 1181, *1191*.

Wilson (Thomas) Woodrow (1856–1924). 28th pres. of the U.S.A., **3333**, 3291; League of Nations, 1908.

Wilson, Mount. *See* Mount Wilson.

Wilton. Tn. in Wiltshire 24 m. N.W. of Southampton; pop. 2,430; Sir Philip Sydney, Holbein, Van Dyck, and Ben Jonson are associated with Wilton House, where Shakespeare said to have played before James I (1603); carpets; 3383.

Wilton carpet, 707.

Wilt'shire, Eng. Co. in s.w., **3383**, 2864; a. 1,350 sq. m.; pop. 303,300; Avebury, 323; Castle Coombe, *1164*; Stonehenge, 3096.

Wim'bledon. Tn. in Surrey, a residential suburb of London; pop. 59,000; supposed scene of defeat of King Ethelbert of Kent by King Ceawlin of Wessex (586); famous tennis courts, scene of All-England Championships, *1906*, 1907.

Wimshurst, James (1832–1903), Eng. eng.; static electric machine, 1131.

Winant, John Gilbert, Hon. O. M. (1889–1947), gov. of New Hampshire 1925–33; director of I.L.O. 1938; Roosevelt's representative in London 1941; U.S. Ambassador to Britain 1941–46; committed suicide.

Winch, winding gear for boats, etc., 3375.

Win'chelsea. Tn. in Sussex, 8 m. N.E. Hastings; cinque port; pop. 700; 3123.

Winchester. Co. tn. and educational centre of Hampshire. 65 m. s.w. of London; pop. 23,000; **3333**, 1571; illuminators of, *1177*, 2092.

Winchester College, Winchester. Public school founded 1382 by William of Wykeham, oldest school in country; connected with New College, Oxford; scholarships for Winchester students; *2833*, *2885*, 3383, 1312.

Wind, 3384, 2149, 3100, *3385*; affects Atlantic Ocean currents, 291, 2419; affects climate, 677, 840, 1232; anemometer measures, *3384*; - Antarctic velocity, 174; Chinooks, 580; cyclones, 949; daily records, *3384*; dew formation, 1000; fogs, 1333; forests damaged, 1351; highest velocity, 3386; monsoons, 1701; oceanic winds, 1232, 2419; and rainfall, 2741; storms, 3100; typhoons, 3100.

Windau (vin'dow). *See* Ventspils.

Windermere, Lake, on w. border of Westmorland in S.E. Lake Dist.); largest lake in Eng., 1164, 3371.

Wind-flowers. *See* Anemones.

Windhoek. Cap. of s.w. Africa; pop. 15,000; *3029*.

Wind-hover. *See* Kestrel.

Wind instruments, 2267; horns, 1643; orchestra, 2445, 2446; organ, 2449.

"Wind in the Willows," by Kenneth Grahame, 1967.

Windischgrätz (vin'-dish-grets), **Prince Alfred** (1787–1862). Austrian field-marshal; served in Napoleonic Wars.

Windmills, 3386; in England, *1168*; in Holland, *2318, plate f. 2320*.

Windpipe. *See* Trachea.

Windrush, tributary of Thames, 3194.

Windsor. Old tn. in Berkshire, on Thames; famous royal castle; pop. 20,000; **3387**, 416, *1318*.

Windsor, Ontario, Canada. Industrial and rly. city on Detroit R.; pop. 105,300; motor-cars and accessories, salt, chemicals, drugs; 3388.

Windsor, Duke of. Title created Dec. 1936 for H.R.H. Prince Edward, after his abdication as King Edward VIII, 3388. *See* Edward VIII.

Windsor, House of, 1442, 2833. *See also* Hanover, House of.

Windsor Castle, Eng. royal home, *3387*.

Wind tunnel, for testing ships and aircraft, 2195, *2196*.

Windward Islands. Brit. group forming s. div. of Lesser Antilles, W. Indies; a. 800 sq. m.; pop. 262,000; produces sugar spices, cocoa, cotton, etc., 3368.

Wines, 3388, 1500; France, 524, 1360; Portugal, 2658, *2660*; Spain, 3032; vinegar from, 3214.

Wingate, Gen. Orde C. (1903–44). Brit. soldier; in Sudan defence force 1928–33; organized and trained Jewish volunteer force in Palestine and Transjordan 1936–38, and restored order in Arab and Syrian disturbances in areas where oil-pipeline ran; in 2nd World War raised guerrilla force to assist Allies in Abyssinian campaign;

raised Chindits, 815, for guerrilla warfare in Burma; killed in aeroplane accident Mar. 1944.

"Winged Victory," celebrated Gk. statue, *1276*, 1538.

Wingfield Sculls. Sculling race which forms the English Amateur Championship. Instituted in 1830, it is rowed annually in July on the Thames, from Putney to Mortlake (4¼ m.).

"Wingless Victory," erroneous designation of temple of Athena Nike, *285*.

Wings, of aeroplanes, *41, 42*, 44; armoured forms in beetles, 398, 1732; of birds, 437, *438*; of flies, *1329*, 1732; of moths and butterflies, 628; in prehistoric birds and reptiles, *437*, 2680; as sense organ in bats, 370.

Winkelried (vin'-kel-rēt), **Arnold von.** Swiss hero who, at battle of Sempach (1386), rushed towards the Austrians, and, gathering many of their spears into his breast, was pierced and fell dead; his act caused a break in the Austrian ranks; 3141.

Winkle or **periwinkle,** a mollusc, 2199.

Winnebagoes. Tribe of N. Amer. Indians formerly residing in cent. Wisconsin, U.S.A., *2757*.

Winnington-Ingram, Arthur Foley (1858–1946). Brit. prelate; Bishop of Stepney and canon of St. Paul's (1897–1901); Bishop of London (1901–39). ("The Church in time of War," "The Potter and the Clay," and "The Spirit of Peace").

Win'nipeg, Canada, cap. of Manitoba, at junction of Red and Assiniboine rivers; pop. about 220,000; 3388, *682*, 2089.

Winnipeg, Lake, Manitoba; a. 8,000 sq. m.; length, 260 m.; drained by Nelson r. into Hudson Bay, 2088.

Winnipego'sis Lake, a lake of Manitoba, Canada, w. of L. Winnipeg; a. 2,000 sq. m.

Winslow, U.S.A., meteorite pit, *2152*.

Winslow, Edward (1595–1655). One of founders of Plymouth colony; governor at intervals (1633–45).

Win'stanley, Henry (1644–1703). Eng. artist and engineer; clerk of works to Charles II; whilst superintending building of first Eddystone lighthouse, which he designed, taken prisoner by French privateer; escaped, and completed it in 1700; swept away with lighthouse in storm of 1703.

Winster, Lord Reginald Thomas (b. 1885). Min. of Civil Aviation 1945–46. Gov. and C.-in-C. Cyprus 1946.

Winston-Salem, North Carolina, U.S.A. Second largest city of state; pop. 79,800; tobacco mfg. centre; chemicals, iron products, flour.

Winter, John Strange (1856–1911). Eng. novelist, pen-name of Mrs. Arthur Stannard; wrote chiefly stories of military life; "Bootle's Baby" and "Houp-La!" most popular.

Winter, fourth season, astron., beginning about Dec. 21; 2914; festivals, 819, 1037; hibernation, 1622; Nature study in, 2289, 3579; solstice, 1221.

Winter-green. A creeping evergreen plant, of the natural order *Ericaceae*; oil from gaultheria leaves gives salicylate, used in rheumatism.

Winterhalter, Franz Xavier (1806–73). Ger. painter; famous for portraits of royalty, including Napoleon III, Queen Victoria and Queen Alexandra.

Winter moths, 3388.

Winter sports, ski-ing, tobogganing, curling, skating; in Canada, 681, *680*; in Norway, 2392; in Sweden, 3131; in Switzerland, 133, 3142; curling, 944; ice hockey, 1683; skating, 2976; ski-ing, 2978.

"Winter's Tale," comedy by Shakespeare, **3389.**

Winterthur (vin'-ter-tōōr), Switzerland; Tn. 12 m. N.E. of Zürich on R. Eulach; pop. 58,800; cambric, printed cotton, machinery; vineyards.

Winthrop, John (1588–1649). Eng. colonist ; first gov. of Massachusetts Colony, a post he held four times.

Winthrop, John (1606–76). Son of preceding ; b. in Eng., gov. of Connecticut most of period 1657–76.

Wire, 3389 ; aerial, 3393 ; cables, 2827 ; gold, *1481* ; manufacture, *3390* ; pins, 2609 ; needles, 2311 ; ropes, 2827 ; tungsten, 1135, 3253 ; nails, 2271.

Wire-glass, 1474.

Wireless or Radio, 3391 ; aerial, 3392 ; amplifiers, 3012 ; beam system, 3396 ; broadcasting, 3398, *3399* ; carrier wave, 3393 ; Clerk-Maxwell, 839, 3391 ; crystal detector, 3394 ; day and night reception, *3395* 3396 ; direction-finding, 2291, 3397 ; facsimile transmission, 3397 ; fading, *3395*, 3397 ; first transatlantic message, *3391* ; frequency modulation, 3397 ; gramophone programmes, 1497 ; Hertz, 1622, 3391 ; high frequency currents, 1623, *3199*, 3393 ; interference (" beat "), 3394 ; interference (" static "), 3397 ; Lodge, 1988 ; loud speaker, *3012* ; Marconi, *2098, 2099*, 3391, 3398 ; microphone, 2162 ; modulation, 3393 ; oscillation, 3393 ; place of waves in spectrum, *plate f. 3057* ; police use, *2649*, 3396 ; radar a form, 2726 ; radio beacon, 2291 ; radiogram, 1497 ; reception, 3393 ; rectifier, 2751 ; remote control, *2301*, 3397 ; schools broadcasts, 2886, 3398 ; short waves, 3396 ; speed of waves, 3359 ; stratosphere, 3102 ; studio, *2446* ; superheterodyne, 3395 ; telegraphy, 3394 ; telephony, 3394 ; television, 3182 ; in transatlantic telephone, 3174 ; thermionic valve, 3198 ; transformers, 3238 ; time switch in receivers, 3214 ; transmission, 2605, *3391, 3392, 3394, 3397, 3399* ; ultra-short waves, 3396 ; " walkie-talkie," 3396 ; waves, 2729, 3396. *See also* **Television ; Thermionic Valve.**

Wire-worm. Larva of click-beetle, 399.

Wisbech. Tn. in Cambridgeshire, 15 m. w. of King's Lynn ; agric. trade, brewing ; pop. 15,900 ; 669.

Wisby, Sweden. *See* **Visby.**

Wiscon'sin. A N.-cent. state of U.S.A. ; a. 56,000 sq. m. ; pop. 3,137,600 ; 3400.

Wisconsin River, U.S.A. Flows s. about 400 m. through centre of Wisconsin into Mississippi r. ; Marquette and Joliet discover, 2107.

" Wisden's Almanack." Handbook devoted to cricket, published annually since 1864.

" Wisdom of Solomon." Apocryphal book of Old Testament, 424.

Wisdom teeth, *3163,* 3164.

Wish'art, George (*c.* 1513–46). Scot. reformer and martyr, converted John Knox ; burned for heresy, 1871.

Wishaw, Scot. Tn. in Lanarkshire, amalgamated with Motherwell in 1920 ; coal mines, iron and steel works, 1890.

Wistar'ia. A flowering vine of the bean family belonging to the climbing order ; it is a native of China but can be grown in almost any part of the world, *1802.*

Wister, Owen (1860–1938). Amer. novelist (" The Virginian " ; " Lady Baltimore " ; " Members of the Family " ; " The Pentecost of Calamity "), 3295.

Witan. Same as **Witenagemot.**

Witchcraft, 3400. *See also* **Magic ; Superstitions.**

Witch-hazel. A shrub of the genus *Hamamelis* ; it has yellow flowers and bears edible seeds ; it is a native of S. Amer. and popular in gardens in Britain. Used in medicine.

Witenagemot (wit'-en-ag-em-ōt). Old Anglo-Saxon assembly, 1488, 2521.

Witham. R. of Rutlandshire and Lincolnshire, flowing 75 m. to the Wash, *529, 1953.*

Wither, George (1588–1667). Eng. lyric poet (" Shepherd's Hunting " ; " Songs of the Old Testament " ; " Psalms of David "), 1211.

Witney. Tn. in Oxfordshire ; 10 m. w. of Oxford ; famous for blankets ; pop. 6,380 ; 2466.

Witte (vit'-ê), **Sergei Julievitch** (1849–1915). Rus. liberal statesman, chief

TERMS USED IN WIRELESS AND TELEVISION

Aerial (or **Antenna**). Elevated wire insulated from the ground but connected through the wireless receiver or transmitter to earth. High frequency oscillations sent out from the transmitting aerial are received on the aerial of the receiving set.

Amplifier. Circuit for magnifying weak electrical impulses.

Atmospherics (or " **Static** "). Electromagnetic waves set up by electrical discharges due to lightning, sunspots or other similar electrical disturbances. Atmospherics cause crackles in the loudspeaker, and interfere with the proper reception of radio signals.

Automatic volume control (A.V.C.). A circuit designed to overcome fading by strengthening or weakening signals as these fade or as they increase above a desirable strength.

Beat and Beat Frequency. When two musical notes are sounded which have a small difference in frequency, they mutually interfere and react to produce a third note of intermediate frequency equal to the difference between the two primary frequencies. This note is called a *beat*, and its frequency is the *beat frequency*. A similar phenomenon is made use of in the superheterodyne radio receiver : incoming signals are made to beat with an oscillation of another frequency set up by an oscillator in the receiving set. The beats are rectified and translated into pulses which operate a loud-speaker in the usual manner.

Choke. A coil introduced into a circuit to oppose or limit the flow of alternating current by inductance and not resistance.

Condenser. Thin alternating layers of conductor and insulator designed to produce capacity effects.

Carrier Wave. Series of high frequency oscillations sent out from a radio transmitter. When modulated by telephony or by the speech and music of broadcasting, a pattern is impressed upon the carrier wave. It is this pattern which, reproduced by a broadcast receiver, gives rise to the received speech or music.

Cathode Ray Tube. Exhausted glass tube in which an electron stream is generated and made to strike a fluorescent screen. Such an electron stream can be modified by electro-magnetic means. Applications are in the oscillograph, the

X-ray tube, and in the television receiving tube. In electron scanning for television, cathode ray tube is embodied in the camera and works in conjunction with a " mosaic " of tiny photo-electric cells.

Crystal (crystal detector). Means of rectifying wireless waves employing a crystal of galena or other minerals which pass a current in one direction only.

Earth. An electrical connexion with the earth, which is regarded as a conductor whose potential is always zero ; often used as part of an electrical circuit, as in wireless, etc.

Emitron (or **Iconoscope**). Apparatus combining a cathode ray tube and a number of tiny photo-electric cells ; used in the television camera of the Marconi-E.M.I. system.

Fading. Periodic reduction in strength of reception in wireless owing to interference.

Frame. One complete still picture from a sequence of movements ; in television, 25 frames are broadcast per second so as to give the illusion of continuous movement. In the Marconi-E.M.I. process the picture is scanned in two frames at the rate of 405 lines per one-twenty-fifth of a second.

Frequency. The number of waves (crest to crest) passing a point per second.

Frequency Modulation. The general method of modulating the carrier wave is to vary the *amplitude* of the wave according to the speech or music pattern being transmitted. In Frequency Modulation, however, the *frequency* of the carrier wave is altered instead of its amplitude, within certain strictly defined limits : this produces the pattern which is " decoded " by the radio receiver.

Grid. A wire spiral or mesh between the cathode and anode of a valve ; controls flow of electrons.

Heaviside layer (or **Kennelly-Heaviside layer**). Upper ionized region of atmosphere causing reflection and refraction of wireless waves.

Inductance. The capacity for electromagnetic induction possessed by a circuit.

Interference. Unwanted wave impulses due to natural disturbances, other transmissions, or near-by electrical apparatus.

Kilocycle (kc.). Practical unit of frequency (1,000 cycles).

Loud speaker. Converts electrical impulses into sound audible from distance.

Microphone. Device for converting

sound vibrations into electrical impulses of the same frequency.

Modulation. Process of superimposing upon a carrier wave the electrical impulses produced by a microphone.

Oscillograph. Form of cathode ray tube in which the pattern produced upon the fluorescent screen varies according to the behaviour of the circuit in which the tube is connected. The track on the screen portrays the shape of the alternating current waves passing through the circuit. Applications are in television, radar, and many forms of recording or detecting instrument.

Raster. Pattern in which the picture or scene to be televised is scanned.

Scanning. The traversing of a scene or picture by a beam or spot of light for the purpose of television or of picture transmission by radio. In television, the light-spot traverses the picture in successive lines (405 lines in 1/25th second), so that all the picture is swept by the spot in sequence. The photo-electric effect of each tiny area of the picture thus scanned is translated eventually into electro-magnetic variations, and at the receiver a picture is built up by a corresponding process (in reverse), so that the scene televised appears on the cathode ray screen.

Superheterodyne Receiver. Receiver in which the principle of *beat frequency* is utilised.

Thermionic Valve. A device allowing a current to pass in one direction only ; a vacuum tube containing two or more electrodes, one of which when heated produces an emission of electrons.

Tuning. Method of adjusting the inductance and capacity of a receiving circuit to receive signals at one definite frequency.

Volume control. A device of variable resistance enabling the output of a loud speaker to be varied.

Wave. Vibration or electro-magnetic disturbance due to the radiation of oscillations, as in a broadcast aerial.

Wavelength. Distance between two adjacent crests (or troughs) in a wave, measured along the direction of the wave ; varies, in wireless, from one to 2,000 metres.

(Many other terms frequently used in wireless and television will be found in the Fact-Index and the list of electrical terms.)

Rus. negotiator of peace with **Japan** (1905), and first Rus. **prime minister** (1905–06); struggled to free Rus. from economic foreign bondage.

Wittekind (d. *c.* 807). Most celebrated leader of the Saxons against Charlemagne; fought Franks for 8 years, but finally accepted Christianity in 785.

Wittelsbach (vit′-els-bahkh), **House of.** Family which ruled Bavaria for a century as kings and for 7 centuries previous as counts or dukes, 378.

Wittenberg (vit′-en-bärkh). Ger. tn. on R. Elbe 58 m. s.w. of Berlin; pop. 25,100; textiles, machinery; home of Luther and cradle of Reformation, 2040, 2041; univ. incorporated with Halle in 1817; captured by Russians, April 1945, and later in Russian occupation zone.

Witwatersrand (vit′-vah-tẽrz-rahnt), or the **Rand.** Gold-mining dist. in the Transvaal, S. Africa, 1479, 1833, *3017*, 3019, 3240; university, *1833.*

Wiz′ard. A magician, 2058.

Woad. A mustard-like plant yielding blue dye; early Britons used, 1193, supplanted by indigo, 1059.

Wodehouse, Pelham Grenville (b. 1881). Eng. humorous writer; created characters of Psmith, Jeeves and Bertie Wooster.

Wo′den. *See* **Odin.**

Wof′fington, Margaret (" **Peg** ") (1718–60). Celebrated Irish actress, heroine of Charles Reade's " Peg Woffington."

Wöhler, Friedrich (1800–82). Ger. chemist; isolated aluminium and opened up entirely new fields in chemistry by his synthesis of urea, the first organic synthesis; and dyes, 1059. *See also* **Urea.**

Wokingham. Tn. in Berkshire, 7 m. s.e. of Reading; agric. trade; pop. 8,400; 416.

Wolf, Hugo (1860–1903). Austrian composer. Works include: " Der Corregidor " (opera), orchestral and choral works, but Wolf's fame rests mainly upon his songs (*lieder*), 2265.

Wolf. A dog-like wild animal, **3400**; dog a descendant, 1025.

Wolf, Tasmanian. A striped carnivorous marsupial of Australasia, 3157.

Wolf Cubs, in Boy Scouts, 538.

Wolfe, Humbert (1885–1940). British poet and critic. Works include: " The Unknown Goddess "; " Requiem "; " Dialogues and Monologues "; " Upward Anguish " (autobiography).

Wolfe, James (1727–59). Brit. soldier, hero of Quebec, **3401**, 759, 2715, *2716*, 2925; monument, *2716*, 2218.

Wolfe-Barry, Sir John Wolfe (1836–1918). Eng. engineer; his work included the Tower Bridge and important docks.

Wolff (volf), **Kaspar Friedrich** (1733–94). Ger. embryologist, lived in Leningrad after 1766; first to advance modern " cell theory " of embryology.

Wolf-fish. A large carnivorous fish of coasts of Europe and N. Amer.; great interlocking front teeth give wolfish appearance: bites savagely when caught.

Wolfram. *See* **Tungsten.**

Wolframite. A tungsten ore, 3254; in Peru, 3024.

Wolfram von Eschenbach (völ′-frahm fon esh′-en-bahkh) (1170–1220). Ger. minnesinger, greatest of Middle High Ger. epic poets; chief works: " Parzifal," " Titurel."

Wolf spider. A hairy running spider, 3065.

Wol′laston, Sir William H. (1766–1828). Eng. chemist, first discoverer of " Fraunhöfer's lines," *plate f. 3057*; also discovered palladium and rhodium; invented camera lucida.

Woll′stonecraft, Mary. *See* **Godwin.**

Wolseley, Garnet Joseph, Viscount (1833–1913). Field marshal and commander-in-chief of Brit. army

(1885–1900); leader of Red River expedition.

Wolsey, Thomas (*c.* 1475–1530). Eng. cardinal and statesman, **3401**, 1612; London residence, 2013; Hampton Court, *3402.*

Wol′verhampton. Mfg. tn. of Staffordshire, 13 m. N.W. of Birmingham; pop. 155,600; tin plate, japanned goods, enamelled ware, various iron products; 3072.

Woman suffrage. The right of women to vote in affairs of govt. granted in England in 1918; age limit extended in 1928; 1241, *3280*, 3330.

Wom′bat. A small bear-like marsupial, 309, 2111.

Women. In anc. Athens, 1523; among Aztecs, 326; in anc. Babylonia, 330; in Burma, 623; foot-binding in China, 807, *809*; in Mahomedan countries, 2066; among N. Amer. Indians, 369, 2754; nursing as a profession, 2406; police, 2648; as warriors, 137; votes for, 3330.

Women's Land Army (W.L.A.). Body which functioned in both World Wars; organized by the Min. of Agriculture for farm and market garden work for a nationally fixed wage; the scheme continued after the 2nd World War; was scheduled to end in Nov. 1950; 86.

Women's Royal Air Force (W.R.A.F.). Official title since Feb. 1949 of the Women's Auxiliary Air Force (W.A.A.F.), formed July 1939 from the section of the A.T.S. attached to the R.A.F.; they replaced men of the R.A.F., 70 per cent being in skilled trades; a permanent part of the R.A.F.; 2833.

Women's Royal Army Corps (W.R.A.C.). Official title from Feb. 1, 1949, of the Auxiliary Territorial Service (A.T.S.) of the 2nd World War, which on that date became part of the regular army.

Women's Royal Naval Service (W.R.N.S.). Women's Auxiliary service of both World Wars; estab. by the Admiralty to free R.N. personnel from shore duties; in Jan. 1949 placed on a permanent basis, remaining a civilian orgn. under the Admiralty.

Women's Voluntary Services (W.V.S.). Brit. orgn. formed May 1938 to co-ordinate all women's voluntary associations for civil defence; also enrolled individuals; max. strength 1,215,000; in May 1947 estab. on perm. basis by govt.

Wonderberry. Cross between raspberry and dewberry, 621.

Wood, Christopher (1901–30). Eng. artist; his works, painted in a naïve and very individual style, include Cornish and Breton vil. landscapes.

Wood, Sir Evelyn (1838–1919). Brit. soldier; in Naval Brigade in the Crimea; exchanged into army (1855); served in Indian Mutiny and in Ashanti, Kaffir, Zulu, and Boer wars; sirdar of Eg. army (1883–5); promoted field-marshal (1903).

Wood, Mrs. Henry (1814–87). Eng. novelist. " Danesbury House " (1860), her first novel, was followed (1861) by the enormously popular " East Lynne "; others include " The Channings," " Mrs. Halliburton's Troubles "; founded and edited the " Argosy " magazine.

Wood, Sir Henry Joseph (1869–1944). Brit. musical composer and conductor; started his career as organist; founded Promenade Concerts at Queen's Hall, London, in 1897, and conducted them until his death. Knighted in 1910; C.H. in 1944.

Wood, Sir (Howard) Kingsley (1881–1943). Eng. politician. Postmaster-General (1931–35); Minister of Health (1935–38); Sec. for Air (1938); Chancellor of Exchequer (1940–43).

Wood. The stiffening tissue in tree trunks and branches, 3245; in aeroplane construction, 3070; baskets and boxes, 368, 3382; bats, 3382; bows, 3434; building timber, 611,

1230; charcoal, 753; combustion, how it produces heat, 1595; durability under water, 395, 1152, 1230; fuel, 1405 436; furniture and cabinet work, 436, 952, 1076, 1409, 2065, 2092, 3162; lumber, 2035; paper pulp, 2497, 3070; pencils, 2541; ships and ship parts, 3162; sleepers and posts, 927; spirit from, 3067; trestles and wharves, 579. *See also* under trees, such as **Ash, Elm, Oak, Pine, Teak,** etc.

Wood or methyl alcohol, 104.

Wood ant. A forest-dwelling ant, *168, 1729.*

Woodbine. Honeysuckle, *1639.*

Wood-borer. American insect, *1731.*

Woodburn, Arthur (b. 1890). Secretary of State for Scotland (1947–50).

Wood-carving, Japanese, 1809; Spanish, *3046*; Grinling Gibbons, 1462.

Woodchuck or ground hog. A burrowing rodent, a species of marmot; hibernation, 1623.

Woodcock. Game bird of snipe family, 3403; protective coloration, 2692.

Wood-engravings or **Wood-cuts,** 1219; Japanese, *1806, 1807,* 1811.

" **Wooden Horse, Story of the,** " 3249.

Wooderson, Sydney C. Eng. runner; winner of world records for 1 mile, ½ mile and ¾ mile. *See* **Records, Running.**

Woodlark, 1893.

Woodlouse, 3403.

Wood owl. Same as Tawny Owl.

Woodpecker, 3403; *plates f. 3404, 3405*; courtship, 441; eggs, 442; feet, *448*; how he got his red crest (Indian legend), 2023; Story, How Goldenwings learned to Fly, 3485.

Wood pigeon, 2606.

Wood pulp, 2497, *2498, 2499*; used for rayon, 2748.

Wood's metal, an alloy containing bismuth, 459.

Wood sorrel. Member of genus *Oxalis,* common in woods in Britain; small white flowers and acid-tasting, clover-like leaves.

Wood′stock. Tn. in Oxfordshire, 8 m. N.W. of Oxford; pop. 1,800; formerly a royal residence; associated with Henry II and " Fair Rosamund "; Elizabeth was imprisoned here by Mary; near by is Blenheim Park.

Wood tar. Dark liquid distilled from wood, 3154.

Woodville, Richard Caton (1856–1927). Eng. artist; Turkish War (1878) and Egyptian War (1882); first exhibited at Royal Academy in 1879; well known for his spirited battle pictures.

Wood warbler, 3341.

Wood-wind instruments, **3404**, 2445.

Woof, or weft, in weaving, 850, 3360.

Wookey Hole. Cavern in Somerset, *733.*

Wool, **3404**; alpaca, 125; artificial, *850*; bleaching, 470; fabrics, 860; felt, 1265; industries, 1918; llama, 1975. *See also* **Loom**; **Sheep**; **Spinning**; **Weaving.**

Woolf (Adeline) **Virginia** (1882–1941). Eng. writer. Works include: " Jacob's Room "; " Mrs. Dalloway "; " Orlando "; " The Common Reader "; " The Years," 1216, 2401, 2403.

Woolley, Sir Charles Leonard (b. 1880). Brit. archaeologist. Made discoveries of the greatest value at Ur (1922–30). Publications include " Excavations at Ur of the Chaldees "; " Digging up the Past "; 208, 2375, *3297.*

Woolley, Frank Edward (b. 1887). Eng. cricketer. Joined Kent team in 1906. Fine all-rounder, especially notable as a left-handed batsman. Retired from county cricket in 1938.

Woolly bear. A caterpillar, *720, 729*.

Woolly or hairy **rhinoceros.** An extinct species, *735.*

Wool′ner, Thomas (1825–92). Eng. sculptor and poet, one of Pre-Raphaelites; became R.A. (1874).

Woolsack. Name given to seat of Lord High Chancellor in the House of Lords—a large square bag of wool covered with red cloth, *2520*.

Woolton, Frederick J. Marquis, 1st Baron (b. 1883). Brit. business man and politician ; director of Lewis's Ltd., Lewis's Investment Trust, etc. ; min. of Food 1940–43 ; Ld. pres. of Council 1945 ; on various govt. cttees. ; chm. of Conservative party after 1945.

Woolwich (wool'ich). Met. bor. S.E. London, on both sides of Thames ; pop. 126,900 ; Royal arsenal ; h.q. of Royal Artillery and R. Military Academy ; ferry across Thames.

Woolworth, Frank Winfield (1852–1919). Amer. business man ; developed system of stores specializing in sale of articles of small cost ; Woolworth Building, in New York, built by him for head office requirements ; left £9,000,000.

Woolworth Building. A New York skyscraper, *plate f. 2352.*

Woomera Rocket Range, Central Australia, from Woomera hamlet, 240 m. N.W. of Adelaide, across desert 1,200 m. to N. coast and across 1,500 m. of Indian Ocean to Christmas Is. ; radar posts check rocket flights ; research centre at Salisbury, nr. Adelaide.

Woonsock′et, Rhode Is., U.S.A. Centre for woollen, cotton, and other mfrs., on R. Blackstone ; pop. 49,000 ; *2770.*

Worcester (woos′-tĕr). Co. tn. of Worcestershire on R. Severn, 25 m. s.w. of Birmingham ; pop. 61,700 ; *3407* ; battle (1651), 1198 ; gloves, 1477 ; pottery, 2670.

Worcester, Massachusetts, U.S.A., 2nd largest city of state ; pop. 193,600 ; mfrs. wire, envelopes, belts, and machinery ; 2118.

Worcester, H.M.S. Former Brit. training ship, at one time moored off Greenhithe. Officially known as Thames Nautical Training College, and established in 1876, the ship was a wooden man-of-war (Frederick William) ; used for training merchant navy officers until 2nd World War, when Admiralty used her as h.q. of Greenhithe section of London auxiliary patrol. In 1945 proved out-of-date ; sunk off Grays, Aug. 29, 1948 ; *2144.*

Worcester College, Oxford. Founded, 2464.

Worcestershire, Eng. Midland co. ; a. 716 sq. m. ; pop. 420,000 ; **3407.**

Words, study of, 2570.

Wordsworth, Dorothy (1771–1855). Eng. writer, sister of William Wordsworth (" Journal ").

Wordsworth, William (1770–1850). Eng. poet, **3408,** *1214* ; friendship with Coleridge, 869.

Work. In physics, moving an object against resistance ; measured by multiplying weight by distance moved ; 1397, 1666, 2700.

Worker bee, 390, *391.*

Workmen's Compensation Acts. Bills by which workmen were entitled to be compensated for injury arising out of their employment ; superseded by National Insurance (Industrial Injuries) Act of 1947.

Works, Min. of. Eng. govt. dept., replacing former Office of Works, **3408.**

World, *map, 3419* ; Ptolemy's map, *2698.*

World Economic Conference, held in London in 1933 to discuss problems connected with adverse conditions that had arisen, particularly the stabilisation of currencies, the reduction of artificial restrictions to trade, and the raising of price levels in basic commodities.

World languages, 1223 ; Latin. 1894.

World War, First (1914–18), **3409** ; chief events and battles, see charts, pp. 4046–47 ; aeroplanes, 46, 47 ; air-ships, 93 ; army, 250 ; balloons, 349 ; blockade and embargo, 473 ; camouflage, 673, *674* ; homing

pigeons, *2606* ; conscription, 250 ; convoy system, 292 ; gas warfare, 3409, 3415 ; international law, 473, 1563, 1905 ; mines, 2185 ; navy, 2293 ; Red Cross, 2752 ; Royal Air Force, 91 ; Royal Flying Corps, 91 ; submarines, 3411 ; tanks, 3151 ; torpedoes, 3226. *See also* under names of chief battles, commanders, statesmen, and countries involved.

World War, Second (1939–1945), **3416** ; *maps, 3073, 3419* ; chief events, battles and operations, see charts pp. 4047–50 ; aeroplanes, 34–39, 48 ; air force, 91 ; antiseptics, 179 ; armour, 242 ; army, 244 ; artillery, 257 ; atom, *299* ; blockade, 473 ; British casualties, 3424 ; broadcasting, 3398 ; conscription, 250 ; flying bomb, 1330 ; gliders, 1476 ; Home Guard, 1637 ; infra-red rays, 1724 ; jet-propelled aircraft, 1827 ; machine-gun, 2050 ; Merchant Navy, 2144 ; mines, 2185 ; Mulberry harbours, 2251 ; National-Socialist party, 2281 ; Navy, 2293, 2295 ; 2296 ; parachute troops, 2509 ; radar, 2293, 2726 ; rocket-bomb, *2792* ; rocket-guns, *2794* ; smoke screens, *2987* ; submarines, 3107 ; tanks, 3151 ; torpedoes, 3227. *See also* under names of chief battles, operations (e.g., **Dunkirk, Normandy Invasion**), commanders, statesmen, countries, and areas (e.g., **Pacific Ocean, Rhine**) involved.

Worms, Ger. mfg. tn. on R. Rhine ; pop. 51,000 ; 11th-cent. cath., 2769.

Worms, Diet of (1521), 2040, 2759.

Worms. Name formerly given to a large conglomeration of members of the animal kingdom ; scientifically vermes (*see* Vermes). Given popularly to the earthworm and its allies ; 3425 ; earthworm, 1070, 2768.

Worms Head, Wales. Promontory at the extreme w. of Glamorganshire.

Worm shell, *2943.*

Worsted goods, 850, 3406.

Wort, in brewing, 3434.

Wor′thing. Tn. and watering place in Sussex, 61 m. s.w. of London ; pop. 67,790 ; 3123.

Worthington-Evans, Sir Laming, Bart. (1868–1931). Brit. solicitor and politician ; entered Parl. in 1910 ; in 1921 became Sec. for War and in 1923 Postmaster-General ; Sec. of State for War (1924–29).

Wounds, bandaging, 1291, 1295.

Wove paper, 2500.

Wrangel (vrang′-gel), **Peter Nicholaievitch, Baron** (1879–1928), Ukrainian general.

Wrangle. Isl. of Arctic Ocean 400 m. N.W. of Bering Strait ; 70 m. by 35 m.

Wrath, Cape. Headland of Sutherlandshire ; extreme N.W. point of Scot. ; has lighthouse, 3124.

Wrekin, The, Eng. Hill in Shropshire, 1,335 ft. high.

Wren, Sir Christopher (1632–1723). Greatest Eng. architect, designer of St. Paul's Cath., **3425,** *3426,* 1538, *2010* ; St. Paul's Cathedral, 2862 ; Sheldonian theatre, 2465.

Wren, Percival Christopher (1873–1941). Eng. author ; wrote stories of life in the Fr. Foreign Legion, notably " Beau Geste " and " Beau Sabreur."

Wren, a very small passerine bird, 3425 ; insect destruction, 438, *439* ; remarkable feeding record, 438.

Wrestling, 3426 ; jujitsu, 1840.

Wrexham, Wales. Tn. in Denbighshire, 12 m. s.w. of Chester ; pop. 29,200 ; medieval church, 990.

Wright, Sir Almroth (1861–1947). Pioneer of immunization.

Wright, Orville (1871–1948), **and Wilbur** (1867–1912). Amer. aviators and inventors ; designers of first successful heavier-than-air flying machine · *45,* **3427,** 1474.

Wright, Philemon (1760–1839), founder of Ottawa, Canada, 2459.

Writing ; alphabetic, 125 ; Assyrian clay tablets, *331* ; Babylonian, *328* ; Braille system, 471 ; Chinese, 807.

808 ; cuneiform, 328 ; early materials for, 509 ; " invisible," 1724 ; Japanese, 1809 ; pens, quills, and reeds, 2539 ; shorthand, 2961.

Wroclaw. Poland. Cap. of Silesia, on Oder, just within Polish frontier ; formerly Ger. Breslau ; rly. and canal centre ; trade in coal, timber, corn ; mfrs. rly. stock, machinery, furniture, carpets, beer, glass, etc. ; pop. est. 96,000 ; taken by Russ. in Koniev's advance on Berlin, May 1945.

Wrought iron. One of the purest forms of iron, containing less than 0·2 p.c. of carbon ; tensile strength 17–25 tons per sq. in. ; 123, 1756, 3362.

Wryneck. Brit. bird of woodpecker family ; one of earliest migrants ; so called from habit of screwing head round.

Wuchang′, China, city adjoining Hankow, 1573 ; with Hankow and Hanyang forms city of Wu-han.

Wuchow (wŏŏ-chow′), China. Treaty port on Sikiang or West r. 125 m. w. of Canton ; pop. 58,100 ; distributing point for 3 provinces.

Wundt (voont), **Wilhelm** (1832–1920). Ger. physiologist, psychologist and philosopher ; called creator of modern experimental psychology.

Wuppertal (voop′-er-tahl). City of Germany, E.N.E. of Düsseldorf, formed by union (1929) of Barmen and Elberfeld ; mfg. centre ; pop. 324,900 ; U.S. took in April 1945 ; 1447.

Württemberg (vürt-em-bărkh). State in s.w. Ger., formerly kingdom in Ger. Empire ; a. 7,350 sq. m. ; pop. 2,696,000 ; 1445 ; ruler abdicates, 3414 ; U.S. entered April 1945 ; in 1946 divided into Württ.-Baden and Württ.-Hohenzollern.

Würzburg (vürts′-bŏŏrkh), Ger. city of Bavaria on Main, 60 m. s.e. of Frankfort ; pop. (1939), 101,000 ; very badly damaged during 2nd World War ; machinery, spirits, scientific instruments ; Univ.

" **Wuthering Heights,** " novel by Emily Brontë, 587.

Wyandotte, a breed of fowls, *2671.*

Wy′at or **Wyatt, Sir Thomas** (1503–42). Eng. poet and statesman, said to have been in love with Anne Boleyn ; introduced sonnet into Eng. from It. ; father of Sir Thomas Wyat the Younger (1520–54) who was executed for leading " Wyat's rebellion " to prevent Sp. marriage of Queen Mary.

Wyatt, John (1700–66). Brit. inventor ; with some mechanical help from Lewis Paul made a machine for spinning thread by rollers revolving at different rates ; 235.

Wychelm, 1152.

Wycherley (wich′-er-li), **William** (*c.* 1640–1716). Eng. wit and dramatist.

Wycliffe (wik′-lif) or **Wyclif, John** (*c.* 1320–84). Eng. churchman and reformer, **3427** ; Bible translation, *425* ; Huss influenced by, 1660 ; influence on Eng. language, 1210 ; Richard II, 2777.

Wye. A river rising on Plynlimmon, Montgomeryshire, Wales ; flows s.e. into Herefordshire, Eng., and turns s. entering the estuary of the Severn a little below the tn. of Chepstow, celebrated for its beautiful scenery, especially at Symonds Yat ; length 130 m. ; *1167, 1311, 1316,* 1476, 2733, 1618.

Wyllie (wī-li), **William Lionel** (1851–1931) ; Eng. artist, painter of many fine marine subjects ; became R.A. (1907).

Wynd′ham, Sir Charles (1841–1919). Eng. actor ; his long series of successes at the Criterion Theatre, London, began in 1874, and were continued at Wyndham's Theatre and the New Theatre ; his wife acted under the name of Mary Moore.

Wyo′ming. A Rocky Mt. state of the U.S.A. ; a. 97,000 sq. m. ; pop. 250,740 ; **3428.**

Wyss (vĕs), **Johann Rudolf** (1781–1830). Swiss professor and author (" The Swiss Family Robinson ").

FIRST WORLD WAR 1914–1918

PRELIMINARY EVENTS

1914

June 28. Archduke Ferdinand assassinated.
July 23. Austria sends ultimatum to Serbia; conciliatory reply (July 25).
July 27. Failure of Conference proposed by England owing to refusal of Germany.
July 28. Austria declares war on Serbia.
July 29. Russia mobilizes against Austria in aid of Serbia.

July 30. Belgrade bombarded. General mobilization in Russia begun.
Aug. 1. Germany declares war on Russia over mobilization.
Aug. 2. Germany demands passage through Belgium.
Aug. 3. Germany declares war against France, Russia's ally.
Aug. 4. Germans invade Belgium when passage is refused.
Aug. 4. England declares war on Germany to protect Belgium.

	WESTERN FRONT	EASTERN FRONT	OTHER FRONTS AND EVENTS	DIPLOMATIC EVENTS
1914	Sept. 6–10. German invasion of France stopped at the Marne. Entrenched line established along the Aisne, north to Belgian coast, and south-east to Switzerland. Oct.–Nov. Germans fail to break line in Flanders (Ypres).	Aug. 26–31. Hindenburg stops Russian offensive at Masurian Lakes (Battle of Tannenberg). Aug.–May 1915. Russians invade Galicia and capture Carpathian passes. Nov.–Dec. Three German attacks on Warsaw beaten off.	Aug. 28. Naval battle at Heligoland; German navy bottled up. Aug.–Sept. Germany loses oversea colonies—in Africa to the British, Pacific Islands to British and Japanese. Aug.–Sept. Austrian invasions of Serbia fail. Nov. 7. Japanese take Tsingtao (Kiaochow) in Shantung, China, from Germans. Nov. 10. German cruiser Emden destroyed at Cocos Islands.	Aug. 7. Montenegro joins the Allies. Aug. 23. Japan joins the Allies. Oct. 29. Turkey openly joins Germany and Austria.
1915	Repeated attempts to break the line by Allies at Neuve-Chapelle (Mar. 10); Germans at Ypres (Apr.–May); Allies above Arras (May–June); Germans in the Argonne (July); Allies in Champagne and Artois (Sept.–Oct.).	May–Sept. "Mackensen's drive" expels Russians from Galicia. June–Oct. Austro-German drive into Russian Poland; capture of Warsaw (Aug. 5); Brest-Litovsk (Aug. 25); Vilna (Sept. 18).	Feb.–Dec. Anglo-French attacks on the Dardanelles fail. May 7. Lusitania sunk; 1,198 lives lost. July. German South-West Africa conquered by General Botha. Oct.–Dec. Austro-German army conquers Serbia; Allied expedition from Salonika defeated at Vardar (Dec. 3–12). Dec.–Jan. Gallipoli expedition abandoned by Allies after enormous losses.	May 23. Italy declares war on Austria. Oct. 13. Bulgaria joins Teutonic allies.
1916	Feb.–July. Terrific German attacks on Verdun fail ("They shall not pass"). July–Nov. Allied gains in Battle of the Somme.	June–Aug. Russian counter-attack on Galicia; penetrates to Halicz. Aug.–Dec. Rumania invades Transylvania; terrific counter-attack of German-Austrian-Bulgarian armies (Mackensen); Bucharest taken and Rumania crushed.	Jan.–Feb. Austro-Bulgarian invasion of Montenegro and Albania. Jan.–July. Russian drive through the Caucasus. Apr. 29. Capture of British forces at Kut-el-Amara. May–June. Austrian offensive against Italy. May 31. Naval battle of Jutland; German fleet withdraws. Aug. 4. Italian counter-offensive begun; gains in the Trentino; Gorizia captured (Aug. 9).	Mar. 9. Portugal joins the Allies. Aug. 27. Rumania joins the Allies. Dec. 6. Lloyd George displaces Asquith as head of British Cabinet.
1917	Mar. Withdrawal of Germans to "Hindenburg line"; wasting of country on 50-mile front. Apr.–Dec. Repeated Allied attempts to break line at Arras (Apr.–June). Vimy Ridge taken (Apr. 9–12); along Aisne (Apr.–Nov.); in Flanders (July–Dec.); at Cambrai (Nov.–Dec.).	Mar. 15. Russian revolution destroys effectiveness of Russian army. July. Russian offensive on east front fails. Sept. 3. Riga captured by Germans.	Feb.–Oct. British Mesopotamia campaign; Kut-el-Amara recaptured (Feb. 24); Baghdad (Mar. 11). Oct.–Dec. Italian disaster at Caporetto; driven back from Isonzo to Piave. Oct.–Dec. Allenby's Palestine campaign; fall of Jerusalem (Dec. 9).	Jan. 31. Germany announces unrestricted submarine warfare. Feb. 3. United States severs diplomatic relations with Germany. Mar. 15. Tsar of Russia dethroned; Kerensky establishes moderate government. Apr. 6. United States enters the war; Panama, Cuba, Liberia, Brazil follow; nine Central and South American states sever relations with Germany but do not declare war. June 12. King Constantine deposed and Greece joins Allies. Aug. 14. China joins the Allies. Nov. 8. Bolsheviks control government in Russia.
1918	Mar.–July. Great drive of Germans fails; Picardy offensive launched (Mar. 21); Lys River (Apr. 9); Aisne and Marne (May 27); Oise (June 9); second battle of the Marne (July 15). July 18. Allied counter-offensive begun; Battle of Amiens (Aug. 8); Americans take St. Mihiel (Sept. 12); Germans lose Lys salient (Aug.–Sept.); Allied and American advance along Argonne-Meuse front (Sept.–Nov.); "Hindenburg line" broken (Oct.); German right flank turned in Belgium (Sept.–Nov.). Germans decide to surrender.	Feb.–Mar. Germany transports forces from Russian front for use on western front. Sept. Allies defeat Bulgarian armies in Macedonia, and Bulgaria sues for peace. Oct.–Nov. Montenegro and Serbia recovered by Allies.	Aug. 6. Allies seize Archangel, Russia, and establish a northern front. Aug. American-Japanese expedition to Siberia. Sept. 19–Oct. 26. Allenby clears Palestine of Turks; cuts Baghdad railway. Turkey sues for peace. Oct. 24–25. New Italian attack drives Austrians back on line from Alps to Adriatic. Austria sues for peace (Oct. 29).	Jan. 5. Lloyd George announces war aims of the Allies. Jan. 8. President Wilson lays down "14 points." Jan.–Feb. Break-up of Russia; Finland, Lithuania, Ukraine, Crimea, Armenia, Siberia, etc., set up independent governments. Mar. 3. Soviet Russia concludes humiliating peace of Brest-Litovsk with Germany. June 30–Sept. Allies recognize independence of Czechoslovakia. Sept. 29. Bulgaria signs armistice. Oct. 5. Germany appeals to President Wilson for restoration of peace. Oct. 31. Turkey signs armistice. Oct. 31. Hungarian independence declared. Nov. 3. Austria signs armistice. Nov. 9. Polish republic announced. Nov. 9. German Emperor flees to Holland; signs abdication (Nov. 28). Nov. 11. Armistice signed by Germany. Nov. 12. Emperor Charles abdicates Austrian throne. Nov. Yugoslav convention proclaims Kingdom of Serbs, Croats, and Slovenes.

NOTABLE BATTLES OF THE FIRST WORLD WAR

1914 Aug. 4–7 .. .. .. **Battle of Liége,** a fortress on the Belgian frontier. The determined stand of the Belgians upset the enemy's programme and made the German army ten days late in reaching the French frontier.

Aug. 21–23 .. .. **Battle of Mons-Charleroi,** in Belgium. The combined forces of the British and French were defeated by the Germans, whose path into France was now open.

Aug. 26–Sept. 1 .. .. **Battle of Tannenberg** in East Prussia, called by the Germans the " Sedan of the East." Hindenburg here crushed one of the Russian armies that had invaded East Prussia.

Sept. 6–10 .. .. **First Battle of the Marne.** The Allied troops stopped the German advance within sight of Paris and turned it into a German retreat.

Sept. 6–10 .. .. **First Battle of the Masurian Lakes,** in East Prussia, resulted in the crushing of the second Russian army by the Germans.

Sept. 12–17 .. .. **Battle of the Aisne** began the trench warfare, which lasted until 1918.

Oct. 16–30 .. .. **Battle of the Yser,** in Belgium ; the Belgians halted the German advance by cutting the dykes.

Oct. 22–Nov. 15 .. .. **First Battle of Ypres** (a city in Belgium), or the **First Battle of Flanders.** The Germans failed in their attempt to pierce the lines and reach Calais.

Nov.–March 22 (1915) .. **Siege of Przemysl.** a strong Austrian fortress in eastern Galicia. 120,000 Austrians were made prisoners when hunger forced Przemysl to surrender to the Russians. The fortress was retaken by the Austrians and Germans on June 2, 1915.

1915 Jan. 24 .. .. .. **Battle of Dogger Bank,** a naval engagement in the North Sea between battle-cruiser squadrons of the British and Germans. The German vessels finally retired to the mine-strewn German waters.

Feb. 4–12 .. .. **Second Battle of the Masurian Lakes** ended in disaster for the Russians.

March 10–12 .. .. **Battle of Neuve-Chapelle,** a little village in northern France, near Lille. The British captured a few miles of territory at a terrific cost.

Apr. 22–26 .. .. **Second Battle of Ypres, or the Second Battle of Flanders.** The Germans for the first time used poison gas (chlorine), through pipes and bombs, and gained two miles on a five-mile front.

Apr. 26–Jan. 8.. (1916) .. **Invasion of Gallipoli,** the peninsula between the Dardanelles and the Aegean Sea. After many months the British forces, made up largely of Dominion troops (Anzacs), and the French army were withdrawn with nothing accomplished.

May 2 .. .. .. **Battle of Dunajec River,** in western Galicia, Austria. Austrian and German troops forced back the Russian line, taking many prisoners. This was the beginning of the drive which expelled the Russians from Galicia and conquered Russian Poland (July 12–Sept. 18).

Sept. 25–Oct. .. .. **Battle of Champagne,** a desperate offensive of the French, British, and Belgians, resulted in some advance and many prisoners, but failed to break the German lines.

1916 Feb. 21–July .. .. **Battle of Verdun,** a fortified city in eastern France. The German Crown Prince sacrificed 500,000 men in the vain attempt to take the city.

May 31 .. .. .. **Battle of Jutland,** in the North Sea, off the Danish coast. The losses on both sides were heavy, but the British remained in control of the sea.

July 1–Nov. 18 .. **First Battle of the Somme,** in northern France. The French and British, using tanks for the first time, drove the Germans back nine miles on a 20-mile front.

1917 July–Nov. .. .. **Third Battle of Ypres, or Third Battle of Flanders** (Passchendaele Ridge) was a slight gain for the British, French, and Belgians over the Germans. Fought in mud, which rendered tanks useless.

Oct.–Nov. .. .. **Battle of Caporetto.** The Austrians began a counter-offensive against the Italians by this surprise attack, which resulted in a terrible rout. The Italians lost 200,000 prisoners.

Nov. 20–Dec. 13 .. **Battle of Cambrai,** a city of northern France on the River Schelde, was begun by the British and French tanks without any artillery preparation. The gains that were made at first were later lost.

1918 March 21–Apr. 21 .. **Second Battle of the Somme, or Battle of Picardy,** on the west front from La Fère to Ypres and beyond, began the German offensive in 1918.

May 27–June .. .. **Third Battle of the Aisne,** a second success for the Germans. When within about 40 miles of Paris, however, they were stopped by the French and the Americans at Chateau-Thierry.

July 15–18 .. .. **Second Battle of the Marne** resulted in some gains by the Germans, but their plans were suddenly upset by the counter-offensive of the Allied troops under Foch.

Aug. 8–Sept. .. .. **Battle of Amiens,** a great gain for the British, French, Belgians, and Americans. The operations spread until the Germans were pushed back beyond the " Hindenburg Line."

Sept. 12–13 .. .. **Battle of St. Mihiel,** the first battle in which the Americans acted independently. The salient which had been held by the Germans since 1914 was wiped out.

Sept. 19–22 .. .. **Battle of Samaria** resulted in the annihilation of the Turkish troops by the British and Arabs.

Oct. 24–31 .. .. **Battle of the Piave** removed Austria from the war and led her to ask for peace.

SECOND WORLD WAR 1939–1945

PRELIMINARY EVENTS

1931 Oct.–Nov. Japan occupied Manchuria.

1933 Jan. 30. Hitler appointed Chancellor of German Reich.

1935 Mar. 16. Conscription revived in Germany.

1936 Mar. 7 Hitler reoccupied Rhineland.

May 9 Abyssinia conquered by Italy.

July 17 Civil war broke out in Spain.

Oct. 25 Rome–Berlin Axis formed.

Nov. 25 Anti-Comintern Pact between Germany and Japan.

1937 July 7 " China Incident " began.

Nov. 6 Italy joined Anti-Comintern.

1938 Mar. 13 Hitler annexed Austria.

Sept. 30 Czechoslovakia dismembered by Munich Agreement.

1939 Mar. 15 Hitler occupied Czechoslovakia.

Mar. 22 Hitler annexed Memel.

31 Spanish Civil War ended, Gen. Franco Dictator of Spain.

Apl. 6 Chamberlain promised British support to Poland.

Apl. 7 Franco adhered to Anti-Comintern Pact. Italy invaded Albania.

28 Germany denounced 1934 Anglo-German Naval Agreement.

Aug. 23 Germany and U.S.S.R. signed Pact of Non-Aggression.

24 Gt. Britain and Poland signed Pact of Mutual Assistance.

Sep. 1 Germany invaded Poland.

3 Britain and France declared war on Germany.

	WESTERN EUROPE	N. AFRICA AND ITALY	RUSSO-GERMAN CAMPAIGNS
1939	Sept. 1–28. Ger. and Russ. invasion, defeat and partition of **Poland**. Nov. 30. Russ. invasion of Finland.		
1940	Mar. 12. Surrender of Finland to Russ. **April–May. Ger. invasion of Denmark, Norway, Netherlands, Belgium, Luxemburg and France ; B.E.F. evacuated at Dunkirk.** June. Italy declares war on Britain and France ; fall of France. **Aug.–Oct. Battle of Britain.** Oct. 28. It. invasion of Greece.	Aug.–Sept. Itals. invade Kenya, Sudan, Brit. Somaliland and Egypt. Dec. 9. Brit. under Wavell advance in Egypt and Libya.	
1941	Mar. 4. Brit. raid on Lofoten Is. **April. Ger. invasion and defeat of Yugoslavia and Greece.** June 1. Crete captured by Gers. **Dec. 11. Ger. and It. declare war on U.S.A.**	Jan.–Feb. Itals. swept from Libya, Kenya and Sudan ; It. Somaliland occupied. Mar.–Apr. Brit. Somaliland liberated, Eritrea occupied and Abyssinia entered. Ger. and It. counter-offensive in Libya opens: Brit. withdraw. **Tobruk besieged** (Apr. 1–Nov. 26). Nov.–Dec. Second Brit. offensive in Libya ; Benghazi taken Dec. 24. With surrender of Gondar by Itals. **Abyssinia freed** (Nov. 27).	**June 22. Ger. invasion of Russ.** June–Dec. Ger. victories force Russ. withdrawal from Baltic States and Poland (June), Smolensk (Aug. 12), Kiev (Sept. 22), Vyazma (Oct. 13), Odessa (Oct. 16), Kharkov (Oct. 29). Dec. 10. Russ. counter-offensive opens.
1942	Brit. Commando raids on Brunéval (Feb. 27), St. Nazaire (Mar. 27), Boulogne (Apr. 22), Dieppe (Aug. 19).	May–July. Second Ger. offensive in Libya ; Tobruk captured (June 21) ; El Alamein reached (July 1). **Oct. 23. Brit. victory of El Alamein ;** third Brit. offensive in Libya opens. **Nov. 8. Allied landings in N.W. Africa.**	Fierce fighting in southern half of front, with victories to both sides (Russ. at Staraya Russa, Feb. 24 ; Ger. at Sevastopol, July 1). Aug.–Sept. Ger. advance in Caucasus and to Stalingrad. **Sept. 16. Decisive battle of Stalingrad opens.** Nov.–Dec. Russ. offensives across Don and in Caucasus.
1943		Eighth Army from east and Allied forces from west advance towards each other, and meet in Tunisia, Apr. 8. **May 12. Surrender of all Axis forces in N. Africa.** July–Aug. Allied conquest of Sicily. **Sept. 3. Allied landings in Italy ; unconditional surrender of Italy**, which on Oct. 13 declares war on Ger.	The tide turns with Russ. victories at **Leningrad** (siege raised Jan. 18) and **Stalingrad** (siege raised Jan. 27 ; Ger. 6th Army destroyed). Feb. Russ. advance, recapturing Kursk (Feb. 8) and Rostov (Feb. 14). Mar.–Aug. Great battles around Kharkov and on Orel-Kursk-Byelgorod front end in victories for Russ. **Sept. Russ. victorious advance begins ;** Gers. cleared from Caucasus, Oct. 9 ; liberation of Smolensk (Sept. 25) and Kiev (Nov. 6).
1944	**June 6. Allied invasion of Normandy (D-day).** **July–Aug. Gigantic battles at Caen and Falaise.** Following Ger. defeats there, Allies spread through France (**Paris** liberated, Aug. 25) and Belgium (**Brussels** liberated, Sept. 3), and enter Germany (**Aachen** taken, Oct. 20). **Sept. 17–25.** Battle for Rhine crossings ; **Arnhem airborne operation.** Oct. Liberation of Greece begun. **Dec.** Desperate **Ger. counter-offensive in Ardennes** defeated.	Dogged fighting all the way up Italy. **June 4. Rome occupied.** Aug. 11. Florence occupied.	Jan.–Aug. Russ. advance continues on whole length of front : liberation of Leningrad (Jan. 27), Odessa (Apr. 10), Sevastopol (May 9), Minsk (July 3), Lublin (July 24), and Brest-Litovsk (July 28). Aug.–Dec. Advance carries Red Army into Lithuania (Kovno taken Aug. 1), Rumania (surrender Aug. 23), Estonia (Tartu taken Aug. 25), Bulgaria (surrender Aug. 26), Finland (cease-fire Sept. 5), Yugoslavia (Belgrade taken Oct. 20), E. Prussia (entered Oct. 23), Norway (Oct. 25), and Hungary (Budapest encircled Dec. 26).
1945	Feb. 22. Liberation of Luxemburg. **Mar.** Offensive in Ger. carries **Allies across Rhine** in force. Apr. Allied offensives in Cent. Ger., Ruhr, and S. Ger. (Leipzig taken, Apr. 20 ; Stuttgart, Apr. 22 ; Allied and Russ. forces meet at Torgau, Apr. 25 ; Munich taken, Apr. 30). May 2. Brit. forces reach Baltic at Wismar. Hamburg taken May 3. May 5. Surrender of all Ger. forces in N.W. Ger., Denmark and Netherlands. **May 7. Unconditional surrender of all Ger. forces.**	Apr. 21. Bologna occupied. Apr. 27. Genoa entered. **Apr. 29. Unconditional surrender of all Ger. forces in Italy.** May 4. U.S. forces enter Italy from Austria. May 6. 5th Army enters Austria from Italy.	Jan. 17. Warsaw liberated. Jan.–Mar. Russ. advances in Prussia, Hungary (Budapest falls Feb. 13), and Poland (Danzig taken Mar. 30). **Apr. Red Army capture Koenigsberg** (9th), **Vienna** (13th), **enters Berlin** (23rd), and meets Allied forces from W. at Torgau (25th). **May 2. Surrender of Berlin.** May 10. Prague liberated.

THE FAR EAST	OTHER FRONTS	HOME AND GENERAL EVENTS
	Sept. 4. " Athenia " sunk. Oct. 14. " Royal Oak " sunk in Scapa Flow. Nov. 21. " Rawalpindi " sunk. **Dec. 13–17. Battle of River Plate.**	Oct. 27. U.S. Senate repeals arms export embargo. Nov. 8. Hitler escapes Munich beer-hall bomb.
	Feb. 16. Rescue of " Altmark " prisoners. May 10. Brit. landing in Iceland. June 30. Gers. occupy Channel Is. July 2. Brit. action against Fr. warships at Oran. July 8. Attack on Dakar. **Sept. 7. London " blitz " opens.** Nov. 5. " Jervis Bay " sunk. Nov. 11. Sea-air victory of Taranto. Nov. 14. Devastation of Coventry by Ger. bombing. Dec. 29–30. Fire raid on City of London.	Jan. 8. Butter, sugar and bacon rationed in U.K. Mar. 21. Reynaud premier of France. **May 10. Winston Churchill prime minister.** May 14. Local Defence Volunteers (later Home Guard) formed. June 16. Pétain premier of France. July 26. Jap. occupies Fr. Indo-China. Sept. 3. U.K. leases Atlantic bases to U.S.A. in exchange for 50 old destroyers. Sept. 23. George Cross and Medal instituted. **Sept. 27. Jap. signs 10-year pact with Ger. and Italy.** Oct. 21. Purchase Tax instituted in U.K.
Dec. Jap. attacks on Pearl Harbour, Siam, Hong Kong, Shanghai, Guam, Wake Is. (7th) ; invasion of Malaya (8th), Philippines (9th) and N. Borneo (17th). Dec. 10. Loss of " Prince of Wales " and " Repulse." **Dec. 25. Surrender of Hong Kong.**	**Mar. 28. Battle of Cape Matapan.** Apr. 3–June. Revolt in Iraq. May 6. Axis occupy Aegean Is. May 24. H.M.S. " Hood " sunk. May 27. " Bismarck " sunk. July 12. Brit. and Free French occupy Syria. Aug. 25. Brit. and Russ. enter Iran. Sept. 8. Allied raid on Spitsbergen. Nov. 14. " Ark Royal " sunk.	**Mar. 11. Lease-Lend Act passed by U.S. Congress.** Mar. 27. Coup d'état in Yugoslavia ; King Peter forms new govt. May 16. Iceland becomes independent. June 1. Clothes rationing in U.K. **Aug. 14. Atlantic Charter drawn up by Churchill and Roosevelt.** Sept. 16. Abdication of Shah of Persia. Oct. 20. Soviet govt. moved to Kuibyshev.
Jan. 23–29. Battle of Macassar Straits. **Feb. 15. Fall of Singapore.** Feb. 27–Mar. 1. Battle of Java Sea : Jap. landings in Java and New Guinea. Mar.–May. Jap. advance in Burma and Brit. evacuation. **May 4–9. Battle of Coral Sea** arrests Jap. progress towards Australia. June 3–6. Battle of Midway Is. ; Japs. land in Aleutian Is. Sept.–Nov. Jap. withdrawal in Papua.	**Feb. 12. Escape of " Scharnhorst "** " Gneisenau " and " Prinz Eugen " up English Channel. Feb. 19. Japs bomb Darwin, Australia. Apr.–May. " Baedeker " raids on Bath, Norwich, York, Exeter and Canterbury. Apr. 18. Tokyo bombed by U.S. carrier-borne planes. May–Nov. Brit. occupation of Madagascar. **May 30. First 1,000-bomber raid—on Cologne.** June 10. Lidice (Czechoslovakia) destroyed. Sept. 25. Mosquito raid on Gestapo h.q. at Oslo. Oct. 7. Commando raid on Sark. Nov. 11. Gers. occupy Vichy France. Nov. 27. Fr. fleet scuttled at Toulon.	Feb. 19. Riom trials begin. Apr. 14. Laval chief of Fr. govt. Apr. 16. Malta awarded George Cross. May 26. Anglo-Soviet Treaty signed. July 26. Sweets rationed in U.K. Aug. 25. Duke of Kent killed in air crash. Dec. 24. Darlan assassinated.
Allies prevent further Jap. advances and begin counter-offensive. Feb. 9. Guadalcanal cleared of Japs. Feb.–May. Chindit operations in Burma. Mar. 5. Battle of Bismarck Sea. July. Battles of Kula Gulf. Aug. 22. Aleutians cleared of Japs. Sept.–Nov. Allied victories in New Guinea and New Georgia ; landings in Solomon and Gilbert Is.	May 17. R.A.F. bomb Mohne and Eder dams. June 19. U.S. planes bomb Rome. Oct. 4. Liberation of Corsica by French. Oct.–Nov. Ger. occupation of Rhodes and Dodecanese Is. Dec. 26. " Scharnhorst " sunk.	**Jan. 14–24. Casablanca conference.** June 8. Comintern dissolved. July 25. Mussolini resigns. July 26. Ital. Fascist party dissolved. **Aug. 17–24. 1st Quebec Conference.** Oct. 12. Portugal grants Azores bases to Allies. Nov. 9. 44 nations agree to set up U.N.R.R.A. **Nov. 22–26. Cairo conference.** **Nov. 28–Dec. 1. Teheran conference.**
Feb.–May. Allied landings in Marshall, Admiralty and Mariana Is. and Dutch New Guinea. Mar. 17. Japs. invade Assam ; Kohima besieged (relieved Apr. 19). **June. Brit. counter-offensive in Assam and Burma.** July–Nov. Allied " island-hopping " continues in Marianas, Moluccas, Palau Is. and Philippines. **Oct. 23–27. Battle for Leyte Gulf.**	Feb. " Little blitz " on London. Mar. 9. 2000 U.S. planes raid Berlin. **June 13. First flying-bombs on England.** **Sept. 8. First rocket bombs on England.** Nov. 12. " Tirpitz " sunk in Alten Fjord. Nov. 24. Tokyo bombed by U.S. Superfortresses from Saipan.	Jan. 11. Ciano shot by Fascists. Mar. 24. Gen. Wingate killed in air crash. July 20. Failure of bomb plot against Hitler. **Sept. 11–16. 2nd Quebec conference.** Oct. 15. Death of F.-M. Rommel. Nov. 1. Home Guard stands down.
Jan.–June. Brit. advance in Burma ; Mandalay retaken (Mar. 20), Rangoon (May 3), U.S. in Philippines retake Manila (Feb. 24). Feb. 19. U.S. landing in Iwo Jima. Apr. 1. U.S. landing on Okinawa. **Aug. 6. Atom bomb on Hiroshima.** Aug. 8. Russ. declares war on Japan. **Aug. 9. Atom bomb on Nagasaki.** **Aug. 14. Unconditional surrender of Japan.**	Jan. 15. Ledo road completed. Feb. 11. Singapore floating dock sunk by U.S. Flying Fortresses. Mar. 27. Last rocket bomb on England. Mar. 29. Last flying-bomb on England. Apr. 9. " Admiral Scheer " sunk by bombs at Kiel.	**Feb. 4–12. Yalta (Crimea) conference.** Apr. 12. Death of Pres. Roosevelt. **Apr. 28. Mussolini executed.** **Apr. 30. Death of Hitler.** **May 8. V-E day.** July 5. General election in U.K. ; Labour govt. formed July 26. July 17–Aug. 1. Potsdam conference. **Aug. 15. V-J day.**

NOTABLE BATTLES OF THE SECOND WORLD WAR

1939–1940 Sept. 1–28 .. **Battle of Poland and 1st Battle of Warsaw.** Germans attacked Poland, took Warsaw on the 27th, partitioned the country with Soviet Union, 28th.

June 5–22 .. .. **Battle of France.** Germans, having turned the Maginot Line, swept across N. France to Paris.

June–July .. .. **Battle of Malta.** First attacked by Italian aircraft, June 11, 1940 ; Luftwaffe joined in attacks, Jan.
(1943) 1941. Allied reconquest of N. Africa freed Malta from danger of isolation and invasion.

Aug. 8–Oct. 31 **Battle of Britain.** Luftwaffe, attempting to prepare for German invasion of Britain, met decisive defeat at hands of R.A.F.

Oct. 28–Nov. 21 **1st Battle of Greece.** Italian invaders of Greece defeated by Greeks with slight British aid.

1941 March 28 .. .. **Battle of Cape Matapan.** British naval victory over Italians in Greek waters.

Jan. 24–Nov. 27 .. **Battle of Abyssinia.** First Axis-enslaved country freed ; by British forces.

April 6–27 .. .. **2nd Battle of Greece.** Germans defeated Greeks and small British and Imperial forces.

May 20–June 1 .. **Battle of Crete.** British, Imperial and Greek forces defeated by first successful use of airborne troops.

Aug. 22–Jan. 27 **Siege of Leningrad.** Leningrad was cut off from outside help except across L. Ladoga until Jan. 18,
(1944) 1943 ; complete relief only on Jan. 27, 1944.

Oct. 6–Dec. 6 .. .. **Battle of Moscow.** State of siege (proclaimed Oct. 19) lifted by Russian offensive beginning Dec. 6.

Nov. 1–July 3 (1942) **Siege of Sevastopol.** Russians held city for eight months ; recaptured it in three days (May 7–9, 1944).

1942 Feb. 8–15 .. .. **Fall of Singapore.** " Greatest disaster to British arms which our history records."—Winston Churchill.

Feb. 27–March 1 .. **Battle of Java Sea.** British, Dutch, U.S. and Australian force of 12 ships wiped out.

May 4–9 .. .. .. **Battle of Coral Sea.** Japanese fleet approaching Solomons defeated with loss of 7 major warships.

June 3–6 .. .. .. **Battle of Midway Island.** Japanese air and naval attack ; 15 enemy warships sunk or damaged.

Aug. 7–Feb. 8 (1943) **Battle of Guadalcanal.** First reconquest of island seized by the Japanese.

Sept. 16–Feb. 2 (1943) **Battle of Stalingrad.** Russian tenacity held the Germans west of the Volga and this marked the turning point of the war in E. Europe.

Oct. 23–Nov. 5 .. **Battle of El Alamein.** Beginning of 8th Army's drive across N. Africa ; turning point of war in west.

1943 March 5 .. .. .. **Battle of the Bismarck Sea.** Japanese convoy of 10 warships ; 12 transports destroyed by air bombing ; " a naval victory won by air power directed by an army general " (MacArthur).

March 20–28 .. .. **Battle of Mareth.** Capture of Mareth Line, last major conflict in N. Africa.

July 10–Aug. 17 **Battle of Sicily.** Sicily fell to the Allies in 38 days.

Nov. 20–23 .. .. **Battle of Betio Atoll, Tarawa.** U.S. Marines lost 1,026 killed, 2,557 wounded on this small atoll in Gilberts.

1944 Feb. 2–May 18.. .. **Battle of Cassino.** Picked German troops on Monte Cassino, lofty strongpoint covering only possible road to Rome and kingpin of so-called Gustav Line, offered stubborn resistance to Allied advance.

May 17–Aug. 4 .. **Siege of Myitkyina.** American and Chinese captured Myitkyina airfields (Burma) on May 17; town, Aug. 4.

June 18–19 .. .. **Battle of the Philippine Sea.** Japanese attack (18th) on American fleet off Saipan beaten off with loss of 353 enemy machines, 21 American, slight damage to 3 U.S. ships ; Japanese fleet driven to retreat by U.S. air attack (19th) ; 7 enemy ships sunk.

Aug. 1–Oct. 3 .. **2nd Battle of Warsaw.** Polish Home Army rose when Soviet artillery could be heard at Praga ; but Germans frustrated Soviet advance and Poles were totally defeated.

Aug. 19–22 .. .. **Battle of " Falaise Gap."** German 7th Army encircled and destroyed by British, Canadian, U.S., Polish and French forces ; first decisive Allied victory in reopened western front.

Sept. 2–21 .. .. **Battle of Rimini.** Victory in Italy in 1944 became impossible owing to stand by Germans at Rimini.

Sept. 17–25 .. .. **Battle of Arnhem.** British 1st Airborne Division, 10,095 strong, stood for 8 days without aid in an effort to hold a bridgehead across the Lower Rhine.

Sept. 21–Nov. 9 .. **Battle of the Scheldt.** Cleared the Scheldt estuary to open Antwerp, essential for invasion of Germany.

Oct. 16–20 .. .. **Battle of Aachen.** First large German town to fall to the Allies.

Oct. 20–Dec. 20 .. **Battle of Leyte.** Americans surprised Japanese by landing first on this central island of the Philippines. Its capture cut in two enemy defence forces in those islands.

Oct. 23–27 .. .. **Battle for Leyte Gulf.** Most important naval battle of war ; U.S. 3rd and 7th Fleets virtually destroyed Japanese Navy ; 24 ships (including 2 battleships) sunk, 13 probably sunk, 19 damaged.

Dec. 16–Feb. 5 (1945) **Battle of the Ardennes.** Last big effort of Germans in the west, who tried to break the Allied line between the U.S. 1st and 3rd Armies. Enemy salient eliminated Jan. 1945.

Dec. 26–Feb. 13 (1945) **Battle of Budapest.** Encircled on Dec. 26, 1944, was defended by the Germans street by street.

1945 Feb. 19–Mar. 16 .. **Battle of Iwo Jima.** In heavy fighting for this important base in Volcano Islands there were 19,938 U.S. casualties ; 21,000 Japanese casualties, mostly dead. First part of Japanese empire invaded.

April 1–June 21 .. **Battle of Okinawa.** Fierce defence of this island, first spot of Japan proper to be invaded, cost Japanese nearly 100,000 dead ; U.S. losses, over 10,000 killed and missing, 34,000 wounded.

April 3–20 .. .. **Battle of the Ruhr.** U.S. 9th Army and 12th and 6th Army Groups encircled German Army Group B ; 21 enemy divisions eliminated (317,000 prisoners).

April 23–May 2 .. **Battle of Berlin.** Russians cleared the city only after severe fighting through its streets.

July 14–Aug. 14 .. **Battle of Japan.** Intensive bombardment of Honshu by U.S. and British fleets and planes.

PEACE TREATIES OF THE SECOND WORLD WAR

Bulgaria. Signed Feb. 10, 1947. S. Dobruja retained (ceded by Rumania in 1940). Reparations by Bulgaria to Yugoslavia (25 million dollars) and Greece (45 million dollars), to be paid in commodities over 8 years.

Finland. Signed Feb. 10, 1947. Cession to U.S.S.R. of Karelian isthmus, Viborg, and territory w. of L. Ladoga, as provided in 1940 peace treaty, confirmed ; Petsamo ceded to U.S.S.R. ; 50 year lease to U.S.S.R. of Porkkala-Udd area, s.w. of Helsinki, as naval base. Reparations to U.S.S.R. of 300 million dollars in commodities over 8 years.

Hungary. Signed Feb. 10, 1947. Return to 1938 frontiers (Transylvania restored to Rumania and Banat to Yugoslavia, Ruthenia ceded to U.S.S.R.) ; small area (the Bratislava bridgehead) ceded to Czechoslovakia. Reparations to U.S.S.R. (200 million dollars) and Czechoslovakia and Yugoslavia (100 million dollars) in commodities over 8 years.

Italy. Signed Feb. 10, 1947. Cession to France of the Little St. Bernard Pass, Mont Cénis plateau, Mont Thabor-Chaberton area, and the Tenda-Briga area of the Maritime Alps, and restoration of Nice, etc. ; cession to Yugoslavia of former It. territory on frontier, Zara, isls. off Dalmatian coast, and Pelagosa isl. ; to Greece of Dodecanese isls. Agrees to estab. of free territory of Trieste. Renounces all rights to African colonies, Ethiopia and Albania. Navy reduced to 2 battleships, 5 cruisers and other vessels ; 3 battleships and 5 cruisers surrendered to Allies. Agreement on Tirol with Austria. Reparations to U.S.S.R. (100 million dollars), Yugoslavia (125 million dollars), Greece (105 million dollars), Ethiopia (25 million dollars) and Albania (5 million dollars) in commodities, etc. over 7 years.

Rumania. Signed Feb. 2, 1947. Cession of Bessarabia and Bukovina to U.S.S.R., and of S. Dobruja to Bulgaria, confirmed. Reparations to U.S.S.R. (300 million dollars) in commodities over 8 years.

Siam. Signed June 1, 1946 ; with Great Britain and India. Restoration of all occupd. territory ; compensation for damage and destruction. Rice surplus (max. 1,500,000 tons) to be handed over to Far East rice organization.

OUR letter X got into the alphabet by starting as a chair back. That is what the sign ▬ represented in the picture-writing of the Egyptians. In the hieratic writing it became ⌐ʃ and the Phoenicians added some more horizontal bars and made it ≢ (*Samekh*), out of which grew the Greek Ξ. The Greeks also developed another form X, which passed to the Romans and from them to us. Just how this form grew out of ≢ is not quite clear, but it is thought that *Samekh*

was sometimes written ⊞ and that from this two characters developed: one Ξ by removing the vertical lines, and the other ✛ by removing the enclosing square. Then the latter was tilted over and became X. In classical Greek the character X came to be used for the letter *Chi* (sounded *kh*), while the ⋍ was used for the *ks* sound. In English we pronounce X in three ways, as *ks* in *extra*, as *gz* in *exact*, and as *z* at the beginning of words, such as *Xanthus*.

Xanadu. In Coleridge's "Kubla Khan." an imaginary city, residence of the Khan Kubla; description based on that of Khan Kubla's palace in Purchas's "Pilgrimage."

Xanthate process, in rayon mfr., 2748.

Xan'thium. A small genus of plants of the family *Ambrosiaceae*, having coarsely toothed leaves and fruit a spiny burr; known as cockle-burr or clot-burr.

Xantippe or **Xanthippe** (zan-tip'-ē). Socrates's shrewish wife.

Xavier (zā'-vi'er), **Saint Francis** (1506–52). Sp. Jesuit missionary, 3429, 1799.

Xenon (Xe). Element of the inert gas group; atomic weight 131·3; occurs in the air in minute traces; is liquefied fairly easily and the solid melts at −169° F.; 3429; properties, 88, 777; in atmosphere, 1420; in miner's lamp, 1135;

discovered by Ramsay and Travers, 2744.

Xenophon (zen'-ō-fon) (*c.* 430–355 B.C.). Gk. historian and general, 3429, 2997.

Xerez de la Frontera. Same as **Jerez de la Frontera.**

Xerophytes (zer'-ō-fītz). Plants adapted to endure scantiness or absence of moisture, as for example cacti, 648. *See also* **Hydrophytes; Mesophytes.**

Xerxes (zērk'-sēz) I (*c.* 519–465 B.C.). King of Persia, 2554, 2555; expedition against Greece, 2555, 2556.

Xeuxis (*fl.* 4th cent. B.C.). Gk. painter, "realist," using light and shadow (then new); legend says, painted grapes at which birds pecked; 1528.

Xi, ξ, Ξ (Rom. x, X). 14th letter of Gk. alphabet.

Ximenes (zim-ē'-nēz) **de Cisneros,**

Francisco (1436–1517). Sp. cardinal and statesman; 427.

Xingu. A large s. tributary of the Amazon, in Brazil; about 1,200 m. long; *map, 551.*

Xochimilco, floating gardens of, *2158.*

X-rays, 3430, *plate f. 3057;* analysis, 3056; angles of deflection measured, 1739; and crystals, 940; cause fluorescence, 2574; Coolidge tube, 3056; resemble gamma rays, 2731; ionize gases, 1739; spectrograph, 3056; tungsten for tubes, 3253; use in art, 2730; in metallurgy, 2148; wavelength of, 1942, 2730.

Xylography (zī-log'-ra-fi), block printing, 512.

Xylol (zī'-lol). A coal-tar product, 857.

Xylonite (zī'-lon-īt). A variety of celluloid.

Xylophone (zī'-lō-fōn). Musical instrument, *2267, 2267.*

THE twenty-fifth letter of the alphabet is one of the four letters (U, V, W, Y) which have developed out of the Greek *Upsilon* Υ. And these are all related to the letter F, being derived from the Egyptian hieroglyphic picture of the horned asp ◄. The two horns and the body of the asp appear even better in Y than in the letter F (read the story of F). In the Middle English period Y was a favourite with penmen on account of its final flourish, and they

frequently used it in place of a final I. That is why today we write " city," " fairy," and " kindly," but where Y is not terminal use I, as in " cities," " fairies," " kindliest." In old English books Y often represents the *th* sound, as in " ye " for " the," because of its resemblance to Anglo-Saxon Þ (called thorn), which had the sound *th*. Printers not having this character replaced it sometimes by *th* and sometimes by *y*, but *the* was never pronounced *ye*.

Yablonoi Mts. A system of S. Siberia, extending from S.W. to N.E. 1,000 m. in the direction of the Stanovoi range; highest point about 8,000 ft.

Yachts and Boats, 481, *1168.*

Yaffle. The green woodpecker, 3404.

Yahoos', in "Gulliver's Travels," 3134.

Yahweh (yah'-vā). See **Jehovah.**

Yahya, Imam. Yemen chief, 196.

Yak. A bovine animal of the Himalayas, **3433,** *266.*

Yakut. Turkic people of Lena basin, E. Siberia; number 250,000; marriage customs, 2108.

Yakutsk. Autonomous republic of Soviet Russia, mainly consisting of the former Siberian prov. of Yakutsk; a. 1,457,000 sq. m.; pop. 400,500; cap. Yakutsk; climate, 841.

Yale, Elihu (1648–1721). Eng. philanthropist; founder of Yale College.

Yale lock, 1980.

Yale University, at New Haven, Connecticut; 3rd eldest univ. in U.S.A.; men, non-sect.; chartered 1701 as Collegiate School of Connecticut, name changed 1718 in honour of Elihu Yale; arts and science, medicine, divinity, law, fine arts, music, forestry.

Yalta. Tn. of R.S.F.S.R., on S.E. coast of Crimea, 35 m. E. of Sevastopol; holiday resort; held by Germans in 2nd World War Nov. 1941–Apr.

1944. Yalta Conference of war held Feb. 4–12, 1945, between Churchill, Stalin, and Roosevelt; plans for 4-fold division of Ger., formation of internat. anti-war charter, 3-power help for liberated Europe, and the drawing of the Curzon Line.

Yam. A vegetable resembling the sweet potato.

Yanaon (yan-a-awn'). Fr. possession in India; a. 9 sq. m.; 1692.

Yangtze. Longest and most important waterway in China; rises in Tibet, flows 3,400 m. to China Sea; **3433,** 265, 807; at Hankow, 1573.

Yankee, 3433.

Yap. One of Caroline Isls. (Pacific), formerly German; important cable station.

Yapura or **Japura** (yah-pūr-ah'). One of chief tributaries of Amazon, rising in Colombian Andes; 1,800 m.; *map, 873.*

Yaqui Indians. Mex. tribe living in Sonora; engaged in agriculture, weaving; highly developed clan system; much reduced in numbers by wars arising from rebellions against Mex. govt.

Yard, a unit of distance. See **Weights and Measures,** *f-i.*

Yare, Eng. A river of Norfolk, flowing 60 m. to the North Sea at Yarmouth, 2375.

Yareta, a woody fungus of S. Amer., 491.

Yarkand. Trade tn. in Chinese Turkistan (Sinkiang), in rich oasis of Yarkand and on Yarkand r., 100 m. S.E. of Kashgar; pop. 118,560; carpets, 3267, 264.

Yarmouth, Great. Spt. and watering place in Norfolk, on E. coast, 19 m. E. of Norwich; pop. 48,560; herring fisheries (Yarmouth bloaters), 2376; fishing fleet, 1621; glut of herring at, *1307;* Scottish fishery workers, *1306.*

Yarn, cotton, 917; wool, *3407.*

Yaroslavl (yah-rō-slaf'), Soviet Russia. Port on Volga r., 160 m. N.E. of Moscow; pop. 298,000; textiles; 13th-cent. cathedral.

Yarra R., Melbourne on, *2137.*

Yarrow, Sir Alfred Fernandez, Bart. (1842–1932). Brit. marine engineer and shipbuilder; pioneer of sternwheel craft of steel; helped largely in the development of torpedo-boats and destroyers; designed the Yarrow water-tube boiler; gave £100,000 for purpose of research to the Royal Society.

Yar'row, flower of the daisy family.

Yaunde. Cap. of Fr. Cameroons; pop. 20,000; *673.*

Yeames (yāmz), **William** (1835–1918). Brit. artist, b. in Russia; painted many fine historical pictures; R.A. 1878; Prince Arthur and Hubert, *254*; Wycliffe sending out his preachers, *425*.

Year, in calendar, 661; beginning dates, 2223; length on other planets, 2617. *See also* each month by name.

Yeast. A microscopic, unicellular plant, **3433**; produces alcohol, 103; in bread-making, 554; produces enzymes, 1220; causes fermentation, 1266.

Yeats (yāts), **Jack Butler** (b. 1871). Irish painter and illustrator, brother of William; wrote "Life in the West of Ireland," illustrated books by Synge and other Irish writers.

Yeats, William Butler (1865–1939). Irish poet and dramatist; connected with Celtic revival and Irish Theatre movement. ("The Land of Heart's Desire"; "Deirdre"; "The Wild Swans of Coole"; "J. M. Synge and the Ireland of His Time"; "Michael Robartes and the Dancer"); *1751, 2375*.

Yed'o, Japan, former name of Tokyo, 3222.

Yellow, pigment, 2478.

Yellow fever. A disease transmitted by mosquitoes, 2236; banished from Panama, 2487, 2488, *2489*.

Yellow-hammer. Common Brit. bird (*Emberiza citrinella*); it is a species of bunting, about 7 in. long, bright in colour, with patches of brown, richly-mottled, brownish-yellow on back; chin, throat, and under part of body bright pure yellow, 616.

Yellow pine, 2609; importance in U.S.A., 3289.

Yellow race. Same as **Mongolian race**.

Yellow River. Same as **Hwang-ho**.

Yellow Sea or **Hwang-hai**. N. portion of China Sea between Korea, Manchuria, and China; length, about 620 m.; greatest breadth, 400 m.; silt deposits, 3433, 809, 1662; *map, 808*.

Yellow spot, of eye, *1252*.

Yellowstone National Park. N.W. of Wyoming, largest and most celebrated national park in U.S.A.; it is a govt. reservation and has an area of 3,350 sq. m.; famous for its wild scenery and geysers, 1259, 3428; buffalo, 602.

Yellowstone River, U.S.A. Trib. of Missouri; rises in N.W. Wyoming, flows N. and N.E. 1,000 m.

Yellow water-lily, 3354.

Yemen (yā'-men). Imamate or principality of S.W. Arabia on Red Sea; a. 75,000 sq. m.; pop. 3,500,000; mountainous country with low plains on coast, 196; coffee, livestock; cap. Sana (pop. 40,000); *map, 197*; Yemenite Jew, *1830*.

Yen. The unit of the Japanese monetary system; sub-divided into 100 sen; 5, 10, and 20 yen pieces coined in gold.

Yenisei (yen-is-ā'-i). One of great rivers of Siberia; rises in N.W. Mongolia, flows N. 3,000 m. to Bay of Yenisei, an inlet of Arctic Ocean; crossed by Trans-Siberian Rly. at Krasnoyarsk; *2966*, 265.

Yeo'manry. Force of volunteer cavalry, since 1907 included in the Territorial Army; the force first came into existence in 1761 for the purpose of quelling local riots, but was not organized until 1794.

Yeomen of the Guard, in Royal Household. *See* **Beefeater**.

"Yeomen of the Guard." Favourite comic opera by Gilbert and Sullivan.

Yeomen Warders of Tower. Distinct from Beefeaters, 396.

Yerba maté. *See* **Maté**.

Yerivan. *See* **Erivan**.

Yerkes, Charles Tyson (1837–1905). Amer. capitalist and munificent patron of science and art; obtained control of and exploited Chicago city railways; gave great Yerkes telescope to Univ. of Chicago.

Yerkes Observatory, 2413; telescope, 3181.

Yer'mak (d. 1584). Cossack outlaw, initiator of Rus. conquest of Siberia:

made prince of Siberia by Ivan the Terrible, 2966.

Yessenin (yes-ān'-yin), **Sergei Aleksandrovich** (1895–1925). Russian poet, 2856.

Yes Tor. Mt. of Devonshire, on Dartmoor; 2,028 ft. high.

Yew, a conifer, **3434**, *2639*.

Yezd, Iran. City 165 m. S.E. of Ispahan; pop. 60,000; on important trade route; cobalt, antimony, and nickel in vicinity, 264.

Yez'o. Same as **Hokushu**.

Yg'drasil. In Norse myth., tree of life.

Yid'dish, Jewish dialect, 1601.

Ymir. In Norse myth., a frost giant, the first being created; slain by Odin and other gods, who formed the earth from his body.

Ymuiden or **Ijmuiden** (ē-mē-den). Tn. of the Netherlands; N. Sea Canal connects it with Amsterdam; fishing; ice and chemical works; pop. 46,000; Ger. base, 1940–45, for light coastal craft.

Yo, river in Africa, 68.

Yodo River, Osaka on, 2454.

Yoga, an Indian cult, **3434**.

Yoho Park, Brit. Columbia.

Yokohama (yō-kō-hah'-mah). Chief spt. of Japan, 17 m. S. of Tokyo; pop. (1941) 968,000; **3435**, 1795.

Yolk, of egg, 1093.

Yom Kip'pur. Jewish day of atonement, in the autumn.

Yonge, Charlotte Mary (1823–1901). Eng. novelist and writer on religious and educational subjects ("The Heir of Redclyffe"; "The Daisy Chain"; "Heartsease"; "The Book of Golden Deeds").

Yon'kers, New York, U.S.A. Mfg. and residential city on Hudson r., adjoining New York City on N.; pop. 142,600; carpets, rugs, hats, lifts, sugar, electrical supplies, clothing.

Yonne (yon). R. in S. Fr., trib. of Seine, 2919.

Yorick. In Shakespeare's "Hamlet" the former jester of the king of Denmark ("Alas, poor Yorick; I knew him, Horatio"). In Sterne's "Tristram Shandy," the parson; name later used as pseudonym by Sterne.

York, House of. Royal line in Eng. founded by Richard, Duke of York; list of rulers, *see* **England**; Richard III, *2777, 2778*; in Wars of the Roses, 2828, 1612.

York, Richard, Duke of (1411–60). Eng. prince; protector of Eng. during illness of Henry VI; claimant for throne, 2828.

York. City and archbishop's see of Yorkshire, near centre on Ouse r.; has cocoa and confectionery factories, iron foundries, carriage works; pop. 106,000; important Rom. settlement, **3435**; cathedral, 1168, 725, 219.

York, Ontario. Former name for Toronto, 3224.

York Cycle, of mystery plays, 1039.

York River, in Virginia, U.S.A.; flowing into Chesapeake Bay, 3326.

Yorkshire, largest co. in Eng.; in N.E., bordering N. Sea; divided into 3 Ridings (E., N. and W.); a. 6,000 sq. m.; pop. 4,304,800; farming, mfg., coal mining, **3435**; Leeds, 1918; Sheffield, 2941; York, 725, 1168, 3435; Wakefield, 3332.

Yorkshire terrier, *plate f. 1024*.

Yorktown, Virginia, U.S.A. Historic tn. on Chesapeake Bay, 60 m. S.E. of Richmond; here, during the War of Amer. Independence, Cornwallis sought shelter with his men; Cornwallis' surrender, 146.

Yosemite (yō-sem'-it-ē) **Falls**, California, U.S.A.

Yosemite National Park, Calif., U.S.A., containing magnificently wild scenery, occupies some 1,500 sq. m.; redwood trees, 2921.

Yosemite Valley, in cent. Calif., U.S.A., part of Yosemite National Park, a great gorge between 7 and 8 miles long; surrounded by scenery of wildest kind; mighty granite for-

mations; Merced riv. flows through it, *663*.

Yoshihito (yō-shē-hē-tō) (1879–1926). Emperor of Japan (1912–26).

Yoshinobu, Prince of Tokugawa. *See* **Tokugawa, Prince Yoshinobu**.

Youghal (yōō'-ahl), Eire. Spt. and watering-place in co. Cork on the Blackwater r., 27 m. E. of Cork; fisheries; has house of Sir Walter Raleigh.

Young, Arthur (1741–1820). Influential Eng. writer on agriculture and social economy; and roads, 2783.

Young, Brigham (1801–77). Successor, as head of Mormon Church, to Joseph Smith, its founder, *2230*, 3300.

Young, Edward (1683–1765). Eng. poet, whose fame rests on "Night Thoughts on Life, Death, and Immortality"; this contains passages of fine imagination and many phrases which have passed into proverbial speech ("Procrastination is the thief of time"), but is marred by its gloomy tone.

Young, Francis Brett (b. 1884). Eng. novelist and poet. ("Cold Harbour"; "Portrait of Clare"; "My Brother Jonathan"; "A Man about the House").

Young, Dr. James (1811–83), Brit. chemist, estab. coal distillation works from *c.* 1850, and produced paraffin, 2426.

Young, Thomas (1773–1829). Eng. physicist and archaeologist, **3436**; discovered interference of light, 1941.

Younghusband, Sir Francis Edward (1863–1942). Eng. soldier and political agent in India; commissioner to Tibet (1902–04).

Young Men's Christian Association (Y.M.C.A.). Christian social service organization, founded 1844; membership 2,000,000; emblem, red triangle.

Young Pretender, *1791*, 2682.

Youngstown. City in Ohio on Mahoning r., 2nd largest steel centre in U.S.A.; pop. 167,700.

"Young Turks," *4099*; policy in Balkans, 345.

Young Women's Christian Association (Y.W.C.A.), founded 1877; Christian social service institution; emblem, blue triangle.

Youth, Iduna, goddess of, in Norse mythology, 2881, *2881*.

Youth Hostels, 3436.

Ypres (ē'-pr), **John Denton Pinkstone French, 1st Earl of** (1852–1925). Brit. soldier, **3437**.

Ypres, Belgium. Tn. 35 m. S. of Ostend; pop. before 1st World War, 200,000; later about 17,000; **3436**, *403, 407*; in 1st World War, 3409.

Ypsilan'ti. A family of Greek soldiers, leaders in Greek struggle for freedom.

Ysaye (ē-zah'-ē), **Eugène** (1858–1931). Belgian violinist, one of the most famous players of his time.

Yser (ē'-zēr) **River**. Fr. and Belgian r. rising 20 m. S.E. of Calais and flowing E. and N. to sea at Nieuport, 403.

Yssel Meer, *see* **Ijssel Lake**.

Ytterbium (Yb). Element of the rare earth metal group; atomic weight 173·04; 3437; properties, 777.

Ytterby or **Ytter**. Swed. village where rare earths were first obtained; gave name to ytterbium, terbium, yttrium, etc.; 3188.

Yttrium (Yt). Rare metallic element of the aluminium group; atomic weight 88·92; 3437; properties, 777.

Yuan Shi-Kai (1859–1916). Chinese soldier and statesman, pres. of republic of China from 1913 until his death, 813.

Yucatan'. Peninsula between Gulf of Mexico and Caribbean Sea, **3437**; Maya ruins, 208, 3438; sisal plant, 2975.

Yucatan, Mexico. State in N. of Yucatan peninsula, on Gulf of Mexico; a. 23,000 sq. m.; pop. 418,200; cap. Merida; sisal exports, 2158.

Yucatan Channel or **Straits**. Between Gulf of Mexico and Caribbean Sea, 701.

Yucca. Plant or tree of lily family, native in N. and Central America and Mexico; "Spanish bayonet" is a species so called from its long sharply pointed leaves; this and other species are frequently grown outdoors in England; flowers, on a long spike in centre of rosette of leaves, are bell-shaped, whitish and very numerous.

Yuen' dynasty. In China (1260–1368).

Yugoslavia (ū-gō-slah'-vi-a), former kingdom of the Serbs, Croats, and Slovenes, declared a republic, Dec. 1945; state formed after 1914–18 war; 99,720 sq. m.; pop. 15,324,500, **3438.** *map, plate f. 1232*; cap. Belgrade, 408; Danube Highway, 972; Montenegro, 2219; people, *345*,

2982; Serbia, 2922; Tito, 3440; in 2nd World War, 1452, 3418, 3424, 3440.

Yu'kon. A large r. of N. Amer., partly in Canada, partly in Alaska; flows to Bering Sea; 1800 m. long; 98, 677, 3287, 3440; 2379; *map, plate f. 680.*

Yukon Territory, Canada. Most northwesterly political division of Canada; a. 207,000 sq. m.; pop. 4,900; gold fields, **3440,** 676.

Yule. The Scandinavian and early Saxon name for Christmas (*q.v.*).

Yuma ("sons of the river"). Chief tribe of Yuman stock of N. Amer. Indians; lived originally about confluence of Gila and Colorado rs., U.S.A.

Yu'man. A linguistic stock of N. Amer. Indians, living in s.w. U.S.A. and

N. Mexico; agric. people; chief tribes grouped among "pueblo" Indians.

Yunca. Name of a Peruvian nation who lived in ancient times on Pacific coast, where great monuments still exist.

Yungas. Bolivian valleys, 102.

Yunnan'. s.w. prov. of China; a. 146,714 sq. m.; pop. 10,853,360; rich copper mines; exports tin; cap. Yunnanfu.

Yuste (yōō'-sta), Sp. Monastery in w. centre near Plasencia; Charles V, 755.

Yusuf ibn Ayyub (yōō'-soof ibn i'-yoob). Original name of Saladin, 2864.

Yvon, Adolphe. Ney with the rearguard, *2360.*

O UR Z comes from the Greek letter *Zeta*, written thus: **Z**. Originally in Egyptian picture-writing it represented a duc!. Written in a running hand (the "hieratic" form), it became the symbol and then in the Phoenician and early Greek alphabets came to look more like the letter I crushed down **I I**. As the letter became more crushed the vertical became diagonal and finally slipped at top and bottom so as to joint the horizontals as in the Z today.

Among the Phoenicians it was the 7th letter and so remained in the Greek and early Latin alphabets, but it was dropped from the Latin in the third century B.C. Later, when the study of Greek became a mark of culture among the Romans, it was restored, but it had lost its place in the alphabet and had to fall in at the tail of the procession, where it still remains. It was called *ézed* in Old French and *ezed* in Early English; and thus evolved the queer old name of *izzard* for the letter Z.

Zacatecas (sah-kah-tā-kahs). State in cent. Mexico; a. 28,000 sq. m.; pop. 565,400; silver, 2157.

Zacatecas, Mexico. Cap. of state of Zacatecas, 350 m. N.W. of Mexico City; pop. 21,000.

Zaghlul (zahg'-lool) **Pasha** (1852–1927), Egypt. Nationalist leader; took part in the rebellion provoked by Arabi Pasha, and arrested; became minister of education in 1906; dismissed from office he inaugurated anti-British campaign; arrested and deported in 1921; permitted to return, he became Prime Minister in 1924.

Zagreb (zah-greb) or **Agram.** City of N.W. Yugoslavia; linen, carpets, leather; pop. 185,000.

Zaharoff, Sir Basil (1849–1936). Gk. financier; acquired vast fortune out of dealings in armaments; made many donations to charity and science.

Za'ma, battle of (202 B.C.), 1574, 2808.

Zambezi (zam-bē'-zi). 4th largest r. of Africa, **3441,** 69, 569, 2772; Victoria Falls, 3321; *plate f. 3016.*

Za'menhof, Lazarus (1859–1917). Inventor of Esperanto, 1223.

Zamora, Alcala (1877–1949). First Spanish president (1931)

Zancle, Greek Messina, 2968.

Zang'will, Israel (1864–1926). Brit. (Jewish) novelist and dramatist, Zionist leader ("Children of the Ghetto"; "Chosen Peoples"; "The Melting Pot").

Zan'zibar. Isl., forming (with Pemba) a Brit. protectorate, off E. coast of Africa; a. (isl.) 640 sq. m. (protectorate, 1,020 sq. m.); pop. (protectorate) 250,000; **3441;** *map, 1073.*

Zanzibar. Cap. of Zanzibar Protectorate; pop. 50,000; 3441.

Zaporozhe, Ukraine (formerly Alexandrovsk). City on R. Dnieper; rly. and waterway junc.; Dnieper dam, constructed here 1932, breached 1941, re-taken 1943; pop. 289,000; *plate f. 961,* 961.

Zara (zah'-ra), or **Zadar.** Adriatic port on Dalmatian coast, 90 m. S.E. of Fiume; pop. 18,600; assigned to It. by Treaty of Rapallo (1920), and to Yugoslavia after 2nd World War, 3440.

Zarathus'tra. Same as **Zoroaster.**

Zealand (zē'-land). Largest of the Danish isls., 991, *map, 992*; Copenhagen, 904, *905.*

Zealand. Prov. of s.w. Netherlands; a. 690 sq. m.; pop. 252,400; cap. Middleburg.

Ze'bra, 3442, *plate f. 73.*

Ze'bu. The Indian ox, having characteristic hump; is of a greyish-white colour and noted for endurance under tropical heat.

Zebulon (zeb'-yōō-lon). Hebrew patriarch, son of Jacob and ancestor of the tribe of Zebulon.

Zechariah (zek-ar-ī'-a) (6th–5th cents. B.C.). Hebrew minor prophet; returned to Palestine from captivity and promoted rebuilding of the temple ("Book of Zechariah"), 2692.

Zedekiah. Youngest son of Joseph and last king of Judah; ended his life blinded and a prisoner in Babylon.

Zeebrugge (zā-broog'-ge). Spt. of N. Belgium; Ger. submarine base (1914–18), 593, 3409; famous British naval raid, April 23, 1918; German base during 1940–44.

Zeeman effect. A strong magnetic field applied to a single line in a spectrum is found to split the line into two; named after the discoverer, Pieter Zeeman (b. 1865), a Dutch physicist and Nobel Prize winner (1902); and sun spots, 3119.

Zeiss planetarium, 2620.

Zemun. Formerly Semlin, tn. of Yugoslavia; pop. 28,080.

Zenana (zā-nah'-na). In India, the women's apartments.

Zend-Aves'ta. Sacred book of Zoroastrians.

Zenel'ophon. The legendary beggarmaid queen, *905.*

Zeno'bia (3rd cent. B.C.). Queen of Palmyra, 2485.

Ze'no of Citium (*c.* 342–*c.* 270 B.C.). Gk. philosopher, founder of the Stoic school of philosophy. *See* Stoicism.

Zeno of Elea (5th cent. B.C.). Gk. philosopher, inventor of many ingenious paradoxes to discredit common beliefs about time, space, and motion; taught the unity of all being, 2551.

Ze'olite, kind of clay in water softeners, **3114, 3351.**

Zephani'ah. A Hebrew minor prophet, said to have lived in 7th cent. B.C.; prophesied punishment of Israel for its sins; 2692.

Zeph'yrus. In Gk. myth., the west wind.

Zep'pelin, Friedrich, Count von (1838–1917). Ger. general and airship builder, **3442,** 93.

Zeppelin. A type of airship, 93; 3442.

Zer'matt. Tourist centre of Switzerland; *map, 3140.*

Ze'ro, origin of word, 233. *See also* **Nought.**

Zero, absolute, 1391, 1594.

Zeta, ζ. Z (Rom. z, Z). 6th letter of Gk. alphabet.

Zetland. Alternative name of the Shetland Is., 2945.

Zetland, Lawrence John Lumley Dundas, 2nd Marquess of (b. 1876). Secretary of State for India 1935–40, for Burma 1937–40.

Zeus (zūs). The supreme deity in Gk. myth., corresponding to Jupiter among the Romans, **3443;** in Aesop's fable of the frogs, 54; and Danaë, 2551; and Europa, 757; Hera his wife, 1614; oracle at Dodona, 989; and Prometheus, 2690; statue at Olympia, *plate f. 1524,* 2923; temple at Athens, 284, *285, 1520, 1528.*

Zhukov, Marshal Gregory. Chief of Soviet General Staff 1941. Dep. Defence Commissar 1942–43; C.-in-C. S. Front 1943–45.

Zic'zac. The "crocodile-bird," *931.*

Ziegfeld, Florenz (1869–1932). American theatrical manager. Famous for his "Ziegfeld Follies" revues.

Zimbabwe. Bantu name for various ancient stone strongholds.

Zinc (Zn). Bluish white metallic element of the mercury group; atomic weight 65·38; its chief ores are *zinc blende,* the sulphide and the carbonate or *calamine*; melts at 788° F.; **3443,** 777; in alloys, 122, 906, 2365; in elec. cell. *376*; in electro-plating, 1139; Poland, 2640; refined by electrolysis, 1136; hydrogen made from, 1673; ores, 2181; poison, 2638; properties, 777; in rubber mfr., 2836; in Russia, 2845; sulphide, 2574, 2731; "trace" metal in diet, 2149; U.S.A., 3285; Wales, 3333.

Zinc etching, 2688.

Zingali. The best known gipsy tribe, about whom George Borrow wrote.

Zinkeisen, Anna Katrina (b. 1901). British artist. Made her name particularly as a poster artist. Her sister Doris became equally well known as a designer of scenery for stage and films.

Zin'nia. A genus of the *Compositae*, native to Mexico and Cent. Amer. ; the garden zinnia (*Zinnia elegans*) is the best-known species.

Zinoviev, Grigory Evseevitch (1883–1936). Russian politician, President of the 3rd International (1919). Name became prominent in Eng. in 1924 when a letter, purporting to be addressed by him to Eng. Communists, whom it urged to rebel, was published in the London press on Oct. 25, just before General Election, and contributed to the defeat of the first Labour government. Sentenced to 10 years' imprisonment in 1935 for conspiracy against Stalin regime. Shot in 1936.

Zi'on. Jebusite stronghold at Jerusalem, captured by David ; name also applied to all Jerusalem, 1819, 1820.

Zi'onicm. Jewish movement for return to Palestine, 1829, 2480.

Zircon, a mineral : silicate of Zirconium, 3444.

Zirco'nium (Zr). Metallic element of the lead group ; atomic weight 91·2 ; melts at *c.* 3,090° F. ; properties, 777.

Zis'ka, John (*c.* 1360–1424). Bohemian Hussite leader, great general, and almost legendary hero ; died at point of apparent triumph over Emperor Sigismund.

Zith'er. Musical instrument, 2267.

Zlin. Town of Czechoslovakia, in district of Moravia ; pop. 42,100 ; factories of the Bata boot and shoe company, 373, 954.

Zloty. Polish coin.

Zo'diac. The zone in the skies traversed by the sun and planets, 3444 ; mapped by Chaldeans, 331.

Zodiacal light. A celestial phenomenon of unknown origin, observable as a cone of faint light in the sky after sunset at the end of March or before sunrise during October.

Zoetrope (zō'-ē-trōp). A toy showing moving pictures.

Zoffany, John (1733–1810). Eng. artist, 1182.

Zog I (b. 1895). Ex-King of Albania, 100. Son of a tribal chief and a Moslem, he was pres. of Albanian republic 1925–28, then becoming king. Escaped to Eng. after Italian occupation of Albania (1939).

Zo'ia, Emile (1840–1902). Fr. novelist, 3444, 1381, 2404.

Zollern (tsol'-ern). Ancestral home of Hohenzollerns, near the Danube in Swabia, s.w. Ger. ; built in 980, rebuilt in 1850–56.

Zollverein (tsol'-fer-īn) (Ger. *Zoll,* "custom," *Verein,* "union "). A union of Ger. states for maintenance of uniform rates of duty on foreign imports and of free trade among themselves, instituted in 1819 ; term is used generally for certain form of customs union.

Zone, of the earth, 1898.

Zone (time). Since 1883 many countries have adopted the system of standard time by zones. In the U.S.A. and Canada five standard times are used, the countries being divided into five zones for the purpose ; 3213.

Zones of occupation, of Germany after 2nd World War, *1453.*

Zoning. Term used to describe allocation of areas of land, in town-planning projects, to specific uses ; residential, commerce, factories, open spaces, etc., 3233.

Zoological Gardens (" Zoo "), 3445, aquarium, *192* ; penguin pool, *885* ; children's zoo, 3446.

Zoological Society of London. Society for the scientific study of animals, founded 1828. Has collection of living animals at Regent's Park, London, and Whipsnade, Bedfordshire, 3446.

Zoology (zōō-ol'-o-ji or zō-ol'-o-ji), 3446 ; classification of animals, 156 ; ecology, 1079, *plate f. 1080* ; nature study, 2283 ; place of man, 2078. *See* **Animals.**

Zorn (tsawn), **Anders Leonhard** (1860–1920). Swedish landscape, figure, and portrait painter ; one of the greatest etchers of his time.

Zorndorf (tsawn'-dorf). Vil. of Prussia, 53 m. N.E. of Berlin ; victory of Frederick the Great over the Rus. under Fermor (Aug. 25, 1758).

Zoroas'ter or **Zarathustra.** Persian teacher, founder of Zoroastrianism, 3447 ; fire worship, 1278. *See also* **Parsees.**

Zoshchenko, Michael (b. 1895). Russ. humorous author, satirised many Soviet institutions ; rebuked by govt. and admitted " errors " in 1948 ; 2856.

Zoser, King. His pyramid, *212, 1114.*

Zouaves. Fr. infantry corps originally recruited in Algeria from the Zouaves, a tribe of Berbers, but later drawn from Fr. ; they wear a picturesque Oriental uniform.

Zug. Lake of Switzerland, 3140.

Zugspitze (tsōōg'-spēts-ê). Highest peak in Ger., 1447.

Zuider or **Zuyder Zee** (zī'-dêr zē). Former arm of North Sea extending s. into Netherlands. By land reclamation it has been reduced to the fresh-water lake **Ijsselmeer** (*q.v.*).

Zuloaga (thōō-lō-ah'-gah), **Ignacio** (1870–1945). Sp. painter, *3048,* 3050.

Zu'luland. Division of Natal, S. Africa, annexed to Natal in 1897 : Brit. territory since 1887.

Zulus. Kaffir tribes of Bantu stock, S. Africa, **3448**, 70, *67* ; African colonization, 70 ; black race, *2723* ; girl, *3016* ; kraal, *3018.*

Zulu Wars, in South Africa, 3019.

Zuñis (zōōn-yēz). Tribe of Pueblo Indians inhabiting w. New Mexico-Arizona region, U.S.A., 2698, *2699.*

Zurbaran, Francisco (1598–1664). Sp. artist. *3049,* 3049.

Zürich (zūr'-ikh). Largest city of Switzerland ; pop. 336,000 ; **3448**, 3138, 3142 ; *map,* 3140.

Zürich, Lake of. Swiss L. chiefly in s. part of canton of Zürich ; a. 34 sq. m. ; city of Zürich at N. end ; *map,* 3140, 3140.

Zutphen (zŭt'-fen). Tn. in S.E. Netherlands, several times taken and sacked ; pop. 21,500 ; held by Germans 1940–45 ; Sir Philip Sidney killed (1586).

Zwickau (tsvik'-ow). Ger. mfg. tn. of Saxony, 60 m. s.w. of Dresden, on R. Mulde ; pop. 84,700 ; old churches ; coal fields ; 1841 ; birthplace of Schumann, 2887.

Zwinger (tsving'-gêr), art gallery, Dresden, 1048.

Zwingli (tsving'-glē), **Ulrich** (1484–1531). Swiss Prot. reformer, **3448**, 818, 2758, 3141.

Zwolle (zvol'-ê), Netherlands. Cap. of prov. of Overyssel, 60 m. N.E. of Amsterdam ; pop. 46,840 ; centre of N. and E. canal systems ; cotton, iron, ships ; cattle and fish market ; near by Thomas à Kempis lived and died.

Zworykin, Vladimir Kosma (b. 1889), U.S. television and electronics expert, Russian-born ; wrote " Television " (1940) ; " Photo-electricity and its Applications " (1948) ; 3184.

Zygomatic process. A prolongation of the temporal bone which supports the malar bone.

Zygospore (zī'-gō-spŏr). A spore resulting from fusion of two cells.

Zymase (zī'-mās). A ferment found in yeast, 1220, 3434.